AMERICAN
COST
OF
LIVING
SURVEY

Second Edition

AMERICAN
COST
OF
LIVING
SURVEY

Second Edition

A Compilation of Price Data
for Nearly 600 Goods and
Services in 445 U.S. Cities
from More Than 90 Sources

HELEN S. FISHER

 **Gale Research Inc.**

An International Thomson Publishing Company

 I⊤P

Changing the Way the World Learns

NEW YORK • LONDON • BONN • BOSTON • DETROIT • MADRID
MELBOURNE • MEXICO CITY • PARIS • SINGAPORE • TOKYO
TORONTO • WASHINGTON • ALBANY NY • BELMONT CA • CINCINNATI OH

Helen S. Fisher, *Editor*

Editorial Code & Data Inc. Staff

Robert S. Lazich, Marlita A. Reddy, and Susan Turner, *Contributing Editors*
Sherae R. Carroll, *Data Entry Associate*
Gary Alampi, *Programmer Analyst*

Gale Research Inc. Staff

Linda Thurn, *Editor*
Mary Beth Trimper, *Production Director*
Deborah L. Milliken, *Production Assistant*

Cynthia D. Baldwin, *Product Design Manager*
Sherrel Hobbs, *Macintosh Artist*

Copyright © 1995
Gale Research Inc.
835 Penobscot Building
Detroit, MI 48226-4094
ISBN 0-8103-4324-x
ISSN 1071-099x

Printed in the United States of America

I(T)P™   Gale Research Inc., an International Thomson Publishing Company.
          ITP logo is a trademark under license.

TABLE OF CONTENTS

STATE LISTING OF CITIES

INTRODUCTION

American Cost of Living Survey, second edition (*ACLS*) is a compilation of reported prices for more than 600 products and services in 445 cities in the United States drawn from more than 90 sources, including federal and state statistical reports, city surveys, association databases, and the periodicals literature. The large number of items and communities covered ensures that cost of living data are now available to individuals, librarians, researchers, and analysts in a single, comprehensive, easy-to-use volume.

ACLS responds to a current need. Curiosity about the state of the economy is prevalent. At the national scale, economic indicators provide an insight into the general performance of the economy. But data at the local level are difficult to obtain; the Consumer Price Index (CPI) covers major cities but does not permit comparisons *between and among* cities and is unavailable for smaller communities. *ACLS* provides a convenient and current bridge between the relatively accessible "global" scale and the "local" scale where, after all, everybody lives.

ACLS is, therefore, an excellent tool for those seeking cost of living information and those asked to supply it (librarians, counselors, employers, analysts, and others).

Uses of *ACLS* are many and varied. For example:

- People considering a move to another part of the United States can use the book to see how the move may affect their standard of living.

- Companies relocating employees can use *ACLS* to determine appropriate levels of compensation adjustment.

- Parents deciding the costs of education for their college-bound offspring can use *ACLS* to determine living costs in other areas.

- Individuals and organizations seeking adjustments in compensation—or organizations defending the levels of compensation they offer—can both use *ACLS* as a basis for analysis.

- Investors, market researchers, developers, and government agencies, similarly, will find well-organized data in *ACLS* to fill in the often missing information on local cost of living.

Making comparisons among locations can bring interesting differences to light. For example, in the fourth quarter of 1994, the price of a bottle of Gallo Chablis Blanc wine in Amarillo, Texas, is $5.55; the same product in Atlanta, Georgia, cost $4.95; and in Albany, New York, $6.17. A comparison of phone line installation charges for businesses in 1993 shows that in Alexandria, Louisiana, the cost was $85; in Allentown, Pennsylvania, $75; and in Akron, Ohio, $55.42. For those considering attending a public university, the total average cost for one year in a four-year public university in Abilene, Texas, is $4935; in Altoona, Pennsylvania, $8278; in Ann Arbor, Michigan, $7642; and in Bloomington, Indiana, $6639. Delivering a child by Cesarean costs $6334 in Allentown, Pennsylvania; $6059 in Anaheim, California; and $5462 in Asheville, North Carolina. Obtaining information on such differences can aid the typical consumer in making decisions on where to live, where to look for employment, where to send children to college, and where to obtain medical care.

*   *   *

The remainder of this introduction presents a discussion of subjects covered, geographical coverage, periods of coverage, methodology of compilation, the consumer price index, arrangement and format, and sources.

SUBJECTS COVERED

ACLS contains more than 90,000 entries for the average prices of more than 600 items in 445 cities in the United States. For each community, if available, items are arranged under the following major topics:

Alcoholic Beverages	Funerals	Personal Services
Charity	Goods and Services	Restaurant Food
Child Care	Groceries	Taxes
Clothing	Health Care	Transportation
Communications	Household Goods	Travel
Construction	Housing	Utilities
Education	Insurance and Pensions	Energy and Fuels
Legal Assistance	Entertainment	Personal Goods
Weddings		

Under each of these major topics, price information for more specific items within the broader topic is provided. A listing of these items, alphabetically arranged within each major topic, is provided in the *List of Items Covered* which appears on p. xxix.

Energy and Fuels. Energy substances—including natural gas, gasoline, and fuel oil—are placed under *Energy and Fuels*. The notable exception is electric power: all entries dealing with electric power have been placed under *Utilities* because, in general, people associate electric power with the "local utility."

Utilities. Included under the heading of *Utilities* are electric power costs as well as costs associated with water and similar services that are regulated or franchised. The chief exception is telephone service, which is classified under *Communications*.

Costs versus Expenditures. The majority of items shown are costs as they would be experienced by people buying the product or service. Some data shown are followed by the abbreviation *exp*. These indicate measured *levels of expenditure* on the item on a per capita basis or annual basis.

Prices for Two or More Periods. In some cases prices for the same item were obtained for more than one period, sometimes from the same sources, sometimes from different sources. In these instances, both prices are shown, with the most recent period shown last. These data may be useful in tracking changes in price over a period of time.

ACCRA Indexes. For cities that are part of the ACCRA cost of living survey (discussed more fully below), the ACCRA composite index is shown as the first item; component indices are also shown under major topics.

The ACCRA indices measure the relative price levels for consumer goods and services in the areas that participate in the ACCRA survey. The average of all participating cities is defined as 100. For each community, the community's index is read as a percentage of the average of all places. The values are always on either side of 100, e.g., 95.6 or 105.2. A value less than 100 indicates an area where the price levels are *less* than the average of all places surveyed. A value greater than 100 indicates that price levels, on average, are *higher* than average prices of all places participating in the ACCRA survey.

GEOGRAPHIC COVERAGE

ACLS provides information on 445 cities. At least one city is covered in every state. For many cities, data are reported for metropolitan areas, e.g., Allentown-Bethlehem-Easton, PA, NJ. In this case, as in others, the cities listed second or third in order are also listed alphabetically in the *Table of Contents*. Thus, Bethlehem, PA and Easton, NJ can both be found separately in alphabetical order; page references, however, are to the Allentown-Bethlehem-Easton metropolitan area.

Geographical access to the data is provided, first, in the *Table of Contents*, where the cities are arranged in alphabetical order. Immediately following the *Table of Contents* is a *List of Cities by State*. Cities are listed alphabetically by state. Cost of living data for some items are only available at the state or regional level. The methods used to "allocate" such data to cities are described below under *Methodology of Compilation*.

Coverage of cities also varies depending on the data available. For most communities, many specific items are available. For others, reporting is more sparse. However, only communities in which data were available for most major categories are included in *ACLS*.

PERIODS OF COVERAGE

ACLS coverage extends from 1991 up to and including mid-1995. The majority of entries, however, are from the period 1991 to 1994. The dates reproduced with each entry refer either to the date of collection or, if not available from the source, the date of the source itself. To the extent possible, the time periods of data collection are reported in the *List of Sources* which concludes *ACLS*.

METHODOLOGY OF COMPILATION

Geographical Selection. The editors initially selected 300 metropolitan statistical areas (MSAs) for coverage using 1990 Census of Population data. All research and data acquisition efforts were then aimed at obtaining information for at least the targeted MSAs. One major source (ACCRA—discussed more fully below) provided data for many (but not all) of the targeted MSAs. ACCRA data were also available for cities that were not on the original target list. These cities were added to the list. Similarly, the number of communities covered grew as other sources came to light. The final list of communities was edited to conform to a single naming convention. Descriptive tags (such as "MSA," "Area," and others) were removed so that the database, once sorted, would not display variants of the same city name. The final result was a "master list" of cities to be included.

Data Acquisition. Data were obtained from a variety of sources using many methods. Data arrived on paper as well as on magnetic media. Mailings, telephone contacts, special arrangements, and literature searches were used to locate and to obtain data. Sources were classified by the geographical level of the data (city, metro area, state, region) and each item within each source was assigned to one of the major topics used.

Data Allocation. Some interesting data were obtainable only at the state level (e.g., auto insurance costs, driver's license fees, education costs), at the Census region level (e.g., funeral costs), and in one case (weddings), at the national level. The editors decided to include the national average costs for wedding because inquiries determined that these costs were fairly consistent across the nation. If alternative sources for such categories could not be located, data were "allocated" to cities on the master list by using the state of each city and the known state composition of regions as a guide.

An obvious consequence of this method is that items marked as having a regional or a state-level source are not as accurate as items that have a city-level source. This is generally true except for those items where the price is controlled at the state level, e.g., driver's license fees or tuition at state educational institutions. In the case of many cities, data from regional/state as well as city-level sources are shown side-by-side, permitting some judgment on the accuracy of the regional/state or regional/city items.

Accuracy of Data. In all cases, data are reported exactly as obtained from the sources. The quality and accuracy of the data are obviously variable and depend on the methods used by the sources themselves. Data assigned from state or regional sources to cities were not changed in the process of allocation in any way.

COST OF LIVING VS. CONSUMER PRICE INDEX

ACLS does **not** report on the Consumer Price Index (CPI). A detailed listing of CPI data is available from another Gale title: *Economic Indicators Handbook.*

The difference between *cost of living* and the CPI is confusing for many people. For this reason, a brief outline of the differences is provided here.

The CPI measures price change from **one period to the next within the same city** (or in the Nation). A cost of living index measures differences in the price of goods and services **between cities within the same period**. To see how prices have changed in Chicago between 1990 and 1994, one would use the CPI. To see how Chicago compares with Dallas in cost of living, one would use a cost of living index or data such as those reported in *ACLS*.

ARRANGEMENT AND FORMAT

ACLS is arranged alphabetically by city. The city name and its state appear in boldface type at the head of a column of entries. The first item under each city name is usually the composite cost of living index attributed to that city by ACCRA.

Major topics covered are sorted alphabetically and appear in boldface print and initial caps, e.g., **Alcoholic Beverages**. Specific items covered within the major topic are arranged alphabetically.

The "Per" column typically contains a measurement, such as pound, month, or hour.

The "Value" column contains average prices represented in dollars or in fractions of dollars.

The "Date" column indicates the date on which that particular price was charged for that item, or in some cases, the date of the source material consulted. In some cases, there are two prices or price ranges given for a particular item; these reflect different dates from different source materials which included some of the same products, or the difference in price between a brand-name product and a generic product.

The "Ref." (for Reference) column contains numbers to be used when consulting the *List of Sources* section of *ACLS*. Each reference number is followed by a letter representing the geographical level for which data were reported in the source materials: s = State, r = Region, c = City or Metropolitan area.

A list of abbreviations used in *ACLS* is provided below.

SOURCES

General. More than 90 sources were used to compile *ACLS*. These included newspapers, magazines, government reports and publications, and surveys or other reports compiled by independent governmental agencies.

In addition to governmental sources, *ACLS* cites significant databases that are copyrighted and are included by special arrangement with the originators or publishers. Some of these sources are mentioned in the acknowledgments below. One source, ACCRA, represents what might well be described as the spine of the *ACLS-2* database by providing a large number of items for a large number of cities.

ACCRA. A large database was obtained by a special arrangement with ACCRA, the association of applied community researchers (formerly the American Chambers of Commerce Research Association). ACCRA is an affiliate of the American Chamber of Commerce Executives and the American Economic Development Council. ACCRA produces the *ACCRA Cost of Living Index* in cooperation with chambers of commerce or analogous organizations in 300 urban areas. Participation in the survey is voluntary and communities covered also change from one reporting period to the next.

In addition to price information, ACCRA provides a weighted ***cost of living index*** for the city as a whole ("composite index") and for components of expenditure (e.g., "grocery items," "utilities," etc.). These indexes are also included in *ACLS*. The user should note that these indexes are specifically built to reflect "differentials for a midmanagement standard of living." The use of ACCRA indexes, therefore, should not be applied indiscriminately to other groupings, e.g., "clerical workers" or "all urban consumers".

All sources are cited by number in each entry of *ACLS* in the column headed by the abbreviation "Ref." The reference numbers can be used as a guide to the sources shown in the *List of Sources*. A given source may be cited more than once if several different issues of the same source were used. This applies especially to periodicals.

Source entries include comments and notes that are useful for further interpretation of the data. Wherever possible, the address and telephone number of the publisher, association, or agency have been provided as a convenience for further research.

ACKNOWLEDGMENTS

A compilation like *ACLS* would not be possible without the help of numerous people who provided information, took time to discuss the availability of data, made useful referrals, and otherwise lent the editors a helping hand.

Furthermore, each source—whether containing many entries or just a few that filled a gap—was valued and appreciated.

The editors, therefore, would like to thank all those who made a contribution. Without intending to slight any contributor, we would like to acknowledge the unusual efforts on our behalf of the following persons/organizations:

- ACCRA
- American Public Transit Association (APTA)
- Bellcore, Inc.
- Health Insurance Association of America (HIAA)
- National Association of Insurance Commissioners (NAIC)
- National Association of Realtors (NAR)
- National Association of Regulatory Utility Commissioners (NARUC)
- National Funeral Directors Association

COMMENTS AND SUGGESTIONS

Comments on *ACLS* and suggestions for improvement of its usefulness, format, and coverage are always welcome. Although every effort is made to maintain accuracy, errors may occasionally occur; the editors would be grateful if these are called to their attention. Please contact:

Editors

American Cost of Living Survey

Gale Research, Inc.

835 Penobscot Building

Detroit, Michigan 48226-4094

Phone: (313) 961-2242 or (800) 347- GALE

Fax: (313) 961-6815

ABBREVIATIONS

The following abbreviations are used throughout *American Cost of Living Survey*, 2nd edition.

<	less than		inc	including
4Q	Fourth Quarter		IPEDS	Integrated Postsecondary Education Data System
ABA	American Bar Association		KWh	Kilowatt hour
addl	additional		lab	labor
APTA	American Public Transit Association		lb	pound
BTU	British Thermal Unit		LOTS	Local Option Taxes
c	city, metro		mg	milligram
CDL	Commercial Driver's License		mi	mile
CES	Consumer Expenditure Survey		mil	million
chg	charge		min	minimum, minute
CPI	Consumer Price Index		misc	miscellaneous
cu ft	cubic foot		ml	milliliter
DL	Driver's License		mo	month
DOE	Department of Energy		NARUC	National Association of Regulatory Utility Commissioners
doz	dozen			
EIA	Energy Information Administration		NFDA	National Funeral Directors Association
exc	except, excluding			
exp	expenditures		oz	ounce
FEC	Family Entertainment Center		pk	package
FHFB	Federal Housing Finance Board		priv	private
FHWA	Federal Highway Administration		r	region
ft	foot		s	state
FTC	Federal Trade Commission		SCETS	State Comprehensive Enhanced Transportation System
gal	gallon			
gov't	government		sq ft	square foot
HMO	Health Maintenance Organization		USDA	United States Department of Agriculture
in	inch		yr	year

LIST OF ITEMS COVERED

This listing shows all categories of items contained in *American Cost of Living Survey, 2nd Edition.* Items are arranged in alphabetical order under topic headings as they appear in the body of the book.

Composite, ACCRA index

Alcoholic Beverages
Beer
Beer, Miller Lite, Bud, 12-oz., ex deposit
J & B Scotch
Wine, Gallo Chablis blanc

Appliances
Appliances (major), expenditures
Appliances (small), misc. housewares, expenditures

Average annual exp.
Food, health care, personal goods, services

Banking
Bank fee, ATM, different bank
Bank fee, ATM, same bank
Bank fee, bad check
Bank fee, banking by personal computer, individuals
Bank fee, banking by personal computer, low balance
Bank fee, banking by personal computer, small businesses
Bank fee, bill paying, phone or ATM
Bank fee, bill paying, phone or ATM, low balance
Bank fees, teller visit

Business Expenses
Car rental, midsized car
Continental breakfast, room service
Dinner and tip, hotel, corporate rate
Hotel room, corporate rate
Lunch, convention center
Photocopies, copy shop
Restaurant meal
Room rate, hotel
Taxicab fare, airport to convention center

Business Fees
Lawyer's license fee

Charity
Cash contributions, expenditures

Child Care
Child care, for-profit daycare center

Clothing
Apparel and services, total expenditures
Apparel products and services, miscellaneous, expenditures
Apparel, boys age 2 to 15, expenditures
Apparel, children under age 2, expenditures
Apparel, girls age 2 to 15, expenditures
Apparel, men age 16 and older, expenditures
Apparel, men and boys, total expenditures
Apparel, women age 16 and older, expenditures
Apparel, women and girls, total expenditures
Footwear, expenditures
Formal wear rental, tuxedo, downtown store
Jeans, man's denim
Shirt, dress, men's
Suit, two-piece, medium weight wool, man's, Armani name
Shirt, man's dress shirt
Undervest, boy's size 10-14, cotton

Communications
Long-distance telephone rate, day, addl. min., 1-10 mi.
Long-distance telephone rate, day, initial min., 1-10 mi.
Newspaper cost, major daily
Newspaper subscription, dly. and Sun. delivery
Phone bill
Phone bill, AT & T Direct Dial plan
Phone bill, MCI Direct Dial plan
Phone bill, Sprint Direct Dian plan
Phone line, single, business, field visit
Phone line, single, business, no field visit
Phone line, single, residence, field visit
Phone line, single, residence, no field visit
Telephone call, to Dallas, Texas, between 9 a.m. and 5 p.m.
Telephone, business, PBX line, touch tone
Telephone, business, addl. line, touch tone
Telephone, business, connection charges, touch tone
Telephone, business, key system line, touch tone
Telephone, business, single ln., touch tone

Telephone, business, touch tone, inside wiring
   maintenance plan
Telephone, residential, flat rate
Telephone bill, family of four
Telephone service, expenditures

Credit Cards
Fee, conventional credit card, bal. carried
Fee, conventional credit card, secured

Drugs
Cocaine, street price
Crack Cocaine, street price
Heroin, street price
LSD, street price
Marijuana, street price
Methamphetamine, street price

Education
Bar examination preparatory course
Board, 4-year private college/university
Board, 4-year public college/university
Clothing, university student
Education, total expenditures
Living expenses, personal miscellaneous,
   university student
Personal grooming expenses, university student
Phone bills, university student
Recreation and entertainment, university student
Room, 4-year private college/university
Room, 4-year public college/university
Student fee, university
Total cost, 4-year private college/university
Total cost, 4-year public college/university
Transportation (campus bus passes; one trip
   home) university student
Tuition, 2-year public college/university, in-state
Tuition, 4-year private college/university, in-state
Tuition, 4-year public college/university, in-state

Energy and Fuels
Electricity
Energy, combined forms, 1800 sq. ft.
Energy, exc. electricity, 1800 sq. ft.
Fuel oil #2
Fuel oil and other fuels, expenditures
Gas
Gas, cooking, 10 therms
Gas, cooking, 30 therms
Gas, cooking, 50 therms
Gas, cooking, winter, 10 therms
Gas, cooking, winter, 30 therms
Gas, cooking, winter, 50 therms
Gas, heating, winter, 100 therms
Gas, heating, winter, average use
Gas, natural, expenditures
Gas, piped
Gas, reg unlead, taxes inc., cash, self-service

Gasoline, all types
Gasoline, unleaded midgrade
Gasoline, unleaded premium
Gasoline, unleaded regular
Gasoline and motor oil purchased

Entertainment
Admission fee, museum
Admission fee, seating, symphony performance
Archery event, Atlanta Olympics
Athletics event (track and field), Atlanta Olympics
Badminton event, Atlanta Olympics
Baseball event, Atlanta Olympics
Baseball game, four-person family
Basketball event, Atlanta Olympics
Boat ride, bumper boat, family entertainment
   center
Bowling, evening rate
Boxing event, Atlanta Olympics
Camping session, summer
Canoeing event (flat water), Atlanta Olympics
Canoeing event (white water), Atlanta Olympics
Ceremonies, opening and closing, Atlanta
   Olympics
Concert ticket, Pearl Jam group
Cycling event, Atlanta Olympics
Diving event, Atlanta Olympics
Entertainment supplies, equipment, and services,
   misc. exp.
Entertainment, total expenditures
Equestrian event, Atlanta Olympics
Fees and admissions, expenditures
Fencing event, Atlanta Olympics
Field hockey event, Atlanta Olympics
Football (soccer) event, Atlanta Olympics
Game tokens, family entertainment center
Go-kart ride, family entertainment center
Golf game, miniature, family entertainment center
Gymnastics (artistic) event, Atlanta Olympics
Gymnastics (rhythmic) event, Atlanta Olympics
Handball event, Atlanta Olympics
Hot dog, family entertainment center
Judo event, Atlanta Olympics
Monopoly game, Parker Brothers', No. 9
Movie
Movie ticket, adult
Pentathlon event, Atlanta Olympics
Pets, toys, playground equipment, expenditures
Reading, expenditures
Rowing event, Atlanta Olympics
Shooting event, Atlanta Olympics
Soft drink, family entertainment center
Softball event, Atlanta Olympics
Souvenir, family entertainment center
Swimming (synchronized) event, Atlanta Olympics

Swimming event, Atlanta Olympics
Televisions, radios, and sound equipment,
   expenditures
Tennis balls, yellow, Wilson or Penn, 3
Tennis (table) event, Atlanta Olympics
Tennis event, Atlanta Olympics
Ticket, basketball game
Volleyball (beach) event, Atlanta Olympics
Volleyball (indoor) event, Atlanta Olympics
Water polo event, Atlanta Olympics
Weightlifting event, Atlanta Olympics

Funerals
Burial vault, two-piece concrete
Burial, immediate, container provided by family
Burial, immediate, container provided by funeral
   home
Cards, acknowledgment
Casket, cloth-covered wood
Casket, hardwood, crepe interior
Casket, minimum alternative
Cosmetology, hair care, etc.
Cremation, direct, container provided by family
Cremation, direct, container provided by funeral
   home
Embalming
Funeral, funeral home
Funeral, other facility
Graveside service
Hearse, local
Limousine, local
Memorial service
Remains transfered to funeral home
Service charge, professional, nondeclinable
Visitation and viewing

Goods and Services
Miscellaneous goods and services, ACCRA Index

Groceries
Groceries, ACCRA Index
Apples, Red Delicious
Baby food, strained vegetables, lowest price
Bacon, sliced
Bacon, sliced, Oscar Mayer brand
Bakery products purchases
Balogna, sliced, Oscar Mayer brand
Bananas
Bananas, brand name
Beef or hamburger, ground
Beef purchases
Beef, stew, boneless
Beverage purchases, alcoholic
Beverage purchases, nonalcoholic
Beverage, Coca Cola
Beverage, Pepsi
Big Mac hamburger

Bologna, all beef or mixed
Bread, Pepperidge Farm white
Bread, local brand
Bread, white
Bread, white, pan
Bread, whole wheat, pan
Butter, Land O'Lakes brand
Butter, private label
Butter, salted, Grade AA, stick
Cabbage
Carrots, short trimmed and topped
Cereal, Corn Flakes, Kellogg's
Cereal, Corn Flakes, local brand
Cereal, Fruit Loops
Cereal, Rice Krispies
Cereals and bakery products purchases
Cereals and cereal products purchases
Cheddar cheese, natural
Cheese, Kraft American Singles brand
Cheese, Kraft grated Parmesan
Chicken
Chicken breast, bone-in
Chicken legs, bone-in
Chicken, fresh, whole
Chicken, whole fryer
Chuck roast, USDA choice, bone-in
Chuck roast, USDA choice, boneless
Chuck roast, graded and ungraded, exc. USDA
   prime and choice
Cigarettes, Winston, Kings
Cilantro
Coffee, 100%, ground roast, all sizes
Coffee, Maxwell House brand, regular grind
Coffee, vacuum-packed
Cookies, chocolate chip
Corn Flakes, Kellogg's or Post Toasties
Corn, frozen, whole kernel, lowest price
Crackers, soda, salted
Cucumbers
Dairy products (other) purchases
Dairy products purchases
Detergent powder, Tide Ultra brand
Dishwashing detergent, Dawn brand
Eggs purchases
Eggs, Grade A large
Eggs, Grade AA large
Eggs, private label, large, white
Fats and oils, eaten at home, purchases
Fish and seafood purchases
Flour, white, all purpose
Food (other than fruit and vegetables), eaten at
   home, purchases
Food purchases
Food purchases, food eaten at home
Food purchases, miscellaneous

Foods purchased and prepared by consumer away from home
Foods purchased away from home, not prepared by consumer
Frankfurters, Oscar Mayer brand
Frankfurters, all meat or all beef
Frozen dinner, Lean Cuisine brand, glazed chicken
Fruits (fresh) purchases
Fruits (processed) purchases
Fruits and vegetables purchases
Grapefruit
Grapes, Thompson seedless
Ground beef, 100% beef
Ground beef, lean and extra lean
Ground chuck, 100% beef
Ham shoulder, picnic, bone-in, smoked
Ham, boneless, exc. canned
Ham, rump or shank half, bone-in, smoked
Ice cream, prepackaged, bulk, regular
Iceberg lettuce
Jelly, Welch's brand, grape
Kale
Ketchup, Heinz brand
Lemons
Lettuce, iceberg
Margarine
Margarine sticks, Parkay brand
Margarine, Blue Bonnet or Parkay cubes
Margarine, stick
Mayonnaise, Hellmann's brand
Meat, ground chuck steak, 80% lean
Meats (other) purchases
Meats, poultry, fish, and eggs purchases
Milk
Milk and cream (fresh) purchases
Milk, 2%
Milk, 2%, brand name
Milk, 2%, local brand
Milk, fresh, whole, fortified
Milk, whole
Milk, whole, private label
Muffins, Thomas's English
Onions
Orange juice, Minute Maid frozen
Orange juice, frozen concentrate 12-oz. can
Oranges, Navel
Paper towels, Bounty brand
Parmesan
Peaches, halves or slices, Hunt's, Del Monte, or Libby's
Peanut butter, Skippy brand, creamy
Peanut butter, creamy, all sizes
Pears, Anjou
Peas, canned, Le Sueur brand

Peas, sweet, Del Monte or Green Giant
Plastic wrap, Saran brand
Pork chops, center cut, bone-in
Pork purchases
Potato chips
Potatoes, frozen, French fried
Potatoes, white
Potatoes, white or red
Poultry purchases
Rental rate, 2-bedroom apartment
Rib roast, USDA choice, bone-in
Rice, white, long grain, uncooked
Round roast, USDA choice, boneless
Round roast, graded & ungraded, exc. USDA prime & choice
Sausage, Jimmy Dean, 100% pork
Sausage, fresh
Shave cream, Barbasol brand
Shortening, vegetable oil blends
Shortening, vegetable, Crisco
Soft drink
Soft drink, Coca Cola, ex deposit
Soup, Campbell's brand, tomato, canned
Spaghetti and macaroni
Spaghetti sauce, Prego brand
Spaghetti, Mueller brand
Steak, T-bone
Steak, T-bone, USDA choice, bone-in
Steak, rib eye, USDA choice, boneless
Steak, round, USDA choice, boneless
Steak, round, graded & ungraded, exc. USDA prime & choice
Steak, sirloin, USDA choice, bone-in
Steak, sirloin, USDA choice, boneless
Steak, sirloin, graded & ungraded, exc. USDA prime & choice
Steak, t-bone
Sugar and other sweets, eaten at home, expenditures
Sugar and other sweets, eaten at home, purchases
Sugar, Domino brand
Sugar, cane or beet
Sugar, white, 33-80-oz. pkg.
Sugar, white, all sizes
Tea, Lipton brand
Tobacco products and smoking supplies, total expenditures
Tomatoes
Tomatoes, Hunt's or Del Monte
Tomatoes, field grown
Tuna
Tuna, chunk, light
Tuna, chunk, light, oil-packed
Turkey, frozen, whole

Vegetables (fresh) purchases
Vegetables (processed) purchases
Yogurt, natural, fruit flavored
Zucchini

Health Care

Health care, ACCRA Index
Adenosine, emergency room
Antibiotic ointment, Polysporin
Appendectomy
Birth, normal delivery
Bladder tap, superpubic, infant, emergency room
Blood analysis, emergency room
Blood count, infant, emergency room
Blood tests, abdominal pain, emergency room
Breast lesion excision (lumpectomy)
Broken arm treatment
Burn dressing, emergency room
Cardiology interpretation, emergency room
Cesarean section delivery
Chest X-ray, emergency room
Childbirth, Cesarean delivery, hospital charge
Childbirth, Cesarean delivery, physician charge
Childbirth, normal delivery, hospital charge
Childbirth, normal delivery, physician charge
Cholecystectomy
Coronary bypass, triple
Defibrillation pads, emergency room
Delivery, uncomplicated, total charge
Delivery, uncomplicated, vaginal, hospital charge
Delivery, uncomplicated, vaginal, physician's
  charge
Dentist's fee, adult teeth cleaning and periodic
  oral exam
Doctor visit, routine
Doctor's fee, routine exam, established patient
Drugs, expenditures
Gastric tube insertion, nasal, emergency room
Health care, total expenditures
Health insurance expenditures
Health insurance premium
Heart monitor, emergency room
Hospital care, semiprivate room
Hospital cost
Hysterectomy, abdominal
Immunization, DTP, measles, mumps, rubella,
  polio
Insurance premium, family medical care
Intravenous catheter, emergency room
Intravenous equipment, including tubing,
  emergency room
Intravenous fluids, emergency room
Intravenous line, central, emergency room
Intravenous pump tubing, emergency room

Liver function tests, abdominal pain, emergency
  room
Medical care charges, total, emergency room,
  abdominal pain
Medical care charges, total, emergency room,
  third-degree burns
Medical care charges, total, emergency, infant
  with fever
Medical care, AIDS patient with intestinal
  blockage, emergency
Medical care, total, emergency room, adolescent
  girl
Medical services expenditures
Medical supplies expenditures
Morphine, emergency room
Nursing care and facilities charges, emergency
  room
Nursing care and facilities charges, emergency,
  abdominal pain
Nursing care and facilities charges, emergency,
  infant with fever
Nursing care and facilities charges, emergency,
  third-degree burns
Nursing facilities, AIDS patient with intestinal
  blockage, emergency
Oophorectomy
Physical exam, well baby
Physical, complete
Physician's charges, emergency, abdominal pain
Physician's charges, emergency, infant with fever
Physician's charges, emergency, third-degree
  burns
Physician's fee, AIDS patient with intestinal
  blockage, emergency
Physician's fee, emergency room
Physician's fee, general practitioner
Salpingo-oophorectomy
Surgery, open-heart
Ultrasound, abdominal, emergency room
Urinalysis, emergency room
Urinalysis, infant, emergency room
X-ray, abdominal, emergency room
X-rays, emergency room

Household Goods

Appl. repair, service call, wash mach
Floor coverings, expenditures
Furniture, expenditures
Household equipment, misc. expenditures
Household expenditures, miscellaneous
Household furnishings and equipment,
  expenditures
Household operations expenditures
Household products, miscellaneous expenditures
Household textiles, expenditures

Housekeeping supplies, expenditures
Laundry and cleaning supplies, expenditures
Laundry detergent, Tide Ultra, Bold, or Cheer
Postage and stationery, expenditures
Tissues, facial, Kleenex brand

Housing

Housing, ACCRA Index
Add garage/carport
Add interior bath
Add room(s)
Add sunroom
Apartment condominium or co-op, median
Bathroom
Bathroom addition, average cost
Bathroom remodeling, average cost
Bedroom, attic addition, average cost
Bedroom, master suite addition, average cost
Car rental
Deck addition, average cost
Dwellings (owned), expenditures
Enclose porch/patio/breezeway
Exterior facelift
Exterior remodeling, average cost
Family room addition, average cost
Finish room in basement/attic
Home
Home repairs, maintenance, and insurance
Home, existing, single-family, median
Home, purchase price
Home, single family, median
Home, three-bedrooms, one-and-a-half baths
Home, vacation
Hotel room
House payment, principal and interest, 25%
   down payment
House, 1800 sq ft, 8000 sq ft lot, new, urban,
   utilities
Housing expenditures, total
Kitchen
Kitchen remodeling, major, average cost
Kitchen remodeling, minor, average cost
Lodgings expenditures (other than homes or
   rental units)
Maintenance, repairs, insurance, and other
   housing expenditures
Mortgage
Mortgage interest and charges expenditures
Mortgage payment
Mortgage rate, 15-year mortgage
Mortgage rate, 30-year mortgage
Mortgage rate, adjustable rate mortgage
Mtge. rate, incl. points and orig. fee, 30-year
   conv. fixed or ARM
Office, home addition, average cost

Princ. & int., mortgage, median-price exist.
   sing.-family home
Property taxes expenditures
Redesign, restructure more than half of home's
   interior
Rent, apartment, 2 br., 1 1/2-2 baths,
   unfurnished, 950 sq ft, water
Rent, office space
Rental unit, two-bedroom
Rental units expenditures
Shelter expenditures
Sun-space addition, average cost
Wing addition, two-story, average cost

Insurance and Pensions

Auto insurance, private passenger
Health insurance, HMO plan, cost to employer
Insurance and pensions, personal, expenditures
Insurance, life and other personal, expenditures
Pensions and Social Security, expenditures

Legal Assistance

Estate planning, law-firm partner
Lawyer's consultation fee
Lawyer's fee, apartment complex mortgage
   closing
Legal work, law firm associate
Legal work, law firm partner

Legal Fees

Legal fee, private attorney for Legal Aid Society
   indigent client

Personal Goods

Personal care products and services, total exp.
Shampoo, Alberto VO5
Toothpaste, Crest or Colgate

Personal Services

Dry cleaning
Haircut, man or child
Haircut, man's barbershop, no styling
Haircut, woman's shampoo, trim, blow-dry
Haircut, styling, blow dry
Manicure
Personal services expenditures
Plumbing service, house call
Dry cleaning, man's 2-pc. suit
Dry cleaning, woman's dress

Restaurant Food

Big Mac, small fries, medium drink
Chicken, fried, thigh and drumstick
Dining expenditures, family
Hamburger with cheese
Pizza, Pizza Hut or Pizza Inn

Taxes

Tax rate, residential property, month
Tax, cigarettes

Taxes, Federal income, expenditures
Taxes, State and local income, expenditures
Taxes, miscellaneous, personal, expenditures
Taxes, personal, expenditures

Transportation
Transportation, ACCRA Index
Bus fare, one-way
Bus fare, up to 10 miles
Cable car fare, one-way
Cars and trucks purchased, new
Cars and trucks purchased, used
Commuter rail (inclined plane) fare, one-way
Commuter rail fare (automated guideway),
    one-way
Driver's learning permit fee
Driver's license fee
Driver's license fee, duplicate
Driver's license reinstatement fee, min.
Driver's license renewal fee
Driving expenses
Ferry boat fare, one-way
Fine, illegal parking, handicapped zone
Fine, safety belt violation
Identification card, nondriver
Mileage fee, mileage traveled over rental
    company limit
Motorcycle learning permit fee
Motorcycle license fee
Motorcycle license fee, duplicate
Motorcycle license renewal fee
Parking, long-term lot, airport
Public transportation expenditures
Railway fare, commuter rail, one-way
Railway fare, heavy rail, one-way
Railway fare, light rail, one-way
Rental car, economy size, unlim. mileage
Shuttle, airport-to-downtown hotel
Taxi fare
Tire balance, computer or spin bal., front
Transportation expenditures, total
Trolley bus, downtown-to-plaza
Trolley fare, one-way
Vehicle expenditures, miscellaneous
Vehicle expenses, miscellaneous
Vehicle finance charges
Vehicle insurance expenditures
Vehicle maintenance and repairs expenditures

Vehicle purchases
Vehicle rental, leases, licenses, etc. expenditures
Vehicles purchased, other than cars and trucks

Travel
Car rental
Car rental, midsize car, 150 fee miles, Hertz
Car rental, midsize car, unlimited mileage
Dinner, restaurant, inc. tax and tips, no drink
Hotel room, two persons, inc. tax
Lodging, hotel suite, with continental breakfast
Taxi fare, airport-to-hotel
Taxi fare, to airport

Utilities
Utilities, ACCRA Index
Electricity
Electricity expenditures
Electricity, (part.), other, 1800 sq. ft., new home
Electricity, 1800 sq. ft., new home
Electricity, summer, 250 KWh
Electricity, summer, 500 KWh
Electricity, summer, 750 KWh
Electricity, summer, 1000 KWh
Fee, water use, industrial
Utilities, fuels, and public services, total
    expenditures
Water and other public services, expenditures

Weddings
Bridal attendants' gowns
Bridal gown
Bridal headpiece and veil
Bride's wedding band
Clergy
Engagement ring
Flowers
Formal wear for groom
Gifts to bridal attendants
Groom's attendants' formal wear
Groom's wedding band
Limousine
Music
Photography
Shoes for bride
Videography
Wedding invitations and announcements
Wedding package, chapel
Wedding reception

Abilene, TX

Item	Per	Value	Date	Ref.
Composite, ACCRA index		92.50	12/94	2c
Alcoholic Beverages				
Beer, Miller Lite, Bud, 12-oz., ex deposit	6	3.96	12/94	2c
J & B Scotch	750-ml.	19.45	12/94	2c
Wine, Gallo Chablis blanc	1.5-lit	5.17	12/94	2c
Appliances				
Appliances (major), expenditures	year	153	91	81r
Average annual exp.				
Food, health care, personal goods, services	year	27020	91	81r
Charity				
Cash contributions, expenditures	year	839	91	81r
Clothing				
Apparel, men and boys, total expenditures	year	380	91	81r
Apparel, women and girls, total expenditures	year	660	91	81r
Footwear, expenditures	year	193	91	81r
Jeans, man's denim		27.59	12/94	2c
Shirt, man's dress shirt		25.12	12/94	2c
Undervest, boy's size 10-14, cotton	3	4.50	12/94	2c
Communications				
Long-distance telephone rate, day, addl. min., 1-10 mi.	min.	0.08	12/93	9s
Long-distance telephone rate, day, initial min., 1-10 mi.	min.	0.10	12/93	9s
Newspaper subscription, dly. and Sun. delivery	month	12.50	12/94	2c
Phone line, single, business, field visit	inst	71.90	12/93	9s
Phone line, single, business, no field visit	inst	57.30	12/93	9s
Phone line, single, residence, field visit	inst	52.95	12/93	9s
Phone line, single, residence, no field visit	inst	38.35	12/93	9s
Telephone bill, family of four	month	15.14	12/94	2c
Telephone service, expenditures	year	616	91	81r
Telephone, residential, flat rate	mo.	8.80	12/93	8c
Education				
Board, 4-year private college/university	year	2084	8/94	80s
Board, 4-year public college/university	year	1675	8/94	80s
Education, total expenditures	year	319	91	81r
Room, 4-year private college/university	year	1840	8/94	80s
Room, 4-year public college/university	year	1756	8/94	80s
Total cost, 4-year private college/university	year	11876	8/94	80s
Total cost, 4-year public college/university	year	4935	8/94	80s
Tuition, 2-year public college/university, in-state	year	625	8/94	80s
Tuition, 4-year private college/university, in-state	year	7952	8/94	80s
Tuition, 4-year public college/university, in-state	year	1503	8/94	80s
Energy and Fuels				
Energy, combined forms, 1800 sq. ft.	mo.	102.94	12/94	2c
Fuel oil and other fuels, expenditures	year	56	91	81r
Gas, natural, expenditures	year	150	91	81r
Gas, reg unlead, taxes inc., cash, self-service	gal	1.20	12/94	2c
Gasoline and motor oil purchased	year	1152	91	81r
Gasoline, unleaded midgrade	gallon	1.21	4/93	82r
Gasoline, unleaded premium	gallon	1.30	4/93	82r
Gasoline, unleaded regular	gallon	1.10	4/93	82r
Entertainment				
Bowling, evening rate	game	1.95	12/94	2c
Concert ticket, Pearl Jam group	perf	20.00	94	50r

Item	Per	Value	Date	Ref.
Entertainment - continued				
Entertainment, total expenditures	year	1266	91	81r
Fees and admissions, expenditures	year	306	91	81r
Monopoly game, Parker Brothers', No. 9	game	11.28	12/94	2c
Movie	adm	5.62	12/94	2c
Pets, toys, playground equipment, expenditures	year	271	91	81r
Reading, expenditures	year	131	91	81r
Televisions, radios, and sound equipment, expenditures	year	439	91	81r
Tennis balls, yellow, Wilson or Penn, 3	can	2.29	12/94	2c
Funerals				
Burial, immediate, container provided by funeral home		1574.60	1/95	54r
Cards, acknowledgment		22.24	1/95	54r
Casket, minimum alternative		239.41	1/95	54r
Cosmetology, hair care, etc.		91.04	1/95	54r
Cremation, direct, container provided by funeral home		1085.15	1/95	54r
Embalming		281.30	1/95	54r
Funeral, funeral home		323.04	1/95	54r
Funeral, other facility		327.58	1/95	54r
Graveside service		355.19	1/95	54r
Hearse, local		141.89	1/95	54r
Limousine, local		99.40	1/95	54r
Memorial service		284.67	1/95	54r
Service charge, professional, nondeclinable		904.06	1/95	54r
Visitation and viewing		187.04	1/95	54r
Groceries				
Groceries, ACCRA Index		89.20	12/94	2c
Apples, Red Delicious	lb.	0.73	12/94	82r
Baby food, strained vegetables, lowest price	4-4.5 oz.	0.23	12/94	2c
Bacon, sliced	lb.	1.67	12/94	82r
Bananas	lb.	0.37	12/94	2c
Bananas	lb.	0.42	12/94	82r
Beef or hamburger, ground	lb.	1.02	12/94	2c
Beef purchases	year	213	91	81r
Beverage purchases, alcoholic	year	249	91	81r
Beverage purchases, nonalcoholic	year	207	91	81r
Bologna, all beef or mixed	lb.	2.27	12/94	82r
Bread, white	24-oz.	0.62	12/94	2c
Bread, white, pan	lb.	0.68	12/94	82r
Cabbage	lb.	0.42	12/94	82r
Carrots, short trimmed and topped	lb.	0.53	12/94	82r
Cereals and bakery products purchases	year	345	91	81r
Cereals and cereals products purchases	year	127	91	81r
Cheddar cheese, natural	lb.	3.58	12/94	82r
Cheese, Kraft grated Parmesan	8-oz.	3.49	12/94	2c
Chicken breast, bone-in	lb.	1.71	12/94	82r
Chicken, fresh, whole	lb.	0.78	12/94	82r
Chicken, whole fryer	lb.	0.71	12/94	2c
Chuck roast, USDA choice, boneless	lb.	2.26	12/94	82r
Cigarettes, Winston, Kings	carton	17.10	12/94	2c
Coffee, vacuum-packed	13 oz.	3.10	12/94	2c
Corn Flakes, Kellogg's or Post Toasties	18 oz.	2.18	12/94	2c
Corn, frozen, whole kernel, lowest price	10 oz.	0.70	12/94	2c
Crackers, soda, salted	lb.	1.27	12/94	82r
Cucumbers	lb.	0.65	12/94	82r
Dairy products (other) purchases	year	141	91	81r
Eggs, Grade A large	dozen	0.73	12/94	2c
Eggs, Grade A large	dozen	0.87	12/94	82r
Fish and seafood purchases	year	72	91	81r
Flour, white, all purpose	lb.	0.23	12/94	82r

Values are in dollars or fractions of dollars. In the column headed *Ref*, references are shown to sources. Each reference is followed by a letter. These refer to the geographical level for which data were reported: s=State, r=Region, and c=City or metro. The abbreviation *ex* is used to mean *except* or *excluding*; *exp* stands for expenditures. For other abbreviations and further explanations, please see the Introduction.

Abilene, TX - continued

Item	Per	Value	Date	Ref.
Groceries				
Food purchases, food eaten at home	year	2381	91	81r
Foods purchased away from home, not prepared by consumer	year	1696	91	81r
Frankfurters, all meat or all beef	lb.	1.74	12/94	82r
Fruits and vegetables purchases	year	380	91	81r
Grapefruit	lb.	0.45	12/94	82r
Grapes, Thompson seedless	lb.	2.30	12/94	82r
Ground beef, 100% beef	lb.	1.37	12/94	82r
Ground chuck, 100% beef	lb.	1.97	12/94	82r
Ham, boneless, exc. canned	lb.	2.54	12/94	82r
Ice cream, prepackaged, bulk, regular	1/2 gal.	2.47	12/94	82r
Lemons	lb.	1.02	12/94	82r
Lettuce, iceberg	lb.	0.96	12/94	82r
Lettuce, iceberg	head	0.81	12/94	2c
Margarine, Blue Bonnet or Parkay cubes	lb.	0.52	12/94	2c
Margarine, stick	lb.	0.77	12/94	82r
Meats, poultry, fish, and eggs purchases	year	655	91	81r
Milk and cream (fresh) purchases	year	130	91	81r
Milk, whole	1/2 gal.	1.23	12/94	2c
Orange juice, frozen concentrate 12-oz. can	16 oz.	1.36	12/94	82r
Orange juice, Minute Maid frozen	12-oz.	1.01	12/94	2c
Oranges, Navel	lb.	0.54	12/94	82r
Peaches, halves or slices, Hunt's, Del Monte, or Libby's	29-oz.	1.30	12/94	2c
Pears, Anjou	lb.	0.81	12/94	82r
Peas, sweet, Del Monte or Green Giant	15-17 oz.	0.43	12/94	2c
Pork chops, center cut, bone-in	lb.	3.07	12/94	82r
Pork purchases	year	142	91	81r
Potato chips	16-oz.	3.15	12/94	82r
Potatoes, frozen, French fried	lb.	0.82	12/94	82r
Potatoes, white	lb.	0.34	12/94	82r
Potatoes, white or red	10-lb. sack	2.31	12/94	2c
Rice, white, long grain, uncooked	lb.	0.48	12/94	82r
Round roast, USDA choice, boneless	lb.	2.91	12/94	82r
Sausage, fresh	lb.	1.82	12/94	82r
Sausage, Jimmy Dean, 100% pork	lb.	2.25	12/94	2c
Shortening, vegetable oil blends	lb.	0.75	12/94	82r
Shortening, vegetable, Crisco	3-lb.	2.20	12/94	2c
Soft drink, Coca Cola, ex deposit	2 lit	1.52	12/94	2c
Spaghetti and macaroni	lb.	0.87	12/94	82r
Steak, rib eye, USDA choice, boneless	lb.	6.85	12/94	82r
Steak, round, graded & ungraded, exc. USDA prime & choice	lb.	2.96	12/94	82r
Steak, round, USDA choice, boneless	lb.	3.17	12/94	82r
Steak, sirloin, USDA choice, boneless	lb.	4.12	12/94	82r
Steak, t-bone	lb.	4.37	12/94	2c
Steak, T-bone, USDA choice, bone-in	lb.	5.63	12/94	82r
Sugar and other sweets, eaten at home, expenditures	year	93	91	81r
Sugar, cane or beet	4 lbs.	1.39	12/94	2c
Sugar, white, all sizes	lb.	0.39	12/94	82r
Tobacco products and smoking supplies, total expenditures	year	286	91	81r
Tomatoes, field grown	lb.	1.36	12/94	82r
Tomatoes, Hunt's or Del Monte	14.5 oz.	0.68	12/94	2c
Tuna, chunk, light	lb.	1.94	12/94	82r
Tuna, chunk, light, oil-packed	6.125-6.5 oz.	0.65	12/94	2c
Turkey, frozen, whole	lb.	0.96	12/94	82r
Yogurt, natural, fruit flavored	8 oz.	0.58	12/94	82r
Goods and Services				
Miscellaneous goods and services, ACCRA Index		94.70	12/94	2c
Health Care				
Health care, ACCRA Index		94.70	12/94	2c
Adenosine, emergency room	treat	100.00	95	23r

Abilene, TX - continued

Item	Per	Value	Date	Ref.
Health Care - continued				
Antibiotic ointment, Polysporin	1.5 oz.	3.89	12/94	2c
Bladder tap, superpubic, infant, emergency room	treat	119.00	95	23r
Blood analysis, emergency room	treat	25.00	95	23r
Blood tests, abdominal pain, emergency room	treat	25.00	95	23r
Burn dressing, emergency room	treat	266.00	95	23r
Cardiology interpretation, emergency room	treat	26.00	95	23r
Chest X-ray, emergency room	treat	78.00	95	23r
Childbirth, Cesarean delivery, hospital charge	birth	5462.00	12/91	69r
Childbirth, Cesarean delivery, physician charge	birth	2228.00	12/91	69r
Childbirth, normal delivery, hospital charge	birth	2943.00	12/91	69r
Childbirth, normal delivery, physician charge	birth	1619.00	12/91	69r
Defibrillation pads, emergency room	treat	6.00	95	23r
Dentist's fee, adult teeth cleaning and periodic oral exam	visit	51.67	12/94	2c
Doctor's fee, routine exam, established patient	visit	35.42	12/94	2c
Drugs, expenditures	year	297	91	81r
Gastric tube insertion, nasal, emergency room	treat	25.00	95	23r
Health care, total expenditures	year	1600	91	81r
Health insurance expenditures	year	637	91	81r
Heart monitor, emergency room	treat	40.00	95	23r
Hospital care, semiprivate room	day	384.50	12/94	2c
Insurance premium, family medical care	month	389.25	1/95	41s
Intravenous fluids, emergency room	treat	130.00	95	23r
Intravenous fluids, emergency room	liter	26.00	95	23r
Intravenous line, central, emergency room	treat	342.00	95	23r
Liver function tests, abdominal pain, emergency room	treat	26.00	95	23r
Medical care charges, total, emergency room, third-degree burns	treat	2101.00	95	23r
Medical care charges, total, emergency, infant with fever	treat	628.00	95	23r
Medical services expenditures	year	573	91	81r
Medical supplies expenditures	year	93	91	81r
Morphine, emergency room	treat	34.00	95	23r
Nursing care and facilities charges, emergency room	treat	252.00	95	23r
Nursing care and facilities charges, emergency, infant with fever	treat	252.00	95	23r
Nursing care and facilities charges, emergency, third-degree burns	treat	861.00	95	23r
Physician's charges, emergency, infant with fever	treat	212.00	95	23r
Physician's charges, emergency, third-degree burns	treat	372.00	95	23r
Physician's fee, emergency room	treat	372.00	95	23r
Physician's fee, general practitioner	visit	51.20	12/93	60r
Surgery, open-heart	proc	42374.00	1/93	14r
Ultrasound, abdominal, emergency room	treat	276.00	95	23r
Urinalysis, emergency room	treat	20.00	95	23r
Urinalysis, infant, emergency room	treat	20.00	95	23r
X-rays, emergency room	treat	78.00	95	23r
Household Goods				
Appl. repair, service call, wash mach	min. lab. chg.	30.10	12/94	2c
Floor coverings, expenditures	year	48	91	81r
Furniture, expenditures	year	280	91	81r
Household equipment, misc. expenditures	year	342	91	81r
Household expenditures, miscellaneous	year	256	91	81r
Household furnishings and equipment, expenditures	year	988	91	81r
Household operations expenditures	year	468	91	81r
Household textiles, expenditures	year	95	91	81r
Housekeeping supplies, expenditures	year	380	91	81r
Laundry and cleaning supplies, expenditures	year	109	91	81r

Values are in dollars or fractions of dollars. In the column headed *Ref*, references are shown to sources. Each reference is followed by a letter. These refer to the geographical level for which data were reported: s=State, r=Region, and c=City or metro. The abbreviation *ex* is used to mean *except* or *excluding*; *exp* stands for *expenditures*. For other abbreviations and further explanations, please see the Introduction.

Abilene, TX - continued

Item	Per	Value	Date	Ref.
Household Goods				
Laundry detergent, Tide Ultra, Bold, or Cheer	42 oz.	2.82	12/94	2c
Postage and stationery, expenditures	year	105	91	81r
Tissues, facial, Kleenex brand	175	0.94	12/94	2c
Housing				
Housing, ACCRA Index		88.00	12/94	2c
Add garage/carport		6,980	3/95	74r
Add room(s)		11,403	3/95	74r
Apartment condominium or co-op, median	unit	68600	12/94	62r
Dwellings (owned), expenditures	year	2428	91	81r
Enclose porch/patio/breezeway		4,572	3/95	74r
Finish room in basement/attic		3,794	3/95	74r
Home, existing, single-family, median	unit	120200	12/94	62r
House payment, principal and interest, 25% down payment	mo.	668	12/94	2c
House, 1800 sq ft, 8000 sq ft lot, new, urban, utilities	total	108000	12/94	2c
Maintenance, repairs, insurance, and other housing expenditures	year	531	91	81r
Mortgage interest and charges expenditures	year	1506	91	81r
Mtge. rate, incl. points and orig. fee, 30-year conv. fixed or ARM	mo.	9.27	12/94	2c
Princ. & int., mortgage, median-price exist. sing.-family home	mo.	540	12/94	62r
Property taxes expenditures	year	391	91	81r
Redesign, restructure more than half of home's interior		17,641	3/95	74r
Rent, apartment, 2 br., 1 1/2-2 baths, unfurnished, 950 sq ft, water	mo.	485	12/94	2c
Rental units expenditures	year	1264	91	81r
Insurance and Pensions				
Auto insurance, private passenger	year	785.78	12/94	71s
Insurance and pensions, personal, expenditures	year	2395	91	81r
Insurance, life and other personal, expenditures	year	368	91	81r
Pensions and Social Security, expenditures	year	2027	91	81r
Personal Goods				
Shampoo, Alberto VO5	15-oz.	0.87	12/94	2c
Toothpaste, Crest or Colgate	6-7 oz.	1.94	12/94	2c
Personal Services				
Dry cleaning, man's 2-pc. suit		5.13	12/94	2c
Haircut, man's barbershop, no styling		7.66	12/94	2c
Haircut, woman's shampoo, trim, blow-dry		17.58	12/94	2c
Personal services expenditures	year	212	91	81r
Restaurant Food				
Chicken, fried, thigh and drumstick		1.88	12/94	2c
Dining expenditures, family	week	33.83	94	73r
Hamburger with cheese	1/4 lb.	1.85	12/94	2c
Pizza, Pizza Hut or Pizza Inn	12-13 in.	8.99	12/94	2c
Taxes				
Tax, cigarettes	year	584.00	10/93	43s
Taxes, Federal income, expenditures	year	2275	91	81r
Taxes, personal, expenditures	year	2715	91	81r
Taxes, State and local income, expenditures	year	365	91	81r
Transportation				
Transportation, ACCRA Index		104.70	12/94	2c
Bus fare, one-way	trip	0.75	12/95	1c
Cars and trucks purchased, new	year	1306	91	81r
Cars and trucks purchased, used	year	942	91	81r
Driver's learning permit fee	perm	5.00	1/94	84s
Driver's license fee	orig	16.00	1/94	84s
Driver's license fee, duplicate	lic	10.00	1/94	84s
Driver's license reinstatement fee, min.	susp	50.00	1/94	85s
Driver's license renewal fee	renew	16.00	1/94	84s
Identification card, nondriver	card	10.00	1/94	83s
Motorcycle learning permit fee	perm	5.00	1/94	84s

Abilene, TX - continued

Item	Per	Value	Date	Ref.
Transportation - continued				
Motorcycle license fee	orig	16.00	1/94	84s
Motorcycle license fee, duplicate	lic	10.00	1/94	84s
Motorcycle license renewal fee	renew	21.00	1/94	84s
Public transportation expenditures	year	249	91	81r
Tire balance, computer or spin bal., front	wheel	6.89	12/94	2c
Transportation expenditures, total	year	5307	91	81r
Vehicle finance charges	year	346	91	81r
Vehicle insurance expenditures	year	544	91	81r
Vehicle maintenance and repairs expenditures	year	600	91	81r
Vehicle purchases	year	2275	91	81r
Vehicle rental, leases, licenses, etc. expenditures	year	141	91	81r
Vehicles purchased, other than cars and trucks	year	27	91	81r
Utilities				
Utilities, ACCRA Index		89.80	12/94	2c
Electricity expenditures	year	950	91	81r
Electricity, 1800 sq. ft., new home	mo.	102.94	12/94	2c
Electricity, summer, 250 KWh	month	26.20	8/93	64c
Electricity, summer, 500 KWh	month	45.90	8/93	64c
Electricity, summer, 750 KWh	month	65.60	8/93	64c
Electricity, summer, 1000 KWh	month	85.30	8/93	64c
Utilities, fuels, and public services, total expenditures	year	2000	91	81r
Water and other public services, expenditures	year	227	91	81r
Weddings				
Bridal attendants' gowns	event	750	10/93	76r
Bridal gown	event	852	10/93	76r
Bridal headpiece and veil	event	167	10/93	76r
Bride's wedding band	event	708	10/93	76r
Clergy	event	224	10/93	76r
Engagement ring	event	2756	10/93	76r
Flowers	event	863	10/93	76r
Formal wear for groom	event	106	10/93	76r
Groom's attendants' formal wear	event	530	10/93	76r
Groom's wedding band	event	402	10/93	76r
Music	event	600	10/93	76r
Photography	event	1088	10/93	76r
Shoes for bride	event	50	10/93	76r
Videography	event	483	10/93	76r
Wedding invitations and announcements	event	342	10/93	76r
Wedding reception	event	7000	10/93	76r

Akron, OH

Item	Per	Value	Date	Ref.
Composite, ACCRA index		94.50	12/94	2c
Alcoholic Beverages				
Beer, Miller Lite, Bud, 12-oz., ex deposit	6	4.05	12/94	2c
J & B Scotch	750-ml.	18.95	12/94	2c
Wine, Gallo Chablis blanc	1.5-lit	4.99	12/94	2c
Appliances				
Appliances (major), expenditures	year	131	91	81r
Average annual exp.				
Food, health care, personal goods, services	year	25935	91	81r
Charity				
Cash contributions, expenditures	year	745	91	81r
Clothing				
Apparel, men and boys, total expenditures	year	332	91	81r
Apparel, women and girls, total expenditures	year	578	91	81r
Footwear, expenditures	year	164	91	81r
Jeans, man's denim		30.79	12/94	2c
Shirt, man's dress shirt		24.59	12/94	2c
Undervest, boy's size 10-14, cotton	3	3.73	12/94	2c

Values are in dollars or fractions of dollars. In the column headed *Ref*, references are shown to sources. Each reference is followed by a letter. These refer to the geographical level for which data were reported: s = State, r = Region, and c = City or metro. The abbreviation *ex* is used to mean *except* or *excluding*; *exp* stands for *expenditures*. For other abbreviations and further explanations, please see the Introduction.

Akron, OH - continued

Item	Per	Value	Date	Ref.
Communications				
Long-distance telephone rate, day, addl. min., 1-10 mi.	min.	0.16	12/93	9s
Long-distance telephone rate, day, initial min., 1-10 mi.	min.	0.32	12/93	9s
Newspaper subscription, dly. and Sun. delivery	month	10.87	12/94	2c
Phone line, single, business, field visit	inst	55.42	12/93	9s
Phone line, single, business, no field visit	inst	55.42	12/93	9s
Phone line, single, residence, field visit	inst	30.38	12/93	9s
Phone line, single, residence, no field visit	inst	30.38	12/93	9s
Telephone bill, family of four	month	22.45	12/94	2c
Telephone service, expenditures	year	547	91	81r
Telephone, residential, flat rate	mo.	15.25	12/93	8c
Education				
Board, 4-year private college/university	year	2241	8/94	80s
Board, 4-year public college/university	year	1625	8/94	80s
Education, total expenditures	year	394	91	81r
Room, 4-year private college/university	year	2118	8/94	80s
Room, 4-year public college/university	year	2103	8/94	80s
Total cost, 4-year private college/university	year	15444	8/94	80s
Total cost, 4-year public college/university	year	6987	8/94	80s
Tuition, 2-year public college/university, in-state	year	2076	8/94	80s
Tuition, 4-year private college/university, in-state	year	11085	8/94	80s
Tuition, 4-year public college/university, in-state	year	3259	8/94	80s
Energy and Fuels				
Energy, combined forms, 1800 sq. ft.	mo.	135.11	12/94	2c
Energy, exc. electricity, 1800 sq. ft.	mo.	52.66	12/94	2c
Fuel oil and other fuels, expenditures	year	83	91	81r
Gas, natural, expenditures	year	373	91	81r
Gas, reg unlead, taxes inc., cash, self-service	gal	1.02	12/94	2c
Gasoline and motor oil purchased	year	1000	91	81r
Gasoline, unleaded midgrade	gallon	1.15	4/93	82r
Gasoline, unleaded premium	gallon	1.23	4/93	82r
Gasoline, unleaded regular	gallon	1.07	4/93	82r
Entertainment				
Bowling, evening rate	game	1.85	12/94	2c
Entertainment, total expenditures	year	1356	91	81r
Fees and admissions, expenditures	year	347	91	81r
Monopoly game, Parker Brothers', No. 9	game	10.97	12/94	2c
Movie	adm	6.50	12/94	2c
Pets, toys, playground equipment, expenditures	year	270	91	81r
Reading, expenditures	year	160	91	81r
Televisions, radios, and sound equipment, expenditures	year	433	91	81r
Tennis balls, yellow, Wilson or Penn, 3	can	2.27	12/94	2c
Funerals				
Burial, immediate, container provided by funeral home		1268.31	1/95	54r
Cards, acknowledgment		26.12	1/95	54r
Casket, minimum alternative		198.03	1/95	54r
Cosmetology, hair care, etc.		122.19	1/95	54r
Cremation, direct, container provided by funeral home		977.81	1/95	54r
Embalming		334.00	1/95	54r
Funeral, funeral home		321.16	1/95	54r
Funeral, other facility		317.73	1/95	54r
Graveside service		292.48	1/95	54r
Hearse, local		153.20	1/95	54r
Limousine, local		123.52	1/95	54r
Memorial service		356.30	1/95	54r
Service charge, professional, nondeclinable		968.24	1/95	54r
Visitation and viewing		332.66	1/95	54r
Groceries				
Groceries, ACCRA Index		96.00	12/94	2c

Akron, OH - continued

Item	Per	Value	Date	Ref.
Groceries - continued				
Apples, Red Delicious	lb.	0.68	12/94	82r
Baby food, strained vegetables, lowest price	4-4.5 oz.	0.35	12/94	2c
Bacon, sliced	lb.	1.88	12/94	82r
Bananas	lb.	0.38	12/94	2c
Bananas	lb.	0.41	12/94	82r
Beef or hamburger, ground	lb.	1.44	12/94	2c
Beef purchases	year	197	91	81r
Beef, stew, boneless	lb.	2.52	12/94	82r
Beverage purchases, alcoholic	year	293	91	81r
Beverage purchases, nonalcoholic	year	203	91	81r
Bologna, all beef or mixed	lb.	2.12	12/94	82r
Bread, white	24-oz.	0.57	12/94	2c
Bread, white, pan	lb.	0.76	12/94	82r
Cabbage	lb.	0.44	12/94	82r
Carrots, short trimmed and topped	lb.	0.44	12/94	82r
Cereals and bakery products purchases	year	347	91	81r
Cereals and cereals products purchases	year	119	91	81r
Cheddar cheese, natural	lb.	3.28	12/94	82r
Cheese, Kraft grated Parmesan	8-oz.	3.04	12/94	2c
Chicken breast, bone-in	lb.	1.61	12/94	82r
Chicken, fresh, whole	lb.	0.89	12/94	82r
Chicken, whole fryer	lb.	0.92	12/94	2c
Chuck roast, USDA choice, boneless	lb.	2.33	12/94	82r
Cigarettes, Winston, Kings	carton	15.09	12/94	2c
Coffee, 100%, ground roast, all sizes	lb.	4.28	12/94	82r
Coffee, vacuum-packed	13 oz.	3.81	12/94	2c
Cookies, chocolate chip	lb.	2.72	12/94	82r
Corn Flakes, Kellogg's or Post Toasties	18 oz.	2.26	12/94	2c
Corn, frozen, whole kernel, lowest price	10 oz.	0.72	12/94	2c
Dairy products (other) purchases	year	148	91	81r
Eggs, Grade A large	dozen	0.58	12/94	2c
Eggs, Grade A large	dozen	0.76	12/94	82r
Fish and seafood purchases	year	61	91	81r
Flour, white, all purpose	lb.	0.22	12/94	82r
Food purchases, food eaten at home	year	2313	91	81r
Foods purchased away from home, not prepared by consumer	year	1709	91	81r
Fruits and vegetables purchases	year	372	91	81r
Grapefruit	lb.	0.47	12/94	82r
Grapes, Thompson seedless	lb.	2.15	12/94	82r
Ground beef, 100% beef	lb.	1.37	12/94	82r
Ground chuck, 100% beef	lb.	1.81	12/94	82r
Ham, boneless, exc. canned	lb.	2.16	12/94	82r
Ice cream, prepackaged, bulk, regular	1/2 gal.	2.48	12/94	82r
Lemons	lb.	1.08	12/94	82r
Lettuce, iceberg	lb.	0.81	12/94	82r
Lettuce, iceberg	head	0.82	12/94	2c
Margarine, Blue Bonnet or Parkay cubes	lb.	0.64	12/94	2c
Margarine, stick	lb.	0.81	12/94	82r
Meats, poultry, fish, and eggs purchases	year	591	91	81r
Milk and cream (fresh) purchases	year	132	91	81r
Milk, whole	1/2 gal.	1.09	12/94	2c
Orange juice, frozen concentrate 12-oz. can	16 oz.	1.41	12/94	82r
Orange juice, Minute Maid frozen	12-oz.	1.28	12/94	2c
Oranges, Navel	lb.	0.56	12/94	82r
Peaches, halves or slices, Hunt's, Del Monte, or Libby's	29-oz.	1.33	12/94	2c
Peanut butter, creamy, all sizes	lb.	1.81	12/94	82r
Peas, sweet, Del Monte or Green Giant	15-17 oz.	0.61	12/94	2c
Pork chops, center cut, bone-in	lb.	2.76	12/94	82r
Pork purchases	year	130	91	81r
Potato chips	16-oz.	2.81	12/94	82r
Potatoes, frozen, French fried	lb.	0.83	12/94	82r
Potatoes, white	lb.	0.28	12/94	82r
Potatoes, white or red	10-lb. sack	2.34	12/94	2c
Round roast, USDA choice, boneless	lb.	2.90	12/94	82r
Sausage, Jimmy Dean, 100% pork	lb.	2.78	12/94	2c

Values are in dollars or fractions of dollars. In the column headed *Ref*, references are shown to sources. Each reference is followed by a letter. These refer to the geographical level for which data were reported: s=State, r=Region, and c=City or metro. The abbreviation *ex* is used to mean *except* or *excluding*; *exp* stands for *expenditures*. For other abbreviations and further explanations, please see the Introduction.

Akron, OH - continued

Item	Per	Value	Date	Ref.
Groceries				
Shortening, vegetable oil blends	lb.	0.88	12/94	82r
Shortening, vegetable, Crisco	3-lb.	2.34	12/94	2c
Soft drink, Coca Cola, ex deposit	2 lit	1.02	12/94	2c
Spaghetti and macaroni	lb.	0.78	12/94	82r
Steak, rib eye, USDA choice, boneless	lb.	6.15	12/94	82r
Steak, round, graded & ungraded, exc. USDA prime & choice	lb.	2.72	12/94	82r
Steak, round, USDA choice, boneless	lb.	3.02	12/94	82r
Steak, sirloin, USDA choice, boneless	lb.	3.85	12/94	82r
Steak, t-bone	lb.	5.16	12/94	2c
Steak, T-bone, USDA choice, bone-in	lb.	5.38	12/94	82r
Sugar and other sweets, eaten at home, expenditures	year	91	91	81r
Sugar, cane or beet	4 lbs.	1.37	12/94	2c
Sugar, white, all sizes	lb.	0.36	12/94	82r
Tobacco products and smoking supplies, total expenditures	year	298	91	81r
Tomatoes, field grown	lb.	1.36	12/94	82r
Tomatoes, Hunt's or Del Monte	14.5 oz.	0.75	12/94	2c
Tuna, chunk, light	lb.	1.94	12/94	82r
Tuna, chunk, light, oil-packed	6.125-6.5 oz.	0.65	12/94	2c
Turkey, frozen, whole	lb.	0.96	12/94	82r
Yogurt, natural, fruit flavored	8 oz.	0.62	12/94	82r
Goods and Services				
Miscellaneous goods and services, ACCRA Index		95.20	12/94	2c
Health Care				
Health care, ACCRA Index		92.90	12/94	2c
Antibiotic ointment, Polysporin	1.5 oz.	3.57	12/94	2c
Childbirth, Cesarean delivery, hospital charge	birth	5101.00	12/91	69r
Childbirth, Cesarean delivery, physician charge	birth	2234.00	12/91	69r
Childbirth, normal delivery, hospital charge	birth	2891.00	12/91	69r
Childbirth, normal delivery, physician charge	birth	1623.00	12/91	69r
Dentist's fee, adult teeth cleaning and periodic oral exam	visit	44.12	12/94	2c
Doctor's fee, routine exam, established patient	visit	38.00	12/94	2c
Drugs, expenditures	year	248	91	81r
Health care, total expenditures	year	1336	91	81r
Health insurance expenditures	year	550	91	81r
Hospital care, semiprivate room	day	422.00	12/94	2c
Insurance premium, family medical care	month	350.73	1/95	41s
Medical services expenditures	year	457	91	81r
Medical supplies expenditures	year	82	91	81r
Household Goods				
Appl. repair, service call, wash mach	min. lab. chg.	30.09	12/94	2c
Floor coverings, expenditures	year	105	91	81r
Furniture, expenditures	year	291	91	81r
Household equipment, misc. expenditures	year	341	91	81r
Household expenditures, miscellaneous	year	162	91	81r
Household furnishings and equipment, expenditures	year	1042	91	81r
Household operations expenditures	year	365	91	81r
Household textiles, expenditures	year	101	91	81r
Housekeeping supplies, expenditures	year	390	91	81r
Laundry and cleaning supplies, expenditures	year	110	91	81r
Laundry detergent, Tide Ultra, Bold, or Cheer	42 oz.	3.16	12/94	2c
Postage and stationery, expenditures	year	115	91	81r
Tissues, facial, Kleenex brand	175	1.01	12/94	2c
Housing				
Housing, ACCRA Index		84.50	12/94	2c
Add garage/carport		8,479	3/95	74r

Item	Per	Value	Date	Ref.
Housing - continued				
Add room(s)		21,347	3/95	74r
Apartment condominium or co-op, median	unit	87100	12/94	62r
Bathroom addition, average cost	add	9734.00	3/95	13r
Bathroom remodeling, average cost	remod	6414.00	3/95	13r
Bedroom, master suite addition, average cost	add	27122.00	3/95	13r
Deck addition, average cost	add	6665.00	3/95	13r
Dwellings (owned), expenditures	year	2566	91	81r
Enclose porch/patio/breezeway		4,556	3/95	74r
Exterior remodeling, average cost	remod	15395.00	3/95	13r
Family room addition, average cost	add	27658.00	3/95	13r
Finish room in basement/attic		5,074	3/95	74r
Home, existing, single-family, median	unit	106500	12/94	62r
Home, existing, single-family, median	unit	83.30	12/94	62c
House payment, principal and interest, 25% down payment	mo.	641	12/94	2c
House, 1800 sq ft, 8000 sq ft lot, new, urban, utilities	total	104600	12/94	2c
Kitchen remodeling, major, average cost	remod	17084.00	3/95	13r
Kitchen remodeling, minor, average cost	remod	5804.00	3/95	13r
Maintenance, repairs, insurance, and other housing expenditures	year	484	91	81r
Mortgage interest and charges expenditures	year	1443	91	81r
Mtge. rate, incl. points and orig. fee, 30-year conv. fixed or ARM	mo.	9.17	12/94	2c
Office, home addition, average cost	add	8121.00	3/95	13r
Princ. & int., mortgage, median-price exist. sing.-family home	mo.	515	12/94	62r
Property taxes expenditures	year	639	91	81r
Redesign, restructure more than half of home's interior		9,114	3/95	74r
Rent, apartment, 2 br., 1 1/2-2 baths, unfurnished, 950 sq ft, water	mo.	464	12/94	2c
Rental units expenditures	year	1200	91	81r
Sun-space addition, average cost	add	23768.00	3/95	13r
Wing addition, two-story, average cost	add	50410.00	3/95	13r
Insurance and Pensions				
Auto insurance, private passenger	year	550.52	12/94	71s
Insurance and pensions, personal, expenditures	year	2408	91	81r
Insurance, life and other personal, expenditures	year	355	91	81r
Pensions and Social Security, expenditures	year	2053	91	81r
Legal Assistance				
Legal work, law firm associate	hour	90		10r
Legal work, law firm partner	hour	139		10r
Personal Goods				
Shampoo, Alberto VO5	15-oz.	0.99	12/94	2c
Toothpaste, Crest or Colgate	6-7 oz.	1.68	12/94	2c
Personal Services				
Dry cleaning, man's 2-pc. suit		5.75	12/94	2c
Haircut, man's barbershop, no styling		8.89	12/94	2c
Haircut, woman's shampoo, trim, blow-dry		20.00	12/94	2c
Personal services expenditures	year	203	91	81r
Restaurant Food				
Chicken, fried, thigh and drumstick		2.08	12/94	2c
Dining expenditures, family	week	30.03	94	73r
Hamburger with cheese	1/4 lb.	1.85	12/94	2c
Pizza, Pizza Hut or Pizza Inn	12-13 in.	8.00	12/94	2c
Taxes				
Taxes, Federal income, expenditures	year	1756	91	81r
Taxes, personal, expenditures	year	2426	91	81r
Taxes, State and local income, expenditures	year	568	91	81r
Transportation				
Transportation, ACCRA Index		99.30	12/94	2c
Bus fare, one-way	trip	0.75	12/95	1c

Values are in dollars or fractions of dollars. In the column headed *Ref*, references are shown to sources. Each reference is followed by a letter. These refer to the geographical level for which data were reported: s=State, r=Region, and c=City or metro. The abbreviation *ex* is used to mean *except* or *excluding*; *exp* stands for *expenditures*. For other abbreviations and further explanations, please see the Introduction.

Akron, OH - continued

Item	Per	Value	Date	Ref.
Transportation				
Bus fare, up to 10 miles	one-way	0.85	12/94	2c
Cars and trucks purchased, new	year	891	91	81r
Cars and trucks purchased, used	year	1155	91	81r
Driver's learning permit fee	perm	3.00	1/94	84s
Driver's license fee	orig	5.00	1/94	84s
Driver's license fee, duplicate	lic	1.50	1/94	84s
Driver's license reinstatement fee, min.	susp	12.50-100.00	1/94	85s
Driver's license renewal fee	renew	5.00	1/94	84s
Identification card, nondriver	card	2.50	1/94	83s
Motorcycle learning permit fee	perm	3.00	1/94	84s
Motorcycle license fee	orig	5.00	1/94	84s
Motorcycle license fee, duplicate	lic	1.50	1/94	84s
Motorcycle license renewal fee	renew	5.00	1/94	84s
Public transportation expenditures	year	209	91	81r
Tire balance, computer or spin bal., front	wheel	7.68	12/94	2c
Transportation expenditures, total	year	4792	91	81r
Vehicle finance charges	year	300	91	81r
Vehicle insurance expenditures	year	485	91	81r
Vehicle maintenance and repairs expenditures	year	534	91	81r
Vehicle purchases	year	2068	91	81r
Vehicle rental, leases, licenses, etc. expenditures	year	197	91	81r
Vehicles purchased, other than cars and trucks	year	22	91	81r
Utilities				
Utilities, ACCRA Index		119.70	12/94	2c
Electricity expenditures	year	668	91	81r
Electricity, (part.), other, 1800 sq. ft., new home	mo.	82.45	12/94	2c
Electricity, summer, 250 KWh	month	32.25	8/93	64c
Electricity, summer, 500 KWh	month	60.47	8/93	64c
Electricity, summer, 750 KWh	month	95.46	8/93	64c
Electricity, summer, 1000 KWh	month	125.94	8/93	64c
Utilities, fuels, and public services, total expenditures	year	1838	91	81r
Water and other public services, expenditures	year	167	91	81r
Weddings				
Bridal attendants' gowns	event	750	10/93	76r
Bridal gown	event	852	10/93	76r
Bridal headpiece and veil	event	167	10/93	76r
Bride's wedding band	event	708	10/93	76r
Clergy	event	224	10/93	76r
Engagement ring	event	2756	10/93	76r
Flowers	event	863	10/93	76r
Formal wear for groom	event	106	10/93	76r
Groom's attendants' formal wear	event	530	10/93	76r
Groom's wedding band	event	402	10/93	76r
Music	event	600	10/93	76r
Photography	event	1088	10/93	76r
Shoes for bride	event	50	10/93	76r
Videography	event	483	10/93	76r
Wedding invitations and announcements	event	342	10/93	76r
Wedding reception	event	7000	10/93	76r

Albany, GA

Item	Per	Value	Date	Ref.
Composite, ACCRA index		92.00	12/94	2c
Alcoholic Beverages				
Beer, Miller Lite, Bud, 12-oz., ex deposit	6	4.36	12/94	2c
J & B Scotch	750-ml.	14.59	12/94	2c
Wine, Gallo Chablis blanc	1.5-lit	6.01	12/94	2c
Appliances				
Appliances (major), expenditures	year	153	91	81r

Albany, GA - continued

Item	Per	Value	Date	Ref.
Average annual exp.				
Food, health care, personal goods, services	year	27020	91	81r
Charity				
Cash contributions, expenditures	year	839	91	81r
Clothing				
Apparel, men and boys, total expenditures	year	380	91	81r
Apparel, women and girls, total expenditures	year	660	91	81r
Footwear, expenditures	year	193	91	81r
Jeans, man's denim		33.19	12/94	2c
Shirt, man's dress shirt		29.83	12/94	2c
Undervest, boy's size 10-14, cotton	3	5.24	12/94	2c
Communications				
Long-distance telephone rate, day, addl. min., 1-10 mi.	min.	0.04	12/93	9s
Long-distance telephone rate, day, initial min., 1-10 mi.	min.	0.08	12/93	9s
Newspaper subscription, dly. and Sun. delivery	month	8.49	12/94	2c
Phone line, single, business, field visit	inst	58.25	12/93	9s
Phone line, single, business, no field visit	inst	52.25	12/93	9s
Phone line, single, residence, field visit	inst	47.50	12/93	9s
Phone line, single, residence, no field visit	inst	42.50	12/93	9s
Telephone bill, family of four	month	20.35	12/94	2c
Telephone service, expenditures	year	616	91	81r
Telephone, residential, flat rate	mo.	13.00	12/93	8c
Education				
Board, 4-year private college/university	year	2288	8/94	80s
Board, 4-year public college/university	year	1723	8/94	80s
Education, total expenditures	year	319	91	81r
Room, 4-year private college/university	year	2409	8/94	80s
Room, 4-year public college/university	year	1459	8/94	80s
Total cost, 4-year private college/university	year	13950	8/94	80s
Total cost, 4-year public college/university	year	5075	8/94	80s
Tuition, 2-year public college/university, in-state	year	972	8/94	80s
Tuition, 4-year private college/university, in-state	year	9253	8/94	80s
Tuition, 4-year public college/university, in-state	year	1894	8/94	80s
Energy and Fuels				
Energy, combined forms, 1800 sq. ft.	mo.	111.22	12/94	2c
Fuel oil and other fuels, expenditures	year	56	91	81r
Gas, natural, expenditures	year	150	91	81r
Gas, reg unlead, taxes inc., cash, self-service	gal	1.00	12/94	2c
Gasoline and motor oil purchased	year	1152	91	81r
Gasoline, unleaded midgrade	gallon	1.21	4/93	82r
Gasoline, unleaded premium	gallon	1.30	4/93	82r
Gasoline, unleaded regular	gallon	1.10	4/93	82r
Entertainment				
Bowling, evening rate	game	2.32	12/94	2c
Concert ticket, Pearl Jam group	perf	20.00	94	50r
Entertainment, total expenditures	year	1266	91	81r
Fees and admissions, expenditures	year	306	91	81r
Monopoly game, Parker Brothers', No. 9	game	11.17	12/94	2c
Movie	adm	5.50	12/94	2c
Pets, toys, playground equipment, expenditures	year	271	91	81r
Reading, expenditures	year	131	91	81r
Televisions, radios, and sound equipment, expenditures	year	439	91	81r
Tennis balls, yellow, Wilson or Penn, 3	can	2.11	12/94	2c
Funerals				
Burial, immediate, container provided by funeral home		1370.36	1/95	54r
Cards, acknowledgment		14.83	1/95	54r
Casket, minimum alternative		192.52	1/95	54r
Cosmetology, hair care, etc.		102.27	1/95	54r

Values are in dollars or fractions of dollars. In the column headed *Ref*, references are shown to sources. Each reference is followed by a letter. These refer to the geographical level for which data were reported: s=State, r=Region, and c=City or metro. The abbreviation *ex* is used to mean *except* or *excluding*; *exp* stands for expenditures. For other abbreviations and further explanations, please see the Introduction.

Albany, GA - continued

Item	Per	Value	Date	Ref.
Funerals				
Cremation, direct, container provided by funeral home		1065.64	1/95	54r
Embalming		304.29	1/95	54r
Funeral, funeral home		287.83	1/95	54r
Funeral, other facility		284.14	1/95	54r
Graveside service		349.13	1/95	54r
Hearse, local		132.27	1/95	54r
Limousine, local		98.45	1/95	54r
Memorial service		270.59	1/95	54r
Service charge, professional, nondeclinable		933.59	1/95	54r
Visitation and viewing		225.83	1/95	54r
Groceries				
Groceries, ACCRA Index		92.60	12/94	2c
Apples, Red Delicious	lb.	0.73	12/94	82r
Baby food, strained vegetables, lowest price	4-4.5 oz.	0.30	12/94	2c
Bacon, sliced	lb.	1.67	12/94	82r
Bananas	lb.	0.41	12/94	2c
Bananas	lb.	0.42	12/94	82r
Beef or hamburger, ground	lb.	1.44	12/94	2c
Beef purchases	year	213	91	81r
Beverage purchases, alcoholic	year	249	91	81r
Beverage purchases, nonalcoholic	year	207	91	81r
Bologna, all beef or mixed	lb.	2.27	12/94	82r
Bread, white	24-oz.	0.64	12/94	2c
Bread, white, pan	lb.	0.68	12/94	82r
Cabbage	lb.	0.42	12/94	82r
Carrots, short trimmed and topped	lb.	0.53	12/94	82r
Cereals and bakery products purchases	year	345	91	81r
Cereals and cereals products purchases	year	127	91	81r
Cheddar cheese, natural	lb.	3.58	12/94	82r
Cheese, Kraft grated Parmesan	8-oz.	3.16	12/94	2c
Chicken breast, bone-in	lb.	1.71	12/94	82r
Chicken, fresh, whole	lb.	0.78	12/94	82r
Chicken, whole fryer	lb.	0.79	12/94	2c
Chuck roast, USDA choice, boneless	lb.	2.26	12/94	82r
Cigarettes, Winston, Kings	carton	12.98	12/94	2c
Coffee, vacuum-packed	13 oz.	3.14	12/94	2c
Corn Flakes, Kellogg's or Post Toasties	18 oz.	2.41	12/94	2c
Corn, frozen, whole kernel, lowest price	10 oz.	0.62	12/94	2c
Crackers, soda, salted	lb.	1.27	12/94	82r
Cucumbers	lb.	0.65	12/94	82r
Dairy products (other) purchases	year	141	91	81r
Eggs, Grade A large	dozen	0.78	12/94	2c
Eggs, Grade A large	dozen	0.87	12/94	82r
Fish and seafood purchases	year	72	91	81r
Flour, white, all purpose	lb.	0.23	12/94	82r
Food purchases, food eaten at home	year	2381	91	81r
Foods purchased away from home, not prepared by consumer	year	1696	91	81r
Frankfurters, all meat or all beef	lb.	1.74	12/94	82r
Fruits and vegetables purchases	year	380	91	81r
Grapefruit	lb.	0.45	12/94	82r
Grapes, Thompson seedless	lb.	2.30	12/94	82r
Ground beef, 100% beef	lb.	1.37	12/94	82r
Ground chuck, 100% beef	lb.	1.97	12/94	82r
Ham, boneless, exc. canned	lb.	2.54	12/94	82r
Ice cream, prepackaged, bulk, regular	1/2 gal.	2.47	12/94	82r
Lemons	lb.	1.02	12/94	82r
Lettuce, iceberg	lb.	0.96	12/94	82r
Lettuce, iceberg	head	0.91	12/94	2c
Margarine, Blue Bonnet or Parkay cubes	lb.	0.55	12/94	2c
Margarine, stick	lb.	0.77	12/94	82r
Meats, poultry, fish, and eggs purchases	year	655	91	81r
Milk and cream (fresh) purchases	year	130	91	81r
Milk, whole	1/2 gal.	1.32	12/94	2c
Orange juice, frozen concentrate 12-oz. can	16 oz.	1.36	12/94	82r
Orange juice, Minute Maid frozen	12-oz.	1.13	12/94	2c
Oranges, Navel	lb.	0.54	12/94	82r

Albany, GA - continued

Item	Per	Value	Date	Ref.
Groceries - continued				
Peaches, halves or slices, Hunt's, Del Monte, or Libby's	29-oz.	1.24	12/94	2c
Pears, Anjou	lb.	0.81	12/94	82r
Peas, sweet, Del Monte or Green Giant	15-17 oz.	0.52	12/94	2c
Pork chops, center cut, bone-in	lb.	3.07	12/94	82r
Pork purchases	year	142	91	81r
Potato chips	16-oz.	3.15	12/94	82r
Potatoes, frozen, French fried	lb.	0.82	12/94	82r
Potatoes, white	lb.	0.34	12/94	82r
Potatoes, white or red	10-lb. sack	2.48	12/94	2c
Rice, white, long grain, uncooked	lb.	0.48	12/94	82r
Round roast, USDA choice, boneless	lb.	2.91	12/94	82r
Sausage, fresh	lb.	1.82	12/94	82r
Sausage, Jimmy Dean, 100% pork	lb.	2.24	12/94	2c
Shortening, vegetable oil blends	lb.	0.75	12/94	82r
Shortening, vegetable, Crisco	3-lb.	2.25	12/94	2c
Soft drink, Coca Cola, ex deposit	2 lit	1.19	12/94	2c
Spaghetti and macaroni	lb.	0.87	12/94	82r
Steak, rib eye, USDA choice, boneless	lb.	6.85	12/94	82r
Steak, round, graded & ungraded, exc. USDA prime & choice	lb.	2.96	12/94	82r
Steak, round, USDA choice, boneless	lb.	3.17	12/94	82r
Steak, sirloin, USDA choice, boneless	lb.	4.12	12/94	82r
Steak, t-bone	lb.	5.98	12/94	2c
Steak, T-bone, USDA choice, bone-in	lb.	5.63	12/94	82r
Sugar and other sweets, eaten at home, expenditures	year	93	91	81r
Sugar, cane or beet	4 lbs.	1.42	12/94	2c
Sugar, white, all sizes	lb.	0.39	12/94	82r
Tobacco products and smoking supplies, total expenditures	year	286	91	81r
Tomatoes, field grown	lb.	1.36	12/94	82r
Tomatoes, Hunt's or Del Monte	14.5 oz.	0.60	12/94	2c
Tuna, chunk, light	lb.	1.94	12/94	82r
Tuna, chunk, light, oil-packed	6.125-6.5 oz.	0.64	12/94	2c
Turkey, frozen, whole	lb.	0.96	12/94	82r
Yogurt, natural, fruit flavored	8 oz.	0.58	12/94	82r
Goods and Services				
Miscellaneous goods and services, ACCRA Index		100.60	12/94	2c
Health Care				
Health care, ACCRA Index		88.20	12/94	2c
Adenosine, emergency room	treat	100.00	95	23r
Antibiotic ointment, Polysporin	1.5 oz.	3.75	12/94	2c
Bladder tap, superpubic, infant, emergency room	treat	119.00	95	23r
Blood analysis, emergency room	treat	25.00	95	23r
Blood tests, abdominal pain, emergency room	treat	25.00	95	23r
Burn dressing, emergency room	treat	266.00	95	23r
Cardiology interpretation, emergency room	treat	26.00	95	23r
Chest X-ray, emergency room	treat	78.00	95	23r
Childbirth, Cesarean delivery, hospital charge	birth	5462.00	12/91	69r
Childbirth, Cesarean delivery, physician charge	birth	2228.00	12/91	69r
Childbirth, normal delivery, hospital charge	birth	2943.00	12/91	69r
Childbirth, normal delivery, physician charge	birth	1619.00	12/91	69r
Defibrillation pads, emergency room	treat	6.00	95	23r
Dentist's fee, adult teeth cleaning and periodic oral exam	visit	41.40	12/94	2c
Doctor's fee, routine exam, established patient	visit	44.00	12/94	2c
Drugs, expenditures	year	297	91	81r
Gastric tube insertion, nasal, emergency room	treat	25.00	95	23r
Health care, total expenditures	year	1600	91	81r

Values are in dollars or fractions of dollars. In the column headed *Ref*, references are shown to sources. Each reference is followed by a letter. These refer to the geographical level for which data were reported: s = State, r = Region, and c = City or metro. The abbreviation *ex* is used to mean *except* or *excluding*; *exp* stands for *expenditures*. For other abbreviations and further explanations, please see the Introduction.

Albany, GA - continued

Item	Per	Value	Date	Ref.
Health Care				
Health insurance expenditures	year	637	91	81r
Heart monitor, emergency room	treat	40.00	95	23r
Hospital care, semiprivate room	day	255.00	12/94	2c
Insurance premium, family medical care	month	320.13	1/95	41s
Intravenous fluids, emergency room	treat	130.00	95	23r
Intravenous fluids, emergency room	liter	26.00	95	23r
Intravenous line, central, emergency room	treat	342.00	95	23r
Liver function tests, abdominal pain, emergency room	treat	26.00	95	23r
Medical care charges, total, emergency room, third-degree burns	treat	2101.00	95	23r
Medical care charges, total, emergency, infant with fever	treat	628.00	95	23r
Medical services expenditures	year	573	91	81r
Medical supplies expenditures	year	93	91	81r
Morphine, emergency room	treat	34.00	95	23r
Nursing care and facilities charges, emergency room	treat	252.00	95	23r
Nursing care and facilities charges, emergency, infant with fever	treat	252.00	95	23r
Nursing care and facilities charges, emergency, third-degree burns	treat	861.00	95	23r
Physician's charges, emergency, infant with fever	treat	212.00	95	23r
Physician's charges, emergency, third-degree burns	treat	372.00	95	23r
Physician's fee, emergency room	treat	372.00	95	23r
Physician's fee, general practitioner	visit	51.20	12/93	60r
Surgery, open-heart	proc	42374.00	1/93	14r
Ultrasound, abdominal, emergency room	treat	276.00	95	23r
Urinalysis, emergency room	treat	20.00	95	23r
Urinalysis, infant, emergency room	treat	20.00	95	23r
X-rays, emergency room	treat	78.00	95	23r
Household Goods				
Appl. repair, service call, wash mach	min. lab. chg.	32.97	12/94	2c
Floor coverings, expenditures	year	48	91	81r
Furniture, expenditures	year	280	91	81r
Household equipment, misc. expenditures	year	342	91	81r
Household expenditures, miscellaneous	year	256	91	81r
Household furnishings and equipment, expenditures	year	988	91	81r
Household operations expenditures	year	468	91	81r
Household textiles, expenditures	year	95	91	81r
Housekeeping supplies, expenditures	year	380	91	81r
Laundry and cleaning supplies, expenditures	year	109	91	81r
Laundry detergent, Tide Ultra, Bold, or Cheer	42 oz.	2.65	12/94	2c
Postage and stationery, expenditures	year	105	91	81r
Tissues, facial, Kleenex brand	175	0.97	12/94	2c
Housing				
Housing, ACCRA Index		77.70	12/94	2c
Add garage/carport		6,980	3/95	74r
Add room(s)		11,403	3/95	74r
Apartment condominium or co-op, median	unit	68600	12/94	62r
Dwellings (owned), expenditures	year	2428	91	81r
Enclose porch/patio/breezeway		4,572	3/95	74r
Finish room in basement/attic		3,794	3/95	74r
Home, existing, single-family, median	unit	120200	12/94	62r
House payment, principal and interest, 25% down payment	mo.	587	12/94	2c
House, 1800 sq ft, 8000 sq ft lot, new, urban, utilities	total	95200	12/94	2c
Maintenance, repairs, insurance, and other housing expenditures	year	531	91	81r
Mortgage interest and charges expenditures	year	1506	91	81r
Mtge. rate, incl. points and orig. fee, 30-year conv. fixed or ARM	mo.	9.24	12/94	2c

Albany, GA - continued

Item	Per	Value	Date	Ref.
Housing - continued				
Princ. & int., mortgage, median-price exist. sing.-family home	mo.	540	12/94	62r
Property taxes expenditures	year	391	91	81r
Redesign, restructure more than half of home's interior		17,641	3/95	74r
Rent, apartment, 2 br., 1 1/2-2 baths, unfurnished, 950 sq ft, water	mo.	435	12/94	2c
Rental units expenditures	year	1264	91	81r
Insurance and Pensions				
Auto insurance, private passenger	year	664.85	12/94	71s
Insurance and pensions, personal, expenditures	year	2395	91	81r
Insurance, life and other personal, expenditures	year	368	91	81r
Pensions and Social Security, expenditures	year	2027	91	81r
Personal Goods				
Shampoo, Alberto VO5	15-oz.	1.00	12/94	2c
Toothpaste, Crest or Colgate	6-7 oz.	1.87	12/94	2c
Personal Services				
Dry cleaning, man's 2-pc. suit		5.30	12/94	2c
Haircut, man's barbershop, no styling		8.00	12/94	2c
Haircut, woman's shampoo, trim, blow-dry		21.20	12/94	2c
Personal services expenditures	year	212	91	81r
Restaurant Food				
Chicken, fried, thigh and drumstick		2.39	12/94	2c
Dining expenditures, family	week	33.83	94	73r
Hamburger with cheese	1/4 lb.	1.80	12/94	2c
Pizza, Pizza Hut or Pizza Inn	12-13 in.	7.99	12/94	2c
Taxes				
Taxes, Federal income, expenditures	year	2275	91	81r
Taxes, personal, expenditures	year	2715	91	81r
Taxes, State and local income, expenditures	year	365	91	81r
Transportation				
Transportation, ACCRA Index		99.70	12/94	2c
Bus fare, one-way	trip	0.60	12/95	1c
Cars and trucks purchased, new	year	1306	91	81r
Cars and trucks purchased, used	year	942	91	81r
Driver's learning permit fee	perm	10.00	1/94	84s
Driver's license fee	orig	15.00	1/94	84s
Driver's license fee, duplicate	lic	10.00	1/94	84s
Driver's license reinstatement fee, min.	susp	25.00	1/94	85s
Driver's license renewal fee	renew	15.00	1/94	84s
Identification card, nondriver	card	3.00	1/94	83s
Motorcycle learning permit fee	perm	10.00	1/94	84s
Motorcycle license fee	orig	15.00	1/94	84s
Motorcycle license fee, duplicate	lic	10.00	1/94	84s
Motorcycle license renewal fee	renew	15.00	1/94	84s
Public transportation expenditures	year	249	91	81r
Tire balance, computer or spin bal., front	wheel	7.75	12/94	2c
Transportation expenditures, total	year	5307	91	81r
Vehicle finance charges	year	346	91	81r
Vehicle insurance expenditures	year	544	91	81r
Vehicle maintenance and repairs expenditures	year	600	91	81r
Vehicle purchases	year	2275	91	81r
Vehicle rental, leases, licenses, etc. expenditures	year	141	91	81r
Vehicles purchased, other than cars and trucks	year	27	91	81r
Utilities				
Utilities, ACCRA Index		99.80	12/94	2c
Electricity expenditures	year	950	91	81r
Electricity, 1800 sq. ft., new home	mo.	111.22	12/94	2c
Utilities, fuels, and public services, total expenditures	year	2000	91	81r
Water and other public services, expenditures	year	227	91	81r

Values are in dollars or fractions of dollars. In the column headed *Ref*, references are shown to sources. Each reference is followed by a letter. These refer to the geographical level for which data were reported: s=State, r=Region, and c=City or metro. The abbreviation *ex* is used to mean *except* or *excluding*; *exp* stands for *expenditures*. For other abbreviations and further explanations, please see the Introduction.

Albany, GA - continued

Weddings

Item	Per	Value	Date	Ref.
Bridal attendants' gowns	event	750	10/93	76r
Bridal gown	event	852	10/93	76r
Bridal headpiece and veil	event	167	10/93	76r
Bride's wedding band	event	708	10/93	76r
Clergy	event	224	10/93	76r
Engagement ring	event	2756	10/93	76r
Flowers	event	863	10/93	76r
Formal wear for groom	event	106	10/93	76r
Groom's attendants' formal wear	event	530	10/93	76r
Groom's wedding band	event	402	10/93	76r
Music	event	600	10/93	76r
Photography	event	1088	10/93	76r
Shoes for bride	event	50	10/93	76r
Videography	event	483	10/93	76r
Wedding invitations and announcements	event	342	10/93	76r
Wedding reception	event	7000	10/93	76r

Albany-Schenectady-Troy, NY

Item	Per	Value	Date	Ref.
Composite, ACCRA index		107.10	12/94	2c
Alcoholic Beverages				
Beer, Miller Lite, Bud, 12-oz., ex deposit	6	4.03	12/94	2c
J & B Scotch	750-ml.	18.45	12/94	2c
Wine, Gallo Chablis blanc	1.5-lit	6.17	12/94	2c
Appliances				
Appliances (major), expenditures	year	145	91	81r
Average annual exp.				
Food, health care, personal goods, services	year	29496	91	81r
Charity				
Cash contributions, expenditures	year	708	91	81r
Clothing				
Apparel, men and boys, total expenditures	year	416	91	81r
Apparel, women and girls, total expenditures	year	744	91	81r
Footwear, expenditures	year	305	91	81r
Jeans, man's denim		34.78	12/94	2c
Shirt, man's dress shirt		31.50	12/94	2c
Undervest, boy's size 10-14, cotton	3	5.43	12/94	2c
Communications				
Long-distance telephone rate, day, addl. min., 1-10 mi.	min.	4.00	12/93	9s
Long-distance telephone rate, day, initial min., 1-10 mi.	min.	14.90	12/93	9s
Newspaper subscription, dly. and Sun. delivery	month	14.57	12/94	2c
Phone line, single, business, field visit	inst	143.26	12/93	9s
Phone line, single, business, no field visit	inst	106.05	12/93	9s
Phone line, single, residence, field visit	inst	85.46	12/93	9s
Phone line, single, residence, no field visit	inst	55.00	12/93	9s
Telephone bill, family of four	month	30.25	12/94	2c
Telephone service, expenditures	year	589	91	81r
Telephone, residential, flat rate	mo.	20.16	12/93	8c
Education				
Board, 4-year private college/university	year	2918	8/94	80s
Board, 4-year public college/university	year	2177	8/94	80s
Education, total expenditures	year	593	91	81r
Room, 4-year private college/university	year	3302	8/94	80s
Room, 4-year public college/university	year	2624	8/94	80s
Total cost, 4-year private college/university	year	18451	8/94	80s
Total cost, 4-year public college/university	year	7723	8/94	80s
Tuition, 2-year public college/university, in-state	year	2112	8/94	80s
Tuition, 4-year private college/university, in-state	year	12231	8/94	80s
Tuition, 4-year public college/university, in-state	year	2921	8/94	80s

Albany-Schenectady-Troy, NY - continued

Item	Per	Value	Date	Ref.
Energy and Fuels				
Energy, combined forms, 1800 sq. ft.	mo.	171.35	12/94	2c
Energy, exc. electricity, 1800 sq. ft.	mo.	74.44	12/94	2c
Fuel oil and other fuels, expenditures	year	257	91	81r
Gas, natural, expenditures	year	285	91	81r
Gas, reg unlead, taxes inc., cash, self-service	gal	1.22	12/94	2c
Gasoline and motor oil purchased	year	867	91	81r
Gasoline, unleaded midgrade	gallon	1.32	4/93	82r
Gasoline, unleaded premium	gallon	1.40	4/93	82r
Gasoline, unleaded regular	gallon	1.19	4/93	82r
Entertainment				
Bowling, evening rate	game	2.36	12/94	2c
Entertainment, total expenditures	year	1331	91	81r
Fees and admissions, expenditures	year	398	91	81r
Monopoly game, Parker Brothers', No. 9	game	10.98	12/94	2c
Movie	adm	7.12	12/94	2c
Pets, toys, playground equipment, expenditures	year	270	91	81r
Reading, expenditures	year	171	91	81r
Televisions, radios, and sound equipment, expenditures	year	429	91	81r
Tennis balls, yellow, Wilson or Penn, 3	can	2.11	12/94	2c
Funerals				
Burial, immediate, container provided by funeral home		1370.36	1/95	54r
Cards, acknowledgment		17.72	1/95	54r
Casket, minimum alternative		192.52	1/95	54r
Cosmetology, hair care, etc.		139.56	1/95	54r
Cremation, direct, container provided by funeral home		1049.24	1/95	54r
Embalming		387.57	1/95	54r
Funeral, funeral home		278.77	1/95	54r
Funeral, other facility		275.85	1/95	54r
Graveside service		213.08	1/95	54r
Hearse, local		157.27	1/95	54r
Limousine, local		146.45	1/95	54r
Memorial service		271.02	1/95	54r
Service charge, professional, nondeclinable		943.58	1/95	54r
Visitation and viewing		322.86	1/95	54r
Groceries				
Groceries, ACCRA Index		104.70	12/94	2c
Apples, Red Delicious	lb.	0.78	12/94	82r
Baby food, strained vegetables, lowest price	4-4.5 oz.	0.34	12/94	2c
Bacon, sliced	lb.	2.24	12/94	82r
Bananas	lb.	0.40	12/94	2c
Bananas	lb.	0.49	12/94	82r
Beef or hamburger, ground	lb.	1.52	12/94	2c
Beef purchases	year	226	91	81r
Beverage purchases, alcoholic	year	332	91	81r
Beverage purchases, nonalcoholic	year	213	91	81r
Bread, white	24-oz.	0.93	12/94	2c
Bread, white, pan	lb.	0.80	12/94	82r
Butter, salted, Grade AA, stick	lb.	1.67	12/94	82r
Carrots, short trimmed and topped	lb.	0.51	12/94	82r
Cereals and bakery products purchases	year	407	91	81r
Cereals and cereals products purchases	year	132	91	81r
Cheese, Kraft grated Parmesan	8-oz.	3.11	12/94	2c
Chicken breast, bone-in	lb.	2.22	12/94	82r
Chicken, fresh, whole	lb.	1.05	12/94	82r
Chicken, whole fryer	lb.	0.93	12/94	2c
Chuck roast, USDA choice, boneless	lb.	2.74	12/94	82r
Cigarettes, Winston, Kings	carton	18.59	12/94	2c
Coffee, 100%, ground roast, all sizes	lb.	4.61	12/94	82r
Coffee, vacuum-packed	13 oz.	3.42	12/94	2c
Corn Flakes, Kellogg's or Post Toasties	18 oz.	2.32	12/94	2c
Corn, frozen, whole kernel, lowest price	10 oz.	0.67	12/94	2c
Dairy products (other) purchases	year	161	91	81r
Eggs, Grade A large	dozen	0.81	12/94	2c
Eggs, Grade A large	dozen	1.12	12/94	82r
Fish and seafood purchases	year	112	91	81r

Values are in dollars or fractions of dollars. In the column headed *Ref*, references are shown to sources. Each reference is followed by a letter. These refer to the geographical level for which data were reported: s=State, r=Region, and c=City or metro. The abbreviation *ex* is used to mean *except* or *excluding*; *exp* stands for expenditures. For other abbreviations and further explanations, please see the Introduction.

9

Albany-Schenectady-Troy, NY - continued

Item	Per	Value	Date	Ref.
Groceries				
Food purchases, food eaten at home	year	2599	91	81r
Foods purchased away from home, not prepared by consumer	year	2024	91	81r
Fruits and vegetables purchases	year	444	91	81r
Grapefruit	lb.	0.44	12/94	82r
Grapes, Thompson seedless	lb.	2.24	12/94	82r
Ground chuck, 100% beef	lb.	1.67	12/94	82r
Ice cream, prepackaged, bulk, regular	1/2 gal.	2.93	12/94	82r
Lemons	lb.	1.06	12/94	82r
Lettuce, iceberg	lb.	0.92	12/94	82r
Lettuce, iceberg	head	0.91	12/94	2c
Margarine, Blue Bonnet or Parkay cubes	lb.	0.58	12/94	2c
Meats, poultry, fish, and eggs purchases	year	751	91	81r
Milk and cream (fresh) purchases	year	152	91	81r
Milk, whole	1/2 gal.	1.18	12/94	2c
Orange juice, frozen concentrate 12-oz. can	16 oz.	1.92	12/94	82r
Orange juice, Minute Maid frozen	12-oz.	1.13	12/94	2c
Oranges, Navel	lb.	0.56	12/94	82r
Peaches, halves or slices, Hunt's, Del Monte, or Libby's	29-oz.	1.53	12/94	2c
Peas, sweet, Del Monte or Green Giant	15-17 oz.	0.52	12/94	2c
Pork chops, center cut, bone-in	lb.	3.09	12/94	82r
Pork purchases	year	130	91	81r
Potatoes, white	lb.	0.37	12/94	82r
Potatoes, white or red	10-lb. sack	2.79	12/94	2c
Rib roast, USDA choice, bone-in	lb.	4.98	12/94	82r
Round roast, USDA choice, boneless	lb.	2.93	12/94	82r
Sausage, Jimmy Dean, 100% pork	lb.	2.84	12/94	2c
Shortening, vegetable oil blends	lb.	1.03	12/94	82r
Shortening, vegetable, Crisco	3-lb.	2.61	12/94	2c
Soft drink, Coca Cola, ex deposit	2 lit	1.33	12/94	2c
Spaghetti and macaroni	lb.	0.84	12/94	82r
Steak, round, USDA choice, boneless	lb.	3.48	12/94	82r
Steak, sirloin, USDA choice, bone-in	lb.	3.38	12/94	82r
Steak, sirloin, USDA choice, boneless	lb.	4.81	12/94	82r
Steak, t-bone	lb.	5.43	12/94	2c
Sugar and other sweets, eaten at home, expenditures	year	89	91	81r
Sugar, cane or beet	4 lbs.	1.41	12/94	2c
Sugar, white, all sizes	lb.	0.46	12/94	82r
Tobacco products and smoking supplies, total expenditures	year	279	91	81r
Tomatoes, field grown	lb.	1.56	12/94	82r
Tomatoes, Hunt's or Del Monte	14.5 oz.	0.78	12/94	2c
Tuna, chunk, light	lb.	2.09	12/94	82r
Tuna, chunk, light, oil-packed	6.125-6.5 oz.	0.77	12/94	2c
Goods and Services				
Miscellaneous goods and services, ACCRA Index		108.50	12/94	2c
Health Care				
Health care, ACCRA Index		104.10	12/94	2c
Antibiotic ointment, Polysporin	1.5 oz.	3.29	12/94	2c
Childbirth, Cesarean delivery, hospital charge	birth	6334.00	12/91	69r
Childbirth, Cesarean delivery, physician charge	birth	2234.00	12/91	69r
Childbirth, normal delivery, hospital charge	birth	3225.00	12/91	69r
Childbirth, normal delivery, physician charge	birth	1623.00	12/91	69r
Dentist's fee, adult teeth cleaning and periodic oral exam	visit	57.60	12/94	2c
Doctor's fee, routine exam, established patient	visit	48.00	12/94	2c
Drugs, expenditures	year	205	91	81r
Health care, total expenditures	year	1396	91	81r
Health insurance expenditures	year	553	91	81r

Albany-Schenectady-Troy, NY - continued

Item	Per	Value	Date	Ref.
Health Care - continued				
Hospital care, semiprivate room	day	311.60	12/94	2c
Insurance premium, family medical care	month	384.24	1/95	41s
Medical services expenditures	year	559	91	81r
Medical supplies expenditures	year	80	91	81r
Household Goods				
Appl. repair, service call, wash mach	min. lab. chg.	38.89	12/94	2c
Floor coverings, expenditures	year	158	91	81r
Furniture, expenditures	year	341	91	81r
Household equipment, misc. expenditures	year	363	91	81r
Household expenditures, miscellaneous	year	194	91	81r
Household furnishings and equipment, expenditures	year	1158	91	81r
Household operations expenditures	year	378	91	81r
Household textiles, expenditures	year	88	91	81r
Housekeeping supplies, expenditures	year	426	91	81r
Laundry and cleaning supplies, expenditures	year	122	91	81r
Laundry detergent, Tide Ultra, Bold, or Cheer	42 oz.	3.60	12/94	2c
Postage and stationery, expenditures	year	134	91	81r
Tissues, facial, Kleenex brand	175	1.03	12/94	2c
Housing				
Housing, ACCRA Index		93.30	12/94	2c
Add garage/carport		11,614	3/95	74r
Add room(s)		16,816	3/95	74r
Apartment condominium or co-op, median	unit	96700	12/94	62r
Dwellings (owned), expenditures	year	3305	91	81r
Enclose porch/patio/breezeway		2,980	3/95	74r
Finish room in basement/attic		4,330	3/95	74r
Home, existing, single-family, median	unit	161600	12/94	62r
Home, existing, single-family, median	unit	112.30	12/94	62c
House payment, principal and interest, 25% down payment	mo.	673	12/94	2c
House, 1800 sq ft, 8000 sq ft lot, new, urban, utilities	total	108793	12/94	2c
Maintenance, repairs, insurance, and other housing expenditures	year	569	91	81r
Mortgage interest and charges expenditures	year	1852	91	81r
Mtge. rate, incl. points and orig. fee, 30-year conv. fixed or ARM	mo.	9.27	12/94	2c
Princ. & int., mortgage, median-price exist. sing.-family home	mo.	765	12/94	62r
Property taxes expenditures	year	884	91	81r
Redesign, restructure more than half of home's interior		2,750	3/95	74r
Rent, apartment, 2 br., 1 1/2-2 baths, unfurnished, 950 sq ft, water	mo.	613	12/94	2c
Rental units expenditures	year	1832	91	81r
Insurance and Pensions				
Auto insurance, private passenger	year	985.07	12/94	71s
Insurance and pensions, personal, expenditures	year	2690	91	81r
Insurance, life and other personal, expenditures	year	341	91	81r
Pensions and Social Security, expenditures	year	2349	91	81r
Legal Assistance				
Estate planning, law-firm partner	hr.	375.00	10/93	12r
Legal work, law firm associate	hour	78		10r
Legal work, law firm partner	hour	183		10r
Personal Goods				
Shampoo, Alberto VO5	15-oz.	1.10	12/94	2c
Toothpaste, Crest or Colgate	6-7 oz.	1.65	12/94	2c
Personal Services				
Dry cleaning, man's 2-pc. suit		7.03	12/94	2c
Haircut, man's barbershop, no styling		8.50	12/94	2c
Haircut, woman's shampoo, trim, blow-dry		17.50	12/94	2c
Personal services expenditures	year	184	91	81r

Values are in dollars or fractions of dollars. In the column headed *Ref*, references are shown to sources. Each reference is followed by a letter. These refer to the geographical level for which data were reported: s = State, r = Region, and c = City or metro. The abbreviation *ex* is used to mean *except* or *excluding*; *exp* stands for expenditures. For other abbreviations and further explanations, please see the Introduction.

Albany-Schenectady-Troy, NY - continued

Item	Per	Value	Date	Ref.
Restaurant Food				
Chicken, fried, thigh and drumstick		2.50	12/94	2c
Dining expenditures, family	week	34.26	94	73r
Hamburger with cheese	1/4 lb.	1.97	12/94	2c
Pizza, Pizza Hut or Pizza Inn	12-13 in.	8.75	12/94	2c
Taxes				
Taxes, Federal income, expenditures	year	2409	91	81r
Taxes, personal, expenditures	year	3094	91	81r
Taxes, State and local income, expenditures	year	620	91	81r
Transportation				
Transportation, ACCRA Index		109.90	12/94	2c
Bus fare, one-way	trip	0.75	12/95	1c
Bus fare, up to 10 miles	one-way	0.75	12/94	2c
Cars and trucks purchased, new	year	1170	91	81r
Cars and trucks purchased, used	year	739	91	81r
Driver's learning permit fee	perm	10.00	1/94	84s
Driver's license fee	orig	32.00-37.00	1/94	84s
Driver's license fee, duplicate	lic	7.25	1/94	84s
Driver's license reinstatement fee, min.	susp	25.00	1/94	85s
Driver's license renewal fee	renew	22.25	1/94	84s
Identification card, nondriver	card	6.25	1/94	83s
Motorcycle license fee	orig	32.00-37.00	1/94	84s
Motorcycle license fee, duplicate	lic	7.25	1/94	84s
Motorcycle license renewal fee	renew	22.25	1/94	84s
Public transportation expenditures	year	430	91	81r
Tire balance, computer or spin bal., front	wheel	8.15	12/94	2c
Transportation expenditures, total	year	4810	91	81r
Vehicle finance charges	year	238	91	81r
Vehicle insurance expenditures	year	630	91	81r
Vehicle maintenance and repairs expenditures	year	532	91	81r
Vehicle purchases	year	1920	91	81r
Vehicle rental, leases, licenses, etc. expenditures	year	193	91	81r
Vehicles purchased, other than cars and trucks	year	11	91	81r
Utilities				
Utilities, ACCRA Index		153.00	12/94	2c
Electricity expenditures	year	695	91	81r
Electricity, (part.), other, 1800 sq. ft., new home	mo.	96.61	12/94	2c
Utilities, fuels, and public services, total expenditures	year	1981	91	81r
Water and other public services, expenditures	year	154	91	81r
Weddings				
Bridal attendants' gowns	event	750	10/93	76r
Bridal gown	event	852	10/93	76r
Bridal headpiece and veil	event	167	10/93	76r
Bride's wedding band	event	708	10/93	76r
Clergy	event	224	10/93	76r
Engagement ring	event	2756	10/93	76r
Flowers	event	863	10/93	76r
Formal wear for groom	event	106	10/93	76r
Groom's attendants' formal wear	event	530	10/93	76r
Groom's wedding band	event	402	10/93	76r
Music	event	600	10/93	76r
Photography	event	1088	10/93	76r
Shoes for bride	event	50	10/93	76r
Videography	event	483	10/93	76r
Wedding invitations and announcements	event	342	10/93	76r
Wedding reception	event	7000	10/93	76r

Albemarle, NC

Item	Per	Value	Date	Ref.
Composite, ACCRA index		89.80	12/94	2c
Alcoholic Beverages				
Beer, Miller Lite, Bud, 12-oz., ex deposit	6	3.53	12/94	2c
J & B Scotch	750-ml.	18.60	12/94	2c
Wine, Gallo Chablis blanc	1.5-lit	4.29	12/94	2c
Clothing				
Jeans, man's denim		21.99	12/94	2c
Shirt, man's dress shirt		35.75	12/94	2c
Undervest, boy's size 10-14, cotton	3	2.99	12/94	2c
Communications				
Newspaper subscription, dly. and Sun. delivery	month	9.75	12/94	2c
Telephone bill, family of four	month	14.82	12/94	2c
Energy and Fuels				
Energy, combined forms, 1800 sq. ft.	mo.	109.31	12/94	2c
Energy, exc. electricity, 1800 sq. ft.	mo.	45.88	12/94	2c
Gas, reg unlead, taxes inc., cash, self-service	gal	1.07	12/94	2c
Entertainment				
Bowling, evening rate	game	1.85	12/94	2c
Monopoly game, Parker Brothers', No. 9	game	11.26	12/94	2c
Movie	adm	5.25	12/94	2c
Tennis balls, yellow, Wilson or Penn, 3	can	2.15	12/94	2c
Groceries				
Groceries, ACCRA Index		96.20	12/94	2c
Baby food, strained vegetables, lowest price	4-4.5 oz.	0.35	12/94	2c
Bananas	lb.	0.45	12/94	2c
Beef or hamburger, ground	lb.	1.46	12/94	2c
Bread, white	24-oz.	0.70	12/94	2c
Cheese, Kraft grated Parmesan	8-oz.	3.19	12/94	2c
Chicken, whole fryer	lb.	0.80	12/94	2c
Cigarettes, Winston, Kings	carton	12.17	12/94	2c
Coffee, vacuum-packed	13 oz.	3.51	12/94	2c
Corn Flakes, Kellogg's or Post Toasties	18 oz.	2.30	12/94	2c
Corn, frozen, whole kernel, lowest price	10 oz.	0.65	12/94	2c
Eggs, Grade A large	dozen	0.84	12/94	2c
Lettuce, iceberg	head	0.99	12/94	2c
Margarine, Blue Bonnet or Parkay cubes	lb.	0.62	12/94	2c
Milk, whole	1/2 gal.	1.48	12/94	2c
Orange juice, Minute Maid frozen	12-oz.	1.10	12/94	2c
Peaches, halves or slices, Hunt's, Del Monte, or Libby's	29-oz.	1.26	12/94	2c
Peas, sweet, Del Monte or Green Giant	15-17 oz.	0.49	12/94	2c
Potatoes, white or red	10-lb. sack	2.54	12/94	2c
Sausage, Jimmy Dean, 100% pork	lb.	2.29	12/94	2c
Shortening, vegetable, Crisco	3-lb.	2.49	12/94	2c
Soft drink, Coca Cola, ex deposit	2 lit	1.26	12/94	2c
Steak, t-bone	lb.	4.92	12/94	2c
Sugar, cane or beet	4 lbs.	1.46	12/94	2c
Tomatoes, Hunt's or Del Monte	14.5 oz.	0.55	12/94	2c
Tuna, chunk, light, oil-packed	6.125-6.5 oz.	0.64	12/94	2c
Goods and Services				
Miscellaneous goods and services, ACCRA Index		94.10	12/94	2c
Health Care				
Health care, ACCRA Index		92.90	12/94	2c
Antibiotic ointment, Polysporin	1.5 oz.	3.77	12/94	2c
Dentist's fee, adult teeth cleaning and periodic oral exam	visit	48.00	12/94	2c
Doctor's fee, routine exam, established patient	visit	40.41	12/94	2c
Hospital care, semiprivate room	day	319.00	12/94	2c

Values are in dollars or fractions of dollars. In the column headed *Ref*, references are shown to sources. Each reference is followed by a letter. These refer to the geographical level for which data were reported: s=State, r=Region, and c=City or metro. The abbreviation *ex* is used to mean *except* or *excluding*; *exp* stands for *expenditures*. For other abbreviations and further explanations, please see the Introduction.

Albemarle, NC - continued

Item	Per	Value	Date	Ref.
Household Goods				
Appl. repair, service call, wash mach	min. lab. chg.	31.67	12/94	2c
Laundry detergent, Tide Ultra, Bold, or Cheer	42 oz.	2.89	12/94	2c
Tissues, facial, Kleenex brand	175	0.96	12/94	2c
Housing				
Housing, ACCRA Index		82.20	12/94	2c
House payment, principal and interest, 25% down payment	mo.	637	12/94	2c
House, 1800 sq ft, 8000 sq ft lot, new, urban, utilities	total	103758	12/94	2c
Mtge. rate, incl. points and orig. fee, 30-year conv. fixed or ARM	mo.	9.19	12/94	2c
Rent, apartment, 2 br., 1 1/2-2 baths, unfurnished, 950 sq ft, water	mo.	414	12/94	2c
Personal Goods				
Shampoo, Alberto VO5	15-oz.	0.98	12/94	2c
Toothpaste, Crest or Colgate	6-7 oz.	1.77	12/94	2c
Personal Services				
Dry cleaning, man's 2-pc. suit		5.75	12/94	2c
Haircut, man's barbershop, no styling		7.00	12/94	2c
Haircut, woman's shampoo, trim, blow-dry		18.00	12/94	2c
Restaurant Food				
Chicken, fried, thigh and drumstick		2.29	12/94	2c
Hamburger with cheese	1/4 lb.	1.89	12/94	2c
Pizza, Pizza Hut or Pizza Inn	12-13 in.	7.75	12/94	2c
Transportation				
Transportation, ACCRA Index		79.90	12/94	2c
Tire balance, computer or spin bal., front	wheel	4.00	12/94	2c
Utilities				
Utilities, ACCRA Index		94.50	12/94	2c
Electricity, (part.), other, 1800 sq. ft., new home	mo.	63.43	12/94	2c

Albuquerque, NM

Item	Per	Value	Date	Ref.
Composite, ACCRA index		103.40	12/94	2c
Alcoholic Beverages				
Beer, Miller Lite, Bud, 12-oz., ex deposit	6	4.01	12/94	2c
J & B Scotch	750-ml.	17.89	12/94	2c
Wine, Gallo Chablis blanc	1.5-lit	5.49	12/94	2c
Appliances				
Appliances (major), expenditures	year	160	91	81r
Average annual exp.				
Food, health care, personal goods, services	year	32461	91	81r
Charity				
Cash contributions, expenditures	year	975	91	81r
Clothing				
Apparel, men and boys, total expenditures	year	467	91	81r
Apparel, women and girls, total expenditures	year	737	91	81r
Footwear, expenditures	year	270	91	81r
Jeans, man's denim		29.56	12/94	2c
Shirt, man's dress shirt		27.96	12/94	2c
Undervest, boy's size 10-14, cotton	3	4.89	12/94	2c
Communications				
Long-distance telephone rate, day, addl. min., 1-10 mi.	min.	0.11	12/93	9s
Long-distance telephone rate, day, initial min., 1-10 mi.	min.	0.19	12/93	9s
Newspaper subscription, dly. and Sun. delivery	month	10.25	12/94	2c
Phone line, single, business, field visit	inst	53.95	12/93	9s

Albuquerque, NM - continued

Item	Per	Value	Date	Ref.
Communications - continued				
Phone line, single, business, no field visit	inst	53.95	12/93	9s
Phone line, single, residence, field visit	inst	30.00	12/93	9s
Phone line, single, residence, no field visit	inst	30.00	12/93	9s
Telephone bill, family of four	month	22.18	12/94	2c
Telephone service, expenditures	year	611	91	81r
Telephone, residential, flat rate	mo.	15.53	12/93	8c
Education				
Board, 4-year private college/university	year	2285	8/94	80s
Board, 4-year public college/university	year	1798	8/94	80s
Education, total expenditures	year	375	91	81r
Room, 4-year private college/university	year	2091	8/94	80s
Room, 4-year public college/university	year	1565	8/94	80s
Total cost, 4-year private college/university	year	14552	8/94	80s
Total cost, 4-year public college/university	year	5094	8/94	80s
Tuition, 2-year public college/university, in-state	year	625	8/94	80s
Tuition, 4-year private college/university, in-state	year	10176	8/94	80s
Tuition, 4-year public college/university, in-state	year	1731	8/94	80s
Energy and Fuels				
Energy, combined forms, 1800 sq. ft.	mo.	105.50	12/94	2c
Energy, exc. electricity, 1800 sq. ft.	mo.	39.80	12/94	2c
Fuel oil and other fuels, expenditures	year	33	91	81r
Gas, cooking, winter, 10 therms	month	13.23	2/94	65c
Gas, cooking, winter, 30 therms	month	21.73	2/94	65c
Gas, cooking, winter, 50 therms	month	30.22	2/94	65c
Gas, heating, winter, 100 therms	month	51.42	2/94	65c
Gas, heating, winter, average use	month	38.69	2/94	65c
Gas, natural, expenditures	year	212	91	81r
Gas, reg unlead, taxes inc., cash, self-service	gal	1.20	12/94	2c
Gasoline and motor oil purchased	year	1115	91	81r
Gasoline, unleaded midgrade	gallon	1.36	4/93	82r
Gasoline, unleaded premium	gallon	1.43	4/93	82r
Gasoline, unleaded regular	gallon	1.23	4/93	82r
Entertainment				
Bowling, evening rate	game	2.07	12/94	2c
Concert ticket, Pearl Jam group	perf	20.00	94	50r
Entertainment, total expenditures	year	1853	91	81r
Fees and admissions, expenditures	year	482	91	81r
Monopoly game, Parker Brothers', No. 9	game	11.14	12/94	2c
Movie	adm	5.90	12/94	2c
Pets, toys, playground equipment, expenditures	year	299	91	81r
Reading, expenditures	year	164	91	81r
Televisions, radios, and sound equipment, expenditures	year	528	91	81r
Tennis balls, yellow, Wilson or Penn, 3	can	2.72	12/94	2c
Funerals				
Burial, immediate, container provided by funeral home		1360.49	1/95	54r
Cards, acknowledgment		11.24	1/95	54r
Casket, minimum alternative		232.73	1/95	54r
Cosmetology, hair care, etc.		114.13	1/95	54r
Cremation, direct, container provided by funeral home		1027.08	1/95	54r
Embalming		286.24	1/95	54r
Funeral, funeral home		315.60	1/95	54r
Funeral, other facility		303.08	1/95	54r
Graveside service		423.83	1/95	54r
Hearse, local		133.12	1/95	54r
Limousine, local		99.10	1/95	54r
Memorial service		442.57	1/95	54r
Service charge, professional, nondeclinable		840.16	1/95	54r
Visitation and viewing		168.50	1/95	54r
Groceries				
Groceries, ACCRA Index		97.70	12/94	2c
Apples, Red Delicious	lb.	0.72	12/94	82r

Values are in dollars or fractions of dollars. In the column headed *Ref*, references are shown to sources. Each reference is followed by a letter. These refer to the geographical level for which data were reported: s = State, r = Region, and c = City or metro. The abbreviation *ex* is used to mean *except* or *excluding*; *exp* stands for *expenditures*. For other abbreviations and further explanations, please see the Introduction.

Albuquerque, NM - continued

Item	Per	Value	Date	Ref.
Groceries				
Baby food, strained vegetables, lowest price	4-4.5 oz.	0.30	12/94	2c
Bacon, sliced	lb.	1.73	12/94	82r
Bananas	lb.	0.43	12/94	2c
Bananas	lb.	0.52	12/94	82r
Beef or hamburger, ground	lb.	1.03	12/94	2c
Beef purchases	year	241	91	81r
Beverage purchases, alcoholic	year	328	91	81r
Beverage purchases, nonalcoholic	year	234	91	81r
Bologna, all beef or mixed	lb.	2.33	12/94	82r
Bread, white	24-oz.	0.71	12/94	2c
Bread, white, pan	lb.	0.81	12/94	82r
Carrots, short trimmed and topped	lb.	0.43	12/94	82r
Cereals and bakery products purchases	year	392	91	81r
Cereals and cereals products purchases	year	139	91	81r
Cheese, Kraft grated Parmesan	8-oz.	3.99	12/94	2c
Chicken breast, bone-in	lb.	2.04	12/94	82r
Chicken, fresh, whole	lb.	0.95	12/94	82r
Chicken, whole fryer	lb.	0.68	12/94	2c
Cigarettes, Winston, Kings	carton	14.67	12/94	2c
Coffee, 100%, ground roast, all sizes	lb.	4.48	12/94	82r
Coffee, vacuum-packed	13 oz.	3.57	12/94	2c
Corn Flakes, Kellogg's or Post Toasties	18 oz.	2.42	12/94	2c
Corn, frozen, whole kernel, lowest price	10 oz.	0.86	12/94	2c
Dairy products (other) purchases	year	182	91	81r
Eggs, Grade A large	dozen	0.74	12/94	2c
Fish and seafood purchases	year	94	91	81r
Flour, white, all purpose	lb.	0.21	12/94	82r
Food purchases, food eaten at home	year	2749	91	81r
Foods purchased away from home, not prepared by consumer	year	1909	91	81r
Fruits and vegetables purchases	year	459	91	81r
Grapefruit	lb.	0.56	12/94	82r
Ground beef, 100% beef	lb.	1.31	12/94	82r
Ham, boneless, exc. canned	lb.	2.46	12/94	82r
Ice cream, prepackaged, bulk, regular	1/2 gal.	2.57	12/94	82r
Lemons	lb.	1.00	12/94	82r
Lettuce, iceberg	lb.	0.93	12/94	82r
Lettuce, iceberg	head	0.69	12/94	2c
Margarine, Blue Bonnet or Parkay cubes	lb.	0.74	12/94	2c
Meats, poultry, fish, and eggs purchases	year	700	91	81r
Milk and cream (fresh) purchases	year	155	91	81r
Milk, whole	1/2 gal.	1.54	12/94	2c
Orange juice, frozen concentrate 12-oz. can	16 oz.	1.52	12/94	82r
Orange juice, Minute Maid frozen	12-oz.	1.13	12/94	2c
Oranges, Navel	lb.	0.56	12/94	82r
Peaches, halves or slices, Hunt's, Del Monte, or Libby's	29-oz.	1.37	12/94	2c
Peas, sweet, Del Monte or Green Giant	15-17 oz.	0.51	12/94	2c
Pork chops, center cut, bone-in	lb.	3.30	12/94	82r
Pork purchases	year	122	91	81r
Potato chips	16-oz.	3.03	12/94	82r
Potatoes, frozen, French fried	lb.	0.77	12/94	82r
Potatoes, white	lb.	0.35	12/94	82r
Potatoes, white or red	10-lb. sack	2.27	12/94	2c
Rice, white, long grain, uncooked	lb.	0.54	12/94	82r
Round roast, USDA choice, boneless	lb.	2.92	12/94	82r
Sausage, Jimmy Dean, 100% pork	lb.	2.43	12/94	2c
Shortening, vegetable oil blends	lb.	0.80	12/94	82r
Shortening, vegetable, Crisco	3-lb.	3.02	12/94	2c
Soft drink, Coca Cola, ex deposit	2 lit	0.86	12/94	2c
Spaghetti and macaroni	lb.	1.02	12/94	82r
Steak, round, graded & ungraded, exc. USDA prime & choice	lb.	3.13	12/94	82r
Steak, sirloin, USDA choice, boneless	lb.	4.07	12/94	82r
Steak, t-bone	lb.	4.49	12/94	2c
Sugar and other sweets, eaten at home, expenditures	year	105	91	81r

Albuquerque, NM - continued

Item	Per	Value	Date	Ref.
Groceries - continued				
Sugar, cane or beet	4 lbs.	1.76	12/94	2c
Sugar, white, all sizes	lb.	0.38	12/94	82r
Tobacco products and smoking supplies, total expenditures	year	221	91	81r
Tomatoes, field grown	lb.	1.45	12/94	82r
Tomatoes, Hunt's or Del Monte	14.5 oz.	0.73	12/94	2c
Tuna, chunk, light	lb.	2.18	12/94	82r
Tuna, chunk, light, oil-packed	6.125-6.5 oz.	0.84	12/94	2c
Goods and Services				
Miscellaneous goods and services, ACCRA Index		102.30	12/94	2c
Health Care				
Health care, ACCRA Index		113.50	12/94	2c
Antibiotic ointment, Polysporin	1.5 oz.	4.43	12/94	2c
Childbirth, Cesarean delivery, hospital charge	birth	6059.00	12/91	69r
Childbirth, Cesarean delivery, physician charge	birth	2248.00	12/91	69r
Childbirth, normal delivery, hospital charge	birth	3006.00	12/91	69r
Childbirth, normal delivery, physician charge	birth	1634.00	12/91	69r
Dentist's fee, adult teeth cleaning and periodic oral exam	visit	67.80	12/94	2c
Doctor's fee, routine exam, established patient	visit	45.55	12/94	2c
Drugs, expenditures	year	230	91	81r
Health care, total expenditures	year	1544	91	81r
Health insurance expenditures	year	558	91	81r
Hospital care, semiprivate room	day	344.00	12/94	2c
Insurance premium, family medical care	month	331.96	1/95	41s
Medical services expenditures	year	676	91	81r
Medical supplies expenditures	year	80	91	81r
Surgery, open-heart	proc	37818.00	1/93	14r
Household Goods				
Appl. repair, service call, wash mach	min. lab. chg.	39.18	12/94	2c
Floor coverings, expenditures	year	79	91	81r
Furniture, expenditures	year	352	91	81r
Household equipment, misc. expenditures	year	614	91	81r
Household expenditures, miscellaneous	year	294	91	81r
Household furnishings and equipment, expenditures	year	1416	91	81r
Household operations expenditures	year	580	91	81r
Household textiles, expenditures	year	113	91	81r
Housekeeping supplies, expenditures	year	447	91	81r
Laundry and cleaning supplies, expenditures	year	114	91	81r
Laundry detergent, Tide Ultra, Bold, or Cheer	42 oz.	3.55	12/94	2c
Postage and stationery, expenditures	year	145	91	81r
Tissues, facial, Kleenex brand	175	1.05	12/94	2c
Housing				
Housing, ACCRA Index		108.50	12/94	2c
Add garage/carport		6,422	3/95	74r
Add room(s)		26,583	3/95	74r
Apartment condominium or co-op, median	unit	105300	12/94	62r
Dwellings (owned), expenditures	year	3932	91	81r
Enclose porch/patio/breezeway		5,382	3/95	74r
Finish room in basement/attic		3,911	3/95	74r
Home, existing, single-family, median	unit	178600	12/94	62r
Home, existing, single-family, median	unit	114.50	12/94	62c
House payment, principal and interest, 25% down payment	mo.	806	12/94	2c
House, 1800 sq ft, 8000 sq ft lot, new, urban, utilities	total	130450	12/94	2c
Maintenance, repairs, insurance, and other housing expenditures	year	591	91	81r
Mortgage interest and charges expenditures	year	2747	91	81r

Values are in dollars or fractions of dollars. In the column headed *Ref*, references are shown to sources. Each reference is followed by a letter. These refer to the geographical level for which data were reported: s=State, r=Region, and c=City or metro. The abbreviation *ex* is used to mean *except* or *excluding*; *exp* stands for *expenditures*. For other abbreviations and further explanations, please see the Introduction.

Albuquerque, NM - continued

Item	Per	Value	Date	Ref.
Housing				
Mtge. rate, incl. points and orig. fee, 30-year conv. fixed or ARM	mo.	9.26	12/94	2c
Princ. & int., mortgage, median-price exist. sing.-family home	mo.	845	12/94	62r
Property taxes expenditures	year	594	91	81r
Redesign, restructure more than half of home's interior		5,467	3/95	74r
Rent, apartment, 2 br., 1 1/2-2 baths, unfurnished, 950 sq ft, water	mo.	645	12/94	2c
Rental units expenditures	year	2077	91	81r
Insurance and Pensions				
Auto insurance, private passenger	year	727.43	12/94	71s
Insurance and pensions, personal, expenditures	year	3042	91	81r
Insurance, life and other personal, expenditures	year	298	91	81r
Pensions and Social Security, expenditures	year	2744	91	81r
Legal Assistance				
Legal work, law firm associate	hour	91		10r
Legal work, law firm partner	hour	151		10r
Personal Goods				
Shampoo, Alberto VO5	15-oz.	1.33	12/94	2c
Toothpaste, Crest or Colgate	6-7 oz.	2.33	12/94	2c
Personal Services				
Dry cleaning, man's 2-pc. suit		6.30	12/94	2c
Haircut, man's barbershop, no styling		7.68	12/94	2c
Haircut, woman's shampoo, trim, blow-dry		18.45	12/94	2c
Personal services expenditures	year	286	91	81r
Restaurant Food				
Chicken, fried, thigh and drumstick		2.08	12/94	2c
Dining expenditures, family	week	32.25	94	73r
Hamburger with cheese	1/4 lb.	2.10	12/94	2c
Pizza, Pizza Hut or Pizza Inn	12-13 in.	8.28	12/94	2c
Taxes				
Tax rate, residential property, month	$100	1.04	1/92	79c
Taxes, Federal income, expenditures	year	2946	91	81r
Taxes, personal, expenditures	year	3791	91	81r
Taxes, State and local income, expenditures	year	791	91	81r
Transportation				
Transportation, ACCRA Index		101.30	12/94	2c
Bus fare, one-way	trip	0.75	12/95	1c
Bus fare, up to 10 miles	one-way	0.75	12/94	2c
Cars and trucks purchased, new	year	1231	91	81r
Cars and trucks purchased, used	year	915	91	81r
Driver's learning permit fee	perm	2.00	1/94	84s
Driver's license fee	orig	10.00	1/94	84s
Driver's license fee, duplicate	lic	10.00	1/94	84s
Driver's license reinstatement fee, min.	susp	25.00	1/94	85s
Driver's license renewal fee	renew	10.00	1/94	84s
Identification card, nondriver	card	5.00	1/94	83s
Motorcycle learning permit fee	perm	2.00	1/94	84s
Motorcycle license fee	orig	10.00	1/94	84s
Motorcycle license fee, duplicate	lic	10.00	1/94	84s
Motorcycle license renewal fee	renew	10.00	1/94	84s
Public transportation expenditures	year	375	91	81r
Tire balance, computer or spin bal., front	wheel	6.78	12/94	2c
Transportation expenditures, total	year	5527	91	81r
Vehicle finance charges	year	287	91	81r
Vehicle insurance expenditures	year	624	91	81r
Vehicle maintenance and repairs expenditures	year	695	91	81r
Vehicle purchases	year	2174	91	81r
Vehicle rental, leases, licenses, etc. expenditures	year	257	91	81r
Vehicles purchased, other than cars and trucks	year	28	91	81r

Albuquerque, NM - continued

Item	Per	Value	Date	Ref.
Utilities				
Utilities, ACCRA Index		96.70	12/94	2c
Electricity expenditures	year	616	91	81r
Electricity, (part.), other, 1800 sq. ft., new home	mo.	65.70	12/94	2c
Electricity, summer, 250 KWh	month	25.21	8/93	64c
Electricity, summer, 500 KWh	month	49.07	8/93	64c
Electricity, summer, 750 KWh	month	72.93	8/93	64c
Electricity, summer, 1000 KWh	month	96.79	8/93	64c
Utilities, fuels, and public services, total expenditures	year	1681	91	81r
Water and other public services, expenditures	year	209	91	81r
Weddings				
Bridal attendants' gowns	event	750	10/93	76r
Bridal gown	event	852	10/93	76r
Bridal headpiece and veil	event	167	10/93	76r
Bride's wedding band	event	708	10/93	76r
Clergy	event	224	10/93	76r
Engagement ring	event	2756	10/93	76r
Flowers	event	863	10/93	76r
Formal wear for groom	event	106	10/93	76r
Groom's attendants' formal wear	event	530	10/93	76r
Groom's wedding band	event	402	10/93	76r
Music	event	600	10/93	76r
Photography	event	1088	10/93	76r
Shoes for bride	event	50	10/93	76r
Videography	event	483	10/93	76r
Wedding invitations and announcements	event	342	10/93	76r
Wedding reception	event	7000	10/93	76r

Alexandria, LA

Item	Per	Value	Date	Ref.
Composite, ACCRA index		90.40	12/94	2c
Alcoholic Beverages				
Beer, Miller Lite, Bud, 12-oz., ex deposit	6	3.80	12/94	2c
J & B Scotch	750-ml.	15.91	12/94	2c
Wine, Gallo Chablis blanc	1.5-lit	4.13	12/94	2c
Appliances				
Appliances (major), expenditures	year	153	91	81r
Average annual exp.				
Food, health care, personal goods, services	year	27020	91	81r
Charity				
Cash contributions, expenditures	year	839	91	81r
Clothing				
Apparel, men and boys, total expenditures	year	380	91	81r
Apparel, women and girls, total expenditures	year	660	91	81r
Footwear, expenditures	year	193	91	81r
Jeans, man's denim		27.97	12/94	2c
Shirt, man's dress shirt		33.98	12/94	2c
Undervest, boy's size 10-14, cotton	3	3.56	12/94	2c
Communications				
Long-distance telephone rate, day, addl. min., 1-10 mi.	min.	0.29	12/93	9s
Long-distance telephone rate, day, initial min., 1-10 mi.	min.	0.41	12/93	9s
Newspaper subscription, dly. and Sun. delivery	month	10.50	12/94	2c
Phone line, single, business, field visit	inst	85.00	12/93	9s
Phone line, single, business, no field visit	inst	85.00	12/93	9s
Phone line, single, residence, field visit	inst	50.00	12/93	9s
Phone line, single, residence, no field visit	inst	50.00	12/93	9s
Telephone bill, family of four	month	20.86	12/94	2c
Telephone service, expenditures	year	616	91	81r
Telephone, residential, flat rate	mo.	12.64	12/93	8c

Values are in dollars or fractions of dollars. In the column headed *Ref*, references are shown to sources. Each reference is followed by a letter. These refer to the geographical level for which data were reported: s = State, r = Region, and c = City or metro. The abbreviation *ex* is used to mean *except* or *excluding*; *exp* stands for expenditures. For other abbreviations and further explanations, please see the Introduction.

Alexandria, LA - continued

Item	Per	Value	Date	Ref.
Education				
Board, 4-year private college/university	year	2436	8/94	80s
Board, 4-year public college/university	year	1638	8/94	80s
Education, total expenditures	year	319	91	81r
Room, 4-year private college/university	year	2558	8/94	80s
Room, 4-year public college/university	year	1405	8/94	80s
Total cost, 4-year private college/university	year	16467	8/94	80s
Total cost, 4-year public college/university	year	5225	8/94	80s
Tuition, 2-year public college/university, in-state	year	956	8/94	80s
Tuition, 4-year private college/university, in-state	year	11473	8/94	80s
Tuition, 4-year public college/university, in-state	year	2182	8/94	80s
Energy and Fuels				
Energy, combined forms, 1800 sq. ft.	mo.	96.08	12/94	2c
Fuel oil and other fuels, expenditures	year	56	91	81r
Gas, natural, expenditures	year	150	91	81r
Gas, reg unlead, taxes inc., cash, self-service	gal	1.08	12/94	2c
Gasoline and motor oil purchased	year	1152	91	81r
Gasoline, unleaded midgrade	gallon	1.21	4/93	82r
Gasoline, unleaded premium	gallon	1.30	4/93	82r
Gasoline, unleaded regular	gallon	1.10	4/93	82r
Entertainment				
Bowling, evening rate	game	2.30	12/94	2c
Concert ticket, Pearl Jam group	perf	20.00	94	50r
Entertainment, total expenditures	year	1266	91	81r
Fees and admissions, expenditures	year	306	91	81r
Monopoly game, Parker Brothers', No. 9	game	10.17	12/94	2c
Movie	adm	5.50	12/94	2c
Pets, toys, playground equipment, expenditures	year	271	91	81r
Reading, expenditures	year	131	91	81r
Televisions, radios, and sound equipment, expenditures	year	439	91	81r
Tennis balls, yellow, Wilson or Penn, 3	can	2.60	12/94	2c
Funerals				
Burial, immediate, container provided by funeral home		1574.60	1/95	54r
Cards, acknowledgment		22.24	1/95	54r
Casket, minimum alternative		239.41	1/95	54r
Cosmetology, hair care, etc.		91.04	1/95	54r
Cremation, direct, container provided by funeral home		1085.15	1/95	54r
Embalming		281.30	1/95	54r
Funeral, funeral home		323.04	1/95	54r
Funeral, other facility		327.58	1/95	54r
Graveside service		355.19	1/95	54r
Hearse, local		141.89	1/95	54r
Limousine, local		99.40	1/95	54r
Memorial service		284.67	1/95	54r
Service charge, professional, nondeclinable		904.06	1/95	54r
Visitation and viewing		187.04	1/95	54r
Groceries				
Groceries, ACCRA Index		96.80	12/94	2c
Apples, Red Delicious	lb.	0.73	12/94	82r
Baby food, strained vegetables, lowest price	4-4.5 oz.	0.27	12/94	2c
Bacon, sliced	lb.	1.67	12/94	82r
Bananas	lb.	0.38	12/94	2c
Bananas	lb.	0.42	12/94	82r
Beef or hamburger, ground	lb.	1.48	12/94	2c
Beef purchases	year	213	91	81r
Beverage purchases, alcoholic	year	249	91	81r
Beverage purchases, nonalcoholic	year	207	91	81r
Bologna, all beef or mixed	lb.	2.27	12/94	82r
Bread, white	24-oz.	0.77	12/94	2c
Bread, white, pan	lb.	0.68	12/94	82r
Cabbage	lb.	0.42	12/94	82r
Carrots, short trimmed and topped	lb.	0.53	12/94	82r

Item	Per	Value	Date	Ref.
Groceries - continued				
Cereals and bakery products purchases	year	345	91	81r
Cereals and cereals products purchases	year	127	91	81r
Cheddar cheese, natural	lb.	3.58	12/94	82r
Cheese, Kraft grated Parmesan	8-oz.	3.59	12/94	2c
Chicken breast, bone-in	lb.	1.71	12/94	82r
Chicken, fresh, whole	lb.	0.78	12/94	82r
Chicken, whole fryer	lb.	0.76	12/94	2c
Chuck roast, USDA choice, boneless	lb.	2.26	12/94	82r
Cigarettes, Winston, Kings	carton	15.04	12/94	2c
Coffee, vacuum-packed	13 oz.	3.52	12/94	2c
Corn Flakes, Kellogg's or Post Toasties	18 oz.	2.23	12/94	2c
Corn, frozen, whole kernel, lowest price	10 oz.	0.78	12/94	2c
Crackers, soda, salted	lb.	1.27	12/94	82r
Cucumbers	lb.	0.65	12/94	82r
Dairy products (other) purchases	year	141	91	81r
Eggs, Grade A large	dozen	0.74	12/94	2c
Eggs, Grade A large	dozen	0.87	12/94	82r
Fish and seafood purchases	year	72	91	81r
Flour, white, all purpose	lb.	0.23	12/94	82r
Food purchases, food eaten at home	year	2381	91	81r
Foods purchased away from home, not prepared by consumer	year	1696	91	81r
Frankfurters, all meat or all beef	lb.	1.74	12/94	82r
Fruits and vegetables purchases	year	380	91	81r
Grapefruit	lb.	0.45	12/94	82r
Grapes, Thompson seedless	lb.	2.30	12/94	82r
Ground beef, 100% beef	lb.	1.37	12/94	82r
Ground chuck, 100% beef	lb.	1.97	12/94	82r
Ham, boneless, exc. canned	lb.	2.54	12/94	82r
Ice cream, prepackaged, bulk, regular	1/2 gal.	2.47	12/94	82r
Lemons	lb.	1.02	12/94	82r
Lettuce, iceberg	lb.	0.96	12/94	82r
Lettuce, iceberg	head	0.88	12/94	2c
Margarine, Blue Bonnet or Parkay cubes	lb.	0.57	12/94	2c
Margarine, stick	lb.	0.77	12/94	82r
Meats, poultry, fish, and eggs purchases	year	655	91	81r
Milk and cream (fresh) purchases	year	130	91	81r
Milk, whole	1/2 gal.	1.33	12/94	2c
Orange juice, frozen concentrate 12-oz. can	16 oz.	1.36	12/94	82r
Orange juice, Minute Maid frozen	12-oz.	1.26	12/94	2c
Oranges, Navel	lb.	0.54	12/94	82r
Peaches, halves or slices, Hunt's, Del Monte, or Libby's	29-oz.	1.41	12/94	2c
Pears, Anjou	lb.	0.81	12/94	82r
Peas, sweet, Del Monte or Green Giant	15-17 oz.	0.48	12/94	2c
Pork chops, center cut, bone-in	lb.	3.07	12/94	82r
Pork purchases	year	142	91	81r
Potato chips	16-oz.	3.15	12/94	82r
Potatoes, frozen, French fried	lb.	0.82	12/94	82r
Potatoes, white	lb.	0.34	12/94	82r
Potatoes, white or red	10-lb. sack	1.91	12/94	2c
Rice, white, long grain, uncooked	lb.	0.48	12/94	82r
Round roast, USDA choice, boneless	lb.	2.91	12/94	82r
Sausage, fresh	lb.	1.82	12/94	82r
Sausage, Jimmy Dean, 100% pork	lb.	2.28	12/94	2c
Shortening, vegetable oil blends	lb.	0.75	12/94	82r
Shortening, vegetable, Crisco	3-lb.	2.42	12/94	2c
Soft drink, Coca Cola, ex deposit	2 lit	1.03	12/94	2c
Spaghetti and macaroni	lb.	0.87	12/94	82r
Steak, rib eye, USDA choice, boneless	lb.	6.85	12/94	82r
Steak, round, graded & ungraded, exc. USDA prime & choice	lb.	2.96	12/94	82r
Steak, round, USDA choice, boneless	lb.	3.17	12/94	82r
Steak, sirloin, USDA choice, boneless	lb.	4.12	12/94	82r
Steak, t-bone	lb.	5.54	12/94	2c
Steak, T-bone, USDA choice, bone-in	lb.	5.63	12/94	82r
Sugar and other sweets, eaten at home, expenditures	year	93	91	81r

Values are in dollars or fractions of dollars. In the column headed *Ref*, references are shown to sources. Each reference is followed by a letter. These refer to the geographical level for which data were reported: s=State, r=Region, and c=City or metro. The abbreviation *ex* is used to mean *except* or *excluding*; *exp* stands for *expenditures*. For other abbreviations and further explanations, please see the Introduction.

Alexandria, LA - continued

Item	Per	Value	Date	Ref.
Groceries				
Sugar, cane or beet	4 lbs.	1.50	12/94	2c
Sugar, white, all sizes	lb.	0.39	12/94	82r
Tobacco products and smoking supplies, total expenditures	year	286	91	81r
Tomatoes, field grown	lb.	1.36	12/94	82r
Tomatoes, Hunt's or Del Monte	14.5 oz.	0.70	12/94	2c
Tuna, chunk, light	lb.	1.94	12/94	82r
Tuna, chunk, light, oil-packed	6.125-6.5 oz.	0.69	12/94	2c
Turkey, frozen, whole	lb.	0.96	12/94	82r
Yogurt, natural, fruit flavored	8 oz.	0.58	12/94	82r
Goods and Services				
Miscellaneous goods and services, ACCRA Index		95.20	12/94	2c
Health Care				
Health care, ACCRA Index		82.00	12/94	2c
Adenosine, emergency room	treat	100.00	95	23r
Antibiotic ointment, Polysporin	1.5 oz.	4.01	12/94	2c
Bladder tap, superpubic, infant, emergency room	treat	119.00	95	23r
Blood analysis, emergency room	treat	25.00	95	23r
Blood tests, abdominal pain, emergency room	treat	25.00	95	23r
Burn dressing, emergency room	treat	266.00	95	23r
Cardiology interpretation, emergency room	treat	26.00	95	23r
Chest X-ray, emergency room	treat	78.00	95	23r
Childbirth, Cesarean delivery, hospital charge	birth	5462.00	12/91	69r
Childbirth, Cesarean delivery, physician charge	birth	2228.00	12/91	69r
Childbirth, normal delivery, hospital charge	birth	2943.00	12/91	69r
Childbirth, normal delivery, physician charge	birth	1619.00	12/91	69r
Defibrillation pads, emergency room	treat	6.00	95	23r
Dentist's fee, adult teeth cleaning and periodic oral exam	visit	39.00	12/94	2c
Doctor's fee, routine exam, established patient	visit	38.00	12/94	2c
Drugs, expenditures	year	297	91	81r
Gastric tube insertion, nasal, emergency room	treat	25.00	95	23r
Health care, total expenditures	year	1600	91	81r
Health insurance expenditures	year	637	91	81r
Heart monitor, emergency room	treat	40.00	95	23r
Hospital care, semiprivate room	day	250.00	12/94	2c
Insurance premium, family medical care	month	394.31	1/95	41s
Intravenous fluids, emergency room	treat	130.00	95	23r
Intravenous fluids, emergency room	liter	26.00	95	23r
Intravenous line, central, emergency room	treat	342.00	95	23r
Liver function tests, abdominal pain, emergency room	treat	26.00	95	23r
Medical care charges, total, emergency room, third-degree burns	treat	2101.00	95	23r
Medical care charges, total, emergency, infant with fever	treat	628.00	95	23r
Medical services expenditures	year	573	91	81r
Medical supplies expenditures	year	93	91	81r
Morphine, emergency room	treat	34.00	95	23r
Nursing care and facilities charges, emergency room	treat	252.00	95	23r
Nursing care and facilities charges, emergency, infant with fever	treat	252.00	95	23r
Nursing care and facilities charges, emergency, third-degree burns	treat	861.00	95	23r
Physician's charges, emergency, infant with fever	treat	212.00	95	23r
Physician's charges, emergency, third-degree burns	treat	372.00	95	23r
Physician's fee, emergency room	treat	372.00	95	23r
Physician's fee, general practitioner	visit	51.20	12/93	60r
Surgery, open-heart	proc	42374.00	1/93	14r

Alexandria, LA - continued

Item	Per	Value	Date	Ref.
Health Care - continued				
Ultrasound, abdominal, emergency room	treat	276.00	95	23r
Urinalysis, emergency room	treat	20.00	95	23r
Urinalysis, infant, emergency room	treat	20.00	95	23r
X-rays, emergency room	treat	78.00	95	23r
Household Goods				
Appl. repair, service call, wash mach	min. lab. chg.	32.20	12/94	2c
Floor coverings, expenditures	year	48	91	81r
Furniture, expenditures	year	280	91	81r
Household equipment, misc. expenditures	year	342	91	81r
Household expenditures, miscellaneous	year	256	91	81r
Household furnishings and equipment, expenditures	year	988	91	81r
Household operations expenditures	year	468	91	81r
Household textiles, expenditures	year	95	91	81r
Housekeeping supplies, expenditures	year	380	91	81r
Laundry and cleaning supplies, expenditures	year	109	91	81r
Laundry detergent, Tide Ultra, Bold, or Cheer	42 oz.	3.66	12/94	2c
Postage and stationery, expenditures	year	105	91	81r
Tissues, facial, Kleenex brand	175	1.04	12/94	2c
Housing				
Housing, ACCRA Index		81.50	12/94	2c
Add garage/carport		6,980	3/95	74r
Add room(s)		11,403	3/95	74r
Apartment condominium or co-op, median	unit	68600	12/94	62r
Dwellings (owned), expenditures	year	2428	91	81r
Enclose porch/patio/breezeway		4,572	3/95	74r
Finish room in basement/attic		3,794	3/95	74r
Home, existing, single-family, median	unit	120200	12/94	62r
House payment, principal and interest, 25% down payment	mo.	622	12/94	2c
House, 1800 sq ft, 8000 sq ft lot, new, urban, utilities	total	99750	12/94	2c
Maintenance, repairs, insurance, and other housing expenditures	year	531	91	81r
Mortgage interest and charges expenditures	year	1506	91	81r
Mtge. rate, incl. points and orig. fee, 30-year conv. fixed or ARM	mo.	9.36	12/94	2c
Princ. & int., mortgage, median-price exist. sing.-family home	mo.	540	12/94	62r
Property taxes expenditures	year	391	91	81r
Redesign, restructure more than half of home's interior		17,641	3/95	74r
Rent, apartment, 2 br., 1 1/2-2 baths, unfurnished, 950 sq ft, water	mo.	437	12/94	2c
Rental units expenditures	year	1264	91	81r
Insurance and Pensions				
Auto insurance, private passenger	year	862.62	12/94	71s
Insurance and pensions, personal, expenditures	year	2395	91	81r
Insurance, life and other personal, expenditures	year	368	91	81r
Pensions and Social Security, expenditures	year	2027	91	81r
Personal Goods				
Shampoo, Alberto VO5	15-oz.	0.97	12/94	2c
Toothpaste, Crest or Colgate	6-7 oz.	1.52	12/94	2c
Personal Services				
Dry cleaning, man's 2-pc. suit		6.14	12/94	2c
Haircut, man's barbershop, no styling		7.20	12/94	2c
Haircut, woman's shampoo, trim, blow-dry		17.60	12/94	2c
Personal services expenditures	year	212	91	81r
Restaurant Food				
Chicken, fried, thigh and drumstick		1.92	12/94	2c
Dining expenditures, family	week	33.83	94	73r
Hamburger with cheese	1/4 lb.	1.89	12/94	2c

Values are in dollars or fractions of dollars. In the column headed *Ref*, references are shown to sources. Each reference is followed by a letter. These refer to the geographical level for which data were reported: s=State, r=Region, and c=City or metro. The abbreviation *ex* is used to mean *except* or *excluding*; *exp* stands for expenditures. For other abbreviations and further explanations, please see the Introduction.

Alexandria, LA - continued

Item	Per	Value	Date	Ref.
Restaurant Food				
Pizza, Pizza Hut or Pizza Inn	12-13 in.	6.50	12/94	2c
Taxes				
Taxes, Federal income, expenditures	year	2275	91	81r
Taxes, personal, expenditures	year	2715	91	81r
Taxes, State and local income, expenditures	year	365	91	81r
Transportation				
Transportation, ACCRA Index		96.50	12/94	2c
Cars and trucks purchased, new	year	1306	91	81r
Cars and trucks purchased, used	year	942	91	81r
Driver's learning permit fee	perm	12.50	1/94	84s
Driver's license fee	orig	12.50	1/94	84s
Driver's license fee, duplicate	lic	5.00	1/94	84s
Driver's license reinstatement fee, min.	susp	60.00	1/94	85s
Driver's license renewal fee	renew	12.50	1/94	84s
Identification card, nondriver	card	7.00	1/94	83s
Motorcycle license fee	orig	8.00	1/94	84s
Motorcycle license renewal fee	renew	8.00	1/94	84s
Public transportation expenditures	year	249	91	81r
Tire balance, computer or spin bal., front	wheel	6.60	12/94	2c
Transportation expenditures, total	year	5307	91	81r
Vehicle finance charges	year	346	91	81r
Vehicle insurance expenditures	year	544	91	81r
Vehicle maintenance and repairs expenditures	year	600	91	81r
Vehicle purchases	year	2275	91	81r
Vehicle rental, leases, licenses, etc. expenditures	year	141	91	81r
Vehicles purchased, other than cars and trucks	year	27	91	81r
Utilities				
Utilities, ACCRA Index		88.50	12/94	2c
Electricity expenditures	year	950	91	81r
Electricity, 1800 sq. ft., new home	mo.	96.08	12/94	2c
Utilities, fuels, and public services, total expenditures	year	2000	91	81r
Water and other public services, expenditures	year	227	91	81r
Weddings				
Bridal attendants' gowns	event	750	10/93	76r
Bridal gown	event	852	10/93	76r
Bridal headpiece and veil	event	167	10/93	76r
Bride's wedding band	event	708	10/93	76r
Clergy	event	224	10/93	76r
Engagement ring	event	2756	10/93	76r
Flowers	event	863	10/93	76r
Formal wear for groom	event	106	10/93	76r
Groom's attendants' formal wear	event	530	10/93	76r
Groom's wedding band	event	402	10/93	76r
Music	event	600	10/93	76r
Photography	event	1088	10/93	76r
Shoes for bride	event	50	10/93	76r
Videography	event	483	10/93	76r
Wedding invitations and announcements	event	342	10/93	76r
Wedding reception	event	7000	10/93	76r

Allentown-Bethlehem-Easton, PA, NJ

Item	Per	Value	Date	Ref.
Composite, ACCRA index		104.60	12/94	2c
Alcoholic Beverages				
Beer, Miller Lite, Bud, 12-oz., ex deposit	6	5.32	12/94	2c
J & B Scotch	750-ml.	16.99	12/94	2c
Wine, Gallo Chablis blanc	1.5-lit	5.99	12/94	2c
Appliances				
Appliances (major), expenditures	year	145	91	81r

Allentown-Bethlehem-Easton, PA, NJ - continued

Item	Per	Value	Date	Ref.
Average annual exp.				
Food, health care, personal goods, services	year	29496	91	81r
Charity				
Cash contributions, expenditures	year	708	91	81r
Clothing				
Apparel, men and boys, total expenditures	year	416	91	81r
Apparel, women and girls, total expenditures	year	744	91	81r
Footwear, expenditures	year	305	91	81r
Jeans, man's denim		34.63	12/94	2c
Shirt, man's dress shirt		28.49	12/94	2c
Undervest, boy's size 10-14, cotton	3	4.76	12/94	2c
Communications				
Long-distance telephone rate, day, addl. min., 1-10 mi.	min.	0.08	12/93	9s
Long-distance telephone rate, day, initial min., 1-10 mi.	min.	0.15	12/93	9s
Newspaper subscription, dly. and Sun. delivery	month	14.13	12/94	2c
Phone line, single, business, field visit	inst	75.00	12/93	9s
Phone line, single, business, no field visit	inst	75.00	12/93	9s
Phone line, single, residence, field visit	inst	40.00	12/93	9s
Phone line, single, residence, no field visit	inst	40.00	12/93	9s
Telephone bill, family of four	month	17.70	12/94	2c
Telephone service, expenditures	year	589	91	81r
Telephone, business, addl. line, touch tone	month	1.90	10/91	25c
Telephone, business, connection charges, touch tone	inst	79.50	10/91	25c
Telephone, business, key system line, touch tone	month	31.53	10/91	25c
Telephone, business, PBX line, touch tone	month	31.47	10/91	25c
Telephone, business, single ln., touch tone	month	32.28	10/91	25c
Telephone, business, touch tone, inside wiring maintenance plan	month	0.95	10/91	25c
Telephone, residential, flat rate	mo.	21.00	12/93	8c
Education				
Board, 4-year private college/university	year	2714	8/94	80s
Board, 4-year public college/university	year	1899	8/94	80s
Education, total expenditures	year	593	91	81r
Room, 4-year private college/university	year	2720	8/94	80s
Room, 4-year public college/university	year	2063	8/94	80s
Total cost, 4-year private college/university	year	18118	8/94	80s
Total cost, 4-year public college/university	year	8278	8/94	80s
Tuition, 2-year public college/university, in-state	year	1671	8/94	80s
Tuition, 4-year private college/university, in-state	year	12684	8/94	80s
Tuition, 4-year public college/university, in-state	year	4316	8/94	80s
Energy and Fuels				
Energy, combined forms, 1800 sq. ft.	mo.	124.08	12/94	2c
Fuel oil and other fuels, expenditures	year	257	91	81r
Gas, cooking, winter, 10 therms	month	13.53	2/94	65c
Gas, cooking, winter, 30 therms	month	27.98	2/94	65c
Gas, cooking, winter, 50 therms	month	42.43	2/94	65c
Gas, heating, winter, average use	month	152.35	2/94	65c
Gas, natural, expenditures	year	285	91	81r
Gas, reg unlead, taxes inc., cash, self-service	gal	1.10	12/94	2c
Gasoline and motor oil purchased	year	867	91	81r
Gasoline, unleaded midgrade	gallon	1.32	4/93	82r
Gasoline, unleaded premium	gallon	1.40	4/93	82r
Gasoline, unleaded regular	gallon	1.19	4/93	82r
Entertainment				
Bowling, evening rate	game	2.18	12/94	2c
Entertainment, total expenditures	year	1331	91	81r
Fees and admissions, expenditures	year	398	91	81r
Monopoly game, Parker Brothers', No. 9	game	10.49	12/94	2c
Movie	adm	5.25	12/94	2c
Pets, toys, playground equipment, expenditures	year	270	91	81r

Values are in dollars or fractions of dollars. In the column headed *Ref*, references are shown to sources. Each reference is followed by a letter. These refer to the geographical level for which data were reported: s=State, r=Region, and c=City or metro. The abbreviation *ex* is used to mean *except* or *excluding*; *exp* stands for expenditures. For other abbreviations and further explanations, please see the Introduction.

Allentown-Bethlehem-Easton, PA, NJ - continued

Item	Per	Value	Date	Ref.
Entertainment				
Reading, expenditures	year	171	91	81r
Televisions, radios, and sound equipment, expenditures	year	429	91	81r
Tennis balls, yellow, Wilson or Penn, 3	can	2.59	12/94	2c
Funerals				
Burial, immediate, container provided by funeral home		1370.36	1/95	54r
Cards, acknowledgment		17.72	1/95	54r
Casket, minimum alternative		192.52	1/95	54r
Cosmetology, hair care, etc.		139.56	1/95	54r
Cremation, direct, container provided by funeral home		1049.24	1/95	54r
Embalming		387.57	1/95	54r
Funeral, funeral home		278.77	1/95	54r
Funeral, other facility		275.85	1/95	54r
Graveside service		213.08	1/95	54r
Hearse, local		157.27	1/95	54r
Limousine, local		146.45	1/95	54r
Memorial service		271.02	1/95	54r
Service charge, professional, nondeclinable		943.58	1/95	54r
Visitation and viewing		322.86	1/95	54r
Groceries				
Groceries, ACCRA Index		112.20	12/94	2c
Apples, Red Delicious	lb.	0.78	12/94	82r
Baby food, strained vegetables, lowest price	4-4.5 oz.	0.38	12/94	2c
Bacon, sliced	lb.	2.24	12/94	82r
Bananas	lb.	0.46	12/94	2c
Bananas	lb.	0.49	12/94	82r
Beef or hamburger, ground	lb.	1.93	12/94	2c
Beef purchases	year	226	91	81r
Beverage purchases, alcoholic	year	332	91	81r
Beverage purchases, nonalcoholic	year	213	91	81r
Bread, white	24-oz.	1.04	12/94	2c
Bread, white, pan	lb.	0.80	12/94	82r
Butter, salted, Grade AA, stick	lb.	1.67	12/94	82r
Carrots, short trimmed and topped	lb.	0.51	12/94	82r
Cereals and bakery products purchases	year	407	91	81r
Cereals and cereals products purchases	year	132	91	81r
Cheese, Kraft grated Parmesan	8-oz.	3.59	12/94	2c
Chicken breast, bone-in	lb.	2.22	12/94	82r
Chicken, fresh, whole	lb.	1.05	12/94	82r
Chicken, whole fryer	lb.	0.89	12/94	2c
Chuck roast, USDA choice, boneless	lb.	2.74	12/94	82r
Cigarettes, Winston, Kings	carton	15.83	12/94	2c
Coffee, 100%, ground roast, all sizes	lb.	4.61	12/94	82r
Coffee, vacuum-packed	13 oz.	3.34	12/94	2c
Corn Flakes, Kellogg's or Post Toasties	18 oz.	2.71	12/94	2c
Corn, frozen, whole kernel, lowest price	10 oz.	0.73	12/94	2c
Dairy products (other) purchases	year	161	91	81r
Eggs, Grade A large	dozen	0.89	12/94	2c
Eggs, Grade A large	dozen	1.12	12/94	82r
Fish and seafood purchases	year	112	91	81r
Food purchases, food eaten at home	year	2599	91	81r
Foods purchased away from home, not prepared by consumer	year	2024	91	81r
Fruits and vegetables purchases	year	444	91	81r
Grapefruit	lb.	0.44	12/94	82r
Grapes, Thompson seedless	lb.	2.24	12/94	82r
Ground chuck, 100% beef	lb.	1.67	12/94	82r
Ice cream, prepackaged, bulk, regular	1/2 gal.	2.93	12/94	82r
Lemons	lb.	1.06	12/94	82r
Lettuce, iceberg	lb.	0.92	12/94	82r
Lettuce, iceberg	head	0.99	12/94	2c
Margarine, Blue Bonnet or Parkay cubes	lb.	0.96	12/94	2c
Meats, poultry, fish, and eggs purchases	year	751	91	81r
Milk and cream (fresh) purchases	year	152	91	81r
Milk, whole	1/2 gal.	1.22	12/94	2c
Orange juice, frozen concentrate 12-oz. can	16 oz.	1.92	12/94	82r

Allentown-Bethlehem-Easton, PA, NJ - continued

Item	Per	Value	Date	Ref.
Groceries - continued				
Orange juice, Minute Maid frozen	12-oz.	1.39	12/94	2c
Oranges, Navel	lb.	0.56	12/94	82r
Peaches, halves or slices, Hunt's, Del Monte, or Libby's	29-oz.	1.32	12/94	2c
Peas, sweet, Del Monte or Green Giant	15-17 oz.	0.63	12/94	2c
Pork chops, center cut, bone-in	lb.	3.09	12/94	82r
Pork purchases	year	130	91	81r
Potatoes, white	lb.	0.37	12/94	82r
Potatoes, white or red	10-lb. sack	2.99	12/94	2c
Rib roast, USDA choice, bone-in	lb.	4.98	12/94	82r
Round roast, USDA choice, boneless	lb.	2.93	12/94	82r
Sausage, Jimmy Dean, 100% pork	lb.	3.12	12/94	2c
Shortening, vegetable oil blends	lb.	1.03	12/94	82r
Shortening, vegetable, Crisco	3-lb.	2.83	12/94	2c
Soft drink, Coca Cola, ex deposit	2 lit	1.20	12/94	2c
Spaghetti and macaroni	lb.	0.84	12/94	82r
Steak, round, USDA choice, boneless	lb.	3.48	12/94	82r
Steak, sirloin, USDA choice, bone-in	lb.	3.38	12/94	82r
Steak, sirloin, USDA choice, boneless	lb.	4.81	12/94	82r
Steak, t-bone	lb.	5.05	12/94	2c
Sugar and other sweets, eaten at home, expenditures	year	89	91	81r
Sugar, cane or beet	4 lbs.	1.54	12/94	2c
Sugar, white, all sizes	lb.	0.46	12/94	82r
Tobacco products and smoking supplies, total expenditures	year	279	91	81r
Tomatoes, field grown	lb.	1.56	12/94	82r
Tomatoes, Hunt's or Del Monte	14.5 oz.	0.75	12/94	2c
Tuna, chunk, light	lb.	2.09	12/94	82r
Tuna, chunk, light, oil-packed	6.125-6.5 oz.	0.81	12/94	2c
Goods and Services				
Miscellaneous goods and services, ACCRA Index		105.30	12/94	2c
Health Care				
Health care, ACCRA Index		98.30	12/94	2c
Antibiotic ointment, Polysporin	1.5 oz.	4.99	12/94	2c
Childbirth, Cesarean delivery, hospital charge	birth	6334.00	12/91	69r
Childbirth, Cesarean delivery, physician charge	birth	2234.00	12/91	69r
Childbirth, normal delivery, hospital charge	birth	3225.00	12/91	69r
Childbirth, normal delivery, physician charge	birth	1623.00	12/91	69r
Dentist's fee, adult teeth cleaning and periodic oral exam	visit	54.40	12/94	2c
Doctor's fee, routine exam, established patient	visit	34.40	12/94	2c
Drugs, expenditures	year	205	91	81r
Health care, total expenditures	year	1396	91	81r
Health insurance expenditures	year	553	91	81r
Hospital care, semiprivate room	day	378.00	12/94	2c
Insurance premium, family medical care	month	349.05	1/95	41s
Medical services expenditures	year	559	91	81r
Medical supplies expenditures	year	80	91	81r
Household Goods				
Appl. repair, service call, wash mach	min. lab. chg.	35.60	12/94	2c
Floor coverings, expenditures	year	158	91	81r
Furniture, expenditures	year	341	91	81r
Household equipment, misc. expenditures	year	363	91	81r
Household expenditures, miscellaneous	year	194	91	81r
Household furnishings and equipment, expenditures	year	1158	91	81r
Household operations expenditures	year	378	91	81r
Household textiles, expenditures	year	88	91	81r
Housekeeping supplies, expenditures	year	426	91	81r

Values are in dollars or fractions of dollars. In the column headed *Ref*, references are shown to sources. Each reference is followed by a letter. These refer to the geographical level for which data were reported: s=State, r=Region, and c=City or metro. The abbreviation *ex* is used to mean *except* or *excluding*; *exp* stands for *expenditures*. For other abbreviations and further explanations, please see the Introduction.

Allentown-Bethlehem-Easton, PA, NJ - continued

Item	Per	Value	Date	Ref.
Household Goods				
Laundry and cleaning supplies, expenditures	year	122	91	81r
Laundry detergent, Tide Ultra, Bold, or Cheer	42 oz.	3.31	12/94	2c
Postage and stationery, expenditures	year	134	91	81r
Tissues, facial, Kleenex brand	175	1.13	12/94	2c
Housing				
Housing, ACCRA Index		103.10	12/94	2c
Add garage/carport		11,614	3/95	74r
Add room(s)		16,816	3/95	74r
Apartment condominium or co-op, median	unit	96700	12/94	62r
Dwellings (owned), expenditures	year	3305	91	81r
Enclose porch/patio/breezeway		2,980	3/95	74r
Finish room in basement/attic		4,330	3/95	74r
Home, existing, single-family, median	unit	161600	12/94	62r
House payment, principal and interest, 25% down payment	mo.	792	12/94	2c
House, 1800 sq ft, 8000 sq ft lot, new, urban, utilities	total	129922	12/94	2c
Maintenance, repairs, insurance, and other housing expenditures	year	569	91	81r
Mortgage interest and charges expenditures	year	1852	91	81r
Mtge. rate, incl. points and orig. fee, 30-year conv. fixed or ARM	mo.	9.11	12/94	2c
Princ. & int., mortgage, median-price exist. sing.-family home	mo.	765	12/94	62r
Property taxes expenditures	year	884	91	81r
Redesign, restructure more than half of home's interior		2,750	3/95	74r
Rent, apartment, 2 br., 1 1/2-2 baths, unfurnished, 950 sq ft, water	mo.	537	12/94	2c
Rental units expenditures	year	1832	91	81r
Insurance and Pensions				
Auto insurance, private passenger	year	721.50	12/94	71s
Insurance and pensions, personal, expenditures	year	2690	91	81r
Insurance, life and other personal, expenditures	year	341	91	81r
Pensions and Social Security, expenditures	year	2349	91	81r
Legal Assistance				
Estate planning, law-firm partner	hr.	375.00	10/93	12r
Legal work, law firm associate	hour	78		10r
Legal work, law firm partner	hour	183		10r
Personal Goods				
Shampoo, Alberto VO5	15-oz.	1.35	12/94	2c
Toothpaste, Crest or Colgate	6-7 oz.	2.26	12/94	2c
Personal Services				
Dry cleaning, man's 2-pc. suit		6.50	12/94	2c
Haircut, man's barbershop, no styling		8.60	12/94	2c
Haircut, woman's shampoo, trim, blow-dry		20.40	12/94	2c
Personal services expenditures	year	184	91	81r
Restaurant Food				
Chicken, fried, thigh and drumstick		2.38	12/94	2c
Dining expenditures, family	week	34.26	94	73r
Hamburger with cheese	1/4 lb.	1.95	12/94	2c
Pizza, Pizza Hut or Pizza Inn	12-13 in.	7.99	12/94	2c
Taxes				
Taxes, Federal income, expenditures	year	2409	91	81r
Taxes, personal, expenditures	year	3094	91	81r
Taxes, State and local income, expenditures	year	620	91	81r
Transportation				
Transportation, ACCRA Index		94.70	12/94	2c
Bus fare, one-way	trip	1.10	12/95	1c
Bus fare, up to 10 miles	one-way	1.00	12/94	2c
Cars and trucks purchased, new	year	1170	91	81r
Cars and trucks purchased, used	year	739	91	81r

Allentown-Bethlehem-Easton, PA, NJ - continued

Item	Per	Value	Date	Ref.
Transportation - continued				
Driver's learning permit fee	perm	27.00	1/94	84s
Driver's license fee	orig	0.00	1/94	84s
Driver's license fee, duplicate	lic	7.00	1/94	84s
Driver's license reinstatement fee, min.	susp	25.00	1/94	85s
Driver's license renewal fee	renew	0.00	1/94	84s
Identification card, nondriver	card	5.00	1/94	83s
Motorcycle learning permit fee	perm	27.00	1/94	84s
Motorcycle license fee	orig	0.00	1/94	84s
Motorcycle license fee, duplicate	lic	7.00	1/94	84s
Motorcycle license renewal fee	renew	0.00	1/94	84s
Public transportation expenditures	year	430	91	81r
Tire balance, computer or spin bal., front	wheel	5.90	12/94	2c
Transportation expenditures, total	year	4810	91	81r
Vehicle finance charges	year	238	91	81r
Vehicle insurance expenditures	year	630	91	81r
Vehicle maintenance and repairs expenditures	year	532	91	81r
Vehicle purchases	year	1920	91	81r
Vehicle rental, leases, licenses, etc. expenditures	year	193	91	81r
Vehicles purchased, other than cars and trucks	year	11	91	81r
Utilities				
Utilities, ACCRA Index		107.90	12/94	2c
Electricity expenditures	year	695	91	81r
Electricity, 1800 sq. ft., new home	mo.	124.08	12/94	2c
Electricity, summer, 250 KWh	month	26.77	8/93	64c
Electricity, summer, 500 KWh	month	45.06	8/93	64c
Electricity, summer, 750 KWh	month	63.35	8/93	64c
Electricity, summer, 1000 KWh	month	81.64	8/93	64c
Utilities, fuels, and public services, total expenditures	year	1981	91	81r
Water and other public services, expenditures	year	154	91	81r
Weddings				
Bridal attendants' gowns	event	750	10/93	76r
Bridal gown	event	852	10/93	76r
Bridal headpiece and veil	event	167	10/93	76r
Bride's wedding band	event	708	10/93	76r
Clergy	event	224	10/93	76r
Engagement ring	event	2756	10/93	76r
Flowers	event	863	10/93	76r
Formal wear for groom	event	106	10/93	76r
Groom's attendants' formal wear	event	530	10/93	76r
Groom's wedding band	event	402	10/93	76r
Music	event	600	10/93	76r
Photography	event	1088	10/93	76r
Shoes for bride	event	50	10/93	76r
Videography	event	483	10/93	76r
Wedding invitations and announcements	event	342	10/93	76r
Wedding reception	event	7000	10/93	76r

Altoona, PA

Item	Per	Value	Date	Ref.
Composite, ACCRA index		101.80	12/94	2c
Alcoholic Beverages				
Beer, Miller Lite, Bud, 12-oz., ex deposit	6	4.82	12/94	2c
J & B Scotch	750-ml.	16.99	12/94	2c
Wine, Gallo Chablis blanc	1.5-lit	5.99	12/94	2c
Appliances				
Appliances (major), expenditures	year	145	91	81r
Average annual exp.				
Food, health care, personal goods, services	year	29496	91	81r
Charity				
Cash contributions, expenditures	year	708	91	81r

Values are in dollars or fractions of dollars. In the column headed *Ref*, references are shown to sources. Each reference is followed by a letter. These refer to the geographical level for which data were reported: s = State, r = Region, and c = City or metro. The abbreviation *ex* is used to mean *except* or *excluding*; *exp* stands for *expenditures*. For other abbreviations and further explanations, please see the Introduction.

Altoona, PA - continued

Item	Per	Value	Date	Ref.
Clothing				
Apparel, men and boys, total expenditures	year	416	91	81r
Apparel, women and girls, total expenditures	year	744	91	81r
Footwear, expenditures	year	305	91	81r
Jeans, man's denim		33.99	12/94	2c
Shirt, man's dress shirt		34.50	12/94	2c
Undervest, boy's size 10-14, cotton	3	3.98	12/94	2c
Communications				
Long-distance telephone rate, day, addl. min., 1-10 mi.	min.	0.08	12/93	9s
Long-distance telephone rate, day, initial min., 1-10 mi.	min.	0.15	12/93	9s
Newspaper subscription, dly. and Sun. delivery	month	9.58	12/94	2c
Phone line, single, business, field visit	inst	75.00	12/93	9s
Phone line, single, business, no field visit	inst	75.00	12/93	9s
Phone line, single, residence, field visit	inst	40.00	12/93	9s
Phone line, single, residence, no field visit	inst	40.00	12/93	9s
Telephone bill, family of four	month	17.10	12/94	2c
Telephone service, expenditures	year	589	91	81r
Telephone, residential, flat rate	mo.	21.00	12/93	8c
Education				
Board, 4-year private college/university	year	2714	8/94	80s
Board, 4-year public college/university	year	1899	8/94	80s
Education, total expenditures	year	593	91	81r
Room, 4-year private college/university	year	2720	8/94	80s
Room, 4-year public college/university	year	2063	8/94	80s
Total cost, 4-year private college/university	year	18118	8/94	80s
Total cost, 4-year public college/university	year	8278	8/94	80s
Tuition, 2-year public college/university, in-state	year	1671	8/94	80s
Tuition, 4-year private college/university, in-state	year	12684	8/94	80s
Tuition, 4-year public college/university, in-state	year	4316	8/94	80s
Energy and Fuels				
Energy, combined forms, 1800 sq. ft.	mo.	130.14	12/94	2c
Energy, exc. electricity, 1800 sq. ft.	mo.	84.39	12/94	2c
Fuel oil and other fuels, expenditures	year	257	91	81r
Gas, natural, expenditures	year	285	91	81r
Gas, reg unlead, taxes inc., cash, self-service	gal	1.06	12/94	2c
Gasoline and motor oil purchased	year	867	91	81r
Gasoline, unleaded midgrade	gallon	1.32	4/93	82r
Gasoline, unleaded premium	gallon	1.40	4/93	82r
Gasoline, unleaded regular	gallon	1.19	4/93	82r
Entertainment				
Bowling, evening rate	game	1.82	12/94	2c
Entertainment, total expenditures	year	1331	91	81r
Fees and admissions, expenditures	year	398	91	81r
Monopoly game, Parker Brothers', No. 9	game	11.18	12/94	2c
Movie	adm	5.75	12/94	2c
Pets, toys, playground equipment, expenditures	year	270	91	81r
Reading, expenditures	year	171	91	81r
Televisions, radios, and sound equipment, expenditures	year	429	91	81r
Tennis balls, yellow, Wilson or Penn, 3	can	2.51	12/94	2c
Funerals				
Burial, immediate, container provided by funeral home		1370.36	1/95	54r
Cards, acknowledgment		17.72	1/95	54r
Casket, minimum alternative		192.52	1/95	54r
Cosmetology, hair care, etc.		139.56	1/95	54r
Cremation, direct, container provided by funeral home		1049.24	1/95	54r
Embalming		387.57	1/95	54r
Funeral, funeral home		278.77	1/95	54r
Funeral, other facility		275.85	1/95	54r
Graveside service		213.08	1/95	54r

Altoona, PA - continued

Item	Per	Value	Date	Ref.
Funerals - continued				
Hearse, local		157.27	1/95	54r
Limousine, local		146.45	1/95	54r
Memorial service		271.02	1/95	54r
Service charge, professional, nondeclinable		943.58	1/95	54r
Visitation and viewing		322.86	1/95	54r
Groceries				
Groceries, ACCRA Index		102.40	12/94	2c
Apples, Red Delicious	lb.	0.78	12/94	82r
Baby food, strained vegetables, lowest price	4-4.5 oz.	0.37	12/94	2c
Bacon, sliced	lb.	2.24	12/94	82r
Bananas	lb.	0.49	12/94	2c
Bananas	lb.	0.49	12/94	82r
Beef or hamburger, ground	lb.	1.49	12/94	2c
Beef purchases	year	226	91	81r
Beverage purchases, alcoholic	year	332	91	81r
Beverage purchases, nonalcoholic	year	213	91	81r
Bread, white	24-oz.	0.66	12/94	2c
Bread, white, pan	lb.	0.80	12/94	82r
Butter, salted, Grade AA, stick	lb.	1.67	12/94	82r
Carrots, short trimmed and topped	lb.	0.51	12/94	82r
Cereals and bakery products purchases	year	407	91	81r
Cereals and cereals products purchases	year	132	91	81r
Cheese, Kraft grated Parmesan	8-oz.	3.33	12/94	2c
Chicken breast, bone-in	lb.	2.22	12/94	82r
Chicken, fresh, whole	lb.	1.05	12/94	82r
Chicken, whole fryer	lb.	0.99	12/94	2c
Chuck roast, USDA choice, boneless	lb.	2.74	12/94	82r
Cigarettes, Winston, Kings	carton	14.76	12/94	2c
Coffee, 100%, ground roast, all sizes	lb.	4.61	12/94	82r
Coffee, vacuum-packed	13 oz.	3.79	12/94	2c
Corn Flakes, Kellogg's or Post Toasties	18 oz.	2.54	12/94	2c
Corn, frozen, whole kernel, lowest price	10 oz.	0.77	12/94	2c
Dairy products (other) purchases	year	161	91	81r
Eggs, Grade A large	dozen	0.75	12/94	2c
Eggs, Grade A large	dozen	1.12	12/94	82r
Fish and seafood purchases	year	112	91	81r
Food purchases, food eaten at home	year	2599	91	81r
Foods purchased away from home, not prepared by consumer	year	2024	91	81r
Fruits and vegetables purchases	year	444	91	81r
Grapefruit	lb.	0.44	12/94	82r
Grapes, Thompson seedless	lb.	2.24	12/94	82r
Ground chuck, 100% beef	lb.	1.67	12/94	82r
Ice cream, prepackaged, bulk, regular	1/2 gal.	2.93	12/94	82r
Lemons	lb.	1.06	12/94	82r
Lettuce, iceberg	lb.	0.92	12/94	82r
Lettuce, iceberg	head	0.94	12/94	2c
Margarine, Blue Bonnet or Parkay cubes	lb.	0.66	12/94	2c
Meats, poultry, fish, and eggs purchases	year	751	91	81r
Milk and cream (fresh) purchases	year	152	91	81r
Milk, whole	1/2 gal.	1.22	12/94	2c
Orange juice, frozen concentrate 12-oz. can	16 oz.	1.92	12/94	82r
Orange juice, Minute Maid frozen	12-oz.	1.34	12/94	2c
Oranges, Navel	lb.	0.56	12/94	82r
Peaches, halves or slices, Hunt's, Del Monte, or Libby's	29-oz.	1.51	12/94	2c
Peas, sweet, Del Monte or Green Giant	15-17 oz.	0.53	12/94	2c
Pork chops, center cut, bone-in	lb.	3.09	12/94	82r
Pork purchases	year	130	91	81r
Potatoes, white	lb.	0.37	12/94	82r
Potatoes, white or red	10-lb. sack	2.05	12/94	2c
Rib roast, USDA choice, bone-in	lb.	4.98	12/94	82r
Round roast, USDA choice, boneless	lb.	2.93	12/94	82r
Sausage, Jimmy Dean, 100% pork	lb.	2.56	12/94	2c
Shortening, vegetable oil blends	lb.	1.03	12/94	82r
Shortening, vegetable, Crisco	3-lb.	2.50	12/94	2c
Soft drink, Coca Cola, ex deposit	2 lit	1.21	12/94	2c

Values are in dollars or fractions of dollars. In the column headed *Ref*, references are shown to sources. Each reference is followed by a letter. These refer to the geographical level for which data were reported: s=State, r=Region, and c=City or metro. The abbreviation *ex* is used to mean *except* or *excluding*; *exp* stands for expenditures. For other abbreviations and further explanations, please see the Introduction.

Altoona, PA - continued

Item	Per	Value	Date	Ref.
Groceries				
Spaghetti and macaroni	lb.	0.84	12/94	82r
Steak, round, USDA choice, boneless	lb.	3.48	12/94	82r
Steak, sirloin, USDA choice, bone-in	lb.	3.38	12/94	82r
Steak, sirloin, USDA choice, boneless	lb.	4.81	12/94	82r
Steak, t-bone	lb.	5.72	12/94	2c
Sugar and other sweets, eaten at home, expenditures	year	89	91	81r
Sugar, cane or beet	4 lbs.	1.47	12/94	2c
Sugar, white, all sizes	lb.	0.46	12/94	82r
Tobacco products and smoking supplies, total expenditures	year	279	91	81r
Tomatoes, field grown	lb.	1.56	12/94	82r
Tomatoes, Hunt's or Del Monte	14.5 oz.	0.72	12/94	2c
Tuna, chunk, light	lb.	2.09	12/94	82r
Tuna, chunk, light, oil-packed	6.125-6.5 oz.	0.80	12/94	2c
Goods and Services				
Miscellaneous goods and services, ACCRA Index		103.10	12/94	2c
Health Care				
Health care, ACCRA Index		89.10	12/94	2c
Antibiotic ointment, Polysporin	1.5 oz.	3.62	12/94	2c
Childbirth, Cesarean delivery, hospital charge	birth	6334.00	12/91	69r
Childbirth, Cesarean delivery, physician charge	birth	2234.00	12/91	69r
Childbirth, normal delivery, hospital charge	birth	3225.00	12/91	69r
Childbirth, normal delivery, physician charge	birth	1623.00	12/91	69r
Dentist's fee, adult teeth cleaning and periodic oral exam	visit	45.00	12/94	2c
Doctor's fee, routine exam, established patient	visit	34.80	12/94	2c
Drugs, expenditures	year	205	91	81r
Health care, total expenditures	year	1396	91	81r
Health insurance expenditures	year	553	91	81r
Hospital care, semiprivate room	day	386.25	12/94	2c
Insurance premium, family medical care	month	349.05	1/95	41s
Medical services expenditures	year	559	91	81r
Medical supplies expenditures	year	80	91	81r
Household Goods				
Appl. repair, service call, wash mach	min. lab. chg.	29.22	12/94	2c
Floor coverings, expenditures	year	158	91	81r
Furniture, expenditures	year	341	91	81r
Household equipment, misc. expenditures	year	363	91	81r
Household expenditures, miscellaneous	year	194	91	81r
Household furnishings and equipment, expenditures	year	1158	91	81r
Household operations expenditures	year	378	91	81r
Household textiles, expenditures	year	88	91	81r
Housekeeping supplies, expenditures	year	426	91	81r
Laundry and cleaning supplies, expenditures	year	122	91	81r
Laundry detergent, Tide Ultra, Bold, or Cheer	42 oz.	3.11	12/94	2c
Postage and stationery, expenditures	year	134	91	81r
Tissues, facial, Kleenex brand	175	1.01	12/94	2c
Housing				
Housing, ACCRA Index		104.00	12/94	2c
Add garage/carport		11,614	3/95	74r
Add room(s)		16,816	3/95	74r
Apartment condominium or co-op, median	unit	96700	12/94	62r
Dwellings (owned), expenditures	year	3305	91	81r
Enclose porch/patio/breezeway		2,980	3/95	74r
Finish room in basement/attic		4,330	3/95	74r
Home, existing, single-family, median	unit	161600	12/94	62r
House payment, principal and interest, 25% down payment	mo.	858	12/94	2c

Altoona, PA - continued

Item	Per	Value	Date	Ref.
Housing - continued				
House, 1800 sq ft, 8000 sq ft lot, new, urban, utilities	total	140000	12/94	2c
Maintenance, repairs, insurance, and other housing expenditures	year	569	91	81r
Mortgage interest and charges expenditures	year	1852	91	81r
Mtge. rate, incl. points and orig. fee, 30-year conv. fixed or ARM	mo.	9.17	12/94	2c
Princ. & int., mortgage, median-price exist. sing.-family home	mo.	765	12/94	62r
Property taxes expenditures	year	884	91	81r
Redesign, restructure more than half of home's interior		2,750	3/95	74r
Rent, apartment, 2 br., 1 1/2-2 baths, unfurnished, 950 sq ft, water	mo.	375	12/94	2c
Rental units expenditures	year	1832	91	81r
Insurance and Pensions				
Auto insurance, private passenger	year	721.50	12/94	71s
Insurance and pensions, personal, expenditures	year	2690	91	81r
Insurance, life and other personal, expenditures	year	341	91	81r
Pensions and Social Security, expenditures	year	2349	91	81r
Legal Assistance				
Estate planning, law-firm partner	hr.	375.00	10/93	12r
Legal work, law firm associate	hour	78		10r
Legal work, law firm partner	hour	183		10r
Personal Goods				
Shampoo, Alberto VO5	15-oz.	1.33	12/94	2c
Toothpaste, Crest or Colgate	6-7 oz.	2.15	12/94	2c
Personal Services				
Dry cleaning, man's 2-pc. suit		6.30	12/94	2c
Haircut, man's barbershop, no styling		7.75	12/94	2c
Haircut, woman's shampoo, trim, blow-dry		17.67	12/94	2c
Personal services expenditures	year	184	91	81r
Restaurant Food				
Chicken, fried, thigh and drumstick		2.26	12/94	2c
Dining expenditures, family	week	34.26	94	73r
Hamburger with cheese	1/4 lb.	1.99	12/94	2c
Pizza, Pizza Hut or Pizza Inn	12-13 in.	7.79	12/94	2c
Taxes				
Taxes, Federal income, expenditures	year	2409	91	81r
Taxes, personal, expenditures	year	3094	91	81r
Taxes, State and local income, expenditures	year	620	91	81r
Transportation				
Transportation, ACCRA Index		88.60	12/94	2c
Bus fare, one-way	trip	1.00	12/95	1c
Cars and trucks purchased, new	year	1170	91	81r
Cars and trucks purchased, used	year	739	91	81r
Driver's learning permit fee	perm	27.00	1/94	84s
Driver's license fee	orig	0.00	1/94	84s
Driver's license fee, duplicate	lic	7.00	1/94	84s
Driver's license reinstatement fee, min.	susp	25.00	1/94	85s
Driver's license renewal fee	renew	0.00	1/94	84s
Identification card, nondriver	card	5.00	1/94	83s
Motorcycle learning permit fee	perm	27.00	1/94	84s
Motorcycle license fee	orig	0.00	1/94	84s
Motorcycle license fee, duplicate	lic	7.00	1/94	84s
Motorcycle license renewal fee	renew	0.00	1/94	84s
Public transportation expenditures	year	430	91	81r
Tire balance, computer or spin bal., front	wheel	5.45	12/94	2c
Transportation expenditures, total	year	4810	91	81r
Vehicle finance charges	year	238	91	81r
Vehicle insurance expenditures	year	630	91	81r
Vehicle maintenance and repairs expenditures	year	532	91	81r
Vehicle purchases	year	1920	91	81r

Values are in dollars or fractions of dollars. In the column headed *Ref*, references are shown to sources. Each reference is followed by a letter. These refer to the geographical level for which data were reported: s=State, r=Region, and c=City or metro. The abbreviation *ex* is used to mean *except* or *excluding*; *exp* stands for *expenditures*. For other abbreviations and further explanations, please see the Introduction.

Altoona, PA - continued

Item	Per	Value	Date	Ref.
Transportation				
Vehicle rental, leases, licenses, etc. expenditures	year	193	91	81r
Vehicles purchased, other than cars and trucks	year	11	91	81r
Utilities				
Utilities, ACCRA Index		112.20	12/94	2c
Electricity expenditures	year	695	91	81r
Electricity, (part.), other, 1800 sq. ft., new home	mo.	45.75	12/94	2c
Utilities, fuels, and public services, total expenditures	year	1981	91	81r
Water and other public services, expenditures	year	154	91	81r
Weddings				
Bridal attendants' gowns	event	750	10/93	76r
Bridal gown	event	852	10/93	76r
Bridal headpiece and veil	event	167	10/93	76r
Bride's wedding band	event	708	10/93	76r
Clergy	event	224	10/93	76r
Engagement ring	event	2756	10/93	76r
Flowers	event	863	10/93	76r
Formal wear for groom	event	106	10/93	76r
Groom's attendants' formal wear	event	530	10/93	76r
Groom's wedding band	event	402	10/93	76r
Music	event	600	10/93	76r
Photography	event	1088	10/93	76r
Shoes for bride	event	50	10/93	76r
Videography	event	483	10/93	76r
Wedding invitations and announcements	event	342	10/93	76r
Wedding reception	event	7000	10/93	76r

Amarillo, TX

Item	Per	Value	Date	Ref.
Composite, ACCRA index		91.10	12/94	2c
Alcoholic Beverages				
Beer, Miller Lite, Bud, 12-oz., ex deposit	6	4.10	12/94	2c
J & B Scotch	750-ml.	17.59	12/94	2c
Wine, Gallo Chablis blanc	1.5-lit	5.55	12/94	2c
Appliances				
Appliances (major), expenditures	year	153	91	81r
Average annual exp.				
Food, health care, personal goods, services	year	27020	91	81r
Charity				
Cash contributions, expenditures	year	839	91	81r
Clothing				
Apparel, men and boys, total expenditures	year	380	91	81r
Apparel, women and girls, total expenditures	year	660	91	81r
Footwear, expenditures	year	193	91	81r
Jeans, man's denim		26.57	12/94	2c
Shirt, man's dress shirt		27.50	12/94	2c
Undervest, boy's size 10-14, cotton	3	3.99	12/94	2c
Communications				
Long-distance telephone rate, day, addl. min., 1-10 mi.	min.	0.08	12/93	9s
Long-distance telephone rate, day, initial min., 1-10 mi.	min.	0.10	12/93	9s
Newspaper subscription, dly. and Sun. delivery	month	8.75	12/94	2c
Phone line, single, business, field visit	inst	71.90	12/93	9s
Phone line, single, business, no field visit	inst	57.30	12/93	9s
Phone line, single, residence, field visit	inst	52.95	12/93	9s
Phone line, single, residence, no field visit	inst	38.35	12/93	9s
Telephone bill, family of four	month	17.73	12/94	2c
Telephone service, expenditures	year	616	91	81r
Telephone, residential, flat rate	mo.	9.10	12/93	8c

Amarillo, TX - continued

Item	Per	Value	Date	Ref.
Education				
Board, 4-year private college/university	year	2084	8/94	80s
Board, 4-year public college/university	year	1675	8/94	80s
Education, total expenditures	year	319	91	81r
Room, 4-year private college/university	year	1840	8/94	80s
Room, 4-year public college/university	year	1756	8/94	80s
Total cost, 4-year private college/university	year	11876	8/94	80s
Total cost, 4-year public college/university	year	4935	8/94	80s
Tuition, 2-year public college/university, in-state	year	625	8/94	80s
Tuition, 4-year private college/university, in-state	year	7952	8/94	80s
Tuition, 4-year private college/university, in-state	year	1503	8/94	80s
Energy and Fuels				
Energy, combined forms, 1800 sq. ft.	mo.	83.49	12/94	2c
Energy, exc. electricity, 1800 sq. ft.	mo.	33.12	12/94	2c
Fuel oil and other fuels, expenditures	year	56	91	81r
Gas, cooking, winter, 10 therms	month	8.53	2/94	65c
Gas, cooking, winter, 30 therms	month	15.30	2/94	65c
Gas, cooking, winter, 50 therms	month	21.97	2/94	65c
Gas, heating, winter, 100 therms	month	38.62	2/94	65c
Gas, heating, winter, average use	month	68.59	2/94	65c
Gas, natural, expenditures	year	150	91	81r
Gas, reg unlead, taxes inc., cash, self-service	gal	1.09	12/94	2c
Gasoline and motor oil purchased	year	1152	91	81r
Gasoline, unleaded midgrade	gallon	1.21	4/93	82r
Gasoline, unleaded premium	gallon	1.30	4/93	82r
Gasoline, unleaded regular	gallon	1.10	4/93	82r
Entertainment				
Bowling, evening rate	game	2.00	12/94	2c
Concert ticket, Pearl Jam group	perf	20.00	94	50r
Entertainment, total expenditures	year	1266	91	81r
Fees and admissions, expenditures	year	306	91	81r
Monopoly game, Parker Brothers', No. 9	game	10.65	12/94	2c
Movie	adm	5.50	12/94	2c
Pets, toys, playground equipment, expenditures	year	271	91	81r
Reading, expenditures	year	131	91	81r
Televisions, radios, and sound equipment, expenditures	year	439	91	81r
Tennis balls, yellow, Wilson or Penn, 3	can	2.29	12/94	2c
Funerals				
Burial, immediate, container provided by funeral home		1574.60	1/95	54r
Cards, acknowledgment		22.24	1/95	54r
Casket, minimum alternative		239.41	1/95	54r
Cosmetology, hair care, etc.		91.04	1/95	54r
Cremation, direct, container provided by funeral home		1085.15	1/95	54r
Embalming		281.30	1/95	54r
Funeral, funeral home		323.04	1/95	54r
Funeral, other facility		327.58	1/95	54r
Graveside service		355.19	1/95	54r
Hearse, local		141.89	1/95	54r
Limousine, local		99.40	1/95	54r
Memorial service		284.67	1/95	54r
Service charge, professional, nondeclinable		904.06	1/95	54r
Visitation and viewing		187.04	1/95	54r
Groceries				
Groceries, ACCRA Index		94.60	12/94	2c
Apples, Red Delicious	lb.	0.73	12/94	82r
Baby food, strained vegetables, lowest price	4-4.5 oz.	0.29	12/94	2c
Bacon, sliced	lb.	1.67	12/94	82r
Bananas	lb.	0.41	12/94	2c
Bananas	lb.	0.42	12/94	82r
Beef or hamburger, ground	lb.	1.23	12/94	2c
Beef purchases	year	213	91	81r
Beverage purchases, alcoholic	year	249	91	81r

Values are in dollars or fractions of dollars. In the column headed *Ref*, references are shown to sources. Each reference is followed by a letter. These refer to the geographical level for which data were reported: s = State, r = Region, and c = City or metro. The abbreviation *ex* is used to mean *except* or *excluding*; *exp* stands for expenditures. For other abbreviations and further explanations, please see the Introduction.

Amarillo, TX - continued

Groceries

Item	Per	Value	Date	Ref.
Beverage purchases, nonalcoholic	year	207	91	81r
Bologna, all beef or mixed	lb.	2.27	12/94	82r
Bread, white	24-oz.	0.54	12/94	2c
Bread, white, pan	lb.	0.68	12/94	82r
Cabbage	lb.	0.42	12/94	82r
Carrots, short trimmed and topped	lb.	0.53	12/94	82r
Cereals and bakery products purchases	year	345	91	81r
Cereals and cereals products purchases	year	127	91	81r
Cheddar cheese, natural	lb.	3.58	12/94	82r
Cheese, Kraft grated Parmesan	8-oz.	3.53	12/94	2c
Chicken breast, bone-in	lb.	1.71	12/94	82r
Chicken, fresh, whole	lb.	0.78	12/94	82r
Chicken, whole fryer	lb.	0.75	12/94	2c
Chuck roast, USDA choice, boneless	lb.	2.26	12/94	82r
Cigarettes, Winston, Kings	carton	16.06	12/94	2c
Coffee, vacuum-packed	13 oz.	3.50	12/94	2c
Corn Flakes, Kellogg's or Post Toasties	18 oz.	2.27	12/94	2c
Corn, frozen, whole kernel, lowest price	10 oz.	0.81	12/94	2c
Crackers, soda, salted	lb.	1.27	12/94	82r
Cucumbers	lb.	0.65	12/94	82r
Dairy products (other) purchases	year	141	91	81r
Eggs, Grade A large	dozen	0.73	12/94	2c
Eggs, Grade A large	dozen	0.87	12/94	82r
Fish and seafood purchases	year	72	91	81r
Flour, white, all purpose	lb.	0.23	12/94	82r
Food purchases, food eaten at home	year	2381	91	81r
Foods purchased away from home, not prepared by consumer	year	1696	91	81r
Frankfurters, all meat or all beef	lb.	1.74	12/94	82r
Fruits and vegetables purchases	year	380	91	81r
Grapefruit	lb.	0.45	12/94	82r
Grapes, Thompson seedless	lb.	2.30	12/94	82r
Ground beef, 100% beef	lb.	1.37	12/94	82r
Ground chuck, 100% beef	lb.	1.97	12/94	82r
Ham, boneless, exc. canned	lb.	2.54	12/94	82r
Ice cream, prepackaged, bulk, regular	1/2 gal.	2.47	12/94	82r
Lemons	lb.	1.02	12/94	82r
Lettuce, iceberg	lb.	0.96	12/94	82r
Lettuce, iceberg	head	0.90	12/94	2c
Margarine, Blue Bonnet or Parkay cubes	lb.	0.63	12/94	2c
Margarine, stick	lb.	0.77	12/94	82r
Meats, poultry, fish, and eggs purchases	year	655	91	81r
Milk and cream (fresh) purchases	year	130	91	81r
Milk, whole	1/2 gal.	1.29	12/94	2c
Orange juice, frozen concentrate 12-oz. can	16 oz.	1.36	12/94	82r
Orange juice, Minute Maid frozen	12-oz.	1.21	12/94	2c
Oranges, Navel	lb.	0.54	12/94	82r
Peaches, halves or slices, Hunt's, Del Monte, or Libby's	29-oz.	1.46	12/94	2c
Pears, Anjou	lb.	0.81	12/94	82r
Peas, sweet, Del Monte or Green Giant	15-17 oz.	0.60	12/94	2c
Pork chops, center cut, bone-in	lb.	3.07	12/94	82r
Pork purchases	year	142	91	81r
Potato chips	16-oz.	3.15	12/94	82r
Potatoes, frozen, French fried	lb.	0.82	12/94	82r
Potatoes, white	lb.	0.34	12/94	82r
Potatoes, white or red	10-lb. sack	2.27	12/94	2c
Rice, white, long grain, uncooked	lb.	0.48	12/94	82r
Round roast, USDA choice, boneless	lb.	2.91	12/94	82r
Sausage, fresh	lb.	1.82	12/94	82r
Sausage, Jimmy Dean, 100% pork	lb.	2.39	12/94	2c
Shortening, vegetable oil blends	lb.	0.75	12/94	82r
Shortening, vegetable, Crisco	3-lb.	2.36	12/94	2c
Soft drink, Coca Cola, ex deposit	2 lit	1.55	12/94	2c
Spaghetti and macaroni	lb.	0.87	12/94	82r
Steak, rib eye, USDA choice, boneless	lb.	6.85	12/94	82r
Steak, round, graded & ungraded, exc. USDA prime & choice	lb.	2.96	12/94	82r

Groceries - continued

Item	Per	Value	Date	Ref.
Steak, round, USDA choice, boneless	lb.	3.17	12/94	82r
Steak, sirloin, USDA choice, boneless	lb.	4.12	12/94	82r
Steak, t-bone	lb.	4.99	12/94	2c
Steak, T-bone, USDA choice, bone-in	lb.	5.63	12/94	82r
Sugar and other sweets, eaten at home, expenditures	year	93	91	81r
Sugar, cane or beet	4 lbs.	1.36	12/94	2c
Sugar, white, all sizes	lb.	0.39	12/94	82r
Tobacco products and smoking supplies, total expenditures	year	286	91	81r
Tomatoes, field grown	lb.	1.36	12/94	82r
Tomatoes, Hunt's or Del Monte	14.5 oz.	0.77	12/94	2c
Tuna, chunk, light	lb.	1.94	12/94	82r
Tuna, chunk, light, oil-packed	6.125-6.5 oz.	0.65	12/94	2c
Turkey, frozen, whole	lb.	0.96	12/94	82r
Yogurt, natural, fruit flavored	8 oz.	0.58	12/94	82r

Goods and Services

Item	Per	Value	Date	Ref.
Miscellaneous goods and services, ACCRA Index		96.20	12/94	2c

Health Care

Item	Per	Value	Date	Ref.
Health care, ACCRA Index		93.50	12/94	2c
Adenosine, emergency room	treat	100.00	95	23r
Antibiotic ointment, Polysporin	1.5 oz.	4.07	12/94	2c
Bladder tap, superpubic, infant, emergency room	treat	119.00	95	23r
Blood analysis, emergency room	treat	25.00	95	23r
Blood tests, abdominal pain, emergency room	treat	25.00	95	23r
Burn dressing, emergency room	treat	266.00	95	23r
Cardiology interpretation, emergency room	treat	26.00	95	23r
Chest X-ray, emergency room	treat	78.00	95	23r
Childbirth, Cesarean delivery, hospital charge	birth	5462.00	12/91	69r
Childbirth, Cesarean delivery, physician charge	birth	2228.00	12/91	69r
Childbirth, normal delivery, hospital charge	birth	2943.00	12/91	69r
Childbirth, normal delivery, physician charge	birth	1619.00	12/91	69r
Defibrillation pads, emergency room	treat	6.00	95	23r
Dentist's fee, adult teeth cleaning and periodic oral exam	visit	45.50	12/94	2c
Doctor's fee, routine exam, established patient	visit	43.00	12/94	2c
Drugs, expenditures	year	297	91	81r
Gastric tube insertion, nasal, emergency room	treat	25.00	95	23r
Health care, total expenditures	year	1600	91	81r
Health insurance expenditures	year	637	91	81r
Heart monitor, emergency room	treat	40.00	95	23r
Hospital care, semiprivate room	day	305.50	12/94	2c
Insurance premium, family medical care	month	389.25	1/95	41s
Intravenous fluids, emergency room	treat	130.00	95	23r
Intravenous fluids, emergency room	liter	26.00	95	23r
Intravenous line, central, emergency room	treat	342.00	95	23r
Liver function tests, abdominal pain, emergency room	treat	26.00	95	23r
Medical care charges, total, emergency room, third-degree burns	treat	2101.00	95	23r
Medical care charges, total, emergency, infant with fever	treat	628.00	95	23r
Medical services expenditures	year	573	91	81r
Medical supplies expenditures	year	93	91	81r
Morphine, emergency room	treat	34.00	95	23r
Nursing care and facilities charges, emergency room	treat	252.00	95	23r
Nursing care and facilities charges, emergency, infant with fever	treat	252.00	95	23r
Nursing care and facilities charges, emergency, third-degree burns	treat	861.00	95	23r

Values are in dollars or fractions of dollars. In the column headed *Ref*, references are shown to sources. Each reference is followed by a letter. These refer to the geographical level for which data were reported: s=State, r=Region, and c=City or metro. The abbreviation *ex* is used to mean *except* or *excluding*; *exp* stands for *expenditures*. For other abbreviations and further explanations, please see the Introduction.

Amarillo, TX - continued

Item	Per	Value	Date	Ref.
Health Care				
Physician's charges, emergency, infant with fever	treat	212.00	95	23r
Physician's charges, emergency, third-degree burns	treat	372.00	95	23r
Physician's fee, emergency room	treat	372.00	95	23r
Physician's fee, general practitioner	visit	51.20	12/93	60r
Surgery, open-heart	proc	42374.00	1/93	14r
Ultrasound, abdominal, emergency room	treat	276.00	95	23r
Urinalysis, emergency room	treat	20.00	95	23r
Urinalysis, infant, emergency room	treat	20.00	95	23r
X-rays, emergency room	treat	78.00	95	23r
Household Goods				
Appl. repair, service call, wash mach	min. lab. chg.	36.28	12/94	2c
Floor coverings, expenditures	year	48	91	81r
Furniture, expenditures	year	280	91	81r
Household equipment, misc. expenditures	year	342	91	81r
Household expenditures, miscellaneous	year	256	91	81r
Household furnishings and equipment, expenditures	year	988	91	81r
Household operations expenditures	year	468	91	81r
Household textiles, expenditures	year	95	91	81r
Housekeeping supplies, expenditures	year	380	91	81r
Laundry and cleaning supplies, expenditures	year	109	91	81r
Laundry detergent, Tide Ultra, Bold, or Cheer	42 oz.	2.92	12/94	2c
Postage and stationery, expenditures	year	105	91	81r
Tissues, facial, Kleenex brand	175	0.99	12/94	2c
Housing				
Housing, ACCRA Index		84.90	12/94	2c
Add garage/carport		6,980	3/95	74r
Add room(s)		11,403	3/95	74r
Apartment condominium or co-op, median	unit	68600	12/94	62r
Dwellings (owned), expenditures	year	2428	91	81r
Enclose porch/patio/breezeway		4,572	3/95	74r
Finish room in basement/attic		3,794	3/95	74r
Home, existing, single-family, median	unit	120200	12/94	62r
Home, existing, single-family, median	unit	63.80	12/94	62c
House payment, principal and interest, 25% down payment	mo.	650	12/94	2c
House, 1800 sq ft, 8000 sq ft lot, new, urban, utilities	total	104700	12/94	2c
Maintenance, repairs, insurance, and other housing expenditures	year	531	91	81r
Mortgage interest and charges expenditures	year	1506	91	81r
Mtge. rate, incl. points and orig. fee, 30-year conv. fixed or ARM	mo.	9.32	12/94	2c
Princ. & int., mortgage, median-price exist. sing.-family home	mo.	540	12/94	62r
Property taxes expenditures	year	391	91	81r
Redesign, restructure more than half of home's interior		17,641	3/95	74r
Rent, apartment, 2 br., 1 1/2-2 baths, unfurnished, 950 sq ft, water	mo.	449	12/94	2c
Rental units expenditures	year	1264	91	81r
Insurance and Pensions				
Auto insurance, private passenger	year	785.78	12/94	71s
Insurance and pensions, personal, expenditures	year	2395	91	81r
Insurance, life and other personal, expenditures	year	368	91	81r
Pensions and Social Security, expenditures	year	2027	91	81r
Personal Goods				
Shampoo, Alberto VO5	15-oz.	0.98	12/94	2c
Toothpaste, Crest or Colgate	6-7 oz.	1.76	12/94	2c
Personal Services				
Dry cleaning, man's 2-pc. suit		5.44	12/94	2c

Amarillo, TX - continued

Item	Per	Value	Date	Ref.
Personal Services - continued				
Haircut, man's barbershop, no styling		8.00	12/94	2c
Haircut, woman's shampoo, trim, blow-dry		19.80	12/94	2c
Personal services expenditures	year	212	91	81r
Restaurant Food				
Chicken, fried, thigh and drumstick		1.99	12/94	2c
Dining expenditures, family	week	33.83	94	73r
Hamburger with cheese	1/4 lb.	1.89	12/94	2c
Pizza, Pizza Hut or Pizza Inn	12-13 in.	9.49	12/94	2c
Taxes				
Tax, cigarettes	year	584.00	10/93	43s
Taxes, Federal income, expenditures	year	2275	91	81r
Taxes, personal, expenditures	year	2715	91	81r
Taxes, State and local income, expenditures	year	365	91	81r
Transportation				
Transportation, ACCRA Index		97.30	12/94	2c
Cars and trucks purchased, new	year	1306	91	81r
Cars and trucks purchased, used	year	942	91	81r
Driver's learning permit fee	perm	5.00	1/94	84s
Driver's license fee	orig	16.00	1/94	84s
Driver's license fee, duplicate	lic	10.00	1/94	84s
Driver's license reinstatement fee, min.	susp	50.00	1/94	85s
Driver's license renewal fee	renew	16.00	1/94	84s
Identification card, nondriver	card	10.00	1/94	83s
Motorcycle learning permit fee	perm	5.00	1/94	84s
Motorcycle license fee	orig	16.00	1/94	84s
Motorcycle license fee, duplicate	lic	10.00	1/94	84s
Motorcycle license renewal fee	renew	21.00	1/94	84s
Public transportation expenditures	year	249	91	81r
Tire balance, computer or spin bal., front	wheel	6.60	12/94	2c
Transportation expenditures, total	year	5307	91	81r
Vehicle finance charges	year	346	91	81r
Vehicle insurance expenditures	year	544	91	81r
Vehicle maintenance and repairs expenditures	year	600	91	81r
Vehicle purchases	year	2275	91	81r
Vehicle rental, leases, licenses, etc. expenditures	year	141	91	81r
Vehicles purchased, other than cars and trucks	year	27	91	81r
Utilities				
Utilities, ACCRA Index		76.60	12/94	2c
Electricity expenditures	year	950	91	81r
Electricity, (part.), other, 1800 sq. ft., new home	mo.	50.37	12/94	2c
Electricity, summer, 250 KWh	month	19.67	8/93	64c
Electricity, summer, 500 KWh	month	34.69	8/93	64c
Electricity, summer, 750 KWh	month	49.70	8/93	64c
Electricity, summer, 1000 KWh	month	64.72	8/93	64c
Utilities, fuels, and public services, total expenditures	year	2000	91	81r
Water and other public services, expenditures	year	227	91	81r
Weddings				
Bridal attendants' gowns	event	750	10/93	76r
Bridal gown	event	852	10/93	76r
Bridal headpiece and veil	event	167	10/93	76r
Bride's wedding band	event	708	10/93	76r
Clergy	event	224	10/93	76r
Engagement ring	event	2756	10/93	76r
Flowers	event	863	10/93	76r
Formal wear for groom	event	106	10/93	76r
Groom's attendants' formal wear	event	530	10/93	76r
Groom's wedding band	event	402	10/93	76r
Music	event	600	10/93	76r
Photography	event	1088	10/93	76r
Shoes for bride	event	50	10/93	76r
Videography	event	483	10/93	76r
Wedding invitations and announcements	event	342	10/93	76r

Values are in dollars or fractions of dollars. In the column headed *Ref*, references are shown to sources. Each reference is followed by a letter. These refer to the geographical level for which data were reported: s=State, r=Region, and c=City or metro. The abbreviation *ex* is used to mean *except* or *excluding*; *exp* stands for expenditures. For other abbreviations and further explanations, please see the Introduction.

Amarillo, TX - continued

Item	Per	Value	Date	Ref.
Weddings				
Wedding reception	event	7000	10/93	76r

Americus, GA

Item	Per	Value	Date	Ref.
Composite, ACCRA index		90.80	12/94	2c
Alcoholic Beverages				
Beer, Miller Lite, Bud, 12-oz., ex deposit	6	4.80	12/94	2c
J & B Scotch	750-ml.	17.04	12/94	2c
Wine, Gallo Chablis blanc	1.5-lit	6.94	12/94	2c
Clothing				
Jeans, man's denim		31.32	12/94	2c
Shirt, man's dress shirt		18.99	12/94	2c
Undervest, boy's size 10-14, cotton	3	4.06	12/94	2c
Communications				
Newspaper subscription, dly. and Sun. delivery	month	14.79	12/94	2c
Telephone bill, family of four	month	17.20	12/94	2c
Telephone, residential, flat rate	mo.	11.20	12/93	8c
Energy and Fuels				
Energy, combined forms, 1800 sq. ft.	mo.	135.71	12/94	2c
Gas, reg unlead, taxes inc., cash, self-service	gal	1.01	12/94	2c
Entertainment				
Bowling, evening rate	game	2.32	12/94	2c
Monopoly game, Parker Brothers', No. 9	game	12.39	12/94	2c
Movie	adm	3.24	12/94	2c
Tennis balls, yellow, Wilson or Penn, 3	can	2.98	12/94	2c
Groceries				
Groceries, ACCRA Index		97.30	12/94	2c
Baby food, strained vegetables, lowest price	4-4.5 oz.	0.29	12/94	2c
Bananas	lb.	0.44	12/94	2c
Beef or hamburger, ground	lb.	1.46	12/94	2c
Bread, white	24-oz.	0.80	12/94	2c
Cheese, Kraft grated Parmesan	8-oz.	3.49	12/94	2c
Chicken, whole fryer	lb.	0.79	12/94	2c
Cigarettes, Winston, Kings	carton	13.98	12/94	2c
Coffee, vacuum-packed	13 oz.	3.59	12/94	2c
Corn Flakes, Kellogg's or Post Toasties	18 oz.	2.23	12/94	2c
Corn, frozen, whole kernel, lowest price	10 oz.	0.66	12/94	2c
Eggs, Grade A large	dozen	0.78	12/94	2c
Lettuce, iceberg	head	0.94	12/94	2c
Margarine, Blue Bonnet or Parkay cubes	lb.	0.63	12/94	2c
Milk, whole	1/2 gal.	1.32	12/94	2c
Orange juice, Minute Maid frozen	12-oz.	1.26	12/94	2c
Peaches, halves or slices, Hunt's, Del Monte, or Libby's	29-oz.	1.29	12/94	2c
Peas, sweet, Del Monte or Green Giant	15-17 oz.	0.52	12/94	2c
Potatoes, white or red	10-lb. sack	2.78	12/94	2c
Sausage, Jimmy Dean, 100% pork	lb.	2.31	12/94	2c
Shortening, vegetable, Crisco	3-lb.	2.61	12/94	2c
Soft drink, Coca Cola, ex deposit	2 lit	1.22	12/94	2c
Steak, t-bone	lb.	4.91	12/94	2c
Sugar, cane or beet	4 lbs.	1.05	12/94	2c
Tomatoes, Hunt's or Del Monte	14.5 oz.	0.69	12/94	2c
Tuna, chunk, light, oil-packed	6.125-6.5 oz.	0.68	12/94	2c
Goods and Services				
Miscellaneous goods and services, ACCRA Index		95.00	12/94	2c

Americus, GA - continued

Item	Per	Value	Date	Ref.
Health Care				
Health care, ACCRA Index		89.00	12/94	2c
Antibiotic ointment, Polysporin	1.5 oz.	3.70	12/94	2c
Dentist's fee, adult teeth cleaning and periodic oral exam	visit	42.20	12/94	2c
Doctor's fee, routine exam, established patient	visit	45.00	12/94	2c
Hospital care, semiprivate room	day	245.00	12/94	2c
Household Goods				
Appl. repair, service call, wash mach	min. lab. chg.	35.00	12/94	2c
Laundry detergent, Tide Ultra, Bold, or Cheer	42 oz.	3.24	12/94	2c
Tissues, facial, Kleenex brand	175	0.97	12/94	2c
Housing				
Housing, ACCRA Index		73.20	12/94	2c
House payment, principal and interest, 25% down payment	mo.	573	12/94	2c
House, 1800 sq ft, 8000 sq ft lot, new, urban, utilities	total	92000	12/94	2c
Mtge. rate, incl. points and orig. fee, 30-year conv. fixed or ARM	mo.	9.37	12/94	2c
Rent, apartment, 2 br., 1 1/2-2 baths, unfurnished, 950 sq ft, water	mo.	351	12/94	2c
Personal Goods				
Shampoo, Alberto VO5	15-oz.	1.16	12/94	2c
Toothpaste, Crest or Colgate	6-7 oz.	2.26	12/94	2c
Personal Services				
Dry cleaning, man's 2-pc. suit		5.07	12/94	2c
Haircut, man's barbershop, no styling		8.60	12/94	2c
Haircut, woman's shampoo, trim, blow-dry		14.83	12/94	2c
Restaurant Food				
Chicken, fried, thigh and drumstick		1.78	12/94	2c
Hamburger with cheese	1/4 lb.	1.69	12/94	2c
Pizza, Pizza Hut or Pizza Inn	12-13 in.	7.99	12/94	2c
Transportation				
Transportation, ACCRA Index		96.90	12/94	2c
Tire balance, computer or spin bal., front	wheel	7.17	12/94	2c
Utilities				
Utilities, ACCRA Index		116.50	12/94	2c
Electricity, 1800 sq. ft., new home	mo.	135.71	12/94	2c

Ames, IA

Item	Per	Value	Date	Ref.
Composite, ACCRA index		101.40	12/94	2c
Alcoholic Beverages				
Beer, Miller Lite, Bud, 12-oz., ex deposit	6	3.91	12/94	2c
J & B Scotch	750-ml.	19.39	12/94	2c
Wine, Gallo Chablis blanc	1.5-lit	5.69	12/94	2c
Clothing				
Jeans, man's denim		30.29	12/94	2c
Shirt, man's dress shirt		33.00	12/94	2c
Undervest, boy's size 10-14, cotton	3	5.99	12/94	2c
Communications				
Newspaper subscription, dly. and Sun. delivery	month	14.13	12/94	2c
Telephone bill, family of four	month	18.20	12/94	2c
Telephone, residential, flat rate	mo.	12.95	12/93	8c
Energy and Fuels				
Energy, combined forms, 1800 sq. ft.	mo.	105.61	12/94	2c
Energy, exc. electricity, 1800 sq. ft.	mo.	47.39	12/94	2c
Gas, cooking, 10 therms	month	12.54	2/94	65c
Gas, cooking, 30 therms	month	22.32	2/94	65c
Gas, cooking, 50 therms	month	32.10	2/94	65c

Values are in dollars or fractions of dollars. In the column headed *Ref*, references are shown to sources. Each reference is followed by a letter. These refer to the geographical level for which data were reported: s = State, r = Region, and c = City or metro. The abbreviation *ex* is used to mean *except* or *excluding*; *exp* stands for *expenditures*. For other abbreviations and further explanations, please see the Introduction.

Ames, IA - continued

Item	Per	Value	Date	Ref.
Energy and Fuels				
Gas, reg unlead, taxes inc., cash, self-service	gal	1.19	12/94	2c
Entertainment				
Bowling, evening rate	game	1.93	12/94	2c
Monopoly game, Parker Brothers', No. 9	game	10.51	12/94	2c
Movie	adm	4.50	12/94	2c
Tennis balls, yellow, Wilson or Penn, 3	can	1.98	12/94	2c
Groceries				
Groceries, ACCRA Index		93.50	12/94	2c
Baby food, strained vegetables, lowest price	4-4.5 oz.	0.34	12/94	2c
Bananas	lb.	0.32	12/94	2c
Beef or hamburger, ground	lb.	1.05	12/94	2c
Bread, white	24-oz.	0.79	12/94	2c
Cheese, Kraft grated Parmesan	8-oz.	3.29	12/94	2c
Chicken, whole fryer	lb.	0.71	12/94	2c
Cigarettes, Winston, Kings	carton	15.82	12/94	2c
Coffee, vacuum-packed	13 oz.	3.22	12/94	2c
Corn Flakes, Kellogg's or Post Toasties	18 oz.	2.32	12/94	2c
Corn, frozen, whole kernel, lowest price	10 oz.	0.64	12/94	2c
Eggs, Grade A large	dozen	0.62	12/94	2c
Lettuce, iceberg	head	0.88	12/94	2c
Margarine, Blue Bonnet or Parkay cubes	lb.	0.51	12/94	2c
Milk, whole	1/2 gal.	1.17	12/94	2c
Orange juice, Minute Maid frozen	12-oz.	1.21	12/94	2c
Peaches, halves or slices, Hunt's, Del Monte, or Libby's	29-oz.	1.36	12/94	2c
Peas, sweet, Del Monte or Green Giant	15-17 oz.	0.57	12/94	2c
Potatoes, white or red	10-lb. sack	2.02	12/94	2c
Sausage, Jimmy Dean, 100% pork	lb.	2.56	12/94	2c
Shortening, vegetable, Crisco	3-lb.	2.11	12/94	2c
Soft drink, Coca Cola, ex deposit	2 lit	0.99	12/94	2c
Steak, t-bone	lb.	4.72	12/94	2c
Sugar, cane or beet	4 lbs.	1.42	12/94	2c
Tomatoes, Hunt's or Del Monte	14.5 oz.	0.63	12/94	2c
Tuna, chunk, light, oil-packed	6.125-6.5 oz.	0.69	12/94	2c
Goods and Services				
Miscellaneous goods and services, ACCRA Index		100.70	12/94	2c
Health Care				
Health care, ACCRA Index		109.70	12/94	2c
Antibiotic ointment, Polysporin	1.5 oz.	4.67	12/94	2c
Dentist's fee, adult teeth cleaning and periodic oral exam	visit	56.67	12/94	2c
Doctor's fee, routine exam, established patient	visit	49.50	12/94	2c
Hospital care, semiprivate room	day	335.00	12/94	2c
Household Goods				
Appl. repair, service call, wash mach	min. lab. chg.	30.98	12/94	2c
Laundry detergent, Tide Ultra, Bold, or Cheer	42 oz.	3.06	12/94	2c
Tissues, facial, Kleenex brand	175	1.04	12/94	2c
Housing				
Housing, ACCRA Index		103.40	12/94	2c
House payment, principal and interest, 25% down payment	mo.	795	12/94	2c
House, 1800 sq ft, 8000 sq ft lot, new, urban, utilities	total	127500	12/94	2c
Mtge. rate, incl. points and orig. fee, 30-year conv. fixed or ARM	mo.	9.38	12/94	2c
Rent, apartment, 2 br., 1 1/2-2 baths, unfurnished, 950 sq ft, water	mo.	537	12/94	2c

Ames, IA - continued

Item	Per	Value	Date	Ref.
Personal Goods				
Shampoo, Alberto VO5	15-oz.	1.19	12/94	2c
Toothpaste, Crest or Colgate	6-7 oz.	2.09	12/94	2c
Personal Services				
Dry cleaning, man's 2-pc. suit		6.60	12/94	2c
Haircut, man's barbershop, no styling		9.30	12/94	2c
Haircut, woman's shampoo, trim, blow-dry		18.30	12/94	2c
Restaurant Food				
Chicken, fried, thigh and drumstick		2.02	12/94	2c
Hamburger with cheese	1/4 lb.	1.95	12/94	2c
Pizza, Pizza Hut or Pizza Inn	12-13 in.	7.99	12/94	2c
Transportation				
Transportation, ACCRA Index		112.30	12/94	2c
Bus fare, one-way	trip	0.75	12/95	1c
Tire balance, computer or spin bal., front	wheel	8.20	12/94	2c
Utilities				
Utilities, ACCRA Index		94.00	12/94	2c
Electricity, (part.), other, 1800 sq. ft., new home	mo.	58.22	12/94	2c

Anaheim-Santa Ana, CA

Item	Per	Value	Date	Ref.
Appliances				
Appliances (major), expenditures	year	160	91	81r
Average annual exp.				
Food, health care, personal goods, services	year	32461	91	81r
Charity				
Cash contributions, expenditures	year	975	91	81r
Clothing				
Apparel, men and boys, total expenditures	year	467	91	81r
Apparel, women and girls, total expenditures	year	737	91	81r
Footwear, expenditures	year	270	91	81r
Communications				
Long-distance telephone rate, day, addl. min., 1-10 mi.	min.	0.07	12/93	9s
Long-distance telephone rate, day, initial min., 1-10 mi.	min.	0.17	12/93	9s
Phone line, single, business, field visit	inst	70.75	12/93	9s
Phone line, single, business, no field visit	inst	70.75	12/93	9s
Phone line, single, residence, field visit	inst	34.75	12/93	9s
Phone line, single, residence, no field visit	inst	34.75	12/93	9s
Telephone service, expenditures	year	611	91	81r
Education				
Board, 4-year private college/university	year	2945	8/94	80s
Board, 4-year public college/university	year	2321	8/94	80s
Education, total expenditures	year	375	91	81r
Room, 4-year private college/university	year	3094	8/94	80s
Room, 4-year public college/university	year	2812	8/94	80s
Student fee, university	year	21.00	93	18s
Total cost, 4-year private college/university	year	19321	8/94	80s
Total cost, 4-year public college/university	year	7511	8/94	80s
Tuition, 2-year public college/university, in-state	year	345	8/94	80s
Tuition, 4-year private college/university, in-state	year	13282	8/94	80s
Tuition, 4-year public college/university, in-state	year	2378	8/94	80s
Energy and Fuels				
Fuel oil and other fuels, expenditures	year	33	91	81r
Gas, natural, expenditures	year	212	91	81r
Gasoline and motor oil purchased	year	1115	91	81r
Gasoline, unleaded midgrade	gallon	1.36	4/93	82r
Gasoline, unleaded premium	gallon	1.43	4/93	82r
Gasoline, unleaded regular	gallon	1.23	4/93	82r

Values are in dollars or fractions of dollars. In the column headed *Ref*, references are shown to sources. Each reference is followed by a letter. These refer to the geographical level for which data were reported: s=State, r=Region, and c=City or metro. The abbreviation *ex* is used to mean *except* or *excluding*; *exp* stands for expenditures. For other abbreviations and further explanations, please see the Introduction.

Anaheim-Santa Ana, CA - continued

Item	Per	Value	Date	Ref.
Entertainment				
Concert ticket, Pearl Jam group	perf	20.00	94	50r
Entertainment, total expenditures	year	1853	91	81r
Fees and admissions, expenditures	year	482	91	81r
Pets, toys, playground equipment, expenditures	year	299	91	81r
Reading, expenditures	year	164	91	81r
Televisions, radios, and sound equipment, expenditures	year	528	91	81r
Funerals				
Burial, immediate, container provided by funeral home		1382.70	1/95	54r
Cards, acknowledgment		21.87	1/95	54r
Casket, minimum alternative		128.54	1/95	54r
Cosmetology, hair care, etc.		119.69	1/95	54r
Cremation, direct, container provided by funeral home		1030.62	1/95	54r
Embalming		255.42	1/95	54r
Funeral, funeral home		437.38	1/95	54r
Funeral, other facility		444.46	1/95	54r
Graveside service		338.46	1/95	54r
Hearse, local		147.50	1/95	54r
Limousine, local		130.33	1/95	54r
Memorial service		553.16	1/95	54r
Service charge, professional, nondeclinable		859.15	1/95	54r
Visitation and viewing		93.23	1/95	54r
Groceries				
Apples, Red Delicious	lb.	0.72	12/94	82r
Bacon, sliced	lb.	1.73	12/94	82r
Bananas	lb.	0.52	12/94	82r
Beef purchases	year	241	91	81r
Beverage purchases, alcoholic	year	328	91	81r
Beverage purchases, nonalcoholic	year	234	91	81r
Bologna, all beef or mixed	lb.	2.33	12/94	82r
Bread, white, pan	lb.	0.81	12/94	82r
Carrots, short trimmed and topped	lb.	0.43	12/94	82r
Cereals and bakery products purchases	year	392	91	81r
Cereals and cereals products purchases	year	139	91	81r
Chicken breast, bone-in	lb.	2.04	12/94	82r
Chicken, fresh, whole	lb.	0.95	12/94	82r
Coffee, 100%, ground roast, all sizes	lb.	4.48	12/94	82r
Dairy products (other) purchases	year	182	91	81r
Fish and seafood purchases	year	94	91	81r
Flour, white, all purpose	lb.	0.21	12/94	82r
Food purchases, food eaten at home	year	2749	91	81r
Foods purchased away from home, not prepared by consumer	year	1909	91	81r
Fruits and vegetables purchases	year	459	91	81r
Grapefruit	lb.	0.56	12/94	82r
Ground beef, 100% beef	lb.	1.31	12/94	82r
Ham, boneless, exc. canned	lb.	2.46	12/94	82r
Ice cream, prepackaged, bulk, regular	1/2 gal.	2.57	12/94	82r
Lemons	lb.	1.00	12/94	82r
Lettuce, iceberg	lb.	0.93	12/94	82r
Meats, poultry, fish, and eggs purchases	year	700	91	81r
Milk and cream (fresh) purchases	year	155	91	81r
Orange juice, frozen concentrate 12-oz. can	16 oz.	1.52	12/94	82r
Oranges, Navel	lb.	0.56	12/94	82r
Pork chops, center cut, bone-in	lb.	3.30	12/94	82r
Pork purchases	year	122	91	81r
Potato chips	16-oz.	3.03	12/94	82r
Potatoes, frozen, French fried	lb.	0.77	12/94	82r
Potatoes, white	lb.	0.35	12/94	82r
Rice, white, long grain, uncooked	lb.	0.54	12/94	82r
Round roast, USDA choice, boneless	lb.	2.92	12/94	82r
Shortening, vegetable oil blends	lb.	0.80	12/94	82r
Spaghetti and macaroni	lb.	1.02	12/94	82r
Steak, round, graded & ungraded, exc. USDA prime & choice	lb.	3.13	12/94	82r
Steak, sirloin, USDA choice, boneless	lb.	4.07	12/94	82r

Item	Per	Value	Date	Ref.
Groceries - continued				
Sugar and other sweets, eaten at home, expenditures	year	105	91	81r
Sugar, white, all sizes	lb.	0.38	12/94	82r
Tobacco products and smoking supplies, total expenditures	year	221	91	81r
Tomatoes, field grown	lb.	1.45	12/94	82r
Tuna, chunk, light	lb.	2.18	12/94	82r
Health Care				
Childbirth, Cesarean delivery, hospital charge	birth	6059.00	12/91	69r
Childbirth, Cesarean delivery, physician charge	birth	2248.00	12/91	69r
Childbirth, normal delivery, hospital charge	birth	3006.00	12/91	69r
Childbirth, normal delivery, physician charge	birth	1634.00	12/91	69r
Drugs, expenditures	year	230	91	81r
Health care, total expenditures	year	1544	91	81r
Health insurance expenditures	year	558	91	81r
Insurance premium, family medical care	month	380.27	1/95	41s
Medical services expenditures	year	676	91	81r
Medical supplies expenditures	year	80	91	81r
Surgery, open-heart	proc	37818.00	1/93	14r
Household Goods				
Floor coverings, expenditures	year	79	91	81r
Furniture, expenditures	year	352	91	81r
Household equipment, misc. expenditures	year	614	91	81r
Household expenditures, miscellaneous	year	294	91	81r
Household furnishings and equipment, expenditures	year	1416	91	81r
Household operations expenditures	year	580	91	81r
Household textiles, expenditures	year	113	91	81r
Housekeeping supplies, expenditures	year	447	91	81r
Laundry and cleaning supplies, expenditures	year	114	91	81r
Postage and stationery, expenditures	year	145	91	81r
Housing				
Add garage/carport		6,422	3/95	74r
Add room(s)		26,583	3/95	74r
Apartment condominium or co-op, median	unit	105300	12/94	62r
Dwellings (owned), expenditures	year	3932	91	81r
Enclose porch/patio/breezeway		5,382	3/95	74r
Finish room in basement/attic		3,911	3/95	74r
Home, existing, single-family, median	unit	178600	12/94	62r
Maintenance, repairs, insurance, and other housing expenditures	year	591	91	81r
Mortgage interest and charges expenditures	year	2747	91	81r
Princ. & int., mortgage, median-price exist. sing.-family home	mo.	845	12/94	62r
Property taxes expenditures	year	594	91	81r
Redesign, restructure more than half of home's interior		5,467	3/95	74r
Rental units expenditures	year	2077	91	81r
Insurance and Pensions				
Auto insurance, private passenger	year	892.80	12/94	71s
Insurance and pensions, personal, expenditures	year	3042	91	81r
Insurance, life and other personal, expenditures	year	298	91	81r
Pensions and Social Security, expenditures	year	2744	91	81r
Legal Assistance				
Legal work, law firm associate	hour	91		10r
Legal work, law firm partner	hour	151		10r
Personal Services				
Personal services expenditures	year	286	91	81r
Restaurant Food				
Dining expenditures, family	week	32.25	94	73r
Taxes				
Taxes, Federal income, expenditures	year	2946	91	81r
Taxes, personal, expenditures	year	3791	91	81r

Values are in dollars or fractions of dollars. In the column headed *Ref*, references are shown to sources. Each reference is followed by a letter. These refer to the geographical level for which data were reported: s=State, r=Region, and c=City or metro. The abbreviation *ex* is used to mean *except* or *excluding*; *exp* stands for *expenditures*. For other abbreviations and further explanations, please see the Introduction.

Anaheim-Santa Ana, CA - continued

Item	Per	Value	Date	Ref.
Taxes				
Taxes, State and local income, expenditures	year	791	91	81r
Transportation				
Cars and trucks purchased, new	year	1231	91	81r
Cars and trucks purchased, used	year	915	91	81r
Driver's learning permit fee	perm	12.00	1/94	84s
Driver's license fee	orig	12.00	1/94	84s
Driver's license fee, duplicate	lic	12.00	1/94	84s
Driver's license reinstatement fee, min.	susp	15.00	1/94	85s
Driver's license renewal fee	renew	12.00	1/94	84s
Identification card, nondriver	card	6.00	1/94	83s
Motorcycle learning permit fee	perm	12.00	1/94	84s
Motorcycle license fee	orig	12.00	1/94	84s
Motorcycle license fee, duplicate	lic	12.00	1/94	84s
Motorcycle license renewal fee	renew	12.00	1/94	84s
Public transportation expenditures	year	375	91	81r
Transportation expenditures, total	year	5527	91	81r
Vehicle finance charges	year	287	91	81r
Vehicle insurance expenditures	year	624	91	81r
Vehicle maintenance and repairs expenditures	year	695	91	81r
Vehicle purchases	year	2174	91	81r
Vehicle rental, leases, licenses, etc. expenditures	year	257	91	81r
Vehicles purchased, other than cars and trucks	year	28	91	81r
Utilities				
Electricity expenditures	year	616	91	81r
Utilities, fuels, and public services, total expenditures	year	1681	91	81r
Water and other public services, expenditures	year	209	91	81r
Weddings				
Bridal attendants' gowns	event	750	10/93	76r
Bridal gown	event	852	10/93	76r
Bridal headpiece and veil	event	167	10/93	76r
Bride's wedding band	event	708	10/93	76r
Clergy	event	224	10/93	76r
Engagement ring	event	2756	10/93	76r
Flowers	event	863	10/93	76r
Formal wear for groom	event	106	10/93	76r
Groom's attendants' formal wear	event	530	10/93	76r
Groom's wedding band	event	402	10/93	76r
Music	event	600	10/93	76r
Photography	event	1088	10/93	76r
Shoes for bride	event	50	10/93	76r
Videography	event	483	10/93	76r
Wedding invitations and announcements	event	342	10/93	76r
Wedding reception	event	7000	10/93	76r

Anchorage, AK

Item	Per	Value	Date	Ref.
Composite, ACCRA index		126.50	12/94	2c
Alcoholic Beverages				
Beer, Miller Lite, Bud, 12-oz., ex deposit	6	4.97	12/94	2c
J & B Scotch	750-ml.	22.71	12/94	2c
Wine, Gallo Chablis blanc	1.5-lit	5.76	12/94	2c
Appliances				
Appliances (major), expenditures	year	241	91	81c
Appliances (major), expenditures	year	160	91	81r
Average annual exp.				
Food, health care, personal goods, services	year	43991	91	81c
Food, health care, personal goods, services	year	32461	91	81r
Charity				
Cash contributions, expenditures	year	1110	91	81c
Cash contributions, expenditures	year	975	91	81r

Anchorage, AK - continued

Item	Per	Value	Date	Ref.
Child Care				
Child care, for-profit daycare center	week	96.00	12/94	28c
Clothing				
Apparel, men and boys, total expenditures	year	449	91	81c
Apparel, men and boys, total expenditures	year	467	91	81r
Apparel, women and girls, total expenditures	year	950	91	81c
Apparel, women and girls, total expenditures	year	737	91	81r
Footwear, expenditures	year	287	91	81c
Footwear, expenditures	year	270	91	81r
Jeans, man's denim		29.16	12/94	2c
Shirt, man's dress shirt		35.44	12/94	2c
Undervest, boy's size 10-14, cotton	3	4.74	12/94	2c
Communications				
Newspaper subscription, dly. and Sun. delivery	month	11.50	12/94	2c
Telephone bill, family of four	month	14.41	12/94	2c
Telephone service, expenditures	year	683	91	81c
Telephone service, expenditures	year	611	91	81r
Education				
Board, 4-year private college/university	year	2668	8/94	80s
Board, 4-year public college/university	year	1884	8/94	80s
Education, total expenditures	year	695	91	81c
Education, total expenditures	year	375	91	81r
Room, 4-year private college/university	year	1859	8/94	80s
Room, 4-year public college/university	year	2193	8/94	80s
Total cost, 4-year private college/university	year	12251	8/94	80s
Total cost, 4-year public college/university	year	5985	8/94	80s
Tuition, 2-year public college/university, in-state	year	1268	8/94	80s
Tuition, 4-year private college/university, in-state	year	7727	8/94	80s
Tuition, 4-year public college/university, in-state	year	1908	8/94	80s
Energy and Fuels				
Energy, combined forms, 1800 sq. ft.	mo.	116.10	12/94	2c
Energy, exc. electricity, 1800 sq. ft.	mo.	44.12	12/94	2c
Fuel oil and other fuels, expenditures	year	18	91	81c
Fuel oil and other fuels, expenditures	year	33	91	81r
Gas, cooking, 10 therms	month	7.88	2/94	65c
Gas, cooking, 30 therms	month	14.61	2/94	65c
Gas, cooking, 50 therms	month	21.34	2/94	65c
Gas, heating, winter, 100 therms	month	38.18	2/94	65c
Gas, heating, winter, average use	month	81.94	2/94	65c
Gas, natural, expenditures	year	524	91	81c
Gas, natural, expenditures	year	212	91	81r
Gas, reg unlead, taxes inc., cash, self-service	gal	1.20	12/94	2c
Gasoline and motor oil purchased	year	1165	91	81c
Gasoline and motor oil purchased	year	1115	91	81r
Gasoline, unleaded midgrade	gallon	1.36	4/93	82r
Gasoline, unleaded premium	gallon	1.43	4/93	82r
Gasoline, unleaded regular	gallon	1.23	4/93	82r
Entertainment				
Bowling, evening rate	game	2.88	12/94	2c
Concert ticket, Pearl Jam group	perf	20.00	94	50r
Entertainment supplies, equipment, and services, misc. expenditures	year	1290	91	81c
Entertainment, total expenditures	year	3172	91	81c
Entertainment, total expenditures	year	1853	91	81r
Fees and admissions, expenditures	year	674	91	81c
Fees and admissions, expenditures	year	482	91	81r
Monopoly game, Parker Brothers', No. 9	game	12.16	12/94	2c
Movie	adm	7.00	12/94	2c
Pets, toys, playground equipment, expenditures	year	361	91	81c
Pets, toys, playground equipment, expenditures	year	299	91	81r
Reading, expenditures	year	264	91	81c
Reading, expenditures	year	164	91	81r

Values are in dollars or fractions of dollars. In the column headed *Ref*, references are shown to sources. Each reference is followed by a letter. These refer to the geographical level for which data were reported: s = State, r = Region, and c = City or metro. The abbreviation *ex* is used to mean *except* or *excluding*; *exp* stands for expenditures. For other abbreviations and further explanations, please see the Introduction.

Anchorage, AK - continued

Item	Per	Value	Date	Ref.
Entertainment				
Televisions, radios, and sound equipment, expenditures	year	846	91	81c
Televisions, radios, and sound equipment, expenditures	year	528	91	81r
Tennis balls, yellow, Wilson or Penn, 3	can	2.80	12/94	2c
Funerals				
Burial, immediate, container provided by funeral home		1382.70	1/95	54r
Cards, acknowledgment		21.87	1/95	54r
Casket, minimum alternative		128.54	1/95	54r
Cosmetology, hair care, etc.		119.69	1/95	54r
Cremation, direct, container provided by funeral home		1030.62	1/95	54r
Embalming		255.42	1/95	54r
Funeral, funeral home		437.38	1/95	54r
Funeral, other facility		444.46	1/95	54r
Graveside service		338.46	1/95	54r
Hearse, local		147.50	1/95	54r
Limousine, local		130.33	1/95	54r
Memorial service		553.16	1/95	54r
Service charge, professional, nondeclinable		859.15	1/95	54r
Visitation and viewing		93.23	1/95	54r
Groceries				
Groceries, ACCRA Index		120.60	12/94	2c
Apples, Red Delicious	lb.	0.72	12/94	82r
Baby food, strained vegetables, lowest price	4-4.5 oz.	0.30	12/94	2c
Bacon, sliced	lb.	1.73	12/94	82r
Bananas	lb.	0.88	12/94	2c
Bananas	lb.	0.52	12/94	82r
Beef or hamburger, ground	lb.	1.68	12/94	2c
Beef purchases	year	254	91	81c
Beef purchases	year	241	91	81r
Beverage purchases, alcoholic	year	608	91	81c
Beverage purchases, alcoholic	year	328	91	81r
Beverage purchases, nonalcoholic	year	313	91	81c
Beverage purchases, nonalcoholic	year	234	91	81r
Bologna, all beef or mixed	lb.	2.33	12/94	82r
Bread, white	24-oz.	0.77	12/94	2c
Bread, white, pan	lb.	0.81	12/94	82r
Carrots, short trimmed and topped	lb.	0.43	12/94	82r
Cereals and bakery products purchases	year	506	91	81c
Cereals and bakery products purchases	year	392	91	81r
Cereals and cereal products purchases	year	154	91	81c
Cereals and cereals products purchases	year	139	91	81r
Cheese, Kraft grated Parmesan	8-oz.	3.27	12/94	2c
Chicken breast, bone-in	lb.	2.04	12/94	82r
Chicken, fresh, whole	lb.	0.95	12/94	2c
Chicken, whole fryer	lb.	1.17	12/94	2c
Cigarettes, Winston, Kings	carton	18.04	12/94	2c
Coffee, 100%, ground roast, all sizes	lb.	4.48	12/94	82r
Coffee, vacuum-packed	13 oz.	4.26	12/94	2c
Corn Flakes, Kellogg's or Post Toasties	18 oz.	2.39	12/94	2c
Corn, frozen, whole kernel, lowest price	10 oz.	0.86	12/94	2c
Dairy products (other) purchases	year	240	91	81c
Dairy products (other) purchases	year	182	91	81r
Eggs, Grade A large	dozen	1.20	12/94	2c
Fish and seafood purchases	year	109	91	81c
Fish and seafood purchases	year	94	91	81r
Flour, white, all purpose	lb.	0.21	12/94	82r
Food purchases, food eaten at home	year	3480	91	81c
Food purchases, food eaten at home	year	2749	91	81r
Foods purchased away from home, not prepared by consumer	year	2097	91	81c
Foods purchased away from home, not prepared by consumer	year	1909	91	81r
Fruits and vegetables purchases	year	601	91	81c
Fruits and vegetables purchases	year	459	91	81r
Grapefruit	lb.	0.56	12/94	82r
Ground beef, 100% beef	lb.	1.31	12/94	82r
Ham, boneless, exc. canned	lb.	2.46	12/94	82r

Anchorage, AK - continued

Item	Per	Value	Date	Ref.
Groceries - continued				
Ice cream, prepackaged, bulk, regular	1/2 gal.	2.57	12/94	82r
Lemons	lb.	1.00	12/94	82r
Lettuce, iceberg	lb.	0.93	12/94	82r
Lettuce, iceberg	head	1.18	12/94	2c
Margarine, Blue Bonnet or Parkay cubes	lb.	0.68	12/94	2c
Meats, poultry, fish, and eggs purchases	year	780	91	81c
Meats, poultry, fish, and eggs purchases	year	700	91	81r
Milk and cream (fresh) purchases	year	196	91	81c
Milk and cream (fresh) purchases	year	155	91	81r
Milk, whole	1/2 gal.	2.11	12/94	2c
Orange juice, frozen concentrate 12-oz. can	16 oz.	1.52	12/94	82r
Orange juice, Minute Maid frozen	12-oz.	1.20	12/94	2c
Oranges, Navel	lb.	0.56	12/94	82r
Peaches, halves or slices, Hunt's, Del Monte, or Libby's	29-oz.	1.57	12/94	2c
Peas, sweet, Del Monte or Green Giant	15-17 oz.	0.61	12/94	2c
Pork chops, center cut, bone-in	lb.	3.30	12/94	82r
Pork purchases	year	141	91	81c
Pork purchases	year	122	91	81r
Potato chips	16-oz.	3.03	12/94	82r
Potatoes, frozen, French fried	lb.	0.77	12/94	82r
Potatoes, white	lb.	0.35	12/94	82r
Potatoes, white or red	10-lb. sack	3.32	12/94	2c
Rice, white, long grain, uncooked	lb.	0.54	12/94	82r
Round roast, USDA choice, boneless	lb.	2.92	12/94	82r
Sausage, Jimmy Dean, 100% pork	lb.	3.39	12/94	2c
Shortening, vegetable oil blends	lb.	0.80	12/94	82r
Shortening, vegetable, Crisco	3-lb.	2.49	12/94	2c
Soft drink, Coca Cola, ex deposit	2 lit	1.85	12/94	2c
Spaghetti and macaroni	lb.	1.02	12/94	82r
Steak, round, graded & ungraded, exc. USDA prime & choice	lb.	3.13	12/94	82r
Steak, sirloin, USDA choice, boneless	lb.	4.07	12/94	82r
Steak, t-bone	lb.	6.32	12/94	2c
Sugar and other sweets, eaten at home, expenditures	year	105	91	81r
Sugar and other sweets, eaten at home, purchases	year	142	91	81c
Sugar, cane or beet	4 lbs.	1.85	12/94	2c
Sugar, white, all sizes	lb.	0.38	12/94	82r
Tobacco products and smoking supplies, total expenditures	year	313	91	81c
Tobacco products and smoking supplies, total expenditures	year	221	91	81r
Tomatoes, field grown	lb.	1.45	12/94	82r
Tomatoes, Hunt's or Del Monte	14.5 oz.	0.70	12/94	2c
Tuna, chunk, light	lb.	2.18	12/94	82r
Tuna, chunk, light, oil-packed	6.125-6.5 oz.	0.72	12/94	2c
Goods and Services				
Miscellaneous goods and services, ACCRA Index		124.10	12/94	2c
Health Care				
Health care, ACCRA Index		158.60	12/94	2c
Antibiotic ointment, Polysporin	1.5 oz.	3.83	12/94	2c
Childbirth, Cesarean delivery, hospital charge	birth	6059.00	12/91	69r
Childbirth, Cesarean delivery, physician charge	birth	2248.00	12/91	69r
Childbirth, normal delivery, hospital charge	birth	3006.00	12/91	69r
Childbirth, normal delivery, physician charge	birth	1634.00	12/91	69r
Dentist's fee, adult teeth cleaning and periodic oral exam	visit	103.20	12/94	2c
Doctor's fee, routine exam, established patient	visit	58.00	12/94	2c
Drugs, expenditures	year	244	91	81c

Values are in dollars or fractions of dollars. In the column headed *Ref*, references are shown to sources. Each reference is followed by a letter. These refer to the geographical level for which data were reported: s=State, r=Region, and c=City or metro. The abbreviation *ex* is used to mean *except* or *excluding*; *exp* stands for *expenditures*. For other abbreviations and further explanations, please see the Introduction.

Anchorage, AK - continued

Item	Per	Value	Date	Ref.
Health Care				
Drugs, expenditures	year	230	91	81r
Health care, total expenditures	year	1730	91	81c
Health care, total expenditures	year	1544	91	81r
Health insurance expenditures	year	463	91	81c
Health insurance expenditures	year	558	91	81r
Hospital care, semiprivate room	day	590.00	12/94	2c
Medical services expenditures	year	915	91	81c
Medical services expenditures	year	676	91	81r
Medical supplies expenditures	year	108	91	81c
Medical supplies expenditures	year	80	91	81r
Surgery, open-heart	proc	37818.00	1/93	14r
Household Goods				
Appl. repair, service call, wash mach	min. lab. chg.	46.67	12/94	2c
Floor coverings, expenditures	year	44	91	81c
Floor coverings, expenditures	year	79	91	81r
Furniture, expenditures	year	409	91	81c
Furniture, expenditures	year	352	91	81r
Household equipment, misc. expenditures	year	614	91	81r
Household equipment, misc., expenditures	year	832	91	81c
Household expenditures, miscellaneous	year	209	91	81c
Household expenditures, miscellaneous	year	294	91	81r
Household furnishings and equipment, expenditures	year	1799	91	81c
Household furnishings and equipment, expenditures	year	1416	91	81r
Household operations expenditures	year	621	91	81c
Household operations expenditures	year	580	91	81r
Household textiles, expenditures	year	110	91	81c
Household textiles, expenditures	year	113	91	81r
Housekeeping supplies, expenditures	year	475	91	81c
Housekeeping supplies, expenditures	year	447	91	81r
Laundry and cleaning supplies, expenditures	year	107	91	81c
Laundry and cleaning supplies, expenditures	year	114	91	81r
Laundry detergent, Tide Ultra, Bold, or Cheer	42 oz.	4.87	12/94	2c
Postage and stationery, expenditures	year	182	91	81c
Postage and stationery, expenditures	year	145	91	81r
Tissues, facial, Kleenex brand	175	0.99	12/94	2c
Housing				
Housing, ACCRA Index		139.10	12/94	2c
Add garage/carport		6,422	3/95	74r
Add room(s)		26,583	3/95	74r
Apartment condominium or co-op, median	unit	105300	12/94	62r
Dwellings (owned), expenditures	year	5109	91	81c
Dwellings (owned), expenditures	year	3932	91	81r
Enclose porch/patio/breezeway		5,382	3/95	74r
Finish room in basement/attic		3,911	3/95	74r
Home, existing, single-family, median	unit	178600	12/94	62r
House payment, principal and interest, 25% down payment	mo.	1069	12/94	2c
House, 1800 sq ft, 8000 sq ft lot, new, urban, utilities	total	171956	12/94	2c
Maintenance, repairs, insurance, and other housing expenditures	year	613	91	81c
Maintenance, repairs, insurance, and other housing expenditures	year	591	91	81r
Mortgage interest and charges expenditures	year	3854	91	81c
Mortgage interest and charges expenditures	year	2747	91	81r
Mtge. rate, incl. points and orig. fee, 30-year conv. fixed or ARM	mo.	9.34	12/94	2c
Princ. & int., mortgage, median-price exist. sing.-family home	mo.	845	12/94	62r
Property taxes expenditures	year	642	91	81c
Property taxes expenditures	year	594	91	81r
Redesign, restructure more than half of home's interior		5,467	3/95	74r

Anchorage, AK - continued

Item	Per	Value	Date	Ref.
Housing - continued				
Rent, apartment, 2 br., 1 1/2-2 baths, unfurnished, 950 sq ft, water	mo.	725	12/94	2c
Rental units expenditures	year	2821	900/00/ 91	81c
Rental units expenditures	year	2077	91	81r
Insurance and Pensions				
Auto insurance, private passenger	year	873.87	12/94	71s
Insurance and pensions, personal, expenditures	year	5307	91	81c
Insurance and pensions, personal, expenditures	year	3042	91	81r
Insurance, life and other personal, expenditures	year	553	91	81c
Insurance, life and other personal, expenditures	year	298	91	81r
Pensions and Social Security, expenditures	year	4754	91	81c
Pensions and Social Security, expenditures	year	2744	91	81r
Legal Assistance				
Legal work, law firm associate	hour	91		10r
Legal work, law firm partner	hour	151		10r
Personal Goods				
Personal care products and services, total expenditures	year	466	91	81c
Shampoo, Alberto VO5	15-oz.	1.04	12/94	2c
Toothpaste, Crest or Colgate	6-7 oz.	1.90	12/94	2c
Personal Services				
Dry cleaning, man's 2-pc. suit		9.38	12/94	2c
Haircut, man's barbershop, no styling		12.62	12/94	2c
Haircut, woman's shampoo, trim, blow-dry		28.43	12/94	2c
Personal services expenditures	year	412	91	81c
Personal services expenditures	year	286	91	81r
Restaurant Food				
Chicken, fried, thigh and drumstick		3.60	12/94	2c
Dining expenditures, family	week	32.25	94	73r
Hamburger with cheese	1/4 lb.	2.44	12/94	2c
Pizza, Pizza Hut or Pizza Inn	12-13 in.	10.99	12/94	2c
Taxes				
Tax rate, residential property, month	$100	1.71	1/92	79c
Tax, cigarettes	year	837.00	10/93	43s
Taxes, Federal income, expenditures	year	6390	91	81c
Taxes, Federal income, expenditures	year	2946	91	81r
Taxes, personal, expenditures	year	6506	91	81c
Taxes, personal, expenditures	year	3791	91	81r
Taxes, State and local income, expenditures	year	29	91	81c
Taxes, State and local income, expenditures	year	791	91	81r
Transportation				
Transportation, ACCRA Index		109.60	12/94	2c
Bus fare, one-way	trip	1.00	12/95	1c
Bus fare, up to 10 miles	one-way	1.00	12/94	2c
Cars and trucks purchased, new	year	2298	91	81c
Cars and trucks purchased, new	year	1231	91	81r
Cars and trucks purchased, used	year	730	91	81c
Cars and trucks purchased, used	year	915	91	81r
Driver's learning permit fee	perm	10.00	1/94	84s
Driver's license fee	orig	15.00	1/94	84s
Driver's license fee, duplicate	lic	10.00	1/94	84s
Driver's license reinstatement fee, min.	susp	100.00	1/94	85s
Driver's license renewal fee	renew	15.00	1/94	84s
Identification card, nondriver	card	15.00	1/94	83s
Motorcycle license fee	orig	15.00	1/94	84s
Motorcycle license fee, duplicate	lic	10.00	1/94	84s
Motorcycle license renewal fee	renew	15.00	1/94	84s
Public transportation expenditures	year	873	91	81c
Public transportation expenditures	year	375	91	81r
Tire balance, computer or spin bal., front	wheel	7.80	12/94	2c
Transportation expenditures, total	year	7531	91	81c

Values are in dollars or fractions of dollars. In the column headed *Ref*, references are shown to sources. Each reference is followed by a letter. These refer to the geographical level for which data were reported: s = State, r = Region, and c = City or metro. The abbreviation *ex* is used to mean *except* or *excluding*; *exp* stands for expenditures. For other abbreviations and further explanations, please see the Introduction.

Anchorage, AK - continued

Item	Per	Value	Date	Ref.
Transportation				
Transportation expenditures, total	year	5527	91	81r
Vehicle expenses, miscellaneous	year	2380	91	81c
Vehicle finance charges	year	553	91	81c
Vehicle finance charges	year	287	91	81r
Vehicle insurance expenditures	year	779	91	81c
Vehicle insurance expenditures	year	624	91	81r
Vehicle maintenance and repairs expenditures	year	824	91	81c
Vehicle maintenance and repairs expenditures	year	695	91	81r
Vehicle purchases	year	3112	91	81c
Vehicle purchases	year	2174	91	81r
Vehicle rental, leases, licenses, etc. expenditures	year	223	91	81c
Vehicle rental, leases, licenses, etc. expenditures	year	257	91	81r
Vehicles purchased, other than cars and trucks	year	83	91	81c
Vehicles purchased, other than cars and trucks	year	28	91	81r
Utilities				
Utilities, ACCRA Index		99.50	12/94	2c
Electricity expenditures	year	605	91	81c
Electricity expenditures	year	616	91	81r
Electricity, (part.), other, 1800 sq. ft., new home	mo.	71.98	12/94	2c
Utilities, fuels, and public services, total expenditures	year	2146	91	81c
Utilities, fuels, and public services, total expenditures	year	1681	91	81r
Water and other public services, expenditures	year	317	91	81c
Water and other public services, expenditures	year	209	91	81r
Weddings				
Bridal attendants' gowns	event	750	10/93	76r
Bridal gown	event	852	10/93	76r
Bridal headpiece and veil	event	167	10/93	76r
Bride's wedding band	event	708	10/93	76r
Clergy	event	224	10/93	76r
Engagement ring	event	2756	10/93	76r
Flowers	event	863	10/93	76r
Formal wear for groom	event	106	10/93	76r
Groom's attendants' formal wear	event	530	10/93	76r
Groom's wedding band	event	402	10/93	76r
Music	event	600	10/93	76r
Photography	event	1088	10/93	76r
Shoes for bride	event	50	10/93	76r
Videography	event	483	10/93	76r
Wedding invitations and announcements	event	342	10/93	76r
Wedding reception	event	7000	10/93	76r

Anderson, IN

Item	Per	Value	Date	Ref.
Composite, ACCRA index		97.40	12/94	2c
Alcoholic Beverages				
Beer, Miller Lite, Bud, 12-oz., ex deposit	6	3.97	12/94	2c
J & B Scotch	750-ml.	15.79	12/94	2c
Wine, Gallo Chablis blanc	1.5-lit	4.47	12/94	2c
Appliances				
Appliances (major), expenditures	year	131	91	81r
Average annual exp.				
Food, health care, personal goods, services	year	25935	91	81r
Charity				
Cash contributions, expenditures	year	745	91	81r

Anderson, IN - continued

Item	Per	Value	Date	Ref.
Clothing				
Apparel, men and boys, total expenditures	year	332	91	81r
Apparel, women and girls, total expenditures	year	578	91	81r
Footwear, expenditures	year	164	91	81r
Jeans, man's denim		28.74	12/94	2c
Shirt, man's dress shirt		29.36	12/94	2c
Undervest, boy's size 10-14, cotton	3	3.41	12/94	2c
Communications				
Long-distance telephone rate, day, addl. min., 1-10 mi.	min.	0.10	12/93	9s
Long-distance telephone rate, day, initial min., 1-10 mi.	min.	0.18	12/93	9s
Newspaper subscription, dly. and Sun. delivery	month	13.04	12/94	2c
Phone line, single, business, field visit	inst	59.00	12/93	9s
Phone line, single, business, no field visit	inst	59.00	12/93	9s
Phone line, single, residence, field visit	inst	47.00	12/93	9s
Phone line, single, residence, no field visit	inst	47.00	12/93	9s
Telephone bill, family of four	month	17.97	12/94	2c
Telephone service, expenditures	year	547	91	81r
Telephone, residential, flat rate	mo.	11.11	12/93	8c
Education				
Board, 4-year private college/university	year	2095	8/94	80s
Board, 4-year public college/university	year	2300	8/94	80s
Education, total expenditures	year	394	91	81r
Room, 4-year private college/university	year	1784	8/94	80s
Room, 4-year public college/university	year	1718	8/94	80s
Total cost, 4-year private college/university	year	15045	8/94	80s
Total cost, 4-year public college/university	year	6639	8/94	80s
Tuition, 2-year public college/university, in-state	year	1737	8/94	80s
Tuition, 4-year private college/university, in-state	year	11165	8/94	80s
Tuition, 4-year public college/university, in-state	year	2621	8/94	80s
Energy and Fuels				
Energy, combined forms, 1800 sq. ft.	mo.	107.17	12/94	2c
Energy, exc. electricity, 1800 sq. ft.	mo.	53.03	12/94	2c
Fuel oil and other fuels, expenditures	year	83	91	81r
Gas, natural, expenditures	year	373	91	81r
Gas, reg unlead, taxes inc., cash, self-service	gal	0.97	12/94	2c
Gasoline and motor oil purchased	year	1000	91	81r
Gasoline, unleaded midgrade	gallon	1.15	4/93	82r
Gasoline, unleaded premium	gallon	1.23	4/93	82r
Gasoline, unleaded regular	gallon	1.07	4/93	82r
Entertainment				
Bowling, evening rate	game	1.83	12/94	2c
Entertainment, total expenditures	year	1356	91	81r
Fees and admissions, expenditures	year	347	91	81r
Monopoly game, Parker Brothers', No. 9	game	10.14	12/94	2c
Movie	adm	5.58	12/94	2c
Pets, toys, playground equipment, expenditures	year	270	91	81r
Reading, expenditures	year	160	91	81r
Televisions, radios, and sound equipment, expenditures	year	433	91	81r
Tennis balls, yellow, Wilson or Penn, 3	can	2.05	12/94	2c
Funerals				
Burial, immediate, container provided by funeral home		1268.31	1/95	54r
Cards, acknowledgment		26.12	1/95	54r
Casket, minimum alternative		198.03	1/95	54r
Cosmetology, hair care, etc.		122.19	1/95	54r
Cremation, direct, container provided by funeral home		977.81	1/95	54r
Embalming		334.00	1/95	54r
Funeral, funeral home		321.16	1/95	54r
Funeral, other facility		317.73	1/95	54r
Graveside service		292.48	1/95	54r

Values are in dollars or fractions of dollars. In the column headed *Ref*, references are shown to sources. Each reference is followed by a letter. These refer to the geographical level for which data were reported: s = State, r = Region, and c = City or metro. The abbreviation *ex* is used to mean *except* or *excluding*; *exp* stands for expenditures. For other abbreviations and further explanations, please see the Introduction.

Anderson, IN - continued

Item	Per	Value	Date	Ref.
Funerals				
Hearse, local		153.20	1/95	54r
Limousine, local		123.52	1/95	54r
Memorial service		356.30	1/95	54r
Service charge, professional, nondeclinable		968.24	1/95	54r
Visitation and viewing		332.66	1/95	54r
Groceries				
Groceries, ACCRA Index		101.50	12/94	2c
Apples, Red Delicious	lb.	0.68	12/94	82r
Baby food, strained vegetables, lowest price	4-4.5 oz.	0.39	12/94	2c
Bacon, sliced	lb.	1.88	12/94	82r
Bananas	lb.	0.41	12/94	2c
Bananas	lb.	0.41	12/94	82r
Beef or hamburger, ground	lb.	1.30	12/94	2c
Beef purchases	year	197	91	81r
Beef, stew, boneless	lb.	2.52	12/94	82r
Beverage purchases, alcoholic	year	293	91	81r
Beverage purchases, nonalcoholic	year	203	91	81r
Bologna, all beef or mixed	lb.	2.12	12/94	82r
Bread, white	24-oz.	0.72	12/94	2c
Bread, white, pan	lb.	0.76	12/94	82r
Cabbage	lb.	0.44	12/94	82r
Carrots, short trimmed and topped	lb.	0.44	12/94	82r
Cereals and bakery products purchases	year	347	91	81r
Cereals and cereals products purchases	year	119	91	81r
Cheddar cheese, natural	lb.	3.28	12/94	82r
Cheese, Kraft grated Parmesan	8-oz.	3.26	12/94	2c
Chicken breast, bone-in	lb.	1.61	12/94	82r
Chicken, fresh, whole	lb.	0.89	12/94	82r
Chicken, whole fryer	lb.	0.74	12/94	2c
Chuck roast, USDA choice, boneless	lb.	2.33	12/94	82r
Cigarettes, Winston, Kings	carton	14.39	12/94	2c
Coffee, 100%, ground roast, all sizes	lb.	4.28	12/94	82r
Coffee, vacuum-packed	13 oz.	3.61	12/94	2c
Cookies, chocolate chip	lb.	2.72	12/94	82r
Corn Flakes, Kellogg's or Post Toasties	18 oz.	2.26	12/94	2c
Corn, frozen, whole kernel, lowest price	10 oz.	0.80	12/94	2c
Dairy products (other) purchases	year	148	91	81r
Eggs, Grade A large	dozen	0.60	12/94	2c
Eggs, Grade A large	dozen	0.76	12/94	82r
Fish and seafood purchases	year	61	91	81r
Flour, white, all purpose	lb.	0.22	12/94	82r
Food purchases, food eaten at home	year	2313	91	81r
Foods purchased away from home, not prepared by consumer	year	1709	91	81r
Fruits and vegetables purchases	year	372	91	81r
Grapefruit	lb.	0.47	12/94	82r
Grapes, Thompson seedless	lb.	2.15	12/94	82r
Ground beef, 100% beef	lb.	1.37	12/94	82r
Ground chuck, 100% beef	lb.	1.81	12/94	82r
Ham, boneless, exc. canned	lb.	2.16	12/94	82r
Ice cream, prepackaged, bulk, regular	1/2 gal.	2.48	12/94	82r
Lemons	lb.	1.08	12/94	82r
Lettuce, iceberg	lb.	0.81	12/94	82r
Lettuce, iceberg	head	0.79	12/94	2c
Margarine, Blue Bonnet or Parkay cubes	lb.	0.64	12/94	2c
Margarine, stick	lb.	0.81	12/94	82r
Meats, poultry, fish, and eggs purchases	year	591	91	81r
Milk and cream (fresh) purchases	year	132	91	81r
Milk, whole	1/2 gal.	1.44	12/94	2c
Orange juice, frozen concentrate 12-oz. can	16 oz.	1.41	12/94	82r
Orange juice, Minute Maid frozen	12-oz.	1.29	12/94	2c
Oranges, Navel	lb.	0.56	12/94	82r
Peaches, halves or slices, Hunt's, Del Monte, or Libby's	29-oz.	1.35	12/94	2c
Peanut butter, creamy, all sizes	lb.	1.81	12/94	82r
Peas, sweet, Del Monte or Green Giant	15-17 oz.	0.59	12/94	2c
Pork chops, center cut, bone-in	lb.	2.76	12/94	82r
Pork purchases	year	130	91	81r

Anderson, IN - continued

Item	Per	Value	Date	Ref.
Groceries - continued				
Potato chips	16-oz.	2.81	12/94	82r
Potatoes, frozen, French fried	lb.	0.83	12/94	82r
Potatoes, white	lb.	0.28	12/94	82r
Potatoes, white or red	10-lb. sack	2.39	12/94	2c
Round roast, USDA choice, boneless	lb.	2.90	12/94	82r
Sausage, Jimmy Dean, 100% pork	lb.	3.05	12/94	2c
Shortening, vegetable oil blends	lb.	0.88	12/94	82r
Shortening, vegetable, Crisco	3-lb.	2.52	12/94	2c
Soft drink, Coca Cola, ex deposit	2 lit	1.22	12/94	2c
Spaghetti and macaroni	lb.	0.78	12/94	82r
Steak, rib eye, USDA choice, boneless	lb.	6.15	12/94	82r
Steak, round, graded & ungraded, exc. USDA prime & choice	lb.	2.72	12/94	82r
Steak, round, USDA choice, boneless	lb.	3.02	12/94	82r
Steak, sirloin, USDA choice, boneless	lb.	3.85	12/94	82r
Steak, t-bone	lb.	4.56	12/94	2c
Steak, T-bone, USDA choice, bone-in	lb.	5.38	12/94	82r
Sugar and other sweets, eaten at home, expenditures	year	91	91	81r
Sugar, cane or beet	4 lbs.	1.52	12/94	2c
Sugar, white, all sizes	lb.	0.36	12/94	82r
Tobacco products and smoking supplies, total expenditures	year	298	91	81r
Tomatoes, field grown	lb.	1.36	12/94	82r
Tomatoes, Hunt's or Del Monte	14.5 oz.	0.76	12/94	2c
Tuna, chunk, light	lb.	1.94	12/94	82r
Tuna, chunk, light, oil-packed	6.125-6.5 oz.	0.82	12/94	2c
Turkey, frozen, whole	lb.	0.96	12/94	82r
Yogurt, natural, fruit flavored	8 oz.	0.62	12/94	82r
Goods and Services				
Miscellaneous goods and services, ACCRA Index		94.20	12/94	2c
Health Care				
Health care, ACCRA Index		91.90	12/94	2c
Antibiotic ointment, Polysporin	1.5 oz.	3.82	12/94	2c
Childbirth, Cesarean delivery, hospital charge	birth	5101.00	12/91	69r
Childbirth, Cesarean delivery, physician charge	birth	2234.00	12/91	69r
Childbirth, normal delivery, hospital charge	birth	2891.00	12/91	69r
Childbirth, normal delivery, physician charge	birth	1623.00	12/91	69r
Dentist's fee, adult teeth cleaning and periodic oral exam	visit	52.17	12/94	2c
Doctor's fee, routine exam, established patient	visit	35.75	12/94	2c
Drugs, expenditures	year	248	91	81r
Health care, total expenditures	year	1336	91	81r
Health insurance expenditures	year	550	91	81r
Hospital care, semiprivate room	day	320.50	12/94	2c
Insurance premium, family medical care	month	353.94	1/95	41s
Medical services expenditures	year	457	91	81r
Medical supplies expenditures	year	82	91	81r
Household Goods				
Appl. repair, service call, wash mach	min. lab. chg.	35.20	12/94	2c
Floor coverings, expenditures	year	105	91	81r
Furniture, expenditures	year	291	91	81r
Household equipment, misc. expenditures	year	341	91	81r
Household expenditures, miscellaneous	year	162	91	81r
Household furnishings and equipment, expenditures	year	1042	91	81r
Household operations expenditures	year	365	91	81r
Household textiles, expenditures	year	101	91	81r
Housekeeping supplies, expenditures	year	390	91	81r
Laundry and cleaning supplies, expenditures	year	110	91	81r

Values are in dollars or fractions of dollars. In the column headed *Ref*, references are shown to sources. Each reference is followed by a letter. These refer to the geographical level for which data were reported: s=State, r=Region, and c=City or metro. The abbreviation *ex* is used to mean *except* or *excluding*; *exp* stands for *expenditures*. For other abbreviations and further explanations, please see the Introduction.

Anderson, IN - continued

Item	Per	Value	Date	Ref.
Household Goods				
Laundry detergent, Tide Ultra, Bold, or Cheer	42 oz.	3.95	12/94	2c
Postage and stationery, expenditures	year	115	91	81r
Tissues, facial, Kleenex brand	175	1.09	12/94	2c
Housing				
Housing, ACCRA Index		102.80	12/94	2c
Add garage/carport		8,479	3/95	74r
Add room(s)		21,347	3/95	74r
Apartment condominium or co-op, median	unit	87100	12/94	62r
Bathroom addition, average cost	add	9734.00	3/95	13r
Bathroom remodeling, average cost	remod	6414.00	3/95	13r
Bedroom, master suite addition, average cost	add	27122.00	3/95	13r
Deck addition, average cost	add	6665.00	3/95	13r
Dwellings (owned), expenditures	year	2566	91	81r
Enclose porch/patio/breezeway		4,556	3/95	74r
Exterior remodeling, average cost	remod	15395.00	3/95	13r
Family room addition, average cost	add	27658.00	3/95	13r
Finish room in basement/attic		5,074	3/95	74r
Home, existing, single-family, median	unit	106500	12/94	62r
House payment, principal and interest, 25% down payment	mo.	818	12/94	2c
House, 1800 sq ft, 8000 sq ft lot, new, urban, utilities	total	130500	12/94	2c
Kitchen remodeling, major, average cost	remod	17084.00	3/95	13r
Kitchen remodeling, minor, average cost	remod	5804.00	3/95	13r
Maintenance, repairs, insurance, and other housing expenditures	year	484	91	81r
Mortgage interest and charges expenditures	year	1443	91	81r
Mtge. rate, incl. points and orig. fee, 30-year conv. fixed or ARM	mo.	9.43	12/94	2c
Office, home addition, average cost	add	8121.00	3/95	13r
Princ. & int., mortgage, median-price exist. sing.-family home	mo.	515	12/94	62r
Property taxes expenditures	year	639	91	81r
Redesign, restructure more than half of home's interior		9,114	3/95	74r
Rent, apartment, 2 br., 1 1/2-2 baths, unfurnished, 950 sq ft, water	mo.	455	12/94	2c
Rental units expenditures	year	1200	91	81r
Sun-space addition, average cost	add	23768.00	3/95	13r
Wing addition, two-story, average cost	add	50410.00	3/95	13r
Insurance and Pensions				
Auto insurance, private passenger	year	586.58	12/94	71s
Insurance and pensions, personal, expenditures	year	2408	91	81r
Insurance, life and other personal, expenditures	year	355	91	81r
Pensions and Social Security, expenditures	year	2053	91	81r
Legal Assistance				
Legal work, law firm associate	hour	90		10r
Legal work, law firm partner	hour	139		10r
Personal Goods				
Shampoo, Alberto VO5	15-oz.	1.15	12/94	2c
Toothpaste, Crest or Colgate	6-7 oz.	1.59	12/94	2c
Personal Services				
Dry cleaning, man's 2-pc. suit		5.70	12/94	2c
Haircut, man's barbershop, no styling		6.80	12/94	2c
Haircut, woman's shampoo, trim, blow-dry		18.80	12/94	2c
Personal services expenditures	year	203	91	81r
Restaurant Food				
Chicken, fried, thigh and drumstick		2.29	12/94	2c
Dining expenditures, family	week	30.03	94	73r
Hamburger with cheese	1/4 lb.	1.69	12/94	2c
Pizza, Pizza Hut or Pizza Inn	12-13 in.	7.50	12/94	2c

Anderson, IN - continued

Item	Per	Value	Date	Ref.
Taxes				
Taxes, Federal income, expenditures	year	1756	91	81r
Taxes, personal, expenditures	year	2426	91	81r
Taxes, State and local income, expenditures	year	568	91	81r
Transportation				
Transportation, ACCRA Index		90.50	12/94	2c
Cars and trucks purchased, new	year	891	91	81r
Cars and trucks purchased, used	year	1155	91	81r
Driver's learning permit fee	perm	2.00	1/94	84s
Driver's license fee	orig	6.00	1/94	84s
Driver's license fee, duplicate	lic	3.00	1/94	84s
Driver's license renewal fee	renew	6.00	1/94	84s
Identification card, nondriver	card	4.00	1/94	83s
Motorcycle learning permit fee	perm	2.00	1/94	84s
Motorcycle license fee	orig	6.00	1/94	84s
Motorcycle license fee, duplicate	lic	3.00	1/94	84s
Motorcycle license renewal fee	renew	6.00	1/94	84s
Public transportation expenditures	year	209	91	81r
Tire balance, computer or spin bal., front	wheel	6.50	12/94	2c
Transportation expenditures, total	year	4792	91	81r
Vehicle finance charges	year	300	91	81r
Vehicle insurance expenditures	year	485	91	81r
Vehicle maintenance and repairs expenditures	year	534	91	81r
Vehicle purchases	year	2068	91	81r
Vehicle rental, leases, licenses, etc. expenditures	year	197	91	81r
Vehicles purchased, other than cars and trucks	year	22	91	81r
Utilities				
Utilities, ACCRA Index		95.00	12/94	2c
Electricity expenditures	year	668	91	81r
Electricity, (part.), other, 1800 sq. ft., new home	mo.	54.14	12/94	2c
Utilities, fuels, and public services, total expenditures	year	1838	91	81r
Water and other public services, expenditures	year	167	91	81r
Weddings				
Bridal attendants' gowns	event	750	10/93	76r
Bridal gown	event	852	10/93	76r
Bridal headpiece and veil	event	167	10/93	76r
Bride's wedding band	event	708	10/93	76r
Clergy	event	224	10/93	76r
Engagement ring	event	2756	10/93	76r
Flowers	event	863	10/93	76r
Formal wear for groom	event	106	10/93	76r
Groom's attendants' formal wear	event	530	10/93	76r
Groom's wedding band	event	402	10/93	76r
Music	event	600	10/93	76r
Photography	event	1088	10/93	76r
Shoes for bride	event	50	10/93	76r
Videography	event	483	10/93	76r
Wedding invitations and announcements	event	342	10/93	76r
Wedding reception	event	7000	10/93	76r

Anderson, SC

Item	Per	Value	Date	Ref.
Appliances				
Appliances (major), expenditures	year	153	91	81r
Average annual exp.				
Food, health care, personal goods, services	year	27020	91	81r
Charity				
Cash contributions, expenditures	year	839	91	81r
Clothing				
Apparel, men and boys, total expenditures	year	380	91	81r
Apparel, women and girls, total expenditures	year	660	91	81r
Footwear, expenditures	year	193	91	81r

Values are in dollars or fractions of dollars. In the column headed *Ref*, references are shown to sources. Each reference is followed by a letter. These refer to the geographical level for which data were reported: s=State, r=Region, and c=City or metro. The abbreviation *ex* is used to mean *except* or *excluding*; *exp* stands for expenditures. For other abbreviations and further explanations, please see the Introduction.

Anderson, SC - continued

Item	Per	Value	Date	Ref.
Communications				
Long-distance telephone rate, day, addl. min., 1-10 mi.	min.	0.13	12/93	9s
Long-distance telephone rate, day, initial min., 1-10 mi.	min.	0.24	12/93	9s
Phone line, single, business, field visit	inst	82.50	12/93	9s
Phone line, single, business, no field visit	inst	64.00	12/93	9s
Phone line, single, residence, field visit	inst	62.50	12/93	9s
Phone line, single, residence, no field visit	inst	44.00	12/93	9s
Telephone service, expenditures	year	616	91	81r
Education				
Board, 4-year private college/university	year	1831	8/94	80s
Board, 4-year public college/university	year	1462	8/94	80s
Education, total expenditures	year	319	91	81r
Room, 4-year private college/university	year	1744	8/94	80s
Room, 4-year public college/university	year	1851	8/94	80s
Total cost, 4-year private college/university	year	12082	8/94	80s
Total cost, 4-year public college/university	year	6203	8/94	80s
Tuition, 2-year public college/university, in-state	year	1061	8/94	80s
Tuition, 4-year private college/university, in-state	year	8507	8/94	80s
Tuition, 4-year public college/university, in-state	year	2891	8/94	80s
Energy and Fuels				
Fuel oil and other fuels, expenditures	year	56	91	81r
Gas, natural, expenditures	year	150	91	81r
Gasoline and motor oil purchased	year	1152	91	81r
Gasoline, unleaded midgrade	gallon	1.21	4/93	82r
Gasoline, unleaded premium	gallon	1.30	4/93	82r
Gasoline, unleaded regular	gallon	1.10	4/93	82r
Entertainment				
Concert ticket, Pearl Jam group	perf	20.00	94	50r
Entertainment, total expenditures	year	1266	91	81r
Fees and admissions, expenditures	year	306	91	81r
Pets, toys, playground equipment, expenditures	year	271	91	81r
Reading, expenditures	year	131	91	81r
Televisions, radios, and sound equipment, expenditures	year	439	91	81r
Funerals				
Burial, immediate, container provided by funeral home		1370.36	1/95	54r
Cards, acknowledgment		14.83	1/95	54r
Casket, minimum alternative		192.52	1/95	54r
Cosmetology, hair care, etc.		102.27	1/95	54r
Cremation, direct, container provided by funeral home		1065.64	1/95	54r
Embalming		304.29	1/95	54r
Funeral, funeral home		287.83	1/95	54r
Funeral, other facility		284.14	1/95	54r
Graveside service		349.13	1/95	54r
Hearse, local		132.27	1/95	54r
Limousine, local		98.45	1/95	54r
Memorial service		270.59	1/95	54r
Service charge, professional, nondeclinable		933.59	1/95	54r
Visitation and viewing		225.83	1/95	54r
Groceries				
Apples, Red Delicious	lb.	0.73	12/94	82r
Bacon, sliced	lb.	1.67	12/94	82r
Bananas	lb.	0.42	12/94	82r
Beef purchases	year	213	91	81r
Beverage purchases, alcoholic	year	249	91	81r
Beverage purchases, nonalcoholic	year	207	91	81r
Bologna, all beef or mixed	lb.	2.27	12/94	82r
Bread, white, pan	lb.	0.68	12/94	82r
Cabbage	lb.	0.42	12/94	82r
Carrots, short trimmed and topped	lb.	0.53	12/94	82r
Cereals and bakery products purchases	year	345	91	81r
Cereals and cereals products purchases	year	127	91	81r

Anderson, SC - continued

Item	Per	Value	Date	Ref.
Groceries - continued				
Cheddar cheese, natural	lb.	3.58	12/94	82r
Chicken breast, bone-in	lb.	1.71	12/94	82r
Chicken, fresh, whole	lb.	0.78	12/94	82r
Chuck roast, USDA choice, boneless	lb.	2.26	12/94	82r
Crackers, soda, salted	lb.	1.27	12/94	82r
Cucumbers	lb.	0.65	12/94	82r
Dairy products (other) purchases	year	141	91	81r
Eggs, Grade A large	dozen	0.87	12/94	82r
Fish and seafood purchases	year	72	91	81r
Flour, white, all purpose	lb.	0.23	12/94	82r
Food purchases, food eaten at home	year	2381	91	81r
Foods purchased away from home, not prepared by consumer	year	1696	91	81r
Frankfurters, all meat or all beef	lb.	1.74	12/94	82r
Fruits and vegetables purchases	year	380	91	81r
Grapefruit	lb.	0.45	12/94	82r
Grapes, Thompson seedless	lb.	2.30	12/94	82r
Ground beef, 100% beef	lb.	1.37	12/94	82r
Ground chuck, 100% beef	lb.	1.97	12/94	82r
Ham, boneless, exc. canned	lb.	2.54	12/94	82r
Ice cream, prepackaged, bulk, regular	1/2 gal.	2.47	12/94	82r
Lemons	lb.	1.02	12/94	82r
Lettuce, iceberg	lb.	0.96	12/94	82r
Margarine, stick	lb.	0.77	12/94	82r
Meats, poultry, fish, and eggs purchases	year	655	91	81r
Milk and cream (fresh) purchases	year	130	91	81r
Orange juice, frozen concentrate 12-oz. can	16 oz.	1.36	12/94	82r
Oranges, Navel	lb.	0.54	12/94	82r
Pears, Anjou	lb.	0.81	12/94	82r
Pork chops, center cut, bone-in	lb.	3.07	12/94	82r
Pork purchases	year	142	91	81r
Potato chips	16-oz.	3.15	12/94	82r
Potatoes, frozen, French fried	lb.	0.82	12/94	82r
Potatoes, white	lb.	0.34	12/94	82r
Rice, white, long grain, uncooked	lb.	0.48	12/94	82r
Round roast, USDA choice, boneless	lb.	2.91	12/94	82r
Sausage, fresh	lb.	1.82	12/94	82r
Shortening, vegetable oil blends	lb.	0.75	12/94	82r
Spaghetti and macaroni	lb.	0.87	12/94	82r
Steak, rib eye, USDA choice, boneless	lb.	6.85	12/94	82r
Steak, round, graded & ungraded, exc. USDA prime & choice	lb.	2.96	12/94	82r
Steak, round, USDA choice, boneless	lb.	3.17	12/94	82r
Steak, sirloin, USDA choice, boneless	lb.	4.12	12/94	82r
Steak, T-bone, USDA choice, bone-in	lb.	5.63	12/94	82r
Sugar and other sweets, eaten at home, expenditures	year	93	91	81r
Sugar, white, all sizes	lb.	0.39	12/94	82r
Tobacco products and smoking supplies, total expenditures	year	286	91	81r
Tomatoes, field grown	lb.	1.36	12/94	82r
Tuna, chunk, light	lb.	1.94	12/94	82r
Turkey, frozen, whole	lb.	0.96	12/94	82r
Yogurt, natural, fruit flavored	8 oz.	0.58	12/94	82r
Health Care				
Adenosine, emergency room	treat	100.00	95	23r
Bladder tap, superpubic, infant, emergency room	treat	119.00	95	23r
Blood analysis, emergency room	treat	25.00	95	23r
Blood tests, abdominal pain, emergency room	treat	25.00	95	23r
Burn dressing, emergency room	treat	266.00	95	23r
Cardiology interpretation, emergency room	treat	26.00	95	23r
Chest X-ray, emergency room	treat	78.00	95	23r
Childbirth, Cesarean delivery, hospital charge	birth	5462.00	12/91	69r
Childbirth, Cesarean delivery, physician charge	birth	2228.00	12/91	69r
Childbirth, normal delivery, hospital charge	birth	2943.00	12/91	69r
Childbirth, normal delivery, physician charge	birth	1619.00	12/91	69r
Defibrillation pads, emergency room	treat	6.00	95	23r

Values are in dollars or fractions of dollars. In the column headed *Ref*, references are shown to sources. Each reference is followed by a letter. These refer to the geographical level for which data were reported: s = State, r = Region, and c = City or metro. The abbreviation *ex* is used to mean *except* or *excluding*; *exp* stands for expenditures. For other abbreviations and further explanations, please see the Introduction.

Anderson, SC - continued

Item	Per	Value	Date	Ref.
Health Care				
Drugs, expenditures	year	297	91	81r
Gastric tube insertion, nasal, emergency room	treat	25.00	95	23r
Health care, total expenditures	year	1600	91	81r
Health insurance expenditures	year	637	91	81r
Heart monitor, emergency room	treat	40.00	95	23r
Insurance premium, family medical care	month	414.49	1/95	41s
Intravenous fluids, emergency room	treat	130.00	95	23r
Intravenous fluids, emergency room	liter	26.00	95	23r
Intravenous line, central, emergency room	treat	342.00	95	23r
Liver function tests, abdominal pain, emergency room	treat	26.00	95	23r
Medical care charges, total, emergency room, third-degree burns	treat	2101.00	95	23r
Medical care charges, total, emergency, infant with fever	treat	628.00	95	23r
Medical services expenditures	year	573	91	81r
Medical supplies expenditures	year	93	91	81r
Morphine, emergency room	treat	34.00	95	23r
Nursing care and facilities charges, emergency room	treat	252.00	95	23r
Nursing care and facilities charges, emergency, infant with fever	treat	252.00	95	23r
Nursing care and facilities charges, emergency, third-degree burns	treat	861.00	95	23r
Physician's charges, emergency, infant with fever	treat	212.00	95	23r
Physician's charges, emergency, third-degree burns	treat	372.00	95	23r
Physician's fee, emergency room	treat	372.00	95	23r
Physician's fee, general practitioner	visit	51.20	12/93	60r
Surgery, open-heart	proc	42374.00	1/93	14r
Ultrasound, abdominal, emergency room	treat	276.00	95	23r
Urinalysis, emergency room	treat	20.00	95	23r
Urinalysis, infant, emergency room	treat	20.00	95	23r
X-rays, emergency room	treat	78.00	95	23r
Household Goods				
Floor coverings, expenditures	year	48	91	81r
Furniture, expenditures	year	280	91	81r
Household equipment, misc. expenditures	year	342	91	81r
Household expenditures, miscellaneous	year	256	91	81r
Household furnishings and equipment, expenditures	year	988	91	81r
Household operations expenditures	year	468	91	81r
Household textiles, expenditures	year	95	91	81r
Housekeeping supplies, expenditures	year	380	91	81r
Laundry and cleaning supplies, expenditures	year	109	91	81r
Postage and stationery, expenditures	year	105	91	81r
Housing				
Add garage/carport		6,980	3/95	74r
Add room(s)		11,403	3/95	74r
Apartment condominium or co-op, median	unit	68600	12/94	62r
Dwellings (owned), expenditures	year	2428	91	81r
Enclose porch/patio/breezeway		4,572	3/95	74r
Finish room in basement/attic		3,794	3/95	74r
Home, existing, single-family, median	unit	120200	12/94	62r
Maintenance, repairs, insurance, and other housing expenditures	year	531	91	81r
Mortgage interest and charges expenditures	year	1506	91	81r
Princ. & int., mortgage, median-price exist. sing.-family home	mo.	540	12/94	62r
Property taxes expenditures	year	391	91	81r
Redesign, restructure more than half of home's interior		17,641	3/95	74r
Rental units expenditures	year	1264	91	81r
Insurance and Pensions				
Auto insurance, private passenger	year	684.10	12/94	71s
Insurance and pensions, personal, expenditures	year	2395	91	81r

Anderson, SC - continued

Item	Per	Value	Date	Ref.
Insurance and Pensions - continued				
Insurance, life and other personal, expenditures	year	368	91	81r
Pensions and Social Security, expenditures	year	2027	91	81r
Personal Services				
Personal services expenditures	year	212	91	81r
Restaurant Food				
Dining expenditures, family	week	33.83	94	73r
Taxes				
Taxes, Federal income, expenditures	year	2275	91	81r
Taxes, personal, expenditures	year	2715	91	81r
Taxes, State and local income, expenditures	year	365	91	81r
Transportation				
Cars and trucks purchased, new	year	1306	91	81r
Cars and trucks purchased, used	year	942	91	81r
Driver's learning permit fee	perm	2.00	1/94	84s
Driver's license fee	orig	10.00	1/94	84s
Driver's license fee, duplicate	lic	0.50	1/94	84s
Driver's license reinstatement fee, min.	susp	30.00	1/94	85s
Driver's license renewal fee	renew	10.00	1/94	84s
Identification card, nondriver	card	5.00	1/94	83s
Motorcycle learning permit fee	perm	2.00	1/94	84s
Motorcycle license fee	orig	10.00	1/94	84s
Motorcycle license fee, duplicate	lic	0.50	1/94	84s
Motorcycle license renewal fee	renew	10.00	1/94	84s
Public transportation expenditures	year	249	91	81r
Transportation expenditures, total	year	5307	91	81r
Vehicle finance charges	year	346	91	81r
Vehicle insurance expenditures	year	544	91	81r
Vehicle maintenance and repairs expenditures	year	600	91	81r
Vehicle purchases	year	2275	91	81r
Vehicle rental, leases, licenses, etc. expenditures	year	141	91	81r
Vehicles purchased, other than cars and trucks	year	27	91	81r
Utilities				
Electricity expenditures	year	950	91	81r
Utilities, fuels, and public services, total expenditures	year	2000	91	81r
Water and other public services, expenditures	year	227	91	81r
Weddings				
Bridal attendants' gowns	event	750	10/93	76r
Bridal gown	event	852	10/93	76r
Bridal headpiece and veil	event	167	10/93	76r
Bride's wedding band	event	708	10/93	76r
Clergy	event	224	10/93	76r
Engagement ring	event	2756	10/93	76r
Flowers	event	863	10/93	76r
Formal wear for groom	event	106	10/93	76r
Groom's attendants' formal wear	event	530	10/93	76r
Groom's wedding band	event	402	10/93	76r
Music	event	600	10/93	76r
Photography	event	1088	10/93	76r
Shoes for bride	event	50	10/93	76r
Videography	event	483	10/93	76r
Wedding invitations and announcements	event	342	10/93	76r
Wedding reception	event	7000	10/93	76r

Ann Arbor, MI

Item	Per	Value	Date	Ref.
Appliances				
Appliances (major), expenditures	year	131	91	81r
Average annual exp.				
Food, health care, personal goods, services	year	25935	91	81r

Values are in dollars or fractions of dollars. In the column headed *Ref*, references are shown to sources. Each reference is followed by a letter. These refer to the geographical level for which data were reported: s=State, r=Region, and c=City or metro. The abbreviation *ex* is used to mean *except* or *excluding*; *exp* stands for *expenditures*. For other abbreviations and further explanations, please see the Introduction.

Ann Arbor, MI - continued

Item	Per	Value	Date	Ref.
Charity				
Cash contributions, expenditures	year	745	91	81r
Clothing				
Apparel, men and boys, total expenditures	year	332	91	81r
Apparel, women and girls, total expenditures	year	578	91	81r
Footwear, expenditures	year	164	91	81r
Communications				
Long-distance telephone rate, day, addl. min., 1-10 mi.	min.	0.08	12/93	9s
Long-distance telephone rate, day, initial min., 1-10 mi.	min.	0.14	12/93	9s
Phone line, single, business, field visit	inst	42.00	12/93	9s
Phone line, single, business, no field visit	inst	42.00	12/93	9s
Phone line, single, residence, field visit	inst	42.00	12/93	9s
Phone line, single, residence, no field visit	inst	42.00	12/93	9s
Telephone service, expenditures	year	547	91	81r
Education				
Board, 4-year private college/university	year	2064	8/94	80s
Board, 4-year public college/university	year	2304	8/94	80s
Education, total expenditures	year	394	91	81r
Room, 4-year private college/university	year	1814	8/94	80s
Room, 4-year public college/university	year	1856	8/94	80s
Total cost, 4-year private college/university	year	12178	8/94	80s
Total cost, 4-year public college/university	year	7642	8/94	80s
Tuition, 2-year public college/university, in-state	year	1358	8/94	80s
Tuition, 4-year private college/university, in-state	year	8300	8/94	80s
Tuition, 4-year public college/university, in-state	year	3481	8/94	80s
Energy and Fuels				
Fuel oil and other fuels, expenditures	year	83	91	81r
Gas, natural, expenditures	year	373	91	81r
Gasoline and motor oil purchased	year	1000	91	81r
Gasoline, unleaded midgrade	gallon	1.15	4/93	82r
Gasoline, unleaded premium	gallon	1.23	4/93	82r
Gasoline, unleaded regular	gallon	1.07	4/93	82r
Entertainment				
Entertainment, total expenditures	year	1356	91	81r
Fees and admissions, expenditures	year	347	91	81r
Pets, toys, playground equipment, expenditures	year	270	91	81r
Reading, expenditures	year	160	91	81r
Televisions, radios, and sound equipment, expenditures	year	433	91	81r
Funerals				
Burial, immediate, container provided by funeral home		1268.31	1/95	54r
Cards, acknowledgment		26.12	1/95	54r
Casket, minimum alternative		198.03	1/95	54r
Cosmetology, hair care, etc.		122.19	1/95	54r
Cremation, direct, container provided by funeral home		977.81	1/95	54r
Embalming		334.00	1/95	54r
Funeral, funeral home		321.16	1/95	54r
Funeral, other facility		317.73	1/95	54r
Graveside service		292.48	1/95	54r
Hearse, local		153.20	1/95	54r
Limousine, local		123.52	1/95	54r
Memorial service		356.30	1/95	54r
Service charge, professional, nondeclinable		968.24	1/95	54r
Visitation and viewing		332.66	1/95	54r
Groceries				
Apples, Red Delicious	lb.	0.68	12/94	82r
Bacon, sliced	lb.	1.88	12/94	82r
Bananas	lb.	0.41	12/94	82r
Beef purchases	year	197	91	81r
Beef, stew, boneless	lb.	2.52	12/94	82r
Beverage purchases, alcoholic	year	293	91	81r

Ann Arbor, MI - continued

Item	Per	Value	Date	Ref.
Groceries - continued				
Beverage purchases, nonalcoholic	year	203	91	81r
Bologna, all beef or mixed	lb.	2.12	12/94	82r
Bread, white, pan	lb.	0.76	12/94	82r
Cabbage	lb.	0.44	12/94	82r
Carrots, short trimmed and topped	lb.	0.44	12/94	82r
Cereals and bakery products purchases	year	347	91	81r
Cereals and cereals products purchases	year	119	91	81r
Cheddar cheese, natural	lb.	3.28	12/94	82r
Chicken breast, bone-in	lb.	1.61	12/94	82r
Chicken, fresh, whole	lb.	0.89	12/94	82r
Chuck roast, USDA choice, boneless	lb.	2.33	12/94	82r
Coffee, 100%, ground roast, all sizes	lb.	4.28	12/94	82r
Cookies, chocolate chip	lb.	2.72	12/94	82r
Dairy products (other) purchases	year	148	91	81r
Eggs, Grade A large	dozen	0.76	12/94	82r
Fish and seafood purchases	year	61	91	81r
Flour, white, all purpose	lb.	0.22	12/94	82r
Food purchases, food eaten at home	year	2313	91	81r
Foods purchased away from home, not prepared by consumer	year	1709	91	81r
Fruits and vegetables purchases	year	372	91	81r
Grapefruit	lb.	0.47	12/94	82r
Grapes, Thompson seedless	lb.	2.15	12/94	82r
Ground beef, 100% beef	lb.	1.37	12/94	82r
Ground chuck, 100% beef	lb.	1.81	12/94	82r
Ham, boneless, exc. canned	lb.	2.16	12/94	82r
Ice cream, prepackaged, bulk, regular	1/2 gal.	2.48	12/94	82r
Lemons	lb.	1.08	12/94	82r
Lettuce, iceberg	lb.	0.81	12/94	82r
Margarine, stick	lb.	0.81	12/94	82r
Meats, poultry, fish, and eggs purchases	year	591	91	81r
Milk and cream (fresh) purchases	year	132	91	81r
Orange juice, frozen concentrate 12-oz. can	16 oz.	1.41	12/94	82r
Oranges, Navel	lb.	0.56	12/94	82r
Peanut butter, creamy, all sizes	lb.	1.81	12/94	82r
Pork chops, center cut, bone-in	lb.	2.76	12/94	82r
Pork purchases	year	130	91	81r
Potato chips	16-oz.	2.81	12/94	82r
Potatoes, frozen, French fried	lb.	0.83	12/94	82r
Potatoes, white	lb.	0.28	12/94	82r
Round roast, USDA choice, boneless	lb.	2.90	12/94	82r
Shortening, vegetable oil blends	lb.	0.88	12/94	82r
Spaghetti and macaroni	lb.	0.78	12/94	82r
Steak, rib eye, USDA choice, boneless	lb.	6.15	12/94	82r
Steak, round, graded & ungraded, exc. USDA prime & choice	lb.	2.72	12/94	82r
Steak, round, USDA choice, boneless	lb.	3.02	12/94	82r
Steak, sirloin, USDA choice, boneless	lb.	3.85	12/94	82r
Steak, T-bone, USDA choice, bone-in	lb.	5.38	12/94	82r
Sugar and other sweets, eaten at home, expenditures	year	91	91	81r
Sugar, white, all sizes	lb.	0.36	12/94	82r
Tobacco products and smoking supplies, total expenditures	year	298	91	81r
Tomatoes, field grown	lb.	1.36	12/94	82r
Tuna, chunk, light	lb.	1.94	12/94	82r
Turkey, frozen, whole	lb.	0.96	12/94	82r
Yogurt, natural, fruit flavored	8 oz.	0.62	12/94	82r
Health Care				
Childbirth, Cesarean delivery, hospital charge	birth	5101.00	12/91	69r
Childbirth, Cesarean delivery, physician charge	birth	2234.00	12/91	69r
Childbirth, normal delivery, hospital charge	birth	2891.00	12/91	69r
Childbirth, normal delivery, physician charge	birth	1623.00	12/91	69r
Drugs, expenditures	year	248	91	81r
Health care, total expenditures	year	1336	91	81r
Health insurance expenditures	year	550	91	81r
Insurance premium, family medical care	month	369.41	1/95	41s
Medical services expenditures	year	457	91	81r
Medical supplies expenditures	year	82	91	81r

Values are in dollars or fractions of dollars. In the column headed *Ref*, references are shown to sources. Each reference is followed by a letter. These refer to the geographical level for which data were reported: s=State, r=Region, and c=City or metro. The abbreviation *ex* is used to mean *except* or *excluding*; *exp* stands for expenditures. For other abbreviations and further explanations, please see the Introduction.

Ann Arbor, MI - continued

Item	Per	Value	Date	Ref.
Household Goods				
Floor coverings, expenditures	year	105	91	81r
Furniture, expenditures	year	291	91	81r
Household equipment, misc. expenditures	year	341	91	81r
Household expenditures, miscellaneous	year	162	91	81r
Household furnishings and equipment, expenditures	year	1042	91	81r
Household operations expenditures	year	365	91	81r
Household textiles, expenditures	year	101	91	81r
Housekeeping supplies, expenditures	year	390	91	81r
Laundry and cleaning supplies, expenditures	year	110	91	81r
Postage and stationery, expenditures	year	115	91	81r
Housing				
Add garage/carport		8,479	3/95	74r
Add room(s)		21,347	3/95	74r
Apartment condominium or co-op, median	unit	87100	12/94	62r
Bathroom addition, average cost	add	9734.00	3/95	13r
Bathroom remodeling, average cost	remod	6414.00	3/95	13r
Bedroom, master suite addition, average cost	add	27122.00	3/95	13r
Deck addition, average cost	add	6665.00	3/95	13r
Dwellings (owned), expenditures	year	2566	91	81r
Enclose porch/patio/breezeway		4,556	3/95	74r
Exterior remodeling, average cost	remod	15395.00	3/95	13r
Family room addition, average cost	add	27658.00	3/95	13r
Finish room in basement/attic		5,074	3/95	74r
Home, existing, single-family, median	unit	106500	12/94	62r
Kitchen remodeling, major, average cost	remod	17084.00	3/95	13r
Kitchen remodeling, minor, average cost	remod	5804.00	3/95	13r
Maintenance, repairs, insurance, and other housing expenditures	year	484	91	81r
Mortgage interest and charges expenditures	year	1443	91	81r
Office, home addition, average cost	add	8121.00	3/95	13r
Princ. & int., mortgage, median-price exist. sing.-family home	mo.	515	12/94	62r
Property taxes expenditures	year	639	91	81r
Redesign, restructure more than half of home's interior		9,114	3/95	74r
Rental units expenditures	year	1200	91	81r
Sun-space addition, average cost	add	23768.00	3/95	13r
Wing addition, two-story, average cost	add	50410.00	3/95	13r
Insurance and Pensions				
Auto insurance, private passenger	year	788.26	12/94	71s
Insurance and pensions, personal, expenditures	year	2408	91	81r
Insurance, life and other personal, expenditures	year	355	91	81r
Pensions and Social Security, expenditures	year	2053	91	81r
Legal Assistance				
Legal work, law firm associate	hour	90		10r
Legal work, law firm partner	hour	139		10r
Personal Services				
Personal services expenditures	year	203	91	81r
Restaurant Food				
Dining expenditures, family	week	30.03	94	73r
Taxes				
Taxes, Federal income, expenditures	year	1756	91	81r
Taxes, personal, expenditures	year	2426	91	81r
Taxes, State and local income, expenditures	year	568	91	81r
Transportation				
Cars and trucks purchased, new	year	891	91	81r
Cars and trucks purchased, used	year	1155	91	81r
Driver's learning permit fee	perm	12.00	1/94	84s
Driver's license fee	orig	12.00	1/94	84s
Driver's license fee, duplicate	lic	6.00	1/94	84s
Driver's license reinstatement fee, min.	susp	125.00	1/94	85s
Driver's license renewal fee	renew	12.00	1/94	84s
Identification card, nondriver	card	6.00	1/94	83s

Ann Arbor, MI - continued

Item	Per	Value	Date	Ref.
Transportation - continued				
Motorcycle license fee	orig	7.50	1/94	84s
Motorcycle license renewal fee	renew	4.00	1/94	84s
Public transportation expenditures	year	209	91	81r
Transportation expenditures, total	year	4792	91	81r
Vehicle finance charges	year	300	91	81r
Vehicle insurance expenditures	year	485	91	81r
Vehicle maintenance and repairs expenditures	year	534	91	81r
Vehicle purchases	year	2068	91	81r
Vehicle rental, leases, licenses, etc. expenditures	year	197	91	81r
Vehicles purchased, other than cars and trucks	year	22	91	81r
Utilities				
Electricity expenditures	year	668	91	81r
Utilities, fuels, and public services, total expenditures	year	1838	91	81r
Water and other public services, expenditures	year	167	91	81r
Weddings				
Bridal attendants' gowns	event	750	10/93	76r
Bridal gown	event	852	10/93	76r
Bridal headpiece and veil	event	167	10/93	76r
Bride's wedding band	event	708	10/93	76r
Clergy	event	224	10/93	76r
Engagement ring	event	2756	10/93	76r
Flowers	event	863	10/93	76r
Formal wear for groom	event	106	10/93	76r
Groom's attendants' formal wear	event	530	10/93	76r
Groom's wedding band	event	402	10/93	76r
Music	event	600	10/93	76r
Photography	event	1088	10/93	76r
Shoes for bride	event	50	10/93	76r
Videography	event	483	10/93	76r
Wedding invitations and announcements	event	342	10/93	76r
Wedding reception	event	7000	10/93	76r

Anniston, AL

Item	Per	Value	Date	Ref.
Composite, ACCRA index		93.50	12/94	2c
Alcoholic Beverages				
Beer, Miller Lite, Bud, 12-oz., ex deposit	6	4.05	12/94	2c
J & B Scotch	750-ml.	20.99	12/94	2c
Wine, Gallo Chablis blanc	1.5-lit	5.41	12/94	2c
Appliances				
Appliances (major), expenditures	year	153	91	81r
Average annual exp.				
Food, health care, personal goods, services	year	27020	91	81r
Charity				
Cash contributions, expenditures	year	839	91	81r
Clothing				
Apparel, men and boys, total expenditures	year	380	91	81r
Apparel, women and girls, total expenditures	year	660	91	81r
Footwear, expenditures	year	193	91	81r
Jeans, man's denim		39.00	12/94	2c
Shirt, man's dress shirt		31.49	12/94	2c
Undervest, boy's size 10-14, cotton	3	2.91	12/94	2c
Communications				
Long-distance telephone rate, day, addl. min., 1-10 mi.	min.	0.09	12/93	9s
Long-distance telephone rate, day, initial min., 1-10 mi.	min.	0.11	12/93	9s
Newspaper subscription, dly. and Sun. delivery	month	8.00	12/94	2c
Phone line, single, business, field visit	inst	69.00	12/93	9s
Phone line, single, business, no field visit	inst	69.00	12/93	9s

Values are in dollars or fractions of dollars. In the column headed *Ref*, references are shown to sources. Each reference is followed by a letter. These refer to the geographical level for which data were reported: s = State, r = Region, and c = City or metro. The abbreviation *ex* is used to mean *except* or *excluding*; *exp* stands for expenditures. For other abbreviations and further explanations, please see the Introduction.

Anniston, AL - continued

Item	Per	Value	Date	Ref.
Communications				
Phone line, single, residence, field visit	inst	40.00	12/93	9s
Phone line, single, residence, no field visit	inst	40.00	12/93	9s
Telephone bill, family of four	month	22.15	12/94	2c
Telephone service, expenditures	year	616	91	81r
Telephone, residential, flat rate	mo.	16.70	12/93	8c
Education				
Board, 4-year private college/university	year	2072	8/94	80s
Board, 4-year public college/university	year	1706	8/94	80s
Education, total expenditures	year	319	91	81r
Room, 4-year private college/university	year	1607	8/94	80s
Room, 4-year public college/university	year	1598	8/94	80s
Total cost, 4-year private college/university	year	10664	8/94	80s
Total cost, 4-year public college/university	year	5287	8/94	80s
Tuition, 2-year public college/university, in-state	year	1110	8/94	80s
Tuition, 4-year private college/university, in-state	year	6985	8/94	80s
Tuition, 4-year public college/university, in-state	year	1983	8/94	80s
Energy and Fuels				
Energy, combined forms, 1800 sq. ft.	mo.	127.67	12/94	2c
Energy, exc. electricity, 1800 sq. ft.	mo.	48.96	12/94	2c
Fuel oil and other fuels, expenditures	year	56	91	81r
Gas, natural, expenditures	year	150	91	81r
Gas, reg unlead, taxes inc., cash, self-service	gal	1.09	12/94	2c
Gasoline and motor oil purchased	year	1152	91	81r
Gasoline, unleaded midgrade	gallon	1.21	4/93	82r
Gasoline, unleaded premium	gallon	1.30	4/93	82r
Gasoline, unleaded regular	gallon	1.10	4/93	82r
Entertainment				
Bowling, evening rate	game	1.88	12/94	2c
Concert ticket, Pearl Jam group	perf	20.00	94	50r
Entertainment, total expenditures	year	1266	91	81r
Fees and admissions, expenditures	year	306	91	81r
Monopoly game, Parker Brothers', No. 9	game	9.00	12/94	2c
Movie	adm	5.50	12/94	2c
Pets, toys, playground equipment, expenditures	year	271	91	81r
Reading, expenditures	year	131	91	81r
Televisions, radios, and sound equipment, expenditures	year	439	91	81r
Tennis balls, yellow, Wilson or Penn, 3	can	1.97	12/94	2c
Funerals				
Burial, immediate, container provided by funeral home		1298.96	1/95	54r
Cards, acknowledgment		21.26	1/95	54r
Casket, minimum alternative		204.95	1/95	54r
Cosmetology, hair care, etc.		85.40	1/95	54r
Cremation, direct, container provided by funeral home		1054.77	1/95	54r
Embalming		287.71	1/95	54r
Funeral, funeral home		269.18	1/95	54r
Funeral, other facility		272.88	1/95	54r
Graveside service		302.54	1/95	54r
Hearse, local		122.08	1/95	54r
Limousine, local		80.31	1/95	54r
Memorial service		277.66	1/95	54r
Service charge, professional, nondeclinable		896.65	1/95	54r
Visitation and viewing		232.39	1/95	54r
Groceries				
Groceries, ACCRA Index		96.80	12/94	2c
Apples, Red Delicious	lb.	0.73	12/94	82r
Baby food, strained vegetables, lowest price	4-4.5 oz.	0.33	12/94	2c
Bacon, sliced	lb.	1.67	12/94	82r
Bananas	lb.	0.48	12/94	2c
Bananas	lb.	0.42	12/94	82r
Beef or hamburger, ground	lb.	1.55	12/94	2c

Anniston, AL - continued

Item	Per	Value	Date	Ref.
Groceries - continued				
Beef purchases	year	213	91	81r
Beverage purchases, alcoholic	year	249	91	81r
Beverage purchases, nonalcoholic	year	207	91	81r
Bologna, all beef or mixed	lb.	2.27	12/94	82r
Bread, white	24-oz.	0.81	12/94	2c
Bread, white, pan	lb.	0.68	12/94	82r
Cabbage	lb.	0.42	12/94	82r
Carrots, short trimmed and topped	lb.	0.53	12/94	82r
Cereals and bakery products purchases	year	345	91	81r
Cereals and cereals products purchases	year	127	91	81r
Cheddar cheese, natural	lb.	3.58	12/94	82r
Cheese, Kraft grated Parmesan	8-oz.	3.41	12/94	2c
Chicken breast, bone-in	lb.	1.71	12/94	82r
Chicken, fresh, whole	lb.	0.78	12/94	82r
Chicken, whole fryer	lb.	0.81	12/94	2c
Chuck roast, USDA choice, boneless	lb.	2.26	12/94	82r
Cigarettes, Winston, Kings	carton	16.16	12/94	2c
Coffee, vacuum-packed	13 oz.	2.99	12/94	2c
Corn Flakes, Kellogg's or Post Toasties	18 oz.	2.05	12/94	2c
Corn, frozen, whole kernel, lowest price	10 oz.	0.77	12/94	2c
Crackers, soda, salted	lb.	1.27	12/94	82r
Cucumbers	lb.	0.65	12/94	82r
Dairy products (other) purchases	year	141	91	81r
Eggs, Grade A large	dozen	0.70	12/94	2c
Eggs, Grade A large	dozen	0.87	12/94	82r
Fish and seafood purchases	year	72	91	81r
Flour, white, all purpose	lb.	0.23	12/94	82r
Food purchases, food eaten at home	year	2381	91	81r
Foods purchased away from home, not prepared by consumer	year	1696	91	81r
Frankfurters, all meat or all beef	lb.	1.74	12/94	82r
Fruits and vegetables purchases	year	380	91	81r
Grapefruit	lb.	0.45	12/94	82r
Grapes, Thompson seedless	lb.	2.30	12/94	82r
Ground beef, 100% beef	lb.	1.37	12/94	82r
Ground chuck, 100% beef	lb.	1.97	12/94	82r
Ham, boneless, exc. canned	lb.	2.54	12/94	82r
Ice cream, prepackaged, bulk, regular	1/2 gal.	2.47	12/94	82r
Lemons	lb.	1.02	12/94	82r
Lettuce, iceberg	lb.	0.96	12/94	82r
Lettuce, iceberg	head	0.91	12/94	2c
Margarine, Blue Bonnet or Parkay cubes	lb.	0.56	12/94	2c
Margarine, stick	lb.	0.77	12/94	82r
Meats, poultry, fish, and eggs purchases	year	655	91	81r
Milk and cream (fresh) purchases	year	130	91	81r
Milk, whole	1/2 gal.	1.35	12/94	2c
Orange juice, frozen concentrate 12-oz. can	16 oz.	1.36	12/94	82r
Orange juice, Minute Maid frozen	12-oz.	1.14	12/94	2c
Oranges, Navel	lb.	0.54	12/94	82r
Peaches, halves or slices, Hunt's, Del Monte, or Libby's	29-oz.	1.23	12/94	2c
Pears, Anjou	lb.	0.81	12/94	82r
Peas, sweet, Del Monte or Green Giant	15-17 oz.	0.51	12/94	2c
Pork chops, center cut, bone-in	lb.	3.07	12/94	82r
Pork purchases	year	142	91	81r
Potato chips	16-oz.	3.15	12/94	82r
Potatoes, frozen, French fried	lb.	0.82	12/94	82r
Potatoes, white	lb.	0.34	12/94	82r
Potatoes, white or red	10-lb. sack	2.77	12/94	2c
Rice, white, long grain, uncooked	lb.	0.48	12/94	82r
Round roast, USDA choice, boneless	lb.	2.91	12/94	82r
Sausage, fresh	lb.	1.82	12/94	82r
Sausage, Jimmy Dean, 100% pork	lb.	2.19	12/94	2c
Shortening, vegetable oil blends	lb.	0.75	12/94	82r
Shortening, vegetable, Crisco	3-lb.	2.49	12/94	2c
Soft drink, Coca Cola, ex deposit	2 lit	1.05	12/94	2c
Spaghetti and macaroni	lb.	0.87	12/94	82r
Steak, rib eye, USDA choice, boneless	lb.	6.85	12/94	82r

Values are in dollars or fractions of dollars. In the column headed *Ref*, references are shown to sources. Each reference is followed by a letter. These refer to the geographical level for which data were reported: s=State, r=Region, and c=City or metro. The abbreviation *ex* is used to mean *except* or *excluding*; *exp* stands for expenditures. For other abbreviations and further explanations, please see the Introduction.

Anniston, AL - continued

Item	Per	Value	Date	Ref.
Groceries				
Steak, round, graded & ungraded, exc. USDA prime & choice	lb.	2.96	12/94	82r
Steak, round, USDA choice, boneless	lb.	3.17	12/94	82r
Steak, sirloin, USDA choice, boneless	lb.	4.12	12/94	82r
Steak, t-bone	lb.	4.56	12/94	2c
Steak, T-bone, USDA choice, bone-in	lb.	5.63	12/94	82r
Sugar and other sweets, eaten at home, expenditures	year	93	91	81r
Sugar, cane or beet	4 lbs.	1.34	12/94	2c
Sugar, white, all sizes	lb.	0.39	12/94	82r
Tobacco products and smoking supplies, total expenditures	year	286	91	81r
Tomatoes, field grown	lb.	1.36	12/94	82r
Tomatoes, Hunt's or Del Monte	14.5 oz.	0.66	12/94	2c
Tuna, chunk, light	lb.	1.94	12/94	82r
Tuna, chunk, light, oil-packed	6.125-6.5 oz.	0.62	12/94	2c
Turkey, frozen, whole	lb.	0.96	12/94	82r
Yogurt, natural, fruit flavored	8 oz.	0.58	12/94	82r
Goods and Services				
Miscellaneous goods and services, ACCRA Index		97.20	12/94	2c
Health Care				
Health care, ACCRA Index		87.50	12/94	2c
Adenosine, emergency room	treat	100.00	95	23r
Antibiotic ointment, Polysporin	1.5 oz.	4.01	12/94	2c
Bladder tap, superpubic, infant, emergency room	treat	119.00	95	23r
Blood analysis, emergency room	treat	25.00	95	23r
Blood tests, abdominal pain, emergency room	treat	25.00	95	23r
Burn dressing, emergency room	treat	266.00	95	23r
Cardiology interpretation, emergency room	treat	26.00	95	23r
Chest X-ray, emergency room	treat	78.00	95	23r
Childbirth, Cesarean delivery, hospital charge	birth	5462.00	12/91	69r
Childbirth, Cesarean delivery, physician charge	birth	2228.00	12/91	69r
Childbirth, normal delivery, hospital charge	birth	2943.00	12/91	69r
Childbirth, normal delivery, physician charge	birth	1619.00	12/91	69r
Defibrillation pads, emergency room	treat	6.00	95	23r
Dentist's fee, adult teeth cleaning and periodic oral exam	visit	40.60	12/94	2c
Doctor's fee, routine exam, established patient	visit	42.20	12/94	2c
Drugs, expenditures	year	297	91	81r
Gastric tube insertion, nasal, emergency room	treat	25.00	95	23r
Health care, total expenditures	year	1600	91	81r
Health insurance expenditures	year	637	91	81r
Heart monitor, emergency room	treat	40.00	95	23r
Hospital care, semiprivate room	day	266.67	12/94	2c
Insurance premium, family medical care	month	360.67	1/95	41s
Intravenous fluids, emergency room	treat	130.00	95	23r
Intravenous fluids, emergency room	liter	26.00	95	23r
Intravenous line, central, emergency room	treat	342.00	95	23r
Liver function tests, abdominal pain, emergency room	treat	26.00	95	23r
Medical care charges, total, emergency room, third-degree burns	treat	2101.00	95	23r
Medical care charges, total, emergency, infant with fever	treat	628.00	95	23r
Medical services expenditures	year	573	91	81r
Medical supplies expenditures	year	93	91	81r
Morphine, emergency room	treat	34.00	95	23r
Nursing care and facilities charges, emergency room	treat	252.00	95	23r
Nursing care and facilities charges, emergency, infant with fever	treat	252.00	95	23r

Anniston, AL - continued

Item	Per	Value	Date	Ref.
Health Care - continued				
Nursing care and facilities charges, emergency, third-degree burns	treat	861.00	95	23r
Physician's charges, emergency, infant with fever	treat	212.00	95	23r
Physician's charges, emergency, third-degree burns	treat	372.00	95	23r
Physician's fee, emergency room	treat	372.00	95	23r
Physician's fee, general practitioner	visit	51.20	12/93	60r
Surgery, open-heart	proc	42374.00	1/93	14r
Ultrasound, abdominal, emergency room	treat	276.00	95	23r
Urinalysis, emergency room	treat	20.00	95	23r
Urinalysis, infant, emergency room	treat	20.00	95	23r
X-rays, emergency room	treat	78.00	95	23r
Household Goods				
Appl. repair, service call, wash mach	min. lab. chg.	33.75	12/94	2c
Floor coverings, expenditures	year	48	91	81r
Furniture, expenditures	year	280	91	81r
Household equipment, misc. expenditures	year	342	91	81r
Household expenditures, miscellaneous	year	256	91	81r
Household furnishings and equipment, expenditures	year	988	91	81r
Household operations expenditures	year	468	91	81r
Household textiles, expenditures	year	95	91	81r
Housekeeping supplies, expenditures	year	380	91	81r
Laundry and cleaning supplies, expenditures	year	109	91	81r
Laundry detergent, Tide Ultra, Bold, or Cheer	42 oz.	3.11	12/94	2c
Postage and stationery, expenditures	year	105	91	81r
Tissues, facial, Kleenex brand	175	1.00	12/94	2c
Housing				
Housing, ACCRA Index		82.20	12/94	2c
Add garage/carport		6,980	3/95	74r
Add room(s)		11,403	3/95	74r
Apartment condominium or co-op, median	unit	68600	12/94	62r
Dwellings (owned), expenditures	year	2428	91	81r
Enclose porch/patio/breezeway		4,572	3/95	74r
Finish room in basement/attic		3,794	3/95	74r
Home, existing, single-family, median	unit	120200	12/94	62r
House payment, principal and interest, 25% down payment	mo.	613	12/94	2c
House, 1800 sq ft, 8000 sq ft lot, new, urban, utilities	total	97800	12/94	2c
Maintenance, repairs, insurance, and other housing expenditures	year	531	91	81r
Mortgage interest and charges expenditures	year	1506	91	81r
Mtge. rate, incl. points and orig. fee, 30-year conv. fixed or ARM	mo.	9.43	12/94	2c
Princ. & int., mortgage, median-price exist. sing.-family home	mo.	540	12/94	62r
Property taxes expenditures	year	391	91	81r
Redesign, restructure more than half of home's interior		17,641	3/95	74r
Rent, apartment, 2 br., 1 1/2-2 baths, unfurnished, 950 sq ft, water	mo.	481	12/94	2c
Rental units expenditures	year	1264	91	81r
Insurance and Pensions				
Auto insurance, private passenger	year	604.07	12/94	71s
Insurance and pensions, personal, expenditures	year	2395	91	81r
Insurance, life and other personal, expenditures	year	368	91	81r
Pensions and Social Security, expenditures	year	2027	91	81r
Personal Goods				
Shampoo, Alberto VO5	15-oz.	0.99	12/94	2c
Toothpaste, Crest or Colgate	6-7 oz.	1.84	12/94	2c

Values are in dollars or fractions of dollars. In the column headed *Ref*, references are shown to sources. Each reference is followed by a letter. These refer to the geographical level for which data were reported: s=State, r=Region, and c=City or metro. The abbreviation *ex* is used to mean *except* or *excluding*; *exp* stands for *expenditures*. For other abbreviations and further explanations, please see the Introduction.

Anniston, AL - continued

Item	Per	Value	Date	Ref.
Personal Services				
Dry cleaning, man's 2-pc. suit		4.97	12/94	2c
Haircut, man's barbershop, no styling		6.00	12/94	2c
Haircut, woman's shampoo, trim, blow-dry		20.75	12/94	2c
Personal services expenditures	year	212	91	81r
Restaurant Food				
Chicken, fried, thigh and drumstick		1.86	12/94	2c
Dining expenditures, family	week	33.83	94	73r
Hamburger with cheese	1/4 lb.	1.72	12/94	2c
Pizza, Pizza Hut or Pizza Inn	12-13 in.	8.76	12/94	2c
Taxes				
Taxes, Federal income, expenditures	year	2275	91	81r
Taxes, personal, expenditures	year	2715	91	81r
Taxes, State and local income, expenditures	year	365	91	81r
Transportation				
Transportation, ACCRA Index		94.80	12/94	2c
Bus fare, up to 10 miles	one-way	1.00	12/94	2c
Cars and trucks purchased, new	year	1306	91	81r
Cars and trucks purchased, used	year	942	91	81r
Driver's learning permit fee	perm	20.00	1/94	84s
Driver's license fee	orig	20.00	1/94	84s
Driver's license fee, duplicate	lic	5.00	1/94	84s
Driver's license reinstatement fee, min.	susp	50.00	1/94	85s
Driver's license renewal fee	renew	20.00	1/94	84s
Identification card, nondriver	card	20.00	1/94	83s
Motorcycle license fee	orig	20.00	1/94	84s
Motorcycle license fee, duplicate	lic	5.00	1/94	84s
Motorcycle license renewal fee	renew	20.00	1/94	84s
Public transportation expenditures	year	249	91	81r
Tire balance, computer or spin bal., front	wheel	6.00	12/94	2c
Transportation expenditures, total	year	5307	91	81r
Vehicle finance charges	year	346	91	81r
Vehicle insurance expenditures	year	544	91	81r
Vehicle maintenance and repairs expenditures	year	600	91	81r
Vehicle purchases	year	2275	91	81r
Vehicle rental, leases, licenses, etc. expenditures	year	141	91	81r
Vehicles purchased, other than cars and trucks	year	27	91	81r
Utilities				
Utilities, ACCRA Index		113.70	12/94	2c
Electricity expenditures	year	950	91	81r
Electricity, (part.), other, 1800 sq. ft., new home	mo.	78.71	12/94	2c
Utilities, fuels, and public services, total expenditures	year	2000	91	81r
Water and other public services, expenditures	year	227	91	81r
Weddings				
Bridal attendants' gowns	event	750	10/93	76r
Bridal gown	event	852	10/93	76r
Bridal headpiece and veil	event	167	10/93	76r
Bride's wedding band	event	708	10/93	76r
Clergy	event	224	10/93	76r
Engagement ring	event	2756	10/93	76r
Flowers	event	863	10/93	76r
Formal wear for groom	event	106	10/93	76r
Groom's attendants' formal wear	event	530	10/93	76r
Groom's wedding band	event	402	10/93	76r
Music	event	600	10/93	76r
Photography	event	1088	10/93	76r
Shoes for bride	event	50	10/93	76r
Videography	event	483	10/93	76r
Wedding invitations and announcements	event	342	10/93	76r
Wedding reception	event	7000	10/93	76r

Appleton-Neenah, WI

Item	Per	Value	Date	Ref.
Composite, ACCRA index		98.50	12/94	2c
Alcoholic Beverages				
Beer, Miller Lite, Bud, 12-oz., ex deposit	6	3.56	12/94	2c
J & B Scotch	750-ml.	14.77	12/94	2c
Wine, Gallo Chablis blanc	1.5-lit	3.08	12/94	2c
Appliances				
Appliances (major), expenditures	year	131	91	81r
Average annual exp.				
Food, health care, personal goods, services	year	25935	91	81r
Charity				
Cash contributions, expenditures	year	745	91	81r
Clothing				
Apparel, men and boys, total expenditures	year	332	91	81r
Apparel, women and girls, total expenditures	year	578	91	81r
Footwear, expenditures	year	164	91	81r
Jeans, man's denim		37.76	12/94	2c
Shirt, man's dress shirt		36.12	12/94	2c
Undervest, boy's size 10-14, cotton	3	3.56	12/94	2c
Communications				
Long-distance telephone rate, day, addl. min., 1-10 mi.	min.	0.10	12/93	9s
Long-distance telephone rate, day, initial min., 1-10 mi.	min.	0.15	12/93	9s
Newspaper subscription, dly. and Sun. delivery	month	14.13	12/94	2c
Phone line, single, business, field visit	inst	64.65	12/93	9s
Phone line, single, business, no field visit	inst	64.65	12/93	9s
Phone line, single, residence, field visit	inst	33.05	12/93	9s
Phone line, single, residence, no field visit	inst	33.05	12/93	9s
Telephone bill, family of four	month	16.36	12/94	2c
Telephone service, expenditures	year	547	91	81r
Telephone, residential, flat rate	mo.	6.00	12/93	8c
Education				
Board, 4-year private college/university	year	2145	8/94	80s
Board, 4-year public college/university	year	1303	8/94	80s
Education, total expenditures	year	394	91	81r
Room, 4-year private college/university	year	1576	8/94	80s
Room, 4-year public college/university	year	1631	8/94	80s
Total cost, 4-year private college/university	year	13902	8/94	80s
Total cost, 4-year public college/university	year	5252	8/94	80s
Tuition, 2-year public college/university, in-state	year	1557	8/94	80s
Tuition, 4-year private college/university, in-state	year	10181	8/94	80s
Tuition, 4-year public college/university, in-state	year	2318	8/94	80s
Energy and Fuels				
Energy, combined forms, 1800 sq. ft.	mo.	93.00	12/94	2c
Energy, exc. electricity, 1800 sq. ft.	mo.	53.39	12/94	2c
Fuel oil and other fuels, expenditures	year	83	91	81r
Gas, natural, expenditures	year	373	91	81r
Gas, reg unlead, taxes inc., cash, self-service	gal	1.13	12/94	2c
Gasoline and motor oil purchased	year	1000	91	81r
Gasoline, unleaded midgrade	gallon	1.15	4/93	82r
Gasoline, unleaded premium	gallon	1.23	4/93	82r
Gasoline, unleaded regular	gallon	1.07	4/93	82r
Entertainment				
Bowling, evening rate	game	1.67	12/94	2c
Entertainment, total expenditures	year	1356	91	81r
Fees and admissions, expenditures	year	347	91	81r
Monopoly game, Parker Brothers', No. 9	game	11.17	12/94	2c
Movie	adm	6.00	12/94	2c
Pets, toys, playground equipment, expenditures	year	270	91	81r
Reading, expenditures	year	160	91	81r

Values are in dollars or fractions of dollars. In the column headed *Ref*, references are shown to sources. Each reference is followed by a letter. These refer to the geographical level for which data were reported: s = State, r = Region, and c = City or metro. The abbreviation *ex* is used to mean *except* or *excluding*; *exp* stands for *expenditures*. For other abbreviations and further explanations, please see the Introduction.

Appleton-Neenah, WI - continued

Item	Per	Value	Date	Ref.
Entertainment				
Televisions, radios, and sound equipment, expenditures	year	433	91	81r
Tennis balls, yellow, Wilson or Penn, 3	can	2.44	12/94	2c
Funerals				
Burial, immediate, container provided by funeral home		1268.31	1/95	54r
Cards, acknowledgment		26.12	1/95	54r
Casket, minimum alternative		198.03	1/95	54r
Cosmetology, hair care, etc.		122.19	1/95	54r
Cremation, direct, container provided by funeral home		977.81	1/95	54r
Embalming		334.00	1/95	54r
Funeral, funeral home		321.16	1/95	54r
Funeral, other facility		317.73	1/95	54r
Graveside service		292.48	1/95	54r
Hearse, local		153.20	1/95	54r
Limousine, local		123.52	1/95	54r
Memorial service		356.30	1/95	54r
Service charge, professional, nondeclinable		968.24	1/95	54r
Visitation and viewing		332.66	1/95	54r
Groceries				
Groceries, ACCRA Index		96.10	12/94	2c
Apples, Red Delicious	lb.	0.68	12/94	82r
Baby food, strained vegetables, lowest price	4-4.5 oz.	0.37	12/94	2c
Bacon, sliced	lb.	1.88	12/94	82r
Bananas	lb.	0.46	12/94	2c
Bananas	lb.	0.41	12/94	82r
Beef or hamburger, ground	lb.	1.71	12/94	2c
Beef purchases	year	197	91	81r
Beef, stew, boneless	lb.	2.52	12/94	82r
Beverage purchases, alcoholic	year	293	91	81r
Beverage purchases, nonalcoholic	year	203	91	81r
Bologna, all beef or mixed	lb.	2.12	12/94	82r
Bread, white	24-oz.	0.53	12/94	2c
Bread, white, pan	lb.	0.76	12/94	82r
Cabbage	lb.	0.44	12/94	82r
Carrots, short trimmed and topped	lb.	0.44	12/94	82r
Cereals and bakery products purchases	year	347	91	81r
Cereals and cereals products purchases	year	119	91	81r
Cheddar cheese, natural	lb.	3.28	12/94	82r
Cheese, Kraft grated Parmesan	8-oz.	3.00	12/94	2c
Chicken breast, bone-in	lb.	1.61	12/94	82r
Chicken, fresh, whole	lb.	0.89	12/94	82r
Chicken, whole fryer	lb.	0.90	12/94	2c
Chuck roast, USDA choice, boneless	lb.	2.33	12/94	82r
Cigarettes, Winston, Kings	carton	16.44	12/94	2c
Coffee, 100%, ground roast, all sizes	lb.	4.28	12/94	82r
Coffee, vacuum-packed	13 oz.	3.45	12/94	2c
Cookies, chocolate chip	lb.	2.72	12/94	82r
Corn Flakes, Kellogg's or Post Toasties	18 oz.	2.46	12/94	2c
Corn, frozen, whole kernel, lowest price	10 oz.	0.64	12/94	2c
Dairy products (other) purchases	year	148	91	81r
Eggs, Grade A large	dozen	0.68	12/94	2c
Eggs, Grade A large	dozen	0.76	12/94	82r
Fish and seafood purchases	year	61	91	81r
Flour, white, all purpose	lb.	0.22	12/94	82r
Food purchases, food eaten at home	year	2313	91	81r
Foods purchased away from home, not prepared by consumer	year	1709	91	81r
Fruits and vegetables purchases	year	372	91	81r
Grapefruit	lb.	0.47	12/94	82r
Grapes, Thompson seedless	lb.	2.15	12/94	82r
Ground beef, 100% beef	lb.	1.37	12/94	82r
Ground chuck, 100% beef	lb.	1.81	12/94	82r
Ham, boneless, exc. canned	lb.	2.16	12/94	82r
Ice cream, prepackaged, bulk, regular	1/2 gal.	2.48	12/94	82r
Lemons	lb.	1.08	12/94	82r
Lettuce, iceberg	lb.	0.81	12/94	82r
Lettuce, iceberg	head	0.82	12/94	2c

Groceries - continued

Item	Per	Value	Date	Ref.
Margarine, Blue Bonnet or Parkay cubes	lb.	0.60	12/94	2c
Margarine, stick	lb.	0.81	12/94	82r
Meats, poultry, fish, and eggs purchases	year	591	91	81r
Milk and cream (fresh) purchases	year	132	91	81r
Milk, whole	1/2 gal.	1.28	12/94	2c
Orange juice, frozen concentrate 12-oz. can	16 oz.	1.41	12/94	82r
Orange juice, Minute Maid frozen	12-oz.	1.09	12/94	2c
Oranges, Navel	lb.	0.56	12/94	82r
Peaches, halves or slices, Hunt's, Del Monte, or Libby's	29-oz.	1.39	12/94	2c
Peanut butter, creamy, all sizes	lb.	1.81	12/94	82r
Peas, sweet, Del Monte or Green Giant	15-17 oz.	0.50	12/94	2c
Pork chops, center cut, bone-in	lb.	2.76	12/94	82r
Pork purchases	year	130	91	81r
Potato chips	16-oz.	2.81	12/94	82r
Potatoes, frozen, French fried	lb.	0.83	12/94	82r
Potatoes, white	lb.	0.28	12/94	82r
Potatoes, white or red	10-lb. sack	1.63	12/94	2c
Round roast, USDA choice, boneless	lb.	2.90	12/94	82r
Sausage, Jimmy Dean, 100% pork	lb.	2.47	12/94	2c
Shortening, vegetable oil blends	lb.	0.88	12/94	82r
Shortening, vegetable, Crisco	3-lb.	2.49	12/94	2c
Soft drink, Coca Cola, ex deposit	2 lit	1.00	12/94	2c
Spaghetti and macaroni	lb.	0.78	12/94	82r
Steak, rib eye, USDA choice, boneless	lb.	6.15	12/94	82r
Steak, round, graded & ungraded, exc. USDA prime & choice	lb.	2.72	12/94	82r
Steak, round, USDA choice, boneless	lb.	3.02	12/94	82r
Steak, sirloin, USDA choice, boneless	lb.	3.85	12/94	82r
Steak, t-bone	lb.	5.10	12/94	2c
Steak, T-bone, USDA choice, bone-in	lb.	5.38	12/94	82r
Sugar and other sweets, eaten at home, expenditures	year	91	91	81r
Sugar, cane or beet	4 lbs.	1.44	12/94	2c
Sugar, white, all sizes	lb.	0.36	12/94	82r
Tobacco products and smoking supplies, total expenditures	year	298	91	81r
Tomatoes, field grown	lb.	1.36	12/94	82r
Tomatoes, Hunt's or Del Monte	14.5 oz.	0.71	12/94	2c
Tuna, chunk, light	lb.	1.94	12/94	82r
Tuna, chunk, light, oil-packed	6.125-6.5 oz.	0.67	12/94	2c
Turkey, frozen, whole	lb.	0.96	12/94	82r
Yogurt, natural, fruit flavored	8 oz.	0.62	12/94	82r
Goods and Services				
Miscellaneous goods and services, ACCRA Index		102.20	12/94	2c
Health Care				
Health care, ACCRA Index		96.10	12/94	2c
Antibiotic ointment, Polysporin	1.5 oz.	3.93	12/94	2c
Childbirth, Cesarean delivery, hospital charge	birth	5101.00	12/91	69r
Childbirth, Cesarean delivery, physician charge	birth	2234.00	12/91	69r
Childbirth, normal delivery, hospital charge	birth	2891.00	12/91	69r
Childbirth, normal delivery, physician charge	birth	1623.00	12/91	69r
Dentist's fee, adult teeth cleaning and periodic oral exam	visit	45.14	12/94	2c
Doctor's fee, routine exam, established patient	visit	50.50	12/94	2c
Drugs, expenditures	year	248	91	81r
Health care, total expenditures	year	1336	91	81r
Health insurance expenditures	year	550	91	81r
Hospital care, semiprivate room	day	243.00	12/94	2c
Insurance premium, family medical care	month	378.79	1/95	41s
Medical services expenditures	year	457	91	81r
Medical supplies expenditures	year	82	91	81r

Values are in dollars or fractions of dollars. In the column headed *Ref*, references are shown to sources. Each reference is followed by a letter. These refer to the geographical level for which data were reported: s = State, r = Region, and c = City or metro. The abbreviation *ex* is used to mean *except* or *excluding*; *exp* stands for expenditures. For other abbreviations and further explanations, please see the Introduction.

Appleton-Neenah, WI - continued

Item	Per	Value	Date	Ref.
Household Goods				
Appl. repair, service call, wash mach	min. lab. chg.	33.52	12/94	2c
Floor coverings, expenditures	year	105	91	81r
Furniture, expenditures	year	291	91	81r
Household equipment, misc. expenditures	year	341	91	81r
Household expenditures, miscellaneous	year	162	91	81r
Household furnishings and equipment, expenditures	year	1042	91	81r
Household operations expenditures	year	365	91	81r
Household textiles, expenditures	year	101	91	81r
Housekeeping supplies, expenditures	year	390	91	81r
Laundry and cleaning supplies, expenditures	year	110	91	81r
Laundry detergent, Tide Ultra, Bold, or Cheer	42 oz.	3.53	12/94	2c
Postage and stationery, expenditures	year	115	91	81r
Tissues, facial, Kleenex brand	175	0.93	12/94	2c
Housing				
Housing, ACCRA Index		100.90	12/94	2c
Add garage/carport		8,479	3/95	74r
Add room(s)		21,347	3/95	74r
Apartment condominium or co-op, median	unit	87100	12/94	62r
Bathroom addition, average cost	add	9734.00	3/95	13r
Bathroom remodeling, average cost	remod	6414.00	3/95	13r
Bedroom, master suite addition, average cost	add	27122.00	3/95	13r
Deck addition, average cost	add	6665.00	3/95	13r
Dwellings (owned), expenditures	year	2566	91	81r
Enclose porch/patio/breezeway		4,556	3/95	74r
Exterior remodeling, average cost	remod	15395.00	3/95	13r
Family room addition, average cost	add	27658.00	3/95	13r
Finish room in basement/attic		5,074	3/95	74r
Home, existing, single-family, median	unit	106500	12/94	62r
Home, existing, single-family, median	unit	80.20	12/94	62c
House payment, principal and interest, 25% down payment	mo.	789	12/94	2c
House, 1800 sq ft, 8000 sq ft lot, new, urban, utilities	total	113714	12/94	2c
Kitchen remodeling, major, average cost	remod	17084.00	3/95	13r
Kitchen remodeling, minor, average cost	remod	5804.00	3/95	13r
Maintenance, repairs, insurance, and other housing expenditures	year	484	91	81r
Mortgage interest and charges expenditures	year	1443	91	81r
Mtge. rate, incl. points and orig. fee, 30-year conv. fixed or ARM	mo.	9.27	12/94	2c
Office, home addition, average cost	add	8121.00	3/95	13r
Princ. & int., mortgage, median-price exist. sing.-family home	mo.	515	12/94	62r
Property taxes expenditures	year	639	91	81r
Redesign, restructure more than half of home's interior		9,114	3/95	74r
Rent, apartment, 2 br., 1 1/2-2 baths, unfurnished, 950 sq ft, water	mo.	494	12/94	2c
Rental units expenditures	year	1200	91	81r
Sun-space addition, average cost	add	23768.00	3/95	13r
Wing addition, two-story, average cost	add	50410.00	3/95	13r
Insurance and Pensions				
Auto insurance, private passenger	year	554.10	12/94	71s
Insurance and pensions, personal, expenditures	year	2408	91	81r
Insurance, life and other personal, expenditures	year	355	91	81r
Pensions and Social Security, expenditures	year	2053	91	81r
Legal Assistance				
Legal work, law firm associate	hour	90		10r
Legal work, law firm partner	hour	139		10r
Personal Goods				
Shampoo, Alberto VO5	15-oz.	1.04	12/94	2c
Toothpaste, Crest or Colgate	6-7 oz.	1.91	12/94	2c

Appleton-Neenah, WI - continued

Item	Per	Value	Date	Ref.
Personal Services				
Dry cleaning, man's 2-pc. suit		7.53	12/94	2c
Haircut, man's barbershop, no styling		7.92	12/94	2c
Haircut, woman's shampoo, trim, blow-dry		18.83	12/94	2c
Personal services expenditures	year	203	91	81r
Restaurant Food				
Chicken, fried, thigh and drumstick		2.09	12/94	2c
Dining expenditures, family	week	30.03	94	73r
Hamburger with cheese	1/4 lb.	1.75	12/94	2c
Pizza, Pizza Hut or Pizza Inn	12-13 in.	7.49	12/94	2c
Taxes				
Taxes, Federal income, expenditures	year	1756	91	81r
Taxes, personal, expenditures	year	2426	91	81r
Taxes, State and local income, expenditures	year	568	91	81r
Transportation				
Transportation, ACCRA Index		97.60	12/94	2c
Cars and trucks purchased, new	year	891	91	81r
Cars and trucks purchased, used	year	1155	91	81r
Driver's learning permit fee	perm	20.00	1/94	84s
Driver's license fee	orig	10.00	1/94	84s
Driver's license fee, duplicate	lic	4.00	1/94	84s
Driver's license reinstatement fee, min.	susp	50.00	1/94	85s
Driver's license renewal fee	renew	10.00	1/94	84s
Identification card, nondriver	card	4.00	1/94	83s
Motorcycle license fee	orig	4.00	1/94	84s
Motorcycle license fee, duplicate	lic	4.00	1/94	84s
Motorcycle license renewal fee	renew	4.00	1/94	84s
Public transportation expenditures	year	209	91	81r
Tire balance, computer or spin bal., front	wheel	6.30	12/94	2c
Transportation expenditures, total	year	4792	91	81r
Vehicle finance charges	year	300	91	81r
Vehicle insurance expenditures	year	485	91	81r
Vehicle maintenance and repairs expenditures	year	534	91	81r
Vehicle purchases	year	2068	91	81r
Vehicle rental, leases, licenses, etc. expenditures	year	197	91	81r
Vehicles purchased, other than cars and trucks	year	22	91	81r
Utilities				
Utilities, ACCRA Index		83.00	12/94	2c
Electricity expenditures	year	668	91	81r
Electricity, (part.), other, 1800 sq. ft., new home	mo.	39.61	12/94	2c
Utilities, fuels, and public services, total expenditures	year	1838	91	81r
Water and other public services, expenditures	year	167	91	81r
Weddings				
Bridal attendants' gowns	event	750	10/93	76r
Bridal gown	event	852	10/93	76r
Bridal headpiece and veil	event	167	10/93	76r
Bride's wedding band	event	708	10/93	76r
Clergy	event	224	10/93	76r
Engagement ring	event	2756	10/93	76r
Flowers	event	863	10/93	76r
Formal wear for groom	event	106	10/93	76r
Groom's attendants' formal wear	event	530	10/93	76r
Groom's wedding band	event	402	10/93	76r
Music	event	600	10/93	76r
Photography	event	1088	10/93	76r
Shoes for bride	event	50	10/93	76r
Videography	event	483	10/93	76r
Wedding invitations and announcements	event	342	10/93	76r
Wedding reception	event	7000	10/93	76r

Values are in dollars or fractions of dollars. In the column headed *Ref*, references are shown to sources. Each reference is followed by a letter. These refer to the geographical level for which data were reported: s=State, r=Region, and c=City or metro. The abbreviation *ex* is used to mean *except* or *excluding*; *exp* stands for *expenditures*. For other abbreviations and further explanations, please see the Introduction.

Ardmore, OK

Item	Per	Value	Date	Ref.
Composite, ACCRA index		90.40	12/94	2c
Alcoholic Beverages				
Beer, Miller Lite, Bud, 12-oz., ex deposit	6	3.94	12/94	2c
J & B Scotch	750-ml.	16.79	12/94	2c
Wine, Gallo Chablis blanc	1.5-lit	6.42	12/94	2c
Clothing				
Jeans, man's denim		25.00	12/94	2c
Shirt, man's dress shirt		35.00	12/94	2c
Undervest, boy's size 10-14, cotton	3	3.12	12/94	2c
Communications				
Newspaper subscription, dly. and Sun. delivery	month	12.85	12/94	2c
Telephone bill, family of four	month	17.88	12/94	2c
Telephone, residential, flat rate	mo.	10.87	12/93	8c
Energy and Fuels				
Energy, combined forms, 1800 sq. ft.	mo.	121.23	12/94	2c
Energy, exc. electricity, 1800 sq. ft.	mo.	41.57	12/94	2c
Gas, reg unlead, taxes inc., cash, self-service	gal	1.06	12/94	2c
Entertainment				
Bowling, evening rate	game	2.00	12/94	2c
Monopoly game, Parker Brothers', No. 9	game	10.36	12/94	2c
Movie	adm	5.25	12/94	2c
Tennis balls, yellow, Wilson or Penn, 3	can	1.88	12/94	2c
Groceries				
Groceries, ACCRA Index		89.20	12/94	2c
Baby food, strained vegetables, lowest price	4-4.5 oz.	0.26	12/94	2c
Bananas	lb.	0.32	12/94	2c
Beef or hamburger, ground	lb.	1.32	12/94	2c
Bread, white	24-oz.	0.54	12/94	2c
Cheese, Kraft grated Parmesan	8-oz.	3.13	12/94	2c
Chicken, whole fryer	lb.	0.71	12/94	2c
Cigarettes, Winston, Kings	carton	15.30	12/94	2c
Coffee, vacuum-packed	13 oz.	3.27	12/94	2c
Corn Flakes, Kellogg's or Post Toasties	18 oz.	2.14	12/94	2c
Corn, frozen, whole kernel, lowest price	10 oz.	0.66	12/94	2c
Eggs, Grade A large	dozen	0.70	12/94	2c
Lettuce, iceberg	head	0.81	12/94	2c
Margarine, Blue Bonnet or Parkay cubes	lb.	0.51	12/94	2c
Milk, whole	1/2 gal.	1.32	12/94	2c
Orange juice, Minute Maid frozen	12-oz.	1.12	12/94	2c
Peaches, halves or slices, Hunt's, Del Monte, or Libby's	29-oz.	1.16	12/94	2c
Peas, sweet, Del Monte or Green Giant	15-17 oz.	0.51	12/94	2c
Potatoes, white or red	10-lb. sack	2.22	12/94	2c
Sausage, Jimmy Dean, 100% pork	lb.	2.46	12/94	2c
Shortening, vegetable, Crisco	3-lb.	2.15	12/94	2c
Soft drink, Coca Cola, ex deposit	2 lit	1.07	12/94	2c
Steak, t-bone	lb.	5.29	12/94	2c
Sugar, cane or beet	4 lbs.	1.41	12/94	2c
Tomatoes, Hunt's or Del Monte	14.5 oz.	0.71	12/94	2c
Tuna, chunk, light, oil-packed	6.125-6.5 oz.	0.67	12/94	2c
Goods and Services				
Miscellaneous goods and services, ACCRA Index		95.00	12/94	2c
Health Care				
Health care, ACCRA Index		85.70	12/94	2c
Antibiotic ointment, Polysporin	1.5 oz.	4.13	12/94	2c
Dentist's fee, adult teeth cleaning and periodic oral exam	visit	41.00	12/94	2c
Doctor's fee, routine exam, established patient	visit	42.50	12/94	2c

Ardmore, OK - continued

Item	Per	Value	Date	Ref.
Health Care - continued				
Hospital care, semiprivate room	day	215.00	12/94	2c
Household Goods				
Appl. repair, service call, wash mach	min. lab. chg.	32.50	12/94	2c
Laundry detergent, Tide Ultra, Bold, or Cheer	42 oz.	3.10	12/94	2c
Tissues, facial, Kleenex brand	175	1.06	12/94	2c
Housing				
Housing, ACCRA Index		81.90	12/94	2c
House payment, principal and interest, 25% down payment	mo.	643	12/94	2c
House, 1800 sq ft, 8000 sq ft lot, new, urban, utilities	total	102000	12/94	2c
Mtge. rate, incl. points and orig. fee, 30-year conv. fixed or ARM	mo.	9.50	12/94	2c
Rent, apartment, 2 br., 1 1/2-2 baths, unfurnished, 950 sq ft, water	mo.	387	12/94	2c
Personal Goods				
Shampoo, Alberto VO5	15-oz.	0.86	12/94	2c
Toothpaste, Crest or Colgate	6-7 oz.	1.67	12/94	2c
Personal Services				
Dry cleaning, man's 2-pc. suit		5.06	12/94	2c
Haircut, man's barbershop, no styling		5.00	12/94	2c
Haircut, woman's shampoo, trim, blow-dry		15.67	12/94	2c
Restaurant Food				
Chicken, fried, thigh and drumstick		2.08	12/94	2c
Hamburger with cheese	1/4 lb.	1.91	12/94	2c
Pizza, Pizza Hut or Pizza Inn	12-13 in.	8.70	12/94	2c
Transportation				
Transportation, ACCRA Index		91.90	12/94	2c
Tire balance, computer or spin bal., front	wheel	6.00	12/94	2c
Utilities				
Utilities, ACCRA Index		105.80	12/94	2c
Electricity, (part.), other, 1800 sq. ft., new home	mo.	79.66	12/94	2c

Asheville, NC

Item	Per	Value	Date	Ref.
Appliances				
Appliances (major), expenditures	year	153	91	81r
Average annual exp.				
Food, health care, personal goods, services	year	27020	91	81r
Charity				
Cash contributions, expenditures	year	839	91	81r
Clothing				
Apparel, men and boys, total expenditures	year	380	91	81r
Apparel, women and girls, total expenditures	year	660	91	81r
Footwear, expenditures	year	193	91	81r
Communications				
Long-distance telephone rate, day, addl. min., 1-10 mi.	min.	0.10	12/93	9s
Long-distance telephone rate, day, initial min., 1-10 mi.	min.	0.16	12/93	9s
Phone line, single, business, field visit	inst	62.50	12/93	9s
Phone line, single, business, no field visit	inst	62.50	12/93	9s
Phone line, single, residence, field visit	inst	42.75	12/93	9s
Phone line, single, residence, no field visit	inst	42.75	12/93	9s
Telephone service, expenditures	year	616	91	81r
Education				
Board, 4-year private college/university	year	2069	8/94	80s
Board, 4-year public college/university	year	1627	8/94	80s
Education, total expenditures	year	319	91	81r

Values are in dollars or fractions of dollars. In the column headed *Ref*, references are shown to sources. Each reference is followed by a letter. These refer to the geographical level for which data were reported: s=State, r=Region, and c=City or metro. The abbreviation *ex* is used to mean *except* or *excluding*; *exp* stands for expenditures. For other abbreviations and further explanations, please see the Introduction.

Asheville, NC - continued

Item	Per	Value	Date	Ref.
Education				
Room, 4-year private college/university	year	1824	8/94	80s
Room, 4-year public college/university	year	1669	8/94	80s
Total cost, 4-year private college/university	year	13505	8/94	80s
Total cost, 4-year public college/university	year	4704	8/94	80s
Tuition, 2-year public college/university, in-state	year	577	8/94	80s
Tuition, 4-year private college/university, in-state	year	9612	8/94	80s
Tuition, 4-year public college/university, in-state	year	1409	8/94	80s
Energy and Fuels				
Fuel oil and other fuels, expenditures	year	56	91	81r
Gas, natural, expenditures	year	150	91	81r
Gasoline and motor oil purchased	year	1152	91	81r
Gasoline, unleaded midgrade	gallon	1.21	4/93	82r
Gasoline, unleaded premium	gallon	1.30	4/93	82r
Gasoline, unleaded regular	gallon	1.10	4/93	82r
Entertainment				
Concert ticket, Pearl Jam group	perf	20.00	94	50r
Entertainment, total expenditures	year	1266	91	81r
Fees and admissions, expenditures	year	306	91	81r
Pets, toys, playground equipment, expenditures	year	271	91	81r
Reading, expenditures	year	131	91	81r
Televisions, radios, and sound equipment, expenditures	year	439	91	81r
Funerals				
Burial, immediate, container provided by funeral home		1370.36	1/95	54r
Cards, acknowledgment		14.83	1/95	54r
Casket, minimum alternative		192.52	1/95	54r
Cosmetology, hair care, etc.		102.27	1/95	54r
Cremation, direct, container provided by funeral home		1065.64	1/95	54r
Embalming		304.29	1/95	54r
Funeral, funeral home		287.83	1/95	54r
Funeral, other facility		284.14	1/95	54r
Graveside service		349.13	1/95	54r
Hearse, local		132.27	1/95	54r
Limousine, local		98.45	1/95	54r
Memorial service		270.59	1/95	54r
Service charge, professional, nondeclinable		933.59	1/95	54r
Visitation and viewing		225.83	1/95	54r
Groceries				
Apples, Red Delicious	lb.	0.73	12/94	82r
Bacon, sliced	lb.	1.67	12/94	82r
Bananas	lb.	0.42	12/94	82r
Beef purchases	year	213	91	81r
Beverage purchases, alcoholic	year	249	91	81r
Beverage purchases, nonalcoholic	year	207	91	81r
Bologna, all beef or mixed	lb.	2.27	12/94	82r
Bread, white, pan	lb.	0.68	12/94	82r
Cabbage	lb.	0.42	12/94	82r
Carrots, short trimmed and topped	lb.	0.53	12/94	82r
Cereals and bakery products purchases	year	345	91	81r
Cereals and cereals products purchases	year	127	91	81r
Cheddar cheese, natural	lb.	3.58	12/94	82r
Chicken breast, bone-in	lb.	1.71	12/94	82r
Chicken, fresh, whole	lb.	0.78	12/94	82r
Chuck roast, USDA choice, boneless	lb.	2.26	12/94	82r
Crackers, soda, salted	lb.	1.27	12/94	82r
Cucumbers	lb.	0.65	12/94	82r
Dairy products (other) purchases	year	141	91	81r
Eggs, Grade A large	dozen	0.87	12/94	82r
Fish and seafood purchases	year	72	91	81r
Flour, white, all purpose	lb.	0.23	12/94	82r
Food purchases, food eaten at home	year	2381	91	81r
Foods purchased away from home, not prepared by consumer	year	1696	91	81r
Frankfurters, all meat or all beef	lb.	1.74	12/94	82r

Asheville, NC - continued

Item	Per	Value	Date	Ref.
Groceries - continued				
Fruits and vegetables purchases	year	380	91	81r
Grapefruit	lb.	0.45	12/94	82r
Grapes, Thompson seedless	lb.	2.30	12/94	82r
Ground beef, 100% beef	lb.	1.37	12/94	82r
Ground chuck, 100% beef	lb.	1.97	12/94	82r
Ham, boneless, exc. canned	lb.	2.54	12/94	82r
Ice cream, prepackaged, bulk, regular	1/2 gal.	2.47	12/94	82r
Lemons	lb.	1.02	12/94	82r
Lettuce, iceberg	lb.	0.96	12/94	82r
Margarine, stick	lb.	0.77	12/94	82r
Meats, poultry, fish, and eggs purchases	year	655	91	81r
Milk and cream (fresh) purchases	year	130	91	81r
Orange juice, frozen concentrate 12-oz. can	16 oz.	1.36	12/94	82r
Oranges, Navel	lb.	0.54	12/94	82r
Pears, Anjou	lb.	0.81	12/94	82r
Pork chops, center cut, bone-in	lb.	3.07	12/94	82r
Pork purchases	year	142	91	81r
Potato chips	16-oz.	3.15	12/94	82r
Potatoes, frozen, French fried	lb.	0.82	12/94	82r
Potatoes, white	lb.	0.34	12/94	82r
Rice, white, long grain, uncooked	lb.	0.48	12/94	82r
Round roast, USDA choice, boneless	lb.	2.91	12/94	82r
Sausage, fresh	lb.	1.82	12/94	82r
Shortening, vegetable oil blends	lb.	0.75	12/94	82r
Spaghetti and macaroni	lb.	0.87	12/94	82r
Steak, rib eye, USDA choice, boneless	lb.	6.85	12/94	82r
Steak, round, graded & ungraded, exc. USDA prime & choice	lb.	2.96	12/94	82r
Steak, round, USDA choice, boneless	lb.	3.17	12/94	82r
Steak, sirloin, USDA choice, boneless	lb.	4.12	12/94	82r
Steak, T-bone, USDA choice, bone-in	lb.	5.63	12/94	82r
Sugar and other sweets, eaten at home, expenditures	year	93	91	81r
Sugar, white, all sizes	lb.	0.39	12/94	82r
Tobacco products and smoking supplies, total expenditures	year	286	91	81r
Tomatoes, field grown	lb.	1.36	12/94	82r
Tuna, chunk, light	lb.	1.94	12/94	82r
Turkey, frozen, whole	lb.	0.96	12/94	82r
Yogurt, natural, fruit flavored	8 oz.	0.58	12/94	82r
Health Care				
Adenosine, emergency room	treat	100.00	95	23r
Bladder tap, superpubic, infant, emergency room	treat	119.00	95	23r
Blood analysis, emergency room	treat	25.00	95	23r
Blood tests, abdominal pain, emergency room	treat	25.00	95	23r
Burn dressing, emergency room	treat	266.00	95	23r
Cardiology interpretation, emergency room	treat	26.00	95	23r
Chest X-ray, emergency room	treat	78.00	95	23r
Childbirth, Cesarean delivery, hospital charge	birth	5462.00	12/91	69r
Childbirth, Cesarean delivery, physician charge	birth	2228.00	12/91	69r
Childbirth, normal delivery, hospital charge	birth	2943.00	12/91	69r
Childbirth, normal delivery, physician charge	birth	1619.00	12/91	69r
Defibrillation pads, emergency room	treat	6.00	95	23r
Drugs, expenditures	year	297	91	81r
Gastric tube insertion, nasal, emergency room	treat	25.00	95	23r
Health care, total expenditures	year	1600	91	81r
Health insurance expenditures	year	637	91	81r
Heart monitor, emergency room	treat	40.00	95	23r
Insurance premium, family medical care	month	405.45	1/95	41s
Intravenous fluids, emergency room	treat	130.00	95	23r
Intravenous fluids, emergency room	liter	26.00	95	23r
Intravenous line, central, emergency room	treat	342.00	95	23r
Liver function tests, abdominal pain, emergency room	treat	26.00	95	23r
Medical care charges, total, emergency room, third-degree burns	treat	2101.00	95	23r

Values are in dollars or fractions of dollars. In the column headed *Ref*, references are shown to sources. Each reference is followed by a letter. These refer to the geographical level for which data were reported: s=State, r=Region, and c=City or metro. The abbreviation *ex* is used to mean *except* or *excluding*; *exp* stands for *expenditures*. For other abbreviations and further explanations, please see the Introduction.

Asheville, NC - continued

Item	Per	Value	Date	Ref.
Health Care				
Medical care charges, total, emergency, infant with fever	treat	628.00	95	23r
Medical services expenditures	year	573	91	81r
Medical supplies expenditures	year	93	91	81r
Morphine, emergency room	treat	34.00	95	23r
Nursing care and facilities charges, emergency room	treat	252.00	95	23r
Nursing care and facilities charges, emergency, infant with fever	treat	252.00	95	23r
Nursing care and facilities charges, emergency, third-degree burns	treat	861.00	95	23r
Physician's charges, emergency, infant with fever	treat	212.00	95	23r
Physician's charges, emergency, third-degree burns	treat	372.00	95	23r
Physician's fee, emergency room	treat	372.00	95	23r
Physician's fee, general practitioner	visit	51.20	12/93	60r
Surgery, open-heart	proc	42374.00	1/93	14r
Ultrasound, abdominal, emergency room	treat	276.00	95	23r
Urinalysis, emergency room	treat	20.00	95	23r
Urinalysis, infant, emergency room	treat	20.00	95	23r
X-rays, emergency room	treat	78.00	95	23r
Household Goods				
Floor coverings, expenditures	year	48	91	81r
Furniture, expenditures	year	280	91	81r
Household equipment, misc. expenditures	year	342	91	81r
Household expenditures, miscellaneous	year	256	91	81r
Household furnishings and equipment, expenditures	year	988	91	81r
Household operations expenditures	year	468	91	81r
Household textiles, expenditures	year	95	91	81r
Housekeeping supplies, expenditures	year	380	91	81r
Laundry and cleaning supplies, expenditures	year	109	91	81r
Postage and stationery, expenditures	year	105	91	81r
Housing				
Add garage/carport		6,980	3/95	74r
Add room(s)		11,403	3/95	74r
Apartment condominium or co-op, median	unit	68600	12/94	62r
Dwellings (owned), expenditures	year	2428	91	81r
Enclose porch/patio/breezeway		4,572	3/95	74r
Finish room in basement/attic		3,794	3/95	74r
Home, existing, single-family, median	unit	120200	12/94	62r
Maintenance, repairs, insurance, and other housing expenditures	year	531	91	81r
Mortgage interest and charges expenditures	year	1506	91	81r
Princ. & int., mortgage, median-price exist. sing.-family home	mo.	540	12/94	62r
Property taxes expenditures	year	391	91	81r
Redesign, restructure more than half of home's interior		17,641	3/95	74r
Rental units expenditures	year	1264	91	81r
Insurance and Pensions				
Auto insurance, private passenger	year	528.43	12/94	71s
Insurance and pensions, personal, expenditures	year	2395	91	81r
Insurance, life and other personal, expenditures	year	368	91	81r
Pensions and Social Security, expenditures	year	2027	91	81r
Personal Services				
Personal services expenditures	year	212	91	81r
Restaurant Food				
Dining expenditures, family	week	33.83	94	73r
Taxes				
Taxes, Federal income, expenditures	year	2275	91	81r
Taxes, personal, expenditures	year	2715	91	81r
Taxes, State and local income, expenditures	year	365	91	81r

Asheville, NC - continued

Item	Per	Value	Date	Ref.
Transportation				
Cars and trucks purchased, new	year	1306	91	81r
Cars and trucks purchased, used	year	942	91	81r
Driver's learning permit fee	perm	10.00	1/94	84s
Driver's license fee	orig	10.00	1/94	84s
Driver's license fee, duplicate	lic	5.00	1/94	84s
Driver's license reinstatement fee, min.	susp	25.00	1/94	85s
Driver's license renewal fee	renew	10.00	1/94	84s
Fine, safety belt violation	ticket	25.00	95	56s
Identification card, nondriver	card	10.00	1/94	83s
Motorcycle license fee	orig	5.00	1/94	84s
Public transportation expenditures	year	249	91	81r
Transportation expenditures, total	year	5307	91	81r
Vehicle finance charges	year	346	91	81r
Vehicle insurance expenditures	year	544	91	81r
Vehicle maintenance and repairs expenditures	year	600	91	81r
Vehicle purchases	year	2275	91	81r
Vehicle rental, leases, licenses, etc. expenditures	year	141	91	81r
Vehicles purchased, other than cars and trucks	year	27	91	81r
Utilities				
Electricity expenditures	year	950	91	81r
Utilities, fuels, and public services, total expenditures	year	2000	91	81r
Water and other public services, expenditures	year	227	91	81r
Weddings				
Bridal attendants' gowns	event	750	10/93	76r
Bridal gown	event	852	10/93	76r
Bridal headpiece and veil	event	167	10/93	76r
Bride's wedding band	event	708	10/93	76r
Clergy	event	224	10/93	76r
Engagement ring	event	2756	10/93	76r
Flowers	event	863	10/93	76r
Formal wear for groom	event	106	10/93	76r
Groom's attendants' formal wear	event	530	10/93	76r
Groom's wedding band	event	402	10/93	76r
Music	event	600	10/93	76r
Photography	event	1088	10/93	76r
Shoes for bride	event	50	10/93	76r
Videography	event	483	10/93	76r
Wedding invitations and announcements	event	342	10/93	76r
Wedding reception	event	7000	10/93	76r

Ashland, KY

Item	Per	Value	Date	Ref.
Composite, ACCRA index		94.70	12/94	2c
Alcoholic Beverages				
Beer, Miller Lite, Bud, 12-oz., ex deposit	6	3.91	12/94	2c
J & B Scotch	750-ml.	17.55	12/94	2c
Wine, Gallo Chablis blanc	1.5-lit	5.30	12/94	2c
Clothing				
Jeans, man's denim		32.16	12/94	2c
Shirt, man's dress shirt		24.09	12/94	2c
Undervest, boy's size 10-14, cotton	3	3.74	12/94	2c
Communications				
Newspaper subscription, dly. and Sun. delivery	month	12.08	12/94	2c
Telephone bill, family of four	month	21.07	12/94	2c
Energy and Fuels				
Energy, combined forms, 1800 sq. ft.	mo.	104.42	12/94	2c
Gas, reg unlead, taxes inc., cash, self-service	gal	1.13	12/94	2c
Entertainment				
Bowling, evening rate	game	1.97	12/94	2c
Monopoly game, Parker Brothers', No. 9	game	10.44	12/94	2c

Values are in dollars or fractions of dollars. In the column headed *Ref*, references are shown to sources. Each reference is followed by a letter. These refer to the geographical level for which data were reported: s = State, r = Region, and c = City or metro. The abbreviation *ex* is used to mean *except* or *excluding*; *exp* stands for *expenditures*. For other abbreviations and further explanations, please see the Introduction.

Ashland, KY - continued

Item	Per	Value	Date	Ref.
Entertainment				
Movie	adm	5.25	12/94	2c
Tennis balls, yellow, Wilson or Penn, 3	can	2.37	12/94	2c
Groceries				
Groceries, ACCRA Index		98.00	12/94	2c
Baby food, strained vegetables, lowest price	4-4.5 oz.	0.24	12/94	2c
Bananas	lb.	0.43	12/94	2c
Beef or hamburger, ground	lb.	1.47	12/94	2c
Bread, white	24-oz.	0.71	12/94	2c
Cheese, Kraft grated Parmesan	8-oz.	2.99	12/94	2c
Chicken, whole fryer	lb.	0.91	12/94	2c
Cigarettes, Winston, Kings	carton	13.08	12/94	2c
Coffee, vacuum-packed	13 oz.	3.72	12/94	2c
Corn Flakes, Kellogg's or Post Toasties	18 oz.	2.47	12/94	2c
Corn, frozen, whole kernel, lowest price	10 oz.	0.69	12/94	2c
Eggs, Grade A large	dozen	0.77	12/94	2c
Lettuce, iceberg	head	0.87	12/94	2c
Margarine, Blue Bonnet or Parkay cubes	lb.	0.63	12/94	2c
Milk, whole	1/2 gal.	1.41	12/94	2c
Orange juice, Minute Maid frozen	12-oz.	1.29	12/94	2c
Peaches, halves or slices, Hunt's, Del Monte, or Libby's	29-oz.	1.44	12/94	2c
Peas, sweet, Del Monte or Green Giant	15-17 oz.	0.65	12/94	2c
Potatoes, white or red	10-lb. sack	2.19	12/94	2c
Sausage, Jimmy Dean, 100% pork	lb.	2.53	12/94	2c
Shortening, vegetable, Crisco	3-lb.	2.45	12/94	2c
Soft drink, Coca Cola, ex deposit	2 lit	1.09	12/94	2c
Steak, t-bone	lb.	4.72	12/94	2c
Sugar, cane or beet	4 lbs.	1.38	12/94	2c
Tomatoes, Hunt's or Del Monte	14.5 oz.	0.73	12/94	2c
Tuna, chunk, light, oil-packed	6.125-6.5 oz.	0.71	12/94	2c
Goods and Services				
Miscellaneous goods and services, ACCRA Index		96.30	12/94	2c
Health Care				
Health care, ACCRA Index		91.40	12/94	2c
Antibiotic ointment, Polysporin	1.5 oz.	4.75	12/94	2c
Dentist's fee, adult teeth cleaning and periodic oral exam	visit	40.00	12/94	2c
Doctor's fee, routine exam, established patient	visit	38.60	12/94	2c
Hospital care, semiprivate room	day	372.50	12/94	2c
Household Goods				
Appl. repair, service call, wash mach	min. lab. chg.	30.99	12/94	2c
Laundry detergent, Tide Ultra, Bold, or Cheer	42 oz.	4.02	12/94	2c
Tissues, facial, Kleenex brand	175	1.15	12/94	2c
Housing				
Housing, ACCRA Index		91.10	12/94	2c
House payment, principal and interest, 25% down payment	mo.	714	12/94	2c
House, 1800 sq ft, 8000 sq ft lot, new, urban, utilities	total	115750	12/94	2c
Mtge. rate, incl. points and orig. fee, 30-year conv. fixed or ARM	mo.	9.24	12/94	2c
Rent, apartment, 2 br., 1 1/2-2 baths, unfurnished, 950 sq ft, water	mo.	435	12/94	2c
Personal Goods				
Shampoo, Alberto VO5	15-oz.	1.45	12/94	2c
Toothpaste, Crest or Colgate	6-7 oz.	2.41	12/94	2c

Ashland, KY - continued

Item	Per	Value	Date	Ref.
Personal Services				
Dry cleaning, man's 2-pc. suit		5.68	12/94	2c
Haircut, man's barbershop, no styling		6.89	12/94	2c
Haircut, woman's shampoo, trim, blow-dry		17.12	12/94	2c
Restaurant Food				
Chicken, fried, thigh and drumstick		2.00	12/94	2c
Hamburger with cheese	1/4 lb.	1.85	12/94	2c
Pizza, Pizza Hut or Pizza Inn	12-13 in.	8.59	12/94	2c
Transportation				
Transportation, ACCRA Index		96.00	12/94	2c
Tire balance, computer or spin bal., front	wheel	6.10	12/94	2c
Utilities				
Utilities, ACCRA Index		95.10	12/94	2c
Electricity, 1800 sq. ft., new home	mo.	104.42	12/94	2c
Electricity, summer, 250 KWh	month	16.73	8/93	64c
Electricity, summer, 500 KWh	month	29.22	8/93	64c
Electricity, summer, 750 KWh	month	30.86	8/93	64c
Electricity, summer, 1000 KWh	month	50.52	8/93	64c

Athens, GA

Item	Per	Value	Date	Ref.
Appliances				
Appliances (major), expenditures	year	153	91	81r
Average annual exp.				
Food, health care, personal goods, services	year	27020	91	81r
Charity				
Cash contributions, expenditures	year	839	91	81r
Clothing				
Apparel, men and boys, total expenditures	year	380	91	81r
Apparel, women and girls, total expenditures	year	660	91	81r
Footwear, expenditures	year	193	91	81r
Communications				
Long-distance telephone rate, day, addl. min., 1-10 mi.	min.	0.04	12/93	9s
Long-distance telephone rate, day, initial min., 1-10 mi.	min.	0.08	12/93	9s
Phone line, single, business, field visit	inst	58.25	12/93	9s
Phone line, single, business, no field visit	inst	52.25	12/93	9s
Phone line, single, residence, field visit	inst	47.50	12/93	9s
Phone line, single, residence, no field visit	inst	42.50	12/93	9s
Telephone service, expenditures	year	616	91	81r
Telephone, residential, flat rate	mo.	13.00	12/93	8c
Education				
Board, 4-year private college/university	year	2288	8/94	80s
Board, 4-year public college/university	year	1723	8/94	80s
Education, total expenditures	year	319	91	81r
Room, 4-year private college/university	year	2409	8/94	80s
Room, 4-year public college/university	year	1459	8/94	80s
Total cost, 4-year private college/university	year	13950	8/94	80s
Total cost, 4-year public college/university	year	5075	8/94	80s
Tuition, 2-year public college/university, in-state	year	972	8/94	80s
Tuition, 4-year private college/university, in-state	year	9253	8/94	80s
Tuition, 4-year public college/university, in-state	year	1894	8/94	80s
Energy and Fuels				
Fuel oil and other fuels, expenditures	year	56	91	81r
Gas, natural, expenditures	year	150	91	81r
Gasoline and motor oil purchased	year	1152	91	81r
Gasoline, unleaded midgrade	gallon	1.21	4/93	82r
Gasoline, unleaded premium	gallon	1.30	4/93	82r
Gasoline, unleaded regular	gallon	1.10	4/93	82r
Entertainment				
Concert ticket, Pearl Jam group	perf	20.00	94	50r
Entertainment, total expenditures	year	1266	91	81r

Values are in dollars or fractions of dollars. In the column headed *Ref*, references are shown to sources. Each reference is followed by a letter. These refer to the geographical level for which data were reported: s = State, r = Region, and c = City or metro. The abbreviation *ex* is used to mean *except* or *excluding*; *exp* stands for expenditures. For other abbreviations and further explanations, please see the Introduction.

Athens, GA - continued

Item	Per	Value	Date	Ref.
Entertainment				
Fees and admissions, expenditures	year	306	91	81r
Pets, toys, playground equipment, expenditures	year	271	91	81r
Reading, expenditures	year	131	91	81r
Televisions, radios, and sound equipment, expenditures	year	439	91	81r
Funerals				
Burial, immediate, container provided by funeral home		1370.36	1/95	54r
Cards, acknowledgment		14.83	1/95	54r
Casket, minimum alternative		192.52	1/95	54r
Cosmetology, hair care, etc.		102.27	1/95	54r
Cremation, direct, container provided by funeral home		1065.64	1/95	54r
Embalming		304.29	1/95	54r
Funeral, funeral home		287.83	1/95	54r
Funeral, other facility		284.14	1/95	54r
Graveside service		349.13	1/95	54r
Hearse, local		132.27	1/95	54r
Limousine, local		98.45	1/95	54r
Memorial service		270.59	1/95	54r
Service charge, professional, nondeclinable		933.59	1/95	54r
Visitation and viewing		225.83	1/95	54r
Groceries				
Apples, Red Delicious	lb.	0.73	12/94	82r
Bacon, sliced	lb.	1.67	12/94	82r
Bananas	lb.	0.42	12/94	82r
Beef purchases	year	213	91	81r
Beverage purchases, alcoholic	year	249	91	81r
Beverage purchases, nonalcoholic	year	207	91	81r
Bologna, all beef or mixed	lb.	2.27	12/94	82r
Bread, white, pan	lb.	0.68	12/94	82r
Cabbage	lb.	0.42	12/94	82r
Carrots, short trimmed and topped	lb.	0.53	12/94	82r
Cereals and bakery products purchases	year	345	91	81r
Cereals and cereals products purchases	year	127	91	81r
Cheddar cheese, natural	lb.	3.58	12/94	82r
Chicken breast, bone-in	lb.	1.71	12/94	82r
Chicken, fresh, whole	lb.	0.78	12/94	82r
Chuck roast, USDA choice, boneless	lb.	2.26	12/94	82r
Crackers, soda, salted	lb.	1.27	12/94	82r
Cucumbers	lb.	0.65	12/94	82r
Dairy products (other) purchases	year	141	91	81r
Eggs, Grade A large	dozen	0.87	12/94	82r
Fish and seafood purchases	year	72	91	81r
Flour, white, all purpose	lb.	0.23	12/94	82r
Food purchases, food eaten at home	year	2381	91	81r
Foods purchased away from home, not prepared by consumer	year	1696	91	81r
Frankfurters, all meat or all beef	lb.	1.74	12/94	82r
Fruits and vegetables purchases	year	380	91	81r
Grapefruit	lb.	0.45	12/94	82r
Grapes, Thompson seedless	lb.	2.30	12/94	82r
Ground beef, 100% beef	lb.	1.37	12/94	82r
Ground chuck, 100% beef	lb.	1.97	12/94	82r
Ham, boneless, exc. canned	lb.	2.54	12/94	82r
Ice cream, prepackaged, bulk, regular	1/2 gal.	2.47	12/94	82r
Lemons	lb.	1.02	12/94	82r
Lettuce, iceberg	lb.	0.96	12/94	82r
Margarine, stick	lb.	0.77	12/94	82r
Meats, poultry, fish, and eggs purchases	year	655	91	81r
Milk and cream (fresh) purchases	year	130	91	81r
Orange juice, frozen concentrate 12-oz. can	16 oz.	1.36	12/94	82r
Oranges, Navel	lb.	0.54	12/94	82r
Pears, Anjou	lb.	0.81	12/94	82r
Pork chops, center cut, bone-in	lb.	3.07	12/94	82r
Pork purchases	year	142	91	81r
Potato chips	16-oz.	3.15	12/94	82r
Potatoes, frozen, French fried	lb.	0.82	12/94	82r
Potatoes, white	lb.	0.34	12/94	82r

Athens, GA - continued

Item	Per	Value	Date	Ref.
Groceries - continued				
Rice, white, long grain, uncooked	lb.	0.48	12/94	82r
Round roast, USDA choice, boneless	lb.	2.91	12/94	82r
Sausage, fresh	lb.	1.82	12/94	82r
Shortening, vegetable oil blends	lb.	0.75	12/94	82r
Spaghetti and macaroni	lb.	0.87	12/94	82r
Steak, rib eye, USDA choice, boneless	lb.	6.85	12/94	82r
Steak, round, graded & ungraded, exc. USDA prime & choice	lb.	2.96	12/94	82r
Steak, round, USDA choice, boneless	lb.	3.17	12/94	82r
Steak, sirloin, USDA choice, boneless	lb.	4.12	12/94	82r
Steak, T-bone, USDA choice, bone-in	lb.	5.63	12/94	82r
Sugar and other sweets, eaten at home, expenditures	year	93	91	81r
Sugar, white, all sizes	lb.	0.39	12/94	82r
Tobacco products and smoking supplies, total expenditures	year	286	91	81r
Tomatoes, field grown	lb.	1.36	12/94	82r
Tuna, chunk, light	lb.	1.94	12/94	82r
Turkey, frozen, whole	lb.	0.96	12/94	82r
Yogurt, natural, fruit flavored	8 oz.	0.58	12/94	82r
Health Care				
Adenosine, emergency room	treat	100.00	95	23r
Bladder tap, superpubic, infant, emergency room	treat	119.00	95	23r
Blood analysis, emergency room	treat	25.00	95	23r
Blood tests, abdominal pain, emergency room	treat	25.00	95	23r
Burn dressing, emergency room	treat	266.00	95	23r
Cardiology interpretation, emergency room	treat	26.00	95	23r
Chest X-ray, emergency room	treat	78.00	95	23r
Childbirth, Cesarean delivery, hospital charge	birth	5462.00	12/91	69r
Childbirth, Cesarean delivery, physician charge	birth	2228.00	12/91	69r
Childbirth, normal delivery, hospital charge	birth	2943.00	12/91	69r
Childbirth, normal delivery, physician charge	birth	1619.00	12/91	69r
Defibrillation pads, emergency room	treat	6.00	95	23r
Drugs, expenditures	year	297	91	81r
Gastric tube insertion, nasal, emergency room	treat	25.00	95	23r
Health care, total expenditures	year	1600	91	81r
Health insurance expenditures	year	637	91	81r
Heart monitor, emergency room	treat	40.00	95	23r
Insurance premium, family medical care	month	320.13	1/95	41s
Intravenous fluids, emergency room	treat	130.00	95	23r
Intravenous fluids, emergency room	liter	26.00	95	23r
Intravenous line, central, emergency room	treat	342.00	95	23r
Liver function tests, abdominal pain, emergency room	treat	26.00	95	23r
Medical care charges, total, emergency room, third-degree burns	treat	2101.00	95	23r
Medical care charges, total, emergency, infant with fever	treat	628.00	95	23r
Medical services expenditures	year	573	91	81r
Medical supplies expenditures	year	93	91	81r
Morphine, emergency room	treat	34.00	95	23r
Nursing care and facilities charges, emergency room	treat	252.00	95	23r
Nursing care and facilities charges, emergency, infant with fever	treat	252.00	95	23r
Nursing care and facilities charges, emergency, third-degree burns	treat	861.00	95	23r
Physician's charges, emergency, infant with fever	treat	212.00	95	23r
Physician's charges, emergency, third-degree burns	treat	372.00	95	23r
Physician's fee, emergency room	treat	372.00	95	23r
Physician's fee, general practitioner	visit	51.20	12/93	60r
Surgery, open-heart	proc	42374.00	1/93	14r
Ultrasound, abdominal, emergency room	treat	276.00	95	23r
Urinalysis, emergency room	treat	20.00	95	23r
Urinalysis, infant, emergency room	treat	20.00	95	23r

Values are in dollars or fractions of dollars. In the column headed *Ref*, references are shown to sources. Each reference is followed by a letter. These refer to the geographical level for which data were reported: s=State, r=Region, and c=City or metro. The abbreviation *ex* is used to mean *except* or *excluding*; *exp* stands for expenditures. For other abbreviations and further explanations, please see the Introduction.

Athens, GA - continued

Item	Per	Value	Date	Ref.
Health Care				
X-rays, emergency room	treat	78.00	95	23r
Household Goods				
Floor coverings, expenditures	year	48	91	81r
Furniture, expenditures	year	280	91	81r
Household equipment, misc. expenditures	year	342	91	81r
Household expenditures, miscellaneous	year	256	91	81r
Household furnishings and equipment, expenditures	year	988	91	81r
Household operations expenditures	year	468	91	81r
Household textiles, expenditures	year	95	91	81r
Housekeeping supplies, expenditures	year	380	91	81r
Laundry and cleaning supplies, expenditures	year	109	91	81r
Postage and stationery, expenditures	year	105	91	81r
Housing				
Add garage/carport		6,980	3/95	74r
Add room(s)		11,403	3/95	74r
Apartment condominium or co-op, median	unit	68600	12/94	62r
Dwellings (owned), expenditures	year	2428	91	81r
Enclose porch/patio/breezeway		4,572	3/95	74r
Finish room in basement/attic		3,794	3/95	74r
Home, existing, single-family, median	unit	120200	12/94	62r
Maintenance, repairs, insurance, and other housing expenditures	year	531	91	81r
Mortgage interest and charges expenditures	year	1506	91	81r
Princ. & int., mortgage, median-price exist. sing.-family home	mo.	540	12/94	62r
Property taxes expenditures	year	391	91	81r
Redesign, restructure more than half of home's interior		17,641	3/95	74r
Rental units expenditures	year	1264	91	81r
Insurance and Pensions				
Auto insurance, private passenger	year	664.85	12/94	71s
Insurance and pensions, personal, expenditures	year	2395	91	81r
Insurance, life and other personal, expenditures	year	368	91	81r
Pensions and Social Security, expenditures	year	2027	91	81r
Personal Services				
Personal services expenditures	year	212	91	81r
Restaurant Food				
Dining expenditures, family	week	33.83	94	73r
Taxes				
Taxes, Federal income, expenditures	year	2275	91	81r
Taxes, personal, expenditures	year	2715	91	81r
Taxes, State and local income, expenditures	year	365	91	81r
Transportation				
Bus fare, one-way	trip	0.75	12/95	1c
Cars and trucks purchased, new	year	1306	91	81r
Cars and trucks purchased, used	year	942	91	81r
Driver's learning permit fee	perm	10.00	1/94	84s
Driver's license fee	orig	15.00	1/94	84s
Driver's license fee, duplicate	lic	10.00	1/94	84s
Driver's license reinstatement fee, min.	susp	25.00	1/94	85s
Driver's license renewal fee	renew	15.00	1/94	84s
Identification card, nondriver	card	3.00	1/94	83s
Motorcycle learning permit fee	perm	10.00	1/94	84s
Motorcycle license fee	orig	15.00	1/94	84s
Motorcycle license fee, duplicate	lic	10.00	1/94	84s
Motorcycle license renewal fee	renew	15.00	1/94	84s
Public transportation expenditures	year	249	91	81r
Transportation expenditures, total	year	5307	91	81r
Vehicle finance charges	year	346	91	81r
Vehicle insurance expenditures	year	544	91	81r
Vehicle maintenance and repairs expenditures	year	600	91	81r
Vehicle purchases	year	2275	91	81r

Athens, GA - continued

Item	Per	Value	Date	Ref.
Transportation - continued				
Vehicle rental, leases, licenses, etc. expenditures	year	141	91	81r
Vehicles purchased, other than cars and trucks	year	27	91	81r
Utilities				
Electricity expenditures	year	950	91	81r
Utilities, fuels, and public services, total expenditures	year	2000	91	81r
Water and other public services, expenditures	year	227	91	81r
Weddings				
Bridal attendants' gowns	event	750	10/93	76r
Bridal gown	event	852	10/93	76r
Bridal headpiece and veil	event	167	10/93	76r
Bride's wedding band	event	708	10/93	76r
Clergy	event	224	10/93	76r
Engagement ring	event	2756	10/93	76r
Flowers	event	863	10/93	76r
Formal wear for groom	event	106	10/93	76r
Groom's attendants' formal wear	event	530	10/93	76r
Groom's wedding band	event	402	10/93	76r
Music	event	600	10/93	76r
Photography	event	1088	10/93	76r
Shoes for bride	event	50	10/93	76r
Videography	event	483	10/93	76r
Wedding invitations and announcements	event	342	10/93	76r
Wedding reception	event	7000	10/93	76r

Atlanta, GA

Item	Per	Value	Date	Ref.
Composite, ACCRA index		97.20	12/94	2c
Alcoholic Beverages				
Beer, Miller Lite, Bud, 12-oz., ex deposit	6	4.23	12/94	2c
J & B Scotch	750-ml.	17.19	12/94	2c
Wine, Gallo Chablis blanc	1.5-lit	4.95	12/94	2c
Appliances				
Appliances (major), expenditures	year	173	91	81c
Appliances (major), expenditures	year	153	91	81r
Average annual exp.				
Food, health care, personal goods, services	year	34163	91	81c
Food, health care, personal goods, services	year	27020	91	81r
Business				
Dinner and tip, hotel, corporate rate	night	32.00	2/94	15c
Hotel room, corporate rate	night	86.00	2/94	15c
Business Expenses				
Car rental, midsized car	day	43.99	92	52c
Continental breakfast, room service	meal	11.00	92	52c
Lunch, convention center	meal	6.00	92	52c
Restaurant meal	meal	49.00	92	52c
Room rate, hotel	day	65.14	92	52c
Taxicab fare, airport to convention center	trip	15.00	92	52c
Charity				
Cash contributions, expenditures	year	1292	91	81c
Cash contributions, expenditures	year	839	91	81r
Clothing				
Apparel, men and boys, total expenditures	year	527	91	81c
Apparel, men and boys, total expenditures	year	380	91	81r
Apparel, women and girls, total expenditures	year	1114	91	81c
Apparel, women and girls, total expenditures	year	660	91	81r
Footwear, expenditures	year	262	91	81c
Footwear, expenditures	year	193	91	81r
Formal wear rental, tuxedo, downtown store	rental	50.00	92	52c
Jeans, man's denim		30.47	12/94	2c
Shirt, dress, men's	shirt	29.95	1/92	44c
Shirt, man's dress shirt		24.74	12/94	2c
Undervest, boy's size 10-14, cotton	3	3.49	12/94	2c

Values are in dollars or fractions of dollars. In the column headed *Ref*, references are shown to sources. Each reference is followed by a letter. These refer to the geographical level for which data were reported: s = State, r = Region, and c = City or metro. The abbreviation *ex* is used to mean *except* or *excluding*; *exp* stands for expenditures. For other abbreviations and further explanations, please see the Introduction.

Atlanta, GA - continued

Item	Per	Value	Date	Ref.
Communications				
Long-distance telephone rate, day, addl. min., 1-10 mi.	min.	0.04	12/93	9s
Long-distance telephone rate, day, initial min., 1-10 mi.	min.	0.08	12/93	9s
Newspaper cost, major daily	1	0.35	92	52c
Newspaper subscription, dly. and Sun. delivery	month	14.26	12/94	2c
Phone line, single, business, field visit	inst	58.25	12/93	9s
Phone line, single, business, no field visit	inst	52.25	12/93	9s
Phone line, single, residence, field visit	inst	47.50	12/93	9s
Phone line, single, residence, no field visit	inst	42.50	12/93	9s
Telephone bill, family of four	month	21.53	12/94	2c
Telephone service, expenditures	year	705	91	81c
Telephone service, expenditures	year	616	91	81r
Telephone, residential, flat rate	mo.	15.90	12/93	8c
Education				
Board, 4-year private college/university	year	2288	8/94	80s
Board, 4-year public college/university	year	1723	8/94	80s
Education, total expenditures	year	626	91	81c
Education, total expenditures	year	319	91	81r
Room, 4-year private college/university	year	2409	8/94	80s
Room, 4-year public college/university	year	1459	8/94	80s
Total cost, 4-year private college/university	year	13950	8/94	80s
Total cost, 4-year public college/university	year	5075	8/94	80s
Tuition, 2-year public college/university, in-state	year	972	8/94	80s
Tuition, 4-year private college/university, in-state	year	9253	8/94	80s
Tuition, 4-year public college/university, in-state	year	1894	8/94	80s
Energy and Fuels				
Energy, combined forms, 1800 sq. ft.	mo.	123.30	12/94	2c
Energy, exc. electricity, 1800 sq. ft.	mo.	50.98	12/94	2c
Fuel oil and other fuels, expenditures	year	49	91	81c
Fuel oil and other fuels, expenditures	year	56	91	81r
Gas	gal.	0.92	1/92	44c
Gas, cooking, 10 therms	month	13.27	2/94	65c
Gas, cooking, 30 therms	month	25.13	2/94	65c
Gas, cooking, 50 therms	month	37.59	2/94	65c
Gas, heating, winter, 100 therms	month	67.99	2/94	65c
Gas, heating, winter, average use	month	77.72	2/94	65c
Gas, natural, expenditures	year	408	91	81c
Gas, natural, expenditures	year	150	91	81r
Gas, reg unlead, taxes inc., cash, self-service	gal	1.01	12/94	2c
Gasoline and motor oil purchased	year	1112	91	81c
Gasoline and motor oil purchased	year	1152	91	81r
Gasoline, unleaded midgrade	gallon	1.21	4/93	82r
Gasoline, unleaded premium	gallon	1.30	4/93	82r
Gasoline, unleaded regular	gallon	1.10	4/93	82r
Entertainment				
Admission fee, museum	visit	5.00	92	52c
Admission fee, seating, symphony performance		37.00	92	52c
Archery event, Atlanta Olympics	ticket	11.00-27.00	4/95	75c
Athletics event (track and field), Atlanta Olympics	ticket	22.00-265.00	4/95	75c
Badminton event, Atlanta Olympics	ticket	16.00-38.00	4/95	75c
Baseball event, Atlanta Olympics	ticket	7.00-64.00	4/95	75c
Baseball game, four-person family	game	112.98	4/94	47c
Basketball event, Atlanta Olympics	ticket	11.00-265.00	4/95	75c
Bowling, evening rate	game	2.68	12/94	2c
Boxing event, Atlanta Olympics	ticket	27.00-186.00	4/95	75c
Canoeing event (flat water), Atlanta Olympics	ticket	11.00-32.00	4/95	75c

Atlanta, GA - continued

Item	Per	Value	Date	Ref.
Entertainment - continued				
Canoeing event (white water), Atlanta Olympics	ticket	26.00-32.00	4/95	75c
Ceremonies, opening and closing, Atlanta Olympics	ticket	212.00-636	4/95	75c
Concert ticket, Pearl Jam group	perf	20.00	94	50r
Cycling event, Atlanta Olympics	ticket	0.00-37.00	4/95	75c
Diving event, Atlanta Olympics	ticket	22.00-159.00	4/95	75c
Entertainment supplies, equipment, and services, misc. expenditures	year	204	91	81c
Entertainment, total expenditures	year	1393	91	81c
Entertainment, total expenditures	year	1266	91	81r
Equestrian event, Atlanta Olympics	ticket	11.00-79.00	4/95	75c
Fees and admissions, expenditures	year	455	91	81c
Fees and admissions, expenditures	year	306	91	81r
Fencing event, Atlanta Olympics	ticket	11.00-27.00	4/95	75c
Field hockey event, Atlanta Olympics	ticket	11.00-27.00	4/95	75c
Football (soccer) event, Atlanta Olympics	ticket	20.00-133.00	4/95	75c
Gymnastics (artistic) event, Atlanta Olympics	ticket	11.00-265.00	4/95	75c
Gymnastics (rhythmic) event, Atlanta Olympics	ticket	25.00-53.00	4/95	75c
Handball event, Atlanta Olympics	ticket	16.00-27.00	4/95	75c
Judo event, Atlanta Olympics	ticket	22.00-43.00	4/95	75c
Monopoly game, Parker Brothers', No. 9	game	11.12	12/94	2c
Movie	adm	6.45	12/94	2c
Movie ticket, adult	ticket	5.50	1/92	44c
Pentathlon event, Atlanta Olympics	ticket	27.00	4/95	75c
Pets, toys, playground equipment, expenditures	year	259	91	81c
Pets, toys, playground equipment, expenditures	year	271	91	81r
Reading, expenditures	year	179	91	81c
Reading, expenditures	year	131	91	81r
Rowing event, Atlanta Olympics	ticket	11.00-32.00	4/95	75c
Shooting event, Atlanta Olympics	ticket	22.00	4/95	75c
Softball event, Atlanta Olympics	ticket	16.00-32.00	4/95	75c
Swimming (synchronized) event, Atlanta Olympics	ticket	11.00-48.00	4/95	75c
Swimming event, Atlanta Olympics	ticket	27.00-159.00	4/95	75c
Televisions, radios, and sound equipment, expenditures	year	474	91	81c
Televisions, radios, and sound equipment, expenditures	year	439	91	81r
Tennis (table) event, Atlanta Olympics	ticket	11.00-27.00	4/95	75c
Tennis balls, yellow, Wilson or Penn, 3	can	2.09	12/94	2c
Tennis event, Atlanta Olympics	ticket	21.00-132.00	4/95	75c
Ticket, basketball game		10.00-30.00	92	52c
Volleyball (beach) event, Atlanta Olympics	ticket	27.00-69.00	4/95	75c
Volleyball (indoor) event, Atlanta Olympics	ticket	16.00-133.00	4/95	75c
Water polo event, Atlanta Olympics	ticket	11.00-53.00	4/95	75c
Weightlifting event, Atlanta Olympics	ticket	22.00-43.00	4/95	75c
Funerals				
Burial, immediate, container provided by funeral home		1370.36	1/95	54r

Values are in dollars or fractions of dollars. In the column headed *Ref*, references are shown to sources. Each reference is followed by a letter. These refer to the geographical level for which data were reported: s = State, r = Region, and c = City or metro. The abbreviation *ex* is used to mean *except* or *excluding*; *exp* stands for *expenditures*. For other abbreviations and further explanations, please see the Introduction.

Atlanta, GA - continued

Item	Per	Value	Date	Ref.
Funerals				
Cards, acknowledgment		14.83	1/95	54r
Casket, minimum alternative		192.52	1/95	54r
Cosmetology, hair care, etc.		102.27	1/95	54r
Cremation, direct, container provided by funeral home		1065.64	1/95	54r
Embalming		304.29	1/95	54r
Funeral, funeral home		287.83	1/95	54r
Funeral, other facility		284.14	1/95	54r
Graveside service		349.13	1/95	54r
Hearse, local		132.27	1/95	54r
Limousine, local		98.45	1/95	54r
Memorial service		270.59	1/95	54r
Service charge, professional, nondeclinable		933.59	1/95	54r
Visitation and viewing		225.83	1/95	54r
Groceries				
Groceries, ACCRA Index		100.30	12/94	2c
Apples, Red Delicious	lb.	0.73	12/94	82r
Baby food, strained vegetables, lowest price	4-4.5 oz.	0.34	12/94	2c
Bacon, sliced	lb.	1.67	12/94	82r
Bananas	lb.	0.46	12/94	2c
Bananas	lb.	0.42	12/94	82r
Beef or hamburger, ground	lb.	1.75	12/94	2c
Beef purchases	year	214	91	81c
Beef purchases	year	213	91	81r
Beverage purchases, alcoholic	year	289	91	81c
Beverage purchases, alcoholic	year	249	91	81r
Beverage purchases, nonalcoholic	year	191	91	81c
Beverage purchases, nonalcoholic	year	207	91	81r
Bologna, all beef or mixed	lb.	2.27	12/94	82r
Bread, white	24-oz.	0.81	12/94	2c
Bread, white, pan	lb.	0.68	12/94	82r
Cabbage	lb.	0.42	12/94	82r
Carrots, short trimmed and topped	lb.	0.53	12/94	82r
Cereals and bakery products purchases	year	334	91	81c
Cereals and bakery products purchases	year	345	91	81r
Cereals and cereal products purchases	year	112	91	81c
Cereals and cereals products purchases	year	127	91	81r
Cheddar cheese, natural	lb.	3.58	12/94	82r
Cheese, Kraft grated Parmesan	8-oz.	3.11	12/94	2c
Chicken breast, bone-in	lb.	1.71	12/94	82r
Chicken, fresh, whole	lb.	0.78	12/94	82r
Chicken, whole fryer	lb.	0.69	12/94	2c
Chuck roast, USDA choice, boneless	lb.	2.26	12/94	82r
Cigarettes, Winston, Kings	carton	14.56	12/94	2c
Coffee, vacuum-packed	13 oz.	3.52	12/94	2c
Corn Flakes, Kellogg's or Post Toasties	18 oz.	2.44	12/94	2c
Corn, frozen, whole kernel, lowest price	10 oz.	0.64	12/94	2c
Crackers, soda, salted	lb.	1.27	12/94	82r
Cucumbers	lb.	0.65	12/94	82r
Dairy products (other) purchases	year	140	91	81c
Dairy products (other) purchases	year	141	91	81r
Eggs, Grade A large	dozen	0.70	12/94	2c
Eggs, Grade A large	dozen	0.87	12/94	82r
Fish and seafood purchases	year	72	91	81c
Fish and seafood purchases	year	72	91	81r
Flour, white, all purpose	lb.	0.23	12/94	82r
Food purchases, food eaten at home	year	2293	91	81c
Food purchases, food eaten at home	year	2381	91	81r
Foods purchased away from home, not prepared by consumer	year	1893	91	81c
Foods purchased away from home, not prepared by consumer	year	1696	91	81r
Frankfurters, all meat or all beef	lb.	1.74	12/94	82r
Fruits and vegetables purchases	year	379	91	81c
Fruits and vegetables purchases	year	380	91	81r
Grapefruit	lb.	0.45	12/94	82r
Grapes, Thompson seedless	lb.	2.30	12/94	82r
Ground beef, 100% beef	lb.	1.37	12/94	82r
Ground chuck, 100% beef	lb.	1.97	12/94	82r
Ham, boneless, exc. canned	lb.	2.54	12/94	82r

Atlanta, GA - continued

Item	Per	Value	Date	Ref.
Grocerals - continued				
Ice cream, prepackaged, bulk, regular	1/2 gal.	2.47	12/94	82r
Lemons	lb.	1.02	12/94	82r
Lettuce, iceberg	lb.	0.96	12/94	82r
Lettuce, iceberg	head	1.01	12/94	2c
Margarine, Blue Bonnet or Parkay cubes	lb.	0.69	12/94	2c
Margarine, stick	lb.	0.77	12/94	82r
Meats, poultry, fish, and eggs purchases	year	620	91	81c
Meats, poultry, fish, and eggs purchases	year	655	91	81r
Milk and cream (fresh) purchases	year	98	91	81c
Milk and cream (fresh) purchases	year	130	91	81r
Milk, 2%	gal.	1.97	1/92	44c
Milk, whole	1/2 gal.	1.38	12/94	2c
Orange juice, frozen concentrate 12-oz. can	16 oz.	1.36	12/94	82r
Orange juice, Minute Maid frozen	12-oz.	1.06	12/94	2c
Oranges, Navel	lb.	0.54	12/94	82r
Peaches, halves or slices, Hunt's, Del Monte, or Libby's	29-oz.	1.35	12/94	2c
Pears, Anjou	lb.	0.81	12/94	82r
Peas, sweet, Del Monte or Green Giant	15-17 oz.	0.58	12/94	2c
Pork chops, center cut, bone-in	lb.	3.07	12/94	82r
Pork purchases	year	134	91	81c
Pork purchases	year	142	91	81r
Potato chips	16-oz.	3.15	12/94	82r
Potatoes, frozen, French fried	lb.	0.82	12/94	82r
Potatoes, white	lb.	0.34	12/94	82r
Potatoes, white or red	10-lb. sack	2.59	12/94	2c
Rental rate, 2-bedroom apartment	month	500.00-600	1/92	44c
Rice, white, long grain, uncooked	lb.	0.48	12/94	82r
Round roast, USDA choice, boneless	lb.	2.91	12/94	82r
Sausage, fresh	lb.	1.82	12/94	82r
Sausage, Jimmy Dean, 100% pork	lb.	2.34	12/94	2c
Shortening, vegetable oil blends	lb.	0.75	12/94	82r
Shortening, vegetable, Crisco	3-lb.	2.74	12/94	2c
Soft drink, Coca Cola, ex deposit	2 lit	1.17	12/94	2c
Spaghetti and macaroni	lb.	0.87	12/94	82r
Steak, rib eye, USDA choice, boneless	lb.	6.85	12/94	82r
Steak, round, graded & ungraded, exc. USDA prime & choice	lb.	2.96	12/94	82r
Steak, round, USDA choice, boneless	lb.	3.17	12/94	82r
Steak, sirloin, USDA choice, boneless	lb.	4.12	12/94	82r
Steak, t-bone	lb.	5.79	12/94	2c
Steak, T-bone, USDA choice, bone-in	lb.	5.63	12/94	82r
Sugar and other sweets, eaten at home, expenditures	year	93	91	81r
Sugar and other sweets, eaten at home, purchases	year	92	91	81c
Sugar, cane or beet	4 lbs.	1.47	12/94	2c
Sugar, white, all sizes	lb.	0.39	12/94	82r
Tobacco products and smoking supplies, total expenditures	year	284	91	81c
Tobacco products and smoking supplies, total expenditures	year	286	91	81r
Tomatoes, field grown	lb.	1.36	12/94	82r
Tomatoes, Hunt's or Del Monte	14.5 oz.	0.68	12/94	2c
Tuna, chunk, light	lb.	1.94	12/94	82r
Tuna, chunk, light, oil-packed	6.125-6.5 oz.	0.67	12/94	2c
Turkey, frozen, whole	lb.	0.96	12/94	82r
Yogurt, natural, fruit flavored	8 oz.	0.58	12/94	82r
Goods and Services				
Miscellaneous goods and services, ACCRA Index		98.10	12/94	2c
Health Care				
Health care, ACCRA Index		108.60	12/94	2c
Adenosine, emergency room	treat	100.00	95	23r

Values are in dollars or fractions of dollars. In the column headed *Ref*, references are shown to sources. Each reference is followed by a letter. These refer to the geographical level for which data were reported: s=State, r=Region, and c=City or metro. The abbreviation *ex* is used to mean *except* or *excluding*; *exp* stands for expenditures. For other abbreviations and further explanations, please see the Introduction.

Atlanta, GA - continued

Item	Per	Value	Date	Ref.
Health Care				
Antibiotic ointment, Polysporin	1.5 oz.	3.46	12/94	2c
Appendectomy	proc	1052.00	12/92	69c
Birth, normal delivery	del	2,150	11/93	93c
Bladder tap, superpubic, infant, emergency room	treat	119.00	95	23r
Blood analysis, emergency room	treat	25.00	95	23r
Blood tests, abdominal pain, emergency room	treat	25.00	95	23r
Breast lesion excision (lumpectomy)	proc	628.00	12/92	69c
Broken arm treatment	treat	402	11/93	93c
Burn dressing, emergency room	treat	266.00	95	23r
Cardiology interpretation, emergency room	treat	26.00	95	23r
Cesarean section delivery	proc	2643.00	12/92	69c
Chest X-ray, emergency room	treat	78.00	95	23r
Childbirth, Cesarean delivery, hospital charge	birth	5462.00	12/91	69r
Childbirth, Cesarean delivery, physician charge	birth	2228.00	12/91	69r
Childbirth, normal delivery, hospital charge	birth	2943.00	12/91	69r
Childbirth, normal delivery, physician charge	birth	1619.00	12/91	69r
Cholecystectomy	proc	2920.00	12/92	69c
Coronary bypass, triple	proc	5733.00	12/92	69c
Defibrillation pads, emergency room	treat	6.00	95	23r
Dentist's fee, adult teeth cleaning and periodic oral exam	visit	69.00	12/94	2c
Doctor visit, routine	visit	15.00-84.00	1/94	88c
Doctor's fee, routine exam, established patient	visit	42.50	12/94	2c
Drugs, expenditures	year	269	91	81c
Drugs, expenditures	year	297	91	81r
Gastric tube insertion, nasal, emergency room	treat	25.00	95	23r
Health care, total expenditures	year	1778	91	81c
Health care, total expenditures	year	1600	91	81r
Health insurance expenditures	year	717	91	81c
Health insurance expenditures	year	637	91	81r
Health insurance premium	month	383.00	7/93	94c
Heart monitor, emergency room	treat	40.00	95	23r
Hospital care, semiprivate room	day	333.20	12/94	2c
Hysterectomy, abdominal	proc	2253.00	12/92	69c
Insurance premium, family medical care	month	320.13	1/95	41s
Intravenous fluids, emergency room	treat	130.00	95	23r
Intravenous fluids, emergency room	liter	26.00	95	23r
Intravenous line, central, emergency room	treat	342.00	95	23r
Liver function tests, abdominal pain, emergency room	treat	26.00	95	23r
Medical care charges, total, emergency room, third-degree burns	treat	2101.00	95	23r
Medical care charges, total, emergency, infant with fever	treat	628.00	95	23r
Medical services expenditures	year	681	91	81c
Medical services expenditures	year	573	91	81r
Medical supplies expenditures	year	110	91	81c
Medical supplies expenditures	year	93	91	81r
Morphine, emergency room	treat	34.00	95	23r
Nursing care and facilities charges, emergency room	treat	252.00	95	23r
Nursing care and facilities charges, emergency, infant with fever	treat	252.00	95	23r
Nursing care and facilities charges, emergency, third-degree burns	treat	861.00	95	23r
Oophorectomy	proc	1488.00	12/92	69c
Physical exam, well baby	check-up	34	11/93	93c
Physical, complete	phys	96	11/93	93c
Physician's charges, emergency, infant with fever	treat	212.00	95	23r
Physician's charges, emergency, third-degree burns	treat	372.00	95	23r
Physician's fee, emergency room	treat	372.00	95	23r
Physician's fee, general practitioner	visit	51.20	12/93	60r

Atlanta, GA - continued

Item	Per	Value	Date	Ref.
Health Care - continued				
Salpingo-oophorectomy	proc	1562.00	12/92	69c
Surgery, open-heart	proc	42374.00	1/93	14r
Surgery, open-heart	surg	6,100	11/93	93c
Ultrasound, abdominal, emergency room	treat	276.00	95	23r
Urinalysis, emergency room	treat	20.00	95	23r
Urinalysis, infant, emergency room	treat	20.00	95	23r
X-rays, emergency room	treat	78.00	95	23r
Household Goods				
Appl. repair, service call, wash mach	min. lab. chg.	34.25	12/94	2c
Floor coverings, expenditures	year	72	91	81c
Floor coverings, expenditures	year	48	91	81r
Furniture, expenditures	year	390	91	81c
Furniture, expenditures	year	280	91	81r
Household equipment, misc. expenditures	year	342	91	81r
Household equipment, misc., expenditures	year	509	91	81c
Household expenditures, miscellaneous	year	260	91	81c
Household expenditures, miscellaneous	year	256	91	81r
Household furnishings and equipment, expenditures	year	1389	91	81c
Household furnishings and equipment, expenditures	year	988	91	81r
Household operations expenditures	year	602	91	81c
Household operations expenditures	year	468	91	81r
Household textiles, expenditures	year	166	91	81c
Household textiles, expenditures	year	95	91	81r
Housekeeping supplies, expenditures	year	403	91	81c
Housekeeping supplies, expenditures	year	380	91	81r
Laundry and cleaning supplies, expenditures	year	83	91	81c
Laundry and cleaning supplies, expenditures	year	109	91	81r
Laundry detergent, Tide Ultra, Bold, or Cheer	42 oz.	3.16	12/94	2c
Postage and stationery, expenditures	year	128	91	81c
Postage and stationery, expenditures	year	105	91	81r
Tissues, facial, Kleenex brand	175	1.00	12/94	2c
Housing				
Housing, ACCRA Index		88.00	12/94	2c
Add garage/carport		6,980	3/95	74r
Add room(s)		11,403	3/95	74r
Apartment condominium or co-op, median	unit	68600	12/94	62r
Car rental	day	53.00	5/95	95c
Dwellings (owned), expenditures	year	3760	91	81c
Dwellings (owned), expenditures	year	2428	91	81r
Enclose porch/patio/breezeway		4,572	3/95	74r
Finish room in basement/attic		3,794	3/95	74r
Home, existing, single-family, median	unit	120200	12/94	62r
Home, existing, single-family, median	unit	93.40	12/94	62c
Home, purchase price	unit	105.80	3/93	26c
Hotel room	day	123.00	5/95	95c
House payment, principal and interest, 25% down payment	mo.	646	12/94	2c
House, 1800 sq ft, 8000 sq ft lot, new, urban, utilities	total	105500	12/94	2c
Maintenance, repairs, insurance, and other housing expenditures	year	719	91	81c
Maintenance, repairs, insurance, and other housing expenditures	year	531	91	81r
Mortgage interest and charges expenditures	year	2385	91	81c
Mortgage interest and charges expenditures	year	1506	91	81r
Mtge. rate, incl. points and orig. fee, 30-year conv. fixed or ARM	mo.	9.17	12/94	2c
Princ. & int., mortgage, median-price exist. sing.-family home	mo.	540	12/94	62r
Property taxes expenditures	year	656	91	81c
Property taxes expenditures	year	391	91	81r
Redesign, restructure more than half of home's interior		17,641	3/95	74r

Values are in dollars or fractions of dollars. In the column headed *Ref*, references are shown to sources. Each reference is followed by a letter. These refer to the geographical level for which data were reported: s=State, r=Region, and c=City or metro. The abbreviation *ex* is used to mean *except* or *excluding*; *exp* stands for expenditures. For other abbreviations and further explanations, please see the Introduction.

Atlanta, GA - continued

Item	Per	Value	Date	Ref.
Housing				
Rent, apartment, 2 br., 1 1/2-2 baths, unfurnished, 950 sq ft, water	mo.	544	12/94	2c
Rent, office space	sq. ft.	10.86	93	57c
Rental units expenditures	year	1753	900/00/91	81c
Rental units expenditures	year	1264	91	81r
Insurance and Pensions				
Auto insurance, private passenger	year	664.85	12/94	71s
Health insurance, HMO plan, cost to employer	year	3311	93	59c
Insurance and pensions, personal, expenditures	year	3595	91	81c
Insurance and pensions, personal, expenditures	year	2395	91	81r
Insurance, life and other personal, expenditures	year	611	91	81c
Insurance, life and other personal, expenditures	year	368	91	81r
Pensions and Social Security, expenditures	year	2985	91	81c
Pensions and Social Security, expenditures	year	2027	91	81r
Personal Goods				
Personal care products and services, total expenditures	year	490	91	81c
Shampoo, Alberto VO5	15-oz.	0.89	12/94	2c
Toothpaste, Crest or Colgate	6-7 oz.	1.60	12/94	2c
Personal Services				
Dry cleaning	serv	9.50	92	52c
Dry cleaning, man's 2-pc. suit		6.06	12/94	2c
Dry cleaning, woman's dress	dress	4.50	1/92	44c
Haircut, man's barbershop, no styling		8.20	12/94	2c
Haircut, woman's shampoo, trim, blow-dry		26.70	12/94	2c
Manicure		15.00	92	52c
Personal services expenditures	year	342	91	81c
Personal services expenditures	year	212	91	81r
Restaurant Food				
Big Mac, small fries, medium drink	meal	3.65	1/92	44c
Chicken, fried, thigh and drumstick		1.99	12/94	2c
Dining expenditures, family	week	33.83	94	73r
Hamburger with cheese	1/4 lb.	2.02	12/94	2c
Pizza, Pizza Hut or Pizza Inn	12-13 in.	7.99	12/94	2c
Taxes				
Tax rate, residential property, month	$100	1.74	1/92	79c
Taxes, Federal income, expenditures	year	3554	91	81c
Taxes, Federal income, expenditures	year	2275	91	81r
Taxes, personal, expenditures	year	4732	91	81c
Taxes, personal, expenditures	year	2715	91	81r
Taxes, State and local income, expenditures	year	1093	91	81c
Taxes, State and local income, expenditures	year	365	91	81r
Transportation				
Transportation, ACCRA Index		98.60	12/94	2c
Bus fare, one-way	trip	1.13	12/95	1c
Bus fare, up to 10 miles	one-way	1.08	12/94	2c
Cars and trucks purchased, new	year	1449	91	81c
Cars and trucks purchased, new	year	1306	91	81r
Cars and trucks purchased, used	year	627	91	81c
Cars and trucks purchased, used	year	942	91	81r
Driver's learning permit fee	perm	10.00	1/94	84s
Driver's license fee	orig	15.00	1/94	84s
Driver's license fee, duplicate	lic	10.00	1/94	84s
Driver's license reinstatement fee, min.	susp	25.00	1/94	85s
Driver's license renewal fee	renew	15.00	1/94	84s
Identification card, nondriver	card	3.00	1/94	83s
Motorcycle learning permit fee	perm	10.00	1/94	84s
Motorcycle license fee	orig	15.00	1/94	84s
Motorcycle license fee, duplicate	lic	10.00	1/94	84s
Motorcycle license renewal fee	renew	15.00	1/94	84s
parking, long-term lot, airport	3 days	12.00	1/92	44c

Atlanta, GA - continued

Item	Per	Value	Date	Ref.
Transportation - continued				
Public transportation expenditures	year	397	91	81c
Public transportation expenditures	year	249	91	81r
Railway fare, heavy rail, one-way	trip	1.25	12/95	1c
Tire balance, computer or spin bal., front	wheel	7.20	12/94	2c
Transportation expenditures, total	year	5807	91	81c
Transportation expenditures, total	year	5307	91	81r
Vehicle expenses, miscellaneous	year	2222	91	81c
Vehicle finance charges	year	362	91	81c
Vehicle finance charges	year	346	91	81r
Vehicle insurance expenditures	year	764	91	81c
Vehicle insurance expenditures	year	544	91	81r
Vehicle maintenance and repairs expenditures	year	828	91	81c
Vehicle maintenance and repairs expenditures	year	600	91	81r
Vehicle purchases	year	2076	91	81c
Vehicle purchases	year	2275	91	81r
Vehicle rental, leases, licenses, etc. expenditures	year	268	91	81c
Vehicle rental, leases, licenses, etc. expenditures	year	141	91	81r
Vehicles purchased, other than cars and trucks	year	27	91	81r
Travel				
Car rental	day	43.99	1/93	49c
Car rental	week	174.99	1/93	49c
Utilities				
Utilities, ACCRA Index		109.90	12/94	2c
Electricity expenditures	year	923	91	81c
Electricity expenditures	year	950	91	81r
Electricity, (part.), other, 1800 sq. ft., new home	mo.	72.32	12/94	2c
Electricity, summer, 250 KWh	month	23.08	8/93	64c
Electricity, summer, 500 KWh	month	38.67	8/93	64c
Electricity, summer, 750 KWh	month	57.41	8/93	64c
Electricity, summer, 1000 KWh	month	80.90	8/93	64c
Utilities, fuels, and public services, total expenditures	year	2343	91	81c
Utilities, fuels, and public services, total expenditures	year	2000	91	81r
Water and other public services, expenditures	year	258	91	81c
Water and other public services, expenditures	year	227	91	81r
Weddings				
Bridal attendants' gowns	event	750	10/93	76r
Bridal gown	event	852	10/93	76r
Bridal headpiece and veil	event	167	10/93	76r
Bride's wedding band	event	708	10/93	76r
Clergy	event	224	10/93	76r
Engagement ring	event	2756	10/93	76r
Flowers	event	863	10/93	76r
Formal wear for groom	event	106	10/93	76r
Groom's attendants' formal wear	event	530	10/93	76r
Groom's wedding band	event	402	10/93	76r
Music	event	600	10/93	76r
Photography	event	1088	10/93	76r
Shoes for bride	event	50	10/93	76r
Videography	event	483	10/93	76r
Wedding invitations and announcements	event	342	10/93	76r
Wedding reception	event	7000	10/93	76r

Atlantic City, NJ

Item	Per	Value	Date	Ref.
Appliances				
Appliances (major), expenditures	year	145	91	81r
Average annual exp.				
Food, health care, personal goods, services	year	29496	91	81r

Values are in dollars or fractions of dollars. In the column headed *Ref*, references are shown to sources. Each reference is followed by a letter. These refer to the geographical level for which data were reported: s=State, r=Region, and c=City or metro. The abbreviation *ex* is used to mean *except* or *excluding*; *exp* stands for expenditures. For other abbreviations and further explanations, please see the Introduction.

Atlantic City, NJ - continued

Item	Per	Value	Date	Ref.
Charity				
Cash contributions, expenditures	year	708	91	81r
Clothing				
Apparel, men and boys, total expenditures	year	416	91	81r
Apparel, women and girls, total expenditures	year	744	91	81r
Footwear, expenditures	year	305	91	81r
Communications				
Long-distance telephone rate, day, addl. min., 1-10 mi.	min.	0.03	12/93	9s
Long-distance telephone rate, day, initial min., 1-10 mi.	min.	0.09	12/93	9s
Phone line, single, business, field visit	inst	98.50	12/93	9s
Phone line, single, business, no field visit	inst	79.50	12/93	9s
Phone line, single, residence, field visit	inst	56.50	12/93	9s
Phone line, single, residence, no field visit	inst	42.00	12/93	9s
Telephone service, expenditures	year	589	91	81r
Telephone, residential, flat rate	mo.	7.45	12/93	8c
Education				
Board, 4-year private college/university	year	2841	8/94	80s
Board, 4-year public college/university	year	1956	8/94	80s
Education, total expenditures	year	593	91	81r
Room, 4-year private college/university	year	2999	8/94	80s
Room, 4-year public college/university	year	2778	8/94	80s
Total cost, 4-year private college/university	year	18264	8/94	80s
Total cost, 4-year public college/university	year	8252	8/94	80s
Tuition, 2-year public college/university, in-state	year	1539	8/94	80s
Tuition, 4-year private college/university, in-state	year	12423	8/94	80s
Tuition, 4-year public college/university, in-state	year	3518	8/94	80s
Energy and Fuels				
Fuel oil and other fuels, expenditures	year	257	91	81r
Gas, cooking, winter, 10 therms	month	12.02	2/94	65c
Gas, cooking, winter, 30 therms	month	23.56	2/94	65c
Gas, cooking, winter, 50 therms	month	35.09	2/94	65c
Gas, heating, winter, 100 therms	month	63.92	2/94	65c
Gas, heating, winter, average use	month	112.94	2/94	65c
Gas, natural, expenditures	year	285	91	81r
Gasoline and motor oil purchased	year	867	91	81r
Gasoline, unleaded midgrade	gallon	1.32	4/93	82r
Gasoline, unleaded premium	gallon	1.40	4/93	82r
Gasoline, unleaded regular	gallon	1.19	4/93	82r
Entertainment				
Entertainment, total expenditures	year	1331	91	81r
Fees and admissions, expenditures	year	398	91	81r
Pets, toys, playground equipment, expenditures	year	270	91	81r
Reading, expenditures	year	171	91	81r
Televisions, radios, and sound equipment, expenditures	year	429	91	81r
Funerals				
Burial, immediate, container provided by funeral home		1370.36	1/95	54r
Cards, acknowledgment		17.72	1/95	54r
Casket, minimum alternative		192.52	1/95	54r
Cosmetology, hair care, etc.		139.56	1/95	54r
Cremation, direct, container provided by funeral home		1049.24	1/95	54r
Embalming		387.57	1/95	54r
Funeral, funeral home		278.77	1/95	54r
Funeral, other facility		275.85	1/95	54r
Graveside service		213.08	1/95	54r
Hearse, local		157.27	1/95	54r
Limousine, local		146.45	1/95	54r
Memorial service		271.02	1/95	54r
Service charge, professional, nondeclinable		943.58	1/95	54r
Visitation and viewing		322.86	1/95	54r

Atlantic City, NJ - continued

Item	Per	Value	Date	Ref.
Groceries				
Apples, Red Delicious	lb.	0.78	12/94	82r
Bacon, sliced	lb.	2.24	12/94	82r
Bananas	lb.	0.49	12/94	82r
Beef purchases	year	226	91	81r
Beverage purchases, alcoholic	year	332	91	81r
Beverage purchases, nonalcoholic	year	213	91	81r
Bread, white, pan	lb.	0.80	12/94	82r
Butter, salted, Grade AA, stick	lb.	1.67	12/94	82r
Carrots, short trimmed and topped	lb.	0.51	12/94	82r
Cereals and bakery products purchases	year	407	91	81r
Cereals and cereals products purchases	year	132	91	81r
Chicken breast, bone-in	lb.	2.22	12/94	82r
Chicken, fresh, whole	lb.	1.05	12/94	82r
Chuck roast, USDA choice, boneless	lb.	2.74	12/94	82r
Coffee, 100%, ground roast, all sizes	lb.	4.61	12/94	82r
Dairy products (other) purchases	year	161	91	81r
Eggs, Grade A large	dozen	1.12	12/94	82r
Fish and seafood purchases	year	112	91	81r
Food purchases, food eaten at home	year	2599	91	81r
Foods purchased away from home, not prepared by consumer	year	2024	91	81r
Fruits and vegetables purchases	year	444	91	81r
Grapefruit	lb.	0.44	12/94	82r
Grapes, Thompson seedless	lb.	2.24	12/94	82r
Ground chuck, 100% beef	lb.	1.67	12/94	82r
Ice cream, prepackaged, bulk, regular	1/2 gal.	2.93	12/94	82r
Lemons	lb.	1.06	12/94	82r
Lettuce, iceberg	lb.	0.92	12/94	82r
Meats, poultry, fish, and eggs purchases	year	751	91	81r
Milk and cream (fresh) purchases	year	152	91	81r
Orange juice, frozen concentrate 12-oz. can	16 oz.	1.92	12/94	82r
Oranges, Navel	lb.	0.56	12/94	82r
Pork chops, center cut, bone-in	lb.	3.09	12/94	82r
Pork purchases	year	130	91	81r
Potatoes, white	lb.	0.37	12/94	82r
Rib roast, USDA choice, bone-in	lb.	4.98	12/94	82r
Round roast, USDA choice, boneless	lb.	2.93	12/94	82r
Shortening, vegetable oil blends	lb.	1.03	12/94	82r
Spaghetti and macaroni	lb.	0.84	12/94	82r
Steak, round, USDA choice, boneless	lb.	3.48	12/94	82r
Steak, sirloin, USDA choice, bone-in	lb.	3.38	12/94	82r
Steak, sirloin, USDA choice, boneless	lb.	4.81	12/94	82r
Sugar and other sweets, eaten at home, expenditures	year	89	91	81r
Sugar, white, all sizes	lb.	0.46	12/94	82r
Tobacco products and smoking supplies, total expenditures	year	279	91	81r
Tomatoes, field grown	lb.	1.56	12/94	82r
Tuna, chunk, light	lb.	2.09	12/94	82r
Health Care				
Childbirth, Cesarean delivery, hospital charge	birth	6334.00	12/91	69r
Childbirth, Cesarean delivery, physician charge	birth	2234.00	12/91	69r
Childbirth, normal delivery, hospital charge	birth	3225.00	12/91	69r
Childbirth, normal delivery, physician charge	birth	1623.00	12/91	69r
Drugs, expenditures	year	205	91	81r
Health care, total expenditures	year	1396	91	81r
Health insurance expenditures	year	553	91	81r
Insurance premium, family medical care	month	396.06	1/95	41s
Medical services expenditures	year	559	91	81r
Medical supplies expenditures	year	80	91	81r
Household Goods				
Floor coverings, expenditures	year	158	91	81r
Furniture, expenditures	year	341	91	81r
Household equipment, misc. expenditures	year	363	91	81r
Household expenditures, miscellaneous	year	194	91	81r
Household furnishings and equipment, expenditures	year	1158	91	81r
Household operations expenditures	year	378	91	81r

Values are in dollars or fractions of dollars. In the column headed *Ref*, references are shown to sources. Each reference is followed by a letter. These refer to the geographical level for which data were reported: s = State, r = Region, and c = City or metro. The abbreviation *ex* is used to mean *except* or *excluding*; *exp* stands for *expenditures*. For other abbreviations and further explanations, please see the Introduction.

Atlantic City, NJ - continued

Item	Per	Value	Date	Ref.
Household Goods				
Household textiles, expenditures	year	88	91	81r
Housekeeping supplies, expenditures	year	426	91	81r
Laundry and cleaning supplies, expenditures	year	122	91	81r
Postage and stationery, expenditures	year	134	91	81r
Housing				
Add garage/carport		11,614	3/95	74r
Add room(s)		16,816	3/95	74r
Apartment condominium or co-op, median	unit	96700	12/94	62r
Dwellings (owned), expenditures	year	3305	91	81r
Enclose porch/patio/breezeway		2,980	3/95	74r
Finish room in basement/attic		4,330	3/95	74r
Home, existing, single-family, median	unit	161600	12/94	62r
Home, existing, single-family, median	unit	107.30	12/94	62c
Maintenance, repairs, insurance, and other housing expenditures	year	569	91	81r
Mortgage interest and charges expenditures	year	1852	91	81r
Princ. & int., mortgage, median-price exist. sing.-family home	mo.	765	12/94	62r
Property taxes expenditures	year	884	91	81r
Redesign, restructure more than half of home's interior		2,750	3/95	74r
Rental units expenditures	year	1832	91	81r
Insurance and Pensions				
Auto insurance, private passenger	year	1094.56	12/94	71s
Insurance and pensions, personal, expenditures	year	2690	91	81r
Insurance, life and other personal, expenditures	year	341	91	81r
Pensions and Social Security, expenditures	year	2349	91	81r
Legal Assistance				
Estate planning, law-firm partner	hr.	375.00	10/93	12r
Legal work, law firm associate	hour	78		10r
Legal work, law firm partner	hour	183		10r
Personal Services				
Personal services expenditures	year	184	91	81r
Restaurant Food				
Dining expenditures, family	week	34.26	94	73r
Taxes				
Taxes, Federal income, expenditures	year	2409	91	81r
Taxes, personal, expenditures	year	3094	91	81r
Taxes, State and local income, expenditures	year	620	91	81r
Transportation				
Bus fare, one-way	trip	1.00	12/95	1c
Cars and trucks purchased, new	year	1170	91	81r
Cars and trucks purchased, used	year	739	91	81r
Driver's learning permit fee	perm	5.00	1/94	84s
Driver's license fee	orig	16.00	1/94	84s
Driver's license fee, duplicate	lic	3.00	1/94	84s
Driver's license reinstatement fee, min.	susp	30.00	1/94	85s
Driver's license renewal fee	renew	16.00	1/94	84s
Identification card, nondriver	card	5.50	1/94	83s
Motorcycle learning permit fee	perm	5.00	1/94	84s
Motorcycle license fee	orig	8.00	1/94	84s
Motorcycle license fee, duplicate	lic	3.00	1/94	84s
Motorcycle license renewal fee	renew	8.00	1/94	84s
Public transportation expenditures	year	430	91	81r
Railway fare, commuter rail, one-way	trip	0.85	12/95	1c
Transportation expenditures, total	year	4810	91	81r
Vehicle finance charges	year	238	91	81r
Vehicle insurance expenditures	year	630	91	81r
Vehicle maintenance and repairs expenditures	year	532	91	81r
Vehicle purchases	year	1920	91	81r
Vehicle rental, leases, licenses, etc. expenditures	year	193	91	81r
Vehicles purchased, other than cars and trucks	year	11	91	81r

Atlantic City, NJ - continued

Item	Per	Value	Date	Ref.
Utilities				
Electricity expenditures	year	695	91	81r
Utilities, fuels, and public services, total expenditures	year	1981	91	81r
Water and other public services, expenditures	year	154	91	81r
Weddings				
Bridal attendants' gowns	event	750	10/93	76r
Bridal gown	event	852	10/93	76r
Bridal headpiece and veil	event	167	10/93	76r
Bride's wedding band	event	708	10/93	76r
Clergy	event	224	10/93	76r
Engagement ring	event	2756	10/93	76r
Flowers	event	863	10/93	76r
Formal wear for groom	event	106	10/93	76r
Groom's attendants' formal wear	event	530	10/93	76r
Groom's wedding band	event	402	10/93	76r
Music	event	600	10/93	76r
Photography	event	1088	10/93	76r
Shoes for bride	event	50	10/93	76r
Videography	event	483	10/93	76r
Wedding invitations and announcements	event	342	10/93	76r
Wedding reception	event	7000	10/93	76r

Augusta, GA, SC

Item	Per	Value	Date	Ref.
Composite, ACCRA index		93.20	12/94	2c
Alcoholic Beverages				
Beer, Miller Lite, Bud, 12-oz., ex deposit	6	4.08	12/94	2c
J & B Scotch	750-ml.	19.28	12/94	2c
Wine, Gallo Chablis blanc	1.5-lit	5.31	12/94	2c
Appliances				
Appliances (major), expenditures	year	153	91	81r
Average annual exp.				
Food, health care, personal goods, services	year	27020	91	81r
Charity				
Cash contributions, expenditures	year	839	91	81r
Clothing				
Apparel, men and boys, total expenditures	year	380	91	81r
Apparel, women and girls, total expenditures	year	660	91	81r
Footwear, expenditures	year	193	91	81r
Jeans, man's denim		29.94	12/94	2c
Shirt, man's dress shirt		29.80	12/94	2c
Undervest, boy's size 10-14, cotton	3	4.09	12/94	2c
Communications				
Long-distance telephone rate, day, addl. min., 1-10 mi.	min.	0.04	12/93	9s
Long-distance telephone rate, day, initial min., 1-10 mi.	min.	0.08	12/93	9s
Newspaper subscription, dly. and Sun. delivery	month	10.00	12/94	2c
Phone line, single, business, field visit	inst	58.25	12/93	9s
Phone line, single, business, no field visit	inst	52.25	12/93	9s
Phone line, single, residence, field visit	inst	47.50	12/93	9s
Phone line, single, residence, no field visit	inst	42.50	12/93	9s
Telephone bill, family of four	month	21.32	12/94	2c
Telephone service, expenditures	year	616	91	81r
Telephone, residential, flat rate	mo.	13.55	12/93	8c
Telephone, residential, flat rate	mo.	16.00	12/93	8c
Education				
Board, 4-year private college/university	year	2288	8/94	80s
Board, 4-year public college/university	year	1723	8/94	80s
Education, total expenditures	year	319	91	81r
Room, 4-year private college/university	year	2409	8/94	80s
Room, 4-year public college/university	year	1459	8/94	80s
Total cost, 4-year private college/university	year	13950	8/94	80s
Total cost, 4-year public college/university	year	5075	8/94	80s

Values are in dollars or fractions of dollars. In the column headed *Ref*, references are shown to sources. Each reference is followed by a letter. These refer to the geographical level for which data were reported: s = State, r = Region, and c = City or metro. The abbreviation *ex* is used to mean *except* or *excluding*; *exp* stands for expenditures. For other abbreviations and further explanations, please see the Introduction.

Augusta, GA, SC - continued

Item	Per	Value	Date	Ref.
Education				
Tuition, 2-year public college/university, in-state	year	972	8/94	80s
Tuition, 4-year private college/university, in-state	year	9253	8/94	80s
Tuition, 4-year public college/university, in-state	year	1894	8/94	80s
Energy and Fuels				
Energy, combined forms, 1800 sq. ft.	mo.	121.88	12/94	2c
Energy, exc. electricity, 1800 sq. ft.	mo.	41.48	12/94	2c
Fuel oil and other fuels, expenditures	year	56	91	81r
Gas, natural, expenditures	year	150	91	81r
Gas, reg unlead, taxes inc., cash, self-service	gal	1.00	12/94	2c
Gasoline and motor oil purchased	year	1152	91	81r
Gasoline, unleaded midgrade	gallon	1.21	4/93	82r
Gasoline, unleaded premium	gallon	1.30	4/93	82r
Gasoline, unleaded regular	gallon	1.10	4/93	82r
Entertainment				
Bowling, evening rate	game	2.40	12/94	2c
Concert ticket, Pearl Jam group	perf	20.00	94	50r
Entertainment, total expenditures	year	1266	91	81r
Fees and admissions, expenditures	year	306	91	81r
Monopoly game, Parker Brothers', No. 9	game	12.49	12/94	2c
Movie	adm	5.65	12/94	2c
Pets, toys, playground equipment, expenditures	year	271	91	81r
Reading, expenditures	year	131	91	81r
Televisions, radios, and sound equipment, expenditures	year	439	91	81r
Tennis balls, yellow, Wilson or Penn, 3	can	1.94	12/94	2c
Funerals				
Burial, immediate, container provided by funeral home		1370.36	1/95	54r
Cards, acknowledgment		14.83	1/95	54r
Casket, minimum alternative		192.52	1/95	54r
Cosmetology, hair care, etc.		102.27	1/95	54r
Cremation, direct, container provided by funeral home		1065.64	1/95	54r
Embalming		304.29	1/95	54r
Funeral, funeral home		287.83	1/95	54r
Funeral, other facility		284.14	1/95	54r
Graveside service		349.13	1/95	54r
Hearse, local		132.27	1/95	54r
Limousine, local		98.45	1/95	54r
Memorial service		270.59	1/95	54r
Service charge, professional, nondeclinable		933.59	1/95	54r
Visitation and viewing		225.83	1/95	54r
Groceries				
Groceries, ACCRA Index		98.70	12/94	2c
Apples, Red Delicious	lb.	0.73	12/94	82r
Baby food, strained vegetables, lowest price	4-4.5 oz.	0.37	12/94	2c
Bacon, sliced	lb.	1.67	12/94	82r
Bananas	lb.	0.47	12/94	2c
Bananas	lb.	0.42	12/94	82r
Beef or hamburger, ground	lb.	1.43	12/94	2c
Beef purchases	year	213	91	81r
Beverage purchases, alcoholic	year	249	91	81r
Beverage purchases, nonalcoholic	year	207	91	81r
Bologna, all beef or mixed	lb.	2.27	12/94	82r
Bread, white	24-oz.	0.76	12/94	2c
Bread, white, pan	lb.	0.68	12/94	82r
Cabbage	lb.	0.42	12/94	82r
Carrots, short trimmed and topped	lb.	0.53	12/94	82r
Cereals and bakery products purchases	year	345	91	81r
Cereals and cereals products purchases	year	127	91	81r
Cheddar cheese, natural	lb.	3.58	12/94	82r
Cheese, Kraft grated Parmesan	8-oz.	3.05	12/94	2c
Chicken breast, bone-in	lb.	1.71	12/94	82r
Chicken, fresh, whole	lb.	0.78	12/94	82r

Augusta, GA, SC - continued

Item	Per	Value	Date	Ref.
Groceries - continued				
Chicken, whole fryer	lb.	0.85	12/94	2c
Chuck roast, USDA choice, boneless	lb.	2.26	12/94	82r
Cigarettes, Winston, Kings	carton	13.39	12/94	2c
Coffee, vacuum-packed	13 oz.	3.15	12/94	2c
Corn Flakes, Kellogg's or Post Toasties	18 oz.	2.32	12/94	2c
Corn, frozen, whole kernel, lowest price	10 oz.	0.60	12/94	2c
Crackers, soda, salted	lb.	1.27	12/94	82r
Cucumbers	lb.	0.65	12/94	82r
Dairy products (other) purchases	year	141	91	81r
Eggs, Grade A large	dozen	0.77	12/94	2c
Eggs, Grade A large	dozen	0.87	12/94	82r
Fish and seafood purchases	year	72	91	81r
Flour, white, all purpose	lb.	0.23	12/94	82r
Food purchases, food eaten at home	year	2381	91	81r
Foods purchased away from home, not prepared by consumer	year	1696	91	81r
Frankfurters, all meat or all beef	lb.	1.74	12/94	82r
Fruits and vegetables purchases	year	380	91	81r
Grapefruit	lb.	0.45	12/94	82r
Grapes, Thompson seedless	lb.	2.30	12/94	82r
Ground beef, 100% beef	lb.	1.37	12/94	82r
Ground chuck, 100% beef	lb.	1.97	12/94	82r
Ham, boneless, exc. canned	lb.	2.54	12/94	82r
Ice cream, prepackaged, bulk, regular	1/2 gal.	2.47	12/94	82r
Lemons	lb.	1.02	12/94	82r
Lettuce, iceberg	lb.	0.96	12/94	82r
Lettuce, iceberg	head	0.99	12/94	2c
Margarine, Blue Bonnet or Parkay cubes	lb.	0.56	12/94	2c
Margarine, stick	lb.	0.77	12/94	82r
Meats, poultry, fish, and eggs purchases	year	655	91	81r
Milk and cream (fresh) purchases	year	130	91	81r
Milk, whole	1/2 gal.	1.41	12/94	2c
Orange juice, frozen concentrate 12-oz. can	16 oz.	1.36	12/94	82r
Orange juice, Minute Maid frozen	12-oz.	1.25	12/94	2c
Oranges, Navel	lb.	0.54	12/94	82r
Peaches, halves or slices, Hunt's, Del Monte, or Libby's	29-oz.	1.28	12/94	2c
Pears, Anjou	lb.	0.81	12/94	82r
Peas, sweet, Del Monte or Green Giant	15-17 oz.	0.55	12/94	2c
Pork chops, center cut, bone-in	lb.	3.07	12/94	82r
Pork purchases	year	142	91	81r
Potato chips	16-oz.	3.15	12/94	2c
Potatoes, frozen, French fried	lb.	0.82	12/94	82r
Potatoes, white	lb.	0.34	12/94	82r
Potatoes, white or red	10-lb. sack	2.89	12/94	2c
Rice, white, long grain, uncooked	lb.	0.48	12/94	82r
Round roast, USDA choice, boneless	lb.	2.91	12/94	82r
Sausage, fresh	lb.	1.82	12/94	82r
Sausage, Jimmy Dean, 100% pork	lb.	2.25	12/94	2c
Shortening, vegetable oil blends	lb.	0.75	12/94	82r
Shortening, vegetable, Crisco	3-lb.	2.55	12/94	2c
Soft drink, Coca Cola, ex deposit	2 lit	1.13	12/94	2c
Spaghetti and macaroni	lb.	0.87	12/94	82r
Steak, rib eye, USDA choice, boneless	lb.	6.85	12/94	82r
Steak, round, graded & ungraded, exc. USDA prime & choice	lb.	2.96	12/94	82r
Steak, round, USDA choice, boneless	lb.	3.17	12/94	82r
Steak, sirloin, USDA choice, boneless	lb.	4.12	12/94	82r
Steak, t-bone	lb.	5.93	12/94	2c
Steak, T-bone, USDA choice, bone-in	lb.	5.63	12/94	82r
Sugar and other sweets, eaten at home, expenditures	year	93	91	81r
Sugar, cane or beet	4 lbs.	1.52	12/94	2c
Sugar, white, all sizes	lb.	0.39	12/94	82r
Tobacco products and smoking supplies, total expenditures	year	286	91	81r
Tomatoes, field grown	lb.	1.36	12/94	82r

Values are in dollars or fractions of dollars. In the column headed *Ref*, references are shown to sources. Each reference is followed by a letter. These refer to the geographical level for which data were reported: s=State, r=Region, and c=City or metro. The abbreviation *ex* is used to mean *except* or *excluding*; *exp* stands for *expenditures*. For other abbreviations and further explanations, please see the Introduction.

Augusta, GA, SC - continued

Item	Per	Value	Date	Ref.
Groceries				
Tomatoes, Hunt's or Del Monte	14.5 oz.	0.57	12/94	2c
Tuna, chunk, light	lb.	1.94	12/94	82r
Tuna, chunk, light, oil-packed	6.125-6.5 oz.	0.69	12/94	2c
Turkey, frozen, whole	lb.	0.96	12/94	82r
Yogurt, natural, fruit flavored	8 oz.	0.58	12/94	82r
Goods and Services				
Miscellaneous goods and services, ACCRA Index		93.30	12/94	2c
Health Care				
Health care, ACCRA Index		97.50	12/94	2c
Adenosine, emergency room	treat	100.00	95	23r
Antibiotic ointment, Polysporin	1.5 oz.	4.61	12/94	2c
Bladder tap, superpubic, infant, emergency room	treat	119.00	95	23r
Blood analysis, emergency room	treat	25.00	95	23r
Blood tests, abdominal pain, emergency room	treat	25.00	95	23r
Burn dressing, emergency room	treat	266.00	95	23r
Cardiology interpretation, emergency room	treat	26.00	95	23r
Chest X-ray, emergency room	treat	78.00	95	23r
Childbirth, Cesarean delivery, hospital charge	birth	5462.00	12/91	69r
Childbirth, Cesarean delivery, physician charge	birth	2228.00	12/91	69r
Childbirth, normal delivery, hospital charge	birth	2943.00	12/91	69r
Childbirth, normal delivery, physician charge	birth	1619.00	12/91	69r
Defibrillation pads, emergency room	treat	6.00	95	23r
Dentist's fee, adult teeth cleaning and periodic oral exam	visit	51.40	12/94	2c
Doctor's fee, routine exam, established patient	visit	41.20	12/94	2c
Drugs, expenditures	year	297	91	81r
Gastric tube insertion, nasal, emergency room	treat	25.00	95	23r
Health care, total expenditures	year	1600	91	81r
Health insurance expenditures	year	637	91	81r
Heart monitor, emergency room	treat	40.00	95	23r
Hospital care, semiprivate room	day	307.75	12/94	2c
Insurance premium, family medical care	month	320.13	1/95	41s
Intravenous fluids, emergency room	treat	130.00	95	23r
Intravenous fluids, emergency room	liter	26.00	95	23r
Intravenous line, central, emergency room	treat	342.00	95	23r
Liver function tests, abdominal pain, emergency room	treat	26.00	95	23r
Medical care charges, total, emergency room, third-degree burns	treat	2101.00	95	23r
Medical care charges, total, emergency, infant with fever	treat	628.00	95	23r
Medical services expenditures	year	573	91	81r
Medical supplies expenditures	year	93	91	81r
Morphine, emergency room	treat	34.00	95	23r
Nursing care and facilities charges, emergency room	treat	252.00	95	23r
Nursing care and facilities charges, emergency, infant with fever	treat	252.00	95	23r
Nursing care and facilities charges, emergency, third-degree burns	treat	861.00	95	23r
Physician's charges, emergency, infant with fever	treat	212.00	95	23r
Physician's charges, emergency, third-degree burns	treat	372.00	95	23r
Physician's fee, emergency room	treat	372.00	95	23r
Physician's fee, general practitioner	visit	51.20	12/93	60r
Surgery, open-heart	proc	42374.00	1/93	14r
Ultrasound, abdominal, emergency room	treat	276.00	95	23r
Urinalysis, emergency room	treat	20.00	95	23r
Urinalysis, infant, emergency room	treat	20.00	95	23r
X-rays, emergency room	treat	78.00	95	23r

Augusta, GA, SC - continued

Item	Per	Value	Date	Ref.
Household Goods				
Appl. repair, service call, wash mach	min. lab. chg.	29.10	12/94	2c
Floor coverings, expenditures	year	48	91	81r
Furniture, expenditures	year	280	91	81r
Household equipment, misc. expenditures	year	342	91	81r
Household expenditures, miscellaneous	year	256	91	81r
Household furnishings and equipment, expenditures	year	988	91	81r
Household operations expenditures	year	468	91	81r
Household textiles, expenditures	year	95	91	81r
Housekeeping supplies, expenditures	year	380	91	81r
Laundry and cleaning supplies, expenditures	year	109	91	81r
Laundry detergent, Tide Ultra, Bold, or Cheer	42 oz.	2.92	12/94	2c
Postage and stationery, expenditures	year	105	91	81r
Tissues, facial, Kleenex brand	175	0.98	12/94	2c
Housing				
Housing, ACCRA Index		83.30	12/94	2c
Add garage/carport		6,980	3/95	74r
Add room(s)		11,403	3/95	74r
Apartment condominium or co-op, median	unit	68600	12/94	62r
Dwellings (owned), expenditures	year	2428	91	81r
Enclose porch/patio/breezeway		4,572	3/95	74r
Finish room in basement/attic		3,794	3/95	74r
Home, existing, single-family, median	unit	120200	12/94	62r
House payment, principal and interest, 25% down payment	mo.	629	12/94	2c
House, 1800 sq ft, 8000 sq ft lot, new, urban, utilities	total	96235	12/94	2c
Maintenance, repairs, insurance, and other housing expenditures	year	531	91	81r
Mortgage interest and charges expenditures	year	1506	91	81r
Mtge. rate, incl. points and orig. fee, 30-year conv. fixed or ARM	mo.	9.21	12/94	2c
Princ. & int., mortgage, median-price exist. sing.-family home	mo.	540	12/94	62r
Property taxes expenditures	year	391	91	81r
Redesign, restructure more than half of home's interior		17,641	3/95	74r
Rent, apartment, 2 br., 1 1/2-2 baths, unfurnished, 950 sq ft, water	mo.	468	12/94	2c
Rental units expenditures	year	1264	91	81r
Insurance and Pensions				
Auto insurance, private passenger	year	664.85	12/94	71s
Insurance and pensions, personal, expenditures	year	2395	91	81r
Insurance, life and other personal, expenditures	year	368	91	81r
Pensions and Social Security, expenditures	year	2027	91	81r
Personal Goods				
Shampoo, Alberto VO5	15-oz.	0.93	12/94	2c
Toothpaste, Crest or Colgate	6-7 oz.	1.77	12/94	2c
Personal Services				
Dry cleaning, man's 2-pc. suit		5.68	12/94	2c
Haircut, man's barbershop, no styling		10.40	12/94	2c
Haircut, woman's shampoo, trim, blow-dry		21.00	12/94	2c
Personal services expenditures	year	212	91	81r
Restaurant Food				
Chicken, fried, thigh and drumstick		2.06	12/94	2c
Dining expenditures, family	week	33.83	94	73r
Hamburger with cheese	1/4 lb.	0.99	12/94	2c
Pizza, Pizza Hut or Pizza Inn	12-13 in.	7.99	12/94	2c
Taxes				
Taxes, Federal income, expenditures	year	2275	91	81r
Taxes, personal, expenditures	year	2715	91	81r
Taxes, State and local income, expenditures	year	365	91	81r

Values are in dollars or fractions of dollars. In the column headed *Ref*, references are shown to sources. Each reference is followed by a letter. These refer to the geographical level for which data were reported: s=State, r=Region, and c=City or metro. The abbreviation *ex* is used to mean *except* or *excluding*; *exp* stands for *expenditures*. For other abbreviations and further explanations, please see the Introduction.

Augusta, GA, SC - continued

Item	Per	Value	Date	Ref.
Transportation				
Transportation, ACCRA Index		97.40	12/94	2c
Bus fare, one-way	trip	0.75	12/95	1c
Cars and trucks purchased, new	year	1306	91	81r
Cars and trucks purchased, used	year	942	91	81r
Driver's learning permit fee	perm	10.00	1/94	84s
Driver's license fee	orig	15.00	1/94	84s
Driver's license fee, duplicate	lic	10.00	1/94	84s
Driver's license reinstatement fee, min.	susp	25.00	1/94	85s
Driver's license renewal fee	renew	15.00	1/94	84s
Identification card, nondriver	card	3.00	1/94	83s
Motorcycle learning permit fee	perm	10.00	1/94	84s
Motorcycle license fee	orig	15.00	1/94	84s
Motorcycle license fee, duplicate	lic	10.00	1/94	84s
Motorcycle license renewal fee	renew	15.00	1/94	84s
Public transportation expenditures	year	249	91	81r
Tire balance, computer or spin bal., front	wheel	7.39	12/94	2c
Transportation expenditures, total	year	5307	91	81r
Vehicle finance charges	year	346	91	81r
Vehicle insurance expenditures	year	544	91	81r
Vehicle maintenance and repairs expenditures	year	600	91	81r
Vehicle purchases	year	2275	91	81r
Vehicle rental, leases, licenses, etc. expenditures	year	141	91	81r
Vehicles purchased, other than cars and trucks	year	27	91	81r
Utilities				
Utilities, ACCRA Index		108.70	12/94	2c
Electricity expenditures	year	950	91	81r
Electricity, (part.), other, 1800 sq. ft., new home	mo.	80.40	12/94	2c
Utilities, fuels, and public services, total expenditures	year	2000	91	81r
Water and other public services, expenditures	year	227	91	81r
Weddings				
Bridal attendants' gowns	event	750	10/93	76r
Bridal gown	event	852	10/93	76r
Bridal headpiece and veil	event	167	10/93	76r
Bride's wedding band	event	708	10/93	76r
Clergy	event	224	10/93	76r
Engagement ring	event	2756	10/93	76r
Flowers	event	863	10/93	76r
Formal wear for groom	event	106	10/93	76r
Groom's attendants' formal wear	event	530	10/93	76r
Groom's wedding band	event	402	10/93	76r
Music	event	600	10/93	76r
Photography	event	1088	10/93	76r
Shoes for bride	event	50	10/93	76r
Videography	event	483	10/93	76r
Wedding invitations and announcements	event	342	10/93	76r
Wedding reception	event	7000	10/93	76r

Aurora-Elgin, IL

Item	Per	Value	Date	Ref.
Appliances				
Appliances (major), expenditures	year	131	91	81r
Average annual exp.				
Food, health care, personal goods, services	year	25935	91	81r
Charity				
Cash contributions, expenditures	year	745	91	81r
Clothing				
Apparel, men and boys, total expenditures	year	332	91	81r
Apparel, women and girls, total expenditures	year	578	91	81r
Footwear, expenditures	year	164	91	81r
Communications				
Long-distance telephone rate, day, addl. min., 1-10 mi.	min.	0.04	12/93	9s

Aurora-Elgin, IL - continued

Item	Per	Value	Date	Ref.
Communications - continued				
Long-distance telephone rate, day, initial min., 1-10 mi.	min.	0.10	12/93	9s
Phone line, single, business, field visit	inst	84.50	12/93	9s
Phone line, single, business, no field visit	inst	84.50	12/93	9s
Phone line, single, residence, field visit	inst	55.00	12/93	9s
Phone line, single, residence, no field visit	inst	55.00	12/93	9s
Telephone service, expenditures	year	547	91	81r
Education				
Board, 4-year private college/university	year	2078	8/94	80s
Board, 4-year public college/university	year	2139	8/94	80s
Education, total expenditures	year	394	91	81r
Room, 4-year private college/university	year	2696	8/94	80s
Room, 4-year public college/university	year	1796	8/94	80s
Total cost, 4-year private college/university	year	15249	8/94	80s
Total cost, 4-year public college/university	year	6964	8/94	80s
Tuition, 2-year public college/university, in-state	year	1135	8/94	80s
Tuition, 4-year private college/university, in-state	year	10474	8/94	80s
Tuition, 4-year public college/university, in-state	year	3029	8/94	80s
Energy and Fuels				
Fuel oil and other fuels, expenditures	year	83	91	81r
Gas, natural, expenditures	year	373	91	81r
Gasoline and motor oil purchased	year	1000	91	81r
Gasoline, unleaded midgrade	gallon	1.15	4/93	82r
Gasoline, unleaded premium	gallon	1.23	4/93	82r
Gasoline, unleaded regular	gallon	1.07	4/93	82r
Entertainment				
Entertainment, total expenditures	year	1356	91	81r
Fees and admissions, expenditures	year	347	91	81r
Pets, toys, playground equipment, expenditures	year	270	91	81r
Reading, expenditures	year	160	91	81r
Televisions, radios, and sound equipment, expenditures	year	433	91	81r
Funerals				
Burial, immediate, container provided by funeral home		1268.31	1/95	54r
Cards, acknowledgment		26.12	1/95	54r
Casket, minimum alternative		198.03	1/95	54r
Cosmetology, hair care, etc.		122.19	1/95	54r
Cremation, direct, container provided by funeral home		977.81	1/95	54r
Embalming		334.00	1/95	54r
Funeral, funeral home		321.16	1/95	54r
Funeral, other facility		317.73	1/95	54r
Graveside service		292.48	1/95	54r
Hearse, local		153.20	1/95	54r
Limousine, local		123.52	1/95	54r
Memorial service		356.30	1/95	54r
Service charge, professional, nondeclinable		968.24	1/95	54r
Visitation and viewing		332.66	1/95	54r
Groceries				
Apples, Red Delicious	lb.	0.68	12/94	82r
Bacon, sliced	lb.	1.88	12/94	82r
Bananas	lb.	0.41	12/94	82r
Beef purchases	year	197	91	81r
Beef, stew, boneless	lb.	2.52	12/94	82r
Beverage purchases, alcoholic	year	293	91	81r
Beverage purchases, nonalcoholic	year	203	91	81r
Bologna, all beef or mixed	lb.	2.12	12/94	82r
Bread, white, pan	lb.	0.76	12/94	82r
Cabbage	lb.	0.44	12/94	82r
Carrots, short trimmed and topped	lb.	0.44	12/94	82r
Cereals and bakery products purchases	year	347	91	81r
Cereals and cereals products purchases	year	119	91	81r
Cheddar cheese, natural	lb.	3.28	12/94	82r
Chicken breast, bone-in	lb.	1.61	12/94	82r

Values are in dollars or fractions of dollars. In the column headed *Ref*, references are shown to sources. Each reference is followed by a letter. These refer to the geographical level for which data were reported: s=State, r=Region, and c=City or metro. The abbreviation *ex* is used to mean *except* or *excluding*; *exp* stands for expenditures. For other abbreviations and further explanations, please see the Introduction.

Aurora-Elgin, IL

Aurora-Elgin, IL - continued

Item	Per	Value	Date	Ref.
Groceries				
Chicken, fresh, whole	lb.	0.89	12/94	82r
Chuck roast, USDA choice, boneless	lb.	2.33	12/94	82r
Coffee, 100%, ground roast, all sizes	lb.	4.28	12/94	82r
Cookies, chocolate chip	lb.	2.72	12/94	82r
Dairy products (other) purchases	year	148	91	81r
Eggs, Grade A large	dozen	0.76	12/94	82r
Fish and seafood purchases	year	61	91	81r
Flour, white, all purpose	lb.	0.22	12/94	82r
Food purchases, food eaten at home	year	2313	91	81r
Foods purchased away from home, not prepared by consumer	year	1709	91	81r
Fruits and vegetables purchases	year	372	91	81r
Grapefruit	lb.	0.47	12/94	82r
Grapes, Thompson seedless	lb.	2.15	12/94	82r
Ground beef, 100% beef	lb.	1.37	12/94	82r
Ground chuck, 100% beef	lb.	1.81	12/94	82r
Ham, boneless, exc. canned	lb.	2.16	12/94	82r
Ice cream, prepackaged, bulk, regular	1/2 gal.	2.48	12/94	82r
Lemons	lb.	1.08	12/94	82r
Lettuce, iceberg	lb.	0.81	12/94	82r
Margarine, stick	lb.	0.81	12/94	82r
Meats, poultry, fish, and eggs purchases	year	591	91	81r
Milk and cream (fresh) purchases	year	132	91	81r
Orange juice, frozen concentrate 12-oz. can	16 oz.	1.41	12/94	82r
Oranges, Navel	lb.	0.56	12/94	82r
Peanut butter, creamy, all sizes	lb.	1.81	12/94	82r
Pork chops, center cut, bone-in	lb.	2.76	12/94	82r
Pork purchases	year	130	91	81r
Potato chips	16-oz.	2.81	12/94	82r
Potatoes, frozen, French fried	lb.	0.83	12/94	82r
Potatoes, white	lb.	0.28	12/94	82r
Round roast, USDA choice, boneless	lb.	2.90	12/94	82r
Shortening, vegetable oil blends	lb.	0.88	12/94	82r
Spaghetti and macaroni	lb.	0.78	12/94	82r
Steak, rib eye, USDA choice, boneless	lb.	6.15	12/94	82r
Steak, round, graded & ungraded, exc. USDA prime & choice	lb.	2.72	12/94	82r
Steak, round, USDA choice, boneless	lb.	3.02	12/94	82r
Steak, sirloin, USDA choice, boneless	lb.	3.85	12/94	82r
Steak, T-bone, USDA choice, bone-in	lb.	5.38	12/94	82r
Sugar and other sweets, eaten at home, expenditures	year	91	91	81r
Sugar, white, all sizes	lb.	0.36	12/94	82r
Tobacco products and smoking supplies, total expenditures	year	298	91	81r
Tomatoes, field grown	lb.	1.36	12/94	82r
Tuna, chunk, light	lb.	1.94	12/94	82r
Turkey, frozen, whole	lb.	0.96	12/94	82r
Yogurt, natural, fruit flavored	8 oz.	0.62	12/94	82r
Health Care				
Childbirth, Cesarean delivery, hospital charge	birth	5101.00	12/91	69r
Childbirth, Cesarean delivery, physician charge	birth	2234.00	12/91	69r
Childbirth, normal delivery, hospital charge	birth	2891.00	12/91	69r
Childbirth, normal delivery, physician charge	birth	1623.00	12/91	69r
Drugs, expenditures	year	248	91	81r
Health care, total expenditures	year	1336	91	81r
Health insurance expenditures	year	550	91	81r
Insurance premium, family medical care	month	363.57	1/95	41s
Medical services expenditures	year	457	91	81r
Medical supplies expenditures	year	82	91	81r
Household Goods				
Floor coverings, expenditures	year	105	91	81r
Furniture, expenditures	year	291	91	81r
Household equipment, misc. expenditures	year	341	91	81r
Household expenditures, miscellaneous	year	162	91	81r
Household furnishings and equipment, expenditures	year	1042	91	81r
Household operations expenditures	year	365	91	81r

Aurora-Elgin, IL - continued

Item	Per	Value	Date	Ref.
Household Goods - continued				
Household textiles, expenditures	year	101	91	81r
Housekeeping supplies, expenditures	year	390	91	81r
Laundry and cleaning supplies, expenditures	year	110	91	81r
Postage and stationery, expenditures	year	115	91	81r
Housing				
Add garage/carport		8,479	3/95	74r
Add room(s)		21,347	3/95	74r
Apartment condominium or co-op, median	unit	87100	12/94	62r
Bathroom addition, average cost	add	9734.00	3/95	13r
Bathroom remodeling, average cost	remod	6414.00	3/95	13r
Bedroom, master suite addition, average cost	add	27122.00	3/95	13r
Deck addition, average cost	add	6665.00	3/95	13r
Dwellings (owned), expenditures	year	2566	91	81r
Enclose porch/patio/breezeway		4,556	3/95	74r
Exterior remodeling, average cost	remod	15395.00	3/95	13r
Family room addition, average cost	add	27658.00	3/95	13r
Finish room in basement/attic		5,074	3/95	74r
Home, existing, single-family, median	unit	106500	12/94	62r
Kitchen remodeling, major, average cost	remod	17084.00	3/95	13r
Kitchen remodeling, minor, average cost	remod	5804.00	3/95	13r
Maintenance, repairs, insurance, and other housing expenditures	year	484	91	81r
Mortgage interest and charges expenditures	year	1443	91	81r
Office, home addition, average cost	add	8121.00	3/95	13r
Princ. & int., mortgage, median-price exist. sing.-family home	mo.	515	12/94	62r
Property taxes expenditures	year	639	91	81r
Redesign, restructure more than half of home's interior		9,114	3/95	74r
Rental units expenditures	year	1200	91	81r
Sun-space addition, average cost	add	23768.00	3/95	13r
Wing addition, two-story, average cost	add	50410.00	3/95	13r
Insurance and Pensions				
Auto insurance, private passenger	year	679.48	12/94	71s
Insurance and pensions, personal, expenditures	year	2408	91	81r
Insurance, life and other personal, expenditures	year	355	91	81r
Pensions and Social Security, expenditures	year	2053	91	81r
Legal Assistance				
Legal work, law firm associate	hour	90		10r
Legal work, law firm partner	hour	139		10r
Personal Services				
Personal services expenditures	year	203	91	81r
Restaurant Food				
Dining expenditures, family	week	30.03	94	73r
Taxes				
Taxes, Federal income, expenditures	year	1756	91	81r
Taxes, personal, expenditures	year	2426	91	81r
Taxes, State and local income, expenditures	year	568	91	81r
Transportation				
Cars and trucks purchased, new	year	891	91	81r
Cars and trucks purchased, used	year	1155	91	81r
Driver's learning permit fee	perm	20.00	1/94	84s
Driver's license fee	orig	10.00	1/94	84s
Driver's license fee, duplicate	lic	5.00	1/94	84s
Driver's license reinstatement fee, min.	susp	30.00	1/94	85s
Driver's license renewal fee	renew	10.00	1/94	84s
Identification card, nondriver	card	4.00	1/94	83s
Motorcycle learning permit fee	perm	20.00	1/94	84s
Motorcycle license fee	orig	10.00	1/94	84s
Motorcycle license fee, duplicate	lic	5.00	1/94	84s
Motorcycle license renewal fee	renew	10.00	1/94	84s
Public transportation expenditures	year	209	91	81r
Transportation expenditures, total	year	4792	91	81r
Vehicle finance charges	year	300	91	81r

Values are in dollars or fractions of dollars. In the column headed *Ref*, references are shown to sources. Each reference is followed by a letter. These refer to the geographical level for which data were reported: s = State, r = Region, and c = City or metro. The abbreviation *ex* is used to mean *except* or *excluding*; *exp* stands for expenditures. For other abbreviations and further explanations, please see the Introduction.

Aurora-Elgin, IL - continued

Item	Per	Value	Date	Ref.
Transportation				
Vehicle insurance expenditures	year	485	91	81r
Vehicle maintenance and repairs expenditures	year	534	91	81r
Vehicle purchases	year	2068	91	81r
Vehicle rental, leases, licenses, etc. expenditures	year	197	91	81r
Vehicles purchased, other than cars and trucks	year	22	91	81r
Utilities				
Electricity expenditures	year	668	91	81r
Utilities, fuels, and public services, total expenditures	year	1838	91	81r
Water and other public services, expenditures	year	167	91	81r
Weddings				
Bridal attendants' gowns	event	750	10/93	76r
Bridal gown	event	852	10/93	76r
Bridal headpiece and veil	event	167	10/93	76r
Bride's wedding band	event	708	10/93	76r
Clergy	event	224	10/93	76r
Engagement ring	event	2756	10/93	76r
Flowers	event	863	10/93	76r
Formal wear for groom	event	106	10/93	76r
Groom's attendants' formal wear	event	530	10/93	76r
Groom's wedding band	event	402	10/93	76r
Music	event	600	10/93	76r
Photography	event	1088	10/93	76r
Shoes for bride	event	50	10/93	76r
Videography	event	483	10/93	76r
Wedding invitations and announcements	event	342	10/93	76r
Wedding reception	event	7000	10/93	76r

Austin, TX

Item	Per	Value	Date	Ref.
Composite, ACCRA index		95.50	12/94	2c
Alcoholic Beverages				
Beer, Miller Lite, Bud, 12-oz., ex deposit	6	3.80	12/94	2c
J & B Scotch	750-ml.	18.46	12/94	2c
Wine, Gallo Chablis blanc	1.5-lit	5.47	12/94	2c
Appliances				
Appliances (major), expenditures	year	153	91	81r
Average annual exp.				
Food, health care, personal goods, services	year	27020	91	81r
Charity				
Cash contributions, expenditures	year	839	91	81r
Clothing				
Apparel, men and boys, total expenditures	year	380	91	81r
Apparel, women and girls, total expenditures	year	660	91	81r
Footwear, expenditures	year	193	91	81r
Jeans, man's denim		28.28	12/94	2c
Shirt, man's dress shirt		27.25	12/94	2c
Undervest, boy's size 10-14, cotton	3	4.21	12/94	2c
Communications				
Long-distance telephone rate, day, addl. min., 1-10 mi.	min.	0.08	12/93	9s
Long-distance telephone rate, day, initial min., 1-10 mi.	min.	0.10	12/93	9s
Newspaper subscription, dly. and Sun. delivery	month	11.30	12/94	2c
Phone line, single, business, field visit	inst	71.90	12/93	9s
Phone line, single, business, no field visit	inst	57.30	12/93	9s
Phone line, single, residence, field visit	inst	52.95	12/93	9s
Phone line, single, residence, no field visit	inst	38.35	12/93	9s
Telephone bill, family of four	month	16.72	12/94	2c
Telephone service, expenditures	year	616	91	81r
Telephone, residential, flat rate	mo.	9.35	12/93	8c

Item	Per	Value	Date	Ref.
Education				
Board, 4-year private college/university	year	2084	8/94	80s
Board, 4-year public college/university	year	1675	8/94	80s
Education, total expenditures	year	319	91	81r
Room, 4-year private college/university	year	1840	8/94	80s
Room, 4-year public college/university	year	1756	8/94	80s
Total cost, 4-year private college/university	year	11876	8/94	80s
Total cost, 4-year public college/university	year	4935	8/94	80s
Tuition, 2-year public college/university, in-state	year	625	8/94	80s
Tuition, 4-year private college/university, in-state	year	7952	8/94	80s
Tuition, 4-year public college/university, in-state	year	1503	8/94	80s
Energy and Fuels				
Energy, combined forms, 1800 sq. ft.	mo.	105.28	12/94	2c
Fuel oil and other fuels, expenditures	year	56	91	81r
Gas, natural, expenditures	year	150	91	81r
Gas, reg unlead, taxes inc., cash, self-service	gal	1.12	12/94	2c
Gasoline and motor oil purchased	year	1152	91	81r
Gasoline, unleaded midgrade	gallon	1.21	4/93	82r
Gasoline, unleaded premium	gallon	1.30	4/93	82r
Gasoline, unleaded regular	gallon	1.10	4/93	82r
Entertainment				
Bowling, evening rate	game	2.68	12/94	2c
Concert ticket, Pearl Jam group	perf	20.00	94	50r
Entertainment, total expenditures	year	1266	91	81r
Fees and admissions, expenditures	year	306	91	81r
Monopoly game, Parker Brothers', No. 9	game	10.43	12/94	2c
Movie	adm	6.18	12/94	2c
Pets, toys, playground equipment, expenditures	year	271	91	81r
Reading, expenditures	year	131	91	81r
Televisions, radios, and sound equipment, expenditures	year	439	91	81r
Tennis balls, yellow, Wilson or Penn, 3	can	2.07	12/94	2c
Funerals				
Burial, immediate, container provided by funeral home		1574.60	1/95	54r
Cards, acknowledgment		22.24	1/95	54r
Casket, minimum alternative		239.41	1/95	54r
Cosmetology, hair care, etc.		91.04	1/95	54r
Cremation, direct, container provided by funeral home		1085.15	1/95	54r
Embalming		281.30	1/95	54r
Funeral, funeral home		323.04	1/95	54r
Funeral, other facility		327.58	1/95	54r
Graveside service		355.19	1/95	54r
Hearse, local		141.89	1/95	54r
Limousine, local		99.40	1/95	54r
Memorial service		284.67	1/95	54r
Service charge, professional, nondeclinable		904.06	1/95	54r
Visitation and viewing		187.04	1/95	54r
Groceries				
Groceries, ACCRA Index		93.30	12/94	2c
Apples, Red Delicious	lb.	0.73	12/94	82r
Baby food, strained vegetables, lowest price	4-4.5 oz.	0.24	12/94	2c
Bacon, sliced	lb.	1.67	12/94	82r
Bananas	lb.	0.38	12/94	2c
Bananas	lb.	0.42	12/94	82r
Beef or hamburger, ground	lb.	1.21	12/94	2c
Beef purchases	year	213	91	81r
Beverage purchases, alcoholic	year	249	91	81r
Beverage purchases, nonalcoholic	year	207	91	81r
Bologna, all beef or mixed	lb.	2.27	12/94	82r
Bread, white	24-oz.	0.75	12/94	2c
Bread, white, pan	lb.	0.68	12/94	82r
Cabbage	lb.	0.42	12/94	82r
Carrots, short trimmed and topped	lb.	0.53	12/94	82r

Values are in dollars or fractions of dollars. In the column headed *Ref*, references are shown to sources. Each reference is followed by a letter. These refer to the geographical level for which data were reported: s = State, r = Region, and c = City or metro. The abbreviation *ex* is used to mean *except* or *excluding*; *exp* stands for *expenditures*. For other abbreviations and further explanations, please see the Introduction.

Austin, TX - continued

Item	Per	Value	Date	Ref.
Groceries				
Cereals and bakery products purchases	year	345	91	81r
Cereals and cereals products purchases	year	127	91	81r
Cheddar cheese, natural	lb.	3.58	12/94	82r
Cheese, Kraft grated Parmesan	8-oz.	3.29	12/94	2c
Chicken breast, bone-in	lb.	1.71	12/94	82r
Chicken, fresh, whole	lb.	0.78	12/94	82r
Chicken, whole fryer	lb.	0.75	12/94	2c
Chuck roast, USDA choice, boneless	lb.	2.26	12/94	82r
Cigarettes, Winston, Kings	carton	14.49	12/94	2c
Coffee, vacuum-packed	13 oz.	3.29	12/94	2c
Corn Flakes, Kellogg's or Post Toasties	18 oz.	2.49	12/94	2c
Corn, frozen, whole kernel, lowest price	10 oz.	0.73	12/94	2c
Crackers, soda, salted	lb.	1.27	12/94	82r
Cucumbers	lb.	0.65	12/94	82r
Dairy products (other) purchases	year	141	91	81r
Eggs, Grade A large	dozen	0.64	12/94	2c
Eggs, Grade A large	dozen	0.87	12/94	82r
Fish and seafood purchases	year	72	91	81r
Flour, white, all purpose	lb.	0.23	12/94	82r
Food purchases, food eaten at home	year	2381	91	81r
Foods purchased away from home, not prepared by consumer	year	1696	91	81r
Frankfurters, all meat or all beef	lb.	1.74	12/94	82r
Fruits and vegetables purchases	year	380	91	81r
Grapefruit	lb.	0.45	12/94	82r
Grapes, Thompson seedless	lb.	2.30	12/94	82r
Ground beef, 100% beef	lb.	1.37	12/94	82r
Ground chuck, 100% beef	lb.	1.97	12/94	82r
Ham, boneless, exc. canned	lb.	2.54	12/94	82r
Ice cream, prepackaged, bulk, regular	1/2 gal.	2.47	12/94	82r
Lemons	lb.	1.02	12/94	82r
Lettuce, iceberg	lb.	0.96	12/94	82r
Lettuce, iceberg	head	0.87	12/94	2c
Margarine, Blue Bonnet or Parkay cubes	lb.	0.64	12/94	2c
Margarine, stick	lb.	0.77	12/94	82r
Meats, poultry, fish, and eggs purchases	year	655	91	81r
Milk and cream (fresh) purchases	year	130	91	81r
Milk, whole	1/2 gal.	1.19	12/94	2c
Orange juice, frozen concentrate 12-oz. can	16 oz.	1.36	12/94	82r
Orange juice, Minute Maid frozen	12-oz.	1.14	12/94	2c
Oranges, Navel	lb.	0.54	12/94	82r
Peaches, halves or slices, Hunt's, Del Monte, or Libby's	29-oz.	1.41	12/94	2c
Pears, Anjou	lb.	0.81	12/94	82r
Peas, sweet, Del Monte or Green Giant	15-17 oz.	0.50	12/94	2c
Pork chops, center cut, bone-in	lb.	3.07	12/94	82r
Pork purchases	year	142	91	81r
Potato chips	16-oz.	3.15	12/94	82r
Potatoes, frozen, French fried	lb.	0.82	12/94	82r
Potatoes, white	lb.	0.34	12/94	82r
Potatoes, white or red	10-lb. sack	2.38	12/94	2c
Rice, white, long grain, uncooked	lb.	0.48	12/94	82r
Round roast, USDA choice, boneless	lb.	2.91	12/94	82r
Sausage, fresh	lb.	1.82	12/94	82r
Sausage, Jimmy Dean, 100% pork	lb.	2.64	12/94	2c
Shortening, vegetable oil blends	lb.	0.75	12/94	82r
Shortening, vegetable, Crisco	3-lb.	2.35	12/94	2c
Soft drink, Coca Cola, ex deposit	2 lit	1.46	12/94	2c
Spaghetti and macaroni	lb.	0.87	12/94	82r
Steak, rib eye, USDA choice, boneless	lb.	6.85	12/94	2c
Steak, round, graded & ungraded, exc. USDA prime & choice	lb.	2.96	12/94	82r
Steak, round, USDA choice, boneless	lb.	3.17	12/94	82r
Steak, sirloin, USDA choice, boneless	lb.	4.12	12/94	82r
Steak, t-bone	lb.	3.19	12/94	2c
Steak, T-bone, USDA choice, bone-in	lb.	5.63	12/94	82r
Sugar and other sweets, eaten at home, expenditures	year	93	91	81r

Austin, TX - continued

Item	Per	Value	Date	Ref.
Groceries - continued				
Sugar, cane or beet	4 lbs.	1.37	12/94	2c
Sugar, white, all sizes	lb.	0.39	12/94	82r
Tobacco products and smoking supplies, total expenditures	year	286	91	81r
Tomatoes, field grown	lb.	1.36	12/94	82r
Tomatoes, Hunt's or Del Monte	14.5 oz.	0.55	12/94	2c
Tuna, chunk, light	lb.	1.94	12/94	82r
Tuna, chunk, light, oil-packed	6.125-6.5 oz.	0.72	12/94	2c
Turkey, frozen, whole	lb.	0.96	12/94	82r
Yogurt, natural, fruit flavored	8 oz.	0.58	12/94	82r
Goods and Services				
Miscellaneous goods and services, ACCRA Index		100.00	12/94	2c
Health Care				
Health care, ACCRA Index		100.90	12/94	2c
Adenosine, emergency room	treat	100.00	95	23r
Antibiotic ointment, Polysporin	1.5 oz.	3.81	12/94	2c
Bladder tap, superpubic, infant, emergency room	treat	119.00	95	23r
Blood analysis, emergency room	treat	25.00	95	23r
Blood tests, abdominal pain, emergency room	treat	25.00	95	23r
Burn dressing, emergency room	treat	266.00	95	23r
Cardiology interpretation, emergency room	treat	26.00	95	23r
Chest X-ray, emergency room	treat	78.00	95	23r
Childbirth, Cesarean delivery, hospital charge	birth	5462.00	12/91	69r
Childbirth, Cesarean delivery, physician charge	birth	2228.00	12/91	69r
Childbirth, normal delivery, hospital charge	birth	2943.00	12/91	69r
Childbirth, normal delivery, physician charge	birth	1619.00	12/91	69r
Defibrillation pads, emergency room	treat	6.00	95	23r
Dentist's fee, adult teeth cleaning and periodic oral exam	visit	52.70	12/94	2c
Doctor's fee, routine exam, established patient	visit	44.60	12/94	2c
Drugs, expenditures	year	297	91	81r
Gastric tube insertion, nasal, emergency room	treat	25.00	95	23r
Health care, total expenditures	year	1600	91	81r
Health insurance expenditures	year	637	91	81r
Heart monitor, emergency room	treat	40.00	95	23r
Hospital care, semiprivate room	day	343.25	12/94	2c
Insurance premium, family medical care	month	389.25	1/95	41s
Intravenous fluids, emergency room	treat	130.00	95	23r
Intravenous fluids, emergency room	liter	26.00	95	23r
Intravenous line, central, emergency room	treat	342.00	95	23r
Liver function tests, abdominal pain, emergency room	treat	26.00	95	23r
Medical care charges, total, emergency room, third-degree burns	treat	2101.00	95	23r
Medical care charges, total, emergency, infant with fever	treat	628.00	95	23r
Medical services expenditures	year	573	91	81r
Medical supplies expenditures	year	93	91	81r
Morphine, emergency room	treat	34.00	95	23r
Nursing care and facilities charges, emergency room	treat	252.00	95	23r
Nursing care and facilities charges, emergency, infant with fever	treat	252.00	95	23r
Nursing care and facilities charges, emergency, third-degree burns	treat	861.00	95	23r
Physician's charges, emergency, infant with fever	treat	212.00	95	23r
Physician's charges, emergency, third-degree burns	treat	372.00	95	23r
Physician's fee, emergency room	treat	372.00	95	23r
Physician's fee, general practitioner	visit	51.20	12/93	60r
Surgery, open-heart	proc	42374.00	1/93	14r

Values are in dollars or fractions of dollars. In the column headed *Ref*, references are shown to sources. Each reference is followed by a letter. These refer to the geographical level for which data were reported: s = State, r = Region, and c = City or metro. The abbreviation *ex* is used to mean *except* or *excluding*; *exp* stands for expenditures. For other abbreviations and further explanations, please see the Introduction.

Austin, TX - continued

Item	Per	Value	Date	Ref.
Health Care				
Ultrasound, abdominal, emergency room	treat	276.00	95	23r
Urinalysis, emergency room	treat	20.00	95	23r
Urinalysis, infant, emergency room	treat	20.00	95	23r
X-rays, emergency room	treat	78.00	95	23r
Household Goods				
Appl. repair, service call, wash mach	min. lab. chg.	35.80	12/94	2c
Floor coverings, expenditures	year	48	91	81r
Furniture, expenditures	year	280	91	81r
Household equipment, misc. expenditures	year	342	91	81r
Household expenditures, miscellaneous	year	256	91	81r
Household furnishings and equipment, expenditures	year	988	91	81r
Household operations expenditures	year	468	91	81r
Household textiles, expenditures	year	95	91	81r
Housekeeping supplies, expenditures	year	380	91	81r
Laundry and cleaning supplies, expenditures	year	109	91	81r
Laundry detergent, Tide Ultra, Bold, or Cheer	42 oz.	2.95	12/94	2c
Postage and stationery, expenditures	year	105	91	81r
Tissues, facial, Kleenex brand	175	1.01	12/94	2c
Housing				
Housing, ACCRA Index		88.70	12/94	2c
Add garage/carport		6,980	3/95	74r
Add room(s)		11,403	3/95	74r
Apartment condominium or co-op, median	unit	68600	12/94	62r
Dwellings (owned), expenditures	year	2428	91	81r
Enclose porch/patio/breezeway		4,572	3/95	74r
Finish room in basement/attic		3,794	3/95	74r
Home, existing, single-family, median	unit	120200	12/94	62r
Home, existing, single-family, median	unit	97.30	12/94	62c
House payment, principal and interest, 25% down payment	mo.	613	12/94	2c
House, 1800 sq ft, 8000 sq ft lot, new, urban, utilities	total	99146	12/94	2c
Maintenance, repairs, insurance, and other housing expenditures	year	531	91	81r
Mortgage interest and charges expenditures	year	1506	91	81r
Mtge. rate, incl. points and orig. fee, 30-year conv. fixed or ARM	mo.	9.27	12/94	2c
Princ. & int., mortgage, median-price exist. sing.-family home	mo.	540	12/94	62c
Property taxes expenditures	year	391	91	81r
Redesign, restructure more than half of home's interior		17,641	3/95	74r
Rent, apartment, 2 br., 1 1/2-2 baths, unfurnished, 950 sq ft, water	mo.	661	12/94	2c
Rental units expenditures	year	1264	91	81r
Insurance and Pensions				
Auto insurance, private passenger	year	785.78	12/94	71s
Insurance and pensions, personal, expenditures	year	2395	91	81r
Insurance, life and other personal, expenditures	year	368	91	81r
Pensions and Social Security, expenditures	year	2027	91	81r
Personal Goods				
Shampoo, Alberto VO5	15-oz.	1.00	12/94	2c
Toothpaste, Crest or Colgate	6-7 oz.	1.71	12/94	2c
Personal Services				
Dry cleaning, man's 2-pc. suit		6.35	12/94	2c
Haircut, man's barbershop, no styling		8.30	12/94	2c
Haircut, woman's shampoo, trim, blow-dry		20.65	12/94	2c
Personal services expenditures	year	212	91	81r
Restaurant Food				
Chicken, fried, thigh and drumstick		2.46	12/94	2c
Dining expenditures, family	week	33.83	94	73r
Hamburger with cheese	1/4 lb.	2.04	12/94	2c

Austin, TX - continued

Item	Per	Value	Date	Ref.
Restaurant Food - continued				
Pizza, Pizza Hut or Pizza Inn	12-13 in.	7.99	12/94	2c
Taxes				
Tax, cigarettes	year	584.00	10/93	43s
Taxes, Federal income, expenditures	year	2275	91	81r
Taxes, personal, expenditures	year	2715	91	81r
Taxes, State and local income, expenditures	year	365	91	81r
Transportation				
Transportation, ACCRA Index		103.40	12/94	2c
Bus fare, one-way	trip	0.50	12/95	1c
Bus fare, up to 10 miles	one-way	1.00	12/94	2c
Cars and trucks purchased, new	year	1306	91	81r
Cars and trucks purchased, used	year	942	91	81r
Driver's learning permit fee	perm	5.00	1/94	84s
Driver's license fee	orig	16.00	1/94	84s
Driver's license fee, duplicate	lic	10.00	1/94	84s
Driver's license reinstatement fee, min.	susp	50.00	1/94	85s
Driver's license renewal fee	renew	16.00	1/94	84s
Identification card, nondriver	card	10.00	1/94	83s
Motorcycle learning permit fee	perm	5.00	1/94	84s
Motorcycle license fee	orig	16.00	1/94	84s
Motorcycle license fee, duplicate	lic	10.00	1/94	84s
Motorcycle license renewal fee	renew	21.00	1/94	84s
Public transportation expenditures	year	249	91	81r
Tire balance, computer or spin bal., front	wheel	7.34	12/94	2c
Transportation expenditures, total	year	5307	91	81r
Vehicle finance charges	year	346	91	81r
Vehicle insurance expenditures	year	544	91	81r
Vehicle maintenance and repairs expenditures	year	600	91	81r
Vehicle purchases	year	2275	91	81r
Vehicle rental, leases, licenses, etc. expenditures	year	141	91	81r
Vehicles purchased, other than cars and trucks	year	27	91	81r
Utilities				
Utilities, ACCRA Index		92.70	12/94	2c
Electricity expenditures	year	950	91	81r
Electricity, 1800 sq. ft., new home	mo.	105.28	12/94	2c
Utilities, fuels, and public services, total expenditures	year	2000	91	81r
Water and other public services, expenditures	year	227	91	81r
Weddings				
Bridal attendants' gowns	event	750	10/93	76r
Bridal gown	event	852	10/93	76r
Bridal headpiece and veil	event	167	10/93	76r
Bride's wedding band	event	708	10/93	76r
Clergy	event	224	10/93	76r
Engagement ring	event	2756	10/93	76r
Flowers	event	863	10/93	76r
Formal wear for groom	event	106	10/93	76r
Groom's attendants' formal wear	event	530	10/93	76r
Groom's wedding band	event	402	10/93	76r
Music	event	600	10/93	76r
Photography	event	1088	10/93	76r
Shoes for bride	event	50	10/93	76r
Videography	event	483	10/93	76r
Wedding invitations and announcements	event	342	10/93	76r
Wedding reception	event	7000	10/93	76r

Bainbridge, GA

Item	Per	Value	Date	Ref.
Composite, ACCRA index		91.00	12/94	2c
Alcoholic Beverages				
Beer, Miller Lite, Bud, 12-oz., ex deposit	6	4.55	12/94	2c

Values are in dollars or fractions of dollars. In the column headed *Ref*, references are shown to sources. Each reference is followed by a letter. These refer to the geographical level for which data were reported: s=State, r=Region, and c=City or metro. The abbreviation *ex* is used to mean *except* or *excluding*; *exp* stands for *expenditures*. For other abbreviations and further explanations, please see the Introduction.

Bainbridge, GA - continued

Item	Per	Value	Date	Ref.
Alcoholic Beverages				
J & B Scotch	750-ml.	15.74	12/94	2c
Wine, Gallo Chablis blanc	1.5-lit	6.51	12/94	2c
Clothing				
Jeans, man's denim		26.32	12/94	2c
Shirt, man's dress shirt		28.16	12/94	2c
Undervest, boy's size 10-14, cotton	3	4.52	12/94	2c
Communications				
Newspaper subscription, dly. and Sun. delivery	month	13.09	12/94	2c
Telephone bill, family of four	month	18.49	12/94	2c
Telephone, residential, flat rate	mo.	11.20	12/93	8c
Energy and Fuels				
Energy, combined forms, 1800 sq. ft.	mo.	124.16	12/94	2c
Gas, reg unlead, taxes inc., cash, self-service	gal	1.02	12/94	2c
Entertainment				
Bowling, evening rate	game	1.50	12/94	2c
Monopoly game, Parker Brothers', No. 9	game	12.59	12/94	2c
Movie	adm	5.50	12/94	2c
Tennis balls, yellow, Wilson or Penn, 3	can	2.71	12/94	2c
Groceries				
Groceries, ACCRA Index		96.50	12/94	2c
Baby food, strained vegetables, lowest price	4-4.5 oz.	0.34	12/94	2c
Bananas	lb.	0.36	12/94	2c
Beef or hamburger, ground	lb.	1.45	12/94	2c
Bread, white	24-oz.	0.79	12/94	2c
Cheese, Kraft grated Parmesan	8-oz.	3.12	12/94	2c
Chicken, whole fryer	lb.	0.65	12/94	2c
Cigarettes, Winston, Kings	carton	14.27	12/94	2c
Coffee, vacuum-packed	13 oz.	3.29	12/94	2c
Corn Flakes, Kellogg's or Post Toasties	18 oz.	2.42	12/94	2c
Corn, frozen, whole kernel, lowest price	10 oz.	0.63	12/94	2c
Eggs, Grade A large	dozen	0.69	12/94	2c
Lettuce, iceberg	head	0.96	12/94	2c
Margarine, Blue Bonnet or Parkay cubes	lb.	0.64	12/94	2c
Milk, whole	1/2 gal.	1.42	12/94	2c
Orange juice, Minute Maid frozen	12-oz.	1.21	12/94	2c
Peaches, halves or slices, Hunt's, Del Monte, or Libby's	29-oz.	1.28	12/94	2c
Peas, sweet, Del Monte or Green Giant	15-17 oz.	0.61	12/94	2c
Potatoes, white or red	10-lb. sack	2.79	12/94	2c
Sausage, Jimmy Dean, 100% pork	lb.	2.39	12/94	2c
Shortening, vegetable, Crisco	3-lb.	2.62	12/94	2c
Soft drink, Coca Cola, ex deposit	2 lit	0.99	12/94	2c
Steak, t-bone	lb.	5.58	12/94	2c
Sugar, cane or beet	4 lbs.	1.50	12/94	2c
Tomatoes, Hunt's or Del Monte	14.5 oz.	0.49	12/94	2c
Tuna, chunk, light, oil-packed	6.125-6.5 oz.	0.66	12/94	2c
Goods and Services				
Miscellaneous goods and services, ACCRA Index		97.80	12/94	2c
Health Care				
Health care, ACCRA Index		84.20	12/94	2c
Antibiotic ointment, Polysporin	1.5 oz.	3.91	12/94	2c
Dentist's fee, adult teeth cleaning and periodic oral exam	visit	50.00	12/94	2c
Doctor's fee, routine exam, established patient	visit	35.62	12/94	2c
Hospital care, semiprivate room	day	195.00	12/94	2c

Bainbridge, GA - continued

Item	Per	Value	Date	Ref.
Household Goods				
Appl. repair, service call, wash mach	min. lab. chg.	28.25	12/94	2c
Laundry detergent, Tide Ultra, Bold, or Cheer	42 oz.	2.72	12/94	2c
Tissues, facial, Kleenex brand	175	0.99	12/94	2c
Housing				
Housing, ACCRA Index		78.50	12/94	2c
House payment, principal and interest, 25% down payment	mo.	613	12/94	2c
House, 1800 sq ft, 8000 sq ft lot, new, urban, utilities	total	98750	12/94	2c
Mtge. rate, incl. points and orig. fee, 30-year conv. fixed or ARM	mo.	9.32	12/94	2c
Rent, apartment, 2 br., 1 1/2-2 baths, unfurnished, 950 sq ft, water	mo.	380	12/94	2c
Personal Goods				
Shampoo, Alberto VO5	15-oz.	1.18	12/94	2c
Toothpaste, Crest or Colgate	6-7 oz.	2.03	12/94	2c
Personal Services				
Dry cleaning, man's 2-pc. suit		5.35	12/94	2c
Haircut, man's barbershop, no styling		8.75	12/94	2c
Haircut, woman's shampoo, trim, blow-dry		18.25	12/94	2c
Restaurant Food				
Chicken, fried, thigh and drumstick		2.18	12/94	2c
Hamburger with cheese	1/4 lb.	1.89	12/94	2c
Pizza, Pizza Hut or Pizza Inn	12-13 in.	7.99	12/94	2c
Transportation				
Transportation, ACCRA Index		83.80	12/94	2c
Tire balance, computer or spin bal., front	wheel	5.00	12/94	2c
Utilities				
Utilities, ACCRA Index		108.50	12/94	2c
Electricity, 1800 sq. ft., new home	mo.	124.16	12/94	2c

Bakersfield, CA

Item	Per	Value	Date	Ref.
Composite, ACCRA index		107.60	12/94	2c
Alcoholic Beverages				
Beer, Miller Lite, Bud, 12-oz., ex deposit	6	3.67	12/94	2c
J & B Scotch	750-ml.	14.65	12/94	2c
Wine, Gallo Chablis blanc	1.5-lit	3.91	12/94	2c
Appliances				
Appliances (major), expenditures	year	160	91	81r
Average annual exp.				
Food, health care, personal goods, services	year	32461	91	81r
Charity				
Cash contributions, expenditures	year	975	91	81r
Clothing				
Apparel, men and boys, total expenditures	year	467	91	81r
Apparel, women and girls, total expenditures	year	737	91	81r
Footwear, expenditures	year	270	91	81r
Jeans, man's denim		33.19	12/94	2c
Shirt, man's dress shirt		32.99	12/94	2c
Undervest, boy's size 10-14, cotton	3	3.57	12/94	2c
Communications				
Long-distance telephone rate, day, addl. min., 1-10 mi.	min.	0.07	12/93	9s
Long-distance telephone rate, day, initial min., 1-10 mi.	min.	0.17	12/93	9s
Newspaper subscription, dly. and Sun. delivery	month	10.50	12/94	2c
Phone line, single, business, field visit	inst	70.75	12/93	9s
Phone line, single, business, no field visit	inst	70.75	12/93	9s

Values are in dollars or fractions of dollars. In the column headed *Ref*, references are shown to sources. Each reference is followed by a letter. These refer to the geographical level for which data were reported: s=State, r=Region, and c=City or metro. The abbreviation *ex* is used to mean *except* or *excluding*; *exp* stands for expenditures. For other abbreviations and further explanations, please see the Introduction.

Bakersfield, CA - continued

Item	Per	Value	Date	Ref.
Communications				
Phone line, single, residence, field visit	inst	34.75	12/93	9s
Phone line, single, residence, no field visit	inst	34.75	12/93	9s
Telephone bill, family of four	month	12.45	12/94	2c
Telephone service, expenditures	year	611	91	81r
Telephone, residential, flat rate	mo.	8.35	12/93	8c
Education				
Board, 4-year private college/university	year	2945	8/94	80s
Board, 4-year public college/university	year	2321	8/94	80s
Education, total expenditures	year	375	91	81r
Room, 4-year private college/university	year	3094	8/94	80s
Room, 4-year public college/university	year	2812	8/94	80s
Student fee, university	year	21.00	93	18s
Total cost, 4-year private college/university	year	19321	8/94	80s
Total cost, 4-year public college/university	year	7511	8/94	80s
Tuition, 2-year public college/university, in-state	year	345	8/94	80s
Tuition, 4-year private college/university, in-state	year	13282	8/94	80s
Tuition, 4-year public college/university, in-state	year	2378	8/94	80s
Energy and Fuels				
Energy, combined forms, 1800 sq. ft.	mo.	143.97	12/94	2c
Energy, exc. electricity, 1800 sq. ft.	mo.	21.64	12/94	2c
Fuel oil and other fuels, expenditures	year	33	91	81r
Gas, natural, expenditures	year	212	91	81r
Gas, reg unlead, taxes inc., cash, self-service	gal	1.24	12/94	2c
Gasoline and motor oil purchased	year	1115	91	81r
Gasoline, unleaded midgrade	gallon	1.36	4/93	82r
Gasoline, unleaded premium	gallon	1.43	4/93	82r
Gasoline, unleaded regular	gallon	1.23	4/93	82r
Entertainment				
Bowling, evening rate	game	2.25	12/94	2c
Concert ticket, Pearl Jam group	perf	20.00	94	50r
Entertainment, total expenditures	year	1853	91	81r
Fees and admissions, expenditures	year	482	91	81r
Monopoly game, Parker Brothers', No. 9	game	12.01	12/94	2c
Movie	adm	6.17	12/94	2c
Pets, toys, playground equipment, expenditures	year	299	91	81r
Reading, expenditures	year	164	91	81r
Televisions, radios, and sound equipment, expenditures	year	528	91	81r
Tennis balls, yellow, Wilson or Penn, 3	can	2.26	12/94	2c
Funerals				
Burial, immediate, container provided by funeral home		1382.70	1/95	54r
Cards, acknowledgment		21.87	1/95	54r
Casket, minimum alternative		128.54	1/95	54r
Cosmetology, hair care, etc.		119.69	1/95	54r
Cremation, direct, container provided by funeral home		1030.62	1/95	54r
Embalming		255.42	1/95	54r
Funeral, funeral home		437.38	1/95	54r
Funeral, other facility		444.46	1/95	54r
Graveside service		338.46	1/95	54r
Hearse, local		147.50	1/95	54r
Limousine, local		130.33	1/95	54r
Memorial service		553.16	1/95	54r
Service charge, professional, nondeclinable		859.15	1/95	54r
Visitation and viewing		93.23	1/95	54r
Groceries				
Groceries, ACCRA Index		106.70	12/94	2c
Apples, Red Delicious	lb.	0.72	12/94	82r
Baby food, strained vegetables, lowest price	4-4.5 oz.	0.35	12/94	2c
Bacon, sliced	lb.	1.73	12/94	82r
Bananas	lb.	0.53	12/94	2c
Bananas	lb.	0.52	12/94	82r

Bakersfield, CA - continued

Item	Per	Value	Date	Ref.
Groceries - continued				
Beef or hamburger, ground	lb.	1.55	12/94	2c
Beef purchases	year	241	91	81r
Beverage purchases, alcoholic	year	328	91	81r
Beverage purchases, nonalcoholic	year	234	91	81r
Bologna, all beef or mixed	lb.	2.33	12/94	82r
Bread, white	24-oz.	0.81	12/94	2c
Bread, white, pan	lb.	0.81	12/94	82r
Carrots, short trimmed and topped	lb.	0.43	12/94	82r
Cereals and bakery products purchases	year	392	91	81r
Cereals and cereals products purchases	year	139	91	81r
Cheese, Kraft grated Parmesan	8-oz.	3.06	12/94	2c
Chicken breast, bone-in	lb.	2.04	12/94	82r
Chicken, fresh, whole	lb.	0.95	12/94	82r
Chicken, whole fryer	lb.	0.99	12/94	2c
Cigarettes, Winston, Kings	carton	16.85	12/94	2c
Coffee, 100%, ground roast, all sizes	lb.	4.48	12/94	82r
Coffee, vacuum-packed	13 oz.	3.57	12/94	2c
Corn Flakes, Kellogg's or Post Toasties	18 oz.	2.21	12/94	2c
Corn, frozen, whole kernel, lowest price	10 oz.	0.77	12/94	2c
Dairy products (other) purchases	year	182	91	81r
Eggs, Grade A large	dozen	1.49	12/94	2c
Fish and seafood purchases	year	94	91	81r
Flour, white, all purpose	lb.	0.21	12/94	82r
Food purchases, food eaten at home	year	2749	91	81r
Foods purchased away from home, not prepared by consumer	year	1909	91	81r
Fruits and vegetables purchases	year	459	91	81r
Grapefruit	lb.	0.56	12/94	82r
Ground beef, 100% beef	lb.	1.31	12/94	82r
Ham, boneless, exc. canned	lb.	2.46	12/94	82r
Ice cream, prepackaged, bulk, regular	1/2 gal.	2.57	12/94	82r
Lemons	lb.	1.00	12/94	82r
Lettuce, iceberg	lb.	0.93	12/94	82r
Lettuce, iceberg	head	0.75	12/94	2c
Margarine, Blue Bonnet or Parkay cubes	lb.	0.80	12/94	2c
Meats, poultry, fish, and eggs purchases	year	700	91	81r
Milk and cream (fresh) purchases	year	155	91	81r
Milk, whole	1/2 gal.	1.44	12/94	2c
Orange juice, frozen concentrate 12-oz. can	16 oz.	1.52	12/94	82r
Orange juice, Minute Maid frozen	12-oz.	1.41	12/94	2c
Oranges, Navel	lb.	0.56	12/94	82r
Peaches, halves or slices, Hunt's, Del Monte, or Libby's	29-oz.	1.23	12/94	2c
Peas, sweet, Del Monte or Green Giant	15-17 oz.	0.51	12/94	2c
Pork chops, center cut, bone-in	lb.	3.30	12/94	82r
Pork purchases	year	122	91	81r
Potato chips	16-oz.	3.03	12/94	82r
Potatoes, frozen, French fried	lb.	0.77	12/94	82r
Potatoes, white	lb.	0.35	12/94	82r
Potatoes, white or red	10-lb. sack	1.99	12/94	2c
Rice, white, long grain, uncooked	lb.	0.54	12/94	82r
Round roast, USDA choice, boneless	lb.	2.92	12/94	82r
Sausage, Jimmy Dean, 100% pork	lb.	3.13	12/94	2c
Shortening, vegetable oil blends	lb.	0.80	12/94	82r
Shortening, vegetable, Crisco	3-lb.	2.82	12/94	2c
Soft drink, Coca Cola, ex deposit	2 lit	1.03	12/94	2c
Spaghetti and macaroni	lb.	1.02	12/94	82r
Steak, round, graded & ungraded, exc. USDA prime & choice	lb.	3.13	12/94	82r
Steak, sirloin, USDA choice, boneless	lb.	4.07	12/94	82r
Steak, t-bone	lb.	4.72	12/94	2c
Sugar and other sweets, eaten at home, expenditures	year	105	91	81r
Sugar, cane or beet	4 lbs.	1.63	12/94	2c
Sugar, white, all sizes	lb.	0.38	12/94	82r
Tobacco products and smoking supplies, total expenditures	year	221	91	81r
Tomatoes, field grown	lb.	1.45	12/94	82r

Values are in dollars or fractions of dollars. In the column headed *Ref*, references are shown to sources. Each reference is followed by a letter. These refer to the geographical level for which data were reported: s=State, r=Region, and c=City or metro. The abbreviation *ex* is used to mean *except* or *excluding*; *exp* stands for *expenditures*. For other abbreviations and further explanations, please see the Introduction.

Bakersfield, CA - continued

Item	Per	Value	Date	Ref.
Groceries				
Tomatoes, Hunt's or Del Monte	14.5 oz.	0.74	12/94	2c
Tuna, chunk, light	lb.	2.18	12/94	82r
Tuna, chunk, light, oil-packed	6.125-6.5 oz.	0.71	12/94	2c
Goods and Services				
Miscellaneous goods and services, ACCRA Index		103.30	12/94	2c
Health Care				
Health care, ACCRA Index		121.60	12/94	2c
Antibiotic ointment, Polysporin	1.5 oz.	4.56	12/94	2c
Childbirth, Cesarean delivery, hospital charge	birth	6059.00	12/91	69r
Childbirth, Cesarean delivery, physician charge	birth	2248.00	12/91	69r
Childbirth, normal delivery, hospital charge	birth	3006.00	12/91	69r
Childbirth, normal delivery, physician charge	birth	1634.00	12/91	69r
Dentist's fee, adult teeth cleaning and periodic oral exam	visit	69.80	12/94	2c
Doctor's fee, routine exam, established patient	visit	43.17	12/94	2c
Drugs, expenditures	year	230	91	81r
Health care, total expenditures	year	1544	91	81r
Health insurance expenditures	year	558	91	81r
Hospital care, semiprivate room	day	510.00	12/94	2c
Insurance premium, family medical care	month	380.27	1/95	41s
Medical services expenditures	year	676	91	81r
Medical supplies expenditures	year	80	91	81r
Surgery, open-heart	proc	37818.00	1/93	14r
Household Goods				
Appl. repair, service call, wash mach	min. lab. chg.	37.19	12/94	2c
Floor coverings, expenditures	year	79	91	81r
Furniture, expenditures	year	352	91	81r
Household equipment, misc. expenditures	year	614	91	81r
Household expenditures, miscellaneous	year	294	91	81r
Household furnishings and equipment, expenditures	year	1416	91	81r
Household operations expenditures	year	580	91	81r
Household textiles, expenditures	year	113	91	81r
Housekeeping supplies, expenditures	year	447	91	81r
Laundry and cleaning supplies, expenditures	year	114	91	81r
Laundry detergent, Tide Ultra, Bold, or Cheer	42 oz.	4.23	12/94	2c
Postage and stationery, expenditures	year	145	91	81r
Tissues, facial, Kleenex brand	175	0.97	12/94	2c
Housing				
Housing, ACCRA Index		104.40	12/94	2c
Add garage/carport		6,422	3/95	74r
Add room(s)		26,583	3/95	74r
Apartment condominium or co-op, median	unit	105300	12/94	62r
Dwellings (owned), expenditures	year	3932	91	81r
Enclose porch/patio/breezeway		5,382	3/95	74r
Finish room in basement/attic		3,911	3/95	74r
Home, existing, single-family, median	unit	178600	12/94	62r
House payment, principal and interest, 25% down payment	mo.	795	12/94	2c
House, 1800 sq ft, 8000 sq ft lot, new, urban, utilities	total	128712	12/94	2c
Maintenance, repairs, insurance, and other housing expenditures	year	591	91	81r
Mortgage interest and charges expenditures	year	2747	91	81r
Mtge. rate, incl. points and orig. fee, 30-year conv. fixed or ARM	mo.	9.26	12/94	2c
Princ. & int., mortgage, median-price exist. sing.-family home	mo.	845	12/94	62r
Property taxes expenditures	year	594	91	81r

Bakersfield, CA - continued

Item	Per	Value	Date	Ref.
Housing - continued				
Redesign, restructure more than half of home's interior		5,467	3/95	74r
Rent, apartment, 2 br., 1 1/2-2 baths, unfurnished, 950 sq ft, water	mo.	566	12/94	2c
Rental units expenditures	year	2077	91	81r
Insurance and Pensions				
Auto insurance, private passenger	year	892.80	12/94	71s
Insurance and pensions, personal, expenditures	year	3042	91	81r
Insurance, life and other personal, expenditures	year	298	91	81r
Pensions and Social Security, expenditures	year	2744	91	81r
Legal Assistance				
Legal work, law firm associate	hour	91		10r
Legal work, law firm partner	hour	151		10r
Personal Goods				
Shampoo, Alberto VO5	15-oz.	1.36	12/94	2c
Toothpaste, Crest or Colgate	6-7 oz.	2.43	12/94	2c
Personal Services				
Dry cleaning, man's 2-pc. suit		8.63	12/94	2c
Haircut, man's barbershop, no styling		7.60	12/94	2c
Haircut, woman's shampoo, trim, blow-dry		26.60	12/94	2c
Personal services expenditures	year	286	91	81r
Restaurant Food				
Chicken, fried, thigh and drumstick		2.09	12/94	2c
Dining expenditures, family	week	32.25	94	73r
Hamburger with cheese	1/4 lb.	1.89	12/94	2c
Pizza, Pizza Hut or Pizza Inn	12-13 in.	7.99	12/94	2c
Taxes				
Taxes, Federal income, expenditures	year	2946	91	81r
Taxes, personal, expenditures	year	3791	91	81r
Taxes, State and local income, expenditures	year	791	91	81r
Transportation				
Transportation, ACCRA Index		114.80	12/94	2c
Bus fare, one-way	trip	0.50	12/95	1c
Bus fare, up to 10 miles	one-way	0.75	12/94	2c
Cars and trucks purchased, new	year	1231	91	81r
Cars and trucks purchased, used	year	915	91	81r
Driver's learning permit fee	perm	12.00	1/94	84s
Driver's license fee	orig	12.00	1/94	84s
Driver's license fee, duplicate	lic	12.00	1/94	84s
Driver's license reinstatement fee, min.	susp	15.00	1/94	85s
Driver's license renewal fee	renew	12.00	1/94	84s
Identification card, nondriver	card	6.00	1/94	83s
Motorcycle learning permit fee	perm	12.00	1/94	84s
Motorcycle license fee	orig	12.00	1/94	84s
Motorcycle license fee, duplicate	lic	12.00	1/94	84s
Motorcycle license renewal fee	renew	12.00	1/94	84s
Public transportation expenditures	year	375	91	81r
Tire balance, computer or spin bal., front	wheel	8.89	12/94	2c
Transportation expenditures, total	year	5527	91	81r
Vehicle finance charges	year	287	91	81r
Vehicle insurance expenditures	year	624	91	81r
Vehicle maintenance and repairs expenditures	year	695	91	81r
Vehicle purchases	year	2174	91	81r
Vehicle rental, leases, licenses, etc.	year	257	91	81r
Vehicles purchased, other than cars and trucks	year	28	91	81r
Utilities				
Utilities, ACCRA Index		119.60	12/94	2c
Electricity expenditures	year	616	91	81r
Electricity, (part.), other, 1800 sq. ft., new home	mo.	122.33	12/94	2c

Values are in dollars or fractions of dollars. In the column headed *Ref*, references are shown to sources. Each reference is followed by a letter. These refer to the geographical level for which data were reported: s=State, r=Region, and c=City or metro. The abbreviation *ex* is used to mean *except* or *excluding*; *exp* stands for expenditures. For other abbreviations and further explanations, please see the Introduction.

Bakersfield, CA - continued

Item	Per	Value	Date	Ref.
Utilities				
Utilities, fuels, and public services, total expenditures	year	1681	91	81r
Water and other public services, expenditures	year	209	91	81r
Weddings				
Bridal attendants' gowns	event	750	10/93	76r
Bridal gown	event	852	10/93	76r
Bridal headpiece and veil	event	167	10/93	76r
Bride's wedding band	event	708	10/93	76r
Clergy	event	224	10/93	76r
Engagement ring	event	2756	10/93	76r
Flowers	event	863	10/93	76r
Formal wear for groom	event	106	10/93	76r
Groom's attendants' formal wear	event	530	10/93	76r
Groom's wedding band	event	402	10/93	76r
Music	event	600	10/93	76r
Photography	event	1088	10/93	76r
Shoes for bride	event	50	10/93	76r
Videography	event	483	10/93	76r
Wedding invitations and announcements	event	342	10/93	76r
Wedding reception	event	7000	10/93	76r

Baltimore, MD

Item	Per	Value	Date	Ref.
Composite, ACCRA index		103.10	12/94	2c
Alcoholic Beverages				
Beer, Miller Lite, Bud, 12-oz., ex deposit	6	4.24	12/94	2c
J & B Scotch	750-ml.	15.37	12/94	2c
Wine, Gallo Chablis blanc	1.5-lit	5.19	12/94	2c
Appliances				
Appliances (major), expenditures	year	137	91	81c
Average annual exp.				
Food, health care, personal goods, services	year	33208	91	81c
Charity				
Cash contributions, expenditures	year	1469	91	81c
Clothing				
Apparel, men and boys, total expenditures	year	465	91	81c
Apparel, women and girls, total expenditures	year	732	91	81c
Footwear, expenditures	year	280	91	81c
Jeans, man's denim		34.79	12/94	2c
Shirt, dress, men's	shirt	35.00	1/92	44c
Shirt, man's dress shirt		28.90	12/94	2c
Undervest, boy's size 10-14, cotton	3	3.49	12/94	2c
Communications				
Long-distance telephone rate, day, addl. min., 1-10 mi.	min.	0.10	12/93	9s
Long-distance telephone rate, day, initial min., 1-10 mi.	min.	0.21	12/93	9s
Newspaper subscription, dly. and Sun. delivery	month	12.95	12/94	2c
Phone line, single, business, field visit	inst	0.00	12/93	9s
Phone line, single, business, no field visit	inst	98.50	12/93	9s
Phone line, single, residence, field visit	inst	0.00	12/93	9s
Phone line, single, residence, no field visit	inst	48.00	12/93	9s
Telephone bill, family of four	month	22.01	12/94	2c
Telephone service, expenditures	year	600	91	81c
Telephone, residential, flat rate	mo.	16.51	12/93	8c
Education				
Board, 4-year private college/university	year	2878	8/94	80s
Board, 4-year public college/university	year	2464	8/94	80s
Education, total expenditures	year	467	91	81c
Room, 4-year private college/university	year	3231	8/94	80s
Room, 4-year public college/university	year	2587	8/94	80s
Total cost, 4-year private college/university	year	19012	8/94	80s
Total cost, 4-year public college/university	year	8171	8/94	80s

Baltimore, MD - continued

Item	Per	Value	Date	Ref.
Education - continued				
Tuition, 2-year public college/university, in-state	year	1676	8/94	80s
Tuition, 4-year private college/university, in-state	year	12903	8/94	80s
Tuition, 4-year public college/university, in-state	year	3120	8/94	80s
Energy and Fuels				
Electricity	500 KWh	47.80	12/94	82c
Energy, combined forms, 1800 sq. ft.	mo.	107.53	12/94	2c
Energy, exc. electricity, 1800 sq. ft.	mo.	42.51	12/94	2c
Fuel oil #2	gallon	1.01	12/94	82c
Fuel oil and other fuels, expenditures	year	88	91	81c
Gas	gal.	1.14	1/92	44c
Gas, cooking, 10 therms	month	13.70	2/94	65c
Gas, cooking, 30 therms	month	25.10	2/94	65c
Gas, cooking, 50 therms	month	36.50	2/94	65c
Gas, heating, winter, 100 therms	month	64.99	2/94	65c
Gas, heating, winter, average use	month	141.93	2/94	65c
Gas, natural, expenditures	year	150	91	81c
Gas, piped	40 therms	26.74	12/94	82c
Gas, piped	100 therms	54.86	12/94	82c
Gas, piped	therm	0.59	12/94	82c
Gas, reg unlead, taxes inc., cash, self-service	gal	1.12	12/94	2c
Gasoline and motor oil purchased	year	1051	91	81c
Gasoline, unleaded midgrade	gallon	1.32	4/93	82c
Gasoline, unleaded premium	gallon	1.40	4/93	82c
Gasoline, unleaded regular	gallon	1.20	4/93	82c
Entertainment				
Baseball game, four-person family	game	104.96	4/94	47c
Bowling, evening rate	game	2.51	12/94	2c
Entertainment supplies, equipment, and services, misc. expenditures	year	271	91	81c
Entertainment, total expenditures	year	1500	91	81c
Fees and admissions, expenditures	year	360	91	81c
Monopoly game, Parker Brothers', No. 9	game	11.01	12/94	2c
Movie	adm	6.00	12/94	2c
Movie ticket, adult	ticket	6.50	1/92	44c
Pets, toys, playground equipment, expenditures	year	373	91	81c
Reading, expenditures	year	162	91	81c
Televisions, radios, and sound equipment, expenditures	year	496	91	81c
Tennis balls, yellow, Wilson or Penn, 3	can	2.10	12/94	2c
Funerals				
Burial, immediate, container provided by funeral home		1370.36	1/95	54r
Cards, acknowledgment		14.83	1/95	54r
Casket, minimum alternative		192.52	1/95	54r
Cosmetology, hair care, etc.		102.27	1/95	54r
Cremation, direct, container provided by funeral home		1065.64	1/95	54r
Embalming		304.29	1/95	54r
Funeral, funeral home		287.83	1/95	54r
Funeral, other facility		284.14	1/95	54r
Graveside service		349.13	1/95	54r
Hearse, local		132.27	1/95	54r
Limousine, local		98.45	1/95	54r
Memorial service		270.59	1/95	54r
Service charge, professional, nondeclinable		933.59	1/95	54r
Visitation and viewing		225.83	1/95	54r
Groceries				
Groceries, ACCRA Index		103.50	12/94	2c
Baby food, strained vegetables, lowest price	4-4.5 oz.	0.39	12/94	2c
Bananas	lb.	0.41	12/94	2c
Beef or hamburger, ground	lb.	1.51	12/94	2c

Values are in dollars or fractions of dollars. In the column headed *Ref*, references are shown to sources. Each reference is followed by a letter. These refer to the geographical level for which data were reported: s=State, r=Region, and c=City or metro. The abbreviation *ex* is used to mean *except* or *excluding*; *exp* stands for expenditures. For other abbreviations and further explanations, please see the Introduction.

Baltimore, MD - continued

Item	Per	Value	Date	Ref.
Groceries				
Beef purchases	year	239	91	81c
Beverage purchases, alcoholic	year	327	91	81c
Beverage purchases, nonalcoholic	year	214	91	81c
Bread, white	24-oz.	0.59	12/94	2c
Cereals and bakery products purchases	year	396	91	81c
Cereals and cereal products purchases	year	135	91	81c
Cheese, Kraft grated Parmesan	8-oz.	3.53	12/94	2c
Chicken, whole fryer	lb.	0.84	12/94	2c
Cigarettes, Winston, Kings	carton	16.79	12/94	2c
Coffee, vacuum-packed	13 oz.	3.43	12/94	2c
Corn Flakes, Kellogg's or Post Toasties	18 oz.	2.65	12/94	2c
Corn, frozen, whole kernel, lowest price	10 oz.	0.64	12/94	2c
Dairy products (other) purchases	year	176	91	81c
Eggs, Grade A large	dozen	0.80	12/94	2c
Fish and seafood purchases	year	140	91	81c
Food purchases, food eaten at home	year	2701	91	81c
Foods purchased away from home, not prepared by consumer	year	1811	91	81c
Fruits and vegetables purchases	year	428	91	81c
Lettuce, iceberg	head	0.80	12/94	2c
Margarine, Blue Bonnet or Parkay cubes	lb.	0.75	12/94	2c
Meats, poultry, fish, and eggs purchases	year	805	91	81c
Milk and cream (fresh) purchases	year	109	91	81c
Milk, 2%	gal.	2.12	1/92	44c
Milk, whole	1/2 gal.	1.42	12/94	2c
Orange juice, Minute Maid frozen	12-oz.	1.48	12/94	2c
Peaches, halves or slices, Hunt's, Del Monte, or Libby's	29-oz.	1.51	12/94	2c
Peas, sweet, Del Monte or Green Giant	15-17 oz.	0.63	12/94	2c
Pork purchases	year	135	91	81c
Potatoes, white or red	10-lb. sack	2.23	12/94	2c
Rental rate, 2-bedroom apartment	month	650.00	1/92	44c
Sausage, Jimmy Dean, 100% pork	lb.	2.63	12/94	2c
Shortening, vegetable, Crisco	3-lb.	3.03	12/94	2c
Soft drink, Coca Cola, ex deposit	2 lit	1.02	12/94	2c
Steak, t-bone	lb.	5.75	12/94	2c
Sugar and other sweets, eaten at home, purchases	year	87	91	81c
Sugar, cane or beet	4 lbs.	1.46	12/94	2c
Tobacco products and smoking supplies, total expenditures	year	273	91	81c
Tomatoes, Hunt's or Del Monte	14.5 oz.	0.78	12/94	2c
Tuna, chunk, light, oil-packed	6.125-6.5 oz.	0.80	12/94	2c
Goods and Services				
Miscellaneous goods and services, ACCRA Index		99.60	12/94	2c
Health Care				
Health care, ACCRA Index		103.00	12/94	2c
Antibiotic ointment, Polysporin	1.5 oz.	4.03	12/94	2c
Delivery, uncomplicated, total charge	birth	6100	1/93	24s
Delivery, uncomplicated, vaginal, hospital charge	birth	2780	1/93	24s
Delivery, uncomplicated, vaginal, physician's charge	birth	3320	1/93	24s
Dentist's fee, adult teeth cleaning and periodic oral exam	visit	52.60	12/94	2c
Doctor's fee, routine exam, established patient	visit	39.40	12/94	2c
Drugs, expenditures	year	177	91	81c
Health care, total expenditures	year	1401	91	81c
Health insurance expenditures	year	596	91	81c
Hospital care, semiprivate room	day	461.00	12/94	2c
Insurance premium, family medical care	month	389.07	1/95	41s
Medical services expenditures	year	562	91	81c
Medical supplies expenditures	year	67	91	81c

Baltimore, MD - continued

Item	Per	Value	Date	Ref.
Household Goods				
Appl. repair, service call, wash mach	min. lab. chg.	35.27	12/94	2c
Floor coverings, expenditures	year	120	91	81c
Furniture, expenditures	year	454	91	81c
Household equipment, misc., expenditures	year	413	91	81c
Household expenditures, miscellaneous	year	181	91	81c
Household furnishings and equipment, expenditures	year	1321	91	81c
Household operations expenditures	year	555	91	81c
Household textiles, expenditures	year	104	91	81c
Housekeeping supplies, expenditures	year	366	91	81c
Laundry and cleaning supplies, expenditures	year	107	91	81c
Laundry detergent, Tide Ultra, Bold, or Cheer	42 oz.	3.57	12/94	2c
Postage and stationery, expenditures	year	123	91	81c
Tissues, facial, Kleenex brand	175	1.11	12/94	2c
Housing				
Housing, ACCRA Index		107.20	12/94	2c
Dwellings (owned), expenditures	year	4701	91	81c
Home, existing, single-family, median	unit	108.80	12/94	62c
Home, purchase price	unit	127.60	3/93	26c
House payment, principal and interest, 25% down payment	mo.	840	12/94	2c
House, 1800 sq ft, 8000 sq ft lot, new, urban, utilities	total	136846	12/94	2c
Maintenance, repairs, insurance, and other housing expenditures	year	823	91	81c
Mortgage interest and charges expenditures	year	3078	91	81c
Mtge. rate, incl. points and orig. fee, 30-year conv. fixed or ARM	mo.	9.19	12/94	2c
Property taxes expenditures	year	801	91	81c
Rent, apartment, 2 br., 1 1/2-2 baths, unfurnished, 950 sq ft, water	mo.	512	12/94	2c
Rental units expenditures	year	1813	900/00/91	81c
Insurance and Pensions				
Auto insurance, private passenger	year	761.57	12/94	71s
Insurance and pensions, personal, expenditures	year	3176	91	81c
Insurance, life and other personal, expenditures	year	464	91	81c
Pensions and Social Security, expenditures	year	2711	91	81c
Personal Goods				
Personal care products and services, total expenditures	year	352	91	81c
Shampoo, Alberto VO5	15-oz.	1.17	12/94	2c
Toothpaste, Crest or Colgate	6-7 oz.	2.03	12/94	2c
Personal Services				
Dry cleaning, man's 2-pc. suit		6.28	12/94	2c
Dry cleaning, woman's dress	dress	6.25	1/92	44c
Haircut, man's barbershop, no styling		7.25	12/94	2c
Haircut, woman's shampoo, trim, blow-dry		25.30	12/94	2c
Personal services expenditures	year	374	91	81c
Restaurant Food				
Big Mac, small fries, medium drink	meal	2.99	1/92	44c
Chicken, fried, thigh and drumstick		1.98	12/94	2c
Hamburger with cheese	1/4 lb.	1.78	12/94	2c
Pizza, Pizza Hut or Pizza Inn	12-13 in.	7.59	12/94	2c
Taxes				
Tax rate, residential property, month	$100	2.44	1/92	79c
Taxes, Federal income, expenditures	year	3581	91	81c
Taxes, personal, expenditures	year	4992	91	81c
Taxes, State and local income, expenditures	year	1410	91	81c

Values are in dollars or fractions of dollars. In the column headed *Ref*, references are shown to sources. Each reference is followed by a letter. These refer to the geographical level for which data were reported: s = State, r = Region, and c = City or metro. The abbreviation *ex* is used to mean *except* or *excluding*; *exp* stands for expenditures. For other abbreviations and further explanations, please see the Introduction.

Baltimore, MD - continued

Item	Per	Value	Date	Ref.
Transportation				
Transportation, ACCRA Index		106.50	12/94	2c
Bus fare, one-way	trip	1.25	12/95	1c
Bus fare, up to 10 miles	one-way	1.25	12/94	2c
Cars and trucks purchased, new	year	1665	91	81c
Cars and trucks purchased, used	year	533	91	81c
Driver's learning permit fee	perm	30.00	1/94	84s
Driver's license fee	orig	30.00	1/94	84s
Driver's license fee, duplicate	lic	10.00	1/94	84s
Driver's license renewal fee	renew	20.00	1/94	84s
Identification card, nondriver	card	5.00	1/94	83s
Motorcycle learning permit fee	perm	30.00	1/94	84s
Motorcycle license fee	orig	30.00	1/94	84s
Motorcycle license fee, duplicate	lic	10.00	1/94	84s
Motorcycle license renewal fee	renew	20.00	1/94	84s
parking, long-term lot, airport	3 days	15.00	1/92	44c
Public transportation expenditures	year	182	91	81c
Railway fare, commuter rail, one-way	trip	3.00	12/95	1c
Railway fare, heavy rail, one-way	trip	1.25	12/95	1c
Railway fare, light rail, one-way	trip	1.25	12/95	1c
Tire balance, computer or spin bal., front	wheel	7.38	12/94	2c
Transportation expenditures, total	year	5498	91	81c
Vehicle expenses, miscellaneous	year	2065	91	81c
Vehicle finance charges	year	439	91	81c
Vehicle insurance expenditures	year	715	91	81c
Vehicle maintenance and repairs expenditures	year	689	91	81c
Vehicle purchases	year	2201	91	81c
Vehicle rental, leases, licenses, etc. expenditures	year	222	91	81c
Vehicles purchased, other than cars and trucks	year	3	91	81c
Utilities				
Utilities, ACCRA Index		98.10	12/94	2c
Electricity	KWh	0.08	12/94	82c
Electricity expenditures	year	979	91	81c
Electricity, (part.), other, 1800 sq. ft., new home	mo.	65.02	12/94	2c
Electricity, summer, 250 KWh	month	29.48	8/93	64c
Electricity, summer, 500 KWh	month	54.48	8/93	64c
Electricity, summer, 750 KWh	month	79.46	8/93	64c
Electricity, summer, 1000 KWh	month	104.43	8/93	64c
Utilities, fuels, and public services, total expenditures	year	1923	91	81c
Water and other public services, expenditures	year	106	91	81c
Weddings				
Bridal attendants' gowns	event	750	10/93	76r
Bridal gown	event	852	10/93	76r
Bridal headpiece and veil	event	167	10/93	76r
Bride's wedding band	event	708	10/93	76r
Clergy	event	224	10/93	76r
Engagement ring	event	2756	10/93	76r
Flowers	event	863	10/93	76r
Formal wear for groom	event	106	10/93	76r
Groom's attendants' formal wear	event	530	10/93	76r
Groom's wedding band	event	402	10/93	76r
Music	event	600	10/93	76r
Photography	event	1088	10/93	76r
Shoes for bride	event	50	10/93	76r
Videography	event	483	10/93	76r
Wedding invitations and announcements	event	342	10/93	76r
Wedding reception	event	7000	10/93	76r

Bangor, ME

Item	Per	Value	Date	Ref.
Appliances				
Appliances (major), expenditures	year	145	91	81r

Bangor, ME - continued

Item	Per	Value	Date	Ref.
Average annual exp.				
Food, health care, personal goods, services	year	29496	91	81r
Charity				
Cash contributions, expenditures	year	708	91	81r
Clothing				
Apparel, men and boys, total expenditures	year	416	91	81r
Apparel, women and girls, total expenditures	year	744	91	81r
Footwear, expenditures	year	305	91	81r
Communications				
Long-distance telephone rate, day, addl. min., 1-10 mi.	min.	0.15	12/93	9s
Long-distance telephone rate, day, initial min., 1-10 mi.	min.	0.19	12/93	9s
Phone line, single, business, field visit	inst	35.00	12/93	9s
Phone line, single, business, no field visit	inst	56.00	12/93	9s
Phone line, single, residence, field visit	inst	26.00	12/93	9s
Phone line, single, residence, no field visit	inst	44.75	12/93	9s
Telephone service, expenditures	year	589	91	81r
Education				
Board, 4-year private college/university	year	2772	8/94	80s
Board, 4-year public college/university	year	2178	8/94	80s
Education, total expenditures	year	593	91	81r
Room, 4-year private college/university	year	2620	8/94	80s
Room, 4-year public college/university	year	2204	8/94	80s
Total cost, 4-year private college/university	year	19658	8/94	80s
Total cost, 4-year public college/university	year	7521	8/94	80s
Tuition, 2-year public college/university, in-state	year	1913	8/94	80s
Tuition, 4-year private college/university, in-state	year	14265	8/94	80s
Tuition, 4-year public college/university, in-state	year	3139	8/94	80s
Energy and Fuels				
Fuel oil and other fuels, expenditures	year	257	91	81r
Gas, natural, expenditures	year	285	91	81r
Gasoline and motor oil purchased	year	867	91	81r
Gasoline, unleaded midgrade	gallon	1.32	4/93	82r
Gasoline, unleaded premium	gallon	1.40	4/93	82r
Gasoline, unleaded regular	gallon	1.19	4/93	82r
Entertainment				
Entertainment, total expenditures	year	1331	91	81r
Fees and admissions, expenditures	year	398	91	81r
Pets, toys, playground equipment, expenditures	year	270	91	81r
Reading, expenditures	year	171	91	81r
Televisions, radios, and sound equipment, expenditures	year	429	91	81r
Funerals				
Burial, immediate, container provided by funeral home		1507.89	1/95	54r
Cards, acknowledgment		18.10	1/95	54r
Casket, minimum alternative		133.03	1/95	54r
Cosmetology, hair care, etc.		114.12	1/95	54r
Cremation, direct, container provided by funeral home		1309.19	1/95	54r
Embalming		320.97	1/95	54r
Funeral, funeral home		327.61	1/95	54r
Funeral, other facility		314.81	1/95	54r
Graveside service		286.11	1/95	54r
Hearse, local		158.95	1/95	54r
Limousine, local		149.45	1/95	54r
Memorial service		315.94	1/95	54r
Service charge, professional, nondeclinable		1148.43	1/95	54r
Visitation and viewing		249.66	1/95	54r
Groceries				
Apples, Red Delicious	lb.	0.78	12/94	82r
Bacon, sliced	lb.	2.24	12/94	82r
Bananas	lb.	0.49	12/94	82r
Beef purchases	year	226	91	81r

Values are in dollars or fractions of dollars. In the column headed *Ref*, references are shown to sources. Each reference is followed by a letter. These refer to the geographical level for which data were reported: s = State, r = Region, and c = City or metro. The abbreviation *ex* is used to mean *except* or *excluding*; *exp* stands for *expenditures*. For other abbreviations and further explanations, please see the Introduction.

Bangor, ME - continued

Item	Per	Value	Date	Ref.
Groceries				
Beverage purchases, alcoholic	year	332	91	81r
Beverage purchases, nonalcoholic	year	213	91	81r
Bread, white, pan	lb.	0.80	12/94	82r
Butter, salted, Grade AA, stick	lb.	1.67	12/94	82r
Carrots, short trimmed and topped	lb.	0.51	12/94	82r
Cereals and bakery products purchases	year	407	91	81r
Cereals and cereals products purchases	year	132	91	81r
Chicken breast, bone-in	lb.	2.22	12/94	82r
Chicken, fresh, whole	lb.	1.05	12/94	82r
Chuck roast, USDA choice, boneless	lb.	2.74	12/94	82r
Coffee, 100%, ground roast, all sizes	lb.	4.61	12/94	82r
Dairy products (other) purchases	year	161	91	81r
Eggs, Grade A large	dozen	1.12	12/94	82r
Fish and seafood purchases	year	112	91	81r
Food purchases, food eaten at home	year	2599	91	81r
Foods purchased away from home, not prepared by consumer	year	2024	91	81r
Fruits and vegetables purchases	year	444	91	81r
Grapefruit	lb.	0.44	12/94	82r
Grapes, Thompson seedless	lb.	2.24	12/94	82r
Ground chuck, 100% beef	lb.	1.67	12/94	82r
Ice cream, prepackaged, bulk, regular	1/2 gal.	2.93	12/94	82r
Lemons	lb.	1.06	12/94	82r
Lettuce, iceberg	lb.	0.92	12/94	82r
Meats, poultry, fish, and eggs purchases	year	751	91	81r
Milk and cream (fresh) purchases	year	152	91	81r
Orange juice, frozen concentrate 12-oz. can	16 oz.	1.92	12/94	82r
Oranges, Navel	lb.	0.56	12/94	82r
Pork chops, center cut, bone-in	lb.	3.09	12/94	82r
Pork purchases	year	130	91	81r
Potatoes, white	lb.	0.37	12/94	82r
Rib roast, USDA choice, bone-in	lb.	4.98	12/94	82r
Round roast, USDA choice, boneless	lb.	2.93	12/94	82r
Shortening, vegetable oil blends	lb.	1.03	12/94	82r
Spaghetti and macaroni	lb.	0.84	12/94	82r
Steak, round, USDA choice, boneless	lb.	3.48	12/94	82r
Steak, sirloin, USDA choice, bone-in	lb.	3.38	12/94	82r
Steak, sirloin, USDA choice, boneless	lb.	4.81	12/94	82r
Sugar and other sweets, eaten at home, expenditures	year	89	91	81r
Sugar, white, all sizes	lb.	0.46	12/94	82r
Tobacco products and smoking supplies, total expenditures	year	279	91	81r
Tomatoes, field grown	lb.	1.56	12/94	82r
Tuna, chunk, light	lb.	2.09	12/94	82r
Health Care				
Childbirth, Cesarean delivery, hospital charge	birth	6334.00	12/91	69r
Childbirth, Cesarean delivery, physician charge	birth	2234.00	12/91	69r
Childbirth, normal delivery, hospital charge	birth	3225.00	12/91	69r
Childbirth, normal delivery, physician charge	birth	1623.00	12/91	69r
Drugs, expenditures	year	205	91	81r
Health care, total expenditures	year	1396	91	81r
Health insurance expenditures	year	553	91	81r
Insurance premium, family medical care	month	473.31	1/95	41s
Medical services expenditures	year	559	91	81r
Medical supplies expenditures	year	80	91	81r
Household Goods				
Floor coverings, expenditures	year	158	91	81r
Furniture, expenditures	year	341	91	81r
Household equipment, misc. expenditures	year	363	91	81r
Household expenditures, miscellaneous	year	194	91	81r
Household furnishings and equipment, expenditures	year	1158	91	81r
Household operations expenditures	year	378	91	81r
Household textiles, expenditures	year	88	91	81r
Housekeeping supplies, expenditures	year	426	91	81r
Laundry and cleaning supplies, expenditures	year	122	91	81r

Item	Per	Value	Date	Ref.
Household Goods - continued				
Postage and stationery, expenditures	year	134	91	81r
Housing				
Add garage/carport		11,614	3/95	74r
Add room(s)		16,816	3/95	74r
Apartment condominium or co-op, median	unit	96700	12/94	62r
Dwellings (owned), expenditures	year	3305	91	81r
Enclose porch/patio/breezeway		2,980	3/95	74r
Finish room in basement/attic		4,330	3/95	74r
Home, existing, single-family, median	unit	161600	12/94	62r
Maintenance, repairs, insurance, and other housing expenditures	year	569	91	81r
Mortgage interest and charges expenditures	year	1852	91	81r
Princ. & int., mortgage, median-price exist. sing.-family home	mo.	765	12/94	62r
Property taxes expenditures	year	884	91	81r
Redesign, restructure more than half of home's interior		2,750	3/95	74r
Rental units expenditures	year	1832	91	81r
Insurance and Pensions				
Auto insurance, private passenger	year	556.67	12/94	71s
Insurance and pensions, personal, expenditures	year	2690	91	81r
Insurance, life and other personal, expenditures	year	341	91	81r
Pensions and Social Security, expenditures	year	2349	91	81r
Legal Assistance				
Estate planning, law-firm partner	hr.	375.00	10/93	12r
Legal work, law firm associate	hour	78		10r
Legal work, law firm partner	hour	183		10r
Personal Services				
Personal services expenditures	year	184	91	81r
Restaurant Food				
Dining expenditures, family	week	34.26	94	73r
Taxes				
Taxes, Federal income, expenditures	year	2409	91	81r
Taxes, personal, expenditures	year	3094	91	81r
Taxes, State and local income, expenditures	year	620	91	81r
Transportation				
Cars and trucks purchased, new	year	1170	91	81r
Cars and trucks purchased, used	year	739	91	81r
Driver's learning permit fee	perm	10.00	1/94	84s
Driver's license fee	orig	29.00	1/94	84s
Driver's license fee, duplicate	lic	4.00	1/94	84s
Driver's license reinstatement fee, min.	susp	25.00	1/94	85s
Driver's license renewal fee	renew	29.00	1/94	84s
Identification card, nondriver	card	5.00	1/94	83s
Motorcycle learning permit fee	perm	10.00	1/94	84s
Motorcycle license fee	orig	29.00	1/94	84s
Motorcycle license fee, duplicate	lic	4.00	1/94	84s
Motorcycle license renewal fee	renew	29.00	1/94	84s
Public transportation expenditures	year	430	91	81r
Transportation expenditures, total	year	4810	91	81r
Vehicle finance charges	year	238	91	81r
Vehicle insurance expenditures	year	630	91	81r
Vehicle maintenance and repairs expenditures	year	532	91	81r
Vehicle purchases	year	1920	91	81r
Vehicle rental, leases, licenses, etc. expenditures	year	193	91	81r
Vehicles purchased, other than cars and trucks	year	11	91	81r
Utilities				
Electricity expenditures	year	695	91	81r
Utilities, fuels, and public services, total expenditures	year	1981	91	81r
Water and other public services, expenditures	year	154	91	81r

Values are in dollars or fractions of dollars. In the column headed *Ref*, references are shown to sources. Each reference is followed by a letter. These refer to the geographical level for which data were reported: s = State, r = Region, and c = City or metro. The abbreviation *ex* is used to mean *except* or *excluding*; *exp* stands for *expenditures*. For other abbreviations and further explanations, please see the Introduction.

Bangor, ME - continued

Item	Per	Value	Date	Ref.
Weddings				
Bridal attendants' gowns	event	750	10/93	76r
Bridal gown	event	852	10/93	76r
Bridal headpiece and veil	event	167	10/93	76r
Bride's wedding band	event	708	10/93	76r
Clergy	event	224	10/93	76r
Engagement ring	event	2756	10/93	76r
Flowers	event	863	10/93	76r
Formal wear for groom	event	106	10/93	76r
Groom's attendants' formal wear	event	530	10/93	76r
Groom's wedding band	event	402	10/93	76r
Music	event	600	10/93	76r
Photography	event	1088	10/93	76r
Shoes for bride	event	50	10/93	76r
Videography	event	483	10/93	76r
Wedding invitations and announcements	event	342	10/93	76r
Wedding reception	event	7000	10/93	76r

Barre-Montpelier, VT

Item	Per	Value	Date	Ref.
Composite, ACCRA index		108.10	12/94	2c
Alcoholic Beverages				
Beer, Miller Lite, Bud, 12-oz., ex deposit	6	3.69	12/94	2c
J & B Scotch	750-ml.	14.95	12/94	2c
Wine, Gallo Chablis blanc	1.5-lit	5.19	12/94	2c
Clothing				
Jeans, man's denim		32.99	12/94	2c
Shirt, man's dress shirt		32.16	12/94	2c
Undervest, boy's size 10-14, cotton	3	4.29	12/94	2c
Communications				
Newspaper subscription, dly. and Sun. delivery	month	10.65	12/94	2c
Telephone bill, family of four	month	28.39	12/94	2c
Telephone, residential, flat rate	mo.	16.10	12/93	8c
Energy and Fuels				
Energy, combined forms, 1800 sq. ft.	mo.	120.53	12/94	2c
Energy, exc. electricity, 1800 sq. ft.	mo.	56.28	12/94	2c
Gas, reg unlead, taxes inc., cash, self-service	gal	1.04	12/94	2c
Entertainment				
Bowling, evening rate	game	2.00	12/94	2c
Monopoly game, Parker Brothers', No. 9	game	13.32	12/94	2c
Movie	adm	6.00	12/94	2c
Tennis balls, yellow, Wilson or Penn, 3	can	3.82	12/94	2c
Groceries				
Groceries, ACCRA Index		112.30	12/94	2c
Baby food, strained vegetables, lowest price	4-4.5 oz.	0.36	12/94	2c
Bananas	lb.	0.61	12/94	2c
Beef or hamburger, ground	lb.	1.75	12/94	2c
Bread, white	24-oz.	0.81	12/94	2c
Cheese, Kraft grated Parmesan	8-oz.	3.32	12/94	2c
Chicken, whole fryer	lb.	0.94	12/94	2c
Cigarettes, Winston, Kings	carton	18.49	12/94	2c
Coffee, vacuum-packed	13 oz.	3.16	12/94	2c
Corn Flakes, Kellogg's or Post Toasties	18 oz.	2.19	12/94	2c
Corn, frozen, whole kernel, lowest price	10 oz.	0.74	12/94	2c
Eggs, Grade A large	dozen	1.10	12/94	2c
Lettuce, iceberg	head	0.96	12/94	2c
Margarine, Blue Bonnet or Parkay cubes	lb.	0.58	12/94	2c
Milk, whole	1/2 gal.	1.23	12/94	2c
Orange juice, Minute Maid frozen	12-oz.	1.16	12/94	2c
Peaches, halves or slices, Hunt's, Del Monte, or Libby's	29-oz.	1.66	12/94	2c
Peas, sweet, Del Monte or Green Giant	15-17 oz.	0.61	12/94	2c

Barre-Montpelier, VT - continued

Item	Per	Value	Date	Ref.
Groceries - continued				
Potatoes, white or red	10-lb. sack	3.09	12/94	2c
Sausage, Jimmy Dean, 100% pork	lb.	3.45	12/94	2c
Shortening, vegetable, Crisco	3-lb.	3.16	12/94	2c
Soft drink, Coca Cola, ex deposit	2 lit	1.26	12/94	2c
Steak, t-bone	lb.	5.66	12/94	2c
Sugar, cane or beet	4 lbs.	1.86	12/94	2c
Tomatoes, Hunt's or Del Monte	14.5 oz.	0.71	12/94	2c
Tuna, chunk, light, oil-packed	6.125-6.5 oz.	1.06	12/94	2c
Goods and Services				
Miscellaneous goods and services, ACCRA Index		109.50	12/94	2c
Health Care				
Health care, ACCRA Index		108.60	12/94	2c
Antibiotic ointment, Polysporin	1.5 oz.	3.96	12/94	2c
Dentist's fee, adult teeth cleaning and periodic oral exam	visit	52.00	12/94	2c
Doctor's fee, routine exam, established patient	visit	39.00	12/94	2c
Hospital care, semiprivate room	day	590.00	12/94	2c
Household Goods				
Appl. repair, service call, wash mach	min. lab. chg.	37.67	12/94	2c
Laundry detergent, Tide Ultra, Bold, or Cheer	42 oz.	4.36	12/94	2c
Tissues, facial, Kleenex brand	175	1.12	12/94	2c
Housing				
Housing, ACCRA Index		108.10	12/94	2c
House payment, principal and interest, 25% down payment	mo.	819	12/94	2c
House, 1800 sq ft, 8000 sq ft lot, new, urban, utilities	total	129667	12/94	2c
Mtge. rate, incl. points and orig. fee, 30-year conv. fixed or ARM	mo.	9.52	12/94	2c
Rent, apartment, 2 br., 1 1/2-2 baths, unfurnished, 950 sq ft, water	mo.	598	12/94	2c
Personal Goods				
Shampoo, Alberto VO5	15-oz.	1.56	12/94	2c
Toothpaste, Crest or Colgate	6-7 oz.	2.39	12/94	2c
Personal Services				
Dry cleaning, man's 2-pc. suit		7.33	12/94	2c
Haircut, man's barbershop, no styling		6.67	12/94	2c
Haircut, woman's shampoo, trim, blow-dry		18.17	12/94	2c
Restaurant Food				
Chicken, fried, thigh and drumstick		2.50	12/94	2c
Hamburger with cheese	1/4 lb.	1.99	12/94	2c
Pizza, Pizza Hut or Pizza Inn	12-13 in.	7.75	12/94	2c
Transportation				
Transportation, ACCRA Index		91.30	12/94	2c
Tire balance, computer or spin bal., front	wheel	6.07	12/94	2c
Utilities				
Utilities, ACCRA Index		112.60	12/94	2c
Electricity, (part.), other, 1800 sq. ft., new home	mo.	64.25	12/94	2c

Bartlesville, OK

Item	Per	Value	Date	Ref.
Composite, ACCRA index		91.60	12/94	2c
Alcoholic Beverages				
Beer, Miller Lite, Bud, 12-oz., ex deposit	6	3.93	12/94	2c

Values are in dollars or fractions of dollars. In the column headed *Ref*, references are shown to sources. Each reference is followed by a letter. These refer to the geographical level for which data were reported: s = State, r = Region, and c = City or metro. The abbreviation *ex* is used to mean *except* or *excluding*; *exp* stands for *expenditures*. For other abbreviations and further explanations, please see the Introduction.

Bartlesville, OK - continued

Item	Per	Value	Date	Ref.
Alcoholic Beverages				
J & B Scotch	750-ml.	15.60	12/94	2c
Wine, Gallo Chablis blanc	1.5-lit	5.56	12/94	2c
Clothing				
Jeans, man's denim		27.50	12/94	2c
Shirt, man's dress shirt		25.00	12/94	2c
Undervest, boy's size 10-14, cotton	3	4.22	12/94	2c
Communications				
Newspaper subscription, dly. and Sun. delivery	month	9.00	12/94	2c
Telephone bill, family of four	month	18.33	12/94	2c
Telephone, residential, flat rate	mo.	11.32	12/93	8c
Energy and Fuels				
Energy, combined forms, 1800 sq. ft.	mo.	91.81	12/94	2c
Energy, exc. electricity, 1800 sq. ft.	mo.	33.92	12/94	2c
Gas, cooking, winter, 10 therms	month	12.37	2/94	65c
Gas, cooking, winter, 30 therms	month	19.80	2/94	65c
Gas, cooking, winter, 50 therms	month	27.23	2/94	65c
Gas, heating, winter, average use	month	67.07	2/94	65c
Gas, reg unlead, taxes inc., cash, self-service	gal	0.99	12/94	2c
Entertainment				
Bowling, evening rate	game	1.75	12/94	2c
Monopoly game, Parker Brothers', No. 9	game	11.34	12/94	2c
Movie	adm	5.25	12/94	2c
Tennis balls, yellow, Wilson or Penn, 3	can	1.97	12/94	2c
Groceries				
Groceries, ACCRA Index		88.90	12/94	2c
Baby food, strained vegetables, lowest price	4-4.5 oz.	0.24	12/94	2c
Bananas	lb.	0.41	12/94	2c
Beef or hamburger, ground	lb.	1.34	12/94	2c
Bread, white	24-oz.	0.48	12/94	2c
Cheese, Kraft grated Parmesan	8-oz.	3.06	12/94	2c
Chicken, whole fryer	lb.	0.63	12/94	2c
Cigarettes, Winston, Kings	carton	14.96	12/94	2c
Coffee, vacuum-packed	13 oz.	3.36	12/94	2c
Corn Flakes, Kellogg's or Post Toasties	18 oz.	1.98	12/94	2c
Corn, frozen, whole kernel, lowest price	10 oz.	0.68	12/94	2c
Eggs, Grade A large	dozen	0.69	12/94	2c
Lettuce, iceberg	head	0.71	12/94	2c
Margarine, Blue Bonnet or Parkay cubes	lb.	0.55	12/94	2c
Milk, whole	1/2 gal.	1.22	12/94	2c
Orange juice, Minute Maid frozen	12-oz.	1.16	12/94	2c
Peaches, halves or slices, Hunt's, Del Monte, or Libby's	29-oz.	1.54	12/94	2c
Peas, sweet, Del Monte or Green Giant	15-17 oz.	0.55	12/94	2c
Potatoes, white or red	10-lb. sack	1.90	12/94	2c
Sausage, Jimmy Dean, 100% pork	lb.	2.61	12/94	2c
Shortening, vegetable, Crisco	3-lb.	2.15	12/94	2c
Soft drink, Coca Cola, ex deposit	2 lit	1.06	12/94	2c
Steak, t-bone	lb.	4.79	12/94	2c
Sugar, cane or beet	4 lbs.	1.38	12/94	2c
Tomatoes, Hunt's or Del Monte	14.5 oz.	0.69	12/94	2c
Tuna, chunk, light, oil-packed	6.125-6.5 oz.	0.76	12/94	2c
Goods and Services				
Miscellaneous goods and services, ACCRA Index		95.50	12/94	2c
Health Care				
Health care, ACCRA Index		96.30	12/94	2c
Antibiotic ointment, Polysporin	1.5 oz.	3.95	12/94	2c
Dentist's fee, adult teeth cleaning and periodic oral exam	visit	52.33	12/94	2c

Bartlesville, OK - continued

Item	Per	Value	Date	Ref.
Health Care - continued				
Doctor's fee, routine exam, established patient	visit	39.75	12/94	2c
Hospital care, semiprivate room	day	330.00	12/94	2c
Household Goods				
Appl. repair, service call, wash mach	min. lab. chg.	34.00	12/94	2c
Laundry detergent, Tide Ultra, Bold, or Cheer	42 oz.	3.74	12/94	2c
Tissues, facial, Kleenex brand	175	0.97	12/94	2c
Housing				
Housing, ACCRA Index		90.60	12/94	2c
House payment, principal and interest, 25% down payment	mo.	706	12/94	2c
House, 1800 sq ft, 8000 sq ft lot, new, urban, utilities	total	114000	12/94	2c
Mtge. rate, incl. points and orig. fee, 30-year conv. fixed or ARM	mo.	9.29	12/94	2c
Rent, apartment, 2 br., 1 1/2-2 baths, unfurnished, 950 sq ft, water	mo.	445	12/94	2c
Personal Goods				
Shampoo, Alberto VO5	15-oz.	1.32	12/94	2c
Toothpaste, Crest or Colgate	6-7 oz.	1.96	12/94	2c
Personal Services				
Dry cleaning, man's 2-pc. suit		6.37	12/94	2c
Haircut, man's barbershop, no styling		7.50	12/94	2c
Haircut, woman's shampoo, trim, blow-dry		17.00	12/94	2c
Restaurant Food				
Chicken, fried, thigh and drumstick		2.68	12/94	2c
Hamburger with cheese	1/4 lb.	1.85	12/94	2c
Pizza, Pizza Hut or Pizza Inn	12-13 in.	7.99	12/94	2c
Transportation				
Transportation, ACCRA Index		89.30	12/94	2c
Tire balance, computer or spin bal., front	wheel	6.17	12/94	2c
Utilities				
Utilities, ACCRA Index		83.50	12/94	2c
Electricity, (part.), other, 1800 sq. ft., new home	mo.	57.89	12/94	2c

Baton Rouge, LA

Item	Per	Value	Date	Ref.
Composite, ACCRA index		100.20	12/94	2c
Alcoholic Beverages				
Beer, Miller Lite, Bud, 12-oz., ex deposit	6	3.97	12/94	2c
J & B Scotch	750-ml.	15.09	12/94	2c
Wine, Gallo Chablis blanc	1.5-lit	5.10	12/94	2c
Appliances				
Appliances (major), expenditures	year	153	91	81r
Average annual exp.				
Food, health care, personal goods, services	year	27020	91	81r
Charity				
Cash contributions, expenditures	year	839	91	81r
Clothing				
Apparel, men and boys, total expenditures	year	380	91	81r
Apparel, women and girls, total expenditures	year	660	91	81r
Footwear, expenditures	year	193	91	81r
Jeans, man's denim		30.79	12/94	2c
Shirt, man's dress shirt		30.60	12/94	2c
Undervest, boy's size 10-14, cotton	3	4.90	12/94	2c
Communications				
Long-distance telephone rate, day, addl. min., 1-10 mi.	min.	0.29	12/93	9s

Values are in dollars or fractions of dollars. In the column headed *Ref*, references are shown to sources. Each reference is followed by a letter. These refer to the geographical level for which data were reported: s = State, r = Region, and c = City or metro. The abbreviation *ex* is used to mean *except* or *excluding*; *exp* stands for *expenditures*. For other abbreviations and further explanations, please see the Introduction.

Baton Rouge, LA - continued

Item	Per	Value	Date	Ref.
Communications				
Long-distance telephone rate, day, initial min., 1-10 mi.	min.	0.41	12/93	9s
Newspaper subscription, dly. and Sun. delivery	month	9.74	12/94	2c
Phone line, single, business, field visit	inst	85.00	12/93	9s
Phone line, single, business, no field visit	inst	85.00	12/93	9s
Phone line, single, residence, field visit	inst	50.00	12/93	9s
Phone line, single, residence, no field visit	inst	50.00	12/93	9s
Telephone bill, family of four	month	20.95	12/94	2c
Telephone service, expenditures	year	616	91	81r
Telephone, residential, flat rate	mo.	13.69	12/93	8c
Education				
Board, 4-year private college/university	year	2436	8/94	80s
Board, 4-year public college/university	year	1638	8/94	80s
Education, total expenditures	year	319	91	81r
Room, 4-year private college/university	year	2558	8/94	80s
Room, 4-year public college/university	year	1405	8/94	80s
Total cost, 4-year private college/university	year	16467	8/94	80s
Total cost, 4-year public college/university	year	5225	8/94	80s
Tuition, 2-year public college/university, in-state	year	956	8/94	80s
Tuition, 4-year private college/university, in-state	year	11473	8/94	80s
Tuition, 4-year public college/university, in-state	year	2182	8/94	80s
Energy and Fuels				
Energy, combined forms, 1800 sq. ft.	mo.	136.37	12/94	2c
Energy, exc. electricity, 1800 sq. ft.	mo.	16.41	12/94	2c
Fuel oil and other fuels, expenditures	year	56	91	81r
Gas, cooking, 10 therms	month	8.16	2/94	65c
Gas, cooking, 30 therms	month	15.96	2/94	65c
Gas, cooking, 50 therms	month	25.15	2/94	65c
Gas, heating, winter, 100 therms	month	48.09	2/94	65c
Gas, heating, winter, average use	month	38.91	2/94	65c
Gas, natural, expenditures	year	150	91	81r
Gas, reg unlead, taxes inc., cash, self-service	gal	1.13	12/94	2c
Gasoline and motor oil purchased	year	1152	91	81r
Gasoline, unleaded midgrade	gallon	1.21	4/93	82r
Gasoline, unleaded premium	gallon	1.30	4/93	82r
Gasoline, unleaded regular	gallon	1.10	4/93	82r
Entertainment				
Bowling, evening rate	game	2.58	12/94	2c
Concert ticket, Pearl Jam group	perf	20.00	94	50r
Entertainment, total expenditures	year	1266	91	81r
Fees and admissions, expenditures	year	306	91	81r
Monopoly game, Parker Brothers', No. 9	game	11.33	12/94	2c
Movie	adm	6.00	12/94	2c
Pets, toys, playground equipment, expenditures	year	271	91	81r
Reading, expenditures	year	131	91	81r
Televisions, radios, and sound equipment, expenditures	year	439	91	81r
Tennis balls, yellow, Wilson or Penn, 3	can	2.43	12/94	2c
Funerals				
Burial, immediate, container provided by funeral home		1574.60	1/95	54r
Cards, acknowledgment		22.24	1/95	54r
Casket, minimum alternative		239.41	1/95	54r
Cosmetology, hair care, etc.		91.04	1/95	54r
Cremation, direct, container provided by funeral home		1085.15	1/95	54r
Embalming		281.30	1/95	54r
Funeral, funeral home		323.04	1/95	54r
Funeral, other facility		327.58	1/95	54r
Graveside service		355.19	1/95	54r
Hearse, local		141.89	1/95	54r
Limousine, local		99.40	1/95	54r
Memorial service		284.67	1/95	54r
Service charge, professional, nondeclinable		904.06	1/95	54r

Baton Rouge, LA - continued

Item	Per	Value	Date	Ref.
Funerals - continued				
Visitation and viewing		187.04	1/95	54r
Groceries				
Groceries, ACCRA Index		98.40	12/94	2c
Apples, Red Delicious	lb.	0.73	12/94	82r
Baby food, strained vegetables, lowest price	4-4.5 oz.	0.25	12/94	2c
Bacon, sliced	lb.	1.67	12/94	82r
Bananas	lb.	0.43	12/94	2c
Bananas	lb.	0.42	12/94	82r
Beef or hamburger, ground	lb.	1.43	12/94	2c
Beef purchases	year	213	91	81r
Beverage purchases, alcoholic	year	249	91	81r
Beverage purchases, nonalcoholic	year	207	91	81r
Bologna, all beef or mixed	lb.	2.27	12/94	82r
Bread, white	24-oz.	0.78	12/94	2c
Bread, white, pan	lb.	0.68	12/94	82r
Cabbage	lb.	0.42	12/94	82r
Carrots, short trimmed and topped	lb.	0.53	12/94	82r
Cereals and bakery products purchases	year	345	91	81r
Cereals and cereals products purchases	year	127	91	81r
Cheddar cheese, natural	lb.	3.58	12/94	82r
Cheese, Kraft grated Parmesan	8-oz.	3.43	12/94	2c
Chicken breast, bone-in	lb.	1.71	12/94	82r
Chicken, fresh, whole	lb.	0.78	12/94	82r
Chicken, whole fryer	lb.	0.86	12/94	2c
Chuck roast, USDA choice, boneless	lb.	2.26	12/94	82r
Cigarettes, Winston, Kings	carton	14.83	12/94	2c
Coffee, vacuum-packed	13 oz.	3.67	12/94	2c
Corn Flakes, Kellogg's or Post Toasties	18 oz.	2.52	12/94	2c
Corn, frozen, whole kernel, lowest price	10 oz.	0.70	12/94	2c
Crackers, soda, salted	lb.	1.27	12/94	82r
Cucumbers	lb.	0.65	12/94	82r
Dairy products (other) purchases	year	141	91	81r
Eggs, Grade A large	dozen	0.73	12/94	2c
Eggs, Grade A large	dozen	0.87	12/94	82r
Fish and seafood purchases	year	72	91	81r
Flour, white, all purpose	lb.	0.23	12/94	82r
Food purchases, food eaten at home	year	2381	91	81r
Foods purchased away from home, not prepared by consumer	year	1696	91	81r
Frankfurters, all meat or all beef	lb.	1.74	12/94	82r
Fruits and vegetables purchases	year	380	91	81r
Grapefruit	lb.	0.45	12/94	82r
Grapes, Thompson seedless	lb.	2.30	12/94	82r
Ground beef, 100% beef	lb.	1.37	12/94	82r
Ground chuck, 100% beef	lb.	1.97	12/94	82r
Ham, boneless, exc. canned	lb.	2.54	12/94	82r
Ice cream, prepackaged, bulk, regular	1/2 gal.	2.47	12/94	82r
Lemons	lb.	1.02	12/94	82r
Lettuce, iceberg	lb.	0.96	12/94	82r
Lettuce, iceberg	head	0.75	12/94	2c
Margarine, Blue Bonnet or Parkay cubes	lb.	0.63	12/94	2c
Margarine, stick	lb.	0.77	12/94	82r
Meats, poultry, fish, and eggs purchases	year	655	91	81r
Milk and cream (fresh) purchases	year	130	91	81r
Milk, whole	1/2 gal.	1.35	12/94	2c
Orange juice, frozen concentrate 12-oz. can	16 oz.	1.36	12/94	82r
Orange juice, Minute Maid frozen	12-oz.	1.20	12/94	2c
Oranges, Navel	lb.	0.54	12/94	82r
Peaches, halves or slices, Hunt's, Del Monte, or Libby's	29-oz.	1.34	12/94	2c
Pears, Anjou	lb.	0.81	12/94	82r
Peas, sweet, Del Monte or Green Giant	15-17 oz.	0.55	12/94	2c
Pork chops, center cut, bone-in	lb.	3.07	12/94	82r
Pork purchases	year	142	91	81r
Potato chips	16-oz.	3.15	12/94	82r
Potatoes, frozen, French fried	lb.	0.82	12/94	82r
Potatoes, white	lb.	0.34	12/94	82r

Values are in dollars or fractions of dollars. In the column headed *Ref*, references are shown to sources. Each reference is followed by a letter. These refer to the geographical level for which data were reported: s = State, r = Region, and c = City or metro. The abbreviation *ex* is used to mean *except* or *excluding*; *exp* stands for expenditures. For other abbreviations and further explanations, please see the Introduction.

Baton Rouge, LA - continued

Item	Per	Value	Date	Ref.
Groceries				
Potatoes, white or red	10-lb. sack	2.09	12/94	2c
Rice, white, long grain, uncooked	lb.	0.48	12/94	82r
Round roast, USDA choice, boneless	lb.	2.91	12/94	82r
Sausage, fresh	lb.	1.82	12/94	82r
Sausage, Jimmy Dean, 100% pork	lb.	2.56	12/94	2c
Shortening, vegetable oil blends	lb.	0.75	12/94	82r
Shortening, vegetable, Crisco	3-lb.	2.24	12/94	2c
Soft drink, Coca Cola, ex deposit	2 lit	1.07	12/94	2c
Spaghetti and macaroni	lb.	0.87	12/94	82r
Steak, rib eye, USDA choice, boneless	lb.	6.85	12/94	82r
Steak, round, graded & ungraded, exc. USDA prime & choice	lb.	2.96	12/94	82r
Steak, round, USDA choice, boneless	lb.	3.17	12/94	82r
Steak, sirloin, USDA choice, boneless	lb.	4.12	12/94	82r
Steak, t-bone	lb.	5.91	12/94	2c
Steak, T-bone, USDA choice, bone-in	lb.	5.63	12/94	82r
Sugar and other sweets, eaten at home, expenditures	year	93	91	81r
Sugar, cane or beet	4 lbs.	1.55	12/94	2c
Sugar, white, all sizes	lb.	0.39	12/94	82r
Tobacco products and smoking supplies, total expenditures	year	286	91	81r
Tomatoes, field grown	lb.	1.36	12/94	82r
Tomatoes, Hunt's or Del Monte	14.5 oz.	0.67	12/94	2c
Tuna, chunk, light	lb.	1.94	12/94	82r
Tuna, chunk, light, oil-packed	6.125-6.5 oz.	0.67	12/94	2c
Turkey, frozen, whole	lb.	0.96	12/94	82r
Yogurt, natural, fruit flavored	8 oz.	0.58	12/94	82r
Goods and Services				
Miscellaneous goods and services, ACCRA Index		100.20	12/94	2c
Health Care				
Health care, ACCRA Index		91.70	12/94	2c
Adenosine, emergency room	treat	100.00	95	23r
Antibiotic ointment, Polysporin	1.5 oz.	3.79	12/94	2c
Bladder tap, superpubic, infant, emergency room	treat	119.00	95	23r
Blood analysis, emergency room	treat	25.00	95	23r
Blood tests, abdominal pain, emergency room	treat	25.00	95	23r
Burn dressing, emergency room	treat	266.00	95	23r
Cardiology interpretation, emergency room	treat	26.00	95	23r
Chest X-ray, emergency room	treat	78.00	95	23r
Childbirth, Cesarean delivery, hospital charge	birth	5462.00	12/91	69r
Childbirth, Cesarean delivery, physician charge	birth	2228.00	12/91	69r
Childbirth, normal delivery, hospital charge	birth	2943.00	12/91	69r
Childbirth, normal delivery, physician charge	birth	1619.00	12/91	69r
Defibrillation pads, emergency room	treat	6.00	95	23r
Dentist's fee, adult teeth cleaning and periodic oral exam	visit	44.58	12/94	2c
Doctor's fee, routine exam, established patient	visit	40.00	12/94	2c
Drugs, expenditures	year	297	91	81r
Gastric tube insertion, nasal, emergency room	treat	25.00	95	23r
Health care, total expenditures	year	1600	91	81r
Health insurance expenditures	year	637	91	81r
Heart monitor, emergency room	treat	40.00	95	23r
Hospital care, semiprivate room	day	346.40	12/94	2c
Insurance premium, family medical care	month	394.31	1/95	41s
Intravenous fluids, emergency room	treat	130.00	95	23r
Intravenous fluids, emergency room	liter	26.00	95	23r
Intravenous line, central, emergency room	treat	342.00	95	23r
Liver function tests, abdominal pain, emergency room	treat	26.00	95	23r

Baton Rouge, LA - continued

Item	Per	Value	Date	Ref.
Health Care - continued				
Medical care charges, total, emergency room, third-degree burns	treat	2101.00	95	23r
Medical care charges, total, emergency, infant with fever	treat	628.00	95	23r
Medical services expenditures	year	573	91	81r
Medical supplies expenditures	year	93	91	81r
Morphine, emergency room	treat	34.00	95	23r
Nursing care and facilities charges, emergency room	treat	252.00	95	23r
Nursing care and facilities charges, emergency, infant with fever	treat	252.00	95	23r
Nursing care and facilities charges, emergency, third-degree burns	treat	861.00	95	23r
Physician's charges, emergency, infant with fever	treat	212.00	95	23r
Physician's charges, emergency, third-degree burns	treat	372.00	95	23r
Physician's fee, emergency room	treat	372.00	95	23r
Physician's fee, general practitioner	visit	51.20	12/93	60r
Surgery, open-heart	proc	42374.00	1/93	14r
Ultrasound, abdominal, emergency room	treat	276.00	95	23r
Urinalysis, emergency room	treat	20.00	95	23r
Urinalysis, infant, emergency room	treat	20.00	95	23r
X-rays, emergency room	treat	78.00	95	23r
Household Goods				
Appl. repair, service call, wash mach	min. lab. chg.	28.41	12/94	2c
Floor coverings, expenditures	year	48	91	81r
Furniture, expenditures	year	280	91	81r
Household equipment, misc. expenditures	year	342	91	81r
Household expenditures, miscellaneous	year	256	91	81r
Household furnishings and equipment, expenditures	year	988	91	81r
Household operations expenditures	year	468	91	81r
Household textiles, expenditures	year	95	91	81r
Housekeeping supplies, expenditures	year	380	91	81r
Laundry and cleaning supplies, expenditures	year	109	91	81r
Laundry detergent, Tide Ultra, Bold, or Cheer	42 oz.	3.65	12/94	2c
Postage and stationery, expenditures	year	105	91	81r
Tissues, facial, Kleenex brand	175	1.03	12/94	2c
Housing				
Housing, ACCRA Index		96.10	12/94	2c
Add garage/carport		6,980	3/95	74r
Add room(s)		11,403	3/95	74r
Apartment condominium or co-op, median	unit	68600	12/94	62r
Dwellings (owned), expenditures	year	2428	91	81r
Enclose porch/patio/breezeway		4,572	3/95	74r
Finish room in basement/attic		3,794	3/95	74r
Home, existing, single-family, median	unit	120200	12/94	62r
Home, existing, single-family, median	unit	77.10	12/94	62c
House payment, principal and interest, 25% down payment	mo.	741	12/94	2c
House, 1800 sq ft, 8000 sq ft lot, new, urban, utilities	total	119760	12/94	2c
Maintenance, repairs, insurance, and other housing expenditures	year	531	91	81r
Mortgage interest and charges expenditures	year	1506	91	81r
Mtge. rate, incl. points and orig. fee, 30-year conv. fixed or ARM	mo.	9.29	12/94	2c
Princ. & int., mortgage, median-price exist. sing.-family home	mo.	540	12/94	62c
Property taxes expenditures	year	391	91	81r
Redesign, restructure more than half of home's interior		17,641	3/95	74r
Rent, apartment, 2 br., 1 1/2-2 baths, unfurnished, 950 sq ft, water	mo.	493	12/94	2c
Rental units expenditures	year	1264	91	81r

Baton Rouge, LA - continued

Item	Per	Value	Date	Ref.
Insurance and Pensions				
Auto insurance, private passenger	year	862.62	12/94	71s
Insurance and pensions, personal, expenditures	year	2395	91	81r
Insurance, life and other personal, expenditures	year	368	91	81r
Pensions and Social Security, expenditures	year	2027	91	81r
Personal Goods				
Shampoo, Alberto VO5	15-oz.	0.98	12/94	2c
Toothpaste, Crest or Colgate	6-7 oz.	1.76	12/94	2c
Personal Services				
Dry cleaning, man's 2-pc. suit		6.46	12/94	2c
Haircut, man's barbershop, no styling		7.60	12/94	2c
Haircut, woman's shampoo, trim, blow-dry		22.00	12/94	2c
Personal services expenditures	year	212	91	81r
Restaurant Food				
Chicken, fried, thigh and drumstick		2.29	12/94	2c
Dining expenditures, family	week	33.83	94	73r
Hamburger with cheese	1/4 lb.	1.75	12/94	2c
Pizza, Pizza Hut or Pizza Inn	12-13 in.	7.99	12/94	2c
Taxes				
Taxes, Federal income, expenditures	year	2275	91	81r
Taxes, personal, expenditures	year	2715	91	81r
Taxes, State and local income, expenditures	year	365	91	81r
Transportation				
Transportation, ACCRA Index		104.70	12/94	2c
Bus fare, up to 10 miles	one-way	1.00	12/94	2c
Cars and trucks purchased, new	year	1306	91	81r
Cars and trucks purchased, used	year	942	91	81r
Driver's learning permit fee	perm	12.50	1/94	84s
Driver's license fee	orig	12.50	1/94	84s
Driver's license fee, duplicate	lic	5.00	1/94	84s
Driver's license reinstatement fee, min.	susp	60.00	1/94	85s
Driver's license renewal fee	renew	12.50	1/94	84s
Identification card, nondriver	card	7.00	1/94	83s
Motorcycle license fee	orig	8.00	1/94	84s
Motorcycle license renewal fee	renew	8.00	1/94	84s
Public transportation expenditures	year	249	91	81r
Tire balance, computer or spin bal., front	wheel	7.49	12/94	2c
Transportation expenditures, total	year	5307	91	81r
Vehicle finance charges	year	346	91	81r
Vehicle insurance expenditures	year	544	91	81r
Vehicle maintenance and repairs expenditures	year	600	91	81r
Vehicle purchases	year	2275	91	81r
Vehicle rental, leases, licenses, etc. expenditures	year	141	91	81r
Vehicles purchased, other than cars and trucks	year	27	91	81r
Utilities				
Utilities, ACCRA Index		119.60	12/94	2c
Electricity expenditures	year	950	91	81r
Electricity, (part.), other, 1800 sq. ft., new home	mo.	119.96	12/94	2c
Electricity, summer, 250 KWh	month	25.45	8/93	64c
Electricity, summer, 500 KWh	month	44.89	8/93	64c
Electricity, summer, 750 KWh	month	64.34	8/93	64c
Electricity, summer, 1000 KWh	month	83.78	8/93	64c
Utilities, fuels, and public services, total expenditures	year	2000	91	81r
Water and other public services, expenditures	year	227	91	81r
Weddings				
Bridal attendants' gowns	event	750	10/93	76r
Bridal gown	event	852	10/93	76r
Bridal headpiece and veil	event	167	10/93	76r
Bride's wedding band	event	708	10/93	76r

Baton Rouge, LA - continued

Item	Per	Value	Date	Ref.
Weddings - continued				
Clergy	event	224	10/93	76r
Engagement ring	event	2756	10/93	76r
Flowers	event	863	10/93	76r
Formal wear for groom	event	106	10/93	76r
Groom's attendants' formal wear	event	530	10/93	76r
Groom's wedding band	event	402	10/93	76r
Music	event	600	10/93	76r
Photography	event	1088	10/93	76r
Shoes for bride	event	50	10/93	76r
Videography	event	483	10/93	76r
Wedding invitations and announcements	event	342	10/93	76r
Wedding reception	event	7000	10/93	76r

Battle Creek, MI

Item	Per	Value	Date	Ref.
Appliances				
Appliances (major), expenditures	year	131	91	81r
Average annual exp.				
Food, health care, personal goods, services	year	25935	91	81r
Charity				
Cash contributions, expenditures	year	745	91	81r
Clothing				
Apparel, men and boys, total expenditures	year	332	91	81r
Apparel, women and girls, total expenditures	year	578	91	81r
Footwear, expenditures	year	164	91	81r
Communications				
Long-distance telephone rate, day, addl. min., 1-10 mi.	min.	0.08	12/93	9s
Long-distance telephone rate, day, initial min., 1-10 mi.	min.	0.14	12/93	9s
Phone line, single, business, field visit	inst	42.00	12/93	9s
Phone line, single, business, no field visit	inst	42.00	12/93	9s
Phone line, single, residence, field visit	inst	42.00	12/93	9s
Phone line, single, residence, no field visit	inst	42.00	12/93	9s
Telephone service, expenditures	year	547	91	81r
Education				
Board, 4-year private college/university	year	2064	8/94	80s
Board, 4-year public college/university	year	2304	8/94	80s
Education, total expenditures	year	394	91	81r
Room, 4-year private college/university	year	1814	8/94	80s
Room, 4-year public college/university	year	1856	8/94	80s
Total cost, 4-year private college/university	year	12178	8/94	80s
Total cost, 4-year public college/university	year	7642	8/94	80s
Tuition, 2-year public college/university, in-state	year	1358	8/94	80s
Tuition, 4-year private college/university, in-state	year	8300	8/94	80s
Tuition, 4-year public college/university, in-state	year	3481	8/94	80s
Energy and Fuels				
Fuel oil and other fuels, expenditures	year	83	91	81r
Gas, natural, expenditures	year	373	91	81r
Gasoline and motor oil purchased	year	1000	91	81r
Gasoline, unleaded midgrade	gallon	1.15	4/93	82r
Gasoline, unleaded premium	gallon	1.23	4/93	82r
Gasoline, unleaded regular	gallon	1.07	4/93	82r
Entertainment				
Entertainment, total expenditures	year	1356	91	81r
Fees and admissions, expenditures	year	347	91	81r
Pets, toys, playground equipment, expenditures	year	270	91	81r
Reading, expenditures	year	160	91	81r
Televisions, radios, and sound equipment, expenditures	year	433	91	81r
Funerals				
Burial, immediate, container provided by funeral home		1268.31	1/95	54r

Values are in dollars or fractions of dollars. In the column headed *Ref*, references are shown to sources. Each reference is followed by a letter. These refer to the geographical level for which data were reported: s=State, r=Region, and c=City or metro. The abbreviation *ex* is used to mean *except* or *excluding*; *exp* stands for expenditures. For other abbreviations and further explanations, please see the Introduction.

Battle Creek, MI - continued

Item	Per	Value	Date	Ref.
Funerals				
Cards, acknowledgment		26.12	1/95	54r
Casket, minimum alternative		198.03	1/95	54r
Cosmetology, hair care, etc.		122.19	1/95	54r
Cremation, direct, container provided by funeral home		977.81	1/95	54r
Embalming		334.00	1/95	54r
Funeral, funeral home		321.16	1/95	54r
Funeral, other facility		317.73	1/95	54r
Graveside service		292.48	1/95	54r
Hearse, local		153.20	1/95	54r
Limousine, local		123.52	1/95	54r
Memorial service		356.30	1/95	54r
Service charge, professional, nondeclinable		968.24	1/95	54r
Visitation and viewing		332.66	1/95	54r
Groceries				
Apples, Red Delicious	lb.	0.68	12/94	82r
Bacon, sliced	lb.	1.88	12/94	82r
Bananas	lb.	0.41	12/94	82r
Beef purchases	year	197	91	81r
Beef, stew, boneless	lb.	2.52	12/94	82r
Beverage purchases, alcoholic	year	293	91	81r
Beverage purchases, nonalcoholic	year	203	91	81r
Bologna, all beef or mixed	lb.	2.12	12/94	82r
Bread, white, pan	lb.	0.76	12/94	82r
Cabbage	lb.	0.44	12/94	82r
Carrots, short trimmed and topped	lb.	0.44	12/94	82r
Cereals and bakery products purchases	year	347	91	81r
Cereals and cereals products purchases	year	119	91	81r
Cheddar cheese, natural	lb.	3.28	12/94	82r
Chicken breast, bone-in	lb.	1.61	12/94	82r
Chicken, fresh, whole	lb.	0.89	12/94	82r
Chuck roast, USDA choice, boneless	lb.	2.33	12/94	82r
Coffee, 100%, ground roast, all sizes	lb.	4.28	12/94	82r
Cookies, chocolate chip	lb.	2.72	12/94	82r
Dairy products (other) purchases	year	148	91	81r
Eggs, Grade A large	dozen	0.76	12/94	82r
Fish and seafood purchases	year	61	91	81r
Flour, white, all purpose	lb.	0.22	12/94	82r
Food purchases, food eaten at home	year	2313	91	81r
Foods purchased away from home, not prepared by consumer	year	1709	91	81r
Fruits and vegetables purchases	year	372	91	81r
Grapefruit	lb.	0.47	12/94	82r
Grapes, Thompson seedless	lb.	2.15	12/94	82r
Ground beef, 100% beef	lb.	1.37	12/94	82r
Ground chuck, 100% beef	lb.	1.81	12/94	82r
Ham, boneless, exc. canned	lb.	2.16	12/94	82r
Ice cream, prepackaged, bulk, regular	1/2 gal.	2.48	12/94	82r
Lemons	lb.	1.08	12/94	82r
Lettuce, iceberg	lb.	0.81	12/94	82r
Margarine, stick	lb.	0.81	12/94	82r
Meats, poultry, fish, and eggs purchases	year	591	91	81r
Milk and cream (fresh) purchases	year	132	91	81r
Orange juice, frozen concentrate 12-oz. can	16 oz.	1.41	12/94	82r
Oranges, Navel	lb.	0.56	12/94	82r
Peanut butter, creamy, all sizes	lb.	1.81	12/94	82r
Pork chops, center cut, bone-in	lb.	2.76	12/94	82r
Pork purchases	year	130	91	81r
Potato chips	16-oz.	2.81	12/94	82r
Potatoes, frozen, French fried	lb.	0.83	12/94	82r
Potatoes, white	lb.	0.28	12/94	82r
Round roast, USDA choice, boneless	lb.	2.90	12/94	82r
Shortening, vegetable oil blends	lb.	0.88	12/94	82r
Spaghetti and macaroni	lb.	0.78	12/94	82r
Steak, rib eye, USDA choice, boneless	lb.	6.15	12/94	82r
Steak, round, graded & ungraded, exc. USDA prime & choice	lb.	2.72	12/94	82r
Steak, round, USDA choice, boneless	lb.	3.02	12/94	82r
Steak, sirloin, USDA choice, boneless	lb.	3.85	12/94	82r
Steak, T-bone, USDA choice, bone-in	lb.	5.38	12/94	82r

Battle Creek, MI - continued

Item	Per	Value	Date	Ref.
Groceries - continued				
Sugar and other sweets, eaten at home, expenditures	year	91	91	81r
Sugar, white, all sizes	lb.	0.36	12/94	82r
Tobacco products and smoking supplies, total expenditures	year	298	91	81r
Tomatoes, field grown	lb.	1.36	12/94	82r
Tuna, chunk, light	lb.	1.94	12/94	82r
Turkey, frozen, whole	lb.	0.96	12/94	82r
Yogurt, natural, fruit flavored	8 oz.	0.62	12/94	82r
Health Care				
Childbirth, Cesarean delivery, hospital charge	birth	5101.00	12/91	69r
Childbirth, Cesarean delivery, physician charge	birth	2234.00	12/91	69r
Childbirth, normal delivery, hospital charge	birth	2891.00	12/91	69r
Childbirth, normal delivery, physician charge	birth	1623.00	12/91	69r
Drugs, expenditures	year	248	91	81r
Health care, total expenditures	year	1336	91	81r
Health insurance expenditures	year	550	91	81r
Insurance premium, family medical care	month	369.41	1/95	41s
Medical services expenditures	year	457	91	81r
Medical supplies expenditures	year	82	91	81r
Household Goods				
Floor coverings, expenditures	year	105	91	81r
Furniture, expenditures	year	291	91	81r
Household equipment, misc. expenditures	year	341	91	81r
Household expenditures, miscellaneous	year	162	91	81r
Household furnishings and equipment, expenditures	year	1042	91	81r
Household operations expenditures	year	365	91	81r
Household textiles, expenditures	year	101	91	81r
Housekeeping supplies, expenditures	year	390	91	81r
Laundry and cleaning supplies, expenditures	year	110	91	81r
Postage and stationery, expenditures	year	115	91	81r
Housing				
Add garage/carport		8,479	3/95	74r
Add room(s)		21,347	3/95	74r
Apartment condominium or co-op, median	unit	87100	12/94	62r
Bathroom addition, average cost	add	9734.00	3/95	13r
Bathroom remodeling, average cost	remod	6414.00	3/95	13r
Bedroom, master suite addition, average cost	add	27122.00	3/95	13r
Deck addition, average cost	add	6665.00	3/95	13r
Dwellings (owned), expenditures	year	2566	91	81r
Enclose porch/patio/breezeway		4,556	3/95	74r
Exterior remodeling, average cost	remod	15395.00	3/95	13r
Family room addition, average cost	add	27658.00	3/95	13r
Finish room in basement/attic		5,074	3/95	74r
Home, existing, single-family, median	unit	106500	12/94	62r
Kitchen remodeling, major, average cost	remod	17084.00	3/95	13r
Kitchen remodeling, minor, average cost	remod	5804.00	3/95	13r
Maintenance, repairs, insurance, and other housing expenditures	year	484	91	81r
Mortgage interest and charges expenditures	year	1443	91	81r
Office, home addition, average cost	add	8121.00	3/95	13r
Princ. & int., mortgage, median-price exist. sing.-family home	mo.	515	12/94	62r
Property taxes expenditures	year	639	91	81r
Redesign, restructure more than half of home's interior		9,114	3/95	74r
Rental units expenditures	year	1200	91	81r
Sun-space addition, average cost	add	23768.00	3/95	13r
Wing addition, two-story, average cost	add	50410.00	3/95	13r
Insurance and Pensions				
Auto insurance, private passenger	year	788.26	12/94	71s
Insurance and pensions, personal, expenditures	year	2408	91	81r
Insurance, life and other personal, expenditures	year	355	91	81r

Values are in dollars or fractions of dollars. In the column headed *Ref*, references are shown to sources. Each reference is followed by a letter. These refer to the geographical level for which data were reported: s=State, r=Region, and c=City or metro. The abbreviation *ex* is used to mean *except* or *excluding*; *exp* stands for *expenditures*. For other abbreviations and further explanations, please see the Introduction.

74

Battle Creek, MI - continued

Item	Per	Value	Date	Ref.
Insurance and Pensions				
Pensions and Social Security, expenditures	year	2053	91	81r
Legal Assistance				
Legal work, law firm associate	hour	90		10r
Legal work, law firm partner	hour	139		10r
Personal Services				
Personal services expenditures	year	203	91	81r
Restaurant Food				
Dining expenditures, family	week	30.03	94	73r
Taxes				
Taxes, Federal income, expenditures	year	1756	91	81r
Taxes, personal, expenditures	year	2426	91	81r
Taxes, State and local income, expenditures	year	568	91	81r
Transportation				
Cars and trucks purchased, new	year	891	91	81r
Cars and trucks purchased, used	year	1155	91	81r
Driver's learning permit fee	perm	12.00	1/94	84s
Driver's license fee	orig	12.00	1/94	84s
Driver's license fee, duplicate	lic	6.00	1/94	84s
Driver's license reinstatement fee, min.	susp	125.00	1/94	85s
Driver's license renewal fee	renew	12.00	1/94	84s
Identification card, nondriver	card	6.00	1/94	83s
Motorcycle license fee	orig	7.50	1/94	84s
Motorcycle license renewal fee	renew	4.00	1/94	84s
Public transportation expenditures	year	209	91	81r
Transportation expenditures, total	year	4792	91	81r
Vehicle finance charges	year	300	91	81r
Vehicle insurance expenditures	year	485	91	81r
Vehicle maintenance and repairs expenditures	year	534	91	81r
Vehicle purchases	year	2068	91	81r
Vehicle rental, leases, licenses, etc. expenditures	year	197	91	81r
Vehicles purchased, other than cars and trucks	year	22	91	81r
Utilities				
Electricity expenditures	year	668	91	81r
Utilities, fuels, and public services, total expenditures	year	1838	91	81r
Water and other public services, expenditures	year	167	91	81r
Weddings				
Bridal attendants' gowns	event	750	10/93	76r
Bridal gown	event	852	10/93	76r
Bridal headpiece and veil	event	167	10/93	76r
Bride's wedding band	event	708	10/93	76r
Clergy	event	224	10/93	76r
Engagement ring	event	2756	10/93	76r
Flowers	event	863	10/93	76r
Formal wear for groom	event	106	10/93	76r
Groom's attendants' formal wear	event	530	10/93	76r
Groom's wedding band	event	402	10/93	76r
Music	event	600	10/93	76r
Photography	event	1088	10/93	76r
Shoes for bride	event	50	10/93	76r
Videography	event	483	10/93	76r
Wedding invitations and announcements	event	342	10/93	76r
Wedding reception	event	7000	10/93	76r

Beaumont-Port Arthur, TX

Item	Per	Value	Date	Ref.
Composite, ACCRA index		93.20	12/94	2c
Alcoholic Beverages				
Beer, Miller Lite, Bud, 12-oz., ex deposit	6	3.83	12/94	2c
J & B Scotch	750-ml.	15.49	12/94	2c
Wine, Gallo Chablis blanc	1.5-lit	4.44	12/94	2c

Beaumont-Port Arthur, TX - continued

Item	Per	Value	Date	Ref.
Appliances				
Appliances (major), expenditures	year	153	91	81r
Average annual exp.				
Food, health care, personal goods, services	year	27020	91	81r
Charity				
Cash contributions, expenditures	year	839	91	81r
Clothing				
Apparel, men and boys, total expenditures	year	380	91	81r
Apparel, women and girls, total expenditures	year	660	91	81r
Footwear, expenditures	year	193	91	81r
Jeans, man's denim		27.66	12/94	2c
Shirt, man's dress shirt		31.33	12/94	2c
Undervest, boy's size 10-14, cotton	3	4.49	12/94	2c
Communications				
Long-distance telephone rate, day, addl. min., 1-10 mi.	min.	0.08	12/93	9s
Long-distance telephone rate, day, initial min., 1-10 mi.	min.	0.10	12/93	9s
Newspaper subscription, dly. and Sun. delivery	month	8.50	12/94	2c
Phone line, single, business, field visit	inst	71.90	12/93	9s
Phone line, single, business, no field visit	inst	57.30	12/93	9s
Phone line, single, residence, field visit	inst	52.95	12/93	9s
Phone line, single, residence, no field visit	inst	38.35	12/93	9s
Telephone bill, family of four	month	16.36	12/94	2c
Telephone service, expenditures	year	616	91	81r
Telephone, residential, flat rate	mo.	9.10	12/93	8c
Education				
Board, 4-year private college/university	year	2084	8/94	80s
Board, 4-year public college/university	year	1675	8/94	80s
Education, total expenditures	year	319	91	81r
Room, 4-year private college/university	year	1840	8/94	80s
Room, 4-year public college/university	year	1756	8/94	80s
Total cost, 4-year private college/university	year	11876	8/94	80s
Total cost, 4-year public college/university	year	4935	8/94	80s
Tuition, 2-year public college/university, in-state	year	625	8/94	80s
Tuition, 4-year private college/university, in-state	year	7952	8/94	80s
Tuition, 4-year public college/university, in-state	year	1503	8/94	80s
Energy and Fuels				
Energy, combined forms, 1800 sq. ft.	mo.	106.35	12/94	2c
Energy, exc. electricity, 1800 sq. ft.	mo.	32.10	12/94	2c
Fuel oil and other fuels, expenditures	year	56	91	81r
Gas, natural, expenditures	year	150	91	81r
Gas, reg unlead, taxes inc., cash, self-service	gal	1.12	12/94	2c
Gasoline and motor oil purchased	year	1152	91	81r
Gasoline, unleaded midgrade	gallon	1.21	4/93	82r
Gasoline, unleaded premium	gallon	1.30	4/93	82r
Gasoline, unleaded regular	gallon	1.10	4/93	82r
Entertainment				
Bowling, evening rate	game	2.45	12/94	2c
Concert ticket, Pearl Jam group	perf	20.00	94	50r
Entertainment, total expenditures	year	1266	91	81r
Fees and admissions, expenditures	year	306	91	81r
Monopoly game, Parker Brothers', No. 9	game	10.49	12/94	2c
Movie	adm	5.75	12/94	2c
Pets, toys, playground equipment, expenditures	year	271	91	81r
Reading, expenditures	year	131	91	81r
Televisions, radios, and sound equipment, expenditures	year	439	91	81r
Tennis balls, yellow, Wilson or Penn, 3	can	2.79	12/94	2c
Funerals				
Burial, immediate, container provided by funeral home		1574.60	1/95	54r
Cards, acknowledgment		22.24	1/95	54r

Values are in dollars or fractions of dollars. In the column headed *Ref*, references are shown to sources. Each reference is followed by a letter. These refer to the geographical level for which data were reported: s = State, r = Region, and c = City or metro. The abbreviation *ex* is used to mean *except* or *excluding*; *exp* stands for *expenditures*. For other abbreviations and further explanations, please see the Introduction.

Beaumont-Port Arthur, TX - continued

Item	Per	Value	Date	Ref.
Funerals				
Casket, minimum alternative		239.41	1/95	54r
Cosmetology, hair care, etc.		91.04	1/95	54r
Cremation, direct, container provided by funeral home		1085.15	1/95	54r
Embalming		281.30	1/95	54r
Funeral, funeral home		323.04	1/95	54r
Funeral, other facility		327.58	1/95	54r
Graveside service		355.19	1/95	54r
Hearse, local		141.89	1/95	54r
Limousine, local		99.40	1/95	54r
Memorial service		284.67	1/95	54r
Service charge, professional, nondeclinable		904.06	1/95	54r
Visitation and viewing		187.04	1/95	54r
Groceries				
Groceries, ACCRA Index		93.80	12/94	2c
Apples, Red Delicious	lb.	0.73	12/94	82r
Baby food, strained vegetables, lowest price	4-4.5 oz.	0.26	12/94	2c
Bacon, sliced	lb.	1.67	12/94	82r
Bananas	lb.	0.37	12/94	2c
Bananas	lb.	0.42	12/94	82r
Beef or hamburger, ground	lb.	1.20	12/94	2c
Beef purchases	year	213	91	81r
Beverage purchases, alcoholic	year	249	91	81r
Beverage purchases, nonalcoholic	year	207	91	81r
Bologna, all beef or mixed	lb.	2.27	12/94	82r
Bread, white	24-oz.	0.63	12/94	2c
Bread, white, pan	lb.	0.68	12/94	82r
Cabbage	lb.	0.42	12/94	82r
Carrots, short trimmed and topped	lb.	0.53	12/94	82r
Cereals and bakery products purchases	year	345	91	81r
Cereals and cereals products purchases	year	127	91	81r
Cheddar cheese, natural	lb.	3.58	12/94	82r
Cheese, Kraft grated Parmesan	8-oz.	3.56	12/94	2c
Chicken breast, bone-in	lb.	1.71	12/94	82r
Chicken, fresh, whole	lb.	0.78	12/94	82r
Chicken, whole fryer	lb.	0.61	12/94	2c
Chuck roast, USDA choice, boneless	lb.	2.26	12/94	82r
Cigarettes, Winston, Kings	carton	17.82	12/94	2c
Coffee, vacuum-packed	13 oz.	3.26	12/94	2c
Corn Flakes, Kellogg's or Post Toasties	18 oz.	2.47	12/94	2c
Corn, frozen, whole kernel, lowest price	10 oz.	0.65	12/94	2c
Crackers, soda, salted	lb.	1.27	12/94	82r
Cucumbers	lb.	0.65	12/94	82r
Dairy products (other) purchases	year	141	91	81r
Eggs, Grade A large	dozen	0.78	12/94	2c
Eggs, Grade A large	dozen	0.87	12/94	82r
Fish and seafood purchases	year	72	91	81r
Flour, white, all purpose	lb.	0.23	12/94	82r
Food purchases, food eaten at home	year	2381	91	81r
Foods purchased away from home, not prepared by consumer	year	1696	91	81r
Frankfurters, all meat or all beef	lb.	1.74	12/94	82r
Fruits and vegetables purchases	year	380	91	81r
Grapefruit	lb.	0.45	12/94	82r
Grapes, Thompson seedless	lb.	2.30	12/94	82r
Ground beef, 100% beef	lb.	1.37	12/94	82r
Ground chuck, 100% beef	lb.	1.97	12/94	82r
Ham, boneless, exc. canned	lb.	2.54	12/94	82r
Ice cream, prepackaged, bulk, regular	1/2 gal.	2.47	12/94	82r
Lemons	lb.	1.02	12/94	82r
Lettuce, iceberg	lb.	0.96	12/94	82r
Lettuce, iceberg	head	0.82	12/94	2c
Margarine, Blue Bonnet or Parkay cubes	lb.	0.61	12/94	2c
Margarine, stick	lb.	0.77	12/94	82r
Meats, poultry, fish, and eggs purchases	year	655	91	81r
Milk and cream (fresh) purchases	year	130	91	81r
Milk, whole	1/2 gal.	1.39	12/94	2c
Orange juice, frozen concentrate 12-oz. can	16 oz.	1.36	12/94	82r
Orange juice, Minute Maid frozen	12-oz.	1.12	12/94	2c

Beaumont-Port Arthur, TX - continued

Item	Per	Value	Date	Ref.
Groceries - continued				
Oranges, Navel	lb.	0.54	12/94	82r
Peaches, halves or slices, Hunt's, Del Monte, or Libby's	29-oz.	1.38	12/94	2c
Pears, Anjou	lb.	0.81	12/94	82r
Peas, sweet, Del Monte or Green Giant	15-17 oz.	0.50	12/94	2c
Pork chops, center cut, bone-in	lb.	3.07	12/94	82r
Pork purchases	year	142	91	81r
Potato chips	16-oz.	3.15	12/94	82r
Potatoes, frozen, French fried	lb.	0.82	12/94	82r
Potatoes, white	lb.	0.34	12/94	82r
Potatoes, white or red	10-lb. sack	2.32	12/94	2c
Rice, white, long grain, uncooked	lb.	0.48	12/94	82r
Round roast, USDA choice, boneless	lb.	2.91	12/94	82r
Sausage, fresh	lb.	1.82	12/94	82r
Sausage, Jimmy Dean, 100% pork	lb.	2.99	12/94	2c
Shortening, vegetable oil blends	lb.	0.75	12/94	82r
Shortening, vegetable, Crisco	3-lb.	2.38	12/94	2c
Soft drink, Coca Cola, ex deposit	2 lit	1.22	12/94	2c
Spaghetti and macaroni	lb.	0.87	12/94	82r
Steak, rib eye, USDA choice, boneless	lb.	6.85	12/94	82r
Steak, round, graded & ungraded, exc. USDA prime & choice	lb.	2.96	12/94	82r
Steak, round, USDA choice, boneless	lb.	3.17	12/94	82r
Steak, sirloin, USDA choice, boneless	lb.	4.12	12/94	82r
Steak, t-bone	lb.	3.68	12/94	2c
Steak, T-bone, USDA choice, bone-in	lb.	5.63	12/94	82r
Sugar and other sweets, eaten at home, expenditures	year	93	91	81r
Sugar, cane or beet	4 lbs.	1.41	12/94	2c
Sugar, white, all sizes	lb.	0.39	12/94	82r
Tobacco products and smoking supplies, total expenditures	year	286	91	81r
Tomatoes, field grown	lb.	1.36	12/94	82r
Tomatoes, Hunt's or Del Monte	14.5 oz.	0.71	12/94	2c
Tuna, chunk, light	lb.	1.94	12/94	82r
Tuna, chunk, light, oil-packed	6.125-6.5 oz.	0.65	12/94	2c
Turkey, frozen, whole	lb.	0.96	12/94	82r
Yogurt, natural, fruit flavored	8 oz.	0.58	12/94	82r
Goods and Services				
Miscellaneous goods and services, ACCRA Index		100.20	12/94	2c
Health Care				
Health care, ACCRA Index		87.00	12/94	2c
Adenosine, emergency room	treat	100.00	95	23r
Antibiotic ointment, Polysporin	1.5 oz.	4.53	12/94	2c
Bladder tap, superpubic, infant, emergency room	treat	119.00	95	23r
Blood analysis, emergency room	treat	25.00	95	23r
Blood tests, abdominal pain, emergency room	treat	25.00	95	23r
Burn dressing, emergency room	treat	266.00	95	23r
Cardiology interpretation, emergency room	treat	26.00	95	23r
Chest X-ray, emergency room	treat	78.00	95	23r
Childbirth, Cesarean delivery, hospital charge	birth	5462.00	12/91	69r
Childbirth, Cesarean delivery, physician charge	birth	2228.00	12/91	69r
Childbirth, normal delivery, hospital charge	birth	2943.00	12/91	69r
Childbirth, normal delivery, physician charge	birth	1619.00	12/91	69r
Defibrillation pads, emergency room	treat	6.00	95	23r
Dentist's fee, adult teeth cleaning and periodic oral exam	visit	43.33	12/94	2c
Doctor's fee, routine exam, established patient	visit	39.00	12/94	2c
Drugs, expenditures	year	297	91	81r
Gastric tube insertion, nasal, emergency room	treat	25.00	95	23r

Values are in dollars or fractions of dollars. In the column headed *Ref*, references are shown to sources. Each reference is followed by a letter. These refer to the geographical level for which data were reported: s=State, r=Region, and c=City or metro. The abbreviation *ex* is used to mean *except* or *excluding*; *exp* stands for *expenditures*. For other abbreviations and further explanations, please see the Introduction.

Beaumont-Port Arthur, TX - continued

Item	Per	Value	Date	Ref.
Health Care				
Health care, total expenditures	year	1600	91	81r
Health insurance expenditures	year	637	91	81r
Heart monitor, emergency room	treat	40.00	95	23r
Hospital care, semiprivate room	day	248.00	12/94	2c
Insurance premium, family medical care	month	389.25	1/95	41s
Intravenous fluids, emergency room	treat	130.00	95	23r
Intravenous fluids, emergency room	liter	26.00	95	23r
Intravenous line, central, emergency room	treat	342.00	95	23r
Liver function tests, abdominal pain, emergency room	treat	26.00	95	23r
Medical care charges, total, emergency room, third-degree burns	treat	2101.00	95	23r
Medical care charges, total, emergency, infant with fever	treat	628.00	95	23r
Medical services expenditures	year	573	91	81r
Medical supplies expenditures	year	93	91	81r
Morphine, emergency room	treat	34.00	95	23r
Nursing care and facilities charges, emergency room	treat	252.00	95	23r
Nursing care and facilities charges, emergency, infant with fever	treat	252.00	95	23r
Nursing care and facilities charges, emergency, third-degree burns	treat	861.00	95	23r
Physician's charges, emergency, infant with fever	treat	212.00	95	23r
Physician's charges, emergency, third-degree burns	treat	372.00	95	23r
Physician's fee, emergency room	treat	372.00	95	23r
Physician's fee, general practitioner	visit	51.20	12/93	60r
Surgery, open-heart	proc	42374.00	1/93	14r
Ultrasound, abdominal, emergency room	treat	276.00	95	23r
Urinalysis, emergency room	treat	20.00	95	23r
Urinalysis, infant, emergency room	treat	20.00	95	23r
X-rays, emergency room	treat	78.00	95	23r
Household Goods				
Appl. repair, service call, wash mach	min. lab. chg.	43.33	12/94	2c
Floor coverings, expenditures	year	48	91	81r
Furniture, expenditures	year	280	91	81r
Household equipment, misc. expenditures	year	342	91	81r
Household expenditures, miscellaneous	year	256	91	81r
Household furnishings and equipment, expenditures	year	988	91	81r
Household operations expenditures	year	468	91	81r
Household textiles, expenditures	year	95	91	81r
Housekeeping supplies, expenditures	year	380	91	81r
Laundry and cleaning supplies, expenditures	year	109	91	81r
Laundry detergent, Tide Ultra, Bold, or Cheer	42 oz.	3.59	12/94	2c
Postage and stationery, expenditures	year	105	91	81r
Tissues, facial, Kleenex brand	175	0.99	12/94	2c
Housing				
Housing, ACCRA Index		80.90	12/94	2c
Add garage/carport		6,980	3/95	74r
Add room(s)		11,403	3/95	74r
Apartment condominium or co-op, median	unit	68600	12/94	62r
Dwellings (owned), expenditures	year	2428	91	81r
Enclose porch/patio/breezeway		4,572	3/95	74r
Finish room in basement/attic		3,794	3/95	74r
Home, existing, single-family, median	unit	120200	12/94	62r
Home, existing, single-family, median	unit	61.80	12/94	62c
House payment, principal and interest, 25% down payment	mo.	592	12/94	2c
House, 1800 sq ft, 8000 sq ft lot, new, urban, utilities	total	93425	12/94	2c
Maintenance, repairs, insurance, and other housing expenditures	year	531	91	81r
Mortgage interest and charges expenditures	year	1506	91	81r

Beaumont-Port Arthur, TX - continued

Item	Per	Value	Date	Ref.
Housing - continued				
Mtge. rate, incl. points and orig. fee, 30-year conv. fixed or ARM	mo.	9.55	12/94	2c
Princ. & int., mortgage, median-price exist. sing.-family home	mo.	540	12/94	62r
Property taxes expenditures	year	391	91	81r
Redesign, restructure more than half of home's interior		17,641	3/95	74r
Rent, apartment, 2 br., 1 1/2-2 baths, unfurnished, 950 sq ft, water	mo.	508	12/94	2c
Rental units expenditures	year	1264	91	81r
Insurance and Pensions				
Auto insurance, private passenger	year	785.78	12/94	71s
Insurance and pensions, personal, expenditures	year	2395	91	81r
Insurance, life and other personal, expenditures	year	368	91	81r
Pensions and Social Security, expenditures	year	2027	91	81r
Personal Goods				
Shampoo, Alberto VO5	15-oz.	1.12	12/94	2c
Toothpaste, Crest or Colgate	6-7 oz.	2.12	12/94	2c
Personal Services				
Dry cleaning, man's 2-pc. suit		5.47	12/94	2c
Haircut, man's barbershop, no styling		8.20	12/94	2c
Haircut, woman's shampoo, trim, blow-dry		24.00	12/94	2c
Personal services expenditures	year	212	91	81r
Restaurant Food				
Chicken, fried, thigh and drumstick		1.87	12/94	2c
Dining expenditures, family	week	33.83	94	73r
Hamburger with cheese	1/4 lb.	1.89	12/94	2c
Pizza, Pizza Hut or Pizza Inn	12-13 in.	7.99	12/94	2c
Taxes				
Tax, cigarettes	year	584.00	10/93	43s
Taxes, Federal income, expenditures	year	2275	91	81r
Taxes, personal, expenditures	year	2715	91	81r
Taxes, State and local income, expenditures	year	365	91	81r
Transportation				
Transportation, ACCRA Index		108.70	12/94	2c
Cars and trucks purchased, new	year	1306	91	81r
Cars and trucks purchased, used	year	942	91	81r
Driver's learning permit fee	perm	5.00	1/94	84s
Driver's license fee	orig	16.00	1/94	84s
Driver's license fee, duplicate	lic	10.00	1/94	84s
Driver's license reinstatement fee, min.	susp	50.00	1/94	85s
Driver's license renewal fee	renew	16.00	1/94	84s
Identification card, nondriver	card	10.00	1/94	83s
Motorcycle learning permit fee	perm	5.00	1/94	84s
Motorcycle license fee	orig	16.00	1/94	84s
Motorcycle license fee, duplicate	lic	10.00	1/94	84s
Motorcycle license renewal fee	renew	21.00	1/94	84s
Public transportation expenditures	year	249	91	81r
Tire balance, computer or spin bal., front	wheel	8.17	12/94	2c
Transportation expenditures, total	year	5307	91	81r
Vehicle finance charges	year	346	91	81r
Vehicle insurance expenditures	year	544	91	81r
Vehicle maintenance and repairs expenditures	year	600	91	81r
Vehicle purchases	year	2275	91	81r
Vehicle rental, leases, licenses, etc. expenditures	year	141	91	81r
Vehicles purchased, other than cars and trucks	year	27	91	81r
Utilities				
Utilities, ACCRA Index		93.30	12/94	2c
Electricity expenditures	year	950	91	81r
Electricity, (part.), other, 1800 sq. ft., new home	mo.	74.25	12/94	2c
Electricity, summer, 250 KWh	month	26.41	8/93	64c

Values are in dollars or fractions of dollars. In the column headed *Ref*, references are shown to sources. Each reference is followed by a letter. These refer to the geographical level for which data were reported: s=State, r=Region, and c=City or metro. The abbreviation *ex* is used to mean *except* or *excluding*; *exp* stands for expenditures. For other abbreviations and further explanations, please see the Introduction.

Beaumont-Port Arthur, TX - continued

Item	Per	Value	Date	Ref.
Utilities				
Electricity, summer, 500 KWh	month	46.58	8/93	64c
Electricity, summer, 750 KWh	month	66.76	8/93	64c
Electricity, summer, 1000 KWh	month	86.93	8/93	64c
Utilities, fuels, and public services, total expenditures	year	2000	91	81r
Water and other public services, expenditures	year	227	91	81r
Weddings				
Bridal attendants' gowns	event	750	10/93	76r
Bridal gown	event	852	10/93	76r
Bridal headpiece and veil	event	167	10/93	76r
Bride's wedding band	event	708	10/93	76r
Clergy	event	224	10/93	76r
Engagement ring	event	2756	10/93	76r
Flowers	event	863	10/93	76r
Formal wear for groom	event	106	10/93	76r
Groom's attendants' formal wear	event	530	10/93	76r
Groom's wedding band	event	402	10/93	76r
Music	event	600	10/93	76r
Photography	event	1088	10/93	76r
Shoes for bride	event	50	10/93	76r
Videography	event	483	10/93	76r
Wedding invitations and announcements	event	342	10/93	76r
Wedding reception	event	7000	10/93	76r

Bellingham, WA

Item	Per	Value	Date	Ref.
Composite, ACCRA index		104.20	12/94	2c
Alcoholic Beverages				
Beer, Miller Lite, Bud, 12-oz., ex deposit	6	3.63	12/94	2c
J & B Scotch	750-ml.	18.95	12/94	2c
Wine, Gallo Chablis blanc	1.5-lit	4.14	12/94	2c
Appliances				
Appliances (major), expenditures	year	160	91	81r
Average annual exp.				
Food, health care, personal goods, services	year	32461	91	81r
Charity				
Cash contributions, expenditures	year	975	91	81r
Clothing				
Apparel, men and boys, total expenditures	year	467	91	81r
Apparel, women and girls, total expenditures	year	737	91	81r
Footwear, expenditures	year	270	91	81r
Jeans, man's denim		32.19	12/94	2c
Shirt, man's dress shirt		34.83	12/94	2c
Undervest, boy's size 10-14, cotton	3	4.95	12/94	2c
Communications				
Long-distance telephone rate, day, addl. min., 1-10 mi.	min.	0.01	12/93	9s
Long-distance telephone rate, day, initial min., 1-10 mi.	min.	0.15	12/93	9s
Newspaper subscription, dly. and Sun. delivery	month	11.25	12/94	2c
Phone line, single, business, field visit	inst	48.00	12/93	9s
Phone line, single, business, no field visit	inst	48.00	12/93	9s
Phone line, single, residence, field visit	inst	31.00	12/93	9s
Phone line, single, residence, no field visit	inst	31.00	12/93	9s
Telephone bill, family of four	month	14.96	12/94	2c
Telephone service, expenditures	year	611	91	81r
Telephone, residential, flat rate	mo.	9.75	12/93	8c
Education				
Board, 4-year private college/university	year	1928	8/94	80s
Board, 4-year public college/university	year	2194	8/94	80s
Education, total expenditures	year	375	91	81r
Room, 4-year private college/university	year	2455	8/94	80s
Room, 4-year public college/university	year	1952	8/94	80s
Total cost, 4-year private college/university	year	16332	8/94	80s

Bellingham, WA - continued

Item	Per	Value	Date	Ref.
Education - continued				
Total cost, 4-year public college/university	year	6483	8/94	80s
Tuition, 2-year public college/university, in-state	year	1141	8/94	80s
Tuition, 4-year private college/university, in-state	year	11949	8/94	80s
Tuition, 4-year public college/university, in-state	year	2337	8/94	80s
Energy and Fuels				
Energy, combined forms, 1800 sq. ft.	mo.	63.68	12/94	2c
Energy, exc. electricity, 1800 sq. ft.	mo.	32.60	12/94	2c
Fuel oil and other fuels, expenditures	year	33	91	81r
Gas, cooking, winter, 10 therms	month	6.60	2/94	65c
Gas, cooking, winter, 30 therms	month	16.63	2/94	65c
Gas, cooking, winter, 50 therms	month	26.65	2/94	65c
Gas, heating, winter, 100 therms	month	49.12	2/94	65c
Gas, heating, winter, average use	month	58.47	2/94	65c
Gas, natural, expenditures	year	212	91	81r
Gas, reg unlead, taxes inc., cash, self-service	gal	1.30	12/94	2c
Gasoline and motor oil purchased	year	1115	91	81r
Gasoline, unleaded midgrade	gallon	1.36	4/93	82r
Gasoline, unleaded premium	gallon	1.43	4/93	82r
Gasoline, unleaded regular	gallon	1.23	4/93	82r
Entertainment				
Bowling, evening rate	game	2.44	12/94	2c
Concert ticket, Pearl Jam group	perf	20.00	94	50r
Entertainment, total expenditures	year	1853	91	81r
Fees and admissions, expenditures	year	482	91	81r
Monopoly game, Parker Brothers', No. 9	game	10.99	12/94	2c
Movie	adm	5.83	12/94	2c
Pets, toys, playground equipment, expenditures	year	299	91	81r
Reading, expenditures	year	164	91	81r
Televisions, radios, and sound equipment, expenditures	year	528	91	81r
Tennis balls, yellow, Wilson or Penn, 3	can	2.38	12/94	2c
Funerals				
Burial, immediate, container provided by funeral home		1382.70	1/95	54r
Cards, acknowledgment		21.87	1/95	54r
Casket, minimum alternative		128.54	1/95	54r
Cosmetology, hair care, etc.		119.69	1/95	54r
Cremation, direct, container provided by funeral home		1030.62	1/95	54r
Embalming		255.42	1/95	54r
Funeral, funeral home		437.38	1/95	54r
Funeral, other facility		444.46	1/95	54r
Graveside service		338.46	1/95	54r
Hearse, local		147.50	1/95	54r
Limousine, local		130.33	1/95	54r
Memorial service		553.16	1/95	54r
Service charge, professional, nondeclinable		859.15	1/95	54r
Visitation and viewing		93.23	1/95	54r
Groceries				
Groceries, ACCRA Index		100.40	12/94	2c
Apples, Red Delicious	lb.	0.72	12/94	82r
Baby food, strained vegetables, lowest price	4-4.5 oz.	0.22	12/94	2c
Bacon, sliced	lb.	1.73	12/94	82r
Bananas	lb.	0.47	12/94	2c
Bananas	lb.	0.52	12/94	82r
Beef or hamburger, ground	lb.	1.59	12/94	2c
Beef purchases	year	241	91	81r
Beverage purchases, alcoholic	year	328	91	81r
Beverage purchases, nonalcoholic	year	234	91	81r
Bologna, all beef or mixed	lb.	2.33	12/94	82r
Bread, white	24-oz.	0.54	12/94	2c
Bread, white, pan	lb.	0.81	12/94	82r
Carrots, short trimmed and topped	lb.	0.43	12/94	82r
Cereals and bakery products purchases	year	392	91	81r

Values are in dollars or fractions of dollars. In the column headed *Ref*, references are shown to sources. Each reference is followed by a letter. These refer to the geographical level for which data were reported: s=State, r=Region, and c=City or metro. The abbreviation *ex* is used to mean *except* or *excluding*; *exp* stands for expenditures. For other abbreviations and further explanations, please see the Introduction.

Bellingham, WA - continued

Item	Per	Value	Date	Ref.
Groceries				
Cereals and cereals products purchases	year	139	91	81r
Cheese, Kraft grated Parmesan	8-oz.	3.39	12/94	2c
Chicken breast, bone-in	lb.	2.04	12/94	82r
Chicken, fresh, whole	lb.	0.95	12/94	82r
Chicken, whole fryer	lb.	1.01	12/94	2c
Cigarettes, Winston, Kings	carton	20.85	12/94	2c
Coffee, 100%, ground roast, all sizes	lb.	4.48	12/94	82r
Coffee, vacuum-packed	13 oz.	3.93	12/94	2c
Corn Flakes, Kellogg's or Post Toasties	18 oz.	2.71	12/94	2c
Corn, frozen, whole kernel, lowest price	10 oz.	0.73	12/94	2c
Dairy products (other) purchases	year	182	91	81r
Eggs, Grade A large	dozen	0.87	12/94	2c
Fish and seafood purchases	year	94	91	81r
Flour, white, all purpose	lb.	0.21	12/94	82r
Food purchases, food eaten at home	year	2749	91	81r
Foods purchased away from home, not prepared by consumer	year	1909	91	81r
Fruits and vegetables purchases	year	459	91	81r
Grapefruit	lb.	0.56	12/94	82r
Ground beef, 100% beef	lb.	1.31	12/94	82r
Ham, boneless, exc. canned	lb.	2.46	12/94	82r
Ice cream, prepackaged, bulk, regular	1/2 gal.	2.57	12/94	82r
Lemons	lb.	1.00	12/94	82r
Lettuce, iceberg	lb.	0.93	12/94	82r
Lettuce, iceberg	head	0.71	12/94	2c
Margarine, Blue Bonnet or Parkay cubes	lb.	0.55	12/94	2c
Meats, poultry, fish, and eggs purchases	year	700	91	81r
Milk and cream (fresh) purchases	year	155	91	81r
Milk, whole	1/2 gal.	1.51	12/94	2c
Orange juice, frozen concentrate 12-oz. can	16 oz.	1.52	12/94	82r
Orange juice, Minute Maid frozen	12-oz.	0.95	12/94	2c
Oranges, Navel	lb.	0.56	12/94	82r
Peaches, halves or slices, Hunt's, Del Monte, or Libby's	29-oz.	1.52	12/94	2c
Peas, sweet, Del Monte or Green Giant	15-17 oz.	0.61	12/94	2c
Pork chops, center cut, bone-in	lb.	3.30	12/94	82r
Pork purchases	year	122	91	81r
Potato chips	16-oz.	3.03	12/94	82r
Potatoes, frozen, French fried	lb.	0.77	12/94	82r
Potatoes, white	lb.	0.35	12/94	82r
Potatoes, white or red	10-lb. sack	1.46	12/94	2c
Rice, white, long grain, uncooked	lb.	0.54	12/94	82r
Round roast, USDA choice, boneless	lb.	2.92	12/94	82r
Sausage, Jimmy Dean, 100% pork	lb.	3.02	12/94	2c
Shortening, vegetable oil blends	lb.	0.80	12/94	82r
Shortening, vegetable, Crisco	3-lb.	1.39	12/94	2c
Soft drink, Coca Cola, ex deposit	2 lit	1.24	12/94	2c
Spaghetti and macaroni	lb.	1.02	12/94	82r
Steak, round, graded & ungraded, exc. USDA prime & choice	lb.	3.13	12/94	82r
Steak, sirloin, USDA choice, boneless	lb.	4.07	12/94	82r
Steak, t-bone	lb.	5.30	12/94	2c
Sugar and other sweets, eaten at home, expenditures	year	105	91	81r
Sugar, cane or beet	4 lbs.	1.13	12/94	2c
Sugar, white, all sizes	lb.	0.38	12/94	82r
Tobacco products and smoking supplies, total expenditures	year	221	91	81r
Tomatoes, field grown	lb.	1.45	12/94	82r
Tomatoes, Hunt's or Del Monte	14.5 oz.	0.65	12/94	2c
Tuna, chunk, light	lb.	2.18	12/94	82r
Tuna, chunk, light, oil-packed	6.125-6.5 oz.	0.87	12/94	2c
Goods and Services				
Miscellaneous goods and services, ACCRA Index		109.10	12/94	2c

Bellingham, WA - continued

Item	Per	Value	Date	Ref.
Health Care				
Health care, ACCRA Index		126.70	12/94	2c
Antibiotic ointment, Polysporin	1.5 oz.	4.06	12/94	2c
Childbirth, Cesarean delivery, hospital charge	birth	6059.00	12/91	69r
Childbirth, Cesarean delivery, physician charge	birth	2248.00	12/91	69r
Childbirth, normal delivery, hospital charge	birth	3006.00	12/91	69r
Childbirth, normal delivery, physician charge	birth	1634.00	12/91	69r
Dentist's fee, adult teeth cleaning and periodic oral exam	visit	75.50	12/94	2c
Doctor's fee, routine exam, established patient	visit	51.48	12/94	2c
Drugs, expenditures	year	230	91	81r
Health care, total expenditures	year	1544	91	81r
Health insurance expenditures	year	558	91	81r
Hospital care, semiprivate room	day	422.00	12/94	2c
Insurance premium, family medical care	month	382.32	1/95	41s
Medical services expenditures	year	676	91	81r
Medical supplies expenditures	year	80	91	81r
Surgery, open-heart	proc	37818.00	1/93	14r
Household Goods				
Appl. repair, service call, wash mach	min. lab. chg.	38.98	12/94	2c
Floor coverings, expenditures	year	79	91	81r
Furniture, expenditures	year	352	91	81r
Household equipment, misc. expenditures	year	614	91	81r
Household expenditures, miscellaneous	year	294	91	81r
Household furnishings and equipment, expenditures	year	1416	91	81r
Household operations expenditures	year	580	91	81r
Household textiles, expenditures	year	113	91	81r
Housekeeping supplies, expenditures	year	447	91	81r
Laundry and cleaning supplies, expenditures	year	114	91	81r
Laundry detergent, Tide Ultra, Bold, or Cheer	42 oz.	4.41	12/94	2c
Postage and stationery, expenditures	year	145	91	81r
Tissues, facial, Kleenex brand	175	1.20	12/94	2c
Housing				
Housing, ACCRA Index		109.90	12/94	2c
Add garage/carport		6,422	3/95	74r
Add room(s)		26,583	3/95	74r
Apartment condominium or co-op, median	unit	105300	12/94	62r
Dwellings (owned), expenditures	year	3932	91	81r
Enclose porch/patio/breezeway		5,382	3/95	74r
Finish room in basement/attic		3,911	3/95	74r
Home, existing, single-family, median	unit	178600	12/94	62r
House payment, principal and interest, 25% down payment	mo.	683	12/94	2c
House, 1800 sq ft, 8000 sq ft lot, new, urban, utilities	total	113217	12/94	2c
Maintenance, repairs, insurance, and other housing expenditures	year	591	91	81r
Mortgage interest and charges expenditures	year	2747	91	81r
Mtge. rate, incl. points and orig. fee, 30-year conv. fixed or ARM	mo.	8.99	12/94	2c
Princ. & int., mortgage, median-price exist. sing.-family home	mo.	845	12/94	62r
Property taxes expenditures	year	594	91	81r
Redesign, restructure more than half of home's interior		5,467	3/95	74r
Rent, apartment, 2 br., 1 1/2-2 baths, unfurnished, 950 sq ft, water	mo.	486	12/94	2c
Rental units expenditures	year	2077	91	81r
Insurance and Pensions				
Auto insurance, private passenger	year	711.57	12/94	71s
Insurance and pensions, personal, expenditures	year	3042	91	81r
Insurance, life and other personal, expenditures	year	298	91	81r

Values are in dollars or fractions of dollars. In the column headed *Ref*, references are shown to sources. Each reference is followed by a letter. These refer to the geographical level for which data were reported: s=State, r=Region, and c=City or metro. The abbreviation *ex* is used to mean *except* or *excluding*; *exp* stands for expenditures. For other abbreviations and further explanations, please see the Introduction.

Bellingham, WA - continued

Item	Per	Value	Date	Ref.
Insurance and Pensions				
Pensions and Social Security, expenditures	year	2744	91	81r
Legal Assistance				
Legal work, law firm associate	hour	91		10r
Legal work, law firm partner	hour	151		10r
Personal Goods				
Shampoo, Alberto VO5	15-oz.	1.26	12/94	2c
Toothpaste, Crest or Colgate	6-7 oz.	2.25	12/94	2c
Personal Services				
Dry cleaning, man's 2-pc. suit		7.45	12/94	2c
Haircut, man's barbershop, no styling		9.89	12/94	2c
Haircut, woman's shampoo, trim, blow-dry		21.90	12/94	2c
Personal services expenditures	year	286	91	81r
Restaurant Food				
Chicken, fried, thigh and drumstick		2.59	12/94	2c
Dining expenditures, family	week	32.25	94	73r
Hamburger with cheese	1/4 lb.	1.99	12/94	2c
Pizza, Pizza Hut or Pizza Inn	12-13 in.	8.90	12/94	2c
Taxes				
Taxes, Federal income, expenditures	year	2946	91	81r
Taxes, personal, expenditures	year	3791	91	81r
Taxes, State and local income, expenditures	year	791	91	81r
Transportation				
Transportation, ACCRA Index		99.90	12/94	2c
Bus fare, one-way	trip	0.35	12/95	1c
Bus fare, up to 10 miles	one-way	0.25	12/94	2c
Cars and trucks purchased, new	year	1231	91	81r
Cars and trucks purchased, used	year	915	91	81r
Driver's learning permit fee	perm	4.00	1/94	84s
Driver's license fee	orig	21.00	1/94	84s
Driver's license fee, duplicate	lic	5.00	1/94	84s
Driver's license reinstatement fee, min.	susp	20.00-50.00	1/94	85s
Driver's license renewal fee	renew	14.00	1/94	84s
Identification card, nondriver	card	4.00	1/94	83s
Motorcycle license fee	orig	8.00	1/94	84s
Motorcycle license renewal fee	renew	7.50	1/94	84s
Public transportation expenditures	year	375	91	81r
Tire balance, computer or spin bal., front	wheel	6.74	12/94	2c
Transportation expenditures, total	year	5527	91	81r
Vehicle finance charges	year	287	91	81r
Vehicle insurance expenditures	year	624	91	81r
Vehicle maintenance and repairs expenditures	year	695	91	81r
Vehicle purchases	year	2174	91	81r
Vehicle rental, leases, licenses, etc. expenditures	year	257	91	81r
Vehicles purchased, other than cars and trucks	year	28	91	81r
Utilities				
Utilities, ACCRA Index		59.40	12/94	2c
Electricity expenditures	year	616	91	81r
Electricity, (part.), other, 1800 sq. ft., new home	mo.	31.08	12/94	2c
Utilities, fuels, and public services, total expenditures	year	1681	91	81r
Water and other public services, expenditures	year	209	91	81r
Weddings				
Bridal attendants' gowns	event	750	10/93	76r
Bridal gown	event	852	10/93	76r
Bridal headpiece and veil	event	167	10/93	76r
Bride's wedding band	event	708	10/93	76r
Clergy	event	224	10/93	76r
Engagement ring	event	2756	10/93	76r
Flowers	event	863	10/93	76r
Formal wear for groom	event	106	10/93	76r

Bellingham, WA - continued

Item	Per	Value	Date	Ref.
Weddings - continued				
Groom's attendants' formal wear	event	530	10/93	76r
Groom's wedding band	event	402	10/93	76r
Music	event	600	10/93	76r
Photography	event	1088	10/93	76r
Shoes for bride	event	50	10/93	76r
Videography	event	483	10/93	76r
Wedding invitations and announcements	event	342	10/93	76r
Wedding reception	event	7000	10/93	76r

Benton Harbor-Saint Joseph, MI

Item	Per	Value	Date	Ref.
Appliances				
Appliances (major), expenditures	year	131	91	81r
Average annual exp.				
Food, health care, personal goods, services	year	25935	91	81r
Charity				
Cash contributions, expenditures	year	745	91	81r
Clothing				
Apparel, men and boys, total expenditures	year	332	91	81r
Apparel, women and girls, total expenditures	year	578	91	81r
Footwear, expenditures	year	164	91	81r
Communications				
Long-distance telephone rate, day, addl. min., 1-10 mi.	min.	0.08	12/93	9s
Long-distance telephone rate, day, initial min., 1-10 mi.	min.	0.14	12/93	9s
Phone line, single, business, field visit	inst	42.00	12/93	9s
Phone line, single, business, no field visit	inst	42.00	12/93	9s
Phone line, single, residence, field visit	inst	42.00	12/93	9s
Phone line, single, residence, no field visit	inst	42.00	12/93	9s
Telephone service, expenditures	year	547	91	81r
Education				
Board, 4-year private college/university	year	2064	8/94	80s
Board, 4-year public college/university	year	2304	8/94	80s
Education, total expenditures	year	394	91	81r
Room, 4-year private college/university	year	1814	8/94	80s
Room, 4-year public college/university	year	1856	8/94	80s
Total cost, 4-year private college/university	year	12178	8/94	80s
Total cost, 4-year public college/university	year	7642	8/94	80s
Tuition, 2-year public college/university, in-state	year	1358	8/94	80s
Tuition, 4-year private college/university, in-state	year	8300	8/94	80s
Tuition, 4-year public college/university, in-state	year	3481	8/94	80s
Energy and Fuels				
Fuel oil and other fuels, expenditures	year	83	91	81r
Gas, natural, expenditures	year	373	91	81r
Gasoline and motor oil purchased	year	1000	91	81r
Gasoline, unleaded midgrade	gallon	1.15	4/93	82r
Gasoline, unleaded premium	gallon	1.23	4/93	82r
Gasoline, unleaded regular	gallon	1.07	4/93	82r
Entertainment				
Entertainment, total expenditures	year	1356	91	81r
Fees and admissions, expenditures	year	347	91	81r
Pets, toys, playground equipment, expenditures	year	270	91	81r
Reading, expenditures	year	160	91	81r
Televisions, radios, and sound equipment, expenditures	year	433	91	81r
Funerals				
Burial, immediate, container provided by funeral home		1268.31	1/95	54r
Cards, acknowledgment		26.12	1/95	54r
Casket, minimum alternative		198.03	1/95	54r
Cosmetology, hair care, etc.		122.19	1/95	54r

Values are in dollars or fractions of dollars. In the column headed *Ref*, references are shown to sources. Each reference is followed by a letter. These refer to the geographical level for which data were reported: s=State, r=Region, and c=City or metro. The abbreviation *ex* is used to mean *except* or *excluding*; *exp* stands for expenditures. For other abbreviations and further explanations, please see the Introduction.

Benton Harbor-Saint Joseph, MI - continued

Item	Per	Value	Date	Ref.
Funerals				
Cremation, direct, container provided by funeral home		977.81	1/95	54r
Embalming		334.00	1/95	54r
Funeral, funeral home		321.16	1/95	54r
Funeral, other facility		317.73	1/95	54r
Graveside service		292.48	1/95	54r
Hearse, local		153.20	1/95	54r
Limousine, local		123.52	1/95	54r
Memorial service		356.30	1/95	54r
Service charge, professional, nondeclinable		968.24	1/95	54r
Visitation and viewing		332.66	1/95	54r
Groceries				
Apples, Red Delicious	lb.	0.68	12/94	82r
Bacon, sliced	lb.	1.88	12/94	82r
Bananas	lb.	0.41	12/94	82r
Beef purchases	year	197	91	81r
Beef, stew, boneless	lb.	2.52	12/94	82r
Beverage purchases, alcoholic	year	293	91	81r
Beverage purchases, nonalcoholic	year	203	91	81r
Bologna, all beef or mixed	lb.	2.12	12/94	82r
Bread, white, pan	lb.	0.76	12/94	82r
Cabbage	lb.	0.44	12/94	82r
Carrots, short trimmed and topped	lb.	0.44	12/94	82r
Cereals and bakery products purchases	year	347	91	81r
Cereals and cereals products purchases	year	119	91	81r
Cheddar cheese, natural	lb.	3.28	12/94	82r
Chicken breast, bone-in	lb.	1.61	12/94	82r
Chicken, fresh, whole	lb.	0.89	12/94	82r
Chuck roast, USDA choice, boneless	lb.	2.33	12/94	82r
Coffee, 100%, ground roast, all sizes	lb.	4.28	12/94	82r
Cookies, chocolate chip	lb.	2.72	12/94	82r
Dairy products (other) purchases	year	148	91	81r
Eggs, Grade A large	dozen	0.76	12/94	82r
Fish and seafood purchases	year	61	91	81r
Flour, white, all purpose	lb.	0.22	12/94	82r
Food purchases, food eaten at home	year	2313	91	81r
Foods purchased away from home, not prepared by consumer	year	1709	91	81r
Fruits and vegetables purchases	year	372	91	81r
Grapefruit	lb.	0.47	12/94	82r
Grapes, Thompson seedless	lb.	2.15	12/94	82r
Ground beef, 100% beef	lb.	1.37	12/94	82r
Ground chuck, 100% beef	lb.	1.81	12/94	82r
Ham, boneless, exc. canned	lb.	2.16	12/94	82r
Ice cream, prepackaged, bulk, regular	1/2 gal.	2.48	12/94	82r
Lemons	lb.	1.08	12/94	82r
Lettuce, iceberg	lb.	0.81	12/94	82r
Margarine, stick	lb.	0.81	12/94	82r
Meats, poultry, fish, and eggs purchases	year	591	91	81r
Milk and cream (fresh) purchases	year	132	91	81r
Orange juice, frozen concentrate 12-oz. can	16 oz.	1.41	12/94	82r
Oranges, Navel	lb.	0.56	12/94	82r
Peanut butter, creamy, all sizes	lb.	1.81	12/94	82r
Pork chops, center cut, bone-in	lb.	2.76	12/94	82r
Pork purchases	year	130	91	81r
Potato chips	16-oz.	2.81	12/94	82r
Potatoes, frozen, French fried	lb.	0.83	12/94	82r
Potatoes, white	lb.	0.28	12/94	82r
Round roast, USDA choice, boneless	lb.	2.90	12/94	82r
Shortening, vegetable oil blends	lb.	0.88	12/94	82r
Spaghetti and macaroni	lb.	0.78	12/94	82r
Steak, rib eye, USDA choice, boneless	lb.	6.15	12/94	82r
Steak, round, graded & ungraded, exc. USDA prime & choice	lb.	2.72	12/94	82r
Steak, round, USDA choice, boneless	lb.	3.02	12/94	82r
Steak, sirloin, USDA choice, boneless	lb.	3.85	12/94	82r
Steak, T-bone, USDA choice, bone-in	lb.	5.38	12/94	82r
Sugar and other sweets, eaten at home, expenditures	year	91	91	81r
Sugar, white, all sizes	lb.	0.36	12/94	82r

Benton Harbor-Saint Joseph, MI - continued

Item	Per	Value	Date	Ref.
Groceries - continued				
Tobacco products and smoking supplies, total expenditures	year	298	91	81r
Tomatoes, field grown	lb.	1.36	12/94	82r
Tuna, chunk, light	lb.	1.94	12/94	82r
Turkey, frozen, whole	lb.	0.96	12/94	82r
Yogurt, natural, fruit flavored	8 oz.	0.62	12/94	82r
Health Care				
Childbirth, Cesarean delivery, hospital charge	birth	5101.00	12/91	69r
Childbirth, Cesarean delivery, physician charge	birth	2234.00	12/91	69r
Childbirth, normal delivery, hospital charge	birth	2891.00	12/91	69r
Childbirth, normal delivery, physician charge	birth	1623.00	12/91	69r
Drugs, expenditures	year	248	91	81r
Health care, total expenditures	year	1336	91	81r
Health insurance expenditures	year	550	91	81r
Insurance premium, family medical care	month	369.41	1/95	41s
Medical services expenditures	year	457	91	81r
Medical supplies expenditures	year	82	91	81r
Household Goods				
Floor coverings, expenditures	year	105	91	81r
Furniture, expenditures	year	291	91	81r
Household equipment, misc. expenditures	year	341	91	81r
Household expenditures, miscellaneous	year	162	91	81r
Household furnishings and equipment, expenditures	year	1042	91	81r
Household operations expenditures	year	365	91	81r
Household textiles, expenditures	year	101	91	81r
Housekeeping supplies, expenditures	year	390	91	81r
Laundry and cleaning supplies, expenditures	year	110	91	81r
Postage and stationery, expenditures	year	115	91	81r
Housing				
Add garage/carport		8,479	3/95	74r
Add room(s)		21,347	3/95	74r
Apartment condominium or co-op, median	unit	87100	12/94	62r
Bathroom addition, average cost	add	9734.00	3/95	13r
Bathroom remodeling, average cost	remod	6414.00	3/95	13r
Bedroom, master suite addition, average cost	add	27122.00	3/95	13r
Deck addition, average cost	add	6665.00	3/95	13r
Dwellings (owned), expenditures	year	2566	91	81r
Enclose porch/patio/breezeway		4,556	3/95	74r
Exterior remodeling, average cost	remod	15395.00	3/95	13r
Family room addition, average cost	add	27658.00	3/95	13r
Finish room in basement/attic		5,074	3/95	74r
Home, existing, single-family, median	unit	106500	12/94	62r
Kitchen remodeling, major, average cost	remod	17084.00	3/95	13r
Kitchen remodeling, minor, average cost	remod	5804.00	3/95	13r
Maintenance, repairs, insurance, and other housing expenditures	year	484	91	81r
Mortgage interest and charges expenditures	year	1443	91	81r
Office, home addition, average cost	add	8121.00	3/95	13r
Princ. & int., mortgage, median-price exist. sing.-family home	mo.	515	12/94	62r
Property taxes expenditures	year	639	91	81r
Redesign, restructure more than half of home's interior		9,114	3/95	74r
Rental units expenditures	year	1200	91	81r
Sun-space addition, average cost	add	23768.00	3/95	13r
Wing addition, two-story, average cost	add	50410.00	3/95	13r
Insurance and Pensions				
Auto insurance, private passenger	year	788.26	12/94	71s
Insurance and pensions, personal, expenditures	year	2408	91	81r
Insurance, life and other personal, expenditures	year	355	91	81r
Pensions and Social Security, expenditures	year	2053	91	81r

Values are in dollars or fractions of dollars. In the column headed *Ref*, references are shown to sources. Each reference is followed by a letter. These refer to the geographical level for which data were reported: s=State, r=Region, and c=City or metro. The abbreviation *ex* is used to mean *except* or *excluding*; *exp* stands for *expenditures*. For other abbreviations and further explanations, please see the Introduction.

Benton Harbor-Saint Joseph, MI - continued

Item	Per	Value	Date	Ref.
Legal Assistance				
Legal work, law firm associate	hour	90		10r
Legal work, law firm partner	hour	139		10r
Personal Services				
Personal services expenditures	year	203	91	81r
Restaurant Food				
Dining expenditures, family	week	30.03	94	73r
Taxes				
Taxes, Federal income, expenditures	year	1756	91	81r
Taxes, personal, expenditures	year	2426	91	81r
Taxes, State and local income, expenditures	year	568	91	81r
Transportation				
Cars and trucks purchased, new	year	891	91	81r
Cars and trucks purchased, used	year	1155	91	81r
Driver's learning permit fee	perm	12.00	1/94	84s
Driver's license fee	orig	12.00	1/94	84s
Driver's license fee, duplicate	lic	6.00	1/94	84s
Driver's license reinstatement fee, min.	susp	125.00	1/94	85s
Driver's license renewal fee	renew	12.00	1/94	84s
Identification card, nondriver	card	6.00	1/94	83s
Motorcycle license fee	orig	7.50	1/94	84s
Motorcycle license renewal fee	renew	4.00	1/94	84s
Public transportation expenditures	year	209	91	81r
Transportation expenditures, total	year	4792	91	81r
Vehicle finance charges	year	300	91	81r
Vehicle insurance expenditures	year	485	91	81r
Vehicle maintenance and repairs expenditures	year	534	91	81r
Vehicle purchases	year	2068	91	81r
Vehicle rental, leases, licenses, etc. expenditures	year	197	91	81r
Vehicles purchased, other than cars and trucks	year	22	91	81r
Utilities				
Electricity expenditures	year	668	91	81r
Utilities, fuels, and public services, total expenditures	year	1838	91	81r
Water and other public services, expenditures	year	167	91	81r
Weddings				
Bridal attendants' gowns	event	750	10/93	76r
Bridal gown	event	852	10/93	76r
Bridal headpiece and veil	event	167	10/93	76r
Bride's wedding band	event	708	10/93	76r
Clergy	event	224	10/93	76r
Engagement ring	event	2756	10/93	76r
Flowers	event	863	10/93	76r
Formal wear for groom	event	106	10/93	76r
Groom's attendants' formal wear	event	530	10/93	76r
Groom's wedding band	event	402	10/93	76r
Music	event	600	10/93	76r
Photography	event	1088	10/93	76r
Shoes for bride	event	50	10/93	76r
Videography	event	483	10/93	76r
Wedding invitations and announcements	event	342	10/93	76r
Wedding reception	event	7000	10/93	76r

Bergen-Passaic, NJ

Item	Per	Value	Date	Ref.
Appliances				
Appliances (major), expenditures	year	145	91	81r
Average annual exp.				
Food, health care, personal goods, services	year	29496	91	81r
Charity				
Cash contributions, expenditures	year	708	91	81r

Bergen-Passaic, NJ - continued

Item	Per	Value	Date	Ref.
Clothing				
Apparel, men and boys, total expenditures	year	416	91	81r
Apparel, women and girls, total expenditures	year	744	91	81r
Footwear, expenditures	year	305	91	81r
Communications				
Long-distance telephone rate, day, addl. min., 1-10 mi.	min.	0.03	12/93	9s
Long-distance telephone rate, day, initial min., 1-10 mi.	min.	0.09	12/93	9s
Phone line, single, business, field visit	inst	98.50	12/93	9s
Phone line, single, business, no field visit	inst	79.50	12/93	9s
Phone line, single, residence, field visit	inst	56.50	12/93	9s
Phone line, single, residence, no field visit	inst	42.00	12/93	9s
Telephone service, expenditures	year	589	91	81r
Education				
Board, 4-year private college/university	year	2841	8/94	80s
Board, 4-year public college/university	year	1956	8/94	80s
Education, total expenditures	year	593	91	81r
Room, 4-year private college/university	year	2999	8/94	80s
Room, 4-year public college/university	year	2778	8/94	80s
Total cost, 4-year private college/university	year	18264	8/94	80s
Total cost, 4-year public college/university	year	8252	8/94	80s
Tuition, 2-year public college/university, in-state	year	1539	8/94	80s
Tuition, 4-year private college/university, in-state	year	12423	8/94	80s
Tuition, 4-year public college/university, in-state	year	3518	8/94	80s
Energy and Fuels				
Fuel oil and other fuels, expenditures	year	257	91	81r
Gas, natural, expenditures	year	285	91	81r
Gasoline and motor oil purchased	year	867	91	81r
Gasoline, unleaded midgrade	gallon	1.32	4/93	82r
Gasoline, unleaded premium	gallon	1.40	4/93	82r
Gasoline, unleaded regular	gallon	1.19	4/93	82r
Entertainment				
Entertainment, total expenditures	year	1331	91	81r
Fees and admissions, expenditures	year	398	91	81r
Pets, toys, playground equipment, expenditures	year	270	91	81r
Reading, expenditures	year	171	91	81r
Televisions, radios, and sound equipment, expenditures	year	429	91	81r
Funerals				
Burial, immediate, container provided by funeral home		1370.36	1/95	54r
Cards, acknowledgment		17.72	1/95	54r
Casket, minimum alternative		192.52	1/95	54r
Cosmetology, hair care, etc.		139.56	1/95	54r
Cremation, direct, container provided by funeral home		1049.24	1/95	54r
Embalming		387.57	1/95	54r
Funeral, funeral home		278.77	1/95	54r
Funeral, other facility		275.85	1/95	54r
Graveside service		213.08	1/95	54r
Hearse, local		157.27	1/95	54r
Limousine, local		146.45	1/95	54r
Memorial service		271.02	1/95	54r
Service charge, professional, nondeclinable		943.58	1/95	54r
Visitation and viewing		322.86	1/95	54r
Groceries				
Apples, Red Delicious	lb.	0.78	12/94	82r
Bacon, sliced	lb.	2.24	12/94	82r
Bananas	lb.	0.49	12/94	82r
Beef purchases	year	226	91	81r
Beverage purchases, alcoholic	year	332	91	81r
Beverage purchases, nonalcoholic	year	213	91	81r
Bread, white, pan	lb.	0.80	12/94	82r
Butter, salted, Grade AA, stick	lb.	1.67	12/94	82r
Carrots, short trimmed and topped	lb.	0.51	12/94	82r

Values are in dollars or fractions of dollars. In the column headed *Ref*, references are shown to sources. Each reference is followed by a letter. These refer to the geographical level for which data were reported: s = State, r = Region, and c = City or metro. The abbreviation *ex* is used to mean *except* or *excluding*; *exp* stands for expenditures. For other abbreviations and further explanations, please see the Introduction.

Bergen-Passaic, NJ - continued

Item	Per	Value	Date	Ref.
Groceries				
Cereals and bakery products purchases	year	407	91	81r
Cereals and cereals products purchases	year	132	91	81r
Chicken breast, bone-in	lb.	2.22	12/94	82r
Chicken, fresh, whole	lb.	1.05	12/94	82r
Chuck roast, USDA choice, boneless	lb.	2.74	12/94	82r
Coffee, 100%, ground roast, all sizes	lb.	4.61	12/94	82r
Dairy products (other) purchases	year	161	91	81r
Eggs, Grade A large	dozen	1.12	12/94	82r
Fish and seafood purchases	year	112	91	81r
Food purchases, food eaten at home	year	2599	91	81r
Foods purchased away from home, not prepared by consumer	year	2024	91	81r
Fruits and vegetables purchases	year	444	91	81r
Grapefruit	lb.	0.44	12/94	82r
Grapes, Thompson seedless	lb.	2.24	12/94	82r
Ground chuck, 100% beef	lb.	1.67	12/94	82r
Ice cream, prepackaged, bulk, regular	1/2 gal.	2.93	12/94	82r
Lemons	lb.	1.06	12/94	82r
Lettuce, iceberg	lb.	0.92	12/94	82r
Meats, poultry, fish, and eggs purchases	year	751	91	81r
Milk and cream (fresh) purchases	year	152	91	81r
Orange juice, frozen concentrate 12-oz. can	16 oz.	1.92	12/94	82r
Oranges, Navel	lb.	0.56	12/94	82r
Pork chops, center cut, bone-in	lb.	3.09	12/94	82r
Pork purchases	year	130	91	81r
Potatoes, white	lb.	0.37	12/94	82r
Rib roast, USDA choice, bone-in	lb.	4.98	12/94	82r
Round roast, USDA choice, boneless	lb.	2.93	12/94	82r
Shortening, vegetable oil blends	lb.	1.03	12/94	82r
Spaghetti and macaroni	lb.	0.84	12/94	82r
Steak, round, USDA choice, boneless	lb.	3.48	12/94	82r
Steak, sirloin, USDA choice, bone-in	lb.	3.38	12/94	82r
Steak, sirloin, USDA choice, boneless	lb.	4.81	12/94	82r
Sugar and other sweets, eaten at home, expenditures	year	89	91	81r
Sugar, white, all sizes	lb.	0.46	12/94	82r
Tobacco products and smoking supplies, total expenditures	year	279	91	81r
Tomatoes, field grown	lb.	1.56	12/94	82r
Tuna, chunk, light	lb.	2.09	12/94	82r
Health Care				
Childbirth, Cesarean delivery, hospital charge	birth	6334.00	12/91	69r
Childbirth, Cesarean delivery, physician charge	birth	2234.00	12/91	69r
Childbirth, normal delivery, hospital charge	birth	3225.00	12/91	69r
Childbirth, normal delivery, physician charge	birth	1623.00	12/91	69r
Drugs, expenditures	year	205	91	81r
Health care, total expenditures	year	1396	91	81r
Health insurance expenditures	year	553	91	81r
Insurance premium, family medical care	month	396.06	1/95	41s
Medical services expenditures	year	559	91	81r
Medical supplies expenditures	year	80	91	81r
Household Goods				
Floor coverings, expenditures	year	158	91	81r
Furniture, expenditures	year	341	91	81r
Household equipment, misc. expenditures	year	363	91	81r
Household expenditures, miscellaneous	year	194	91	81r
Household furnishings and equipment, expenditures	year	1158	91	81r
Household operations expenditures	year	378	91	81r
Household textiles, expenditures	year	88	91	81r
Housekeeping supplies, expenditures	year	426	91	81r
Laundry and cleaning supplies, expenditures	year	122	91	81r
Postage and stationery, expenditures	year	134	91	81r
Housing				
Add garage/carport		11,614	3/95	74r
Add room(s)		16,816	3/95	74r
Apartment condominium or co-op, median	unit	96700	12/94	62r

Bergen-Passaic, NJ - continued

Item	Per	Value	Date	Ref.
Housing - continued				
Dwellings (owned), expenditures	year	3305	91	81r
Enclose porch/patio/breezeway		2,980	3/95	74r
Finish room in basement/attic		4,330	3/95	74r
Home, existing, single-family, median	unit	161600	12/94	62r
Maintenance, repairs, insurance, and other housing expenditures	year	569	91	81r
Mortgage interest and charges expenditures	year	1852	91	81r
Princ. & int., mortgage, median-price exist. sing.-family home	mo.	765	12/94	62r
Property taxes expenditures	year	884	91	81r
Redesign, restructure more than half of home's interior		2,750	3/95	74r
Rental units expenditures	year	1832	91	81r
Insurance and Pensions				
Auto insurance, private passenger	year	1094.56	12/94	71s
Insurance and pensions, personal, expenditures	year	2690	91	81r
Insurance, life and other personal, expenditures	year	341	91	81r
Pensions and Social Security, expenditures	year	2349	91	81r
Legal Assistance				
Estate planning, law-firm partner	hr.	375.00	10/93	12r
Legal work, law firm associate	hour	78		10r
Legal work, law firm partner	hour	183		10r
Personal Services				
Personal services expenditures	year	184	91	81r
Restaurant Food				
Dining expenditures, family	week	34.26	94	73r
Taxes				
Taxes, Federal income, expenditures	year	2409	91	81r
Taxes, personal, expenditures	year	3094	91	81r
Taxes, State and local income, expenditures	year	620	91	81r
Transportation				
Cars and trucks purchased, new	year	1170	91	81r
Cars and trucks purchased, used	year	739	91	81r
Driver's learning permit fee	perm	5.00	1/94	84s
Driver's license fee	orig	16.00	1/94	84s
Driver's license fee, duplicate	lic	3.00	1/94	84s
Driver's license reinstatement fee, min.	susp	30.00	1/94	85s
Driver's license renewal fee	renew	16.00	1/94	84s
Identification card, nondriver	card	5.50	1/94	83s
Motorcycle learning permit fee	perm	5.00	1/94	84s
Motorcycle license fee	orig	8.00	1/94	84s
Motorcycle license fee, duplicate	lic	3.00	1/94	84s
Motorcycle license renewal fee	renew	8.00	1/94	84s
Public transportation expenditures	year	430	91	81r
Transportation expenditures, total	year	4810	91	81r
Vehicle finance charges	year	238	91	81r
Vehicle insurance expenditures	year	630	91	81r
Vehicle maintenance and repairs expenditures	year	532	91	81r
Vehicle purchases	year	1920	91	81r
Vehicle rental, leases, licenses, etc. expenditures	year	193	91	81r
Vehicles purchased, other than cars and trucks	year	11	91	81r
Utilities				
Electricity expenditures	year	695	91	81r
Utilities, fuels, and public services, total expenditures	year	1981	91	81r
Water and other public services, expenditures	year	154	91	81r
Weddings				
Bridal attendants' gowns	event	750	10/93	76r
Bridal gown	event	852	10/93	76r
Bridal headpiece and veil	event	167	10/93	76r
Bride's wedding band	event	708	10/93	76r
Clergy	event	224	10/93	76r

Values are in dollars or fractions of dollars. In the column headed *Ref*, references are shown to sources. Each reference is followed by a letter. These refer to the geographical level for which data were reported: s=State, r=Region, and c=City or metro. The abbreviation *ex* is used to mean *except* or *excluding*; *exp* stands for *expenditures*. For other abbreviations and further explanations, please see the Introduction.

Bergen-Passaic, NJ - continued

Item	Per	Value	Date	Ref.
Weddings				
Engagement ring	event	2756	10/93	76r
Flowers	event	863	10/93	76r
Formal wear for groom	event	106	10/93	76r
Groom's attendants' formal wear	event	530	10/93	76r
Groom's wedding band	event	402	10/93	76r
Music	event	600	10/93	76r
Photography	event	1088	10/93	76r
Shoes for bride	event	50	10/93	76r
Videography	event	483	10/93	76r
Wedding invitations and announcements	event	342	10/93	76r
Wedding reception	event	7000	10/93	76r

Billings, MT

Item	Per	Value	Date	Ref.
Composite, ACCRA index		103.40	12/94	2c
Alcoholic Beverages				
Beer, Miller Lite, Bud, 12-oz., ex deposit	6	4.47	12/94	2c
J & B Scotch	750-ml.	18.85	12/94	2c
Wine, Gallo Chablis blanc	1.5-lit	5.17	12/94	2c
Appliances				
Appliances (major), expenditures	year	160	91	81r
Average annual exp.				
Food, health care, personal goods, services	year	32461	91	81r
Charity				
Cash contributions, expenditures	year	975	91	81r
Clothing				
Apparel, men and boys, total expenditures	year	467	91	81r
Apparel, women and girls, total expenditures	year	737	91	81r
Footwear, expenditures	year	270	91	81r
Jeans, man's denim		31.79	12/94	2c
Shirt, man's dress shirt		34.50	12/94	2c
Undervest, boy's size 10-14, cotton	3	5.54	12/94	2c
Communications				
Long-distance telephone rate, day, addl. min., 1-10 mi.	min.	0.04	12/93	9s
Long-distance telephone rate, day, initial min., 1-10 mi.	min.	0.13	12/93	9s
Newspaper subscription, dly. and Sun. delivery	month	17.39	12/94	2c
Phone line, single, business, field visit	inst	61.40	12/93	9s
Phone line, single, business, no field visit	inst	61.40	12/93	9s
Phone line, single, residence, field visit	inst	35.30	12/93	9s
Phone line, single, residence, no field visit	inst	35.30	12/93	9s
Telephone bill, family of four	month	18.22	12/94	2c
Telephone service, expenditures	year	611	91	81r
Education				
Board, 4-year private college/university	year	2014	8/94	80s
Board, 4-year public college/university	year	2064	8/94	80s
Education, total expenditures	year	375	91	81r
Room, 4-year private college/university	year	1355	8/94	80s
Room, 4-year public college/university	year	1710	8/94	80s
Total cost, 4-year private college/university	year	10474	8/94	80s
Total cost, 4-year public college/university	year	5665	8/94	80s
Tuition, 2-year public college/university, in-state	year	1171	8/94	80s
Tuition, 4-year private college/university, in-state	year	7104	8/94	80s
Tuition, 4-year public college/university, in-state	year	1890	8/94	80s
Energy and Fuels				
Energy, combined forms, 1800 sq. ft.	mo.	88.94	12/94	2c
Energy, exc. electricity, 1800 sq. ft.	mo.	46.02	12/94	2c
Fuel oil and other fuels, expenditures	year	33	91	81r
Gas, cooking, 10 therms	month	9.20	2/94	65c
Gas, cooking, 30 therms	month	18.60	2/94	65c
Gas, cooking, 50 therms	month	27.99	2/94	65c

Item	Per	Value	Date	Ref.
Energy and Fuels - continued				
Gas, heating, winter, 100 therms	month	51.47	2/94	65c
Gas, heating, winter, average use	month	79.65	2/94	65c
Gas, natural, expenditures	year	212	91	81r
Gas, reg unlead, taxes inc., cash, self-service	gal	1.30	12/94	2c
Gasoline and motor oil purchased	year	1115	91	81r
Gasoline, unleaded midgrade	gallon	1.36	4/93	82r
Gasoline, unleaded premium	gallon	1.43	4/93	82r
Gasoline, unleaded regular	gallon	1.23	4/93	82r
Entertainment				
Bowling, evening rate	game	1.70	12/94	2c
Concert ticket, Pearl Jam group	perf	20.00	94	50r
Entertainment, total expenditures	year	1853	91	81r
Fees and admissions, expenditures	year	482	91	81r
Monopoly game, Parker Brothers', No. 9	game	10.38	12/94	2c
Movie	adm	5.50	12/94	2c
Pets, toys, playground equipment, expenditures	year	299	91	81r
Reading, expenditures	year	164	91	81r
Televisions, radios, and sound equipment, expenditures	year	528	91	81r
Tennis balls, yellow, Wilson or Penn, 3	can	2.28	12/94	2c
Funerals				
Burial, immediate, container provided by funeral home		1360.49	1/95	54r
Cards, acknowledgment		11.24	1/95	54r
Casket, minimum alternative		232.73	1/95	54r
Cosmetology, hair care, etc.		114.13	1/95	54r
Cremation, direct, container provided by funeral home		1027.08	1/95	54r
Embalming		286.24	1/95	54r
Funeral, funeral home		315.60	1/95	54r
Funeral, other facility		303.08	1/95	54r
Graveside service		423.83	1/95	54r
Hearse, local		133.12	1/95	54r
Limousine, local		99.10	1/95	54r
Memorial service		442.57	1/95	54r
Service charge, professional, nondeclinable		840.16	1/95	54r
Visitation and viewing		168.50	1/95	54r
Groceries				
Groceries, ACCRA Index		102.30	12/94	2c
Apples, Red Delicious	lb.	0.72	12/94	82r
Baby food, strained vegetables, lowest price	4-4.5 oz.	0.27	12/94	2c
Bacon, sliced	lb.	1.73	12/94	82r
Bananas	lb.	0.47	12/94	2c
Bananas	lb.	0.52	12/94	82r
Beef or hamburger, ground	lb.	0.99	12/94	2c
Beef purchases	year	241	91	81r
Beverage purchases, alcoholic	year	328	91	81r
Beverage purchases, nonalcoholic	year	234	91	81r
Bologna, all beef or mixed	lb.	2.33	12/94	82r
Bread, white	24-oz.	0.96	12/94	2c
Bread, white, pan	lb.	0.81	12/94	82r
Carrots, short trimmed and topped	lb.	0.43	12/94	82r
Cereals and bakery products purchases	year	392	91	81r
Cereals and cereals products purchases	year	139	91	81r
Cheese, Kraft grated Parmesan	8-oz.	3.54	12/94	2c
Chicken breast, bone-in	lb.	2.04	12/94	82r
Chicken, fresh, whole	lb.	0.95	12/94	82r
Chicken, whole fryer	lb.	0.93	12/94	2c
Cigarettes, Winston, Kings	carton	15.12	12/94	2c
Coffee, 100%, ground roast, all sizes	lb.	4.48	12/94	82r
Coffee, vacuum-packed	13 oz.	3.85	12/94	2c
Corn Flakes, Kellogg's or Post Toasties	18 oz.	2.32	12/94	2c
Corn, frozen, whole kernel, lowest price	10 oz.	0.71	12/94	2c
Dairy products (other) purchases	year	182	91	81r
Eggs, Grade A large	dozen	0.73	12/94	2c
Fish and seafood purchases	year	94	91	81r
Flour, white, all purpose	lb.	0.21	12/94	82r
Food purchases, food eaten at home	year	2749	91	81r

Values are in dollars or fractions of dollars. In the column headed *Ref*, references are shown to sources. Each reference is followed by a letter. These refer to the geographical level for which data were reported: s = State, r = Region, and c = City or metro. The abbreviation *ex* is used to mean *except* or *excluding*; *exp* stands for expenditures. For other abbreviations and further explanations, please see the Introduction.

Billings, MT - continued

Item	Per	Value	Date	Ref.
Groceries				
Foods purchased away from home, not prepared by consumer	year	1909	91	81r
Fruits and vegetables purchases	year	459	91	81r
Grapefruit	lb.	0.56	12/94	82r
Ground beef, 100% beef	lb.	1.31	12/94	82r
Ham, boneless, exc. canned	lb.	2.46	12/94	82r
Ice cream, prepackaged, bulk, regular	1/2 gal.	2.57	12/94	82r
Lemons	lb.	1.00	12/94	82r
Lettuce, iceberg	lb.	0.93	12/94	82r
Lettuce, iceberg	head	0.70	12/94	2c
Margarine, Blue Bonnet or Parkay cubes	lb.	0.65	12/94	2c
Meats, poultry, fish, and eggs purchases	year	700	91	81r
Milk and cream (fresh) purchases	year	155	91	81r
Milk, whole	1/2 gal.	1.45	12/94	2c
Orange juice, frozen concentrate 12-oz. can	16 oz.	1.52	12/94	82r
Orange juice, Minute Maid frozen	12-oz.	1.26	12/94	2c
Oranges, Navel	lb.	0.56	12/94	82r
Peaches, halves or slices, Hunt's, Del Monte, or Libby's	29-oz.	1.43	12/94	2c
Peas, sweet, Del Monte or Green Giant	15-17 oz.	0.52	12/94	2c
Pork chops, center cut, bone-in	lb.	3.30	12/94	82r
Pork purchases	year	122	91	81r
Potato chips	16-oz.	3.03	12/94	82r
Potatoes, frozen, French fried	lb.	0.77	12/94	82r
Potatoes, white	lb.	0.35	12/94	82r
Potatoes, white or red	10-lb. sack	1.92	12/94	2c
Rice, white, long grain, uncooked	lb.	0.54	12/94	82r
Round roast, USDA choice, boneless	lb.	2.92	12/94	82r
Sausage, Jimmy Dean, 100% pork	lb.	3.51	12/94	2c
Shortening, vegetable oil blends	lb.	0.80	12/94	82r
Shortening, vegetable, Crisco	3-lb.	2.04	12/94	2c
Soft drink, Coca Cola, ex deposit	2 lit	1.37	12/94	2c
Spaghetti and macaroni	lb.	1.02	12/94	82r
Steak, round, graded & ungraded, exc. USDA prime & choice	lb.	3.13	12/94	82r
Steak, sirloin, USDA choice, boneless	lb.	4.07	12/94	82r
Steak, t-bone	lb.	4.77	12/94	2c
Sugar and other sweets, eaten at home, expenditures	year	105	91	81r
Sugar, cane or beet	4 lbs.	1.19	12/94	2c
Sugar, white, all sizes	lb.	0.38	12/94	82r
Tobacco products and smoking supplies, total expenditures	year	221	91	81r
Tomatoes, field grown	lb.	1.45	12/94	82r
Tomatoes, Hunt's or Del Monte	14.5 oz.	0.72	12/94	2c
Tuna, chunk, light	lb.	2.18	12/94	82r
Tuna, chunk, light, oil-packed	6.125-6.5 oz.	0.79	12/94	2c
Goods and Services				
Miscellaneous goods and services, ACCRA Index		105.00	12/94	2c
Health Care				
Health care, ACCRA Index		101.30	12/94	2c
Antibiotic ointment, Polysporin	1.5 oz.	3.59	12/94	2c
Childbirth, Cesarean delivery, hospital charge	birth	6059.00	12/91	69r
Childbirth, Cesarean delivery, physician charge	birth	2248.00	12/91	69r
Childbirth, normal delivery, hospital charge	birth	3006.00	12/91	69r
Childbirth, normal delivery, physician charge	birth	1634.00	12/91	69r
Dentist's fee, adult teeth cleaning and periodic oral exam	visit	50.60	12/94	2c
Doctor's fee, routine exam, established patient	visit	43.20	12/94	2c
Drugs, expenditures	year	230	91	81r
Health care, total expenditures	year	1544	91	81r

Billings, MT - continued

Item	Per	Value	Date	Ref.
Health Care - continued				
Health insurance expenditures	year	558	91	81r
Hospital care, semiprivate room	day	414.00	12/94	2c
Medical services expenditures	year	676	91	81r
Medical supplies expenditures	year	80	91	81r
Surgery, open-heart	proc	37818.00	1/93	14r
Household Goods				
Appl. repair, service call, wash mach	min. lab. chg.	34.08	12/94	2c
Floor coverings, expenditures	year	79	91	81r
Furniture, expenditures	year	352	91	81r
Household equipment, misc. expenditures	year	614	91	81r
Household expenditures, miscellaneous	year	294	91	81r
Household furnishings and equipment, expenditures	year	1416	91	81r
Household operations expenditures	year	580	91	81r
Household textiles, expenditures	year	113	91	81r
Housekeeping supplies, expenditures	year	447	91	81r
Laundry and cleaning supplies, expenditures	year	114	91	81r
Laundry detergent, Tide Ultra, Bold, or Cheer	42 oz.	3.45	12/94	2c
Postage and stationery, expenditures	year	145	91	81r
Tissues, facial, Kleenex brand	175	0.97	12/94	2c
Housing				
Housing, ACCRA Index		107.10	12/94	2c
Add garage/carport		6,422	3/95	74r
Add room(s)		26,583	3/95	74r
Apartment condominium or co-op, median	unit	105300	12/94	62r
Dwellings (owned), expenditures	year	3932	91	81r
Enclose porch/patio/breezeway		5,382	3/95	74r
Finish room in basement/attic		3,911	3/95	74r
Home, existing, single-family, median	unit	178600	12/94	62r
House payment, principal and interest, 25% down payment	mo.	887	12/94	2c
House, 1800 sq ft, 8000 sq ft lot, new, urban, utilities	total	142500	12/94	2c
Maintenance, repairs, insurance, and other housing expenditures	year	591	91	81r
Mortgage interest and charges expenditures	year	2747	91	81r
Mtge. rate, incl. points and orig. fee, 30-year conv. fixed or ARM	mo.	9.35	12/94	2c
Princ. & int., mortgage, median-price exist. sing.-family home	mo.	845	12/94	62r
Property taxes expenditures	year	594	91	81r
Redesign, restructure more than half of home's interior		5,467	3/95	74r
Rent, apartment, 2 br., 1 1/2-2 baths, unfurnished, 950 sq ft, water	mo.	375	12/94	2c
Rental units expenditures	year	2077	91	81r
Insurance and Pensions				
Auto insurance, private passenger	year	551.37	12/94	71s
Insurance and pensions, personal, expenditures	year	3042	91	81r
Insurance, life and other personal, expenditures	year	298	91	81r
Pensions and Social Security, expenditures	year	2744	91	81r
Legal Assistance				
Legal work, law firm associate	hour	91		10r
Legal work, law firm partner	hour	151		10r
Personal Goods				
Shampoo, Alberto VO5	15-oz.	1.32	12/94	2c
Toothpaste, Crest or Colgate	6-7 oz.	2.32	12/94	2c
Personal Services				
Dry cleaning, man's 2-pc. suit		7.55	12/94	2c
Haircut, man or child	cut	8.00	12/93	60c
Haircut, man's barbershop, no styling		8.60	12/94	2c
Haircut, woman's shampoo, trim, blow-dry		17.00	12/94	2c
Personal services expenditures	year	286	91	81r

Values are in dollars or fractions of dollars. In the column headed *Ref*, references are shown to sources. Each reference is followed by a letter. These refer to the geographical level for which data were reported: s = State, r = Region, and c = City or metro. The abbreviation *ex* is used to mean *except* or *excluding*; *exp* stands for *expenditures*. For other abbreviations and further explanations, please see the Introduction.

Billings, MT - continued

Item	Per	Value	Date	Ref.
Restaurant Food				
Chicken, fried, thigh and drumstick		2.18	12/94	2c
Dining expenditures, family	week	32.25	94	73r
Hamburger with cheese	1/4 lb.	1.85	12/94	2c
Pizza, Pizza Hut or Pizza Inn	12-13 in.	8.39	12/94	2c
Taxes				
Tax rate, residential property, month	$100	1.47	1/92	79c
Taxes, Federal income, expenditures	year	2946	91	81r
Taxes, personal, expenditures	year	3791	91	81r
Taxes, State and local income, expenditures	year	791	91	81r
Transportation				
Transportation, ACCRA Index		109.20	12/94	2c
Cars and trucks purchased, new	year	1231	91	81r
Cars and trucks purchased, used	year	915	91	81r
Driver's learning permit fee	perm	16.00	1/94	84s
Driver's license fee	orig	16.00	1/94	84s
Driver's license fee, duplicate	lic	5.00	1/94	84s
Driver's license reinstatement fee, min.	susp	100.00	1/94	85s
Driver's license renewal fee	renew	16.00	1/94	84s
Identification card, nondriver	card	8.00	1/94	83s
Motorcycle learning permit fee	perm	2.00	1/94	84s
Motorcycle license fee	orig	2.00	1/94	84s
Public transportation expenditures	year	375	91	81r
Tire balance, computer or spin bal., front	wheel	6.80	12/94	2c
Transportation expenditures, total	year	5527	91	81r
Vehicle finance charges	year	287	91	81r
Vehicle insurance expenditures	year	624	91	81r
Vehicle maintenance and repairs expenditures	year	695	91	81r
Vehicle purchases	year	2174	91	81r
Vehicle rental, leases, licenses, etc. expenditures	year	257	91	81r
Vehicles purchased, other than cars and trucks	year	28	91	81r
Utilities				
Utilities, ACCRA Index		81.20	12/94	2c
Electricity expenditures	year	616	91	81r
Electricity, (part.), other, 1800 sq. ft., new home	mo.	42.92	12/94	2c
Electricity, summer, 250 KWh	month	15.36	8/93	64c
Electricity, summer, 500 KWh	month	27.37	8/93	64c
Electricity, summer, 750 KWh	month	39.38	8/93	64c
Electricity, summer, 1000 KWh	month	51.39	8/93	64c
Utilities, fuels, and public services, total expenditures	year	1681	91	81r
Water and other public services, expenditures	year	209	91	81r
Weddings				
Bridal attendants' gowns	event	750	10/93	76r
Bridal gown	event	852	10/93	76r
Bridal headpiece and veil	event	167	10/93	76r
Bride's wedding band	event	708	10/93	76r
Clergy	event	224	10/93	76r
Engagement ring	event	2756	10/93	76r
Flowers	event	863	10/93	76r
Formal wear for groom	event	106	10/93	76r
Groom's attendants' formal wear	event	530	10/93	76r
Groom's wedding band	event	402	10/93	76r
Music	event	600	10/93	76r
Photography	event	1088	10/93	76r
Shoes for bride	event	50	10/93	76r
Videography	event	483	10/93	76r
Wedding invitations and announcements	event	342	10/93	76r
Wedding reception	event	7000	10/93	76r

Biloxi, MS

Item	Per	Value	Date	Ref.
Appliances				
Appliances (major), expenditures	year	153	91	81r
Average annual exp.				
Food, health care, personal goods, services	year	27020	91	81r
Charity				
Cash contributions, expenditures	year	839	91	81r
Clothing				
Apparel, men and boys, total expenditures	year	380	91	81r
Apparel, women and girls, total expenditures	year	660	91	81r
Footwear, expenditures	year	193	91	81r
Communications				
Long-distance telephone rate, day, addl. min., 1-10 mi.	min.	0.11	12/93	9s
Long-distance telephone rate, day, initial min., 1-10 mi.	min.	0.19	12/93	9s
Phone line, single, business, field visit	inst	67.00	12/93	9s
Phone line, single, business, no field visit	inst	67.00	12/93	9s
Phone line, single, residence, field visit	inst	46.00	12/93	9s
Phone line, single, residence, no field visit	inst	46.00	12/93	9s
Telephone service, expenditures	year	616	91	81r
Telephone, residential, flat rate	mo.	17.95	12/93	8c
Education				
Board, 4-year private college/university	year	1394	8/94	80s
Board, 4-year public college/university	year	1380	8/94	80s
Education, total expenditures	year	319	91	81r
Room, 4-year private college/university	year	1400	8/94	80s
Room, 4-year public college/university	year	1343	8/94	80s
Total cost, 4-year private college/university	year	8754	8/94	80s
Total cost, 4-year public college/university	year	5093	8/94	80s
Tuition, 2-year public college/university, in-state	year	939	8/94	80s
Tuition, 4-year private college/university, in-state	year	5959	8/94	80s
Tuition, 4-year public college/university, in-state	year	2370	8/94	80s
Energy and Fuels				
Fuel oil and other fuels, expenditures	year	56	91	81r
Gas, cooking, 10 therms	month	10.79	2/94	65c
Gas, cooking, 30 therms	month	20.90	2/94	65c
Gas, cooking, 50 therms	month	29.71	2/94	65c
Gas, heating, winter, 100 therms	month	51.73	2/94	65c
Gas, heating, winter, average use	month	45.56	2/94	65c
Gas, natural, expenditures	year	150	91	81r
Gasoline and motor oil purchased	year	1152	91	81r
Gasoline, unleaded midgrade	gallon	1.21	4/93	82r
Gasoline, unleaded premium	gallon	1.30	4/93	82r
Gasoline, unleaded regular	gallon	1.10	4/93	82r
Entertainment				
Concert ticket, Pearl Jam group	perf	20.00	94	50r
Entertainment, total expenditures	year	1266	91	81r
Fees and admissions, expenditures	year	306	91	81r
Pets, toys, playground equipment, expenditures	year	271	91	81r
Reading, expenditures	year	131	91	81r
Televisions, radios, and sound equipment, expenditures	year	439	91	81r
Funerals				
Burial, immediate, container provided by funeral home		1298.96	1/95	54r
Cards, acknowledgment		21.26	1/95	54r
Casket, minimum alternative		204.95	1/95	54r
Cosmetology, hair care, etc.		85.40	1/95	54r
Cremation, direct, container provided by funeral home		1054.77	1/95	54r
Embalming		287.71	1/95	54r
Funeral, funeral home		269.18	1/95	54r
Funeral, other facility		272.88	1/95	54r
Graveside service		302.54	1/95	54r

Values are in dollars or fractions of dollars. In the column headed *Ref*, references are shown to sources. Each reference is followed by a letter. These refer to the geographical level for which data were reported: s=State, r=Region, and c=City or metro. The abbreviation *ex* is used to mean *except* or *excluding*; *exp* stands for expenditures. For other abbreviations and further explanations, please see the Introduction.

Biloxi, MS - continued

Item	Per	Value	Date	Ref.
Funerals				
Hearse, local		122.08	1/95	54r
Limousine, local		80.31	1/95	54r
Memorial service		277.66	1/95	54r
Service charge, professional, nondeclinable		896.65	1/95	54r
Visitation and viewing		232.39	1/95	54r
Groceries				
Apples, Red Delicious	lb.	0.73	12/94	82r
Bacon, sliced	lb.	1.67	12/94	82r
Bananas	lb.	0.42	12/94	82r
Beef purchases	year	213	91	81r
Beverage purchases, alcoholic	year	249	91	81r
Beverage purchases, nonalcoholic	year	207	91	81r
Bologna, all beef or mixed	lb.	2.27	12/94	82r
Bread, white, pan	lb.	0.68	12/94	82r
Cabbage	lb.	0.42	12/94	82r
Carrots, short trimmed and topped	lb.	0.53	12/94	82r
Cereals and bakery products purchases	year	345	91	81r
Cereals and cereals products purchases	year	127	91	81r
Cheddar cheese, natural	lb.	3.58	12/94	82r
Chicken breast, bone-in	lb.	1.71	12/94	82r
Chicken, fresh, whole	lb.	0.78	12/94	82r
Chuck roast, USDA choice, boneless	lb.	2.26	12/94	82r
Crackers, soda, salted	lb.	1.27	12/94	82r
Cucumbers	lb.	0.65	12/94	82r
Dairy products (other) purchases	year	141	91	81r
Eggs, Grade A large	dozen	0.87	12/94	82r
Fish and seafood purchases	year	72	91	81r
Flour, white, all purpose	lb.	0.23	12/94	82r
Food purchases, food eaten at home	year	2381	91	81r
Foods purchased away from home, not prepared by consumer	year	1696	91	81r
Frankfurters, all meat or all beef	lb.	1.74	12/94	82r
Fruits and vegetables purchases	year	380	91	81r
Grapefruit	lb.	0.45	12/94	82r
Grapes, Thompson seedless	lb.	2.30	12/94	82r
Ground beef, 100% beef	lb.	1.37	12/94	82r
Ground chuck, 100% beef	lb.	1.97	12/94	82r
Ham, boneless, exc. canned	lb.	2.54	12/94	82r
Ice cream, prepackaged, bulk, regular	1/2 gal.	2.47	12/94	82r
Lemons	lb.	1.02	12/94	82r
Lettuce, iceberg	lb.	0.96	12/94	82r
Margarine, stick	lb.	0.77	12/94	82r
Meats, poultry, fish, and eggs purchases	year	655	91	81r
Milk and cream (fresh) purchases	year	130	91	81r
Orange juice, frozen concentrate 12-oz. can	16 oz.	1.36	12/94	82r
Oranges, Navel	lb.	0.54	12/94	82r
Pears, Anjou	lb.	0.81	12/94	82r
Pork chops, center cut, bone-in	lb.	3.07	12/94	82r
Pork purchases	year	142	91	81r
Potato chips	16-oz.	3.15	12/94	82r
Potatoes, frozen, French fried	lb.	0.82	12/94	82r
Potatoes, white	lb.	0.34	12/94	82r
Rice, white, long grain, uncooked	lb.	0.48	12/94	82r
Round roast, USDA choice, boneless	lb.	2.91	12/94	82r
Sausage, fresh	lb.	1.82	12/94	82r
Shortening, vegetable oil blends	lb.	0.75	12/94	82r
Spaghetti and macaroni	lb.	0.87	12/94	82r
Steak, rib eye, USDA choice, boneless	lb.	6.85	12/94	82r
Steak, round, graded & ungraded, exc. USDA prime & choice	lb.	2.96	12/94	82r
Steak, round, USDA choice, boneless	lb.	3.17	12/94	82r
Steak, sirloin, USDA choice, boneless	lb.	4.12	12/94	82r
Steak, T-bone, USDA choice, bone-in	lb.	5.63	12/94	82r
Sugar and other sweets, eaten at home, expenditures	year	93	91	81r
Sugar, white, all sizes	lb.	0.39	12/94	82r
Tobacco products and smoking supplies, total expenditures	year	286	91	81r
Tomatoes, field grown	lb.	1.36	12/94	82r
Tuna, chunk, light	lb.	1.94	12/94	82r
Turkey, frozen, whole	lb.	0.96	12/94	82r

Biloxi, MS - continued

Item	Per	Value	Date	Ref.
Groceries - continued				
Yogurt, natural, fruit flavored	8 oz.	0.58	12/94	82r
Health Care				
Adenosine, emergency room	treat	100.00	95	23r
Bladder tap, superpubic, infant, emergency room	treat	119.00	95	23r
Blood analysis, emergency room	treat	25.00	95	23r
Blood tests, abdominal pain, emergency room	treat	25.00	95	23r
Burn dressing, emergency room	treat	266.00	95	23r
Cardiology interpretation, emergency room	treat	26.00	95	23r
Chest X-ray, emergency room	treat	78.00	95	23r
Childbirth, Cesarean delivery, hospital charge	birth	5462.00	12/91	69r
Childbirth, Cesarean delivery, physician charge	birth	2228.00	12/91	69r
Childbirth, normal delivery, hospital charge	birth	2943.00	12/91	69r
Childbirth, normal delivery, physician charge	birth	1619.00	12/91	69r
Defibrillation pads, emergency room	treat	6.00	95	23r
Drugs, expenditures	year	297	91	81r
Gastric tube insertion, nasal, emergency room	treat	25.00	95	23r
Health care, total expenditures	year	1600	91	81r
Health insurance expenditures	year	637	91	81r
Heart monitor, emergency room	treat	40.00	95	23r
Intravenous fluids, emergency room	treat	130.00	95	23r
Intravenous fluids, emergency room	liter	26.00	95	23r
Intravenous line, central, emergency room	treat	342.00	95	23r
Liver function tests, abdominal pain, emergency room	treat	26.00	95	23r
Medical care charges, total, emergency room, third-degree burns	treat	2101.00	95	23r
Medical care charges, total, emergency, infant with fever	treat	628.00	95	23r
Medical services expenditures	year	573	91	81r
Medical supplies expenditures	year	93	91	81r
Morphine, emergency room	treat	34.00	95	23r
Nursing care and facilities charges, emergency room	treat	252.00	95	23r
Nursing care and facilities charges, emergency, infant with fever	treat	252.00	95	23r
Nursing care and facilities charges, emergency, third-degree burns	treat	861.00	95	23r
Physician's charges, emergency, infant with fever	treat	212.00	95	23r
Physician's charges, emergency, third-degree burns	treat	372.00	95	23r
Physician's fee, emergency room	treat	372.00	95	23r
Physician's fee, general practitioner	visit	51.20	12/93	60r
Surgery, open-heart	proc	42374.00	1/93	14r
Ultrasound, abdominal, emergency room	treat	276.00	95	23r
Urinalysis, emergency room	treat	20.00	95	23r
Urinalysis, infant, emergency room	treat	20.00	95	23r
X-rays, emergency room	treat	78.00	95	23r
Household Goods				
Floor coverings, expenditures	year	48	91	81r
Furniture, expenditures	year	280	91	81r
Household equipment, misc. expenditures	year	342	91	81r
Household expenditures, miscellaneous	year	256	91	81r
Household furnishings and equipment, expenditures	year	988	91	81r
Household operations expenditures	year	468	91	81r
Household textiles, expenditures	year	95	91	81r
Housekeeping supplies, expenditures	year	380	91	81r
Laundry and cleaning supplies, expenditures	year	109	91	81r
Postage and stationery, expenditures	year	105	91	81r
Housing				
Add garage/carport		6,980	3/95	74r
Add room(s)		11,403	3/95	74r
Apartment condominium or co-op, median	unit	68600	12/94	62r
Dwellings (owned), expenditures	year	2428	91	81r

Values are in dollars or fractions of dollars. In the column headed *Ref*, references are shown to sources. Each reference is followed by a letter. These refer to the geographical level for which data were reported: s=State, r=Region, and c=City or metro. The abbreviation *ex* is used to mean *except* or *excluding*; *exp* stands for *expenditures*. For other abbreviations and further explanations, please see the Introduction.

Biloxi, MS - continued

Item	Per	Value	Date	Ref.
Housing				
Enclose porch/patio/breezeway		4,572	3/95	74r
Finish room in basement/attic		3,794	3/95	74r
Home, existing, single-family, median	unit	120200	12/94	62r
Home, existing, single-family, median	unit	72.90	12/94	62c
Maintenance, repairs, insurance, and other housing expenditures	year	531	91	81r
Mortgage interest and charges expenditures	year	1506	91	81r
Princ. & int., mortgage, median-price exist. sing.-family home	mo.	540	12/94	62r
Property taxes expenditures	year	391	91	81r
Redesign, restructure more than half of home's interior		17,641	3/95	74r
Rental units expenditures	year	1264	91	81r
Insurance and Pensions				
Auto insurance, private passenger	year	643.74	12/94	71s
Insurance and pensions, personal, expenditures	year	2395	91	81r
Insurance, life and other personal, expenditures	year	368	91	81r
Pensions and Social Security, expenditures	year	2027	91	81r
Personal Services				
Personal services expenditures	year	212	91	81r
Restaurant Food				
Dining expenditures, family	week	33.83	94	73r
Taxes				
Taxes, Federal income, expenditures	year	2275	91	81r
Taxes, personal, expenditures	year	2715	91	81r
Taxes, State and local income, expenditures	year	365	91	81r
Transportation				
Cars and trucks purchased, new	year	1306	91	81r
Cars and trucks purchased, used	year	942	91	81r
Driver's learning permit fee	perm	1.00	1/94	84s
Driver's license fee	orig	20.00	1/94	84s
Driver's license fee, duplicate	lic	5.00	1/94	84s
Driver's license renewal fee	renew	20.00	1/94	84s
Identification card, nondriver	card	13.00	1/94	83s
Motorcycle license fee	orig	5.00	1/94	84s
Public transportation expenditures	year	249	91	81r
Transportation expenditures, total	year	5307	91	81r
Vehicle finance charges	year	346	91	81r
Vehicle insurance expenditures	year	544	91	81r
Vehicle maintenance and repairs expenditures	year	600	91	81r
Vehicle purchases	year	2275	91	81r
Vehicle rental, leases, licenses, etc. expenditures	year	141	91	81r
Vehicles purchased, other than cars and trucks	year	27	91	81r
Utilities				
Electricity expenditures	year	950	91	81r
Electricity, summer, 250 KWh	month	20.10	8/93	64c
Electricity, summer, 500 KWh	month	34.43	8/93	64c
Electricity, summer, 750 KWh	month	48.78	8/93	64c
Electricity, summer, 1000 KWh	month	63.12	8/93	64c
Utilities, fuels, and public services, total expenditures	year	2000	91	81r
Water and other public services, expenditures	year	227	91	81r
Weddings				
Bridal attendants' gowns	event	750	10/93	76r
Bridal gown	event	852	10/93	76r
Bridal headpiece and veil	event	167	10/93	76r
Bride's wedding band	event	708	10/93	76r
Clergy	event	224	10/93	76r
Engagement ring	event	2756	10/93	76r
Flowers	event	863	10/93	76r
Formal wear for groom	event	106	10/93	76r
Groom's attendants' formal wear	event	530	10/93	76r

Biloxi, MS - continued

Item	Per	Value	Date	Ref.
Weddings - continued				
Groom's wedding band	event	402	10/93	76r
Music	event	600	10/93	76r
Photography	event	1088	10/93	76r
Shoes for bride	event	50	10/93	76r
Videography	event	483	10/93	76r
Wedding invitations and announcements	event	342	10/93	76r
Wedding reception	event	7000	10/93	76r

Binghamton, NY

Item	Per	Value	Date	Ref.
Composite, ACCRA index		97.10	12/94	2c
Alcoholic Beverages				
Beer, Miller Lite, Bud, 12-oz., ex deposit	6	3.97	12/94	2c
J & B Scotch	750-ml.	18.21	12/94	2c
Wine, Gallo Chablis blanc	1.5-lit	5.99	12/94	2c
Appliances				
Appliances (major), expenditures	year	145	91	81r
Average annual exp.				
Food, health care, personal goods, services	year	29496	91	81r
Charity				
Cash contributions, expenditures	year	708	91	81r
Clothing				
Apparel, men and boys, total expenditures	year	416	91	81r
Apparel, women and girls, total expenditures	year	744	91	81r
Footwear, expenditures	year	305	91	81r
Jeans, man's denim		29.59	12/94	2c
Shirt, man's dress shirt		28.38	12/94	2c
Undervest, boy's size 10-14, cotton	3	5.55	12/94	2c
Communications				
Long-distance telephone rate, day, addl. min., 1-10 mi.	min.	4.00	12/93	9s
Long-distance telephone rate, day, initial min., 1-10 mi.	min.	14.90	12/93	9s
Newspaper subscription, dly. and Sun. delivery	month	14.35	12/94	2c
Phone line, single, business, field visit	inst	143.26	12/93	9s
Phone line, single, business, no field visit	inst	106.05	12/93	9s
Phone line, single, residence, field visit	inst	85.46	12/93	9s
Phone line, single, residence, no field visit	inst	55.00	12/93	9s
Telephone bill, family of four	month	25.73	12/94	2c
Telephone service, expenditures	year	589	91	81r
Telephone, business, addl. line, touch tone	month	4.74	10/91	25c
Telephone, business, connection charges, touch tone	inst	146.63	10/91	25c
Telephone, business, key system line, touch tone	month	49.22	10/91	25c
Telephone, business, PBX line, touch tone	month	49.32	10/91	25c
Telephone, business, single ln., touch tone	month	50.50	10/91	25c
Telephone, business, touch tone, inside wiring maintenance plan	month	5.97	10/91	25c
Telephone, residential, flat rate	mo.	16.65	12/93	8c
Education				
Board, 4-year private college/university	year	2918	8/94	80s
Board, 4-year public college/university	year	2177	8/94	80s
Education, total expenditures	year	593	91	81r
Room, 4-year private college/university	year	3302	8/94	80s
Room, 4-year public college/university	year	2624	8/94	80s
Total cost, 4-year private college/university	year	18451	8/94	80s
Total cost, 4-year public college/university	year	7723	8/94	80s
Tuition, 2-year public college/university, in-state	year	2112	8/94	80s
Tuition, 4-year private college/university, in-state	year	12231	8/94	80s
Tuition, 4-year public college/university, in-state	year	2921	8/94	80s

Values are in dollars or fractions of dollars. In the column headed *Ref*, references are shown to sources. Each reference is followed by a letter. These refer to the geographical level for which data were reported: s=State, r=Region, and c=City or metro. The abbreviation *ex* is used to mean *except* or *excluding*; *exp* stands for *expenditures*. For other abbreviations and further explanations, please see the Introduction.

Binghamton, NY - continued

Item	Per	Value	Date	Ref.
Energy and Fuels				
Energy, combined forms, 1800 sq. ft.	mo.	138.03	12/94	2c
Energy, exc. electricity, 1800 sq. ft.	mo.	59.63	12/94	2c
Fuel oil and other fuels, expenditures	year	257	91	81r
Gas, cooking, winter, 10 therms	month	11.62	2/94	65c
Gas, cooking, winter, 30 therms	month	23.54	2/94	65c
Gas, cooking, winter, 50 therms	month	35.45	2/94	65c
Gas, heating, winter, 100 therms	month	65.26	2/94	65c
Gas, heating, winter, average use	month	100.78	2/94	65c
Gas, natural, expenditures	year	285	91	81r
Gas, reg unlead, taxes inc., cash, self-service	gal	1.20	12/94	2c
Gasoline and motor oil purchased	year	867	91	81r
Gasoline, unleaded midgrade	gallon	1.32	4/93	82r
Gasoline, unleaded premium	gallon	1.40	4/93	82r
Gasoline, unleaded regular	gallon	1.19	4/93	82r
Entertainment				
Bowling, evening rate	game	1.59	12/94	2c
Entertainment, total expenditures	year	1331	91	81r
Fees and admissions, expenditures	year	398	91	81r
Monopoly game, Parker Brothers', No. 9	game	11.35	12/94	2c
Movie	adm	6.50	12/94	2c
Pets, toys, playground equipment, expenditures	year	270	91	81r
Reading, expenditures	year	171	91	81r
Televisions, radios, and sound equipment, expenditures	year	429	91	81r
Tennis balls, yellow, Wilson or Penn, 3	can	2.25	12/94	2c
Funerals				
Burial, immediate, container provided by funeral home		1370.36	1/95	54r
Cards, acknowledgment		17.72	1/95	54r
Casket, minimum alternative		192.52	1/95	54r
Cosmetology, hair care, etc.		139.56	1/95	54r
Cremation, direct, container provided by funeral home		1049.24	1/95	54r
Embalming		387.57	1/95	54r
Funeral, funeral home		278.77	1/95	54r
Funeral, other facility		275.85	1/95	54r
Graveside service		213.08	1/95	54r
Hearse, local		157.27	1/95	54r
Limousine, local		146.45	1/95	54r
Memorial service		271.02	1/95	54r
Service charge, professional, nondeclinable		943.58	1/95	54r
Visitation and viewing		322.86	1/95	54r
Groceries				
Groceries, ACCRA Index		103.70	12/94	2c
Apples, Red Delicious	lb.	0.78	12/94	82r
Baby food, strained vegetables, lowest price	4-4.5 oz.	0.33	12/94	2c
Bacon, sliced	lb.	2.24	12/94	82r
Bananas	lb.	0.50	12/94	2c
Bananas	lb.	0.49	12/94	82r
Beef or hamburger, ground	lb.	1.67	12/94	2c
Beef purchases	year	226	91	81r
Beverage purchases, alcoholic	year	332	91	81r
Beverage purchases, nonalcoholic	year	213	91	81r
Bread, white	24-oz.	0.84	12/94	2c
Bread, white, pan	lb.	0.80	12/94	82r
Butter, salted, Grade AA, stick	lb.	1.67	12/94	82r
Carrots, short trimmed and topped	lb.	0.51	12/94	82r
Cereals and bakery products purchases	year	407	91	81r
Cereals and cereals products purchases	year	132	91	81r
Cheese, Kraft grated Parmesan	8-oz.	3.11	12/94	2c
Chicken breast, bone-in	lb.	2.22	12/94	82r
Chicken, fresh, whole	lb.	1.05	12/94	82r
Chicken, whole fryer	lb.	0.88	12/94	2c
Chuck roast, USDA choice, boneless	lb.	2.74	12/94	82r
Cigarettes, Winston, Kings	carton	18.90	12/94	2c
Coffee, 100%, ground roast, all sizes	lb.	4.61	12/94	82r
Coffee, vacuum-packed	13 oz.	2.97	12/94	2c
Corn Flakes, Kellogg's or Post Toasties	18 oz.	2.11	12/94	2c

Binghamton, NY - continued

Item	Per	Value	Date	Ref.
Groceries - continued				
Corn, frozen, whole kernel, lowest price	10 oz.	0.68	12/94	2c
Dairy products (other) purchases	year	161	91	81r
Eggs, Grade A large	dozen	0.80	12/94	2c
Eggs, Grade A large	dozen	1.12	12/94	82r
Fish and seafood purchases	year	112	91	81r
Food purchases, food eaten at home	year	2599	91	81r
Foods purchased away from home, not prepared by consumer	year	2024	91	81r
Fruits and vegetables purchases	year	444	91	81r
Grapefruit	lb.	0.44	12/94	82r
Grapes, Thompson seedless	lb.	2.24	12/94	82r
Ground chuck, 100% beef	lb.	1.67	12/94	82r
Ice cream, prepackaged, bulk, regular	1/2 gal.	2.93	12/94	82r
Lemons	lb.	1.06	12/94	82r
Lettuce, iceberg	lb.	0.92	12/94	82r
Lettuce, iceberg	head	0.90	12/94	2c
Margarine, Blue Bonnet or Parkay cubes	lb.	0.51	12/94	2c
Meats, poultry, fish, and eggs purchases	year	751	91	81r
Milk and cream (fresh) purchases	year	152	91	81r
Milk, whole	1/2 gal.	1.21	12/94	2c
Orange juice, frozen concentrate 12-oz. can	16 oz.	1.92	12/94	82r
Orange juice, Minute Maid frozen	12-oz.	1.12	12/94	2c
Oranges, Navel	lb.	0.56	12/94	82r
Peaches, halves or slices, Hunt's, Del Monte, or Libby's	29-oz.	1.28	12/94	2c
Peas, sweet, Del Monte or Green Giant	15-17 oz.	0.54	12/94	2c
Pork chops, center cut, bone-in	lb.	3.09	12/94	82r
Pork purchases	year	130	91	81r
Potatoes, white	lb.	0.37	12/94	82r
Potatoes, white or red	10-lb. sack	2.21	12/94	2c
Rib roast, USDA choice, bone-in	lb.	4.98	12/94	82r
Round roast, USDA choice, boneless	lb.	2.93	12/94	82r
Sausage, Jimmy Dean, 100% pork	lb.	3.15	12/94	2c
Shortening, vegetable oil blends	lb.	1.03	12/94	82r
Shortening, vegetable, Crisco	3-lb.	2.39	12/94	2c
Soft drink, Coca Cola, ex deposit	2 lit	1.21	12/94	2c
Spaghetti and macaroni	lb.	0.84	12/94	82r
Steak, round, USDA choice, boneless	lb.	3.48	12/94	82r
Steak, sirloin, USDA choice, bone-in	lb.	3.38	12/94	82r
Steak, sirloin, USDA choice, boneless	lb.	4.81	12/94	82r
Steak, t-bone	lb.	6.49	12/94	2c
Sugar and other sweets, eaten at home, expenditures	year	89	91	81r
Sugar, cane or beet	4 lbs.	1.43	12/94	2c
Sugar, white, all sizes	lb.	0.46	12/94	82r
Tobacco products and smoking supplies, total expenditures	year	279	91	81r
Tomatoes, field grown	lb.	1.56	12/94	82r
Tomatoes, Hunt's or Del Monte	14.5 oz.	0.73	12/94	2c
Tuna, chunk, light	lb.	2.09	12/94	82r
Tuna, chunk, light, oil-packed	6.125-6.5 oz.	0.82	12/94	2c
Goods and Services				
Miscellaneous goods and services, ACCRA Index		99.80	12/94	2c
Health Care				
Health care, ACCRA Index		91.40	12/94	2c
Antibiotic ointment, Polysporin	1.5 oz.	4.04	12/94	2c
Childbirth, Cesarean delivery, hospital charge	birth	6334.00	12/91	69r
Childbirth, Cesarean delivery, physician charge	birth	2234.00	12/91	69r
Childbirth, normal delivery, hospital charge	birth	3225.00	12/91	69r
Childbirth, normal delivery, physician charge	birth	1623.00	12/91	69r
Dentist's fee, adult teeth cleaning and periodic oral exam	visit	47.20	12/94	2c

Values are in dollars or fractions of dollars. In the column headed *Ref*, references are shown to sources. Each reference is followed by a letter. These refer to the geographical level for which data were reported: s = State, r = Region, and c = City or metro. The abbreviation *ex* is used to mean *except* or *excluding*; *exp* stands for *expenditures*. For other abbreviations and further explanations, please see the Introduction.

Binghamton, NY - continued

Item	Per	Value	Date	Ref.
Health Care				
Doctor's fee, routine exam, established patient	visit	41.60	12/94	2c
Drugs, expenditures	year	205	91	81r
Health care, total expenditures	year	1396	91	81r
Health insurance expenditures	year	553	91	81r
Hospital care, semiprivate room	day	265.00	12/94	2c
Insurance premium, family medical care	month	384.24	1/95	41s
Medical services expenditures	year	559	91	81r
Medical supplies expenditures	year	80	91	81r
Household Goods				
Appl. repair, service call, wash mach	min. lab. chg.	33.77	12/94	2c
Floor coverings, expenditures	year	158	91	81r
Furniture, expenditures	year	341	91	81r
Household equipment, misc. expenditures	year	363	91	81r
Household expenditures, miscellaneous	year	194	91	81r
Household furnishings and equipment, expenditures	year	1158	91	81r
Household operations expenditures	year	378	91	81r
Household textiles, expenditures	year	88	91	81r
Housekeeping supplies, expenditures	year	426	91	81r
Laundry and cleaning supplies, expenditures	year	122	91	81r
Laundry detergent, Tide Ultra, Bold, or Cheer	42 oz.	3.78	12/94	2c
Postage and stationery, expenditures	year	134	91	81r
Tissues, facial, Kleenex brand	175	1.09	12/94	2c
Housing				
Housing, ACCRA Index		81.80	12/94	2c
Add garage/carport		11,614	3/95	74r
Add room(s)		16,816	3/95	74r
Apartment condominium or co-op, median	unit	96700	12/94	62r
Dwellings (owned), expenditures	year	3305	91	81r
Enclose porch/patio/breezeway		2,980	3/95	74r
Finish room in basement/attic		4,330	3/95	74r
Home, existing, single-family, median	unit	161600	12/94	62r
House payment, principal and interest, 25% down payment	mo.	613	12/94	2c
House, 1800 sq ft, 8000 sq ft lot, new, urban, utilities	total	97525	12/94	2c
Maintenance, repairs, insurance, and other housing expenditures	year	569	91	81r
Mortgage interest and charges expenditures	year	1852	91	81r
Mtge. rate, incl. points and orig. fee, 30-year conv. fixed or ARM	mo.	9.46	12/94	2c
Princ. & int., mortgage, median-price exist. sing.-family home	mo.	765	12/94	62r
Property taxes expenditures	year	884	91	81r
Redesign, restructure more than half of home's interior		2,750	3/95	74r
Rent, apartment, 2 br., 1 1/2-2 baths, unfurnished, 950 sq ft, water	mo.	472	12/94	2c
Rental units expenditures	year	1832	91	81r
Insurance and Pensions				
Auto insurance, private passenger	year	985.07	12/94	71s
Insurance and pensions, personal, expenditures	year	2690	91	81r
Insurance, life and other personal, expenditures	year	341	91	81r
Pensions and Social Security, expenditures	year	2349	91	81r
Legal Assistance				
Estate planning, law-firm partner	hr.	375.00	10/93	12r
Legal work, law firm associate	hour	78		10r
Legal work, law firm partner	hour	183		10r
Personal Goods				
Shampoo, Alberto VO5	15-oz.	1.44	12/94	2c
Toothpaste, Crest or Colgate	6-7 oz.	2.03	12/94	2c

Binghamton, NY - continued

Item	Per	Value	Date	Ref.
Personal Services				
Dry cleaning, man's 2-pc. suit		6.90	12/94	2c
Haircut, man's barbershop, no styling		6.50	12/94	2c
Haircut, woman's shampoo, trim, blow-dry		19.27	12/94	2c
Personal services expenditures	year	184	91	81r
Restaurant Food				
Chicken, fried, thigh and drumstick		2.00	12/94	2c
Dining expenditures, family	week	34.26	94	73r
Hamburger with cheese	1/4 lb.	1.99	12/94	2c
Pizza, Pizza Hut or Pizza Inn	12-13 in.	7.49	12/94	2c
Taxes				
Taxes, Federal income, expenditures	year	2409	91	81r
Taxes, personal, expenditures	year	3094	91	81r
Taxes, State and local income, expenditures	year	620	91	81r
Transportation				
Transportation, ACCRA Index		102.50	12/94	2c
Bus fare, up to 10 miles	one-way	0.80	12/94	2c
Cars and trucks purchased, new	year	1170	91	81r
Cars and trucks purchased, used	year	739	91	81r
Driver's learning permit fee	perm	10.00	1/94	84s
Driver's license fee	orig	32.00-37.00	1/94	84s
Driver's license fee, duplicate	lic	7.25	1/94	84s
Driver's license reinstatement fee, min.	susp	25.00	1/94	85s
Driver's license renewal fee	renew	22.25	1/94	84s
Identification card, nondriver	card	6.25	1/94	83s
Motorcycle license fee	orig	32.00-37.00	1/94	84s
Motorcycle license fee, duplicate	lic	7.25	1/94	84s
Motorcycle license renewal fee	renew	22.25	1/94	84s
Public transportation expenditures	year	430	91	81r
Tire balance, computer or spin bal., front	wheel	6.88	12/94	2c
Transportation expenditures, total	year	4810	91	81r
Vehicle finance charges	year	238	91	81r
Vehicle insurance expenditures	year	630	91	81r
Vehicle maintenance and repairs expenditures	year	532	91	81r
Vehicle purchases	year	1920	91	81r
Vehicle rental, leases, licenses, etc. expenditures	year	193	91	81r
Vehicles purchased, other than cars and trucks	year	11	91	81r
Utilities				
Utilities, ACCRA Index		124.20	12/94	2c
Electricity expenditures	year	695	91	81r
Electricity, (part.), other, 1800 sq. ft., new home	mo.	78.40	12/94	2c
Electricity, summer, 250 KWh	month	33.84	8/93	64c
Electricity, summer, 500 KWh	month	61.45	8/93	64c
Electricity, summer, 750 KWh	month	89.07	8/93	64c
Electricity, summer, 1000 KWh	month	116.68	8/93	64c
Utilities, fuels, and public services, total expenditures	year	1981	91	81r
Water and other public services, expenditures	year	154	91	81r
Weddings				
Bridal attendants' gowns	event	750	10/93	76r
Bridal gown	event	852	10/93	76r
Bridal headpiece and veil	event	167	10/93	76r
Bride's wedding band	event	708	10/93	76r
Clergy	event	224	10/93	76r
Engagement ring	event	2756	10/93	76r
Flowers	event	863	10/93	76r
Formal wear for groom	event	106	10/93	76r
Groom's attendants' formal wear	event	530	10/93	76r
Groom's wedding band	event	402	10/93	76r
Music	event	600	10/93	76r
Photography	event	1088	10/93	76r

Values are in dollars or fractions of dollars. In the column headed *Ref*, references are shown to sources. Each reference is followed by a letter. These refer to the geographical level for which data were reported: s = State, r = Region, and c = City or metro. The abbreviation *ex* is used to mean *except* or *excluding*; *exp* stands for expenditures. For other abbreviations and further explanations, please see the Introduction.

Binghamton, NY - continued

Item	Per	Value	Date	Ref.
Weddings				
Shoes for bride	event	50	10/93	76r
Videography	event	483	10/93	76r
Wedding invitations and announcements	event	342	10/93	76r
Wedding reception	event	7000	10/93	76r

Birmingham, AL

Item	Per	Value	Date	Ref.
Composite, ACCRA index		99.10	12/94	2c
Alcoholic Beverages				
Beer, Miller Lite, Bud, 12-oz., ex deposit	6	3.80	12/94	2c
J & B Scotch	750-ml.	20.99	12/94	2c
Wine, Gallo Chablis blanc	1.5-lit	5.02	12/94	2c
Appliances				
Appliances (major), expenditures	year	153	91	81r
Average annual exp.				
Food, health care, personal goods, services	year	27020	91	81r
Charity				
Cash contributions, expenditures	year	839	91	81r
Clothing				
Apparel, men and boys, total expenditures	year	380	91	81r
Apparel, women and girls, total expenditures	year	660	91	81r
Footwear, expenditures	year	193	91	81r
Jeans, man's denim		30.84	12/94	2c
Shirt, man's dress shirt		30.30	12/94	2c
Undervest, boy's size 10-14, cotton	3	5.04	12/94	2c
Communications				
Long-distance telephone rate, day, addl. min., 1-10 mi.	min.	0.09	12/93	9s
Long-distance telephone rate, day, initial min., 1-10 mi.	min.	0.11	12/93	9s
Newspaper subscription, dly. and Sun. delivery	month	11.96	12/94	2c
Phone line, single, business, field visit	inst	69.00	12/93	9s
Phone line, single, business, no field visit	inst	69.00	12/93	9s
Phone line, single, residence, field visit	inst	40.00	12/93	9s
Phone line, single, residence, no field visit	inst	40.00	12/93	9s
Telephone bill, family of four	month	25.98	12/94	2c
Telephone service, expenditures	year	616	91	81r
Telephone, residential, flat rate	mo.	20.10	12/93	8c
Education				
Board, 4-year private college/university	year	2072	8/94	80s
Board, 4-year public college/university	year	1706	8/94	80s
Education, total expenditures	year	319	91	81r
Room, 4-year private college/university	year	1607	8/94	80s
Room, 4-year public college/university	year	1598	8/94	80s
Total cost, 4-year private college/university	year	10664	8/94	80s
Total cost, 4-year public college/university	year	5287	8/94	80s
Tuition, 2-year public college/university, in-state	year	1110	8/94	80s
Tuition, 4-year private college/university, in-state	year	6985	8/94	80s
Tuition, 4-year public college/university, in-state	year	1983	8/94	80s
Energy and Fuels				
Energy, combined forms, 1800 sq. ft.	mo.	127.17	12/94	2c
Energy, exc. electricity, 1800 sq. ft.	mo.	48.46	12/94	2c
Fuel oil and other fuels, expenditures	year	56	91	81r
Gas, cooking, 10 therms	month	14.58	2/94	65c
Gas, cooking, 30 therms	month	27.74	2/94	65c
Gas, cooking, 50 therms	month	40.88	2/94	65c
Gas, heating, winter, 100 therms	month	68.71	2/94	65c
Gas, heating, winter, average use	month	103.23	2/94	65c
Gas, natural, expenditures	year	150	91	81r
Gas, reg unlead, taxes inc., cash, self-service	gal	1.10	12/94	2c
Gasoline and motor oil purchased	year	1152	91	81r

Birmingham, AL - continued

Item	Per	Value	Date	Ref.
Energy and Fuels - continued				
Gasoline, unleaded midgrade	gallon	1.21	4/93	82r
Gasoline, unleaded premium	gallon	1.30	4/93	82r
Gasoline, unleaded regular	gallon	1.10	4/93	82r
Entertainment				
Bowling, evening rate	game	2.37	12/94	2c
Concert ticket, Pearl Jam group	perf	20.00	94	50r
Entertainment, total expenditures	year	1266	91	81r
Fees and admissions, expenditures	year	306	91	81r
Monopoly game, Parker Brothers', No. 9	game	11.74	12/94	2c
Movie	adm	5.75	12/94	2c
Pets, toys, playground equipment, expenditures	year	271	91	81r
Reading, expenditures	year	131	91	81r
Televisions, radios, and sound equipment, expenditures	year	439	91	81r
Tennis balls, yellow, Wilson or Penn, 3	can	2.22	12/94	2c
Funerals				
Burial, immediate, container provided by funeral home		1298.96	1/95	54r
Cards, acknowledgment		21.26	1/95	54r
Casket, minimum alternative		204.95	1/95	54r
Cosmetology, hair care, etc.		85.40	1/95	54r
Cremation, direct, container provided by funeral home		1054.77	1/95	54r
Embalming		287.71	1/95	54r
Funeral, funeral home		269.18	1/95	54r
Funeral, other facility		272.88	1/95	54r
Graveside service		302.54	1/95	54r
Hearse, local		122.08	1/95	54r
Limousine, local		80.31	1/95	54r
Memorial service		277.66	1/95	54r
Service charge, professional, nondeclinable		896.65	1/95	54r
Visitation and viewing		232.39	1/95	54r
Groceries				
Groceries, ACCRA Index		94.60	12/94	2c
Apples, Red Delicious	lb.	0.73	12/94	82r
Baby food, strained vegetables, lowest price	4-4.5 oz.	0.31	12/94	2c
Bacon, sliced	lb.	1.67	12/94	82r
Bananas	lb.	0.45	12/94	2c
Bananas	lb.	0.42	12/94	82r
Beef or hamburger, ground	lb.	1.53	12/94	2c
Beef purchases	year	213	91	81r
Beverage purchases, alcoholic	year	249	91	81r
Beverage purchases, nonalcoholic	year	207	91	81r
Bologna, all beef or mixed	lb.	2.27	12/94	82r
Bread, white	24-oz.	0.74	12/94	2c
Bread, white, pan	lb.	0.68	12/94	82r
Cabbage	lb.	0.42	12/94	82r
Carrots, short trimmed and topped	lb.	0.53	12/94	82r
Cereals and bakery products purchases	year	345	91	81r
Cereals and cereals products purchases	year	127	91	81r
Cheddar cheese, natural	lb.	3.58	12/94	82r
Cheese, Kraft grated Parmesan	8-oz.	3.25	12/94	2c
Chicken breast, bone-in	lb.	1.71	12/94	82r
Chicken, fresh, whole	lb.	0.78	12/94	82r
Chicken, whole fryer	lb.	0.67	12/94	2c
Chuck roast, USDA choice, boneless	lb.	2.26	12/94	82r
Cigarettes, Winston, Kings	carton	14.44	12/94	2c
Coffee, vacuum-packed	13 oz.	3.06	12/94	2c
Corn Flakes, Kellogg's or Post Toasties	18 oz.	2.08	12/94	2c
Corn, frozen, whole kernel, lowest price	10 oz.	0.69	12/94	2c
Crackers, soda, salted	lb.	1.27	12/94	82r
Cucumbers	lb.	0.65	12/94	82r
Dairy products (other) purchases	year	141	91	81r
Eggs, Grade A large	dozen	0.72	12/94	2c
Eggs, Grade A large	dozen	0.87	12/94	82r
Fish and seafood purchases	year	72	91	81r
Flour, white, all purpose	lb.	0.23	12/94	82r
Food purchases, food eaten at home	year	2381	91	81r

Values are in dollars or fractions of dollars. In the column headed *Ref*, references are shown to sources. Each reference is followed by a letter. These refer to the geographical level for which data were reported: s=State, r=Region, and c=City or metro. The abbreviation *ex* is used to mean *except* or *excluding*; *exp* stands for *expenditures*. For other abbreviations and further explanations, please see the Introduction.

Birmingham, AL - continued

Item	Per	Value	Date	Ref.
Groceries				
Foods purchased away from home, not prepared by consumer	year	1696	91	81r
Frankfurters, all meat or all beef	lb.	1.74	12/94	82r
Fruits and vegetables purchases	year	380	91	81r
Grapefruit	lb.	0.45	12/94	82r
Grapes, Thompson seedless	lb.	2.30	12/94	82r
Ground beef, 100% beef	lb.	1.37	12/94	82r
Ground chuck, 100% beef	lb.	1.97	12/94	82r
Ham, boneless, exc. canned	lb.	2.54	12/94	82r
Ice cream, prepackaged, bulk, regular	1/2 gal.	2.47	12/94	82r
Lemons	lb.	1.02	12/94	82r
Lettuce, iceberg	lb.	0.96	12/94	82r
Lettuce, iceberg	head	0.91	12/94	2c
Margarine, Blue Bonnet or Parkay cubes	lb.	0.60	12/94	2c
Margarine, stick	lb.	0.77	12/94	82r
Meats, poultry, fish, and eggs purchases	year	655	91	81r
Milk and cream (fresh) purchases	year	130	91	81r
Milk, whole	1/2 gal.	1.35	12/94	2c
Orange juice, frozen concentrate 12-oz. can	16 oz.	1.36	12/94	82r
Orange juice, Minute Maid frozen	12-oz.	1.14	12/94	2c
Oranges, Navel	lb.	0.54	12/94	82r
Peaches, halves or slices, Hunt's, Del Monte, or Libby's	29-oz.	1.23	12/94	2c
Pears, Anjou	lb.	0.81	12/94	82r
Peas, sweet, Del Monte or Green Giant	15-17 oz.	0.48	12/94	2c
Pork chops, center cut, bone-in	lb.	3.07	12/94	82r
Pork purchases	year	142	91	81r
Potato chips	16-oz.	3.15	12/94	82r
Potatoes, frozen, French fried	lb.	0.82	12/94	82r
Potatoes, white	lb.	0.34	12/94	82r
Potatoes, white or red	10-lb. sack	2.67	12/94	2c
Rice, white, long grain, uncooked	lb.	0.48	12/94	82r
Round roast, USDA choice, boneless	lb.	2.91	12/94	82r
Sausage, fresh	lb.	1.82	12/94	82r
Sausage, Jimmy Dean, 100% pork	lb.	2.22	12/94	2c
Shortening, vegetable oil blends	lb.	0.75	12/94	82r
Shortening, vegetable, Crisco	3-lb.	2.46	12/94	2c
Soft drink, Coca Cola, ex deposit	2 lit	1.04	12/94	2c
Spaghetti and macaroni	lb.	0.87	12/94	82r
Steak, rib eye, USDA choice, boneless	lb.	6.85	12/94	82r
Steak, round, graded & ungraded, exc. USDA prime & choice	lb.	2.96	12/94	82r
Steak, round, USDA choice, boneless	lb.	3.17	12/94	82r
Steak, sirloin, USDA choice, boneless	lb.	4.12	12/94	82r
Steak, t-bone	lb.	5.74	12/94	2c
Steak, T-bone, USDA choice, bone-in	lb.	5.63	12/94	82r
Sugar and other sweets, eaten at home, expenditures	year	93	91	81r
Sugar, cane or beet	4 lbs.	1.42	12/94	2c
Sugar, white, all sizes	lb.	0.39	12/94	82r
Tobacco products and smoking supplies, total expenditures	year	286	91	81r
Tomatoes, field grown	lb.	1.36	12/94	82r
Tomatoes, Hunt's or Del Monte	14.5 oz.	0.66	12/94	2c
Tuna, chunk, light	lb.	1.94	12/94	82r
Tuna, chunk, light, oil-packed	6.125-6.5 oz.	0.64	12/94	2c
Turkey, frozen, whole	lb.	0.96	12/94	82r
Yogurt, natural, fruit flavored	8 oz.	0.58	12/94	82r
Goods and Services				
Miscellaneous goods and services, ACCRA Index		98.90	12/94	2c
Health Care				
Health care, ACCRA Index		95.00	12/94	2c
Adenosine, emergency room	treat	100.00	95	23r
Antibiotic ointment, Polysporin	1.5 oz.	3.65	12/94	2c

Birmingham, AL - continued

Item	Per	Value	Date	Ref.
Health Care - continued				
Bladder tap, superpubic, infant, emergency room	treat	119.00	95	23r
Blood analysis, emergency room	treat	25.00	95	23r
Blood tests, abdominal pain, emergency room	treat	25.00	95	23r
Burn dressing, emergency room	treat	266.00	95	23r
Cardiology interpretation, emergency room	treat	26.00	95	23r
Chest X-ray, emergency room	treat	78.00	95	23r
Childbirth, Cesarean delivery, hospital charge	birth	5462.00	12/91	69r
Childbirth, Cesarean delivery, physician charge	birth	2228.00	12/91	69r
Childbirth, normal delivery, hospital charge	birth	2943.00	12/91	69r
Childbirth, normal delivery, physician charge	birth	1619.00	12/91	69r
Defibrillation pads, emergency room	treat	6.00	95	23r
Dentist's fee, adult teeth cleaning and periodic oral exam	visit	46.50	12/94	2c
Doctor's fee, routine exam, established patient	visit	38.50	12/94	2c
Drugs, expenditures	year	297	91	81r
Gastric tube insertion, nasal, emergency room	treat	25.00	95	23r
Health care, total expenditures	year	1600	91	81r
Health insurance expenditures	year	637	91	81r
Heart monitor, emergency room	treat	40.00	95	23r
Hospital care, semiprivate room	day	419.00	12/94	2c
Insurance premium, family medical care	month	360.67	1/95	41s
Intravenous fluids, emergency room	treat	130.00	95	23r
Intravenous fluids, emergency room	liter	26.00	95	23r
Intravenous line, central, emergency room	treat	342.00	95	23r
Liver function tests, abdominal pain, emergency room	treat	26.00	95	23r
Medical care charges, total, emergency room, third-degree burns	treat	2101.00	95	23r
Medical care charges, total, emergency, infant with fever	treat	628.00	95	23r
Medical services expenditures	year	573	91	81r
Medical supplies expenditures	year	93	91	81r
Morphine, emergency room	treat	34.00	95	23r
Nursing care and facilities charges, emergency room	treat	252.00	95	23r
Nursing care and facilities charges, emergency, infant with fever	treat	252.00	95	23r
Nursing care and facilities charges, emergency, third-degree burns	treat	861.00	95	23r
Physician's charges, emergency, infant with fever	treat	212.00	95	23r
Physician's charges, emergency, third-degree burns	treat	372.00	95	23r
Physician's fee, emergency room	treat	372.00	95	23r
Physician's fee, general practitioner	visit	51.20	12/93	60r
Surgery, open-heart	proc	42374.00	1/93	14r
Ultrasound, abdominal, emergency room	treat	276.00	95	23r
Urinalysis, emergency room	treat	20.00	95	23r
Urinalysis, infant, emergency room	treat	20.00	95	23r
X-rays, emergency room	treat	78.00	95	23r
Household Goods				
Appl. repair, service call, wash mach	min. lab. chg.	35.00	12/94	2c
Floor coverings, expenditures	year	48	91	81r
Furniture, expenditures	year	280	91	81r
Household equipment, misc. expenditures	year	342	91	81r
Household expenditures, miscellaneous	year	256	91	81r
Household furnishings and equipment, expenditures	year	988	91	81r
Household operations expenditures	year	468	91	81r
Household textiles, expenditures	year	95	91	81r
Housekeeping supplies, expenditures	year	380	91	81r
Laundry and cleaning supplies, expenditures	year	109	91	81r

Values are in dollars or fractions of dollars. In the column headed *Ref*, references are shown to sources. Each reference is followed by a letter. These refer to the geographical level for which data were reported: s=State, r=Region, and c=City or metro. The abbreviation *ex* is used to mean *except* or *excluding*; *exp* stands for expenditures. For other abbreviations and further explanations, please see the Introduction.

Birmingham, AL - continued

Item	Per	Value	Date	Ref.
Household Goods				
Laundry detergent, Tide Ultra, Bold, or Cheer	42 oz.	3.02	12/94	2c
Postage and stationery, expenditures	year	105	91	81r
Tissues, facial, Kleenex brand	175	0.99	12/94	2c
Housing				
Housing, ACCRA Index		99.40	12/94	2c
Add garage/carport		6,980	3/95	74r
Add room(s)		11,403	3/95	74r
Apartment condominium or co-op, median	unit	68600	12/94	62r
Dwellings (owned), expenditures	year	2428	91	81r
Enclose porch/patio/breezeway		4,572	3/95	74r
Finish room in basement/attic		3,794	3/95	74r
Home, existing, single-family, median	unit	120200	12/94	62r
Home, existing, single-family, median	unit	100.10	12/94	62c
House payment, principal and interest, 25% down payment	mo.	768	12/94	2c
House, 1800 sq ft, 8000 sq ft lot, new, urban, utilities	total	123500	12/94	2c
Maintenance, repairs, insurance, and other housing expenditures	year	531	91	81r
Mortgage interest and charges expenditures	year	1506	91	81r
Mtge. rate, incl. points and orig. fee, 30-year conv. fixed or ARM	mo.	9.33	12/94	2c
Princ. & int., mortgage, median-price exist. sing.-family home	mo.	540	12/94	62r
Property taxes expenditures	year	391	91	81r
Redesign, restructure more than half of home's interior		17,641	3/95	74r
Rent, apartment, 2 br., 1 1/2-2 baths, unfurnished, 950 sq ft, water	mo.	507	12/94	2c
Rental units expenditures	year	1264	91	81r
Insurance and Pensions				
Auto insurance, private passenger	year	604.07	12/94	71s
Insurance and pensions, personal, expenditures	year	2395	91	81r
Insurance, life and other personal, expenditures	year	368	91	81r
Pensions and Social Security, expenditures	year	2027	91	81r
Personal Goods				
Shampoo, Alberto VO5	15-oz.	0.97	12/94	2c
Toothpaste, Crest or Colgate	6-7 oz.	2.01	12/94	2c
Personal Services				
Dry cleaning, man's 2-pc. suit		6.40	12/94	2c
Haircut, man's barbershop, no styling		8.33	12/94	2c
Haircut, woman's shampoo, trim, blow-dry		20.60	12/94	2c
Personal services expenditures	year	212	91	81r
Restaurant Food				
Chicken, fried, thigh and drumstick		1.89	12/94	2c
Dining expenditures, family	week	33.83	94	73r
Hamburger with cheese	1/4 lb.	1.59	12/94	2c
Pizza, Pizza Hut or Pizza Inn	12-13 in.	7.99	12/94	2c
Taxes				
Tax rate, residential property, month	$100	0.70	1/92	79c
Taxes, Federal income, expenditures	year	2275	91	81r
Taxes, personal, expenditures	year	2715	91	81r
Taxes, State and local income, expenditures	year	365	91	81r
Transportation				
Transportation, ACCRA Index		94.10	12/94	2c
Bus fare, one-way	trip	0.80	12/95	1c
Bus fare, up to 10 miles	one-way	0.80	12/94	2c
Cars and trucks purchased, new	year	1306	91	81r
Cars and trucks purchased, used	year	942	91	81r
Driver's learning permit fee	perm	20.00	1/94	84s
Driver's license fee	orig	20.00	1/94	84s
Driver's license fee, duplicate	lic	5.00	1/94	84s
Driver's license reinstatement fee, min.	susp	50.00	1/94	85s

Birmingham, AL - continued

Item	Per	Value	Date	Ref.
Transportation - continued				
Driver's license renewal fee	renew	20.00	1/94	84s
Identification card, nondriver	card	20.00	1/94	83s
Motorcycle license fee	orig	20.00	1/94	84s
Motorcycle license fee, duplicate	lic	5.00	1/94	84s
Motorcycle license renewal fee	renew	20.00	1/94	84s
Public transportation expenditures	year	249	91	81r
Tire balance, computer or spin bal., front	wheel	6.25	12/94	2c
Transportation expenditures, total	year	5307	91	81r
Vehicle finance charges	year	346	91	81r
Vehicle insurance expenditures	year	544	91	81r
Vehicle maintenance and repairs expenditures	year	600	91	81r
Vehicle purchases	year	2275	91	81r
Vehicle rental, leases, licenses, etc. expenditures	year	141	91	81r
Vehicles purchased, other than cars and trucks	year	27	91	81r
Utilities				
Utilities, ACCRA Index		116.00	12/94	2c
Electricity expenditures	year	950	91	81r
Electricity, (part.), other, 1800 sq. ft., new home	mo.	78.71	12/94	2c
Electricity, summer, 250 KWh	month	24.26	8/93	64c
Electricity, summer, 500 KWh	month	41.31	8/93	64c
Electricity, summer, 750 KWh	month	58.35	8/93	64c
Electricity, summer, 1000 KWh	month	75.37	8/93	64c
Utilities, fuels, and public services, total expenditures	year	2000	91	81r
Water and other public services, expenditures	year	227	91	81r
Weddings				
Bridal attendants' gowns	event	750	10/93	76r
Bridal gown	event	852	10/93	76r
Bridal headpiece and veil	event	167	10/93	76r
Bride's wedding band	event	708	10/93	76r
Clergy	event	224	10/93	76r
Engagement ring	event	2756	10/93	76r
Flowers	event	863	10/93	76r
Formal wear for groom	event	106	10/93	76r
Groom's attendants' formal wear	event	530	10/93	76r
Groom's wedding band	event	402	10/93	76r
Music	event	600	10/93	76r
Photography	event	1088	10/93	76r
Shoes for bride	event	50	10/93	76r
Videography	event	483	10/93	76r
Wedding invitations and announcements	event	342	10/93	76r
Wedding reception	event	7000	10/93	76r

Bismarck, ND

Item	Per	Value	Date	Ref.
Composite, ACCRA index		102.10	12/94	2c
Alcoholic Beverages				
Beer, Miller Lite, Bud, 12-oz., ex deposit	6	3.81	12/94	2c
J & B Scotch	750-ml.	17.32	12/94	2c
Wine, Gallo Chablis blanc	1.5-lit	5.41	12/94	2c
Appliances				
Appliances (major), expenditures	year	131	91	81r
Average annual exp.				
Food, health care, personal goods, services	year	25935	91	81r
Charity				
Cash contributions, expenditures	year	745	91	81r
Clothing				
Apparel, men and boys, total expenditures	year	332	91	81r
Apparel, women and girls, total expenditures	year	578	91	81r
Footwear, expenditures	year	164	91	81r
Jeans, man's denim		37.50	12/94	2c
Shirt, man's dress shirt		34.14	12/94	2c

Values are in dollars or fractions of dollars. In the column headed *Ref*, references are shown to sources. Each reference is followed by a letter. These refer to the geographical level for which data were reported: s = State, r = Region, and c = City or metro. The abbreviation *ex* is used to mean *except* or *excluding*; *exp* stands for expenditures. For other abbreviations and further explanations, please see the Introduction.

Bismarck, ND - continued

Item	Per	Value	Date	Ref.
Clothing				
Undervest, boy's size 10-14, cotton	3	5.53	12/94	2c
Communications				
Long-distance telephone rate, day, addl. min., 1-10 mi.	min.	0.10	12/93	9s
Long-distance telephone rate, day, initial min., 1-10 mi.	min.	0.24	12/93	9s
Newspaper subscription, dly. and Sun. delivery	month	13.50	12/94	2c
Phone line, single, business, field visit	inst	52.67	12/93	9s
Phone line, single, business, no field visit	inst	52.67	12/93	9s
Phone line, single, residence, field visit	inst	31.79	12/93	9s
Phone line, single, residence, no field visit	inst	31.79	12/93	9s
Telephone bill, family of four	month	18.48	12/94	2c
Telephone service, expenditures	year	547	91	81r
Telephone, residential, flat rate	mo.	11.54	12/93	8c
Education				
Board, 4-year private college/university	year	1582	8/94	80s
Board, 4-year public college/university	year	2259	8/94	80s
Education, total expenditures	year	394	91	81r
Room, 4-year private college/university	year	1183	8/94	80s
Room, 4-year public college/university	year	908	8/94	80s
Total cost, 4-year private college/university	year	9188	8/94	80s
Total cost, 4-year public college/university	year	5294	8/94	80s
Tuition, 2-year public college/university, in-state	year	1634	8/94	80s
Tuition, 4-year private college/university, in-state	year	6422	8/94	80s
Tuition, 4-year public college/university, in-state	year	2128	8/94	80s
Energy and Fuels				
Energy, combined forms, 1800 sq. ft.	mo.	91.72	12/94	2c
Energy, exc. electricity, 1800 sq. ft.	mo.	44.36	12/94	2c
Fuel oil and other fuels, expenditures	year	83	91	81r
Gas, cooking, winter, 10 therms	month	10.36	2/94	65c
Gas, cooking, winter, 30 therms	month	20.06	2/94	65c
Gas, cooking, winter, 50 therms	month	29.76	2/94	65c
Gas, heating, winter, 100 therms	month	51.77	2/94	65c
Gas, heating, winter, average use	month	78.18	2/94	65c
Gas, natural, expenditures	year	373	91	81r
Gas, reg unlead, taxes inc., cash, self-service	gal	1.20	12/94	2c
Gasoline and motor oil purchased	year	1000	91	81r
Gasoline, unleaded midgrade	gallon	1.15	4/93	82r
Gasoline, unleaded premium	gallon	1.23	4/93	82r
Gasoline, unleaded regular	gallon	1.07	4/93	82r
Entertainment				
Bowling, evening rate	game	1.78	12/94	2c
Entertainment, total expenditures	year	1356	91	81r
Fees and admissions, expenditures	year	347	91	81r
Monopoly game, Parker Brothers', No. 9	game	10.98	12/94	2c
Movie	adm	5.50	12/94	2c
Pets, toys, playground equipment, expenditures	year	270	91	81r
Reading, expenditures	year	160	91	81r
Televisions, radios, and sound equipment, expenditures	year	433	91	81r
Tennis balls, yellow, Wilson or Penn, 3	can	2.77	12/94	2c
Funerals				
Burial, immediate, container provided by funeral home		1348.78	1/95	54r
Cards, acknowledgment		21.20	1/95	54r
Casket, minimum alternative		182.83	1/95	54r
Cosmetology, hair care, etc.		133.11	1/95	54r
Cremation, direct, container provided by funeral home		1101.95	1/95	54r
Embalming		314.45	1/95	54r
Funeral, funeral home		304.88	1/95	54r
Funeral, other facility		301.37	1/95	54r
Graveside service		290.59	1/95	54r

Bismarck, ND - continued

Item	Per	Value	Date	Ref.
Funerals - continued				
Hearse, local		137.37	1/95	54r
Limousine, local		82.84	1/95	54r
Memorial service		316.57	1/95	54r
Service charge, professional, nondeclinable		1099.00	1/95	54r
Visitation and viewing		209.25	1/95	54r
Groceries				
Groceries, ACCRA Index		107.70	12/94	2c
Apples, Red Delicious	lb.	0.68	12/94	82r
Baby food, strained vegetables, lowest price	4-4.5 oz.	0.46	12/94	2c
Bacon, sliced	lb.	1.88	12/94	82r
Bananas	lb.	0.52	12/94	2c
Bananas	lb.	0.41	12/94	82r
Beef or hamburger, ground	lb.	1.42	12/94	2c
Beef purchases	year	197	91	81r
Beef, stew, boneless	lb.	2.52	12/94	82r
Beverage purchases, alcoholic	year	293	91	81r
Beverage purchases, nonalcoholic	year	203	91	81r
Bologna, all beef or mixed	lb.	2.12	12/94	82r
Bread, white	24-oz.	0.89	12/94	2c
Bread, white, pan	lb.	0.76	12/94	82r
Cabbage	lb.	0.44	12/94	82r
Carrots, short trimmed and topped	lb.	0.44	12/94	82r
Cereals and bakery products purchases	year	347	91	81r
Cereals and cereals products purchases	year	119	91	81r
Cheddar cheese, natural	lb.	3.28	12/94	82r
Cheese, Kraft grated Parmesan	8-oz.	3.52	12/94	2c
Chicken breast, bone-in	lb.	1.61	12/94	82r
Chicken, fresh, whole	lb.	0.89	12/94	82r
Chicken, whole fryer	lb.	0.89	12/94	2c
Chuck roast, USDA choice, boneless	lb.	2.33	12/94	82r
Cigarettes, Winston, Kings	carton	17.11	12/94	2c
Coffee, 100%, ground roast, all sizes	lb.	4.28	12/94	82r
Coffee, vacuum-packed	13 oz.	3.88	12/94	2c
Cookies, chocolate chip	lb.	2.72	12/94	82r
Corn Flakes, Kellogg's or Post Toasties	18 oz.	2.25	12/94	2c
Corn, frozen, whole kernel, lowest price	10 oz.	0.81	12/94	2c
Dairy products (other) purchases	year	148	91	81r
Eggs, Grade A large	dozen	0.67	12/94	2c
Eggs, Grade A large	dozen	0.76	12/94	82r
Fish and seafood purchases	year	61	91	81r
Flour, white, all purpose	lb.	0.22	12/94	82r
Food purchases, food eaten at home	year	2313	91	81r
Foods purchased away from home, not prepared by consumer	year	1709	91	81r
Fruits and vegetables purchases	year	372	91	81r
Grapefruit	lb.	0.47	12/94	82r
Grapes, Thompson seedless	lb.	2.15	12/94	82r
Ground beef, 100% beef	lb.	1.37	12/94	82r
Ground chuck, 100% beef	lb.	1.81	12/94	82r
Ham, boneless, exc. canned	lb.	2.16	12/94	82r
Ice cream, prepackaged, bulk, regular	1/2 gal.	2.48	12/94	82r
Lemons	lb.	1.08	12/94	82r
Lettuce, iceberg	lb.	0.81	12/94	82r
Lettuce, iceberg	head	0.89	12/94	2c
Margarine, Blue Bonnet or Parkay cubes	lb.	0.72	12/94	2c
Margarine, stick	lb.	0.81	12/94	82r
Meats, poultry, fish, and eggs purchases	year	591	91	81r
Milk and cream (fresh) purchases	year	132	91	81r
Milk, whole	1/2 gal.	1.42	12/94	2c
Orange juice, frozen concentrate 12-oz. can	16 oz.	1.41	12/94	82r
Orange juice, Minute Maid frozen	12-oz.	1.29	12/94	2c
Oranges, Navel	lb.	0.56	12/94	82r
Peaches, halves or slices, Hunt's, Del Monte, or Libby's	29-oz.	1.40	12/94	2c
Peanut butter, creamy, all sizes	lb.	1.81	12/94	82r
Peas, sweet, Del Monte or Green Giant	15-17 oz.	0.62	12/94	2c
Pork chops, center cut, bone-in	lb.	2.76	12/94	82r
Pork purchases	year	130	91	81r

Values are in dollars or fractions of dollars. In the column headed *Ref*, references are shown to sources. Each reference is followed by a letter. These refer to the geographical level for which data were reported: s=State, r=Region, and c=City or metro. The abbreviation *ex* is used to mean *except* or *excluding*; *exp* stands for expenditures. For other abbreviations and further explanations, please see the Introduction.

Bismarck, ND - continued

Item	Per	Value	Date	Ref.
Groceries				
Potato chips	16-oz.	2.81	12/94	82r
Potatoes, frozen, French fried	lb.	0.83	12/94	82r
Potatoes, white	lb.	0.28	12/94	82r
Potatoes, white or red	10-lb. sack	2.09	12/94	2c
Round roast, USDA choice, boneless	lb.	2.90	12/94	82r
Sausage, Jimmy Dean, 100% pork	lb.	2.64	12/94	2c
Shortening, vegetable oil blends	lb.	0.88	12/94	82r
Shortening, vegetable, Crisco	3-lb.	2.79	12/94	2c
Soft drink, Coca Cola, ex deposit	2 lit	1.02	12/94	2c
Spaghetti and macaroni	lb.	0.78	12/94	82r
Steak, rib eye, USDA choice, boneless	lb.	6.15	12/94	82r
Steak, round, graded & ungraded, exc. USDA prime & choice	lb.	2.72	12/94	82r
Steak, round, USDA choice, boneless	lb.	3.02	12/94	82r
Steak, sirloin, USDA choice, boneless	lb.	3.85	12/94	82r
Steak, t-bone	lb.	4.66	12/94	2c
Steak, T-bone, USDA choice, bone-in	lb.	5.38	12/94	82r
Sugar and other sweets, eaten at home, expenditures	year	91	91	81r
Sugar, cane or beet	4 lbs.	1.54	12/94	2c
Sugar, white, all sizes	lb.	0.36	12/94	82r
Tobacco products and smoking supplies, total expenditures	year	298	91	81r
Tomatoes, field grown	lb.	1.36	12/94	82r
Tomatoes, Hunt's or Del Monte	14.5 oz.	0.82	12/94	2c
Tuna, chunk, light	lb.	1.94	12/94	82r
Tuna, chunk, light, oil-packed	6.125-6.5 oz.	0.73	12/94	2c
Turkey, frozen, whole	lb.	0.96	12/94	82r
Yogurt, natural, fruit flavored	8 oz.	0.62	12/94	82r
Goods and Services				
Miscellaneous goods and services, ACCRA Index		105.40	12/94	2c
Health Care				
Health care, ACCRA Index		91.10	12/94	2c
Antibiotic ointment, Polysporin	1.5 oz.	4.48	12/94	2c
Childbirth, Cesarean delivery, hospital charge	birth	5101.00	12/91	69r
Childbirth, Cesarean delivery, physician charge	birth	2234.00	12/91	69r
Childbirth, normal delivery, hospital charge	birth	2891.00	12/91	69r
Childbirth, normal delivery, physician charge	birth	1623.00	12/91	69r
Dentist's fee, adult teeth cleaning and periodic oral exam	visit	52.17	12/94	2c
Doctor's fee, routine exam, established patient	visit	36.00	12/94	2c
Drugs, expenditures	year	248	91	81r
Health care, total expenditures	year	1336	91	81r
Health insurance expenditures	year	550	91	81r
Hospital care, semiprivate room	day	264.50	12/94	2c
Insurance premium, family medical care	month	379.10	1/95	41s
Medical services expenditures	year	457	91	81r
Medical supplies expenditures	year	82	91	81r
Household Goods				
Appl. repair, service call, wash mach	min. lab. chg.	24.69	12/94	2c
Floor coverings, expenditures	year	105	91	81r
Furniture, expenditures	year	291	91	81r
Household equipment, misc. expenditures	year	341	91	81r
Household expenditures, miscellaneous	year	162	91	81r
Household furnishings and equipment, expenditures	year	1042	91	81r
Household operations expenditures	year	365	91	81r
Household textiles, expenditures	year	101	91	81r
Housekeeping supplies, expenditures	year	390	91	81r
Laundry and cleaning supplies, expenditures	year	110	91	81r

Bismarck, ND - continued

Item	Per	Value	Date	Ref.
Household Goods - continued				
Laundry detergent, Tide Ultra, Bold, or Cheer	42 oz.	3.75	12/94	2c
Postage and stationery, expenditures	year	115	91	81r
Tissues, facial, Kleenex brand	175	0.98	12/94	2c
Housing				
Housing, ACCRA Index		102.10	12/94	2c
Add garage/carport		8,479	3/95	74r
Add room(s)		21,347	3/95	74r
Apartment condominium or co-op, median	unit	87100	12/94	62r
Bathroom addition, average cost	add	9734.00	3/95	13r
Bathroom remodeling, average cost	remod	6414.00	3/95	13r
Bedroom, master suite addition, average cost	add	27122.00	3/95	13r
Deck addition, average cost	add	6665.00	3/95	13r
Dwellings (owned), expenditures	year	2566	91	81r
Enclose porch/patio/breezeway		4,556	3/95	74r
Exterior remodeling, average cost	remod	15395.00	3/95	13r
Family room addition, average cost	add	27658.00	3/95	13r
Finish room in basement/attic		5,074	3/95	74r
Home, existing, single-family, median	unit	106500	12/94	62r
House payment, principal and interest, 25% down payment	mo.	807	12/94	2c
House, 1800 sq ft, 8000 sq ft lot, new, urban, utilities	total	129500	12/94	2c
Kitchen remodeling, major, average cost	remod	17084.00	3/95	13r
Kitchen remodeling, minor, average cost	remod	5804.00	3/95	13r
Maintenance, repairs, insurance, and other housing expenditures	year	484	91	81r
Mortgage interest and charges expenditures	year	1443	91	81r
Mtge. rate, incl. points and orig. fee, 30-year conv. fixed or ARM	mo.	9.36	12/94	2c
Office, home addition, average cost	add	8121.00	3/95	13r
Princ. & int., mortgage, median-price exist. sing.-family home	mo.	515	12/94	62r
Property taxes expenditures	year	639	91	81r
Redesign, restructure more than half of home's interior		9,114	3/95	74r
Rent, apartment, 2 br., 1 1/2-2 baths, unfurnished, 950 sq ft, water	mo.	467	12/94	2c
Rental units expenditures	year	1200	91	81r
Sun-space addition, average cost	add	23768.00	3/95	13r
Wing addition, two-story, average cost	add	50410.00	3/95	13r
Insurance and Pensions				
Auto insurance, private passenger	year	448.24	12/94	71s
Insurance and pensions, personal, expenditures	year	2408	91	81r
Insurance, life and other personal, expenditures	year	355	91	81r
Pensions and Social Security, expenditures	year	2053	91	81r
Legal Assistance				
Legal work, law firm associate	hour	90		10r
Legal work, law firm partner	hour	139		10r
Personal Goods				
Shampoo, Alberto VO5	15-oz.	1.09	12/94	2c
Toothpaste, Crest or Colgate	6-7 oz.	1.71	12/94	2c
Personal Services				
Dry cleaning, man's 2-pc. suit		6.49	12/94	2c
Haircut, man's barbershop, no styling		8.72	12/94	2c
Haircut, woman's shampoo, trim, blow-dry		17.25	12/94	2c
Personal services expenditures	year	203	91	81r
Restaurant Food				
Chicken, fried, thigh and drumstick		2.15	12/94	2c
Dining expenditures, family	week	30.03	94	73r
Hamburger with cheese	1/4 lb.	1.89	12/94	2c
Pizza, Pizza Hut or Pizza Inn	12-13 in.	8.49	12/94	2c

Values are in dollars or fractions of dollars. In the column headed *Ref*, references are shown to sources. Each reference is followed by a letter. These refer to the geographical level for which data were reported: s=State, r=Region, and c=City or metro. The abbreviation *ex* is used to mean *except* or *excluding*; *exp* stands for *expenditures*. For other abbreviations and further explanations, please see the Introduction.

Bismarck, ND - continued

Item	Per	Value	Date	Ref.
Taxes				
Taxes, Federal income, expenditures	year	1756	91	81r
Taxes, personal, expenditures	year	2426	91	81r
Taxes, State and local income, expenditures	year	568	91	81r
Transportation				
Transportation, ACCRA Index		103.40	12/94	2c
Cars and trucks purchased, new	year	891	91	81r
Cars and trucks purchased, used	year	1155	91	81r
Driver's learning permit fee	perm	10.00	1/94	84s
Driver's license fee	orig	10.00	1/94	84s
Driver's license fee, duplicate	lic	8.00	1/94	84s
Driver's license reinstatement fee, min.	susp	25.00	1/94	85s
Driver's license renewal fee	renew	10.00	1/94	84s
Driving expenses	mile	36.30	5/95	89c
Identification card, nondriver	card	8.00	1/94	83s
Motorcycle learning permit fee	perm	10.00	1/94	84s
Motorcycle license fee	orig	10.00	1/94	84s
Motorcycle license fee, duplicate	lic	8.00	1/94	84s
Motorcycle license renewal fee	renew	10.00	1/94	84s
Public transportation expenditures	year	209	91	81r
Tire balance, computer or spin bal., front	wheel	6.69	12/94	2c
Transportation expenditures, total	year	4792	91	81r
Vehicle finance charges	year	300	91	81r
Vehicle insurance expenditures	year	485	91	81r
Vehicle maintenance and repairs expenditures	year	534	91	81r
Vehicle purchases	year	2068	91	81r
Vehicle rental, leases, licenses, etc. expenditures	year	197	91	81r
Vehicles purchased, other than cars and trucks	year	22	91	81r
Utilities				
Utilities, ACCRA Index		83.50	12/94	2c
Electricity expenditures	year	668	91	81r
Electricity, (part.), other, 1800 sq. ft., new home	mo.	47.36	12/94	2c
Electricity, summer, 250 KWh	month	20.34	8/93	64c
Electricity, summer, 500 KWh	month	36.97	8/93	64c
Electricity, summer, 750 KWh	month	52.81	8/93	64c
Electricity, summer, 1000 KWh	month	67.14	8/93	64c
Utilities, fuels, and public services, total expenditures	year	1838	91	81r
Water and other public services, expenditures	year	167	91	81r
Weddings				
Bridal attendants' gowns	event	750	10/93	76r
Bridal gown	event	852	10/93	76r
Bridal headpiece and veil	event	167	10/93	76r
Bride's wedding band	event	708	10/93	76r
Clergy	event	224	10/93	76r
Engagement ring	event	2756	10/93	76r
Flowers	event	863	10/93	76r
Formal wear for groom	event	106	10/93	76r
Groom's attendants' formal wear	event	530	10/93	76r
Groom's wedding band	event	402	10/93	76r
Music	event	600	10/93	76r
Photography	event	1088	10/93	76r
Shoes for bride	event	50	10/93	76r
Videography	event	483	10/93	76r
Wedding invitations and announcements	event	342	10/93	76r
Wedding reception	event	7000	10/93	76r

Bloomington, IN

Item	Per	Value	Date	Ref.
Composite, ACCRA index		99.90	12/94	2c
Alcoholic Beverages				
Beer, Miller Lite, Bud, 12-oz., ex deposit	6	3.87	12/94	2c
J & B Scotch	750-ml.	17.12	12/94	2c
Wine, Gallo Chablis blanc	1.5-lit	4.27	12/94	2c

Bloomington, IN - continued

Item	Per	Value	Date	Ref.
Appliances				
Appliances (major), expenditures	year	131	91	81r
Average annual exp.				
Food, health care, personal goods, services	year	25935	91	81r
Charity				
Cash contributions, expenditures	year	745	91	81r
Clothing				
Apparel, men and boys, total expenditures	year	332	91	81r
Apparel, women and girls, total expenditures	year	578	91	81r
Footwear, expenditures	year	164	91	81r
Jeans, man's denim		31.99	12/94	2c
Shirt, man's dress shirt		24.99	12/94	2c
Undervest, boy's size 10-14, cotton	3	3.64	12/94	2c
Communications				
Long-distance telephone rate, day, addl. min., 1-10 mi.	min.	0.10	12/93	9s
Long-distance telephone rate, day, initial min., 1-10 mi.	min.	0.18	12/93	9s
Newspaper subscription, dly. and Sun. delivery	month	10.65	12/94	2c
Phone line, single, business, field visit	inst	59.00	12/93	9s
Phone line, single, business, no field visit	inst	59.00	12/93	9s
Phone line, single, residence, field visit	inst	47.00	12/93	9s
Phone line, single, residence, no field visit	inst	47.00	12/93	9s
Telephone bill, family of four	month	17.48	12/94	2c
Telephone service, expenditures	year	547	91	81r
Telephone, residential, flat rate	mo.	9.85	12/93	8c
Education				
Board, 4-year private college/university	year	2095	8/94	80s
Board, 4-year public college/university	year	2300	8/94	80s
Education, total expenditures	year	394	91	81r
Room, 4-year private college/university	year	1784	8/94	80s
Room, 4-year public college/university	year	1718	8/94	80s
Total cost, 4-year private college/university	year	15045	8/94	80s
Total cost, 4-year public college/university	year	6639	8/94	80s
Tuition, 2-year public college/university, in-state	year	1737	8/94	80s
Tuition, 4-year private college/university, in-state	year	11165	8/94	80s
Tuition, 4-year public college/university, in-state	year	2621	8/94	80s
Energy and Fuels				
Energy, combined forms, 1800 sq. ft.	mo.	118.05	12/94	2c
Energy, exc. electricity, 1800 sq. ft.	mo.	50.73	12/94	2c
Fuel oil and other fuels, expenditures	year	83	91	81r
Gas, natural, expenditures	year	373	91	81r
Gas, reg unlead, taxes inc., cash, self-service	gal	1.00	12/94	2c
Gasoline and motor oil purchased	year	1000	91	81r
Gasoline, unleaded midgrade	gallon	1.15	4/93	82r
Gasoline, unleaded premium	gallon	1.23	4/93	82r
Gasoline, unleaded regular	gallon	1.07	4/93	82r
Entertainment				
Bowling, evening rate	game	2.00	12/94	2c
Entertainment, total expenditures	year	1356	91	81r
Fees and admissions, expenditures	year	347	91	81r
Monopoly game, Parker Brothers', No. 9	game	12.28	12/94	2c
Movie	adm	5.50	12/94	2c
Pets, toys, playground equipment, expenditures	year	270	91	81r
Reading, expenditures	year	160	91	81r
Televisions, radios, and sound equipment, expenditures	year	433	91	81r
Tennis balls, yellow, Wilson or Penn, 3	can	2.56	12/94	2c
Funerals				
Burial, immediate, container provided by funeral home		1268.31	1/95	54r
Cards, acknowledgment		26.12	1/95	54r
Casket, minimum alternative		198.03	1/95	54r

Values are in dollars or fractions of dollars. In the column headed *Ref*, references are shown to sources. Each reference is followed by a letter. These refer to the geographical level for which data were reported: s = State, r = Region, and c = City or metro. The abbreviation *ex* is used to mean *except* or *excluding*; *exp* stands for expenditures. For other abbreviations and further explanations, please see the Introduction.

Bloomington, IN - continued

Item	Per	Value	Date	Ref.
Funerals				
Cosmetology, hair care, etc.		122.19	1/95	54r
Cremation, direct, container provided by funeral home		977.81	1/95	54r
Embalming		334.00	1/95	54r
Funeral, funeral home		321.16	1/95	54r
Funeral, other facility		317.73	1/95	54r
Graveside service		292.48	1/95	54r
Hearse, local		153.20	1/95	54r
Limousine, local		123.52	1/95	54r
Memorial service		356.30	1/95	54r
Service charge, professional, nondeclinable		968.24	1/95	54r
Visitation and viewing		332.66	1/95	54r
Groceries				
Groceries, ACCRA Index		101.60	12/94	2c
Apples, Red Delicious	lb.	0.68	12/94	82r
Baby food, strained vegetables, lowest price	4-4.5 oz.	0.37	12/94	2c
Bacon, sliced	lb.	1.88	12/94	82r
Bananas	lb.	0.39	12/94	2c
Bananas	lb.	0.41	12/94	82r
Beef or hamburger, ground	lb.	1.45	12/94	2c
Beef purchases	year	197	91	81r
Beef, stew, boneless	lb.	2.52	12/94	82r
Beverage purchases, alcoholic	year	293	91	81r
Beverage purchases, nonalcoholic	year	203	91	81r
Bologna, all beef or mixed	lb.	2.12	12/94	82r
Bread, white	24-oz.	0.64	12/94	2c
Bread, white, pan	lb.	0.76	12/94	82r
Cabbage	lb.	0.44	12/94	82r
Carrots, short trimmed and topped	lb.	0.44	12/94	82r
Cereals and bakery products purchases	year	347	91	81r
Cereals and cereals products purchases	year	119	91	81r
Cheddar cheese, natural	lb.	3.28	12/94	82r
Cheese, Kraft grated Parmesan	8-oz.	3.23	12/94	2c
Chicken breast, bone-in	lb.	1.61	12/94	82r
Chicken, fresh, whole	lb.	0.89	12/94	82r
Chicken, whole fryer	lb.	0.91	12/94	2c
Chuck roast, USDA choice, boneless	lb.	2.33	12/94	82r
Cigarettes, Winston, Kings	carton	14.71	12/94	2c
Coffee, 100%, ground roast, all sizes	lb.	4.28	12/94	82r
Coffee, vacuum-packed	13 oz.	3.75	12/94	2c
Cookies, chocolate chip	lb.	2.72	12/94	82r
Corn Flakes, Kellogg's or Post Toasties	18 oz.	2.19	12/94	2c
Corn, frozen, whole kernel, lowest price	10 oz.	0.73	12/94	2c
Dairy products (other) purchases	year	148	91	81r
Eggs, Grade A large	dozen	0.80	12/94	2c
Eggs, Grade A large	dozen	0.76	12/94	82r
Fish and seafood purchases	year	61	91	81r
Flour, white, all purpose	lb.	0.22	12/94	82r
Food purchases, food eaten at home	year	2313	91	81r
Foods purchased away from home, not prepared by consumer	year	1709	91	81r
Fruits and vegetables purchases	year	372	91	81r
Grapefruit	lb.	0.47	12/94	82r
Grapes, Thompson seedless	lb.	2.15	12/94	82r
Ground beef, 100% beef	lb.	1.37	12/94	82r
Ground chuck, 100% beef	lb.	1.81	12/94	82r
Ham, boneless, exc. canned	lb.	2.16	12/94	82r
Ice cream, prepackaged, bulk, regular	1/2 gal.	2.48	12/94	82r
Lemons	lb.	1.08	12/94	82r
Lettuce, iceberg	lb.	0.81	12/94	82r
Lettuce, iceberg	head	0.97	12/94	2c
Margarine, Blue Bonnet or Parkay cubes	lb.	0.67	12/94	2c
Margarine, stick	lb.	0.81	12/94	82r
Meats, poultry, fish, and eggs purchases	year	591	91	81r
Milk and cream (fresh) purchases	year	132	91	81r
Milk, whole	1/2 gal.	1.60	12/94	2c
Orange juice, frozen concentrate 12-oz. can	16 oz.	1.41	12/94	82r
Orange juice, Minute Maid frozen	12-oz.	1.30	12/94	2c
Oranges, Navel	lb.	0.56	12/94	82r

Bloomington, IN - continued

Item	Per	Value	Date	Ref.
Groceries - continued				
Peaches, halves or slices, Hunt's, Del Monte, or Libby's	29-oz.	1.27	12/94	2c
Peanut butter, creamy, all sizes	lb.	1.81	12/94	82r
Peas, sweet, Del Monte or Green Giant	15-17 oz.	0.58	12/94	2c
Pork chops, center cut, bone-in	lb.	2.76	12/94	82r
Pork purchases	year	130	91	81r
Potato chips	16-oz.	2.81	12/94	82r
Potatoes, frozen, French fried	lb.	0.83	12/94	82r
Potatoes, white	lb.	0.28	12/94	82r
Potatoes, white or red	10-lb. sack	3.79	12/94	2c
Round roast, USDA choice, boneless	lb.	2.90	12/94	82r
Sausage, Jimmy Dean, 100% pork	lb.	2.51	12/94	2c
Shortening, vegetable oil blends	lb.	0.88	12/94	82r
Shortening, vegetable, Crisco	3-lb.	2.45	12/94	2c
Soft drink, Coca Cola, ex deposit	2 lit	1.19	12/94	2c
Spaghetti and macaroni	lb.	0.78	12/94	82r
Steak, rib eye, USDA choice, boneless	lb.	6.15	12/94	82r
Steak, round, graded & ungraded, exc. USDA prime & choice	lb.	2.72	12/94	82r
Steak, round, USDA choice, boneless	lb.	3.02	12/94	82r
Steak, sirloin, USDA choice, boneless	lb.	3.85	12/94	82r
Steak, t-bone	lb.	5.69	12/94	2c
Steak, T-bone, USDA choice, bone-in	lb.	5.38	12/94	82r
Sugar and other sweets, eaten at home, expenditures	year	91	91	81r
Sugar, cane or beet	4 lbs.	1.13	12/94	2c
Sugar, white, all sizes	lb.	0.36	12/94	82r
Tobacco products and smoking supplies, total expenditures	year	298	91	81r
Tomatoes, field grown	lb.	1.36	12/94	82r
Tomatoes, Hunt's or Del Monte	14.5 oz.	0.75	12/94	2c
Tuna, chunk, light	lb.	1.94	12/94	82r
Tuna, chunk, light, oil-packed	6.125-6.5 oz.	0.65	12/94	2c
Turkey, frozen, whole	lb.	0.96	12/94	82r
Yogurt, natural, fruit flavored	8 oz.	0.62	12/94	82r
Goods and Services				
Miscellaneous goods and services, ACCRA Index		98.60	12/94	2c
Health Care				
Health care, ACCRA Index		96.10	12/94	2c
Antibiotic ointment, Polysporin	1.5 oz.	4.31	12/94	2c
Childbirth, Cesarean delivery, hospital charge	birth	5101.00	12/91	69r
Childbirth, Cesarean delivery, physician charge	birth	2234.00	12/91	69r
Childbirth, normal delivery, hospital charge	birth	2891.00	12/91	69r
Childbirth, normal delivery, physician charge	birth	1623.00	12/91	69r
Dentist's fee, adult teeth cleaning and periodic oral exam	visit	44.80	12/94	2c
Doctor's fee, routine exam, established patient	visit	36.00	12/94	2c
Drugs, expenditures	year	248	91	81r
Health care, total expenditures	year	1336	91	81r
Health insurance expenditures	year	550	91	81r
Hospital care, semiprivate room	day	470.00	12/94	2c
Insurance premium, family medical care	month	353.94	1/95	41s
Medical services expenditures	year	457	91	81r
Medical supplies expenditures	year	82	91	81r
Household Goods				
Appl. repair, service call, wash mach	min. lab. chg.	40.69	12/94	2c
Floor coverings, expenditures	year	105	91	81r
Furniture, expenditures	year	291	91	81r
Household equipment, misc. expenditures	year	341	91	81r
Household expenditures, miscellaneous	year	162	91	81r

Values are in dollars or fractions of dollars. In the column headed *Ref*, references are shown to sources. Each reference is followed by a letter. These refer to the geographical level for which data were reported: s=State, r=Region, and c=City or metro. The abbreviation *ex* is used to mean *except* or *excluding*; *exp* stands for expenditures. For other abbreviations and further explanations, please see the Introduction.

Bloomington, IN - continued

Item	Per	Value	Date	Ref.
Household Goods				
Household furnishings and equipment, expenditures	year	1042	91	81r
Household operations expenditures	year	365	91	81r
Household textiles, expenditures	year	101	91	81r
Housekeeping supplies, expenditures	year	390	91	81r
Laundry and cleaning supplies, expenditures	year	110	91	81r
Laundry detergent, Tide Ultra, Bold, or Cheer	42 oz.	3.89	12/94	2c
Postage and stationery, expenditures	year	115	91	81r
Tissues, facial, Kleenex brand	175	1.03	12/94	2c
Housing				
Housing, ACCRA Index		101.20	12/94	2c
Add garage/carport		8,479	3/95	74r
Add room(s)		21,347	3/95	74r
Apartment condominium or co-op, median	unit	87100	12/94	62r
Bathroom addition, average cost	add	9734.00	3/95	13r
Bathroom remodeling, average cost	remod	6414.00	3/95	13r
Bedroom, master suite addition, average cost	add	27122.00	3/95	13r
Deck addition, average cost	add	6665.00	3/95	13r
Dwellings (owned), expenditures	year	2566	91	81r
Enclose porch/patio/breezeway		4,556	3/95	74r
Exterior remodeling, average cost	remod	15395.00	3/95	13r
Family room addition, average cost	add	27658.00	3/95	13r
Finish room in basement/attic		5,074	3/95	74r
Home, existing, single-family, median	unit	106500	12/94	62r
House payment, principal and interest, 25% down payment	mo.	775	12/94	2c
House, 1800 sq ft, 8000 sq ft lot, new, urban, utilities	total	121392	12/94	2c
Kitchen remodeling, major, average cost	remod	17084.00	3/95	13r
Kitchen remodeling, minor, average cost	remod	5804.00	3/95	13r
Maintenance, repairs, insurance, and other housing expenditures	year	484	91	81r
Mortgage interest and charges expenditures	year	1443	91	81r
Mtge. rate, incl. points and orig. fee, 30-year conv. fixed or ARM	mo.	9.27	12/94	2c
Office, home addition, average cost	add	8121.00	3/95	13r
Princ. & int., mortgage, median-price exist. sing.-family home	mo.	515	12/94	62r
Property taxes expenditures	year	639	91	81r
Redesign, restructure more than half of home's interior		9,114	3/95	74r
Rent, apartment, 2 br., 1 1/2-2 baths, unfurnished, 950 sq ft, water	mo.	534	12/94	2c
Rental units expenditures	year	1200	91	81r
Sun-space addition, average cost	add	23768.00	3/95	13r
Wing addition, two-story, average cost	add	50410.00	3/95	13r
Insurance and Pensions				
Auto insurance, private passenger	year	586.58	12/94	71s
Insurance and pensions, personal, expenditures	year	2408	91	81r
Insurance, life and other personal, expenditures	year	355	91	81r
Pensions and Social Security, expenditures	year	2053	91	81r
Legal Assistance				
Legal work, law firm associate	hour	90		10r
Legal work, law firm partner	hour	139		10r
Personal Goods				
Shampoo, Alberto VO5	15-oz.	1.39	12/94	2c
Toothpaste, Crest or Colgate	6-7 oz.	2.09	12/94	2c
Personal Services				
Dry cleaning, man's 2-pc. suit		6.56	12/94	2c
Haircut, man's barbershop, no styling		7.85	12/94	2c
Haircut, woman's shampoo, trim, blow-dry		18.40	12/94	2c
Personal services expenditures	year	203	91	81r

Bloomington, IN - continued

Item	Per	Value	Date	Ref.
Restaurant Food				
Chicken, fried, thigh and drumstick		1.99	12/94	2c
Dining expenditures, family	week	30.03	94	73r
Hamburger with cheese	1/4 lb.	1.85	12/94	2c
Pizza, Pizza Hut or Pizza Inn	12-13 in.	8.29	12/94	2c
Taxes				
Taxes, Federal income, expenditures	year	1756	91	81r
Taxes, personal, expenditures	year	2426	91	81r
Taxes, State and local income, expenditures	year	568	91	81r
Transportation				
Transportation, ACCRA Index		97.40	12/94	2c
Bus fare, one-way	trip	0.50	12/95	1c
Cars and trucks purchased, new	year	891	91	81r
Cars and trucks purchased, used	year	1155	91	81r
Driver's learning permit fee	perm	2.00	1/94	84s
Driver's license fee	orig	6.00	1/94	84s
Driver's license fee, duplicate	lic	3.00	1/94	84s
Driver's license renewal fee	renew	6.00	1/94	84s
Identification card, nondriver	card	4.00	1/94	83s
Motorcycle learning permit fee	perm	2.00	1/94	84s
Motorcycle license fee	orig	6.00	1/94	84s
Motorcycle license fee, duplicate	lic	3.00	1/94	84s
Motorcycle license renewal fee	renew	6.00	1/94	84s
Public transportation expenditures	year	209	91	81r
Tire balance, computer or spin bal., front	wheel	7.40	12/94	2c
Transportation expenditures, total	year	4792	91	81r
Vehicle finance charges	year	300	91	81r
Vehicle insurance expenditures	year	485	91	81r
Vehicle maintenance and repairs expenditures	year	534	91	81r
Vehicle purchases	year	2068	91	81r
Vehicle rental, leases, licenses, etc. expenditures	year	197	91	81r
Vehicles purchased, other than cars and trucks	year	22	91	81r
Utilities				
Utilities, ACCRA Index		103.10	12/94	2c
Electricity expenditures	year	668	91	81r
Electricity, (part.), other, 1800 sq. ft., new home	mo.	67.32	12/94	2c
Utilities, fuels, and public services, total expenditures	year	1838	91	81r
Water and other public services, expenditures	year	167	91	81r
Weddings				
Bridal attendants' gowns	event	750	10/93	76r
Bridal gown	event	852	10/93	76r
Bridal headpiece and veil	event	167	10/93	76r
Bride's wedding band	event	708	10/93	76r
Clergy	event	224	10/93	76r
Engagement ring	event	2756	10/93	76r
Flowers	event	863	10/93	76r
Formal wear for groom	event	106	10/93	76r
Groom's attendants' formal wear	event	530	10/93	76r
Groom's wedding band	event	402	10/93	76r
Music	event	600	10/93	76r
Photography	event	1088	10/93	76r
Shoes for bride	event	50	10/93	76r
Videography	event	483	10/93	76r
Wedding invitations and announcements	event	342	10/93	76r
Wedding reception	event	7000	10/93	76r

Bloomington-Normal, IL

Item	Per	Value	Date	Ref.
Composite, ACCRA index		102.80	12/94	2c
Alcoholic Beverages				
Beer, Miller Lite, Bud, 12-oz., ex deposit	6	3.95	12/94	2c

Values are in dollars or fractions of dollars. In the column headed *Ref*, references are shown to sources. Each reference is followed by a letter. These refer to the geographical level for which data were reported: s=State, r=Region, and c=City or metro. The abbreviation *ex* is used to mean *except* or *excluding*; *exp* stands for expenditures. For other abbreviations and further explanations, please see the Introduction.

Bloomington-Normal, IL - continued

Item	Per	Value	Date	Ref.
Alcoholic Beverages				
J & B Scotch	750-ml.	14.95	12/94	2c
Wine, Gallo Chablis blanc	1.5-lit	4.41	12/94	2c
Appliances				
Appliances (major), expenditures	year	131	91	81r
Average annual exp.				
Food, health care, personal goods, services	year	25935	91	81r
Charity				
Cash contributions, expenditures	year	745	91	81r
Clothing				
Apparel, men and boys, total expenditures	year	332	91	81r
Apparel, women and girls, total expenditures	year	578	91	81r
Footwear, expenditures	year	164	91	81r
Jeans, man's denim		34.09	12/94	2c
Shirt, man's dress shirt		31.10	12/94	2c
Undervest, boy's size 10-14, cotton	3	4.08	12/94	2c
Communications				
Long-distance telephone rate, day, addl. min., 1-10 mi.	min.	0.04	12/93	9s
Long-distance telephone rate, day, initial min., 1-10 mi.	min.	0.10	12/93	9s
Newspaper subscription, dly. and Sun. delivery	month	13.04	12/94	2c
Phone line, single, business, field visit	inst	84.50	12/93	9s
Phone line, single, business, no field visit	inst	84.50	12/93	9s
Phone line, single, residence, field visit	inst	55.00	12/93	9s
Phone line, single, residence, no field visit	inst	55.00	12/93	9s
Telephone bill, family of four	month	21.05	12/94	2c
Telephone service, expenditures	year	547	91	81r
Education				
Board, 4-year private college/university	year	2078	8/94	80s
Board, 4-year public college/university	year	2139	8/94	80s
Education, total expenditures	year	394	91	81r
Room, 4-year private college/university	year	2696	8/94	80s
Room, 4-year public college/university	year	1796	8/94	80s
Total cost, 4-year private college/university	year	15249	8/94	80s
Total cost, 4-year public college/university	year	6964	8/94	80s
Tuition, 2-year public college/university, in-state	year	1135	8/94	80s
Tuition, 4-year private college/university, in-state	year	10474	8/94	80s
Tuition, 4-year public college/university, in-state	year	3029	8/94	80s
Energy and Fuels				
Energy, combined forms, 1800 sq. ft.	mo.	137.87	12/94	2c
Energy, exc. electricity, 1800 sq. ft.	mo.	50.46	12/94	2c
Fuel oil and other fuels, expenditures	year	83	91	81r
Gas, natural, expenditures	year	373	91	81r
Gas, reg unlead, taxes inc., cash, self-service	gal	1.17	12/94	2c
Gasoline and motor oil purchased	year	1000	91	81r
Gasoline, unleaded midgrade	gallon	1.15	4/93	82r
Gasoline, unleaded premium	gallon	1.23	4/93	82r
Gasoline, unleaded regular	gallon	1.07	4/93	82r
Entertainment				
Bowling, evening rate	game	2.37	12/94	2c
Entertainment, total expenditures	year	1356	91	81r
Fees and admissions, expenditures	year	347	91	81r
Monopoly game, Parker Brothers', No. 9	game	12.01	12/94	2c
Movie	adm	5.50	12/94	2c
Pets, toys, playground equipment, expenditures	year	270	91	81r
Reading, expenditures	year	160	91	81r
Televisions, radios, and sound equipment, expenditures	year	433	91	81r
Tennis balls, yellow, Wilson or Penn, 3	can	2.14	12/94	2c

Bloomington-Normal, IL - continued

Item	Per	Value	Date	Ref.
Funerals				
Burial, immediate, container provided by funeral home		1268.31	1/95	54r
Cards, acknowledgment		26.12	1/95	54r
Casket, minimum alternative		198.03	1/95	54r
Cosmetology, hair care, etc.		122.19	1/95	54r
Cremation, direct, container provided by funeral home		977.81	1/95	54r
Embalming		334.00	1/95	54r
Funeral, funeral home		321.16	1/95	54r
Funeral, other facility		317.73	1/95	54r
Graveside service		292.48	1/95	54r
Hearse, local		153.20	1/95	54r
Limousine, local		123.52	1/95	54r
Memorial service		356.30	1/95	54r
Service charge, professional, nondeclinable		968.24	1/95	54r
Visitation and viewing		332.66	1/95	54r
Groceries				
Groceries, ACCRA Index		102.00	12/94	2c
Apples, Red Delicious	lb.	0.68	12/94	82r
Baby food, strained vegetables, lowest price	4-4.5 oz.	0.33	12/94	2c
Bacon, sliced	lb.	1.88	12/94	82r
Bananas	lb.	0.51	12/94	2c
Bananas	lb.	0.41	12/94	82r
Beef or hamburger, ground	lb.	1.49	12/94	2c
Beef purchases	year	197	91	81r
Beef, stew, boneless	lb.	2.52	12/94	82r
Beverage purchases, alcoholic	year	293	91	81r
Beverage purchases, nonalcoholic	year	203	91	81r
Bologna, all beef or mixed	lb.	2.12	12/94	82r
Bread, white	24-oz.	0.54	12/94	2c
Bread, white, pan	lb.	0.76	12/94	82r
Cabbage	lb.	0.44	12/94	82r
Carrots, short trimmed and topped	lb.	0.44	12/94	82r
Cereals and bakery products purchases	year	347	91	81r
Cereals and cereals products purchases	year	119	91	81r
Cheddar cheese, natural	lb.	3.28	12/94	82r
Cheese, Kraft grated Parmesan	8-oz.	3.41	12/94	2c
Chicken breast, bone-in	lb.	1.61	12/94	82r
Chicken, fresh, whole	lb.	0.89	12/94	82r
Chicken, whole fryer	lb.	0.65	12/94	2c
Chuck roast, USDA choice, boneless	lb.	2.33	12/94	82r
Cigarettes, Winston, Kings	carton	17.26	12/94	2c
Coffee, 100%, ground roast, all sizes	lb.	4.28	12/94	82r
Coffee, vacuum-packed	13 oz.	3.57	12/94	2c
Cookies, chocolate chip	lb.	2.72	12/94	82r
Corn Flakes, Kellogg's or Post Toasties	18 oz.	2.30	12/94	2c
Corn, frozen, whole kernel, lowest price	10 oz.	0.66	12/94	2c
Dairy products (other) purchases	year	148	91	81r
Eggs, Grade A large	dozen	0.81	12/94	2c
Eggs, Grade A large	dozen	0.76	12/94	82r
Fish and seafood purchases	year	61	91	81r
Flour, white, all purpose	lb.	0.22	12/94	82r
Food purchases, food eaten at home	year	2313	91	81r
Foods purchased away from home, not prepared by consumer	year	1709	91	81r
Fruits and vegetables purchases	year	372	91	81r
Grapefruit	lb.	0.47	12/94	82r
Grapes, Thompson seedless	lb.	2.15	12/94	82r
Ground beef, 100% beef	lb.	1.37	12/94	82r
Ground chuck, 100% beef	lb.	1.81	12/94	82r
Ham, boneless, exc. canned	lb.	2.16	12/94	82r
Ice cream, prepackaged, bulk, regular	1/2 gal.	2.48	12/94	82r
Lemons	lb.	1.08	12/94	82r
Lettuce, iceberg	lb.	0.81	12/94	82r
Lettuce, iceberg	head	0.92	12/94	2c
Margarine, Blue Bonnet or Parkay cubes	lb.	0.63	12/94	2c
Margarine, stick	lb.	0.81	12/94	82r
Meats, poultry, fish, and eggs purchases	year	591	91	81r
Milk and cream (fresh) purchases	year	132	91	81r

Values are in dollars or fractions of dollars. In the column headed *Ref*, references are shown to sources. Each reference is followed by a letter. These refer to the geographical level for which data were reported: s=State, r=Region, and c=City or metro. The abbreviation *ex* is used to mean *except* or *excluding*; *exp* stands for *expenditures*. For other abbreviations and further explanations, please see the Introduction.

Bloomington-Normal, IL - continued

Item	Per	Value	Date	Ref.
Groceries				
Milk, whole	1/2 gal.	1.55	12/94	2c
Orange juice, frozen concentrate 12-oz. can	16 oz.	1.41	12/94	82r
Orange juice, Minute Maid frozen	12-oz.	1.46	12/94	2c
Oranges, Navel	lb.	0.56	12/94	82r
Peaches, halves or slices, Hunt's, Del Monte, or Libby's	29-oz.	1.42	12/94	2c
Peanut butter, creamy, all sizes	lb.	1.81	12/94	82r
Peas, sweet, Del Monte or Green Giant	15-17 oz.	0.67	12/94	2c
Pork chops, center cut, bone-in	lb.	2.76	12/94	82r
Pork purchases	year	130	91	81r
Potato chips	16-oz.	2.81	12/94	82r
Potatoes, frozen, French fried	lb.	0.83	12/94	82r
Potatoes, white	lb.	0.28	12/94	82r
Potatoes, white or red	10-lb. sack	3.29	12/94	2c
Round roast, USDA choice, boneless	lb.	2.90	12/94	82r
Sausage, Jimmy Dean, 100% pork	lb.	2.97	12/94	2c
Shortening, vegetable oil blends	lb.	0.88	12/94	82r
Shortening, vegetable, Crisco	3-lb.	2.33	12/94	2c
Soft drink, Coca Cola, ex deposit	2 lit	1.19	12/94	2c
Spaghetti and macaroni	lb.	0.78	12/94	82r
Steak, rib eye, USDA choice, boneless	lb.	6.15	12/94	82r
Steak, round, graded & ungraded, exc. USDA prime & choice	lb.	2.72	12/94	82r
Steak, round, USDA choice, boneless	lb.	3.02	12/94	82r
Steak, sirloin, USDA choice, boneless	lb.	3.85	12/94	82r
Steak, t-bone	lb.	5.89	12/94	2c
Steak, T-bone, USDA choice, bone-in	lb.	5.38	12/94	82r
Sugar and other sweets, eaten at home, expenditures	year	91	91	81r
Sugar, cane or beet	4 lbs.	1.45	12/94	2c
Sugar, white, all sizes	lb.	0.36	12/94	82r
Tobacco products and smoking supplies, total expenditures	year	298	91	81r
Tomatoes, field grown	lb.	1.36	12/94	82r
Tomatoes, Hunt's or Del Monte	14.5 oz.	0.79	12/94	2c
Tuna, chunk, light	lb.	1.94	12/94	82r
Tuna, chunk, light, oil-packed	6.125-6.5 oz.	0.75	12/94	2c
Turkey, frozen, whole	lb.	0.96	12/94	82r
Yogurt, natural, fruit flavored	8 oz.	0.62	12/94	82r
Goods and Services				
Miscellaneous goods and services, ACCRA Index		103.20	12/94	2c
Health Care				
Health care, ACCRA Index		96.50	12/94	2c
Antibiotic ointment, Polysporin	1.5 oz.	3.54	12/94	2c
Childbirth, Cesarean delivery, hospital charge	birth	5101.00	12/91	69r
Childbirth, Cesarean delivery, physician charge	birth	2234.00	12/91	69r
Childbirth, normal delivery, hospital charge	birth	2891.00	12/91	69r
Childbirth, normal delivery, physician charge	birth	1623.00	12/91	69r
Dentist's fee, adult teeth cleaning and periodic oral exam	visit	52.60	12/94	2c
Doctor's fee, routine exam, established patient	visit	40.00	12/94	2c
Drugs, expenditures	year	248	91	81r
Health care, total expenditures	year	1336	91	81r
Health insurance expenditures	year	550	91	81r
Hospital care, semiprivate room	day	348.50	12/94	2c
Insurance premium, family medical care	month	363.57	1/95	41s
Medical services expenditures	year	457	91	81r
Medical supplies expenditures	year	82	91	81r
Household Goods				
Appl. repair, service call, wash mach	min. lab. chg.	33.79	12/94	2c

Bloomington-Normal, IL - continued

Item	Per	Value	Date	Ref.
Household Goods - continued				
Floor coverings, expenditures	year	105	91	81r
Furniture, expenditures	year	291	91	81r
Household equipment, misc. expenditures	year	341	91	81r
Household expenditures, miscellaneous	year	162	91	81r
Household furnishings and equipment, expenditures	year	1042	91	81r
Household operations expenditures	year	365	91	81r
Household textiles, expenditures	year	101	91	81r
Housekeeping supplies, expenditures	year	390	91	81r
Laundry and cleaning supplies, expenditures	year	110	91	81r
Laundry detergent, Tide Ultra, Bold, or Cheer	42 oz.	3.64	12/94	2c
Postage and stationery, expenditures	year	115	91	81r
Tissues, facial, Kleenex brand	175	1.01	12/94	2c
Housing				
Housing, ACCRA Index		99.40	12/94	2c
Add garage/carport		8,479	3/95	74r
Add room(s)		21,347	3/95	74r
Apartment condominium or co-op, median	unit	87100	12/94	62r
Bathroom addition, average cost	add	9734.00	3/95	13r
Bathroom remodeling, average cost	remod	6414.00	3/95	13r
Bedroom, master suite addition, average cost	add	27122.00	3/95	13r
Deck addition, average cost	add	6665.00	3/95	13r
Dwellings (owned), expenditures	year	2566	91	81r
Enclose porch/patio/breezeway		4,556	3/95	74r
Exterior remodeling, average cost	remod	15395.00	3/95	13r
Family room addition, average cost	add	27658.00	3/95	13r
Finish room in basement/attic		5,074	3/95	74r
Home, existing, single-family, median	unit	106500	12/94	62r
House payment, principal and interest, 25% down payment	mo.	751	12/94	2c
House, 1800 sq ft, 8000 sq ft lot, new, urban, utilities	total	121982	12/94	2c
Kitchen remodeling, major, average cost	remod	17084.00	3/95	13r
Kitchen remodeling, minor, average cost	remod	5804.00	3/95	13r
Maintenance, repairs, insurance, and other housing expenditures	year	484	91	81r
Mortgage interest and charges expenditures	year	1443	91	81r
Mtge. rate, incl. points and orig. fee, 30-year conv. fixed or ARM	mo.	9.22	12/94	2c
Office, home addition, average cost	add	8121.00	3/95	13r
Princ. & int., mortgage, median-price exist. sing.-family home	mo.	515	12/94	62r
Property taxes expenditures	year	639	91	81r
Redesign, restructure more than half of home's interior		9,114	3/95	74r
Rent, apartment, 2 br., 1 1/2-2 baths, unfurnished, 950 sq ft, water	mo.	555	12/94	2c
Rental units expenditures	year	1200	91	81r
Sun-space addition, average cost	add	23768.00	3/95	13r
Wing addition, two-story, average cost	add	50410.00	3/95	13r
Insurance and Pensions				
Auto insurance, private passenger	year	679.48	12/94	71s
Insurance and pensions, personal, expenditures	year	2408	91	81r
Insurance, life and other personal, expenditures	year	355	91	81r
Pensions and Social Security, expenditures	year	2053	91	81r
Legal Assistance				
Legal work, law firm associate	hour	90		10r
Legal work, law firm partner	hour	139		10r
Personal Goods				
Shampoo, Alberto VO5	15-oz.	1.34	12/94	2c
Toothpaste, Crest or Colgate	6-7 oz.	1.97	12/94	2c
Personal Services				
Dry cleaning, man's 2-pc. suit		6.54	12/94	2c
Haircut, man's barbershop, no styling		8.60	12/94	2c

Values are in dollars or fractions of dollars. In the column headed *Ref*, references are shown to sources. Each reference is followed by a letter. These refer to the geographical level for which data were reported: s=State, r=Region, and c=City or metro. The abbreviation *ex* is used to mean *except* or *excluding*; *exp* stands for expenditures. For other abbreviations and further explanations, please see the Introduction.

Bloomington-Normal, IL - continued

Item	Per	Value	Date	Ref.
Personal Services				
Haircut, woman's shampoo, trim, blow-dry		22.20	12/94	2c
Personal services expenditures	year	203	91	81r
Restaurant Food				
Chicken, fried, thigh and drumstick		2.30	12/94	2c
Dining expenditures, family	week	30.03	94	73r
Hamburger with cheese	1/4 lb.	1.96	12/94	2c
Pizza, Pizza Hut or Pizza Inn	12-13 in.	7.99	12/94	2c
Taxes				
Taxes, Federal income, expenditures	year	1756	91	81r
Taxes, personal, expenditures	year	2426	91	81r
Taxes, State and local income, expenditures	year	568	91	81r
Transportation				
Transportation, ACCRA Index		101.30	12/94	2c
Cars and trucks purchased, new	year	891	91	81r
Cars and trucks purchased, used	year	1155	91	81r
Driver's learning permit fee	perm	20.00	1/94	84s
Driver's license fee	orig	10.00	1/94	84s
Driver's license fee, duplicate	lic	5.00	1/94	84s
Driver's license reinstatement fee, min.	susp	30.00	1/94	85s
Driver's license renewal fee	renew	10.00	1/94	84s
Identification card, nondriver	card	4.00	1/94	83s
Motorcycle learning permit fee	perm	20.00	1/94	84s
Motorcycle license fee	orig	10.00	1/94	84s
Motorcycle license fee, duplicate	lic	5.00	1/94	84s
Motorcycle license renewal fee	renew	10.00	1/94	84s
Public transportation expenditures	year	209	91	81r
Tire balance, computer or spin bal., front	wheel	6.59	12/94	2c
Transportation expenditures, total	year	4792	91	81r
Vehicle finance charges	year	300	91	81r
Vehicle insurance expenditures	year	485	91	81r
Vehicle maintenance and repairs expenditures	year	534	91	81r
Vehicle purchases	year	2068	91	81r
Vehicle rental, leases, licenses, etc. expenditures	year	197	91	81r
Vehicles purchased, other than cars and trucks	year	22	91	81r
Utilities				
Utilities, ACCRA Index		120.80	12/94	2c
Electricity expenditures	year	668	91	81r
Electricity, (part.), other, 1800 sq. ft., new home	mo.	87.41	12/94	2c
Utilities, fuels, and public services, total expenditures	year	1838	91	81r
Water and other public services, expenditures	year	167	91	81r
Weddings				
Bridal attendants' gowns	event	750	10/93	76r
Bridal gown	event	852	10/93	76r
Bridal headpiece and veil	event	167	10/93	76r
Bride's wedding band	event	708	10/93	76r
Clergy	event	224	10/93	76r
Engagement ring	event	2756	10/93	76r
Flowers	event	863	10/93	76r
Formal wear for groom	event	106	10/93	76r
Groom's attendants' formal wear	event	530	10/93	76r
Groom's wedding band	event	402	10/93	76r
Music	event	600	10/93	76r
Photography	event	1088	10/93	76r
Shoes for bride	event	50	10/93	76r
Videography	event	483	10/93	76r
Wedding invitations and announcements	event	342	10/93	76r
Wedding reception	event	7000	10/93	76r

Boise, ID

Item	Per	Value	Date	Ref.
Composite, ACCRA index		101.40	12/94	2c
Alcoholic Beverages				
Beer, Miller Lite, Bud, 12-oz., ex deposit	6	4.03	12/94	2c
J & B Scotch	750-ml.	18.85	12/94	2c
Wine, Gallo Chablis blanc	1.5-lit	4.75	12/94	2c
Appliances				
Appliances (major), expenditures	year	160	91	81r
Average annual exp.				
Food, health care, personal goods, services	year	32461	91	81r
Business				
Dinner and tip, hotel, corporate rate	night	28.00	2/94	15c
Hotel room, corporate rate	night	66.00	2/94	15c
Charity				
Cash contributions, expenditures	year	975	91	81r
Clothing				
Apparel, men and boys, total expenditures	year	467	91	81r
Apparel, women and girls, total expenditures	year	737	91	81r
Footwear, expenditures	year	270	91	81r
Jeans, man's denim		31.98	12/94	2c
Shirt, man's dress shirt		30.55	12/94	2c
Undervest, boy's size 10-14, cotton	3	3.93	12/94	2c
Communications				
Long-distance telephone rate, day, addl. min., 1-10 mi.	min.	0.07	12/93	9s
Long-distance telephone rate, day, initial min., 1-10 mi.	min.	0.14	12/93	9s
Newspaper subscription, dly. and Sun. delivery	month	12.39	12/94	2c
Phone line, single, business, field visit	inst	47.50	12/93	9s
Phone line, single, business, no field visit	inst	47.50	12/93	9s
Phone line, single, residence, field visit	inst	28.50	12/93	9s
Phone line, single, residence, no field visit	inst	28.50	12/93	9s
Telephone bill, family of four	month	16.75	12/94	2c
Telephone service, expenditures	year	611	91	81r
Telephone, residential, flat rate	mo.	12.03	12/93	8c
Education				
Board, 4-year private college/university	year	2824	8/94	80s
Board, 4-year public college/university	year	2007	8/94	80s
Education, total expenditures	year	375	91	81r
Room, 4-year private college/university	year	1212	8/94	80s
Room, 4-year public college/university	year	1479	8/94	80s
Total cost, 4-year private college/university	year	14044	8/94	80s
Total cost, 4-year public college/university	year	4983	8/94	80s
Tuition, 2-year public college/university, in-state	year	914	8/94	80s
Tuition, 4-year private college/university, in-state	year	10007	8/94	80s
Tuition, 4-year public college/university, in-state	year	1498	8/94	80s
Energy and Fuels				
Energy, combined forms, 1800 sq. ft.	mo.	83.80	12/94	2c
Energy, exc. electricity, 1800 sq. ft.	mo.	44.13	12/94	2c
Fuel oil and other fuels, expenditures	year	33	91	81r
Gas, cooking, 10 therms	month	11.84	2/94	65c
Gas, cooking, 30 therms	month	22.53	2/94	65c
Gas, cooking, 50 therms	month	33.21	2/94	65c
Gas, heating, winter, 100 therms	month	59.93	2/94	65c
Gas, heating, winter, average use	month	86.64	2/94	65c
Gas, natural, expenditures	year	212	91	81r
Gas, reg unlead, taxes inc., cash, self-service	gal	1.26	12/94	2c
Gasoline and motor oil purchased	year	1115	91	81r
Gasoline, unleaded midgrade	gallon	1.36	4/93	82r
Gasoline, unleaded premium	gallon	1.43	4/93	82r
Gasoline, unleaded regular	gallon	1.23	4/93	82r

Values are in dollars or fractions of dollars. In the column headed *Ref*, references are shown to sources. Each reference is followed by a letter. These refer to the geographical level for which data were reported: s=State, r=Region, and c=City or metro. The abbreviation *ex* is used to mean *except* or *excluding*; *exp* stands for expenditures. For other abbreviations and further explanations, please see the Introduction.

Boise, ID - continued

Item	Per	Value	Date	Ref.
Entertainment				
Bowling, evening rate	game	1.96	12/94	2c
Concert ticket, Pearl Jam group	perf	20.00	94	50r
Entertainment, total expenditures	year	1853	91	81r
Fees and admissions, expenditures	year	482	91	81r
Monopoly game, Parker Brothers', No. 9	game	10.59	12/94	2c
Movie	adm	5.90	12/94	2c
Pets, toys, playground equipment, expenditures	year	299	91	81r
Reading, expenditures	year	164	91	81r
Televisions, radios, and sound equipment, expenditures	year	528	91	81r
Tennis balls, yellow, Wilson or Penn, 3	can	2.20	12/94	2c
Funerals				
Burial, immediate, container provided by funeral home		1360.49	1/95	54r
Cards, acknowledgment		11.24	1/95	54r
Casket, minimum alternative		232.73	1/95	54r
Cosmetology, hair care, etc.		114.13	1/95	54r
Cremation, direct, container provided by funeral home		1027.08	1/95	54r
Embalming		286.24	1/95	54r
Funeral, funeral home		315.60	1/95	54r
Funeral, other facility		303.08	1/95	54r
Graveside service		423.83	1/95	54r
Hearse, local		133.12	1/95	54r
Limousine, local		99.10	1/95	54r
Memorial service		442.57	1/95	54r
Service charge, professional, nondeclinable		840.16	1/95	54r
Visitation and viewing		168.50	1/95	54r
Groceries				
Groceries, ACCRA Index		96.30	12/94	2c
Apples, Red Delicious	lb.	0.72	12/94	82r
Baby food, strained vegetables, lowest price	4-4.5 oz.	0.27	12/94	2c
Bacon, sliced	lb.	1.73	12/94	82r
Bananas	lb.	0.55	12/94	2c
Bananas	lb.	0.52	12/94	82r
Beef or hamburger, ground	lb.	1.41	12/94	2c
Beef purchases	year	241	91	81r
Beverage purchases, alcoholic	year	328	91	81r
Beverage purchases, nonalcoholic	year	234	91	81r
Bologna, all beef or mixed	lb.	2.33	12/94	82r
Bread, white	24-oz.	0.68	12/94	2c
Bread, white, pan	lb.	0.81	12/94	82r
Carrots, short trimmed and topped	lb.	0.43	12/94	82r
Cereals and bakery products purchases	year	392	91	81r
Cereals and cereals products purchases	year	139	91	81r
Cheese, Kraft grated Parmesan	8-oz.	3.52	12/94	2c
Chicken breast, bone-in	lb.	2.04	12/94	82r
Chicken, fresh, whole	lb.	0.95	12/94	2c
Chicken, whole fryer	lb.	0.77	12/94	2c
Cigarettes, Winston, Kings	carton	15.87	12/94	2c
Coffee, 100%, ground roast, all sizes	lb.	4.48	12/94	82r
Coffee, vacuum-packed	13 oz.	4.05	12/94	2c
Corn Flakes, Kellogg's or Post Toasties	18 oz.	1.93	12/94	2c
Corn, frozen, whole kernel, lowest price	10 oz.	0.66	12/94	2c
Dairy products (other) purchases	year	182	91	81r
Eggs, Grade A large	dozen	0.74	12/94	2c
Fish and seafood purchases	year	94	91	81r
Flour, white, all purpose	lb.	0.21	12/94	82r
Food purchases, food eaten at home	year	2749	91	81r
Foods purchased away from home, not prepared by consumer	year	1909	91	81r
Fruits and vegetables purchases	year	459	91	81r
Grapefruit	lb.	0.56	12/94	82r
Ground beef, 100% beef	lb.	1.31	12/94	82r
Ham, boneless, exc. canned	lb.	2.46	12/94	82r
Ice cream, prepackaged, bulk, regular	1/2 gal.	2.57	12/94	82r
Lemons	lb.	1.00	12/94	82r
Lettuce, iceberg	lb.	0.93	12/94	82r

Boise, ID - continued

Item	Per	Value	Date	Ref.
Groceries - continued				
Lettuce, iceberg	head	0.59	12/94	2c
Margarine, Blue Bonnet or Parkay cubes	lb.	0.52	12/94	2c
Meats, poultry, fish, and eggs purchases	year	700	91	81r
Milk and cream (fresh) purchases	year	155	91	81r
Milk, whole	1/2 gal.	1.37	12/94	2c
Orange juice, frozen concentrate 12-oz. can	16 oz.	1.52	12/94	82r
Orange juice, Minute Maid frozen	12-oz.	1.10	12/94	2c
Oranges, Navel	lb.	0.56	12/94	82r
Peaches, halves or slices, Hunt's, Del Monte, or Libby's	29-oz.	1.34	12/94	2c
Peas, sweet, Del Monte or Green Giant	15-17 oz.	0.57	12/94	2c
Pork chops, center cut, bone-in	lb.	3.30	12/94	82r
Pork purchases	year	122	91	81r
Potato chips	16-oz.	3.03	12/94	82r
Potatoes, frozen, French fried	lb.	0.77	12/94	82r
Potatoes, white	lb.	0.35	12/94	82r
Potatoes, white or red	10-lb. sack	1.63	12/94	2c
Rice, white, long grain, uncooked	lb.	0.54	12/94	82r
Round roast, USDA choice, boneless	lb.	2.92	12/94	82r
Sausage, Jimmy Dean, 100% pork	lb.	3.15	12/94	2c
Shortening, vegetable oil blends	lb.	0.80	12/94	82r
Shortening, vegetable, Crisco	3-lb.	2.30	12/94	2c
Soft drink, Coca Cola, ex deposit	2 lit	1.06	12/94	2c
Spaghetti and macaroni	lb.	1.02	12/94	82r
Steak, round, graded & ungraded, exc. USDA prime & choice	lb.	3.13	12/94	82r
Steak, sirloin, USDA choice, boneless	lb.	4.07	12/94	82r
Steak, t-bone	lb.	4.11	12/94	2c
Sugar and other sweets, eaten at home, expenditures	year	105	91	81r
Sugar, cane or beet	4 lbs.	1.25	12/94	2c
Sugar, white, all sizes	lb.	0.38	12/94	82r
Tobacco products and smoking supplies, total expenditures	year	221	91	81r
Tomatoes, field grown	lb.	1.45	12/94	82r
Tomatoes, Hunt's or Del Monte	14.5 oz.	0.76	12/94	2c
Tuna, chunk, light	lb.	2.18	12/94	82r
Tuna, chunk, light, oil-packed	6.125-6.5 oz.	0.72	12/94	2c
Goods and Services				
Miscellaneous goods and services, ACCRA Index		101.80	12/94	2c
Health Care				
Health care, ACCRA Index		113.40	12/94	2c
Antibiotic ointment, Polysporin	1.5 oz.	4.11	12/94	2c
Childbirth, Cesarean delivery, hospital charge	birth	6059.00	12/91	69r
Childbirth, Cesarean delivery, physician charge	birth	2248.00	12/91	69r
Childbirth, normal delivery, hospital charge	birth	3006.00	12/91	69r
Childbirth, normal delivery, physician charge	birth	1634.00	12/91	69r
Dentist's fee, adult teeth cleaning and periodic oral exam	visit	62.80	12/94	2c
Doctor's fee, routine exam, established patient	visit	47.40	12/94	2c
Drugs, expenditures	year	230	91	81r
Health care, total expenditures	year	1544	91	81r
Health insurance expenditures	year	558	91	81r
Hospital care, semiprivate room	day	393.00	12/94	2c
Insurance premium, family medical care	month	314.95	1/95	41s
Medical services expenditures	year	676	91	81r
Medical supplies expenditures	year	80	91	81r
Surgery, open-heart	proc	37818.00	1/93	14r
Household Goods				
Appl. repair, service call, wash mach	min. lab. chg.	36.40	12/94	2c

Values are in dollars or fractions of dollars. In the column headed *Ref*, references are shown to sources. Each reference is followed by a letter. These refer to the geographical level for which data were reported: s = State, r = Region, and c = City or metro. The abbreviation *ex* is used to mean *except* or *excluding*; *exp* stands for *expenditures*. For other abbreviations and further explanations, please see the Introduction.

Boise, ID - continued

Item	Per	Value	Date	Ref.
Household Goods				
Floor coverings, expenditures	year	79	91	81r
Furniture, expenditures	year	352	91	81r
Household equipment, misc. expenditures	year	614	91	81r
Household expenditures, miscellaneous	year	294	91	81r
Household furnishings and equipment, expenditures	year	1416	91	81r
Household operations expenditures	year	580	91	81r
Household textiles, expenditures	year	113	91	81r
Housekeeping supplies, expenditures	year	447	91	81r
Laundry and cleaning supplies, expenditures	year	114	91	81r
Laundry detergent, Tide Ultra, Bold, or Cheer	42 oz.	3.92	12/94	2c
Postage and stationery, expenditures	year	145	91	81r
Tissues, facial, Kleenex brand	175	1.03	12/94	2c
Housing				
Housing, ACCRA Index		107.60	12/94	2c
Add garage/carport		6,422	3/95	74r
Add room(s)		26,583	3/95	74r
Apartment condominium or co-op, median	unit	105300	12/94	62r
Dwellings (owned), expenditures	year	3932	91	81r
Enclose porch/patio/breezeway		5,382	3/95	74r
Finish room in basement/attic		3,911	3/95	74r
Home, existing, single-family, median	unit	178600	12/94	62r
Home, existing, single-family, median	unit	101.00	12/94	62c
House payment, principal and interest, 25% down payment	mo.	772	12/94	2c
House, 1800 sq ft, 8000 sq ft lot, new, urban, utilities	total	122000	12/94	2c
Maintenance, repairs, insurance, and other housing expenditures	year	591	91	81r
Mortgage interest and charges expenditures	year	2747	91	81r
Mtge. rate, incl. points and orig. fee, 30-year conv. fixed or ARM	mo.	9.54	12/94	2c
Princ. & int., mortgage, median-price exist. sing.-family home	mo.	845	12/94	62r
Property taxes expenditures	year	594	91	81r
Redesign, restructure more than half of home's interior		5,467	3/95	74r
Rent, apartment, 2 br., 1 1/2-2 baths, unfurnished, 950 sq ft, water	mo.	717	12/94	2c
Rental units expenditures	year	2077	91	81r
Insurance and Pensions				
Auto insurance, private passenger	year	513.32	12/94	71s
Insurance and pensions, personal, expenditures	year	3042	91	81r
Insurance, life and other personal, expenditures	year	298	91	81r
Pensions and Social Security, expenditures	year	2744	91	81r
Legal Assistance				
Legal work, law firm associate	hour	91		10r
Legal work, law firm partner	hour	151		10r
Personal Goods				
Shampoo, Alberto VO5	15-oz.	1.20	12/94	2c
Toothpaste, Crest or Colgate	6-7 oz.	2.29	12/94	2c
Personal Services				
Dry cleaning, man's 2-pc. suit		6.57	12/94	2c
Haircut, man's barbershop, no styling		8.05	12/94	2c
Haircut, woman's shampoo, trim, blow-dry		22.40	12/94	2c
Personal services expenditures	year	286	91	81r
Plumbing service, house call	hr.	39.00	12/93	60c
Restaurant Food				
Chicken, fried, thigh and drumstick		2.09	12/94	2c
Dining expenditures, family	week	32.25	94	73r
Hamburger with cheese	1/4 lb.	1.94	12/94	2c
Pizza, Pizza Hut or Pizza Inn	12-13 in.	8.95	12/94	2c

Boise, ID - continued

Item	Per	Value	Date	Ref.
Taxes				
Tax rate, residential property, month	$100	1.98	1/92	79c
Taxes, Federal income, expenditures	year	2946	91	81r
Taxes, personal, expenditures	year	3791	91	81r
Taxes, State and local income, expenditures	year	791	91	81r
Transportation				
Transportation, ACCRA Index		104.30	12/94	2c
Bus fare, one-way	trip	0.75	12/95	1c
Bus fare, up to 10 miles	one-way	0.75	12/94	2c
Cars and trucks purchased, new	year	1231	91	81r
Cars and trucks purchased, used	year	915	91	81r
Driver's learning permit fee	perm	11.50	1/94	84s
Driver's license fee	orig	19.50	1/94	84s
Driver's license fee, duplicate	lic	11.50	1/94	84s
Driver's license reinstatement fee, min.	susp	15.00	1/94	85s
Driver's license renewal fee	renew	19.50	1/94	84s
Driving expenses	mile	36.70	5/95	89c
Identification card, nondriver	card	7.50	1/94	83s
Motorcycle learning permit fee	perm	11.50	1/94	84s
Motorcycle license fee	orig	19.50	1/94	84s
Motorcycle license fee, duplicate	lic	11.50	1/94	84s
Motorcycle license renewal fee	renew	19.50	1/94	84s
Public transportation expenditures	year	375	91	81r
Tire balance, computer or spin bal., front	wheel	6.80	12/94	2c
Transportation expenditures, total	year	5527	91	81r
Vehicle finance charges	year	287	91	81r
Vehicle insurance expenditures	year	624	91	81r
Vehicle maintenance and repairs expenditures	year	695	91	81r
Vehicle purchases	year	2174	91	81r
Vehicle rental, leases, licenses, etc. expenditures	year	257	91	81r
Vehicles purchased, other than cars and trucks	year	28	91	81r
Utilities				
Utilities, ACCRA Index		76.20	12/94	2c
Electricity expenditures	year	616	91	81r
Electricity, (part.), other, 1800 sq. ft., new home	mo.	39.67	12/94	2c
Electricity, summer, 250 KWh	month	11.88	8/93	64c
Electricity, summer, 500 KWh	month	23.75	8/93	64c
Electricity, summer, 750 KWh	month	35.63	8/93	64c
Electricity, summer, 1000 KWh	month	47.50	8/93	64c
Utilities, fuels, and public services, total expenditures	year	1681	91	81r
Water and other public services, expenditures	year	209	91	81r
Weddings				
Bridal attendants' gowns	event	750	10/93	76r
Bridal gown	event	852	10/93	76r
Bridal headpiece and veil	event	167	10/93	76r
Bride's wedding band	event	708	10/93	76r
Clergy	event	224	10/93	76r
Engagement ring	event	2756	10/93	76r
Flowers	event	863	10/93	76r
Formal wear for groom	event	106	10/93	76r
Groom's attendants' formal wear	event	530	10/93	76r
Groom's wedding band	event	402	10/93	76r
Music	event	600	10/93	76r
Photography	event	1088	10/93	76r
Shoes for bride	event	50	10/93	76r
Videography	event	483	10/93	76r
Wedding invitations and announcements	event	342	10/93	76r
Wedding reception	event	7000	10/93	76r

Values are in dollars or fractions of dollars. In the column headed *Ref*, references are shown to sources. Each reference is followed by a letter. These refer to the geographical level for which data were reported: s=State, r=Region, and c=City or metro. The abbreviation *ex* is used to mean *except* or *excluding*; *exp* stands for expenditures. For other abbreviations and further explanations, please see the Introduction.

Boston, MA

Item	Per	Value	Date	Ref.
Composite, ACCRA index		137.70	12/94	2c
Alcoholic Beverages				
Beer	bottle	3.00	94	34c
Beer, Miller Lite, Bud, 12-oz., ex deposit	6	4.72	12/94	2c
J & B Scotch	750-ml.	16.55	12/94	2c
Wine, Gallo Chablis blanc	1.5-lit	5.07	12/94	2c
Appliances				
Appliances (major), expenditures	year	139	91	81c
Appliances (major), expenditures	year	145	91	81r
Average annual exp.				
Food, health care, personal goods, services	year	30835	91	81c
Food, health care, personal goods, services	year	29496	91	81r
Business				
Dinner and tip, hotel, corporate rate	night	33.00	2/94	15c
Hotel room, corporate rate	night	112.00	2/94	15c
Charity				
Cash contributions, expenditures	year	434	91	81c
Cash contributions, expenditures	year	708	91	81r
Child Care				
Child care, for-profit daycare center	week	122.00	12/94	28c
Clothing				
Apparel, men and boys, total expenditures	year	451	91	81c
Apparel, men and boys, total expenditures	year	416	91	81r
Apparel, women and girls, total expenditures	year	715	91	81c
Apparel, women and girls, total expenditures	year	744	91	81r
Footwear, expenditures	year	361	91	81c
Footwear, expenditures	year	305	91	81r
Jeans, man's denim		30.79	12/94	2c
Shirt, man's dress shirt		31.49	12/94	2c
Undervest, boy's size 10-14, cotton	3	3.49	12/94	2c
Communications				
Long-distance telephone rate, day, addl. min., 1-10 mi.	min.	0.09	12/93	9s
Long-distance telephone rate, day, initial min., 1-10 mi.	min.	0.19	12/93	9s
Newspaper subscription, dly. and Sun. delivery	month	17.39	12/94	2c
Phone line, single, business, field visit	inst	27.50	12/93	9s
Phone line, single, business, no field visit	inst	93.02	12/93	9s
Phone line, single, residence, field visit	inst	27.50	12/93	9s
Phone line, single, residence, no field visit	inst	37.07	12/93	9s
Telephone bill, family of four	month	22.89	12/94	2c
Telephone service, expenditures	year	584	91	81c
Telephone service, expenditures	year	589	91	81r
Telephone, residential, flat rate	mo.	16.85	12/93	8c
Education				
Board, 4-year private college/university	year	3179	8/94	80s
Board, 4-year public college/university	year	2035	8/94	80s
Education, total expenditures	year	814	91	81c
Education, total expenditures	year	593	91	81r
Room, 4-year private college/university	year	3369	8/94	80s
Room, 4-year public college/university	year	2290	8/94	80s
Total cost, 4-year private college/university	year	21346	8/94	80s
Total cost, 4-year public college/university	year	8467	8/94	80s
Tuition, 2-year public college/university, in-state	year	2361	8/94	80s
Tuition, 4-year private college/university, in-state	year	14797	8/94	80s
Tuition, 4-year public college/university, in-state	year	4142	8/94	80s
Energy and Fuels				
Electricity	500 KWh	60.89	12/94	82c
Energy, combined forms, 1800 sq. ft.	mo.	228.19	12/94	2c
Energy, exc. electricity, 1800 sq. ft.	mo.	114.77	12/94	2c
Fuel oil #2	gallon	0.91	12/94	82c
Fuel oil and other fuels, expenditures	year	150	91	81c

Boston, MA - continued

Item	Per	Value	Date	Ref.
Energy and Fuels - continued				
Fuel oil and other fuels, expenditures	year	257	91	81r
Gas, cooking, 10 therms	month	17.85	2/94	65c
Gas, cooking, 30 therms	month	35.25	2/94	65c
Gas, cooking, 50 therms	month	48.71	2/94	65c
Gas, heating, winter, 100 therms	month	94.19	2/94	65c
Gas, heating, winter, average use	month	220.81	2/94	65c
Gas, natural, expenditures	year	293	91	81c
Gas, natural, expenditures	year	285	91	81r
Gas, piped	40 therms	44.35	12/94	82c
Gas, piped	100 therms	97.40	12/94	82c
Gas, piped	therm	1.03	12/94	82c
Gas, reg unlead, taxes inc., cash, self-service	gal	1.16	12/94	2c
Gasoline and motor oil purchased	year	881	91	81c
Gasoline and motor oil purchased	year	867	91	81r
Gasoline, unleaded midgrade	gallon	1.26	4/93	82c
Gasoline, unleaded midgrade	gallon	1.32	4/93	82r
Gasoline, unleaded premium	gallon	1.36	4/93	82c
Gasoline, unleaded premium	gallon	1.40	4/93	82r
Gasoline, unleaded regular	gallon	1.16	4/93	82c
Gasoline, unleaded regular	gallon	1.19	4/93	82r
Entertainment				
Baseball game, four-person family	game	102.55	4/94	47c
Bowling, evening rate	game	2.25	12/94	2c
Entertainment supplies, equipment, and services, misc. expenditures	year	179	91	81c
Entertainment, total expenditures	year	1341	91	81c
Entertainment, total expenditures	year	1331	91	81r
Fees and admissions, expenditures	year	410	91	81c
Fees and admissions, expenditures	year	398	91	81r
Monopoly game, Parker Brothers', No. 9	game	11.58	12/94	2c
Movie	adm	7.00	12/94	2c
Pets, toys, playground equipment, expenditures	year	296	91	81c
Pets, toys, playground equipment, expenditures	year	270	91	81r
Reading, expenditures	year	204	91	81c
Reading, expenditures	year	171	91	81r
Televisions, radios, and sound equipment, expenditures	year	456	91	81c
Televisions, radios, and sound equipment, expenditures	year	429	91	81r
Tennis balls, yellow, Wilson or Penn, 3	can	2.08	12/94	2c
Funerals				
Burial, immediate, container provided by funeral home		1507.89	1/95	54r
Cards, acknowledgment		18.10	1/95	54r
Casket, minimum alternative		133.03	1/95	54r
Cosmetology, hair care, etc.		114.12	1/95	54r
Cremation, direct, container provided by funeral home		1309.19	1/95	54r
Embalming		320.97	1/95	54r
Funeral, funeral home		327.61	1/95	54r
Funeral, other facility		314.81	1/95	54r
Graveside service		286.11	1/95	54r
Hearse, local		158.95	1/95	54r
Limousine, local		149.45	1/95	54r
Memorial service		315.94	1/95	54r
Service charge, professional, nondeclinable		1148.43	1/95	54r
Visitation and viewing		249.66	1/95	54r
Groceries				
Groceries, ACCRA Index		123.10	12/94	2c
Apples, Red Delicious	lb.	0.78	12/94	82r
Baby food, strained vegetables, lowest price	4-4.5 oz.	0.42	12/94	2c
Bacon, sliced	lb.	2.24	12/94	82r
Bananas	lb.	0.69	12/94	2c
Bananas	lb.	0.49	12/94	82r
Beef or hamburger, ground	lb.	1.65	12/94	2c

Values are in dollars or fractions of dollars. In the column headed *Ref*, references are shown to sources. Each reference is followed by a letter. These refer to the geographical level for which data were reported: s = State, r = Region, and c = City or metro. The abbreviation *ex* is used to mean *except* or *excluding*; *exp* stands for expenditures. For other abbreviations and further explanations, please see the Introduction.

Boston, MA - continued

Item	Per	Value	Date	Ref.
Groceries				
Beef purchases	year	204	91	81c
Beef purchases	year	226	91	81r
Beverage purchases, alcoholic	year	429	91	81c
Beverage purchases, alcoholic	year	332	91	81r
Beverage purchases, nonalcoholic	year	168	91	81c
Beverage purchases, nonalcoholic	year	213	91	81r
Big Mac hamburger	burger	2.09	94	34c
Bread, white	24-oz.	1.03	12/94	2c
Bread, white, pan	lb.	0.80	12/94	82r
Butter, salted, Grade AA, stick	lb.	1.67	12/94	82r
Carrots, short trimmed and topped	lb.	0.51	12/94	82r
Cereals and bakery products purchases	year	377	91	81c
Cereals and bakery products purchases	year	407	91	81r
Cereals and cereal products purchases	year	107	91	81c
Cereals and cereals products purchases	year	132	91	81r
Cheese, Kraft grated Parmesan	8-oz.	3.19	12/94	2c
Chicken breast, bone-in	lb.	2.22	12/94	82r
Chicken, fresh, whole	lb.	1.05	12/94	82r
Chicken, whole fryer	lb.	1.17	12/94	2c
Chuck roast, USDA choice, boneless	lb.	2.74	12/94	82r
Cigarettes, Winston, Kings	carton	19.42	12/94	2c
Coffee, 100%, ground roast, all sizes	lb.	4.61	12/94	82r
Coffee, vacuum-packed	13 oz.	3.79	12/94	2c
Corn Flakes, Kellogg's or Post Toasties	18 oz.	2.61	12/94	2c
Corn, frozen, whole kernel, lowest price	10 oz.	0.57	12/94	2c
Dairy products (other) purchases	year	122	91	81c
Dairy products (other) purchases	year	161	91	81r
Eggs, Grade A large	dozen	1.08	12/94	2c
Eggs, Grade A large	dozen	1.12	12/94	82r
Fish and seafood purchases	year	77	91	81c
Fish and seafood purchases	year	112	91	81r
Food purchases, food eaten at home	year	2169	91	81c
Food purchases, food eaten at home	year	2599	91	81r
Foods purchased away from home, not prepared by consumer	year	2014	91	81c
Foods purchased away from home, not prepared by consumer	year	2024	91	81r
Fruits and vegetables purchases	year	394	91	81c
Fruits and vegetables purchases	year	444	91	81r
Grapefruit	lb.	0.44	12/94	82r
Grapes, Thompson seedless	lb.	2.24	12/94	82r
Ground chuck, 100% beef	lb.	1.67	12/94	82r
Ice cream, prepackaged, bulk, regular	1/2 gal.	2.93	12/94	82r
Lemons	lb.	1.06	12/94	82r
Lettuce, iceberg	lb.	0.92	12/94	82r
Lettuce, iceberg	head	1.29	12/94	2c
Margarine, Blue Bonnet or Parkay cubes	lb.	0.78	12/94	2c
Meats, poultry, fish, and eggs purchases	year	590	91	81c
Meats, poultry, fish, and eggs purchases	year	751	91	81r
Milk and cream (fresh) purchases	year	136	91	81c
Milk and cream (fresh) purchases	year	152	91	81r
Milk, whole	1/2 gal.	1.47	12/94	2c
Orange juice, frozen concentrate 12-oz. can	16 oz.	1.92	12/94	82r
Orange juice, Minute Maid frozen	12-oz.	1.47	12/94	2c
Oranges, Navel	lb.	0.56	12/94	82r
Peaches, halves or slices, Hunt's, Del Monte, or Libby's	29-oz.	1.69	12/94	2c
Peas, sweet, Del Monte or Green Giant	15-17 oz.	0.70	12/94	2c
Pork chops, center cut, bone-in	lb.	3.09	12/94	82r
Pork purchases	year	71	91	81c
Pork purchases	year	130	91	81r
Potatoes, white	lb.	0.37	12/94	82r
Potatoes, white or red	10-lb. sack	2.35	12/94	2c
Rib roast, USDA choice, bone-in	lb.	4.98	12/94	82r
Round roast, USDA choice, boneless	lb.	2.93	12/94	82r
Sausage, Jimmy Dean, 100% pork	lb.	3.49	12/94	2c
Shortening, vegetable oil blends	lb.	1.03	12/94	82r
Shortening, vegetable, Crisco	3-lb.	3.15	12/94	2c

Boston, MA - continued

Item	Per	Value	Date	Ref.
Groceries - continued				
Soft drink, Coca Cola, ex deposit	2 lit	1.49	12/94	2c
Spaghetti and macaroni	lb.	0.84	12/94	82r
Steak, round, USDA choice, boneless	lb.	3.48	12/94	82r
Steak, sirloin, USDA choice, bone-in	lb.	3.38	12/94	82r
Steak, sirloin, USDA choice, boneless	lb.	4.81	12/94	82r
Steak, t-bone	lb.	6.21	12/94	2c
Sugar and other sweets, eaten at home, expenditures	year	89	91	81r
Sugar and other sweets, eaten at home, purchases	year	68	91	81c
Sugar, cane or beet	4 lbs.	1.43	12/94	2c
Sugar, white, all sizes	lb.	0.46	12/94	82r
Tobacco products and smoking supplies, total expenditures	year	262	91	81c
Tobacco products and smoking supplies, total expenditures	year	279	91	81r
Tomatoes, field grown	lb.	1.56	12/94	82r
Tomatoes, Hunt's or Del Monte	14.5 oz.	0.83	12/94	2c
Tuna, chunk, light	lb.	2.09	12/94	82r
Tuna, chunk, light, oil-packed	6.125-6.5 oz.	0.87	12/94	2c
Goods and Services				
Miscellaneous goods and services, ACCRA Index		108.30	12/94	2c
Health Care				
Health care, ACCRA Index		139.80	12/94	2c
Antibiotic ointment, Polysporin	1.5 oz.	4.47	12/94	2c
Childbirth, Cesarean delivery, hospital charge	birth	6334.00	12/91	69r
Childbirth, Cesarean delivery, physician charge	birth	2234.00	12/91	69r
Childbirth, normal delivery, hospital charge	birth	3225.00	12/91	69r
Childbirth, normal delivery, physician charge	birth	1623.00	12/91	69r
Dentist's fee, adult teeth cleaning and periodic oral exam	visit	72.00	12/94	2c
Doctor's fee, routine exam, established patient	visit	58.17	12/94	2c
Drugs, expenditures	year	199	91	81c
Drugs, expenditures	year	205	91	81r
Health care, total expenditures	year	1498	91	81c
Health care, total expenditures	year	1396	91	81r
Health insurance expenditures	year	735	91	81c
Health insurance expenditures	year	553	91	81r
Health insurance premium	month	495.00	7/93	94c
Hospital care, semiprivate room	day	593.00	12/94	2c
Hospital cost	adm	7,420	2/94	72c
Insurance premium, family medical care	month	457.38	1/95	41s
Medical services expenditures	year	461	91	81c
Medical services expenditures	year	559	91	81r
Medical supplies expenditures	year	103	91	81c
Medical supplies expenditures	year	80	91	81r
Household Goods				
Appl. repair, service call, wash mach	min. lab. chg.	31.87	12/94	2c
Floor coverings, expenditures	year	58	91	81c
Floor coverings, expenditures	year	158	91	81r
Furniture, expenditures	year	308	91	81c
Furniture, expenditures	year	341	91	81r
Household equipment, misc. expenditures	year	363	91	81r
Household equipment, misc., expenditures	year	392	91	81c
Household expenditures, miscellaneous	year	206	91	81c
Household expenditures, miscellaneous	year	194	91	81r
Household furnishings and equipment, expenditures	year	1037	91	81c
Household furnishings and equipment, expenditures	year	1158	91	81r
Household operations expenditures	year	405	91	81c
Household operations expenditures	year	378	91	81r
Household textiles, expenditures	year	77	91	81c

Values are in dollars or fractions of dollars. In the column headed *Ref*, references are shown to sources. Each reference is followed by a letter. These refer to the geographical level for which data were reported: s = State, r = Region, and c = City or metro. The abbreviation *ex* is used to mean *except* or *excluding*; *exp* stands for *expenditures*. For other abbreviations and further explanations, please see the Introduction.

Boston, MA - continued

Item	Per	Value	Date	Ref.
Household Goods				
Household textiles, expenditures	year	88	91	81r
Housekeeping supplies, expenditures	year	364	91	81c
Housekeeping supplies, expenditures	year	426	91	81r
Laundry and cleaning supplies, expenditures	year	94	91	81c
Laundry and cleaning supplies, expenditures	year	122	91	81r
Laundry detergent, Tide Ultra, Bold, or Cheer	42 oz.	4.47	12/94	2c
Postage and stationery, expenditures	year	137	91	81c
Postage and stationery, expenditures	year	134	91	81r
Tissues, facial, Kleenex brand	175	1.19	12/94	2c
Housing				
Housing, ACCRA Index		171.00	12/94	2c
Add garage/carport		11,614	3/95	74r
Add room(s)		16,816	3/95	74r
Apartment condominium or co-op, median	unit	96700	12/94	62r
Car rental	day	38.00	5/95	95c
Dwellings (owned), expenditures	year	4531	91	81c
Dwellings (owned), expenditures	year	3305	91	81r
Enclose porch/patio/breezeway		2,980	3/95	74r
Finish room in basement/attic		4,330	3/95	74r
Home, existing, single-family, median	unit	161600	12/94	62r
Home, existing, single-family, median	unit	177.60	12/94	62c
Home, purchase price	unit	165.00	3/93	26c
Hotel room	day	183.00	5/95	95c
House payment, principal and interest, 25% down payment	mo.	1259	12/94	2c
House, 1800 sq ft, 8000 sq ft lot, new, urban, utilities	total	199600	12/94	2c
Maintenance, repairs, insurance, and other housing expenditures	year	540	91	81c
Maintenance, repairs, insurance, and other housing expenditures	year	569	91	81r
Mortgage interest and charges expenditures	year	2837	91	81c
Mortgage interest and charges expenditures	year	1852	91	81r
Mtge. rate, incl. points and orig. fee, 30-year conv. fixed or ARM	mo.	9.50	12/94	2c
Princ. & int., mortgage, median-price exist. sing.-family home	mo.	765	12/94	62r
Property taxes expenditures	year	1154	91	81c
Property taxes expenditures	year	884	91	81r
Redesign, restructure more than half of home's interior		2,750	3/95	74r
Rent, apartment, 2 br., 1 1/2-2 baths, unfurnished, 950 sq ft, water	mo.	1051	12/94	2c
Rent, office space	sq. ft.	9.87	93	57c
Rental units expenditures	year	2264	900/00/91	81c
Rental units expenditures	year	1832	91	81r
Insurance and Pensions				
Auto insurance, private passenger	year	1009.56	12/94	71s
Insurance and pensions, personal, expenditures	year	2787	91	81c
Insurance and pensions, personal, expenditures	year	2690	91	81r
Insurance, life and other personal, expenditures	year	360	91	81c
Insurance, life and other personal, expenditures	year	341	91	81r
Pensions and Social Security, expenditures	year	2428	91	81c
Pensions and Social Security, expenditures	year	2349	91	81r
Legal Assistance				
Estate planning, law-firm partner	hr.	375.00	10/93	12r
Legal work, law firm associate	hour	78		10r
Legal work, law firm partner	hour	183		10r
Personal Goods				
Personal care products and services, total expenditures	year	340	91	81c
Shampoo, Alberto VO5	15-oz.	1.57	12/94	2c

Boston, MA - continued

Item	Per	Value	Date	Ref.
Personal Goods - continued				
Toothpaste, Crest or Colgate	6-7 oz.	2.61	12/94	2c
Personal Services				
Dry cleaning, man's 2-pc. suit		6.73	12/94	2c
Haircut, man's barbershop, no styling		9.60	12/94	2c
Haircut, woman's shampoo, trim, blow-dry		19.80	12/94	2c
Personal services expenditures	year	199	91	81c
Personal services expenditures	year	184	91	81r
Restaurant Food				
Chicken, fried, thigh and drumstick		2.91	12/94	2c
Dining expenditures, family	week	34.26	94	73r
Hamburger with cheese	1/4 lb.	2.19	12/94	2c
Pizza, Pizza Hut or Pizza Inn	12-13 in.	8.09	12/94	2c
Taxes				
Tax rate, residential property, month	$100	1.12	1/92	79c
Taxes, Federal income, expenditures	year	2187	91	81c
Taxes, Federal income, expenditures	year	2409	91	81r
Taxes, personal, expenditures	year	2989	91	81c
Taxes, personal, expenditures	year	3094	91	81r
Taxes, State and local income, expenditures	year	789	91	81c
Taxes, State and local income, expenditures	year	620	91	81r
Transportation				
Transportation, ACCRA Index		118.30	12/94	2c
Bus fare, one-way	trip	0.60	12/95	1c
Bus fare, up to 10 miles	one-way	1.81	12/94	2c
Cars and trucks purchased, new	year	1257	91	81c
Cars and trucks purchased, new	year	1170	91	81r
Cars and trucks purchased, used	year	482	91	81c
Cars and trucks purchased, used	year	739	91	81r
Driver's learning permit fee	perm	15.00	1/94	84s
Driver's license fee	orig	50.00	1/94	84s
Driver's license fee, duplicate	lic	15.00	1/94	84s
Driver's license renewal fee	renew	43.75	1/94	84s
Driving expenses	mile	49.80	5/95	86c
Ferry boat fare, one-way	trip	4.00	12/95	1c
Identification card, nondriver	card	15.00	1/94	83s
Mileage fee, mileage traveled over rental company limit	mile	0.25	95	7c
Motorcycle license fee	orig	50.00	1/94	84s
Motorcycle license fee, duplicate	lic	15.00	1/94	84s
Motorcycle license renewal fee	renew	43.75	1/94	84s
Public transportation expenditures	year	360	91	81c
Public transportation expenditures	year	430	91	81r
Railway fare, commuter rail, one-way	trip	0.85	12/95	1c
Railway fare, heavy rail, one-way	trip	0.85	12/95	1c
Railway fare, light rail, one-way	trip	0.85	12/95	1c
Tire balance, computer or spin bal., front	wheel	8.00	12/94	2c
Transportation expenditures, total	year	4696	91	81c
Transportation expenditures, total	year	4810	91	81r
Trolley fare, one-way	trip	0.60	12/95	1c
Vehicle expenses, miscellaneous	year	1715	91	81c
Vehicle finance charges	year	321	91	81c
Vehicle finance charges	year	238	91	81r
Vehicle insurance expenditures	year	708	91	81c
Vehicle insurance expenditures	year	630	91	81r
Vehicle maintenance and repairs expenditures	year	470	91	81c
Vehicle maintenance and repairs expenditures	year	532	91	81r
Vehicle purchases	year	1739	91	81c
Vehicle purchases	year	1920	91	81r
Vehicle rental, leases, licenses, etc. expenditures	year	216	91	81c
Vehicle rental, leases, licenses, etc. expenditures	year	193	91	81r
Vehicles purchased, other than cars and trucks	year	11	91	81r

Values are in dollars or fractions of dollars. In the column headed *Ref*, references are shown to sources. Each reference is followed by a letter. These refer to the geographical level for which data were reported: s=State, r=Region, and c=City or metro. The abbreviation *ex* is used to mean *except* or *excluding*; *exp* stands for expenditures. For other abbreviations and further explanations, please see the Introduction.

Boston, MA - continued

Utilities

Item	Per	Value	Date	Ref.
Utilities, ACCRA Index		191.80	12/94	2c
Electricity	KWh	0.11	12/94	82c
Electricity expenditures	year	644	91	81c
Electricity expenditures	year	695	91	81r
Electricity, (part.), other, 1800 sq. ft., new home	mo.	113.42	12/94	2c
Electricity, summer, 250 KWh	month	32.35	8/93	64c
Electricity, summer, 500 KWh	month	58.93	8/93	64c
Electricity, summer, 750 KWh	month	85.49	8/93	64c
Electricity, summer, 1000 KWh	month	112.06	8/93	64c
Fee, water use, industrial	month	1650.82	1/95	16c
Utilities, fuels, and public services, total expenditures	year	1952	91	81c
Utilities, fuels, and public services, total expenditures	year	1981	91	81r
Water and other public services, expenditures	year	265	91	81c
Water and other public services, expenditures	year	154	91	81r

Weddings

Item	Per	Value	Date	Ref.
Bridal attendants' gowns	event	750	10/93	76r
Bridal gown	event	852	10/93	76r
Bridal headpiece and veil	event	167	10/93	76r
Bride's wedding band	event	708	10/93	76r
Clergy	event	224	10/93	76r
Engagement ring	event	2756	10/93	76r
Flowers	event	863	10/93	76r
Formal wear for groom	event	106	10/93	76r
Groom's attendants' formal wear	event	530	10/93	76r
Groom's wedding band	event	402	10/93	76r
Music	event	600	10/93	76r
Photography	event	1088	10/93	76r
Shoes for bride	event	50	10/93	76r
Videography	event	483	10/93	76r
Wedding invitations and announcements	event	342	10/93	76r
Wedding reception	event	7000	10/93	76r

Boulder, CO

Item	Per	Value	Date	Ref.
Composite, ACCRA index		111.80	12/94	2c

Alcoholic Beverages

Item	Per	Value	Date	Ref.
Beer, Miller Lite, Bud, 12-oz., ex deposit	6	3.94	12/94	2c
J & B Scotch	750-ml.	18.12	12/94	2c
Wine, Gallo Chablis blanc	1.5-lit	4.17	12/94	2c

Appliances

Item	Per	Value	Date	Ref.
Appliances (major), expenditures	year	160	91	81r

Average annual exp.

Item	Per	Value	Date	Ref.
Food, health care, personal goods, services	year	32461	91	81r

Charity

Item	Per	Value	Date	Ref.
Cash contributions, expenditures	year	975	91	81r

Clothing

Item	Per	Value	Date	Ref.
Apparel, men and boys, total expenditures	year	467	91	81r
Apparel, women and girls, total expenditures	year	737	91	81r
Footwear, expenditures	year	270	91	81r
Jeans, man's denim		30.69	12/94	2c
Shirt, man's dress shirt		32.99	12/94	2c
Undervest, boy's size 10-14, cotton	3	3.72	12/94	2c

Communications

Item	Per	Value	Date	Ref.
Long-distance telephone rate, day, addl. min., 1-10 mi.	min.	0.13	12/93	9s
Long-distance telephone rate, day, initial min., 1-10 mi.	min.	0.17	12/93	9s
Newspaper subscription, dly. and Sun. delivery	month	10.00	12/94	2c
Phone line, single, business, field visit	inst	70.00	12/93	9s
Phone line, single, business, no field visit	inst	70.00	12/93	9s
Phone line, single, residence, field visit	inst	35.00	12/93	9s

Boulder, CO - continued

Communications - continued

Item	Per	Value	Date	Ref.
Phone line, single, residence, no field visit	inst	35.00	12/93	9s
Telephone bill, family of four	month	21.30	12/94	2c
Telephone service, expenditures	year	611	91	81r
Telephone, residential, flat rate	mo.	14.48	12/93	8c

Education

Item	Per	Value	Date	Ref.
Board, 4-year private college/university	year	2468	8/94	80s
Board, 4-year public college/university	year	2148	8/94	80s
Education, total expenditures	year	375	91	81r
Room, 4-year private college/university	year	2492	8/94	80s
Room, 4-year public college/university	year	1772	8/94	80s
Total cost, 4-year private college/university	year	16064	8/94	80s
Total cost, 4-year public college/university	year	6183	8/94	80s
Tuition, 2-year public college/university, in-state	year	1193	8/94	80s
Tuition, 4-year private college/university, in-state	year	11104	8/94	80s
Tuition, 4-year public college/university, in-state	year	2262	8/94	80s

Energy and Fuels

Item	Per	Value	Date	Ref.
Energy, combined forms, 1800 sq. ft.	mo.	101.91	12/94	2c
Energy, exc. electricity, 1800 sq. ft.	mo.	40.87	12/94	2c
Fuel oil and other fuels, expenditures	year	33	91	81r
Gas, natural, expenditures	year	212	91	81r
Gas, reg unlead, taxes inc., cash, self-service	gal	1.22	12/94	2c
Gasoline and motor oil purchased	year	1115	91	81r
Gasoline, unleaded midgrade	gallon	1.36	4/93	82r
Gasoline, unleaded premium	gallon	1.43	4/93	82r
Gasoline, unleaded regular	gallon	1.23	4/93	82r

Entertainment

Item	Per	Value	Date	Ref.
Bowling, evening rate	game	2.23	12/94	2c
Concert ticket, Pearl Jam group	perf	20.00	94	50r
Entertainment, total expenditures	year	1853	91	81r
Fees and admissions, expenditures	year	482	91	81r
Monopoly game, Parker Brothers', No. 9	game	10.61	12/94	2c
Movie	adm	6.08	12/94	2c
Pets, toys, playground equipment, expenditures	year	299	91	81r
Reading, expenditures	year	164	91	81r
Televisions, radios, and sound equipment, expenditures	year	528	91	81r
Tennis balls, yellow, Wilson or Penn, 3	can	2.33	12/94	2c

Funerals

Item	Per	Value	Date	Ref.
Burial, immediate, container provided by funeral home		1360.49	1/95	54r
Cards, acknowledgment		11.24	1/95	54r
Casket, minimum alternative		232.73	1/95	54r
Cosmetology, hair care, etc.		114.13	1/95	54r
Cremation, direct, container provided by funeral home		1027.08	1/95	54r
Embalming		286.24	1/95	54r
Funeral, funeral home		315.60	1/95	54r
Funeral, other facility		303.08	1/95	54r
Graveside service		423.83	1/95	54r
Hearse, local		133.12	1/95	54r
Limousine, local		99.10	1/95	54r
Memorial service		442.57	1/95	54r
Service charge, professional, nondeclinable		840.16	1/95	54r
Visitation and viewing		168.50	1/95	54r

Groceries

Item	Per	Value	Date	Ref.
Groceries, ACCRA Index		104.50	12/94	2c
Apples, Red Delicious	lb.	0.72	12/94	82r
Baby food, strained vegetables, lowest price	4-4.5 oz.	0.36	12/94	2c
Bacon, sliced	lb.	1.73	12/94	82r
Bananas	lb.	0.55	12/94	2c
Bananas	lb.	0.52	12/94	82r
Beef or hamburger, ground	lb.	1.11	12/94	2c
Beef purchases	year	241	91	81r

Values are in dollars or fractions of dollars. In the column headed *Ref*, references are shown to sources. Each reference is followed by a letter. These refer to the geographical level for which data were reported: s = State, r = Region, and c = City or metro. The abbreviation *ex* is used to mean *except* or *excluding*; *exp* stands for *expenditures*. For other abbreviations and further explanations, please see the Introduction.

Boulder, CO - continued

Groceries

Item	Per	Value	Date	Ref.
Beverage purchases, alcoholic	year	328	91	81r
Beverage purchases, nonalcoholic	year	234	91	81r
Bologna, all beef or mixed	lb.	2.33	12/94	82r
Bread, white	24-oz.	0.80	12/94	2c
Bread, white, pan	lb.	0.81	12/94	82r
Carrots, short trimmed and topped	lb.	0.43	12/94	82r
Cereals and bakery products purchases	year	392	91	81r
Cereals and cereals products purchases	year	139	91	81r
Cheese, Kraft grated Parmesan	8-oz.	3.02	12/94	2c
Chicken breast, bone-in	lb.	2.04	12/94	82r
Chicken, fresh, whole	lb.	0.95	12/94	82r
Chicken, whole fryer	lb.	0.77	12/94	2c
Cigarettes, Winston, Kings	carton	14.85	12/94	2c
Coffee, 100%, ground roast, all sizes	lb.	4.48	12/94	82r
Coffee, vacuum-packed	13 oz.	3.79	12/94	2c
Corn Flakes, Kellogg's or Post Toasties	18 oz.	2.69	12/94	2c
Corn, frozen, whole kernel, lowest price	10 oz.	0.84	12/94	2c
Dairy products (other) purchases	year	182	91	81r
Eggs, Grade A large	dozen	0.84	12/94	2c
Fish and seafood purchases	year	94	91	81r
Flour, white, all purpose	lb.	0.21	12/94	82r
Food purchases, food eaten at home	year	2749	91	81r
Foods purchased away from home, not prepared by consumer	year	1909	91	81r
Fruits and vegetables purchases	year	459	91	81r
Grapefruit	lb.	0.56	12/94	82r
Ground beef, 100% beef	lb.	1.31	12/94	82r
Ham, boneless, exc. canned	lb.	2.46	12/94	82r
Ice cream, prepackaged, bulk, regular	1/2 gal.	2.57	12/94	82r
Lemons	lb.	1.00	12/94	82r
Lettuce, iceberg	lb.	0.93	12/94	82r
Lettuce, iceberg	head	0.73	12/94	2c
Margarine, Blue Bonnet or Parkay cubes	lb.	0.67	12/94	2c
Meats, poultry, fish, and eggs purchases	year	700	91	81r
Milk and cream (fresh) purchases	year	155	91	81r
Milk, whole	1/2 gal.	1.67	12/94	2c
Orange juice, frozen concentrate 12-oz. can	16 oz.	1.52	12/94	82r
Orange juice, Minute Maid frozen	12-oz.	1.39	12/94	2c
Oranges, Navel	lb.	0.56	12/94	82r
Peaches, halves or slices, Hunt's, Del Monte, or Libby's	29-oz.	1.48	12/94	2c
Peas, sweet, Del Monte or Green Giant	15-17 oz.	0.82	12/94	2c
Pork chops, center cut, bone-in	lb.	3.30	12/94	82r
Pork purchases	year	122	91	81r
Potato chips	16-oz.	3.03	12/94	82r
Potatoes, frozen, French fried	lb.	0.77	12/94	82r
Potatoes, white	lb.	0.35	12/94	82r
Potatoes, white or red	10-lb. sack	1.85	12/94	2c
Rice, white, long grain, uncooked	lb.	0.54	12/94	82r
Round roast, USDA choice, boneless	lb.	2.92	12/94	82r
Sausage, Jimmy Dean, 100% pork	lb.	3.55	12/94	2c
Shortening, vegetable oil blends	lb.	0.80	12/94	82r
Shortening, vegetable, Crisco	3-lb.	2.91	12/94	2c
Soft drink, Coca Cola, ex deposit	2 lit	0.81	12/94	2c
Spaghetti and macaroni	lb.	1.02	12/94	82r
Steak, round, graded & ungraded, exc. USDA prime & choice	lb.	3.13	12/94	82r
Steak, sirloin, USDA choice, boneless	lb.	4.07	12/94	82r
Steak, t-bone	lb.	5.09	12/94	2c
Sugar and other sweets, eaten at home, expenditures	year	105	91	81r
Sugar, cane or beet	4 lbs.	1.24	12/94	2c
Sugar, white, all sizes	lb.	0.38	12/94	82r
Tobacco products and smoking supplies, total expenditures	year	221	91	81r
Tomatoes, field grown	lb.	1.45	12/94	82r
Tomatoes, Hunt's or Del Monte	14.5 oz.	0.93	12/94	2c

Boulder, CO - continued

Groceries - continued

Item	Per	Value	Date	Ref.
Tuna, chunk, light	lb.	2.18	12/94	82r
Tuna, chunk, light, oil-packed	6.125-6.5 oz.	0.83	12/94	2c

Goods and Services

Item	Per	Value	Date	Ref.
Miscellaneous goods and services, ACCRA Index		99.80	12/94	2c

Health Care

Item	Per	Value	Date	Ref.
Health care, ACCRA Index		121.70	12/94	2c
Antibiotic ointment, Polysporin	1.5 oz.	3.88	12/94	2c
Childbirth, Cesarean delivery, hospital charge	birth	6059.00	12/91	69r
Childbirth, Cesarean delivery, physician charge	birth	2248.00	12/91	69r
Childbirth, normal delivery, hospital charge	birth	3006.00	12/91	69r
Childbirth, normal delivery, physician charge	birth	1634.00	12/91	69r
Dentist's fee, adult teeth cleaning and periodic oral exam	visit	69.40	12/94	2c
Doctor's fee, routine exam, established patient	visit	52.30	12/94	2c
Drugs, expenditures	year	230	91	81r
Health care, total expenditures	year	1544	91	81r
Health insurance expenditures	year	558	91	81r
Hospital care, semiprivate room	day	400.00	12/94	2c
Insurance premium, family medical care	month	362.55	1/95	41s
Medical services expenditures	year	676	91	81r
Medical supplies expenditures	year	80	91	81r
Surgery, open-heart	proc	37818.00	1/93	14r

Household Goods

Item	Per	Value	Date	Ref.
Appl. repair, service call, wash mach	min. lab. chg.	27.08	12/94	2c
Floor coverings, expenditures	year	79	91	81r
Furniture, expenditures	year	352	91	81r
Household equipment, misc. expenditures	year	614	91	81r
Household expenditures, miscellaneous	year	294	91	81r
Household furnishings and equipment, expenditures	year	1416	91	81r
Household operations expenditures	year	580	91	81r
Household textiles, expenditures	year	113	91	81r
Housekeeping supplies, expenditures	year	447	91	81r
Laundry and cleaning supplies, expenditures	year	114	91	81r
Laundry detergent, Tide Ultra, Bold, or Cheer	42 oz.	3.67	12/94	2c
Postage and stationery, expenditures	year	145	91	81r
Tissues, facial, Kleenex brand	175	0.99	12/94	2c

Housing

Item	Per	Value	Date	Ref.
Housing, ACCRA Index		136.30	12/94	2c
Add garage/carport		6,422	3/95	74r
Add room(s)		26,583	3/95	74r
Apartment condominium or co-op, median	unit	105300	12/94	62r
Dwellings (owned), expenditures	year	3932	91	81r
Enclose porch/patio/breezeway		5,382	3/95	74r
Finish room in basement/attic		3,911	3/95	74r
Home, existing, single-family, median	unit	178600	12/94	62r
House payment, principal and interest, 25% down payment	mo.	1047	12/94	2c
House, 1800 sq ft, 8000 sq ft lot, new, urban, utilities	total	170734	12/94	2c
Maintenance, repairs, insurance, and other housing expenditures	year	591	91	81r
Mortgage interest and charges expenditures	year	2747	91	81r
Mtge. rate, incl. points and orig. fee, 30-year conv. fixed or ARM	mo.	9.18	12/94	2c
Princ. & int., mortgage, median-price exist. sing.-family home	mo.	845	12/94	62r
Property taxes expenditures	year	594	91	81r
Redesign, restructure more than half of home's interior		5,467	3/95	74r

Values are in dollars or fractions of dollars. In the column headed *Ref*, references are shown to sources. Each reference is followed by a letter. These refer to the geographical level for which data were reported: s=State, r=Region, and c=City or metro. The abbreviation *ex* is used to mean *except* or *excluding*; *exp* stands for *expenditures*. For other abbreviations and further explanations, please see the Introduction.

Boulder, CO - continued

Item	Per	Value	Date	Ref.
Housing				
Rent, apartment, 2 br., 1 1/2-2 baths, unfurnished, 950 sq ft, water	mo.	710	12/94	2c
Rental units expenditures	year	2077	91	81r
Insurance and Pensions				
Auto insurance, private passenger	year	804.17	12/94	71s
Insurance and pensions, personal, expenditures	year	3042	91	81r
Insurance, life and other personal, expenditures	year	298	91	81r
Pensions and Social Security, expenditures	year	2744	91	81r
Legal Assistance				
Legal work, law firm associate	hour	91		10r
Legal work, law firm partner	hour	151		10r
Personal Goods				
Shampoo, Alberto VO5	15-oz.	1.23	12/94	2c
Toothpaste, Crest or Colgate	6-7 oz.	2.12	12/94	2c
Personal Services				
Dry cleaning, man's 2-pc. suit		7.79	12/94	2c
Haircut, man's barbershop, no styling		9.70	12/94	2c
Haircut, woman's shampoo, trim, blow-dry		21.20	12/94	2c
Personal services expenditures	year	286	91	81r
Restaurant Food				
Chicken, fried, thigh and drumstick		1.99	12/94	2c
Dining expenditures, family	week	32.25	94	73r
Hamburger with cheese	1/4 lb.	2.04	12/94	2c
Pizza, Pizza Hut or Pizza Inn	12-13 in.	7.49	12/94	2c
Taxes				
Taxes, Federal income, expenditures	year	2946	91	81r
Taxes, personal, expenditures	year	3791	91	81r
Taxes, State and local income, expenditures	year	791	91	81r
Transportation				
Transportation, ACCRA Index		102.30	12/94	2c
Bus fare, one-way	trip	0.60	12/95	1c
Bus fare, up to 10 miles	one-way	0.65	12/94	2c
Cars and trucks purchased, new	year	1231	91	81r
Cars and trucks purchased, used	year	915	91	81r
Driver's learning permit fee	perm	10.00	1/94	84s
Driver's license fee	orig	15.00	1/94	84s
Driver's license fee, duplicate	lic	5.00	1/94	84s
Driver's license reinstatement fee, min.	susp	40.00	1/94	85s
Driver's license renewal fee	renew	15.00	1/94	84s
Identification card, nondriver	card	3.50	1/94	83s
Motorcycle license fee	orig	16.00	1/94	84s
Public transportation expenditures	year	375	91	81r
Tire balance, computer or spin bal., front	wheel	7.00	12/94	2c
Transportation expenditures, total	year	5527	91	81r
Vehicle finance charges	year	287	91	81r
Vehicle insurance expenditures	year	624	91	81r
Vehicle maintenance and repairs expenditures	year	695	91	81r
Vehicle purchases	year	2174	91	81r
Vehicle rental, leases, licenses, etc. expenditures	year	257	91	81r
Vehicles purchased, other than cars and trucks	year	28	91	81r
Utilities				
Utilities, ACCRA Index		93.30	12/94	2c
Electricity expenditures	year	616	91	81r
Electricity, (part.), other, 1800 sq. ft., new home	mo.	61.04	12/94	2c
Utilities, fuels, and public services, total expenditures	year	1681	91	81r
Water and other public services, expenditures	year	209	91	81r

Boulder, CO - continued

Item	Per	Value	Date	Ref.
Weddings				
Bridal attendants' gowns	event	750	10/93	76r
Bridal gown	event	852	10/93	76r
Bridal headpiece and veil	event	167	10/93	76r
Bride's wedding band	event	708	10/93	76r
Clergy	event	224	10/93	76r
Engagement ring	event	2756	10/93	76r
Flowers	event	863	10/93	76r
Formal wear for groom	event	106	10/93	76r
Groom's attendants' formal wear	event	530	10/93	76r
Groom's wedding band	event	402	10/93	76r
Music	event	600	10/93	76r
Photography	event	1088	10/93	76r
Shoes for bride	event	50	10/93	76r
Videography	event	483	10/93	76r
Wedding invitations and announcements	event	342	10/93	76r
Wedding reception	event	7000	10/93	76r

Bowling Green, KY

Item	Per	Value	Date	Ref.
Composite, ACCRA index		95.30	12/94	2c
Alcoholic Beverages				
Beer, Miller Lite, Bud, 12-oz., ex deposit	6	3.95	12/94	2c
J & B Scotch	750-ml.	17.83	12/94	2c
Wine, Gallo Chablis blanc	1.5-lit	5.16	12/94	2c
Clothing				
Jeans, man's denim		24.99	12/94	2c
Shirt, man's dress shirt		32.99	12/94	2c
Undervest, boy's size 10-14, cotton	3	3.25	12/94	2c
Communications				
Newspaper subscription, dly. and Sun. delivery	month	13.50	12/94	2c
Telephone bill, family of four	month	19.83	12/94	2c
Telephone, residential, flat rate	mo.	12.69	12/93	8c
Energy and Fuels				
Energy, combined forms, 1800 sq. ft.	mo.	105.25	12/94	2c
Energy, exc. electricity, 1800 sq. ft.	mo.	42.11	12/94	2c
Gas, reg unlead, taxes inc., cash, self-service	gal	1.20	12/94	2c
Entertainment				
Bowling, evening rate	game	2.10	12/94	2c
Monopoly game, Parker Brothers', No. 9	game	11.99	12/94	2c
Movie	adm	5.50	12/94	2c
Tennis balls, yellow, Wilson or Penn, 3	can	1.99	12/94	2c
Groceries				
Groceries, ACCRA Index		93.90	12/94	2c
Baby food, strained vegetables, lowest price	4-4.5 oz.	0.27	12/94	2c
Bananas	lb.	0.37	12/94	2c
Beef or hamburger, ground	lb.	1.59	12/94	2c
Bread, white	24-oz.	0.78	12/94	2c
Cheese, Kraft grated Parmesan	8-oz.	3.14	12/94	2c
Chicken, whole fryer	lb.	0.80	12/94	2c
Cigarettes, Winston, Kings	carton	13.15	12/94	2c
Coffee, vacuum-packed	13 oz.	3.55	12/94	2c
Corn Flakes, Kellogg's or Post Toasties	18 oz.	1.60	12/94	2c
Corn, frozen, whole kernel, lowest price	10 oz.	0.73	12/94	2c
Eggs, Grade A large	dozen	0.76	12/94	2c
Lettuce, iceberg	head	0.99	12/94	2c
Margarine, Blue Bonnet or Parkay cubes	lb.	0.44	12/94	2c
Milk, whole	1/2 gal.	1.42	12/94	2c
Orange juice, Minute Maid frozen	12-oz.	1.03	12/94	2c
Peaches, halves or slices, Hunt's, Del Monte, or Libby's	29-oz.	1.29	12/94	2c
Peas, sweet, Del Monte or Green Giant	15-17 oz.	0.44	12/94	2c

Values are in dollars or fractions of dollars. In the column headed *Ref*, references are shown to sources. Each reference is followed by a letter. These refer to the geographical level for which data were reported: s = State, r = Region, and c = City or metro. The abbreviation *ex* is used to mean *except* or *excluding*; *exp* stands for *expenditures*. For other abbreviations and further explanations, please see the Introduction.

Bowling Green, KY - continued

Item	Per	Value	Date	Ref.
Groceries				
Potatoes, white or red	10-lb. sack	3.59	12/94	2c
Sausage, Jimmy Dean, 100% pork	lb.	2.09	12/94	2c
Shortening, vegetable, Crisco	3-lb.	2.19	12/94	2c
Soft drink, Coca Cola, ex deposit	2 lit	1.02	12/94	2c
Steak, t-bone	lb.	5.52	12/94	2c
Sugar, cane or beet	4 lbs.	1.27	12/94	2c
Tomatoes, Hunt's or Del Monte	14.5 oz.	0.67	12/94	2c
Tuna, chunk, light, oil-packed	6.125-6.5 oz.	0.71	12/94	2c
Goods and Services				
Miscellaneous goods and services, ACCRA Index		95.10	12/94	2c
Health Care				
Health care, ACCRA Index		92.90	12/94	2c
Antibiotic ointment, Polysporin	1.5 oz.	3.98	12/94	2c
Dentist's fee, adult teeth cleaning and periodic oral exam	visit	52.67	12/94	2c
Doctor's fee, routine exam, established patient	visit	35.00	12/94	2c
Hospital care, semiprivate room	day	337.00	12/94	2c
Household Goods				
Appl. repair, service call, wash mach	min. lab. chg.	26.50	12/94	2c
Laundry detergent, Tide Ultra, Bold, or Cheer	42 oz.	3.38	12/94	2c
Tissues, facial, Kleenex brand	175	1.02	12/94	2c
Housing				
Housing, ACCRA Index		95.30	12/94	2c
House payment, principal and interest, 25% down payment	mo.	746	12/94	2c
House, 1800 sq ft, 8000 sq ft lot, new, urban, utilities	total	120000	12/94	2c
Mtge. rate, incl. points and orig. fee, 30-year conv. fixed or ARM	mo.	9.33	12/94	2c
Rent, apartment, 2 br., 1 1/2-2 baths, unfurnished, 950 sq ft, water	mo.	460	12/94	2c
Personal Goods				
Shampoo, Alberto VO5	15-oz.	1.22	12/94	2c
Toothpaste, Crest or Colgate	6-7 oz.	1.98	12/94	2c
Personal Services				
Dry cleaning, man's 2-pc. suit		5.50	12/94	2c
Haircut, man's barbershop, no styling		7.00	12/94	2c
Haircut, woman's shampoo, trim, blow-dry		18.50	12/94	2c
Restaurant Food				
Chicken, fried, thigh and drumstick		2.00	12/94	2c
Hamburger with cheese	1/4 lb.	1.89	12/94	2c
Pizza, Pizza Hut or Pizza Inn	12-13 in.	7.99	12/94	2c
Transportation				
Transportation, ACCRA Index		100.30	12/94	2c
Tire balance, computer or spin bal., front	wheel	6.17	12/94	2c
Utilities				
Utilities, ACCRA Index		94.90	12/94	2c
Electricity, (part.), other, 1800 sq. ft., new home	mo.	63.14	12/94	2c

Bozeman, MT

Item	Per	Value	Date	Ref.
Composite, ACCRA index		107.30	12/94	2c
Alcoholic Beverages				
Beer, Miller Lite, Bud, 12-oz., ex deposit	6	4.46	12/94	2c

Bozeman, MT - continued

Item	Per	Value	Date	Ref.
Alcoholic Beverages - continued				
J & B Scotch	750-ml.	18.85	12/94	2c
Wine, Gallo Chablis blanc	1.5-lit	5.49	12/94	2c
Clothing				
Jeans, man's denim		31.99	12/94	2c
Shirt, man's dress shirt		30.00	12/94	2c
Undervest, boy's size 10-14, cotton	3	4.50	12/94	2c
Communications				
Newspaper subscription, dly. and Sun. delivery	month	14.13	12/94	2c
Telephone bill, family of four	month	18.22	12/94	2c
Energy and Fuels				
Energy, combined forms, 1800 sq. ft.	mo.	98.34	12/94	2c
Energy, exc. electricity, 1800 sq. ft.	mo.	53.80	12/94	2c
Gas, reg unlead, taxes inc., cash, self-service	gal	1.37	12/94	2c
Entertainment				
Bowling, evening rate	game	1.70	12/94	2c
Monopoly game, Parker Brothers', No. 9	game	10.89	12/94	2c
Movie	adm	5.25	12/94	2c
Tennis balls, yellow, Wilson or Penn, 3	can	1.97	12/94	2c
Groceries				
Groceries, ACCRA Index		104.50	12/94	2c
Baby food, strained vegetables, lowest price	4-4.5 oz.	0.38	12/94	2c
Bananas	lb.	0.52	12/94	2c
Beef or hamburger, ground	lb.	1.24	12/94	2c
Bread, white	24-oz.	0.72	12/94	2c
Cheese, Kraft grated Parmesan	8-oz.	3.70	12/94	2c
Chicken, whole fryer	lb.	0.83	12/94	2c
Cigarettes, Winston, Kings	carton	15.14	12/94	2c
Coffee, vacuum-packed	13 oz.	3.99	12/94	2c
Corn Flakes, Kellogg's or Post Toasties	18 oz.	1.92	12/94	2c
Corn, frozen, whole kernel, lowest price	10 oz.	0.70	12/94	2c
Eggs, Grade A large	dozen	0.84	12/94	2c
Lettuce, iceberg	head	0.81	12/94	2c
Margarine, Blue Bonnet or Parkay cubes	lb.	0.65	12/94	2c
Milk, whole	1/2 gal.	1.46	12/94	2c
Orange juice, Minute Maid frozen	12-oz.	1.31	12/94	2c
Peaches, halves or slices, Hunt's, Del Monte, or Libby's	29-oz.	1.48	12/94	2c
Peas, sweet, Del Monte or Green Giant	15-17 oz.	0.58	12/94	2c
Potatoes, white or red	10-lb. sack	2.04	12/94	2c
Sausage, Jimmy Dean, 100% pork	lb.	3.50	12/94	2c
Shortening, vegetable, Crisco	3-lb.	2.39	12/94	2c
Soft drink, Coca Cola, ex deposit	2 lit	1.42	12/94	2c
Steak, t-bone	lb.	4.92	12/94	2c
Sugar, cane or beet	4 lbs.	1.43	12/94	2c
Tomatoes, Hunt's or Del Monte	14.5 oz.	0.74	12/94	2c
Tuna, chunk, light, oil-packed	6.125-6.5 oz.	0.69	12/94	2c
Goods and Services				
Miscellaneous goods and services, ACCRA Index		102.10	12/94	2c
Health Care				
Health care, ACCRA Index		97.80	12/94	2c
Antibiotic ointment, Polysporin	1.5 oz.	4.22	12/94	2c
Dentist's fee, adult teeth cleaning and periodic oral exam	visit	56.00	12/94	2c
Doctor's fee, routine exam, established patient	visit	39.00	12/94	2c
Hospital care, semiprivate room	day	310.00	12/94	2c

Values are in dollars or fractions of dollars. In the column headed *Ref*, references are shown to sources. Each reference is followed by a letter. These refer to the geographical level for which data were reported: s=State, r=Region, and c=City or metro. The abbreviation *ex* is used to mean *except* or *excluding*; *exp* stands for expenditures. For other abbreviations and further explanations, please see the Introduction.

Bozeman, MT - continued

Item	Per	Value	Date	Ref.
Household Goods				
Appl. repair, service call, wash mach	min. lab. chg.	33.98	12/94	2c
Laundry detergent, Tide Ultra, Bold, or Cheer	42 oz.	4.06	12/94	2c
Tissues, facial, Kleenex brand	175	1.11	12/94	2c
Housing				
Housing, ACCRA Index		116.50	12/94	2c
House payment, principal and interest, 25% down payment	mo.	898	12/94	2c
House, 1800 sq ft, 8000 sq ft lot, new, urban, utilities	total	142767	12/94	2c
Mtge. rate, incl. points and orig. fee, 30-year conv. fixed or ARM	mo.	9.46	12/94	2c
Rent, apartment, 2 br., 1 1/2-2 baths, unfurnished, 950 sq ft, water	mo.	601	12/94	2c
Personal Goods				
Shampoo, Alberto VO5	15-oz.	1.13	12/94	2c
Toothpaste, Crest or Colgate	6-7 oz.	2.36	12/94	2c
Personal Services				
Dry cleaning, man's 2-pc. suit		7.07	12/94	2c
Haircut, man's barbershop, no styling		9.40	12/94	2c
Haircut, woman's shampoo, trim, blow-dry		18.00	12/94	2c
Restaurant Food				
Chicken, fried, thigh and drumstick		2.45	12/94	2c
Hamburger with cheese	1/4 lb.	1.95	12/94	2c
Pizza, Pizza Hut or Pizza Inn	12-13 in.	8.39	12/94	2c
Transportation				
Transportation, ACCRA Index		126.10	12/94	2c
Tire balance, computer or spin bal., front	wheel	8.93	12/94	2c
Utilities				
Utilities, ACCRA Index		88.40	12/94	2c
Electricity, (part.), other, 1800 sq. ft., new home	mo.	44.54	12/94	2c

Bradenton, FL

Item	Per	Value	Date	Ref.
Appliances				
Appliances (major), expenditures	year	153	91	81r
Average annual exp.				
Food, health care, personal goods, services	year	27020	91	81r
Charity				
Cash contributions, expenditures	year	839	91	81r
Clothing				
Apparel, men and boys, total expenditures	year	380	91	81r
Apparel, women and girls, total expenditures	year	660	91	81r
Footwear, expenditures	year	193	91	81r
Communications				
Long-distance telephone rate, day, addl. min., 1-10 mi.	min.	0.08	12/93	9s
Long-distance telephone rate, day, initial min., 1-10 mi.	min.	0.15	12/93	9s
Phone line, single, business, field visit	inst	86.00	12/93	9s
Phone line, single, business, no field visit	inst	54.50	12/93	9s
Phone line, single, residence, field visit	inst	76.00	12/93	9s
Phone line, single, residence, no field visit	inst	44.50	12/93	9s
Telephone service, expenditures	year	616	91	81r
Education				
Bar examinination preparatory course	course	500.00-100	94	17s
Board, 4-year private college/university	year	2123	8/94	80s
Board, 4-year public college/university	year	2101	8/94	80s
Education, total expenditures	year	319	91	81r
Room, 4-year private college/university	year	2242	8/94	80s

Bradenton, FL - continued

Item	Per	Value	Date	Ref.
Education - continued				
Room, 4-year public college/university	year	1970	8/94	80s
Total cost, 4-year private college/university	year	13853	8/94	80s
Total cost, 4-year public college/university	year	5855	8/94	80s
Tuition, 2-year public college/university, in-state	year	1076	8/94	80s
Tuition, 4-year private college/university, in-state	year	9287	8/94	80s
Tuition, 4-year public college/university, in-state	year	1784	8/94	80s
Energy and Fuels				
Fuel oil and other fuels, expenditures	year	56	91	81r
Gas, natural, expenditures	year	150	91	81r
Gasoline and motor oil purchased	year	1152	91	81r
Gasoline, unleaded midgrade	gallon	1.21	4/93	82r
Gasoline, unleaded premium	gallon	1.30	4/93	82r
Gasoline, unleaded regular	gallon	1.10	4/93	82r
Entertainment				
Concert ticket, Pearl Jam group	perf	20.00	94	50r
Entertainment, total expenditures	year	1266	91	81r
Fees and admissions, expenditures	year	306	91	81r
Pets, toys, playground equipment, expenditures	year	271	91	81r
Reading, expenditures	year	131	91	81r
Televisions, radios, and sound equipment, expenditures	year	439	91	81r
Funerals				
Burial, immediate, container provided by funeral home		1370.36	1/95	54r
Cards, acknowledgment		14.83	1/95	54r
Casket, minimum alternative		192.52	1/95	54r
Cosmetology, hair care, etc.		102.27	1/95	54r
Cremation, direct, container provided by funeral home		1065.64	1/95	54r
Embalming		304.29	1/95	54r
Funeral, funeral home		287.83	1/95	54r
Funeral, other facility		284.14	1/95	54r
Graveside service		349.13	1/95	54r
Hearse, local		132.27	1/95	54r
Limousine, local		98.45	1/95	54r
Memorial service		270.59	1/95	54r
Service charge, professional, nondeclinable		933.59	1/95	54r
Visitation and viewing		225.83	1/95	54r
Groceries				
Apples, Red Delicious	lb.	0.73	12/94	82r
Bacon, sliced	lb.	1.67	12/94	82r
Bananas	lb.	0.42	12/94	82r
Beef purchases	year	213	91	81r
Beverage purchases, alcoholic	year	249	91	81r
Beverage purchases, nonalcoholic	year	207	91	81r
Bologna, all beef or mixed	lb.	2.27	12/94	82r
Bread, white, pan	lb.	0.68	12/94	82r
Cabbage	lb.	0.42	12/94	82r
Carrots, short trimmed and topped	lb.	0.53	12/94	82r
Cereals and bakery products purchases	year	345	91	81r
Cereals and cereals products purchases	year	127	91	81r
Cheddar cheese, natural	lb.	3.58	12/94	82r
Chicken breast, bone-in	lb.	1.71	12/94	82r
Chicken, fresh, whole	lb.	0.78	12/94	82r
Chuck roast, USDA choice, boneless	lb.	2.26	12/94	82r
Crackers, soda, salted	lb.	1.27	12/94	82r
Cucumbers	lb.	0.65	12/94	82r
Dairy products (other) purchases	year	141	91	81r
Eggs, Grade A large	dozen	0.87	12/94	82r
Fish and seafood purchases	year	72	91	81r
Flour, white, all purpose	lb.	0.23	12/94	82r
Food purchases, food eaten at home	year	2381	91	81r
Foods purchased away from home, not prepared by consumer	year	1696	91	81r
Frankfurters, all meat or all beef	lb.	1.74	12/94	82r
Fruits and vegetables purchases	year	380	91	81r

Values are in dollars or fractions of dollars. In the column headed *Ref*, references are shown to sources. Each reference is followed by a letter. These refer to the geographical level for which data were reported: s=State, r=Region, and c=City or metro. The abbreviation *ex* is used to mean *except* or *excluding*; *exp* stands for *expenditures*. For other abbreviations and further explanations, please see the Introduction.

Bradenton, FL - continued

Item	Per	Value	Date	Ref.
Groceries				
Grapefruit	lb.	0.45	12/94	82r
Grapes, Thompson seedless	lb.	2.30	12/94	82r
Ground beef, 100% beef	lb.	1.37	12/94	82r
Ground chuck, 100% beef	lb.	1.97	12/94	82r
Ham, boneless, exc. canned	lb.	2.54	12/94	82r
Ice cream, prepackaged, bulk, regular	1/2 gal.	2.47	12/94	82r
Lemons	lb.	1.02	12/94	82r
Lettuce, iceberg	lb.	0.96	12/94	82r
Margarine, stick	lb.	0.77	12/94	82r
Meats, poultry, fish, and eggs purchases	year	655	91	81r
Milk and cream (fresh) purchases	year	130	91	81r
Orange juice, frozen concentrate 12-oz. can	16 oz.	1.36	12/94	82r
Oranges, Navel	lb.	0.54	12/94	82r
Pears, Anjou	lb.	0.81	12/94	82r
Pork chops, center cut, bone-in	lb.	3.07	12/94	82r
Pork purchases	year	142	91	81r
Potato chips	16-oz.	3.15	12/94	82r
Potatoes, frozen, French fried	lb.	0.82	12/94	82r
Potatoes, white	lb.	0.34	12/94	82r
Rice, white, long grain, uncooked	lb.	0.48	12/94	82r
Round roast, USDA choice, boneless	lb.	2.91	12/94	82r
Sausage, fresh	lb.	1.82	12/94	82r
Shortening, vegetable oil blends	lb.	0.75	12/94	82r
Spaghetti and macaroni	lb.	0.87	12/94	82r
Steak, rib eye, USDA choice, boneless	lb.	6.85	12/94	82r
Steak, round, graded & ungraded, exc. USDA prime & choice	lb.	2.96	12/94	82r
Steak, round, USDA choice, boneless	lb.	3.17	12/94	82r
Steak, sirloin, USDA choice, boneless	lb.	4.12	12/94	82r
Steak, T-bone, USDA choice, bone-in	lb.	5.63	12/94	82r
Sugar and other sweets, eaten at home, expenditures	year	93	91	81r
Sugar, white, all sizes	lb.	0.39	12/94	82r
Tobacco products and smoking supplies, total expenditures	year	286	91	81r
Tomatoes, field grown	lb.	1.36	12/94	82r
Tuna, chunk, light	lb.	1.94	12/94	82r
Turkey, frozen, whole	lb.	0.96	12/94	82r
Yogurt, natural, fruit flavored	8 oz.	0.58	12/94	82r
Health Care				
Adenosine, emergency room	treat	100.00	95	23r
Bladder tap, superpubic, infant, emergency room	treat	119.00	95	23r
Blood analysis, emergency room	treat	25.00	95	23r
Blood tests, abdominal pain, emergency room	treat	25.00	95	23r
Burn dressing, emergency room	treat	266.00	95	23r
Cardiology interpretation, emergency room	treat	26.00	95	23r
Chest X-ray, emergency room	treat	78.00	95	23r
Childbirth, Cesarean delivery, hospital charge	birth	5462.00	12/91	69r
Childbirth, Cesarean delivery, physician charge	birth	2228.00	12/91	69r
Childbirth, normal delivery, hospital charge	birth	2943.00	12/91	69r
Childbirth, normal delivery, physician charge	birth	1619.00	12/91	69r
Defibrillation pads, emergency room	treat	6.00	95	23r
Drugs, expenditures	year	297	91	81r
Gastric tube insertion, nasal, emergency room	treat	25.00	95	23r
Health care, total expenditures	year	1600	91	81r
Health insurance expenditures	year	637	91	81r
Heart monitor, emergency room	treat	40.00	95	23r
Insurance premium, family medical care	month	301.92	1/95	41s
Intravenous fluids, emergency room	treat	130.00	95	23r
Intravenous fluids, emergency room	liter	26.00	95	23r
Intravenous line, central, emergency room	treat	342.00	95	23r
Liver function tests, abdominal pain, emergency room	treat	26.00	95	23r
Medical care charges, total, emergency room, third-degree burns	treat	2101.00	95	23r

Bradenton, FL - continued

Item	Per	Value	Date	Ref.
Health Care - continued				
Medical care charges, total, emergency, infant with fever	treat	628.00	95	23r
Medical services expenditures	year	573	91	81r
Medical supplies expenditures	year	93	91	81r
Morphine, emergency room	treat	34.00	95	23r
Nursing care and facilities charges, emergency room	treat	252.00	95	23r
Nursing care and facilities charges, emergency, infant with fever	treat	252.00	95	23r
Nursing care and facilities charges, emergency, third-degree burns	treat	861.00	95	23r
Physician's charges, emergency, infant with fever	treat	212.00	95	23r
Physician's charges, emergency, third-degree burns	treat	372.00	95	23r
Physician's fee, emergency room	treat	372.00	95	23r
Physician's fee, general practitioner	visit	51.20	12/93	60r
Surgery, open-heart	proc	42374.00	1/93	14r
Ultrasound, abdominal, emergency room	treat	276.00	95	23r
Urinalysis, emergency room	treat	20.00	95	23r
Urinalysis, infant, emergency room	treat	20.00	95	23r
X-rays, emergency room	treat	78.00	95	23r
Household Goods				
Floor coverings, expenditures	year	48	91	81r
Furniture, expenditures	year	280	91	81r
Household equipment, misc. expenditures	year	342	91	81r
Household expenditures, miscellaneous	year	256	91	81r
Household furnishings and equipment, expenditures	year	988	91	81r
Household operations expenditures	year	468	91	81r
Household textiles, expenditures	year	95	91	81r
Housekeeping supplies, expenditures	year	380	91	81r
Laundry and cleaning supplies, expenditures	year	109	91	81r
Postage and stationery, expenditures	year	105	91	81r
Housing				
Add garage/carport		6,980	3/95	74r
Add room(s)		11,403	3/95	74r
Apartment condominium or co-op, median	unit	68600	12/94	62r
Dwellings (owned), expenditures	year	2428	91	81r
Enclose porch/patio/breezeway		4,572	3/95	74r
Finish room in basement/attic		3,794	3/95	74r
Home, existing, single-family, median	unit	120200	12/94	62r
Maintenance, repairs, insurance, and other housing expenditures	year	531	91	81r
Mortgage interest and charges expenditures	year	1506	91	81r
Princ. & int., mortgage, median-price exist. sing.-family home	mo.	540	12/94	62r
Property taxes expenditures	year	391	91	81r
Redesign, restructure more than half of home's interior		17,641	3/95	74r
Rental units expenditures	year	1264	91	81r
Insurance and Pensions				
Auto insurance, private passenger	year	753.93	12/94	71s
Insurance and pensions, personal, expenditures	year	2395	91	81r
Insurance, life and other personal, expenditures	year	368	91	81r
Pensions and Social Security, expenditures	year	2027	91	81r
Personal Services				
Personal services expenditures	year	212	91	81r
Restaurant Food				
Dining expenditures, family	week	33.83	94	73r
Taxes				
Taxes, Federal income, expenditures	year	2275	91	81r
Taxes, personal, expenditures	year	2715	91	81r
Taxes, State and local income, expenditures	year	365	91	81r

Values are in dollars or fractions of dollars. In the column headed *Ref*, references are shown to sources. Each reference is followed by a letter. These refer to the geographical level for which data were reported: s = State, r = Region, and c = City or metro. The abbreviation *ex* is used to mean *except* or *excluding*; *exp* stands for *expenditures*. For other abbreviations and further explanations, please see the Introduction.

Bradenton, FL - continued

Item	Per	Value	Date	Ref.
Transportation				
Cars and trucks purchased, new	year	1306	91	81r
Cars and trucks purchased, used	year	942	91	81r
Driver's learning permit fee	perm	20.00	1/94	84s
Driver's license fee	orig	20.00	1/94	84s
Driver's license fee, duplicate	lic	10.00	1/94	84s
Driver's license reinstatement fee, min.	susp	25.00	1/94	85s
Driver's license renewal fee	renew	15.00	1/94	84s
Identification card, nondriver	card	3.00	1/94	83s
Motorcycle learning permit fee	perm	20.00	1/94	84s
Motorcycle license fee	orig	20.00	1/94	84s
Motorcycle license fee, duplicate	lic	10.00	1/94	84s
Motorcycle license renewal fee	renew	15.00	1/94	84s
Public transportation expenditures	year	249	91	81r
Transportation expenditures, total	year	5307	91	81r
Vehicle finance charges	year	346	91	81r
Vehicle insurance expenditures	year	544	91	81r
Vehicle maintenance and repairs expenditures	year	600	91	81r
Vehicle purchases	year	2275	91	81r
Vehicle rental, leases, licenses, etc. expenditures	year	141	91	81r
Vehicles purchased, other than cars and trucks	year	27	91	81r
Utilities				
Electricity expenditures	year	950	91	81r
Utilities, fuels, and public services, total expenditures	year	2000	91	81r
Water and other public services, expenditures	year	227	91	81r
Weddings				
Bridal attendants' gowns	event	750	10/93	76r
Bridal gown	event	852	10/93	76r
Bridal headpiece and veil	event	167	10/93	76r
Bride's wedding band	event	708	10/93	76r
Clergy	event	224	10/93	76r
Engagement ring	event	2756	10/93	76r
Flowers	event	863	10/93	76r
Formal wear for groom	event	106	10/93	76r
Groom's attendants' formal wear	event	530	10/93	76r
Groom's wedding band	event	402	10/93	76r
Music	event	600	10/93	76r
Photography	event	1088	10/93	76r
Shoes for bride	event	50	10/93	76r
Videography	event	483	10/93	76r
Wedding invitations and announcements	event	342	10/93	76r
Wedding reception	event	7000	10/93	76r

Brazoria, TX

Item	Per	Value	Date	Ref.
Appliances				
Appliances (major), expenditures	year	153	91	81r
Average annual exp.				
Food, health care, personal goods, services	year	27020	91	81r
Charity				
Cash contributions, expenditures	year	839	91	81r
Clothing				
Apparel, men and boys, total expenditures	year	380	91	81r
Apparel, women and girls, total expenditures	year	660	91	81r
Footwear, expenditures	year	193	91	81r
Communications				
Long-distance telephone rate, day, addl. min., 1-10 mi.	min.	0.08	12/93	9s
Long-distance telephone rate, day, initial min., 1-10 mi.	min.	0.10	12/93	9s
Phone line, single, business, field visit	inst	71.90	12/93	9s
Phone line, single, business, no field visit	inst	57.30	12/93	9s
Phone line, single, residence, field visit	inst	52.95	12/93	9s
Phone line, single, residence, no field visit	inst	38.35	12/93	9s

Brazoria, TX - continued

Item	Per	Value	Date	Ref.
Communications - continued				
Telephone service, expenditures	year	616	91	81r
Education				
Board, 4-year private college/university	year	2084	8/94	80s
Board, 4-year public college/university	year	1675	8/94	80s
Education, total expenditures	year	319	91	81r
Room, 4-year private college/university	year	1840	8/94	80s
Room, 4-year public college/university	year	1756	8/94	80s
Total cost, 4-year private college/university	year	11876	8/94	80s
Total cost, 4-year public college/university	year	4935	8/94	80s
Tuition, 2-year public college/university, in-state	year	625	8/94	80s
Tuition, 4-year private college/university, in-state	year	7952	8/94	80s
Tuition, 4-year public college/university, in-state	year	1503	8/94	80s
Energy and Fuels				
Fuel oil and other fuels, expenditures	year	56	91	81r
Gas, natural, expenditures	year	150	91	81r
Gasoline and motor oil purchased	year	1152	91	81r
Gasoline, unleaded midgrade	gallon	1.21	4/93	82r
Gasoline, unleaded premium	gallon	1.30	4/93	82r
Gasoline, unleaded regular	gallon	1.10	4/93	82r
Entertainment				
Concert ticket, Pearl Jam group	perf	20.00	94	50r
Entertainment, total expenditures	year	1266	91	81r
Fees and admissions, expenditures	year	306	91	81r
Pets, toys, playground equipment, expenditures	year	271	91	81r
Reading, expenditures	year	131	91	81r
Televisions, radios, and sound equipment, expenditures	year	439	91	81r
Funerals				
Burial, immediate, container provided by funeral home		1574.60	1/95	54r
Cards, acknowledgment		22.24	1/95	54r
Casket, minimum alternative		239.41	1/95	54r
Cosmetology, hair care, etc.		91.04	1/95	54r
Cremation, direct, container provided by funeral home		1085.15	1/95	54r
Embalming		281.30	1/95	54r
Funeral, funeral home		323.04	1/95	54r
Funeral, other facility		327.58	1/95	54r
Graveside service		355.19	1/95	54r
Hearse, local		141.89	1/95	54r
Limousine, local		99.40	1/95	54r
Memorial service		284.67	1/95	54r
Service charge, professional, nondeclinable		904.06	1/95	54r
Visitation and viewing		187.04	1/95	54r
Groceries				
Apples, Red Delicious	lb.	0.73	12/94	82r
Bacon, sliced	lb.	1.67	12/94	82r
Bananas	lb.	0.42	12/94	82r
Beef purchases	year	213	91	81r
Beverage purchases, alcoholic	year	249	91	81r
Beverage purchases, nonalcoholic	year	207	91	81r
Bologna, all beef or mixed	lb.	2.27	12/94	82r
Bread, white, pan	lb.	0.68	12/94	82r
Cabbage	lb.	0.42	12/94	82r
Carrots, short trimmed and topped	lb.	0.53	12/94	82r
Cereals and bakery products purchases	year	345	91	81r
Cereals and cereals products purchases	year	127	91	81r
Cheddar cheese, natural	lb.	3.58	12/94	82r
Chicken breast, bone-in	lb.	1.71	12/94	82r
Chicken, fresh, whole	lb.	0.78	12/94	82r
Chuck roast, USDA choice, boneless	lb.	2.26	12/94	82r
Crackers, soda, salted	lb.	1.27	12/94	82r
Cucumbers	lb.	0.65	12/94	82r
Dairy products (other) purchases	year	141	91	81r
Eggs, Grade A large	dozen	0.87	12/94	82r

Values are in dollars or fractions of dollars. In the column headed *Ref*, references are shown to sources. Each reference is followed by a letter. These refer to the geographical level for which data were reported: s=State, r=Region, and c=City or metro. The abbreviation *ex* is used to mean *except* or *excluding*; *exp* stands for expenditures. For other abbreviations and further explanations, please see the Introduction.

Brazoria, TX - continued

Item	Per	Value	Date	Ref.
Groceries				
Fish and seafood purchases	year	72	91	81r
Flour, white, all purpose	lb.	0.23	12/94	82r
Food purchases, food eaten at home	year	2381	91	81r
Foods purchased away from home, not prepared by consumer	year	1696	91	81r
Frankfurters, all meat or all beef	lb.	1.74	12/94	82r
Fruits and vegetables purchases	year	380	91	81r
Grapefruit	lb.	0.45	12/94	82r
Grapes, Thompson seedless	lb.	2.30	12/94	82r
Ground beef, 100% beef	lb.	1.37	12/94	82r
Ground chuck, 100% beef	lb.	1.97	12/94	82r
Ham, boneless, exc. canned	lb.	2.54	12/94	82r
Ice cream, prepackaged, bulk, regular	1/2 gal.	2.47	12/94	82r
Lemons	lb.	1.02	12/94	82r
Lettuce, iceberg	lb.	0.96	12/94	82r
Margarine, stick	lb.	0.77	12/94	82r
Meats, poultry, fish, and eggs purchases	year	655	91	81r
Milk and cream (fresh) purchases	year	130	91	81r
Orange juice, frozen concentrate 12-oz. can	16 oz.	1.36	12/94	82r
Oranges, Navel	lb.	0.54	12/94	82r
Pears, Anjou	lb.	0.81	12/94	82r
Pork chops, center cut, bone-in	lb.	3.07	12/94	82r
Pork purchases	year	142	91	81r
Potato chips	16-oz.	3.15	12/94	82r
Potatoes, frozen, French fried	lb.	0.82	12/94	82r
Potatoes, white	lb.	0.34	12/94	82r
Rice, white, long grain, uncooked	lb.	0.48	12/94	82r
Round roast, USDA choice, boneless	lb.	2.91	12/94	82r
Sausage, fresh	lb.	1.82	12/94	82r
Shortening, vegetable oil blends	lb.	0.75	12/94	82r
Spaghetti and macaroni	lb.	0.87	12/94	82r
Steak, rib eye, USDA choice, boneless	lb.	6.85	12/94	82r
Steak, round, graded & ungraded, exc. USDA prime & choice	lb.	2.96	12/94	82r
Steak, round, USDA choice, boneless	lb.	3.17	12/94	82r
Steak, sirloin, USDA choice, boneless	lb.	4.12	12/94	82r
Steak, T-bone, USDA choice, bone-in	lb.	5.63	12/94	82r
Sugar and other sweets, eaten at home, expenditures	year	93	91	81r
Sugar, white, all sizes	lb.	0.39	12/94	82r
Tobacco products and smoking supplies, total expenditures	year	286	91	81r
Tomatoes, field grown	lb.	1.36	12/94	82r
Tuna, chunk, light	lb.	1.94	12/94	82r
Turkey, frozen, whole	lb.	0.96	12/94	82r
Yogurt, natural, fruit flavored	8 oz.	0.58	12/94	82r
Health Care				
Adenosine, emergency room	treat	100.00	95	23r
Bladder tap, superpubic, infant, emergency room	treat	119.00	95	23r
Blood analysis, emergency room	treat	25.00	95	23r
Blood tests, abdominal pain, emergency room	treat	25.00	95	23r
Burn dressing, emergency room	treat	266.00	95	23r
Cardiology interpretation, emergency room	treat	26.00	95	23r
Chest X-ray, emergency room	treat	78.00	95	23r
Childbirth, Cesarean delivery, hospital charge	birth	5462.00	12/91	69r
Childbirth, Cesarean delivery, physician charge	birth	2228.00	12/91	69r
Childbirth, normal delivery, hospital charge	birth	2943.00	12/91	69r
Childbirth, normal delivery, physician charge	birth	1619.00	12/91	69r
Defibrillation pads, emergency room	treat	6.00	95	23r
Drugs, expenditures	year	297	91	81r
Gastric tube insertion, nasal, emergency room	treat	25.00	95	23r
Health care, total expenditures	year	1600	91	81r
Health insurance expenditures	year	637	91	81r
Heart monitor, emergency room	treat	40.00	95	23r
Insurance premium, family medical care	month	389.25	1/95	41s
Intravenous fluids, emergency room	treat	130.00	95	23r

Item	Per	Value	Date	Ref.
Health Care - continued				
Intravenous fluids, emergency room	liter	26.00	95	23r
Intravenous line, central, emergency room	treat	342.00	95	23r
Liver function tests, abdominal pain, emergency room	treat	26.00	95	23r
Medical care charges, total, emergency room, third-degree burns	treat	2101.00	95	23r
Medical care charges, total, emergency, infant with fever	treat	628.00	95	23r
Medical services expenditures	year	573	91	81r
Medical supplies expenditures	year	93	91	81r
Morphine, emergency room	treat	34.00	95	23r
Nursing care and facilities charges, emergency room	treat	252.00	95	23r
Nursing care and facilities charges, emergency, infant with fever	treat	252.00	95	23r
Nursing care and facilities charges, emergency, third-degree burns	treat	861.00	95	23r
Physician's charges, emergency, infant with fever	treat	212.00	95	23r
Physician's charges, emergency, third-degree burns	treat	372.00	95	23r
Physician's fee, emergency room	treat	372.00	95	23r
Physician's fee, general practitioner	visit	51.20	12/93	60r
Surgery, open-heart	proc	42374.00	1/93	14r
Ultrasound, abdominal, emergency room	treat	276.00	95	23r
Urinalysis, emergency room	treat	20.00	95	23r
Urinalysis, infant, emergency room	treat	20.00	95	23r
X-rays, emergency room	treat	78.00	95	23r
Household Goods				
Floor coverings, expenditures	year	48	91	81r
Furniture, expenditures	year	280	91	81r
Household equipment, misc. expenditures	year	342	91	81r
Household expenditures, miscellaneous	year	256	91	81r
Household furnishings and equipment, expenditures	year	988	91	81r
Household operations expenditures	year	468	91	81r
Household textiles, expenditures	year	95	91	81r
Housekeeping supplies, expenditures	year	380	91	81r
Laundry and cleaning supplies, expenditures	year	109	91	81r
Postage and stationery, expenditures	year	105	91	81r
Housing				
Add garage/carport		6,980	3/95	74r
Add room(s)		11,403	3/95	74r
Apartment condominium or co-op, median	unit	68600	12/94	62r
Dwellings (owned), expenditures	year	2428	91	81r
Enclose porch/patio/breezeway		4,572	3/95	74r
Finish room in basement/attic		3,794	3/95	74r
Home, existing, single-family, median	unit	120200	12/94	62r
Maintenance, repairs, insurance, and other housing expenditures	year	531	91	81r
Mortgage interest and charges expenditures	year	1506	91	81r
Princ. & int., mortgage, median-price exist. sing.-family home	mo.	540	12/94	62r
Property taxes expenditures	year	391	91	81r
Redesign, restructure more than half of home's interior		17,641	3/95	74r
Rental units expenditures	year	1264	91	81r
Insurance and Pensions				
Auto insurance, private passenger	year	785.78	12/94	71s
Insurance and pensions, personal, expenditures	year	2395	91	81r
Insurance, life and other personal, expenditures	year	368	91	81r
Pensions and Social Security, expenditures	year	2027	91	81r
Personal Services				
Personal services expenditures	year	212	91	81r
Restaurant Food				
Dining expenditures, family	week	33.83	94	73r

Values are in dollars or fractions of dollars. In the column headed *Ref*, references are shown to sources. Each reference is followed by a letter. These refer to the geographical level for which data were reported: s = State, r = Region, and c = City or metro. The abbreviation *ex* is used to mean *except* or *excluding*; *exp* stands for *expenditures*. For other abbreviations and further explanations, please see the Introduction.

Brazoria, TX - continued

Item	Per	Value	Date	Ref.
Taxes				
Tax, cigarettes	year	584.00	10/93	43s
Taxes, Federal income, expenditures	year	2275	91	81r
Taxes, personal, expenditures	year	2715	91	81r
Taxes, State and local income, expenditures	year	365	91	81r
Transportation				
Cars and trucks purchased, new	year	1306	91	81r
Cars and trucks purchased, used	year	942	91	81r
Driver's learning permit fee	perm	5.00	1/94	84s
Driver's license fee	orig	16.00	1/94	84s
Driver's license fee, duplicate	lic	10.00	1/94	84s
Driver's license reinstatement fee, min.	susp	50.00	1/94	85s
Driver's license renewal fee	renew	16.00	1/94	84s
Identification card, nondriver	card	10.00	1/94	83s
Motorcycle learning permit fee	perm	5.00	1/94	84s
Motorcycle license fee	orig	16.00	1/94	84s
Motorcycle license fee, duplicate	lic	10.00	1/94	84s
Motorcycle license renewal fee	renew	21.00	1/94	84s
Public transportation expenditures	year	249	91	81r
Transportation expenditures, total	year	5307	91	81r
Vehicle finance charges	year	346	91	81r
Vehicle insurance expenditures	year	544	91	81r
Vehicle maintenance and repairs expenditures	year	600	91	81r
Vehicle purchases	year	2275	91	81r
Vehicle rental, leases, licenses, etc. expenditures	year	141	91	81r
Vehicles purchased, other than cars and trucks	year	27	91	81r
Utilities				
Electricity expenditures	year	950	91	81r
Utilities, fuels, and public services, total expenditures	year	2000	91	81r
Water and other public services, expenditures	year	227	91	81r
Weddings				
Bridal attendants' gowns	event	750	10/93	76r
Bridal gown	event	852	10/93	76r
Bridal headpiece and veil	event	167	10/93	76r
Bride's wedding band	event	708	10/93	76r
Clergy	event	224	10/93	76r
Engagement ring	event	2756	10/93	76r
Flowers	event	863	10/93	76r
Formal wear for groom	event	106	10/93	76r
Groom's attendants' formal wear	event	530	10/93	76r
Groom's wedding band	event	402	10/93	76r
Music	event	600	10/93	76r
Photography	event	1088	10/93	76r
Shoes for bride	event	50	10/93	76r
Videography	event	483	10/93	76r
Wedding invitations and announcements	event	342	10/93	76r
Wedding reception	event	7000	10/93	76r

Bremerton, WA

Item	Per	Value	Date	Ref.
Appliances				
Appliances (major), expenditures	year	160	91	81r
Average annual exp.				
Food, health care, personal goods, services	year	32461	91	81r
Charity				
Cash contributions, expenditures	year	975	91	81r
Clothing				
Apparel, men and boys, total expenditures	year	467	91	81r
Apparel, women and girls, total expenditures	year	737	91	81r
Footwear, expenditures	year	270	91	81r
Communications				
Long-distance telephone rate, day, addl. min., 1-10 mi.	min.	0.01	12/93	9s

Bremerton, WA - continued

Item	Per	Value	Date	Ref.
Communications - continued				
Long-distance telephone rate, day, initial min., 1-10 mi.	min.	0.15	12/93	9s
Phone line, single, business, field visit	inst	48.00	12/93	9s
Phone line, single, business, no field visit	inst	48.00	12/93	9s
Phone line, single, residence, field visit	inst	31.00	12/93	9s
Phone line, single, residence, no field visit	inst	31.00	12/93	9s
Telephone service, expenditures	year	611	91	81r
Education				
Board, 4-year private college/university	year	1928	8/94	80s
Board, 4-year public college/university	year	2194	8/94	80s
Education, total expenditures	year	375	91	81r
Room, 4-year private college/university	year	2455	8/94	80s
Room, 4-year public college/university	year	1952	8/94	80s
Total cost, 4-year private college/university	year	16332	8/94	80s
Total cost, 4-year public college/university	year	6483	8/94	80s
Tuition, 2-year public college/university, in-state	year	1141	8/94	80s
Tuition, 4-year private college/university, in-state	year	11949	8/94	80s
Tuition, 4-year public college/university, in-state	year	2337	8/94	80s
Energy and Fuels				
Fuel oil and other fuels, expenditures	year	33	91	81r
Gas, natural, expenditures	year	212	91	81r
Gasoline and motor oil purchased	year	1115	91	81r
Gasoline, unleaded midgrade	gallon	1.36	4/93	82r
Gasoline, unleaded premium	gallon	1.43	4/93	82r
Gasoline, unleaded regular	gallon	1.23	4/93	82r
Entertainment				
Concert ticket, Pearl Jam group	perf	20.00	94	50r
Entertainment, total expenditures	year	1853	91	81r
Fees and admissions, expenditures	year	482	91	81r
Pets, toys, playground equipment, expenditures	year	299	91	81r
Reading, expenditures	year	164	91	81r
Televisions, radios, and sound equipment, expenditures	year	528	91	81r
Funerals				
Burial, immediate, container provided by funeral home		1382.70	1/95	54r
Cards, acknowledgment		21.87	1/95	54r
Casket, minimum alternative		128.54	1/95	54r
Cosmetology, hair care, etc.		119.69	1/95	54r
Cremation, direct, container provided by funeral home		1030.62	1/95	54r
Embalming		255.42	1/95	54r
Funeral, funeral home		437.38	1/95	54r
Funeral, other facility		444.46	1/95	54r
Graveside service		338.46	1/95	54r
Hearse, local		147.50	1/95	54r
Limousine, local		130.33	1/95	54r
Memorial service		553.16	1/95	54r
Service charge, professional, nondeclinable		859.15	1/95	54r
Visitation and viewing		93.23	1/95	54r
Groceries				
Apples, Red Delicious	lb.	0.72	12/94	82r
Bacon, sliced	lb.	1.73	12/94	82r
Bananas	lb.	0.52	12/94	82r
Beef purchases	year	241	91	81r
Beverage purchases, alcoholic	year	328	91	81r
Beverage purchases, nonalcoholic	year	234	91	81r
Bologna, all beef or mixed	lb.	2.33	12/94	82r
Bread, white, pan	lb.	0.81	12/94	82r
Carrots, short trimmed and topped	lb.	0.43	12/94	82r
Cereals and bakery products purchases	year	392	91	81r
Cereals and cereals products purchases	year	139	91	81r
Chicken breast, bone-in	lb.	2.04	12/94	82r
Chicken, fresh, whole	lb.	0.95	12/94	82r
Coffee, 100%, ground roast, all sizes	lb.	4.48	12/94	82r

Values are in dollars or fractions of dollars. In the column headed *Ref*, references are shown to sources. Each reference is followed by a letter. These refer to the geographical level for which data were reported: s=State, r=Region, and c=City or metro. The abbreviation *ex* is used to mean *except* or *excluding*; *exp* stands for expenditures. For other abbreviations and further explanations, please see the Introduction.

Bremerton, WA - continued

Item	Per	Value	Date	Ref.
Groceries				
Dairy products (other) purchases	year	182	91	81r
Fish and seafood purchases	year	94	91	81r
Flour, white, all purpose	lb.	0.21	12/94	82r
Food purchases, food eaten at home	year	2749	91	81r
Foods purchased away from home, not prepared by consumer	year	1909	91	81r
Fruits and vegetables purchases	year	459	91	81r
Grapefruit	lb.	0.56	12/94	82r
Ground beef, 100% beef	lb.	1.31	12/94	82r
Ham, boneless, exc. canned	lb.	2.46	12/94	82r
Ice cream, prepackaged, bulk, regular	1/2 gal.	2.57	12/94	82r
Lemons	lb.	1.00	12/94	82r
Lettuce, iceberg	lb.	0.93	12/94	82r
Meats, poultry, fish, and eggs purchases	year	700	91	81r
Milk and cream (fresh) purchases	year	155	91	81r
Orange juice, frozen concentrate 12-oz. can	16 oz.	1.52	12/94	82r
Oranges, Navel	lb.	0.56	12/94	82r
Pork chops, center cut, bone-in	lb.	3.30	12/94	82r
Pork purchases	year	122	91	81r
Potato chips	16-oz.	3.03	12/94	82r
Potatoes, frozen, French fried	lb.	0.77	12/94	82r
Potatoes, white	lb.	0.35	12/94	82r
Rice, white, long grain, uncooked	lb.	0.54	12/94	82r
Round roast, USDA choice, boneless	lb.	2.92	12/94	82r
Shortening, vegetable oil blends	lb.	0.80	12/94	82r
Spaghetti and macaroni	lb.	1.02	12/94	82r
Steak, round, graded & ungraded, exc. USDA prime & choice	lb.	3.13	12/94	82r
Steak, sirloin, USDA choice, boneless	lb.	4.07	12/94	82r
Sugar and other sweets, eaten at home, expenditures	year	105	91	81r
Sugar, white, all sizes	lb.	0.38	12/94	82r
Tobacco products and smoking supplies, total expenditures	year	221	91	81r
Tomatoes, field grown	lb.	1.45	12/94	82r
Tuna, chunk, light	lb.	2.18	12/94	82r
Health Care				
Childbirth, Cesarean delivery, hospital charge	birth	6059.00	12/91	69r
Childbirth, Cesarean delivery, physician charge	birth	2248.00	12/91	69r
Childbirth, normal delivery, hospital charge	birth	3006.00	12/91	69r
Childbirth, normal delivery, physician charge	birth	1634.00	12/91	69r
Drugs, expenditures	year	230	91	81r
Health care, total expenditures	year	1544	91	81r
Health insurance expenditures	year	558	91	81r
Insurance premium, family medical care	month	382.32	1/95	41s
Medical services expenditures	year	676	91	81r
Medical supplies expenditures	year	80	91	81r
Surgery, open-heart	proc	37818.00	1/93	14r
Household Goods				
Floor coverings, expenditures	year	79	91	81r
Furniture, expenditures	year	352	91	81r
Household equipment, misc. expenditures	year	614	91	81r
Household expenditures, miscellaneous	year	294	91	81r
Household furnishings and equipment, expenditures	year	1416	91	81r
Household operations expenditures	year	580	91	81r
Household textiles, expenditures	year	113	91	81r
Housekeeping supplies, expenditures	year	447	91	81r
Laundry and cleaning supplies, expenditures	year	114	91	81r
Postage and stationery, expenditures	year	145	91	81r
Housing				
Add garage/carport		6,422	3/95	74r
Add room(s)		26,583	3/95	74r
Apartment condominium or co-op, median	unit	105300	12/94	62r
Dwellings (owned), expenditures	year	3932	91	81r
Enclose porch/patio/breezeway		5,382	3/95	74r
Finish room in basement/attic		3,911	3/95	74r

Bremerton, WA - continued

Item	Per	Value	Date	Ref.
Housing - continued				
Home, existing, single-family, median	unit	178600	12/94	62r
Maintenance, repairs, insurance, and other housing expenditures	year	591	91	81r
Mortgage interest and charges expenditures	year	2747	91	81r
Princ. & int., mortgage, median-price exist. sing.-family home	mo.	845	12/94	62r
Property taxes expenditures	year	594	91	81r
Redesign, restructure more than half of home's interior		5,467	3/95	74r
Rental units expenditures	year	2077	91	81r
Insurance and Pensions				
Auto insurance, private passenger	year	711.57	12/94	71s
Insurance and pensions, personal, expenditures	year	3042	91	81r
Insurance, life and other personal, expenditures	year	298	91	81r
Pensions and Social Security, expenditures	year	2744	91	81r
Legal Assistance				
Legal work, law firm associate	hour	91		10r
Legal work, law firm partner	hour	151		10r
Personal Services				
Personal services expenditures	year	286	91	81r
Restaurant Food				
Dining expenditures, family	week	32.25	94	73r
Taxes				
Taxes, Federal income, expenditures	year	2946	91	81r
Taxes, personal, expenditures	year	3791	91	81r
Taxes, State and local income, expenditures	year	791	91	81r
Transportation				
Cars and trucks purchased, new	year	1231	91	81r
Cars and trucks purchased, used	year	915	91	81r
Driver's learning permit fee	perm	4.00	1/94	84s
Driver's license fee	orig	21.00	1/94	84s
Driver's license fee, duplicate	lic	5.00	1/94	84s
Driver's license reinstatement fee, min.	susp	20.00-50.00	1/94	85s
Driver's license renewal fee	renew	14.00	1/94	84s
Identification card, nondriver	card	4.00	1/94	83s
Motorcycle license fee	orig	8.00	1/94	84s
Motorcycle license renewal fee	renew	7.50	1/94	84s
Public transportation expenditures	year	375	91	81r
Transportation expenditures, total	year	5527	91	81r
Vehicle finance charges	year	287	91	81r
Vehicle insurance expenditures	year	624	91	81r
Vehicle maintenance and repairs expenditures	year	695	91	81r
Vehicle purchases	year	2174	91	81r
Vehicle rental, leases, licenses, etc. expenditures	year	257	91	81r
Vehicles purchased, other than cars and trucks	year	28	91	81r
Utilities				
Electricity expenditures	year	616	91	81r
Utilities, fuels, and public services, total expenditures	year	1681	91	81r
Water and other public services, expenditures	year	209	91	81r
Weddings				
Bridal attendants' gowns	event	750	10/93	76r
Bridal gown	event	852	10/93	76r
Bridal headpiece and veil	event	167	10/93	76r
Bride's wedding band	event	708	10/93	76r
Clergy	event	224	10/93	76r
Engagement ring	event	2756	10/93	76r
Flowers	event	863	10/93	76r
Formal wear for groom	event	106	10/93	76r
Groom's attendants' formal wear	event	530	10/93	76r
Groom's wedding band	event	402	10/93	76r

Values are in dollars or fractions of dollars. In the column headed *Ref*, references are shown to sources. Each reference is followed by a letter. These refer to the geographical level for which data were reported: s=State, r=Region, and c=City or metro. The abbreviation *ex* is used to mean *except* or *excluding*; *exp* stands for expenditures. For other abbreviations and further explanations, please see the Introduction.

Bremerton, WA - continued

Item	Per	Value	Date	Ref.
Weddings				
Music	event	600	10/93	76r
Photography	event	1088	10/93	76r
Shoes for bride	event	50	10/93	76r
Videography	event	483	10/93	76r
Wedding invitations and announcements	event	342	10/93	76r
Wedding reception	event	7000	10/93	76r

Bridgeport, CT

Item	Per	Value	Date	Ref.
Appliances				
Appliances (major), expenditures	year	145	91	81r
Average annual exp.				
Food, health care, personal goods, services	year	29496	91	81r
Charity				
Cash contributions, expenditures	year	708	91	81r
Clothing				
Apparel, men and boys, total expenditures	year	416	91	81r
Apparel, women and girls, total expenditures	year	744	91	81r
Footwear, expenditures	year	305	91	81r
Communications				
Long-distance telephone rate, day, addl. min., 1-10 mi.	min.	0.09	12/93	9s
Long-distance telephone rate, day, initial min., 1-10 mi.	min.	0.09	12/93	9s
Phone line, single, business, field visit	inst	127.44	12/93	9s
Phone line, single, business, no field visit	inst	95.58	12/93	9s
Phone line, single, residence, field visit	inst	64.85	12/93	9s
Phone line, single, residence, no field visit	inst	38.27	12/93	9s
Telephone service, expenditures	year	589	91	81r
Telephone, residential, flat rate	mo.	12.27	12/93	8c
Credit Cards				
Fee, conventional credit card, secured	year	45.00	1/95	96c
Education				
Board, 4-year private college/university	year	2664	8/94	80s
Board, 4-year public college/university	year	2137	8/94	80s
Education, total expenditures	year	593	91	81r
Room, 4-year private college/university	year	3287	8/94	80s
Room, 4-year public college/university	year	2310	8/94	80s
Total cost, 4-year private college/university	year	20726	8/94	80s
Total cost, 4-year public college/university	year	7926	8/94	80s
Tuition, 2-year public college/university, in-state	year	1398	8/94	80s
Tuition, 4-year private college/university, in-state	year	14775	8/94	80s
Tuition, 4-year public college/university, in-state	year	3479	8/94	80s
Energy and Fuels				
Fuel oil and other fuels, expenditures	year	257	91	81r
Gas, cooking, 10 therms	month	17.85	2/94	65c
Gas, cooking, 30 therms	month	37.06	2/94	65c
Gas, cooking, 50 therms	month	56.27	2/94	65c
Gas, heating, winter, 100 therms	month	104.29	2/94	65c
Gas, heating, winter, average use	month	235.77	2/94	65c
Gas, natural, expenditures	year	285	91	81r
Gasoline and motor oil purchased	year	867	91	81r
Gasoline, unleaded midgrade	gallon	1.32	4/93	82r
Gasoline, unleaded premium	gallon	1.40	4/93	82r
Gasoline, unleaded regular	gallon	1.19	4/93	82r
Entertainment				
Entertainment, total expenditures	year	1331	91	81r
Fees and admissions, expenditures	year	398	91	81r
Pets, toys, playground equipment, expenditures	year	270	91	81r
Reading, expenditures	year	171	91	81r
Televisions, radios, and sound equipment, expenditures	year	429	91	81r

Bridgeport, CT - continued

Item	Per	Value	Date	Ref.
Funerals				
Burial, immediate, container provided by funeral home		1507.89	1/95	54r
Cards, acknowledgment		18.10	1/95	54r
Casket, minimum alternative		133.03	1/95	54r
Cosmetology, hair care, etc.		114.12	1/95	54r
Cremation, direct, container provided by funeral home		1309.19	1/95	54r
Embalming		320.97	1/95	54r
Funeral, funeral home		327.61	1/95	54r
Funeral, other facility		314.81	1/95	54r
Graveside service		286.11	1/95	54r
Hearse, local		158.95	1/95	54r
Limousine, local		149.45	1/95	54r
Memorial service		315.94	1/95	54r
Service charge, professional, nondeclinable		1148.43	1/95	54r
Visitation and viewing		249.66	1/95	54r
Groceries				
Apples, Red Delicious	lb.	0.78	12/94	82r
Bacon, sliced	lb.	2.24	12/94	82r
Bananas	lb.	0.49	12/94	82r
Beef purchases	year	226	91	81r
Beverage purchases, alcoholic	year	332	91	81r
Beverage purchases, nonalcoholic	year	213	91	81r
Bread, white, pan	lb.	0.80	12/94	82r
Butter, salted, Grade AA, stick	lb.	1.67	12/94	82r
Carrots, short trimmed and topped	lb.	0.51	12/94	82r
Cereals and bakery products purchases	year	407	91	81r
Cereals and cereals products purchases	year	132	91	81r
Chicken breast, bone-in	lb.	2.22	12/94	82r
Chicken, fresh, whole	lb.	1.05	12/94	82r
Chuck roast, USDA choice, boneless	lb.	2.74	12/94	82r
Coffee, 100%, ground roast, all sizes	lb.	4.61	12/94	82r
Dairy products (other) purchases	year	161	91	81r
Eggs, Grade A large	dozen	1.12	12/94	82r
Fish and seafood purchases	year	112	91	81r
Food purchases, food eaten at home	year	2599	91	81r
Foods purchased away from home, not prepared by consumer	year	2024	91	81r
Fruits and vegetables purchases	year	444	91	81r
Grapefruit	lb.	0.44	12/94	82r
Grapes, Thompson seedless	lb.	2.24	12/94	82r
Ground chuck, 100% beef	lb.	1.67	12/94	82r
Ice cream, prepackaged, bulk, regular	1/2 gal.	2.93	12/94	82r
Lemons	lb.	1.06	12/94	82r
Lettuce, iceberg	lb.	0.92	12/94	82r
Meats, poultry, fish, and eggs purchases	year	751	91	81r
Milk and cream (fresh) purchases	year	152	91	81r
Orange juice, frozen concentrate 12-oz. can	16 oz.	1.92	12/94	82r
Oranges, Navel	lb.	0.56	12/94	82r
Pork chops, center cut, bone-in	lb.	3.09	12/94	82r
Pork purchases	year	130	91	81r
Potatoes, white	lb.	0.37	12/94	82r
Rib roast, USDA choice, bone-in	lb.	4.98	12/94	82r
Round roast, USDA choice, boneless	lb.	2.93	12/94	82r
Shortening, vegetable oil blends	lb.	1.03	12/94	82r
Spaghetti and macaroni	lb.	0.84	12/94	82r
Steak, round, USDA choice, boneless	lb.	3.48	12/94	82r
Steak, sirloin, USDA choice, bone-in	lb.	3.38	12/94	82r
Steak, sirloin, USDA choice, boneless	lb.	4.81	12/94	82r
Sugar and other sweets, eaten at home, expenditures	year	89	91	81r
Sugar, white, all sizes	lb.	0.46	12/94	82r
Tobacco products and smoking supplies, total expenditures	year	279	91	81r
Tomatoes, field grown	lb.	1.56	12/94	82r
Tuna, chunk, light	lb.	2.09	12/94	82r
Health Care				
Childbirth, Cesarean delivery, hospital charge	birth	6334.00	12/91	69r

Values are in dollars or fractions of dollars. In the column headed *Ref*, references are shown to sources. Each reference is followed by a letter. These refer to the geographical level for which data were reported: s=State, r=Region, and c=City or metro. The abbreviation *ex* is used to mean *except* or *excluding*; *exp* stands for expenditures. For other abbreviations and further explanations, please see the Introduction.

Bridgeport, CT - continued

Item	Per	Value	Date	Ref.
Health Care				
Childbirth, Cesarean delivery, physician charge	birth	2234.00	12/91	69r
Childbirth, normal delivery, hospital charge	birth	3225.00	12/91	69r
Childbirth, normal delivery, physician charge	birth	1623.00	12/91	69r
Drugs, expenditures	year	205	91	81r
Health care, total expenditures	year	1396	91	81r
Health insurance expenditures	year	553	91	81r
Insurance premium, family medical care	month	500.40	1/95	41s
Medical services expenditures	year	559	91	81r
Medical supplies expenditures	year	80	91	81r
Household Goods				
Floor coverings, expenditures	year	158	91	81r
Furniture, expenditures	year	341	91	81r
Household equipment, misc. expenditures	year	363	91	81r
Household expenditures, miscellaneous	year	194	91	81r
Household furnishings and equipment, expenditures	year	1158	91	81r
Household operations expenditures	year	378	91	81r
Household textiles, expenditures	year	88	91	81r
Housekeeping supplies, expenditures	year	426	91	81r
Laundry and cleaning supplies, expenditures	year	122	91	81r
Postage and stationery, expenditures	year	134	91	81r
Housing				
Add garage/carport		11,614	3/95	74r
Add room(s)		16,816	3/95	74r
Apartment condominium or co-op, median	unit	96700	12/94	62r
Dwellings (owned), expenditures	year	3305	91	81r
Enclose porch/patio/breezeway		2,980	3/95	74r
Finish room in basement/attic		4,330	3/95	74r
Home, existing, single-family, median	unit	161600	12/94	62r
Maintenance, repairs, insurance, and other housing expenditures	year	569	91	81r
Mortgage interest and charges expenditures	year	1852	91	81r
Princ. & int., mortgage, median-price exist. sing.-family home	mo.	765	12/94	62r
Property taxes expenditures	year	884	91	81r
Redesign, restructure more than half of home's interior		2,750	3/95	74r
Rental units expenditures	year	1832	91	81r
Insurance and Pensions				
Auto insurance, private passenger	year	1002.84	12/94	71s
Insurance and pensions, personal, expenditures	year	2690	91	81r
Insurance, life and other personal, expenditures	year	341	91	81r
Pensions and Social Security, expenditures	year	2349	91	81r
Legal Assistance				
Estate planning, law-firm partner	hr.	375.00	10/93	12r
Legal work, law firm associate	hour	78		10r
Legal work, law firm partner	hour	183		10r
Personal Services				
Personal services expenditures	year	184	91	81r
Restaurant Food				
Dining expenditures, family	week	34.26	94	73r
Taxes				
Tax rate, residential property, month	$100	2.49	1/92	79c
Taxes, Federal income, expenditures	year	2409	91	81r
Taxes, personal, expenditures	year	3094	91	81r
Taxes, State and local income, expenditures	year	620	91	81r
Transportation				
Bus fare, one-way	trip	0.85	12/95	1c
Cars and trucks purchased, new	year	1170	91	81r
Cars and trucks purchased, used	year	739	91	81r
Driver's learning permit fee	perm	3.50	1/94	84s
Driver's license fee	orig	38.00	1/94	84s
Driver's license fee, duplicate	lic	5.00	1/94	84s
Driver's license reinstatement fee, min.	susp	30.00	1/94	85s

Bridgeport, CT - continued

Item	Per	Value	Date	Ref.
Transportation - continued				
Driver's license renewal fee	renew	31.00	1/94	84s
Identification card, nondriver	card	4.00	1/94	83s
Motorcycle learning permit fee	perm	3.50	1/94	84s
Motorcycle license fee	orig	38.00	1/94	84s
Motorcycle license fee, duplicate	lic	5.00	1/94	84s
Motorcycle license renewal fee	renew	31.00	1/94	84s
Public transportation expenditures	year	430	91	81r
Transportation expenditures, total	year	4810	91	81r
Vehicle finance charges	year	238	91	81r
Vehicle insurance expenditures	year	630	91	81r
Vehicle maintenance and repairs expenditures	year	532	91	81r
Vehicle purchases	year	1920	91	81r
Vehicle rental, leases, licenses, etc. expenditures	year	193	91	81r
Vehicles purchased, other than cars and trucks	year	11	91	81r
Utilities				
Electricity expenditures	year	695	91	81r
Electricity, summer, 250 KWh	month	37.09	8/93	64c
Electricity, summer, 500 KWh	month	65.68	8/93	64c
Electricity, summer, 750 KWh	month	101.36	8/93	64c
Electricity, summer, 1000 KWh	month	137.04	8/93	64c
Utilities, fuels, and public services, total expenditures	year	1981	91	81r
Water and other public services, expenditures	year	154	91	81r
Weddings				
Bridal attendants' gowns	event	750	10/93	76r
Bridal gown	event	852	10/93	76r
Bridal headpiece and veil	event	167	10/93	76r
Bride's wedding band	event	708	10/93	76r
Clergy	event	224	10/93	76r
Engagement ring	event	2756	10/93	76r
Flowers	event	863	10/93	76r
Formal wear for groom	event	106	10/93	76r
Groom's attendants' formal wear	event	530	10/93	76r
Groom's wedding band	event	402	10/93	76r
Music	event	600	10/93	76r
Photography	event	1088	10/93	76r
Shoes for bride	event	50	10/93	76r
Videography	event	483	10/93	76r
Wedding invitations and announcements	event	342	10/93	76r
Wedding reception	event	7000	10/93	76r

Bristol, CT

Item	Per	Value	Date	Ref.
Appliances				
Appliances (major), expenditures	year	145	91	81r
Average annual exp.				
Food, health care, personal goods, services	year	29496	91	81r
Charity				
Cash contributions, expenditures	year	708	91	81r
Clothing				
Apparel, men and boys, total expenditures	year	416	91	81r
Apparel, women and girls, total expenditures	year	744	91	81r
Footwear, expenditures	year	305	91	81r
Communications				
Long-distance telephone rate, day, addl. min., 1-10 mi.	min.	0.09	12/93	9s
Long-distance telephone rate, day, initial min., 1-10 mi.	min.	0.09	12/93	9s
Phone line, single, business, field visit	inst	127.44	12/93	9s
Phone line, single, business, no field visit	inst	95.58	12/93	9s
Phone line, single, residence, field visit	inst	64.85	12/93	9s
Phone line, single, residence, no field visit	inst	38.27	12/93	9s
Telephone service, expenditures	year	589	91	81r

Values are in dollars or fractions of dollars. In the column headed *Ref*, references are shown to sources. Each reference is followed by a letter. These refer to the geographical level for which data were reported: s=State, r=Region, and c=City or metro. The abbreviation *ex* is used to mean *except* or *excluding*; *exp* stands for *expenditures*. For other abbreviations and further explanations, please see the Introduction.

Bristol, CT - continued

Item	Per	Value	Date	Ref.
Education				
Board, 4-year private college/university	year	2664	8/94	80s
Board, 4-year public college/university	year	2137	8/94	80s
Education, total expenditures	year	593	91	81r
Room, 4-year private college/university	year	3287	8/94	80s
Room, 4-year public college/university	year	2310	8/94	80s
Total cost, 4-year private college/university	year	20726	8/94	80s
Total cost, 4-year public college/university	year	7926	8/94	80s
Tuition, 2-year public college/university, in-state	year	1398	8/94	80s
Tuition, 4-year private college/university, in-state	year	14775	8/94	80s
Tuition, 4-year public college/university, in-state	year	3479	8/94	80s
Energy and Fuels				
Fuel oil and other fuels, expenditures	year	257	91	81r
Gas, natural, expenditures	year	285	91	81r
Gasoline and motor oil purchased	year	867	91	81r
Gasoline, unleaded midgrade	gallon	1.32	4/93	82r
Gasoline, unleaded premium	gallon	1.40	4/93	82r
Gasoline, unleaded regular	gallon	1.19	4/93	82r
Entertainment				
Entertainment, total expenditures	year	1331	91	81r
Fees and admissions, expenditures	year	398	91	81r
Pets, toys, playground equipment, expenditures	year	270	91	81r
Reading, expenditures	year	171	91	81r
Televisions, radios, and sound equipment, expenditures	year	429	91	81r
Funerals				
Burial, immediate, container provided by funeral home		1507.89	1/95	54r
Cards, acknowledgment		18.10	1/95	54r
Casket, minimum alternative		133.03	1/95	54r
Cosmetology, hair care, etc.		114.12	1/95	54r
Cremation, direct, container provided by funeral home		1309.19	1/95	54r
Embalming		320.97	1/95	54r
Funeral, funeral home		327.61	1/95	54r
Funeral, other facility		314.81	1/95	54r
Graveside service		286.11	1/95	54r
Hearse, local		158.95	1/95	54r
Limousine, local		149.45	1/95	54r
Memorial service		315.94	1/95	54r
Service charge, professional, nondeclinable		1148.43	1/95	54r
Visitation and viewing		249.66	1/95	54r
Groceries				
Apples, Red Delicious	lb.	0.78	12/94	82r
Bacon, sliced	lb.	2.24	12/94	82r
Bananas	lb.	0.49	12/94	82r
Beef purchases	year	226	91	81r
Beverage purchases, alcoholic	year	332	91	81r
Beverage purchases, nonalcoholic	year	213	91	81r
Bread, white, pan	lb.	0.80	12/94	82r
Butter, salted, Grade AA, stick	lb.	1.67	12/94	82r
Carrots, short trimmed and topped	lb.	0.51	12/94	82r
Cereals and bakery products purchases	year	407	91	81r
Cereals and cereals products purchases	year	132	91	81r
Chicken breast, bone-in	lb.	2.22	12/94	82r
Chicken, fresh, whole	lb.	1.05	12/94	82r
Chuck roast, USDA choice, boneless	lb.	2.74	12/94	82r
Coffee, 100%, ground roast, all sizes	lb.	4.61	12/94	82r
Dairy products (other) purchases	year	161	91	81r
Eggs, Grade A large	dozen	1.12	12/94	82r
Fish and seafood purchases	year	112	91	81r
Food purchases, food eaten at home	year	2599	91	81r
Foods purchased away from home, not prepared by consumer	year	2024	91	81r
Fruits and vegetables purchases	year	444	91	81r
Grapefruit	lb.	0.44	12/94	82r
Grapes, Thompson seedless	lb.	2.24	12/94	82r

Bristol, CT - continued

Item	Per	Value	Date	Ref.
Groceries - continued				
Ground chuck, 100% beef	lb.	1.67	12/94	82r
Ice cream, prepackaged, bulk, regular	1/2 gal.	2.93	12/94	82r
Lemons	lb.	1.06	12/94	82r
Lettuce, iceberg	lb.	0.92	12/94	82r
Meats, poultry, fish, and eggs purchases	year	751	91	81r
Milk and cream (fresh) purchases	year	152	91	81r
Orange juice, frozen concentrate 12-oz. can	16 oz.	1.92	12/94	82r
Oranges, Navel	lb.	0.56	12/94	82r
Pork chops, center cut, bone-in	lb.	3.09	12/94	82r
Pork purchases	year	130	91	81r
Potatoes, white	lb.	0.37	12/94	82r
Rib roast, USDA choice, bone-in	lb.	4.98	12/94	82r
Round roast, USDA choice, boneless	lb.	2.93	12/94	82r
Shortening, vegetable oil blends	lb.	1.03	12/94	82r
Spaghetti and macaroni	lb.	0.84	12/94	82r
Steak, round, USDA choice, boneless	lb.	3.48	12/94	82r
Steak, sirloin, USDA choice, bone-in	lb.	3.38	12/94	82r
Steak, sirloin, USDA choice, boneless	lb.	4.81	12/94	82r
Sugar and other sweets, eaten at home, expenditures	year	89	91	81r
Sugar, white, all sizes	lb.	0.46	12/94	82r
Tobacco products and smoking supplies, total expenditures	year	279	91	81r
Tomatoes, field grown	lb.	1.56	12/94	82r
Tuna, chunk, light	lb.	2.09	12/94	82r
Health Care				
Childbirth, Cesarean delivery, hospital charge	birth	6334.00	12/91	69r
Childbirth, Cesarean delivery, physician charge	birth	2234.00	12/91	69r
Childbirth, normal delivery, hospital charge	birth	3225.00	12/91	69r
Childbirth, normal delivery, physician charge	birth	1623.00	12/91	69r
Drugs, expenditures	year	205	91	81r
Health care, total expenditures	year	1396	91	81r
Health insurance expenditures	year	553	91	81r
Insurance premium, family medical care	month	500.40	1/95	41s
Medical services expenditures	year	559	91	81r
Medical supplies expenditures	year	80	91	81r
Household Goods				
Floor coverings, expenditures	year	158	91	81r
Furniture, expenditures	year	341	91	81r
Household equipment, misc. expenditures	year	363	91	81r
Household expenditures, miscellaneous	year	194	91	81r
Household furnishings and equipment, expenditures	year	1158	91	81r
Household operations expenditures	year	378	91	81r
Household textiles, expenditures	year	88	91	81r
Housekeeping supplies, expenditures	year	426	91	81r
Laundry and cleaning supplies, expenditures	year	122	91	81r
Postage and stationery, expenditures	year	134	91	81r
Housing				
Add garage/carport		11,614	3/95	74r
Add room(s)		16,816	3/95	74r
Apartment condominium or co-op, median	unit	96700	12/94	62r
Dwellings (owned), expenditures	year	3305	91	81r
Enclose porch/patio/breezeway		2,980	3/95	74r
Finish room in basement/attic		4,330	3/95	74r
Home, existing, single-family, median	unit	161600	12/94	62r
Maintenance, repairs, insurance, and other housing expenditures	year	569	91	81r
Mortgage interest and charges expenditures	year	1852	91	81r
Princ. & int., mortgage, median-price exist. sing.-family home	mo.	765	12/94	62r
Property taxes expenditures	year	884	91	81r
Redesign, restructure more than half of home's interior		2,750	3/95	74r
Rental units expenditures	year	1832	91	81r

Values are in dollars or fractions of dollars. In the column headed *Ref*, references are shown to sources. Each reference is followed by a letter. These refer to the geographical level for which data were reported: s = State, r = Region, and c = City or metro. The abbreviation *ex* is used to mean *except* or *excluding*; *exp* stands for *expenditures*. For other abbreviations and further explanations, please see the Introduction.

Bristol, CT - continued

Item	Per	Value	Date	Ref.
Insurance and Pensions				
Auto insurance, private passenger	year	1002.84	12/94	71s
Insurance and pensions, personal, expenditures	year	2690	91	81r
Insurance, life and other personal, expenditures	year	341	91	81r
Pensions and Social Security, expenditures	year	2349	91	81r
Legal Assistance				
Estate planning, law-firm partner	hr.	375.00	10/93	12r
Legal work, law firm associate	hour	78		10r
Legal work, law firm partner	hour	183		10r
Personal Services				
Personal services expenditures	year	184	91	81r
Restaurant Food				
Dining expenditures, family	week	34.26	94	73r
Taxes				
Taxes, Federal income, expenditures	year	2409	91	81r
Taxes, personal, expenditures	year	3094	91	81r
Taxes, State and local income, expenditures	year	620	91	81r
Transportation				
Cars and trucks purchased, new	year	1170	91	81r
Cars and trucks purchased, used	year	739	91	81r
Driver's learning permit fee	perm	3.50	1/94	84s
Driver's license fee	orig	38.00	1/94	84s
Driver's license fee, duplicate	lic	5.00	1/94	84s
Driver's license reinstatement fee, min.	susp	30.00	1/94	85s
Driver's license renewal fee	renew	31.00	1/94	84s
Identification card, nondriver	card	4.00	1/94	83s
Motorcycle learning permit fee	perm	3.50	1/94	84s
Motorcycle license fee	orig	38.00	1/94	84s
Motorcycle license fee, duplicate	lic	5.00	1/94	84s
Motorcycle license renewal fee	renew	31.00	1/94	84s
Public transportation expenditures	year	430	91	81r
Transportation expenditures, total	year	4810	91	81r
Vehicle finance charges	year	238	91	81r
Vehicle insurance expenditures	year	630	91	81r
Vehicle maintenance and repairs expenditures	year	532	91	81r
Vehicle purchases	year	1920	91	81r
Vehicle rental, leases, licenses, etc. expenditures	year	193	91	81r
Vehicles purchased, other than cars and trucks	year	11	91	81r
Utilities				
Electricity expenditures	year	695	91	81r
Utilities, fuels, and public services, total expenditures	year	1981	91	81r
Water and other public services, expenditures	year	154	91	81r
Weddings				
Bridal attendants' gowns	event	750	10/93	76r
Bridal gown	event	852	10/93	76r
Bridal headpiece and veil	event	167	10/93	76r
Bride's wedding band	event	708	10/93	76r
Clergy	event	224	10/93	76r
Engagement ring	event	2756	10/93	76r
Flowers	event	863	10/93	76r
Formal wear for groom	event	106	10/93	76r
Groom's attendants' formal wear	event	530	10/93	76r
Groom's wedding band	event	402	10/93	76r
Music	event	600	10/93	76r
Photography	event	1088	10/93	76r
Shoes for bride	event	50	10/93	76r
Videography	event	483	10/93	76r
Wedding invitations and announcements	event	342	10/93	76r
Wedding reception	event	7000	10/93	76r

Bristol, VA

Item	Per	Value	Date	Ref.
Composite, ACCRA index		87.40	12/94	2c
Alcoholic Beverages				
Beer, Miller Lite, Bud, 12-oz., ex deposit	6	3.53	12/94	2c
J & B Scotch	750-ml.	18.45	12/94	2c
Wine, Gallo Chablis blanc	1.5-lit	4.96	12/94	2c
Clothing				
Jeans, man's denim		35.30	12/94	2c
Shirt, man's dress shirt		39.37	12/94	2c
Undervest, boy's size 10-14, cotton	3	5.37	12/94	2c
Communications				
Newspaper subscription, dly. and Sun. delivery	month	9.50	12/94	2c
Telephone bill, family of four	month	20.54	12/94	2c
Energy and Fuels				
Energy, combined forms, 1800 sq. ft.	mo.	105.80	12/94	2c
Gas, cooking, winter, 10 therms	month	11.34	2/94	65c
Gas, cooking, winter, 30 therms	month	21.72	2/94	65c
Gas, cooking, winter, 50 therms	month	32.71	2/94	65c
Gas, heating, winter, 100 therms	month	59.41	2/94	65c
Gas, heating, winter, average use	month	91.99	2/94	65c
Gas, reg unlead, taxes inc., cash, self-service	gal	1.03	12/94	2c
Entertainment				
Bowling, evening rate	game	1.75	12/94	2c
Monopoly game, Parker Brothers', No. 9	game	8.97	12/94	2c
Movie	adm	5.50	12/94	2c
Tennis balls, yellow, Wilson or Penn, 3	can	1.93	12/94	2c
Groceries				
Groceries, ACCRA Index		94.90	12/94	2c
Baby food, strained vegetables, lowest price	4-4.5 oz.	0.31	12/94	2c
Bananas	lb.	0.47	12/94	2c
Beef or hamburger, ground	lb.	1.37	12/94	2c
Bread, white	24-oz.	0.66	12/94	2c
Cheese, Kraft grated Parmesan	8-oz.	3.04	12/94	2c
Chicken, whole fryer	lb.	0.83	12/94	2c
Cigarettes, Winston, Kings	carton	13.42	12/94	2c
Coffee, vacuum-packed	13 oz.	3.05	12/94	2c
Corn Flakes, Kellogg's or Post Toasties	18 oz.	2.40	12/94	2c
Corn, frozen, whole kernel, lowest price	10 oz.	0.56	12/94	2c
Eggs, Grade A large	dozen	0.77	12/94	2c
Lettuce, iceberg	head	0.97	12/94	2c
Margarine, Blue Bonnet or Parkay cubes	lb.	0.57	12/94	2c
Milk, whole	1/2 gal.	1.39	12/94	2c
Orange juice, Minute Maid frozen	12-oz.	1.13	12/94	2c
Peaches, halves or slices, Hunt's, Del Monte, or Libby's	29-oz.	1.15	12/94	2c
Peas, sweet, Del Monte or Green Giant	15-17 oz.	0.44	12/94	2c
Potatoes, white or red	10-lb. sack	2.49	12/94	2c
Sausage, Jimmy Dean, 100% pork	lb.	2.39	12/94	2c
Shortening, vegetable, Crisco	3-lb.	2.49	12/94	2c
Soft drink, Coca Cola, ex deposit	2 lit	0.97	12/94	2c
Steak, t-bone	lb.	5.33	12/94	2c
Sugar, cane or beet	4 lbs.	1.59	12/94	2c
Tomatoes, Hunt's or Del Monte	14.5 oz.	0.66	12/94	2c
Tuna, chunk, light, oil-packed	6.125-6.5 oz.	0.67	12/94	2c
Goods and Services				
Miscellaneous goods and services, ACCRA Index		95.20	12/94	2c
Health Care				
Health care, ACCRA Index		79.90	12/94	2c
Antibiotic ointment, Polysporin	1.5 oz.	4.06	12/94	2c

Values are in dollars or fractions of dollars. In the column headed *Ref*, references are shown to sources. Each reference is followed by a letter. These refer to the geographical level for which data were reported: s = State, r = Region, and c = City or metro. The abbreviation *ex* is used to mean *except* or *excluding*; *exp* stands for expenditures. For other abbreviations and further explanations, please see the Introduction.

Bristol, VA - continued

Item	Per	Value	Date	Ref.
Health Care				
Dentist's fee, adult teeth cleaning and periodic oral exam	visit	40.80	12/94	2c
Doctor's fee, routine exam, established patient	visit	34.40	12/94	2c
Hospital care, semiprivate room	day	244.00	12/94	2c
Household Goods				
Appl. repair, service call, wash mach	min. lab. chg.	36.00	12/94	2c
Laundry detergent, Tide Ultra, Bold, or Cheer	42 oz.	3.29	12/94	2c
Tissues, facial, Kleenex brand	175	1.07	12/94	2c
Housing				
Housing, ACCRA Index		73.00	12/94	2c
House payment, principal and interest, 25% down payment	mo.	548	12/94	2c
House, 1800 sq ft, 8000 sq ft lot, new, urban, utilities	total	90150	12/94	2c
Mtge. rate, incl. points and orig. fee, 30-year conv. fixed or ARM	mo.	9.07	12/94	2c
Rent, apartment, 2 br., 1 1/2-2 baths, unfurnished, 950 sq ft, water	mo.	418	12/94	2c
Personal Goods				
Shampoo, Alberto VO5	15-oz.	1.21	12/94	2c
Toothpaste, Crest or Colgate	6-7 oz.	2.03	12/94	2c
Personal Services				
Dry cleaning, man's 2-pc. suit		5.50	12/94	2c
Haircut, man's barbershop, no styling		6.50	12/94	2c
Haircut, woman's shampoo, trim, blow-dry		12.75	12/94	2c
Restaurant Food				
Chicken, fried, thigh and drumstick		1.60	12/94	2c
Hamburger with cheese	1/4 lb.	0.99	12/94	2c
Pizza, Pizza Hut or Pizza Inn	12-13 in.	7.75	12/94	2c
Transportation				
Transportation, ACCRA Index		87.80	12/94	2c
Bus fare, up to 10 miles	one-way	0.70	12/94	2c
Tire balance, computer or spin bal., front	wheel	5.88	12/94	2c
Utilities				
Utilities, ACCRA Index		95.80	12/94	2c
Electricity, 1800 sq. ft., new home	mo.	105.80	12/94	2c

Brockton, MA

Item	Per	Value	Date	Ref.
Appliances				
Appliances (major), expenditures	year	145	91	81r
Average annual exp.				
Food, health care, personal goods, services	year	29496	91	81r
Charity				
Cash contributions, expenditures	year	708	91	81r
Clothing				
Apparel, men and boys, total expenditures	year	416	91	81r
Apparel, women and girls, total expenditures	year	744	91	81r
Footwear, expenditures	year	305	91	81r
Communications				
Long-distance telephone rate, day, addl. min., 1-10 mi.	min.	0.09	12/93	9s
Long-distance telephone rate, day, initial min., 1-10 mi.	min.	0.19	12/93	9s
Phone line, single, business, field visit	inst	27.50	12/93	9s
Phone line, single, business, no field visit	inst	93.02	12/93	9s
Phone line, single, residence, field visit	inst	27.50	12/93	9s
Phone line, single, residence, no field visit	inst	37.07	12/93	9s
Telephone service, expenditures	year	589	91	81r

Brockton, MA - continued

Item	Per	Value	Date	Ref.
Education				
Board, 4-year private college/university	year	3179	8/94	80s
Board, 4-year public college/university	year	2035	8/94	80s
Education, total expenditures	year	593	91	81r
Room, 4-year private college/university	year	3369	8/94	80s
Room, 4-year public college/university	year	2290	8/94	80s
Total cost, 4-year private college/university	year	21346	8/94	80s
Total cost, 4-year public college/university	year	8467	8/94	80s
Tuition, 2-year public college/university, in-state	year	2361	8/94	80s
Tuition, 4-year private college/university, in-state	year	14797	8/94	80s
Tuition, 4-year public college/university, in-state	year	4142	8/94	80s
Energy and Fuels				
Fuel oil and other fuels, expenditures	year	257	91	81r
Gas, natural, expenditures	year	285	91	81r
Gasoline and motor oil purchased	year	867	91	81r
Gasoline, unleaded midgrade	gallon	1.32	4/93	82r
Gasoline, unleaded premium	gallon	1.40	4/93	82r
Gasoline, unleaded regular	gallon	1.19	4/93	82r
Entertainment				
Entertainment, total expenditures	year	1331	91	81r
Fees and admissions, expenditures	year	398	91	81r
Pets, toys, playground equipment, expenditures	year	270	91	81r
Reading, expenditures	year	171	91	81r
Televisions, radios, and sound equipment, expenditures	year	429	91	81r
Funerals				
Burial, immediate, container provided by funeral home		1507.89	1/95	54r
Cards, acknowledgment		18.10	1/95	54r
Casket, minimum alternative		133.03	1/95	54r
Cosmetology, hair care, etc.		114.12	1/95	54r
Cremation, direct, container provided by funeral home		1309.19	1/95	54r
Embalming		320.97	1/95	54r
Funeral, funeral home		327.61	1/95	54r
Funeral, other facility		314.81	1/95	54r
Graveside service		286.11	1/95	54r
Hearse, local		158.95	1/95	54r
Limousine, local		149.45	1/95	54r
Memorial service		315.94	1/95	54r
Service charge, professional, nondeclinable		1148.43	1/95	54r
Visitation and viewing		249.66	1/95	54r
Groceries				
Apples, Red Delicious	lb.	0.78	12/94	82r
Bacon, sliced	lb.	2.24	12/94	82r
Bananas	lb.	0.49	12/94	82r
Beef purchases	year	226	91	81r
Beverage purchases, alcoholic	year	332	91	81r
Beverage purchases, nonalcoholic	year	213	91	81r
Bread, white, pan	lb.	0.80	12/94	82r
Butter, salted, Grade AA, stick	lb.	1.67	12/94	82r
Carrots, short trimmed and topped	lb.	0.51	12/94	82r
Cereals and bakery products purchases	year	407	91	81r
Cereals and cereals products purchases	year	132	91	81r
Chicken breast, bone-in	lb.	2.22	12/94	82r
Chicken, fresh, whole	lb.	1.05	12/94	82r
Chuck roast, USDA choice, boneless	lb.	2.74	12/94	82r
Coffee, 100%, ground roast, all sizes	lb.	4.61	12/94	82r
Dairy products (other) purchases	year	161	91	81r
Eggs, Grade A large	dozen	1.12	12/94	82r
Fish and seafood purchases	year	112	91	81r
Food purchases, food eaten at home	year	2599	91	81r
Foods purchased away from home, not prepared by consumer	year	2024	91	81r
Fruits and vegetables purchases	year	444	91	81r
Grapefruit	lb.	0.44	12/94	82r
Grapes, Thompson seedless	lb.	2.24	12/94	82r

Values are in dollars or fractions of dollars. In the column headed *Ref*, references are shown to sources. Each reference is followed by a letter. These refer to the geographical level for which data were reported: s=State, r=Region, and c=City or metro. The abbreviation *ex* is used to mean *except* or *excluding*; *exp* stands for *expenditures*. For other abbreviations and further explanations, please see the Introduction.

Brockton, MA - continued

Item	Per	Value	Date	Ref.
Groceries				
Ground chuck, 100% beef	lb.	1.67	12/94	82r
Ice cream, prepackaged, bulk, regular	1/2 gal.	2.93	12/94	82r
Lemons	lb.	1.06	12/94	82r
Lettuce, iceberg	lb.	0.92	12/94	82r
Meats, poultry, fish, and eggs purchases	year	751	91	81r
Milk and cream (fresh) purchases	year	152	91	81r
Orange juice, frozen concentrate 12-oz. can	16 oz.	1.92	12/94	82r
Oranges, Navel	lb.	0.56	12/94	82r
Pork chops, center cut, bone-in	lb.	3.09	12/94	82r
Pork purchases	year	130	91	81r
Potatoes, white	lb.	0.37	12/94	82r
Rib roast, USDA choice, bone-in	lb.	4.98	12/94	82r
Round roast, USDA choice, boneless	lb.	2.93	12/94	82r
Shortening, vegetable oil blends	lb.	1.03	12/94	82r
Spaghetti and macaroni	lb.	0.84	12/94	82r
Steak, round, USDA choice, boneless	lb.	3.48	12/94	82r
Steak, sirloin, USDA choice, bone-in	lb.	3.38	12/94	82r
Steak, sirloin, USDA choice, boneless	lb.	4.81	12/94	82r
Sugar and other sweets, eaten at home, expenditures	year	89	91	81r
Sugar, white, all sizes	lb.	0.46	12/94	82r
Tobacco products and smoking supplies, total expenditures	year	279	91	81r
Tomatoes, field grown	lb.	1.56	12/94	82r
Tuna, chunk, light	lb.	2.09	12/94	82r
Health Care				
Childbirth, Cesarean delivery, hospital charge	birth	6334.00	12/91	69r
Childbirth, Cesarean delivery, physician charge	birth	2234.00	12/91	69r
Childbirth, normal delivery, hospital charge	birth	3225.00	12/91	69r
Childbirth, normal delivery, physician charge	birth	1623.00	12/91	69r
Drugs, expenditures	year	205	91	81r
Health care, total expenditures	year	1396	91	81r
Health insurance expenditures	year	553	91	81r
Insurance premium, family medical care	month	457.38	1/95	41s
Medical services expenditures	year	559	91	81r
Medical supplies expenditures	year	80	91	81r
Household Goods				
Floor coverings, expenditures	year	158	91	81r
Furniture, expenditures	year	341	91	81r
Household equipment, misc. expenditures	year	363	91	81r
Household expenditures, miscellaneous	year	194	91	81r
Household furnishings and equipment, expenditures	year	1158	91	81r
Household operations expenditures	year	378	91	81r
Household textiles, expenditures	year	88	91	81r
Housekeeping supplies, expenditures	year	426	91	81r
Laundry and cleaning supplies, expenditures	year	122	91	81r
Postage and stationery, expenditures	year	134	91	81r
Housing				
Add garage/carport		11,614	3/95	74r
Add room(s)		16,816	3/95	74r
Apartment condominium or co-op, median	unit	96700	12/94	62r
Dwellings (owned), expenditures	year	3305	91	81r
Enclose porch/patio/breezeway		2,980	3/95	74r
Finish room in basement/attic		4,330	3/95	74r
Home, existing, single-family, median	unit	161600	12/94	62r
Maintenance, repairs, insurance, and other housing expenditures	year	569	91	81r
Mortgage interest and charges expenditures	year	1852	91	81r
Princ. & int., mortgage, median-price exist. sing.-family home	mo.	765	12/94	62r
Property taxes expenditures	year	884	91	81r
Redesign, restructure more than half of home's interior		2,750	3/95	74r
Rental units expenditures	year	1832	91	81r

Brockton, MA - continued

Item	Per	Value	Date	Ref.
Insurance and Pensions				
Auto insurance, private passenger	year	1009.56	12/94	71s
Insurance and pensions, personal, expenditures	year	2690	91	81r
Insurance, life and other personal, expenditures	year	341	91	81r
Pensions and Social Security, expenditures	year	2349	91	81r
Legal Assistance				
Estate planning, law-firm partner	hr.	375.00	10/93	12r
Legal work, law firm associate	hour	78		10r
Legal work, law firm partner	hour	183		10r
Personal Services				
Personal services expenditures	year	184	91	81r
Restaurant Food				
Dining expenditures, family	week	34.26	94	73r
Taxes				
Taxes, Federal income, expenditures	year	2409	91	81r
Taxes, personal, expenditures	year	3094	91	81r
Taxes, State and local income, expenditures	year	620	91	81r
Transportation				
Cars and trucks purchased, new	year	1170	91	81r
Cars and trucks purchased, used	year	739	91	81r
Driver's learning permit fee	perm	15.00	1/94	84s
Driver's license fee	orig	50.00	1/94	84s
Driver's license fee, duplicate	lic	15.00	1/94	84s
Driver's license renewal fee	renew	43.75	1/94	84s
Identification card, nondriver	card	15.00	1/94	83s
Motorcycle license fee	orig	50.00	1/94	84s
Motorcycle license fee, duplicate	lic	15.00	1/94	84s
Motorcycle license renewal fee	renew	43.75	1/94	84s
Public transportation expenditures	year	430	91	81r
Transportation expenditures, total	year	4810	91	81r
Vehicle finance charges	year	238	91	81r
Vehicle insurance expenditures	year	630	91	81r
Vehicle maintenance and repairs expenditures	year	532	91	81r
Vehicle purchases	year	1920	91	81r
Vehicle rental, leases, licenses, etc. expenditures	year	193	91	81r
Vehicles purchased, other than cars and trucks	year	11	91	81r
Utilities				
Electricity expenditures	year	695	91	81r
Utilities, fuels, and public services, total expenditures	year	1981	91	81r
Water and other public services, expenditures	year	154	91	81r
Weddings				
Bridal attendants' gowns	event	750	10/93	76r
Bridal gown	event	852	10/93	76r
Bridal headpiece and veil	event	167	10/93	76r
Bride's wedding band	event	708	10/93	76r
Clergy	event	224	10/93	76r
Engagement ring	event	2756	10/93	76r
Flowers	event	863	10/93	76r
Formal wear for groom	event	106	10/93	76r
Groom's attendants' formal wear	event	530	10/93	76r
Groom's wedding band	event	402	10/93	76r
Music	event	600	10/93	76r
Photography	event	1088	10/93	76r
Shoes for bride	event	50	10/93	76r
Videography	event	483	10/93	76r
Wedding invitations and announcements	event	342	10/93	76r
Wedding reception	event	7000	10/93	76r

Values are in dollars or fractions of dollars. In the column headed *Ref*, references are shown to sources. Each reference is followed by a letter. These refer to the geographical level for which data were reported: s = State, r = Region, and c = City or metro. The abbreviation *ex* is used to mean *except* or *excluding*; *exp* stands for expenditures. For other abbreviations and further explanations, please see the Introduction.

Brownsville-Harlingen, TX

Item	Per	Value	Date	Ref.
Appliances				
Appliances (major), expenditures	year	153	91	81r
Average annual exp.				
Food, health care, personal goods, services	year	27020	91	81r
Charity				
Cash contributions, expenditures	year	839	91	81r
Clothing				
Apparel, men and boys, total expenditures	year	380	91	81r
Apparel, women and girls, total expenditures	year	660	91	81r
Footwear, expenditures	year	193	91	81r
Communications				
Long-distance telephone rate, day, addl. min., 1-10 mi.	min.	0.08	12/93	9s
Long-distance telephone rate, day, initial min., 1-10 mi.	min.	0.10	12/93	9s
Phone line, single, business, field visit	inst	71.90	12/93	9s
Phone line, single, business, no field visit	inst	57.30	12/93	9s
Phone line, single, residence, field visit	inst	52.95	12/93	9s
Phone line, single, residence, no field visit	inst	38.35	12/93	9s
Telephone service, expenditures	year	616	91	81r
Education				
Board, 4-year private college/university	year	2084	8/94	80s
Board, 4-year public college/university	year	1675	8/94	80s
Education, total expenditures	year	319	91	81r
Room, 4-year private college/university	year	1840	8/94	80s
Room, 4-year public college/university	year	1756	8/94	80s
Total cost, 4-year private college/university	year	11876	8/94	80s
Total cost, 4-year public college/university	year	4935	8/94	80s
Tuition, 2-year public college/university, in-state	year	625	8/94	80s
Tuition, 4-year private college/university, in-state	year	7952	8/94	80s
Tuition, 4-year public college/university, in-state	year	1503	8/94	80s
Energy and Fuels				
Fuel oil and other fuels, expenditures	year	56	91	81r
Gas, natural, expenditures	year	150	91	81r
Gasoline and motor oil purchased	year	1152	91	81r
Gasoline, unleaded midgrade	gallon	1.21	4/93	82r
Gasoline, unleaded premium	gallon	1.30	4/93	82r
Gasoline, unleaded regular	gallon	1.10	4/93	82r
Entertainment				
Concert ticket, Pearl Jam group	perf	20.00	94	50r
Entertainment, total expenditures	year	1266	91	81r
Fees and admissions, expenditures	year	306	91	81r
Pets, toys, playground equipment, expenditures	year	271	91	81r
Reading, expenditures	year	131	91	81r
Televisions, radios, and sound equipment, expenditures	year	439	91	81r
Funerals				
Burial, immediate, container provided by funeral home		1574.60	1/95	54r
Cards, acknowledgment		22.24	1/95	54r
Casket, minimum alternative		239.41	1/95	54r
Cosmetology, hair care, etc.		91.04	1/95	54r
Cremation, direct, container provided by funeral home		1085.15	1/95	54r
Embalming		281.30	1/95	54r
Funeral, funeral home		323.04	1/95	54r
Funeral, other facility		327.58	1/95	54r
Graveside service		355.19	1/95	54r
Hearse, local		141.89	1/95	54r
Limousine, local		99.40	1/95	54r
Memorial service		284.67	1/95	54r
Service charge, professional, nondeclinable		904.06	1/95	54r
Visitation and viewing		187.04	1/95	54r

Brownsville-Harlingen, TX - continued

Item	Per	Value	Date	Ref.
Groceries				
Apples, Red Delicious	lb.	0.73	12/94	82r
Bacon, sliced	lb.	1.67	12/94	82r
Bananas	lb.	0.42	12/94	82r
Beef purchases	year	213	91	81r
Beverage purchases, alcoholic	year	249	91	81r
Beverage purchases, nonalcoholic	year	207	91	81r
Bologna, all beef or mixed	lb.	2.27	12/94	82r
Bread, white, pan	lb.	0.68	12/94	82r
Cabbage	lb.	0.42	12/94	82r
Carrots, short trimmed and topped	lb.	0.53	12/94	82r
Cereals and bakery products purchases	year	345	91	81r
Cereals and cereals products purchases	year	127	91	81r
Cheddar cheese, natural	lb.	3.58	12/94	82r
Chicken breast, bone-in	lb.	1.71	12/94	82r
Chicken, fresh, whole	lb.	0.78	12/94	82r
Chuck roast, USDA choice, boneless	lb.	2.26	12/94	82r
Crackers, soda, salted	lb.	1.27	12/94	82r
Cucumbers	lb.	0.65	12/94	82r
Dairy products (other) purchases	year	141	91	81r
Eggs, Grade A large	dozen	0.87	12/94	82r
Fish and seafood purchases	year	72	91	81r
Flour, white, all purpose	lb.	0.23	12/94	82r
Food purchases, food eaten at home	year	2381	91	81r
Foods purchased away from home, not prepared by consumer	year	1696	91	81r
Frankfurters, all meat or all beef	lb.	1.74	12/94	82r
Fruits and vegetables purchases	year	380	91	81r
Grapefruit	lb.	0.45	12/94	82r
Grapes, Thompson seedless	lb.	2.30	12/94	82r
Ground beef, 100% beef	lb.	1.37	12/94	82r
Ground chuck, 100% beef	lb.	1.97	12/94	82r
Ham, boneless, exc. canned	lb.	2.54	12/94	82r
Ice cream, prepackaged, bulk, regular	1/2 gal.	2.47	12/94	82r
Lemons	lb.	1.02	12/94	82r
Lettuce, iceberg	lb.	0.96	12/94	82r
Margarine, stick	lb.	0.77	12/94	82r
Meats, poultry, fish, and eggs purchases	year	655	91	81r
Milk and cream (fresh) purchases	year	130	91	81r
Orange juice, frozen concentrate 12-oz. can	16 oz.	1.36	12/94	82r
Oranges, Navel	lb.	0.54	12/94	82r
Pears, Anjou	lb.	0.81	12/94	82r
Pork chops, center cut, bone-in	lb.	3.07	12/94	82r
Pork purchases	year	142	91	81r
Potato chips	16-oz.	3.15	12/94	82r
Potatoes, frozen, French fried	lb.	0.82	12/94	82r
Potatoes, white	lb.	0.34	12/94	82r
Rice, white, long grain, uncooked	lb.	0.48	12/94	82r
Round roast, USDA choice, boneless	lb.	2.91	12/94	82r
Sausage, fresh	lb.	1.82	12/94	82r
Shortening, vegetable oil blends	lb.	0.75	12/94	82r
Spaghetti and macaroni	lb.	0.87	12/94	82r
Steak, rib eye, USDA choice, boneless	lb.	6.85	12/94	82r
Steak, round, graded & ungraded, exc. USDA prime & choice	lb.	2.96	12/94	82r
Steak, round, USDA choice, boneless	lb.	3.17	12/94	82r
Steak, sirloin, USDA choice, boneless	lb.	4.12	12/94	82r
Steak, T-bone, USDA choice, bone-in	lb.	5.63	12/94	82r
Sugar and other sweets, eaten at home, expenditures	year	93	91	81r
Sugar, white, all sizes	lb.	0.39	12/94	82r
Tobacco products and smoking supplies, total expenditures	year	286	91	81r
Tomatoes, field grown	lb.	1.36	12/94	82r
Tuna, chunk, light	lb.	1.94	12/94	82r
Turkey, frozen, whole	lb.	0.96	12/94	82r
Yogurt, natural, fruit flavored	8 oz.	0.58	12/94	82r
Health Care				
Adenosine, emergency room	treat	100.00	95	23r
Bladder tap, superpubic, infant, emergency room	treat	119.00	95	23r
Blood analysis, emergency room	treat	25.00	95	23r

Values are in dollars or fractions of dollars. In the column headed *Ref*, references are shown to sources. Each reference is followed by a letter. These refer to the geographical level for which data were reported: s = State, r = Region, and c = City or metro. The abbreviation *ex* is used to mean *except* or *excluding*; *exp* stands for *expenditures*. For other abbreviations and further explanations, please see the Introduction.

Brownsville-Harlingen, TX - continued

Item	Per	Value	Date	Ref.
Health Care				
Blood tests, abdominal pain, emergency room	treat	25.00	95	23r
Burn dressing, emergency room	treat	266.00	95	23r
Cardiology interpretation, emergency room	treat	26.00	95	23r
Chest X-ray, emergency room	treat	78.00	95	23r
Childbirth, Cesarean delivery, hospital charge	birth	5462.00	12/91	69r
Childbirth, Cesarean delivery, physician charge	birth	2228.00	12/91	69r
Childbirth, normal delivery, hospital charge	birth	2943.00	12/91	69r
Childbirth, normal delivery, physician charge	birth	1619.00	12/91	69r
Defibrillation pads, emergency room	treat	6.00	95	23r
Drugs, expenditures	year	297	91	81r
Gastric tube insertion, nasal, emergency room	treat	25.00	95	23r
Health care, total expenditures	year	1600	91	81r
Health insurance expenditures	year	637	91	81r
Heart monitor, emergency room	treat	40.00	95	23r
Insurance premium, family medical care	month	389.25	1/95	41s
Intravenous fluids, emergency room	treat	130.00	95	23r
Intravenous fluids, emergency room	liter	26.00	95	23r
Intravenous line, central, emergency room	treat	342.00	95	23r
Liver function tests, abdominal pain, emergency room	treat	26.00	95	23r
Medical care charges, total, emergency room, third-degree burns	treat	2101.00	95	23r
Medical care charges, total, emergency, infant with fever	treat	628.00	95	23r
Medical services expenditures	year	573	91	81r
Medical supplies expenditures	year	93	91	81r
Morphine, emergency room	treat	34.00	95	23r
Nursing care and facilities charges, emergency room	treat	252.00	95	23r
Nursing care and facilities charges, emergency, infant with fever	treat	252.00	95	23r
Nursing care and facilities charges, emergency, third-degree burns	treat	861.00	95	23r
Physician's charges, emergency, infant with fever	treat	212.00	95	23r
Physician's charges, emergency, third-degree burns	treat	372.00	95	23r
Physician's fee, emergency room	treat	372.00	95	23r
Physician's fee, general practitioner	visit	51.20	12/93	60r
Surgery, open-heart	proc	42374.00	1/93	14r
Ultrasound, abdominal, emergency room	treat	276.00	95	23r
Urinalysis, emergency room	treat	20.00	95	23r
Urinalysis, infant, emergency room	treat	20.00	95	23r
X-rays, emergency room	treat	78.00	95	23r
Household Goods				
Floor coverings, expenditures	year	48	91	81r
Furniture, expenditures	year	280	91	81r
Household equipment, misc. expenditures	year	342	91	81r
Household expenditures, miscellaneous	year	256	91	81r
Household furnishings and equipment, expenditures	year	988	91	81r
Household operations expenditures	year	468	91	81r
Household textiles, expenditures	year	95	91	81r
Housekeeping supplies, expenditures	year	380	91	81r
Laundry and cleaning supplies, expenditures	year	109	91	81r
Postage and stationery, expenditures	year	105	91	81r
Housing				
Add garage/carport		6,980	3/95	74r
Add room(s)		11,403	3/95	74r
Apartment condominium or co-op, median	unit	68600	12/94	62r
Dwellings (owned), expenditures	year	2428	91	81r
Enclose porch/patio/breezeway		4,572	3/95	74r
Finish room in basement/attic		3,794	3/95	74r
Home, existing, single-family, median	unit	120200	12/94	62r
Maintenance, repairs, insurance, and other housing expenditures	year	531	91	81r

Brownsville-Harlingen, TX - continued

Item	Per	Value	Date	Ref.
Housing - continued				
Mortgage interest and charges expenditures	year	1506	91	81r
Princ. & int., mortgage, median-price exist. sing.-family home	mo.	540	12/94	62r
Property taxes expenditures	year	391	91	81r
Redesign, restructure more than half of home's interior		17,641	3/95	74r
Rental units expenditures	year	1264	91	81r
Insurance and Pensions				
Auto insurance, private passenger	year	785.78	12/94	71s
Insurance and pensions, personal, expenditures	year	2395	91	81r
Insurance, life and other personal, expenditures	year	368	91	81r
Pensions and Social Security, expenditures	year	2027	91	81r
Personal Services				
Personal services expenditures	year	212	91	81r
Restaurant Food				
Dining expenditures, family	week	33.83	94	73r
Taxes				
Tax, cigarettes	year	584.00	10/93	43s
Taxes, Federal income, expenditures	year	2275	91	81r
Taxes, personal, expenditures	year	2715	91	81r
Taxes, State and local income, expenditures	year	365	91	81r
Transportation				
Cars and trucks purchased, new	year	1306	91	81r
Cars and trucks purchased, used	year	942	91	81r
Driver's learning permit fee	perm	5.00	1/94	84s
Driver's license fee	orig	16.00	1/94	84s
Driver's license fee, duplicate	lic	10.00	1/94	84s
Driver's license reinstatement fee, min.	susp	50.00	1/94	85s
Driver's license renewal fee	renew	16.00	1/94	84s
Identification card, nondriver	card	10.00	1/94	83s
Motorcycle learning permit fee	perm	5.00	1/94	84s
Motorcycle license fee	orig	16.00	1/94	84s
Motorcycle license fee, duplicate	lic	10.00	1/94	84s
Motorcycle license renewal fee	renew	21.00	1/94	84s
Public transportation expenditures	year	249	91	81r
Transportation expenditures, total	year	5307	91	81r
Vehicle finance charges	year	346	91	81r
Vehicle insurance expenditures	year	544	91	81r
Vehicle maintenance and repairs expenditures	year	600	91	81r
Vehicle purchases	year	2275	91	81r
Vehicle rental, leases, licenses, etc. expenditures	year	141	91	81r
Vehicles purchased, other than cars and trucks	year	27	91	81r
Utilities				
Electricity expenditures	year	950	91	81r
Utilities, fuels, and public services, total expenditures	year	2000	91	81r
Water and other public services, expenditures	year	227	91	81r
Weddings				
Bridal attendants' gowns	event	750	10/93	76r
Bridal gown	event	852	10/93	76r
Bridal headpiece and veil	event	167	10/93	76r
Bride's wedding band	event	708	10/93	76r
Clergy	event	224	10/93	76r
Engagement ring	event	2756	10/93	76r
Flowers	event	863	10/93	76r
Formal wear for groom	event	106	10/93	76r
Groom's attendants' formal wear	event	530	10/93	76r
Groom's wedding band	event	402	10/93	76r
Music	event	600	10/93	76r
Photography	event	1088	10/93	76r
Shoes for bride	event	50	10/93	76r
Videography	event	483	10/93	76r

Values are in dollars or fractions of dollars. In the column headed *Ref*, references are shown to sources. Each reference is followed by a letter. These refer to the geographical level for which data were reported: s = State, r = Region, and c = City or metro. The abbreviation *ex* is used to mean *except* or *excluding*; *exp* stands for expenditures. For other abbreviations and further explanations, please see the Introduction.

Brownsville-Harlingen, TX - continued

Item	Per	Value	Date	Ref.
Weddings				
Wedding invitations and announcements	event	342	10/93	76r
Wedding reception	event	7000	10/93	76r

Bryan-College Station, TX

Item	Per	Value	Date	Ref.
Composite, ACCRA index		89.90	12/94	2c
Alcoholic Beverages				
Beer, Miller Lite, Bud, 12-oz., ex deposit	6	3.78	12/94	2c
J & B Scotch	750-ml.	17.56	12/94	2c
Wine, Gallo Chablis blanc	1.5-lit	4.71	12/94	2c
Appliances				
Appliances (major), expenditures	year	153	91	81r
Average annual exp.				
Food, health care, personal goods, services	year	27020	91	81r
Charity				
Cash contributions, expenditures	year	839	91	81r
Clothing				
Apparel, men and boys, total expenditures	year	380	91	81r
Apparel, women and girls, total expenditures	year	660	91	81r
Footwear, expenditures	year	193	91	81r
Jeans, man's denim		25.74	12/94	2c
Shirt, man's dress shirt		26.17	12/94	2c
Undervest, boy's size 10-14, cotton	3	3.24	12/94	2c
Communications				
Long-distance telephone rate, day, addl. min., 1-10 mi.	min.	0.08	12/93	9s
Long-distance telephone rate, day, initial min., 1-10 mi.	min.	0.10	12/93	9s
Newspaper subscription, dly. and Sun. delivery	month	8.79	12/94	2c
Phone line, single, business, field visit	inst	71.90	12/93	9s
Phone line, single, business, no field visit	inst	57.30	12/93	9s
Phone line, single, residence, field visit	inst	52.95	12/93	9s
Phone line, single, residence, no field visit	inst	38.35	12/93	9s
Telephone bill, family of four	month	16.13	12/94	2c
Telephone service, expenditures	year	616	91	81r
Education				
Board, 4-year private college/university	year	2084	8/94	80s
Board, 4-year public college/university	year	1675	8/94	80s
Education, total expenditures	year	319	91	81r
Room, 4-year private college/university	year	1840	8/94	80s
Room, 4-year public college/university	year	1756	8/94	80s
Total cost, 4-year private college/university	year	11876	8/94	80s
Total cost, 4-year public college/university	year	4935	8/94	80s
Tuition, 2-year public college/university, in-state	year	625	8/94	80s
Tuition, 4-year private college/university, in-state	year	7952	8/94	80s
Tuition, 4-year public college/university, in-state	year	1503	8/94	80s
Energy and Fuels				
Energy, combined forms, 1800 sq. ft.	mo.	104.53	12/94	2c
Energy, exc. electricity, 1800 sq. ft.	mo.	28.19	12/94	2c
Fuel oil and other fuels, expenditures	year	56	91	81r
Gas, natural, expenditures	year	150	91	81r
Gas, reg unlead, taxes inc., cash, self-service	gal	1.07	12/94	2c
Gasoline and motor oil purchased	year	1152	91	81r
Gasoline, unleaded midgrade	gallon	1.21	4/93	82r
Gasoline, unleaded premium	gallon	1.30	4/93	82r
Gasoline, unleaded regular	gallon	1.10	4/93	82r
Entertainment				
Bowling, evening rate	game	2.25	12/94	2c
Concert ticket, Pearl Jam group	perf	20.00	94	50r
Entertainment, total expenditures	year	1266	91	81r
Fees and admissions, expenditures	year	306	91	81r

Bryan-College Station, TX - continued

Item	Per	Value	Date	Ref.
Entertainment - continued				
Monopoly game, Parker Brothers', No. 9	game	10.06	12/94	2c
Movie	adm	5.17	12/94	2c
Pets, toys, playground equipment, expenditures	year	271	91	81r
Reading, expenditures	year	131	91	81r
Televisions, radios, and sound equipment, expenditures	year	439	91	81r
Tennis balls, yellow, Wilson or Penn, 3	can	2.01	12/94	2c
Funerals				
Burial, immediate, container provided by funeral home		1574.60	1/95	54r
Cards, acknowledgment		22.24	1/95	54r
Casket, minimum alternative		239.41	1/95	54r
Cosmetology, hair care, etc.		91.04	1/95	54r
Cremation, direct, container provided by funeral home		1085.15	1/95	54r
Embalming		281.30	1/95	54r
Funeral, funeral home		323.04	1/95	54r
Funeral, other facility		327.58	1/95	54r
Graveside service		355.19	1/95	54r
Hearse, local		141.89	1/95	54r
Limousine, local		99.40	1/95	54r
Memorial service		284.67	1/95	54r
Service charge, professional, nondeclinable		904.06	1/95	54r
Visitation and viewing		187.04	1/95	54r
Groceries				
Groceries, ACCRA Index		87.00	12/94	2c
Apples, Red Delicious	lb.	0.73	12/94	82r
Baby food, strained vegetables, lowest price	4-4.5 oz.	0.25	12/94	2c
Bacon, sliced	lb.	1.67	12/94	82r
Bananas	lb.	0.33	12/94	2c
Bananas	lb.	0.42	12/94	82r
Beef or hamburger, ground	lb.	1.15	12/94	2c
Beef purchases	year	213	91	81r
Beverage purchases, alcoholic	year	249	91	81r
Beverage purchases, nonalcoholic	year	207	91	81r
Bologna, all beef or mixed	lb.	2.27	12/94	82r
Bread, white	24-oz.	0.53	12/94	2c
Bread, white, pan	lb.	0.68	12/94	82r
Cabbage	lb.	0.42	12/94	82r
Carrots, short trimmed and topped	lb.	0.53	12/94	82r
Cereals and bakery products purchases	year	345	91	81r
Cereals and cereals products purchases	year	127	91	81r
Cheddar cheese, natural	lb.	3.58	12/94	82r
Cheese, Kraft grated Parmesan	8-oz.	3.14	12/94	2c
Chicken breast, bone-in	lb.	1.71	12/94	82r
Chicken, fresh, whole	lb.	0.78	12/94	82r
Chicken, whole fryer	lb.	0.66	12/94	2c
Chuck roast, USDA choice, boneless	lb.	2.26	12/94	82r
Cigarettes, Winston, Kings	carton	16.97	12/94	2c
Coffee, vacuum-packed	13 oz.	3.33	12/94	2c
Corn Flakes, Kellogg's or Post Toasties	18 oz.	1.84	12/94	2c
Corn, frozen, whole kernel, lowest price	10 oz.	0.64	12/94	2c
Crackers, soda, salted	lb.	1.27	12/94	82r
Cucumbers	lb.	0.65	12/94	82r
Dairy products (other) purchases	year	141	91	81r
Eggs, Grade A large	dozen	0.73	12/94	2c
Eggs, Grade A large	dozen	0.87	12/94	82r
Fish and seafood purchases	year	72	91	81r
Flour, white, all purpose	lb.	0.23	12/94	82r
Food purchases, food eaten at home	year	2381	91	81r
Foods purchased away from home, not prepared by consumer	year	1696	91	81r
Frankfurters, all meat or all beef	lb.	1.74	12/94	82r
Fruits and vegetables purchases	year	380	91	81r
Grapefruit	lb.	0.45	12/94	82r
Grapes, Thompson seedless	lb.	2.30	12/94	82r
Ground beef, 100% beef	lb.	1.37	12/94	82r
Ground chuck, 100% beef	lb.	1.97	12/94	82r
Ham, boneless, exc. canned	lb.	2.54	12/94	82r

Values are in dollars or fractions of dollars. In the column headed *Ref*, references are shown to sources. Each reference is followed by a letter. These refer to the geographical level for which data were reported: s=State, r=Region, and c=City or metro. The abbreviation *ex* is used to mean *except* or *excluding*; *exp* stands for expenditures. For other abbreviations and further explanations, please see the Introduction.

Bryan-College Station, TX - continued

Item	Per	Value	Date	Ref.
Groceries				
Ice cream, prepackaged, bulk, regular	1/2 gal.	2.47	12/94	82r
Lemons	lb.	1.02	12/94	82r
Lettuce, iceberg	lb.	0.96	12/94	82r
Lettuce, iceberg	head	0.88	12/94	2c
Margarine, Blue Bonnet or Parkay cubes	lb.	0.52	12/94	2c
Margarine, stick	lb.	0.77	12/94	82r
Meats, poultry, fish, and eggs purchases	year	655	91	81r
Milk and cream (fresh) purchases	year	130	91	81r
Milk, whole	1/2 gal.	1.29	12/94	2c
Orange juice, frozen concentrate 12-oz. can	16 oz.	1.36	12/94	82r
Orange juice, Minute Maid frozen	12-oz.	1.08	12/94	2c
Oranges, Navel	lb.	0.54	12/94	82r
Peaches, halves or slices, Hunt's, Del Monte, or Libby's	29-oz.	1.32	12/94	2c
Pears, Anjou	lb.	0.81	12/94	82r
Peas, sweet, Del Monte or Green Giant	15-17 oz.	0.52	12/94	2c
Pork chops, center cut, bone-in	lb.	3.07	12/94	82r
Pork purchases	year	142	91	81r
Potato chips	16-oz.	3.15	12/94	82r
Potatoes, frozen, French fried	lb.	0.82	12/94	82r
Potatoes, white	lb.	0.34	12/94	82r
Potatoes, white or red	10-lb. sack	2.27	12/94	2c
Rice, white, long grain, uncooked	lb.	0.48	12/94	82r
Round roast, USDA choice, boneless	lb.	2.91	12/94	82r
Sausage, fresh	lb.	1.82	12/94	82r
Sausage, Jimmy Dean, 100% pork	lb.	2.44	12/94	2c
Shortening, vegetable oil blends	lb.	0.75	12/94	82r
Shortening, vegetable, Crisco	3-lb.	2.25	12/94	2c
Soft drink, Coca Cola, ex deposit	2 lit	1.12	12/94	2c
Spaghetti and macaroni	lb.	0.87	12/94	82r
Steak, rib eye, USDA choice, boneless	lb.	6.85	12/94	82r
Steak, round, graded & ungraded, exc. USDA prime & choice	lb.	2.96	12/94	82r
Steak, round, USDA choice, boneless	lb.	3.17	12/94	82r
Steak, sirloin, USDA choice, boneless	lb.	4.12	12/94	82r
Steak, t-bone	lb.	4.86	12/94	2c
Steak, T-bone, USDA choice, bone-in	lb.	5.63	12/94	82r
Sugar and other sweets, eaten at home, expenditures	year	93	91	81r
Sugar, cane or beet	4 lbs.	1.30	12/94	2c
Sugar, white, all sizes	lb.	0.39	12/94	82r
Tobacco products and smoking supplies, total expenditures	year	286	91	81r
Tomatoes, field grown	lb.	1.36	12/94	82r
Tomatoes, Hunt's or Del Monte	14.5 oz.	0.65	12/94	2c
Tuna, chunk, light	lb.	1.94	12/94	82r
Tuna, chunk, light, oil-packed	6.125-6.5 oz.	0.59	12/94	2c
Turkey, frozen, whole	lb.	0.96	12/94	82r
Yogurt, natural, fruit flavored	8 oz.	0.58	12/94	82r
Goods and Services				
Miscellaneous goods and services, ACCRA Index		92.90	12/94	2c
Health Care				
Health care, ACCRA Index		89.90	12/94	2c
Adenosine, emergency room	treat	100.00	95	23r
Antibiotic ointment, Polysporin	1.5 oz.	3.99	12/94	2c
Bladder tap, superpubic, infant, emergency room	treat	119.00	95	23r
Blood analysis, emergency room	treat	25.00	95	23r
Blood tests, abdominal pain, emergency room	treat	25.00	95	23r
Burn dressing, emergency room	treat	266.00	95	23r
Cardiology interpretation, emergency room	treat	26.00	95	23r
Chest X-ray, emergency room	treat	78.00	95	23r

Bryan-College Station, TX - continued

Item	Per	Value	Date	Ref.
Health Care - continued				
Childbirth, Cesarean delivery, hospital charge	birth	5462.00	12/91	69r
Childbirth, Cesarean delivery, physician charge	birth	2228.00	12/91	69r
Childbirth, normal delivery, hospital charge	birth	2943.00	12/91	69r
Childbirth, normal delivery, physician charge	birth	1619.00	12/91	69r
Defibrillation pads, emergency room	treat	6.00	95	23r
Dentist's fee, adult teeth cleaning and periodic oral exam	visit	54.00	12/94	2c
Doctor's fee, routine exam, established patient	visit	32.20	12/94	2c
Drugs, expenditures	year	297	91	81r
Gastric tube insertion, nasal, emergency room	treat	25.00	95	23r
Health care, total expenditures	year	1600	91	81r
Health insurance expenditures	year	637	91	81r
Heart monitor, emergency room	treat	40.00	95	23r
Hospital care, semiprivate room	day	306.50	12/94	2c
Insurance premium, family medical care	month	389.25	1/95	41s
Intravenous fluids, emergency room	treat	130.00	95	23r
Intravenous fluids, emergency room	liter	26.00	95	23r
Intravenous line, central, emergency room	treat	342.00	95	23r
Liver function tests, abdominal pain, emergency room	treat	26.00	95	23r
Medical care charges, total, emergency room, third-degree burns	treat	2101.00	95	23r
Medical care charges, total, emergency, infant with fever	treat	628.00	95	23r
Medical services expenditures	year	573	91	81r
Medical supplies expenditures	year	93	91	81r
Morphine, emergency room	treat	34.00	95	23r
Nursing care and facilities charges, emergency room	treat	252.00	95	23r
Nursing care and facilities charges, emergency, infant with fever	treat	252.00	95	23r
Nursing care and facilities charges, emergency, third-degree burns	treat	861.00	95	23r
Physician's charges, emergency, infant with fever	treat	212.00	95	23r
Physician's charges, emergency, third-degree burns	treat	372.00	95	23r
Physician's fee, emergency room	treat	372.00	95	23r
Physician's fee, general practitioner	visit	51.20	12/93	60r
Surgery, open-heart	proc	42374.00	1/93	14r
Ultrasound, abdominal, emergency room	treat	276.00	95	23r
Urinalysis, emergency room	treat	20.00	95	23r
Urinalysis, infant, emergency room	treat	20.00	95	23r
X-rays, emergency room	treat	78.00	95	23r
Household Goods				
Appl. repair, service call, wash mach	min. lab. chg.	33.83	12/94	2c
Floor coverings, expenditures	year	48	91	81r
Furniture, expenditures	year	280	91	81r
Household equipment, misc. expenditures	year	342	91	81r
Household expenditures, miscellaneous	year	256	91	81r
Household furnishings and equipment, expenditures	year	988	91	81r
Household operations expenditures	year	468	91	81r
Household textiles, expenditures	year	95	91	81r
Housekeeping supplies, expenditures	year	380	91	81r
Laundry and cleaning supplies, expenditures	year	109	91	81r
Laundry detergent, Tide Ultra, Bold, or Cheer	42 oz.	2.76	12/94	2c
Postage and stationery, expenditures	year	105	91	81r
Tissues, facial, Kleenex brand	175	0.90	12/94	2c
Housing				
Housing, ACCRA Index		86.30	12/94	2c
Add garage/carport		6,980	3/95	74r
Add room(s)		11,403	3/95	74r

Values are in dollars or fractions of dollars. In the column headed *Ref*, references are shown to sources. Each reference is followed by a letter. These refer to the geographical level for which data were reported: s=State, r=Region, and c=City or metro. The abbreviation *ex* is used to mean *except* or *excluding*; *exp* stands for expenditures. For other abbreviations and further explanations, please see the Introduction.

Bryan-College Station, TX - continued

Item	Per	Value	Date	Ref.
Housing				
Apartment condominium or co-op, median	unit	68600	12/94	62r
Dwellings (owned), expenditures	year	2428	91	81r
Enclose porch/patio/breezeway		4,572	3/95	74r
Finish room in basement/attic		3,794	3/95	74r
Home, existing, single-family, median	unit	120200	12/94	62r
House payment, principal and interest, 25% down payment	mo.	639	12/94	2c
House, 1800 sq ft, 8000 sq ft lot, new, urban, utilities	total	105395	12/94	2c
Maintenance, repairs, insurance, and other housing expenditures	year	531	91	81r
Mortgage interest and charges expenditures	year	1506	91	81r
Mtge. rate, incl. points and orig. fee, 30-year conv. fixed or ARM	mo.	9.04	12/94	2c
Princ. & int., mortgage, median-price exist. sing.-family home	mo.	540	12/94	62r
Property taxes expenditures	year	391	91	81r
Redesign, restructure more than half of home's interior		17,641	3/95	74r
Rent, apartment, 2 br., 1 1/2-2 baths, unfurnished, 950 sq ft, water	mo.	520	12/94	2c
Rental units expenditures	year	1264	91	81r
Insurance and Pensions				
Auto insurance, private passenger	year	785.78	12/94	71s
Insurance and pensions, personal, expenditures	year	2395	91	81r
Insurance, life and other personal, expenditures	year	368	91	81r
Pensions and Social Security, expenditures	year	2027	91	81r
Personal Goods				
Shampoo, Alberto VO5	15-oz.	1.05	12/94	2c
Toothpaste, Crest or Colgate	6-7 oz.	1.85	12/94	2c
Personal Services				
Dry cleaning, man's 2-pc. suit		5.36	12/94	2c
Haircut, man's barbershop, no styling		7.82	12/94	2c
Haircut, woman's shampoo, trim, blow-dry		21.40	12/94	2c
Personal services expenditures	year	212	91	81r
Restaurant Food				
Chicken, fried, thigh and drumstick		1.99	12/94	2c
Dining expenditures, family	week	33.83	94	73r
Hamburger with cheese	1/4 lb.	1.95	12/94	2c
Pizza, Pizza Hut or Pizza Inn	12-13 in.	8.99	12/94	2c
Taxes				
Tax, cigarettes	year	584.00	10/93	43s
Taxes, Federal income, expenditures	year	2275	91	81r
Taxes, personal, expenditures	year	2715	91	81r
Taxes, State and local income, expenditures	year	365	91	81r
Transportation				
Transportation, ACCRA Index		93.20	12/94	2c
Bus fare, one-way	trip	0.50	12/95	1c
Cars and trucks purchased, new	year	1306	91	81r
Cars and trucks purchased, used	year	942	91	81r
Driver's learning permit fee	perm	5.00	1/94	84s
Driver's license fee	orig	16.00	1/94	84s
Driver's license fee, duplicate	lic	10.00	1/94	84s
Driver's license reinstatement fee, min.	susp	50.00	1/94	85s
Driver's license renewal fee	renew	16.00	1/94	84s
Identification card, nondriver	card	10.00	1/94	83s
Motorcycle learning permit fee	perm	5.00	1/94	84s
Motorcycle license fee	orig	16.00	1/94	84s
Motorcycle license fee, duplicate	lic	10.00	1/94	84s
Motorcycle license renewal fee	renew	21.00	1/94	84s
Public transportation expenditures	year	249	91	81r
Tire balance, computer or spin bal., front	wheel	6.10	12/94	2c
Transportation expenditures, total	year	5307	91	81r
Vehicle finance charges	year	346	91	81r
Vehicle insurance expenditures	year	544	91	81r

Bryan-College Station, TX - continued

Item	Per	Value	Date	Ref.
Transportation - continued				
Vehicle maintenance and repairs expenditures	year	600	91	81r
Vehicle purchases	year	2275	91	81r
Vehicle rental, leases, licenses, etc. expenditures	year	141	91	81r
Vehicles purchased, other than cars and trucks	year	27	91	81r
Utilities				
Utilities, ACCRA Index		91.70	12/94	2c
Electricity expenditures	year	950	91	81r
Electricity, (part.), other, 1800 sq. ft., new home	mo.	76.34	12/94	2c
Utilities, fuels, and public services, total expenditures	year	2000	91	81r
Water and other public services, expenditures	year	227	91	81r
Weddings				
Bridal attendants' gowns	event	750	10/93	76r
Bridal gown	event	852	10/93	76r
Bridal headpiece and veil	event	167	10/93	76r
Bride's wedding band	event	708	10/93	76r
Clergy	event	224	10/93	76r
Engagement ring	event	2756	10/93	76r
Flowers	event	863	10/93	76r
Formal wear for groom	event	106	10/93	76r
Groom's attendants' formal wear	event	530	10/93	76r
Groom's wedding band	event	402	10/93	76r
Music	event	600	10/93	76r
Photography	event	1088	10/93	76r
Shoes for bride	event	50	10/93	76r
Videography	event	483	10/93	76r
Wedding invitations and announcements	event	342	10/93	76r
Wedding reception	event	7000	10/93	76r

Buffalo, NY

Item	Per	Value	Date	Ref.
Appliances				
Appliances (major), expenditures	year	154	91	81c
Appliances (major), expenditures	year	145	91	81r
Average annual exp.				
Food, health care, personal goods, services	year	25119	91	81c
Food, health care, personal goods, services	year	29496	91	81r
Charity				
Cash contributions, expenditures	year	681	91	81c
Cash contributions, expenditures	year	708	91	81r
Child Care				
Child care, for-profit daycare center	week	91.00	12/94	28c
Clothing				
Apparel, men and boys, total expenditures	year	395	91	81c
Apparel, men and boys, total expenditures	year	416	91	81r
Apparel, women and girls, total expenditures	year	632	91	81c
Apparel, women and girls, total expenditures	year	744	91	81r
Footwear, expenditures	year	158	91	81c
Footwear, expenditures	year	305	91	81r
Communications				
Long-distance telephone rate, day, addl. min., 1-10 mi.	min.	4.00	12/93	9s
Long-distance telephone rate, day, initial min., 1-10 mi.	min.	14.90	12/93	9s
Phone line, single, business, field visit	inst	143.26	12/93	9s
Phone line, single, business, no field visit	inst	106.05	12/93	9s
Phone line, single, residence, field visit	inst	85.46	12/93	9s
Phone line, single, residence, no field visit	inst	55.00	12/93	9s
Telephone service, expenditures	year	539	91	81c
Telephone service, expenditures	year	589	91	81r
Telephone, business, addl. line, touch tone	month	4.82	10/91	25c

Values are in dollars or fractions of dollars. In the column headed *Ref*, references are shown to sources. Each reference is followed by a letter. These refer to the geographical level for which data were reported: s=State, r=Region, and c=City or metro. The abbreviation *ex* is used to mean *except* or *excluding*; *exp* stands for expenditures. For other abbreviations and further explanations, please see the Introduction.

Buffalo, NY - continued

Item	Per	Value	Date	Ref.
Communications				
Telephone, business, connection charges, touch tone	inst	150.61	10/91	25c
Telephone, business, key system line, touch tone	month	50.69	10/91	25c
Telephone, business, PBX line, touch tone	month	50.80	10/91	25c
Telephone, business, single ln., touch tone	month	51.95	10/91	25c
Telephone, business, touch tone, inside wiring maintenance plan	month	5.97	10/91	25c
Telephone, residential, flat rate	mo.	22.27	12/93	8c
Education				
Board, 4-year private college/university	year	2918	8/94	80s
Board, 4-year public college/university	year	2177	8/94	80s
Education, total expenditures	year	373	91	81c
Education, total expenditures	year	593	91	81r
Room, 4-year private college/university	year	3302	8/94	80s
Room, 4-year public college/university	year	2624	8/94	80s
Total cost, 4-year private college/university	year	18451	8/94	80s
Total cost, 4-year public college/university	year	7723	8/94	80s
Tuition, 2-year public college/university, in-state	year	2112	8/94	80s
Tuition, 4-year private college/university, in-state	year	12231	8/94	80s
Tuition, 4-year public college/university, in-state	year	2921	8/94	80s
Energy and Fuels				
Fuel oil and other fuels, expenditures	year	28	91	81c
Fuel oil and other fuels, expenditures	year	257	91	81r
Gas, cooking, winter, 10 therms	month	17.12	2/94	65c
Gas, cooking, winter, 30 therms	month	31.64	2/94	65c
Gas, cooking, winter, 50 therms	month	46.17	2/94	65c
Gas, heating, winter, 100 therms	month	80.85	2/94	65c
Gas, heating, winter, average use	month	172.36	2/94	65c
Gas, natural, expenditures	year	678	91	81c
Gas, natural, expenditures	year	285	91	81r
Gasoline and motor oil purchased	year	768	91	81c
Gasoline and motor oil purchased	year	867	91	81r
Gasoline, unleaded midgrade	gallon	1.32	4/93	82r
Gasoline, unleaded premium	gallon	1.40	4/93	82r
Gasoline, unleaded regular	gallon	1.19	4/93	82r
Entertainment				
Entertainment supplies, equipment, and services, misc. expenditures	year	186	91	81c
Entertainment, total expenditures	year	1090	91	81c
Entertainment, total expenditures	year	1331	91	81r
Fees and admissions, expenditures	year	293	91	81c
Fees and admissions, expenditures	year	398	91	81r
Pets, toys, playground equipment, expenditures	year	204	91	81c
Pets, toys, playground equipment, expenditures	year	270	91	81r
Reading, expenditures	year	151	91	81c
Reading, expenditures	year	171	91	81r
Televisions, radios, and sound equipment, expenditures	year	408	91	81c
Televisions, radios, and sound equipment, expenditures	year	429	91	81r
Funerals				
Burial, immediate, container provided by funeral home		1370.36	1/95	54r
Cards, acknowledgment		17.72	1/95	54r
Casket, minimum alternative		192.52	1/95	54r
Cosmetology, hair care, etc.		139.56	1/95	54r
Cremation, direct, container provided by funeral home		1049.24	1/95	54r
Embalming		387.57	1/95	54r
Funeral, funeral home		278.77	1/95	54r
Funeral, other facility		275.85	1/95	54r
Graveside service		213.08	1/95	54r
Hearse, local		157.27	1/95	54r
Limousine, local		146.45	1/95	54r

Buffalo, NY - continued

Item	Per	Value	Date	Ref.
Funerals - continued				
Memorial service		271.02	1/95	54r
Service charge, professional, nondeclinable		943.58	1/95	54r
Visitation and viewing		322.86	1/95	54r
Groceries				
Apples, Red Delicious	lb.	0.78	12/94	82r
Bacon, sliced	lb.	2.24	12/94	82r
Bananas	lb.	0.49	12/94	82r
Beef purchases	year	274	91	81c
Beef purchases	year	226	91	81r
Beverage purchases, alcoholic	year	369	91	81c
Beverage purchases, alcoholic	year	332	91	81r
Beverage purchases, nonalcoholic	year	231	91	81c
Beverage purchases, nonalcoholic	year	213	91	81r
Bread, white, pan	lb.	0.80	12/94	82r
Butter, salted, Grade AA, stick	lb.	1.67	12/94	82r
Carrots, short trimmed and topped	lb.	0.51	12/94	82
Cereals and bakery products purchases	year	454	91	81c
Cereals and bakery products purchases	year	407	91	81r
Cereals and cereal products purchases	year	148	91	81c
Cereals and cereals products purchases	year	132	91	81r
Chicken breast, bone-in	lb.	2.22	12/94	82r
Chicken, fresh, whole	lb.	1.05	12/94	82r
Chuck roast, USDA choice, boneless	lb.	2.74	12/94	82r
Coffee, 100%, ground roast, all sizes	lb.	4.61	12/94	82r
Dairy products (other) purchases	year	176	91	81c
Dairy products (other) purchases	year	161	91	81r
Eggs, Grade A large	dozen	1.12	12/94	82r
Fish and seafood purchases	year	107	91	81c
Fish and seafood purchases	year	112	91	81r
Food purchases, food eaten at home	year	3012	91	81c
Food purchases, food eaten at home	year	2599	91	81r
Foods purchased away from home, not prepared by consumer	year	1544	91	81c
Foods purchased away from home, not prepared by consumer	year	2024	91	81r
Fruits and vegetables purchases	year	478	91	81c
Fruits and vegetables purchases	year	444	91	81r
Grapefruit	lb.	0.44	12/94	82r
Grapes, Thompson seedless	lb.	2.24	12/94	82r
Ground chuck, 100% beef	lb.	1.67	12/94	82r
Ice cream, prepackaged, bulk, regular	1/2 gal.	2.93	12/94	82r
Lemons	lb.	1.06	12/94	82r
Lettuce, iceberg	lb.	0.92	12/94	82r
Meats, poultry, fish, and eggs purchases	year	899	91	81c
Meats, poultry, fish, and eggs purchases	year	751	91	81r
Milk and cream (fresh) purchases	year	123	91	81c
Milk and cream (fresh) purchases	year	152	91	81r
Orange juice, frozen concentrate 12-oz. can	16 oz.	1.92	12/94	82r
Oranges, Navel	lb.	0.56	12/94	82r
Pork chops, center cut, bone-in	lb.	3.09	12/94	82r
Pork purchases	year	202	91	81c
Pork purchases	year	130	91	81r
Potatoes, white	lb.	0.37	12/94	82r
Rib roast, USDA choice, bone-in	lb.	4.98	12/94	82r
Round roast, USDA choice, boneless	lb.	2.93	12/94	82r
Shortening, vegetable oil blends	lb.	1.03	12/94	82r
Spaghetti and macaroni	lb.	0.84	12/94	82r
Steak, round, USDA choice, boneless	lb.	3.48	12/94	82r
Steak, sirloin, USDA choice, bone-in	lb.	3.38	12/94	82r
Steak, sirloin, USDA choice, boneless	lb.	4.81	12/94	82r
Sugar and other sweets, eaten at home, expenditures	year	89	91	81r
Sugar and other sweets, eaten at home, purchases	year	122	91	81c
Sugar, white, all sizes	lb.	0.46	12/94	82r
Tobacco products and smoking supplies, total expenditures	year	250	91	81c
Tobacco products and smoking supplies, total expenditures	year	279	91	81r
Tomatoes, field grown	lb.	1.56	12/94	82r
Tuna, chunk, light	lb.	2.09	12/94	82r

Values are in dollars or fractions of dollars. In the column headed *Ref*, references are shown to sources. Each reference is followed by a letter. These refer to the geographical level for which data were reported: s=State, r=Region, and c=City or metro. The abbreviation *ex* is used to mean *except* or *excluding*; *exp* stands for *expenditures*. For other abbreviations and further explanations, please see the Introduction.

Buffalo, NY - continued

Item	Per	Value	Date	Ref.
Health Care				
Childbirth, Cesarean delivery, hospital charge	birth	6334.00	12/91	69r
Childbirth, Cesarean delivery, physician charge	birth	2234.00	12/91	69r
Childbirth, normal delivery, hospital charge	birth	3225.00	12/91	69r
Childbirth, normal delivery, physician charge	birth	1623.00	12/91	69r
Drugs, expenditures	year	142	91	81c
Drugs, expenditures	year	205	91	81r
Health care, total expenditures	year	1149	91	81c
Health care, total expenditures	year	1396	91	81r
Health insurance expenditures	year	565	91	81c
Health insurance expenditures	year	553	91	81r
Insurance premium, family medical care	month	384.24	1/95	41s
Medical services expenditures	year	365	91	81c
Medical services expenditures	year	559	91	81r
Medical supplies expenditures	year	76	91	81c
Medical supplies expenditures	year	80	91	81r
Household Goods				
Floor coverings, expenditures	year	194	91	81c
Floor coverings, expenditures	year	158	91	81r
Furniture, expenditures	year	233	91	81c
Furniture, expenditures	year	341	91	81r
Household equipment, misc. expenditures	year	363	91	81r
Household equipment, misc., expenditures	year	254	91	81c
Household expenditures, miscellaneous	year	122	91	81c
Household expenditures, miscellaneous	year	194	91	81r
Household furnishings and equipment, expenditures	year	1009	91	81c
Household furnishings and equipment, expenditures	year	1158	91	81r
Household operations expenditures	year	199	91	81c
Household operations expenditures	year	378	91	81r
Household textiles, expenditures	year	108	91	81c
Household textiles, expenditures	year	88	91	81r
Housekeeping supplies, expenditures	year	299	91	81c
Housekeeping supplies, expenditures	year	426	91	81r
Laundry and cleaning supplies, expenditures	year	87	91	81c
Laundry and cleaning supplies, expenditures	year	122	91	81r
Postage and stationery, expenditures	year	113	91	81c
Postage and stationery, expenditures	year	134	91	81r
Housing				
Add garage/carport		11,614	3/95	74r
Add room(s)		16,816	3/95	74r
Apartment condominium or co-op, median	unit	96700	12/94	62r
Dwellings (owned), expenditures	year	2745	91	81c
Dwellings (owned), expenditures	year	3305	91	81r
Enclose porch/patio/breezeway		2,980	3/95	74r
Finish room in basement/attic		4,330	3/95	74r
Home, existing, single-family, median	unit	161600	12/94	62r
Home, existing, single-family, median	unit	83.70	12/94	62c
Maintenance, repairs, insurance, and other housing expenditures	year	438	91	81c
Maintenance, repairs, insurance, and other housing expenditures	year	569	91	81r
Mortgage interest and charges expenditures	year	1347	91	81c
Mortgage interest and charges expenditures	year	1852	91	81r
Princ. & int., mortgage, median-price exist. sing.-family home	mo.	765	12/94	62r
Property taxes expenditures	year	960	91	81c
Property taxes expenditures	year	884	91	81r
Redesign, restructure more than half of home's interior		2,750	3/95	74r
Rental units expenditures	year	1442	900/00/ 91	81c
Rental units expenditures	year	1832	91	81r
Insurance and Pensions				
Auto insurance, private passenger	year	985.07	12/94	71s
Insurance and pensions, personal, expenditures	year	1538	91	81c

Buffalo, NY - continued

Item	Per	Value	Date	Ref.
Insurance and Pensions - continued				
Insurance and pensions, personal, expenditures	year	2690	91	81r
Insurance, life and other personal, expenditures	year	273	91	81c
Insurance, life and other personal, expenditures	year	341	91	81r
Pensions and Social Security, expenditures	year	1265	91	81c
Pensions and Social Security, expenditures	year	2349	91	81r
Legal Assistance				
Estate planning, law-firm partner	hr.	375.00	10/93	12r
Legal work, law firm associate	hour	78		10r
Legal work, law firm partner	hour	183		10r
Personal Goods				
Personal care products and services, total expenditures	year	360	91	81c
Personal Services				
Personal services expenditures	year	78	91	81c
Personal services expenditures	year	184	91	81r
Restaurant Food				
Dining expenditures, family	week	34.26	94	73r
Taxes				
Taxes, Federal income, expenditures	year	203	91	81c
Taxes, Federal income, expenditures	year	2409	91	81r
Taxes, personal, expenditures	year	352	91	81c
Taxes, personal, expenditures	year	3094	91	81r
Taxes, State and local income, expenditures	year	149	91	81c
Taxes, State and local income, expenditures	year	620	91	81r
Transportation				
Bus fare, one-way	trip	1.10	12/95	1c
Cars and trucks purchased, new	year	1293	91	81c
Cars and trucks purchased, new	year	1170	91	81r
Cars and trucks purchased, used	year	646	91	81c
Cars and trucks purchased, used	year	739	91	81r
Driver's learning permit fee	perm	10.00	1/94	84s
Driver's license fee	orig	32.00-37.00	1/94	84s
Driver's license fee, duplicate	lic	7.25	1/94	84s
Driver's license reinstatement fee, min.	susp	25.00	1/94	85s
Driver's license renewal fee	renew	22.25	1/94	84s
Identification card, nondriver	card	6.25	1/94	83s
Motorcycle license fee	orig	32.00-37.00	1/94	84s
Motorcycle license fee, duplicate	lic	7.25	1/94	84s
Motorcycle license renewal fee	renew	22.25	1/94	84s
Public transportation expenditures	year	233	91	81c
Public transportation expenditures	year	430	91	81r
Railway fare, light rail, one-way	trip	1.10	12/95	1c
Transportation expenditures, total	year	4521	91	81c
Transportation expenditures, total	year	4810	91	81r
Vehicle expenses, miscellaneous	year	1580	91	81c
Vehicle finance charges	year	272	91	81c
Vehicle finance charges	year	238	91	81r
Vehicle insurance expenditures	year	518	91	81c
Vehicle insurance expenditures	year	630	91	81r
Vehicle maintenance and repairs expenditures	year	637	91	81c
Vehicle maintenance and repairs expenditures	year	532	91	81r
Vehicle purchases	year	1940	91	81c
Vehicle purchases	year	1920	91	81r
Vehicle rental, leases, licenses, etc. expenditures	year	152	91	81c
Vehicle rental, leases, licenses, etc. expenditures	year	193	91	81r
Vehicles purchased, other than cars and trucks	year	1	91	81c
Vehicles purchased, other than cars and trucks	year	11	91	81r

Values are in dollars or fractions of dollars. In the column headed *Ref*, references are shown to sources. Each reference is followed by a letter. These refer to the geographical level for which data were reported: s=State, r=Region, and c=City or metro. The abbreviation *ex* is used to mean *except* or *excluding*; *exp* stands for *expenditures*. For other abbreviations and further explanations, please see the Introduction.

Buffalo, NY - continued

Item	Per	Value	Date	Ref.
Utilities				
Electricity expenditures	year	572	91	81c
Electricity expenditures	year	695	91	81r
Electricity, summer, 250 KWh	month	32.04	8/93	64c
Electricity, summer, 500 KWh	month	58.86	8/93	64c
Electricity, summer, 750 KWh	month	84.56	8/93	64c
Electricity, summer, 1000 KWh	month	110.27	8/93	64c
Utilities, fuels, and public services, total expenditures	year	1931	91	81c
Utilities, fuels, and public services, total expenditures	year	1981	91	81r
Water and other public services, expenditures	year	114	91	81c
Water and other public services, expenditures	year	154	91	81r
Weddings				
Bridal attendants' gowns	event	750	10/93	76r
Bridal gown	event	852	10/93	76r
Bridal headpiece and veil	event	167	10/93	76r
Bride's wedding band	event	708	10/93	76r
Clergy	event	224	10/93	76r
Engagement ring	event	2756	10/93	76r
Flowers	event	863	10/93	76r
Formal wear for groom	event	106	10/93	76r
Groom's attendants' formal wear	event	530	10/93	76r
Groom's wedding band	event	402	10/93	76r
Music	event	600	10/93	76r
Photography	event	1088	10/93	76r
Shoes for bride	event	50	10/93	76r
Videography	event	483	10/93	76r
Wedding invitations and announcements	event	342	10/93	76r
Wedding reception	event	7000	10/93	76r

Burlington, NC

Item	Per	Value	Date	Ref.
Composite, ACCRA index		94.00	12/94	2c
Alcoholic Beverages				
Beer, Miller Lite, Bud, 12-oz., ex deposit	6	3.59	12/94	2c
J & B Scotch	750-ml.	18.60	12/94	2c
Wine, Gallo Chablis blanc	1.5-lit	4.37	12/94	2c
Appliances				
Appliances (major), expenditures	year	153	91	81r
Average annual exp.				
Food, health care, personal goods, services	year	27020	91	81r
Charity				
Cash contributions, expenditures	year	839	91	81r
Clothing				
Apparel, men and boys, total expenditures	year	380	91	81r
Apparel, women and girls, total expenditures	year	660	91	81r
Footwear, expenditures	year	193	91	81r
Jeans, man's denim		31.75	12/94	2c
Shirt, man's dress shirt		28.72	12/94	2c
Undervest, boy's size 10-14, cotton	3	3.17	12/94	2c
Communications				
Long-distance telephone rate, day, addl. min., 1-10 mi.	min.	0.10	12/93	9s
Long-distance telephone rate, day, initial min., 1-10 mi.	min.	0.16	12/93	9s
Newspaper subscription, dly. and Sun. delivery	month	8.70	12/94	2c
Phone line, single, business, field visit	inst	62.50	12/93	9s
Phone line, single, business, no field visit	inst	62.50	12/93	9s
Phone line, single, residence, field visit	inst	42.75	12/93	9s
Phone line, single, residence, no field visit	inst	42.75	12/93	9s
Telephone bill, family of four	month	16.64	12/94	2c
Telephone service, expenditures	year	616	91	81r
Telephone, residential, flat rate	mo.	11.34	12/93	8c

Burlington, NC - continued

Item	Per	Value	Date	Ref.
Education				
Board, 4-year private college/university	year	2069	8/94	80s
Board, 4-year public college/university	year	1627	8/94	80s
Education, total expenditures	year	319	91	81r
Room, 4-year private college/university	year	1824	8/94	80s
Room, 4-year public college/university	year	1669	8/94	80s
Total cost, 4-year private college/university	year	13505	8/94	80s
Total cost, 4-year public college/university	year	4704	8/94	80s
Tuition, 2-year public college/university, in-state	year	577	8/94	80s
Tuition, 4-year private college/university, in-state	year	9612	8/94	80s
Tuition, 4-year public college/university, in-state	year	1409	8/94	80s
Energy and Fuels				
Energy, combined forms, 1800 sq. ft.	mo.	112.27	12/94	2c
Fuel oil and other fuels, expenditures	year	56	91	81r
Gas, natural, expenditures	year	150	91	81r
Gas, reg unlead, taxes inc., cash, self-service	gal	1.00	12/94	2c
Gasoline and motor oil purchased	year	1152	91	81r
Gasoline, unleaded midgrade	gallon	1.21	4/93	82r
Gasoline, unleaded premium	gallon	1.30	4/93	82r
Gasoline, unleaded regular	gallon	1.10	4/93	82r
Entertainment				
Bowling, evening rate	game	2.25	12/94	2c
Concert ticket, Pearl Jam group	perf	20.00	94	50r
Entertainment, total expenditures	year	1266	91	81r
Fees and admissions, expenditures	year	306	91	81r
Monopoly game, Parker Brothers', No. 9	game	10.84	12/94	2c
Movie	adm	4.50	12/94	2c
Pets, toys, playground equipment, expenditures	year	271	91	81r
Reading, expenditures	year	131	91	81r
Televisions, radios, and sound equipment, expenditures	year	439	91	81r
Tennis balls, yellow, Wilson or Penn, 3	can	2.03	12/94	2c
Funerals				
Burial, immediate, container provided by funeral home		1370.36	1/95	54r
Cards, acknowledgment		14.83	1/95	54r
Casket, minimum alternative		192.52	1/95	54r
Cosmetology, hair care, etc.		102.27	1/95	54r
Cremation, direct, container provided by funeral home		1065.64	1/95	54r
Embalming		304.29	1/95	54r
Funeral, funeral home		287.83	1/95	54r
Funeral, other facility		284.14	1/95	54r
Graveside service		349.13	1/95	54r
Hearse, local		132.27	1/95	54r
Limousine, local		98.45	1/95	54r
Memorial service		270.59	1/95	54r
Service charge, professional, nondeclinable		933.59	1/95	54r
Visitation and viewing		225.83	1/95	54r
Groceries				
Groceries, ACCRA Index		96.30	12/94	2c
Apples, Red Delicious	lb.	0.73	12/94	82r
Baby food, strained vegetables, lowest price	4-4.5 oz.	0.35	12/94	2c
Bacon, sliced	lb.	1.67	12/94	82r
Bananas	lb.	0.49	12/94	2c
Bananas	lb.	0.42	12/94	82r
Beef or hamburger, ground	lb.	1.68	12/94	2c
Beef purchases	year	213	91	81r
Beverage purchases, alcoholic	year	249	91	81r
Beverage purchases, nonalcoholic	year	207	91	81r
Bologna, all beef or mixed	lb.	2.27	12/94	82r
Bread, white	24-oz.	0.69	12/94	2c
Bread, white, pan	lb.	0.68	12/94	82r
Cabbage	lb.	0.42	12/94	82r
Carrots, short trimmed and topped	lb.	0.53	12/94	82r

Values are in dollars or fractions of dollars. In the column headed *Ref*, references are shown to sources. Each reference is followed by a letter. These refer to the geographical level for which data were reported: s = State, r = Region, and c = City or metro. The abbreviation *ex* is used to mean *except* or *excluding*; *exp* stands for expenditures. For other abbreviations and further explanations, please see the Introduction.

Burlington, NC - continued

Item	Per	Value	Date	Ref.
Groceries				
Cereals and bakery products purchases	year	345	91	81r
Cereals and cereals products purchases	year	127	91	81r
Cheddar cheese, natural	lb.	3.58	12/94	82r
Cheese, Kraft grated Parmesan	8-oz.	3.26	12/94	2c
Chicken breast, bone-in	lb.	1.71	12/94	82r
Chicken, fresh, whole	lb.	0.78	12/94	82r
Chicken, whole fryer	lb.	0.86	12/94	2c
Chuck roast, USDA choice, boneless	lb.	2.26	12/94	82r
Cigarettes, Winston, Kings	carton	12.99	12/94	2c
Coffee, vacuum-packed	13 oz.	3.33	12/94	2c
Corn Flakes, Kellogg's or Post Toasties	18 oz.	2.33	12/94	2c
Corn, frozen, whole kernel, lowest price	10 oz.	0.65	12/94	2c
Crackers, soda, salted	lb.	1.27	12/94	82r
Cucumbers	lb.	0.65	12/94	82r
Dairy products (other) purchases	year	141	91	81r
Eggs, Grade A large	dozen	0.83	12/94	2c
Eggs, Grade A large	dozen	0.87	12/94	82r
Fish and seafood purchases	year	72	91	81r
Flour, white, all purpose	lb.	0.23	12/94	82r
Food purchases, food eaten at home	year	2381	91	81r
Foods purchased away from home, not prepared by consumer	year	1696	91	81r
Frankfurters, all meat or all beef	lb.	1.74	12/94	82r
Fruits and vegetables purchases	year	380	91	81r
Grapefruit	lb.	0.45	12/94	82r
Grapes, Thompson seedless	lb.	2.30	12/94	82r
Ground beef, 100% beef	lb.	1.37	12/94	82r
Ground chuck, 100% beef	lb.	1.97	12/94	82r
Ham, boneless, exc. canned	lb.	2.54	12/94	82r
Ice cream, prepackaged, bulk, regular	1/2 gal.	2.47	12/94	82r
Lemons	lb.	1.02	12/94	82r
Lettuce, iceberg	lb.	0.96	12/94	82r
Lettuce, iceberg	head	0.93	12/94	2c
Margarine, Blue Bonnet or Parkay cubes	lb.	0.56	12/94	2c
Margarine, stick	lb.	0.77	12/94	82r
Meats, poultry, fish, and eggs purchases	year	655	91	81r
Milk and cream (fresh) purchases	year	130	91	81r
Milk, whole	1/2 gal.	1.40	12/94	2c
Orange juice, frozen concentrate 12-oz. can	16 oz.	1.36	12/94	82r
Orange juice, Minute Maid frozen	12-oz.	0.99	12/94	2c
Oranges, Navel	lb.	0.54	12/94	82r
Peaches, halves or slices, Hunt's, Del Monte, or Libby's	29-oz.	1.32	12/94	2c
Pears, Anjou	lb.	0.81	12/94	82r
Peas, sweet, Del Monte or Green Giant	15-17 oz.	0.50	12/94	2c
Pork chops, center cut, bone-in	lb.	3.07	12/94	82r
Pork purchases	year	142	91	81r
Potato chips	16-oz.	3.15	12/94	82r
Potatoes, frozen, French fried	lb.	0.82	12/94	82r
Potatoes, white	lb.	0.34	12/94	82r
Potatoes, white or red	10-lb. sack	2.37	12/94	2c
Rice, white, long grain, uncooked	lb.	0.48	12/94	82r
Round roast, USDA choice, boneless	lb.	2.91	12/94	82r
Sausage, fresh	lb.	1.82	12/94	82r
Sausage, Jimmy Dean, 100% pork	lb.	2.13	12/94	2c
Shortening, vegetable oil blends	lb.	0.75	12/94	82r
Shortening, vegetable, Crisco	3-lb.	2.53	12/94	2c
Soft drink, Coca Cola, ex deposit	2 lit	1.34	12/94	2c
Spaghetti and macaroni	lb.	0.87	12/94	82r
Steak, rib eye, USDA choice, boneless	lb.	6.85	12/94	82r
Steak, round, graded & ungraded, exc. USDA prime & choice	lb.	2.96	12/94	82r
Steak, round, USDA choice, boneless	lb.	3.17	12/94	82r
Steak, sirloin, USDA choice, boneless	lb.	4.12	12/94	82r
Steak, t-bone	lb.	5.27	12/94	2c
Steak, T-bone, USDA choice, bone-in	lb.	5.63	12/94	82r
Sugar and other sweets, eaten at home, expenditures	year	93	91	81r

Burlington, NC - continued

Item	Per	Value	Date	Ref.
Groceries - continued				
Sugar, cane or beet	4 lbs.	1.51	12/94	2c
Sugar, white, all sizes	lb.	0.39	12/94	82r
Tobacco products and smoking supplies, total expenditures	year	286	91	81r
Tomatoes, field grown	lb.	1.36	12/94	82r
Tomatoes, Hunt's or Del Monte	14.5 oz.	0.51	12/94	2c
Tuna, chunk, light	lb.	1.94	12/94	82r
Tuna, chunk, light, oil-packed	6.125-6.5 oz.	0.65	12/94	2c
Turkey, frozen, whole	lb.	0.96	12/94	82r
Yogurt, natural, fruit flavored	8 oz.	0.58	12/94	82r
Goods and Services				
Miscellaneous goods and services, ACCRA Index		97.00	12/94	2c
Health Care				
Health care, ACCRA Index		90.00	12/94	2c
Adenosine, emergency room	treat	100.00	95	23r
Antibiotic ointment, Polysporin	1.5 oz.	3.77	12/94	2c
Bladder tap, superpubic, infant, emergency room	treat	119.00	95	23r
Blood analysis, emergency room	treat	25.00	95	23r
Blood tests, abdominal pain, emergency room	treat	25.00	95	23r
Burn dressing, emergency room	treat	266.00	95	23r
Cardiology interpretation, emergency room	treat	26.00	95	23r
Chest X-ray, emergency room	treat	78.00	95	23r
Childbirth, Cesarean delivery, hospital charge	birth	5462.00	12/91	69r
Childbirth, Cesarean delivery, physician charge	birth	2228.00	12/91	69r
Childbirth, normal delivery, hospital charge	birth	2943.00	12/91	69r
Childbirth, normal delivery, physician charge	birth	1619.00	12/91	69r
Defibrillation pads, emergency room	treat	6.00	95	23r
Dentist's fee, adult teeth cleaning and periodic oral exam	visit	48.00	12/94	2c
Doctor's fee, routine exam, established patient	visit	34.80	12/94	2c
Drugs, expenditures	year	297	91	81r
Gastric tube insertion, nasal, emergency room	treat	25.00	95	23r
Health care, total expenditures	year	1600	91	81r
Health insurance expenditures	year	637	91	81r
Heart monitor, emergency room	treat	40.00	95	23r
Hospital care, semiprivate room	day	356.00	12/94	2c
Insurance premium, family medical care	month	405.45	1/95	41s
Intravenous fluids, emergency room	treat	130.00	95	23r
Intravenous fluids, emergency room	liter	26.00	95	23r
Intravenous line, central, emergency room	treat	342.00	95	23r
Liver function tests, abdominal pain, emergency room	treat	26.00	95	23r
Medical care charges, total, emergency room, third-degree burns	treat	2101.00	95	23r
Medical care charges, total, emergency, infant with fever	treat	628.00	95	23r
Medical services expenditures	year	573	91	81r
Medical supplies expenditures	year	93	91	81r
Morphine, emergency room	treat	34.00	95	23r
Nursing care and facilities charges, emergency room	treat	252.00	95	23r
Nursing care and facilities charges, emergency, infant with fever	treat	252.00	95	23r
Nursing care and facilities charges, emergency, third-degree burns	treat	861.00	95	23r
Physician's charges, emergency, infant with fever	treat	212.00	95	23r
Physician's charges, emergency, third-degree burns	treat	372.00	95	23r
Physician's fee, emergency room	treat	372.00	95	23r
Physician's fee, general practitioner	visit	51.20	12/93	60r
Surgery, open-heart	proc	42374.00	1/93	14r

Values are in dollars or fractions of dollars. In the column headed *Ref*, references are shown to sources. Each reference is followed by a letter. These refer to the geographical level for which data were reported: s=State, r=Region, and c=City or metro. The abbreviation *ex* is used to mean *except* or *excluding*; *exp* stands for *expenditures*. For other abbreviations and further explanations, please see the Introduction.

Burlington, NC - continued

Item	Per	Value	Date	Ref.
Health Care				
Ultrasound, abdominal, emergency room	treat	276.00	95	23r
Urinalysis, emergency room	treat	20.00	95	23r
Urinalysis, infant, emergency room	treat	20.00	95	23r
X-rays, emergency room	treat	78.00	95	23r
Household Goods				
Appl. repair, service call, wash mach	min. lab. chg.	39.50	12/94	2c
Floor coverings, expenditures	year	48	91	81r
Furniture, expenditures	year	280	91	81r
Household equipment, misc. expenditures	year	342	91	81r
Household expenditures, miscellaneous	year	256	91	81r
Household furnishings and equipment, expenditures	year	988	91	81r
Household operations expenditures	year	468	91	81r
Household textiles, expenditures	year	95	91	81r
Housekeeping supplies, expenditures	year	380	91	81r
Laundry and cleaning supplies, expenditures	year	109	91	81r
Laundry detergent, Tide Ultra, Bold, or Cheer	42 oz.	2.70	12/94	2c
Postage and stationery, expenditures	year	105	91	81r
Tissues, facial, Kleenex brand	175	0.93	12/94	2c
Housing				
Housing, ACCRA Index		91.60	12/94	2c
Add garage/carport		6,980	3/95	74r
Add room(s)		11,403	3/95	74r
Apartment condominium or co-op, median	unit	68600	12/94	62r
Dwellings (owned), expenditures	year	2428	91	81r
Enclose porch/patio/breezeway		4,572	3/95	74r
Finish room in basement/attic		3,794	3/95	74r
Home, existing, single-family, median	unit	120200	12/94	62r
House payment, principal and interest, 25% down payment	mo.	713	12/94	2c
House, 1800 sq ft, 8000 sq ft lot, new, urban, utilities	total	115650	12/94	2c
Maintenance, repairs, insurance, and other housing expenditures	year	531	91	81r
Mortgage interest and charges expenditures	year	1506	91	81r
Mtge. rate, incl. points and orig. fee, 30-year conv. fixed or ARM	mo.	9.24	12/94	2c
Princ. & int., mortgage, median-price exist. sing.-family home	mo.	540	12/94	62r
Property taxes expenditures	year	391	91	81r
Redesign, restructure more than half of home's interior		17,641	3/95	74r
Rent, apartment, 2 br., 1 1/2-2 baths, unfurnished, 950 sq ft, water	mo.	453	12/94	2c
Rental units expenditures	year	1264	91	81r
Insurance and Pensions				
Auto insurance, private passenger	year	528.43	12/94	71s
Insurance and pensions, personal, expenditures	year	2395	91	81r
Insurance, life and other personal, expenditures	year	368	91	81r
Pensions and Social Security, expenditures	year	2027	91	81r
Personal Goods				
Shampoo, Alberto VO5	15-oz.	0.90	12/94	2c
Toothpaste, Crest or Colgate	6-7 oz.	1.60	12/94	2c
Personal Services				
Dry cleaning, man's 2-pc. suit		6.50	12/94	2c
Haircut, man's barbershop, no styling		6.80	12/94	2c
Haircut, woman's shampoo, trim, blow-dry		18.00	12/94	2c
Personal services expenditures	year	212	91	81r
Restaurant Food				
Chicken, fried, thigh and drumstick		2.49	12/94	2c
Dining expenditures, family	week	33.83	94	73r
Hamburger with cheese	1/4 lb.	1.89	12/94	2c

Burlington, NC - continued

Item	Per	Value	Date	Ref.
Restaurant Food - continued				
Pizza, Pizza Hut or Pizza Inn	12-13 in.	7.99	12/94	2c
Taxes				
Taxes, Federal income, expenditures	year	2275	91	81r
Taxes, personal, expenditures	year	2715	91	81r
Taxes, State and local income, expenditures	year	365	91	81r
Transportation				
Transportation, ACCRA Index		85.00	12/94	2c
Cars and trucks purchased, new	year	1306	91	81r
Cars and trucks purchased, used	year	942	91	81r
Driver's learning permit fee	perm	10.00	1/94	84s
Driver's license fee	orig	10.00	1/94	84s
Driver's license fee, duplicate	lic	5.00	1/94	84s
Driver's license reinstatement fee, min.	susp	25.00	1/94	85s
Driver's license renewal fee	renew	10.00	1/94	84s
Fine, safety belt violation	ticket	25.00	95	56s
Identification card, nondriver	card	10.00	1/94	83s
Motorcycle license fee	orig	5.00	1/94	84s
Public transportation expenditures	year	249	91	81r
Tire balance, computer or spin bal., front	wheel	5.40	12/94	2c
Transportation expenditures, total	year	5307	91	81r
Vehicle finance charges	year	346	91	81r
Vehicle insurance expenditures	year	544	91	81r
Vehicle maintenance and repairs expenditures	year	600	91	81r
Vehicle purchases	year	2275	91	81r
Vehicle rental, leases, licenses, etc. expenditures	year	141	91	81r
Vehicles purchased, other than cars and trucks	year	27	91	81r
Utilities				
Utilities, ACCRA Index		98.10	12/94	2c
Electricity expenditures	year	950	91	81r
Electricity, 1800 sq. ft., new home	mo.	112.27	12/94	2c
Utilities, fuels, and public services, total expenditures	year	2000	91	81r
Water and other public services, expenditures	year	227	91	81r
Weddings				
Bridal attendants' gowns	event	750	10/93	76r
Bridal gown	event	852	10/93	76r
Bridal headpiece and veil	event	167	10/93	76r
Bride's wedding band	event	708	10/93	76r
Clergy	event	224	10/93	76r
Engagement ring	event	2756	10/93	76r
Flowers	event	863	10/93	76r
Formal wear for groom	event	106	10/93	76r
Groom's attendants' formal wear	event	530	10/93	76r
Groom's wedding band	event	402	10/93	76r
Music	event	600	10/93	76r
Photography	event	1088	10/93	76r
Shoes for bride	event	50	10/93	76r
Videography	event	483	10/93	76r
Wedding invitations and announcements	event	342	10/93	76r
Wedding reception	event	7000	10/93	76r

Burlington, VT

Item	Per	Value	Date	Ref.
Composite, ACCRA index		113.20	12/94	2c
Alcoholic Beverages				
Beer, Miller Lite, Bud, 12-oz., ex deposit	6	4.24	12/94	2c
J & B Scotch	750-ml.	15.99	12/94	2c
Wine, Gallo Chablis blanc	1.5-lit	6.59	12/94	2c
Appliances				
Appliances (major), expenditures	year	145	91	81r

Values are in dollars or fractions of dollars. In the column headed *Ref*, references are shown to sources. Each reference is followed by a letter. These refer to the geographical level for which data were reported: s = State, r = Region, and c = City or metro. The abbreviation *ex* is used to mean *except* or *excluding*; *exp* stands for *expenditures*. For other abbreviations and further explanations, please see the Introduction.

Burlington, VT - continued

Item	Per	Value	Date	Ref.
Average annual exp.				
Food, health care, personal goods, services	year	29496	91	81r
Charity				
Cash contributions, expenditures	year	708	91	81r
Clothing				
Apparel, men and boys, total expenditures	year	416	91	81r
Apparel, women and girls, total expenditures	year	744	91	81r
Footwear, expenditures	year	305	91	81r
Jeans, man's denim		27.59	12/94	2c
Shirt, man's dress shirt		27.66	12/94	2c
Undervest, boy's size 10-14, cotton	3	4.63	12/94	2c
Communications				
Long-distance telephone rate, day, addl. min., 1-10 mi.	min.	0.15	12/93	9s
Long-distance telephone rate, day, initial min., 1-10 mi.	min.	0.29	12/93	9s
Newspaper subscription, dly. and Sun. delivery	month	13.04	12/94	2c
Phone line, single, business, field visit	inst	30.00	12/93	9s
Phone line, single, business, no field visit	inst	46.00	12/93	9s
Phone line, single, residence, field visit	inst	20.00	12/93	9s
Phone line, single, residence, no field visit	inst	33.00	12/93	9s
Telephone bill, family of four	month	35.84	12/94	2c
Telephone service, expenditures	year	589	91	81r
Telephone, residential, flat rate	mo.	16.99	12/93	8c
Education				
Board, 4-year private college/university	year	2433	8/94	80s
Board, 4-year public college/university	year	1740	8/94	80s
Education, total expenditures	year	593	91	81r
Room, 4-year private college/university	year	2768	8/94	80s
Room, 4-year public college/university	year	2781	8/94	80s
Total cost, 4-year private college/university	year	19412	8/94	80s
Total cost, 4-year public college/university	year	10057	8/94	80s
Tuition, 2-year public college/university, in-state	year	2793	8/94	80s
Tuition, 4-year private college/university, in-state	year	14210	8/94	80s
Tuition, 4-year public college/university, in-state	year	5536	8/94	80s
Energy and Fuels				
Energy, combined forms, 1800 sq. ft.	mo.	110.55	12/94	2c
Energy, exc. electricity, 1800 sq. ft.	mo.	57.78	12/94	2c
Fuel oil and other fuels, expenditures	year	257	91	81r
Gas, cooking, winter, 10 therms	month	13.29	2/94	65c
Gas, cooking, winter, 30 therms	month	25.73	2/94	65c
Gas, cooking, winter, 50 therms	month	38.16	2/94	65c
Gas, heating, winter, 100 therms	month	69.26	2/94	65c
Gas, heating, winter, average use	month	141.39	2/94	65c
Gas, natural, expenditures	year	285	91	81r
Gas, reg unlead, taxes inc., cash, self-service	gal	1.18	12/94	2c
Gasoline and motor oil purchased	year	867	91	81r
Gasoline, unleaded midgrade	gallon	1.32	4/93	82r
Gasoline, unleaded premium	gallon	1.40	4/93	82r
Gasoline, unleaded regular	gallon	1.19	4/93	82r
Entertainment				
Bowling, evening rate	game	2.13	12/94	2c
Entertainment, total expenditures	year	1331	91	81r
Fees and admissions, expenditures	year	398	91	81r
Monopoly game, Parker Brothers', No. 9	game	13.32	12/94	2c
Movie	adm	6.50	12/94	2c
Pets, toys, playground equipment, expenditures	year	270	91	81r
Reading, expenditures	year	171	91	81r
Televisions, radios, and sound equipment, expenditures	year	429	91	81r
Tennis balls, yellow, Wilson or Penn, 3	can	2.81	12/94	2c

Burlington, VT - continued

Item	Per	Value	Date	Ref.
Funerals				
Burial, immediate, container provided by funeral home		1507.89	1/95	54r
Cards, acknowledgment		18.10	1/95	54r
Casket, minimum alternative		133.03	1/95	54r
Cosmetology, hair care, etc.		114.12	1/95	54r
Cremation, direct, container provided by funeral home		1309.19	1/95	54r
Embalming		320.97	1/95	54r
Funeral, funeral home		327.61	1/95	54r
Funeral, other facility		314.81	1/95	54r
Graveside service		286.11	1/95	54r
Hearse, local		158.95	1/95	54r
Limousine, local		149.45	1/95	54r
Memorial service		315.94	1/95	54r
Service charge, professional, nondeclinable		1148.43	1/95	54r
Visitation and viewing		249.66	1/95	54r
Groceries				
Groceries, ACCRA Index		106.90	12/94	2c
Apples, Red Delicious	lb.	0.78	12/94	82r
Baby food, strained vegetables, lowest price	4-4.5 oz.	0.35	12/94	2c
Bacon, sliced	lb.	2.24	12/94	82r
Bananas	lb.	0.59	12/94	2c
Bananas	lb.	0.49	12/94	82r
Beef or hamburger, ground	lb.	1.65	12/94	2c
Beef purchases	year	226	91	81r
Beverage purchases, alcoholic	year	332	91	81r
Beverage purchases, nonalcoholic	year	213	91	81r
Bread, white	24-oz.	0.84	12/94	2c
Bread, white, pan	lb.	0.80	12/94	82r
Butter, salted, Grade AA, stick	lb.	1.67	12/94	82r
Carrots, short trimmed and topped	lb.	0.51	12/94	82r
Cereals and bakery products purchases	year	407	91	81r
Cereals and cereals products purchases	year	132	91	81r
Cheese, Kraft grated Parmesan	8-oz.	3.24	12/94	2c
Chicken breast, bone-in	lb.	2.22	12/94	82r
Chicken, fresh, whole	lb.	1.05	12/94	82r
Chicken, whole fryer	lb.	1.11	12/94	2c
Chuck roast, USDA choice, boneless	lb.	2.74	12/94	82r
Cigarettes, Winston, Kings	carton	15.94	12/94	2c
Coffee, 100%, ground roast, all sizes	lb.	4.61	12/94	82r
Coffee, vacuum-packed	13 oz.	3.58	12/94	2c
Corn Flakes, Kellogg's or Post Toasties	18 oz.	2.07	12/94	2c
Corn, frozen, whole kernel, lowest price	10 oz.	0.71	12/94	2c
Dairy products (other) purchases	year	161	91	81r
Eggs, Grade A large	dozen	1.02	12/94	2c
Eggs, Grade A large	dozen	1.12	12/94	82r
Fish and seafood purchases	year	112	91	81r
Food purchases, food eaten at home	year	2599	91	81r
Foods purchased away from home, not prepared by consumer	year	2024	91	81r
Fruits and vegetables purchases	year	444	91	81r
Grapefruit	lb.	0.44	12/94	82r
Grapes, Thompson seedless	lb.	2.24	12/94	82r
Ground chuck, 100% beef	lb.	1.67	12/94	82r
Ice cream, prepackaged, bulk, regular	1/2 gal.	2.93	12/94	82r
Lemons	lb.	1.06	12/94	82r
Lettuce, iceberg	lb.	0.92	12/94	82r
Lettuce, iceberg	head	0.99	12/94	2c
Margarine, Blue Bonnet or Parkay cubes	lb.	0.63	12/94	2c
Meats, poultry, fish, and eggs purchases	year	751	91	81r
Milk and cream (fresh) purchases	year	152	91	81r
Milk, whole	1/2 gal.	1.29	12/94	2c
Orange juice, frozen concentrate 12-oz. can	16 oz.	1.92	12/94	82r
Orange juice, Minute Maid frozen	12-oz.	1.21	12/94	2c
Oranges, Navel	lb.	0.56	12/94	82r
Peaches, halves or slices, Hunt's, Del Monte, or Libby's	29-oz.	1.47	12/94	2c
Peas, sweet, Del Monte or Green Giant	15-17 oz.	0.63	12/94	2c

Values are in dollars or fractions of dollars. In the column headed *Ref*, references are shown to sources. Each reference is followed by a letter. These refer to the geographical level for which data were reported: s=State, r=Region, and c=City or metro. The abbreviation *ex* is used to mean *except* or *excluding*; *exp* stands for expenditures. For other abbreviations and further explanations, please see the Introduction.

Burlington, VT - continued

Item	Per	Value	Date	Ref.
Groceries				
Pork chops, center cut, bone-in	lb.	3.09	12/94	82r
Pork purchases	year	130	91	81r
Potatoes, white	lb.	0.37	12/94	82r
Potatoes, white or red	10-lb. sack	2.17	12/94	2c
Rib roast, USDA choice, bone-in	lb.	4.98	12/94	82r
Round roast, USDA choice, boneless	lb.	2.93	12/94	82r
Sausage, Jimmy Dean, 100% pork	lb.	3.43	12/94	2c
Shortening, vegetable oil blends	lb.	1.03	12/94	82r
Shortening, vegetable, Crisco	3-lb.	2.81	12/94	2c
Soft drink, Coca Cola, ex deposit	2 lit	0.99	12/94	2c
Spaghetti and macaroni	lb.	0.84	12/94	82r
Steak, round, USDA choice, boneless	lb.	3.48	12/94	82r
Steak, sirloin, USDA choice, bone-in	lb.	3.38	12/94	82r
Steak, sirloin, USDA choice, boneless	lb.	4.81	12/94	82r
Steak, t-bone	lb.	5.83	12/94	2c
Sugar and other sweets, eaten at home, expenditures	year	89	91	81r
Sugar, cane or beet	4 lbs.	1.16	12/94	2c
Sugar, white, all sizes	lb.	0.46	12/94	82r
Tobacco products and smoking supplies, total expenditures	year	279	91	81r
Tomatoes, field grown	lb.	1.56	12/94	82r
Tomatoes, Hunt's or Del Monte	14.5 oz.	0.81	12/94	2c
Tuna, chunk, light	lb.	2.09	12/94	82r
Tuna, chunk, light, oil-packed	6.125-6.5 oz.	0.74	12/94	2c
Goods and Services				
Miscellaneous goods and services, ACCRA Index		105.80	12/94	2c
Health Care				
Health care, ACCRA Index		116.50	12/94	2c
Antibiotic ointment, Polysporin	1.5 oz.	4.01	12/94	2c
Childbirth, Cesarean delivery, hospital charge	birth	6334.00	12/91	69r
Childbirth, Cesarean delivery, physician charge	birth	2234.00	12/91	69r
Childbirth, normal delivery, hospital charge	birth	3225.00	12/91	69r
Childbirth, normal delivery, physician charge	birth	1623.00	12/91	69r
Dentist's fee, adult teeth cleaning and periodic oral exam	visit	53.40	12/94	2c
Doctor's fee, routine exam, established patient	visit	50.80	12/94	2c
Drugs, expenditures	year	205	91	81r
Health care, total expenditures	year	1396	91	81r
Health insurance expenditures	year	553	91	81r
Hospital care, semiprivate room	day	526.00	12/94	2c
Medical services expenditures	year	559	91	81r
Medical supplies expenditures	year	80	91	81r
Household Goods				
Appl. repair, service call, wash mach	min. lab. chg.	37.80	12/94	2c
Floor coverings, expenditures	year	158	91	81r
Furniture, expenditures	year	341	91	81r
Household equipment, misc. expenditures	year	363	91	81r
Household expenditures, miscellaneous	year	194	91	81r
Household furnishings and equipment, expenditures	year	1158	91	81r
Household operations expenditures	year	378	91	81r
Household textiles, expenditures	year	88	91	81r
Housekeeping supplies, expenditures	year	426	91	81r
Laundry and cleaning supplies, expenditures	year	122	91	81r
Laundry detergent, Tide Ultra, Bold, or Cheer	42 oz.	3.64	12/94	2c
Postage and stationery, expenditures	year	134	91	81r
Tissues, facial, Kleenex brand	175	1.13	12/94	2c

Burlington, VT - continued

Item	Per	Value	Date	Ref.
Housing				
Housing, ACCRA Index		127.60	12/94	2c
Add garage/carport		11,614	3/95	74r
Add room(s)		16,816	3/95	74r
Apartment condominium or co-op, median	unit	96700	12/94	62r
Dwellings (owned), expenditures	year	3305	91	81r
Enclose porch/patio/breezeway		2,980	3/95	74r
Finish room in basement/attic		4,330	3/95	74r
Home, existing, single-family, median	unit	161600	12/94	62r
House payment, principal and interest, 25% down payment	mo.	961	12/94	2c
House, 1800 sq ft, 8000 sq ft lot, new, urban, utilities	total	154828	12/94	2c
Maintenance, repairs, insurance, and other housing expenditures	year	569	91	81r
Mortgage interest and charges expenditures	year	1852	91	81r
Mtge. rate, incl. points and orig. fee, 30-year conv. fixed or ARM	mo.	9.32	12/94	2c
Princ. & int., mortgage, median-price exist. sing.-family home	mo.	765	12/94	62r
Property taxes expenditures	year	884	91	81r
Redesign, restructure more than half of home's interior		2,750	3/95	74r
Rent, apartment, 2 br., 1 1/2-2 baths, unfurnished, 950 sq ft, water	mo.	720	12/94	2c
Rental units expenditures	year	1832	91	81r
Insurance and Pensions				
Auto insurance, private passenger	year	577.94	12/94	71s
Insurance and pensions, personal, expenditures	year	2690	91	81r
Insurance, life and other personal, expenditures	year	341	91	81r
Pensions and Social Security, expenditures	year	2349	91	81r
Legal Assistance				
Estate planning, law-firm partner	hr.	375.00	10/93	12r
Legal work, law firm associate	hour	78		10r
Legal work, law firm partner	hour	183		10r
Personal Goods				
Shampoo, Alberto VO5	15-oz.	1.45	12/94	2c
Toothpaste, Crest or Colgate	6-7 oz.	2.54	12/94	2c
Personal Services				
Dry cleaning, man's 2-pc. suit		6.79	12/94	2c
Haircut, man's barbershop, no styling		8.65	12/94	2c
Haircut, woman's shampoo, trim, blow-dry		18.50	12/94	2c
Personal services expenditures	year	184	91	81r
Restaurant Food				
Chicken, fried, thigh and drumstick		2.51	12/94	2c
Dining expenditures, family	week	34.26	94	73r
Hamburger with cheese	1/4 lb.	2.13	12/94	2c
Pizza, Pizza Hut or Pizza Inn	12-13 in.	7.75	12/94	2c
Taxes				
Tax rate, residential property, month	$100	1.51	1/92	79c
Taxes, Federal income, expenditures	year	2409	91	81r
Taxes, personal, expenditures	year	3094	91	81r
Taxes, State and local income, expenditures	year	620	91	81r
Transportation				
Transportation, ACCRA Index		107.60	12/94	2c
Bus fare, one-way	trip	0.75	12/95	1c
Cars and trucks purchased, new	year	1170	91	81r
Cars and trucks purchased, used	year	739	91	81r
Driver's learning permit fee	perm	7.00	1/94	84s
Driver's license fee	orig	0.00	1/94	84s
Driver's license fee, duplicate	lic	5.00	1/94	84s
Driver's license reinstatement fee, min.	susp	30.00	1/94	85s
Driver's license renewal fee	renew	0.00	1/94	84s
Driving expenses	mile	36.40	5/95	89c
Identification card, nondriver	card	10.00	1/94	83s
Motorcycle license fee	orig	0.00	1/94	84s

Values are in dollars or fractions of dollars. In the column headed *Ref*, references are shown to sources. Each reference is followed by a letter. These refer to the geographical level for which data were reported: s = State, r = Region, and c = City or metro. The abbreviation *ex* is used to mean *except* or *excluding*; *exp* stands for *expenditures*. For other abbreviations and further explanations, please see the Introduction.

Burlington, VT - continued

Item	Per	Value	Date	Ref.
Transportation				
Motorcycle license fee, duplicate	lic	5.00	1/94	84s
Public transportation expenditures	year	430	91	81r
Tire balance, computer or spin bal., front	wheel	7.50	12/94	2c
Transportation expenditures, total	year	4810	91	81r
Vehicle finance charges	year	238	91	81r
Vehicle insurance expenditures	year	630	91	81r
Vehicle maintenance and repairs expenditures	year	532	91	81r
Vehicle purchases	year	1920	91	81r
Vehicle rental, leases, licenses, etc. expenditures	year	193	91	81r
Vehicles purchased, other than cars and trucks	year	11	91	81r
Utilities				
Utilities, ACCRA Index		110.00	12/94	2c
Electricity expenditures	year	695	91	81r
Electricity, (part.), other, 1800 sq. ft., new home	mo.	52.77	12/94	2c
Fee, water use, industrial	month	1636.31	1/95	16c
Utilities, fuels, and public services, total expenditures	year	1981	91	81r
Water and other public services, expenditures	year	154	91	81r
Weddings				
Bridal attendants' gowns	event	750	10/93	76r
Bridal gown	event	852	10/93	76r
Bridal headpiece and veil	event	167	10/93	76r
Bride's wedding band	event	708	10/93	76r
Clergy	event	224	10/93	76r
Engagement ring	event	2756	10/93	76r
Flowers	event	863	10/93	76r
Formal wear for groom	event	106	10/93	76r
Groom's attendants' formal wear	event	530	10/93	76r
Groom's wedding band	event	402	10/93	76r
Music	event	600	10/93	76r
Photography	event	1088	10/93	76r
Shoes for bride	event	50	10/93	76r
Videography	event	483	10/93	76r
Wedding invitations and announcements	event	342	10/93	76r
Wedding reception	event	7000	10/93	76r

Canton, OH

Item	Per	Value	Date	Ref.
Composite, ACCRA index		104.60	12/94	2c
Alcoholic Beverages				
Beer, Miller Lite, Bud, 12-oz., ex deposit	6	4.09	12/94	2c
J & B Scotch	750-ml.	18.70	12/94	2c
Wine, Gallo Chablis blanc	1.5-lit	5.24	12/94	2c
Appliances				
Appliances (major), expenditures	year	131	91	81r
Average annual exp.				
Food, health care, personal goods, services	year	25935	91	81r
Charity				
Cash contributions, expenditures	year	745	91	81r
Clothing				
Apparel, men and boys, total expenditures	year	332	91	81r
Apparel, women and girls, total expenditures	year	578	91	81r
Footwear, expenditures	year	164	91	81r
Jeans, man's denim		31.39	12/94	2c
Shirt, man's dress shirt		32.75	12/94	2c
Undervest, boy's size 10-14, cotton	3	5.89	12/94	2c
Communications				
Long-distance telephone rate, day, addl. min., 1-10 mi.	min.	0.16	12/93	9s
Long-distance telephone rate, day, initial min., 1-10 mi.	min.	0.32	12/93	9s

Canton, OH - continued

Item	Per	Value	Date	Ref.
Communications - continued				
Newspaper subscription, dly. and Sun. delivery	month	10.65	12/94	2c
Phone line, single, business, field visit	inst	55.42	12/93	9s
Phone line, single, business, no field visit	inst	55.42	12/93	9s
Phone line, single, residence, field visit	inst	30.38	12/93	9s
Phone line, single, residence, no field visit	inst	30.38	12/93	9s
Telephone bill, family of four	month	21.70	12/94	2c
Telephone service, expenditures	year	547	91	81r
Telephone, business, addl. line, touch tone	month	3.25	10/91	25c
Telephone, business, connection charges, touch tone	inst	72.15	10/91	25c
Telephone, business, key system line, touch tone	month	44.71	10/91	25c
Telephone, business, PBX line, touch tone	month	44.84	10/91	25c
Telephone, business, single ln., touch tone	month	41.01	10/91	25c
Telephone, business, touch tone, inside wiring maintenance plan	month	1.50	10/91	25c
Telephone, residential, flat rate	mo.	15.25	12/93	8c
Education				
Board, 4-year private college/university	year	2241	8/94	80s
Board, 4-year public college/university	year	1625	8/94	80s
Education, total expenditures	year	394	91	81r
Room, 4-year private college/university	year	2118	8/94	80s
Room, 4-year public college/university	year	2103	8/94	80s
Total cost, 4-year private college/university	year	15444	8/94	80s
Total cost, 4-year public college/university	year	6987	8/94	80s
Tuition, 2-year public college/university, in-state	year	2076	8/94	80s
Tuition, 4-year private college/university, in-state	year	11085	8/94	80s
Tuition, 4-year public college/university, in-state	year	3259	8/94	80s
Energy and Fuels				
Energy, combined forms, 1800 sq. ft.	mo.	126.13	12/94	2c
Energy, exc. electricity, 1800 sq. ft.	mo.	53.83	12/94	2c
Fuel oil and other fuels, expenditures	year	83	91	81r
Gas, natural, expenditures	year	373	91	81r
Gas, reg unlead, taxes inc., cash, self-service	gal	1.09	12/94	2c
Gasoline and motor oil purchased	year	1000	91	81r
Gasoline, unleaded midgrade	gallon	1.15	4/93	82r
Gasoline, unleaded premium	gallon	1.23	4/93	82r
Gasoline, unleaded regular	gallon	1.07	4/93	82r
Entertainment				
Bowling, evening rate	game	1.46	12/94	2c
Entertainment, total expenditures	year	1356	91	81r
Fees and admissions, expenditures	year	347	91	81r
Monopoly game, Parker Brothers', No. 9	game	11.76	12/94	2c
Movie	adm	6.00	12/94	2c
Pets, toys, playground equipment, expenditures	year	270	91	81r
Reading, expenditures	year	160	91	81r
Televisions, radios, and sound equipment, expenditures	year	433	91	81r
Tennis balls, yellow, Wilson or Penn, 3	can	2.68	12/94	2c
Funerals				
Burial, immediate, container provided by funeral home		1268.31	1/95	54r
Cards, acknowledgment		26.12	1/95	54r
Casket, minimum alternative		198.03	1/95	54r
Cosmetology, hair care, etc.		122.19	1/95	54r
Cremation, direct, container provided by funeral home		977.81	1/95	54r
Embalming		334.00	1/95	54r
Funeral, funeral home		321.16	1/95	54r
Funeral, other facility		317.73	1/95	54r
Graveside service		292.48	1/95	54r
Hearse, local		153.20	1/95	54r
Limousine, local		123.52	1/95	54r
Memorial service		356.30	1/95	54r

Values are in dollars or fractions of dollars. In the column headed *Ref*, references are shown to sources. Each reference is followed by a letter. These refer to the geographical level for which data were reported: s = State, r = Region, and c = City or metro. The abbreviation *ex* is used to mean *except* or *excluding*; *exp* stands for expenditures. For other abbreviations and further explanations, please see the Introduction.

Canton, OH - continued

Item	Per	Value	Date	Ref.
Funerals				
Service charge, professional, nondeclinable		968.24	1/95	54r
Visitation and viewing		332.66	1/95	54r
Groceries				
Groceries, ACCRA Index		97.00	12/94	2c
Apples, Red Delicious	lb.	0.68	12/94	82r
Baby food, strained vegetables, lowest price	4-4.5 oz.	0.35	12/94	2c
Bacon, sliced	lb.	1.88	12/94	82r
Bananas	lb.	0.35	12/94	2c
Bananas	lb.	0.41	12/94	82r
Beef or hamburger, ground	lb.	1.47	12/94	2c
Beef purchases	year	197	91	81r
Beef, stew, boneless	lb.	2.52	12/94	82r
Beverage purchases, alcoholic	year	293	91	81r
Beverage purchases, nonalcoholic	year	203	91	81r
Bologna, all beef or mixed	lb.	2.12	12/94	82r
Bread, white	24-oz.	0.62	12/94	2c
Bread, white, pan	lb.	0.76	12/94	82r
Cabbage	lb.	0.44	12/94	82r
Carrots, short trimmed and topped	lb.	0.44	12/94	82r
Cereals and bakery products purchases	year	347	91	81r
Cereals and cereals products purchases	year	119	91	81r
Cheddar cheese, natural	lb.	3.28	12/94	82r
Cheese, Kraft grated Parmesan	8-oz.	3.10	12/94	2c
Chicken breast, bone-in	lb.	1.61	12/94	82r
Chicken, fresh, whole	lb.	0.89	12/94	82r
Chicken, whole fryer	lb.	0.91	12/94	2c
Chuck roast, USDA choice, boneless	lb.	2.33	12/94	82r
Cigarettes, Winston, Kings	carton	14.86	12/94	2c
Coffee, 100%, ground roast, all sizes	lb.	4.28	12/94	82r
Coffee, vacuum-packed	13 oz.	3.88	12/94	2c
Cookies, chocolate chip	lb.	2.72	12/94	82r
Corn Flakes, Kellogg's or Post Toasties	18 oz.	2.15	12/94	2c
Corn, frozen, whole kernel, lowest price	10 oz.	0.73	12/94	2c
Dairy products (other) purchases	year	148	91	81r
Eggs, Grade A large	dozen	0.69	12/94	2c
Eggs, Grade A large	dozen	0.76	12/94	82r
Fish and seafood purchases	year	61	91	81r
Flour, white, all purpose	lb.	0.22	12/94	82r
Food purchases, food eaten at home	year	2313	91	81r
Foods purchased away from home, not prepared by consumer	year	1709	91	81r
Fruits and vegetables purchases	year	372	91	81r
Grapefruit	lb.	0.47	12/94	82r
Grapes, Thompson seedless	lb.	2.15	12/94	82r
Ground beef, 100% beef	lb.	1.37	12/94	82r
Ground chuck, 100% beef	lb.	1.81	12/94	82r
Ham, boneless, exc. canned	lb.	2.16	12/94	82r
Ice cream, prepackaged, bulk, regular	1/2 gal.	2.48	12/94	82r
Lemons	lb.	1.08	12/94	82r
Lettuce, iceberg	lb.	0.81	12/94	82r
Lettuce, iceberg	head	0.82	12/94	2c
Margarine, Blue Bonnet or Parkay cubes	lb.	0.69	12/94	2c
Margarine, stick	lb.	0.81	12/94	82r
Meats, poultry, fish, and eggs purchases	year	591	91	81r
Milk and cream (fresh) purchases	year	132	91	81r
Milk, whole	1/2 gal.	1.27	12/94	2c
Orange juice, frozen concentrate 12-oz. can	16 oz.	1.41	12/94	82r
Orange juice, Minute Maid frozen	12-oz.	1.17	12/94	2c
Oranges, Navel	lb.	0.56	12/94	82r
Peaches, halves or slices, Hunt's, Del Monte, or Libby's	29-oz.	1.27	12/94	2c
Peanut butter, creamy, all sizes	lb.	1.81	12/94	82r
Peas, sweet, Del Monte or Green Giant	15-17 oz.	0.58	12/94	2c
Pork chops, center cut, bone-in	lb.	2.76	12/94	82r
Pork purchases	year	130	91	81r
Potato chips	16-oz.	2.81	12/94	82r
Potatoes, frozen, French fried	lb.	0.83	12/94	82r
Potatoes, white	lb.	0.28	12/94	2c

Canton, OH - continued

Item	Per	Value	Date	Ref.
Groceries - continued				
Potatoes, white or red	10-lb. sack	1.99	12/94	2c
Round roast, USDA choice, boneless	lb.	2.90	12/94	82r
Sausage, Jimmy Dean, 100% pork	lb.	2.72	12/94	2c
Shortening, vegetable oil blends	lb.	0.88	12/94	82r
Shortening, vegetable, Crisco	3-lb.	2.33	12/94	2c
Soft drink, Coca Cola, ex deposit	2 lit	1.00	12/94	2c
Spaghetti and macaroni	lb.	0.78	12/94	82r
Steak, rib eye, USDA choice, boneless	lb.	6.15	12/94	82r
Steak, round, graded & ungraded, exc. USDA prime & choice	lb.	2.72	12/94	82r
Steak, round, USDA choice, boneless	lb.	3.02	12/94	82r
Steak, sirloin, USDA choice, boneless	lb.	3.85	12/94	82r
Steak, t-bone	lb.	6.15	12/94	2c
Steak, T-bone, USDA choice, bone-in	lb.	5.38	12/94	82r
Sugar and other sweets, eaten at home, expenditures	year	91	91	81r
Sugar, cane or beet	4 lbs.	1.43	12/94	2c
Sugar, white, all sizes	lb.	0.36	12/94	82r
Tobacco products and smoking supplies, total expenditures	year	298	91	81r
Tomatoes, field grown	lb.	1.36	12/94	82r
Tomatoes, Hunt's or Del Monte	14.5 oz.	0.72	12/94	2c
Tuna, chunk, light	lb.	1.94	12/94	82r
Tuna, chunk, light, oil-packed	6.125-6.5 oz.	0.69	12/94	2c
Turkey, frozen, whole	lb.	0.96	12/94	82r
Yogurt, natural, fruit flavored	8 oz.	0.62	12/94	82r
Goods and Services				
Miscellaneous goods and services, ACCRA Index		101.40	12/94	2c
Health Care				
Health care, ACCRA Index		88.50	12/94	2c
Antibiotic ointment, Polysporin	1.5 oz.	3.74	12/94	2c
Childbirth, Cesarean delivery, hospital charge	birth	5101.00	12/91	69r
Childbirth, Cesarean delivery, physician charge	birth	2234.00	12/91	69r
Childbirth, normal delivery, hospital charge	birth	2891.00	12/91	69r
Childbirth, normal delivery, physician charge	birth	1623.00	12/91	69r
Dentist's fee, adult teeth cleaning and periodic oral exam	visit	51.70	12/94	2c
Doctor's fee, routine exam, established patient	visit	37.75	12/94	2c
Drugs, expenditures	year	248	91	81r
Health care, total expenditures	year	1336	91	81r
Health insurance expenditures	year	550	91	81r
Hospital care, semiprivate room	day	229.40	12/94	2c
Insurance premium, family medical care	month	350.73	1/95	41s
Medical services expenditures	year	457	91	81r
Medical supplies expenditures	.year	82	91	81r
Household Goods				
Appl. repair, service call, wash mach	min. lab. chg.	32.57	12/94	2c
Floor coverings, expenditures	year	105	91	81r
Furniture, expenditures	year	291	91	81r
Household equipment, misc. expenditures	year	341	91	81r
Household expenditures, miscellaneous	year	162	91	81r
Household furnishings and equipment, expenditures	year	1042	91	81r
Household operations expenditures	year	365	91	81r
Household textiles, expenditures	year	101	91	81r
Housekeeping supplies, expenditures	year	390	91	81r
Laundry and cleaning supplies, expenditures	year	110	91	81r
Laundry detergent, Tide Ultra, Bold, or Cheer	42 oz.	3.30	12/94	2c
Postage and stationery, expenditures	year	115	91	81r
Tissues, facial, Kleenex brand	175	0.97	12/94	2c

Values are in dollars or fractions of dollars. In the column headed *Ref*, references are shown to sources. Each reference is followed by a letter. These refer to the geographical level for which data were reported: s=State, r=Region, and c=City or metro. The abbreviation *ex* is used to mean *except* or *excluding*; *exp* stands for *expenditures*. For other abbreviations and further explanations, please see the Introduction.

Canton, OH - continued

Item	Per	Value	Date	Ref.
Housing				
Housing, ACCRA Index		115.80	12/94	2c
Add garage/carport		8,479	3/95	74r
Add room(s)		21,347	3/95	74r
Apartment condominium or co-op, median	unit	87100	12/94	62r
Bathroom addition, average cost	add	9734.00	3/95	13r
Bathroom remodeling, average cost	remod	6414.00	3/95	13r
Bedroom, master suite addition, average cost	add	27122.00	3/95	13r
Deck addition, average cost	add	6665.00	3/95	13r
Dwellings (owned), expenditures	year	2566	91	81r
Enclose porch/patio/breezeway		4,556	3/95	74r
Exterior remodeling, average cost	remod	15395.00	3/95	13r
Family room addition, average cost	add	27658.00	3/95	13r
Finish room in basement/attic		5,074	3/95	74r
Home, existing, single-family, median	unit	106500	12/94	62r
Home, existing, single-family, median	unit	80.10	12/94	62c
House payment, principal and interest, 25% down payment	mo.	939	12/94	2c
House, 1800 sq ft, 8000 sq ft lot, new, urban, utilities	total	153237	12/94	2c
Kitchen remodeling, major, average cost	remod	17084.00	3/95	13r
Kitchen remodeling, minor, average cost	remod	5804.00	3/95	13r
Maintenance, repairs, insurance, and other housing expenditures	year	484	91	81r
Mortgage interest and charges expenditures	year	1443	91	81r
Mtge. rate, incl. points and orig. fee, 30-year conv. fixed or ARM	mo.	9.18	12/94	2c
Office, home addition, average cost	add	8121.00	3/95	13r
Princ. & int., mortgage, median-price exist. sing.-family home	mo.	515	12/94	62r
Property taxes expenditures	year	639	91	81r
Redesign, restructure more than half of home's interior		9,114	3/95	74r
Rent, apartment, 2 br., 1 1/2-2 baths, unfurnished, 950 sq ft, water	mo.	462	12/94	2c
Rental units expenditures	year	1200	91	81r
Sun-space addition, average cost	add	23768.00	3/95	13r
Wing addition, two-story, average cost	add	50410.00	3/95	13r
Insurance and Pensions				
Auto insurance, private passenger	year	550.52	12/94	71s
Insurance and pensions, personal, expenditures	year	2408	91	81r
Insurance, life and other personal, expenditures	year	355	91	81r
Pensions and Social Security, expenditures	year	2053	91	81r
Legal Assistance				
Legal work, law firm associate	hour	90		10r
Legal work, law firm partner	hour	139		10r
Personal Goods				
Shampoo, Alberto VO5	15-oz.	1.15	12/94	2c
Toothpaste, Crest or Colgate	6-7 oz.	1.92	12/94	2c
Personal Services				
Dry cleaning, man's 2-pc. suit		6.30	12/94	2c
Haircut, man's barbershop, no styling		7.90	12/94	2c
Haircut, woman's shampoo, trim, blow-dry		20.30	12/94	2c
Personal services expenditures	year	203	91	81r
Restaurant Food				
Chicken, fried, thigh and drumstick		1.91	12/94	2c
Dining expenditures, family	week	30.03	94	73r
Hamburger with cheese	1/4 lb.	1.82	12/94	2c
Pizza, Pizza Hut or Pizza Inn	12-13 in.	8.00	12/94	2c
Taxes				
Taxes, Federal income, expenditures	year	1756	91	81r
Taxes, personal, expenditures	year	2426	91	81r
Taxes, State and local income, expenditures	year	568	91	81r

Canton, OH - continued

Item	Per	Value	Date	Ref.
Transportation				
Transportation, ACCRA Index		99.30	12/94	2c
Bus fare, one-way	trip	0.70	12/95	1c
Cars and trucks purchased, new	year	891	91	81r
Cars and trucks purchased, used	year	1155	91	81r
Driver's learning permit fee	perm	3.00	1/94	84s
Driver's license fee	orig	5.00	1/94	84s
Driver's license fee, duplicate	lic	1.50	1/94	84s
Driver's license reinstatement fee, min.	susp	12.50-100.00	1/94	85s
Driver's license renewal fee	renew	5.00	1/94	84s
Identification card, nondriver	card	2.50	1/94	83s
Motorcycle learning permit fee	perm	3.00	1/94	84s
Motorcycle license fee	orig	5.00	1/94	84s
Motorcycle license fee, duplicate	lic	1.50	1/94	84s
Motorcycle license renewal fee	renew	5.00	1/94	84s
Public transportation expenditures	year	209	91	81r
Tire balance, computer or spin bal., front	wheel	6.96	12/94	2c
Transportation expenditures, total	year	4792	91	81r
Vehicle finance charges	year	300	91	81r
Vehicle insurance expenditures	year	485	91	81r
Vehicle maintenance and repairs expenditures	year	534	91	81r
Vehicle purchases	year	2068	91	81r
Vehicle rental, leases, licenses, etc. expenditures	year	197	91	81r
Vehicles purchased, other than cars and trucks	year	22	91	81r
Utilities				
Utilities, ACCRA Index		112.20	12/94	2c
Electricity expenditures	year	668	91	81r
Electricity, (part.), other, 1800 sq. ft., new home	mo.	72.30	12/94	2c
Electricity, summer, 250 KWh	month	19.32	8/93	64c
Electricity, summer, 500 KWh	month	35.39	8/93	64c
Electricity, summer, 750 KWh	month	51.45	8/93	64c
Electricity, summer, 1000 KWh	month	51.74	8/93	64c
Utilities, fuels, and public services, total expenditures	year	1838	91	81r
Water and other public services, expenditures	year	167	91	81r
Weddings				
Bridal attendants' gowns	event	750	10/93	76r
Bridal gown	event	852	10/93	76r
Bridal headpiece and veil	event	167	10/93	76r
Bride's wedding band	event	708	10/93	76r
Clergy	event	224	10/93	76r
Engagement ring	event	2756	10/93	76r
Flowers	event	863	10/93	76r
Formal wear for groom	event	106	10/93	76r
Groom's attendants' formal wear	event	530	10/93	76r
Groom's wedding band	event	402	10/93	76r
Music	event	600	10/93	76r
Photography	event	1088	10/93	76r
Shoes for bride	event	50	10/93	76r
Videography	event	483	10/93	76r
Wedding invitations and announcements	event	342	10/93	76r
Wedding reception	event	7000	10/93	76r

Carlsbad, NM

Item	Per	Value	Date	Ref.
Composite, ACCRA index		93.50	12/94	2c
Alcoholic Beverages				
Beer, Miller Lite, Bud, 12-oz., ex deposit	6	3.99	12/94	2c
J & B Scotch	750-ml.	16.82	12/94	2c
Wine, Gallo Chablis blanc	1.5-lit	5.49	12/94	2c
Clothing				
Jeans, man's denim		25.66	12/94	2c
Shirt, man's dress shirt		32.00	12/94	2c
Undervest, boy's size 10-14, cotton	3	3.70	12/94	2c

Values are in dollars or fractions of dollars. In the column headed *Ref*, references are shown to sources. Each reference is followed by a letter. These refer to the geographical level for which data were reported: s=State, r=Region, and c=City or metro. The abbreviation *ex* is used to mean *except* or *excluding*; *exp* stands for expenditures. For other abbreviations and further explanations, please see the Introduction.

Carlsbad, NM - continued

Item	Per	Value	Date	Ref.
Communications				
Newspaper subscription, dly. and Sun. delivery	month	8.25	12/94	2c
Telephone bill, family of four	month	20.74	12/94	2c
Energy and Fuels				
Energy, combined forms, 1800 sq. ft.	mo.	69.65	12/94	2c
Gas, reg unlead, taxes inc., cash, self-service	gal	1.20	12/94	2c
Entertainment				
Bowling, evening rate	game	1.90	12/94	2c
Monopoly game, Parker Brothers', No. 9	game	12.16	12/94	2c
Movie	adm	5.00	12/94	2c
Tennis balls, yellow, Wilson or Penn, 3	can	2.25	12/94	2c
Groceries				
Groceries, ACCRA Index		100.10	12/94	2c
Baby food, strained vegetables, lowest price	4-4.5 oz.	0.32	12/94	2c
Bananas	lb.	0.40	12/94	2c
Beef or hamburger, ground	lb.	0.89	12/94	2c
Bread, white	24-oz.	0.68	12/94	2c
Cheese, Kraft grated Parmesan	8-oz.	3.62	12/94	2c
Chicken, whole fryer	lb.	0.70	12/94	2c
Cigarettes, Winston, Kings	carton	15.16	12/94	2c
Coffee, vacuum-packed	13 oz.	3.88	12/94	2c
Corn Flakes, Kellogg's or Post Toasties	18 oz.	2.56	12/94	2c
Corn, frozen, whole kernel, lowest price	10 oz.	0.72	12/94	2c
Eggs, Grade A large	dozen	0.76	12/94	2c
Lettuce, iceberg	head	0.89	12/94	2c
Margarine, Blue Bonnet or Parkay cubes	lb.	0.78	12/94	2c
Milk, whole	1/2 gal.	1.31	12/94	2c
Orange juice, Minute Maid frozen	12-oz.	1.42	12/94	2c
Peaches, halves or slices, Hunt's, Del Monte, or Libby's	29-oz.	1.50	12/94	2c
Peas, sweet, Del Monte or Green Giant	15-17 oz.	0.57	12/94	2c
Potatoes, white or red	10-lb. sack	2.16	12/94	2c
Sausage, Jimmy Dean, 100% pork	lb.	2.21	12/94	2c
Shortening, vegetable, Crisco	3-lb.	2.88	12/94	2c
Soft drink, Coca Cola, ex deposit	2 lit	1.42	12/94	2c
Steak, t-bone	lb.	4.69	12/94	2c
Sugar, cane or beet	4 lbs.	1.79	12/94	2c
Tomatoes, Hunt's or Del Monte	14.5 oz.	0.78	12/94	2c
Tuna, chunk, light, oil-packed	6.125-6.5 oz.	0.78	12/94	2c
Goods and Services				
Miscellaneous goods and services, ACCRA Index		97.80	12/94	2c
Health Care				
Health care, ACCRA Index		100.00	12/94	2c
Antibiotic ointment, Polysporin	1.5 oz.	4.01	12/94	2c
Dentist's fee, adult teeth cleaning and periodic oral exam	visit	65.38	12/94	2c
Doctor's fee, routine exam, established patient	visit	32.91	12/94	2c
Hospital care, semiprivate room	day	344.00	12/94	2c
Household Goods				
Appl. repair, service call, wash mach	min. lab. chg.	32.17	12/94	2c
Laundry detergent, Tide Ultra, Bold, or Cheer	42 oz.	3.26	12/94	2c
Tissues, facial, Kleenex brand	175	1.08	12/94	2c
Housing				
Housing, ACCRA Index		88.40	12/94	2c
House payment, principal and interest, 25% down payment	mo.	699	12/94	2c

Carlsbad, NM - continued

Item	Per	Value	Date	Ref.
Housing - continued				
House, 1800 sq ft, 8000 sq ft lot, new, urban, utilities	total	112000	12/94	2c
Mtge. rate, incl. points and orig. fee, 30-year conv. fixed or ARM	mo.	9.38	12/94	2c
Rent, apartment, 2 br., 1 1/2-2 baths, unfurnished, 950 sq ft, water	mo.	404	12/94	2c
Personal Goods				
Shampoo, Alberto VO5	15-oz.	1.11	12/94	2c
Toothpaste, Crest or Colgate	6-7 oz.	2.03	12/94	2c
Personal Services				
Dry cleaning, man's 2-pc. suit		5.42	12/94	2c
Haircut, man's barbershop, no styling		6.50	12/94	2c
Haircut, woman's shampoo, trim, blow-dry		21.33	12/94	2c
Restaurant Food				
Chicken, fried, thigh and drumstick		2.44	12/94	2c
Hamburger with cheese	1/4 lb.	2.04	12/94	2c
Pizza, Pizza Hut or Pizza Inn	12-13 in.	8.06	12/94	2c
Transportation				
Transportation, ACCRA Index		100.30	12/94	
Tire balance, computer or spin bal., front	wheel	6.17	12/94	2c
Utilities				
Utilities, ACCRA Index		68.00	12/94	2c
Electricity, 1800 sq. ft., new home	mo.	69.65	12/94	2c

Carrollton, GA

Item	Per	Value	Date	Ref.
Composite, ACCRA index		93.50	12/94	2c
Alcoholic Beverages				
Beer, Miller Lite, Bud, 12-oz., ex deposit	6	4.23	12/94	2c
J & B Scotch	750-ml.	19.38	12/94	2c
Wine, Gallo Chablis blanc	1.5-lit	5.00	12/94	2c
Clothing				
Jeans, man's denim		37.00	12/94	2c
Shirt, man's dress shirt		29.50	12/94	2c
Undervest, boy's size 10-14, cotton	3	3.89	12/94	2c
Communications				
Newspaper subscription, dly. and Sun. delivery	month	13.26	12/94	2c
Telephone bill, family of four	month	19.18	12/94	2c
Telephone, residential, flat rate	mo.	11.20	12/93	8c
Energy and Fuels				
Energy, combined forms, 1800 sq. ft.	mo.	126.01	12/94	2c
Energy, exc. electricity, 1800 sq. ft.	mo.	49.55	12/94	2c
Gas, reg unlead, taxes inc., cash, self-service	gal	1.00	12/94	2c
Entertainment				
Bowling, evening rate	game	2.25	12/94	2c
Monopoly game, Parker Brothers', No. 9	game	10.36	12/94	2c
Movie	adm	5.50	12/94	2c
Tennis balls, yellow, Wilson or Penn, 3	can	2.31	12/94	2c
Groceries				
Groceries, ACCRA Index		94.70	12/94	2c
Baby food, strained vegetables, lowest price	4-4.5 oz.	0.31	12/94	2c
Bananas	lb.	0.47	12/94	2c
Beef or hamburger, ground	lb.	1.46	12/94	2c
Bread, white	24-oz.	0.80	12/94	2c
Cheese, Kraft grated Parmesan	8-oz.	3.18	12/94	2c
Chicken, whole fryer	lb.	0.76	12/94	2c
Cigarettes, Winston, Kings	carton	14.18	12/94	2c
Coffee, vacuum-packed	13 oz.	3.21	12/94	2c
Corn Flakes, Kellogg's or Post Toasties	18 oz.	2.27	12/94	2c
Corn, frozen, whole kernel, lowest price	10 oz.	0.62	12/94	2c
Eggs, Grade A large	dozen	0.73	12/94	2c

Values are in dollars or fractions of dollars. In the column headed *Ref*, references are shown to sources. Each reference is followed by a letter. These refer to the geographical level for which data were reported: s = State, r = Region, and c = City or metro. The abbreviation *ex* is used to mean *except* or *excluding*; *exp* stands for expenditures. For other abbreviations and further explanations, please see the Introduction.

Carrollton, GA - continued

Item	Per	Value	Date	Ref.
Groceries				
Lettuce, iceberg	head	0.79	12/94	2c
Margarine, Blue Bonnet or Parkay cubes	lb.	0.54	12/94	2c
Milk, whole	1/2 gal.	1.39	12/94	2c
Orange juice, Minute Maid frozen	12-oz.	1.08	12/94	2c
Peaches, halves or slices, Hunt's, Del Monte, or Libby's	29-oz.	1.29	12/94	2c
Peas, sweet, Del Monte or Green Giant	15-17 oz.	0.47	12/94	2c
Potatoes, white or red	10-lb. sack	1.98	12/94	2c
Sausage, Jimmy Dean, 100% pork	lb.	2.26	12/94	2c
Shortening, vegetable, Crisco	3-lb.	2.63	12/94	2c
Soft drink, Coca Cola, ex deposit	2 lit	1.16	12/94	2c
Steak, t-bone	lb.	4.66	12/94	2c
Sugar, cane or beet	4 lbs.	1.43	12/94	2c
Tomatoes, Hunt's or Del Monte	14.5 oz.	0.62	12/94	2c
Tuna, chunk, light, oil-packed	6.125-6.5 oz.	0.64	12/94	2c
Goods and Services				
Miscellaneous goods and services, ACCRA Index		101.20	12/94	2c
Health Care				
Health care, ACCRA Index		87.80	12/94	2c
Antibiotic ointment, Polysporin	1.5 oz.	3.98	12/94	2c
Antibiotic ointment, Polysporin	1.5 oz.	4.90	12/94	2c
Dentist's fee, adult teeth cleaning and periodic oral exam	visit	48.00	12/94	2c
Dentist's fee, adult teeth cleaning and periodic oral exam	visit	49.80	12/94	2c
Doctor's fee, routine exam, established patient	visit	37.00	12/94	2c
Doctor's fee, routine exam, established patient	visit	37.75	12/94	2c
Hospital care, semiprivate room	day	265.00	12/94	2c
Hospital care, semiprivate room	day	292.00	12/94	2c
Household Goods				
Appl. repair, service call, wash mach	min. lab. chg.	35.00	12/94	2c
Laundry detergent, Tide Ultra, Bold, or Cheer	42 oz.	2.86	12/94	2c
Tissues, facial, Kleenex brand	175	1.04	12/94	2c
Housing				
Housing, ACCRA Index		81.40	12/94	2c
House payment, principal and interest, 25% down payment	mo.	627	12/94	2c
House, 1800 sq ft, 8000 sq ft lot, new, urban, utilities	total	101250	12/94	2c
Mtge. rate, incl. points and orig. fee, 30-year conv. fixed or ARM	mo.	9.29	12/94	2c
Rent, apartment, 2 br., 1 1/2-2 baths, unfurnished, 950 sq ft, water	mo.	418	12/94	2c
Personal Goods				
Shampoo, Alberto VO5	15-oz.	1.05	12/94	2c
Toothpaste, Crest or Colgate	6-7 oz.	1.77	12/94	2c
Personal Services				
Dry cleaning, man's 2-pc. suit		6.80	12/94	2c
Haircut, man's barbershop, no styling		6.67	12/94	2c
Haircut, woman's shampoo, trim, blow-dry		17.50	12/94	2c
Restaurant Food				
Chicken, fried, thigh and drumstick		2.09	12/94	2c
Hamburger with cheese	1/4 lb.	1.85	12/94	2c
Pizza, Pizza Hut or Pizza Inn	12-13 in.	7.99	12/94	2c

Carrollton, GA - continued

Item	Per	Value	Date	Ref.
Transportation				
Transportation, ACCRA Index		90.00	12/94	2c
Tire balance, computer or spin bal., front	wheel	6.19	12/94	2c
Utilities				
Utilities, ACCRA Index		110.40	12/94	2c
Electricity, (part.), other, 1800 sq. ft., new home	mo.	76.46	12/94	2c

Carson City, NV

Item	Per	Value	Date	Ref.
Composite, ACCRA index		105.10	12/94	2c
Alcoholic Beverages				
Beer, Miller Lite, Bud, 12-oz., ex deposit	6	4.10	12/94	2c
J & B Scotch	750-ml.	17.19	12/94	2c
Wine, Gallo Chablis blanc	1.5-lit	4.37	12/94	2c
Clothing				
Jeans, man's denim		29.49	12/94	2c
Shirt, man's dress shirt		28.00	12/94	2c
Undervest, boy's size 10-14, cotton	3	4.29	12/94	2c
Communications				
Newspaper subscription, dly. and Sun. delivery	month	9.02	12/94	2c
Telephone bill, family of four	month	14.41	12/94	2c
Telephone, residential, flat rate	mo.	10.50	12/93	8c
Energy and Fuels				
Energy, combined forms, 1800 sq. ft.	mo.	108.38	12/94	2c
Energy, exc. electricity, 1800 sq. ft.	mo.	55.69	12/94	2c
Gas, cooking, winter, 10 therms	month	11.39	2/94	65c
Gas, cooking, winter, 30 therms	month	22.98	2/94	65c
Gas, cooking, winter, 50 therms	month	34.55	2/94	65c
Gas, heating, winter, 100 therms	month	63.51	2/94	65c
Gas, heating, winter, average use	month	77.99	2/94	65c
Gas, reg unlead, taxes inc., cash, self-service	gal	1.21	12/94	2c
Entertainment				
Bowling, evening rate	game	2.30	12/94	2c
Monopoly game, Parker Brothers', No. 9	game	10.92	12/94	2c
Movie	adm	6.00	12/94	2c
Tennis balls, yellow, Wilson or Penn, 3	can	2.55	12/94	2c
Groceries				
Groceries, ACCRA Index		102.90	12/94	2c
Baby food, strained vegetables, lowest price	4-4.5 oz.	0.35	12/94	2c
Bananas	lb.	0.45	12/94	2c
Beef or hamburger, ground	lb.	1.21	12/94	2c
Bread, white	24-oz.	0.81	12/94	2c
Cheese, Kraft grated Parmesan	8-oz.	3.79	12/94	2c
Chicken, whole fryer	lb.	0.79	12/94	2c
Cigarettes, Winston, Kings	carton	17.45	12/94	2c
Coffee, vacuum-packed	13 oz.	3.81	12/94	2c
Corn Flakes, Kellogg's or Post Toasties	18 oz.	2.70	12/94	2c
Corn, frozen, whole kernel, lowest price	10 oz.	0.68	12/94	2c
Eggs, Grade A large	dozen	0.79	12/94	2c
Lettuce, iceberg	head	0.63	12/94	2c
Margarine, Blue Bonnet or Parkay cubes	lb.	0.71	12/94	2c
Milk, whole	1/2 gal.	1.27	12/94	2c
Orange juice, Minute Maid frozen	12-oz.	1.41	12/94	2c
Peaches, halves or slices, Hunt's, Del Monte, or Libby's	29-oz.	0.99	12/94	2c
Peas, sweet, Del Monte or Green Giant	15-17 oz.	0.61	12/94	2c
Potatoes, white or red	10-lb. sack	1.75	12/94	2c
Sausage, Jimmy Dean, 100% pork	lb.	3.23	12/94	2c
Shortening, vegetable, Crisco	3-lb.	2.84	12/94	2c
Soft drink, Coca Cola, ex deposit	2 lit	1.21	12/94	2c
Steak, t-bone	lb.	4.85	12/94	2c

Values are in dollars or fractions of dollars. In the column headed *Ref*, references are shown to sources. Each reference is followed by a letter. These refer to the geographical level for which data were reported: s=State, r=Region, and c=City or metro. The abbreviation *ex* is used to mean *except* or *excluding*; *exp* stands for *expenditures*. For other abbreviations and further explanations, please see the Introduction.

Carson City, NV - continued

Item	Per	Value	Date	Ref.
Groceries				
Sugar, cane or beet	4 lbs.	1.37	12/94	2c
Tomatoes, Hunt's or Del Monte	14.5 oz.	0.67	12/94	2c
Tuna, chunk, light, oil-packed	6.125-6.5 oz.	0.72	12/94	2c
Goods and Services				
Miscellaneous goods and services, ACCRA Index		101.00	12/94	2c
Health Care				
Health care, ACCRA Index		122.70	12/94	2c
Antibiotic ointment, Polysporin	1.5 oz.	4.35	12/94	2c
Dentist's fee, adult teeth cleaning and periodic oral exam	visit	78.60	12/94	2c
Doctor's fee, routine exam, established patient	visit	42.40	12/94	2c
Hospital care, semiprivate room	day	440.00	12/94	2c
Household Goods				
Appl. repair, service call, wash mach	min. lab. chg.	31.99	12/94	2c
Laundry detergent, Tide Ultra, Bold, or Cheer	42 oz.	3.25	12/94	2c
Tissues, facial, Kleenex brand	175	1.03	12/94	2c
Housing				
Housing, ACCRA Index		109.60	12/94	2c
House payment, principal and interest, 25% down payment	mo.	845	12/94	2c
House, 1800 sq ft, 8000 sq ft lot, new, urban, utilities	total	136776	12/94	2c
Mtge. rate, incl. points and orig. fee, 30-year conv. fixed or ARM	mo.	9.27	12/94	2c
Rent, apartment, 2 br., 1 1/2-2 baths, unfurnished, 950 sq ft, water	mo.	562	12/94	2c
Personal Goods				
Shampoo, Alberto VO5	15-oz.	1.35	12/94	2c
Toothpaste, Crest or Colgate	6-7 oz.	1.95	12/94	2c
Personal Services				
Dry cleaning, man's 2-pc. suit		7.89	12/94	2c
Haircut, man's barbershop, no styling		9.19	12/94	2c
Haircut, woman's shampoo, trim, blow-dry		24.00	12/94	2c
Restaurant Food				
Chicken, fried, thigh and drumstick		2.10	12/94	2c
Hamburger with cheese	1/4 lb.	1.98	12/94	2c
Pizza, Pizza Hut or Pizza Inn	12-13 in.	8.78	12/94	2c
Transportation				
Transportation, ACCRA Index		108.60	12/94	2c
Tire balance, computer or spin bal., front	wheel	7.40	12/94	2c
Utilities				
Utilities, ACCRA Index		93.50	12/94	2c
Electricity, (part.), other, 1800 sq. ft., new home	mo.	52.69	12/94	2c

Casper, WY

Item	Per	Value	Date	Ref.
Composite, ACCRA index		104.00	12/94	2c
Alcoholic Beverages				
Beer, Miller Lite, Bud, 12-oz., ex deposit	6	4.68	12/94	2c
J & B Scotch	750-ml.	18.00	12/94	2c
Wine, Gallo Chablis blanc	1.5-lit	5.47	12/94	2c
Appliances				
Appliances (major), expenditures	year	160	91	81r

Casper, WY - continued

Item	Per	Value	Date	Ref.
Average annual exp.				
Food, health care, personal goods, services	year	32461	91	81r
Charity				
Cash contributions, expenditures	year	975	91	81r
Clothing				
Apparel, men and boys, total expenditures	year	467	91	81r
Apparel, women and girls, total expenditures	year	737	91	81r
Footwear, expenditures	year	270	91	81r
Jeans, man's denim		34.19	12/94	2c
Shirt, man's dress shirt		39.50	12/94	2c
Undervest, boy's size 10-14, cotton	3	5.66	12/94	2c
Communications				
Long-distance telephone rate, day, addl. min., 1-10 mi.	min.	0.09	12/93	9s
Long-distance telephone rate, day, initial min., 1-10 mi.	min.	0.19	12/93	9s
Newspaper subscription, dly. and Sun. delivery	month	12.83	12/94	2c
Phone line, single, business, field visit	inst	86.25	12/93	9s
Phone line, single, business, no field visit	inst	86.25	12/93	9s
Phone line, single, residence, field visit	inst	41.25	12/93	9s
Phone line, single, residence, no field visit	inst	41.25	12/93	9s
Telephone bill, family of four	month	18.97	12/94	2c
Telephone service, expenditures	year	611	91	81r
Telephone, residential, flat rate	mo.	11.96	12/93	8c
Education				
Board, 4-year public college/university	year	1830	8/94	80s
Education, total expenditures	year	375	91	81r
Room, 4-year public college/university	year	1422	8/94	80s
Total cost, 4-year public college/university	year	4900	8/94	80s
Tuition, 4-year public college/university, in-state	year	1648	8/94	80s
Energy and Fuels				
Energy, combined forms, 1800 sq. ft.	mo.	82.77	12/94	2c
Energy, exc. electricity, 1800 sq. ft.	mo.	40.70	12/94	2c
Fuel oil and other fuels, expenditures	year	33	91	81r
Gas, cooking, winter, 10 therms	month	4.43	2/94	65c
Gas, cooking, winter, 30 therms	month	13.30	2/94	65c
Gas, cooking, winter, 50 therms	month	22.17	2/94	65c
Gas, heating, winter, 100 therms	month	44.30	2/94	65c
Gas, heating, winter, average use	month	88.69	2/94	65c
Gas, natural, expenditures	year	212	91	81r
Gas, reg unlead, taxes inc., cash, self-service	gal	1.09	12/94	2c
Gasoline and motor oil purchased	year	1115	91	81r
Gasoline, unleaded midgrade	gallon	1.36	4/93	82r
Gasoline, unleaded premium	gallon	1.43	4/93	82r
Gasoline, unleaded regular	gallon	1.23	4/93	82r
Entertainment				
Bowling, evening rate	game	1.68	12/94	2c
Concert ticket, Pearl Jam group	perf	20.00	94	50r
Entertainment, total expenditures	year	1853	91	81r
Fees and admissions, expenditures	year	482	91	81r
Monopoly game, Parker Brothers', No. 9	game	11.67	12/94	2c
Movie	adm	5.25	12/94	2c
Pets, toys, playground equipment, expenditures	year	299	91	81r
Reading, expenditures	year	164	91	81r
Televisions, radios, and sound equipment, expenditures	year	528	91	81r
Tennis balls, yellow, Wilson or Penn, 3	can	2.73	12/94	2c
Funerals				
Burial, immediate, container provided by funeral home		1360.49	1/95	54r
Cards, acknowledgment		11.24	1/95	54r
Casket, minimum alternative		232.73	1/95	54r
Cosmetology, hair care, etc.		114.13	1/95	54r
Cremation, direct, container provided by funeral home		1027.08	1/95	54r

Values are in dollars or fractions of dollars. In the column headed *Ref*, references are shown to sources. Each reference is followed by a letter. These refer to the geographical level for which data were reported: s = State, r = Region, and c = City or metro. The abbreviation *ex* is used to mean *except* or *excluding*; *exp* stands for *expenditures*. For other abbreviations and further explanations, please see the Introduction.

Casper, WY - continued

Item	Per	Value	Date	Ref.
Funerals				
Embalming		286.24	1/95	54r
Funeral, funeral home		315.60	1/95	54r
Funeral, other facility		303.08	1/95	54r
Graveside service		423.83	1/95	54r
Hearse, local		133.12	1/95	54r
Limousine, local		99.10	1/95	54r
Memorial service		442.57	1/95	54r
Service charge, professional, nondeclinable		840.16	1/95	54r
Visitation and viewing		168.50	1/95	54r
Groceries				
Groceries, ACCRA Index		101.80	12/94	2c
Apples, Red Delicious	lb.	0.72	12/94	82r
Baby food, strained vegetables, lowest price	4-4.5 oz.	0.28	12/94	2c
Bacon, sliced	lb.	1.73	12/94	82r
Bananas	lb.	0.59	12/94	2c
Bananas	lb.	0.52	12/94	82r
Beef or hamburger, ground	lb.	1.39	12/94	2c
Beef purchases	year	241	91	81r
Beverage purchases, alcoholic	year	328	91	81r
Beverage purchases, nonalcoholic	year	234	91	81r
Bologna, all beef or mixed	lb.	2.33	12/94	82r
Bread, white	24-oz.	0.72	12/94	2c
Bread, white, pan	lb.	0.81	12/94	82r
Carrots, short trimmed and topped	lb.	0.43	12/94	82r
Cereals and bakery products purchases	year	392	91	81r
Cereals and cereals products purchases	year	139	91	81r
Cheese, Kraft grated Parmesan	8-oz.	3.32	12/94	2c
Chicken breast, bone-in	lb.	2.04	12/94	82r
Chicken, fresh, whole	lb.	0.95	12/94	82r
Chicken, whole fryer	lb.	0.79	12/94	2c
Cigarettes, Winston, Kings	carton	13.49	12/94	2c
Coffee, 100%, ground roast, all sizes	lb.	4.48	12/94	82r
Coffee, vacuum-packed	13 oz.	3.91	12/94	2c
Corn Flakes, Kellogg's or Post Toasties	18 oz.	2.44	12/94	2c
Corn, frozen, whole kernel, lowest price	10 oz.	0.69	12/94	2c
Dairy products (other) purchases	year	182	91	81r
Eggs, Grade A large	dozen	0.71	12/94	2c
Fish and seafood purchases	year	94	91	81r
Flour, white, all purpose	lb.	0.21	12/94	82r
Food purchases, food eaten at home	year	2749	91	81r
Foods purchased away from home, not prepared by consumer	year	1909	91	81r
Fruits and vegetables purchases	year	459	91	81r
Grapefruit	lb.	0.56	12/94	82r
Ground beef, 100% beef	lb.	1.31	12/94	82r
Ham, boneless, exc. canned	lb.	2.46	12/94	82r
Ice cream, prepackaged, bulk, regular	1/2 gal.	2.57	12/94	82r
Lemons	lb.	1.00	12/94	82r
Lettuce, iceberg	lb.	0.93	12/94	82r
Lettuce, iceberg	head	0.94	12/94	2c
Margarine, Blue Bonnet or Parkay cubes	lb.	0.65	12/94	2c
Meats, poultry, fish, and eggs purchases	year	700	91	81r
Milk and cream (fresh) purchases	year	155	91	81r
Milk, whole	1/2 gal.	1.35	12/94	2c
Orange juice, frozen concentrate 12-oz. can	16 oz.	1.52	12/94	82r
Orange juice, Minute Maid frozen	12-oz.	1.15	12/94	2c
Oranges, Navel	lb.	0.56	12/94	82r
Peaches, halves or slices, Hunt's, Del Monte, or Libby's	29-oz.	1.37	12/94	2c
Peas, sweet, Del Monte or Green Giant	15-17 oz.	0.62	12/94	2c
Pork chops, center cut, bone-in	lb.	3.30	12/94	82r
Pork purchases	year	122	91	81r
Potato chips	16-oz.	3.03	12/94	82r
Potatoes, frozen, French fried	lb.	0.77	12/94	82r
Potatoes, white	lb.	0.35	12/94	82r
Potatoes, white or red	10-lb. sack	1.42	12/94	2c
Rice, white, long grain, uncooked	lb.	0.54	12/94	82r

Casper, WY - continued

Item	Per	Value	Date	Ref.
Groceries - continued				
Round roast, USDA choice, boneless	lb.	2.92	12/94	82r
Sausage, Jimmy Dean, 100% pork	lb.	3.39	12/94	2c
Shortening, vegetable oil blends	lb.	0.80	12/94	82r
Shortening, vegetable, Crisco	3-lb.	2.51	12/94	2c
Soft drink, Coca Cola, ex deposit	2 lit	1.87	12/94	2c
Spaghetti and macaroni	lb.	1.02	12/94	82r
Steak, round, graded & ungraded, exc. USDA prime & choice	lb.	3.13	12/94	82r
Steak, sirloin, USDA choice, boneless	lb.	4.07	12/94	82r
Steak, t-bone	lb.	4.66	12/94	2c
Sugar and other sweets, eaten at home, expenditures	year	105	91	81r
Sugar, cane or beet	4 lbs.	1.41	12/94	2c
Sugar, white, all sizes	lb.	0.38	12/94	82r
Tobacco products and smoking supplies, total expenditures	year	221	91	81r
Tomatoes, field grown	lb.	1.45	12/94	82r
Tomatoes, Hunt's or Del Monte	14.5 oz.	0.65	12/94	2c
Tuna, chunk, light	lb.	2.18	12/94	82r
Tuna, chunk, light, oil-packed	6.125-6.5 oz.	0.76	12/94	2c
Goods and Services				
Miscellaneous goods and services, ACCRA Index		109.10	12/94	2c
Health Care				
Health care, ACCRA Index		101.50	12/94	2c
Antibiotic ointment, Polysporin	1.5 oz.	3.32	12/94	2c
Childbirth, Cesarean delivery, hospital charge	birth	6059.00	12/91	69r
Childbirth, Cesarean delivery, physician charge	birth	2248.00	12/91	69r
Childbirth, normal delivery, hospital charge	birth	3006.00	12/91	69r
Childbirth, normal delivery, physician charge	birth	1634.00	12/91	69r
Dentist's fee, adult teeth cleaning and periodic oral exam	visit	52.75	12/94	2c
Doctor's fee, routine exam, established patient	visit	39.80	12/94	2c
Drugs, expenditures	year	230	91	81r
Health care, total expenditures	year	1544	91	81r
Health insurance expenditures	year	558	91	81r
Hospital care, semiprivate room	day	460.00	12/94	2c
Medical services expenditures	year	676	91	81r
Medical supplies expenditures	year	80	91	81r
Surgery, open-heart	proc	37818.00	1/93	14r
Household Goods				
Appl. repair, service call, wash mach	min. lab. chg.	29.38	12/94	2c
Floor coverings, expenditures	year	79	91	81r
Furniture, expenditures	year	352	91	81r
Household equipment, misc. expenditures	year	614	91	81r
Household expenditures, miscellaneous	year	294	91	81r
Household furnishings and equipment, expenditures	year	1416	91	81r
Household operations expenditures	year	580	91	81r
Household textiles, expenditures	year	113	91	81r
Housekeeping supplies, expenditures	year	447	91	81r
Laundry and cleaning supplies, expenditures	year	114	91	81r
Laundry detergent, Tide Ultra, Bold, or Cheer	42 oz.	3.39	12/94	2c
Postage and stationery, expenditures	year	145	91	81r
Tissues, facial, Kleenex brand	175	1.03	12/94	2c
Housing				
Housing, ACCRA Index		108.80	12/94	2c
Add garage/carport		6,422	3/95	74r
Add room(s)		26,583	3/95	74r
Apartment condominium or co-op, median	unit	105300	12/94	62r
Dwellings (owned), expenditures	year	3932	91	81r

Values are in dollars or fractions of dollars. In the column headed *Ref*, references are shown to sources. Each reference is followed by a letter. These refer to the geographical level for which data were reported: s=State, r=Region, and c=City or metro. The abbreviation *ex* is used to mean *except* or *excluding*; *exp* stands for *expenditures*. For other abbreviations and further explanations, please see the Introduction.

Casper, WY - continued

Item	Per	Value	Date	Ref.
Housing				
Enclose porch/patio/breezeway		5,382	3/95	74r
Finish room in basement/attic		3,911	3/95	74r
Home, existing, single-family, median	unit	178600	12/94	62r
House payment, principal and interest, 25% down payment	mo.	909	12/94	2c
House, 1800 sq ft, 8000 sq ft lot, new, urban, utilities	total	144200	12/94	2c
Maintenance, repairs, insurance, and other housing expenditures	year	591	91	81r
Mortgage interest and charges expenditures	year	2747	91	81r
Mtge. rate, incl. points and orig. fee, 30-year conv. fixed or ARM	mo.	9.49	12/94	2c
Princ. & int., mortgage, median-price exist. sing.-family home	mo.	845	12/94	62r
Property taxes expenditures	year	594	91	81r
Redesign, restructure more than half of home's interior		5,467	3/95	74r
Rent, apartment, 2 br., 1 1/2-2 baths, unfurnished, 950 sq ft, water	mo.	358	12/94	2c
Rental units expenditures	year	2077	91	81r
Insurance and Pensions				
Auto insurance, private passenger	year	531.91	12/94	71s
Insurance and pensions, personal, expenditures	year	3042	91	81r
Insurance, life and other personal, expenditures	year	298	91	81r
Pensions and Social Security, expenditures	year	2744	91	81r
Legal Assistance				
Legal work, law firm associate	hour	91		10r
Legal work, law firm partner	hour	151		10r
Personal Goods				
Shampoo, Alberto VO5	15-oz.	1.32	12/94	2c
Toothpaste, Crest or Colgate	6-7 oz.	2.12	12/94	2c
Personal Services				
Dry cleaning, man's 2-pc. suit		5.91	12/94	2c
Haircut, man's barbershop, no styling		7.75	12/94	2c
Haircut, woman's shampoo, trim, blow-dry		20.00	12/94	2c
Personal services expenditures	year	286	91	81r
Restaurant Food				
Chicken, fried, thigh and drumstick		2.49	12/94	2c
Dining expenditures, family	week	32.25	94	73r
Hamburger with cheese	1/4 lb.	1.88	12/94	2c
Pizza, Pizza Hut or Pizza Inn	12-13 in.	8.39	12/94	2c
Taxes				
Tax, cigarettes	year	609.00	10/93	43s
Taxes, Federal income, expenditures	year	2946	91	81r
Taxes, personal, expenditures	year	3791	91	81r
Taxes, State and local income, expenditures	year	791	91	81r
Transportation				
Transportation, ACCRA Index		99.80	12/94	2c
Cars and trucks purchased, new	year	1231	91	81r
Cars and trucks purchased, used	year	915	91	81r
Driver's learning permit fee	perm	10.00	1/94	84s
Driver's license fee	orig	20.00	1/94	84s
Driver's license fee, duplicate	lic	15.00	1/94	84s
Driver's license reinstatement fee, min.	susp	50.00	1/94	85s
Driver's license renewal fee	renew	15.00	1/94	84s
Identification card, nondriver	card	10.00	1/94	83s
Motorcycle learning permit fee	perm	10.00	1/94	84s
Motorcycle license fee	orig	20.00	1/94	84s
Motorcycle license fee, duplicate	lic	15.00	1/94	84s
Motorcycle license renewal fee	renew	15.00	1/94	84s
Public transportation expenditures	year	375	91	81r
Tire balance, computer or spin bal., front	wheel	6.99	12/94	2c
Transportation expenditures, total	year	5527	91	81r
Vehicle finance charges	year	287	91	81r
Vehicle insurance expenditures	year	624	91	81r

Casper, WY - continued

Item	Per	Value	Date	Ref.
Transportation - continued				
Vehicle maintenance and repairs expenditures	year	695	91	81r
Vehicle purchases	year	2174	91	81r
Vehicle rental, leases, licenses, etc. expenditures	year	257	91	81r
Vehicles purchased, other than cars and trucks	year	28	91	81r
Utilities				
Utilities, ACCRA Index		76.90	12/94	2c
Electricity expenditures	year	616	91	81r
Electricity, (part.), other, 1800 sq. ft., new home	mo.	42.07	12/94	2c
Electricity, summer, 250 KWh	month	15.03	8/93	64c
Electricity, summer, 500 KWh	month	30.03	8/93	64c
Electricity, summer, 750 KWh	month	41.93	8/93	64c
Electricity, summer, 1000 KWh	month	54.56	8/93	64c
Utilities, fuels, and public services, total expenditures	year	1681	91	81r
Water and other public services, expenditures	year	209	91	81r
Weddings				
Bridal attendants' gowns	event	750	10/93	76r
Bridal gown	event	852	10/93	76r
Bridal headpiece and veil	event	167	10/93	76r
Bride's wedding band	event	708	10/93	76r
Clergy	event	224	10/93	76r
Engagement ring	event	2756	10/93	76r
Flowers	event	863	10/93	76r
Formal wear for groom	event	106	10/93	76r
Groom's attendants' formal wear	event	530	10/93	76r
Groom's wedding band	event	402	10/93	76r
Music	event	600	10/93	76r
Photography	event	1088	10/93	76r
Shoes for bride	event	50	10/93	76r
Videography	event	483	10/93	76r
Wedding invitations and announcements	event	342	10/93	76r
Wedding reception	event	7000	10/93	76r

Cedar City, UT

Item	Per	Value	Date	Ref.
Composite, ACCRA index		92.70	12/94	2c
Alcoholic Beverages				
Beer, Miller Lite, Bud, 12-oz., ex deposit	6	4.24	12/94	2c
J & B Scotch	750-ml.	19.95	12/94	2c
Wine, Gallo Chablis blanc	1.5-lit	4.95	12/94	2c
Clothing				
Jeans, man's denim		24.98	12/94	2c
Shirt, man's dress shirt		26.00	12/94	2c
Undervest, boy's size 10-14, cotton	3	3.22	12/94	2c
Communications				
Newspaper subscription, dly. and Sun. delivery	month	10.50	12/94	2c
Telephone bill, family of four	month	13.52	12/94	2c
Telephone, residential, flat rate	mo.	7.98	12/93	8c
Energy and Fuels				
Energy, combined forms, 1800 sq. ft.	mo.	101.30	12/94	2c
Energy, exc. electricity, 1800 sq. ft.	mo.	43.47	12/94	2c
Gas, reg unlead, taxes inc., cash, self-service	gal	1.20	12/94	2c
Entertainment				
Bowling, evening rate	game	2.00	12/94	2c
Monopoly game, Parker Brothers', No. 9	game	12.23	12/94	2c
Movie	adm	5.00	12/94	2c
Tennis balls, yellow, Wilson or Penn, 3	can	1.95	12/94	2c

Values are in dollars or fractions of dollars. In the column headed *Ref*, references are shown to sources. Each reference is followed by a letter. These refer to the geographical level for which data were reported: s = State, r = Region, and c = City or metro. The abbreviation *ex* is used to mean *except* or *excluding*; *exp* stands for expenditures. For other abbreviations and further explanations, please see the Introduction.

Cedar City, UT - continued

Item	Per	Value	Date	Ref.
Groceries				
Groceries, ACCRA Index		101.40	12/94	2c
Baby food, strained vegetables, lowest price	4-4.5 oz.	0.40	12/94	2c
Bananas	lb.	0.38	12/94	2c
Beef or hamburger, ground	lb.	1.22	12/94	2c
Bread, white	24-oz.	0.72	12/94	2c
Cheese, Kraft grated Parmesan	8-oz.	3.82	12/94	2c
Chicken, whole fryer	lb.	0.82	12/94	2c
Cigarettes, Winston, Kings	carton	16.66	12/94	2c
Coffee, vacuum-packed	13 oz.	3.78	12/94	2c
Corn Flakes, Kellogg's or Post Toasties	18 oz.	2.29	12/94	2c
Corn, frozen, whole kernel, lowest price	10 oz.	0.63	12/94	2c
Eggs, Grade A large	dozen	0.78	12/94	2c
Lettuce, iceberg	head	0.68	12/94	2c
Margarine, Blue Bonnet or Parkay cubes	lb.	0.66	12/94	2c
Milk, whole	1/2 gal.	1.55	12/94	2c
Orange juice, Minute Maid frozen	12-oz.	1.16	12/94	2c
Peaches, halves or slices, Hunt's, Del Monte, or Libby's	29-oz.	1.36	12/94	2c
Peas, sweet, Del Monte or Green Giant	15-17 oz.	0.59	12/94	2c
Potatoes, white or red	10-lb. sack	1.69	12/94	2c
Sausage, Jimmy Dean, 100% pork	lb.	3.01	12/94	2c
Shortening, vegetable, Crisco	3-lb.	2.83	12/94	2c
Soft drink, Coca Cola, ex deposit	2 lit	1.19	12/94	2c
Steak, t-bone	lb.	4.26	12/94	2c
Sugar, cane or beet	4 lbs.	1.49	12/94	2c
Tomatoes, Hunt's or Del Monte	14.5 oz.	0.69	12/94	2c
Tuna, chunk, light, oil-packed	6.125-6.5 oz.	0.82	12/94	2c
Goods and Services				
Miscellaneous goods and services, ACCRA Index		93.20	12/94	2c
Health Care				
Health care, ACCRA Index		98.80	12/94	2c
Antibiotic ointment, Polysporin	1.5 oz.	4.69	12/94	2c
Dentist's fee, adult teeth cleaning and periodic oral exam	visit	49.20	12/94	2c
Doctor's fee, routine exam, established patient	visit	40.40	12/94	2c
Hospital care, semiprivate room	day	370.00	12/94	2c
Household Goods				
Appl. repair, service call, wash mach	min. lab. chg.	26.63	12/94	2c
Laundry detergent, Tide Ultra, Bold, or Cheer	42 oz.	3.39	12/94	2c
Tissues, facial, Kleenex brand	175	1.09	12/94	2c
Housing				
Housing, ACCRA Index		84.50	12/94	2c
House payment, principal and interest, 25% down payment	mo.	668	12/94	2c
House, 1800 sq ft, 8000 sq ft lot, new, urban, utilities	total	107400	12/94	2c
Mtge. rate, incl. points and orig. fee, 30-year conv. fixed or ARM	mo.	9.33	12/94	2c
Rent, apartment, 2 br., 1 1/2-2 baths, unfurnished, 950 sq ft, water	mo.	387	12/94	2c
Personal Goods				
Shampoo, Alberto VO5	15-oz.	1.42	12/94	2c
Toothpaste, Crest or Colgate	6-7 oz.	2.40	12/94	2c
Personal Services				
Dry cleaning, man's 2-pc. suit		7.45	12/94	2c
Haircut, man's barbershop, no styling		8.00	12/94	2c
Haircut, woman's shampoo, trim, blow-dry		14.33	12/94	2c

Cedar City, UT - continued

Item	Per	Value	Date	Ref.
Restaurant Food				
Chicken, fried, thigh and drumstick		2.00	12/94	2c
Hamburger with cheese	1/4 lb.	2.09	12/94	2c
Pizza, Pizza Hut or Pizza Inn	12-13 in.	7.99	12/94	2c
Transportation				
Transportation, ACCRA Index		101.70	12/94	2c
Tire balance, computer or spin bal., front	wheel	6.40	12/94	2c
Utilities				
Utilities, ACCRA Index		97.40	12/94	2c
Electricity, (part.), other, 1800 sq. ft., new home	mo.	57.83	12/94	2c

Cedar Rapids, IA

Item	Per	Value	Date	Ref.
Composite, ACCRA index		100.80	12/94	2c
Alcoholic Beverages				
Beer, Miller Lite, Bud, 12-oz., ex deposit	6	3.68	12/94	2c
J & B Scotch	750-ml.	18.83	12/94	2c
Wine, Gallo Chablis blanc	1.5-lit	5.34	12/94	2c
Appliances				
Appliances (major), expenditures	year	131	91	81r
Average annual exp.				
Food, health care, personal goods, services	year	25935	91	81r
Charity				
Cash contributions, expenditures	year	745	91	81r
Clothing				
Apparel, men and boys, total expenditures	year	332	91	81r
Apparel, women and girls, total expenditures	year	578	91	81r
Footwear, expenditures	year	164	91	81r
Jeans, man's denim		29.99	12/94	2c
Shirt, man's dress shirt		34.60	12/94	2c
Undervest, boy's size 10-14, cotton	3	3.72	12/94	2c
Communications				
Long-distance telephone rate, day, addl. min., 1-10 mi.	min.	0.11	12/93	9s
Long-distance telephone rate, day, initial min., 1-10 mi.	min.	0.21	12/93	9s
Newspaper subscription, dly. and Sun. delivery	month	14.52	12/94	2c
Phone line, single, business, field visit	inst	50.00	12/93	9s
Phone line, single, business, no field visit	inst	50.00	12/93	9s
Phone line, single, residence, field visit	inst	35.00	12/93	9s
Phone line, single, residence, no field visit	inst	35.00	12/93	9s
Telephone bill, family of four	month	24.25	12/94	2c
Telephone service, expenditures	year	547	91	81r
Telephone, residential, flat rate	mo.	14.95	12/93	8c
Education				
Board, 4-year private college/university	year	1971	8/94	80s
Board, 4-year public college/university	year	1562	8/94	80s
Education, total expenditures	year	394	91	81r
Room, 4-year private college/university	year	1707	8/94	80s
Room, 4-year public college/university	year	1526	8/94	80s
Total cost, 4-year private college/university	year	14510	8/94	80s
Total cost, 4-year public college/university	year	5440	8/94	80s
Tuition, 2-year public college/university, in-state	year	1612	8/94	80s
Tuition, 4-year private college/university, in-state	year	10832	8/94	80s
Tuition, 4-year public college/university, in-state	year	2352	8/94	80s
Energy and Fuels				
Energy, combined forms, 1800 sq. ft.	mo.	115.14	12/94	2c
Energy, exc. electricity, 1800 sq. ft.	mo.	45.42	12/94	2c
Fuel oil and other fuels, expenditures	year	83	91	81r
Gas, cooking, 10 therms	month	13.00	2/94	65c

Values are in dollars or fractions of dollars. In the column headed *Ref*, references are shown to sources. Each reference is followed by a letter. These refer to the geographical level for which data were reported: s=State, r=Region, and c=City or metro. The abbreviation *ex* is used to mean *except* or *excluding*; *exp* stands for expenditures. For other abbreviations and further explanations, please see the Introduction.

Cedar Rapids, IA - continued

Item	Per	Value	Date	Ref.
Energy and Fuels				
Gas, cooking, 30 therms	month	22.01	2/94	65c
Gas, cooking, 50 therms	month	31.01	2/94	65c
Gas, natural, expenditures	year	373	91	81r
Gas, reg unlead, taxes inc., cash, self-service	gal	1.21	12/94	2c
Gasoline and motor oil purchased	year	1000	91	81r
Gasoline, unleaded midgrade	gallon	1.15	4/93	82r
Gasoline, unleaded premium	gallon	1.23	4/93	82r
Gasoline, unleaded regular	gallon	1.07	4/93	82r
Entertainment				
Bowling, evening rate	game	1.98	12/94	2c
Entertainment, total expenditures	year	1356	91	81r
Fees and admissions, expenditures	year	347	91	81r
Monopoly game, Parker Brothers', No. 9	game	11.04	12/94	2c
Movie	adm	5.75	12/94	2c
Pets, toys, playground equipment, expenditures	year	270	91	81r
Reading, expenditures	year	160	91	81r
Televisions, radios, and sound equipment, expenditures	year	433	91	81r
Tennis balls, yellow, Wilson or Penn, 3	can	2.29	12/94	2c
Funerals				
Burial, immediate, container provided by funeral home		1348.78	1/95	54r
Cards, acknowledgment		21.20	1/95	54r
Casket, minimum alternative		182.83	1/95	54r
Cosmetology, hair care, etc.		133.11	1/95	54r
Cremation, direct, container provided by funeral home		1101.95	1/95	54r
Embalming		314.45	1/95	54r
Funeral, funeral home		304.88	1/95	54r
Funeral, other facility		301.37	1/95	54r
Graveside service		290.59	1/95	54r
Hearse, local		137.37	1/95	54r
Limousine, local		82.84	1/95	54r
Memorial service		316.57	1/95	54r
Service charge, professional, nondeclinable		1099.00	1/95	54r
Visitation and viewing		209.25	1/95	54r
Groceries				
Groceries, ACCRA Index		93.70	12/94	2c
Apples, Red Delicious	lb.	0.68	12/94	82r
Baby food, strained vegetables, lowest price	4-4.5 oz.	0.36	12/94	2c
Bacon, sliced	lb.	1.88	12/94	82r
Bananas	lb.	0.36	12/94	2c
Bananas	lb.	0.41	12/94	82r
Beef or hamburger, ground	lb.	1.15	12/94	2c
Beef purchases	year	197	91	81r
Beef, stew, boneless	lb.	2.52	12/94	82r
Beverage purchases, alcoholic	year	293	91	81r
Beverage purchases, nonalcoholic	year	203	91	81r
Bologna, all beef or mixed	lb.	2.12	12/94	82r
Bread, white	24-oz.	0.61	12/94	2c
Bread, white, pan	lb.	0.76	12/94	82r
Cabbage	lb.	0.44	12/94	82r
Carrots, short trimmed and topped	lb.	0.44	12/94	82r
Cereals and bakery products purchases	year	347	91	81r
Cereals and cereals products purchases	year	119	91	81r
Cheddar cheese, natural	lb.	3.28	12/94	82r
Cheese, Kraft grated Parmesan	8-oz.	3.30	12/94	2c
Chicken breast, bone-in	lb.	1.61	12/94	82r
Chicken, fresh, whole	lb.	0.89	12/94	82r
Chicken, whole fryer	lb.	0.83	12/94	2c
Chuck roast, USDA choice, boneless	lb.	2.33	12/94	82r
Cigarettes, Winston, Kings	carton	16.01	12/94	2c
Coffee, 100% ground roast, all sizes	lb.	4.28	12/94	82r
Coffee, vacuum-packed	13 oz.	3.23	12/94	2c
Cookies, chocolate chip	lb.	2.72	12/94	82r
Corn Flakes, Kellogg's or Post Toasties	18 oz.	2.24	12/94	2c
Corn, frozen, whole kernel, lowest price	10 oz.	0.76	12/94	2c
Dairy products (other) purchases	year	148	91	81r

Cedar Rapids, IA - continued

Item	Per	Value	Date	Ref.
Groceries - continued				
Eggs, Grade A large	dozen	0.68	12/94	2c
Eggs, Grade A large	dozen	0.76	12/94	82r
Fish and seafood purchases	year	61	91	81r
Flour, white, all purpose	lb.	0.22	12/94	82r
Food purchases, food eaten at home	year	2313	91	81r
Foods purchased away from home, not prepared by consumer	year	1709	91	81r
Fruits and vegetables purchases	year	372	91	81r
Grapefruit	lb.	0.47	12/94	82r
Grapes, Thompson seedless	lb.	2.15	12/94	82r
Ground beef, 100% beef	lb.	1.37	12/94	82r
Ground chuck, 100% beef	lb.	1.81	12/94	82r
Ham, boneless, exc. canned	lb.	2.16	12/94	82r
Ice cream, prepackaged, bulk, regular	1/2 gal.	2.48	12/94	82r
Lemons	lb.	1.08	12/94	82r
Lettuce, iceberg	lb.	0.81	12/94	82r
Lettuce, iceberg	head	0.67	12/94	2c
Margarine, Blue Bonnet or Parkay cubes	lb.	0.53	12/94	2c
Margarine, stick	lb.	0.81	12/94	82r
Meats, poultry, fish, and eggs purchases	year	591	91	81r
Milk and cream (fresh) purchases	year	132	91	81r
Milk, whole	1/2 gal.	1.25	12/94	2c
Orange juice, frozen concentrate 12-oz. can	16 oz.	1.41	12/94	82r
Orange juice, Minute Maid frozen	12-oz.	1.30	12/94	2c
Oranges, Navel	lb.	0.56	12/94	82r
Peaches, halves or slices, Hunt's, Del Monte, or Libby's	29-oz.	1.31	12/94	2c
Peanut butter, creamy, all sizes	lb.	1.81	12/94	82r
Peas, sweet, Del Monte or Green Giant	15-17 oz.	0.52	12/94	2c
Pork chops, center cut, bone-in	lb.	2.76	12/94	82r
Pork purchases	year	130	91	81r
Potato chips	16-oz.	2.81	12/94	82r
Potatoes, frozen, French fried	lb.	0.83	12/94	82r
Potatoes, white	lb.	0.28	12/94	82r
Potatoes, white or red	10-lb. sack	2.09	12/94	2c
Round roast, USDA choice, boneless	lb.	2.90	12/94	82r
Sausage, Jimmy Dean, 100% pork	lb.	2.51	12/94	2c
Shortening, vegetable oil blends	lb.	0.88	12/94	82r
Shortening, vegetable, Crisco	3-lb.	2.55	12/94	2c
Soft drink, Coca Cola, ex deposit	2 lit	1.29	12/94	2c
Spaghetti and macaroni	lb.	0.78	12/94	82r
Steak, rib eye, USDA choice, boneless	lb.	6.15	12/94	82r
Steak, round, graded & ungraded, exc. USDA prime & choice	lb.	2.72	12/94	82r
Steak, round, USDA choice, boneless	lb.	3.02	12/94	82r
Steak, sirloin, USDA choice, boneless	lb.	3.85	12/94	82r
Steak, t-bone	lb.	4.35	12/94	2c
Steak, T-bone, USDA choice, bone-in	lb.	5.38	12/94	82r
Sugar and other sweets, eaten at home, expenditures	year	91	91	81r
Sugar, cane or beet	4 lbs.	1.41	12/94	2c
Sugar, white, all sizes	lb.	0.36	12/94	82r
Tobacco products and smoking supplies, total expenditures	year	298	91	81r
Tomatoes, field grown	lb.	1.36	12/94	82r
Tomatoes, Hunt's or Del Monte	14.5 oz.	0.70	12/94	2c
Tuna, chunk, light	lb.	1.94	12/94	82r
Tuna, chunk, light, oil-packed	6.125-6.5 oz.	0.66	12/94	2c
Turkey, frozen, whole	lb.	0.96	12/94	82r
Yogurt, natural, fruit flavored	8 oz.	0.62	12/94	82r
Goods and Services				
Miscellaneous goods and services, ACCRA Index		102.40	12/94	2c

Values are in dollars or fractions of dollars. In the column headed *Ref*, references are shown to sources. Each reference is followed by a letter. These refer to the geographical level for which data were reported: s = State, r = Region, and c = City or metro. The abbreviation *ex* is used to mean *except* or *excluding*; *exp* stands for *expenditures*. For other abbreviations and further explanations, please see the Introduction.

Cedar Rapids, IA - continued

Item	Per	Value	Date	Ref.
Health Care				
Health care, ACCRA Index		92.40	12/94	2c
Antibiotic ointment, Polysporin	1.5 oz.	3.55	12/94	2c
Childbirth, Cesarean delivery, hospital charge	birth	5101.00	12/91	69r
Childbirth, Cesarean delivery, physician charge	birth	2234.00	12/91	69r
Childbirth, normal delivery, hospital charge	birth	2891.00	12/91	69r
Childbirth, normal delivery, physician charge	birth	1623.00	12/91	69r
Dentist's fee, adult teeth cleaning and periodic oral exam	visit	48.80	12/94	2c
Doctor's fee, routine exam, established patient	visit	38.72	12/94	2c
Drugs, expenditures	year	248	91	81r
Health care, total expenditures	year	1336	91	81r
Health insurance expenditures	year	550	91	81r
Hospital care, semiprivate room	day	338.50	12/94	2c
Insurance premium, family medical care	month	395.98	1/95	41s
Medical services expenditures	year	457	91	81r
Medical supplies expenditures	year	82	91	81r
Household Goods				
Appl. repair, service call, wash mach	min. lab. chg.	34.36	12/94	2c
Floor coverings, expenditures	year	105	91	81r
Furniture, expenditures	year	291	91	81r
Household equipment, misc. expenditures	year	341	91	81r
Household expenditures, miscellaneous	year	162	91	81r
Household furnishings and equipment, expenditures	year	1042	91	81r
Household operations expenditures	year	365	91	81r
Household textiles, expenditures	year	101	91	81r
Housekeeping supplies, expenditures	year	390	91	81r
Laundry and cleaning supplies, expenditures	year	110	91	81r
Laundry detergent, Tide Ultra, Bold, or Cheer	42 oz.	2.75	12/94	2c
Postage and stationery, expenditures	year	115	91	81r
Tissues, facial, Kleenex brand	175	1.01	12/94	2c
Housing				
Housing, ACCRA Index		103.30	12/94	2c
Add garage/carport		8,479	3/95	74r
Add room(s)		21,347	3/95	74r
Apartment condominium or co-op, median	unit	87100	12/94	62r
Bathroom addition, average cost	add	9734.00	3/95	13r
Bathroom remodeling, average cost	remod	6414.00	3/95	13r
Bedroom, master suite addition, average cost	add	27122.00	3/95	13r
Deck addition, average cost	add	6665.00	3/95	13r
Dwellings (owned), expenditures	year	2566	91	81r
Enclose porch/patio/breezeway		4,556	3/95	74r
Exterior remodeling, average cost	remod	15395.00	3/95	13r
Family room addition, average cost	add	27658.00	3/95	13r
Finish room in basement/attic		5,074	3/95	74r
Home, existing, single-family, median	unit	106500	12/94	62r
Home, existing, single-family, median	unit	84.90	12/94	62c
House payment, principal and interest, 25% down payment	mo.	819	12/94	2c
House, 1800 sq ft, 8000 sq ft lot, new, urban, utilities	total	130592	12/94	2c
Kitchen remodeling, major, average cost	remod	17084.00	3/95	13r
Kitchen remodeling, minor, average cost	remod	5804.00	3/95	13r
Maintenance, repairs, insurance, and other housing expenditures	year	484	91	81r
Mortgage interest and charges expenditures	year	1443	91	81r
Mtge. rate, incl. points and orig. fee, 30-year conv. fixed or ARM	mo.	9.43	12/94	2c
Office, home addition, average cost	add	8121.00	3/95	13r
Princ. & int., mortgage, median-price exist. sing.-family home	mo.	515	12/94	62c
Property taxes expenditures	year	639	91	81r

Cedar Rapids, IA - continued

Item	Per	Value	Date	Ref.
Housing - continued				
Redesign, restructure more than half of home's interior		9,114	3/95	74r
Rent, apartment, 2 br., 1 1/2-2 baths, unfurnished, 950 sq ft, water	mo.	467	12/94	2c
Rental units expenditures	year	1200	91	81r
Sun-space addition, average cost	add	23768.00	3/95	13r
Wing addition, two-story, average cost	add	50410.00	3/95	13r
Insurance and Pensions				
Auto insurance, private passenger	year	467.45	12/94	71s
Insurance and pensions, personal, expenditures	year	2408	91	81r
Insurance, life and other personal, expenditures	year	355	91	81r
Pensions and Social Security, expenditures	year	2053	91	81r
Legal Assistance				
Legal work, law firm associate	hour	90		10r
Legal work, law firm partner	hour	139		10r
Personal Goods				
Shampoo, Alberto VO5	15-oz.	1.29	12/94	2c
Toothpaste, Crest or Colgate	6-7 oz.	1.84	12/94	2c
Personal Services				
Dry cleaning, man's 2-pc. suit		6.66	12/94	2c
Haircut, man's barbershop, no styling		7.90	12/94	2c
Haircut, woman's shampoo, trim, blow-dry		18.69	12/94	2c
Personal services expenditures	year	203	91	81r
Restaurant Food				
Chicken, fried, thigh and drumstick		2.32	12/94	2c
Dining expenditures, family	week	30.03	94	73r
Hamburger with cheese	1/4 lb.	1.99	12/94	2c
Pizza, Pizza Hut or Pizza Inn	12-13 in.	7.79	12/94	2c
Taxes				
Taxes, Federal income, expenditures	year	1756	91	81r
Taxes, personal, expenditures	year	2426	91	81r
Taxes, State and local income, expenditures	year	568	91	81r
Transportation				
Transportation, ACCRA Index		101.50	12/94	2c
Cars and trucks purchased, new	year	891	91	81r
Cars and trucks purchased, used	year	1155	91	81r
Driver's learning permit fee	perm	6.00	1/94	84s
Driver's license fee	orig	0.00	1/94	84s
Driver's license fee, duplicate	lic	3.00	1/94	84s
Driver's license reinstatement fee, min.	susp	20.00	1/94	85s
Driver's license renewal fee	renew	0.00	1/94	84s
Identification card, nondriver	card	5.00	1/94	83s
Motorcycle learning permit fee	perm	8.00	1/94	84s
Motorcycle license fee	orig	8.00	1/94	84s
Motorcycle license fee, duplicate	lic	3.00	1/94	84s
Motorcycle license renewal fee	renew	8.00	1/94	84s
Public transportation expenditures	year	209	91	81r
Tire balance, computer or spin bal., front	wheel	6.30	12/94	2c
Transportation expenditures, total	year	4792	91	81r
Vehicle finance charges	year	300	91	81r
Vehicle insurance expenditures	year	485	91	81r
Vehicle maintenance and repairs expenditures	year	534	91	81r
Vehicle purchases	year	2068	91	81r
Vehicle rental, leases, licenses, etc. expenditures	year	197	91	81r
Vehicles purchased, other than cars and trucks	year	22	91	81r
Utilities				
Utilities, ACCRA Index		105.50	12/94	2c
Electricity expenditures	year	668	91	81r
Electricity, (part.), other, 1800 sq. ft., new home	mo.	69.72	12/94	2c
Electricity, summer, 250 KWh	month	36.83	8/93	64c
Electricity, summer, 500 KWh	month	64.65	8/93	64c

Values are in dollars or fractions of dollars. In the column headed *Ref*, references are shown to sources. Each reference is followed by a letter. These refer to the geographical level for which data were reported: s = State, r = Region, and c = City or metro. The abbreviation *ex* is used to mean *except* or *excluding*; *exp* stands for expenditures. For other abbreviations and further explanations, please see the Introduction.

Cedar Rapids, IA - continued

Item	Per	Value	Date	Ref.
Utilities				
Electricity, summer, 750 KWh	month	90.43	8/93	64c
Electricity, summer, 1000 KWh	month	116.20	8/93	64c
Utilities, fuels, and public services, total expenditures	year	1838	91	81r
Water and other public services, expenditures	year	167	91	81r
Weddings				
Bridal attendants' gowns	event	750	10/93	76r
Bridal gown	event	852	10/93	76r
Bridal headpiece and veil	event	167	10/93	76r
Bride's wedding band	event	708	10/93	76r
Clergy	event	224	10/93	76r
Engagement ring	event	2756	10/93	76r
Flowers	event	863	10/93	76r
Formal wear for groom	event	106	10/93	76r
Groom's attendants' formal wear	event	530	10/93	76r
Groom's wedding band	event	402	10/93	76r
Music	event	600	10/93	76r
Photography	event	1088	10/93	76r
Shoes for bride	event	50	10/93	76r
Videography	event	483	10/93	76r
Wedding invitations and announcements	event	342	10/93	76r
Wedding reception	event	7000	10/93	76r

Champaign-Urbana, IL

Item	Per	Value	Date	Ref.
Composite, ACCRA index		102.30	12/94	2c
Alcoholic Beverages				
Beer, Miller Lite, Bud, 12-oz., ex deposit	6	3.94	12/94	2c
J & B Scotch	750-ml.	14.99	12/94	2c
Wine, Gallo Chablis blanc	1.5-lit	4.19	12/94	2c
Appliances				
Appliances (major), expenditures	year	131	91	81r
Average annual exp.				
Food, health care, personal goods, services	year	25935	91	81r
Charity				
Cash contributions, expenditures	year	745	91	81r
Clothing				
Apparel, men and boys, total expenditures	year	332	91	81r
Apparel, women and girls, total expenditures	year	578	91	81r
Footwear, expenditures	year	164	91	81r
Jeans, man's denim		29.49	12/94	2c
Shirt, man's dress shirt		34.00	12/94	2c
Undervest, boy's size 10-14, cotton	3	4.85	12/94	2c
Communications				
Long-distance telephone rate, day, addl. min., 1-10 mi.	min.	0.04	12/93	9s
Long-distance telephone rate, day, initial min., 1-10 mi.	min.	0.10	12/93	9s
Newspaper subscription, dly. and Sun. delivery	month	12.61	12/94	2c
Phone line, single, business, field visit	inst	84.50	12/93	9s
Phone line, single, business, no field visit	inst	84.50	12/93	9s
Phone line, single, residence, field visit	inst	55.00	12/93	9s
Phone line, single, residence, no field visit	inst	55.00	12/93	9s
Telephone bill, family of four	month	20.94	12/94	2c
Telephone service, expenditures	year	547	91	81r
Telephone, residential, flat rate	mo.	9.00	12/93	8c
Education				
Board, 4-year private college/university	year	2078	8/94	80s
Board, 4-year public college/university	year	2139	8/94	80s
Education, total expenditures	year	394	91	81r
Room, 4-year private college/university	year	2696	8/94	80s
Room, 4-year public college/university	year	1796	8/94	80s
Total cost, 4-year private college/university	year	15249	8/94	80s
Total cost, 4-year public college/university	year	6964	8/94	80s

Champaign-Urbana, IL - continued

Item	Per	Value	Date	Ref.
Education - continued				
Tuition, 2-year public college/university, in-state	year	1135	8/94	80s
Tuition, 4-year private college/university, in-state	year	10474	8/94	80s
Tuition, 4-year public college/university, in-state	year	3029	8/94	80s
Energy and Fuels				
Energy, combined forms, 1800 sq. ft.	mo.	122.08	12/94	2c
Energy, exc. electricity, 1800 sq. ft.	mo.	44.80	12/94	2c
Fuel oil and other fuels, expenditures	year	83	91	81r
Gas, natural, expenditures	year	373	91	81r
Gas, reg unlead, taxes inc., cash, self-service	gal	1.09	12/94	2c
Gasoline and motor oil purchased	year	1000	91	81r
Gasoline, unleaded midgrade	gallon	1.15	4/93	82r
Gasoline, unleaded premium	gallon	1.23	4/93	82r
Gasoline, unleaded regular	gallon	1.07	4/93	82r
Entertainment				
Bowling, evening rate	game	2.55	12/94	2c
Entertainment, total expenditures	year	1356	91	81r
Fees and admissions, expenditures	year	347	91	81r
Monopoly game, Parker Brothers', No. 9	game	9.98	12/94	2c
Movie	adm	5.44	12/94	2c
Pets, toys, playground equipment, expenditures	year	270	91	81r
Reading, expenditures	year	160	91	81r
Televisions, radios, and sound equipment, expenditures	year	433	91	81r
Tennis balls, yellow, Wilson or Penn, 3	can	2.52	12/94	2c
Funerals				
Burial, immediate, container provided by funeral home		1268.31	1/95	54r
Cards, acknowledgment		26.12	1/95	54r
Casket, minimum alternative		198.03	1/95	54r
Cosmetology, hair care, etc.		122.19	1/95	54r
Cremation, direct, container provided by funeral home		977.81	1/95	54r
Embalming		334.00	1/95	54r
Funeral, funeral home		321.16	1/95	54r
Funeral, other facility		317.73	1/95	54r
Graveside service		292.48	1/95	54r
Hearse, local		153.20	1/95	54r
Limousine, local		123.52	1/95	54r
Memorial service		356.30	1/95	54r
Service charge, professional, nondeclinable		968.24	1/95	54r
Visitation and viewing		332.66	1/95	54r
Groceries				
Groceries, ACCRA Index		102.90	12/94	2c
Apples, Red Delicious	lb.	0.68	12/94	82r
Baby food, strained vegetables, lowest price	4-4.5 oz.	0.37	12/94	2c
Bacon, sliced	lb.	1.88	12/94	82r
Bananas	lb.	0.52	12/94	2c
Bananas	lb.	0.41	12/94	82r
Beef or hamburger, ground	lb.	1.15	12/94	2c
Beef purchases	year	197	91	81r
Beef, stew, boneless	lb.	2.52	12/94	82r
Beverage purchases, alcoholic	year	293	91	81r
Beverage purchases, nonalcoholic	year	203	91	81r
Bologna, all beef or mixed	lb.	2.12	12/94	82r
Bread, white	24-oz.	0.64	12/94	2c
Bread, white, pan	lb.	0.76	12/94	82r
Cabbage	lb.	0.44	12/94	82r
Carrots, short trimmed and topped	lb.	0.44	12/94	82r
Cereals and bakery products purchases	year	347	91	81r
Cereals and cereals products purchases	year	119	91	81r
Cheddar cheese, natural	lb.	3.28	12/94	82r
Cheese, Kraft grated Parmesan	8-oz.	3.20	12/94	2c
Chicken breast, bone-in	lb.	1.61	12/94	82r
Chicken, fresh, whole	lb.	0.89	12/94	82r

Values are in dollars or fractions of dollars. In the column headed *Ref*, references are shown to sources. Each reference is followed by a letter. These refer to the geographical level for which data were reported: s=State, r=Region, and c=City or metro. The abbreviation *ex* is used to mean *except* or *excluding*; *exp* stands for expenditures. For other abbreviations and further explanations, please see the Introduction.

Champaign-Urbana, IL - continued

Item	Per	Value	Date	Ref.
Groceries				
Chicken, whole fryer	lb.	0.71	12/94	2c
Chuck roast, USDA choice, boneless	lb.	2.33	12/94	82r
Cigarettes, Winston, Kings	carton	18.14	12/94	2c
Coffee, 100%, ground roast, all sizes	lb.	4.28	12/94	82r
Coffee, vacuum-packed	13 oz.	3.55	12/94	2c
Cookies, chocolate chip	lb.	2.72	12/94	82r
Corn Flakes, Kellogg's or Post Toasties	18 oz.	2.30	12/94	2c
Corn, frozen, whole kernel, lowest price	10 oz.	0.68	12/94	2c
Dairy products (other) purchases	year	148	91	81r
Eggs, Grade A large	dozen	0.78	12/94	2c
Eggs, Grade A large	dozen	0.76	12/94	82r
Fish and seafood purchases	year	61	91	81r
Flour, white, all purpose	lb.	0.22	12/94	82r
Food purchases, food eaten at home	year	2313	91	81r
Foods purchased away from home, not prepared by consumer	year	1709	91	81r
Fruits and vegetables purchases	year	372	91	81r
Grapefruit	lb.	0.47	12/94	82r
Grapes, Thompson seedless	lb.	2.15	12/94	82r
Ground beef, 100% beef	lb.	1.37	12/94	82r
Ground chuck, 100% beef	lb.	1.81	12/94	82r
Ham, boneless, exc. canned	lb.	2.16	12/94	82r
Ice cream, prepackaged, bulk, regular	1/2 gal.	2.48	12/94	82r
Lemons	lb.	1.08	12/94	82r
Lettuce, iceberg	lb.	0.81	12/94	82r
Lettuce, iceberg	head	0.85	12/94	2c
Margarine, Blue Bonnet or Parkay cubes	lb.	0.71	12/94	2c
Margarine, stick	lb.	0.81	12/94	82r
Meats, poultry, fish, and eggs purchases	year	591	91	81r
Milk and cream (fresh) purchases	year	132	91	81r
Milk, whole	1/2 gal.	1.66	12/94	2c
Orange juice, frozen concentrate 12-oz. can	16 oz.	1.41	12/94	82r
Orange juice, Minute Maid frozen	12-oz.	1.38	12/94	2c
Oranges, Navel	lb.	0.56	12/94	82r
Peaches, halves or slices, Hunt's, Del Monte, or Libby's	29-oz.	1.49	12/94	2c
Peanut butter, creamy, all sizes	lb.	1.81	12/94	82r
Peas, sweet, Del Monte or Green Giant	15-17 oz.	0.56	12/94	2c
Pork chops, center cut, bone-in	lb.	2.76	12/94	82r
Pork purchases	year	130	91	81r
Potato chips	16-oz.	2.81	12/94	82r
Potatoes, frozen, French fried	lb.	0.83	12/94	82r
Potatoes, white	lb.	0.28	12/94	82r
Potatoes, white or red	10-lb. sack	2.57	12/94	2c
Round roast, USDA choice, boneless	lb.	2.90	12/94	82r
Sausage, Jimmy Dean, 100% pork	lb.	2.85	12/94	2c
Shortening, vegetable oil blends	lb.	0.88	12/94	82r
Shortening, vegetable, Crisco	3-lb.	2.54	12/94	2c
Soft drink, Coca Cola, ex deposit	2 lit	1.21	12/94	2c
Spaghetti and macaroni	lb.	0.78	12/94	82r
Steak, rib eye, USDA choice, boneless	lb.	6.15	12/94	82r
Steak, round, graded & ungraded, exc. USDA prime & choice	lb.	2.72	12/94	82r
Steak, round, USDA choice, boneless	lb.	3.02	12/94	82r
Steak, sirloin, USDA choice, boneless	lb.	3.85	12/94	82r
Steak, t-bone	lb.	5.77	12/94	2c
Steak, T-bone, USDA choice, bone-in	lb.	5.38	12/94	82r
Sugar and other sweets, eaten at home, expenditures	year	91	91	81r
Sugar, cane or beet	4 lbs.	1.38	12/94	2c
Sugar, white, all sizes	lb.	0.36	12/94	82r
Tobacco products and smoking supplies, total expenditures	year	298	91	81r
Tomatoes, field grown	lb.	1.36	12/94	82r
Tomatoes, Hunt's or Del Monte	14.5 oz.	0.78	12/94	2c
Tuna, chunk, light	lb.	1.94	12/94	82r

Item	Per	Value	Date	Ref.
Groceries - continued				
Tuna, chunk, light, oil-packed	6.125-6.5 oz.	0.77	12/94	2c
Turkey, frozen, whole	lb.	0.96	12/94	82r
Yogurt, natural, fruit flavored	8 oz.	0.62	12/94	82r
Goods and Services				
Miscellaneous goods and services, ACCRA Index		102.90	12/94	2c
Health Care				
Health care, ACCRA Index		106.00	12/94	2c
Antibiotic ointment, Polysporin	1.5 oz.	4.42	12/94	2c
Childbirth, Cesarean delivery, hospital charge	birth	5101.00	12/91	69r
Childbirth, Cesarean delivery, physician charge	birth	2234.00	12/91	69r
Childbirth, normal delivery, hospital charge	birth	2891.00	12/91	69r
Childbirth, normal delivery, physician charge	birth	1623.00	12/91	69r
Dentist's fee, adult teeth cleaning and periodic oral exam	visit	57.00	12/94	2c
Doctor's fee, routine exam, established patient	visit	39.00	12/94	2c
Drugs, expenditures	year	248	91	81r
Health care, total expenditures	year	1336	91	81r
Health insurance expenditures	year	550	91	81r
Hospital care, semiprivate room	day	447.00	12/94	2c
Insurance premium, family medical care	month	363.57	1/95	41s
Medical services expenditures	year	457	91	81r
Medical supplies expenditures	year	82	91	81r
Household Goods				
Appl. repair, service call, wash mach	min. lab. chg.	39.15	12/94	2c
Floor coverings, expenditures	year	105	91	81r
Furniture, expenditures	year	291	91	81r
Household equipment, misc. expenditures	year	341	91	81r
Household expenditures, miscellaneous	year	162	91	81r
Household furnishings and equipment, expenditures	year	1042	91	81r
Household operations expenditures	year	365	91	81r
Household textiles, expenditures	year	101	91	81r
Housekeeping supplies, expenditures	year	390	91	81r
Laundry and cleaning supplies, expenditures	year	110	91	81r
Laundry detergent, Tide Ultra, Bold, or Cheer	42 oz.	3.63	12/94	2c
Postage and stationery, expenditures	year	115	91	81r
Tissues, facial, Kleenex brand	175	0.95	12/94	2c
Housing				
Housing, ACCRA Index		100.10	12/94	2c
Add garage/carport		8,479	3/95	74r
Add room(s)		21,347	3/95	74r
Apartment condominium or co-op, median	unit	87100	12/94	62r
Bathroom addition, average cost	add	9734.00	3/95	13r
Bathroom remodeling, average cost	remod	6414.00	3/95	13r
Bedroom, master suite addition, average cost	add	27122.00	3/95	13r
Deck addition, average cost	add	6665.00	3/95	13r
Dwellings (owned), expenditures	year	2566	91	81r
Enclose porch/patio/breezeway		4,556	3/95	74r
Exterior remodeling, average cost	remod	15395.00	3/95	13r
Family room addition, average cost	add	27658.00	3/95	13r
Finish room in basement/attic		5,074	3/95	74r
Home, existing, single-family, median	unit	106500	12/94	62r
Home, existing, single-family, median	unit	73.10	12/94	62c
House payment, principal and interest, 25% down payment	mo.	755	12/94	2c
House, 1800 sq ft, 8000 sq ft lot, new, urban, utilities	total	123833	12/94	2c
Kitchen remodeling, major, average cost	remod	17084.00	3/95	13r
Kitchen remodeling, minor, average cost	remod	5804.00	3/95	13r

Values are in dollars or fractions of dollars. In the column headed *Ref*, references are shown to sources. Each reference is followed by a letter. These refer to the geographical level for which data were reported: s=State, r=Region, and c=City or metro. The abbreviation *ex* is used to mean *except* or *excluding*; *exp* stands for *expenditures*. For other abbreviations and further explanations, please see the Introduction.

Champaign-Urbana, IL - continued

Item	Per	Value	Date	Ref.
Housing				
Maintenance, repairs, insurance, and other housing expenditures	year	484	91	81r
Mortgage interest and charges expenditures	year	1443	91	81r
Mtge. rate, incl. points and orig. fee, 30-year conv. fixed or ARM	mo.	9.42	12/94	2c
Office, home addition, average cost	add	8121.00	3/95	13r
Princ. & int., mortgage, median-price exist. sing.-family home	mo.	515	12/94	62r
Property taxes expenditures	year	639	91	81r
Redesign, restructure more than half of home's interior		9,114	3/95	74r
Rent, apartment, 2 br., 1 1/2-2 baths, unfurnished, 950 sq ft, water	mo.	506	12/94	2c
Rental units expenditures	year	1200	91	81r
Sun-space addition, average cost	add	23768.00	3/95	13r
Wing addition, two-story, average cost	add	50410.00	3/95	13r
Insurance and Pensions				
Auto insurance, private passenger	year	679.48	12/94	71s
Insurance and pensions, personal, expenditures	year	2408	91	81r
Insurance, life and other personal, expenditures	year	355	91	81r
Pensions and Social Security, expenditures	year	2053	91	81r
Legal Assistance				
Legal work, law firm associate	hour	90		10r
Legal work, law firm partner	hour	139		10r
Personal Goods				
Shampoo, Alberto VO5	15-oz.	1.37	12/94	2c
Toothpaste, Crest or Colgate	6-7 oz.	2.15	12/94	2c
Personal Services				
Dry cleaning, man's 2-pc. suit		7.30	12/94	2c
Haircut, man's barbershop, no styling		8.88	12/94	2c
Haircut, woman's shampoo, trim, blow-dry		20.59	12/94	2c
Personal services expenditures	year	203	91	81r
Restaurant Food				
Chicken, fried, thigh and drumstick		2.15	12/94	2c
Dining expenditures, family	week	30.03	94	73r
Hamburger with cheese	1/4 lb.	1.79	12/94	2c
Pizza, Pizza Hut or Pizza Inn	12-13 in.	7.66	12/94	2c
Taxes				
Taxes, Federal income, expenditures	year	1756	91	81r
Taxes, personal, expenditures	year	2426	91	81r
Taxes, State and local income, expenditures	year	568	91	81r
Transportation				
Transportation, ACCRA Index		98.20	12/94	2c
Bus fare, one-way	trip	0.75	12/95	1c
Bus fare, up to 10 miles	one-way	0.75	12/94	2c
Cars and trucks purchased, new	year	891	91	81r
Cars and trucks purchased, used	year	1155	91	81r
Driver's learning permit fee	perm	20.00	1/94	84s
Driver's license fee	orig	10.00	1/94	84s
Driver's license fee, duplicate	lic	5.00	1/94	84s
Driver's license reinstatement fee, min.	susp	30.00	1/94	85s
Driver's license renewal fee	renew	10.00	1/94	84s
Identification card, nondriver	card	4.00	1/94	83s
Motorcycle learning permit fee	perm	20.00	1/94	84s
Motorcycle license fee	orig	10.00	1/94	84s
Motorcycle license fee, duplicate	lic	5.00	1/94	84s
Motorcycle license renewal fee	renew	10.00	1/94	84s
Public transportation expenditures	year	209	91	81r
Tire balance, computer or spin bal., front	wheel	7.17	12/94	2c
Transportation expenditures, total	year	4792	91	81r
Vehicle finance charges	year	300	91	81r
Vehicle insurance expenditures	year	485	91	81r
Vehicle maintenance and repairs expenditures	year	534	91	81r

Champaign-Urbana, IL - continued

Item	Per	Value	Date	Ref.
Transportation - continued				
Vehicle purchases	year	2068	91	81r
Vehicle rental, leases, licenses, etc. expenditures	year	197	91	81r
Vehicles purchased, other than cars and trucks	year	22	91	81r
Utilities				
Utilities, ACCRA Index		108.60	12/94	2c
Electricity expenditures	year	668	91	81r
Electricity, (part.), other, 1800 sq. ft., new home	mo.	77.28	12/94	2c
Utilities, fuels, and public services, total expenditures	year	1838	91	81r
Water and other public services, expenditures	year	167	91	81r
Weddings				
Bridal attendants' gowns	event	750	10/93	76r
Bridal gown	event	852	10/93	76r
Bridal headpiece and veil	event	167	10/93	76r
Bride's wedding band	event	708	10/93	76r
Clergy	event	224	10/93	76r
Engagement ring	event	2756	10/93	76r
Flowers	event	863	10/93	76r
Formal wear for groom	event	106	10/93	76r
Groom's attendants' formal wear	event	530	10/93	76r
Groom's wedding band	event	402	10/93	76r
Music	event	600	10/93	76r
Photography	event	1088	10/93	76r
Shoes for bride	event	50	10/93	76r
Videography	event	483	10/93	76r
Wedding invitations and announcements	event	342	10/93	76r
Wedding reception	event	7000	10/93	76r

Charleston, SC

Item	Per	Value	Date	Ref.
Composite, ACCRA index		98.10	12/94	2c
Alcoholic Beverages				
Beer, Miller Lite, Bud, 12-oz., ex deposit	6	3.97	12/94	2c
J & B Scotch	750-ml.	16.18	12/94	2c
Wine, Gallo Chablis blanc	1.5-lit	4.89	12/94	2c
Appliances				
Appliances (major), expenditures	year	153	91	81r
Average annual exp.				
Food, health care, personal goods, services	year	27020	91	81r
Charity				
Cash contributions, expenditures	year	839	91	81r
Clothing				
Apparel, men and boys, total expenditures	year	380	91	81r
Apparel, women and girls, total expenditures	year	660	91	81r
Footwear, expenditures	year	193	91	81r
Jeans, man's denim		35.37	12/94	2c
Shirt, man's dress shirt		29.49	12/94	2c
Undervest, boy's size 10-14, cotton	3	5.23	12/94	2c
Communications				
Long-distance telephone rate, day, addl. min., 1-10 mi.	min.	0.13	12/93	9s
Long-distance telephone rate, day, initial min., 1-10 mi.	min.	0.24	12/93	9s
Newspaper subscription, dly. and Sun. delivery	month	9.95	12/94	2c
Phone line, single, business, field visit	inst	82.50	12/93	9s
Phone line, single, business, no field visit	inst	64.00	12/93	9s
Phone line, single, residence, field visit	inst	62.50	12/93	9s
Phone line, single, residence, no field visit	inst	44.00	12/93	9s
Telephone bill, family of four	month	25.79	12/94	2c
Telephone service, expenditures	year	616	91	81r
Telephone, residential, flat rate	mo.	16.90	12/93	8c

Values are in dollars or fractions of dollars. In the column headed *Ref*, references are shown to sources. Each reference is followed by a letter. These refer to the geographical level for which data were reported: s=State, r=Region, and c=City or metro. The abbreviation *ex* is used to mean *except* or *excluding*; *exp* stands for *expenditures*. For other abbreviations and further explanations, please see the Introduction.

Charleston, SC - continued

Item	Per	Value	Date	Ref.
Education				
Board, 4-year private college/university	year	1831	8/94	80s
Board, 4-year public college/university	year	1462	8/94	80s
Education, total expenditures	year	319	91	81r
Room, 4-year private college/university	year	1744	8/94	80s
Room, 4-year public college/university	year	1851	8/94	80s
Total cost, 4-year private college/university	year	12082	8/94	80s
Total cost, 4-year public college/university	year	6203	8/94	80s
Tuition, 2-year public college/university, in-state	year	1061	8/94	80s
Tuition, 4-year private college/university, in-state	year	8507	8/94	80s
Tuition, 4-year public college/university, in-state	year	2891	8/94	80s
Energy and Fuels				
Energy, combined forms, 1800 sq. ft.	mo.	109.21	12/94	2c
Fuel oil and other fuels, expenditures	year	56	91	81r
Gas, natural, expenditures	year	150	91	81r
Gas, reg unlead, taxes inc., cash, self-service	gal	1.01	12/94	2c
Gasoline and motor oil purchased	year	1152	91	81r
Gasoline, unleaded midgrade	gallon	1.21	4/93	82r
Gasoline, unleaded premium	gallon	1.30	4/93	82r
Gasoline, unleaded regular	gallon	1.10	4/93	82r
Entertainment				
Bowling, evening rate	game	2.48	12/94	2c
Concert ticket, Pearl Jam group	perf	20.00	94	50r
Entertainment, total expenditures	year	1266	91	81r
Fees and admissions, expenditures	year	306	91	81r
Monopoly game, Parker Brothers', No. 9	game	11.94	12/94	2c
Movie	adm	5.71	12/94	2c
Pets, toys, playground equipment, expenditures	year	271	91	81r
Reading, expenditures	year	131	91	81r
Televisions, radios, and sound equipment, expenditures	year	439	91	81r
Tennis balls, yellow, Wilson or Penn, 3	can	2.38	12/94	2c
Funerals				
Burial, immediate, container provided by funeral home		1370.36	1/95	54r
Cards, acknowledgment		14.83	1/95	54r
Casket, minimum alternative		192.52	1/95	54r
Cosmetology, hair care, etc.		102.27	1/95	54r
Cremation, direct, container provided by funeral home		1065.64	1/95	54r
Embalming		304.29	1/95	54r
Funeral, funeral home		287.83	1/95	54r
Funeral, other facility		284.14	1/95	54r
Graveside service		349.13	1/95	54r
Hearse, local		132.27	1/95	54r
Limousine, local		98.45	1/95	54r
Memorial service		270.59	1/95	54r
Service charge, professional, nondeclinable		933.59	1/95	54r
Visitation and viewing		225.83	1/95	54r
Groceries				
Groceries, ACCRA Index		94.50	12/94	2c
Apples, Red Delicious	lb.	0.73	12/94	82r
Baby food, strained vegetables, lowest price	4-4.5 oz.	0.34	12/94	2c
Bacon, sliced	lb.	1.67	12/94	82r
Bananas	lb.	0.44	12/94	2c
Bananas	lb.	0.42	12/94	82r
Beef or hamburger, ground	lb.	1.33	12/94	2c
Beef purchases	year	213	91	81r
Beverage purchases, alcoholic	year	249	91	81r
Beverage purchases, nonalcoholic	year	207	91	81r
Bologna, all beef or mixed	lb.	2.27	12/94	82r
Bread, white	24-oz.	0.62	12/94	2c
Bread, white, pan	lb.	0.68	12/94	82r
Cabbage	lb.	0.42	12/94	82r
Carrots, short trimmed and topped	lb.	0.53	12/94	82r

Charleston, SC - continued

Item	Per	Value	Date	Ref.
Groceries - continued				
Cereals and bakery products purchases	year	345	91	81r
Cereals and cereals products purchases	year	127	91	81r
Cheddar cheese, natural	lb.	3.58	12/94	82r
Cheese, Kraft grated Parmesan	8-oz.	3.21	12/94	2c
Chicken breast, bone-in	lb.	1.71	12/94	82r
Chicken, fresh, whole	lb.	0.78	12/94	82r
Chicken, whole fryer	lb.	0.89	12/94	2c
Chuck roast, USDA choice, boneless	lb.	2.26	12/94	82r
Cigarettes, Winston, Kings	carton	13.32	12/94	2c
Coffee, vacuum-packed	13 oz.	3.07	12/94	2c
Corn Flakes, Kellogg's or Post Toasties	18 oz.	2.28	12/94	2c
Corn, frozen, whole kernel, lowest price	10 oz.	0.63	12/94	2c
Crackers, soda, salted	lb.	1.27	12/94	82r
Cucumbers	lb.	0.65	12/94	82r
Dairy products (other) purchases	year	141	91	81r
Eggs, Grade A large	dozen	0.87	12/94	2c
Eggs, Grade A large	dozen	0.87	12/94	82r
Fish and seafood purchases	year	72	91	81r
Flour, white, all purpose	lb.	0.23	12/94	82r
Food purchases, food eaten at home	year	2381	91	81r
Foods purchased away from home, not prepared by consumer	year	1696	91	81r
Frankfurters, all meat or all beef	lb.	1.74	12/94	82r
Fruits and vegetables purchases	year	380	91	81r
Grapefruit	lb.	0.45	12/94	82r
Grapes, Thompson seedless	lb.	2.30	12/94	82r
Ground beef, 100% beef	lb.	1.37	12/94	82r
Ground chuck, 100% beef	lb.	1.97	12/94	82r
Ham, boneless, exc. canned	lb.	2.54	12/94	82r
Ice cream, prepackaged, bulk, regular	1/2 gal.	2.47	12/94	82r
Lemons	lb.	1.02	12/94	82r
Lettuce, iceberg	lb.	0.96	12/94	82r
Lettuce, iceberg	head	1.01	12/94	2c
Margarine, Blue Bonnet or Parkay cubes	lb.	0.59	12/94	2c
Margarine, stick	lb.	0.77	12/94	82r
Meats, poultry, fish, and eggs purchases	year	655	91	81r
Milk and cream (fresh) purchases	year	130	91	81r
Milk, whole	1/2 gal.	1.45	12/94	2c
Orange juice, frozen concentrate 12-oz. can	16 oz.	1.36	12/94	82r
Orange juice, Minute Maid frozen	12-oz.	1.20	12/94	2c
Oranges, Navel	lb.	0.54	12/94	82r
Peaches, halves or slices, Hunt's, Del Monte, or Libby's	29-oz.	1.31	12/94	2c
Pears, Anjou	lb.	0.81	12/94	82r
Peas, sweet, Del Monte or Green Giant	15-17 oz.	0.49	12/94	2c
Pork chops, center cut, bone-in	lb.	3.07	12/94	82r
Pork purchases	year	142	91	81r
Potato chips	16-oz.	3.15	12/94	82r
Potatoes, frozen, French fried	lb.	0.82	12/94	82r
Potatoes, white	lb.	0.34	12/94	82r
Potatoes, white or red	10-lb. sack	2.45	12/94	2c
Rice, white, long grain, uncooked	lb.	0.48	12/94	82r
Round roast, USDA choice, boneless	lb.	2.91	12/94	82r
Sausage, fresh	lb.	1.82	12/94	82r
Sausage, Jimmy Dean, 100% pork	lb.	2.21	12/94	2c
Shortening, vegetable oil blends	lb.	0.75	12/94	82r
Shortening, vegetable, Crisco	3-lb.	2.51	12/94	2c
Soft drink, Coca Cola, ex deposit	2 lit	1.07	12/94	2c
Spaghetti and macaroni	lb.	0.87	12/94	82r
Steak, rib eye, USDA choice, boneless	lb.	6.85	12/94	82r
Steak, round, graded & ungraded, exc. USDA prime & choice	lb.	2.96	12/94	82r
Steak, round, USDA choice, boneless	lb.	3.17	12/94	82r
Steak, sirloin, USDA choice, boneless	lb.	4.12	12/94	82r
Steak, t-bone	lb.	6.07	12/94	2c
Steak, T-bone, USDA choice, bone-in	lb.	5.63	12/94	82r
Sugar and other sweets, eaten at home, expenditures	year	93	91	81r

Values are in dollars or fractions of dollars. In the column headed *Ref*, references are shown to sources. Each reference is followed by a letter. These refer to the geographical level for which data were reported: s=State, r=Region, and c=City or metro. The abbreviation *ex* is used to mean *except* or *excluding*; *exp* stands for expenditures. For other abbreviations and further explanations, please see the Introduction.

Charleston, SC - continued

Item	Per	Value	Date	Ref.
Groceries				
Sugar, cane or beet	4 lbs.	1.48	12/94	2c
Sugar, white, all sizes	lb.	0.39	12/94	82r
Tobacco products and smoking supplies, total expenditures	year	286	91	81r
Tomatoes, field grown	lb.	1.36	12/94	82r
Tomatoes, Hunt's or Del Monte	14.5 oz.	0.54	12/94	2c
Tuna, chunk, light	lb.	1.94	12/94	82r
Tuna, chunk, light, oil-packed	6.125-6.5 oz.	0.66	12/94	2c
Turkey, frozen, whole	lb.	0.96	12/94	82r
Yogurt, natural, fruit flavored	8 oz.	0.58	12/94	82r
Goods and Services				
Miscellaneous goods and services, ACCRA Index		102.80	12/94	2c
Health Care				
Health care, ACCRA Index		107.20	12/94	2c
Adenosine, emergency room	treat	100.00	95	23r
Antibiotic ointment, Polysporin	1.5 oz.	4.01	12/94	2c
Bladder tap, superpubic, infant, emergency room	treat	119.00	95	23r
Blood analysis, emergency room	treat	25.00	95	23r
Blood tests, abdominal pain, emergency room	treat	25.00	95	23r
Burn dressing, emergency room	treat	266.00	95	23r
Cardiology interpretation, emergency room	treat	26.00	95	23r
Chest X-ray, emergency room	treat	78.00	95	23r
Childbirth, Cesarean delivery, hospital charge	birth	5462.00	12/91	69r
Childbirth, Cesarean delivery, physician charge	birth	2228.00	12/91	69r
Childbirth, normal delivery, hospital charge	birth	2943.00	12/91	69r
Childbirth, normal delivery, physician charge	birth	1619.00	12/91	69r
Defibrillation pads, emergency room	treat	6.00	95	23r
Dentist's fee, adult teeth cleaning and periodic oral exam	visit	55.14	12/94	2c
Doctor's fee, routine exam, established patient	visit	49.67	12/94	2c
Drugs, expenditures	year	297	91	81r
Gastric tube insertion, nasal, emergency room	treat	25.00	95	23r
Health care, total expenditures	year	1600	91	81r
Health insurance expenditures	year	637	91	81r
Heart monitor, emergency room	treat	40.00	95	23r
Hospital care, semiprivate room	day	339.25	12/94	2c
Insurance premium, family medical care	month	414.49	1/95	41s
Intravenous fluids, emergency room	treat	130.00	95	23r
Intravenous fluids, emergency room	liter	26.00	95	23r
Intravenous line, central, emergency room	treat	342.00	95	23r
Liver function tests, abdominal pain, emergency room	treat	26.00	95	23r
Medical care charges, total, emergency room, third-degree burns	treat	2101.00	95	23r
Medical care charges, total, emergency, infant with fever	treat	628.00	95	23r
Medical services expenditures	year	573	91	81r
Medical supplies expenditures	year	93	91	81r
Morphine, emergency room	treat	34.00	95	23r
Nursing care and facilities charges, emergency room	treat	252.00	95	23r
Nursing care and facilities charges, emergency, infant with fever	treat	252.00	95	23r
Nursing care and facilities charges, emergency, third-degree burns	treat	861.00	95	23r
Physician's charges, emergency, infant with fever	treat	212.00	95	23r
Physician's charges, emergency, third-degree burns	treat	372.00	95	23r
Physician's fee, emergency room	treat	372.00	95	23r
Physician's fee, general practitioner	visit	51.20	12/93	60r
Surgery, open-heart	proc	42374.00	1/93	14r

Charleston, SC - continued

Item	Per	Value	Date	Ref.
Health Care - continued				
Ultrasound, abdominal, emergency room	treat	276.00	95	23r
Urinalysis, emergency room	treat	20.00	95	23r
Urinalysis, infant, emergency room	treat	20.00	95	23r
X-rays, emergency room	treat	78.00	95	23r
Household Goods				
Appl. repair, service call, wash mach	min. lab. chg.	38.25	12/94	2c
Floor coverings, expenditures	year	48	91	81r
Furniture, expenditures	year	280	91	81r
Household equipment, misc. expenditures	year	342	91	81r
Household expenditures, miscellaneous	year	256	91	81r
Household furnishings and equipment, expenditures	year	988	91	81r
Household operations expenditures	year	468	91	81r
Household textiles, expenditures	year	95	91	81r
Housekeeping supplies, expenditures	year	380	91	81r
Laundry and cleaning supplies, expenditures	year	109	91	81r
Laundry detergent, Tide Ultra, Bold, or Cheer	42 oz.	2.62	12/94	2c
Postage and stationery, expenditures	year	105	91	81r
Tissues, facial, Kleenex brand	175	0.89	12/94	2c
Housing				
Housing, ACCRA Index		93.80	12/94	2c
Add garage/carport		6,980	3/95	74r
Add room(s)		11,403	3/95	74r
Apartment condominium or co-op, median	unit	68600	12/94	62r
Dwellings (owned), expenditures	year	2428	91	81r
Enclose porch/patio/breezeway		4,572	3/95	74r
Finish room in basement/attic		3,794	3/95	74r
Home, existing, single-family, median	unit	120200	12/94	62r
Home, existing, single-family, median	unit	92.00	12/94	62c
House payment, principal and interest, 25% down payment	mo.	698	12/94	2c
House, 1800 sq ft, 8000 sq ft lot, new, urban, utilities	total	114567	12/94	2c
Maintenance, repairs, insurance, and other housing expenditures	year	531	91	81r
Mortgage interest and charges expenditures	year	1506	91	81r
Mtge. rate, incl. points and orig. fee, 30-year conv. fixed or ARM	mo.	9.11	12/94	2c
Princ. & int., mortgage, median-price exist. sing.-family home	mo.	540	12/94	62r
Property taxes expenditures	year	391	91	81r
Redesign, restructure more than half of home's interior		17,641	3/95	74r
Rent, apartment, 2 br., 1 1/2-2 baths, unfurnished, 950 sq ft, water	mo.	555	12/94	2c
Rental units expenditures	year	1264	91	81r
Insurance and Pensions				
Auto insurance, private passenger	year	684.10	12/94	71s
Insurance and pensions, personal, expenditures	year	2395	91	81r
Insurance, life and other personal, expenditures	year	368	91	81r
Pensions and Social Security, expenditures	year	2027	91	81r
Personal Goods				
Shampoo, Alberto VO5	15-oz.	1.02	12/94	2c
Toothpaste, Crest or Colgate	6-7 oz.	1.85	12/94	2c
Personal Services				
Dry cleaning, man's 2-pc. suit		6.57	12/94	2c
Haircut, man's barbershop, no styling		9.17	12/94	2c
Haircut, woman's shampoo, trim, blow-dry		25.00	12/94	2c
Personal services expenditures	year	212	91	81r
Restaurant Food				
Chicken, fried, thigh and drumstick		1.99	12/94	2c
Dining expenditures, family	week	33.83	94	73r
Hamburger with cheese	1/4 lb.	1.79	12/94	2c

Values are in dollars or fractions of dollars. In the column headed *Ref*, references are shown to sources. Each reference is followed by a letter. These refer to the geographical level for which data were reported: s = State, r = Region, and c = City or metro. The abbreviation *ex* is used to mean *except* or *excluding*; *exp* stands for *expenditures*. For other abbreviations and further explanations, please see the Introduction.

Charleston, SC - continued

Item	Per	Value	Date	Ref.
Restaurant Food				
Pizza, Pizza Hut or Pizza Inn	12-13 in.	7.89	12/94	2c
Taxes				
Taxes, Federal income, expenditures	year	2275	91	81r
Taxes, personal, expenditures	year	2715	91	81r
Taxes, State and local income, expenditures	year	365	91	81r
Transportation				
Transportation, ACCRA Index		90.80	12/94	2c
Bus fare, one-way	trip	0.75	12/95	1c
Bus fare, up to 10 miles	one-way	0.75	12/94	2c
Cars and trucks purchased, new	year	1306	91	81r
Cars and trucks purchased, used	year	942	91	81r
Driver's learning permit fee	perm	2.00	1/94	84s
Driver's license fee	orig	10.00	1/94	84s
Driver's license fee, duplicate	lic	0.50	1/94	84s
Driver's license reinstatement fee, min.	susp	30.00	1/94	85s
Driver's license renewal fee	renew	10.00	1/94	84s
Identification card, nondriver	card	5.00	1/94	83s
Motorcycle learning permit fee	perm	2.00	1/94	84s
Motorcycle license fee	orig	10.00	1/94	84s
Motorcycle license fee, duplicate	lic	0.50	1/94	84s
Motorcycle license renewal fee	renew	10.00	1/94	84s
Public transportation expenditures	year	249	91	81r
Tire balance, computer or spin bal., front	wheel	6.48	12/94	2c
Transportation expenditures, total	year	5307	91	81r
Vehicle finance charges	year	346	91	81r
Vehicle insurance expenditures	year	544	91	81r
Vehicle maintenance and repairs expenditures	year	600	91	81r
Vehicle purchases	year	2275	91	81r
Vehicle rental, leases, licenses, etc. expenditures	year	141	91	81r
Vehicles purchased, other than cars and trucks	year	27	91	81r
Utilities				
Utilities, ACCRA Index		102.00	12/94	2c
Electricity expenditures	year	950	91	81r
Electricity, 1800 sq. ft., new home	mo.	109.21	12/94	2c
Fee, water use, industrial	month	1093.05	1/95	16c
Utilities, fuels, and public services, total expenditures	year	2000	91	81r
Water and other public services, expenditures	year	227	91	81r
Weddings				
Bridal attendants' gowns	event	750	10/93	76r
Bridal gown	event	852	10/93	76r
Bridal headpiece and veil	event	167	10/93	76r
Bride's wedding band	event	708	10/93	76r
Clergy	event	224	10/93	76r
Engagement ring	event	2756	10/93	76r
Flowers	event	863	10/93	76r
Formal wear for groom	event	106	10/93	76r
Groom's attendants' formal wear	event	530	10/93	76r
Groom's wedding band	event	402	10/93	76r
Music	event	600	10/93	76r
Photography	event	1088	10/93	76r
Shoes for bride	event	50	10/93	76r
Videography	event	483	10/93	76r
Wedding invitations and announcements	event	342	10/93	76r
Wedding reception	event	7000	10/93	76r

Charleston, WV

Item	Per	Value	Date	Ref.
Composite, ACCRA index		98.00	12/94	2c
Alcoholic Beverages				
Beer, Miller Lite, Bud, 12-oz., ex deposit	6	4.31	12/94	2c

Charleston, WV - continued

Item	Per	Value	Date	Ref.
Alcoholic Beverages - continued				
J & B Scotch	750-ml.	16.87	12/94	2c
Wine, Gallo Chablis blanc	1.5-lit	6.03	12/94	2c
Appliances				
Appliances (major), expenditures	year	153	91	81r
Average annual exp.				
Food, health care, personal goods, services	year	27020	91	81r
Charity				
Cash contributions, expenditures	year	839	91	81r
Clothing				
Apparel, men and boys, total expenditures	year	380	91	81r
Apparel, women and girls, total expenditures	year	660	91	81r
Footwear, expenditures	year	193	91	81r
Jeans, man's denim		28.51	12/94	2c
Shirt, man's dress shirt		33.50	12/94	2c
Undervest, boy's size 10-14, cotton	3	3.00	12/94	2c
Communications				
Long-distance telephone rate, day, addl. min., 1-10 mi.	min.	0.13	12/93	9s
Long-distance telephone rate, day, initial min., 1-10 mi.	min.	0.26	12/93	9s
Newspaper subscription, dly. and Sun. delivery	month	11.30	12/94	2c
Phone line, single, business, field visit	inst	0.00	12/93	9s
Phone line, single, business, no field visit	inst	96.90	12/93	9s
Phone line, single, residence, field visit	inst	0.00	12/93	9s
Phone line, single, residence, no field visit	inst	42.00	12/93	9s
Telephone bill, family of four	month	29.93	12/94	2c
Telephone service, expenditures	year	616	91	81r
Telephone, residential, flat rate	mo.	6.00	12/93	8c
Education				
Board, 4-year private college/university	year	2166	8/94	80s
Board, 4-year public college/university	year	1968	8/94	80s
Education, total expenditures	year	319	91	81r
Room, 4-year private college/university	year	1745	8/94	80s
Room, 4-year public college/university	year	1847	8/94	80s
Total cost, 4-year private college/university	year	13220	8/94	80s
Total cost, 4-year public college/university	year	5691	8/94	80s
Tuition, 2-year public college/university, in-state	year	1247	8/94	80s
Tuition, 4-year private college/university, in-state	year	9310	8/94	80s
Tuition, 4-year public college/university, in-state	year	1875	8/94	80s
Energy and Fuels				
Energy, combined forms, 1800 sq. ft.	mo.	105.58	12/94	2c
Fuel oil and other fuels, expenditures	year	56	91	81r
Gas, cooking, winter, 10 therms	month	11.17	2/94	65c
Gas, cooking, winter, 30 therms	month	23.51	2/94	65c
Gas, cooking, winter, 50 therms	month	35.85	2/94	65c
Gas, heating, winter, 100 therms	month	66.70	2/94	65c
Gas, heating, winter, average use	month	122.23	2/94	65c
Gas, natural, expenditures	year	150	91	81r
Gas, reg unlead, taxes inc., cash, self-service	gal	1.20	12/94	2c
Gasoline and motor oil purchased	year	1152	91	81r
Gasoline, unleaded midgrade	gallon	1.21	4/93	82r
Gasoline, unleaded premium	gallon	1.30	4/93	82r
Gasoline, unleaded regular	gallon	1.10	4/93	82r
Entertainment				
Bowling, evening rate	game	2.01	12/94	2c
Concert ticket, Pearl Jam group	perf	20.00	94	50r
Entertainment, total expenditures	year	1266	91	81r
Fees and admissions, expenditures	year	306	91	81r
Monopoly game, Parker Brothers', No. 9	game	9.28	12/94	2c
Movie	adm	5.50	12/94	2c
Pets, toys, playground equipment, expenditures	year	271	91	81r

Values are in dollars or fractions of dollars. In the column headed *Ref*, references are shown to sources. Each reference is followed by a letter. These refer to the geographical level for which data were reported: s=State, r=Region, and c=City or metro. The abbreviation *ex* is used to mean *except* or *excluding*; *exp* stands for expenditures. For other abbreviations and further explanations, please see the Introduction.

Item	Per	Value	Date	Ref.
Entertainment				
Reading, expenditures	year	131	91	81r
Televisions, radios, and sound equipment, expenditures	year	439	91	81r
Tennis balls, yellow, Wilson or Penn, 3	can	2.09	12/94	2c
Funerals				
Burial, immediate, container provided by funeral home		1370.36	1/95	54r
Cards, acknowledgment		14.83	1/95	54r
Casket, minimum alternative		192.52	1/95	54r
Cosmetology, hair care, etc.		102.27	1/95	54r
Cremation, direct, container provided by funeral home		1065.64	1/95	54r
Embalming		304.29	1/95	54r
Funeral, funeral home		287.83	1/95	54r
Funeral, other facility		284.14	1/95	54r
Graveside service		349.13	1/95	54r
Hearse, local		132.27	1/95	54r
Limousine, local		98.45	1/95	54r
Memorial service		270.59	1/95	54r
Service charge, professional, nondeclinable		933.59	1/95	54r
Visitation and viewing		225.83	1/95	54r
Groceries				
Groceries, ACCRA Index		99.30	12/94	2c
Apples, Red Delicious	lb.	0.73	12/94	82r
Baby food, strained vegetables, lowest price	4-4.5 oz.	0.21	12/94	2c
Bacon, sliced	lb.	1.67	12/94	82r
Bananas	lb.	0.58	12/94	2c
Bananas	lb.	0.42	12/94	82r
Beef or hamburger, ground	lb.	1.45	12/94	2c
Beef purchases	year	213	91	81r
Beverage purchases, alcoholic	year	249	91	81r
Beverage purchases, nonalcoholic	year	207	91	81r
Bologna, all beef or mixed	lb.	2.27	12/94	82r
Bread, white	24-oz.	0.58	12/94	2c
Bread, white, pan	lb.	0.68	12/94	82r
Cabbage	lb.	0.42	12/94	82r
Carrots, short trimmed and topped	lb.	0.53	12/94	82r
Cereals and bakery products purchases	year	345	91	81r
Cereals and cereals products purchases	year	127	91	81r
Cheddar cheese, natural	lb.	3.58	12/94	82r
Cheese, Kraft grated Parmesan	8-oz.	3.49	12/94	2c
Chicken breast, bone-in	lb.	1.71	12/94	82r
Chicken, fresh, whole	lb.	0.78	12/94	82r
Chicken, whole fryer	lb.	0.93	12/94	2c
Chuck roast, USDA choice, boneless	lb.	2.26	12/94	82r
Cigarettes, Winston, Kings	carton	14.99	12/94	2c
Coffee, vacuum-packed	13 oz.	3.67	12/94	2c
Corn Flakes, Kellogg's or Post Toasties	18 oz.	3.01	12/94	2c
Corn, frozen, whole kernel, lowest price	10 oz.	0.81	12/94	2c
Crackers, soda, salted	lb.	1.27	12/94	82r
Cucumbers	lb.	0.65	12/94	82r
Dairy products (other) purchases	year	141	91	81r
Eggs, Grade A large	dozen	0.93	12/94	2c
Eggs, Grade A large	dozen	0.87	12/94	82r
Fish and seafood purchases	year	72	91	81r
Flour, white, all purpose	lb.	0.23	12/94	82r
Food purchases, food eaten at home	year	2381	91	81r
Foods purchased away from home, not prepared by consumer	year	1696	91	81r
Frankfurters, all meat or all beef	lb.	1.74	12/94	82r
Fruits and vegetables purchases	year	380	91	81r
Grapefruit	lb.	0.45	12/94	82r
Grapes, Thompson seedless	lb.	2.30	12/94	82r
Ground beef, 100% beef	lb.	1.37	12/94	82r
Ground chuck, 100% beef	lb.	1.97	12/94	82r
Ham, boneless, exc. canned	lb.	2.54	12/94	82r
Ice cream, prepackaged, bulk, regular	1/2 gal.	2.47	12/94	82r
Lemons	lb.	1.02	12/94	82r
Lettuce, iceberg	lb.	0.96	12/94	82r

Item	Per	Value	Date	Ref.
Groceries - continued				
Lettuce, iceberg	head	0.76	12/94	2c
Margarine, Blue Bonnet or Parkay cubes	lb.	0.54	12/94	2c
Margarine, stick	lb.	0.77	12/94	82r
Meats, poultry, fish, and eggs purchases	year	655	91	81r
Milk and cream (fresh) purchases	year	130	91	81r
Milk, whole	1/2 gal.	1.39	12/94	2c
Orange juice, frozen concentrate 12-oz. can	16 oz.	1.36	12/94	82r
Orange juice, Minute Maid frozen	12-oz.	1.39	12/94	2c
Oranges, Navel	lb.	0.54	12/94	82r
Peaches, halves or slices, Hunt's, Del Monte, or Libby's	29-oz.	1.54	12/94	2c
Pears, Anjou	lb.	0.81	12/94	82r
Peas, sweet, Del Monte or Green Giant	15-17 oz.	0.44	12/94	2c
Pork chops, center cut, bone-in	lb.	3.07	12/94	82r
Pork purchases	year	142	91	81r
Potato chips	16-oz.	3.15	12/94	82r
Potatoes, frozen, French fried	lb.	0.82	12/94	82r
Potatoes, white	lb.	0.34	12/94	82r
Potatoes, white or red	10-lb. sack	2.59	12/94	2c
Rice, white, long grain, uncooked	lb.	0.48	12/94	82r
Round roast, USDA choice, boneless	lb.	2.91	12/94	82r
Sausage, fresh	lb.	1.82	12/94	82r
Sausage, Jimmy Dean, 100% pork	lb.	2.77	12/94	2c
Shortening, vegetable oil blends	lb.	0.75	12/94	82r
Shortening, vegetable, Crisco	3-lb.	2.48	12/94	2c
Soft drink, Coca Cola, ex deposit	2 lit	1.29	12/94	2c
Spaghetti and macaroni	lb.	0.87	12/94	82r
Steak, rib eye, USDA choice, boneless	lb.	6.85	12/94	82r
Steak, round, graded & ungraded, exc. USDA prime & choice	lb.	2.96	12/94	82r
Steak, round, USDA choice, boneless	lb.	3.17	12/94	82r
Steak, sirloin, USDA choice, boneless	lb.	4.12	12/94	82r
Steak, t-bone	lb.	5.39	12/94	2c
Steak, T-bone, USDA choice, bone-in	lb.	5.63	12/94	82r
Sugar and other sweets, eaten at home, expenditures	year	93	91	81r
Sugar, cane or beet	4 lbs.	1.30	12/94	2c
Sugar, white, all sizes	lb.	0.39	12/94	82r
Tobacco products and smoking supplies, total expenditures	year	286	91	81r
Tomatoes, field grown	lb.	1.36	12/94	82r
Tomatoes, Hunt's or Del Monte	14.5 oz.	0.77	12/94	2c
Tuna, chunk, light	lb.	1.94	12/94	82r
Tuna, chunk, light, oil-packed	6.125-6.5 oz.	0.69	12/94	2c
Turkey, frozen, whole	lb.	0.96	12/94	82r
Yogurt, natural, fruit flavored	8 oz.	0.58	12/94	82r
Goods and Services				
Miscellaneous goods and services, ACCRA Index		93.20	12/94	2c
Health Care				
Health care, ACCRA Index		92.20	12/94	2c
Adenosine, emergency room	treat	100.00	95	23r
Antibiotic ointment, Polysporin	1.5 oz.	3.81	12/94	2c
Bladder tap, superpubic, infant, emergency room	treat	119.00	95	23r
Blood analysis, emergency room	treat	25.00	95	23r
Blood tests, abdominal pain, emergency room	treat	25.00	95	23r
Burn dressing, emergency room	treat	266.00	95	23r
Cardiology interpretation, emergency room	treat	26.00	95	23r
Chest X-ray, emergency room	treat	78.00	95	23r
Childbirth, Cesarean delivery, hospital charge	birth	5462.00	12/91	69r
Childbirth, Cesarean delivery, physician charge	birth	2228.00	12/91	69r
Childbirth, normal delivery, hospital charge	birth	2943.00	12/91	69r

Values are in dollars or fractions of dollars. In the column headed *Ref*, references are shown to sources. Each reference is followed by a letter. These refer to the geographical level for which data were reported: s=State, r=Region, and c=City or metro. The abbreviation *ex* is used to mean *except* or *excluding*; *exp* stands for *expenditures*. For other abbreviations and further explanations, please see the Introduction.

Charleston, WV - continued

Item	Per	Value	Date	Ref.
Health Care				
Childbirth, normal delivery, physician charge	birth	1619.00	12/91	69r
Defibrillation pads, emergency room	treat	6.00	95	23r
Dentist's fee, adult teeth cleaning and periodic oral exam	visit	46.20	12/94	2c
Doctor's fee, routine exam, established patient	visit	43.60	12/94	2c
Drugs, expenditures	year	297	91	81r
Gastric tube insertion, nasal, emergency room	treat	25.00	95	23r
Health care, total expenditures	year	1600	91	81r
Health insurance expenditures	year	637	91	81r
Heart monitor, emergency room	treat	40.00	95	23r
Hospital care, semiprivate room	day	274.40	12/94	2c
Intravenous fluids, emergency room	treat	130.00	95	23r
Intravenous fluids, emergency room	liter	26.00	95	23r
Intravenous line, central, emergency room	treat	342.00	95	23r
Liver function tests, abdominal pain, emergency room	treat	26.00	95	23r
Medical care charges, total, emergency room, third-degree burns	treat	2101.00	95	23r
Medical care charges, total, emergency, infant with fever	treat	628.00	95	23r
Medical services expenditures	year	573	91	81r
Medical supplies expenditures	year	93	91	81r
Morphine, emergency room	treat	34.00	95	23r
Nursing care and facilities charges, emergency room	treat	252.00	95	23r
Nursing care and facilities charges, emergency, infant with fever	treat	252.00	95	23r
Nursing care and facilities charges, emergency, third-degree burns	treat	861.00	95	23r
Physician's charges, emergency, infant with fever	treat	212.00	95	23r
Physician's charges, emergency, third-degree burns	treat	372.00	95	23r
Physician's fee, emergency room	treat	372.00	95	23r
Physician's fee, general practitioner	visit	51.20	12/93	60r
Surgery, open-heart	proc	42374.00	1/93	14r
Ultrasound, abdominal, emergency room	treat	276.00	95	23r
Urinalysis, emergency room	treat	20.00	95	23r
Urinalysis, infant, emergency room	treat	20.00	95	23r
X-rays, emergency room	treat	78.00	95	23r
Household Goods				
Appl. repair, service call, wash mach	min. lab. chg.	37.58	12/94	2c
Floor coverings, expenditures	year	48	91	81r
Furniture, expenditures	year	280	91	81r
Household equipment, misc. expenditures	year	342	91	81r
Household expenditures, miscellaneous	year	256	91	81r
Household furnishings and equipment, expenditures	year	988	91	81r
Household operations expenditures	year	468	91	81r
Household textiles, expenditures	year	95	91	81r
Housekeeping supplies, expenditures	year	380	91	81r
Laundry and cleaning supplies, expenditures	year	109	91	81r
Laundry detergent, Tide Ultra, Bold, or Cheer	42 oz.	3.17	12/94	2c
Postage and stationery, expenditures	year	105	91	81r
Tissues, facial, Kleenex brand	175	0.99	12/94	2c
Housing				
Housing, ACCRA Index		101.10	12/94	2c
Add garage/carport		6,980	3/95	74r
Add room(s)		11,403	3/95	74r
Apartment condominium or co-op, median	unit	68600	12/94	62r
Dwellings (owned), expenditures	year	2428	91	81r
Enclose porch/patio/breezeway		4,572	3/95	74r
Finish room in basement/attic		3,794	3/95	74r
Home, existing, single-family, median	unit	120200	12/94	62r
Home, existing, single-family, median	unit	78.10	12/94	62c

Charleston, WV - continued

Item	Per	Value	Date	Ref.
Housing - continued				
House payment, principal and interest, 25% down payment	mo.	918	12/94	2c
House, 1800 sq ft, 8000 sq ft lot, new, urban, utilities	total	149300	12/94	2c
Maintenance, repairs, insurance, and other housing expenditures	year	531	91	81r
Mortgage interest and charges expenditures	year	1506	91	81r
Mtge. rate, incl. points and orig. fee, 30-year conv. fixed or ARM	mo.	9.21	12/94	2c
Princ. & int., mortgage, median-price exist. sing.-family home	mo.	540	12/94	62r
Property taxes expenditures	year	391	91	81r
Redesign, restructure more than half of home's interior		17,641	3/95	74r
Rent, apartment, 2 br., 1 1/2-2 baths, unfurnished, 950 sq ft, water	mo.	530	12/94	2c
Rental units expenditures	year	1264	91	81r
Insurance and Pensions				
Auto insurance, private passenger	year	696.89	12/94	71s
Insurance and pensions, personal, expenditures	year	2395	91	81r
Insurance, life and other personal, expenditures	year	368	91	81r
Pensions and Social Security, expenditures	year	2027	91	81r
Personal Goods				
Shampoo, Alberto VO5	15-oz.	0.88	12/94	2c
Toothpaste, Crest or Colgate	6-7 oz.	1.54	12/94	2c
Personal Services				
Dry cleaning, man's 2-pc. suit		6.24	12/94	2c
Haircut, man's barbershop, no styling		6.80	12/94	2c
Haircut, woman's shampoo, trim, blow-dry		20.40	12/94	2c
Personal services expenditures	year	212	91	81r
Restaurant Food				
Chicken, fried, thigh and drumstick		1.84	12/94	2c
Dining expenditures, family	week	33.83	94	73r
Hamburger with cheese	1/4 lb.	1.81	12/94	2c
Pizza, Pizza Hut or Pizza Inn	12-13 in.	6.24	12/94	2c
Taxes				
Tax rate, residential property, month	$100	0.68	1/92	79c
Taxes, Federal income, expenditures	year	2275	91	81r
Taxes, personal, expenditures	year	2715	91	81r
Taxes, State and local income, expenditures	year	365	91	81r
Transportation				
Transportation, ACCRA Index		103.70	12/94	2c
Bus fare, up to 10 miles	one-way	1.00	12/94	2c
Cars and trucks purchased, new	year	1306	91	81r
Cars and trucks purchased, used	year	942	91	81r
Driver's learning permit fee	perm	4.00	1/94	84s
Driver's license fee	orig	10.50	1/94	84s
Driver's license fee, duplicate	lic	5.00	1/94	84s
Driver's license renewal fee	renew	10.50	1/94	84s
Identification card, nondriver	card	5.00	1/94	83s
Motorcycle learning permit fee	perm	5.00	1/94	84s
Motorcycle license fee	orig	10.00	1/94	84s
Motorcycle license fee, duplicate	lic	5.00	1/94	84s
Motorcycle license renewal fee	renew	10.00	1/94	84s
Public transportation expenditures	year	249	91	81r
Tire balance, computer or spin bal., front	wheel	6.71	12/94	2c
Transportation expenditures, total	year	5307	91	81r
Vehicle finance charges	year	346	91	81r
Vehicle insurance expenditures	year	544	91	81r
Vehicle maintenance and repairs expenditures	year	600	91	81r
Vehicle purchases	year	2275	91	81r
Vehicle rental, leases, licenses, etc. expenditures	year	141	91	81r

Values are in dollars or fractions of dollars. In the column headed *Ref*, references are shown to sources. Each reference is followed by a letter. These refer to the geographical level for which data were reported: s=State, r=Region, and c=City or metro. The abbreviation *ex* is used to mean *except* or *excluding*; *exp* stands for *expenditures*. For other abbreviations and further explanations, please see the Introduction.

Charleston, WV - continued

Item	Per	Value	Date	Ref.
Transportation				
Vehicles purchased, other than cars and trucks	year	27	91	81r
Utilities				
Utilities, ACCRA Index		102.10	12/94	2c
Electricity expenditures	year	950	91	81r
Electricity, 1800 sq. ft., new home	mo.	105.58	12/94	2c
Electricity, summer, 250 KWh	month	27.23	8/93	64s
Electricity, summer, 500 KWh	month	36.96	8/93	64s
Electricity, summer, 750 KWh	month	52.76	8/93	64s
Electricity, summer, 1000 KWh	month	68.52	8/93	64s
Utilities, fuels, and public services, total expenditures	year	2000	91	81r
Water and other public services, expenditures	year	227	91	81r
Weddings				
Bridal attendants' gowns	event	750	10/93	76r
Bridal gown	event	852	10/93	76r
Bridal headpiece and veil	event	167	10/93	76r
Bride's wedding band	event	708	10/93	76r
Clergy	event	224	10/93	76r
Engagement ring	event	2756	10/93	76r
Flowers	event	863	10/93	76r
Formal wear for groom	event	106	10/93	76r
Groom's attendants' formal wear	event	530	10/93	76r
Groom's wedding band	event	402	10/93	76r
Music	event	600	10/93	76r
Photography	event	1088	10/93	76r
Shoes for bride	event	50	10/93	76r
Videography	event	483	10/93	76r
Wedding invitations and announcements	event	342	10/93	76r
Wedding reception	event	7000	10/93	76r

Charlotte, NC

Item	Per	Value	Date	Ref.
Composite, ACCRA index		98.70	12/94	2c
Alcoholic Beverages				
Beer, Miller Lite, Bud, 12-oz., ex deposit	6	3.86	12/94	2c
J & B Scotch	750-ml.	18.60	12/94	2c
Wine, Gallo Chablis blanc	1.5-lit	4.29	12/94	2c
Appliances				
Appliances (major), expenditures	year	153	91	81r
Average annual exp.				
Food, health care, personal goods, services	year	27020	91	81r
Charity				
Cash contributions, expenditures	year	839	91	81r
Clothing				
Apparel, men and boys, total expenditures	year	380	91	81r
Apparel, women and girls, total expenditures	year	660	91	81r
Footwear, expenditures	year	193	91	81r
Jeans, man's denim		33.60	12/94	2c
Shirt, dress, men's	shirt	35.00	1/92	44c
Shirt, man's dress shirt		25.60	12/94	2c
Undervest, boy's size 10-14, cotton	3	4.75	12/94	2c
Communications				
Long-distance telephone rate, day, addl. min., 1-10 mi.	min.	0.10	12/93	9s
Long-distance telephone rate, day, initial min., 1-10 mi.	min.	0.16	12/93	9s
Newspaper subscription, dly. and Sun. delivery	month	10.80	12/94	2c
Phone line, single, business, field visit	inst	62.50	12/93	9s
Phone line, single, business, no field visit	inst	62.50	12/93	9s
Phone line, single, residence, field visit	inst	42.75	12/93	9s
Phone line, single, residence, no field visit	inst	42.75	12/93	9s
Telephone bill, family of four	month	18.12	12/94	2c
Telephone service, expenditures	year	616	91	81r

Charlotte, NC - continued

Item	Per	Value	Date	Ref.
Communications - continued				
Telephone, residential, flat rate	mo.	11.66	12/93	8c
Credit Cards				
Fee, conventional credit card, bal. carried	year	39.00	1/95	96c
Education				
Board, 4-year private college/university	year	2069	8/94	80s
Board, 4-year public college/university	year	1627	8/94	80s
Education, total expenditures	year	319	91	81r
Room, 4-year private college/university	year	1824	8/94	80s
Room, 4-year public college/university	year	1669	8/94	80s
Total cost, 4-year private college/university	year	13505	8/94	80s
Total cost, 4-year public college/university	year	4704	8/94	80s
Tuition, 2-year public college/university, in-state	year	577	8/94	80s
Tuition, 4-year private college/university, in-state	year	9612	8/94	80s
Tuition, 4-year public college/university, in-state	year	1409	8/94	80s
Energy and Fuels				
Energy, combined forms, 1800 sq. ft.	mo.	112.27	12/94	2c
Fuel oil and other fuels, expenditures	year	56	91	81r
Gas	gal.	1.09	1/92	44c
Gas, cooking, winter, 10 therms	month	12.56	2/94	65c
Gas, cooking, winter, 30 therms	month	23.69	2/94	65c
Gas, cooking, winter, 50 therms	month	34.82	2/94	65c
Gas, heating, winter, 100 therms	month	62.63	2/94	65c
Gas, heating, winter, average use	month	99.46	2/94	65c
Gas, natural, expenditures	year	150	91	81r
Gas, reg unlead, taxes inc., cash, self-service	gal	1.09	12/94	2c
Gasoline and motor oil purchased	year	1152	91	81r
Gasoline, unleaded midgrade	gallon	1.21	4/93	82r
Gasoline, unleaded premium	gallon	1.30	4/93	82r
Gasoline, unleaded regular	gallon	1.10	4/93	82r
Entertainment				
Bowling, evening rate	game	2.56	12/94	2c
Concert ticket, Pearl Jam group	perf	20.00	94	50r
Entertainment, total expenditures	year	1266	91	81r
Fees and admissions, expenditures	year	306	91	81r
Monopoly game, Parker Brothers', No. 9	game	10.18	12/94	2c
Movie	adm	5.90	12/94	2c
Movie ticket, adult	ticket	5.75	1/92	44c
Pets, toys, playground equipment, expenditures	year	271	91	81r
Reading, expenditures	year	131	91	81r
Televisions, radios, and sound equipment, expenditures	year	439	91	81r
Tennis balls, yellow, Wilson or Penn, 3	can	1.80	12/94	2c
Funerals				
Burial, immediate, container provided by funeral home		1370.36	1/95	54r
Cards, acknowledgment		14.83	1/95	54r
Casket, minimum alternative		192.52	1/95	54r
Cosmetology, hair care, etc.		102.27	1/95	54r
Cremation, direct, container provided by funeral home		1065.64	1/95	54r
Embalming		304.29	1/95	54r
Funeral, funeral home		287.83	1/95	54r
Funeral, other facility		284.14	1/95	54r
Graveside service		349.13	1/95	54r
Hearse, local		132.27	1/95	54r
Limousine, local		98.45	1/95	54r
Memorial service		270.59	1/95	54r
Service charge, professional, nondeclinable		933.59	1/95	54r
Visitation and viewing		225.83	1/95	54r
Groceries				
Groceries, ACCRA Index		97.40	12/94	2c
Apples, Red Delicious	lb.	0.73	12/94	82r
Baby food, strained vegetables, lowest price	4-4.5 oz.	0.36	12/94	2c

Values are in dollars or fractions of dollars. In the column headed *Ref*, references are shown to sources. Each reference is followed by a letter. These refer to the geographical level for which data were reported: s = State, r = Region, and c = City or metro. The abbreviation *ex* is used to mean *except* or *excluding*; *exp* stands for *expenditures*. For other abbreviations and further explanations, please see the Introduction.

Charlotte, NC - continued

Item	Per	Value	Date	Ref.
Groceries				
Bacon, sliced	lb.	1.67	12/94	82r
Bacon, sliced, Oscar Mayer brand	lb.	2.67	3/94	58c
Balogna, sliced, Oscar Mayer brand	8 oz.	1.64	3/94	58c
Bananas	lb.	0.42	12/94	82r
Bananas	lb.	0.53	12/94	2c
Beef or hamburger, ground	lb.	1.47	12/94	2c
Beef purchases	year	213	91	81r
Beverage purchases, alcoholic	year	249	91	81r
Beverage purchases, nonalcoholic	year	207	91	81r
Beverage, Coca Cola	2 lit	1.06	3/94	58c
Beverage, Pepsi	2 lit	1.17	3/94	58c
Bologna, all beef or mixed	lb.	2.27	12/94	82r
Bread, local brand	1 lb. 8 oz.	1.36	3/94	58c
Bread, Pepperidge Farm white	lb.	1.68	3/94	58c
Bread, white	24-oz.	0.71	12/94	2c
Bread, white, pan	lb.	0.68	12/94	82r
Butter, Land O'Lakes brand	lb.	1.35	3/94	58c
Butter, private label	lb.	1.24	3/94	58c
Cabbage	lb.	0.42	12/94	82r
Carrots, short trimmed and topped	lb.	0.53	12/94	82r
Cereals and bakery products purchases	year	345	91	81r
Cereals and cereals products purchases	year	127	91	81r
Cheddar cheese, natural	lb.	3.58	12/94	82r
Cheese, Kraft American Singles brand	16 oz.	2.62	3/94	58c
Cheese, Kraft grated Parmesan	8-oz.	2.97	12/94	2c
Chicken breast, bone-in	lb.	1.71	12/94	82r
Chicken, fresh, whole	lb.	0.78	12/94	82r
Chicken, whole fryer	lb.	0.90	12/94	2c
Chuck roast, USDA choice, boneless	lb.	2.26	12/94	82r
Cigarettes, Winston, Kings	carton	12.89	12/94	2c
Coffee, Maxwell House brand, regular grind	13 oz.	2.07	3/94	58c
Coffee, vacuum-packed	13 oz.	3.31	12/94	2c
Corn Flakes, Kellogg's or Post Toasties	18 oz.	2.45	12/94	2c
Corn, frozen, whole kernel, lowest price	10 oz.	0.69	12/94	2c
Crackers, soda, salted	lb.	1.27	12/94	82r
Cucumbers	lb.	0.65	12/94	82r
Dairy products (other) purchases	year	141	91	81r
Detergent powder, Tide Ultra brand	42 oz.	3.21	3/94	58c
Eggs, Grade A large	dozen	0.87	12/94	2c
Eggs, Grade A large	dozen	0.87	12/94	82r
Eggs, private label, large, white	doz.	0.86	3/94	58c
Fish and seafood purchases	year	72	91	81r
Flour, white, all purpose	lb.	0.23	12/94	82r
Food purchases, food eaten at home	year	2381	91	81r
Foods purchased away from home, not prepared by consumer	year	1696	91	81r
Frankfurters, all meat or all beef	lb.	1.74	12/94	82r
Frankfurters, Oscar Mayer brand	lb.	1.99	3/94	58c
Fruits and vegetables purchases	year	380	91	81r
Grapefruit	lb.	0.45	12/94	82r
Grapes, Thompson seedless	lb.	2.30	12/94	82r
Ground beef, 100% beef	lb.	1.37	12/94	82r
Ground chuck, 100% beef	lb.	1.97	12/94	82r
Ham, boneless, exc. canned	lb.	2.54	12/94	82r
Ice cream, prepackaged, bulk, regular	1/2 gal.	2.47	12/94	82r
Jelly, Welch's brand, grape	32 oz.	1.39	3/94	58c
Ketchup, Heinz brand	14 oz.	0.83	3/94	58c
Lemons	lb.	1.02	12/94	82r
Lettuce, iceberg	lb.	0.96	12/94	82r
Lettuce, iceberg	head	0.99	12/94	2c
Margarine sticks, Parkay brand	lb.	0.45	3/94	58c
Margarine, Blue Bonnet or Parkay cubes	lb.	0.56	12/94	2c
Margarine, stick	lb.	0.77	12/94	82r
Mayonnaise, Hellmann's brand	quart	2.42	3/94	58c
Meat, ground chuck steak, 80% lean	lb.	1.94	3/94	58c
Meats, poultry, fish, and eggs purchases	year	655	91	81r
Milk and cream (fresh) purchases	year	130	91	81r
Milk, 2%	gal.	2.37	1/92	44c
Milk, whole	1/2 gal.	1.43	12/94	2c

Charlotte, NC - continued

Item	Per	Value	Date	Ref.
Groceries - continued				
Milk, whole, private label	gallon	2.48	3/94	58c
Muffins, Thomas's English	6	1.82	3/94	58c
Orange juice, frozen concentrate 12-oz. can	16 oz.	1.36	12/94	82r
Orange juice, Minute Maid frozen	12-oz.	1.17	12/94	2c
Oranges, Navel	lb.	0.54	12/94	82r
Peaches, halves or slices, Hunt's, Del Monte, or Libby's	29-oz.	1.19	12/94	2c
Peanut butter, Skippy brand, creamy	18 oz.	1.87	3/94	58c
Pears, Anjou	lb.	0.81	12/94	82r
Peas, sweet, Del Monte or Green Giant	15-17 oz.	0.52	12/94	2c
Pork chops, center cut, bone-in	lb.	3.07	12/94	82r
Pork purchases	year	142	91	81r
Potato chips	16-oz.	3.15	12/94	82r
Potatoes, frozen, French fried	lb.	0.82	12/94	82r
Potatoes, white	lb.	0.34	12/94	82r
Potatoes, white or red	10-lb. sack	2.67	12/94	2c
Rental rate, 2-bedroom apartment	month	550.00-650	1/92	44c
Rice, white, long grain, uncooked	lb.	0.48	12/94	82r
Round roast, USDA choice, boneless	lb.	2.91	12/94	82r
Sausage, fresh	lb.	1.82	12/94	82r
Sausage, Jimmy Dean, 100% pork	lb.	2.47	12/94	2c
Shortening, vegetable oil blends	lb.	0.75	12/94	82r
Shortening, vegetable, Crisco	3-lb.	2.51	12/94	2c
Soft drink, Coca Cola, ex deposit	2 lit	1.01	12/94	2c
Soup, Campbell's brand, tomato, canned	10 3/4 oz.	0.45	3/94	58c
Spaghetti and macaroni	lb.	0.87	12/94	82r
Steak, rib eye, USDA choice, boneless	lb.	6.85	12/94	82r
Steak, round, graded & ungraded, exc. USDA prime & choice	lb.	2.96	12/94	82r
Steak, round, USDA choice, boneless	lb.	3.17	12/94	82r
Steak, sirloin, USDA choice, boneless	lb.	4.12	12/94	82r
Steak, t-bone	lb.	5.19	12/94	2c
Steak, T-bone, USDA choice, bone-in	lb.	5.63	12/94	82r
Sugar and other sweets, eaten at home, expenditures	year	93	91	81r
Sugar, cane or beet	4 lbs.	1.49	12/94	2c
Sugar, Domino brand	5 lbs.	1.94	3/94	58c
Sugar, white, all sizes	lb.	0.39	12/94	82r
Tea, Lipton brand	100 bags	2.54	3/94	58c
Tobacco products and smoking supplies, total expenditures	year	286	91	81r
Tomatoes, field grown	lb.	1.36	12/94	82r
Tomatoes, Hunt's or Del Monte	14.5 oz.	0.55	12/94	2c
Tuna, chunk, light	lb.	1.94	12/94	82r
Tuna, chunk, light, oil-packed	6.125-6.5 oz.	0.67	12/94	2c
Turkey, frozen, whole	lb.	0.96	12/94	82r
Yogurt, natural, fruit flavored	8 oz.	0.58	12/94	82r
Goods and Services				
Miscellaneous goods and services, ACCRA Index		98.90	12/94	2c
Health Care				
Health care, ACCRA Index		110.20	12/94	2c
Adenosine, emergency room	treat	100.00	95	23r
Antibiotic ointment, Polysporin	1.5 oz.	3.73	12/94	2c
Bladder tap, superpubic, infant, emergency room	treat	119.00	95	23r
Blood analysis, emergency room	treat	25.00	95	23r
Blood tests, abdominal pain, emergency room	treat	25.00	95	23r
Burn dressing, emergency room	treat	266.00	95	23r
Cardiology interpretation, emergency room	treat	26.00	95	23r
Chest X-ray, emergency room	treat	78.00	95	23r
Childbirth, Cesarean delivery, hospital charge	birth	5462.00	12/91	69r

Values are in dollars or fractions of dollars. In the column headed *Ref*, references are shown to sources. Each reference is followed by a letter. These refer to the geographical level for which data were reported: s=State, r=Region, and c=City or metro. The abbreviation *ex* is used to mean *except* or *excluding*; *exp* stands for *expenditures*. For other abbreviations and further explanations, please see the Introduction.

Charlotte, NC - continued

Item	Per	Value	Date	Ref.
Health Care				
Childbirth, Cesarean delivery, physician charge	birth	2228.00	12/91	69r
Childbirth, normal delivery, hospital charge	birth	2943.00	12/91	69r
Childbirth, normal delivery, physician charge	birth	1619.00	12/91	69r
Defibrillation pads, emergency room	treat	6.00	95	23r
Dentist's fee, adult teeth cleaning and periodic oral exam	visit	54.40	12/94	2c
Doctor's fee, routine exam, established patient	visit	55.80	12/94	2c
Drugs, expenditures	year	297	91	81r
Gastric tube insertion, nasal, emergency room	treat	25.00	95	23r
Health care, total expenditures	year	1600	91	81r
Health insurance expenditures	year	637	91	81r
Heart monitor, emergency room	treat	40.00	95	23r
Hospital care, semiprivate room	day	320.67	12/94	2c
Insurance premium, family medical care	month	405.45	1/95	41s
Intravenous fluids, emergency room	treat	130.00	95	23r
Intravenous fluids, emergency room	liter	26.00	95	23r
Intravenous line, central, emergency room	treat	342.00	95	23r
Liver function tests, abdominal pain, emergency room	treat	26.00	95	23r
Medical care charges, total, emergency room, third-degree burns	treat	2101.00	95	23r
Medical care charges, total, emergency, infant with fever	treat	628.00	95	23r
Medical services expenditures	year	573	91	81r
Medical supplies expenditures	year	93	91	81r
Morphine, emergency room	treat	34.00	95	23r
Nursing care and facilities charges, emergency room	treat	252.00	95	23r
Nursing care and facilities charges, emergency, infant with fever	treat	252.00	95	23r
Nursing care and facilities charges, emergency, third-degree burns	treat	861.00	95	23r
Physician's charges, emergency, infant with fever	treat	212.00	95	23r
Physician's charges, emergency, third-degree burns	treat	372.00	95	23r
Physician's fee, emergency room	treat	372.00	95	23r
Physician's fee, general practitioner	visit	51.20	12/93	60r
Surgery, open-heart	proc	42374.00	1/93	14r
Ultrasound, abdominal, emergency room	treat	276.00	95	23r
Urinalysis, emergency room	treat	20.00	95	23r
Urinalysis, infant, emergency room	treat	20.00	95	23r
X-rays, emergency room	treat	78.00	95	23r
Household Goods				
Appl. repair, service call, wash mach	min. lab. chg.	31.30	12/94	2c
Floor coverings, expenditures	year	48	91	81r
Furniture, expenditures	year	280	91	81r
Household equipment, misc. expenditures	year	342	91	81r
Household expenditures, miscellaneous	year	256	91	81r
Household furnishings and equipment, expenditures	year	988	91	81r
Household operations expenditures	year	468	91	81r
Household textiles, expenditures	year	95	91	81r
Housekeeping supplies, expenditures	year	380	91	81r
Laundry and cleaning supplies, expenditures	year	109	91	81r
Laundry detergent, Tide Ultra, Bold, or Cheer	42 oz.	2.59	12/94	2c
Postage and stationery, expenditures	year	105	91	81r
Tissues, facial, Kleenex brand	175	0.93	12/94	2c
Housing				
Housing, ACCRA Index		97.70	12/94	2c
Add garage/carport		6,980	3/95	74r
Add room(s)		11,403	3/95	74r
Apartment condominium or co-op, median	unit	68600	12/94	62r
Dwellings (owned), expenditures	year	2428	91	81r

Charlotte, NC - continued

Item	Per	Value	Date	Ref.
Housing - continued				
Enclose porch/patio/breezeway		4,572	3/95	74r
Finish room in basement/attic		3,794	3/95	74r
Home, existing, single-family, median	unit	120200	12/94	62r
Home, existing, single-family, median	unit	104.60	12/94	62c
House payment, principal and interest, 25% down payment	mo.	764	12/94	2c
House, 1800 sq ft, 8000 sq ft lot, new, urban, utilities	total	126000	12/94	2c
Maintenance, repairs, insurance, and other housing expenditures	year	531	91	81r
Mortgage interest and charges expenditures	year	1506	91	81r
Mtge. rate, incl. points and orig. fee, 30-year conv. fixed or ARM	mo.	9.06	12/94	2c
Princ. & int., mortgage, median-price exist. sing.-family home	mo.	540	12/94	62r
Property taxes expenditures	year	391	91	81r
Redesign, restructure more than half of home's interior		17,641	3/95	74r
Rent, apartment, 2 br., 1 1/2-2 baths, unfurnished, 950 sq ft, water	mo.	471	12/94	2c
Rental units expenditures	year	1264	91	81r
Insurance and Pensions				
Auto insurance, private passenger	year	528.43	12/94	71s
Insurance and pensions, personal, expenditures	year	2395	91	81r
Insurance, life and other personal, expenditures	year	368	91	81r
Pensions and Social Security, expenditures	year	2027	91	81r
Personal Goods				
Shampoo, Alberto VO5	15-oz.	1.16	12/94	2c
Toothpaste, Crest or Colgate	6-7 oz.	2.18	12/94	2c
Personal Services				
Dry cleaning, man's 2-pc. suit		5.94	12/94	2c
Dry cleaning, woman's dress	dress	9.50	1/92	44c
Haircut, man's barbershop, no styling		10.40	12/94	2c
Haircut, woman's shampoo, trim, blow-dry		21.60	12/94	2c
Personal services expenditures	year	212	91	81r
Restaurant Food				
Big Mac, small fries, medium drink	meal	3.25	1/92	44c
Chicken, fried, thigh and drumstick		2.24	12/94	2c
Dining expenditures, family	week	33.83	94	73r
Hamburger with cheese	1/4 lb.	1.99	12/94	2c
Pizza, Pizza Hut or Pizza Inn	12-13 in.	7.49	12/94	2c
Taxes				
Tax rate, residential property, month	$100	1.17	1/92	79c
Taxes, Federal income, expenditures	year	2275	91	81r
Taxes, personal, expenditures	year	2715	91	81r
Taxes, State and local income, expenditures	year	365	91	81r
Transportation				
Transportation, ACCRA Index		95.70	12/94	2c
Bus fare, one-way	trip	0.80	12/95	1c
Bus fare, up to 10 miles	one-way	0.80	12/94	2c
Cars and trucks purchased, new	year	1306	91	81r
Cars and trucks purchased, used	year	942	91	81r
Driver's learning permit fee	perm	10.00	1/94	84s
Driver's license fee	orig	10.00	1/94	84s
Driver's license fee, duplicate	lic	5.00	1/94	84s
Driver's license reinstatement fee, min.	susp	25.00	1/94	85s
Driver's license renewal fee	renew	10.00	1/94	84s
Fine, safety belt violation	ticket	25.00	95	56s
Identification card, nondriver	card	10.00	1/94	83s
Motorcycle license fee	orig	5.00	1/94	84s
parking, long-term lot, airport	3 days	8.25	1/92	44c
Public transportation expenditures	year	249	91	81r
Tire balance, computer or spin bal., front	wheel	6.60	12/94	2c
Transportation expenditures, total	year	5307	91	81r
Vehicle finance charges	year	346	91	81r

Values are in dollars or fractions of dollars. In the column headed *Ref*, references are shown to sources. Each reference is followed by a letter. These refer to the geographical level for which data were reported: s = State, r = Region, and c = City or metro. The abbreviation *ex* is used to mean *except* or *excluding*; *exp* stands for *expenditures*. For other abbreviations and further explanations, please see the Introduction.

Charlotte, NC - continued

Item	Per	Value	Date	Ref.
Transportation				
Vehicle insurance expenditures	year	544	91	81r
Vehicle maintenance and repairs expenditures	year	600	91	81r
Vehicle purchases	year	2275	91	81r
Vehicle rental, leases, licenses, etc. expenditures	year	141	91	81r
Vehicles purchased, other than cars and trucks	year	27	91	81r
Utilities				
Utilities, ACCRA Index		99.10	12/94	2c
Electricity expenditures	year	950	91	81r
Electricity, 1800 sq. ft., new home	mo.	112.27	12/94	2c
Electricity, summer, 250 KWh	month	24.20	8/93	64c
Electricity, summer, 500 KWh	month	41.66	8/93	64c
Electricity, summer, 750 KWh	month	59.86	8/93	64c
Electricity, summer, 1000 KWh	month	78.07	8/93	64c
Utilities, fuels, and public services, total expenditures	year	2000	91	81r
Water and other public services, expenditures	year	227	91	81r
Weddings				
Bridal attendants' gowns	event	750	10/93	76r
Bridal gown	event	852	10/93	76r
Bridal headpiece and veil	event	167	10/93	76r
Bride's wedding band	event	708	10/93	76r
Clergy	event	224	10/93	76r
Engagement ring	event	2756	10/93	76r
Flowers	event	863	10/93	76r
Formal wear for groom	event	106	10/93	76r
Groom's attendants' formal wear	event	530	10/93	76r
Groom's wedding band	event	402	10/93	76r
Music	event	600	10/93	76r
Photography	event	1088	10/93	76r
Shoes for bride	event	50	10/93	76r
Videography	event	483	10/93	76r
Wedding invitations and announcements	event	342	10/93	76r
Wedding reception	event	7000	10/93	76r

Charlottesville, VA

Item	Per	Value	Date	Ref.
Appliances				
Appliances (major), expenditures	year	153	91	81r
Average annual exp.				
Food, health care, personal goods, services	year	27020	91	81r
Charity				
Cash contributions, expenditures	year	839	91	81r
Clothing				
Apparel, men and boys, total expenditures	year	380	91	81r
Apparel, women and girls, total expenditures	year	660	91	81r
Footwear, expenditures	year	193	91	81r
Communications				
Long-distance telephone rate, day, addl. min., 1-10 mi.	min.	0.12	12/93	9s
Long-distance telephone rate, day, initial min., 1-10 mi.	min.	0.21	12/93	9s
Phone line, single, business, field visit	inst	0.00	12/93	9s
Phone line, single, business, no field visit	inst	64.00	12/93	9s
Phone line, single, residence, field visit	inst	0.00	12/93	9s
Phone line, single, residence, no field visit	inst	38.50	12/93	9s
Telephone service, expenditures	year	616	91	81r
Education				
Board, 4-year private college/university	year	2242	8/94	80s
Board, 4-year public college/university	year	1901	8/94	80s
Education, total expenditures	year	319	91	81r
Room, 4-year private college/university	year	2022	8/94	80s
Room, 4-year public college/university	year	2186	8/94	80s
Total cost, 4-year private college/university	year	14043	8/94	80s

Charlottesville, VA - continued

Item	Per	Value	Date	Ref.
Education - continued				
Total cost, 4-year public college/university	year	7726	8/94	80s
Tuition, 2-year public college/university, in-state	year	1332	8/94	80s
Tuition, 4-year private college/university, in-state	year	9778	8/94	80s
Tuition, 4-year public college/university, in-state	year	3639	8/94	80s
Energy and Fuels				
Fuel oil and other fuels, expenditures	year	56	91	81r
Gas, natural, expenditures	year	150	91	81r
Gasoline and motor oil purchased	year	1152	91	81r
Gasoline, unleaded midgrade	gallon	1.21	4/93	82r
Gasoline, unleaded premium	gallon	1.30	4/93	82r
Gasoline, unleaded regular	gallon	1.10	4/93	82r
Entertainment				
Concert ticket, Pearl Jam group	perf	20.00	94	50r
Entertainment, total expenditures	year	1266	91	81r
Fees and admissions, expenditures	year	306	91	81r
Pets, toys, playground equipment, expenditures	year	271	91	81r
Reading, expenditures	year	131	91	81r
Televisions, radios, and sound equipment, expenditures	year	439	91	81r
Funerals				
Burial, immediate, container provided by funeral home		1370.36	1/95	54r
Cards, acknowledgment		14.83	1/95	54r
Casket, minimum alternative		192.52	1/95	54r
Cosmetology, hair care, etc.		102.27	1/95	54r
Cremation, direct, container provided by funeral home		1065.64	1/95	54r
Embalming		304.29	1/95	54r
Funeral, funeral home		287.83	1/95	54r
Funeral, other facility		284.14	1/95	54r
Graveside service		349.13	1/95	54r
Hearse, local		132.27	1/95	54r
Limousine, local		98.45	1/95	54r
Memorial service		270.59	1/95	54r
Service charge, professional, nondeclinable		933.59	1/95	54r
Visitation and viewing		225.83	1/95	54r
Groceries				
Apples, Red Delicious	lb.	0.73	12/94	82r
Bacon, sliced	lb.	1.67	12/94	82r
Bananas	lb.	0.42	12/94	82r
Beef purchases	year	213	91	81r
Beverage purchases, alcoholic	year	249	91	81r
Beverage purchases, nonalcoholic	year	207	91	81r
Bologna, all beef or mixed	lb.	2.27	12/94	82r
Bread, white, pan	lb.	0.68	12/94	82r
Cabbage	lb.	0.42	12/94	82r
Carrots, short trimmed and topped	lb.	0.53	12/94	82r
Cereals and bakery products purchases	year	345	91	81r
Cereals and cereals products purchases	year	127	91	81r
Cheddar cheese, natural	lb.	3.58	12/94	82r
Chicken breast, bone-in	lb.	1.71	12/94	82r
Chicken, fresh, whole	lb.	0.78	12/94	82r
Chuck roast, USDA choice, boneless	lb.	2.26	12/94	82r
Crackers, soda, salted	lb.	1.27	12/94	82r
Cucumbers	lb.	0.65	12/94	82r
Dairy products (other) purchases	year	141	91	81r
Eggs, Grade A large	dozen	0.87	12/94	82r
Fish and seafood purchases	year	72	91	81r
Flour, white, all purpose	lb.	0.23	12/94	82r
Food purchases, food eaten at home	year	2381	91	81r
Foods purchased away from home, not prepared by consumer	year	1696	91	81r
Frankfurters, all meat or all beef	lb.	1.74	12/94	82r
Fruits and vegetables purchases	year	380	91	81r
Grapefruit	lb.	0.45	12/94	82r
Grapes, Thompson seedless	lb.	2.30	12/94	82r

Values are in dollars or fractions of dollars. In the column headed *Ref*, references are shown to sources. Each reference is followed by a letter. These refer to the geographical level for which data were reported: s=State, r=Region, and c=City or metro. The abbreviation *ex* is used to mean *except* or *excluding*; *exp* stands for expenditures. For other abbreviations and further explanations, please see the Introduction.

Charlottesville, VA - continued

Item	Per	Value	Date	Ref.
Groceries				
Ground beef, 100% beef	lb.	1.37	12/94	82r
Ground chuck, 100% beef	lb.	1.97	12/94	82r
Ham, boneless, exc. canned	lb.	2.54	12/94	82r
Ice cream, prepackaged, bulk, regular	1/2 gal.	2.47	12/94	82r
Lemons	lb.	1.02	12/94	82r
Lettuce, iceberg	lb.	0.96	12/94	82r
Margarine, stick	lb.	0.77	12/94	82r
Meats, poultry, fish, and eggs purchases	year	655	91	81r
Milk and cream (fresh) purchases	year	130	91	81r
Orange juice, frozen concentrate 12-oz. can	16 oz.	1.36	12/94	82r
Oranges, Navel	lb.	0.54	12/94	82r
Pears, Anjou	lb.	0.81	12/94	82r
Pork chops, center cut, bone-in	lb.	3.07	12/94	82r
Pork purchases	year	142	91	81r
Potato chips	16-oz.	3.15	12/94	82r
Potatoes, frozen, French fried	lb.	0.82	12/94	82r
Potatoes, white	lb.	0.34	12/94	82r
Rice, white, long grain, uncooked	lb.	0.48	12/94	82r
Round roast, USDA choice, boneless	lb.	2.91	12/94	82r
Sausage, fresh	lb.	1.82	12/94	82r
Shortening, vegetable oil blends	lb.	0.75	12/94	82r
Spaghetti and macaroni	lb.	0.87	12/94	82r
Steak, rib eye, USDA choice, boneless	lb.	6.85	12/94	82r
Steak, round, graded & ungraded, exc. USDA prime & choice	lb.	2.96	12/94	82r
Steak, round, USDA choice, boneless	lb.	3.17	12/94	82r
Steak, sirloin, USDA choice, boneless	lb.	4.12	12/94	82r
Steak, T-bone, USDA choice, bone-in	lb.	5.63	12/94	82r
Sugar and other sweets, eaten at home, expenditures	year	93	91	81r
Sugar, white, all sizes	lb.	0.39	12/94	82r
Tobacco products and smoking supplies, total expenditures	year	286	91	81r
Tomatoes, field grown	lb.	1.36	12/94	82r
Tuna, chunk, light	lb.	1.94	12/94	82r
Turkey, frozen, whole	lb.	0.96	12/94	82r
Yogurt, natural, fruit flavored	8 oz.	0.58	12/94	82r
Health Care				
Adenosine, emergency room	treat	100.00	95	23r
Bladder tap, superpubic, infant, emergency room	treat	119.00	95	23r
Blood analysis, emergency room	treat	25.00	95	23r
Blood tests, abdominal pain, emergency room	treat	25.00	95	23r
Burn dressing, emergency room	treat	266.00	95	23r
Cardiology interpretation, emergency room	treat	26.00	95	23r
Chest X-ray, emergency room	treat	78.00	95	23r
Childbirth, Cesarean delivery, hospital charge	birth	5462.00	12/91	69r
Childbirth, Cesarean delivery, physician charge	birth	2228.00	12/91	69r
Childbirth, normal delivery, hospital charge	birth	2943.00	12/91	69r
Childbirth, normal delivery, physician charge	birth	1619.00	12/91	69r
Defibrillation pads, emergency room	treat	6.00	95	23r
Delivery, uncomplicated, total charge	birth	6180	1/93	24s
Delivery, uncomplicated, vaginal, hospital charge	birth	3380	1/93	24s
Delivery, uncomplicated, vaginal, physician's charge	birth	2800	1/93	24s
Drugs, expenditures	year	297	91	81r
Gastric tube insertion, nasal, emergency room	treat	25.00	95	23r
Health care, total expenditures	year	1600	91	81r
Health insurance expenditures	year	637	91	81r
Heart monitor, emergency room	treat	40.00	95	23r
Insurance premium, family medical care	month	386.57	1/95	41s
Intravenous fluids, emergency room	treat	130.00	95	23r
Intravenous fluids, emergency room	liter	26.00	95	23r
Intravenous line, central, emergency room	treat	342.00	95	23r
Liver function tests, abdominal pain, emergency room	treat	26.00	95	23r

Charlottesville, VA - continued

Item	Per	Value	Date	Ref.
Health Care - continued				
Medical care charges, total, emergency room, third-degree burns	treat	2101.00	95	23r
Medical care charges, total, emergency, infant with fever	treat	628.00	95	23r
Medical services expenditures	year	573	91	81r
Medical supplies expenditures	year	93	91	81r
Morphine, emergency room	treat	34.00	95	23r
Nursing care and facilities charges, emergency room	treat	252.00	95	23r
Nursing care and facilities charges, emergency, infant with fever	treat	252.00	95	23r
Nursing care and facilities charges, emergency, third-degree burns	treat	861.00	95	23r
Physician's charges, emergency, infant with fever	treat	212.00	95	23r
Physician's charges, emergency, third-degree burns	treat	372.00	95	23r
Physician's fee, emergency room	treat	372.00	95	23r
Physician's fee, general practitioner	visit	51.20	12/93	60r
Surgery, open-heart	proc	42374.00	1/93	14r
Ultrasound, abdominal, emergency room	treat	276.00	95	23r
Urinalysis, emergency room	treat	20.00	95	23r
Urinalysis, infant, emergency room	treat	20.00	95	23r
X-rays, emergency room	treat	78.00	95	23r
Household Goods				
Floor coverings, expenditures	year	48	91	81r
Furniture, expenditures	year	280	91	81r
Household equipment, misc. expenditures	year	342	91	81r
Household expenditures, miscellaneous	year	256	91	81r
Household furnishings and equipment, expenditures	year	988	91	81r
Household operations expenditures	year	468	91	81r
Household textiles, expenditures	year	95	91	81r
Housekeeping supplies, expenditures	year	380	91	81r
Laundry and cleaning supplies, expenditures	year	109	91	81r
Postage and stationery, expenditures	year	105	91	81r
Housing				
Add garage/carport		6,980	3/95	74r
Add room(s)		11,403	3/95	74r
Apartment condominium or co-op, median	unit	68600	12/94	62r
Dwellings (owned), expenditures	year	2428	91	81r
Enclose porch/patio/breezeway		4,572	3/95	74r
Finish room in basement/attic		3,794	3/95	74r
Home, existing, single-family, median	unit	120200	12/94	62r
Maintenance, repairs, insurance, and other housing expenditures	year	531	91	81r
Mortgage interest and charges expenditures	year	1506	91	81r
Princ. & int., mortgage, median-price exist. sing.-family home	mo.	540	12/94	62r
Property taxes expenditures	year	391	91	81r
Redesign, restructure more than half of home's interior		17,641	3/95	74r
Rental units expenditures	year	1264	91	81r
Insurance and Pensions				
Auto insurance, private passenger	year	564.07	12/94	71s
Insurance and pensions, personal, expenditures	year	2395	91	81r
Insurance, life and other personal, expenditures	year	368	91	81r
Pensions and Social Security, expenditures	year	2027	91	81r
Personal Services				
Personal services expenditures	year	212	91	81r
Restaurant Food				
Dining expenditures, family	week	33.83	94	73r
Taxes				
Taxes, Federal income, expenditures	year	2275	91	81r
Taxes, personal, expenditures	year	2715	91	81r
Taxes, State and local income, expenditures	year	365	91	81r

Values are in dollars or fractions of dollars. In the column headed *Ref*, references are shown to sources. Each reference is followed by a letter. These refer to the geographical level for which data were reported: s=State, r=Region, and c=City or metro. The abbreviation *ex* is used to mean *except* or *excluding*; *exp* stands for expenditures. For other abbreviations and further explanations, please see the Introduction.

Charlottesville, VA - continued

Item	Per	Value	Date	Ref.
Transportation				
Cars and trucks purchased, new	year	1306	91	81r
Cars and trucks purchased, used	year	942	91	81r
Driver's learning permit fee	perm	3.00	1/94	84s
Driver's license fee	orig	12.00	1/94	84s
Driver's license fee, duplicate	lic	5.00	1/94	84s
Driver's license reinstatement fee, min.	susp	30.00	1/94	85s
Driver's license renewal fee	renew	12.00	1/94	84s
Identification card, nondriver	card	5.00	1/94	83s
Motorcycle license fee	orig	5.00	1/94	84s
Motorcycle license renewal fee	renew	5.00	1/94	84s
Public transportation expenditures	year	249	91	81r
Transportation expenditures, total	year	5307	91	81r
Vehicle finance charges	year	346	91	81r
Vehicle insurance expenditures	year	544	91	81r
Vehicle maintenance and repairs expenditures	year	600	91	81r
Vehicle purchases	year	2275	91	81r
Vehicle rental, leases, licenses, etc. expenditures	year	141	91	81r
Vehicles purchased, other than cars and trucks	year	27	91	81r
Utilities				
Electricity expenditures	year	950	91	81r
Utilities, fuels, and public services, total expenditures	year	2000	91	81r
Water and other public services, expenditures	year	227	91	81r
Weddings				
Bridal attendants' gowns	event	750	10/93	76r
Bridal gown	event	852	10/93	76r
Bridal headpiece and veil	event	167	10/93	76r
Bride's wedding band	event	708	10/93	76r
Clergy	event	224	10/93	76r
Engagement ring	event	2756	10/93	76r
Flowers	event	863	10/93	76r
Formal wear for groom	event	106	10/93	76r
Groom's attendants' formal wear	event	530	10/93	76r
Groom's wedding band	event	402	10/93	76r
Music	event	600	10/93	76r
Photography	event	1088	10/93	76r
Shoes for bride	event	50	10/93	76r
Videography	event	483	10/93	76r
Wedding invitations and announcements	event	342	10/93	76r
Wedding reception	event	7000	10/93	76r

Chattanooga, TN

Item	Per	Value	Date	Ref.
Composite, ACCRA index		94.50	12/94	2c
Alcoholic Beverages				
Beer, Miller Lite, Bud, 12-oz., ex deposit	6	4.19	12/94	2c
J & B Scotch	750-ml.	18.18	12/94	2c
Wine, Gallo Chablis blanc	1.5-lit	5.86	12/94	2c
Appliances				
Appliances (major), expenditures	year	153	91	81r
Average annual exp.				
Food, health care, personal goods, services	year	27020	91	81r
Charity				
Cash contributions, expenditures	year	839	91	81r
Clothing				
Apparel, men and boys, total expenditures	year	380	91	81r
Apparel, women and girls, total expenditures	year	660	91	81r
Footwear, expenditures	year	193	91	81r
Jeans, man's denim		33.19	12/94	2c
Shirt, man's dress shirt		32.50	12/94	2c
Undervest, boy's size 10-14, cotton	3	3.27	12/94	2c

Chattanooga, TN - continued

Item	Per	Value	Date	Ref.
Communications				
Long-distance telephone rate, day, addl. min., 1-10 mi.	min.	0.10	12/93	9s
Long-distance telephone rate, day, initial min., 1-10 mi.	min.	0.10	12/93	9s
Newspaper subscription, dly. and Sun. delivery	month	11.05	12/94	2c
Phone line, single, business, field visit	inst	58.50	12/93	9s
Phone line, single, business, no field visit	inst	58.50	12/93	9s
Phone line, single, residence, field visit	inst	41.50	12/93	9s
Phone line, single, residence, no field visit	inst	41.50	12/93	9s
Telephone bill, family of four	month	20.74	12/94	2c
Telephone service, expenditures	year	616	91	81r
Telephone, residential, flat rate	mo.	11.85	12/93	8c
Education				
Board, 4-year private college/university	year	1846	8/94	80s
Board, 4-year public college/university	year	1700	8/94	80s
Education, total expenditures	year	319	91	81r
Room, 4-year private college/university	year	1553	8/94	80s
Room, 4-year public college/university	year	1524	8/94	80s
Total cost, 4-year private college/university	year	12025	8/94	80s
Total cost, 4-year public college/university	year	5021	8/94	80s
Tuition, 2-year public college/university, in-state	year	950	8/94	80s
Tuition, 4-year private college/university, in-state	year	8627	8/94	80s
Tuition, 4-year public college/university, in-state	year	1797	8/94	80s
Energy and Fuels				
Energy, combined forms, 1800 sq. ft.	mo.	117.20	12/94	2c
Energy, exc. electricity, 1800 sq. ft.	mo.	41.56	12/94	2c
Fuel oil and other fuels, expenditures	year	56	91	81r
Gas, cooking, winter, 10 therms	month	14.00	2/94	65c
Gas, cooking, winter, 30 therms	month	27.50	2/94	65c
Gas, cooking, winter, 50 therms	month	39.55	2/94	65c
Gas, heating, winter, 100 therms	month	68.71	2/94	65c
Gas, heating, winter, average use	month	47.13	2/94	65c
Gas, natural, expenditures	year	150	91	81r
Gas, reg unlead, taxes inc., cash, self-service	gal	1.08	12/94	2c
Gasoline and motor oil purchased	year	1152	91	81r
Gasoline, unleaded midgrade	gallon	1.21	4/93	82r
Gasoline, unleaded premium	gallon	1.30	4/93	82r
Gasoline, unleaded regular	gallon	1.10	4/93	82r
Entertainment				
Bowling, evening rate	game	2.53	12/94	2c
Concert ticket, Pearl Jam group	perf	20.00	94	50r
Entertainment, total expenditures	year	1266	91	81r
Fees and admissions, expenditures	year	306	91	81r
Monopoly game, Parker Brothers', No. 9	game	10.74	12/94	2c
Movie	adm	5.60	12/94	2c
Pets, toys, playground equipment, expenditures	year	271	91	81r
Reading, expenditures	year	131	91	81r
Televisions, radios, and sound equipment, expenditures	year	439	91	81r
Tennis balls, yellow, Wilson or Penn, 3	can	2.08	12/94	2c
Funerals				
Burial, immediate, container provided by funeral home		1298.96	1/95	54r
Cards, acknowledgment		21.26	1/95	54r
Casket, minimum alternative		204.95	1/95	54r
Cosmetology, hair care, etc.		85.40	1/95	54r
Cremation, direct, container provided by funeral home		1054.77	1/95	54r
Embalming		287.71	1/95	54r
Funeral, funeral home		269.18	1/95	54r
Funeral, other facility		272.88	1/95	54r
Graveside service		302.54	1/95	54r
Hearse, local		122.08	1/95	54r
Limousine, local		80.31	1/95	54r

Values are in dollars or fractions of dollars. In the column headed *Ref*, references are shown to sources. Each reference is followed by a letter. These refer to the geographical level for which data were reported: s=State, r=Region, and c=City or metro. The abbreviation *ex* is used to mean *except* or *excluding*; *exp* stands for *expenditures*. For other abbreviations and further explanations, please see the Introduction.

Chattanooga, TN - continued

Item	Per	Value	Date	Ref.
Funerals				
Memorial service		277.66	1/95	54r
Service charge, professional, nondeclinable		896.65	1/95	54r
Visitation and viewing		232.39	1/95	54r
Groceries				
Groceries, ACCRA Index		94.90	12/94	2c
Apples, Red Delicious	lb.	0.73	12/94	82r
Baby food, strained vegetables, lowest price	4-4.5 oz.	0.29	12/94	2c
Bacon, sliced	lb.	1.67	12/94	82r
Bananas	lb.	0.44	12/94	2c
Bananas	lb.	0.42	12/94	82r
Beef or hamburger, ground	lb.	1.61	12/94	2c
Beef purchases	year	213	91	81r
Beverage purchases, alcoholic	year	249	91	81r
Beverage purchases, nonalcoholic	year	207	91	81r
Bologna, all beef or mixed	lb.	2.27	12/94	82r
Bread, white	24-oz.	0.64	12/94	2c
Bread, white, pan	lb.	0.68	12/94	82r
Cabbage	lb.	0.42	12/94	82r
Carrots, short trimmed and topped	lb.	0.53	12/94	82r
Cereals and bakery products purchases	year	345	91	81r
Cereals and cereals products purchases	year	127	91	81r
Cheddar cheese, natural	lb.	3.58	12/94	82r
Cheese, Kraft grated Parmesan	8-oz.	3.11	12/94	2c
Chicken breast, bone-in	lb.	1.71	12/94	82r
Chicken, fresh, whole	lb.	0.78	12/94	82r
Chicken, whole fryer	lb.	0.87	12/94	2c
Chuck roast, USDA choice, boneless	lb.	2.26	12/94	82r
Cigarettes, Winston, Kings	carton	14.44	12/94	2c
Coffee, vacuum-packed	13 oz.	3.02	12/94	2c
Corn Flakes, Kellogg's or Post Toasties	18 oz.	2.46	12/94	2c
Corn, frozen, whole kernel, lowest price	10 oz.	0.63	12/94	2c
Crackers, soda, salted	lb.	1.27	12/94	82r
Cucumbers	lb.	0.65	12/94	82r
Dairy products (other) purchases	year	141	91	81r
Eggs, Grade A large	dozen	0.70	12/94	2c
Eggs, Grade A large	dozen	0.87	12/94	82r
Fish and seafood purchases	year	72	91	81r
Flour, white, all purpose	lb.	0.23	12/94	82r
Food purchases, food eaten at home	year	2381	91	81r
Foods purchased away from home, not prepared by consumer	year	1696	91	81r
Frankfurters, all meat or all beef	lb.	1.74	12/94	82r
Fruits and vegetables purchases	year	380	91	81r
Grapefruit	lb.	0.45	12/94	82r
Grapes, Thompson seedless	lb.	2.30	12/94	82r
Ground beef, 100% beef	lb.	1.37	12/94	82r
Ground chuck, 100% beef	lb.	1.97	12/94	82r
Ham, boneless, exc. canned	lb.	2.54	12/94	82r
Ice cream, prepackaged, bulk, regular	1/2 gal.	2.47	12/94	82r
Lemons	lb.	1.02	12/94	82r
Lettuce, iceberg	lb.	0.96	12/94	82r
Lettuce, iceberg	head	0.97	12/94	2c
Margarine, Blue Bonnet or Parkay cubes	lb.	0.55	12/94	2c
Margarine, stick	lb.	0.77	12/94	82r
Meats, poultry, fish, and eggs purchases	year	655	91	81r
Milk and cream (fresh) purchases	year	130	91	81r
Milk, whole	1/2 gal.	1.34	12/94	2c
Orange juice, frozen concentrate 12-oz. can	16 oz.	1.36	12/94	82r
Orange juice, Minute Maid frozen	12-oz.	1.15	12/94	2c
Oranges, Navel	lb.	0.54	12/94	82r
Peaches, halves or slices, Hunt's, Del Monte, or Libby's	29-oz.	1.25	12/94	2c
Pears, Anjou	lb.	0.81	12/94	82r
Peas, sweet, Del Monte or Green Giant	15-17 oz.	0.53	12/94	2c
Pork chops, center cut, bone-in	lb.	3.07	12/94	82r
Pork purchases	year	142	91	81r
Potato chips	16-oz.	3.15	12/94	82r
Potatoes, frozen, French fried	lb.	0.82	12/94	82r

Chattanooga, TN - continued

Item	Per	Value	Date	Ref.
Groceries - continued				
Potatoes, white	lb.	0.34	12/94	82r
Potatoes, white or red	10-lb. sack	1.99	12/94	2c
Rice, white, long grain, uncooked	lb.	0.48	12/94	82r
Round roast, USDA choice, boneless	lb.	2.91	12/94	82r
Sausage, fresh	lb.	1.82	12/94	82r
Sausage, Jimmy Dean, 100% pork	lb.	2.31	12/94	2c
Shortening, vegetable oil blends	lb.	0.75	12/94	82r
Shortening, vegetable, Crisco	3-lb.	2.55	12/94	2c
Soft drink, Coca Cola, ex deposit	2 lit	1.19	12/94	2c
Spaghetti and macaroni	lb.	0.87	12/94	82r
Steak, rib eye, USDA choice, boneless	lb.	6.85	12/94	82r
Steak, round, graded & ungraded, exc. USDA prime & choice	lb.	2.96	12/94	82r
Steak, round, USDA choice, boneless	lb.	3.17	12/94	82r
Steak, sirloin, USDA choice, boneless	lb.	4.12	12/94	82r
Steak, t-bone	lb.	5.89	12/94	2c
Steak, T-bone, USDA choice, bone-in	lb.	5.63	12/94	82r
Sugar and other sweets, eaten at home, expenditures	year	93	91	81r
Sugar, cane or beet	4 lbs.	1.45	12/94	2c
Sugar, white, all sizes	lb.	0.39	12/94	82r
Tobacco products and smoking supplies, total expenditures	year	286	91	81r
Tomatoes, field grown	lb.	1.36	12/94	82r
Tomatoes, Hunt's or Del Monte	14.5 oz.	0.64	12/94	2c
Tuna, chunk, light	lb.	1.94	12/94	82r
Tuna, chunk, light, oil-packed	6.125-6.5 oz.	0.64	12/94	2c
Turkey, frozen, whole	lb.	0.96	12/94	82r
Yogurt, natural, fruit flavored	8 oz.	0.58	12/94	82r
Goods and Services				
Miscellaneous goods and services, ACCRA Index		99.50	12/94	2c
Health Care				
Health care, ACCRA Index		88.30	12/94	2c
Adenosine, emergency room	treat	100.00	95	23r
Antibiotic ointment, Polysporin	1.5 oz.	4.21	12/94	2c
Bladder tap, superpubic, infant, emergency room	treat	119.00	95	23r
Blood analysis, emergency room	treat	25.00	95	23r
Blood tests, abdominal pain, emergency room	treat	25.00	95	23r
Burn dressing, emergency room	treat	266.00	95	23r
Cardiology interpretation, emergency room	treat	26.00	95	23r
Chest X-ray, emergency room	treat	78.00	95	23r
Childbirth, Cesarean delivery, hospital charge	birth	5462.00	12/91	69r
Childbirth, Cesarean delivery, physician charge	birth	2228.00	12/91	69r
Childbirth, normal delivery, hospital charge	birth	2943.00	12/91	69r
Childbirth, normal delivery, physician charge	birth	1619.00	12/91	69r
Defibrillation pads, emergency room	treat	6.00	95	23r
Dentist's fee, adult teeth cleaning and periodic oral exam	visit	45.40	12/94	2c
Doctor's fee, routine exam, established patient	visit	36.20	12/94	2c
Drugs, expenditures	year	297	91	81r
Gastric tube insertion, nasal, emergency room	treat	25.00	95	23r
Health care, total expenditures	year	1600	91	81r
Health insurance expenditures	year	637	91	81r
Heart monitor, emergency room	treat	40.00	95	23r
Hospital care, semiprivate room	day	310.00	12/94	2c
Insurance premium, family medical care	month	344.21	1/95	41s
Intravenous fluids, emergency room	treat	130.00	95	23r
Intravenous fluids, emergency room	liter	26.00	95	23r
Intravenous line, central, emergency room	treat	342.00	95	23r
Liver function tests, abdominal pain, emergency room	treat	26.00	95	23r

Values are in dollars or fractions of dollars. In the column headed *Ref*, references are shown to sources. Each reference is followed by a letter. These refer to the geographical level for which data were reported: s=State, r=Region, and c=City or metro. The abbreviation *ex* is used to mean *except* or *excluding*; *exp* stands for *expenditures*. For other abbreviations and further explanations, please see the Introduction.

Chattanooga, TN - continued

Item	Per	Value	Date	Ref.
Health Care				
Medical care charges, total, emergency room, third-degree burns	treat	2101.00	95	23r
Medical care charges, total, emergency, infant with fever	treat	628.00	95	23r
Medical services expenditures	year	573	91	81r
Medical supplies expenditures	year	93	91	81r
Morphine, emergency room	treat	34.00	95	23r
Nursing care and facilities charges, emergency room	treat	252.00	95	23r
Nursing care and facilities charges, emergency, infant with fever	treat	252.00	95	23r
Nursing care and facilities charges, emergency, third-degree burns	treat	861.00	95	23r
Physician's charges, emergency, infant with fever	treat	212.00	95	23r
Physician's charges, emergency, third-degree burns	treat	372.00	95	23r
Physician's fee, emergency room	treat	372.00	95	23r
Physician's fee, general practitioner	visit	51.20	12/93	60r
Surgery, open-heart	proc	42374.00	1/93	14r
Ultrasound, abdominal, emergency room	treat	276.00	95	23r
Urinalysis, emergency room	treat	20.00	95	23r
Urinalysis, infant, emergency room	treat	20.00	95	23r
X-rays, emergency room	treat	78.00	95	23r
Household Goods				
Appl. repair, service call, wash mach	min. lab. chg.	29.98	12/94	2c
Floor coverings, expenditures	year	48	91	81r
Furniture, expenditures	year	280	91	81r
Household equipment, misc. expenditures	year	342	91	81r
Household expenditures, miscellaneous	year	256	91	81r
Household furnishings and equipment, expenditures	year	988	91	81r
Household operations expenditures	year	468	91	81r
Household textiles, expenditures	year	95	91	81r
Housekeeping supplies, expenditures	year	380	91	81r
Laundry and cleaning supplies, expenditures	year	109	91	81r
Laundry detergent, Tide Ultra, Bold, or Cheer	42 oz.	3.17	12/94	2c
Postage and stationery, expenditures	year	105	91	81r
Tissues, facial, Kleenex brand	175	0.97	12/94	2c
Housing				
Housing, ACCRA Index		87.80	12/94	2c
Add garage/carport		6,980	3/95	74r
Add room(s)		11,403	3/95	74r
Apartment condominium or co-op, median	unit	68600	12/94	62r
Dwellings (owned), expenditures	year	2428	91	81r
Enclose porch/patio/breezeway		4,572	3/95	74r
Finish room in basement/attic		3,794	3/95	74r
Home, existing, single-family, median	unit	120200	12/94	62r
Home, existing, single-family, median	unit	77.70	12/94	62c
House payment, principal and interest, 25% down payment	mo.	633	12/94	2c
House, 1800 sq ft, 8000 sq ft lot, new, urban, utilities	total	101410	12/94	2c
Maintenance, repairs, insurance, and other housing expenditures	year	531	91	81r
Mortgage interest and charges expenditures	year	1506	91	81r
Mtge. rate, incl. points and orig. fee, 30-year conv. fixed or ARM	mo.	9.38	12/94	2c
Princ. & int., mortgage, median-price exist. sing.-family home	mo.	540	12/94	62r
Property taxes expenditures	year	391	91	81r
Redesign, restructure more than half of home's interior		17,641	3/95	74r
Rent, apartment, 2 br., 1 1/2-2 baths, unfurnished, 950 sq ft, water	mo.	578	12/94	2c
Rental units expenditures	year	1264	91	81r

Chattanooga, TN - continued

Item	Per	Value	Date	Ref.
Insurance and Pensions				
Auto insurance, private passenger	year	574.08	12/94	71s
Insurance and pensions, personal, expenditures	year	2395	91	81r
Insurance, life and other personal, expenditures	year	368	91	81r
Pensions and Social Security, expenditures	year	2027	91	81r
Personal Goods				
Shampoo, Alberto VO5	15-oz.	0.97	12/94	2c
Toothpaste, Crest or Colgate	6-7 oz.	1.83	12/94	2c
Personal Services				
Dry cleaning, man's 2-pc. suit		5.51	12/94	2c
Haircut, man's barbershop, no styling		8.00	12/94	2c
Haircut, woman's shampoo, trim, blow-dry		22.40	12/94	2c
Personal services expenditures	year	212	91	81r
Restaurant Food				
Chicken, fried, thigh and drumstick		2.07	12/94	2c
Dining expenditures, family	week	33.83	94	73r
Hamburger with cheese	1/4 lb.	1.85	12/94	2c
Pizza, Pizza Hut or Pizza Inn	12-13 in.	7.99	12/94	2c
Taxes				
Tax, cigarettes	year	379.00	10/93	43s
Taxes, Federal income, expenditures	year	2275	91	81r
Taxes, personal, expenditures	year	2715	91	81r
Taxes, State and local income, expenditures	year	365	91	81r
Transportation				
Transportation, ACCRA Index		91.30	12/94	2c
Bus fare, one-way	trip	0.75	12/95	1c
Bus fare, up to 10 miles	one-way	0.75	12/94	2c
Cars and trucks purchased, new	year	1306	91	81r
Cars and trucks purchased, used	year	942	91	81r
Commuter rail (inclined plane) fare, one-way	trip	6.00	12/95	1c
Driver's learning permit fee	perm	5.50	1/94	84s
Driver's license fee	orig	16.00	1/94	84s
Driver's license fee, duplicate	lic	8.00	1/94	84s
Driver's license reinstatement fee, min.	susp	65.00	1/94	85s
Driver's license renewal fee	renew	14.00	1/94	84s
Identification card, nondriver	card	7.50	1/94	83s
Motorcycle learning permit fee	perm	6.50	1/94	84s
Motorcycle license fee	orig	17.00	1/94	84s
Motorcycle license fee, duplicate	lic	8.00	1/94	84s
Motorcycle license renewal fee	renew	15.00	1/94	84s
Public transportation expenditures	year	249	91	81r
Tire balance, computer or spin bal., front	wheel	6.00	12/94	2c
Transportation expenditures, total	year	5307	91	81r
Vehicle finance charges	year	346	91	81r
Vehicle insurance expenditures	year	544	91	81r
Vehicle maintenance and repairs expenditures	year	600	91	81r
Vehicle purchases	year	2275	91	81r
Vehicle rental, leases, licenses, etc. expenditures	year	141	91	81r
Vehicles purchased, other than cars and trucks	year	27	91	81r
Utilities				
Utilities, ACCRA Index		104.70	12/94	2c
Electricity expenditures	year	950	91	81r
Electricity, (part.), other, 1800 sq. ft., new home	mo.	75.64	12/94	2c
Utilities, fuels, and public services, total expenditures	year	2000	91	81r
Water and other public services, expenditures	year	227	91	81r
Weddings				
Bridal attendants' gowns	event	750	10/93	76r
Bridal gown	event	852	10/93	76r
Bridal headpiece and veil	event	167	10/93	76r

Values are in dollars or fractions of dollars. In the column headed *Ref*, references are shown to sources. Each reference is followed by a letter. These refer to the geographical level for which data were reported: s=State, r=Region, and c=City or metro. The abbreviation *ex* is used to mean *except* or *excluding*; *exp* stands for expenditures. For other abbreviations and further explanations, please see the Introduction.

Chattanooga, TN - continued

Item	Per	Value	Date	Ref.
Weddings				
Bride's wedding band	event	708	10/93	76r
Clergy	event	224	10/93	76r
Engagement ring	event	2756	10/93	76r
Flowers	event	863	10/93	76r
Formal wear for groom	event	106	10/93	76r
Groom's attendants' formal wear	event	530	10/93	76r
Groom's wedding band	event	402	10/93	76r
Music	event	600	10/93	76r
Photography	event	1088	10/93	76r
Shoes for bride	event	50	10/93	76r
Videography	event	483	10/93	76r
Wedding invitations and announcements	event	342	10/93	76r
Wedding reception	event	7000	10/93	76r

Cheyenne, WY

Item	Per	Value	Date	Ref.
Composite, ACCRA index		96.60	12/94	2c
Alcoholic Beverages				
Beer, Miller Lite, Bud, 12-oz., ex deposit	6	4.25	12/94	2c
J & B Scotch	750-ml.	16.57	12/94	2c
Wine, Gallo Chablis blanc	1.5-lit	5.27	12/94	2c
Appliances				
Appliances (major), expenditures	year	160	91	81r
Average annual exp.				
Food, health care, personal goods, services	year	32461	91	81r
Charity				
Cash contributions, expenditures	year	975	91	81r
Clothing				
Apparel, men and boys, total expenditures	year	467	91	81r
Apparel, women and girls, total expenditures	year	737	91	81r
Footwear, expenditures	year	270	91	81r
Jeans, man's denim		30.99	12/94	2c
Shirt, man's dress shirt		27.00	12/94	2c
Undervest, boy's size 10-14, cotton	3	3.80	12/94	2c
Communications				
Long-distance telephone rate, day, addl. min., 1-10 mi.	min.	0.09	12/93	9s
Long-distance telephone rate, day, initial min., 1-10 mi.	min.	0.19	12/93	9s
Newspaper subscription, dly. and Sun. delivery	month	6.00	12/94	2c
Phone line, single, business, field visit	inst	86.25	12/93	9s
Phone line, single, business, no field visit	inst	86.25	12/93	9s
Phone line, single, residence, field visit	inst	41.25	12/93	9s
Phone line, single, residence, no field visit	inst	41.25	12/93	9s
Telephone bill, family of four	month	21.77	12/94	2c
Telephone service, expenditures	year	611	91	81r
Telephone, residential, flat rate	mo.	11.96	12/93	8c
Education				
Board, 4-year public college/university	year	1830	8/94	80s
Education, total expenditures	year	375	91	81r
Room, 4-year public college/university	year	1422	8/94	80s
Total cost, 4-year public college/university	year	4900	8/94	80s
Tuition, 4-year public college/university, in-state	year	1648	8/94	80s
Energy and Fuels				
Energy, combined forms, 1800 sq. ft.	mo.	87.86	12/94	2c
Energy, exc. electricity, 1800 sq. ft.	mo.	46.70	12/94	2c
Fuel oil and other fuels, expenditures	year	33	91	81r
Gas, cooking, winter, 10 therms	month	3.14	2/94	65c
Gas, cooking, winter, 30 therms	month	9.42	2/94	65c
Gas, cooking, winter, 50 therms	month	15.71	2/94	65c
Gas, heating, winter, 100 therms	month	31.41	2/94	65c
Gas, heating, winter, average use	month	62.82	2/94	65c
Gas, natural, expenditures	year	212	91	81r

Cheyenne, WY - continued

Item	Per	Value	Date	Ref.
Energy and Fuels - continued				
Gas, reg unlead, taxes inc., cash, self-service	gal	1.07	12/94	2c
Gasoline and motor oil purchased	year	1115	91	81r
Gasoline, unleaded midgrade	gallon	1.36	4/93	82r
Gasoline, unleaded premium	gallon	1.43	4/93	82r
Gasoline, unleaded regular	gallon	1.23	4/93	82r
Entertainment				
Bowling, evening rate	game	2.10	12/94	2c
Concert ticket, Pearl Jam group	perf	20.00	94	50r
Entertainment, total expenditures	year	1853	91	81r
Fees and admissions, expenditures	year	482	91	81r
Monopoly game, Parker Brothers', No. 9	game	9.15	12/94	2c
Movie	adm	5.25	12/94	2c
Pets, toys, playground equipment, expenditures	year	299	91	81r
Reading, expenditures	year	164	91	81r
Televisions, radios, and sound equipment, expenditures	year	528	91	81r
Tennis balls, yellow, Wilson or Penn, 3	can	2.28	12/94	2c
Funerals				
Burial, immediate, container provided by funeral home		1360.49	1/95	54r
Cards, acknowledgment		11.24	1/95	54r
Casket, minimum alternative		232.73	1/95	54r
Cosmetology, hair care, etc.		114.13	1/95	54r
Cremation, direct, container provided by funeral home		1027.08	1/95	54r
Embalming		286.24	1/95	54r
Funeral, funeral home		315.60	1/95	54r
Funeral, other facility		303.08	1/95	54r
Graveside service		423.83	1/95	54r
Hearse, local		133.12	1/95	54r
Limousine, local		99.10	1/95	54r
Memorial service		442.57	1/95	54r
Service charge, professional, nondeclinable		840.16	1/95	54r
Visitation and viewing		168.50	1/95	54r
Groceries				
Groceries, ACCRA Index		101.90	12/94	2c
Apples, Red Delicious	lb.	0.72	12/94	82r
Baby food, strained vegetables, lowest price	4-4.5 oz.	0.34	12/94	2c
Bacon, sliced	lb.	1.73	12/94	82r
Bananas	lb.	0.51	12/94	2c
Bananas	lb.	0.52	12/94	82r
Beef or hamburger, ground	lb.	1.19	12/94	2c
Beef purchases	year	241	91	81r
Beverage purchases, alcoholic	year	328	91	81r
Beverage purchases, nonalcoholic	year	234	91	81r
Bologna, all beef or mixed	lb.	2.33	12/94	82r
Bread, white	24-oz.	0.69	12/94	2c
Bread, white, pan	lb.	0.81	12/94	82r
Carrots, short trimmed and topped	lb.	0.43	12/94	82r
Cereals and bakery products purchases	year	392	91	81r
Cereals and cereals products purchases	year	139	91	81r
Cheese, Kraft grated Parmesan	8-oz.	3.16	12/94	2c
Chicken breast, bone-in	lb.	2.04	12/94	82r
Chicken, fresh, whole	lb.	0.95	12/94	82r
Chicken, whole fryer	lb.	0.78	12/94	2c
Cigarettes, Winston, Kings	carton	13.51	12/94	2c
Coffee, 100%, ground roast, all sizes	lb.	4.48	12/94	82r
Coffee, vacuum-packed	13 oz.	3.77	12/94	2c
Corn Flakes, Kellogg's or Post Toasties	18 oz.	2.55	12/94	2c
Corn, frozen, whole kernel, lowest price	10 oz.	0.75	12/94	2c
Dairy products (other) purchases	year	182	91	81r
Eggs, Grade A large	dozen	0.81	12/94	2c
Fish and seafood purchases	year	94	91	81r
Flour, white, all purpose	lb.	0.21	12/94	82r
Food purchases, food eaten at home	year	2749	91	81r
Foods purchased away from home, not prepared by consumer	year	1909	91	81r
Fruits and vegetables purchases	year	459	91	81r

Values are in dollars or fractions of dollars. In the column headed *Ref*, references are shown to sources. Each reference is followed by a letter. These refer to the geographical level for which data were reported: s=State, r=Region, and c=City or metro. The abbreviation *ex* is used to mean *except* or *excluding*; *exp* stands for expenditures. For other abbreviations and further explanations, please see the Introduction.

Cheyenne, WY - continued

Item	Per	Value	Date	Ref.
Groceries				
Grapefruit	lb.	0.56	12/94	82r
Ground beef, 100% beef	lb.	1.31	12/94	82r
Ham, boneless, exc. canned	lb.	2.46	12/94	82r
Ice cream, prepackaged, bulk, regular	1/2 gal.	2.57	12/94	82r
Lemons	lb.	1.00	12/94	82r
Lettuce, iceberg	lb.	0.93	12/94	82r
Lettuce, iceberg	head	0.96	12/94	2c
Margarine, Blue Bonnet or Parkay cubes	lb.	0.81	12/94	2c
Meats, poultry, fish, and eggs purchases	year	700	91	81r
Milk and cream (fresh) purchases	year	155	91	81r
Milk, whole	1/2 gal.	1.31	12/94	2c
Orange juice, frozen concentrate 12-oz. can	16 oz.	1.52	12/94	82r
Orange juice, Minute Maid frozen	12-oz.	1.20	12/94	2c
Oranges, Navel	lb.	0.56	12/94	82r
Peaches, halves or slices, Hunt's, Del Monte, or Libby's	29-oz.	1.51	12/94	2c
Peas, sweet, Del Monte or Green Giant	15-17 oz.	0.62	12/94	2c
Pork chops, center cut, bone-in	lb.	3.30	12/94	82r
Pork purchases	year	122	91	81r
Potato chips	16-oz.	3.03	12/94	82r
Potatoes, frozen, French fried	lb.	0.77	12/94	82r
Potatoes, white	lb.	0.35	12/94	82r
Potatoes, white or red	10-lb. sack	2.21	12/94	2c
Rice, white, long grain, uncooked	lb.	0.54	12/94	82r
Round roast, USDA choice, boneless	lb.	2.92	12/94	82r
Sausage, Jimmy Dean, 100% pork	lb.	3.45	12/94	2c
Shortening, vegetable oil blends	lb.	0.80	12/94	82r
Shortening, vegetable, Crisco	3-lb.	2.21	12/94	2c
Soft drink, Coca Cola, ex deposit	2 lit	1.27	12/94	2c
Spaghetti and macaroni	lb.	1.02	12/94	82r
Steak, round, graded & ungraded, exc. USDA prime & choice	lb.	3.13	12/94	82r
Steak, sirloin, USDA choice, boneless	lb.	4.07	12/94	82r
Steak, t-bone	lb.	4.55	12/94	2c
Sugar and other sweets, eaten at home, expenditures	year	105	91	81r
Sugar, cane or beet	4 lbs.	1.43	12/94	2c
Sugar, white, all sizes	lb.	0.38	12/94	82r
Tobacco products and smoking supplies, total expenditures	year	221	91	81r
Tomatoes, field grown	lb.	1.45	12/94	82r
Tomatoes, Hunt's or Del Monte	14.5 oz.	0.68	12/94	2c
Tuna, chunk, light	lb.	2.18	12/94	82r
Tuna, chunk, light, oil-packed	6.125-6.5 oz.	0.83	12/94	2c
Goods and Services				
Miscellaneous goods and services, ACCRA Index		98.40	12/94	2c
Health Care				
Health care, ACCRA Index		95.00	12/94	2c
Antibiotic ointment, Polysporin	1.5 oz.	3.75	12/94	2c
Childbirth, Cesarean delivery, hospital charge	birth	6059.00	12/91	69r
Childbirth, Cesarean delivery, physician charge	birth	2248.00	12/91	69r
Childbirth, normal delivery, hospital charge	birth	3006.00	12/91	69r
Childbirth, normal delivery, physician charge	birth	1634.00	12/91	69r
Dentist's fee, adult teeth cleaning and periodic oral exam	visit	53.00	12/94	2c
Doctor's fee, routine exam, established patient	visit	34.80	12/94	2c
Drugs, expenditures	year	230	91	81r
Health care, total expenditures	year	1544	91	81r
Health insurance expenditures	year	558	91	81r
Hospital care, semiprivate room	day	349.00	12/94	2c
Medical services expenditures	year	676	91	81r

Cheyenne, WY - continued

Item	Per	Value	Date	Ref.
Health Care - continued				
Medical supplies expenditures	year	80	91	81r
Surgery, open-heart	proc	37818.00	1/93	14r
Household Goods				
Appl. repair, service call, wash mach	min. lab. chg.	33.58	12/94	2c
Floor coverings, expenditures	year	79	91	81r
Furniture, expenditures	year	352	91	81r
Household equipment, misc. expenditures	year	614	91	81r
Household expenditures, miscellaneous	year	294	91	81r
Household furnishings and equipment, expenditures	year	1416	91	81r
Household operations expenditures	year	580	91	81r
Household textiles, expenditures	year	113	91	81r
Housekeeping supplies, expenditures	year	447	91	81r
Laundry and cleaning supplies, expenditures	year	114	91	81r
Laundry detergent, Tide Ultra, Bold, or Cheer	42 oz.	3.75	12/94	2c
Postage and stationery, expenditures	year	145	91	81r
Tissues, facial, Kleenex brand	175	1.01	12/94	2c
Housing				
Housing, ACCRA Index		94.80	12/94	2c
Add garage/carport		6,422	3/95	74r
Add room(s)		26,583	3/95	74r
Apartment condominium or co-op, median	unit	105300	12/94	62r
Dwellings (owned), expenditures	year	3932	91	81r
Enclose porch/patio/breezeway		5,382	3/95	74r
Finish room in basement/attic		3,911	3/95	74r
Home, existing, single-family, median	unit	178600	12/94	62r
House payment, principal and interest, 25% down payment	mo.	725	12/94	2c
House, 1800 sq ft, 8000 sq ft lot, new, urban, utilities	total	115500	12/94	2c
Maintenance, repairs, insurance, and other housing expenditures	year	591	91	81r
Mortgage interest and charges expenditures	year	2747	91	81r
Mtge. rate, incl. points and orig. fee, 30-year conv. fixed or ARM	mo.	9.44	12/94	2c
Princ. & int., mortgage, median-price exist. sing.-family home	mo.	845	12/94	62r
Property taxes expenditures	year	594	91	81r
Redesign, restructure more than half of home's interior		5,467	3/95	74r
Rent, apartment, 2 br., 1 1/2-2 baths, unfurnished, 950 sq ft, water	mo.	505	12/94	2c
Rental units expenditures	year	2077	91	81r
Insurance and Pensions				
Auto insurance, private passenger	year	531.91	12/94	71s
Insurance and pensions, personal, expenditures	year	3042	91	81r
Insurance, life and other personal, expenditures	year	298	91	81r
Pensions and Social Security, expenditures	year	2744	91	81r
Legal Assistance				
Legal work, law firm associate	hour	91		10r
Legal work, law firm partner	hour	151		10r
Personal Goods				
Shampoo, Alberto VO5	15-oz.	0.94	12/94	2c
Toothpaste, Crest or Colgate	6-7 oz.	1.76	12/94	2c
Personal Services				
Dry cleaning, man's 2-pc. suit		6.25	12/94	2c
Haircut, man's barbershop, no styling		8.90	12/94	2c
Haircut, woman's shampoo, trim, blow-dry		20.40	12/94	2c
Personal services expenditures	year	286	91	81r
Restaurant Food				
Chicken, fried, thigh and drumstick		2.49	12/94	2c
Dining expenditures, family	week	32.25	94	73r

Values are in dollars or fractions of dollars. In the column headed *Ref*, references are shown to sources. Each reference is followed by a letter. These refer to the geographical level for which data were reported: s=State, r=Region, and c=City or metro. The abbreviation *ex* is used to mean *except* or *excluding*; *exp* stands for *expenditures*. For other abbreviations and further explanations, please see the Introduction.

Cheyenne, WY - continued

Item	Per	Value	Date	Ref.
Restaurant Food				
Hamburger with cheese	1/4 lb.	1.99	12/94	2c
Pizza, Pizza Hut or Pizza Inn	12-13 in.	9.05	12/94	2c
Taxes				
Tax rate, residential property, month	$100	0.74	1/92	79c
Tax, cigarettes	year	609.00	10/93	43s
Taxes, Federal income, expenditures	year	2946	91	81r
Taxes, personal, expenditures	year	3791	91	81r
Taxes, State and local income, expenditures	year	791	91	81r
Transportation				
Transportation, ACCRA Index		99.80	12/94	2c
Bus fare, up to 10 miles	one-way	1.00	12/94	2c
Cars and trucks purchased, new	year	1231	91	81r
Cars and trucks purchased, used	year	915	91	81r
Driver's learning permit fee	perm	10.00	1/94	84s
Driver's license fee	orig	20.00	1/94	84s
Driver's license fee, duplicate	lic	15.00	1/94	84s
Driver's license reinstatement fee, min.	susp	50.00	1/94	85s
Driver's license renewal fee	renew	15.00	1/94	84s
Identification card, nondriver	card	10.00	1/94	83s
Motorcycle learning permit fee	perm	10.00	1/94	84s
Motorcycle license fee	orig	20.00	1/94	84s
Motorcycle license fee, duplicate	lic	15.00	1/94	84s
Motorcycle license renewal fee	renew	15.00	1/94	84s
Public transportation expenditures	year	375	91	81r
Tire balance, computer or spin bal., front	wheel	7.05	12/94	2c
Transportation expenditures, total	year	5527	91	81r
Vehicle finance charges	year	287	91	81r
Vehicle insurance expenditures	year	624	91	81r
Vehicle maintenance and repairs expenditures	year	695	91	81r
Vehicle purchases	year	2174	91	81r
Vehicle rental, leases, licenses, etc. expenditures	year	257	91	81r
Vehicles purchased, other than cars and trucks	year	28	91	81r
Utilities				
Utilities, ACCRA Index		82.80	12/94	2c
Electricity expenditures	year	616	91	81r
Electricity, (part.), other, 1800 sq. ft., new home	mo.	41.16	12/94	2c
Electricity, summer, 250 KWh	month	14.43	8/93	64c
Electricity, summer, 500 KWh	month	28.85	8/93	64c
Electricity, summer, 750 KWh	month	39.60	8/93	64c
Electricity, summer, 1000 KWh	month	51.20	8/93	64c
Utilities, fuels, and public services, total expenditures	year	1681	91	81r
Water and other public services, expenditures	year	209	91	81r
Weddings				
Bridal attendants' gowns	event	750	10/93	76r
Bridal gown	event	852	10/93	76r
Bridal headpiece and veil	event	167	10/93	76r
Bride's wedding band	event	708	10/93	76r
Clergy	event	224	10/93	76r
Engagement ring	event	2756	10/93	76r
Flowers	event	863	10/93	76r
Formal wear for groom	event	106	10/93	76r
Groom's attendants' formal wear	event	530	10/93	76r
Groom's wedding band	event	402	10/93	76r
Music	event	600	10/93	76r
Photography	event	1088	10/93	76r
Shoes for bride	event	50	10/93	76r
Videography	event	483	10/93	76r
Wedding invitations and announcements	event	342	10/93	76r
Wedding reception	event	7000	10/93	76r

Chicago, IL

Item	Per	Value	Date	Ref.
Appliances				
Appliances (major), expenditures	year	106	91	81c
Appliances (major), expenditures	year	131	91	81r
Average annual exp.				
Food, health care, personal goods, services	year	32568	91	81c
Food, health care, personal goods, services	year	25935	91	81r
Banking				
Bank fees, teller visit	visit	3.00	95	38c
Business				
Dinner and tip, hotel, corporate rate	night	25.00	2/94	15c
Hotel room, corporate rate	night	101.00	2/94	15c
Photocopies, copy shop	10 copies	0.50	7/95	4c
Photocopies, copy shop	100 copies	2.00	7/95	4c
Photocopies, copy shop	500 copies	9.50	7/95	4c
Photocopies, copy shop	1000 copies	19.00	7/95	4c
Photocopies, copy shop	5000 copies	95.00	7/95	4c
Business Expenses				
Car rental, midsized car	day	47.99	92	52c
Continental breakfast, room service	meal	6.50	92	52c
Lunch, convention center	meal	7.07	92	52c
Restaurant meal	meal	66.00	92	52c
Room rate, hotel	day	78.82	92	52c
Taxicab fare, airport to convention center	trip	15.00-20.00	92	52c
Charity				
Cash contributions, expenditures	year	947	91	81c
Cash contributions, expenditures	year	745	91	81r
Child Care				
Child care, for-profit daycare center	week	91.00	12/94	28c
Clothing				
Apparel, men and boys, total expenditures	year	580	91	81c
Apparel, men and boys, total expenditures	year	332	91	81r
Apparel, women and girls, total expenditures	year	921	91	81c
Apparel, women and girls, total expenditures	year	578	91	81r
Footwear, expenditures	year	326	91	81c
Footwear, expenditures	year	164	91	81r
Formal wear rental, tuxedo, downtown store	rental	60.00	92	52c
Communications				
Long-distance telephone rate, day, addl. min., 1-10 mi.	min.	0.04	12/93	9s
Long-distance telephone rate, day, initial min., 1-10 mi.	min.	0.10	12/93	9s
Newspaper cost, major daily	1	0.50	92	52c
Phone bill	month	55.00	93	37c
Phone line, single, business, field visit	inst	84.50	12/93	9s
Phone line, single, business, no field visit	inst	84.50	12/93	9s
Phone line, single, residence, field visit	inst	55.00	12/93	9s
Phone line, single, residence, no field visit	inst	55.00	12/93	9s
Telephone call, to Dallas, Texas, between 9 a.m. and 5 p.m.	15 min.	3.60	12/93	60c
Telephone service, expenditures	year	660	91	81c
Telephone service, expenditures	year	547	91	81r
Credit Cards				
Fee, conventional credit card, bal. carried	year	37.00	1/95	96c
Education				
Board, 4-year private college/university	year	2078	8/94	80s
Board, 4-year public college/university	year	2139	8/94	80s
Education, total expenditures	year	413	91	81c
Education, total expenditures	year	394	91	81r
Room, 4-year private college/university	year	2696	8/94	80s
Room, 4-year public college/university	year	1796	8/94	80s
Total cost, 4-year private college/university	year	15249	8/94	80s

Values are in dollars or fractions of dollars. In the column headed *Ref*, references are shown to sources. Each reference is followed by a letter. These refer to the geographical level for which data were reported: s = State, r = Region, and c = City or metro. The abbreviation *ex* is used to mean *except* or *excluding*; *exp* stands for expenditures. For other abbreviations and further explanations, please see the Introduction.

Chicago, IL - continued

Item	Per	Value	Date	Ref.
Education				
Total cost, 4-year public college/university	year	6964	8/94	80s
Tuition, 2-year public college/university, in-state	year	1135	8/94	80s
Tuition, 4-year private college/university, in-state	year	10474	8/94	80s
Tuition, 4-year public college/university, in-state	year	3029	8/94	80s
Energy and Fuels				
Electricity	500 KWh	56.02	12/94	82c
Fuel oil #2	gallon	1.03	12/94	82c
Fuel oil and other fuels, expenditures	year	12	91	81c
Fuel oil and other fuels, expenditures	year	83	91	81r
Gas, cooking, 10 therms	month	14.97	2/94	65c
Gas, cooking, 30 therms	month	28.91	2/94	65c
Gas, cooking, 50 therms	month	42.85	2/94	65c
Gas, heating, winter, 100 therms	month	66.41	2/94	65c
Gas, heating, winter, average use	month	147.94	2/94	65c
Gas, natural, expenditures	year	504	91	81c
Gas, natural, expenditures	year	373	91	81r
Gas, piped	40 therms	33.32	12/94	82c
Gas, piped	100 therms	62.83	12/94	82c
Gas, piped	therm	0.48	12/94	82c
Gasoline and motor oil purchased	year	1015	91	81c
Gasoline and motor oil purchased	year	1000	91	81r
Gasoline, unleaded midgrade	gallon	1.31	4/93	82c
Gasoline, unleaded midgrade	gallon	1.15	4/93	82r
Gasoline, unleaded premium	gallon	1.40	4/93	82c
Gasoline, unleaded premium	gallon	1.23	4/93	82r
Gasoline, unleaded regular	gallon	1.22	4/93	82c
Gasoline, unleaded regular	gallon	1.07	4/93	82r
Entertainment				
Admission fee, museum	visit	4.00	92	52c
Admission fee, seating, symphony performance		63.00	92	52c
Baseball game, four-person family	game	108.97	4/94	47c
Baseball game, four-person family	game	106.13	4/94	47c
Entertainment supplies, equipment, and services, misc. expenditures	year	213	91	81c
Entertainment, total expenditures	year	1637	91	81c
Entertainment, total expenditures	year	1356	91	81r
Fees and admissions, expenditures	year	510	91	81c
Fees and admissions, expenditures	year	347	91	81r
Pets, toys, playground equipment, expenditures	year	367	91	81c
Pets, toys, playground equipment, expenditures	year	270	91	81r
Reading, expenditures	year	192	91	81c
Reading, expenditures	year	160	91	81r
Televisions, radios, and sound equipment, expenditures	year	548	91	81c
Televisions, radios, and sound equipment, expenditures	year	433	91	81r
Ticket, basketball game		17.00-275.00	92	52c
Funerals				
Burial, immediate, container provided by funeral home		1268.31	1/95	54r
Cards, acknowledgment		26.12	1/95	54r
Casket, minimum alternative		198.03	1/95	54r
Cosmetology, hair care, etc.		122.19	1/95	54r
Cremation, direct, container provided by funeral home		977.81	1/95	54r
Embalming		334.00	1/95	54r
Funeral, funeral home		321.16	1/95	54r
Funeral, other facility		317.73	1/95	54r
Graveside service		292.48	1/95	54r
Hearse, local		153.20	1/95	54r
Limousine, local		123.52	1/95	54r

Chicago, IL - continued

Item	Per	Value	Date	Ref.
Funerals - continued				
Memorial service		356.30	1/95	54r
Service charge, professional, nondeclinable		968.24	1/95	54r
Visitation and viewing		332.66	1/95	54r
Groceries				
Apples, Red Delicious	lb.	0.68	12/94	82r
Bacon, sliced	lb.	1.88	12/94	82r
Bananas	lb.	0.41	12/94	82r
Beef purchases	year	229	91	81c
Beef purchases	year	197	91	81r
Beef, stew, boneless	lb.	2.52	12/94	82r
Beverage purchases, alcoholic	year	391	91	81c
Beverage purchases, alcoholic	year	293	91	81r
Beverage purchases, nonalcoholic	year	245	91	81c
Beverage purchases, nonalcoholic	year	203	91	81r
Bologna, all beef or mixed	lb.	2.12	12/94	82r
Bread, white, pan	lb.	0.76	12/94	82r
Cabbage	lb.	0.44	12/94	82r
Carrots, short trimmed and topped	lb.	0.44	12/94	82r
Cereals and bakery products purchases	year	425	91	81c
Cereals and bakery products purchases	year	347	91	81r
Cereals and cereal products purchases	year	148	91	81c
Cereals and cereals products purchases	year	119	91	81r
Cheddar cheese, natural	lb.	3.28	12/94	82r
Chicken breast, bone-in	lb.	1.61	12/94	82r
Chicken, fresh, whole	lb.	0.89	12/94	82r
Chuck roast, USDA choice, boneless	lb.	2.33	12/94	82r
Coffee, 100%, ground roast, all sizes	lb.	4.28	12/94	82r
Cookies, chocolate chip	lb.	2.72	12/94	82r
Dairy products (other) purchases	year	177	91	81c
Dairy products (other) purchases	year	148	91	81r
Eggs, Grade A large	dozen	0.76	12/94	82r
Fish and seafood purchases	year	104	91	81c
Fish and seafood purchases	year	61	91	81r
Flour, white, all purpose	lb.	0.22	12/94	82r
Food purchases, food eaten at home	year	2909	91	81c
Food purchases, food eaten at home	year	2313	91	81r
Foods purchased away from home, not prepared by consumer	year	2199	91	81c
Foods purchased away from home, not prepared by consumer	year	1709	91	81r
Fruits and vegetables purchases	year	511	91	81c
Fruits and vegetables purchases	year	372	91	81r
Grapefruit	lb.	0.47	12/94	82r
Grapes, Thompson seedless	lb.	2.15	12/94	82r
Ground beef, 100% beef	lb.	1.37	12/94	82r
Ground chuck, 100% beef	lb.	1.81	12/94	82r
Ham, boneless, exc. canned	lb.	2.16	12/94	82r
Ice cream, prepackaged, bulk, regular	1/2 gal.	2.48	12/94	82r
Lemons	lb.	1.08	12/94	82r
Lettuce, iceberg	lb.	0.81	12/94	82r
Margarine, stick	lb.	0.81	12/94	82r
Meats, poultry, fish, and eggs purchases	year	758	91	81c
Meats, poultry, fish, and eggs purchases	year	591	91	81r
Milk and cream (fresh) purchases	year	144	91	81c
Milk and cream (fresh) purchases	year	132	91	81r
Orange juice, frozen concentrate 12-oz. can	16 oz.	1.41	12/94	82r
Oranges, Navel	lb.	0.56	12/94	82r
Peanut butter, creamy, all sizes	lb.	1.81	12/94	82r
Pork chops, center cut, bone-in	lb.	2.76	12/94	82r
Pork purchases	year	175	91	81c
Pork purchases	year	130	91	81r
Potato chips	16-oz.	2.81	12/94	82r
Potatoes, frozen, French fried	lb.	0.83	12/94	82r
Potatoes, white	lb.	0.28	12/94	82r
Round roast, USDA choice, boneless	lb.	2.90	12/94	82r
Shortening, vegetable oil blends	lb.	0.88	12/94	82r
Spaghetti and macaroni	lb.	0.78	12/94	82r
Steak, rib eye, USDA choice, boneless	lb.	6.15	12/94	82r
Steak, round, graded & ungraded, exc. USDA prime & choice	lb.	2.72	12/94	82r
Steak, round, USDA choice, boneless	lb.	3.02	12/94	82r

Values are in dollars or fractions of dollars. In the column headed *Ref*, references are shown to sources. Each reference is followed by a letter. These refer to the geographical level for which data were reported: s=State, r=Region, and c=City or metro. The abbreviation *ex* is used to mean *except* or *excluding*; *exp* stands for *expenditures*. For other abbreviations and further explanations, please see the Introduction.

Chicago, IL - continued

Item	Per	Value	Date	Ref.
Groceries				
Steak, sirloin, USDA choice, boneless	lb.	3.85	12/94	82r
Steak, T-bone, USDA choice, bone-in	lb.	5.38	12/94	82r
Sugar and other sweets, eaten at home, expenditures	year	91	91	81r
Sugar and other sweets, eaten at home, purchases	year	107	91	81c
Sugar, white, all sizes	lb.	0.36	12/94	82r
Tobacco products and smoking supplies, total expenditures	year	376	91	81c
Tobacco products and smoking supplies, total expenditures	year	298	91	81r
Tomatoes, field grown	lb.	1.36	12/94	82r
Tuna, chunk, light	lb.	1.94	12/94	82r
Turkey, frozen, whole	lb.	0.96	12/94	82r
Yogurt, natural, fruit flavored	8 oz.	0.62	12/94	82r
Health Care				
Appendectomy	proc	1150.00	12/92	69c
Birth, normal delivery	del	2,189	11/93	93c
Breast lesion excision (lumpectomy)	proc	656.00	12/92	69c
Broken arm treatment	treat	518	11/93	93c
Cesarean section delivery	proc	2539.00	12/92	69c
Childbirth, Cesarean delivery, hospital charge	birth	5101.00	12/91	69r
Childbirth, Cesarean delivery, physician charge	birth	2234.00	12/91	69r
Childbirth, normal delivery, hospital charge	birth	2891.00	12/91	69r
Childbirth, normal delivery, physician charge	birth	1623.00	12/91	69r
Cholecystectomy	proc	1899.00	12/92	69c
Coronary bypass, triple	proc	6063.00	12/92	69c
Drugs, expenditures	year	220	91	81c
Drugs, expenditures	year	248	91	81r
Health care, total expenditures	year	1439	91	81c
Health care, total expenditures	year	1336	91	81r
Health insurance expenditures	year	459	91	81c
Health insurance expenditures	year	550	91	81r
Hospital cost	adm	6,637	2/94	72c
Hysterectomy, abdominal	proc	2543.00	12/92	69c
Immunization, DTP, measles, mumps, rubella, polio	inject	130.00	8/93	90c
Insurance premium, family medical care	month	363.57	1/95	41s
Medical services expenditures	year	680	91	81c
Medical services expenditures	year	457	91	81r
Medical supplies expenditures	year	80	91	81c
Medical supplies expenditures	year	82	91	81r
Oophorectomy	proc	1576.00	12/92	69c
Physical exam, well baby	check-up	48	11/93	93c
Physical, complete	phys	113	11/93	93c
Salpingo-oophorectomy	proc	1570.00	12/92	69c
Surgery, open-heart	surg	7,254	11/93	93c
Household Goods				
Floor coverings, expenditures	year	146	91	81c
Floor coverings, expenditures	year	105	91	81r
Furniture, expenditures	year	393	91	81c
Furniture, expenditures	year	291	91	81r
Household equipment, misc. expenditures	year	341	91	81r
Household equipment, misc., expenditures	year	329	91	81c
Household expenditures, miscellaneous	year	214	91	81c
Household expenditures, miscellaneous	year	162	91	81r
Household furnishings and equipment, expenditures	year	1178	91	81c
Household furnishings and equipment, expenditures	year	1042	91	81r
Household operations expenditures	year	450	91	81c
Household operations expenditures	year	365	91	81r
Household textiles, expenditures	year	115	91	81c
Household textiles, expenditures	year	101	91	81r
Housekeeping supplies, expenditures	year	477	91	81c
Housekeeping supplies, expenditures	year	390	91	81r
Laundry and cleaning supplies, expenditures	year	141	91	81c

Chicago, IL - continued

Item	Per	Value	Date	Ref.
Household Goods - continued				
Laundry and cleaning supplies, expenditures	year	110	91	81r
Postage and stationery, expenditures	year	122	91	81c
Postage and stationery, expenditures	year	115	91	81r
Housing				
Add garage/carport		8,479	3/95	74r
Add room(s)		21,347	3/95	74r
Apartment condominium or co-op, median	unit	87100	12/94	62r
Bathroom addition, average cost	add	9734.00	3/95	13r
Bathroom remodeling, average cost	remod	6414.00	3/95	13r
Bedroom, master suite addition, average cost	add	27122.00	3/95	13r
Car rental	day	54.00	5/95	95c
Deck addition, average cost	add	6665.00	3/95	13r
Dwellings (owned), expenditures	year	4138	91	81c
Dwellings (owned), expenditures	year	2566	91	81r
Enclose porch/patio/breezeway		4,556	3/95	74r
Exterior remodeling, average cost	remod	15395.00	3/95	13r
Family room addition, average cost	add	27658.00	3/95	13r
Finish room in basement/attic		5,074	3/95	74r
Home repairs, maintenance, and insurance	year	693.00	93	37c
Home, existing, single-family, median	unit	106500	12/94	62r
Home, existing, single-family, median	unit	141.60	12/94	62c
Home, purchase price	unit	174.30	3/93	26c
Hotel room	day	167.00	5/95	95c
Kitchen remodeling, major, average cost	remod	17084.00	3/95	13r
Kitchen remodeling, minor, average cost	remod	5804.00	3/95	13r
Maintenance, repairs, insurance, and other housing expenditures	year	693	91	81c
Maintenance, repairs, insurance, and other housing expenditures	year	484	91	81r
Mortgage interest and charges expenditures	year	2473	91	81c
Mortgage interest and charges expenditures	year	1443	91	81r
Office, home addition, average cost	add	8121.00	3/95	13r
Princ. & int., mortgage, median-price exist. sing.-family home	mo.	515	12/94	62r
Property taxes expenditures	year	972	91	81c
Property taxes expenditures	year	639	91	81r
Redesign, restructure more than half of home's interior		9,114	3/95	74r
Rent, office space	sq. ft.	1.32	93	57c
Rental units expenditures	year	1883	900/00/ 91	81c
Rental units expenditures	year	1200	91	81r
Sun-space addition, average cost	add	23768.00	3/95	13r
Wing addition, two-story, average cost	add	50410.00	3/95	13r
Insurance and Pensions				
Auto insurance, private passenger	year	679.48	12/94	71s
Health insurance, HMO plan, cost to employer	year	3088	93	59c
Insurance and pensions, personal, expenditures	year	2788	91	81c
Insurance and pensions, personal, expenditures	year	2408	91	81r
Insurance, life and other personal, expenditures	year	315	91	81c
Insurance, life and other personal, expenditures	year	355	91	81r
Pensions and Social Security, expenditures	year	2473	91	81c
Pensions and Social Security, expenditures	year	2053	91	81r
Legal Assistance				
Legal work, law firm associate	hour	90		10r
Legal work, law firm partner	hour	139		10r
Personal Goods				
Personal care products and services, total expenditures	year	442	91	81c
Personal Services				
Dry cleaning	serv	7.00	92	52c
Manicure		15.00	92	52c

Values are in dollars or fractions of dollars. In the column headed *Ref*, references are shown to sources. Each reference is followed by a letter. These refer to the geographical level for which data were reported: s=State, r=Region, and c=City or metro. The abbreviation *ex* is used to mean *except* or *excluding*; *exp* stands for *expenditures*. For other abbreviations and further explanations, please see the Introduction.

Chicago, IL - continued

Item	Per	Value	Date	Ref.
Personal Services				
Personal services expenditures	year	236	91	81c
Personal services expenditures	year	203	91	81r
Restaurant Food				
Dining expenditures, family	week	30.03	94	73r
Taxes				
Tax rate, residential property, month	$100	1.49	1/92	79c
Taxes, Federal income, expenditures	year	2819	91	81c
Taxes, Federal income, expenditures	year	1756	91	81r
Taxes, personal, expenditures	year	3420	91	81c
Taxes, personal, expenditures	year	2426	91	81r
Taxes, State and local income, expenditures	year	583	91	81c
Taxes, State and local income, expenditures	year	568	91	81r
Transportation				
Bus fare, one-way	trip	1.16	12/95	1c
Cars and trucks purchased, new	year	1095	91	81c
Cars and trucks purchased, new	year	891	91	81r
Cars and trucks purchased, used	year	615	91	81c
Cars and trucks purchased, used	year	1155	91	81r
Driver's learning permit fee	perm	20.00	1/94	84s
Driver's license fee	orig	10.00	1/94	84s
Driver's license fee, duplicate	lic	5.00	1/94	84s
Driver's license reinstatement fee, min.	susp	30.00	1/94	85s
Driver's license renewal fee	renew	10.00	1/94	84s
Identification card, nondriver	card	4.00	1/94	83s
Motorcycle learning permit fee	perm	20.00	1/94	84s
Motorcycle license fee	orig	10.00	1/94	84s
Motorcycle license fee, duplicate	lic	5.00	1/94	84s
Motorcycle license renewal fee	renew	10.00	1/94	84s
Public transportation expenditures	year	533	91	81c
Public transportation expenditures	year	209	91	81r
Railway fare, commuter rail, one-way	trip	2.35	12/95	1c
Railway fare, heavy rail, one-way	trip	1.50	12/95	1c
Transportation expenditures, total	year	4955	91	81c
Transportation expenditures, total	year	4792	91	81r
Vehicle expenses, miscellaneous	year	1678	91	81c
Vehicle finance charges	year	288	91	81c
Vehicle finance charges	year	300	91	81r
Vehicle insurance expenditures	year	514	91	81c
Vehicle insurance expenditures	year	485	91	81r
Vehicle maintenance and repairs expenditures	year	641	91	81c
Vehicle maintenance and repairs expenditures	year	534	91	81r
Vehicle purchases	year	1728	91	81c
Vehicle purchases	year	2068	91	81r
Vehicle rental, leases, licenses, etc. expenditures	year	235	91	81c
Vehicle rental, leases, licenses, etc. expenditures	year	197	91	81r
Vehicles purchased, other than cars and trucks	year	18	91	81c
Vehicles purchased, other than cars and trucks	year	22	91	81r
Utilities				
Electricity	KWh	0.10	12/94	82c
Electricity expenditures	year	704	91	81c
Electricity expenditures	year	668	91	81r
Electricity, summer, 250 KWh	month	35.72	8/93	64c
Electricity, summer, 500 KWh	month	62.38	8/93	64c
Electricity, summer, 750 KWh	month	89.04	8/93	64c
Electricity, summer, 1000 KWh	month	115.70	8/93	64c
Utilities, fuels, and public services, total expenditures	year	2059	91	81c
Utilities, fuels, and public services, total expenditures	year	1838	91	81r
Water and other public services, expenditures	year	179	91	81c
Water and other public services, expenditures	year	167	91	81r

Chicago, IL - continued

Item	Per	Value	Date	Ref.
Weddings				
Bridal attendants' gowns	event	750	10/93	76r
Bridal gown	event	852	10/93	76r
Bridal headpiece and veil	event	167	10/93	76r
Bride's wedding band	event	708	10/93	76r
Clergy	event	224	10/93	76r
Engagement ring	event	2756	10/93	76r
Flowers	event	863	10/93	76r
Formal wear for groom	event	106	10/93	76r
Groom's attendants' formal wear	event	530	10/93	76r
Groom's wedding band	event	402	10/93	76r
Music	event	600	10/93	76r
Photography	event	1088	10/93	76r
Shoes for bride	event	50	10/93	76r
Videography	event	483	10/93	76r
Wedding invitations and announcements	event	342	10/93	76r
Wedding reception	event	7000	10/93	76r

Chico, CA

Item	Per	Value	Date	Ref.
Appliances				
Appliances (major), expenditures	year	160	91	81r
Average annual exp.				
Food, health care, personal goods, services	year	32461	91	81r
Charity				
Cash contributions, expenditures	year	975	91	81r
Clothing				
Apparel, men and boys, total expenditures	year	467	91	81r
Apparel, women and girls, total expenditures	year	737	91	81r
Footwear, expenditures	year	270	91	81r
Communications				
Long-distance telephone rate, day, addl. min., 1-10 mi.	min.	0.07	12/93	9s
Long-distance telephone rate, day, initial min., 1-10 mi.	min.	0.17	12/93	9s
Phone line, single, business, field visit	inst	70.75	12/93	9s
Phone line, single, business, no field visit	inst	70.75	12/93	9s
Phone line, single, residence, field visit	inst	34.75	12/93	9s
Phone line, single, residence, no field visit	inst	34.75	12/93	9s
Telephone service, expenditures	year	611	91	81r
Education				
Board, 4-year private college/university	year	2945	8/94	80s
Board, 4-year public college/university	year	2321	8/94	80s
Education, total expenditures	year	375	91	81r
Room, 4-year private college/university	year	3094	8/94	80s
Room, 4-year public college/university	year	2812	8/94	80s
Student fee, university	year	21.00	93	18s
Total cost, 4-year private college/university	year	19321	8/94	80s
Total cost, 4-year public college/university	year	7511	8/94	80s
Tuition, 2-year public college/university, in-state	year	345	8/94	80s
Tuition, 4-year private college/university, in-state	year	13282	8/94	80s
Tuition, 4-year public college/university, in-state	year	2378	8/94	80s
Energy and Fuels				
Fuel oil and other fuels, expenditures	year	33	91	81r
Gas, natural, expenditures	year	212	91	81r
Gasoline and motor oil purchased	year	1115	91	81r
Gasoline, unleaded midgrade	gallon	1.36	4/93	82r
Gasoline, unleaded premium	gallon	1.43	4/93	82r
Gasoline, unleaded regular	gallon	1.23	4/93	82r
Entertainment				
Concert ticket, Pearl Jam group	perf	20.00	94	50r
Entertainment, total expenditures	year	1853	91	81r
Fees and admissions, expenditures	year	482	91	81r
Pets, toys, playground equipment, expenditures	year	299	91	81r

Values are in dollars or fractions of dollars. In the column headed *Ref*, references are shown to sources. Each reference is followed by a letter. These refer to the geographical level for which data were reported: s=State, r=Region, and c=City or metro. The abbreviation *ex* is used to mean *except* or *excluding*; *exp* stands for *expenditures*. For other abbreviations and further explanations, please see the Introduction.

Chico, CA - continued

Item	Per	Value	Date	Ref.
Entertainment				
Reading, expenditures	year	164	91	81r
Televisions, radios, and sound equipment, expenditures	year	528	91	81r
Funerals				
Burial, immediate, container provided by funeral home		1382.70	1/95	54r
Cards, acknowledgment		21.87	1/95	54r
Casket, minimum alternative		128.54	1/95	54r
Cosmetology, hair care, etc.		119.69	1/95	54r
Cremation, direct, container provided by funeral home		1030.62	1/95	54r
Embalming		255.42	1/95	54r
Funeral, funeral home		437.38	1/95	54r
Funeral, other facility		444.46	1/95	54r
Graveside service		338.46	1/95	54r
Hearse, local		147.50	1/95	54r
Limousine, local		130.33	1/95	54r
Memorial service		553.16	1/95	54r
Service charge, professional, nondeclinable		859.15	1/95	54r
Visitation and viewing		93.23	1/95	54r
Groceries				
Apples, Red Delicious	lb.	0.72	12/94	82r
Bacon, sliced	lb.	1.73	12/94	82r
Bananas	lb.	0.52	12/94	82r
Beef purchases	year	241	91	81r
Beverage purchases, alcoholic	year	328	91	81r
Beverage purchases, nonalcoholic	year	234	91	81r
Bologna, all beef or mixed	lb.	2.33	12/94	82r
Bread, white, pan	lb.	0.81	12/94	82r
Carrots, short trimmed and topped	lb.	0.43	12/94	82r
Cereals and bakery products purchases	year	392	91	81r
Cereals and cereals products purchases	year	139	91	81r
Chicken breast, bone-in	lb.	2.04	12/94	82r
Chicken, fresh, whole	lb.	0.95	12/94	82r
Coffee, 100%, ground roast, all sizes	lb.	4.48	12/94	82r
Dairy products (other) purchases	year	182	91	81r
Fish and seafood purchases	year	94	91	81r
Flour, white, all purpose	lb.	0.21	12/94	82r
Food purchases, food eaten at home	year	2749	91	81r
Foods purchased away from home, not prepared by consumer	year	1909	91	81r
Fruits and vegetables purchases	year	459	91	81r
Grapefruit	lb.	0.56	12/94	82r
Ground beef, 100% beef	lb.	1.31	12/94	82r
Ham, boneless, exc. canned	lb.	2.46	12/94	82r
Ice cream, prepackaged, bulk, regular	1/2 gal.	2.57	12/94	82r
Lemons	lb.	1.00	12/94	82r
Lettuce, iceberg	lb.	0.93	12/94	82r
Meats, poultry, fish, and eggs purchases	year	700	91	81r
Milk and cream (fresh) purchases	year	155	91	81r
Orange juice, frozen concentrate 12-oz. can	16 oz.	1.52	12/94	82r
Oranges, Navel	lb.	0.56	12/94	82r
Pork chops, center cut, bone-in	lb.	3.30	12/94	82r
Pork purchases	year	122	91	81r
Potato chips	16-oz.	3.03	12/94	82r
Potatoes, frozen, French fried	lb.	0.77	12/94	82r
Potatoes, white	lb.	0.35	12/94	82r
Rice, white, long grain, uncooked	lb.	0.54	12/94	82r
Round roast, USDA choice, boneless	lb.	2.92	12/94	82r
Shortening, vegetable oil blends	lb.	0.80	12/94	82r
Spaghetti and macaroni	lb.	1.02	12/94	82r
Steak, round, graded & ungraded, exc. USDA prime & choice	lb.	3.13	12/94	82r
Steak, sirloin, USDA choice, boneless	lb.	4.07	12/94	82r
Sugar and other sweets, eaten at home, expenditures	year	105	91	81r
Sugar, white, all sizes	lb.	0.38	12/94	82r
Tobacco products and smoking supplies, total expenditures	year	221	91	81r
Tomatoes, field grown	lb.	1.45	12/94	82r

Chico, CA - continued

Item	Per	Value	Date	Ref.
Groceries - continued				
Tuna, chunk, light	lb.	2.18	12/94	82r
Health Care				
Childbirth, Cesarean delivery, hospital charge	birth	6059.00	12/91	69r
Childbirth, Cesarean delivery, physician charge	birth	2248.00	12/91	69r
Childbirth, normal delivery, hospital charge	birth	3006.00	12/91	69r
Childbirth, normal delivery, physician charge	birth	1634.00	12/91	69r
Drugs, expenditures	year	230	91	81r
Health care, total expenditures	year	1544	91	81r
Health insurance expenditures	year	558	91	81r
Insurance premium, family medical care	month	380.27	1/95	41s
Medical services expenditures	year	676	91	81r
Medical supplies expenditures	year	80	91	81r
Surgery, open-heart	proc	37818.00	1/93	14r
Household Goods				
Floor coverings, expenditures	year	79	91	81r
Furniture, expenditures	year	352	91	81r
Household equipment, misc. expenditures	year	614	91	81r
Household expenditures, miscellaneous	year	294	91	81r
Household furnishings and equipment, expenditures	year	1416	91	81r
Household operations expenditures	year	580	91	81r
Household textiles, expenditures	year	113	91	81r
Housekeeping supplies, expenditures	year	447	91	81r
Laundry and cleaning supplies, expenditures	year	114	91	81r
Postage and stationery, expenditures	year	145	91	81r
Housing				
Add garage/carport		6,422	3/95	74r
Add room(s)		26,583	3/95	74r
Apartment condominium or co-op, median	unit	105300	12/94	62r
Dwellings (owned), expenditures	year	3932	91	81r
Enclose porch/patio/breezeway		5,382	3/95	74r
Finish room in basement/attic		3,911	3/95	74r
Home, existing, single-family, median	unit	178600	12/94	62r
Maintenance, repairs, insurance, and other housing expenditures	year	591	91	81r
Mortgage interest and charges expenditures	year	2747	91	81r
Princ. & int., mortgage, median-price exist. sing.-family home	mo.	845	12/94	62r
Property taxes expenditures	year	594	91	81r
Redesign, restructure more than half of home's interior		5,467	3/95	74r
Rental units expenditures	year	2077	91	81r
Insurance and Pensions				
Auto insurance, private passenger	year	892.80	12/94	71s
Insurance and pensions, personal, expenditures	year	3042	91	81r
Insurance, life and other personal, expenditures	year	298	91	81r
Pensions and Social Security, expenditures	year	2744	91	81r
Legal Assistance				
Legal work, law firm associate	hour	91		10r
Legal work, law firm partner	hour	151		10r
Personal Services				
Personal services expenditures	year	286	91	81r
Restaurant Food				
Dining expenditures, family	week	32.25	94	73r
Taxes				
Taxes, Federal income, expenditures	year	2946	91	81r
Taxes, personal, expenditures	year	3791	91	81r
Taxes, State and local income, expenditures	year	791	91	81r
Transportation				
Cars and trucks purchased, new	year	1231	91	81r
Cars and trucks purchased, used	year	915	91	81r
Driver's learning permit fee	perm	12.00	1/94	84s

Values are in dollars or fractions of dollars. In the column headed *Ref*, references are shown to sources. Each reference is followed by a letter. These refer to the geographical level for which data were reported: s=State, r=Region, and c=City or metro. The abbreviation *ex* is used to mean *except* or *excluding*; *exp* stands for expenditures. For other abbreviations and further explanations, please see the Introduction.

Chico, CA - continued

Transportation

Item	Per	Value	Date	Ref.
Driver's license fee	orig	12.00	1/94	84s
Driver's license fee, duplicate	lic	12.00	1/94	84s
Driver's license reinstatement fee, min.	susp	15.00	1/94	85s
Driver's license renewal fee	renew	12.00	1/94	84s
Identification card, nondriver	card	6.00	1/94	83s
Motorcycle learning permit fee	perm	12.00	1/94	84s
Motorcycle license fee	orig	12.00	1/94	84s
Motorcycle license fee, duplicate	lic	12.00	1/94	84s
Motorcycle license renewal fee	renew	12.00	1/94	84s
Public transportation expenditures	year	375	91	81r
Transportation expenditures, total	year	5527	91	81r
Vehicle finance charges	year	287	91	81r
Vehicle insurance expenditures	year	624	91	81r
Vehicle maintenance and repairs expenditures	year	695	91	81r
Vehicle purchases	year	2174	91	81r
Vehicle rental, leases, licenses, etc. expenditures	year	257	91	81r
Vehicles purchased, other than cars and trucks	year	28	91	81r

Utilities

Item	Per	Value	Date	Ref.
Electricity expenditures	year	616	91	81r
Utilities, fuels, and public services, total expenditures	year	1681	91	81r
Water and other public services, expenditures	year	209	91	81r

Weddings

Item	Per	Value	Date	Ref.
Bridal attendants' gowns	event	750	10/93	76r
Bridal gown	event	852	10/93	76r
Bridal headpiece and veil	event	167	10/93	76r
Bride's wedding band	event	708	10/93	76r
Clergy	event	224	10/93	76r
Engagement ring	event	2756	10/93	76r
Flowers	event	863	10/93	76r
Formal wear for groom	event	106	10/93	76r
Groom's attendants' formal wear	event	530	10/93	76r
Groom's wedding band	event	402	10/93	76r
Music	event	600	10/93	76r
Photography	event	1088	10/93	76r
Shoes for bride	event	50	10/93	76r
Videography	event	483	10/93	76r
Wedding invitations and announcements	event	342	10/93	76r
Wedding reception	event	7000	10/93	76r

Cincinnati, OH

Item	Per	Value	Date	Ref.
Composite, ACCRA index		101.00	12/94	2c

Alcoholic Beverages

Item	Per	Value	Date	Ref.
Beer, Miller Lite, Bud, 12-oz., ex deposit	6	3.99	12/94	2c
J & B Scotch	750-ml.	18.80	12/94	2c
Wine, Gallo Chablis blanc	1.5-lit	4.99	12/94	2c

Appliances

Item	Per	Value	Date	Ref.
Appliances (major), expenditures	year	142	91	81c
Appliances (major), expenditures	year	131	91	81r

Average annual exp.

Item	Per	Value	Date	Ref.
Food, health care, personal goods, services	year	27781	91	81c
Food, health care, personal goods, services	year	25935	91	81r

Charity

Item	Per	Value	Date	Ref.
Cash contributions, expenditures	year	675	91	81c
Cash contributions, expenditures	year	745	91	81r

Clothing

Item	Per	Value	Date	Ref.
Apparel, men and boys, total expenditures	year	341	91	81c
Apparel, men and boys, total expenditures	year	332	91	81r
Apparel, women and girls, total expenditures	year	777	91	81c
Apparel, women and girls, total expenditures	year	578	91	81r
Footwear, expenditures	year	275	91	81c
Footwear, expenditures	year	164	91	81r

Cincinnati, OH - continued

Clothing - continued

Item	Per	Value	Date	Ref.
Jeans, man's denim		37.79	12/94	2c
Shirt, dress, men's	shirt	25.00	1/92	44c
Shirt, man's dress shirt		24.87	12/94	2c
Undervest, boy's size 10-14, cotton	3	4.95	12/94	2c

Communications

Item	Per	Value	Date	Ref.
Long-distance telephone rate, day, addl. min., 1-10 mi.	min.	0.16	12/93	9s
Long-distance telephone rate, day, initial min., 1-10 mi.	min.	0.32	12/93	9s
Newspaper subscription, dly. and Sun. delivery	month	14.25	12/94	2c
Phone line, single, business, field visit	inst	55.42	12/93	9s
Phone line, single, business, no field visit	inst	55.42	12/93	9s
Phone line, single, residence, field visit	inst	30.38	12/93	9s
Phone line, single, residence, no field visit	inst	30.38	12/93	9s
Telephone bill, family of four	month	20.30	12/94	2c
Telephone service, expenditures	year	528	91	81c
Telephone service, expenditures	year	547	91	81r
Telephone, business, addl. line, touch tone	month	2.35	10/91	25c
Telephone, business, connection charges, touch tone	inst	54.00	10/91	25c
Telephone, business, key system line, touch tone	month	59.45	10/91	25c
Telephone, business, PBX line, touch tone	month	59.80	10/91	25c
Telephone, business, single ln., touch tone	month	48.25	10/91	25c
Telephone, business, touch tone, inside wiring maintenance plan	month	1.00	10/91	25c
Telephone, residential, flat rate	mo.	15.25	12/93	8c

Education

Item	Per	Value	Date	Ref.
Board, 4-year private college/university	year	2241	8/94	80s
Board, 4-year public college/university	year	1625	8/94	80s
Education, total expenditures	year	358	91	81c
Education, total expenditures	year	394	91	81r
Room, 4-year private college/university	year	2118	8/94	80s
Room, 4-year public college/university	year	2103	8/94	80s
Total cost, 4-year private college/university	year	15444	8/94	80s
Total cost, 4-year public college/university	year	6987	8/94	80s
Tuition, 2-year public college/university, in-state	year	2076	8/94	80s
Tuition, 4-year private college/university, in-state	year	11085	8/94	80s
Tuition, 4-year public college/university, in-state	year	3259	8/94	80s

Energy and Fuels

Item	Per	Value	Date	Ref.
Energy, combined forms, 1800 sq. ft.	mo.	115.81	12/94	2c
Energy, exc. electricity, 1800 sq. ft.	mo.	39.31	12/94	2c
Fuel oil and other fuels, expenditures	year	84	91	81c
Fuel oil and other fuels, expenditures	year	83	91	81r
Gas	gal.	1.00	1/92	44c
Gas, cooking, winter, 10 therms	month	11.41	2/94	65c
Gas, cooking, winter, 30 therms	month	23.23	2/94	65c
Gas, cooking, winter, 50 therms	month	35.05	2/94	65c
Gas, heating, winter, 100 therms	month	64.60	2/94	65c
Gas, heating, winter, average use	month	132.86	2/94	65c
Gas, natural, expenditures	year	174	91	81c
Gas, natural, expenditures	year	373	91	81r
Gas, reg unlead, taxes inc., cash, self-service	gal	1.08	12/94	2c
Gasoline and motor oil purchased	year	1054	91	81c
Gasoline and motor oil purchased	year	1000	91	81r
Gasoline, unleaded midgrade	gallon	1.15	4/93	82r
Gasoline, unleaded premium	gallon	1.23	4/93	82r
Gasoline, unleaded regular	gallon	1.07	4/93	82r

Entertainment

Item	Per	Value	Date	Ref.
Baseball game, four-person family	game	79.31	4/94	47c
Bowling, evening rate	game	2.00	12/94	2c
Entertainment supplies, equipment, and services, misc. expenditures	year	211	91	81c
Entertainment, total expenditures	year	1501	91	81c
Entertainment, total expenditures	year	1356	91	81r

Values are in dollars or fractions of dollars. In the column headed *Ref*, references are shown to sources. Each reference is followed by a letter. These refer to the geographical level for which data were reported: s=State, r=Region, and c=City or metro. The abbreviation *ex* is used to mean *except* or *excluding*; *exp* stands for expenditures. For other abbreviations and further explanations, please see the Introduction.

Cincinnati, OH - continued

Item	Per	Value	Date	Ref.
Entertainment				
Fees and admissions, expenditures	year	394	91	81c
Fees and admissions, expenditures	year	347	91	81r
Monopoly game, Parker Brothers', No. 9	game	14.39	12/94	2c
Movie	adm	6.75	12/94	2c
Movie ticket, adult	ticket	6.50	1/92	44c
Pets, toys, playground equipment, expenditures	year	308	91	81c
Pets, toys, playground equipment, expenditures	year	270	91	81r
Reading, expenditures	year	182	91	81c
Reading, expenditures	year	160	91	81r
Televisions, radios, and sound equipment, expenditures	year	588	91	81c
Televisions, radios, and sound equipment, expenditures	year	433	91	81r
Tennis balls, yellow, Wilson or Penn, 3	can	2.67	12/94	2c
Funerals				
Burial, immediate, container provided by funeral home		1268.31	1/95	54r
Cards, acknowledgment		26.12	1/95	54r
Casket, minimum alternative		198.03	1/95	54r
Cosmetology, hair care, etc.		122.19	1/95	54r
Cremation, direct, container provided by funeral home		977.81	1/95	54r
Embalming		334.00	1/95	54r
Funeral, funeral home		321.16	1/95	54r
Funeral, other facility		317.73	1/95	54r
Graveside service		292.48	1/95	54r
Hearse, local		153.20	1/95	54r
Limousine, local		123.52	1/95	54r
Memorial service		356.30	1/95	54r
Service charge, professional, nondeclinable		968.24	1/95	54r
Visitation and viewing		332.66	1/95	54r
Groceries				
Groceries, ACCRA Index		95.60	12/94	2c
Apples, Red Delicious	lb.	0.68	12/94	82r
Baby food, strained vegetables, lowest price	4-4.5 oz.	0.27	12/94	2c
Bacon, sliced	lb.	1.88	12/94	82r
Bananas	lb.	0.49	12/94	2c
Bananas	lb.	0.41	12/94	82r
Beef or hamburger, ground	lb.	1.11	12/94	2c
Beef purchases	year	222	91	81c
Beef purchases	year	197	91	81r
Beef, stew, boneless	lb.	2.52	12/94	82r
Beverage purchases, alcoholic	year	247	91	81c
Beverage purchases, alcoholic	year	293	91	81r
Beverage purchases, nonalcoholic	year	235	91	81c
Beverage purchases, nonalcoholic	year	203	91	81r
Bologna, all beef or mixed	lb.	2.12	12/94	82r
Bread, white	24-oz.	0.58	12/94	2c
Bread, white, pan	lb.	0.76	12/94	82r
Cabbage	lb.	0.44	12/94	82r
Carrots, short trimmed and topped	lb.	0.44	12/94	82r
Cereals and bakery products purchases	year	403	91	81c
Cereals and bakery products purchases	year	347	91	81r
Cereals and cereal products purchases	year	141	91	81c
Cereals and cereals products purchases	year	119	91	81r
Cheddar cheese, natural	lb.	3.28	12/94	82r
Cheese, Kraft grated Parmesan	8-oz.	3.19	12/94	2c
Chicken breast, bone-in	lb.	1.61	12/94	82r
Chicken, fresh, whole	lb.	0.89	12/94	82r
Chicken, whole fryer	lb.	0.68	12/94	2c
Chuck roast, USDA choice, boneless	lb.	2.33	12/94	82r
Cigarettes, Winston, Kings	carton	14.78	12/94	2c
Coffee, 100%, ground roast, all sizes	lb.	4.28	12/94	82r
Coffee, vacuum-packed	13 oz.	3.71	12/94	2c
Cookies, chocolate chip	lb.	2.72	12/94	82r
Corn Flakes, Kellogg's or Post Toasties	18 oz.	2.29	12/94	2c
Corn, frozen, whole kernel, lowest price	10 oz.	0.65	12/94	2c
Dairy products (other) purchases	year	168	91	81c

Cincinnati, OH - continued

Item	Per	Value	Date	Ref.
Groceries - continued				
Dairy products (other) purchases	year	148	91	81r
Eggs, Grade A large	dozen	0.91	12/94	2c
Eggs, Grade A large	dozen	0.76	12/94	82r
Fish and seafood purchases	year	77	91	81c
Fish and seafood purchases	year	61	91	81r
Flour, white, all purpose	lb.	0.22	12/94	82r
Food purchases, food eaten at home	year	2670	91	81c
Food purchases, food eaten at home	year	2313	91	81r
Foods purchased away from home, not prepared by consumer	year	2018	91	81c
Foods purchased away from home, not prepared by consumer	year	1709	91	81r
Fruits and vegetables purchases	year	411	91	81c
Fruits and vegetables purchases	year	372	91	81r
Grapefruit	lb.	0.47	12/94	82r
Grapes, Thompson seedless	lb.	2.15	12/94	82r
Ground beef, 100% beef	lb.	1.37	12/94	82r
Ground chuck, 100% beef	lb.	1.81	12/94	82r
Ham, boneless, exc. canned	lb.	2.16	12/94	82r
Ice cream, prepackaged, bulk, regular	1/2 gal.	2.48	12/94	82r
Lemons	lb.	1.08	12/94	82r
Lettuce, iceberg	lb.	0.81	12/94	82r
Lettuce, iceberg	head	0.95	12/94	2c
Margarine, Blue Bonnet or Parkay cubes	lb.	0.63	12/94	2c
Margarine, stick	lb.	0.81	12/94	82r
Meats, poultry, fish, and eggs purchases	year	701	91	81c
Meats, poultry, fish, and eggs purchases	year	591	91	81r
Milk and cream (fresh) purchases	year	134	91	81c
Milk and cream (fresh) purchases	year	132	91	81r
Milk, 2%	gal.	1.90	1/92	44c
Milk, whole	1/2 gal.	1.49	12/94	2c
Orange juice, frozen concentrate 12-oz. can	16 oz.	1.41	12/94	82r
Orange juice, Minute Maid frozen	12-oz.	1.23	12/94	2c
Oranges, Navel	lb.	0.56	12/94	82r
Peaches, halves or slices, Hunt's, Del Monte, or Libby's	29-oz.	1.55	12/94	2c
Peanut butter, creamy, all sizes	lb.	1.81	12/94	82r
Peas, sweet, Del Monte or Green Giant	15-17 oz.	0.59	12/94	2c
Pork chops, center cut, bone-in	lb.	2.76	12/94	82r
Pork purchases	year	175	91	81c
Pork purchases	year	130	91	81r
Potato chips	16-oz.	2.81	12/94	82r
Potatoes, frozen, French fried	lb.	0.83	12/94	82r
Potatoes, white	lb.	0.28	12/94	82r
Potatoes, white or red	10-lb. sack	2.23	12/94	2c
Rental rate, 2-bedroom apartment	month	525.00	1/92	44c
Round roast, USDA choice, boneless	lb.	2.90	12/94	82r
Sausage, Jimmy Dean, 100% pork	lb.	2.73	12/94	2c
Shortening, vegetable oil blends	lb.	0.88	12/94	82r
Shortening, vegetable, Crisco	3-lb.	2.99	12/94	2c
Soft drink, Coca Cola, ex deposit	2 lit	0.99	12/94	2c
Spaghetti and macaroni	lb.	0.78	12/94	82r
Steak, rib eye, USDA choice, boneless	lb.	6.15	12/94	82r
Steak, round, graded & ungraded, exc. USDA prime & choice	lb.	2.72	12/94	82r
Steak, round, USDA choice, boneless	lb.	3.02	12/94	82r
Steak, sirloin, USDA choice, boneless	lb.	3.85	12/94	82r
Steak, t-bone	lb.	3.67	12/94	2c
Steak, T-bone, USDA choice, bone-in	lb.	5.38	12/94	82r
Sugar and other sweets, eaten at home, expenditures	year	91	91	81r
Sugar and other sweets, eaten at home, purchases	year	111	91	81c
Sugar, cane or beet	4 lbs.	1.65	12/94	2c
Sugar, white, all sizes	lb.	0.36	12/94	82r
Tobacco products and smoking supplies, total expenditures	year	309	91	81c

Values are in dollars or fractions of dollars. In the column headed *Ref*, references are shown to sources. Each reference is followed by a letter. These refer to the geographical level for which data were reported: s = State, r = Region, and c = City or metro. The abbreviation *ex* is used to mean *except* or *excluding*; *exp* stands for expenditures. For other abbreviations and further explanations, please see the Introduction.

Cincinnati, OH - continued

Item	Per	Value	Date	Ref.
Groceries				
Tobacco products and smoking supplies, total expenditures	year	298	91	81r
Tomatoes, field grown	lb.	1.36	12/94	82r
Tomatoes, Hunt's or Del Monte	14.5 oz.	0.81	12/94	2c
Tuna, chunk, light	lb.	1.94	12/94	82r
Tuna, chunk, light, oil-packed	6.125-6.5 oz.	0.79	12/94	2c
Turkey, frozen, whole	lb.	0.96	12/94	82r
Yogurt, natural, fruit flavored	8 oz.	0.62	12/94	82r
Goods and Services				
Miscellaneous goods and services, ACCRA Index		104.40	12/94	2c
Health Care				
Health care, ACCRA Index		95.50	12/94	2c
Antibiotic ointment, Polysporin	1.5 oz.	4.06	12/94	2c
Childbirth, Cesarean delivery, hospital charge	birth	5101.00	12/91	69r
Childbirth, Cesarean delivery, physician charge	birth	2234.00	12/91	69r
Childbirth, normal delivery, hospital charge	birth	2891.00	12/91	69r
Childbirth, normal delivery, physician charge	birth	1623.00	12/91	69r
Dentist's fee, adult teeth cleaning and periodic oral exam	visit	50.20	12/94	2c
Doctor's fee, routine exam, established patient	visit	38.80	12/94	2c
Drugs, expenditures	year	289	91	81c
Drugs, expenditures	year	248	91	81r
Health care, total expenditures	year	1583	91	81c
Health care, total expenditures	year	1336	91	81r
Health insurance expenditures	year	729	91	81c
Health insurance expenditures	year	550	91	81r
Health insurance premium	month	406.00	7/93	94c
Hospital care, semiprivate room	day	354.00	12/94	2c
Insurance premium, family medical care	month	350.73	1/95	41s
Medical services expenditures	year	497	91	81c
Medical services expenditures	year	457	91	81r
Medical supplies expenditures	year	68	91	81c
Medical supplies expenditures	year	82	91	81r
Household Goods				
Appl. repair, service call, wash mach	min. lab. chg.	36.48	12/94	2c
Floor coverings, expenditures	year	118	91	81c
Floor coverings, expenditures	year	105	91	81r
Furniture, expenditures	year	286	91	81c
Furniture, expenditures	year	291	91	81r
Household equipment, misc. expenditures	year	341	91	81r
Household equipment, misc., expenditures	year	424	91	81c
Household expenditures, miscellaneous	year	174	91	81c
Household expenditures, miscellaneous	year	162	91	81r
Household furnishings and equipment, expenditures	year	1134	91	81c
Household furnishings and equipment, expenditures	year	1042	91	81r
Household operations expenditures	year	307	91	81c
Household operations expenditures	year	365	91	81r
Household textiles, expenditures	year	93	91	81c
Household textiles, expenditures	year	101	91	81r
Housekeeping supplies, expenditures	year	380	91	81c
Housekeeping supplies, expenditures	year	390	91	81r
Laundry and cleaning supplies, expenditures	year	108	91	81c
Laundry and cleaning supplies, expenditures	year	110	91	81r
Laundry detergent, Tide Ultra, Bold, or Cheer	42 oz.	3.29	12/94	2c
Postage and stationery, expenditures	year	118	91	81c
Postage and stationery, expenditures	year	115	91	81r
Tissues, facial, Kleenex brand	175	0.99	12/94	2c

Cincinnati, OH - continued

Item	Per	Value	Date	Ref.
Housing				
Housing, ACCRA Index		99.50	12/94	2c
Add garage/carport		8,479	3/95	74r
Add room(s)		21,347	3/95	74r
Apartment condominium or co-op, median	unit	87100	12/94	62r
Bathroom addition, average cost	add	9734.00	3/95	13r
Bathroom remodeling, average cost	remod	6414.00	3/95	13r
Bedroom, master suite addition, average cost	add	27122.00	3/95	13r
Deck addition, average cost	add	6665.00	3/95	13r
Dwellings (owned), expenditures	year	2976	91	81c
Dwellings (owned), expenditures	year	2566	91	81r
Enclose porch/patio/breezeway		4,556	3/95	74r
Exterior remodeling, average cost	remod	15395.00	3/95	13r
Family room addition, average cost	add	27658.00	3/95	13r
Finish room in basement/attic		5,074	3/95	74r
Home, existing, single-family, median	unit	106500	12/94	62r
Home, existing, single-family, median	unit	96.40	12/94	62c
House payment, principal and interest, 25% down payment	mo.	748	12/94	2c
House, 1800 sq ft, 8000 sq ft lot, new, urban, utilities	total	123365	12/94	2c
Kitchen remodeling, major, average cost	remod	17084.00	3/95	13r
Kitchen remodeling, minor, average cost	remod	5804.00	3/95	13r
Maintenance, repairs, insurance, and other housing expenditures	year	515	91	81c
Maintenance, repairs, insurance, and other housing expenditures	year	484	91	81r
Mortgage interest and charges expenditures	year	1797	91	81c
Mortgage interest and charges expenditures	year	1443	91	81r
Mtge. rate, incl. points and orig. fee, 30-year conv. fixed or ARM	mo.	9.05	12/94	2c
Office, home addition, average cost	add	8121.00	3/95	13r
Princ. & int., mortgage, median-price exist. sing.-family home	mo.	515	12/94	62r
Property taxes expenditures	year	665	91	81c
Property taxes expenditures	year	639	91	81r
Redesign, restructure more than half of home's interior		9,114	3/95	74r
Rent, apartment, 2 br., 1 1/2-2 baths, unfurnished, 950 sq ft, water	mo.	568	12/94	2c
Rental units expenditures	year	1271	900/00/91	81c
Rental units expenditures	year	1200	91	81r
Sun-space addition, average cost	add	23768.00	3/95	13r
Wing addition, two-story, average cost	add	50410.00	3/95	13r
Insurance and Pensions				
Auto insurance, private passenger	year	550.52	12/94	71s
Insurance and pensions, personal, expenditures	year	2258	91	81c
Insurance and pensions, personal, expenditures	year	2408	91	81r
Insurance, life and other personal, expenditures	year	303	91	81c
Insurance, life and other personal, expenditures	year	355	91	81r
Pensions and Social Security, expenditures	year	1955	91	81c
Pensions and Social Security, expenditures	year	2053	91	81r
Legal Assistance				
Legal work, law firm associate	hour	90		10r
Legal work, law firm partner	hour	139		10r
Personal Goods				
Personal care products and services, total expenditures	year	369	91	81c
Shampoo, Alberto VO5	15-oz.	1.09	12/94	2c
Toothpaste, Crest or Colgate	6-7 oz.	1.69	12/94	2c
Personal Services				
Dry cleaning, man's 2-pc. suit		6.88	12/94	2c
Dry cleaning, woman's dress	dress	6.50	1/92	44c
Haircut, man's barbershop, no styling		7.00	12/94	2c
Haircut, woman's shampoo, trim, blow-dry		20.59	12/94	2c

Values are in dollars or fractions of dollars. In the column headed *Ref*, references are shown to sources. Each reference is followed by a letter. These refer to the geographical level for which data were reported: s=State, r=Region, and c=City or metro. The abbreviation *ex* is used to mean *except* or *excluding*; *exp* stands for *expenditures*. For other abbreviations and further explanations, please see the Introduction.

Cincinnati, OH - continued

Item	Per	Value	Date	Ref.
Personal Services				
Personal services expenditures	year	133	91	81c
Personal services expenditures	year	203	91	81r
Restaurant Food				
Big Mac, small fries, medium drink	meal	3.35	1/92	44c
Chicken, fried, thigh and drumstick		2.29	12/94	2c
Dining expenditures, family	week	30.03	94	73r
Hamburger with cheese	1/4 lb.	1.75	12/94	2c
Pizza, Pizza Hut or Pizza Inn	12-13 in.	7.69	12/94	2c
Taxes				
Taxes, Federal income, expenditures	year	1011	91	81c
Taxes, Federal income, expenditures	year	1756	91	81r
Taxes, personal, expenditures	year	1573	91	81c
Taxes, personal, expenditures	year	2426	91	81r
Taxes, State and local income, expenditures	year	435	91	81c
Taxes, State and local income, expenditures	year	568	91	81r
Transportation				
Transportation, ACCRA Index		104.30	12/94	2c
Bus fare, one-way	trip	0.70	12/95	1c
Bus fare, up to 10 miles	one-way	0.80	12/94	2c
Cars and trucks purchased, new	year	986	91	81c
Cars and trucks purchased, new	year	891	91	81r
Cars and trucks purchased, used	year	910	91	81c
Cars and trucks purchased, used	year	1155	91	81r
Driver's learning permit fee	perm	3.00	1/94	84s
Driver's license fee	orig	5.00	1/94	84s
Driver's license fee, duplicate	lic	1.50	1/94	84s
Driver's license reinstatement fee, min.	susp	12.50-100.00	1/94	85s
Driver's license renewal fee	renew	5.00	1/94	84s
Identification card, nondriver	card	2.50	1/94	83s
Motorcycle learning permit fee	perm	3.00	1/94	84s
Motorcycle license fee	orig	5.00	1/94	84s
Motorcycle license fee, duplicate	lic	1.50	1/94	84s
Motorcycle license renewal fee	renew	5.00	1/94	84s
parking, long-term lot, airport	3 days	10.00	1/92	44c
Public transportation expenditures	year	185	91	81c
Public transportation expenditures	year	209	91	81r
Tire balance, computer or spin bal., front	wheel	8.17	12/94	2c
Transportation expenditures, total	year	4857	91	81c
Transportation expenditures, total	year	4792	91	81r
Vehicle expenses, miscellaneous	year	1715	91	81c
Vehicle finance charges	year	313	91	81c
Vehicle finance charges	year	300	91	81r
Vehicle insurance expenditures	year	520	91	81c
Vehicle insurance expenditures	year	485	91	81r
Vehicle maintenance and repairs expenditures	year	623	91	81c
Vehicle maintenance and repairs expenditures	year	534	91	81r
Vehicle purchases	year	1904	91	81c
Vehicle purchases	year	2068	91	81r
Vehicle rental, leases, licenses, etc. expenditures	year	260	91	81c
Vehicle rental, leases, licenses, etc. expenditures	year	197	91	81r
Vehicles purchased, other than cars and trucks	year	8	91	81c
Vehicles purchased, other than cars and trucks	year	22	91	81r
Utilities				
Utilities, ACCRA Index		103.30	12/94	2c
Electricity expenditures	year	868	91	81c
Electricity expenditures	year	668	91	81r
Electricity, (part.), other, 1800 sq. ft., new home	mo.	76.50	12/94	2c
Electricity, summer, 250 KWh	month	22.73	8/93	64c
Electricity, summer, 500 KWh	month	41.44	8/93	64c
Electricity, summer, 750 KWh	month	60.17	8/93	64c

Cincinnati, OH - continued

Item	Per	Value	Date	Ref.
Utilities - continued				
Electricity, summer, 1000 KWh	month	78.88	8/93	64c
Utilities, fuels, and public services, total expenditures	year	1848	91	81c
Utilities, fuels, and public services, total expenditures	year	1838	91	81r
Water and other public services, expenditures	year	193	91	81c
Water and other public services, expenditures	year	167	91	81r
Weddings				
Bridal attendants' gowns	event	750	10/93	76r
Bridal gown	event	852	10/93	76r
Bridal headpiece and veil	event	167	10/93	76r
Bride's wedding band	event	708	10/93	76r
Clergy	event	224	10/93	76r
Engagement ring	event	2756	10/93	76r
Flowers	event	863	10/93	76r
Formal wear for groom	event	106	10/93	76r
Groom's attendants' formal wear	event	530	10/93	76r
Groom's wedding band	event	402	10/93	76r
Music	event	600	10/93	76r
Photography	event	1088	10/93	76r
Shoes for bride	event	50	10/93	76r
Videography	event	483	10/93	76r
Wedding invitations and announcements	event	342	10/93	76r
Wedding reception	event	7000	10/93	76r

Clarksville, TN

Item	Per	Value	Date	Ref.
Appliances				
Appliances (major), expenditures	year	153	91	81r
Average annual exp.				
Food, health care, personal goods, services	year	27020	91	81r
Charity				
Cash contributions, expenditures	year	839	91	81r
Clothing				
Apparel, men and boys, total expenditures	year	380	91	81r
Apparel, women and girls, total expenditures	year	660	91	81r
Footwear, expenditures	year	193	91	81r
Communications				
Long-distance telephone rate, day, addl. min., 1-10 mi.	min.	0.10	12/93	9s
Long-distance telephone rate, day, initial min., 1-10 mi.	min.	0.10	12/93	9s
Phone line, single, business, field visit	inst	58.50	12/93	9s
Phone line, single, business, no field visit	inst	58.50	12/93	9s
Phone line, single, residence, field visit	inst	41.50	12/93	9s
Phone line, single, residence, no field visit	inst	41.50	12/93	9s
Telephone service, expenditures	year	616	91	81r
Education				
Board, 4-year private college/university	year	1846	8/94	80s
Board, 4-year public college/university	year	1700	8/94	80s
Education, total expenditures	year	319	91	81r
Room, 4-year private college/university	year	1553	8/94	80s
Room, 4-year public college/university	year	1524	8/94	80s
Total cost, 4-year private college/university	year	12025	8/94	80s
Total cost, 4-year public college/university	year	5021	8/94	80s
Tuition, 2-year public college/university, in-state	year	950	8/94	80s
Tuition, 4-year private college/university, in-state	year	8627	8/94	80s
Tuition, 4-year public college/university, in-state	year	1797	8/94	80s
Energy and Fuels				
Fuel oil and other fuels, expenditures	year	56	91	81r
Gas, natural, expenditures	year	150	91	81r
Gasoline and motor oil purchased	year	1152	91	81r

Values are in dollars or fractions of dollars. In the column headed *Ref*, references are shown to sources. Each reference is followed by a letter. These refer to the geographical level for which data were reported: s = State, r = Region, and c = City or metro. The abbreviation *ex* is used to mean *except* or *excluding*; *exp* stands for expenditures. For other abbreviations and further explanations, please see the Introduction.

Clarksville, TN - continued

Item	Per	Value	Date	Ref.
Energy and Fuels				
Gasoline, unleaded midgrade	gallon	1.21	4/93	82r
Gasoline, unleaded premium	gallon	1.30	4/93	82r
Gasoline, unleaded regular	gallon	1.10	4/93	82r
Entertainment				
Concert ticket, Pearl Jam group	perf	20.00	94	50r
Entertainment, total expenditures	year	1266	91	81r
Fees and admissions, expenditures	year	306	91	81r
Pets, toys, playground equipment, expenditures	year	271	91	81r
Reading, expenditures	year	131	91	81r
Televisions, radios, and sound equipment, expenditures	year	439	91	81r
Funerals				
Burial, immediate, container provided by funeral home		1298.96	1/95	54r
Cards, acknowledgment		21.26	1/95	54r
Casket, minimum alternative		204.95	1/95	54r
Cosmetology, hair care, etc.		85.40	1/95	54r
Cremation, direct, container provided by funeral home		1054.77	1/95	54r
Embalming		287.71	1/95	54r
Funeral, funeral home		269.18	1/95	54r
Funeral, other facility		272.88	1/95	54r
Graveside service		302.54	1/95	54r
Hearse, local		122.08	1/95	54r
Limousine, local		80.31	1/95	54r
Memorial service		277.66	1/95	54r
Service charge, professional, nondeclinable		896.65	1/95	54r
Visitation and viewing		232.39	1/95	54r
Groceries				
Apples, Red Delicious	lb.	0.73	12/94	82r
Bacon, sliced	lb.	1.67	12/94	82r
Bananas	lb.	0.42	12/94	82r
Beef purchases	year	213	91	81r
Beverage purchases, alcoholic	year	249	91	81r
Beverage purchases, nonalcoholic	year	207	91	81r
Bologna, all beef or mixed	lb.	2.27	12/94	82r
Bread, white, pan	lb.	0.68	12/94	82r
Cabbage	lb.	0.42	12/94	82r
Carrots, short trimmed and topped	lb.	0.53	12/94	82r
Cereals and bakery products purchases	year	345	91	81r
Cereals and cereals products purchases	year	127	91	81r
Cheddar cheese, natural	lb.	3.58	12/94	82r
Chicken breast, bone-in	lb.	1.71	12/94	82r
Chicken, fresh, whole	lb.	0.78	12/94	82r
Chuck roast, USDA choice, boneless	lb.	2.26	12/94	82r
Crackers, soda, salted	lb.	1.27	12/94	82r
Cucumbers	lb.	0.65	12/94	82r
Dairy products (other) purchases	year	141	91	81r
Eggs, Grade A large	dozen	0.87	12/94	82r
Fish and seafood purchases	year	72	91	81r
Flour, white, all purpose	lb.	0.23	12/94	82r
Food purchases, food eaten at home	year	2381	91	81r
Foods purchased away from home, not prepared by consumer	year	1696	91	81r
Frankfurters, all meat or all beef	lb.	1.74	12/94	82r
Fruits and vegetables purchases	year	380	91	81r
Grapefruit	lb.	0.45	12/94	82r
Grapes, Thompson seedless	lb.	2.30	12/94	82r
Ground beef, 100% beef	lb.	1.37	12/94	82r
Ground chuck, 100% beef	lb.	1.97	12/94	82r
Ham, boneless, exc. canned	lb.	2.54	12/94	82r
Ice cream, prepackaged, bulk, regular	1/2 gal.	2.47	12/94	82r
Lemons	lb.	1.02	12/94	82r
Lettuce, iceberg	lb.	0.96	12/94	82r
Margarine, stick	lb.	0.77	12/94	82r
Meats, poultry, fish, and eggs purchases	year	655	91	81r
Milk and cream (fresh) purchases	year	130	91	81r
Orange juice, frozen concentrate 12-oz. can	16 oz.	1.36	12/94	82r
Oranges, Navel	lb.	0.54	12/94	82r

Clarksville, TN - continued

Item	Per	Value	Date	Ref.
Groceries - continued				
Pears, Anjou	lb.	0.81	12/94	82r
Pork chops, center cut, bone-in	lb.	3.07	12/94	82r
Pork purchases	year	142	91	81r
Potato chips	16-oz.	3.15	12/94	82r
Potatoes, frozen, French fried	lb.	0.82	12/94	82r
Potatoes, white	lb.	0.34	12/94	82r
Rice, white, long grain, uncooked	lb.	0.48	12/94	82r
Round roast, USDA choice, boneless	lb.	2.91	12/94	82r
Sausage, fresh	lb.	1.82	12/94	82r
Shortening, vegetable oil blends	lb.	0.75	12/94	82r
Spaghetti and macaroni	lb.	0.87	12/94	82r
Steak, rib eye, USDA choice, boneless	lb.	6.85	12/94	82r
Steak, round, graded & ungraded, exc. USDA prime & choice	lb.	2.96	12/94	82r
Steak, round, USDA choice, boneless	lb.	3.17	12/94	82r
Steak, sirloin, USDA choice, boneless	lb.	4.12	12/94	82r
Steak, T-bone, USDA choice, bone-in	lb.	5.63	12/94	82r
Sugar and other sweets, eaten at home, expenditures	year	93	91	81r
Sugar, white, all sizes	lb.	0.39	12/94	82r
Tobacco products and smoking supplies, total expenditures	year	286	91	81r
Tomatoes, field grown	lb.	1.36	12/94	82r
Tuna, chunk, light	lb.	1.94	12/94	82r
Turkey, frozen, whole	lb.	0.96	12/94	82r
Yogurt, natural, fruit flavored	8 oz.	0.58	12/94	82r
Health Care				
Adenosine, emergency room	treat	100.00	95	23r
Bladder tap, superpubic, infant, emergency room	treat	119.00	95	23r
Blood analysis, emergency room	treat	25.00	95	23r
Blood tests, abdominal pain, emergency room	treat	25.00	95	23r
Burn dressing, emergency room	treat	266.00	95	23r
Cardiology interpretation, emergency room	treat	26.00	95	23r
Chest X-ray, emergency room	treat	78.00	95	23r
Childbirth, Cesarean delivery, hospital charge	birth	5462.00	12/91	69r
Childbirth, Cesarean delivery, physician charge	birth	2228.00	12/91	69r
Childbirth, normal delivery, hospital charge	birth	2943.00	12/91	69r
Childbirth, normal delivery, physician charge	birth	1619.00	12/91	69r
Defibrillation pads, emergency room	treat	6.00	95	23r
Drugs, expenditures	year	297	91	81r
Gastric tube insertion, nasal, emergency room	treat	25.00	95	23r
Health care, total expenditures	year	1600	91	81r
Health insurance expenditures	year	637	91	81r
Heart monitor, emergency room	treat	40.00	95	23r
Insurance premium, family medical care	month	344.21	1/95	41s
Intravenous fluids, emergency room	treat	130.00	95	23r
Intravenous fluids, emergency room	liter	26.00	95	23r
Intravenous line, central, emergency room	treat	342.00	95	23r
Liver function tests, abdominal pain, emergency room	treat	26.00	95	23r
Medical care charges, total, emergency room, third-degree burns	treat	2101.00	95	23r
Medical care charges, total, emergency, infant with fever	treat	628.00	95	23r
Medical services expenditures	year	573	91	81r
Medical supplies expenditures	year	93	91	81r
Morphine, emergency room	treat	34.00	95	23r
Nursing care and facilities charges, emergency room	treat	252.00	95	23r
Nursing care and facilities charges, emergency, infant with fever	treat	252.00	95	23r
Nursing care and facilities charges, emergency, third-degree burns	treat	861.00	95	23r
Physician's charges, emergency, infant with fever	treat	212.00	95	23r
Physician's charges, emergency, third-degree burns	treat	372.00	95	23r

Values are in dollars or fractions of dollars. In the column headed *Ref*, references are shown to sources. Each reference is followed by a letter. These refer to the geographical level for which data were reported: s = State, r = Region, and c = City or metro. The abbreviation *ex* is used to mean *except* or *excluding*; *exp* stands for expenditures. For other abbreviations and further explanations, please see the Introduction.

Clarksville, TN - continued

Item	Per	Value	Date	Ref.
Health Care				
Physician's fee, emergency room	treat	372.00	95	23r
Physician's fee, general practitioner	visit	51.20	12/93	60r
Surgery, open-heart	proc	42374.00	1/93	14r
Ultrasound, abdominal, emergency room	treat	276.00	95	23r
Urinalysis, emergency room	treat	20.00	95	23r
Urinalysis, infant, emergency room	treat	20.00	95	23r
X-rays, emergency room	treat	78.00	95	23r
Household Goods				
Floor coverings, expenditures	year	48	91	81r
Furniture, expenditures	year	280	91	81r
Household equipment, misc. expenditures	year	342	91	81r
Household expenditures, miscellaneous	year	256	91	81r
Household furnishings and equipment, expenditures	year	988	91	81r
Household operations expenditures	year	468	91	81r
Household textiles, expenditures	year	95	91	81r
Housekeeping supplies, expenditures	year	380	91	81r
Laundry and cleaning supplies, expenditures	year	109	91	81r
Postage and stationery, expenditures	year	105	91	81r
Housing				
Add garage/carport		6,980	3/95	74r
Add room(s)		11,403	3/95	74r
Apartment condominium or co-op, median	unit	68600	12/94	62r
Dwellings (owned), expenditures	year	2428	91	81r
Enclose porch/patio/breezeway		4,572	3/95	74r
Finish room in basement/attic		3,794	3/95	74r
Home, existing, single-family, median	unit	120200	12/94	62r
Maintenance, repairs, insurance, and other housing expenditures	year	531	91	81r
Mortgage interest and charges expenditures	year	1506	91	81r
Princ. & int., mortgage, median-price exist. sing.-family home	mo.	540	12/94	62r
Property taxes expenditures	year	391	91	81r
Redesign, restructure more than half of home's interior		17,641	3/95	74r
Rental units expenditures	year	1264	91	81r
Insurance and Pensions				
Auto insurance, private passenger	year	574.08	12/94	71s
Insurance and pensions, personal, expenditures	year	2395	91	81r
Insurance, life and other personal, expenditures	year	368	91	81r
Pensions and Social Security, expenditures	year	2027	91	81r
Personal Services				
Personal services expenditures	year	212	91	81r
Restaurant Food				
Dining expenditures, family	week	33.83	94	73r
Taxes				
Tax, cigarettes	year	379.00	10/93	43s
Taxes, Federal income, expenditures	year	2275	91	81r
Taxes, personal, expenditures	year	2715	91	81r
Taxes, State and local income, expenditures	year	365	91	81r
Transportation				
Cars and trucks purchased, new	year	1306	91	81r
Cars and trucks purchased, used	year	942	91	81r
Driver's learning permit fee	perm	5.50	1/94	84s
Driver's license fee	orig	16.00	1/94	84s
Driver's license fee, duplicate	lic	8.00	1/94	84s
Driver's license reinstatement fee, min.	susp	65.00	1/94	85s
Driver's license renewal fee	renew	14.00	1/94	84s
Identification card, nondriver	card	7.50	1/94	83s
Motorcycle learning permit fee	perm	6.50	1/94	84s
Motorcycle license fee	orig	17.00	1/94	84s
Motorcycle license fee, duplicate	lic	8.00	1/94	84s
Motorcycle license renewal fee	renew	15.00	1/94	84s
Public transportation expenditures	year	249	91	81r
Transportation expenditures, total	year	5307	91	81r

Clarksville, TN - continued

Item	Per	Value	Date	Ref.
Transportation - continued				
Vehicle finance charges	year	346	91	81r
Vehicle insurance expenditures	year	544	91	81r
Vehicle maintenance and repairs expenditures	year	600	91	81r
Vehicle purchases	year	2275	91	81r
Vehicle rental, leases, licenses, etc. expenditures	year	141	91	81r
Vehicles purchased, other than cars and trucks	year	27	91	81r
Utilities				
Electricity expenditures	year	950	91	81r
Utilities, fuels, and public services, total expenditures	year	2000	91	81r
Water and other public services, expenditures	year	227	91	81r
Weddings				
Bridal attendants' gowns	event	750	10/93	76r
Bridal gown	event	852	10/93	76r
Bridal headpiece and veil	event	167	10/93	76r
Bride's wedding band	event	708	10/93	76r
Clergy	event	224	10/93	76r
Engagement ring	event	2756	10/93	76r
Flowers	event	863	10/93	76r
Formal wear for groom	event	106	10/93	76r
Groom's attendants' formal wear	event	530	10/93	76r
Groom's wedding band	event	402	10/93	76r
Music	event	600	10/93	76r
Photography	event	1088	10/93	76r
Shoes for bride	event	50	10/93	76r
Videography	event	483	10/93	76r
Wedding invitations and announcements	event	342	10/93	76r
Wedding reception	event	7000	10/93	76r

Cleveland, OH

Item	Per	Value	Date	Ref.
Composite, ACCRA index		104.30	12/94	2c
Alcoholic Beverages				
Beer, Miller Lite, Bud, 12-oz., ex deposit	6	4.09	12/94	2c
J & B Scotch	750-ml.	19.65	12/94	2c
Wine, Gallo Chablis blanc	1.5-lit	6.24	12/94	2c
Appliances				
Appliances (major), expenditures	year	104	91	81c
Appliances (major), expenditures	year	131	91	81r
Average annual exp.				
Food, health care, personal goods, services	year	26960	91	81c
Food, health care, personal goods, services	year	25935	91	81r
Charity				
Cash contributions, expenditures	year	780	91	81c
Cash contributions, expenditures	year	745	91	81r
Clothing				
Apparel, men and boys, total expenditures	year	434	91	81c
Apparel, men and boys, total expenditures	year	332	91	81r
Apparel, women and girls, total expenditures	year	1140	91	81c
Apparel, women and girls, total expenditures	year	578	91	81r
Footwear, expenditures	year	281	91	81c
Footwear, expenditures	year	164	91	81r
Jeans, man's denim		29.32	12/94	2c
Shirt, man's dress shirt		26.55	12/94	2c
Undervest, boy's size 10-14, cotton	3	4.03	12/94	2c
Communications				
Long-distance telephone rate, day, addl. min., 1-10 mi.	min.	0.16	12/93	9s
Long-distance telephone rate, day, initial min., 1-10 mi.	min.	0.32	12/93	9s
Newspaper subscription, dly. and Sun. delivery	month	9.78	12/94	2c

Values are in dollars or fractions of dollars. In the column headed *Ref*, references are shown to sources. Each reference is followed by a letter. These refer to the geographical level for which data were reported: s = State, r = Region, and c = City or metro. The abbreviation *ex* is used to mean *except* or *excluding*; *exp* stands for expenditures. For other abbreviations and further explanations, please see the Introduction.

Cleveland, OH - continued

Item	Per	Value	Date	Ref.
Communications				
Phone line, single, business, field visit	inst	55.42	12/93	9s
Phone line, single, business, no field visit	inst	55.42	12/93	9s
Phone line, single, residence, field visit	inst	30.38	12/93	9s
Phone line, single, residence, no field visit	inst	30.38	12/93	9s
Telephone bill, family of four	month	21.29	12/94	2c
Telephone service, expenditures	year	525	91	81c
Telephone service, expenditures	year	547	91	81r
Telephone, business, addl. line, touch tone	month	3.25	10/91	25c
Telephone, business, connection charges, touch tone	inst	72.15	10/91	25c
Telephone, business, key system line, touch tone	month	44.71	10/91	25c
Telephone, business, PBX line, touch tone	month	44.84	10/91	25c
Telephone, business, single ln., touch tone	month	41.01	10/91	25c
Telephone, business, touch tone, inside wiring maintenance plan	month	1.50	10/91	25c
Telephone, residential, flat rate	mo.	15.25	12/93	8c
Education				
Board, 4-year private college/university	year	2241	8/94	80s
Board, 4-year public college/university	year	1625	8/94	80s
Education, total expenditures	year	375	91	81c
Education, total expenditures	year	394	91	81r
Room, 4-year private college/university	year	2118	8/94	80s
Room, 4-year public college/university	year	2103	8/94	80s
Total cost, 4-year private college/university	year	15444	8/94	80s
Total cost, 4-year public college/university	year	6987	8/94	80s
Tuition, 2-year public college/university, in-state	year	2076	8/94	80s
Tuition, 4-year private college/university, in-state	year	11085	8/94	80s
Tuition, 4-year public college/university, in-state	year	3259	8/94	80s
Energy and Fuels				
Electricity	500 KWh	54.93	12/94	82c
Energy, combined forms, 1800 sq. ft.	mo.	150.78	12/94	2c
Energy, exc. electricity, 1800 sq. ft.	mo.	64.62	12/94	2c
Fuel oil and other fuels, expenditures	year	42	91	81c
Fuel oil and other fuels, expenditures	year	83	91	81r
Gas, cooking, winter, 10 therms	month	9.54	2/94	65c
Gas, cooking, winter, 30 therms	month	20.07	2/94	65c
Gas, cooking, winter, 50 therms	month	30.60	2/94	65c
Gas, heating, winter, 100 therms	month	56.91	2/94	65c
Gas, heating, winter, average use	month	127.96	2/94	65c
Gas, natural, expenditures	year	430	91	81c
Gas, natural, expenditures	year	373	91	81r
Gas, piped	40 therms	24.84	12/94	82c
Gas, piped	100 therms	53.42	12/94	82c
Gas, piped	therm	0.54	12/94	82c
Gas, reg unlead, taxes inc., cash, self-service	gal	1.12	12/94	2c
Gasoline and motor oil purchased	year	893	91	81c
Gasoline and motor oil purchased	year	1000	91	81r
Gasoline, unleaded midgrade	gallon	1.12	4/93	82c
Gasoline, unleaded midgrade	gallon	1.15	4/93	82r
Gasoline, unleaded premium	gallon	1.22	4/93	82c
Gasoline, unleaded premium	gallon	1.23	4/93	82r
Gasoline, unleaded regular	gallon	1.03	4/93	82c
Gasoline, unleaded regular	gallon	1.07	4/93	82r
Entertainment				
Baseball game, four-person family	game	103.75	4/94	47c
Bowling, evening rate	game	2.04	12/94	2c
Entertainment supplies, equipment, and services, misc. expenditures	year	196	91	81c
Entertainment, total expenditures	year	1271	91	81c
Entertainment, total expenditures	year	1356	91	81r
Fees and admissions, expenditures	year	341	91	81c
Fees and admissions, expenditures	year	347	91	81r
Monopoly game, Parker Brothers', No. 9	game	10.85	12/94	2c

Cleveland, OH - continued

Item	Per	Value	Date	Ref.
Entertainment - continued				
Movie	adm	6.50	12/94	2c
Pets, toys, playground equipment, expenditures	year	272	91	81c
Pets, toys, playground equipment, expenditures	year	270	91	81r
Reading, expenditures	year	143	91	81c
Reading, expenditures	year	160	91	81r
Televisions, radios, and sound equipment, expenditures	year	462	91	81c
Televisions, radios, and sound equipment, expenditures	year	433	91	81r
Tennis balls, yellow, Wilson or Penn, 3	can	2.85	12/94	2c
Funerals				
Burial, immediate, container provided by funeral home		1268.31	1/95	54r
Cards, acknowledgment		26.12	1/95	54r
Casket, minimum alternative		198.03	1/95	54r
Cosmetology, hair care, etc.		122.19	1/95	54r
Cremation, direct, container provided by funeral home		977.81	1/95	54r
Embalming		334.00	1/95	54r
Funeral, funeral home		321.16	1/95	54r
Funeral, other facility		317.73	1/95	54r
Graveside service		292.48	1/95	54r
Hearse, local		153.20	1/95	54r
Limousine, local		123.52	1/95	54r
Memorial service		356.30	1/95	54r
Service charge, professional, nondeclinable		968.24	1/95	54r
Visitation and viewing		332.66	1/95	54r
Groceries				
Groceries, ACCRA Index		97.20	12/94	2c
Apples, Red Delicious	lb.	0.68	12/94	82r
Baby food, strained vegetables, lowest price	4-4.5 oz.	0.36	12/94	2c
Bacon, sliced	lb.	1.88	12/94	82r
Bananas	lb.	0.50	12/94	2c
Bananas	lb.	0.41	12/94	82r
Beef or hamburger, ground	lb.	0.96	12/94	2c
Beef purchases	year	186	91	81c
Beef purchases	year	197	91	81r
Beef, stew, boneless	lb.	2.52	12/94	82r
Beverage purchases, alcoholic	year	330	91	81c
Beverage purchases, alcoholic	year	293	91	81r
Beverage purchases, nonalcoholic	year	205	91	81c
Beverage purchases, nonalcoholic	year	203	91	81r
Bologna, all beef or mixed	lb.	2.12	12/94	82r
Bread, white	24-oz.	0.61	12/94	2c
Bread, white, pan	lb.	0.76	12/94	82r
Cabbage	lb.	0.44	12/94	82r
Carrots, short trimmed and topped	lb.	0.44	12/94	82r
Cereals and bakery products purchases	year	372	91	81c
Cereals and bakery products purchases	year	347	91	81r
Cereals and cereal products purchases	year	130	91	81c
Cereals and cereals products purchases	year	119	91	81r
Cheddar cheese, natural	lb.	3.28	12/94	82r
Cheese, Kraft grated Parmesan	8-oz.	2.93	12/94	2c
Chicken breast, bone-in	lb.	1.61	12/94	82r
Chicken, fresh, whole	lb.	0.89	12/94	82r
Chicken, whole fryer	lb.	0.98	12/94	2c
Chuck roast, USDA choice, boneless	lb.	2.33	12/94	82r
Cigarettes, Winston, Kings	carton	16.05	12/94	2c
Coffee, 100%, ground roast, all sizes	lb.	4.28	12/94	82r
Coffee, vacuum-packed	13 oz.	3.86	12/94	2c
Cookies, chocolate chip	lb.	2.72	12/94	82r
Corn Flakes, Kellogg's or Post Toasties	18 oz.	2.15	12/94	2c
Corn, frozen, whole kernel, lowest price	10 oz.	0.68	12/94	2c
Dairy products (other) purchases	year	161	91	81c
Dairy products (other) purchases	year	148	91	81r
Eggs, Grade A large	dozen	0.58	12/94	2c
Eggs, Grade A large	dozen	0.76	12/94	82r
Fish and seafood purchases	year	71	91	81c

Values are in dollars or fractions of dollars. In the column headed *Ref*, references are shown to sources. Each reference is followed by a letter. These refer to the geographical level for which data were reported: s=State, r=Region, and c=City or metro. The abbreviation *ex* is used to mean *except* or *excluding*; *exp* stands for expenditures. For other abbreviations and further explanations, please see the Introduction.

Cleveland, OH - continued

Item	Per	Value	Date	Ref.
Groceries				
Fish and seafood purchases	year	61	91	81r
Flour, white, all purpose	lb.	0.22	12/94	82r
Food purchases, food eaten at home	year	2434	91	81c
Food purchases, food eaten at home	year	2313	91	81r
Foods purchased away from home, not prepared by consumer	year	1799	91	81c
Foods purchased away from home, not prepared by consumer	year	1709	91	81r
Fruits and vegetables purchases	year	382	91	81c
Fruits and vegetables purchases	year	372	91	81r
Grapefruit	lb.	0.47	12/94	82r
Grapes, Thompson seedless	lb.	2.15	12/94	82r
Ground beef, 100% beef	lb.	1.37	12/94	82r
Ground chuck, 100% beef	lb.	1.81	12/94	82r
Ham, boneless, exc. canned	lb.	2.16	12/94	82r
Ice cream, prepackaged, bulk, regular	1/2 gal.	2.48	12/94	82r
Lemons	lb.	1.08	12/94	82r
Lettuce, iceberg	lb.	0.81	12/94	82r
Lettuce, iceberg	head	0.73	12/94	2c
Margarine, Blue Bonnet or Parkay cubes	lb.	0.61	12/94	2c
Margarine, stick	lb.	0.81	12/94	82r
Meats, poultry, fish, and eggs purchases	year	651	91	81c
Meats, poultry, fish, and eggs purchases	year	591	91	81r
Milk and cream (fresh) purchases	year	118	91	81c
Milk and cream (fresh) purchases	year	132	91	81r
Milk, whole	1/2 gal.	1.03	12/94	2c
Orange juice, frozen concentrate 12-oz. can	16 oz.	1.41	12/94	82r
Orange juice, Minute Maid frozen	12-oz.	1.37	12/94	2c
Oranges, Navel	lb.	0.56	12/94	82r
Peaches, halves or slices, Hunt's, Del Monte, or Libby's	29-oz.	1.36	12/94	2c
Peanut butter, creamy, all sizes	lb.	1.81	12/94	82r
Peas, sweet, Del Monte or Green Giant	15-17 oz.	0.62	12/94	2c
Pork chops, center cut, bone-in	lb.	2.76	12/94	82r
Pork purchases	year	153	91	81c
Pork purchases	year	130	91	81r
Potato chips	16-oz.	2.81	12/94	82r
Potatoes, frozen, French fried	lb.	0.83	12/94	82r
Potatoes, white	lb.	0.28	12/94	82r
Potatoes, white or red	10-lb. sack	1.90	12/94	2c
Round roast, USDA choice, boneless	lb.	2.90	12/94	82r
Sausage, Jimmy Dean, 100% pork	lb.	2.45	12/94	2c
Shortening, vegetable oil blends	lb.	0.88	12/94	82r
Shortening, vegetable, Crisco	3-lb.	2.45	12/94	2c
Soft drink, Coca Cola, ex deposit	2 lit	0.94	12/94	2c
Spaghetti and macaroni	lb.	0.78	12/94	82r
Steak, rib eye, USDA choice, boneless	lb.	6.15	12/94	82r
Steak, round, graded & ungraded, exc. USDA prime & choice	lb.	2.72	12/94	82r
Steak, round, USDA choice, boneless	lb.	3.02	12/94	82r
Steak, sirloin, USDA choice, boneless	lb.	3.85	12/94	82r
Steak, t-bone	lb.	6.43	12/94	2c
Steak, T-bone, USDA choice, bone-in	lb.	5.38	12/94	82r
Sugar and other sweets, eaten at home, expenditures	year	91	91	81r
Sugar and other sweets, eaten at home, purchases	year	101	91	81c
Sugar, cane or beet	4 lbs.	1.48	12/94	2c
Sugar, white, all sizes	lb.	0.36	12/94	82r
Tobacco products and smoking supplies, total expenditures	year	347	91	81c
Tobacco products and smoking supplies, total expenditures	year	298	91	81r
Tomatoes, field grown	lb.	1.36	12/94	82r
Tomatoes, Hunt's or Del Monte	14.5 oz.	0.60	12/94	2c
Tuna, chunk, light	lb.	1.94	12/94	82r

Cleveland, OH - continued

Item	Per	Value	Date	Ref.
Groceries - continued				
Tuna, chunk, light, oil-packed	6.125-6.5 oz.	0.65	12/94	2c
Turkey, frozen, whole	lb.	0.96	12/94	82r
Yogurt, natural, fruit flavored	8 oz.	0.62	12/94	82r
Goods and Services				
Miscellaneous goods and services, ACCRA Index		99.40	12/94	2c
Health Care				
Health care, ACCRA Index		105.60	12/94	2c
Antibiotic ointment, Polysporin	1.5 oz.	3.79	12/94	2c
Childbirth, Cesarean delivery, hospital charge	birth	5101.00	12/91	69r
Childbirth, Cesarean delivery, physician charge	birth	2234.00	12/91	69r
Childbirth, normal delivery, hospital charge	birth	2891.00	12/91	69r
Childbirth, normal delivery, physician charge	birth	1623.00	12/91	69r
Dentist's fee, adult teeth cleaning and periodic oral exam	visit	50.17	12/94	2c
Doctor's fee, routine exam, established patient	visit	38.83	12/94	2c
Drugs, expenditures	year	233	91	81c
Drugs, expenditures	year	248	91	81r
Health care, total expenditures	year	1430	91	81c
Health care, total expenditures	year	1336	91	81r
Health insurance expenditures	year	609	91	81c
Health insurance expenditures	year	550	91	81r
Hospital care, semiprivate room	day	566.00	12/94	2c
Insurance premium, family medical care	month	350.73	1/95	41s
Medical services expenditures	year	491	91	81c
Medical services expenditures	year	457	91	81r
Medical supplies expenditures	year	97	91	81c
Medical supplies expenditures	year	82	91	81r
Household Goods				
Appl. repair, service call, wash mach	min. lab. chg.	29.98	12/94	2c
Floor coverings, expenditures	year	38	91	81c
Floor coverings, expenditures	year	105	91	81r
Furniture, expenditures	year	239	91	81c
Furniture, expenditures	year	291	91	81r
Household equipment, misc. expenditures	year	341	91	81r
Household equipment, misc., expenditures	year	481	91	81c
Household expenditures, miscellaneous	year	150	91	81c
Household expenditures, miscellaneous	year	162	91	81r
Household furnishings and equipment, expenditures	year	1069	91	81c
Household furnishings and equipment, expenditures	year	1042	91	81r
Household operations expenditures	year	335	91	81c
Household operations expenditures	year	365	91	81r
Household textiles, expenditures	year	134	91	81c
Household textiles, expenditures	year	101	91	81r
Housekeeping supplies, expenditures	year	527	91	81c
Housekeeping supplies, expenditures	year	390	91	81r
Laundry and cleaning supplies, expenditures	year	131	91	81c
Laundry and cleaning supplies, expenditures	year	110	91	81r
Laundry detergent, Tide Ultra, Bold, or Cheer	42 oz.	3.59	12/94	2c
Postage and stationery, expenditures	year	150	91	81c
Postage and stationery, expenditures	year	115	91	81r
Tissues, facial, Kleenex brand	175	0.96	12/94	2c
Housing				
Housing, ACCRA Index		106.10	12/94	2c
Add garage/carport		8,479	3/95	74r
Add room(s)		21,347	3/95	74r
Apartment condominium or co-op, median	unit	87100	12/94	62r
Bathroom addition, average cost	add	9734.00	3/95	13r
Bathroom remodeling, average cost	remod	6414.00	3/95	13r

Values are in dollars or fractions of dollars. In the column headed *Ref*, references are shown to sources. Each reference is followed by a letter. These refer to the geographical level for which data were reported: s = State, r = Region, and c = City or metro. The abbreviation *ex* is used to mean *except* or *excluding*; *exp* stands for *expenditures*. For other abbreviations and further explanations, please see the Introduction.

Cleveland, OH - continued

Item	Per	Value	Date	Ref.
Housing				
Bedroom, master suite addition, average cost	add	27122.00	3/95	13r
Car rental	day	54.00	5/95	95c
Deck addition, average cost	add	6665.00	3/95	13r
Dwellings (owned), expenditures	year	2168	91	81c
Dwellings (owned), expenditures	year	2566	91	81r
Enclose porch/patio/breezeway		4,556	3/95	74r
Exterior remodeling, average cost	remod	15395.00	3/95	13r
Family room addition, average cost	add	27658.00	3/95	13r
Finish room in basement/attic		5,074	3/95	74r
Home, existing, single-family, median	unit	106500	12/94	62r
Home, existing, single-family, median	unit	98.10	12/94	62c
Home, purchase price	unit	124.70	3/93	26c
Hotel room	day	120.00	5/95	95c
House payment, principal and interest, 25% down payment	mo.	814	12/94	2c
House, 1800 sq ft, 8000 sq ft lot, new, urban, utilities	total	135716	12/94	2c
Kitchen remodeling, major, average cost	remod	17084.00	3/95	13r
Kitchen remodeling, minor, average cost	remod	5804.00	3/95	13r
Maintenance, repairs, insurance, and other housing expenditures	year	570	91	81c
Maintenance, repairs, insurance, and other housing expenditures	year	484	91	81r
Mortgage interest and charges expenditures	year	1135	91	81c
Mortgage interest and charges expenditures	year	1443	91	81r
Mortgage payment	month	659.00	1/94	78c
Mtge. rate, incl. points and orig. fee, 30-year conv. fixed or ARM	mo.	8.94	12/94	2c
Office, home addition, average cost	add	8121.00	3/95	13r
Princ. & int., mortgage, median-price exist. sing.-family home	mo.	515	12/94	62r
Property taxes expenditures	year	463	91	81c
Property taxes expenditures	year	639	91	81r
Redesign, restructure more than half of home's interior		9,114	3/95	74r
Rent, apartment, 2 br., 1 1/2-2 baths, unfurnished, 950 sq ft, water	mo.	556	12/94	2c
Rental units expenditures	year	1590	900/00/91	81c
Rental units expenditures	year	1200	91	81r
Sun-space addition, average cost	add	23768.00	3/95	13r
Wing addition, two-story, average cost	add	50410.00	3/95	13r
Insurance and Pensions				
Auto insurance, private passenger	year	550.52	12/94	71s
Health insurance, HMO plan, cost to employer	year	3727	93	59c
Insurance and pensions, personal, expenditures	year	2384	91	81c
Insurance and pensions, personal, expenditures	year	2408	91	81r
Insurance, life and other personal, expenditures	year	290	91	81c
Insurance, life and other personal, expenditures	year	355	91	81r
Pensions and Social Security, expenditures	year	2094	91	81c
Pensions and Social Security, expenditures	year	2053	91	81r
Legal Assistance				
Legal work, law firm associate	hour	90		10r
Legal work, law firm partner	hour	139		10r
Personal Goods				
Personal care products and services, total expenditures	year	394	91	81c
Shampoo, Alberto VO5	15-oz.	1.12	12/94	2c
Toothpaste, Crest or Colgate	6-7 oz.	2.19	12/94	2c
Personal Services				
Dry cleaning, man's 2-pc. suit		7.06	12/94	2c
Haircut, man's barbershop, no styling		9.71	12/94	2c
Haircut, woman's shampoo, trim, blow-dry		19.33	12/94	2c
Personal services expenditures	year	185	91	81c

Cleveland, OH - continued

Item	Per	Value	Date	Ref.
Personal Services - continued				
Personal services expenditures	year	203	91	81r
Restaurant Food				
Chicken, fried, thigh and drumstick		2.20	12/94	2c
Dining expenditures, family	week	30.03	94	73r
Hamburger with cheese	1/4 lb.	1.87	12/94	2c
Pizza, Pizza Hut or Pizza Inn	12-13 in.	7.69	12/94	2c
Taxes				
Taxes, Federal income, expenditures	year	1254	91	81c
Taxes, Federal income, expenditures	year	1756	91	81r
Taxes, personal, expenditures	year	1785	91	81c
Taxes, personal, expenditures	year	2426	91	81r
Taxes, State and local income, expenditures	year	526	91	81c
Taxes, State and local income, expenditures	year	568	91	81r
Transportation				
Transportation, ACCRA Index		104.50	12/94	2c
Bus fare, one-way	trip	1.00	12/95	1c
Bus fare, up to 10 miles	one-way	1.50	12/94	2c
Cars and trucks purchased, new	year	1037	91	81c
Cars and trucks purchased, new	year	891	91	81r
Cars and trucks purchased, used	year	711	91	81c
Cars and trucks purchased, used	year	1155	91	81r
Driver's learning permit fee	perm	3.00	1/94	84s
Driver's license fee	orig	5.00	1/94	84s
Driver's license fee, duplicate	lic	1.50	1/94	84s
Driver's license reinstatement fee, min.	susp	12.50-100.00	1/94	85s
Driver's license renewal fee	renew	5.00	1/94	84s
Identification card, nondriver	card	2.50	1/94	83s
Motorcycle learning permit fee	perm	3.00	1/94	84s
Motorcycle license fee	orig	5.00	1/94	84s
Motorcycle license fee, duplicate	lic	1.50	1/94	84s
Motorcycle license renewal fee	renew	5.00	1/94	84s
Public transportation expenditures	year	165	91	81c
Public transportation expenditures	year	209	91	81r
Railway fare, heavy rail, one-way	trip	1.50	12/95	1c
Railway fare, light rail, one-way	trip	1.50	12/95	1c
Tire balance, computer or spin bal., front	wheel	6.47	12/94	2c
Transportation expenditures, total	year	4555	91	81c
Transportation expenditures, total	year	4792	91	81r
Vehicle expenses, miscellaneous	year	1748	91	81c
Vehicle finance charges	year	305	91	81c
Vehicle finance charges	year	300	91	81r
Vehicle insurance expenditures	year	546	91	81c
Vehicle insurance expenditures	year	485	91	81r
Vehicle maintenance and repairs expenditures	year	648	91	81c
Vehicle maintenance and repairs expenditures	year	534	91	81r
Vehicle purchases	year	1748	91	81c
Vehicle purchases	year	2068	91	81r
Vehicle rental, leases, licenses, etc. expenditures	year	249	91	81c
Vehicle rental, leases, licenses, etc. expenditures	year	197	91	81r
Vehicles purchased, other than cars and trucks	year	22	91	81r
Utilities				
Utilities, ACCRA Index		131.00	12/94	2c
Electricity	KWh	0.11	12/94	82c
Electricity expenditures	year	675	91	81c
Electricity expenditures	year	668	91	81r
Electricity, (part.), other, 1800 sq. ft., new home	mo.	86.16	12/94	2c
Electricity, summer, 250 KWh	month	33.73	8/93	64c
Electricity, summer, 500 KWh	month	67.46	8/93	64c
Electricity, summer, 750 KWh	month	96.56	8/93	64c
Electricity, summer, 1000 KWh	month	128.75	8/93	64c

Values are in dollars or fractions of dollars. In the column headed *Ref*, references are shown to sources. Each reference is followed by a letter. These refer to the geographical level for which data were reported: s=State, r=Region, and c=City or metro. The abbreviation *ex* is used to mean *except* or *excluding*; *exp* stands for expenditures. For other abbreviations and further explanations, please see the Introduction.

Cleveland, OH - continued

Item	Per	Value	Date	Ref.
Utilities				
Utilities, fuels, and public services, total expenditures	year	1842	91	81c
Utilities, fuels, and public services, total expenditures	year	1838	91	81r
Water and other public services, expenditures	year	170	91	81c
Water and other public services, expenditures	year	167	91	81r
Weddings				
Bridal attendants' gowns	event	750	10/93	76r
Bridal gown	event	852	10/93	76r
Bridal headpiece and veil	event	167	10/93	76r
Bride's wedding band	event	708	10/93	76r
Clergy	event	224	10/93	76r
Engagement ring	event	2756	10/93	76r
Flowers	event	863	10/93	76r
Formal wear for groom	event	106	10/93	76r
Groom's attendants' formal wear	event	530	10/93	76r
Groom's wedding band	event	402	10/93	76r
Music	event	600	10/93	76r
Photography	event	1088	10/93	76r
Shoes for bride	event	50	10/93	76r
Videography	event	483	10/93	76r
Wedding invitations and announcements	event	342	10/93	76r
Wedding reception	event	7000	10/93	76r

Cleveland, TN

Item	Per	Value	Date	Ref.
Composite, ACCRA index		92.50	12/94	2c
Alcoholic Beverages				
Beer, Miller Lite, Bud, 12-oz., ex deposit	6	4.27	12/94	2c
J & B Scotch	750-ml.	18.18	12/94	2c
Wine, Gallo Chablis blanc	1.5-lit	5.86	12/94	2c
Clothing				
Jeans, man's denim		34.29	12/94	2c
Shirt, man's dress shirt		30.67	12/94	2c
Undervest, boy's size 10-14, cotton	3	3.12	12/94	2c
Communications				
Newspaper subscription, dly. and Sun. delivery	month	11.09	12/94	2c
Telephone bill, family of four	month	18.67	12/94	2c
Telephone, residential, flat rate	mo.	11.85	12/93	8c
Energy and Fuels				
Energy, combined forms, 1800 sq. ft.	mo.	109.62	12/94	2c
Energy, exc. electricity, 1800 sq. ft.	mo.	43.32	12/94	2c
Gas, reg unlead, taxes inc., cash, self-service	gal	1.10	12/94	2c
Entertainment				
Bowling, evening rate	game	2.00	12/94	2c
Monopoly game, Parker Brothers', No. 9	game	6.72	12/94	2c
Movie	adm	5.33	12/94	2c
Tennis balls, yellow, Wilson or Penn, 3	can	2.18	12/94	2c
Groceries				
Groceries, ACCRA Index		95.70	12/94	2c
Baby food, strained vegetables, lowest price	4-4.5 oz.	0.34	12/94	2c
Bananas	lb.	0.41	12/94	2c
Beef or hamburger, ground	lb.	1.46	12/94	2c
Bread, white	24-oz.	0.69	12/94	2c
Cheese, Kraft grated Parmesan	8-oz.	3.46	12/94	2c
Chicken, whole fryer	lb.	0.82	12/94	2c
Cigarettes, Winston, Kings	carton	14.35	12/94	2c
Coffee, vacuum-packed	13 oz.	3.28	12/94	2c
Corn Flakes, Kellogg's or Post Toasties	18 oz.	2.42	12/94	2c
Corn, frozen, whole kernel, lowest price	10 oz.	0.68	12/94	2c
Eggs, Grade A large	dozen	0.76	12/94	2c
Lettuce, iceberg	head	0.84	12/94	2c

Cleveland, TN - continued

Item	Per	Value	Date	Ref.
Groceries - continued				
Margarine, Blue Bonnet or Parkay cubes	lb.	0.67	12/94	2c
Milk, whole	1/2 gal.	1.38	12/94	2c
Orange juice, Minute Maid frozen	12-oz.	1.19	12/94	2c
Peaches, halves or slices, Hunt's, Del Monte, or Libby's	29-oz.	1.14	12/94	2c
Peas, sweet, Del Monte or Green Giant	15-17 oz.	0.56	12/94	2c
Potatoes, white or red	10-lb. sack	2.12	12/94	2c
Sausage, Jimmy Dean, 100% pork	lb.	2.04	12/94	2c
Shortening, vegetable, Crisco	3-lb.	2.46	12/94	2c
Soft drink, Coca Cola, ex deposit	2 lit	1.02	12/94	2c
Steak, t-bone	lb.	5.92	12/94	2c
Sugar, cane or beet	4 lbs.	1.08	12/94	2c
Tomatoes, Hunt's or Del Monte	14.5 oz.	0.68	12/94	2c
Tuna, chunk, light, oil-packed	6.125-6.5 oz.	0.63	12/94	2c
Goods and Services				
Miscellaneous goods and services, ACCRA Index		98.60	12/94	2c
Health Care				
Health care, ACCRA Index		85.00	12/94	2c
Antibiotic ointment, Polysporin	1.5 oz.	3.64	12/94	2c
Dentist's fee, adult teeth cleaning and periodic oral exam	visit	49.00	12/94	2c
Doctor's fee, routine exam, established patient	visit	38.20	12/94	2c
Hospital care, semiprivate room	day	193.75	12/94	2c
Household Goods				
Appl. repair, service call, wash mach	min. lab. chg.	36.98	12/94	2c
Laundry detergent, Tide Ultra, Bold, or Cheer	42 oz.	3.57	12/94	2c
Tissues, facial, Kleenex brand	175	1.02	12/94	2c
Housing				
Housing, ACCRA Index		84.20	12/94	2c
House payment, principal and interest, 25% down payment	mo.	641	12/94	2c
House, 1800 sq ft, 8000 sq ft lot, new, urban, utilities	total	102100	12/94	2c
Mtge. rate, incl. points and orig. fee, 30-year conv. fixed or ARM	mo.	9.44	12/94	2c
Rent, apartment, 2 br., 1 1/2-2 baths, unfurnished, 950 sq ft, water	mo.	458	12/94	2c
Personal Goods				
Shampoo, Alberto VO5	15-oz.	1.09	12/94	2c
Toothpaste, Crest or Colgate	6-7 oz.	2.09	12/94	2c
Personal Services				
Dry cleaning, man's 2-pc. suit		5.22	12/94	2c
Haircut, man's barbershop, no styling		7.98	12/94	2c
Haircut, woman's shampoo, trim, blow-dry		16.80	12/94	2c
Restaurant Food				
Chicken, fried, thigh and drumstick		2.19	12/94	2c
Hamburger with cheese	1/4 lb.	1.89	12/94	2c
Pizza, Pizza Hut or Pizza Inn	12-13 in.	8.49	12/94	2c
Transportation				
Transportation, ACCRA Index		90.80	12/94	2c
Tire balance, computer or spin bal., front	wheel	5.50	12/94	2c
Utilities				
Utilities, ACCRA Index		97.40	12/94	2c
Electricity, (part.), other, 1800 sq. ft., new home	mo.	66.30	12/94	2c

Values are in dollars or fractions of dollars. In the column headed *Ref*, references are shown to sources. Each reference is followed by a letter. These refer to the geographical level for which data were reported: s = State, r = Region, and c = City or metro. The abbreviation *ex* is used to mean *except* or *excluding*; *exp* stands for *expenditures*. For other abbreviations and further explanations, please see the Introduction.

Clovis-Portales, NM

Item	Per	Value	Date	Ref.
Composite, ACCRA index		92.60	12/94	2c
Alcoholic Beverages				
Beer, Miller Lite, Bud, 12-oz., ex deposit	6	4.09	12/94	2c
J & B Scotch	750-ml.	18.26	12/94	2c
Wine, Gallo Chablis blanc	1.5-lit	5.66	12/94	2c
Clothing				
Jeans, man's denim		26.49	12/94	2c
Shirt, man's dress shirt		31.50	12/94	2c
Undervest, boy's size 10-14, cotton	3	4.24	12/94	2c
Communications				
Newspaper subscription, dly. and Sun. delivery	month	10.25	12/94	2c
Telephone bill, family of four	month	17.96	12/94	2c
Telephone, residential, flat rate	mo.	13.91	12/93	8c
Energy and Fuels				
Energy, combined forms, 1800 sq. ft.	mo.	103.96	12/94	2c
Gas, reg unlead, taxes inc., cash, self-service	gal	1.15	12/94	2c
Entertainment				
Bowling, evening rate	game	1.75	12/94	2c
Monopoly game, Parker Brothers', No. 9	game	12.91	12/94	2c
Movie	adm	4.67	12/94	2c
Tennis balls, yellow, Wilson or Penn, 3	can	2.63	12/94	2c
Groceries				
Groceries, ACCRA Index		97.70	12/94	2c
Baby food, strained vegetables, lowest price	4-4.5 oz.	0.30	12/94	2c
Bananas	lb.	0.35	12/94	2c
Beef or hamburger, ground	lb.	1.07	12/94	2c
Bread, white	24-oz.	0.69	12/94	2c
Cheese, Kraft grated Parmesan	8-oz.	3.94	12/94	2c
Chicken, whole fryer	lb.	0.65	12/94	2c
Cigarettes, Winston, Kings	carton	15.49	12/94	2c
Coffee, vacuum-packed	13 oz.	3.50	12/94	2c
Corn Flakes, Kellogg's or Post Toasties	18 oz.	2.60	12/94	2c
Corn, frozen, whole kernel, lowest price	10 oz.	0.80	12/94	2c
Eggs, Grade A large	dozen	0.87	12/94	2c
Lettuce, iceberg	head	0.68	12/94	2c
Margarine, Blue Bonnet or Parkay cubes	lb.	0.80	12/94	2c
Milk, whole	1/2 gal.	1.26	12/94	2c
Orange juice, Minute Maid frozen	12-oz.	1.30	12/94	2c
Peaches, halves or slices, Hunt's, Del Monte, or Libby's	29-oz.	1.39	12/94	2c
Peas, sweet, Del Monte or Green Giant	15-17 oz.	0.60	12/94	2c
Potatoes, white or red	10-lb. sack	1.63	12/94	2c
Sausage, Jimmy Dean, 100% pork	lb.	2.28	12/94	2c
Shortening, vegetable, Crisco	3-lb.	2.80	12/94	2c
Soft drink, Coca Cola, ex deposit	2 lit	1.69	12/94	2c
Steak, t-bone	lb.	4.39	12/94	2c
Sugar, cane or beet	4 lbs.	1.55	12/94	2c
Tomatoes, Hunt's or Del Monte	14.5 oz.	0.80	12/94	2c
Tuna, chunk, light, oil-packed	6.125-6.5 oz.	0.72	12/94	2c
Goods and Services				
Miscellaneous goods and services, ACCRA Index		101.90	12/94	2c
Health Care				
Health care, ACCRA Index		85.20	12/94	2c
Antibiotic ointment, Polysporin	1.5 oz.	3.98	12/94	2c
Dentist's fee, adult teeth cleaning and periodic oral exam	visit	45.50	12/94	2c
Doctor's fee, routine exam, established patient	visit	37.97	12/94	2c
Hospital care, semiprivate room	day	230.00	12/94	2c

Clovis-Portales, NM - continued

Item	Per	Value	Date	Ref.
Household Goods				
Appl. repair, service call, wash mach	min. lab. chg.	32.74	12/94	2c
Laundry detergent, Tide Ultra, Bold, or Cheer	42 oz.	3.27	12/94	2c
Tissues, facial, Kleenex brand	175	1.11	12/94	2c
Housing				
Housing, ACCRA Index		80.00	12/94	2c
House payment, principal and interest, 25% down payment	mo.	565	12/94	2c
House, 1800 sq ft, 8000 sq ft lot, new, urban, utilities	total	91150	12/94	2c
Mtge. rate, incl. points and orig. fee, 30-year conv. fixed or ARM	mo.	9.30	12/94	2c
Rent, apartment, 2 br., 1 1/2-2 baths, unfurnished, 950 sq ft, water	mo.	560	12/94	2c
Personal Goods				
Shampoo, Alberto VO5	15-oz.	1.15	12/94	2c
Toothpaste, Crest or Colgate	6-7 oz.	2.28	12/94	2c
Personal Services				
Dry cleaning, man's 2-pc. suit		5.61	12/94	2c
Haircut, man's barbershop, no styling		7.88	12/94	2c
Haircut, woman's shampoo, trim, blow-dry		18.42	12/94	2c
Restaurant Food				
Chicken, fried, thigh and drumstick		2.69	12/94	2c
Hamburger with cheese	1/4 lb.	1.89	12/94	2c
Pizza, Pizza Hut or Pizza Inn	12-13 in.	8.90	12/94	2c
Transportation				
Transportation, ACCRA Index		93.50	12/94	2c
Tire balance, computer or spin bal., front	wheel	5.50	12/94	2c
Utilities				
Utilities, ACCRA Index		92.60	12/94	2c
Electricity, 1800 sq. ft., new home	mo.	103.96	12/94	2c

Colorado Springs, CO

Item	Per	Value	Date	Ref.
Composite, ACCRA index		96.80	12/94	2c
Alcoholic Beverages				
Beer, Miller Lite, Bud, 12-oz., ex deposit	6	4.17	12/94	2c
J & B Scotch	750-ml.	17.87	12/94	2c
Wine, Gallo Chablis blanc	1.5-lit	4.24	12/94	2c
Appliances				
Appliances (major), expenditures	year	160	91	81r
Average annual exp.				
Food, health care, personal goods, services	year	32461	91	81r
Charity				
Cash contributions, expenditures	year	975	91	81r
Clothing				
Apparel, men and boys, total expenditures	year	467	91	81r
Apparel, women and girls, total expenditures	year	737	91	81r
Footwear, expenditures	year	270	91	81r
Jeans, man's denim		27.39	12/94	2c
Shirt, man's dress shirt		24.19	12/94	2c
Undervest, boy's size 10-14, cotton	3	4.07	12/94	2c
Communications				
Long-distance telephone rate, day, addl. min., 1-10 mi.	min.	0.13	12/93	9s
Long-distance telephone rate, day, initial min., 1-10 mi.	min.	0.17	12/93	9s
Newspaper subscription, dly. and Sun. delivery	month	9.50	12/94	2c
Phone line, single, business, field visit	inst	70.00	12/93	9s
Phone line, single, business, no field visit	inst	70.00	12/93	9s

Values are in dollars or fractions of dollars. In the column headed *Ref*, references are shown to sources. Each reference is followed by a letter. These refer to the geographical level for which data were reported: s = State, r = Region, and c = City or metro. The abbreviation *ex* is used to mean *except* or *excluding*; *exp* stands for expenditures. For other abbreviations and further explanations, please see the Introduction.

Colorado Springs, CO - continued

Item	Per	Value	Date	Ref.
Communications				
Phone line, single, residence, field visit	inst	35.00	12/93	9s
Phone line, single, residence, no field visit	inst	35.00	12/93	9s
Telephone bill, family of four	month	20.36	12/94	2c
Telephone service, expenditures	year	611	91	81r
Telephone, residential, flat rate	mo.	14.48	12/93	8c
Credit Cards				
Fee, conventional credit card, bal. carried	year	35.00	1/95	96c
Education				
Board, 4-year private college/university	year	2468	8/94	80s
Board, 4-year public college/university	year	2148	8/94	80s
Education, total expenditures	year	375	91	81r
Room, 4-year private college/university	year	2492	8/94	80s
Room, 4-year public college/university	year	1772	8/94	80s
Total cost, 4-year private college/university	year	16064	8/94	80s
Total cost, 4-year public college/university	year	6183	8/94	80s
Tuition, 2-year public college/university, in-state	year	1193	8/94	80s
Tuition, 4-year private college/university, in-state	year	11104	8/94	80s
Tuition, 4-year public college/university, in-state	year	2262	8/94	80s
Energy and Fuels				
Energy, combined forms, 1800 sq. ft.	mo.	79.99	12/94	2c
Energy, exc. electricity, 1800 sq. ft.	mo.	32.95	12/94	2c
Fuel oil and other fuels, expenditures	year	33	91	81r
Gas, natural, expenditures	year	212	91	81r
Gas, reg unlead, taxes inc., cash, self-service	gal	1.14	12/94	2c
Gasoline and motor oil purchased	year	1115	91	81r
Gasoline, unleaded midgrade	gallon	1.36	4/93	82r
Gasoline, unleaded premium	gallon	1.43	4/93	82r
Gasoline, unleaded regular	gallon	1.23	4/93	82r
Entertainment				
Bowling, evening rate	game	1.60	12/94	2c
Concert ticket, Pearl Jam group	perf	20.00	94	50r
Entertainment, total expenditures	year	1853	91	81r
Fees and admissions, expenditures	year	482	91	81r
Monopoly game, Parker Brothers', No. 9	game	11.30	12/94	2c
Movie	adm	5.79	12/94	2c
Pets, toys, playground equipment, expenditures	year	299	91	81r
Reading, expenditures	year	164	91	81r
Televisions, radios, and sound equipment, expenditures	year	528	91	81r
Tennis balls, yellow, Wilson or Penn, 3	can	2.19	12/94	2c
Funerals				
Burial, immediate, container provided by funeral home		1360.49	1/95	54r
Cards, acknowledgment		11.24	1/95	54r
Casket, minimum alternative		232.73	1/95	54r
Cosmetology, hair care, etc.		114.13	1/95	54r
Cremation, direct, container provided by funeral home		1027.08	1/95	54r
Embalming		286.24	1/95	54r
Funeral, funeral home		315.60	1/95	54r
Funeral, other facility		303.08	1/95	54r
Graveside service		423.83	1/95	54r
Hearse, local		133.12	1/95	54r
Limousine, local		99.10	1/95	54r
Memorial service		442.57	1/95	54r
Service charge, professional, nondeclinable		840.16	1/95	54r
Visitation and viewing		168.50	1/95	54r
Groceries				
Groceries, ACCRA Index		98.20	12/94	2c
Apples, Red Delicious	lb.	0.72	12/94	82r
Baby food, strained vegetables, lowest price	4-4.5 oz.	0.32	12/94	2c
Bacon, sliced	lb.	1.73	12/94	82r
Bananas	lb.	0.44	12/94	2c

Colorado Springs, CO - continued

Item	Per	Value	Date	Ref.
Groceries - continued				
Bananas	lb.	0.52	12/94	82r
Beef or hamburger, ground	lb.	1.22	12/94	2c
Beef purchases	year	241	91	81r
Beverage purchases, alcoholic	year	328	91	81r
Beverage purchases, nonalcoholic	year	234	91	81r
Bologna, all beef or mixed	lb.	2.33	12/94	82r
Bread, white	24-oz.	0.66	12/94	2c
Bread, white, pan	lb.	0.81	12/94	82r
Carrots, short trimmed and topped	lb.	0.43	12/94	82r
Cereals and bakery products purchases	year	392	91	81r
Cereals and cereals products purchases	year	139	91	81r
Cheese, Kraft grated Parmesan	8-oz.	3.03	12/94	2c
Chicken breast, bone-in	lb.	2.04	12/94	82r
Chicken, fresh, whole	lb.	0.95	12/94	82r
Chicken, whole fryer	lb.	0.78	12/94	2c
Cigarettes, Winston, Kings	carton	13.54	12/94	2c
Coffee, 100% ground roast, all sizes	lb.	4.48	12/94	82r
Coffee, vacuum-packed	13 oz.	3.83	12/94	2c
Corn Flakes, Kellogg's or Post Toasties	18 oz.	2.08	12/94	2c
Corn, frozen, whole kernel, lowest price	10 oz.	0.79	12/94	2c
Dairy products (other) purchases	year	182	91	81r
Eggs, Grade A large	dozen	0.81	12/94	2c
Fish and seafood purchases	year	94	91	81r
Flour, white, all purpose	lb.	0.21	12/94	82r
Food purchases, food eaten at home	year	2749	91	81r
Foods purchased away from home, not prepared by consumer	year	1909	91	81r
Fruits and vegetables purchases	year	459	91	81r
Grapefruit	lb.	0.56	12/94	82r
Ground beef, 100% beef	lb.	1.31	12/94	82r
Ham, boneless, exc. canned	lb.	2.46	12/94	82r
Ice cream, prepackaged, bulk, regular	1/2 gal.	2.57	12/94	82r
Lemons	lb.	1.00	12/94	82r
Lettuce, iceberg	lb.	0.93	12/94	82r
Lettuce, iceberg	head	0.85	12/94	2c
Margarine, Blue Bonnet or Parkay cubes	lb.	0.63	12/94	2c
Meats, poultry, fish, and eggs purchases	year	700	91	81r
Milk and cream (fresh) purchases	year	155	91	81r
Milk, whole	1/2 gal.	1.67	12/94	2c
Orange juice, frozen concentrate 12-oz. can	16 oz.	1.52	12/94	82r
Orange juice, Minute Maid frozen	12-oz.	1.21	12/94	2c
Oranges, Navel	lb.	0.56	12/94	82r
Peaches, halves or slices, Hunt's, Del Monte, or Libby's	29-oz.	1.39	12/94	2c
Peas, sweet, Del Monte or Green Giant	15-17 oz.	0.67	12/94	2c
Pork chops, center cut, bone-in	lb.	3.30	12/94	82r
Pork purchases	year	122	91	81r
Potato chips	16-oz.	3.03	12/94	82r
Potatoes, frozen, French fried	lb.	0.77	12/94	82r
Potatoes, white	lb.	0.35	12/94	82r
Potatoes, white or red	10-lb. sack	1.71	12/94	2c
Rice, white, long grain, uncooked	lb.	0.54	12/94	82r
Round roast, USDA choice, boneless	lb.	2.92	12/94	82r
Sausage, Jimmy Dean, 100% pork	lb.	3.31	12/94	2c
Shortening, vegetable oil blends	lb.	0.80	12/94	82r
Shortening, vegetable, Crisco	3-lb.	2.81	12/94	2c
Soft drink, Coca Cola, ex deposit	2 lit	1.08	12/94	2c
Spaghetti and macaroni	lb.	1.02	12/94	82r
Steak, round, graded & ungraded, exc. USDA prime & choice	lb.	3.13	12/94	82r
Steak, sirloin, USDA choice, boneless	lb.	4.07	12/94	82r
Steak, t-bone	lb.	4.90	12/94	2c
Sugar and other sweets, eaten at home, expenditures	year	105	91	81r
Sugar, cane or beet	4 lbs.	1.31	12/94	2c
Sugar, white, all sizes	lb.	0.38	12/94	82r
Tobacco products and smoking supplies, total expenditures	year	221	91	81r

Values are in dollars or fractions of dollars. In the column headed *Ref*, references are shown to sources. Each reference is followed by a letter. These refer to the geographical level for which data were reported: s=State, r=Region, and c=City or metro. The abbreviation *ex* is used to mean *except* or *excluding*; *exp* stands for *expenditures*. For other abbreviations and further explanations, please see the Introduction.

Colorado Springs, CO - continued

Item	Per	Value	Date	Ref.
Groceries				
Tomatoes, field grown	lb.	1.45	12/94	82r
Tomatoes, Hunt's or Del Monte	14.5 oz.	0.84	12/94	2c
Tuna, chunk, light	lb.	2.18	12/94	82r
Tuna, chunk, light, oil-packed	6.125-6.5 oz.	0.87	12/94	2c
Goods and Services				
Miscellaneous goods and services, ACCRA Index		90.00	12/94	2c
Health Care				
Health care, ACCRA Index		123.60	12/94	2c
Antibiotic ointment, Polysporin	1.5 oz.	3.80	12/94	2c
Childbirth, Cesarean delivery, hospital charge	birth	6059.00	12/91	69r
Childbirth, Cesarean delivery, physician charge	birth	2248.00	12/91	69r
Childbirth, normal delivery, hospital charge	birth	3006.00	12/91	69r
Childbirth, normal delivery, physician charge	birth	1634.00	12/91	69r
Dentist's fee, adult teeth cleaning and periodic oral exam	visit	59.80	12/94	2c
Doctor's fee, routine exam, established patient	visit	57.96	12/94	2c
Drugs, expenditures	year	230	91	81r
Health care, total expenditures	year	1544	91	81r
Health insurance expenditures	year	558	91	81r
Hospital care, semiprivate room	day	523.75	12/94	2c
Insurance premium, family medical care	month	362.55	1/95	41s
Medical services expenditures	year	676	91	81r
Medical supplies expenditures	year	80	91	81r
Surgery, open-heart	proc	37818.00	1/93	14r
Household Goods				
Appl. repair, service call, wash mach	min. lab. chg.	23.80	12/94	2c
Floor coverings, expenditures	year	79	91	81r
Furniture, expenditures	year	352	91	81r
Household equipment, misc. expenditures	year	614	91	81r
Household expenditures, miscellaneous	year	294	91	81r
Household furnishings and equipment, expenditures	year	1416	91	81r
Household operations expenditures	year	580	91	81r
Household textiles, expenditures	year	113	91	81r
Housekeeping supplies, expenditures	year	447	91	81r
Laundry and cleaning supplies, expenditures	year	114	91	81r
Laundry detergent, Tide Ultra, Bold, or Cheer	42 oz.	3.08	12/94	2c
Postage and stationery, expenditures	year	145	91	81r
Tissues, facial, Kleenex brand	175	1.01	12/94	2c
Housing				
Housing, ACCRA Index		103.00	12/94	2c
Add garage/carport		6,422	3/95	74r
Add room(s)		26,583	3/95	74r
Apartment condominium or co-op, median	unit	105300	12/94	62r
Dwellings (owned), expenditures	year	3932	91	81r
Enclose porch/patio/breezeway		5,382	3/95	74r
Finish room in basement/attic		3,911	3/95	74r
Home, existing, single-family, median	unit	178600	12/94	62r
Home, existing, single-family, median	unit	105.50	12/94	62c
House payment, principal and interest, 25% down payment	mo.	794	12/94	2c
House, 1800 sq ft, 8000 sq ft lot, new, urban, utilities	total	127580	12/94	2c
Maintenance, repairs, insurance, and other housing expenditures	year	591	91	81r
Mortgage interest and charges expenditures	year	2747	91	81r
Mtge. rate, incl. points and orig. fee, 30-year conv. fixed or ARM	mo.	9.34	12/94	2c
Princ. & int., mortgage, median-price exist. sing.-family home	mo.	845	12/94	62r

Colorado Springs, CO - continued

Item	Per	Value	Date	Ref.
Housing - continued				
Property taxes expenditures	year	594	91	81r
Redesign, restructure more than half of home's interior		5,467	3/95	74r
Rent, apartment, 2 br., 1 1/2-2 baths, unfurnished, 950 sq ft, water	mo.	532	12/94	2c
Rental units expenditures	year	2077	91	81r
Insurance and Pensions				
Auto insurance, private passenger	year	804.17	12/94	71s
Insurance and pensions, personal, expenditures	year	3042	91	81r
Insurance, life and other personal, expenditures	year	298	91	81r
Pensions and Social Security, expenditures	year	2744	91	81r
Legal Assistance				
Legal work, law firm associate	hour	91		10r
Legal work, law firm partner	hour	151		10r
Personal Goods				
Shampoo, Alberto VO5	15-oz.	1.18	12/94	2c
Toothpaste, Crest or Colgate	6-7 oz.	1.75	12/94	2c
Personal Services				
Dry cleaning, man's 2-pc. suit		4.54	12/94	2c
Haircut, man's barbershop, no styling		8.00	12/94	2c
Haircut, woman's shampoo, trim, blow-dry		17.00	12/94	2c
Personal services expenditures	year	286	91	81r
Restaurant Food				
Chicken, fried, thigh and drumstick		1.99	12/94	2c
Dining expenditures, family	week	32.25	94	73r
Hamburger with cheese	1/4 lb.	1.99	12/94	2c
Pizza, Pizza Hut or Pizza Inn	12-13 in.	6.99	12/94	2c
Taxes				
Taxes, Federal income, expenditures	year	2946	91	81r
Taxes, personal, expenditures	year	3791	91	81r
Taxes, State and local income, expenditures	year	791	91	81r
Transportation				
Transportation, ACCRA Index		100.50	12/94	2c
Cars and trucks purchased, new	year	1231	91	81r
Cars and trucks purchased, used	year	915	91	81r
Driver's learning permit fee	perm	10.00	1/94	84s
Driver's license fee	orig	15.00	1/94	84s
Driver's license fee, duplicate	lic	5.00	1/94	84s
Driver's license reinstatement fee, min.	susp	40.00	1/94	85s
Driver's license renewal fee	renew	15.00	1/94	84s
Identification card, nondriver	card	3.50	1/94	83s
Motorcycle license fee	orig	16.00	1/94	84s
Public transportation expenditures	year	375	91	81r
Tire balance, computer or spin bal., front	wheel	6.69	12/94	2c
Transportation expenditures, total	year	5527	91	81r
Vehicle finance charges	year	287	91	81r
Vehicle insurance expenditures	year	624	91	81r
Vehicle maintenance and repairs expenditures	year	695	91	81r
Vehicle purchases	year	2174	91	81r
Vehicle rental, leases, licenses, etc. expenditures	year	257	91	81r
Vehicles purchased, other than cars and trucks	year	28	91	81r
Utilities				
Utilities, ACCRA Index		75.70	12/94	2c
Electricity expenditures	year	616	91	81r
Electricity, (part.), other, 1800 sq. ft., new home	mo.	47.04	12/94	2c
Utilities, fuels, and public services, total expenditures	year	1681	91	81r
Water and other public services, expenditures	year	209	91	81r

Values are in dollars or fractions of dollars. In the column headed *Ref*, references are shown to sources. Each reference is followed by a letter. These refer to the geographical level for which data were reported: s=State, r=Region, and c=City or metro. The abbreviation *ex* is used to mean *except* or *excluding*; *exp* stands for expenditures. For other abbreviations and further explanations, please see the Introduction.

Colorado Springs, CO - continued

Item	Per	Value	Date	Ref.
Weddings				
Bridal attendants' gowns	event	750	10/93	76r
Bridal gown	event	852	10/93	76r
Bridal headpiece and veil	event	167	10/93	76r
Bride's wedding band	event	708	10/93	76r
Clergy	event	224	10/93	76r
Engagement ring	event	2756	10/93	76r
Flowers	event	863	10/93	76r
Formal wear for groom	event	106	10/93	76r
Groom's attendants' formal wear	event	530	10/93	76r
Groom's wedding band	event	402	10/93	76r
Music	event	600	10/93	76r
Photography	event	1088	10/93	76r
Shoes for bride	event	50	10/93	76r
Videography	event	483	10/93	76r
Wedding invitations and announcements	event	342	10/93	76r
Wedding reception	event	7000	10/93	76r

Columbia, MO

Item	Per	Value	Date	Ref.
Composite, ACCRA index		94.30	12/94	2c
Alcoholic Beverages				
Beer, Miller Lite, Bud, 12-oz., ex deposit	6	3.91	12/94	2c
J & B Scotch	750-ml.	15.97	12/94	2c
Wine, Gallo Chablis blanc	1.5-lit	5.04	12/94	2c
Appliances				
Appliances (major), expenditures	year	131	91	81r
Average annual exp.				
Food, health care, personal goods, services	year	25935	91	81r
Charity				
Cash contributions, expenditures	year	745	91	81r
Clothing				
Apparel, men and boys, total expenditures	year	332	91	81r
Apparel, women and girls, total expenditures	year	578	91	81r
Footwear, expenditures	year	164	91	81r
Jeans, man's denim		31.05	12/94	2c
Shirt, man's dress shirt		30.50	12/94	2c
Undervest, boy's size 10-14, cotton	3	4.03	12/94	2c
Communications				
Long-distance telephone rate, day, addl. min., 1-10 mi.	min.	0.08	12/93	9s
Long-distance telephone rate, day, initial min., 1-10 mi.	min.	0.10	12/93	9s
Newspaper subscription, dly. and Sun. delivery	month	7.94	12/94	2c
Phone line, single, business, field visit	inst	52.25	12/93	9s
Phone line, single, business, no field visit	inst	52.25	12/93	9s
Phone line, single, residence, field visit	inst	36.50	12/93	9s
Phone line, single, residence, no field visit	inst	36.50	12/93	9s
Telephone bill, family of four	month	12.63	12/94	2c
Telephone service, expenditures	year	547	91	81r
Education				
Board, 4-year private college/university	year	2296	8/94	80s
Board, 4-year public college/university	year	1544	8/94	80s
Education, total expenditures	year	394	91	81r
Room, 4-year private college/university	year	2012	8/94	80s
Room, 4-year public college/university	year	1817	8/94	80s
Total cost, 4-year private college/university	year	13053	8/94	80s
Total cost, 4-year public college/university	year	5836	8/94	80s
Tuition, 2-year public college/university, in-state	year	1152	8/94	80s
Tuition, 4-year private college/university, in-state	year	8745	8/94	80s
Tuition, 4-year public college/university, in-state	year	2475	8/94	80s

Columbia, MO - continued

Item	Per	Value	Date	Ref.
Energy and Fuels				
Energy, combined forms, 1800 sq. ft.	mo.	86.57	12/94	2c
Energy, exc. electricity, 1800 sq. ft.	mo.	40.33	12/94	2c
Fuel oil and other fuels, expenditures	year	83	91	81r
Gas, natural, expenditures	year	373	91	81r
Gas, reg unlead, taxes inc., cash, self-service	gal	1.03	12/94	2c
Gasoline and motor oil purchased	year	1000	91	81r
Gasoline, unleaded midgrade	gallon	1.15	4/93	82r
Gasoline, unleaded premium	gallon	1.23	4/93	82r
Gasoline, unleaded regular	gallon	1.07	4/93	82r
Entertainment				
Bowling, evening rate	game	2.17	12/94	2c
Entertainment, total expenditures	year	1356	91	81r
Fees and admissions, expenditures	year	347	91	81r
Monopoly game, Parker Brothers', No. 9	game	11.25	12/94	2c
Movie	adm	5.00	12/94	2c
Pets, toys, playground equipment, expenditures	year	270	91	81r
Reading, expenditures	year	160	91	81r
Televisions, radios, and sound equipment, expenditures	year	433	91	81r
Tennis balls, yellow, Wilson or Penn, 3	can	2.27	12/94	2c
Funerals				
Burial, immediate, container provided by funeral home		1348.78	1/95	54r
Cards, acknowledgment		21.20	1/95	54r
Casket, minimum alternative		182.83	1/95	54r
Cosmetology, hair care, etc.		133.11	1/95	54r
Cremation, direct, container provided by funeral home		1101.95	1/95	54r
Embalming		314.45	1/95	54r
Funeral, funeral home		304.88	1/95	54r
Funeral, other facility		301.37	1/95	54r
Graveside service		290.59	1/95	54r
Hearse, local		137.37	1/95	54r
Limousine, local		82.84	1/95	54r
Memorial service		316.57	1/95	54r
Service charge, professional, nondeclinable		1099.00	1/95	54r
Visitation and viewing		209.25	1/95	54r
Groceries				
Groceries, ACCRA Index		97.10	12/94	2c
Apples, Red Delicious	lb.	0.68	12/94	82r
Baby food, strained vegetables, lowest price	4-4.5 oz.	0.32	12/94	2c
Bacon, sliced	lb.	1.88	12/94	82r
Bananas	lb.	0.39	12/94	2c
Bananas	lb.	0.41	12/94	82r
Beef or hamburger, ground	lb.	1.17	12/94	2c
Beef purchases	year	197	91	81r
Beef, stew, boneless	lb.	2.52	12/94	82r
Beverage purchases, alcoholic	year	293	91	81r
Beverage purchases, nonalcoholic	year	203	91	81r
Bologna, all beef or mixed	lb.	2.12	12/94	82r
Bread, white	24-oz.	0.67	12/94	2c
Bread, white, pan	lb.	0.76	12/94	82r
Cabbage	lb.	0.44	12/94	82r
Carrots, short trimmed and topped	lb.	0.44	12/94	82r
Cereals and bakery products purchases	year	347	91	81r
Cereals and cereals products purchases	year	119	91	81r
Cheddar cheese, natural	lb.	3.28	12/94	82r
Cheese, Kraft grated Parmesan	8-oz.	2.95	12/94	2c
Chicken breast, bone-in	lb.	1.61	12/94	82r
Chicken, fresh, whole	lb.	0.89	12/94	82r
Chicken, whole fryer	lb.	0.73	12/94	2c
Chuck roast, USDA choice, boneless	lb.	2.33	12/94	82r
Cigarettes, Winston, Kings	carton	15.40	12/94	2c
Coffee, 100%, ground roast, all sizes	lb.	4.28	12/94	82r
Coffee, vacuum-packed	13 oz.	3.66	12/94	2c
Cookies, chocolate chip	lb.	2.72	12/94	82r
Corn Flakes, Kellogg's or Post Toasties	18 oz.	1.97	12/94	2c
Corn, frozen, whole kernel, lowest price	10 oz.	0.66	12/94	2c

Values are in dollars or fractions of dollars. In the column headed *Ref*, references are shown to sources. Each reference is followed by a letter. These refer to the geographical level for which data were reported: s = State, r = Region, and c = City or metro. The abbreviation *ex* is used to mean *except* or *excluding*; *exp* stands for expenditures. For other abbreviations and further explanations, please see the Introduction.

Columbia, MO - continued

Item	Per	Value	Date	Ref.
Groceries				
Dairy products (other) purchases	year	148	91	81r
Eggs, Grade A large	dozen	0.71	12/94	2c
Eggs, Grade A large	dozen	0.76	12/94	82r
Fish and seafood purchases	year	61	91	81r
Flour, white, all purpose	lb.	0.22	12/94	82r
Food purchases, food eaten at home	year	2313	91	81r
Foods purchased away from home, not prepared by consumer	year	1709	91	81r
Fruits and vegetables purchases	year	372	91	81r
Grapefruit	lb.	0.47	12/94	82r
Grapes, Thompson seedless	lb.	2.15	12/94	82r
Ground beef, 100% beef	lb.	1.37	12/94	82r
Ground chuck, 100% beef	lb.	1.81	12/94	82r
Ham, boneless, exc. canned	lb.	2.16	12/94	82r
Ice cream, prepackaged, bulk, regular	1/2 gal.	2.48	12/94	82r
Lemons	lb.	1.08	12/94	82r
Lettuce, iceberg	lb.	0.81	12/94	82r
Lettuce, iceberg	head	0.89	12/94	2c
Margarine, Blue Bonnet or Parkay cubes	lb.	0.68	12/94	2c
Margarine, stick	lb.	0.81	12/94	82r
Meats, poultry, fish, and eggs purchases	year	591	91	81r
Milk and cream (fresh) purchases	year	132	91	81r
Milk, whole	1/2 gal.	1.35	12/94	2c
Orange juice, frozen concentrate 12-oz. can	16 oz.	1.41	12/94	82r
Orange juice, Minute Maid frozen	12-oz.	1.30	12/94	2c
Oranges, Navel	lb.	0.56	12/94	82r
Peaches, halves or slices, Hunt's, Del Monte, or Libby's	29-oz.	1.42	12/94	2c
Peanut butter, creamy, all sizes	lb.	1.81	12/94	82r
Peas, sweet, Del Monte or Green Giant	15-17 oz.	0.62	12/94	2c
Pork chops, center cut, bone-in	lb.	2.76	12/94	82r
Pork purchases	year	130	91	81r
Potato chips	16-oz.	2.81	12/94	82r
Potatoes, frozen, French fried	lb.	0.83	12/94	82r
Potatoes, white	lb.	0.28	12/94	82r
Potatoes, white or red	10-lb. sack	2.37	12/94	2c
Round roast, USDA choice, boneless	lb.	2.90	12/94	82r
Sausage, Jimmy Dean, 100% pork	lb.	2.83	12/94	2c
Shortening, vegetable oil blends	lb.	0.88	12/94	82r
Shortening, vegetable, Crisco	3-lb.	2.85	12/94	2c
Soft drink, Coca Cola, ex deposit	2 lit	1.11	12/94	2c
Spaghetti and macaroni	lb.	0.78	12/94	82r
Steak, rib eye, USDA choice, boneless	lb.	6.15	12/94	82r
Steak, round, graded & ungraded, exc. USDA prime & choice	lb.	2.72	12/94	82r
Steak, round, USDA choice, boneless	lb.	3.02	12/94	82r
Steak, sirloin, USDA choice, boneless	lb.	3.85	12/94	82r
Steak, t-bone	lb.	5.55	12/94	2c
Steak, T-bone, USDA choice, bone-in	lb.	5.38	12/94	82r
Sugar and other sweets, eaten at home, expenditures	year	91	91	81r
Sugar, cane or beet	4 lbs.	1.36	12/94	2c
Sugar, white, all sizes	lb.	0.36	12/94	82r
Tobacco products and smoking supplies, total expenditures	year	298	91	81r
Tomatoes, field grown	lb.	1.36	12/94	82r
Tomatoes, Hunt's or Del Monte	14.5 oz.	0.77	12/94	2c
Tuna, chunk, light	lb.	1.94	12/94	82r
Tuna, chunk, light, oil-packed	6.125-6.5 oz.	0.68	12/94	2c
Turkey, frozen, whole	lb.	0.96	12/94	82r
Yogurt, natural, fruit flavored	8 oz.	0.62	12/94	82r
Goods and Services				
Miscellaneous goods and services, ACCRA Index		100.70	12/94	2c

Columbia, MO - continued

Item	Per	Value	Date	Ref.
Health Care				
Health care, ACCRA Index		102.30	12/94	2c
Antibiotic ointment, Polysporin	1.5 oz.	4.02	12/94	2c
Childbirth, Cesarean delivery, hospital charge	birth	5101.00	12/91	69r
Childbirth, Cesarean delivery, physician charge	birth	2234.00	12/91	69r
Childbirth, normal delivery, hospital charge	birth	2891.00	12/91	69r
Childbirth, normal delivery, physician charge	birth	1623.00	12/91	69r
Dentist's fee, adult teeth cleaning and periodic oral exam	visit	54.22	12/94	2c
Doctor's fee, routine exam, established patient	visit	43.50	12/94	2c
Drugs, expenditures	year	248	91	81r
Health care, total expenditures	year	1336	91	81r
Health insurance expenditures	year	550	91	81r
Hospital care, semiprivate room	day	357.67	12/94	2c
Insurance premium, family medical care	month	390.73	1/95	41s
Medical services expenditures	year	457	91	81r
Medical supplies expenditures	year	82	91	81r
Household Goods				
Appl. repair, service call, wash mach	min. lab. chg.	37.59	12/94	2c
Floor coverings, expenditures	year	105	91	81r
Furniture, expenditures	year	291	91	81r
Household equipment, misc. expenditures	year	341	91	81r
Household expenditures, miscellaneous	year	162	91	81r
Household furnishings and equipment, expenditures	year	1042	91	81r
Household operations expenditures	year	365	91	81r
Household textiles, expenditures	year	101	91	81r
Housekeeping supplies, expenditures	year	390	91	81r
Laundry and cleaning supplies, expenditures	year	110	91	81r
Laundry detergent, Tide Ultra, Bold, or Cheer	42 oz.	3.10	12/94	2c
Postage and stationery, expenditures	year	115	91	81r
Tissues, facial, Kleenex brand	175	1.15	12/94	2c
Housing				
Housing, ACCRA Index		88.20	12/94	2c
Add garage/carport		8,479	3/95	74r
Add room(s)		21,347	3/95	74r
Apartment condominium or co-op, median	unit	87100	12/94	62r
Bathroom addition, average cost	add	9734.00	3/95	13r
Bathroom remodeling, average cost	remod	6414.00	3/95	13r
Bedroom, master suite addition, average cost	add	27122.00	3/95	13r
Deck addition, average cost	add	6665.00	3/95	13r
Dwellings (owned), expenditures	year	2566	91	81r
Enclose porch/patio/breezeway		4,556	3/95	74r
Exterior remodeling, average cost	remod	15395.00	3/95	13r
Family room addition, average cost	add	27658.00	3/95	13r
Finish room in basement/attic		5,074	3/95	74r
Home, existing, single-family, median	unit	106500	12/94	62r
Home, single family, median	home	86000	4/94	11c
House payment, principal and interest, 25% down payment	mo.	700	12/94	2c
House, 1800 sq ft, 8000 sq ft lot, new, urban, utilities	total	110500	12/94	2c
Kitchen remodeling, major, average cost	remod	17084.00	3/95	13r
Kitchen remodeling, minor, average cost	remod	5804.00	3/95	13r
Maintenance, repairs, insurance, and other housing expenditures	year	484	91	81r
Mortgage interest and charges expenditures	year	1443	91	81r
Mtge. rate, incl. points and orig. fee, 30-year conv. fixed or ARM	mo.	9.55	12/94	2c
Office, home addition, average cost	add	8121.00	3/95	13r
Princ. & int., mortgage, median-price exist. sing.-family home	mo.	515	12/94	62r
Property taxes expenditures	year	639	91	81r

Values are in dollars or fractions of dollars. In the column headed *Ref*, references are shown to sources. Each reference is followed by a letter. These refer to the geographical level for which data was reported: s=State, r=Region, and c=City or metro. The abbreviation *ex* is used to mean *except* or *excluding*; *exp* stands for *expenditures*. For other abbreviations and further explanations, please see the Introduction.

Columbia, MO - continued

Item	Per	Value	Date	Ref.
Housing				
Redesign, restructure more than half of home's interior		9,114	3/95	74r
Rent, apartment, 2 br., 1 1/2-2 baths, unfurnished, 950 sq ft, water	mo.	396	12/94	2c
Rental units expenditures	year	1200	91	81r
Sun-space addition, average cost	add	23768.00	3/95	13r
Wing addition, two-story, average cost	add	50410.00	3/95	13r
Insurance and Pensions				
Auto insurance, private passenger	year	600.64	12/94	71s
Insurance and pensions, personal, expenditures	year	2408	91	81r
Insurance, life and other personal, expenditures	year	355	91	81r
Pensions and Social Security, expenditures	year	2053	91	81r
Legal Assistance				
Legal work, law firm associate	hour	90		10r
Legal work, law firm partner	hour	139		10r
Personal Goods				
Shampoo, Alberto VO5	15-oz.	1.25	12/94	2c
Toothpaste, Crest or Colgate	6-7 oz.	1.52	12/94	2c
Personal Services				
Dry cleaning, man's 2-pc. suit		6.22	12/94	2c
Haircut, man's barbershop, no styling		7.88	12/94	2c
Haircut, woman's shampoo, trim, blow-dry		22.80	12/94	2c
Personal services expenditures	year	203	91	81r
Restaurant Food				
Chicken, fried, thigh and drumstick		2.48	12/94	2c
Dining expenditures, family	week	30.03	94	73r
Hamburger with cheese	1/4 lb.	1.84	12/94	2c
Pizza, Pizza Hut or Pizza Inn	12-13 in.	8.70	12/94	2c
Taxes				
Taxes, Federal income, expenditures	year	1756	91	81r
Taxes, personal, expenditures	year	2426	91	81r
Taxes, State and local income, expenditures	year	568	91	81r
Transportation				
Transportation, ACCRA Index		96.40	12/94	2c
Cars and trucks purchased, new	year	891	91	81r
Cars and trucks purchased, used	year	1155	91	81r
Driver's learning permit fee	perm	1.00	1/94	84s
Driver's license fee	orig	7.50	1/94	84s
Driver's license fee, duplicate	lic	7.50	1/94	84s
Driver's license reinstatement fee, min.	susp	20.00	1/94	85s
Driver's license renewal fee	renew	7.50	1/94	84s
Identification card, nondriver	card	7.50	1/94	83s
Motorcycle license fee	orig	7.50	1/94	84s
Motorcycle license fee, duplicate	lic	7.50	1/94	84s
Motorcycle license renewal fee	renew	7.50	1/94	84s
Public transportation expenditures	year	209	91	81r
Tire balance, computer or spin bal., front	wheel	7.00	12/94	2c
Transportation expenditures, total	year	4792	91	81r
Vehicle finance charges	year	300	91	81r
Vehicle insurance expenditures	year	485	91	81r
Vehicle maintenance and repairs expenditures	year	534	91	81r
Vehicle purchases	year	2068	91	81r
Vehicle rental, leases, licenses, etc. expenditures	year	197	91	81r
Vehicles purchased, other than cars and trucks	year	22	91	81r
Utilities				
Utilities, ACCRA Index		75.50	12/94	2c
Electricity expenditures	year	668	91	81r
Electricity, (part.), other, 1800 sq. ft., new home	mo.	46.24	12/94	2c
Utilities, fuels, and public services, total expenditures	year	1838	91	81r

Columbia, MO - continued

Item	Per	Value	Date	Ref.
Utilities - continued				
Water and other public services, expenditures	year	167	91	81r
Weddings				
Bridal attendants' gowns	event	750	10/93	76r
Bridal gown	event	852	10/93	76r
Bridal headpiece and veil	event	167	10/93	76r
Bride's wedding band	event	708	10/93	76r
Clergy	event	224	10/93	76r
Engagement ring	event	2756	10/93	76r
Flowers	event	863	10/93	76r
Formal wear for groom	event	106	10/93	76r
Groom's attendants' formal wear	event	530	10/93	76r
Groom's wedding band	event	402	10/93	76r
Music	event	600	10/93	76r
Photography	event	1088	10/93	76r
Shoes for bride	event	50	10/93	76r
Videography	event	483	10/93	76r
Wedding invitations and announcements	event	342	10/93	76r
Wedding reception	event	7000	10/93	76r

Columbia, SC

Item	Per	Value	Date	Ref.
Composite, ACCRA index		92.70	12/94	2c
Alcoholic Beverages				
Beer, Miller Lite, Bud, 12-oz., ex deposit	6	3.83	12/94	2c
J & B Scotch	750-ml.	18.51	12/94	2c
Wine, Gallo Chablis blanc	1.5-lit	4.87	12/94	2c
Appliances				
Appliances (major), expenditures	year	153	91	81r
Average annual exp.				
Food, health care, personal goods, services	year	27020	91	81r
Charity				
Cash contributions, expenditures	year	839	91	81r
Clothing				
Apparel, men and boys, total expenditures	year	380	91	81r
Apparel, women and girls, total expenditures	year	660	91	81r
Footwear, expenditures	year	193	91	81r
Jeans, man's denim		29.57	12/94	2c
Shirt, man's dress shirt		27.00	12/94	2c
Undervest, boy's size 10-14, cotton	3	4.69	12/94	2c
Communications				
Long-distance telephone rate, day, addl. min., 1-10 mi.	min.	0.13	12/93	9s
Long-distance telephone rate, day, initial min., 1-10 mi.	min.	0.24	12/93	9s
Newspaper subscription, dly. and Sun. delivery	month	12.92	12/94	2c
Phone line, single, business, field visit	inst	82.50	12/93	9s
Phone line, single, business, no field visit	inst	64.00	12/93	9s
Phone line, single, residence, field visit	inst	62.50	12/93	9s
Phone line, single, residence, no field visit	inst	44.00	12/93	9s
Telephone bill, family of four	month	23.05	12/94	2c
Telephone service, expenditures	year	616	91	81r
Telephone, residential, flat rate	mo.	16.90	12/93	8c
Education				
Board, 4-year private college/university	year	1831	8/94	80s
Board, 4-year public college/university	year	1462	8/94	80s
Education, total expenditures	year	319	91	81r
Room, 4-year private college/university	year	1744	8/94	80s
Room, 4-year public college/university	year	1851	8/94	80s
Total cost, 4-year private college/university	year	12082	8/94	80s
Total cost, 4-year public college/university	year	6203	8/94	80s
Tuition, 2-year public college/university, in-state	year	1061	8/94	80s
Tuition, 4-year private college/university, in-state	year	8507	8/94	80s

Values are in dollars or fractions of dollars. In the column headed *Ref*, references are shown to sources. Each reference is followed by a letter. These refer to the geographical level for which data were reported: s=State, r=Region, and c=City or metro. The abbreviation *ex* is used to mean *except* or *excluding*; *exp* stands for expenditures. For other abbreviations and further explanations, please see the Introduction.

Columbia, SC - continued

Item	Per	Value	Date	Ref.
Education				
Tuition, 4-year public college/university, in-state	year	2891	8/94	80s
Energy and Fuels				
Energy, combined forms, 1800 sq. ft.	mo.	105.79	12/94	2c
Fuel oil and other fuels, expenditures	year	56	91	81r
Gas, cooking, winter, 10 therms	month	9.90	2/94	65c
Gas, cooking, winter, 30 therms	month	24.02	2/94	65c
Gas, cooking, winter, 50 therms	month	39.12	2/94	65c
Gas, heating, winter, 100 therms	month	76.87	2/94	65c
Gas, heating, winter, average use	month	85.93	2/94	65c
Gas, natural, expenditures	year	150	91	81r
Gas, reg unlead, taxes inc., cash, self-service	gal	1.05	12/94	2c
Gasoline and motor oil purchased	year	1152	91	81r
Gasoline, unleaded midgrade	gallon	1.21	4/93	82r
Gasoline, unleaded premium	gallon	1.30	4/93	82r
Gasoline, unleaded regular	gallon	1.10	4/93	82r
Entertainment				
Bowling, evening rate	game	1.63	12/94	2c
Concert ticket, Pearl Jam group	perf	20.00	94	50r
Entertainment, total expenditures	year	1266	91	81r
Fees and admissions, expenditures	year	306	91	81r
Monopoly game, Parker Brothers', No. 9	game	10.18	12/94	2c
Movie	adm	5.75	12/94	2c
Pets, toys, playground equipment, expenditures	year	271	91	81r
Reading, expenditures	year	131	91	81r
Televisions, radios, and sound equipment, expenditures	year	439	91	81r
Tennis balls, yellow, Wilson or Penn, 3	can	2.66	12/94	2c
Funerals				
Burial, immediate, container provided by funeral home		1370.36	1/95	54r
Cards, acknowledgment		14.83	1/95	54r
Casket, minimum alternative		192.52	1/95	54r
Cosmetology, hair care, etc.		102.27	1/95	54r
Cremation, direct, container provided by funeral home		1065.64	1/95	54r
Embalming		304.29	1/95	54r
Funeral, funeral home		287.83	1/95	54r
Funeral, other facility		284.14	1/95	54r
Graveside service		349.13	1/95	54r
Hearse, local		132.27	1/95	54r
Limousine, local		98.45	1/95	54r
Memorial service		270.59	1/95	54r
Service charge, professional, nondeclinable		933.59	1/95	54r
Visitation and viewing		225.83	1/95	54r
Groceries				
Groceries, ACCRA Index		97.40	12/94	2c
Apples, Red Delicious	lb.	0.73	12/94	82r
Baby food, strained vegetables, lowest price	4-4.5 oz.	0.37	12/94	2c
Bacon, sliced	lb.	1.67	12/94	82r
Bananas	lb.	0.47	12/94	2c
Bananas	lb.	0.42	12/94	82r
Beef or hamburger, ground	lb.	1.71	12/94	2c
Beef purchases	year	213	91	81r
Beverage purchases, alcoholic	year	249	91	81r
Beverage purchases, nonalcoholic	year	207	91	81r
Bologna, all beef or mixed	lb.	2.27	12/94	82r
Bread, white	24-oz.	0.72	12/94	2c
Bread, white, pan	lb.	0.68	12/94	82r
Cabbage	lb.	0.42	12/94	82r
Carrots, short trimmed and topped	lb.	0.53	12/94	82r
Cereals and bakery products purchases	year	345	91	81r
Cereals and cereals products purchases	year	127	91	81r
Cheddar cheese, natural	lb.	3.58	12/94	82r
Cheese, Kraft grated Parmesan	8-oz.	3.13	12/94	2c
Chicken breast, bone-in	lb.	1.71	12/94	82r
Chicken, fresh, whole	lb.	0.78	12/94	82r

Columbia, SC - continued

Item	Per	Value	Date	Ref.
Groceries - continued				
Chicken, whole fryer	lb.	0.89	12/94	2c
Chuck roast, USDA choice, boneless	lb.	2.26	12/94	82r
Cigarettes, Winston, Kings	carton	12.89	12/94	2c
Coffee, vacuum-packed	13 oz.	3.31	12/94	2c
Corn Flakes, Kellogg's or Post Toasties	18 oz.	2.40	12/94	2c
Corn, frozen, whole kernel, lowest price	10 oz.	0.66	12/94	2c
Crackers, soda, salted	lb.	1.27	12/94	82r
Cucumbers	lb.	0.65	12/94	82r
Dairy products (other) purchases	year	141	91	81r
Eggs, Grade A large	dozen	0.85	12/94	2c
Eggs, Grade A large	dozen	0.87	12/94	82r
Fish and seafood purchases	year	72	91	81r
Flour, white, all purpose	lb.	0.23	12/94	82r
Food purchases, food eaten at home	year	2381	91	81r
Foods purchased away from home, not prepared by consumer	year	1696	91	81r
Frankfurters, all meat or all beef	lb.	1.74	12/94	82r
Fruits and vegetables purchases	year	380	91	81r
Grapefruit	lb.	0.45	12/94	82r
Grapes, Thompson seedless	lb.	2.30	12/94	82r
Ground beef, 100% beef	lb.	1.37	12/94	82r
Ground chuck, 100% beef	lb.	1.97	12/94	82r
Ham, boneless, exc. canned	lb.	2.54	12/94	82r
Ice cream, prepackaged, bulk, regular	1/2 gal.	2.47	12/94	82r
Lemons	lb.	1.02	12/94	82r
Lettuce, iceberg	lb.	0.96	12/94	82r
Lettuce, iceberg	head	0.99	12/94	2c
Margarine, Blue Bonnet or Parkay cubes	lb.	0.57	12/94	2c
Margarine, stick	lb.	0.77	12/94	82r
Meats, poultry, fish, and eggs purchases	year	655	91	81r
Milk and cream (fresh) purchases	year	130	91	81r
Milk, whole	1/2 gal.	1.43	12/94	2c
Orange juice, frozen concentrate 12-oz. can	16 oz.	1.36	12/94	82r
Orange juice, Minute Maid frozen	12-oz.	1.13	12/94	2c
Oranges, Navel	lb.	0.54	12/94	82r
Peaches, halves or slices, Hunt's, Del Monte, or Libby's	29-oz.	1.26	12/94	2c
Pears, Anjou	lb.	0.81	12/94	82r
Peas, sweet, Del Monte or Green Giant	15-17 oz.	0.56	12/94	2c
Pork chops, center cut, bone-in	lb.	3.07	12/94	82r
Pork purchases	year	142	91	81r
Potato chips	16-oz.	3.15	12/94	82r
Potatoes, frozen, French fried	lb.	0.82	12/94	82r
Potatoes, white	lb.	0.34	12/94	82r
Potatoes, white or red	10-lb. sack	2.19	12/94	2c
Rice, white, long grain, uncooked	lb.	0.48	12/94	82r
Round roast, USDA choice, boneless	lb.	2.91	12/94	82r
Sausage, fresh	lb.	1.82	12/94	82r
Sausage, Jimmy Dean, 100% pork	lb.	2.11	12/94	2c
Shortening, vegetable oil blends	lb.	0.75	12/94	82r
Shortening, vegetable, Crisco	3-lb.	2.53	12/94	2c
Soft drink, Coca Cola, ex deposit	2 lit	1.19	12/94	2c
Spaghetti and macaroni	lb.	0.87	12/94	82r
Steak, rib eye, USDA choice, boneless	lb.	6.85	12/94	82r
Steak, round, graded & ungraded, exc. USDA prime & choice	lb.	2.96	12/94	82r
Steak, round, USDA choice, boneless	lb.	3.17	12/94	82r
Steak, sirloin, USDA choice, boneless	lb.	4.12	12/94	82r
Steak, t-bone	lb.	4.45	12/94	2c
Steak, T-bone, USDA choice, bone-in	lb.	5.63	12/94	82r
Sugar and other sweets, eaten at home, expenditures	year	93	91	81r
Sugar, cane or beet	4 lbs.	1.48	12/94	2c
Sugar, white, all sizes	lb.	0.39	12/94	82r
Tobacco products and smoking supplies, total expenditures	year	286	91	81r
Tomatoes, field grown	lb.	1.36	12/94	82r

Values are in dollars or fractions of dollars. In the column headed *Ref*, references are shown to sources. Each reference is followed by a letter. These refer to the geographical level for which data were reported: s = State, r = Region, and c = City or metro. The abbreviation *ex* is used to mean *except* or *excluding*; *exp* stands for *expenditures*. For other abbreviations and further explanations, please see the Introduction.

Columbia, SC - continued

Item	Per	Value	Date	Ref.
Groceries				
Tomatoes, Hunt's or Del Monte	14.5 oz.	0.57	12/94	2c
Tuna, chunk, light	lb.	1.94	12/94	82r
Tuna, chunk, light, oil-packed	6.125-6.5 oz.	0.67	12/94	2c
Turkey, frozen, whole	lb.	0.96	12/94	82r
Yogurt, natural, fruit flavored	8 oz.	0.58	12/94	82r
Goods and Services				
Miscellaneous goods and services, ACCRA Index		91.60	12/94	2c
Health Care				
Health care, ACCRA Index		93.70	12/94	2c
Adenosine, emergency room	treat	100.00	95	23r
Antibiotic ointment, Polysporin	1.5 oz.	4.04	12/94	2c
Bladder tap, superpubic, infant, emergency room	treat	119.00	95	23r
Blood analysis, emergency room	treat	25.00	95	23r
Blood tests, abdominal pain, emergency room	treat	25.00	95	23r
Burn dressing, emergency room	treat	266.00	95	23r
Cardiology interpretation, emergency room	treat	26.00	95	23r
Chest X-ray, emergency room	treat	78.00	95	23r
Childbirth, Cesarean delivery, hospital charge	birth	5462.00	12/91	69r
Childbirth, Cesarean delivery, physician charge	birth	2228.00	12/91	69r
Childbirth, normal delivery, hospital charge	birth	2943.00	12/91	69r
Childbirth, normal delivery, physician charge	birth	1619.00	12/91	69r
Defibrillation pads, emergency room	treat	6.00	95	23r
Dentist's fee, adult teeth cleaning and periodic oral exam	visit	51.00	12/94	2c
Doctor's fee, routine exam, established patient	visit	36.00	12/94	2c
Drugs, expenditures	year	297	91	81r
Gastric tube insertion, nasal, emergency room	treat	25.00	95	23r
Health care, total expenditures	year	1600	91	81r
Health insurance expenditures	year	637	91	81r
Heart monitor, emergency room	treat	40.00	95	23r
Hospital care, semiprivate room	day	355.00	12/94	2c
Insurance premium, family medical care	month	414.49	1/95	41s
Intravenous fluids, emergency room	treat	130.00	95	23r
Intravenous fluids, emergency room	liter	26.00	95	23r
Intravenous line, central, emergency room	treat	342.00	95	23r
Liver function tests, abdominal pain, emergency room	treat	26.00	95	23r
Medical care charges, total, emergency room, third-degree burns	treat	2101.00	95	23r
Medical care charges, total, emergency, infant with fever	treat	628.00	95	23r
Medical services expenditures	year	573	91	81r
Medical supplies expenditures	year	93	91	81r
Morphine, emergency room	treat	34.00	95	23r
Nursing care and facilities charges, emergency room	treat	252.00	95	23r
Nursing care and facilities charges, emergency, infant with fever	treat	252.00	95	23r
Nursing care and facilities charges, emergency, third-degree burns	treat	861.00	95	23r
Physician's charges, emergency, infant with fever	treat	212.00	95	23r
Physician's charges, emergency, third-degree burns	treat	372.00	95	23r
Physician's fee, emergency room	treat	372.00	95	23r
Physician's fee, general practitioner	visit	51.20	12/93	60r
Surgery, open-heart	proc	42374.00	1/93	14r
Ultrasound, abdominal, emergency room	treat	276.00	95	23r
Urinalysis, emergency room	treat	20.00	95	23r
Urinalysis, infant, emergency room	treat	20.00	95	23r
X-rays, emergency room	treat	78.00	95	23r

Columbia, SC - continued

Item	Per	Value	Date	Ref.
Household Goods				
Appl. repair, service call, wash mach	min. lab. chg.	34.00	12/94	2c
Floor coverings, expenditures	year	48	91	81r
Furniture, expenditures	year	280	91	81r
Household equipment, misc. expenditures	year	342	91	81r
Household expenditures, miscellaneous	year	256	91	81r
Household furnishings and equipment, expenditures	year	988	91	81r
Household operations expenditures	year	468	91	81r
Household textiles, expenditures	year	95	91	81r
Housekeeping supplies, expenditures	year	380	91	81r
Laundry and cleaning supplies, expenditures	year	109	91	81r
Laundry detergent, Tide Ultra, Bold, or Cheer	42 oz.	3.11	12/94	2c
Postage and stationery, expenditures	year	105	91	81r
Tissues, facial, Kleenex brand	175	0.95	12/94	2c
Housing				
Housing, ACCRA Index		90.50	12/94	2c
Add garage/carport		6,980	3/95	74r
Add room(s)		11,403	3/95	74r
Apartment condominium or co-op, median	unit	68600	12/94	62r
Dwellings (owned), expenditures	year	2428	91	81r
Enclose porch/patio/breezeway		4,572	3/95	74r
Finish room in basement/attic		3,794	3/95	74r
Home, existing, single-family, median	unit	120200	12/94	62r
Home, existing, single-family, median	unit	84.90	12/94	62c
House payment, principal and interest, 25% down payment	mo.	670	12/94	2c
House, 1800 sq ft, 8000 sq ft lot, new, urban, utilities	total	108380	12/94	2c
Maintenance, repairs, insurance, and other housing expenditures	year	531	91	81r
Mortgage interest and charges expenditures	year	1506	91	81r
Mtge. rate, incl. points and orig. fee, 30-year conv. fixed or ARM	mo.	9.27	12/94	2c
Princ. & int., mortgage, median-price exist. sing.-family home	mo.	540	12/94	62r
Property taxes expenditures	year	391	91	81r
Redesign, restructure more than half of home's interior		17,641	3/95	74r
Rent, apartment, 2 br., 1 1/2-2 baths, unfurnished, 950 sq ft, water	mo.	547	12/94	2c
Rental units expenditures	year	1264	91	81r
Insurance and Pensions				
Auto insurance, private passenger	year	684.10	12/94	71s
Insurance and pensions, personal, expenditures	year	2395	91	81r
Insurance, life and other personal, expenditures	year	368	91	81r
Pensions and Social Security, expenditures	year	2027	91	81r
Personal Goods				
Shampoo, Alberto VO5	15-oz.	0.99	12/94	2c
Toothpaste, Crest or Colgate	6-7 oz.	1.83	12/94	2c
Personal Services				
Dry cleaning, man's 2-pc. suit		6.22	12/94	2c
Haircut, man's barbershop, no styling		9.00	12/94	2c
Haircut, woman's shampoo, trim, blow-dry		15.19	12/94	2c
Personal services expenditures	year	212	91	81r
Restaurant Food				
Chicken, fried, thigh and drumstick		1.89	12/94	2c
Dining expenditures, family	week	33.83	94	73r
Hamburger with cheese	1/4 lb.	0.99	12/94	2c
Pizza, Pizza Hut or Pizza Inn	12-13 in.	7.59	12/94	2c
Taxes				
Tax rate, residential property, month	$100	1.25	1/92	79c
Taxes, Federal income, expenditures	year	2275	91	81r

Values are in dollars or fractions of dollars. In the column headed *Ref*, references are shown to sources. Each reference is followed by a letter. These refer to the geographical level for which data were reported: s=State, r=Region, and c=City or metro. The abbreviation *ex* is used to mean *except* or *excluding*; *exp* stands for *expenditures*. For other abbreviations and further explanations, please see the Introduction.

Columbia, SC - continued

Item	Per	Value	Date	Ref.
Taxes				
Taxes, personal, expenditures	year	2715	91	81r
Taxes, State and local income, expenditures	year	365	91	81r
Transportation				
Transportation, ACCRA Index		90.20	12/94	2c
Cars and trucks purchased, new	year	1306	91	81r
Cars and trucks purchased, used	year	942	91	81r
Driver's learning permit fee	perm	2.00	1/94	84s
Driver's license fee	orig	10.00	1/94	84s
Driver's license fee, duplicate	lic	0.50	1/94	84s
Driver's license reinstatement fee, min.	susp	30.00	1/94	85s
Driver's license renewal fee	renew	10.00	1/94	84s
Identification card, nondriver	card	5.00	1/94	83s
Motorcycle learning permit fee	perm	2.00	1/94	84s
Motorcycle license fee	orig	10.00	1/94	84s
Motorcycle license fee, duplicate	lic	0.50	1/94	84s
Motorcycle license renewal fee	renew	10.00	1/94	84s
Public transportation expenditures	year	249	91	81r
Tire balance, computer or spin bal., front	wheel	5.80	12/94	2c
Transportation expenditures, total	year	5307	91	81r
Vehicle finance charges	year	346	91	81r
Vehicle insurance expenditures	year	544	91	81r
Vehicle maintenance and repairs expenditures	year	600	91	81r
Vehicle purchases	year	2275	91	81r
Vehicle rental, leases, licenses, etc. expenditures	year	141	91	81r
Vehicles purchased, other than cars and trucks	year	27	91	81r
Utilities				
Utilities, ACCRA Index		97.50	12/94	2c
Electricity expenditures	year	950	91	81r
Electricity, 1800 sq. ft., new home	mo.	105.79	12/94	2c
Electricity, summer, 250 KWh	month	22.59	8/93	64c
Electricity, summer, 500 KWh	month	39.17	8/93	64c
Electricity, summer, 750 KWh	month	55.76	8/93	64c
Electricity, summer, 1000 KWh	month	74.07	8/93	64c
Utilities, fuels, and public services, total expenditures	year	2000	91	81r
Water and other public services, expenditures	year	227	91	81r
Weddings				
Bridal attendants' gowns	event	750	10/93	76r
Bridal gown	event	852	10/93	76r
Bridal headpiece and veil	event	167	10/93	76r
Bride's wedding band	event	708	10/93	76r
Clergy	event	224	10/93	76r
Engagement ring	event	2756	10/93	76r
Flowers	event	863	10/93	76r
Formal wear for groom	event	106	10/93	76r
Groom's attendants' formal wear	event	530	10/93	76r
Groom's wedding band	event	402	10/93	76r
Music	event	600	10/93	76r
Photography	event	1088	10/93	76r
Shoes for bride	event	50	10/93	76r
Videography	event	483	10/93	76r
Wedding invitations and announcements	event	342	10/93	76r
Wedding reception	event	7000	10/93	76r

Columbus, GA

Item	Per	Value	Date	Ref.
Composite, ACCRA index		92.30	12/94	2c
Alcoholic Beverages				
Beer, Miller Lite, Bud, 12-oz., ex deposit	6	4.09	12/94	2c
J & B Scotch	750-ml.	15.56	12/94	2c
Wine, Gallo Chablis blanc	1.5-lit	5.37	12/94	2c
Clothing				
Jeans, man's denim		29.31	12/94	2c
Shirt, man's dress shirt		33.00	12/94	2c

Columbus, GA - continued

Item	Per	Value	Date	Ref.
Clothing - continued				
Undervest, boy's size 10-14, cotton	3	4.99	12/94	2c
Communications				
Newspaper subscription, dly. and Sun. delivery	month	13.26	12/94	2c
Telephone bill, family of four	month	21.35	12/94	2c
Telephone, residential, flat rate	mo.	13.55	12/93	8c
Credit Cards				
Fee, conventional credit card, bal. carried	year	29.00	1/95	96c
Energy and Fuels				
Energy, combined forms, 1800 sq. ft.	mo.	101.55	12/94	2c
Energy, exc. electricity, 1800 sq. ft.	mo.	33.04	12/94	2c
Gas, cooking, 10 therms	month	11.48	2/94	65c
Gas, cooking, 30 therms	month	22.43	2/94	65c
Gas, cooking, 50 therms	month	33.38	2/94	65c
Gas, heating, winter, 100 therms	month	60.75	2/94	65c
Gas, heating, winter, average use	month	69.51	2/94	65c
Gas, reg unlead, taxes inc., cash, self-service	gal	1.03	12/94	2c
Entertainment				
Bowling, evening rate	game	2.40	12/94	2c
Monopoly game, Parker Brothers', No. 9	game	10.23	12/94	2c
Movie	adm	5.50	12/94	2c
Tennis balls, yellow, Wilson or Penn, 3	can	2.71	12/94	2c
Groceries				
Groceries, ACCRA Index		94.10	12/94	2c
Baby food, strained vegetables, lowest price	4-4.5 oz.	0.32	12/94	2c
Bananas	lb.	0.44	12/94	2c
Beef or hamburger, ground	lb.	1.46	12/94	2c
Bread, white	24-oz.	0.76	12/94	2c
Cheese, Kraft grated Parmesan	8-oz.	3.33	12/94	2c
Chicken, whole fryer	lb.	0.83	12/94	2c
Cigarettes, Winston, Kings	carton	14.26	12/94	2c
Coffee, vacuum-packed	13 oz.	2.91	12/94	2c
Corn Flakes, Kellogg's or Post Toasties	18 oz.	1.90	12/94	2c
Corn, frozen, whole kernel, lowest price	10 oz.	0.68	12/94	2c
Eggs, Grade A large	dozen	0.73	12/94	2c
Lettuce, iceberg	head	0.97	12/94	2c
Margarine, Blue Bonnet or Parkay cubes	lb.	0.60	12/94	2c
Milk, whole	1/2 gal.	1.35	12/94	2c
Orange juice, Minute Maid frozen	12-oz.	1.12	12/94	2c
Peaches, halves or slices, Hunt's, Del Monte, or Libby's	29-oz.	1.23	12/94	2c
Peas, sweet, Del Monte or Green Giant	15-17 oz.	0.60	12/94	2c
Potatoes, white or red	10-lb. sack	2.54	12/94	2c
Sausage, Jimmy Dean, 100% pork	lb.	2.23	12/94	2c
Shortening, vegetable, Crisco	3-lb.	2.53	12/94	2c
Soft drink, Coca Cola, ex deposit	2 lit	1.01	12/94	2c
Steak, t-bone	lb.	4.88	12/94	2c
Sugar, cane or beet	4 lbs.	1.33	12/94	2c
Tomatoes, Hunt's or Del Monte	14.5 oz.	0.71	12/94	2c
Tuna, chunk, light, oil-packed	6.125-6.5 oz.	0.63	12/94	2c
Goods and Services				
Miscellaneous goods and services, ACCRA Index		100.90		2c
Health Care				
Health care, ACCRA Index		93.50	12/94	2c
Household Goods				
Appl. repair, service call, wash mach	min. lab. chg.	35.00	12/94	2c
Laundry detergent, Tide Ultra, Bold, or Cheer	42 oz.	3.03	12/94	2c

Values are in dollars or fractions of dollars. In the column headed *Ref*, references are shown to sources. Each reference is followed by a letter. These refer to the geographical level for which data were reported: s=State, r=Region, and c=City or metro. The abbreviation *ex* is used to mean *except* or *excluding*; *exp* stands for expenditures. For other abbreviations and further explanations, please see the Introduction.

Columbus, GA - continued

Item	Per	Value	Date	Ref.
Household Goods				
Tissues, facial, Kleenex brand	175	0.94	12/94	2c
Housing				
Housing, ACCRA Index		80.20	12/94	2c
House payment, principal and interest, 25% down payment	mo.	601	12/94	2c
House, 1800 sq ft, 8000 sq ft lot, new, urban, utilities	total	96440	12/94	2c
Mtge. rate, incl. points and orig. fee, 30-year conv. fixed or ARM	mo.	9.37	12/94	2c
Rent, apartment, 2 br., 1 1/2-2 baths, unfurnished, 950 sq ft, water	mo.	462	12/94	2c
Personal Goods				
Shampoo, Alberto VO5	15-oz.	0.98	12/94	2c
Toothpaste, Crest or Colgate	6-7 oz.	1.94	12/94	2c
Personal Services				
Dry cleaning, man's 2-pc. suit		5.89	12/94	2c
Haircut, man's barbershop, no styling		6.75	12/94	2c
Haircut, woman's shampoo, trim, blow-dry		22.00	12/94	2c
Restaurant Food				
Chicken, fried, thigh and drumstick		1.75	12/94	2c
Hamburger with cheese	1/4 lb.	1.95	12/94	2c
Pizza, Pizza Hut or Pizza Inn	12-13 in.	7.99	12/94	2c
Transportation				
Transportation, ACCRA Index		93.50	12/94	2c
Bus fare, one-way	trip	0.80	12/95	1c
Bus fare, up to 10 miles	one-way	0.80	12/94	2c
Tire balance, computer or spin bal., front	wheel	6.70	12/94	2c
Utilities				
Utilities, ACCRA Index		93.10	12/94	2c
Electricity, (part.), other, 1800 sq. ft., new home	mo.	68.51	12/94	2c

Columbus, OH

Item	Per	Value	Date	Ref.
Composite, ACCRA index		104.30	12/94	2c
Alcoholic Beverages				
Beer, Miller Lite, Bud, 12-oz., ex deposit	6	4.00	12/94	2c
J & B Scotch	750-ml.	18.85	12/94	2c
Wine, Gallo Chablis blanc	1.5-lit	4.99	12/94	2c
Appliances				
Appliances (major), expenditures	year	131	91	81r
Average annual exp.				
Food, health care, personal goods, services	year	25935	91	81r
Charity				
Cash contributions, expenditures	year	745	91	81r
Clothing				
Apparel, men and boys, total expenditures	year	332	91	81r
Apparel, women and girls, total expenditures	year	578	91	81r
Footwear, expenditures	year	164	91	81r
Jeans, man's denim		34.99	12/94	2c
Shirt, man's dress shirt		29.50	12/94	2c
Undervest, boy's size 10-14, cotton	3	5.59	12/94	2c
Communications				
Long-distance telephone rate, day, addl. min., 1-10 mi.	min.	0.16	12/93	9s
Long-distance telephone rate, day, initial min., 1-10 mi.	min.	0.32	12/93	9s
Newspaper subscription, dly. and Sun. delivery	month	12.39	12/94	2c
Phone line, single, business, field visit	inst	55.42	12/93	9s
Phone line, single, business, no field visit	inst	55.42	12/93	9s
Phone line, single, residence, field visit	inst	30.38	12/93	9s

Columbus, OH - continued

Item	Per	Value	Date	Ref.
Communications - continued				
Phone line, single, residence, no field visit	inst	30.38	12/93	9s
Telephone bill, family of four	month	20.67	12/94	2c
Telephone service, expenditures	year	547	91	81r
Telephone, business, addl. line, touch tone	month	3.25	10/91	25c
Telephone, business, connection charges, touch tone	inst	72.15	10/91	25c
Telephone, business, key system line, touch tone	month	44.71	10/91	25c
Telephone, business, PBX line, touch tone	month	44.84	10/91	25c
Telephone, business, single ln., touch tone	month	41.01	10/91	25c
Telephone, business, touch tone, inside wiring maintenance plan	month	1.50	10/91	25c
Telephone, residential, flat rate	mo.	15.25	12/93	8c
Education				
Board, 4-year private college/university	year	2241	8/94	80s
Board, 4-year public college/university	year	1625	8/94	80s
Education, total expenditures	year	394	91	81r
Room, 4-year private college/university	year	2118	8/94	80s
Room, 4-year public college/university	year	2103	8/94	80s
Total cost, 4-year private college/university	year	15444	8/94	80s
Total cost, 4-year public college/university	year	6987	8/94	80s
Tuition, 2-year public college/university, in-state	year	2076	8/94	80s
Tuition, 4-year private college/university, in-state	year	11085	8/94	80s
Tuition, 4-year public college/university, in-state	year	3259	8/94	80s
Energy and Fuels				
Energy, combined forms, 1800 sq. ft.	mo.	152.11	12/94	2c
Energy, exc. electricity, 1800 sq. ft.	mo.	62.27	12/94	2c
Fuel oil and other fuels, expenditures	year	83	91	81r
Gas, cooking, winter, 10 therms	month	11.88	2/94	65c
Gas, cooking, winter, 30 therms	month	22.65	2/94	65c
Gas, cooking, winter, 50 therms	month	33.42	2/94	65c
Gas, heating, winter, 100 therms	month	60.33	2/94	65c
Gas, heating, winter, average use	month	115.77	2/94	65c
Gas, natural, expenditures	year	373	91	81r
Gas, reg unlead, taxes inc., cash, self-service	gal	1.09	12/94	2c
Gasoline and motor oil purchased	year	1000	91	81r
Gasoline, unleaded midgrade	gallon	1.15	4/93	82r
Gasoline, unleaded premium	gallon	1.23	4/93	82r
Gasoline, unleaded regular	gallon	1.07	4/93	82r
Entertainment				
Bowling, evening rate	game	1.82	12/94	2c
Entertainment, total expenditures	year	1356	91	81r
Fees and admissions, expenditures	year	347	91	81r
Monopoly game, Parker Brothers', No. 9	game	9.99	12/94	2c
Movie	adm	5.80	12/94	2c
Pets, toys, playground equipment, expenditures	year	270	91	81r
Reading, expenditures	year	160	91	81r
Televisions, radios, and sound equipment, expenditures	year	433	91	81r
Tennis balls, yellow, Wilson or Penn, 3	can	3.48	12/94	2c
Funerals				
Burial, immediate, container provided by funeral home		1268.31	1/95	54r
Cards, acknowledgment		26.12	1/95	54r
Casket, minimum alternative		198.03	1/95	54r
Cosmetology, hair care, etc.		122.19	1/95	54r
Cremation, direct, container provided by funeral home		977.81	1/95	54r
Embalming		334.00	1/95	54r
Funeral, funeral home		321.16	1/95	54r
Funeral, other facility		317.73	1/95	54r
Graveside service		292.48	1/95	54r
Hearse, local		153.20	1/95	54r
Limousine, local		123.52	1/95	54r
Memorial service		356.30	1/95	54r

Values are in dollars or fractions of dollars. In the column headed *Ref*, references are shown to sources. Each reference is followed by a letter. These refer to the geographical level for which data were reported: s=State, r=Region, and c=City or metro. The abbreviation *ex* is used to mean *except* or *excluding*; *exp* stands for expenditures. For other abbreviations and further explanations, please see the Introduction.

Columbus, OH - continued

Item	Per	Value	Date	Ref.
Funerals				
Service charge, professional, nondeclinable		968.24	1/95	54r
Visitation and viewing		332.66	1/95	54r
Groceries				
Groceries, ACCRA Index		101.80	12/94	2c
Apples, Red Delicious	lb.	0.68	12/94	82r
Baby food, strained vegetables, lowest price	4-4.5 oz.	0.19	12/94	2c
Bacon, sliced	lb.	1.88	12/94	82r
Bananas	lb.	0.40	12/94	2c
Bananas	lb.	0.41	12/94	82r
Beef or hamburger, ground	lb.	1.46	12/94	2c
Beef purchases	year	197	91	81r
Beef, stew, boneless	lb.	2.52	12/94	82r
Beverage purchases, alcoholic	year	293	91	81r
Beverage purchases, nonalcoholic	year	203	91	81r
Bologna, all beef or mixed	lb.	2.12	12/94	82r
Bread, white	24-oz.	0.87	12/94	2c
Bread, white, pan	lb.	0.76	12/94	82r
Cabbage	lb.	0.44	12/94	82r
Carrots, short trimmed and topped	lb.	0.44	12/94	82r
Cereals and bakery products purchases	year	347	91	81r
Cereals and cereals products purchases	year	119	91	81r
Cheddar cheese, natural	lb.	3.28	12/94	82r
Cheese, Kraft grated Parmesan	8-oz.	3.31	12/94	2c
Chicken breast, bone-in	lb.	1.61	12/94	82r
Chicken, fresh, whole	lb.	0.89	12/94	82r
Chicken, whole fryer	lb.	0.93	12/94	2c
Chuck roast, USDA choice, boneless	lb.	2.33	12/94	82r
Cigarettes, Winston, Kings	carton	15.99	12/94	2c
Coffee, 100%, ground roast, all sizes	lb.	4.28	12/94	82r
Coffee, vacuum-packed	13 oz.	3.99	12/94	2c
Cookies, chocolate chip	lb.	2.72	12/94	82r
Corn Flakes, Kellogg's or Post Toasties	18 oz.	2.65	12/94	2c
Corn, frozen, whole kernel, lowest price	10 oz.	0.75	12/94	2c
Dairy products (other) purchases	year	148	91	81r
Eggs, Grade A large	dozen	0.77	12/94	2c
Eggs, Grade A large	dozen	0.76	12/94	82r
Fish and seafood purchases	year	61	91	81r
Flour, white, all purpose	lb.	0.22	12/94	82r
Food purchases, food eaten at home	year	2313	91	81r
Foods purchased away from home, not prepared by consumer	year	1709	91	81r
Fruits and vegetables purchases	year	372	91	81r
Grapefruit	lb.	0.47	12/94	82r
Grapes, Thompson seedless	lb.	2.15	12/94	82r
Ground beef, 100% beef	lb.	1.37	12/94	82r
Ground chuck, 100% beef	lb.	1.81	12/94	82r
Ham, boneless, exc. canned	lb.	2.16	12/94	82r
Ice cream, prepackaged, bulk, regular	1/2 gal.	2.48	12/94	82r
Lemons	lb.	1.08	12/94	82r
Lettuce, iceberg	lb.	0.81	12/94	82r
Lettuce, iceberg	head	0.92	12/94	2c
Margarine, Blue Bonnet or Parkay cubes	lb.	0.64	12/94	2c
Margarine, stick	lb.	0.81	12/94	82r
Meats, poultry, fish, and eggs purchases	year	591	91	81r
Milk and cream (fresh) purchases	year	132	91	81r
Milk, whole	1/2 gal.	1.37	12/94	2c
Orange juice, frozen concentrate 12-oz. can	16 oz.	1.41	12/94	82r
Orange juice, Minute Maid frozen	12-oz.	1.29	12/94	2c
Oranges, Navel	lb.	0.56	12/94	82r
Peaches, halves or slices, Hunt's, Del Monte, or Libby's	29-oz.	1.51	12/94	2c
Peanut butter, creamy, all sizes	lb.	1.81	12/94	82r
Peas, sweet, Del Monte or Green Giant	15-17 oz.	0.59	12/94	2c
Pork chops, center cut, bone-in	lb.	2.76	12/94	82r
Pork purchases	year	130	91	81r
Potato chips	16-oz.	2.81	12/94	82r
Potatoes, frozen, French fried	lb.	0.83	12/94	82r
Potatoes, white	lb.	0.28	12/94	82r

Columbus, OH - continued

Item	Per	Value	Date	Ref.
Groceries - continued				
Potatoes, white or red	10-lb. sack	1.81	12/94	2c
Round roast, USDA choice, boneless	lb.	2.90	12/94	82r
Sausage, Jimmy Dean, 100% pork	lb.	2.89	12/94	2c
Shortening, vegetable oil blends	lb.	0.88	12/94	82r
Shortening, vegetable, Crisco	3-lb.	2.39	12/94	2c
Soft drink, Coca Cola, ex deposit	2 lit	1.09	12/94	2c
Spaghetti and macaroni	lb.	0.78	12/94	82r
Steak, rib eye, USDA choice, boneless	lb.	6.15	12/94	82r
Steak, round, graded & ungraded, exc. USDA prime & choice	lb.	2.72	12/94	82r
Steak, round, USDA choice, boneless	lb.	3.02	12/94	82r
Steak, sirloin, USDA choice, boneless	lb.	3.85	12/94	82r
Steak, t-bone	lb.	6.19	12/94	2c
Steak, T-bone, USDA choice, bone-in	lb.	5.38	12/94	82r
Sugar and other sweets, eaten at home, expenditures	year	91	91	81r
Sugar, cane or beet	4 lbs.	1.28	12/94	2c
Sugar, white, all sizes	lb.	0.36	12/94	82r
Tobacco products and smoking supplies, total expenditures	year	298	91	81r
Tomatoes, field grown	lb.	1.36	12/94	82r
Tomatoes, Hunt's or Del Monte	14.5 oz.	0.73	12/94	2c
Tuna, chunk, light	lb.	1.94	12/94	82r
Tuna, chunk, light, oil-packed	6.125-6.5 oz.	0.72	12/94	2c
Turkey, frozen, whole	lb.	0.96	12/94	82r
Yogurt, natural, fruit flavored	8 oz.	0.62	12/94	82r
Goods and Services				
Miscellaneous goods and services, ACCRA Index		105.10	12/94	2c
Health Care				
Health care, ACCRA Index		96.40	12/94	2c
Antibiotic ointment, Polysporin	1.5 oz.	4.11	12/94	2c
Childbirth, Cesarean delivery, hospital charge	birth	5101.00	12/91	69r
Childbirth, Cesarean delivery, physician charge	birth	2234.00	12/91	69r
Childbirth, normal delivery, hospital charge	birth	2891.00	12/91	69r
Childbirth, normal delivery, physician charge	birth	1623.00	12/91	69r
Dentist's fee, adult teeth cleaning and periodic oral exam	visit	55.00	12/94	2c
Doctor's fee, routine exam, established patient	visit	39.40	12/94	2c
Drugs, expenditures	year	248	91	81r
Health care, total expenditures	year	1336	91	81r
Health insurance expenditures	year	550	91	81r
Hospital care, semiprivate room	day	295.00	12/94	2c
Immunization, DTP, measles, mumps, rubella, polio	inject	69.00	8/93	90c
Insurance premium, family medical care	month	350.73	1/95	41s
Medical services expenditures	year	457	91	81r
Medical supplies expenditures	year	82	91	81r
Household Goods				
Appl. repair, service call, wash mach	min. lab. chg.	32.98	12/94	2c
Floor coverings, expenditures	year	105	91	81r
Furniture, expenditures	year	291	91	81r
Household equipment, misc. expenditures	year	341	91	81r
Household expenditures, miscellaneous	year	162	91	81r
Household furnishings and equipment, expenditures	year	1042	91	81r
Household operations expenditures	year	365	91	81r
Household textiles, expenditures	year	101	91	81r
Housekeeping supplies, expenditures	year	390	91	81r
Laundry and cleaning supplies, expenditures	year	110	91	81r
Laundry detergent, Tide Ultra, Bold, or Cheer	42 oz.	4.12	12/94	2c

Values are in dollars or fractions of dollars. In the column headed *Ref*, references are shown to sources. Each reference is followed by a letter. These refer to the geographical level for which data were reported: s = State, r = Region, and c = City or metro. The abbreviation *ex* is used to mean *except* or *excluding*; *exp* stands for expenditures. For other abbreviations and further explanations, please see the Introduction.

Columbus, OH - continued

Item	Per	Value	Date	Ref.
Household Goods				
Postage and stationery, expenditures	year	115	91	81r
Tissues, facial, Kleenex brand	175	0.97	12/94	2c
Housing				
Housing, ACCRA Index		97.60	12/94	2c
Add garage/carport		8,479	3/95	74r
Add room(s)		21,347	3/95	74r
Apartment condominium or co-op, median	unit	87100	12/94	62r
Bathroom addition, average cost	add	9734.00	3/95	13r
Bathroom remodeling, average cost	remod	6414.00	3/95	13r
Bedroom, master suite addition, average cost	add	27122.00	3/95	13r
Deck addition, average cost	add	6665.00	3/95	13r
Dwellings (owned), expenditures	year	2566	91	81r
Enclose porch/patio/breezeway		4,556	3/95	74r
Exterior remodeling, average cost	remod	15395.00	3/95	13r
Family room addition, average cost	add	27658.00	3/95	13r
Finish room in basement/attic		5,074	3/95	74r
Home, existing, single-family, median	unit	106500	12/94	62r
Home, existing, single-family, median	unit	93.60	12/94	62c
Home, purchase price	unit	128.10	3/93	26c
House payment, principal and interest, 25% down payment	mo.	720	12/94	2c
House, 1800 sq ft, 8000 sq ft lot, new, urban, utilities	total	116380	12/94	2c
Kitchen remodeling, major, average cost	remod	17084.00	3/95	13r
Kitchen remodeling, minor, average cost	remod	5804.00	3/95	13r
Maintenance, repairs, insurance, and other housing expenditures	year	484	91	81r
Mortgage interest and charges expenditures	year	1443	91	81r
Mtge. rate, incl. points and orig. fee, 30-year conv. fixed or ARM	mo.	9.27	12/94	2c
Office, home addition, average cost	add	8121.00	3/95	13r
Princ. & int., mortgage, median-price exist. sing.-family home	mo.	515	12/94	62r
Property taxes expenditures	year	639	91	81r
Redesign, restructure more than half of home's interior		9,114	3/95	74r
Rent, apartment, 2 br., 1 1/2-2 baths, unfurnished, 950 sq ft, water	mo.	595	12/94	2c
Rental units expenditures	year	1200	91	81r
Sun-space addition, average cost	add	23768.00	3/95	13r
Wing addition, two-story, average cost	add	50410.00	3/95	13r
Insurance and Pensions				
Auto insurance, private passenger	year	550.52	12/94	71s
Insurance and pensions, personal, expenditures	year	2408	91	81r
Insurance, life and other personal, expenditures	year	355	91	81r
Pensions and Social Security, expenditures	year	2053	91	81r
Legal Assistance				
Legal work, law firm associate	hour	90		10r
Legal work, law firm partner	hour	139		10r
Personal Goods				
Shampoo, Alberto VO5	15-oz.	1.36	12/94	2c
Toothpaste, Crest or Colgate	6-7 oz.	1.76	12/94	2c
Personal Services				
Dry cleaning, man's 2-pc. suit		7.61	12/94	2c
Haircut, man's barbershop, no styling		8.45	12/94	2c
Haircut, woman's shampoo, trim, blow-dry		22.70	12/94	2c
Personal services expenditures	year	203	91	81r
Restaurant Food				
Chicken, fried, thigh and drumstick		2.09	12/94	2c
Dining expenditures, family	week	30.03	94	73r
Hamburger with cheese	1/4 lb.	1.81	12/94	2c
Pizza, Pizza Hut or Pizza Inn	12-13 in.	7.69	12/94	2c

Columbus, OH - continued

Item	Per	Value	Date	Ref.
Taxes				
Tax rate, residential property, month	$100	1.80	1/92	79c
Taxes, Federal income, expenditures	year	1756	91	81r
Taxes, personal, expenditures	year	2426	91	81r
Taxes, State and local income, expenditures	year	568	91	81r
Transportation				
Transportation, ACCRA Index		108.10	12/94	2c
Bus fare, one-way	trip	1.00	12/95	1c
Bus fare, up to 10 miles	one-way	1.00	12/94	2c
Cars and trucks purchased, new	year	891	91	81r
Cars and trucks purchased, used	year	1155	91	81r
Driver's learning permit fee	perm	3.00	1/94	84s
Driver's license fee	orig	5.00	1/94	84s
Driver's license fee, duplicate	lic	1.50	1/94	84s
Driver's license reinstatement fee, min.	susp	12.50-100.00	1/94	85s
Driver's license renewal fee	renew	5.00	1/94	84s
Identification card, nondriver	card	2.50	1/94	83s
Motorcycle learning permit fee	perm	3.00	1/94	84s
Motorcycle license fee	orig	5.00	1/94	84s
Motorcycle license fee, duplicate	lic	1.50	1/94	84s
Motorcycle license renewal fee	renew	5.00	1/94	84s
Public transportation expenditures	year	209	91	81r
Tire balance, computer or spin bal., front	wheel	8.37	12/94	2c
Transportation expenditures, total	year	4792	91	81r
Vehicle finance charges	year	300	91	81r
Vehicle insurance expenditures	year	485	91	81r
Vehicle maintenance and repairs expenditures	year	534	91	81r
Vehicle purchases	year	2068	91	81r
Vehicle rental, leases, licenses, etc. expenditures	year	197	91	81r
Vehicles purchased, other than cars and trucks	year	22	91	81r
Utilities				
Utilities, ACCRA Index		131.60	12/94	2c
Electricity expenditures	year	668	91	81r
Electricity, (part.), other, 1800 sq. ft., new home	mo.	89.84	12/94	2c
Electricity, summer, 250 KWh	month	25.43	8/93	64c
Electricity, summer, 500 KWh	month	46.11	8/93	64c
Electricity, summer, 750 KWh	month	66.80	8/93	64c
Electricity, summer, 1000 KWh	month	87.48	8/93	64c
Utilities, fuels, and public services, total expenditures	year	1838	91	81r
Water and other public services, expenditures	year	167	91	81r
Weddings				
Bridal attendants' gowns	event	750	10/93	76r
Bridal gown	event	852	10/93	76r
Bridal headpiece and veil	event	167	10/93	76r
Bride's wedding band	event	708	10/93	76r
Clergy	event	224	10/93	76r
Engagement ring	event	2756	10/93	76r
Flowers	event	863	10/93	76r
Formal wear for groom	event	106	10/93	76r
Groom's attendants' formal wear	event	530	10/93	76r
Groom's wedding band	event	402	10/93	76r
Music	event	600	10/93	76r
Photography	event	1088	10/93	76r
Shoes for bride	event	50	10/93	76r
Videography	event	483	10/93	76r
Wedding invitations and announcements	event	342	10/93	76r
Wedding reception	event	7000	10/93	76r

Values are in dollars or fractions of dollars. In the column headed *Ref*, references are shown to sources. Each reference is followed by a letter. These refer to the geographical level for which data were reported: s = State, r = Region, and c = City or metro. The abbreviation *ex* is used to mean *except* or *excluding*; *exp* stands for *expenditures*. For other abbreviations and further explanations, please see the Introduction.

Corpus Christi, TX

Item	Per	Value	Date	Ref.
Composite, ACCRA index		94.00	12/94	2c
Alcoholic Beverages				
Beer, Miller Lite, Bud, 12-oz., ex deposit	6	3.89	12/94	2c
J & B Scotch	750-ml.	17.47	12/94	2c
Wine, Gallo Chablis blanc	1.5-lit	4.85	12/94	2c
Appliances				
Appliances (major), expenditures	year	153	91	81r
Average annual exp.				
Food, health care, personal goods, services	year	27020	91	81r
Charity				
Cash contributions, expenditures	year	839	91	81r
Clothing				
Apparel, men and boys, total expenditures	year	380	91	81r
Apparel, women and girls, total expenditures	year	660	91	81r
Footwear, expenditures	year	193	91	81r
Jeans, man's denim		25.00	12/94	2c
Shirt, man's dress shirt		32.10	12/94	2c
Undervest, boy's size 10-14, cotton	3	5.48	12/94	2c
Communications				
Long-distance telephone rate, day, addl. min., 1-10 mi.	min.	0.08	12/93	9s
Long-distance telephone rate, day, initial min., 1-10 mi.	min.	0.10	12/93	9s
Newspaper subscription, dly. and Sun. delivery	month	10.95	12/94	2c
Phone line, single, business, field visit	inst	71.90	12/93	9s
Phone line, single, business, no field visit	inst	57.30	12/93	9s
Phone line, single, residence, field visit	inst	52.95	12/93	9s
Phone line, single, residence, no field visit	inst	38.35	12/93	9s
Telephone bill, family of four	month	17.82	12/94	2c
Telephone service, expenditures	year	616	91	81r
Telephone, business, addl. line, touch tone	month	1.75	10/91	25c
Telephone, business, connection charges, touch tone	inst	69.31	10/91	25c
Telephone, business, key system line, touch tone	month	31.65	10/91	25c
Telephone, business, PBX line, touch tone	month	32.47	10/91	25c
Telephone, business, single ln., touch tone	month	27.55	10/91	25c
Telephone, business, touch tone, inside wiring maintenance plan	month	2.25	10/91	25c
Telephone, residential, flat rate	mo.	9.10	12/93	8c
Education				
Board, 4-year private college/university	year	2084	8/94	80s
Board, 4-year public college/university	year	1675	8/94	80s
Education, total expenditures	year	319	91	81r
Room, 4-year private college/university	year	1840	8/94	80s
Room, 4-year public college/university	year	1756	8/94	80s
Total cost, 4-year private college/university	year	11876	8/94	80s
Total cost, 4-year public college/university	year	4935	8/94	80s
Tuition, 2-year public college/university, in-state	year	625	8/94	80s
Tuition, 4-year private college/university, in-state	year	7952	8/94	80s
Tuition, 4-year public college/university, in-state	year	1503	8/94	80s
Energy and Fuels				
Energy, combined forms, 1800 sq. ft.	mo.	123.38	12/94	2c
Energy, exc. electricity, 1800 sq. ft.	mo.	23.44	12/94	2c
Fuel oil and other fuels, expenditures	year	56	91	81r
Gas, natural, expenditures	year	150	91	81r
Gas, reg unlead, taxes inc., cash, self-service	gal	1.05	12/94	2c
Gasoline and motor oil purchased	year	1152	91	81r
Gasoline, unleaded midgrade	gallon	1.21	4/93	82r
Gasoline, unleaded premium	gallon	1.30	4/93	82r
Gasoline, unleaded regular	gallon	1.10	4/93	82r

Corpus Christi, TX - continued

Item	Per	Value	Date	Ref.
Entertainment				
Bowling, evening rate	game	2.55	12/94	2c
Concert ticket, Pearl Jam group	perf	20.00	94	50r
Entertainment, total expenditures	year	1266	91	81r
Fees and admissions, expenditures	year	306	91	81r
Monopoly game, Parker Brothers', No. 9	game	11.81	12/94	2c
Movie	adm	5.44	12/94	2c
Pets, toys, playground equipment, expenditures	year	271	91	81r
Reading, expenditures	year	131	91	81r
Televisions, radios, and sound equipment, expenditures	year	439	91	81r
Tennis balls, yellow, Wilson or Penn, 3	can	2.28	12/94	2c
Funerals				
Burial, immediate, container provided by funeral home		1574.60	1/95	54r
Cards, acknowledgment		22.24	1/95	54r
Casket, minimum alternative		239.41	1/95	54r
Cosmetology, hair care, etc.		91.04	1/95	54r
Cremation, direct, container provided by funeral home		1085.15	1/95	54r
Embalming		281.30	1/95	54r
Funeral, funeral home		323.04	1/95	54r
Funeral, other facility		327.58	1/95	54r
Graveside service		355.19	1/95	54r
Hearse, local		141.89	1/95	54r
Limousine, local		99.40	1/95	54r
Memorial service		284.67	1/95	54r
Service charge, professional, nondeclinable		904.06	1/95	54r
Visitation and viewing		187.04	1/95	54r
Groceries				
Groceries, ACCRA Index		81.90	12/94	2c
Apples, Red Delicious	lb.	0.73	12/94	82r
Baby food, strained vegetables, lowest price	4-4.5 oz.	0.23	12/94	2c
Bacon, sliced	lb.	1.67	12/94	82r
Bananas	lb.	0.38	12/94	2c
Bananas	lb.	0.42	12/94	82r
Beef or hamburger, ground	lb.	1.07	12/94	2c
Beef purchases	year	213	91	81r
Beverage purchases, alcoholic	year	249	91	81r
Beverage purchases, nonalcoholic	year	207	91	81r
Bologna, all beef or mixed	lb.	2.27	12/94	82r
Bread, white	24-oz.	0.51	12/94	2c
Bread, white, pan	lb.	0.68	12/94	82r
Cabbage	lb.	0.42	12/94	82r
Carrots, short trimmed and topped	lb.	0.53	12/94	82r
Cereals and bakery products purchases	year	345	91	81r
Cereals and cereals products purchases	year	127	91	81r
Cheddar cheese, natural	lb.	3.58	12/94	82r
Cheese, Kraft grated Parmesan	8-oz.	2.99	12/94	2c
Chicken breast, bone-in	lb.	1.71	12/94	82r
Chicken, fresh, whole	lb.	0.78	12/94	82r
Chicken, whole fryer	lb.	0.51	12/94	2c
Chuck roast, USDA choice, boneless	lb.	2.26	12/94	82r
Cigarettes, Winston, Kings	carton	17.49	12/94	2c
Coffee, vacuum-packed	13 oz.	2.98	12/94	2c
Corn Flakes, Kellogg's or Post Toasties	18 oz.	2.03	12/94	2c
Corn, frozen, whole kernel, lowest price	10 oz.	0.64	12/94	2c
Crackers, soda, salted	lb.	1.27	12/94	82r
Cucumbers	lb.	0.65	12/94	82r
Dairy products (other) purchases	year	141	91	81r
Eggs, Grade A large	dozen	0.65	12/94	2c
Eggs, Grade A large	dozen	0.87	12/94	82r
Fish and seafood purchases	year	72	91	81r
Flour, white, all purpose	lb.	0.23	12/94	82r
Food purchases, food eaten at home	year	2381	91	81r
Foods purchased away from home, not prepared by consumer	year	1696	91	81r
Frankfurters, all meat or all beef	lb.	1.74	12/94	82r
Fruits and vegetables purchases	year	380	91	81r
Grapefruit	lb.	0.45	12/94	82r

Values are in dollars or fractions of dollars. In the column headed *Ref*, references are shown to sources. Each reference is followed by a letter. These refer to the geographical level for which data were reported: s = State, r = Region, and c = City or metro. The abbreviation *ex* is used to mean *except* or *excluding*; *exp* stands for expenditures. For other abbreviations and further explanations, please see the Introduction.

Corpus Christi, TX - continued

Item	Per	Value	Date	Ref.
Groceries				
Grapes, Thompson seedless	lb.	2.30	12/94	82r
Ground beef, 100% beef	lb.	1.37	12/94	82r
Ground chuck, 100% beef	lb.	1.97	12/94	82r
Ham, boneless, exc. canned	lb.	2.54	12/94	82r
Ice cream, prepackaged, bulk, regular	1/2 gal.	2.47	12/94	82r
Lemons	lb.	1.02	12/94	82r
Lettuce, iceberg	lb.	0.96	12/94	82r
Lettuce, iceberg	head	0.94	12/94	2c
Margarine, Blue Bonnet or Parkay cubes	lb.	0.50	12/94	2c
Margarine, stick	lb.	0.77	12/94	82r
Meats, poultry, fish, and eggs purchases	year	655	91	81r
Milk and cream (fresh) purchases	year	130	91	81r
Milk, whole	1/2 gal.	1.08	12/94	2c
Orange juice, frozen concentrate 12-oz. can	16 oz.	1.36	12/94	82r
Orange juice, Minute Maid frozen	12-oz.	1.04	12/94	2c
Oranges, Navel	lb.	0.54	12/94	82r
Peaches, halves or slices, Hunt's, Del Monte, or Libby's	29-oz.	1.16	12/94	2c
Pears, Anjou	lb.	0.81	12/94	82r
Peas, sweet, Del Monte or Green Giant	15-17 oz.	0.33	12/94	2c
Pork chops, center cut, bone-in	lb.	3.07	12/94	82r
Pork purchases	year	142	91	81r
Potato chips	16-oz.	3.15	12/94	82r
Potatoes, frozen, French fried	lb.	0.82	12/94	82r
Potatoes, white	lb.	0.34	12/94	82r
Potatoes, white or red	10-lb. sack	2.12	12/94	2c
Rice, white, long grain, uncooked	lb.	0.48	12/94	82r
Round roast, USDA choice, boneless	lb.	2.91	12/94	82r
Sausage, fresh	lb.	1.82	12/94	82r
Sausage, Jimmy Dean, 100% pork	lb.	2.41	12/94	2c
Shortening, vegetable oil blends	lb.	0.75	12/94	82r
Shortening, vegetable, Crisco	3-lb.	2.23	12/94	2c
Soft drink, Coca Cola, ex deposit	2 lit	0.92	12/94	2c
Spaghetti and macaroni	lb.	0.87	12/94	82r
Steak, rib eye, USDA choice, boneless	lb.	6.85	12/94	82r
Steak, round, graded & ungraded, exc. USDA prime & choice	lb.	2.96	12/94	82r
Steak, round, USDA choice, boneless	lb.	3.17	12/94	82r
Steak, sirloin, USDA choice, boneless	lb.	4.12	12/94	82r
Steak, t-bone	lb.	2.64	12/94	2c
Steak, T-bone, USDA choice, bone-in	lb.	5.63	12/94	82r
Sugar and other sweets, eaten at home, expenditures	year	93	91	81r
Sugar, cane or beet	4 lbs.	1.37	12/94	2c
Sugar, white, all sizes	lb.	0.39	12/94	82r
Tobacco products and smoking supplies, total expenditures	year	286	91	81r
Tomatoes, field grown	lb.	1.36	12/94	82r
Tomatoes, Hunt's or Del Monte	14.5 oz.	0.51	12/94	2c
Tuna, chunk, light	lb.	1.94	12/94	82r
Tuna, chunk, light, oil-packed	6.125-6.5 oz.	0.62	12/94	2c
Turkey, frozen, whole	lb.	0.96	12/94	82r
Yogurt, natural, fruit flavored	8 oz.	0.58	12/94	82r
Goods and Services				
Miscellaneous goods and services, ACCRA Index		100.80	12/94	2c
Health Care				
Health care, ACCRA Index		95.00	12/94	2c
Adenosine, emergency room	treat	100.00	95	23r
Antibiotic ointment, Polysporin	1.5 oz.	3.67	12/94	2c
Bladder tap, superpubic, infant, emergency room	treat	119.00	95	23r
Blood analysis, emergency room	treat	25.00	95	23r
Blood tests, abdominal pain, emergency room	treat	25.00	95	23r

Corpus Christi, TX - continued

Item	Per	Value	Date	Ref.
Health Care - continued				
Burn dressing, emergency room	treat	266.00	95	23r
Cardiology interpretation, emergency room	treat	26.00	95	23r
Chest X-ray, emergency room	treat	78.00	95	23r
Childbirth, Cesarean delivery, hospital charge	birth	5462.00	12/91	69r
Childbirth, Cesarean delivery, physician charge	birth	2228.00	12/91	69r
Childbirth, normal delivery, hospital charge	birth	2943.00	12/91	69r
Childbirth, normal delivery, physician charge	birth	1619.00	12/91	69r
Defibrillation pads, emergency room	treat	6.00	95	23r
Dentist's fee, adult teeth cleaning and periodic oral exam	visit	48.40	12/94	2c
Doctor's fee, routine exam, established patient	visit	42.00	12/94	2c
Drugs, expenditures	year	297	91	81r
Gastric tube insertion, nasal, emergency room	treat	25.00	95	23r
Health care, total expenditures	year	1600	91	81r
Health insurance expenditures	year	637	91	81r
Heart monitor, emergency room	treat	40.00	95	23r
Hospital care, semiprivate room	day	335.00	12/94	2c
Insurance premium, family medical care	month	389.25	1/95	41s
Intravenous fluids, emergency room	treat	130.00	95	23r
Intravenous fluids, emergency room	liter	26.00	95	23r
Intravenous line, central, emergency room	treat	342.00	95	23r
Liver function tests, abdominal pain, emergency room	treat	26.00	95	23r
Medical care charges, total, emergency room, third-degree burns	treat	2101.00	95	23r
Medical care charges, total, emergency, infant with fever	treat	628.00	95	23r
Medical services expenditures	year	573	91	81r
Medical supplies expenditures	year	93	91	81r
Morphine, emergency room	treat	34.00	95	23r
Nursing care and facilities charges, emergency room	treat	252.00	95	23r
Nursing care and facilities charges, emergency, infant with fever	treat	252.00	95	23r
Nursing care and facilities charges, emergency, third-degree burns	treat	861.00	95	23r
Physician's charges, emergency, infant with fever	treat	212.00	95	23r
Physician's charges, emergency, third-degree burns	treat	372.00	95	23r
Physician's fee, emergency room	treat	372.00	95	23r
Physician's fee, general practitioner	visit	51.20	12/93	60r
Surgery, open-heart	proc	42374.00	1/93	14r
Ultrasound, abdominal, emergency room	treat	276.00	95	23r
Urinalysis, emergency room	treat	20.00	95	23r
Urinalysis, infant, emergency room	treat	20.00	95	23r
X-rays, emergency room	treat	78.00	95	23r
Household Goods				
Appl. repair, service call, wash mach	min. lab. chg.	34.50	12/94	2c
Floor coverings, expenditures	year	48	91	81r
Furniture, expenditures	year	280	91	81r
Household equipment, misc. expenditures	year	342	91	81r
Household expenditures, miscellaneous	year	256	91	81r
Household furnishings and equipment, expenditures	year	988	91	81r
Household operations expenditures	year	468	91	81r
Household textiles, expenditures	year	95	91	81r
Housekeeping supplies, expenditures	year	380	91	81r
Laundry and cleaning supplies, expenditures	year	109	91	81r
Laundry detergent, Tide Ultra, Bold, or Cheer	42 oz.	2.85	12/94	2c
Postage and stationery, expenditures	year	105	91	81r
Tissues, facial, Kleenex brand	175	0.81	12/94	2c

Values are in dollars or fractions of dollars. In the column headed *Ref*, references are shown to sources. Each reference is followed by a letter. These refer to the geographical level for which data were reported: s = State, r = Region, and c = City or metro. The abbreviation *ex* is used to mean *except* or *excluding*; *exp* stands for expenditures. For other abbreviations and further explanations, please see the Introduction.

Corpus Christi, TX - continued

Item	Per	Value	Date	Ref.
Housing				
Housing, ACCRA Index		88.40	12/94	2c
Add garage/carport		6,980	3/95	74r
Add room(s)		11,403	3/95	74r
Apartment condominium or co-op, median	unit	68600	12/94	62r
Dwellings (owned), expenditures	year	2428	91	81r
Enclose porch/patio/breezeway		4,572	3/95	74r
Finish room in basement/attic		3,794	3/95	74r
Home, existing, single-family, median	unit	120200	12/94	62r
Home, existing, single-family, median	unit	75.10	12/94	62c
House payment, principal and interest, 25% down payment	mo.	666	12/94	2c
House, 1800 sq ft, 8000 sq ft lot, new, urban, utilities	total	107600	12/94	2c
Maintenance, repairs, insurance, and other housing expenditures	year	531	91	81r
Mortgage interest and charges expenditures	year	1506	91	81r
Mtge. rate, incl. points and orig. fee, 30-year conv. fixed or ARM	mo.	9.28	12/94	2c
Princ. & int., mortgage, median-price exist. sing.-family home	mo.	540	12/94	62r
Property taxes expenditures	year	391	91	81r
Redesign, restructure more than half of home's interior		17,641	3/95	74r
Rent, apartment, 2 br., 1 1/2-2 baths, unfurnished, 950 sq ft, water	mo.	501	12/94	2c
Rental units expenditures	year	1264	91	81r
Insurance and Pensions				
Auto insurance, private passenger	year	785.78	12/94	71s
Insurance and pensions, personal, expenditures	year	2395	91	81r
Insurance, life and other personal, expenditures	year	368	91	81r
Pensions and Social Security, expenditures	year	2027	91	81r
Personal Goods				
Shampoo, Alberto VO5	15-oz.	0.87	12/94	2c
Toothpaste, Crest or Colgate	6-7 oz.	1.55	12/94	2c
Personal Services				
Dry cleaning, man's 2-pc. suit		6.75	12/94	2c
Haircut, man's barbershop, no styling		7.80	12/94	2c
Haircut, woman's shampoo, trim, blow-dry		25.00	12/94	2c
Personal services expenditures	year	212	91	81r
Restaurant Food				
Chicken, fried, thigh and drumstick		2.29	12/94	2c
Dining expenditures, family	week	33.83	94	73r
Hamburger with cheese	1/4 lb.	1.90	12/94	2c
Pizza, Pizza Hut or Pizza Inn	12-13 in.	8.39	12/94	2c
Taxes				
Tax, cigarettes	year	584.00	10/93	43s
Taxes, Federal income, expenditures	year	2275	91	81r
Taxes, personal, expenditures	year	2715	91	81r
Taxes, State and local income, expenditures	year	365	91	81r
Transportation				
Transportation, ACCRA Index		95.10	12/94	2c
Bus fare, one-way	trip	0.50	12/95	1c
Cars and trucks purchased, new	year	1306	91	81r
Cars and trucks purchased, used	year	942	91	81r
Driver's learning permit fee	perm	5.00	1/94	84s
Driver's license fee	orig	16.00	1/94	84s
Driver's license fee, duplicate	lic	10.00	1/94	84s
Driver's license reinstatement fee, min.	susp	50.00	1/94	85s
Driver's license renewal fee	renew	16.00	1/94	84s
Identification card, nondriver	card	10.00	1/94	83s
Motorcycle learning permit fee	perm	5.00	1/94	84s
Motorcycle license fee	orig	16.00	1/94	84s
Motorcycle license fee, duplicate	lic	10.00	1/94	84s
Motorcycle license renewal fee	renew	21.00	1/94	84s
Public transportation expenditures	year	249	91	81r
Tire balance, computer or spin bal., front	wheel	6.62	12/94	2c

Corpus Christi, TX - continued

Item	Per	Value	Date	Ref.
Transportation - continued				
Transportation expenditures, total	year	5307	91	81r
Vehicle finance charges	year	346	91	81r
Vehicle insurance expenditures	year	544	91	81r
Vehicle maintenance and repairs expenditures	year	600	91	81r
Vehicle purchases	year	2275	91	81r
Vehicle rental, leases, licenses, etc. expenditures	year	141	91	81r
Vehicles purchased, other than cars and trucks	year	27	91	81r
Utilities				
Utilities, ACCRA Index		107.40	12/94	2c
Electricity expenditures	year	950	91	81r
Electricity, (part.), other, 1800 sq. ft., new home	mo.	99.94	12/94	2c
Electricity, summer, 250 KWh	month	27.12	8/93	64c
Electricity, summer, 500 KWh	month	46.97	8/93	64c
Electricity, summer, 750 KWh	month	66.82	8/93	64c
Electricity, summer, 1000 KWh	month	86.66	8/93	64c
Utilities, fuels, and public services, total expenditures	year	2000	91	81r
Water and other public services, expenditures	year	227	91	81r
Weddings				
Bridal attendants' gowns	event	750	10/93	76r
Bridal gown	event	852	10/93	76r
Bridal headpiece and veil	event	167	10/93	76r
Bride's wedding band	event	708	10/93	76r
Clergy	event	224	10/93	76r
Engagement ring	event	2756	10/93	76r
Flowers	event	863	10/93	76r
Formal wear for groom	event	106	10/93	76r
Groom's attendants' formal wear	event	530	10/93	76r
Groom's wedding band	event	402	10/93	76r
Music	event	600	10/93	76r
Photography	event	1088	10/93	76r
Shoes for bride	event	50	10/93	76r
Videography	event	483	10/93	76r
Wedding invitations and announcements	event	342	10/93	76r
Wedding reception	event	7000	10/93	76r

Cortland, NY

Item	Per	Value	Date	Ref.
Composite, ACCRA index		109.40	12/94	2c
Alcoholic Beverages				
Beer, Miller Lite, Bud, 12-oz., ex deposit	6	3.93	12/94	2c
J & B Scotch	750-ml.	17.77	12/94	2c
Wine, Gallo Chablis blanc	1.5-lit	5.76	12/94	2c
Clothing				
Jeans, man's denim		32.61	12/94	2c
Shirt, man's dress shirt		33.50	12/94	2c
Undervest, boy's size 10-14, cotton	3	3.80	12/94	2c
Communications				
Newspaper subscription, dly. and Sun. delivery	month	15.65	12/94	2c
Telephone bill, family of four	month	26.08	12/94	2c
Telephone, residential, flat rate	mo.	15.28	12/93	8c
Energy and Fuels				
Energy, combined forms, 1800 sq. ft.	mo.	152.22	12/94	2c
Energy, exc. electricity, 1800 sq. ft.	mo.	65.86	12/94	2c
Gas, reg unlead, taxes inc., cash, self-service	gal	1.19	12/94	2c
Entertainment				
Bowling, evening rate	game	1.82	12/94	2c
Monopoly game, Parker Brothers', No. 9	game	11.93	12/94	2c
Movie	adm	5.50	12/94	2c
Tennis balls, yellow, Wilson or Penn, 3	can	2.01	12/94	2c

Values are in dollars or fractions of dollars. In the column headed *Ref*, references are shown to sources. Each reference is followed by a letter. These refer to the geographical level for which data were reported: s=State, r=Region, and c=City or metro. The abbreviation *ex* is used to mean *except* or *excluding*; *exp* stands for expenditures. For other abbreviations and further explanations, please see the Introduction.

Cortland, NY - continued

Item	Per	Value	Date	Ref.
Groceries				
Groceries, ACCRA Index		104.90	12/94	2c
Baby food, strained vegetables, lowest price	4-4.5 oz.	0.40	12/94	2c
Bananas	lb.	0.59	12/94	2c
Beef or hamburger, ground	lb.	1.99	12/94	2c
Bread, white	24-oz.	0.47	12/94	2c
Cheese, Kraft grated Parmesan	8-oz.	3.19	12/94	2c
Chicken, whole fryer	lb.	0.72	12/94	2c
Cigarettes, Winston, Kings	carton	17.12	12/94	2c
Coffee, vacuum-packed	13 oz.	3.46	12/94	2c
Corn Flakes, Kellogg's or Post Toasties	18 oz.	2.29	12/94	2c
Corn, frozen, whole kernel, lowest price	10 oz.	0.75	12/94	2c
Eggs, Grade A large	dozen	0.76	12/94	2c
Lettuce, iceberg	head	0.59	12/94	2c
Margarine, Blue Bonnet or Parkay cubes	lb.	0.59	12/94	2c
Milk, whole	1/2 gal.	1.26	12/94	2c
Orange juice, Minute Maid frozen	12-oz.	1.59	12/94	2c
Peaches, halves or slices, Hunt's, Del Monte, or Libby's	29-oz.	1.66	12/94	2c
Peas, sweet, Del Monte or Green Giant	15-17 oz.	0.70	12/94	2c
Potatoes, white or red	10-lb. sack	1.69	12/94	2c
Sausage, Jimmy Dean, 100% pork	lb.	2.72	12/94	2c
Shortening, vegetable, Crisco	3-lb.	2.65	12/94	2c
Soft drink, Coca Cola, ex deposit	2 lit	1.43	12/94	2c
Steak, t-bone	lb.	5.99	12/94	2c
Sugar, cane or beet	4 lbs.	1.65	12/94	2c
Tomatoes, Hunt's or Del Monte	14.5 oz.	0.90	12/94	2c
Tuna, chunk, light, oil-packed	6.125-6.5 oz.	0.80	12/94	2c
Goods and Services				
Miscellaneous goods and services, ACCRA Index		101.30	12/94	2c
Health Care				
Health care, ACCRA Index		83.80	12/94	2c
Antibiotic ointment, Polysporin	1.5 oz.	3.76	12/94	2c
Dentist's fee, adult teeth cleaning and periodic oral exam	visit	47.20	12/94	2c
Doctor's fee, routine exam, established patient	visit	36.00	12/94	2c
Hospital care, semiprivate room	day	225.00	12/94	2c
Household Goods				
Appl. repair, service call, wash mach	min. lab. chg.	28.33	12/94	2c
Laundry detergent, Tide Ultra, Bold, or Cheer	42 oz.	4.16	12/94	2c
Tissues, facial, Kleenex brand	175	1.19	12/94	2c
Housing				
Housing, ACCRA Index		121.30	12/94	2c
House payment, principal and interest, 25% down payment	mo.	965	12/94	2c
House, 1800 sq ft, 8000 sq ft lot, new, urban, utilities	total	154900	12/94	2c
Mtge. rate, incl. points and orig. fee, 30-year conv. fixed or ARM	mo.	9.36	12/94	2c
Rent, apartment, 2 br., 1 1/2-2 baths, unfurnished, 950 sq ft, water	mo.	537	12/94	2c
Personal Goods				
Shampoo, Alberto VO5	15-oz.	1.10	12/94	2c
Toothpaste, Crest or Colgate	6-7 oz.	1.87	12/94	2c
Personal Services				
Dry cleaning, man's 2-pc. suit		8.08	12/94	2c
Haircut, man's barbershop, no styling		7.10	12/94	2c
Haircut, woman's shampoo, trim, blow-dry		13.50	12/94	2c

Cortland, NY - continued

Item	Per	Value	Date	Ref.
Restaurant Food				
Chicken, fried, thigh and drumstick		2.49	12/94	2c
Hamburger with cheese	1/4 lb.	1.94	12/94	2c
Pizza, Pizza Hut or Pizza Inn	12-13 in.	7.49	12/94	2c
Transportation				
Transportation, ACCRA Index		104.40	12/94	2c
Bus fare, up to 10 miles	one-way	1.00	12/94	2c
Tire balance, computer or spin bal., front	wheel	6.90	12/94	2c
Utilities				
Utilities, ACCRA Index		135.40	12/94	2c
Electricity, (part.), other, 1800 sq. ft., new home	mo.	86.36	12/94	2c

Covington, KY

Item	Per	Value	Date	Ref.
Composite, ACCRA index		91.50	12/94	2c
Alcoholic Beverages				
Beer, Miller Lite, Bud, 12-oz., ex deposit	6	3.59	12/94	2c
J & B Scotch	750-ml.	15.39	12/94	2c
Wine, Gallo Chablis blanc	1.5-lit	5.39	12/94	2c
Clothing				
Jeans, man's denim		25.39	12/94	2c
Shirt, man's dress shirt		23.66	12/94	2c
Undervest, boy's size 10-14, cotton	3	3.79	12/94	2c
Communications				
Newspaper subscription, dly. and Sun. delivery	month	16.00	12/94	2c
Telephone bill, family of four	month	20.38	12/94	2c
Energy and Fuels				
Energy, combined forms, 1800 sq. ft.	mo.	109.65	12/94	2c
Energy, exc. electricity, 1800 sq. ft.	mo.	32.44	12/94	2c
Gas, reg unlead, taxes inc., cash, self-service	gal	0.98	12/94	2c
Entertainment				
Bowling, evening rate	game	2.05	12/94	2c
Monopoly game, Parker Brothers', No. 9	game	9.98	12/94	2c
Movie	adm	6.55	12/94	2c
Tennis balls, yellow, Wilson or Penn, 3	can	2.33	12/94	2c
Groceries				
Groceries, ACCRA Index		92.30	12/94	2c
Baby food, strained vegetables, lowest price	4-4.5 oz.	0.24	12/94	2c
Bananas	lb.	0.40	12/94	2c
Beef or hamburger, ground	lb.	1.12	12/94	2c
Bread, white	24-oz.	0.57	12/94	2c
Cheese, Kraft grated Parmesan	8-oz.	3.15	12/94	2c
Chicken, whole fryer	lb.	0.70	12/94	2c
Cigarettes, Winston, Kings	carton	12.86	12/94	2c
Coffee, vacuum-packed	13 oz.	3.76	12/94	2c
Corn Flakes, Kellogg's or Post Toasties	18 oz.	2.25	12/94	2c
Corn, frozen, whole kernel, lowest price	10 oz.	0.65	12/94	2c
Eggs, Grade A large	dozen	0.76	12/94	2c
Lettuce, iceberg	head	0.90	12/94	2c
Margarine, Blue Bonnet or Parkay cubes	lb.	0.59	12/94	2c
Milk, whole	1/2 gal.	1.47	12/94	2c
Orange juice, Minute Maid frozen	12-oz.	1.22	12/94	2c
Peaches, halves or slices, Hunt's, Del Monte, or Libby's	29-oz.	1.46	12/94	2c
Peas, sweet, Del Monte or Green Giant	15-17 oz.	0.58	12/94	2c
Potatoes, white or red	10-lb. sack	2.23	12/94	2c
Sausage, Jimmy Dean, 100% pork	lb.	2.59	12/94	2c
Shortening, vegetable, Crisco	3-lb.	2.59	12/94	2c

Values are in dollars or fractions of dollars. In the column headed *Ref*, references are shown to sources. Each reference is followed by a letter. These refer to the geographical level for which data were reported: s=State, r=Region, and c=City or metro. The abbreviation *ex* is used to mean *except* or *excluding*; *exp* stands for *expenditures*. For other abbreviations and further explanations, please see the Introduction.

Covington, KY - continued

Item	Per	Value	Date	Ref.
Groceries				
Soft drink, Coca Cola, ex deposit	2 lit	0.98	12/94	2c
Steak, t-bone	lb.	5.85	12/94	2c
Sugar, cane or beet	4 lbs.	1.41	12/94	2c
Tomatoes, Hunt's or Del Monte	14.5 oz.	0.76	12/94	2c
Tuna, chunk, light, oil-packed	6.125-6.5 oz.	0.72	12/94	2c
Goods and Services				
Miscellaneous goods and services, ACCRA Index		90.50	12/94	2c
Health Care				
Health care, ACCRA Index		100.80	12/94	2c
Antibiotic ointment, Polysporin	1.5 oz.	3.95	12/94	2c
Dentist's fee, adult teeth cleaning and periodic oral exam	visit	50.33	12/94	2c
Doctor's fee, routine exam, established patient	visit	44.20	12/94	2c
Hospital care, semiprivate room	day	370.17	12/94	2c
Household Goods				
Appl. repair, service call, wash mach	min. lab. chg.	22.49	12/94	2c
Laundry detergent, Tide Ultra, Bold, or Cheer	42 oz.	3.40	12/94	2c
Tissues, facial, Kleenex brand	175	0.92	12/94	2c
Housing				
Housing, ACCRA Index		88.70	12/94	2c
House payment, principal and interest, 25% down payment	mo.	656	12/94	2c
House, 1800 sq ft, 8000 sq ft lot, new, urban, utilities	total	108667	12/94	2c
Mtge. rate, incl. points and orig. fee, 30-year conv. fixed or ARM	mo.	9.00	12/94	2c
Rent, apartment, 2 br., 1 1/2-2 baths, unfurnished, 950 sq ft, water	mo.	537	12/94	2c
Personal Goods				
Shampoo, Alberto VO5	15-oz.	1.03	12/94	2c
Toothpaste, Crest or Colgate	6-7 oz.	1.72	12/94	2c
Personal Services				
Dry cleaning, man's 2-pc. suit		5.80	12/94	2c
Haircut, man's barbershop, no styling		7.20	12/94	2c
Haircut, woman's shampoo, trim, blow-dry		14.50	12/94	2c
Restaurant Food				
Chicken, fried, thigh and drumstick		2.02	12/94	2c
Hamburger with cheese	1/4 lb.	1.75	12/94	2c
Pizza, Pizza Hut or Pizza Inn	12-13 in.	7.59	12/94	2c
Transportation				
Transportation, ACCRA Index		89.60	12/94	2c
Bus fare, up to 10 miles	one-way	0.75	12/94	2c
Tire balance, computer or spin bal., front	wheel	6.50	12/94	2c
Utilities				
Utilities, ACCRA Index		98.60	12/94	2c
Electricity, (part.), other, 1800 sq. ft., new home	mo.	77.21	12/94	2c
Electricity, summer, 250 KWh	month	19.98	8/93	64c
Electricity, summer, 500 KWh	month	36.23	8/93	64c
Electricity, summer, 750 KWh	month	52.48	8/93	64c
Electricity, summer, 1000 KWh	month	68.72	8/93	64c

Cullman County, AL

Item	Per	Value	Date	Ref.
Composite, ACCRA index		91.60	12/94	2c
Alcoholic Beverages				
Beer, Miller Lite, Bud, 12-oz., ex deposit	6	4.12	12/94	2c
J & B Scotch	750-ml.	20.99	12/94	2c
Wine, Gallo Chablis blanc	1.5-lit	5.54	12/94	2c
Clothing				
Jeans, man's denim		31.79	12/94	2c
Shirt, man's dress shirt		32.19	12/94	2c
Undervest, boy's size 10-14, cotton	3	3.95	12/94	2c
Communications				
Newspaper subscription, dly. and Sun. delivery	month	10.30	12/94	2c
Telephone bill, family of four	month	23.44	12/94	2c
Telephone, residential, flat rate	mo.	16.40	12/93	8c
Energy and Fuels				
Energy, combined forms, 1800 sq. ft.	mo.	107.88	12/94	2c
Gas, reg unlead, taxes inc., cash, self-service	gal	1.20	12/94	2c
Entertainment				
Bowling, evening rate	game	2.50	12/94	2c
Monopoly game, Parker Brothers', No. 9	game	8.97	12/94	2c
Movie	adm	5.25	12/94	2c
Tennis balls, yellow, Wilson or Penn, 3	can	2.60	12/94	2c
Groceries				
Groceries, ACCRA Index		96.50	12/94	2c
Baby food, strained vegetables, lowest price	4-4.5 oz.	0.35	12/94	2c
Bananas	lb.	0.42	12/94	2c
Beef or hamburger, ground	lb.	1.51	12/94	2c
Bread, white	24-oz.	0.71	12/94	2c
Cheese, Kraft grated Parmesan	8-oz.	3.27	12/94	2c
Chicken, whole fryer	lb.	0.79	12/94	2c
Cigarettes, Winston, Kings	carton	14.49	12/94	2c
Coffee, vacuum-packed	13 oz.	2.87	12/94	2c
Corn Flakes, Kellogg's or Post Toasties	18 oz.	2.17	12/94	2c
Corn, frozen, whole kernel, lowest price	10 oz.	0.65	12/94	2c
Eggs, Grade A large	dozen	0.73	12/94	2c
Lettuce, iceberg	head	0.98	12/94	2c
Margarine, Blue Bonnet or Parkay cubes	lb.	0.57	12/94	2c
Milk, whole	1/2 gal.	1.51	12/94	2c
Orange juice, Minute Maid frozen	12-oz.	1.11	12/94	2c
Peaches, halves or slices, Hunt's, Del Monte, or Libby's	29-oz.	1.21	12/94	2c
Peas, sweet, Del Monte or Green Giant	15-17 oz.	0.51	12/94	2c
Potatoes, white or red	10-lb. sack	3.19	12/94	2c
Sausage, Jimmy Dean, 100% pork	lb.	2.27	12/94	2c
Shortening, vegetable, Crisco	3-lb.	2.46	12/94	2c
Soft drink, Coca Cola, ex deposit	2 lit	1.19	12/94	2c
Steak, t-bone	lb.	5.32	12/94	2c
Sugar, cane or beet	4 lbs.	1.36	12/94	2c
Tomatoes, Hunt's or Del Monte	14.5 oz.	0.62	12/94	2c
Tuna, chunk, light, oil-packed	6.125-6.5 oz.	0.65	12/94	2c
Goods and Services				
Miscellaneous goods and services, ACCRA Index		101.80	12/94	2c
Health Care				
Health care, ACCRA Index		85.30	12/94	2c
Antibiotic ointment, Polysporin	1.5 oz.	3.67	12/94	2c
Dentist's fee, adult teeth cleaning and periodic oral exam	visit	43.75	12/94	2c
Doctor's fee, routine exam, established patient	visit	39.83	12/94	2c
Hospital care, semiprivate room	day	241.00	12/94	2c

Values are in dollars or fractions of dollars. In the column headed *Ref*, references are shown to sources. Each reference is followed by a letter. These refer to the geographical level for which data were reported: s=State, r=Region, and c=City or metro. The abbreviation *ex* is used to mean *except* or *excluding*; *exp* stands for *expenditures*. For other abbreviations and further explanations, please see the Introduction.

Cullman County, AL - continued

Item	Per	Value	Date	Ref.
Household Goods				
Appl. repair, service call, wash mach	min. lab. chg.	31.60	12/94	2c
Laundry detergent, Tide Ultra, Bold, or Cheer	42 oz.	3.28	12/94	2c
Tissues, facial, Kleenex brand	175	1.00	12/94	2c
Housing				
Housing, ACCRA Index		73.10	12/94	2c
House payment, principal and interest, 25% down payment	mo.	561	12/94	2c
House, 1800 sq ft, 8000 sq ft lot, new, urban, utilities	total	90800	12/94	2c
Mtge. rate, incl. points and orig. fee, 30-year conv. fixed or ARM	mo.	9.27	12/94	2c
Personal Goods				
Shampoo, Alberto VO5	15-oz.	1.00	12/94	2c
Toothpaste, Crest or Colgate	6-7 oz.	2.12	12/94	2c
Personal Services				
Dry cleaning, man's 2-pc. suit		5.67	12/94	2c
Haircut, man's barbershop, no styling		7.67	12/94	2c
Haircut, woman's shampoo, trim, blow-dry		15.33	12/94	2c
Restaurant Food				
Chicken, fried, thigh and drumstick		1.99	12/94	2c
Hamburger with cheese	1/4 lb.	1.95	12/94	2c
Pizza, Pizza Hut or Pizza Inn	12-13 in.	9.70	12/94	2c
Transportation				
Transportation, ACCRA Index		100.30	12/94	2c
Tire balance, computer or spin bal., front	wheel	6.21	12/94	2c
Utilities				
Utilities, ACCRA Index		99.40	12/94	2c
Electricity, 1800 sq. ft., new home	mo.	107.88	12/94	2c

Cumberland, MD

Item	Per	Value	Date	Ref.
Composite, ACCRA index		101.00	12/94	2c
Alcoholic Beverages				
Beer, Miller Lite, Bud, 12-oz., ex deposit	6	4.35	12/94	2c
J & B Scotch	750-ml.	15.79	12/94	2c
Wine, Gallo Chablis blanc	1.5-lit	5.34	12/94	2c
Clothing				
Jeans, man's denim		29.20	12/94	2c
Shirt, man's dress shirt		25.25	12/94	2c
Undervest, boy's size 10-14, cotton	3	4.33	12/94	2c
Communications				
Long-distance telephone rate, day, addl. min., 1-10 mi.	min.	0.10	12/93	9s
Long-distance telephone rate, day, initial min., 1-10 mi.	min.	0.21	12/93	9s
Newspaper subscription, dly. and Sun. delivery	month	11.23	12/94	2c
Phone line, single, business, field visit	inst	0.00	12/93	9s
Phone line, single, business, no field visit	inst	98.50	12/93	9s
Phone line, single, residence, field visit	inst	0.00	12/93	9s
Phone line, single, residence, no field visit	inst	48.00	12/93	9s
Telephone bill, family of four	month	26.83	12/94	2c
Telephone, residential, flat rate	mo.	15.24	12/93	8c
Education				
Board, 4-year private college/university	year	2878	8/94	80s
Board, 4-year public college/university	year	2464	8/94	80s
Room, 4-year private college/university	year	3231	8/94	80s
Room, 4-year public college/university	year	2587	8/94	80s
Total cost, 4-year private college/university	year	19012	8/94	80s
Total cost, 4-year public college/university	year	8171	8/94	80s

Cumberland, MD - continued

Item	Per	Value	Date	Ref.
Education - continued				
Tuition, 2-year public college/university, in-state	year	1676	8/94	80s
Tuition, 4-year private college/university, in-state	year	12903	8/94	80s
Tuition, 4-year public college/university, in-state	year	3120	8/94	80s
Energy and Fuels				
Energy, combined forms, 1800 sq. ft.	mo.	122.98	12/94	2c
Gas, cooking, 10 therms	month	14.57	2/94	65c
Gas, cooking, 30 therms	month	27.38	2/94	65c
Gas, cooking, 50 therms	month	40.19	2/94	65c
Gas, heating, winter, 100 therms	month	72.20	2/94	65c
Gas, heating, winter, average use	month	133.68	2/94	65c
Gas, reg unlead, taxes inc., cash, self-service	gal	1.17	12/94	2c
Entertainment				
Bowling, evening rate	game	1.95	12/94	2c
Monopoly game, Parker Brothers', No. 9	game	10.66	12/94	2c
Movie	adm	4.50	12/94	2c
Tennis balls, yellow, Wilson or Penn, 3	can	2.85	12/94	2c
Funerals				
Burial, immediate, container provided by funeral home		1370.36	1/95	54r
Cards, acknowledgment		14.83	1/95	54r
Casket, minimum alternative		192.52	1/95	54r
Cosmetology, hair care, etc.		102.27	1/95	54r
Cremation, direct, container provided by funeral home		1065.64	1/95	54r
Embalming		304.29	1/95	54r
Funeral, funeral home		287.83	1/95	54r
Funeral, other facility		284.14	1/95	54r
Graveside service		349.13	1/95	54r
Hearse, local		132.27	1/95	54r
Limousine, local		98.45	1/95	54r
Memorial service		270.59	1/95	54r
Service charge, professional, nondeclinable		933.59	1/95	54r
Visitation and viewing		225.83	1/95	54r
Groceries				
Groceries, ACCRA Index		98.70	12/94	2c
Baby food, strained vegetables, lowest price	4-4.5 oz.	0.38	12/94	2c
Bananas	lb.	0.40	12/94	2c
Beef or hamburger, ground	lb.	1.25	12/94	2c
Bread, white	24-oz.	0.69	12/94	2c
Cheese, Kraft grated Parmesan	8-oz.	3.28	12/94	2c
Chicken, whole fryer	lb.	0.87	12/94	2c
Cigarettes, Winston, Kings	carton	16.46	12/94	2c
Coffee, vacuum-packed	13 oz.	3.49	12/94	2c
Corn Flakes, Kellogg's or Post Toasties	18 oz.	2.53	12/94	2c
Corn, frozen, whole kernel, lowest price	10 oz.	0.70	12/94	2c
Eggs, Grade A large	dozen	0.84	12/94	2c
Lettuce, iceberg	head	0.86	12/94	2c
Margarine, Blue Bonnet or Parkay cubes	lb.	0.71	12/94	2c
Milk, whole	1/2 gal.	1.22	12/94	2c
Orange juice, Minute Maid frozen	12-oz.	1.35	12/94	2c
Peaches, halves or slices, Hunt's, Del Monte, or Libby's	29-oz.	1.35	12/94	2c
Peas, sweet, Del Monte or Green Giant	15-17 oz.	0.49	12/94	2c
Potatoes, white or red	10-lb. sack	2.04	12/94	2c
Sausage, Jimmy Dean, 100% pork	lb.	2.48	12/94	2c
Shortening, vegetable, Crisco	3-lb.	2.51	12/94	2c
Soft drink, Coca Cola, ex deposit	2 lit	0.85	12/94	2c
Steak, t-bone	lb.	4.73	12/94	2c
Sugar, cane or beet	4 lbs.	1.45	12/94	2c
Tomatoes, Hunt's or Del Monte	14.5 oz.	0.58	12/94	2c

Values are in dollars or fractions of dollars. In the column headed *Ref*, references are shown to sources. Each reference is followed by a letter. These refer to the geographical level for which data were reported: s = State, r = Region, and c = City or metro. The abbreviation *ex* is used to mean *except* or *excluding*; *exp* stands for expenditures. For other abbreviations and further explanations, please see the Introduction.

Cumberland, MD - continued

Item	Per	Value	Date	Ref.
Groceries				
Tuna, chunk, light, oil-packed	6.125-6.5 oz.	0.70	12/94	2c
Goods and Services				
Miscellaneous goods and services, ACCRA Index		96.30	12/94	2c
Health Care				
Health care, ACCRA Index		82.10	12/94	2c
Antibiotic ointment, Polysporin	1.5 oz.	3.68	12/94	2c
Delivery, uncomplicated, total charge	birth	6100	1/93	24s
Delivery, uncomplicated, vaginal, hospital charge	birth	2780	1/93	24s
Delivery, uncomplicated, vaginal, physician's charge	birth	3320	1/93	24s
Dentist's fee, adult teeth cleaning and periodic oral exam	visit	41.40	12/94	2c
Doctor's fee, routine exam, established patient	visit	36.20	12/94	2c
Hospital care, semiprivate room	day	267.75	12/94	2c
Insurance premium, family medical care	month	389.07	1/95	41s
Household Goods				
Appl. repair, service call, wash mach	min. lab. chg.	24.00	12/94	2c
Laundry detergent, Tide Ultra, Bold, or Cheer	42 oz.	3.59	12/94	2c
Tissues, facial, Kleenex brand	175	1.01	12/94	2c
Housing				
Housing, ACCRA Index		109.60	12/94	2c
House payment, principal and interest, 25% down payment	mo.	856	12/94	2c
House, 1800 sq ft, 8000 sq ft lot, new, urban, utilities	total	137000	12/94	2c
Mtge. rate, incl. points and orig. fee, 30-year conv. fixed or ARM	mo.	9.40	12/94	2c
Rent, apartment, 2 br., 1 1/2-2 baths, unfurnished, 950 sq ft, water	mo.	532	12/94	2c
Insurance and Pensions				
Auto insurance, private passenger	year	761.57	12/94	71s
Personal Goods				
Shampoo, Alberto VO5	15-oz.	1.28	12/94	2c
Toothpaste, Crest or Colgate	6-7 oz.	1.99	12/94	2c
Personal Services				
Dry cleaning, man's 2-pc. suit		5.96	12/94	2c
Haircut, man's barbershop, no styling		7.10	12/94	2c
Haircut, woman's shampoo, trim, blow-dry		18.80	12/94	2c
Restaurant Food				
Chicken, fried, thigh and drumstick		2.29	12/94	2c
Hamburger with cheese	1/4 lb.	1.89	12/94	2c
Pizza, Pizza Hut or Pizza Inn	12-13 in.	7.99	12/94	2c
Transportation				
Transportation, ACCRA Index		96.90	12/94	2c
Driver's learning permit fee	perm	30.00	1/94	84s
Driver's license fee	orig	30.00	1/94	84s
Driver's license fee, duplicate	lic	10.00	1/94	84s
Driver's license renewal fee	renew	20.00	1/94	84s
Identification card, nondriver	card	5.00	1/94	83s
Motorcycle learning permit fee	perm	30.00	1/94	84s
Motorcycle license fee	orig	30.00	1/94	84s
Motorcycle license fee, duplicate	lic	10.00	1/94	84s
Motorcycle license renewal fee	renew	20.00	1/94	84s
Tire balance, computer or spin bal., front	wheel	5.90	12/94	2c
Utilities				
Utilities, ACCRA Index		113.40	12/94	2c
Electricity, 1800 sq. ft., new home	mo.	122.98	12/94	2c

Cumberland, MD - continued

Item	Per	Value	Date	Ref.
Weddings				
Bridal attendants' gowns	event	750	10/93	76r
Bridal gown	event	852	10/93	76r
Bridal headpiece and veil	event	167	10/93	76r
Bride's wedding band	event	708	10/93	76r
Clergy	event	224	10/93	76r
Engagement ring	event	2756	10/93	76r
Flowers	event	863	10/93	76r
Formal wear for groom	event	106	10/93	76r
Groom's attendants' formal wear	event	530	10/93	76r
Groom's wedding band	event	402	10/93	76r
Music	event	600	10/93	76r
Photography	event	1088	10/93	76r
Shoes for bride	event	50	10/93	76r
Videography	event	483	10/93	76r
Wedding invitations and announcements	event	342	10/93	76r
Wedding reception	event	7000	10/93	76r

Dallas-Fort Worth, TX

Item	Per	Value	Date	Ref.
Composite, ACCRA index		101.90	12/94	2c
Alcoholic Beverages				
Beer, Miller Lite, Bud, 12-oz., ex deposit	6	4.53	12/94	2c
J & B Scotch	750-ml.	18.59	12/94	2c
Wine, Gallo Chablis blanc	1.5-lit	5.09	12/94	2c
Appliances				
Appliances (major), expenditures	year	195	91	81c
Appliances (major), expenditures	year	153	91	81r
Average annual exp.				
Food, health care, personal goods, services	year	33500	91	81c
Food, health care, personal goods, services	year	27020	91	81r
Business				
Dinner and tip, hotel, corporate rate	night	37.00	2/94	15c
Hotel room, corporate rate	night	73.00	2/94	15c
Charity				
Cash contributions, expenditures	year	988	91	81c
Cash contributions, expenditures	year	839	91	81r
Clothing				
Apparel, men and boys, total expenditures	year	466	91	81c
Apparel, men and boys, total expenditures	year	380	91	81r
Apparel, women and girls, total expenditures	year	852	91	81c
Apparel, women and girls, total expenditures	year	660	91	81r
Footwear, expenditures	year	197	91	81c
Footwear, expenditures	year	193	91	81r
Jeans, man's denim		31.14	12/94	2c
Shirt, dress, men's	shirt	29.00	1/92	44c
Shirt, man's dress shirt		32.50	12/94	2c
Undervest, boy's size 10-14, cotton	3	6.39	12/94	2c
Communications				
Long-distance telephone rate, day, addl. min., 1-10 mi.	min.	0.08	12/93	9s
Long-distance telephone rate, day, initial min., 1-10 mi.	min.	0.10	12/93	9s
Newspaper subscription, dly. and Sun. delivery	month	10.50	12/94	2c
Phone bill	month	55.75	93	37c
Phone line, single, business, field visit	inst	71.90	12/93	9s
Phone line, single, business, no field visit	inst	57.30	12/93	9s
Phone line, single, residence, field visit	inst	52.95	12/93	9s
Phone line, single, residence, no field visit	inst	38.35	12/93	9s
Telephone bill, family of four	month	16.29	12/94	2c
Telephone service, expenditures	year	669	91	81c
Telephone service, expenditures	year	616	91	81r
Telephone, business, addl. line, touch tone	month	1.75	10/91	25c
Telephone, business, connection charges, touch tone	inst	73.60	10/91	25c
Telephone, business, key system line, touch tone	month	39.33	10/91	25c

Values are in dollars or fractions of dollars. In the column headed *Ref*, references are shown to sources. Each reference is followed by a letter. These refer to the geographical level for which data were reported: s = State, r = Region, and c = City or metro. The abbreviation *ex* is used to mean *except* or *excluding*; *exp* stands for expenditures. For other abbreviations and further explanations, please see the Introduction.

Dallas-Fort Worth, TX - continued

Item	Per	Value	Date	Ref.
Communications				
Telephone, business, PBX line, touch tone	month	40.76	10/91	25c
Telephone, business, single ln., touch tone	month	34.23	10/91	25c
Telephone, business, touch tone, inside wiring maintenance plan	month	2.25	10/91	25c
Telephone, residential, flat rate	mo.	10.40	12/93	8c
Education				
Board, 4-year private college/university	year	2084	8/94	80s
Board, 4-year public college/university	year	1675	8/94	80s
Education, total expenditures	year	345	91	81c
Education, total expenditures	year	319	91	81r
Room, 4-year private college/university	year	1840	8/94	80s
Room, 4-year public college/university	year	1756	8/94	80s
Total cost, 4-year private college/university	year	11876	8/94	80s
Total cost, 4-year public college/university	year	4935	8/94	80s
Tuition, 2-year public college/university, in-state	year	625	8/94	80s
Tuition, 4-year private college/university, in-state	year	7952	8/94	80s
Tuition, 4-year public college/university, in-state	year	1503	8/94	80s
Energy and Fuels				
Electricity	500 KWh	45.19	12/94	82c
Energy, combined forms, 1800 sq. ft.	mo.	146.71	12/94	2c
Energy, exc. electricity, 1800 sq. ft.	mo.	36.98	12/94	2c
Fuel oil and other fuels, expenditures	year	23	91	81c
Fuel oil and other fuels, expenditures	year	56	91	81r
Gas	gal.	1.10	1/92	44c
Gas, cooking, winter, 10 therms	month	10.32	2/94	65c
Gas, cooking, winter, 30 therms	month	19.98	2/94	65c
Gas, cooking, winter, 50 therms	month	29.63	2/94	65c
Gas, heating, winter, 100 therms	month	53.76	2/94	65c
Gas, heating, winter, average use	month	78.86	2/94	65c
Gas, natural, expenditures	year	239	91	81c
Gas, natural, expenditures	year	150	91	81r
Gas, piped	40 therms	25.77	12/94	82c
Gas, piped	100 therms	56.10	12/94	82c
Gas, piped	therm	0.72	12/94	82c
Gas, reg unlead, taxes inc., cash, self-service	gal	1.16	12/94	2c
Gasoline and motor oil purchased	year	1293	91	81c
Gasoline and motor oil purchased	year	1152	91	81r
Gasoline, unleaded midgrade	gallon	1.25	4/93	82c
Gasoline, unleaded midgrade	gallon	1.21	4/93	82r
Gasoline, unleaded premium	gallon	1.34	4/93	82c
Gasoline, unleaded premium	gallon	1.30	4/93	82r
Gasoline, unleaded regular	gallon	1.15	4/93	82c
Gasoline, unleaded regular	gallon	1.10	4/93	82r
Entertainment				
Bowling, evening rate	game	2.64	12/94	2c
Concert ticket, Pearl Jam group	perf	20.00	94	50r
Entertainment supplies, equipment, and services, misc. expenditures	year	248	91	81c
Entertainment, total expenditures	year	1509	91	81c
Entertainment, total expenditures	year	1266	91	81r
Fees and admissions, expenditures	year	479	91	81c
Fees and admissions, expenditures	year	306	91	81r
Monopoly game, Parker Brothers', No. 9	game	9.99	12/94	2c
Movie	adm	6.12	12/94	2c
Movie ticket, adult	ticket	6.00	1/92	44c
Pets, toys, playground equipment, expenditures	year	344	91	81c
Pets, toys, playground equipment, expenditures	year	271	91	81r
Reading, expenditures	year	176	91	81c
Reading, expenditures	year	131	91	81r
Televisions, radios, and sound equipment, expenditures	year	437	91	81c

Dallas-Fort Worth, TX - continued

Item	Per	Value	Date	Ref.
Entertainment - continued				
Televisions, radios, and sound equipment, expenditures	year	439	91	81r
Tennis balls, yellow, Wilson or Penn, 3	can	1.99	12/94	2c
Funerals				
Burial, immediate, container provided by funeral home		1574.60	1/95	54r
Cards, acknowledgment		22.24	1/95	54r
Casket, minimum alternative		239.41	1/95	54r
Cosmetology, hair care, etc.		91.04	1/95	54r
Cremation, direct, container provided by funeral home		1085.15	1/95	54r
Embalming		281.30	1/95	54r
Funeral, funeral home		323.04	1/95	54r
Funeral, other facility		327.58	1/95	54r
Graveside service		355.19	1/95	54r
Hearse, local		141.89	1/95	54r
Limousine, local		99.40	1/95	54r
Memorial service		284.67	1/95	54r
Service charge, professional, nondeclinable		904.06	1/95	54r
Visitation and viewing		187.04	1/95	54r
Groceries				
Groceries, ACCRA Index		99.20	12/94	2c
Apples, Red Delicious	lb.	0.73	12/94	82r
Baby food, strained vegetables, lowest price	4-4.5 oz.	0.30	12/94	2c
Bacon, sliced	lb.	1.67	12/94	82r
Bananas	lb.	0.40	12/94	2c
Bananas	lb.	0.42	12/94	82r
Beef or hamburger, ground	lb.	1.32	12/94	2c
Beef purchases	year	258	91	81c
Beef purchases	year	213	91	81r
Beverage purchases, alcoholic	year	284	91	81c
Beverage purchases, alcoholic	year	249	91	81r
Beverage purchases, nonalcoholic	year	220	91	81c
Beverage purchases, nonalcoholic	year	207	91	81r
Bologna, all beef or mixed	lb.	2.27	12/94	82r
Bread, white	24-oz.	0.74	12/94	2c
Bread, white, pan	lb.	0.68	12/94	82r
Cabbage	lb.	0.42	12/94	82r
Carrots, short trimmed and topped	lb.	0.53	12/94	82r
Cereals and bakery products purchases	year	404	91	81c
Cereals and bakery products purchases	year	345	91	81r
Cereals and cereal products purchases	year	144	91	81c
Cereals and cereals products purchases	year	127	91	81r
Cheddar cheese, natural	lb.	3.58	12/94	82r
Cheese, Kraft grated Parmesan	8-oz.	3.47	12/94	2c
Chicken breast, bone-in	lb.	1.71	12/94	82r
Chicken, fresh, whole	lb.	0.78	12/94	82r
Chicken, whole fryer	lb.	0.69	12/94	2c
Chuck roast, USDA choice, boneless	lb.	2.26	12/94	82r
Cigarettes, Winston, Kings	carton	18.35	12/94	2c
Coffee, vacuum-packed	13 oz.	3.37	12/94	2c
Corn Flakes, Kellogg's or Post Toasties	18 oz.	2.31	12/94	2c
Corn, frozen, whole kernel, lowest price	10 oz.	0.76	12/94	2c
Crackers, soda, salted	lb.	1.27	12/94	82r
Cucumbers	lb.	0.65	12/94	82r
Dairy products (other) purchases	year	187	91	81c
Dairy products (other) purchases	year	141	91	81r
Eggs, Grade A large	dozen	0.84	12/94	2c
Eggs, Grade A large	dozen	0.87	12/94	82r
Fish and seafood purchases	year	96	91	81c
Fish and seafood purchases	year	72	91	81r
Flour, white, all purpose	lb.	0.23	12/94	82r
Food purchases, food eaten at home	year	2825	91	81c
Food purchases, food eaten at home	year	2381	91	81r
Foods purchased away from home, not prepared by consumer	year	1916	91	81c
Foods purchased away from home, not prepared by consumer	year	1696	91	81r
Frankfurters, all meat or all beef	lb.	1.74	12/94	82r
Fruits and vegetables purchases	year	475	91	81c

Values are in dollars or fractions of dollars. In the column headed *Ref*, references are shown to sources. Each reference is followed by a letter. These refer to the geographical level for which data were reported: s = State, r = Region, and c = City or metro. The abbreviation *ex* is used to mean *except* or *excluding*; *exp* stands for expenditures. For other abbreviations and further explanations, please see the Introduction.

Dallas-Fort Worth, TX - continued

Item	Per	Value	Date	Ref.
Groceries				
Fruits and vegetables purchases	year	380	91	81r
Grapefruit	lb.	0.45	12/94	82r
Grapes, Thompson seedless	lb.	2.30	12/94	82r
Ground beef, 100% beef	lb.	1.37	12/94	82r
Ground chuck, 100% beef	lb.	1.97	12/94	82r
Ham, boneless, exc. canned	lb.	2.54	12/94	82r
Ice cream, prepackaged, bulk, regular	1/2 gal.	2.47	12/94	82r
Lemons	lb.	1.02	12/94	82r
Lettuce, iceberg	lb.	0.96	12/94	82r
Lettuce, iceberg	head	0.93	12/94	2c
Margarine, Blue Bonnet or Parkay cubes	lb.	0.60	12/94	2c
Margarine, stick	lb.	0.77	12/94	82r
Meats, poultry, fish, and eggs purchases	year	756	91	81c
Meats, poultry, fish, and eggs purchases	year	655	91	81r
Milk and cream (fresh) purchases	year	125	91	81c
Milk and cream (fresh) purchases	year	130	91	81r
Milk, 2%	gal.	2.20	1/92	44c
Milk, whole	1/2 gal.	1.51	12/94	2c
Orange juice, frozen concentrate 12-oz. can	16 oz.	1.36	12/94	82r
Orange juice, Minute Maid frozen	12-oz.	1.22	12/94	2c
Oranges, Navel	lb.	0.54	12/94	82r
Peaches, halves or slices, Hunt's, Del Monte, or Libby's	29-oz.	1.49	12/94	2c
Pears, Anjou	lb.	0.81	12/94	82r
Peas, sweet, Del Monte or Green Giant	15-17 oz.	0.55	12/94	2c
Pork chops, center cut, bone-in	lb.	3.07	12/94	82r
Pork purchases	year	144	91	81c
Pork purchases	year	142	91	81r
Potato chips	16-oz.	3.15	12/94	82r
Potatoes, frozen, French fried	lb.	0.82	12/94	82r
Potatoes, white	lb.	0.34	12/94	82r
Potatoes, white or red	10-lb. sack	2.53	12/94	2c
Rental rate, 2-bedroom apartment	month	560.00	1/92	44c
Rice, white, long grain, uncooked	lb.	0.48	12/94	82r
Round roast, USDA choice, boneless	lb.	2.91	12/94	82r
Sausage, fresh	lb.	1.82	12/94	82r
Sausage, Jimmy Dean, 100% pork	lb.	2.47	12/94	2c
Shortening, vegetable oil blends	lb.	0.75	12/94	82r
Shortening, vegetable, Crisco	3-lb.	2.53	12/94	2c
Soft drink, Coca Cola, ex deposit	2 lit	1.13	12/94	2c
Spaghetti and macaroni	lb.	0.87	12/94	82r
Steak, rib eye, USDA choice, boneless	lb.	6.85	12/94	82r
Steak, round, graded & ungraded, exc. USDA prime & choice	lb.	2.96	12/94	82r
Steak, round, USDA choice, boneless	lb.	3.17	12/94	82r
Steak, sirloin, USDA choice, boneless	lb.	4.12	12/94	82r
Steak, t-bone	lb.	5.88	12/94	2c
Steak, T-bone, USDA choice, bone-in	lb.	5.63	12/94	82r
Sugar and other sweets, eaten at home, expenditures	year	93	91	81r
Sugar and other sweets, eaten at home, purchases	year	114	91	81c
Sugar, cane or beet	4 lbs.	1.46	12/94	2c
Sugar, white, all sizes	lb.	0.39	12/94	82r
Tobacco products and smoking supplies, total expenditures	year	301	91	81c
Tobacco products and smoking supplies, total expenditures	year	286	91	81r
Tomatoes, field grown	lb.	1.36	12/94	82r
Tomatoes, Hunt's or Del Monte	14.5 oz.	0.74	12/94	2c
Tuna, chunk, light	lb.	1.94	12/94	82r
Tuna, chunk, light, oil-packed	6.125-6.5 oz.	0.69	12/94	2c
Turkey, frozen, whole	lb.	0.96	12/94	82r
Yogurt, natural, fruit flavored	8 oz.	0.58	12/94	82r

Dallas-Fort Worth, TX - continued

Item	Per	Value	Date	Ref.
Goods and Services				
Miscellaneous goods and services, ACCRA Index		102.70	12/94	2c
Health Care				
Health care, ACCRA Index		108.30	12/94	2c
Adenosine, emergency room	treat	100.00	95	23r
Antibiotic ointment, Polysporin	1.5 oz.	3.91	12/94	2c
Appendectomy	proc	1091.00	12/92	69c
Bladder tap, superpubic, infant, emergency room	treat	119.00	95	23r
Blood analysis, emergency room	treat	25.00	95	23r
Blood tests, abdominal pain, emergency room	treat	25.00	95	23r
Breast lesion excision (lumpectomy)	proc	631.00	12/92	69c
Burn dressing, emergency room	treat	266.00	95	23r
Cardiology interpretation, emergency room	treat	26.00	95	23r
Cesarean section delivery	proc	2253.00	12/92	69c
Chest X-ray, emergency room	treat	78.00	95	23r
Childbirth, Cesarean delivery, hospital charge	birth	5462.00	12/91	69r
Childbirth, Cesarean delivery, physician charge	birth	2228.00	12/91	69r
Childbirth, normal delivery, hospital charge	birth	2943.00	12/91	69r
Childbirth, normal delivery, physician charge	birth	1619.00	12/91	69r
Cholecystectomy	proc	1802.00	12/92	69c
Coronary bypass, triple	proc	5661.00	12/92	69c
Defibrillation pads, emergency room	treat	6.00	95	23r
Dentist's fee, adult teeth cleaning and periodic oral exam	visit	56.00	12/94	2c
Doctor's fee, routine exam, established patient	visit	47.60	12/94	2c
Drugs, expenditures	year	262	91	81c
Drugs, expenditures	year	297	91	81r
Gastric tube insertion, nasal, emergency room	treat	25.00	95	23r
Health care, total expenditures	year	1543	91	81c
Health care, total expenditures	year	1600	91	81r
Health insurance expenditures	year	644	91	81c
Health insurance expenditures	year	637	91	81r
Heart monitor, emergency room	treat	40.00	95	23r
Hospital care, semiprivate room	day	390.00	12/94	2c
Hysterectomy, abdominal	proc	2133.00	12/92	69c
Insurance premium, family medical care	month	389.25	1/95	41s
Intravenous fluids, emergency room	treat	130.00	95	23r
Intravenous fluids, emergency room	liter	26.00	95	23r
Intravenous line, central, emergency room	treat	342.00	95	23r
Liver function tests, abdominal pain, emergency room	treat	26.00	95	23r
Medical care charges, total, emergency room, third-degree burns	treat	2101.00	95	23r
Medical care charges, total, emergency, infant with fever	treat	628.00	95	23r
Medical services expenditures	year	548	91	81c
Medical services expenditures	year	573	91	81r
Medical supplies expenditures	year	89	91	81c
Medical supplies expenditures	year	93	91	81r
Morphine, emergency room	treat	34.00	95	23r
Nursing care and facilities charges, emergency room	treat	252.00	95	23r
Nursing care and facilities charges, emergency, infant with fever	treat	252.00	95	23r
Nursing care and facilities charges, emergency, third-degree burns	treat	861.00	95	23r
Oophorectomy	proc	1494.00	12/92	69c
Physician's charges, emergency, infant with fever	treat	212.00	95	23r
Physician's charges, emergency, third-degree burns	treat	372.00	95	23r
Physician's fee, emergency room	treat	372.00	95	23r
Physician's fee, general practitioner	visit	51.20	12/93	60r
Salpingo-oophorectomy	proc	1579.00	12/92	69c
Surgery, open-heart	proc	42374.00	1/93	14r
Ultrasound, abdominal, emergency room	treat	276.00	95	23r

Values are in dollars or fractions of dollars. In the column headed *Ref*, references are shown to sources. Each reference is followed by a letter. These refer to the geographical level for which data were reported: s = State, r = Region, and c = City or metro. The abbreviation *ex* is used to mean *except* or *excluding*; *exp* stands for *expenditures*. For other abbreviations and further explanations, please see the Introduction.

Dallas-Fort Worth, TX - continued

Item	Per	Value	Date	Ref.
Health Care				
Urinalysis, emergency room	treat	20.00	95	23r
Urinalysis, infant, emergency room	treat	20.00	95	23r
X-rays, emergency room	treat	78.00	95	23r
Household Goods				
Appl. repair, service call, wash mach	min. lab. chg.	32.78	12/94	2c
Floor coverings, expenditures	year	16	91	81c
Floor coverings, expenditures	year	48	91	81r
Furniture, expenditures	year	278	91	81c
Furniture, expenditures	year	280	91	81r
Household equipment, misc. expenditures	year	342	91	81r
Household equipment, misc., expenditures	year	503	91	81c
Household expenditures, miscellaneous	year	449	91	81c
Household expenditures, miscellaneous	year	256	91	81r
Household furnishings and equipment, expenditures	year	1295	91	81c
Household furnishings and equipment, expenditures	year	988	91	81r
Household operations expenditures	year	820	91	81c
Household operations expenditures	year	468	91	81r
Household textiles, expenditures	year	205	91	81c
Household textiles, expenditures	year	95	91	81r
Housekeeping supplies, expenditures	year	495	91	81c
Housekeeping supplies, expenditures	year	380	91	81r
Laundry and cleaning supplies, expenditures	year	166	91	81c
Laundry and cleaning supplies, expenditures	year	109	91	81r
Laundry detergent, Tide Ultra, Bold, or Cheer	42 oz.	3.29	12/94	2c
Postage and stationery, expenditures	year	121	91	81c
Postage and stationery, expenditures	year	105	91	81r
Tissues, facial, Kleenex brand	175	0.98	12/94	2c
Housing				
Housing, ACCRA Index		93.50	12/94	2c
Add garage/carport		6,980	3/95	74r
Add room(s)		11,403	3/95	74r
Apartment condominium or co-op, median	unit	68600	12/94	62r
Car rental	day	39.00	5/95	95c
Dwellings (owned), expenditures	year	2870	91	81c
Dwellings (owned), expenditures	year	2428	91	81r
Enclose porch/patio/breezeway		4,572	3/95	74r
Finish room in basement/attic		3,794	3/95	74r
Home, existing, single-family, median	unit	120200	12/94	62r
Home, existing, single-family, median	unit	92.30	12/94	62c
Home, purchase price	unit	141.40	3/93	26c
Hotel room	day	107.00	5/95	95c
House payment, principal and interest, 25% down payment	mo.	663	12/94	2c
House, 1800 sq ft, 8000 sq ft lot, new, urban, utilities	total	106820	12/94	2c
Maintenance, repairs, insurance, and other housing expenditures	year	518	91	81c
Maintenance, repairs, insurance, and other housing expenditures	year	531	91	81r
Mortgage interest and charges expenditures	year	1730	91	81c
Mortgage interest and charges expenditures	year	1506	91	81r
Mtge. rate, incl. points and orig. fee, 30-year conv. fixed or ARM	mo.	9.32	12/94	2c
Princ. & int., mortgage, median-price exist. sing.-family home	mo.	540	12/94	62r
Property taxes expenditures	year	622	91	81c
Property taxes expenditures	year	391	91	81r
Redesign, restructure more than half of home's interior		17,641	3/95	74r
Rent, apartment, 2 br., 1 1/2-2 baths, unfurnished, 950 sq ft, water	mo.	647	12/94	2c
Rental units expenditures	year	2248	900/00/ 91	81c
Rental units expenditures	year	1264	91	81r

Item	Per	Value	Date	Ref.
Insurance and Pensions				
Auto insurance, private passenger	year	785.78	12/94	71s
Health insurance, HMO plan, cost to employer	year	3330	93	59c
Insurance and pensions, personal, expenditures	year	3874	91	81c
Insurance and pensions, personal, expenditures	year	2395	91	81r
Insurance, life and other personal, expenditures	year	358	91	81c
Insurance, life and other personal, expenditures	year	368	91	81r
Pensions and Social Security, expenditures	year	3516	91	81c
Pensions and Social Security, expenditures	year	2027	91	81r
Personal Goods				
Personal care products and services, total expenditures	year	520	91	81c
Shampoo, Alberto VO5	15-oz.	1.15	12/94	2c
Toothpaste, Crest or Colgate	6-7 oz.	2.35	12/94	2c
Personal Services				
Dry cleaning, man's 2-pc. suit		7.14	12/94	2c
Dry cleaning, woman's dress	dress	6.00	1/92	44c
Haircut, man's barbershop, no styling		9.22	12/94	2c
Haircut, woman's shampoo, trim, blow-dry		30.67	12/94	2c
Personal services expenditures	year	370	91	81c
Personal services expenditures	year	212	91	81r
Restaurant Food				
Big Mac, small fries, medium drink	meal	3.70	1/92	44c
Chicken, fried, thigh and drumstick		1.71	12/94	2c
Dining expenditures, family	week	33.83	94	73r
Hamburger with cheese	1/4 lb.	1.88	12/94	2c
Pizza, Pizza Hut or Pizza Inn	12-13 in.	7.89	12/94	2c
Taxes				
Tax, cigarettes	year	584.00	10/93	43s
Taxes, Federal income, expenditures	year	4715	91	81c
Taxes, Federal income, expenditures	year	2275	91	81r
Taxes, personal, expenditures	year	4754	91	81c
Taxes, personal, expenditures	year	2715	91	81r
Taxes, State and local income, expenditures	year	2	91	81c
Taxes, State and local income, expenditures	year	365	91	81r
Transportation				
Transportation, ACCRA Index		105.10	12/94	2c
Bus fare, one-way	trip	0.90	12/95	1c
Bus fare, up to 10 miles	one-way	1.25	12/94	2c
Cars and trucks purchased, new	year	1332	91	81c
Cars and trucks purchased, new	year	1306	91	81r
Cars and trucks purchased, used	year	1270	91	81c
Cars and trucks purchased, used	year	942	91	81r
Driver's learning permit fee	perm	5.00	1/94	84s
Driver's license fee	orig	16.00	1/94	84s
Driver's license fee, duplicate	lic	10.00	1/94	84s
Driver's license reinstatement fee, min.	susp	50.00	1/94	85s
Driver's license renewal fee	renew	16.00	1/94	84s
Identification card, nondriver	card	10.00	1/94	83s
Motorcycle learning permit fee	perm	5.00	1/94	84s
Motorcycle license fee	orig	16.00	1/94	84s
Motorcycle license fee, duplicate	lic	10.00	1/94	84s
Motorcycle license renewal fee	renew	21.00	1/94	84s
parking, long-term lot, airport	3 days	22.50	1/92	44c
Public transportation expenditures	year	310	91	81c
Public transportation expenditures	year	249	91	81r
Tire balance, computer or spin bal., front	wheel	6.81	12/94	2c
Transportation expenditures, total	year	6413	91	81c
Transportation expenditures, total	year	5307	91	81r
Vehicle expenses, miscellaneous	year	2199	91	81c
Vehicle finance charges	year	416	91	81c
Vehicle finance charges	year	346	91	81r
Vehicle insurance expenditures	year	729	91	81c

Values are in dollars or fractions of dollars. In the column headed *Ref*, references are shown to sources. Each reference is followed by a letter. These refer to the geographical level for which data were reported: s = State, r = Region, and c = City or metro. The abbreviation *ex* is used to mean *except* or *excluding*; *exp* stands for expenditures. For other abbreviations and further explanations, please see the Introduction.

Dallas-Fort Worth, TX - continued

Item	Per	Value	Date	Ref.
Transportation				
Vehicle insurance expenditures	year	544	91	81r
Vehicle maintenance and repairs expenditures	year	796	91	81c
Vehicle maintenance and repairs expenditures	year	600	91	81r
Vehicle purchases	year	2612	91	81c
Vehicle purchases	year	2275	91	81r
Vehicle rental, leases, licenses, etc. expenditures	year	258	91	81c
Vehicle rental, leases, licenses, etc. expenditures	year	141	91	81r
Vehicles purchased, other than cars and trucks	year	9	91	81c
Vehicles purchased, other than cars and trucks	year	27	91	81r
Travel				
Car rental	day	46.99	1/93	49c
Car rental	week	159.99	1/93	49c
Utilities				
Utilities, ACCRA Index		124.40	12/94	2c
Electricity	KWh	0.07	12/94	82c
Electricity expenditures	year	890	91	81c
Electricity expenditures	year	950	91	81r
Electricity, (part.), other, 1800 sq. ft., new home	mo.	109.73	12/94	2c
Electricity, summer, 250 KWh	month	24.54	8/93	64c
Electricity, summer, 500 KWh	month	43.09	8/93	64c
Electricity, summer, 750 KWh	month	61.62	8/93	64c
Electricity, summer, 1000 KWh	month	80.16	8/93	64c
Utilities, fuels, and public services, total expenditures	year	2130	91	81c
Utilities, fuels, and public services, total expenditures	year	2000	91	81r
Water and other public services, expenditures	year	309	91	81c
Water and other public services, expenditures	year	227	91	81r
Weddings				
Bridal attendants' gowns	event	750	10/93	76r
Bridal gown	event	852	10/93	76r
Bridal headpiece and veil	event	167	10/93	76r
Bride's wedding band	event	708	10/93	76r
Clergy	event	224	10/93	76r
Engagement ring	event	2756	10/93	76r
Flowers	event	863	10/93	76r
Formal wear for groom	event	106	10/93	76r
Groom's attendants' formal wear	event	530	10/93	76r
Groom's wedding band	event	402	10/93	76r
Music	event	600	10/93	76r
Photography	event	1088	10/93	76r
Shoes for bride	event	50	10/93	76r
Videography	event	483	10/93	76r
Wedding invitations and announcements	event	342	10/93	76r
Wedding reception	event	7000	10/93	76r

Danbury, CT

Item	Per	Value	Date	Ref.
Appliances				
Appliances (major), expenditures	year	145	91	81r
Average annual exp.				
Food, health care, personal goods, services	year	29496	91	81r
Charity				
Cash contributions, expenditures	year	708	91	81r
Clothing				
Apparel, men and boys, total expenditures	year	416	91	81r
Apparel, women and girls, total expenditures	year	744	91	81r
Footwear, expenditures	year	305	91	81r

Danbury, CT - continued

Item	Per	Value	Date	Ref.
Communications				
Long-distance telephone rate, day, addl. min., 1-10 mi.	min.	0.09	12/93	9s
Long-distance telephone rate, day, initial min., 1-10 mi.	min.	0.09	12/93	9s
Phone line, single, business, field visit	inst	127.44	12/93	9s
Phone line, single, business, no field visit	inst	95.58	12/93	9s
Phone line, single, residence, field visit	inst	64.85	12/93	9s
Phone line, single, residence, no field visit	inst	38.27	12/93	9s
Telephone service, expenditures	year	589	91	81r
Education				
Board, 4-year private college/university	year	2664	8/94	80s
Board, 4-year public college/university	year	2137	8/94	80s
Education, total expenditures	year	593	91	81r
Room, 4-year private college/university	year	3287	8/94	80s
Room, 4-year public college/university	year	2310	8/94	80s
Total cost, 4-year private college/university	year	20726	8/94	80s
Total cost, 4-year public college/university	year	7926	8/94	80s
Tuition, 2-year public college/university, in-state	year	1398	8/94	80s
Tuition, 4-year private college/university, in-state	year	14775	8/94	80s
Tuition, 4-year public college/university, in-state	year	3479	8/94	80s
Energy and Fuels				
Fuel oil and other fuels, expenditures	year	257	91	81r
Gas, natural, expenditures	year	285	91	81r
Gasoline and motor oil purchased	year	867	91	81r
Gasoline, unleaded midgrade	gallon	1.32	4/93	82r
Gasoline, unleaded premium	gallon	1.40	4/93	82r
Gasoline, unleaded regular	gallon	1.19	4/93	82r
Entertainment				
Entertainment, total expenditures	year	1331	91	81r
Fees and admissions, expenditures	year	398	91	81r
Pets, toys, playground equipment, expenditures	year	270	91	81r
Reading, expenditures	year	171	91	81r
Televisions, radios, and sound equipment, expenditures	year	429	91	81r
Funerals				
Burial, immediate, container provided by funeral home		1507.89	1/95	54r
Cards, acknowledgment		18.10	1/95	54r
Casket, minimum alternative		133.03	1/95	54r
Cosmetology, hair care, etc.		114.12	1/95	54r
Cremation, direct, container provided by funeral home		1309.19	1/95	54r
Embalming		320.97	1/95	54r
Funeral, funeral home		327.61	1/95	54r
Funeral, other facility		314.81	1/95	54r
Graveside service		286.11	1/95	54r
Hearse, local		158.95	1/95	54r
Limousine, local		149.45	1/95	54r
Memorial service		315.94	1/95	54r
Service charge, professional, nondeclinable		1148.43	1/95	54r
Visitation and viewing		249.66	1/95	54r
Groceries				
Apples, Red Delicious	lb.	0.78	12/94	82r
Bacon, sliced	lb.	2.24	12/94	82r
Bananas	lb.	0.49	12/94	82r
Beef purchases	year	226	91	81r
Beverage purchases, alcoholic	year	332	91	81r
Beverage purchases, nonalcoholic	year	213	91	81r
Bread, white, pan	lb.	0.80	12/94	82r
Butter, salted, Grade AA, stick	lb.	1.67	12/94	82r
Carrots, short trimmed and topped	lb.	0.51	12/94	82r
Cereals and bakery products purchases	year	407	91	81r
Cereals and cereals products purchases	year	132	91	81r
Chicken breast, bone-in	lb.	2.22	12/94	82r
Chicken, fresh, whole	lb.	1.05	12/94	82r

Values are in dollars or fractions of dollars. In the column headed *Ref*, references are shown to sources. Each reference is followed by a letter. These refer to the geographical level for which data were reported: s = State, r = Region, and c = City or metro. The abbreviation *ex* is used to mean *except* or *excluding*; *exp* stands for expenditures. For other abbreviations and further explanations, please see the Introduction.

Danbury, CT - continued

Item	Per	Value	Date	Ref.
Groceries				
Chuck roast, USDA choice, boneless	lb.	2.74	12/94	82r
Coffee, 100%, ground roast, all sizes	lb.	4.61	12/94	82r
Dairy products (other) purchases	year	161	91	81r
Eggs, Grade A large	dozen	1.12	12/94	82r
Fish and seafood purchases	year	112	91	81r
Food purchases, food eaten at home	year	2599	91	81r
Foods purchased away from home, not prepared by consumer	year	2024	91	81r
Fruits and vegetables purchases	year	444	91	81r
Grapefruit	lb.	0.44	12/94	82r
Grapes, Thompson seedless	lb.	2.24	12/94	82r
Ground chuck, 100% beef	lb.	1.67	12/94	82r
Ice cream, prepackaged, bulk, regular	1/2 gal.	2.93	12/94	82r
Lemons	lb.	1.06	12/94	82r
Lettuce, iceberg	lb.	0.92	12/94	82r
Meats, poultry, fish, and eggs purchases	year	751	91	81r
Milk and cream (fresh) purchases	year	152	91	81r
Orange juice, frozen concentrate 12-oz. can	16 oz.	1.92	12/94	82r
Oranges, Navel	lb.	0.56	12/94	82r
Pork chops, center cut, bone-in	lb.	3.09	12/94	82r
Pork purchases	year	130	91	81r
Potatoes, white	lb.	0.37	12/94	82r
Rib roast, USDA choice, bone-in	lb.	4.98	12/94	82r
Round roast, USDA choice, boneless	lb.	2.93	12/94	82r
Shortening, vegetable oil blends	lb.	1.03	12/94	82r
Spaghetti and macaroni	lb.	0.84	12/94	82r
Steak, round, USDA choice, boneless	lb.	3.48	12/94	82r
Steak, sirloin, USDA choice, bone-in	lb.	3.38	12/94	82r
Steak, sirloin, USDA choice, boneless	lb.	4.81	12/94	82r
Sugar and other sweets, eaten at home, expenditures	year	89	91	81r
Sugar, white, all sizes	lb.	0.46	12/94	82r
Tobacco products and smoking supplies, total expenditures	year	279	91	81r
Tomatoes, field grown	lb.	1.56	12/94	82r
Tuna, chunk, light	lb.	2.09	12/94	82r
Health Care				
Childbirth, Cesarean delivery, hospital charge	birth	6334.00	12/91	69r
Childbirth, Cesarean delivery, physician charge	birth	2234.00	12/91	69r
Childbirth, normal delivery, hospital charge	birth	3225.00	12/91	69r
Childbirth, normal delivery, physician charge	birth	1623.00	12/91	69r
Drugs, expenditures	year	205	91	81r
Health care, total expenditures	year	1396	91	81r
Health insurance expenditures	year	553	91	81r
Insurance premium, family medical care	month	500.40	1/95	41s
Medical services expenditures	year	559	91	81r
Medical supplies expenditures	year	80	91	81r
Household Goods				
Floor coverings, expenditures	year	158	91	81r
Furniture, expenditures	year	341	91	81r
Household equipment, misc. expenditures	year	363	91	81r
Household expenditures, miscellaneous	year	194	91	81r
Household furnishings and equipment, expenditures	year	1158	91	81r
Household operations expenditures	year	378	91	81r
Household textiles, expenditures	year	88	91	81r
Housekeeping supplies, expenditures	year	426	91	81r
Laundry and cleaning supplies, expenditures	year	122	91	81r
Postage and stationery, expenditures	year	134	91	81r
Housing				
Add garage/carport		11,614	3/95	74r
Add room(s)		16,816	3/95	74r
Apartment condominium or co-op, median	unit	96700	12/94	62r
Dwellings (owned), expenditures	year	3305	91	81r
Enclose porch/patio/breezeway		2,980	3/95	74r
Finish room in basement/attic		4,330	3/95	74r
Home, existing, single-family, median	unit	161600	12/94	62r

Danbury, CT - continued

Item	Per	Value	Date	Ref.
Housing - continued				
Maintenance, repairs, insurance, and other housing expenditures	year	569	91	81r
Mortgage interest and charges expenditures	year	1852	91	81r
Princ. & int., mortgage, median-price exist. sing.-family home	mo.	765	12/94	62r
Property taxes expenditures	year	884	91	81r
Redesign, restructure more than half of home's interior		2,750	3/95	74r
Rental units expenditures	year	1832	91	81r
Insurance and Pensions				
Auto insurance, private passenger	year	1002.84	12/94	71s
Insurance and pensions, personal, expenditures	year	2690	91	81r
Insurance, life and other personal, expenditures	year	341	91	81r
Pensions and Social Security, expenditures	year	2349	91	81r
Legal Assistance				
Estate planning, law-firm partner	hr.	375.00	10/93	12r
Legal work, law firm associate	hour	78		10r
Legal work, law firm partner	hour	183		10r
Personal Services				
Personal services expenditures	year	184	91	81r
Restaurant Food				
Dining expenditures, family	week	34.26	94	73r
Taxes				
Taxes, Federal income, expenditures	year	2409	91	81r
Taxes, personal, expenditures	year	3094	91	81r
Taxes, State and local income, expenditures	year	620	91	81r
Transportation				
Cars and trucks purchased, new	year	1170	91	81r
Cars and trucks purchased, used	year	739	91	81r
Driver's learning permit fee	perm	3.50	1/94	84s
Driver's license fee	orig	38.00	1/94	84s
Driver's license fee, duplicate	lic	5.00	1/94	84s
Driver's license reinstatement fee, min.	susp	30.00	1/94	85s
Driver's license renewal fee	renew	31.00	1/94	84s
Identification card, nondriver	card	4.00	1/94	83s
Motorcycle learning permit fee	perm	3.50	1/94	84s
Motorcycle license fee	orig	38.00	1/94	84s
Motorcycle license fee, duplicate	lic	5.00	1/94	84s
Motorcycle license renewal fee	renew	31.00	1/94	84s
Public transportation expenditures	year	430	91	81r
Transportation expenditures, total	year	4810	91	81r
Vehicle finance charges	year	238	91	81r
Vehicle insurance expenditures	year	630	91	81r
Vehicle maintenance and repairs expenditures	year	532	91	81r
Vehicle purchases	year	1920	91	81r
Vehicle rental, leases, licenses, etc. expenditures	year	193	91	81r
Vehicles purchased, other than cars and trucks	year	11	91	81r
Utilities				
Electricity expenditures	year	695	91	81r
Utilities, fuels, and public services, total expenditures	year	1981	91	81r
Water and other public services, expenditures	year	154	91	81r
Weddings				
Bridal attendants' gowns	event	750	10/93	76r
Bridal gown	event	852	10/93	76r
Bridal headpiece and veil	event	167	10/93	76r
Bride's wedding band	event	708	10/93	76r
Clergy	event	224	10/93	76r
Engagement ring	event	2756	10/93	76r
Flowers	event	863	10/93	76r
Formal wear for groom	event	106	10/93	76r
Groom's attendants' formal wear	event	530	10/93	76r

Values are in dollars or fractions of dollars. In the column headed *Ref*, references are shown to sources. Each reference is followed by a letter. These refer to the geographical level for which data were reported: s=State, r=Region, and c=City or metro. The abbreviation *ex* is used to mean *except* or *excluding*; *exp* stands for expenditures. For other abbreviations and further explanations, please see the Introduction.

Danbury, CT - continued

Item	Per	Value	Date	Ref.
Weddings				
Groom's wedding band	event	402	10/93	76r
Music	event	600	10/93	76r
Photography	event	1088	10/93	76r
Shoes for bride	event	50	10/93	76r
Videography	event	483	10/93	76r
Wedding invitations and announcements	event	342	10/93	76r
Wedding reception	event	7000	10/93	76r

Danville, IL

Item	Per	Value	Date	Ref.
Composite, ACCRA index		94.20	12/94	2c
Alcoholic Beverages				
Beer, Miller Lite, Bud, 12-oz., ex deposit	6	3.96	12/94	2c
J & B Scotch	750-ml.	15.39	12/94	2c
Wine, Gallo Chablis blanc	1.5-lit	4.93	12/94	2c
Clothing				
Jeans, man's denim		33.49	12/94	2c
Shirt, man's dress shirt		29.50	12/94	2c
Undervest, boy's size 10-14, cotton	3	3.99	12/94	2c
Communications				
Newspaper subscription, dly. and Sun. delivery	month	11.30	12/94	2c
Telephone bill, family of four	month	21.00	12/94	2c
Energy and Fuels				
Energy, combined forms, 1800 sq. ft.	mo.	122.08	12/94	2c
Energy, exc. electricity, 1800 sq. ft.	mo.	44.80	12/94	2c
Gas, reg unlead, taxes inc., cash, self-service	gal	1.05	12/94	2c
Entertainment				
Bowling, evening rate	game	1.70	12/94	2c
Monopoly game, Parker Brothers', No. 9	game	9.99	12/94	2c
Movie	adm	5.00	12/94	2c
Tennis balls, yellow, Wilson or Penn, 3	can	1.99	12/94	2c
Groceries				
Groceries, ACCRA Index		104.60	12/94	2c
Baby food, strained vegetables, lowest price	4-4.5 oz.	0.41	12/94	2c
Bananas	lb.	0.44	12/94	2c
Beef or hamburger, ground	lb.	1.29	12/94	2c
Bread, white	24-oz.	0.76	12/94	2c
Cheese, Kraft grated Parmesan	8-oz.	3.08	12/94	2c
Chicken, whole fryer	lb.	0.82	12/94	2c
Cigarettes, Winston, Kings	carton	18.23	12/94	2c
Coffee, vacuum-packed	13 oz.	3.47	12/94	2c
Corn Flakes, Kellogg's or Post Toasties	18 oz.	2.78	12/94	2c
Corn, frozen, whole kernel, lowest price	10 oz.	0.83	12/94	2c
Eggs, Grade A large	dozen	0.80	12/94	2c
Lettuce, iceberg	head	0.84	12/94	2c
Margarine, Blue Bonnet or Parkay cubes	lb.	0.76	12/94	2c
Milk, whole	1/2 gal.	1.52	12/94	2c
Orange juice, Minute Maid frozen	12-oz.	1.23	12/94	2c
Peaches, halves or slices, Hunt's, Del Monte, or Libby's	29-oz.	1.39	12/94	2c
Peas, sweet, Del Monte or Green Giant	15-17 oz.	0.66	12/94	2c
Potatoes, white or red	10-lb. sack	2.19	12/94	2c
Sausage, Jimmy Dean, 100% pork	lb.	2.76	12/94	2c
Shortening, vegetable, Crisco	3-lb.	2.46	12/94	2c
Soft drink, Coca Cola, ex deposit	2 lit	1.16	12/94	2c
Steak, t-bone	lb.	5.74	12/94	2c
Sugar, cane or beet	4 lbs.	1.28	12/94	2c
Tomatoes, Hunt's or Del Monte	14.5 oz.	0.83	12/94	2c
Tuna, chunk, light, oil-packed	6.125-6.5 oz.	0.72	12/94	2c

Danville, IL - continued

Item	Per	Value	Date	Ref.
Goods and Services				
Miscellaneous goods and services, ACCRA Index		94.70	12/94	2c
Health Care				
Health care, ACCRA Index		92.50	12/94	2c
Antibiotic ointment, Polysporin	1.5 oz.	4.37	12/94	2c
Dentist's fee, adult teeth cleaning and periodic oral exam	visit	42.00	12/94	2c
Doctor's fee, routine exam, established patient	visit	36.75	12/94	2c
Hospital care, semiprivate room	day	420.00	12/94	2c
Household Goods				
Appl. repair, service call, wash mach	min. lab. chg.	33.75	12/94	2c
Laundry detergent, Tide Ultra, Bold, or Cheer	42 oz.	3.62	12/94	2c
Tissues, facial, Kleenex brand	175	1.02	12/94	2c
Housing				
Housing, ACCRA Index		81.80	12/94	2c
House payment, principal and interest, 25% down payment	mo.	622	12/94	2c
House, 1800 sq ft, 8000 sq ft lot, new, urban, utilities	total	100000	12/94	2c
Mtge. rate, incl. points and orig. fee, 30-year conv. fixed or ARM	mo.	9.34	12/94	2c
Rent, apartment, 2 br., 1 1/2-2 baths, unfurnished, 950 sq ft, water	mo.	447	12/94	2c
Personal Goods				
Shampoo, Alberto VO5	15-oz.	1.32	12/94	2c
Toothpaste, Crest or Colgate	6-7 oz.	2.26	12/94	2c
Personal Services				
Dry cleaning, man's 2-pc. suit		5.26	12/94	2c
Haircut, man's barbershop, no styling		7.00	12/94	2c
Haircut, woman's shampoo, trim, blow-dry		14.00	12/94	2c
Restaurant Food				
Chicken, fried, thigh and drumstick		2.18	12/94	2c
Hamburger with cheese	1/4 lb.	2.00	12/94	2c
Pizza, Pizza Hut or Pizza Inn	12-13 in.	5.99	12/94	2c
Transportation				
Transportation, ACCRA Index		100.70	12/94	2c
Tire balance, computer or spin bal., front	wheel	7.50	12/94	2c
Utilities				
Utilities, ACCRA Index		108.60	12/94	2c
Electricity, (part.), other, 1800 sq. ft., new home	mo.	77.28	12/94	2c

Danville, VA

Item	Per	Value	Date	Ref.
Composite, ACCRA index		96.00	12/94	2c
Alcoholic Beverages				
Beer, Miller Lite, Bud, 12-oz., ex deposit	6	3.66	12/94	2c
J & B Scotch	750-ml.	18.45	12/94	2c
Wine, Gallo Chablis blanc	1.5-lit	5.42	12/94	2c
Appliances				
Appliances (major), expenditures	year	153	91	81r
Average annual exp.				
Food, health care, personal goods, services	year	27020	91	81r
Charity				
Cash contributions, expenditures	year	839	91	81r
Clothing				
Apparel, men and boys, total expenditures	year	380	91	81r
Apparel, women and girls, total expenditures	year	660	91	81r

Values are in dollars or fractions of dollars. In the column headed *Ref*, references are shown to sources. Each reference is followed by a letter. These refer to the geographical level for which data were reported: s=State, r=Region, and c=City or metro. The abbreviation *ex* is used to mean *except* or *excluding*; *exp* stands for expenditures. For other abbreviations and further explanations, please see the Introduction.

Danville, VA - continued

Item	Per	Value	Date	Ref.
Clothing				
Footwear, expenditures	year	193	91	81r
Jeans, man's denim		31.97	12/94	2c
Shirt, man's dress shirt		38.00	12/94	2c
Undervest, boy's size 10-14, cotton	3	3.78	12/94	2c
Communications				
Long-distance telephone rate, day, addl. min., 1-10 mi.	min.	0.12	12/93	9s
Long-distance telephone rate, day, initial min., 1-10 mi.	min.	0.21	12/93	9s
Newspaper subscription, dly. and Sun. delivery	month	7.50	12/94	2c
Phone line, single, business, field visit	inst	0.00	12/93	9s
Phone line, single, business, no field visit	inst	64.00	12/93	9s
Phone line, single, residence, field visit	inst	0.00	12/93	9s
Phone line, single, residence, no field visit	inst	38.50	12/93	9s
Telephone bill, family of four	month	28.35	12/94	2c
Telephone service, expenditures	year	616	91	81r
Education				
Board, 4-year private college/university	year	2242	8/94	80s
Board, 4-year public college/university	year	1901	8/94	80s
Education, total expenditures	year	319	91	81r
Room, 4-year private college/university	year	2022	8/94	80s
Room, 4-year public college/university	year	2186	8/94	80s
Total cost, 4-year private college/university	year	14043	8/94	80s
Total cost, 4-year public college/university	year	7726	8/94	80s
Tuition, 2-year public college/university, in-state	year	1332	8/94	80s
Tuition, 4-year private college/university, in-state	year	9778	8/94	80s
Tuition, 4-year public college/university, in-state	year	3639	8/94	80s
Energy and Fuels				
Energy, combined forms, 1800 sq. ft.	mo.	104.50	12/94	2c
Fuel oil and other fuels, expenditures	year	56	91	81r
Gas, natural, expenditures	year	150	91	81r
Gas, reg unlead, taxes inc., cash, self-service	gal	1.10	12/94	2c
Gasoline and motor oil purchased	year	1152	91	81r
Gasoline, unleaded midgrade	gallon	1.21	4/93	82r
Gasoline, unleaded premium	gallon	1.30	4/93	82r
Gasoline, unleaded regular	gallon	1.10	4/93	82r
Entertainment				
Bowling, evening rate	game	2.25	12/94	2c
Concert ticket, Pearl Jam group	perf	20.00	94	50r
Entertainment, total expenditures	year	1266	91	81r
Fees and admissions, expenditures	year	306	91	81r
Monopoly game, Parker Brothers', No. 9	game	10.14	12/94	2c
Movie	adm	5.00	12/94	2c
Pets, toys, playground equipment, expenditures	year	271	91	81r
Reading, expenditures	year	131	91	81r
Televisions, radios, and sound equipment, expenditures	year	439	91	81r
Tennis balls, yellow, Wilson or Penn, 3	can	1.93	12/94	2c
Funerals				
Burial, immediate, container provided by funeral home		1370.36	1/95	54r
Cards, acknowledgment		14.83	1/95	54r
Casket, minimum alternative		192.52	1/95	54r
Cosmetology, hair care, etc.		102.27	1/95	54r
Cremation, direct, container provided by funeral home		1065.64	1/95	54r
Embalming		304.29	1/95	54r
Funeral, funeral home		287.83	1/95	54r
Funeral, other facility		284.14	1/95	54r
Graveside service		349.13	1/95	54r
Hearse, local		132.27	1/95	54r
Limousine, local		98.45	1/95	54r
Memorial service		270.59	1/95	54r

Danville, VA - continued

Item	Per	Value	Date	Ref.
Funerals - continued				
Service charge, professional, nondeclinable		933.59	1/95	54r
Visitation and viewing		225.83	1/95	54r
Groceries				
Groceries, ACCRA Index		102.60	12/94	2c
Apples, Red Delicious	lb.	0.73	12/94	82r
Baby food, strained vegetables, lowest price	4-4.5 oz.	0.37	12/94	2c
Bacon, sliced	lb.	1.67	12/94	82r
Bananas	lb.	0.47	12/94	2c
Bananas	lb.	0.42	12/94	82r
Beef or hamburger, ground	lb.	1.49	12/94	2c
Beef purchases	year	213	91	81r
Beverage purchases, alcoholic	year	249	91	81r
Beverage purchases, nonalcoholic	year	207	91	81r
Bologna, all beef or mixed	lb.	2.27	12/94	82r
Bread, white	24-oz.	0.89	12/94	2c
Bread, white, pan	lb.	0.68	12/94	82r
Cabbage	lb.	0.42	12/94	82r
Carrots, short trimmed and topped	lb.	0.53	12/94	82r
Cereals and bakery products purchases	year	345	91	81r
Cereals and cereals products purchases	year	127	91	81r
Cheddar cheese, natural	lb.	3.58	12/94	82r
Cheese, Kraft grated Parmesan	8-oz.	2.95	12/94	2c
Chicken breast, bone-in	lb.	1.71	12/94	82r
Chicken, fresh, whole	lb.	0.78	12/94	82r
Chicken, whole fryer	lb.	1.05	12/94	2c
Chuck roast, USDA choice, boneless	lb.	2.26	12/94	82r
Cigarettes, Winston, Kings	carton	12.88	12/94	2c
Coffee, vacuum-packed	13 oz.	3.19	12/94	2c
Corn Flakes, Kellogg's or Post Toasties	18 oz.	2.51	12/94	2c
Corn, frozen, whole kernel, lowest price	10 oz.	0.80	12/94	2c
Crackers, soda, salted	lb.	1.27	12/94	82r
Cucumbers	lb.	0.65	12/94	82r
Dairy products (other) purchases	year	141	91	81r
Eggs, Grade A large	dozen	0.92	12/94	2c
Eggs, Grade A large	dozen	0.87	12/94	82r
Fish and seafood purchases	year	72	91	81r
Flour, white, all purpose	lb.	0.23	12/94	82r
Food purchases, food eaten at home	year	2381	91	81r
Foods purchased away from home, not prepared by consumer	year	1696	91	81r
Frankfurters, all meat or all beef	lb.	1.74	12/94	82r
Fruits and vegetables purchases	year	380	91	81r
Grapefruit	lb.	0.45	12/94	82r
Grapes, Thompson seedless	lb.	2.30	12/94	82r
Ground beef, 100% beef	lb.	1.37	12/94	82r
Ground chuck, 100% beef	lb.	1.97	12/94	82r
Ham, boneless, exc. canned	lb.	2.54	12/94	82r
Ice cream, prepackaged, bulk, regular	1/2 gal.	2.47	12/94	82r
Lemons	lb.	1.02	12/94	82r
Lettuce, iceberg	lb.	0.96	12/94	82r
Lettuce, iceberg	head	0.99	12/94	2c
Margarine, Blue Bonnet or Parkay cubes	lb.	0.59	12/94	2c
Margarine, stick	lb.	0.77	12/94	82r
Meats, poultry, fish, and eggs purchases	year	655	91	81r
Milk and cream (fresh) purchases	year	130	91	81r
Milk, whole	1/2 gal.	1.37	12/94	2c
Orange juice, frozen concentrate 12-oz. can	16 oz.	1.36	12/94	82r
Orange juice, Minute Maid frozen	12-oz.	1.06	12/94	2c
Oranges, Navel	lb.	0.54	12/94	82r
Peaches, halves or slices, Hunt's, Del Monte, or Libby's	29-oz.	1.42	12/94	2c
Pears, Anjou	lb.	0.81	12/94	82r
Peas, sweet, Del Monte or Green Giant	15-17 oz.	0.48	12/94	2c
Pork chops, center cut, bone-in	lb.	3.07	12/94	82r
Pork purchases	year	142	91	81r
Potato chips	16-oz.	3.15	12/94	82r
Potatoes, frozen, French fried	lb.	0.82	12/94	82r
Potatoes, white	lb.	0.34	12/94	82r

Values are in dollars or fractions of dollars. In the column headed *Ref*, references are shown to sources. Each reference is followed by a letter. These refer to the geographical level for which data were reported: s=State, r=Region, and c=City or metro. The abbreviation *ex* is used to mean *except* or *excluding*; *exp* stands for *expenditures*. For other abbreviations and further explanations, please see the Introduction.

Danville, VA - continued

Item	Per	Value	Date	Ref.
Groceries				
Potatoes, white or red	10-lb. sack	2.95	12/94	2c
Rice, white, long grain, uncooked	lb.	0.48	12/94	82r
Round roast, USDA choice, boneless	lb.	2.91	12/94	82r
Sausage, fresh	lb.	1.82	12/94	82r
Sausage, Jimmy Dean, 100% pork	lb.	2.45	12/94	2c
Shortening, vegetable oil blends	lb.	0.75	12/94	82r
Shortening, vegetable, Crisco	3-lb.	2.52	12/94	2c
Soft drink, Coca Cola, ex deposit	2 lit	1.07	12/94	2c
Spaghetti and macaroni	lb.	0.87	12/94	82r
Steak, rib eye, USDA choice, boneless	lb.	6.85	12/94	82r
Steak, round, graded & ungraded, exc. USDA prime & choice	lb.	2.96	12/94	82r
Steak, round, USDA choice, boneless	lb.	3.17	12/94	82r
Steak, sirloin, USDA choice, boneless	lb.	4.12	12/94	82r
Steak, t-bone	lb.	5.51	12/94	2c
Steak, T-bone, USDA choice, bone-in	lb.	5.63	12/94	82r
Sugar and other sweets, eaten at home, expenditures	year	93	91	81r
Sugar, cane or beet	4 lbs.	1.60	12/94	2c
Sugar, white, all sizes	lb.	0.39	12/94	82r
Tobacco products and smoking supplies, total expenditures	year	286	91	81r
Tomatoes, field grown	lb.	1.36	12/94	82r
Tomatoes, Hunt's or Del Monte	14.5 oz.	0.71	12/94	2c
Tuna, chunk, light	lb.	1.94	12/94	82r
Tuna, chunk, light, oil-packed	6.125-6.5 oz.	0.69	12/94	2c
Turkey, frozen, whole	lb.	0.96	12/94	82r
Yogurt, natural, fruit flavored	8 oz.	0.58	12/94	82r
Goods and Services				
Miscellaneous goods and services, ACCRA Index		100.50	12/94	2c
Health Care				
Health care, ACCRA Index		87.90	12/94	2c
Adenosine, emergency room	treat	100.00	95	23r
Antibiotic ointment, Polysporin	1.5 oz.	4.13	12/94	2c
Bladder tap, superpubic, infant, emergency room	treat	119.00	95	23r
Blood analysis, emergency room	treat	25.00	95	23r
Blood tests, abdominal pain, emergency room	treat	25.00	95	23r
Burn dressing, emergency room	treat	266.00	95	23r
Cardiology interpretation, emergency room	treat	26.00	95	23r
Chest X-ray, emergency room	treat	78.00	95	23r
Childbirth, Cesarean delivery, hospital charge	birth	5462.00	12/91	69r
Childbirth, Cesarean delivery, physician charge	birth	2228.00	12/91	69r
Childbirth, normal delivery, hospital charge	birth	2943.00	12/91	69r
Childbirth, normal delivery, physician charge	birth	1619.00	12/91	69r
Defibrillation pads, emergency room	treat	6.00	95	23r
Delivery, uncomplicated, total charge	birth	6180	1/93	24s
Delivery, uncomplicated, vaginal, hospital charge	birth	3380	1/93	24s
Delivery, uncomplicated, vaginal, physician's charge	birth	2800	1/93	24s
Dentist's fee, adult teeth cleaning and periodic oral exam	visit	47.60	12/94	2c
Doctor's fee, routine exam, established patient	visit	34.60	12/94	2c
Drugs, expenditures	year	297	91	81r
Gastric tube insertion, nasal, emergency room	treat	25.00	95	23r
Health care, total expenditures	year	1600	91	81r
Health insurance expenditures	year	637	91	81r
Heart monitor, emergency room	treat	40.00	95	23r
Hospital care, semiprivate room	day	304.00	12/94	2c
Insurance premium, family medical care	month	386.57	1/95	41s
Intravenous fluids, emergency room	treat	130.00	95	23r

Danville, VA - continued

Item	Per	Value	Date	Ref.
Health Care - continued				
Intravenous fluids, emergency room	liter	26.00	95	23r
Intravenous line, central, emergency room	treat	342.00	95	23r
Liver function tests, abdominal pain, emergency room	treat	26.00	95	23r
Medical care charges, total, emergency room, third-degree burns	treat	2101.00	95	23r
Medical care charges, total, emergency, infant with fever	treat	628.00	95	23r
Medical services expenditures	year	573	91	81r
Medical supplies expenditures	year	93	91	81r
Morphine, emergency room	treat	34.00	95	23r
Nursing care and facilities charges, emergency room	treat	252.00	95	23r
Nursing care and facilities charges, emergency, infant with fever	treat	252.00	95	23r
Nursing care and facilities charges, emergency, third-degree burns	treat	861.00	95	23r
Physician's charges, emergency, infant with fever	treat	212.00	95	23r
Physician's charges, emergency, third-degree burns	treat	372.00	95	23r
Physician's fee, emergency room	treat	372.00	95	23r
Physician's fee, general practitioner	visit	51.20	12/93	60r
Surgery, open-heart	proc	42374.00	1/93	14r
Ultrasound, abdominal, emergency room	treat	276.00	95	23r
Urinalysis, emergency room	treat	20.00	95	23r
Urinalysis, infant, emergency room	treat	20.00	95	23r
X-rays, emergency room	treat	78.00	95	23r
Household Goods				
Appl. repair, service call, wash mach	min. lab. chg.	33.50	12/94	2c
Floor coverings, expenditures	year	48	91	81r
Furniture, expenditures	year	280	91	81r
Household equipment, misc. expenditures	year	342	91	81r
Household expenditures, miscellaneous	year	256	91	81r
Household furnishings and equipment, expenditures	year	988	91	81r
Household operations expenditures	year	468	91	81r
Household textiles, expenditures	year	95	91	81r
Housekeeping supplies, expenditures	year	380	91	81r
Laundry and cleaning supplies, expenditures	year	109	91	81r
Laundry detergent, Tide Ultra, Bold, or Cheer	42 oz.	3.47	12/94	2c
Postage and stationery, expenditures	year	105	91	81r
Tissues, facial, Kleenex brand	175	1.02	12/94	2c
Housing				
Housing, ACCRA Index		88.60	12/94	2c
Add garage/carport		6,980	3/95	74r
Add room(s)		11,403	3/95	74r
Apartment condominium or co-op, median	unit	68600	12/94	62r
Dwellings (owned), expenditures	year	2428	91	81r
Enclose porch/patio/breezeway		4,572	3/95	74r
Finish room in basement/attic		3,794	3/95	74r
Home, existing, single-family, median	unit	120200	12/94	62r
Maintenance, repairs, insurance, and other housing expenditures	year	531	91	81r
Mortgage interest and charges expenditures	year	1506	91	81r
Princ. & int., mortgage, median-price exist. sing.-family home	mo.	540	12/94	62r
Property taxes expenditures	year	391	91	81r
Redesign, restructure more than half of home's interior		17,641	3/95	74r
Rental units expenditures	year	1264	91	81r
Insurance and Pensions				
Auto insurance, private passenger	year	564.07	12/94	71s
Insurance and pensions, personal, expenditures	year	2395	91	81r
Insurance, life and other personal, expenditures	year	368	91	81r

Values are in dollars or fractions of dollars. In the column headed *Ref*, references are shown to sources. Each reference is followed by a letter. These refer to the geographical level for which data were reported: s=State, r=Region, and c=City or metro. The abbreviation *ex* is used to mean *except* or *excluding*; *exp* stands for expenditures. For other abbreviations and further explanations, please see the Introduction.

Danville, VA - continued

Item	Per	Value	Date	Ref.
Insurance and Pensions				
Pensions and Social Security, expenditures	year	2027	91	81r
Personal Goods				
Shampoo, Alberto VO5	15-oz.	1.07	12/94	2c
Toothpaste, Crest or Colgate	6-7 oz.	1.67	12/94	2c
Personal Services				
Dry cleaning, man's 2-pc. suit		6.16	12/94	2c
Haircut, man's barbershop, no styling		8.98	12/94	2c
Haircut, woman's shampoo, trim, blow-dry		18.20	12/94	2c
Personal services expenditures	year	212	91	81r
Restaurant Food				
Chicken, fried, thigh and drumstick		2.29	12/94	2c
Dining expenditures, family	week	33.83	94	73r
Hamburger with cheese	1/4 lb.	1.99	12/94	2c
Pizza, Pizza Hut or Pizza Inn	12-13 in.	7.49	12/94	2c
Taxes				
Taxes, Federal income, expenditures	year	2275	91	81r
Taxes, personal, expenditures	year	2715	91	81r
Taxes, State and local income, expenditures	year	365	91	81r
Transportation				
Transportation, ACCRA Index		92.80	12/94	2c
Bus fare, up to 10 miles	one-way	1.00	12/94	2c
Cars and trucks purchased, new	year	1306	91	81r
Cars and trucks purchased, used	year	942	91	81r
Driver's learning permit fee	perm	3.00	1/94	84s
Driver's license fee	orig	12.00	1/94	84s
Driver's license fee, duplicate	lic	5.00	1/94	84s
Driver's license reinstatement fee, min.	susp	30.00	1/94	85s
Driver's license renewal fee	renew	12.00	1/94	84s
Identification card, nondriver	card	5.00	1/94	83s
Motorcycle license fee	orig	5.00	1/94	84s
Motorcycle license renewal fee	renew	5.00	1/94	84s
Public transportation expenditures	year	249	91	81r
Tire balance, computer or spin bal., front	wheel	5.59	12/94	2c
Transportation expenditures, total	year	5307	91	81r
Vehicle finance charges	year	346	91	81r
Vehicle insurance expenditures	year	544	91	81r
Vehicle maintenance and repairs expenditures	year	600	91	81r
Vehicle purchases	year	2275	91	81r
Vehicle rental, leases, licenses, etc. expenditures	year	141	91	81r
Vehicles purchased, other than cars and trucks	year	27	91	81r
Utilities				
Utilities, ACCRA Index		100.20	12/94	2c
Electricity expenditures	year	950	91	81r
Electricity, 1800 sq. ft., new home	mo.	104.50	12/94	2c
Utilities, fuels, and public services, total expenditures	year	2000	91	81r
Water and other public services, expenditures	year	227	91	81r
Weddings				
Bridal attendants' gowns	event	750	10/93	76r
Bridal gown	event	852	10/93	76r
Bridal headpiece and veil	event	167	10/93	76r
Bride's wedding band	event	708	10/93	76r
Clergy	event	224	10/93	76r
Engagement ring	event	2756	10/93	76r
Flowers	event	863	10/93	76r
Formal wear for groom	event	106	10/93	76r
Groom's attendants' formal wear	event	530	10/93	76r
Groom's wedding band	event	402	10/93	76r
Music	event	600	10/93	76r
Photography	event	1088	10/93	76r
Shoes for bride	event	50	10/93	76r
Videography	event	483	10/93	76r

Danville, VA - continued

Item	Per	Value	Date	Ref.
Weddings - continued				
Wedding invitations and announcements	event	342	10/93	76r
Wedding reception	event	7000	10/93	76r

Dare County, NC

Item	Per	Value	Date	Ref.
Composite, ACCRA index		102.10	12/94	2c
Alcoholic Beverages				
Beer, Miller Lite, Bud, 12-oz., ex deposit	6	3.54	12/94	2c
J & B Scotch	750-ml.	18.60	12/94	2c
Wine, Gallo Chablis blanc	1.5-lit	5.82	12/94	2c
Clothing				
Jeans, man's denim		34.49	12/94	2c
Shirt, man's dress shirt		35.00	12/94	2c
Undervest, boy's size 10-14, cotton	3	3.38	12/94	2c
Communications				
Newspaper subscription, dly. and Sun. delivery	month	11.79	12/94	2c
Telephone bill, family of four	month	16.80	12/94	2c
Energy and Fuels				
Energy, combined forms, 1800 sq. ft.	mo.	146.00	12/94	2c
Gas, reg unlead, taxes inc., cash, self-service	gal	1.13	12/94	2c
Entertainment				
Bowling, evening rate	game	2.50	12/94	2c
Monopoly game, Parker Brothers', No. 9	game	9.97	12/94	2c
Movie	adm	5.00	12/94	2c
Tennis balls, yellow, Wilson or Penn, 3	can	2.97	12/94	2c
Groceries				
Groceries, ACCRA Index		101.10	12/94	2c
Baby food, strained vegetables, lowest price	4-4.5 oz.	0.33	12/94	2c
Bananas	lb.	0.55	12/94	2c
Beef or hamburger, ground	lb.	1.37	12/94	2c
Bread, white	24-oz.	0.86	12/94	2c
Cheese, Kraft grated Parmesan	8-oz.	3.46	12/94	2c
Chicken, whole fryer	lb.	0.59	12/94	2c
Cigarettes, Winston, Kings	carton	12.89	12/94	2c
Coffee, vacuum-packed	13 oz.	3.95	12/94	2c
Corn Flakes, Kellogg's or Post Toasties	18 oz.	2.53	12/94	2c
Corn, frozen, whole kernel, lowest price	10 oz.	0.67	12/94	2c
Eggs, Grade A large	dozen	0.82	12/94	2c
Lettuce, iceberg	head	1.13	12/94	2c
Margarine, Blue Bonnet or Parkay cubes	lb.	0.83	12/94	2c
Milk, whole	1/2 gal.	1.40	12/94	2c
Orange juice, Minute Maid frozen	12-oz.	1.11	12/94	2c
Peaches, halves or slices, Hunt's, Del Monte or Libby's	29-oz.	1.24	12/94	2c
Peas, sweet, Del Monte or Green Giant	15-17 oz.	0.53	12/94	2c
Potatoes, white or red	10-lb. sack	2.39	12/94	2c
Sausage, Jimmy Dean, 100% pork	lb.	2.07	12/94	2c
Shortening, vegetable, Crisco	3-lb.	2.51	12/94	2c
Soft drink, Coca Cola, ex deposit	2 lit	1.01	12/94	2c
Steak, t-bone	lb.	4.75	12/94	2c
Sugar, cane or beet	4 lbs.	1.49	12/94	2c
Tomatoes, Hunt's or Del Monte	14.5 oz.	0.63	12/94	2c
Tuna, chunk, light, oil-packed	6.125-6.5 oz.	0.71	12/94	2c
Goods and Services				
Miscellaneous goods and services, ACCRA Index		101.40	12/94	2c

Values are in dollars or fractions of dollars. In the column headed *Ref*, references are shown to sources. Each reference is followed by a letter. These refer to the geographical level for which data were reported: s = State, r = Region, and c = City or metro. The abbreviation *ex* is used to mean *except* or *excluding*; *exp* stands for *expenditures*. For other abbreviations and further explanations, please see the Introduction.

Dare County, NC - continued

Item	Per	Value	Date	Ref.
Health Care				
Health care, ACCRA Index		85.50	12/94	2c
Antibiotic ointment, Polysporin	1.5 oz.	3.55	12/94	2c
Dentist's fee, adult teeth cleaning and periodic oral exam	visit	44.60	12/94	2c
Doctor's fee, routine exam, established patient	visit	35.75	12/94	2c
Hospital care, semiprivate room	day	309.00	12/94	2c
Household Goods				
Appl. repair, service call, wash mach	min. lab. chg.	36.09	12/94	2c
Laundry detergent, Tide Ultra, Bold, or Cheer	42 oz.	3.53	12/94	2c
Tissues, facial, Kleenex brand	175	1.20	12/94	2c
Housing				
Housing, ACCRA Index		101.70	12/94	2c
House payment, principal and interest, 25% down payment	mo.	780	12/94	2c
House, 1800 sq ft, 8000 sq ft lot, new, urban, utilities	total	126850	12/94	2c
Mtge. rate, incl. points and orig. fee, 30-year conv. fixed or ARM	mo.	9.21	12/94	2c
Personal Goods				
Shampoo, Alberto VO5	15-oz.	1.10	12/94	2c
Toothpaste, Crest or Colgate	6-7 oz.	1.94	12/94	2c
Personal Services				
Dry cleaning, man's 2-pc. suit		6.62	12/94	2c
Haircut, man's barbershop, no styling		8.80	12/94	2c
Haircut, woman's shampoo, trim, blow-dry		16.40	12/94	2c
Restaurant Food				
Chicken, fried, thigh and drumstick		2.52	12/94	2c
Hamburger with cheese	1/4 lb.	0.99	12/94	2c
Pizza, Pizza Hut or Pizza Inn	12-13 in.	7.75	12/94	2c
Transportation				
Transportation, ACCRA Index		99.10	12/94	2c
Tire balance, computer or spin bal., front	wheel	6.58	12/94	2c
Utilities				
Utilities, ACCRA Index		124.20	12/94	2c
Electricity, 1800 sq. ft., new home	mo.	146.00	12/94	2c

Davenport, IA

Item	Per	Value	Date	Ref.
Appliances				
Appliances (major), expenditures	year	131	91	81r
Average annual exp.				
Food, health care, personal goods, services	year	25935	91	81r
Charity				
Cash contributions, expenditures	year	745	91	81r
Clothing				
Apparel, men and boys, total expenditures	year	332	91	81r
Apparel, women and girls, total expenditures	year	578	91	81r
Footwear, expenditures	year	164	91	81r
Communications				
Long-distance telephone rate, day, addl. min., 1-10 mi.	min.	0.11	12/93	9s
Long-distance telephone rate, day, initial min., 1-10 mi.	min.	0.21	12/93	9s
Phone line, single, business, field visit	inst	50.00	12/93	9s
Phone line, single, business, no field visit	inst	50.00	12/93	9s
Phone line, single, residence, field visit	inst	35.00	12/93	9s
Phone line, single, residence, no field visit	inst	35.00	12/93	9s
Telephone service, expenditures	year	547	91	81r

Davenport, IA - continued

Item	Per	Value	Date	Ref.
Education				
Board, 4-year private college/university	year	1971	8/94	80s
Board, 4-year public college/university	year	1562	8/94	80s
Education, total expenditures	year	394	91	81r
Room, 4-year private college/university	year	1707	8/94	80s
Room, 4-year public college/university	year	1526	8/94	80s
Total cost, 4-year private college/university	year	14510	8/94	80s
Total cost, 4-year public college/university	year	5440	8/94	80s
Tuition, 2-year public college/university, in-state	year	1612	8/94	80s
Tuition, 4-year private college/university, in-state	year	10832	8/94	80s
Tuition, 4-year public college/university, in-state	year	2352	8/94	80s
Energy and Fuels				
Fuel oil and other fuels, expenditures	year	83	91	81r
Gas, natural, expenditures	year	373	91	81r
Gasoline and motor oil purchased	year	1000	91	81r
Gasoline, unleaded midgrade	gallon	1.15	4/93	82r
Gasoline, unleaded premium	gallon	1.23	4/93	82r
Gasoline, unleaded regular	gallon	1.07	4/93	82r
Entertainment				
Entertainment, total expenditures	year	1356	91	81r
Fees and admissions, expenditures	year	347	91	81r
Pets, toys, playground equipment, expenditures	year	270	91	81r
Reading, expenditures	year	160	91	81r
Televisions, radios, and sound equipment, expenditures	year	433	91	81r
Funerals				
Burial, immediate, container provided by funeral home		1348.78	1/95	54r
Cards, acknowledgment		21.20	1/95	54r
Casket, minimum alternative		182.83	1/95	54r
Cosmetology, hair care, etc.		133.11	1/95	54r
Cremation, direct, container provided by funeral home		1101.95	1/95	54r
Embalming		314.45	1/95	54r
Funeral, funeral home		304.88	1/95	54r
Funeral, other facility		301.37	1/95	54r
Graveside service		290.59	1/95	54r
Hearse, local		137.37	1/95	54r
Limousine, local		82.84	1/95	54r
Memorial service		316.57	1/95	54r
Service charge, professional, nondeclinable		1099.00	1/95	54r
Visitation and viewing		209.25	1/95	54r
Groceries				
Apples, Red Delicious	lb.	0.68	12/94	82r
Bacon, sliced	lb.	1.88	12/94	82r
Bananas	lb.	0.41	12/94	82r
Beef purchases	year	197	91	81r
Beef, stew, boneless	lb.	2.52	12/94	82r
Beverage purchases, alcoholic	year	293	91	81r
Beverage purchases, nonalcoholic	year	203	91	81r
Bologna, all beef or mixed	lb.	2.12	12/94	82r
Bread, white, pan	lb.	0.76	12/94	82r
Cabbage	lb.	0.44	12/94	82r
Carrots, short trimmed and topped	lb.	0.44	12/94	82r
Cereals and bakery products purchases	year	347	91	81r
Cereals and cereals products purchases	year	119	91	81r
Cheddar cheese, natural	lb.	3.28	12/94	82r
Chicken breast, bone-in	lb.	1.61	12/94	82r
Chicken, fresh, whole	lb.	0.89	12/94	82r
Chuck roast, USDA choice, boneless	lb.	2.33	12/94	82r
Coffee, 100%, ground roast, all sizes	lb.	4.28	12/94	82r
Cookies, chocolate chip	lb.	2.72	12/94	82r
Dairy products (other) purchases	year	148	91	81r
Eggs, Grade A large	dozen	0.76	12/94	82r
Fish and seafood purchases	year	61	91	81r
Flour, white, all purpose	lb.	0.22	12/94	82r
Food purchases, food eaten at home	year	2313	91	81r

Values are in dollars or fractions of dollars. In the column headed *Ref*, references are shown to sources. Each reference is followed by a letter. These refer to the geographical level for which data were reported: s=State, r=Region, and c=City or metro. The abbreviation *ex* is used to mean *except* or *excluding*; *exp* stands for *expenditures*. For other abbreviations and further explanations, please see the Introduction.

Davenport, IA - continued

Item	Per	Value	Date	Ref.
Groceries				
Foods purchased away from home, not prepared by consumer	year	1709	91	81r
Fruits and vegetables purchases	year	372	91	81r
Grapefruit	lb.	0.47	12/94	82r
Grapes, Thompson seedless	lb.	2.15	12/94	82r
Ground beef, 100% beef	lb.	1.37	12/94	82r
Ground chuck, 100% beef	lb.	1.81	12/94	82r
Ham, boneless, exc. canned	lb.	2.16	12/94	82r
Ice cream, prepackaged, bulk, regular	1/2 gal.	2.48	12/94	82r
Lemons	lb.	1.08	12/94	82r
Lettuce, iceberg	lb.	0.81	12/94	82r
Margarine, stick	lb.	0.81	12/94	82r
Meats, poultry, fish, and eggs purchases	year	591	91	81r
Milk and cream (fresh) purchases	year	132	91	81r
Orange juice, frozen concentrate 12-oz. can	16 oz.	1.41	12/94	82r
Oranges, Navel	lb.	0.56	12/94	82r
Peanut butter, creamy, all sizes	lb.	1.81	12/94	82r
Pork chops, center cut, bone-in	lb.	2.76	12/94	82r
Pork purchases	year	130	91	81r
Potato chips	16-oz.	2.81	12/94	82r
Potatoes, frozen, French fried	lb.	0.83	12/94	82r
Potatoes, white	lb.	0.28	12/94	82r
Round roast, USDA choice, boneless	lb.	2.90	12/94	82r
Shortening, vegetable oil blends	lb.	0.88	12/94	82r
Spaghetti and macaroni	lb.	0.78	12/94	82r
Steak, rib eye, USDA choice, boneless	lb.	6.15	12/94	82r
Steak, round, graded & ungraded, exc. USDA prime & choice	lb.	2.72	12/94	82r
Steak, round, USDA choice, boneless	lb.	3.02	12/94	82r
Steak, sirloin, USDA choice, boneless	lb.	3.85	12/94	82r
Steak, T-bone, USDA choice, bone-in	lb.	5.38	12/94	82r
Sugar and other sweets, eaten at home, expenditures	year	91	91	81r
Sugar, white, all sizes	lb.	0.36	12/94	82r
Tobacco products and smoking supplies, total expenditures	year	298	91	81r
Tomatoes, field grown	lb.	1.36	12/94	82r
Tuna, chunk, light	lb.	1.94	12/94	82r
Turkey, frozen, whole	lb.	0.96	12/94	82r
Yogurt, natural, fruit flavored	8 oz.	0.62	12/94	82r
Health Care				
Childbirth, Cesarean delivery, hospital charge	birth	5101.00	12/91	69r
Childbirth, Cesarean delivery, physician charge	birth	2234.00	12/91	69r
Childbirth, normal delivery, hospital charge	birth	2891.00	12/91	69r
Childbirth, normal delivery, physician charge	birth	1623.00	12/91	69r
Drugs, expenditures	year	248	91	81r
Health care, total expenditures	year	1336	91	81r
Health insurance expenditures	year	550	91	81r
Insurance premium, family medical care	month	395.98	1/95	41s
Medical services expenditures	year	457	91	81r
Medical supplies expenditures	year	82	91	81r
Household Goods				
Floor coverings, expenditures	year	105	91	81r
Furniture, expenditures	year	291	91	81r
Household equipment, misc. expenditures	year	341	91	81r
Household expenditures, miscellaneous	year	162	91	81r
Household furnishings and equipment, expenditures	year	1042	91	81r
Household operations expenditures	year	365	91	81r
Household textiles, expenditures	year	101	91	81r
Housekeeping supplies, expenditures	year	390	91	81r
Laundry and cleaning supplies, expenditures	year	110	91	81r
Postage and stationery, expenditures	year	115	91	81r
Housing				
Add garage/carport		8,479	3/95	74r
Add room(s)		21,347	3/95	74r
Apartment condominium or co-op, median	unit	87100	12/94	62r

Davenport, IA - continued

Item	Per	Value	Date	Ref.
Housing - continued				
Bathroom addition, average cost	add	9734.00	3/95	13r
Bathroom remodeling, average cost	remod	6414.00	3/95	13r
Bedroom, master suite addition, average cost	add	27122.00	3/95	13r
Deck addition, average cost	add	6665.00	3/95	13r
Dwellings (owned), expenditures	year	2566	91	81r
Enclose porch/patio/breezeway		4,556	3/95	74r
Exterior remodeling, average cost	remod	15395.00	3/95	13r
Family room addition, average cost	add	27658.00	3/95	13r
Finish room in basement/attic		5,074	3/95	74r
Home, existing, single-family, median	unit	106500	12/94	62r
Home, existing, single-family, median	unit	61.90	12/94	62c
Kitchen remodeling, major, average cost	remod	17084.00	3/95	13r
Kitchen remodeling, minor, average cost	remod	5804.00	3/95	13r
Maintenance, repairs, insurance, and other housing expenditures	year	484	91	81r
Mortgage interest and charges expenditures	year	1443	91	81r
Office, home addition, average cost	add	8121.00	3/95	13r
Princ. & int., mortgage, median-price exist. sing.-family home	mo.	515	12/94	62r
Property taxes expenditures	year	639	91	81r
Redesign, restructure more than half of home's interior		9,114	3/95	74r
Rental units expenditures	year	1200	91	81r
Sun-space addition, average cost	add	23768.00	3/95	13r
Wing addition, two-story, average cost	add	50410.00	3/95	13r
Insurance and Pensions				
Auto insurance, private passenger	year	467.45	12/94	71s
Insurance and pensions, personal, expenditures	year	2408	91	81r
Insurance, life and other personal, expenditures	year	355	91	81r
Pensions and Social Security, expenditures	year	2053	91	81r
Legal Assistance				
Legal work, law firm associate	hour	90		10r
Legal work, law firm partner	hour	139		10r
Personal Services				
Personal services expenditures	year	203	91	81r
Restaurant Food				
Dining expenditures, family	week	30.03	94	73r
Taxes				
Taxes, Federal income, expenditures	year	1756	91	81r
Taxes, personal, expenditures	year	2426	91	81r
Taxes, State and local income, expenditures	year	568	91	81r
Transportation				
Bus fare, one-way	trip	0.70	12/95	1c
Cars and trucks purchased, new	year	891	91	81r
Cars and trucks purchased, used	year	1155	91	81r
Driver's learning permit fee	perm	6.00	1/94	84s
Driver's license fee	orig	0.00	1/94	84s
Driver's license fee, duplicate	lic	3.00	1/94	84s
Driver's license reinstatement fee, min.	susp	20.00	1/94	85s
Driver's license renewal fee	renew	0.00	1/94	84s
Identification card, nondriver	card	5.00	1/94	83s
Motorcycle learning permit fee	perm	8.00	1/94	84s
Motorcycle license fee	orig	8.00	1/94	84s
Motorcycle license fee, duplicate	lic	3.00	1/94	84s
Motorcycle license renewal fee	renew	8.00	1/94	84s
Public transportation expenditures	year	209	91	81r
Transportation expenditures, total	year	4792	91	81r
Vehicle finance charges	year	300	91	81r
Vehicle insurance expenditures	year	485	91	81r
Vehicle maintenance and repairs expenditures	year	534	91	81r
Vehicle purchases	year	2068	91	81r
Vehicle rental, leases, licenses, etc. expenditures	year	197	91	81r
Vehicles purchased, other than cars and trucks	year	22	91	81r

Values are in dollars or fractions of dollars. In the column headed *Ref*, references are shown to sources. Each reference is followed by a letter. These refer to the geographical level for which data were reported: s =State, r =Region, and c =City or metro. The abbreviation *ex* is used to mean *except* or *excluding*; *exp* stands for *expenditures*. For other abbreviations and further explanations, please see the Introduction.

Davenport, IA - continued

Item	Per	Value	Date	Ref.
Utilities				
Electricity expenditures	year	668	91	81r
Electricity, summer, 250 KWh	month	30.32	8/93	64c
Electricity, summer, 500 KWh	month	55.43	8/93	64c
Electricity, summer, 750 KWh	month	80.53	8/93	64c
Electricity, summer, 1000 KWh	month	105.63	8/93	64c
Utilities, fuels, and public services, total expenditures	year	1838	91	81r
Water and other public services, expenditures	year	167	91	81r
Weddings				
Bridal attendants' gowns	event	750	10/93	76r
Bridal gown	event	852	10/93	76r
Bridal headpiece and veil	event	167	10/93	76r
Bride's wedding band	event	708	10/93	76r
Clergy	event	224	10/93	76r
Engagement ring	event	2756	10/93	76r
Flowers	event	863	10/93	76r
Formal wear for groom	event	106	10/93	76r
Groom's attendants' formal wear	event	530	10/93	76r
Groom's wedding band	event	402	10/93	76r
Music	event	600	10/93	76r
Photography	event	1088	10/93	76r
Shoes for bride	event	50	10/93	76r
Videography	event	483	10/93	76r
Wedding invitations and announcements	event	342	10/93	76r
Wedding reception	event	7000	10/93	76r

Davenport, IL

Item	Per	Value	Date	Ref.
Appliances				
Appliances (major), expenditures	year	131	91	81r
Average annual exp.				
Food, health care, personal goods, services	year	25935	91	81r
Charity				
Cash contributions, expenditures	year	745	91	81r
Clothing				
Apparel, men and boys, total expenditures	year	332	91	81r
Apparel, women and girls, total expenditures	year	578	91	81r
Footwear, expenditures	year	164	91	81r
Communications				
Long-distance telephone rate, day, addl. min., 1-10 mi.	min.	0.04	12/93	9s
Long-distance telephone rate, day, initial min., 1-10 mi.	min.	0.10	12/93	9s
Phone line, single, business, field visit	inst	84.50	12/93	9s
Phone line, single, business, no field visit	inst	84.50	12/93	9s
Phone line, single, residence, field visit	inst	55.00	12/93	9s
Phone line, single, residence, no field visit	inst	55.00	12/93	9s
Telephone service, expenditures	year	547	91	81r
Education				
Board, 4-year private college/university	year	2078	8/94	80s
Board, 4-year public college/university	year	2139	8/94	80s
Education, total expenditures	year	394	91	81r
Room, 4-year private college/university	year	2696	8/94	80s
Room, 4-year public college/university	year	1796	8/94	80s
Total cost, 4-year private college/university	year	15249	8/94	80s
Total cost, 4-year public college/university	year	6964	8/94	80s
Tuition, 2-year public college/university, in-state	year	1135	8/94	80s
Tuition, 4-year private college/university, in-state	year	10474	8/94	80s
Tuition, 4-year public college/university, in-state	year	3029	8/94	80s
Energy and Fuels				
Fuel oil and other fuels, expenditures	year	83	91	81r
Gas, natural, expenditures	year	373	91	81r
Gasoline and motor oil purchased	year	1000	91	81r

Davenport, IL - continued

Item	Per	Value	Date	Ref.
Energy and Fuels - continued				
Gasoline, unleaded midgrade	gallon	1.15	4/93	82r
Gasoline, unleaded premium	gallon	1.23	4/93	82r
Gasoline, unleaded regular	gallon	1.07	4/93	82r
Entertainment				
Entertainment, total expenditures	year	1356	91	81r
Fees and admissions, expenditures	year	347	91	81r
Pets, toys, playground equipment, expenditures	year	270	91	81r
Reading, expenditures	year	160	91	81r
Televisions, radios, and sound equipment, expenditures	year	433	91	81r
Funerals				
Burial, immediate, container provided by funeral home		1268.31	1/95	54r
Cards, acknowledgment		26.12	1/95	54r
Casket, minimum alternative		198.03	1/95	54r
Cosmetology, hair care, etc.		122.19	1/95	54r
Cremation, direct, container provided by funeral home		977.81	1/95	54r
Embalming		334.00	1/95	54r
Funeral, funeral home		321.16	1/95	54r
Funeral, other facility		317.73	1/95	54r
Graveside service		292.48	1/95	54r
Hearse, local		153.20	1/95	54r
Limousine, local		123.52	1/95	54r
Memorial service		356.30	1/95	54r
Service charge, professional, nondeclinable		968.24	1/95	54r
Visitation and viewing		332.66	1/95	54r
Groceries				
Apples, Red Delicious	lb.	0.68	12/94	82r
Bacon, sliced	lb.	1.88	12/94	82r
Bananas	lb.	0.41	12/94	82r
Beef purchases	year	197	91	81r
Beef, stew, boneless	lb.	2.52	12/94	82r
Beverage purchases, alcoholic	year	293	91	81r
Beverage purchases, nonalcoholic	year	203	91	81r
Bologna, all beef or mixed	lb.	2.12	12/94	82r
Bread, white, pan	lb.	0.76	12/94	82r
Cabbage	lb.	0.44	12/94	82r
Carrots, short trimmed and topped	lb.	0.44	12/94	82r
Cereals and bakery products purchases	year	347	91	81r
Cereals and cereals products purchases	year	119	91	81r
Cheddar cheese, natural	lb.	3.28	12/94	82r
Chicken breast, bone-in	lb.	1.61	12/94	82r
Chicken, fresh, whole	lb.	0.89	12/94	82r
Chuck roast, USDA choice, boneless	lb.	2.33	12/94	82r
Coffee, 100%, ground roast, all sizes	lb.	4.28	12/94	82r
Cookies, chocolate chip	lb.	2.72	12/94	82r
Dairy products (other) purchases	year	148	91	81r
Eggs, Grade A large	dozen	0.76	12/94	82r
Fish and seafood purchases	year	61	91	81r
Flour, white, all purpose	lb.	0.22	12/94	82r
Food purchases, food eaten at home	year	2313	91	81r
Foods purchased away from home, not prepared by consumer	year	1709	91	81r
Fruits and vegetables purchases	year	372	91	81r
Grapefruit	lb.	0.47	12/94	82r
Grapes, Thompson seedless	lb.	2.15	12/94	82r
Ground beef, 100% beef	lb.	1.37	12/94	82r
Ground chuck, 100% beef	lb.	1.81	12/94	82r
Ham, boneless, exc. canned	lb.	2.16	12/94	82r
Ice cream, prepackaged, bulk, regular	1/2 gal.	2.48	12/94	82r
Lemons	lb.	1.08	12/94	82r
Lettuce, iceberg	lb.	0.81	12/94	82r
Margarine, stick	lb.	0.81	12/94	82r
Meats, poultry, fish, and eggs purchases	year	591	91	81r
Milk and cream (fresh) purchases	year	132	91	81r
Orange juice, frozen concentrate 12-oz. can	16 oz.	1.41	12/94	82r
Oranges, Navel	lb.	0.56	12/94	82r
Peanut butter, creamy, all sizes	lb.	1.81	12/94	82r

Values are in dollars or fractions of dollars. In the column headed *Ref*, references are shown to sources. Each reference is followed by a letter. These refer to the geographical level for which data were reported: s = State, r = Region, and c = City or metro. The abbreviation *ex* is used to mean *except* or *excluding*; *exp* stands for expenditures. For other abbreviations and further explanations, please see the Introduction.

Davenport, IL - continued

Item	Per	Value	Date	Ref.
Groceries				
Pork chops, center cut, bone-in	lb.	2.76	12/94	82r
Pork purchases	year	130	91	81r
Potato chips	16-oz.	2.81	12/94	82r
Potatoes, frozen, French fried	lb.	0.83	12/94	82r
Potatoes, white	lb.	0.28	12/94	82r
Round roast, USDA choice, boneless	lb.	2.90	12/94	82r
Shortening, vegetable oil blends	lb.	0.88	12/94	82r
Spaghetti and macaroni	lb.	0.78	12/94	82r
Steak, rib eye, USDA choice, boneless	lb.	6.15	12/94	82r
Steak, round, graded & ungraded, exc. USDA prime & choice	lb.	2.72	12/94	82r
Steak, round, USDA choice, boneless	lb.	3.02	12/94	82r
Steak, sirloin, USDA choice, boneless	lb.	3.85	12/94	82r
Steak, T-bone, USDA choice, bone-in	lb.	5.38	12/94	82r
Sugar and other sweets, eaten at home, expenditures	year	91	91	81r
Sugar, white, all sizes	lb.	0.36	12/94	82r
Tobacco products and smoking supplies, total expenditures	year	298	91	81r
Tomatoes, field grown	lb.	1.36	12/94	82r
Tuna, chunk, light	lb.	1.94	12/94	82r
Turkey, frozen, whole	lb.	0.96	12/94	82r
Yogurt, natural, fruit flavored	8 oz.	0.62	12/94	82r
Health Care				
Childbirth, Cesarean delivery, hospital charge	birth	5101.00	12/91	69r
Childbirth, Cesarean delivery, physician charge	birth	2234.00	12/91	69r
Childbirth, normal delivery, hospital charge	birth	2891.00	12/91	69r
Childbirth, normal delivery, physician charge	birth	1623.00	12/91	69r
Drugs, expenditures	year	248	91	81r
Health care, total expenditures	year	1336	91	81r
Health insurance expenditures	year	550	91	81r
Insurance premium, family medical care	month	363.57	1/95	41s
Medical services expenditures	year	457	91	81r
Medical supplies expenditures	year	82	91	81r
Household Goods				
Floor coverings, expenditures	year	105	91	81r
Furniture, expenditures	year	291	91	81r
Household equipment, misc. expenditures	year	341	91	81r
Household expenditures, miscellaneous	year	162	91	81r
Household furnishings and equipment, expenditures	year	1042	91	81r
Household operations expenditures	year	365	91	81r
Household textiles, expenditures	year	101	91	81r
Housekeeping supplies, expenditures	year	390	91	81r
Laundry and cleaning supplies, expenditures	year	110	91	81r
Postage and stationery, expenditures	year	115	91	81r
Housing				
Add garage/carport		8,479	3/95	74r
Add room(s)		21,347	3/95	74r
Apartment condominium or co-op, median	unit	87100	12/94	62r
Bathroom addition, average cost	add	9734.00	3/95	13r
Bathroom remodeling, average cost	remod	6414.00	3/95	13r
Bedroom, master suite addition, average cost	add	27122.00	3/95	13r
Deck addition, average cost	add	6665.00	3/95	13r
Dwellings (owned), expenditures	year	2566	91	81r
Enclose porch/patio/breezeway		4,556	3/95	74r
Exterior remodeling, average cost	remod	15395.00	3/95	13r
Family room addition, average cost	add	27658.00	3/95	13r
Finish room in basement/attic		5,074	3/95	74r
Home, existing, single-family, median	unit	106500	12/94	62r
Kitchen remodeling, major, average cost	remod	17084.00	3/95	13r
Kitchen remodeling, minor, average cost	remod	5804.00	3/95	13r
Maintenance, repairs, insurance, and other housing expenditures	year	484	91	81r
Mortgage interest and charges expenditures	year	1443	91	81r
Office, home addition, average cost	add	8121.00	3/95	13r

Davenport, IL - continued

Item	Per	Value	Date	Ref.
Housing - continued				
Princ. & int., mortgage, median-price exist. sing.-family home	mo.	515	12/94	62r
Property taxes expenditures	year	639	91	81r
Redesign, restructure more than half of home's interior		9,114	3/95	74r
Rental units expenditures	year	1200	91	81r
Sun-space addition, average cost	add	23768.00	3/95	13r
Wing addition, two-story, average cost	add	50410.00	3/95	13r
Insurance and Pensions				
Auto insurance, private passenger	year	679.48	12/94	71s
Insurance and pensions, personal, expenditures	year	2408	91	81r
Insurance, life and other personal, expenditures	year	355	91	81r
Pensions and Social Security, expenditures	year	2053	91	81r
Legal Assistance				
Legal work, law firm associate	hour	90		10r
Legal work, law firm partner	hour	139		10r
Personal Services				
Personal services expenditures	year	203	91	81r
Restaurant Food				
Dining expenditures, family	week	30.03	94	73r
Taxes				
Taxes, Federal income, expenditures	year	1756	91	81r
Taxes, personal, expenditures	year	2426	91	81r
Taxes, State and local income, expenditures	year	568	91	81r
Transportation				
Cars and trucks purchased, new	year	891	91	81r
Cars and trucks purchased, used	year	1155	91	81r
Driver's learning permit fee	perm	20.00	1/94	84s
Driver's license fee	orig	10.00	1/94	84s
Driver's license fee, duplicate	lic	5.00	1/94	84s
Driver's license reinstatement fee, min.	susp	30.00	1/94	85s
Driver's license renewal fee	renew	10.00	1/94	84s
Identification card, nondriver	card	4.00	1/94	83s
Motorcycle learning permit fee	perm	20.00	1/94	84s
Motorcycle license fee	orig	10.00	1/94	84s
Motorcycle license fee, duplicate	lic	5.00	1/94	84s
Motorcycle license renewal fee	renew	10.00	1/94	84s
Public transportation expenditures	year	209	91	81r
Transportation expenditures, total	year	4792	91	81r
Vehicle finance charges	year	300	91	81r
Vehicle insurance expenditures	year	485	91	81r
Vehicle maintenance and repairs expenditures	year	534	91	81r
Vehicle purchases	year	2068	91	81r
Vehicle rental, leases, licenses, etc. expenditures	year	197	91	81r
Vehicles purchased, other than cars and trucks	year	22	91	81r
Utilities				
Electricity expenditures	year	668	91	81r
Utilities, fuels, and public services, total expenditures	year	1838	91	81r
Water and other public services, expenditures	year	167	91	81r
Weddings				
Bridal attendants' gowns	event	750	10/93	76r
Bridal gown	event	852	10/93	76r
Bridal headpiece and veil	event	167	10/93	76r
Bride's wedding band	event	708	10/93	76r
Clergy	event	224	10/93	76r
Engagement ring	event	2756	10/93	76r
Flowers	event	863	10/93	76r
Formal wear for groom	event	106	10/93	76r
Groom's attendants' formal wear	event	530	10/93	76r
Groom's wedding band	event	402	10/93	76r
Music	event	600	10/93	76r

Values are in dollars or fractions of dollars. In the column headed *Ref*, references are shown to sources. Each reference is followed by a letter. These refer to the geographical level for which data were reported: s=State, r=Region, and c=City or metro. The abbreviation *ex* is used to mean *except* or *excluding*; *exp* stands for *expenditures*. For other abbreviations and further explanations, please see the Introduction.

Davenport, IL - continued

Item	Per	Value	Date	Ref.
Weddings				
Photography	event	1088	10/93	76r
Shoes for bride	event	50	10/93	76r
Videography	event	483	10/93	76r
Wedding invitations and announcements	event	342	10/93	76r
Wedding reception	event	7000	10/93	76r

Dayton, OH

Item	Per	Value	Date	Ref.
Composite, ACCRA index		99.10	12/94	2c
Alcoholic Beverages				
Beer, Miller Lite, Bud, 12-oz., ex deposit	6	4.01	12/94	2c
J & B Scotch	750-ml.	19.00	12/94	2c
Wine, Gallo Chablis blanc	1.5-lit	5.19	12/94	2c
Appliances				
Appliances (major), expenditures	year	131	91	81r
Average annual exp.				
Food, health care, personal goods, services	year	25935	91	81r
Charity				
Cash contributions, expenditures	year	745	91	81r
Clothing				
Apparel, men and boys, total expenditures	year	332	91	81r
Apparel, women and girls, total expenditures	year	578	91	81r
Footwear, expenditures	year	164	91	81r
Jeans, man's denim		28.48	12/94	2c
Shirt, man's dress shirt		32.10	12/94	2c
Undervest, boy's size 10-14, cotton	3	3.68	12/94	2c
Communications				
Long-distance telephone rate, day, addl. min., 1-10 mi.	min.	0.16	12/93	9s
Long-distance telephone rate, day, initial min., 1-10 mi.	min.	0.32	12/93	9s
Newspaper subscription, dly. and Sun. delivery	month	14.78	12/94	2c
Phone line, single, business, field visit	inst	55.42	12/93	9s
Phone line, single, business, no field visit	inst	55.42	12/93	9s
Phone line, single, residence, field visit	inst	30.38	12/93	9s
Phone line, single, residence, no field visit	inst	30.38	12/93	9s
Telephone bill, family of four	month	22.01	12/94	2c
Telephone service, expenditures	year	547	91	81r
Telephone, residential, flat rate	mo.	15.25	12/93	8c
Education				
Board, 4-year private college/university	year	2241	8/94	80s
Board, 4-year public college/university	year	1625	8/94	80s
Education, total expenditures	year	394	91	81r
Room, 4-year private college/university	year	2118	8/94	80s
Room, 4-year public college/university	year	2103	8/94	80s
Total cost, 4-year private college/university	year	15444	8/94	80s
Total cost, 4-year public college/university	year	6987	8/94	80s
Tuition, 2-year public college/university, in-state	year	2076	8/94	80s
Tuition, 4-year private college/university, in-state	year	11085	8/94	80s
Tuition, 4-year public college/university, in-state	year	3259	8/94	80s
Energy and Fuels				
Energy, combined forms, 1800 sq. ft.	mo.	116.62	12/94	2c
Energy, exc. electricity, 1800 sq. ft.	mo.	44.31	12/94	2c
Fuel oil and other fuels, expenditures	year	83	91	81r
Gas, cooking, winter, 10 therms	month	9.08	2/94	65c
Gas, cooking, winter, 30 therms	month	19.24	2/94	65c
Gas, cooking, winter, 50 therms	month	29.41	2/94	65c
Gas, heating, winter, 100 therms	month	54.82	2/94	65c
Gas, heating, winter, average use	month	93.44	2/94	65c
Gas, natural, expenditures	year	373	91	81r
Gas, reg unlead, taxes inc., cash, self-service	gal	1.09	12/94	2c

Dayton, OH - continued

Item	Per	Value	Date	Ref.
Energy and Fuels - continued				
Gasoline and motor oil purchased	year	1000	91	81r
Gasoline, unleaded midgrade	gallon	1.15	4/93	82r
Gasoline, unleaded premium	gallon	1.23	4/93	82r
Gasoline, unleaded regular	gallon	1.07	4/93	82r
Entertainment				
Bowling, evening rate	game	2.31	12/94	2c
Entertainment, total expenditures	year	1356	91	81r
Fees and admissions, expenditures	year	347	91	81r
Monopoly game, Parker Brothers', No. 9	game	9.14	12/94	2c
Movie	adm	6.50	12/94	2c
Pets, toys, playground equipment, expenditures	year	270	91	81r
Reading, expenditures	year	160	91	81r
Televisions, radios, and sound equipment, expenditures	year	433	91	81r
Tennis balls, yellow, Wilson or Penn, 3	can	2.18	12/94	2c
Funerals				
Burial, immediate, container provided by funeral home		1268.31	1/95	54r
Cards, acknowledgment		26.12	1/95	54r
Casket, minimum alternative		198.03	1/95	54r
Cosmetology, hair care, etc.		122.19	1/95	54r
Cremation, direct, container provided by funeral home		977.81	1/95	54r
Embalming		334.00	1/95	54r
Funeral, funeral home		321.16	1/95	54r
Funeral, other facility		317.73	1/95	54r
Graveside service		292.48	1/95	54r
Hearse, local		153.20	1/95	54r
Limousine, local		123.52	1/95	54r
Memorial service		356.30	1/95	54r
Service charge, professional, nondeclinable		968.24	1/95	54r
Visitation and viewing		332.66	1/95	54r
Groceries				
Groceries, ACCRA Index		88.90	12/94	2c
Apples, Red Delicious	lb.	0.68	12/94	82r
Baby food, strained vegetables, lowest price	4-4.5 oz.	0.23	12/94	2c
Bacon, sliced	lb.	1.88	12/94	82r
Bananas	lb.	0.36	12/94	2c
Bananas	lb.	0.41	12/94	82r
Beef or hamburger, ground	lb.	1.31	12/94	2c
Beef purchases	year	197	91	81r
Beef, stew, boneless	lb.	2.52	12/94	82r
Beverage purchases, alcoholic	year	293	91	81r
Beverage purchases, nonalcoholic	year	203	91	81r
Bologna, all beef or mixed	lb.	2.12	12/94	82r
Bread, white	24-oz.	0.47	12/94	2c
Bread, white, pan	lb.	0.76	12/94	82r
Cabbage	lb.	0.44	12/94	82r
Carrots, short trimmed and topped	lb.	0.44	12/94	82r
Cereals and bakery products purchases	year	347	91	81r
Cereals and cereals products purchases	year	119	91	81r
Cheddar cheese, natural	lb.	3.28	12/94	82r
Cheese, Kraft grated Parmesan	8-oz.	3.17	12/94	2c
Chicken breast, bone-in	lb.	1.61	12/94	82r
Chicken, fresh, whole	lb.	0.89	12/94	82r
Chicken, whole fryer	lb.	0.75	12/94	2c
Chuck roast, USDA choice, boneless	lb.	2.33	12/94	82r
Cigarettes, Winston, Kings	carton	14.70	12/94	2c
Coffee, 100%, ground roast, all sizes	lb.	4.28	12/94	82r
Coffee, vacuum-packed	13 oz.	3.73	12/94	2c
Cookies, chocolate chip	lb.	2.72	12/94	82r
Corn Flakes, Kellogg's or Post Toasties	18 oz.	1.97	12/94	2c
Corn, frozen, whole kernel, lowest price	10 oz.	0.61	12/94	2c
Dairy products (other) purchases	year	148	91	81r
Eggs, Grade A large	dozen	0.77	12/94	2c
Eggs, Grade A large	dozen	0.76	12/94	82r
Fish and seafood purchases	year	61	91	81r
Flour, white, all purpose	lb.	0.22	12/94	82r
Food purchases, food eaten at home	year	2313	91	81r

Values are in dollars or fractions of dollars. In the column headed *Ref*, references are shown to sources. Each reference is followed by a letter. These refer to the geographical level for which data were reported: s=State, r=Region, and c=City or metro. The abbreviation *ex* is used to mean *except* or *excluding*; *exp* stands for expenditures. For other abbreviations and further explanations, please see the Introduction.

Dayton, OH - continued

Item	Per	Value	Date	Ref.
Groceries				
Foods purchased away from home, not prepared by consumer	year	1709	91	81r
Fruits and vegetables purchases	year	372	91	81r
Grapefruit	lb.	0.47	12/94	82r
Grapes, Thompson seedless	lb.	2.15	12/94	82r
Ground beef, 100% beef	lb.	1.37	12/94	82r
Ground chuck, 100% beef	lb.	1.81	12/94	82r
Ham, boneless, exc. canned	lb.	2.16	12/94	82r
Ice cream, prepackaged, bulk, regular	1/2 gal.	2.48	12/94	82r
Lemons	lb.	1.08	12/94	82r
Lettuce, iceberg	lb.	0.81	12/94	82r
Lettuce, iceberg	head	0.83	12/94	2c
Margarine, Blue Bonnet or Parkay cubes	lb.	0.55	12/94	2c
Margarine, stick	lb.	0.81	12/94	82r
Meats, poultry, fish, and eggs purchases	year	591	91	81r
Milk and cream (fresh) purchases	year	132	91	81r
Milk, whole	1/2 gal.	1.39	12/94	2c
Orange juice, frozen concentrate 12-oz. can	16 oz.	1.41	12/94	82r
Orange juice, Minute Maid frozen	12-oz.	1.21	12/94	2c
Oranges, Navel	lb.	0.56	12/94	82r
Peaches, halves or slices, Hunt's, Del Monte, or Libby's	29-oz.	1.49	12/94	2c
Peanut butter, creamy, all sizes	lb.	1.81	12/94	82r
Peas, sweet, Del Monte or Green Giant	15-17 oz.	0.60	12/94	2c
Pork chops, center cut, bone-in	lb.	2.76	12/94	82r
Pork purchases	year	130	91	81r
Potato chips	16-oz.	2.81	12/94	82r
Potatoes, frozen, French fried	lb.	0.83	12/94	82r
Potatoes, white	lb.	0.28	12/94	82r
Potatoes, white or red	10-lb. sack	1.81	12/94	2c
Round roast, USDA choice, boneless	lb.	2.90	12/94	82r
Sausage, Jimmy Dean, 100% pork	lb.	2.27	12/94	2c
Shortening, vegetable oil blends	lb.	0.88	12/94	82r
Shortening, vegetable, Crisco	3-lb.	2.55	12/94	2c
Soft drink, Coca Cola, ex deposit	2 lit	1.13	12/94	2c
Spaghetti and macaroni	lb.	0.78	12/94	82r
Steak, rib eye, USDA choice, boneless	lb.	6.15	12/94	82r
Steak, round, graded & ungraded, exc. USDA prime & choice	lb.	2.72	12/94	82r
Steak, round, USDA choice, boneless	lb.	3.02	12/94	82r
Steak, sirloin, USDA choice, boneless	lb.	3.85	12/94	82r
Steak, t-bone	lb.	5.31	12/94	2c
Steak, T-bone, USDA choice, bone-in	lb.	5.38	12/94	82r
Sugar and other sweets, eaten at home, expenditures	year	91	91	81r
Sugar, cane or beet	4 lbs.	1.34	12/94	2c
Sugar, white, all sizes	lb.	0.36	12/94	82r
Tobacco products and smoking supplies, total expenditures	year	298	91	81r
Tomatoes, field grown	lb.	1.36	12/94	82r
Tomatoes, Hunt's or Del Monte	14.5 oz.	0.77	12/94	2c
Tuna, chunk, light	lb.	1.94	12/94	82r
Tuna, chunk, light, oil-packed	6.125-6.5 oz.	0.60	12/94	2c
Turkey, frozen, whole	lb.	0.96	12/94	82r
Yogurt, natural, fruit flavored	8 oz.	0.62	12/94	82r
Goods and Services				
Miscellaneous goods and services, ACCRA Index		98.10	12/94	2c
Health Care				
Health care, ACCRA Index		94.60	12/94	2c
Antibiotic ointment, Polysporin	1.5 oz.	4.13	12/94	2c
Childbirth, Cesarean delivery, hospital charge	birth	5101.00	12/91	69r
Childbirth, Cesarean delivery, physician charge	birth	2234.00	12/91	69r

Dayton, OH - continued

Item	Per	Value	Date	Ref.
Health Care - continued				
Childbirth, normal delivery, hospital charge	birth	2891.00	12/91	69r
Childbirth, normal delivery, physician charge	birth	1623.00	12/91	69r
Dentist's fee, adult teeth cleaning and periodic oral exam	visit	51.80	12/94	2c
Doctor's fee, routine exam, established patient	visit	34.60	12/94	2c
Drugs, expenditures	year	248	91	81r
Health care, total expenditures	year	1336	91	81r
Health insurance expenditures	year	550	91	81r
Hospital care, semiprivate room	day	381.20	12/94	2c
Insurance premium, family medical care	month	350.73	1/95	41s
Medical services expenditures	year	457	91	81r
Medical supplies expenditures	year	82	91	81r
Household Goods				
Appl. repair, service call, wash mach	min. lab. chg.	39.78	12/94	2c
Floor coverings, expenditures	year	105	91	81r
Furniture, expenditures	year	291	91	81r
Household equipment, misc. expenditures	year	341	91	81r
Household expenditures, miscellaneous	year	162	91	81r
Household furnishings and equipment, expenditures	year	1042	91	81r
Household operations expenditures	year	365	91	81r
Household textiles, expenditures	year	101	91	81r
Housekeeping supplies, expenditures	year	390	91	81r
Laundry and cleaning supplies, expenditures	year	110	91	81r
Laundry detergent, Tide Ultra, Bold, or Cheer	42 oz.	3.18	12/94	2c
Postage and stationery, expenditures	year	115	91	81r
Tissues, facial, Kleenex brand	175	0.92	12/94	2c
Housing				
Housing, ACCRA Index		105.80	12/94	2c
Add garage/carport		8,479	3/95	74r
Add room(s)		21,347	3/95	74r
Apartment condominium or co-op, median	unit	87100	12/94	62r
Bathroom addition, average cost	add	9734.00	3/95	13r
Bathroom remodeling, average cost	remod	6414.00	3/95	13r
Bedroom, master suite addition, average cost	add	27122.00	3/95	13r
Deck addition, average cost	add	6665.00	3/95	13r
Dwellings (owned), expenditures	year	2566	91	81r
Enclose porch/patio/breezeway		4,556	3/95	74r
Exterior remodeling, average cost	remod	15395.00	3/95	13r
Family room addition, average cost	add	27658.00	3/95	13r
Finish room in basement/attic		5,074	3/95	74r
Home, existing, single-family, median	unit	106500	12/94	62r
Home, existing, single-family, median	unit	81.90	12/94	62c
House payment, principal and interest, 25% down payment	mo.	836	12/94	2c
House, 1800 sq ft, 8000 sq ft lot, new, urban, utilities	total	134850	12/94	2c
Kitchen remodeling, major, average cost	remod	17084.00	3/95	13r
Kitchen remodeling, minor, average cost	remod	5804.00	3/95	13r
Maintenance, repairs, insurance, and other housing expenditures	year	484	91	81r
Mortgage interest and charges expenditures	year	1443	91	81r
Mtge. rate, incl. points and orig. fee, 30-year conv. fixed or ARM	mo.	9.30	12/94	2c
Office, home addition, average cost	add	8121.00	3/95	13r
Princ. & int., mortgage, median-price exist. sing.-family home	mo.	515	12/94	62r
Property taxes expenditures	year	639	91	81r
Redesign, restructure more than half of home's interior		9,114	3/95	74r
Rent, apartment, 2 br., 1 1/2-2 baths, unfurnished, 950 sq ft, water	mo.	486	12/94	2c
Rental units expenditures	year	1200	91	81r
Sun-space addition, average cost	add	23768.00	3/95	13r
Wing addition, two-story, average cost	add	50410.00	3/95	13r

Values are in dollars or fractions of dollars. In the column headed *Ref,* references are shown to sources. Each reference is followed by a letter. These refer to the geographical level for which data were reported: s=State, r=Region, and c=City or metro. The abbreviation *ex* is used to mean *except* or *excluding*; *exp* stands for expenditures. For other abbreviations and further explanations, please see the Introduction.

Dayton, OH - continued

Item	Per	Value	Date	Ref.
Insurance and Pensions				
Auto insurance, private passenger	year	550.52	12/94	71s
Insurance and pensions, personal, expenditures	year	2408	91	81r
Insurance, life and other personal, expenditures	year	355	91	81r
Pensions and Social Security, expenditures	year	2053	91	81r
Legal Assistance				
Legal work, law firm associate	hour	90		10r
Legal work, law firm partner	hour	139		10r
Personal Goods				
Shampoo, Alberto VO5	15-oz.	0.97	12/94	2c
Toothpaste, Crest or Colgate	6-7 oz.	1.39	12/94	2c
Personal Services				
Dry cleaning, man's 2-pc. suit		6.32	12/94	2c
Haircut, man's barbershop, no styling		7.99	12/94	2c
Haircut, woman's shampoo, trim, blow-dry		19.80	12/94	2c
Personal services expenditures	year	203	91	81r
Restaurant Food				
Chicken, fried, thigh and drumstick		1.99	12/94	2c
Dining expenditures, family	week	30.03	94	73r
Hamburger with cheese	1/4 lb.	1.75	12/94	2c
Pizza, Pizza Hut or Pizza Inn	12-13 in.	7.69	12/94	2c
Taxes				
Taxes, Federal income, expenditures	year	1756	91	81r
Taxes, personal, expenditures	year	2426	91	81r
Taxes, State and local income, expenditures	year	568	91	81r
Transportation				
Transportation, ACCRA Index		97.30	12/94	2c
Bus fare, one-way	trip	0.90	12/95	1c
Bus fare, up to 10 miles	one-way	0.90	12/94	2c
Cars and trucks purchased, new	year	891	91	81r
Cars and trucks purchased, used	year	1155	91	81r
Driver's learning permit fee	perm	3.00	1/94	84s
Driver's license fee	orig	5.00	1/94	84s
Driver's license fee, duplicate	lic	1.50	1/94	84s
Driver's license reinstatement fee, min.	susp	12.50-100.00	1/94	85s
Driver's license renewal fee	renew	5.00	1/94	84s
Identification card, nondriver	card	2.50	1/94	83s
Motorcycle learning permit fee	perm	3.00	1/94	84s
Motorcycle license fee	orig	5.00	1/94	84s
Motorcycle license fee, duplicate	lic	1.50	1/94	84s
Motorcycle license renewal fee	renew	5.00	1/94	84s
Public transportation expenditures	year	209	91	81r
Tire balance, computer or spin bal., front	wheel	6.70	12/94	2c
Transportation expenditures, total	year	4792	91	81r
Trolley fare, one-way	trip	0.90	12/95	1c
Vehicle finance charges	year	300	91	81r
Vehicle insurance expenditures	year	485	91	81r
Vehicle maintenance and repairs expenditures	year	534	91	81r
Vehicle purchases	year	2068	91	81r
Vehicle rental, leases, licenses, etc. expenditures	year	197	91	81r
Vehicles purchased, other than cars and trucks	year	22	91	81r
Utilities				
Utilities, ACCRA Index		105.10	12/94	2c
Electricity expenditures	year	668	91	81r
Electricity, (part.), other, 1800 sq. ft., new home	mo.	72.31	12/94	2c
Electricity, summer, 250 KWh	month	29.95	8/93	64c
Electricity, summer, 500 KWh	month	47.15	8/93	64c
Electricity, summer, 750 KWh	month	57.87	8/93	64c
Electricity, summer, 1000 KWh	month	75.75	8/93	64c

Dayton, OH - continued

Item	Per	Value	Date	Ref.
Utilities - continued				
Utilities, fuels, and public services, total expenditures	year	1838	91	81r
Water and other public services, expenditures	year	167	91	81r
Weddings				
Bridal attendants' gowns	event	750	10/93	76r
Bridal gown	event	852	10/93	76r
Bridal headpiece and veil	event	167	10/93	76r
Bride's wedding band	event	708	10/93	76r
Clergy	event	224	10/93	76r
Engagement ring	event	2756	10/93	76r
Flowers	event	863	10/93	76r
Formal wear for groom	event	106	10/93	76r
Groom's attendants' formal wear	event	530	10/93	76r
Groom's wedding band	event	402	10/93	76r
Music	event	600	10/93	76r
Photography	event	1088	10/93	76r
Shoes for bride	event	50	10/93	76r
Videography	event	483	10/93	76r
Wedding invitations and announcements	event	342	10/93	76r
Wedding reception	event	7000	10/93	76r

Daytona Beach, FL

Item	Per	Value	Date	Ref.
Appliances				
Appliances (major), expenditures	year	153	91	81r
Average annual exp.				
Food, health care, personal goods, services	year	27020	91	81r
Charity				
Cash contributions, expenditures	year	839	91	81r
Clothing				
Apparel, men and boys, total expenditures	year	380	91	81r
Apparel, women and girls, total expenditures	year	660	91	81r
Footwear, expenditures	year	193	91	81r
Communications				
Long-distance telephone rate, day, addl. min., 1-10 mi.	min.	0.08	12/93	9s
Long-distance telephone rate, day, initial min., 1-10 mi.	min.	0.15	12/93	9s
Phone line, single, business, field visit	inst	86.00	12/93	9s
Phone line, single, business, no field visit	inst	54.50	12/93	9s
Phone line, single, residence, field visit	inst	76.00	12/93	9s
Phone line, single, residence, no field visit	inst	44.50	12/93	9s
Telephone service, expenditures	year	616	91	81r
Education				
Bar examination preparatory course	course	500.00-100	94	17s
Board, 4-year private college/university	year	2123	8/94	80s
Board, 4-year public college/university	year	2101	8/94	80s
Education, total expenditures	year	319	91	81r
Room, 4-year private college/university	year	2242	8/94	80s
Room, 4-year public college/university	year	1970	8/94	80s
Total cost, 4-year private college/university	year	13853	8/94	80s
Total cost, 4-year public college/university	year	5855	8/94	80s
Tuition, 2-year public college/university, in-state	year	1076	8/94	80s
Tuition, 4-year private college/university, in-state	year	9287	8/94	80s
Tuition, 4-year public college/university, in-state	year	1784	8/94	80s
Energy and Fuels				
Fuel oil and other fuels, expenditures	year	56	91	81r
Gas, natural, expenditures	year	150	91	81r
Gasoline and motor oil purchased	year	1152	91	81r
Gasoline, unleaded midgrade	gallon	1.21	4/93	82r
Gasoline, unleaded premium	gallon	1.30	4/93	82r
Gasoline, unleaded regular	gallon	1.10	4/93	82r

Values are in dollars or fractions of dollars. In the column headed *Ref*, references are shown to sources. Each reference is followed by a letter. These refer to the geographical level for which data were reported: s=State, r=Region, and c=City or metro. The abbreviation *ex* is used to mean *except* or *excluding*; *exp* stands for expenditures. For other abbreviations and further explanations, please see the Introduction.

Daytona Beach, FL - continued

Item	Per	Value	Date	Ref.
Entertainment				
Concert ticket, Pearl Jam group	perf	20.00	94	50r
Entertainment, total expenditures	year	1266	91	81r
Fees and admissions, expenditures	year	306	91	81r
Pets, toys, playground equipment, expenditures	year	271	91	81r
Reading, expenditures	year	131	91	81r
Televisions, radios, and sound equipment, expenditures	year	439	91	81r
Funerals				
Burial, immediate, container provided by funeral home		1370.36	1/95	54r
Cards, acknowledgment		14.83	1/95	54r
Casket, minimum alternative		192.52	1/95	54r
Cosmetology, hair care, etc.		102.27	1/95	54r
Cremation, direct, container provided by funeral home		1065.64	1/95	54r
Embalming		304.29	1/95	54r
Funeral, funeral home		287.83	1/95	54r
Funeral, other facility		284.14	1/95	54r
Graveside service		349.13	1/95	54r
Hearse, local		132.27	1/95	54r
Limousine, local		98.45	1/95	54r
Memorial service		270.59	1/95	54r
Service charge, professional, nondeclinable		933.59	1/95	54r
Visitation and viewing		225.83	1/95	54r
Groceries				
Apples, Red Delicious	lb.	0.73	12/94	82r
Bacon, sliced	lb.	1.67	12/94	82r
Bananas	lb.	0.42	12/94	82r
Beef purchases	year	213	91	81r
Beverage purchases, alcoholic	year	249	91	81r
Beverage purchases, nonalcoholic	year	207	91	81r
Bologna, all beef or mixed	lb.	2.27	12/94	82r
Bread, white, pan	lb.	0.68	12/94	82r
Cabbage	lb.	0.42	12/94	82r
Carrots, short trimmed and topped	lb.	0.53	12/94	82r
Cereals and bakery products purchases	year	345	91	81r
Cereals and cereals products purchases	year	127	91	81r
Cheddar cheese, natural	lb.	3.58	12/94	82r
Chicken breast, bone-in	lb.	1.71	12/94	82r
Chicken, fresh, whole	lb.	0.78	12/94	82r
Chuck roast, USDA choice, boneless	lb.	2.26	12/94	82r
Crackers, soda, salted	lb.	1.27	12/94	82r
Cucumbers	lb.	0.65	12/94	82r
Dairy products (other) purchases	year	141	91	81r
Eggs, Grade A large	dozen	0.87	12/94	82r
Fish and seafood purchases	year	72	91	81r
Flour, white, all purpose	lb.	0.23	12/94	82r
Food purchases, food eaten at home	year	2381	91	81r
Foods purchased away from home, not prepared by consumer	year	1696	91	81r
Frankfurters, all meat or all beef	lb.	1.74	12/94	82r
Fruits and vegetables purchases	year	380	91	81r
Grapefruit	lb.	0.45	12/94	82r
Grapes, Thompson seedless	lb.	2.30	12/94	82r
Ground beef, 100% beef	lb.	1.37	12/94	82r
Ground chuck, 100% beef	lb.	1.97	12/94	82r
Ham, boneless, exc. canned	lb.	2.54	12/94	82r
Ice cream, prepackaged, bulk, regular	1/2 gal.	2.47	12/94	82r
Lemons	lb.	1.02	12/94	82r
Lettuce, iceberg	lb.	0.96	12/94	82r
Margarine, stick	lb.	0.77	12/94	82r
Meats, poultry, fish, and eggs purchases	year	655	91	81r
Milk and cream (fresh) purchases	year	130	91	81r
Orange juice, frozen concentrate 12-oz. can	16 oz.	1.36	12/94	82r
Oranges, Navel	lb.	0.54	12/94	82r
Pears, Anjou	lb.	0.81	12/94	82r
Pork chops, center cut, bone-in	lb.	3.07	12/94	82r
Pork purchases	year	142	91	81r
Potato chips	16-oz.	3.15	12/94	82r

Daytona Beach, FL - continued

Item	Per	Value	Date	Ref.
Groceries - continued				
Potatoes, frozen, French fried	lb.	0.82	12/94	82r
Potatoes, white	lb.	0.34	12/94	82r
Rice, white, long grain, uncooked	lb.	0.48	12/94	82r
Round roast, USDA choice, boneless	lb.	2.91	12/94	82r
Sausage, fresh	lb.	1.82	12/94	82r
Shortening, vegetable oil blends	lb.	0.75	12/94	82r
Spaghetti and macaroni	lb.	0.87	12/94	82r
Steak, rib eye, USDA choice, boneless	lb.	6.85	12/94	82r
Steak, round, graded & ungraded, exc. USDA prime & choice	lb.	2.96	12/94	82r
Steak, round, USDA choice, boneless	lb.	3.17	12/94	82r
Steak, sirloin, USDA choice, boneless	lb.	4.12	12/94	82r
Steak, T-bone, USDA choice, bone-in	lb.	5.63	12/94	82r
Sugar and other sweets, eaten at home, expenditures	year	93	91	81r
Sugar, white, all sizes	lb.	0.39	12/94	82r
Tobacco products and smoking supplies, total expenditures	year	286	91	81r
Tomatoes, field grown	lb.	1.36	12/94	82r
Tuna, chunk, light	lb.	1.94	12/94	82r
Turkey, frozen, whole	lb.	0.96	12/94	82r
Yogurt, natural, fruit flavored	8 oz.	0.58	12/94	82r
Health Care				
Adenosine, emergency room	treat	100.00	95	23r
Bladder tap, superpubic, infant, emergency room	treat	119.00	95	23r
Blood analysis, emergency room	treat	25.00	95	23r
Blood tests, abdominal pain, emergency room	treat	25.00	95	23r
Burn dressing, emergency room	treat	266.00	95	23r
Cardiology interpretation, emergency room	treat	26.00	95	23r
Chest X-ray, emergency room	treat	78.00	95	23r
Childbirth, Cesarean delivery, hospital charge	birth	5462.00	12/91	69r
Childbirth, Cesarean delivery, physician charge	birth	2228.00	12/91	69r
Childbirth, normal delivery, hospital charge	birth	2943.00	12/91	69r
Childbirth, normal delivery, physician charge	birth	1619.00	12/91	69r
Defibrillation pads, emergency room	treat	6.00	95	23r
Drugs, expenditures	year	297	91	81r
Gastric tube insertion, nasal, emergency room	treat	25.00	95	23r
Health care, total expenditures	year	1600	91	81r
Health insurance expenditures	year	637	91	81r
Heart monitor, emergency room	treat	40.00	95	23r
Insurance premium, family medical care	month	301.92	1/95	41s
Intravenous fluids, emergency room	treat	130.00	95	23r
Intravenous fluids, emergency room	liter	26.00	95	23r
Intravenous line, central, emergency room	treat	342.00	95	23r
Liver function tests, abdominal pain, emergency room	treat	26.00	95	23r
Medical care charges, total, emergency room, third-degree burns	treat	2101.00	95	23r
Medical care charges, total, emergency, infant with fever	treat	628.00	95	23r
Medical services expenditures	year	573	91	81r
Medical supplies expenditures	year	93	91	81r
Morphine, emergency room	treat	34.00	95	23r
Nursing care and facilities charges, emergency room	treat	252.00	95	23r
Nursing care and facilities charges, emergency, infant with fever	treat	252.00	95	23r
Nursing care and facilities charges, emergency, third-degree burns	treat	861.00	95	23r
Physician's charges, emergency, infant with fever	treat	212.00	95	23r
Physician's charges, emergency, third-degree burns	treat	372.00	95	23r
Physician's fee, emergency room	treat	372.00	95	23r
Physician's fee, general practitioner	visit	51.20	12/93	60r
Surgery, open-heart	proc	42374.00	1/93	14r
Ultrasound, abdominal, emergency room	treat	276.00	95	23r

Values are in dollars or fractions of dollars. In the column headed *Ref*, references are shown to sources. Each reference is followed by a letter. These refer to the geographical level for which data were reported: s=State, r=Region, and c=City or metro. The abbreviation *ex* is used to mean *except* or *excluding*; *exp* stands for *expenditures*. For other abbreviations and further explanations, please see the Introduction.

Daytona Beach, FL - continued

Item	Per	Value	Date	Ref.
Health Care				
Urinalysis, emergency room	treat	20.00	95	23r
Urinalysis, infant, emergency room	treat	20.00	95	23r
X-rays, emergency room	treat	78.00	95	23r
Household Goods				
Floor coverings, expenditures	year	48	91	81r
Furniture, expenditures	year	280	91	81r
Household equipment, misc. expenditures	year	342	91	81r
Household expenditures, miscellaneous	year	256	91	81r
Household furnishings and equipment, expenditures	year	988	91	81r
Household operations expenditures	year	468	91	81r
Household textiles, expenditures	year	95	91	81r
Housekeeping supplies, expenditures	year	380	91	81r
Laundry and cleaning supplies, expenditures	year	109	91	81r
Postage and stationery, expenditures	year	105	91	81r
Housing				
Add garage/carport		6,980	3/95	74r
Add room(s)		11,403	3/95	74r
Apartment condominium or co-op, median	unit	68600	12/94	62r
Dwellings (owned), expenditures	year	2428	91	81r
Enclose porch/patio/breezeway		4,572	3/95	74r
Finish room in basement/attic		3,794	3/95	74r
Home, existing, single-family, median	unit	120200	12/94	62r
Maintenance, repairs, insurance, and other housing expenditures	year	531	91	81r
Mortgage interest and charges expenditures	year	1506	91	81r
Princ. & int., mortgage, median-price exist. sing.-family home	mo.	540	12/94	62r
Property taxes expenditures	year	391	91	81r
Redesign, restructure more than half of home's interior		17,641	3/95	74r
Rental units expenditures	year	1264	91	81r
Insurance and Pensions				
Auto insurance, private passenger	year	753.93	12/94	71s
Insurance and pensions, personal, expenditures	year	2395	91	81r
Insurance, life and other personal, expenditures	year	368	91	81r
Pensions and Social Security, expenditures	year	2027	91	81r
Personal Services				
Personal services expenditures	year	212	91	81r
Restaurant Food				
Dining expenditures, family	week	33.83	94	73r
Taxes				
Taxes, Federal income, expenditures	year	2275	91	81r
Taxes, personal, expenditures	year	2715	91	81r
Taxes, State and local income, expenditures	year	365	91	81r
Transportation				
Cars and trucks purchased, new	year	1306	91	81r
Cars and trucks purchased, used	year	942	91	81r
Driver's learning permit fee	perm	20.00	1/94	84s
Driver's license fee	orig	20.00	1/94	84s
Driver's license fee, duplicate	lic	10.00	1/94	84s
Driver's license reinstatement fee, min.	susp	25.00	1/94	85s
Driver's license renewal fee	renew	15.00	1/94	84s
Identification card, nondriver	card	3.00	1/94	83s
Motorcycle learning permit fee	perm	20.00	1/94	84s
Motorcycle license fee	orig	20.00	1/94	84s
Motorcycle license fee, duplicate	lic	10.00	1/94	84s
Motorcycle license renewal fee	renew	15.00	1/94	84s
Public transportation expenditures	year	249	91	81r
Transportation expenditures, total	year	5307	91	81r
Vehicle finance charges	year	346	91	81r
Vehicle insurance expenditures	year	544	91	81r
Vehicle maintenance and repairs expenditures	year	600	91	81r
Vehicle purchases	year	2275	91	81r

Daytona Beach, FL - continued

Item	Per	Value	Date	Ref.
Transportation - continued				
Vehicle rental, leases, licenses, etc. expenditures	year	141	91	81r
Vehicles purchased, other than cars and trucks	year	27	91	81r
Utilities				
Electricity expenditures	year	950	91	81r
Utilities, fuels, and public services, total expenditures	year	2000	91	81r
Water and other public services, expenditures	year	227	91	81r
Weddings				
Bridal attendants' gowns	event	750	10/93	76r
Bridal gown	event	852	10/93	76r
Bridal headpiece and veil	event	167	10/93	76r
Bride's wedding band	event	708	10/93	76r
Clergy	event	224	10/93	76r
Engagement ring	event	2756	10/93	76r
Flowers	event	863	10/93	76r
Formal wear for groom	event	106	10/93	76r
Groom's attendants' formal wear	event	530	10/93	76r
Groom's wedding band	event	402	10/93	76r
Music	event	600	10/93	76r
Photography	event	1088	10/93	76r
Shoes for bride	event	50	10/93	76r
Videography	event	483	10/93	76r
Wedding invitations and announcements	event	342	10/93	76r
Wedding reception	event	7000	10/93	76r

Decatur, IL

Item	Per	Value	Date	Ref.
Composite, ACCRA index		90.40	12/94	2c
Alcoholic Beverages				
Beer, Miller Lite, Bud, 12-oz., ex deposit	6	3.76	12/94	2c
J & B Scotch	750-ml.	14.82	12/94	2c
Wine, Gallo Chablis blanc	1.5-lit	4.69	12/94	2c
Appliances				
Appliances (major), expenditures	year	131	91	81r
Average annual exp.				
Food, health care, personal goods, services	year	25935	91	81r
Charity				
Cash contributions, expenditures	year	745	91	81r
Clothing				
Apparel, men and boys, total expenditures	year	332	91	81r
Apparel, women and girls, total expenditures	year	578	91	81r
Footwear, expenditures	year	164	91	81r
Jeans, man's denim		29.99	12/94	2c
Shirt, man's dress shirt		16.36	12/94	2c
Undervest, boy's size 10-14, cotton	3	2.92	12/94	2c
Communications				
Long-distance telephone rate, day, addl. min., 1-10 mi.	min.	0.04	12/93	9s
Long-distance telephone rate, day, initial min., 1-10 mi.	min.	0.10	12/93	9s
Newspaper subscription, dly. and Sun. delivery	month	12.50	12/94	2c
Phone line, single, business, field visit	inst	84.50	12/93	9s
Phone line, single, business, no field visit	inst	84.50	12/93	9s
Phone line, single, residence, field visit	inst	55.00	12/93	9s
Phone line, single, residence, no field visit	inst	55.00	12/93	9s
Telephone bill, family of four	month	17.32	12/94	2c
Telephone service, expenditures	year	547	91	81r
Telephone, residential, flat rate	mo.	9.00	12/93	8c
Education				
Board, 4-year private college/university	year	2078	8/94	80s
Board, 4-year public college/university	year	2139	8/94	80s
Education, total expenditures	year	394	91	81r

Values are in dollars or fractions of dollars. In the column headed *Ref*, references are shown to sources. Each reference is followed by a letter. These refer to the geographical level for which data were reported: s=State, r=Region, and c=City or metro. The abbreviation *ex* is used to mean *except* or *excluding*; *exp* stands for expenditures. For other abbreviations and further explanations, please see the Introduction.

Decatur, IL - continued

Item	Per	Value	Date	Ref.
Education				
Room, 4-year private college/university	year	2696	8/94	80s
Room, 4-year public college/university	year	1796	8/94	80s
Total cost, 4-year private college/university	year	15249	8/94	80s
Total cost, 4-year public college/university	year	6964	8/94	80s
Tuition, 2-year public college/university, in-state	year	1135	8/94	80s
Tuition, 4-year private college/university, in-state	year	10474	8/94	80s
Tuition, 4-year public college/university, in-state	year	3029	8/94	80s
Energy and Fuels				
Energy, combined forms, 1800 sq. ft.	mo.	122.08	12/94	2c
Energy, exc. electricity, 1800 sq. ft.	mo.	44.80	12/94	2c
Fuel oil and other fuels, expenditures	year	83	91	81r
Gas, cooking, 10 therms	month	12.94	2/94	65c
Gas, cooking, 30 therms	month	21.83	2/94	65c
Gas, cooking, 50 therms	month	30.72	2/94	65c
Gas, heating, winter, 100 therms	month	52.06	2/94	65c
Gas, heating, winter, average use	month	91.38	2/94	65c
Gas, natural, expenditures	year	373	91	81r
Gas, reg unlead, taxes inc., cash, self-service	gal	1.12	12/94	2c
Gasoline and motor oil purchased	year	1000	91	81r
Gasoline, unleaded midgrade	gallon	1.15	4/93	82r
Gasoline, unleaded premium	gallon	1.23	4/93	82r
Gasoline, unleaded regular	gallon	1.07	4/93	82r
Entertainment				
Bowling, evening rate	game	1.72	12/94	2c
Entertainment, total expenditures	year	1356	91	81r
Fees and admissions, expenditures	year	347	91	81r
Monopoly game, Parker Brothers', No. 9	game	10.20	12/94	2c
Movie	adm	5.00	12/94	2c
Pets, toys, playground equipment, expenditures	year	270	91	81r
Reading, expenditures	year	160	91	81r
Televisions, radios, and sound equipment, expenditures	year	433	91	81r
Tennis balls, yellow, Wilson or Penn, 3	can	1.80	12/94	2c
Funerals				
Burial, immediate, container provided by funeral home		1268.31	1/95	54r
Cards, acknowledgment		26.12	1/95	54r
Casket, minimum alternative		198.03	1/95	54r
Cosmetology, hair care, etc.		122.19	1/95	54r
Cremation, direct, container provided by funeral home		977.81	1/95	54r
Embalming		334.00	1/95	54r
Funeral, funeral home		321.16	1/95	54r
Funeral, other facility		317.73	1/95	54r
Graveside service		292.48	1/95	54r
Hearse, local		153.20	1/95	54r
Limousine, local		123.52	1/95	54r
Memorial service		356.30	1/95	54r
Service charge, professional, nondeclinable		968.24	1/95	54r
Visitation and viewing		332.66	1/95	54r
Groceries				
Groceries, ACCRA Index		101.10	12/94	2c
Apples, Red Delicious	lb.	0.68	12/94	82r
Baby food, strained vegetables, lowest price	4-4.5 oz.	0.30	12/94	2c
Bacon, sliced	lb.	1.88	12/94	82r
Bananas	lb.	0.52	12/94	2c
Bananas	lb.	0.41	12/94	82r
Beef or hamburger, ground	lb.	1.19	12/94	2c
Beef purchases	year	197	91	81r
Beef, stew, boneless	lb.	2.52	12/94	82r
Beverage purchases, alcoholic	year	293	91	81r
Beverage purchases, nonalcoholic	year	203	91	81r
Bologna, all beef or mixed	lb.	2.12	12/94	82r
Bread, white	24-oz.	0.76	12/94	2c

Decatur, IL - continued

Item	Per	Value	Date	Ref.
Groceries - continued				
Bread, white, pan	lb.	0.76	12/94	82r
Cabbage	lb.	0.44	12/94	82r
Carrots, short trimmed and topped	lb.	0.44	12/94	82r
Cereals and bakery products purchases	year	347	91	81r
Cereals and cereals products purchases	year	119	91	81r
Cheddar cheese, natural	lb.	3.28	12/94	82r
Cheese, Kraft grated Parmesan	8-oz.	3.51	12/94	2c
Chicken breast, bone-in	lb.	1.61	12/94	82r
Chicken, fresh, whole	lb.	0.89	12/94	82r
Chicken, whole fryer	lb.	0.79	12/94	2c
Chuck roast, USDA choice, boneless	lb.	2.33	12/94	82r
Cigarettes, Winston, Kings	carton	18.30	12/94	2c
Coffee, 100%, ground roast, all sizes	lb.	4.28	12/94	82r
Coffee, vacuum-packed	13 oz.	3.77	12/94	2c
Cookies, chocolate chip	lb.	2.72	12/94	82r
Corn Flakes, Kellogg's or Post Toasties	18 oz.	2.19	12/94	2c
Corn, frozen, whole kernel, lowest price	10 oz.	0.69	12/94	2c
Dairy products (other) purchases	year	148	91	81r
Eggs, Grade A large	dozen	0.74	12/94	2c
Eggs, Grade A large	dozen	0.76	12/94	82r
Fish and seafood purchases	year	61	91	81r
Flour, white, all purpose	lb.	0.22	12/94	82r
Food purchases, food eaten at home	year	2313	91	81r
Foods purchased away from home, not prepared by consumer	year	1709	91	81r
Fruits and vegetables purchases	year	372	91	81r
Grapefruit	lb.	0.47	12/94	82r
Grapes, Thompson seedless	lb.	2.15	12/94	82r
Ground beef, 100% beef	lb.	1.37	12/94	82r
Ground chuck, 100% beef	lb.	1.81	12/94	82r
Ham, boneless, exc. canned	lb.	2.16	12/94	82r
Ice cream, prepackaged, bulk, regular	1/2 gal.	2.48	12/94	82r
Lemons	lb.	1.08	12/94	82r
Lettuce, iceberg	lb.	0.81	12/94	82r
Lettuce, iceberg	head	0.79	12/94	2c
Margarine, Blue Bonnet or Parkay cubes	lb.	0.65	12/94	2c
Margarine, stick	lb.	0.81	12/94	82r
Meats, poultry, fish, and eggs purchases	year	591	91	81r
Milk and cream (fresh) purchases	year	132	91	81r
Milk, whole	1/2 gal.	1.52	12/94	2c
Orange juice, frozen concentrate 12-oz. can	16 oz.	1.41	12/94	82r
Orange juice, Minute Maid frozen	12-oz.	1.24	12/94	2c
Oranges, Navel	lb.	0.56	12/94	82r
Peaches, halves or slices, Hunt's, Del Monte, or Libby's	29-oz.	1.32	12/94	2c
Peanut butter, creamy, all sizes	lb.	1.81	12/94	82r
Peas, sweet, Del Monte or Green Giant	15-17 oz.	0.47	12/94	2c
Pork chops, center cut, bone-in	lb.	2.76	12/94	82r
Pork purchases	year	130	91	81r
Potato chips	16-oz.	2.81	12/94	82r
Potatoes, frozen, French fried	lb.	0.83	12/94	82r
Potatoes, white	lb.	0.28	12/94	82r
Potatoes, white or red	10-lb. sack	2.69	12/94	2c
Round roast, USDA choice, boneless	lb.	2.90	12/94	82r
Sausage, Jimmy Dean, 100% pork	lb.	2.49	12/94	2c
Shortening, vegetable oil blends	lb.	0.88	12/94	82r
Shortening, vegetable, Crisco	3-lb.	2.24	12/94	2c
Soft drink, Coca Cola, ex deposit	2 lit	1.16	12/94	2c
Spaghetti and macaroni	lb.	0.78	12/94	82r
Steak, rib eye, USDA choice, boneless	lb.	6.15	12/94	82r
Steak, round, graded & ungraded, exc. USDA prime & choice	lb.	2.72	12/94	82r
Steak, round, USDA choice, boneless	lb.	3.02	12/94	82r
Steak, sirloin, USDA choice, boneless	lb.	3.85	12/94	82r
Steak, t-bone	lb.	5.82	12/94	2c
Steak, T-bone, USDA choice, bone-in	lb.	5.38	12/94	82r
Sugar and other sweets, eaten at home, expenditures	year	91	91	81r

Values are in dollars or fractions of dollars. In the column headed *Ref*, references are shown to sources. Each reference is followed by a letter. These refer to the geographical level for which data were reported: s = State, r = Region, and c = City or metro. The abbreviation *ex* is used to mean *except* or *excluding*; *exp* stands for *expenditures*. For other abbreviations and further explanations, please see the Introduction.

Decatur, IL - continued

Item	Per	Value	Date	Ref.
Groceries				
Sugar, cane or beet	4 lbs.	1.27	12/94	2c
Sugar, white, all sizes	lb.	0.36	12/94	82r
Tobacco products and smoking supplies, total expenditures	year	298	91	81r
Tomatoes, field grown	lb.	1.36	12/94	82r
Tomatoes, Hunt's or Del Monte	14.5 oz.	0.79	12/94	2c
Tuna, chunk, light	lb.	1.94	12/94	82r
Tuna, chunk, light, oil-packed	6.125-6.5 oz.	0.67	12/94	2c
Turkey, frozen, whole	lb.	0.96	12/94	82r
Yogurt, natural, fruit flavored	8 oz.	0.62	12/94	82r
Goods and Services				
Miscellaneous goods and services, ACCRA Index		87.60	12/94	2c
Health Care				
Health care, ACCRA Index		86.70	12/94	2c
Antibiotic ointment, Polysporin	1.5 oz.	3.66	12/94	2c
Childbirth, Cesarean delivery, hospital charge	birth	5101.00	12/91	69r
Childbirth, Cesarean delivery, physician charge	birth	2234.00	12/91	69r
Childbirth, normal delivery, hospital charge	birth	2891.00	12/91	69r
Childbirth, normal delivery, physician charge	birth	1623.00	12/91	69r
Dentist's fee, adult teeth cleaning and periodic oral exam	visit	45.50	12/94	2c
Doctor's fee, routine exam, established patient	visit	35.75	12/94	2c
Drugs, expenditures	year	248	91	81r
Health care, total expenditures	year	1336	91	81r
Health insurance expenditures	year	550	91	81r
Hospital care, semiprivate room	day	313.50	12/94	2c
Insurance premium, family medical care	month	363.57	1/95	41s
Medical services expenditures	year	457	91	81r
Medical supplies expenditures	year	82	91	81r
Household Goods				
Appl. repair, service call, wash mach	min. lab. chg.	28.68	12/94	2c
Floor coverings, expenditures	year	105	91	81r
Furniture, expenditures	year	291	91	81r
Household equipment, misc. expenditures	year	341	91	81r
Household expenditures, miscellaneous	year	162	91	81r
Household furnishings and equipment, expenditures	year	1042	91	81r
Household operations expenditures	year	365	91	81r
Household textiles, expenditures	year	101	91	81r
Housekeeping supplies, expenditures	year	390	91	81r
Laundry and cleaning supplies, expenditures	year	110	91	81r
Laundry detergent, Tide Ultra, Bold, or Cheer	42 oz.	3.62	12/94	2c
Postage and stationery, expenditures	year	115	91	81r
Tissues, facial, Kleenex brand	175	1.05	12/94	2c
Housing				
Housing, ACCRA Index		81.10	12/94	2c
Add garage/carport		8,479	3/95	74r
Add room(s)		21,347	3/95	74r
Apartment condominium or co-op, median	unit	87100	12/94	62r
Bathroom addition, average cost	add	9734.00	3/95	13r
Bathroom remodeling, average cost	remod	6414.00	3/95	13r
Bedroom, master suite addition, average cost	add	27122.00	3/95	13r
Deck addition, average cost	add	6665.00	3/95	13r
Dwellings (owned), expenditures	year	2566	91	81r
Enclose porch/patio/breezeway		4,556	3/95	74r
Exterior remodeling, average cost	remod	15395.00	3/95	13r
Family room addition, average cost	add	27658.00	3/95	13r
Finish room in basement/attic		5,074	3/95	74r
Home, existing, single-family, median	unit	106500	12/94	62r

Decatur, IL - continued

Item	Per	Value	Date	Ref.
Housing - continued				
House payment, principal and interest, 25% down payment	mo.	616	12/94	2c
House, 1800 sq ft, 8000 sq ft lot, new, urban, utilities	total	99650	12/94	2c
Kitchen remodeling, major, average cost	remod	17084.00	3/95	13r
Kitchen remodeling, minor, average cost	remod	5804.00	3/95	13r
Maintenance, repairs, insurance, and other housing expenditures	year	484	91	81r
Mortgage interest and charges expenditures	year	1443	91	81r
Mtge. rate, incl. points and orig. fee, 30-year conv. fixed or ARM	mo.	9.26	12/94	2c
Office, home addition, average cost	add	8121.00	3/95	13r
Princ. & int., mortgage, median-price exist. sing.-family home	mo.	515	12/94	62r
Property taxes expenditures	year	639	91	81r
Redesign, restructure more than half of home's interior		9,114	3/95	74r
Rent, apartment, 2 br., 1 1/2-2 baths, unfurnished, 950 sq ft, water	mo.	445	12/94	2c
Rental units expenditures	year	1200	91	81r
Sun-space addition, average cost	add	23768.00	3/95	13r
Wing addition, two-story, average cost	add	50410.00	3/95	13r
Insurance and Pensions				
Auto insurance, private passenger	year	679.48	12/94	71s
Insurance and pensions, personal, expenditures	year	2408	91	81r
Insurance, life and other personal, expenditures	year	355	91	81r
Pensions and Social Security, expenditures	year	2053	91	81r
Legal Assistance				
Legal work, law firm associate	hour	90		10r
Legal work, law firm partner	hour	139		10r
Personal Goods				
Shampoo, Alberto VO5	15-oz.	1.00	12/94	2c
Toothpaste, Crest or Colgate	6-7 oz.	1.52	12/94	2c
Personal Services				
Dry cleaning, man's 2-pc. suit		7.11	12/94	2c
Haircut, man's barbershop, no styling		8.19	12/94	2c
Haircut, woman's shampoo, trim, blow-dry		16.60	12/94	2c
Personal services expenditures	year	203	91	81r
Restaurant Food				
Chicken, fried, thigh and drumstick		2.29	12/94	2c
Dining expenditures, family	week	30.03	94	73r
Hamburger with cheese	1/4 lb.	1.79	12/94	2c
Pizza, Pizza Hut or Pizza Inn	12-13 in.	7.99	12/94	2c
Taxes				
Taxes, Federal income, expenditures	year	1756	91	81r
Taxes, personal, expenditures	year	2426	91	81r
Taxes, State and local income, expenditures	year	568	91	81r
Transportation				
Transportation, ACCRA Index		99.10	12/94	2c
Bus fare, one-way	trip	0.50	12/95	1c
Cars and trucks purchased, new	year	891	91	81r
Cars and trucks purchased, used	year	1155	91	81r
Driver's learning permit fee	perm	20.00	1/94	84s
Driver's license fee	orig	10.00	1/94	84s
Driver's license fee, duplicate	lic	5.00	1/94	84s
Driver's license reinstatement fee, min.	susp	30.00	1/94	85s
Driver's license renewal fee	renew	10.00	1/94	84s
Identification card, nondriver	card	4.00	1/94	83s
Motorcycle learning permit fee	perm	20.00	1/94	84s
Motorcycle license fee	orig	10.00	1/94	84s
Motorcycle license fee, duplicate	lic	5.00	1/94	84s
Motorcycle license renewal fee	renew	10.00	1/94	84s
Public transportation expenditures	year	209	91	81r
Tire balance, computer or spin bal., front	wheel	6.62	12/94	2c
Transportation expenditures, total	year	4792	91	81r

Values are in dollars or fractions of dollars. In the column headed *Ref*, references are shown to sources. Each reference is followed by a letter. These refer to the geographical level for which data were reported: s = State, r = Region, and c = City or metro. The abbreviation *ex* is used to mean *except* or *excluding*; *exp* stands for expenditures. For other abbreviations and further explanations, please see the Introduction.

Decatur, IL - continued

Item	Per	Value	Date	Ref.
Transportation				
Vehicle finance charges	year	300	91	81r
Vehicle insurance expenditures	year	485	91	81r
Vehicle maintenance and repairs expenditures	year	534	91	81r
Vehicle purchases	year	2068	91	81r
Vehicle rental, leases, licenses, etc. expenditures	year	197	91	81r
Vehicles purchased, other than cars and trucks	year	22	91	81r
Utilities				
Utilities, ACCRA Index		106.10	12/94	2c
Electricity expenditures	year	668	91	81r
Electricity, (part.), other, 1800 sq. ft., new home	mo.	77.28	12/94	2c
Electricity, summer, 250 KWh	month	36.73	8/93	64c
Electricity, summer, 500 KWh	month	61.51	8/93	64c
Electricity, summer, 750 KWh	month	85.78	8/93	64c
Electricity, summer, 1000 KWh	month	110.06	8/93	64c
Utilities, fuels, and public services, total expenditures	year	1838	91	81r
Water and other public services, expenditures	year	167	91	81r
Weddings				
Bridal attendants' gowns	event	750	10/93	76r
Bridal gown	event	852	10/93	76r
Bridal headpiece and veil	event	167	10/93	76r
Bride's wedding band	event	708	10/93	76r
Clergy	event	224	10/93	76r
Engagement ring	event	2756	10/93	76r
Flowers	event	863	10/93	76r
Formal wear for groom	event	106	10/93	76r
Groom's attendants' formal wear	event	530	10/93	76r
Groom's wedding band	event	402	10/93	76r
Music	event	600	10/93	76r
Photography	event	1088	10/93	76r
Shoes for bride	event	50	10/93	76r
Videography	event	483	10/93	76r
Wedding invitations and announcements	event	342	10/93	76r
Wedding reception	event	7000	10/93	76r

Decatur-Hartselle, AL

Item	Per	Value	Date	Ref.
Composite, ACCRA index		92.80	12/94	2c
Alcoholic Beverages				
Beer, Miller Lite, Bud, 12-oz., ex deposit	6	4.12	12/94	2c
J & B Scotch	750-ml.	20.99	12/94	2c
Wine, Gallo Chablis blanc	1.5-lit	5.54	12/94	2c
Appliances				
Appliances (major), expenditures	year	153	91	81r
Average annual exp.				
Food, health care, personal goods, services	year	27020	91	81r
Charity				
Cash contributions, expenditures	year	839	91	81r
Clothing				
Apparel, men and boys, total expenditures	year	380	91	81r
Apparel, women and girls, total expenditures	year	660	91	81r
Footwear, expenditures	year	193	91	81r
Jeans, man's denim		32.59	12/94	2c
Shirt, man's dress shirt		30.39	12/94	2c
Undervest, boy's size 10-14, cotton	3	3.37	12/94	2c
Communications				
Long-distance telephone rate, day, addl. min., 1-10 mi.	min.	0.09	12/93	9s
Long-distance telephone rate, day, initial min., 1-10 mi.	min.	0.11	12/93	9s

Decatur-Hartselle, AL - continued

Item	Per	Value	Date	Ref.
Communications - continued				
Newspaper subscription, dly. and Sun. delivery	month	9.00	12/94	2c
Phone line, single, business, field visit	inst	69.00	12/93	9s
Phone line, single, business, no field visit	inst	69.00	12/93	9s
Phone line, single, residence, field visit	inst	40.00	12/93	9s
Phone line, single, residence, no field visit	inst	40.00	12/93	9s
Telephone bill, family of four	month	23.53	12/94	2c
Telephone service, expenditures	year	616	91	81r
Telephone, residential, flat rate	mo.	16.70	12/93	8c
Education				
Board, 4-year private college/university	year	2072	8/94	80s
Board, 4-year public college/university	year	1706	8/94	80s
Education, total expenditures	year	319	91	81r
Room, 4-year private college/university	year	1607	8/94	80s
Room, 4-year public college/university	year	1598	8/94	80s
Total cost, 4-year private college/university	year	10664	8/94	80s
Total cost, 4-year public college/university	year	5287	8/94	80s
Tuition, 2-year public college/university, in-state	year	1110	8/94	80s
Tuition, 4-year private college/university, in-state	year	6985	8/94	80s
Tuition, 4-year public college/university, in-state	year	1983	8/94	80s
Energy and Fuels				
Energy, combined forms, 1800 sq. ft.	mo.	106.39	12/94	2c
Fuel oil and other fuels, expenditures	year	56	91	81r
Gas, natural, expenditures	year	150	91	81r
Gas, reg unlead, taxes inc., cash, self-service	gal	1.15	12/94	2c
Gasoline and motor oil purchased	year	1152	91	81r
Gasoline, unleaded midgrade	gallon	1.21	4/93	82r
Gasoline, unleaded premium	gallon	1.30	4/93	82r
Gasoline, unleaded regular	gallon	1.10	4/93	82r
Entertainment				
Bowling, evening rate	game	2.40	12/94	2c
Concert ticket, Pearl Jam group	perf	20.00	94	50r
Entertainment, total expenditures	year	1266	91	81r
Fees and admissions, expenditures	year	306	91	81r
Monopoly game, Parker Brothers', No. 9	game	12.08	12/94	2c
Movie	adm	5.25	12/94	2c
Pets, toys, playground equipment, expenditures	year	271	91	81r
Reading, expenditures	year	131	91	81r
Televisions, radios, and sound equipment, expenditures	year	439	91	81r
Tennis balls, yellow, Wilson or Penn, 3	can	1.90	12/94	2c
Funerals				
Burial, immediate, container provided by funeral home		1298.96	1/95	54r
Cards, acknowledgment		21.26	1/95	54r
Casket, minimum alternative		204.95	1/95	54r
Cosmetology, hair care, etc.		85.40	1/95	54r
Cremation, direct, container provided by funeral home		1054.77	1/95	54r
Embalming		287.71	1/95	54r
Funeral, funeral home		269.18	1/95	54r
Funeral, other facility		272.88	1/95	54r
Graveside service		302.54	1/95	54r
Hearse, local		122.08	1/95	54r
Limousine, local		80.31	1/95	54r
Memorial service		277.66	1/95	54r
Service charge, professional, nondeclinable		896.65	1/95	54r
Visitation and viewing		232.39	1/95	54r
Groceries				
Groceries, ACCRA Index		94.20	12/94	2c
Apples, Red Delicious	lb.	0.73	12/94	82r
Baby food, strained vegetables, lowest price	4-4.5 oz.	0.33	12/94	2c
Bacon, sliced	lb.	1.67	12/94	82r

Values are in dollars or fractions of dollars. In the column headed *Ref*, references are shown to sources. Each reference is followed by a letter. These refer to the geographical level for which data were reported: s=State, r=Region, and c=City or metro. The abbreviation *ex* is used to mean *except* or *excluding*; *exp* stands for *expenditures*. For other abbreviations and further explanations, please see the Introduction.

Decatur-Hartselle, AL - continued

Item	Per	Value	Date	Ref.
Groceries				
Bananas	lb.	0.44	12/94	2c
Bananas	lb.	0.42	12/94	82r
Beef or hamburger, ground	lb.	1.29	12/94	2c
Beef purchases	year	213	91	81r
Beverage purchases, alcoholic	year	249	91	81r
Beverage purchases, nonalcoholic	year	207	91	81r
Bologna, all beef or mixed	lb.	2.27	12/94	82r
Bread, white	24-oz.	0.69	12/94	2c
Bread, white, pan	lb.	0.68	12/94	82r
Cabbage	lb.	0.42	12/94	82r
Carrots, short trimmed and topped	lb.	0.53	12/94	82r
Cereals and bakery products purchases	year	345	91	81r
Cereals and cereals products purchases	year	127	91	81r
Cheddar cheese, natural	lb.	3.58	12/94	82r
Cheese, Kraft grated Parmesan	8-oz.	3.07	12/94	2c
Chicken breast, bone-in	lb.	1.71	12/94	82r
Chicken, fresh, whole	lb.	0.78	12/94	82r
Chicken, whole fryer	lb.	0.65	12/94	2c
Chuck roast, USDA choice, boneless	lb.	2.26	12/94	82r
Cigarettes, Winston, Kings	carton	14.17	12/94	2c
Coffee, vacuum-packed	13 oz.	3.21	12/94	2c
Corn Flakes, Kellogg's or Post Toasties	18 oz.	1.95	12/94	2c
Corn, frozen, whole kernel, lowest price	10 oz.	0.64	12/94	2c
Crackers, soda, salted	lb.	1.27	12/94	82r
Cucumbers	lb.	0.65	12/94	82r
Dairy products (other) purchases	year	141	91	81r
Eggs, Grade A large	dozen	0.72	12/94	2c
Eggs, Grade A large	dozen	0.87	12/94	82r
Fish and seafood purchases	year	72	91	81r
Flour, white, all purpose	lb.	0.23	12/94	82r
Food purchases, food eaten at home	year	2381	91	81r
Foods purchased away from home, not prepared by consumer	year	1696	91	81r
Frankfurters, all meat or all beef	lb.	1.74	12/94	82r
Fruits and vegetables purchases	year	380	91	81r
Grapefruit	lb.	0.45	12/94	82r
Grapes, Thompson seedless	lb.	2.30	12/94	82r
Ground beef, 100% beef	lb.	1.37	12/94	82r
Ground chuck, 100% beef	lb.	1.97	12/94	82r
Ham, boneless, exc. canned	lb.	2.54	12/94	82r
Ice cream, prepackaged, bulk, regular	1/2 gal.	2.47	12/94	82r
Lemons	lb.	1.02	12/94	82r
Lettuce, iceberg	lb.	0.96	12/94	82r
Lettuce, iceberg	head	0.89	12/94	2c
Margarine, Blue Bonnet or Parkay cubes	lb.	0.54	12/94	2c
Margarine, stick	lb.	0.77	12/94	82r
Meats, poultry, fish, and eggs purchases	year	655	91	81r
Milk and cream (fresh) purchases	year	130	91	81r
Milk, whole	1/2 gal.	1.42	12/94	2c
Orange juice, frozen concentrate 12-oz. can	16 oz.	1.36	12/94	82r
Orange juice, Minute Maid frozen	12-oz.	1.08	12/94	2c
Oranges, Navel	lb.	0.54	12/94	82r
Peaches, halves or slices, Hunt's, Del Monte, or Libby's	29-oz.	1.25	12/94	2c
Pears, Anjou	lb.	0.81	12/94	82r
Peas, sweet, Del Monte or Green Giant	15-17 oz.	0.48	12/94	2c
Pork chops, center cut, bone-in	lb.	3.07	12/94	82r
Pork purchases	year	142	91	81r
Potato chips	16-oz.	3.15	12/94	82r
Potatoes, frozen, French fried	lb.	0.82	12/94	82r
Potatoes, white	lb.	0.34	12/94	82r
Potatoes, white or red	10-lb. sack	3.04	12/94	2c
Rice, white, long grain, uncooked	lb.	0.48	12/94	82r
Round roast, USDA choice, boneless	lb.	2.91	12/94	82r
Sausage, fresh	lb.	1.82	12/94	82r
Sausage, Jimmy Dean, 100% pork	lb.	2.55	12/94	2c
Shortening, vegetable oil blends	lb.	0.75	12/94	82r
Shortening, vegetable, Crisco	3-lb.	2.61	12/94	2c

Decatur-Hartselle, AL - continued

Item	Per	Value	Date	Ref.
Groceries - continued				
Soft drink, Coca Cola, ex deposit	2 lit	1.06	12/94	2c
Spaghetti and macaroni	lb.	0.87	12/94	82r
Steak, rib eye, USDA choice, boneless	lb.	6.85	12/94	82r
Steak, round, graded & ungraded, exc. USDA prime & choice	lb.	2.96	12/94	82r
Steak, round, USDA choice, boneless	lb.	3.17	12/94	82r
Steak, sirloin, USDA choice, boneless	lb.	4.12	12/94	82r
Steak, t-bone	lb.	5.87	12/94	2c
Steak, T-bone, USDA choice, bone-in	lb.	5.63	12/94	82r
Sugar and other sweets, eaten at home, expenditures	year	93	91	81r
Sugar, cane or beet	4 lbs.	1.21	12/94	2c
Sugar, white, all sizes	lb.	0.39	12/94	82r
Tobacco products and smoking supplies, total expenditures	year	286	91	81r
Tomatoes, field grown	lb.	1.36	12/94	82r
Tomatoes, Hunt's or Del Monte	14.5 oz.	0.63	12/94	2c
Tuna, chunk, light	lb.	1.94	12/94	82r
Tuna, chunk, light, oil-packed	6.125-6.5 oz.	0.71	12/94	2c
Turkey, frozen, whole	lb.	0.96	12/94	82r
Yogurt, natural, fruit flavored	8 oz.	0.58	12/94	82r
Goods and Services				
Miscellaneous goods and services, ACCRA Index		96.80	12/94	2c
Health Care				
Health care, ACCRA Index		88.20	12/94	2c
Adenosine, emergency room	treat	100.00	95	23r
Antibiotic ointment, Polysporin	1.5 oz.	4.10	12/94	2c
Bladder tap, superpubic, infant, emergency room	treat	119.00	95	23r
Blood analysis, emergency room	treat	25.00	95	23r
Blood tests, abdominal pain, emergency room	treat	25.00	95	23r
Burn dressing, emergency room	treat	266.00	95	23r
Cardiology interpretation, emergency room	treat	26.00	95	23r
Chest X-ray, emergency room	treat	78.00	95	23r
Childbirth, Cesarean delivery, hospital charge	birth	5462.00	12/91	69r
Childbirth, Cesarean delivery, physician charge	birth	2228.00	12/91	69r
Childbirth, normal delivery, hospital charge	birth	2943.00	12/91	69r
Childbirth, normal delivery, physician charge	birth	1619.00	12/91	69r
Defibrillation pads, emergency room	treat	6.00	95	23r
Dentist's fee, adult teeth cleaning and periodic oral exam	visit	46.60	12/94	2c
Doctor's fee, routine exam, established patient	visit	37.60	12/94	2c
Drugs, expenditures	year	297	91	81r
Gastric tube insertion, nasal, emergency room	treat	25.00	95	23r
Health care, total expenditures	year	1600	91	81r
Health insurance expenditures	year	637	91	81r
Heart monitor, emergency room	treat	40.00	95	23r
Hospital care, semiprivate room	day	275.00	12/94	2c
Insurance premium, family medical care	month	360.67	1/95	41s
Intravenous fluids, emergency room	treat	130.00	95	23r
Intravenous fluids, emergency room	liter	26.00	95	23r
Intravenous line, central, emergency room	treat	342.00	95	23r
Liver function tests, abdominal pain, emergency room	treat	26.00	95	23r
Medical care charges, total, emergency room, third-degree burns	treat	2101.00	95	23r
Medical care charges, total, emergency, infant with fever	treat	628.00	95	23r
Medical services expenditures	year	573	91	81r
Medical supplies expenditures	year	93	91	81r
Morphine, emergency room	treat	34.00	95	23r
Nursing care and facilities charges, emergency room	treat	252.00	95	23r

Values are in dollars or fractions of dollars. In the column headed *Ref*, references are shown to sources. Each reference is followed by a letter. These refer to the geographical level for which data were reported: s=State, r=Region, and c=City or metro. The abbreviation *ex* is used to mean *except* or *excluding*; *exp* stands for *expenditures*. For other abbreviations and further explanations, please see the Introduction.

Decatur-Hartselle, AL - continued

Item	Per	Value	Date	Ref.
Health Care				
Nursing care and facilities charges, emergency, infant with fever	treat	252.00	95	23r
Nursing care and facilities charges, emergency, third-degree burns	treat	861.00	95	23r
Physician's charges, emergency, infant with fever	treat	212.00	95	23r
Physician's charges, emergency, third-degree burns	treat	372.00	95	23r
Physician's fee, emergency room	treat	372.00	95	23r
Physician's fee, general practitioner	visit	51.20	12/93	60r
Surgery, open-heart	proc	42374.00	1/93	14r
Ultrasound, abdominal, emergency room	treat	276.00	95	23r
Urinalysis, emergency room	treat	20.00	95	23r
Urinalysis, infant, emergency room	treat	20.00	95	23r
X-rays, emergency room	treat	78.00	95	23r
Household Goods				
Appl. repair, service call, wash mach	min. lab. chg.	30.99	12/94	2c
Floor coverings, expenditures	year	48	91	81r
Furniture, expenditures	year	280	91	81r
Household equipment, misc. expenditures	year	342	91	81r
Household expenditures, miscellaneous	year	256	91	81r
Household furnishings and equipment, expenditures	year	988	91	81r
Household operations expenditures	year	468	91	81r
Household textiles, expenditures	year	95	91	81r
Housekeeping supplies, expenditures	year	380	91	81r
Laundry and cleaning supplies, expenditures	year	109	91	81r
Laundry detergent, Tide Ultra, Bold, or Cheer	42 oz.	3.23	12/94	2c
Postage and stationery, expenditures	year	105	91	81r
Tissues, facial, Kleenex brand	175	1.02	12/94	2c
Housing				
Housing, ACCRA Index		84.30	12/94	2c
Add garage/carport		6,980	3/95	74r
Add room(s)		11,403	3/95	74r
Apartment condominium or co-op, median	unit	68600	12/94	62r
Dwellings (owned), expenditures	year	2428	91	81r
Enclose porch/patio/breezeway		4,572	3/95	74r
Finish room in basement/attic		3,794	3/95	74r
Home, existing, single-family, median	unit	120200	12/94	62r
House payment, principal and interest, 25% down payment	mo.	664	12/94	2c
House, 1800 sq ft, 8000 sq ft lot, new, urban, utilities	total	106000	12/94	2c
Maintenance, repairs, insurance, and other housing expenditures	year	531	91	81r
Mortgage interest and charges expenditures	year	1506	91	81r
Mtge. rate, incl. points and orig. fee, 30-year conv. fixed or ARM	mo.	9.41	12/94	2c
Princ. & int., mortgage, median-price exist. sing.-family home	mo.	540	12/94	62r
Property taxes expenditures	year	391	91	81r
Redesign, restructure more than half of home's interior		17,641	3/95	74r
Rent, apartment, 2 br., 1 1/2-2 baths, unfurnished, 950 sq ft, water	mo.	394	12/94	2c
Rental units expenditures	year	1264	91	81r
Insurance and Pensions				
Auto insurance, private passenger	year	604.07	12/94	71s
Insurance and pensions, personal, expenditures	year	2395	91	81r
Insurance, life and other personal, expenditures	year	368	91	81r
Pensions and Social Security, expenditures	year	2027	91	81r
Personal Goods				
Shampoo, Alberto VO5	15-oz.	1.06	12/94	2c
Toothpaste, Crest or Colgate	6-7 oz.	1.67	12/94	2c

Decatur-Hartselle, AL - continued

Item	Per	Value	Date	Ref.
Personal Services				
Dry cleaning, man's 2-pc. suit		6.04	12/94	2c
Haircut, man's barbershop, no styling		7.20	12/94	2c
Haircut, woman's shampoo, trim, blow-dry		18.10	12/94	2c
Personal services expenditures	year	212	91	81r
Restaurant Food				
Chicken, fried, thigh and drumstick		1.96	12/94	2c
Dining expenditures, family	week	33.83	94	73r
Hamburger with cheese	1/4 lb.	1.86	12/94	2c
Pizza, Pizza Hut or Pizza Inn	12-13 in.	7.99	12/94	2c
Taxes				
Taxes, Federal income, expenditures	year	2275	91	81r
Taxes, personal, expenditures	year	2715	91	81r
Taxes, State and local income, expenditures	year	365	91	81r
Transportation				
Transportation, ACCRA Index		100.50	12/94	2c
Cars and trucks purchased, new	year	1306	91	81r
Cars and trucks purchased, used	year	942	91	81r
Driver's learning permit fee	perm	20.00	1/94	84s
Driver's license fee	orig	20.00	1/94	84s
Driver's license fee, duplicate	lic	5.00	1/94	84s
Driver's license reinstatement fee, min.	susp	50.00	1/94	85s
Driver's license renewal fee	renew	20.00	1/94	84s
Identification card, nondriver	card	20.00	1/94	83s
Motorcycle license fee	orig	20.00	1/94	84s
Motorcycle license fee, duplicate	lic	5.00	1/94	84s
Motorcycle license renewal fee	renew	20.00	1/94	84s
Public transportation expenditures	year	249	91	81r
Tire balance, computer or spin bal., front	wheel	6.65	12/94	2c
Transportation expenditures, total	year	5307	91	81r
Vehicle finance charges	year	346	91	81r
Vehicle insurance expenditures	year	544	91	81r
Vehicle maintenance and repairs expenditures	year	600	91	81r
Vehicle purchases	year	2275	91	81r
Vehicle rental, leases, licenses, etc. expenditures	year	141	91	81r
Vehicles purchased, other than cars and trucks	year	27	91	81r
Utilities				
Utilities, ACCRA Index		98.30	12/94	2c
Electricity expenditures	year	950	91	81r
Electricity, 1800 sq. ft., new home	mo.	106.39	12/94	2c
Utilities, fuels, and public services, total expenditures	year	2000	91	81r
Water and other public services, expenditures	year	227	91	81r
Weddings				
Bridal attendants' gowns	event	750	10/93	76r
Bridal gown	event	852	10/93	76r
Bridal headpiece and veil	event	167	10/93	76r
Bride's wedding band	event	708	10/93	76r
Clergy	event	224	10/93	76r
Engagement ring	event	2756	10/93	76r
Flowers	event	863	10/93	76r
Formal wear for groom	event	106	10/93	76r
Groom's attendants' formal wear	event	530	10/93	76r
Groom's wedding band	event	402	10/93	76r
Music	event	600	10/93	76r
Photography	event	1088	10/93	76r
Shoes for bride	event	50	10/93	76r
Videography	event	483	10/93	76r
Wedding invitations and announcements	event	342	10/93	76r
Wedding reception	event	7000	10/93	76r

Values are in dollars or fractions of dollars. In the column headed *Ref*, references are shown to sources. Each reference is followed by a letter. These refer to the geographical level for which data were reported: s = State, r = Region, and c = City or metro. The abbreviation *ex* is used to mean *except* or *excluding*; *exp* stands for *expenditures*. For other abbreviations and further explanations, please see the Introduction.

Denver, CO

Item	Per	Value	Date	Ref.
Composite, ACCRA index		104.50	12/94	2c
Alcoholic Beverages				
Beer, Miller Lite, Bud, 12-oz., ex deposit	6	3.94	12/94	2c
J & B Scotch	750-ml.	17.77	12/94	2c
Wine, Gallo Chablis blanc	1.5-lit	4.13	12/94	2c
Appliances				
Appliances (major), expenditures	year	160	91	81r
Average annual exp.				
Food, health care, personal goods, services	year	32461	91	81r
Business				
Dinner and tip, hotel, corporate rate	night	31.00	2/94	15c
Hotel room, corporate rate	night	79.00	2/94	15c
Charity				
Cash contributions, expenditures	year	975	91	81r
Clothing				
Apparel, men and boys, total expenditures	year	467	91	81r
Apparel, women and girls, total expenditures	year	737	91	81r
Footwear, expenditures	year	270	91	81r
Jeans, man's denim		30.42	12/94	2c
Shirt, man's dress shirt		25.08	12/94	2c
Undervest, boy's size 10-14, cotton	3	5.38	12/94	2c
Communications				
Long-distance telephone rate, day, addl. min., 1-10 mi.	min.	0.13	12/93	9s
Long-distance telephone rate, day, initial min., 1-10 mi.	min.	0.17	12/93	9s
Newspaper subscription, dly. and Sun. delivery	month	8.61	12/94	2c
Phone line, single, business, field visit	inst	70.00	12/93	9s
Phone line, single, business, no field visit	inst	70.00	12/93	9s
Phone line, single, residence, field visit	inst	35.00	12/93	9s
Phone line, single, residence, no field visit	inst	35.00	12/93	9s
Telephone bill, family of four	month	20.47	12/94	2c
Telephone service, expenditures	year	611	91	81r
Telephone, residential, flat rate	mo.	14.48	12/93	8c
Education				
Board, 4-year private college/university	year	2468	8/94	80s
Board, 4-year public college/university	year	2148	8/94	80s
Education, total expenditures	year	375	91	81r
Room, 4-year private college/university	year	2492	8/94	80s
Room, 4-year public college/university	year	1772	8/94	80s
Total cost, 4-year private college/university	year	16064	8/94	80s
Total cost, 4-year public college/university	year	6183	8/94	80s
Tuition, 2-year public college/university, in-state	year	1193	8/94	80s
Tuition, 4-year private college/university, in-state	year	11104	8/94	80s
Tuition, 4-year public college/university, in-state	year	2262	8/94	80s
Energy and Fuels				
Energy, combined forms, 1800 sq. ft.	mo.	101.91	12/94	2c
Energy, exc. electricity, 1800 sq. ft.	mo.	40.87	12/94	2c
Fuel oil and other fuels, expenditures	year	33	91	81r
Gas, cooking, 10 therms	month	13.82	2/94	65c
Gas, cooking, 30 therms	month	18.72	2/94	65c
Gas, cooking, 50 therms	month	24.67	2/94	65c
Gas, heating, winter, average use	month	67.86	2/94	65c
Gas, natural, expenditures	year	212	91	81r
Gas, reg unlead, taxes inc., cash, self-service	gal	1.16	12/94	2c
Gasoline and motor oil purchased	year	1115	91	81r
Gasoline, unleaded midgrade	gallon	1.36	4/93	82r
Gasoline, unleaded premium	gallon	1.43	4/93	82r
Gasoline, unleaded regular	gallon	1.23	4/93	82r
Entertainment				
Bowling, evening rate	game	1.88	12/94	2c
Concert ticket, Pearl Jam group	perf	20.00	94	50r

Denver, CO - continued

Item	Per	Value	Date	Ref.
Entertainment - continued				
Entertainment, total expenditures	year	1853	91	81r
Fees and admissions, expenditures	year	482	91	81r
Monopoly game, Parker Brothers', No. 9	game	10.35	12/94	2c
Movie	adm	6.00	12/94	2c
Pets, toys, playground equipment, expenditures	year	299	91	81r
Reading, expenditures	year	164	91	81r
Televisions, radios, and sound equipment, expenditures	year	528	91	81r
Tennis balls, yellow, Wilson or Penn, 3	can	2.18	12/94	2c
Funerals				
Burial, immediate, container provided by funeral home		1360.49	1/95	54r
Cards, acknowledgment		11.24	1/95	54r
Casket, minimum alternative		232.73	1/95	54r
Cosmetology, hair care, etc.		114.13	1/95	54r
Cremation, direct, container provided by funeral home		1027.08	1/95	54r
Embalming		286.24	1/95	54r
Funeral, funeral home		315.60	1/95	54r
Funeral, other facility		303.08	1/95	54r
Graveside service		423.83	1/95	54r
Hearse, local		133.12	1/95	54r
Limousine, local		99.10	1/95	54r
Memorial service		442.57	1/95	54r
Service charge, professional, nondeclinable		840.16	1/95	54r
Visitation and viewing		168.50	1/95	54r
Groceries				
Groceries, ACCRA Index		100.00	12/94	2c
Apples, Red Delicious	lb.	0.72	12/94	82r
Baby food, strained vegetables, lowest price	4-4.5 oz.	0.33	12/94	2c
Bacon, sliced	lb.	1.73	12/94	82r
Bananas	lb.	0.53	12/94	2c
Bananas	lb.	0.52	12/94	82r
Beef or hamburger, ground	lb.	1.43	12/94	2c
Beef purchases	year	241	91	81r
Beverage purchases, alcoholic	year	328	91	81r
Beverage purchases, nonalcoholic	year	234	91	81r
Beverage, Coca Cola	2 lit	0.85	4/95	30c
Beverage, Pepsi	2 lit	0.85	4/95	30c
Bologna, all beef or mixed	lb.	2.33	12/94	82r
Bread, white	24-oz.	0.69	12/94	2c
Bread, white, pan	lb.	0.81	12/94	82r
Carrots, short trimmed and topped	lb.	0.43	12/94	82r
Cereal, Corn Flakes, Kellogg's brand	18 oz.	2.71	4/95	30c
Cereal, Corn Flakes, local brand	18 oz.	1.45	4/95	30c
Cereals and bakery products purchases	year	392	91	81r
Cereals and cereals products purchases	year	139	91	81r
Cheese, Kraft grated Parmesan	8-oz.	2.99	12/94	2c
Chicken breast, bone-in	lb.	2.04	12/94	82r
Chicken, fresh, whole	lb.	0.95	12/94	82r
Chicken, whole fryer	lb.	0.78	12/94	2c
Cigarettes, Winston, Kings	carton	14.94	12/94	2c
Coffee, 100%, ground roast, all sizes	lb.	4.48	12/94	82r
Coffee, vacuum-packed	13 oz.	3.80	12/94	2c
Corn Flakes, Kellogg's or Post Toasties	18 oz.	2.14	12/94	2c
Corn, frozen, whole kernel, lowest price	10 oz.	0.82	12/94	2c
Dairy products (other) purchases	year	182	91	81r
Eggs, Grade A large	dozen	0.84	12/94	2c
Fish and seafood purchases	year	94	91	81r
Flour, white, all purpose	lb.	0.21	12/94	82r
Food purchases, food eaten at home	year	2749	91	81r
Foods purchased away from home, not prepared by consumer	year	1909	91	81r
Frozen dinner, Lean Cuisine brand, glazed chicken	pkg.	2.55	4/95	30c
Fruits and vegetables purchases	year	459	91	81r
Grapefruit	lb.	0.56	12/94	82r
Ground beef, 100% beef	lb.	1.31	12/94	82r
Ham, boneless, exc. canned	lb.	2.46	12/94	82r

Values are in dollars or fractions of dollars. In the column headed *Ref*, references are shown to sources. Each reference is followed by a letter. These refer to the geographical level for which data were reported: s=State, r=Region, and c=City or metro. The abbreviation *ex* is used to mean *except* or *excluding*; *exp* stands for expenditures. For other abbreviations and further explanations, please see the Introduction.

Denver, CO - continued

Item	Per	Value	Date	Ref.
Groceries				
Ice cream, prepackaged, bulk, regular	1/2 gal.	2.57	12/94	82r
Lemons	lb.	1.00	12/94	82r
Lettuce, iceberg	lb.	0.93	12/94	82r
Lettuce, iceberg	head	0.88	12/94	2c
Margarine, Blue Bonnet or Parkay cubes	lb.	0.56	12/94	2c
Meats, poultry, fish, and eggs purchases	year	700	91	81r
Milk and cream (fresh) purchases	year	155	91	81r
Milk, 2%, brand name	gallon	2.78	4/95	30c
Milk, 2%, local brand	gallon	2.41	4/95	30c
Milk, whole	1/2 gal.	1.68	12/94	2c
Orange juice, frozen concentrate 12-oz. can	16 oz.	1.52	12/94	82r
Orange juice, Minute Maid frozen	12-oz.	1.31	12/94	2c
Oranges, Navel	lb.	0.56	12/94	82r
Peaches, halves or slices, Hunt's, Del Monte, or Libby's	29-oz.	1.54	12/94	2c
Peas, Le Sueur brand, canned	8.5 oz.	0.64	4/95	30c
Peas, sweet, Del Monte or Green Giant	15-17 oz.	0.73	12/94	2c
Pork chops, center cut, bone-in	lb.	3.30	12/94	82r
Pork purchases	year	122	91	81r
Potato chips	16-oz.	3.03	12/94	82r
Potatoes, frozen, French fried	lb.	0.77	12/94	82r
Potatoes, white	lb.	0.35	12/94	82r
Potatoes, white or red	10-lb. sack	1.67	12/94	2c
Rice, white, long grain, uncooked	lb.	0.54	12/94	82r
Round roast, USDA choice, boneless	lb.	2.92	12/94	82r
Sausage, Jimmy Dean, 100% pork	lb.	3.54	12/94	2c
Shortening, vegetable oil blends	lb.	0.80	12/94	82r
Shortening, vegetable, Crisco	3-lb.	2.86	12/94	2c
Soft drink, Coca Cola, ex deposit	2 lit	0.81	12/94	2c
Spaghetti and macaroni	lb.	1.02	12/94	82r
Steak, round, graded & ungraded, exc. USDA prime & choice	lb.	3.13	12/94	82r
Steak, sirloin, USDA choice, boneless	lb.	4.07	12/94	82r
Steak, t-bone	lb.	4.97	12/94	2c
Sugar and other sweets, eaten at home, expenditures	year	105	91	81r
Sugar, cane or beet	4 lbs.	1.24	12/94	2c
Sugar, white, all sizes	lb.	0.38	12/94	82r
Tobacco products and smoking supplies, total expenditures	year	221	91	81r
Tomatoes, field grown	lb.	1.45	12/94	82r
Tomatoes, Hunt's or Del Monte	14.5 oz.	0.89	12/94	2c
Tuna, chunk, light	lb.	2.18	12/94	82r
Tuna, chunk, light, oil-packed	6.125-6.5 oz.	0.82	12/94	2c
Goods and Services				
Miscellaneous goods and services, ACCRA Index		95.50	12/94	2c
Health Care				
Health care, ACCRA Index		124.00	12/94	2c
Antibiotic ointment, Polysporin	1.5 oz.	4.08	12/94	2c
Appendectomy	proc	932.00	12/92	69c
Breast lesion excision (lumpectomy)	proc	482.00	12/92	69c
Cesarean section delivery	proc	1505.00	12/92	69c
Childbirth, Cesarean delivery, hospital charge	birth	6059.00	12/91	69r
Childbirth, Cesarean delivery, physician charge	birth	2248.00	12/91	69r
Childbirth, normal delivery, hospital charge	birth	3006.00	12/91	69r
Childbirth, normal delivery, physician charge	birth	1634.00	12/91	69r
Cholecystectomy	proc	1450.00	12/92	69c
Coronary bypass, triple	proc	5146.00	12/92	69c
Dentist's fee, adult teeth cleaning and periodic oral exam	visit	64.86	12/94	2c
Doctor's fee, routine exam, established patient	visit	55.00	12/94	2c

Denver, CO - continued

Item	Per	Value	Date	Ref.
Health Care - continued				
Drugs, expenditures	year	230	91	81r
Health care, total expenditures	year	1544	91	81r
Health insurance expenditures	year	558	91	81r
Hospital care, semiprivate room	day	448.40	12/94	2c
Hysterectomy, abdominal	proc	1852.00	12/92	69c
Insurance premium, family medical care	month	362.55	1/95	41s
Medical services expenditures	year	676	91	81r
Medical supplies expenditures	year	80	91	81r
Oophorectomy	proc	1036.00	12/92	69c
Salpingo-oophorectomy	proc	1095.00	12/92	69c
Surgery, open-heart	proc	37818.00	1/93	14r
Household Goods				
Appl. repair, service call, wash mach	min. lab. chg.	29.29	12/94	2c
Floor coverings, expenditures	year	79	91	81r
Furniture, expenditures	year	352	91	81r
Household equipment, misc. expenditures	year	614	91	81r
Household expenditures, miscellaneous	year	294	91	81r
Household furnishings and equipment, expenditures	year	1416	91	81r
Household operations expenditures	year	580	91	81r
Household textiles, expenditures	year	113	91	81r
Housekeeping supplies, expenditures	year	447	91	81r
Laundry and cleaning supplies, expenditures	year	114	91	81r
Laundry detergent, Tide Ultra, Bold, or Cheer	42 oz.	2.98	12/94	2c
Postage and stationery, expenditures	year	145	91	81r
Tissues, facial, Kleenex brand	175	0.87	12/94	2c
Housing				
Housing, ACCRA Index		116.30	12/94	2c
Add garage/carport		6,422	3/95	74r
Add room(s)		26,583	3/95	74r
Apartment condominium or co-op, median	unit	105300	12/94	62r
Car rental	day	35.00	5/95	95c
Dwellings (owned), expenditures	year	3932	91	81r
Enclose porch/patio/breezeway		5,382	3/95	74r
Finish room in basement/attic		3,911	3/95	74r
Home, existing, single-family, median	unit	178600	12/94	62r
Home, existing, single-family, median	unit	119.00	12/94	62c
Home, purchase price	unit	137.10	3/93	26c
Hotel room	day	88.00	5/95	95c
House payment, principal and interest, 25% down payment	mo.	872	12/94	2c
House, 1800 sq ft, 8000 sq ft lot, new, urban, utilities	total	143359	12/94	2c
Maintenance, repairs, insurance, and other housing expenditures	year	591	91	81r
Mortgage interest and charges expenditures	year	2747	91	81r
Mtge. rate, incl. points and orig. fee, 30-year conv. fixed or ARM	mo.	9.09	12/94	2c
Princ. & int., mortgage, median-price exist. sing.-family home	mo.	845	12/94	62r
Property taxes expenditures	year	594	91	81r
Redesign, restructure more than half of home's interior		5,467	3/95	74r
Rent, apartment, 2 br., 1 1/2-2 baths, unfurnished, 950 sq ft, water	mo.	670	12/94	2c
Rental units expenditures	year	2077	91	81r
Insurance and Pensions				
Auto insurance, private passenger	year	804.17	12/94	71s
Insurance and pensions, personal, expenditures	year	3042	91	81r
Insurance, life and other personal, expenditures	year	298	91	81r
Pensions and Social Security, expenditures	year	2744	91	81r
Legal Assistance				
Lawyer's consultation fee	hour	160.00	93	45c
Legal work, law firm associate	hour	91		10r

Values are in dollars or fractions of dollars. In the column headed *Ref*, references are shown to sources. Each reference is followed by a letter. These refer to the geographical level for which data were reported: s=State, r=Region, and c=City or metro. The abbreviation *ex* is used to mean *except* or *excluding*; *exp* stands for expenditures. For other abbreviations and further explanations, please see the Introduction.

Denver, CO - continued

Item	Per	Value	Date	Ref.
Legal Assistance				
Legal work, law firm partner	hour	151		10r
Personal Goods				
Shampoo, Alberto VO5	15-oz.	1.20	12/94	2c
Toothpaste, Crest or Colgate	6-7 oz.	1.97	12/94	2c
Personal Services				
Dry cleaning, man's 2-pc. suit		6.76	12/94	2c
Haircut, man's barbershop, no styling		8.13	12/94	2c
Haircut, woman's shampoo, trim, blow-dry		20.94	12/94	2c
Personal services expenditures	year	286	91	81r
Restaurant Food				
Chicken, fried, thigh and drumstick		1.97	12/94	2c
Dining expenditures, family	week	32.25	94	73r
Hamburger with cheese	1/4 lb.	2.01	12/94	2c
Pizza, Pizza Hut or Pizza Inn	12-13 in.	7.49	12/94	2c
Taxes				
Tax rate, residential property, month	$100	0.97	1/92	79c
Taxes, Federal income, expenditures	year	2946	91	81r
Taxes, personal, expenditures	year	3791	91	81r
Taxes, State and local income, expenditures	year	791	91	81r
Transportation				
Transportation, ACCRA Index		106.10	12/94	2c
Bus fare, one-way	trip	0.50	12/95	1c
Bus fare, up to 10 miles	one-way	1.25	12/94	2c
Cars and trucks purchased, new	year	1231	91	81r
Cars and trucks purchased, used	year	915	91	81r
Driver's learning permit fee	perm	10.00	1/94	84s
Driver's license fee	orig	15.00	1/94	84s
Driver's license fee, duplicate	lic	5.00	1/94	84s
Driver's license reinstatement fee, min.	susp	40.00	1/94	85s
Driver's license renewal fee	renew	15.00	1/94	84s
Identification card, nondriver	card	3.50	1/94	83s
Motorcycle license fee	orig	16.00	1/94	84s
Public transportation expenditures	year	375	91	81r
Railway fare, light rail, one-way	trip	0.50	12/95	1c
Tire balance, computer or spin bal., front	wheel	6.94	12/94	2c
Transportation expenditures, total	year	5527	91	81r
Vehicle finance charges	year	287	91	81r
Vehicle insurance expenditures	year	624	91	81r
Vehicle maintenance and repairs expenditures	year	695	91	81r
Vehicle purchases	year	2174	91	81r
Vehicle rental, leases, licenses, etc. expenditures	year	257	91	81r
Vehicles purchased, other than cars and trucks	year	28	91	81r
Utilities				
Utilities, ACCRA Index		92.70	12/94	2c
Electricity expenditures	year	616	91	81r
Electricity, (part.), other, 1800 sq. ft., new home	mo.	61.04	12/94	2c
Electricity, summer, 250 KWh	month	20.52	8/93	64c
Electricity, summer, 500 KWh	month	35.99	8/93	64c
Electricity, summer, 750 KWh	month	51.46	8/93	64c
Electricity, summer, 1000 KWh	month	66.94	8/93	64c
Utilities, fuels, and public services, total expenditures	year	1681	91	81r
Water and other public services, expenditures	year	209	91	81r
Weddings				
Bridal attendants' gowns	event	750	10/93	76r
Bridal gown	event	852	10/93	76r
Bridal headpiece and veil	event	167	10/93	76r
Bride's wedding band	event	708	10/93	76r
Clergy	event	224	10/93	76r
Engagement ring	event	2756	10/93	76r
Flowers	event	863	10/93	76r

Denver, CO - continued

Item	Per	Value	Date	Ref.
Weddings - continued				
Formal wear for groom	event	106	10/93	76r
Groom's attendants' formal wear	event	530	10/93	76r
Groom's wedding band	event	402	10/93	76r
Music	event	600	10/93	76r
Photography	event	1088	10/93	76r
Shoes for bride	event	50	10/93	76r
Videography	event	483	10/93	76r
Wedding invitations and announcements	event	342	10/93	76r
Wedding reception	event	7000	10/93	76r

Des Moines, IA

Item	Per	Value	Date	Ref.
Composite, ACCRA index		96.90	12/94	2c
Alcoholic Beverages				
Beer, Miller Lite, Bud, 12-oz., ex deposit	6	3.67	12/94	2c
J & B Scotch	750-ml.	18.85	12/94	2c
Wine, Gallo Chablis blanc	1.5-lit	5.11	12/94	2c
Appliances				
Appliances (major), expenditures	year	131	91	81r
Average annual exp.				
Food, health care, personal goods, services	year	25935	91	81r
Charity				
Cash contributions, expenditures	year	745	91	81r
Clothing				
Apparel, men and boys, total expenditures	year	332	91	81r
Apparel, women and girls, total expenditures	year	578	91	81r
Footwear, expenditures	year	164	91	81r
Jeans, man's denim		29.41	12/94	2c
Shirt, dress, men's	shirt	25.00	1/92	44c
Shirt, man's dress shirt		22.50	12/94	2c
Undervest, boy's size 10-14, cotton	3	3.48	12/94	2c
Communications				
Long-distance telephone rate, day, addl. min., 1-10 mi.	min.	0.11	12/93	9s
Long-distance telephone rate, day, initial min., 1-10 mi.	min.	0.21	12/93	9s
Newspaper subscription, dly. and Sun. delivery	month	14.13	12/94	2c
Phone line, single, business, field visit	inst	50.00	12/93	9s
Phone line, single, business, no field visit	inst	50.00	12/93	9s
Phone line, single, residence, field visit	inst	35.00	12/93	9s
Phone line, single, residence, no field visit	inst	35.00	12/93	9s
Telephone bill, family of four	month	19.76	12/94	2c
Telephone service, expenditures	year	547	91	81r
Telephone, residential, flat rate	mo.	14.95	12/93	8c
Education				
Board, 4-year private college/university	year	1971	8/94	80s
Board, 4-year public college/university	year	1562	8/94	80s
Education, total expenditures	year	394	91	81r
Room, 4-year private college/university	year	1707	8/94	80s
Room, 4-year public college/university	year	1526	8/94	80s
Total cost, 4-year private college/university	year	14510	8/94	80s
Total cost, 4-year public college/university	year	5440	8/94	80s
Tuition, 2-year public college/university, in-state	year	1612	8/94	80s
Tuition, 4-year private college/university, in-state	year	10832	8/94	80s
Tuition, 4-year public college/university, in-state	year	2352	8/94	80s
Energy and Fuels				
Energy, combined forms, 1800 sq. ft.	mo.	120.95	12/94	2c
Energy, exc. electricity, 1800 sq. ft.	mo.	48.95	12/94	2c
Fuel oil and other fuels, expenditures	year	83	91	81r
Gas	gal.	1.10	1/92	44c
Gas, cooking, 10 therms	month	13.24	2/94	65c
Gas, cooking, 30 therms	month	22.23	2/94	65c

Values are in dollars or fractions of dollars. In the column headed *Ref*, references are shown to sources. Each reference is followed by a letter. These refer to the geographical level for which data were reported: s = State, r = Region, and c = City or metro. The abbreviation *ex* is used to mean *except* or *excluding*; *exp* stands for *expenditures*. For other abbreviations and further explanations, please see the Introduction.

Des Moines, IA - continued

Item	Per	Value	Date	Ref.
Energy and Fuels				
Gas, cooking, 50 therms	month	31.22	2/94	65c
Gas, natural, expenditures	year	373	91	81r
Gas, reg unlead, taxes inc., cash, self-service	gal	1.15	12/94	2c
Gasoline and motor oil purchased	year	1000	91	81r
Gasoline, unleaded midgrade	gallon	1.15	4/93	82r
Gasoline, unleaded premium	gallon	1.23	4/93	82r
Gasoline, unleaded regular	gallon	1.07	4/93	82r
Entertainment				
Bowling, evening rate	game	2.75	12/94	2c
Entertainment, total expenditures	year	1356	91	81r
Fees and admissions, expenditures	year	347	91	81r
Monopoly game, Parker Brothers', No. 9	game	10.29	12/94	2c
Movie	adm	5.40	12/94	2c
Movie ticket, adult	ticket	5.50	1/92	44c
Pets, toys, playground equipment, expenditures	year	270	91	81r
Reading, expenditures	year	160	91	81r
Televisions, radios, and sound equipment, expenditures	year	433	91	81r
Tennis balls, yellow, Wilson or Penn, 3	can	2.07	12/94	2c
Funerals				
Burial, immediate, container provided by funeral home		1348.78	1/95	54r
Cards, acknowledgment		21.20	1/95	54r
Casket, minimum alternative		182.83	1/95	54r
Cosmetology, hair care, etc.		133.11	1/95	54r
Cremation, direct, container provided by funeral home		1101.95	1/95	54r
Embalming		314.45	1/95	54r
Funeral, funeral home		304.88	1/95	54r
Funeral, other facility		301.37	1/95	54r
Graveside service		290.59	1/95	54r
Hearse, local		137.37	1/95	54r
Limousine, local		82.84	1/95	54r
Memorial service		316.57	1/95	54r
Service charge, professional, nondeclinable		1099.00	1/95	54r
Visitation and viewing		209.25	1/95	54r
Groceries				
Groceries, ACCRA Index		96.60	12/94	2c
Apples, Red Delicious	lb.	0.68	12/94	82r
Baby food, strained vegetables, lowest price	4-4.5 oz.	0.26	12/94	2c
Bacon, sliced	lb.	1.88	12/94	82r
Bananas	lb.	0.35	12/94	2c
Bananas	lb.	0.41	12/94	82r
Beef or hamburger, ground	lb.	1.06	12/94	2c
Beef purchases	year	197	91	81r
Beef, stew, boneless	lb.	2.52	12/94	82r
Beverage purchases, alcoholic	year	293	91	81r
Beverage purchases, nonalcoholic	year	203	91	81r
Bologna, all beef or mixed	lb.	2.12	12/94	82r
Bread, white	24-oz.	0.97	12/94	2c
Bread, white, pan	lb.	0.76	12/94	82r
Cabbage	lb.	0.44	12/94	82r
Carrots, short trimmed and topped	lb.	0.44	12/94	82r
Cereals and bakery products purchases	year	347	91	81r
Cereals and cereals products purchases	year	119	91	81r
Cheddar cheese, natural	lb.	3.28	12/94	82r
Cheese, Kraft grated Parmesan	8-oz.	3.26	12/94	2c
Chicken breast, bone-in	lb.	1.61	12/94	82r
Chicken, fresh, whole	lb.	0.89	12/94	82r
Chicken, whole fryer	lb.	0.80	12/94	2c
Chuck roast, USDA choice, boneless	lb.	2.33	12/94	82r
Cigarettes, Winston, Kings	carton	16.58	12/94	2c
Coffee, 100%, ground roast, all sizes	lb.	4.28	12/94	82r
Coffee, vacuum-packed	13 oz.	3.27	12/94	2c
Cookies, chocolate chip	lb.	2.72	12/94	82r
Corn Flakes, Kellogg's or Post Toasties	18 oz.	2.34	12/94	2c
Corn, frozen, whole kernel, lowest price	10 oz.	0.82	12/94	2c
Dairy products (other) purchases	year	148	91	81r

Des Moines, IA - continued

Item	Per	Value	Date	Ref.
Groceries - continued				
Eggs, Grade A large	dozen	0.67	12/94	2c
Eggs, Grade A large	dozen	0.76	12/94	82r
Fish and seafood purchases	year	61	91	81r
Flour, white, all purpose	lb.	0.22	12/94	82r
Food purchases, food eaten at home	year	2313	91	81r
Foods purchased away from home, not prepared by consumer	year	1709	91	81r
Fruits and vegetables purchases	year	372	91	81r
Grapefruit	lb.	0.47	12/94	82r
Grapes, Thompson seedless	lb.	2.15	12/94	82r
Ground beef, 100% beef	lb.	1.37	12/94	82r
Ground chuck, 100% beef	lb.	1.81	12/94	82r
Ham, boneless, exc. canned	lb.	2.16	12/94	82r
Ice cream, prepackaged, bulk, regular	1/2 gal.	2.48	12/94	82r
Lemons	lb.	1.08	12/94	82r
Lettuce, iceberg	lb.	0.81	12/94	82r
Lettuce, iceberg	head	0.77	12/94	2c
Margarine, Blue Bonnet or Parkay cubes	lb.	0.59	12/94	2c
Margarine, stick	lb.	0.81	12/94	82r
Meats, poultry, fish, and eggs purchases	year	591	91	81r
Milk and cream (fresh) purchases	year	132	91	81r
Milk, 2%	gal.	2.15	1/92	44c
Milk, whole	1/2 gal.	1.18	12/94	2c
Orange juice, frozen concentrate 12-oz. can	16 oz.	1.41	12/94	82r
Orange juice, Minute Maid frozen	12-oz.	1.18	12/94	2c
Oranges, Navel	lb.	0.56	12/94	82r
Peaches, halves or slices, Hunt's, Del Monte, or Libby's	29-oz.	1.44	12/94	2c
Peanut butter, creamy, all sizes	lb.	1.81	12/94	82r
Peas, sweet, Del Monte or Green Giant	15-17 oz.	0.57	12/94	2c
Pork chops, center cut, bone-in	lb.	2.76	12/94	82r
Pork purchases	year	130	91	81r
Potato chips	16-oz.	2.81	12/94	82r
Potatoes, frozen, French fried	lb.	0.83	12/94	82r
Potatoes, white	lb.	0.28	12/94	82r
Potatoes, white or red	10-lb. sack	2.30	12/94	2c
Rental rate, 2-bedroom apartment	month	500.00	1/92	44c
Round roast, USDA choice, boneless	lb.	2.90	12/94	82r
Sausage, Jimmy Dean, 100% pork	lb.	3.07	12/94	2c
Shortening, vegetable oil blends	lb.	0.88	12/94	82r
Shortening, vegetable, Crisco	3-lb.	2.13	12/94	2c
Soft drink, Coca Cola, ex deposit	2 lit	0.96	12/94	2c
Spaghetti and macaroni	lb.	0.78	12/94	82r
Steak, rib eye, USDA choice, boneless	lb.	6.15	12/94	82r
Steak, round, graded & ungraded, exc. USDA prime & choice	lb.	2.72	12/94	82r
Steak, round, USDA choice, boneless	lb.	3.02	12/94	82r
Steak, sirloin, USDA choice, boneless	lb.	3.85	12/94	82r
Steak, t-bone	lb.	4.20	12/94	2c
Steak, T-bone, USDA choice, bone-in	lb.	5.38	12/94	82r
Sugar and other sweets, eaten at home, expenditures	year	91	91	81r
Sugar, cane or beet	4 lbs.	1.43	12/94	2c
Sugar, white, all sizes	lb.	0.36	12/94	82r
Tobacco products and smoking supplies, total expenditures	year	298	91	81r
Tomatoes, field grown	lb.	1.36	12/94	82r
Tomatoes, Hunt's or Del Monte	14.5 oz.	0.76	12/94	2c
Tuna, chunk, light	lb.	1.94	12/94	82r
Tuna, chunk, light, oil-packed	6.125-6.5 oz.	0.62	12/94	2c
Turkey, frozen, whole	lb.	0.96	12/94	82r
Yogurt, natural, fruit flavored	8 oz.	0.62	12/94	82r
Goods and Services				
Miscellaneous goods and services, ACCRA Index		95.80	12/94	2c

Values are in dollars or fractions of dollars. In the column headed *Ref*, references are shown to sources. Each reference is followed by a letter. These refer to the geographical level for which data were reported: s=State, r=Region, and c=City or metro. The abbreviation *ex* is used to mean *except* or *excluding*; *exp* stands for *expenditures*. For other abbreviations and further explanations, please see the Introduction.

Des Moines, IA - continued

Item	Per	Value	Date	Ref.
Health Care				
Health care, ACCRA Index		93.70	12/94	2c
Antibiotic ointment, Polysporin	1.5 oz.	3.12	12/94	2c
Childbirth, Cesarean delivery, hospital charge	birth	5101.00	12/91	69r
Childbirth, Cesarean delivery, physician charge	birth	2234.00	12/91	69r
Childbirth, normal delivery, hospital charge	birth	2891.00	12/91	69r
Childbirth, normal delivery, physician charge	birth	1623.00	12/91	69r
Dentist's fee, adult teeth cleaning and periodic oral exam	visit	47.60	12/94	2c
Doctor's fee, routine exam, established patient	visit	39.10	12/94	2c
Drugs, expenditures	year	248	91	81r
Health care, total expenditures	year	1336	91	81r
Health insurance expenditures	year	550	91	81r
Hospital care, semiprivate room	day	396.40	12/94	2c
Insurance premium, family medical care	month	395.98	1/95	41s
Medical services expenditures	year	457	91	81r
Medical supplies expenditures	year	82	91	81r
Household Goods				
Appl. repair, service call, wash mach	min. lab. chg.	40.00	12/94	2c
Floor coverings, expenditures	year	105	91	81r
Furniture, expenditures	year	291	91	81r
Household equipment, misc. expenditures	year	341	91	81r
Household expenditures, miscellaneous	year	162	91	81r
Household furnishings and equipment, expenditures	year	1042	91	81r
Household operations expenditures	year	365	91	81r
Household textiles, expenditures	year	101	91	81r
Housekeeping supplies, expenditures	year	390	91	81r
Laundry and cleaning supplies, expenditures	year	110	91	81r
Laundry detergent, Tide Ultra, Bold, or Cheer	42 oz.	3.60	12/94	2c
Postage and stationery, expenditures	year	115	91	81r
Tissues, facial, Kleenex brand	175	0.92	12/94	2c
Housing				
Housing, ACCRA Index		95.20	12/94	2c
Add garage/carport		8,479	3/95	74r
Add room(s)		21,347	3/95	74r
Apartment condominium or co-op, median	unit	87100	12/94	62r
Bathroom addition, average cost	add	9734.00	3/95	13r
Bathroom remodeling, average cost	remod	6414.00	3/95	13r
Bedroom, master suite addition, average cost	add	27122.00	3/95	13r
Deck addition, average cost	add	6665.00	3/95	13r
Dwellings (owned), expenditures	year	2566	91	81r
Enclose porch/patio/breezeway		4,556	3/95	74r
Exterior remodeling, average cost	remod	15395.00	3/95	13r
Family room addition, average cost	add	27658.00	3/95	13r
Finish room in basement/attic		5,074	3/95	74r
Home, existing, single-family, median	unit	106500	12/94	62r
Home, existing, single-family, median	unit	82.00	12/94	62c
House payment, principal and interest, 25% down payment	mo.	739	12/94	2c
House, 1800 sq ft, 8000 sq ft lot, new, urban, utilities	total	122750	12/94	2c
Kitchen remodeling, major, average cost	remod	17084.00	3/95	13r
Kitchen remodeling, minor, average cost	remod	5804.00	3/95	13r
Maintenance, repairs, insurance, and other housing expenditures	year	484	91	81r
Mortgage interest and charges expenditures	year	1443	91	81r
Mtge. rate, incl. points and orig. fee, 30-year conv. fixed or ARM	mo.	8.98	12/94	2c
Office, home addition, average cost	add	8121.00	3/95	13r
Princ. & int., mortgage, median-price exist. sing.-family home	mo.	515	12/94	62r
Property taxes expenditures	year	639	91	81r

Des Moines, IA - continued

Item	Per	Value	Date	Ref.
Housing - continued				
Redesign, restructure more than half of home's interior		9,114	3/95	74r
Rent, apartment, 2 br., 1 1/2-2 baths, unfurnished, 950 sq ft, water	mo.	474	12/94	2c
Rental units expenditures	year	1200	91	81r
Sun-space addition, average cost	add	23768.00	3/95	13r
Wing addition, two-story, average cost	add	50410.00	3/95	13r
Insurance and Pensions				
Auto insurance, private passenger	year	467.45	12/94	71s
Insurance and pensions, personal, expenditures	year	2408	91	81r
Insurance, life and other personal, expenditures	year	355	91	81r
Pensions and Social Security, expenditures	year	2053	91	81r
Legal Assistance				
Legal work, law firm associate	hour	90		10r
Legal work, law firm partner	hour	139		10r
Personal Goods				
Shampoo, Alberto VO5	15-oz.	0.95	12/94	2c
Toothpaste, Crest or Colgate	6-7 oz.	1.66	12/94	2c
Personal Services				
Dry cleaning, man's 2-pc. suit		6.36	12/94	2c
Dry cleaning, woman's dress	dress	6.25	1/92	44c
Haircut, man's barbershop, no styling		8.41	12/94	2c
Haircut, woman's shampoo, trim, blow-dry		18.67	12/94	2c
Personal services expenditures	year	203	91	81r
Restaurant Food				
Big Mac, small fries, medium drink	meal	3.73	1/92	44c
Chicken, fried, thigh and drumstick		2.43	12/94	2c
Dining expenditures, family	week	30.03	94	73r
Hamburger with cheese	1/4 lb.	1.59	12/94	2c
Pizza, Pizza Hut or Pizza Inn	12-13 in.	8.05	12/94	2c
Taxes				
Tax rate, residential property, month	$100	2.66	1/92	79c
Taxes, Federal income, expenditures	year	1756	91	81r
Taxes, personal, expenditures	year	2426	91	81r
Taxes, State and local income, expenditures	year	568	91	81r
Transportation				
Transportation, ACCRA Index		99.80	12/94	2c
Bus fare, one-way	trip	0.75	12/95	1c
Bus fare, up to 10 miles	one-way	0.75	12/94	2c
Cars and trucks purchased, new	year	891	91	81r
Cars and trucks purchased, used	year	1155	91	81r
Driver's learning permit fee	perm	6.00	1/94	84s
Driver's license fee	orig	0.00	1/94	84s
Driver's license fee, duplicate	lic	3.00	1/94	84s
Driver's license reinstatement fee, min.	susp	20.00	1/94	85s
Driver's license renewal fee	renew	0.00	1/94	84s
Identification card, nondriver	card	5.00	1/94	83s
Motorcycle learning permit fee	perm	8.00	1/94	84s
Motorcycle license fee	orig	8.00	1/94	84s
Motorcycle license fee, duplicate	lic	3.00	1/94	84s
Motorcycle license renewal fee	renew	8.00	1/94	84s
parking, long-term lot, airport	3 days	12.00	1/92	44c
Public transportation expenditures	year	209	91	81r
Tire balance, computer or spin bal., front	wheel	6.93	12/94	2c
Transportation expenditures, total	year	4792	91	81r
Vehicle finance charges	year	300	91	81r
Vehicle insurance expenditures	year	485	91	81r
Vehicle maintenance and repairs expenditures	year	534	91	81r
Vehicle purchases	year	2068	91	81r
Vehicle rental, leases, licenses, etc. expenditures	year	197	91	81r
Vehicles purchased, other than cars and trucks	year	22	91	81r

Values are in dollars or fractions of dollars. In the column headed *Ref*, references are shown to sources. Each reference is followed by a letter. These refer to the geographical level for which data were reported: s=State, r=Region, and c=City or metro. The abbreviation *ex* is used to mean *except* or *excluding*; *exp* stands for expenditures. For other abbreviations and further explanations, please see the Introduction.

Des Moines, IA - continued

Item	Per	Value	Date	Ref.
Utilities				
Utilities, ACCRA Index		106.90	12/94	2c
Electricity expenditures	year	668	91	81r
Electricity, (part.), other, 1800 sq. ft., new home	mo.	72.00	12/94	2c
Electricity, summer, 250 KWh	month	32.86	8/93	64c
Electricity, summer, 500 KWh	month	55.80	8/93	64c
Electricity, summer, 750 KWh	month	78.76	8/93	64c
Electricity, summer, 1000 KWh	month	101.71	8/93	64c
Utilities, fuels, and public services, total expenditures	year	1838	91	81r
Water and other public services, expenditures	year	167	91	81r
Weddings				
Bridal attendants' gowns	event	750	10/93	76r
Bridal gown	event	852	10/93	76r
Bridal headpiece and veil	event	167	10/93	76r
Bride's wedding band	event	708	10/93	76r
Clergy	event	224	10/93	76r
Engagement ring	event	2756	10/93	76r
Flowers	event	863	10/93	76r
Formal wear for groom	event	106	10/93	76r
Groom's attendants' formal wear	event	530	10/93	76r
Groom's wedding band	event	402	10/93	76r
Music	event	600	10/93	76r
Photography	event	1088	10/93	76r
Shoes for bride	event	50	10/93	76r
Videography	event	483	10/93	76r
Wedding invitations and announcements	event	342	10/93	76r
Wedding reception	event	7000	10/93	76r

Detroit-Ann Arbor, MI

Item	Per	Value	Date	Ref.
Appliances				
Appliances (major), expenditures	year	106	91	81c
Appliances (major), expenditures	year	131	91	81r
Average annual exp.				
Food, health care, personal goods, services	year	29732	91	81c
Food, health care, personal goods, services	year	25935	91	81r
Business Expenses				
Car rental, midsized car	day	44.99	92	52c
Continental breakfast, room service	meal	10.30	92	52c
Lunch, convention center	meal	6.25	92	52c
Restaurant meal	meal	45.00	92	52c
Room rate, hotel	day	64.59	92	52c
Taxicab fare, airport to convention center	trip	25.00	92	52c
Charity				
Cash contributions, expenditures	year	763	91	81c
Cash contributions, expenditures	year	745	91	81r
Clothing				
Apparel, men and boys, total expenditures	year	416	91	81c
Apparel, men and boys, total expenditures	year	332	91	81r
Apparel, women and girls, total expenditures	year	651	91	81c
Apparel, women and girls, total expenditures	year	578	91	81r
Footwear, expenditures	year	220	91	81c
Footwear, expenditures	year	164	91	81r
Formal wear rental, tuxedo, downtown store	rental	64.00	92	52c
Communications				
Long-distance telephone rate, day, addl. min., 1-10 mi.	min.	0.08	12/93	9s
Long-distance telephone rate, day, initial min., 1-10 mi.	min.	0.14	12/93	9s
Newspaper cost, major daily	1	0.35	92	52c
Phone line, single, business, field visit	inst	42.00	12/93	9s
Phone line, single, business, no field visit	inst	42.00	12/93	9s
Phone line, single, residence, field visit	inst	42.00	12/93	9s
Phone line, single, residence, no field visit	inst	42.00	12/93	9s
Telephone service, expenditures	year	665	91	81c
Telephone service, expenditures	year	547	91	81r

Detroit-Ann Arbor, MI - continued

Item	Per	Value	Date	Ref.
Communications - continued				
Telephone, residential, flat rate	mo.	11.95	12/93	8c
Education				
Board, 4-year private college/university	year	2064	8/94	80s
Board, 4-year public college/university	year	2304	8/94	80s
Education, total expenditures	year	409	91	81c
Education, total expenditures	year	394	91	81r
Living expenses, personal miscellaneous, university student	year	1656.00	5/96	22c
Room, 4-year private college/university	year	1814	8/94	80s
Room, 4-year public college/university	year	1856	8/94	80s
Total cost, 4-year private college/university	year	12178	8/94	80s
Total cost, 4-year public college/university	year	7642	8/94	80s
Tuition, 2-year public college/university, in-state	year	1358	8/94	80s
Tuition, 4-year private college/university, in-state	year	8300	8/94	80s
Tuition, 4-year public college/university, in-state	year	3481	8/94	80s
Energy and Fuels				
Electricity	500 KWh	49.35	12/94	82c
Fuel oil #2	gallon	0.92	12/94	82c
Fuel oil and other fuels, expenditures	year	53	91	81c
Fuel oil and other fuels, expenditures	year	83	91	81r
Gas, cooking, 10 therms	month	11.92	2/94	65c
Gas, cooking, 30 therms	month	20.75	2/94	65c
Gas, cooking, 50 therms	month	29.58	2/94	65c
Gas, heating, winter, 100 therms	month	51.66	2/94	65c
Gas, heating, winter, average use	month	118.09	2/94	65c
Gas, natural, expenditures	year	512	91	81c
Gas, natural, expenditures	year	373	91	81r
Gas, piped	40 therms	23.29	12/94	82c
Gas, piped	100 therms	48.20	12/94	82c
Gas, piped	therm	0.48	12/94	82c
Gasoline and motor oil purchased	year	1114	91	81c
Gasoline and motor oil purchased	year	1000	91	81r
Gasoline, unleaded midgrade	gallon	1.10	4/93	82c
Gasoline, unleaded midgrade	gallon	1.15	4/93	82r
Gasoline, unleaded premium	gallon	1.19	4/93	82c
Gasoline, unleaded premium	gallon	1.23	4/93	82r
Gasoline, unleaded regular	gallon	1.02	4/93	82c
Gasoline, unleaded regular	gallon	1.07	4/93	82r
Entertainment				
Admission fee, museum	visit	4.00	92	52c
Admission fee, seating, symphony performance		28.00	92	52c
Baseball game, four-person family	game	103.45	4/94	47c
Camping session, summer	week	45.00	8/95	48c
Entertainment supplies, equipment, and services, misc. expenditures	year	500	91	81c
Entertainment, total expenditures	year	1580	91	81c
Entertainment, total expenditures	year	1356	91	81r
Fees and admissions, expenditures	year	355	91	81c
Fees and admissions, expenditures	year	347	91	81r
Pets, toys, playground equipment, expenditures	year	223	91	81c
Pets, toys, playground equipment, expenditures	year	270	91	81r
Reading, expenditures	year	155	91	81c
Reading, expenditures	year	160	91	81r
Televisions, radios, and sound equipment, expenditures	year	503	91	81c
Televisions, radios, and sound equipment, expenditures	year	433	91	81r
Ticket, basketball game		16.50-50.00	92	52c

Values are in dollars or fractions of dollars. In the column headed *Ref*, references are shown to sources. Each reference is followed by a letter. These refer to the geographical level for which data were reported: s = State, r = Region, and c = City or metro. The abbreviation *ex* is used to mean *except* or *excluding*; *exp* stands for *expenditures*. For other abbreviations and further explanations, please see the Introduction.

Detroit-Ann Arbor, MI - continued

Item	Per	Value	Date	Ref.
Funerals				
Burial, immediate, container provided by funeral home		1268.31	1/95	54r
Cards, acknowledgment		26.12	1/95	54r
Casket, minimum alternative		198.03	1/95	54r
Cosmetology, hair care, etc.		122.19	1/95	54r
Cremation, direct, container provided by funeral home		977.81	1/95	54r
Embalming		334.00	1/95	54r
Funeral, funeral home		321.16	1/95	54r
Funeral, other facility		317.73	1/95	54r
Graveside service		292.48	1/95	54r
Hearse, local		153.20	1/95	54r
Limousine, local		123.52	1/95	54r
Memorial service		356.30	1/95	54r
Service charge, professional, nondeclinable		968.24	1/95	54r
Visitation and viewing		332.66	1/95	54r
Groceries				
Apples, Red Delicious	lb.	0.68	12/94	82r
Bacon, sliced	lb.	1.88	12/94	82r
Bananas	lb.	0.41	12/94	82r
Beef purchases	year	209	91	81c
Beef purchases	year	197	91	81r
Beef, stew, boneless	lb.	2.52	12/94	82r
Beverage purchases, alcoholic	year	323	91	81c
Beverage purchases, alcoholic	year	293	91	81r
Beverage purchases, nonalcoholic	year	186	91	81c
Beverage purchases, nonalcoholic	year	203	91	81r
Bologna, all beef or mixed	lb.	2.12	12/94	82r
Bread, white, pan	lb.	0.76	12/94	82r
Cabbage	lb.	0.44	12/94	82r
Carrots, short trimmed and topped	lb.	0.44	12/94	82r
Cereals and bakery products purchases	year	364	91	81c
Cereals and bakery products purchases	year	347	91	81r
Cereals and cereal products purchases	year	124	91	81c
Cereals and cereals products purchases	year	119	91	81r
Cheddar cheese, natural	lb.	3.28	12/94	82r
Chicken breast, bone-in	lb.	1.61	12/94	82r
Chicken, fresh, whole	lb.	0.89	12/94	82r
Chuck roast, USDA choice, boneless	lb.	2.33	12/94	82r
Cilantro	3	1.00	6/95	29c
Coffee, 100%, ground roast, all sizes	lb.	4.28	12/94	82r
Cookies, chocolate chip	lb.	2.72	12/94	82r
Dairy products (other) purchases	year	129	91	81c
Dairy products (other) purchases	year	148	91	81r
Eggs, Grade A large	dozen	0.76	12/94	82r
Fish and seafood purchases	year	71	91	81c
Fish and seafood purchases	year	61	91	81r
Flour, white, all purpose	lb.	0.22	12/94	82r
Food purchases, food eaten at home	year	2406	91	81c
Food purchases, food eaten at home	year	2313	91	81r
Foods purchased away from home, not prepared by consumer	year	1716	91	81c
Foods purchased away from home, not prepared by consumer	year	1709	91	81r
Fruits and vegetables purchases	year	449	91	81c
Fruits and vegetables purchases	year	372	91	81r
Grapefruit	lb.	0.47	12/94	82r
Grapefruit	22	3.00	6/95	29c
Grapes, Thompson seedless	lb.	2.15	12/94	82r
Ground beef, 100% beef	lb.	1.37	12/94	82r
Ground chuck, 100% beef	lb.	1.81	12/94	82r
Ham, boneless, exc. canned	lb.	2.16	12/94	82r
Ice cream, prepackaged, bulk, regular	1/2 gal.	2.48	12/94	82r
Kale	20 lbs.	1.00	6/95	29c
Lemons	lb.	1.08	12/94	82r
Lettuce, iceberg	lb.	0.81	12/94	82r
Margarine, stick	lb.	0.81	12/94	82r
Meats, poultry, fish, and eggs purchases	year	681	91	81c
Meats, poultry, fish, and eggs purchases	year	591	91	81r
Milk and cream (fresh) purchases	year	116	91	81c
Milk and cream (fresh) purchases	year	132	91	81r

Detroit-Ann Arbor, MI - continued

Item	Per	Value	Date	Ref.
Groceries - continued				
Onions	50 lbs.	2.00	6/95	29c
Orange juice, frozen concentrate 12-oz. can	16 oz.	1.41	12/94	82r
Oranges, Navel	lb.	0.56	12/94	82r
Peanut butter, creamy, all sizes	lb.	1.81	12/94	82r
Pork chops, center cut, bone-in	lb.	2.76	12/94	82r
Pork purchases	year	144	91	81c
Pork purchases	year	130	91	81r
Potato chips	16-oz.	2.81	12/94	82r
Potatoes, frozen, French fried	lb.	0.83	12/94	82r
Potatoes, white	lb.	0.28	12/94	82r
Round roast, USDA choice, boneless	lb.	2.90	12/94	82r
Shortening, vegetable oil blends	lb.	0.88	12/94	82r
Spaghetti and macaroni	lb.	0.78	12/94	82r
Steak, rib eye, USDA choice, boneless	lb.	6.15	12/94	82r
Steak, round, graded & ungraded, exc. USDA prime & choice	lb.	2.72	12/94	82r
Steak, round, USDA choice, boneless	lb.	3.02	12/94	82r
Steak, sirloin, USDA choice, boneless	lb.	3.85	12/94	82r
Steak, T-bone, USDA choice, bone-in	lb.	5.38	12/94	82r
Sugar and other sweets, eaten at home, expenditures	year	91	91	81r
Sugar and other sweets, eaten at home, purchases	year	74	91	81c
Sugar, white, all sizes	lb.	0.36	12/94	82r
Tobacco products and smoking supplies, total expenditures	year	273	91	81c
Tobacco products and smoking supplies, total expenditures	year	298	91	81r
Tomatoes	23 lbs.	3.00	6/95	29c
Tomatoes, field grown	lb.	1.36	12/94	82r
Tuna, chunk, light	lb.	1.94	12/94	82r
Turkey, frozen, whole	lb.	0.96	12/94	82r
Yogurt, natural, fruit flavored	8 oz.	0.62	12/94	82r
Zucchini	12 lbs.	1.50	6/95	29c
Health Care				
Childbirth, Cesarean delivery, hospital charge	birth	5101.00	12/91	69r
Childbirth, Cesarean delivery, physician charge	birth	2234.00	12/91	69r
Childbirth, normal delivery, hospital charge	birth	2891.00	12/91	69r
Childbirth, normal delivery, physician charge	birth	1623.00	12/91	69r
Drugs, expenditures	year	175	91	81c
Drugs, expenditures	year	248	91	81r
Health care, total expenditures	year	1304	91	81c
Health care, total expenditures	year	1336	91	81r
Health insurance expenditures	year	523	91	81c
Health insurance expenditures	year	550	91	81r
Hospital cost	adm	6,346	2/94	72c
Insurance premium, family medical care	month	369.41	1/95	41s
Medical services expenditures	year	526	91	81c
Medical services expenditures	year	457	91	81r
Medical supplies expenditures	year	80	91	81c
Medical supplies expenditures	year	82	91	81r
Household Goods				
Floor coverings, expenditures	year	94	91	81c
Floor coverings, expenditures	year	105	91	81r
Furniture, expenditures	year	453	91	81c
Furniture, expenditures	year	291	91	81r
Household equipment, misc. expenditures	year	341	91	81r
Household equipment, misc., expenditures	year	353	91	81c
Household expenditures, miscellaneous	year	202	91	81c
Household expenditures, miscellaneous	year	162	91	81r
Household furnishings and equipment, expenditures	year	1226	91	81c
Household furnishings and equipment, expenditures	year	1042	91	81r
Household operations expenditures	year	363	91	81c
Household operations expenditures	year	365	91	81r
Household textiles, expenditures	year	146	91	81c
Household textiles, expenditures	year	101	91	81r
Housekeeping supplies, expenditures	year	434	91	81c

Values are in dollars or fractions of dollars. In the column headed *Ref*, references are shown to sources. Each reference is followed by a letter. These refer to the geographical level for which data were reported: s = State, r = Region, and c = City or metro. The abbreviation *ex* is used to mean *except* or *excluding*; *exp* stands for *expenditures*. For other abbreviations and further explanations, please see the Introduction.

Detroit-Ann Arbor, MI - continued

Item	Per	Value	Date	Ref.
Household Goods				
Housekeeping supplies, expenditures	year	390	91	81r
Laundry and cleaning supplies, expenditures	year	109	91	81c
Laundry and cleaning supplies, expenditures	year	110	91	81r
Postage and stationery, expenditures	year	127	91	81c
Postage and stationery, expenditures	year	115	91	81r
Housing				
Add garage/carport		8,479	3/95	74r
Add room(s)		21,347	3/95	74r
Apartment condominium or co-op, median	unit	87100	12/94	62r
Bathroom addition, average cost	add	9734.00	3/95	13r
Bathroom addition, average cost	add	10786.00	3/95	13c
Bathroom remodeling, average cost	remod	6414.00	3/95	13r
Bathroom remodeling, average cost	remod	6998.00	3/95	13c
Bedroom, master suite addition, average cost	add	27122.00	3/95	13r
Bedroom, master suite addition, average cost	add	29942.00	3/95	13c
Car rental	day	52.00	5/95	95c
Deck addition, average cost	add	6665.00	3/95	13r
Deck addition, average cost	add	7457.00	95	13c
Dwellings (owned), expenditures	year	3763	91	81c
Dwellings (owned), expenditures	year	2566	91	81r
Enclose porch/patio/breezeway		4,556	3/95	74r
Exterior remodeling, average cost	remod	15395.00	3/95	13r
Exterior remodeling, average cost	remod	17510.00	95	13c
Family room addition, average cost	add	27658.00	3/95	13r
Family room addition, average cost	add	30866.00	95	13c
Finish room in basement/attic		5,074	3/95	74r
Home, existing, single-family, median	unit	106500	12/94	62r
Home, existing, single-family, median	unit	85.80	12/94	62c
Home, purchase price	unit	134.80	3/93	26c
Hotel room	day	112.00	5/95	95c
Kitchen remodeling, major, average cost	remod	17084.00	3/95	13r
Kitchen remodeling, major, average cost	remod	18510.00	3/95	13c
Kitchen remodeling, minor, average cost	remod	5804.00	3/95	13r
Kitchen remodeling, minor, average cost	remod	6261.00	3/95	13c
Maintenance, repairs, insurance, and other housing expenditures	year	523	91	81c
Maintenance, repairs, insurance, and other housing expenditures	year	484	91	81r
Mortgage interest and charges expenditures	year	1968	91	81c
Mortgage interest and charges expenditures	year	1443	91	81r
Mortgage payment	month	810.00	1/94	78c
Mortgage rate, 15-year mortgage	month	7.11	6/95	63c
Mortgage rate, 30-year mortgage	month	7.62	6/95	63c
Mortgage rate, adjustable rate mortgage	month	5.68	6/95	63c
Office, home addition, average cost	add	8121.00	3/95	13r
Office, home addition, average cost	add	9001.00	95	13c
Princ. & int., mortgage, median-price exist. sing.-family home	mo.	515	12/94	62r
Property taxes expenditures	year	1272	91	81c
Property taxes expenditures	year	639	91	81r
Redesign, restructure more than half of home's interior		9,114	3/95	74r
Rental units expenditures	year	1530	900/00/91	81c
Rental units expenditures	year	1200	91	81r
Sun-space addition, average cost	add	23768.00	3/95	13r
Sun-space addition, average cost	add	26616.00	95	13c
Wing addition, two-story, average cost	add	50410.00	3/95	13r
Wing addition, two-story, average cost	add	55893.00	95	13c
Insurance and Pensions				
Auto insurance, private passenger	year	788.26	12/94	71s
Insurance and pensions, personal, expenditures	year	2655	91	81c
Insurance and pensions, personal, expenditures	year	2408	91	81r
Insurance, life and other personal, expenditures	year	314	91	81c

Detroit-Ann Arbor, MI - continued

Item	Per	Value	Date	Ref.
Insurance and Pensions - continued				
Insurance, life and other personal, expenditures	year	355	91	81r
Pensions and Social Security, expenditures	year	2341	91	81c
Pensions and Social Security, expenditures	year	2053	91	81r
Legal Assistance				
Legal work, law firm associate	hour	90		10r
Legal work, law firm partner	hour	139		10r
Personal Goods				
Personal care products and services, total expenditures	year	386	91	81c
Personal Services				
Dry cleaning	serv	5.00	92	52c
Manicure		13.00	92	52c
Personal services expenditures	year	161	91	81c
Personal services expenditures	year	203	91	81r
Restaurant Food				
Dining expenditures, family	week	30.03	94	73r
Taxes				
Tax rate, residential property, month	$100	4.53	1/92	79c
Taxes, Federal income, expenditures	year	1357	91	81c
Taxes, Federal income, expenditures	year	1756	91	81r
Taxes, personal, expenditures	year	1963	91	81c
Taxes, personal, expenditures	year	2426	91	81r
Taxes, State and local income, expenditures	year	504	91	81c
Taxes, State and local income, expenditures	year	568	91	81r
Transportation				
Bus fare, one-way	trip	1.00	12/95	1c
Cars and trucks purchased, new	year	1239	91	81c
Cars and trucks purchased, new	year	891	91	81r
Cars and trucks purchased, used	year	1157	91	81c
Cars and trucks purchased, used	year	1155	91	81r
Driver's learning permit fee	perm	12.00	1/94	84s
Driver's license fee	orig	12.00	1/94	84s
Driver's license fee, duplicate	lic	6.00	1/94	84s
Driver's license reinstatement fee, min.	susp	125.00	1/94	85s
Driver's license renewal fee	renew	12.00	1/94	84s
Identification card, nondriver	card	6.00	1/94	83s
Mileage fee, mileage traveled over rental company limit	mile	0.23	95	77c
Motorcycle license fee	orig	7.50	1/94	84s
Motorcycle license renewal fee	renew	4.00	1/94	84s
Public transportation expenditures	year	313	91	81c
Public transportation expenditures	year	209	91	81r
Transportation expenditures, total	year	5748	91	81c
Transportation expenditures, total	year	4792	91	81r
Vehicle expenses, miscellaneous	year	1924	91	81c
Vehicle finance charges	year	330	91	81c
Vehicle finance charges	year	300	91	81r
Vehicle insurance expenditures	year	745	91	81c
Vehicle insurance expenditures	year	485	91	81r
Vehicle maintenance and repairs expenditures	year	559	91	81c
Vehicle maintenance and repairs expenditures	year	534	91	81r
Vehicle purchases	year	2398	91	81c
Vehicle purchases	year	2068	91	81r
Vehicle rental, leases, licenses, etc. expenditures	year	290	91	81c
Vehicle rental, leases, licenses, etc. expenditures	year	197	91	81r
Vehicles purchased, other than cars and trucks	year	2	91	81c
Vehicles purchased, other than cars and trucks	year	22	91	81r
Utilities				
Electricity	KWh	0.10	12/94	82c
Electricity expenditures	year	610	91	81c
Electricity expenditures	year	668	91	81r

Values are in dollars or fractions of dollars. In the column headed *Ref*, references are shown to sources. Each reference is followed by a letter. These refer to the geographical level for which data were reported: s = State, r = Region, and c = City or metro. The abbreviation *ex* is used to mean *except* or *excluding*; *exp* stands for expenditures. For other abbreviations and further explanations, please see the Introduction.

Detroit-Ann Arbor, MI - continued

Item	Per	Value	Date	Ref.
Utilities				
Electricity, summer, 250 KWh	month	23.29	8/93	64c
Electricity, summer, 500 KWh	month	46.58	8/93	64c
Electricity, summer, 750 KWh	month	73.51	8/93	64c
Electricity, summer, 1000 KWh	month	100.60	8/93	64c
Utilities, fuels, and public services, total expenditures	year	1986	91	81c
Utilities, fuels, and public services, total expenditures	year	1838	91	81r
Water and other public services, expenditures	year	147	91	81c
Water and other public services, expenditures	year	167	91	81r
Weddings				
Bridal attendants' gowns	event	750	10/93	76r
Bridal gown	event	852	10/93	76r
Bridal headpiece and veil	event	167	10/93	76r
Bride's wedding band	event	708	10/93	76r
Clergy	event	224	10/93	76r
Engagement ring	event	2756	10/93	76r
Flowers	event	863	10/93	76r
Formal wear for groom	event	106	10/93	76r
Groom's attendants' formal wear	event	530	10/93	76r
Groom's wedding band	event	402	10/93	76r
Music	event	600	10/93	76r
Photography	event	1088	10/93	76r
Shoes for bride	event	50	10/93	76r
Videography	event	483	10/93	76r
Wedding invitations and announcements	event	342	10/93	76r
Wedding package, chapel	event	85.00-395.00	6/95	51c
Wedding reception	event	7000	10/93	76r

Dothan, AL

Item	Per	Value	Date	Ref.
Appliances				
Appliances (major), expenditures	year	153	91	81r
Average annual exp.				
Food, health care, personal goods, services	year	27020	91	81r
Charity				
Cash contributions, expenditures	year	839	91	81r
Clothing				
Apparel, men and boys, total expenditures	year	380	91	81r
Apparel, women and girls, total expenditures	year	660	91	81r
Footwear, expenditures	year	193	91	81r
Communications				
Long-distance telephone rate, day, addl. min., 1-10 mi.	min.	0.09	12/93	9s
Long-distance telephone rate, day, initial min., 1-10 mi.	min.	0.11	12/93	9s
Phone line, single, business, field visit	inst	69.00	12/93	9s
Phone line, single, business, no field visit	inst	69.00	12/93	9s
Phone line, single, residence, field visit	inst	40.00	12/93	9s
Phone line, single, residence, no field visit	inst	40.00	12/93	9s
Telephone service, expenditures	year	616	91	81r
Education				
Board, 4-year private college/university	year	2072	8/94	80s
Board, 4-year public college/university	year	1706	8/94	80s
Education, total expenditures	year	319	91	81r
Room, 4-year private college/university	year	1607	8/94	80s
Room, 4-year public college/university	year	1598	8/94	80s
Total cost, 4-year private college/university	year	10664	8/94	80s
Total cost, 4-year public college/university	year	5287	8/94	80s
Tuition, 2-year public college/university, in-state	year	1110	8/94	80s
Tuition, 4-year private college/university, in-state	year	6985	8/94	80s
Tuition, 4-year public college/university, in-state	year	1983	8/94	80s

Dothan, AL - continued

Item	Per	Value	Date	Ref.
Energy and Fuels				
Fuel oil and other fuels, expenditures	year	56	91	81r
Gas, natural, expenditures	year	150	91	81r
Gasoline and motor oil purchased	year	1152	91	81r
Gasoline, unleaded midgrade	gallon	1.21	4/93	82r
Gasoline, unleaded premium	gallon	1.30	4/93	82r
Gasoline, unleaded regular	gallon	1.10	4/93	82r
Entertainment				
Concert ticket, Pearl Jam group	perf	20.00	94	50r
Entertainment, total expenditures	year	1266	91	81r
Fees and admissions, expenditures	year	306	91	81r
Pets, toys, playground equipment, expenditures	year	271	91	81r
Reading, expenditures	year	131	91	81r
Televisions, radios, and sound equipment, expenditures	year	439	91	81r
Funerals				
Burial, immediate, container provided by funeral home		1298.96	1/95	54r
Cards, acknowledgment		21.26	1/95	54r
Casket, minimum alternative		204.95	1/95	54r
Cosmetology, hair care, etc.		85.40	1/95	54r
Cremation, direct, container provided by funeral home		1054.77	1/95	54r
Embalming		287.71	1/95	54r
Funeral, funeral home		269.18	1/95	54r
Funeral, other facility		272.88	1/95	54r
Graveside service		302.54	1/95	54r
Hearse, local		122.08	1/95	54r
Limousine, local		80.31	1/95	54r
Memorial service		277.66	1/95	54r
Service charge, professional, nondeclinable		896.65	1/95	54r
Visitation and viewing		232.39	1/95	54r
Groceries				
Apples, Red Delicious	lb.	0.73	12/94	82r
Bacon, sliced	lb.	1.67	12/94	82r
Bananas	lb.	0.42	12/94	82r
Beef purchases	year	213	91	81r
Beverage purchases, alcoholic	year	249	91	81r
Beverage purchases, nonalcoholic	year	207	91	81r
Bologna, all beef or mixed	lb.	2.27	12/94	82r
Bread, white, pan	lb.	0.68	12/94	82r
Cabbage	lb.	0.42	12/94	82r
Carrots, short trimmed and topped	lb.	0.53	12/94	82r
Cereals and bakery products purchases	year	345	91	81r
Cereals and cereals products purchases	year	127	91	81r
Cheddar cheese, natural	lb.	3.58	12/94	82r
Chicken breast, bone-in	lb.	1.71	12/94	82r
Chicken, fresh, whole	lb.	0.78	12/94	82r
Chuck roast, USDA choice, boneless	lb.	2.26	12/94	82r
Crackers, soda, salted	lb.	1.27	12/94	82r
Cucumbers	lb.	0.65	12/94	82r
Dairy products (other) purchases	year	141	91	81r
Eggs, Grade A large	dozen	0.87	12/94	82r
Fish and seafood purchases	year	72	91	81r
Flour, white, all purpose	lb.	0.23	12/94	82r
Food purchases, food eaten at home	year	2381	91	81r
Foods purchased away from home, not prepared by consumer	year	1696	91	81r
Frankfurters, all meat or all beef	lb.	1.74	12/94	82r
Fruits and vegetables purchases	year	380	91	81r
Grapefruit	lb.	0.45	12/94	82r
Grapes, Thompson seedless	lb.	2.30	12/94	82r
Ground beef, 100% beef	lb.	1.37	12/94	82r
Ground chuck, 100% beef	lb.	1.97	12/94	82r
Ham, boneless, exc. canned	lb.	2.54	12/94	82r
Ice cream, prepackaged, bulk, regular	1/2 gal.	2.47	12/94	82r
Lemons	lb.	1.02	12/94	82r
Lettuce, iceberg	lb.	0.96	12/94	82r
Margarine, stick	lb.	0.77	12/94	82r
Meats, poultry, fish, and eggs purchases	year	655	91	81r

Values are in dollars or fractions of dollars. In the column headed *Ref*, references are shown to sources. Each reference is followed by a letter. These refer to the geographical level for which data were reported: s=State, r=Region, and c=City or metro. The abbreviation *ex* is used to mean *except* or *excluding*; *exp* stands for expenditures. For other abbreviations and further explanations, please see the Introduction.

Dothan, AL - continued

Item	Per	Value	Date	Ref.
Groceries				
Milk and cream (fresh) purchases	year	130	91	81r
Orange juice, frozen concentrate 12-oz. can	16 oz.	1.36	12/94	82r
Oranges, Navel	lb.	0.54	12/94	82r
Pears, Anjou	lb.	0.81	12/94	82r
Pork chops, center cut, bone-in	lb.	3.07	12/94	82r
Pork purchases	year	142	91	81r
Potato chips	16-oz.	3.15	12/94	82r
Potatoes, frozen, French fried	lb.	0.82	12/94	82r
Potatoes, white	lb.	0.34	12/94	82r
Rice, white, long grain, uncooked	lb.	0.48	12/94	82r
Round roast, USDA choice, boneless	lb.	2.91	12/94	82r
Sausage, fresh	lb.	1.82	12/94	82r
Shortening, vegetable oil blends	lb.	0.75	12/94	82r
Spaghetti and macaroni	lb.	0.87	12/94	82r
Steak, rib eye, USDA choice, boneless	lb.	6.85	12/94	82r
Steak, round, graded & ungraded, exc. USDA prime & choice	lb.	2.96	12/94	82r
Steak, round, USDA choice, boneless	lb.	3.17	12/94	82r
Steak, sirloin, USDA choice, boneless	lb.	4.12	12/94	82r
Steak, T-bone, USDA choice, bone-in	lb.	5.63	12/94	82r
Sugar and other sweets, eaten at home, expenditures	year	93	91	81r
Sugar, white, all sizes	lb.	0.39	12/94	82r
Tobacco products and smoking supplies, total expenditures	year	286	91	81r
Tomatoes, field grown	lb.	1.36	12/94	82r
Tuna, chunk, light	lb.	1.94	12/94	82r
Turkey, frozen, whole	lb.	0.96	12/94	82r
Yogurt, natural, fruit flavored	8 oz.	0.58	12/94	82r
Health Care				
Adenosine, emergency room	treat	100.00	95	23r
Bladder tap, superpubic, infant, emergency room	treat	119.00	95	23r
Blood analysis, emergency room	treat	25.00	95	23r
Blood tests, abdominal pain, emergency room	treat	25.00	95	23r
Burn dressing, emergency room	treat	266.00	95	23r
Cardiology interpretation, emergency room	treat	26.00	95	23r
Chest X-ray, emergency room	treat	78.00	95	23r
Childbirth, Cesarean delivery, hospital charge	birth	5462.00	12/91	69r
Childbirth, Cesarean delivery, physician charge	birth	2228.00	12/91	69r
Childbirth, normal delivery, hospital charge	birth	2943.00	12/91	69r
Childbirth, normal delivery, physician charge	birth	1619.00	12/91	69r
Defibrillation pads, emergency room	treat	6.00	95	23r
Drugs, expenditures	year	297	91	81r
Gastric tube insertion, nasal, emergency room	treat	25.00	95	23r
Health care, total expenditures	year	1600	91	81r
Health insurance expenditures	year	637	91	81r
Heart monitor, emergency room	treat	40.00	95	23r
Insurance premium, family medical care	month	360.67	1/95	41s
Intravenous fluids, emergency room	treat	130.00	95	23r
Intravenous fluids, emergency room	liter	26.00	95	23r
Intravenous line, central, emergency room	treat	342.00	95	23r
Liver function tests, abdominal pain, emergency room	treat	26.00	95	23r
Medical care charges, total, emergency room, third-degree burns	treat	2101.00	95	23r
Medical care charges, total, emergency, infant with fever	treat	628.00	95	23r
Medical services expenditures	year	573	91	81r
Medical supplies expenditures	year	93	91	81r
Morphine, emergency room	treat	34.00	95	23r
Nursing care and facilities charges, emergency room	treat	252.00	95	23r
Nursing care and facilities charges, emergency, infant with fever	treat	252.00	95	23r
Nursing care and facilities charges, emergency, third-degree burns	treat	861.00	95	23r

Dothan, AL - continued

Item	Per	Value	Date	Ref.
Health Care - continued				
Physician's charges, emergency, infant with fever	treat	212.00	95	23r
Physician's charges, emergency, third-degree burns	treat	372.00	95	23r
Physician's fee, emergency room	treat	372.00	95	23r
Physician's fee, general practitioner	visit	51.20	12/93	60r
Surgery, open-heart	proc	42374.00	1/93	14r
Ultrasound, abdominal, emergency room	treat	276.00	95	23r
Urinalysis, emergency room	treat	20.00	95	23r
Urinalysis, infant, emergency room	treat	20.00	95	23r
X-rays, emergency room	treat	78.00	95	23r
Household Goods				
Floor coverings, expenditures	year	48	91	81r
Furniture, expenditures	year	280	91	81r
Household equipment, misc. expenditures	year	342	91	81r
Household expenditures, miscellaneous	year	256	91	81r
Household furnishings and equipment, expenditures	year	988	91	81r
Household operations expenditures	year	468	91	81r
Household textiles, expenditures	year	95	91	81r
Housekeeping supplies, expenditures	year	380	91	81r
Laundry and cleaning supplies, expenditures	year	109	91	81r
Postage and stationery, expenditures	year	105	91	81r
Housing				
Add garage/carport		6,980	3/95	74r
Add room(s)		11,403	3/95	74r
Apartment condominium or co-op, median	unit	68600	12/94	62r
Dwellings (owned), expenditures	year	2428	91	81r
Enclose porch/patio/breezeway		4,572	3/95	74r
Finish room in basement/attic		3,794	3/95	74r
Home, existing, single-family, median	unit	120200	12/94	62r
Maintenance, repairs, insurance, and other housing expenditures	year	531	91	81r
Mortgage interest and charges expenditures	year	1506	91	81r
Princ. & int., mortgage, median-price exist. sing.-family home	mo.	540	12/94	62r
Property taxes expenditures	year	391	91	81r
Redesign, restructure more than half of home's interior		17,641	3/95	74r
Rental units expenditures	year	1264	91	81r
Insurance and Pensions				
Auto insurance, private passenger	year	604.07	12/94	71s
Insurance and pensions, personal, expenditures	year	2395	91	81r
Insurance, life and other personal, expenditures	year	368	91	81r
Pensions and Social Security, expenditures	year	2027	91	81r
Personal Services				
Personal services expenditures	year	212	91	81r
Restaurant Food				
Dining expenditures, family	week	33.83	94	73r
Taxes				
Taxes, Federal income, expenditures	year	2275	91	81r
Taxes, personal, expenditures	year	2715	91	81r
Taxes, State and local income, expenditures	year	365	91	81r
Transportation				
Cars and trucks purchased, new	year	1306	91	81r
Cars and trucks purchased, used	year	942	91	81r
Driver's learning permit fee	perm	20.00	1/94	84s
Driver's license fee	orig	20.00	1/94	84s
Driver's license fee, duplicate	lic	5.00	1/94	84s
Driver's license reinstatement fee, min.	susp	50.00	1/94	85s
Driver's license renewal fee	renew	20.00	1/94	84s
Identification card, nondriver	card	20.00	1/94	83s
Motorcycle license fee	orig	20.00	1/94	84s
Motorcycle license fee, duplicate	lic	5.00	1/94	84s
Motorcycle license renewal fee	renew	20.00	1/94	84s

Values are in dollars or fractions of dollars. In the column headed *Ref*, references are shown to sources. Each reference is followed by a letter. These refer to the geographical level for which data were reported: s = State, r = Region, and c = City or metro. The abbreviation *ex* is used to mean *except* or *excluding*; *exp* stands for *expenditures*. For other abbreviations and further explanations, please see the Introduction.

Dothan, AL - continued

Item	Per	Value	Date	Ref.
Transportation				
Public transportation expenditures	year	249	91	81r
Transportation expenditures, total	year	5307	91	81r
Vehicle finance charges	year	346	91	81r
Vehicle insurance expenditures	year	544	91	81r
Vehicle maintenance and repairs expenditures	year	600	91	81r
Vehicle purchases	year	2275	91	81r
Vehicle rental, leases, licenses, etc. expenditures	year	141	91	81r
Vehicles purchased, other than cars and trucks	year	27	91	81r
Utilities				
Electricity expenditures	year	950	91	81r
Utilities, fuels, and public services, total expenditures	year	2000	91	81r
Water and other public services, expenditures	year	227	91	81r
Weddings				
Bridal attendants' gowns	event	750	10/93	76r
Bridal gown	event	852	10/93	76r
Bridal headpiece and veil	event	167	10/93	76r
Bride's wedding band	event	708	10/93	76r
Clergy	event	224	10/93	76r
Engagement ring	event	2756	10/93	76r
Flowers	event	863	10/93	76r
Formal wear for groom	event	106	10/93	76r
Groom's attendants' formal wear	event	530	10/93	76r
Groom's wedding band	event	402	10/93	76r
Music	event	600	10/93	76r
Photography	event	1088	10/93	76r
Shoes for bride	event	50	10/93	76r
Videography	event	483	10/93	76r
Wedding invitations and announcements	event	342	10/93	76r
Wedding reception	event	7000	10/93	76r

Douglas, GA

Item	Per	Value	Date	Ref.
Composite, ACCRA index		92.40	12/94	2c
Alcoholic Beverages				
Beer, Miller Lite, Bud, 12-oz., ex deposit	6	4.61	12/94	2c
J & B Scotch	750-ml.	17.72	12/94	2c
Wine, Gallo Chablis blanc	1.5-lit	5.65	12/94	2c
Clothing				
Jeans, man's denim		39.00	12/94	2c
Shirt, man's dress shirt		33.50	12/94	2c
Undervest, boy's size 10-14, cotton	3	3.59	12/94	2c
Communications				
Newspaper subscription, dly. and Sun. delivery	month	10.44	12/94	2c
Telephone bill, family of four	month	21.49	12/94	2c
Energy and Fuels				
Energy, combined forms, 1800 sq. ft.	mo.	131.69	12/94	2c
Gas, reg unlead, taxes inc., cash, self-service	gal	1.00	12/94	2c
Entertainment				
Bowling, evening rate	game	2.05	12/94	2c
Monopoly game, Parker Brothers', No. 9	game	9.88	12/94	2c
Movie	adm	5.00	12/94	2c
Tennis balls, yellow, Wilson or Penn, 3	can	2.97	12/94	2c
Groceries				
Groceries, ACCRA Index		99.90	12/94	2c
Baby food, strained vegetables, lowest price	4-4.5 oz.	0.35	12/94	2c
Bananas	lb.	0.41	12/94	2c
Beef or hamburger, ground	lb.	1.55	12/94	2c
Bread, white	24-oz.	0.80	12/94	2c

Douglas, GA - continued

Item	Per	Value	Date	Ref.
Groceries - continued				
Cheese, Kraft grated Parmesan	8-oz.	3.32	12/94	2c
Chicken, whole fryer	lb.	0.79	12/94	2c
Cigarettes, Winston, Kings	carton	13.10	12/94	2c
Coffee, vacuum-packed	13 oz.	3.62	12/94	2c
Corn Flakes, Kellogg's or Post Toasties	18 oz.	2.14	12/94	2c
Corn, frozen, whole kernel, lowest price	10 oz.	0.65	12/94	2c
Eggs, Grade A large	dozen	0.79	12/94	2c
Lettuce, iceberg	head	0.87	12/94	2c
Margarine, Blue Bonnet or Parkay cubes	lb.	0.65	12/94	2c
Milk, whole	1/2 gal.	1.46	12/94	2c
Orange juice, Minute Maid frozen	12-oz.	1.27	12/94	2c
Peaches, halves or slices, Hunt's, Del Monte, or Libby's	29-oz.	1.31	12/94	2c
Peas, sweet, Del Monte or Green Giant	15-17 oz.	0.55	12/94	2c
Potatoes, white or red	10-lb. sack	2.61	12/94	2c
Sausage, Jimmy Dean, 100% pork	lb.	2.46	12/94	2c
Shortening, vegetable, Crisco	3-lb.	2.65	12/94	2c
Soft drink, Coca Cola, ex deposit	2 lit	1.22	12/94	2c
Steak, t-bone	lb.	5.65	12/94	2c
Sugar, cane or beet	4 lbs.	1.51	12/94	2c
Tomatoes, Hunt's or Del Monte	14.5 oz.	0.52	12/94	2c
Tuna, chunk, light, oil-packed	6.125-6.5 oz.	0.67	12/94	2c
Goods and Services				
Miscellaneous goods and services, ACCRA Index		104.10	12/94	2c
Health Care				
Health care, ACCRA Index		79.60	12/94	2c
Antibiotic ointment, Polysporin	1.5 oz.	3.81	12/94	2c
Dentist's fee, adult teeth cleaning and periodic oral exam	visit	49.33	12/94	2c
Doctor's fee, routine exam, established patient	visit	31.00	12/94	2c
Hospital care, semiprivate room	day	195.00	12/94	2c
Household Goods				
Appl. repair, service call, wash mach	min. lab. chg.	34.00	12/94	2c
Laundry detergent, Tide Ultra, Bold, or Cheer	42 oz.	3.35	12/94	2c
Tissues, facial, Kleenex brand	175	0.98	12/94	2c
Housing				
Housing, ACCRA Index		69.00	12/94	2c
House payment, principal and interest, 25% down payment	mo.	524	12/94	2c
House, 1800 sq ft, 8000 sq ft lot, new, urban, utilities	total	84987	12/94	2c
Mtge. rate, incl. points and orig. fee, 30-year conv. fixed or ARM	mo.	9.24	12/94	2c
Rent, apartment, 2 br., 1 1/2-2 baths, unfurnished, 950 sq ft, water	mo.	377	12/94	2c
Personal Goods				
Shampoo, Alberto VO5	15-oz.	1.16	12/94	2c
Toothpaste, Crest or Colgate	6-7 oz.	2.14	12/94	2c
Personal Services				
Dry cleaning, man's 2-pc. suit		5.26	12/94	2c
Haircut, man's barbershop, no styling		6.50	12/94	2c
Haircut, woman's shampoo, trim, blow-dry		13.75	12/94	2c
Restaurant Food				
Chicken, fried, thigh and drumstick		2.19	12/94	2c
Hamburger with cheese	1/4 lb.	1.89	12/94	2c
Pizza, Pizza Hut or Pizza Inn	12-13 in.	7.99	12/94	2c

Values are in dollars or fractions of dollars. In the column headed *Ref*, references are shown to sources. Each reference is followed by a letter. These refer to the geographical level for which data were reported: s=State, r=Region, and c=City or metro. The abbreviation *ex* is used to mean *except* or *excluding*; *exp* stands for *expenditures*. For other abbreviations and further explanations, please see the Introduction.

Douglas, GA - continued

Item	Per	Value	Date	Ref.
Transportation				
Transportation, ACCRA Index		96.60	12/94	2c
Tire balance, computer or spin bal., front	wheel	7.25	12/94	2c
Utilities				
Utilities, ACCRA Index		116.40	12/94	2c
Electricity, 1800 sq. ft., new home	mo.	131.69	12/94	2c

Dover, DE

Item	Per	Value	Date	Ref.
Composite, ACCRA index		102.70	12/94	2c
Alcoholic Beverages				
Beer, Miller Lite, Bud, 12-oz., ex deposit	6	4.73	12/94	2c
J & B Scotch	750-ml.	13.99	12/94	2c
Wine, Gallo Chablis blanc	1.5-lit	5.88	12/94	2c
Clothing				
Jeans, man's denim		32.39	12/94	2c
Shirt, man's dress shirt		30.62	12/94	2c
Undervest, boy's size 10-14, cotton	3	4.06	12/94	2c
Communications				
Newspaper subscription, dly. and Sun. delivery	month	9.78	12/94	2c
Telephone bill, family of four	month	13.89	12/94	2c
Telephone, residential, flat rate	mo.	9.40	12/93	8c
Energy and Fuels				
Energy, combined forms, 1800 sq. ft.	mo.	127.53	12/94	2c
Energy, exc. electricity, 1800 sq. ft.	mo.	54.81	12/94	2c
Gas, reg unlead, taxes inc., cash, self-service	gal	1.09	12/94	2c
Entertainment				
Bowling, evening rate	game	2.52	12/94	2c
Monopoly game, Parker Brothers', No. 9	game	10.51	12/94	2c
Movie	adm	6.25	12/94	2c
Tennis balls, yellow, Wilson or Penn, 3	can	2.21	12/94	2c
Groceries				
Groceries, ACCRA Index		108.40	12/94	2c
Baby food, strained vegetables, lowest price	4-4.5 oz.	0.33	12/94	2c
Bananas	lb.	0.40	12/94	2c
Beef or hamburger, ground	lb.	1.48	12/94	2c
Bread, white	24-oz.	0.78	12/94	2c
Cheese, Kraft grated Parmesan	8-oz.	3.84	12/94	2c
Chicken, whole fryer	lb.	0.98	12/94	2c
Cigarettes, Winston, Kings	carton	15.02	12/94	2c
Coffee, vacuum-packed	13 oz.	3.89	12/94	2c
Corn Flakes, Kellogg's or Post Toasties	18 oz.	2.59	12/94	2c
Corn, frozen, whole kernel, lowest price	10 oz.	0.70	12/94	2c
Eggs, Grade A large	dozen	0.91	12/94	2c
Lettuce, iceberg	head	0.83	12/94	2c
Margarine, Blue Bonnet or Parkay cubes	lb.	0.89	12/94	2c
Milk, whole	1/2 gal.	1.11	12/94	2c
Orange juice, Minute Maid frozen	12-oz.	1.66	12/94	2c
Peaches, halves or slices, Hunt's, Del Monte, or Libby's	29-oz.	1.58	12/94	2c
Peas, sweet, Del Monte or Green Giant	15-17 oz.	0.62	12/94	2c
Potatoes, white or red	10-lb. sack	3.08	12/94	2c
Sausage, Jimmy Dean, 100% pork	lb.	3.37	12/94	2c
Shortening, vegetable, Crisco	3-lb.	3.11	12/94	2c
Soft drink, Coca Cola, ex deposit	2 lit	0.98	12/94	2c
Steak, t-bone	lb.	5.94	12/94	2c
Sugar, cane or beet	4 lbs.	1.74	12/94	2c
Tomatoes, Hunt's or Del Monte	14.5 oz.	0.84	12/94	2c
Tuna, chunk, light, oil-packed	6.125-6.5 oz.	0.69	12/94	2c

Dover, DE - continued

Item	Per	Value	Date	Ref.
Goods and Services				
Miscellaneous goods and services, ACCRA Index		103.90	12/94	2c
Health Care				
Health care, ACCRA Index		108.10	12/94	2c
Antibiotic ointment, Polysporin	1.5 oz.	4.19	12/94	2c
Dentist's fee, adult teeth cleaning and periodic oral exam	visit	61.20	12/94	2c
Doctor's fee, routine exam, established patient	visit	39.00	12/94	2c
Hospital care, semiprivate room	day	447.00	12/94	2c
Household Goods				
Appl. repair, service call, wash mach	min. lab. chg.	40.50	12/94	2c
Laundry detergent, Tide Ultra, Bold, or Cheer	42 oz.	3.28	12/94	2c
Tissues, facial, Kleenex brand	175	1.14	12/94	2c
Housing				
Housing, ACCRA Index		97.40	12/94	2c
House payment, principal and interest, 25% down payment	mo.	733	12/94	2c
House, 1800 sq ft, 8000 sq ft lot, new, urban, utilities	total	121875	12/94	2c
Mtge. rate, incl. points and orig. fee, 30-year conv. fixed or ARM	mo.	8.96	12/94	2c
Rent, apartment, 2 br., 1 1/2-2 baths, unfurnished, 950 sq ft, water	mo.	553	12/94	2c
Personal Goods				
Shampoo, Alberto VO5	15-oz.	1.22	12/94	2c
Toothpaste, Crest or Colgate	6-7 oz.	2.26	12/94	2c
Personal Services				
Dry cleaning, man's 2-pc. suit		6.66	12/94	2c
Haircut, man's barbershop, no styling		6.95	12/94	2c
Haircut, woman's shampoo, trim, blow-dry		19.75	12/94	2c
Restaurant Food				
Chicken, fried, thigh and drumstick		2.29	12/94	2c
Hamburger with cheese	1/4 lb.	1.91	12/94	2c
Pizza, Pizza Hut or Pizza Inn	12-13 in.	8.99	12/94	2c
Transportation				
Transportation, ACCRA Index		96.70	12/94	2c
Bus fare, one-way	trip	0.75	12/95	1c
Tire balance, computer or spin bal., front	wheel	6.50	12/94	2c
Utilities				
Utilities, ACCRA Index		107.90	12/94	2c
Electricity, (part.), other, 1800 sq. ft., new home	mo.	72.72	12/94	2c

Dubuque, IA

Item	Per	Value	Date	Ref.
Composite, ACCRA index		106.50	12/94	2c
Alcoholic Beverages				
Beer	bottle	2.00	94	34c
Beer, Miller Lite, Bud, 12-oz., ex deposit	6	3.62	12/94	2c
J & B Scotch	750-ml.	18.88	12/94	2c
Wine, Gallo Chablis blanc	1.5-lit	5.11	12/94	2c
Appliances				
Appliances (major), expenditures	year	131	91	81r
Average annual exp.				
Food, health care, personal goods, services	year	25935	91	81r
Charity				
Cash contributions, expenditures	year	745	91	81r

Values are in dollars or fractions of dollars. In the column headed *Ref*, references are shown to sources. Each reference is followed by a letter. These refer to the geographical level for which data were reported: s=State, r=Region, and c=City or metro. The abbreviation *ex* is used to mean *except* or *excluding*; *exp* stands for expenditures. For other abbreviations and further explanations, please see the Introduction.

Dubuque, IA - continued

Item	Per	Value	Date	Ref.
Clothing				
Apparel, men and boys, total expenditures	year	332	91	81r
Apparel, women and girls, total expenditures	year	578	91	81r
Footwear, expenditures	year	164	91	81r
Jeans, man's denim		30.32	12/94	2c
Shirt, man's dress shirt		32.00	12/94	2c
Undervest, boy's size 10-14, cotton	3	4.11	12/94	2c
Communications				
Long-distance telephone rate, day, addl. min., 1-10 mi.	min.	0.11	12/93	9s
Long-distance telephone rate, day, initial min., 1-10 mi.	min.	0.21	12/93	9s
Newspaper subscription, dly. and Sun. delivery	month	13.04	12/94	2c
Phone line, single, business, field visit	inst	50.00	12/93	9s
Phone line, single, business, no field visit	inst	50.00	12/93	9s
Phone line, single, residence, field visit	inst	35.00	12/93	9s
Phone line, single, residence, no field visit	inst	35.00	12/93	9s
Telephone bill, family of four	month	18.34	12/94	2c
Telephone service, expenditures	year	547	91	81r
Telephone, residential, flat rate	mo.	13.45	12/93	8c
Education				
Board, 4-year private college/university	year	1971	8/94	80s
Board, 4-year public college/university	year	1562	8/94	80s
Education, total expenditures	year	394	91	81r
Room, 4-year private college/university	year	1707	8/94	80s
Room, 4-year public college/university	year	1526	8/94	80s
Total cost, 4-year private college/university	year	14510	8/94	80s
Total cost, 4-year public college/university	year	5440	8/94	80s
Tuition, 2-year public college/university, in-state	year	1612	8/94	80s
Tuition, 4-year private college/university, in-state	year	10832	8/94	80s
Tuition, 4-year public college/university, in-state	year	2352	8/94	80s
Energy and Fuels				
Energy, combined forms, 1800 sq. ft.	mo.	107.44	12/94	2c
Energy, exc. electricity, 1800 sq. ft.	mo.	44.79	12/94	2c
Fuel oil and other fuels, expenditures	year	83	91	81r
Gas, natural, expenditures	year	373	91	81r
Gas, reg unlead, taxes inc., cash, self-service	gal	1.20	12/94	2c
Gasoline and motor oil purchased	year	1000	91	81r
Gasoline, unleaded midgrade	gallon	1.15	4/93	82r
Gasoline, unleaded premium	gallon	1.23	4/93	82r
Gasoline, unleaded regular	gallon	1.07	4/93	82r
Entertainment				
Bowling, evening rate	game	1.69	12/94	2c
Entertainment, total expenditures	year	1356	91	81r
Fees and admissions, expenditures	year	347	91	81r
Monopoly game, Parker Brothers', No. 9	game	10.19	12/94	2c
Movie	adm	5.50	12/94	2c
Pets, toys, playground equipment, expenditures	year	270	91	81r
Reading, expenditures	year	160	91	81r
Televisions, radios, and sound equipment, expenditures	year	433	91	81r
Tennis balls, yellow, Wilson or Penn, 3	can	2.26	12/94	2c
Funerals				
Burial, immediate, container provided by funeral home		1348.78	1/95	54r
Cards, acknowledgment		21.20	1/95	54r
Casket, minimum alternative		182.83	1/95	54r
Cosmetology, hair care, etc.		133.11	1/95	54r
Cremation, direct, container provided by funeral home		1101.95	1/95	54r
Embalming		314.45	1/95	54r
Funeral, funeral home		304.88	1/95	54r
Funeral, other facility		301.37	1/95	54r
Graveside service		290.59	1/95	54r

Dubuque, IA - continued

Item	Per	Value	Date	Ref.
Funerals - continued				
Hearse, local		137.37	1/95	54r
Limousine, local		82.84	1/95	54r
Memorial service		316.57	1/95	54r
Service charge, professional, nondeclinable		1099.00	1/95	54r
Visitation and viewing		209.25	1/95	54r
Groceries				
Groceries, ACCRA Index		95.30	12/94	2c
Apples, Red Delicious	lb.	0.68	12/94	82r
Baby food, strained vegetables, lowest price	4-4.5 oz.	0.35	12/94	2c
Bacon, sliced	lb.	1.88	12/94	82r
Bananas	lb.	0.43	12/94	2c
Bananas	lb.	0.41	12/94	82r
Beef or hamburger, ground	lb.	1.05	12/94	2c
Beef purchases	year	197	91	81r
Beef, stew, boneless	lb.	2.52	12/94	82r
Beverage purchases, alcoholic	year	293	91	81r
Beverage purchases, nonalcoholic	year	203	91	81r
Big Mac hamburger	burger	2.01	94	34c
Bologna, all beef or mixed	lb.	2.12	12/94	82r
Bread, white	24-oz.	0.67	12/94	2c
Bread, white, pan	lb.	0.76	12/94	82r
Cabbage	lb.	0.44	12/94	82r
Carrots, short trimmed and topped	lb.	0.44	12/94	82r
Cereals and bakery products purchases	year	347	91	81r
Cereals and cereals products purchases	year	119	91	81r
Cheddar cheese, natural	lb.	3.28	12/94	82r
Cheese, Kraft grated Parmesan	8-oz.	3.34	12/94	2c
Chicken breast, bone-in	lb.	1.61	12/94	82r
Chicken, fresh, whole	lb.	0.89	12/94	82r
Chicken, whole fryer	lb.	0.71	12/94	2c
Chuck roast, USDA choice, boneless	lb.	2.33	12/94	82r
Cigarettes, Winston, Kings	carton	15.97	12/94	2c
Coffee, 100%, ground roast, all sizes	lb.	4.28	12/94	82r
Coffee, vacuum-packed	13 oz.	3.45	12/94	2c
Cookies, chocolate chip	lb.	2.72	12/94	82r
Corn Flakes, Kellogg's or Post Toasties	18 oz.	2.27	12/94	2c
Corn, frozen, whole kernel, lowest price	10 oz.	0.79	12/94	2c
Dairy products (other) purchases	year	148	91	81r
Eggs, Grade A large	dozen	0.60	12/94	2c
Eggs, Grade A large	dozen	0.76	12/94	82r
Fish and seafood purchases	year	61	91	81r
Flour, white, all purpose	lb.	0.22	12/94	82r
Food purchases, food eaten at home	year	2313	91	81r
Foods purchased away from home, not prepared by consumer	year	1709	91	81r
Fruits and vegetables purchases	year	372	91	81r
Grapefruit	lb.	0.47	12/94	82r
Grapes, Thompson seedless	lb.	2.15	12/94	82r
Ground beef, 100% beef	lb.	1.37	12/94	82r
Ground chuck, 100% beef	lb.	1.81	12/94	82r
Ham, boneless, exc. canned	lb.	2.16	12/94	82r
Ice cream, prepackaged, bulk, regular	1/2 gal.	2.48	12/94	82r
Lemons	lb.	1.08	12/94	82r
Lettuce, iceberg	lb.	0.81	12/94	82r
Lettuce, iceberg	head	0.76	12/94	2c
Margarine, Blue Bonnet or Parkay cubes	lb.	0.58	12/94	2c
Margarine, stick	lb.	0.81	12/94	82r
Meats, poultry, fish, and eggs purchases	year	591	91	81r
Milk and cream (fresh) purchases	year	132	91	81r
Milk, whole	1/2 gal.	1.26	12/94	2c
Orange juice, frozen concentrate 12-oz. can	16 oz.	1.41	12/94	82r
Orange juice, Minute Maid frozen	12-oz.	1.16	12/94	2c
Oranges, Navel	lb.	0.56	12/94	82r
Peaches, halves or slices, Hunt's, Del Monte, or Libby's	29-oz.	1.46	12/94	2c
Peanut butter, creamy, all sizes	lb.	1.81	12/94	82r
Peas, sweet, Del Monte or Green Giant	15-17 oz.	0.63	12/94	2c
Pork chops, center cut, bone-in	lb.	2.76	12/94	82r

Values are in dollars or fractions of dollars. In the column headed *Ref*, references are shown to sources. Each reference is followed by a letter. These refer to the geographical level for which data were reported: s=State, r=Region, and c=City or metro. The abbreviation *ex* is used to mean *except* or *excluding*; *exp* stands for *expenditures*. For other abbreviations and further explanations, please see the Introduction.

Dubuque, IA - continued

Item	Per	Value	Date	Ref.
Groceries				
Pork purchases	year	130	91	81r
Potato chips	16-oz.	2.81	12/94	82r
Potatoes, frozen, French fried	lb.	0.83	12/94	82r
Potatoes, white	lb.	0.28	12/94	82r
Potatoes, white or red	10-lb. sack	2.69	12/94	2c
Round roast, USDA choice, boneless	lb.	2.90	12/94	82r
Sausage, Jimmy Dean, 100% pork	lb.	2.82	12/94	2c
Shortening, vegetable oil blends	lb.	0.88	12/94	82r
Shortening, vegetable, Crisco	3-lb.	2.57	12/94	2c
Soft drink, Coca Cola, ex deposit	2 lit	1.21	12/94	2c
Spaghetti and macaroni	lb.	0.78	12/94	82r
Steak, rib eye, USDA choice, boneless	lb.	6.15	12/94	82r
Steak, round, graded & ungraded, exc. USDA prime & choice	lb.	2.72	12/94	82r
Steak, round, USDA choice, boneless	lb.	3.02	12/94	82r
Steak, sirloin, USDA choice, boneless	lb.	3.85	12/94	82r
Steak, t-bone	lb.	4.19	12/94	2c
Steak, T-bone, USDA choice, bone-in	lb.	5.38	12/94	82r
Sugar and other sweets, eaten at home, expenditures	year	91	91	81r
Sugar, cane or beet	4 lbs.	1.30	12/94	2c
Sugar, white, all sizes	lb.	0.36	12/94	82r
Tobacco products and smoking supplies, total expenditures	year	298	91	81r
Tomatoes, field grown	lb.	1.36	12/94	82r
Tomatoes, Hunt's or Del Monte	14.5 oz.	0.79	12/94	2c
Tuna, chunk, light	lb.	1.94	12/94	82r
Tuna, chunk, light, oil-packed	6.125-6.5 oz.	0.62	12/94	2c
Turkey, frozen, whole	lb.	0.96	12/94	82r
Yogurt, natural, fruit flavored	8 oz.	0.62	12/94	82r
Goods and Services				
Miscellaneous goods and services, ACCRA Index		99.70	12/94	2c
Health Care				
Health care, ACCRA Index		94.30	12/94	2c
Antibiotic ointment, Polysporin	1.5 oz.	3.89	12/94	2c
Childbirth, Cesarean delivery, hospital charge	birth	5101.00	12/91	69r
Childbirth, Cesarean delivery, physician charge	birth	2234.00	12/91	69r
Childbirth, normal delivery, hospital charge	birth	2891.00	12/91	69r
Childbirth, normal delivery, physician charge	birth	1623.00	12/91	69r
Dentist's fee, adult teeth cleaning and periodic oral exam	visit	45.00	12/94	2c
Doctor's fee, routine exam, established patient	visit	47.75	12/94	2c
Drugs, expenditures	year	248	91	81r
Health care, total expenditures	year	1336	91	81r
Health insurance expenditures	year	550	91	81r
Hospital care, semiprivate room	day	257.50	12/94	2c
Insurance premium, family medical care	month	395.98	1/95	41s
Medical services expenditures	year	457	91	81r
Medical supplies expenditures	year	82	91	81r
Household Goods				
Appl. repair, service call, wash mach	min. lab. chg.	35.50	12/94	2c
Floor coverings, expenditures	year	105	91	81r
Furniture, expenditures	year	291	91	81r
Household equipment, misc. expenditures	year	341	91	81r
Household expenditures, miscellaneous	year	162	91	81r
Household furnishings and equipment, expenditures	year	1042	91	81r
Household operations expenditures	year	365	91	81r
Household textiles, expenditures	year	101	91	81r
Housekeeping supplies, expenditures	year	390	91	81r
Laundry and cleaning supplies, expenditures	year	110	91	81r

Dubuque, IA - continued

Item	Per	Value	Date	Ref.
Household Goods - continued				
Laundry detergent, Tide Ultra, Bold, or Cheer	42 oz.	3.10	12/94	2c
Postage and stationery, expenditures	year	115	91	81r
Tissues, facial, Kleenex brand	175	0.96	12/94	2c
Housing				
Housing, ACCRA Index		128.70	12/94	2c
Add garage/carport		8,479	3/95	74r
Add room(s)		21,347	3/95	74r
Apartment condominium or co-op, median	unit	87100	12/94	62r
Bathroom addition, average cost	add	9734.00	3/95	13r
Bathroom remodeling, average cost	remod	6414.00	3/95	13r
Bedroom, master suite addition, average cost	add	27122.00	3/95	13r
Deck addition, average cost	add	6665.00	3/95	13r
Dwellings (owned), expenditures	year	2566	91	81r
Enclose porch/patio/breezeway		4,556	3/95	74r
Exterior remodeling, average cost	remod	15395.00	3/95	13r
Family room addition, average cost	add	27658.00	3/95	13r
Finish room in basement/attic		5,074	3/95	74r
Home, existing, single-family, median	unit	106500	12/94	62r
House payment, principal and interest, 25% down payment	mo.	1043	12/94	2c
House, 1800 sq ft, 8000 sq ft lot, new, urban, utilities	total	166500	12/94	2c
Kitchen remodeling, major, average cost	remod	17084.00	3/95	13r
Kitchen remodeling, minor, average cost	remod	5804.00	3/95	13r
Maintenance, repairs, insurance, and other housing expenditures	year	484	91	81r
Mortgage interest and charges expenditures	year	1443	91	81r
Mtge. rate, incl. points and orig. fee, 30-year conv. fixed or ARM	mo.	9.42	12/94	2c
Office, home addition, average cost	add	8121.00	3/95	13r
Princ. & int., mortgage, median-price exist. sing.-family home	mo.	515	12/94	62r
Property taxes expenditures	year	639	91	81r
Redesign, restructure more than half of home's interior		9,114	3/95	74r
Rent, apartment, 2 br., 1 1/2-2 baths, unfurnished, 950 sq ft, water	mo.	518	12/94	2c
Rental units expenditures	year	1200	91	81r
Sun-space addition, average cost	add	23768.00	3/95	13r
Wing addition, two-story, average cost	add	50410.00	3/95	13r
Insurance and Pensions				
Auto insurance, private passenger	year	467.45	12/94	71s
Insurance and pensions, personal, expenditures	year	2408	91	81r
Insurance, life and other personal, expenditures	year	355	91	81r
Pensions and Social Security, expenditures	year	2053	91	81r
Legal Assistance				
Legal work, law firm associate	hour	90		10r
Legal work, law firm partner	hour	139		10r
Personal Goods				
Shampoo, Alberto VO5	15-oz.	1.12	12/94	2c
Toothpaste, Crest or Colgate	6-7 oz.	2.26	12/94	2c
Personal Services				
Dry cleaning, man's 2-pc. suit		6.00	12/94	2c
Haircut, man's barbershop, no styling		7.60	12/94	2c
Haircut, woman's shampoo, trim, blow-dry		14.79	12/94	2c
Personal services expenditures	year	203	91	81r
Restaurant Food				
Chicken, fried, thigh and drumstick		2.25	12/94	2c
Dining expenditures, family	week	30.03	94	73r
Hamburger with cheese	1/4 lb.	2.00	12/94	2c
Pizza, Pizza Hut or Pizza Inn	12-13 in.	7.85	12/94	2c

Values are in dollars or fractions of dollars. In the column headed *Ref*, references are shown to sources. Each reference is followed by a letter. These refer to the geographical level for which data were reported: s = State, r = Region, and c = City or metro. The abbreviation *ex* is used to mean *except* or *excluding*; *exp* stands for expenditures. For other abbreviations and further explanations, please see the Introduction.

Dubuque, IA - continued

Item	Per	Value	Date	Ref.
Taxes				
Taxes, Federal income, expenditures	year	1756	91	81r
Taxes, personal, expenditures	year	2426	91	81r
Taxes, State and local income, expenditures	year	568	91	81r
Transportation				
Transportation, ACCRA Index		100.00	12/94	2c
Bus fare, up to 10 miles	one-way	0.80	12/94	2c
Cars and trucks purchased, new	year	891	91	81r
Cars and trucks purchased, used	year	1155	91	81r
Driver's learning permit fee	perm	6.00	1/94	84s
Driver's license fee	orig	0.00	1/94	84s
Driver's license fee, duplicate	lic	3.00	1/94	84s
Driver's license reinstatement fee, min.	susp	20.00	1/94	85s
Driver's license renewal fee	renew	0.00	1/94	84s
Identification card, nondriver	card	5.00	1/94	83s
Motorcycle learning permit fee	perm	8.00	1/94	84s
Motorcycle license fee	orig	8.00	1/94	84s
Motorcycle license fee, duplicate	lic	3.00	1/94	84s
Motorcycle license renewal fee	renew	8.00	1/94	84s
Public transportation expenditures	year	209	91	81r
Tire balance, computer or spin bal., front	wheel	6.45	12/94	2c
Transportation expenditures, total	year	4792	91	81r
Vehicle finance charges	year	300	91	81r
Vehicle insurance expenditures	year	485	91	81r
Vehicle maintenance and repairs expenditures	year	534	91	81r
Vehicle purchases	year	2068	91	81r
Vehicle rental, leases, licenses, etc. expenditures	year	197	91	81r
Vehicles purchased, other than cars and trucks	year	22	91	81r
Utilities				
Utilities, ACCRA Index		95.50	12/94	2c
Electricity expenditures	year	668	91	81r
Electricity, (part.), other, 1800 sq. ft., new home	mo.	62.65	12/94	2c
Electricity, summer, 250 KWh	month	22.35	8/93	64c
Electricity, summer, 500 KWh	month	39.64	8/93	64c
Electricity, summer, 750 KWh	month	56.93	8/93	64c
Electricity, summer, 1000 KWh	month	74.22	8/93	64c
Utilities, fuels, and public services, total expenditures	year	1838	91	81r
Water and other public services, expenditures	year	167	91	81r
Weddings				
Bridal attendants' gowns	event	750	10/93	76r
Bridal gown	event	852	10/93	76r
Bridal headpiece and veil	event	167	10/93	76r
Bride's wedding band	event	708	10/93	76r
Clergy	event	224	10/93	76r
Engagement ring	event	2756	10/93	76r
Flowers	event	863	10/93	76r
Formal wear for groom	event	106	10/93	76r
Groom's attendants' formal wear	event	530	10/93	76r
Groom's wedding band	event	402	10/93	76r
Music	event	600	10/93	76r
Photography	event	1088	10/93	76r
Shoes for bride	event	50	10/93	76r
Videography	event	483	10/93	76r
Wedding invitations and announcements	event	342	10/93	76r
Wedding reception	event	7000	10/93	76r

Duluth, MN

Item	Per	Value	Date	Ref.
Appliances				
Appliances (major), expenditures	year	131	91	81r
Average annual exp.				
Food, health care, personal goods, services	year	25935	91	81r

Duluth, MN - continued

Item	Per	Value	Date	Ref.
Charity				
Cash contributions, expenditures	year	745	91	81r
Clothing				
Apparel, men and boys, total expenditures	year	332	91	81r
Apparel, women and girls, total expenditures	year	578	91	81r
Footwear, expenditures	year	164	91	81r
Communications				
Long-distance telephone rate, day, addl. min., 1-10 mi.	min.	0.05	12/93	9s
Long-distance telephone rate, day, initial min., 1-10 mi.	min.	0.14	12/93	9s
Phone line, single, business, field visit	inst	45.00	12/93	9s
Phone line, single, business, no field visit	inst	45.00	12/93	9s
Phone line, single, residence, field visit	inst	16.25	12/93	9s
Phone line, single, residence, no field visit	inst	16.25	12/93	9s
Telephone service, expenditures	year	547	91	81r
Education				
Board, 4-year private college/university	year	2070	8/94	80s
Board, 4-year public college/university	year	1545	8/94	80s
Education, total expenditures	year	394	91	81r
Living expenses, personal miscellaneous, university student	year	4200.00	5/96	22s
Room, 4-year private college/university	year	1894	8/94	80s
Room, 4-year public college/university	year	1580	8/94	80s
Total cost, 4-year private college/university	year	15556	8/94	80s
Total cost, 4-year public college/university	year	5904	8/94	80s
Tuition, 2-year public college/university, in-state	year	1858	8/94	80s
Tuition, 4-year private college/university, in-state	year	11592	8/94	80s
Tuition, 4-year public college/university, in-state	year	2780	8/94	80s
Energy and Fuels				
Fuel oil and other fuels, expenditures	year	83	91	81r
Gas, natural, expenditures	year	373	91	81r
Gasoline and motor oil purchased	year	1000	91	81r
Gasoline, unleaded midgrade	gallon	1.15	4/93	82r
Gasoline, unleaded premium	gallon	1.23	4/93	82r
Gasoline, unleaded regular	gallon	1.07	4/93	82r
Entertainment				
Entertainment, total expenditures	year	1356	91	81r
Fees and admissions, expenditures	year	347	91	81r
Pets, toys, playground equipment, expenditures	year	270	91	81r
Reading, expenditures	year	160	91	81r
Televisions, radios, and sound equipment, expenditures	year	433	91	81r
Funerals				
Burial, immediate, container provided by funeral home		1348.78	1/95	54r
Cards, acknowledgment		21.20	1/95	54r
Casket, minimum alternative		182.83	1/95	54r
Cosmetology, hair care, etc.		133.11	1/95	54r
Cremation, direct, container provided by funeral home		1101.95	1/95	54r
Embalming		314.45	1/95	54r
Funeral, funeral home		304.88	1/95	54r
Funeral, other facility		301.37	1/95	54r
Graveside service		290.59	1/95	54r
Hearse, local		137.37	1/95	54r
Limousine, local		82.84	1/95	54r
Memorial service		316.57	1/95	54r
Service charge, professional, nondeclinable		1099.00	1/95	54r
Visitation and viewing		209.25	1/95	54r
Groceries				
Apples, Red Delicious	lb.	0.68	12/94	82r
Bacon, sliced	lb.	1.88	12/94	82r
Bananas	lb.	0.41	12/94	82r
Beef purchases	year	197	91	81r

Values are in dollars or fractions of dollars. In the column headed *Ref*, references are shown to sources. Each reference is followed by a letter. These refer to the geographical level for which data were reported: s = State, r = Region, and c = City or metro. The abbreviation *ex* is used to mean *except* or *excluding*; *exp* stands for expenditures. For other abbreviations and further explanations, please see the Introduction.

Duluth, MN - continued

Item	Per	Value	Date	Ref.
Groceries				
Beef, stew, boneless	lb.	2.52	12/94	82r
Beverage purchases, alcoholic	year	293	91	81r
Beverage purchases, nonalcoholic	year	203	91	81r
Bologna, all beef or mixed	lb.	2.12	12/94	82r
Bread, white, pan	lb.	0.76	12/94	82r
Cabbage	lb.	0.44	12/94	82r
Carrots, short trimmed and topped	lb.	0.44	12/94	82r
Cereals and bakery products purchases	year	347	91	81r
Cereals and cereals products purchases	year	119	91	81r
Cheddar cheese, natural	lb.	3.28	12/94	82r
Chicken breast, bone-in	lb.	1.61	12/94	82r
Chicken, fresh, whole	lb.	0.89	12/94	82r
Chuck roast, USDA choice, boneless	lb.	2.33	12/94	82r
Coffee, 100%, ground roast, all sizes	lb.	4.28	12/94	82r
Cookies, chocolate chip	lb.	2.72	12/94	82r
Dairy products (other) purchases	year	148	91	81r
Eggs, Grade A large	dozen	0.76	12/94	82r
Fish and seafood purchases	year	61	91	81r
Flour, white, all purpose	lb.	0.22	12/94	82r
Food purchases, food eaten at home	year	2313	91	81r
Foods purchased away from home, not prepared by consumer	year	1709	91	81r
Fruits and vegetables purchases	year	372	91	81r
Grapefruit	lb.	0.47	12/94	82r
Grapes, Thompson seedless	lb.	2.15	12/94	82r
Ground beef, 100% beef	lb.	1.37	12/94	82r
Ground chuck, 100% beef	lb.	1.81	12/94	82r
Ham, boneless, exc. canned	lb.	2.16	12/94	82r
Ice cream, prepackaged, bulk, regular	1/2 gal.	2.48	12/94	82r
Lemons	lb.	1.08	12/94	82r
Lettuce, iceberg	lb.	0.81	12/94	82r
Margarine, stick	lb.	0.81	12/94	82r
Meats, poultry, fish, and eggs purchases	year	591	91	81r
Milk and cream (fresh) purchases	year	132	91	81r
Orange juice, frozen concentrate 12-oz. can	16 oz.	1.41	12/94	82r
Oranges, Navel	lb.	0.56	12/94	82r
Peanut butter, creamy, all sizes	lb.	1.81	12/94	82r
Pork chops, center cut, bone-in	lb.	2.76	12/94	82r
Pork purchases	year	130	91	81r
Potato chips	16-oz.	2.81	12/94	82r
Potatoes, frozen, French fried	lb.	0.83	12/94	82r
Potatoes, white	lb.	0.28	12/94	82r
Round roast, USDA choice, boneless	lb.	2.90	12/94	82r
Shortening, vegetable oil blends	lb.	0.88	12/94	82r
Spaghetti and macaroni	lb.	0.78	12/94	82r
Steak, rib eye, USDA choice, boneless	lb.	6.15	12/94	82r
Steak, round, graded & ungraded, exc. USDA prime & choice	lb.	2.72	12/94	82r
Steak, round, USDA choice, boneless	lb.	3.02	12/94	82r
Steak, sirloin, USDA choice, boneless	lb.	3.85	12/94	82r
Steak, T-bone, USDA choice, bone-in	lb.	5.38	12/94	82r
Sugar and other sweets, eaten at home, expenditures	year	91	91	81r
Sugar, white, all sizes	lb.	0.36	12/94	82r
Tobacco products and smoking supplies, total expenditures	year	298	91	81r
Tomatoes, field grown	lb.	1.36	12/94	82r
Tuna, chunk, light	lb.	1.94	12/94	82r
Turkey, frozen, whole	lb.	0.96	12/94	82r
Yogurt, natural, fruit flavored	8 oz.	0.62	12/94	82r
Health Care				
Childbirth, Cesarean delivery, hospital charge	birth	5101.00	12/91	69r
Childbirth, Cesarean delivery, physician charge	birth	2234.00	12/91	69r
Childbirth, normal delivery, hospital charge	birth	2891.00	12/91	69r
Childbirth, normal delivery, physician charge	birth	1623.00	12/91	69r
Drugs, expenditures	year	248	91	81r
Health care, total expenditures	year	1336	91	81r
Health insurance expenditures	year	550	91	81r
Insurance premium, family medical care	month	375.35	1/95	41s

Duluth, MN - continued

Item	Per	Value	Date	Ref.
Health Care - continued				
Medical services expenditures	year	457	91	81r
Medical supplies expenditures	year	82	91	81r
Household Goods				
Floor coverings, expenditures	year	105	91	81r
Furniture, expenditures	year	291	91	81r
Household equipment, misc. expenditures	year	341	91	81r
Household expenditures, miscellaneous	year	162	91	81r
Household furnishings and equipment, expenditures	year	1042	91	81r
Household operations expenditures	year	365	91	81r
Household textiles, expenditures	year	101	91	81r
Housekeeping supplies, expenditures	year	390	91	81r
Laundry and cleaning supplies, expenditures	year	110	91	81r
Postage and stationery, expenditures	year	115	91	81r
Housing				
Add garage/carport		8,479	3/95	74r
Add room(s)		21,347	3/95	74r
Apartment condominium or co-op, median	unit	87100	12/94	62r
Bathroom addition, average cost	add	9734.00	3/95	13r
Bathroom remodeling, average cost	remod	6414.00	3/95	13r
Bedroom, master suite addition, average cost	add	27122.00	3/95	13r
Deck addition, average cost	add	6665.00	3/95	13r
Dwellings (owned), expenditures	year	2566	91	81r
Enclose porch/patio/breezeway		4,556	3/95	74r
Exterior remodeling, average cost	remod	15395.00	3/95	13r
Family room addition, average cost	add	27658.00	3/95	13r
Finish room in basement/attic		5,074	3/95	74r
Home, existing, single-family, median	unit	106500	12/94	62r
Kitchen remodeling, major, average cost	remod	17084.00	3/95	13r
Kitchen remodeling, minor, average cost	remod	5804.00	3/95	13r
Maintenance, repairs, insurance, and other housing expenditures	year	484	91	81r
Mortgage interest and charges expenditures	year	1443	91	81r
Office, home addition, average cost	add	8121.00	3/95	13r
Princ. & int., mortgage, median-price exist. sing.-family home	mo.	515	12/94	62r
Property taxes expenditures	year	639	91	81r
Redesign, restructure more than half of home's interior		9,114	3/95	74r
Rental units expenditures	year	1200	91	81r
Sun-space addition, average cost	add	23768.00	3/95	13r
Wing addition, two-story, average cost	add	50410.00	3/95	13r
Insurance and Pensions				
Auto insurance, private passenger	year	656.87	12/94	71s
Insurance and pensions, personal, expenditures	year	2408	91	81r
Insurance, life and other personal, expenditures	year	355	91	81r
Pensions and Social Security, expenditures	year	2053	91	81r
Legal Assistance				
Legal work, law firm associate	hour	90		10r
Legal work, law firm partner	hour	139		10r
Personal Services				
Personal services expenditures	year	203	91	81r
Restaurant Food				
Dining expenditures, family	week	30.03	94	73r
Taxes				
Tax, cigarettes	year	400.00	10/93	43s
Taxes, Federal income, expenditures	year	1756	91	81r
Taxes, personal, expenditures	year	2426	91	81r
Taxes, State and local income, expenditures	year	568	91	81r
Transportation				
Cars and trucks purchased, new	year	891	91	81r
Cars and trucks purchased, used	year	1155	91	81r
Driver's learning permit fee	perm	6.00	1/94	84s
Driver's license fee	orig	15.00	1/94	84s

Values are in dollars or fractions of dollars. In the column headed *Ref*, references are shown to sources. Each reference is followed by a letter. These refer to the geographical level for which data were reported: s = State, r = Region, and c = City or metro. The abbreviation *ex* is used to mean *except* or *excluding*; *exp* stands for expenditures. For other abbreviations and further explanations, please see the Introduction.

Duluth, MN - continued

Item	Per	Value	Date	Ref.
Transportation				
Driver's license fee, duplicate	lic	4.50	1/94	84s
Driver's license reinstatement fee, min.	susp	20.00	1/94	85s
Driver's license renewal fee	renew	15.00	1/94	84s
Identification card, nondriver	card	9.00	1/94	83s
Public transportation expenditures	year	209	91	81r
Transportation expenditures, total	year	4792	91	81r
Vehicle finance charges	year	300	91	81r
Vehicle insurance expenditures	year	485	91	81r
Vehicle maintenance and repairs expenditures	year	534	91	81r
Vehicle purchases	year	2068	91	81r
Vehicle rental, leases, licenses, etc. expenditures	year	197	91	81r
Vehicles purchased, other than cars and trucks	year	22	91	81r
Utilities				
Electricity expenditures	year	668	91	81r
Utilities, fuels, and public services, total expenditures	year	1838	91	81r
Water and other public services, expenditures	year	167	91	81r
Weddings				
Bridal attendants' gowns	event	750	10/93	76r
Bridal gown	event	852	10/93	76r
Bridal headpiece and veil	event	167	10/93	76r
Bride's wedding band	event	708	10/93	76r
Clergy	event	224	10/93	76r
Engagement ring	event	2756	10/93	76r
Flowers	event	863	10/93	76r
Formal wear for groom	event	106	10/93	76r
Groom's attendants' formal wear	event	530	10/93	76r
Groom's wedding band	event	402	10/93	76r
Music	event	600	10/93	76r
Photography	event	1088	10/93	76r
Shoes for bride	event	50	10/93	76r
Videography	event	483	10/93	76r
Wedding invitations and announcements	event	342	10/93	76r
Wedding reception	event	7000	10/93	76r

Dyersburg, TN

Item	Per	Value	Date	Ref.
Composite, ACCRA index		92.00	12/94	2c
Alcoholic Beverages				
Beer, Miller Lite, Bud, 12-oz., ex deposit	6	3.99	12/94	2c
J & B Scotch	750-ml.	19.60	12/94	2c
Wine, Gallo Chablis blanc	1.5-lit	7.95	12/94	2c
Clothing				
Jeans, man's denim		33.98	12/94	2c
Shirt, man's dress shirt		39.97	12/94	2c
Undervest, boy's size 10-14, cotton	3	3.99	12/94	2c
Communications				
Newspaper subscription, dly. and Sun. delivery	month	15.16	12/94	2c
Telephone bill, family of four	month	15.63	12/94	2c
Telephone, residential, flat rate	mo.	8.50	12/93	8c
Energy and Fuels				
Energy, combined forms, 1800 sq. ft.	mo.	102.70	12/94	2c
Energy, exc. electricity, 1800 sq. ft.	mo.	29.42	12/94	2c
Gas, reg unlead, taxes inc., cash, self-service	gal	1.09	12/94	2c
Entertainment				
Bowling, evening rate	game	2.00	12/94	2c
Monopoly game, Parker Brothers', No. 9	game	14.99	12/94	2c
Movie	adm	5.00	12/94	2c
Tennis balls, yellow, Wilson or Penn, 3	can	2.11	12/94	2c

Dyersburg, TN - continued

Item	Per	Value	Date	Ref.
Groceries				
Groceries, ACCRA Index		99.60	12/94	2c
Baby food, strained vegetables, lowest price	4-4.5 oz.	0.36	12/94	2c
Bananas	lb.	0.44	12/94	2c
Beef or hamburger, ground	lb.	1.46	12/94	2c
Bread, white	24-oz.	0.64	12/94	2c
Cheese, Kraft grated Parmesan	8-oz.	3.64	12/94	2c
Chicken, whole fryer	lb.	0.84	12/94	2c
Cigarettes, Winston, Kings	carton	14.92	12/94	2c
Coffee, vacuum-packed	13 oz.	3.67	12/94	2c
Corn Flakes, Kellogg's or Post Toasties	18 oz.	2.72	12/94	2c
Corn, frozen, whole kernel, lowest price	10 oz.	0.86	12/94	2c
Eggs, Grade A large	dozen	0.68	12/94	2c
Lettuce, iceberg	head	0.59	12/94	2c
Margarine, Blue Bonnet or Parkay cubes	lb.	0.53	12/94	2c
Milk, whole	1/2 gal.	1.53	12/94	2c
Orange juice, Minute Maid frozen	12-oz.	1.47	12/94	2c
Peaches, halves or slices, Hunt's, Del Monte, or Libby's	29-oz.	1.16	12/94	2c
Peas, sweet, Del Monte or Green Giant	15-17 oz.	0.70	12/94	2c
Potatoes, white or red	10-lb. sack	1.99	12/94	2c
Sausage, Jimmy Dean, 100% pork	lb.	2.25	12/94	2c
Shortening, vegetable, Crisco	3-lb.	2.71	12/94	2c
Soft drink, Coca Cola, ex deposit	2 lit	0.99	12/94	2c
Steak, t-bone	lb.	4.27	12/94	2c
Sugar, cane or beet	4 lbs.	1.44	12/94	2c
Tomatoes, Hunt's or Del Monte	14.5 oz.	0.82	12/94	2c
Tuna, chunk, light, oil-packed	6.125-6.5 oz.	0.71	12/94	2c
Goods and Services				
Miscellaneous goods and services, ACCRA Index		103.10	12/94	2c
Health Care				
Health care, ACCRA Index		84.60	12/94	2c
Antibiotic ointment, Polysporin	1.5 oz.	3.99	12/94	2c
Dentist's fee, adult teeth cleaning and periodic oral exam	visit	46.00	12/94	2c
Doctor's fee, routine exam, established patient	visit	38.00	12/94	2c
Hospital care, semiprivate room	day	210.00	12/94	2c
Household Goods				
Appl. repair, service call, wash mach	min. lab. chg.	26.88	12/94	2c
Laundry detergent, Tide Ultra, Bold, or Cheer	42 oz.	4.18	12/94	2c
Tissues, facial, Kleenex brand	175	1.04	12/94	2c
Housing				
Housing, ACCRA Index		76.40	12/94	2c
House payment, principal and interest, 25% down payment	mo.	582	12/94	2c
House, 1800 sq ft, 8000 sq ft lot, new, urban, utilities	total	93903	12/94	2c
Mtge. rate, incl. points and orig. fee, 30-year conv. fixed or ARM	mo.	9.31	12/94	2c
Rent, apartment, 2 br., 1 1/2-2 baths, unfurnished, 950 sq ft, water	mo.	413	12/94	2c
Personal Goods				
Shampoo, Alberto VO5	15-oz.	1.18	12/94	2c
Toothpaste, Crest or Colgate	6-7 oz.	2.39	12/94	2c
Personal Services				
Dry cleaning, man's 2-pc. suit		6.77	12/94	2c
Haircut, man's barbershop, no styling		7.00	12/94	2c
Haircut, woman's shampoo, trim, blow-dry		14.00	12/94	2c

Values are in dollars or fractions of dollars. In the column headed *Ref*, references are shown to sources. Each reference is followed by a letter. These refer to the geographical level for which data were reported: s=State, r=Region, and c=City or metro. The abbreviation *ex* is used to mean *except* or *excluding*; *exp* stands for expenditures. For other abbreviations and further explanations, please see the Introduction.

Dyersburg, TN - continued

Item	Per	Value	Date	Ref.
Restaurant Food				
Chicken, fried, thigh and drumstick		1.85	12/94	2c
Hamburger with cheese	1/4 lb.	1.89	12/94	2c
Pizza, Pizza Hut or Pizza Inn	12-13 in.	6.50	12/94	2c
Transportation				
Transportation, ACCRA Index		92.80	12/94	2c
Tire balance, computer or spin bal., front	wheel	5.90	12/94	2c
Utilities				
Utilities, ACCRA Index		90.00	12/94	2c
Electricity, (part.), other, 1800 sq. ft., new home	mo.	73.28	12/94	2c

Eau Claire, WI

Item	Per	Value	Date	Ref.
Composite, ACCRA index		103.40	12/94	2c
Alcoholic Beverages				
Beer, Miller Lite, Bud, 12-oz., ex deposit	6	3.51	12/94	2c
J & B Scotch	750-ml.	16.91	12/94	2c
Wine, Gallo Chablis blanc	1.5-lit	4.86	12/94	2c
Appliances				
Appliances (major), expenditures	year	131	91	81r
Average annual exp.				
Food, health care, personal goods, services	year	25935	91	81r
Charity				
Cash contributions, expenditures	year	745	91	81r
Clothing				
Apparel, men and boys, total expenditures	year	332	91	81r
Apparel, women and girls, total expenditures	year	578	91	81r
Footwear, expenditures	year	164	91	81r
Jeans, man's denim		38.33	12/94	2c
Shirt, man's dress shirt		34.50	12/94	2c
Undervest, boy's size 10-14, cotton	3	2.64	12/94	2c
Communications				
Long-distance telephone rate, day, addl. min., 1-10 mi.	min.	0.10	12/93	9s
Long-distance telephone rate, day, initial min., 1-10 mi.	min.	0.15	12/93	9s
Newspaper subscription, dly. and Sun. delivery	month	10.47	12/94	2c
Phone line, single, business, field visit	inst	64.65	12/93	9s
Phone line, single, business, no field visit	inst	64.65	12/93	9s
Phone line, single, residence, field visit	inst	33.05	12/93	9s
Phone line, single, residence, no field visit	inst	33.05	12/93	9s
Telephone bill, family of four	month	15.80	12/94	2c
Telephone service, expenditures	year	547	91	81r
Telephone, residential, flat rate	mo.	6.00	12/93	8c
Education				
Board, 4-year private college/university	year	2145	8/94	80s
Board, 4-year public college/university	year	1303	8/94	80s
Education, total expenditures	year	394	91	81r
Room, 4-year private college/university	year	1576	8/94	80s
Room, 4-year public college/university	year	1631	8/94	80s
Total cost, 4-year private college/university	year	13902	8/94	80s
Total cost, 4-year public college/university	year	5252	8/94	80s
Tuition, 2-year public college/university, in-state	year	1557	8/94	80s
Tuition, 4-year private college/university, in-state	year	10181	8/94	80s
Tuition, 4-year public college/university, in-state	year	2318	8/94	80s
Energy and Fuels				
Energy, combined forms, 1800 sq. ft.	mo.	109.19	12/94	2c
Energy, exc. electricity, 1800 sq. ft.	mo.	63.01	12/94	2c
Fuel oil and other fuels, expenditures	year	83	91	81r
Gas, cooking, winter, 10 therms	month	10.18	2/94	65c

Eau Claire, WI - continued

Item	Per	Value	Date	Ref.
Energy and Fuels - continued				
Gas, cooking, winter, 30 therms	month	22.54	2/94	65c
Gas, cooking, winter, 50 therms	month	34.91	2/94	65c
Gas, heating, winter, 100 therms	month	68.81	2/94	65c
Gas, heating, winter, average use	month	123.29	2/94	65c
Gas, natural, expenditures	year	373	91	81r
Gas, reg unlead, taxes inc., cash, self-service	gal	1.16	12/94	2c
Gasoline and motor oil purchased	year	1000	91	81r
Gasoline, unleaded midgrade	gallon	1.15	4/93	82r
Gasoline, unleaded premium	gallon	1.23	4/93	82r
Gasoline, unleaded regular	gallon	1.07	4/93	82r
Entertainment				
Bowling, evening rate	game	2.04	12/94	2c
Entertainment, total expenditures	year	1356	91	81r
Fees and admissions, expenditures	year	347	91	81r
Monopoly game, Parker Brothers', No. 9	game	8.77	12/94	2c
Movie	adm	5.50	12/94	2c
Pets, toys, playground equipment, expenditures	year	270	91	81r
Reading, expenditures	year	160	91	81r
Televisions, radios, and sound equipment, expenditures	year	433	91	81r
Tennis balls, yellow, Wilson or Penn, 3	can	2.65	12/94	2c
Funerals				
Burial, immediate, container provided by funeral home		1268.31	1/95	54r
Cards, acknowledgment		26.12	1/95	54r
Casket, minimum alternative		198.03	1/95	54r
Cosmetology, hair care, etc.		122.19	1/95	54r
Cremation, direct, container provided by funeral home		977.81	1/95	54r
Embalming		334.00	1/95	54r
Funeral, funeral home		321.16	1/95	54r
Funeral, other facility		317.73	1/95	54r
Graveside service		292.48	1/95	54r
Hearse, local		153.20	1/95	54r
Limousine, local		123.52	1/95	54r
Memorial service		356.30	1/95	54r
Service charge, professional, nondeclinable		968.24	1/95	54r
Visitation and viewing		332.66	1/95	54r
Groceries				
Groceries, ACCRA Index		104.90	12/94	2c
Apples, Red Delicious	lb.	0.68	12/94	82r
Baby food, strained vegetables, lowest price	4-4.5 oz.	0.40	12/94	2c
Bacon, sliced	lb.	1.88	12/94	82r
Bananas	lb.	0.39	12/94	2c
Bananas	lb.	0.41	12/94	82r
Beef or hamburger, ground	lb.	1.66	12/94	2c
Beef purchases	year	197	91	81r
Beef, stew, boneless	lb.	2.52	12/94	82r
Beverage purchases, alcoholic	year	293	91	81r
Beverage purchases, nonalcoholic	year	203	91	81r
Bologna, all beef or mixed	lb.	2.12	12/94	82r
Bread, white	24-oz.	0.92	12/94	2c
Bread, white, pan	lb.	0.76	12/94	82r
Cabbage	lb.	0.44	12/94	82r
Carrots, short trimmed and topped	lb.	0.44	12/94	82r
Cereals and bakery products purchases	year	347	91	81r
Cereals and cereals products purchases	year	119	91	81r
Cheddar cheese, natural	lb.	3.28	12/94	82r
Cheese, Kraft grated Parmesan	8-oz.	3.22	12/94	2c
Chicken breast, bone-in	lb.	1.61	12/94	82r
Chicken, fresh, whole	lb.	0.89	12/94	82r
Chicken, whole fryer	lb.	0.87	12/94	2c
Chuck roast, USDA choice, boneless	lb.	2.33	12/94	82r
Cigarettes, Winston, Kings	carton	16.54	12/94	2c
Coffee, 100%, ground roast, all sizes	lb.	4.28	12/94	82r
Coffee, vacuum-packed	13 oz.	3.57	12/94	2c
Cookies, chocolate chip	lb.	2.72	12/94	82r
Corn Flakes, Kellogg's or Post Toasties	18 oz.	2.56	12/94	2c

Values are in dollars or fractions of dollars. In the column headed *Ref*, references are shown to sources. Each reference is followed by a letter. These refer to the geographical level for which data were reported: s=State, r=Region, and c=City or metro. The abbreviation *ex* is used to mean *except* or *excluding*; *exp* stands for expenditures. For other abbreviations and further explanations, please see the Introduction.

Eau Claire, WI - continued

Item	Per	Value	Date	Ref.
Groceries				
Corn, frozen, whole kernel, lowest price	10 oz.	0.74	12/94	2c
Dairy products (other) purchases	year	148	91	81r
Eggs, Grade A large	dozen	0.65	12/94	2c
Eggs, Grade A large	dozen	0.76	12/94	82r
Fish and seafood purchases	year	61	91	81r
Flour, white, all purpose	lb.	0.22	12/94	82r
Food purchases, food eaten at home	year	2313	91	81r
Foods purchased away from home, not prepared by consumer	year	1709	91	81r
Fruits and vegetables purchases	year	372	91	81r
Grapefruit	lb.	0.47	12/94	82r
Grapes, Thompson seedless	lb.	2.15	12/94	82r
Ground beef, 100% beef	lb.	1.37	12/94	82r
Ground chuck, 100% beef	lb.	1.81	12/94	82r
Ham, boneless, exc. canned	lb.	2.16	12/94	82r
Ice cream, prepackaged, bulk, regular	1/2 gal.	2.48	12/94	82r
Lemons	lb.	1.08	12/94	82r
Lettuce, iceberg	lb.	0.81	12/94	82r
Lettuce, iceberg	head	0.79	12/94	2c
Margarine, Blue Bonnet or Parkay cubes	lb.	0.67	12/94	2c
Margarine, stick	lb.	0.81	12/94	82r
Meats, poultry, fish, and eggs purchases	year	591	91	81r
Milk and cream (fresh) purchases	year	132	91	81r
Milk, whole	1/2 gal.	1.48	12/94	2c
Orange juice, frozen concentrate 12-oz. can	16 oz.	1.41	12/94	82r
Orange juice, Minute Maid frozen	12-oz.	1.19	12/94	2c
Oranges, Navel	lb.	0.56	12/94	82r
Peaches, halves or slices, Hunt's, Del Monte, or Libby's	29-oz.	1.38	12/94	2c
Peanut butter, creamy, all sizes	lb.	1.81	12/94	82r
Peas, sweet, Del Monte or Green Giant	15-17 oz.	0.58	12/94	2c
Pork chops, center cut, bone-in	lb.	2.76	12/94	82r
Pork purchases	year	130	91	81r
Potato chips	16-oz.	2.81	12/94	82r
Potatoes, frozen, French fried	lb.	0.83	12/94	82r
Potatoes, white	lb.	0.28	12/94	82r
Potatoes, white or red	10-lb. sack	1.67	12/94	2c
Round roast, USDA choice, boneless	lb.	2.90	12/94	82r
Sausage, Jimmy Dean, 100% pork	lb.	2.74	12/94	2c
Shortening, vegetable oil blends	lb.	0.88	12/94	82r
Shortening, vegetable, Crisco	3-lb.	2.81	12/94	2c
Soft drink, Coca Cola, ex deposit	2 lit	1.13	12/94	2c
Spaghetti and macaroni	lb.	0.78	12/94	82r
Steak, rib eye, USDA choice, boneless	lb.	6.15	12/94	82r
Steak, round, graded & ungraded, exc. USDA prime & choice	lb.	2.72	12/94	82r
Steak, round, USDA choice, boneless	lb.	3.02	12/94	82r
Steak, sirloin, USDA choice, boneless	lb.	3.85	12/94	82r
Steak, t-bone	lb.	5.33	12/94	2c
Steak, T-bone, USDA choice, bone-in	lb.	5.38	12/94	82r
Sugar and other sweets, eaten at home, expenditures	year	91	91	81r
Sugar, cane or beet	4 lbs.	1.34	12/94	2c
Sugar, white, all sizes	lb.	0.36	12/94	82r
Tobacco products and smoking supplies, total expenditures	year	298	91	81r
Tomatoes, field grown	lb.	1.36	12/94	82r
Tomatoes, Hunt's or Del Monte	14.5 oz.	0.74	12/94	2c
Tuna, chunk, light	lb.	1.94	12/94	82r
Tuna, chunk, light, oil-packed	6.125- 6.5 oz.	0.76	12/94	2c
Turkey, frozen, whole	lb.	0.96	12/94	82r
Yogurt, natural, fruit flavored	8 oz.	0.62	12/94	82r
Goods and Services				
Miscellaneous goods and services, ACCRA Index		102.40	12/94	2c

Eau Claire, WI - continued

Item	Per	Value	Date	Ref.
Health Care				
Health care, ACCRA Index		107.40	12/94	2c
Antibiotic ointment, Polysporin	1.5 oz.	4.27	12/94	2c
Childbirth, Cesarean delivery, hospital charge	birth	5101.00	12/91	69r
Childbirth, Cesarean delivery, physician charge	birth	2234.00	12/91	69r
Childbirth, normal delivery, hospital charge	birth	2891.00	12/91	69r
Childbirth, normal delivery, physician charge	birth	1623.00	12/91	69r
Dentist's fee, adult teeth cleaning and periodic oral exam	visit	52.00	12/94	2c
Doctor's fee, routine exam, established patient	visit	55.00	12/94	2c
Drugs, expenditures	year	248	91	81r
Health care, total expenditures	year	1336	91	81r
Health insurance expenditures	year	550	91	81r
Hospital care, semiprivate room	day	280.00	12/94	2c
Insurance premium, family medical care	month	378.79	1/95	41s
Medical services expenditures	year	457	91	81r
Medical supplies expenditures	year	82	91	81r
Household Goods				
Appl. repair, service call, wash mach	min. lab. chg.	29.90	12/94	2c
Floor coverings, expenditures	year	105	91	81r
Furniture, expenditures	year	291	91	81r
Household equipment, misc. expenditures	year	341	91	81r
Household expenditures, miscellaneous	year	162	91	81r
Household furnishings and equipment, expenditures	year	1042	91	81r
Household operations expenditures	year	365	91	81r
Household textiles, expenditures	year	101	91	81r
Housekeeping supplies, expenditures	year	390	91	81r
Laundry and cleaning supplies, expenditures	year	110	91	81r
Laundry detergent, Tide Ultra, Bold, or Cheer	42 oz.	3.80	12/94	2c
Postage and stationery, expenditures	year	115	91	81r
Tissues, facial, Kleenex brand	175	0.99	12/94	2c
Housing				
Housing, ACCRA Index		107.80	12/94	2c
Add garage/carport		8,479	3/95	74r
Add room(s)		21,347	3/95	74r
Apartment condominium or co-op, median	unit	87100	12/94	62r
Bathroom addition, average cost	add	9734.00	3/95	13r
Bathroom remodeling, average cost	remod	6414.00	3/95	13r
Bedroom, master suite addition, average cost	add	27122.00	3/95	13r
Deck addition, average cost	add	6665.00	3/95	13r
Dwellings (owned), expenditures	year	2566	91	81r
Enclose porch/patio/breezeway		4,556	3/95	74r
Exterior remodeling, average cost	remod	15395.00	3/95	13r
Family room addition, average cost	add	27658.00	3/95	13r
Finish room in basement/attic		5,074	3/95	74r
Home, existing, single-family, median	unit	106500	12/94	62r
House payment, principal and interest, 25% down payment	mo.	837	12/94	2c
House, 1800 sq ft, 8000 sq ft lot, new, urban, utilities	total	133500	12/94	2c
Kitchen remodeling, major, average cost	remod	17084.00	3/95	13r
Kitchen remodeling, minor, average cost	remod	5804.00	3/95	13r
Maintenance, repairs, insurance, and other housing expenditures	year	484	91	81r
Mortgage interest and charges expenditures	year	1443	91	81r
Mtge. rate, incl. points and orig. fee, 30-year conv. fixed or ARM	mo.	9.44	12/94	2c
Office, home addition, average cost	add	8121.00	3/95	13r
Princ. & int., mortgage, median-price exist. sing.-family home	mo.	515	12/94	62r
Property taxes expenditures	year	639	91	81r
Redesign, restructure more than half of home's interior		9,114	3/95	74r

Values are in dollars or fractions of dollars. In the column headed *Ref*, references are shown to sources. Each reference is followed by a letter. These refer to the geographical level for which data were reported: s = State, r = Region, and c = City or metro. The abbreviation *ex* is used to mean *except* or *excluding*; *exp* stands for *expenditures*. For other abbreviations and further explanations, please see the Introduction.

Eau Claire, WI - continued

Item	Per	Value	Date	Ref.
Housing				
Rent, apartment, 2 br., 1 1/2-2 baths, unfurnished, 950 sq ft, water	mo.	536	12/94	2c
Rental units expenditures	year	1200	91	81r
Sun-space addition, average cost	add	23768.00	3/95	13r
Wing addition, two-story, average cost	add	50410.00	3/95	13r
Insurance and Pensions				
Auto insurance, private passenger	year	554.10	12/94	71s
Insurance and pensions, personal, expenditures	year	2408	91	81r
Insurance, life and other personal, expenditures	year	355	91	81r
Pensions and Social Security, expenditures	year	2053	91	81r
Legal Assistance				
Legal work, law firm associate	hour	90		10r
Legal work, law firm partner	hour	139		10r
Personal Goods				
Shampoo, Alberto VO5	15-oz.	1.17	12/94	2c
Toothpaste, Crest or Colgate	6-7 oz.	2.28	12/94	2c
Personal Services				
Dry cleaning, man's 2-pc. suit		6.75	12/94	2c
Haircut, man's barbershop, no styling		8.49	12/94	2c
Haircut, woman's shampoo, trim, blow-dry		15.75	12/94	2c
Personal services expenditures	year	203	91	81r
Restaurant Food				
Chicken, fried, thigh and drumstick		2.09	12/94	2c
Dining expenditures, family	week	30.03	94 .	73r
Hamburger with cheese	1/4 lb.	1.80	12/94	2c
Pizza, Pizza Hut or Pizza Inn	12-13 in.	8.99	12/94	2c
Taxes				
Taxes, Federal income, expenditures	year	1756	91	81r
Taxes, personal, expenditures	year	2426	91	81r
Taxes, State and local income, expenditures	year	568	91	81r
Transportation				
Transportation, ACCRA Index		95.10	12/94	2c
Bus fare, up to 10 miles	one-way	0.75	12/94	2c
Cars and trucks purchased, new	year	891	91	81r
Cars and trucks purchased, used	year	1155	91	81r
Driver's learning permit fee	perm	20.00	1/94	84s
Driver's license fee	orig	10.00	1/94	84s
Driver's license fee, duplicate	lic	4.00	1/94	84s
Driver's license reinstatement fee, min.	susp	50.00	1/94	85s
Driver's license renewal fee	renew	10.00	1/94	84s
Identification card, nondriver	card	4.00	1/94	83s
Motorcycle license fee	orig	4.00	1/94	84s
Motorcycle license fee, duplicate	lic	4.00	1/94	84s
Motorcycle license renewal fee	renew	4.00	1/94	84s
Public transportation expenditures	year	209	91	81r
Tire balance, computer or spin bal., front	wheel	6.00	12/94	2c
Transportation expenditures, total	year	4792	91	81r
Vehicle finance charges	year	300	91	81r
Vehicle insurance expenditures	year	485	91	81r
Vehicle maintenance and repairs expenditures	year	534	91	81r
Vehicle purchases	year	2068	91	81r
Vehicle rental, leases, licenses, etc. expenditures	year	197	91	81r
Vehicles purchased, other than cars and trucks	year	22	91	81r
Utilities				
Utilities, ACCRA Index		95.10	12/94	2c
Electricity expenditures	year	668	91	81r
Electricity, (part.), other, 1800 sq. ft., new home	mo.	46.18	12/94	2c
Electricity, summer, 250 KWH	month	20.41	8/93	64c
Electricity, summer, 500 KWH	month	37.32	8/93	64c
Electricity, summer, 750 KWH	month	54.23	8/93	64c

Eau Claire, WI - continued

Item	Per	Value	Date	Ref.
Utilities - continued				
Electricity, summer, 1000 KWh	month	71.14	8/93	64c
Utilities, fuels, and public services, total expenditures	year	1838	91	81r
Water and other public services, expenditures	year	167	91	81r
Weddings				
Bridal attendants' gowns	event	750	10/93	76r
Bridal gown	event	852	10/93	76r
Bridal headpiece and veil	event	167	10/93	76r
Bride's wedding band	event	708	10/93	76r
Clergy	event	224	10/93	76r
Engagement ring	event	2756	10/93	76r
Flowers	event	863	10/93	76r
Formal wear for groom	event	106	10/93	76r
Groom's attendants' formal wear	event	530	10/93	76r
Groom's wedding band	event	402	10/93	76r
Music	event	600	10/93	76r
Photography	event	1088	10/93	76r
Shoes for bride	event	50	10/93	76r
Videography	event	483	10/93	76r
Wedding invitations and announcements	event	342	10/93	76r
Wedding reception	event	7000	10/93	76r

El Paso, TX

Item	Per	Value	Date	Ref.
Composite, ACCRA index		94.20	12/94	2c
Alcoholic Beverages				
Beer, Miller Lite, Bud, 12-oz., ex deposit	6	3.95	12/94	2c
J & B Scotch	750-ml.	18.89	12/94	2c
Wine, Gallo Chablis blanc	1.5-lit	4.65	12/94	2c
Appliances				
Appliances (major), expenditures	year	153	91	81r
Average annual exp.				
Food, health care, personal goods, services	year	27020	91	81r
Charity				
Cash contributions, expenditures	year	839	91	81r
Clothing				
Apparel, men and boys, total expenditures	year	380	91	81r
Apparel, women and girls, total expenditures	year	660	91	81r
Footwear, expenditures	year	193	91	81r
Jeans, man's denim		27.77	12/94	2c
Shirt, man's dress shirt		31.98	12/94	2c
Undervest, boy's size 10-14, cotton	3	4.69	12/94	2c
Communications				
Long-distance telephone rate, day, addl. min., 1-10 mi.	min.	0.08	12/93	9s
Long-distance telephone rate, day, initial min., 1-10 mi.	min.	0.10	12/93	9s
Newspaper subscription, dly. and Sun. delivery	month	10.50	12/94	2c
Phone line, single, business, field visit	inst	71.90	12/93	9s
Phone line, single, business, no field visit	inst	57.30	12/93	9s
Phone line, single, residence, field visit	inst	52.95	12/93	9s
Phone line, single, residence, no field visit	inst	38.35	12/93	9s
Telephone bill, family of four	month	16.53	12/94	2c
Telephone service, expenditures	year	616	91	81r
Telephone, residential, flat rate	mo.	9.35	12/93	8c
Education				
Board, 4-year private college/university	year	2084	8/94	80s
Board, 4-year public college/university	year	1675	8/94	80s
Education, total expenditures	year	319	91	81r
Room, 4-year private college/university	year	1840	8/94	80s
Room, 4-year public college/university	year	1756	8/94	80s
Total cost, 4-year private college/university	year	11876	8/94	80s
Total cost, 4-year public college/university	year	4935	8/94	80s

Values are in dollars or fractions of dollars. In the column headed *Ref*, references are shown to sources. Each reference is followed by a letter. These refer to the geographical level for which data were reported: s=State, r=Region, and c=City or metro. The abbreviation *ex* is used to mean *except* or *excluding*; *exp* stands for expenditures. For other abbreviations and further explanations, please see the Introduction.

El Paso, TX - continued

Item	Per	Value	Date	Ref.
Education				
Tuition, 2-year public college/university, in-state	year	625	8/94	80s
Tuition, 4-year private college/university, in-state	year	7952	8/94	80s
Tuition, 4-year public college/university, in-state	year	1503	8/94	80s
Energy and Fuels				
Energy, combined forms, 1800 sq. ft.	mo.	104.32	12/94	2c
Energy, exc. electricity, 1800 sq. ft.	mo.	23.57	12/94	2c
Fuel oil and other fuels, expenditures	year	56	91	81r
Gas, cooking, winter, 10 therms	month	8.09	2/94	65c
Gas, cooking, winter, 30 therms	month	14.26	2/94	65c
Gas, cooking, winter, 50 therms	month	20.44	2/94	65c
Gas, heating, winter, 100 therms	month	35.87	2/94	65c
Gas, heating, winter, average use	month	42.04	2/94	65c
Gas, natural, expenditures	year	150	91	81r
Gas, reg unlead, taxes inc., cash, self-service	gal	1.25	12/94	2c
Gasoline and motor oil purchased	year	1152	91	81r
Gasoline, unleaded midgrade	gallon	1.21	4/93	82r
Gasoline, unleaded premium	gallon	1.30	4/93	82r
Gasoline, unleaded regular	gallon	1.10	4/93	82r
Entertainment				
Boat ride, bumper boat, family entertainment center	1 turn	3.25	5/94	91c
Bowling, evening rate	game	2.04	12/94	2c
Concert ticket, Pearl Jam group	perf	20.00	94	50r
Entertainment, total expenditures	year	1266	91	81r
Fees and admissions, expenditures	year	306	91	81r
Game tokens, family entertainment center	4	1.00	5/94	91c
Go-kart ride, family entertainment center	1 ride	3.50	5/94	91c
Golf game, miniature, family entertainment center	1 round	4.00	5/94	91c
Hot dog, family entertainment center	one	1.00	5/94	91c
Monopoly game, Parker Brothers', No. 9	game	11.68	12/94	2c
Movie	adm	6.17	12/94	2c
Pets, toys, playground equipment, expenditures	year	271	91	81r
Reading, expenditures	year	131	91	81r
Soft drink, family entertainment center	one	1.00	5/94	91c
Souvenir, family entertainment center	one	7.00	5/94	91c
Televisions, radios, and sound equipment, expenditures	year	439	91	81r
Tennis balls, yellow, Wilson or Penn, 3	can	2.63	12/94	2c
Funerals				
Burial, immediate, container provided by funeral home		1574.60	1/95	54r
Cards, acknowledgment		22.24	1/95	54r
Casket, minimum alternative		239.41	1/95	54r
Cosmetology, hair care, etc.		91.04	1/95	54r
Cremation, direct, container provided by funeral home		1085.15	1/95	54r
Embalming		281.30	1/95	54r
Funeral, funeral home		323.04	1/95	54r
Funeral, other facility		327.58	1/95	54r
Graveside service		355.19	1/95	54r
Hearse, local		141.89	1/95	54r
Limousine, local		99.40	1/95	54r
Memorial service		284.67	1/95	54r
Service charge, professional, nondeclinable		904.06	1/95	54r
Visitation and viewing		187.04	1/95	54r
Groceries				
Groceries, ACCRA Index		93.80	12/94	2c
Apples, Red Delicious	lb.	0.73	12/94	82r
Baby food, strained vegetables, lowest price	4-4.5 oz.	0.24	12/94	2c
Bacon, sliced	lb.	1.67	12/94	82r
Bananas	lb.	0.42	12/94	2c
Bananas	lb.	0.42	12/94	82r
Beef or hamburger, ground	lb.	1.05	12/94	2c

El Paso, TX - continued

Item	Per	Value	Date	Ref.
Groceries - continued				
Beef purchases	year	213	91	81r
Beverage purchases, alcoholic	year	249	91	81r
Beverage purchases, nonalcoholic	year	207	91	81r
Bologna, all beef or mixed	lb.	2.27	12/94	82r
Bread, white	24-oz.	0.63	12/94	2c
Bread, white, pan	lb.	0.68	12/94	82r
Cabbage	lb.	0.42	12/94	82r
Carrots, short trimmed and topped	lb.	0.53	12/94	82r
Cereals and bakery products purchases	year	345	91	81r
Cereals and cereals products purchases	year	127	91	81r
Cheddar cheese, natural	lb.	3.58	12/94	82r
Cheese, Kraft grated Parmesan	8-oz.	3.53	12/94	2c
Chicken breast, bone-in	lb.	1.71	12/94	82r
Chicken, fresh, whole	lb.	0.78	12/94	82r
Chicken, whole fryer	lb.	0.59	12/94	2c
Chuck roast, USDA choice, boneless	lb.	2.26	12/94	82r
Cigarettes, Winston, Kings	carton	17.19	12/94	2c
Coffee, vacuum-packed	13 oz.	3.68	12/94	2c
Corn Flakes, Kellogg's or Post Toasties	18 oz.	2.39	12/94	2c
Corn, frozen, whole kernel, lowest price	10 oz.	0.76	12/94	2c
Crackers, soda, salted	lb.	1.27	12/94	82r
Cucumbers	lb.	0.65	12/94	82r
Dairy products (other) purchases	year	141	91	81r
Eggs, Grade A large	dozen	0.82	12/94	2c
Eggs, Grade A large	dozen	0.87	12/94	82r
Fish and seafood purchases	year	72	91	81r
Flour, white, all purpose	lb.	0.23	12/94	82r
Food purchases, food eaten at home	year	2381	91	81r
Foods purchased away from home, not prepared by consumer	year	1696	91	81r
Frankfurters, all meat or all beef	lb.	1.74	12/94	82r
Fruits and vegetables purchases	year	380	91	81r
Grapefruit	lb.	0.45	12/94	82r
Grapes, Thompson seedless	lb.	2.30	12/94	82r
Ground beef, 100% beef	lb.	1.37	12/94	82r
Ground chuck, 100% beef	lb.	1.97	12/94	82r
Ham, boneless, exc. canned	lb.	2.54	12/94	82r
Ice cream, prepackaged, bulk, regular	1/2 gal.	2.47	12/94	82r
Lemons	lb.	1.02	12/94	82r
Lettuce, iceberg	lb.	0.96	12/94	82r
Lettuce, iceberg	head	0.73	12/94	2c
Margarine, Blue Bonnet or Parkay cubes	lb.	0.71	12/94	2c
Margarine, stick	lb.	0.77	12/94	82r
Meats, poultry, fish, and eggs purchases	year	655	91	81r
Milk and cream (fresh) purchases	year	130	91	81r
Milk, whole	1/2 gal.	1.53	12/94	2c
Orange juice, frozen concentrate 12-oz. can	16 oz.	1.36	12/94	82r
Orange juice, Minute Maid frozen	12-oz.	1.07	12/94	2c
Oranges, Navel	lb.	0.54	12/94	82r
Peaches, halves or slices, Hunt's, Del Monte, or Libby's	29-oz.	1.18	12/94	2c
Pears, Anjou	lb.	0.81	12/94	82r
Peas, sweet, Del Monte or Green Giant	15-17 oz.	0.49	12/94	2c
Pork chops, center cut, bone-in	lb.	3.07	12/94	82r
Pork purchases	year	142	91	81r
Potato chips	16-oz.	3.15	12/94	82r
Potatoes, frozen, French fried	lb.	0.82	12/94	82r
Potatoes, white	lb.	0.34	12/94	82r
Potatoes, white or red	10-lb. sack	2.03	12/94	2c
Rice, white, long grain, uncooked	lb.	0.48	12/94	82r
Round roast, USDA choice, boneless	lb.	2.91	12/94	82r
Sausage, fresh	lb.	1.82	12/94	82r
Sausage, Jimmy Dean, 100% pork	lb.	1.91	12/94	2c
Shortening, vegetable oil blends	lb.	0.75	12/94	82r
Shortening, vegetable, Crisco	3-lb.	2.99	12/94	2c
Soft drink, Coca Cola, ex deposit	2 lit	1.26	12/94	2c
Spaghetti and macaroni	lb.	0.87	12/94	82r
Steak, rib eye, USDA choice, boneless	lb.	6.85	12/94	82r

Values are in dollars or fractions of dollars. In the column headed *Ref*, references are shown to sources. Each reference is followed by a letter. These refer to the geographical level for which data were reported: s = State, r = Region, and c = City or metro. The abbreviation *ex* is used to mean *except* or *excluding*; *exp* stands for expenditures. For other abbreviations and further explanations, please see the Introduction.

El Paso, TX - continued

Item	Per	Value	Date	Ref.
Groceries				
Steak, round, graded & ungraded, exc. USDA prime & choice	lb.	2.96	12/94	82r
Steak, round, USDA choice, boneless	lb.	3.17	12/94	82r
Steak, sirloin, USDA choice, boneless	lb.	4.12	12/94	82r
Steak, t-bone	lb.	4.57	12/94	2c
Steak, T-bone, USDA choice, bone-in	lb.	5.63	12/94	82r
Sugar and other sweets, eaten at home, expenditures	year	93	91	81r
Sugar, cane or beet	4 lbs.	1.37	12/94	2c
Sugar, white, all sizes	lb.	0.39	12/94	82r
Tobacco products and smoking supplies, total expenditures	year	286	91	81r
Tomatoes, field grown	lb.	1.36	12/94	82r
Tomatoes, Hunt's or Del Monte	14.5 oz.	0.74	12/94	2c
Tuna, chunk, light	lb.	1.94	12/94	82r
Tuna, chunk, light, oil-packed	6.125-6.5 oz.	0.82	12/94	2c
Turkey, frozen, whole	lb.	0.96	12/94	82r
Yogurt, natural, fruit flavored	8 oz.	0.58	12/94	82r
Goods and Services				
Miscellaneous goods and services, ACCRA Index		99.00	12/94	2c
Health Care				
Health care, ACCRA Index		93.40	12/94	2c
Adenosine, emergency room	treat	100.00	95	23r
Antibiotic ointment, Polysporin	1.5 oz.	4.67	12/94	2c
Bladder tap, superpubic, infant, emergency room	treat	119.00	95	23r
Blood analysis, emergency room	treat	25.00	95	23r
Blood tests, abdominal pain, emergency room	treat	25.00	95	23r
Burn dressing, emergency room	treat	266.00	95	23r
Cardiology interpretation, emergency room	treat	26.00	95	23r
Chest X-ray, emergency room	treat	78.00	95	23r
Childbirth, Cesarean delivery, hospital charge	birth	5462.00	12/91	69r
Childbirth, Cesarean delivery, physician charge	birth	2228.00	12/91	69r
Childbirth, normal delivery, hospital charge	birth	2943.00	12/91	69r
Childbirth, normal delivery, physician charge	birth	1619.00	12/91	69r
Defibrillation pads, emergency room	treat	6.00	95	23r
Dentist's fee, adult teeth cleaning and periodic oral exam	visit	48.60	12/94	2c
Doctor's fee, routine exam, established patient	visit	37.80	12/94	2c
Drugs, expenditures	year	297	91	81r
Gastric tube insertion, nasal, emergency room	treat	25.00	95	23r
Health care, total expenditures	year	1600	91	81r
Health insurance expenditures	year	637	91	81r
Heart monitor, emergency room	treat	40.00	95	23r
Hospital care, semiprivate room	day	316.40	12/94	2c
Insurance premium, family medical care	month	389.25	1/95	41s
Intravenous fluids, emergency room	treat	130.00	95	23r
Intravenous fluids, emergency room	liter	26.00	95	23r
Intravenous line, central, emergency room	treat	342.00	95	23r
Liver function tests, abdominal pain, emergency room	treat	26.00	95	23r
Medical care charges, total, emergency room, third-degree burns	treat	2101.00	95	23r
Medical care charges, total, emergency, infant with fever	treat	628.00	95	23r
Medical services expenditures	year	573	91	81r
Medical supplies expenditures	year	93	91	81r
Morphine, emergency room	treat	34.00	95	23r
Nursing care and facilities charges, emergency room	treat	252.00	95	23r
Nursing care and facilities charges, emergency, infant with fever	treat	252.00	95	23r

El Paso, TX - continued

Item	Per	Value	Date	Ref.
Health Care - continued				
Nursing care and facilities charges, emergency, third-degree burns	treat	861.00	95	23r
Physician's charges, emergency, infant with fever	treat	212.00	95	23r
Physician's charges, emergency, third-degree burns	treat	372.00	95	23r
Physician's fee, emergency room	treat	372.00	95	23r
Physician's fee, general practitioner	visit	51.20	12/93	60r
Surgery, open-heart	proc	42374.00	1/93	14r
Ultrasound, abdominal, emergency room	treat	276.00	95	23r
Urinalysis, emergency room	treat	20.00	95	23r
Urinalysis, infant, emergency room	treat	20.00	95	23r
X-rays, emergency room	treat	78.00	95	23r
Household Goods				
Appl. repair, service call, wash mach	min. lab. chg.	32.88	12/94	2c
Floor coverings, expenditures	year	48	91	81r
Furniture, expenditures	year	280	91	81r
Household equipment, misc. expenditures	year	342	91	81r
Household expenditures, miscellaneous	year	256	91	81r
Household furnishings and equipment, expenditures	year	988	91	81r
Household operations expenditures	year	468	91	81r
Household textiles, expenditures	year	95	91	81r
Housekeeping supplies, expenditures	year	380	91	81r
Laundry and cleaning supplies, expenditures	year	109	91	81r
Laundry detergent, Tide Ultra, Bold, or Cheer	42 oz.	3.19	12/94	2c
Postage and stationery, expenditures	year	105	91	81r
Tissues, facial, Kleenex brand	175	1.07	12/94	2c
Housing				
Housing, ACCRA Index		84.30	12/94	2c
Add garage/carport		6,980	3/95	74r
Add room(s)		11,403	3/95	74r
Apartment condominium or co-op, median	unit	68600	12/94	62r
Dwellings (owned), expenditures	year	2428	91	81r
Enclose porch/patio/breezeway		4,572	3/95	74r
Finish room in basement/attic		3,794	3/95	74r
Home, existing, single-family, median	unit	120200	12/94	62r
Home, existing, single-family, median	unit	75.40	12/94	62c
House payment, principal and interest, 25% down payment	mo.	622	12/94	2c
House, 1800 sq ft, 8000 sq ft lot, new, urban, utilities	total	99773	12/94	2c
Maintenance, repairs, insurance, and other housing expenditures	year	531	91	81r
Mortgage interest and charges expenditures	year	1506	91	81r
Mtge. rate, incl. points and orig. fee, 30-year conv. fixed or ARM	mo.	9.37	12/94	2c
Princ. & int., mortgage, median-price exist. sing.-family home	mo.	540	12/94	62r
Property taxes expenditures	year	391	91	81r
Redesign, restructure more than half of home's interior		17,641	3/95	74r
Rent, apartment, 2 br., 1 1/2-2 baths, unfurnished, 950 sq ft, water	mo.	515	12/94	2c
Rental units expenditures	year	1264	91	81r
Insurance and Pensions				
Auto insurance, private passenger	year	785.78	12/94	71s
Insurance and pensions, personal, expenditures	year	2395	91	81r
Insurance, life and other personal, expenditures	year	368	91	81r
Pensions and Social Security, expenditures	year	2027	91	81r
Personal Goods				
Shampoo, Alberto VO5	15-oz.	1.31	12/94	2c
Toothpaste, Crest or Colgate	6-7 oz.	2.21	12/94	2c

Values are in dollars or fractions of dollars. In the column headed *Ref*, references are shown to sources. Each reference is followed by a letter. These refer to the geographical level for which data were reported: s = State, r = Region, and c = City or metro. The abbreviation *ex* is used to mean *except* or *excluding*; *exp* stands for *expenditures*. For other abbreviations and further explanations, please see the Introduction.

El Paso, TX - continued

Item	Per	Value	Date	Ref.
Personal Services				
Dry cleaning, man's 2-pc. suit		5.80	12/94	2c
Haircut, man's barbershop, no styling		7.20	12/94	2c
Haircut, woman's shampoo, trim, blow-dry		26.40	12/94	2c
Personal services expenditures	year	212	91	81r
Restaurant Food				
Chicken, fried, thigh and drumstick		1.74	12/94	2c
Dining expenditures, family	week	33.83	94	73r
Hamburger with cheese	1/4 lb.	1.77	12/94	2c
Pizza, Pizza Hut or Pizza Inn	12-13 in.	7.97	12/94	2c
Taxes				
Tax, cigarettes	year	584.00	10/93	43s
Taxes, Federal income, expenditures	year	2275	91	81r
Taxes, personal, expenditures	year	2715	91	81r
Taxes, State and local income, expenditures	year	365	91	81r
Transportation				
Transportation, ACCRA Index		110.70	12/94	2c
Bus fare, one-way	trip	0.85	12/95	1c
Bus fare, up to 10 miles	one-way	0.75	12/94	2c
Cars and trucks purchased, new	year	1306	91	81r
Cars and trucks purchased, used	year	942	91	81r
Driver's learning permit fee	perm	5.00	1/94	84s
Driver's license fee	orig	16.00	1/94	84s
Driver's license fee, duplicate	lic	10.00	1/94	84s
Driver's license reinstatement fee, min.	susp	50.00	1/94	85s
Driver's license renewal fee	renew	16.00	1/94	84s
Identification card, nondriver	card	10.00	1/94	83s
Motorcycle learning permit fee	perm	5.00	1/94	84s
Motorcycle license fee	orig	16.00	1/94	84s
Motorcycle license fee, duplicate	lic	10.00	1/94	84s
Motorcycle license renewal fee	renew	21.00	1/94	84s
Public transportation expenditures	year	249	91	81r
Tire balance, computer or spin bal., front	wheel	8.05	12/94	2c
Transportation expenditures, total	year	5307	91	81r
Vehicle finance charges	year	346	91	81r
Vehicle insurance expenditures	year	544	91	81r
Vehicle maintenance and repairs expenditures	year	600	91	81r
Vehicle purchases	year	2275	91	81r
Vehicle rental, leases, licenses, etc. expenditures	year	141	91	81r
Vehicles purchased, other than cars and trucks	year	27	91	81r
Utilities				
Utilities, ACCRA Index		91.90	12/94	2c
Electricity expenditures	year	950	91	81r
Electricity, (part.), other, 1800 sq. ft., new home	mo.	80.75	12/94	2c
Electricity, summer, 250 KWh	month	28.68	8/93	64c
Electricity, summer, 500 KWh	month	52.85	8/93	64c
Electricity, summer, 750 KWh	month	77.02	8/93	64c
Electricity, summer, 1000 KWh	month	101.19	8/93	64c
Utilities, fuels, and public services, total expenditures	year	2000	91	81r
Water and other public services, expenditures	year	227	91	81r
Weddings				
Bridal attendants' gowns	event	750	10/93	76r
Bridal gown	event	852	10/93	76r
Bridal headpiece and veil	event	167	10/93	76r
Bride's wedding band	event	708	10/93	76r
Clergy	event	224	10/93	76r
Engagement ring	event	2756	10/93	76r
Flowers	event	863	10/93	76r
Formal wear for groom	event	106	10/93	76r
Groom's attendants' formal wear	event	530	10/93	76r
Groom's wedding band	event	402	10/93	76r
Music	event	600	10/93	76r

El Paso, TX - continued

Item	Per	Value	Date	Ref.
Weddings - continued				
Photography	event	1088	10/93	76r
Shoes for bride	event	50	10/93	76r
Videography	event	483	10/93	76r
Wedding invitations and announcements	event	342	10/93	76r
Wedding reception	event	7000	10/93	76r

Elkhart-Goshen, IN

Item	Per	Value	Date	Ref.
Appliances				
Appliances (major), expenditures	year	131	91	81r
Average annual exp.				
Food, health care, personal goods, services	year	25935	91	81r
Charity				
Cash contributions, expenditures	year	745	91	81r
Clothing				
Apparel, men and boys, total expenditures	year	332	91	81r
Apparel, women and girls, total expenditures	year	578	91	81r
Footwear, expenditures	year	164	91	81r
Communications				
Long-distance telephone rate, day, addl. min., 1-10 mi.	min.	0.10	12/93	9s
Long-distance telephone rate, day, initial min., 1-10 mi.	min.	0.18	12/93	9s
Phone line, single, business, field visit	inst	59.00	12/93	9s
Phone line, single, business, no field visit	inst	59.00	12/93	9s
Phone line, single, residence, field visit	inst	47.00	12/93	9s
Phone line, single, residence, no field visit	inst	47.00	12/93	9s
Telephone service, expenditures	year	547	91	81r
Education				
Board, 4-year private college/university	year	2095	8/94	80s
Board, 4-year public college/university	year	2300	8/94	80s
Education, total expenditures	year	394	91	81r
Room, 4-year private college/university	year	1784	8/94	80s
Room, 4-year public college/university	year	1718	8/94	80s
Total cost, 4-year private college/university	year	15045	8/94	80s
Total cost, 4-year public college/university	year	6639	8/94	80s
Tuition, 2-year public college/university, in-state	year	1737	8/94	80s
Tuition, 4-year private college/university, in-state	year	11165	8/94	80s
Tuition, 4-year public college/university, in-state	year	2621	8/94	80s
Energy and Fuels				
Fuel oil and other fuels, expenditures	year	83	91	81r
Gas, natural, expenditures	year	373	91	81r
Gasoline and motor oil purchased	year	1000	91	81r
Gasoline, unleaded midgrade	gallon	1.15	4/93	82r
Gasoline, unleaded premium	gallon	1.23	4/93	82r
Gasoline, unleaded regular	gallon	1.07	4/93	82r
Entertainment				
Entertainment, total expenditures	year	1356	91	81r
Fees and admissions, expenditures	year	347	91	81r
Pets, toys, playground equipment, expenditures	year	270	91	81r
Reading, expenditures	year	160	91	81r
Televisions, radios, and sound equipment, expenditures	year	433	91	81r
Funerals				
Burial, immediate, container provided by funeral home		1268.31	1/95	54r
Cards, acknowledgment		26.12	1/95	54r
Casket, minimum alternative		198.03	1/95	54r
Cosmetology, hair care, etc.		122.19	1/95	54r
Cremation, direct, container provided by funeral home		977.81	1/95	54r
Embalming		334.00	1/95	54r
Funeral, funeral home		321.16	1/95	54r

Values are in dollars or fractions of dollars. In the column headed *Ref*, references are shown to sources. Each reference is followed by a letter. These refer to the geographical level for which data were reported: s=State, r=Region, and c=City or metro. The abbreviation *ex* is used to mean *except* or *excluding*; *exp* stands for expenditures. For other abbreviations and further explanations, please see the Introduction.

Elkhart-Goshen, IN - continued

Item	Per	Value	Date	Ref.
Funerals				
Funeral, other facility		317.73	1/95	54r
Graveside service		292.48	1/95	54r
Hearse, local		153.20	1/95	54r
Limousine, local		123.52	1/95	54r
Memorial service		356.30	1/95	54r
Service charge, professional, nondeclinable		968.24	1/95	54r
Visitation and viewing		332.66	1/95	54r
Groceries				
Apples, Red Delicious	lb.	0.68	12/94	82r
Bacon, sliced	lb.	1.88	12/94	82r
Bananas	lb.	0.41	12/94	82r
Beef purchases	year	197	91	81r
Beef, stew, boneless	lb.	2.52	12/94	82r
Beverage purchases, alcoholic	year	293	91	81r
Beverage purchases, nonalcoholic	year	203	91	81r
Bologna, all beef or mixed	lb.	2.12	12/94	82r
Bread, white, pan	lb.	0.76	12/94	82r
Cabbage	lb.	0.44	12/94	82r
Carrots, short trimmed and topped	lb.	0.44	12/94	82r
Cereals and bakery products purchases	year	347	91	81r
Cereals and cereals products purchases	year	119	91	81r
Cheddar cheese, natural	lb.	3.28	12/94	82r
Chicken breast, bone-in	lb.	1.61	12/94	82r
Chicken, fresh, whole	lb.	0.89	12/94	82r
Chuck roast, USDA choice, boneless	lb.	2.33	12/94	82r
Coffee, 100%, ground roast, all sizes	lb.	4.28	12/94	82r
Cookies, chocolate chip	lb.	2.72	12/94	82r
Dairy products (other) purchases	year	148	91	81r
Eggs, Grade A large	dozen	0.76	12/94	82r
Fish and seafood purchases	year	61	91	81r
Flour, white, all purpose	lb.	0.22	12/94	82r
Food purchases, food eaten at home	year	2313	91	81r
Foods purchased away from home, not prepared by consumer	year	1709	91	81r
Fruits and vegetables purchases	year	372	91	81r
Grapefruit	lb.	0.47	12/94	82r
Grapes, Thompson seedless	lb.	2.15	12/94	82r
Ground beef, 100% beef	lb.	1.37	12/94	82r
Ground chuck, 100% beef	lb.	1.81	12/94	82r
Ham, boneless, exc. canned	lb.	2.16	12/94	82r
Ice cream, prepackaged, bulk, regular	1/2 gal.	2.48	12/94	82r
Lemons	lb.	1.08	12/94	82r
Lettuce, iceberg	lb.	0.81	12/94	82r
Margarine, stick	lb.	0.81	12/94	82r
Meats, poultry, fish, and eggs purchases	year	591	91	81r
Milk and cream (fresh) purchases	year	132	91	81r
Orange juice, frozen concentrate 12-oz. can	16 oz.	1.41	12/94	82r
Oranges, Navel	lb.	0.56	12/94	82r
Peanut butter, creamy, all sizes	lb.	1.81	12/94	82r
Pork chops, center cut, bone-in	lb.	2.76	12/94	82r
Pork purchases	year	130	91	81r
Potato chips	16-oz.	2.81	12/94	82r
Potatoes, frozen, French fried	lb.	0.83	12/94	82r
Potatoes, white	lb.	0.28	12/94	82r
Round roast, USDA choice, boneless	lb.	2.90	12/94	82r
Shortening, vegetable oil blends	lb.	0.88	12/94	82r
Spaghetti and macaroni	lb.	0.78	12/94	82r
Steak, rib eye, USDA choice, boneless	lb.	6.15	12/94	82r
Steak, round, graded & ungraded, exc. USDA prime & choice	lb.	2.72	12/94	82r
Steak, round, USDA choice, boneless	lb.	3.02	12/94	82r
Steak, sirloin, USDA choice, boneless	lb.	3.85	12/94	82r
Steak, T-bone, USDA choice, bone-in	lb.	5.38	12/94	82r
Sugar and other sweets, eaten at home, expenditures	year	91	91	81r
Sugar, white, all sizes	lb.	0.36	12/94	82r
Tobacco products and smoking supplies, total expenditures	year	298	91	81r
Tomatoes, field grown	lb.	1.36	12/94	82r
Tuna, chunk, light	lb.	1.94	12/94	82r
Turkey, frozen, whole	lb.	0.96	12/94	82r

Elkhart-Goshen, IN - continued

Item	Per	Value	Date	Ref.
Groceries - continued				
Yogurt, natural, fruit flavored	8 oz.	0.62	12/94	82r
Health Care				
Childbirth, Cesarean delivery, hospital charge	birth	5101.00	12/91	69r
Childbirth, Cesarean delivery, physician charge	birth	2234.00	12/91	69r
Childbirth, normal delivery, hospital charge	birth	2891.00	12/91	69r
Childbirth, normal delivery, physician charge	birth	1623.00	12/91	69r
Drugs, expenditures	year	248	91	81r
Health care, total expenditures	year	1336	91	81r
Health insurance expenditures	year	550	91	81r
Insurance premium, family medical care	month	353.94	1/95	41s
Medical services expenditures	year	457	91	81r
Medical supplies expenditures	year	82	91	81r
Household Goods				
Floor coverings, expenditures	year	105	91	81r
Furniture, expenditures	year	291	91	81r
Household equipment, misc. expenditures	year	341	91	81r
Household expenditures, miscellaneous	year	162	91	81r
Household furnishings and equipment, expenditures	year	1042	91	81r
Household operations expenditures	year	365	91	81r
Household textiles, expenditures	year	101	91	81r
Housekeeping supplies, expenditures	year	390	91	81r
Laundry and cleaning supplies, expenditures	year	110	91	81r
Postage and stationery, expenditures	year	115	91	81r
Housing				
Add garage/carport		8,479	3/95	74r
Add room(s)		21,347	3/95	74r
Apartment condominium or co-op, median	unit	87100	12/94	62r
Bathroom addition, average cost	add	9734.00	3/95	13r
Bathroom remodeling, average cost	remod	6414.00	3/95	13r
Bedroom, master suite addition, average cost	add	27122.00	3/95	13r
Deck addition, average cost	add	6665.00	3/95	13r
Dwellings (owned), expenditures	year	2566	91	81r
Enclose porch/patio/breezeway		4,556	3/95	74r
Exterior remodeling, average cost	remod	15395.00	3/95	13r
Family room addition, average cost	add	27658.00	3/95	13r
Finish room in basement/attic		5,074	3/95	74r
Home, existing, single-family, median	unit	106500	12/94	62r
Kitchen remodeling, major, average cost	remod	17084.00	3/95	13r
Kitchen remodeling, minor, average cost	remod	5804.00	3/95	13r
Maintenance, repairs, insurance, and other housing expenditures	year	484	91	81r
Mortgage interest and charges expenditures	year	1443	91	81r
Office, home addition, average cost	add	8121.00	3/95	13r
Princ. & int., mortgage, median-price exist. sing.-family home	mo.	515	12/94	62r
Property taxes expenditures	year	639	91	81r
Redesign, restructure more than half of home's interior		9,114	3/95	74r
Rental units expenditures	year	1200	91	81r
Sun-space addition, average cost	add	23768.00	3/95	13r
Wing addition, two-story, average cost	add	50410.00	3/95	13r
Insurance and Pensions				
Auto insurance, private passenger	year	586.58	12/94	71s
Insurance and pensions, personal, expenditures	year	2408	91	81r
Insurance, life and other personal, expenditures	year	355	91	81r
Pensions and Social Security, expenditures	year	2053	91	81r
Legal Assistance				
Legal work, law firm associate	hour	90		10r
Legal work, law firm partner	hour	139		10r
Personal Services				
Personal services expenditures	year	203	91	81r

Values are in dollars or fractions of dollars. In the column headed *Ref*, references are shown to sources. Each reference is followed by a letter. These refer to the geographical level for which data were reported: s = State, r = Region, and c = City or metro. The abbreviation *ex* is used to mean *except* or *excluding*; *exp* stands for *expenditures*. For other abbreviations and further explanations, please see the Introduction.

Elkhart-Goshen, IN - continued

Item	Per	Value	Date	Ref.
Restaurant Food				
Dining expenditures, family	week	30.03	94	73r
Taxes				
Taxes, Federal income, expenditures	year	1756	91	81r
Taxes, personal, expenditures	year	2426	91	81r
Taxes, State and local income, expenditures	year	568	91	81r
Transportation				
Cars and trucks purchased, new	year	891	91	81r
Cars and trucks purchased, used	year	1155	91	81r
Driver's learning permit fee	perm	2.00	1/94	84s
Driver's license fee	orig	6.00	1/94	84s
Driver's license fee, duplicate	lic	3.00	1/94	84s
Driver's license renewal fee	renew	6.00	1/94	84s
Identification card, nondriver	card	4.00	1/94	83s
Motorcycle learning permit fee	perm	2.00	1/94	84s
Motorcycle license fee	orig	6.00	1/94	84s
Motorcycle license fee, duplicate	lic	3.00	1/94	84s
Motorcycle license renewal fee	renew	6.00	1/94	84s
Public transportation expenditures	year	209	91	81r
Transportation expenditures, total	year	4792	91	81r
Vehicle finance charges	year	300	91	81r
Vehicle insurance expenditures	year	485	91	81r
Vehicle maintenance and repairs expenditures	year	534	91	81r
Vehicle purchases	year	2068	91	81r
Vehicle rental, leases, licenses, etc. expenditures	year	197	91	81r
Vehicles purchased, other than cars and trucks	year	22	91	81r
Utilities				
Electricity expenditures	year	668	91	81r
Utilities, fuels, and public services, total expenditures	year	1838	91	81r
Water and other public services, expenditures	year	167	91	81r
Weddings				
Bridal attendants' gowns	event	750	10/93	76r
Bridal gown	event	852	10/93	76r
Bridal headpiece and veil	event	167	10/93	76r
Bride's wedding band	event	708	10/93	76r
Clergy	event	224	10/93	76r
Engagement ring	event	2756	10/93	76r
Flowers	event	863	10/93	76r
Formal wear for groom	event	106	10/93	76r
Groom's attendants' formal wear	event	530	10/93	76r
Groom's wedding band	event	402	10/93	76r
Music	event	600	10/93	76r
Photography	event	1088	10/93	76r
Shoes for bride	event	50	10/93	76r
Videography	event	483	10/93	76r
Wedding invitations and announcements	event	342	10/93	76r
Wedding reception	event	7000	10/93	76r

Elko, NV

Item	Per	Value	Date	Ref.
Composite, ACCRA index		104.00	12/94	2c
Alcoholic Beverages				
Beer, Miller Lite, Bud, 12-oz., ex deposit	6	3.99	12/94	2c
J & B Scotch	750-ml.	17.09	12/94	2c
Wine, Gallo Chablis blanc	1.5-lit	5.58	12/94	2c
Clothing				
Jeans, man's denim		28.65	12/94	2c
Shirt, man's dress shirt		29.74	12/94	2c
Undervest, boy's size 10-14, cotton	3	4.66	12/94	2c
Communications				
Newspaper subscription, dly. and Sun. delivery	month	16.30	12/94	2c
Telephone bill, family of four	month	14.23	12/94	2c

Elko, NV - continued

Item	Per	Value	Date	Ref.
Communications - continued				
Telephone, residential, flat rate	mo.	10.50	12/93	8c
Energy and Fuels				
Energy, combined forms, 1800 sq. ft.	mo.	91.28	12/94	2c
Energy, exc. electricity, 1800 sq. ft.	mo.	44.40	12/94	2c
Gas, reg unlead, taxes inc., cash, self-service	gal	1.30	12/94	2c
Entertainment				
Bowling, evening rate	game	1.83	12/94	2c
Monopoly game, Parker Brothers', No. 9	game	12.49	12/94	2c
Movie	adm	6.00	12/94	2c
Tennis balls, yellow, Wilson or Penn, 3	can	2.45	12/94	2c
Groceries				
Groceries, ACCRA Index		113.40	12/94	2c
Baby food, strained vegetables, lowest price	4-4.5 oz.	0.30	12/94	2c
Bananas	lb.	0.56	12/94	2c
Beef or hamburger, ground	lb.	1.69	12/94	2c
Bread, white	24-oz.	0.96	12/94	2c
Cheese, Kraft grated Parmesan	8-oz.	3.99	12/94	2c
Chicken, whole fryer	lb.	1.06	12/94	2c
Cigarettes, Winston, Kings	carton	19.42	12/94	2c
Coffee, vacuum-packed	13 oz.	3.62	12/94	2c
Corn Flakes, Kellogg's or Post Toasties	18 oz.	2.38	12/94	2c
Corn, frozen, whole kernel, lowest price	10 oz.	0.59	12/94	2c
Eggs, Grade A large	dozen	1.19	12/94	2c
Lettuce, iceberg	head	0.82	12/94	2c
Margarine, Blue Bonnet or Parkay cubes	lb.	0.76	12/94	2c
Milk, whole	1/2 gal.	1.69	12/94	2c
Orange juice, Minute Maid frozen	12-oz.	1.40	12/94	2c
Peaches, halves or slices, Hunt's, Del Monte, or Libby's	29-oz.	1.32	12/94	2c
Peas, sweet, Del Monte or Green Giant	15-17 oz.	0.61	12/94	2c
Potatoes, white or red	10-lb. sack	3.05	12/94	2c
Sausage, Jimmy Dean, 100% pork	lb.	3.32	12/94	2c
Shortening, vegetable, Crisco	3-lb.	2.19	12/94	2c
Soft drink, Coca Cola, ex deposit	2 lit	1.09	12/94	2c
Steak, t-bone	lb.	5.39	12/94	2c
Sugar, cane or beet	4 lbs.	1.34	12/94	2c
Tomatoes, Hunt's or Del Monte	14.5 oz.	1.19	12/94	2c
Tuna, chunk, light, oil-packed	6.125-6.5 oz.	0.94	12/94	2c
Goods and Services				
Miscellaneous goods and services, ACCRA Index		104.10	12/94	2c
Health Care				
Health care, ACCRA Index		111.00	12/94	2c
Antibiotic ointment, Polysporin	1.5 oz.	4.46	12/94	2c
Dentist's fee, adult teeth cleaning and periodic oral exam	visit	62.40	12/94	2c
Doctor's fee, routine exam, established patient	visit	43.33	12/94	2c
Hospital care, semiprivate room	day	400.00	12/94	2c
Household Goods				
Appl. repair, service call, wash mach	min. lab. chg.	57.65	12/94	2c
Laundry detergent, Tide Ultra, Bold, or Cheer	42 oz.	3.99	12/94	2c
Tissues, facial, Kleenex brand	175	1.02	12/94	2c
Housing				
Housing, ACCRA Index		100.80	12/94	2c
House payment, principal and interest, 25% down payment	mo.	751	12/94	2c

Values are in dollars or fractions of dollars. In the column headed *Ref*, references are shown to sources. Each reference is followed by a letter. These refer to the geographical level for which data were reported: s=State, r=Region, and c=City or metro. The abbreviation *ex* is used to mean *except* or *excluding*; *exp* stands for *expenditures*. For other abbreviations and further explanations, please see the Introduction.

Elko, NV - continued

Item	Per	Value	Date	Ref.
Housing				
House, 1800 sq ft, 8000 sq ft lot, new, urban, utilities	total	120967	12/94	2c
Mtge. rate, incl. points and orig. fee, 30-year conv. fixed or ARM	mo.	9.32	12/94	2c
Rent, apartment, 2 br., 1 1/2-2 baths, unfurnished, 950 sq ft, water	mo.	593	12/94	2c
Personal Goods				
Shampoo, Alberto VO5	15-oz.	1.26	12/94	2c
Toothpaste, Crest or Colgate	6-7 oz.	2.34	12/94	2c
Personal Services				
Dry cleaning, man's 2-pc. suit		9.08	12/94	2c
Haircut, man's barbershop, no styling		10.80	12/94	2c
Haircut, woman's shampoo, trim, blow-dry		15.90	12/94	2c
Restaurant Food				
Chicken, fried, thigh and drumstick		1.32	12/94	2c
Hamburger with cheese	1/4 lb.	1.99	12/94	2c
Pizza, Pizza Hut or Pizza Inn	12-13 in.	9.00	12/94	2c
Transportation				
Transportation, ACCRA Index		113.70	12/94	2c
Tire balance, computer or spin bal., front	wheel	7.50	12/94	2c
Utilities				
Utilities, ACCRA Index		80.20	12/94	2c
Electricity, (part.), other, 1800 sq. ft., new home	mo.	46.88	12/94	2c

Elmira, NY

Item	Per	Value	Date	Ref.
Appliances				
Appliances (major), expenditures	year	145	91	81r
Average annual exp.				
Food, health care, personal goods, services	year	29496	91	81r
Charity				
Cash contributions, expenditures	year	708	91	81r
Clothing				
Apparel, men and boys, total expenditures	year	416	91	81r
Apparel, women and girls, total expenditures	year	744	91	81r
Footwear, expenditures	year	305	91	81r
Communications				
Long-distance telephone rate, day, addl. min., 1-10 mi.	min.	4.00	12/93	9s
Long-distance telephone rate, day, initial min., 1-10 mi.	min.	14.90	12/93	9s
Phone line, single, business, field visit	inst	143.26	12/93	9s
Phone line, single, business, no field visit	inst	106.05	12/93	9s
Phone line, single, residence, field visit	inst	85.46	12/93	9s
Phone line, single, residence, no field visit	inst	55.00	12/93	9s
Telephone service, expenditures	year	589	91	81r
Education				
Board, 4-year private college/university	year	2918	8/94	80s
Board, 4-year public college/university	year	2177	8/94	80s
Education, total expenditures	year	593	91	81r
Room, 4-year private college/university	year	3302	8/94	80s
Room, 4-year public college/university	year	2624	8/94	80s
Total cost, 4-year private college/university	year	18451	8/94	80s
Total cost, 4-year public college/university	year	7723	8/94	80s
Tuition, 2-year public college/university, in-state	year	2112	8/94	80s
Tuition, 4-year private college/university, in-state	year	12231	8/94	80s
Tuition, 4-year public college/university, in-state	year	2921	8/94	80s
Energy and Fuels				
Fuel oil and other fuels, expenditures	year	257	91	81r
Gas, natural, expenditures	year	285	91	81r

Elmira, NY - continued

Item	Per	Value	Date	Ref.
Energy and Fuels - continued				
Gasoline and motor oil purchased	year	867	91	81r
Gasoline, unleaded midgrade	gallon	1.32	4/93	82r
Gasoline, unleaded premium	gallon	1.40	4/93	82r
Gasoline, unleaded regular	gallon	1.19	4/93	82r
Entertainment				
Entertainment, total expenditures	year	1331	91	81r
Fees and admissions, expenditures	year	398	91	81r
Pets, toys, playground equipment, expenditures	year	270	91	81r
Reading, expenditures	year	171	91	81r
Televisions, radios, and sound equipment, expenditures	year	429	91	81r
Funerals				
Burial, immediate, container provided by funeral home		1370.36	1/95	54r
Cards, acknowledgment		17.72	1/95	54r
Casket, minimum alternative		192.52	1/95	54r
Cosmetology, hair care, etc.		139.56	1/95	54r
Cremation, direct, container provided by funeral home		1049.24	1/95	54r
Embalming		387.57	1/95	54r
Funeral, funeral home		278.77	1/95	54r
Funeral, other facility		275.85	1/95	54r
Graveside service		213.08	1/95	54r
Hearse, local		157.27	1/95	54r
Limousine, local		146.45	1/95	54r
Memorial service		271.02	1/95	54r
Service charge, professional, nondeclinable		943.58	1/95	54r
Visitation and viewing		322.86	1/95	54r
Groceries				
Apples, Red Delicious	lb.	0.78	12/94	82r
Bacon, sliced	lb.	2.24	12/94	82r
Bananas	lb.	0.49	12/94	82r
Beef purchases	year	226	91	81r
Beverage purchases, alcoholic	year	332	91	81r
Beverage purchases, nonalcoholic	year	213	91	81r
Bread, white, pan	lb.	0.80	12/94	82r
Butter, salted, Grade AA, stick	lb.	1.67	12/94	82r
Carrots, short trimmed and topped	lb.	0.51	12/94	82r
Cereals and bakery products purchases	year	407	91	81r
Cereals and cereals products purchases	year	132	91	81r
Chicken breast, bone-in	lb.	2.22	12/94	82r
Chicken, fresh, whole	lb.	1.05	12/94	82r
Chuck roast, USDA choice, boneless	lb.	2.74	12/94	82r
Coffee, 100%, ground roast, all sizes	lb.	4.61	12/94	82r
Dairy products (other) purchases	year	161	91	81r
Eggs, Grade A large	dozen	1.12	12/94	82r
Fish and seafood purchases	year	112	91	81r
Food purchases, food eaten at home	year	2599	91	81r
Foods purchased away from home, not prepared by consumer	year	2024	91	81r
Fruits and vegetables purchases	year	444	91	81r
Grapefruit	lb.	0.44	12/94	82r
Grapes, Thompson seedless	lb.	2.24	12/94	82r
Ground chuck, 100% beef	lb.	1.67	12/94	82r
Ice cream, prepackaged, bulk, regular	1/2 gal.	2.93	12/94	82r
Lemons	lb.	1.06	12/94	82r
Lettuce, iceberg	lb.	0.92	12/94	82r
Meats, poultry, fish, and eggs purchases	year	751	91	81r
Milk and cream (fresh) purchases	year	152	91	81r
Orange juice, frozen concentrate 12-oz. can	16 oz.	1.92	12/94	82r
Oranges, Navel	lb.	0.56	12/94	82r
Pork chops, center cut, bone-in	lb.	3.09	12/94	82r
Pork purchases	year	130	91	81r
Potatoes, white	lb.	0.37	12/94	82r
Rib roast, USDA choice, bone-in	lb.	4.98	12/94	82r
Round roast, USDA choice, boneless	lb.	2.93	12/94	82r
Shortening, vegetable oil blends	lb.	1.03	12/94	82r
Spaghetti and macaroni	lb.	0.84	12/94	82r
Steak, round, USDA choice, boneless	lb.	3.48	12/94	82r

Values are in dollars or fractions of dollars. In the column headed *Ref*, references are shown to sources. Each reference is followed by a letter. These refer to the geographical level for which data were reported: s=State, r=Region, and c=City or metro. The abbreviation *ex* is used to mean *except* or *excluding*; *exp* stands for *expenditures*. For other abbreviations and further explanations, please see the Introduction.

Elmira, NY - continued

Item	Per	Value	Date	Ref.
Groceries				
Steak, sirloin, USDA choice, bone-in	lb.	3.38	12/94	82r
Steak, sirloin, USDA choice, boneless	lb.	4.81	12/94	82r
Sugar and other sweets, eaten at home, expenditures	year	89	91	81r
Sugar, white, all sizes	lb.	0.46	12/94	82r
Tobacco products and smoking supplies, total expenditures	year	279	91	81r
Tomatoes, field grown	lb.	1.56	12/94	82r
Tuna, chunk, light	lb.	2.09	12/94	82r
Health Care				
Childbirth, Cesarean delivery, hospital charge	birth	6334.00	12/91	69r
Childbirth, Cesarean delivery, physician charge	birth	2234.00	12/91	69r
Childbirth, normal delivery, hospital charge	birth	3225.00	12/91	69r
Childbirth, normal delivery, physician charge	birth	1623.00	12/91	69r
Drugs, expenditures	year	205	91	81r
Health care, total expenditures	year	1396	91	81r
Health insurance expenditures	year	553	91	81r
Insurance premium, family medical care	month	384.24	1/95	41s
Medical services expenditures	year	559	91	81r
Medical supplies expenditures	year	80	91	81r
Household Goods				
Floor coverings, expenditures	year	158	91	81r
Furniture, expenditures	year	341	91	81r
Household equipment, misc. expenditures	year	363	91	81r
Household expenditures, miscellaneous	year	194	91	81r
Household furnishings and equipment, expenditures	year	1158	91	81r
Household operations expenditures	year	378	91	81r
Household textiles, expenditures	year	88	91	81r
Housekeeping supplies, expenditures	year	426	91	81r
Laundry and cleaning supplies, expenditures	year	122	91	81r
Postage and stationery, expenditures	year	134	91	81r
Housing				
Add garage/carport		11,614	3/95	74r
Add room(s)		16,816	3/95	74r
Apartment condominium or co-op, median	unit	96700	12/94	62r
Dwellings (owned), expenditures	year	3305	91	81r
Enclose porch/patio/breezeway		2,980	3/95	74r
Finish room in basement/attic		4,330	3/95	74r
Home, existing, single-family, median	unit	161600	12/94	62r
Maintenance, repairs, insurance, and other housing expenditures	year	569	91	81r
Mortgage interest and charges expenditures	year	1852	91	81r
Princ. & int., mortgage, median-price exist. sing.-family home	mo.	765	12/94	62r
Property taxes expenditures	year	884	91	81r
Redesign, restructure more than half of home's interior		2,750	3/95	74r
Rental units expenditures	year	1832	91	81r
Insurance and Pensions				
Auto insurance, private passenger	year	985.07	12/94	71s
Insurance and pensions, personal, expenditures	year	2690	91	81r
Insurance, life and other personal, expenditures	year	341	91	81r
Pensions and Social Security, expenditures	year	2349	91	81r
Legal Assistance				
Estate planning, law-firm partner	hr.	375.00	10/93	12r
Legal work, law firm associate	hour	78		10r
Legal work, law firm partner	hour	183		10r
Personal Services				
Personal services expenditures	year	184	91	81r
Restaurant Food				
Dining expenditures, family	week	34.26	94	73r

Elmira, NY - continued

Item	Per	Value	Date	Ref.
Taxes				
Taxes, Federal income, expenditures	year	2409	91	81r
Taxes, personal, expenditures	year	3094	91	81r
Taxes, State and local income, expenditures	year	620	91	81r
Transportation				
Cars and trucks purchased, new	year	1170	91	81r
Cars and trucks purchased, used	year	739	91	81r
Driver's learning permit fee	perm	10.00	1/94	84s
Driver's license fee	orig	32.00-37.00	1/94	84s
Driver's license fee, duplicate	lic	7.25	1/94	84s
Driver's license reinstatement fee, min.	susp	25.00	1/94	85s
Driver's license renewal fee	renew	22.25	1/94	84s
Identification card, nondriver	card	6.25	1/94	83s
Motorcycle license fee	orig	32.00-37.00	1/94	84s
Motorcycle license fee, duplicate	lic	7.25	1/94	84s
Motorcycle license renewal fee	renew	22.25	1/94	84s
Public transportation expenditures	year	430	91	81r
Transportation expenditures, total	year	4810	91	81r
Vehicle finance charges	year	238	91	81r
Vehicle insurance expenditures	year	630	91	81r
Vehicle maintenance and repairs expenditures	year	532	91	81r
Vehicle purchases	year	1920	91	81r
Vehicle rental, leases, licenses, etc. expenditures	year	193	91	81r
Vehicles purchased, other than cars and trucks	year	11	91	81r
Utilities				
Electricity expenditures	year	695	91	81r
Utilities, fuels, and public services, total expenditures	year	1981	91	81r
Water and other public services, expenditures	year	154	91	81r
Weddings				
Bridal attendants' gowns	event	750	10/93	76r
Bridal gown	event	852	10/93	76r
Bridal headpiece and veil	event	167	10/93	76r
Bride's wedding band	event	708	10/93	76r
Clergy	event	224	10/93	76r
Engagement ring	event	2756	10/93	76r
Flowers	event	863	10/93	76r
Formal wear for groom	event	106	10/93	76r
Groom's attendants' formal wear	event	530	10/93	76r
Groom's wedding band	event	402	10/93	76r
Music	event	600	10/93	76r
Photography	event	1088	10/93	76r
Shoes for bride	event	50	10/93	76r
Videography	event	483	10/93	76r
Wedding invitations and announcements	event	342	10/93	76r
Wedding reception	event	7000	10/93	76r

Enid, OK

Item	Per	Value	Date	Ref.
Appliances				
Appliances (major), expenditures	year	153	91	81r
Average annual exp.				
Food, health care, personal goods, services	year	27020	91	81r
Charity				
Cash contributions, expenditures	year	839	91	81r
Clothing				
Apparel, men and boys, total expenditures	year	380	91	81r
Apparel, women and girls, total expenditures	year	660	91	81r
Footwear, expenditures	year	193	91	81r
Communications				
Long-distance telephone rate, day, addl. min., 1-10 mi.	min.	0.07	12/93	9s

Values are in dollars or fractions of dollars. In the column headed *Ref*, references are shown to sources. Each reference is followed by a letter. These refer to the geographical level for which data were reported: s=State, r=Region, and c=City or metro. The abbreviation *ex* is used to mean *except* or *excluding*; *exp* stands for expenditures. For other abbreviations and further explanations, please see the Introduction.

Enid, OK - continued

Item	Per	Value	Date	Ref.
Communications				
Long-distance telephone rate, day, initial min., 1-10 mi.	min.	0.12	12/93	9s
Phone line, single, business, field visit	inst	82.75	12/93	9s
Phone line, single, business, no field visit	inst	82.75	12/93	9s
Phone line, single, residence, field visit	inst	44.45	12/93	9s
Phone line, single, residence, no field visit	inst	44.45	12/93	9s
Telephone service, expenditures	year	616	91	81r
Education				
Board, 4-year private college/university	year	1974	8/94	80s
Board, 4-year public college/university	year	1502	8/94	80s
Education, total expenditures	year	319	91	81r
Room, 4-year private college/university	year	1618	8/94	80s
Room, 4-year public college/university	year	876	8/94	80s
Total cost, 4-year private college/university	year	10801	8/94	80s
Total cost, 4-year public college/university	year	4023	8/94	80s
Tuition, 2-year public college/university, in-state	year	1095	8/94	80s
Tuition, 4-year private college/university, in-state	year	7210	8/94	80s
Tuition, 4-year public college/university, in-state	year	1645	8/94	80s
Energy and Fuels				
Fuel oil and other fuels, expenditures	year	56	91	81r
Gas, natural, expenditures	year	150	91	81r
Gasoline and motor oil purchased	year	1152	91	81r
Gasoline, unleaded midgrade	gallon	1.21	4/93	82r
Gasoline, unleaded premium	gallon	1.30	4/93	82r
Gasoline, unleaded regular	gallon	1.10	4/93	82r
Entertainment				
Concert ticket, Pearl Jam group	perf	20.00	94	50r
Entertainment, total expenditures	year	1266	91	81r
Fees and admissions, expenditures	year	306	91	81r
Pets, toys, playground equipment, expenditures	year	271	91	81r
Reading, expenditures	year	131	91	81r
Televisions, radios, and sound equipment, expenditures	year	439	91	81r
Funerals				
Burial, immediate, container provided by funeral home		1574.60	1/95	54r
Cards, acknowledgment		22.24	1/95	54r
Casket, minimum alternative		239.41	1/95	54r
Cosmetology, hair care, etc.		91.04	1/95	54r
Cremation, direct, container provided by funeral home		1085.15	1/95	54r
Embalming		281.30	1/95	54r
Funeral, funeral home		323.04	1/95	54r
Funeral, other facility		327.58	1/95	54r
Graveside service		355.19	1/95	54r
Hearse, local		141.89	1/95	54r
Limousine, local		99.40	1/95	54r
Memorial service		284.67	1/95	54r
Service charge, professional, nondeclinable		904.06	1/95	54r
Visitation and viewing		187.04	1/95	54r
Groceries				
Apples, Red Delicious	lb.	0.73	12/94	82r
Bacon, sliced	lb.	1.67	12/94	82r
Bananas	lb.	0.42	12/94	82r
Beef purchases	year	213	91	81r
Beverage purchases, alcoholic	year	249	91	81r
Beverage purchases, nonalcoholic	year	207	91	81r
Bologna, all beef or mixed	lb.	2.27	12/94	82r
Bread, white, pan	lb.	0.68	12/94	82r
Cabbage	lb.	0.42	12/94	82r
Carrots, short trimmed and topped	lb.	0.53	12/94	82r
Cereals and bakery products purchases	year	345	91	81r
Cereals and cereals products purchases	year	127	91	81r
Cheddar cheese, natural	lb.	3.58	12/94	82r
Chicken breast, bone-in	lb.	1.71	12/94	82r

Enid, OK - continued

Item	Per	Value	Date	Ref.
Groceries - continued				
Chicken, fresh, whole	lb.	0.78	12/94	82r
Chuck roast, USDA choice, boneless	lb.	2.26	12/94	82r
Crackers, soda, salted	lb.	1.27	12/94	82r
Cucumbers	lb.	0.65	12/94	82r
Dairy products (other) purchases	year	141	91	81r
Eggs, Grade A large	dozen	0.87	12/94	82r
Fish and seafood purchases	year	72	91	81r
Flour, white, all purpose	lb.	0.23	12/94	82r
Food purchases, food eaten at home	year	2381	91	81r
Foods purchased away from home, not prepared by consumer	year	1696	91	81r
Frankfurters, all meat or all beef	lb.	1.74	12/94	82r
Fruits and vegetables purchases	year	380	91	81r
Grapefruit	lb.	0.45	12/94	82r
Grapes, Thompson seedless	lb.	2.30	12/94	82r
Ground beef, 100% beef	lb.	1.37	12/94	82r
Ground chuck, 100% beef	lb.	1.97	12/94	82r
Ham, boneless, exc. canned	lb.	2.54	12/94	82r
Ice cream, prepackaged, bulk, regular	1/2 gal.	2.47	12/94	82r
Lemons	lb.	1.02	12/94	82r
Lettuce, iceberg	lb.	0.96	12/94	82r
Margarine, stick	lb.	0.77	12/94	82r
Meats, poultry, fish, and eggs purchases	year	655	91	81r
Milk and cream (fresh) purchases	year	130	91	81r
Orange juice, frozen concentrate 12-oz. can	16 oz.	1.36	12/94	82r
Oranges, Navel	lb.	0.54	12/94	82r
Pears, Anjou	lb.	0.81	12/94	82r
Pork chops, center cut, bone-in	lb.	3.07	12/94	82r
Pork purchases	year	142	91	81r
Potato chips	16-oz.	3.15	12/94	82r
Potatoes, frozen, French fried	lb.	0.82	12/94	82r
Potatoes, white	lb.	0.34	12/94	82r
Rice, white, long grain, uncooked	lb.	0.48	12/94	82r
Round roast, USDA choice, boneless	lb.	2.91	12/94	82r
Sausage, fresh	lb.	1.82	12/94	82r
Shortening, vegetable oil blends	lb.	0.75	12/94	82r
Spaghetti and macaroni	lb.	0.87	12/94	82r
Steak, rib eye, USDA choice, boneless	lb.	6.85	12/94	82r
Steak, round, graded & ungraded, exc. USDA prime & choice	lb.	2.96	12/94	82r
Steak, round, USDA choice, boneless	lb.	3.17	12/94	82r
Steak, sirloin, USDA choice, boneless	lb.	4.12	12/94	82r
Steak, T-bone, USDA choice, bone-in	lb.	5.63	12/94	82r
Sugar and other sweets, eaten at home, expenditures	year	93	91	81r
Sugar, white, all sizes	lb.	0.39	12/94	82r
Tobacco products and smoking supplies, total expenditures	year	286	91	81r
Tomatoes, field grown	lb.	1.36	12/94	82r
Tuna, chunk, light	lb.	1.94	12/94	82r
Turkey, frozen, whole	lb.	0.96	12/94	82r
Yogurt, natural, fruit flavored	8 oz.	0.58	12/94	82r
Health Care				
Adenosine, emergency room	treat	100.00	95	23r
Bladder tap, superpubic, infant, emergency room	treat	119.00	95	23r
Blood analysis, emergency room	treat	25.00	95	23r
Blood tests, abdominal pain, emergency room	treat	25.00	95	23r
Burn dressing, emergency room	treat	266.00	95	23r
Cardiology interpretation, emergency room	treat	26.00	95	23r
Chest X-ray, emergency room	treat	78.00	95	23r
Childbirth, Cesarean delivery, hospital charge	birth	5462.00	12/91	69r
Childbirth, Cesarean delivery, physician charge	birth	2228.00	12/91	69r
Childbirth, normal delivery, hospital charge	birth	2943.00	12/91	69r
Childbirth, normal delivery, physician charge	birth	1619.00	12/91	69r
Defibrillation pads, emergency room	treat	6.00	95	23r
Drugs, expenditures	year	297	91	81r

Values are in dollars or fractions of dollars. In the column headed *Ref*, references are shown to sources. Each reference is followed by a letter. These refer to the geographical level for which data were reported: s = State, r = Region, and c = City or metro. The abbreviation *ex* is used to mean *except* or *excluding*; *exp* stands for *expenditures*. For other abbreviations and further explanations, please see the Introduction.

Enid, OK - continued

Item	Per	Value	Date	Ref.
Health Care				
Gastric tube insertion, nasal, emergency room	treat	25.00	95	23r
Health care, total expenditures	year	1600	91	81r
Health insurance expenditures	year	637	91	81r
Heart monitor, emergency room	treat	40.00	95	23r
Insurance premium, family medical care	month	373.98	1/95	41s
Intravenous fluids, emergency room	treat	130.00	95	23r
Intravenous fluids, emergency room	liter	26.00	95	23r
Intravenous line, central, emergency room	treat	342.00	95	23r
Liver function tests, abdominal pain, emergency room	treat	26.00	95	23r
Medical care charges, total, emergency room, third-degree burns	treat	2101.00	95	23r
Medical care charges, total, emergency, infant with fever	treat	628.00	95	23r
Medical services expenditures	year	573	91	81r
Medical supplies expenditures	year	93	91	81r
Morphine, emergency room	treat	34.00	95	23r
Nursing care and facilities charges, emergency room	treat	252.00	95	23r
Nursing care and facilities charges, emergency, infant with fever	treat	252.00	95	23r
Nursing care and facilities charges, emergency, third-degree burns	treat	861.00	95	23r
Physician's charges, emergency, infant with fever	treat	212.00	95	23r
Physician's charges, emergency, third-degree burns	treat	372.00	95	23r
Physician's fee, emergency room	treat	372.00	95	23r
Physician's fee, general practitioner	visit	51.20	12/93	60r
Surgery, open-heart	proc	42374.00	1/93	14r
Ultrasound, abdominal, emergency room	treat	276.00	95	23r
Urinalysis, emergency room	treat	20.00	95	23r
Urinalysis, infant, emergency room	treat	20.00	95	23r
X-rays, emergency room	treat	78.00	95	23r
Household Goods				
Floor coverings, expenditures	year	48	91	81r
Furniture, expenditures	year	280	91	81r
Household equipment, misc. expenditures	year	342	91	81r
Household expenditures, miscellaneous	year	256	91	81r
Household furnishings and equipment, expenditures	year	988	91	81r
Household operations expenditures	year	468	91	81r
Household textiles, expenditures	year	95	91	81r
Housekeeping supplies, expenditures	year	380	91	81r
Laundry and cleaning supplies, expenditures	year	109	91	81r
Postage and stationery, expenditures	year	105	91	81r
Housing				
Add garage/carport		6,980	3/95	74r
Add room(s)		11,403	3/95	74r
Apartment condominium or co-op, median	unit	68600	12/94	62r
Dwellings (owned), expenditures	year	2428	91	81r
Enclose porch/patio/breezeway		4,572	3/95	74r
Finish room in basement/attic		3,794	3/95	74r
Home, existing, single-family, median	unit	120200	12/94	62r
Maintenance, repairs, insurance, and other housing expenditures	year	531	91	81r
Mortgage interest and charges expenditures	year	1506	91	81r
Princ. & int., mortgage, median-price exist. sing.-family home	mo.	540	12/94	62r
Property taxes expenditures	year	391	91	81r
Redesign, restructure more than half of home's interior		17,641	3/95	74r
Rental units expenditures	year	1264	91	81r
Insurance and Pensions				
Auto insurance, private passenger	year	604.38	12/94	71s
Insurance and pensions, personal, expenditures	year	2395	91	81r
Insurance, life and other personal, expenditures	year	368	91	81r

Enid, OK - continued

Item	Per	Value	Date	Ref.
Insurance and Pensions - continued				
Pensions and Social Security, expenditures	year	2027	91	81r
Personal Services				
Personal services expenditures	year	212	91	81r
Restaurant Food				
Dining expenditures, family	week	33.83	94	73r
Taxes				
Tax, cigarettes	year	382.00	10/93	43s
Taxes, Federal income, expenditures	year	2275	91	81r
Taxes, personal, expenditures	year	2715	91	81r
Taxes, State and local income, expenditures	year	365	91	81r
Transportation				
Cars and trucks purchased, new	year	1306	91	81r
Cars and trucks purchased, used	year	942	91	81r
Driver's learning permit fee	perm	19.00	1/94	84s
Driver's license fee	orig	19.00	1/94	84s
Driver's license fee, duplicate	lic	5.00	1/94	84s
Driver's license reinstatement fee, min.	susp	75.00	1/94	85s
Driver's license renewal fee	renew	15.00	1/94	84s
Identification card, nondriver	card	7.00	1/94	83s
Motorcycle license fee	orig	19.00	1/94	84s
Motorcycle license fee, duplicate	lic	5.00	1/94	84s
Motorcycle license renewal fee	renew	15.00	1/94	84s
Public transportation expenditures	year	249	91	81r
Transportation expenditures, total	year	5307	91	81r
Vehicle finance charges	year	346	91	81r
Vehicle insurance expenditures	year	544	91	81r
Vehicle maintenance and repairs expenditures	year	600	91	81r
Vehicle purchases	year	2275	91	81r
Vehicle rental, leases, licenses, etc. expenditures	year	141	91	81r
Vehicles purchased, other than cars and trucks	year	27	91	81r
Utilities				
Electricity expenditures	year	950	91	81r
Utilities, fuels, and public services, total expenditures	year	2000	91	81r
Water and other public services, expenditures	year	227	91	81r
Weddings				
Bridal attendants' gowns	event	750	10/93	76r
Bridal gown	event	852	10/93	76r
Bridal headpiece and veil	event	167	10/93	76r
Bride's wedding band	event	708	10/93	76r
Clergy	event	224	10/93	76r
Engagement ring	event	2756	10/93	76r
Flowers	event	863	10/93	76r
Formal wear for groom	event	106	10/93	76r
Groom's attendants' formal wear	event	530	10/93	76r
Groom's wedding band	event	402	10/93	76r
Music	event	600	10/93	76r
Photography	event	1088	10/93	76r
Shoes for bride	event	50	10/93	76r
Videography	event	483	10/93	76r
Wedding invitations and announcements	event	342	10/93	76r
Wedding reception	event	7000	10/93	76r

Erie, PA

Item	Per	Value	Date	Ref.
Composite, ACCRA index		107.60	12/94	2c
Alcoholic Beverages				
Beer, Miller Lite, Bud, 12-oz., ex deposit	6	4.66	12/94	2c
J & B Scotch	750-ml.	16.99	12/94	2c
Wine, Gallo Chablis blanc	1.5-lit	5.99	12/94	2c

Values are in dollars or fractions of dollars. In the column headed *Ref*, references are shown to sources. Each reference is followed by a letter. These refer to the geographical level for which data were reported: s=State, r=Region, and c=City or metro. The abbreviation *ex* is used to mean *except* or *excluding*; *exp* stands for *expenditures*. For other abbreviations and further explanations, please see the Introduction.

Erie, PA - continued

Item	Per	Value	Date	Ref.
Appliances				
Appliances (major), expenditures	year	145	91	81r
Average annual exp.				
Food, health care, personal goods, services	year	29496	91	81r
Charity				
Cash contributions, expenditures	year	708	91	81r
Clothing				
Apparel, men and boys, total expenditures	year	416	91	81r
Apparel, women and girls, total expenditures	year	744	91	81r
Footwear, expenditures	year	305	91	81r
Jeans, man's denim		30.98	12/94	2c
Shirt, man's dress shirt		31.25	12/94	2c
Undervest, boy's size 10-14, cotton	3	3.37	12/94	2c
Communications				
Long-distance telephone rate, day, addl. min., 1-10 mi.	min.	0.08	12/93	9s
Long-distance telephone rate, day, initial min., 1-10 mi.	min.	0.15	12/93	9s
Newspaper subscription, dly. and Sun. delivery	month	13.04	12/94	2c
Phone line, single, business, field visit	inst	75.00	12/93	9s
Phone line, single, business, no field visit	inst	75.00	12/93	9s
Phone line, single, residence, field visit	inst	40.00	12/93	9s
Phone line, single, residence, no field visit	inst	40.00	12/93	9s
Telephone bill, family of four	month	22.03	12/94	2c
Telephone service, expenditures	year	589	91	81r
Telephone, residential, flat rate	mo.	21.00	12/93	8c
Education				
Board, 4-year private college/university	year	2714	8/94	80s
Board, 4-year public college/university	year	1899	8/94	80s
Education, total expenditures	year	593	91	81r
Room, 4-year private college/university	year	2720	8/94	80s
Room, 4-year public college/university	year	2063	8/94	80s
Total cost, 4-year private college/university	year	18118	8/94	80s
Total cost, 4-year public college/university	year	8278	8/94	80s
Tuition, 2-year public college/university, in-state	year	1671	8/94	80s
Tuition, 4-year private college/university, in-state	year	12684	8/94	80s
Tuition, 4-year public college/university, in-state	year	4316	8/94	80s
Energy and Fuels				
Energy, combined forms, 1800 sq. ft.	mo.	132.63	12/94	2c
Energy, exc. electricity, 1800 sq. ft.	mo.	82.68	12/94	2c
Fuel oil and other fuels, expenditures	year	257	91	81r
Gas, cooking, winter, 10 therms	month	17.81	2/94	65c
Gas, cooking, winter, 30 therms	month	30.06	2/94	65c
Gas, cooking, winter, 50 therms	month	42.32	2/94	65c
Gas, heating, winter, 100 therms	month	71.38	2/94	65c
Gas, heating, winter, average use	month	151.57	2/94	65c
Gas, natural, expenditures	year	285	91	81r
Gas, reg unlead, taxes inc., cash, self-service	gal	1.08	12/94	2c
Gasoline and motor oil purchased	year	867	91	81r
Gasoline, unleaded midgrade	gallon	1.32	4/93	82r
Gasoline, unleaded premium	gallon	1.40	4/93	82r
Gasoline, unleaded regular	gallon	1.19	4/93	82r
Entertainment				
Bowling, evening rate	game	1.63	12/94	2c
Entertainment, total expenditures	year	1331	91	81r
Fees and admissions, expenditures	year	398	91	81r
Monopoly game, Parker Brothers', No. 9	game	9.99	12/94	2c
Movie	adm	4.85	12/94	2c
Pets, toys, playground equipment, expenditures	year	270	91	81r
Reading, expenditures	year	171	91	81r
Televisions, radios, and sound equipment, expenditures	year	429	91	81r
Tennis balls, yellow, Wilson or Penn, 3	can	2.99	12/94	2c

Erie, PA - continued

Item	Per	Value	Date	Ref.
Funerals				
Burial, immediate, container provided by funeral home		1370.36	1/95	54r
Cards, acknowledgment		17.72	1/95	54r
Casket, minimum alternative		192.52	1/95	54r
Cosmetology, hair care, etc.		139.56	1/95	54r
Cremation, direct, container provided by funeral home		1049.24	1/95	54r
Embalming		387.57	1/95	54r
Funeral, funeral home		278.77	1/95	54r
Funeral, other facility		275.85	1/95	54r
Graveside service		213.08	1/95	54r
Hearse, local		157.27	1/95	54r
Limousine, local		146.45	1/95	54r
Memorial service		271.02	1/95	54r
Service charge, professional, nondeclinable		943.58	1/95	54r
Visitation and viewing		322.86	1/95	54r
Groceries				
Groceries, ACCRA Index		98.10	12/94	2c
Apples, Red Delicious	lb.	0.78	12/94	82r
Baby food, strained vegetables, lowest price	4-4.5 oz.	0.32	12/94	2c
Bacon, sliced	lb.	2.24	12/94	82r
Bananas	lb.	0.47	12/94	2c
Bananas	lb.	0.49	12/94	82r
Beef or hamburger, ground	lb.	1.43	12/94	2c
Beef purchases	year	226	91	81r
Beverage purchases, alcoholic	year	332	91	81r
Beverage purchases, nonalcoholic	year	213	91	81r
Bread, white	24-oz.	0.64	12/94	2c
Bread, white, pan	lb.	0.80	12/94	82r
Butter, salted, Grade AA, stick	lb.	1.67	12/94	82r
Carrots, short trimmed and topped	lb.	0.51	12/94	82r
Cereals and bakery products purchases	year	407	91	81r
Cereals and cereals products purchases	year	132	91	81r
Cheese, Kraft grated Parmesan	8-oz.	3.21	12/94	2c
Chicken breast, bone-in	lb.	2.22	12/94	82r
Chicken, fresh, whole	lb.	1.05	12/94	82r
Chicken, whole fryer	lb.	0.79	12/94	2c
Chuck roast, USDA choice, boneless	lb.	2.74	12/94	82r
Cigarettes, Winston, Kings	carton	17.83	12/94	2c
Coffee, 100%, ground roast, all sizes	lb.	4.61	12/94	82r
Coffee, vacuum-packed	13 oz.	3.50	12/94	2c
Corn Flakes, Kellogg's or Post Toasties	18 oz.	2.15	12/94	2c
Corn, frozen, whole kernel, lowest price	10 oz.	0.71	12/94	2c
Dairy products (other) purchases	year	161	91	81r
Eggs, Grade A large	dozen	0.58	12/94	2c
Eggs, Grade A large	dozen	1.12	12/94	82r
Fish and seafood purchases	year	112	91	81r
Food purchases, food eaten at home	year	2599	91	81r
Foods purchased away from home, not prepared by consumer	year	2024	91	81r
Fruits and vegetables purchases	year	444	91	81r
Grapefruit	lb.	0.44	12/94	82r
Grapes, Thompson seedless	lb.	2.24	12/94	82r
Ground chuck, 100% beef	lb.	1.67	12/94	82r
Ice cream, prepackaged, bulk, regular	1/2 gal.	2.93	12/94	82r
Lemons	lb.	1.06	12/94	82r
Lettuce, iceberg	lb.	0.92	12/94	82r
Lettuce, iceberg	head	0.79	12/94	2c
Margarine, Blue Bonnet or Parkay cubes	lb.	0.61	12/94	2c
Meats, poultry, fish, and eggs purchases	year	751	91	81r
Milk and cream (fresh) purchases	year	152	91	81r
Milk, whole	1/2 gal.	1.22	12/94	2c
Orange juice, frozen concentrate 12-oz. can	16 oz.	1.92	12/94	82r
Orange juice, Minute Maid frozen	12-oz.	1.14	12/94	2c
Oranges, Navel	lb.	0.56	12/94	82r
Peaches, halves or slices, Hunt's, Del Monte, or Libby's	29-oz.	1.51	12/94	2c
Peas, sweet, Del Monte or Green Giant	15-17 oz.	0.68	12/94	2c

Values are in dollars or fractions of dollars. In the column headed *Ref*, references are shown to sources. Each reference is followed by a letter. These refer to the geographical level for which data were reported: s=State, r=Region, and c=City or metro. The abbreviation *ex* is used to mean *except* or *excluding*; *exp* stands for expenditures. For other abbreviations and further explanations, please see the Introduction.

Erie, PA - continued

Item	Per	Value	Date	Ref.
Groceries				
Pork chops, center cut, bone-in	lb.	3.09	12/94	82r
Pork purchases	year	130	91	81r
Potatoes, white	lb.	0.37	12/94	82r
Potatoes, white or red	10-lb. sack	1.80	12/94	2c
Rib roast, USDA choice, bone-in	lb.	4.98	12/94	82r
Round roast, USDA choice, boneless	lb.	2.93	12/94	82r
Sausage, Jimmy Dean, 100% pork	lb.	2.79	12/94	2c
Shortening, vegetable oil blends	lb.	1.03	12/94	82r
Shortening, vegetable, Crisco	3-lb.	2.50	12/94	2c
Soft drink, Coca Cola, ex deposit	2 lit	0.99	12/94	2c
Spaghetti and macaroni	lb.	0.84	12/94	82r
Steak, round, USDA choice, boneless	lb.	3.48	12/94	82r
Steak, sirloin, USDA choice, bone-in	lb.	3.38	12/94	82r
Steak, sirloin, USDA choice, boneless	lb.	4.81	12/94	82r
Steak, t-bone	lb.	6.55	12/94	2c
Sugar and other sweets, eaten at home, expenditures	year	89	91	81r
Sugar, cane or beet	4 lbs.	1.58	12/94	2c
Sugar, white, all sizes	lb.	0.46	12/94	82r
Tobacco products and smoking supplies, total expenditures	year	279	91	81r
Tomatoes, field grown	lb.	1.56	12/94	82r
Tomatoes, Hunt's or Del Monte	14.5 oz.	0.92	12/94	2c
Tuna, chunk, light	lb.	2.09	12/94	82r
Tuna, chunk, light, oil-packed	6.125-6.5 oz.	0.66	12/94	2c
Goods and Services				
Miscellaneous goods and services, ACCRA Index		102.30	12/94	2c
Health Care				
Health care, ACCRA Index		97.80	12/94	2c
Antibiotic ointment, Polysporin	1.5 oz.	4.19	12/94	2c
Childbirth, Cesarean delivery, hospital charge	birth	6334.00	12/91	69r
Childbirth, Cesarean delivery, physician charge	birth	2234.00	12/91	69r
Childbirth, normal delivery, hospital charge	birth	3225.00	12/91	69r
Childbirth, normal delivery, physician charge	birth	1623.00	12/91	69r
Dentist's fee, adult teeth cleaning and periodic oral exam	visit	50.60	12/94	2c
Doctor's fee, routine exam, established patient	visit	34.20	12/94	2c
Drugs, expenditures	year	205	91	81r
Health care, total expenditures	year	1396	91	81r
Health insurance expenditures	year	553	91	81r
Hospital care, semiprivate room	day	462.50	12/94	2c
Insurance premium, family medical care	month	349.05	1/95	41s
Medical services expenditures	year	559	91	81r
Medical supplies expenditures	year	80	91	81r
Household Goods				
Appl. repair, service call, wash mach	min. lab. chg.	29.20	12/94	2c
Floor coverings, expenditures	year	158	91	81r
Furniture, expenditures	year	341	91	81r
Household equipment, misc. expenditures	year	363	91	81r
Household expenditures, miscellaneous	year	194	91	81r
Household furnishings and equipment, expenditures	year	1158	91	81r
Household operations expenditures	year	378	91	81r
Household textiles, expenditures	year	88	91	81r
Housekeeping supplies, expenditures	year	426	91	81r
Laundry and cleaning supplies, expenditures	year	122	91	81r
Laundry detergent, Tide Ultra, Bold, or Cheer	42 oz.	3.69	12/94	2c
Postage and stationery, expenditures	year	134	91	81r
Tissues, facial, Kleenex brand	175	0.90	12/94	2c

Erie, PA - continued

Item	Per	Value	Date	Ref.
Housing				
Housing, ACCRA Index		121.70	12/94	2c
Add garage/carport		11,614	3/95	74r
Add room(s)		16,816	3/95	74r
Apartment condominium or co-op, median	unit	96700	12/94	62r
Dwellings (owned), expenditures	year	3305	91	81r
Enclose porch/patio/breezeway		2,980	3/95	74r
Finish room in basement/attic		4,330	3/95	74r
Home, existing, single-family, median	unit	161600	12/94	62r
House payment, principal and interest, 25% down payment	mo.	949	12/94	2c
House, 1800 sq ft, 8000 sq ft lot, new, urban, utilities	total	154933	12/94	2c
Maintenance, repairs, insurance, and other housing expenditures	year	569	91	81r
Mortgage interest and charges expenditures	year	1852	91	81r
Mtge. rate, incl. points and orig. fee, 30-year conv. fixed or ARM	mo.	9.17	12/94	2c
Princ. & int., mortgage, median-price exist. sing.-family home	mo.	765	12/94	62r
Property taxes expenditures	year	884	91	81r
Redesign, restructure more than half of home's interior		2,750	3/95	74r
Rent, apartment, 2 br., 1 1/2-2 baths, unfurnished, 950 sq ft, water	mo.	595	12/94	2c
Rental units expenditures	year	1832	91	81r
Insurance and Pensions				
Auto insurance, private passenger	year	721.50	12/94	71s
Insurance and pensions, personal, expenditures	year	2690	91	81r
Insurance, life and other personal, expenditures	year	341	91	81r
Pensions and Social Security, expenditures	year	2349	91	81r
Legal Assistance				
Estate planning, law-firm partner	hr.	375.00	10/93	12r
Legal work, law firm associate	hour	78		10r
Legal work, law firm partner	hour	183		10r
Personal Goods				
Shampoo, Alberto VO5	15-oz.	1.54	12/94	2c
Toothpaste, Crest or Colgate	6-7 oz.	1.96	12/94	2c
Personal Services				
Dry cleaning, man's 2-pc. suit		7.52	12/94	2c
Haircut, man's barbershop, no styling		6.80	12/94	2c
Haircut, woman's shampoo, trim, blow-dry		16.80	12/94	2c
Personal services expenditures	year	184	91	81r
Restaurant Food				
Chicken, fried, thigh and drumstick		2.50	12/94	2c
Dining expenditures, family	week	34.26	94	73r
Hamburger with cheese	1/4 lb.	1.80	12/94	2c
Pizza, Pizza Hut or Pizza Inn	12-13 in.	8.99	12/94	2c
Taxes				
Taxes, Federal income, expenditures	year	2409	91	81r
Taxes, personal, expenditures	year	3094	91	81r
Taxes, State and local income, expenditures	year	620	91	81r
Transportation				
Transportation, ACCRA Index		98.30	12/94	2c
Bus fare, one-way	trip	1.00	12/95	1c
Bus fare, up to 10 miles	one-way	1.00	12/94	2c
Cars and trucks purchased, new	year	1170	91	81r
Cars and trucks purchased, used	year	739	91	81r
Driver's learning permit fee	perm	27.00	1/94	84s
Driver's license fee	orig	0.00	1/94	84s
Driver's license fee, duplicate	lic	7.00	1/94	84s
Driver's license reinstatement fee, min.	susp	25.00	1/94	85s
Driver's license renewal fee	renew	0.00	1/94	84s
Identification card, nondriver	card	5.00	1/94	83s
Motorcycle learning permit fee	perm	27.00	1/94	84s

Values are in dollars or fractions of dollars. In the column headed *Ref*, references are shown to sources. Each reference is followed by a letter. These refer to the geographical level for which data were reported: s=State, r=Region, and c=City or metro. The abbreviation *ex* is used to mean *except* or *excluding*; *exp* stands for expenditures. For other abbreviations and further explanations, please see the Introduction.

Erie, PA - continued

Item	Per	Value	Date	Ref.
Transportation				
Motorcycle license fee	orig	0.00	1/94	84s
Motorcycle license fee, duplicate	lic	7.00	1/94	84s
Motorcycle license renewal fee	renew	0.00	1/94	84s
Public transportation expenditures	year	430	91	81r
Tire balance, computer or spin bal., front	wheel	6.73	12/94	2c
Transportation expenditures, total	year	4810	91	81r
Vehicle finance charges	year	238	91	81r
Vehicle insurance expenditures	year	630	91	81r
Vehicle maintenance and repairs expenditures	year	532	91	81r
Vehicle purchases	year	1920	91	81r
Vehicle rental, leases, licenses, etc. expenditures	year	193	91	81r
Vehicles purchased, other than cars and trucks	year	11	91	81r
Utilities				
Utilities, ACCRA Index		117.50	12/94	2c
Electricity expenditures	year	695	91	81r
Electricity, (part.), other, 1800 sq. ft., new home	mo.	49.95	12/94	2c
Electricity, summer, 250 KWh	month	25.27	8/93	64c
Electricity, summer, 500 KWh	month	48.71	8/93	64c
Electricity, summer, 750 KWh	month	62.17	8/93	64c
Electricity, summer, 1000 KWh	month	75.04	8/93	64c
Utilities, fuels, and public services, total expenditures	year	1981	91	81r
Water and other public services, expenditures	year	154	91	81r
Weddings				
Bridal attendants' gowns	event	750	10/93	76r
Bridal gown	event	852	10/93	76r
Bridal headpiece and veil	event	167	10/93	76r
Bride's wedding band	event	708	10/93	76r
Clergy	event	224	10/93	76r
Engagement ring	event	2756	10/93	76r
Flowers	event	863	10/93	76r
Formal wear for groom	event	106	10/93	76r
Groom's attendants' formal wear	event	530	10/93	76r
Groom's wedding band	event	402	10/93	76r
Music	event	600	10/93	76r
Photography	event	1088	10/93	76r
Shoes for bride	event	50	10/93	76r
Videography	event	483	10/93	76r
Wedding invitations and announcements	event	342	10/93	76r
Wedding reception	event	7000	10/93	76r

Eugene, OR

Item	Per	Value	Date	Ref.
Composite, ACCRA index		11.80	12/94	2c
Alcoholic Beverages				
Beer, Miller Lite, Bud, 12-oz., ex deposit	6	4.26	12/94	2c
J & B Scotch	750-ml.	20.95	12/94	2c
Wine, Gallo Chablis blanc	1.5-lit	4.44	12/94	2c
Appliances				
Appliances (major), expenditures	year	160	91	81r
Average annual exp.				
Food, health care, personal goods, services	year	32461	91	81r
Charity				
Cash contributions, expenditures	year	975	91	81r
Clothing				
Apparel, men and boys, total expenditures	year	467	91	81r
Apparel, women and girls, total expenditures	year	737	91	81r
Footwear, expenditures	year	270	91	81r
Jeans, man's denim		30.97	12/94	2c
Shirt, man's dress shirt		36.50	12/94	2c
Undervest, boy's size 10-14, cotton	3	3.47	12/94	2c

Eugene, OR - continued

Item	Per	Value	Date	Ref.
Communications				
Long-distance telephone rate, day, addl. min., 1-10 mi.	min.	0.10	12/93	9s
Long-distance telephone rate, day, initial min., 1-10 mi.	min.	0.13	12/93	9s
Newspaper subscription, dly. and Sun. delivery	month	9.75	12/94	2c
Phone line, single, business, field visit	inst	31.00	12/93	9s
Phone line, single, business, no field visit	inst	31.00	12/93	9s
Phone line, single, residence, field visit	inst	12.00	12/93	9s
Phone line, single, residence, no field visit	inst	12.00	12/93	9s
Telephone bill, family of four	month	18.28	12/94	2c
Telephone service, expenditures	year	611	91	81r
Telephone, residential, flat rate	mo.	12.80	12/93	8c
Education				
Board, 4-year private college/university	year	2338	8/94	80s
Board, 4-year public college/university	year	2211	8/94	80s
Education, total expenditures	year	375	91	81r
Room, 4-year private college/university	year	1959	8/94	80s
Room, 4-year public college/university	year	1604	8/94	80s
Total cost, 4-year private college/university	year	16622	8/94	80s
Total cost, 4-year public college/university	year	6648	8/94	80s
Tuition, 2-year public college/university, in-state	year	1186	8/94	80s
Tuition, 4-year private college/university, in-state	year	12325	8/94	80s
Tuition, 4-year public college/university, in-state	year	2833	8/94	80s
Energy and Fuels				
Energy, combined forms, 1800 sq. ft.	mo.	82.84	12/94	2c
Fuel oil and other fuels, expenditures	year	33	91	81r
Gas, natural, expenditures	year	212	91	81r
Gas, reg unlead, taxes inc., cash, self-service	gal	1.30	12/94	2c
Gasoline and motor oil purchased	year	1115	91	81r
Gasoline, unleaded midgrade	gallon	1.36	4/93	82r
Gasoline, unleaded premium	gallon	1.43	4/93	82r
Gasoline, unleaded regular	gallon	1.23	4/93	82r
Entertainment				
Bowling, evening rate	game	1.75	12/94	2c
Concert ticket, Pearl Jam group	perf	20.00	94	50r
Entertainment, total expenditures	year	1853	91	81r
Fees and admissions, expenditures	year	482	91	81r
Monopoly game, Parker Brothers', No. 9	game	9.99	12/94	2c
Movie	adm	5.63	12/94	2c
Pets, toys, playground equipment, expenditures	year	299	91	81r
Reading, expenditures	year	164	91	81r
Televisions, radios, and sound equipment, expenditures	year	528	91	81r
Tennis balls, yellow, Wilson or Penn, 3	can	2.16	12/94	2c
Funerals				
Burial, immediate, container provided by funeral home		1382.70	1/95	54r
Cards, acknowledgment		21.87	1/95	54r
Casket, minimum alternative		128.54	1/95	54r
Cosmetology, hair care, etc.		119.69	1/95	54r
Cremation, direct, container provided by funeral home		1030.62	1/95	54r
Embalming		255.42	1/95	54r
Funeral, funeral home		437.38	1/95	54r
Funeral, other facility		444.46	1/95	54r
Graveside service		338.46	1/95	54r
Hearse, local		147.50	1/95	54r
Limousine, local		130.33	1/95	54r
Memorial service		553.16	1/95	54r
Service charge, professional, nondeclinable		859.15	1/95	54r
Visitation and viewing		93.23	1/95	54r
Groceries				
Groceries, ACCRA Index		0.80	12/94	2c

Values are in dollars or fractions of dollars. In the column headed *Ref*, references are shown to sources. Each reference is followed by a letter. These refer to the geographical level for which data were reported: s=State, r=Region, and c=City or metro. The abbreviation *ex* is used to mean *except* or *excluding*; *exp* stands for *expenditures*. For other abbreviations and further explanations, please see the Introduction.

Eugene, OR - continued

Item	Per	Value	Date	Ref.
Groceries				
Apples, Red Delicious	lb.	0.72	12/94	82r
Baby food, strained vegetables, lowest price	4-4.5 oz.	0.22	12/94	2c
Bacon, sliced	lb.	1.73	12/94	82r
Bananas	lb.	0.46	12/94	2c
Bananas	lb.	0.52	12/94	82r
Beef or hamburger, ground	lb.	1.50	12/94	2c
Beef purchases	year	241	91	81r
Beverage purchases, alcoholic	year	328	91	81r
Beverage purchases, nonalcoholic	year	234	91	81r
Bologna, all beef or mixed	lb.	2.33	12/94	82r
Bread, white	24-oz.	0.95	12/94	2c
Bread, white, pan	lb.	0.81	12/94	82r
Carrots, short trimmed and topped	lb.	0.43	12/94	82r
Cereals and bakery products purchases	year	392	91	81r
Cereals and cereals products purchases	year	139	91	81r
Cheese, Kraft grated Parmesan	8-oz.	3.17	12/94	2c
Chicken breast, bone-in	lb.	2.04	12/94	82r
Chicken, fresh, whole	lb.	0.95	12/94	82r
Chicken, whole fryer	lb.	1.06	12/94	2c
Cigarettes, Winston, Kings	carton	17.99	12/94	2c
Coffee, 100%, ground roast, all sizes	lb.	4.48	12/94	82r
Coffee, vacuum-packed	13 oz.	4.01	12/94	2c
Corn Flakes, Kellogg's or Post Toasties	18 oz.	1.82	12/94	2c
Corn, frozen, whole kernel, lowest price	10 oz.	0.71	12/94	2c
Dairy products (other) purchases	year	182	91	81r
Eggs, Grade A large	dozen	0.83	12/94	2c
Fish and seafood purchases	year	94	91	81r
Flour, white, all purpose	lb.	0.21	12/94	82r
Food purchases, food eaten at home	year	2749	91	81r
Foods purchased away from home, not prepared by consumer	year	1909	91	81r
Fruits and vegetables purchases	year	459	91	81r
Grapefruit	lb.	0.56	12/94	82r
Ground beef, 100% beef	lb.	1.31	12/94	82r
Ham, boneless, exc. canned	lb.	2.46	12/94	82r
Ice cream, prepackaged, bulk, regular	1/2 gal.	2.57	12/94	82r
Lemons	lb.	1.00	12/94	82r
Lettuce, iceberg	lb.	0.93	12/94	82r
Lettuce, iceberg	head	0.74	12/94	2c
Margarine, Blue Bonnet or Parkay cubes	lb.	0.50	12/94	2c
Meats, poultry, fish, and eggs purchases	year	700	91	81r
Milk and cream (fresh) purchases	year	155	91	81r
Milk, whole	1/2 gal.	1.28	12/94	2c
Orange juice, frozen concentrate 12-oz. can	16 oz.	1.52	12/94	82r
Orange juice, Minute Maid frozen	12-oz.	1.00	12/94	2c
Oranges, Navel	lb.	0.56	12/94	82r
Peaches, halves or slices, Hunt's, Del Monte, or Libby's	29-oz.	1.63	12/94	2c
Peas, sweet, Del Monte or Green Giant	15-17 oz.	0.58	12/94	2c
Pork chops, center cut, bone-in	lb.	3.30	12/94	82r
Pork purchases	year	122	91	81r
Potato chips	16-oz.	3.03	12/94	82r
Potatoes, frozen, French fried	lb.	0.77	12/94	82r
Potatoes, white	lb.	0.35	12/94	82r
Potatoes, white or red	10-lb. sack	1.44	12/94	2c
Rice, white, long grain, uncooked	lb.	0.54	12/94	82r
Round roast, USDA choice, boneless	lb.	2.92	12/94	82r
Sausage, Jimmy Dean, 100% pork	lb.	3.31	12/94	2c
Shortening, vegetable oil blends	lb.	0.80	12/94	82r
Shortening, vegetable, Crisco	3-lb.	1.72	12/94	2c
Soft drink, Coca Cola, ex deposit	2 lit	1.21	12/94	2c
Spaghetti and macaroni	lb.	1.02	12/94	82r
Steak, round, graded & ungraded, exc. USDA prime & choice	lb.	3.13	12/94	82r
Steak, sirloin, USDA choice, boneless	lb.	4.07	12/94	82r
Steak, t-bone	lb.	4.32	12/94	2c

Eugene, OR - continued

Item	Per	Value	Date	Ref.
Groceries - continued				
Sugar and other sweets, eaten at home, expenditures	year	105	91	81r
Sugar, cane or beet	4 lbs.	1.12	12/94	2c
Sugar, white, all sizes	lb.	0.38	12/94	82r
Tobacco products and smoking supplies, total expenditures	year	221	91	81r
Tomatoes, field grown	lb.	1.45	12/94	82r
Tomatoes, Hunt's or Del Monte	14.5 oz.	0.76	12/94	2c
Tuna, chunk, light	lb.	2.18	12/94	82r
Tuna, chunk, light, oil-packed	6.125-6.5 oz.	0.72	12/94	2c
Goods and Services				
Miscellaneous goods and services, ACCRA Index		103.30	12/94	2c
Health Care				
Health care, ACCRA Index		18.80	12/94	2c
Antibiotic ointment, Polysporin	1.5 oz.	3.99	12/94	2c
Childbirth, Cesarean delivery, hospital charge	birth	6059.00	12/91	69r
Childbirth, Cesarean delivery, physician charge	birth	2248.00	12/91	69r
Childbirth, normal delivery, hospital charge	birth	3006.00	12/91	69r
Childbirth, normal delivery, physician charge	birth	1634.00	12/91	69r
Dentist's fee, adult teeth cleaning and periodic oral exam	visit	67.25	12/94	2c
Doctor's fee, routine exam, established patient	visit	48.75	12/94	2c
Drugs, expenditures	year	230	91	81r
Health care, total expenditures	year	1544	91	81r
Health insurance expenditures	year	558	91	81r
Hospital care, semiprivate room	day	424.50	12/94	2c
Insurance premium, family medical care	month	331.06	1/95	41s
Medical services expenditures	year	676	91	81r
Medical supplies expenditures	year	80	91	81r
Surgery, open-heart	proc	37818.00	1/93	14r
Household Goods				
Appl. repair, service call, wash mach	min. lab. chg.	37.25	12/94	2c
Floor coverings, expenditures	year	79	91	81r
Furniture, expenditures	year	352	91	81r
Household equipment, misc. expenditures	year	614	91	81r
Household expenditures, miscellaneous	year	294	91	81r
Household furnishings and equipment, expenditures	year	1416	91	81r
Household operations expenditures	year	580	91	81r
Household textiles, expenditures	year	113	91	81r
Housekeeping supplies, expenditures	year	447	91	81r
Laundry and cleaning supplies, expenditures	year	114	91	81r
Laundry detergent, Tide Ultra, Bold, or Cheer	42 oz.	4.16	12/94	2c
Postage and stationery, expenditures	year	145	91	81r
Tissues, facial, Kleenex brand	175	1.15	12/94	2c
Housing				
Housing, ACCRA Index		37.10	12/94	2c
Add garage/carport		6,422	3/95	74r
Add room(s)		26,583	3/95	74r
Apartment condominium or co-op, median	unit	105300	12/94	62r
Dwellings (owned), expenditures	year	3932	91	81r
Enclose porch/patio/breezeway		5,382	3/95	74r
Finish room in basement/attic		3,911	3/95	74r
Home, existing, single-family, median	unit	178600	12/94	62r
Home, existing, single-family, median	unit	96.70	12/94	62c
House payment, principal and interest, 25% down payment	mo.	1091	12/94	2c
House, 1800 sq ft, 8000 sq ft lot, new, urban, utilities	total	177167	12/94	2c

Values are in dollars or fractions of dollars. In the column headed *Ref*, references are shown to sources. Each reference is followed by a letter. These refer to the geographical level for which data were reported: s=State, r=Region, and c=City or metro. The abbreviation *ex* is used to mean *except* or *excluding*; *exp* stands for expenditures. For other abbreviations and further explanations, please see the Introduction.

Eugene, OR - continued

Item	Per	Value	Date	Ref.
Housing				
Maintenance, repairs, insurance, and other housing expenditures	year	591	91	81r
Mortgage interest and charges expenditures	year	2747	91	81r
Mtge. rate, incl. points and orig. fee, 30-year conv. fixed or ARM	mo.	9.22	12/94	2c
Princ. & int., mortgage, median-price exist. sing.-family home	mo.	845	12/94	62r
Property taxes expenditures	year	594	91	81r
Redesign, restructure more than half of home's interior		5,467	3/95	74r
Rent, apartment, 2 br., 1 1/2-2 baths, unfurnished, 950 sq ft, water	mo.	607	12/94	2c
Rental units expenditures	year	2077	91	81r
Insurance and Pensions				
Auto insurance, private passenger	year	632.21	12/94	71s
Insurance and pensions, personal, expenditures	year	3042	91	81r
Insurance, life and other personal, expenditures	year	298	91	81r
Pensions and Social Security, expenditures	year	2744	91	81r
Legal Assistance				
Legal work, law firm associate	hour	91		10r
Legal work, law firm partner	hour	151		10r
Personal Goods				
Shampoo, Alberto VO5	15-oz.	1.22	12/94	2c
Toothpaste, Crest or Colgate	6-7 oz.	2.04	12/94	2c
Personal Services				
Dry cleaning, man's 2-pc. suit		7.24	12/94	2c
Haircut, man's barbershop, no styling		9.31	12/94	2c
Haircut, woman's shampoo, trim, blow-dry		21.75	12/94	2c
Personal services expenditures	year	286	91	81r
Restaurant Food				
Chicken, fried, thigh and drumstick		2.19	12/94	2c
Dining expenditures, family	week	32.25	94	73r
Hamburger with cheese	1/4 lb.	2.04	12/94	2c
Pizza, Pizza Hut or Pizza Inn	12-13 in.	8.90	12/94	2c
Taxes				
Taxes, Federal income, expenditures	year	2946	91	81r
Taxes, personal, expenditures	year	3791	91	81r
Taxes, State and local income, expenditures	year	791	91	81r
Transportation				
Transportation, ACCRA Index		10.20	12/94	2c
Bus fare, up to 10 miles	one-way	0.75	12/94	2c
Cars and trucks purchased, new	year	1231	91	81r
Cars and trucks purchased, used	year	915	91	81r
Driver's learning permit fee	perm	13.00	1/94	84s
Driver's license fee	orig	26.25	1/94	84s
Driver's license fee, duplicate	lic	11.00	1/94	84s
Driver's license reinstatement fee, min.	susp	53.00	1/94	85s
Driver's license renewal fee	renew	16.25	1/94	84s
Identification card, nondriver	card	13.00	1/94	83s
Motorcycle learning permit fee	perm	13.00	1/94	84s
Motorcycle license fee	orig	30.00	1/94	84s
Motorcycle license fee, duplicate	lic	11.00	1/94	84s
Motorcycle license renewal fee	renew	7.00	1/94	84s
Public transportation expenditures	year	375	91	81r
Tire balance, computer or spin bal., front	wheel	7.56	12/94	2c
Transportation expenditures, total	year	5527	91	81r
Vehicle finance charges	year	287	91	81r
Vehicle insurance expenditures	year	624	91	81r
Vehicle maintenance and repairs expenditures	year	695	91	81r
Vehicle purchases	year	2174	91	81r
Vehicle rental, leases, licenses, etc. expenditures	year	257	91	81r

Eugene, OR - continued

Item	Per	Value	Date	Ref.
Transportation - continued				
Vehicles purchased, other than cars and trucks	year	28	91	81r
Utilities				
Utilities, ACCRA Index		6.50	12/94	2c
Electricity expenditures	year	616	91	81r
Electricity, 1800 sq. ft., new home	mo.	82.84	12/94	2c
Utilities, fuels, and public services, total expenditures	year	1681	91	81r
Water and other public services, expenditures	year	209	91	81r
Weddings				
Bridal attendants' gowns	event	750	10/93	76r
Bridal gown	event	852	10/93	76r
Bridal headpiece and veil	event	167	10/93	76r
Bride's wedding band	event	708	10/93	76r
Clergy	event	224	10/93	76r
Engagement ring	event	2756	10/93	76r
Flowers	event	863	10/93	76r
Formal wear for groom	event	106	10/93	76r
Groom's attendants' formal wear	event	530	10/93	76r
Groom's wedding band	event	402	10/93	76r
Music	event	600	10/93	76r
Photography	event	1088	10/93	76r
Shoes for bride	event	50	10/93	76r
Videography	event	483	10/93	76r
Wedding invitations and announcements	event	342	10/93	76r
Wedding reception	event	7000	10/93	76r

Evansville, IN

Item	Per	Value	Date	Ref.
Composite, ACCRA index		94.90	12/94	2c
Alcoholic Beverages				
Beer, Miller Lite, Bud, 12-oz., ex deposit	6	3.74	12/94	2c
J & B Scotch	750-ml.	16.73	12/94	2c
Wine, Gallo Chablis blanc	1.5-lit	5.14	12/94	2c
Appliances				
Appliances (major), expenditures	year	131	91	81r
Average annual exp.				
Food, health care, personal goods, services	year	25935	91	81r
Charity				
Cash contributions, expenditures	year	745	91	81r
Clothing				
Apparel, men and boys, total expenditures	year	332	91	81r
Apparel, women and girls, total expenditures	year	578	91	81r
Footwear, expenditures	year	164	91	81r
Jeans, man's denim		29.96	12/94	2c
Shirt, man's dress shirt		27.05	12/94	2c
Undervest, boy's size 10-14, cotton	3	2.73	12/94	2c
Communications				
Long-distance telephone rate, day, addl. min., 1-10 mi.	min.	0.10	12/93	9s
Long-distance telephone rate, day, initial min., 1-10 mi.	min.	0.18	12/93	9s
Newspaper subscription, dly. and Sun. delivery	month	14.25	12/94	2c
Phone line, single, business, field visit	inst	59.00	12/93	9s
Phone line, single, business, no field visit	inst	59.00	12/93	9s
Phone line, single, residence, field visit	inst	47.00	12/93	9s
Phone line, single, residence, no field visit	inst	47.00	12/93	9s
Telephone bill, family of four	month	22.13	12/94	2c
Telephone service, expenditures	year	547	91	81r
Telephone, residential, flat rate	mo.	11.11	12/93	8c
Education				
Board, 4-year private college/university	year	2095	8/94	80s
Board, 4-year public college/university	year	2300	8/94	80s
Education, total expenditures	year	394	91	81r

Values are in dollars or fractions of dollars. In the column headed *Ref*, references are shown to sources. Each reference is followed by a letter. These refer to the geographical level for which data were reported: s = State, r = Region, and c = City or metro. The abbreviation *ex* is used to mean *except* or *excluding*; *exp* stands for expenditures. For other abbreviations and further explanations, please see the Introduction.

Evansville, IN - continued

Item	Per	Value	Date	Ref.
Education				
Room, 4-year private college/university	year	1784	8/94	80s
Room, 4-year public college/university	year	1718	8/94	80s
Total cost, 4-year private college/university	year	15045	8/94	80s
Total cost, 4-year public college/university	year	6639	8/94	80s
Tuition, 2-year public college/university, in-state	year	1737	8/94	80s
Tuition, 4-year private college/university, in-state	year	11165	8/94	80s
Tuition, 4-year public college/university, in-state	year	2621	8/94	80s
Energy and Fuels				
Energy, combined forms, 1800 sq. ft.	mo.	105.40	12/94	2c
Energy, exc. electricity, 1800 sq. ft.	mo.	35.84	12/94	2c
Fuel oil and other fuels, expenditures	year	83	91	81r
Gas, cooking, 10 therms	month	9.06	2/94	65c
Gas, cooking, 30 therms	month	17.00	2/94	65c
Gas, cooking, 50 therms	month	24.94	2/94	65c
Gas, heating, winter, 100 therms	month	43.54	2/94	65c
Gas, heating, winter, average use	month	85.93	2/94	65c
Gas, natural, expenditures	year	373	91	81r
Gas, reg unlead, taxes inc., cash, self-service	gal	1.12	12/94	2c
Gasoline and motor oil purchased	year	1000	91	81r
Gasoline, unleaded midgrade	gallon	1.15	4/93	82r
Gasoline, unleaded premium	gallon	1.23	4/93	82r
Gasoline, unleaded regular	gallon	1.07	4/93	82r
Entertainment				
Bowling, evening rate	game	1.96	12/94	2c
Entertainment, total expenditures	year	1356	91	81r
Fees and admissions, expenditures	year	347	91	81r
Monopoly game, Parker Brothers', No. 9	game	10.15	12/94	2c
Movie	adm	5.44	12/94	2c
Pets, toys, playground equipment, expenditures	year	270	91	81r
Reading, expenditures	year	160	91	81r
Televisions, radios, and sound equipment, expenditures	year	433	91	81r
Tennis balls, yellow, Wilson or Penn, 3	can	2.00	12/94	2c
Funerals				
Burial, immediate, container provided by funeral home		1268.31	1/95	54r
Cards, acknowledgment		26.12	1/95	54r
Casket, minimum alternative		198.03	1/95	54r
Cosmetology, hair care, etc.		122.19	1/95	54r
Cremation, direct, container provided by funeral home		977.81	1/95	54r
Embalming		334.00	1/95	54r
Funeral, funeral home		321.16	1/95	54r
Funeral, other facility		317.73	1/95	54r
Graveside service		292.48	1/95	54r
Hearse, local		153.20	1/95	54r
Limousine, local		123.52	1/95	54r
Memorial service		356.30	1/95	54r
Service charge, professional, nondeclinable		968.24	1/95	54r
Visitation and viewing		332.66	1/95	54r
Groceries				
Groceries, ACCRA Index		96.20	12/94	2c
Apples, Red Delicious	lb.	0.68	12/94	82r
Baby food, strained vegetables, lowest price	4-4.5 oz.	0.29	12/94	2c
Bacon, sliced	lb.	1.88	12/94	82r
Bananas	lb.	0.33	12/94	2c
Bananas	lb.	0.41	12/94	82r
Beef or hamburger, ground	lb.	1.04	12/94	2c
Beef purchases	year	197	91	81r
Beef, stew, boneless	lb.	2.52	12/94	82r
Beverage purchases, alcoholic	year	293	91	81r
Beverage purchases, nonalcoholic	year	203	91	81r
Bologna, all beef or mixed	lb.	2.12	12/94	82r
Bread, white	24-oz.	0.84	12/94	2c

Evansville, IN - continued

Item	Per	Value	Date	Ref.
Groceries - continued				
Bread, white, pan	lb.	0.76	12/94	82r
Cabbage	lb.	0.44	12/94	82r
Carrots, short trimmed and topped	lb.	0.44	12/94	82r
Cereals and bakery products purchases	year	347	91	81r
Cereals and cereals products purchases	year	119	91	81r
Cheddar cheese, natural	lb.	3.28	12/94	82r
Cheese, Kraft grated Parmesan	8-oz.	3.11	12/94	2c
Chicken breast, bone-in	lb.	1.61	12/94	82r
Chicken, fresh, whole	lb.	0.89	12/94	82r
Chicken, whole fryer	lb.	0.81	12/94	2c
Chuck roast, USDA choice, boneless	lb.	2.33	12/94	82r
Cigarettes, Winston, Kings	carton	14.07	12/94	2c
Coffee, 100%, ground roast, all sizes	lb.	4.28	12/94	82r
Coffee, vacuum-packed	13 oz.	3.77	12/94	2c
Cookies, chocolate chip	lb.	2.72	12/94	82r
Corn Flakes, Kellogg's or Post Toasties	18 oz.	2.26	12/94	2c
Corn, frozen, whole kernel, lowest price	10 oz.	0.70	12/94	2c
Dairy products (other) purchases	year	148	91	81r
Eggs, Grade A large	dozen	0.78	12/94	2c
Eggs, Grade A large	dozen	0.76	12/94	82r
Fish and seafood purchases	year	61	91	81r
Flour, white, all purpose	lb.	0.22	12/94	82r
Food purchases, food eaten at home	year	2313	91	81r
Foods purchased away from home, not prepared by consumer	year	1709	91	81r
Fruits and vegetables purchases	year	372	91	81r
Grapefruit	lb.	0.47	12/94	82r
Grapes, Thompson seedless	lb.	2.15	12/94	82r
Ground beef, 100% beef	lb.	1.37	12/94	82r
Ground chuck, 100% beef	lb.	1.81	12/94	82r
Ham, boneless, exc. canned	lb.	2.16	12/94	82r
Ice cream, prepackaged, bulk, regular	1/2 gal.	2.48	12/94	82r
Lemons	lb.	1.08	12/94	82r
Lettuce, iceberg	lb.	0.81	12/94	82r
Lettuce, iceberg	head	0.90	12/94	2c
Margarine, Blue Bonnet or Parkay cubes	lb.	0.60	12/94	2c
Margarine, stick	lb.	0.81	12/94	82r
Meats, poultry, fish, and eggs purchases	year	591	91	81r
Milk and cream (fresh) purchases	year	132	91	81r
Milk, whole	1/2 gal.	1.54	12/94	2c
Orange juice, frozen concentrate 12-oz. can	16 oz.	1.41	12/94	82r
Orange juice, Minute Maid frozen	12-oz.	1.20	12/94	2c
Oranges, Navel	lb.	0.56	12/94	82r
Peaches, halves or slices, Hunt's, Del Monte, or Libby's	29-oz.	1.43	12/94	2c
Peanut butter, creamy, all sizes	lb.	1.81	12/94	82r
Peas, sweet, Del Monte or Green Giant	15-17 oz.	0.58	12/94	2c
Pork chops, center cut, bone-in	lb.	2.76	12/94	82r
Pork purchases	year	130	91	81r
Potato chips	16-oz.	2.81	12/94	82r
Potatoes, frozen, French fried	lb.	0.83	12/94	82r
Potatoes, white	lb.	0.28	12/94	82r
Potatoes, white or red	10-lb. sack	1.56	12/94	2c
Round roast, USDA choice, boneless	lb.	2.90	12/94	82r
Sausage, Jimmy Dean, 100% pork	lb.	2.66	12/94	2c
Shortening, vegetable oil blends	lb.	0.88	12/94	82r
Shortening, vegetable, Crisco	3-lb.	2.36	12/94	2c
Soft drink, Coca Cola, ex deposit	2 lit	1.23	12/94	2c
Spaghetti and macaroni	lb.	0.78	12/94	82r
Steak, rib eye, USDA choice, boneless	lb.	6.15	12/94	82r
Steak, round, graded & ungraded, exc. USDA prime & choice	lb.	2.72	12/94	82r
Steak, round, USDA choice, boneless	lb.	3.02	12/94	82r
Steak, sirloin, USDA choice, boneless	lb.	3.85	12/94	82r
Steak, t-bone	lb.	5.62	12/94	2c
Steak, T-bone, USDA choice, bone-in	lb.	5.38	12/94	82r
Sugar and other sweets, eaten at home, expenditures	year	91	91	81r

Values are in dollars or fractions of dollars. In the column headed *Ref*, references are shown to sources. Each reference is followed by a letter. These refer to the geographical level for which data were reported: s=State, r=Region, and c=City or metro. The abbreviation *ex* is used to mean *except* or *excluding*; *exp* stands for *expenditures*. For other abbreviations and further explanations, please see the Introduction.

Evansville, IN - continued

Item	Per	Value	Date	Ref.
Groceries				
Sugar, cane or beet	4 lbs.	1.28	12/94	2c
Sugar, white, all sizes	lb.	0.36	12/94	82r
Tobacco products and smoking supplies, total expenditures	year	298	91	81r
Tomatoes, field grown	lb.	1.36	12/94	82r
Tomatoes, Hunt's or Del Monte	14.5 oz.	0.75	12/94	2c
Tuna, chunk, light	lb.	1.94	12/94	82r
Tuna, chunk, light, oil-packed	6.125-6.5 oz.	0.64	12/94	2c
Turkey, frozen, whole	lb.	0.96	12/94	82r
Yogurt, natural, fruit flavored	8 oz.	0.62	12/94	82r
Goods and Services				
Miscellaneous goods and services, ACCRA Index		95.90	12/94	2c
Health Care				
Health care, ACCRA Index		88.00	12/94	2c
Antibiotic ointment, Polysporin	1.5 oz.	3.70	12/94	2c
Childbirth, Cesarean delivery, hospital charge	birth	5101.00	12/91	69r
Childbirth, Cesarean delivery, physician charge	birth	2234.00	12/91	69r
Childbirth, normal delivery, hospital charge	birth	2891.00	12/91	69r
Childbirth, normal delivery, physician charge	birth	1623.00	12/91	69r
Dentist's fee, adult teeth cleaning and periodic oral exam	visit	41.38	12/94	2c
Doctor's fee, routine exam, established patient	visit	37.31	12/94	2c
Drugs, expenditures	year	248	91	81r
Health care, total expenditures	year	1336	91	81r
Health insurance expenditures	year	550	91	81r
Hospital care, semiprivate room	day	365.33	12/94	2c
Insurance premium, family medical care	month	353.94	1/95	41s
Medical services expenditures	year	457	91	81r
Medical supplies expenditures	year	82	91	81r
Household Goods				
Appl. repair, service call, wash mach	min. lab. chg.	29.59	12/94	2c
Floor coverings, expenditures	year	105	91	81r
Furniture, expenditures	year	291	91	81r
Household equipment, misc. expenditures	year	341	91	81r
Household expenditures, miscellaneous	year	162	91	81r
Household furnishings and equipment, expenditures	year	1042	91	81r
Household operations expenditures	year	365	91	81r
Household textiles, expenditures	year	101	91	81r
Housekeeping supplies, expenditures	year	390	91	81r
Laundry and cleaning supplies, expenditures	year	110	91	81r
Laundry detergent, Tide Ultra, Bold, or Cheer	42 oz.	3.14	12/94	2c
Postage and stationery, expenditures	year	115	91	81r
Tissues, facial, Kleenex brand	175	0.96	12/94	2c
Housing				
Housing, ACCRA Index		94.30	12/94	2c
Add garage/carport		8,479	3/95	74r
Add room(s)		21,347	3/95	74r
Apartment condominium or co-op, median	unit	87100	12/94	62r
Bathroom addition, average cost	add	9734.00	3/95	13r
Bathroom remodeling, average cost	remod	6414.00	3/95	13r
Bedroom, master suite addition, average cost	add	27122.00	3/95	13r
Deck addition, average cost	add	6665.00	3/95	13r
Dwellings (owned), expenditures	year	2566	91	81r
Enclose porch/patio/breezeway		4,556	3/95	74r
Exterior remodeling, average cost	remod	15395.00	3/95	13r
Family room addition, average cost	add	27658.00	3/95	13r
Finish room in basement/attic		5,074	3/95	74r
Home, existing, single-family, median	unit	106500	12/94	62r

Evansville, IN - continued

Item	Per	Value	Date	Ref.
Housing - continued				
House payment, principal and interest, 25% down payment	mo.	746	12/94	2c
House, 1800 sq ft, 8000 sq ft lot, new, urban, utilities	total	119667	12/94	2c
Kitchen remodeling, major, average cost	remod	17084.00	3/95	13r
Kitchen remodeling, minor, average cost	remod	5804.00	3/95	13r
Maintenance, repairs, insurance, and other housing expenditures	year	484	91	81r
Mortgage interest and charges expenditures	year	1443	91	81r
Mtge. rate, incl. points and orig. fee, 30-year conv. fixed or ARM	mo.	9.37	12/94	2c
Office, home addition, average cost	add	8121.00	3/95	13r
Princ. & int., mortgage, median-price exist. sing.-family home	mo.	515	12/94	62r
Property taxes expenditures	year	639	91	81r
Redesign, restructure more than half of home's interior		9,114	3/95	74r
Rent, apartment, 2 br., 1 1/2-2 baths, unfurnished, 950 sq ft, water	mo.	430	12/94	2c
Rental units expenditures	year	1200	91	81r
Sun-space addition, average cost	add	23768.00	3/95	13r
Wing addition, two-story, average cost	add	50410.00	3/95	13r
Insurance and Pensions				
Auto insurance, private passenger	year	586.58	12/94	71s
Insurance and pensions, personal, expenditures	year	2408	91	81r
Insurance, life and other personal, expenditures	year	355	91	81r
Pensions and Social Security, expenditures	year	2053	91	81r
Legal Assistance				
Legal work, law firm associate	hour	90		10r
Legal work, law firm partner	hour	139		10r
Personal Goods				
Shampoo, Alberto VO5	15-oz.	0.94	12/94	2c
Toothpaste, Crest or Colgate	6-7 oz.	1.61	12/94	2c
Personal Services				
Dry cleaning, man's 2-pc. suit		7.08	12/94	2c
Haircut, man's barbershop, no styling		7.00	12/94	2c
Haircut, woman's shampoo, trim, blow-dry		19.30	12/94	2c
Personal services expenditures	year	203	91	81r
Restaurant Food				
Chicken, fried, thigh and drumstick		2.23	12/94	2c
Dining expenditures, family	week	30.03	94	73r
Hamburger with cheese	1/4 lb.	1.75	12/94	2c
Pizza, Pizza Hut or Pizza Inn	12-13 in.	10.00	12/94	2c
Taxes				
Taxes, Federal income, expenditures	year	1756	91	81r
Taxes, personal, expenditures	year	2426	91	81r
Taxes, State and local income, expenditures	year	568	91	81r
Transportation				
Transportation, ACCRA Index		94.20	12/94	2c
Cars and trucks purchased, new	year	891	91	81r
Cars and trucks purchased, used	year	1155	91	81r
Driver's learning permit fee	perm	2.00	1/94	84s
Driver's license fee	orig	6.00	1/94	84s
Driver's license fee, duplicate	lic	3.00	1/94	84s
Driver's license renewal fee	renew	6.00	1/94	84s
Identification card, nondriver	card	4.00	1/94	83s
Motorcycle learning permit fee	perm	2.00	1/94	84s
Motorcycle license fee	orig	6.00	1/94	84s
Motorcycle license fee, duplicate	lic	3.00	1/94	84s
Motorcycle license renewal fee	renew	6.00	1/94	84s
Public transportation expenditures	year	209	91	81r
Tire balance, computer or spin bal., front	wheel	5.89	12/94	2c
Transportation expenditures, total	year	4792	91	81r
Vehicle finance charges	year	300	91	81r
Vehicle insurance expenditures	year	485	91	81r

Values are in dollars or fractions of dollars. In the column headed *Ref*, references are shown to sources. Each reference is followed by a letter. These refer to the geographical level for which data were reported: s = State, r = Region, and c = City or metro. The abbreviation *ex* is used to mean *except* or *excluding*; *exp* stands for *expenditures*. For other abbreviations and further explanations, please see the Introduction.

Evansville, IN - continued

Item	Per	Value	Date	Ref.
Transportation				
Vehicle maintenance and repairs expenditures	year	534	91	81r
Vehicle purchases	year	2068	91	81r
Vehicle rental, leases, licenses, etc. expenditures	year	197	91	81r
Vehicles purchased, other than cars and trucks	year	22	91	81r
Utilities				
Utilities, ACCRA Index		96.60	12/94	2c
Electricity expenditures	year	668	91	81r
Electricity, (part.), other, 1800 sq. ft., new home	mo.	69.56	12/94	2c
Electricity, summer, 250 KWh	month	22.41	8/93	64c
Electricity, summer, 500 KWh	month	38.15	8/93	64c
Electricity, summer, 750 KWh	month	53.89	8/93	64c
Electricity, summer, 1000 KWh	month	69.63	8/93	64c
Utilities, fuels, and public services, total expenditures	year	1838	91	81r
Water and other public services, expenditures	year	167	91	81r
Weddings				
Bridal attendants' gowns	event	750	10/93	76r
Bridal gown	event	852	10/93	76r
Bridal headpiece and veil	event	167	10/93	76r
Bride's wedding band	event	708	10/93	76r
Clergy	event	224	10/93	76r
Engagement ring	event	2756	10/93	76r
Flowers	event	863	10/93	76r
Formal wear for groom	event	106	10/93	76r
Groom's attendants' formal wear	event	530	10/93	76r
Groom's wedding band	event	402	10/93	76r
Music	event	600	10/93	76r
Photography	event	1088	10/93	76r
Shoes for bride	event	50	10/93	76r
Videography	event	483	10/93	76r
Wedding invitations and announcements	event	342	10/93	76r
Wedding reception	event	7000	10/93	76r

Fairbanks, AK

Item	Per	Value	Date	Ref.
Composite, ACCRA index		127.90	12/94	2c
Alcoholic Beverages				
Beer, Miller Lite, Bud, 12-oz., ex deposit	6	5.00	12/94	2c
J & B Scotch	750-ml.	20.45	12/94	2c
Wine, Gallo Chablis blanc	1.5-lit	6.17	12/94	2c
Clothing				
Jeans, man's denim		34.13	12/94	2c
Shirt, man's dress shirt		32.33	12/94	2c
Undervest, boy's size 10-14, cotton	3	4.54	12/94	2c
Communications				
Newspaper subscription, dly. and Sun. delivery	month	12.00	12/94	2c
Telephone bill, family of four	month	16.49	12/94	2c
Energy and Fuels				
Energy, combined forms, 1800 sq. ft.	mo.	157.54	12/94	2c
Energy, exc. electricity, 1800 sq. ft.	mo.	89.00	12/94	2c
Gas, reg unlead, taxes inc., cash, self-service	gal	1.27	12/94	2c
Entertainment				
Bowling, evening rate	game	3.00	12/94	2c
Monopoly game, Parker Brothers', No. 9	game	11.65	12/94	2c
Movie	adm	6.75	12/94	2c
Tennis balls, yellow, Wilson or Penn, 3	can	2.93	12/94	2c
Groceries				
Groceries, ACCRA Index		130.00	12/94	2c

Fairbanks, AK - continued

Item	Per	Value	Date	Ref.
Groceries - continued				
Baby food, strained vegetables, lowest price	4-4.5 oz.	0.36	12/94	2c
Bananas	lb.	0.88	12/94	2c
Beef or hamburger, ground	lb.	1.75	12/94	2c
Bread, white	24-oz.	1.15	12/94	2c
Cheese, Kraft grated Parmesan	8-oz.	3.29	12/94	2c
Chicken, whole fryer	lb.	1.19	12/94	2c
Cigarettes, Winston, Kings	carton	18.67	12/94	2c
Coffee, vacuum-packed	13 oz.	4.23	12/94	2c
Corn Flakes, Kellogg's or Post Toasties	18 oz.	2.46	12/94	2c
Corn, frozen, whole kernel, lowest price	10 oz.	0.99	12/94	2c
Eggs, Grade A large	dozen	1.44	12/94	2c
Lettuce, iceberg	head	1.24	12/94	2c
Margarine, Blue Bonnet or Parkay cubes	lb.	0.72	12/94	2c
Milk, whole	1/2 gal.	1.99	12/94	2c
Orange juice, Minute Maid frozen	12-oz.	1.17	12/94	2c
Peaches, halves or slices, Hunt's, Del Monte, or Libby's	29-oz.	1.53	12/94	2c
Peas, sweet, Del Monte or Green Giant	15-17 oz.	0.68	12/94	2c
Potatoes, white or red	10-lb. sack	3.54	12/94	2c
Sausage, Jimmy Dean, 100% pork	lb.	3.84	12/94	2c
Shortening, vegetable, Crisco	3-lb.	2.55	12/94	2c
Soft drink, Coca Cola, ex deposit	2 lit	1.80	12/94	2c
Steak, t-bone	lb.	6.34	12/94	2c
Sugar, cane or beet	4 lbs.	2.00	12/94	2c
Tomatoes, Hunt's or Del Monte	14.5 oz.	0.85	12/94	2c
Tuna, chunk, light, oil-packed	6.125-6.5 oz.	0.83	12/94	2c
Goods and Services				
Miscellaneous goods and services, ACCRA Index		121.30	12/94	2c
Health Care				
Health care, ACCRA Index		177.00	12/94	2c
Antibiotic ointment, Polysporin	1.5 oz.	4.12	12/94	2c
Dentist's fee, adult teeth cleaning and periodic oral exam	visit	121.50	12/94	2c
Doctor's fee, routine exam, established patient	visit	72.25	12/94	2c
Hospital care, semiprivate room	day	456.00	12/94	2c
Household Goods				
Appl. repair, service call, wash mach	min. lab. chg.	43.67	12/94	2c
Laundry detergent, Tide Ultra, Bold, or Cheer	42 oz.	4.67	12/94	2c
Tissues, facial, Kleenex brand	175	1.17	12/94	2c
Housing				
Housing, ACCRA Index		127.80	12/94	2c
House payment, principal and interest, 25% down payment	mo.	961	12/94	2c
House, 1800 sq ft, 8000 sq ft lot, new, urban, utilities	total	153000	12/94	2c
Mtge. rate, incl. points and orig. fee, 30-year conv. fixed or ARM	mo.	9.46	12/94	2c
Rent, apartment, 2 br., 1 1/2-2 baths, unfurnished, 950 sq ft, water	mo.	725	12/94	2c
Personal Goods				
Shampoo, Alberto VO5	15-oz.	1.17	12/94	2c
Toothpaste, Crest or Colgate	6-7 oz.	2.21	12/94	2c
Personal Services				
Dry cleaning, man's 2-pc. suit		9.55	12/94	2c
Haircut, man's barbershop, no styling		13.09	12/94	2c
Haircut, woman's shampoo, trim, blow-dry		21.88	12/94	2c

Values are in dollars or fractions of dollars. In the column headed *Ref*, references are shown to sources. Each reference is followed by a letter. These refer to the geographical level for which data were reported: s=State, r=Region, and c=City or metro. The abbreviation *ex* is used to mean *except* or *excluding*; *exp* stands for *expenditures*. For other abbreviations and further explanations, please see the Introduction.

Fairbanks, AK - continued

Item	Per	Value	Date	Ref.
Restaurant Food				
Chicken, fried, thigh and drumstick		3.00	12/94	2c
Hamburger with cheese	1/4 lb.	2.32	12/94	2c
Pizza, Pizza Hut or Pizza Inn	12-13 in.	10.99	12/94	2c
Transportation				
Transportation, ACCRA Index		111.40	12/94	2c
Tire balance, computer or spin bal., front	wheel	7.39	12/94	2c
Utilities				
Utilities, ACCRA Index		132.90	12/94	2c
Electricity, (part.), other, 1800 sq. ft., new home	mo.	68.54	12/94	2c

Fall River, MA

Item	Per	Value	Date	Ref.
Appliances				
Appliances (major), expenditures	year	145	91	81r
Average annual exp.				
Food, health care, personal goods, services	year	29496	91	81r
Charity				
Cash contributions, expenditures	year	708	91	81r
Clothing				
Apparel, men and boys, total expenditures	year	416	91	81r
Apparel, women and girls, total expenditures	year	744	91	81r
Footwear, expenditures	year	305	91	81r
Communications				
Long-distance telephone rate, day, addl. min., 1-10 mi.	min.	0.09	12/93	9s
Long-distance telephone rate, day, initial min., 1-10 mi.	min.	0.19	12/93	9s
Phone line, single, business, field visit	inst	27.50	12/93	9s
Phone line, single, business, no field visit	inst	93.02	12/93	9s
Phone line, single, residence, field visit	inst	27.50	12/93	9s
Phone line, single, residence, no field visit	inst	37.07	12/93	9s
Telephone service, expenditures	year	589	91	81r
Education				
Board, 4-year private college/university	year	3179	8/94	80s
Board, 4-year public college/university	year	2035	8/94	80s
Education, total expenditures	year	593	91	81r
Room, 4-year private college/university	year	3369	8/94	80s
Room, 4-year public college/university	year	2290	8/94	80s
Total cost, 4-year private college/university	year	21346	8/94	80s
Total cost, 4-year public college/university	year	8467	8/94	80s
Tuition, 2-year public college/university, in-state	year	2361	8/94	80s
Tuition, 4-year private college/university, in-state	year	14797	8/94	80s
Tuition, 4-year public college/university, in-state	year	4142	8/94	80s
Energy and Fuels				
Fuel oil and other fuels, expenditures	year	257	91	81r
Gas, natural, expenditures	year	285	91	81r
Gasoline and motor oil purchased	year	867	91	81r
Gasoline, unleaded midgrade	gallon	1.32	4/93	82r
Gasoline, unleaded premium	gallon	1.40	4/93	82r
Gasoline, unleaded regular	gallon	1.19	4/93	82r
Entertainment				
Entertainment, total expenditures	year	1331	91	81r
Fees and admissions, expenditures	year	398	91	81r
Pets, toys, playground equipment, expenditures	year	270	91	81r
Reading, expenditures	year	171	91	81r
Televisions, radios, and sound equipment, expenditures	year	429	91	81r
Funerals				
Burial, immediate, container provided by funeral home		1507.89	1/95	54r

Fall River, MA - continued

Item	Per	Value	Date	Ref.
Funerals - continued				
Cards, acknowledgment		18.10	1/95	54r
Casket, minimum alternative		133.03	1/95	54r
Cosmetology, hair care, etc.		114.12	1/95	54r
Cremation, direct, container provided by funeral home		1309.19	1/95	54r
Embalming		320.97	1/95	54r
Funeral, funeral home		327.61	1/95	54r
Funeral, other facility		314.81	1/95	54r
Graveside service		286.11	1/95	54r
Hearse, local		158.95	1/95	54r
Limousine, local		149.45	1/95	54r
Memorial service		315.94	1/95	54r
Service charge, professional, nondeclinable		1148.43	1/95	54r
Visitation and viewing		249.66	1/95	54r
Groceries				
Apples, Red Delicious	lb.	0.78	12/94	82r
Bacon, sliced	lb.	2.24	12/94	82r
Bananas	lb.	0.49	12/94	82r
Beef purchases	year	226	91	81r
Beverage purchases, alcoholic	year	332	91	81r
Beverage purchases, nonalcoholic	year	213	91	81r
Bread, white, pan	lb.	0.80	12/94	82r
Butter, salted, Grade AA, stick	lb.	1.67	12/94	82r
Carrots, short trimmed and topped	lb.	0.51	12/94	82r
Cereals and bakery products purchases	year	407	91	81r
Cereals and cereals products purchases	year	132	91	81r
Chicken breast, bone-in	lb.	2.22	12/94	82r
Chicken, fresh, whole	lb.	1.05	12/94	82r
Chuck roast, USDA choice, boneless	lb.	2.74	12/94	82r
Coffee, 100%, ground roast, all sizes	lb.	4.61	12/94	82r
Dairy products (other) purchases	year	161	91	81r
Eggs, Grade A large	dozen	1.12	12/94	82r
Fish and seafood purchases	year	112	91	81r
Food purchases, food eaten at home	year	2599	91	81r
Foods purchased away from home, not prepared by consumer	year	2024	91	81r
Fruits and vegetables purchases	year	444	91	81r
Grapefruit	lb.	0.44	12/94	82r
Grapes, Thompson seedless	lb.	2.24	12/94	82r
Ground chuck, 100% beef	lb.	1.67	12/94	82r
Ice cream, prepackaged, bulk, regular	1/2 gal.	2.93	12/94	82r
Lemons	lb.	1.06	12/94	82r
Lettuce, iceberg	lb.	0.92	12/94	82r
Meats, poultry, fish, and eggs purchases	year	751	91	81r
Milk and cream (fresh) purchases	year	152	91	81r
Orange juice, frozen concentrate 12-oz. can	16 oz.	1.92	12/94	82r
Oranges, Navel	lb.	0.56	12/94	82r
Pork chops, center cut, bone-in	lb.	3.09	12/94	82r
Pork purchases	year	130	91	81r
Potatoes, white	lb.	0.37	12/94	82r
Rib roast, USDA choice, bone-in	lb.	4.98	12/94	82r
Round roast, USDA choice, boneless	lb.	2.93	12/94	82r
Shortening, vegetable oil blends	lb.	1.03	12/94	82r
Spaghetti and macaroni	lb.	0.84	12/94	82r
Steak, round, USDA choice, boneless	lb.	3.48	12/94	82r
Steak, sirloin, USDA choice, bone-in	lb.	3.38	12/94	82r
Steak, sirloin, USDA choice, boneless	lb.	4.81	12/94	82r
Sugar and other sweets, eaten at home, expenditures	year	89	91	81r
Sugar, white, all sizes	lb.	0.46	12/94	82r
Tobacco products and smoking supplies, total expenditures	year	279	91	81r
Tomatoes, field grown	lb.	1.56	12/94	82r
Tuna, chunk, light	lb.	2.09	12/94	82r
Health Care				
Childbirth, Cesarean delivery, hospital charge	birth	6334.00	12/91	69r
Childbirth, Cesarean delivery, physician charge	birth	2234.00	12/91	69r
Childbirth, normal delivery, hospital charge	birth	3225.00	12/91	69r

Values are in dollars or fractions of dollars. In the column headed *Ref*, references are shown to sources. Each reference is followed by a letter. These refer to the geographical level for which data were reported: s = State, r = Region, and c = City or metro. The abbreviation *ex* is used to mean *except* or *excluding*; *exp* stands for expenditures. For other abbreviations and further explanations, please see the Introduction.

Fall River, MA - continued

Item	Per	Value	Date	Ref.
Health Care				
Childbirth, normal delivery, physician charge	birth	1623.00	12/91	69r
Drugs, expenditures	year	205	91	81r
Health care, total expenditures	year	1396	91	81r
Health insurance expenditures	year	553	91	81r
Insurance premium, family medical care	month	457.38	1/95	41s
Medical services expenditures	year	559	91	81r
Medical supplies expenditures	year	80	91	81r
Household Goods				
Floor coverings, expenditures	year	158	91	81r
Furniture, expenditures	year	341	91	81r
Household equipment, misc. expenditures	year	363	91	81r
Household expenditures, miscellaneous	year	194	91	81r
Household furnishings and equipment, expenditures	year	1158	91	81r
Household operations expenditures	year	378	91	81r
Household textiles, expenditures	year	88	91	81r
Housekeeping supplies, expenditures	year	426	91	81r
Laundry and cleaning supplies, expenditures	year	122	91	81r
Postage and stationery, expenditures	year	134	91	81r
Housing				
Add garage/carport		11,614	3/95	74r
Add room(s)		16,816	3/95	74r
Apartment condominium or co-op, median	unit	96700	12/94	62r
Dwellings (owned), expenditures	year	3305	91	81r
Enclose porch/patio/breezeway		2,980	3/95	74r
Finish room in basement/attic		4,330	3/95	74r
Home, existing, single-family, median	unit	161600	12/94	62r
Maintenance, repairs, insurance, and other housing expenditures	year	569	91	81r
Mortgage interest and charges expenditures	year	1852	91	81r
Princ. & int., mortgage, median-price exist. sing.-family home	mo.	765	12/94	62r
Property taxes expenditures	year	884	91	81r
Redesign, restructure more than half of home's interior		2,750	3/95	74r
Rental units expenditures	year	1832	91	81r
Insurance and Pensions				
Auto insurance, private passenger	year	1009.56	12/94	71s
Insurance and pensions, personal, expenditures	year	2690	91	81r
Insurance, life and other personal, expenditures	year	341	91	81r
Pensions and Social Security, expenditures	year	2349	91	81r
Legal Assistance				
Estate planning, law-firm partner	hr.	375.00	10/93	12r
Legal work, law firm associate	hour	78		10r
Legal work, law firm partner	hour	183		10r
Personal Services				
Personal services expenditures	year	184	91	81r
Restaurant Food				
Dining expenditures, family	week	34.26	94	73r
Taxes				
Taxes, Federal income, expenditures	year	2409	91	81r
Taxes, personal, expenditures	year	3094	91	81r
Taxes, State and local income, expenditures	year	620	91	81r
Transportation				
Cars and trucks purchased, new	year	1170	91	81r
Cars and trucks purchased, used	year	739	91	81r
Driver's learning permit fee	perm	15.00	1/94	84s
Driver's license fee	orig	50.00	1/94	84s
Driver's license fee, duplicate	lic	15.00	1/94	84s
Driver's license renewal fee	renew	43.75	1/94	84s
Identification card, nondriver	card	15.00	1/94	83s
Motorcycle license fee	orig	50.00	1/94	84s
Motorcycle license fee, duplicate	lic	15.00	1/94	84s
Motorcycle license renewal fee	renew	43.75	1/94	84s
Public transportation expenditures	year	430	91	81r

Fall River, MA - continued

Item	Per	Value	Date	Ref.
Transportation - continued				
Transportation expenditures, total	year	4810	91	81r
Vehicle finance charges	year	238	91	81r
Vehicle insurance expenditures	year	630	91	81r
Vehicle maintenance and repairs expenditures	year	532	91	81r
Vehicle purchases	year	1920	91	81r
Vehicle rental, leases, licenses, etc. expenditures	year	193	91	81r
Vehicles purchased, other than cars and trucks	year	11	91	81r
Utilities				
Electricity expenditures	year	695	91	81r
Utilities, fuels, and public services, total expenditures	year	1981	91	81r
Water and other public services, expenditures	year	154	91	81r
Weddings				
Bridal attendants' gowns	event	750	10/93	76r
Bridal gown	event	852	10/93	76r
Bridal headpiece and veil	event	167	10/93	76r
Bride's wedding band	event	708	10/93	76r
Clergy	event	224	10/93	76r
Engagement ring	event	2756	10/93	76r
Flowers	event	863	10/93	76r
Formal wear for groom	event	106	10/93	76r
Groom's attendants' formal wear	event	530	10/93	76r
Groom's wedding band	event	402	10/93	76r
Music	event	600	10/93	76r
Photography	event	1088	10/93	76r
Shoes for bride	event	50	10/93	76r
Videography	event	483	10/93	76r
Wedding invitations and announcements	event	342	10/93	76r
Wedding reception	event	7000	10/93	76r

Fargo-Moorhead, ND, MN

Item	Per	Value	Date	Ref.
Composite, ACCRA index		102.80	12/94	2c
Alcoholic Beverages				
Beer, Miller Lite, Bud, 12-oz., ex deposit	6	4.14	12/94	2c
J & B Scotch	750-ml.	16.69	12/94	2c
Wine, Gallo Chablis blanc	1.5-lit	5.09	12/94	2c
Appliances				
Appliances (major), expenditures	year	131	91	81r
Average annual exp.				
Food, health care, personal goods, services	year	25935	91	81r
Charity				
Cash contributions, expenditures	year	745	91	81r
Clothing				
Apparel, men and boys, total expenditures	year	332	91	81r
Apparel, women and girls, total expenditures	year	578	91	81r
Footwear, expenditures	year	164	91	81r
Jeans, man's denim		32.99	12/94	2c
Shirt, man's dress shirt		36.10	12/94	2c
Undervest, boy's size 10-14, cotton	3	6.53	12/94	2c
Communications				
Long-distance telephone rate, day, addl. min., 1-10 mi.	min.	0.10	12/93	9s
Long-distance telephone rate, day, initial min., 1-10 mi.	min.	0.24	12/93	9s
Newspaper subscription, dly. and Sun. delivery	month	14.00	12/94	2c
Phone line, single, business, field visit	inst	52.67	12/93	9s
Phone line, single, business, no field visit	inst	52.67	12/93	9s
Phone line, single, residence, field visit	inst	31.79	12/93	9s
Phone line, single, residence, no field visit	inst	31.79	12/93	9s
Telephone bill, family of four	month	19.68	12/94	2c

Values are in dollars or fractions of dollars. In the column headed *Ref*, references are shown to sources. Each reference is followed by a letter. These refer to the geographical level for which data were reported: s=State, r=Region, and c=City or metro. The abbreviation *ex* is used to mean *except* or *excluding*; *exp* stands for *expenditures*. For other abbreviations and further explanations, please see the Introduction.

Fargo-Moorhead, ND, MN - continued

Item	Per	Value	Date	Ref.
Communications				
Telephone service, expenditures	year	547	91	81r
Telephone, residential, flat rate	mo.	14.58	12/93	8c
Telephone, residential, flat rate	mo.	12.73	12/93	8c
Education				
Board, 4-year private college/university	year	1582	8/94	80s
Board, 4-year public college/university	year	2259	8/94	80s
Education, total expenditures	year	394	91	81r
Room, 4-year private college/university	year	1183	8/94	80s
Room, 4-year public college/university	year	908	8/94	80s
Total cost, 4-year private college/university	year	9188	8/94	80s
Total cost, 4-year public college/university	year	5294	8/94	80s
Tuition, 2-year public college/university, in-state	year	1634	8/94	80s
Tuition, 4-year private college/university, in-state	year	6422	8/94	80s
Tuition, 4-year public college/university, in-state	year	2128	8/94	80s
Energy and Fuels				
Energy, combined forms, 1800 sq. ft.	mo.	110.44	12/94	2c
Energy, exc. electricity, 1800 sq. ft.	mo.	34.50	12/94	2c
Fuel oil and other fuels, expenditures	year	83	91	81r
Gas, cooking, winter, 10 therms	month	4.91	2/94	65c
Gas, cooking, winter, 30 therms	month	14.73	2/94	65c
Gas, cooking, winter, 50 therms	month	23.55	2/94	65c
Gas, heating, winter, 100 therms	month	45.60	2/94	65c
Gas, heating, winter, average use	month	99.91	2/94	65c
Gas, natural, expenditures	year	373	91	81r
Gas, reg unlead, taxes inc., cash, self-service	gal	1.22	12/94	2c
Gasoline and motor oil purchased	year	1000	91	81r
Gasoline, unleaded midgrade	gallon	1.15	4/93	82r
Gasoline, unleaded premium	gallon	1.23	4/93	82r
Gasoline, unleaded regular	gallon	1.07	4/93	82r
Entertainment				
Bowling, evening rate	game	1.85	12/94	2c
Entertainment, total expenditures	year	1356	91	81r
Fees and admissions, expenditures	year	347	91	81r
Monopoly game, Parker Brothers', No. 9	game	11.47	12/94	2c
Movie	adm	5.38	12/94	2c
Pets, toys, playground equipment, expenditures	year	270	91	81r
Reading, expenditures	year	160	91	81r
Televisions, radios, and sound equipment, expenditures	year	433	91	81r
Tennis balls, yellow, Wilson or Penn, 3	can	1.92	12/94	2c
Funerals				
Burial, immediate, container provided by funeral home		1348.78	1/95	54r
Cards, acknowledgment		21.20	1/95	54r
Casket, minimum alternative		182.83	1/95	54r
Cosmetology, hair care, etc.		133.11	1/95	54r
Cremation, direct, container provided by funeral home		1101.95	1/95	54r
Embalming		314.45	1/95	54r
Funeral, funeral home		304.88	1/95	54r
Funeral, other facility		301.37	1/95	54r
Graveside service		290.59	1/95	54r
Hearse, local		137.37	1/95	54r
Limousine, local		82.84	1/95	54r
Memorial service		316.57	1/95	54r
Service charge, professional, nondeclinable		1099.00	1/95	54r
Visitation and viewing		209.25	1/95	54r
Groceries				
Groceries, ACCRA Index		103.00	12/94	2c
Apples, Red Delicious	lb.	0.68	12/94	82r
Baby food, strained vegetables, lowest price	4-4.5 oz.	0.35	12/94	2c
Bacon, sliced	lb.	1.88	12/94	82r
Bananas	lb.	0.33	12/94	2c

Fargo-Moorhead, ND, MN - continued

Item	Per	Value	Date	Ref.
Groceries - continued				
Bananas	lb.	0.41	12/94	82r
Beef or hamburger, ground	lb.	1.60	12/94	2c
Beef purchases	year	197	91	81r
Beef, stew, boneless	lb.	2.52	12/94	82r
Beverage purchases, alcoholic	year	293	91	81r
Beverage purchases, nonalcoholic	year	203	91	81r
Bologna, all beef or mixed	lb.	2.12	12/94	82r
Bread, white	24-oz.	0.95	12/94	2c
Bread, white, pan	lb.	0.76	12/94	82r
Cabbage	lb.	0.44	12/94	82r
Carrots, short trimmed and topped	lb.	0.44	12/94	82r
Cereals and bakery products purchases	year	347	91	81r
Cereals and cereals products purchases	year	119	91	81r
Cheddar cheese, natural	lb.	3.28	12/94	82r
Cheese, Kraft grated Parmesan	8-oz.	2.78	12/94	2c
Chicken breast, bone-in	lb.	1.61	12/94	82r
Chicken, fresh, whole	lb.	0.89	12/94	82r
Chicken, whole fryer	lb.	0.82	12/94	2c
Chuck roast, USDA choice, boneless	lb.	2.33	12/94	82r
Cigarettes, Winston, Kings	carton	17.55	12/94	2c
Coffee, 100%, ground roast, all sizes	lb.	4.28	12/94	82r
Coffee, vacuum-packed	13 oz.	3.42	12/94	2c
Cookies, chocolate chip	lb.	2.72	12/94	82r
Corn Flakes, Kellogg's or Post Toasties	18 oz.	2.60	12/94	2c
Corn, frozen, whole kernel, lowest price	10 oz.	0.79	12/94	2c
Dairy products (other) purchases	year	148	91	81r
Eggs, Grade A large	dozen	0.69	12/94	2c
Eggs, Grade A large	dozen	0.76	12/94	82r
Fish and seafood purchases	year	61	91	81r
Flour, white, all purpose	lb.	0.22	12/94	82r
Food purchases, food eaten at home	year	2313	91	81r
Foods purchased away from home, not prepared by consumer	year	1709	91	81r
Fruits and vegetables purchases	year	372	91	81r
Grapefruit	lb.	0.47	12/94	82r
Grapes, Thompson seedless	lb.	2.15	12/94	82r
Ground beef, 100% beef	lb.	1.37	12/94	82r
Ground chuck, 100% beef	lb.	1.81	12/94	82r
Ham, boneless, exc. canned	lb.	2.16	12/94	82r
Ice cream, prepackaged, bulk, regular	1/2 gal.	2.48	12/94	82r
Lemons	lb.	1.08	12/94	82r
Lettuce, iceberg	lb.	0.81	12/94	82r
Lettuce, iceberg	head	0.69	12/94	2c
Margarine, Blue Bonnet or Parkay cubes	lb.	0.52	12/94	2c
Margarine, stick	lb.	0.81	12/94	82r
Meats, poultry, fish, and eggs purchases	year	591	91	81r
Milk and cream (fresh) purchases	year	132	91	81r
Milk, whole	1/2 gal.	1.48	12/94	2c
Orange juice, frozen concentrate 12-oz. can	16 oz.	1.41	12/94	82r
Orange juice, Minute Maid frozen	12-oz.	1.29	12/94	2c
Oranges, Navel	lb.	0.56	12/94	82r
Peaches, halves or slices, Hunt's, Del Monte, or Libby's	29-oz.	1.32	12/94	2c
Peanut butter, creamy, all sizes	lb.	1.81	12/94	82r
Peas, sweet, Del Monte or Green Giant	15-17 oz.	0.57	12/94	2c
Pork chops, center cut, bone-in	lb.	2.76	12/94	82r
Pork purchases	year	130	91	81r
Potato chips	16-oz.	2.81	12/94	82r
Potatoes, frozen, French fried	lb.	0.83	12/94	82r
Potatoes, white	lb.	0.28	12/94	82r
Potatoes, white or red	10-lb. sack	1.89	12/94	2c
Round roast, USDA choice, boneless	lb.	2.90	12/94	82r
Sausage, Jimmy Dean, 100% pork	lb.	3.18	12/94	2c
Shortening, vegetable oil blends	lb.	0.88	12/94	82r
Shortening, vegetable, Crisco	3-lb.	2.32	12/94	2c
Soft drink, Coca Cola, ex deposit	2 lit	1.15	12/94	2c
Spaghetti and macaroni	lb.	0.78	12/94	82r
Steak, rib eye, USDA choice, boneless	lb.	6.15	12/94	82r

Values are in dollars or fractions of dollars. In the column headed *Ref*, references are shown to sources. Each reference is followed by a letter. These refer to the geographical level for which data were reported: s=State, r=Region, and c=City or metro. The abbreviation *ex* is used to mean *except* or *excluding*; *exp* stands for *expenditures*. For other abbreviations and further explanations, please see the Introduction.

Item	Per	Value	Date	Ref.
Groceries				
Steak, round, graded & ungraded, exc. USDA prime & choice	lb.	2.72	12/94	82r
Steak, round, USDA choice, boneless	lb.	3.02	12/94	82r
Steak, sirloin, USDA choice, boneless	lb.	3.85	12/94	82r
Steak, t-bone	lb.	5.29	12/94	2c
Steak, T-bone, USDA choice, bone-in	lb.	5.38	12/94	82r
Sugar and other sweets, eaten at home, expenditures	year	91	91	81r
Sugar, cane or beet	4 lbs.	1.49	12/94	2c
Sugar, white, all sizes	lb.	0.36	12/94	82r
Tobacco products and smoking supplies, total expenditures	year	298	91	81r
Tomatoes, field grown	lb.	1.36	12/94	82r
Tomatoes, Hunt's or Del Monte	14.5 oz.	0.74	12/94	2c
Tuna, chunk, light	lb.	1.94	12/94	82r
Tuna, chunk, light, oil-packed	6.125-6.5 oz.	0.65	12/94	2c
Turkey, frozen, whole	lb.	0.96	12/94	82r
Yogurt, natural, fruit flavored	8 oz.	0.62	12/94	82r
Goods and Services				
Miscellaneous goods and services, ACCRA Index		103.00	12/94	2c
Health Care				
Health care, ACCRA Index		102.20	12/94	2c
Antibiotic ointment, Polysporin	1.5 oz.	4.36	12/94	2c
Childbirth, Cesarean delivery, hospital charge	birth	5101.00	12/91	69r
Childbirth, Cesarean delivery, physician charge	birth	2234.00	12/91	69r
Childbirth, normal delivery, hospital charge	birth	2891.00	12/91	69r
Childbirth, normal delivery, physician charge	birth	1623.00	12/91	69r
Dentist's fee, adult teeth cleaning and periodic oral exam	visit	52.20	12/94	2c
Doctor's fee, routine exam, established patient	visit	45.30	12/94	2c
Drugs, expenditures	year	248	91	81r
Health care, total expenditures	year	1336	91	81r
Health insurance expenditures	year	550	91	81r
Hospital care, semiprivate room	day	334.67	12/94	2c
Insurance premium, family medical care	month	379.10	1/95	41s
Medical services expenditures	year	457	91	81r
Medical supplies expenditures	year	82	91	81r
Household Goods				
Appl. repair, service call, wash mach	min. lab. chg.	31.19	12/94	2c
Floor coverings, expenditures	year	105	91	81r
Furniture, expenditures	year	291	91	81r
Household equipment, misc. expenditures	year	341	91	81r
Household expenditures, miscellaneous	year	162	91	81r
Household furnishings and equipment, expenditures	year	1042	91	81r
Household operations expenditures	year	365	91	81r
Household textiles, expenditures	year	101	91	81r
Housekeeping supplies, expenditures	year	390	91	81r
Laundry and cleaning supplies, expenditures	year	110	91	81r
Laundry detergent, Tide Ultra, Bold, or Cheer	42 oz.	3.71	12/94	2c
Postage and stationery, expenditures	year	115	91	81r
Tissues, facial, Kleenex brand	175	1.04	12/94	2c
Housing				
Housing, ACCRA Index		105.60	12/94	2c
Add garage/carport		8,479	3/95	74r
Add room(s)		21,347	3/95	74r
Apartment condominium or co-op, median	unit	87100	12/94	62r
Bathroom addition, average cost	add	9734.00	3/95	13r
Bathroom remodeling, average cost	remod	6414.00	3/95	13r

Item	Per	Value	Date	Ref.
Housing - continued				
Bedroom, master suite addition, average cost	add	27122.00	3/95	13r
Deck addition, average cost	add	6665.00	3/95	13r
Dwellings (owned), expenditures	year	2566	91	81r
Enclose porch/patio/breezeway		4,556	3/95	74r
Exterior remodeling, average cost	remod	15395.00	3/95	13r
Family room addition, average cost	add	27658.00	3/95	13r
Finish room in basement/attic		5,074	3/95	74r
Home, existing, single-family, median	unit	106500	12/94	62r
Home, existing, single-family, median	unit	78.30	12/94	62c
House payment, principal and interest, 25% down payment	mo.	829	12/94	2c
House, 1800 sq ft, 8000 sq ft lot, new, urban, utilities	total	131888	12/94	2c
Kitchen remodeling, major, average cost	remod	17084.00	3/95	13r
Kitchen remodeling, minor, average cost	remod	5804.00	3/95	13r
Maintenance, repairs, insurance, and other housing expenditures	year	484	91	81r
Mortgage interest and charges expenditures	year	1443	91	81r
Mtge. rate, incl. points and orig. fee, 30-year conv. fixed or ARM	mo.	9.46	12/94	2c
Office, home addition, average cost	add	8121.00	3/95	13r
Princ. & int., mortgage, median-price exist. sing.-family home	mo.	515	12/94	62r
Property taxes expenditures	year	639	91	81r
Redesign, restructure more than half of home's interior		9,114	3/95	74r
Rent, apartment, 2 br., 1 1/2-2 baths, unfurnished, 950 sq ft, water	mo.	499	12/94	2c
Rental units expenditures	year	1200	91	81r
Sun-space addition, average cost	add	23768.00	3/95	13r
Wing addition, two-story, average cost	add	50410.00	3/95	13r
Insurance and Pensions				
Auto insurance, private passenger	year	448.24	12/94	71s
Insurance and pensions, personal, expenditures	year	2408	91	81r
Insurance, life and other personal, expenditures	year	355	91	81r
Pensions and Social Security, expenditures	year	2053	91	81r
Legal Assistance				
Legal work, law firm associate	hour	90		10r
Legal work, law firm partner	hour	139		10r
Personal Goods				
Shampoo, Alberto VO5	15-oz.	0.99	12/94	2c
Toothpaste, Crest or Colgate	6-7 oz.	1.77	12/94	2c
Personal Services				
Dry cleaning, man's 2-pc. suit		6.79	12/94	2c
Haircut, man's barbershop, no styling		10.30	12/94	2c
Haircut, woman's shampoo, trim, blow-dry		18.20	12/94	2c
Personal services expenditures	year	203	91	81r
Restaurant Food				
Chicken, fried, thigh and drumstick		2.00	12/94	2c
Dining expenditures, family	week	30.03	94	73r
Hamburger with cheese	1/4 lb.	1.95	12/94	2c
Pizza, Pizza Hut or Pizza Inn	12-13 in.	7.49	12/94	2c
Taxes				
Tax rate, residential property, month	$100	1.78	1/92	79c
Taxes, Federal income, expenditures	year	1756	91	81r
Taxes, personal, expenditures	year	2426	91	81r
Taxes, State and local income, expenditures	year	568	91	81r
Transportation				
Transportation, ACCRA Index		96.70	12/94	2c
Bus fare, one-way	trip	0.70	12/95	1c
Cars and trucks purchased, new	year	891	91	81r
Cars and trucks purchased, used	year	1155	91	81r
Driver's learning permit fee	perm	10.00	1/94	84s
Driver's license fee	orig	10.00	1/94	84s

Values are in dollars or fractions of dollars. In the column headed *Ref*, references are shown to sources. Each reference is followed by a letter. These refer to the geographical level for which data were reported: s = State, r = Region, and c = City or metro. The abbreviation *ex* is used to mean *except* or *excluding*; *exp* stands for *expenditures*. For other abbreviations and further explanations, please see the Introduction.

Fargo-Moorhead, ND, MN - continued

Item	Per	Value	Date	Ref.
Transportation				
Driver's license fee, duplicate	lic	8.00	1/94	84s
Driver's license reinstatement fee, min.	susp	25.00	1/94	85s
Driver's license renewal fee	renew	10.00	1/94	84s
Identification card, nondriver	card	8.00	1/94	83s
Motorcycle learning permit fee	perm	10.00	1/94	84s
Motorcycle license fee	orig	10.00	1/94	84s
Motorcycle license fee, duplicate	lic	8.00	1/94	84s
Motorcycle license renewal fee	renew	10.00	1/94	84s
Public transportation expenditures	year	209	91	81r
Tire balance, computer or spin bal., front	wheel	5.45	12/94	2c
Transportation expenditures, total	year	4792	91	81r
Vehicle finance charges	year	300	91	81r
Vehicle insurance expenditures	year	485	91	81r
Vehicle maintenance and repairs expenditures	year	534	91	81r
Vehicle purchases	year	2068	91	81r
Vehicle rental, leases, licenses, etc. expenditures	year	197	91	81r
Vehicles purchased, other than cars and trucks	year	22	91	81r
Utilities				
Utilities, ACCRA Index		98.80	12/94	2c
Electricity expenditures	year	668	91	81r
Electricity, (part.), other, 1800 sq. ft., new home	mo.	75.94	12/94	2c
Electricity, summer, 250 KWh	month	20.16	8/93	64c
Electricity, summer, 500 KWh	month	36.21	8/93	64c
Electricity, summer, 750 KWh	month	52.29	8/93	64c
Electricity, summer, 1000 KWh	month	64.27	8/93	64c
Utilities, fuels, and public services, total expenditures	year	1838	91	81r
Water and other public services, expenditures	year	167	91	81r
Weddings				
Bridal attendants' gowns	event	750	10/93	76r
Bridal gown	event	852	10/93	76r
Bridal headpiece and veil	event	167	10/93	76r
Bride's wedding band	event	708	10/93	76r
Clergy	event	224	10/93	76r
Engagement ring	event	2756	10/93	76r
Flowers	event	863	10/93	76r
Formal wear for groom	event	106	10/93	76r
Groom's attendants' formal wear	event	530	10/93	76r
Groom's wedding band	event	402	10/93	76r
Music	event	600	10/93	76r
Photography	event	1088	10/93	76r
Shoes for bride	event	50	10/93	76r
Videography	event	483	10/93	76r
Wedding invitations and announcements	event	342	10/93	76r
Wedding reception	event	7000	10/93	76r

Farmington, NM

Item	Per	Value	Date	Ref.
Composite, ACCRA index		98.70	12/94	2c
Alcoholic Beverages				
Beer, Miller Lite, Bud, 12-oz., ex deposit	6	3.94	12/94	2c
J & B Scotch	750-ml.	18.04	12/94	2c
Wine, Gallo Chablis blanc	1.5-lit	5.47	12/94	2c
Clothing				
Jeans, man's denim		29.99	12/94	2c
Shirt, man's dress shirt		30.00	12/94	2c
Undervest, boy's size 10-14, cotton	3	5.09	12/94	2c
Communications				
Newspaper subscription, dly. and Sun. delivery	month	10.25	12/94	2c
Telephone bill, family of four	month	19.65	12/94	2c
Telephone, residential, flat rate	mo.	13.91	12/93	8c

Farmington, NM - continued

Item	Per	Value	Date	Ref.
Energy and Fuels				
Energy, combined forms, 1800 sq. ft.	mo.	104.23	12/94	2c
Energy, exc. electricity, 1800 sq. ft.	mo.	41.26	12/94	2c
Gas, reg unlead, taxes inc., cash, self-service	gal	1.26	12/94	2c
Entertainment				
Bowling, evening rate	game	1.85	12/94	2c
Monopoly game, Parker Brothers', No. 9	game	10.70	12/94	2c
Movie	adm	5.00	12/94	2c
Tennis balls, yellow, Wilson or Penn, 3	can	2.38	12/94	2c
Groceries				
Groceries, ACCRA Index		99.80	12/94	2c
Baby food, strained vegetables, lowest price	4-4.5 oz.	0.27	12/94	2c
Bananas	lb.	0.50	12/94	2c
Beef or hamburger, ground	lb.	1.55	12/94	2c
Bread, white	24-oz.	0.74	12/94	2c
Cheese, Kraft grated Parmesan	8-oz.	3.35	12/94	2c
Chicken, whole fryer	lb.	0.60	12/94	2c
Cigarettes, Winston, Kings	carton	14.79	12/94	2c
Coffee, vacuum-packed	13 oz.	3.95	12/94	2c
Corn Flakes, Kellogg's or Post Toasties	18 oz.	2.45	12/94	2c
Corn, frozen, whole kernel, lowest price	10 oz.	0.71	12/94	2c
Eggs, Grade A large	dozen	0.82	12/94	2c
Lettuce, iceberg	head	0.75	12/94	2c
Margarine, Blue Bonnet or Parkay cubes	lb.	0.73	12/94	2c
Milk, whole	1/2 gal.	1.65	12/94	2c
Orange juice, Minute Maid frozen	12-oz.	1.15	12/94	2c
Peaches, halves or slices, Hunt's, Del Monte, or Libby's	29-oz.	1.50	12/94	2c
Peas, sweet, Del Monte or Green Giant	15-17 oz.	0.57	12/94	2c
Potatoes, white or red	10-lb. sack	1.93	12/94	2c
Sausage, Jimmy Dean, 100% pork	lb.	2.35	12/94	2c
Shortening, vegetable, Crisco	3-lb.	2.76	12/94	2c
Soft drink, Coca Cola, ex deposit	2 lit	1.33	12/94	2c
Steak, t-bone	lb.	4.75	12/94	2c
Sugar, cane or beet	4 lbs.	1.43	12/94	2c
Tomatoes, Hunt's or Del Monte	14.5 oz.	0.79	12/94	2c
Tuna, chunk, light, oil-packed	6.125-6.5 oz.	0.85	12/94	2c
Goods and Services				
Miscellaneous goods and services, ACCRA Index		100.90	12/94	2c
Health Care				
Health care, ACCRA Index		109.00	12/94	2c
Antibiotic ointment, Polysporin	1.5 oz.	4.40	12/94	2c
Dentist's fee, adult teeth cleaning and periodic oral exam	visit	57.75	12/94	2c
Doctor's fee, routine exam, established patient	visit	49.35	12/94	2c
Hospital care, semiprivate room	day	325.00	12/94	2c
Household Goods				
Appl. repair, service call, wash mach	min. lab. chg.	36.60	12/94	2c
Laundry detergent, Tide Ultra, Bold, or Cheer	42 oz.	3.51	12/94	2c
Tissues, facial, Kleenex brand	175	0.97	12/94	2c
Housing				
Housing, ACCRA Index		93.60	12/94	2c
House payment, principal and interest, 25% down payment	mo.	730	12/94	2c
House, 1800 sq ft, 8000 sq ft lot, new, urban, utilities	total	119100	12/94	2c
Mtge. rate, incl. points and orig. fee, 30-year conv. fixed or ARM	mo.	9.18	12/94	2c

Values are in dollars or fractions of dollars. In the column headed *Ref*, references are shown to sources. Each reference is followed by a letter. These refer to the geographical level for which data were reported: s = State, r = Region, and c = City or metro. The abbreviation *ex* is used to mean *except* or *excluding*; *exp* stands for *expenditures*. For other abbreviations and further explanations, please see the Introduction.

Farmington, NM - continued

Item	Per	Value	Date	Ref.
Housing				
Rent, apartment, 2 br., 1 1/2-2 baths, unfurnished, 950 sq ft, water	mo.	456	12/94	2c
Personal Goods				
Shampoo, Alberto VO5	15-oz.	1.25	12/94	2c
Toothpaste, Crest or Colgate	6-7 oz.	2.22	12/94	2c
Personal Services				
Dry cleaning, man's 2-pc. suit		6.19	12/94	2c
Haircut, man's barbershop, no styling		7.60	12/94	2c
Haircut, woman's shampoo, trim, blow-dry		18.40	12/94	2c
Restaurant Food				
Chicken, fried, thigh and drumstick		2.45	12/94	2c
Hamburger with cheese	1/4 lb.	2.09	12/94	2c
Pizza, Pizza Hut or Pizza Inn	12-13 in.	7.19	12/94	2c
Transportation				
Transportation, ACCRA Index		102.00	12/94	2c
Tire balance, computer or spin bal., front	wheel	6.00	12/94	2c
Utilities				
Utilities, ACCRA Index		93.90	12/94	2c
Electricity, (part.), other, 1800 sq. ft., new home	mo.	62.97	12/94	2c

Fayetteville, AR

Item	Per	Value	Date	Ref.
Appliances				
Appliances (major), expenditures	year	153	91	81r
Average annual exp.				
Food, health care, personal goods, services	year	27020	91	81r
Charity				
Cash contributions, expenditures	year	839	91	81r
Clothing				
Apparel, men and boys, total expenditures	year	380	91	81r
Apparel, women and girls, total expenditures	year	660	91	81r
Footwear, expenditures	year	193	91	81r
Communications				
Long-distance telephone rate, day, addl. min., 1-10 mi.	min.	0.08	12/93	9s
Long-distance telephone rate, day, initial min., 1-10 mi.	min.	0.10	12/93	9s
Phone line, single, business, field visit	inst	84.00	12/93	9s
Phone line, single, business, no field visit	inst	84.00	12/93	9s
Phone line, single, residence, field visit	inst	39.70	12/93	9s
Phone line, single, residence, no field visit	inst	39.70	12/93	9s
Telephone service, expenditures	year	616	91	81r
Education				
Board, 4-year private college/university	year	1801	8/94	80s
Board, 4-year public college/university	year	1774	8/94	80s
Education, total expenditures	year	319	91	81r
Room, 4-year private college/university	year	1349	8/94	80s
Room, 4-year public college/university	year	1752	8/94	80s
Total cost, 4-year private college/university	year	8866	8/94	80s
Total cost, 4-year public college/university	year	5334	8/94	80s
Tuition, 2-year public college/university, in-state	year	833	8/94	80s
Tuition, 4-year private college/university, in-state	year	5716	8/94	80s
Tuition, 4-year public college/university, in-state	year	1808	8/94	80s
Energy and Fuels				
Fuel oil and other fuels, expenditures	year	56	91	81r
Gas, natural, expenditures	year	150	91	81r
Gasoline and motor oil purchased	year	1152	91	81r
Gasoline, unleaded midgrade	gallon	1.21	4/93	82r
Gasoline, unleaded premium	gallon	1.30	4/93	82r
Gasoline, unleaded regular	gallon	1.10	4/93	82r

Fayetteville, AR - continued

Item	Per	Value	Date	Ref.
Entertainment				
Concert ticket, Pearl Jam group	perf	20.00	94	50r
Entertainment, total expenditures	year	1266	91	81r
Fees and admissions, expenditures	year	306	91	81r
Pets, toys, playground equipment, expenditures	year	271	91	81r
Reading, expenditures	year	131	91	81r
Televisions, radios, and sound equipment, expenditures	year	439	91	81r
Funerals				
Burial, immediate, container provided by funeral home		1574.60	1/95	54r
Cards, acknowledgment		22.24	1/95	54r
Casket, minimum alternative		239.41	1/95	54r
Cosmetology, hair care, etc.		91.04	1/95	54r
Cremation, direct, container provided by funeral home		1085.15	1/95	54r
Embalming		281.30	1/95	54r
Funeral, funeral home		323.04	1/95	54r
Funeral, other facility		327.58	1/95	54r
Graveside service		355.19	1/95	54r
Hearse, local		141.89	1/95	54r
Limousine, local		99.40	1/95	54r
Memorial service		284.67	1/95	54r
Service charge, professional, nondeclinable		904.06	1/95	54r
Visitation and viewing		187.04	1/95	54r
Groceries				
Apples, Red Delicious	lb.	0.73	12/94	82r
Bacon, sliced	lb.	1.67	12/94	82r
Bananas	lb.	0.42	12/94	82r
Beef purchases	year	213	91	81r
Beverage purchases, alcoholic	year	249	91	81r
Beverage purchases, nonalcoholic	year	207	91	81r
Bologna, all beef or mixed	lb.	2.27	12/94	82r
Bread, white, pan	lb.	0.68	12/94	82r
Cabbage	lb.	0.42	12/94	82r
Carrots, short trimmed and topped	lb.	0.53	12/94	82r
Cereals and bakery products purchases	year	345	91	81r
Cereals and cereals products purchases	year	127	91	81r
Cheddar cheese, natural	lb.	3.58	12/94	82r
Chicken breast, bone-in	lb.	1.71	12/94	82r
Chicken, fresh, whole	lb.	0.78	12/94	82r
Chuck roast, USDA choice, boneless	lb.	2.26	12/94	82r
Crackers, soda, salted	lb.	1.27	12/94	82r
Cucumbers	lb.	0.65	12/94	82r
Dairy products (other) purchases	year	141	91	81r
Eggs, Grade A large	dozen	0.87	12/94	82r
Fish and seafood purchases	year	72	91	81r
Flour, white, all purpose	lb.	0.23	12/94	82r
Food purchases, food eaten at home	year	2381	91	81r
Foods purchased away from home, not prepared by consumer	year	1696	91	81r
Frankfurters, all meat or all beef	lb.	1.74	12/94	82r
Fruits and vegetables purchases	year	380	91	81r
Grapefruit	lb.	0.45	12/94	82r
Grapes, Thompson seedless	lb.	2.30	12/94	82r
Ground beef, 100% beef	lb.	1.37	12/94	82r
Ground chuck, 100% beef	lb.	1.97	12/94	82r
Ham, boneless, exc. canned	lb.	2.54	12/94	82r
Ice cream, prepackaged, bulk, regular	1/2 gal.	2.47	12/94	82r
Lemons	lb.	1.02	12/94	82r
Lettuce, iceberg	lb.	0.96	12/94	82r
Margarine, stick	lb.	0.77	12/94	82r
Meats, poultry, fish, and eggs purchases	year	655	91	81r
Milk and cream (fresh) purchases	year	130	91	81r
Orange juice, frozen concentrate 12-oz. can	16 oz.	1.36	12/94	82r
Oranges, Navel	lb.	0.54	12/94	82r
Pears, Anjou	lb.	0.81	12/94	82r
Pork chops, center cut, bone-in	lb.	3.07	12/94	82r
Pork purchases	year	142	91	81r
Potato chips	16-oz.	3.15	12/94	82r

Values are in dollars or fractions of dollars. In the column headed *Ref*, references are shown to sources. Each reference is followed by a letter. These refer to the geographical level for which data were reported: s = State, r = Region, and c = City or metro. The abbreviation *ex* is used to mean *except* or *excluding*; *exp* stands for *expenditures*. For other abbreviations and further explanations, please see the Introduction.

Fayetteville, AR - continued

Item	Per	Value	Date	Ref.
Groceries				
Potatoes, frozen, French fried	lb.	0.82	12/94	82r
Potatoes, white	lb.	0.34	12/94	82r
Rice, white, long grain, uncooked	lb.	0.48	12/94	82r
Round roast, USDA choice, boneless	lb.	2.91	12/94	82r
Sausage, fresh	lb.	1.82	12/94	82r
Shortening, vegetable oil blends	lb.	0.75	12/94	82r
Spaghetti and macaroni	lb.	0.87	12/94	82r
Steak, rib eye, USDA choice, boneless	lb.	6.85	12/94	82r
Steak, round, graded & ungraded, exc. USDA prime & choice	lb.	2.96	12/94	82r
Steak, round, USDA choice, boneless	lb.	3.17	12/94	82r
Steak, sirloin, USDA choice, boneless	lb.	4.12	12/94	82r
Steak, T-bone, USDA choice, bone-in	lb.	5.63	12/94	82r
Sugar and other sweets, eaten at home, expenditures	year	93	91	81r
Sugar, white, all sizes	lb.	0.39	12/94	82r
Tobacco products and smoking supplies, total expenditures	year	286	91	81r
Tomatoes, field grown	lb.	1.36	12/94	82r
Tuna, chunk, light	lb.	1.94	12/94	82r
Turkey, frozen, whole	lb.	0.96	12/94	82r
Yogurt, natural, fruit flavored	8 oz.	0.58	12/94	82r
Health Care				
Adenosine, emergency room	treat	100.00	95	23r
Bladder tap, superpubic, infant, emergency room	treat	119.00	95	23r
Blood analysis, emergency room	treat	25.00	95	23r
Blood tests, abdominal pain, emergency room	treat	25.00	95	23r
Burn dressing, emergency room	treat	266.00	95	23r
Cardiology interpretation, emergency room	treat	26.00	95	23r
Chest X-ray, emergency room	treat	78.00	95	23r
Childbirth, Cesarean delivery, hospital charge	birth	5462.00	12/91	69r
Childbirth, Cesarean delivery, physician charge	birth	2228.00	12/91	69r
Childbirth, normal delivery, hospital charge	birth	2943.00	12/91	69r
Childbirth, normal delivery, physician charge	birth	1619.00	12/91	69r
Defibrillation pads, emergency room	treat	6.00	95	23r
Drugs, expenditures	year	297	91	81r
Gastric tube insertion, nasal, emergency room	treat	25.00	95	23r
Health care, total expenditures	year	1600	91	81r
Health insurance expenditures	year	637	91	81r
Heart monitor, emergency room	treat	40.00	95	23r
Insurance premium, family medical care	month	326.03	1/95	41s
Intravenous fluids, emergency room	treat	130.00	95	23r
Intravenous fluids, emergency room	liter	26.00	95	23r
Intravenous line, central, emergency room	treat	342.00	95	23r
Liver function tests, abdominal pain, emergency room	treat	26.00	95	23r
Medical care charges, total, emergency room, third-degree burns	treat	2101.00	95	23r
Medical care charges, total, emergency, infant with fever	treat	628.00	95	23r
Medical services expenditures	year	573	91	81r
Medical supplies expenditures	year	93	91	81r
Morphine, emergency room	treat	34.00	95	23r
Nursing care and facilities charges, emergency room	treat	252.00	95	23r
Nursing care and facilities charges, emergency, infant with fever	treat	252.00	95	23r
Nursing care and facilities charges, emergency, third-degree burns	treat	861.00	95	23r
Physician's charges, emergency, infant with fever	treat	212.00	95	23r
Physician's charges, emergency, third-degree burns	treat	372.00	95	23r
Physician's fee, emergency room	treat	372.00	95	23r
Physician's fee, general practitioner	visit	51.20	12/93	60r
Surgery, open-heart	proc	42374.00	1/93	14r
Ultrasound, abdominal, emergency room	treat	276.00	95	23r

Fayetteville, AR - continued

Item	Per	Value	Date	Ref.
Health Care - continued				
Urinalysis, emergency room	treat	20.00	95	23r
Urinalysis, infant, emergency room	treat	20.00	95	23r
X-rays, emergency room	treat	78.00	95	23r
Household Goods				
Floor coverings, expenditures	year	48	91	81r
Furniture, expenditures	year	280	91	81r
Household equipment, misc. expenditures	year	342	91	81r
Household expenditures, miscellaneous	year	256	91	81r
Household furnishings and equipment, expenditures	year	988	91	81r
Household operations expenditures	year	468	91	81r
Household textiles, expenditures	year	95	91	81r
Housekeeping supplies, expenditures	year	380	91	81r
Laundry and cleaning supplies, expenditures	year	109	91	81r
Postage and stationery, expenditures	year	105	91	81r
Housing				
Add garage/carport		6,980	3/95	74r
Add room(s)		11,403	3/95	74r
Apartment condominium or co-op, median	unit	68600	12/94	62r
Dwellings (owned), expenditures	year	2428	91	81r
Enclose porch/patio/breezeway		4,572	3/95	74r
Finish room in basement/attic		3,794	3/95	74r
Home, existing, single-family, median	unit	120200	12/94	62r
Home, single family, median	home	75000	4/94	11c
Maintenance, repairs, insurance, and other housing expenditures	year	531	91	81r
Mortgage interest and charges expenditures	year	1506	91	81r
Princ. & int., mortgage, median-price exist. sing.-family home	mo.	540	12/94	62r
Property taxes expenditures	year	391	91	81r
Redesign, restructure more than half of home's interior		17,641	3/95	74r
Rental units expenditures	year	1264	91	81r
Insurance and Pensions				
Auto insurance, private passenger	year	565.35	12/94	71s
Insurance and pensions, personal, expenditures	year	2395	91	81r
Insurance, life and other personal, expenditures	year	368	91	81r
Pensions and Social Security, expenditures	year	2027	91	81r
Personal Services				
Personal services expenditures	year	212	91	81r
Restaurant Food				
Dining expenditures, family	week	33.83	94	73r
Taxes				
Taxes, Federal income, expenditures	year	2275	91	81r
Taxes, personal, expenditures	year	2715	91	81r
Taxes, State and local income, expenditures	year	365	91	81r
Transportation				
Cars and trucks purchased, new	year	1306	91	81r
Cars and trucks purchased, used	year	942	91	81r
Driver's license fee	orig	14.00	1/94	84s
Driver's license fee, duplicate	lic	5.00	1/94	84s
Driver's license renewal fee	renew	14.00	1/94	84s
Identification card, nondriver	card	5.00	1/94	83s
Motorcycle license fee	orig	4.00	1/94	84s
Motorcycle license fee, duplicate	lic	5.00	1/94	84s
Public transportation expenditures	year	249	91	81r
Transportation expenditures, total	year	5307	91	81r
Vehicle finance charges	year	346	91	81r
Vehicle insurance expenditures	year	544	91	81r
Vehicle maintenance and repairs expenditures	year	600	91	81r
Vehicle purchases	year	2275	91	81r
Vehicle rental, leases, licenses, etc. expenditures	year	141	91	81r

Values are in dollars or fractions of dollars. In the column headed *Ref*, references are shown to sources. Each reference is followed by a letter. These refer to the geographical level for which data were reported: s=State, r=Region, and c=City or metro. The abbreviation *ex* is used to mean *except* or *excluding*; *exp* stands for expenditures. For other abbreviations and further explanations, please see the Introduction.

Fayetteville, AR - continued

Item	Per	Value	Date	Ref.
Transportation				
Vehicles purchased, other than cars and trucks	year	27	91	81r
Utilities				
Electricity expenditures	year	950	91	81r
Utilities, fuels, and public services, total expenditures	year	2000	91	81r
Water and other public services, expenditures	year	227	91	81r
Weddings				
Bridal attendants' gowns	event	750	10/93	76r
Bridal gown	event	852	10/93	76r
Bridal headpiece and veil	event	167	10/93	76r
Bride's wedding band	event	708	10/93	76r
Clergy	event	224	10/93	76r
Engagement ring	event	2756	10/93	76r
Flowers	event	863	10/93	76r
Formal wear for groom	event	106	10/93	76r
Groom's attendants' formal wear	event	530	10/93	76r
Groom's wedding band	event	402	10/93	76r
Music	event	600	10/93	76r
Photography	event	1088	10/93	76r
Shoes for bride	event	50	10/93	76r
Videography	event	483	10/93	76r
Wedding invitations and announcements	event	342	10/93	76r
Wedding reception	event	7000	10/93	76r

Fayetteville, NC

Item	Per	Value	Date	Ref.
Composite, ACCRA index		93.50	12/94	2c
Alcoholic Beverages				
Beer, Miller Lite, Bud, 12-oz., ex deposit	6	3.55	12/94	2c
J & B Scotch	750-ml.	18.60	12/94	2c
Wine, Gallo Chablis blanc	1.5-lit	4.79	12/94	2c
Appliances				
Appliances (major), expenditures	year	153	91	81r
Average annual exp.				
Food, health care, personal goods, services	year	27020	91	81r
Charity				
Cash contributions, expenditures	year	839	91	81r
Clothing				
Apparel, men and boys, total expenditures	year	380	91	81r
Apparel, women and girls, total expenditures	year	660	91	81r
Footwear, expenditures	year	193	91	81r
Jeans, man's denim		35.66	12/94	2c
Shirt, man's dress shirt		27.00	12/94	2c
Undervest, boy's size 10-14, cotton	3	4.99	12/94	2c
Communications				
Long-distance telephone rate, day, addl. min., 1-10 mi.	min.	0.10	12/93	9s
Long-distance telephone rate, day, initial min., 1-10 mi.	min.	0.16	12/93	9s
Newspaper subscription, dly. and Sun. delivery	month	9.50	12/94	2c
Phone line, single, business, field visit	inst	62.50	12/93	9s
Phone line, single, business, no field visit	inst	62.50	12/93	9s
Phone line, single, residence, field visit	inst	42.75	12/93	9s
Phone line, single, residence, no field visit	inst	42.75	12/93	9s
Telephone bill, family of four	month	18.16	12/94	2c
Telephone service, expenditures	year	616	91	81r
Education				
Board, 4-year private college/university	year	2069	8/94	80s
Board, 4-year public college/university	year	1627	8/94	80s
Education, total expenditures	year	319	91	81r
Room, 4-year private college/university	year	1824	8/94	80s
Room, 4-year public college/university	year	1669	8/94	80s
Total cost, 4-year private college/university	year	13505	8/94	80s

Fayetteville, NC - continued

Item	Per	Value	Date	Ref.
Education - continued				
Total cost, 4-year public college/university	year	4704	8/94	80s
Tuition, 2-year public college/university, in-state	year	577	8/94	80s
Tuition, 4-year private college/university, in-state	year	9612	8/94	80s
Tuition, 4-year public college/university, in-state	year	1409	8/94	80s
Energy and Fuels				
Energy, combined forms, 1800 sq. ft.	mo.	116.32	12/94	2c
Fuel oil and other fuels, expenditures	year	56	91	81r
Gas, cooking, winter, 10 therms	month	12.27	2/94	65c
Gas, cooking, winter, 30 therms	month	22.62	2/94	65c
Gas, cooking, winter, 50 therms	month	32.97	2/94	65c
Gas, heating, winter, 100 therms	month	58.85	2/94	65c
Gas, heating, winter, average use	month	80.43	2/94	65c
Gas, natural, expenditures	year	150	91	81r
Gas, reg unlead, taxes inc., cash, self-service	gal	1.09	12/94	2c
Gasoline and motor oil purchased	year	1152	91	81r
Gasoline, unleaded midgrade	gallon	1.21	4/93	82r
Gasoline, unleaded premium	gallon	1.30	4/93	82r
Gasoline, unleaded regular	gallon	1.10	4/93	82r
Entertainment				
Bowling, evening rate	game	1.94	12/94	2c
Concert ticket, Pearl Jam group	perf	20.00	94	50r
Entertainment, total expenditures	year	1266	91	81r
Fees and admissions, expenditures	year	306	91	81r
Monopoly game, Parker Brothers', No. 9	game	11.24	12/94	2c
Movie	adm	5.88	12/94	2c
Pets, toys, playground equipment, expenditures	year	271	91	81r
Reading, expenditures	year	131	91	81r
Televisions, radios, and sound equipment, expenditures	year	439	91	81r
Tennis balls, yellow, Wilson or Penn, 3	can	2.74	12/94	2c
Funerals				
Burial, immediate, container provided by funeral home		1370.36	1/95	54r
Cards, acknowledgment		14.83	1/95	54r
Casket, minimum alternative		192.52	1/95	54r
Cosmetology, hair care, etc.		102.27	1/95	54r
Cremation, direct, container provided by funeral home		1065.64	1/95	54r
Embalming		304.29	1/95	54r
Funeral, funeral home		287.83	1/95	54r
Funeral, other facility		284.14	1/95	54r
Graveside service		349.13	1/95	54r
Hearse, local		132.27	1/95	54r
Limousine, local		98.45	1/95	54r
Memorial service		270.59	1/95	54r
Service charge, professional, nondeclinable		933.59	1/95	54r
Visitation and viewing		225.83	1/95	54r
Groceries				
Groceries, ACCRA Index		94.40	12/94	2c
Apples, Red Delicious	lb.	0.73	12/94	82r
Baby food, strained vegetables, lowest price	4-4.5 oz.	0.39	12/94	2c
Bacon, sliced	lb.	1.67	12/94	82r
Bananas	lb.	0.53	12/94	2c
Bananas	lb.	0.42	12/94	82r
Beef or hamburger, ground	lb.	1.06	12/94	2c
Beef purchases	year	213	91	81r
Beverage purchases, alcoholic	year	249	91	81r
Beverage purchases, nonalcoholic	year	207	91	81r
Bologna, all beef or mixed	lb.	2.27	12/94	82r
Bread, white	24-oz.	0.54	12/94	2c
Bread, white, pan	lb.	0.68	12/94	82r
Cabbage	lb.	0.42	12/94	82r
Carrots, short trimmed and topped	lb.	0.53	12/94	82r
Cereals and bakery products purchases	year	345	91	81r

Values are in dollars or fractions of dollars. In the column headed *Ref*, references are shown to sources. Each reference is followed by a letter. These refer to the geographical level for which data were reported: s=State, r=Region, and c=City or metro. The abbreviation *ex* is used to mean *except* or *excluding*; *exp* stands for *expenditures*. For other abbreviations and further explanations, please see the Introduction.

Fayetteville, NC - continued

Item	Per	Value	Date	Ref.
Groceries				
Cereals and cereals products purchases	year	127	91	81r
Cheddar cheese, natural	lb.	3.58	12/94	82r
Cheese, Kraft grated Parmesan	8-oz.	3.13	12/94	2c
Chicken breast, bone-in	lb.	1.71	12/94	82r
Chicken, fresh, whole	lb.	0.78	12/94	82r
Chicken, whole fryer	lb.	0.67	12/94	2c
Chuck roast, USDA choice, boneless	lb.	2.26	12/94	82r
Cigarettes, Winston, Kings	carton	13.12	12/94	2c
Coffee, vacuum-packed	13 oz.	3.20	12/94	2c
Corn Flakes, Kellogg's or Post Toasties	18 oz.	2.31	12/94	2c
Corn, frozen, whole kernel, lowest price	10 oz.	0.77	12/94	2c
Crackers, soda, salted	lb.	1.27	12/94	82r
Cucumbers	lb.	0.65	12/94	82r
Dairy products (other) purchases	year	141	91	81r
Eggs, Grade A large	dozen	0.88	12/94	2c
Eggs, Grade A large	dozen	0.87	12/94	82r
Fish and seafood purchases	year	72	91	81r
Flour, white, all purpose	lb.	0.23	12/94	82r
Food purchases, food eaten at home	year	2381	91	81r
Foods purchased away from home, not prepared by consumer	year	1696	91	81r
Frankfurters, all meat or all beef	lb.	1.74	12/94	82r
Fruits and vegetables purchases	year	380	91	81r
Grapefruit	lb.	0.45	12/94	82r
Grapes, Thompson seedless	lb.	2.30	12/94	82r
Ground beef, 100% beef	lb.	1.37	12/94	82r
Ground chuck, 100% beef	lb.	1.97	12/94	82r
Ham, boneless, exc. canned	lb.	2.54	12/94	82r
Ice cream, prepackaged, bulk, regular	1/2 gal.	2.47	12/94	82r
Lemons	lb.	1.02	12/94	82r
Lettuce, iceberg	lb.	0.96	12/94	82r
Lettuce, iceberg	head	1.17	12/94	2c
Margarine, Blue Bonnet or Parkay cubes	lb.	0.58	12/94	2c
Margarine, stick	lb.	0.77	12/94	82r
Meats, poultry, fish, and eggs purchases	year	655	91	81r
Milk and cream (fresh) purchases	year	130	91	81r
Milk, whole	1/2 gal.	1.41	12/94	2c
Orange juice, frozen concentrate 12-oz. can	16 oz.	1.36	12/94	82r
Orange juice, Minute Maid frozen	12-oz.	1.16	12/94	2c
Oranges, Navel	lb.	0.54	12/94	82r
Peaches, halves or slices, Hunt's, Del Monte, or Libby's	29-oz.	1.32	12/94	2c
Pears, Anjou	lb.	0.81	12/94	82r
Peas, sweet, Del Monte or Green Giant	15-17 oz.	0.49	12/94	2c
Pork chops, center cut, bone-in	lb.	3.07	12/94	82r
Pork purchases	year	142	91	81r
Potato chips	16-oz.	3.15	12/94	82r
Potatoes, frozen, French fried	lb.	0.82	12/94	82r
Potatoes, white	lb.	0.34	12/94	82r
Potatoes, white or red	10-lb. sack	2.91	12/94	2c
Rice, white, long grain, uncooked	lb.	0.48	12/94	82r
Round roast, USDA choice, boneless	lb.	2.91	12/94	82r
Sausage, fresh	lb.	1.82	12/94	82r
Sausage, Jimmy Dean, 100% pork	lb.	2.29	12/94	2c
Shortening, vegetable oil blends	lb.	0.75	12/94	82r
Shortening, vegetable, Crisco	3-lb.	2.49	12/94	2c
Soft drink, Coca Cola, ex deposit	2 lit	1.06	12/94	2c
Spaghetti and macaroni	lb.	0.87	12/94	82r
Steak, rib eye, USDA choice, boneless	lb.	6.85	12/94	82r
Steak, round, graded & ungraded, exc. USDA prime & choice	lb.	2.96	12/94	82r
Steak, round, USDA choice, boneless	lb.	3.17	12/94	82r
Steak, sirloin, USDA choice, boneless	lb.	4.12	12/94	82r
Steak, t-bone	lb.	5.34	12/94	2c
Steak, T-bone, USDA choice, bone-in	lb.	5.63	12/94	82r
Sugar and other sweets, eaten at home, expenditures	year	93	91	81r
Sugar, cane or beet	4 lbs.	1.51	12/94	2c

Groceries - continued

Item	Per	Value	Date	Ref.
Sugar, white, all sizes	lb.	0.39	12/94	82r
Tobacco products and smoking supplies, total expenditures	year	286	91	81r
Tomatoes, field grown	lb.	1.36	12/94	82r
Tomatoes, Hunt's or Del Monte	14.5 oz.	0.55	12/94	2c
Tuna, chunk, light	lb.	1.94	12/94	82r
Tuna, chunk, light, oil-packed	6.125-6.5 oz.	0.66	12/94	2c
Turkey, frozen, whole	lb.	0.96	12/94	82r
Yogurt, natural, fruit flavored	8 oz.	0.58	12/94	82r
Goods and Services				
Miscellaneous goods and services, ACCRA Index		100.70	12/94	2c
Health Care				
Health care, ACCRA Index		93.60	12/94	2c
Adenosine, emergency room	treat	100.00	95	23r
Antibiotic ointment, Polysporin	1.5 oz.	4.05	12/94	2c
Bladder tap, superpubic, infant, emergency room	treat	119.00	95	23r
Blood analysis, emergency room	treat	25.00	95	23r
Blood tests, abdominal pain, emergency room	treat	25.00	95	23r
Burn dressing, emergency room	treat	266.00	95	23r
Cardiology interpretation, emergency room	treat	26.00	95	23r
Chest X-ray, emergency room	treat	78.00	95	23r
Childbirth, Cesarean delivery, hospital charge	birth	5462.00	12/91	69r
Childbirth, Cesarean delivery, physician charge	birth	2228.00	12/91	69r
Childbirth, normal delivery, hospital charge	birth	2943.00	12/91	69r
Childbirth, normal delivery, physician charge	birth	1619.00	12/91	69r
Defibrillation pads, emergency room	treat	6.00	95	23r
Dentist's fee, adult teeth cleaning and periodic oral exam	visit	45.67	12/94	2c
Doctor's fee, routine exam, established patient	visit	40.33	12/94	2c
Drugs, expenditures	year	297	91	81r
Gastric tube insertion, nasal, emergency room	treat	25.00	95	23r
Health care, total expenditures	year	1600	91	81r
Health insurance expenditures	year	637	91	81r
Heart monitor, emergency room	treat	40.00	95	23r
Hospital care, semiprivate room	day	350.00	12/94	2c
Insurance premium, family medical care	month	405.45	1/95	41s
Intravenous fluids, emergency room	treat	130.00	95	23r
Intravenous fluids, emergency room	liter	26.00	95	23r
Intravenous line, central, emergency room	treat	342.00	95	23r
Liver function tests, abdominal pain, emergency room	treat	26.00	95	23r
Medical care charges, total, emergency room, third-degree burns	treat	2101.00	95	23r
Medical care charges, total, emergency, infant with fever	treat	628.00	95	23r
Medical services expenditures	year	573	91	81r
Medical supplies expenditures	year	93	91	81r
Morphine, emergency room	treat	34.00	95	23r
Nursing care and facilities charges, emergency room	treat	252.00	95	23r
Nursing care and facilities charges, emergency, infant with fever	treat	252.00	95	23r
Nursing care and facilities charges, emergency, third-degree burns	treat	861.00	95	23r
Physician's charges, emergency, infant with fever	treat	212.00	95	23r
Physician's charges, emergency, third-degree burns	treat	372.00	95	23r
Physician's fee, emergency room	treat	372.00	95	23r
Physician's fee, general practitioner	visit	51.20	12/93	60r
Surgery, open-heart	proc	42374.00	1/93	14r
Ultrasound, abdominal, emergency room	treat	276.00	95	23r

Values are in dollars or fractions of dollars. In the column headed *Ref*, references are shown to sources. Each reference is followed by a letter. These refer to the geographical level for which data were reported: s = State, r = Region, and c = City or metro. The abbreviation *ex* is used to mean *except* or *excluding*; *exp* stands for *expenditures*. For other abbreviations and further explanations, please see the Introduction.

Fayetteville, NC - continued

Item	Per	Value	Date	Ref.
Health Care				
Urinalysis, emergency room	treat	20.00	95	23r
Urinalysis, infant, emergency room	treat	20.00	95	23r
X-rays, emergency room	treat	78.00	95	23r
Household Goods				
Appl. repair, service call, wash mach	min. lab. chg.	33.32	12/94	2c
Floor coverings, expenditures	year	48	91	81r
Furniture, expenditures	year	280	91	81r
Household equipment, misc. expenditures	year	342	91	81r
Household expenditures, miscellaneous	year	256	91	81r
Household furnishings and equipment, expenditures	year	988	91	81r
Household operations expenditures	year	468	91	81r
Household textiles, expenditures	year	95	91	81r
Housekeeping supplies, expenditures	year	380	91	81r
Laundry and cleaning supplies, expenditures	year	109	91	81r
Laundry detergent, Tide Ultra, Bold, or Cheer	42 oz.	2.63	12/94	2c
Postage and stationery, expenditures	year	105	91	81r
Tissues, facial, Kleenex brand	175	0.99	12/94	2c
Housing				
Housing, ACCRA Index		80.90	12/94	2c
Add garage/carport		6,980	3/95	74r
Add room(s)		11,403	3/95	74r
Apartment condominium or co-op, median	unit	68600	12/94	62r
Dwellings (owned), expenditures	year	2428	91	81r
Enclose porch/patio/breezeway		4,572	3/95	74r
Finish room in basement/attic		3,794	3/95	74r
Home, existing, single-family, median	unit	120200	12/94	62r
House payment, principal and interest, 25% down payment	mo.	614	12/94	2c
House, 1800 sq ft, 8000 sq ft lot, new, urban, utilities	total	100000	12/94	2c
Maintenance, repairs, insurance, and other housing expenditures	year	531	91	81r
Mortgage interest and charges expenditures	year	1506	91	81r
Mtge. rate, incl. points and orig. fee, 30-year conv. fixed or ARM	mo.	9.19	12/94	2c
Princ. & int., mortgage, median-price exist. sing.-family home	mo.	540	12/94	62r
Property taxes expenditures	year	391	91	81r
Redesign, restructure more than half of home's interior		17,641	3/95	74r
Rent, apartment, 2 br., 1 1/2-2 baths, unfurnished, 950 sq ft, water	mo.	446	12/94	2c
Rental units expenditures	year	1264	91	81r
Insurance and Pensions				
Auto insurance, private passenger	year	528.43	12/94	71s
Insurance and pensions, personal, expenditures	year	2395	91	81r
Insurance, life and other personal, expenditures	year	368	91	81r
Pensions and Social Security, expenditures	year	2027	91	81r
Personal Goods				
Shampoo, Alberto VO5	15-oz.	1.08	12/94	2c
Toothpaste, Crest or Colgate	6-7 oz.	1.91	12/94	2c
Personal Services				
Dry cleaning, man's 2-pc. suit		6.34	12/94	2c
Haircut, man's barbershop, no styling		6.90	12/94	2c
Haircut, woman's shampoo, trim, blow-dry		20.00	12/94	2c
Personal services expenditures	year	212	91	81r
Restaurant Food				
Chicken, fried, thigh and drumstick		1.99	12/94	2c
Dining expenditures, family	week	33.83	94	73r
Hamburger with cheese	1/4 lb.	1.92	12/94	2c
Pizza, Pizza Hut or Pizza Inn	12-13 in.	8.07	12/94	2c

Fayetteville, NC - continued

Item	Per	Value	Date	Ref.
Taxes				
Taxes, Federal income, expenditures	year	2275	91	81r
Taxes, personal, expenditures	year	2715	91	81r
Taxes, State and local income, expenditures	year	365	91	81r
Transportation				
Transportation, ACCRA Index		96.70	12/94	2c
Cars and trucks purchased, new	year	1306	91	81r
Cars and trucks purchased, used	year	942	91	81r
Driver's learning permit fee	perm	10.00	1/94	84s
Driver's license fee	orig	10.00	1/94	84s
Driver's license fee, duplicate	lic	5.00	1/94	84s
Driver's license reinstatement fee, min.	susp	25.00	1/94	85s
Driver's license renewal fee	renew	10.00	1/94	84s
Fine, safety belt violation	ticket	25.00	95	56s
Identification card, nondriver	card	10.00	1/94	83s
Motorcycle license fee	orig	5.00	1/94	84s
Public transportation expenditures	year	249	91	81r
Tire balance, computer or spin bal., front	wheel	6.50	12/94	2c
Transportation expenditures, total	year	5307	91	81r
Vehicle finance charges	year	346	91	81r
Vehicle insurance expenditures	year	544	91	81r
Vehicle maintenance and repairs expenditures	year	600	91	81r
Vehicle purchases	year	2275	91	81r
Vehicle rental, leases, licenses, etc. expenditures	year	141	91	81r
Vehicles purchased, other than cars and trucks	year	27	91	81r
Utilities				
Utilities, ACCRA Index		102.20	12/94	2c
Electricity expenditures	year	950	91	81r
Electricity, 1800 sq. ft., new home	mo.	116.32	12/94	2c
Utilities, fuels, and public services, total expenditures	year	2000	91	81r
Water and other public services, expenditures	year	227	91	81r
Weddings				
Bridal attendants' gowns	event	750	10/93	76r
Bridal gown	event	852	10/93	76r
Bridal headpiece and veil	event	167	10/93	76r
Bride's wedding band	event	708	10/93	76r
Clergy	event	224	10/93	76r
Engagement ring	event	2756	10/93	76r
Flowers	event	863	10/93	76r
Formal wear for groom	event	106	10/93	76r
Groom's attendants' formal wear	event	530	10/93	76r
Groom's wedding band	event	402	10/93	76r
Music	event	600	10/93	76r
Photography	event	1088	10/93	76r
Shoes for bride	event	50	10/93	76r
Videography	event	483	10/93	76r
Wedding invitations and announcements	event	342	10/93	76r
Wedding reception	event	7000	10/93	76r

Findlay, OH

Item	Per	Value	Date	Ref.
Composite, ACCRA index		97.00	12/94	2c
Alcoholic Beverages				
Beer, Miller Lite, Bud, 12-oz., ex deposit	6	3.99	12/94	2c
J & B Scotch	750-ml.	18.80	12/94	2c
Wine, Gallo Chablis blanc	1.5-lit	5.24	12/94	2c
Clothing				
Jeans, man's denim		29.20	12/94	2c
Shirt, man's dress shirt		32.17	12/94	2c
Undervest, boy's size 10-14, cotton	3	3.36	12/94	2c
Communications				
Newspaper subscription, dly. and Sun. delivery	month	11.30	12/94	2c

Values are in dollars or fractions of dollars. In the column headed *Ref*, references are shown to sources. Each reference is followed by a letter. These refer to the geographical level for which data were reported: s=State, r=Region, and c=City or metro. The abbreviation *ex* is used to mean *except* or *excluding*; *exp* stands for *expenditures*. For other abbreviations and further explanations, please see the Introduction.

Findlay, OH - continued

Item	Per	Value	Date	Ref.
Communications				
Telephone bill, family of four	month	21.29	12/94	2c
Telephone, residential, flat rate	mo.	15.25	12/93	8c
Energy and Fuels				
Energy, combined forms, 1800 sq. ft.	mo.	117.09	12/94	2c
Energy, exc. electricity, 1800 sq. ft.	mo.	61.72	12/94	2c
Gas, reg unlead, taxes inc., cash, self-service	gal	1.12	12/94	2c
Entertainment				
Bowling, evening rate	game	2.40	12/94	2c
Monopoly game, Parker Brothers', No. 9	game	10.86	12/94	2c
Movie	adm	6.00	12/94	2c
Tennis balls, yellow, Wilson or Penn, 3	can	2.10	12/94	2c
Groceries				
Groceries, ACCRA Index		95.50	12/94	2c
Baby food, strained vegetables, lowest price	4-4.5 oz.	0.21	12/94	2c
Bananas	lb.	0.39	12/94	2c
Beef or hamburger, ground	lb.	1.74	12/94	2c
Bread, white	24-oz.	0.50	12/94	2c
Cheese, Kraft grated Parmesan	8-oz.	3.16	12/94	2c
Chicken, whole fryer	lb.	0.82	12/94	2c
Cigarettes, Winston, Kings	carton	15.60	12/94	2c
Coffee, vacuum-packed	13 oz.	4.22	12/94	2c
Corn Flakes, Kellogg's or Post Toasties	18 oz.	2.44	12/94	2c
Corn, frozen, whole kernel, lowest price	10 oz.	0.76	12/94	2c
Eggs, Grade A large	dozen	0.75	12/94	2c
Lettuce, iceberg	head	0.89	12/94	2c
Margarine, Blue Bonnet or Parkay cubes	lb.	0.66	12/94	2c
Milk, whole	1/2 gal.	1.41	12/94	2c
Orange juice, Minute Maid frozen	12-oz.	1.22	12/94	2c
Peaches, halves or slices, Hunt's, Del Monte, or Libby's	29-oz.	1.42	12/94	2c
Peas, sweet, Del Monte or Green Giant	15-17 oz.	0.58	12/94	2c
Potatoes, white or red	10-lb. sack	2.08	12/94	2c
Sausage, Jimmy Dean, 100% pork	lb.	2.49	12/94	2c
Shortening, vegetable, Crisco	3-lb.	2.39	12/94	2c
Soft drink, Coca Cola, ex deposit	2 lit	0.94	12/94	2c
Steak, t-bone	lb.	4.29	12/94	2c
Sugar, cane or beet	4 lbs.	1.29	12/94	2c
Tomatoes, Hunt's or Del Monte	14.5 oz.	0.94	12/94	2c
Tuna, chunk, light, oil-packed	6.125-6.5 oz.	0.73	12/94	2c
Goods and Services				
Miscellaneous goods and services, ACCRA Index		98.10	12/94	2c
Health Care				
Health care, ACCRA Index		89.70	12/94	2c
Antibiotic ointment, Polysporin	1.5 oz.	3.71	12/94	2c
Dentist's fee, adult teeth cleaning and periodic oral exam	visit	48.00	12/94	2c
Doctor's fee, routine exam, established patient	visit	37.12	12/94	2c
Hospital care, semiprivate room	day	315.00	12/94	2c
Household Goods				
Appl. repair, service call, wash mach	min. lab. chg.	38.95	12/94	2c
Laundry detergent, Tide Ultra, Bold, or Cheer	42 oz.	4.34	12/94	2c
Tissues, facial, Kleenex brand	175	1.04	12/94	2c
Housing				
Housing, ACCRA Index		94.60	12/94	2c
House payment, principal and interest, 25% down payment	mo.	752	12/94	2c

Findlay, OH - continued

Item	Per	Value	Date	Ref.
Housing - continued				
House, 1800 sq ft, 8000 sq ft lot, new, urban, utilities	total	119500	12/94	2c
Mtge. rate, incl. points and orig. fee, 30-year conv. fixed or ARM	mo.	9.47	12/94	2c
Rent, apartment, 2 br., 1 1/2-2 baths, unfurnished, 950 sq ft, water	mo.	422	12/94	2c
Personal Goods				
Shampoo, Alberto VO5	15-oz.	1.04	12/94	2c
Toothpaste, Crest or Colgate	6-7 oz.	1.78	12/94	2c
Personal Services				
Dry cleaning, man's 2-pc. suit		6.96	12/94	2c
Haircut, man's barbershop, no styling		7.69	12/94	2c
Haircut, woman's shampoo, trim, blow-dry		16.75	12/94	2c
Restaurant Food				
Chicken, fried, thigh and drumstick		1.98	12/94	2c
Hamburger with cheese	1/4 lb.	1.90	12/94	2c
Pizza, Pizza Hut or Pizza Inn	12-13 in.	7.49	12/94	2c
Transportation				
Transportation, ACCRA Index		100.60	12/94	2c
Tire balance, computer or spin bal., front	wheel	6.88	12/94	2c
Utilities				
Utilities, ACCRA Index		105.00	12/94	2c
Electricity, (part.), other, 1800 sq. ft., new home	mo.	55.37	12/94	2c

Fitchburg-Leominster, MA

Item	Per	Value	Date	Ref.
Appliances				
Appliances (major), expenditures	year	145	91	81r
Average annual exp.				
Food, health care, personal goods, services	year	29496	91	81r
Charity				
Cash contributions, expenditures	year	708	91	81r
Clothing				
Apparel, men and boys, total expenditures	year	416	91	81r
Apparel, women and girls, total expenditures	year	744	91	81r
Footwear, expenditures	year	305	91	81r
Communications				
Long-distance telephone rate, day, addl. min., 1-10 mi.	min.	0.09	12/93	9s
Long-distance telephone rate, day, initial min., 1-10 mi.	min.	0.19	12/93	9s
Phone line, single, business, field visit	inst	27.50	12/93	9s
Phone line, single, business, no field visit	inst	93.02	12/93	9s
Phone line, single, residence, field visit	inst	27.50	12/93	9s
Phone line, single, residence, no field visit	inst	37.07	12/93	9s
Telephone service, expenditures	year	589	91	81r
Telephone, residential, flat rate	mo.	16.85	12/93	8c
Education				
Board, 4-year private college/university	year	3179	8/94	80s
Board, 4-year public college/university	year	2035	8/94	80s
Education, total expenditures	year	593	91	81r
Room, 4-year private college/university	year	3369	8/94	80s
Room, 4-year public college/university	year	2290	8/94	80s
Total cost, 4-year private college/university	year	21346	8/94	80s
Total cost, 4-year public college/university	year	8467	8/94	80s
Tuition, 2-year public college/university, in-state	year	2361	8/94	80s
Tuition, 4-year private college/university, in-state	year	14797	8/94	80s
Tuition, 4-year public college/university, in-state	year	4142	8/94	80s

Values are in dollars or fractions of dollars. In the column headed *Ref*, references are shown to sources. Each reference is followed by a letter. These refer to the geographical level for which data were reported: s=State, r=Region, and c=City or metro. The abbreviation *ex* is used to mean *except* or *excluding*; *exp* stands for *expenditures*. For other abbreviations and further explanations, please see the Introduction.

Fitchburg-Leominster, MA - continued

Item	Per	Value	Date	Ref.
Energy and Fuels				
Fuel oil and other fuels, expenditures	year	257	91	81r
Gas, cooking, 10 therms	month	12.70	2/94	65c
Gas, cooking, 30 therms	month	28.31	2/94	65c
Gas, cooking, 50 therms	month	43.91	2/94	65c
Gas, heating, winter, 100 therms	month	82.56	2/94	65c
Gas, heating, winter, average use	month	167.99	2/94	65c
Gas, natural, expenditures	year	285	91	81r
Gasoline and motor oil purchased	year	867	91	81r
Gasoline, unleaded midgrade	gallon	1.32	4/93	82r
Gasoline, unleaded premium	gallon	1.40	4/93	82r
Gasoline, unleaded regular	gallon	1.19	4/93	82r
Entertainment				
Entertainment, total expenditures	year	1331	91	81r
Fees and admissions, expenditures	year	398	91	81r
Pets, toys, playground equipment, expenditures	year	270	91	81r
Reading, expenditures	year	171	91	81r
Televisions, radios, and sound equipment, expenditures	year	429	91	81r
Funerals				
Burial, immediate, container provided by funeral home		1507.89	1/95	54r
Cards, acknowledgment		18.10	1/95	54r
Casket, minimum alternative		133.03	1/95	54r
Cosmetology, hair care, etc.		114.12	1/95	54r
Cremation, direct, container provided by funeral home		1309.19	1/95	54r
Embalming		320.97	1/95	54r
Funeral, funeral home		327.61	1/95	54r
Funeral, other facility		314.81	1/95	54r
Graveside service		286.11	1/95	54r
Hearse, local		158.95	1/95	54r
Limousine, local		149.45	1/95	54r
Memorial service		315.94	1/95	54r
Service charge, professional, nondeclinable		1148.43	1/95	54r
Visitation and viewing		249.66	1/95	54r
Groceries				
Apples, Red Delicious	lb.	0.78	12/94	82r
Bacon, sliced	lb.	2.24	12/94	82r
Bananas	lb.	0.49	12/94	82r
Beef purchases	year	226	91	81r
Beverage purchases, alcoholic	year	332	91	81r
Beverage purchases, nonalcoholic	year	213	91	81r
Bread, white, pan	lb.	0.80	12/94	82r
Butter, salted, Grade AA, stick	lb.	1.67	12/94	82r
Carrots, short trimmed and topped	lb.	0.51	12/94	82r
Cereals and bakery products purchases	year	407	91	81r
Cereals and cereals products purchases	year	132	91	81r
Chicken breast, bone-in	lb.	2.22	12/94	82r
Chicken, fresh, whole	lb.	1.05	12/94	82r
Chuck roast, USDA choice, boneless	lb.	2.74	12/94	82r
Coffee, 100%, ground roast, all sizes	lb.	4.61	12/94	82r
Dairy products (other) purchases	year	161	91	81r
Eggs, Grade A large	dozen	1.12	12/94	82r
Fish and seafood purchases	year	112	91	81r
Food purchases, food eaten at home	year	2599	91	81r
Foods purchased away from home, not prepared by consumer	year	2024	91	81r
Fruits and vegetables purchases	year	444	91	81r
Grapefruit	lb.	0.44	12/94	82r
Grapes, Thompson seedless	lb.	2.24	12/94	82r
Ground chuck, 100% beef	lb.	1.67	12/94	82r
Ice cream, prepackaged, bulk, regular	1/2 gal.	2.93	12/94	82r
Lemons	lb.	1.06	12/94	82r
Lettuce, iceberg	lb.	0.92	12/94	82r
Meats, poultry, fish, and eggs purchases	year	751	91	81r
Milk and cream (fresh) purchases	year	152	91	81r
Orange juice, frozen concentrate 12-oz. can	16 oz.	1.92	12/94	82r
Oranges, Navel	lb.	0.56	12/94	82r
Pork chops, center cut, bone-in	lb.	3.09	12/94	82r

Fitchburg-Leominster, MA - continued

Item	Per	Value	Date	Ref.
Groceries - continued				
Pork purchases	year	130	91	81r
Potatoes, white	lb.	0.37	12/94	82r
Rib roast, USDA choice, bone-in	lb.	4.98	12/94	82r
Round roast, USDA choice, boneless	lb.	2.93	12/94	82r
Shortening, vegetable oil blends	lb.	1.03	12/94	82r
Spaghetti and macaroni	lb.	0.84	12/94	82r
Steak, round, USDA choice, boneless	lb.	3.48	12/94	82r
Steak, sirloin, USDA choice, bone-in	lb.	3.38	12/94	82r
Steak, sirloin, USDA choice, boneless	lb.	4.81	12/94	82r
Sugar and other sweets, eaten at home, expenditures	year	89	91	81r
Sugar, white, all sizes	lb.	0.46	12/94	82r
Tobacco products and smoking supplies, total expenditures	year	279	91	81r
Tomatoes, field grown	lb.	1.56	12/94	82r
Tuna, chunk, light	lb.	2.09	12/94	82r
Health Care				
Childbirth, Cesarean delivery, hospital charge	birth	6334.00	12/91	69r
Childbirth, Cesarean delivery, physician charge	birth	2234.00	12/91	69r
Childbirth, normal delivery, hospital charge	birth	3225.00	12/91	69r
Childbirth, normal delivery, physician charge	birth	1623.00	12/91	69r
Drugs, expenditures	year	205	91	81r
Health care, total expenditures	year	1396	91	81r
Health insurance expenditures	year	553	91	81r
Insurance premium, family medical care	month	457.38	1/95	41s
Medical services expenditures	year	559	91	81r
Medical supplies expenditures	year	80	91	81r
Household Goods				
Floor coverings, expenditures	year	158	91	81r
Furniture, expenditures	year	341	91	81r
Household equipment, misc. expenditures	year	363	91	81r
Household expenditures, miscellaneous	year	194	91	81r
Household furnishings and equipment, expenditures	year	1158	91	81r
Household operations expenditures	year	378	91	81r
Household textiles, expenditures	year	88	91	81r
Housekeeping supplies, expenditures	year	426	91	81r
Laundry and cleaning supplies, expenditures	year	122	91	81r
Postage and stationery, expenditures	year	134	91	81r
Housing				
Add garage/carport		11,614	3/95	74r
Add room(s)		16,816	3/95	74r
Apartment condominium or co-op, median	unit	96700	12/94	62r
Dwellings (owned), expenditures	year	3305	91	81r
Enclose porch/patio/breezeway		2,980	3/95	74r
Finish room in basement/attic		4,330	3/95	74r
Home, existing, single-family, median	unit	161600	12/94	62r
Maintenance, repairs, insurance, and other housing expenditures	year	569	91	81r
Mortgage interest and charges expenditures	year	1852	91	81r
Princ. & int., mortgage, median-price exist. sing.-family home	mo.	765	12/94	62r
Property taxes expenditures	year	884	91	81r
Redesign, restructure more than half of home's interior		2,750	3/95	74r
Rental units expenditures	year	1832	91	81r
Insurance and Pensions				
Auto insurance, private passenger	year	1009.56	12/94	71s
Insurance and pensions, personal, expenditures	year	2690	91	81r
Insurance, life and other personal, expenditures	year	341	91	81r
Pensions and Social Security, expenditures	year	2349	91	81r
Legal Assistance				
Estate planning, law-firm partner	hr.	375.00	10/93	12r
Legal work, law firm associate	hour	78		10r

Values are in dollars or fractions of dollars. In the column headed *Ref*, references are shown to sources. Each reference is followed by a letter. These refer to the geographical level for which data were reported: s=State, r=Region, and c=City or metro. The abbreviation *ex* is used to mean *except* or *excluding*; *exp* stands for *expenditures*. For other abbreviations and further explanations, please see the Introduction.

Fitchburg-Leominster, MA - continued

Item	Per	Value	Date	Ref.
Legal Assistance				
Legal work, law firm partner	hour	183		10r
Personal Services				
Personal services expenditures	year	184	91	81r
Restaurant Food				
Dining expenditures, family	week	34.26	94	73r
Taxes				
Taxes, Federal income, expenditures	year	2409	91	81r
Taxes, personal, expenditures	year	3094	91	81r
Taxes, State and local income, expenditures	year	620	91	81r
Transportation				
Bus fare, one-way	trip	0.50	12/95	1c
Cars and trucks purchased, new	year	1170	91	81r
Cars and trucks purchased, used	year	739	91	81r
Driver's learning permit fee	perm	15.00	1/94	84s
Driver's license fee	orig	50.00	1/94	84s
Driver's license fee, duplicate	lic	15.00	1/94	84s
Driver's license renewal fee	renew	43.75	1/94	84s
Identification card, nondriver	card	15.00	1/94	83s
Motorcycle license fee	orig	50.00	1/94	84s
Motorcycle license fee, duplicate	lic	15.00	1/94	84s
Motorcycle license renewal fee	renew	43.75	1/94	84s
Public transportation expenditures	year	430	91	81r
Transportation expenditures, total	year	4810	91	81r
Vehicle finance charges	year	238	91	81r
Vehicle insurance expenditures	year	630	91	81r
Vehicle maintenance and repairs expenditures	year	532	91	81r
Vehicle purchases	year	1920	91	81r
Vehicle rental, leases, licenses, etc. expenditures	year	193	91	81r
Vehicles purchased, other than cars and trucks	year	11	91	81r
Utilities				
Electricity expenditures	year	695	91	81r
Electricity, summer, 250 KWh	month	33.23	8/93	64c
Electricity, summer, 500 KWh	month	63.22	8/93	64c
Electricity, summer, 750 KWh	month	93.19	8/93	64c
Electricity, summer, 1000 KWh	month	123.17	8/93	64c
Utilities, fuels, and public services, total expenditures	year	1981	91	81r
Water and other public services, expenditures	year	154	91	81r
Weddings				
Bridal attendants' gowns	event	750	10/93	76r
Bridal gown	event	852	10/93	76r
Bridal headpiece and veil	event	167	10/93	76r
Bride's wedding band	event	708	10/93	76r
Clergy	event	224	10/93	76r
Engagement ring	event	2756	10/93	76r
Flowers	event	863	10/93	76r
Formal wear for groom	event	106	10/93	76r
Groom's attendants' formal wear	event	530	10/93	76r
Groom's wedding band	event	402	10/93	76r
Music	event	600	10/93	76r
Photography	event	1088	10/93	76r
Shoes for bride	event	50	10/93	76r
Videography	event	483	10/93	76r
Wedding invitations and announcements	event	342	10/93	76r
Wedding reception	event	7000	10/93	76r

Flagstaff, AZ

Item	Per	Value	Date	Ref.
Composite, ACCRA index		108.90	12/94	2c
Alcoholic Beverages				
Beer, Miller Lite, Bud, 12-oz., ex deposit	6	3.71	12/94	2c
J & B Scotch	750-ml.	15.74	12/94	2c
Wine, Gallo Chablis blanc	1.5-lit	4.76	12/94	2c

Flagstaff, AZ - continued

Item	Per	Value	Date	Ref.
Clothing				
Jeans, man's denim		31.99	12/94	2c
Shirt, man's dress shirt		31.93	12/94	2c
Undervest, boy's size 10-14, cotton	3	4.91	12/94	2c
Communications				
Newspaper subscription, dly. and Sun. delivery	month	9.00	12/94	2c
Telephone bill, family of four	month	18.14	12/94	2c
Telephone, residential, flat rate	mo.	12.40	12/93	8c
Energy and Fuels				
Energy, combined forms, 1800 sq. ft.	mo.	101.28	12/94	2c
Energy, exc. electricity, 1800 sq. ft.	mo.	44.52	12/94	2c
Gas, cooking, 10 therms	month	9.05	2/94	65c
Gas, cooking, 30 therms	month	18.15	2/94	65c
Gas, cooking, 50 therms	month	27.25	2/94	65c
Gas, heating, winter, 100 therms	month	49.99	2/94	65c
Gas, heating, winter, average use	month	54.08	2/94	65c
Gas, reg unlead, taxes inc., cash, self-service	gal	1.30	12/94	2c
Entertainment				
Bowling, evening rate	game	1.98	12/94	2c
Monopoly game, Parker Brothers', No. 9	game	12.13	12/94	2c
Movie	adm	5.25	12/94	2c
Tennis balls, yellow, Wilson or Penn, 3	can	2.56	12/94	2c
Groceries				
Groceries, ACCRA Index		101.40	12/94	2c
Baby food, strained vegetables, lowest price	4-4.5 oz.	0.31	12/94	2c
Bananas	lb.	0.44	12/94	2c
Beef or hamburger, ground	lb.	1.32	12/94	2c
Bread, white	24-oz.	0.67	12/94	2c
Cheese, Kraft grated Parmesan	8-oz.	3.67	12/94	2c
Chicken, whole fryer	lb.	0.77	12/94	2c
Cigarettes, Winston, Kings	carton	14.84	12/94	2c
Coffee, vacuum-packed	13 oz.	3.67	12/94	2c
Corn Flakes, Kellogg's or Post Toasties	18 oz.	2.90	12/94	2c
Corn, frozen, whole kernel, lowest price	10 oz.	0.69	12/94	2c
Eggs, Grade A large	dozen	0.77	12/94	2c
Lettuce, iceberg	head	0.67	12/94	2c
Margarine, Blue Bonnet or Parkay cubes	lb.	0.77	12/94	2c
Milk, whole	1/2 gal.	1.54	12/94	2c
Orange juice, Minute Maid frozen	12-oz.	1.30	12/94	2c
Peaches, halves or slices, Hunt's, Del Monte, or Libby's	29-oz.	1.41	12/94	2c
Peas, sweet, Del Monte or Green Giant	15-17 oz.	0.53	12/94	2c
Potatoes, white or red	10-lb. sack	1.39	12/94	2c
Sausage, Jimmy Dean, 100% pork	lb.	3.32	12/94	2c
Shortening, vegetable, Crisco	3-lb.	2.82	12/94	2c
Soft drink, Coca Cola, ex deposit	2 lit	1.30	12/94	2c
Steak, t-bone	lb.	4.47	12/94	2c
Sugar, cane or beet	4 lbs.	1.55	12/94	2c
Tomatoes, Hunt's or Del Monte	14.5 oz.	0.77	12/94	2c
Tuna, chunk, light, oil-packed	6.125-6.5 oz.	0.78	12/94	2c
Goods and Services				
Miscellaneous goods and services, ACCRA Index		104.50	12/94	2c
Health Care				
Health care, ACCRA Index		110.80	12/94	2c
Antibiotic ointment, Polysporin	1.5 oz.	4.52	12/94	2c
Dentist's fee, adult teeth cleaning and periodic oral exam	visit	61.80	12/94	2c
Doctor's fee, routine exam, established patient	visit	45.50	12/94	2c
Hospital care, semiprivate room	day	366.00	12/94	2c

Values are in dollars or fractions of dollars. In the column headed *Ref*, references are shown to sources. Each reference is followed by a letter. These refer to the geographical level for which data were reported: s = State, r = Region, and c = City or metro. The abbreviation *ex* is used to mean *except* or *excluding*; *exp* stands for *expenditures*. For other abbreviations and further explanations, please see the Introduction.

Flagstaff, AZ - continued

Item	Per	Value	Date	Ref.
Household Goods				
Appl. repair, service call, wash mach	min. lab. chg.	36.58	12/94	2c
Laundry detergent, Tide Ultra, Bold, or Cheer	42 oz.	3.25	12/94	2c
Tissues, facial, Kleenex brand	175	1.14	12/94	2c
Housing				
Housing, ACCRA Index		120.70	12/94	2c
House payment, principal and interest, 25% down payment	mo.	927	12/94	2c
House, 1800 sq ft, 8000 sq ft lot, new, urban, utilities	total	148800	12/94	2c
Mtge. rate, incl. points and orig. fee, 30-year conv. fixed or ARM	mo.	9.36	12/94	2c
Rent, apartment, 2 br., 1 1/2-2 baths, unfurnished, 950 sq ft, water	mo.	630	12/94	2c
Personal Goods				
Shampoo, Alberto VO5	15-oz.	1.14	12/94	2c
Toothpaste, Crest or Colgate	6-7 oz.	1.92	12/94	2c
Personal Services				
Dry cleaning, man's 2-pc. suit		7.97	12/94	2c
Haircut, man's barbershop, no styling		8.90	12/94	2c
Haircut, woman's shampoo, trim, blow-dry		20.70	12/94	2c
Restaurant Food				
Chicken, fried, thigh and drumstick		2.49	12/94	2c
Hamburger with cheese	1/4 lb.	1.99	12/94	2c
Pizza, Pizza Hut or Pizza Inn	12-13 in.	8.19	12/94	2c
Transportation				
Transportation, ACCRA Index		116.30	12/94	2c
Tire balance, computer or spin bal., front	wheel	7.97	12/94	2c
Utilities				
Utilities, ACCRA Index		90.60	12/94	2c
Electricity, (part.), other, 1800 sq. ft., new home	mo.	56.76	12/94	2c

Flint, MI

Item	Per	Value	Date	Ref.
Appliances				
Appliances (major), expenditures	year	131	91	81r
Average annual exp.				
Food, health care, personal goods, services	year	25935	91	81r
Charity				
Cash contributions, expenditures	year	745	91	81r
Clothing				
Apparel, men and boys, total expenditures	year	332	91	81r
Apparel, women and girls, total expenditures	year	578	91	81r
Footwear, expenditures	year	164	91	81r
Communications				
Long-distance telephone rate, day, addl. min., 1-10 mi.	min.	0.08	12/93	9s
Long-distance telephone rate, day, initial min., 1-10 mi.	min.	0.14	12/93	9s
Phone line, single, business, field visit	inst	42.00	12/93	9s
Phone line, single, business, no field visit	inst	42.00	12/93	9s
Phone line, single, residence, field visit	inst	42.00	12/93	9s
Phone line, single, residence, no field visit	inst	42.00	12/93	9s
Telephone service, expenditures	year	547	91	81r
Education				
Board, 4-year private college/university	year	2064	8/94	80s
Board, 4-year public college/university	year	2304	8/94	80s
Education, total expenditures	year	394	91	81r
Room, 4-year private college/university	year	1814	8/94	80s
Room, 4-year public college/university	year	1856	8/94	80s
Total cost, 4-year private college/university	year	12178	8/94	80s

Flint, MI - continued

Item	Per	Value	Date	Ref.
Education - continued				
Total cost, 4-year public college/university	year	7642	8/94	80s
Tuition, 2-year public college/university, in-state	year	1358	8/94	80s
Tuition, 4-year private college/university, in-state	year	8300	8/94	80s
Tuition, 4-year public college/university, in-state	year	3481	8/94	80s
Energy and Fuels				
Fuel oil and other fuels, expenditures	year	83	91	81r
Gas, natural, expenditures	year	373	91	81r
Gasoline and motor oil purchased	year	1000	91	81r
Gasoline, unleaded midgrade	gallon	1.15	4/93	82r
Gasoline, unleaded premium	gallon	1.23	4/93	82r
Gasoline, unleaded regular	gallon	1.07	4/93	82r
Entertainment				
Entertainment, total expenditures	year	1356	91	81r
Fees and admissions, expenditures	year	347	91	81r
Pets, toys, playground equipment, expenditures	year	270	91	81r
Reading, expenditures	year	160	91	81r
Televisions, radios, and sound equipment, expenditures	year	433	91	81r
Funerals				
Burial, immediate, container provided by funeral home		1268.31	1/95	54r
Cards, acknowledgment		26.12	1/95	54r
Casket, minimum alternative		198.03	1/95	54r
Cosmetology, hair care, etc.		122.19	1/95	54r
Cremation, direct, container provided by funeral home		977.81	1/95	54r
Embalming		334.00	1/95	54r
Funeral, funeral home		321.16	1/95	54r
Funeral, other facility		317.73	1/95	54r
Graveside service		292.48	1/95	54r
Hearse, local		153.20	1/95	54r
Limousine, local		123.52	1/95	54r
Memorial service		356.30	1/95	54r
Service charge, professional, nondeclinable		968.24	1/95	54r
Visitation and viewing		332.66	1/95	54r
Groceries				
Apples, Red Delicious	lb.	0.68	12/94	82r
Bacon, sliced	lb.	1.88	12/94	82r
Bananas	lb.	0.41	12/94	82r
Beef purchases	year	197	91	81r
Beef, stew, boneless	lb.	2.52	12/94	82r
Beverage purchases, alcoholic	year	293	91	81r
Beverage purchases, nonalcoholic	year	203	91	81r
Bologna, all beef or mixed	lb.	2.12	12/94	82r
Bread, white, pan	lb.	0.76	12/94	82r
Cabbage	lb.	0.44	12/94	82r
Carrots, short trimmed and topped	lb.	0.44	12/94	82r
Cereals and bakery products purchases	year	347	91	81r
Cereals and cereals products purchases	year	119	91	81r
Cheddar cheese, natural	lb.	3.28	12/94	82r
Chicken breast, bone-in	lb.	1.61	12/94	82r
Chicken, fresh, whole	lb.	0.89	12/94	82r
Chuck roast, USDA choice, boneless	lb.	2.33	12/94	82r
Coffee, 100%, ground roast, all sizes	lb.	4.28	12/94	82r
Cookies, chocolate chip	lb.	2.72	12/94	82r
Dairy products (other) purchases	year	148	91	81r
Eggs, Grade A large	dozen	0.76	12/94	82r
Fish and seafood purchases	year	61	91	81r
Flour, white, all purpose	lb.	0.22	12/94	82r
Food purchases, food eaten at home	year	2313	91	81r
Foods purchased away from home, not prepared by consumer	year	1709	91	81r
Fruits and vegetables purchases	year	372	91	81r
Grapefruit	lb.	0.47	12/94	82r
Grapes, Thompson seedless	lb.	2.15	12/94	82r
Ground beef, 100% beef	lb.	1.37	12/94	82r

Values are in dollars or fractions of dollars. In the column headed *Ref*, references are shown to sources. Each reference is followed by a letter. These refer to the geographical level for which data were reported: s=State, r=Region, and c=City or metro. The abbreviation *ex* is used to mean *except* or *excluding*; *exp* stands for expenditures. For other abbreviations and further explanations, please see the Introduction.

Flint, MI - continued

Item	Per	Value	Date	Ref.
Groceries				
Ground chuck, 100% beef	lb.	1.81	12/94	82r
Ham, boneless, exc. canned	lb.	2.16	12/94	82r
Ice cream, prepackaged, bulk, regular	1/2 gal.	2.48	12/94	82r
Lemons	lb.	1.08	12/94	82r
Lettuce, iceberg	lb.	0.81	12/94	82r
Margarine, stick	lb.	0.81	12/94	82r
Meats, poultry, fish, and eggs purchases	year	591	91	81r
Milk and cream (fresh) purchases	year	132	91	81r
Orange juice, frozen concentrate 12-oz. can	16 oz.	1.41	12/94	82r
Oranges, Navel	lb.	0.56	12/94	82r
Peanut butter, creamy, all sizes	lb.	1.81	12/94	82r
Pork chops, center cut, bone-in	lb.	2.76	12/94	82r
Pork purchases	year	130	91	81r
Potato chips	16-oz.	2.81	12/94	82r
Potatoes, frozen, French fried	lb.	0.83	12/94	82r
Potatoes, white	lb.	0.28	12/94	82r
Round roast, USDA choice, boneless	lb.	2.90	12/94	82r
Shortening, vegetable oil blends	lb.	0.88	12/94	82r
Spaghetti and macaroni	lb.	0.78	12/94	82r
Steak, rib eye, USDA choice, boneless	lb.	6.15	12/94	82r
Steak, round, graded & ungraded, exc. USDA prime & choice	lb.	2.72	12/94	82r
Steak, round, USDA choice, boneless	lb.	3.02	12/94	82r
Steak, sirloin, USDA choice, boneless	lb.	3.85	12/94	82r
Steak, T-bone, USDA choice, bone-in	lb.	5.38	12/94	82r
Sugar and other sweets, eaten at home, expenditures	year	91	91	81r
Sugar, white, all sizes	lb.	0.36	12/94	82r
Tobacco products and smoking supplies, total expenditures	year	298	91	81r
Tomatoes, field grown	lb.	1.36	12/94	82r
Tuna, chunk, light	lb.	1.94	12/94	82r
Turkey, frozen, whole	lb.	0.96	12/94	82r
Yogurt, natural, fruit flavored	8 oz.	0.62	12/94	82r
Health Care				
Childbirth, Cesarean delivery, hospital charge	birth	5101.00	12/91	69r
Childbirth, Cesarean delivery, physician charge	birth	2234.00	12/91	69r
Childbirth, normal delivery, hospital charge	birth	2891.00	12/91	69r
Childbirth, normal delivery, physician charge	birth	1623.00	12/91	69r
Drugs, expenditures	year	248	91	81r
Health care, total expenditures	year	1336	91	81r
Health insurance expenditures	year	550	91	81r
Insurance premium, family medical care	month	369.41	1/95	41s
Medical services expenditures	year	457	91	81r
Medical supplies expenditures	year	82	91	81r
Household Goods				
Floor coverings, expenditures	year	105	91	81r
Furniture, expenditures	year	291	91	81r
Household equipment, misc. expenditures	year	341	91	81r
Household expenditures, miscellaneous	year	162	91	81r
Household furnishings and equipment, expenditures	year	1042	91	81r
Household operations expenditures	year	365	91	81r
Household textiles, expenditures	year	101	91	81r
Housekeeping supplies, expenditures	year	390	91	81r
Laundry and cleaning supplies, expenditures	year	110	91	81r
Postage and stationery, expenditures	year	115	91	81r
Housing				
Add garage/carport		8,479	3/95	74r
Add room(s)		21,347	3/95	74r
Apartment condominium or co-op, median	unit	87100	12/94	62r
Bathroom addition, average cost	add	9734.00	3/95	13r
Bathroom remodeling, average cost	remod	6414.00	3/95	13r
Bedroom, master suite addition, average cost	add	27122.00	3/95	13r
Deck addition, average cost	add	6665.00	3/95	13r
Dwellings (owned), expenditures	year	2566	91	81r

Flint, MI - continued

Item	Per	Value	Date	Ref.
Housing - continued				
Enclose porch/patio/breezeway		4,556	3/95	74r
Exterior remodeling, average cost	remod	15395.00	3/95	13r
Family room addition, average cost	add	27658.00	3/95	13r
Finish room in basement/attic		5,074	3/95	74r
Home, existing, single-family, median	unit	106500	12/94	62r
Kitchen remodeling, major, average cost	remod	17084.00	3/95	13r
Kitchen remodeling, minor, average cost	remod	5804.00	3/95	13r
Maintenance, repairs, insurance, and other housing expenditures	year	484	91	81r
Mortgage interest and charges expenditures	year	1443	91	81r
Office, home addition, average cost	add	8121.00	3/95	13r
Princ. & int., mortgage, median-price exist. sing.-family home	mo.	515	12/94	62r
Property taxes expenditures	year	639	91	81r
Redesign, restructure more than half of home's interior		9,114	3/95	74r
Rental units expenditures	year	1200	91	81r
Sun-space addition, average cost	add	23768.00	3/95	13r
Wing addition, two-story, average cost	add	50410.00	3/95	13r
Insurance and Pensions				
Auto insurance, private passenger	year	788.26	12/94	71s
Insurance and pensions, personal, expenditures	year	2408	91	81r
Insurance, life and other personal, expenditures	year	355	91	81r
Pensions and Social Security, expenditures	year	2053	91	81r
Legal Assistance				
Legal work, law firm associate	hour	90		10r
Legal work, law firm partner	hour	139		10r
Personal Services				
Personal services expenditures	year	203	91	81r
Restaurant Food				
Dining expenditures, family	week	30.03	94	73r
Taxes				
Taxes, Federal income, expenditures	year	1756	91	81r
Taxes, personal, expenditures	year	2426	91	81r
Taxes, State and local income, expenditures	year	568	91	81r
Transportation				
Cars and trucks purchased, new	year	891	91	81r
Cars and trucks purchased, used	year	1155	91	81r
Driver's learning permit fee	perm	12.00	1/94	84s
Driver's license fee	orig	12.00	1/94	84s
Driver's license fee, duplicate	lic	6.00	1/94	84s
Driver's license reinstatement fee, min.	susp	125.00	1/94	85s
Driver's license renewal fee	renew	12.00	1/94	84s
Identification card, nondriver	card	6.00	1/94	83s
Motorcycle license fee	orig	7.50	1/94	84s
Motorcycle license renewal fee	renew	4.00	1/94	84s
Public transportation expenditures	year	209	91	81r
Transportation expenditures, total	year	4792	91	81r
Vehicle finance charges	year	300	91	81r
Vehicle insurance expenditures	year	485	91	81r
Vehicle maintenance and repairs expenditures	year	534	91	81r
Vehicle purchases	year	2068	91	81r
Vehicle rental, leases, licenses, etc. expenditures	year	197	91	81r
Vehicles purchased, other than cars and trucks	year	22	91	81r
Utilities				
Electricity expenditures	year	668	91	81r
Utilities, fuels, and public services, total expenditures	year	1838	91	81r
Water and other public services, expenditures	year	167	91	81r
Weddings				
Bridal attendants' gowns	event	750	10/93	76r
Bridal gown	event	852	10/93	76r

Values are in dollars or fractions of dollars. In the column headed *Ref*, references are shown to sources. Each reference is followed by a letter. These refer to the geographical level for which data were reported: s = State, r = Region, and c = City or metro. The abbreviation *ex* is used to mean *except* or *excluding*; *exp* stands for *expenditures*. For other abbreviations and further explanations, please see the Introduction.

Flint, MI - continued

Item	Per	Value	Date	Ref.
Weddings				
Bridal headpiece and veil	event	167	10/93	76r
Bride's wedding band	event	708	10/93	76r
Clergy	event	224	10/93	76r
Engagement ring	event	2756	10/93	76r
Flowers	event	863	10/93	76r
Formal wear for groom	event	106	10/93	76r
Groom's attendants' formal wear	event	530	10/93	76r
Groom's wedding band	event	402	10/93	76r
Music	event	600	10/93	76r
Photography	event	1088	10/93	76r
Shoes for bride	event	50	10/93	76r
Videography	event	483	10/93	76r
Wedding invitations and announcements	event	342	10/93	76r
Wedding reception	event	7000	10/93	76r

Florence, AL

Item	Per	Value	Date	Ref.
Appliances				
Appliances (major), expenditures	year	153	91	81r
Average annual exp.				
Food, health care, personal goods, services	year	27020	91	81r
Charity				
Cash contributions, expenditures	year	839	91	81r
Clothing				
Apparel, men and boys, total expenditures	year	380	91	81r
Apparel, women and girls, total expenditures	year	660	91	81r
Footwear, expenditures	year	193	91	81r
Communications				
Long-distance telephone rate, day, addl. min., 1-10 mi.	min.	0.09	12/93	9s
Long-distance telephone rate, day, initial min., 1-10 mi.	min.	0.11	12/93	9s
Phone line, single, business, field visit	inst	69.00	12/93	9s
Phone line, single, business, no field visit	inst	69.00	12/93	9s
Phone line, single, residence, field visit	inst	40.00	12/93	9s
Phone line, single, residence, no field visit	inst	40.00	12/93	9s
Telephone service, expenditures	year	616	91	81r
Education				
Board, 4-year private college/university	year	2072	8/94	80s
Board, 4-year public college/university	year	1706	8/94	80s
Education, total expenditures	year	319	91	81r
Room, 4-year private college/university	year	1607	8/94	80s
Room, 4-year public college/university	year	1598	8/94	80s
Total cost, 4-year private college/university	year	10664	8/94	80s
Total cost, 4-year public college/university	year	5287	8/94	80s
Tuition, 2-year public college/university, in-state	year	1110	8/94	80s
Tuition, 4-year private college/university, in-state	year	6985	8/94	80s
Tuition, 4-year public college/university, in-state	year	1983	8/94	80s
Energy and Fuels				
Fuel oil and other fuels, expenditures	year	56	91	81r
Gas, natural, expenditures	year	150	91	81r
Gasoline and motor oil purchased	year	1152	91	81r
Gasoline, unleaded midgrade	gallon	1.21	4/93	82r
Gasoline, unleaded premium	gallon	1.30	4/93	82r
Gasoline, unleaded regular	gallon	1.10	4/93	82r
Entertainment				
Concert ticket, Pearl Jam group	perf	20.00	94	50r
Entertainment, total expenditures	year	1266	91	81r
Fees and admissions, expenditures	year	306	91	81r
Pets, toys, playground equipment, expenditures	year	271	91	81r
Reading, expenditures	year	131	91	81r
Televisions, radios, and sound equipment, expenditures	year	439	91	81r

Florence, AL - continued

Item	Per	Value	Date	Ref.
Funerals				
Burial, immediate, container provided by funeral home		1298.96	1/95	54r
Cards, acknowledgment		21.26	1/95	54r
Casket, minimum alternative		204.95	1/95	54r
Cosmetology, hair care, etc.		85.40	1/95	54r
Cremation, direct, container provided by funeral home		1054.77	1/95	54r
Embalming		287.71	1/95	54r
Funeral, funeral home		269.18	1/95	54r
Funeral, other facility		272.88	1/95	54r
Graveside service		302.54	1/95	54r
Hearse, local		122.08	1/95	54r
Limousine, local		80.31	1/95	54r
Memorial service		277.66	1/95	54r
Service charge, professional, nondeclinable		896.65	1/95	54r
Visitation and viewing		232.39	1/95	54r
Groceries				
Apples, Red Delicious	lb.	0.73	12/94	82r
Bacon, sliced	lb.	1.67	12/94	82r
Bananas	lb.	0.42	12/94	82r
Beef purchases	year	213	91	81r
Beverage purchases, alcoholic	year	249	91	81r
Beverage purchases, nonalcoholic	year	207	91	81r
Bologna, all beef or mixed	lb.	2.27	12/94	82r
Bread, white, pan	lb.	0.68	12/94	82r
Cabbage	lb.	0.42	12/94	82r
Carrots, short trimmed and topped	lb.	0.53	12/94	82r
Cereals and bakery products purchases	year	345	91	81r
Cereals and cereals products purchases	year	127	91	81r
Cheddar cheese, natural	lb.	3.58	12/94	82r
Chicken breast, bone-in	lb.	1.71	12/94	82r
Chicken, fresh, whole	lb.	0.78	12/94	82r
Chuck roast, USDA choice, boneless	lb.	2.26	12/94	82r
Crackers, soda, salted	lb.	1.27	12/94	82r
Cucumbers	lb.	0.65	12/94	82r
Dairy products (other) purchases	year	141	91	81r
Eggs, Grade A large	dozen	0.87	12/94	82r
Fish and seafood purchases	year	72	91	81r
Flour, white, all purpose	lb.	0.23	12/94	82r
Food purchases, food eaten at home	year	2381	91	81r
Foods purchased away from home, not prepared by consumer	year	1696	91	81r
Frankfurters, all meat or all beef	lb.	1.74	12/94	82r
Fruits and vegetables purchases	year	380	91	81r
Grapefruit	lb.	0.45	12/94	82r
Grapes, Thompson seedless	lb.	2.30	12/94	82r
Ground beef, 100% beef	lb.	1.37	12/94	82r
Ground chuck, 100% beef	lb.	1.97	12/94	82r
Ham, boneless, exc. canned	lb.	2.54	12/94	82r
Ice cream, prepackaged, bulk, regular	1/2 gal.	2.47	12/94	82r
Lemons	lb.	1.02	12/94	82r
Lettuce, iceberg	lb.	0.96	12/94	82r
Margarine, stick	lb.	0.77	12/94	82r
Meats, poultry, fish, and eggs purchases	year	655	91	81r
Milk and cream (fresh) purchases	year	130	91	81r
Orange juice, frozen concentrate 12-oz. can	16 oz.	1.36	12/94	82r
Oranges, Navel	lb.	0.54	12/94	82r
Pears, Anjou	lb.	0.81	12/94	82r
Pork chops, center cut, bone-in	lb.	3.07	12/94	82r
Pork purchases	year	142	91	81r
Potato chips	16-oz.	3.15	12/94	82r
Potatoes, frozen, French fried	lb.	0.82	12/94	82r
Potatoes, white	lb.	0.34	12/94	82r
Rice, white, long grain, uncooked	lb.	0.48	12/94	82r
Round roast, USDA choice, boneless	lb.	2.91	12/94	82r
Sausage, fresh	lb.	1.82	12/94	82r
Shortening, vegetable oil blends	lb.	0.75	12/94	82r
Spaghetti and macaroni	lb.	0.87	12/94	82r
Steak, rib eye, USDA choice, boneless	lb.	6.85	12/94	82r
Steak, round, graded & ungraded, exc. USDA prime & choice	lb.	2.96	12/94	82r

Values are in dollars or fractions of dollars. In the column headed *Ref*, references are shown to sources. Each reference is followed by a letter. These refer to the geographical level for which data were reported: s=State, r=Region, and c=City or metro. The abbreviation *ex* is used to mean *except* or *excluding*; *exp* stands for expenditures. For other abbreviations and further explanations, please see the Introduction.

Florence, AL - continued

Item	Per	Value	Date	Ref.
Groceries				
Steak, round, USDA choice, boneless	lb.	3.17	12/94	82r
Steak, sirloin, USDA choice, boneless	lb.	4.12	12/94	82r
Steak, T-bone, USDA choice, bone-in	lb.	5.63	12/94	82r
Sugar and other sweets, eaten at home, expenditures	year	93	91	81r
Sugar, white, all sizes	lb.	0.39	12/94	82r
Tobacco products and smoking supplies, total expenditures	year	286	91	81r
Tomatoes, field grown	lb.	1.36	12/94	82r
Tuna, chunk, light	lb.	1.94	12/94	82r
Turkey, frozen, whole	lb.	0.96	12/94	82r
Yogurt, natural, fruit flavored	8 oz.	0.58	12/94	82r
Health Care				
Adenosine, emergency room	treat	100.00	95	23r
Bladder tap, superpubic, infant, emergency room	treat	119.00	95	23r
Blood analysis, emergency room	treat	25.00	95	23r
Blood tests, abdominal pain, emergency room	treat	25.00	95	23r
Burn dressing, emergency room	treat	266.00	95	23r
Cardiology interpretation, emergency room	treat	26.00	95	23r
Chest X-ray, emergency room	treat	78.00	95	23r
Childbirth, Cesarean delivery, hospital charge	birth	5462.00	12/91	69r
Childbirth, Cesarean delivery, physician charge	birth	2228.00	12/91	69r
Childbirth, normal delivery, hospital charge	birth	2943.00	12/91	69r
Childbirth, normal delivery, physician charge	birth	1619.00	12/91	69r
Defibrillation pads, emergency room	treat	6.00	95	23r
Drugs, expenditures	year	297	91	81r
Gastric tube insertion, nasal, emergency room	treat	25.00	95	23r
Health care, total expenditures	year	1600	91	81r
Health insurance expenditures	year	637	91	81r
Heart monitor, emergency room	treat	40.00	95	23r
Insurance premium, family medical care	month	360.67	1/95	41s
Intravenous fluids, emergency room	treat	130.00	95	23r
Intravenous fluids, emergency room	liter	26.00	95	23r
Intravenous line, central, emergency room	treat	342.00	95	23r
Liver function tests, abdominal pain, emergency room	treat	26.00	95	23r
Medical care charges, total, emergency room, third-degree burns	treat	2101.00	95	23r
Medical care charges, total, emergency, infant with fever	treat	628.00	95	23r
Medical services expenditures	year	573	91	81r
Medical supplies expenditures	year	93	91	81r
Morphine, emergency room	treat	34.00	95	23r
Nursing care and facilities charges, emergency room	treat	252.00	95	23r
Nursing care and facilities charges, emergency, infant with fever	treat	252.00	95	23r
Nursing care and facilities charges, emergency, third-degree burns	treat	861.00	95	23r
Physician's charges, emergency, infant with fever	treat	212.00	95	23r
Physician's charges, emergency, third-degree burns	treat	372.00	95	23r
Physician's fee, emergency room	treat	372.00	95	23r
Physician's fee, general practitioner	visit	51.20	12/93	60r
Surgery, open-heart	proc	42374.00	1/93	14r
Ultrasound, abdominal, emergency room	treat	276.00	95	23r
Urinalysis, emergency room	treat	20.00	95	23r
Urinalysis, infant, emergency room	treat	20.00	95	23r
X-rays, emergency room	treat	78.00	95	23r
Household Goods				
Floor coverings, expenditures	year	48	91	81r
Furniture, expenditures	year	280	91	81r
Household equipment, misc. expenditures	year	342	91	81r
Household expenditures, miscellaneous	year	256	91	81r

Florence, AL - continued

Item	Per	Value	Date	Ref.
Household Goods - continued				
Household furnishings and equipment, expenditures	year	988	91	81r
Household operations expenditures	year	468	91	81r
Household textiles, expenditures	year	95	91	81r
Housekeeping supplies, expenditures	year	380	91	81r
Laundry and cleaning supplies, expenditures	year	109	91	81r
Postage and stationery, expenditures	year	105	91	81r
Housing				
Add garage/carport		6,980	3/95	74r
Add room(s)		11,403	3/95	74r
Apartment condominium or co-op, median	unit	68600	12/94	62r
Dwellings (owned), expenditures	year	2428	91	81r
Enclose porch/patio/breezeway		4,572	3/95	74r
Finish room in basement/attic		3,794	3/95	74r
Home, existing, single-family, median	unit	120200	12/94	62r
Maintenance, repairs, insurance, and other housing expenditures	year	531	91	81r
Mortgage interest and charges expenditures	year	1506	91	81r
Princ. & int., mortgage, median-price exist. sing.-family home	mo.	540	12/94	62r
Property taxes expenditures	year	391	91	81r
Redesign, restructure more than half of home's interior		17,641	3/95	74r
Rental units expenditures	year	1264	91	81r
Insurance and Pensions				
Auto insurance, private passenger	year	604.07	12/94	71s
Insurance and pensions, personal, expenditures	year	2395	91	81r
Insurance, life and other personal, expenditures	year	368	91	81r
Pensions and Social Security, expenditures	year	2027	91	81r
Personal Services				
Personal services expenditures	year	212	91	81r
Restaurant Food				
Dining expenditures, family	week	33.83	94	73r
Taxes				
Taxes, Federal income, expenditures	year	2275	91	81r
Taxes, personal, expenditures	year	2715	91	81r
Taxes, State and local income, expenditures	year	365	91	81r
Transportation				
Cars and trucks purchased, new	year	1306	91	81r
Cars and trucks purchased, used	year	942	91	81r
Driver's learning permit fee	perm	20.00	1/94	84s
Driver's license fee	orig	20.00	1/94	84s
Driver's license fee, duplicate	lic	5.00	1/94	84s
Driver's license reinstatement fee, min.	susp	50.00	1/94	85s
Driver's license renewal fee	renew	20.00	1/94	84s
Identification card, nondriver	card	20.00	1/94	83s
Motorcycle license fee	orig	20.00	1/94	84s
Motorcycle license fee, duplicate	lic	5.00	1/94	84s
Motorcycle license renewal fee	renew	20.00	1/94	84s
Public transportation expenditures	year	249	91	81r
Transportation expenditures, total	year	5307	91	81r
Vehicle finance charges	year	346	91	81r
Vehicle insurance expenditures	year	544	91	81r
Vehicle maintenance and repairs expenditures	year	600	91	81r
Vehicle purchases	year	2275	91	81r
Vehicle rental, leases, licenses, etc. expenditures	year	141	91	81r
Vehicles purchased, other than cars and trucks	year	27	91	81r
Utilities				
Electricity expenditures	year	950	91	81r
Utilities, fuels, and public services, total expenditures	year	2000	91	81r

Values are in dollars or fractions of dollars. In the column headed *Ref*, references are shown to sources. Each reference is followed by a letter. These refer to the geographical level for which data were reported: s = State, r = Region, and c = City or metro. The abbreviation *ex* is used to mean *except* or *excluding*; *exp* stands for *expenditures*. For other abbreviations and further explanations, please see the Introduction.

Florence, AL - continued

Item	Per	Value	Date	Ref.
Utilities				
Water and other public services, expenditures	year	227	91	81r
Weddings				
Bridal attendants' gowns	event	750	10/93	76r
Bridal gown	event	852	10/93	76r
Bridal headpiece and veil	event	167	10/93	76r
Bride's wedding band	event	708	10/93	76r
Clergy	event	224	10/93	76r
Engagement ring	event	2756	10/93	76r
Flowers	event	863	10/93	76r
Formal wear for groom	event	106	10/93	76r
Groom's attendants' formal wear	event	530	10/93	76r
Groom's wedding band	event	402	10/93	76r
Music	event	600	10/93	76r
Photography	event	1088	10/93	76r
Shoes for bride	event	50	10/93	76r
Videography	event	483	10/93	76r
Wedding invitations and announcements	event	342	10/93	76r
Wedding reception	event	7000	10/93	76r

Florence, SC

Item	Per	Value	Date	Ref.
Composite, ACCRA index		92.70	12/94	2c
Alcoholic Beverages				
Beer, Miller Lite, Bud, 12-oz., ex deposit	6	3.87	12/94	2c
J & B Scotch	750-ml.	17.54	12/94	2c
Wine, Gallo Chablis blanc	1.5-lit	4.57	12/94	2c
Appliances				
Appliances (major), expenditures	year	153	91	81r
Average annual exp.				
Food, health care, personal goods, services	year	27020	91	81r
Charity				
Cash contributions, expenditures	year	839	91	81r
Clothing				
Apparel, men and boys, total expenditures	year	380	91	81r
Apparel, women and girls, total expenditures	year	660	91	81r
Footwear, expenditures	year	193	91	81r
Jeans, man's denim		32.99	12/94	2c
Shirt, man's dress shirt		26.59	12/94	2c
Undervest, boy's size 10-14, cotton	3	3.62	12/94	2c
Communications				
Long-distance telephone rate, day, addl. min., 1-10 mi.	min.	0.13	12/93	9s
Long-distance telephone rate, day, initial min., 1-10 mi.	min.	0.24	12/93	9s
Newspaper subscription, dly. and Sun. delivery	month	9.50	12/94	2c
Phone line, single, business, field visit	inst	82.50	12/93	9s
Phone line, single, business, no field visit	inst	64.00	12/93	9s
Phone line, single, residence, field visit	inst	62.50	12/93	9s
Phone line, single, residence, no field visit	inst	44.00	12/93	9s
Telephone bill, family of four	month	23.26	12/94	2c
Telephone service, expenditures	year	616	91	81r
Education				
Board, 4-year private college/university	year	1831	8/94	80s
Board, 4-year public college/university	year	1462	8/94	80s
Education, total expenditures	year	319	91	81r
Room, 4-year private college/university	year	1744	8/94	80s
Room, 4-year public college/university	year	1851	8/94	80s
Total cost, 4-year private college/university	year	12082	8/94	80s
Total cost, 4-year public college/university	year	6203	8/94	80s
Tuition, 2-year public college/university, in-state	year	1061	8/94	80s
Tuition, 4-year private college/university, in-state	year	8507	8/94	80s

Florence, SC - continued

Item	Per	Value	Date	Ref.
Education - continued				
Tuition, 4-year public college/university, in-state	year	2891	8/94	80s
Energy and Fuels				
Energy, combined forms, 1800 sq. ft.	mo.	111.04	12/94	2c
Fuel oil and other fuels, expenditures	year	56	91	81r
Gas, natural, expenditures	year	150	91	81r
Gas, reg unlead, taxes inc., cash, self-service	gal	1.02	12/94	2c
Gasoline and motor oil purchased	year	1152	91	81r
Gasoline, unleaded midgrade	gallon	1.21	4/93	82r
Gasoline, unleaded premium	gallon	1.30	4/93	82r
Gasoline, unleaded regular	gallon	1.10	4/93	82r
Entertainment				
Bowling, evening rate	game	1.92	12/94	2c
Concert ticket, Pearl Jam group	perf	20.00	94	50r
Entertainment, total expenditures	year	1266	91	81r
Fees and admissions, expenditures	year	306	91	81r
Monopoly game, Parker Brothers', No. 9	game	11.14	12/94	2c
Movie	adm	5.50	12/94	2c
Pets, toys, playground equipment, expenditures	year	271	91	81r
Reading, expenditures	year	131	91	81r
Televisions, radios, and sound equipment, expenditures	year	439	91	81r
Tennis balls, yellow, Wilson or Penn, 3	can	1.97	12/94	2c
Funerals				
Burial, immediate, container provided by funeral home		1370.36	1/95	54r
Cards, acknowledgment		14.83	1/95	54r
Casket, minimum alternative		192.52	1/95	54r
Cosmetology, hair care, etc.		102.27	1/95	54r
Cremation, direct, container provided by funeral home		1065.64	1/95	54r
Embalming		304.29	1/95	54r
Funeral, funeral home		287.83	1/95	54r
Funeral, other facility		284.14	1/95	54r
Graveside service		349.13	1/95	54r
Hearse, local		132.27	1/95	54r
Limousine, local		98.45	1/95	54r
Memorial service		270.59	1/95	54r
Service charge, professional, nondeclinable		933.59	1/95	54r
Visitation and viewing		225.83	1/95	54r
Groceries				
Groceries, ACCRA Index		96.00	12/94	2c
Apples, Red Delicious	lb.	0.73	12/94	82r
Baby food, strained vegetables, lowest price	4-4.5 oz.	0.32	12/94	2c
Bacon, sliced	lb.	1.67	12/94	82r
Bananas	lb.	0.49	12/94	2c
Bananas	lb.	0.42	12/94	82r
Beef or hamburger, ground	lb.	1.46	12/94	2c
Beef purchases	year	213	91	81r
Beverage purchases, alcoholic	year	249	91	81r
Beverage purchases, nonalcoholic	year	207	91	81r
Bologna, all beef or mixed	lb.	2.27	12/94	82r
Bread, white	24-oz.	0.74	12/94	2c
Bread, white, pan	lb.	0.68	12/94	82r
Cabbage	lb.	0.42	12/94	82r
Carrots, short trimmed and topped	lb.	0.53	12/94	82r
Cereals and bakery products purchases	year	345	91	81r
Cereals and cereals products purchases	year	127	91	81r
Cheddar cheese, natural	lb.	3.58	12/94	82r
Cheese, Kraft grated Parmesan	8-oz.	3.19	12/94	2c
Chicken breast, bone-in	lb.	1.71	12/94	82r
Chicken, fresh, whole	lb.	0.78	12/94	82r
Chicken, whole fryer	lb.	0.90	12/94	2c
Chuck roast, USDA choice, boneless	lb.	2.26	12/94	82r
Cigarettes, Winston, Kings	carton	13.25	12/94	2c
Coffee, vacuum-packed	13 oz.	3.21	12/94	2c
Corn Flakes, Kellogg's or Post Toasties	18 oz.	2.32	12/94	2c

Values are in dollars or fractions of dollars. In the column headed *Ref*, references are shown to sources. Each reference is followed by a letter. These refer to the geographical level for which data were reported: s = State, r = Region, and c = City or metro. The abbreviation *ex* is used to mean *except* or *excluding*; *exp* stands for expenditures. For other abbreviations and further explanations, please see the Introduction.

Florence, SC - continued

Item	Per	Value	Date	Ref.
Groceries				
Corn, frozen, whole kernel, lowest price	10 oz.	0.64	12/94	2c
Crackers, soda, salted	lb.	1.27	12/94	82r
Cucumbers	lb.	0.65	12/94	82r
Dairy products (other) purchases	year	141	91	81r
Eggs, Grade A large	dozen	0.85	12/94	2c
Eggs, Grade A large	dozen	0.87	12/94	82r
Fish and seafood purchases	year	72	91	81r
Flour, white, all purpose	lb.	0.23	12/94	82r
Food purchases, food eaten at home	year	2381	91	81r
Foods purchased away from home, not prepared by consumer	year	1696	91	81r
Frankfurters, all meat or all beef	lb.	1.74	12/94	82r
Fruits and vegetables purchases	year	380	91	81r
Grapefruit	lb.	0.45	12/94	82r
Grapes, Thompson seedless	lb.	2.30	12/94	82r
Ground beef, 100% beef	lb.	1.37	12/94	82r
Ground chuck, 100% beef	lb.	1.97	12/94	82r
Ham, boneless, exc. canned	lb.	2.54	12/94	82r
Ice cream, prepackaged, bulk, regular	1/2 gal.	2.47	12/94	82r
Lemons	lb.	1.02	12/94	82r
Lettuce, iceberg	lb.	0.96	12/94	82r
Lettuce, iceberg	head	0.99	12/94	2c
Margarine, Blue Bonnet or Parkay cubes	lb.	0.58	12/94	2c
Margarine, stick	lb.	0.77	12/94	82r
Meats, poultry, fish, and eggs purchases	year	655	91	81r
Milk and cream (fresh) purchases	year	130	91	81r
Milk, whole	1/2 gal.	1.50	12/94	2c
Orange juice, frozen concentrate 12-oz. can	16 oz.	1.36	12/94	82r
Orange juice, Minute Maid frozen	12-oz.	1.15	12/94	2c
Oranges, Navel	lb.	0.54	12/94	82r
Peaches, halves or slices, Hunt's, Del Monte, or Libby's	29-oz.	1.19	12/94	2c
Pears, Anjou	lb.	0.81	12/94	82r
Peas, sweet, Del Monte or Green Giant	15-17 oz.	0.49	12/94	2c
Pork chops, center cut, bone-in	lb.	3.07	12/94	82r
Pork purchases	year	142	91	81r
Potato chips	16-oz.	3.15	12/94	82r
Potatoes, frozen, French fried	lb.	0.82	12/94	82r
Potatoes, white	lb.	0.34	12/94	82r
Potatoes, white or red	10-lb. sack	2.17	12/94	2c
Rice, white, long grain, uncooked	lb.	0.48	12/94	82r
Round roast, USDA choice, boneless	lb.	2.91	12/94	82r
Sausage, fresh	lb.	1.82	12/94	82r
Sausage, Jimmy Dean, 100% pork	lb.	2.19	12/94	2c
Shortening, vegetable oil blends	lb.	0.75	12/94	82r
Shortening, vegetable, Crisco	3-lb.	2.51	12/94	2c
Soft drink, Coca Cola, ex deposit	2 lit	1.05	12/94	2c
Spaghetti and macaroni	lb.	0.87	12/94	82r
Steak, rib eye, USDA choice, boneless	lb.	6.85	12/94	82r
Steak, round, graded & ungraded, exc. USDA prime & choice	lb.	2.96	12/94	82r
Steak, round, USDA choice, boneless	lb.	3.17	12/94	82r
Steak, sirloin, USDA choice, boneless	lb.	4.12	12/94	82r
Steak, t-bone	lb.	5.57	12/94	2c
Steak, T-bone, USDA choice, bone-in	lb.	5.63	12/94	82r
Sugar and other sweets, eaten at home, expenditures	year	93	91	81r
Sugar, cane or beet	4 lbs.	1.51	12/94	2c
Sugar, white, all sizes	lb.	0.39	12/94	82r
Tobacco products and smoking supplies, total expenditures	year	286	91	81r
Tomatoes, field grown	lb.	1.36	12/94	82r
Tomatoes, Hunt's or Del Monte	14.5 oz.	0.57	12/94	2c
Tuna, chunk, light	lb.	1.94	12/94	82r
Tuna, chunk, light, oil-packed	6.125-6.5 oz.	0.66	12/94	2c
Turkey, frozen, whole	lb.	0.96	12/94	82r

Florence, SC - continued

Item	Per	Value	Date	Ref.
Groceries - continued				
Yogurt, natural, fruit flavored	8 oz.	0.58	12/94	82r
Goods and Services				
Miscellaneous goods and services, ACCRA Index		97.30	12/94	2c
Health Care				
Health care, ACCRA Index		92.70	12/94	2c
Adenosine, emergency room	treat	100.00	95	23r
Antibiotic ointment, Polysporin	1.5 oz.	3.96	12/94	2c
Bladder tap, superpubic, infant, emergency room	treat	119.00	95	23r
Blood analysis, emergency room	treat	25.00	95	23r
Blood tests, abdominal pain, emergency room	treat	25.00	95	23r
Burn dressing, emergency room	treat	266.00	95	23r
Cardiology interpretation, emergency room	treat	26.00	95	23r
Chest X-ray, emergency room	treat	78.00	95	23r
Childbirth, Cesarean delivery, hospital charge	birth	5462.00	12/91	69r
Childbirth, Cesarean delivery, physician charge	birth	2228.00	12/91	69r
Childbirth, normal delivery, hospital charge	birth	2943.00	12/91	69r
Childbirth, normal delivery, physician charge	birth	1619.00	12/91	69r
Defibrillation pads, emergency room	treat	6.00	95	23r
Dentist's fee, adult teeth cleaning and periodic oral exam	visit	44.80	12/94	2c
Doctor's fee, routine exam, established patient	visit	40.20	12/94	2c
Drugs, expenditures	year	297	91	81r
Gastric tube insertion, nasal, emergency room	treat	25.00	95	23r
Health care, total expenditures	year	1600	91	81r
Health insurance expenditures	year	637	91	81r
Heart monitor, emergency room	treat	40.00	95	23r
Hospital care, semiprivate room	day	351.67	12/94	2c
Insurance premium, family medical care	month	414.49	1/95	41s
Intravenous fluids, emergency room	treat	130.00	95	23r
Intravenous fluids, emergency room	liter	26.00	95	23r
Intravenous line, central, emergency room	treat	342.00	95	23r
Liver function tests, abdominal pain, emergency room	treat	26.00	95	23r
Medical care charges, total, emergency room, third-degree burns	treat	2101.00	95	23r
Medical care charges, total, emergency, infant with fever	treat	628.00	95	23r
Medical services expenditures	year	573	91	81r
Medical supplies expenditures	year	93	91	81r
Morphine, emergency room	treat	34.00	95	23r
Nursing care and facilities charges, emergency room	treat	252.00	95	23r
Nursing care and facilities charges, emergency, infant with fever	treat	252.00	95	23r
Nursing care and facilities charges, emergency, third-degree burns	treat	861.00	95	23r
Physician's charges, emergency, infant with fever	treat	212.00	95	23r
Physician's charges, emergency, third-degree burns	treat	372.00	95	23r
Physician's fee, emergency room	treat	372.00	95	23r
Physician's fee, general practitioner	visit	51.20	12/93	60r
Surgery, open-heart	proc	42374.00	1/93	14r
Ultrasound, abdominal, emergency room	treat	276.00	95	23r
Urinalysis, emergency room	treat	20.00	95	23r
Urinalysis, infant, emergency room	treat	20.00	95	23r
X-rays, emergency room	treat	78.00	95	23r
Household Goods				
Appl. repair, service call, wash mach	min. lab. chg.	38.30	12/94	2c
Floor coverings, expenditures	year	48	91	81r
Furniture, expenditures	year	280	91	81r
Household equipment, misc. expenditures	year	342	91	81r

Values are in dollars or fractions of dollars. In the column headed *Ref*, references are shown to sources. Each reference is followed by a letter. These refer to the geographical level for which data were reported: s=State, r=Region, and c=City or metro. The abbreviation *ex* is used to mean *except* or *excluding*; *exp* stands for *expenditures*. For other abbreviations and further explanations, please see the Introduction.

Florence, SC - continued

Item	Per	Value	Date	Ref.
Household Goods				
Household expenditures, miscellaneous	year	256	91	81r
Household furnishings and equipment, expenditures	year	988	91	81r
Household operations expenditures	year	468	91	81r
Household textiles, expenditures	year	95	91	81r
Housekeeping supplies, expenditures	year	380	91	81r
Laundry and cleaning supplies, expenditures	year	109	91	81r
Laundry detergent, Tide Ultra, Bold, or Cheer	42 oz.	2.72	12/94	2c
Postage and stationery, expenditures	year	105	91	81r
Tissues, facial, Kleenex brand	175	0.91	12/94	2c
Housing				
Housing, ACCRA Index		83.90	12/94	2c
Add garage/carport		6,980	3/95	74r
Add room(s)		11,403	3/95	74r
Apartment condominium or co-op, median	unit	68600	12/94	62r
Dwellings (owned), expenditures	year	2428	91	81r
Enclose porch/patio/breezeway		4,572	3/95	74r
Finish room in basement/attic		3,794	3/95	74r
Home, existing, single-family, median	unit	120200	12/94	62r
House payment, principal and interest, 25% down payment	mo.	652	12/94	2c
House, 1800 sq ft, 8000 sq ft lot, new, urban, utilities	total	108225	12/94	2c
Maintenance, repairs, insurance, and other housing expenditures	year	531	91	81r
Mortgage interest and charges expenditures	year	1506	91	81r
Mtge. rate, incl. points and orig. fee, 30-year conv. fixed or ARM	mo.	8.97	12/94	2c
Princ. & int., mortgage, median-price exist. sing.-family home	mo.	540	12/94	62r
Property taxes expenditures	year	391	91	81r
Redesign, restructure more than half of home's interior		17,641	3/95	74r
Rent, apartment, 2 br., 1 1/2-2 baths, unfurnished, 950 sq ft, water	mo.	416	12/94	2c
Rental units expenditures	year	1264	91	81r
Insurance and Pensions				
Auto insurance, private passenger	year	684.10	12/94	71s
Insurance and pensions, personal, expenditures	year	2395	91	81r
Insurance, life and other personal, expenditures	year	368	91	81r
Pensions and Social Security, expenditures	year	2027	91	81r
Personal Goods				
Shampoo, Alberto VO5	15-oz.	0.95	12/94	2c
Toothpaste, Crest or Colgate	6-7 oz.	1.70	12/94	2c
Personal Services				
Dry cleaning, man's 2-pc. suit		5.80	12/94	2c
Haircut, man's barbershop, no styling		7.40	12/94	2c
Haircut, woman's shampoo, trim, blow-dry		21.20	12/94	2c
Personal services expenditures	year	212	91	81r
Restaurant Food				
Chicken, fried, thigh and drumstick		2.15	12/94	2c
Dining expenditures, family	week	33.83	94	73r
Hamburger with cheese	1/4 lb.	2.02	12/94	2c
Pizza, Pizza Hut or Pizza Inn	12-13 in.	8.34	12/94	2c
Taxes				
Taxes, Federal income, expenditures	year	2275	91	81r
Taxes, personal, expenditures	year	2715	91	81r
Taxes, State and local income, expenditures	year	365	91	81r
Transportation				
Transportation, ACCRA Index		89.90	12/94	2c
Cars and trucks purchased, new	year	1306	91	81r
Cars and trucks purchased, used	year	942	91	81r
Driver's learning permit fee	perm	2.00	1/94	84s

Florence, SC - continued

Item	Per	Value	Date	Ref.
Transportation - continued				
Driver's license fee	orig	10.00	1/94	84s
Driver's license fee, duplicate	lic	0.50	1/94	84s
Driver's license reinstatement fee, min.	susp	30.00	1/94	85s
Driver's license renewal fee	renew	10.00	1/94	84s
Identification card, nondriver	card	5.00	1/94	83s
Motorcycle learning permit fee	perm	2.00	1/94	84s
Motorcycle license fee	orig	10.00	1/94	84s
Motorcycle license fee, duplicate	lic	0.50	1/94	84s
Motorcycle license renewal fee	renew	10.00	1/94	84s
Public transportation expenditures	year	249	91	81r
Tire balance, computer or spin bal., front	wheel	5.98	12/94	2c
Transportation expenditures, total	year	5307	91	81r
Vehicle finance charges	year	346	91	81r
Vehicle insurance expenditures	year	544	91	81r
Vehicle maintenance and repairs expenditures	year	600	91	81r
Vehicle purchases	year	2275	91	81r
Vehicle rental, leases, licenses, etc. expenditures	year	141	91	81r
Vehicles purchased, other than cars and trucks	year	27	91	81r
Utilities				
Utilities, ACCRA Index		101.70	12/94	2c
Electricity expenditures	year	950	91	81r
Electricity, 1800 sq. ft., new home	mo.	111.04	12/94	2c
Electricity, summer, 250 KWh	month	26.19	8/93	64c
Electricity, summer, 500 KWh	month	45.87	8/93	64c
Electricity, summer, 750 KWh	month	65.56	8/93	64c
Electricity, summer, 1000 KWh	month	85.24	8/93	64c
Utilities, fuels, and public services, total expenditures	year	2000	91	81r
Water and other public services, expenditures	year	227	91	81r
Weddings				
Bridal attendants' gowns	event	750	10/93	76r
Bridal gown	event	852	10/93	76r
Bridal headpiece and veil	event	167	10/93	76r
Bride's wedding band	event	708	10/93	76r
Clergy	event	224	10/93	76r
Engagement ring	event	2756	10/93	76r
Flowers	event	863	10/93	76r
Formal wear for groom	event	106	10/93	76r
Groom's attendants' formal wear	event	530	10/93	76r
Groom's wedding band	event	402	10/93	76r
Music	event	600	10/93	76r
Photography	event	1088	10/93	76r
Shoes for bride	event	50	10/93	76r
Videography	event	483	10/93	76r
Wedding invitations and announcements	event	342	10/93	76r
Wedding reception	event	7000	10/93	76r

Fond du Lac, WI

Item	Per	Value	Date	Ref.
Composite, ACCRA index		101.20	12/94	2c
Alcoholic Beverages				
Beer, Miller Lite, Bud, 12-oz., ex deposit	6	3.50	12/94	2c
J & B Scotch	750-ml.	16.91	12/94	2c
Wine, Gallo Chablis blanc	1.5-lit	4.04	12/94	2c
Clothing				
Jeans, man's denim		38.59	12/94	2c
Shirt, man's dress shirt		32.25	12/94	2c
Undervest, boy's size 10-14, cotton	3	4.52	12/94	2c
Communications				
Newspaper subscription, dly. and Sun. delivery	month	13.91	12/94	2c
Telephone bill, family of four	month	16.31	12/94	2c
Telephone, residential, flat rate	mo.	6.00	12/93	8c

Values are in dollars or fractions of dollars. In the column headed *Ref*, references are shown to sources. Each reference is followed by a letter. These refer to the geographical level for which data were reported: s = State, r = Region, and c = City or metro. The abbreviation *ex* is used to mean *except* or *excluding*; *exp* stands for *expenditures*. For other abbreviations and further explanations, please see the Introduction.

Fond du Lac, WI - continued

Item	Per	Value	Date	Ref.
Energy and Fuels				
Energy, combined forms, 1800 sq. ft.	mo.	112.70	12/94	2c
Energy, exc. electricity, 1800 sq. ft.	mo.	68.34	12/94	2c
Gas, reg unlead, taxes inc., cash, self-service	gal	1.19	12/94	2c
Entertainment				
Bowling, evening rate	game	1.50	12/94	2c
Monopoly game, Parker Brothers', No. 9	game	9.86	12/94	2c
Movie	adm	5.50	12/94	2c
Tennis balls, yellow, Wilson or Penn, 3	can	2.10	12/94	2c
Groceries				
Groceries, ACCRA Index		101.50	12/94	2c
Baby food, strained vegetables, lowest price	4-4.5 oz.	0.42	12/94	2c
Bananas	lb.	0.46	12/94	2c
Beef or hamburger, ground	lb.	1.05	12/94	2c
Bread, white	24-oz.	0.64	12/94	2c
Cheese, Kraft grated Parmesan	8-oz.	3.22	12/94	2c
Chicken, whole fryer	lb.	0.94	12/94	2c
Cigarettes, Winston, Kings	carton	17.28	12/94	2c
Coffee, vacuum-packed	13 oz.	3.50	12/94	2c
Corn Flakes, Kellogg's or Post Toasties	18 oz.	2.52	12/94	2c
Corn, frozen, whole kernel, lowest price	10 oz.	0.66	12/94	2c
Eggs, Grade A large	dozen	0.69	12/94	2c
Lettuce, iceberg	head	0.80	12/94	2c
Margarine, Blue Bonnet or Parkay cubes	lb.	0.64	12/94	2c
Milk, whole	1/2 gal.	1.48	12/94	2c
Orange juice, Minute Maid frozen	12-oz.	1.23	12/94	2c
Peaches, halves or slices, Hunt's, Del Monte, or Libby's	29-oz.	1.55	12/94	2c
Peas, sweet, Del Monte or Green Giant	15-17 oz.	0.51	12/94	2c
Potatoes, white or red	10-lb. sack	2.07	12/94	2c
Sausage, Jimmy Dean, 100% pork	lb.	2.79	12/94	2c
Shortening, vegetable, Crisco	3-lb.	2.66	12/94	2c
Soft drink, Coca Cola, ex deposit	2 lit	1.03	12/94	2c
Steak, t-bone	lb.	4.31	12/94	2c
Sugar, cane or beet	4 lbs.	1.60	12/94	2c
Tomatoes, Hunt's or Del Monte	14.5 oz.	0.76	12/94	2c
Tuna, chunk, light, oil-packed	6.125-6.5 oz.	0.68	12/94	2c
Goods and Services				
Miscellaneous goods and services, ACCRA Index		96.90	12/94	2c
Health Care				
Health care, ACCRA Index		89.00	12/94	2c
Antibiotic ointment, Polysporin	1.5 oz.	4.10	12/94	2c
Dentist's fee, adult teeth cleaning and periodic oral exam	visit	48.50	12/94	2c
Doctor's fee, routine exam, established patient	visit	34.00	12/94	2c
Hospital care, semiprivate room	day	325.00	12/94	2c
Household Goods				
Appl. repair, service call, wash mach	min. lab. chg.	23.45	12/94	2c
Laundry detergent, Tide Ultra, Bold, or Cheer	42 oz.	3.78	12/94	2c
Tissues, facial, Kleenex brand	175	1.12	12/94	2c
Housing				
Housing, ACCRA Index		110.30	12/94	2c
House payment, principal and interest, 25% down payment	mo.	869	12/94	2c
House, 1800 sq ft, 8000 sq ft lot, new, urban, utilities	total	139000	12/94	2c
Mtge. rate, incl. points and orig. fee, 30-year conv. fixed or ARM	mo.	9.40	12/94	2c

Fond du Lac, WI - continued

Item	Per	Value	Date	Ref.
Housing - continued				
Rent, apartment, 2 br., 1 1/2-2 baths, unfurnished, 950 sq ft, water	mo.	515	12/94	2c
Personal Goods				
Shampoo, Alberto VO5	15-oz.	0.99	12/94	2c
Toothpaste, Crest or Colgate	6-7 oz.	1.36	12/94	2c
Personal Services				
Dry cleaning, man's 2-pc. suit		7.72	12/94	2c
Haircut, man's barbershop, no styling		8.75	12/94	2c
Haircut, woman's shampoo, trim, blow-dry		13.60	12/94	2c
Restaurant Food				
Chicken, fried, thigh and drumstick		2.00	12/94	2c
Hamburger with cheese	1/4 lb.	1.75	12/94	2c
Pizza, Pizza Hut or Pizza Inn	12-13 in.	7.20	12/94	2c
Transportation				
Transportation, ACCRA Index		98.90	12/94	2c
Bus fare, one-way	trip	0.60	12/95	1c
Bus fare, up to 10 miles	one-way	0.60	12/94	.
Tire balance, computer or spin bal., front	wheel	6.74	12/94	2c
Utilities				
Utilities, ACCRA Index		98.20	12/94	2c
Electricity, (part.), other, 1800 sq. ft., new home	mo.	44.34	12/94	2c

Fort Collins, CO

Item	Per	Value	Date	Ref.
Composite, ACCRA index		111.10	12/94	2c
Alcoholic Beverages				
Beer, Miller Lite, Bud, 12-oz., ex deposit	6	4.07	12/94	2c
J & B Scotch	750-ml.	18.99	12/94	2c
Wine, Gallo Chablis blanc	1.5-lit	4.33	12/94	2c
Appliances				
Appliances (major), expenditures	year	160	91	81r
Average annual exp.				
Food, health care, personal goods, services	year	32461	91	81r
Charity				
Cash contributions, expenditures	year	975	91	81r
Clothing				
Apparel, men and boys, total expenditures	year	467	91	81r
Apparel, women and girls, total expenditures	year	737	91	81r
Footwear, expenditures	year	270	91	81r
Jeans, man's denim		34.97	12/94	2c
Shirt, man's dress shirt		34.57	12/94	2c
Undervest, boy's size 10-14, cotton	3	4.73	12/94	2c
Communications				
Long-distance telephone rate, day, addl. min., 1-10 mi.	min.	0.13	12/93	9s
Long-distance telephone rate, day, initial min., 1-10 mi.	min.	0.17	12/93	9s
Newspaper subscription, dly. and Sun. delivery	month	8.70	12/94	2c
Phone line, single, business, field visit	inst	70.00	12/93	9s
Phone line, single, business, no field visit	inst	70.00	12/93	9s
Phone line, single, residence, field visit	inst	35.00	12/93	9s
Phone line, single, residence, no field visit	inst	35.00	12/93	9s
Telephone bill, family of four	month	21.13	12/94	2c
Telephone service, expenditures	year	611	91	81r
Telephone, residential, flat rate	mo.	14.68	12/93	8c
Education				
Board, 4-year private college/university	year	2468	8/94	80s
Board, 4-year public college/university	year	2148	8/94	80s
Education, total expenditures	year	375	91	81r
Room, 4-year private college/university	year	2492	8/94	80s

Values are in dollars or fractions of dollars. In the column headed *Ref*, references are shown to sources. Each reference is followed by a letter. These refer to the geographical level for which data were reported: s = State, r = Region, and c = City or metro. The abbreviation *ex* is used to mean *except* or *excluding*; *exp* stands for expenditures. For other abbreviations and further explanations, please see the Introduction.

Fort Collins, CO - continued

Item	Per	Value	Date	Ref.
Education				
Room, 4-year public college/university	year	1772	8/94	80s
Total cost, 4-year private college/university	year	16064	8/94	80s
Total cost, 4-year public college/university	year	6183	8/94	80s
Tuition, 2-year public college/university, in-state	year	1193	8/94	80s
Tuition, 4-year private college/university, in-state	year	11104	8/94	80s
Tuition, 4-year public college/university, in-state	year	2262	8/94	80s
Energy and Fuels				
Energy, combined forms, 1800 sq. ft.	mo.	81.10	12/94	2c
Energy, exc. electricity, 1800 sq. ft.	mo.	36.36	12/94	2c
Fuel oil and other fuels, expenditures	year	33	91	81r
Gas, natural, expenditures	year	212	91	81r
Gas, reg unlead, taxes inc., cash, self-service	gal	1.25	12/94	2c
Gasoline and motor oil purchased	year	1115	91	81r
Gasoline, unleaded midgrade	gallon	1.36	4/93	82r
Gasoline, unleaded premium	gallon	1.43	4/93	82r
Gasoline, unleaded regular	gallon	1.23	4/93	82r
Entertainment				
Bowling, evening rate	game	2.17	12/94	2c
Concert ticket, Pearl Jam group	perf	20.00	94	50r
Entertainment, total expenditures	year	1853	91	81r
Fees and admissions, expenditures	year	482	91	81r
Monopoly game, Parker Brothers', No. 9	game	12.98	12/94	2c
Movie	adm	6.10	12/94	2c
Pets, toys, playground equipment, expenditures	year	299	91	81r
Reading, expenditures	year	164	91	81r
Televisions, radios, and sound equipment, expenditures	year	528	91	81r
Tennis balls, yellow, Wilson or Penn, 3	can	2.77	12/94	2c
Funerals				
Burial, immediate, container provided by funeral home		1360.49	1/95	54r
Cards, acknowledgment		11.24	1/95	54r
Casket, minimum alternative		232.73	1/95	54r
Cosmetology, hair care, etc.		114.13	1/95	54r
Cremation, direct, container provided by funeral home		1027.08	1/95	54r
Embalming		286.24	1/95	54r
Funeral, funeral home		315.60	1/95	54r
Funeral, other facility		303.08	1/95	54r
Graveside service		423.83	1/95	54r
Hearse, local		133.12	1/95	54r
Limousine, local		99.10	1/95	54r
Memorial service		442.57	1/95	54r
Service charge, professional, nondeclinable		840.16	1/95	54r
Visitation and viewing		168.50	1/95	54r
Groceries				
Groceries, ACCRA Index		102.80	12/94	2c
Apples, Red Delicious	lb.	0.72	12/94	82r
Baby food, strained vegetables, lowest price	4-4.5 oz.	0.30	12/94	2c
Bacon, sliced	lb.	1.73	12/94	82r
Bananas	lb.	0.59	12/94	2c
Bananas	lb.	0.52	12/94	82r
Beef or hamburger, ground	lb.	1.41	12/94	2c
Beef purchases	year	241	91	81r
Beverage purchases, alcoholic	year	328	91	81r
Beverage purchases, nonalcoholic	year	234	91	81r
Bologna, all beef or mixed	lb.	2.33	12/94	82r
Bread, white	24-oz.	0.69	12/94	2c
Bread, white, pan	lb.	0.81	12/94	82r
Carrots, short trimmed and topped	lb.	0.43	12/94	82r
Cereals and bakery products purchases	year	392	91	81r
Cereals and cereals products purchases	year	139	91	81r
Cheese, Kraft grated Parmesan	8-oz.	3.04	12/94	2c
Chicken breast, bone-in	lb.	2.04	12/94	82r

Fort Collins, CO - continued

Item	Per	Value	Date	Ref.
Groceries - continued				
Chicken, fresh, whole	lb.	0.95	12/94	82r
Chicken, whole fryer	lb.	0.81	12/94	2c
Cigarettes, Winston, Kings	carton	14.99	12/94	2c
Coffee, 100%, ground roast, all sizes	lb.	4.48	12/94	82r
Coffee, vacuum-packed	13 oz.	3.56	12/94	2c
Corn Flakes, Kellogg's or Post Toasties	18 oz.	2.53	12/94	2c
Corn, frozen, whole kernel, lowest price	10 oz.	0.75	12/94	2c
Dairy products (other) purchases	year	182	91	81r
Eggs, Grade A large	dozen	0.82	12/94	2c
Fish and seafood purchases	year	94	91	81r
Flour, white, all purpose	lb.	0.21	12/94	82r
Food purchases, food eaten at home	year	2749	91	81r
Foods purchased away from home, not prepared by consumer	year	1909	91	81r
Fruits and vegetables purchases	year	459	91	81r
Grapefruit	lb.	0.56	12/94	82r
Ground beef, 100% beef	lb.	1.31	12/94	82r
Ham, boneless, exc. canned	lb.	2.46	12/94	82r
Ice cream, prepackaged, bulk, regular	1/2 gal.	2.57	12/94	82r
Lemons	lb.	1.00	12/94	82r
Lettuce, iceberg	lb.	0.93	12/94	82r
Lettuce, iceberg	head	0.76	12/94	2c
Margarine, Blue Bonnet or Parkay cubes	lb.	0.59	12/94	2c
Meats, poultry, fish, and eggs purchases	year	700	91	81r
Milk and cream (fresh) purchases	year	155	91	81r
Milk, whole	1/2 gal.	1.66	12/94	2c
Orange juice, frozen concentrate 12-oz. can	16 oz.	1.52	12/94	82r
Orange juice, Minute Maid frozen	12-oz.	1.33	12/94	2c
Oranges, Navel	lb.	0.56	12/94	82r
Peaches, halves or slices, Hunt's, Del Monte, or Libby's	29-oz.	1.52	12/94	2c
Peas, sweet, Del Monte or Green Giant	15-17 oz.	0.73	12/94	2c
Pork chops, center cut, bone-in	lb.	3.30	12/94	82r
Pork purchases	year	122	91	81r
Potato chips	16-oz.	3.03	12/94	82r
Potatoes, frozen, French fried	lb.	0.77	12/94	82r
Potatoes, white	lb.	0.35	12/94	82r
Potatoes, white or red	10-lb. sack	1.87	12/94	2c
Rice, white, long grain, uncooked	lb.	0.54	12/94	82r
Round roast, USDA choice, boneless	lb.	2.92	12/94	82r
Sausage, Jimmy Dean, 100% pork	lb.	3.66	12/94	2c
Shortening, vegetable oil blends	lb.	0.80	12/94	82r
Shortening, vegetable, Crisco	3-lb.	2.91	12/94	2c
Soft drink, Coca Cola, ex deposit	2 lit	0.82	12/94	2c
Spaghetti and macaroni	lb.	1.02	12/94	82r
Steak, round, graded & ungraded, exc. USDA prime & choice	lb.	3.13	12/94	82r
Steak, sirloin, USDA choice, boneless	lb.	4.07	12/94	82r
Steak, t-bone	lb.	5.05	12/94	2c
Sugar and other sweets, eaten at home, expenditures	year	105	91	81r
Sugar, cane or beet	4 lbs.	1.51	12/94	2c
Sugar, white, all sizes	lb.	0.38	12/94	82r
Tobacco products and smoking supplies, total expenditures	year	221	91	81r
Tomatoes, field grown	lb.	1.45	12/94	82r
Tomatoes, Hunt's or Del Monte	14.5 oz.	0.87	12/94	2c
Tuna, chunk, light	lb.	2.18	12/94	82r
Tuna, chunk, light, oil-packed	6.125-6.5 oz.	0.87	12/94	2c
Goods and Services				
Miscellaneous goods and services, ACCRA Index		106.10	12/94	2c
Health Care				
Health care, ACCRA Index		117.40	12/94	2c
Antibiotic ointment, Polysporin	1.5 oz.	4.29	12/94	2c

Values are in dollars or fractions of dollars. In the column headed *Ref*, references are shown to sources. Each reference is followed by a letter. These refer to the geographical level for which data were reported: s=State, r=Region, and c=City or metro. The abbreviation *ex* is used to mean *except* or *excluding*; *exp* stands for expenditures. For other abbreviations and further explanations, please see the Introduction.

Fort Collins, CO - continued

Item	Per	Value	Date	Ref.
Health Care				
Childbirth, Cesarean delivery, hospital charge	birth	6059.00	12/91	69r
Childbirth, Cesarean delivery, physician charge	birth	2248.00	12/91	69r
Childbirth, normal delivery, hospital charge	birth	3006.00	12/91	69r
Childbirth, normal delivery, physician charge	birth	1634.00	12/91	69r
Dentist's fee, adult teeth cleaning and periodic oral exam	visit	54.40	12/94	2c
Doctor's fee, routine exam, established patient	visit	55.00	12/94	2c
Drugs, expenditures	year	230	91	81r
Health care, total expenditures	year	1544	91	81r
Health insurance expenditures	year	558	91	81r
Hospital care, semiprivate room	day	445.00	12/94	2c
Insurance premium, family medical care	month	362.55	1/95	41s
Medical services expenditures	year	676	91	81r
Medical supplies expenditures	year	80	91	81r
Surgery, open-heart	proc	37818.00	1/93	14r
Household Goods				
Appl. repair, service call, wash mach	min. lab. chg.	36.30	12/94	2c
Floor coverings, expenditures	year	79	91	81r
Furniture, expenditures	year	352	91	81r
Household equipment, misc. expenditures	year	614	91	81r
Household expenditures, miscellaneous	year	294	91	81r
Household furnishings and equipment, expenditures	year	1416	91	81r
Household operations expenditures	year	580	91	81r
Household textiles, expenditures	year	113	91	81r
Housekeeping supplies, expenditures	year	447	91	81r
Laundry and cleaning supplies, expenditures	year	114	91	81r
Laundry detergent, Tide Ultra, Bold, or Cheer	42 oz.	3.71	12/94	2c
Postage and stationery, expenditures	year	145	91	81r
Tissues, facial, Kleenex brand	175	0.98	12/94	2c
Housing				
Housing, ACCRA Index		130.30	12/94	2c
Add garage/carport		6,422	3/95	74r
Add room(s)		26,583	3/95	74r
Apartment condominium or co-op, median	unit	105300	12/94	62r
Dwellings (owned), expenditures	year	3932	91	81r
Enclose porch/patio/breezeway		5,382	3/95	74r
Finish room in basement/attic		3,911	3/95	74r
Home, existing, single-family, median	unit	178600	12/94	62r
House payment, principal and interest, 25% down payment	mo.	1011	12/94	2c
House, 1800 sq ft, 8000 sq ft lot, new, urban, utilities	total	161387	12/94	2c
Maintenance, repairs, insurance, and other housing expenditures	year	591	91	81r
Mortgage interest and charges expenditures	year	2747	91	81r
Mtge. rate, incl. points and orig. fee, 30-year conv. fixed or ARM	mo.	9.43	12/94	2c
Princ. & int., mortgage, median-price exist. sing.-family home	mo.	845	12/94	62r
Property taxes expenditures	year	594	91	81r
Redesign, restructure more than half of home's interior		5,467	3/95	74r
Rent, apartment, 2 br., 1 1/2-2 baths, unfurnished, 950 sq ft, water	mo.	651	12/94	2c
Rental units expenditures	year	2077	91	81r
Insurance and Pensions				
Auto insurance, private passenger	year	804.17	12/94	71s
Insurance and pensions, personal, expenditures	year	3042	91	81r
Insurance, life and other personal, expenditures	year	298	91	81r
Pensions and Social Security, expenditures	year	2744	91	81r

Fort Collins, CO - continued

Item	Per	Value	Date	Ref.
Legal Assistance				
Legal work, law firm associate	hour	91		10r
Legal work, law firm partner	hour	151		10r
Personal Goods				
Shampoo, Alberto VO5	15-oz.	1.30	12/94	2c
Toothpaste, Crest or Colgate	6-7 oz.	2.08	12/94	2c
Personal Services				
Dry cleaning, man's 2-pc. suit		7.08	12/94	2c
Haircut, man's barbershop, no styling		8.53	12/94	2c
Haircut, woman's shampoo, trim, blow-dry		20.50	12/94	2c
Personal services expenditures	year	286	91	81r
Restaurant Food				
Chicken, fried, thigh and drumstick		1.99	12/94	2c
Dining expenditures, family	week	32.25	94	73r
Hamburger with cheese	1/4 lb.	1.98	12/94	2c
Pizza, Pizza Hut or Pizza Inn	12-13 in.	7.69	12/94	2c
Taxes				
Taxes, Federal income, expenditures	year	2946	91	81r
Taxes, personal, expenditures	year	3791	91	81r
Taxes, State and local income, expenditures	year	791	91	81r
Transportation				
Transportation, ACCRA Index		110.60	12/94	2c
Bus fare, one-way	trip	0.80	12/95	1c
Cars and trucks purchased, new	year	1231	91	81r
Cars and trucks purchased, used	year	915	91	81r
Driver's learning permit fee	perm	10.00	1/94	84s
Driver's license fee	orig	15.00	1/94	84s
Driver's license fee, duplicate	lic	5.00	1/94	84s
Driver's license reinstatement fee, min.	susp	40.00	1/94	85s
Driver's license renewal fee	renew	15.00	1/94	84s
Identification card, nondriver	card	3.50	1/94	83s
Motorcycle license fee	orig	16.00	1/94	84s
Public transportation expenditures	year	375	91	81r
Tire balance, computer or spin bal., front	wheel	7.38	12/94	2c
Transportation expenditures, total	year	5527	91	81r
Vehicle finance charges	year	287	91	81r
Vehicle insurance expenditures	year	624	91	81r
Vehicle maintenance and repairs expenditures	year	695	91	81r
Vehicle purchases	year	2174	91	81r
Vehicle rental, leases, licenses, etc. expenditures	year	257	91	81r
Vehicles purchased, other than cars and trucks	year	28	91	81r
Utilities				
Utilities, ACCRA Index		77.10	12/94	2c
Electricity expenditures	year	616	91	81r
Electricity, (part.), other, 1800 sq. ft., new home	mo.	44.73	12/94	2c
Utilities, fuels, and public services, total expenditures	year	1681	91	81r
Water and other public services, expenditures	year	209	91	81r
Weddings				
Bridal attendants' gowns	event	750	10/93	76r
Bridal gown	event	852	10/93	76r
Bridal headpiece and veil	event	167	10/93	76r
Bride's wedding band	event	708	10/93	76r
Clergy	event	224	10/93	76r
Engagement ring	event	2756	10/93	76r
Flowers	event	863	10/93	76r
Formal wear for groom	event	106	10/93	76r
Groom's attendants' formal wear	event	530	10/93	76r
Groom's wedding band	event	402	10/93	76r
Music	event	600	10/93	76r
Photography	event	1088	10/93	76r
Shoes for bride	event	50	10/93	76r
Videography	event	483	10/93	76r

Values are in dollars or fractions of dollars. In the column headed *Ref*, references are shown to sources. Each reference is followed by a letter. These refer to the geographical level for which data were reported: s = State, r = Region, and c = City or metro. The abbreviation *ex* is used to mean *except* or *excluding*; *exp* stands for *expenditures*. For other abbreviations and further explanations, please see the Introduction.

Fort Collins, CO - continued

Item	Per	Value	Date	Ref.
Weddings				
Wedding invitations and announcements	event	342	10/93	76r
Wedding reception	event	7000	10/93	76r

Fort Lauderdale-Hollywood-Pompano Beach, FL

Item	Per	Value	Date	Ref.
Appliances				
Appliances (major), expenditures	year	153	91	81r
Average annual exp.				
Food, health care, personal goods, services	year	27020	91	81r
Charity				
Cash contributions, expenditures	year	839	91	81r
Clothing				
Apparel, men and boys, total expenditures	year	380	91	81r
Apparel, women and girls, total expenditures	year	660	91	81r
Footwear, expenditures	year	193	91	81r
Communications				
Long-distance telephone rate, day, addl. min., 1-10 mi.	min.	0.08	12/93	9s
Long-distance telephone rate, day, initial min., 1-10 mi.	min.	0.15	12/93	9s
Phone line, single, business, field visit	inst	86.00	12/93	9s
Phone line, single, business, no field visit	inst	54.50	12/93	9s
Phone line, single, residence, field visit	inst	76.00	12/93	9s
Phone line, single, residence, no field visit	inst	44.50	12/93	9s
Telephone service, expenditures	year	616	91	81r
Education				
Bar examinination preparatory course	course	500.00-100	94	17s
Board, 4-year private college/university	year	2123	8/94	80s
Board, 4-year public college/university	year	2101	8/94	80s
Education, total expenditures	year	319	91	81r
Room, 4-year private college/university	year	2242	8/94	80s
Room, 4-year public college/university	year	1970	8/94	80s
Total cost, 4-year private college/university	year	13853	8/94	80s
Total cost, 4-year public college/university	year	5855	8/94	80s
Tuition, 2-year public college/university, in-state	year	1076	8/94	80s
Tuition, 4-year private college/university, in-state	year	9287	8/94	80s
Tuition, 4-year public college/university, in-state	year	1784	8/94	80s
Energy and Fuels				
Fuel oil and other fuels, expenditures	year	56	91	81r
Gas, natural, expenditures	year	150	91	81r
Gasoline and motor oil purchased	year	1152	91	81r
Gasoline, unleaded midgrade	gallon	1.21	4/93	82r
Gasoline, unleaded premium	gallon	1.30	4/93	82r
Gasoline, unleaded regular	gallon	1.10	4/93	82r
Entertainment				
Concert ticket, Pearl Jam group	perf	20.00	94	50r
Entertainment, total expenditures	year	1266	91	81r
Fees and admissions, expenditures	year	306	91	81r
Pets, toys, playground equipment, expenditures	year	271	91	81r
Reading, expenditures	year	131	91	81r
Televisions, radios, and sound equipment, expenditures	year	439	91	81r
Funerals				
Burial, immediate, container provided by funeral home		1370.36	1/95	54r
Cards, acknowledgment		14.83	1/95	54r
Casket, minimum alternative		192.52	1/95	54r
Cosmetology, hair care, etc.		102.27	1/95	54r
Cremation, direct, container provided by funeral home		1065.64	1/95	54r
Embalming		304.29	1/95	54r
Funeral, funeral home		287.83	1/95	54r

Fort Lauderdale-Hollywood-Pompano Beach, FL - continued

Item	Per	Value	Date	Ref.
Funerals - continued				
Funeral, other facility		284.14	1/95	54r
Graveside service		349.13	1/95	54r
Hearse, local		132.27	1/95	54r
Limousine, local		98.45	1/95	54r
Memorial service		270.59	1/95	54r
Service charge, professional, nondeclinable		933.59	1/95	54r
Visitation and viewing		225.83	1/95	54r
Groceries				
Apples, Red Delicious	lb.	0.73	12/94	82r
Bacon, sliced	lb.	1.67	12/94	82r
Bananas	lb.	0.42	12/94	82r
Beef purchases	year	213	91	81r
Beverage purchases, alcoholic	year	249	91	81r
Beverage purchases, nonalcoholic	year	207	91	81r
Bologna, all beef or mixed	lb.	2.27	12/94	82r
Bread, white, pan	lb.	0.68	12/94	82r
Cabbage	lb.	0.42	12/94	82r
Carrots, short trimmed and topped	lb.	0.53	12/94	82r
Cereals and bakery products purchases	year	345	91	81r
Cereals and cereals products purchases	year	127	91	81r
Cheddar cheese, natural	lb.	3.58	12/94	82r
Chicken breast, bone-in	lb.	1.71	12/94	82r
Chicken, fresh, whole	lb.	0.78	12/94	82r
Chuck roast, USDA choice, boneless	lb.	2.26	12/94	82r
Crackers, soda, salted	lb.	1.27	12/94	82r
Cucumbers	lb.	0.65	12/94	82r
Dairy products (other) purchases	year	141	91	81r
Eggs, Grade A large	dozen	0.87	12/94	82r
Fish and seafood purchases	year	72	91	81r
Flour, white, all purpose	lb.	0.23	12/94	82r
Food purchases, food eaten at home	year	2381	91	81r
Foods purchased away from home, not prepared by consumer	year	1696	91	81r
Frankfurters, all meat or all beef	lb.	1.74	12/94	82r
Fruits and vegetables purchases	year	380	91	81r
Grapefruit	lb.	0.45	12/94	82r
Grapes, Thompson seedless	lb.	2.30	12/94	82r
Ground beef, 100% beef	lb.	1.37	12/94	82r
Ground chuck, 100% beef	lb.	1.97	12/94	82r
Ham, boneless, exc. canned	lb.	2.54	12/94	82r
Ice cream, prepackaged, bulk, regular	1/2 gal.	2.47	12/94	82r
Lemons	lb.	1.02	12/94	82r
Lettuce, iceberg	lb.	0.96	12/94	82r
Margarine, stick	lb.	0.77	12/94	82r
Meats, poultry, fish, and eggs purchases	year	655	91	81r
Milk and cream (fresh) purchases	year	130	91	81r
Orange juice, frozen concentrate 12-oz. can	16 oz.	1.36	12/94	82r
Oranges, Navel	lb.	0.54	12/94	82r
Pears, Anjou	lb.	0.81	12/94	82r
Pork chops, center cut, bone-in	lb.	3.07	12/94	82r
Pork purchases	year	142	91	81r
Potato chips	16-oz.	3.15	12/94	82r
Potatoes, frozen, French fried	lb.	0.82	12/94	82r
Potatoes, white	lb.	0.34	12/94	82r
Rice, white, long grain, uncooked	lb.	0.48	12/94	82r
Round roast, USDA choice, boneless	lb.	2.91	12/94	82r
Sausage, fresh	lb.	1.82	12/94	82r
Shortening, vegetable oil blends	lb.	0.75	12/94	82r
Spaghetti and macaroni	lb.	0.87	12/94	82r
Steak, rib eye, USDA choice, boneless	lb.	6.85	12/94	82r
Steak, round, graded & ungraded, exc. USDA prime & choice	lb.	2.96	12/94	82r
Steak, round, USDA choice, boneless	lb.	3.17	12/94	82r
Steak, sirloin, USDA choice, boneless	lb.	4.12	12/94	82r
Steak, T-bone, USDA choice, bone-in	lb.	5.63	12/94	82r
Sugar and other sweets, eaten at home, expenditures	year	93	91	81r
Sugar, white, all sizes	lb.	0.39	12/94	82r
Tobacco products and smoking supplies, total expenditures	year	286	91	81r
Tomatoes, field grown	lb.	1.36	12/94	82r

Values are in dollars or fractions of dollars. In the column headed *Ref*, references are shown to sources. Each reference is followed by a letter. These refer to the geographical level for which data were reported: s=State, r=Region, and c=City or metro. The abbreviation *ex* is used to mean *except* or *excluding*; *exp* stands for expenditures. For other abbreviations and further explanations, please see the Introduction.

Fort Lauderdale-Hollywood-Pompano Beach, FL - continued

Item	Per	Value	Date	Ref.
Groceries				
Tuna, chunk, light	lb.	1.94	12/94	82r
Turkey, frozen, whole	lb.	0.96	12/94	82r
Yogurt, natural, fruit flavored	8 oz.	0.58	12/94	82r
Health Care				
Adenosine, emergency room	treat	100.00	95	23r
Bladder tap, superpubic, infant, emergency room	treat	119.00	95	23r
Blood analysis, emergency room	treat	25.00	95	23r
Blood tests, abdominal pain, emergency room	treat	25.00	95	23r
Burn dressing, emergency room	treat	266.00	95	23r
Cardiology interpretation, emergency room	treat	26.00	95	23r
Chest X-ray, emergency room	treat	78.00	95	23r
Childbirth, Cesarean delivery, hospital charge	birth	5462.00	12/91	69r
Childbirth, Cesarean delivery, physician charge	birth	2228.00	12/91	69r
Childbirth, normal delivery, hospital charge	birth	2943.00	12/91	69r
Childbirth, normal delivery, physician charge	birth	1619.00	12/91	69r
Defibrillation pads, emergency room	treat	6.00	95	23r
Drugs, expenditures	year	297	91	81r
Gastric tube insertion, nasal, emergency room	treat	25.00	95	23r
Health care, total expenditures	year	1600	91	81r
Health insurance expenditures	year	637	91	81r
Heart monitor, emergency room	treat	40.00	95	23r
Insurance premium, family medical care	month	301.92	1/95	41s
Intravenous fluids, emergency room	treat	130.00	95	23r
Intravenous fluids, emergency room	liter	26.00	95	23r
Intravenous line, central, emergency room	treat	342.00	95	23r
Liver function tests, abdominal pain, emergency room	treat	26.00	95	23r
Medical care charges, total, emergency room, third-degree burns	treat	2101.00	95	23r
Medical care charges, total, emergency, infant with fever	treat	628.00	95	23r
Medical services expenditures	year	573	91	81r
Medical supplies expenditures	year	93	91	81r
Morphine, emergency room	treat	34.00	95	23r
Nursing care and facilities charges, emergency room	treat	252.00	95	23r
Nursing care and facilities charges, emergency, infant with fever	treat	252.00	95	23r
Nursing care and facilities charges, emergency, third-degree burns	treat	861.00	95	23r
Physician's charges, emergency, infant with fever	treat	212.00	95	23r
Physician's charges, emergency, third-degree burns	treat	372.00	95	23r
Physician's fee, emergency room	treat	372.00	95	23r
Physician's fee, general practitioner	visit	51.20	12/93	60r
Surgery, open-heart	proc	42374.00	1/93	14r
Ultrasound, abdominal, emergency room	treat	276.00	95	23r
Urinalysis, emergency room	treat	20.00	95	23r
Urinalysis, infant, emergency room	treat	20.00	95	23r
X-rays, emergency room	treat	78.00	95	23r
Household Goods				
Floor coverings, expenditures	year	48	91	81r
Furniture, expenditures	year	280	91	81r
Household equipment, misc. expenditures	year	342	91	81r
Household expenditures, miscellaneous	year	256	91	81r
Household furnishings and equipment, expenditures	year	988	91	81r
Household operations expenditures	year	468	91	81r
Household textiles, expenditures	year	95	91	81r
Housekeeping supplies, expenditures	year	380	91	81r
Laundry and cleaning supplies, expenditures	year	109	91	81r
Postage and stationery, expenditures	year	105	91	81r

Fort Lauderdale-Hollywood-Pompano Beach, FL - continued

Item	Per	Value	Date	Ref.
Housing				
Add garage/carport		6,980	3/95	74r
Add room(s)		11,403	3/95	74r
Apartment condominium or co-op, median	unit	68600	12/94	62r
Dwellings (owned), expenditures	year	2428	91	81r
Enclose porch/patio/breezeway		4,572	3/95	74r
Finish room in basement/attic		3,794	3/95	74r
Home, existing, single-family, median	unit	120200	12/94	62r
Maintenance, repairs, insurance, and other housing expenditures	year	531	91	81r
Mortgage interest and charges expenditures	year	1506	91	81r
Princ. & int., mortgage, median-price exist. sing.-family home	mo.	540	12/94	62r
Property taxes expenditures	year	391	91	81r
Redesign, restructure more than half of home's interior		17,641	3/95	74r
Rental units expenditures	year	1264	91	81r
Insurance and Pensions				
Auto insurance, private passenger	year	753.93	12/94	71s
Insurance and pensions, personal, expenditures	year	2395	91	81r
Insurance, life and other personal, expenditures	year	368	91	81r
Pensions and Social Security, expenditures	year	2027	91	81r
Personal Services				
Personal services expenditures	year	212	91	81r
Restaurant Food				
Dining expenditures, family	week	33.83	94	73r
Taxes				
Taxes, Federal income, expenditures	year	2275	91	81r
Taxes, personal, expenditures	year	2715	91	81r
Taxes, State and local income, expenditures	year	365	91	81r
Transportation				
Cars and trucks purchased, new	year	1306	91	81r
Cars and trucks purchased, used	year	942	91	81r
Driver's learning permit fee	perm	20.00	1/94	84s
Driver's license fee	orig	20.00	1/94	84s
Driver's license fee, duplicate	lic	10.00	1/94	84s
Driver's license reinstatement fee, min.	susp	25.00	1/94	85s
Driver's license renewal fee	renew	15.00	1/94	84s
Identification card, nondriver	card	3.00	1/94	83s
Motorcycle learning permit fee	perm	20.00	1/94	84s
Motorcycle license fee	orig	20.00	1/94	84s
Motorcycle license fee, duplicate	lic	10.00	1/94	84s
Motorcycle license renewal fee	renew	15.00	1/94	84s
Public transportation expenditures	year	249	91	81r
Transportation expenditures, total	year	5307	91	81r
Vehicle finance charges	year	346	91	81r
Vehicle insurance expenditures	year	544	91	81r
Vehicle maintenance and repairs expenditures	year	600	91	81r
Vehicle purchases	year	2275	91	81r
Vehicle rental, leases, licenses, etc. expenditures	year	141	91	81r
Vehicles purchased, other than cars and trucks	year	27	91	81r
Utilities				
Electricity expenditures	year	950	91	81r
Utilities, fuels, and public services, total expenditures	year	2000	91	81r
Water and other public services, expenditures	year	227	91	81r
Weddings				
Bridal attendants' gowns	event	750	10/93	76r
Bridal gown	event	852	10/93	76r
Bridal headpiece and veil	event	167	10/93	76r
Bride's wedding band	event	708	10/93	76r
Clergy	event	224	10/93	76r
Engagement ring	event	2756	10/93	76r

Values are in dollars or fractions of dollars. In the column headed *Ref*, references are shown to sources. Each reference is followed by a letter. These refer to the geographical level for which data were reported: s = State, r = Region, and c = City or metro. The abbreviation *ex* is used to mean *except* or *excluding*; *exp* stands for *expenditures*. For other abbreviations and further explanations, please see the Introduction.

Fort Lauderdale-Hollywood-Pompano Beach, FL - continued

Item	Per	Value	Date	Ref.
Weddings				
Flowers	event	863	10/93	76r
Formal wear for groom	event	106	10/93	76r
Groom's attendants' formal wear	event	530	10/93	76r
Groom's wedding band	event	402	10/93	76r
Music	event	600	10/93	76r
Photography	event	1088	10/93	76r
Shoes for bride	event	50	10/93	76r
Videography	event	483	10/93	76r
Wedding invitations and announcements	event	342	10/93	76r
Wedding reception	event	7000	10/93	76r

Fort Myers-Cape Coral, FL

Item	Per	Value	Date	Ref.
Composite, ACCRA index		97.20	12/94	2c
Alcoholic Beverages				
Beer, Miller Lite, Bud, 12-oz., ex deposit	6	3.56	12/94	2c
J & B Scotch	750-ml.	16.69	12/94	2c
Wine, Gallo Chablis blanc	1.5-lit	4.87	12/94	2c
Appliances				
Appliances (major), expenditures	year	153	91	81r
Average annual exp.				
Food, health care, personal goods, services	year	27020	91	81r
Charity				
Cash contributions, expenditures	year	839	91	81r
Clothing				
Apparel, men and boys, total expenditures	year	380	91	81r
Apparel, women and girls, total expenditures	year	660	91	81r
Footwear, expenditures	year	193	91	81r
Jeans, man's denim		29.24	12/94	2c
Shirt, man's dress shirt		28.93	12/94	2c
Undervest, boy's size 10-14, cotton	3	3.09	12/94	2c
Communications				
Long-distance telephone rate, day, addl. min., 1-10 mi.	min.	0.08	12/93	9s
Long-distance telephone rate, day, initial min., 1-10 mi.	min.	0.15	12/93	9s
Newspaper subscription, dly. and Sun. delivery	month	13.32	12/94	2c
Phone line, single, business, field visit	inst	86.00	12/93	9s
Phone line, single, business, no field visit	inst	54.50	12/93	9s
Phone line, single, residence, field visit	inst	76.00	12/93	9s
Phone line, single, residence, no field visit	inst	44.50	12/93	9s
Telephone bill, family of four	month	15.62	12/94	2c
Telephone service, expenditures	year	616	91	81r
Education				
Bar examinination preparatory course	course	500.00-100	94	17s
Board, 4-year private college/university	year	2123	8/94	80s
Board, 4-year public college/university	year	2101	8/94	80s
Education, total expenditures	year	319	91	81r
Room, 4-year private college/university	year	2242	8/94	80s
Room, 4-year public college/university	year	1970	8/94	80s
Total cost, 4-year private college/university	year	13853	8/94	80s
Total cost, 4-year public college/university	year	5855	8/94	80s
Tuition, 2-year public college/university, in-state	year	1076	8/94	80s
Tuition, 4-year private college/university, in-state	year	9287	8/94	80s
Tuition, 4-year public college/university, in-state	year	1784	8/94	80s
Energy and Fuels				
Energy, combined forms, 1800 sq. ft.	mo.	114.23	12/94	2c
Fuel oil and other fuels, expenditures	year	56	91	81r
Gas, natural, expenditures	year	150	91	81r
Gas, reg unlead, taxes inc., cash, self-service	gal	1.21	12/94	2c

Fort Myers-Cape Coral, FL - continued

Item	Per	Value	Date	Ref.
Energy and Fuels - continued				
Gasoline and motor oil purchased	year	1152	91	81r
Gasoline, unleaded midgrade	gallon	1.21	4/93	82r
Gasoline, unleaded premium	gallon	1.30	4/93	82r
Gasoline, unleaded regular	gallon	1.10	4/93	82r
Entertainment				
Bowling, evening rate	game	2.26	12/94	2c
Concert ticket, Pearl Jam group	perf	20.00	94	50r
Entertainment, total expenditures	year	1266	91	81r
Fees and admissions, expenditures	year	306	91	81r
Monopoly game, Parker Brothers', No. 9	game	10.20	12/94	2c
Movie	adm	6.00	12/94	2c
Pets, toys, playground equipment, expenditures	year	271	91	81r
Reading, expenditures	year	131	91	81r
Televisions, radios, and sound equipment, expenditures	year	439	91	81r
Tennis balls, yellow, Wilson or Penn, 3	can	1.88	12/94	2c
Funerals				
Burial, immediate, container provided by funeral home		1370.36	1/95	54r
Cards, acknowledgment		14.83	1/95	54r
Casket, minimum alternative		192.52	1/95	54r
Cosmetology, hair care, etc.		102.27	1/95	54r
Cremation, direct, container provided by funeral home		1065.64	1/95	54r
Embalming		304.29	1/95	54r
Funeral, funeral home		287.83	1/95	54r
Funeral, other facility		284.14	1/95	54r
Graveside service		349.13	1/95	54r
Hearse, local		132.27	1/95	54r
Limousine, local		98.45	1/95	54r
Memorial service		270.59	1/95	54r
Service charge, professional, nondeclinable		933.59	1/95	54r
Visitation and viewing		225.83	1/95	54r
Groceries				
Groceries, ACCRA Index		94.80	12/94	2c
Apples, Red Delicious	lb.	0.73	12/94	82r
Baby food, strained vegetables, lowest price	4-4.5 oz.	0.35	12/94	2c
Bacon, sliced	lb.	1.67	12/94	82r
Bananas	lb.	0.38	12/94	2c
Bananas	lb.	0.42	12/94	82r
Beef or hamburger, ground	lb.	1.24	12/94	2c
Beef purchases	year	213	91	81r
Beverage purchases, alcoholic	year	249	91	81r
Beverage purchases, nonalcoholic	year	207	91	81r
Bologna, all beef or mixed	lb.	2.27	12/94	82r
Bread, white	24-oz.	0.79	12/94	2c
Bread, white, pan	lb.	0.68	12/94	82r
Cabbage	lb.	0.42	12/94	82r
Carrots, short trimmed and topped	lb.	0.53	12/94	82r
Cereals and bakery products purchases	year	345	91	81r
Cereals and cereals products purchases	year	127	91	81r
Cheddar cheese, natural	lb.	3.58	12/94	82r
Cheese, Kraft grated Parmesan	8-oz.	3.07	12/94	2c
Chicken breast, bone-in	lb.	1.71	12/94	82r
Chicken, fresh, whole	lb.	0.78	12/94	82r
Chicken, whole fryer	lb.	0.90	12/94	2c
Chuck roast, USDA choice, boneless	lb.	2.26	12/94	82r
Cigarettes, Winston, Kings	carton	16.01	12/94	2c
Coffee, vacuum-packed	13 oz.	2.84	12/94	2c
Corn Flakes, Kellogg's or Post Toasties	18 oz.	2.18	12/94	2c
Corn, frozen, whole kernel, lowest price	10 oz.	0.59	12/94	2c
Crackers, soda, salted	lb.	1.27	12/94	82r
Cucumbers	lb.	0.65	12/94	82r
Dairy products (other) purchases	year	141	91	81r
Eggs, Grade A large	dozen	0.75	12/94	2c
Eggs, Grade A large	dozen	0.87	12/94	82r
Fish and seafood purchases	year	72	91	81r
Flour, white, all purpose	lb.	0.23	12/94	82r
Food purchases, food eaten at home	year	2381	91	81r

Values are in dollars or fractions of dollars. In the column headed *Ref*, references are shown to sources. Each reference is followed by a letter. These refer to the geographical level for which data were reported: s=State, r=Region, and c=City or metro. The abbreviation *ex* is used to mean *except* or *excluding*; *exp* stands for expenditures. For other abbreviations and further explanations, please see the Introduction.

Fort Myers-Cape Coral, FL - continued

Item	Per	Value	Date	Ref.
Groceries				
Foods purchased away from home, not prepared by consumer	year	1696	91	81r
Frankfurters, all meat or all beef	lb.	1.74	12/94	82r
Fruits and vegetables purchases	year	380	91	81r
Grapefruit	lb.	0.45	12/94	82r
Grapes, Thompson seedless	lb.	2.30	12/94	82r
Ground beef, 100% beef	lb.	1.37	12/94	82r
Ground chuck, 100% beef	lb.	1.97	12/94	82r
Ham, boneless, exc. canned	lb.	2.54	12/94	82r
Ice cream, prepackaged, bulk, regular	1/2 gal.	2.47	12/94	82r
Lemons	lb.	1.02	12/94	82r
Lettuce, iceberg	lb.	0.96	12/94	82r
Lettuce, iceberg	head	0.81	12/94	2c
Margarine, Blue Bonnet or Parkay cubes	lb.	0.55	12/94	2c
Margarine, stick	lb.	0.77	12/94	82r
Meats, poultry, fish, and eggs purchases	year	655	91	81r
Milk and cream (fresh) purchases	year	130	91	81r
Milk, whole	1/2 gal.	1.39	12/94	2c
Orange juice, frozen concentrate 12-oz. can	16 oz.	1.36	12/94	82r
Orange juice, Minute Maid frozen	12-oz.	1.13	12/94	2c
Oranges, Navel	lb.	0.54	12/94	82r
Peaches, halves or slices, Hunt's, Del Monte, or Libby's	29-oz.	1.36	12/94	2c
Pears, Anjou	lb.	0.81	12/94	82r
Peas, sweet, Del Monte or Green Giant	15-17 oz.	0.52	12/94	2c
Pork chops, center cut, bone-in	lb.	3.07	12/94	82r
Pork purchases	year	142	91	81r
Potato chips	16-oz.	3.15	12/94	82r
Potatoes, frozen, French fried	lb.	0.82	12/94	82r
Potatoes, white	lb.	0.34	12/94	82r
Potatoes, white or red	10-lb. sack	1.88	12/94	2c
Rice, white, long grain, uncooked	lb.	0.48	12/94	82r
Round roast, USDA choice, boneless	lb.	2.91	12/94	82r
Sausage, fresh	lb.	1.82	12/94	82r
Sausage, Jimmy Dean, 100% pork	lb.	2.25	12/94	2c
Shortening, vegetable oil blends	lb.	0.75	12/94	82r
Shortening, vegetable, Crisco	3-lb.	2.64	12/94	2c
Soft drink, Coca Cola, ex deposit	2 lit	1.05	12/94	2c
Spaghetti and macaroni	lb.	0.87	12/94	82r
Steak, rib eye, USDA choice, boneless	lb.	6.85	12/94	82r
Steak, round, graded & ungraded, exc. USDA prime & choice	lb.	2.96	12/94	82r
Steak, round, USDA choice, boneless	lb.	3.17	12/94	82r
Steak, sirloin, USDA choice, boneless	lb.	4.12	12/94	82r
Steak, t-bone	lb.	5.44	12/94	2c
Steak, T-bone, USDA choice, bone-in	lb.	5.63	12/94	82r
Sugar and other sweets, eaten at home, expenditures	year	93	91	81r
Sugar, cane or beet	4 lbs.	1.46	12/94	2c
Sugar, white, all sizes	lb.	0.39	12/94	82r
Tobacco products and smoking supplies, total expenditures	year	286	91	81r
Tomatoes, field grown	lb.	1.36	12/94	82r
Tomatoes, Hunt's or Del Monte	14.5 oz.	0.71	12/94	2c
Tuna, chunk, light	lb.	1.94	12/94	82r
Tuna, chunk, light, oil-packed	6.125-6.5 oz.	0.64	12/94	2c
Turkey, frozen, whole	lb.	0.96	12/94	82r
Yogurt, natural, fruit flavored	8 oz.	0.58	12/94	82r
Goods and Services				
Miscellaneous goods and services, ACCRA Index		93.70	12/94	2c
Health Care				
Health care, ACCRA Index		94.30	12/94	2c
Adenosine, emergency room	treat	100.00	95	23r
Antibiotic ointment, Polysporin	1.5 oz.	4.31	12/94	2c

Fort Myers-Cape Coral, FL - continued

Item	Per	Value	Date	Ref.
Health Care - continued				
Bladder tap, superpubic, infant, emergency room	treat	119.00	95	23r
Blood analysis, emergency room	treat	25.00	95	23r
Blood tests, abdominal pain, emergency room	treat	25.00	95	23r
Burn dressing, emergency room	treat	266.00	95	23r
Cardiology interpretation, emergency room	treat	26.00	95	23r
Chest X-ray, emergency room	treat	78.00	95	23r
Childbirth, Cesarean delivery, hospital charge	birth	5462.00	12/91	69r
Childbirth, Cesarean delivery, physician charge	birth	2228.00	12/91	69r
Childbirth, normal delivery, hospital charge	birth	2943.00	12/91	69r
Childbirth, normal delivery, physician charge	birth	1619.00	12/91	69r
Defibrillation pads, emergency room	treat	6.00	95	23r
Dentist's fee, adult teeth cleaning and periodic oral exam	visit	42.10	12/94	2c
Doctor's fee, routine exam, established patient	visit	42.80	12/94	2c
Drugs, expenditures	year	297	91	81r
Gastric tube insertion, nasal, emergency room	treat	25.00	95	23r
Health care, total expenditures	year	1600	91	81r
Health insurance expenditures	year	637	91	81r
Heart monitor, emergency room	treat	40.00	95	23r
Hospital care, semiprivate room	day	354.97	12/94	2c
Insurance premium, family medical care	month	301.92	1/95	41s
Intravenous fluids, emergency room	treat	130.00	95	23r
Intravenous fluids, emergency room	liter	26.00	95	23r
Intravenous line, central, emergency room	treat	342.00	95	23r
Liver function tests, abdominal pain, emergency room	treat	26.00	95	23r
Medical care charges, total, emergency room, third-degree burns	treat	2101.00	95	23r
Medical care charges, total, emergency, infant with fever	treat	628.00	95	23r
Medical services expenditures	year	573	91	81r
Medical supplies expenditures	year	93	91	81r
Morphine, emergency room	treat	34.00	95	23r
Nursing care and facilities charges, emergency room	treat	252.00	95	23r
Nursing care and facilities charges, emergency, infant with fever	treat	252.00	95	23r
Nursing care and facilities charges, emergency, third-degree burns	treat	861.00	95	23r
Physician's charges, emergency, infant with fever	treat	212.00	95	23r
Physician's charges, emergency, third-degree burns	treat	372.00	95	23r
Physician's fee, emergency room	treat	372.00	95	23r
Physician's fee, general practitioner	visit	51.20	12/93	60r
Surgery, open-heart	proc	42374.00	1/93	14r
Ultrasound, abdominal, emergency room	treat	276.00	95	23r
Urinalysis, emergency room	treat	20.00	95	23r
Urinalysis, infant, emergency room	treat	20.00	95	23r
X-rays, emergency room	treat	78.00	95	23r
Household Goods				
Appl. repair, service call, wash mach	min. lab. chg.	37.08	12/94	2c
Floor coverings, expenditures	year	48	91	81r
Furniture, expenditures	year	280	91	81r
Household equipment, misc. expenditures	year	342	91	81r
Household expenditures, miscellaneous	year	256	91	81r
Household furnishings and equipment, expenditures	year	988	91	81r
Household operations expenditures	year	468	91	81r
Household textiles, expenditures	year	95	91	81r
Housekeeping supplies, expenditures	year	380	91	81r
Laundry and cleaning supplies, expenditures	year	109	91	81r

Values are in dollars or fractions of dollars. In the column headed *Ref*, references are shown to sources. Each reference is followed by a letter. These refer to the geographical level for which data were reported: s = State, r = Region, and c = City or metro. The abbreviation *ex* is used to mean *except* or *excluding*; *exp* stands for *expenditures*. For other abbreviations and further explanations, please see the Introduction.

Fort Myers-Cape Coral, FL - continued

Item	Per	Value	Date	Ref.
Household Goods				
Laundry detergent, Tide Ultra, Bold, or Cheer	42 oz.	2.75	12/94	2c
Postage and stationery, expenditures	year	105	91	81r
Tissues, facial, Kleenex brand	175	0.96	12/94	2c
Housing				
Housing, ACCRA Index		99.90	12/94	2c
Add garage/carport		6,980	3/95	74r
Add room(s)		11,403	3/95	74r
Apartment condominium or co-op, median	unit	68600	12/94	62r
Dwellings (owned), expenditures	year	2428	91	81r
Enclose porch/patio/breezeway		4,572	3/95	74r
Finish room in basement/attic		3,794	3/95	74r
Home, existing, single-family, median	unit	120200	12/94	62r
Home, existing, single-family, median	unit	76.90	12/94	62c
House payment, principal and interest, 25% down payment	mo.	762	12/94	2c
House, 1800 sq ft, 8000 sq ft lot, new, urban, utilities	total	122378	12/94	2c
Maintenance, repairs, insurance, and other housing expenditures	year	531	91	81r
Mortgage interest and charges expenditures	year	1506	91	81r
Mtge. rate, incl. points and orig. fee, 30-year conv. fixed or ARM	mo.	9.36	12/94	2c
Princ. & int., mortgage, median-price exist. sing.-family home	mo.	540	12/94	62r
Property taxes expenditures	year	391	91	81r
Redesign, restructure more than half of home's interior		17,641	3/95	74r
Rent, apartment, 2 br., 1 1/2-2 baths, unfurnished, 950 sq ft, water	mo.	537	12/94	2c
Rental units expenditures	year	1264	91	81r
Insurance and Pensions				
Auto insurance, private passenger	year	753.93	12/94	71s
Insurance and pensions, personal, expenditures	year	2395	91	81r
Insurance, life and other personal, expenditures	year	368	91	81r
Pensions and Social Security, expenditures	year	2027	91	81r
Personal Goods				
Shampoo, Alberto VO5	15-oz.	0.97	12/94	2c
Toothpaste, Crest or Colgate	6-7 oz.	1.72	12/94	2c
Personal Services				
Dry cleaning, man's 2-pc. suit		7.30	12/94	2c
Haircut, man's barbershop, no styling		7.30	12/94	2c
Haircut, woman's shampoo, trim, blow-dry		20.40	12/94	2c
Personal services expenditures	year	212	91	81r
Restaurant Food				
Chicken, fried, thigh and drumstick		1.82	12/94	2c
Dining expenditures, family	week	33.83	94	73r
Hamburger with cheese	1/4 lb.	1.96	12/94	2c
Pizza, Pizza Hut or Pizza Inn	12-13 in.	6.50	12/94	2c
Taxes				
Taxes, Federal income, expenditures	year	2275	91	81r
Taxes, personal, expenditures	year	2715	91	81r
Taxes, State and local income, expenditures	year	365	91	81r
Transportation				
Transportation, ACCRA Index		106.70	12/94	2c
Cars and trucks purchased, new	year	1306	91	81r
Cars and trucks purchased, used	year	942	91	81r
Driver's learning permit fee	perm	20.00	1/94	84s
Driver's license fee	orig	20.00	1/94	84s
Driver's license fee, duplicate	lic	10.00	1/94	84s
Driver's license reinstatement fee, min.	susp	25.00	1/94	85s
Driver's license renewal fee	renew	15.00	1/94	84s
Identification card, nondriver	card	3.00	1/94	83s
Motorcycle learning permit fee	perm	20.00	1/94	84s
Motorcycle license fee	orig	20.00	1/94	84s

Fort Myers-Cape Coral, FL - continued

Item	Per	Value	Date	Ref.
Transportation - continued				
Motorcycle license fee, duplicate	lic	10.00	1/94	84s
Motorcycle license renewal fee	renew	15.00	1/94	84s
Public transportation expenditures	year	249	91	81r
Tire balance, computer or spin bal., front	wheel	7.09	12/94	2c
Transportation expenditures, total	year	5307	91	81r
Vehicle finance charges	year	346	91	81r
Vehicle insurance expenditures	year	544	91	81r
Vehicle maintenance and repairs expenditures	year	600	91	81r
Vehicle purchases	year	2275	91	81r
Vehicle rental, leases, licenses, etc. expenditures	year	141	91	81r
Vehicles purchased, other than cars and trucks	year	27	91	81r
Utilities				
Utilities, ACCRA Index		98.90	12/94	2c
Electricity expenditures	year	950	91	81r
Electricity, 1800 sq. ft., new home	mo.	114.23	12/94	2c
Utilities, fuels, and public services, total expenditures	year	2000	91	81r
Water and other public services, expenditures	year	227	91	81r
Weddings				
Bridal attendants' gowns	event	750	10/93	76r
Bridal gown	event	852	10/93	76r
Bridal headpiece and veil	event	167	10/93	76r
Bride's wedding band	event	708	10/93	76r
Clergy	event	224	10/93	76r
Engagement ring	event	2756	10/93	76r
Flowers	event	863	10/93	76r
Formal wear for groom	event	106	10/93	76r
Groom's attendants' formal wear	event	530	10/93	76r
Groom's wedding band	event	402	10/93	76r
Music	event	600	10/93	76r
Photography	event	1088	10/93	76r
Shoes for bride	event	50	10/93	76r
Videography	event	483	10/93	76r
Wedding invitations and announcements	event	342	10/93	76r
Wedding reception	event	7000	10/93	76r

Fort Pierce, FL

Item	Per	Value	Date	Ref.
Appliances				
Appliances (major), expenditures	year	153	91	81r
Average annual exp.				
Food, health care, personal goods, services	year	27020	91	81r
Charity				
Cash contributions, expenditures	year	839	91	81r
Clothing				
Apparel, men and boys, total expenditures	year	380	91	81r
Apparel, women and girls, total expenditures	year	660	91	81r
Footwear, expenditures	year	193	91	81r
Communications				
Long-distance telephone rate, day, addl. min., 1-10 mi.	min.	0.08	12/93	9s
Long-distance telephone rate, day, initial min., 1-10 mi.	min.	0.15	12/93	9s
Phone line, single, business, field visit	inst	86.00	12/93	9s
Phone line, single, business, no field visit	inst	54.50	12/93	9s
Phone line, single, residence, field visit	inst	76.00	12/93	9s
Phone line, single, residence, no field visit	inst	44.50	12/93	9s
Telephone service, expenditures	year	616	91	81r
Education				
Bar examination preparatory course	course	500.00-100	94	17s
Board, 4-year private college/university	year	2123	8/94	80s
Board, 4-year public college/university	year	2101	8/94	80s

Values are in dollars or fractions of dollars. In the column headed *Ref*, references are shown to sources. Each reference is followed by a letter. These refer to the geographical level for which data were reported: s=State, r=Region, and c=City or metro. The abbreviation *ex* is used to mean *except* or *excluding*; *exp* stands for *expenditures*. For other abbreviations and further explanations, please see the Introduction.

Fort Pierce, FL - continued

Item	Per	Value	Date	Ref.
Education				
Education, total expenditures	year	319	91	81r
Room, 4-year private college/university	year	2242	8/94	80s
Room, 4-year public college/university	year	1970	8/94	80s
Total cost, 4-year private college/university	year	13853	8/94	80s
Total cost, 4-year public college/university	year	5855	8/94	80s
Tuition, 2-year public college/university, in-state	year	1076	8/94	80s
Tuition, 4-year private college/university, in-state	year	9287	8/94	80s
Tuition, 4-year public college/university, in-state	year	1784	8/94	80s
Energy and Fuels				
Fuel oil and other fuels, expenditures	year	56	91	81r
Gas, natural, expenditures	year	150	91	81r
Gasoline and motor oil purchased	year	1152	91	81r
Gasoline, unleaded midgrade	gallon	1.21	4/93	82r
Gasoline, unleaded premium	gallon	1.30	4/93	82r
Gasoline, unleaded regular	gallon	1.10	4/93	82r
Entertainment				
Concert ticket, Pearl Jam group	perf	20.00	94	50r
Entertainment, total expenditures	year	1266	91	81r
Fees and admissions, expenditures	year	306	91	81r
Pets, toys, playground equipment, expenditures	year	271	91	81r
Reading, expenditures	year	131	91	81r
Televisions, radios, and sound equipment, expenditures	year	439	91	81r
Funerals				
Burial, immediate, container provided by funeral home		1370.36	1/95	54r
Cards, acknowledgment		14.83	1/95	54r
Casket, minimum alternative		192.52	1/95	54r
Cosmetology, hair care, etc.		102.27	1/95	54r
Cremation, direct, container provided by funeral home		1065.64	1/95	54r
Embalming		304.29	1/95	54r
Funeral, funeral home		287.83	1/95	54r
Funeral, other facility		284.14	1/95	54r
Graveside service		349.13	1/95	54r
Hearse, local		132.27	1/95	54r
Limousine, local		98.45	1/95	54r
Memorial service		270.59	1/95	54r
Service charge, professional, nondeclinable		933.59	1/95	54r
Visitation and viewing		225.83	1/95	54r
Groceries				
Apples, Red Delicious	lb.	0.73	12/94	82r
Bacon, sliced	lb.	1.67	12/94	82r
Bananas	lb.	0.42	12/94	82r
Beef purchases	year	213	91	81r
Beverage purchases, alcoholic	year	249	91	81r
Beverage purchases, nonalcoholic	year	207	91	81r
Bologna, all beef or mixed	lb.	2.27	12/94	82r
Bread, white, pan	lb.	0.68	12/94	82r
Cabbage	lb.	0.42	12/94	82r
Carrots, short trimmed and topped	lb.	0.53	12/94	82r
Cereals and bakery products purchases	year	345	91	81r
Cereals and cereals products purchases	year	127	91	81r
Cheddar cheese, natural	lb.	3.58	12/94	82r
Chicken breast, bone-in	lb.	1.71	12/94	82r
Chicken, fresh, whole	lb.	0.78	12/94	82r
Chuck roast, USDA choice, boneless	lb.	2.26	12/94	82r
Crackers, soda, salted	lb.	1.27	12/94	82r
Cucumbers	lb.	0.65	12/94	82r
Dairy products (other) purchases	year	141	91	81r
Eggs, Grade A large	dozen	0.87	12/94	82r
Fish and seafood purchases	year	72	91	81r
Flour, white, all purpose	lb.	0.23	12/94	82r
Food purchases, food eaten at home	year	2381	91	81r
Foods purchased away from home, not prepared by consumer	year	1696	91	81r

Fort Pierce, FL - continued

Item	Per	Value	Date	Ref.
Groceries - continued				
Frankfurters, all meat or all beef	lb.	1.74	12/94	82r
Fruits and vegetables purchases	year	380	91	81r
Grapefruit	lb.	0.45	12/94	82r
Grapes, Thompson seedless	lb.	2.30	12/94	82r
Ground beef, 100% beef	lb.	1.37	12/94	82r
Ground chuck, 100% beef	lb.	1.97	12/94	82r
Ham, boneless, exc. canned	lb.	2.54	12/94	82r
Ice cream, prepackaged, bulk, regular	1/2 gal.	2.47	12/94	82r
Lemons	lb.	1.02	12/94	82r
Lettuce, iceberg	lb.	0.96	12/94	82r
Margarine, stick	lb.	0.77	12/94	82r
Meats, poultry, fish, and eggs purchases	year	655	91	81r
Milk and cream (fresh) purchases	year	130	91	81r
Orange juice, frozen concentrate 12-oz. can	16 oz.	1.36	12/94	82r
Oranges, Navel	lb.	0.54	12/94	82r
Pears, Anjou	lb.	0.81	12/94	82r
Pork chops, center cut, bone-in	lb.	3.07	12/94	82r
Pork purchases	year	142	91	81r
Potato chips	16-oz.	3.15	12/94	82r
Potatoes, frozen, French fried	lb.	0.82	12/94	82r
Potatoes, white	lb.	0.34	12/94	82r
Rice, white, long grain, uncooked	lb.	0.48	12/94	82r
Round roast, USDA choice, boneless	lb.	2.91	12/94	82r
Sausage, fresh	lb.	1.82	12/94	82r
Shortening, vegetable oil blends	lb.	0.75	12/94	82r
Spaghetti and macaroni	lb.	0.87	12/94	82r
Steak, rib eye, USDA choice, boneless	lb.	6.85	12/94	82r
Steak, round, graded & ungraded, exc. USDA prime & choice	lb.	2.96	12/94	82r
Steak, round, USDA choice, boneless	lb.	3.17	12/94	82r
Steak, sirloin, USDA choice, boneless	lb.	4.12	12/94	82r
Steak, T-bone, USDA choice, bone-in	lb.	5.63	12/94	82r
Sugar and other sweets, eaten at home, expenditures	year	93	91	81r
Sugar, white, all sizes	lb.	0.39	12/94	82r
Tobacco products and smoking supplies, total expenditures	year	286	91	81r
Tomatoes, field grown	lb.	1.36	12/94	82r
Tuna, chunk, light	lb.	1.94	12/94	82r
Turkey, frozen, whole	lb.	0.96	12/94	82r
Yogurt, natural, fruit flavored	8 oz.	0.58	12/94	82r
Health Care				
Adenosine, emergency room	treat	100.00	95	23r
Bladder tap, superpubic, infant, emergency room	treat	119.00	95	23r
Blood analysis, emergency room	treat	25.00	95	23r
Blood tests, abdominal pain, emergency room	treat	25.00	95	23r
Burn dressing, emergency room	treat	266.00	95	23r
Cardiology interpretation, emergency room	treat	26.00	95	23r
Chest X-ray, emergency room	treat	78.00	95	23r
Childbirth, Cesarean delivery, hospital charge	birth	5462.00	12/91	69r
Childbirth, Cesarean delivery, physician charge	birth	2228.00	12/91	69r
Childbirth, normal delivery, hospital charge	birth	2943.00	12/91	69r
Childbirth, normal delivery, physician charge	birth	1619.00	12/91	69r
Defibrillation pads, emergency room	treat	6.00	95	23r
Drugs, expenditures	year	297	91	81r
Gastric tube insertion, nasal, emergency room	treat	25.00	95	23r
Health care, total expenditures	year	1600	91	81r
Health insurance expenditures	year	637	91	81r
Heart monitor, emergency room	treat	40.00	95	23r
Insurance premium, family medical care	month	301.92	1/95	41s
Intravenous fluids, emergency room	treat	130.00	95	23r
Intravenous fluids, emergency room	liter	26.00	95	23r
Intravenous line, central, emergency room	treat	342.00	95	23r
Liver function tests, abdominal pain, emergency room	treat	26.00	95	23r

Values are in dollars or fractions of dollars. In the column headed *Ref*, references are shown to sources. Each reference is followed by a letter. These refer to the geographical level for which data were reported: s = State, r = Region, and c = City or metro. The abbreviation *ex* is used to mean *except* or *excluding*; *exp* stands for *expenditures*. For other abbreviations and further explanations, please see the Introduction.

Fort Pierce, FL - continued

Item	Per	Value	Date	Ref.
Health Care				
Medical care charges, total, emergency room, third-degree burns	treat	2101.00	95	23r
Medical care charges, total, emergency, infant with fever	treat	628.00	95	23r
Medical services expenditures	year	573	91	81r
Medical supplies expenditures	year	93	91	81r
Morphine, emergency room	treat	34.00	95	23r
Nursing care and facilities charges, emergency room	treat	252.00	95	23r
Nursing care and facilities charges, emergency, infant with fever	treat	252.00	95	23r
Nursing care and facilities charges, emergency, third-degree burns	treat	861.00	95	23r
Physician's charges, emergency, infant with fever	treat	212.00	95	23r
Physician's charges, emergency, third-degree burns	treat	372.00	95	23r
Physician's fee, emergency room	treat	372.00	95	23r
Physician's fee, general practitioner	visit	51.20	12/93	60r
Surgery, open-heart	proc	42374.00	1/93	14r
Ultrasound, abdominal, emergency room	treat	276.00	95	23r
Urinalysis, emergency room	treat	20.00	95	23r
Urinalysis, infant, emergency room	treat	20.00	95	23r
X-rays, emergency room	treat	78.00	95	23r
Household Goods				
Floor coverings, expenditures	year	48	91	81r
Furniture, expenditures	year	280	91	81r
Household equipment, misc. expenditures	year	342	91	81r
Household expenditures, miscellaneous	year	256	91	81r
Household furnishings and equipment, expenditures	year	988	91	81r
Household operations expenditures	year	468	91	81r
Household textiles, expenditures	year	95	91	81r
Housekeeping supplies, expenditures	year	380	91	81r
Laundry and cleaning supplies, expenditures	year	109	91	81r
Postage and stationery, expenditures	year	105	91	81r
Housing				
Add garage/carport		6,980	3/95	74r
Add room(s)		11,403	3/95	74r
Apartment condominium or co-op, median	unit	68600	12/94	62r
Dwellings (owned), expenditures	year	2428	91	81r
Enclose porch/patio/breezeway		4,572	3/95	74r
Finish room in basement/attic		3,794	3/95	74r
Home, existing, single-family, median	unit	120200	12/94	62r
Maintenance, repairs, insurance, and other housing expenditures	year	531	91	81r
Mortgage interest and charges expenditures	year	1506	91	81r
Princ. & int., mortgage, median-price exist. sing.-family home	mo.	540	12/94	62r
Property taxes expenditures	year	391	91	81r
Redesign, restructure more than half of home's interior		17,641	3/95	74r
Rental units expenditures	year	1264	91	81r
Insurance and Pensions				
Auto insurance, private passenger	year	753.93	12/94	71s
Insurance and pensions, personal, expenditures	year	2395	91	81r
Insurance, life and other personal, expenditures	year	368	91	81r
Pensions and Social Security, expenditures	year	2027	91	81r
Personal Services				
Personal services expenditures	year	212	91	81r
Restaurant Food				
Dining expenditures, family	week	33.83	94	73r
Taxes				
Taxes, Federal income, expenditures	year	2275	91	81r
Taxes, personal, expenditures	year	2715	91	81r
Taxes, State and local income, expenditures	year	365	91	81r

Fort Pierce, FL - continued

Item	Per	Value	Date	Ref.
Transportation				
Cars and trucks purchased, new	year	1306	91	81r
Cars and trucks purchased, used	year	942	91	81r
Driver's learning permit fee	perm	20.00	1/94	84s
Driver's license fee	orig	20.00	1/94	84s
Driver's license fee, duplicate	lic	10.00	1/94	84s
Driver's license reinstatement fee, min.	susp	25.00	1/94	85s
Driver's license renewal fee	renew	15.00	1/94	84s
Identification card, nondriver	card	3.00	1/94	83s
Motorcycle learning permit fee	perm	20.00	1/94	84s
Motorcycle license fee	orig	20.00	1/94	84s
Motorcycle license fee, duplicate	lic	10.00	1/94	84s
Motorcycle license renewal fee	renew	15.00	1/94	84s
Public transportation expenditures	year	249	91	81r
Transportation expenditures, total	year	5307	91	81r
Vehicle finance charges	year	346	91	81r
Vehicle insurance expenditures	year	544	91	81r
Vehicle maintenance and repairs expenditures	year	600	91	81r
Vehicle purchases	year	2275	91	81r
Vehicle rental, leases, licenses, etc. expenditures	year	141	91	81r
Vehicles purchased, other than cars and trucks	year	27	91	81r
Utilities				
Electricity expenditures	year	950	91	81r
Utilities, fuels, and public services, total expenditures	year	2000	91	81r
Water and other public services, expenditures	year	227	91	81r
Weddings				
Bridal attendants' gowns	event	750	10/93	76r
Bridal gown	event	852	10/93	76r
Bridal headpiece and veil	event	167	10/93	76r
Bride's wedding band	event	708	10/93	76r
Clergy	event	224	10/93	76r
Engagement ring	event	2756	10/93	76r
Flowers	event	863	10/93	76r
Formal wear for groom	event	106	10/93	76r
Groom's attendants' formal wear	event	530	10/93	76r
Groom's wedding band	event	402	10/93	76r
Music	event	600	10/93	76r
Photography	event	1088	10/93	76r
Shoes for bride	event	50	10/93	76r
Videography	event	483	10/93	76r
Wedding invitations and announcements	event	342	10/93	76r
Wedding reception	event	7000	10/93	76r

Fort Smith, AR

Item	Per	Value	Date	Ref.
Composite, ACCRA index		89.90	12/94	2c
Alcoholic Beverages				
Beer, Miller Lite, Bud, 12-oz., ex deposit	6	4.53	12/94	2c
J & B Scotch	750-ml.	17.33	12/94	2c
Wine, Gallo Chablis blanc	1.5-lit	5.89	12/94	2c
Appliances				
Appliances (major), expenditures	year	153	91	81r
Average annual exp.				
Food, health care, personal goods, services	year	27020	91	81r
Charity				
Cash contributions, expenditures	year	839	91	81r
Clothing				
Apparel, men and boys, total expenditures	year	380	91	81r
Apparel, women and girls, total expenditures	year	660	91	81r
Footwear, expenditures	year	193	91	81r
Jeans, man's denim		35.66	12/94	2c
Shirt, man's dress shirt		33.83	12/94	2c
Undervest, boy's size 10-14, cotton	3	3.43	12/94	2c

Values are in dollars or fractions of dollars. In the column headed *Ref*, references are shown to sources. Each reference is followed by a letter. These refer to the geographical level for which data were reported: s=State, r=Region, and c=City or metro. The abbreviation *ex* is used to mean *except* or *excluding*; *exp* stands for expenditures. For other abbreviations and further explanations, please see the Introduction.

Fort Smith, AR - continued

Item	Per	Value	Date	Ref.
Communications				
Long-distance telephone rate, day, addl. min., 1-10 mi.	min.	0.08	12/93	9s
Long-distance telephone rate, day, initial min., 1-10 mi.	min.	0.10	12/93	9s
Newspaper subscription, dly. and Sun. delivery	month	8.00	12/94	2c
Phone line, single, business, field visit	inst	84.00	12/93	9s
Phone line, single, business, no field visit	inst	84.00	12/93	9s
Phone line, single, residence, field visit	inst	39.70	12/93	9s
Phone line, single, residence, no field visit	inst	39.70	12/93	9s
Telephone bill, family of four	month	22.30	12/94	2c
Telephone service, expenditures	year	616	91	81r
Telephone, residential, flat rate	mo.	13.91	12/93	8c
Education				
Board, 4-year private college/university	year	1801	8/94	80s
Board, 4-year public college/university	year	1774	8/94	80s
Education, total expenditures	year	319	91	81r
Room, 4-year private college/university	year	1349	8/94	80s
Room, 4-year public college/university	year	1752	8/94	80s
Total cost, 4-year private college/university	year	8866	8/94	80s
Total cost, 4-year public college/university	year	5334	8/94	80s
Tuition, 2-year public college/university, in-state	year	833	8/94	80s
Tuition, 4-year private college/university, in-state	year	5716	8/94	80s
Tuition, 4-year public college/university, in-state	year	1808	8/94	80s
Energy and Fuels				
Energy, combined forms, 1800 sq. ft.	mo.	102.77	12/94	2c
Energy, exc. electricity, 1800 sq. ft.	mo.	34.64	12/94	2c
Fuel oil and other fuels, expenditures	year	56	91	81r
Gas, cooking, 10 therms	month	10.95	2/94	65c
Gas, cooking, 30 therms	month	17.09	2/94	65c
Gas, cooking, 50 therms	month	25.56	2/94	65c
Gas, heating, winter, 100 therms	month	42.37	2/94	65c
Gas, heating, winter, average use	month	68.26	2/94	65c
Gas, natural, expenditures	year	150	91	81r
Gas, reg unlead, taxes inc., cash, self-service	gal	1.00	12/94	2c
Gasoline and motor oil purchased	year	1152	91	81r
Gasoline, unleaded midgrade	gallon	1.21	4/93	82r
Gasoline, unleaded premium	gallon	1.30	4/93	82r
Gasoline, unleaded regular	gallon	1.10	4/93	82r
Entertainment				
Bowling, evening rate	game	2.18	12/94	2c
Concert ticket, Pearl Jam group	perf	20.00	94	50r
Entertainment, total expenditures	year	1266	91	81r
Fees and admissions, expenditures	year	306	91	81r
Monopoly game, Parker Brothers', No. 9	game	10.58	12/94	2c
Movie	adm	5.50	12/94	2c
Pets, toys, playground equipment, expenditures	year	271	91	81r
Reading, expenditures	year	131	91	81r
Televisions, radios, and sound equipment, expenditures	year	439	91	81r
Tennis balls, yellow, Wilson or Penn, 3	can	2.18	12/94	2c
Funerals				
Burial, immediate, container provided by funeral home		1574.60	1/95	54r
Cards, acknowledgment		22.24	1/95	54r
Casket, minimum alternative		239.41	1/95	54r
Cosmetology, hair care, etc.		91.04	1/95	54r
Cremation, direct, container provided by funeral home		1085.15	1/95	54r
Embalming		281.30	1/95	54r
Funeral, funeral home		323.04	1/95	54r
Funeral, other facility		327.58	1/95	54r
Graveside service		355.19	1/95	54r
Hearse, local		141.89	1/95	54r
Limousine, local		99.40	1/95	54r

Fort Smith, AR - continued

Item	Per	Value	Date	Ref.
Funerals - continued				
Memorial service		284.67	1/95	54r
Service charge, professional, nondeclinable		904.06	1/95	54r
Visitation and viewing		187.04	1/95	54r
Groceries				
Groceries, ACCRA Index		95.30	12/94	2c
Apples, Red Delicious	lb.	0.73	12/94	82r
Baby food, strained vegetables, lowest price	4-4.5 oz.	0.31	12/94	2c
Bacon, sliced	lb.	1.67	12/94	82r
Bananas	lb.	0.50	12/94	2c
Bananas	lb.	0.42	12/94	82r
Beef or hamburger, ground	lb.	1.31	12/94	2c
Beef purchases	year	213	91	81r
Beverage purchases, alcoholic	year	249	91	81r
Beverage purchases, nonalcoholic	year	207	91	81r
Bologna, all beef or mixed	lb.	2.27	12/94	82r
Bread, white	24-oz.	0.67	12/94	2c
Bread, white, pan	lb.	0.68	12/94	82r
Cabbage	lb.	0.42	12/94	82r
Carrots, short trimmed and topped	lb.	0.53	12/94	82r
Cereals and bakery products purchases	year	345	91	81r
Cereals and cereals products purchases	year	127	91	81r
Cheddar cheese, natural	lb.	3.58	12/94	82r
Cheese, Kraft grated Parmesan	8-oz.	3.26	12/94	2c
Chicken breast, bone-in	lb.	1.71	12/94	82r
Chicken, fresh, whole	lb.	0.78	12/94	82r
Chicken, whole fryer	lb.	0.75	12/94	2c
Chuck roast, USDA choice, boneless	lb.	2.26	12/94	82r
Cigarettes, Winston, Kings	carton	15.67	12/94	2c
Coffee, vacuum-packed	13 oz.	2.99	12/94	2c
Corn Flakes, Kellogg's or Post Toasties	18 oz.	2.22	12/94	2c
Corn, frozen, whole kernel, lowest price	10 oz.	0.79	12/94	2c
Crackers, soda, salted	lb.	1.27	12/94	82r
Cucumbers	lb.	0.65	12/94	82r
Dairy products (other) purchases	year	141	91	81r
Eggs, Grade A large	dozen	0.69	12/94	2c
Eggs, Grade A large	dozen	0.87	12/94	82r
Fish and seafood purchases	year	72	91	81r
Flour, white, all purpose	lb.	0.23	12/94	82r
Food purchases, food eaten at home	year	2381	91	81r
Foods purchased away from home, not prepared by consumer	year	1696	91	81r
Frankfurters, all meat or all beef	lb.	1.74	12/94	82r
Fruits and vegetables purchases	year	380	91	81r
Grapefruit	lb.	0.45	12/94	82r
Grapes, Thompson seedless	lb.	2.30	12/94	82r
Ground beef, 100% beef	lb.	1.37	12/94	82r
Ground chuck, 100% beef	lb.	1.97	12/94	82r
Ham, boneless, exc. canned	lb.	2.54	12/94	82r
Ice cream, prepackaged, bulk, regular	1/2 gal.	2.47	12/94	82r
Lemons	lb.	1.02	12/94	82r
Lettuce, iceberg	lb.	0.96	12/94	82r
Lettuce, iceberg	head	0.88	12/94	2c
Margarine, Blue Bonnet or Parkay cubes	lb.	0.61	12/94	2c
Margarine, stick	lb.	0.77	12/94	82r
Meats, poultry, fish, and eggs purchases	year	655	91	81r
Milk and cream (fresh) purchases	year	130	91	81r
Milk, whole	1/2 gal.	1.21	12/94	2c
Orange juice, frozen concentrate 12-oz. can	16 oz.	1.36	12/94	82r
Orange juice, Minute Maid frozen	12-oz.	1.09	12/94	2c
Oranges, Navel	lb.	0.54	12/94	82r
Peaches, halves or slices, Hunt's, Del Monte, or Libby's	29-oz.	1.15	12/94	2c
Pears, Anjou	lb.	0.81	12/94	82r
Peas, sweet, Del Monte or Green Giant	15-17 oz.	0.54	12/94	2c
Pork chops, center cut, bone-in	lb.	3.07	12/94	82r
Pork purchases	year	142	91	81r
Potato chips	16-oz.	3.15	12/94	82r
Potatoes, frozen, French fried	lb.	0.82	12/94	82r

Values are in dollars or fractions of dollars. In the column headed *Ref*, references are shown to sources. Each reference is followed by a letter. These refer to the geographical level for which data were reported: s=State, r=Region, and c=City or metro. The abbreviation *ex* is used to mean *except* or *excluding*; *exp* stands for *expenditures*. For other abbreviations and further explanations, please see the Introduction.

Fort Smith, AR - continued

Item	Per	Value	Date	Ref.
Groceries				
Potatoes, white	lb.	0.34	12/94	82r
Potatoes, white or red	10-lb. sack	2.45	12/94	2c
Rice, white, long grain, uncooked	lb.	0.48	12/94	82r
Round roast, USDA choice, boneless	lb.	2.91	12/94	82r
Sausage, fresh	lb.	1.82	12/94	82r
Sausage, Jimmy Dean, 100% pork	lb.	2.51	12/94	2c
Shortening, vegetable oil blends	lb.	0.75	12/94	82r
Shortening, vegetable, Crisco	3-lb.	2.34	12/94	2c
Soft drink, Coca Cola, ex deposit	2 lit	1.15	12/94	2c
Spaghetti and macaroni	lb.	0.87	12/94	82r
Steak, rib eye, USDA choice, boneless	lb.	6.85	12/94	82r
Steak, round, graded & ungraded, exc. USDA prime & choice	lb.	2.96	12/94	82r
Steak, round, USDA choice, boneless	lb.	3.17	12/94	82r
Steak, sirloin, USDA choice, boneless	lb.	4.12	12/94	82r
Steak, t-bone	lb.	5.40	12/94	2c
Steak, T-bone, USDA choice, bone-in	lb.	5.63	12/94	82r
Sugar and other sweets, eaten at home, expenditures	year	93	91	81r
Sugar, cane or beet	4 lbs.	1.47	12/94	2c
Sugar, white, all sizes	lb.	0.39	12/94	82r
Tobacco products and smoking supplies, total expenditures	year	286	91	81r
Tomatoes, field grown	lb.	1.36	12/94	82r
Tomatoes, Hunt's or Del Monte	14.5 oz.	0.67	12/94	2c
Tuna, chunk, light	lb.	1.94	12/94	82r
Tuna, chunk, light, oil-packed	6.125-6.5 oz.	0.62	12/94	2c
Turkey, frozen, whole	lb.	0.96	12/94	82r
Yogurt, natural, fruit flavored	8 oz.	0.58	12/94	82r
Goods and Services				
Miscellaneous goods and services, ACCRA Index		101.00	12/94	2c
Health Care				
Health care, ACCRA Index		88.20	12/94	2c
Adenosine, emergency room	treat	100.00	95	23r
Antibiotic ointment, Polysporin	1.5 oz.	3.82	12/94	2c
Bladder tap, superpubic, infant, emergency room	treat	119.00	95	23r
Blood analysis, emergency room	treat	25.00	95	23r
Blood tests, abdominal pain, emergency room	treat	25.00	95	23r
Burn dressing, emergency room	treat	266.00	95	23r
Cardiology interpretation, emergency room	treat	26.00	95	23r
Chest X-ray, emergency room	treat	78.00	95	23r
Childbirth, Cesarean delivery, hospital charge	birth	5462.00	12/91	69r
Childbirth, Cesarean delivery, physician charge	birth	2228.00	12/91	69r
Childbirth, normal delivery, hospital charge	birth	2943.00	12/91	69r
Childbirth, normal delivery, physician charge	birth	1619.00	12/91	69r
Defibrillation pads, emergency room	treat	6.00	95	23r
Dentist's fee, adult teeth cleaning and periodic oral exam	visit	51.20	12/94	2c
Doctor's fee, routine exam, established patient	visit	38.60	12/94	2c
Drugs, expenditures	year	297	91	81r
Gastric tube insertion, nasal, emergency room	treat	25.00	95	23r
Health care, total expenditures	year	1600	91	81r
Health insurance expenditures	year	637	91	81r
Heart monitor, emergency room	treat	40.00	95	23r
Hospital care, semiprivate room	day	211.50	12/94	2c
Insurance premium, family medical care	month	326.03	1/95	41s
Intravenous fluids, emergency room	treat	130.00	95	23r
Intravenous fluids, emergency room	liter	26.00	95	23r
Intravenous line, central, emergency room	treat	342.00	95	23r
Liver function tests, abdominal pain, emergency room	treat	26.00	95	23r

Fort Smith, AR - continued

Item	Per	Value	Date	Ref.
Health Care - continued				
Medical care charges, total, emergency room, third-degree burns	treat	2101.00	95	23r
Medical care charges, total, emergency, infant with fever	treat	628.00	95	23r
Medical services expenditures	year	573	91	81r
Medical supplies expenditures	year	93	91	81r
Morphine, emergency room	treat	34.00	95	23r
Nursing care and facilities charges, emergency room	treat	252.00	95	23r
Nursing care and facilities charges, emergency, infant with fever	treat	252.00	95	23r
Nursing care and facilities charges, emergency, third-degree burns	treat	861.00	95	23r
Physician's charges, emergency, infant with fever	treat	212.00	95	23r
Physician's charges, emergency, third-degree burns	treat	372.00	95	23r
Physician's fee, emergency room	treat	372.00	95	23r
Physician's fee, general practitioner	visit	51.20	12/93	60r
Surgery, open-heart	proc	42374.00	1/93	14r
Ultrasound, abdominal, emergency room	treat	276.00	95	23r
Urinalysis, emergency room	treat	20.00	95	23r
Urinalysis, infant, emergency room	treat	20.00	95	23r
X-rays, emergency room	treat	78.00	95	23r
Household Goods				
Appl. repair, service call, wash mach	min. lab. chg.	36.65	12/94	2c
Floor coverings, expenditures	year	48	91	81r
Furniture, expenditures	year	280	91	81r
Household equipment, misc. expenditures	year	342	91	81r
Household expenditures, miscellaneous	year	256	91	81r
Household furnishings and equipment, expenditures	year	988	91	81r
Household operations expenditures	year	468	91	81r
Household textiles, expenditures	year	95	91	81r
Housekeeping supplies, expenditures	year	380	91	81r
Laundry and cleaning supplies, expenditures	year	109	91	81r
Laundry detergent, Tide Ultra, Bold, or Cheer	42 oz.	3.75	12/94	2c
Postage and stationery, expenditures	year	105	91	81r
Tissues, facial, Kleenex brand	175	0.96	12/94	2c
Housing				
Housing, ACCRA Index		72.80	12/94	2c
Add garage/carport		6,980	3/95	74r
Add room(s)		11,403	3/95	74r
Apartment condominium or co-op, median	unit	68600	12/94	62r
Dwellings (owned), expenditures	year	2428	91	81r
Enclose porch/patio/breezeway		4,572	3/95	74r
Finish room in basement/attic		3,794	3/95	74r
Home, existing, single-family, median	unit	120200	12/94	62r
House payment, principal and interest, 25% down payment	mo.	568	12/94	2c
House, 1800 sq ft, 8000 sq ft lot, new, urban, utilities	total	92200	12/94	2c
Maintenance, repairs, insurance, and other housing expenditures	year	531	91	81r
Mortgage interest and charges expenditures	year	1506	91	81r
Mtge. rate, incl. points and orig. fee, 30-year conv. fixed or ARM	mo.	9.24	12/94	2c
Princ. & int., mortgage, median-price exist. sing.-family home	mo.	540	12/94	62r
Property taxes expenditures	year	391	91	81r
Redesign, restructure more than half of home's interior		17,641	3/95	74r
Rent, apartment, 2 br., 1 1/2-2 baths, unfurnished, 950 sq ft, water	mo.	354	12/94	2c
Rental units expenditures	year	1264	91	81r

Values are in dollars or fractions of dollars. In the column headed *Ref*, references are shown to sources. Each reference is followed by a letter. These refer to the geographical level for which data were reported: s = State, r = Region, and c = City or metro. The abbreviation *ex* is used to mean *except* or *excluding*; *exp* stands for expenditures. For other abbreviations and further explanations, please see the Introduction.

Fort Smith, AR - continued

Item	Per	Value	Date	Ref.
Insurance and Pensions				
Auto insurance, private passenger	year	565.35	12/94	71s
Insurance and pensions, personal, expenditures	year	2395	91	81r
Insurance, life and other personal, expenditures	year	368	91	81r
Pensions and Social Security, expenditures	year	2027	91	81r
Personal Goods				
Shampoo, Alberto VO5	15-oz.	1.54	12/94	2c
Toothpaste, Crest or Colgate	6-7 oz.	1.86	12/94	2c
Personal Services				
Dry cleaning, man's 2-pc. suit		5.20	12/94	2c
Haircut, man's barbershop, no styling		8.40	12/94	2c
Haircut, woman's shampoo, trim, blow-dry		17.20	12/94	2c
Personal services expenditures	year	212	91	81r
Restaurant Food				
Chicken, fried, thigh and drumstick		2.39	12/94	2c
Dining expenditures, family	week	33.83	94	73r
Hamburger with cheese	1/4 lb.	1.89	12/94	2c
Pizza, Pizza Hut or Pizza Inn	12-13 in.	6.25	12/94	2c
Taxes				
Taxes, Federal income, expenditures	year	2275	91	81r
Taxes, personal, expenditures	year	2715	91	81r
Taxes, State and local income, expenditures	year	365	91	81r
Transportation				
Transportation, ACCRA Index		89.40	12/94	2c
Cars and trucks purchased, new	year	1306	91	81r
Cars and trucks purchased, used	year	942	91	81r
Driver's license fee	orig	14.00	1/94	84s
Driver's license fee, duplicate	lic	5.00	1/94	84s
Driver's license renewal fee	renew	14.00	1/94	84s
Identification card, nondriver	card	5.00	1/94	83s
Motorcycle license fee	orig	4.00	1/94	84s
Motorcycle license fee, duplicate	lic	5.00	1/94	84s
Public transportation expenditures	year	249	91	81r
Tire balance, computer or spin bal., front	wheel	6.08	12/94	2c
Transportation expenditures, total	year	5307	91	81r
Vehicle finance charges	year	346	91	81r
Vehicle insurance expenditures	year	544	91	81r
Vehicle maintenance and repairs expenditures	year	600	91	81r
Vehicle purchases	year	2275	91	81r
Vehicle rental, leases, licenses, etc. expenditures	year	141	91	81r
Vehicles purchased, other than cars and trucks	year	27	91	81r
Utilities				
Utilities, ACCRA Index		94.60	12/94	2c
Electricity expenditures	year	950	91	81r
Electricity, (part.), other, 1800 sq. ft., new home	mo.	68.13	12/94	2c
Electricity, summer, 250 KWh	month	23.24	8/93	64c
Electricity, summer, 500 KWh	month	40.54	8/93	64c
Electricity, summer, 750 KWh	month	57.83	8/93	64c
Electricity, summer, 1000 KWh	month	75.13	8/93	64c
Utilities, fuels, and public services, total expenditures	year	2000	91	81r
Water and other public services, expenditures	year	227	91	81r
Weddings				
Bridal attendants' gowns	event	750	10/93	76r
Bridal gown	event	852	10/93	76r
Bridal headpiece and veil	event	167	10/93	76r
Bride's wedding band	event	708	10/93	76r
Clergy	event	224	10/93	76r
Engagement ring	event	2756	10/93	76r
Flowers	event	863	10/93	76r
Formal wear for groom	event	106	10/93	76r

Fort Smith, AR - continued

Item	Per	Value	Date	Ref.
Weddings - continued				
Groom's attendants' formal wear	event	530	10/93	76r
Groom's wedding band	event	402	10/93	76r
Music	event	600	10/93	76r
Photography	event	1088	10/93	76r
Shoes for bride	event	50	10/93	76r
Videography	event	483	10/93	76r
Wedding invitations and announcements	event	342	10/93	76r
Wedding reception	event	7000	10/93	76r

Fort Walton Beach, FL

Item	Per	Value	Date	Ref.
Composite, ACCRA index		94.10	12/94	2c
Alcoholic Beverages				
Beer, Miller Lite, Bud, 12-oz., ex deposit	6	3.91	12/94	2c
J & B Scotch	750-ml.	17.29	12/94	2c
Wine, Gallo Chablis blanc	1.5-lit	4.97	12/94	2c
Appliances				
Appliances (major), expenditures	year	153	91	81r
Average annual exp.				
Food, health care, personal goods, services	year	27020	91	81r
Charity				
Cash contributions, expenditures	year	839	91	81r
Clothing				
Apparel, men and boys, total expenditures	year	380	91	81r
Apparel, women and girls, total expenditures	year	660	91	81r
Footwear, expenditures	year	193	91	81r
Jeans, man's denim		34.09	12/94	2c
Shirt, man's dress shirt		28.10	12/94	2c
Undervest, boy's size 10-14, cotton	3	5.41	12/94	2c
Communications				
Long-distance telephone rate, day, addl. min., 1-10 mi.	min.	0.08	12/93	9s
Long-distance telephone rate, day, initial min., 1-10 mi.	min.	0.15	12/93	9s
Newspaper subscription, dly. and Sun. delivery	month	9.78	12/94	2c
Phone line, single, business, field visit	inst	86.00	12/93	9s
Phone line, single, business, no field visit	inst	54.50	12/93	9s
Phone line, single, residence, field visit	inst	76.00	12/93	9s
Phone line, single, residence, no field visit	inst	44.50	12/93	9s
Telephone bill, family of four	month	14.27	12/94	2c
Telephone service, expenditures	year	616	91	81r
Education				
Bar examination preparatory course	course	500.00-100	94	17s
Board, 4-year private college/university	year	2123	8/94	80s
Board, 4-year public college/university	year	2101	8/94	80s
Education, total expenditures	year	319	91	81r
Room, 4-year private college/university	year	2242	8/94	80s
Room, 4-year public college/university	year	1970	8/94	80s
Total cost, 4-year private college/university	year	13853	8/94	80s
Total cost, 4-year public college/university	year	5855	8/94	80s
Tuition, 2-year public college/university, in-state	year	1076	8/94	80s
Tuition, 4-year private college/university, in-state	year	9287	8/94	80s
Tuition, 4-year public college/university, in-state	year	1784	8/94	80s
Energy and Fuels				
Energy, combined forms, 1800 sq. ft.	mo.	127.68	12/94	2c
Fuel oil and other fuels, expenditures	year	56	91	81r
Gas, natural, expenditures	year	150	91	81r
Gas, reg unlead, taxes inc., cash, self-service	gal	1.18	12/94	2c
Gasoline and motor oil purchased	year	1152	91	81r
Gasoline, unleaded midgrade	gallon	1.21	4/93	82r

Values are in dollars or fractions of dollars. In the column headed *Ref*, references are shown to sources. Each reference is followed by a letter. These refer to the geographical level for which data were reported: s=State, r=Region, and c=City or metro. The abbreviation *ex* is used to mean *except* or *excluding*; *exp* stands for *expenditures*. For other abbreviations and further explanations, please see the Introduction.

Fort Walton Beach, FL - continued

Item	Per	Value	Date	Ref.
Energy and Fuels				
Gasoline, unleaded premium	gallon	1.30	4/93	82r
Gasoline, unleaded regular	gallon	1.10	4/93	82r
Entertainment				
Bowling, evening rate	game	1.87	12/94	2c
Concert ticket, Pearl Jam group	perf	20.00	94	50r
Entertainment, total expenditures	year	1266	91	81r
Fees and admissions, expenditures	year	306	91	81r
Monopoly game, Parker Brothers', No. 9	game	8.75	12/94	2c
Movie	adm	5.45	12/94	2c
Pets, toys, playground equipment, expenditures	year	271	91	81r
Reading, expenditures	year	131	91	81r
Televisions, radios, and sound equipment, expenditures	year	439	91	81r
Tennis balls, yellow, Wilson or Penn, 3	can	1.95	12/94	2c
Funerals				
Burial, immediate, container provided by funeral home		1370.36	1/95	54r
Cards, acknowledgment		14.83	1/95	54r
Casket, minimum alternative		192.52	1/95	54r
Cosmetology, hair care, etc.		102.27	1/95	54r
Cremation, direct, container provided by funeral home		1065.64	1/95	54r
Embalming		304.29	1/95	54r
Funeral, funeral home		287.83	1/95	54r
Funeral, other facility		284.14	1/95	54r
Graveside service		349.13	1/95	54r
Hearse, local		132.27	1/95	54r
Limousine, local		98.45	1/95	54r
Memorial service		270.59	1/95	54r
Service charge, professional, nondeclinable		933.59	1/95	54r
Visitation and viewing		225.83	1/95	54r
Groceries				
Groceries, ACCRA Index		95.20	12/94	2c
Apples, Red Delicious	lb.	0.73	12/94	82r
Baby food, strained vegetables, lowest price	4-4.5 oz.	0.36	12/94	2c
Bacon, sliced	lb.	1.67	12/94	82r
Bananas	lb.	0.41	12/94	2c
Bananas	lb.	0.42	12/94	82r
Beef or hamburger, ground	lb.	1.28	12/94	2c
Beef purchases	year	213	91	81r
Beverage purchases, alcoholic	year	249	91	81r
Beverage purchases, nonalcoholic	year	207	91	81r
Bologna, all beef or mixed	lb.	2.27	12/94	82r
Bread, white	24-oz.	0.78	12/94	2c
Bread, white, pan	lb.	0.68	12/94	82r
Cabbage	lb.	0.42	12/94	82r
Carrots, short trimmed and topped	lb.	0.53	12/94	82r
Cereals and bakery products purchases	year	345	91	81r
Cereals and cereals products purchases	year	127	91	81r
Cheddar cheese, natural	lb.	3.58	12/94	82r
Cheese, Kraft grated Parmesan	8-oz.	3.38	12/94	2c
Chicken breast, bone-in	lb.	1.71	12/94	82r
Chicken, fresh, whole	lb.	0.78	12/94	82r
Chicken, whole fryer	lb.	0.62	12/94	2c
Chuck roast, USDA choice, boneless	lb.	2.26	12/94	82r
Cigarettes, Winston, Kings	carton	16.16	12/94	2c
Coffee, vacuum-packed	13 oz.	3.02	12/94	2c
Corn Flakes, Kellogg's or Post Toasties	18 oz.	1.89	12/94	2c
Corn, frozen, whole kernel, lowest price	10 oz.	0.66	12/94	2c
Crackers, soda, salted	lb.	1.27	12/94	82r
Cucumbers	lb.	0.65	12/94	82r
Dairy products (other) purchases	year	141	91	81r
Eggs, Grade A large	dozen	0.70	12/94	2c
Eggs, Grade A large	dozen	0.87	12/94	82r
Fish and seafood purchases	year	72	91	81r
Flour, white, all purpose	lb.	0.23	12/94	82r
Food purchases, food eaten at home	year	2381	91	81r
Foods purchased away from home, not prepared by consumer	year	1696	91	81r

Fort Walton Beach, FL - continued

Item	Per	Value	Date	Ref.
Groceries - continued				
Frankfurters, all meat or all beef	lb.	1.74	12/94	82r
Fruits and vegetables purchases	year	380	91	81r
Grapefruit	lb.	0.45	12/94	82r
Grapes, Thompson seedless	lb.	2.30	12/94	82r
Ground beef, 100% beef	lb.	1.37	12/94	82r
Ground chuck, 100% beef	lb.	1.97	12/94	82r
Ham, boneless, exc. canned	lb.	2.54	12/94	82r
Ice cream, prepackaged, bulk, regular	1/2 gal.	2.47	12/94	82r
Lemons	lb.	1.02	12/94	82r
Lettuce, iceberg	lb.	0.96	12/94	82r
Lettuce, iceberg	head	0.89	12/94	2c
Margarine, Blue Bonnet or Parkay cubes	lb.	0.54	12/94	2c
Margarine, stick	lb.	0.77	12/94	82r
Meats, poultry, fish, and eggs purchases	year	655	91	81r
Milk and cream (fresh) purchases	year	130	91	81r
Milk, whole	1/2 gal.	1.35	12/94	2c
Orange juice, frozen concentrate 12-oz. can	16 oz.	1.36	12/94	82r
Orange juice, Minute Maid frozen	12-oz.	1.11	12/94	2c
Oranges, Navel	lb.	0.54	12/94	82r
Peaches, halves or slices, Hunt's, Del Monte, or Libby's	29-oz.	1.30	12/94	2c
Pears, Anjou	lb.	0.81	12/94	82r
Peas, sweet, Del Monte or Green Giant	15-17 oz.	0.56	12/94	2c
Pork chops, center cut, bone-in	lb.	3.07	12/94	82r
Pork purchases	year	142	91	81r
Potato chips	16-oz.	3.15	12/94	82r
Potatoes, frozen, French fried	lb.	0.82	12/94	82r
Potatoes, white	lb.	0.34	12/94	82r
Potatoes, white or red	10-lb. sack	2.65	12/94	2c
Rice, white, long grain, uncooked	lb.	0.48	12/94	82r
Round roast, USDA choice, boneless	lb.	2.91	12/94	82r
Sausage, fresh	lb.	1.82	12/94	82r
Sausage, Jimmy Dean, 100% pork	lb.	2.19	12/94	2c
Shortening, vegetable oil blends	lb.	0.75	12/94	82r
Shortening, vegetable, Crisco	3-lb.	2.41	12/94	2c
Soft drink, Coca Cola, ex deposit	2 lit	1.06	12/94	2c
Spaghetti and macaroni	lb.	0.87	12/94	82r
Steak, rib eye, USDA choice, boneless	lb.	6.85	12/94	82r
Steak, round, graded & ungraded, exc. USDA prime & choice	lb.	2.96	12/94	82r
Steak, round, USDA choice, boneless	lb.	3.17	12/94	82r
Steak, sirloin, USDA choice, boneless	lb.	4.12	12/94	82r
Steak, t-bone	lb.	5.58	12/94	2c
Steak, T-bone, USDA choice, bone-in	lb.	5.63	12/94	82r
Sugar and other sweets, eaten at home, expenditures	year	93	91	81r
Sugar, cane or beet	4 lbs.	1.59	12/94	2c
Sugar, white, all sizes	lb.	0.39	12/94	82r
Tobacco products and smoking supplies, total expenditures	year	286	91	81r
Tomatoes, field grown	lb.	1.36	12/94	82r
Tomatoes, Hunt's or Del Monte	14.5 oz.	0.65	12/94	2c
Tuna, chunk, light	lb.	1.94	12/94	82r
Tuna, chunk, light, oil-packed	6.125-6.5 oz.	0.63	12/94	2c
Turkey, frozen, whole	lb.	0.96	12/94	82r
Yogurt, natural, fruit flavored	8 oz.	0.58	12/94	82r
Goods and Services				
Miscellaneous goods and services, ACCRA Index		97.10	12/94	2c
Health Care				
Health care, ACCRA Index		113.70	12/94	2c
Adenosine, emergency room	treat	100.00	95	23r
Antibiotic ointment, Polysporin	1.5 oz.	3.49	12/94	2c
Bladder tap, superpubic, infant, emergency room	treat	119.00	95	23r

Values are in dollars or fractions of dollars. In the column headed *Ref*, references are shown to sources. Each reference is followed by a letter. These refer to the geographical level for which data were reported: s = State, r = Region, and c = City or metro. The abbreviation *ex* is used to mean *except* or *excluding*; *exp* stands for *expenditures*. For other abbreviations and further explanations, please see the Introduction.

Fort Walton Beach, FL - continued

Item	Per	Value	Date	Ref.
Health Care				
Blood analysis, emergency room	treat	25.00	95	23r
Blood tests, abdominal pain, emergency room	treat	25.00	95	23r
Burn dressing, emergency room	treat	266.00	95	23r
Cardiology interpretation, emergency room	treat	26.00	95	23r
Chest X-ray, emergency room	treat	78.00	95	23r
Childbirth, Cesarean delivery, hospital charge	birth	5462.00	12/91	69r
Childbirth, Cesarean delivery, physician charge	birth	2228.00	12/91	69r
Childbirth, normal delivery, hospital charge	birth	2943.00	12/91	69r
Childbirth, normal delivery, physician charge	birth	1619.00	12/91	69r
Defibrillation pads, emergency room	treat	6.00	95	23r
Dentist's fee, adult teeth cleaning and periodic oral exam	visit	57.80	12/94	2c
Doctor's fee, routine exam, established patient	visit	57.00	12/94	2c
Drugs, expenditures	year	297	91	81r
Gastric tube insertion, nasal, emergency room	treat	25.00	95	23r
Health care, total expenditures	year	1600	91	81r
Health insurance expenditures	year	637	91	81r
Heart monitor, emergency room	treat	40.00	95	23r
Hospital care, semiprivate room	day	336.67	12/94	2c
Insurance premium, family medical care	month	301.92	1/95	41s
Intravenous fluids, emergency room	treat	130.00	95	23r
Intravenous fluids, emergency room	liter	26.00	95	23r
Intravenous line, central, emergency room	treat	342.00	95	23r
Liver function tests, abdominal pain, emergency room	treat	26.00	95	23r
Medical care charges, total, emergency room, third-degree burns	treat	2101.00	95	23r
Medical care charges, total, emergency, infant with fever	treat	628.00	95	23r
Medical services expenditures	year	573	91	81r
Medical supplies expenditures	year	93	91	81r
Morphine, emergency room	treat	34.00	95	23r
Nursing care and facilities charges, emergency room	treat	252.00	95	23r
Nursing care and facilities charges, emergency, infant with fever	treat	252.00	95	23r
Nursing care and facilities charges, emergency, third-degree burns	treat	861.00	95	23r
Physician's charges, emergency, infant with fever	treat	212.00	95	23r
Physician's charges, emergency, third-degree burns	treat	372.00	95	23r
Physician's fee, emergency room	treat	372.00	95	23r
Physician's fee, general practitioner	visit	51.20	12/93	60r
Surgery, open-heart	proc	42374.00	1/93	14r
Ultrasound, abdominal, emergency room	treat	276.00	95	23r
Urinalysis, emergency room	treat	20.00	95	23r
Urinalysis, infant, emergency room	treat	20.00	95	23r
X-rays, emergency room	treat	78.00	95	23r
Household Goods				
Appl. repair, service call, wash mach	min. lab. chg.	35.40	12/94	2c
Floor coverings, expenditures	year	48	91	81r
Furniture, expenditures	year	280	91	81r
Household equipment, misc. expenditures	year	342	91	81r
Household expenditures, miscellaneous	year	256	91	81r
Household furnishings and equipment, expenditures	year	988	91	81r
Household operations expenditures	year	468	91	81r
Household textiles, expenditures	year	95	91	81r
Housekeeping supplies, expenditures	year	380	91	81r
Laundry and cleaning supplies, expenditures	year	109	91	81r
Laundry detergent, Tide Ultra, Bold, or Cheer	42 oz.	3.38	12/94	2c
Postage and stationery, expenditures	year	105	91	81r

Fort Walton Beach, FL - continued

Item	Per	Value	Date	Ref.
Household Goods - continued				
Tissues, facial, Kleenex brand	175	0.95	12/94	2c
Housing				
Housing, ACCRA Index		79.80	12/94	2c
Add garage/carport		6,980	3/95	74r
Add room(s)		11,403	3/95	74r
Apartment condominium or co-op, median	unit	68600	12/94	62r
Dwellings (owned), expenditures	year	2428	91	81r
Enclose porch/patio/breezeway		4,572	3/95	74r
Finish room in basement/attic		3,794	3/95	74r
Home, existing, single-family, median	unit	120200	12/94	62r
House payment, principal and interest, 25% down payment	mo.	623	12/94	2c
House, 1800 sq ft, 8000 sq ft lot, new, urban, utilities	total	100500	12/94	2c
Maintenance, repairs, insurance, and other housing expenditures	year	531	91	81r
Mortgage interest and charges expenditures	year	1506	91	81r
Mtge. rate, incl. points and orig. fee, 30-year conv. fixed or ARM	mo.	9.30	12/94	2c
Princ. & int., mortgage, median-price exist. sing.-family home	mo.	540	12/94	62r
Property taxes expenditures	year	391	91	81r
Redesign, restructure more than half of home's interior		17,641	3/95	74r
Rent, apartment, 2 br., 1 1/2-2 baths, unfurnished, 950 sq ft, water	mo.	389	12/94	2c
Rental units expenditures	year	1264	91	81r
Insurance and Pensions				
Auto insurance, private passenger	year	753.93	12/94	71s
Insurance and pensions, personal, expenditures	year	2395	91	81r
Insurance, life and other personal, expenditures	year	368	91	81r
Pensions and Social Security, expenditures	year	2027	91	81r
Personal Goods				
Shampoo, Alberto VO5	15-oz.	0.85	12/94	2c
Toothpaste, Crest or Colgate	6-7 oz.	2.09	12/94	2c
Personal Services				
Dry cleaning, man's 2-pc. suit		5.95	12/94	2c
Haircut, man's barbershop, no styling		8.25	12/94	2c
Haircut, woman's shampoo, trim, blow-dry		17.95	12/94	2c
Personal services expenditures	year	212	91	81r
Restaurant Food				
Chicken, fried, thigh and drumstick		1.83	12/94	2c
Dining expenditures, family	week	33.83	94	73r
Hamburger with cheese	1/4 lb.	1.88	12/94	2c
Pizza, Pizza Hut or Pizza Inn	12-13 in.	8.68	12/94	2c
Taxes				
Taxes, Federal income, expenditures	year	2275	91	81r
Taxes, personal, expenditures	year	2715	91	81r
Taxes, State and local income, expenditures	year	365	91	81r
Transportation				
Transportation, ACCRA Index		99.70	12/94	2c
Cars and trucks purchased, new	year	1306	91	81r
Cars and trucks purchased, used	year	942	91	81r
Driver's learning permit fee	perm	20.00	1/94	84s
Driver's license fee	orig	20.00	1/94	84s
Driver's license fee, duplicate	lic	10.00	1/94	84s
Driver's license reinstatement fee, min.	susp	25.00	1/94	85s
Driver's license renewal fee	renew	15.00	1/94	84s
Identification card, nondriver	card	3.00	1/94	83s
Motorcycle learning permit fee	perm	20.00	1/94	84s
Motorcycle license fee	orig	20.00	1/94	84s
Motorcycle license fee, duplicate	lic	10.00	1/94	84s
Motorcycle license renewal fee	renew	15.00	1/94	84s
Public transportation expenditures	year	249	91	81r
Tire balance, computer or spin bal., front	wheel	6.25	12/94	2c

Values are in dollars or fractions of dollars. In the column headed *Ref*, references are shown to sources. Each reference is followed by a letter. These refer to the geographical level for which data were reported: s = State, r = Region, and c = City or metro. The abbreviation *ex* is used to mean *except* or *excluding*; *exp* stands for *expenditures*. For other abbreviations and further explanations, please see the Introduction.

Fort Walton Beach, FL - continued

Item	Per	Value	Date	Ref.
Transportation				
Transportation expenditures, total	year	5307	91	81r
Vehicle finance charges	year	346	91	81r
Vehicle insurance expenditures	year	544	91	81r
Vehicle maintenance and repairs expenditures	year	600	91	81r
Vehicle purchases	year	2275	91	81r
Vehicle rental, leases, licenses, etc. expenditures	year	141	91	81r
Vehicles purchased, other than cars and trucks	year	27	91	81r
Utilities				
Utilities, ACCRA Index		108.30	12/94	2c
Electricity expenditures	year	950	91	81r
Electricity, 1800 sq. ft., new home	mo.	127.68	12/94	2c
Utilities, fuels, and public services, total expenditures	year	2000	91	81r
Water and other public services, expenditures	year	227	91	81r
Weddings				
Bridal attendants' gowns	event	750	10/93	76r
Bridal gown	event	852	10/93	76r
Bridal headpiece and veil	event	167	10/93	76r
Bride's wedding band	event	708	10/93	76r
Clergy	event	224	10/93	76r
Engagement ring	event	2756	10/93	76r
Flowers	event	863	10/93	76r
Formal wear for groom	event	106	10/93	76r
Groom's attendants' formal wear	event	530	10/93	76r
Groom's wedding band	event	402	10/93	76r
Music	event	600	10/93	76r
Photography	event	1088	10/93	76r
Shoes for bride	event	50	10/93	76r
Videography	event	483	10/93	76r
Wedding invitations and announcements	event	342	10/93	76r
Wedding reception	event	7000	10/93	76r

Fort Wayne, IN

Item	Per	Value	Date	Ref.
Composite, ACCRA index		94.00	12/94	2c
Alcoholic Beverages				
Beer, Miller Lite, Bud, 12-oz., ex deposit	6	3.72	12/94	2c
J & B Scotch	750-ml.	15.55	12/94	2c
Wine, Gallo Chablis blanc	1.5-lit	4.64	12/94	2c
Appliances				
Appliances (major), expenditures	year	131	91	81r
Average annual exp.				
Food, health care, personal goods, services	year	25935	91	81r
Charity				
Cash contributions, expenditures	year	745	91	81r
Clothing				
Apparel, men and boys, total expenditures	year	332	91	81r
Apparel, women and girls, total expenditures	year	578	91	81r
Footwear, expenditures	year	164	91	81r
Jeans, man's denim		33.39	12/94	2c
Shirt, man's dress shirt		29.90	12/94	2c
Undervest, boy's size 10-14, cotton	3	3.04	12/94	2c
Communications				
Long-distance telephone rate, day, addl. min., 1-10 mi.	min.	0.10	12/93	9s
Long-distance telephone rate, day, initial min., 1-10 mi.	min.	0.18	12/93	9s
Newspaper subscription, dly. and Sun. delivery	month	13.04	12/94	2c
Phone line, single, business, field visit	inst	59.00	12/93	9s
Phone line, single, business, no field visit	inst	59.00	12/93	9s
Phone line, single, residence, field visit	inst	47.00	12/93	9s

Fort Wayne, IN - continued

Item	Per	Value	Date	Ref.
Communications - continued				
Phone line, single, residence, no field visit	inst	47.00	12/93	9s
Telephone bill, family of four	month	20.26	12/94	2c
Telephone service, expenditures	year	547	91	81r
Education				
Board, 4-year private college/university	year	2095	8/94	80s
Board, 4-year public college/university	year	2300	8/94	80s
Education, total expenditures	year	394	91	81r
Room, 4-year private college/university	year	1784	8/94	80s
Room, 4-year public college/university	year	1718	8/94	80s
Total cost, 4-year private college/university	year	15045	8/94	80s
Total cost, 4-year public college/university	year	6639	8/94	80s
Tuition, 2-year public college/university, in-state	year	1737	8/94	80s
Tuition, 4-year private college/university, in-state	year	11165	8/94	80s
Tuition, 4-year public college/university, in-state	year	2621	8/94	80s
Energy and Fuels				
Energy, combined forms, 1800 sq. ft.	mo.	118.60	12/94	2c
Energy, exc. electricity, 1800 sq. ft.	mo.	51.95	12/94	2c
Fuel oil and other fuels, expenditures	year	83	91	81r
Gas, natural, expenditures	year	373	91	81r
Gas, reg unlead, taxes inc., cash, self-service	gal	0.99	12/94	2c
Gasoline and motor oil purchased	year	1000	91	81r
Gasoline, unleaded midgrade	gallon	1.15	4/93	82r
Gasoline, unleaded premium	gallon	1.23	4/93	82r
Gasoline, unleaded regular	gallon	1.07	4/93	82r
Entertainment				
Bowling, evening rate	game	1.79	12/94	2c
Entertainment, total expenditures	year	1356	91	81r
Fees and admissions, expenditures	year	347	91	81r
Monopoly game, Parker Brothers', No. 9	game	9.63	12/94	2c
Movie	adm	5.56	12/94	2c
Pets, toys, playground equipment, expenditures	year	270	91	81r
Reading, expenditures	year	160	91	81r
Televisions, radios, and sound equipment, expenditures	year	433	91	81r
Tennis balls, yellow, Wilson or Penn, 3	can	1.93	12/94	2c
Funerals				
Burial, immediate, container provided by funeral home		1268.31	1/95	54r
Cards, acknowledgment		26.12	1/95	54r
Casket, minimum alternative		198.03	1/95	54r
Cosmetology, hair care, etc.		122.19	1/95	54r
Cremation, direct, container provided by funeral home		977.81	1/95	54r
Embalming		334.00	1/95	54r
Funeral, funeral home		321.16	1/95	54r
Funeral, other facility		317.73	1/95	54r
Graveside service		292.48	1/95	54r
Hearse, local		153.20	1/95	54r
Limousine, local		123.52	1/95	54r
Memorial service		356.30	1/95	54r
Service charge, professional, nondeclinable		968.24	1/95	54r
Visitation and viewing		332.66	1/95	54r
Groceries				
Groceries, ACCRA Index		94.40	12/94	2c
Apples, Red Delicious	lb.	0.68	12/94	82r
Baby food, strained vegetables, lowest price	4-4.5 oz.	0.36	12/94	2c
Bacon, sliced	lb.	1.88	12/94	82r
Bananas	lb.	0.39	12/94	2c
Bananas	lb.	0.41	12/94	82r
Beef or hamburger, ground	lb.	1.37	12/94	2c
Beef purchases	year	197	91	81r
Beef, stew, boneless	lb.	2.52	12/94	82r
Beverage purchases, alcoholic	year	293	91	81r

Values are in dollars or fractions of dollars. In the column headed *Ref*, references are shown to sources. Each reference is followed by a letter. These refer to the geographical level for which data were reported: s = State, r = Region, and c = City or metro. The abbreviation *ex* is used to mean *except* or *excluding*; *exp* stands for expenditures. For other abbreviations and further explanations, please see the Introduction.

Fort Wayne, IN - continued

Item	Per	Value	Date	Ref.
Groceries				
Beverage purchases, nonalcoholic	year	203	91	81r
Bologna, all beef or mixed	lb.	2.12	12/94	82r
Bread, white	24-oz.	0.52	12/94	2c
Bread, white, pan	lb.	0.76	12/94	82r
Cabbage	lb.	0.44	12/94	82r
Carrots, short trimmed and topped	lb.	0.44	12/94	82r
Cereals and bakery products purchases	year	347	91	81r
Cereals and cereals products purchases	year	119	91	81r
Cheddar cheese, natural	lb.	3.28	12/94	82r
Cheese, Kraft grated Parmesan	8-oz.	2.88	12/94	2c
Chicken breast, bone-in	lb.	1.61	12/94	82r
Chicken, fresh, whole	lb.	0.89	12/94	82r
Chicken, whole fryer	lb.	0.92	12/94	2c
Chuck roast, USDA choice, boneless	lb.	2.33	12/94	82r
Cigarettes, Winston, Kings	carton	13.98	12/94	2c
Coffee, 100%, ground roast, all sizes	lb.	4.28	12/94	82r
Coffee, vacuum-packed	13 oz.	3.75	12/94	2c
Cookies, chocolate chip	lb.	2.72	12/94	82r
Corn Flakes, Kellogg's or Post Toasties	18 oz.	3.11	12/94	2c
Corn, frozen, whole kernel, lowest price	10 oz.	0.73	12/94	2c
Dairy products (other) purchases	year	148	91	81r
Eggs, Grade A large	dozen	0.51	12/94	2c
Eggs, Grade A large	dozen	0.76	12/94	82r
Fish and seafood purchases	year	61	91	81r
Flour, white, all purpose	lb.	0.22	12/94	82r
Food purchases, food eaten at home	year	2313	91	81r
Foods purchased away from home, not prepared by consumer	year	1709	91	81r
Fruits and vegetables purchases	year	372	91	81r
Grapefruit	lb.	0.47	12/94	82r
Grapes, Thompson seedless	lb.	2.15	12/94	82r
Ground beef, 100% beef	lb.	1.37	12/94	82r
Ground chuck, 100% beef	lb.	1.81	12/94	82r
Ham, boneless, exc. canned	lb.	2.16	12/94	82r
Ice cream, prepackaged, bulk, regular	1/2 gal.	2.48	12/94	82r
Lemons	lb.	1.08	12/94	82r
Lettuce, iceberg	lb.	0.81	12/94	82r
Lettuce, iceberg	head	0.79	12/94	2c
Margarine, Blue Bonnet or Parkay cubes	lb.	0.64	12/94	2c
Margarine, stick	lb.	0.81	12/94	82r
Meats, poultry, fish, and eggs purchases	year	591	91	81r
Milk and cream (fresh) purchases	year	132	91	81r
Milk, whole	1/2 gal.	1.32	12/94	2c
Orange juice, frozen concentrate 12-oz. can	16 oz.	1.41	12/94	82r
Orange juice, Minute Maid frozen	12-oz.	1.13	12/94	2c
Oranges, Navel	lb.	0.56	12/94	82r
Peaches, halves or slices, Hunt's, Del Monte, or Libby's	29-oz.	1.27	12/94	2c
Peanut butter, creamy, all sizes	lb.	1.81	12/94	82r
Peas, sweet, Del Monte or Green Giant	15-17 oz.	0.49	12/94	2c
Pork chops, center cut, bone-in	lb.	2.76	12/94	82r
Pork purchases	year	130	91	81r
Potato chips	16-oz.	2.81	12/94	82r
Potatoes, frozen, French fried	lb.	0.83	12/94	82r
Potatoes, white	lb.	0.28	12/94	82r
Potatoes, white or red	10-lb. sack	1.83	12/94	2c
Round roast, USDA choice, boneless	lb.	2.90	12/94	82r
Sausage, Jimmy Dean, 100% pork	lb.	2.85	12/94	2c
Shortening, vegetable oil blends	lb.	0.88	12/94	82r
Shortening, vegetable, Crisco	3-lb.	2.29	12/94	2c
Soft drink, Coca Cola, ex deposit	2 lit	0.98	12/94	2c
Spaghetti and macaroni	lb.	0.78	12/94	82r
Steak, rib eye, USDA choice, boneless	lb.	6.15	12/94	82r
Steak, round, graded & ungraded, exc. USDA prime & choice	lb.	2.72	12/94	82r
Steak, round, USDA choice, boneless	lb.	3.02	12/94	82r
Steak, sirloin, USDA choice, boneless	lb.	3.85	12/94	82r
Steak, t-bone	lb.	3.31	12/94	2c

Fort Wayne, IN - continued

Item	Per	Value	Date	Ref.
Groceries - continued				
Steak, T-bone, USDA choice, bone-in	lb.	5.38	12/94	82r
Sugar and other sweets, eaten at home, expenditures	year	91	91	81r
Sugar, cane or beet	4 lbs.	1.33	12/94	2c
Sugar, white, all sizes	lb.	0.36	12/94	82r
Tobacco products and smoking supplies, total expenditures	year	298	91	81r
Tomatoes, field grown	lb.	1.36	12/94	82r
Tomatoes, Hunt's or Del Monte	14.5 oz.	0.74	12/94	2c
Tuna, chunk, light	lb.	1.94	12/94	82r
Tuna, chunk, light, oil-packed	6.125-6.5 oz.	0.61	12/94	2c
Turkey, frozen, whole	lb.	0.96	12/94	82r
Yogurt, natural, fruit flavored	8 oz.	0.62	12/94	82r
Goods and Services				
Miscellaneous goods and services, ACCRA Index		93.30	12/94	2c
Health Care				
Health care, ACCRA Index		87.60	12/94	2c
Antibiotic ointment, Polysporin	1.5 oz.	3.98	12/94	2c
Childbirth, Cesarean delivery, hospital charge	birth	5101.00	12/91	69r
Childbirth, Cesarean delivery, physician charge	birth	2234.00	12/91	69r
Childbirth, normal delivery, hospital charge	birth	2891.00	12/91	69r
Childbirth, normal delivery, physician charge	birth	1623.00	12/91	69r
Dentist's fee, adult teeth cleaning and periodic oral exam	visit	44.00	12/94	2c
Doctor's fee, routine exam, established patient	visit	35.00	12/94	2c
Drugs, expenditures	year	248	91	81r
Health care, total expenditures	year	1336	91	81r
Health insurance expenditures	year	550	91	81r
Hospital care, semiprivate room	day	346.67	12/94	2c
Immunization, DTP, measles, mumps, rubella, polio	inject	74.00	8/93	90c
Insurance premium, family medical care	month	353.94	1/95	41s
Medical services expenditures	year	457	91	81r
Medical supplies expenditures	year	82	91	81r
Household Goods				
Appl. repair, service call, wash mach	min. lab. chg.	31.36	12/94	2c
Floor coverings, expenditures	year	105	91	81r
Furniture, expenditures	year	291	91	81r
Household equipment, misc. expenditures	year	341	91	81r
Household expenditures, miscellaneous	year	162	91	81r
Household furnishings and equipment, expenditures	year	1042	91	81r
Household operations expenditures	year	365	91	81r
Household textiles, expenditures	year	101	91	81r
Housekeeping supplies, expenditures	year	390	91	81r
Laundry and cleaning supplies, expenditures	year	110	91	81r
Laundry detergent, Tide Ultra, Bold, or Cheer	42 oz.	3.33	12/94	2c
Postage and stationery, expenditures	year	115	91	81r
Tissues, facial, Kleenex brand	175	1.09	12/94	2c
Housing				
Housing, ACCRA Index		94.00	12/94	2c
Add garage/carport		8,479	3/95	74r
Add room(s)		21,347	3/95	74r
Apartment condominium or co-op, median	unit	87100	12/94	62r
Bathroom addition, average cost	add	9734.00	3/95	13r
Bathroom remodeling, average cost	remod	6414.00	3/95	13r
Bedroom, master suite addition, average cost	add	27122.00	3/95	13r
Deck addition, average cost	add	6665.00	3/95	13r
Dwellings (owned), expenditures	year	2566	91	81r

Values are in dollars or fractions of dollars. In the column headed *Ref*, references are shown to sources. Each reference is followed by a letter. These refer to the geographical level for which data were reported: s = State, r = Region, and c = City or metro. The abbreviation *ex* is used to mean *except* or *excluding*; *exp* stands for *expenditures*. For other abbreviations and further explanations, please see the Introduction.

Fort Wayne, IN - continued

Item	Per	Value	Date	Ref.
Housing				
Enclose porch/patio/breezeway		4,556	3/95	74r
Exterior remodeling, average cost	remod	15395.00	3/95	13r
Family room addition, average cost	add	27658.00	3/95	13r
Finish room in basement/attic		5,074	3/95	74r
Home, existing, single-family, median	unit	106500	12/94	62r
House payment, principal and interest, 25% down payment	mo.	707	12/94	2c
House, 1800 sq ft, 8000 sq ft lot, new, urban, utilities	total	112925	12/94	2c
Kitchen remodeling, major, average cost	remod	17084.00	3/95	13r
Kitchen remodeling, minor, average cost	remod	5804.00	3/95	13r
Maintenance, repairs, insurance, and other housing expenditures	year	484	91	81r
Mortgage interest and charges expenditures	year	1443	91	81r
Mtge. rate, incl. points and orig. fee, 30-year conv. fixed or ARM	mo.	9.41	12/94	2c
Office, home addition, average cost	add	8121.00	3/95	13r
Princ. & int., mortgage, median-price exist. sing.-family home	mo.	515	12/94	62r
Property taxes expenditures	year	639	91	81r
Redesign, restructure more than half of home's interior		9,114	3/95	74r
Rent, apartment, 2 br., 1 1/2-2 baths, unfurnished, 950 sq ft, water	mo.	536	12/94	2c
Rental units expenditures	year	1200	91	81r
Sun-space addition, average cost	add	23768.00	3/95	13r
Wing addition, two-story, average cost	add	50410.00	3/95	13r
Insurance and Pensions				
Auto insurance, private passenger	year	586.58	12/94	71s
Insurance and pensions, personal, expenditures	year	2408	91	81r
Insurance, life and other personal, expenditures	year	355	91	81r
Pensions and Social Security, expenditures	year	2053	91	81r
Legal Assistance				
Legal work, law firm associate	hour	90		10r
Legal work, law firm partner	hour	139		10r
Personal Goods				
Shampoo, Alberto VO5	15-oz.	0.84	12/94	2c
Toothpaste, Crest or Colgate	6-7 oz.	1.85	12/94	2c
Personal Services				
Dry cleaning, man's 2-pc. suit		6.55	12/94	2c
Haircut, man's barbershop, no styling		8.35	12/94	2c
Haircut, woman's shampoo, trim, blow-dry		19.90	12/94	2c
Personal services expenditures	year	203	91	81r
Restaurant Food				
Chicken, fried, thigh and drumstick		1.98	12/94	2c
Dining expenditures, family	week	30.03	94	73r
Hamburger with cheese	1/4 lb.	1.74	12/94	2c
Pizza, Pizza Hut or Pizza Inn	12-13 in.	6.80	12/94	2c
Taxes				
Taxes, Federal income, expenditures	year	1756	91	81r
Taxes, personal, expenditures	year	2426	91	81r
Taxes, State and local income, expenditures	year	568	91	81r
Transportation				
Transportation, ACCRA Index		89.50	12/94	2c
Bus fare, one-way	trip	1.00	12/95	1c
Bus fare, up to 10 miles	one-way	1.00	12/94	2c
Cars and trucks purchased, new	year	891	91	81r
Cars and trucks purchased, used	year	1155	91	81r
Driver's learning permit fee	perm	2.00	1/94	84s
Driver's license fee	orig	6.00	1/94	84s
Driver's license fee, duplicate	lic	3.00	1/94	84s
Driver's license renewal fee	renew	6.00	1/94	84s
Identification card, nondriver	card	4.00	1/94	83s
Motorcycle learning permit fee	perm	2.00	1/94	84s

Fort Wayne, IN - continued

Item	Per	Value	Date	Ref.
Transportation - continued				
Motorcycle license fee	orig	6.00	1/94	84s
Motorcycle license fee, duplicate	lic	3.00	1/94	84s
Motorcycle license renewal fee	renew	6.00	1/94	84s
Public transportation expenditures	year	209	91	81r
Tire balance, computer or spin bal., front	wheel	5.90	12/94	2c
Transportation expenditures, total	year	4792	91	81r
Vehicle finance charges	year	300	91	81r
Vehicle insurance expenditures	year	485	91	81r
Vehicle maintenance and repairs expenditures	year	534	91	81r
Vehicle purchases	year	2068	91	81r
Vehicle rental, leases, licenses, etc. expenditures	year	197	91	81r
Vehicles purchased, other than cars and trucks	year	22	91	81r
Utilities				
Utilities, ACCRA Index		105.40	12/94	2c
Electricity expenditures	year	668	91	81r
Electricity, (part.), other, 1800 sq. ft., new home	mo.	66.65	12/94	2c
Electricity, summer, 250 KWh	month	22.69	8/93	64c
Electricity, summer, 500 KWh	month	36.60	8/93	64c
Electricity, summer, 750 KWh	month	49.22	8/93	64c
Electricity, summer, 1000 KWh	month	61.84	8/93	64c
Utilities, fuels, and public services, total expenditures	year	1838	91	81r
Water and other public services, expenditures	year	167	91	81r
Weddings				
Bridal attendants' gowns	event	750	10/93	76r
Bridal gown	event	852	10/93	76r
Bridal headpiece and veil	event	167	10/93	76r
Bride's wedding band	event	708	10/93	76r
Clergy	event	224	10/93	76r
Engagement ring	event	2756	10/93	76r
Flowers	event	863	10/93	76r
Formal wear for groom	event	106	10/93	76r
Groom's attendants' formal wear	event	530	10/93	76r
Groom's wedding band	event	402	10/93	76r
Music	event	600	10/93	76r
Photography	event	1088	10/93	76r
Shoes for bride	event	50	10/93	76r
Videography	event	483	10/93	76r
Wedding invitations and announcements	event	342	10/93	76r
Wedding reception	event	7000	10/93	76r

Fort Worth, TX

Item	Per	Value	Date	Ref.
Composite, ACCRA index		93.70	12/94	2c
Alcoholic Beverages				
Beer, Miller Lite, Bud, 12-oz., ex deposit	6	4.21	12/94	2c
J & B Scotch	750-ml.	18.03	12/94	2c
Wine, Gallo Chablis blanc	1.5-lit	4.53	12/94	2c
Appliances				
Appliances (major), expenditures	year	153	91	81r
Average annual exp.				
Food, health care, personal goods, services	year	27020	91	81r
Charity				
Cash contributions, expenditures	year	839	91	81r
Clothing				
Apparel, men and boys, total expenditures	year	380	91	81r
Apparel, women and girls, total expenditures	year	660	91	81r
Footwear, expenditures	year	193	91	81r
Jeans, man's denim		25.76	12/94	2c
Shirt, man's dress shirt		30.09	12/94	2c
Undervest, boy's size 10-14, cotton	3	3.96	12/94	2c

Values are in dollars or fractions of dollars. In the column headed *Ref*, references are shown to sources. Each reference is followed by a letter. These refer to the geographical level for which data were reported: s = State, r = Region, and c = City or metro. The abbreviation *ex* is used to mean *except* or *excluding*; *exp* stands for expenditures. For other abbreviations and further explanations, please see the Introduction.

Fort Worth, TX - continued

Item	Per	Value	Date	Ref.
Communications				
Long-distance telephone rate, day, addl. min., 1-10 mi.	min.	0.08	12/93	9s
Long-distance telephone rate, day, initial min., 1-10 mi.	min.	0.10	12/93	9s
Newspaper subscription, dly. and Sun. delivery	month	10.95	12/94	2c
Phone line, single, business, field visit	inst	71.90	12/93	9s
Phone line, single, business, no field visit	inst	57.30	12/93	9s
Phone line, single, residence, field visit	inst	52.95	12/93	9s
Phone line, single, residence, no field visit	inst	38.35	12/93	9s
Telephone bill, family of four	month	16.62	12/94	2c
Telephone service, expenditures	year	616	91	81r
Telephone, business, addl. line, touch tone	month	1.75	10/91	25c
Telephone, business, connection charges, touch tone	inst	69.13	10/91	25c
Telephone, business, key system line, touch tone	month	34.11	10/91	25c
Telephone, business, PBX line, touch tone	month	35.09	10/91	25c
Telephone, business, single ln., touch tone	month	29.61	10/91	25c
Telephone, business, touch tone, inside wiring maintenance plan	month	2.25	10/91	25c
Telephone, residential, flat rate	mo.	9.85	12/93	8c
Education				
Board, 4-year private college/university	year	2084	8/94	80s
Board, 4-year public college/university	year	1675	8/94	80s
Education, total expenditures	year	319	91	81r
Room, 4-year private college/university	year	1840	8/94	80s
Room, 4-year public college/university	year	1756	8/94	80s
Total cost, 4-year private college/university	year	11876	8/94	80s
Total cost, 4-year public college/university	year	4935	8/94	80s
Tuition, 2-year public college/university, in-state	year	625	8/94	80s
Tuition, 4-year private college/university, in-state	year	7952	8/94	80s
Tuition, 4-year public college/university, in-state	year	1503	8/94	80s
Energy and Fuels				
Energy, combined forms, 1800 sq. ft.	mo.	128.34	12/94	2c
Energy, exc. electricity, 1800 sq. ft.	mo.	18.61	12/94	2c
Fuel oil and other fuels, expenditures	year	56	91	81r
Gas, natural, expenditures	year	150	91	81r
Gas, reg unlead, taxes inc., cash, self-service	gal	1.14	12/94	2c
Gasoline and motor oil purchased	year	1152	91	81r
Gasoline, unleaded midgrade	gallon	1.21	4/93	82r
Gasoline, unleaded premium	gallon	1.30	4/93	82r
Gasoline, unleaded regular	gallon	1.10	4/93	82r
Entertainment				
Bowling, evening rate	game	2.14	12/94	2c
Concert ticket, Pearl Jam group	perf	20.00	94	50r
Entertainment, total expenditures	year	1266	91	81r
Fees and admissions, expenditures	year	306	91	81r
Monopoly game, Parker Brothers', No. 9	game	10.76	12/94	2c
Movie	adm	6.00	12/94	2c
Pets, toys, playground equipment, expenditures	year	271	91	81r
Reading, expenditures	year	131	91	81r
Televisions, radios, and sound equipment, expenditures	year	439	91	81r
Tennis balls, yellow, Wilson or Penn, 3	can	1.95	12/94	2c
Funerals				
Burial, immediate, container provided by funeral home		1574.60	1/95	54r
Cards, acknowledgment		22.24	1/95	54r
Casket, minimum alternative		239.41	1/95	54r
Cosmetology, hair care, etc.		91.04	1/95	54r
Cremation, direct, container provided by funeral home		1085.15	1/95	54r
Embalming		281.30	1/95	54r
Funeral, funeral home		323.04	1/95	54r

Fort Worth, TX - continued

Item	Per	Value	Date	Ref.
Funerals - continued				
Funeral, other facility		327.58	1/95	54r
Graveside service		355.19	1/95	54r
Hearse, local		141.89	1/95	54r
Limousine, local		99.40	1/95	54r
Memorial service		284.67	1/95	54r
Service charge, professional, nondeclinable		904.06	1/95	54r
Visitation and viewing		187.04	1/95	54r
Groceries				
Groceries, ACCRA Index		100.00	12/94	2c
Apples, Red Delicious	lb.	0.73	12/94	82r
Baby food, strained vegetables, lowest price	4-4.5 oz.	0.30	12/94	2c
Bacon, sliced	lb.	1.67	12/94	82r
Bananas	lb.	0.42	12/94	2c
Bananas	lb.	0.42	12/94	82r
Beef or hamburger, ground	lb.	1.75	12/94	2c
Beef purchases	year	213	91	81r
Beverage purchases, alcoholic	year	249	91	81r
Beverage purchases, nonalcoholic	year	207	91	81r
Bologna, all beef or mixed	lb.	2.27	12/94	82r
Bread, white	24-oz.	0.65	12/94	2c
Bread, white, pan	lb.	0.68	12/94	82r
Cabbage	lb.	0.42	12/94	82r
Carrots, short trimmed and topped	lb.	0.53	12/94	82r
Cereals and bakery products purchases	year	345	91	81r
Cereals and cereals products purchases	year	127	91	81r
Cheddar cheese, natural	lb.	3.58	12/94	82r
Cheese, Kraft grated Parmesan	8-oz.	3.47	12/94	2c
Chicken breast, bone-in	lb.	1.71	12/94	82r
Chicken, fresh, whole	lb.	0.78	12/94	82r
Chicken, whole fryer	lb.	0.63	12/94	2c
Chuck roast, USDA choice, boneless	lb.	2.26	12/94	82r
Cigarettes, Winston, Kings	carton	17.94	12/94	2c
Coffee, vacuum-packed	13 oz.	3.44	12/94	2c
Corn Flakes, Kellogg's or Post Toasties	18 oz.	2.50	12/94	2c
Corn, frozen, whole kernel, lowest price	10 oz.	0.78	12/94	2c
Crackers, soda, salted	lb.	1.27	12/94	82r
Cucumbers	lb.	0.65	12/94	82r
Dairy products (other) purchases	year	141	91	81r
Eggs, Grade A large	dozen	0.86	12/94	2c
Eggs, Grade A large	dozen	0.87	12/94	82r
Fish and seafood purchases	year	72	91	81r
Flour, white, all purpose	lb.	0.23	12/94	82r
Food purchases, food eaten at home	year	2381	91	81r
Foods purchased away from home, not prepared by consumer	year	1696	91	81r
Frankfurters, all meat or all beef	lb.	1.74	12/94	82r
Fruits and vegetables purchases	year	380	91	81r
Grapefruit	lb.	0.45	12/94	82r
Grapes, Thompson seedless	lb.	2.30	12/94	82r
Ground beef, 100% beef	lb.	1.37	12/94	82r
Ground chuck, 100% beef	lb.	1.97	12/94	82r
Ham, boneless, exc. canned	lb.	2.54	12/94	82r
Ice cream, prepackaged, bulk, regular	1/2 gal.	2.47	12/94	82r
Lemons	lb.	1.02	12/94	82r
Lettuce, iceberg	lb.	0.96	12/94	82r
Lettuce, iceberg	head	1.01	12/94	2c
Margarine, Blue Bonnet or Parkay cubes	lb.	0.66	12/94	2c
Margarine, stick	lb.	0.77	12/94	82r
Meats, poultry, fish, and eggs purchases	year	655	91	81r
Milk and cream (fresh) purchases	year	130	91	81r
Milk, whole	1/2 gal.	1.58	12/94	2c
Orange juice, frozen concentrate 12-oz. can	16 oz.	1.36	12/94	82r
Orange juice, Minute Maid frozen	12-oz.	1.20	12/94	2c
Oranges, Navel	lb.	0.54	12/94	82r
Peaches, halves or slices, Hunt's, Del Monte, or Libby's	29-oz.	1.55	12/94	2c
Pears, Anjou	lb.	0.81	12/94	82r
Peas, sweet, Del Monte or Green Giant	15-17 oz.	0.56	12/94	2c

Values are in dollars or fractions of dollars. In the column headed *Ref*, references are shown to sources. Each reference is followed by a letter. These refer to the geographical level for which data were reported: s=State, r=Region, and c=City or metro. The abbreviation *ex* is used to mean *except* or *excluding*; *exp* stands for expenditures. For other abbreviations and further explanations, please see the Introduction.

Fort Worth, TX - continued

Item	Per	Value	Date	Ref.
Groceries				
Pork chops, center cut, bone-in	lb.	3.07	12/94	82r
Pork purchases	year	142	91	81r
Potato chips	16-oz.	3.15	12/94	82r
Potatoes, frozen, French fried	lb.	0.82	12/94	82r
Potatoes, white	lb.	0.34	12/94	82r
Potatoes, white or red	10-lb. sack	2.77	12/94	2c
Rice, white, long grain, uncooked	lb.	0.48	12/94	82r
Round roast, USDA choice, boneless	lb.	2.91	12/94	82r
Sausage, fresh	lb.	1.82	12/94	82r
Sausage, Jimmy Dean, 100% pork	lb.	2.31	12/94	2c
Shortening, vegetable oil blends	lb.	0.75	12/94	82r
Shortening, vegetable, Crisco	3-lb.	2.49	12/94	2c
Soft drink, Coca Cola, ex deposit	2 lit	1.01	12/94	2c
Spaghetti and macaroni	lb.	0.87	12/94	82r
Steak, rib eye, USDA choice, boneless	lb.	6.85	12/94	82r
Steak, round, graded & ungraded, exc. USDA prime & choice	lb.	2.96	12/94	82r
Steak, round, USDA choice, boneless	lb.	3.17	12/94	82r
Steak, sirloin, USDA choice, boneless	lb.	4.12	12/94	82r
Steak, t-bone	lb.	5.55	12/94	2c
Steak, T-bone, USDA choice, bone-in	lb.	5.63	12/94	82r
Sugar and other sweets, eaten at home, expenditures	year	93	91	81r
Sugar, cane or beet	4 lbs.	1.45	12/94	2c
Sugar, white, all sizes	lb.	0.39	12/94	82r
Tobacco products and smoking supplies, total expenditures	year	286	91	81r
Tomatoes, field grown	lb.	1.36	12/94	82r
Tomatoes, Hunt's or Del Monte	14.5 oz.	0.83	12/94	2c
Tuna, chunk, light	lb.	1.94	12/94	82r
Tuna, chunk, light, oil-packed	6.125-6.5 oz.	0.69	12/94	2c
Turkey, frozen, whole	lb.	0.96	12/94	82r
Yogurt, natural, fruit flavored	8 oz.	0.58	12/94	82r
Goods and Services				
Miscellaneous goods and services, ACCRA Index		94.70	12/94	2c
Health Care				
Health care, ACCRA Index		101.60	12/94	2c
Adenosine, emergency room	treat	100.00	95	23r
Antibiotic ointment, Polysporin	1.5 oz.	4.25	12/94	2c
Bladder tap, superpubic, infant, emergency room	treat	119.00	95	23r
Blood analysis, emergency room	treat	25.00	95	23r
Blood tests, abdominal pain, emergency room	treat	25.00	95	23r
Burn dressing, emergency room	treat	266.00	95	23r
Cardiology interpretation, emergency room	treat	26.00	95	23r
Chest X-ray, emergency room	treat	78.00	95	23r
Childbirth, Cesarean delivery, hospital charge	birth	5462.00	12/91	69r
Childbirth, Cesarean delivery, physician charge	birth	2228.00	12/91	69r
Childbirth, normal delivery, hospital charge	birth	2943.00	12/91	69r
Childbirth, normal delivery, physician charge	birth	1619.00	12/91	69r
Defibrillation pads, emergency room	treat	6.00	95	23r
Dentist's fee, adult teeth cleaning and periodic oral exam	visit	54.80	12/94	2c
Doctor's fee, routine exam, established patient	visit	43.19	12/94	2c
Drugs, expenditures	year	297	91	81r
Gastric tube insertion, nasal, emergency room	treat	25.00	95	23r
Health care, total expenditures	year	1600	91	81r
Health insurance expenditures	year	637	91	81r
Heart monitor, emergency room	treat	40.00	95	23r
Hospital care, semiprivate room	day	328.60	12/94	2c
Insurance premium, family medical care	month	389.25	1/95	41s
Intravenous fluids, emergency room	treat	130.00	95	23r

Fort Worth, TX - continued

Item	Per	Value	Date	Ref.
Health Care - continued				
Intravenous fluids, emergency room	liter	26.00	95	23r
Intravenous line, central, emergency room	treat	342.00	95	23r
Liver function tests, abdominal pain, emergency room	treat	26.00	95	23r
Medical care charges, total, emergency room, third-degree burns	treat	2101.00	95	23r
Medical care charges, total, emergency, infant with fever	treat	628.00	95	23r
Medical services expenditures	year	573	91	81r
Medical supplies expenditures	year	93	91	81r
Morphine, emergency room	treat	34.00	95	23r
Nursing care and facilities charges, emergency room	treat	252.00	95	23r
Nursing care and facilities charges, emergency, infant with fever	treat	252.00	95	23r
Nursing care and facilities charges, emergency, third-degree burns	treat	861.00	95	23r
Physician's charges, emergency, infant with fever	treat	212.00	95	23r
Physician's charges, emergency, third-degree burns	treat	372.00	95	23r
Physician's fee, emergency room	treat	372.00	95	23r
Physician's fee, general practitioner	visit	51.20	12/93	60r
Surgery, open-heart	proc	42374.00	1/93	14r
Ultrasound, abdominal, emergency room	treat	276.00	95	23r
Urinalysis, emergency room	treat	20.00	95	23r
Urinalysis, infant, emergency room	treat	20.00	95	23r
X-rays, emergency room	treat	78.00	95	23r
Household Goods				
Appl. repair, service call, wash mach	min. lab. chg.	35.60	12/94	2c
Floor coverings, expenditures	year	48	91	81r
Furniture, expenditures	year	280	91	81r
Household equipment, misc. expenditures	year	342	91	81r
Household expenditures, miscellaneous	year	256	91	81r
Household furnishings and equipment, expenditures	year	988	91	81r
Household operations expenditures	year	468	91	81r
Household textiles, expenditures	year	95	91	81r
Housekeeping supplies, expenditures	year	380	91	81r
Laundry and cleaning supplies, expenditures	year	109	91	81r
Laundry detergent, Tide Ultra, Bold, or Cheer	42 oz.	3.61	12/94	2c
Postage and stationery, expenditures	year	105	91	81r
Tissues, facial, Kleenex brand	175	1.01	12/94	2c
Housing				
Housing, ACCRA Index		80.10	12/94	2c
Add garage/carport		6,980	3/95	74r
Add room(s)		11,403	3/95	74r
Apartment condominium or co-op, median	unit	68600	12/94	62r
Dwellings (owned), expenditures	year	2428	91	81r
Enclose porch/patio/breezeway		4,572	3/95	74r
Finish room in basement/attic		3,794	3/95	74r
Home, existing, single-family, median	unit	120200	12/94	62r
Home, existing, single-family, median	unit	81.50	12/94	62c
House payment, principal and interest, 25% down payment	mo.	574	12/94	2c
House, 1800 sq ft, 8000 sq ft lot, new, urban, utilities	total	93077	12/94	2c
Maintenance, repairs, insurance, and other housing expenditures	year	531	91	81r
Mortgage interest and charges expenditures	year	1506	91	81r
Mtge. rate, incl. points and orig. fee, 30-year conv. fixed or ARM	mo.	9.24	12/94	2c
Princ. & int., mortgage, median-price exist. sing.-family home	mo.	540	12/94	62c
Property taxes expenditures	year	391	91	81r
Redesign, restructure more than half of home's interior		17,641	3/95	74r

Values are in dollars or fractions of dollars. In the column headed *Ref*, references are shown to sources. Each reference is followed by a letter. These refer to the geographical level for which data were reported: s = State, r = Region, and c = City or metro. The abbreviation *ex* is used to mean *except* or *excluding*; *exp* stands for expenditures. For other abbreviations and further explanations, please see the Introduction.

Fort Worth, TX - continued

Item	Per	Value	Date	Ref.
Housing				
Rent, apartment, 2 br., 1 1/2-2 baths, unfurnished, 950 sq ft, water	mo.	537	12/94	2c
Rental units expenditures	year	1264	91	81r
Insurance and Pensions				
Auto insurance, private passenger	year	785.78	12/94	71s
Insurance and pensions, personal, expenditures	year	2395	91	81r
Insurance, life and other personal, expenditures	year	368	91	81r
Pensions and Social Security, expenditures	year	2027	91	81r
Personal Goods				
Shampoo, Alberto VO5	15-oz.	1.23	12/94	2c
Toothpaste, Crest or Colgate	6-7 oz.	2.49	12/94	2c
Personal Services				
Dry cleaning, man's 2-pc. suit		6.34	12/94	2c
Haircut, man's barbershop, no styling		7.00	12/94	2c
Haircut, woman's shampoo, trim, blow-dry		13.59	12/94	2c
Personal services expenditures	year	212	91	81r
Restaurant Food				
Chicken, fried, thigh and drumstick		1.87	12/94	2c
Dining expenditures, family	week	33.83	94	73r
Hamburger with cheese	1/4 lb.	1.88	12/94	2c
Pizza, Pizza Hut or Pizza Inn	12-13 in.	7.79	12/94	2c
Taxes				
Tax, cigarettes	year	584.00	10/93	43s
Taxes, Federal income, expenditures	year	2275	91	81r
Taxes, personal, expenditures	year	2715	91	81r
Taxes, State and local income, expenditures	year	365	91	81r
Transportation				
Transportation, ACCRA Index		100.50	12/94	2c
Bus fare, up to 10 miles	one-way	0.80	12/94	2c
Cars and trucks purchased, new	year	1306	91	81r
Cars and trucks purchased, used	year	942	91	81r
Driver's learning permit fee	perm	5.00	1/94	84s
Driver's license fee	orig	16.00	1/94	84s
Driver's license fee, duplicate	lic	10.00	1/94	84s
Driver's license reinstatement fee, min.	susp	50.00	1/94	85s
Driver's license renewal fee	renew	16.00	1/94	84s
Identification card, nondriver	card	10.00	1/94	83s
Motorcycle learning permit fee	perm	5.00	1/94	84s
Motorcycle license fee	orig	16.00	1/94	84s
Motorcycle license fee, duplicate	lic	10.00	1/94	84s
Motorcycle license renewal fee	renew	21.00	1/94	84s
Public transportation expenditures	year	249	91	81r
Tire balance, computer or spin bal., front	wheel	7.08	12/94	2c
Transportation expenditures, total	year	5307	91	81r
Vehicle finance charges	year	346	91	81r
Vehicle insurance expenditures	year	544	91	81r
Vehicle maintenance and repairs expenditures	year	600	91	81r
Vehicle purchases	year	2275	91	81r
Vehicle rental, leases, licenses, etc. expenditures	year	141	91	81r
Vehicles purchased, other than cars and trucks	year	27	91	81r
Utilities				
Utilities, ACCRA Index		110.40	12/94	2c
Electricity expenditures	year	950	91	81r
Electricity, (part.), other, 1800 sq. ft., new home	mo.	109.73	12/94	2c
Utilities, fuels, and public services, total expenditures	year	2000	91	81r
Water and other public services, expenditures	year	227	91	81r

Fort Worth, TX - continued

Item	Per	Value	Date	Ref.
Weddings				
Bridal attendants' gowns	event	750	10/93	76r
Bridal gown	event	852	10/93	76r
Bridal headpiece and veil	event	167	10/93	76r
Bride's wedding band	event	708	10/93	76r
Clergy	event	224	10/93	76r
Engagement ring	event	2756	10/93	76r
Flowers	event	863	10/93	76r
Formal wear for groom	event	106	10/93	76r
Groom's attendants' formal wear	event	530	10/93	76r
Groom's wedding band	event	402	10/93	76r
Music	event	600	10/93	76r
Photography	event	1088	10/93	76r
Shoes for bride	event	50	10/93	76r
Videography	event	483	10/93	76r
Wedding invitations and announcements	event	342	10/93	76r
Wedding reception	event	7000	10/93	76r

Freeport, IL

Item	Per	Value	Date	Ref.
Composite, ACCRA index		97.30	12/94	2c
Alcoholic Beverages				
Beer, Miller Lite, Bud, 12-oz., ex deposit	6	3.89	12/94	2c
J & B Scotch	750-ml.	14.24	12/94	2c
Wine, Gallo Chablis blanc	1.5-lit	5.17	12/94	2c
Clothing				
Jeans, man's denim		39.99	12/94	2c
Shirt, man's dress shirt		38.75	12/94	2c
Undervest, boy's size 10-14, cotton	3	3.53	12/94	2c
Communications				
Newspaper subscription, dly. and Sun. delivery	month	9.57	12/94	2c
Telephone bill, family of four	month	24.52	12/94	2c
Energy and Fuels				
Energy, combined forms, 1800 sq. ft.	mo.	114.16	12/94	2c
Energy, exc. electricity, 1800 sq. ft.	mo.	51.32	12/94	2c
Gas, reg unlead, taxes inc., cash, self-service	gal	1.18	12/94	2c
Entertainment				
Bowling, evening rate	game	1.50	12/94	2c
Monopoly game, Parker Brothers', No. 9	game	10.74	12/94	2c
Movie	adm	4.00	12/94	2c
Tennis balls, yellow, Wilson or Penn, 3	can	2.31	12/94	2c
Groceries				
Groceries, ACCRA Index		97.10	12/94	2c
Baby food, strained vegetables, lowest price	4-4.5 oz.	0.36	12/94	2c
Bananas	lb.	0.42	12/94	2c
Beef or hamburger, ground	lb.	1.46	12/94	2c
Bread, white	24-oz.	0.49	12/94	2c
Cheese, Kraft grated Parmesan	8-oz.	3.29	12/94	2c
Chicken, whole fryer	lb.	0.76	12/94	2c
Cigarettes, Winston, Kings	carton	17.81	12/94	2c
Coffee, vacuum-packed	13 oz.	2.49	12/94	2c
Corn Flakes, Kellogg's or Post Toasties	18 oz.	2.42	12/94	2c
Corn, frozen, whole kernel, lowest price	10 oz.	0.90	12/94	2c
Eggs, Grade A large	dozen	0.71	12/94	2c
Lettuce, iceberg	head	0.91	12/94	2c
Margarine, Blue Bonnet or Parkay cubes	lb.	0.61	12/94	2c
Milk, whole	1/2 gal.	1.38	12/94	2c
Orange juice, Minute Maid frozen	12-oz.	1.36	12/94	2c
Peaches, halves or slices, Hunt's, Del Monte, or Libby's	29-oz.	1.40	12/94	2c
Peas, sweet, Del Monte or Green Giant	15-17 oz.	0.60	12/94	2c
Potatoes, white or red	10-lb. sack	2.66	12/94	2c

Values are in dollars or fractions of dollars. In the column headed *Ref*, references are shown to sources. Each reference is followed by a letter. These refer to the geographical level for which data were reported: s = State, r = Region, and c = City or metro. The abbreviation *ex* is used to mean *except* or *excluding*; *exp* stands for *expenditures*. For other abbreviations and further explanations, please see the Introduction.

Freeport, IL - continued

Item	Per	Value	Date	Ref.
Groceries				
Sausage, Jimmy Dean, 100% pork	lb.	2.74	12/94	2c
Shortening, vegetable, Crisco	3-lb.	2.18	12/94	2c
Soft drink, Coca Cola, ex deposit	2 lit	1.28	12/94	2c
Steak, t-bone	lb.	5.72	12/94	2c
Sugar, cane or beet	4 lbs.	1.34	12/94	2c
Tomatoes, Hunt's or Del Monte	14.5 oz.	0.74	12/94	2c
Tuna, chunk, light, oil-packed	6.125-6.5 oz.	0.66	12/94	2c
Goods and Services				
Miscellaneous goods and services, ACCRA Index		100.10	12/94	2c
Health Care				
Health care, ACCRA Index		92.20	12/94	2c
Antibiotic ointment, Polysporin	1.5 oz.	4.42	12/94	2c
Dentist's fee, adult teeth cleaning and periodic oral exam	visit	51.75	12/94	2c
Doctor's fee, routine exam, established patient	visit	40.69	12/94	2c
Hospital care, semiprivate room	day	217.00	12/94	2c
Household Goods				
Appl. repair, service call, wash mach	min. lab. chg.	26.98	12/94	2c
Laundry detergent, Tide Ultra, Bold, or Cheer	42 oz.	3.28	12/94	2c
Tissues, facial, Kleenex brand	175	1.04	12/94	2c
Housing				
Housing, ACCRA Index		89.70	12/94	2c
House payment, principal and interest, 25% down payment	mo.	716	12/94	2c
House, 1800 sq ft, 8000 sq ft lot, new, urban, utilities	total	114750	12/94	2c
Mtge. rate, incl. points and orig. fee, 30-year conv. fixed or ARM	mo.	9.37	12/94	2c
Rent, apartment, 2 br., 1 1/2-2 baths, unfurnished, 950 sq ft, water	mo.	393	12/94	2c
Personal Goods				
Shampoo, Alberto VO5	15-oz.	1.49	12/94	2c
Toothpaste, Crest or Colgate	6-7 oz.	2.12	12/94	2c
Personal Services				
Dry cleaning, man's 2-pc. suit		6.22	12/94	2c
Haircut, man's barbershop, no styling		6.49	12/94	2c
Haircut, woman's shampoo, trim, blow-dry		16.60	12/94	2c
Restaurant Food				
Chicken, fried, thigh and drumstick		2.09	12/94	2c
Hamburger with cheese	1/4 lb.	1.70	12/94	2c
Pizza, Pizza Hut or Pizza Inn	12-13 in.	7.46	12/94	2c
Transportation				
Transportation, ACCRA Index		107.10	12/94	2c
Tire balance, computer or spin bal., front	wheel	7.45	12/94	2c
Utilities				
Utilities, ACCRA Index		105.00	12/94	2c
Electricity, (part.), other, 1800 sq. ft., new home	mo.	62.84	12/94	2c

Fresno, CA

Item	Per	Value	Date	Ref.
Composite, ACCRA index		107.70	12/94	2c
Alcoholic Beverages				
Beer, Miller Lite, Bud, 12-oz., ex deposit	6	3.98	12/94	2c
J & B Scotch	750-ml.	15.54	12/94	2c
Wine, Gallo Chablis blanc	1.5-lit	4.27	12/94	2c

Fresno, CA - continued

Item	Per	Value	Date	Ref.
Appliances				
Appliances (major), expenditures	year	160	91	81r
Average annual exp.				
Food, health care, personal goods, services	year	32461	91	81r
Charity				
Cash contributions, expenditures	year	975	91	81r
Clothing				
Apparel, men and boys, total expenditures	year	467	91	81r
Apparel, women and girls, total expenditures	year	737	91	81r
Footwear, expenditures	year	270	91	81r
Jeans, man's denim		31.08	12/94	2c
Shirt, man's dress shirt		24.89	12/94	2c
Undervest, boy's size 10-14, cotton	3	6.28	12/94	2c
Communications				
Long-distance telephone rate, day, addl. min., 1-10 mi.	min.	0.07	12/93	9s
Long-distance telephone rate, day, initial min., 1-10 mi.	min.	0.17	12/93	9s
Newspaper subscription, dly. and Sun. delivery	month	10.50	12/94	2c
Phone line, single, business, field visit	inst	70.75	12/93	9s
Phone line, single, business, no field visit	inst	70.75	12/93	9s
Phone line, single, residence, field visit	inst	34.75	12/93	9s
Phone line, single, residence, no field visit	inst	34.75	12/93	9s
Telephone bill, family of four	month	12.56	12/94	2c
Telephone service, expenditures	year	611	91	81r
Telephone, residential, flat rate	mo.	8.35	12/93	8c
Education				
Board, 4-year private college/university	year	2945	8/94	80s
Board, 4-year public college/university	year	2321	8/94	80s
Education, total expenditures	year	375	91	81r
Room, 4-year private college/university	year	3094	8/94	80s
Room, 4-year public college/university	year	2812	8/94	80s
Student fee, university	year	21.00	93	18s
Total cost, 4-year private college/university	year	19321	8/94	80s
Total cost, 4-year public college/university	year	7511	8/94	80s
Tuition, 2-year public college/university, in-state	year	345	8/94	80s
Tuition, 4-year private college/university, in-state	year	13282	8/94	80s
Tuition, 4-year public college/university, in-state	year	2378	8/94	80s
Energy and Fuels				
Energy, combined forms, 1800 sq. ft.	mo.	120.00	12/94	2c
Energy, exc. electricity, 1800 sq. ft.	mo.	25.00	12/94	2c
Fuel oil and other fuels, expenditures	year	33	91	81r
Gas, natural, expenditures	year	212	91	81r
Gas, reg unlead, taxes inc., cash, self-service	gal	1.26	12/94	2c
Gasoline and motor oil purchased	year	1115	91	81r
Gasoline, unleaded midgrade	gallon	1.36	4/93	82r
Gasoline, unleaded premium	gallon	1.43	4/93	82r
Gasoline, unleaded regular	gallon	1.23	4/93	82r
Entertainment				
Bowling, evening rate	game	2.17	12/94	2c
Concert ticket, Pearl Jam group	perf	20.00	94	50r
Entertainment, total expenditures	year	1853	91	81r
Fees and admissions, expenditures	year	482	91	81r
Monopoly game, Parker Brothers', No. 9	game	11.49	12/94	2c
Movie	adm	7.00	12/94	2c
Pets, toys, playground equipment, expenditures	year	299	91	81r
Reading, expenditures	year	164	91	81r
Televisions, radios, and sound equipment, expenditures	year	528	91	81r
Tennis balls, yellow, Wilson or Penn, 3	can	2.49	12/94	2c
Funerals				
Burial, immediate, container provided by funeral home		1382.70	1/95	54r

Values are in dollars or fractions of dollars. In the column headed *Ref*, references are shown to sources. Each reference is followed by a letter. These refer to the geographical level for which data were reported: s=State, r=Region, and c=City or metro. The abbreviation *ex* is used to mean *except* or *excluding*; *exp* stands for expenditures. For other abbreviations and further explanations, please see the Introduction.

Fresno, CA - continued

Item	Per	Value	Date	Ref.
Funerals				
Cards, acknowledgment		21.87	1/95	54r
Casket, minimum alternative		128.54	1/95	54r
Cosmetology, hair care, etc.		119.69	1/95	54r
Cremation, direct, container provided by funeral home		1030.62	1/95	54r
Embalming		255.42	1/95	54r
Funeral, funeral home		437.38	1/95	54r
Funeral, other facility		444.46	1/95	54r
Graveside service		338.46	1/95	54r
Hearse, local		147.50	1/95	54r
Limousine, local		130.33	1/95	54r
Memorial service		553.16	1/95	54r
Service charge, professional, nondeclinable		859.15	1/95	54r
Visitation and viewing		93.23	1/95	54r
Groceries				
Groceries, ACCRA Index		104.50	12/94	2c
Apples, Red Delicious	lb.	0.72	12/94	82r
Baby food, strained vegetables, lowest price	4-4.5 oz.	0.36	12/94	2c
Bacon, sliced	lb.	1.73	12/94	82r
Bananas	lb.	0.42	12/94	2c
Bananas	lb.	0.52	12/94	82r
Beef or hamburger, ground	lb.	1.07	12/94	2c
Beef purchases	year	241	91	81r
Beverage purchases, alcoholic	year	328	91	81r
Beverage purchases, nonalcoholic	year	234	91	81r
Bologna, all beef or mixed	lb.	2.33	12/94	82r
Bread, white	24-oz.	0.78	12/94	2c
Bread, white, pan	lb.	0.81	12/94	82r
Carrots, short trimmed and topped	lb.	0.43	12/94	82r
Cereals and bakery products purchases	year	392	91	81r
Cereals and cereals products purchases	year	139	91	81r
Cheese, Kraft grated Parmesan	8-oz.	3.32	12/94	2c
Chicken breast, bone-in	lb.	2.04	12/94	82r
Chicken, fresh, whole	lb.	0.95	12/94	82r
Chicken, whole fryer	lb.	0.94	12/94	2c
Cigarettes, Winston, Kings	carton	17.06	12/94	2c
Coffee, 100%, ground roast, all sizes	lb.	4.48	12/94	82r
Coffee, vacuum-packed	13 oz.	3.65	12/94	2c
Corn Flakes, Kellogg's or Post Toasties	18 oz.	2.57	12/94	2c
Corn, frozen, whole kernel, lowest price	10 oz.	0.69	12/94	2c
Dairy products (other) purchases	year	182	91	81r
Eggs, Grade A large	dozen	1.27	12/94	2c
Fish and seafood purchases	year	94	91	81r
Flour, white, all purpose	lb.	0.21	12/94	82r
Food purchases, food eaten at home	year	2749	91	81r
Foods purchased away from home, not prepared by consumer	year	1909	91	81r
Fruits and vegetables purchases	year	459	91	81r
Grapefruit	lb.	0.56	12/94	82r
Ground beef, 100% beef	lb.	1.31	12/94	82r
Ham, boneless, exc. canned	lb.	2.46	12/94	82r
Ice cream, prepackaged, bulk, regular	1/2 gal.	2.57	12/94	82r
Lemons	lb.	1.00	12/94	82r
Lettuce, iceberg	lb.	0.93	12/94	82r
Lettuce, iceberg	head	0.65	12/94	2c
Margarine, Blue Bonnet or Parkay cubes	lb.	0.64	12/94	2c
Meats, poultry, fish, and eggs purchases	year	700	91	81r
Milk and cream (fresh) purchases	year	155	91	81r
Milk, whole	1/2 gal.	1.49	12/94	2c
Orange juice, frozen concentrate 12-oz. can	16 oz.	1.52	12/94	82r
Orange juice, Minute Maid frozen	12-oz.	1.36	12/94	2c
Oranges, Navel	lb.	0.56	12/94	82r
Peaches, halves or slices, Hunt's, Del Monte, or Libby's	29-oz.	1.33	12/94	2c
Peas, sweet, Del Monte or Green Giant	15-17 oz.	0.57	12/94	2c
Pork chops, center cut, bone-in	lb.	3.30	12/94	82r
Pork purchases	year	122	91	81r
Potato chips	16-oz.	3.03	12/94	82r

Fresno, CA - continued

Item	Per	Value	Date	Ref.
Groceries - continued				
Potatoes, frozen, French fried	lb.	0.77	12/94	82r
Potatoes, white	lb.	0.35	12/94	82r
Potatoes, white or red	10-lb. sack	2.45	12/94	2c
Rice, white, long grain, uncooked	lb.	0.54	12/94	82r
Round roast, USDA choice, boneless	lb.	2.92	12/94	82r
Sausage, Jimmy Dean, 100% pork	lb.	3.45	12/94	2c
Shortening, vegetable oil blends	lb.	0.80	12/94	82r
Shortening, vegetable, Crisco	3-lb.	2.70	12/94	2c
Soft drink, Coca Cola, ex deposit	2 lit	1.22	12/94	2c
Spaghetti and macaroni	lb.	1.02	12/94	82r
Steak, round, graded & ungraded, exc. USDA prime & choice	lb.	3.13	12/94	82r
Steak, sirloin, USDA choice, boneless	lb.	4.07	12/94	82r
Steak, t-bone	lb.	4.48	12/94	2c
Sugar and other sweets, eaten at home, expenditures	year	105	91	81r
Sugar, cane or beet	4 lbs.	1.51	12/94	2c
Sugar, white, all sizes	lb.	0.38	12/94	82r
Tobacco products and smoking supplies, total expenditures	year	221	91	81r
Tomatoes, field grown	lb.	1.45	12/94	82r
Tomatoes, Hunt's or Del Monte	14.5 oz.	0.77	12/94	2c
Tuna, chunk, light	lb.	2.18	12/94	82r
Tuna, chunk, light, oil-packed	6.125-6.5 oz.	0.67	12/94	2c
Goods and Services				
Miscellaneous goods and services, ACCRA Index		103.30	12/94	2c
Health Care				
Health care, ACCRA Index		122.10	12/94	2c
Antibiotic ointment, Polysporin	1.5 oz.	4.35	12/94	2c
Childbirth, Cesarean delivery, hospital charge	birth	6059.00	12/91	69r
Childbirth, Cesarean delivery, physician charge	birth	2248.00	12/91	69r
Childbirth, normal delivery, hospital charge	birth	3006.00	12/91	69r
Childbirth, normal delivery, physician charge	birth	1634.00	12/91	69r
Dentist's fee, adult teeth cleaning and periodic oral exam	visit	74.38	12/94	2c
Doctor's fee, routine exam, established patient	visit	46.25	12/94	2c
Drugs, expenditures	year	230	91	81r
Health care, total expenditures	year	1544	91	81r
Health insurance expenditures	year	558	91	81r
Hospital care, semiprivate room	day	418.75	12/94	2c
Insurance premium, family medical care	month	380.27	1/95	41s
Medical services expenditures	year	676	91	81r
Medical supplies expenditures	year	80	91	81r
Surgery, open-heart	proc	37818.00	1/93	14r
Household Goods				
Appl. repair, service call, wash mach	min. lab. chg.	38.14	12/94	2c
Floor coverings, expenditures	year	79	91	81r
Furniture, expenditures	year	352	91	81r
Household equipment, misc. expenditures	year	614	91	81r
Household expenditures, miscellaneous	year	294	91	81r
Household furnishings and equipment, expenditures	year	1416	91	81r
Household operations expenditures	year	580	91	81r
Household textiles, expenditures	year	113	91	81r
Housekeeping supplies, expenditures	year	447	91	81r
Laundry and cleaning supplies, expenditures	year	114	91	81r
Laundry detergent, Tide Ultra, Bold, or Cheer	42 oz.	3.87	12/94	2c
Postage and stationery, expenditures	year	145	91	81r
Tissues, facial, Kleenex brand	175	1.05	12/94	2c

Values are in dollars or fractions of dollars. In the column headed *Ref*, references are shown to sources. Each reference is followed by a letter. These refer to the geographical level for which data were reported: s=State, r=Region, and c=City or metro. The abbreviation *ex* is used to mean *except* or *excluding*; *exp* stands for *expenditures*. For other abbreviations and further explanations, please see the Introduction.

Fresno, CA - continued

Item	Per	Value	Date	Ref.
Housing				
Housing, ACCRA Index		110.20	12/94	2c
Add garage/carport		6,422	3/95	74r
Add room(s)		26,583	3/95	74r
Apartment condominium or co-op, median	unit	105300	12/94	62r
Dwellings (owned), expenditures	year	3932	91	81r
Enclose porch/patio/breezeway		5,382	3/95	74r
Finish room in basement/attic		3,911	3/95	74r
Home, existing, single-family, median	unit	178600	12/94	62r
House payment, principal and interest, 25% down payment	mo.	834	12/94	2c
House, 1800 sq ft, 8000 sq ft lot, new, urban, utilities	total	136975	12/94	2c
Maintenance, repairs, insurance, and other housing expenditures	year	591	91	81r
Mortgage interest and charges expenditures	year	2747	91	81r
Mtge. rate, incl. points and orig. fee, 30-year conv. fixed or ARM	mo.	9.11	12/94	2c
Princ. & int., mortgage, median-price exist. sing.-family home	mo.	845	12/94	62r
Property taxes expenditures	year	594	91	81r
Redesign, restructure more than half of home's interior		5,467	3/95	74r
Rent, apartment, 2 br., 1 1/2-2 baths, unfurnished, 950 sq ft, water	mo.	610	12/94	2c
Rental units expenditures	year	2077	91	81r
Insurance and Pensions				
Auto insurance, private passenger	year	892.80	12/94	71s
Insurance and pensions, personal, expenditures	year	3042	91	81r
Insurance, life and other personal, expenditures	year	298	91	81r
Pensions and Social Security, expenditures	year	2744	91	81r
Legal Assistance				
Legal work, law firm associate	hour	91		10r
Legal work, law firm partner	hour	151		10r
Personal Goods				
Shampoo, Alberto VO5	15-oz.	1.39	12/94	2c
Toothpaste, Crest or Colgate	6-7 oz.	2.33	12/94	2c
Personal Services				
Dry cleaning, man's 2-pc. suit		6.44	12/94	2c
Haircut, man's barbershop, no styling		9.40	12/94	2c
Haircut, woman's shampoo, trim, blow-dry		26.30	12/94	2c
Personal services expenditures	year	286	91	81r
Restaurant Food				
Chicken, fried, thigh and drumstick		2.29	12/94	2c
Dining expenditures, family	week	32.25	94	73r
Hamburger with cheese	1/4 lb.	1.77	12/94	2c
Pizza, Pizza Hut or Pizza Inn	12-13 in.	8.29	12/94	2c
Taxes				
Taxes, Federal income, expenditures	year	2946	91	81r
Taxes, personal, expenditures	year	3791	91	81r
Taxes, State and local income, expenditures	year	791	91	81r
Transportation				
Transportation, ACCRA Index		117.80	12/94	2c
Bus fare, one-way	trip	0.75	12/95	1c
Cars and trucks purchased, new	year	1231	91	81r
Cars and trucks purchased, used	year	915	91	81r
Driver's learning permit fee	perm	12.00	1/94	84s
Driver's license fee	orig	12.00	1/94	84s
Driver's license fee, duplicate	lic	12.00	1/94	84s
Driver's license reinstatement fee, min.	susp	15.00	1/94	85s
Driver's license renewal fee	renew	12.00	1/94	84s
Identification card, nondriver	card	6.00	1/94	83s
Motorcycle learning permit fee	perm	12.00	1/94	84s
Motorcycle license fee	orig	12.00	1/94	84s
Motorcycle license fee, duplicate	lic	12.00	1/94	84s
Motorcycle license renewal fee	renew	12.00	1/94	84s

Fresno, CA - continued

Item	Per	Value	Date	Ref.
Transportation - continued				
Public transportation expenditures	year	375	91	81r
Tire balance, computer or spin bal., front	wheel	8.50	12/94	2c
Transportation expenditures, total	year	5527	91	81r
Vehicle finance charges	year	287	91	81r
Vehicle insurance expenditures	year	624	91	81r
Vehicle maintenance and repairs expenditures	year	695	91	81r
Vehicle purchases	year	2174	91	81r
Vehicle rental, leases, licenses, etc. expenditures	year	257	91	81r
Vehicles purchased, other than cars and trucks	year	28	91	81r
Utilities				
Utilities, ACCRA Index		101.20	12/94	2c
Electricity expenditures	year	616	91	81r
Electricity, (part.), other, 1800 sq. ft., new home	mo.	95.00	12/94	2c
Utilities, fuels, and public services, total expenditures	year	1681	91	81r
Water and other public services, expenditures	year	209	91	81r
Weddings				
Bridal attendants' gowns	event	750	10/93	76r
Bridal gown	event	852	10/93	76r
Bridal headpiece and veil	event	167	10/93	76r
Bride's wedding band	event	708	10/93	76r
Clergy	event	224	10/93	76r
Engagement ring	event	2756	10/93	76r
Flowers	event	863	10/93	76r
Formal wear for groom	event	106	10/93	76r
Groom's attendants' formal wear	event	530	10/93	76r
Groom's wedding band	event	402	10/93	76r
Music	event	600	10/93	76r
Photography	event	1088	10/93	76r
Shoes for bride	event	50	10/93	76r
Videography	event	483	10/93	76r
Wedding invitations and announcements	event	342	10/93	76r
Wedding reception	event	7000	10/93	76r

Gadsden, AL

Item	Per	Value	Date	Ref.
Composite, ACCRA index		95.30	12/94	2c
Alcoholic Beverages				
Beer, Miller Lite, Bud, 12-oz., ex deposit	6	4.48	12/94	2c
J & B Scotch	750-ml.	20.99	12/94	2c
Wine, Gallo Chablis blanc	1.5-lit	4.99	12/94	2c
Appliances				
Appliances (major), expenditures	year	153	91	81r
Average annual exp.				
Food, health care, personal goods, services	year	27020	91	81r
Charity				
Cash contributions, expenditures	year	839	91	81r
Clothing				
Apparel, men and boys, total expenditures	year	380	91	81r
Apparel, women and girls, total expenditures	year	660	91	81r
Footwear, expenditures	year	193	91	81r
Jeans, man's denim		31.66	12/94	2c
Shirt, man's dress shirt		31.60	12/94	2c
Undervest, boy's size 10-14, cotton	3	4.44	12/94	2c
Communications				
Long-distance telephone rate, day, addl. min., 1-10 mi.	min.	0.09	12/93	9s
Long-distance telephone rate, day, initial min., 1-10 mi.	min.	0.11	12/93	9s
Newspaper subscription, dly. and Sun. delivery	month	9.46	12/94	2c

Values are in dollars or fractions of dollars. In the column headed *Ref*, references are shown to sources. Each reference is followed by a letter. These refer to the geographical level for which data were reported: s=State, r=Region, and c=City or metro. The abbreviation *ex* is used to mean *except* or *excluding*; *exp* stands for expenditures. For other abbreviations and further explanations, please see the Introduction.

Gadsden, AL - continued

Item	Per	Value	Date	Ref.
Communications				
Phone line, single, business, field visit	inst	69.00	12/93	9s
Phone line, single, business, no field visit	inst	69.00	12/93	9s
Phone line, single, residence, field visit	inst	40.00	12/93	9s
Phone line, single, residence, no field visit	inst	40.00	12/93	9s
Telephone bill, family of four	month	23.14	12/94	2c
Telephone service, expenditures	year	616	91	81r
Telephone, residential, flat rate	mo.	16.70	12/93	8c
Education				
Board, 4-year private college/university	year	2072	8/94	80s
Board, 4-year public college/university	year	1706	8/94	80s
Education, total expenditures	year	319	91	81r
Room, 4-year private college/university	year	1607	8/94	80s
Room, 4-year public college/university	year	1598	8/94	80s
Total cost, 4-year private college/university	year	10664	8/94	80s
Total cost, 4-year public college/university	year	5287	8/94	80s
Tuition, 2-year public college/university, in-state	year	1110	8/94	80s
Tuition, 4-year private college/university, in-state	year	6985	8/94	80s
Tuition, 4-year public college/university, in-state	year	1983	8/94	80s
Energy and Fuels				
Energy, combined forms, 1800 sq. ft.	mo.	127.17	12/94	2c
Energy, exc. electricity, 1800 sq. ft.	mo.	48.46	12/94	2c
Fuel oil and other fuels, expenditures	year	56	91	81r
Gas, natural, expenditures	year	150	91	81r
Gas, reg unlead, taxes inc., cash, self-service	gal	1.16	12/94	2c
Gasoline and motor oil purchased	year	1152	91	81r
Gasoline, unleaded midgrade	gallon	1.21	4/93	82r
Gasoline, unleaded premium	gallon	1.30	4/93	82r
Gasoline, unleaded regular	gallon	1.10	4/93	82r
Entertainment				
Bowling, evening rate	game	2.60	12/94	2c
Concert ticket, Pearl Jam group	perf	20.00	94	50r
Entertainment, total expenditures	year	1266	91	81r
Fees and admissions, expenditures	year	306	91	81r
Monopoly game, Parker Brothers', No. 9	game	11.99	12/94	2c
Movie	adm	5.25	12/94	2c
Pets, toys, playground equipment, expenditures	year	271	91	81r
Reading, expenditures	year	131	91	81r
Televisions, radios, and sound equipment, expenditures	year	439	91	81r
Tennis balls, yellow, Wilson or Penn, 3	can	2.88	12/94	2c
Funerals				
Burial, immediate, container provided by funeral home		1298.96	1/95	54r
Cards, acknowledgment		21.26	1/95	54r
Casket, minimum alternative		204.95	1/95	54r
Cosmetology, hair care, etc.		85.40	1/95	54r
Cremation, direct, container provided by funeral home		1054.77	1/95	54r
Embalming		287.71	1/95	54r
Funeral, funeral home		269.18	1/95	54r
Funeral, other facility		272.88	1/95	54r
Graveside service		302.54	1/95	54r
Hearse, local		122.08	1/95	54r
Limousine, local		80.31	1/95	54r
Memorial service		277.66	1/95	54r
Service charge, professional, nondeclinable		896.65	1/95	54r
Visitation and viewing		232.39	1/95	54r
Groceries				
Groceries, ACCRA Index		95.00	12/94	2c
Apples, Red Delicious	lb.	0.73	12/94	82r
Baby food, strained vegetables, lowest price	4-4.5 oz.	0.35	12/94	2c
Bacon, sliced	lb.	1.67	12/94	82r
Bananas	lb.	0.47	12/94	2c

Gadsden, AL - continued

Item	Per	Value	Date	Ref.
Groceries - continued				
Bananas	lb.	0.42	12/94	82r
Beef or hamburger, ground	lb.	1.59	12/94	2c
Beef purchases	year	213	91	81r
Beverage purchases, alcoholic	year	249	91	81r
Beverage purchases, nonalcoholic	year	207	91	81r
Bologna, all beef or mixed	lb.	2.27	12/94	82r
Bread, white	24-oz.	0.76	12/94	2c
Bread, white, pan	lb.	0.68	12/94	82r
Cabbage	lb.	0.42	12/94	82r
Carrots, short trimmed and topped	lb.	0.53	12/94	82r
Cereals and bakery products purchases	year	345	91	81r
Cereals and cereals products purchases	year	127	91	81r
Cheddar cheese, natural	lb.	3.58	12/94	82r
Cheese, Kraft grated Parmesan	8-oz.	3.27	12/94	2c
Chicken breast, bone-in	lb.	1.71	12/94	82r
Chicken, fresh, whole	lb.	0.78	12/94	82r
Chicken, whole fryer	lb.	0.69	12/94	2c
Chuck roast, USDA choice, boneless	lb.	2.26	12/94	82r
Cigarettes, Winston, Kings	carton	15.14	12/94	2c
Coffee, vacuum-packed	13 oz.	3.02	12/94	2c
Corn Flakes, Kellogg's or Post Toasties	18 oz.	2.22	12/94	2c
Corn, frozen, whole kernel, lowest price	10 oz.	0.60	12/94	2c
Crackers, soda, salted	lb.	1.27	12/94	82r
Cucumbers	lb.	0.65	12/94	82r
Dairy products (other) purchases	year	141	91	81r
Eggs, Grade A large	dozen	0.76	12/94	2c
Eggs, Grade A large	dozen	0.87	12/94	82r
Fish and seafood purchases	year	72	91	81r
Flour, white, all purpose	lb.	0.23	12/94	82r
Food purchases, food eaten at home	year	2381	91	81r
Foods purchased away from home, not prepared by consumer	year	1696	91	81r
Frankfurters, all meat or all beef	lb.	1.74	12/94	82r
Fruits and vegetables purchases	year	380	91	81r
Grapefruit	lb.	0.45	12/94	82r
Grapes, Thompson seedless	lb.	2.30	12/94	82r
Ground beef, 100% beef	lb.	1.37	12/94	82r
Ground chuck, 100% beef	lb.	1.97	12/94	82r
Ham, boneless, exc. canned	lb.	2.54	12/94	82r
Ice cream, prepackaged, bulk, regular	1/2 gal.	2.47	12/94	82r
Lemons	lb.	1.02	12/94	82r
Lettuce, iceberg	lb.	0.96	12/94	82r
Lettuce, iceberg	head	0.99	12/94	2c
Margarine, Blue Bonnet or Parkay cubes	lb.	0.59	12/94	2c
Margarine, stick	lb.	0.77	12/94	82r
Meats, poultry, fish, and eggs purchases	year	655	91	81r
Milk and cream (fresh) purchases	year	130	91	81r
Milk, whole	1/2 gal.	1.29	12/94	2c
Orange juice, frozen concentrate 12-oz. can	16 oz.	1.36	12/94	82r
Orange juice, Minute Maid frozen	12-oz.	1.12	12/94	2c
Oranges, Navel	lb.	0.54	12/94	82r
Peaches, halves or slices, Hunt's, Del Monte, or Libby's	29-oz.	1.19	12/94	2c
Pears, Anjou	lb.	0.81	12/94	82r
Peas, sweet, Del Monte or Green Giant	15-17 oz.	0.44	12/94	2c
Pork chops, center cut, bone-in	lb.	3.07	12/94	82r
Pork purchases	year	142	91	81r
Potato chips	16-oz.	3.15	12/94	82r
Potatoes, frozen, French fried	lb.	0.82	12/94	82r
Potatoes, white	lb.	0.34	12/94	82r
Potatoes, white or red	10-lb. sack	2.91	12/94	2c
Rice, white, long grain, uncooked	lb.	0.48	12/94	82r
Round roast, USDA choice, boneless	lb.	2.91	12/94	82r
Sausage, fresh	lb.	1.82	12/94	82r
Sausage, Jimmy Dean, 100% pork	lb.	2.32	12/94	2c
Shortening, vegetable oil blends	lb.	0.75	12/94	82r
Shortening, vegetable, Crisco	3-lb.	2.65	12/94	2c
Soft drink, Coca Cola, ex deposit	2 lit	0.99	12/94	2c

Values are in dollars or fractions of dollars. In the column headed *Ref*, references are shown to sources. Each reference is followed by a letter. These refer to the geographical level for which data were reported: s=State, r=Region, and c=City or metro. The abbreviation *ex* is used to mean *except* or *excluding*; *exp* stands for expenditures. For other abbreviations and further explanations, please see the Introduction.

Gadsden, AL - continued

Item	Per	Value	Date	Ref.
Groceries				
Spaghetti and macaroni	lb.	0.87	12/94	82r
Steak, rib eye, USDA choice, boneless	lb.	6.85	12/94	82r
Steak, round, graded & ungraded, exc. USDA prime & choice	lb.	2.96	12/94	82r
Steak, round, USDA choice, boneless	lb.	3.17	12/94	82r
Steak, sirloin, USDA choice, boneless	lb.	4.12	12/94	82r
Steak, t-bone	lb.	4.21	12/94	2c
Steak, T-bone, USDA choice, bone-in	lb.	5.63	12/94	82r
Sugar and other sweets, eaten at home, expenditures	year	93	91	81r
Sugar, cane or beet	4 lbs.	1.34	12/94	2c
Sugar, white, all sizes	lb.	0.39	12/94	82r
Tobacco products and smoking supplies, total expenditures	year	286	91	81r
Tomatoes, field grown	lb.	1.36	12/94	82r
Tomatoes, Hunt's or Del Monte	14.5 oz.	0.64	12/94	2c
Tuna, chunk, light	lb.	1.94	12/94	82r
Tuna, chunk, light, oil-packed	6.125-6.5 oz.	0.63	12/94	2c
Turkey, frozen, whole	lb.	0.96	12/94	82r
Yogurt, natural, fruit flavored	8 oz.	0.58	12/94	82r
Goods and Services				
Miscellaneous goods and services, ACCRA Index		99.90	12/94	2c
Health Care				
Health care, ACCRA Index		101.80	12/94	2c
Adenosine, emergency room	treat	100.00	95	23r
Antibiotic ointment, Polysporin	1.5 oz.	3.98	12/94	2c
Bladder tap, superpubic, infant, emergency room	treat	119.00	95	23r
Blood analysis, emergency room	treat	25.00	95	23r
Blood tests, abdominal pain, emergency room	treat	25.00	95	23r
Burn dressing, emergency room	treat	266.00	95	23r
Cardiology interpretation, emergency room	treat	26.00	95	23r
Chest X-ray, emergency room	treat	78.00	95	23r
Childbirth, Cesarean delivery, hospital charge	birth	5462.00	12/91	69r
Childbirth, Cesarean delivery, physician charge	birth	2228.00	12/91	69r
Childbirth, normal delivery, hospital charge	birth	2943.00	12/91	69r
Childbirth, normal delivery, physician charge	birth	1619.00	12/91	69r
Defibrillation pads, emergency room	treat	6.00	95	23r
Dentist's fee, adult teeth cleaning and periodic oral exam	visit	43.67	12/94	2c
Doctor's fee, routine exam, established patient	visit	48.33	12/94	2c
Drugs, expenditures	year	297	91	81r
Gastric tube insertion, nasal, emergency room	treat	25.00	95	23r
Health care, total expenditures	year	1600	91	81r
Health insurance expenditures	year	637	91	81r
Heart monitor, emergency room	treat	40.00	95	23r
Hospital care, semiprivate room	day	407.50	12/94	2c
Insurance premium, family medical care	month	360.67	1/95	41s
Intravenous fluids, emergency room	treat	130.00	95	23r
Intravenous fluids, emergency room	liter	26.00	95	23r
Intravenous line, central, emergency room	treat	342.00	95	23r
Liver function tests, abdominal pain, emergency room	treat	26.00	95	23r
Medical care charges, total, emergency room, third-degree burns	treat	2101.00	95	23r
Medical care charges, total, emergency, infant with fever	treat	628.00	95	23r
Medical services expenditures	year	573	91	81r
Medical supplies expenditures	year	93	91	81r
Morphine, emergency room	treat	34.00	95	23r
Nursing care and facilities charges, emergency room	treat	252.00	95	23r

Gadsden, AL - continued

Item	Per	Value	Date	Ref.
Health Care - continued				
Nursing care and facilities charges, emergency, infant with fever	treat	252.00	95	23r
Nursing care and facilities charges, emergency, third-degree burns	treat	861.00	95	23r
Physician's charges, emergency, infant with fever	treat	212.00	95	23r
Physician's charges, emergency, third-degree burns	treat	372.00	95	23r
Physician's fee, emergency room	treat	372.00	95	23r
Physician's fee, general practitioner	visit	51.20	12/93	60r
Surgery, open-heart	proc	42374.00	1/93	14r
Ultrasound, abdominal, emergency room	treat	276.00	95	23r
Urinalysis, emergency room	treat	20.00	95	23r
Urinalysis, infant, emergency room	treat	20.00	95	23r
X-rays, emergency room	treat	78.00	95	23r
Household Goods				
Appl. repair, service call, wash mach	min. lab. chg.	31.67	12/94	2c
Floor coverings, expenditures	year	48	91	81r
Furniture, expenditures	year	280	91	81r
Household equipment, misc. expenditures	year	342	91	81r
Household expenditures, miscellaneous	year	256	91	81r
Household furnishings and equipment, expenditures	year	988	91	81r
Household operations expenditures	year	468	91	81r
Household textiles, expenditures	year	95	91	81r
Housekeeping supplies, expenditures	year	380	91	81r
Laundry and cleaning supplies, expenditures	year	109	91	81r
Laundry detergent, Tide Ultra, Bold, or Cheer	42 oz.	2.89	12/94	2c
Postage and stationery, expenditures	year	105	91	81r
Tissues, facial, Kleenex brand	175	0.91	12/94	2c
Housing				
Housing, ACCRA Index		82.60	12/94	2c
Add garage/carport		6,980	3/95	74r
Add room(s)		11,403	3/95	74r
Apartment condominium or co-op, median	unit	68600	12/94	62r
Dwellings (owned), expenditures	year	2428	91	81r
Enclose porch/patio/breezeway		4,572	3/95	74r
Finish room in basement/attic		3,794	3/95	74r
Home, existing, single-family, median	unit	120000	12/94	62r
House payment, principal and interest, 25% down payment	mo.	629	12/94	2c
House, 1800 sq ft, 8000 sq ft lot, new, urban, utilities	total	102000	12/94	2c
Maintenance, repairs, insurance, and other housing expenditures	year	531	91	81r
Mortgage interest and charges expenditures	year	1506	91	81r
Mtge. rate, incl. points and orig. fee, 30-year conv. fixed or ARM	mo.	9.24	12/94	2c
Princ. & int., mortgage, median-price exist. sing.-family home	mo.	540	12/94	62r
Property taxes expenditures	year	391	91	81r
Redesign, restructure more than half of home's interior		17,641	3/95	74r
Rent, apartment, 2 br., 1 1/2-2 baths, unfurnished, 950 sq ft, water	mo.	447	12/94	2c
Rental units expenditures	year	1264	91	81r
Insurance and Pensions				
Auto insurance, private passenger	year	604.07	12/94	71s
Insurance and pensions, personal, expenditures	year	2395	91	81r
Insurance, life and other personal, expenditures	year	368	91	81r
Pensions and Social Security, expenditures	year	2027	91	81r
Personal Goods				
Shampoo, Alberto VO5	15-oz.	1.07	12/94	2c
Toothpaste, Crest or Colgate	6-7 oz.	2.01	12/94	2c

Values are in dollars or fractions of dollars. In the column headed *Ref*, references are shown to sources. Each reference is followed by a letter. These refer to the geographical level for which data were reported: s = State, r = Region, and c = City or metro. The abbreviation *ex* is used to mean *except* or *excluding*; *exp* stands for expenditures. For other abbreviations and further explanations, please see the Introduction.

Gadsden, AL - continued

Item	Per	Value	Date	Ref.
Personal Services				
Dry cleaning, man's 2-pc. suit		5.50	12/94	2c
Haircut, man's barbershop, no styling		6.67	12/94	2c
Haircut, woman's shampoo, trim, blow-dry		19.00	12/94	2c
Personal services expenditures	year	212	91	81r
Restaurant Food				
Chicken, fried, thigh and drumstick		1.89	12/94	2c
Dining expenditures, family	week	33.83	94	73r
Hamburger with cheese	1/4 lb.	1.59	12/94	2c
Pizza, Pizza Hut or Pizza Inn	12-13 in.	7.99	12/94	2c
Taxes				
Taxes, Federal income, expenditures	year	2275	91	81r
Taxes, personal, expenditures	year	2715	91	81r
Taxes, State and local income, expenditures	year	365	91	81r
Transportation				
Transportation, ACCRA Index		97.00	12/94	2c
Cars and trucks purchased, new	year	1306	91	81r
Cars and trucks purchased, used	year	942	91	81r
Driver's learning permit fee	perm	20.00	1/94	84s
Driver's license fee	orig	20.00	1/94	84s
Driver's license fee, duplicate	lic	5.00	1/94	84s
Driver's license reinstatement fee, min.	susp	50.00	1/94	85s
Driver's license renewal fee	renew	20.00	1/94	84s
Identification card, nondriver	card	20.00	1/94	83s
Motorcycle license fee	orig	20.00	1/94	84s
Motorcycle license fee, duplicate	lic	5.00	1/94	84s
Motorcycle license renewal fee	renew	20.00	1/94	84s
Public transportation expenditures	year	249	91	81r
Tire balance, computer or spin bal., front	wheel	6.00	12/94	2c
Transportation expenditures, total	year	5307	91	81r
Vehicle finance charges	year	346	91	81r
Vehicle insurance expenditures	year	544	91	81r
Vehicle maintenance and repairs expenditures	year	600	91	81r
Vehicle purchases	year	2275	91	81r
Vehicle rental, leases, licenses, etc. expenditures	year	141	91	81r
Vehicles purchased, other than cars and trucks	year	27	91	81r
Utilities				
Utilities, ACCRA Index		114.00	12/94	2c
Electricity expenditures	year	950	91	81r
Electricity, (part.), other, 1800 sq. ft., new home	mo.	78.71	12/94	2c
Utilities, fuels, and public services, total expenditures	year	2000	91	81r
Water and other public services, expenditures	year	227	91	81r
Weddings				
Bridal attendants' gowns	event	750	10/93	76r
Bridal gown	event	852	10/93	76r
Bridal headpiece and veil	event	167	10/93	76r
Bride's wedding band	event	708	10/93	76r
Clergy	event	224	10/93	76r
Engagement ring	event	2756	10/93	76r
Flowers	event	863	10/93	76r
Formal wear for groom	event	106	10/93	76r
Groom's attendants' formal wear	event	530	10/93	76r
Groom's wedding band	event	402	10/93	76r
Music	event	600	10/93	76r
Photography	event	1088	10/93	76r
Shoes for bride	event	50	10/93	76r
Videography	event	483	10/93	76r
Wedding invitations and announcements	event	342	10/93	76r
Wedding reception	event	7000	10/93	76r

Gainesville, FL

Item	Per	Value	Date	Ref.
Appliances				
Appliances (major), expenditures	year	153	91	81r
Average annual exp.				
Food, health care, personal goods, services	year	27020	91	81r
Charity				
Cash contributions, expenditures	year	839	91	81r
Clothing				
Apparel, men and boys, total expenditures	year	380	91	81r
Apparel, women and girls, total expenditures	year	660	91	81r
Footwear, expenditures	year	193	91	81r
Communications				
Long-distance telephone rate, day, addl. min., 1-10 mi.	min.	0.08	12/93	9s
Long-distance telephone rate, day, initial min., 1-10 mi.	min.	0.15	12/93	9s
Phone line, single, business, field visit	inst	86.00	12/93	9s
Phone line, single, business, no field visit	inst	54.50	12/93	9s
Phone line, single, residence, field visit	inst	76.00	12/93	9s
Phone line, single, residence, no field visit	inst	44.50	12/93	9s
Telephone service, expenditures	year	616	91	81r
Telephone, residential, flat rate	mo.	8.80	12/93	8c
Education				
Bar examination preparatory course	course	500.00-100	94	17s
Board, 4-year private college/university	year	2123	8/94	80s
Board, 4-year public college/university	year	2101	8/94	80s
Education, total expenditures	year	319	91	81r
Room, 4-year private college/university	year	2242	8/94	80s
Room, 4-year public college/university	year	1970	8/94	80s
Total cost, 4-year private college/university	year	13853	8/94	80s
Total cost, 4-year public college/university	year	5855	8/94	80s
Tuition, 2-year public college/university, in-state	year	1076	8/94	80s
Tuition, 4-year private college/university, in-state	year	9287	8/94	80s
Tuition, 4-year public college/university, in-state	year	1784	8/94	80s
Energy and Fuels				
Fuel oil and other fuels, expenditures	year	56	91	81r
Gas, natural, expenditures	year	150	91	81r
Gasoline and motor oil purchased	year	1152	91	81r
Gasoline, unleaded midgrade	gallon	1.21	4/93	82r
Gasoline, unleaded premium	gallon	1.30	4/93	82r
Gasoline, unleaded regular	gallon	1.10	4/93	82r
Entertainment				
Concert ticket, Pearl Jam group	perf	20.00	94	50r
Entertainment, total expenditures	year	1266	91	81r
Fees and admissions, expenditures	year	306	91	81r
Pets, toys, playground equipment, expenditures	year	271	91	81r
Reading, expenditures	year	131	91	81r
Televisions, radios, and sound equipment, expenditures	year	439	91	81r
Funerals				
Burial, immediate, container provided by funeral home		1370.36	1/95	54r
Cards, acknowledgment		14.83	1/95	54r
Casket, minimum alternative		192.52	1/95	54r
Cosmetology, hair care, etc.		102.27	1/95	54r
Cremation, direct, container provided by funeral home		1065.64	1/95	54r
Embalming		304.29	1/95	54r
Funeral, funeral home		287.83	1/95	54r
Funeral, other facility		284.14	1/95	54r
Graveside service		349.13	1/95	54r
Hearse, local		132.27	1/95	54r
Limousine, local		98.45	1/95	54r
Memorial service		270.59	1/95	54r

Values are in dollars or fractions of dollars. In the column headed *Ref*, references are shown to sources. Each reference is followed by a letter. These refer to the geographical level for which data were reported: s=State, r=Region, and c=City or metro. The abbreviation *ex* is used to mean *except* or *excluding*; *exp* stands for expenditures. For other abbreviations and further explanations, please see the Introduction.

Gainesville, FL - continued

Item	Per	Value	Date	Ref.
Funerals				
Service charge, professional, nondeclinable		933.59	1/95	54r
Visitation and viewing		225.83	1/95	54r
Groceries				
Apples, Red Delicious	lb.	0.73	12/94	82r
Bacon, sliced	lb.	1.67	12/94	82r
Bananas	lb.	0.42	12/94	82r
Beef purchases	year	213	91	81r
Beverage purchases, alcoholic	year	249	91	81r
Beverage purchases, nonalcoholic	year	207	91	81r
Bologna, all beef or mixed	lb.	2.27	12/94	82r
Bread, white, pan	lb.	0.68	12/94	82r
Cabbage	lb.	0.42	12/94	82r
Carrots, short trimmed and topped	lb.	0.53	12/94	82r
Cereals and bakery products purchases	year	345	91	81r
Cereals and cereals products purchases	year	127	91	81r
Cheddar cheese, natural	lb.	3.58	12/94	82r
Chicken breast, bone-in	lb.	1.71	12/94	82r
Chicken, fresh, whole	lb.	0.78	12/94	82r
Chuck roast, USDA choice, boneless	lb.	2.26	12/94	82r
Crackers, soda, salted	lb.	1.27	12/94	82r
Cucumbers	lb.	0.65	12/94	82r
Dairy products (other) purchases	year	141	91	81r
Eggs, Grade A large	dozen	0.87	12/94	82r
Fish and seafood purchases	year	72	91	81r
Flour, white, all purpose	lb.	0.23	12/94	82r
Food purchases, food eaten at home	year	2381	91	81r
Foods purchased away from home, not prepared by consumer	year	1696	91	81r
Frankfurters, all meat or all beef	lb.	1.74	12/94	82r
Fruits and vegetables purchases	year	380	91	81r
Grapefruit	lb.	0.45	12/94	82r
Grapes, Thompson seedless	lb.	2.30	12/94	82r
Ground beef, 100% beef	lb.	1.37	12/94	82r
Ground chuck, 100% beef	lb.	1.97	12/94	82r
Ham, boneless, exc. canned	lb.	2.54	12/94	82r
Ice cream, prepackaged, bulk, regular	1/2 gal.	2.47	12/94	82r
Lemons	lb.	1.02	12/94	82r
Lettuce, iceberg	lb.	0.96	12/94	82r
Margarine, stick	lb.	0.77	12/94	82r
Meats, poultry, fish, and eggs purchases	year	655	91	81r
Milk and cream (fresh) purchases	year	130	91	81r
Orange juice, frozen concentrate 12-oz. can	16 oz.	1.36	12/94	82r
Oranges, Navel	lb.	0.54	12/94	82r
Pears, Anjou	lb.	0.81	12/94	82r
Pork chops, center cut, bone-in	lb.	3.07	12/94	82r
Pork purchases	year	142	91	81r
Potato chips	16-oz.	3.15	12/94	82r
Potatoes, frozen, French fried	lb.	0.82	12/94	82r
Potatoes, white	lb.	0.34	12/94	82r
Rice, white, long grain, uncooked	lb.	0.48	12/94	82r
Round roast, USDA choice, boneless	lb.	2.91	12/94	82r
Sausage, fresh	lb.	1.82	12/94	82r
Shortening, vegetable oil blends	lb.	0.75	12/94	82r
Spaghetti and macaroni	lb.	0.87	12/94	82r
Steak, rib eye, USDA choice, boneless	lb.	6.85	12/94	82r
Steak, round, graded & ungraded, exc. USDA prime & choice	lb.	2.96	12/94	82r
Steak, round, USDA choice, boneless	lb.	3.17	12/94	82r
Steak, sirloin, USDA choice, boneless	lb.	4.12	12/94	82r
Steak, T-bone, USDA choice, bone-in	lb.	5.63	12/94	82r
Sugar and other sweets, eaten at home, expenditures	year	93	91	81r
Sugar, white, all sizes	lb.	0.39	12/94	82r
Tobacco products and smoking supplies, total expenditures	year	286	91	81r
Tomatoes, field grown	lb.	1.36	12/94	82r
Tuna, chunk, light	lb.	1.94	12/94	82r
Turkey, frozen, whole	lb.	0.96	12/94	82r
Yogurt, natural, fruit flavored	8 oz.	0.58	12/94	82r

Gainesville, FL - continued

Item	Per	Value	Date	Ref.
Health Care				
Adenosine, emergency room	treat	100.00	95	23r
Bladder tap, superpubic, infant, emergency room	treat	119.00	95	23r
Blood analysis, emergency room	treat	25.00	95	23r
Blood tests, abdominal pain, emergency room	treat	25.00	95	23r
Burn dressing, emergency room	treat	266.00	95	23r
Cardiology interpretation, emergency room	treat	26.00	95	23r
Chest X-ray, emergency room	treat	78.00	95	23r
Childbirth, Cesarean delivery, hospital charge	birth	5462.00	12/91	69r
Childbirth, Cesarean delivery, physician charge	birth	2228.00	12/91	69r
Childbirth, normal delivery, hospital charge	birth	2943.00	12/91	69r
Childbirth, normal delivery, physician charge	birth	1619.00	12/91	69r
Defibrillation pads, emergency room	treat	6.00	95	23r
Drugs, expenditures	year	297	91	81r
Gastric tube insertion, nasal, emergency room	treat	25.00	95	23r
Health care, total expenditures	year	1600	91	81r
Health insurance expenditures	year	637	91	81r
Heart monitor, emergency room	treat	40.00	95	23r
Insurance premium, family medical care	month	301.92	1/95	41s
Intravenous fluids, emergency room	treat	130.00	95	23r
Intravenous fluids, emergency room	liter	26.00	95	23r
Intravenous line, central, emergency room	treat	342.00	95	23r
Liver function tests, abdominal pain, emergency room	treat	26.00	95	23r
Medical care charges, total, emergency room, third-degree burns	treat	2101.00	95	23r
Medical care charges, total, emergency, infant with fever	treat	628.00	95	23r
Medical services expenditures	year	573	91	81r
Medical supplies expenditures	year	93	91	81r
Morphine, emergency room	treat	34.00	95	23r
Nursing care and facilities charges, emergency room	treat	252.00	95	23r
Nursing care and facilities charges, emergency, infant with fever	treat	252.00	95	23r
Nursing care and facilities charges, emergency, third-degree burns	treat	861.00	95	23r
Physician's charges, emergency, infant with fever	treat	212.00	95	23r
Physician's charges, emergency, third-degree burns	treat	372.00	95	23r
Physician's fee, emergency room	treat	372.00	95	23r
Physician's fee, general practitioner	visit	51.20	12/93	60r
Surgery, open-heart	proc	42374.00	1/93	14r
Ultrasound, abdominal, emergency room	treat	276.00	95	23r
Urinalysis, emergency room	treat	20.00	95	23r
Urinalysis, infant, emergency room	treat	20.00	95	23r
X-rays, emergency room	treat	78.00	95	23r
Household Goods				
Floor coverings, expenditures	year	48	91	81r
Furniture, expenditures	year	280	91	81r
Household equipment, misc. expenditures	year	342	91	81r
Household expenditures, miscellaneous	year	256	91	81r
Household furnishings and equipment, expenditures	year	988	91	81r
Household operations expenditures	year	468	91	81r
Household textiles, expenditures	year	95	91	81r
Housekeeping supplies, expenditures	year	380	91	81r
Laundry and cleaning supplies, expenditures	year	109	91	81r
Postage and stationery, expenditures	year	105	91	81r
Housing				
Add garage/carport		6,980	3/95	74r
Add room(s)		11,403	3/95	74r
Apartment condominium or co-op, median	unit	68600	12/94	62r
Dwellings (owned), expenditures	year	2428	91	81r
Enclose porch/patio/breezeway		4,572	3/95	74r

Values are in dollars or fractions of dollars. In the column headed *Ref*, references are shown to sources. Each reference is followed by a letter. These refer to the geographical level for which data were reported: s=State, r=Region, and c=City or metro. The abbreviation *ex* is used to mean *except* or *excluding*; *exp* stands for *expenditures*. For other abbreviations and further explanations, please see the Introduction.

Gainesville, FL - continued

Item	Per	Value	Date	Ref.
Housing				
Finish room in basement/attic		3,794	3/95	74r
Home, existing, single-family, median	unit	120200	12/94	62r
Home, existing, single-family, median	unit	89.30	12/94	62c
Maintenance, repairs, insurance, and other housing expenditures	year	531	91	81r
Mortgage interest and charges expenditures	year	1506	91	81r
Princ. & int., mortgage, median-price exist. sing.-family home	mo.	540	12/94	62r
Property taxes expenditures	year	391	91	81r
Redesign, restructure more than half of home's interior		17,641	3/95	74r
Rental units expenditures	year	1264	91	81r
Insurance and Pensions				
Auto insurance, private passenger	year	753.93	12/94	71s
Insurance and pensions, personal, expenditures	year	2395	91	81r
Insurance, life and other personal, expenditures	year	368	91	81r
Pensions and Social Security, expenditures	year	2027	91	81r
Personal Services				
Personal services expenditures	year	212	91	81r
Restaurant Food				
Dining expenditures, family	week	33.83	94	73r
Taxes				
Taxes, Federal income, expenditures	year	2275	91	81r
Taxes, personal, expenditures	year	2715	91	81r
Taxes, State and local income, expenditures	year	365	91	81r
Transportation				
Cars and trucks purchased, new	year	1306	91	81r
Cars and trucks purchased, used	year	942	91	81r
Driver's learning permit fee	perm	20.00	1/94	84s
Driver's license fee	orig	20.00	1/94	84s
Driver's license fee, duplicate	lic	10.00	1/94	84s
Driver's license reinstatement fee, min.	susp	25.00	1/94	85s
Driver's license renewal fee	renew	15.00	1/94	84s
Identification card, nondriver	card	3.00	1/94	83s
Motorcycle learning permit fee	perm	20.00	1/94	84s
Motorcycle license fee	orig	20.00	1/94	84s
Motorcycle license fee, duplicate	lic	10.00	1/94	84s
Motorcycle license renewal fee	renew	15.00	1/94	84s
Public transportation expenditures	year	249	91	81r
Transportation expenditures, total	year	5307	91	81r
Vehicle finance charges	year	346	91	81r
Vehicle insurance expenditures	year	544	91	81r
Vehicle maintenance and repairs expenditures	year	600	91	81r
Vehicle purchases	year	2275	91	81r
Vehicle rental, leases, licenses, etc. expenditures	year	141	91	81r
Vehicles purchased, other than cars and trucks	year	27	91	81r
Utilities				
Electricity expenditures	year	950	91	81r
Utilities, fuels, and public services, total expenditures	year	2000	91	81r
Water and other public services, expenditures	year	227	91	81r
Weddings				
Bridal attendants' gowns	event	750	10/93	76r
Bridal gown	event	852	10/93	76r
Bridal headpiece and veil	event	167	10/93	76r
Bride's wedding band	event	708	10/93	76r
Clergy	event	224	10/93	76r
Engagement ring	event	2756	10/93	76r
Flowers	event	863	10/93	76r
Formal wear for groom	event	106	10/93	76r
Groom's attendants' formal wear	event	530	10/93	76r
Groom's wedding band	event	402	10/93	76r

Gainesville, FL - continued

Item	Per	Value	Date	Ref.
Weddings - continued				
Music	event	600	10/93	76r
Photography	event	1088	10/93	76r
Shoes for bride	event	50	10/93	76r
Videography	event	483	10/93	76r
Wedding invitations and announcements	event	342	10/93	76r
Wedding reception	event	7000	10/93	76r

Galveston-Texas City, TX

Item	Per	Value	Date	Ref.
Appliances				
Appliances (major), expenditures	year	153	91	81r
Average annual exp.				
Food, health care, personal goods, services	year	27020	91	81r
Charity				
Cash contributions, expenditures	year	839	91	81r
Clothing				
Apparel, men and boys, total expenditures	year	380	91	81r
Apparel, women and girls, total expenditures	year	660	91	81r
Footwear, expenditures	year	193	91	81r
Communications				
Long-distance telephone rate, day, addl. min., 1-10 mi.	min.	0.08	12/93	9s
Long-distance telephone rate, day, initial min., 1-10 mi.	min.	0.10	12/93	9s
Phone line, single, business, field visit	inst	71.90	12/93	9s
Phone line, single, business, no field visit	inst	57.30	12/93	9s
Phone line, single, residence, field visit	inst	52.95	12/93	9s
Phone line, single, residence, no field visit	inst	38.35	12/93	9s
Telephone service, expenditures	year	616	91	81r
Education				
Board, 4-year private college/university	year	2084	8/94	80s
Board, 4-year public college/university	year	1675	8/94	80s
Education, total expenditures	year	319	91	81r
Room, 4-year private college/university	year	1840	8/94	80s
Room, 4-year public college/university	year	1756	8/94	80s
Total cost, 4-year private college/university	year	11876	8/94	80s
Total cost, 4-year public college/university	year	4935	8/94	80s
Tuition, 2-year public college/university, in-state	year	625	8/94	80s
Tuition, 4-year private college/university, in-state	year	7952	8/94	80s
Tuition, 4-year public college/university, in-state	year	1503	8/94	80s
Energy and Fuels				
Fuel oil and other fuels, expenditures	year	56	91	81r
Gas, natural, expenditures	year	150	91	81r
Gasoline and motor oil purchased	year	1152	91	81r
Gasoline, unleaded midgrade	gallon	1.21	4/93	82r
Gasoline, unleaded premium	gallon	1.30	4/93	82r
Gasoline, unleaded regular	gallon	1.10	4/93	82r
Entertainment				
Concert ticket, Pearl Jam group	perf	20.00	94	50r
Entertainment, total expenditures	year	1266	91	81r
Fees and admissions, expenditures	year	306	91	81r
Pets, toys, playground equipment, expenditures	year	271	91	81r
Reading, expenditures	year	131	91	81r
Televisions, radios, and sound equipment, expenditures	year	439	91	81r
Funerals				
Burial, immediate, container provided by funeral home		1574.60	1/95	54r
Cards, acknowledgment		22.24	1/95	54r
Casket, minimum alternative		239.41	1/95	54r
Cosmetology, hair care, etc.		91.04	1/95	54r
Cremation, direct, container provided by funeral home		1085.15	1/95	54r

Values are in dollars or fractions of dollars. In the column headed *Ref*, references are shown to sources. Each reference is followed by a letter. These refer to the geographical level for which data were reported: s=State, r=Region, and c=City or metro. The abbreviation *ex* is used to mean *except* or *excluding*; *exp* stands for expenditures. For other abbreviations and further explanations, please see the Introduction.

Galveston-Texas City, TX - continued

Item	Per	Value	Date	Ref.
Funerals				
Embalming		281.30	1/95	54r
Funeral, funeral home		323.04	1/95	54r
Funeral, other facility		327.58	1/95	54r
Graveside service		355.19	1/95	54r
Hearse, local		141.89	1/95	54r
Limousine, local		99.40	1/95	54r
Memorial service		284.67	1/95	54r
Service charge, professional, nondeclinable		904.06	1/95	54r
Visitation and viewing		187.04	1/95	54r
Groceries				
Apples, Red Delicious	lb.	0.73	12/94	82r
Bacon, sliced	lb.	1.67	12/94	82r
Bananas	lb.	0.42	12/94	82r
Beef purchases	year	213	91	81r
Beverage purchases, alcoholic	year	249	91	81r
Beverage purchases, nonalcoholic	year	207	91	81r
Bologna, all beef or mixed	lb.	2.27	12/94	82r
Bread, white, pan	lb.	0.68	12/94	82r
Cabbage	lb.	0.42	12/94	82r
Carrots, short trimmed and topped	lb.	0.53	12/94	82r
Cereals and bakery products purchases	year	345	91	81r
Cereals and cereals products purchases	year	127	91	81r
Cheddar cheese, natural	lb.	3.58	12/94	82r
Chicken breast, bone-in	lb.	1.71	12/94	82r
Chicken, fresh, whole	lb.	0.78	12/94	82r
Chuck roast, USDA choice, boneless	lb.	2.26	12/94	82r
Crackers, soda, salted	lb.	1.27	12/94	82r
Cucumbers	lb.	0.65	12/94	82r
Dairy products (other) purchases	year	141	91	81r
Eggs, Grade A large	dozen	0.87	12/94	82r
Fish and seafood purchases	year	72	91	81r
Flour, white, all purpose	lb.	0.23	12/94	82r
Food purchases, food eaten at home	year	2381	91	81r
Foods purchased away from home, not prepared by consumer	year	1696	91	81r
Frankfurters, all meat or all beef	lb.	1.74	12/94	82r
Fruits and vegetables purchases	year	380	91	81r
Grapefruit	lb.	0.45	12/94	82r
Grapes, Thompson seedless	lb.	2.30	12/94	82r
Ground beef, 100% beef	lb.	1.37	12/94	82r
Ground chuck, 100% beef	lb.	1.97	12/94	82r
Ham, boneless, exc. canned	lb.	2.54	12/94	82r
Ice cream, prepackaged, bulk, regular	1/2 gal.	2.47	12/94	82r
Lemons	lb.	1.02	12/94	82r
Lettuce, iceberg	lb.	0.96	12/94	82r
Margarine, stick	lb.	0.77	12/94	82r
Meats, poultry, fish, and eggs purchases	year	655	91	81r
Milk and cream (fresh) purchases	year	130	91	81r
Orange juice, frozen concentrate 12-oz. can	16 oz.	1.36	12/94	82r
Oranges, Navel	lb.	0.54	12/94	82r
Pears, Anjou	lb.	0.81	12/94	82r
Pork chops, center cut, bone-in	lb.	3.07	12/94	82r
Pork purchases	year	142	91	81r
Potato chips	16-oz.	3.15	12/94	82r
Potatoes, frozen, French fried	lb.	0.82	12/94	82r
Potatoes, white	lb.	0.34	12/94	82r
Rice, white, long grain, uncooked	lb.	0.48	12/94	82r
Round roast, USDA choice, boneless	lb.	2.91	12/94	82r
Sausage, fresh	lb.	1.82	12/94	82r
Shortening, vegetable oil blends	lb.	0.75	12/94	82r
Spaghetti and macaroni	lb.	0.87	12/94	82r
Steak, rib eye, USDA choice, boneless	lb.	6.85	12/94	82r
Steak, round, graded & ungraded, exc. USDA prime & choice	lb.	2.96	12/94	82r
Steak, round, USDA choice, boneless	lb.	3.17	12/94	82r
Steak, sirloin, USDA choice, boneless	lb.	4.12	12/94	82r
Steak, T-bone, USDA choice, bone-in	lb.	5.63	12/94	82r
Sugar and other sweets, eaten at home, expenditures	year	93	91	81r
Sugar, white, all sizes	lb.	0.39	12/94	82r

Galveston-Texas City, TX - continued

Item	Per	Value	Date	Ref.
Groceries - continued				
Tobacco products and smoking supplies, total expenditures	year	286	91	81r
Tomatoes, field grown	lb.	1.36	12/94	82r
Tuna, chunk, light	lb.	1.94	12/94	82r
Turkey, frozen, whole	lb.	0.96	12/94	82r
Yogurt, natural, fruit flavored	8 oz.	0.58	12/94	82r
Health Care				
Adenosine, emergency room	treat	100.00	95	23r
Bladder tap, superpubic, infant, emergency room	treat	119.00	95	23r
Blood analysis, emergency room	treat	25.00	95	23r
Blood tests, abdominal pain, emergency room	treat	25.00	95	23r
Burn dressing, emergency room	treat	266.00	95	23r
Cardiology interpretation, emergency room	treat	26.00	95	23r
Chest X-ray, emergency room	treat	78.00	95	23r
Childbirth, Cesarean delivery, hospital charge	birth	5462.00	12/91	69r
Childbirth, Cesarean delivery, physician charge	birth	2228.00	12/91	69r
Childbirth, normal delivery, hospital charge	birth	2943.00	12/91	69r
Childbirth, normal delivery, physician charge	birth	1619.00	12/91	69r
Defibrillation pads, emergency room	treat	6.00	95	23r
Drugs, expenditures	year	297	91	81r
Gastric tube insertion, nasal, emergency room	treat	25.00	95	23r
Health care, total expenditures	year	1600	91	81r
Health insurance expenditures	year	637	91	81r
Heart monitor, emergency room	treat	40.00	95	23r
Insurance premium, family medical care	month	389.25	1/95	41s
Intravenous fluids, emergency room	treat	130.00	95	23r
Intravenous fluids, emergency room	liter	26.00	95	23r
Intravenous line, central, emergency room	treat	342.00	95	23r
Liver function tests, abdominal pain, emergency room	treat	26.00	95	23r
Medical care charges, total, emergency room, third-degree burns	treat	2101.00	95	23r
Medical care charges, total, emergency, infant with fever	treat	628.00	95	23r
Medical services expenditures	year	573	91	81r
Medical supplies expenditures	year	93	91	81r
Morphine, emergency room	treat	34.00	95	23r
Nursing care and facilities charges, emergency room	treat	252.00	95	23r
Nursing care and facilities charges, emergency, infant with fever	treat	252.00	95	23r
Nursing care and facilities charges, emergency, third-degree burns	treat	861.00	95	23r
Physician's charges, emergency, infant with fever	treat	212.00	95	23r
Physician's charges, emergency, third-degree burns	treat	372.00	95	23r
Physician's fee, emergency room	treat	372.00	95	23r
Physician's fee, general practitioner	visit	51.20	12/93	60r
Surgery, open-heart	proc	42374.00	1/93	14r
Ultrasound, abdominal, emergency room	treat	276.00	95	23r
Urinalysis, emergency room	treat	20.00	95	23r
Urinalysis, infant, emergency room	treat	20.00	95	23r
X-rays, emergency room	treat	78.00	95	23r
Household Goods				
Floor coverings, expenditures	year	48	91	81r
Furniture, expenditures	year	280	91	81r
Household equipment, misc. expenditures	year	342	91	81r
Household expenditures, miscellaneous	year	256	91	81r
Household furnishings and equipment, expenditures	year	988	91	81r
Household operations expenditures	year	468	91	81r
Household textiles, expenditures	year	95	91	81r
Housekeeping supplies, expenditures	year	380	91	81r
Laundry and cleaning supplies, expenditures	year	109	91	81r

Values are in dollars or fractions of dollars. In the column headed *Ref*, references are shown to sources. Each reference is followed by a letter. These refer to the geographical level for which data were reported: s=State, r=Region, and c=City or metro. The abbreviation *ex* is used to mean *except* or *excluding*; *exp* stands for *expenditures*. For other abbreviations and further explanations, please see the Introduction.

Galveston-Texas City, TX - continued

Item	Per	Value	Date	Ref.
Household Goods				
Postage and stationery, expenditures	year	105	91	81r
Housing				
Add garage/carport		6,980	3/95	74r
Add room(s)		11,403	3/95	74r
Apartment condominium or co-op, median	unit	68600	12/94	62r
Dwellings (owned), expenditures	year	2428	91	81r
Enclose porch/patio/breezeway		4,572	3/95	74r
Finish room in basement/attic		3,794	3/95	74r
Home, existing, single-family, median	unit	120200	12/94	62r
Maintenance, repairs, insurance, and other housing expenditures	year	531	91	81r
Mortgage interest and charges expenditures	year	1506	91	81r
Princ. & int., mortgage, median-price exist. sing.-family home	mo.	540	12/94	62r
Property taxes expenditures	year	391	91	81r
Redesign, restructure more than half of home's interior		17,641	3/95	74r
Rental units expenditures	year	1264	91	81r
Insurance and Pensions				
Auto insurance, private passenger	year	785.78	12/94	71s
Insurance and pensions, personal, expenditures	year	2395	91	81r
Insurance, life and other personal, expenditures	year	368	91	81r
Pensions and Social Security, expenditures	year	2027	91	81r
Personal Services				
Personal services expenditures	year	212	91	81r
Restaurant Food				
Dining expenditures, family	week	33.83	94	73r
Taxes				
Tax, cigarettes	year	584.00	10/93	43s
Taxes, Federal income, expenditures	year	2275	91	81r
Taxes, personal, expenditures	year	2715	91	81r
Taxes, State and local income, expenditures	year	365	91	81r
Transportation				
Cars and trucks purchased, new	year	1306	91	81r
Cars and trucks purchased, used	year	942	91	81r
Driver's learning permit fee	perm	5.00	1/94	84s
Driver's license fee	orig	16.00	1/94	84s
Driver's license fee, duplicate	lic	10.00	1/94	84s
Driver's license reinstatement fee, min.	susp	50.00	1/94	85s
Driver's license renewal fee	renew	16.00	1/94	84s
Identification fee, nondriver	card	10.00	1/94	83s
Motorcycle learning permit fee	perm	5.00	1/94	84s
Motorcycle license fee	orig	16.00	1/94	84s
Motorcycle license fee, duplicate	lic	10.00	1/94	84s
Motorcycle license renewal fee	renew	21.00	1/94	84s
Public transportation expenditures	year	249	91	81r
Transportation expenditures, total	year	5307	91	81r
Vehicle finance charges	year	346	91	81r
Vehicle insurance expenditures	year	544	91	81r
Vehicle maintenance and repairs expenditures	year	600	91	81r
Vehicle purchases	year	2275	91	81r
Vehicle rental, leases, licenses, etc. expenditures	year	141	91	81r
Vehicles purchased, other than cars and trucks	year	27	91	81r
Utilities				
Electricity expenditures	year	950	91	81r
Utilities, fuels, and public services, total expenditures	year	2000	91	81r
Water and other public services, expenditures	year	227	91	81r
Weddings				
Bridal attendants' gowns	event	750	10/93	76r
Bridal gown	event	852	10/93	76r
Bridal headpiece and veil	event	167	10/93	76r

Galveston-Texas City, TX - continued

Item	Per	Value	Date	Ref.
Weddings - continued				
Bride's wedding band	event	708	10/93	76r
Clergy	event	224	10/93	76r
Engagement ring	event	2756	10/93	76r
Flowers	event	863	10/93	76r
Formal wear for groom	event	106	10/93	76r
Groom's attendants' formal wear	event	530	10/93	76r
Groom's wedding band	event	402	10/93	76r
Music	event	600	10/93	76r
Photography	event	1088	10/93	76r
Shoes for bride	event	50	10/93	76r
Videography	event	483	10/93	76r
Wedding invitations and announcements	event	342	10/93	76r
Wedding reception	event	7000	10/93	76r

Garden City, KS

Item	Per	Value	Date	Ref.
Composite, ACCRA index		96.60	12/94	2c
Alcoholic Beverages				
Beer, Miller Lite, Bud, 12-oz., ex deposit	6	3.93	12/94	2c
J & B Scotch	750-ml.	18.42	12/94	2c
Wine, Gallo Chablis blanc	1.5-lit	5.13	12/94	2c
Clothing				
Jeans, man's denim		28.08	12/94	2c
Shirt, man's dress shirt		33.00	12/94	2c
Undervest, boy's size 10-14, cotton	3	3.35	12/94	2c
Communications				
Newspaper subscription, dly. and Sun. delivery	month	16.04	12/94	2c
Telephone bill, family of four	month	16.23	12/94	2c
Telephone, residential, flat rate	mo.	10.05	12/93	8c
Energy and Fuels				
Energy, combined forms, 1800 sq. ft.	mo.	116.44	12/94	2c
Energy, exc. electricity, 1800 sq. ft.	mo.	33.84	12/94	2c
Gas, cooking, 10 therms	month	9.18	2/94	65c
Gas, cooking, 30 therms	month	15.54	2/94	65c
Gas, cooking, 50 therms	month	21.90	2/94	65c
Gas, heating, winter, 100 therms	month	37.80	2/94	65c
Gas, heating, winter, average use	month	69.60	2/94	65c
Gas, reg unlead, taxes inc., cash, self-service	gal	1.20	12/94	2c
Entertainment				
Bowling, evening rate	game	2.05	12/94	2c
Monopoly game, Parker Brothers', No. 9	game	11.35	12/94	2c
Movie	adm	4.50	12/94	2c
Tennis balls, yellow, Wilson or Penn, 3	can	2.24	12/94	2c
Groceries				
Groceries, ACCRA Index		96.60	12/94	2c
Baby food, strained vegetables, lowest price	4-4.5 oz.	0.29	12/94	2c
Bananas	lb.	0.36	12/94	2c
Beef or hamburger, ground	lb.	1.11	12/94	2c
Bread, white	24-oz.	0.60	12/94	2c
Cheese, Kraft grated Parmesan	8-oz.	3.88	12/94	2c
Chicken, whole fryer	lb.	0.75	12/94	2c
Cigarettes, Winston, Kings	carton	15.79	12/94	2c
Coffee, vacuum-packed	13 oz.	3.36	12/94	2c
Corn Flakes, Kellogg's or Post Toasties	18 oz.	2.90	12/94	2c
Corn, frozen, whole kernel, lowest price	10 oz.	0.69	12/94	2c
Eggs, Grade A large	dozen	0.66	12/94	2c
Lettuce, iceberg	head	0.99	12/94	2c
Margarine, Blue Bonnet or Parkay cubes	lb.	0.47	12/94	2c
Milk, whole	1/2 gal.	1.35	12/94	2c
Orange juice, Minute Maid frozen	12-oz.	1.41	12/94	2c
Peaches, halves or slices, Hunt's, Del Monte, or Libby's	29-oz.	1.39	12/94	2c

Values are in dollars or fractions of dollars. In the column headed *Ref*, references are shown to sources. Each reference is followed by a letter. These refer to the geographical level for which data were reported: s=State, r=Region, and c=City or metro. The abbreviation *ex* is used to mean *except* or *excluding*; *exp* stands for expenditures. For other abbreviations and further explanations, please see the Introduction.

Garden City, KS - continued

Item	Per	Value	Date	Ref.
Groceries				
Peas, sweet, Del Monte or Green Giant	15-17 oz.	0.64	12/94	2c
Potatoes, white or red	10-lb. sack	1.79	12/94	2c
Sausage, Jimmy Dean, 100% pork	lb.	2.82	12/94	2c
Shortening, vegetable, Crisco	3-lb.	2.79	12/94	2c
Soft drink, Coca Cola, ex deposit	2 lit	0.96	12/94	2c
Steak, t-bone	lb.	5.49	12/94	2c
Sugar, cane or beet	4 lbs.	1.27	12/94	2c
Tomatoes, Hunt's or Del Monte	14.5 oz.	0.76	12/94	2c
Tuna, chunk, light, oil-packed	6.125-6.5 oz.	0.74	12/94	2c
Goods and Services				
Miscellaneous goods and services, ACCRA Index		103.00	12/94	2c
Health Care				
Health care, ACCRA Index		96.80	12/94	2c
Antibiotic ointment, Polysporin	1.5 oz.	4.24	12/94	2c
Dentist's fee, adult teeth cleaning and periodic oral exam	visit	48.40	12/94	2c
Doctor's fee, routine exam, established patient	visit	45.00	12/94	2c
Hospital care, semiprivate room	day	280.00	12/94	2c
Household Goods				
Appl. repair, service call, wash mach	min. lab. chg.	39.83	12/94	2c
Laundry detergent, Tide Ultra, Bold, or Cheer	42 oz.	3.92	12/94	2c
Tissues, facial, Kleenex brand	175	0.99	12/94	2c
Housing				
Housing, ACCRA Index		82.40	12/94	2c
House payment, principal and interest, 25% down payment	mo.	617	12/94	2c
House, 1800 sq ft, 8000 sq ft lot, new, urban, utilities	total	97333	12/94	2c
Mtge. rate, incl. points and orig. fee, 30-year conv. fixed or ARM	mo.	8.56	12/94	2c
Rent, apartment, 2 br., 1 1/2-2 baths, unfurnished, 950 sq ft, water	mo.	475	12/94	2c
Personal Goods				
Shampoo, Alberto VO5	15-oz.	1.17	12/94	2c
Toothpaste, Crest or Colgate	6-7 oz.	1.81	12/94	2c
Personal Services				
Dry cleaning, man's 2-pc. suit		5.67	12/94	2c
Haircut, man's barbershop, no styling		8.00	12/94	2c
Haircut, woman's shampoo, trim, blow-dry		19.80	12/94	2c
Restaurant Food				
Chicken, fried, thigh and drumstick		2.50	12/94	2c
Hamburger with cheese	1/4 lb.	1.74	12/94	2c
Pizza, Pizza Hut or Pizza Inn	12-13 in.	10.29	12/94	2c
Transportation				
Transportation, ACCRA Index		112.90	12/94	2c
Tire balance, computer or spin bal., front	wheel	8.22	12/94	2c
Utilities				
Utilities, ACCRA Index		101.00	12/94	2c
Electricity, (part.), other, 1800 sq. ft., new home	mo.	82.60	12/94	2c

Gary-Hammond, IN

Item	Per	Value	Date	Ref.
Appliances				
Appliances (major), expenditures	year	131	91	81r
Average annual exp.				
Food, health care, personal goods, services	year	25935	91	81r
Charity				
Cash contributions, expenditures	year	745	91	81r
Clothing				
Apparel, men and boys, total expenditures	year	332	91	81r
Apparel, women and girls, total expenditures	year	578	91	81r
Footwear, expenditures	year	164	91	81r
Communications				
Long-distance telephone rate, day, addl. min., 1-10 mi.	min.	0.10	12/93	9s
Long-distance telephone rate, day, initial min., 1-10 mi.	min.	0.18	12/93	9s
Phone line, single, business, field visit	inst	59.00	12/93	9s
Phone line, single, business, no field visit	inst	59.00	12/93	9s
Phone line, single, residence, field visit	inst	47.00	12/93	9s
Phone line, single, residence, no field visit	inst	47.00	12/93	9s
Telephone service, expenditures	year	547	91	81r
Education				
Board, 4-year private college/university	year	2095	8/94	80s
Board, 4-year public college/university	year	2300	8/94	80s
Education, total expenditures	year	394	91	81r
Room, 4-year private college/university	year	1784	8/94	80s
Room, 4-year public college/university	year	1718	8/94	80s
Total cost, 4-year private college/university	year	15045	8/94	80s
Total cost, 4-year public college/university	year	6639	8/94	80s
Tuition, 2-year public college/university, in-state	year	1737	8/94	80s
Tuition, 4-year private college/university, in-state	year	11165	8/94	80s
Tuition, 4-year public college/university, in-state	year	2621	8/94	80s
Energy and Fuels				
Fuel oil and other fuels, expenditures	year	83	91	81r
Gas, natural, expenditures	year	373	91	81r
Gasoline and motor oil purchased	year	1000	91	81r
Gasoline, unleaded midgrade	gallon	1.15	4/93	82r
Gasoline, unleaded premium	gallon	1.23	4/93	82r
Gasoline, unleaded regular	gallon	1.07	4/93	82r
Entertainment				
Entertainment, total expenditures	year	1356	91	81r
Fees and admissions, expenditures	year	347	91	81r
Pets, toys, playground equipment, expenditures	year	270	91	81r
Reading, expenditures	year	160	91	81r
Televisions, radios, and sound equipment, expenditures	year	433	91	81r
Funerals				
Burial, immediate, container provided by funeral home		1268.31	1/95	54r
Cards, acknowledgment		26.12	1/95	54r
Casket, minimum alternative		198.03	1/95	54r
Cosmetology, hair care, etc.		122.19	1/95	54r
Cremation, direct, container provided by funeral home		977.81	1/95	54r
Embalming		334.00	1/95	54r
Funeral, funeral home		321.16	1/95	54r
Funeral, other facility		317.73	1/95	54r
Graveside service		292.48	1/95	54r
Hearse, local		153.20	1/95	54r
Limousine, local		123.52	1/95	54r
Memorial service		356.30	1/95	54r
Service charge, professional, nondeclinable		968.24	1/95	54r
Visitation and viewing		332.66	1/95	54r

Values are in dollars or fractions of dollars. In the column headed *Ref*, references are shown to sources. Each reference is followed by a letter. These refer to the geographical level for which data were reported: s=State, r=Region, and c=City or metro. The abbreviation *ex* is used to mean *except* or *excluding*; *exp* stands for expenditures. For other abbreviations and further explanations, please see the Introduction.

Gary-Hammond, IN - continued

Item	Per	Value	Date	Ref.
Groceries				
Apples, Red Delicious	lb.	0.68	12/94	82r
Bacon, sliced	lb.	1.88	12/94	82r
Bananas	lb.	0.41	12/94	82r
Beef purchases	year	197	91	81r
Beef, stew, boneless	lb.	2.52	12/94	82r
Beverage purchases, alcoholic	year	293	91	81r
Beverage purchases, nonalcoholic	year	203	91	81r
Bologna, all beef or mixed	lb.	2.12	12/94	82r
Bread, white, pan	lb.	0.76	12/94	82r
Cabbage	lb.	0.44	12/94	82r
Carrots, short trimmed and topped	lb.	0.44	12/94	82r
Cereals and bakery products purchases	year	347	91	81r
Cereals and cereals products purchases	year	119	91	81r
Cheddar cheese, natural	lb.	3.28	12/94	82r
Chicken breast, bone-in	lb.	1.61	12/94	82r
Chicken, fresh, whole	lb.	0.89	12/94	82r
Chuck roast, USDA choice, boneless	lb.	2.33	12/94	82r
Coffee, 100%, ground roast, all sizes	lb.	4.28	12/94	82r
Cookies, chocolate chip	lb.	2.72	12/94	82r
Dairy products (other) purchases	year	148	91	81r
Eggs, Grade A large	dozen	0.76	12/94	82r
Fish and seafood purchases	year	61	91	81r
Flour, white, all purpose	lb.	0.22	12/94	82r
Food purchases, food eaten at home	year	2313	91	81r
Foods purchased away from home, not prepared by consumer	year	1709	91	81r
Fruits and vegetables purchases	year	372	91	81r
Grapefruit	lb.	0.47	12/94	82r
Grapes, Thompson seedless	lb.	2.15	12/94	82r
Ground beef, 100% beef	lb.	1.37	12/94	82r
Ground chuck, 100% beef	lb.	1.81	12/94	82r
Ham, boneless, exc. canned	lb.	2.16	12/94	82r
Ice cream, prepackaged, bulk, regular	1/2 gal.	2.48	12/94	82r
Lemons	lb.	1.08	12/94	82r
Lettuce, iceberg	lb.	0.81	12/94	82r
Margarine, stick	lb.	0.81	12/94	82r
Meats, poultry, fish, and eggs purchases	year	591	91	81r
Milk and cream (fresh) purchases	year	132	91	81r
Orange juice, frozen concentrate 12-oz. can	16 oz.	1.41	12/94	82r
Oranges, Navel	lb.	0.56	12/94	82r
Peanut butter, creamy, all sizes	lb.	1.81	12/94	82r
Pork chops, center cut, bone-in	lb.	2.76	12/94	82r
Pork purchases	year	130	91	81r
Potato chips	16-oz.	2.81	12/94	82r
Potatoes, frozen, French fried	lb.	0.83	12/94	82r
Potatoes, white	lb.	0.28	12/94	82r
Round roast, USDA choice, boneless	lb.	2.90	12/94	82r
Shortening, vegetable oil blends	lb.	0.88	12/94	82r
Spaghetti and macaroni	lb.	0.78	12/94	82r
Steak, rib eye, USDA choice, boneless	lb.	6.15	12/94	82r
Steak, round, graded & ungraded, exc. USDA prime & choice	lb.	2.72	12/94	82r
Steak, round, USDA choice, boneless	lb.	3.02	12/94	82r
Steak, sirloin, USDA choice, boneless	lb.	3.85	12/94	82r
Steak, T-bone, USDA choice, bone-in	lb.	5.38	12/94	82r
Sugar and other sweets, eaten at home, expenditures	year	91	91	81r
Sugar, white, all sizes	lb.	0.36	12/94	82r
Tobacco products and smoking supplies, total expenditures	year	298	91	81r
Tomatoes, field grown	lb.	1.36	12/94	82r
Tuna, chunk, light	lb.	1.94	12/94	82r
Turkey, frozen, whole	lb.	0.96	12/94	82r
Yogurt, natural, fruit flavored	8 oz.	0.62	12/94	82r
Health Care				
Childbirth, Cesarean delivery, hospital charge	birth	5101.00	12/91	69r
Childbirth, Cesarean delivery, physician charge	birth	2234.00	12/91	69r
Childbirth, normal delivery, hospital charge	birth	2891.00	12/91	69r
Childbirth, normal delivery, physician charge	birth	1623.00	12/91	69r

Gary-Hammond, IN - continued

Item	Per	Value	Date	Ref.
Health Care - continued				
Drugs, expenditures	year	248	91	81r
Health care, total expenditures	year	1336	91	81r
Health insurance expenditures	year	550	91	81r
Insurance premium, family medical care	month	353.94	1/95	41s
Medical services expenditures	year	457	91	81r
Medical supplies expenditures	year	82	91	81r
Household Goods				
Floor coverings, expenditures	year	105	91	81r
Furniture, expenditures	year	291	91	81r
Household equipment, misc. expenditures	year	341	91	81r
Household expenditures, miscellaneous	year	162	91	81r
Household furnishings and equipment, expenditures	year	1042	91	81r
Household operations expenditures	year	365	91	81r
Household textiles, expenditures	year	101	91	81r
Housekeeping supplies, expenditures	year	390	91	81r
Laundry and cleaning supplies, expenditures	year	110	91	81r
Postage and stationery, expenditures	year	115	91	81r
Housing				
Add garage/carport		8,479	3/95	74r
Add room(s)		21,347	3/95	74r
Apartment condominium or co-op, median	unit	87100	12/94	62r
Bathroom addition, average cost	add	9734.00	3/95	13r
Bathroom remodeling, average cost	remod	6414.00	3/95	13r
Bedroom, master suite addition, average cost	add	27122.00	3/95	13r
Deck addition, average cost	add	6665.00	3/95	13r
Dwellings (owned), expenditures	year	2566	91	81r
Enclose porch/patio/breezeway		4,556	3/95	74r
Exterior remodeling, average cost	remod	15395.00	3/95	13r
Family room addition, average cost	add	27658.00	3/95	13r
Finish room in basement/attic		5,074	3/95	74r
Home, existing, single-family, median	unit	106500	12/94	62r
Kitchen remodeling, major, average cost	remod	17084.00	3/95	13r
Kitchen remodeling, minor, average cost	remod	5804.00	3/95	13r
Maintenance, repairs, insurance, and other housing expenditures	year	484	91	81r
Mortgage interest and charges expenditures	year	1443	91	81r
Office, home addition, average cost	add	8121.00	3/95	13r
Princ. & int., mortgage, median-price exist. sing.-family home	mo.	515	12/94	62r
Property taxes expenditures	year	639	91	81r
Redesign, restructure more than half of home's interior		9,114	3/95	74r
Rental units expenditures	year	1200	91	81r
Sun-space addition, average cost	add	23768.00	3/95	13r
Wing addition, two-story, average cost	add	50410.00	3/95	13r
Insurance and Pensions				
Auto insurance, private passenger	year	586.58	12/94	71s
Insurance and pensions, personal, expenditures	year	2408	91	81r
Insurance, life and other personal, expenditures	year	355	91	81r
Pensions and Social Security, expenditures	year	2053	91	81r
Legal Assistance				
Legal work, law firm associate	hour	90		10r
Legal work, law firm partner	hour	139		10r
Personal Services				
Personal services expenditures	year	203	91	81r
Restaurant Food				
Dining expenditures, family	week	30.03	94	73r
Taxes				
Taxes, Federal income, expenditures	year	1756	91	81r
Taxes, personal, expenditures	year	2426	91	81r
Taxes, State and local income, expenditures	year	568	91	81r

Values are in dollars or fractions of dollars. In the column headed *Ref*, references are shown to sources. Each reference is followed by a letter. These refer to the geographical level for which data were reported: s = State, r = Region, and c = City or metro. The abbreviation *ex* is used to mean *except* or *excluding*; *exp* stands for *expenditures*. For other abbreviations and further explanations, please see the Introduction.

Gary-Hammond, IN - continued

Item	Per	Value	Date	Ref.
Transportation				
Cars and trucks purchased, new	year	891	91	81r
Cars and trucks purchased, used	year	1155	91	81r
Driver's learning permit fee	perm	2.00	1/94	84s
Driver's license fee	orig	6.00	1/94	84s
Driver's license fee, duplicate	lic	3.00	1/94	84s
Driver's license renewal fee	renew	6.00	1/94	84s
Identification card, nondriver	card	4.00	1/94	83s
Motorcycle learning permit fee	perm	2.00	1/94	84s
Motorcycle license fee	orig	6.00	1/94	84s
Motorcycle license fee, duplicate	lic	3.00	1/94	84s
Motorcycle license renewal fee	renew	6.00	1/94	84s
Public transportation expenditures	year	209	91	81r
Transportation expenditures, total	year	4792	91	81r
Vehicle finance charges	year	300	91	81r
Vehicle insurance expenditures	year	485	91	81r
Vehicle maintenance and repairs expenditures	year	534	91	81r
Vehicle purchases	year	2068	91	81r
Vehicle rental, leases, licenses, etc. expenditures	year	197	91	81r
Vehicles purchased, other than cars and trucks	year	22	91	81r
Utilities				
Electricity expenditures	year	668	91	81r
Utilities, fuels, and public services, total expenditures	year	1838	91	81r
Water and other public services, expenditures	year	167	91	81r
Weddings				
Bridal attendants' gowns	event	750	10/93	76r
Bridal gown	event	852	10/93	76r
Bridal headpiece and veil	event	167	10/93	76r
Bride's wedding band	event	708	10/93	76r
Clergy	event	224	10/93	76r
Engagement ring	event	2756	10/93	76r
Flowers	event	863	10/93	76r
Formal wear for groom	event	106	10/93	76r
Groom's attendants' formal wear	event	530	10/93	76r
Groom's wedding band	event	402	10/93	76r
Music	event	600	10/93	76r
Photography	event	1088	10/93	76r
Shoes for bride	event	50	10/93	76r
Videography	event	483	10/93	76r
Wedding invitations and announcements	event	342	10/93	76r
Wedding reception	event	7000	10/93	76r

Georgetown, TX

Item	Per	Value	Date	Ref.
Composite, ACCRA index		96.60	12/94	2c
Alcoholic Beverages				
Beer, Miller Lite, Bud, 12-oz., ex deposit	6	3.92	12/94	2c
J & B Scotch	750-ml.	17.42	12/94	2c
Wine, Gallo Chablis blanc	1.5-lit	5.49	12/94	2c
Clothing				
Jeans, man's denim		29.97	12/94	2c
Shirt, man's dress shirt		28.48	12/94	2c
Undervest, boy's size 10-14, cotton	3	3.56	12/94	2c
Communications				
Newspaper subscription, dly. and Sun. delivery	month	11.76	12/94	2c
Telephone bill, family of four	month	13.73	12/94	2c
Energy and Fuels				
Energy, combined forms, 1800 sq. ft.	mo.	108.73	12/94	2c
Energy, exc. electricity, 1800 sq. ft.	mo.	27.00	12/94	2c
Gas, reg unlead, taxes inc., cash, self-service	gal	1.12	12/94	2c

Georgetown, TX - continued

Item	Per	Value	Date	Ref.
Entertainment				
Bowling, evening rate	game	2.40	12/94	2c
Monopoly game, Parker Brothers', No. 9	game	11.48	12/94	2c
Movie	adm	5.50	12/94	2c
Tennis balls, yellow, Wilson or Penn, 3	can	1.97	12/94	2c
Groceries				
Groceries, ACCRA Index		96.60	12/94	2c
Baby food, strained vegetables, lowest price	4-4.5 oz.	0.26	12/94	2c
Bananas	lb.	0.39	12/94	2c
Beef or hamburger, ground	lb.	1.81	12/94	2c
Bread, white	24-oz.	0.62	12/94	2c
Cheese, Kraft grated Parmesan	8-oz.	3.38	12/94	2c
Chicken, whole fryer	lb.	0.86	12/94	2c
Cigarettes, Winston, Kings	carton	18.85	12/94	2c
Coffee, vacuum-packed	13 oz.	3.36	12/94	2c
Corn Flakes, Kellogg's or Post Toasties	18 oz.	2.55	12/94	2c
Corn, frozen, whole kernel, lowest price	10 oz.	0.63	12/94	2c
Eggs, Grade A large	dozen	0.71	12/94	2c
Lettuce, iceberg	head	0.73	12/94	2c
Margarine, Blue Bonnet or Parkay cubes	lb.	0.59	12/94	2c
Milk, whole	1/2 gal.	1.24	12/94	2c
Orange juice, Minute Maid frozen	12-oz.	1.09	12/94	2c
Peaches, halves or slices, Hunt's, Del Monte, or Libby's	29-oz.	1.39	12/94	2c
Peas, sweet, Del Monte or Green Giant	15-17 oz.	0.70	12/94	2c
Potatoes, white or red	10-lb. sack	2.11	12/94	2c
Sausage, Jimmy Dean, 100% pork	lb.	2.72	12/94	2c
Shortening, vegetable, Crisco	3-lb.	2.29	12/94	2c
Soft drink, Coca Cola, ex deposit	2 lit	1.61	12/94	2c
Steak, t-bone	lb.	2.98	12/94	2c
Sugar, cane or beet	4 lbs.	1.42	12/94	2c
Tomatoes, Hunt's or Del Monte	14.5 oz.	0.55	12/94	2c
Tuna, chunk, light, oil-packed	6.125-6.5 oz.	0.73	12/94	2c
Goods and Services				
Miscellaneous goods and services, ACCRA Index		98.50	12/94	2c
Health Care				
Health care, ACCRA Index		101.60	12/94	2c
Antibiotic ointment, Polysporin	1.5 oz.	4.32	12/94	2c
Dentist's fee, adult teeth cleaning and periodic oral exam	visit	49.33	12/94	2c
Doctor's fee, routine exam, established patient	visit	47.50	12/94	2c
Hospital care, semiprivate room	day	325.00	12/94	2c
Household Goods				
Appl. repair, service call, wash mach	min. lab. chg.	37.45	12/94	2c
Laundry detergent, Tide Ultra, Bold, or Cheer	42 oz.	3.20	12/94	2c
Tissues, facial, Kleenex brand	175	0.99	12/94	2c
Housing				
Housing, ACCRA Index		92.40	12/94	2c
House payment, principal and interest, 25% down payment	mo.	699	12/94	2c
House, 1800 sq ft, 8000 sq ft lot, new, urban, utilities	total	116100	12/94	2c
Mtge. rate, incl. points and orig. fee, 30-year conv. fixed or ARM	mo.	8.98	12/94	2c
Rent, apartment, 2 br., 1 1/2-2 baths, unfurnished, 950 sq ft, water	mo.	513	12/94	2c
Personal Goods				
Shampoo, Alberto VO5	15-oz.	1.12	12/94	2c
Toothpaste, Crest or Colgate	6-7 oz.	2.12	12/94	2c

Values are in dollars or fractions of dollars. In the column headed *Ref*, references are shown to sources. Each reference is followed by a letter. These refer to the geographical level for which data were reported: s=State, r=Region, and c=City or metro. The abbreviation *ex* is used to mean *except* or *excluding*; *exp* stands for *expenditures*. For other abbreviations and further explanations, please see the Introduction.

Georgetown, TX - continued

Item	Per	Value	Date	Ref.
Personal Services				
Dry cleaning, man's 2-pc. suit		6.38	12/94	2c
Haircut, man's barbershop, no styling		6.25	12/94	2c
Haircut, woman's shampoo, trim, blow-dry		23.50	12/94	2c
Restaurant Food				
Chicken, fried, thigh and drumstick		2.19	12/94	2c
Hamburger with cheese	1/4 lb.	1.89	12/94	2c
Pizza, Pizza Hut or Pizza Inn	12-13 in.	7.99	12/94	2c
Transportation				
Transportation, ACCRA Index		102.10	12/94	2c
Tire balance, computer or spin bal., front	wheel	7.17	12/94	2c
Utilities				
Utilities, ACCRA Index		93.30	12/94	2c
Electricity, (part.), other, 1800 sq. ft., new home	mo.	81.73	12/94	2c

Gillette, WY

Item	Per	Value	Date	Ref.
Composite, ACCRA index		98.90	12/94	2c
Alcoholic Beverages				
Beer, Miller Lite, Bud, 12-oz., ex deposit	6	4.55	12/94	2c
J & B Scotch	750-ml.	19.16	12/94	2c
Wine, Gallo Chablis blanc	1.5-lit	6.02	12/94	2c
Clothing				
Jeans, man's denim		29.30	12/94	2c
Shirt, man's dress shirt		25.99	12/94	2c
Undervest, boy's size 10-14, cotton	3	3.94	12/94	2c
Communications				
Newspaper subscription, dly. and Sun. delivery	month	12.83	12/94	2c
Telephone bill, family of four	month	19.79	12/94	2c
Telephone, residential, flat rate	mo.	11.22	12/93	8c
Energy and Fuels				
Energy, combined forms, 1800 sq. ft.	mo.	120.15	12/94	2c
Gas, reg unlead, taxes inc., cash, self-service	gal	1.21	12/94	2c
Entertainment				
Bowling, evening rate	game	1.95	12/94	2c
Monopoly game, Parker Brothers', No. 9	game	10.36	12/94	2c
Movie	adm	5.25	12/94	2c
Tennis balls, yellow, Wilson or Penn, 3	can	2.14	12/94	2c
Groceries				
Groceries, ACCRA Index		105.40	12/94	2c
Baby food, strained vegetables, lowest price	4-4.5 oz.	0.35	12/94	2c
Bananas	lb.	0.52	12/94	2c
Beef or hamburger, ground	lb.	1.02	12/94	2c
Bread, white	24-oz.	0.84	12/94	2c
Cheese, Kraft grated Parmesan	8-oz.	3.02	12/94	2c
Chicken, whole fryer	lb.	0.84	12/94	2c
Cigarettes, Winston, Kings	carton	14.40	12/94	2c
Coffee, vacuum-packed	13 oz.	4.20	12/94	2c
Corn Flakes, Kellogg's or Post Toasties	18 oz.	2.69	12/94	2c
Corn, frozen, whole kernel, lowest price	10 oz.	0.77	12/94	2c
Eggs, Grade A large	dozen	0.82	12/94	2c
Lettuce, iceberg	head	0.85	12/94	2c
Margarine, Blue Bonnet or Parkay cubes	lb.	0.74	12/94	2c
Milk, whole	1/2 gal.	1.68	12/94	2c
Orange juice, Minute Maid frozen	12-oz.	1.29	12/94	2c
Peaches, halves or slices, Hunt's, Del Monte, or Libby's	29-oz.	1.53	12/94	2c
Peas, sweet, Del Monte or Green Giant	15-17 oz.	0.59	12/94	2c
Potatoes, white or red	10-lb. sack	1.78	12/94	2c

Gillette, WY - continued

Item	Per	Value	Date	Ref.
Groceries - continued				
Sausage, Jimmy Dean, 100% pork	lb.	3.32	12/94	2c
Shortening, vegetable, Crisco	3-lb.	2.90	12/94	2c
Soft drink, Coca Cola, ex deposit	2 lit	1.14	12/94	2c
Steak, t-bone	lb.	4.94	12/94	2c
Sugar, cane or beet	4 lbs.	1.45	12/94	2c
Tomatoes, Hunt's or Del Monte	14.5 oz.	0.71	12/94	2c
Tuna, chunk, light, oil-packed	6.125-6.5 oz.	0.76	12/94	2c
Goods and Services				
Miscellaneous goods and services, ACCRA Index		99.90	12/94	2c
Health Care				
Health care, ACCRA Index		99.10	12/94	2c
Antibiotic ointment, Polysporin	1.5 oz.	3.98	12/94	2c
Dentist's fee, adult teeth cleaning and periodic oral exam	visit	58.50	12/94	2c
Doctor's fee, routine exam, established patient	visit	37.00	12/94	2c
Hospital care, semiprivate room	day	349.00	12/94	2c
Household Goods				
Appl. repair, service call, wash mach	min. lab. chg.	35.50	12/94	2c
Laundry detergent, Tide Ultra, Bold, or Cheer	42 oz.	3.68	12/94	2c
Tissues, facial, Kleenex brand	175	0.93	12/94	2c
Housing				
Housing, ACCRA Index		90.50	12/94	2c
House payment, principal and interest, 25% down payment	mo.	726	12/94	2c
House, 1800 sq ft, 8000 sq ft lot, new, urban, utilities	total	115250	12/94	2c
Mtge. rate, incl. points and orig. fee, 30-year conv. fixed or ARM	mo.	9.49	12/94	2c
Rent, apartment, 2 br., 1 1/2-2 baths, unfurnished, 950 sq ft, water	mo.	383	12/94	2c
Personal Goods				
Shampoo, Alberto VO5	15-oz.	1.20	12/94	2c
Toothpaste, Crest or Colgate	6-7 oz.	2.10	12/94	2c
Personal Services				
Dry cleaning, man's 2-pc. suit		5.77	12/94	2c
Haircut, man's barbershop, no styling		10.50	12/94	2c
Haircut, woman's shampoo, trim, blow-dry		12.50	12/94	2c
Restaurant Food				
Chicken, fried, thigh and drumstick		2.69	12/94	2c
Hamburger with cheese	1/4 lb.	1.97	12/94	2c
Pizza, Pizza Hut or Pizza Inn	12-13 in.	8.39	12/94	2c
Transportation				
Transportation, ACCRA Index		102.60	12/94	2c
Tire balance, computer or spin bal., front	wheel	6.50	12/94	2c
Utilities				
Utilities, ACCRA Index		106.30	12/94	2c
Electricity, 1800 sq. ft., new home	mo.	120.15	12/94	2c

Glens Falls, NY

Item	Per	Value	Date	Ref.
Composite, ACCRA index		107.00	12/94	2c
Alcoholic Beverages				
Beer, Miller Lite, Bud, 12-oz., ex deposit	6	4.07	12/94	2c
J & B Scotch	750-ml.	18.39	12/94	2c
Wine, Gallo Chablis blanc	1.5-lit	5.76	12/94	2c

Values are in dollars or fractions of dollars. In the column headed *Ref*, references are shown to sources. Each reference is followed by a letter. These refer to the geographical level for which data were reported: s=State, r=Region, and c=City or metro. The abbreviation *ex* is used to mean *except* or *excluding*; *exp* stands for *expenditures*. For other abbreviations and further explanations, please see the Introduction.

Glens Falls, NY - continued

Item	Per	Value	Date	Ref.
Appliances				
Appliances (major), expenditures	year	145	91	81r
Average annual exp.				
Food, health care, personal goods, services	year	29496	91	81r
Charity				
Cash contributions, expenditures	year	708	91	81r
Clothing				
Apparel, men and boys, total expenditures	year	416	91	81r
Apparel, women and girls, total expenditures	year	744	91	81r
Footwear, expenditures	year	305	91	81r
Jeans, man's denim		32.99	12/94	2c
Shirt, man's dress shirt		25.89	12/94	2c
Undervest, boy's size 10-14, cotton	3	5.06	12/94	2c
Communications				
Long-distance telephone rate, day, addl. min., 1-10 mi.	min.	4.00	12/93	9s
Long-distance telephone rate, day, initial min., 1-10 mi.	min.	14.90	12/93	9s
Newspaper subscription, dly. and Sun. delivery	month	12.61	12/94	2c
Phone line, single, business, field visit	inst	143.26	12/93	9s
Phone line, single, business, no field visit	inst	106.05	12/93	9s
Phone line, single, residence, field visit	inst	85.46	12/93	9s
Phone line, single, residence, no field visit	inst	55.00	12/93	9s
Telephone bill, family of four	month	25.68	12/94	2c
Telephone service, expenditures	year	589	91	81r
Telephone, residential, flat rate	mo.	16.65	12/93	8c
Education				
Board, 4-year private college/university	year	2918	8/94	80s
Board, 4-year public college/university	year	2177	8/94	80s
Education, total expenditures	year	593	91	81r
Room, 4-year private college/university	year	3302	8/94	80s
Room, 4-year public college/university	year	2624	8/94	80s
Total cost, 4-year private college/university	year	18451	8/94	80s
Total cost, 4-year public college/university	year	7723	8/94	80s
Tuition, 2-year public college/university, in-state	year	2112	8/94	80s
Tuition, 4-year private college/university, in-state	year	12231	8/94	80s
Tuition, 4-year public college/university, in-state	year	2921	8/94	80s
Energy and Fuels				
Energy, combined forms, 1800 sq. ft.	mo.	138.48	12/94	2c
Energy, exc. electricity, 1800 sq. ft.	mo.	60.08	12/94	2c
Fuel oil and other fuels, expenditures	year	257	91	81r
Gas, natural, expenditures	year	285	91	81r
Gas, reg unlead, taxes inc., cash, self-service	gal	1.19	12/94	2c
Gasoline and motor oil purchased	year	867	91	81r
Gasoline, unleaded midgrade	gallon	1.32	4/93	82r
Gasoline, unleaded premium	gallon	1.40	4/93	82r
Gasoline, unleaded regular	gallon	1.19	4/93	82r
Entertainment				
Bowling, evening rate	game	2.14	12/94	2c
Entertainment, total expenditures	year	1331	91	81r
Fees and admissions, expenditures	year	398	91	81r
Monopoly game, Parker Brothers', No. 9	game	12.66	12/94	2c
Movie	adm	6.75	12/94	2c
Pets, toys, playground equipment, expenditures	year	270	91	81r
Reading, expenditures	year	171	91	81r
Televisions, radios, and sound equipment, expenditures	year	429	91	81r
Tennis balls, yellow, Wilson or Penn, 3	can	2.82	12/94	2c
Funerals				
Burial, immediate, container provided by funeral home		1370.36	1/95	54r
Cards, acknowledgment		17.72	1/95	54r
Casket, minimum alternative		192.52	1/95	54r

Glens Falls, NY - continued

Item	Per	Value	Date	Ref.
Funerals - continued				
Cosmetology, hair care, etc.		139.56	1/95	54r
Cremation, direct, container provided by funeral home		1049.24	1/95	54r
Embalming		387.57	1/95	54r
Funeral, funeral home		278.77	1/95	54r
Funeral, other facility		275.85	1/95	54r
Graveside service		213.08	1/95	54r
Hearse, local		157.27	1/95	54r
Limousine, local		146.45	1/95	54r
Memorial service		271.02	1/95	54r
Service charge, professional, nondeclinable		943.58	1/95	54r
Visitation and viewing		322.86	1/95	54r
Groceries				
Groceries, ACCRA Index		112.40	12/94	2c
Apples, Red Delicious	lb.	0.78	12/94	82r
Baby food, strained vegetables, lowest price	4-4.5 oz.	0.36	12/94	2c
Bacon, sliced	lb.	2.24	12/94	82r
Bananas	lb.	0.50	12/94	2c
Bananas	lb.	0.49	12/94	82r
Beef or hamburger, ground	lb.	1.91	12/94	2c
Beef purchases	year	226	91	81r
Beverage purchases, alcoholic	year	332	91	81r
Beverage purchases, nonalcoholic	year	213	91	81r
Bread, white	24-oz.	0.97	12/94	2c
Bread, white, pan	lb.	0.80	12/94	82r
Butter, salted, Grade AA, stick	lb.	1.67	12/94	82r
Carrots, short trimmed and topped	lb.	0.51	12/94	82r
Cereals and bakery products purchases	year	407	91	81r
Cereals and cereals products purchases	year	132	91	81r
Cheese, Kraft grated Parmesan	8-oz.	3.31	12/94	2c
Chicken breast, bone-in	lb.	2.22	12/94	82r
Chicken, fresh, whole	lb.	1.05	12/94	82r
Chicken, whole fryer	lb.	0.99	12/94	2c
Chuck roast, USDA choice, boneless	lb.	2.74	12/94	82r
Cigarettes, Winston, Kings	carton	21.35	12/94	2c
Coffee, 100%, ground roast, all sizes	lb.	4.61	12/94	82r
Coffee, vacuum-packed	13 oz.	3.85	12/94	2c
Corn Flakes, Kellogg's or Post Toasties	18 oz.	2.20	12/94	2c
Corn, frozen, whole kernel, lowest price	10 oz.	0.63	12/94	2c
Dairy products (other) purchases	year	161	91	81r
Eggs, Grade A large	dozen	1.07	12/94	2c
Eggs, Grade A large	dozen	1.12	12/94	82r
Fish and seafood purchases	year	112	91	81r
Food purchases, food eaten at home	year	2599	91	81r
Foods purchased away from home, not prepared by consumer	year	2024	91	81r
Fruits and vegetables purchases	year	444	91	81r
Grapefruit	lb.	0.44	12/94	82r
Grapes, Thompson seedless	lb.	2.24	12/94	82r
Ground chuck, 100% beef	lb.	1.67	12/94	82r
Ice cream, prepackaged, bulk, regular	1/2 gal.	2.93	12/94	82r
Lemons	lb.	1.06	12/94	82r
Lettuce, iceberg	lb.	0.92	12/94	82r
Lettuce, iceberg	head	0.99	12/94	2c
Margarine, Blue Bonnet or Parkay cubes	lb.	0.61	12/94	2c
Meats, poultry, fish, and eggs purchases	year	751	91	81r
Milk and cream (fresh) purchases	year	152	91	81r
Milk, whole	1/2 gal.	1.25	12/94	2c
Orange juice, frozen concentrate 12-oz. can	16 oz.	1.92	12/94	82r
Orange juice, Minute Maid frozen	12-oz.	1.15	12/94	2c
Oranges, Navel	lb.	0.56	12/94	82r
Peaches, halves or slices, Hunt's, Del Monte, or Libby's	29-oz.	1.61	12/94	2c
Peas, sweet, Del Monte or Green Giant	15-17 oz.	0.55	12/94	2c
Pork chops, center cut, bone-in	lb.	3.09	12/94	82r
Pork purchases	year	130	91	81r
Potatoes, white	lb.	0.37	12/94	82r

Values are in dollars or fractions of dollars. In the column headed *Ref*, references are shown to sources. Each reference is followed by a letter. These refer to the geographical level for which data were reported: s = State, r = Region, and c = City or metro. The abbreviation *ex* is used to mean *except* or *excluding*; *exp* stands for expenditures. For other abbreviations and further explanations, please see the Introduction.

Glens Falls, NY - continued

Item	Per	Value	Date	Ref.
Groceries				
Potatoes, white or red	10-lb. sack	2.29	12/94	2c
Rib roast, USDA choice, bone-in	lb.	4.98	12/94	82r
Round roast, USDA choice, boneless	lb.	2.93	12/94	82r
Sausage, Jimmy Dean, 100% pork	lb.	2.65	12/94	2c
Shortening, vegetable oil blends	lb.	1.03	12/94	82r
Shortening, vegetable, Crisco	3-lb.	2.78	12/94	2c
Soft drink, Coca Cola, ex deposit	2 lit	1.55	12/94	2c
Spaghetti and macaroni	lb.	0.84	12/94	82r
Steak, round, USDA choice, boneless	lb.	3.48	12/94	82r
Steak, sirloin, USDA choice, bone-in	lb.	3.38	12/94	82r
Steak, sirloin, USDA choice, boneless	lb.	4.81	12/94	82r
Steak, t-bone	lb.	5.99	12/94	2c
Sugar and other sweets, eaten at home, expenditures	year	89	91	81r
Sugar, cane or beet	4 lbs.	1.57	12/94	2c
Sugar, white, all sizes	lb.	0.46	12/94	82r
Tobacco products and smoking supplies, total expenditures	year	279	91	81r
Tomatoes, field grown	lb.	1.56	12/94	82r
Tomatoes, Hunt's or Del Monte	14.5 oz.	0.93	12/94	2c
Tuna, chunk, light	lb.	2.09	12/94	82r
Tuna, chunk, light, oil-packed	6.125-6.5 oz.	0.79	12/94	2c
Goods and Services				
Miscellaneous goods and services, ACCRA Index		104.90	12/94	2c
Health Care				
Health care, ACCRA Index		103.80	12/94	2c
Antibiotic ointment, Polysporin	1.5 oz.	4.23	12/94	2c
Childbirth, Cesarean delivery, hospital charge	birth	6334.00	12/91	69r
Childbirth, Cesarean delivery, physician charge	birth	2234.00	12/91	69r
Childbirth, normal delivery, hospital charge	birth	3225.00	12/91	69r
Childbirth, normal delivery, physician charge	birth	1623.00	12/91	69r
Dentist's fee, adult teeth cleaning and periodic oral exam	visit	62.40	12/94	2c
Doctor's fee, routine exam, established patient	visit	42.60	12/94	2c
Drugs, expenditures	year	205	91	81r
Health care, total expenditures	year	1396	91	81r
Health insurance expenditures	year	553	91	81r
Hospital care, semiprivate room	day	284.00	12/94	2c
Insurance premium, family medical care	month	384.24	1/95	41s
Medical services expenditures	year	559	91	81r
Medical supplies expenditures	year	80	91	81r
Household Goods				
Appl. repair, service call, wash mach	min. lab. chg.	29.30	12/94	2c
Floor coverings, expenditures	year	158	91	81r
Furniture, expenditures	year	341	91	81r
Household equipment, misc. expenditures	year	363	91	81r
Household expenditures, miscellaneous	year	194	91	81r
Household furnishings and equipment, expenditures	year	1158	91	81r
Household operations expenditures	year	378	91	81r
Household textiles, expenditures	year	88	91	81r
Housekeeping supplies, expenditures	year	426	91	81r
Laundry and cleaning supplies, expenditures	year	122	91	81r
Laundry detergent, Tide Ultra, Bold, or Cheer	42 oz.	3.67	12/94	2c
Postage and stationery, expenditures	year	134	91	81r
Tissues, facial, Kleenex brand	175	1.11	12/94	2c
Housing				
Housing, ACCRA Index		102.20	12/94	2c
Add garage/carport		11,614	3/95	74r

Glens Falls, NY - continued

Item	Per	Value	Date	Ref.
Housing - continued				
Add room(s)		16,816	3/95	74r
Apartment condominium or co-op, median	unit	96700	12/94	62r
Dwellings (owned), expenditures	year	3305	91	81r
Enclose porch/patio/breezeway		2,980	3/95	74r
Finish room in basement/attic		4,330	3/95	74r
Home, existing, single-family, median	unit	161600	12/94	62r
House payment, principal and interest, 25% down payment	mo.	790	12/94	2c
House, 1800 sq ft, 8000 sq ft lot, new, urban, utilities	total	128025	12/94	2c
Maintenance, repairs, insurance, and other housing expenditures	year	569	91	81r
Mortgage interest and charges expenditures	year	1852	91	81r
Mtge. rate, incl. points and orig. fee, 30-year conv. fixed or ARM	mo.	9.25	12/94	2c
Princ. & int., mortgage, median-price exist. sing.-family home	mo.	765	12/94	62r
Property taxes expenditures	year	884	91	81r
Redesign, restructure more than half of home's interior		2,750	3/95	74r
Rent, apartment, 2 br., 1 1/2-2 baths, unfurnished, 950 sq ft, water	mo.	521	12/94	2c
Rental units expenditures	year	1832	91	81r
Insurance and Pensions				
Auto insurance, private passenger	year	985.07	12/94	71s
Insurance and pensions, personal, expenditures	year	2690	91	81r
Insurance, life and other personal, expenditures	year	341	91	81r
Pensions and Social Security, expenditures	year	2349	91	81r
Legal Assistance				
Estate planning, law-firm partner	hr.	375.00	10/93	12r
Legal work, law firm associate	hour	78		10r
Legal work, law firm partner	hour	183		10r
Personal Goods				
Shampoo, Alberto VO5	15-oz.	1.23	12/94	2c
Toothpaste, Crest or Colgate	6-7 oz.	2.31	12/94	2c
Personal Services				
Dry cleaning, man's 2-pc. suit		6.74	12/94	2c
Haircut, man's barbershop, no styling		8.40	12/94	2c
Haircut, woman's shampoo, trim, blow-dry		18.60	12/94	2c
Personal services expenditures	year	184	91	81r
Restaurant Food				
Chicken, fried, thigh and drumstick		2.39	12/94	2c
Dining expenditures, family	week	34.26	94	73r
Hamburger with cheese	1/4 lb.	2.05	12/94	2c
Pizza, Pizza Hut or Pizza Inn	12-13 in.	7.99	12/94	2c
Taxes				
Taxes, Federal income, expenditures	year	2409	91	81r
Taxes, personal, expenditures	year	3094	91	81r
Taxes, State and local income, expenditures	year	620	91	81r
Transportation				
Transportation, ACCRA Index		106.90	12/94	2c
Bus fare, one-way	trip	0.50	12/95	1c
Cars and trucks purchased, new	year	1170	91	81r
Cars and trucks purchased, used	year	739	91	81r
Driver's learning permit fee	perm	10.00	1/94	84s
Driver's license fee	orig	32.00-37.00	1/94	84s
Driver's license fee, duplicate	lic	7.25	1/94	84s
Driver's license reinstatement fee, min.	susp	25.00	1/94	85s
Driver's license renewal fee	renew	22.25	1/94	84s
Identification card, nondriver	card	6.25	1/94	83s
Motorcycle license fee	orig	32.00-37.00	1/94	84s
Motorcycle license fee, duplicate	lic	7.25	1/94	84s
Motorcycle license renewal fee	renew	22.25	1/94	84s

Values are in dollars or fractions of dollars. In the column headed *Ref*, references are shown to sources. Each reference is followed by a letter. These refer to the geographical level for which data were reported: s = State, r = Region, and c = City or metro. The abbreviation *ex* is used to mean *except* or *excluding*; *exp* stands for *expenditures*. For other abbreviations and further explanations, please see the Introduction.

Glens Falls, NY - continued

Item	Per	Value	Date	Ref.
Transportation				
Public transportation expenditures	year	430	91	81r
Tire balance, computer or spin bal., front	wheel	7.30	12/94	2c
Transportation expenditures, total	year	4810	91	81r
Vehicle finance charges	year	238	91	81r
Vehicle insurance expenditures	year	630	91	81r
Vehicle maintenance and repairs expenditures	year	532	91	81r
Vehicle purchases	year	1920	91	81r
Vehicle rental, leases, licenses, etc. expenditures	year	193	91	81r
Vehicles purchased, other than cars and trucks	year	11	91	81r
Utilities				
Utilities, ACCRA Index		124.50	12/94	2c
Electricity expenditures	year	695	91	81r
Electricity, (part.), other, 1800 sq. ft., new home	mo.	78.40	12/94	2c
Utilities, fuels, and public services, total expenditures	year	1981	91	81r
Water and other public services, expenditures	year	154	91	81r
Weddings				
Bridal attendants' gowns	event	750	10/93	76r
Bridal gown	event	852	10/93	76r
Bridal headpiece and veil	event	167	10/93	76r
Bride's wedding band	event	708	10/93	76r
Clergy	event	224	10/93	76r
Engagement ring	event	2756	10/93	76r
Flowers	event	863	10/93	76r
Formal wear for groom	event	106	10/93	76r
Groom's attendants' formal wear	event	530	10/93	76r
Groom's wedding band	event	402	10/93	76r
Music	event	600	10/93	76r
Photography	event	1088	10/93	76r
Shoes for bride	event	50	10/93	76r
Videography	event	483	10/93	76r
Wedding invitations and announcements	event	342	10/93	76r
Wedding reception	event	7000	10/93	76r

Glenwood Springs, CO

Item	Per	Value	Date	Ref.
Composite, ACCRA index		117.20	12/94	2c
Alcoholic Beverages				
Beer, Miller Lite, Bud, 12-oz., ex deposit	6	4.53	12/94	2c
J & B Scotch	750-ml.	19.49	12/94	2c
Wine, Gallo Chablis blanc	1.5-lit	6.99	12/94	2c
Clothing				
Jeans, man's denim		26.95	12/94	2c
Shirt, man's dress shirt		39.25	12/94	2c
Undervest, boy's size 10-14, cotton	3	3.72	12/94	2c
Communications				
Newspaper subscription, dly. and Sun. delivery	month	8.75	12/94	2c
Telephone bill, family of four	month	20.65	12/94	2c
Telephone, residential, flat rate	mo.	14.68	12/93	8c
Energy and Fuels				
Energy, combined forms, 1800 sq. ft.	mo.	125.06	12/94	2c
Energy, exc. electricity, 1800 sq. ft.	mo.	72.67	12/94	2c
Gas, reg unlead, taxes inc., cash, self-service	gal	1.39	12/94	2c
Entertainment				
Bowling, evening rate	game	2.00	12/94	2c
Monopoly game, Parker Brothers', No. 9	game	10.73	12/94	2c
Movie	adm	5.50	12/94	2c
Tennis balls, yellow, Wilson or Penn, 3	can	2.12	12/94	2c

Glenwood Springs, CO - continued

Item	Per	Value	Date	Ref.
Groceries				
Groceries, ACCRA Index		102.70	12/94	2c
Baby food, strained vegetables, lowest price	4-4.5 oz.	0.35	12/94	2c
Bananas	lb.	0.35	12/94	2c
Beef or hamburger, ground	lb.	1.39	12/94	2c
Bread, white	24-oz.	0.59	12/94	2c
Cheese, Kraft grated Parmesan	8-oz.	3.44	12/94	2c
Chicken, whole fryer	lb.	0.79	12/94	2c
Cigarettes, Winston, Kings	carton	14.05	12/94	2c
Coffee, vacuum-packed	13 oz.	3.76	12/94	2c
Corn Flakes, Kellogg's or Post Toasties	18 oz.	2.34	12/94	2c
Corn, frozen, whole kernel, lowest price	10 oz.	0.69	12/94	2c
Eggs, Grade A large	dozen	0.78	12/94	2c
Lettuce, iceberg	head	0.74	12/94	2c
Margarine, Blue Bonnet or Parkay cubes	lb.	0.69	12/94	2c
Milk, whole	1/2 gal.	1.49	12/94	2c
Orange juice, Minute Maid frozen	12-oz.	1.19	12/94	2c
Peaches, halves or slices, Hunt's, Del Monte, or Libby's	29-oz.	1.43	12/94	2c
Peas, sweet, Del Monte or Green Giant	15-17 oz.	0.57	12/94	2c
Potatoes, white or red	10-lb. sack	3.34	12/94	2c
Sausage, Jimmy Dean, 100% pork	lb.	3.32	12/94	2c
Shortening, vegetable, Crisco	3-lb.	2.92	12/94	2c
Soft drink, Coca Cola, ex deposit	2 lit	1.84	12/94	2c
Steak, t-bone	lb.	5.09	12/94	2c
Sugar, cane or beet	4 lbs.	1.43	12/94	2c
Tomatoes, Hunt's or Del Monte	14.5 oz.	0.83	12/94	2c
Tuna, chunk, light, oil-packed	6.125-6.5 oz.	0.79	12/94	2c
Goods and Services				
Miscellaneous goods and services, ACCRA Index		109.00	12/94	2c
Health Care				
Health care, ACCRA Index		106.60	12/94	2c
Antibiotic ointment, Polysporin	1.5 oz.	4.04	12/94	2c
Dentist's fee, adult teeth cleaning and periodic oral exam	visit	60.33	12/94	2c
Doctor's fee, routine exam, established patient	visit	41.50	12/94	2c
Hospital care, semiprivate room	day	395.00	12/94	2c
Household Goods				
Appl. repair, service call, wash mach	min. lab. chg.	41.25	12/94	2c
Laundry detergent, Tide Ultra, Bold, or Cheer	42 oz.	3.46	12/94	2c
Tissues, facial, Kleenex brand	175	1.18	12/94	2c
Housing				
Housing, ACCRA Index		141.70	12/94	2c
House payment, principal and interest, 25% down payment	mo.	1124	12/94	2c
House, 1800 sq ft, 8000 sq ft lot, new, urban, utilities	total	183500	12/94	2c
Mtge. rate, incl. points and orig. fee, 30-year conv. fixed or ARM	mo.	9.17	12/94	2c
Rent, apartment, 2 br., 1 1/2-2 baths, unfurnished, 950 sq ft, water	mo.	637	12/94	2c
Personal Goods				
Shampoo, Alberto VO5	15-oz.	1.23	12/94	2c
Toothpaste, Crest or Colgate	6-7 oz.	1.94	12/94	2c
Personal Services				
Dry cleaning, man's 2-pc. suit		8.31	12/94	2c
Haircut, man's barbershop, no styling		12.00	12/94	2c
Haircut, woman's shampoo, trim, blow-dry		19.67	12/94	2c

Values are in dollars or fractions of dollars. In the column headed *Ref*, references are shown to sources. Each reference is followed by a letter. These refer to the geographical level for which data were reported: s = State, r = Region, and c = City or metro. The abbreviation *ex* is used to mean *except* or *excluding*; *exp* stands for *expenditures*. For other abbreviations and further explanations, please see the Introduction.

Glenwood Springs, CO - continued

Item	Per	Value	Date	Ref.
Restaurant Food				
Chicken, fried, thigh and drumstick		2.88	12/94	2c
Hamburger with cheese	1/4 lb.	2.39	12/94	2c
Pizza, Pizza Hut or Pizza Inn	12-13 in.	7.99	12/94	2c
Transportation				
Transportation, ACCRA Index		109.80	12/94	2c
Tire balance, computer or spin bal., front	wheel	6.17	12/94	2c
Utilities				
Utilities, ACCRA Index		110.70	12/94	2c
Electricity, (part.), other, 1800 sq. ft., new home	mo.	52.39	12/94	2c

Grand Forks, ND

Item	Per	Value	Date	Ref.
Composite, ACCRA index		95.50	12/94	2c
Alcoholic Beverages				
Beer, Miller Lite, Bud, 12-oz., ex deposit	6	3.93	12/94	2c
J & B Scotch	750-ml.	15.94	12/94	2c
Wine, Gallo Chablis blanc	1.5-lit	4.99	12/94	2c
Appliances				
Appliances (major), expenditures	year	131	91	81r
Average annual exp.				
Food, health care, personal goods, services	year	25935	91	81r
Charity				
Cash contributions, expenditures	year	745	91	81r
Clothing				
Apparel, men and boys, total expenditures	year	332	91	81r
Apparel, women and girls, total expenditures	year	578	91	81r
Footwear, expenditures	year	164	91	81r
Jeans, man's denim		30.71	12/94	2c
Shirt, man's dress shirt		34.73	12/94	2c
Undervest, boy's size 10-14, cotton	3	3.89	12/94	2c
Communications				
Long-distance telephone rate, day, addl. min., 1-10 mi.	min.	0.10	12/93	9s
Long-distance telephone rate, day, initial min., 1-10 mi.	min.	0.24	12/93	9s
Newspaper subscription, dly. and Sun. delivery	month	14.13	12/94	2c
Phone line, single, business, field visit	inst	52.67	12/93	9s
Phone line, single, business, no field visit	inst	52.67	12/93	9s
Phone line, single, residence, field visit	inst	31.79	12/93	9s
Phone line, single, residence, no field visit	inst	31.79	12/93	9s
Telephone bill, family of four	month	18.54	12/94	2c
Telephone service, expenditures	year	547	91	81r
Telephone, residential, flat rate	mo.	11.54	12/93	8c
Education				
Board, 4-year private college/university	year	1582	8/94	80s
Board, 4-year public college/university	year	2259	8/94	80s
Education, total expenditures	year	394	91	81r
Room, 4-year private college/university	year	1183	8/94	80s
Room, 4-year public college/university	year	908	8/94	80s
Total cost, 4-year private college/university	year	9188	8/94	80s
Total cost, 4-year public college/university	year	5294	8/94	80s
Tuition, 2-year public college/university, in-state	year	1634	8/94	80s
Tuition, 4-year private college/university, in-state	year	6422	8/94	80s
Tuition, 4-year public college/university, in-state	year	2128	8/94	80s
Energy and Fuels				
Energy, combined forms, 1800 sq. ft.	mo.	86.38	12/94	2c
Energy, exc. electricity, 1800 sq. ft.	mo.	47.07	12/94	2c
Fuel oil and other fuels, expenditures	year	83	91	81r
Gas, natural, expenditures	year	373	91	81r

Grand Forks, ND - continued

Item	Per	Value	Date	Ref.
Energy and Fuels - continued				
Gas, reg unlead, taxes inc., cash, self-service	gal	1.25	12/94	2c
Gasoline and motor oil purchased	year	1000	91	81r
Gasoline, unleaded midgrade	gallon	1.15	4/93	82r
Gasoline, unleaded premium	gallon	1.23	4/93	82r
Gasoline, unleaded regular	gallon	1.07	4/93	82r
Entertainment				
Bowling, evening rate	game	2.10	12/94	2c
Entertainment, total expenditures	year	1356	91	81r
Fees and admissions, expenditures	year	347	91	81r
Monopoly game, Parker Brothers', No. 9	game	8.41	12/94	2c
Movie	adm	5.50	12/94	2c
Pets, toys, playground equipment, expenditures	year	270	91	81r
Reading, expenditures	year	160	91	81r
Televisions, radios, and sound equipment, expenditures	year	433	91	81r
Tennis balls, yellow, Wilson or Penn, 3	can	1.77	12/94	2c
Funerals				
Burial, immediate, container provided by funeral home		1348.78	1/95	54r
Cards, acknowledgment		21.20	1/95	54r
Casket, minimum alternative		182.83	1/95	54r
Cosmetology, hair care, etc.		133.11	1/95	54r
Cremation, direct, container provided by funeral home		1101.95	1/95	54r
Embalming		314.45	1/95	54r
Funeral, funeral home		304.88	1/95	54r
Funeral, other facility		301.37	1/95	54r
Graveside service		290.59	1/95	54r
Hearse, local		137.37	1/95	54r
Limousine, local		82.84	1/95	54r
Memorial service		316.57	1/95	54r
Service charge, professional, nondeclinable		1099.00	1/95	54r
Visitation and viewing		209.25	1/95	54r
Groceries				
Groceries, ACCRA Index		99.60	12/94	2c
Apples, Red Delicious	lb.	0.68	12/94	82r
Baby food, strained vegetables, lowest price	4-4.5 oz.	0.34	12/94	2c
Bacon, sliced	lb.	1.88	12/94	82r
Bananas	lb.	0.49	12/94	2c
Bananas	lb.	0.41	12/94	82r
Beef or hamburger, ground	lb.	1.52	12/94	2c
Beef purchases	year	197	91	81r
Beef, stew, boneless	lb.	2.52	12/94	82r
Beverage purchases, alcoholic	year	293	91	81r
Beverage purchases, nonalcoholic	year	203	91	81r
Bologna, all beef or mixed	lb.	2.12	12/94	82r
Bread, white	24-oz.	0.77	12/94	2c
Bread, white, pan	lb.	0.76	12/94	82r
Cabbage	lb.	0.44	12/94	82r
Carrots, short trimmed and topped	lb.	0.44	12/94	82r
Cereals and bakery products purchases	year	347	91	81r
Cereals and cereals products purchases	year	119	91	81r
Cheddar cheese, natural	lb.	3.28	12/94	82r
Cheese, Kraft grated Parmesan	8-oz.	3.28	12/94	2c
Chicken breast, bone-in	lb.	1.61	12/94	82r
Chicken, fresh, whole	lb.	0.89	12/94	82r
Chicken, whole fryer	lb.	0.89	12/94	2c
Chuck roast, USDA choice, boneless	lb.	2.33	12/94	82r
Cigarettes, Winston, Kings	carton	16.89	12/94	2c
Coffee, 100%, ground roast, all sizes	lb.	4.28	12/94	82r
Coffee, vacuum-packed	13 oz.	3.28	12/94	2c
Cookies, chocolate chip	lb.	2.72	12/94	82r
Corn Flakes, Kellogg's or Post Toasties	18 oz.	2.15	12/94	2c
Corn, frozen, whole kernel, lowest price	10 oz.	0.70	12/94	2c
Dairy products (other) purchases	year	148	91	81r
Eggs, Grade A large	dozen	0.68	12/94	2c
Eggs, Grade A large	dozen	0.76	12/94	82r
Fish and seafood purchases	year	61	91	81r

Values are in dollars or fractions of dollars. In the column headed *Ref*, references are shown to sources. Each reference is followed by a letter. These refer to the geographical level for which data were reported: s = State, r = Region, and c = City or metro. The abbreviation *ex* is used to mean *except* or *excluding*; *exp* stands for expenditures. For other abbreviations and further explanations, please see the Introduction.

Grand Forks, ND - continued

Item	Per	Value	Date	Ref.
Groceries				
Flour, white, all purpose	lb.	0.22	12/94	82r
Food purchases, food eaten at home	year	2313	91	81r
Foods purchased away from home, not prepared by consumer	year	1709	91	81r
Fruits and vegetables purchases	year	372	91	81r
Grapefruit	lb.	0.47	12/94	82r
Grapes, Thompson seedless	lb.	2.15	12/94	82r
Ground beef, 100% beef	lb.	1.37	12/94	82r
Ground chuck, 100% beef	lb.	1.81	12/94	82r
Ham, boneless, exc. canned	lb.	2.16	12/94	82r
Ice cream, prepackaged, bulk, regular	1/2 gal.	2.48	12/94	82r
Lemons	lb.	1.08	12/94	82r
Lettuce, iceberg	lb.	0.81	12/94	82r
Lettuce, iceberg	head	0.53	12/94	2c
Margarine, Blue Bonnet or Parkay cubes	lb.	0.61	12/94	2c
Margarine, stick	lb.	0.81	12/94	82r
Meats, poultry, fish, and eggs purchases	year	591	91	81r
Milk and cream (fresh) purchases	year	132	91	81r
Milk, whole	1/2 gal.	1.41	12/94	2c
Orange juice, frozen concentrate 12-oz. can	16 oz.	1.41	12/94	82r
Orange juice, Minute Maid frozen	12-oz.	1.19	12/94	2c
Oranges, Navel	lb.	0.56	12/94	82r
Peaches, halves or slices, Hunt's, Del Monte, or Libby's	29-oz.	1.24	12/94	2c
Peanut butter, creamy, all sizes	lb.	1.81	12/94	82r
Peas, sweet, Del Monte or Green Giant	15-17 oz.	0.49	12/94	2c
Pork chops, center cut, bone-in	lb.	2.76	12/94	82r
Pork purchases	year	130	91	81r
Potato chips	16-oz.	2.81	12/94	82r
Potatoes, frozen, French fried	lb.	0.83	12/94	82r
Potatoes, white	lb.	0.28	12/94	82r
Potatoes, white or red	10-lb. sack	1.52	12/94	2c
Round roast, USDA choice, boneless	lb.	2.90	12/94	82r
Sausage, Jimmy Dean, 100% pork	lb.	3.28	12/94	2c
Shortening, vegetable oil blends	lb.	0.88	12/94	82r
Shortening, vegetable, Crisco	3-lb.	2.63	12/94	2c
Soft drink, Coca Cola, ex deposit	2 lit	1.12	12/94	2c
Spaghetti and macaroni	lb.	0.78	12/94	82r
Steak, rib eye, USDA choice, boneless	lb.	6.15	12/94	82r
Steak, round, graded & ungraded, exc. USDA prime & choice	lb.	2.72	12/94	82r
Steak, round, USDA choice, boneless	lb.	3.02	12/94	82r
Steak, sirloin, USDA choice, boneless	lb.	3.85	12/94	82r
Steak, t-bone	lb.	5.19	12/94	2c
Steak, T-bone, USDA choice, bone-in	lb.	5.38	12/94	82r
Sugar and other sweets, eaten at home, expenditures	year	91	91	81r
Sugar, cane or beet	4 lbs.	1.44	12/94	2c
Sugar, white, all sizes	lb.	0.36	12/94	82r
Tobacco products and smoking supplies, total expenditures	year	298	91	81r
Tomatoes, field grown	lb.	1.36	12/94	82r
Tomatoes, Hunt's or Del Monte	14.5 oz.	0.72	12/94	2c
Tuna, chunk, light	lb.	1.94	12/94	82r
Tuna, chunk, light, oil-packed	6.125-6.5 oz.	0.63	12/94	2c
Turkey, frozen, whole	lb.	0.96	12/94	82r
Yogurt, natural, fruit flavored	8 oz.	0.62	12/94	82r
Goods and Services				
Miscellaneous goods and services, ACCRA Index		97.50	12/94	2c
Health Care				
Health care, ACCRA Index		98.90	12/94	2c
Antibiotic ointment, Polysporin	1.5 oz.	4.28	12/94	2c
Childbirth, Cesarean delivery, hospital charge	birth	5101.00	12/91	69r

Grand Forks, ND - continued

Item	Per	Value	Date	Ref.
Health Care - continued				
Childbirth, Cesarean delivery, physician charge	birth	2234.00	12/91	69r
Childbirth, normal delivery, hospital charge	birth	2891.00	12/91	69r
Childbirth, normal delivery, physician charge	birth	1623.00	12/91	69r
Dentist's fee, adult teeth cleaning and periodic oral exam	visit	49.40	12/94	2c
Doctor's fee, routine exam, established patient	visit	43.33	12/94	2c
Drugs, expenditures	year	248	91	81r
Health care, total expenditures	year	1336	91	81r
Health insurance expenditures	year	550	91	81r
Hospital care, semiprivate room	day	342.00	12/94	2c
Insurance premium, family medical care	month	379.10	1/95	41s
Medical services expenditures	year	457	91	81r
Medical supplies expenditures	year	82	91	81r
Household Goods				
Appl. repair, service call, wash mach	min. lab. chg.	34.98	12/94	2c
Floor coverings, expenditures	year	105	91	81r
Furniture, expenditures	year	291	91	81r
Household equipment, misc. expenditures	year	341	91	81r
Household expenditures, miscellaneous	year	162	91	81r
Household furnishings and equipment, expenditures	year	1042	91	81r
Household operations expenditures	year	365	91	81r
Household textiles, expenditures	year	101	91	81r
Housekeeping supplies, expenditures	year	390	91	81r
Laundry and cleaning supplies, expenditures	year	110	91	81r
Laundry detergent, Tide Ultra, Bold, or Cheer	42 oz.	3.62	12/94	2c
Postage and stationery, expenditures	year	115	91	81r
Tissues, facial, Kleenex brand	175	0.93	12/94	2c
Housing				
Housing, ACCRA Index		91.30	12/94	2c
Add garage/carport		8,479	3/95	74r
Add room(s)		21,347	3/95	74r
Apartment condominium or co-op, median	unit	87100	12/94	62r
Bathroom addition, average cost	add	9734.00	3/95	13r
Bathroom remodeling, average cost	remod	6414.00	3/95	13r
Bedroom, master suite addition, average cost	add	27122.00	3/95	13r
Deck addition, average cost	add	6665.00	3/95	13r
Dwellings (owned), expenditures	year	2566	91	81r
Enclose porch/patio/breezeway		4,556	3/95	74r
Exterior remodeling, average cost	remod	15395.00	3/95	13r
Family room addition, average cost	add	27658.00	3/95	13r
Finish room in basement/attic		5,074	3/95	74r
Home, existing, single-family, median	unit	106500	12/94	62r
House payment, principal and interest, 25% down payment	mo.	690	12/94	2c
House, 1800 sq ft, 8000 sq ft lot, new, urban, utilities	total	108300	12/94	2c
Kitchen remodeling, major, average cost	remod	17084.00	3/95	13r
Kitchen remodeling, minor, average cost	remod	5804.00	3/95	13r
Maintenance, repairs, insurance, and other housing expenditures	year	484	91	81r
Mortgage interest and charges expenditures	year	1443	91	81r
Mtge. rate, incl. points and orig. fee, 30-year conv. fixed or ARM	mo.	9.62	12/94	2c
Office, home addition, average cost	add	8121.00	3/95	13r
Princ. & int., mortgage, median-price exist. sing.-family home	mo.	515	12/94	62r
Property taxes expenditures	year	639	91	81r
Redesign, restructure more than half of home's interior		9,114	3/95	74r
Rent, apartment, 2 br., 1 1/2-2 baths, unfurnished, 950 sq ft, water	mo.	509	12/94	2c
Rental units expenditures	year	1200	91	81r
Sun-space addition, average cost	add	23768.00	3/95	13r

Values are in dollars or fractions of dollars. In the column headed *Ref*, references are shown to sources. Each reference is followed by a letter. These refer to the geographical level for which data were reported: s=State, r=Region, and c=City or metro. The abbreviation *ex* is used to mean *except* or *excluding*; *exp* stands for expenditures. For other abbreviations and further explanations, please see the Introduction.

Grand Forks, ND - continued

Item	Per	Value	Date	Ref.
Housing				
Wing addition, two-story, average cost	add	50410.00	3/95	13r
Insurance and Pensions				
Auto insurance, private passenger	year	448.24	12/94	71s
Insurance and pensions, personal, expenditures	year	2408	91	81r
Insurance, life and other personal, expenditures	year	355	91	81r
Pensions and Social Security, expenditures	year	2053	91	81r
Legal Assistance				
Legal work, law firm associate	hour	90		10r
Legal work, law firm partner	hour	139		10r
Personal Goods				
Shampoo, Alberto VO5	15-oz.	1.11	12/94	2c
Toothpaste, Crest or Colgate	6-7 oz.	1.71	12/94	2c
Personal Services				
Dry cleaning, man's 2-pc. suit		6.30	12/94	2c
Haircut, man's barbershop, no styling		9.00	12/94	2c
Haircut, woman's shampoo, trim, blow-dry		13.83	12/94	2c
Personal services expenditures	year	203	91	81r
Restaurant Food				
Chicken, fried, thigh and drumstick		2.10	12/94	2c
Dining expenditures, family	week	30.03	94	73r
Hamburger with cheese	1/4 lb.	1.89	12/94	2c
Pizza, Pizza Hut or Pizza Inn	12-13 in.	7.49	12/94	2c
Taxes				
Taxes, Federal income, expenditures	year	1756	91	81r
Taxes, personal, expenditures	year	2426	91	81r
Taxes, State and local income, expenditures	year	568	91	81r
Transportation				
Transportation, ACCRA Index		105.80	12/94	2c
Bus fare, one-way	trip	1.00	12/95	1c
Cars and trucks purchased, new	year	891	91	81r
Cars and trucks purchased, used	year	1155	91	81r
Driver's learning permit fee	perm	10.00	1/94	84s
Driver's license fee	orig	10.00	1/94	84s
Driver's license fee, duplicate	lic	8.00	1/94	84s
Driver's license reinstatement fee, min.	susp	25.00	1/94	85s
Driver's license renewal fee	renew	10.00	1/94	84s
Identification card, nondriver	card	8.00	1/94	83s
Motorcycle learning permit fee	perm	10.00	1/94	84s
Motorcycle license fee	orig	10.00	1/94	84s
Motorcycle license fee, duplicate	lic	8.00	1/94	84s
Motorcycle license renewal fee	renew	10.00	1/94	84s
Public transportation expenditures	year	209	91	81r
Tire balance, computer or spin bal., front	wheel	6.67	12/94	2c
Transportation expenditures, total	year	4792	91	81r
Vehicle finance charges	year	300	91	81r
Vehicle insurance expenditures	year	485	91	81r
Vehicle maintenance and repairs expenditures	year	534	91	81r
Vehicle purchases	year	2068	91	81r
Vehicle rental, leases, licenses, etc. expenditures	year	197	91	81r
Vehicles purchased, other than cars and trucks	year	22	91	81r
Utilities				
Utilities, ACCRA Index		79.40	12/94	2c
Electricity expenditures	year	668	91	81r
Electricity, (part.), other, 1800 sq. ft., new home	mo.	39.31	12/94	2c
Utilities, fuels, and public services, total expenditures	year	1838	91	81r
Water and other public services, expenditures	year	167	91	81r

Grand Forks, ND - continued

Item	Per	Value	Date	Ref.
Weddings				
Bridal attendants' gowns	event	750	10/93	76r
Bridal gown	event	852	10/93	76r
Bridal headpiece and veil	event	167	10/93	76r
Bride's wedding band	event	708	10/93	76r
Clergy	event	224	10/93	76r
Engagement ring	event	2756	10/93	76r
Flowers	event	863	10/93	76r
Formal wear for groom	event	106	10/93	76r
Groom's attendants' formal wear	event	530	10/93	76r
Groom's wedding band	event	402	10/93	76r
Music	event	600	10/93	76r
Photography	event	1088	10/93	76r
Shoes for bride	event	50	10/93	76r
Videography	event	483	10/93	76r
Wedding invitations and announcements	event	342	10/93	76r
Wedding reception	event	7000	10/93	76r

Grand Island, NE

Item	Per	Value	Date	Ref.
Composite, ACCRA index		97.20	12/94	2c
Alcoholic Beverages				
Beer, Miller Lite, Bud, 12-oz., ex deposit	6	4.03	12/94	2c
J & B Scotch	750-ml.	18.77	12/94	2c
Wine, Gallo Chablis blanc	1.5-lit	5.33	12/94	2c
Clothing				
Jeans, man's denim		32.59	12/94	2c
Shirt, man's dress shirt		32.20	12/94	2c
Undervest, boy's size 10-14, cotton	3	3.52	12/94	2c
Communications				
Newspaper subscription, dly. and Sun. delivery	month	8.50	12/94	2c
Telephone bill, family of four	month	21.84	12/94	2c
Telephone, residential, flat rate	mo.	14.90	12/93	8c
Energy and Fuels				
Energy, combined forms, 1800 sq. ft.	mo.	99.90	12/94	2c
Energy, exc. electricity, 1800 sq. ft.	mo.	47.82	12/94	2c
Gas, reg unlead, taxes inc., cash, self-service	gal	1.14	12/94	2c
Entertainment				
Bowling, evening rate	game	2.18	12/94	2c
Monopoly game, Parker Brothers', No. 9	game	11.39	12/94	2c
Movie	adm	5.00	12/94	2c
Tennis balls, yellow, Wilson or Penn, 3	can	2.26	12/94	2c
Groceries				
Groceries, ACCRA Index		101.00	12/94	2c
Baby food, strained vegetables, lowest price	4-4.5 oz.	0.37	12/94	2c
Bananas	lb.	0.50	12/94	2c
Beef or hamburger, ground	lb.	1.43	12/94	2c
Bread, white	24-oz.	0.93	12/94	2c
Cheese, Kraft grated Parmesan	8-oz.	3.09	12/94	2c
Chicken, whole fryer	lb.	0.80	12/94	2c
Cigarettes, Winston, Kings	carton	16.25	12/94	2c
Coffee, vacuum-packed	13 oz.	3.35	12/94	2c
Corn Flakes, Kellogg's or Post Toasties	18 oz.	1.88	12/94	2c
Corn, frozen, whole kernel, lowest price	10 oz.	0.70	12/94	2c
Eggs, Grade A large	dozen	0.57	12/94	2c
Lettuce, iceberg	head	0.77	12/94	2c
Margarine, Blue Bonnet or Parkay cubes	lb.	0.55	12/94	2c
Milk, whole	1/2 gal.	1.29	12/94	2c
Orange juice, Minute Maid frozen	12-oz.	1.27	12/94	2c
Peaches, halves or slices, Hunt's, Del Monte, or Libby's	29-oz.	1.24	12/94	2c
Peas, sweet, Del Monte or Green Giant	15-17 oz.	0.51	12/94	2c

Values are in dollars or fractions of dollars. In the column headed *Ref*, references are shown to sources. Each reference is followed by a letter. These refer to the geographical level for which data were reported: s=State, r=Region, and c=City or metro. The abbreviation *ex* is used to mean *except* or *excluding*; *exp* stands for expenditures. For other abbreviations and further explanations, please see the Introduction.

Grand Island, NE - continued

Item	Per	Value	Date	Ref.
Groceries				
Potatoes, white or red	10-lb. sack	2.11	12/94	2c
Sausage, Jimmy Dean, 100% pork	lb.	2.96	12/94	2c
Shortening, vegetable, Crisco	3-lb.	2.56	12/94	2c
Soft drink, Coca Cola, ex deposit	2 lit	1.33	12/94	2c
Steak, t-bone	lb.	5.35	12/94	2c
Sugar, cane or beet	4 lbs.	1.13	12/94	2c
Tomatoes, Hunt's or Del Monte	14.5 oz.	0.75	12/94	2c
Tuna, chunk, light, oil-packed	6.125-6.5 oz.	0.62	12/94	2c
Goods and Services				
Miscellaneous goods and services, ACCRA Index		97.50	12/94	2c
Health Care				
Health care, ACCRA Index		85.70	12/94	2c
Antibiotic ointment, Polysporin	1.5 oz.	4.27	12/94	2c
Dentist's fee, adult teeth cleaning and periodic oral exam	visit	44.60	12/94	2c
Doctor's fee, routine exam, established patient	visit	34.20	12/94	2c
Hospital care, semiprivate room	day	299.00	12/94	2c
Household Goods				
Appl. repair, service call, wash mach	min. lab. chg.	34.33	12/94	2c
Laundry detergent, Tide Ultra, Bold, or Cheer	42 oz.	3.51	12/94	2c
Tissues, facial, Kleenex brand	175	0.99	12/94	2c
Housing				
Housing, ACCRA Index		98.50	12/94	2c
House payment, principal and interest, 25% down payment	mo.	795	12/94	2c
House, 1800 sq ft, 8000 sq ft lot, new, urban, utilities	total	126900	12/94	2c
Mtge. rate, incl. points and orig. fee, 30-year conv. fixed or ARM	mo.	9.43	12/94	2c
Rent, apartment, 2 br., 1 1/2-2 baths, unfurnished, 950 sq ft, water	mo.	405	12/94	2c
Personal Goods				
Shampoo, Alberto VO5	15-oz.	1.23	12/94	2c
Toothpaste, Crest or Colgate	6-7 oz.	1.99	12/94	2c
Personal Services				
Dry cleaning, man's 2-pc. suit		7.07	12/94	2c
Haircut, man's barbershop, no styling		9.30	12/94	2c
Haircut, woman's shampoo, trim, blow-dry		16.00	12/94	2c
Restaurant Food				
Chicken, fried, thigh and drumstick		1.80	12/94	2c
Hamburger with cheese	1/4 lb.	1.80	12/94	2c
Pizza, Pizza Hut or Pizza Inn	12-13 in.	7.49	12/94	2c
Transportation				
Transportation, ACCRA Index		97.20	12/94	2c
Tire balance, computer or spin bal., front	wheel	6.19	12/94	2c
Utilities				
Utilities, ACCRA Index		92.10	12/94	2c
Electricity, (part.), other, 1800 sq. ft., new home	mo.	52.08	12/94	2c

Grand Junction, CO

Item	Per	Value	Date	Ref.
Composite, ACCRA index		94.90	12/94	2c
Alcoholic Beverages				
Beer, Miller Lite, Bud, 12-oz., ex deposit	6	4.21	12/94	2c

Grand Junction, CO - continued

Item	Per	Value	Date	Ref.
Alcoholic Beverages - continued				
J & B Scotch	750-ml.	18.98	12/94	2c
Wine, Gallo Chablis blanc	1.5-lit	4.63	12/94	2c
Clothing				
Jeans, man's denim		26.74	12/94	2c
Shirt, man's dress shirt		32.33	12/94	2c
Undervest, boy's size 10-14, cotton	3	3.64	12/94	2c
Communications				
Newspaper subscription, dly. and Sun. delivery	month	9.78	12/94	2c
Telephone bill, family of four	month	19.69	12/94	2c
Telephone, residential, flat rate	mo.	14.68	12/93	8c
Energy and Fuels				
Energy, combined forms, 1800 sq. ft.	mo.	77.49	12/94	2c
Energy, exc. electricity, 1800 sq. ft.	mo.	31.26	12/94	2c
Gas, reg unlead, taxes inc., cash, self-service	gal	1.28	12/94	2c
Entertainment				
Bowling, evening rate	game	2.05	12/94	2c
Monopoly game, Parker Brothers', No. 9	game	11.26	12/94	2c
Movie	adm	5.50	12/94	2c
Tennis balls, yellow, Wilson or Penn, 3	can	2.48	12/94	2c
Groceries				
Groceries, ACCRA Index		105.90	12/94	2c
Baby food, strained vegetables, lowest price	4-4.5 oz.	0.38	12/94	2c
Bananas	lb.	0.59	12/94	2c
Beef or hamburger, ground	lb.	1.15	12/94	2c
Bread, white	24-oz.	0.76	12/94	2c
Cheese, Kraft grated Parmesan	8-oz.	3.02	12/94	2c
Chicken, whole fryer	lb.	0.79	12/94	2c
Cigarettes, Winston, Kings	carton	14.55	12/94	2c
Coffee, vacuum-packed	13 oz.	3.81	12/94	2c
Corn Flakes, Kellogg's or Post Toasties	18 oz.	2.14	12/94	2c
Corn, frozen, whole kernel, lowest price	10 oz.	0.79	12/94	2c
Eggs, Grade A large	dozen	0.83	12/94	2c
Lettuce, iceberg	head	0.76	12/94	2c
Margarine, Blue Bonnet or Parkay cubes	lb.	0.64	12/94	2c
Milk, whole	1/2 gal.	1.49	12/94	2c
Orange juice, Minute Maid frozen	12-oz.	1.19	12/94	2c
Peaches, halves or slices, Hunt's, Del Monte, or Libby's	29-oz.	1.55	12/94	2c
Peas, sweet, Del Monte or Green Giant	15-17 oz.	0.71	12/94	2c
Potatoes, white or red	10-lb. sack	2.19	12/94	2c
Sausage, Jimmy Dean, 100% pork	lb.	3.66	12/94	2c
Shortening, vegetable, Crisco	3-lb.	3.00	12/94	2c
Soft drink, Coca Cola, ex deposit	2 lit	1.59	12/94	2c
Steak, t-bone	lb.	5.06	12/94	2c
Sugar, cane or beet	4 lbs.	1.71	12/94	2c
Tomatoes, Hunt's or Del Monte	14.5 oz.	0.78	12/94	2c
Tuna, chunk, light, oil-packed	6.125-6.5 oz.	0.80	12/94	2c
Goods and Services				
Miscellaneous goods and services, ACCRA Index		100.40	12/94	2c
Health Care				
Health care, ACCRA Index		99.00	12/94	2c
Antibiotic ointment, Polysporin	1.5 oz.	3.94	12/94	2c
Dentist's fee, adult teeth cleaning and periodic oral exam	visit	52.29	12/94	2c
Doctor's fee, routine exam, established patient	visit	40.93	12/94	2c
Hospital care, semiprivate room	day	364.93	12/94	2c

Values are in dollars or fractions of dollars. In the column headed *Ref*, references are shown to sources. Each reference is followed by a letter. These refer to the geographical level for which data were reported: s = State, r = Region, and c = City or metro. The abbreviation *ex* is used to mean *except* or *excluding*; *exp* stands for *expenditures*. For other abbreviations and further explanations, please see the Introduction.

Grand Junction, CO - continued

Item	Per	Value	Date	Ref.
Household Goods				
Appl. repair, service call, wash mach	min. lab. chg.	29.33	12/94	2c
Laundry detergent, Tide Ultra, Bold, or Cheer	42 oz.	3.74	12/94	2c
Tissues, facial, Kleenex brand	175	0.91	12/94	2c
Housing				
Housing, ACCRA Index		84.30	12/94	2c
House payment, principal and interest, 25% down payment	mo.	674	12/94	2c
House, 1800 sq ft, 8000 sq ft lot, new, urban, utilities	total	103780	12/94	2c
Mtge. rate, incl. points and orig. fee, 30-year conv. fixed or ARM	mo.	9.37	12/94	2c
Personal Goods				
Shampoo, Alberto VO5	15-oz.	1.16	12/94	2c
Toothpaste, Crest or Colgate	6-7 oz.	1.99	12/94	2c
Personal Services				
Dry cleaning, man's 2-pc. suit		5.88	12/94	2c
Haircut, man's barbershop, no styling		7.00	12/94	2c
Haircut, woman's shampoo, trim, blow-dry		16.00	12/94	2c
Restaurant Food				
Chicken, fried, thigh and drumstick		2.59	12/94	2c
Hamburger with cheese	1/4 lb.	2.09	12/94	2c
Pizza, Pizza Hut or Pizza Inn	12-13 in.	8.49	12/94	2c
Transportation				
Transportation, ACCRA Index		105.00	12/94	2c
Tire balance, computer or spin bal., front	wheel	6.25	12/94	2c
Utilities				
Utilities, ACCRA Index		73.40	12/94	2c
Electricity, (part.), other, 1800 sq. ft., new home	mo.	46.23	12/94	2c

Grand Rapids, MI

Item	Per	Value	Date	Ref.
Appliances				
Appliances (major), expenditures	year	131	91	81r
Average annual exp.				
Food, health care, personal goods, services	year	25935	91	81r
Charity				
Cash contributions, expenditures	year	745	91	81r
Clothing				
Apparel, men and boys, total expenditures	year	332	91	81r
Apparel, women and girls, total expenditures	year	578	91	81r
Footwear, expenditures	year	164	91	81r
Communications				
Long-distance telephone rate, day, addl. min., 1-10 mi.	min.	0.08	12/93	9s
Long-distance telephone rate, day, initial min., 1-10 mi.	min.	0.14	12/93	9s
Phone line, single, business, field visit	inst	42.00	12/93	9s
Phone line, single, business, no field visit	inst	42.00	12/93	9s
Phone line, single, residence, field visit	inst	42.00	12/93	9s
Phone line, single, residence, no field visit	inst	42.00	12/93	9s
Telephone service, expenditures	year	547	91	81r
Telephone, residential, flat rate	mo.	10.93	12/93	8c
Education				
Board, 4-year private college/university	year	2064	8/94	80s
Board, 4-year public college/university	year	2304	8/94	80s
Education, total expenditures	year	394	91	81r
Room, 4-year private college/university	year	1814	8/94	80s
Room, 4-year public college/university	year	1856	8/94	80s
Total cost, 4-year private college/university	year	12178	8/94	80s
Total cost, 4-year public college/university	year	7642	8/94	80s

Grand Rapids, MI - continued

Item	Per	Value	Date	Ref.
Education - continued				
Tuition, 2-year public college/university, in-state	year	1358	8/94	80s
Tuition, 4-year private college/university, in-state	year	8300	8/94	80s
Tuition, 4-year public college/university, in-state	year	3481	8/94	80s
Energy and Fuels				
Fuel oil and other fuels, expenditures	year	83	91	81r
Gas, natural, expenditures	year	373	91	81r
Gasoline and motor oil purchased	year	1000	91	81r
Gasoline, unleaded midgrade	gallon	1.15	4/93	82r
Gasoline, unleaded premium	gallon	1.23	4/93	82r
Gasoline, unleaded regular	gallon	1.07	4/93	82r
Entertainment				
Camping session, summer	week	100.00	8/95	48c
Entertainment, total expenditures	year	1356	91	81r
Fees and admissions, expenditures	year	347	91	81r
Pets, toys, playground equipment, expenditures	year	270	91	81r
Reading, expenditures	year	160	91	81r
Televisions, radios, and sound equipment, expenditures	year	433	91	81r
Funerals				
Burial, immediate, container provided by funeral home		1268.31	1/95	54r
Cards, acknowledgment		26.12	1/95	54r
Casket, minimum alternative		198.03	1/95	54r
Cosmetology, hair care, etc.		122.19	1/95	54r
Cremation, direct, container provided by funeral home		977.81	1/95	54r
Embalming		334.00	1/95	54r
Funeral, funeral home		321.16	1/95	54r
Funeral, other facility		317.73	1/95	54r
Graveside service		292.48	1/95	54r
Hearse, local		153.20	1/95	54r
Limousine, local		123.52	1/95	54r
Memorial service		356.30	1/95	54r
Service charge, professional, nondeclinable		968.24	1/95	54r
Visitation and viewing		332.66	1/95	54r
Groceries				
Apples, Red Delicious	lb.	0.68	12/94	82r
Bacon, sliced	lb.	1.88	12/94	82r
Bananas	lb.	0.41	12/94	82r
Beef purchases	year	197	91	81r
Beef, stew, boneless	lb.	2.52	12/94	82r
Beverage purchases, alcoholic	year	293	91	81r
Beverage purchases, nonalcoholic	year	203	91	81r
Bologna, all beef or mixed	lb.	2.12	12/94	82r
Bread, white, pan	lb.	0.76	12/94	82r
Cabbage	lb.	0.44	12/94	82r
Carrots, short trimmed and topped	lb.	0.44	12/94	82r
Cereals and bakery products purchases	year	347	91	81r
Cereals and cereals products purchases	year	119	91	81r
Cheddar cheese, natural	lb.	3.28	12/94	82r
Chicken breast, bone-in	lb.	1.61	12/94	82r
Chicken, fresh, whole	lb.	0.89	12/94	82r
Chuck roast, USDA choice, boneless	lb.	2.33	12/94	82r
Coffee, 100%, ground roast, all sizes	lb.	4.28	12/94	82r
Cookies, chocolate chip	lb.	2.72	12/94	82r
Dairy products (other) purchases	year	148	91	81r
Eggs, Grade A large	dozen	0.76	12/94	82r
Fish and seafood purchases	year	61	91	81r
Flour, white, all purpose	lb.	0.22	12/94	82r
Food purchases, food eaten at home	year	2313	91	81r
Foods purchased away from home, not prepared by consumer	year	1709	91	81r
Fruits and vegetables purchases	year	372	91	81r
Grapefruit	lb.	0.47	12/94	82r
Grapes, Thompson seedless	lb.	2.15	12/94	82r
Ground beef, 100% beef	lb.	1.37	12/94	82r

Values are in dollars or fractions of dollars. In the column headed *Ref*, references are shown to sources. Each reference is followed by a letter. These refer to the geographical level for which data were reported: s = State, r = Region, and c = City or metro. The abbreviation *ex* is used to mean *except* or *excluding*; *exp* stands for expenditures. For other abbreviations and further explanations, please see the Introduction.

Grand Rapids, MI - continued

Item	Per	Value	Date	Ref.
Groceries				
Ground chuck, 100% beef	lb.	1.81	12/94	82r
Ham, boneless, exc. canned	lb.	2.16	12/94	82r
Ice cream, prepackaged, bulk, regular	1/2 gal.	2.48	12/94	82r
Lemons	lb.	1.08	12/94	82r
Lettuce, iceberg	lb.	0.81	12/94	82r
Margarine, stick	lb.	0.81	12/94	82r
Meats, poultry, fish, and eggs purchases	year	591	91	81r
Milk and cream (fresh) purchases	year	132	91	81r
Orange juice, frozen concentrate 12-oz. can	16 oz.	1.41	12/94	82r
Oranges, Navel	lb.	0.56	12/94	82r
Peanut butter, creamy, all sizes	lb.	1.81	12/94	82r
Pork chops, center cut, bone-in	lb.	2.76	12/94	82r
Pork purchases	year	130	91	81r
Potato chips	16-oz.	2.81	12/94	82r
Potatoes, frozen, French fried	lb.	0.83	12/94	82r
Potatoes, white	lb.	0.28	12/94	82r
Round roast, USDA choice, boneless	lb.	2.90	12/94	82r
Shortening, vegetable oil blends	lb.	0.88	12/94	82r
Spaghetti and macaroni	lb.	0.78	12/94	82r
Steak, rib eye, USDA choice, boneless	lb.	6.15	12/94	82r
Steak, round, graded & ungraded, exc. USDA prime & choice	lb.	2.72	12/94	82r
Steak, round, USDA choice, boneless	lb.	3.02	12/94	82r
Steak, sirloin, USDA choice, boneless	lb.	3.85	12/94	82r
Steak, T-bone, USDA choice, bone-in	lb.	5.38	12/94	82r
Sugar and other sweets, eaten at home, expenditures	year	91	91	81r
Sugar, white, all sizes	lb.	0.36	12/94	82r
Tobacco products and smoking supplies, total expenditures	year	298	91	81r
Tomatoes, field grown	lb.	1.36	12/94	82r
Tuna, chunk, light	lb.	1.94	12/94	82r
Turkey, frozen, whole	lb.	0.96	12/94	82r
Yogurt, natural, fruit flavored	8 oz.	0.62	12/94	82r
Health Care				
Childbirth, Cesarean delivery, hospital charge	birth	5101.00	12/91	69r
Childbirth, Cesarean delivery, physician charge	birth	2234.00	12/91	69r
Childbirth, normal delivery, hospital charge	birth	2891.00	12/91	69r
Childbirth, normal delivery, physician charge	birth	1623.00	12/91	69r
Drugs, expenditures	year	248	91	81r
Health care, total expenditures	year	1336	91	81r
Health insurance expenditures	year	550	91	81r
Insurance premium, family medical care	month	369.41	1/95	41s
Medical services expenditures	year	457	91	81r
Medical supplies expenditures	year	82	91	81r
Household Goods				
Floor coverings, expenditures	year	105	91	81r
Furniture, expenditures	year	291	91	81r
Household equipment, misc. expenditures	year	341	91	81r
Household expenditures, miscellaneous	year	162	91	81r
Household furnishings and equipment, expenditures	year	1042	91	81r
Household operations expenditures	year	365	91	81r
Household textiles, expenditures	year	101	91	81r
Housekeeping supplies, expenditures	year	390	91	81r
Laundry and cleaning supplies, expenditures	year	110	91	81r
Postage and stationery, expenditures	year	115	91	81r
Housing				
Add garage/carport		8,479	3/95	74r
Add room(s)		21,347	3/95	74r
Apartment condominium or co-op, median	unit	87100	12/94	62r
Bathroom addition, average cost	add	9734.00	3/95	13r
Bathroom remodeling, average cost	remod	6414.00	3/95	13r
Bedroom, master suite addition, average cost	add	27122.00	3/95	13r
Deck addition, average cost	add	6665.00	3/95	13r
Dwellings (owned), expenditures	year	2566	91	81r

Grand Rapids, MI - continued

Item	Per	Value	Date	Ref.
Housing - continued				
Enclose porch/patio/breezeway		4,556	3/95	74r
Exterior remodeling, average cost	remod	15395.00	3/95	13r
Family room addition, average cost	add	27658.00	3/95	13r
Finish room in basement/attic		5,074	3/95	74r
Home, existing, single-family, median	unit	106500	12/94	62r
Home, existing, single-family, median	unit	76.90	12/94	62c
Home, vacation	unit	42600.00	1/93	27c
Kitchen remodeling, major, average cost	remod	17084.00	3/95	13r
Kitchen remodeling, minor, average cost	remod	5804.00	3/95	13r
Maintenance, repairs, insurance, and other housing expenditures	year	484	91	81r
Mortgage interest and charges expenditures	year	1443	91	81r
Office, home addition, average cost	add	8121.00	3/95	13r
Princ. & int., mortgage, median-price exist. sing.-family home	mo.	515	12/94	62r
Property taxes expenditures	year	639	91	81r
Redesign, restructure more than half of home's interior		9,114	3/95	74r
Rental units expenditures	year	1200	91	81r
Sun-space addition, average cost	add	23768.00	3/95	13r
Wing addition, two-story, average cost	add	50410.00	3/95	13r
Insurance and Pensions				
Auto insurance, private passenger	year	788.26	12/94	71s
Insurance and pensions, personal, expenditures	year	2408	91	81r
Insurance, life and other personal, expenditures	year	355	91	81r
Pensions and Social Security, expenditures	year	2053	91	81r
Legal Assistance				
Legal work, law firm associate	hour	90		10r
Legal work, law firm partner	hour	139		10r
Personal Services				
Personal services expenditures	year	203	91	81r
Restaurant Food				
Dining expenditures, family	week	30.03	94	73r
Taxes				
Taxes, Federal income, expenditures	year	1756	91	81r
Taxes, personal, expenditures	year	2426	91	81r
Taxes, State and local income, expenditures	year	568	91	81r
Transportation				
Cars and trucks purchased, new	year	891	91	81r
Cars and trucks purchased, used	year	1155	91	81r
Driver's learning permit fee	perm	12.00	1/94	84s
Driver's license fee	orig	12.00	1/94	84s
Driver's license fee, duplicate	lic	6.00	1/94	84s
Driver's license reinstatement fee, min.	susp	125.00	1/94	85s
Driver's license renewal fee	renew	12.00	1/94	84s
Identification card, nondriver	card	6.00	1/94	83s
Motorcycle license fee	orig	7.50	1/94	84s
Motorcycle license renewal fee	renew	4.00	1/94	84s
Public transportation expenditures	year	209	91	81r
Transportation expenditures, total	year	4792	91	81r
Vehicle finance charges	year	300	91	81r
Vehicle insurance expenditures	year	485	91	81r
Vehicle maintenance and repairs expenditures	year	534	91	81r
Vehicle purchases	year	2068	91	81r
Vehicle rental, leases, licenses, etc. expenditures	year	197	91	81r
Vehicles purchased, other than cars and trucks	year	22	91	81r
Utilities				
Electricity expenditures	year	668	91	81r
Electricity, summer, 250 KWh	month	17.74	8/93	64c
Electricity, summer, 500 KWh	month	35.48	8/93	64c
Electricity, summer, 750 KWh	month	56.16	8/93	64c
Electricity, summer, 1000 KWh	month	78.80	8/93	64c

Values are in dollars or fractions of dollars. In the column headed *Ref*, references are shown to sources. Each reference is followed by a letter. These refer to the geographical level for which data were reported: s=State, r=Region, and c=City or metro. The abbreviation *ex* is used to mean *except* or *excluding*; *exp* stands for expenditures. For other abbreviations and further explanations, please see the Introduction.

Grand Rapids, MI - continued

Item	Per	Value	Date	Ref.
Utilities				
Utilities, fuels, and public services, total expenditures	year	1838	91	81r
Water and other public services, expenditures	year	167	91	81r
Weddings				
Bridal attendants' gowns	event	750	10/93	76r
Bridal gown	event	852	10/93	76r
Bridal headpiece and veil	event	167	10/93	76r
Bride's wedding band	event	708	10/93	76r
Clergy	event	224	10/93	76r
Engagement ring	event	2756	10/93	76r
Flowers	event	863	10/93	76r
Formal wear for groom	event	106	10/93	76r
Groom's attendants' formal wear	event	530	10/93	76r
Groom's wedding band	event	402	10/93	76r
Music	event	600	10/93	76r
Photography	event	1088	10/93	76r
Shoes for bride	event	50	10/93	76r
Videography	event	483	10/93	76r
Wedding invitations and announcements	event	342	10/93	76r
Wedding reception	event	7000	10/93	76r

Great Falls, MT

Item	Per	Value	Date	Ref.
Composite, ACCRA index		100.00	12/94	2c
Alcoholic Beverages				
Beer, Miller Lite, Bud, 12-oz., ex deposit	6	4.44	12/94	2c
J & B Scotch	750-ml.	18.85	12/94	2c
Wine, Gallo Chablis blanc	1.5-lit	7.27	12/94	2c
Appliances				
Appliances (major), expenditures	year	160	91	81r
Average annual exp.				
Food, health care, personal goods, services	year	32461	91	81r
Charity				
Cash contributions, expenditures	year	975	91	81r
Clothing				
Apparel, men and boys, total expenditures	year	467	91	81r
Apparel, women and girls, total expenditures	year	737	91	81r
Footwear, expenditures	year	270	91	81r
Jeans, man's denim		34.75	12/94	2c
Shirt, man's dress shirt		38.50	12/94	2c
Undervest, boy's size 10-14, cotton	3	4.42	12/94	2c
Communications				
Long-distance telephone rate, day, addl. min., 1-10 mi.	min.	0.04	12/93	9s
Long-distance telephone rate, day, initial min., 1-10 mi.	min.	0.13	12/93	9s
Newspaper subscription, dly. and Sun. delivery	month	13.26	12/94	2c
Phone line, single, business, field visit	inst	61.40	12/93	9s
Phone line, single, business, no field visit	inst	61.40	12/93	9s
Phone line, single, residence, field visit	inst	35.30	12/93	9s
Phone line, single, residence, no field visit	inst	35.30	12/93	9s
Telephone bill, family of four	month	18.22	12/94	2c
Telephone service, expenditures	year	611	91	81r
Education				
Board, 4-year private college/university	year	2014	8/94	80s
Board, 4-year public college/university	year	2064	8/94	80s
Education, total expenditures	year	375	91	81r
Room, 4-year private college/university	year	1355	8/94	80s
Room, 4-year public college/university	year	1710	8/94	80s
Total cost, 4-year private college/university	year	10474	8/94	80s
Total cost, 4-year public college/university	year	5665	8/94	80s
Tuition, 2-year public college/university, in-state	year	1171	8/94	80s

Great Falls, MT - continued

Item	Per	Value	Date	Ref.
Education - continued				
Tuition, 4-year private college/university, in-state	year	7104	8/94	80s
Tuition, 4-year public college/university, in-state	year	1890	8/94	80s
Energy and Fuels				
Energy, combined forms, 1800 sq. ft.	mo.	102.16	12/94	2c
Energy, exc. electricity, 1800 sq. ft.	mo.	51.43	12/94	2c
Fuel oil and other fuels, expenditures	year	33	91	81r
Gas, cooking, 10 therms	month	7.66	2/94	65c
Gas, cooking, 30 therms	month	14.98	2/94	65c
Gas, cooking, 50 therms	month	22.30	2/94	65c
Gas, heating, winter, 100 therms	month	34.00	2/94	65c
Gas, heating, winter, average use	month	47.60	2/94	65c
Gas, natural, expenditures	year	212	91	81r
Gas, reg unlead, taxes inc., cash, self-service	gal	1.32	12/94	2c
Gasoline and motor oil purchased	year	1115	91	81r
Gasoline, unleaded midgrade	gallon	1.36	4/93	82r
Gasoline, unleaded premium	gallon	1.43	4/93	82r
Gasoline, unleaded regular	gallon	1.23	4/93	82r
Entertainment				
Bowling, evening rate	game	1.83	12/94	2c
Concert ticket, Pearl Jam group	perf	20.00	94	50r
Entertainment, total expenditures	year	1853	91	81r
Fees and admissions, expenditures	year	482	91	81r
Monopoly game, Parker Brothers', No. 9	game	9.99	12/94	2c
Movie	adm	5.25	12/94	2c
Pets, toys, playground equipment, expenditures	year	299	91	81r
Reading, expenditures	year	164	91	81r
Televisions, radios, and sound equipment, expenditures	year	528	91	81r
Tennis balls, yellow, Wilson or Penn, 3	can	2.22	12/94	2c
Funerals				
Burial, immediate, container provided by funeral home		1360.49	1/95	54r
Cards, acknowledgment		11.24	1/95	54r
Casket, minimum alternative		232.73	1/95	54r
Cosmetology, hair care, etc.		114.13	1/95	54r
Cremation, direct, container provided by funeral home		1027.08	1/95	54r
Embalming		286.24	1/95	54r
Funeral, funeral home		315.60	1/95	54r
Funeral, other facility		303.08	1/95	54r
Graveside service		423.83	1/95	54r
Hearse, local		133.12	1/95	54r
Limousine, local		99.10	1/95	54r
Memorial service		442.57	1/95	54r
Service charge, professional, nondeclinable		840.16	1/95	54r
Visitation and viewing		168.50	1/95	54r
Groceries				
Groceries, ACCRA Index		105.20	12/94	2c
Apples, Red Delicious	lb.	0.72	12/94	82r
Baby food, strained vegetables, lowest price	4-4.5 oz.	0.25	12/94	2c
Bacon, sliced	lb.	1.73	12/94	82r
Bananas	lb.	0.56	12/94	2c
Bananas	lb.	0.52	12/94	82r
Beef or hamburger, ground	lb.	1.48	12/94	2c
Beef purchases	year	241	91	81r
Beverage purchases, alcoholic	year	328	91	81r
Beverage purchases, nonalcoholic	year	234	91	81r
Bologna, all beef or mixed	lb.	2.33	12/94	82r
Bread, white	24-oz.	0.88	12/94	2c
Bread, white, pan	lb.	0.81	12/94	82r
Carrots, short trimmed and topped	lb.	0.43	12/94	82r
Cereals and bakery products purchases	year	392	91	81r
Cereals and cereals products purchases	year	139	91	81r
Cheese, Kraft grated Parmesan	8-oz.	3.67	12/94	2c
Chicken breast, bone-in	lb.	2.04	12/94	82r

Values are in dollars or fractions of dollars. In the column headed *Ref*, references are shown to sources. Each reference is followed by a letter. These refer to the geographical level for which data were reported: s=State, r=Region, and c=City or metro. The abbreviation *ex* is used to mean *except* or *excluding*; *exp* stands for *expenditures*. For other abbreviations and further explanations, please see the Introduction.

Great Falls, MT - continued

Item	Per	Value	Date	Ref.
Groceries				
Chicken, fresh, whole	lb.	0.95	12/94	82r
Chicken, whole fryer	lb.	0.89	12/94	2c
Cigarettes, Winston, Kings	carton	15.12	12/94	2c
Coffee, 100%, ground roast, all sizes	lb.	4.48	12/94	82r
Coffee, vacuum-packed	13 oz.	3.80	12/94	2c
Corn Flakes, Kellogg's or Post Toasties	18 oz.	2.62	12/94	2c
Corn, frozen, whole kernel, lowest price	10 oz.	0.64	12/94	2c
Dairy products (other) purchases	year	182	91	81r
Eggs, Grade A large	dozen	0.74	12/94	2c
Fish and seafood purchases	year	94	91	81r
Flour, white, all purpose	lb.	0.21	12/94	82r
Food purchases, food eaten at home	year	2749	91	81r
Foods purchased away from home, not prepared by consumer	year	1909	91	81r
Fruits and vegetables purchases	year	459	91	81r
Grapefruit	lb.	0.56	12/94	82r
Ground beef, 100% beef	lb.	1.31	12/94	82r
Ham, boneless, exc. canned	lb.	2.46	12/94	82r
Ice cream, prepackaged, bulk, regular	1/2 gal.	2.57	12/94	82r
Lemons	lb.	1.00	12/94	82r
Lettuce, iceberg	lb.	0.93	12/94	82r
Lettuce, iceberg	head	0.75	12/94	2c
Margarine, Blue Bonnet or Parkay cubes	lb.	0.64	12/94	2c
Meats, poultry, fish, and eggs purchases	year	700	91	81r
Milk and cream (fresh) purchases	year	155	91	81r
Milk, whole	1/2 gal.	1.44	12/94	2c
Orange juice, frozen concentrate 12-oz. can	16 oz.	1.52	12/94	82r
Orange juice, Minute Maid frozen	12-oz.	1.38	12/94	2c
Oranges, Navel	lb.	0.56	12/94	82r
Peaches, halves or slices, Hunt's, Del Monte, or Libby's	29-oz.	1.46	12/94	2c
Peas, sweet, Del Monte or Green Giant	15-17 oz.	0.69	12/94	2c
Pork chops, center cut, bone-in	lb.	3.30	12/94	82r
Pork purchases	year	122	91	81r
Potato chips	16-oz.	3.03	12/94	82r
Potatoes, frozen, French fried	lb.	0.77	12/94	82r
Potatoes, white	lb.	0.35	12/94	82r
Potatoes, white or red	10-lb. sack	1.23	12/94	2c
Rice, white, long grain, uncooked	lb.	0.54	12/94	82r
Round roast, USDA choice, boneless	lb.	2.92	12/94	82r
Sausage, Jimmy Dean, 100% pork	lb.	3.27	12/94	2c
Shortening, vegetable oil blends	lb.	0.80	12/94	82r
Shortening, vegetable, Crisco	3-lb.	2.33	12/94	2c
Soft drink, Coca Cola, ex deposit	2 lit	1.53	12/94	2c
Spaghetti and macaroni	lb.	1.02	12/94	82r
Steak, round, graded & ungraded, exc. USDA prime & choice	lb.	3.13	12/94	82r
Steak, sirloin, USDA choice, boneless	lb.	4.07	12/94	82r
Steak, t-bone	lb.	5.16	12/94	2c
Sugar and other sweets, eaten at home, expenditures	year	105	91	81r
Sugar, cane or beet	4 lbs.	1.17	12/94	2c
Sugar, white, all sizes	lb.	0.38	12/94	82r
Tobacco products and smoking supplies, total expenditures	year	221	91	81r
Tomatoes, field grown	lb.	1.45	12/94	82r
Tomatoes, Hunt's or Del Monte	14.5 oz.	0.70	12/94	2c
Tuna, chunk, light	lb.	2.18	12/94	82r
Tuna, chunk, light, oil-packed	6.125-6.5 oz.	0.82	12/94	2c
Goods and Services				
Miscellaneous goods and services, ACCRA Index		106.00	12/94	2c
Health Care				
Health care, ACCRA Index		104.80	12/94	2c
Antibiotic ointment, Polysporin	1.5 oz.	5.08	12/94	2c

Great Falls, MT - continued

Item	Per	Value	Date	Ref.
Health Care - continued				
Childbirth, Cesarean delivery, hospital charge	birth	6059.00	12/91	69r
Childbirth, Cesarean delivery, physician charge	birth	2248.00	12/91	69r
Childbirth, normal delivery, hospital charge	birth	3006.00	12/91	69r
Childbirth, normal delivery, physician charge	birth	1634.00	12/91	69r
Dentist's fee, adult teeth cleaning and periodic oral exam	visit	58.33	12/94	2c
Doctor's fee, routine exam, established patient	visit	37.00	12/94	2c
Drugs, expenditures	year	230	91	81r
Health care, total expenditures	year	1544	91	81r
Health insurance expenditures	year	558	91	81r
Hospital care, semiprivate room	day	406.00	12/94	2c
Medical services expenditures	year	676	91	81r
Medical supplies expenditures	year	80	91	81r
Surgery, open-heart	proc	37818.00	1/93	14r
Household Goods				
Appl. repair, service call, wash mach	min. lab. chg.	34.86	12/94	2c
Floor coverings, expenditures	year	79	91	81r
Furniture, expenditures	year	352	91	81r
Household equipment, misc. expenditures	year	614	91	81r
Household expenditures, miscellaneous	year	294	91	81r
Household furnishings and equipment, expenditures	year	1416	91	81r
Household operations expenditures	year	580	91	81r
Household textiles, expenditures	year	113	91	81r
Housekeeping supplies, expenditures	year	447	91	81r
Laundry and cleaning supplies, expenditures	year	114	91	81r
Laundry detergent, Tide Ultra, Bold, or Cheer	42 oz.	3.83	12/94	2c
Postage and stationery, expenditures	year	145	91	81r
Tissues, facial, Kleenex brand	175	1.16	12/94	2c
Housing				
Housing, ACCRA Index		88.80	12/94	2c
Add garage/carport		6,422	3/95	74r
Add room(s)		26,583	3/95	74r
Apartment condominium or co-op, median	unit	105300	12/94	62r
Dwellings (owned), expenditures	year	3932	91	81r
Enclose porch/patio/breezeway		5,382	3/95	74r
Finish room in basement/attic		3,911	3/95	74r
Home, existing, single-family, median	unit	178600	12/94	62r
House payment, principal and interest, 25% down payment	mo.	689	12/94	2c
House, 1800 sq ft, 8000 sq ft lot, new, urban, utilities	total	111500	12/94	2c
Maintenance, repairs, insurance, and other housing expenditures	year	591	91	81r
Mortgage interest and charges expenditures	year	2747	91	81r
Mtge. rate, incl. points and orig. fee, 30-year conv. fixed or ARM	mo.	9.27	12/94	2c
Princ. & int., mortgage, median-price exist. sing.-family home	mo.	845	12/94	62r
Property taxes expenditures	year	594	91	81r
Redesign, restructure more than half of home's interior		5,467	3/95	74r
Rent, apartment, 2 br., 1 1/2-2 baths, unfurnished, 950 sq ft, water	mo.	443	12/94	2c
Rental units expenditures	year	2077	91	81r
Insurance and Pensions				
Auto insurance, private passenger	year	551.37	12/94	71s
Insurance and pensions, personal, expenditures	year	3042	91	81r
Insurance, life and other personal, expenditures	year	298	91	81r
Pensions and Social Security, expenditures	year	2744	91	81r

Values are in dollars or fractions of dollars. In the column headed *Ref*, references are shown to sources. Each reference is followed by a letter. These refer to the geographical level for which data were reported: s=State, r=Region, and c=City or metro. The abbreviation *ex* is used to mean *except* or *excluding*; *exp* stands for expenditures. For other abbreviations and further explanations, please see the Introduction.

Great Falls, MT - continued

Item	Per	Value	Date	Ref.
Legal Assistance				
Legal work, law firm associate	hour	91		10r
Legal work, law firm partner	hour	151		10r
Personal Goods				
Shampoo, Alberto VO5	15-oz.	1.38	12/94	2c
Toothpaste, Crest or Colgate	6-7 oz.	2.53	12/94	2c
Personal Services				
Dry cleaning, man's 2-pc. suit		6.75	12/94	2c
Haircut, man's barbershop, no styling		7.67	12/94	2c
Haircut, woman's shampoo, trim, blow-dry		11.33	12/94	2c
Personal services expenditures	year	286	91	81r
Restaurant Food				
Chicken, fried, thigh and drumstick		1.95	12/94	2c
Dining expenditures, family	week	32.25	94	73r
Hamburger with cheese	1/4 lb.	1.95	12/94	2c
Pizza, Pizza Hut or Pizza Inn	12-13 in.	9.00	12/94	2c
Taxes				
Taxes, Federal income, expenditures	year	2946	91	81r
Taxes, personal, expenditures	year	3791	91	81r
Taxes, State and local income, expenditures	year	791	91	81r
Transportation				
Transportation, ACCRA Index		107.50	12/94	2c
Cars and trucks purchased, new	year	1231	91	81r
Cars and trucks purchased, used	year	915	91	81r
Driver's learning permit fee	perm	16.00	1/94	84s
Driver's license fee	orig	16.00	1/94	84s
Driver's license fee, duplicate	lic	5.00	1/94	84s
Driver's license reinstatement fee, min.	susp	100.00	1/94	85s
Driver's license renewal fee	renew	16.00	1/94	84s
Identification card, nondriver	card	8.00	1/94	83s
Motorcycle learning permit fee	perm	2.00	1/94	84s
Motorcycle license fee	orig	2.00	1/94	84s
Public transportation expenditures	year	375	91	81r
Tire balance, computer or spin bal., front	wheel	6.33	12/94	2c
Transportation expenditures, total	year	5527	91	81r
Vehicle finance charges	year	287	91	81r
Vehicle insurance expenditures	year	624	91	81r
Vehicle maintenance and repairs expenditures	year	695	91	81r
Vehicle purchases	year	2174	91	81r
Vehicle rental, leases, licenses, etc. expenditures	year	257	91	81r
Vehicles purchased, other than cars and trucks	year	28	91	81r
Utilities				
Utilities, ACCRA Index		91.40	12/94	2c
Electricity expenditures	year	616	91	81r
Electricity, (part.), other, 1800 sq. ft., new home	mo.	50.73	12/94	2c
Utilities, fuels, and public services, total expenditures	year	1681	91	81r
Water and other public services, expenditures	year	209	91	81r
Weddings				
Bridal attendants' gowns	event	750	10/93	76r
Bridal gown	event	852	10/93	76r
Bridal headpiece and veil	event	167	10/93	76r
Bride's wedding band	event	708	10/93	76r
Clergy	event	224	10/93	76r
Engagement ring	event	2756	10/93	76r
Flowers	event	863	10/93	76r
Formal wear for groom	event	106	10/93	76r
Groom's attendants' formal wear	event	530	10/93	76r
Groom's wedding band	event	402	10/93	76r
Music	event	600	10/93	76r
Photography	event	1088	10/93	76r
Shoes for bride	event	50	10/93	76r
Videography	event	483	10/93	76r

Great Falls, MT - continued

Item	Per	Value	Date	Ref.
Weddings - continued				
Wedding invitations and announcements	event	342	10/93	76r
Wedding reception	event	7000	10/93	76r

Greeley, CO

Item	Per	Value	Date	Ref.
Appliances				
Appliances (major), expenditures	year	160	91	81r
Average annual exp.				
Food, health care, personal goods, services	year	32461	91	81r
Charity				
Cash contributions, expenditures	year	975	91	81r
Clothing				
Apparel, men and boys, total expenditures	year	467	91	81r
Apparel, women and girls, total expenditures	year	737	91	81r
Footwear, expenditures	year	270	91	81r
Communications				
Long-distance telephone rate, day, addl. min., 1-10 mi.	min.	0.13	12/93	9s
Long-distance telephone rate, day, initial min., 1-10 mi.	min.	0.17	12/93	9s
Phone line, single, business, field visit	inst	70.00	12/93	9s
Phone line, single, business, no field visit	inst	70.00	12/93	9s
Phone line, single, residence, field visit	inst	35.00	12/93	9s
Phone line, single, residence, no field visit	inst	35.00	12/93	9s
Telephone service, expenditures	year	611	91	81r
Education				
Board, 4-year private college/university	year	2468	8/94	80s
Board, 4-year public college/university	year	2148	8/94	80s
Education, total expenditures	year	375	91	81r
Room, 4-year private college/university	year	2492	8/94	80s
Room, 4-year public college/university	year	1772	8/94	80s
Total cost, 4-year private college/university	year	16064	8/94	80s
Total cost, 4-year public college/university	year	6183	8/94	80s
Tuition, 2-year public college/university, in-state	year	1193	8/94	80s
Tuition, 4-year private college/university, in-state	year	11104	8/94	80s
Tuition, 4-year public college/university, in-state	year	2262	8/94	80s
Energy and Fuels				
Fuel oil and other fuels, expenditures	year	33	91	81r
Gas, natural, expenditures	year	212	91	81r
Gasoline and motor oil purchased	year	1115	91	81r
Gasoline, unleaded midgrade	gallon	1.36	4/93	82r
Gasoline, unleaded premium	gallon	1.43	4/93	82r
Gasoline, unleaded regular	gallon	1.23	4/93	82r
Entertainment				
Concert ticket, Pearl Jam group	perf	20.00	94	50r
Entertainment, total expenditures	year	1853	91	81r
Fees and admissions, expenditures	year	482	91	81r
Pets, toys, playground equipment, expenditures	year	299	91	81r
Reading, expenditures	year	164	91	81r
Televisions, radios, and sound equipment, expenditures	year	528	91	81r
Funerals				
Burial, immediate, container provided by funeral home		1360.49	1/95	54r
Cards, acknowledgment		11.24	1/95	54r
Casket, minimum alternative		232.73	1/95	54r
Cosmetology, hair care, etc.		114.13	1/95	54r
Cremation, direct, container provided by funeral home		1027.08	1/95	54r
Embalming		286.24	1/95	54r
Funeral, funeral home		315.60	1/95	54r
Funeral, other facility		303.08	1/95	54r
Graveside service		423.83	1/95	54r

Values are in dollars or fractions of dollars. In the column headed *Ref*, references are shown to sources. Each reference is followed by a letter. These refer to the geographical level for which data were reported: s = State, r = Region, and c = City or metro. The abbreviation *ex* is used to mean *except* or *excluding*; *exp* stands for expenditures. For other abbreviations and further explanations, please see the Introduction.

Greeley, CO - continued

Item	Per	Value	Date	Ref.
Funerals				
Hearse, local		133.12	1/95	54r
Limousine, local		99.10	1/95	54r
Memorial service		442.57	1/95	54r
Service charge, professional, nondeclinable		840.16	1/95	54r
Visitation and viewing		168.50	1/95	54r
Groceries				
Apples, Red Delicious	lb.	0.72	12/94	82r
Bacon, sliced	lb.	1.73	12/94	82r
Bananas	lb.	0.52	12/94	82r
Beef purchases	year	241	91	81r
Beverage purchases, alcoholic	year	328	91	81r
Beverage purchases, nonalcoholic	year	234	91	81r
Bologna, all beef or mixed	lb.	2.33	12/94	82r
Bread, white, pan	lb.	0.81	12/94	82r
Carrots, short trimmed and topped	lb.	0.43	12/94	82r
Cereals and bakery products purchases	year	392	91	81r
Cereals and cereals products purchases	year	139	91	81r
Chicken breast, bone-in	lb.	2.04	12/94	82r
Chicken, fresh, whole	lb.	0.95	12/94	82r
Coffee, 100%, ground roast, all sizes	lb.	4.48	12/94	82r
Dairy products (other) purchases	year	182	91	81r
Fish and seafood purchases	year	94	91	81r
Flour, white, all purpose	lb.	0.21	12/94	82r
Food purchases, food eaten at home	year	2749	91	81r
Foods purchased away from home, not prepared by consumer	year	1909	91	81r
Fruits and vegetables purchases	year	459	91	81r
Grapefruit	lb.	0.56	12/94	82r
Ground beef, 100% beef	lb.	1.31	12/94	82r
Ham, boneless, exc. canned	lb.	2.46	12/94	82r
Ice cream, prepackaged, bulk, regular	1/2 gal.	2.57	12/94	82r
Lemons	lb.	1.00	12/94	82r
Lettuce, iceberg	lb.	0.93	12/94	82r
Meats, poultry, fish, and eggs purchases	year	700	91	81r
Milk and cream (fresh) purchases	year	155	91	81r
Orange juice, frozen concentrate 12-oz. can	16 oz.	1.52	12/94	82r
Oranges, Navel	lb.	0.56	12/94	82r
Pork chops, center cut, bone-in	lb.	3.30	12/94	82r
Pork purchases	year	122	91	81r
Potato chips	16-oz.	3.03	12/94	82r
Potatoes, frozen, French fried	lb.	0.77	12/94	82r
Potatoes, white	lb.	0.35	12/94	82r
Rice, white, long grain, uncooked	lb.	0.54	12/94	82r
Round roast, USDA choice, boneless	lb.	2.92	12/94	82r
Shortening, vegetable oil blends	lb.	0.80	12/94	82r
Spaghetti and macaroni	lb.	1.02	12/94	82r
Steak, round, graded & ungraded, exc. USDA prime & choice	lb.	3.13	12/94	82r
Steak, sirloin, USDA choice, boneless	lb.	4.07	12/94	82r
Sugar and other sweets, eaten at home, expenditures	year	105	91	81r
Sugar, white, all sizes	lb.	0.38	12/94	82r
Tobacco products and smoking supplies, total expenditures	year	221	91	81r
Tomatoes, field grown	lb.	1.45	12/94	82r
Tuna, chunk, light	lb.	2.18	12/94	82r
Health Care				
Childbirth, Cesarean delivery, hospital charge	birth	6059.00	12/91	69r
Childbirth, Cesarean delivery, physician charge	birth	2248.00	12/91	69r
Childbirth, normal delivery, hospital charge	birth	3006.00	12/91	69r
Childbirth, normal delivery, physician charge	birth	1634.00	12/91	69r
Drugs, expenditures	year	230	91	81r
Health care, total expenditures	year	1544	91	81r
Health insurance expenditures	year	558	91	81r
Insurance premium, family medical care	month	362.55	1/95	41s
Medical services expenditures	year	676	91	81r
Medical supplies expenditures	year	80	91	81r
Surgery, open-heart	proc	37818.00	1/93	14r

Greeley, CO - continued

Item	Per	Value	Date	Ref.
Household Goods				
Floor coverings, expenditures	year	79	91	81r
Furniture, expenditures	year	352	91	81r
Household equipment, misc. expenditures	year	614	91	81r
Household expenditures, miscellaneous	year	294	91	81r
Household furnishings and equipment, expenditures	year	1416	91	81r
Household operations expenditures	year	580	91	81r
Household textiles, expenditures	year	113	91	81r
Housekeeping supplies, expenditures	year	447	91	81r
Laundry and cleaning supplies, expenditures	year	114	91	81r
Postage and stationery, expenditures	year	145	91	81r
Housing				
Add garage/carport		6,422	3/95	74r
Add room(s)		26,583	3/95	74r
Apartment condominium or co-op, median	unit	105300	12/94	62r
Dwellings (owned), expenditures	year	3932	91	81r
Enclose porch/patio/breezeway		5,382	3/95	74r
Finish room in basement/attic		3,911	3/95	74r
Home, existing, single-family, median	unit	178600	12/94	62r
Maintenance, repairs, insurance, and other housing expenditures	year	591	91	81r
Mortgage interest and charges expenditures	year	2747	91	81r
Princ. & int., mortgage, median-price exist. sing.-family home	mo.	845	12/94	62r
Property taxes expenditures	year	594	91	81r
Redesign, restructure more than half of home's interior		5,467	3/95	74r
Rental units expenditures	year	2077	91	81r
Insurance and Pensions				
Auto insurance, private passenger	year	804.17	12/94	71s
Insurance and pensions, personal, expenditures	year	3042	91	81r
Insurance, life and other personal, expenditures	year	298	91	81r
Pensions and Social Security, expenditures	year	2744	91	81r
Legal Assistance				
Legal work, law firm associate	hour	91		10r
Legal work, law firm partner	hour	151		10r
Personal Services				
Personal services expenditures	year	286	91	81r
Restaurant Food				
Dining expenditures, family	week	32.25	94	73r
Taxes				
Taxes, Federal income, expenditures	year	2946	91	81r
Taxes, personal, expenditures	year	3791	91	81r
Taxes, State and local income, expenditures	year	791	91	81r
Transportation				
Cars and trucks purchased, new	year	1231	91	81r
Cars and trucks purchased, used	year	915	91	81r
Driver's learning permit fee	perm	10.00	1/94	84s
Driver's license fee	orig	15.00	1/94	84s
Driver's license fee, duplicate	lic	5.00	1/94	84s
Driver's license reinstatement fee, min.	susp	40.00	1/94	85s
Driver's license renewal fee	renew	15.00	1/94	84s
Identification card, nondriver	card	3.50	1/94	83s
Motorcycle license fee	orig	16.00	1/94	84s
Public transportation expenditures	year	375	91	81r
Transportation expenditures, total	year	5527	91	81r
Vehicle finance charges	year	287	91	81r
Vehicle insurance expenditures	year	624	91	81r
Vehicle maintenance and repairs expenditures	year	695	91	81r
Vehicle purchases	year	2174	91	81r
Vehicle rental, leases, licenses, etc. expenditures	year	257	91	81r
Vehicles purchased, other than cars and trucks	year	28	91	81r

Values are in dollars or fractions of dollars. In the column headed *Ref*, references are shown to sources. Each reference is followed by a letter. These refer to the geographical level for which data were reported: s=State, r=Region, and c=City or metro. The abbreviation *ex* is used to mean *except* or *excluding*; *exp* stands for expenditures. For other abbreviations and further explanations, please see the Introduction.

Greeley, CO - continued

Item	Per	Value	Date	Ref.
Utilities				
Electricity expenditures	year	616	91	81r
Utilities, fuels, and public services, total expenditures	year	1681	91	81r
Water and other public services, expenditures	year	209	91	81r
Weddings				
Bridal attendants' gowns	event	750	10/93	76r
Bridal gown	event	852	10/93	76r
Bridal headpiece and veil	event	167	10/93	76r
Bride's wedding band	event	708	10/93	76r
Clergy	event	224	10/93	76r
Engagement ring	event	2756	10/93	76r
Flowers	event	863	10/93	76r
Formal wear for groom	event	106	10/93	76r
Groom's attendants' formal wear	event	530	10/93	76r
Groom's wedding band	event	402	10/93	76r
Music	event	600	10/93	76r
Photography	event	1088	10/93	76r
Shoes for bride	event	50	10/93	76r
Videography	event	483	10/93	76r
Wedding invitations and announcements	event	342	10/93	76r
Wedding reception	event	7000	10/93	76r

Green Bay, WI

Item	Per	Value	Date	Ref.
Composite, ACCRA index		96.90	12/94	2c
Alcoholic Beverages				
Beer, Miller Lite, Bud, 12-oz., ex deposit	6	3.65	12/94	2c
J & B Scotch	750-ml.	16.63	12/94	2c
Wine, Gallo Chablis blanc	1.5-lit	5.01	12/94	2c
Appliances				
Appliances (major), expenditures	year	131	91	81r
Average annual exp.				
Food, health care, personal goods, services	year	25935	91	81r
Charity				
Cash contributions, expenditures	year	745	91	81r
Clothing				
Apparel, men and boys, total expenditures	year	332	91	81r
Apparel, women and girls, total expenditures	year	578	91	81r
Footwear, expenditures	year	164	91	81r
Jeans, man's denim		29.59	12/94	2c
Shirt, man's dress shirt		32.53	12/94	2c
Undervest, boy's size 10-14, cotton	3	3.18	12/94	2c
Communications				
Long-distance telephone rate, day, addl. min., 1-10 mi.	min.	0.10	12/93	9s
Long-distance telephone rate, day, initial min., 1-10 mi.	min.	0.15	12/93	9s
Newspaper subscription, dly. and Sun. delivery	month	14.13	12/94	2c
Phone line, single, business, field visit	inst	64.65	12/93	9s
Phone line, single, business, no field visit	inst	64.65	12/93	9s
Phone line, single, residence, field visit	inst	33.05	12/93	9s
Phone line, single, residence, no field visit	inst	33.05	12/93	9s
Telephone bill, family of four	month	15.94	12/94	2c
Telephone service, expenditures	year	547	91	81r
Telephone, residential, flat rate	mo.	6.00	12/93	8c
Education				
Board, 4-year private college/university	year	2145	8/94	80s
Board, 4-year public college/university	year	1303	8/94	80s
Education, total expenditures	year	394	91	81r
Room, 4-year private college/university	year	1576	8/94	80s
Room, 4-year public college/university	year	1631	8/94	80s
Total cost, 4-year private college/university	year	13902	8/94	80s
Total cost, 4-year public college/university	year	5252	8/94	80s

Green Bay, WI - continued

Item	Per	Value	Date	Ref.
Education - continued				
Tuition, 2-year public college/university, in-state	year	1557	8/94	80s
Tuition, 4-year private college/university, in-state	year	10181	8/94	80s
Tuition, 4-year public college/university, in-state	year	2318	8/94	80s
Energy and Fuels				
Energy, combined forms, 1800 sq. ft.	mo.	81.86	12/94	2c
Energy, exc. electricity, 1800 sq. ft.	mo.	40.55	12/94	2c
Fuel oil and other fuels, expenditures	year	83	91	81r
Gas, cooking, winter, 10 therms	month	9.73	2/94	65c
Gas, cooking, winter, 30 therms	month	21.19	2/94	65c
Gas, cooking, winter, 50 therms	month	32.65	2/94	65c
Gas, heating, winter, 100 therms	month	61.30	2/94	65c
Gas, heating, winter, average use	month	132.36	2/94	65c
Gas, natural, expenditures	year	373	91	81r
Gas, reg unlead, taxes inc., cash, self-service	gal	1.22	12/94	2c
Gasoline and motor oil purchased	year	1000	91	81r
Gasoline, unleaded midgrade	gallon	1.15	4/93	82r
Gasoline, unleaded premium	gallon	1.23	4/93	82r
Gasoline, unleaded regular	gallon	1.07	4/93	82r
Entertainment				
Bowling, evening rate	game	1.45	12/94	2c
Entertainment, total expenditures	year	1356	91	81r
Fees and admissions, expenditures	year	347	91	81r
Monopoly game, Parker Brothers', No. 9	game	10.54	12/94	2c
Movie	adm	5.94	12/94	2c
Pets, toys, playground equipment, expenditures	year	270	91	81r
Reading, expenditures	year	160	91	81r
Televisions, radios, and sound equipment, expenditures	year	433	91	81r
Tennis balls, yellow, Wilson or Penn, 3	can	1.96	12/94	2c
Funerals				
Burial, immediate, container provided by funeral home		1268.31	1/95	54r
Cards, acknowledgment		26.12	1/95	54r
Casket, minimum alternative		198.03	1/95	54r
Cosmetology, hair care, etc.		122.19	1/95	54r
Cremation, direct, container provided by funeral home		977.81	1/95	54r
Embalming		334.00	1/95	54r
Funeral, funeral home		321.16	1/95	54r
Funeral, other facility		317.73	1/95	54r
Graveside service		292.48	1/95	54r
Hearse, local		153.20	1/95	54r
Limousine, local		123.52	1/95	54r
Memorial service		356.30	1/95	54r
Service charge, professional, nondeclinable		968.24	1/95	54r
Visitation and viewing		332.66	1/95	54r
Groceries				
Groceries, ACCRA Index		96.20	12/94	2c
Apples, Red Delicious	lb.	0.68	12/94	82r
Baby food, strained vegetables, lowest price	4-4.5 oz.	0.41	12/94	2c
Bacon, sliced	lb.	1.88	12/94	82r
Bananas	lb.	0.41	12/94	2c
Bananas	lb.	0.41	12/94	82r
Beef or hamburger, ground	lb.	1.29	12/94	2c
Beef purchases	year	197	91	81r
Beef, stew, boneless	lb.	2.52	12/94	82r
Beverage purchases, alcoholic	year	293	91	81r
Beverage purchases, nonalcoholic	year	203	91	81r
Bologna, all beef or mixed	lb.	2.12	12/94	82r
Bread, white	24-oz.	0.57	12/94	2c
Bread, white, pan	lb.	0.76	12/94	82r
Cabbage	lb.	0.44	12/94	82r
Carrots, short trimmed and topped	lb.	0.44	12/94	82r
Cereals and bakery products purchases	year	347	91	81r

Values are in dollars or fractions of dollars. In the column headed *Ref*, references are shown to sources. Each reference is followed by a letter. These refer to the geographical level for which data were reported: s = State, r = Region, and c = City or metro. The abbreviation *ex* is used to mean *except* or *excluding*; *exp* stands for *expenditures*. For other abbreviations and further explanations, please see the Introduction.

Green Bay, WI - continued

Item	Per	Value	Date	Ref.
Groceries				
Cereals and cereals products purchases	year	119	91	81r
Cheddar cheese, natural	lb.	3.28	12/94	82r
Cheese, Kraft grated Parmesan	8-oz.	3.27	12/94	2c
Chicken breast, bone-in	lb.	1.61	12/94	82r
Chicken, fresh, whole	lb.	0.89	12/94	82r
Chicken, whole fryer	lb.	1.00	12/94	2c
Chuck roast, USDA choice, boneless	lb.	2.33	12/94	82r
Cigarettes, Winston, Kings	carton	16.98	12/94	2c
Coffee, 100%, ground roast, all sizes	lb.	4.28	12/94	82r
Coffee, vacuum-packed	13 oz.	3.38	12/94	2c
Cookies, chocolate chip	lb.	2.72	12/94	82r
Corn Flakes, Kellogg's or Post Toasties	18 oz.	1.99	12/94	2c
Corn, frozen, whole kernel, lowest price	10 oz.	0.65	12/94	2c
Dairy products (other) purchases	year	148	91	81r
Eggs, Grade A large	dozen	0.66	12/94	2c
Eggs, Grade A large	dozen	0.76	12/94	82r
Fish and seafood purchases	year	61	91	81r
Flour, white, all purpose	lb.	0.22	12/94	82r
Food purchases, food eaten at home	year	2313	91	81r
Foods purchased away from home, not prepared by consumer	year	1709	91	81r
Fruits and vegetables purchases	year	372	91	81r
Grapefruit	lb.	0.47	12/94	82r
Grapes, Thompson seedless	lb.	2.15	12/94	82r
Ground beef, 100% beef	lb.	1.37	12/94	82r
Ground chuck, 100% beef	lb.	1.81	12/94	82r
Ham, boneless, exc. canned	lb.	2.16	12/94	82r
Ice cream, prepackaged, bulk, regular	1/2 gal.	2.48	12/94	82r
Lemons	lb.	1.08	12/94	82r
Lettuce, iceberg	lb.	0.81	12/94	82r
Lettuce, iceberg	head	0.75	12/94	2c
Margarine, Blue Bonnet or Parkay cubes	lb.	0.56	12/94	2c
Margarine, stick	lb.	0.81	12/94	82r
Meats, poultry, fish, and eggs purchases	year	591	91	81r
Milk and cream (fresh) purchases	year	132	91	81r
Milk, whole	1/2 gal.	1.43	12/94	2c
Orange juice, frozen concentrate 12-oz. can	16 oz.	1.41	12/94	82r
Orange juice, Minute Maid frozen	12-oz.	1.17	12/94	2c
Oranges, Navel	lb.	0.56	12/94	82r
Peaches, halves or slices, Hunt's, Del Monte, or Libby's	29-oz.	1.33	12/94	2c
Peanut butter, creamy, all sizes	lb.	1.81	12/94	82r
Peas, sweet, Del Monte or Green Giant	15-17 oz.	0.45	12/94	2c
Pork chops, center cut, bone-in	lb.	2.76	12/94	82r
Pork purchases	year	130	91	81r
Potato chips	16-oz.	2.81	12/94	82r
Potatoes, frozen, French fried	lb.	0.83	12/94	82r
Potatoes, white	lb.	0.28	12/94	82r
Potatoes, white or red	10-lb. sack	2.11	12/94	2c
Round roast, USDA choice, boneless	lb.	2.90	12/94	82r
Sausage, Jimmy Dean, 100% pork	lb.	2.71	12/94	2c
Shortening, vegetable oil blends	lb.	0.88	12/94	82r
Shortening, vegetable, Crisco	3-lb.	2.85	12/94	2c
Soft drink, Coca Cola, ex deposit	2 lit	0.93	12/94	2c
Spaghetti and macaroni	lb.	0.78	12/94	82r
Steak, rib eye, USDA choice, boneless	lb.	6.15	12/94	82r
Steak, round, graded & ungraded, exc. USDA prime & choice	lb.	2.72	12/94	82r
Steak, round, USDA choice, boneless	lb.	3.02	12/94	82r
Steak, sirloin, USDA choice, boneless	lb.	3.85	12/94	82r
Steak, t-bone	lb.	5.17	12/94	2c
Steak, T-bone, USDA choice, bone-in	lb.	5.38	12/94	82r
Sugar and other sweets, eaten at home, expenditures	year	91	91	81r
Sugar, cane or beet	4 lbs.	1.47	12/94	2c
Sugar, white, all sizes	lb.	0.36	12/94	82r
Tobacco products and smoking supplies, total expenditures	year	298	91	81r

Green Bay, WI - continued

Item	Per	Value	Date	Ref.
Groceries - continued				
Tomatoes, field grown	lb.	1.36	12/94	82r
Tomatoes, Hunt's or Del Monte	14.5 oz.	0.76	12/94	2c
Tuna, chunk, light	lb.	1.94	12/94	82r
Tuna, chunk, light, oil-packed	6.125-6.5 oz.	0.64	12/94	2c
Turkey, frozen, whole	lb.	0.96	12/94	82r
Yogurt, natural, fruit flavored	8 oz.	0.62	12/94	82r
Goods and Services				
Miscellaneous goods and services, ACCRA Index		97.40	12/94	2c
Health Care				
Health care, ACCRA Index		100.10	12/94	2c
Antibiotic ointment, Polysporin	1.5 oz.	4.27	12/94	2c
Childbirth, Cesarean delivery, hospital charge	birth	5101.00	12/91	69r
Childbirth, Cesarean delivery, physician charge	birth	2234.00	12/91	69r
Childbirth, normal delivery, hospital charge	birth	2891.00	12/91	69r
Childbirth, normal delivery, physician charge	birth	1623.00	12/91	69r
Dentist's fee, adult teeth cleaning and periodic oral exam	visit	54.20	12/94	2c
Doctor's fee, routine exam, established patient	visit	43.05	12/94	2c
Drugs, expenditures	year	248	91	81r
Health care, total expenditures	year	1336	91	81r
Health insurance expenditures	year	550	91	81r
Hospital care, semiprivate room	day	308.67	12/94	2c
Insurance premium, family medical care	month	378.79	1/95	41s
Medical services expenditures	year	457	91	81r
Medical supplies expenditures	year	82	91	81r
Household Goods				
Appl. repair, service call, wash mach	min. lab. chg.	34.75	12/94	2c
Floor coverings, expenditures	year	105	91	81r
Furniture, expenditures	year	291	91	81r
Household equipment, misc. expenditures	year	341	91	81r
Household expenditures, miscellaneous	year	162	91	81r
Household furnishings and equipment, expenditures	year	1042	91	81r
Household operations expenditures	year	365	91	81r
Household textiles, expenditures	year	101	91	81r
Housekeeping supplies, expenditures	year	390	91	81r
Laundry and cleaning supplies, expenditures	year	110	91	81r
Laundry detergent, Tide Ultra, Bold, or Cheer	42 oz.	3.20	12/94	2c
Postage and stationery, expenditures	year	115	91	81r
Tissues, facial, Kleenex brand	175	0.78	12/94	2c
Housing				
Housing, ACCRA Index		102.20	12/94	2c
Add garage/carport		8,479	3/95	74r
Add room(s)		21,347	3/95	74r
Apartment condominium or co-op, median	unit	87100	12/94	62r
Bathroom addition, average cost	add	9734.00	3/95	13r
Bathroom remodeling, average cost	remod	6414.00	3/95	13r
Bedroom, master suite addition, average cost	add	27122.00	3/95	13r
Deck addition, average cost	add	6665.00	3/95	13r
Dwellings (owned), expenditures	year	2566	91	81r
Enclose porch/patio/breezeway		4,556	3/95	74r
Exterior remodeling, average cost	remod	15395.00	3/95	13r
Family room addition, average cost	add	27658.00	3/95	13r
Finish room in basement/attic		5,074	3/95	74r
Home, existing, single-family, median	unit	106500	12/94	62r
Home, existing, single-family, median	unit	86.30	12/94	62c
House payment, principal and interest, 25% down payment	mo.	787	12/94	2c

Values are in dollars or fractions of dollars. In the column headed *Ref*, references are shown to sources. Each reference is followed by a letter. These refer to the geographical level for which data were reported: s = State, r = Region, and c = City or metro. The abbreviation *ex* is used to mean *except* or *excluding*; *exp* stands for expenditures. For other abbreviations and further explanations, please see the Introduction.

Green Bay, WI - continued

Item	Per	Value	Date	Ref.
Housing				
House, 1800 sq ft, 8000 sq ft lot, new, urban, utilities	total	125300	12/94	2c
Kitchen remodeling, major, average cost	remod	17084.00	3/95	13r
Kitchen remodeling, minor, average cost	remod	5804.00	3/95	13r
Maintenance, repairs, insurance, and other housing expenditures	year	484	91	81r
Mortgage interest and charges expenditures	year	1443	91	81r
Mtge. rate, incl. points and orig. fee, 30-year conv. fixed or ARM	mo.	9.45	12/94	2c
Office, home addition, average cost	add	8121.00	3/95	13r
Princ. & int., mortgage, median-price exist. sing.-family home	mo.	515	12/94	62r
Property taxes expenditures	year	639	91	81r
Redesign, restructure more than half of home's interior		9,114	3/95	74r
Rent, apartment, 2 br., 1 1/2-2 baths, unfurnished, 950 sq ft, water	mo.	529	12/94	2c
Rental units expenditures	year	1200	91	81r
Sun-space addition, average cost	add	23768.00	3/95	13r
Wing addition, two-story, average cost	add	50410.00	3/95	13r
Insurance and Pensions				
Auto insurance, private passenger	year	554.10	12/94	71s
Insurance and pensions, personal, expenditures	year	2408	91	81r
Insurance, life and other personal, expenditures	year	355	91	81r
Pensions and Social Security, expenditures	year	2053	91	81r
Legal Assistance				
Legal work, law firm associate	hour	90		10r
Legal work, law firm partner	hour	139		10r
Personal Goods				
Shampoo, Alberto VO5	15-oz.	0.98	12/94	2c
Toothpaste, Crest or Colgate	6-7 oz.	1.76	12/94	2c
Personal Services				
Dry cleaning, man's 2-pc. suit		6.99	12/94	2c
Haircut, man's barbershop, no styling		8.15	12/94	2c
Haircut, woman's shampoo, trim, blow-dry		17.60	12/94	2c
Personal services expenditures	year	203	91	81r
Restaurant Food				
Chicken, fried, thigh and drumstick		2.48	12/94	2c
Dining expenditures, family	week	30.03	94	73r
Hamburger with cheese	1/4 lb.	1.83	12/94	2c
Pizza, Pizza Hut or Pizza Inn	12-13 in.	7.49	12/94	2c
Taxes				
Taxes, Federal income, expenditures	year	1756	91	81r
Taxes, personal, expenditures	year	2426	91	81r
Taxes, State and local income, expenditures	year	568	91	81r
Transportation				
Transportation, ACCRA Index		98.30	12/94	2c
Bus fare, up to 10 miles	one-way	0.60	12/94	2c
Cars and trucks purchased, new	year	891	91	81r
Cars and trucks purchased, used	year	1155	91	81r
Driver's learning permit fee	perm	20.00	1/94	84s
Driver's license fee	orig	10.00	1/94	84s
Driver's license fee, duplicate	lic	4.00	1/94	84s
Driver's license reinstatement fee, min.	susp	50.00	1/94	85s
Driver's license renewal fee	renew	10.00	1/94	84s
Identification card, nondriver	card	4.00	1/94	83s
Motorcycle license fee	orig	4.00	1/94	84s
Motorcycle license fee, duplicate	lic	4.00	1/94	84s
Motorcycle license renewal fee	renew	4.00	1/94	84s
Public transportation expenditures	year	209	91	81r
Tire balance, computer or spin bal., front	wheel	6.39	12/94	2c
Transportation expenditures, total	year	4792	91	81r
Vehicle finance charges	year	300	91	81r
Vehicle insurance expenditures	year	485	91	81r

Green Bay, WI - continued

Item	Per	Value	Date	Ref.
Transportation - continued				
Vehicle maintenance and repairs expenditures	year	534	91	81r
Vehicle purchases	year	2068	91	81r
Vehicle rental, leases, licenses, etc. expenditures	year	197	91	81r
Vehicles purchased, other than cars and trucks	year	22	91	81r
Utilities				
Utilities, ACCRA Index		74.10	12/94	2c
Electricity expenditures	year	668	91	81r
Electricity, (part.), other, 1800 sq. ft., new home	mo.	41.31	12/94	2c
Electricity, summer, 250 KWh	month	19.60	8/93	64c
Electricity, summer, 500 KWh	month	35.60	8/93	64c
Electricity, summer, 750 KWh	month	51.60	8/93	64c
Electricity, summer, 1000 KWh	month	67.60	8/93	64c
Utilities, fuels, and public services, total expenditures	year	1838	91	81r
Water and other public services, expenditures	year	167	91	81r
Weddings				
Bridal attendants' gowns	event	750	10/93	76r
Bridal gown	event	852	10/93	76r
Bridal headpiece and veil	event	167	10/93	76r
Bride's wedding band	event	708	10/93	76r
Clergy	event	224	10/93	76r
Engagement ring	event	2756	10/93	76r
Flowers	event	863	10/93	76r
Formal wear for groom	event	106	10/93	76r
Groom's attendants' formal wear	event	530	10/93	76r
Groom's wedding band	event	402	10/93	76r
Music	event	600	10/93	76r
Photography	event	1088	10/93	76r
Shoes for bride	event	50	10/93	76r
Videography	event	483	10/93	76r
Wedding invitations and announcements	event	342	10/93	76r
Wedding reception	event	7000	10/93	76r

Greensboro, NC

Item	Per	Value	Date	Ref.
Appliances				
Appliances (major), expenditures	year	153	91	81r
Average annual exp.				
Food, health care, personal goods, services	year	27020	91	81r
Charity				
Cash contributions, expenditures	year	839	91	81r
Clothing				
Apparel, men and boys, total expenditures	year	380	91	81r
Apparel, women and girls, total expenditures	year	660	91	81r
Footwear, expenditures	year	193	91	81r
Communications				
Long-distance telephone rate, day, addl. min., 1-10 mi.	min.	0.10	12/93	9s
Long-distance telephone rate, day, initial min., 1-10 mi.	min.	0.16	12/93	9s
Phone line, single, business, field visit	inst	62.50	12/93	9s
Phone line, single, business, no field visit	inst	62.50	12/93	9s
Phone line, single, residence, field visit	inst	42.75	12/93	9s
Phone line, single, residence, no field visit	inst	42.75	12/93	9s
Telephone service, expenditures	year	616	91	81r
Education				
Board, 4-year private college/university	year	2069	8/94	80s
Board, 4-year public college/university	year	1627	8/94	80s
Education, total expenditures	year	319	91	81r
Room, 4-year private college/university	year	1824	8/94	80s
Room, 4-year public college/university	year	1669	8/94	80s
Total cost, 4-year private college/university	year	13505	8/94	80s

Values are in dollars or fractions of dollars. In the column headed *Ref*, references are shown to sources. Each reference is followed by a letter. These refer to the geographical level for which data were reported: s = State, r = Region, and c = City or metro. The abbreviation *ex* is used to mean *except* or *excluding*; *exp* stands for expenditures. For other abbreviations and further explanations, please see the Introduction.

Greensboro, NC - continued

Item	Per	Value	Date	Ref.
Education				
Total cost, 4-year public college/university	year	4704	8/94	80s
Tuition, 2-year public college/university, in-state	year	577	8/94	80s
Tuition, 4-year private college/university, in-state	year	9612	8/94	80s
Tuition, 4-year public college/university, in-state	year	1409	8/94	80s
Energy and Fuels				
Fuel oil and other fuels, expenditures	year	56	91	81r
Gas, natural, expenditures	year	150	91	81r
Gasoline and motor oil purchased	year	1152	91	81r
Gasoline, unleaded midgrade	gallon	1.21	4/93	82r
Gasoline, unleaded premium	gallon	1.30	4/93	82r
Gasoline, unleaded regular	gallon	1.10	4/93	82r
Entertainment				
Concert ticket, Pearl Jam group	perf	20.00	94	50r
Entertainment, total expenditures	year	1266	91	81r
Fees and admissions, expenditures	year	306	91	81r
Pets, toys, playground equipment, expenditures	year	271	91	81r
Reading, expenditures	year	131	91	81r
Televisions, radios, and sound equipment, expenditures	year	439	91	81r
Funerals				
Burial, immediate, container provided by funeral home		1370.36	1/95	54r
Cards, acknowledgment		14.83	1/95	54r
Casket, minimum alternative		192.52	1/95	54r
Cosmetology, hair care, etc.		102.27	1/95	54r
Cremation, direct, container provided by funeral home		1065.64	1/95	54r
Embalming		304.29	1/95	54r
Funeral, funeral home		287.83	1/95	54r
Funeral, other facility		284.14	1/95	54r
Graveside service		349.13	1/95	54r
Hearse, local		132.27	1/95	54r
Limousine, local		98.45	1/95	54r
Memorial service		270.59	1/95	54r
Service charge, professional, nondeclinable		933.59	1/95	54r
Visitation and viewing		225.83	1/95	54r
Groceries				
Apples, Red Delicious	lb.	0.73	12/94	82r
Bacon, sliced	lb.	1.67	12/94	82r
Bananas	lb.	0.42	12/94	82r
Beef purchases	year	213	91	81r
Beverage purchases, alcoholic	year	249	91	81r
Beverage purchases, nonalcoholic	year	207	91	81r
Bologna, all beef or mixed	lb.	2.27	12/94	82r
Bread, white, pan	lb.	0.68	12/94	82r
Cabbage	lb.	0.42	12/94	82r
Carrots, short trimmed and topped	lb.	0.53	12/94	82r
Cereals and bakery products purchases	year	345	91	81r
Cereals and cereals products purchases	year	127	91	81r
Cheddar cheese, natural	lb.	3.58	12/94	82r
Chicken breast, bone-in	lb.	1.71	12/94	82r
Chicken, fresh, whole	lb.	0.78	12/94	82r
Chuck roast, USDA choice, boneless	lb.	2.26	12/94	82r
Crackers, soda, salted	lb.	1.27	12/94	82r
Cucumbers	lb.	0.65	12/94	82r
Dairy products (other) purchases	year	141	91	81r
Eggs, Grade A large	dozen	0.87	12/94	82r
Fish and seafood purchases	year	72	91	81r
Flour, white, all purpose	lb.	0.23	12/94	82r
Food purchases, food eaten at home	year	2381	91	81r
Foods purchased away from home, not prepared by consumer	year	1696	91	81r
Frankfurters, all meat or all beef	lb.	1.74	12/94	82r
Fruits and vegetables purchases	year	380	91	81r
Grapefruit	lb.	0.45	12/94	82r
Grapes, Thompson seedless	lb.	2.30	12/94	82r

Greensboro, NC - continued

Item	Per	Value	Date	Ref.
Groceries - continued				
Ground beef, 100% beef	lb.	1.37	12/94	82r
Ground chuck, 100% beef	lb.	1.97	12/94	82r
Ham, boneless, exc. canned	lb.	2.54	12/94	82r
Ice cream, prepackaged, bulk, regular	1/2 gal.	2.47	12/94	82r
Lemons	lb.	1.02	12/94	82r
Lettuce, iceberg	lb.	0.96	12/94	82r
Margarine, stick	lb.	0.77	12/94	82r
Meats, poultry, fish, and eggs purchases	year	655	91	81r
Milk and cream (fresh) purchases	year	130	91	81r
Orange juice, frozen concentrate 12-oz. can	16 oz.	1.36	12/94	82r
Oranges, Navel	lb.	0.54	12/94	82r
Pears, Anjou	lb.	0.81	12/94	82r
Pork chops, center cut, bone-in	lb.	3.07	12/94	82r
Pork purchases	year	142	91	81r
Potato chips	16-oz.	3.15	12/94	82r
Potatoes, frozen, French fried	lb.	0.82	12/94	82r
Potatoes, white	lb.	0.34	12/94	82r
Rice, white, long grain, uncooked	lb.	0.48	12/94	82r
Round roast, USDA choice, boneless	lb.	2.91	12/94	82r
Sausage, fresh	lb.	1.82	12/94	82r
Shortening, vegetable oil blends	lb.	0.75	12/94	82r
Spaghetti and macaroni	lb.	0.87	12/94	82r
Steak, rib eye, USDA choice, boneless	lb.	6.85	12/94	82r
Steak, round, graded & ungraded, exc. USDA prime & choice	lb.	2.96	12/94	82r
Steak, round, USDA choice, boneless	lb.	3.17	12/94	82r
Steak, sirloin, USDA choice, boneless	lb.	4.12	12/94	82r
Steak, T-bone, USDA choice, bone-in	lb.	5.63	12/94	82r
Sugar and other sweets, eaten at home, expenditures	year	93	91	81r
Sugar, white, all sizes	lb.	0.39	12/94	82r
Tobacco products and smoking supplies, total expenditures	year	286	91	81r
Tomatoes, field grown	lb.	1.36	12/94	82r
Tuna, chunk, light	lb.	1.94	12/94	82r
Turkey, frozen, whole	lb.	0.96	12/94	82r
Yogurt, natural, fruit flavored	8 oz.	0.58	12/94	82r
Health Care				
Adenosine, emergency room	treat	100.00	95	23r
Bladder tap, superpubic, infant, emergency room	treat	119.00	95	23r
Blood analysis, emergency room	treat	25.00	95	23r
Blood tests, abdominal pain, emergency room	treat	25.00	95	23r
Burn dressing, emergency room	treat	266.00	95	23r
Cardiology interpretation, emergency room	treat	26.00	95	23r
Chest X-ray, emergency room	treat	78.00	95	23r
Childbirth, Cesarean delivery, hospital charge	birth	5462.00	12/91	69r
Childbirth, Cesarean delivery, physician charge	birth	2228.00	12/91	69r
Childbirth, normal delivery, hospital charge	birth	2943.00	12/91	69r
Childbirth, normal delivery, physician charge	birth	1619.00	12/91	69r
Defibrillation pads, emergency room	treat	6.00	95	23r
Drugs, expenditures	year	297	91	81r
Gastric tube insertion, nasal, emergency room	treat	25.00	95	23r
Health care, total expenditures	year	1600	91	81r
Health insurance expenditures	year	637	91	81r
Heart monitor, emergency room	treat	40.00	95	23r
Insurance premium, family medical care	month	405.45	1/95	41s
Intravenous fluids, emergency room	treat	130.00	95	23r
Intravenous fluids, emergency room	liter	26.00	95	23r
Intravenous line, central, emergency room	treat	342.00	95	23r
Liver function tests, abdominal pain, emergency room	treat	26.00	95	23r
Medical care charges, total, emergency room, third-degree burns	treat	2101.00	95	23r
Medical care charges, total, emergency, infant with fever	treat	628.00	95	23r
Medical services expenditures	year	573	91	81r

Values are in dollars or fractions of dollars. In the column headed *Ref*, references are shown to sources. Each reference is followed by a letter. These refer to the geographical level for which data were reported: s=State, r=Region, and c=City or metro. The abbreviation *ex* is used to mean *except* or *excluding*; *exp* stands for *expenditures*. For other abbreviations and further explanations, please see the Introduction.

Greensboro, NC - continued

Item	Per	Value	Date	Ref.
Health Care				
Medical supplies expenditures	year	93	91	81r
Morphine, emergency room	treat	34.00	95	23r
Nursing care and facilities charges, emergency room	treat	252.00	95	23r
Nursing care and facilities charges, emergency, infant with fever	treat	252.00	95	23r
Nursing care and facilities charges, emergency, third-degree burns	treat	861.00	95	23r
Physician's charges, emergency, infant with fever	treat	212.00	95	23r
Physician's charges, emergency, third-degree burns	treat	372.00	95	23r
Physician's fee, emergency room	treat	372.00	95	23r
Physician's fee, general practitioner	visit	51.20	12/93	60r
Surgery, open-heart	proc	42374.00	1/93	14r
Ultrasound, abdominal, emergency room	treat	276.00	95	23r
Urinalysis, emergency room	treat	20.00	95	23r
Urinalysis, infant, emergency room	treat	20.00	95	23r
X-rays, emergency room	treat	78.00	95	23r
Household Goods				
Floor coverings, expenditures	year	48	91	81r
Furniture, expenditures	year	280	91	81r
Household equipment, misc. expenditures	year	342	91	81r
Household expenditures, miscellaneous	year	256	91	81r
Household furnishings and equipment, expenditures	year	988	91	81r
Household operations expenditures	year	468	91	81r
Household textiles, expenditures	year	95	91	81r
Housekeeping supplies, expenditures	year	380	91	81r
Laundry and cleaning supplies, expenditures	year	109	91	81r
Postage and stationery, expenditures	year	105	91	81r
Housing				
Add garage/carport		6,980	3/95	74r
Add room(s)		11,403	3/95	74r
Apartment condominium or co-op, median	unit	68600	12/94	62r
Dwellings (owned), expenditures	year	2428	91	81r
Enclose porch/patio/breezeway		4,572	3/95	74r
Finish room in basement/attic		3,794	3/95	74r
Home, existing, single-family, median	unit	120200	12/94	62r
Maintenance, repairs, insurance, and other housing expenditures	year	531	91	81r
Mortgage interest and charges expenditures	year	1506	91	81r
Princ. & int., mortgage, median-price exist. sing.-family home	mo.	540	12/94	62r
Property taxes expenditures	year	391	91	81r
Redesign, restructure more than half of home's interior		17,641	3/95	74r
Rental units expenditures	year	1264	91	81r
Insurance and Pensions				
Auto insurance, private passenger	year	528.43	12/94	71s
Insurance and pensions, personal, expenditures	year	2395	91	81r
Insurance, life and other personal, expenditures	year	368	91	81r
Pensions and Social Security, expenditures	year	2027	91	81r
Personal Services				
Personal services expenditures	year	212	91	81r
Restaurant Food				
Dining expenditures, family	week	33.83	94	73r
Taxes				
Taxes, Federal income, expenditures	year	2275	91	81r
Taxes, personal, expenditures	year	2715	91	81r
Taxes, State and local income, expenditures	year	365	91	81r
Transportation				
Cars and trucks purchased, new	year	1306	91	81r
Cars and trucks purchased, used	year	942	91	81r
Driver's learning permit fee	perm	10.00	1/94	84s

Greensboro, NC - continued

Item	Per	Value	Date	Ref.
Transportation - continued				
Driver's license fee	orig	10.00	1/94	84s
Driver's license fee, duplicate	lic	5.00	1/94	84s
Driver's license reinstatement fee, min.	susp	25.00	1/94	85s
Driver's license renewal fee	renew	10.00	1/94	84s
Fine, safety belt violation	ticket	25.00	95	56s
Identification card, nondriver	card	10.00	1/94	83s
Motorcycle license fee	orig	5.00	1/94	84s
Public transportation expenditures	year	249	91	81r
Transportation expenditures, total	year	5307	91	81r
Vehicle finance charges	year	346	91	81r
Vehicle insurance expenditures	year	544	91	81r
Vehicle maintenance and repairs expenditures	year	600	91	81r
Vehicle purchases	year	2275	91	81r
Vehicle rental, leases, licenses, etc. expenditures	year	141	91	81r
Vehicles purchased, other than cars and trucks	year	27	91	81r
Utilities				
Electricity expenditures	year	950	91	81r
Utilities, fuels, and public services, total expenditures	year	2000	91	81r
Water and other public services, expenditures	year	227	91	81r
Weddings				
Bridal attendants' gowns	event	750	10/93	76r
Bridal gown	event	852	10/93	76r
Bridal headpiece and veil	event	167	10/93	76r
Bride's wedding band	event	708	10/93	76r
Clergy	event	224	10/93	76r
Engagement ring	event	2756	10/93	76r
Flowers	event	863	10/93	76r
Formal wear for groom	event	106	10/93	76r
Groom's attendants' formal wear	event	530	10/93	76r
Groom's wedding band	event	402	10/93	76r
Music	event	600	10/93	76r
Photography	event	1088	10/93	76r
Shoes for bride	event	50	10/93	76r
Videography	event	483	10/93	76r
Wedding invitations and announcements	event	342	10/93	76r
Wedding reception	event	7000	10/93	76r

Greenville, NC

Item	Per	Value	Date	Ref.
Composite, ACCRA index		96.70	12/94	2c
Alcoholic Beverages				
Beer, Miller Lite, Bud, 12-oz., ex deposit	6	3.59	12/94	2c
J & B Scotch	750-ml.	18.60	12/94	2c
Wine, Gallo Chablis blanc	1.5-lit	4.45	12/94	2c
Clothing				
Jeans, man's denim		32.49	12/94	2c
Shirt, man's dress shirt		29.50	12/94	2c
Undervest, boy's size 10-14, cotton	3	3.92	12/94	2c
Communications				
Newspaper subscription, dly. and Sun. delivery	month	8.00	12/94	2c
Telephone bill, family of four	month	16.66	12/94	2c
Energy and Fuels				
Energy, combined forms, 1800 sq. ft.	mo.	124.41	12/94	2c
Gas, reg unlead, taxes inc., cash, self-service	gal	0.99	12/94	2c
Entertainment				
Bowling, evening rate	game	2.90	12/94	2c
Monopoly game, Parker Brothers', No. 9	game	8.97	12/94	2c
Movie	adm	5.00	12/94	2c
Tennis balls, yellow, Wilson or Penn, 3	can	2.20	12/94	2c

Values are in dollars or fractions of dollars. In the column headed *Ref*, references are shown to sources. Each reference is followed by a letter. These refer to the geographical level for which data were reported: s=State, r=Region, and c=City or metro. The abbreviation *ex* is used to mean *except* or *excluding*; *exp* stands for expenditures. For other abbreviations and further explanations, please see the Introduction.

Greenville, NC - continued

Item	Per	Value	Date	Ref.
Groceries				
Groceries, ACCRA Index		95.10	12/94	2c
Baby food, strained vegetables, lowest price	4-4.5 oz.	0.35	12/94	2c
Bananas	lb.	0.50	12/94	2c
Beef or hamburger, ground	lb.	1.37	12/94	2c
Bread, white	24-oz.	0.68	12/94	2c
Cheese, Kraft grated Parmesan	8-oz.	3.14	12/94	2c
Chicken, whole fryer	lb.	0.89	12/94	2c
Cigarettes, Winston, Kings	carton	12.55	12/94	2c
Coffee, vacuum-packed	13 oz.	3.07	12/94	2c
Corn Flakes, Kellogg's or Post Toasties	18 oz.	2.19	12/94	2c
Corn, frozen, whole kernel, lowest price	10 oz.	0.65	12/94	2c
Eggs, Grade A large	dozen	0.86	12/94	2c
Lettuce, iceberg	head	0.77	12/94	2c
Margarine, Blue Bonnet or Parkay cubes	lb.	0.54	12/94	2c
Milk, whole	1/2 gal.	1.43	12/94	2c
Orange juice, Minute Maid frozen	12-oz.	1.14	12/94	2c
Peaches, halves or slices, Hunt's, Del Monte, or Libby's	29-oz.	1.32	12/94	2c
Peas, sweet, Del Monte or Green Giant	15-17 oz.	0.45	12/94	2c
Potatoes, white or red	10-lb. sack	2.53	12/94	2c
Sausage, Jimmy Dean, 100% pork	lb.	2.31	12/94	2c
Shortening, vegetable, Crisco	3-lb.	2.55	12/94	2c
Soft drink, Coca Cola, ex deposit	2 lit	1.17	12/94	2c
Steak, t-bone	lb.	5.35	12/94	2c
Sugar, cane or beet	4 lbs.	1.51	12/94	2c
Tomatoes, Hunt's or Del Monte	14.5 oz.	0.63	12/94	2c
Tuna, chunk, light, oil-packed	6.125-6.5 oz.	0.66	12/94	2c
Goods and Services				
Miscellaneous goods and services, ACCRA Index		100.90	12/94	2c
Health Care				
Health care, ACCRA Index		104.00	12/94	2c
Antibiotic ointment, Polysporin	1.5 oz.	3.96	12/94	2c
Dentist's fee, adult teeth cleaning and periodic oral exam	visit	57.75	12/94	2c
Doctor's fee, routine exam, established patient	visit	46.00	12/94	2c
Hospital care, semiprivate room	day	305.00	12/94	2c
Household Goods				
Appl. repair, service call, wash mach	min. lab. chg.	38.30	12/94	2c
Laundry detergent, Tide Ultra, Bold, or Cheer	42 oz.	2.65	12/94	2c
Tissues, facial, Kleenex brand	175	0.99	12/94	2c
Housing				
Housing, ACCRA Index		92.20	12/94	2c
House payment, principal and interest, 25% down payment	mo.	718	12/94	2c
House, 1800 sq ft, 8000 sq ft lot, new, urban, utilities	total	115200	12/94	2c
Mtge. rate, incl. points and orig. fee, 30-year conv. fixed or ARM	mo.	9.37	12/94	2c
Rent, apartment, 2 br., 1 1/2-2 baths, unfurnished, 950 sq ft, water	mo.	453	12/94	2c
Personal Goods				
Shampoo, Alberto VO5	15-oz.	1.05	12/94	2c
Toothpaste, Crest or Colgate	6-7 oz.	1.95	12/94	2c
Personal Services				
Dry cleaning, man's 2-pc. suit		7.18	12/94	2c
Haircut, man's barbershop, no styling		8.80	12/94	2c
Haircut, woman's shampoo, trim, blow-dry		18.80	12/94	2c

Greenville, NC - continued

Item	Per	Value	Date	Ref.
Restaurant Food				
Chicken, fried, thigh and drumstick		2.49	12/94	2c
Hamburger with cheese	1/4 lb.	1.89	12/94	2c
Pizza, Pizza Hut or Pizza Inn	12-13 in.	8.15	12/94	2c
Transportation				
Transportation, ACCRA Index		83.60	12/94	2c
Tire balance, computer or spin bal., front	wheel	5.20	12/94	2c
Utilities				
Utilities, ACCRA Index		107.40	12/94	2c
Electricity, 1800 sq. ft., new home	mo.	124.41	12/94	2c

Greenville, SC

Item	Per	Value	Date	Ref.
Composite, ACCRA index		97.30	12/94	2c
Alcoholic Beverages				
Beer, Miller Lite, Bud, 12-oz., ex deposit	6	3.88	12/94	2c
J & B Scotch	750-ml.	16.90	12/94	2c
Wine, Gallo Chablis blanc	1.5-lit	4.62	12/94	2c
Appliances				
Appliances (major), expenditures	year	153	91	81r
Average annual exp.				
Food, health care, personal goods, services	year	27020	91	81r
Charity				
Cash contributions, expenditures	year	839	91	81r
Clothing				
Apparel, men and boys, total expenditures	year	380	91	81r
Apparel, women and girls, total expenditures	year	660	91	81r
Footwear, expenditures	year	193	91	81r
Jeans, man's denim		30.59	12/94	2c
Shirt, man's dress shirt		36.40	12/94	2c
Undervest, boy's size 10-14, cotton	3	4.54	12/94	2c
Communications				
Long-distance telephone rate, day, addl. min., 1-10 mi.	min.	0.13	12/93	9s
Long-distance telephone rate, day, initial min., 1-10 mi.	min.	0.24	12/93	9s
Newspaper subscription, dly. and Sun. delivery	month	12.00	12/94	2c
Phone line, single, business, field visit	inst	82.50	12/93	9s
Phone line, single, business, no field visit	inst	64.00	12/93	9s
Phone line, single, residence, field visit	inst	62.50	12/93	9s
Phone line, single, residence, no field visit	inst	44.00	12/93	9s
Telephone bill, family of four	month	24.07	12/94	2c
Telephone service, expenditures	year	616	91	81r
Telephone, residential, flat rate	mo.	16.90	12/93	8c
Education				
Board, 4-year private college/university	year	1831	8/94	80s
Board, 4-year public college/university	year	1462	8/94	80s
Education, total expenditures	year	319	91	81r
Room, 4-year private college/university	year	1744	8/94	80s
Room, 4-year public college/university	year	1851	8/94	80s
Total cost, 4-year private college/university	year	12082	8/94	80s
Total cost, 4-year public college/university	year	6203	8/94	80s
Tuition, 2-year public college/university, in-state	year	1061	8/94	80s
Tuition, 4-year private college/university, in-state	year	8507	8/94	80s
Tuition, 4-year public college/university, in-state	year	2891	8/94	80s
Energy and Fuels				
Energy, combined forms, 1800 sq. ft.	mo.	108.16	12/94	2c
Fuel oil and other fuels, expenditures	year	56	91	81r
Gas, cooking, winter, 10 therms	month	9.17	2/94	65c
Gas, cooking, winter, 30 therms	month	21.50	2/94	65c
Gas, cooking, winter, 50 therms	month	33.83	2/94	65c

Values are in dollars or fractions of dollars. In the column headed *Ref*, references are shown to sources. Each reference is followed by a letter. These refer to the geographical level for which data were reported: s=State, r=Region, and c=City or metro. The abbreviation *ex* is used to mean *except* or *excluding*; *exp* stands for expenditures. For other abbreviations and further explanations, please see the Introduction.

Greenville, SC - continued

Item	Per	Value	Date	Ref.
Energy and Fuels				
Gas, heating, winter, 100 therms	month	64.65	2/94	65c
Gas, heating, winter, average use	month	87.46	2/94	65c
Gas, natural, expenditures	year	150	91	81r
Gas, reg unlead, taxes inc., cash, self-service	gal	1.02	12/94	2c
Gasoline and motor oil purchased	year	1152	91	81r
Gasoline, unleaded midgrade	gallon	1.21	4/93	82r
Gasoline, unleaded premium	gallon	1.30	4/93	82r
Gasoline, unleaded regular	gallon	1.10	4/93	82r
Entertainment				
Bowling, evening rate	game	2.40	12/94	2c
Concert ticket, Pearl Jam group	perf	20.00	94	50r
Entertainment, total expenditures	year	1266	91	81r
Fees and admissions, expenditures	year	306	91	81r
Monopoly game, Parker Brothers', No. 9	game	11.98	12/94	2c
Movie	adm	5.50	12/94	2c
Pets, toys, playground equipment, expenditures	year	271	91	81r
Reading, expenditures	year	131	91	81r
Televisions, radios, and sound equipment, expenditures	year	439	91	81r
Tennis balls, yellow, Wilson or Penn, 3	can	1.93	12/94	2c
Funerals				
Burial, immediate, container provided by funeral home		1370.36	1/95	54r
Cards, acknowledgment		14.83	1/95	54r
Casket, minimum alternative		192.52	1/95	54r
Cosmetology, hair care, etc.		102.27	1/95	54r
Cremation, direct, container provided by funeral home		1065.64	1/95	54r
Embalming		304.29	1/95	54r
Funeral, funeral home		287.83	1/95	54r
Funeral, other facility		284.14	1/95	54r
Graveside service		349.13	1/95	54r
Hearse, local		132.27	1/95	54r
Limousine, local		98.45	1/95	54r
Memorial service		270.59	1/95	54r
Service charge, professional, nondeclinable		933.59	1/95	54r
Visitation and viewing		225.83	1/95	54r
Groceries				
Groceries, ACCRA Index		98.70	12/94	2c
Apples, Red Delicious	lb.	0.73	12/94	82r
Baby food, strained vegetables, lowest price	4-4.5 oz.	0.35	12/94	2c
Bacon, sliced	lb.	1.67	12/94	82r
Bananas	lb.	0.45	12/94	2c
Bananas	lb.	0.42	12/94	82r
Beef or hamburger, ground	lb.	1.72	12/94	2c
Beef purchases	year	213	91	81r
Beverage purchases, alcoholic	year	249	91	81r
Beverage purchases, nonalcoholic	year	207	91	81r
Bologna, all beef or mixed	lb.	2.27	12/94	82r
Bread, white	24-oz.	0.70	12/94	2c
Bread, white, pan	lb.	0.68	12/94	82r
Cabbage	lb.	0.42	12/94	82r
Carrots, short trimmed and topped	lb.	0.53	12/94	82r
Cereals and bakery products purchases	year	345	91	81r
Cereals and cereals products purchases	year	127	91	81r
Cheddar cheese, natural	lb.	3.58	12/94	82r
Cheese, Kraft grated Parmesan	8-oz.	3.06	12/94	2c
Chicken breast, bone-in	lb.	1.71	12/94	82r
Chicken, fresh, whole	lb.	0.78	12/94	82r
Chicken, whole fryer	lb.	0.86	12/94	2c
Chuck roast, USDA choice, boneless	lb.	2.26	12/94	82r
Cigarettes, Winston, Kings	carton	13.26	12/94	2c
Coffee, vacuum-packed	13 oz.	3.34	12/94	2c
Corn Flakes, Kellogg's or Post Toasties	18 oz.	2.29	12/94	2c
Corn, frozen, whole kernel, lowest price	10 oz.	0.64	12/94	2c
Crackers, soda, salted	lb.	1.27	12/94	82r
Cucumbers	lb.	0.65	12/94	82r
Dairy products (other) purchases	year	141	91	81r

Greenville, SC - continued

Item	Per	Value	Date	Ref.
Groceries - continued				
Eggs, Grade A large	dozen	0.86	12/94	2c
Eggs, Grade A large	dozen	0.87	12/94	82r
Fish and seafood purchases	year	72	91	81r
Flour, white, all purpose	lb.	0.23	12/94	82r
Food purchases	year	2381	91	81r
Foods purchased away from home, not prepared by consumer	year	1696	91	81r
Frankfurters, all meat or all beef	lb.	1.74	12/94	82r
Fruits and vegetables purchases	year	380	91	81r
Grapefruit	lb.	0.45	12/94	82r
Grapes, Thompson seedless	lb.	2.30	12/94	82r
Ground beef, 100% beef	lb.	1.37	12/94	82r
Ground chuck, 100% beef	lb.	1.97	12/94	82r
Ham, boneless, exc. canned	lb.	2.54	12/94	82r
Ice cream, prepackaged, bulk, regular	1/2 gal.	2.47	12/94	82r
Lemons	lb.	1.02	12/94	82r
Lettuce, iceberg	lb.	0.96	12/94	82r
Lettuce, iceberg	head	0.99	12/94	2c
Margarine, Blue Bonnet or Parkay cubes	lb.	0.57	12/94	2c
Margarine, stick	lb.	0.77	12/94	82r
Meats, poultry, fish, and eggs purchases	year	655	91	81r
Milk and cream (fresh) purchases	year	130	91	81r
Milk, whole	1/2 gal.	1.46	12/94	2c
Orange juice, frozen concentrate 12-oz. can	16 oz.	1.36	12/94	82r
Orange juice, Minute Maid frozen	12-oz.	1.18	12/94	2c
Oranges, Navel	lb.	0.54	12/94	82r
Peaches, halves or slices, Hunt's, Del Monte, or Libby's	29-oz.	1.32	12/94	2c
Pears, Anjou	lb.	0.81	12/94	82r
Peas, sweet, Del Monte or Green Giant	15-17 oz.	0.56	12/94	2c
Pork chops, center cut, bone-in	lb.	3.07	12/94	82r
Pork purchases	year	142	91	81r
Potato chips	16-oz.	3.15	12/94	82r
Potatoes, frozen, French fried	lb.	0.82	12/94	82r
Potatoes, white	lb.	0.34	12/94	82r
Potatoes, white or red	10-lb. sack	2.89	12/94	2c
Rice, white, long grain, uncooked	lb.	0.48	12/94	82r
Round roast, USDA choice, boneless	lb.	2.91	12/94	82r
Sausage, fresh	lb.	1.82	12/94	82r
Sausage, Jimmy Dean, 100% pork	lb.	2.44	12/94	2c
Shortening, vegetable oil blends	lb.	0.75	12/94	82r
Shortening, vegetable, Crisco	3-lb.	2.56	12/94	2c
Soft drink, Coca Cola, ex deposit	2 lit	1.06	12/94	2c
Spaghetti and macaroni	lb.	0.87	12/94	82r
Steak, rib eye, USDA choice, boneless	lb.	6.85	12/94	82r
Steak, round, graded & ungraded, exc. USDA prime & choice	lb.	2.96	12/94	82r
Steak, round, USDA choice, boneless	lb.	3.17	12/94	82r
Steak, sirloin, USDA choice, boneless	lb.	4.12	12/94	82r
Steak, t-bone	lb.	6.19	12/94	2c
Steak, T-bone, USDA choice, bone-in	lb.	5.63	12/94	82r
Sugar and other sweets, eaten at home, expenditures	year	93	91	81r
Sugar, cane or beet	4 lbs.	1.42	12/94	2c
Sugar, white, all sizes	lb.	0.39	12/94	82r
Tobacco products and smoking supplies, total expenditures	year	286	91	81r
Tomatoes, field grown	lb.	1.36	12/94	82r
Tomatoes, Hunt's or Del Monte	14.5 oz.	0.58	12/94	2c
Tuna, chunk, light	lb.	1.94	12/94	82r
Tuna, chunk, light, oil-packed	6.125-6.5 oz.	0.69	12/94	2c
Turkey, frozen, whole	lb.	0.96	12/94	82r
Yogurt, natural, fruit flavored	8 oz.	0.58	12/94	82r
Goods and Services				
Miscellaneous goods and services, ACCRA Index		102.50	12/94	2c

Values are in dollars or fractions of dollars. In the column headed *Ref*, references are shown to sources. Each reference is followed by a letter. These refer to the geographical level for which data were reported: s = State, r = Region, and c = City or metro. The abbreviation *ex* is used to mean *except* or *excluding*; *exp* stands for *expenditures*. For other abbreviations and further explanations, please see the Introduction.

Greenville, SC - continued

Item	Per	Value	Date	Ref.
Health Care				
Health care, ACCRA Index		95.40	12/94	2c
Adenosine, emergency room	treat	100.00	95	23r
Antibiotic ointment, Polysporin	1.5 oz.	3.90	12/94	2c
Bladder tap, superpubic, infant, emergency room	treat	119.00	95	23r
Blood analysis, emergency room	treat	25.00	95	23r
Blood tests, abdominal pain, emergency room	treat	25.00	95	23r
Burn dressing, emergency room	treat	266.00	95	23r
Cardiology interpretation, emergency room	treat	26.00	95	23r
Chest X-ray, emergency room	treat	78.00	95	23r
Childbirth, Cesarean delivery, hospital charge	birth	5462.00	12/91	69r
Childbirth, Cesarean delivery, physician charge	birth	2228.00	12/91	69r
Childbirth, normal delivery, hospital charge	birth	2943.00	12/91	69r
Childbirth, normal delivery, physician charge	birth	1619.00	12/91	69r
Defibrillation pads, emergency room	treat	6.00	95	23r
Dentist's fee, adult teeth cleaning and periodic oral exam	visit	52.40	12/94	2c
Doctor's fee, routine exam, established patient	visit	41.88	12/94	2c
Drugs, expenditures	year	297	91	81r
Gastric tube insertion, nasal, emergency room	treat	25.00	95	23r
Health care, total expenditures	year	1600	91	81r
Health insurance expenditures	year	637	91	81r
Heart monitor, emergency room	treat	40.00	95	23r
Hospital care, semiprivate room	day	268.33	12/94	2c
Insurance premium, family medical care	month	414.49	1/95	41s
Intravenous fluids, emergency room	treat	130.00	95	23r
Intravenous fluids, emergency room	liter	26.00	95	23r
Intravenous line, central, emergency room	treat	342.00	95	23r
Liver function tests, abdominal pain, emergency room	treat	26.00	95	23r
Medical care charges, total, emergency room, third-degree burns	treat	2101.00	95	23r
Medical care charges, total, emergency, infant with fever	treat	628.00	95	23r
Medical services expenditures	year	573	91	81r
Medical supplies expenditures	year	93	91	81r
Morphine, emergency room	treat	34.00	95	23r
Nursing care and facilities charges, emergency room	treat	252.00	95	23r
Nursing care and facilities charges, emergency, infant with fever	treat	252.00	95	23r
Nursing care and facilities charges, emergency, third-degree burns	treat	861.00	95	23r
Physician's charges, emergency, infant with fever	treat	212.00	95	23r
Physician's charges, emergency, third-degree burns	treat	372.00	95	23r
Physician's fee, emergency room	treat	372.00	95	23r
Physician's fee, general practitioner	visit	51.20	12/93	60r
Surgery, open-heart	proc	42374.00	1/93	14r
Ultrasound, abdominal, emergency room	treat	276.00	95	23r
Urinalysis, emergency room	treat	20.00	95	23r
Urinalysis, infant, emergency room	treat	20.00	95	23r
X-rays, emergency room	treat	78.00	95	23r
Household Goods				
Appl. repair, service call, wash mach	min. lab. chg.	34.00	12/94	2c
Floor coverings, expenditures	year	48	91	81r
Furniture, expenditures	year	280	91	81r
Household equipment, misc. expenditures	year	342	91	81r
Household expenditures, miscellaneous	year	256	91	81r
Household furnishings and equipment, expenditures	year	988	91	81r
Household operations expenditures	year	468	91	81r
Household textiles, expenditures	year	95	91	81r
Housekeeping supplies, expenditures	year	380	91	81r

Greenville, SC - continued

Item	Per	Value	Date	Ref.
Household Goods - continued				
Laundry and cleaning supplies, expenditures	year	109	91	81r
Laundry detergent, Tide Ultra, Bold, or Cheer	42 oz.	3.12	12/94	2c
Postage and stationery, expenditures	year	105	91	81r
Tissues, facial, Kleenex brand	175	0.92	12/94	2c
Housing				
Housing, ACCRA Index		91.90	12/94	2c
Add garage/carport		6,980	3/95	74r
Add room(s)		11,403	3/95	74r
Apartment condominium or co-op, median	unit	68600	12/94	62r
Dwellings (owned), expenditures	year	2428	91	81r
Enclose porch/patio/breezeway		4,572	3/95	74r
Finish room in basement/attic		3,794	3/95	74r
Home, existing, single-family, median	unit	120200	12/94	62r
Home, existing, single-family, median	unit	88.50	12/94	62c
House payment, principal and interest, 25% down payment	mo.	680	12/94	2c
House, 1800 sq ft, 8000 sq ft lot, new, urban, utilities	total	109483	12/94	2c
Maintenance, repairs, insurance, and other housing expenditures	year	531	91	81r
Mortgage interest and charges expenditures	year	1506	91	81r
Mtge. rate, incl. points and orig. fee, 30-year conv. fixed or ARM	mo.	9.33	12/94	2c
Princ. & int., mortgage, median-price exist. sing.-family home	mo.	540	12/94	62r
Property taxes expenditures	year	391	91	81r
Redesign, restructure more than half of home's interior		17,641	3/95	74r
Rent, apartment, 2 br., 1 1/2-2 baths, unfurnished, 950 sq ft, water	mo.	554	12/94	2c
Rental units expenditures	year	1264	91	81r
Insurance and Pensions				
Auto insurance, private passenger	year	684.10	12/94	71s
Insurance and pensions, personal, expenditures	year	2395	91	81r
Insurance, life and other personal, expenditures	year	368	91	81r
Pensions and Social Security, expenditures	year	2027	91	81r
Personal Goods				
Shampoo, Alberto VO5	15-oz.	0.96	12/94	2c
Toothpaste, Crest or Colgate	6-7 oz.	1.66	12/94	2c
Personal Services				
Dry cleaning, man's 2-pc. suit		6.02	12/94	2c
Haircut, man's barbershop, no styling		10.00	12/94	2c
Haircut, woman's shampoo, trim, blow-dry		28.40	12/94	2c
Personal services expenditures	year	212	91	81r
Restaurant Food				
Chicken, fried, thigh and drumstick		2.09	12/94	2c
Dining expenditures, family	week	33.83	94	73r
Hamburger with cheese	1/4 lb.	1.89	12/94	2c
Pizza, Pizza Hut or Pizza Inn	12-13 in.	7.99	12/94	2c
Taxes				
Taxes, Federal income, expenditures	year	2275	91	81r
Taxes, personal, expenditures	year	2715	91	81r
Taxes, State and local income, expenditures	year	365	91	81r
Transportation				
Transportation, ACCRA Index		90.90	12/94	2c
Bus fare, one-way	trip	1.00	12/95	1c
Cars and trucks purchased, new	year	1306	91	81r
Cars and trucks purchased, used	year	942	91	81r
Driver's learning permit fee	perm	2.00	1/94	84s
Driver's license fee	orig	10.00	1/94	84s
Driver's license fee, duplicate	lic	0.50	1/94	84s
Driver's license reinstatement fee, min.	susp	30.00	1/94	85s
Driver's license renewal fee	renew	10.00	1/94	84s

Values are in dollars or fractions of dollars. In the column headed *Ref*, references are shown to sources. Each reference is followed by a letter. These refer to the geographical level for which data were reported: s = State, r = Region, and c = City or metro. The abbreviation *ex* is used to mean *except* or *excluding*; *exp* stands for expenditures. For other abbreviations and further explanations, please see the Introduction.

Greenville, SC - continued

Item	Per	Value	Date	Ref.
Transportation				
Identification card, nondriver	card	5.00	1/94	83s
Motorcycle learning permit fee	perm	2.00	1/94	84s
Motorcycle license fee	orig	10.00	1/94	84s
Motorcycle license fee, duplicate	lic	0.50	1/94	84s
Motorcycle license renewal fee	renew	10.00	1/94	84s
Public transportation expenditures	year	249	91	81r
Tire balance, computer or spin bal., front	wheel	6.12	12/94	2c
Transportation expenditures, total	year	5307	91	81r
Vehicle finance charges	year	346	91	81r
Vehicle insurance expenditures	year	544	91	81r
Vehicle maintenance and repairs expenditures	year	600	91	81r
Vehicle purchases	year	2275	91	81r
Vehicle rental, leases, licenses, etc. expenditures	year	141	91	81r
Vehicles purchased, other than cars and trucks	year	27	91	81r
Utilities				
Utilities, ACCRA Index		100.00	12/94	2c
Electricity expenditures	year	950	91	81r
Electricity, 1800 sq. ft., new home	mo.	108.16	12/94	2c
Electricity, summer, 250 KWh	month	23.51	8/93	64c
Electricity, summer, 500 KWh	month	40.87	8/93	64c
Electricity, summer, 750 KWh	month	58.22	8/93	64c
Electricity, summer, 1000 KWh	month	75.57	8/93	64c
Utilities, fuels, and public services, total expenditures	year	2000	91	81r
Water and other public services, expenditures	year	227	91	81r
Weddings				
Bridal attendants' gowns	event	750	10/93	76r
Bridal gown	event	852	10/93	76r
Bridal headpiece and veil	event	167	10/93	76r
Bride's wedding band	event	708	10/93	76r
Clergy	event	224	10/93	76r
Engagement ring	event	2756	10/93	76r
Flowers	event	863	10/93	76r
Formal wear for groom	event	106	10/93	76r
Groom's attendants' formal wear	event	530	10/93	76r
Groom's wedding band	event	402	10/93	76r
Music	event	600	10/93	76r
Photography	event	1088	10/93	76r
Shoes for bride	event	50	10/93	76r
Videography	event	483	10/93	76r
Wedding invitations and announcements	event	342	10/93	76r
Wedding reception	event	7000	10/93	76r

Gunnison, CO

Item	Per	Value	Date	Ref.
Composite, ACCRA index		102.90	12/94	2c
Alcoholic Beverages				
Beer, Miller Lite, Bud, 12-oz., ex deposit	6	4.53	12/94	2c
J & B Scotch	750-ml.	18.74	12/94	2c
Wine, Gallo Chablis blanc	1.5-lit	5.62	12/94	2c
Clothing				
Jeans, man's denim		27.99	12/94	2c
Shirt, man's dress shirt		27.00	12/94	2c
Undervest, boy's size 10-14, cotton	3	3.56	12/94	2c
Communications				
Newspaper subscription, dly. and Sun. delivery	month	9.25	12/94	2c
Telephone bill, family of four	month	20.69	12/94	2c
Telephone, residential, flat rate	mo.	14.68	12/93	8c
Energy and Fuels				
Energy, combined forms, 1800 sq. ft.	mo.	127.17	12/94	2c
Energy, exc. electricity, 1800 sq. ft.	mo.	45.89	12/94	2c

Gunnison, CO - continued

Item	Per	Value	Date	Ref.
Energy and Fuels - continued				
Gas, reg unlead, taxes inc., cash, self-service	gal	1.33	12/94	2c
Entertainment				
Bowling, evening rate	game	1.75	12/94	2c
Monopoly game, Parker Brothers', No. 9	game	10.74	12/94	2c
Movie	adm	5.00	12/94	2c
Tennis balls, yellow, Wilson or Penn, 3	can	2.24	12/94	2c
Groceries				
Groceries, ACCRA Index		110.50	12/94	2c
Baby food, strained vegetables, lowest price	4-4.5 oz.	0.46	12/94	2c
Bananas	lb.	0.59	12/94	2c
Beef or hamburger, ground	lb.	1.29	12/94	2c
Bread, white	24-oz.	0.58	12/94	2c
Cheese, Kraft grated Parmesan	8-oz.	3.24	12/94	2c
Chicken, whole fryer	lb.	0.79	12/94	2c
Cigarettes, Winston, Kings	carton	14.95	12/94	2c
Coffee, vacuum-packed	13 oz.	4.29	12/94	2c
Corn Flakes, Kellogg's or Post Toasties	18 oz.	2.72	12/94	2c
Corn, frozen, whole kernel, lowest price	10 oz.	0.96	12/94	2c
Eggs, Grade A large	dozen	0.88	12/94	2c
Lettuce, iceberg	head	0.74	12/94	2c
Margarine, Blue Bonnet or Parkay cubes	lb.	0.56	12/94	2c
Milk, whole	1/2 gal.	1.66	12/94	2c
Orange juice, Minute Maid frozen	12-oz.	1.29	12/94	2c
Peaches, halves or slices, Hunt's, Del Monte, or Libby's	29-oz.	1.67	12/94	2c
Peas, sweet, Del Monte or Green Giant	15-17 oz.	0.75	12/94	2c
Potatoes, white or red	10-lb. sack	2.19	12/94	2c
Sausage, Jimmy Dean, 100% pork	lb.	3.32	12/94	2c
Shortening, vegetable, Crisco	3-lb.	3.57	12/94	2c
Soft drink, Coca Cola, ex deposit	2 lit	1.99	12/94	2c
Steak, t-bone	lb.	5.09	12/94	2c
Sugar, cane or beet	4 lbs.	1.56	12/94	2c
Tomatoes, Hunt's or Del Monte	14.5 oz.	0.73	12/94	2c
Tuna, chunk, light, oil-packed	6.125-6.5 oz.	0.98	12/94	2c
Goods and Services				
Miscellaneous goods and services, ACCRA Index		94.20	12/94	2c
Health Care				
Health care, ACCRA Index		91.30	12/94	2c
Antibiotic ointment, Polysporin	1.5 oz.	3.58	12/94	2c
Dentist's fee, adult teeth cleaning and periodic oral exam	visit	43.80	12/94	2c
Doctor's fee, routine exam, established patient	visit	40.00	12/94	2c
Hospital care, semiprivate room	day	360.00	12/94	2c
Household Goods				
Appl. repair, service call, wash mach	min. lab. chg.	22.50	12/94	2c
Laundry detergent, Tide Ultra, Bold, or Cheer	42 oz.	3.07	12/94	2c
Tissues, facial, Kleenex brand	175	1.10	12/94	2c
Housing				
Housing, ACCRA Index		107.80	12/94	2c
House payment, principal and interest, 25% down payment	mo.	817	12/94	2c
House, 1800 sq ft, 8000 sq ft lot, new, urban, utilities	total	125200	12/94	2c
Mtge. rate, incl. points and orig. fee, 30-year conv. fixed or ARM	mo.	9.90	12/94	2c
Rent, apartment, 2 br., 1 1/2-2 baths, unfurnished, 950 sq ft, water	mo.	594	12/94	2c

Values are in dollars or fractions of dollars. In the column headed *Ref*, references are shown to sources. Each reference is followed by a letter. These refer to the geographical level for which data were reported: s = State, r = Region, and c = City or metro. The abbreviation *ex* is used to mean *except* or *excluding*; *exp* stands for *expenditures*. For other abbreviations and further explanations, please see the Introduction.

Gunnison, CO - continued

Item	Per	Value	Date	Ref.
Personal Goods				
Shampoo, Alberto VO5	15-oz.	1.18	12/94	2c
Toothpaste, Crest or Colgate	6-7 oz.	1.88	12/94	2c
Personal Services				
Dry cleaning, man's 2-pc. suit		8.45	12/94	2c
Haircut, man's barbershop, no styling		7.00	12/94	2c
Haircut, woman's shampoo, trim, blow-dry		12.30	12/94	2c
Restaurant Food				
Chicken, fried, thigh and drumstick		2.00	12/94	2c
Hamburger with cheese	1/4 lb.	2.19	12/94	2c
Pizza, Pizza Hut or Pizza Inn	12-13 in.	8.39	12/94	2c
Transportation				
Transportation, ACCRA Index		105.70	12/94	2c
Tire balance, computer or spin bal., front	wheel	5.99	12/94	2c
Utilities				
Utilities, ACCRA Index		112.30	12/94	2c
Electricity, (part.), other, 1800 sq. ft., new home	mo.	81.28	12/94	2c

Hagerstown, MD

Item	Per	Value	Date	Ref.
Composite, ACCRA index		97.80	12/94	2c
Alcoholic Beverages				
Beer, Miller Lite, Bud, 12-oz., ex deposit	6	4.41	12/94	2c
J & B Scotch	750-ml.	15.63	12/94	2c
Wine, Gallo Chablis blanc	1.5-lit	5.20	12/94	2c
Clothing				
Jeans, man's denim		30.99	12/94	2c
Shirt, man's dress shirt		24.49	12/94	2c
Undervest, boy's size 10-14, cotton	3	3.41	12/94	2c
Communications				
Long-distance telephone rate, day, addl. min., 1-10 mi.	min.	0.10	12/93	9s
Long-distance telephone rate, day, initial min., 1-10 mi.	min.	0.21	12/93	9s
Newspaper subscription, dly. and Sun. delivery	month	9.25	12/94	2c
Phone line, single, business, field visit	inst	0.00	12/93	9s
Phone line, single, business, no field visit	inst	98.50	12/93	9s
Phone line, single, residence, field visit	inst	0.00	12/93	9s
Phone line, single, residence, no field visit	inst	48.00	12/93	9s
Telephone bill, family of four	month	19.82	12/94	2c
Telephone, residential, flat rate	mo.	15.24	12/93	8c
Education				
Board, 4-year private college/university	year	2878	8/94	80s
Board, 4-year public college/university	year	2464	8/94	80s
Room, 4-year private college/university	year	3231	8/94	80s
Room, 4-year public college/university	year	2587	8/94	80s
Total cost, 4-year private college/university	year	19012	8/94	80s
Total cost, 4-year public college/university	year	8171	8/94	80s
Tuition, 2-year public college/university, in-state	year	1676	8/94	80s
Tuition, 4-year private college/university, in-state	year	12903	8/94	80s
Tuition, 4-year public college/university, in-state	year	3120	8/94	80s
Energy and Fuels				
Energy, combined forms, 1800 sq. ft.	mo.	102.36	12/94	2c
Energy, exc. electricity, 1800 sq. ft.	mo.	50.92	12/94	2c
Gas, reg unlead, taxes inc., cash, self-service	gal	1.16	12/94	2c
Entertainment				
Bowling, evening rate	game	2.18	12/94	2c
Monopoly game, Parker Brothers', No. 9	game	11.74	12/94	2c
Movie	adm	5.75	12/94	2c

Hagerstown, MD - continued

Item	Per	Value	Date	Ref.
Entertainment - continued				
Tennis balls, yellow, Wilson or Penn, 3	can	2.58	12/94	2c
Funerals				
Burial, immediate, container provided by funeral home		1370.36	1/95	54r
Cards, acknowledgment		14.83	1/95	54r
Casket, minimum alternative		192.52	1/95	54r
Cosmetology, hair care, etc.		102.27	1/95	54r
Cremation, direct, container provided by funeral home		1065.64	1/95	54r
Embalming		304.29	1/95	54r
Funeral, funeral home		287.83	1/95	54r
Funeral, other facility		284.14	1/95	54r
Graveside service		349.13	1/95	54r
Hearse, local		132.27	1/95	54r
Limousine, local		98.45	1/95	54r
Memorial service		270.59	1/95	54r
Service charge, professional, nondeclinable		933.59	1/95	54r
Visitation and viewing		225.83	1/95	54r
Groceries				
Groceries, ACCRA Index		93.40	12/94	2c
Baby food, strained vegetables, lowest price	4-4.5 oz.	0.35	12/94	2c
Bananas	lb.	0.36	12/94	2c
Beef or hamburger, ground	lb.	1.53	12/94	2c
Bread, white	24-oz.	0.64	12/94	2c
Cheese, Kraft grated Parmesan	8-oz.	3.37	12/94	2c
Chicken, whole fryer	lb.	0.71	12/94	2c
Cigarettes, Winston, Kings	carton	16.22	12/94	2c
Coffee, vacuum-packed	13 oz.	3.28	12/94	2c
Corn Flakes, Kellogg's or Post Toasties	18 oz.	2.37	12/94	2c
Corn, frozen, whole kernel, lowest price	10 oz.	0.62	12/94	2c
Eggs, Grade A large	dozen	0.76	12/94	2c
Lettuce, iceberg	head	0.89	12/94	2c
Margarine, Blue Bonnet or Parkay cubes	lb.	0.58	12/94	2c
Milk, whole	1/2 gal.	1.02	12/94	2c
Orange juice, Minute Maid frozen	12-oz.	1.10	12/94	2c
Peaches, halves or slices, Hunt's, Del Monte, or Libby's	29-oz.	1.29	12/94	2c
Peas, sweet, Del Monte or Green Giant	15-17 oz.	0.44	12/94	2c
Potatoes, white or red	10-lb. sack	2.12	12/94	2c
Sausage, Jimmy Dean, 100% pork	lb.	2.32	12/94	2c
Shortening, vegetable, Crisco	3-lb.	2.49	12/94	2c
Soft drink, Coca Cola, ex deposit	2 lit	1.07	12/94	2c
Steak, t-bone	lb.	5.56	12/94	2c
Sugar, cane or beet	4 lbs.	1.43	12/94	2c
Tomatoes, Hunt's or Del Monte	14.5 oz.	0.64	12/94	2c
Tuna, chunk, light, oil-packed	6.125-6.5 oz.	0.68	12/94	2c
Goods and Services				
Miscellaneous goods and services, ACCRA Index		97.80	12/94	2c
Health Care				
Health care, ACCRA Index		98.70	12/94	2c
Antibiotic ointment, Polysporin	1.5 oz.	3.92	12/94	2c
Delivery, uncomplicated, total charge	birth	6100	1/93	24s
Delivery, uncomplicated, vaginal, hospital charge	birth	2780	1/93	24s
Delivery, uncomplicated, vaginal, physician's charge	birth	3320	1/93	24s
Dentist's fee, adult teeth cleaning and periodic oral exam	visit	49.00	12/94	2c
Doctor's fee, routine exam, established patient	visit	42.00	12/94	2c
Hospital care, semiprivate room	day	385.00	12/94	2c
Insurance premium, family medical care	month	389.07	1/95	41s

Values are in dollars or fractions of dollars. In the column headed *Ref*, references are shown to sources. Each reference is followed by a letter. These refer to the geographical level for which data were reported: s = State, r = Region, and c = City or metro. The abbreviation *ex* is used to mean *except* or *excluding*; *exp* stands for expenditures. For other abbreviations and further explanations, please see the Introduction.

Hagerstown, MD - continued

Item	Per	Value	Date	Ref.
Household Goods				
Appl. repair, service call, wash mach	min. lab. chg.	37.49	12/94	2c
Laundry detergent, Tide Ultra, Bold, or Cheer	42 oz.	2.73	12/94	2c
Tissues, facial, Kleenex brand	175	0.97	12/94	2c
Housing				
Housing, ACCRA Index		101.10	12/94	2c
House payment, principal and interest, 25% down payment	mo.	796	12/94	2c
House, 1800 sq ft, 8000 sq ft lot, new, urban, utilities	total	126985	12/94	2c
Mtge. rate, incl. points and orig. fee, 30-year conv. fixed or ARM	mo.	9.43	12/94	2c
Rent, apartment, 2 br., 1 1/2-2 baths, unfurnished, 950 sq ft, water	mo.	472	12/94	2c
Insurance and Pensions				
Auto insurance, private passenger	year	761.57	12/94	71s
Personal Goods				
Shampoo, Alberto VO5	15-oz.	1.14	12/94	2c
Toothpaste, Crest or Colgate	6-7 oz.	2.01	12/94	2c
Personal Services				
Dry cleaning, man's 2-pc. suit		6.20	12/94	2c
Haircut, man's barbershop, no styling		4.82	12/94	2c
Haircut, woman's shampoo, trim, blow-dry		17.36	12/94	2c
Restaurant Food				
Chicken, fried, thigh and drumstick		2.29	12/94	2c
Hamburger with cheese	1/4 lb.	1.97	12/94	2c
Pizza, Pizza Hut or Pizza Inn	12-13 in.	7.99	12/94	2c
Transportation				
Transportation, ACCRA Index		99.10	12/94	2c
Driver's learning permit fee	perm	30.00	1/94	84s
Driver's license fee	orig	30.00	1/94	84s
Driver's license fee, duplicate	lic	10.00	1/94	84s
Driver's license renewal fee	renew	20.00	1/94	84s
Identification card, nondriver	card	5.00	1/94	83s
Motorcycle learning permit fee	perm	30.00	1/94	84s
Motorcycle license fee	orig	30.00	1/94	84s
Motorcycle license fee, duplicate	lic	10.00	1/94	84s
Motorcycle license renewal fee	renew	20.00	1/94	84s
Tire balance, computer or spin bal., front	wheel	6.31	12/94	2c
Utilities				
Utilities, ACCRA Index		92.60	12/94	2c
Electricity, (part.), other, 1800 sq. ft., new home	mo.	51.44	12/94	2c
Weddings				
Bridal attendants' gowns	event	750	10/93	76r
Bridal gown	event	852	10/93	76r
Bridal headpiece and veil	event	167	10/93	76r
Bride's wedding band	event	708	10/93	76r
Clergy	event	224	10/93	76r
Engagement ring	event	2756	10/93	76r
Flowers	event	863	10/93	76r
Formal wear for groom	event	106	10/93	76r
Groom's attendants' formal wear	event	530	10/93	76r
Groom's wedding band	event	402	10/93	76r
Music	event	600	10/93	76r
Photography	event	1088	10/93	76r
Shoes for bride	event	50	10/93	76r
Videography	event	483	10/93	76r
Wedding invitations and announcements	event	342	10/93	76r
Wedding reception	event	7000	10/93	76r

Hamilton, OH

Item	Per	Value	Date	Ref.
Appliances				
Appliances (major), expenditures	year	131	91	81r
Average annual exp.				
Food, health care, personal goods, services	year	25935	91	81r
Charity				
Cash contributions, expenditures	year	745	91	81r
Clothing				
Apparel, men and boys, total expenditures	year	332	91	81r
Apparel, women and girls, total expenditures	year	578	91	81r
Footwear, expenditures	year	164	91	81r
Communications				
Long-distance telephone rate, day, addl. min., 1-10 mi.	min.	0.16	12/93	9s
Long-distance telephone rate, day, initial min., 1-10 mi.	min.	0.32	12/93	9s
Phone line, single, business, field visit	inst	55.42	12/93	9s
Phone line, single, business, no field visit	inst	55.42	12/93	9s
Phone line, single, residence, field visit	inst	30.38	12/93	9s
Phone line, single, residence, no field visit	inst	30.38	12/93	9s
Telephone service, expenditures	year	547	91	81r
Education				
Board, 4-year private college/university	year	2241	8/94	80s
Board, 4-year public college/university	year	1625	8/94	80s
Education, total expenditures	year	394	91	81r
Room, 4-year private college/university	year	2118	8/94	80s
Room, 4-year public college/university	year	2103	8/94	80s
Total cost, 4-year private college/university	year	15444	8/94	80s
Total cost, 4-year public college/university	year	6987	8/94	80s
Tuition, 2-year public college/university, in-state	year	2076	8/94	80s
Tuition, 4-year private college/university, in-state	year	11085	8/94	80s
Tuition, 4-year public college/university, in-state	year	3259	8/94	80s
Energy and Fuels				
Fuel oil and other fuels, expenditures	year	83	91	81r
Gas, natural, expenditures	year	373	91	81r
Gasoline and motor oil purchased	year	1000	91	81r
Gasoline, unleaded midgrade	gallon	1.15	4/93	82r
Gasoline, unleaded premium	gallon	1.23	4/93	82r
Gasoline, unleaded regular	gallon	1.07	4/93	82r
Entertainment				
Entertainment, total expenditures	year	1356	91	81r
Fees and admissions, expenditures	year	347	91	81r
Pets, toys, playground equipment, expenditures	year	270	91	81r
Reading, expenditures	year	160	91	81r
Televisions, radios, and sound equipment, expenditures	year	433	91	81r
Funerals				
Burial, immediate, container provided by funeral home		1268.31	1/95	54r
Cards, acknowledgment		26.12	1/95	54r
Casket, minimum alternative		198.03	1/95	54r
Cosmetology, hair care, etc.		122.19	1/95	54r
Cremation, direct, container provided by funeral home		977.81	1/95	54r
Embalming		334.00	1/95	54r
Funeral, funeral home		321.16	1/95	54r
Funeral, other facility		317.73	1/95	54r
Graveside service		292.48	1/95	54r
Hearse, local		153.20	1/95	54r
Limousine, local		123.52	1/95	54r
Memorial service		356.30	1/95	54r
Service charge, professional, nondeclinable		968.24	1/95	54r
Visitation and viewing		332.66	1/95	54r

Values are in dollars or fractions of dollars. In the column headed *Ref*, references are shown to sources. Each reference is followed by a letter. These refer to the geographical level for which data were reported: s = State, r = Region, and c = City or metro. The abbreviation *ex* is used to mean *except* or *excluding*; *exp* stands for expenditures. For other abbreviations and further explanations, please see the Introduction.

Hamilton, OH - continued

Item	Per	Value	Date	Ref.
Groceries				
Apples, Red Delicious	lb.	0.68	12/94	82r
Bacon, sliced	lb.	1.88	12/94	82r
Bananas	lb.	0.41	12/94	82r
Beef purchases	year	197	91	81r
Beef, stew, boneless	lb.	2.52	12/94	82r
Beverage purchases, alcoholic	year	293	91	81r
Beverage purchases, nonalcoholic	year	203	91	81r
Bologna, all beef or mixed	lb.	2.12	12/94	82r
Bread, white, pan	lb.	0.76	12/94	82r
Cabbage	lb.	0.44	12/94	82r
Carrots, short trimmed and topped	lb.	0.44	12/94	82r
Cereals and bakery products purchases	year	347	91	81r
Cereals and cereals products purchases	year	119	91	81r
Cheddar cheese, natural	lb.	3.28	12/94	82r
Chicken breast, bone-in	lb.	1.61	12/94	82r
Chicken, fresh, whole	lb.	0.89	12/94	82r
Chuck roast, USDA choice, boneless	lb.	2.33	12/94	82r
Coffee, 100%, ground roast, all sizes	lb.	4.28	12/94	82r
Cookies, chocolate chip	lb.	2.72	12/94	82r
Dairy products (other) purchases	year	148	91	81r
Eggs, Grade A large	dozen	0.76	12/94	82r
Fish and seafood purchases	year	61	91	81r
Flour, white, all purpose	lb.	0.22	12/94	82r
Food purchases, food eaten at home	year	2313	91	81r
Foods purchased away from home, not prepared by consumer	year	1709	91	81r
Fruits and vegetables purchases	year	372	91	81r
Grapefruit	lb.	0.47	12/94	82r
Grapes, Thompson seedless	lb.	2.15	12/94	82r
Ground beef, 100% beef	lb.	1.37	12/94	82r
Ground chuck, 100% beef	lb.	1.81	12/94	82r
Ham, boneless, exc. canned	lb.	2.16	12/94	82r
Ice cream, prepackaged, bulk, regular	1/2 gal.	2.48	12/94	82r
Lemons	lb.	1.08	12/94	82r
Lettuce, iceberg	lb.	0.81	12/94	82r
Margarine, stick	lb.	0.81	12/94	82r
Meats, poultry, fish, and eggs purchases	year	591	91	81r
Milk and cream (fresh) purchases	year	132	91	81r
Orange juice, frozen concentrate 12-oz. can	16 oz.	1.41	12/94	82r
Oranges, Navel	lb.	0.56	12/94	82r
Peanut butter, creamy, all sizes	lb.	1.81	12/94	82r
Pork chops, center cut, bone-in	lb.	2.76	12/94	82r
Pork purchases	year	130	91	81r
Potato chips	16-oz.	2.81	12/94	82r
Potatoes, frozen, French fried	lb.	0.83	12/94	82r
Potatoes, white	lb.	0.28	12/94	82r
Round roast, USDA choice, boneless	lb.	2.90	12/94	82r
Shortening, vegetable oil blends	lb.	0.88	12/94	82r
Spaghetti and macaroni	lb.	0.78	12/94	82r
Steak, rib eye, USDA choice, boneless	lb.	6.15	12/94	82r
Steak, round, graded & ungraded, exc. USDA prime & choice	lb.	2.72	12/94	82r
Steak, round, USDA choice, boneless	lb.	3.02	12/94	82r
Steak, sirloin, USDA choice, boneless	lb.	3.85	12/94	82r
Steak, T-bone, USDA choice, bone-in	lb.	5.38	12/94	82r
Sugar and other sweets, eaten at home, expenditures	year	91	91	81r
Sugar, white, all sizes	lb.	0.36	12/94	82r
Tobacco products and smoking supplies, total expenditures	year	298	91	81r
Tomatoes, field grown	lb.	1.36	12/94	82r
Tuna, chunk, light	lb.	1.94	12/94	82r
Turkey, frozen, whole	lb.	0.96	12/94	82r
Yogurt, natural, fruit flavored	8 oz.	0.62	12/94	82r
Health Care				
Childbirth, Cesarean delivery, hospital charge	birth	5101.00	12/91	69r
Childbirth, Cesarean delivery, physician charge	birth	2234.00	12/91	69r
Childbirth, normal delivery, hospital charge	birth	2891.00	12/91	69r
Childbirth, normal delivery, physician charge	birth	1623.00	12/91	69r

Hamilton, OH - continued

Item	Per	Value	Date	Ref.
Health Care - continued				
Drugs, expenditures	year	248	91	81r
Health care, total expenditures	year	1336	91	81r
Health insurance expenditures	year	550	91	81r
Insurance premium, family medical care	month	350.73	1/95	41s
Medical services expenditures	year	457	91	81r
Medical supplies expenditures	year	82	91	81r
Household Goods				
Floor coverings, expenditures	year	105	91	81r
Furniture, expenditures	year	291	91	81r
Household equipment, misc. expenditures	year	341	91	81r
Household expenditures, miscellaneous	year	162	91	81r
Household furnishings and equipment, expenditures	year	1042	91	81r
Household operations expenditures	year	365	91	81r
Household textiles, expenditures	year	101	91	81r
Housekeeping supplies, expenditures	year	390	91	81r
Laundry and cleaning supplies, expenditures	year	110	91	81r
Postage and stationery, expenditures	year	115	91	81r
Housing				
Add garage/carport		8,479	3/95	74r
Add room(s)		21,347	3/95	74r
Apartment condominium or co-op, median	unit	87100	12/94	62r
Bathroom addition, average cost	add	9734.00	3/95	13r
Bathroom remodeling, average cost	remod	6414.00	3/95	13r
Bedroom, master suite addition, average cost	add	27122.00	3/95	13r
Deck addition, average cost	add	6665.00	3/95	13r
Dwellings (owned), expenditures	year	2566	91	81r
Enclose porch/patio/breezeway		4,556	3/95	74r
Exterior remodeling, average cost	remod	15395.00	3/95	13r
Family room addition, average cost	add	27658.00	3/95	13r
Finish room in basement/attic		5,074	3/95	74r
Home, existing, single-family, median	unit	106500	12/94	62r
Kitchen remodeling, major, average cost	remod	17084.00	3/95	13r
Kitchen remodeling, minor, average cost	remod	5804.00	3/95	13r
Maintenance, repairs, insurance, and other housing expenditures	year	484	91	81r
Mortgage interest and charges expenditures	year	1443	91	81r
Office, home addition, average cost	add	8121.00	3/95	13r
Princ. & int., mortgage, median-price exist. sing.-family home	mo.	515	12/94	62r
Property taxes expenditures	year	639	91	81r
Redesign, restructure more than half of home's interior		9,114	3/95	74r
Rental units expenditures	year	1200	91	81r
Sun-space addition, average cost	add	23768.00	3/95	13r
Wing addition, two-story, average cost	add	50410.00	3/95	13r
Insurance and Pensions				
Auto insurance, private passenger	year	550.52	12/94	71s
Insurance and pensions, personal, expenditures	year	2408	91	81r
Insurance, life and other personal, expenditures	year	355	91	81r
Pensions and Social Security, expenditures	year	2053	91	81r
Legal Assistance				
Legal work, law firm associate	hour	90		10r
Legal work, law firm partner	hour	139		10r
Personal Services				
Personal services expenditures	year	203	91	81r
Restaurant Food				
Dining expenditures, family	week	30.03	94	73r
Taxes				
Taxes, Federal income, expenditures	year	1756	91	81r
Taxes, personal, expenditures	year	2426	91	81r
Taxes, State and local income, expenditures	year	568	91	81r

Values are in dollars or fractions of dollars. In the column headed *Ref*, references are shown to sources. Each reference is followed by a letter. These refer to the geographical level for which data were reported: s = State, r = Region, and c = City or metro. The abbreviation *ex* is used to mean *except* or *excluding*; *exp* stands for *expenditures*. For other abbreviations and further explanations, please see the Introduction.

Hamilton, OH - continued

Item	Per	Value	Date	Ref.
Transportation				
Cars and trucks purchased, new	year	891	91	81r
Cars and trucks purchased, used	year	1155	91	81r
Driver's learning permit fee	perm	3.00	1/94	84s
Driver's license fee	orig	5.00	1/94	84s
Driver's license fee, duplicate	lic	1.50	1/94	84s
Driver's license reinstatement fee, min.	susp	12.50-100.00	1/94	85s
Driver's license renewal fee	renew	5.00	1/94	84s
Identification card, nondriver	card	2.50	1/94	83s
Motorcycle learning permit fee	perm	3.00	1/94	84s
Motorcycle license fee	orig	5.00	1/94	84s
Motorcycle license fee, duplicate	lic	1.50	1/94	84s
Motorcycle license renewal fee	renew	5.00	1/94	84s
Public transportation expenditures	year	209	91	81r
Transportation expenditures, total	year	4792	91	81r
Vehicle finance charges	year	300	91	81r
Vehicle insurance expenditures	year	485	91	81r
Vehicle maintenance and repairs expenditures	year	534	91	81r
Vehicle purchases	year	2068	91	81r
Vehicle rental, leases, licenses, etc. expenditures	year	197	91	81r
Vehicles purchased, other than cars and trucks	year	22	91	81r
Utilities				
Electricity expenditures	year	668	91	81r
Utilities, fuels, and public services, total expenditures	year	1838	91	81r
Water and other public services, expenditures	year	167	91	81r
Weddings				
Bridal attendants' gowns	event	750	10/93	76r
Bridal gown	event	852	10/93	76r
Bridal headpiece and veil	event	167	10/93	76r
Bride's wedding band	event	708	10/93	76r
Clergy	event	224	10/93	76r
Engagement ring	event	2756	10/93	76r
Flowers	event	863	10/93	76r
Formal wear for groom	event	106	10/93	76r
Groom's attendants' formal wear	event	530	10/93	76r
Groom's wedding band	event	402	10/93	76r
Music	event	600	10/93	76r
Photography	event	1088	10/93	76r
Shoes for bride	event	50	10/93	76r
Videography	event	483	10/93	76r
Wedding invitations and announcements	event	342	10/93	76r
Wedding reception	event	7000	10/93	76r

Hanover, PA

Item	Per	Value	Date	Ref.
Composite, ACCRA index		101.10	12/94	2c
Alcoholic Beverages				
Beer, Miller Lite, Bud, 12-oz., ex deposit	6	5.08	12/94	2c
J & B Scotch	750-ml.	16.99	12/94	2c
Wine, Gallo Chablis blanc	1.5-lit	5.99	12/94	2c
Clothing				
Jeans, man's denim		32.99	12/94	2c
Shirt, man's dress shirt		35.67	12/94	2c
Undervest, boy's size 10-14, cotton	3	4.99	12/94	2c
Communications				
Newspaper subscription, dly. and Sun. delivery	month	8.70	12/94	2c
Telephone bill, family of four	month	16.10	12/94	2c
Telephone, residential, flat rate	mo.	21.00	12/93	8c
Energy and Fuels				
Energy, combined forms, 1800 sq. ft.	mo.	114.75	12/94	2c
Energy, exc. electricity, 1800 sq. ft.	mo.	59.58	12/94	2c

Hanover, PA - continued

Item	Per	Value	Date	Ref.
Energy and Fuels - continued				
Gas, reg unlead, taxes inc., cash, self-service	gal	1.08	12/94	2c
Entertainment				
Bowling, evening rate	game	2.25	12/94	2c
Monopoly game, Parker Brothers', No. 9	game	9.61	12/94	2c
Movie	adm	5.75	12/94	2c
Tennis balls, yellow, Wilson or Penn, 3	can	2.08	12/94	2c
Groceries				
Groceries, ACCRA Index		102.60	12/94	2c
Baby food, strained vegetables, lowest price	4-4.5 oz.	0.39	12/94	2c
Bananas	lb.	0.41	12/94	2c
Beef or hamburger, ground	lb.	1.59	12/94	2c
Bread, white	24-oz.	0.79	12/94	2c
Cheese, Kraft grated Parmesan	8-oz.	3.33	12/94	2c
Chicken, whole fryer	lb.	0.83	12/94	2c
Cigarettes, Winston, Kings	carton	15.76	12/94	2c
Coffee, vacuum-packed	13 oz.	4.23	12/94	2c
Corn Flakes, Kellogg's or Post Toasties	18 oz.	2.70	12/94	2c
Corn, frozen, whole kernel, lowest price	10 oz.	0.64	12/94	2c
Eggs, Grade A large	dozen	0.78	12/94	2c
Lettuce, iceberg	head	0.89	12/94	2c
Margarine, Blue Bonnet or Parkay cubes	lb.	0.74	12/94	2c
Milk, whole	1/2 gal.	1.21	12/94	2c
Orange juice, Minute Maid frozen	12-oz.	1.18	12/94	2c
Peaches, halves or slices, Hunt's, Del Monte, or Libby's	29-oz.	1.27	12/94	2c
Peas, sweet, Del Monte or Green Giant	15-17 oz.	0.39	12/94	2c
Potatoes, white or red	10-lb. sack	2.13	12/94	2c
Sausage, Jimmy Dean, 100% pork	lb.	2.69	12/94	2c
Shortening, vegetable, Crisco	3-lb.	2.49	12/94	2c
Soft drink, Coca Cola, ex deposit	2 lit	1.11	12/94	2c
Steak, t-bone	lb.	5.52	12/94	2c
Sugar, cane or beet	4 lbs.	1.46	12/94	2c
Tomatoes, Hunt's or Del Monte	14.5 oz.	0.73	12/94	2c
Tuna, chunk, light, oil-packed	6.125-6.5 oz.	0.59	12/94	2c
Goods and Services				
Miscellaneous goods and services, ACCRA Index		100.70	12/94	2c
Health Care				
Health care, ACCRA Index		83.50	12/94	2c
Antibiotic ointment, Polysporin	1.5 oz.	3.56	12/94	2c
Dentist's fee, adult teeth cleaning and periodic oral exam	visit	42.60	12/94	2c
Doctor's fee, routine exam, established patient	visit	33.00	12/94	2c
Hospital care, semiprivate room	day	340.00	12/94	2c
Household Goods				
Appl. repair, service call, wash mach	min. lab. chg.	33.67	12/94	2c
Laundry detergent, Tide Ultra, Bold, or Cheer	42 oz.	3.39	12/94	2c
Tissues, facial, Kleenex brand	175	0.96	12/94	2c
Housing				
Housing, ACCRA Index		107.00	12/94	2c
House payment, principal and interest, 25% down payment	mo.	839	12/94	2c
House, 1800 sq ft, 8000 sq ft lot, new, urban, utilities	total	137250	12/94	2c
Mtge. rate, incl. points and orig. fee, 30-year conv. fixed or ARM	mo.	9.15	12/94	2c
Rent, apartment, 2 br., 1 1/2-2 baths, unfurnished, 950 sq ft, water	mo.	510	12/94	2c

Values are in dollars or fractions of dollars. In the column headed *Ref*, references are shown to sources. Each reference is followed by a letter. These refer to the geographical level for which data were reported: s = State, r = Region, and c = City or metro. The abbreviation *ex* is used to mean *except* or *excluding*; *exp* stands for expenditures. For other abbreviations and further explanations, please see the Introduction.

Hanover, PA - continued

Item	Per	Value	Date	Ref.
Personal Goods				
Shampoo, Alberto VO5	15-oz.	1.08	12/94	2c
Toothpaste, Crest or Colgate	6-7 oz.	2.59	12/94	2c
Personal Services				
Dry cleaning, man's 2-pc. suit		7.00	12/94	2c
Haircut, man's barbershop, no styling		6.75	12/94	2c
Haircut, woman's shampoo, trim, blow-dry		16.00	12/94	2c
Restaurant Food				
Chicken, fried, thigh and drumstick		2.24	12/94	2c
Hamburger with cheese	1/4 lb.	1.89	12/94	2c
Pizza, Pizza Hut or Pizza Inn	12-13 in.	5.99	12/94	2c
Transportation				
Transportation, ACCRA Index		95.10	12/94	2c
Tire balance, computer or spin bal., front	wheel	6.36	12/94	2c
Utilities				
Utilities, ACCRA Index		99.60	12/94	2c
Electricity, (part.), other, 1800 sq. ft., new home	mo.	55.17	12/94	2c

Harlingen, TX

Item	Per	Value	Date	Ref.
Composite, ACCRA index		88.70	12/94	2c
Alcoholic Beverages				
Beer, Miller Lite, Bud, 12-oz., ex deposit	6	3.92	12/94	2c
J & B Scotch	750-ml.	17.62	12/94	2c
Wine, Gallo Chablis blanc	1.5-lit	5.68	12/94	2c
Clothing				
Jeans, man's denim		27.32	12/94	2c
Shirt, man's dress shirt		29.17	12/94	2c
Undervest, boy's size 10-14, cotton	3	3.85	12/94	2c
Communications				
Newspaper subscription, dly. and Sun. delivery	month	7.50	12/94	2c
Telephone bill, family of four	month	15.34	12/94	2c
Telephone, residential, flat rate	mo.	8.80	12/93	8c
Energy and Fuels				
Energy, combined forms, 1800 sq. ft.	mo.	123.25	12/94	2c
Gas, reg unlead, taxes inc., cash, self-service	gal	1.05	12/94	2c
Entertainment				
Bowling, evening rate	game	1.99	12/94	2c
Monopoly game, Parker Brothers', No. 9	game	10.67	12/94	2c
Movie	adm	5.00	12/94	2c
Tennis balls, yellow, Wilson or Penn, 3	can	1.99	12/94	2c
Groceries				
Groceries, ACCRA Index		87.60	12/94	2c
Baby food, strained vegetables, lowest price	4-4.5 oz.	0.29	12/94	2c
Bananas	lb.	0.33	12/94	2c
Beef or hamburger, ground	lb.	1.11	12/94	2c
Bread, white	24-oz.	0.55	12/94	2c
Cheese, Kraft grated Parmesan	8-oz.	3.12	12/94	2c
Chicken, whole fryer	lb.	0.67	12/94	2c
Cigarettes, Winston, Kings	carton	17.32	12/94	2c
Coffee, vacuum-packed	13 oz.	3.36	12/94	2c
Corn Flakes, Kellogg's or Post Toasties	18 oz.	2.20	12/94	2c
Corn, frozen, whole kernel, lowest price	10 oz.	0.63	12/94	2c
Eggs, Grade A large	dozen	0.65	12/94	2c
Lettuce, iceberg	head	0.85	12/94	2c
Margarine, Blue Bonnet or Parkay cubes	lb.	0.55	12/94	2c
Milk, whole	1/2 gal.	1.21	12/94	2c
Orange juice, Minute Maid frozen	12-oz.	1.16	12/94	2c
Peaches, halves or slices, Hunt's, Del Monte, or Libby's	29-oz.	1.09	12/94	2c

Harlingen, TX - continued

Item	Per	Value	Date	Ref.
Groceries - continued				
Peas, sweet, Del Monte or Green Giant	15-17 oz.	0.43	12/94	2c
Potatoes, white or red	10-lb. sack	1.94	12/94	2c
Sausage, Jimmy Dean, 100% pork	lb.	2.12	12/94	2c
Shortening, vegetable, Crisco	3-lb.	2.28	12/94	2c
Soft drink, Coca Cola, ex deposit	2 lit	1.38	12/94	2c
Steak, t-bone	lb.	3.36	12/94	2c
Sugar, cane or beet	4 lbs.	1.36	12/94	2c
Tomatoes, Hunt's or Del Monte	14.5 oz.	0.54	12/94	2c
Tuna, chunk, light, oil-packed	6.125-6.5 oz.	0.59	12/94	2c
Goods and Services				
Miscellaneous goods and services, ACCRA Index		92.90	12/94	2c
Health Care				
Health care, ACCRA Index		90.50	12/94	2c
Antibiotic ointment, Polysporin	1.5 oz.	3.74	12/94	2c
Dentist's fee, adult teeth cleaning and periodic oral exam	visit	45.33	12/94	2c
Doctor's fee, routine exam, established patient	visit	41.50	12/94	2c
Hospital care, semiprivate room	day	290.00	12/94	2c
Household Goods				
Appl. repair, service call, wash mach	min. lab. chg.	26.25	12/94	2c
Laundry detergent, Tide Ultra, Bold, or Cheer	42 oz.	3.04	12/94	2c
Tissues, facial, Kleenex brand	175	0.82	12/94	2c
Housing				
Housing, ACCRA Index		77.70	12/94	2c
House payment, principal and interest, 25% down payment	mo.	589	12/94	2c
House, 1800 sq ft, 8000 sq ft lot, new, urban, utilities	total	94833	12/94	2c
Mtge. rate, incl. points and orig. fee, 30-year conv. fixed or ARM	mo.	9.32	12/94	2c
Rent, apartment, 2 br., 1 1/2-2 baths, unfurnished, 950 sq ft, water	mo.	428	12/94	2c
Personal Goods				
Shampoo, Alberto VO5	15-oz.	0.90	12/94	2c
Toothpaste, Crest or Colgate	6-7 oz.	1.67	12/94	2c
Personal Services				
Dry cleaning, man's 2-pc. suit		6.48	12/94	2c
Haircut, man's barbershop, no styling		5.87	12/94	2c
Haircut, woman's shampoo, trim, blow-dry		20.33	12/94	2c
Restaurant Food				
Chicken, fried, thigh and drumstick		2.06	12/94	2c
Hamburger with cheese	1/4 lb.	2.09	12/94	2c
Pizza, Pizza Hut or Pizza Inn	12-13 in.	7.69	12/94	2c
Transportation				
Transportation, ACCRA Index		93.60	12/94	2c
Tire balance, computer or spin bal., front	wheel	6.33	12/94	2c
Utilities				
Utilities, ACCRA Index		105.60	12/94	2c
Electricity, 1800 sq. ft., new home	mo.	123.25	12/94	2c

Harrisburg, PA

Item	Per	Value	Date	Ref.
Composite, ACCRA index		104.90	12/94	2c
Alcoholic Beverages				
Beer, Miller Lite, Bud, 12-oz., ex deposit	6	5.44	12/94	2c

Values are in dollars or fractions of dollars. In the column headed *Ref*, references are shown to sources. Each reference is followed by a letter. These refer to the geographical level for which data were reported: s=State, r=Region, and c=City or metro. The abbreviation *ex* is used to mean *except* or *excluding*; *exp* stands for *expenditures*. For other abbreviations and further explanations, please see the Introduction.

Harrisburg, PA - continued

Item	Per	Value	Date	Ref.
Alcoholic Beverages				
J & B Scotch	750-ml.	16.99	12/94	2c
Wine, Gallo Chablis blanc	1.5-lit	5.99	12/94	2c
Appliances				
Appliances (major), expenditures	year	145	91	81r
Average annual exp.				
Food, health care, personal goods, services	year	29496	91	81r
Charity				
Cash contributions, expenditures	year	708	91	81r
Clothing				
Apparel, men and boys, total expenditures	year	416	91	81r
Apparel, women and girls, total expenditures	year	744	91	81r
Footwear, expenditures	year	305	91	81r
Jeans, man's denim		34.74	12/94	2c
Shirt, man's dress shirt		30.25	12/94	2c
Undervest, boy's size 10-14, cotton	3	7.12	12/94	2c
Communications				
Long-distance telephone rate, day, addl. min., 1-10 mi.	min.	0.08	12/93	9s
Long-distance telephone rate, day, initial min., 1-10 mi.	min.	0.15	12/93	9s
Newspaper subscription, dly. and Sun. delivery	month	14.35	12/94	2c
Phone line, single, business, field visit	inst	75.00	12/93	9s
Phone line, single, business, no field visit	inst	75.00	12/93	9s
Phone line, single, residence, field visit	inst	40.00	12/93	9s
Phone line, single, residence, no field visit	inst	40.00	12/93	9s
Telephone bill, family of four	month	20.29	12/94	2c
Telephone service, expenditures	year	589	91	81r
Telephone, residential, flat rate	mo.	21.00	12/93	8c
Education				
Board, 4-year private college/university	year	2714	8/94	80s
Board, 4-year public college/university	year	1899	8/94	80s
Education, total expenditures	year	593	91	81r
Room, 4-year private college/university	year	2720	8/94	80s
Room, 4-year public college/university	year	2063	8/94	80s
Total cost, 4-year private college/university	year	18118	8/94	80s
Total cost, 4-year public college/university	year	8278	8/94	80s
Tuition, 2-year public college/university, in-state	year	1671	8/94	80s
Tuition, 4-year private college/university, in-state	year	12684	8/94	80s
Tuition, 4-year public college/university, in-state	year	4316	8/94	80s
Energy and Fuels				
Energy, combined forms, 1800 sq. ft.	mo.	153.00	12/94	2c
Fuel oil and other fuels, expenditures	year	257	91	81r
Gas, natural, expenditures	year	285	91	81r
Gas, reg unlead, taxes inc., cash, self-service	gal	1.09	12/94	2c
Gasoline and motor oil purchased	year	867	91	81r
Gasoline, unleaded midgrade	gallon	1.32	4/93	82r
Gasoline, unleaded premium	gallon	1.40	4/93	82r
Gasoline, unleaded regular	gallon	1.19	4/93	82r
Entertainment				
Bowling, evening rate	game	2.14	12/94	2c
Entertainment, total expenditures	year	1331	91	81r
Fees and admissions, expenditures	year	398	91	81r
Monopoly game, Parker Brothers', No. 9	game	11.43	12/94	2c
Movie	adm	4.85	12/94	2c
Pets, toys, playground equipment, expenditures	year	270	91	81r
Reading, expenditures	year	171	91	81r
Televisions, radios, and sound equipment, expenditures	year	429	91	81r
Tennis balls, yellow, Wilson or Penn, 3	can	2.82	12/94	2c

Harrisburg, PA - continued

Item	Per	Value	Date	Ref.
Funerals				
Burial, immediate, container provided by funeral home		1370.36	1/95	54r
Cards, acknowledgment		17.72	1/95	54r
Casket, minimum alternative		192.52	1/95	54r
Cosmetology, hair care, etc.		139.56	1/95	54r
Cremation, direct, container provided by funeral home		1049.24	1/95	54r
Embalming		387.57	1/95	54r
Funeral, funeral home		278.77	1/95	54r
Funeral, other facility		275.85	1/95	54r
Graveside service		213.08	1/95	54r
Hearse, local		157.27	1/95	54r
Limousine, local		146.45	1/95	54r
Memorial service		271.02	1/95	54r
Service charge, professional, nondeclinable		943.58	1/95	54r
Visitation and viewing		322.86	1/95	54r
Groceries				
Groceries, ACCRA Index		103.80	12/94	2c
Apples, Red Delicious	lb.	0.78	12/94	82r
Baby food, strained vegetables, lowest price	4-4.5 oz.	0.38	12/94	2c
Bacon, sliced	lb.	2.24	12/94	82r
Bananas	lb.	0.40	12/94	2c
Bananas	lb.	0.49	12/94	82r
Beef or hamburger, ground	lb.	1.57	12/94	2c
Beef purchases	year	226	91	81r
Beverage purchases, alcoholic	year	332	91	81r
Beverage purchases, nonalcoholic	year	213	91	81r
Bread, white	24-oz.	0.84	12/94	2c
Bread, white, pan	lb.	0.80	12/94	82r
Butter, salted, Grade AA, stick	lb.	1.67	12/94	82r
Carrots, short trimmed and topped	lb.	0.51	12/94	82r
Cereals and bakery products purchases	year	407	91	81r
Cereals and cereals products purchases	year	132	91	81r
Cheese, Kraft grated Parmesan	8-oz.	3.34	12/94	2c
Chicken breast, bone-in	lb.	2.22	12/94	82r
Chicken, fresh, whole	lb.	1.05	12/94	82r
Chicken, whole fryer	lb.	0.76	12/94	2c
Chuck roast, USDA choice, boneless	lb.	2.74	12/94	82r
Cigarettes, Winston, Kings	carton	15.36	12/94	2c
Coffee, 100%, ground roast, all sizes	lb.	4.61	12/94	82r
Coffee, vacuum-packed	13 oz.	3.55	12/94	2c
Corn Flakes, Kellogg's or Post Toasties	18 oz.	2.61	12/94	2c
Corn, frozen, whole kernel, lowest price	10 oz.	0.65	12/94	2c
Dairy products (other) purchases	year	161	91	81r
Eggs, Grade A large	dozen	0.77	12/94	2c
Eggs, Grade A large	dozen	1.12	12/94	82r
Fish and seafood purchases	year	112	91	81r
Food purchases, food eaten at home	year	2599	91	81r
Foods purchased away from home, not prepared by consumer	year	2024	91	81r
Fruits and vegetables purchases	year	444	91	81r
Grapefruit	lb.	0.44	12/94	82r
Grapes, Thompson seedless	lb.	2.24	12/94	82r
Ground chuck, 100% beef	lb.	1.67	12/94	82r
Ice cream, prepackaged, bulk, regular	1/2 gal.	2.93	12/94	82r
Lemons	lb.	1.06	12/94	82r
Lettuce, iceberg	lb.	0.92	12/94	82r
Lettuce, iceberg	head	0.91	12/94	2c
Margarine, Blue Bonnet or Parkay cubes	lb.	0.67	12/94	2c
Meats, poultry, fish, and eggs purchases	year	751	91	81r
Milk and cream (fresh) purchases	year	152	91	81r
Milk, whole	1/2 gal.	1.21	12/94	2c
Orange juice, frozen concentrate 12-oz. can	16 oz.	1.92	12/94	82r
Orange juice, Minute Maid frozen	12-oz.	1.25	12/94	2c
Oranges, Navel	lb.	0.56	12/94	82r
Peaches, halves or slices, Hunt's, Del Monte, or Libby's	29-oz.	1.30	12/94	2c
Peas, sweet, Del Monte or Green Giant	15-17 oz.	0.45	12/94	2c

Values are in dollars or fractions of dollars. In the column headed *Ref*, references are shown to sources. Each reference is followed by a letter. These refer to the geographical level for which data were reported: s = State, r = Region, and c = City or metro. The abbreviation *ex* is used to mean *except* or *excluding*; *exp* stands for *expenditures*. For other abbreviations and further explanations, please see the Introduction.

Harrisburg, PA - continued

Item	Per	Value	Date	Ref.
Groceries				
Pork chops, center cut, bone-in	lb.	3.09	12/94	82r
Pork purchases	year	130	91	81r
Potatoes, white	lb.	0.37	12/94	82r
Potatoes, white or red	10-lb. sack	2.27	12/94	2c
Rib roast, USDA choice, bone-in	lb.	4.98	12/94	82r
Round roast, USDA choice, boneless	lb.	2.93	12/94	82r
Sausage, Jimmy Dean, 100% pork	lb.	3.20	12/94	2c
Shortening, vegetable oil blends	lb.	1.03	12/94	82r
Shortening, vegetable, Crisco	3-lb.	2.58	12/94	2c
Soft drink, Coca Cola, ex deposit	2 lit	1.13	12/94	2c
Spaghetti and macaroni	lb.	0.84	12/94	82r
Steak, round, USDA choice, boneless	lb.	3.48	12/94	82r
Steak, sirloin, USDA choice, bone-in	lb.	3.38	12/94	82r
Steak, sirloin, USDA choice, boneless	lb.	4.81	12/94	82r
Steak, t-bone	lb.	5.37	12/94	2c
Sugar and other sweets, eaten at home, expenditures	year	89	91	81r
Sugar, cane or beet	4 lbs.	1.63	12/94	2c
Sugar, white, all sizes	lb.	0.46	12/94	82r
Tobacco products and smoking supplies, total expenditures	year	279	91	81r
Tomatoes, field grown	lb.	1.56	12/94	82r
Tomatoes, Hunt's or Del Monte	14.5 oz.	0.70	12/94	2c
Tuna, chunk, light	lb.	2.09	12/94	82r
Tuna, chunk, light, oil-packed	6.125-6.5 oz.	0.71	12/94	2c
Goods and Services				
Miscellaneous goods and services, ACCRA Index		105.60	12/94	2c
Health Care				
Health care, ACCRA Index		106.20	12/94	2c
Antibiotic ointment, Polysporin	1.5 oz.	4.17	12/94	2c
Childbirth, Cesarean delivery, hospital charge	birth	6334.00	12/91	69r
Childbirth, Cesarean delivery, physician charge	birth	2234.00	12/91	69r
Childbirth, normal delivery, hospital charge	birth	3225.00	12/91	69r
Childbirth, normal delivery, physician charge	birth	1623.00	12/91	69r
Dentist's fee, adult teeth cleaning and periodic oral exam	visit	53.50	12/94	2c
Doctor's fee, routine exam, established patient	visit	38.20	12/94	2c
Drugs, expenditures	year	205	91	81r
Health care, total expenditures	year	1396	91	81r
Health insurance expenditures	year	553	91	81r
Hospital care, semiprivate room	day	523.75	12/94	2c
Insurance premium, family medical care	month	349.05	1/95	41s
Medical services expenditures	year	559	91	81r
Medical supplies expenditures	year	80	91	81r
Household Goods				
Appl. repair, service call, wash mach	min. lab. chg.	30.97	12/94	2c
Floor coverings, expenditures	year	158	91	81r
Furniture, expenditures	year	341	91	81r
Household equipment, misc. expenditures	year	363	91	81r
Household expenditures, miscellaneous	year	194	91	81r
Household furnishings and equipment, expenditures	year	1158	91	81r
Household operations expenditures	year	378	91	81r
Household textiles, expenditures	year	88	91	81r
Housekeeping supplies, expenditures	year	426	91	81r
Laundry and cleaning supplies, expenditures	year	122	91	81r
Laundry detergent, Tide Ultra, Bold, or Cheer	42 oz.	3.53	12/94	2c
Postage and stationery, expenditures	year	134	91	81r
Tissues, facial, Kleenex brand	175	1.05	12/94	2c

Harrisburg, PA - continued

Item	Per	Value	Date	Ref.
Housing				
Housing, ACCRA Index		94.30	12/94	2c
Add garage/carport		11,614	3/95	74r
Add room(s)		16,816	3/95	74r
Apartment condominium or co-op, median	unit	96700	12/94	62r
Dwellings (owned), expenditures	year	3305	91	81r
Enclose porch/patio/breezeway		2,980	3/95	74r
Finish room in basement/attic		4,330	3/95	74r
Home, existing, single-family, median	unit	161600	12/94	62r
House payment, principal and interest, 25% down payment	mo.	701	12/94	2c
House, 1800 sq ft, 8000 sq ft lot, new, urban, utilities	total	115320	12/94	2c
Maintenance, repairs, insurance, and other housing expenditures	year	569	91	81r
Mortgage interest and charges expenditures	year	1852	91	81r
Mtge. rate, incl. points and orig. fee, 30-year conv. fixed or ARM	mo.	9.08	12/94	2c
Princ. & int., mortgage, median-price exist. sing.-family home	mo.	765	12/94	62r
Property taxes expenditures	year	884	91	81r
Redesign, restructure more than half of home's interior		2,750	3/95	74r
Rent, apartment, 2 br., 1 1/2-2 baths, unfurnished, 950 sq ft, water	mo.	559	12/94	2c
Rental units expenditures	year	1832	91	81r
Insurance and Pensions				
Auto insurance, private passenger	year	721.50	12/94	71s
Insurance and pensions, personal, expenditures	year	2690	91	81r
Insurance, life and other personal, expenditures	year	341	91	81r
Pensions and Social Security, expenditures	year	2349	91	81r
Legal Assistance				
Estate planning, law-firm partner	hr.	375.00	10/93	12r
Legal work, law firm associate	hour	78		10r
Legal work, law firm partner	hour	183		10r
Personal Goods				
Shampoo, Alberto VO5	15-oz.	1.33	12/94	2c
Toothpaste, Crest or Colgate	6-7 oz.	2.37	12/94	2c
Personal Services				
Dry cleaning, man's 2-pc. suit		6.70	12/94	2c
Haircut, man's barbershop, no styling		7.40	12/94	2c
Haircut, woman's shampoo, trim, blow-dry		20.25	12/94	2c
Personal services expenditures	year	184	91	81r
Restaurant Food				
Chicken, fried, thigh and drumstick		2.19	12/94	2c
Dining expenditures, family	week	34.26	94	73r
Hamburger with cheese	1/4 lb.	1.90	12/94	2c
Pizza, Pizza Hut or Pizza Inn	12-13 in.	6.49	12/94	2c
Taxes				
Taxes, Federal income, expenditures	year	2409	91	81r
Taxes, personal, expenditures	year	3094	91	81r
Taxes, State and local income, expenditures	year	620	91	81r
Transportation				
Transportation, ACCRA Index		111.80	12/94	2c
Bus fare, one-way	trip	1.10	12/95	1c
Bus fare, up to 10 miles	one-way	1.40	12/94	2c
Cars and trucks purchased, new	year	1170	91	81r
Cars and trucks purchased, used	year	739	91	81r
Driver's learning permit fee	perm	27.00	1/94	84s
Driver's license fee	orig	0.00	1/94	84s
Driver's license fee, duplicate	lic	7.00	1/94	84s
Driver's license reinstatement fee, min.	susp	25.00	1/94	85s
Driver's license renewal fee	renew	0.00	1/94	84s
Identification card, nondriver	card	5.00	1/94	83s
Motorcycle learning permit fee	perm	27.00	1/94	84s

Values are in dollars or fractions of dollars. In the column headed *Ref*, references are shown to sources. Each reference is followed by a letter. These refer to the geographical level for which data were reported: s=State, r=Region, and c=City or metro. The abbreviation *ex* is used to mean *except* or *excluding*; *exp* stands for expenditures. For other abbreviations and further explanations, please see the Introduction.

Harrisburg, PA - continued

Item	Per	Value	Date	Ref.
Transportation				
Motorcycle license fee	orig	0.00	1/94	84s
Motorcycle license fee, duplicate	lic	7.00	1/94	84s
Motorcycle license renewal fee	renew	0.00	1/94	84s
Public transportation expenditures	year	430	91	81r
Tire balance, computer or spin bal., front	wheel	8.30	12/94	2c
Transportation expenditures, total	year	4810	91	81r
Vehicle finance charges	year	238	91	81r
Vehicle insurance expenditures	year	630	91	81r
Vehicle maintenance and repairs expenditures	year	532	91	81r
Vehicle purchases	year	1920	91	81r
Vehicle rental, leases, licenses, etc. expenditures	year	193	91	81r
Vehicles purchased, other than cars and trucks	year	11	91	81r
Utilities				
Utilities, ACCRA Index		132.00	12/94	2c
Electricity expenditures	year	695	91	81r
Electricity, 1800 sq. ft., new home	mo.	153.00	12/94	2c
Utilities, fuels, and public services, total expenditures	year	1981	91	81r
Water and other public services, expenditures	year	154	91	81r
Weddings				
Bridal attendants' gowns	event	750	10/93	76r
Bridal gown	event	852	10/93	76r
Bridal headpiece and veil	event	167	10/93	76r
Bride's wedding band	event	708	10/93	76r
Clergy	event	224	10/93	76r
Engagement ring	event	2756	10/93	76r
Flowers	event	863	10/93	76r
Formal wear for groom	event	106	10/93	76r
Groom's attendants' formal wear	event	530	10/93	76r
Groom's wedding band	event	402	10/93	76r
Music	event	600	10/93	76r
Photography	event	1088	10/93	76r
Shoes for bride	event	50	10/93	76r
Videography	event	483	10/93	76r
Wedding invitations and announcements	event	342	10/93	76r
Wedding reception	event	7000	10/93	76r

Hartford, CT

Item	Per	Value	Date	Ref.
Composite, ACCRA index		123.70	12/94	2c
Alcoholic Beverages				
Beer, Miller Lite, Bud, 12-oz., ex deposit	6	4.37	12/94	2c
J & B Scotch	750-ml.	18.11	12/94	2c
Wine, Gallo Chablis blanc	1.5-lit	5.19	12/94	2c
Appliances				
Appliances (major), expenditures	year	145	91	81r
Average annual exp.				
Food, health care, personal goods, services	year	29496	91	81r
Charity				
Cash contributions, expenditures	year	708	91	81r
Child Care				
Child care, for-profit daycare center	week	92.00	12/94	28c
Clothing				
Apparel, men and boys, total expenditures	year	416	91	81r
Apparel, women and girls, total expenditures	year	744	91	81r
Footwear, expenditures	year	305	91	81r
Jeans, man's denim		29.39	12/94	2c
Shirt, man's dress shirt		26.29	12/94	2c
Undervest, boy's size 10-14, cotton	3	5.12	12/94	2c
Communications				
Long-distance telephone rate, day, addl. min., 1-10 mi.	min.	0.09	12/93	9s

Hartford, CT - continued

Item	Per	Value	Date	Ref.
Communications - continued				
Long-distance telephone rate, day, initial min., 1-10 mi.	min.	0.09	12/93	9s
Newspaper subscription, dly. and Sun. delivery	month	15.22	12/94	2c
Phone line, single, business, field visit	inst	127.44	12/93	9s
Phone line, single, business, no field visit	inst	95.58	12/93	9s
Phone line, single, residence, field visit	inst	64.85	12/93	9s
Phone line, single, residence, no field visit	inst	38.27	12/93	9s
Telephone bill, family of four	month	18.03	12/94	2c
Telephone service, expenditures	year	589	91	81r
Telephone, residential, flat rate	mo.	14.27	12/93	8c
Education				
Board, 4-year private college/university	year	2664	8/94	80s
Board, 4-year public college/university	year	2137	8/94	80s
Education, total expenditures	year	593	91	81r
Room, 4-year private college/university	year	3287	8/94	80s
Room, 4-year public college/university	year	2310	8/94	80s
Total cost, 4-year private college/university	year	20726	8/94	80s
Total cost, 4-year public college/university	year	7926	8/94	80s
Tuition, 2-year public college/university, in-state	year	1398	8/94	80s
Tuition, 4-year private college/university, in-state	year	14775	8/94	80s
Tuition, 4-year public college/university, in-state	year	3479	8/94	80s
Energy and Fuels				
Energy, combined forms, 1800 sq. ft.	mo.	134.03	12/94	2c
Energy, exc. electricity, 1800 sq. ft.	mo.	74.20	12/94	2c
Fuel oil and other fuels, expenditures	year	257	91	81r
Gas, cooking, 10 therms	month	15.98	2/94	65c
Gas, cooking, 30 therms	month	32.44	2/94	65c
Gas, cooking, 50 therms	month	48.90	2/94	65c
Gas, heating, winter, 100 therms	month	90.04	2/94	65c
Gas, heating, winter, average use	month	216.77	2/94	65c
Gas, natural, expenditures	year	285	91	81r
Gas, reg unlead, taxes inc., cash, self-service	gal	1.26	12/94	2c
Gasoline and motor oil purchased	year	867	91	81r
Gasoline, unleaded midgrade	gallon	1.32	4/93	82r
Gasoline, unleaded premium	gallon	1.40	4/93	82r
Gasoline, unleaded regular	gallon	1.19	4/93	82r
Entertainment				
Bowling, evening rate	game	2.71	12/94	2c
Entertainment, total expenditures	year	1331	91	81r
Fees and admissions, expenditures	year	398	91	81r
Monopoly game, Parker Brothers', No. 9	game	14.39	12/94	2c
Movie	adm	6.50	12/94	2c
Pets, toys, playground equipment, expenditures	year	270	91	81r
Reading, expenditures	year	171	91	81r
Televisions, radios, and sound equipment, expenditures	year	429	91	81r
Tennis balls, yellow, Wilson or Penn, 3	can	2.74	12/94	2c
Funerals				
Burial, immediate, container provided by funeral home		1507.89	1/95	54r
Cards, acknowledgment		18.10	1/95	54r
Casket, minimum alternative		133.03	1/95	54r
Cosmetology, hair care, etc.		114.12	1/95	54r
Cremation, direct, container provided by funeral home		1309.19	1/95	54r
Embalming		320.97	1/95	54r
Funeral, funeral home		327.61	1/95	54r
Funeral, other facility		314.81	1/95	54r
Graveside service		286.11	1/95	54r
Hearse, local		158.95	1/95	54r
Limousine, local		149.45	1/95	54r
Memorial service		315.94	1/95	54r
Service charge, professional, nondeclinable		1148.43	1/95	54r
Visitation and viewing		249.66	1/95	54r

Values are in dollars or fractions of dollars. In the column headed *Ref*, references are shown to sources. Each reference is followed by a letter. These refer to the geographical level for which data were reported: s=State, r=Region, and c=City or metro. The abbreviation *ex* is used to mean *except* or *excluding*; *exp* stands for expenditures. For other abbreviations and further explanations, please see the Introduction.

Hartford, CT - continued

Item	Per	Value	Date	Ref.
Groceries				
Groceries, ACCRA Index		117.20	12/94	2c
Apples, Red Delicious	lb.	0.78	12/94	82r
Baby food, strained vegetables, lowest price	4-4.5 oz.	0.44	12/94	2c
Bacon, sliced	lb.	2.24	12/94	82r
Bananas	lb.	0.67	12/94	2c
Bananas	lb.	0.49	12/94	82r
Beef or hamburger, ground	lb.	1.69	12/94	2c
Beef purchases	year	226	91	81r
Beverage purchases, alcoholic	year	332	91	81r
Beverage purchases, nonalcoholic	year	213	91	81r
Bread, white	24-oz.	1.11	12/94	2c
Bread, white, pan	lb.	0.80	12/94	82r
Butter, salted, Grade AA, stick	lb.	1.67	12/94	82r
Carrots, short trimmed and topped	lb.	0.51	12/94	82r
Cereals and bakery products purchases	year	407	91	81r
Cereals and cereals products purchases	year	132	91	81r
Cheese, Kraft grated Parmesan	8-oz.	3.57	12/94	2c
Chicken breast, bone-in	lb.	2.22	12/94	82r
Chicken, fresh, whole	lb.	1.05	12/94	82r
Chicken, whole fryer	lb.	0.85	12/94	2c
Chuck roast, USDA choice, boneless	lb.	2.74	12/94	82r
Cigarettes, Winston, Kings	carton	19.21	12/94	2c
Coffee, 100%, ground roast, all sizes	lb.	4.61	12/94	82r
Coffee, vacuum-packed	13 oz.	4.35	12/94	2c
Corn Flakes, Kellogg's or Post Toasties	18 oz.	2.13	12/94	2c
Corn, frozen, whole kernel, lowest price	10 oz.	0.66	12/94	2c
Dairy products (other) purchases	year	161	91	81r
Eggs, Grade A large	dozen	0.97	12/94	2c
Eggs, Grade A large	dozen	1.12	12/94	82r
Fish and seafood purchases	year	112	91	81r
Food purchases, food eaten at home	year	2599	91	81r
Foods purchased away from home, not prepared by consumer	year	2024	91	81r
Fruits and vegetables purchases	year	444	91	81r
Grapefruit	lb.	0.44	12/94	82r
Grapes, Thompson seedless	lb.	2.24	12/94	82r
Ground chuck, 100% beef	lb.	1.67	12/94	82r
Ice cream, prepackaged, bulk, regular	1/2 gal.	2.93	12/94	82r
Lemons	lb.	1.06	12/94	82r
Lettuce, iceberg	lb.	0.92	12/94	82r
Lettuce, iceberg	head	1.21	12/94	2c
Margarine, Blue Bonnet or Parkay cubes	lb.	0.59	12/94	2c
Meats, poultry, fish, and eggs purchases	year	751	91	81r
Milk and cream (fresh) purchases	year	152	91	81r
Milk, whole	1/2 gal.	1.33	12/94	2c
Orange juice, frozen concentrate 12-oz. can	16 oz.	1.92	12/94	82r
Orange juice, Minute Maid frozen	12-oz.	1.36	12/94	2c
Oranges, Navel	lb.	0.56	12/94	82r
Peaches, halves or slices, Hunt's, Del Monte, or Libby's	29-oz.	1.31	12/94	2c
Peas, sweet, Del Monte or Green Giant	15-17 oz.	0.65	12/94	2c
Pork chops, center cut, bone-in	lb.	3.09	12/94	82r
Pork purchases	year	130	91	81r
Potatoes, white	lb.	0.37	12/94	82r
Potatoes, white or red	10-lb. sack	2.76	12/94	2c
Rib roast, USDA choice, bone-in	lb.	4.98	12/94	82r
Round roast, USDA choice, boneless	lb.	2.93	12/94	82r
Sausage, Jimmy Dean, 100% pork	lb.	3.30	12/94	2c
Shortening, vegetable oil blends	lb.	1.03	12/94	82r
Shortening, vegetable, Crisco	3-lb.	2.94	12/94	2c
Soft drink, Coca Cola, ex deposit	2 lit	1.13	12/94	2c
Spaghetti and macaroni	lb.	0.84	12/94	82r
Steak, round, USDA choice, boneless	lb.	3.48	12/94	82r
Steak, sirloin, USDA choice, bone-in	lb.	3.38	12/94	82r
Steak, sirloin, USDA choice, boneless	lb.	4.81	12/94	82r
Steak, t-bone	lb.	5.23	12/94	2c

Hartford, CT - continued

Item	Per	Value	Date	Ref.
Groceries - continued				
Sugar and other sweets, eaten at home, expenditures	year	89	91	81r
Sugar, cane or beet	4 lbs.	1.71	12/94	2c
Sugar, white, all sizes	lb.	0.46	12/94	82r
Tobacco products and smoking supplies, total expenditures	year	279	91	81r
Tomatoes, field grown	lb.	1.56	12/94	82r
Tomatoes, Hunt's or Del Monte	14.5 oz.	0.79	12/94	2c
Tuna, chunk, light	lb.	2.09	12/94	82r
Tuna, chunk, light, oil-packed	6.125-6.5 oz.	0.72	12/94	2c
Goods and Services				
Miscellaneous goods and services, ACCRA Index		109.70	12/94	2c
Health Care				
Health care, ACCRA Index		138.20	12/94	2c
Antibiotic ointment, Polysporin	1.5 oz.	5.09	12/94	2c
Childbirth, Cesarean delivery, hospital charge	birth	6334.00	12/91	69r
Childbirth, Cesarean delivery, physician charge	birth	2234.00	12/91	69r
Childbirth, normal delivery, hospital charge	birth	3225.00	12/91	69r
Childbirth, normal delivery, physician charge	birth	1623.00	12/91	69r
Dentist's fee, adult teeth cleaning and periodic oral exam	visit	71.00	12/94	2c
Doctor's fee, routine exam, established patient	visit	56.29	12/94	2c
Drugs, expenditures	year	205	91	81r
Health care, total expenditures	year	1396	91	81r
Health insurance expenditures	year	553	91	81r
Hospital care, semiprivate room	day	572.72	12/94	2c
Insurance premium, family medical care	month	500.40	1/95	41s
Medical services expenditures	year	559	91	81r
Medical supplies expenditures	year	80	91	81r
Household Goods				
Appl. repair, service call, wash mach	min. lab. chg.	40.97	12/94	2c
Floor coverings, expenditures	year	158	91	81r
Furniture, expenditures	year	341	91	81r
Household equipment, misc. expenditures	year	363	91	81r
Household expenditures, miscellaneous	year	194	91	81r
Household furnishings and equipment, expenditures	year	1158	91	81r
Household operations expenditures	year	378	91	81r
Household textiles, expenditures	year	88	91	81r
Housekeeping supplies, expenditures	year	426	91	81r
Laundry and cleaning supplies, expenditures	year	122	91	81r
Laundry detergent, Tide Ultra, Bold, or Cheer	42 oz.	3.81	12/94	2c
Postage and stationery, expenditures	year	134	91	81r
Tissues, facial, Kleenex brand	175	1.08	12/94	2c
Housing				
Housing, ACCRA Index		145.40	12/94	2c
Add garage/carport		11,614	3/95	74r
Add room(s)		16,816	3/95	74r
Apartment condominium or co-op, median	unit	96700	12/94	62r
Dwellings (owned), expenditures	year	3305	91	81r
Enclose porch/patio/breezeway		2,980	3/95	74r
Finish room in basement/attic		4,330	3/95	74r
Home, existing, single-family, median	unit	161600	12/94	62r
Home, existing, single-family, median	unit	130.80	12/94	62c
House payment, principal and interest, 25% down payment	mo.	1116	12/94	2c
House, 1800 sq ft, 8000 sq ft lot, new, urban, utilities	total	184333	12/94	2c
Maintenance, repairs, insurance, and other housing expenditures	year	569	91	81r

Values are in dollars or fractions of dollars. In the column headed *Ref*, references are shown to sources. Each reference is followed by a letter. These refer to the geographical level for which data were reported: s=State, r=Region, and c=City or metro. The abbreviation *ex* is used to mean *except* or *excluding*; *exp* stands for *expenditures*. For other abbreviations and further explanations, please see the Introduction.

Hartford, CT - continued

Item	Per	Value	Date	Ref.
Housing				
Mortgage interest and charges expenditures	year	1852	91	81r
Mtge. rate, incl. points and orig. fee, 30-year conv. fixed or ARM	mo.	9.04	12/94	2c
Princ. & int., mortgage, median-price exist. sing.-family home	mo.	765	12/94	62r
Property taxes expenditures	year	884	91	81r
Redesign, restructure more than half of home's interior		2,750	3/95	74r
Rent, apartment, 2 br., 1 1/2-2 baths, unfurnished, 950 sq ft, water	mo.	762	12/94	2c
Rental units expenditures	year	1832	91	81r
Insurance and Pensions				
Auto insurance, private passenger	year	1002.84	12/94	71s
Insurance and pensions, personal, expenditures	year	2690	91	81r
Insurance, life and other personal, expenditures	year	341	91	81r
Pensions and Social Security, expenditures	year	2349	91	81r
Legal Assistance				
Estate planning, law-firm partner	hr.	375.00	10/93	12r
Legal work, law firm associate	hour	78		10r
Legal work, law firm partner	hour	183		10r
Personal Goods				
Shampoo, Alberto VO5	15-oz.	1.50	12/94	2c
Toothpaste, Crest or Colgate	6-7 oz.	2.27	12/94	2c
Personal Services				
Dry cleaning, man's 2-pc. suit		8.55	12/94	2c
Haircut, man's barbershop, no styling		10.86	12/94	2c
Haircut, woman's shampoo, trim, blow-dry		26.00	12/94	2c
Personal services expenditures	year	184	91	81r
Restaurant Food				
Chicken, fried, thigh and drumstick		2.53	12/94	2c
Dining expenditures, family	week	34.26	94	73r
Hamburger with cheese	1/4 lb.	1.97	12/94	2c
Pizza, Pizza Hut or Pizza Inn	12-13 in.	7.99	12/94	2c
Taxes				
Taxes, Federal income, expenditures	year	2409	91	81r
Taxes, personal, expenditures	year	3094	91	81r
Taxes, State and local income, expenditures	year	620	91	81r
Transportation				
Transportation, ACCRA Index		116.30	12/94	2c
Bus fare, one-way	trip	0.98	12/95	1c
Bus fare, up to 10 miles	one-way	1.70	12/94	2c
Cars and trucks purchased, new	year	1170	91	81r
Cars and trucks purchased, used	year	739	91	81r
Driver's learning permit fee	perm	3.50	1/94	84s
Driver's license fee	orig	38.00	1/94	84s
Driver's license fee, duplicate	lic	5.00	1/94	84s
Driver's license reinstatement fee, min.	susp	30.00	1/94	85s
Driver's license renewal fee	renew	31.00	1/94	84s
Driving expenses	mile	48.00	5/95	86c
Identification card, nondriver	card	4.00	1/94	83s
Motorcycle learning permit fee	perm	3.50	1/94	84s
Motorcycle license fee	orig	38.00	1/94	84s
Motorcycle license fee, duplicate	lic	5.00	1/94	84s
Motorcycle license renewal fee	renew	31.00	1/94	84s
Public transportation expenditures	year	430	91	81r
Tire balance, computer or spin bal., front	wheel	7.06	12/94	2c
Transportation expenditures, total	year	4810	91	81r
Vehicle finance charges	year	238	91	81r
Vehicle insurance expenditures	year	630	91	81r
Vehicle maintenance and repairs expenditures	year	532	91	81r
Vehicle purchases	year	1920	91	81r
Vehicle rental, leases, licenses, etc. expenditures	year	193	91	81r

Hartford, CT - continued

Item	Per	Value	Date	Ref.
Transportation - continued				
Vehicles purchased, other than cars and trucks	year	11	91	81r
Travel				
Car rental	day	41.99	1/93	49c
Car rental	week	174.99	1/93	49c
Utilities				
Utilities, ACCRA Index		115.80	12/94	2c
Electricity expenditures	year	695	91	81r
Electricity, (part.), other, 1800 sq. ft., new home	mo.	59.83	12/94	2c
Electricity, summer, 250 KWh	month	34.58	8/93	64c
Electricity, summer, 500 KWh	month	60.69	8/93	64c
Electricity, summer, 750 KWh	month	86.77	8/93	64c
Electricity, summer, 1000 KWh	month	112.85	8/93	64c
Utilities, fuels, and public services, total expenditures	year	1981	91	81r
Water and other public services, expenditures	year	154	91	81r
Weddings				
Bridal attendants' gowns	event	750	10/93	76r
Bridal gown	event	852	10/93	76r
Bridal headpiece and veil	event	167	10/93	76r
Bride's wedding band	event	708	10/93	76r
Clergy	event	224	10/93	76r
Engagement ring	event	2756	10/93	76r
Flowers	event	863	10/93	76r
Formal wear for groom	event	106	10/93	76r
Groom's attendants' formal wear	event	530	10/93	76r
Groom's wedding band	event	402	10/93	76r
Music	event	600	10/93	76r
Photography	event	1088	10/93	76r
Shoes for bride	event	50	10/93	76r
Videography	event	483	10/93	76r
Wedding invitations and announcements	event	342	10/93	76r
Wedding reception	event	7000	10/93	76r

Hastings, NE

Item	Per	Value	Date	Ref.
Composite, ACCRA index		91.90	12/94	2c
Alcoholic Beverages				
Beer, Miller Lite, Bud, 12-oz., ex deposit	6	4.15	12/94	2c
J & B Scotch	750-ml.	17.73	12/94	2c
Wine, Gallo Chablis blanc	1.5-lit	5.79	12/94	2c
Clothing				
Jeans, man's denim		27.62	12/94	2c
Shirt, man's dress shirt		38.75	12/94	2c
Undervest, boy's size 10-14, cotton	3	2.46	12/94	2c
Communications				
Newspaper subscription, dly. and Sun. delivery	month	8.70	12/94	2c
Telephone bill, family of four	month	17.70	12/94	2c
Energy and Fuels				
Energy, combined forms, 1800 sq. ft.	mo.	101.92	12/94	2c
Energy, exc. electricity, 1800 sq. ft.	mo.	43.48	12/94	2c
Gas, reg unlead, taxes inc., cash, self-service	gal	1.17	12/94	2c
Entertainment				
Bowling, evening rate	game	1.93	12/94	2c
Monopoly game, Parker Brothers', No. 9	game	9.92	12/94	2c
Movie	adm	4.94	12/94	2c
Tennis balls, yellow, Wilson or Penn, 3	can	2.18	12/94	2c
Groceries				
Groceries, ACCRA Index		103.60	12/94	2c
Baby food, strained vegetables, lowest price	4-4.5 oz.	0.40	12/94	2c
Bananas	lb.	0.52	12/94	2c

Values are in dollars or fractions of dollars. In the column headed *Ref*, references are shown to sources. Each reference is followed by a letter. These refer to the geographical level for which data were reported: s = State, r = Region, and c = City or metro. The abbreviation *ex* is used to mean *except* or *excluding*; *exp* stands for expenditures. For other abbreviations and further explanations, please see the Introduction.

American Cost of Living Survey, 2nd Edition

Hattiesburg, MS

Hastings, NE - continued

Item	Per	Value	Date	Ref.
Groceries				
Beef or hamburger, ground	lb.	1.13	12/94	2c
Bread, white	24-oz.	1.01	12/94	2c
Cheese, Kraft grated Parmesan	8-oz.	2.98	12/94	2c
Chicken, whole fryer	lb.	0.89	12/94	2c
Cigarettes, Winston, Kings	carton	15.78	12/94	2c
Coffee, vacuum-packed	13 oz.	3.46	12/94	2c
Corn Flakes, Kellogg's or Post Toasties	18 oz.	2.38	12/94	2c
Corn, frozen, whole kernel, lowest price	10 oz.	0.63	12/94	2c
Eggs, Grade A large	dozen	0.71	12/94	2c
Lettuce, iceberg	head	0.79	12/94	2c
Margarine, Blue Bonnet or Parkay cubes	lb.	0.58	12/94	2c
Milk, whole	1/2 gal.	1.32	12/94	2c
Orange juice, Minute Maid frozen	12-oz.	1.27	12/94	2c
Peaches, halves or slices, Hunt's, Del Monte, or Libby's	29-oz.	1.34	12/94	2c
Peas, sweet, Del Monte or Green Giant	15-17 oz.	0.49	12/94	2c
Potatoes, white or red	10-lb. sack	1.94	12/94	2c
Sausage, Jimmy Dean, 100% pork	lb.	3.05	12/94	2c
Shortening, vegetable, Crisco	3-lb.	2.54	12/94	2c
Soft drink, Coca Cola, ex deposit	2 lit	1.17	12/94	2c
Steak, t-bone	lb.	5.34	12/94	2c
Sugar, cane or beet	4 lbs.	1.36	12/94	2c
Tomatoes, Hunt's or Del Monte	14.5 oz.	0.83	12/94	2c
Tuna, chunk, light, oil-packed	6.125-6.5 oz.	0.65	12/94	2c
Goods and Services				
Miscellaneous goods and services, ACCRA Index		94.30	12/94	2c
Health Care				
Health care, ACCRA Index		83.70	12/94	2c
Antibiotic ointment, Polysporin	1.5 oz.	4.11	12/94	2c
Dentist's fee, adult teeth cleaning and periodic oral exam	visit	45.33	12/94	2c
Doctor's fee, routine exam, established patient	visit	33.20	12/94	2c
Hospital care, semiprivate room	day	277.00	12/94	2c
Household Goods				
Appl. repair, service call, wash mach	min. lab. chg.	33.50	12/94	2c
Laundry detergent, Tide Ultra, Bold, or Cheer	42 oz.	3.65	12/94	2c
Tissues, facial, Kleenex brand	175	0.82	12/94	2c
Housing				
Housing, ACCRA Index		84.40	12/94	2c
House payment, principal and interest, 25% down payment	mo.	663	12/94	2c
House, 1800 sq ft, 8000 sq ft lot, new, urban, utilities	total	106518	12/94	2c
Mtge. rate, incl. points and orig. fee, 30-year conv. fixed or ARM	mo.	9.35	12/94	2c
Rent, apartment, 2 br., 1 1/2-2 baths, unfurnished, 950 sq ft, water	mo.	399	12/94	2c
Personal Goods				
Shampoo, Alberto VO5	15-oz.	1.01	12/94	2c
Toothpaste, Crest or Colgate	6-7 oz.	1.32	12/94	2c
Personal Services				
Dry cleaning, man's 2-pc. suit		8.05	12/94	2c
Haircut, man's barbershop, no styling		7.42	12/94	2c
Haircut, woman's shampoo, trim, blow-dry		18.75	12/94	2c
Restaurant Food				
Chicken, fried, thigh and drumstick		1.91	12/94	2c
Hamburger with cheese	1/4 lb.	1.80	12/94	2c

Hastings, NE - continued

Item	Per	Value	Date	Ref.
Restaurant Food - continued				
Pizza, Pizza Hut or Pizza Inn	12-13 in.	6.50	12/94	2c
Transportation				
Transportation, ACCRA Index		92.20	12/94	2c
Tire balance, computer or spin bal., front	wheel	5.17	12/94	2c
Utilities				
Utilities, ACCRA Index		90.80	12/94	2c
Electricity, (part.), other, 1800 sq. ft., new home	mo.	58.44	12/94	2c

Hattiesburg, MS

Item	Per	Value	Date	Ref.
Composite, ACCRA index		92.00	12/94	2c
Alcoholic Beverages				
Beer, Miller Lite, Bud, 12-oz., ex deposit	6	4.19	12/94	2c
J & B Scotch	750-ml.	17.44	12/94	2c
Wine, Gallo Chablis blanc	1.5-lit	5.71	12/94	2c
Clothing				
Jeans, man's denim		34.99	12/94	2c
Shirt, man's dress shirt		35.00	12/94	2c
Undervest, boy's size 10-14, cotton	3	6.43	12/94	2c
Communications				
Newspaper subscription, dly. and Sun. delivery	month	10.00	12/94	2c
Telephone bill, family of four	month	24.78	12/94	2c
Telephone, residential, flat rate	mo.	17.25	12/93	8c
Energy and Fuels				
Energy, combined forms, 1800 sq. ft.	mo.	96.67	12/94	2c
Gas, reg unlead, taxes inc., cash, self-service	gal	1.10	12/94	2c
Entertainment				
Bowling, evening rate	game	2.29	12/94	2c
Monopoly game, Parker Brothers', No. 9	game	10.98	12/94	2c
Movie	adm	5.38	12/94	2c
Tennis balls, yellow, Wilson or Penn, 3	can	2.28	12/94	2c
Groceries				
Groceries, ACCRA Index		97.70	12/94	2c
Baby food, strained vegetables, lowest price	4-4.5 oz.	0.30	12/94	2c
Bananas	lb.	0.45	12/94	2c
Beef or hamburger, ground	lb.	1.52	12/94	2c
Bread, white	24-oz.	0.67	12/94	2c
Cheese, Kraft grated Parmesan	8-oz.	3.34	12/94	2c
Chicken, whole fryer	lb.	0.70	12/94	2c
Cigarettes, Winston, Kings	carton	14.63	12/94	2c
Coffee, vacuum-packed	13 oz.	3.94	12/94	2c
Corn Flakes, Kellogg's or Post Toasties	18 oz.	2.63	12/94	2c
Corn, frozen, whole kernel, lowest price	10 oz.	0.80	12/94	2c
Eggs, Grade A large	dozen	0.71	12/94	2c
Lettuce, iceberg	head	0.91	12/94	2c
Margarine, Blue Bonnet or Parkay cubes	lb.	0.55	12/94	2c
Milk, whole	1/2 gal.	1.19	12/94	2c
Orange juice, Minute Maid frozen	12-oz.	1.27	12/94	2c
Peaches, halves or slices, Hunt's, Del Monte, or Libby's	29-oz.	1.40	12/94	2c
Peas, sweet, Del Monte or Green Giant	15-17 oz.	0.63	12/94	2c
Potatoes, white or red	10-lb. sack	2.52	12/94	2c
Sausage, Jimmy Dean, 100% pork	lb.	2.34	12/94	2c
Shortening, vegetable, Crisco	3-lb.	2.36	12/94	2c
Soft drink, Coca Cola, ex deposit	2 lit	0.98	12/94	2c
Steak, t-bone	lb.	5.82	12/94	2c
Sugar, cane or beet	4 lbs.	1.55	12/94	2c

Values are in dollars or fractions of dollars. In the column headed *Ref*, references are shown to sources. Each reference is followed by a letter. These refer to the geographical level for which data were reported: s=State, r=Region, and c=City or metro. The abbreviation *ex* is used to mean *except* or *excluding*; *exp* stands for expenditures. For other abbreviations and further explanations, please see the Introduction.

Hattiesburg, MS - continued

Item	Per	Value	Date	Ref.
Groceries				
Tomatoes, Hunt's or Del Monte	14.5 oz.	0.66	12/94	2c
Tuna, chunk, light, oil-packed	6.125-6.5 oz.	0.63	12/94	2c
Goods and Services				
Miscellaneous goods and services, ACCRA Index		104.60	12/94	2c
Health Care				
Health care, ACCRA Index		89.40	12/94	2c
Antibiotic ointment, Polysporin	1.5 oz.	4.67	12/94	2c
Dentist's fee, adult teeth cleaning and periodic oral exam	visit	49.88	12/94	2c
Doctor's fee, routine exam, established patient	visit	38.33	12/94	2c
Hospital care, semiprivate room	day	212.50	12/94	2c
Household Goods				
Appl. repair, service call, wash mach	min. lab. chg.	35.00	12/94	2c
Laundry detergent, Tide Ultra, Bold, or Cheer	42 oz.	2.93	12/94	2c
Tissues, facial, Kleenex brand	175	1.19	12/94	2c
Housing				
Housing, ACCRA Index		72.30	12/94	2c
House payment, principal and interest, 25% down payment	mo.	541	12/94	2c
House, 1800 sq ft, 8000 sq ft lot, new, urban, utilities	total	85300	12/94	2c
Mtge. rate, incl. points and orig. fee, 30-year conv. fixed or ARM	mo.	9.56	12/94	2c
Rent, apartment, 2 br., 1 1/2-2 baths, unfurnished, 950 sq ft, water	mo.	419	12/94	2c
Personal Goods				
Shampoo, Alberto VO5	15-oz.	1.23	12/94	2c
Toothpaste, Crest or Colgate	6-7 oz.	2.17	12/94	2c
Personal Services				
Dry cleaning, man's 2-pc. suit		5.63	12/94	2c
Haircut, man's barbershop, no styling		8.40	12/94	2c
Haircut, woman's shampoo, trim, blow-dry		18.40	12/94	2c
Restaurant Food				
Chicken, fried, thigh and drumstick		1.92	12/94	2c
Hamburger with cheese	1/4 lb.	1.85	12/94	2c
Pizza, Pizza Hut or Pizza Inn	12-13 in.	7.99	12/94	2c
Transportation				
Transportation, ACCRA Index		99.20	12/94	2c
Tire balance, computer or spin bal., front	wheel	6.85	12/94	2c
Utilities				
Utilities, ACCRA Index		91.70	12/94	2c
Electricity, 1800 sq. ft., new home	mo.	96.67	12/94	2c

Hays, KS

Item	Per	Value	Date	Ref.
Composite, ACCRA index		101.00	12/94	2c
Alcoholic Beverages				
Beer, Miller Lite, Bud, 12-oz., ex deposit	6	4.10	12/94	2c
J & B Scotch	750-ml.	17.97	12/94	2c
Wine, Gallo Chablis blanc	1.5-lit	5.00	12/94	2c
Clothing				
Jeans, man's denim		32.99	12/94	2c
Shirt, man's dress shirt		26.66	12/94	2c
Undervest, boy's size 10-14, cotton	3	3.31	12/94	2c

Hays, KS - continued

Item	Per	Value	Date	Ref.
Communications				
Newspaper subscription, dly. and Sun. delivery	month	12.50	12/94	2c
Telephone bill, family of four	month	17.24	12/94	2c
Telephone, residential, flat rate	mo.	10.05	12/93	8c
Energy and Fuels				
Energy, combined forms, 1800 sq. ft.	mo.	127.27	12/94	2c
Energy, exc. electricity, 1800 sq. ft.	mo.	38.29	12/94	2c
Gas, reg unlead, taxes inc., cash, self-service	gal	1.04	12/94	2c
Entertainment				
Bowling, evening rate	game	2.10	12/94	2c
Monopoly game, Parker Brothers', No. 9	game	9.98	12/94	2c
Movie	adm	5.00	12/94	2c
Tennis balls, yellow, Wilson or Penn, 3	can	1.97	12/94	2c
Groceries				
Groceries, ACCRA Index		100.70	12/94	2c
Baby food, strained vegetables, lowest price	4-4.5 oz.	0.43	12/94	2c
Bananas	lb.	0.36	12/94	2c
Beef or hamburger, ground	lb.	1.65	12/94	2c
Bread, white	24-oz.	0.64	12/94	2c
Cheese, Kraft grated Parmesan	8-oz.	3.73	12/94	2c
Chicken, whole fryer	lb.	0.71	12/94	2c
Cigarettes, Winston, Kings	carton	14.58	12/94	2c
Coffee, vacuum-packed	13 oz.	3.45	12/94	2c
Corn Flakes, Kellogg's or Post Toasties	18 oz.	2.52	12/94	2c
Corn, frozen, whole kernel, lowest price	10 oz.	0.71	12/94	2c
Eggs, Grade A large	dozen	0.63	12/94	2c
Lettuce, iceberg	head	0.79	12/94	2c
Margarine, Blue Bonnet or Parkay cubes	lb.	0.52	12/94	2c
Milk, whole	1/2 gal.	1.44	12/94	2c
Orange juice, Minute Maid frozen	12-oz.	1.30	12/94	2c
Peaches, halves or slices, Hunt's, Del Monte, or Libby's	29-oz.	1.37	12/94	2c
Peas, sweet, Del Monte or Green Giant	15-17 oz.	0.50	12/94	2c
Potatoes, white or red	10-lb. sack	2.62	12/94	2c
Sausage, Jimmy Dean, 100% pork	lb.	2.82	12/94	2c
Shortening, vegetable, Crisco	3-lb.	2.81	12/94	2c
Soft drink, Coca Cola, ex deposit	2 lit	1.16	12/94	2c
Steak, t-bone	lb.	5.79	12/94	2c
Sugar, cane or beet	4 lbs.	1.30	12/94	2c
Tomatoes, Hunt's or Del Monte	14.5 oz.	0.72	12/94	2c
Tuna, chunk, light, oil-packed	6.125-6.5 oz.	0.70	12/94	2c
Goods and Services				
Miscellaneous goods and services, ACCRA Index		96.00	12/94	2c
Health Care				
Health care, ACCRA Index		107.40	12/94	2c
Antibiotic ointment, Polysporin	1.5 oz.	4.46	12/94	2c
Dentist's fee, adult teeth cleaning and periodic oral exam	visit	56.67	12/94	2c
Doctor's fee, routine exam, established patient	visit	43.00	12/94	2c
Hospital care, semiprivate room	day	410.00	12/94	2c
Household Goods				
Appl. repair, service call, wash mach	min. lab. chg.	29.83	12/94	2c
Laundry detergent, Tide Ultra, Bold, or Cheer	42 oz.	3.78	12/94	2c
Tissues, facial, Kleenex brand	175	1.01	12/94	2c

Values are in dollars or fractions of dollars. In the column headed *Ref*, references are shown to sources. Each reference is followed by a letter. These refer to the geographical level for which data were reported: s = State, r = Region, and c = City or metro. The abbreviation *ex* is used to mean *except* or *excluding*; *exp* stands for expenditures. For other abbreviations and further explanations, please see the Introduction.

Hays, KS - continued

Item	Per	Value	Date	Ref.
Housing				
Housing, ACCRA Index		107.10	12/94	2c
House payment, principal and interest, 25% down payment	mo.	822	12/94	2c
House, 1800 sq ft, 8000 sq ft lot, new, urban, utilities	total	134000	12/94	2c
Mtge. rate, incl. points and orig. fee, 30-year conv. fixed or ARM	mo.	9.18	12/94	2c
Personal Goods				
Shampoo, Alberto VO5	15-oz.	1.29	12/94	2c
Toothpaste, Crest or Colgate	6-7 oz.	1.36	12/94	2c
Personal Services				
Dry cleaning, man's 2-pc. suit		7.00	12/94	2c
Haircut, man's barbershop, no styling		10.33	12/94	2c
Haircut, woman's shampoo, trim, blow-dry		12.33	12/94	2c
Restaurant Food				
Chicken, fried, thigh and drumstick		2.11	12/94	2c
Hamburger with cheese	1/4 lb.	2.00	12/94	2c
Pizza, Pizza Hut or Pizza Inn	12-13 in.	7.99	12/94	2c
Transportation				
Transportation, ACCRA Index		88.70	12/94	2c
Tire balance, computer or spin bal., front	wheel	5.67	12/94	2c
Utilities				
Utilities, ACCRA Index		110.00	12/94	2c
Electricity, (part.), other, 1800 sq. ft., new home	mo.	88.98	12/94	2c

Helena, MT

Item	Per	Value	Date	Ref.
Composite, ACCRA index		109.20	12/94	2c
Alcoholic Beverages				
Beer, Miller Lite, Bud, 12-oz., ex deposit	6	3.80	12/94	2c
J & B Scotch	750-ml.	18.85	12/94	2c
Wine, Gallo Chablis blanc	1.5-lit	4.00	12/94	2c
Clothing				
Jeans, man's denim		33.00	12/94	2c
Shirt, man's dress shirt		27.25	12/94	2c
Undervest, boy's size 10-14, cotton	3	6.81	12/94	2c
Communications				
Newspaper subscription, dly. and Sun. delivery	month	13.04	12/94	2c
Telephone bill, family of four	month	18.22	12/94	2c
Energy and Fuels				
Energy, combined forms, 1800 sq. ft.	mo.	109.79	12/94	2c
Energy, exc. electricity, 1800 sq. ft.	mo.	66.19	12/94	2c
Gas, reg unlead, taxes inc., cash, self-service	gal	1.30	12/94	2c
Entertainment				
Bowling, evening rate	game	1.50	12/94	2c
Monopoly game, Parker Brothers', No. 9	game	10.05	12/94	2c
Movie	adm	5.25	12/94	2c
Tennis balls, yellow, Wilson or Penn, 3	can	2.13	12/94	2c
Groceries				
Groceries, ACCRA Index		111.20	12/94	2c
Baby food, strained vegetables, lowest price	4-4.5 oz.	0.42	12/94	2c
Bananas	lb.	0.56	12/94	2c
Beef or hamburger, ground	lb.	1.20	12/94	2c
Bread, white	24-oz.	1.05	12/94	2c
Cheese, Kraft grated Parmesan	8-oz.	3.67	12/94	2c
Chicken, whole fryer	lb.	0.86	12/94	2c
Cigarettes, Winston, Kings	carton	15.14	12/94	2c
Coffee, vacuum-packed	13 oz.	3.92	12/94	2c
Corn Flakes, Kellogg's or Post Toasties	18 oz.	2.64	12/94	2c
Corn, frozen, whole kernel, lowest price	10 oz.	0.67	12/94	2c

Helena, MT - continued

Item	Per	Value	Date	Ref.
Groceries - continued				
Eggs, Grade A large	dozen	0.77	12/94	2c
Lettuce, iceberg	head	1.11	12/94	2c
Margarine, Blue Bonnet or Parkay cubes	lb.	0.68	12/94	2c
Milk, whole	1/2 gal.	1.44	12/94	2c
Orange juice, Minute Maid frozen	12-oz.	1.27	12/94	2c
Peaches, halves or slices, Hunt's, Del Monte, or Libby's	29-oz.	1.42	12/94	2c
Peas, sweet, Del Monte or Green Giant	15-17 oz.	0.62	12/94	2c
Potatoes, white or red	10-lb. sack	2.04	12/94	2c
Sausage, Jimmy Dean, 100% pork	lb.	3.39	12/94	2c
Shortening, vegetable, Crisco	3-lb.	2.19	12/94	2c
Soft drink, Coca Cola, ex deposit	2 lit	1.33	12/94	2c
Steak, t-bone	lb.	4.50	12/94	2c
Sugar, cane or beet	4 lbs.	1.43	12/94	2c
Tomatoes, Hunt's or Del Monte	14.5 oz.	0.76	12/94	2c
Tuna, chunk, light, oil-packed	6.125-6.5 oz.	0.81	12/94	2c
Goods and Services				
Miscellaneous goods and services, ACCRA Index		100.70	12/94	2c
Health Care				
Health care, ACCRA Index		101.90	12/94	2c
Antibiotic ointment, Polysporin	1.5 oz.	4.40	12/94	2c
Dentist's fee, adult teeth cleaning and periodic oral exam	visit	58.00	12/94	2c
Doctor's fee, routine exam, established patient	visit	36.91	12/94	2c
Hospital care, semiprivate room	day	390.00	12/94	2c
Household Goods				
Appl. repair, service call, wash mach	min. lab. chg.	25.00	12/94	2c
Laundry detergent, Tide Ultra, Bold, or Cheer	42 oz.	3.70	12/94	2c
Tissues, facial, Kleenex brand	175	1.16	12/94	2c
Housing				
Housing, ACCRA Index		123.80	12/94	2c
House payment, principal and interest, 25% down payment	mo.	1019	12/94	2c
House, 1800 sq ft, 8000 sq ft lot, new, urban, utilities	total	160000	12/94	2c
Mtge. rate, incl. points and orig. fee, 30-year conv. fixed or ARM	mo.	9.62	12/94	2c
Rent, apartment, 2 br., 1 1/2-2 baths, unfurnished, 950 sq ft, water	mo.	450	12/94	2c
Personal Goods				
Shampoo, Alberto VO5	15-oz.	1.16	12/94	2c
Toothpaste, Crest or Colgate	6-7 oz.	1.82	12/94	2c
Personal Services				
Dry cleaning, man's 2-pc. suit		8.15	12/94	2c
Haircut, man's barbershop, no styling		8.75	12/94	2c
Haircut, woman's shampoo, trim, blow-dry		16.00	12/94	2c
Restaurant Food				
Chicken, fried, thigh and drumstick		2.30	12/94	2c
Hamburger with cheese	1/4 lb.	1.99	12/94	2c
Pizza, Pizza Hut or Pizza Inn	12-13 in.	9.00	12/94	2c
Transportation				
Transportation, ACCRA Index		107.40	12/94	2c
Tire balance, computer or spin bal., front	wheel	6.50	12/94	2c
Utilities				
Utilities, ACCRA Index		97.20	12/94	2c

Values are in dollars or fractions of dollars. In the column headed *Ref*, references are shown to sources. Each reference is followed by a letter. These refer to the geographical level for which data were reported: s = State, r = Region, and c = City or metro. The abbreviation *ex* is used to mean *except* or *excluding*; *exp* stands for *expenditures*. For other abbreviations and further explanations, please see the Introduction.

Helena, MT - continued

Item	Per	Value	Date	Ref.
Utilities				
Electricity, (part.), other, 1800 sq. ft., new home	mo.	43.60	12/94	2c

Hickory, NC

Item	Per	Value	Date	Ref.
Composite, ACCRA index		96.50	12/94	2c
Alcoholic Beverages				
Beer, Miller Lite, Bud, 12-oz., ex deposit	6	3.58	12/94	2c
J & B Scotch	750-ml.	18.60	12/94	2c
Wine, Gallo Chablis blanc	1.5-lit	4.39	12/94	2c
Appliances				
Appliances (major), expenditures	year	153	91	81r
Average annual exp.				
Food, health care, personal goods, services	year	27020	91	81r
Charity				
Cash contributions, expenditures	year	839	91	81r
Clothing				
Apparel, men and boys, total expenditures	year	380	91	81r
Apparel, women and girls, total expenditures	year	660	91	81r
Footwear, expenditures	year	193	91	81r
Jeans, man's denim		35.39	12/94	2c
Shirt, man's dress shirt		35.12	12/94	2c
Undervest, boy's size 10-14, cotton	3	3.06	12/94	2c
Communications				
Long-distance telephone rate, day, addl. min., 1-10 mi.	min.	0.10	12/93	9s
Long-distance telephone rate, day, initial min., 1-10 mi.	min.	0.16	12/93	9s
Newspaper subscription, dly. and Sun. delivery	month	9.75	12/94	2c
Phone line, single, business, field visit	inst	62.50	12/93	9s
Phone line, single, business, no field visit	inst	62.50	12/93	9s
Phone line, single, residence, field visit	inst	42.75	12/93	9s
Phone line, single, residence, no field visit	inst	42.75	12/93	9s
Telephone bill, family of four	month	17.45	12/94	2c
Telephone service, expenditures	year	616	91	81r
Education				
Board, 4-year private college/university	year	2069	8/94	80s
Board, 4-year public college/university	year	1627	8/94	80s
Education, total expenditures	year	319	91	81r
Room, 4-year private college/university	year	1824	8/94	80s
Room, 4-year public college/university	year	1669	8/94	80s
Total cost, 4-year private college/university	year	13505	8/94	80s
Total cost, 4-year public college/university	year	4704	8/94	80s
Tuition, 2-year public college/university, in-state	year	577	8/94	80s
Tuition, 4-year private college/university, in-state	year	9612	8/94	80s
Tuition, 4-year public college/university, in-state	year	1409	8/94	80s
Energy and Fuels				
Energy, combined forms, 1800 sq. ft.	mo.	112.27	12/94	2c
Fuel oil and other fuels, expenditures	year	56	91	81r
Gas, natural, expenditures	year	150	91	81r
Gas, reg unlead, taxes inc., cash, self-service	gal	1.15	12/94	2c
Gasoline and motor oil purchased	year	1152	91	81r
Gasoline, unleaded midgrade	gallon	1.21	4/93	82r
Gasoline, unleaded premium	gallon	1.30	4/93	82r
Gasoline, unleaded regular	gallon	1.10	4/93	82r
Entertainment				
Bowling, evening rate	game	2.95	12/94	2c
Concert ticket, Pearl Jam group	perf	20.00	94	50r
Entertainment, total expenditures	year	1266	91	81r
Fees and admissions, expenditures	year	306	91	81r
Monopoly game, Parker Brothers', No. 9	game	10.22	12/94	2c

Hickory, NC - continued

Item	Per	Value	Date	Ref.
Entertainment - continued				
Movie	adm	5.50	12/94	2c
Pets, toys, playground equipment, expenditures	year	271	91	81r
Reading, expenditures	year	131	91	81r
Televisions, radios, and sound equipment, expenditures	year	439	91	81r
Tennis balls, yellow, Wilson or Penn, 3	can	1.92	12/94	2c
Funerals				
Burial, immediate, container provided by funeral home		1370.36	1/95	54r
Cards, acknowledgment		14.83	1/95	54r
Casket, minimum alternative		192.52	1/95	54r
Cosmetology, hair care, etc.		102.27	1/95	54r
Cremation, direct, container provided by funeral home		1065.64	1/95	54r
Embalming		304.29	1/95	54r
Funeral, funeral home		287.83	1/95	54r
Funeral, other facility		284.14	1/95	54r
Graveside service		349.13	1/95	54r
Hearse, local		132.27	1/95	54r
Limousine, local		98.45	1/95	54r
Memorial service		270.59	1/95	54r
Service charge, professional, nondeclinable		933.59	1/95	54r
Visitation and viewing		225.83	1/95	54r
Groceries				
Groceries, ACCRA Index		95.80	12/94	2c
Apples, Red Delicious	lb.	0.73	12/94	82r
Baby food, strained vegetables, lowest price	4-4.5 oz.	0.34	12/94	2c
Bacon, sliced	lb.	1.67	12/94	82r
Bananas	lb.	0.55	12/94	2c
Bananas	lb.	0.42	12/94	82r
Beef or hamburger, ground	lb.	0.97	12/94	2c
Beef purchases	year	213	91	81r
Beverage purchases, alcoholic	year	249	91	81r
Beverage purchases, nonalcoholic	year	207	91	81r
Bologna, all beef or mixed	lb.	2.27	12/94	82r
Bread, white	24-oz.	0.69	12/94	2c
Bread, white, pan	lb.	0.68	12/94	82r
Cabbage	lb.	0.42	12/94	82r
Carrots, short trimmed and topped	lb.	0.53	12/94	82r
Cereals and bakery products purchases	year	345	91	81r
Cereals and cereals products purchases	year	127	91	81r
Cheddar cheese, natural	lb.	3.58	12/94	82r
Cheese, Kraft grated Parmesan	8-oz.	3.28	12/94	2c
Chicken breast, bone-in	lb.	1.71	12/94	82r
Chicken, fresh, whole	lb.	0.78	12/94	82r
Chicken, whole fryer	lb.	0.92	12/94	2c
Chuck roast, USDA choice, boneless	lb.	2.26	12/94	82r
Cigarettes, Winston, Kings	carton	13.08	12/94	2c
Coffee, vacuum-packed	13 oz.	2.83	12/94	2c
Corn Flakes, Kellogg's or Post Toasties	18 oz.	2.21	12/94	2c
Corn, frozen, whole kernel, lowest price	10 oz.	0.60	12/94	2c
Crackers, soda, salted	lb.	1.27	12/94	82r
Cucumbers	lb.	0.65	12/94	82r
Dairy products (other) purchases	year	141	91	81r
Eggs, Grade A large	dozen	0.87	12/94	2c
Eggs, Grade A large	dozen	0.87	12/94	82r
Fish and seafood purchases	year	72	91	81r
Flour, white, all purpose	lb.	0.23	12/94	82r
Food purchases, food eaten at home	year	2381	91	81r
Foods purchased away from home, not prepared by consumer	year	1696	91	81r
Frankfurters, all meat or all beef	lb.	1.74	12/94	82r
Fruits and vegetables purchases	year	380	91	81r
Grapefruit	lb.	0.45	12/94	82r
Grapes, Thompson seedless	lb.	2.30	12/94	82r
Ground beef, 100% beef	lb.	1.37	12/94	82r
Ground chuck, 100% beef	lb.	1.97	12/94	82r
Ham, boneless, exc. canned	lb.	2.54	12/94	82r

Values are in dollars or fractions of dollars. In the column headed *Ref*, references are shown to sources. Each reference is followed by a letter. These refer to the geographical level for which data were reported: s=State, r=Region, and c=City or metro. The abbreviation *ex* is used to mean *except* or *excluding*; *exp* stands for expenditures. For other abbreviations and further explanations, please see the Introduction.

Hickory, NC - continued

Item	Per	Value	Date	Ref.
Groceries				
Ice cream, prepackaged, bulk, regular	1/2 gal.	2.47	12/94	82r
Lemons	lb.	1.02	12/94	82r
Lettuce, iceberg	lb.	0.96	12/94	82r
Lettuce, iceberg	head	0.87	12/94	2c
Margarine, Blue Bonnet or Parkay cubes	lb.	0.51	12/94	2c
Margarine, stick	lb.	0.77	12/94	82r
Meats, poultry, fish, and eggs purchases	year	655	91	81r
Milk and cream (fresh) purchases	year	130	91	81r
Milk, whole	1/2 gal.	1.35	12/94	2c
Orange juice, frozen concentrate 12-oz. can	16 oz.	1.36	12/94	82r
Orange juice, Minute Maid frozen	12-oz.	1.15	12/94	2c
Oranges, Navel	lb.	0.54	12/94	82r
Peaches, halves or slices, Hunt's, Del Monte, or Libby's	29-oz.	1.31	12/94	2c
Pears, Anjou	lb.	0.81	12/94	82r
Peas, sweet, Del Monte or Green Giant	15-17 oz.	0.51	12/94	2c
Pork chops, center cut, bone-in	lb.	3.07	12/94	82r
Pork purchases	year	142	91	81r
Potato chips	16-oz.	3.15	12/94	82r
Potatoes, frozen, French fried	lb.	0.82	12/94	82r
Potatoes, white	lb.	0.34	12/94	82r
Potatoes, white or red	10-lb. sack	3.05	12/94	2c
Rice, white, long grain, uncooked	lb.	0.48	12/94	82r
Round roast, USDA choice, boneless	lb.	2.91	12/94	82r
Sausage, fresh	lb.	1.82	12/94	82r
Sausage, Jimmy Dean, 100% pork	lb.	2.35	12/94	2c
Shortening, vegetable oil blends	lb.	0.75	12/94	82r
Shortening, vegetable, Crisco	3-lb.	2.59	12/94	2c
Soft drink, Coca Cola, ex deposit	2 lit	1.01	12/94	2c
Spaghetti and macaroni	lb.	0.87	12/94	82r
Steak, rib eye, USDA choice, boneless	lb.	6.85	12/94	82r
Steak, round, graded & ungraded, exc. USDA prime & choice	lb.	2.96	12/94	82r
Steak, round, USDA choice, boneless	lb.	3.17	12/94	82r
Steak, sirloin, USDA choice, boneless	lb.	4.12	12/94	82r
Steak, t-bone	lb.	5.93	12/94	2c
Steak, T-bone, USDA choice, bone-in	lb.	5.63	12/94	82r
Sugar and other sweets, eaten at home, expenditures	year	93	91	81r
Sugar, cane or beet	4 lbs.	1.61	12/94	2c
Sugar, white, all sizes	lb.	0.39	12/94	82r
Tobacco products and smoking supplies, total expenditures	year	286	91	81r
Tomatoes, field grown	lb.	1.36	12/94	82r
Tomatoes, Hunt's or Del Monte	14.5 oz.	0.51	12/94	2c
Tuna, chunk, light	lb.	1.94	12/94	82r
Tuna, chunk, light, oil-packed	6.125-6.5 oz.	0.66	12/94	2c
Turkey, frozen, whole	lb.	0.96	12/94	82r
Yogurt, natural, fruit flavored	8 oz.	0.58	12/94	82r
Goods and Services				
Miscellaneous goods and services, ACCRA Index		103.10	12/94	2c
Health Care				
Health care, ACCRA Index		85.20	12/94	2c
Adenosine, emergency room	treat	100.00	95	23r
Antibiotic ointment, Polysporin	1.5 oz.	3.49	12/94	2c
Bladder tap, superpubic, infant, emergency room	treat	119.00	95	23r
Blood analysis, emergency room	treat	25.00	95	23r
Blood tests, abdominal pain, emergency room	treat	25.00	95	23r
Burn dressing, emergency room	treat	266.00	95	23r
Cardiology interpretation, emergency room	treat	26.00	95	23r
Chest X-ray, emergency room	treat	78.00	95	23r

Hickory, NC - continued

Item	Per	Value	Date	Ref.
Health Care - continued				
Childbirth, Cesarean delivery, hospital charge	birth	5462.00	12/91	69r
Childbirth, Cesarean delivery, physician charge	birth	2228.00	12/91	69r
Childbirth, normal delivery, hospital charge	birth	2943.00	12/91	69r
Childbirth, normal delivery, physician charge	birth	1619.00	12/91	69r
Defibrillation pads, emergency room	treat	6.00	95	23r
Dentist's fee, adult teeth cleaning and periodic oral exam	visit	42.40	12/94	2c
Doctor's fee, routine exam, established patient	visit	39.00	12/94	2c
Drugs, expenditures	year	297	91	81r
Gastric tube insertion, nasal, emergency room	treat	25.00	95	23r
Health care, total expenditures	year	1600	91	81r
Health insurance expenditures	year	637	91	81r
Heart monitor, emergency room	treat	40.00	95	23r
Hospital care, semiprivate room	day	280.00	12/94	2c
Insurance premium, family medical care	month	405.45	1/95	41s
Intravenous fluids, emergency room	treat	130.00	95	23r
Intravenous fluids, emergency room	liter	26.00	95	23r
Intravenous line, central, emergency room	treat	342.00	95	23r
Liver function tests, abdominal pain, emergency room	treat	26.00	95	23r
Medical care charges, total, emergency room, third-degree burns	treat	2101.00	95	23r
Medical care charges, total, emergency, infant with fever	treat	628.00	95	23r
Medical services expenditures	year	573	91	81r
Medical supplies expenditures	year	93	91	81r
Morphine, emergency room	treat	34.00	95	23r
Nursing care and facilities charges, emergency room	treat	252.00	95	23r
Nursing care and facilities charges, emergency, infant with fever	treat	252.00	95	23r
Nursing care and facilities charges, emergency, third-degree burns	treat	861.00	95	23r
Physician's charges, emergency, infant with fever	treat	212.00	95	23r
Physician's charges, emergency, third-degree burns	treat	372.00	95	23r
Physician's fee, emergency room	treat	372.00	95	23r
Physician's fee, general practitioner	visit	51.20	12/93	60r
Surgery, open-heart	proc	42374.00	1/93	14r
Ultrasound, abdominal, emergency room	treat	276.00	95	23r
Urinalysis, emergency room	treat	20.00	95	23r
Urinalysis, infant, emergency room	treat	20.00	95	23r
X-rays, emergency room	treat	78.00	95	23r
Household Goods				
Appl. repair, service call, wash mach	min. lab. chg.	40.50	12/94	2c
Floor coverings, expenditures	year	48	91	81r
Furniture, expenditures	year	280	91	81r
Household equipment, misc. expenditures	year	342	91	81r
Household expenditures, miscellaneous	year	256	91	81r
Household furnishings and equipment, expenditures	year	988	91	81r
Household operations expenditures	year	468	91	81r
Household textiles, expenditures	year	95	91	81r
Housekeeping supplies, expenditures	year	380	91	81r
Laundry and cleaning supplies, expenditures	year	109	91	81r
Laundry detergent, Tide Ultra, Bold, or Cheer	42 oz.	3.23	12/94	2c
Postage and stationery, expenditures	year	105	91	81r
Tissues, facial, Kleenex brand	175	0.99	12/94	2c
Housing				
Housing, ACCRA Index		91.80	12/94	2c
Add garage/carport		6,980	3/95	74r
Add room(s)		11,403	3/95	74r

Values are in dollars or fractions of dollars. In the column headed *Ref*, references are shown to sources. Each reference is followed by a letter. These refer to the geographical level for which data were reported: s=State, r=Region, and c=City or metro. The abbreviation *ex* is used to mean *except* or *excluding*; *exp* stands for expenditures. For other abbreviations and further explanations, please see the Introduction.

Hickory, NC - continued

Item	Per	Value	Date	Ref.
Housing				
Apartment condominium or co-op, median	unit	68600	12/94	62r
Dwellings (owned), expenditures	year	2428	91	81r
Enclose porch/patio/breezeway		4,572	3/95	74r
Finish room in basement/attic		3,794	3/95	74r
Home, existing, single-family, median	unit	120200	12/94	62r
House payment, principal and interest, 25% down payment	mo.	700	12/94	2c
House, 1800 sq ft, 8000 sq ft lot, new, urban, utilities	total	114250	12/94	2c
Maintenance, repairs, insurance, and other housing expenditures	year	531	91	81r
Mortgage interest and charges expenditures	year	1506	91	81r
Mtge. rate, incl. points and orig. fee, 30-year conv. fixed or ARM	mo.	9.18	12/94	2c
Princ. & int., mortgage, median-price exist. sing.-family home	mo.	540	12/94	62r
Property taxes expenditures	year	391	91	81r
Redesign, restructure more than half of home's interior		17,641	3/95	74r
Rent, apartment, 2 br., 1 1/2-2 baths, unfurnished, 950 sq ft, water	mo.	494	12/94	2c
Rental units expenditures	year	1264	91	81r
Insurance and Pensions				
Auto insurance, private passenger	year	528.43	12/94	71s
Insurance and pensions, personal, expenditures	year	2395	91	81r
Insurance, life and other personal, expenditures	year	368	91	81r
Pensions and Social Security, expenditures	year	2027	91	81r
Personal Goods				
Shampoo, Alberto VO5	15-oz.	1.04	12/94	2c
Toothpaste, Crest or Colgate	6-7 oz.	1.97	12/94	2c
Personal Services				
Dry cleaning, man's 2-pc. suit		5.71	12/94	2c
Haircut, man's barbershop, no styling		8.36	12/94	2c
Haircut, woman's shampoo, trim, blow-dry		18.74	12/94	2c
Personal services expenditures	year	212	91	81r
Restaurant Food				
Chicken, fried, thigh and drumstick		2.19	12/94	2c
Dining expenditures, family	week	33.83	94	73r
Hamburger with cheese	1/4 lb.	2.00	12/94	2c
Pizza, Pizza Hut or Pizza Inn	12-13 in.	7.95	12/94	2c
Taxes				
Taxes, Federal income, expenditures	year	2275	91	81r
Taxes, personal, expenditures	year	2715	91	81r
Taxes, State and local income, expenditures	year	365	91	81r
Transportation				
Transportation, ACCRA Index		93.30	12/94	2c
Cars and trucks purchased, new	year	1306	91	81r
Cars and trucks purchased, used	year	942	91	81r
Driver's learning permit fee	perm	10.00	1/94	84s
Driver's license fee	orig	10.00	1/94	84s
Driver's license fee, duplicate	lic	5.00	1/94	84s
Driver's license reinstatement fee, min.	susp	25.00		85s
Driver's license renewal fee	renew	10.00	1/94	84s
Fine, safety belt violation	ticket	25.00	95	56s
Identification card, nondriver	card	10.00	1/94	83s
Motorcycle license fee	orig	5.00	1/94	84s
Public transportation expenditures	year	249	91	81r
Tire balance, computer or spin bal., front	wheel	5.49	12/94	2c
Transportation expenditures, total	year	5307	91	81r
Vehicle finance charges	year	346	91	81r
Vehicle insurance expenditures	year	544	91	81r
Vehicle maintenance and repairs expenditures	year	600	91	81r
Vehicle purchases	year	2275	91	81r
Vehicle rental, leases, licenses, etc. expenditures	year	141	91	81r

Hickory, NC - continued

Item	Per	Value	Date	Ref.
Transportation - continued				
Vehicles purchased, other than cars and trucks	year	27	91	81r
Utilities				
Utilities, ACCRA Index		98.60	12/94	2c
Electricity expenditures	year	950	91	81r
Electricity, 1800 sq. ft., new home	mo.	112.27	12/94	2c
Utilities, fuels, and public services, total expenditures	year	2000	91	81r
Water and other public services, expenditures	year	227	91	81r
Weddings				
Bridal attendants' gowns	event	750	10/93	76r
Bridal gown	event	852	10/93	76r
Bridal headpiece and veil	event	167	10/93	76r
Bride's wedding band	event	708	10/93	76r
Clergy	event	224	10/93	76r
Engagement ring	event	2756	10/93	76r
Flowers	event	863	10/93	76r
Formal wear for groom	event	106	10/93	76r
Groom's attendants' formal wear	event	530	10/93	76r
Groom's wedding band	event	402	10/93	76r
Music	event	600	10/93	76r
Photography	event	1088	10/93	76r
Shoes for bride	event	50	10/93	76r
Videography	event	483	10/93	76r
Wedding invitations and announcements	event	342	10/93	76r
Wedding reception	event	7000	10/93	76r

Hilton Head Island, SC

Item	Per	Value	Date	Ref.
Composite, ACCRA index		112.70	12/94	2c
Alcoholic Beverages				
Beer, Miller Lite, Bud, 12-oz., ex deposit	6	3.89	12/94	2c
J & B Scotch	750-ml.	18.15	12/94	2c
Wine, Gallo Chablis blanc	1.5-lit	4.83	12/94	2c
Clothing				
Jeans, man's denim		33.70	12/94	2c
Shirt, man's dress shirt		31.40	12/94	2c
Undervest, boy's size 10-14, cotton	3	5.02	12/94	2c
Communications				
Newspaper subscription, dly. and Sun. delivery	month	7.25	12/94	2c
Telephone bill, family of four	month	14.40	12/94	2c
Energy and Fuels				
Energy, combined forms, 1800 sq. ft.	mo.	98.27	12/94	2c
Gas, reg unlead, taxes inc., cash, self-service	gal	1.12	12/94	2c
Entertainment				
Bowling, evening rate	game	2.75	12/94	2c
Monopoly game, Parker Brothers', No. 9	game	12.91	12/94	2c
Movie	adm	6.17	12/94	2c
Tennis balls, yellow, Wilson or Penn, 3	can	2.05	12/94	2c
Groceries				
Groceries, ACCRA Index		100.30	12/94	2c
Baby food, strained vegetables, lowest price	4-4.5 oz.	0.35	12/94	2c
Bananas	lb.	0.45	12/94	2c
Beef or hamburger, ground	lb.	1.93	12/94	2c
Bread, white	24-oz.	0.89	12/94	2c
Cheese, Kraft grated Parmesan	8-oz.	3.21	12/94	2c
Chicken, whole fryer	lb.	0.89	12/94	2c
Cigarettes, Winston, Kings	carton	13.35	12/94	2c
Coffee, vacuum-packed	13 oz.	3.13	12/94	2c
Corn Flakes, Kellogg's or Post Toasties	18 oz.	2.32	12/94	2c
Corn, frozen, whole kernel, lowest price	10 oz.	0.63	12/94	2c
Eggs, Grade A large	dozen	0.94	12/94	2c

Values are in dollars or fractions of dollars. In the column headed *Ref*, references are shown to sources. Each reference is followed by a letter. These refer to the geographical level for which data were reported: s = State, r = Region, and c = City or metro. The abbreviation *ex* is used to mean *except* or *excluding*; *exp* stands for expenditures. For other abbreviations and further explanations, please see the Introduction.

Hilton Head Island, SC - continued

Item	Per	Value	Date	Ref.
Groceries				
Lettuce, iceberg	head	0.97	12/94	2c
Margarine, Blue Bonnet or Parkay cubes	lb.	0.60	12/94	2c
Milk, whole	1/2 gal.	1.44	12/94	2c
Orange juice, Minute Maid frozen	12-oz.	1.27	12/94	2c
Peaches, halves or slices, Hunt's, Del Monte, or Libby's	29-oz.	1.27	12/94	2c
Peas, sweet, Del Monte or Green Giant	15-17 oz.	0.55	12/94	2c
Potatoes, white or red	10-lb. sack	1.99	12/94	2c
Sausage, Jimmy Dean, 100% pork	lb.	2.23	12/94	2c
Shortening, vegetable, Crisco	3-lb.	2.49	12/94	2c
Soft drink, Coca Cola, ex deposit	2 lit	1.03	12/94	2c
Steak, t-bone	lb.	5.65	12/94	2c
Sugar, cane or beet	4 lbs.	1.49	12/94	2c
Tomatoes, Hunt's or Del Monte	14.5 oz.	0.54	12/94	2c
Tuna, chunk, light, oil-packed	6.125-6.5 oz.	0.66	12/94	2c
Goods and Services				
Miscellaneous goods and services, ACCRA Index		105.10	12/94	2c
Health Care				
Health care, ACCRA Index		95.20	12/94	2c
Antibiotic ointment, Polysporin	1.5 oz.	3.84	12/94	2c
Dentist's fee, adult teeth cleaning and periodic oral exam	visit	53.00	12/94	2c
Doctor's fee, routine exam, established patient	visit	38.40	12/94	2c
Hospital care, semiprivate room	day	325.00	12/94	2c
Household Goods				
Appl. repair, service call, wash mach	min. lab. chg.	34.90	12/94	2c
Laundry detergent, Tide Ultra, Bold, or Cheer	42 oz.	3.15	12/94	2c
Tissues, facial, Kleenex brand	175	0.95	12/94	2c
Housing				
Housing, ACCRA Index		144.60	12/94	2c
House payment, principal and interest, 25% down payment	mo.	1149	12/94	2c
House, 1800 sq ft, 8000 sq ft lot, new, urban, utilities	total	185000	12/94	2c
Mtge. rate, incl. points and orig. fee, 30-year conv. fixed or ARM	mo.	9.32	12/94	2c
Rent, apartment, 2 br., 1 1/2-2 baths, unfurnished, 950 sq ft, water	mo.	645	12/94	2c
Personal Goods				
Shampoo, Alberto VO5	15-oz.	1.02	12/94	2c
Toothpaste, Crest or Colgate	6-7 oz.	1.92	12/94	2c
Personal Services				
Dry cleaning, man's 2-pc. suit		6.87	12/94	2c
Haircut, man's barbershop, no styling		10.00	12/94	2c
Haircut, woman's shampoo, trim, blow-dry		30.40	12/94	2c
Restaurant Food				
Chicken, fried, thigh and drumstick		2.25	12/94	2c
Hamburger with cheese	1/4 lb.	1.99	12/94	2c
Pizza, Pizza Hut or Pizza Inn	12-13 in.	7.99	12/94	2c
Transportation				
Transportation, ACCRA Index		99.40	12/94	2c
Tire balance, computer or spin bal., front	wheel	6.70	12/94	2c
Utilities				
Utilities, ACCRA Index		85.70	12/94	2c
Electricity, 1800 sq. ft., new home	mo.	98.27	12/94	2c

Hobbs, NM

Item	Per	Value	Date	Ref.
Composite, ACCRA index		92.10	12/94	2c
Alcoholic Beverages				
Beer, Miller Lite, Bud, 12-oz., ex deposit	6	4.09	12/94	2c
J & B Scotch	750-ml.	17.99	12/94	2c
Wine, Gallo Chablis blanc	1.5-lit	5.99	12/94	2c
Clothing				
Jeans, man's denim		23.99	12/94	2c
Shirt, man's dress shirt		28.99	12/94	2c
Undervest, boy's size 10-14, cotton	3	4.50	12/94	2c
Communications				
Newspaper subscription, dly. and Sun. delivery	month	6.75	12/94	2c
Telephone bill, family of four	month	21.24	12/94	2c
Energy and Fuels				
Energy, combined forms, 1800 sq. ft.	mo.	107.03	12/94	2c
Energy, exc. electricity, 1800 sq. ft.	mo.	31.86	12/94	2c
Gas, reg unlead, taxes inc., cash, self-service	gal	1.22	12/94	2c
Entertainment				
Bowling, evening rate	game	1.80	12/94	2c
Monopoly game, Parker Brothers', No. 9	game	9.98	12/94	2c
Movie	adm	5.00	12/94	2c
Tennis balls, yellow, Wilson or Penn, 3	can	2.19	12/94	2c
Groceries				
Groceries, ACCRA Index		105.50	12/94	2c
Baby food, strained vegetables, lowest price	4-4.5 oz.	0.36	12/94	2c
Bananas	lb.	0.49	12/94	2c
Beef or hamburger, ground	lb.	1.29	12/94	2c
Bread, white	24-oz.	0.79	12/94	2c
Cheese, Kraft grated Parmesan	8-oz.	3.96	12/94	2c
Chicken, whole fryer	lb.	0.60	12/94	2c
Cigarettes, Winston, Kings	carton	15.89	12/94	2c
Coffee, vacuum-packed	13 oz.	3.86	12/94	2c
Corn Flakes, Kellogg's or Post Toasties	18 oz.	2.74	12/94	2c
Corn, frozen, whole kernel, lowest price	10 oz.	0.74	12/94	2c
Eggs, Grade A large	dozen	0.81	12/94	2c
Lettuce, iceberg	head	0.79	12/94	2c
Margarine, Blue Bonnet or Parkay cubes	lb.	0.81	12/94	2c
Milk, whole	1/2 gal.	1.54	12/94	2c
Orange juice, Minute Maid frozen	12-oz.	1.07	12/94	2c
Peaches, halves or slices, Hunt's, Del Monte, or Libby's	29-oz.	1.58	12/94	2c
Peas, sweet, Del Monte or Green Giant	15-17 oz.	0.62	12/94	2c
Potatoes, white or red	10-lb. sack	1.36	12/94	2c
Sausage, Jimmy Dean, 100% pork	lb.	2.62	12/94	2c
Shortening, vegetable, Crisco	3-lb.	2.78	12/94	2c
Soft drink, Coca Cola, ex deposit	2 lit	1.36	12/94	2c
Steak, t-bone	lb.	4.16	12/94	2c
Sugar, cane or beet	4 lbs.	1.81	12/94	2c
Tomatoes, Hunt's or Del Monte	14.5 oz.	0.79	12/94	2c
Tuna, chunk, light, oil-packed	6.125-6.5 oz.	0.99	12/94	2c
Goods and Services				
Miscellaneous goods and services, ACCRA Index		95.70	12/94	2c
Health Care				
Health care, ACCRA Index		98.70	12/94	2c
Antibiotic ointment, Polysporin	1.5 oz.	3.73	12/94	2c
Dentist's fee, adult teeth cleaning and periodic oral exam	visit	46.00	12/94	2c
Doctor's fee, routine exam, established patient	visit	49.50	12/94	2c
Hospital care, semiprivate room	day	310.00	12/94	2c

Values are in dollars or fractions of dollars. In the column headed *Ref*, references are shown to sources. Each reference is followed by a letter. These refer to the geographical level for which data were reported: s = State, r = Region, and c = City or metro. The abbreviation *ex* is used to mean *except* or *excluding*; *exp* stands for expenditures. For other abbreviations and further explanations, please see the Introduction.

Hobbs, NM - continued

Item	Per	Value	Date	Ref.
Household Goods				
Appl. repair, service call, wash mach	min. lab. chg.	31.33	12/94	2c
Laundry detergent, Tide Ultra, Bold, or Cheer	42 oz.	4.19	12/94	2c
Tissues, facial, Kleenex brand	175	1.11	12/94	2c
Housing				
Housing, ACCRA Index		75.50	12/94	2c
House payment, principal and interest, 25% down payment	mo.	578	12/94	2c
House, 1800 sq ft, 8000 sq ft lot, new, urban, utilities	total	95400	12/94	2c
Mtge. rate, incl. points and orig. fee, 30-year conv. fixed or ARM	mo.	9.05	12/94	2c
Rent, apartment, 2 br., 1 1/2-2 baths, unfurnished, 950 sq ft, water	mo.	400	12/94	2c
Personal Goods				
Shampoo, Alberto VO5	15-oz.	1.12	12/94	2c
Toothpaste, Crest or Colgate	6-7 oz.	2.07	12/94	2c
Personal Services				
Dry cleaning, man's 2-pc. suit		5.97	12/94	2c
Haircut, man's barbershop, no styling		8.17	12/94	2c
Haircut, woman's shampoo, trim, blow-dry		19.00	12/94	2c
Restaurant Food				
Chicken, fried, thigh and drumstick		2.27	12/94	2c
Hamburger with cheese	1/4 lb.	2.09	12/94	2c
Pizza, Pizza Hut or Pizza Inn	12-13 in.	8.64	12/94	2c
Transportation				
Transportation, ACCRA Index		97.90	12/94	2c
Tire balance, computer or spin bal., front	wheel	5.67	12/94	2c
Utilities				
Utilities, ACCRA Index		97.20	12/94	2c
Electricity, (part.), other, 1800 sq. ft., new home	mo.	75.17	12/94	2c

Holland, MI

Item	Per	Value	Date	Ref.
Composite, ACCRA index		102.10	12/94	2c
Alcoholic Beverages				
Beer, Miller Lite, Bud, 12-oz., ex deposit	6	4.17	12/94	2c
J & B Scotch	750-ml.	20.32	12/94	2c
Wine, Gallo Chablis blanc	1.5-lit	5.64	12/94	2c
Clothing				
Jeans, man's denim		36.23	12/94	2c
Shirt, man's dress shirt		30.75	12/94	2c
Undervest, boy's size 10-14, cotton	3	3.25	12/94	2c
Communications				
Newspaper subscription, dly. and Sun. delivery	month	11.00	12/94	2c
Telephone bill, family of four	month	16.03	12/94	2c
Telephone, residential, flat rate	mo.	9.91	12/93	8c
Energy and Fuels				
Energy, combined forms, 1800 sq. ft.	mo.	91.09	12/94	2c
Energy, exc. electricity, 1800 sq. ft.	mo.	48.44	12/94	2c
Gas, cooking, 10 therms	month	11.79	2/94	65c
Gas, cooking, 30 therms	month	21.36	2/94	65c
Gas, cooking, 50 therms	month	30.94	2/94	65c
Gas, heating, winter, 100 therms	month	54.88	2/94	65c
Gas, heating, winter, average use	month	100.27	2/94	65c
Gas, reg unlead, taxes inc., cash, self-service	gal	1.09	12/94	2c
Entertainment				
Bowling, evening rate	game	2.25	12/94	2c
Monopoly game, Parker Brothers', No. 9	game	10.17	12/94	2c

Holland, MI - continued

Item	Per	Value	Date	Ref.
Entertainment - continued				
Movie	adm	5.88	12/94	2c
Tennis balls, yellow, Wilson or Penn, 3	can	2.05	12/94	2c
Groceries				
Groceries, ACCRA Index		108.20	12/94	2c
Baby food, strained vegetables, lowest price	4-4.5 oz.	0.43	12/94	2c
Bananas	lb.	0.46	12/94	2c
Beef or hamburger, ground	lb.	1.61	12/94	2c
Bread, white	24-oz.	0.91	12/94	2c
Cheese, Kraft grated Parmesan	8-oz.	3.37	12/94	2c
Chicken, whole fryer	lb.	0.99	12/94	2c
Cigarettes, Winston, Kings	carton	19.97	12/94	2c
Coffee, vacuum-packed	13 oz.	3.72	12/94	2c
Corn Flakes, Kellogg's or Post Toasties	18 oz.	2.45	12/94	2c
Corn, frozen, whole kernel, lowest price	10 oz.	0.70	12/94	2c
Eggs, Grade A large	dozen	0.70	12/94	2c
Lettuce, iceberg	head	0.81	12/94	2c
Margarine, Blue Bonnet or Parkay cubes	lb.	0.79	12/94	2c
Milk, whole	1/2 gal.	1.63	12/94	2c
Orange juice, Minute Maid frozen	12-oz.	1.29	12/94	2c
Peaches, halves or slices, Hunt's, Del Monte, or Libby's	29-oz.	1.39	12/94	2c
Peas, sweet, Del Monte or Green Giant	15-17 oz.	0.65	12/94	2c
Potatoes, white or red	10-lb. sack	1.67	12/94	2c
Sausage, Jimmy Dean, 100% pork	lb.	2.79	12/94	2c
Shortening, vegetable, Crisco	3-lb.	2.59	12/94	2c
Soft drink, Coca Cola, ex deposit	2 lit	1.09	12/94	2c
Steak, t-bone	lb.	4.93	12/94	2c
Sugar, cane or beet	4 lbs.	1.22	12/94	2c
Tomatoes, Hunt's or Del Monte	14.5 oz.	0.76	12/94	2c
Tuna, chunk, light, oil-packed	6.125-6.5 oz.	0.77	12/94	2c
Goods and Services				
Miscellaneous goods and services, ACCRA Index		100.90	12/94	2c
Health Care				
Health care, ACCRA Index		89.10	12/94	2c
Antibiotic ointment, Polysporin	1.5 oz.	4.10	12/94	2c
Dentist's fee, adult teeth cleaning and periodic oral exam	visit	50.00	12/94	2c
Doctor's fee, routine exam, established patient	visit	39.25	12/94	2c
Hospital care, semiprivate room	day	220.00	12/94	2c
Household Goods				
Appl. repair, service call, wash mach	min. lab. chg.	39.00	12/94	2c
Laundry detergent, Tide Ultra, Bold, or Cheer	42 oz.	3.06	12/94	2c
Tissues, facial, Kleenex brand	175	0.99	12/94	2c
Housing				
Housing, ACCRA Index		109.60	12/94	2c
House payment, principal and interest, 25% down payment	mo.	882	12/94	2c
House, 1800 sq ft, 8000 sq ft lot, new, urban, utilities	total	140698	12/94	2c
Mtge. rate, incl. points and orig. fee, 30-year conv. fixed or ARM	mo.	9.43	12/94	2c
Rent, apartment, 2 br., 1 1/2-2 baths, unfurnished, 950 sq ft, water	mo.	457	12/94	2c
Personal Goods				
Shampoo, Alberto VO5	15-oz.	0.91	12/94	2c
Toothpaste, Crest or Colgate	6-7 oz.	1.69	12/94	2c

Values are in dollars or fractions of dollars. In the column headed *Ref*, references are shown to sources. Each reference is followed by a letter. These refer to the geographical level for which data were reported: s = State, r = Region, and c = City or metro. The abbreviation *ex* is used to mean *except* or *excluding*; *exp* stands for expenditures. For other abbreviations and further explanations, please see the Introduction.

Holland, MI - continued

Item	Per	Value	Date	Ref.
Personal Services				
Dry cleaning, man's 2-pc. suit		7.21	12/94	2c
Haircut, man's barbershop, no styling		9.62	12/94	2c
Haircut, woman's shampoo, trim, blow-dry		16.10	12/94	2c
Restaurant Food				
Chicken, fried, thigh and drumstick		2.09	12/94	2c
Hamburger with cheese	1/4 lb.	1.86	12/94	2c
Pizza, Pizza Hut or Pizza Inn	12-13 in.	7.99	12/94	2c
Transportation				
Transportation, ACCRA Index		99.80	12/94	2c
Tire balance, computer or spin bal., front	wheel	7.04	12/94	2c
Utilities				
Utilities, ACCRA Index		81.30	12/94	2c
Electricity, (part.), other, 1800 sq. ft., new home	mo.	42.65	12/94	2c

Honolulu, HI

Item	Per	Value	Date	Ref.
Appliances				
Appliances (major), expenditures	year	317	91	81c
Appliances (major), expenditures	year	160	91	81r
Average annual exp.				
Food, health care, personal goods, services	year	36394	91	81c
Food, health care, personal goods, services	year	32461	91	81r
Charity				
Cash contributions, expenditures	year	1179	91	81c
Cash contributions, expenditures	year	975	91	81r
Clothing				
Apparel, men and boys, total expenditures	year	393	91	81c
Apparel, men and boys, total expenditures	year	467	91	81r
Apparel, women and girls, total expenditures	year	753	91	81c
Apparel, women and girls, total expenditures	year	737	91	81r
Footwear, expenditures	year	154	91	81c
Footwear, expenditures	year	270	91	81r
Communications				
Telephone service, expenditures	year	533	91	81c
Telephone service, expenditures	year	611	91	81r
Education				
Board, 4-year private college/university	year	2009	8/94	80s
Education, total expenditures	year	693	91	81c
Education, total expenditures	year	375	91	81r
Room, 4-year private college/university	year	2560	8/94	80s
Total cost, 4-year private college/university	year	10091	8/94	80s
Tuition, 2-year public college/university, in-state	year	479	8/94	80s
Tuition, 4-year private college/university, in-state	year	5522	8/94	80s
Tuition, 4-year public college/university, in-state	year	1455	8/94	80s
Energy and Fuels				
Fuel oil and other fuels, expenditures	year	6	91	81c
Fuel oil and other fuels, expenditures	year	33	91	81r
Gas, cooking, 10 therms	month	22.38	2/94	65c
Gas, cooking, 30 therms	month	55.14	2/94	65c
Gas, cooking, 50 therms	month	87.90	2/94	65c
Gas, heating, winter, 100 therms	month	169.80	2/94	65c
Gas, heating, winter, average use	month	32.86	2/94	65c
Gas, natural, expenditures	year	32	91	81c
Gas, natural, expenditures	year	212	91	81r
Gasoline and motor oil purchased	year	852	91	81c
Gasoline and motor oil purchased	year	1115	91	81r
Gasoline, unleaded midgrade	gallon	1.36	4/93	82r
Gasoline, unleaded premium	gallon	1.43	4/93	82r
Gasoline, unleaded regular	gallon	1.23	4/93	82r

Honolulu, HI - continued

Item	Per	Value	Date	Ref.
Entertainment				
Concert ticket, Pearl Jam group	perf	20.00	94	50r
Entertainment supplies, equipment, and services, misc. expenditures	year	320	91	81c
Entertainment, total expenditures	year	1618	91	81c
Entertainment, total expenditures	year	1853	91	81r
Fees and admissions, expenditures	year	470	91	81c
Fees and admissions, expenditures	year	482	91	81r
Pets, toys, playground equipment, expenditures	year	219	91	81c
Pets, toys, playground equipment, expenditures	year	299	91	81r
Reading, expenditures	year	209	91	81c
Reading, expenditures	year	164	91	81r
Televisions, radios, and sound equipment, expenditures	year	609	91	81c
Televisions, radios, and sound equipment, expenditures	year	528	91	81r
Funerals				
Burial, immediate, container provided by funeral home		1382.70	1/95	54r
Cards, acknowledgment		21.87	1/95	54r
Casket, minimum alternative		128.54	1/95	54r
Cosmetology, hair care, etc.		119.69	1/95	54r
Cremation, direct, container provided by funeral home		1030.62	1/95	54r
Embalming		255.42	1/95	54r
Funeral, funeral home		437.38	1/95	54r
Funeral, other facility		444.46	1/95	54r
Graveside service		338.46	1/95	54r
Hearse, local		147.50	1/95	54r
Limousine, local		130.33	1/95	54r
Memorial service		553.16	1/95	54r
Service charge, professional, nondeclinable		859.15	1/95	54r
Visitation and viewing		93.23	1/95	54r
Groceries				
Apples, Red Delicious	lb.	0.72	12/94	82r
Bacon, sliced	lb.	1.73	12/94	82r
Bananas	lb.	0.52	12/94	82r
Beef purchases	year	223	91	81c
Beef purchases	year	241	91	81r
Beverage purchases, alcoholic	year	470	91	81c
Beverage purchases, alcoholic	year	328	91	81r
Beverage purchases, nonalcoholic	year	220	91	81c
Beverage purchases, nonalcoholic	year	234	91	81r
Bologna, all beef or mixed	lb.	2.33	12/94	82r
Bread, white, pan	lb.	0.81	12/94	82r
Carrots, short trimmed and topped	lb.	0.43	12/94	82r
Cereals and bakery products purchases	year	451	91	81c
Cereals and bakery products purchases	year	392	91	81r
Cereals and cereal products purchases	year	148	91	81c
Cereals and cereals products purchases	year	139	91	81r
Chicken breast, bone-in	lb.	2.04	12/94	82r
Chicken, fresh, whole	lb.	0.95	12/94	82r
Coffee, 100%, ground roast, all sizes	lb.	4.48	12/94	82r
Dairy products (other) purchases	year	153	91	81c
Dairy products (other) purchases	year	182	91	81r
Fish and seafood purchases	year	254	91	81c
Fish and seafood purchases	year	94	91	81r
Flour, white, all purpose	lb.	0.21	12/94	82r
Food purchases, food eaten at home	year	3163	91	81c
Food purchases, food eaten at home	year	2749	91	81r
Foods purchased away from home, not prepared by consumer	year	2471	91	81c
Foods purchased away from home, not prepared by consumer	year	1909	91	81r
Fruits and vegetables purchases	year	611	91	81c
Fruits and vegetables purchases	year	459	91	81r
Grapefruit	lb.	0.56	12/94	82r
Ground beef, 100% beef	lb.	1.31	12/94	82r
Ham, boneless, exc. canned	lb.	2.46	12/94	82r

Values are in dollars or fractions of dollars. In the column headed *Ref*, references are shown to sources. Each reference is followed by a letter. These refer to the geographical level for which data were reported: s=State, r=Region, and c=City or metro. The abbreviation *ex* is used to mean *except* or *excluding*; *exp* stands for expenditures. For other abbreviations and further explanations, please see the Introduction.

Honolulu, HI - continued

Item	Per	Value	Date	Ref.
Groceries				
Ice cream, prepackaged, bulk, regular	1/2 gal.	2.57	12/94	82r
Lemons	lb.	1.00	12/94	82r
Lettuce, iceberg	lb.	0.93	12/94	82r
Meats, poultry, fish, and eggs purchases	year	875	91	81c
Meats, poultry, fish, and eggs purchases	year	700	91	81r
Milk and cream (fresh) purchases	year	117	91	81c
Milk and cream (fresh) purchases	year	155	91	81r
Orange juice, frozen concentrate 12-oz. can	16 oz.	1.52	12/94	82r
Oranges, Navel	lb.	0.56	12/94	82r
Pork chops, center cut, bone-in	lb.	3.30	12/94	82r
Pork purchases	year	117	91	81c
Pork purchases	year	122	91	81r
Potato chips	16-oz.	3.03	12/94	82r
Potatoes, frozen, French fried	lb.	0.77	12/94	82r
Potatoes, white	lb.	0.35	12/94	82r
Rice, white, long grain, uncooked	lb.	0.54	12/94	82r
Round roast, USDA choice, boneless	lb.	2.92	12/94	82r
Shortening, vegetable oil blends	lb.	0.80	12/94	82r
Spaghetti and macaroni	lb.	1.02	12/94	82r
Steak, round, graded & ungraded, exc. USDA prime & choice	lb.	3.13	12/94	82r
Steak, sirloin, USDA choice, boneless	lb.	4.07	12/94	82r
Sugar and other sweets, eaten at home, expenditures	year	105	91	81r
Sugar and other sweets, eaten at home, purchases	year	112	91	81c
Sugar, white, all sizes	lb.	0.38	12/94	82r
Tobacco products and smoking supplies, total expenditures	year	181	91	81c
Tobacco products and smoking supplies, total expenditures	year	221	91	81r
Tomatoes, field grown	lb.	1.45	12/94	82r
Tuna, chunk, light	lb.	2.18	12/94	82r
Health Care				
Childbirth, Cesarean delivery, hospital charge	birth	6059.00	12/91	69r
Childbirth, Cesarean delivery, physician charge	birth	2248.00	12/91	69r
Childbirth, normal delivery, hospital charge	birth	3006.00	12/91	69r
Childbirth, normal delivery, physician charge	birth	1634.00	12/91	69r
Drugs, expenditures	year	217	91	81c
Drugs, expenditures	year	230	91	81r
Health care, total expenditures	year	1623	91	81c
Health care, total expenditures	year	1544	91	81r
Health insurance expenditures	year	701	91	81c
Health insurance expenditures	year	558	91	81r
Immunization, DTP, measles, mumps, rubella, polio	inject	137.00	8/93	90c
Insurance premium, family medical care	month	366.26	1/95	41s
Medical services expenditures	year	585	91	81c
Medical services expenditures	year	676	91	81r
Medical supplies expenditures	year	120	91	81c
Medical supplies expenditures	year	80	91	81r
Surgery, open-heart	proc	37818.00	1/93	14r
Household Goods				
Floor coverings, expenditures	year	43	91	81c
Floor coverings, expenditures	year	79	91	81r
Furniture, expenditures	year	311	91	81c
Furniture, expenditures	year	352	91	81r
Household equipment, misc. expenditures	year	614	91	81r
Household equipment, misc., expenditures	year	601	91	81c
Household expenditures, miscellaneous	year	338	91	81c
Household expenditures, miscellaneous	year	294	91	81r
Household furnishings and equipment, expenditures	year	1451	91	81c
Household furnishings and equipment, expenditures	year	1416	91	81r
Household operations expenditures	year	552	91	81c
Household operations expenditures	year	580	91	81r
Household textiles, expenditures	year	86	91	81c

Honolulu, HI - continued

Item	Per	Value	Date	Ref.
Household Goods - continued				
Household textiles, expenditures	year	113	91	81r
Housekeeping supplies, expenditures	year	488	91	81c
Housekeeping supplies, expenditures	year	447	91	81r
Laundry and cleaning supplies, expenditures	year	124	91	81c
Laundry and cleaning supplies, expenditures	year	114	91	81r
Postage and stationery, expenditures	year	169	91	81c
Postage and stationery, expenditures	year	145	91	81r
Housing				
Add garage/carport		6,422	3/95	74r
Add room(s)		26,583	3/95	74r
Apartment condominium or co-op, median	unit	105300	12/94	62r
Dwellings (owned), expenditures	year	3744	91	81c
Dwellings (owned), expenditures	year	3932	91	81r
Enclose porch/patio/breezeway		5,382	3/95	74r
Finish room in basement/attic		3,911	3/95	74r
Home, existing, single-family, median	unit	178600	12/94	62r
Home, existing, single-family, median	unit	357.00	12/94	62c
Home, purchase price	unit	327.70	3/93	26c
Maintenance, repairs, insurance, and other housing expenditures	year	429	91	81c
Maintenance, repairs, insurance, and other housing expenditures	year	591	91	81r
Mortgage interest and charges expenditures	year	2741	91	81c
Mortgage interest and charges expenditures	year	2747	91	81r
Princ. & int., mortgage, median-price exist. sing.-family home	mo.	845	12/94	62r
Property taxes expenditures	year	573	91	81c
Property taxes expenditures	year	594	91	81r
Redesign, restructure more than half of home's interior		5,467	3/95	74r
Rental units expenditures	year	3369	900/00/ 91	81c
Rental units expenditures	year	2077	91	81r
Insurance and Pensions				
Auto insurance, private passenger	year	1078.32	12/94	71s
Insurance and pensions, personal, expenditures	year	3459	91	81c
Insurance and pensions, personal, expenditures	year	3042	91	81r
Insurance, life and other personal, expenditures	year	581	91	81c
Insurance, life and other personal, expenditures	year	298	91	81r
Pensions and Social Security, expenditures	year	2878	91	81c
Pensions and Social Security, expenditures	year	2744	91	81r
Legal Assistance				
Legal work, law firm associate	hour	91		10r
Legal work, law firm partner	hour	151		10r
Personal Goods				
Personal care products and services, total expenditures	year	498	91	81c
Personal Services				
Personal services expenditures	year	215	91	81c
Personal services expenditures	year	286	91	81r
Restaurant Food				
Dining expenditures, family	week	32.25	94	73r
Taxes				
Tax rate, residential property, month	$100	0.30	1/92	79c
Taxes, Federal income, expenditures	year	2704	91	81c
Taxes, Federal income, expenditures	year	2946	91	81r
Taxes, personal, expenditures	year	3705	91	81c
Taxes, personal, expenditures	year	3791	91	81r
Taxes, State and local income, expenditures	year	939	91	81c
Taxes, State and local income, expenditures	year	791	91	81r

Values are in dollars or fractions of dollars. In the column headed *Ref*, references are shown to sources. Each reference is followed by a letter. These refer to the geographical level for which data were reported: s=State, r=Region, and c=City or metro. The abbreviation *ex* is used to mean *except* or *excluding*; *exp* stands for *expenditures*. For other abbreviations and further explanations, please see the Introduction.

Honolulu, HI - continued

Item	Per	Value	Date	Ref.
Transportation				
Bus fare, one-way	trip	0.85	12/95	1c
Cars and trucks purchased, new	year	1380	91	81c
Cars and trucks purchased, new	year	1231	91	81r
Cars and trucks purchased, used	year	1140	91	81c
Cars and trucks purchased, used	year	915	91	81r
Driver's learning permit fee	perm	3.00-5.00	1/94	84s
Driver's license fee	orig	5.25-12.00	1/94	84s
Driver's license fee, duplicate	lic	3.00-6.00	1/94	84s
Driver's license reinstatement fee, min.	susp	18.00	1/94	85s
Driver's license renewal fee	renew	5.25-12.00	1/94	84s
Identification card, nondriver	card	10.00	1/94	83s
Motorcycle learning permit fee	perm	3.00-5.00	1/94	84s
Motorcycle license fee	orig	5.25-12.00	1/94	84s
Motorcycle license fee, duplicate	lic	3.00-6.00	1/94	84s
Motorcycle license renewal fee	renew	5.25-12.00	1/94	84s
Public transportation expenditures	year	859	91	81c
Public transportation expenditures	year	375	91	81r
Transportation expenditures, total	year	6052	91	81c
Transportation expenditures, total	year	5527	91	81r
Vehicle expenses, miscellaneous	year	1818	91	81c
Vehicle finance charges	year	263	91	81c
Vehicle finance charges	year	287	91	81r
Vehicle insurance expenditures	year	668	91	81c
Vehicle insurance expenditures	year	624	91	81r
Vehicle maintenance and repairs expenditures	year	659	91	81c
Vehicle maintenance and repairs expenditures	year	695	91	81r
Vehicle purchases	year	2523	91	81c
Vehicle purchases	year	2174	91	81r
Vehicle rental, leases, licenses, etc. expenditures	year	228	91	81c
Vehicle rental, leases, licenses, etc. expenditures	year	257	91	81r
Vehicles purchased, other than cars and trucks	year	3	91	81c
Vehicles purchased, other than cars and trucks	year	28	91	81r
Utilities				
Electricity expenditures	year	543	91	81c
Electricity expenditures	year	616	91	81r
Electricity, summer, 250 KWh	month	34.64	8/93	64c
Electricity, summer, 500 KWh	month	62.24	8/93	64c
Electricity, summer, 750 KWh	month	89.83	8/93	64c
Electricity, summer, 1000 KWh	month	117.42	8/93	64c
Utilities, fuels, and public services, total expenditures	year	1272	91	81c
Utilities, fuels, and public services, total expenditures	year	1681	91	81r
Water and other public services, expenditures	year	159	91	81c
Water and other public services, expenditures	year	209	91	81r
Weddings				
Bridal attendants' gowns	event	750	10/93	76r
Bridal gown	event	852	10/93	76r
Bridal headpiece and veil	event	167	10/93	76r
Bride's wedding band	event	708	10/93	76r
Clergy	event	224	10/93	76r
Engagement ring	event	2756	10/93	76r
Flowers	event	863	10/93	76r
Formal wear for groom	event	106	10/93	76r
Groom's attendants' formal wear	event	530	10/93	76r
Groom's wedding band	event	402	10/93	76r
Music	event	600	10/93	76r
Photography	event	1088	10/93	76r
Shoes for bride	event	50	10/93	76r

Honolulu, HI - continued

Item	Per	Value	Date	Ref.
Weddings - continued				
Videography	event	483	10/93	76r
Wedding invitations and announcements	event	342	10/93	76r
Wedding reception	event	7000	10/93	76r

Hopkinsville, KY

Item	Per	Value	Date	Ref.
Composite, ACCRA index		94.00	12/94	2c
Alcoholic Beverages				
Beer, Miller Lite, Bud, 12-oz., ex deposit	6	3.98	12/94	2c
J & B Scotch	750-ml.	19.70	12/94	2c
Wine, Gallo Chablis blanc	1.5-lit	6.46	12/94	2c
Clothing				
Jeans, man's denim		31.31	12/94	2c
Shirt, man's dress shirt		34.50	12/94	2c
Undervest, boy's size 10-14, cotton	3	3.39	12/94	2c
Communications				
Newspaper subscription, dly. and Sun. delivery	month	14.25	12/94	2c
Telephone bill, family of four	month	20.16	12/94	2c
Telephone, residential, flat rate	mo.	12.69	12/93	8c
Energy and Fuels				
Energy, combined forms, 1800 sq. ft.	mo.	85.53	12/94	2c
Energy, exc. electricity, 1800 sq. ft.	mo.	37.37	12/94	2c
Gas, reg unlead, taxes inc., cash, self-service	gal	1.01	12/94	2c
Entertainment				
Bowling, evening rate	game	1.75	12/94	2c
Monopoly game, Parker Brothers', No. 9	game	13.29	12/94	2c
Movie	adm	5.50	12/94	2c
Tennis balls, yellow, Wilson or Penn, 3	can	2.85	12/94	2c
Groceries				
Groceries, ACCRA Index		106.60	12/94	2c
Baby food, strained vegetables, lowest price	4-4.5 oz.	0.34	12/94	2c
Bananas	lb.	0.41	12/94	2c
Beef or hamburger, ground	lb.	1.51	12/94	2c
Bread, white	24-oz.	1.26	12/94	2c
Cheese, Kraft grated Parmesan	8-oz.	3.24	12/94	2c
Chicken, whole fryer	lb.	0.85	12/94	2c
Cigarettes, Winston, Kings	carton	12.95	12/94	2c
Coffee, vacuum-packed	13 oz.	4.00	12/94	2c
Corn Flakes, Kellogg's or Post Toasties	18 oz.	2.08	12/94	2c
Corn, frozen, whole kernel, lowest price	10 oz.	0.78	12/94	2c
Eggs, Grade A large	dozen	0.82	12/94	2c
Lettuce, iceberg	head	0.99	12/94	2c
Margarine, Blue Bonnet or Parkay cubes	lb.	0.56	12/94	2c
Milk, whole	1/2 gal.	1.36	12/94	2c
Orange juice, Minute Maid frozen	12-oz.	1.25	12/94	2c
Peaches, halves or slices, Hunt's, Del Monte, or Libby's	29-oz.	1.27	12/94	2c
Peas, sweet, Del Monte or Green Giant	15-17 oz.	0.56	12/94	2c
Potatoes, white or red	10-lb. sack	2.87	12/94	2c
Sausage, Jimmy Dean, 100% pork	lb.	2.23	12/94	2c
Shortening, vegetable, Crisco	3-lb.	2.45	12/94	2c
Soft drink, Coca Cola, ex deposit	2 lit	1.10	12/94	2c
Steak, t-bone	lb.	5.08	12/94	2c
Sugar, cane or beet	4 lbs.	1.60	12/94	2c
Tomatoes, Hunt's or Del Monte	14.5 oz.	0.78	12/94	2c
Tuna, chunk, light, oil-packed	6.125-6.5 oz.	0.76	12/94	2c
Goods and Services				
Miscellaneous goods and services, ACCRA Index		101.10	12/94	2c

Values are in dollars or fractions of dollars. In the column headed *Ref*, references are shown to sources. Each reference is followed by a letter. These refer to the geographical level for which data were reported: s=State, r=Region, and c=City or metro. The abbreviation *ex* is used to mean *except* or *excluding*; *exp* stands for expenditures. For other abbreviations and further explanations, please see the Introduction.

Hopkinsville, KY - continued

Item	Per	Value	Date	Ref.
Health Care				
Health care, ACCRA Index		84.80	12/94	2c
Antibiotic ointment, Polysporin	1.5 oz.	4.46	12/94	2c
Dentist's fee, adult teeth cleaning and periodic oral exam	visit	42.40	12/94	2c
Doctor's fee, routine exam, established patient	visit	37.20	12/94	2c
Hospital care, semiprivate room	day	250.00	12/94	2c
Household Goods				
Appl. repair, service call, wash mach	min. lab. chg.	38.00	12/94	2c
Laundry detergent, Tide Ultra, Bold, or Cheer	42 oz.	3.67	12/94	2c
Tissues, facial, Kleenex brand	175	1.11	12/94	2c
Housing				
Housing, ACCRA Index		86.60	12/94	2c
House payment, principal and interest, 25% down payment	mo.	696	12/94	2c
House, 1800 sq ft, 8000 sq ft lot, new, urban, utilities	total	111472	12/94	2c
Mtge. rate, incl. points and orig. fee, 30-year conv. fixed or ARM	mo.	9.38	12/94	2c
Rent, apartment, 2 br., 1 1/2-2 baths, unfurnished, 950 sq ft, water	mo.	365	12/94	2c
Personal Goods				
Shampoo, Alberto VO5	15-oz.	1.10	12/94	2c
Toothpaste, Crest or Colgate	6-7 oz.	2.31	12/94	2c
Personal Services				
Dry cleaning, man's 2-pc. suit		5.52	12/94	2c
Haircut, man's barbershop, no styling		7.60	12/94	2c
Haircut, woman's shampoo, trim, blow-dry		19.59	12/94	2c
Restaurant Food				
Chicken, fried, thigh and drumstick		1.84	12/94	2c
Hamburger with cheese	1/4 lb.	1.89	12/94	2c
Pizza, Pizza Hut or Pizza Inn	12-13 in.	6.24	12/94	2c
Transportation				
Transportation, ACCRA Index		87.00	12/94	2c
Tire balance, computer or spin bal., front	wheel	5.60	12/94	2c
Utilities				
Utilities, ACCRA Index		79.90	12/94	2c
Electricity, (part.), other, 1800 sq. ft., new home	mo.	48.16	12/94	2c

Hot Springs, AR

Item	Per	Value	Date	Ref.
Composite, ACCRA index		91.50	12/94	2c
Alcoholic Beverages				
Beer, Miller Lite, Bud, 12-oz., ex deposit	6	3.83	12/94	2c
J & B Scotch	750-ml.	17.90	12/94	2c
Wine, Gallo Chablis blanc	1.5-lit	5.29	12/94	2c
Clothing				
Jeans, man's denim		28.99	12/94	2c
Shirt, man's dress shirt		25.50	12/94	2c
Undervest, boy's size 10-14, cotton	3	4.49	12/94	2c
Communications				
Newspaper subscription, dly. and Sun. delivery	month	8.50	12/94	2c
Telephone bill, family of four	month	19.61	12/94	2c
Telephone, residential, flat rate	mo.	13.91	12/93	8c
Energy and Fuels				
Energy, combined forms, 1800 sq. ft.	mo.	123.46	12/94	2c
Gas, reg unlead, taxes inc., cash, self-service	gal	1.10	12/94	2c

Hot Springs, AR - continued

Item	Per	Value	Date	Ref.
Entertainment				
Bowling, evening rate	game	1.50	12/94	2c
Monopoly game, Parker Brothers', No. 9	game	9.66	12/94	2c
Movie	adm	5.00	12/94	2c
Tennis balls, yellow, Wilson or Penn, 3	can	1.91	12/94	2c
Groceries				
Groceries, ACCRA Index		99.50	12/94	2c
Baby food, strained vegetables, lowest price	4-4.5 oz.	0.30	12/94	2c
Bananas	lb.	0.49	12/94	2c
Beef or hamburger, ground	lb.	1.49	12/94	2c
Bread, white	24-oz.	0.72	12/94	2c
Cheese, Kraft grated Parmesan	8-oz.	3.49	12/94	2c
Chicken, whole fryer	lb.	0.81	12/94	2c
Cigarettes, Winston, Kings	carton	17.04	12/94	2c
Coffee, vacuum-packed	13 oz.	3.77	12/94	2c
Corn Flakes, Kellogg's or Post Toasties	18 oz.	2.06	12/94	2c
Corn, frozen, whole kernel, lowest price	10 oz.	0.84	12/94	2c
Eggs, Grade A large	dozen	0.73	12/94	2c
Lettuce, iceberg	head	0.86	12/94	2c
Margarine, Blue Bonnet or Parkay cubes	lb.	0.55	12/94	2c
Milk, whole	1/2 gal.	1.52	12/94	2c
Orange juice, Minute Maid frozen	12-oz.	0.98	12/94	2c
Peaches, halves or slices, Hunt's, Del Monte, or Libby's	29-oz.	1.34	12/94	2c
Peas, sweet, Del Monte or Green Giant	15-17 oz.	0.59	12/94	2c
Potatoes, white or red	10-lb. sack	1.97	12/94	2c
Sausage, Jimmy Dean, 100% pork	lb.	2.24	12/94	2c
Shortening, vegetable, Crisco	3-lb.	2.42	12/94	2c
Soft drink, Coca Cola, ex deposit	2 lit	1.34	12/94	2c
Steak, t-bone	lb.	5.28	12/94	2c
Sugar, cane or beet	4 lbs.	1.63	12/94	2c
Tomatoes, Hunt's or Del Monte	14.5 oz.	0.76	12/94	2c
Tuna, chunk, light, oil-packed	6.125-6.5 oz.	0.56	12/94	2c
Goods and Services				
Miscellaneous goods and services, ACCRA Index		94.00	12/94	2c
Health Care				
Health care, ACCRA Index		79.60	12/94	2c
Antibiotic ointment, Polysporin	1.5 oz.	3.88	12/94	2c
Dentist's fee, adult teeth cleaning and periodic oral exam	visit	39.00	12/94	2c
Doctor's fee, routine exam, established patient	visit	38.00	12/94	2c
Hospital care, semiprivate room	day	210.00	12/94	2c
Household Goods				
Appl. repair, service call, wash mach	min. lab. chg.	30.00	12/94	2c
Laundry detergent, Tide Ultra, Bold, or Cheer	42 oz.	4.17	12/94	2c
Tissues, facial, Kleenex brand	175	1.03	12/94	2c
Housing				
Housing, ACCRA Index		80.30	12/94	2c
Home, vacation	unit	128800	1/93	27c
House payment, principal and interest, 25% down payment	mo.	607	12/94	2c
House, 1800 sq ft, 8000 sq ft lot, new, urban, utilities	total	97333	12/94	2c
Mtge. rate, incl. points and orig. fee, 30-year conv. fixed or ARM	mo.	9.36	12/94	2c
Rent, apartment, 2 br., 1 1/2-2 baths, unfurnished, 950 sq ft, water	mo.	450	12/94	2c

Values are in dollars or fractions of dollars. In the column headed *Ref*, references are shown to sources. Each reference is followed by a letter. These refer to the geographical level for which data were reported: s=State, r=Region, and c=City or metro. The abbreviation *ex* is used to mean *except* or *excluding*; *exp* stands for expenditures. For other abbreviations and further explanations, please see the Introduction.

Hot Springs, AR - continued

Item	Per	Value	Date	Ref.
Personal Goods				
Shampoo, Alberto VO5	15-oz.	1.15	12/94	2c
Toothpaste, Crest or Colgate	6-7 oz.	1.68	12/94	2c
Personal Services				
Dry cleaning, man's 2-pc. suit		4.47	12/94	2c
Haircut, man's barbershop, no styling		8.00	12/94	2c
Haircut, woman's shampoo, trim, blow-dry		20.00	12/94	2c
Restaurant Food				
Chicken, fried, thigh and drumstick		2.39	12/94	2c
Hamburger with cheese	1/4 lb.	1.90	12/94	2c
Pizza, Pizza Hut or Pizza Inn	12-13 in.	8.99	12/94	2c
Transportation				
Transportation, ACCRA Index		95.50	12/94	2c
Tire balance, computer or spin bal., front	wheel	6.25	12/94	2c
Utilities				
Utilities, ACCRA Index		108.70	12/94	2c
Electricity, 1800 sq. ft., new home	mo.	123.46	12/94	2c

Houma-Thibodaux, LA

Item	Per	Value	Date	Ref.
Appliances				
Appliances (major), expenditures	year	153	91	81r
Average annual exp.				
Food, health care, personal goods, services	year	27020	91	81r
Charity				
Cash contributions, expenditures	year	839	91	81r
Clothing				
Apparel, men and boys, total expenditures	year	380	91	81r
Apparel, women and girls, total expenditures	year	660	91	81r
Footwear, expenditures	year	193	91	81r
Communications				
Long-distance telephone rate, day, addl. min., 1-10 mi.	min.	0.29	12/93	9s
Long-distance telephone rate, day, initial min., 1-10 mi.	min.	0.41	12/93	9s
Phone line, single, business, field visit	inst	85.00	12/93	9s
Phone line, single, business, no field visit	inst	85.00	12/93	9s
Phone line, single, residence, field visit	inst	50.00	12/93	9s
Phone line, single, residence, no field visit	inst	50.00	12/93	9s
Telephone service, expenditures	year	616	91	81r
Education				
Board, 4-year private college/university	year	2436	8/94	80s
Board, 4-year public college/university	year	1638	8/94	80s
Education, total expenditures	year	319	91	81r
Room, 4-year private college/university	year	2558	8/94	80s
Room, 4-year public college/university	year	1405	8/94	80s
Total cost, 4-year private college/university	year	16467	8/94	80s
Total cost, 4-year public college/university	year	5225	8/94	80s
Tuition, 2-year public college/university, in-state	year	956	8/94	80s
Tuition, 4-year private college/university, in-state	year	11473	8/94	80s
Tuition, 4-year public college/university, in-state	year	2182	8/94	80s
Energy and Fuels				
Fuel oil and other fuels, expenditures	year	56	91	81r
Gas, natural, expenditures	year	150	91	81r
Gasoline and motor oil purchased	year	1152	91	81r
Gasoline, unleaded midgrade	gallon	1.21	4/93	82r
Gasoline, unleaded premium	gallon	1.30	4/93	82r
Gasoline, unleaded regular	gallon	1.10	4/93	82r
Entertainment				
Concert ticket, Pearl Jam group	perf	20.00	94	50r
Entertainment, total expenditures	year	1266	91	81r
Fees and admissions, expenditures	year	306	91	81r

Houma-Thibodaux, LA - continued

Item	Per	Value	Date	Ref.
Entertainment - continued				
Pets, toys, playground equipment, expenditures	year	271	91	81r
Reading, expenditures	year	131	91	81r
Televisions, radios, and sound equipment, expenditures	year	439	91	81r
Funerals				
Burial, immediate, container provided by funeral home		1574.60	1/95	54r
Cards, acknowledgment		22.24	1/95	54r
Casket, minimum alternative		239.41	1/95	54r
Cosmetology, hair care, etc.		91.04	1/95	54r
Cremation, direct, container provided by funeral home		1085.15	1/95	54r
Embalming		281.30	1/95	54r
Funeral, funeral home		323.04	1/95	54r
Funeral, other facility		327.58	1/95	54r
Graveside service		355.19	1/95	54r
Hearse, local		141.89	1/95	54r
Limousine, local		99.40	1/95	54r
Memorial service		284.67	1/95	54r
Service charge, professional, nondeclinable		904.06	1/95	54r
Visitation and viewing		187.04	1/95	54r
Groceries				
Apples, Red Delicious	lb.	0.73	12/94	82r
Bacon, sliced	lb.	1.67	12/94	82r
Bananas	lb.	0.42	12/94	82r
Beef purchases	year	213	91	81r
Beverage purchases, alcoholic	year	249	91	81r
Beverage purchases, nonalcoholic	year	207	91	81r
Bologna, all beef or mixed	lb.	2.27	12/94	82r
Bread, white, pan	lb.	0.68	12/94	82r
Cabbage	lb.	0.42	12/94	82r
Carrots, short trimmed and topped	lb.	0.53	12/94	82r
Cereals and bakery products purchases	year	345	91	81r
Cereals and cereals products purchases	year	127	91	81r
Cheddar cheese, natural	lb.	3.58	12/94	82r
Chicken breast, bone-in	lb.	1.71	12/94	82r
Chicken, fresh, whole	lb.	0.78	12/94	82r
Chuck roast, USDA choice, boneless	lb.	2.26	12/94	82r
Crackers, soda, salted	lb.	1.27	12/94	82r
Cucumbers	lb.	0.65	12/94	82r
Dairy products (other) purchases	year	141	91	81r
Eggs, Grade A large	dozen	0.87	12/94	82r
Fish and seafood purchases	year	72	91	81r
Flour, white, all purpose	lb.	0.23	12/94	82r
Food purchases, food eaten at home	year	2381	91	81r
Foods purchased away from home, not prepared by consumer	year	1696	91	81r
Frankfurters, all meat or all beef	lb.	1.74	12/94	82r
Fruits and vegetables purchases	year	380	91	81r
Grapefruit	lb.	0.45	12/94	82r
Grapes, Thompson seedless	lb.	2.30	12/94	82r
Ground beef, 100% beef	lb.	1.37	12/94	82r
Ground chuck, 100% beef	lb.	1.97	12/94	82r
Ham, boneless, exc. canned	lb.	2.54	12/94	82r
Ice cream, prepackaged, bulk, regular	1/2 gal.	2.47	12/94	82r
Lemons	lb.	1.02	12/94	82r
Lettuce, iceberg	lb.	0.96	12/94	82r
Margarine, stick	lb.	0.77	12/94	82r
Meats, poultry, fish, and eggs purchases	year	655	91	81r
Milk and cream (fresh) purchases	year	130	91	81r
Orange juice, frozen concentrate 12-oz. can	16 oz.	1.36	12/94	82r
Oranges, Navel	lb.	0.54	12/94	82r
Pears, Anjou	lb.	0.81	12/94	82r
Pork chops, center cut, bone-in	lb.	3.07	12/94	82r
Pork purchases	year	142	91	81r
Potato chips	16-oz.	3.15	12/94	82r
Potatoes, frozen, French fried	lb.	0.82	12/94	82r
Potatoes, white	lb.	0.34	12/94	82r
Rice, white, long grain, uncooked	lb.	0.48	12/94	82r

Values are in dollars or fractions of dollars. In the column headed *Ref*, references are shown to sources. Each reference is followed by a letter. These refer to the geographical level for which data were reported: s=State, r=Region, and c=City or metro. The abbreviation *ex* is used to mean *except* or *excluding*; *exp* stands for expenditures. For other abbreviations and further explanations, please see the Introduction.

Houma-Thibodaux, LA - continued

Item	Per	Value	Date	Ref.
Groceries				
Round roast, USDA choice, boneless	lb.	2.91	12/94	82r
Sausage, fresh	lb.	1.82	12/94	82r
Shortening, vegetable oil blends	lb.	0.75	12/94	82r
Spaghetti and macaroni	lb.	0.87	12/94	82r
Steak, rib eye, USDA choice, boneless	lb.	6.85	12/94	82r
Steak, round, graded & ungraded, exc. USDA prime & choice	lb.	2.96	12/94	82r
Steak, round, USDA choice, boneless	lb.	3.17	12/94	82r
Steak, sirloin, USDA choice, boneless	lb.	4.12	12/94	82r
Steak, T-bone, USDA choice, bone-in	lb.	5.63	12/94	82r
Sugar and other sweets, eaten at home, expenditures	year	93	91	81r
Sugar, white, all sizes	lb.	0.39	12/94	82r
Tobacco products and smoking supplies, total expenditures	year	286	91	81r
Tomatoes, field grown	lb.	1.36	12/94	82r
Tuna, chunk, light	lb.	1.94	12/94	82r
Turkey, frozen, whole	lb.	0.96	12/94	82r
Yogurt, natural, fruit flavored	8 oz.	0.58	12/94	82r
Health Care				
Adenosine, emergency room	treat	100.00	95	23r
Bladder tap, superpubic, infant, emergency room	treat	119.00	95	23r
Blood analysis, emergency room	treat	25.00	95	23r
Blood tests, abdominal pain, emergency room	treat	25.00	95	23r
Burn dressing, emergency room	treat	266.00	95	23r
Cardiology interpretation, emergency room	treat	26.00	95	23r
Chest X-ray, emergency room	treat	78.00	95	23r
Childbirth, Cesarean delivery, hospital charge	birth	5462.00	12/91	69r
Childbirth, Cesarean delivery, physician charge	birth	2228.00	12/91	69r
Childbirth, normal delivery, hospital charge	birth	2943.00	12/91	69r
Childbirth, normal delivery, physician charge	birth	1619.00	12/91	69r
Defibrillation pads, emergency room	treat	6.00	95	23r
Drugs, expenditures	year	297	91	81r
Gastric tube insertion, nasal, emergency room	treat	25.00	95	23r
Health care, total expenditures	year	1600	91	81r
Health insurance expenditures	year	637	91	81r
Heart monitor, emergency room	treat	40.00	95	23r
Insurance premium, family medical care	month	394.31	1/95	41s
Intravenous fluids, emergency room	treat	130.00	95	23r
Intravenous fluids, emergency room	liter	26.00	95	23r
Intravenous line, central, emergency room	treat	342.00	95	23r
Liver function tests, abdominal pain, emergency room	treat	26.00	95	23r
Medical care charges, total, emergency room, third-degree burns	treat	2101.00	95	23r
Medical care charges, total, emergency, infant with fever	treat	628.00	95	23r
Medical services expenditures	year	573	91	81r
Medical supplies expenditures	year	93	91	81r
Morphine, emergency room	treat	34.00	95	23r
Nursing care and facilities charges, emergency room	treat	252.00	95	23r
Nursing care and facilities charges, emergency, infant with fever	treat	252.00	95	23r
Nursing care and facilities charges, emergency, third-degree burns	treat	861.00	95	23r
Physician's charges, emergency, infant with fever	treat	212.00	95	23r
Physician's charges, emergency, third-degree burns	treat	372.00	95	23r
Physician's fee, emergency room	treat	372.00	95	23r
Physician's fee, general practitioner	visit	51.20	12/93	60r
Surgery, open-heart	proc	42374.00	1/93	14r
Ultrasound, abdominal, emergency room	treat	276.00	95	23r
Urinalysis, emergency room	treat	20.00	95	23r
Urinalysis, infant, emergency room	treat	20.00	95	23r
X-rays, emergency room	treat	78.00	95	23r

Houma-Thibodaux, LA - continued

Item	Per	Value	Date	Ref.
Household Goods				
Floor coverings, expenditures	year	48	91	81r
Furniture, expenditures	year	280	91	81r
Household equipment, misc. expenditures	year	342	91	81r
Household expenditures, miscellaneous	year	256	91	81r
Household furnishings and equipment, expenditures	year	988	91	81r
Household operations expenditures	year	468	91	81r
Household textiles, expenditures	year	95	91	81r
Housekeeping supplies, expenditures	year	380	91	81r
Laundry and cleaning supplies, expenditures	year	109	91	81r
Postage and stationery, expenditures	year	105	91	81r
Housing				
Add garage/carport		6,980	3/95	74r
Add room(s)		11,403	3/95	74r
Apartment condominium or co-op, median	unit	68600	12/94	62r
Dwellings (owned), expenditures	year	2428	91	81r
Enclose porch/patio/breezeway		4,572	3/95	74r
Finish room in basement/attic		3,794	3/95	74r
Home, existing, single-family, median	unit	120200	12/94	62r
Maintenance, repairs, insurance, and other housing expenditures	year	531	91	81r
Mortgage interest and charges expenditures	year	1506	91	81r
Princ. & int., mortgage, median-price exist. sing.-family home	mo.	540	12/94	62r
Property taxes expenditures	year	391	91	81r
Redesign, restructure more than half of home's interior		17,641	3/95	74r
Rental units expenditures	year	1264	91	81r
Insurance and Pensions				
Auto insurance, private passenger	year	862.62	12/94	71s
Insurance and pensions, personal, expenditures	year	2395	91	81r
Insurance, life and other personal, expenditures	year	368	91	81r
Pensions and Social Security, expenditures	year	2027	91	81r
Personal Services				
Personal services expenditures	year	212	91	81r
Restaurant Food				
Dining expenditures, family	week	33.83	94	73r
Taxes				
Taxes, Federal income, expenditures	year	2275	91	81r
Taxes, personal, expenditures	year	2715	91	81r
Taxes, State and local income, expenditures	year	365	91	81r
Transportation				
Cars and trucks purchased, new	year	1306	91	81r
Cars and trucks purchased, used	year	942	91	81r
Driver's learning permit fee	perm	12.50	1/94	84s
Driver's license fee	orig	12.50	1/94	84s
Driver's license fee, duplicate	lic	5.00	1/94	84s
Driver's license reinstatement fee, min.	susp	60.00	1/94	85s
Driver's license renewal fee	renew	12.50	1/94	84s
Identification card, nondriver	card	7.00	1/94	83s
Motorcycle license fee	orig	8.00	1/94	84s
Motorcycle license renewal fee	renew	8.00	1/94	84s
Public transportation expenditures	year	249	91	81r
Transportation expenditures, total	year	5307	91	81r
Vehicle finance charges	year	346	91	81r
Vehicle insurance expenditures	year	544	91	81r
Vehicle maintenance and repairs expenditures	year	600	91	81r
Vehicle purchases	year	2275	91	81r
Vehicle rental, leases, licenses, etc. expenditures	year	141	91	81r
Vehicles purchased, other than cars and trucks	year	27	91	81r

Values are in dollars or fractions of dollars. In the column headed *Ref*, references are shown to sources. Each reference is followed by a letter. These refer to the geographical level for which data were reported: s = State, r = Region, and c = City or metro. The abbreviation *ex* is used to mean *except* or *excluding*; *exp* stands for *expenditures*. For other abbreviations and further explanations, please see the Introduction.

Houma-Thibodaux, LA - continued

Item	Per	Value	Date	Ref.
Utilities				
Electricity expenditures	year	950	91	81r
Utilities, fuels, and public services, total expenditures	year	2000	91	81r
Water and other public services, expenditures	year	227	91	81r
Weddings				
Bridal attendants' gowns	event	750	10/93	76r
Bridal gown	event	852	10/93	76r
Bridal headpiece and veil	event	167	10/93	76r
Bride's wedding band	event	708	10/93	76r
Clergy	event	224	10/93	76r
Engagement ring	event	2756	10/93	76r
Flowers	event	863	10/93	76r
Formal wear for groom	event	106	10/93	76r
Groom's attendants' formal wear	event	530	10/93	76r
Groom's wedding band	event	402	10/93	76r
Music	event	600	10/93	76r
Photography	event	1088	10/93	76r
Shoes for bride	event	50	10/93	76r
Videography	event	483	10/93	76r
Wedding invitations and announcements	event	342	10/93	76r
Wedding reception	event	7000	10/93	76r

Houston, TX

Item	Per	Value	Date	Ref.
Composite, ACCRA index		97.00	12/94	2c
Alcoholic Beverages				
Beer	bottle	2.50	94	36c
Beer, Miller Lite, Bud, 12-oz., ex deposit	6	3.97	12/94	2c
J & B Scotch	750-ml.	16.02	12/94	2c
Wine, Gallo Chablis blanc	1.5-lit	4.85	12/94	2c
Appliances				
Appliances (major), expenditures	year	152	91	81c
Appliances (major), expenditures	year	153	91	81r
Average annual exp.				
Food, health care, personal goods, services	year	32298	91	81c
Food, health care, personal goods, services	year	27020	91	81r
Business				
Dinner and tip, hotel, corporate rate	night	40.00	2/94	15c
Hotel room, corporate rate	night	83.00	2/94	15c
Charity				
Cash contributions, expenditures	year	1004	91	81c
Cash contributions, expenditures	year	839	91	81r
Clothing				
Apparel, men and boys, total expenditures	year	507	91	81c
Apparel, men and boys, total expenditures	year	380	91	81r
Apparel, women and girls, total expenditures	year	763	91	81c
Apparel, women and girls, total expenditures	year	660	91	81r
Footwear, expenditures	year	276	91	81c
Footwear, expenditures	year	193	91	81r
Jeans, man's denim		26.78	12/94	2c
Shirt, dress, men's	shirt	35.00	1/92	44c
Shirt, man's dress shirt		28.50	12/94	2c
Undervest, boy's size 10-14, cotton	3	4.89	12/94	2c
Communications				
Long-distance telephone rate, day, addl. min., 1-10 mi.	min.	0.08	12/93	9s
Long-distance telephone rate, day, initial min., 1-10 mi.	min.	0.10	12/93	9s
Newspaper subscription, dly. and Sun. delivery	month	9.00	12/94	2c
Phone line, single, business, field visit	inst	71.90	12/93	9s
Phone line, single, business, no field visit	inst	57.30	12/93	9s
Phone line, single, residence, field visit	inst	52.95	12/93	9s
Phone line, single, residence, no field visit	inst	38.35	12/93	9s
Telephone bill, family of four	month	17.48	12/94	2c

Houston, TX - continued

Item	Per	Value	Date	Ref.
Communications - continued				
Telephone service, expenditures	year	686	91	81c
Telephone service, expenditures	year	616	91	81r
Telephone, business, addl. line, touch tone	month	1.75	10/91	25c
Telephone, business, connection charges, touch tone	inst	73.67	10/91	25c
Telephone, business, key system line, touch tone	month	43.69	10/91	25c
Telephone, business, PBX line, touch tone	month	45.37	10/91	25c
Telephone, business, single ln., touch tone	month	38.14	10/91	25c
Telephone, business, touch tone, inside wiring maintenance plan	month	2.25	10/91	25c
Telephone, residential, flat rate	mo.	11.05	12/93	8c
Education				
Board, 4-year private college/university	year	2084	8/94	80s
Board, 4-year public college/university	year	1675	8/94	80s
Education, total expenditures	year	269	91	81c
Education, total expenditures	year	319	91	81r
Room, 4-year private college/university	year	1840	8/94	80s
Room, 4-year public college/university	year	1756	8/94	80s
Total cost, 4-year private college/university	year	11876	8/94	80s
Total cost, 4-year public college/university	year	4935	8/94	80s
Tuition, 2-year public college/university, in-state	year	625	8/94	80s
Tuition, 4-year private college/university, in-state	year	7952	8/94	80s
Tuition, 4-year public college/university, in-state	year	1503	8/94	80s
Energy and Fuels				
Electricity	500 KWh	43.77	12/94	82c
Energy, combined forms, 1800 sq. ft.	mo.	113.82	12/94	2c
Energy, exc. electricity, 1800 sq. ft.	mo.	24.17	12/94	2c
Fuel oil and other fuels, expenditures	year	11	91	81c
Fuel oil and other fuels, expenditures	year	56	91	81r
Gas	gal.	1.15	1/92	44c
Gas, cooking, winter, 10 therms	month	14.10	2/94	65c
Gas, cooking, winter, 30 therms	month	23.10	2/94	65c
Gas, cooking, winter, 50 therms	month	32.12	2/94	65c
Gas, heating, winter, 100 therms	month	54.62	2/94	65c
Gas, heating, winter, average use	month	57.83	2/94	65c
Gas, natural, expenditures	year	186	91	81c
Gas, natural, expenditures	year	150	91	81r
Gas, piped	40 therms	25.41	12/94	82c
Gas, piped	100 therms	48.99	12/94	82c
Gas, piped	therm	0.59	12/94	82c
Gas, reg unlead, taxes inc., cash, self-service	gal	1.06	12/94	2c
Gasoline and motor oil purchased	year	1237	91	81c
Gasoline and motor oil purchased	year	1152	91	81r
Gasoline, unleaded midgrade	gallon	1.24	4/93	82c
Gasoline, unleaded midgrade	gallon	1.21	4/93	82r
Gasoline, unleaded premium	gallon	1.30	4/93	82c
Gasoline, unleaded premium	gallon	1.30	4/93	82r
Gasoline, unleaded regular	gallon	1.10	4/93	82c
Gasoline, unleaded regular	gallon	1.10	4/93	82r
Entertainment				
Bowling, evening rate	game	2.39	12/94	2c
Concert ticket, Pearl Jam group	perf	20.00	94	50r
Entertainment supplies, equipment, and services, misc. expenditures	year	310	91	81c
Entertainment, total expenditures	year	1587	91	81c
Entertainment, total expenditures	year	1266	91	81r
Fees and admissions, expenditures	year	513	91	81c
Fees and admissions, expenditures	year	306	91	81r
Monopoly game, Parker Brothers', No. 9	game	12.03	12/94	2c
Movie	adm	6.06	12/94	2c
Movie ticket, adult	ticket	6.00	1/92	44c
Pets, toys, playground equipment, expenditures	year	313	91	81c

Values are in dollars or fractions of dollars. In the column headed *Ref*, references are shown to sources. Each reference is followed by a letter. These refer to the geographical level for which data were reported: s = State, r = Region, and c = City or metro. The abbreviation *ex* is used to mean *except* or *excluding*; *exp* stands for expenditures. For other abbreviations and further explanations, please see the Introduction.

Houston, TX - continued

Item	Per	Value	Date	Ref.
Entertainment				
Pets, toys, playground equipment, expenditures	year	271	91	81r
Reading, expenditures	year	159	91	81c
Reading, expenditures	year	131	91	81r
Televisions, radios, and sound equipment, expenditures	year	452	91	81c
Televisions, radios, and sound equipment, expenditures	year	439	91	81r
Tennis balls, yellow, Wilson or Penn, 3	can	2.29	12/94	2c
Funerals				
Burial, immediate, container provided by funeral home		1574.60	1/95	54r
Cards, acknowledgment		22.24	1/95	54r
Casket, minimum alternative		239.41	1/95	54r
Cosmetology, hair care, etc.		91.04	1/95	54r
Cremation, direct, container provided by funeral home		1085.15	1/95	54r
Embalming		281.30	1/95	54r
Funeral, funeral home		323.04	1/95	54r
Funeral, other facility		327.58	1/95	54r
Graveside service		355.19	1/95	54r
Hearse, local		141.89	1/95	54r
Limousine, local		99.40	1/95	54r
Memorial service		284.67	1/95	54r
Service charge, professional, nondeclinable		904.06	1/95	54r
Visitation and viewing		187.04	1/95	54r
Groceries				
Groceries, ACCRA Index		95.70	12/94	2c
Apples, Red Delicious	lb.	0.73	12/94	82r
Baby food, strained vegetables, lowest price	4-4.5 oz.	0.23	12/94	2c
Bacon, sliced	lb.	1.67	12/94	82r
Bananas	lb.	0.40	12/94	2c
Bananas	lb.	0.42	12/94	82r
Beef or hamburger, ground	lb.	1.48	12/94	2c
Beef purchases	year	237	91	81c
Beef purchases	year	213	91	81r
Beverage purchases, alcoholic	year	330	91	81c
Beverage purchases, alcoholic	year	249	91	81r
Beverage purchases, nonalcoholic	year	237	91	81c
Beverage purchases, nonalcoholic	year	207	91	81r
Big Mac hamburger	burger	2.11	94	36c
Bologna, all beef or mixed	lb.	2.27	12/94	82r
Bread, white	24-oz.	0.63	12/94	2c
Bread, white, pan	lb.	0.68	12/94	82r
Cabbage	lb.	0.42	12/94	82r
Carrots, short trimmed and topped	lb.	0.53	12/94	82r
Cereals and bakery products purchases	year	375	91	81c
Cereals and bakery products purchases	year	345	91	81r
Cereals and cereal products purchases	year	135	91	81c
Cereals and cereals products purchases	year	127	91	81r
Cheddar cheese, natural	lb.	3.58	12/94	82r
Cheese, Kraft grated Parmesan	8-oz.	3.28	12/94	2c
Chicken breast, bone-in	lb.	1.71	12/94	82r
Chicken, fresh, whole	lb.	0.78	12/94	82r
Chicken, whole fryer	lb.	0.81	12/94	2c
Chuck roast, USDA choice, boneless	lb.	2.26	12/94	82r
Cigarettes, Winston, Kings	carton	17.17	12/94	2c
Coffee, vacuum-packed	13 oz.	3.47	12/94	2c
Corn Flakes, Kellogg's or Post Toasties	18 oz.	2.34	12/94	2c
Corn, frozen, whole kernel, lowest price	10 oz.	0.73	12/94	2c
Crackers, soda, salted	lb.	1.27	12/94	82r
Cucumbers	lb.	0.65	12/94	82r
Dairy products (other) purchases	year	147	91	81c
Dairy products (other) purchases	year	141	91	81r
Eggs, Grade A large	dozen	0.78	12/94	2c
Eggs, Grade A large	dozen	0.87	12/94	82r
Fish and seafood purchases	year	76	91	81c
Fish and seafood purchases	year	72	91	81r
Flour, white, all purpose	lb.	0.23	12/94	82r
Food purchases, food eaten at home	year	2629	91	81c

Houston, TX - continued

Item	Per	Value	Date	Ref.
Groceries - continued				
Food purchases, food eaten at home	year	2381	91	81r
Foods purchased away from home, not prepared by consumer	year	2051	91	81c
Foods purchased away from home, not prepared by consumer	year	1696	91	81r
Frankfurters, all meat or all beef	lb.	1.74	12/94	82r
Fruits and vegetables purchases	year	399	91	81c
Fruits and vegetables purchases	year	380	91	81r
Grapefruit	lb.	0.45	12/94	82r
Grapes, Thompson seedless	lb.	2.30	12/94	82r
Ground beef, 100% beef	lb.	1.37	12/94	82r
Ground chuck, 100% beef	lb.	1.97	12/94	82r
Ham, boneless, exc. canned	lb.	2.54	12/94	82r
Ice cream, prepackaged, bulk, regular	1/2 gal.	2.47	12/94	82r
Lemons	lb.	1.02	12/94	82r
Lettuce, iceberg	lb.	0.96	12/94	82r
Lettuce, iceberg	head	0.99	12/94	2c
Margarine, Blue Bonnet or Parkay cubes	lb.	0.69	12/94	2c
Margarine, stick	lb.	0.77	12/94	82r
Meats, poultry, fish, and eggs purchases	year	737	91	81c
Meats, poultry, fish, and eggs purchases	year	655	91	81r
Milk and cream (fresh) purchases	year	124	91	81c
Milk and cream (fresh) purchases	year	130	91	81r
Milk, 2%	gal.	2.49	1/92	44c
Milk, whole	1/2 gal.	1.41	12/94	2c
Orange juice, frozen concentrate 12-oz. can	16 oz.	1.36	12/94	82r
Orange juice, Minute Maid frozen	12-oz.	1.35	12/94	2c
Oranges, Navel	lb.	0.54	12/94	82r
Peaches, halves or slices, Hunt's, Del Monte, or Libby's	29-oz.	1.37	12/94	2c
Pears, Anjou	lb.	0.81	12/94	82r
Peas, sweet, Del Monte or Green Giant	15-17 oz.	0.57	12/94	2c
Pork chops, center cut, bone-in	lb.	3.07	12/94	82r
Pork purchases	year	161	91	81c
Pork purchases	year	142	91	81r
Potato chips	16-oz.	3.15	12/94	82r
Potatoes, frozen, French fried	lb.	0.82	12/94	82r
Potatoes, white	lb.	0.34	12/94	82r
Potatoes, white or red	10-lb. sack	2.31	12/94	2c
Rental rate, 2-bedroom apartment	month	575.00	1/92	44c
Rice, white, long grain, uncooked	lb.	0.48	12/94	82r
Round roast, USDA choice, boneless	lb.	2.91	12/94	82r
Sausage, fresh	lb.	1.82	12/94	82r
Sausage, Jimmy Dean, 100% pork	lb.	2.23	12/94	2c
Shortening, vegetable oil blends	lb.	0.75	12/94	82r
Shortening, vegetable, Crisco	3-lb.	2.42	12/94	2c
Soft drink, Coca Cola, ex deposit	2 lit	0.97	12/94	2c
Spaghetti and macaroni	lb.	0.87	12/94	82r
Steak, rib eye, USDA choice, boneless	lb.	6.85	12/94	82r
Steak, round, graded & ungraded, exc. USDA prime & choice	lb.	2.96	12/94	82r
Steak, round, USDA choice, boneless	lb.	3.17	12/94	82r
Steak, sirloin, USDA choice, boneless	lb.	4.12	12/94	82r
Steak, t-bone	lb.	5.37	12/94	2c
Steak, T-bone, USDA choice, bone-in	lb.	5.63	12/94	82r
Sugar and other sweets, eaten at home, expenditures	year	93	91	81r
Sugar and other sweets, eaten at home, purchases	year	97	91	81c
Sugar, cane or beet	4 lbs.	1.23	12/94	2c
Sugar, white, all sizes	lb.	0.39	12/94	82r
Tobacco products and smoking supplies, total expenditures	year	309	91	81c
Tobacco products and smoking supplies, total expenditures	year	286	91	81r
Tomatoes, field grown	lb.	1.36	12/94	82r
Tomatoes, Hunt's or Del Monte	14.5 oz.	0.63	12/94	2c

Values are in dollars or fractions of dollars. In the column headed *Ref*, references are shown to sources. Each reference is followed by a letter. These refer to the geographical level for which data were reported: s = State, r = Region, and c = City or metro. The abbreviation *ex* is used to mean *except* or *excluding*; *exp* stands for expenditures. For other abbreviations and further explanations, please see the Introduction.

Houston, TX - continued

Item	Per	Value	Date	Ref.
Groceries				
Tuna, chunk, light	lb.	1.94	12/94	82r
Tuna, chunk, light, oil-packed	6.125-6.5 oz.	0.68	12/94	2c
Turkey, frozen, whole	lb.	0.96	12/94	82r
Yogurt, natural, fruit flavored	8 oz.	0.58	12/94	82r
Goods and Services				
Miscellaneous goods and services, ACCRA Index		98.00	12/94	2c
Health Care				
Health care, ACCRA Index		104.20	12/94	2c
Adenosine, emergency room	treat	100.00	95	23r
Antibiotic ointment, Polysporin	1.5 oz.	4.55	12/94	2c
Bladder tap, superpubic, infant, emergency room	treat	119.00	95	23r
Blood analysis, emergency room	treat	25.00	95	23r
Blood tests, abdominal pain, emergency room	treat	25.00	95	23r
Burn dressing, emergency room	treat	266.00	95	23r
Cardiology interpretation, emergency room	treat	26.00	95	23r
Chest X-ray, emergency room	treat	78.00	95	23r
Childbirth, Cesarean delivery, hospital charge	birth	5462.00	12/91	69r
Childbirth, Cesarean delivery, physician charge	birth	2228.00	12/91	69r
Childbirth, normal delivery, hospital charge	birth	2943.00	12/91	69r
Childbirth, normal delivery, physician charge	birth	1619.00	12/91	69r
Defibrillation pads, emergency room	treat	6.00	95	23r
Dentist's fee, adult teeth cleaning and periodic oral exam	visit	56.58	12/94	2c
Doctor's fee, routine exam, established patient	visit	42.27	12/94	2c
Drugs, expenditures	year	224	91	81c
Drugs, expenditures	year	297	91	81r
Gastric tube insertion, nasal, emergency room	treat	25.00	95	23r
Health care, total expenditures	year	1458	91	81c
Health care, total expenditures	year	1600	91	81r
Health insurance expenditures	year	545	91	81c
Health insurance expenditures	year	637	91	81r
Heart monitor, emergency room	treat	40.00	95	23r
Hospital care, semiprivate room	day	356.00	12/94	2c
Hospital cost	adm	6,984	2/94	72c
Insurance premium, family medical care	month	389.25	1/95	41s
Intravenous fluids, emergency room	treat	130.00	95	23r
Intravenous fluids, emergency room	liter	26.00	95	23r
Intravenous line, central, emergency room	treat	342.00	95	23r
Liver function tests, abdominal pain, emergency room	treat	26.00	95	23r
Medical care charges, total, emergency room, third-degree burns	treat	2101.00	95	23r
Medical care charges, total, emergency, infant with fever	treat	628.00	95	23r
Medical services expenditures	year	603	91	81c
Medical services expenditures	year	573	91	81r
Medical supplies expenditures	year	85	91	81c
Medical supplies expenditures	year	93	91	81r
Morphine, emergency room	treat	34.00	95	23r
Nursing care and facilities charges, emergency room	treat	252.00	95	23r
Nursing care and facilities charges, emergency, infant with fever	treat	252.00	95	23r
Nursing care and facilities charges, emergency, third-degree burns	treat	861.00	95	23r
Physician's charges, emergency, infant with fever	treat	212.00	95	23r
Physician's charges, emergency, third-degree burns	treat	372.00	95	23r
Physician's fee, emergency room	treat	372.00	95	23r
Physician's fee, general practitioner	visit	51.20	12/93	60r
Surgery, open-heart	proc	42374.00	1/93	14r
Ultrasound, abdominal, emergency room	treat	276.00	95	23r

Houston, TX - continued

Item	Per	Value	Date	Ref.
Health Care - continued				
Urinalysis, emergency room	treat	20.00	95	23r
Urinalysis, infant, emergency room	treat	20.00	95	23r
X-rays, emergency room	treat	78.00	95	23r
Household Goods				
Appl. repair, service call, wash mach	min. lab. chg.	35.54	12/94	2c
Floor coverings, expenditures	year	63	91	81c
Floor coverings, expenditures	year	48	91	81r
Furniture, expenditures	year	276	91	81c
Furniture, expenditures	year	280	91	81r
Household equipment, misc. expenditures	year	342	91	81r
Household equipment, misc., expenditures	year	552	91	81c
Household expenditures, miscellaneous	year	242	91	81c
Household expenditures, miscellaneous	year	256	91	81r
Household furnishings and equipment, expenditures	year	1229	91	81c
Household furnishings and equipment, expenditures	year	988	91	81r
Household operations expenditures	year	475	91	81c
Household operations expenditures	year	468	91	81r
Household textiles, expenditures	year	93	91	81c
Household textiles, expenditures	year	95	91	81r
Housekeeping supplies, expenditures	year	479	91	81c
Housekeeping supplies, expenditures	year	380	91	81r
Laundry and cleaning supplies, expenditures	year	127	91	81c
Laundry and cleaning supplies, expenditures	year	109	91	81r
Laundry detergent, Tide Ultra, Bold, or Cheer	42 oz.	3.24	12/94	2c
Postage and stationery, expenditures	year	159	91	81c
Postage and stationery, expenditures	year	105	91	81r
Tissues, facial, Kleenex brand	175	1.03	12/94	2c
Housing				
Housing, ACCRA Index		90.80	12/94	2c
Add garage/carport		6,980	3/95	74r
Add room(s)		11,403	3/95	74r
Apartment condominium or co-op, median	unit	68600	12/94	62r
Car rental	day	45.00	5/95	95c
Dwellings (owned), expenditures	year	2594	91	81c
Dwellings (owned), expenditures	year	2428	91	81r
Enclose porch/patio/breezeway		4,572	3/95	74r
Finish room in basement/attic		3,794	3/95	74r
Home, existing, single-family, median	unit	120200	12/94	62r
Home, existing, single-family, median	unit	77.60	12/94	62c
Home, purchase price	unit	124.10	3/93	26c
Hotel room	day	121.00	5/95	95c
House payment, principal and interest, 25% down payment	mo.	650	12/94	2c
House, 1800 sq ft, 8000 sq ft lot, new, urban, utilities	total	107561	12/94	2c
Maintenance, repairs, insurance, and other housing expenditures	year	622	91	81c
Maintenance, repairs, insurance, and other housing expenditures	year	531	91	81r
Mortgage interest and charges expenditures	year	1482	91	81c
Mortgage interest and charges expenditures	year	1506	91	81r
Mtge. rate, incl. points and orig. fee, 30-year conv. fixed or ARM	mo.	9.02	12/94	2c
Princ. & int., mortgage, median-price exist. sing.-family home	mo.	540	12/94	62r
Property taxes expenditures	year	489	91	81c
Property taxes expenditures	year	391	91	81r
Redesign, restructure more than half of home's interior		17,641	3/95	74r
Rent, apartment, 2 br., 1 1/2-2 baths, unfurnished, 950 sq ft, water	mo.	608	12/94	2c
Rent, office space	sq. ft.	7.60	93	57c
Rental units expenditures	year	1832	900/00/91	81c

Values are in dollars or fractions of dollars. In the column headed *Ref*, references are shown to sources. Each reference is followed by a letter. These refer to the geographical level for which data were reported: s=State, r=Region, and c=City or metro. The abbreviation *ex* is used to mean *except* or *excluding*; *exp* stands for expenditures. For other abbreviations and further explanations, please see the Introduction.

Houston, TX - continued

Item	Per	Value	Date	Ref.
Housing				
Rental units expenditures	year	1264	91	81r
Insurance and Pensions				
Auto insurance, private passenger	year	785.78	12/94	71s
Health insurance, HMO plan, cost to employer	year	3575	93	59c
Insurance and pensions, personal, expenditures	year	3213	91	81c
Insurance and pensions, personal, expenditures	year	2395	91	81r
Insurance, life and other personal, expenditures	year	332	91	81c
Insurance, life and other personal, expenditures	year	368	91	81r
Pensions and Social Security, expenditures	year	2881	91	81c
Pensions and Social Security, expenditures	year	2027	91	81r
Personal Goods				
Personal care products and services, total expenditures	year	485	91	81c
Shampoo, Alberto VO5	15-oz.	1.15	12/94	2c
Toothpaste, Crest or Colgate	6-7 oz.	2.16	12/94	2c
Personal Services				
Dry cleaning, man's 2-pc. suit		5.50	12/94	2c
Dry cleaning, woman's dress	dress	10.00	1/92	44c
Haircut, man's barbershop, no styling		9.05	12/94	2c
Haircut, woman's shampoo, trim, blow-dry		26.56	12/94	2c
Personal services expenditures	year	232	91	81c
Personal services expenditures	year	212	91	81r
Restaurant Food				
Big Mac, small fries, medium drink	meal	3.80	1/92	44c
Chicken, fried, thigh and drumstick		1.99	12/94	2c
Dining expenditures, family	week	33.83	94	73r
Hamburger with cheese	1/4 lb.	1.88	12/94	2c
Pizza, Pizza Hut or Pizza Inn	12-13 in.	7.54	12/94	2c
Taxes				
Tax rate, residential property, month	$100	2.00	1/92	79c
Tax, cigarettes	year	584.00	10/93	43s
Taxes, Federal income, expenditures	year	3323	91	81c
Taxes, Federal income, expenditures	year	2275	91	81r
Taxes, personal, expenditures	year	3344	91	81c
Taxes, personal, expenditures	year	2715	91	81r
Taxes, State and local income, expenditures	year	4	91	81c
Taxes, State and local income, expenditures	year	365	91	81r
Transportation				
Transportation, ACCRA Index		108.10	12/94	2c
Bus fare, one-way	trip	0.85	12/95	1c
Bus fare, up to 10 miles	one-way	1.46	12/94	2c
Cars and trucks purchased, new	year	1740	91	81c
Cars and trucks purchased, new	year	1306	91	81r
Cars and trucks purchased, used	year	919	91	81c
Cars and trucks purchased, used	year	942	91	81r
Driver's learning permit fee	perm	5.00	1/94	84s
Driver's license fee	orig	16.00	1/94	84s
Driver's license fee, duplicate	lic	10.00	1/94	84s
Driver's license reinstatement fee, min.	susp	50.00	1/94	85s
Driver's license renewal fee	renew	16.00	1/94	84s
Fine, illegal parking, handicapped zone	event	75.00	12/93	87c
Identification card, nondriver	card	10.00	1/94	83s
Motorcycle learning permit fee	perm	5.00	1/94	84s
Motorcycle license fee	orig	16.00	1/94	84s
Motorcycle license fee, duplicate	lic	10.00	1/94	84s
Motorcycle license renewal fee	renew	21.00	1/94	84s
parking, long-term lot, airport	3 days	10.80	1/92	44c
Public transportation expenditures	year	264	91	81c
Public transportation expenditures	year	249	91	81r
Tire balance, computer or spin bal., front	wheel	7.72	12/94	2c
Transportation expenditures, total	year	6692	91	81c
Transportation expenditures, total	year	5307	91	81r

Houston, TX - continued

Item	Per	Value	Date	Ref.
Transportation - continued				
Vehicle expenses, miscellaneous	year	2418	91	81c
Vehicle finance charges	year	279	91	81c
Vehicle finance charges	year	346	91	81r
Vehicle insurance expenditures	year	731	91	81c
Vehicle insurance expenditures	year	544	91	81r
Vehicle maintenance and repairs expenditures	year	1122	91	81c
Vehicle maintenance and repairs expenditures	year	600	91	81r
Vehicle purchases	year	2774	91	81c
Vehicle purchases	year	2275	91	81r
Vehicle rental, leases, licenses, etc. expenditures	year	285	91	81c
Vehicle rental, leases, licenses, etc. expenditures	year	141	91	81r
Vehicles purchased, other than cars and trucks	year	114	91	81c
Vehicles purchased, other than cars and trucks	year	27	91	81r
Utilities				
Utilities, ACCRA Index		99.80	12/94	2c
Electricity	KWh	0.08	12/94	82c
Electricity expenditures	year	1054	91	81c
Electricity expenditures	year	950	91	81r
Electricity, (part.), other, 1800 sq. ft., new home	mo.	89.65	12/94	2c
Electricity, summer, 250 KWh	month	17.94	8/93	64c
Electricity, summer, 500 KWh	month	43.82	8/93	64c
Electricity, summer, 750 KWh	month	69.70	8/93	64c
Electricity, summer, 1000 KWh	month	95.58	8/93	64c
Fee, water use, industrial	month	1372.44	1/95	16c
Utilities, fuels, and public services, total expenditures	year	2183	91	81c
Utilities, fuels, and public services, total expenditures	year	2000	91	81r
Water and other public services, expenditures	year	245	91	81c
Water and other public services, expenditures	year	227	91	81r
Weddings				
Bridal attendants' gowns	event	750	10/93	76r
Bridal gown	event	852	10/93	76r
Bridal headpiece and veil	event	167	10/93	76r
Bride's wedding band	event	708	10/93	76r
Clergy	event	224	10/93	76r
Engagement ring	event	2756	10/93	76r
Flowers	event	863	10/93	76r
Formal wear for groom	event	106	10/93	76r
Groom's attendants' formal wear	event	530	10/93	76r
Groom's wedding band	event	402	10/93	76r
Music	event	600	10/93	76r
Photography	event	1088	10/93	76r
Shoes for bride	event	50	10/93	76r
Videography	event	483	10/93	76r
Wedding invitations and announcements	event	342	10/93	76r
Wedding reception	event	7000	10/93	76r

Huntington, WV

Item	Per	Value	Date	Ref.
Composite, ACCRA index		99.90	12/94	2c
Alcoholic Beverages				
Beer, Miller Lite, Bud, 12-oz., ex deposit	6	4.22	12/94	2c
J & B Scotch	750-ml.	17.08	12/94	2c
Wine, Gallo Chablis blanc	1.5-lit	5.94	12/94	2c
Appliances				
Appliances (major), expenditures	year	153	91	81r

Values are in dollars or fractions of dollars. In the column headed *Ref*, references are shown to sources. Each reference is followed by a letter. These refer to the geographical level for which data were reported: s=State, r=Region, and c=City or metro. The abbreviation *ex* is used to mean *except* or *excluding*; *exp* stands for expenditures. For other abbreviations and further explanations, please see the Introduction.

Huntington, WV - continued

Item	Per	Value	Date	Ref.
Average annual exp.				
Food, health care, personal goods, services	year	27020	91	81r
Charity				
Cash contributions, expenditures	year	839	91	81r
Clothing				
Apparel, men and boys, total expenditures	year	380	91	81r
Apparel, women and girls, total expenditures	year	660	91	81r
Footwear, expenditures	year	193	91	81r
Jeans, man's denim		38.59	12/94	2c
Shirt, man's dress shirt		39.00	12/94	2c
Undervest, boy's size 10-14, cotton	3	5.59	12/94	2c
Communications				
Long-distance telephone rate, day, addl. min., 1-10 mi.	min.	0.13	12/93	9s
Long-distance telephone rate, day, initial min., 1-10 mi.	min.	0.26	12/93	9s
Newspaper subscription, dly. and Sun. delivery	month	14.08	12/94	2c
Phone line, single, business, field visit	inst	0.00	12/93	9s
Phone line, single, business, no field visit	inst	96.90	12/93	9s
Phone line, single, residence, field visit	inst	0.00	12/93	9s
Phone line, single, residence, no field visit	inst	42.00	12/93	9s
Telephone bill, family of four	month	28.17	12/94	2c
Telephone service, expenditures	year	616	91	81r
Telephone, business, addl. line, touch tone	month	2.75	10/91	25c
Telephone, business, connection charges, touch tone	inst	96.90	10/91	25c
Telephone, business, key system line, touch tone	month	67.76	10/91	25c
Telephone, business, PBX line, touch tone	month	67.96	10/91	25c
Telephone, business, single In., touch tone	month	66.36	10/91	25c
Telephone, business, touch tone, inside wiring maintenance plan	month	3.00	10/91	25c
Telephone, residential, flat rate	mo.	6.00	12/93	8c
Education				
Board, 4-year private college/university	year	2166	8/94	80s
Board, 4-year public college/university	year	1968	8/94	80s
Education, total expenditures	year	319	91	81r
Room, 4-year private college/university	year	1745	8/94	80s
Room, 4-year public college/university	year	1847	8/94	80s
Total cost, 4-year private college/university	year	13220	8/94	80s
Total cost, 4-year public college/university	year	5691	8/94	80s
Tuition, 2-year public college/university, in-state	year	1247	8/94	80s
Tuition, 4-year private college/university, in-state	year	9310	8/94	80s
Tuition, 4-year public college/university, in-state	year	1875	8/94	80s
Energy and Fuels				
Energy, combined forms, 1800 sq. ft.	mo.	111.33	12/94	2c
Fuel oil and other fuels, expenditures	year	56	91	81r
Gas, natural, expenditures	year	150	91	81r
Gas, reg unlead, taxes inc., cash, self-service	gal	1.22	12/94	2c
Gasoline and motor oil purchased	year	1152	91	81r
Gasoline, unleaded midgrade	gallon	1.21	4/93	82r
Gasoline, unleaded premium	gallon	1.30	4/93	82r
Gasoline, unleaded regular	gallon	1.10	4/93	82r
Entertainment				
Bowling, evening rate	game	2.37	12/94	2c
Concert ticket, Pearl Jam group	perf	20.00	94	50r
Entertainment, total expenditures	year	1266	91	81r
Fees and admissions, expenditures	year	306	91	81r
Monopoly game, Parker Brothers', No. 9	game	10.45	12/94	2c
Movie	adm	5.56	12/94	2c
Pets, toys, playground equipment, expenditures	year	271	91	81r
Reading, expenditures	year	131	91	81r
Televisions, radios, and sound equipment, expenditures	year	439	91	81r

Huntington, WV - continued

Item	Per	Value	Date	Ref.
Entertainment - continued				
Tennis balls, yellow, Wilson or Penn, 3	can	2.66	12/94	2c
Funerals				
Burial, immediate, container provided by funeral home		1370.36	1/95	54r
Cards, acknowledgment		14.83	1/95	54r
Casket, minimum alternative		192.52	1/95	54r
Cosmetology, hair care, etc.		102.27	1/95	54r
Cremation, direct, container provided by funeral home		1065.64	1/95	54r
Embalming		304.29	1/95	54r
Funeral, funeral home		287.83	1/95	54r
Funeral, other facility		284.14	1/95	54r
Graveside service		349.13	1/95	54r
Hearse, local		132.27	1/95	54r
Limousine, local		98.45	1/95	54r
Memorial service		270.59	1/95	54r
Service charge, professional, nondeclinable		933.59	1/95	54r
Visitation and viewing		225.83	1/95	54r
Groceries				
Groceries, ACCRA Index		99.40	12/94	2c
Apples, Red Delicious	lb.	0.73	12/94	82r
Baby food, strained vegetables, lowest price	4-4.5 oz.	0.21	12/94	2c
Bacon, sliced	lb.	1.67	12/94	82r
Bananas	lb.	0.54	12/94	2c
Bananas	lb.	0.42	12/94	82r
Beef or hamburger, ground	lb.	1.27	12/94	2c
Beef purchases	year	213	91	81r
Beverage purchases, alcoholic	year	249	91	81r
Beverage purchases, nonalcoholic	year	207	91	81r
Bologna, all beef or mixed	lb.	2.27	12/94	82r
Bread, white	24-oz.	0.69	12/94	2c
Bread, white, pan	lb.	0.68	12/94	82r
Cabbage	lb.	0.42	12/94	82r
Carrots, short trimmed and topped	lb.	0.53	12/94	82r
Cereals and bakery products purchases	year	345	91	81r
Cereals and cereals products purchases	year	127	91	81r
Cheddar cheese, natural	lb.	3.58	12/94	82r
Cheese, Kraft grated Parmesan	8-oz.	3.18	12/94	2c
Chicken breast, bone-in	lb.	1.71	12/94	82r
Chicken, fresh, whole	lb.	0.78	12/94	82r
Chicken, whole fryer	lb.	0.91	12/94	2c
Chuck roast, USDA choice, boneless	lb.	2.26	12/94	82r
Cigarettes, Winston, Kings	carton	14.41	12/94	2c
Coffee, vacuum-packed	13 oz.	3.75	12/94	2c
Corn Flakes, Kellogg's or Post Toasties	18 oz.	2.48	12/94	2c
Corn, frozen, whole kernel, lowest price	10 oz.	0.67	12/94	2c
Crackers, soda, salted	lb.	1.27	12/94	82r
Cucumbers	lb.	0.65	12/94	82r
Dairy products (other) purchases	year	141	91	81r
Eggs, Grade A large	dozen	0.85	12/94	2c
Eggs, Grade A large	dozen	0.87	12/94	82r
Fish and seafood purchases	year	72	91	81r
Flour, white, all purpose	lb.	0.23	12/94	82r
Food purchases, food eaten at home	year	2381	91	81r
Foods purchased away from home, not prepared by consumer	year	1696	91	81r
Frankfurters, all meat or all beef	lb.	1.74	12/94	82r
Fruits and vegetables purchases	year	380	91	81r
Grapefruit	lb.	0.45	12/94	82r
Grapes, Thompson seedless	lb.	2.30	12/94	82r
Ground beef, 100% beef	lb.	1.37	12/94	82r
Ground chuck, 100% beef	lb.	1.97	12/94	82r
Ham, boneless, exc. canned	lb.	2.54	12/94	82r
Ice cream, prepackaged, bulk, regular	1/2 gal.	2.47	12/94	82r
Lemons	lb.	1.02	12/94	82r
Lettuce, iceberg	lb.	0.96	12/94	82r
Lettuce, iceberg	head	0.99	12/94	2c
Margarine, Blue Bonnet or Parkay cubes	lb.	0.59	12/94	2c
Margarine, stick	lb.	0.77	12/94	82r

Values are in dollars or fractions of dollars. In the column headed *Ref*, references are shown to sources. Each reference is followed by a letter. These refer to the geographical level for which data were reported: s = State, r = Region, and c = City or metro. The abbreviation *ex* is used to mean *except* or *excluding*; *exp* stands for expenditures. For other abbreviations and further explanations, please see the Introduction.

Huntington, WV - continued

Item	Per	Value	Date	Ref.
Groceries				
Meats, poultry, fish, and eggs purchases	year	655	91	81r
Milk and cream (fresh) purchases	year	130	91	81r
Milk, whole	1/2 gal.	1.43	12/94	2c
Orange juice, frozen concentrate 12-oz. can	16 oz.	1.36	12/94	82r
Orange juice, Minute Maid frozen	12-oz.	1.31	12/94	2c
Oranges, Navel	lb.	0.54	12/94	82r
Peaches, halves or slices, Hunt's, Del Monte, or Libby's	29-oz.	1.48	12/94	2c
Pears, Anjou	lb.	0.81	12/94	82r
Peas, sweet, Del Monte or Green Giant	15-17 oz.	0.43	12/94	2c
Pork chops, center cut, bone-in	lb.	3.07	12/94	82r
Pork purchases	year	142	91	81r
Potato chips	16-oz.	3.15	12/94	82r
Potatoes, frozen, French fried	lb.	0.82	12/94	82r
Potatoes, white	lb.	0.34	12/94	82r
Potatoes, white or red	10-lb. sack	2.99	12/94	2c
Rice, white, long grain, uncooked	lb.	0.48	12/94	82r
Round roast, USDA choice, boneless	lb.	2.91	12/94	82r
Sausage, fresh	lb.	1.82	12/94	82r
Sausage, Jimmy Dean, 100% pork	lb.	2.65	12/94	2c
Shortening, vegetable oil blends	lb.	0.75	12/94	82r
Shortening, vegetable, Crisco	3-lb.	2.30	12/94	2c
Soft drink, Coca Cola, ex deposit	2 lit	1.16	12/94	2c
Spaghetti and macaroni	lb.	0.87	12/94	82r
Steak, rib eye, USDA choice, boneless	lb.	6.85	12/94	82r
Steak, round, graded & ungraded, exc. USDA prime & choice	lb.	2.96	12/94	82r
Steak, round, USDA choice, boneless	lb.	3.17	12/94	82r
Steak, sirloin, USDA choice, boneless	lb.	4.12	12/94	82r
Steak, t-bone	lb.	5.99	12/94	2c
Steak, T-bone, USDA choice, bone-in	lb.	5.63	12/94	82r
Sugar and other sweets, eaten at home, expenditures	year	93	91	81r
Sugar, cane or beet	4 lbs.	1.09	12/94	2c
Sugar, white, all sizes	lb.	0.39	12/94	82r
Tobacco products and smoking supplies, total expenditures	year	286	91	81r
Tomatoes, field grown	lb.	1.36	12/94	82r
Tomatoes, Hunt's or Del Monte	14.5 oz.	0.82	12/94	2c
Tuna, chunk, light	lb.	1.94	12/94	82r
Tuna, chunk, light, oil-packed	6.125-6.5 oz.	0.73	12/94	2c
Turkey, frozen, whole	lb.	0.96	12/94	82r
Yogurt, natural, fruit flavored	8 oz.	0.58	12/94	82r
Goods and Services				
Miscellaneous goods and services, ACCRA Index		107.10	12/94	2c
Health Care				
Health care, ACCRA Index		100.00	12/94	2c
Adenosine, emergency room	treat	100.00	95	23r
Antibiotic ointment, Polysporin	1.5 oz.	4.25	12/94	2c
Bladder tap, superpubic, infant, emergency room	treat	119.00	95	23r
Blood analysis, emergency room	treat	25.00	95	23r
Blood tests, abdominal pain, emergency room	treat	25.00	95	23r
Burn dressing, emergency room	treat	266.00	95	23r
Cardiology interpretation, emergency room	treat	26.00	95	23r
Chest X-ray, emergency room	treat	78.00	95	23r
Childbirth, Cesarean delivery, hospital charge	birth	5462.00	12/91	69r
Childbirth, Cesarean delivery, physician charge	birth	2228.00	12/91	69r
Childbirth, normal delivery, hospital charge	birth	2943.00	12/91	69r
Childbirth, normal delivery, physician charge	birth	1619.00	12/91	69r
Defibrillation pads, emergency room	treat	6.00	95	23r

Huntington, WV - continued

Item	Per	Value	Date	Ref.
Health Care - continued				
Dentist's fee, adult teeth cleaning and periodic oral exam	visit	56.60	12/94	2c
Doctor's fee, routine exam, established patient	visit	40.00	12/94	2c
Drugs, expenditures	year	297	91	81r
Gastric tube insertion, nasal, emergency room	treat	25.00	95	23r
Health care, total expenditures	year	1600	91	81r
Health insurance expenditures	year	637	91	81r
Heart monitor, emergency room	treat	40.00	95	23r
Hospital care, semiprivate room	day	328.00	12/94	2c
Intravenous fluids, emergency room	treat	130.00	95	23r
Intravenous fluids, emergency room	liter	26.00	95	23r
Intravenous line, central, emergency room	treat	342.00	95	23r
Liver function tests, abdominal pain, emergency room	treat	26.00	95	23r
Medical care charges, total, emergency room, third-degree burns	treat	2101.00	95	23r
Medical care charges, total, emergency, infant with fever	treat	628.00	95	23r
Medical services expenditures	year	573	91	81r
Medical supplies expenditures	year	93	91	81r
Morphine, emergency room	treat	34.00	95	23r
Nursing care and facilities charges, emergency room	treat	252.00	95	23r
Nursing care and facilities charges, emergency, infant with fever	treat	252.00	95	23r
Nursing care and facilities charges, emergency, third-degree burns	treat	861.00	95	23r
Physician's charges, emergency, infant with fever	treat	212.00	95	23r
Physician's charges, emergency, third-degree burns	treat	372.00	95	23r
Physician's fee, emergency room	treat	372.00	95	23r
Physician's fee, general practitioner	visit	51.20	12/93	60r
Surgery, open-heart	proc	42374.00	1/93	14r
Ultrasound, abdominal, emergency room	treat	276.00	95	23r
Urinalysis, emergency room	treat	20.00	95	23r
Urinalysis, infant, emergency room	treat	20.00	95	23r
X-rays, emergency room	treat	78.00	95	23r
Household Goods				
Appl. repair, service call, wash mach	min. lab. chg.	30.64	12/94	2c
Floor coverings, expenditures	year	48	91	81r
Furniture, expenditures	year	280	91	81r
Household equipment, misc. expenditures	year	342	91	81r
Household expenditures, miscellaneous	year	256	91	81r
Household furnishings and equipment, expenditures	year	988	91	81r
Household operations expenditures	year	468	91	81r
Household textiles, expenditures	year	95	91	81r
Housekeeping supplies, expenditures	year	380	91	81r
Laundry and cleaning supplies, expenditures	year	109	91	81r
Laundry detergent, Tide Ultra, Bold, or Cheer	42 oz.	3.98	12/94	2c
Postage and stationery, expenditures	year	105	91	81r
Tissues, facial, Kleenex brand	175	0.99	12/94	2c
Housing				
Housing, ACCRA Index		90.20	12/94	2c
Add garage/carport		6,980	3/95	74r
Add room(s)		11,403	3/95	74r
Apartment condominium or co-op, median	unit	68600	12/94	62r
Dwellings (owned), expenditures	year	2428	91	81r
Enclose porch/patio/breezeway		4,572	3/95	74r
Finish room in basement/attic		3,794	3/95	74r
Home, existing, single-family, median	unit	120200	12/94	62r
House payment, principal and interest, 25% down payment	mo.	788	12/94	2c

Values are in dollars or fractions of dollars. In the column headed *Ref*, references are shown to sources. Each reference is followed by a letter. These refer to the geographical level for which data were reported: s=State, r=Region, and c=City or metro. The abbreviation *ex* is used to mean *except* or *excluding*; *exp* stands for expenditures. For other abbreviations and further explanations, please see the Introduction.

Huntington, WV - continued

Item	Per	Value	Date	Ref.
Housing				
House, 1800 sq ft, 8000 sq ft lot, new, urban, utilities	total	128297	12/94	2c
Maintenance, repairs, insurance, and other housing expenditures	year	531	91	81r
Mortgage interest and charges expenditures	year	1506	91	81r
Mtge. rate, incl. points and orig. fee, 30-year conv. fixed or ARM	mo.	9.20	12/94	2c
Princ. & int., mortgage, median-price exist. sing.-family home	mo.	540	12/94	62r
Property taxes expenditures	year	391	91	81r
Redesign, restructure more than half of home's interior		17,641	3/95	74r
Rent, apartment, 2 br., 1 1/2-2 baths, unfurnished, 950 sq ft, water	mo.	494	12/94	2c
Rental units expenditures	year	1264	91	81r
Insurance and Pensions				
Auto insurance, private passenger	year	696.89	12/94	71s
Insurance and pensions, personal, expenditures	year	2395	91	81r
Insurance, life and other personal, expenditures	year	368	91	81r
Pensions and Social Security, expenditures	year	2027	91	81r
Personal Goods				
Shampoo, Alberto VO5	15-oz.	1.07	12/94	2c
Toothpaste, Crest or Colgate	6-7 oz.	2.08	12/94	2c
Personal Services				
Dry cleaning, man's 2-pc. suit		6.85	12/94	2c
Haircut, man's barbershop, no styling		6.75	12/94	2c
Haircut, woman's shampoo, trim, blow-dry		15.60	12/94	2c
Personal services expenditures	year	212	91	81r
Restaurant Food				
Chicken, fried, thigh and drumstick		2.19	12/94	2c
Dining expenditures, family	week	33.83	94	73r
Hamburger with cheese	1/4 lb.	1.85	12/94	2c
Pizza, Pizza Hut or Pizza Inn	12-13 in.	6.25	12/94	2c
Taxes				
Taxes, Federal income, expenditures	year	2275	91	81r
Taxes, personal, expenditures	year	2715	91	81r
Taxes, State and local income, expenditures	year	365	91	81r
Transportation				
Transportation, ACCRA Index		99.50	12/94	2c
Cars and trucks purchased, new	year	1306	91	81r
Cars and trucks purchased, used	year	942	91	81r
Driver's learning permit fee	perm	4.00	1/94	84s
Driver's license fee	orig	10.50	1/94	84s
Driver's license fee, duplicate	lic	5.00	1/94	84s
Driver's license renewal fee	renew	10.50	1/94	84s
Identification card, nondriver	card	5.00	1/94	83s
Motorcycle learning permit fee	perm	5.00	1/94	84s
Motorcycle license fee	orig	10.00	1/94	84s
Motorcycle license fee, duplicate	lic	5.00	1/94	84s
Motorcycle license renewal fee	renew	10.00	1/94	84s
Public transportation expenditures	year	249	91	81r
Tire balance, computer or spin bal., front	wheel	5.90	12/94	2c
Transportation expenditures, total	year	5307	91	81r
Vehicle finance charges	year	346	91	81r
Vehicle insurance expenditures	year	544	91	81r
Vehicle maintenance and repairs expenditures	year	600	91	81r
Vehicle purchases	year	2275	91	81r
Vehicle rental, leases, licenses, etc. expenditures	year	141	91	81r
Vehicles purchased, other than cars and trucks	year	27	91	81r
Utilities				
Utilities, ACCRA Index		105.30	12/94	2c
Electricity expenditures	year	950	91	81r

Huntington, WV - continued

Item	Per	Value	Date	Ref.
Utilities - continued				
Electricity, 1800 sq. ft., new home	mo.	111.33	12/94	2c
Electricity, summer, 250 KWh	month	27.23	8/93	64s
Electricity, summer, 500 KWh	month	36.96	8/93	64s
Electricity, summer, 750 KWh	month	52.76	8/93	64s
Electricity, summer, 1000 KWh	month	68.52	8/93	64s
Utilities, fuels, and public services, total expenditures	year	2000	91	81r
Water and other public services, expenditures	year	227	91	81r
Weddings				
Bridal attendants' gowns	event	750	10/93	76r
Bridal gown	event	852	10/93	76r
Bridal headpiece and veil	event	167	10/93	76r
Bride's wedding band	event	708	10/93	76r
Clergy	event	224	10/93	76r
Engagement ring	event	2756	10/93	76r
Flowers	event	863	10/93	76r
Formal wear for groom	event	106	10/93	76r
Groom's attendants' formal wear	event	530	10/93	76r
Groom's wedding band	event	402	10/93	76r
Music	event	600	10/93	76r
Photography	event	1088	10/93	76r
Shoes for bride	event	50	10/93	76r
Videography	event	483	10/93	76r
Wedding invitations and announcements	event	342	10/93	76r
Wedding reception	event	7000	10/93	76r

Huntsville, AL

Item	Per	Value	Date	Ref.
Composite, ACCRA index		95.10	12/94	2c
Alcoholic Beverages				
Beer, Miller Lite, Bud, 12-oz., ex deposit	6	3.94	12/94	2c
J & B Scotch	750-ml.	20.99	12/94	2c
Wine, Gallo Chablis blanc	1.5-lit	4.99	12/94	2c
Appliances				
Appliances (major), expenditures	year	153	91	81r
Average annual exp.				
Food, health care, personal goods, services	year	27020	91	81r
Charity				
Cash contributions, expenditures	year	839	91	81r
Clothing				
Apparel, men and boys, total expenditures	year	380	91	81r
Apparel, women and girls, total expenditures	year	660	91	81r
Footwear, expenditures	year	193	91	81r
Jeans, man's denim		29.73	12/94	2c
Shirt, man's dress shirt		30.30	12/94	2c
Undervest, boy's size 10-14, cotton	3	5.72	12/94	2c
Communications				
Long-distance telephone rate, day, addl. min., 1-10 mi.	min.	0.09	12/93	9s
Long-distance telephone rate, day, initial min., 1-10 mi.	min.	0.11	12/93	9s
Newspaper subscription, dly. and Sun. delivery	month	9.85	12/94	2c
Phone line, single, business, field visit	inst	69.00	12/93	9s
Phone line, single, business, no field visit	inst	69.00	12/93	9s
Phone line, single, residence, field visit	inst	40.00	12/93	9s
Phone line, single, residence, no field visit	inst	40.00	12/93	9s
Telephone bill, family of four	month	25.40	12/94	2c
Telephone service, expenditures	year	616	91	81r
Telephone, residential, flat rate	mo.	18.10	12/93	8c
Education				
Board, 4-year private college/university	year	2072	8/94	80s
Board, 4-year public college/university	year	1706	8/94	80s
Education, total expenditures	year	319	91	81r
Room, 4-year private college/university	year	1607	8/94	80s

Values are in dollars or fractions of dollars. In the column headed *Ref*, references are shown to sources. Each reference is followed by a letter. These refer to the geographical level for which data were reported: s = State, r = Region, and c = City or metro. The abbreviation *ex* is used to mean *except* or *excluding*; *exp* stands for *expenditures*. For other abbreviations and further explanations, please see the Introduction.

Huntsville, AL - continued

Item	Per	Value	Date	Ref.
Education				
Room, 4-year public college/university	year	1598	8/94	80s
Total cost, 4-year private college/university	year	10664	8/94	80s
Total cost, 4-year public college/university	year	5287	8/94	80s
Tuition, 2-year public college/university, in-state	year	1110	8/94	80s
Tuition, 4-year private college/university, in-state	year	6985	8/94	80s
Tuition, 4-year public college/university, in-state	year	1983	8/94	80s
Energy and Fuels				
Energy, combined forms, 1800 sq. ft.	mo.	107.28	12/94	2c
Fuel oil and other fuels, expenditures	year	56	91	81r
Gas, natural, expenditures	year	150	91	81r
Gas, reg unlead, taxes inc., cash, self-service	gal	1.16	12/94	2c
Gasoline and motor oil purchased	year	1152	91	81r
Gasoline, unleaded midgrade	gallon	1.21	4/93	82r
Gasoline, unleaded premium	gallon	1.30	4/93	82r
Gasoline, unleaded regular	gallon	1.10	4/93	82r
Entertainment				
Bowling, evening rate	game	2.28	12/94	2c
Concert ticket, Pearl Jam group	perf	20.00	94	50r
Entertainment, total expenditures	year	1266	91	81r
Fees and admissions, expenditures	year	306	91	81r
Monopoly game, Parker Brothers', No. 9	game	10.98	12/94	2c
Movie	adm	5.75	12/94	2c
Pets, toys, playground equipment, expenditures	year	271	91	81r
Reading, expenditures	year	131	91	81r
Televisions, radios, and sound equipment, expenditures	year	439	91	81r
Tennis balls, yellow, Wilson or Penn, 3	can	2.43	12/94	2c
Funerals				
Burial, immediate, container provided by funeral home		1298.96	1/95	54r
Cards, acknowledgment		21.26	1/95	54r
Casket, minimum alternative		204.95	1/95	54r
Cosmetology, hair care, etc.		85.40	1/95	54r
Cremation, direct, container provided by funeral home		1054.77	1/95	54r
Embalming		287.71	1/95	54r
Funeral, funeral home		269.18	1/95	54r
Funeral, other facility		272.88	1/95	54r
Graveside service		302.54	1/95	54r
Hearse, local		122.08	1/95	54r
Limousine, local		80.31	1/95	54r
Memorial service		277.66	1/95	54r
Service charge, professional, nondeclinable		896.65	1/95	54r
Visitation and viewing		232.39	1/95	54r
Groceries				
Groceries, ACCRA Index		95.40	12/94	2c
Apples, Red Delicious	lb.	0.73	12/94	82r
Baby food, strained vegetables, lowest price	4-4.5 oz.	0.32	12/94	2c
Bacon, sliced	lb.	1.67	12/94	82r
Bananas	lb.	0.45	12/94	2c
Bananas	lb.	0.42	12/94	82r
Beef or hamburger, ground	lb.	1.67	12/94	2c
Beef purchases	year	213	91	81r
Beverage purchases, alcoholic	year	249	91	81r
Beverage purchases, nonalcoholic	year	207	91	81r
Bologna, all beef or mixed	lb.	2.27	12/94	82r
Bread, white	24-oz.	0.71	12/94	2c
Bread, white, pan	lb.	0.68	12/94	82r
Cabbage	lb.	0.42	12/94	82r
Carrots, short trimmed and topped	lb.	0.53	12/94	82r
Cereals and bakery products purchases	year	345	91	81r
Cereals and cereals products purchases	year	127	91	81r
Cheddar cheese, natural	lb.	3.58	12/94	82r
Cheese, Kraft grated Parmesan	8-oz.	3.06	12/94	2c

Huntsville, AL - continued

Item	Per	Value	Date	Ref.
Groceries - continued				
Chicken breast, bone-in	lb.	1.71	12/94	82r
Chicken, fresh, whole	lb.	0.78	12/94	82r
Chicken, whole fryer	lb.	0.67	12/94	2c
Chuck roast, USDA choice, boneless	lb.	2.26	12/94	82r
Cigarettes, Winston, Kings	carton	14.19	12/94	2c
Coffee, vacuum-packed	13 oz.	3.27	12/94	2c
Corn Flakes, Kellogg's or Post Toasties	18 oz.	2.17	12/94	2c
Corn, frozen, whole kernel, lowest price	10 oz.	0.65	12/94	2c
Crackers, soda, salted	lb.	1.27	12/94	82r
Cucumbers	lb.	0.65	12/94	82r
Dairy products (other) purchases	year	141	91	81r
Eggs, Grade A large	dozen	0.71	12/94	2c
Eggs, Grade A large	dozen	0.87	12/94	82r
Fish and seafood purchases	year	72	91	81r
Flour, white, all purpose	lb.	0.23	12/94	82r
Food purchases, food eaten at home	year	2381	91	81r
Foods purchased away from home, not prepared by consumer	year	1696	91	81r
Frankfurters, all meat or all beef	lb.	1.74	12/94	82r
Fruits and vegetables purchases	year	380	91	81r
Grapefruit	lb.	0.45	12/94	82r
Grapes, Thompson seedless	lb.	2.30	12/94	82r
Ground beef, 100% beef	lb.	1.37	12/94	82r
Ground chuck, 100% beef	lb.	1.97	12/94	82r
Ham, boneless, exc. canned	lb.	2.54	12/94	82r
Ice cream, prepackaged, bulk, regular	1/2 gal.	2.47	12/94	82r
Lemons	lb.	1.02	12/94	82r
Lettuce, iceberg	lb.	0.96	12/94	82r
Lettuce, iceberg	head	0.99	12/94	2c
Margarine, Blue Bonnet or Parkay cubes	lb.	0.53	12/94	2c
Margarine, stick	lb.	0.77	12/94	82r
Meats, poultry, fish, and eggs purchases	year	655	91	81r
Milk and cream (fresh) purchases	year	130	91	81r
Milk, whole	1/2 gal.	1.31	12/94	2c
Orange juice, frozen concentrate 12-oz. can	16 oz.	1.36	12/94	82r
Orange juice, Minute Maid frozen	12-oz.	1.09	12/94	2c
Oranges, Navel	lb.	0.54	12/94	82r
Peaches, halves or slices, Hunt's, Del Monte, or Libby's	29-oz.	1.19	12/94	2c
Pears, Anjou	lb.	0.81	12/94	82r
Peas, sweet, Del Monte or Green Giant	15-17 oz.	0.45	12/94	2c
Pork chops, center cut, bone-in	lb.	3.07	12/94	82r
Pork purchases	year	142	91	81r
Potato chips	16-oz.	3.15	12/94	82r
Potatoes, frozen, French fried	lb.	0.82	12/94	82r
Potatoes, white	lb.	0.34	12/94	82r
Potatoes, white or red	10-lb. sack	2.94	12/94	2c
Rice, white, long grain, uncooked	lb.	0.48	12/94	82r
Round roast, USDA choice, boneless	lb.	2.91	12/94	82r
Sausage, fresh	lb.	1.82	12/94	82r
Sausage, Jimmy Dean, 100% pork	lb.	2.57	12/94	2c
Shortening, vegetable oil blends	lb.	0.75	12/94	82r
Shortening, vegetable, Crisco	3-lb.	2.59	12/94	2c
Soft drink, Coca Cola, ex deposit	2 lit	1.00	12/94	2c
Spaghetti and macaroni	lb.	0.87	12/94	82r
Steak, rib eye, USDA choice, boneless	lb.	6.85	12/94	82r
Steak, round, graded & ungraded, exc. USDA prime & choice	lb.	2.96	12/94	82r
Steak, round, USDA choice, boneless	lb.	3.17	12/94	82r
Steak, sirloin, USDA choice, boneless	lb.	4.12	12/94	82r
Steak, t-bone	lb.	5.19	12/94	2c
Steak, T-bone, USDA choice, bone-in	lb.	5.63	12/94	82r
Sugar and other sweets, eaten at home, expenditures	year	93	91	81r
Sugar, cane or beet	4 lbs.	1.49	12/94	2c
Sugar, white, all sizes	lb.	0.39	12/94	82r
Tobacco products and smoking supplies, total expenditures	year	286	91	81r

Values are in dollars or fractions of dollars. In the column headed *Ref,* references are shown to sources. Each reference is followed by a letter. These refer to the geographical level for which data were reported: s=State, r=Region, and c=City or metro. The abbreviation *ex* is used to mean *except* or *excluding*; *exp* stands for *expenditures*. For other abbreviations and further explanations, please see the Introduction.

Huntsville, AL - continued

Item	Per	Value	Date	Ref.
Groceries				
Tomatoes, field grown	lb.	1.36	12/94	82r
Tomatoes, Hunt's or Del Monte	14.5 oz.	0.66	12/94	2c
Tuna, chunk, light	lb.	1.94	12/94	82r
Tuna, chunk, light, oil-packed	6.125-6.5 oz.	0.67	12/94	2c
Turkey, frozen, whole	lb.	0.96	12/94	82r
Yogurt, natural, fruit flavored	8 oz.	0.58	12/94	82r
Goods and Services				
Miscellaneous goods and services, ACCRA Index		100.30	12/94	2c
Health Care				
Health care, ACCRA Index		98.00	12/94	2c
Adenosine, emergency room	treat	100.00	95	23r
Antibiotic ointment, Polysporin	1.5 oz.	4.28	12/94	2c
Bladder tap, superpubic, infant, emergency room	treat	119.00	95	23r
Blood analysis, emergency room	treat	25.00	95	23r
Blood tests, abdominal pain, emergency room	treat	25.00	95	23r
Burn dressing, emergency room	treat	266.00	95	23r
Cardiology interpretation, emergency room	treat	26.00	95	23r
Chest X-ray, emergency room	treat	78.00	95	23r
Childbirth, Cesarean delivery, hospital charge	birth	5462.00	12/91	69r
Childbirth, Cesarean delivery, physician charge	birth	2228.00	12/91	69r
Childbirth, normal delivery, hospital charge	birth	2943.00	12/91	69r
Childbirth, normal delivery, physician charge	birth	1619.00	12/91	69r
Defibrillation pads, emergency room	treat	6.00	95	23r
Dentist's fee, adult teeth cleaning and periodic oral exam	visit	53.43	12/94	2c
Doctor's fee, routine exam, established patient	visit	40.43	12/94	2c
Drugs, expenditures	year	297	91	81r
Gastric tube insertion, nasal, emergency room	treat	25.00	95	23r
Health care, total expenditures	year	1600	91	81r
Health insurance expenditures	year	637	91	81r
Heart monitor, emergency room	treat	40.00	95	23r
Hospital care, semiprivate room	day	321.50	12/94	2c
Insurance premium, family medical care	month	360.67	1/95	41s
Intravenous fluids, emergency room	treat	130.00	95	23r
Intravenous fluids, emergency room	liter	26.00	95	23r
Intravenous line, central, emergency room	treat	342.00	95	23r
Liver function tests, abdominal pain, emergency room	treat	26.00	95	23r
Medical care charges, total, emergency room, third-degree burns	treat	2101.00	95	23r
Medical care charges, total, emergency, infant with fever	treat	628.00	95	23r
Medical services expenditures	year	573	91	81r
Medical supplies expenditures	year	93	91	81r
Morphine, emergency room	treat	34.00	95	23r
Nursing care and facilities charges, emergency room	treat	252.00	95	23r
Nursing care and facilities charges, emergency, infant with fever	treat	252.00	95	23r
Nursing care and facilities charges, emergency, third-degree burns	treat	861.00	95	23r
Physician's charges, emergency, infant with fever	treat	212.00	95	23r
Physician's charges, emergency, third-degree burns	treat	372.00	95	23r
Physician's fee, emergency room	treat	372.00	95	23r
Physician's fee, general practitioner	visit	51.20	12/93	60r
Surgery, open-heart	proc	42374.00	1/93	14r
Ultrasound, abdominal, emergency room	treat	276.00	95	23r
Urinalysis, emergency room	treat	20.00	95	23r
Urinalysis, infant, emergency room	treat	20.00	95	23r
X-rays, emergency room	treat	78.00	95	23r

Huntsville, AL - continued

Item	Per	Value	Date	Ref.
Household Goods				
Appl. repair, service call, wash mach	min. lab. chg.	32.19	12/94	2c
Floor coverings, expenditures	year	48	91	81r
Furniture, expenditures	year	280	91	81r
Household equipment, misc. expenditures	year	342	91	81r
Household expenditures, miscellaneous	year	256	91	81r
Household furnishings and equipment, expenditures	year	988	91	81r
Household operations expenditures	year	468	91	81r
Household textiles, expenditures	year	95	91	81r
Housekeeping supplies, expenditures	year	380	91	81r
Laundry and cleaning supplies, expenditures	year	109	91	81r
Laundry detergent, Tide Ultra, Bold, or Cheer	42 oz.	3.08	12/94	2c
Postage and stationery, expenditures	year	105	91	81r
Tissues, facial, Kleenex brand	175	1.02	12/94	2c
Housing				
Housing, ACCRA Index		86.40	12/94	2c
Add garage/carport		6,980	3/95	74r
Add room(s)		11,403	3/95	74r
Apartment condominium or co-op, median	unit	68600	12/94	62r
Dwellings (owned), expenditures	year	2428	91	81r
Enclose porch/patio/breezeway		4,572	3/95	74r
Finish room in basement/attic		3,794	3/95	74r
Home, existing, single-family, median	unit	120200	12/94	62r
House payment, principal and interest, 25% down payment	mo.	668	12/94	2c
House, 1800 sq ft, 8000 sq ft lot, new, urban, utilities	total	108606	12/94	2c
Maintenance, repairs, insurance, and other housing expenditures	year	531	91	81r
Mortgage interest and charges expenditures	year	1506	91	81r
Mtge. rate, incl. points and orig. fee, 30-year conv. fixed or ARM	mo.	9.22	12/94	2c
Princ. & int., mortgage, median-price exist. sing.-family home	mo.	540	12/94	62r
Property taxes expenditures	year	391	91	81r
Redesign, restructure more than half of home's interior		17,641	3/95	74r
Rent, apartment, 2 br., 1 1/2-2 baths, unfurnished, 950 sq ft, water	mo.	437	12/94	2c
Rental units expenditures	year	1264	91	81r
Insurance and Pensions				
Auto insurance, private passenger	year	604.07	12/94	71s
Insurance and pensions, personal, expenditures	year	2395	91	81r
Insurance, life and other personal, expenditures	year	368	91	81r
Pensions and Social Security, expenditures	year	2027	91	81r
Personal Goods				
Shampoo, Alberto VO5	15-oz.	1.03	12/94	2c
Toothpaste, Crest or Colgate	6-7 oz.	1.57	12/94	2c
Personal Services				
Dry cleaning, man's 2-pc. suit		5.63	12/94	2c
Haircut, man's barbershop, no styling		7.67	12/94	2c
Haircut, woman's shampoo, trim, blow-dry		22.00	12/94	2c
Personal services expenditures	year	212	91	81r
Restaurant Food				
Chicken, fried, thigh and drumstick		2.09	12/94	2c
Dining expenditures, family	week	33.83	94	73r
Hamburger with cheese	1/4 lb.	1.92	12/94	2c
Pizza, Pizza Hut or Pizza Inn	12-13 in.	7.99	12/94	2c
Taxes				
Taxes, Federal income, expenditures	year	2275	91	81r
Taxes, personal, expenditures	year	2715	91	81r
Taxes, State and local income, expenditures	year	365	91	81r

Values are in dollars or fractions of dollars. In the column headed *Ref*, references are shown to sources. Each reference is followed by a letter. These refer to the geographical level for which data were reported: s=State, r=Region, and c=City or metro. The abbreviation *ex* is used to mean *except* or *excluding*; *exp* stands for expenditures. For other abbreviations and further explanations, please see the Introduction.

Huntsville, AL - continued

Item	Per	Value	Date	Ref.
Transportation				
Transportation, ACCRA Index		96.10	12/94	2c
Cars and trucks purchased, new	year	1306	91	81r
Cars and trucks purchased, used	year	942	91	81r
Driver's learning permit fee	perm	20.00	1/94	84s
Driver's license fee	orig	20.00	1/94	84s
Driver's license fee, duplicate	lic	5.00	1/94	84s
Driver's license reinstatement fee, min.	susp	50.00	1/94	85s
Driver's license renewal fee	renew	20.00	1/94	84s
Identification card, nondriver	card	20.00	1/94	83s
Motorcycle license fee	orig	20.00	1/94	84s
Motorcycle license fee, duplicate	lic	5.00	1/94	84s
Motorcycle license renewal fee	renew	20.00	1/94	84s
Public transportation expenditures	year	249	91	81r
Tire balance, computer or spin bal., front	wheel	5.83	12/94	2c
Transportation expenditures, total	year	5307	91	81r
Vehicle finance charges	year	346	91	81r
Vehicle insurance expenditures	year	544	91	81r
Vehicle maintenance and repairs expenditures	year	600	91	81r
Vehicle purchases	year	2275	91	81r
Vehicle rental, leases, licenses, etc. expenditures	year	141	91	81r
Vehicles purchased, other than cars and trucks	year	27	91	81r
Utilities				
Utilities, ACCRA Index		100.30	12/94	2c
Electricity expenditures	year	950	91	81r
Electricity, 1800 sq. ft., new home	mo.	107.28	12/94	2c
Utilities, fuels, and public services, total expenditures	year	2000	91	81r
Water and other public services, expenditures	year	227	91	81r
Weddings				
Bridal attendants' gowns	event	750	10/93	76r
Bridal gown	event	852	10/93	76r
Bridal headpiece and veil	event	167	10/93	76r
Bride's wedding band	event	708	10/93	76r
Clergy	event	224	10/93	76r
Engagement ring	event	2756	10/93	76r
Flowers	event	863	10/93	76r
Formal wear for groom	event	106	10/93	76r
Groom's attendants' formal wear	event	530	10/93	76r
Groom's wedding band	event	402	10/93	76r
Music	event	600	10/93	76r
Photography	event	1088	10/93	76r
Shoes for bride	event	50	10/93	76r
Videography	event	483	10/93	76r
Wedding invitations and announcements	event	342	10/93	76r
Wedding reception	event	7000	10/93	76r

Indianapolis, IN

Item	Per	Value	Date	Ref.
Composite, ACCRA index		94.70	12/94	2c
Alcoholic Beverages				
Beer, Miller Lite, Bud, 12-oz., ex deposit	6	3.58	12/94	2c
J & B Scotch	750-ml.	15.61	12/94	2c
Wine, Gallo Chablis blanc	1.5-lit	4.32	12/94	2c
Appliances				
Appliances (major), expenditures	year	131	91	81r
Average annual exp.				
Food, health care, personal goods, services	year	25935	91	81r
Charity				
Cash contributions, expenditures	year	745	91	81r
Clothing				
Apparel, men and boys, total expenditures	year	332	91	81r
Apparel, women and girls, total expenditures	year	578	91	81r
Footwear, expenditures	year	164	91	81r

Indianapolis, IN - continued

Item	Per	Value	Date	Ref.
Clothing - continued				
Jeans, man's denim		29.19	12/94	2c
Shirt, dress, men's	shirt	32.00-85.00	1/92	44c
Shirt, man's dress shirt		25.49	12/94	2c
Undervest, boy's size 10-14, cotton	3	4.05	12/94	2c
Communications				
Long-distance telephone rate, day, addl. min., 1-10 mi.	min.	0.10	12/93	9s
Long-distance telephone rate, day, initial min., 1-10 mi.	min.	0.18	12/93	9s
Newspaper subscription, dly. and Sun. delivery	month	13.04	12/94	2c
Phone line, single, business, field visit	inst	59.00	12/93	9s
Phone line, single, business, no field visit	inst	59.00	12/93	9s
Phone line, single, residence, field visit	inst	47.00	12/93	9s
Phone line, single, residence, no field visit	inst	47.00	12/93	9s
Telephone bill, family of four	month	19.66	12/94	2c
Telephone service, expenditures	year	547	91	81r
Telephone, residential, flat rate	mo.	13.17	12/93	8c
Drugs				
Cocaine, street price	500 grams (000)	15000-2500	93	19c
Crack Cocaine, street price	gram	100	93	19c
Heroin, street price	100 grams	3000-5000	93	19c
LSD, street price	dose	3-5	93	19c
Marijuana, street price	100 kilo (000)	300000-600	93	19c
Methamphetamine, street price	10 grams	500	93	19c
Education				
Board, 4-year private college/university	year	2095	8/94	80s
Board, 4-year public college/university	year	2300	8/94	80s
Education, total expenditures	year	394	91	81r
Room, 4-year private college/university	year	1784	8/94	80s
Room, 4-year public college/university	year	1718	8/94	80s
Total cost, 4-year private college/university	year	15045	8/94	80s
Total cost, 4-year public college/university	year	6639	8/94	80s
Tuition, 2-year public college/university, in-state	year	1737	8/94	80s
Tuition, 4-year private college/university, in-state	year	11165	8/94	80s
Tuition, 4-year public college/university, in-state	year	2621	8/94	80s
Energy and Fuels				
Energy, combined forms, 1800 sq. ft.	mo.	103.17	12/94	2c
Energy, exc. electricity, 1800 sq. ft.	mo.	53.84	12/94	2c
Fuel oil and other fuels, expenditures	year	83	91	81r
Gas	gal.	0.99	1/92	44c
Gas, cooking, 10 therms	month	10.81	2/94	65c
Gas, cooking, 30 therms	month	20.44	2/94	65c
Gas, cooking, 50 therms	month	30.07	2/94	65c
Gas, heating, winter, 100 therms	month	60.78	2/94	65c
Gas, heating, winter, average use	month	107.08	2/94	65c
Gas, natural, expenditures	year	373	91	81r
Gas, reg unlead, taxes inc., cash, self-service	gal	1.00	12/94	2c
Gasoline and motor oil purchased	year	1000	91	81r
Gasoline, unleaded midgrade	gallon	1.15	4/93	82r
Gasoline, unleaded premium	gallon	1.23	4/93	82r
Gasoline, unleaded regular	gallon	1.07	4/93	82r
Entertainment				
Bowling, evening rate	game	2.14	12/94	2c
Entertainment, total expenditures	year	1356	91	81r
Fees and admissions, expenditures	year	347	91	81r
Monopoly game, Parker Brothers', No. 9	game	11.04	12/94	2c
Movie	adm	6.50	12/94	2c

Values are in dollars or fractions of dollars. In the column headed *Ref*, references are shown to sources. Each reference is followed by a letter. These refer to the geographical level for which data were reported: s=State, r=Region, and c=City or metro. The abbreviation *ex* is used to mean *except* or *excluding*; *exp* stands for *expenditures*. For other abbreviations and further explanations, please see the Introduction.

Indianapolis, IN - continued

Item	Per	Value	Date	Ref.
Entertainment				
Movie ticket, adult	ticket	6.25	1/92	44c
Pets, toys, playground equipment, expenditures	year	270	91	81r
Reading, expenditures	year	160	91	81r
Televisions, radios, and sound equipment, expenditures	year	433	91	81r
Tennis balls, yellow, Wilson or Penn, 3	can	2.39	12/94	2c
Funerals				
Burial, immediate, container provided by funeral home		1268.31	1/95	54r
Cards, acknowledgment		26.12	1/95	54r
Casket, minimum alternative		198.03	1/95	54r
Cosmetology, hair care, etc.		122.19	1/95	54r
Cremation, direct, container provided by funeral home		977.81	1/95	54r
Embalming		334.00	1/95	54r
Funeral, funeral home		321.16	1/95	54r
Funeral, other facility		317.73	1/95	54r
Graveside service		292.48	1/95	54r
Hearse, local		153.20	1/95	54r
Limousine, local		123.52	1/95	54r
Memorial service		356.30	1/95	54r
Service charge, professional, nondeclinable		968.24	1/95	54r
Visitation and viewing		332.66	1/95	54r
Groceries				
Groceries, ACCRA Index		93.90	12/94	2c
Apples, Red Delicious	lb.	0.68	12/94	82r
Baby food, strained vegetables, lowest price	4-4.5 oz.	0.30	12/94	2c
Bacon, sliced	lb.	1.88	12/94	82r
Bananas	lb.	0.39	12/94	2c
Bananas	lb.	0.41	12/94	82r
Beef or hamburger, ground	lb.	1.50	12/94	2c
Beef purchases	year	197	91	81r
Beef, stew, boneless	lb.	2.52	12/94	82r
Beverage purchases, alcoholic	year	293	91	81r
Beverage purchases, nonalcoholic	year	203	91	81r
Bologna, all beef or mixed	lb.	2.12	12/94	82r
Bread, white	24-oz.	0.56	12/94	2c
Bread, white, pan	lb.	0.76	12/94	82r
Cabbage	lb.	0.44	12/94	82r
Carrots, short trimmed and topped	lb.	0.44	12/94	82r
Cereals and bakery products purchases	year	347	91	81r
Cereals and cereals products purchases	year	119	91	81r
Cheddar cheese, natural	lb.	3.28	12/94	82r
Cheese, Kraft grated Parmesan	8-oz.	3.08	12/94	2c
Chicken breast, bone-in	lb.	1.61	12/94	82r
Chicken, fresh, whole	lb.	0.89	12/94	82r
Chicken, whole fryer	lb.	0.72	12/94	2c
Chuck roast, USDA choice, boneless	lb.	2.33	12/94	82r
Cigarettes, Winston, Kings	carton	14.78	12/94	2c
Coffee, 100%, ground roast, all sizes	lb.	4.28	12/94	82r
Coffee, vacuum-packed	13 oz.	3.67	12/94	2c
Cookies, chocolate chip	lb.	2.72	12/94	82r
Corn Flakes, Kellogg's or Post Toasties	18 oz.	2.06	12/94	2c
Corn, frozen, whole kernel, lowest price	10 oz.	0.74	12/94	2c
Dairy products (other) purchases	year	148	91	81r
Eggs, Grade A large	dozen	0.66	12/94	2c
Eggs, Grade A large	dozen	0.76	12/94	82r
Fish and seafood purchases	year	61	91	81r
Flour, white, all purpose	lb.	0.22	12/94	82r
Food purchases, food eaten at home	year	2313	91	81r
Foods purchased away from home, not prepared by consumer	year	1709	91	81r
Fruits and vegetables purchases	year	372	91	81r
Grapefruit	lb.	0.47	12/94	82r
Grapes, Thompson seedless	lb.	2.15	12/94	82r
Ground beef, 100% beef	lb.	1.37	12/94	82r
Ground chuck, 100% beef	lb.	1.81	12/94	82r
Ham, boneless, exc. canned	lb.	2.16	12/94	82r

Indianapolis, IN - continued

Item	Per	Value	Date	Ref.
Groceries - continued				
Ice cream, prepackaged, bulk, regular	1/2 gal.	2.48	12/94	82r
Lemons	lb.	1.08	12/94	82r
Lettuce, iceberg	lb.	0.81	12/94	82r
Lettuce, iceberg	head	0.82	12/94	2c
Margarine, Blue Bonnet or Parkay cubes	lb.	0.57	12/94	2c
Margarine, stick	lb.	0.81	12/94	82r
Meats, poultry, fish, and eggs purchases	year	591	91	81r
Milk and cream (fresh) purchases	year	132	91	81r
Milk, 2%	gal.	1.99	1/92	44c
Milk, whole	1/2 gal.	1.62	12/94	2c
Orange juice, frozen concentrate 12-oz. can	16 oz.	1.41	12/94	82r
Orange juice, Minute Maid frozen	12-oz.	1.17	12/94	2c
Oranges, Navel	lb.	0.56	12/94	82r
Peaches, halves or slices, Hunt's, Del Monte, or Libby's	29-oz.	1.27	12/94	2c
Peanut butter, creamy, all sizes	lb.	1.81	12/94	82r
Peas, sweet, Del Monte or Green Giant	15-17 oz.	0.59	12/94	2c
Pork chops, center cut, bone-in	lb.	2.76	12/94	82r
Pork purchases	year	130	91	81r
Potato chips	16-oz.	2.81	12/94	82r
Potatoes, frozen, French fried	lb.	0.83	12/94	82r
Potatoes, white	lb.	0.28	12/94	82r
Potatoes, white or red	10-lb. sack	2.49	12/94	2c
Rental rate, 2-bedroom apartment	month	450.00-700	1/92	44c
Round roast, USDA choice, boneless	lb.	2.90	12/94	82r
Sausage, Jimmy Dean, 100% pork	lb.	2.63	12/94	2c
Shortening, vegetable oil blends	lb.	0.88	12/94	82r
Shortening, vegetable, Crisco	3-lb.	2.06	12/94	2c
Soft drink, Coca Cola, ex deposit	2 lit	1.12	12/94	2c
Spaghetti and macaroni	lb.	0.78	12/94	82r
Steak, rib eye, USDA choice, boneless	lb.	6.15	12/94	82r
Steak, round, graded & ungraded, exc. USDA prime & choice	lb.	2.72	12/94	82r
Steak, round, USDA choice, boneless	lb.	3.02	12/94	82r
Steak, sirloin, USDA choice, boneless	lb.	3.85	12/94	82r
Steak, t-bone	lb.	5.08	12/94	2c
Steak, T-bone, USDA choice, bone-in	lb.	5.38	12/94	82r
Sugar and other sweets, eaten at home, expenditures	year	91	91	81r
Sugar, cane or beet	4 lbs.	1.25	12/94	2c
Sugar, white, all sizes	lb.	0.36	12/94	82r
Tobacco products and smoking supplies, total expenditures	year	298	91	81r
Tomatoes, field grown	lb.	1.36	12/94	82r
Tomatoes, Hunt's or Del Monte	14.5 oz.	0.80	12/94	2c
Tuna, chunk, light	lb.	1.94	12/94	82r
Tuna, chunk, light, oil-packed	6.125-6.5 oz.	0.63	12/94	2c
Turkey, frozen, whole	lb.	0.96	12/94	82r
Yogurt, natural, fruit flavored	8 oz.	0.62	12/94	82r
Goods and Services				
Miscellaneous goods and services, ACCRA Index		96.80	12/94	2c
Health Care				
Health care, ACCRA Index		96.90	12/94	2c
Antibiotic ointment, Polysporin	1.5 oz.	4.31	12/94	2c
Childbirth, Cesarean delivery, hospital charge	birth	5101.00	12/91	69r
Childbirth, Cesarean delivery, physician charge	birth	2234.00	12/91	69r
Childbirth, normal delivery, hospital charge	birth	2891.00	12/91	69r
Childbirth, normal delivery, physician charge	birth	1623.00	12/91	69r
Dentist's fee, adult teeth cleaning and periodic oral exam	visit	51.60	12/94	2c

Values are in dollars or fractions of dollars. In the column headed *Ref*, references are shown to sources. Each reference is followed by a letter. These refer to the geographical level for which data were reported: s=State, r=Region, and c=City or metro. The abbreviation *ex* is used to mean *except* or *excluding*; *exp* stands for expenditures. For other abbreviations and further explanations, please see the Introduction.

Indianapolis, IN - continued

Item	Per	Value	Date	Ref.
Health Care				
Doctor's fee, routine exam, established patient	visit	38.20	12/94	2c
Drugs, expenditures	year	248	91	81r
Health care, total expenditures	year	1336	91	81r
Health insurance expenditures	year	550	91	81r
Hospital care, semiprivate room	day	358.53	12/94	2c
Insurance premium, family medical care	month	353.94	1/95	41s
Medical services expenditures	year	457	91	81r
Medical supplies expenditures	year	82	91	81r
Household Goods				
Appl. repair, service call, wash mach	min. lab. chg.	28.49	12/94	2c
Floor coverings, expenditures	year	105	91	81r
Furniture, expenditures	year	291	91	81r
Household equipment, misc. expenditures	year	341	91	81r
Household expenditures, miscellaneous	year	162	91	81r
Household furnishings and equipment, expenditures	year	1042	91	81r
Household operations expenditures	year	365	91	81r
Household textiles, expenditures	year	101	91	81r
Housekeeping supplies, expenditures	year	390	91	81r
Laundry and cleaning supplies, expenditures	year	110	91	81r
Laundry detergent, Tide Ultra, Bold, or Cheer	42 oz.	3.49	12/94	2c
Postage and stationery, expenditures	year	115	91	81r
Tissues, facial, Kleenex brand	175	1.03	12/94	2c
Housing				
Housing, ACCRA Index		92.90	12/94	2c
Add garage/carport		8,479	3/95	74r
Add room(s)		21,347	3/95	74r
Apartment condominium or co-op, median	unit	87100	12/94	62r
Bathroom addition, average cost	add	9734.00	3/95	13r
Bathroom remodeling, average cost	remod	6414.00	3/95	13r
Bedroom, master suite addition, average cost	add	27122.00	3/95	13r
Deck addition, average cost	add	6665.00	3/95	13r
Dwellings (owned), expenditures	year	2566	91	81r
Enclose porch/patio/breezeway		4,556	3/95	74r
Exterior remodeling, average cost	remod	15395.00	3/95	13r
Family room addition, average cost	add	27658.00	3/95	13r
Finish room in basement/attic		5,074	3/95	74r
Home, existing, single-family, median	unit	106500	12/94	62r
Home, existing, single-family, median	unit	89.20	12/94	62c
Home, purchase price	unit	128.90	3/93	26c
House payment, principal and interest, 25% down payment	mo.	698	12/94	2c
House, 1800 sq ft, 8000 sq ft lot, new, urban, utilities	total	116125	12/94	2c
Kitchen remodeling, major, average cost	remod	17084.00	3/95	13r
Kitchen remodeling, minor, average cost	remod	5804.00	3/95	13r
Maintenance, repairs, insurance, and other housing expenditures	year	484	91	81r
Mortgage interest and charges expenditures	year	1443	91	81r
Mtge. rate, incl. points and orig. fee, 30-year conv. fixed or ARM	mo.	8.96	12/94	2c
Office, home addition, average cost	add	8121.00	3/95	13r
Princ. & int., mortgage, median-price exist. sing.-family home	mo.	515	12/94	62r
Property taxes expenditures	year	639	91	81r
Redesign, restructure more than half of home's interior		9,114	3/95	74r
Rent, apartment, 2 br., 1 1/2-2 baths, unfurnished, 950 sq ft, water	mo.	531	12/94	2c
Rental units expenditures	year	1200	91	81r
Sun-space addition, average cost	add	23768.00	3/95	13r
Wing addition, two-story, average cost	add	50410.00	3/95	13r
Insurance and Pensions				
Auto insurance, private passenger	year	586.58	12/94	71s

Indianapolis, IN - continued

Item	Per	Value	Date	Ref.
Insurance and Pensions - continued				
Insurance and pensions, personal, expenditures	year	2408	91	81r
Insurance, life and other personal, expenditures	year	355	91	81r
Pensions and Social Security, expenditures	year	2053	91	81r
Legal Assistance				
Legal work, law firm associate	hour	90		10r
Legal work, law firm partner	hour	139		10r
Personal Goods				
Shampoo, Alberto VO5	15-oz.	1.35	12/94	2c
Toothpaste, Crest or Colgate	6-7 oz.	2.13	12/94	2c
Personal Services				
Dry cleaning, man's 2-pc. suit		6.67	12/94	2c
Dry cleaning, woman's dress	dress	6.50	1/92	44c
Haircut, man's barbershop, no styling		8.60	12/94	2c
Haircut, woman's shampoo, trim, blow-dry		17.70	12/94	2c
Personal services expenditures	year	203	91	81r
Restaurant Food				
Big Mac, small fries, medium drink	meal	3.42	1/92	44c
Chicken, fried, thigh and drumstick		2.14	12/94	2c
Dining expenditures, family	week	30.03	94	73r
Hamburger with cheese	1/4 lb.	1.81	12/94	2c
Pizza, Pizza Hut or Pizza Inn	12-13 in.	7.99	12/94	2c
Taxes				
Tax rate, residential property, month	$100	1.75	1/92	79c
Taxes, Federal income, expenditures	year	1756	91	81r
Taxes, personal, expenditures	year	2426	91	81r
Taxes, State and local income, expenditures	year	568	91	81r
Transportation				
Transportation, ACCRA Index		93.90	12/94	2c
Bus fare, one-way	trip	0.75	12/95	1c
Bus fare, up to 10 miles	one-way	1.25	12/94	2c
Cars and trucks purchased, new	year	891	91	81r
Cars and trucks purchased, used	year	1155	91	81r
Driver's learning permit fee	perm	2.00	1/94	84s
Driver's license fee	orig	6.00	1/94	84s
Driver's license fee, duplicate	lic	3.00	1/94	84s
Driver's license renewal fee	renew	6.00	1/94	84s
Identification card, nondriver	card	4.00	1/94	83s
Motorcycle learning permit fee	perm	2.00	1/94	84s
Motorcycle license fee	orig	6.00	1/94	84s
Motorcycle license fee, duplicate	lic	3.00	1/94	84s
Motorcycle license renewal fee	renew	6.00	1/94	84s
parking, long-term lot, airport	3 days	10.50	1/92	44c
Public transportation expenditures	year	209	91	81r
Tire balance, computer or spin bal., front	wheel	6.12	12/94	2c
Transportation expenditures, total	year	4792	91	81r
Vehicle finance charges	year	300	91	81r
Vehicle insurance expenditures	year	485	91	81r
Vehicle maintenance and repairs expenditures	year	534	91	81r
Vehicle purchases	year	2068	91	81r
Vehicle rental, leases, licenses, etc. expenditures	year	197	91	81r
Vehicles purchased, other than cars and trucks	year	22	91	81r
Utilities				
Utilities, ACCRA Index		93.10	12/94	2c
Electricity expenditures	year	668	91	81r
Electricity, (part.), other, 1800 sq. ft., new home	mo.	49.33	12/94	2c
Electricity, summer, 250 KWh	month	20.52	8/93	64c
Electricity, summer, 500 KWh	month	40.39	8/93	64c
Electricity, summer, 750 KWh	month	49.80	8/93	64c
Electricity, summer, 1000 KWh	month	59.22	8/93	64c

Values are in dollars or fractions of dollars. In the column headed *Ref*, references are shown to sources. Each reference is followed by a letter. These refer to the geographical level for which data were reported: s = State, r = Region, and c = City or metro. The abbreviation *ex* is used to mean *except* or *excluding*; *exp* stands for expenditures. For other abbreviations and further explanations, please see the Introduction.

Indianapolis, IN - continued

Item	Per	Value	Date	Ref.
Utilities				
Utilities, fuels, and public services, total expenditures	year	1838	91	81r
Water and other public services, expenditures	year	167	91	81r
Weddings				
Bridal attendants' gowns	event	750	10/93	76r
Bridal gown	event	852	10/93	76r
Bridal headpiece and veil	event	167	10/93	76r
Bride's wedding band	event	708	10/93	76r
Clergy	event	224	10/93	76r
Engagement ring	event	2756	10/93	76r
Flowers	event	863	10/93	76r
Formal wear for groom	event	106	10/93	76r
Groom's attendants' formal wear	event	530	10/93	76r
Groom's wedding band	event	402	10/93	76r
Music	event	600	10/93	76r
Photography	event	1088	10/93	76r
Shoes for bride	event	50	10/93	76r
Videography	event	483	10/93	76r
Wedding invitations and announcements	event	342	10/93	76r
Wedding reception	event	7000	10/93	76r

Iowa City-Coralville, IA

Item	Per	Value	Date	Ref.
Appliances				
Appliances (major), expenditures	year	131	91	81r
Average annual exp.				
Food, health care, personal goods, services	year	25935	91	81r
Charity				
Cash contributions, expenditures	year	745	91	81r
Clothing				
Apparel, men and boys, total expenditures	year	332	91	81r
Apparel, women and girls, total expenditures	year	578	91	81r
Footwear, expenditures	year	164	91	81r
Communications				
Long-distance telephone rate, day, addl. min., 1-10 mi.	min.	0.11	12/93	9s
Long-distance telephone rate, day, initial min., 1-10 mi.	min.	0.21	12/93	9s
Phone line, single, business, field visit	inst	50.00	12/93	9s
Phone line, single, business, no field visit	inst	50.00	12/93	9s
Phone line, single, residence, field visit	inst	35.00	12/93	9s
Phone line, single, residence, no field visit	inst	35.00	12/93	9s
Telephone service, expenditures	year	547	91	81r
Education				
Board, 4-year private college/university	year	1971	8/94	80s
Board, 4-year public college/university	year	1562	8/94	80s
Education, total expenditures	year	394	91	81r
Room, 4-year private college/university	year	1707	8/94	80s
Room, 4-year public college/university	year	1526	8/94	80s
Total cost, 4-year private college/university	year	14510	8/94	80s
Total cost, 4-year public college/university	year	5440	8/94	80s
Tuition, 2-year public college/university, in-state	year	1612	8/94	80s
Tuition, 4-year private college/university, in-state	year	10832	8/94	80s
Tuition, 4-year public college/university, in-state	year	2352	8/94	80s
Energy and Fuels				
Fuel oil and other fuels, expenditures	year	83	91	81r
Gas, natural, expenditures	year	373	91	81r
Gasoline and motor oil purchased	year	1000	91	81r
Gasoline, unleaded midgrade	gallon	1.15	4/93	82r
Gasoline, unleaded premium	gallon	1.23	4/93	82r
Gasoline, unleaded regular	gallon	1.07	4/93	82r

Iowa City-Coralville, IA - continued

Item	Per	Value	Date	Ref.
Entertainment				
Entertainment, total expenditures	year	1356	91	81r
Fees and admissions, expenditures	year	347	91	81r
Pets, toys, playground equipment, expenditures	year	270	91	81r
Reading, expenditures	year	160	91	81r
Televisions, radios, and sound equipment, expenditures	year	433	91	81r
Funerals				
Burial, immediate, container provided by funeral home		1348.78	1/95	54r
Cards, acknowledgment		21.20	1/95	54r
Casket, minimum alternative		182.83	1/95	54r
Cosmetology, hair care, etc.		133.11	1/95	54r
Cremation, direct, container provided by funeral home		1101.95	1/95	54r
Embalming		314.45	1/95	54r
Funeral, funeral home		304.88	1/95	54r
Funeral, other facility		301.37	1/95	54r
Graveside service		290.59	1/95	54r
Hearse, local		137.37	1/95	54r
Limousine, local		82.84	1/95	54r
Memorial service		316.57	1/95	54r
Service charge, professional, nondeclinable		1099.00	1/95	54r
Visitation and viewing		209.25	1/95	54r
Groceries				
Apples, Red Delicious	lb.	0.68	12/94	82r
Bacon, sliced	lb.	1.88	12/94	82r
Bananas	lb.	0.41	12/94	82r
Beef purchases	year	197	91	81r
Beef, stew, boneless	lb.	2.52	12/94	82r
Beverage purchases, alcoholic	year	293	91	81r
Beverage purchases, nonalcoholic	year	203	91	81r
Bologna, all beef or mixed	lb.	2.12	12/94	82r
Bread, white, pan	lb.	0.76	12/94	82r
Cabbage	lb.	0.44	12/94	82r
Carrots, short trimmed and topped	lb.	0.44	12/94	82r
Cereals and bakery products purchases	year	347	91	81r
Cereals and cereals products purchases	year	119	91	81r
Cheddar cheese, natural	lb.	3.28	12/94	82r
Chicken breast, bone-in	lb.	1.61	12/94	82r
Chicken, fresh, whole	lb.	0.89	12/94	82r
Chuck roast, USDA choice, boneless	lb.	2.33	12/94	82r
Coffee, 100%, ground roast, all sizes	lb.	4.28	12/94	82r
Cookies, chocolate chip	lb.	2.72	12/94	82r
Dairy products (other) purchases	year	148	91	81r
Eggs, Grade A large	dozen	0.76	12/94	82r
Fish and seafood purchases	year	61	91	81r
Flour, white, all purpose	lb.	0.22	12/94	82r
Food purchases, food eaten at home	year	2313	91	81r
Foods purchased away from home, not prepared by consumer	year	1709	91	81r
Fruits and vegetables purchases	year	372	91	81r
Grapefruit	lb.	0.47	12/94	82r
Grapes, Thompson seedless	lb.	2.15	12/94	82r
Ground beef, 100% beef	lb.	1.37	12/94	82r
Ground chuck, 100% beef	lb.	1.81	12/94	82r
Ham, boneless, exc. canned	lb.	2.16	12/94	82r
Ice cream, prepackaged, bulk, regular	1/2 gal.	2.48	12/94	82r
Lemons	lb.	1.08	12/94	82r
Lettuce, iceberg	lb.	0.81	12/94	82r
Margarine, stick	lb.	0.81	12/94	82r
Meats, poultry, fish, and eggs purchases	year	591	91	81r
Milk and cream (fresh) purchases	year	132	91	81r
Orange juice, frozen concentrate 12-oz. can	16 oz.	1.41	12/94	82r
Oranges, Navel	lb.	0.56	12/94	82r
Peanut butter, creamy, all sizes	lb.	1.81	12/94	82r
Pork chops, center cut, bone-in	lb.	2.76	12/94	82r
Pork purchases	year	130	91	81r
Potato chips	16-oz.	2.81	12/94	82r
Potatoes, frozen, French fried	lb.	0.83	12/94	82r

Values are in dollars or fractions of dollars. In the column headed *Ref*, references are shown to sources. Each reference is followed by a letter. These refer to the geographical level for which data were reported: s=State, r=Region, and c=City or metro. The abbreviation *ex* is used to mean *except* or *excluding*; *exp* stands for *expenditures*. For other abbreviations and further explanations, please see the Introduction.

Iowa City-Coralville, IA - continued

Item	Per	Value	Date	Ref.
Groceries				
Potatoes, white	lb.	0.28	12/94	82r
Round roast, USDA choice, boneless	lb.	2.90	12/94	82r
Shortening, vegetable oil blends	lb.	0.88	12/94	82r
Spaghetti and macaroni	lb.	0.78	12/94	82r
Steak, rib eye, USDA choice, boneless	lb.	6.15	12/94	82r
Steak, round, graded & ungraded, exc. USDA prime & choice	lb.	2.72	12/94	82r
Steak, round, USDA choice, boneless	lb.	3.02	12/94	82r
Steak, sirloin, USDA choice, boneless	lb.	3.85	12/94	82r
Steak, T-bone, USDA choice, bone-in	lb.	5.38	12/94	82r
Sugar and other sweets, eaten at home, expenditures	year	91	91	81r
Sugar, white, all sizes	lb.	0.36	12/94	82r
Tobacco products and smoking supplies, total expenditures	year	298	91	81r
Tomatoes, field grown	lb.	1.36	12/94	82r
Tuna, chunk, light	lb.	1.94	12/94	82r
Turkey, frozen, whole	lb.	0.96	12/94	82r
Yogurt, natural, fruit flavored	8 oz.	0.62	12/94	82r
Health Care				
Childbirth, Cesarean delivery, hospital charge	birth	5101.00	12/91	69r
Childbirth, Cesarean delivery, physician charge	birth	2234.00	12/91	69r
Childbirth, normal delivery, hospital charge	birth	2891.00	12/91	69r
Childbirth, normal delivery, physician charge	birth	1623.00	12/91	69r
Drugs, expenditures	year	248	91	81r
Health care, total expenditures	year	1336	91	81r
Health insurance expenditures	year	550	91	81r
Insurance premium, family medical care	month	395.98	1/95	41s
Medical services expenditures	year	457	91	81r
Medical supplies expenditures	year	82	91	81r
Household Goods				
Floor coverings, expenditures	year	105	91	81r
Furniture, expenditures	year	291	91	81r
Household equipment, misc. expenditures	year	341	91	81r
Household expenditures, miscellaneous	year	162	91	81r
Household furnishings and equipment, expenditures	year	1042	91	81r
Household operations expenditures	year	365	91	81r
Household textiles, expenditures	year	101	91	81r
Housekeeping supplies, expenditures	year	390	91	81r
Laundry and cleaning supplies, expenditures	year	110	91	81r
Postage and stationery, expenditures	year	115	91	81r
Housing				
Add garage/carport		8,479	3/95	74r
Add room(s)		21,347	3/95	74r
Apartment condominium or co-op, median	unit	87100	12/94	62r
Bathroom addition, average cost	add	9734.00	3/95	13r
Bathroom remodeling, average cost	remod	6414.00	3/95	13r
Bedroom, master suite addition, average cost	add	27122.00	3/95	13r
Deck addition, average cost	add	6665.00	3/95	13r
Dwellings (owned), expenditures	year	2566	91	81r
Enclose porch/patio/breezeway		4,556	3/95	74r
Exterior remodeling, average cost	remod	15395.00	3/95	13r
Family room addition, average cost	add	27658.00	3/95	13r
Finish room in basement/attic		5,074	3/95	74r
Home, existing, single-family, median	unit	106500	12/94	62r
Kitchen remodeling, major, average cost	remod	17084.00	3/95	13r
Kitchen remodeling, minor, average cost	remod	5804.00	3/95	13r
Maintenance, repairs, insurance, and other housing expenditures	year	484	91	81r
Mortgage interest and charges expenditures	year	1443	91	81r
Office, home addition, average cost	add	8121.00	3/95	13r
Princ. & int., mortgage, median-price exist. sing.-family home	mo.	515	12/94	62r
Property taxes expenditures	year	639	91	81r
Redesign, restructure more than half of home's interior		9,114	3/95	74r

Iowa City-Coralville, IA - continued

Item	Per	Value	Date	Ref.
Housing - continued				
Rental units expenditures	year	1200	91	81r
Sun-space addition, average cost	add	23768.00	3/95	13r
Wing addition, two-story, average cost	add	50410.00	3/95	13r
Insurance and Pensions				
Auto insurance, private passenger	year	467.45	12/94	71s
Insurance and pensions, personal, expenditures	year	2408	91	81r
Insurance, life and other personal, expenditures	year	355	91	81r
Pensions and Social Security, expenditures	year	2053	91	81r
Legal Assistance				
Legal work, law firm associate	hour	90		10r
Legal work, law firm partner	hour	139		10r
Personal Services				
Personal services expenditures	year	203	91	81r
Restaurant Food				
Dining expenditures, family	week	30.03	94	73r
Taxes				
Taxes, Federal income, expenditures	year	1756	91	81r
Taxes, personal, expenditures	year	2426	91	81r
Taxes, State and local income, expenditures	year	568	91	81r
Transportation				
Cars and trucks purchased, new	year	891	91	81r
Cars and trucks purchased, used	year	1155	91	81r
Driver's learning permit fee	perm	6.00	1/94	84s
Driver's license fee	orig	0.00	1/94	84s
Driver's license fee, duplicate	lic	3.00	1/94	84s
Driver's license reinstatement fee, min.	susp	20.00	1/94	85s
Driver's license renewal fee	renew	0.00	1/94	84s
Identification card, nondriver	card	5.00	1/94	83s
Motorcycle learning permit fee	perm	8.00	1/94	84s
Motorcycle license fee	orig	8.00	1/94	84s
Motorcycle license fee, duplicate	lic	3.00	1/94	84s
Motorcycle license renewal fee	renew	8.00	1/94	84s
Public transportation expenditures	year	209	91	81r
Transportation expenditures, total	year	4792	91	81r
Vehicle finance charges	year	300	91	81r
Vehicle insurance expenditures	year	485	91	81r
Vehicle maintenance and repairs expenditures	year	534	91	81r
Vehicle purchases	year	2068	91	81r
Vehicle rental, leases, licenses, etc. expenditures	year	197	91	81r
Vehicles purchased, other than cars and trucks	year	22	91	81r
Utilities				
Electricity expenditures	year	668	91	81r
Utilities, fuels, and public services, total expenditures	year	1838	91	81r
Water and other public services, expenditures	year	167	91	81r
Weddings				
Bridal attendants' gowns	event	750	10/93	76r
Bridal gown	event	852	10/93	76r
Bridal headpiece and veil	event	167	10/93	76r
Bride's wedding band	event	708	10/93	76r
Clergy	event	224	10/93	76r
Engagement ring	event	2756	10/93	76r
Flowers	event	863	10/93	76r
Formal wear for groom	event	106	10/93	76r
Groom's attendants' formal wear	event	530	10/93	76r
Groom's wedding band	event	402	10/93	76r
Music	event	600	10/93	76r
Photography	event	1088	10/93	76r
Shoes for bride	event	50	10/93	76r
Videography	event	483	10/93	76r
Wedding invitations and announcements	event	342	10/93	76r
Wedding reception	event	7000	10/93	76r

Values are in dollars or fractions of dollars. In the column headed *Ref*, references are shown to sources. Each reference is followed by a letter. These refer to the geographical level for which data were reported: s = State, r = Region, and c = City or metro. The abbreviation *ex* is used to mean *except* or *excluding*; *exp* stands for *expenditures*. For other abbreviations and further explanations, please see the Introduction.

Jackson, MI

Item	Per	Value	Date	Ref.
Appliances				
Appliances (major), expenditures	year	131	91	81r
Average annual exp.				
Food, health care, personal goods, services	year	25935	91	81r
Charity				
Cash contributions, expenditures	year	745	91	81r
Clothing				
Apparel, men and boys, total expenditures	year	332	91	81r
Apparel, women and girls, total expenditures	year	578	91	81r
Footwear, expenditures	year	164	91	81r
Communications				
Long-distance telephone rate, day, addl. min., 1-10 mi.	min.	0.08	12/93	9s
Long-distance telephone rate, day, initial min., 1-10 mi.	min.	0.14	12/93	9s
Phone line, single, business, field visit	inst	42.00	12/93	9s
Phone line, single, business, no field visit	inst	42.00	12/93	9s
Phone line, single, residence, field visit	inst	42.00	12/93	9s
Phone line, single, residence, no field visit	inst	42.00	12/93	9s
Telephone service, expenditures	year	547	91	81r
Education				
Board, 4-year private college/university	year	2064	8/94	80s
Board, 4-year public college/university	year	2304	8/94	80s
Education, total expenditures	year	394	91	81r
Room, 4-year private college/university	year	1814	8/94	80s
Room, 4-year public college/university	year	1856	8/94	80s
Total cost, 4-year private college/university	year	12178	8/94	80s
Total cost, 4-year public college/university	year	7642	8/94	80s
Tuition, 2-year public college/university, in-state	year	1358	8/94	80s
Tuition, 4-year private college/university, in-state	year	8300	8/94	80s
Tuition, 4-year public college/university, in-state	year	3481	8/94	80s
Energy and Fuels				
Fuel oil and other fuels, expenditures	year	83	91	81r
Gas, natural, expenditures	year	373	91	81r
Gasoline and motor oil purchased	year	1000	91	81r
Gasoline, unleaded midgrade	gallon	1.15	4/93	82r
Gasoline, unleaded premium	gallon	1.23	4/93	82r
Gasoline, unleaded regular	gallon	1.07	4/93	82r
Entertainment				
Entertainment, total expenditures	year	1356	91	81r
Fees and admissions, expenditures	year	347	91	81r
Pets, toys, playground equipment, expenditures	year	270	91	81r
Reading, expenditures	year	160	91	81r
Televisions, radios, and sound equipment, expenditures	year	433	91	81r
Funerals				
Burial, immediate, container provided by funeral home		1268.31	1/95	54r
Cards, acknowledgment		26.12	1/95	54r
Casket, minimum alternative		198.03	1/95	54r
Cosmetology, hair care, etc.		122.19	1/95	54r
Cremation, direct, container provided by funeral home		977.81	1/95	54r
Embalming		334.00	1/95	54r
Funeral, funeral home		321.16	1/95	54r
Funeral, other facility		317.73	1/95	54r
Graveside service		292.48	1/95	54r
Hearse, local		153.20	1/95	54r
Limousine, local		123.52	1/95	54r
Memorial service		356.30	1/95	54r
Service charge, professional, nondeclinable		968.24	1/95	54r
Visitation and viewing		332.66	1/95	54r

Jackson, MI - continued

Item	Per	Value	Date	Ref.
Groceries				
Apples, Red Delicious	lb.	0.68	12/94	82r
Bacon, sliced	lb.	1.88	12/94	82r
Bananas	lb.	0.41	12/94	82r
Beef purchases	year	197	91	81r
Beef, stew, boneless	lb.	2.52	12/94	82r
Beverage purchases, alcoholic	year	293	91	81r
Beverage purchases, nonalcoholic	year	203	91	81r
Bologna, all beef or mixed	lb.	2.12	12/94	82r
Bread, white, pan	lb.	0.76	12/94	82r
Cabbage	lb.	0.44	12/94	82r
Carrots, short trimmed and topped	lb.	0.44	12/94	82r
Cereals and bakery products purchases	year	347	91	81r
Cereals and cereals products purchases	year	119	91	81r
Cheddar cheese, natural	lb.	3.28	12/94	82r
Chicken breast, bone-in	lb.	1.61	12/94	82r
Chicken, fresh, whole	lb.	0.89	12/94	82r
Chuck roast, USDA choice, boneless	lb.	2.33	12/94	82r
Coffee, 100%, ground roast, all sizes	lb.	4.28	12/94	82r
Cookies, chocolate chip	lb.	2.72	12/94	82r
Dairy products (other) purchases	year	148	91	81r
Eggs, Grade A large	dozen	0.76	12/94	82r
Fish and seafood purchases	year	61	91	81r
Flour, white, all purpose	lb.	0.22	12/94	82r
Food purchases, food eaten at home	year	2313	91	81r
Foods purchased away from home, not prepared by consumer	year	1709	91	81r
Fruits and vegetables purchases	year	372	91	81r
Grapefruit	lb.	0.47	12/94	82r
Grapes, Thompson seedless	lb.	2.15	12/94	82r
Ground beef, 100% beef	lb.	1.37	12/94	82r
Ground chuck, 100% beef	lb.	1.81	12/94	82r
Ham, boneless, exc. canned	lb.	2.16	12/94	82r
Ice cream, prepackaged, bulk, regular	1/2 gal.	2.48	12/94	82r
Lemons	lb.	1.08	12/94	82r
Lettuce, iceberg	lb.	0.81	12/94	82r
Margarine, stick	lb.	0.81	12/94	82r
Meats, poultry, fish, and eggs purchases	year	591	91	81r
Milk and cream (fresh) purchases	year	132	91	81r
Orange juice, frozen concentrate 12-oz. can	16 oz.	1.41	12/94	82r
Oranges, Navel	lb.	0.56	12/94	82r
Peanut butter, creamy, all sizes	lb.	1.81	12/94	82r
Pork chops, center cut, bone-in	lb.	2.76	12/94	82r
Pork purchases	year	130	91	81r
Potato chips	16-oz.	2.81	12/94	82r
Potatoes, frozen, French fried	lb.	0.83	12/94	82r
Potatoes, white	lb.	0.28	12/94	82r
Round roast, USDA choice, boneless	lb.	2.90	12/94	82r
Shortening, vegetable oil blends	lb.	0.88	12/94	82r
Spaghetti and macaroni	lb.	0.78	12/94	82r
Steak, rib eye, USDA choice, boneless	lb.	6.15	12/94	82r
Steak, round, graded & ungraded, exc. USDA prime & choice	lb.	2.72	12/94	82r
Steak, round, USDA choice, boneless	lb.	3.02	12/94	82r
Steak, sirloin, USDA choice, boneless	lb.	3.85	12/94	82r
Steak, T-bone, USDA choice, bone-in	lb.	5.38	12/94	82r
Sugar and other sweets, eaten at home, expenditures	year	91	91	81r
Sugar, white, all sizes	lb.	0.36	12/94	82r
Tobacco products and smoking supplies, total expenditures	year	298	91	81r
Tomatoes, field grown	lb.	1.36	12/94	82r
Tuna, chunk, light	lb.	1.94	12/94	82r
Turkey, frozen, whole	lb.	0.96	12/94	82r
Yogurt, natural, fruit flavored	8 oz.	0.62	12/94	82r
Health Care				
Childbirth, Cesarean delivery, hospital charge	birth	5101.00	12/91	69r
Childbirth, Cesarean delivery, physician charge	birth	2234.00	12/91	69r
Childbirth, normal delivery, hospital charge	birth	2891.00	12/91	69r
Childbirth, normal delivery, physician charge	birth	1623.00	12/91	69r

Values are in dollars or fractions of dollars. In the column headed *Ref*, references are shown to sources. Each reference is followed by a letter. These refer to the geographical level for which data were reported: s = State, r = Region, and c = City or metro. The abbreviation *ex* is used to mean *except* or *excluding*; *exp* stands for expenditures. For other abbreviations and further explanations, please see the Introduction.

Jackson, MI - continued

Item	Per	Value	Date	Ref.
Health Care				
Drugs, expenditures	year	248	91	81r
Health care, total expenditures	year	1336	91	81r
Health insurance expenditures	year	550	91	81r
Insurance premium, family medical care	month	369.41	1/95	41s
Medical services expenditures	year	457	91	81r
Medical supplies expenditures	year	82	91	81r
Household Goods				
Floor coverings, expenditures	year	105	91	81r
Furniture, expenditures	year	291	91	81r
Household equipment, misc. expenditures	year	341	91	81r
Household expenditures, miscellaneous	year	162	91	81r
Household furnishings and equipment, expenditures	year	1042	91	81r
Household operations expenditures	year	365	91	81r
Household textiles, expenditures	year	101	91	81r
Housekeeping supplies, expenditures	year	390	91	81r
Laundry and cleaning supplies, expenditures	year	110	91	81r
Postage and stationery, expenditures	year	115	91	81r
Housing				
Add garage/carport		8,479	3/95	74r
Add room(s)		21,347	3/95	74r
Apartment condominium or co-op, median	unit	87100	12/94	62r
Bathroom addition, average cost	add	9734.00	3/95	13r
Bathroom remodeling, average cost	remod	6414.00	3/95	13r
Bedroom, master suite addition, average cost	add	27122.00	3/95	13r
Deck addition, average cost	add	6665.00	3/95	13r
Dwellings (owned), expenditures	year	2566	91	81r
Enclose porch/patio/breezeway		4,556	3/95	74r
Exterior remodeling, average cost	remod	15395.00	3/95	13r
Family room addition, average cost	add	27658.00	3/95	13r
Finish room in basement/attic		5,074	3/95	74r
Home, existing, single-family, median	unit	106500	12/94	62r
Kitchen remodeling, major, average cost	remod	17084.00	3/95	13r
Kitchen remodeling, minor, average cost	remod	5804.00	3/95	13r
Maintenance, repairs, insurance, and other housing expenditures	year	484	91	81r
Mortgage interest and charges expenditures	year	1443	91	81r
Office, home addition, average cost	add	8121.00	3/95	13r
Princ. & int., mortgage, median-price exist. sing.-family home	mo.	515	12/94	62r
Property taxes expenditures	year	639	91	81r
Redesign, restructure more than half of home's interior		9,114	3/95	74r
Rental units expenditures	year	1200	91	81r
Sun-space addition, average cost	add	23768.00	3/95	13r
Wing addition, two-story, average cost	add	50410.00	3/95	13r
Insurance and Pensions				
Auto insurance, private passenger	year	788.26	12/94	71s
Insurance and pensions, personal, expenditures	year	2408	91	81r
Insurance, life and other personal, expenditures	year	355	91	81r
Pensions and Social Security, expenditures	year	2053	91	81r
Legal Assistance				
Legal work, law firm associate	hour	90		10r
Legal work, law firm partner	hour	139		10r
Personal Services				
Personal services expenditures	year	203	91	81r
Restaurant Food				
Dining expenditures, family	week	30.03	94	73r
Taxes				
Taxes, Federal income, expenditures	year	1756	91	81r
Taxes, personal, expenditures	year	2426	91	81r
Taxes, State and local income, expenditures	year	568	91	81r

Jackson, MI - continued

Item	Per	Value	Date	Ref.
Transportation				
Cars and trucks purchased, new	year	891	91	81r
Cars and trucks purchased, used	year	1155	91	81r
Driver's learning permit fee	perm	12.00	1/94	84s
Driver's license fee	orig	12.00	1/94	84s
Driver's license fee, duplicate	lic	6.00	1/94	84s
Driver's license reinstatement fee, min.	susp	125.00	1/94	85s
Driver's license renewal fee	renew	12.00	1/94	84s
Identification card, nondriver	card	6.00	1/94	83s
Motorcycle license fee	orig	7.50	1/94	84s
Motorcycle license renewal fee	renew	4.00	1/94	84s
Public transportation expenditures	year	209	91	81r
Transportation expenditures, total	year	4792	91	81r
Vehicle finance charges	year	300	91	81r
Vehicle insurance expenditures	year	485	91	81r
Vehicle maintenance and repairs expenditures	year	534	91	81r
Vehicle purchases	year	2068	91	81r
Vehicle rental, leases, licenses, etc. expenditures	year	197	91	81r
Vehicles purchased, other than cars and trucks	year	22	91	81r
Utilities				
Electricity expenditures	year	668	91	81r
Utilities, fuels, and public services, total expenditures	year	1838	91	81r
Water and other public services, expenditures	year	167	91	81r
Weddings				
Bridal attendants' gowns	event	750	10/93	76r
Bridal gown	event	852	10/93	76r
Bridal headpiece and veil	event	167	10/93	76r
Bride's wedding band	event	708	10/93	76r
Clergy	event	224	10/93	76r
Engagement ring	event	2756	10/93	76r
Flowers	event	863	10/93	76r
Formal wear for groom	event	106	10/93	76r
Groom's attendants' formal wear	event	530	10/93	76r
Groom's wedding band	event	402	10/93	76r
Music	event	600	10/93	76r
Photography	event	1088	10/93	76r
Shoes for bride	event	50	10/93	76r
Videography	event	483	10/93	76r
Wedding invitations and announcements	event	342	10/93	76r
Wedding reception	event	7000	10/93	76r

Jackson, MS

Item	Per	Value	Date	Ref.
Composite, ACCRA index		95.20	12/94	2c
Alcoholic Beverages				
Beer, Miller Lite, Bud, 12-oz., ex deposit	6	3.90	12/94	2c
J & B Scotch	750-ml.	16.83	12/94	2c
Wine, Gallo Chablis blanc	1.5-lit	5.59	12/94	2c
Appliances				
Appliances (major), expenditures	year	153	91	81r
Average annual exp.				
Food, health care, personal goods, services	year	27020	91	81r
Charity				
Cash contributions, expenditures	year	839	91	81r
Clothing				
Apparel, men and boys, total expenditures	year	380	91	81r
Apparel, women and girls, total expenditures	year	660	91	81r
Footwear, expenditures	year	193	91	81r
Jeans, man's denim		28.32	12/94	2c
Shirt, man's dress shirt		26.87	12/94	2c
Undervest, boy's size 10-14, cotton	3	2.91	12/94	2c

Values are in dollars or fractions of dollars. In the column headed *Ref*, references are shown to sources. Each reference is followed by a letter. These refer to the geographical level for which data were reported: s = State, r = Region, and c = City or metro. The abbreviation *ex* is used to mean *except* or *excluding*; *exp* stands for expenditures. For other abbreviations and further explanations, please see the Introduction.

Jackson, MS - continued

Item	Per	Value	Date	Ref.
Communications				
Long-distance telephone rate, day, addl. min., 1-10 mi.	min.	0.11	12/93	9s
Long-distance telephone rate, day, initial min., 1-10 mi.	min.	0.19	12/93	9s
Newspaper subscription, dly. and Sun. delivery	month	13.50	12/94	2c
Phone line, single, business, field visit	inst	67.00	12/93	9s
Phone line, single, business, no field visit	inst	67.00	12/93	9s
Phone line, single, residence, field visit	inst	46.00	12/93	9s
Phone line, single, residence, no field visit	inst	46.00	12/93	9s
Telephone bill, family of four	month	27.29	12/94	2c
Telephone service, expenditures	year	616	91	81r
Telephone, residential, flat rate	mo.	19.01	12/93	8c
Education				
Board, 4-year private college/university	year	1394	8/94	80s
Board, 4-year public college/university	year	1380	8/94	80s
Education, total expenditures	year	319	91	81r
Room, 4-year private college/university	year	1400	8/94	80s
Room, 4-year public college/university	year	1343	8/94	80s
Total cost, 4-year private college/university	year	8754	8/94	80s
Total cost, 4-year public college/university	year	5093	8/94	80s
Tuition, 2-year public college/university, in-state	year	939	8/94	80s
Tuition, 4-year private college/university, in-state	year	5959	8/94	80s
Tuition, 4-year public college/university, in-state	year	2370	8/94	80s
Energy and Fuels				
Energy, combined forms, 1800 sq. ft.	mo.	105.55	12/94	2c
Energy, exc. electricity, 1800 sq. ft.	mo.	30.83	12/94	2c
Fuel oil and other fuels, expenditures	year	56	91	81r
Gas, cooking, 10 therms	month	8.14	2/94	65c
Gas, cooking, 30 therms	month	18.01	2/94	65c
Gas, cooking, 50 therms	month	27.88	2/94	65c
Gas, heating, winter, 100 therms	month	52.56	2/94	65c
Gas, heating, winter, average use	month	65.78	2/94	65c
Gas, natural, expenditures	year	150	91	81r
Gas, reg unlead, taxes inc., cash, self-service	gal	1.09	12/94	2c
Gasoline and motor oil purchased	year	1152	91	81r
Gasoline, unleaded midgrade	gallon	1.21	4/93	82r
Gasoline, unleaded premium	gallon	1.30	4/93	82r
Gasoline, unleaded regular	gallon	1.10	4/93	82r
Entertainment				
Bowling, evening rate	game	2.50	12/94	2c
Concert ticket, Pearl Jam group	perf	20.00	94	50r
Entertainment, total expenditures	year	1266	91	81r
Fees and admissions, expenditures	year	306	91	81r
Monopoly game, Parker Brothers', No. 9	game	10.74	12/94	2c
Movie	adm	5.50	12/94	2c
Pets, toys, playground equipment, expenditures	year	271	91	81r
Reading, expenditures	year	131	91	81r
Televisions, radios, and sound equipment, expenditures	year	439	91	81r
Tennis balls, yellow, Wilson or Penn, 3	can	1.94	12/94	2c
Funerals				
Burial, immediate, container provided by funeral home		1298.96	1/95	54r
Cards, acknowledgment		21.26	1/95	54r
Casket, minimum alternative		204.95	1/95	54r
Cosmetology, hair care, etc.		85.40	1/95	54r
Cremation, direct, container provided by funeral home		1054.77	1/95	54r
Embalming		287.71	1/95	54r
Funeral, funeral home		269.18	1/95	54r
Funeral, other facility		272.88	1/95	54r
Graveside service		302.54	1/95	54r
Hearse, local		122.08	1/95	54r
Limousine, local		80.31	1/95	54r

Jackson, MS - continued

Item	Per	Value	Date	Ref.
Funerals - continued				
Memorial service		277.66	1/95	54r
Service charge, professional, nondeclinable		896.65	1/95	54r
Visitation and viewing		232.39	1/95	54r
Groceries				
Groceries, ACCRA Index		96.10	12/94	2c
Apples, Red Delicious	lb.	0.73	12/94	82r
Baby food, strained vegetables, lowest price	4-4.5 oz.	0.25	12/94	2c
Bacon, sliced	lb.	1.67	12/94	82r
Bananas	lb.	0.51	12/94	2c
Bananas	lb.	0.42	12/94	82r
Beef or hamburger, ground	lb.	1.40	12/94	2c
Beef purchases	year	213	91	81r
Beverage purchases, alcoholic	year	249	91	81r
Beverage purchases, nonalcoholic	year	207	91	81r
Bologna, all beef or mixed	lb.	2.27	12/94	82r
Bread, white	24-oz.	0.58	12/94	2c
Bread, white, pan	lb.	0.68	12/94	82r
Cabbage	lb.	0.42	12/94	82r
Carrots, short trimmed and topped	lb.	0.53	12/94	82r
Cereals and bakery products purchases	year	345	91	81r
Cereals and cereals products purchases	year	127	91	81r
Cheddar cheese, natural	lb.	3.58	12/94	82r
Cheese, Kraft grated Parmesan	8-oz.	3.30	12/94	2c
Chicken breast, bone-in	lb.	1.71	12/94	82r
Chicken, fresh, whole	lb.	0.78	12/94	82r
Chicken, whole fryer	lb.	0.83	12/94	2c
Chuck roast, USDA choice, boneless	lb.	2.26	12/94	82r
Cigarettes, Winston, Kings	carton	15.65	12/94	2c
Coffee, vacuum-packed	13 oz.	3.67	12/94	2c
Corn Flakes, Kellogg's or Post Toasties	18 oz.	2.36	12/94	2c
Corn, frozen, whole kernel, lowest price	10 oz.	0.83	12/94	2c
Crackers, soda, salted	lb.	1.27	12/94	82r
Cucumbers	lb.	0.65	12/94	82r
Dairy products (other) purchases	year	141	91	81r
Eggs, Grade A large	dozen	0.75	12/94	2c
Eggs, Grade A large	dozen	0.87	12/94	82r
Fish and seafood purchases	year	72	91	81r
Flour, white, all purpose	lb.	0.23	12/94	82r
Food purchases, food eaten at home	year	2381	91	81r
Foods purchased away from home, not prepared by consumer	year	1696	91	81r
Frankfurters, all meat or all beef	lb.	1.74	12/94	82r
Fruits and vegetables purchases	year	380	91	81r
Grapefruit	lb.	0.45	12/94	82r
Grapes, Thompson seedless	lb.	2.30	12/94	82r
Ground beef, 100% beef	lb.	1.37	12/94	82r
Ground chuck, 100% beef	lb.	1.97	12/94	82r
Ham, boneless, exc. canned	lb.	2.54	12/94	82r
Ice cream, prepackaged, bulk, regular	1/2 gal.	2.47	12/94	82r
Lemons	lb.	1.02	12/94	82r
Lettuce, iceberg	lb.	0.96	12/94	82r
Lettuce, iceberg	head	0.82	12/94	2c
Margarine, Blue Bonnet or Parkay cubes	lb.	0.58	12/94	2c
Margarine, stick	lb.	0.77	12/94	82r
Meats, poultry, fish, and eggs purchases	year	655	91	81r
Milk and cream (fresh) purchases	year	130	91	81r
Milk, whole	1/2 gal.	1.40	12/94	2c
Orange juice, frozen concentrate 12-oz. can	16 oz.	1.36	12/94	82r
Orange juice, Minute Maid frozen	12-oz.	1.43	12/94	2c
Oranges, Navel	lb.	0.54	12/94	82r
Peaches, halves or slices, Hunt's, Del Monte, or Libby's	29-oz.	1.39	12/94	2c
Pears, Anjou	lb.	0.81	12/94	82r
Peas, sweet, Del Monte or Green Giant	15-17 oz.	0.64	12/94	2c
Pork chops, center cut, bone-in	lb.	3.07	12/94	82r
Pork purchases	year	142	91	81r
Potato chips	16-oz.	3.15	12/94	82r
Potatoes, frozen, French fried	lb.	0.82	12/94	82r

Values are in dollars or fractions of dollars. In the column headed *Ref*, references are shown to sources. Each reference is followed by a letter. These refer to the geographical level for which data were reported: s = State, r = Region, and c = City or metro. The abbreviation *ex* is used to mean *except* or *excluding*; *exp* stands for *expenditures*. For other abbreviations and further explanations, please see the Introduction.

Jackson, MS - continued

Item	Per	Value	Date	Ref.
Groceries				
Potatoes, white	lb.	0.34	12/94	82r
Potatoes, white or red	10-lb. sack	2.12	12/94	2c
Rice, white, long grain, uncooked	lb.	0.48	12/94	82r
Round roast, USDA choice, boneless	lb.	2.91	12/94	82r
Sausage, fresh	lb.	1.82	12/94	82r
Sausage, Jimmy Dean, 100% pork	lb.	2.23	12/94	2c
Shortening, vegetable oil blends	lb.	0.75	12/94	82r
Shortening, vegetable, Crisco	3-lb.	2.42	12/94	2c
Soft drink, Coca Cola, ex deposit	2 lit	0.94	12/94	2c
Spaghetti and macaroni	lb.	0.87	12/94	82r
Steak, rib eye, USDA choice, boneless	lb.	6.85	12/94	82r
Steak, round, graded & ungraded, exc. USDA prime & choice	lb.	2.96	12/94	82r
Steak, round, USDA choice, boneless	lb.	3.17	12/94	82r
Steak, sirloin, USDA choice, boneless	lb.	4.12	12/94	82r
Steak, t-bone	lb.	4.83	12/94	2c
Steak, T-bone, USDA choice, bone-in	lb.	5.63	12/94	82r
Sugar and other sweets, eaten at home, expenditures	year	93	91	81r
Sugar, cane or beet	4 lbs.	1.59	12/94	2c
Sugar, white, all sizes	lb.	0.39	12/94	82r
Tobacco products and smoking supplies, total expenditures	year	286	91	81r
Tomatoes, field grown	lb.	1.36	12/94	82r
Tomatoes, Hunt's or Del Monte	14.5 oz.	0.82	12/94	2c
Tuna, chunk, light	lb.	1.94	12/94	82r
Tuna, chunk, light, oil-packed	6.125-6.5 oz.	0.59	12/94	2c
Turkey, frozen, whole	lb.	0.96	12/94	82r
Yogurt, natural, fruit flavored	8 oz.	0.58	12/94	82r
Goods and Services				
Miscellaneous goods and services, ACCRA Index		92.10	12/94	2c
Health Care				
Health care, ACCRA Index		80.00	12/94	2c
Adenosine, emergency room	treat	100.00	95	23r
Antibiotic ointment, Polysporin	1.5 oz.	3.89	95	2c
Bladder tap, superpubic, infant, emergency room	treat	119.00	95	23r
Blood analysis, emergency room	treat	25.00	95	23r
Blood tests, abdominal pain, emergency room	treat	25.00	95	23r
Burn dressing, emergency room	treat	266.00	95	23r
Cardiology interpretation, emergency room	treat	26.00	95	23r
Chest X-ray, emergency room	treat	78.00	95	23r
Childbirth, Cesarean delivery, hospital charge	birth	5462.00	12/91	69r
Childbirth, Cesarean delivery, physician charge	birth	2228.00	12/91	69r
Childbirth, normal delivery, hospital charge	birth	2943.00	12/91	69r
Childbirth, normal delivery, physician charge	birth	1619.00	12/91	69r
Defibrillation pads, emergency room	treat	6.00	95	23r
Dentist's fee, adult teeth cleaning and periodic oral exam	visit	41.80	12/94	2c
Doctor's fee, routine exam, established patient	visit	36.20	12/94	2c
Drugs, expenditures	year	297	91	81r
Gastric tube insertion, nasal, emergency room	treat	25.00	95	23r
Health care, total expenditures	year	1600	91	81r
Health insurance expenditures	year	637	91	81r
Heart monitor, emergency room	treat	40.00	95	23r
Hospital care, semiprivate room	day	211.87	12/94	2c
Intravenous fluids, emergency room	treat	130.00	95	23r
Intravenous fluids, emergency room	liter	26.00	95	23r
Intravenous line, central, emergency room	treat	342.00	95	23r
Liver function tests, abdominal pain, emergency room	treat	26.00	95	23r

Jackson, MS - continued

Item	Per	Value	Date	Ref.
Health Care - continued				
Medical care charges, total, emergency room, third-degree burns	treat	2101.00	95	23r
Medical care charges, total, emergency, infant with fever	treat	628.00	95	23r
Medical services expenditures	year	573	91	81r
Medical supplies expenditures	year	93	91	81r
Morphine, emergency room	treat	34.00	95	23r
Nursing care and facilities charges, emergency room	treat	252.00	95	23r
Nursing care and facilities charges, emergency, infant with fever	treat	252.00	95	23r
Nursing care and facilities charges, emergency, third-degree burns	treat	861.00	95	23r
Physician's charges, emergency, infant with fever	treat	212.00	95	23r
Physician's charges, emergency, third-degree burns	treat	372.00	95	23r
Physician's fee, emergency room	treat	372.00	95	23r
Physician's fee, general practitioner	visit	51.20	12/93	60r
Surgery, open-heart	proc	42374.00	1/93	14r
Ultrasound, abdominal, emergency room	treat	276.00	95	23r
Urinalysis, emergency room	treat	20.00	95	23r
Urinalysis, infant, emergency room	treat	20.00	95	23r
X-rays, emergency room	treat	78.00	95	23r
Household Goods				
Appl. repair, service call, wash mach	min. lab. chg.	31.83	12/94	2c
Floor coverings, expenditures	year	48	91	81r
Furniture, expenditures	year	280	91	81r
Household equipment, misc. expenditures	year	342	91	81r
Household expenditures, miscellaneous	year	256	91	81r
Household furnishings and equipment, expenditures	year	988	91	81r
Household operations expenditures	year	468	91	81r
Household textiles, expenditures	year	95	91	81r
Housekeeping supplies, expenditures	year	380	91	81r
Laundry and cleaning supplies, expenditures	year	109	91	81r
Laundry detergent, Tide Ultra, Bold, or Cheer	42 oz.	3.45	12/94	2c
Postage and stationery, expenditures	year	105	91	81r
Tissues, facial, Kleenex brand	175	1.09	12/94	2c
Housing				
Housing, ACCRA Index		101.60	12/94	2c
Add garage/carport		6,980	3/95	74r
Add room(s)		11,403	3/95	74r
Apartment condominium or co-op, median	unit	68600	12/94	62r
Dwellings (owned), expenditures	year	2428	91	81r
Enclose porch/patio/breezeway		4,572	3/95	74r
Finish room in basement/attic		3,794	3/95	74r
Home, existing, single-family, median	unit	120200	12/94	62r
House payment, principal and interest, 25% down payment	mo.	789	12/94	2c
House, 1800 sq ft, 8000 sq ft lot, new, urban, utilities	total	126660	12/94	2c
Maintenance, repairs, insurance, and other housing expenditures	year	531	91	81r
Mortgage interest and charges expenditures	year	1506	91	81r
Mtge. rate, incl. points and orig. fee, 30-year conv. fixed or ARM	mo.	9.36	12/94	2c
Princ. & int., mortgage, median-price exist. sing.-family home	mo.	540	12/94	62r
Property taxes expenditures	year	391	91	81r
Redesign, restructure more than half of home's interior		17,641	3/95	74r
Rent, apartment, 2 br., 1 1/2-2 baths, unfurnished, 950 sq ft, water	mo.	506	12/94	2c
Rental units expenditures	year	1264	91	81r

Values are in dollars or fractions of dollars. In the column headed *Ref*, references are shown to sources. Each reference is followed by a letter. These refer to the geographical level for which data were reported: s = State, r = Region, and c = City or metro. The abbreviation *ex* is used to mean *except* or *excluding*; *exp* stands for *expenditures*. For other abbreviations and further explanations, please see the Introduction.

American Cost of Living Survey, 2nd Edition

Jackson, TN

Jackson, MS - continued

Item	Per	Value	Date	Ref.
Insurance and Pensions				
Auto insurance, private passenger	year	643.74	12/94	71s
Insurance and pensions, personal, expenditures	year	2395	91	81r
Insurance, life and other personal, expenditures	year	368	91	81r
Pensions and Social Security, expenditures	year	2027	91	81r
Personal Goods				
Shampoo, Alberto VO5	15-oz.	0.98	12/94	2c
Toothpaste, Crest or Colgate	6-7 oz.	1.83	12/94	2c
Personal Services				
Dry cleaning, man's 2-pc. suit		4.58	12/94	2c
Haircut, man's barbershop, no styling		8.10	12/94	2c
Haircut, woman's shampoo, trim, blow-dry		22.00	12/94	2c
Personal services expenditures	year	212	91	81r
Restaurant Food				
Chicken, fried, thigh and drumstick		1.49	12/94	2c
Dining expenditures, family	week	33.83	94	73r
Hamburger with cheese	1/4 lb.	1.88	12/94	2c
Pizza, Pizza Hut or Pizza Inn	12-13 in.	7.99	12/94	2c
Taxes				
Tax rate, residential property, month	$100	1.47	1/92	79c
Taxes, Federal income, expenditures	year	2275	91	81r
Taxes, personal, expenditures	year	2715	91	81r
Taxes, State and local income, expenditures	year	365	91	81r
Transportation				
Transportation, ACCRA Index		91.20	12/94	2c
Bus fare, one-way	trip	0.75	12/95	1c
Bus fare, up to 10 miles	one-way	0.75	12/94	2c
Cars and trucks purchased, new	year	1306	91	81r
Cars and trucks purchased, used	year	942	91	81r
Driver's learning permit fee	perm	1.00	1/94	84s
Driver's license fee	orig	20.00	1/94	84s
Driver's license fee, duplicate	lic	5.00	1/94	84s
Driver's license renewal fee	renew	20.00	1/94	84s
Identification card, nondriver	card	13.00	1/94	83s
Motorcycle license fee	orig	5.00	1/94	84s
Public transportation expenditures	year	249	91	81r
Tire balance, computer or spin bal., front	wheel	5.90	12/94	2c
Transportation expenditures, total	year	5307	91	81r
Vehicle finance charges	year	346	91	81r
Vehicle insurance expenditures	year	544	91	81r
Vehicle maintenance and repairs expenditures	year	600	91	81r
Vehicle purchases	year	2275	91	81r
Vehicle rental, leases, licenses, etc. expenditures	year	141	91	81r
Vehicles purchased, other than cars and trucks	year	27	91	81r
Utilities				
Utilities, ACCRA Index		100.20	12/94	2c
Electricity expenditures	year	950	91	81r
Electricity, (part.), other, 1800 sq. ft., new home	mo.	74.72	12/94	2c
Electricity, summer, 250 KWh	month	31.34	8/93	64c
Electricity, summer, 500 KWh	month	56.39	8/93	64c
Electricity, summer, 750 KWh	month	76.26	8/93	64c
Electricity, summer, 1000 KWh	month	96.13	8/93	64c
Utilities, fuels, and public services, total expenditures	year	2000	91	81r
Water and other public services, expenditures	year	227	91	81r
Weddings				
Bridal attendants' gowns	event	750	10/93	76r
Bridal gown	event	852	10/93	76r
Bridal headpiece and veil	event	167	10/93	76r
Bride's wedding band	event	708	10/93	76r

Jackson, MS - continued

Item	Per	Value	Date	Ref.
Weddings - continued				
Clergy	event	224	10/93	76r
Engagement ring	event	2756	10/93	76r
Flowers	event	863	10/93	76r
Formal wear for groom	event	106	10/93	76r
Groom's attendants' formal wear	event	530	10/93	76r
Groom's wedding band	event	402	10/93	76r
Music	event	600	10/93	76r
Photography	event	1088	10/93	76r
Shoes for bride	event	50	10/93	76r
Videography	event	483	10/93	76r
Wedding invitations and announcements	event	342	10/93	76r
Wedding reception	event	7000	10/93	76r

Jackson, TN

Item	Per	Value	Date	Ref.
Composite, ACCRA index		92.00	12/94	2c
Alcoholic Beverages				
Beer, Miller Lite, Bud, 12-oz., ex deposit	6	4.00	12/94	2c
J & B Scotch	750-ml.	19.09	12/94	2c
Wine, Gallo Chablis blanc	1.5-lit	6.71	12/94	2c
Appliances				
Appliances (major), expenditures	year	153	91	81r
Average annual exp.				
Food, health care, personal goods, services	year	27020	91	81r
Charity				
Cash contributions, expenditures	year	839	91	81r
Clothing				
Apparel, men and boys, total expenditures	year	380	91	81r
Apparel, women and girls, total expenditures	year	660	91	81r
Footwear, expenditures	year	193	91	81r
Jeans, man's denim		33.99	12/94	2c
Shirt, man's dress shirt		38.10	12/94	2c
Undervest, boy's size 10-14, cotton	3	3.22	12/94	2c
Communications				
Long-distance telephone rate, day, addl. min., 1-10 mi.	min.	0.10	12/93	9s
Long-distance telephone rate, day, initial min., 1-10 mi.	min.	0.10	12/93	9s
Newspaper subscription, dly. and Sun. delivery	month	10.50	12/94	2c
Phone line, single, business, field visit	inst	58.50	12/93	9s
Phone line, single, business, no field visit	inst	58.50	12/93	9s
Phone line, single, residence, field visit	inst	41.50	12/93	9s
Phone line, single, residence, no field visit	inst	41.50	12/93	9s
Telephone bill, family of four	month	18.77	12/94	2c
Telephone service, expenditures	year	616	91	81r
Telephone, residential, flat rate	mo.	9.05	12/93	8c
Education				
Board, 4-year private college/university	year	1846	8/94	80s
Board, 4-year public college/university	year	1700	8/94	80s
Education, total expenditures	year	319	91	81r
Room, 4-year private college/university	year	1553	8/94	80s
Room, 4-year public college/university	year	1524	8/94	80s
Total cost, 4-year private college/university	year	12025	8/94	80s
Total cost, 4-year public college/university	year	5021	8/94	80s
Tuition, 2-year public college/university, in-state	year	950	8/94	80s
Tuition, 4-year private college/university, in-state	year	8627	8/94	80s
Tuition, 4-year public college/university, in-state	year	1797	8/94	80s
Energy and Fuels				
Energy, combined forms, 1800 sq. ft.	mo.	98.17	12/94	2c
Fuel oil and other fuels, expenditures	year	56	91	81r
Gas, natural, expenditures	year	150	91	81r

Values are in dollars or fractions of dollars. In the column headed *Ref*, references are shown to sources. Each reference is followed by a letter. These refer to the geographical level for which data were reported: s=State, r=Region, and c=City or metro. The abbreviation *ex* is used to mean *except* or *excluding*; *exp* stands for expenditures. For other abbreviations and further explanations, please see the Introduction.

377

Jackson, TN - continued

Item	Per	Value	Date	Ref.
Energy and Fuels				
Gas, reg unlead, taxes inc., cash, self-service	gal	1.18	12/94	2c
Gasoline and motor oil purchased	year	1152	91	81r
Gasoline, unleaded midgrade	gallon	1.21	4/93	82r
Gasoline, unleaded premium	gallon	1.30	4/93	82r
Gasoline, unleaded regular	gallon	1.10	4/93	82r
Entertainment				
Bowling, evening rate	game	2.00	12/94	2c
Concert ticket, Pearl Jam group	perf	20.00	94	50r
Entertainment, total expenditures	year	1266	91	81r
Fees and admissions, expenditures	year	306	91	81r
Monopoly game, Parker Brothers', No. 9	game	9.92	12/94	2c
Movie	adm	5.50	12/94	2c
Pets, toys, playground equipment, expenditures	year	271	91	81r
Reading, expenditures	year	131	91	81r
Televisions, radios, and sound equipment, expenditures	year	439	91	81r
Tennis balls, yellow, Wilson or Penn, 3	can	1.92	12/94	2c
Funerals				
Burial, immediate, container provided by funeral home		1298.96	1/95	54r
Cards, acknowledgment		21.26	1/95	54r
Casket, minimum alternative		204.95	1/95	54r
Cosmetology, hair care, etc.		85.40	1/95	54r
Cremation, direct, container provided by funeral home		1054.77	1/95	54r
Embalming		287.71	1/95	54r
Funeral, funeral home		269.18	1/95	54r
Funeral, other facility		272.88	1/95	54r
Graveside service		302.54	1/95	54r
Hearse, local		122.08	1/95	54r
Limousine, local		80.31	1/95	54r
Memorial service		277.66	1/95	54r
Service charge, professional, nondeclinable		896.65	1/95	54r
Visitation and viewing		232.39	1/95	54r
Groceries				
Groceries, ACCRA Index		96.50	12/94	2c
Apples, Red Delicious	lb.	0.73	12/94	82r
Baby food, strained vegetables, lowest price	4-4.5 oz.	0.33	12/94	2c
Bacon, sliced	lb.	1.67	12/94	82r
Bananas	lb.	0.45	12/94	2c
Bananas	lb.	0.42	12/94	82r
Beef or hamburger, ground	lb.	1.52	12/94	2c
Beef purchases	year	213	91	81r
Beverage purchases, alcoholic	year	249	91	81r
Beverage purchases, nonalcoholic	year	207	91	81r
Bologna, all beef or mixed	lb.	2.27	12/94	82r
Bread, white	24-oz.	0.71	12/94	2c
Bread, white, pan	lb.	0.68	12/94	82r
Cabbage	lb.	0.42	12/94	82r
Carrots, short trimmed and topped	lb.	0.53	12/94	82r
Cereals and bakery products purchases	year	345	91	81r
Cereals and cereals products purchases	year	127	91	81r
Cheddar cheese, natural	lb.	3.58	12/94	82r
Cheese, Kraft grated Parmesan	8-oz.	3.53	12/94	2c
Chicken breast, bone-in	lb.	1.71	12/94	82r
Chicken, fresh, whole	lb.	0.78	12/94	82r
Chicken, whole fryer	lb.	0.54	12/94	2c
Chuck roast, USDA choice, boneless	lb.	2.26	12/94	82r
Cigarettes, Winston, Kings	carton	14.68	12/94	2c
Coffee, vacuum-packed	13 oz.	3.82	12/94	2c
Corn Flakes, Kellogg's or Post Toasties	18 oz.	2.80	12/94	2c
Corn, frozen, whole kernel, lowest price	10 oz.	1.03	12/94	2c
Crackers, soda, salted	lb.	1.27	12/94	82r
Cucumbers	lb.	0.65	12/94	82r
Dairy products (other) purchases	year	141	91	81r
Eggs, Grade A large	dozen	0.58	12/94	2c
Eggs, Grade A large	dozen	0.87	12/94	82r
Fish and seafood purchases	year	72	91	81r

Jackson, TN - continued

Item	Per	Value	Date	Ref.
Groceries - continued				
Flour, white, all purpose	lb.	0.23	12/94	82r
Food purchases, food eaten at home	year	2381	91	81r
Foods purchased away from home, not prepared by consumer	year	1696	91	81r
Frankfurters, all meat or all beef	lb.	1.74	12/94	82r
Fruits and vegetables purchases	year	380	91	81r
Grapefruit	lb.	0.45	12/94	82r
Grapes, Thompson seedless	lb.	2.30	12/94	82r
Ground beef, 100% beef	lb.	1.37	12/94	82r
Ground chuck, 100% beef	lb.	1.97	12/94	82r
Ham, boneless, exc. canned	lb.	2.54	12/94	82r
Ice cream, prepackaged, bulk, regular	1/2 gal.	2.47	12/94	82r
Lemons	lb.	1.02	12/94	82r
Lettuce, iceberg	lb.	0.96	12/94	82r
Lettuce, iceberg	head	0.55	12/94	2c
Margarine, Blue Bonnet or Parkay cubes	lb.	0.48	12/94	2c
Margarine, stick	lb.	0.77	12/94	82r
Meats, poultry, fish, and eggs purchases	year	655	91	81r
Milk and cream (fresh) purchases	year	130	91	81r
Milk, whole	1/2 gal.	1.24	12/94	2c
Orange juice, frozen concentrate 12-oz. can	16 oz.	1.36	12/94	82r
Orange juice, Minute Maid frozen	12-oz.	1.43	12/94	2c
Oranges, Navel	lb.	0.54	12/94	82r
Peaches, halves or slices, Hunt's, Del Monte, or Libby's	29-oz.	1.24	12/94	2c
Pears, Anjou	lb.	0.81	12/94	82r
Peas, sweet, Del Monte or Green Giant	15-17 oz.	0.61	12/94	2c
Pork chops, center cut, bone-in	lb.	3.07	12/94	82r
Pork purchases	year	142	91	81r
Potato chips	16-oz.	3.15	12/94	82r
Potatoes, frozen, French fried	lb.	0.82	12/94	82r
Potatoes, white	lb.	0.34	12/94	82r
Potatoes, white or red	10-lb. sack	1.99	12/94	2c
Rice, white, long grain, uncooked	lb.	0.48	12/94	82r
Round roast, USDA choice, boneless	lb.	2.91	12/94	82r
Sausage, fresh	lb.	1.82	12/94	82r
Sausage, Jimmy Dean, 100% pork	lb.	2.12	12/94	2c
Shortening, vegetable oil blends	lb.	0.75	12/94	82r
Shortening, vegetable, Crisco	3-lb.	2.70	12/94	2c
Soft drink, Coca Cola, ex deposit	2 lit	0.87	12/94	2c
Spaghetti and macaroni	lb.	0.87	12/94	82r
Steak, rib eye, USDA choice, boneless	lb.	6.85	12/94	82r
Steak, round, graded & ungraded, exc. USDA prime & choice	lb.	2.96	12/94	82r
Steak, round, USDA choice, boneless	lb.	3.17	12/94	82r
Steak, sirloin, USDA choice, boneless	lb.	4.12	12/94	82r
Steak, t-bone	lb.	4.65	12/94	2c
Steak, T-bone, USDA choice, bone-in	lb.	5.63	12/94	82r
Sugar and other sweets, eaten at home, expenditures	year	93	91	81r
Sugar, cane or beet	4 lbs.	1.48	12/94	2c
Sugar, white, all sizes	lb.	0.39	12/94	82r
Tobacco products and smoking supplies, total expenditures	year	286	91	81r
Tomatoes, field grown	lb.	1.36	12/94	82r
Tomatoes, Hunt's or Del Monte	14.5 oz.	0.77	12/94	2c
Tuna, chunk, light	lb.	1.94	12/94	82r
Tuna, chunk, light, oil-packed	6.125-6.5 oz.	0.63	12/94	2c
Turkey, frozen, whole	lb.	0.96	12/94	82r
Yogurt, natural, fruit flavored	8 oz.	0.58	12/94	82r
Goods and Services				
Miscellaneous goods and services, ACCRA Index		100.40	12/94	2c

Values are in dollars or fractions of dollars. In the column headed *Ref*, references are shown to sources. Each reference is followed by a letter. These refer to the geographical level for which data were reported: s=State, r=Region, and c=City or metro. The abbreviation *ex* is used to mean *except* or *excluding*; *exp* stands for *expenditures*. For other abbreviations and further explanations, please see the Introduction.

Jackson, TN - continued

Item	Per	Value	Date	Ref.
Health Care				
Health care, ACCRA Index		78.60	12/94	2c
Adenosine, emergency room	treat	100.00	95	23r
Antibiotic ointment, Polysporin	1.5 oz.	3.74	12/94	2c
Bladder tap, superpubic, infant, emergency room	treat	119.00	95	23r
Blood analysis, emergency room	treat	25.00	95	23r
Blood tests, abdominal pain, emergency room	treat	25.00	95	23r
Burn dressing, emergency room	treat	266.00	95	23r
Cardiology interpretation, emergency room	treat	26.00	95	23r
Chest X-ray, emergency room	treat	78.00	95	23r
Childbirth, Cesarean delivery, hospital charge	birth	5462.00	12/91	69r
Childbirth, Cesarean delivery, physician charge	birth	2228.00	12/91	69r
Childbirth, normal delivery, hospital charge	birth	2943.00	12/91	69r
Childbirth, normal delivery, physician charge	birth	1619.00	12/91	69r
Defibrillation pads, emergency room	treat	6.00	95	23r
Dentist's fee, adult teeth cleaning and periodic oral exam	visit	44.40	12/94	2c
Doctor's fee, routine exam, established patient	visit	30.60	12/94	2c
Drugs, expenditures	year	297	91	81r
Gastric tube insertion, nasal, emergency room	treat	25.00	95	23r
Health care, total expenditures	year	1600	91	81r
Health insurance expenditures	year	637	91	81r
Heart monitor, emergency room	treat	40.00	95	23r
Hospital care, semiprivate room	day	251.00	12/94	2c
Insurance premium, family medical care	month	344.21	1/95	41s
Intravenous fluids, emergency room	treat	130.00	95	23r
Intravenous fluids, emergency room	liter	26.00	95	23r
Intravenous line, central, emergency room	treat	342.00	95	23r
Liver function tests, abdominal pain, emergency room	treat	26.00	95	23r
Medical care charges, total, emergency room, third-degree burns	treat	2101.00	95	23r
Medical care charges, total, emergency, infant with fever	treat	628.00	95	23r
Medical services expenditures	year	573	91	81r
Medical supplies expenditures	year	93	91	81r
Morphine, emergency room	treat	34.00	95	23r
Nursing care and facilities charges, emergency room	treat	252.00	95	23r
Nursing care and facilities charges, emergency, infant with fever	treat	252.00	95	23r
Nursing care and facilities charges, emergency, third-degree burns	treat	861.00	95	23r
Physician's charges, emergency, infant with fever	treat	212.00	95	23r
Physician's charges, emergency, third-degree burns	treat	372.00	95	23r
Physician's fee, emergency room	treat	372.00	95	23r
Physician's fee, general practitioner	visit	51.20	12/93	60r
Surgery, open-heart	proc	42374.00	1/93	14r
Ultrasound, abdominal, emergency room	treat	276.00	95	23r
Urinalysis, emergency room	treat	20.00	95	23r
Urinalysis, infant, emergency room	treat	20.00	95	23r
X-rays, emergency room	treat	78.00	95	23r
Household Goods				
Appl. repair, service call, wash mach	min. lab. chg.	35.50	12/94	2c
Floor coverings, expenditures	year	48	91	81r
Furniture, expenditures	year	280	91	81r
Household equipment, misc. expenditures	year	342	91	81r
Household expenditures, miscellaneous	year	256	91	81r
Household furnishings and equipment, expenditures	year	988	91	81r
Household operations expenditures	year	468	91	81r
Household textiles, expenditures	year	95	91	81r
Housekeeping supplies, expenditures	year	380	91	81r

Jackson, TN - continued

Item	Per	Value	Date	Ref.
Household Goods - continued				
Laundry and cleaning supplies, expenditures	year	109	91	81r
Laundry detergent, Tide Ultra, Bold, or Cheer	42 oz.	4.08	12/94	2c
Postage and stationery, expenditures	year	105	91	81r
Tissues, facial, Kleenex brand	175	0.97	12/94	2c
Housing				
Housing, ACCRA Index		81.90	12/94	2c
Add garage/carport		6,980	3/95	74r
Add room(s)		11,403	3/95	74r
Apartment condominium or co-op, median	unit	68600	12/94	62r
Dwellings (owned), expenditures	year	2428	91	81r
Enclose porch/patio/breezeway		4,572	3/95	74r
Finish room in basement/attic		3,794	3/95	74r
Home, existing, single-family, median	unit	120200	12/94	62r
House payment, principal and interest, 25% down payment	mo.	607	12/94	2c
House, 1800 sq ft, 8000 sq ft lot, new, urban, utilities	total	98750	12/94	2c
Maintenance, repairs, insurance, and other housing expenditures	year	531	91	81r
Mortgage interest and charges expenditures	year	1506	91	81r
Mtge. rate, incl. points and orig. fee, 30-year conv. fixed or ARM	mo.	9.22	12/94	2c
Princ. & int., mortgage, median-price exist. sing.-family home	mo.	540	12/94	62r
Property taxes expenditures	year	391	91	81r
Redesign, restructure more than half of home's interior		17,641	3/95	74r
Rent, apartment, 2 br., 1 1/2-2 baths, unfurnished, 950 sq ft, water	mo.	490	12/94	2c
Rental units expenditures	year	1264	91	81r
Insurance and Pensions				
Auto insurance, private passenger	year	574.08	12/94	71s
Insurance and pensions, personal, expenditures	year	2395	91	81r
Insurance, life and other personal, expenditures	year	368	91	81r
Pensions and Social Security, expenditures	year	2027	91	81r
Personal Goods				
Shampoo, Alberto VO5	15-oz.	0.92	12/94	2c
Toothpaste, Crest or Colgate	6-7 oz.	1.71	12/94	2c
Personal Services				
Dry cleaning, man's 2-pc. suit		6.25	12/94	2c
Haircut, man's barbershop, no styling		7.35	12/94	2c
Haircut, woman's shampoo, trim, blow-dry		19.00	12/94	2c
Personal services expenditures	year	212	91	81r
Restaurant Food				
Chicken, fried, thigh and drumstick		2.02	12/94	2c
Dining expenditures, family	week	33.83	94	73r
Hamburger with cheese	1/4 lb.	1.85	12/94	2c
Pizza, Pizza Hut or Pizza Inn	12-13 in.	7.93	12/94	2c
Taxes				
Tax, cigarettes	year	379.00	10/93	43s
Taxes, Federal income, expenditures	year	2275	91	81r
Taxes, personal, expenditures	year	2715	91	81r
Taxes, State and local income, expenditures	year	365	91	81r
Transportation				
Transportation, ACCRA Index		96.20	12/94	2c
Cars and trucks purchased, new	year	1306	91	81r
Cars and trucks purchased, used	year	942	91	81r
Driver's learning permit fee	perm	5.50	1/94	84s
Driver's license fee	orig	16.00	1/94	84s
Driver's license fee, duplicate	lic	8.00	1/94	84s
Driver's license reinstatement fee, min.	susp	65.00	1/94	85s
Driver's license renewal fee	renew	14.00	1/94	84s
Identification card, nondriver	card	7.50	1/94	83s

Values are in dollars or fractions of dollars. In the column headed *Ref*, references are shown to sources. Each reference is followed by a letter. These refer to the geographical level for which data were reported: s=State, r=Region, and c=City or metro. The abbreviation *ex* is used to mean *except* or *excluding*; *exp* stands for expenditures. For other abbreviations and further explanations, please see the Introduction.

Jackson, TN - continued

Item	Per	Value	Date	Ref.
Transportation				
Motorcycle learning permit fee	perm	6.50	1/94	84s
Motorcycle license fee	orig	17.00	1/94	84s
Motorcycle license fee, duplicate	lic	8.00	1/94	84s
Motorcycle license renewal fee	renew	15.00	1/94	84s
Public transportation expenditures	year	249	91	81r
Tire balance, computer or spin bal., front	wheel	5.70	12/94	2c
Transportation expenditures, total	year	5307	91	81r
Vehicle finance charges	year	346	91	81r
Vehicle insurance expenditures	year	544	91	81r
Vehicle maintenance and repairs expenditures	year	600	91	81r
Vehicle purchases	year	2275	91	81r
Vehicle rental, leases, licenses, etc. expenditures	year	141	91	81r
Vehicles purchased, other than cars and trucks	year	27	91	81r
Utilities				
Utilities, ACCRA Index		88.70	12/94	2c
Electricity expenditures	year	950	91	81r
Electricity, 1800 sq. ft., new home	mo.	98.17	12/94	2c
Utilities, fuels, and public services, total expenditures	year	2000	91	81r
Water and other public services, expenditures	year	227	91	81r
Weddings				
Bridal attendants' gowns	event	750	10/93	76r
Bridal gown	event	852	10/93	76r
Bridal headpiece and veil	event	167	10/93	76r
Bride's wedding band	event	708	10/93	76r
Clergy	event	224	10/93	76r
Engagement ring	event	2756	10/93	76r
Flowers	event	863	10/93	76r
Formal wear for groom	event	106	10/93	76r
Groom's attendants' formal wear	event	530	10/93	76r
Groom's wedding band	event	402	10/93	76r
Music	event	600	10/93	76r
Photography	event	1088	10/93	76r
Shoes for bride	event	50	10/93	76r
Videography	event	483	10/93	76r
Wedding invitations and announcements	event	342	10/93	76r
Wedding reception	event	7000	10/93	76r

Jacksonville, FL

Item	Per	Value	Date	Ref.
Composite, ACCRA index		94.90	12/94	2c
Alcoholic Beverages				
Beer, Miller Lite, Bud, 12-oz., ex deposit	6	3.86	12/94	2c
J & B Scotch	750-ml.	17.20	12/94	2c
Wine, Gallo Chablis blanc	1.5-lit	4.69	12/94	2c
Appliances				
Appliances (major), expenditures	year	153	91	81r
Average annual exp.				
Food, health care, personal goods, services	year	27020	91	81r
Charity				
Cash contributions, expenditures	year	839	91	81r
Clothing				
Apparel, men and boys, total expenditures	year	380	91	81r
Apparel, women and girls, total expenditures	year	660	91	81r
Footwear, expenditures	year	193	91	81r
Jeans, man's denim		30.49	12/94	2c
Shirt, man's dress shirt		29.62	12/94	2c
Undervest, boy's size 10-14, cotton	3	3.67	12/94	2c
Communications				
Long-distance telephone rate, day, addl. min., 1-10 mi.	min.	0.08	12/93	9s

Jacksonville, FL - continued

Item	Per	Value	Date	Ref.
Communications - continued				
Long-distance telephone rate, day, initial min., 1-10 min.	min.	0.15	12/93	9s
Newspaper subscription, dly. and Sun. delivery	month	10.44	12/94	2c
Phone line, single, business, field visit	inst	86.00	12/93	9s
Phone line, single, business, no field visit	inst	54.50	12/93	9s
Phone line, single, residence, field visit	inst	76.00	12/93	9s
Phone line, single, residence, no field visit	inst	44.50	12/93	9s
Telephone bill, family of four	month	16.98	12/94	2c
Telephone service, expenditures	year	616	91	81r
Telephone, residential, flat rate	mo.	10.05	12/93	8c
Education				
Bar examinination preparatory course	course	500.00-100	94	17s
Board, 4-year private college/university	year	2123	8/94	80s
Board, 4-year public college/university	year	2101	8/94	80s
Education, total expenditures	year	319	91	81r
Room, 4-year private college/university	year	2242	8/94	80s
Room, 4-year public college/university	year	1970	8/94	80s
Total cost, 4-year private college/university	year	13853	8/94	80s
Total cost, 4-year public college/university	year	5855	8/94	80s
Tuition, 2-year public college/university, in-state	year	1076	8/94	80s
Tuition, 4-year private college/university, in-state	year	9287	8/94	80s
Tuition, 4-year public college/university, in-state	year	1784	8/94	80s
Energy and Fuels				
Energy, combined forms, 1800 sq. ft.	mo.	113.71	12/94	2c
Fuel oil and other fuels, expenditures	year	56	91	81r
Gas, natural, expenditures	year	150	91	81r
Gas, reg unlead, taxes inc., cash, self-service	gal	1.14	12/94	2c
Gasoline and motor oil purchased	year	1152	91	81r
Gasoline, unleaded midgrade	gallon	1.21	4/93	82r
Gasoline, unleaded premium	gallon	1.30	4/93	82r
Gasoline, unleaded regular	gallon	1.10	4/93	82r
Entertainment				
Bowling, evening rate	game	2.60	12/94	2c
Concert ticket, Pearl Jam group	perf	20.00	94	50r
Entertainment, total expenditures	year	1266	91	81r
Fees and admissions, expenditures	year	306	91	81r
Monopoly game, Parker Brothers', No. 9	game	10.94	12/94	2c
Movie	adm	5.58	12/94	2c
Pets, toys, playground equipment, expenditures	year	271	91	81r
Reading, expenditures	year	131	91	81r
Televisions, radios, and sound equipment, expenditures	year	439	91	81r
Tennis balls, yellow, Wilson or Penn, 3	can	2.36	12/94	2c
Funerals				
Burial, immediate, container provided by funeral home		1370.36	1/95	54r
Cards, acknowledgment		14.83	1/95	54r
Casket, minimum alternative		192.52	1/95	54r
Cosmetology, hair care, etc.		102.27	1/95	54r
Cremation, direct, container provided by funeral home		1065.64	1/95	54r
Embalming		304.29	1/95	54r
Funeral, funeral home		287.83	1/95	54r
Funeral, other facility		284.14	1/95	54r
Graveside service		349.13	1/95	54r
Hearse, local		132.27	1/95	54r
Limousine, local		98.45	1/95	54r
Memorial service		270.59	1/95	54r
Service charge, professional, nondeclinable		933.59	1/95	54r
Visitation and viewing		225.83	1/95	54r
Groceries				
Groceries, ACCRA Index		98.30	12/94	2c

Values are in dollars or fractions of dollars. In the column headed *Ref*, references are shown to sources. Each reference is followed by a letter. These refer to the geographical level for which data were reported: s = State, r = Region, and c = City or metro. The abbreviation *ex* is used to mean *except* or *excluding*; *exp* stands for expenditures. For other abbreviations and further explanations, please see the Introduction.

Jacksonville, FL - continued

Item	Per	Value	Date	Ref.
Groceries				
Apples, Red Delicious	lb.	0.73	12/94	82r
Baby food, strained vegetables, lowest price	4-4.5 oz.	0.34	12/94	2c
Bacon, sliced	lb.	1.67	12/94	82r
Bananas	lb.	0.32	12/94	2c
Bananas	lb.	0.42	12/94	82r
Beef or hamburger, ground	lb.	1.43	12/94	2c
Beef purchases	year	213	91	81r
Beverage purchases, alcoholic	year	249	91	81r
Beverage purchases, nonalcoholic	year	207	91	81r
Bologna, all beef or mixed	lb.	2.27	12/94	82r
Bread, white	24-oz.	0.87	12/94	2c
Bread, white, pan	lb.	0.68	12/94	82r
Cabbage	lb.	0.42	12/94	82r
Carrots, short trimmed and topped	lb.	0.53	12/94	82r
Cereals and bakery products purchases	year	345	91	81r
Cereals and cereals products purchases	year	127	91	81r
Cheddar cheese, natural	lb.	3.58	12/94	82r
Cheese, Kraft grated Parmesan	8-oz.	3.27	12/94	2c
Chicken breast, bone-in	lb.	1.71	12/94	82r
Chicken, fresh, whole	lb.	0.78	12/94	82r
Chicken, whole fryer	lb.	0.91	12/94	2c
Chuck roast, USDA choice, boneless	lb.	2.26	12/94	82r
Cigarettes, Winston, Kings	carton	16.96	12/94	2c
Coffee, vacuum-packed	13 oz.	3.31	12/94	2c
Corn Flakes, Kellogg's or Post Toasties	18 oz.	2.28	12/94	2c
Corn, frozen, whole kernel, lowest price	10 oz.	0.62	12/94	2c
Crackers, soda, salted	lb.	1.27	12/94	82r
Cucumbers	lb.	0.65	12/94	82r
Dairy products (other) purchases	year	141	91	81r
Eggs, Grade A large	dozen	0.74	12/94	2c
Eggs, Grade A large	dozen	0.87	12/94	82r
Fish and seafood purchases	year	72	91	81r
Flour, white, all purpose	lb.	0.23	12/94	82r
Food purchases, food eaten at home	year	2381	91	81r
Foods purchased away from home, not prepared by consumer	year	1696	91	81r
Frankfurters, all meat or all beef	lb.	1.74	12/94	82r
Fruits and vegetables purchases	year	380	91	81r
Grapefruit	lb.	0.45	12/94	82r
Grapes, Thompson seedless	lb.	2.30	12/94	82r
Ground beef, 100% beef	lb.	1.37	12/94	82r
Ground chuck, 100% beef	lb.	1.97	12/94	82r
Ham, boneless, exc. canned	lb.	2.54	12/94	82r
Ice cream, prepackaged, bulk, regular	1/2 gal.	2.47	12/94	82r
Lemons	lb.	1.02	12/94	82r
Lettuce, iceberg	lb.	0.96	12/94	82r
Lettuce, iceberg	head	0.91	12/94	2c
Margarine, Blue Bonnet or Parkay cubes	lb.	0.56	12/94	2c
Margarine, stick	lb.	0.77	12/94	82r
Meats, poultry, fish, and eggs purchases	year	655	91	81r
Milk and cream (fresh) purchases	year	130	91	81r
Milk, whole	1/2 gal.	1.39	12/94	2c
Orange juice, frozen concentrate 12-oz. can	16 oz.	1.36	12/94	82r
Orange juice, Minute Maid frozen	12-oz.	1.11	12/94	2c
Oranges, Navel	lb.	0.54	12/94	82r
Peaches, halves or slices, Hunt's, Del Monte, or Libby's	29-oz.	1.28	12/94	2c
Pears, Anjou	lb.	0.81	12/94	82r
Peas, sweet, Del Monte or Green Giant	15-17 oz.	0.47	12/94	2c
Pork chops, center cut, bone-in	lb.	3.07	12/94	82r
Pork purchases	year	142	91	81r
Potato chips	16-oz.	3.15	12/94	82r
Potatoes, frozen, French fried	lb.	0.82	12/94	82r
Potatoes, white	lb.	0.34	12/94	82r
Potatoes, white or red	10-lb. sack	2.59	12/94	2c
Rice, white, long grain, uncooked	lb.	0.48	12/94	82r
Round roast, USDA choice, boneless	lb.	2.91	12/94	82r

Jacksonville, FL - continued

Item	Per	Value	Date	Ref.
Groceries - continued				
Sausage, fresh	lb.	1.82	12/94	82r
Sausage, Jimmy Dean, 100% pork	lb.	2.31	12/94	2c
Shortening, vegetable oil blends	lb.	0.75	12/94	82r
Shortening, vegetable, Crisco	3-lb.	2.45	12/94	2c
Soft drink, Coca Cola, ex deposit	2 lit	1.13	12/94	2c
Spaghetti and macaroni	lb.	0.87	12/94	82r
Steak, rib eye, USDA choice, boneless	lb.	6.85	12/94	82r
Steak, round, graded & ungraded, exc. USDA prime & choice	lb.	2.96	12/94	82r
Steak, round, USDA choice, boneless	lb.	3.17	12/94	82r
Steak, sirloin, USDA choice, boneless	lb.	4.12	12/94	82r
Steak, t-bone	lb.	5.95	12/94	2c
Steak, T-bone, USDA choice, bone-in	lb.	5.63	12/94	82r
Sugar and other sweets, eaten at home, expenditures	year	93	91	81r
Sugar, cane or beet	4 lbs.	1.50	12/94	2c
Sugar, white, all sizes	lb.	0.39	12/94	82r
Tobacco products and smoking supplies, total expenditures	year	286	91	81r
Tomatoes, field grown	lb.	1.36	12/94	82r
Tomatoes, Hunt's or Del Monte	14.5 oz.	0.67	12/94	2c
Tuna, chunk, light	lb.	1.94	12/94	82r
Tuna, chunk, light, oil-packed	6.125-6.5 oz.	0.64	12/94	2c
Turkey, frozen, whole	lb.	0.96	12/94	82r
Yogurt, natural, fruit flavored	8 oz.	0.58	12/94	82r
Goods and Services				
Miscellaneous goods and services, ACCRA Index		98.00	12/94	2c
Health Care				
Health care, ACCRA Index		104.80	12/94	2c
Adenosine, emergency room	treat	100.00	95	23r
Antibiotic ointment, Polysporin	1.5 oz.	3.71	12/94	2c
Bladder tap, superpubic, infant, emergency room	treat	119.00	95	23r
Blood analysis, emergency room	treat	25.00	95	23r
Blood tests, abdominal pain, emergency room	treat	25.00	95	23r
Burn dressing, emergency room	treat	266.00	95	23r
Cardiology interpretation, emergency room	treat	26.00	95	23r
Chest X-ray, emergency room	treat	78.00	95	23r
Childbirth, Cesarean delivery, hospital charge	birth	5462.00	12/91	69r
Childbirth, Cesarean delivery, physician charge	birth	2228.00	12/91	69r
Childbirth, normal delivery, hospital charge	birth	2943.00	12/91	69r
Childbirth, normal delivery, physician charge	birth	1619.00	12/91	69r
Defibrillation pads, emergency room	treat	6.00	95	23r
Dentist's fee, adult teeth cleaning and periodic oral exam	visit	54.20	12/94	2c
Doctor's fee, routine exam, established patient	visit	50.60	12/94	2c
Drugs, expenditures	year	297	91	81r
Gastric tube insertion, nasal, emergency room	treat	25.00	95	23r
Health care, total expenditures	year	1600	91	81r
Health insurance expenditures	year	637	91	81r
Heart monitor, emergency room	treat	40.00	95	23r
Hospital care, semiprivate room	day	304.20	12/94	2c
Insurance premium, family medical care	month	301.92	1/95	41s
Intravenous fluids, emergency room	treat	130.00	95	23r
Intravenous fluids, emergency room	liter	26.00	95	23r
Intravenous line, central, emergency room	treat	342.00	95	23r
Liver function tests, abdominal pain, emergency room	treat	26.00	95	23r
Medical care charges, total, emergency room, third-degree burns	treat	2101.00	95	23r
Medical care charges, total, emergency, infant with fever	treat	628.00	95	23r
Medical services expenditures	year	573	91	81r

Values are in dollars or fractions of dollars. In the column headed *Ref*, references are shown to sources. Each reference is followed by a letter. These refer to the geographical level for which data were reported: s=State, r=Region, and c=City or metro. The abbreviation *ex* is used to mean *except* or *excluding*; *exp* stands for expenditures. For other abbreviations and further explanations, please see the Introduction.

Jacksonville, FL - continued

Item	Per	Value	Date	Ref.
Health Care				
Medical supplies expenditures	year	93	91	81r
Morphine, emergency room	treat	34.00	95	23r
Nursing care and facilities charges, emergency room	treat	252.00	95	23r
Nursing care and facilities charges, emergency, infant with fever	treat	252.00	95	23r
Nursing care and facilities charges, emergency, third-degree burns	treat	861.00	95	23r
Physician's charges, emergency, infant with fever	treat	212.00	95	23r
Physician's charges, emergency, third-degree burns	treat	372.00	95	23r
Physician's fee, emergency room	treat	372.00	95	23r
Physician's fee, general practitioner	visit	51.20	12/93	60r
Surgery, open-heart	proc	42374.00	1/93	14r
Ultrasound, abdominal, emergency room	treat	276.00	95	23r
Urinalysis, emergency room	treat	20.00	95	23r
Urinalysis, infant, emergency room	treat	20.00	95	23r
X-rays, emergency room	treat	78.00	95	23r
Household Goods				
Appl. repair, service call, wash mach	min. lab. chg.	33.27	12/94	2c
Floor coverings, expenditures	year	48	91	81r
Furniture, expenditures	year	280	91	81r
Household equipment, misc. expenditures	year	342	91	81r
Household expenditures, miscellaneous	year	256	91	81r
Household furnishings and equipment, expenditures	year	988	91	81r
Household operations expenditures	year	468	91	81r
Household textiles, expenditures	year	95	91	81r
Housekeeping supplies, expenditures	year	380	91	81r
Laundry and cleaning supplies, expenditures	year	109	91	81r
Laundry detergent, Tide Ultra, Bold, or Cheer	42 oz.	2.73	12/94	2c
Postage and stationery, expenditures	year	105	91	81r
Tissues, facial, Kleenex brand	175	0.88	12/94	2c
Housing				
Housing, ACCRA Index		81.30	12/94	2c
Add garage/carport		6,980	3/95	74r
Add room(s)		11,403	3/95	74r
Apartment condominium or co-op, median	unit	68600	12/94	62r
Dwellings (owned), expenditures	year	2428	91	81r
Enclose porch/patio/breezeway		4,572	3/95	74r
Finish room in basement/attic		3,794	3/95	74r
Home, existing, single-family, median	unit	120200	12/94	62r
House payment, principal and interest, 25% down payment	mo.	604	12/94	2c
House, 1800 sq ft, 8000 sq ft lot, new, urban, utilities	total	98960	12/94	2c
Maintenance, repairs, insurance, and other housing expenditures	year	531	91	81r
Mortgage interest and charges expenditures	year	1506	91	81r
Mtge. rate, incl. points and orig. fee, 30-year conv. fixed or ARM	mo.	9.13	12/94	2c
Princ. & int., mortgage, median-price exist. sing.-family home	mo.	540	12/94	62r
Property taxes expenditures	year	391	91	81r
Redesign, restructure more than half of home's interior		17,641	3/95	74r
Rent, apartment, 2 br., 1 1/2-2 baths, unfurnished, 950 sq ft, water	mo.	483	12/94	2c
Rental units expenditures	year	1264	91	81r
Insurance and Pensions				
Auto insurance, private passenger	year	753.93	12/94	71s
Insurance and pensions, personal, expenditures	year	2395	91	81r
Insurance, life and other personal, expenditures	year	368	91	81r
Pensions and Social Security, expenditures	year	2027	91	81r

Jacksonville, FL - continued

Item	Per	Value	Date	Ref.
Personal Goods				
Shampoo, Alberto VO5	15-oz.	0.89	12/94	2c
Toothpaste, Crest or Colgate	6-7 oz.	1.67	12/94	2c
Personal Services				
Dry cleaning, man's 2-pc. suit		6.10	12/94	2c
Haircut, man's barbershop, no styling		7.00	12/94	2c
Haircut, woman's shampoo, trim, blow-dry		23.85	12/94	2c
Personal services expenditures	year	212	91	81r
Restaurant Food				
Chicken, fried, thigh and drumstick		2.09	12/94	2c
Dining expenditures, family	week	33.83	94	73r
Hamburger with cheese	1/4 lb.	1.84	12/94	2c
Pizza, Pizza Hut or Pizza Inn	12-13 in.	7.99	12/94	2c
Taxes				
Tax rate, residential property, month	$100	2.15	1/92	79c
Taxes, Federal income, expenditures	year	2275	91	81r
Taxes, personal, expenditures	year	2715	91	81r
Taxes, State and local income, expenditures	year	365	91	81r
Transportation				
Transportation, ACCRA Index		109.30	12/94	2c
Bus fare, one-way	trip	0.60	12/95	1c
Cars and trucks purchased, new	year	1306	91	81r
Cars and trucks purchased, used	year	942	91	81r
Commuter rail fare (automated guideway), one-way	trip	0.25	12/95	1c
Driver's learning permit fee	perm	20.00	1/94	84s
Driver's license fee	orig	20.00	1/94	84s
Driver's license fee, duplicate	lic	10.00	1/94	84s
Driver's license reinstatement fee, min.	susp	25.00	1/94	85s
Driver's license renewal fee	renew	15.00	1/94	84s
Identification card, nondriver	card	3.00	1/94	83s
Motorcycle learning permit fee	perm	20.00	1/94	84s
Motorcycle license fee	orig	20.00	1/94	84s
Motorcycle license fee, duplicate	lic	10.00	1/94	84s
Motorcycle license renewal fee	renew	15.00	1/94	84s
Public transportation expenditures	year	249	91	81r
Tire balance, computer or spin bal., front	wheel	8.09	12/94	2c
Transportation expenditures, total	year	5307	91	81r
Vehicle finance charges	year	346	91	81r
Vehicle insurance expenditures	year	544	91	81r
Vehicle maintenance and repairs expenditures	year	600	91	81r
Vehicle purchases	year	2275	91	81r
Vehicle rental, leases, licenses, etc. expenditures	year	141	91	81r
Vehicles purchased, other than cars and trucks	year	27	91	81r
Utilities				
Utilities, ACCRA Index		99.40	12/94	2c
Electricity expenditures	year	950	91	81r
Electricity, 1800 sq. ft., new home	mo.	113.71	12/94	2c
Utilities, fuels, and public services, total expenditures	year	2000	91	81r
Water and other public services, expenditures	year	227	91	81r
Weddings				
Bridal attendants' gowns	event	750	10/93	76r
Bridal gown	event	852	10/93	76r
Bridal headpiece and veil	event	167	10/93	76r
Bride's wedding band	event	708	10/93	76r
Clergy	event	224	10/93	76r
Engagement ring	event	2756	10/93	76r
Flowers	event	863	10/93	76r
Formal wear for groom	event	106	10/93	76r
Groom's attendants' formal wear	event	530	10/93	76r
Groom's wedding band	event	402	10/93	76r
Music	event	600	10/93	76r
Photography	event	1088	10/93	76r
Shoes for bride	event	50	10/93	76r

Values are in dollars or fractions of dollars. In the column headed *Ref*, references are shown to sources. Each reference is followed by a letter. These refer to the geographical level for which data were reported: s=State, r=Region, and c=City or metro. The abbreviation *ex* is used to mean *except* or *excluding*; *exp* stands for expenditures. For other abbreviations and further explanations, please see the Introduction.

Jacksonville, FL - continued

Item	Per	Value	Date	Ref.
Weddings				
Videography	event	483	10/93	76r
Wedding invitations and announcements	event	342	10/93	76r
Wedding reception	event	7000	10/93	76r

Jacksonville, NC

Item	Per	Value	Date	Ref.
Appliances				
Appliances (major), expenditures	year	153	91	81r
Average annual exp.				
Food, health care, personal goods, services	year	27020	91	81r
Charity				
Cash contributions, expenditures	year	839	91	81r
Clothing				
Apparel, men and boys, total expenditures	year	380	91	81r
Apparel, women and girls, total expenditures	year	660	91	81r
Footwear, expenditures	year	193	91	81r
Communications				
Long-distance telephone rate, day, addl. min., 1-10 mi.	min.	0.10	12/93	9s
Long-distance telephone rate, day, initial min., 1-10 mi.	min.	0.16	12/93	9s
Phone line, single, business, field visit	inst	62.50	12/93	9s
Phone line, single, business, no field visit	inst	62.50	12/93	9s
Phone line, single, residence, field visit	inst	42.75	12/93	9s
Phone line, single, residence, no field visit	inst	42.75	12/93	9s
Telephone service, expenditures	year	616	91	81r
Education				
Board, 4-year private college/university	year	2069	8/94	80s
Board, 4-year public college/university	year	1627	8/94	80s
Education, total expenditures	year	319	91	81r
Room, 4-year private college/university	year	1824	8/94	80s
Room, 4-year public college/university	year	1669	8/94	80s
Total cost, 4-year private college/university	year	13505	8/94	80s
Total cost, 4-year public college/university	year	4704	8/94	80s
Tuition, 2-year public college/university, in-state	year	577	8/94	80s
Tuition, 4-year private college/university, in-state	year	9612	8/94	80s
Tuition, 4-year public college/university, in-state	year	1409	8/94	80s
Energy and Fuels				
Fuel oil and other fuels, expenditures	year	56	91	81r
Gas, natural, expenditures	year	150	91	81r
Gasoline and motor oil purchased	year	1152	91	81r
Gasoline, unleaded midgrade	gallon	1.21	4/93	82r
Gasoline, unleaded premium	gallon	1.30	4/93	82r
Gasoline, unleaded regular	gallon	1.10	4/93	82r
Entertainment				
Concert ticket, Pearl Jam group	perf	20.00	94	50r
Entertainment, total expenditures	year	1266	91	81r
Fees and admissions, expenditures	year	306	91	81r
Pets, toys, playground equipment, expenditures	year	271	91	81r
Reading, expenditures	year	131	91	81r
Televisions, radios, and sound equipment, expenditures	year	439	91	81r
Funerals				
Burial, immediate, container provided by funeral home		1370.36	1/95	54r
Cards, acknowledgment		14.83	1/95	54r
Casket, minimum alternative		192.52	1/95	54r
Cosmetology, hair care, etc.		102.27	1/95	54r
Cremation, direct, container provided by funeral home		1065.64	1/95	54r
Embalming		304.29	1/95	54r
Funeral, funeral home		287.83	1/95	54r
Funeral, other facility		284.14	1/95	54r

Jacksonville, NC - continued

Item	Per	Value	Date	Ref.
Funerals - continued				
Graveside service		349.13	1/95	54r
Hearse, local		132.27	1/95	54r
Limousine, local		98.45	1/95	54r
Memorial service		270.59	1/95	54r
Service charge, professional, nondeclinable		933.59	1/95	54r
Visitation and viewing		225.83	1/95	54r
Groceries				
Apples, Red Delicious	lb.	0.73	12/94	82r
Bacon, sliced	lb.	1.67	12/94	82r
Bananas	lb.	0.42	12/94	82r
Beef purchases	year	213	91	81r
Beverage purchases, alcoholic	year	249	91	81r
Beverage purchases, nonalcoholic	year	207	91	81r
Bologna, all beef or mixed	lb.	2.27	12/94	82r
Bread, white, pan	lb.	0.68	12/94	82r
Cabbage	lb.	0.42	12/94	82r
Carrots, short trimmed and topped	lb.	0.53	12/94	82r
Cereals and bakery products purchases	year	345	91	81r
Cereals and cereals products purchases	year	127	91	81r
Cheddar cheese, natural	lb.	3.58	12/94	82r
Chicken breast, bone-in	lb.	1.71	12/94	82r
Chicken, fresh, whole	lb.	0.78	12/94	82r
Chuck roast, USDA choice, boneless	lb.	2.26	12/94	82r
Crackers, soda, salted	lb.	1.27	12/94	82r
Cucumbers	lb.	0.65	12/94	82r
Dairy products (other) purchases	year	141	91	81r
Eggs, Grade A large	dozen	0.87	12/94	82r
Fish and seafood purchases	year	72	91	81r
Flour, white, all purpose	lb.	0.23	12/94	82r
Food purchases, food eaten at home	year	2381	91	81r
Foods purchased away from home, not prepared by consumer	year	1696	91	81r
Frankfurters, all meat or all beef	lb.	1.74	12/94	82r
Fruits and vegetables purchases	year	380	91	81r
Grapefruit	lb.	0.45	12/94	82r
Grapes, Thompson seedless	lb.	2.30	12/94	82r
Ground beef, 100% beef	lb.	1.37	12/94	82r
Ground chuck, 100% beef	lb.	1.97	12/94	82r
Ham, boneless, exc. canned	lb.	2.54	12/94	82r
Ice cream, prepackaged, bulk, regular	1/2 gal.	2.47	12/94	82r
Lemons	lb.	1.02	12/94	82r
Lettuce, iceberg	lb.	0.96	12/94	82r
Margarine, stick	lb.	0.77	12/94	82r
Meats, poultry, fish, and eggs purchases	year	655	91	81r
Milk and cream (fresh) purchases	year	130	91	81r
Orange juice, frozen concentrate 12-oz. can	16 oz.	1.36	12/94	82r
Oranges, Navel	lb.	0.54	12/94	82r
Pears, Anjou	lb.	0.81	12/94	82r
Pork chops, center cut, bone-in	lb.	3.07	12/94	82r
Pork purchases	year	142	91	81r
Potato chips	16-oz.	3.15	12/94	82r
Potatoes, frozen, French fried	lb.	0.82	12/94	82r
Potatoes, white	lb.	0.34	12/94	82r
Rice, white, long grain, uncooked	lb.	0.48	12/94	82r
Round roast, USDA choice, boneless	lb.	2.91	12/94	82r
Sausage, fresh	lb.	1.82	12/94	82r
Shortening, vegetable oil blends	lb.	0.75	12/94	82r
Spaghetti and macaroni	lb.	0.87	12/94	82r
Steak, rib eye, USDA choice, boneless	lb.	6.85	12/94	82r
Steak, round, graded & ungraded, exc. USDA prime & choice	lb.	2.96	12/94	82r
Steak, round, USDA choice, boneless	lb.	3.17	12/94	82r
Steak, sirloin, USDA choice, boneless	lb.	4.12	12/94	82r
Steak, T-bone, USDA choice, bone-in	lb.	5.63	12/94	82r
Sugar and other sweets, eaten at home, expenditures	year	93	91	81r
Sugar, white, all sizes	lb.	0.39	12/94	82r
Tobacco products and smoking supplies, total expenditures	year	286	91	81r
Tomatoes, field grown	lb.	1.36	12/94	82r
Tuna, chunk, light	lb.	1.94	12/94	82r

Values are in dollars or fractions of dollars. In the column headed *Ref*, references are shown to sources. Each reference is followed by a letter. These refer to the geographical level for which data were reported: s=State, r=Region, and c=City or metro. The abbreviation *ex* is used to mean *except* or *excluding*; *exp* stands for expenditures. For other abbreviations and further explanations, please see the Introduction.

Jacksonville, NC - continued

Item	Per	Value	Date	Ref.
Groceries				
Turkey, frozen, whole	lb.	0.96	12/94	82r
Yogurt, natural, fruit flavored	8 oz.	0.58	12/94	82r
Health Care				
Adenosine, emergency room	treat	100.00	95	23r
Bladder tap, superpubic, infant, emergency room	treat	119.00	95	23r
Blood analysis, emergency room	treat	25.00	95	23r
Blood tests, abdominal pain, emergency room	treat	25.00	95	23r
Burn dressing, emergency room	treat	266.00	95	23r
Cardiology interpretation, emergency room	treat	26.00	95	23r
Chest X-ray, emergency room	treat	78.00	95	23r
Childbirth, Cesarean delivery, hospital charge	birth	5462.00	12/91	69r
Childbirth, Cesarean delivery, physician charge	birth	2228.00	12/91	69r
Childbirth, normal delivery, hospital charge	birth	2943.00	12/91	69r
Childbirth, normal delivery, physician charge	birth	1619.00	12/91	69r
Defibrillation pads, emergency room	treat	6.00	95	23r
Drugs, expenditures	year	297	91	81r
Gastric tube insertion, nasal, emergency room	treat	25.00	95	23r
Health care, total expenditures	year	1600	91	81r
Health insurance expenditures	year	637	91	81r
Heart monitor, emergency room	treat	40.00	95	23r
Insurance premium, family medical care	month	405.45	1/95	41s
Intravenous fluids, emergency room	treat	130.00	95	23r
Intravenous fluids, emergency room	liter	26.00	95	23r
Intravenous line, central, emergency room	treat	342.00	95	23r
Liver function tests, abdominal pain, emergency room	treat	26.00	95	23r
Medical care charges, total, emergency room, third-degree burns	treat	2101.00	95	23r
Medical care charges, total, emergency, infant with fever	treat	628.00	95	23r
Medical services expenditures	year	573	91	81r
Medical supplies expenditures	year	93	91	81r
Morphine, emergency room	treat	34.00	95	23r
Nursing care and facilities charges, emergency room	treat	252.00	95	23r
Nursing care and facilities charges, emergency, infant with fever	treat	252.00	95	23r
Nursing care and facilities charges, emergency, third-degree burns	treat	861.00	95	23r
Physician's charges, emergency, infant with fever	treat	212.00	95	23r
Physician's charges, emergency, third-degree burns	treat	372.00	95	23r
Physician's fee, emergency room	treat	372.00	95	23r
Physician's fee, general practitioner	visit	51.20	12/93	60r
Surgery, open-heart	proc	42374.00	1/93	14r
Ultrasound, abdominal, emergency room	treat	276.00	95	23r
Urinalysis, emergency room	treat	20.00	95	23r
Urinalysis, infant, emergency room	treat	20.00	95	23r
X-rays, emergency room	treat	78.00	95	23r
Household Goods				
Floor coverings, expenditures	year	48	91	81r
Furniture, expenditures	year	280	91	81r
Household equipment, misc. expenditures	year	342	91	81r
Household expenditures, miscellaneous	year	256	91	81r
Household furnishings and equipment, expenditures	year	988	91	81r
Household operations expenditures	year	468	91	81r
Household textiles, expenditures	year	95	91	81r
Housekeeping supplies, expenditures	year	380	91	81r
Laundry and cleaning supplies, expenditures	year	109	91	81r
Postage and stationery, expenditures	year	105	91	81r
Housing				
Add garage/carport		6,980	3/95	74r
Add room(s)		11,403	3/95	74r

Jacksonville, NC - continued

Item	Per	Value	Date	Ref.
Housing - continued				
Apartment condominium or co-op, median	unit	68600	12/94	62r
Dwellings (owned), expenditures	year	2428	91	81r
Enclose porch/patio/breezeway		4,572	3/95	74r
Finish room in basement/attic		3,794	3/95	74r
Home, existing, single-family, median	unit	120200	12/94	62r
Maintenance, repairs, insurance, and other housing expenditures	year	531	91	81r
Mortgage interest and charges expenditures	year	1506	91	81r
Princ. & int., mortgage, median-price exist. sing.-family home	mo.	540	12/94	62r
Property taxes expenditures	year	391	91	81r
Redesign, restructure more than half of home's interior		17,641	3/95	74r
Rental units expenditures	year	1264	91	81r
Insurance and Pensions				
Auto insurance, private passenger	year	528.43	12/94	71s
Insurance and pensions, personal, expenditures	year	2395	91	81r
Insurance, life and other personal, expenditures	year	368	91	81r
Pensions and Social Security, expenditures	year	2027	91	81r
Personal Services				
Personal services expenditures	year	212	91	81r
Restaurant Food				
Dining expenditures, family	week	33.83	94	73r
Taxes				
Taxes, Federal income, expenditures	year	2275	91	81r
Taxes, personal, expenditures	year	2715	91	81r
Taxes, State and local income, expenditures	year	365	91	81r
Transportation				
Cars and trucks purchased, new	year	1306	91	81r
Cars and trucks purchased, used	year	942	91	81r
Driver's learning permit fee	perm	10.00	1/94	84s
Driver's license fee	orig	10.00	1/94	84s
Driver's license fee, duplicate	lic	5.00	1/94	84s
Driver's license reinstatement fee, min.	susp	25.00	1/94	85s
Driver's license renewal fee	renew	10.00	1/94	84s
Fine, safety belt violation	ticket	25.00	95	56s
Identification card, nondriver	card	10.00	1/94	83s
Motorcycle license fee	orig	5.00	1/94	84s
Public transportation expenditures	year	249	91	81r
Transportation expenditures, total	year	5307	91	81r
Vehicle finance charges	year	346	91	81r
Vehicle insurance expenditures	year	544	91	81r
Vehicle maintenance and repairs expenditures	year	600	91	81r
Vehicle purchases	year	2275	91	81r
Vehicle rental, leases, licenses, etc. expenditures	year	141	91	81r
Vehicles purchased, other than cars and trucks	year	27	91	81r
Utilities				
Electricity expenditures	year	950	91	81r
Utilities, fuels, and public services, total expenditures	year	2000	91	81r
Water and other public services, expenditures	year	227	91	81r
Weddings				
Bridal attendants' gowns	event	750	10/93	76r
Bridal gown	event	852	10/93	76r
Bridal headpiece and veil	event	167	10/93	76r
Bride's wedding band	event	708	10/93	76r
Clergy	event	224	10/93	76r
Engagement ring	event	2756	10/93	76r
Flowers	event	863	10/93	76r
Formal wear for groom	event	106	10/93	76r
Groom's attendants' formal wear	event	530	10/93	76r
Groom's wedding band	event	402	10/93	76r

Values are in dollars or fractions of dollars. In the column headed *Ref*, references are shown to sources. Each reference is followed by a letter. These refer to the geographical level for which data were reported: s = State, r = Region, and c = City or metro. The abbreviation *ex* is used to mean *except* or *excluding*; *exp* stands for *expenditures*. For other abbreviations and further explanations, please see the Introduction.

Jacksonville, NC - continued

Item	Per	Value	Date	Ref.
Weddings				
Music	event	600	10/93	76r
Photography	event	1088	10/93	76r
Shoes for bride	event	50	10/93	76r
Videography	event	483	10/93	76r
Wedding invitations and announcements	event	342	10/93	76r
Wedding reception	event	7000	10/93	76r

Jamestown, NY

Item	Per	Value	Date	Ref.
Composite, ACCRA index		101.30	12/94	2c
Alcoholic Beverages				
Beer, Miller Lite, Bud, 12-oz., ex deposit	6	4.06	12/94	2c
J & B Scotch	750-ml.	18.49	12/94	2c
Wine, Gallo Chablis blanc	1.5-lit	5.71	12/94	2c
Clothing				
Jeans, man's denim		34.59	12/94	2c
Shirt, man's dress shirt		29.50	12/94	2c
Undervest, boy's size 10-14, cotton	3	3.91	12/94	2c
Communications				
Newspaper subscription, dly. and Sun. delivery	month	8.48	12/94	2c
Telephone bill, family of four	month	17.44	12/94	2c
Energy and Fuels				
Energy, combined forms, 1800 sq. ft.	mo.	128.75	12/94	2c
Energy, exc. electricity, 1800 sq. ft.	mo.	60.00	12/94	2c
Gas, reg unlead, taxes inc., cash, self-service	gal	1.25	12/94	2c
Entertainment				
Bowling, evening rate	game	1.83	12/94	2c
Monopoly game, Parker Brothers', No. 9	game	11.09	12/94	2c
Movie	adm	5.50	12/94	2c
Tennis balls, yellow, Wilson or Penn, 3	can	3.36	12/94	2c
Groceries				
Groceries, ACCRA Index		115.40	12/94	2c
Baby food, strained vegetables, lowest price	4-4.5 oz.	0.45	12/94	2c
Bananas	lb.	0.59	12/94	2c
Beef or hamburger, ground	lb.	1.59	12/94	2c
Bread, white	24-oz.	0.76	12/94	2c
Cheese, Kraft grated Parmesan	8-oz.	3.34	12/94	2c
Chicken, whole fryer	lb.	1.01	12/94	2c
Cigarettes, Winston, Kings	carton	18.75	12/94	2c
Coffee, vacuum-packed	13 oz.	4.04	12/94	2c
Corn Flakes, Kellogg's or Post Toasties	18 oz.	2.59	12/94	2c
Corn, frozen, whole kernel, lowest price	10 oz.	0.76	12/94	2c
Eggs, Grade A large	dozen	0.79	12/94	2c
Lettuce, iceberg	head	0.99	12/94	2c
Margarine, Blue Bonnet or Parkay cubes	lb.	0.76	12/94	2c
Milk, whole	1/2 gal.	1.24	12/94	2c
Orange juice, Minute Maid frozen	12-oz.	1.52	12/94	2c
Peaches, halves or slices, Hunt's, Del Monte, or Libby's	29-oz.	1.42	12/94	2c
Peas, sweet, Del Monte or Green Giant	15-17 oz.	0.72	12/94	2c
Potatoes, white or red	10-lb. sack	2.46	12/94	2c
Sausage, Jimmy Dean, 100% pork	lb.	2.62	12/94	2c
Shortening, vegetable, Crisco	3-lb.	3.14	12/94	2c
Soft drink, Coca Cola, ex deposit	2 lit	1.42	12/94	2c
Steak, t-bone	lb.	6.04	12/94	2c
Sugar, cane or beet	4 lbs.	1.59	12/94	2c
Tomatoes, Hunt's or Del Monte	14.5 oz.	0.90	12/94	2c
Tuna, chunk, light, oil-packed	6.125-6.5 oz.	0.86	12/94	2c

Jamestown, NY - continued

Item	Per	Value	Date	Ref.
Goods and Services				
Miscellaneous goods and services, ACCRA Index		102.60	12/94	2c
Health Care				
Health care, ACCRA Index		87.00	12/94	2c
Antibiotic ointment, Polysporin	1.5 oz.	4.05	12/94	2c
Dentist's fee, adult teeth cleaning and periodic oral exam	visit	41.33	12/94	2c
Doctor's fee, routine exam, established patient	visit	38.17	12/94	2c
Hospital care, semiprivate room	day	313.75	12/94	2c
Household Goods				
Appl. repair, service call, wash mach	min. lab. chg.	29.98	12/94	2c
Laundry detergent, Tide Ultra, Bold, or Cheer	42 oz.	4.24	12/94	2c
Tissues, facial, Kleenex brand	175	1.25	12/94	2c
Housing				
Housing, ACCRA Index		90.70	12/94	2c
House payment, principal and interest, 25% down payment	mo.	683	12/94	2c
House, 1800 sq ft, 8000 sq ft lot, new, urban, utilities	total	10900	12/94	2c
Mtge. rate, incl. points and orig. fee, 30-year conv. fixed or ARM	mo.	9.43	12/94	2c
Rent, apartment, 2 br., 1 1/2-2 baths, unfurnished, 950 sq ft, water	mo.	513	12/94	2c
Personal Goods				
Shampoo, Alberto VO5	15-oz.	1.69	12/94	2c
Toothpaste, Crest or Colgate	6-7 oz.	2.48	12/94	2c
Personal Services				
Dry cleaning, man's 2-pc. suit		6.00	12/94	2c
Haircut, man's barbershop, no styling		8.13	12/94	2c
Haircut, woman's shampoo, trim, blow-dry		12.29	12/94	2c
Restaurant Food				
Chicken, fried, thigh and drumstick		2.10	12/94	2c
Hamburger with cheese	1/4 lb.	1.98	12/94	2c
Pizza, Pizza Hut or Pizza Inn	12-13 in.	7.69	12/94	2c
Transportation				
Transportation, ACCRA Index		105.10	12/94	2c
Tire balance, computer or spin bal., front	wheel	6.56	12/94	2c
Utilities				
Utilities, ACCRA Index		111.30	12/94	2c
Electricity, (part.), other, 1800 sq. ft., new home	mo.	68.75	12/94	2c

Jamestown-Dunkirk, NY

Item	Per	Value	Date	Ref.
Appliances				
Appliances (major), expenditures	year	145	91	81r
Average annual exp.				
Food, health care, personal goods, services	year	29496	91	81r
Charity				
Cash contributions, expenditures	year	708	91	81r
Clothing				
Apparel, men and boys, total expenditures	year	416	91	81r
Apparel, women and girls, total expenditures	year	744	91	81r
Footwear, expenditures	year	305	91	81r
Communications				
Long-distance telephone rate, day, addl. min., 1-10 mi.	min.	4.00	12/93	9s
Long-distance telephone rate, day, initial min., 1-10 mi.	min.	14.90	12/93	9s

Values are in dollars or fractions of dollars. In the column headed *Ref*, references are shown to sources. Each reference is followed by a letter. These refer to the geographical level for which data were reported: s=State, r=Region, and c=City or metro. The abbreviation *ex* is used to mean *except* or *excluding*; *exp* stands for expenditures. For other abbreviations and further explanations, please see the Introduction.

Jamestown-Dunkirk, NY - continued

Item	Per	Value	Date	Ref.
Communications				
Phone line, single, business, field visit	inst	143.26	12/93	9s
Phone line, single, business, no field visit	inst	106.05	12/93	9s
Phone line, single, residence, field visit	inst	85.46	12/93	9s
Phone line, single, residence, no field visit	inst	55.00	12/93	9s
Telephone service, expenditures	year	589	91	81r
Education				
Board, 4-year private college/university	year	2918	8/94	80s
Board, 4-year public college/university	year	2177	8/94	80s
Education, total expenditures	year	593	91	81r
Room, 4-year private college/university	year	3302	8/94	80s
Room, 4-year public college/university	year	2624	8/94	80s
Total cost, 4-year private college/university	year	18451	8/94	80s
Total cost, 4-year public college/university	year	7723	8/94	80s
Tuition, 2-year public college/university, in-state	year	2112	8/94	80s
Tuition, 4-year private college/university, in-state	year	12231	8/94	80s
Tuition, 4-year public college/university, in-state	year	2921	8/94	80s
Energy and Fuels				
Fuel oil and other fuels, expenditures	year	257	91	81r
Gas, natural, expenditures	year	285	91	81r
Gasoline and motor oil purchased	year	867	91	81r
Gasoline, unleaded midgrade	gallon	1.32	4/93	82r
Gasoline, unleaded premium	gallon	1.40	4/93	82r
Gasoline, unleaded regular	gallon	1.19	4/93	82r
Entertainment				
Entertainment, total expenditures	year	1331	91	81r
Fees and admissions, expenditures	year	398	91	81r
Pets, toys, playground equipment, expenditures	year	270	91	81r
Reading, expenditures	year	171	91	81r
Televisions, radios, and sound equipment, expenditures	year	429	91	81r
Funerals				
Burial, immediate, container provided by funeral home		1370.36	1/95	54r
Cards, acknowledgment		17.72	1/95	54r
Casket, minimum alternative		192.52	1/95	54r
Cosmetology, hair care, etc.		139.56	1/95	54r
Cremation, direct, container provided by funeral home		1049.24	1/95	54r
Embalming		387.57	1/95	54r
Funeral, funeral home		278.77	1/95	54r
Funeral, other facility		275.85	1/95	54r
Graveside service		213.08	1/95	54r
Hearse, local		157.27	1/95	54r
Limousine, local		146.45	1/95	54r
Memorial service		271.02	1/95	54r
Service charge, professional, nondeclinable		943.58	1/95	54r
Visitation and viewing		322.86	1/95	54r
Groceries				
Apples, Red Delicious	lb.	0.78	12/94	82r
Bacon, sliced	lb.	2.24	12/94	82r
Bananas	lb.	0.49	12/94	82r
Beef purchases	year	226	91	81r
Beverage purchases, alcoholic	year	332	91	81r
Beverage purchases, nonalcoholic	year	213	91	81r
Bread, white, pan	lb.	0.80	12/94	82r
Butter, salted, Grade AA, stick	lb.	1.67	12/94	82r
Carrots, short trimmed and topped	lb.	0.51	12/94	82r
Cereals and bakery products purchases	year	407	91	81r
Cereals and cereals products purchases	year	132	91	81r
Chicken breast, bone-in	lb.	2.22	12/94	82r
Chicken, fresh, whole	lb.	1.05	12/94	82r
Chuck roast, USDA choice, boneless	lb.	2.74	12/94	82r
Coffee, 100%, ground roast, all sizes	lb.	4.61	12/94	82r
Dairy products (other) purchases	year	161	91	81r
Eggs, Grade A large	dozen	1.12	12/94	82r

Jamestown-Dunkirk, NY - continued

Item	Per	Value	Date	Ref.
Groceries - continued				
Fish and seafood purchases	year	112	91	81r
Food purchases, food eaten at home	year	2599	91	81r
Foods purchased away from home, not prepared by consumer	year	2024	91	81r
Fruits and vegetables purchases	year	444	91	81r
Grapefruit	lb.	0.44	12/94	82r
Grapes, Thompson seedless	lb.	2.24	12/94	82r
Ground chuck, 100% beef	lb.	1.67	12/94	82r
Ice cream, prepackaged, bulk, regular	1/2 gal.	2.93	12/94	82r
Lemons	lb.	1.06	12/94	82r
Lettuce, iceberg	lb.	0.92	12/94	82r
Meats, poultry, fish, and eggs purchases	year	751	91	81r
Milk and cream (fresh) purchases	year	152	91	81r
Orange juice, frozen concentrate 12-oz. can	16 oz.	1.92	12/94	82r
Oranges, Navel	lb.	0.56	12/94	82r
Pork chops, center cut, bone-in	lb.	3.09	12/94	82r
Pork purchases	year	130	91	81r
Potatoes, white	lb.	0.37	12/94	82r
Rib roast, USDA choice, bone-in	lb.	4.98	12/94	82r
Round roast, USDA choice, boneless	lb.	2.93	12/94	82r
Shortening, vegetable oil blends	lb.	1.03	12/94	82r
Spaghetti and macaroni	lb.	0.84	12/94	82r
Steak, round, USDA choice, boneless	lb.	3.48	12/94	82r
Steak, sirloin, USDA choice, bone-in	lb.	3.38	12/94	82r
Steak, sirloin, USDA choice, boneless	lb.	4.81	12/94	82r
Sugar and other sweets, eaten at home, expenditures	year	89	91	81r
Sugar, white, all sizes	lb.	0.46	12/94	82r
Tobacco products and smoking supplies, total expenditures	year	279	91	81r
Tomatoes, field grown	lb.	1.56	12/94	82r
Tuna, chunk, light	lb.	2.09	12/94	82r
Health Care				
Childbirth, Cesarean delivery, hospital charge	birth	6334.00	12/91	69r
Childbirth, Cesarean delivery, physician charge	birth	2234.00	12/91	69r
Childbirth, normal delivery, hospital charge	birth	3225.00	12/91	69r
Childbirth, normal delivery, physician charge	birth	1623.00	12/91	69r
Drugs, expenditures	year	205	91	81r
Health care, total expenditures	year	1396	91	81r
Health insurance expenditures	year	553	91	81r
Insurance premium, family medical care	month	384.24	1/95	41s
Medical services expenditures	year	559	91	81r
Medical supplies expenditures	year	80	91	81r
Household Goods				
Floor coverings, expenditures	year	158	91	81r
Furniture, expenditures	year	341	91	81r
Household equipment, misc. expenditures	year	363	91	81r
Household expenditures, miscellaneous	year	194	91	81r
Household furnishings and equipment, expenditures	year	1158	91	81r
Household operations expenditures	year	378	91	81r
Household textiles, expenditures	year	88	91	81r
Housekeeping supplies, expenditures	year	426	91	81r
Laundry and cleaning supplies, expenditures	year	122	91	81r
Postage and stationery, expenditures	year	134	91	81r
Housing				
Add garage/carport		11,614	3/95	74r
Add room(s)		16,816	3/95	74r
Apartment condominium or co-op, median	unit	96700	12/94	62r
Dwellings (owned), expenditures	year	3305	91	81r
Enclose porch/patio/breezeway		2,980	3/95	74r
Finish room in basement/attic		4,330	3/95	74r
Home, existing, single-family, median	unit	161600	12/94	62r
Maintenance, repairs, insurance, and other housing expenditures	year	569	91	81r
Mortgage interest and charges expenditures	year	1852	91	81r

Values are in dollars or fractions of dollars. In the column headed *Ref*, references are shown to sources. Each reference is followed by a letter. These refer to the geographical level for which data were reported: s = State, r = Region, and c = City or metro. The abbreviation *ex* is used to mean *except* or *excluding*; *exp* stands for expenditures. For other abbreviations and further explanations, please see the Introduction.

Jamestown-Dunkirk, NY - continued

Item	Per	Value	Date	Ref.
Housing				
Princ. & int., mortgage, median-price exist. sing.-family home	mo.	765	12/94	62r
Property taxes expenditures	year	884	91	81r
Redesign, restructure more than half of home's interior		2,750	3/95	74r
Rental units expenditures	year	1832	91	81r
Insurance and Pensions				
Auto insurance, private passenger	year	985.07	12/94	71s
Insurance and pensions, personal, expenditures	year	2690	91	81r
Insurance, life and other personal, expenditures	year	341	91	81r
Pensions and Social Security, expenditures	year	2349	91	81r
Legal Assistance				
Estate planning, law-firm partner	hr.	375.00	10/93	12r
Legal work, law firm associate	hour	78		10r
Legal work, law firm partner	hour	183		10r
Personal Services				
Personal services expenditures	year	184	91	81r
Restaurant Food				
Dining expenditures, family	week	34.26	94	73r
Taxes				
Taxes, Federal income, expenditures	year	2409	91	81r
Taxes, personal, expenditures	year	3094	91	81r
Taxes, State and local income, expenditures	year	620	91	81r
Transportation				
Cars and trucks purchased, new	year	1170	91	81r
Cars and trucks purchased, used	year	739	91	81r
Driver's learning permit fee	perm	10.00	1/94	84s
Driver's license fee	orig	32.00-37.00	1/94	84s
Driver's license fee, duplicate	lic	7.25	1/94	84s
Driver's license reinstatement fee, min.	susp	25.00	1/94	85s
Driver's license renewal fee	renew	22.25	1/94	84s
Identification card, nondriver	card	6.25	1/94	83s
Motorcycle license fee	orig	32.00-37.00	1/94	84s
Motorcycle license fee, duplicate	lic	7.25	1/94	84s
Motorcycle license renewal fee	renew	22.25	1/94	84s
Public transportation expenditures	year	430	91	81r
Transportation expenditures, total	year	4810	91	81r
Vehicle finance charges	year	238	91	81r
Vehicle insurance expenditures	year	630	91	81r
Vehicle maintenance and repairs expenditures	year	532	91	81r
Vehicle purchases	year	1920	91	81r
Vehicle rental, leases, licenses, etc. expenditures	year	193	91	81r
Vehicles purchased, other than cars and trucks	year	11	91	81r
Utilities				
Electricity expenditures	year	695	91	81r
Utilities, fuels, and public services, total expenditures	year	1981	91	81r
Water and other public services, expenditures	year	154	91	81r
Weddings				
Bridal attendants' gowns	event	750	10/93	76r
Bridal gown	event	852	10/93	76r
Bridal headpiece and veil	event	167	10/93	76r
Bride's wedding band	event	708	10/93	76r
Clergy	event	224	10/93	76r
Engagement ring	event	2756	10/93	76r
Flowers	event	863	10/93	76r
Formal wear for groom	event	106	10/93	76r
Groom's attendants' formal wear	event	530	10/93	76r
Groom's wedding band	event	402	10/93	76r
Music	event	600	10/93	76r

Jamestown-Dunkirk, NY - continued

Item	Per	Value	Date	Ref.
Weddings - continued				
Photography	event	1088	10/93	76r
Shoes for bride	event	50	10/93	76r
Videography	event	483	10/93	76r
Wedding invitations and announcements	event	342	10/93	76r
Wedding reception	event	7000	10/93	76r

Janesville, WI

Item	Per	Value	Date	Ref.
Composite, ACCRA index		103.90	12/94	2c
Alcoholic Beverages				
Beer, Miller Lite, Bud, 12-oz., ex deposit	6	3.60	12/94	2c
J & B Scotch	750-ml.	17.39	12/94	2c
Wine, Gallo Chablis blanc	1.5-lit	4.42	12/94	2c
Appliances				
Appliances (major), expenditures	year	131	91	81r
Average annual exp.				
Food, health care, personal goods, services	year	25935	91	81r
Charity				
Cash contributions, expenditures	year	745	91	81r
Clothing				
Apparel, men and boys, total expenditures	year	332	91	81r
Apparel, women and girls, total expenditures	year	578	91	81r
Footwear, expenditures	year	164	91	81r
Jeans, man's denim		27.49	12/94	2c
Shirt, man's dress shirt		29.82	12/94	2c
Undervest, boy's size 10-14, cotton	3	4.32	12/94	2c
Communications				
Long-distance telephone rate, day, addl. min., 1-10 mi.	min.	0.10	12/93	9s
Long-distance telephone rate, day, initial min., 1-10 mi.	min.	0.15	12/93	9s
Newspaper subscription, dly. and Sun. delivery	month	14.04	12/94	2c
Phone line, single, business, field visit	inst	64.65	12/93	9s
Phone line, single, business, no field visit	inst	64.65	12/93	9s
Phone line, single, residence, field visit	inst	33.05	12/93	9s
Phone line, single, residence, no field visit	inst	33.05	12/93	9s
Telephone bill, family of four	month	15.96	12/94	2c
Telephone service, expenditures	year	547	91	81r
Telephone, residential, flat rate	mo.	6.00	12/93	8c
Education				
Board, 4-year private college/university	year	2145	8/94	80s
Board, 4-year public college/university	year	1303	8/94	80s
Education, total expenditures	year	394	91	81r
Room, 4-year private college/university	year	1576	8/94	80s
Room, 4-year public college/university	year	1631	8/94	80s
Total cost, 4-year private college/university	year	13902	8/94	80s
Total cost, 4-year public college/university	year	5252	8/94	80s
Tuition, 2-year public college/university, in-state	year	1557	8/94	80s
Tuition, 4-year private college/university, in-state	year	10181	8/94	80s
Tuition, 4-year public college/university, in-state	year	2318	8/94	80s
Energy and Fuels				
Energy, combined forms, 1800 sq. ft.	mo.	110.36	12/94	2c
Energy, exc. electricity, 1800 sq. ft.	mo.	47.44	12/94	2c
Fuel oil and other fuels, expenditures	year	83	91	81r
Gas, cooking, winter, 10 therms	month	9.28	2/94	65c
Gas, cooking, winter, 30 therms	month	20.83	2/94	65c
Gas, cooking, winter, 50 therms	month	32.39	2/94	65c
Gas, heating, winter, 100 therms	month	61.27	2/94	65c
Gas, heating, winter, average use	month	124.59	2/94	65c
Gas, natural, expenditures	year	373	91	81r
Gas, reg unlead, taxes inc., cash, self-service	gal	1.16	12/94	2c

Values are in dollars or fractions of dollars. In the column headed *Ref*, references are shown to sources. Each reference is followed by a letter. These refer to the geographical level for which data were reported: s=State, r=Region, and c=City or metro. The abbreviation *ex* is used to mean *except* or *excluding*; *exp* stands for expenditures. For other abbreviations and further explanations, please see the Introduction.

Janesville, WI - continued

Item	Per	Value	Date	Ref.
Energy and Fuels				
Gasoline and motor oil purchased	year	1000	91	81r
Gasoline, unleaded midgrade	gallon	1.15	4/93	82r
Gasoline, unleaded premium	gallon	1.23	4/93	82r
Gasoline, unleaded regular	gallon	1.07	4/93	82r
Entertainment				
Bowling, evening rate	game	1.91	12/94	2c
Entertainment, total expenditures	year	1356	91	81r
Fees and admissions, expenditures	year	347	91	81r
Monopoly game, Parker Brothers', No. 9	game	8.43	12/94	2c
Movie	adm	4.83	12/94	2c
Pets, toys, playground equipment, expenditures	year	270	91	81r
Reading, expenditures	year	160	91	81r
Televisions, radios, and sound equipment, expenditures	year	433	91	81r
Tennis balls, yellow, Wilson or Penn, 3	can	2.03	12/94	2c
Funerals				
Burial, immediate, container provided by funeral home		1268.31	1/95	54r
Cards, acknowledgment		26.12	1/95	54r
Casket, minimum alternative		198.03	1/95	54r
Cosmetology, hair care, etc.		122.19	1/95	54r
Cremation, direct, container provided by funeral home		977.81	1/95	54r
Embalming		334.00	1/95	54r
Funeral, funeral home		321.16	1/95	54r
Funeral, other facility		317.73	1/95	54r
Graveside service		292.48	1/95	54r
Hearse, local		153.20	1/95	54r
Limousine, local		123.52	1/95	54r
Memorial service		356.30	1/95	54r
Service charge, professional, nondeclinable		968.24	1/95	54r
Visitation and viewing		332.66	1/95	54r
Groceries				
Groceries, ACCRA Index		101.90	12/94	2c
Apples, Red Delicious	lb.	0.68	12/94	82r
Baby food, strained vegetables, lowest price	4-4.5 oz.	0.42	12/94	2c
Bacon, sliced	lb.	1.88	12/94	82r
Bananas	lb.	0.44	12/94	2c
Bananas	lb.	0.41	12/94	82r
Beef or hamburger, ground	lb.	1.45	12/94	2c
Beef purchases	year	197	91	81r
Beef, stew, boneless	lb.	2.52	12/94	82r
Beverage purchases, alcoholic	year	293	91	81r
Beverage purchases, nonalcoholic	year	203	91	81r
Bologna, all beef or mixed	lb.	2.12	12/94	82r
Bread, white	24-oz.	0.63	12/94	2c
Bread, white, pan	lb.	0.76	12/94	82r
Cabbage	lb.	0.44	12/94	82r
Carrots, short trimmed and topped	lb.	0.44	12/94	82r
Cereals and bakery products purchases	year	347	91	81r
Cereals and cereals products purchases	year	119	91	81r
Cheddar cheese, natural	lb.	3.28	12/94	82r
Cheese, Kraft grated Parmesan	8-oz.	3.04	12/94	2c
Chicken breast, bone-in	lb.	1.61	12/94	82r
Chicken, fresh, whole	lb.	0.89	12/94	82r
Chicken, whole fryer	lb.	0.92	12/94	2c
Chuck roast, USDA choice, boneless	lb.	2.33	12/94	82r
Cigarettes, Winston, Kings	carton	16.79	12/94	2c
Coffee, 100%, ground roast, all sizes	lb.	4.28	12/94	82r
Coffee, vacuum-packed	13 oz.	3.64	12/94	2c
Cookies, chocolate chip	lb.	2.72	12/94	82r
Corn Flakes, Kellogg's or Post Toasties	18 oz.	2.65	12/94	2c
Corn, frozen, whole kernel, lowest price	10 oz.	0.72	12/94	2c
Dairy products (other) purchases	year	148	91	81r
Eggs, Grade A large	dozen	0.55	12/94	2c
Eggs, Grade A large	dozen	0.76	12/94	82r
Fish and seafood purchases	year	61	91	81r
Flour, white, all purpose	lb.	0.22	12/94	82r
Food purchases, food eaten at home	year	2313	91	81r

Janesville, WI - continued

Item	Per	Value	Date	Ref.
Groceries - continued				
Foods purchased away from home, not prepared by consumer	year	1709	91	81r
Fruits and vegetables purchases	year	372	91	81r
Grapefruit	lb.	0.47	12/94	82r
Grapes, Thompson seedless	lb.	2.15	12/94	82r
Ground beef, 100% beef	lb.	1.37	12/94	82r
Ground chuck, 100% beef	lb.	1.81	12/94	82r
Ham, boneless, exc. canned	lb.	2.16	12/94	82r
Ice cream, prepackaged, bulk, regular	1/2 gal.	2.48	12/94	82r
Lemons	lb.	1.08	12/94	82r
Lettuce, iceberg	lb.	0.81	12/94	82r
Lettuce, iceberg	head	0.86	12/94	2c
Margarine, Blue Bonnet or Parkay cubes	lb.	0.61	12/94	2c
Margarine, stick	lb.	0.81	12/94	82r
Meats, poultry, fish, and eggs purchases	year	591	91	81r
Milk and cream (fresh) purchases	year	132	91	81r
Milk, whole	1/2 gal.	1.19	12/94	2c
Orange juice, frozen concentrate 12-oz. can	16 oz.	1.41	12/94	82r
Orange juice, Minute Maid frozen	12-oz.	1.19	12/94	2c
Oranges, Navel	lb.	0.56	12/94	82r
Peaches, halves or slices, Hunt's, Del Monte, or Libby's	29-oz.	1.58	12/94	2c
Peanut butter, creamy, all sizes	lb.	1.81	12/94	82r
Peas, sweet, Del Monte or Green Giant	15-17 oz.	0.59	12/94	2c
Pork chops, center cut, bone-in	lb.	2.76	12/94	82r
Pork purchases	year	130	91	81r
Potato chips	16-oz.	2.81	12/94	82r
Potatoes, frozen, French fried	lb.	0.83	12/94	82r
Potatoes, white	lb.	0.28	12/94	82r
Potatoes, white or red	10-lb. sack	2.08	12/94	2c
Round roast, USDA choice, boneless	lb.	2.90	12/94	82r
Sausage, Jimmy Dean, 100% pork	lb.	2.73	12/94	2c
Shortening, vegetable oil blends	lb.	0.88	12/94	82r
Shortening, vegetable, Crisco	3-lb.	2.71	12/94	2c
Soft drink, Coca Cola, ex deposit	2 lit	1.13	12/94	2c
Spaghetti and macaroni	lb.	0.78	12/94	82r
Steak, rib eye, USDA choice, boneless	lb.	6.15	12/94	82r
Steak, round, graded & ungraded, exc. USDA prime & choice	lb.	2.72	12/94	82r
Steak, round, USDA choice, boneless	lb.	3.02	12/94	82r
Steak, sirloin, USDA choice, boneless	lb.	3.85	12/94	82r
Steak, t-bone	lb.	5.55	12/94	2c
Steak, T-bone, USDA choice, bone-in	lb.	5.38	12/94	82r
Sugar and other sweets, eaten at home, expenditures	year	91	91	81r
Sugar, cane or beet	4 lbs.	1.40	12/94	2c
Sugar, white, all sizes	lb.	0.36	12/94	82r
Tobacco products and smoking supplies, total expenditures	year	298	91	81r
Tomatoes, field grown	lb.	1.36	12/94	82r
Tomatoes, Hunt's or Del Monte	14.5 oz.	0.77	12/94	2c
Tuna, chunk, light	lb.	1.94	12/94	82r
Tuna, chunk, light, oil-packed	6.125-6.5 oz.	0.66	12/94	2c
Turkey, frozen, whole	lb.	0.96	12/94	82r
Yogurt, natural, fruit flavored	8 oz.	0.62	12/94	82r
Goods and Services				
Miscellaneous goods and services, ACCRA Index		96.60	12/94	2c
Health Care				
Health care, ACCRA Index		100.00	12/94	2c
Antibiotic ointment, Polysporin	1.5 oz.	4.08	12/94	2c
Childbirth, Cesarean delivery, hospital charge	birth	5101.00	12/91	69r
Childbirth, Cesarean delivery, physician charge	birth	2234.00	12/91	69r

Values are in dollars or fractions of dollars. In the column headed *Ref*, references are shown to sources. Each reference is followed by a letter. These refer to the geographical level for which data were reported: s = State, r = Region, and c = City or metro. The abbreviation *ex* is used to mean *except* or *excluding*; *exp* stands for *expenditures*. For other abbreviations and further explanations, please see the Introduction.

Janesville, WI - continued

Item	Per	Value	Date	Ref.
Health Care				
Childbirth, normal delivery, hospital charge	birth	2891.00	12/91	69r
Childbirth, normal delivery, physician charge	birth	1623.00	12/91	69r
Dentist's fee, adult teeth cleaning and periodic oral exam	visit	47.71	12/94	2c
Doctor's fee, routine exam, established patient	visit	53.00	12/94	2c
Drugs, expenditures	year	248	91	81r
Health care, total expenditures	year	1336	91	81r
Health insurance expenditures	year	550	91	81r
Hospital care, semiprivate room	day	235.00	12/94	2c
Insurance premium, family medical care	month	378.79	1/95	41s
Medical services expenditures	year	457	91	81r
Medical supplies expenditures	year	82	91	81r
Household Goods				
Appl. repair, service call, wash mach	min. lab. chg.	32.75	12/94	2c
Floor coverings, expenditures	year	105	91	81r
Furniture, expenditures	year	291	91	81r
Household equipment, misc. expenditures	year	341	91	81r
Household expenditures, miscellaneous	year	162	91	81r
Household furnishings and equipment, expenditures	year	1042	91	81r
Household operations expenditures	year	365	91	81r
Household textiles, expenditures	year	101	91	81r
Housekeeping supplies, expenditures	year	390	91	81r
Laundry and cleaning supplies, expenditures	year	110	91	81r
Laundry detergent, Tide Ultra, Bold, or Cheer	42 oz.	3.78	12/94	2c
Postage and stationery, expenditures	year	115	91	81r
Tissues, facial, Kleenex brand	175	1.11	12/94	2c
Housing				
Housing, ACCRA Index		118.70	12/94	2c
Add garage/carport		8,479	3/95	74r
Add room(s)		21,347	3/95	74r
Apartment condominium or co-op, median	unit	87100	12/94	62r
Bathroom addition, average cost	add	9734.00	3/95	13r
Bathroom remodeling, average cost	remod	6414.00	3/95	13r
Bedroom, master suite addition, average cost	add	27122.00	3/95	13r
Deck addition, average cost	add	6665.00	3/95	13r
Dwellings (owned), expenditures	year	2566	91	81r
Enclose porch/patio/breezeway		4,556	3/95	74r
Exterior remodeling, average cost	remod	15395.00	3/95	13r
Family room addition, average cost	add	27658.00	3/95	13r
Finish room in basement/attic		5,074	3/95	74r
Home, existing, single-family, median	unit	106500	12/94	62r
House payment, principal and interest, 25% down payment	mo.	955	12/94	2c
House, 1800 sq ft, 8000 sq ft lot, new, urban, utilities	total	152200	12/94	2c
Kitchen remodeling, major, average cost	remod	17084.00	3/95	13r
Kitchen remodeling, minor, average cost	remod	5804.00	3/95	13r
Maintenance, repairs, insurance, and other housing expenditures	year	484	91	81r
Mortgage interest and charges expenditures	year	1443	91	81r
Mtge. rate, incl. points and orig. fee, 30-year conv. fixed or ARM	mo.	9.45	12/94	2c
Office, home addition, average cost	add	8121.00	3/95	13r
Princ. & int., mortgage, median-price exist. sing.-family home	mo.	515	12/94	62r
Property taxes expenditures	year	639	91	81r
Redesign, restructure more than half of home's interior		9,114	3/95	74r
Rent, apartment, 2 br., 1 1/2-2 baths, unfurnished, 950 sq ft, water	mo.	496	12/94	2c
Rental units expenditures	year	1200	91	81r
Sun-space addition, average cost	add	23768.00	3/95	13r
Wing addition, two-story, average cost	add	50410.00	3/95	13r

Janesville, WI - continued

Item	Per	Value	Date	Ref.
Insurance and Pensions				
Auto insurance, private passenger	year	554.10	12/94	71s
Insurance and pensions, personal, expenditures	year	2408	91	81r
Insurance, life and other personal, expenditures	year	355	91	81r
Pensions and Social Security, expenditures	year	2053	91	81r
Legal Assistance				
Legal work, law firm associate	hour	90		10r
Legal work, law firm partner	hour	139		10r
Personal Goods				
Shampoo, Alberto VO5	15-oz.	1.16	12/94	2c
Toothpaste, Crest or Colgate	6-7 oz.	2.86	12/94	2c
Personal Services				
Dry cleaning, man's 2-pc. suit		8.33	12/94	2c
Haircut, man's barbershop, no styling		7.95	12/94	2c
Haircut, woman's shampoo, trim, blow-dry		17.00	12/94	2c
Personal services expenditures	year	203	91	81r
Restaurant Food				
Chicken, fried, thigh and drumstick		2.30	12/94	2c
Dining expenditures, family	week	30.03	94	73r
Hamburger with cheese	1/4 lb.	1.84	12/94	2c
Pizza, Pizza Hut or Pizza Inn	12-13 in.	7.74	12/94	2c
Taxes				
Taxes, Federal income, expenditures	year	1756	91	81r
Taxes, personal, expenditures	year	2426	91	81r
Taxes, State and local income, expenditures	year	568	91	81r
Transportation				
Transportation, ACCRA Index		97.50	12/94	2c
Bus fare, up to 10 miles	one-way	0.75	12/94	2c
Cars and trucks purchased, new	year	891	91	81r
Cars and trucks purchased, used	year	1155	91	81r
Driver's learning permit fee	perm	20.00	1/94	84s
Driver's license fee	orig	10.00	1/94	84s
Driver's license fee, duplicate	lic	4.00	1/94	84s
Driver's license reinstatement fee, min.	susp	50.00	1/94	85s
Driver's license renewal fee	renew	10.00	1/94	84s
Identification card, nondriver	card	4.00	1/94	83s
Motorcycle license fee	orig	4.00	1/94	84s
Motorcycle license fee, duplicate	lic	4.00	1/94	84s
Motorcycle license renewal fee	renew	4.00	1/94	84s
Public transportation expenditures	year	209	91	81r
Tire balance, computer or spin bal., front	wheel	6.40	12/94	2c
Transportation expenditures, total	year	4792	91	81r
Vehicle finance charges	year	300	91	81r
Vehicle insurance expenditures	year	485	91	81r
Vehicle maintenance and repairs expenditures	year	534	91	81r
Vehicle purchases	year	2068	91	81r
Vehicle rental, leases, licenses, etc. expenditures	year	197	91	81r
Vehicles purchased, other than cars and trucks	year	22	91	81r
Utilities				
Utilities, ACCRA Index		96.10	12/94	2c
Electricity expenditures	year	668	91	81r
Electricity, (part.), other, 1800 sq. ft., new home	mo.	62.92	12/94	2c
Electricity, summer, 250 KWh	month	18.87	8/93	64c
Electricity, summer, 500 KWh	month	34.23	8/93	64c
Electricity, summer, 750 KWh	month	49.60	8/93	64c
Electricity, summer, 1000 KWh	month	64.96	8/93	64c
Utilities, fuels, and public services, total expenditures	year	1838	91	81r
Water and other public services, expenditures	year	167	91	81r

Values are in dollars or fractions of dollars. In the column headed *Ref*, references are shown to sources. Each reference is followed by a letter. These refer to the geographical level for which data were reported: s=State, r=Region, and c=City or metro. The abbreviation *ex* is used to mean *except* or *excluding*; *exp* stands for *expenditures*. For other abbreviations and further explanations, please see the Introduction.

Janesville, WI - continued

Item	Per	Value	Date	Ref.
Weddings				
Bridal attendants' gowns	event	750	10/93	76r
Bridal gown	event	852	10/93	76r
Bridal headpiece and veil	event	167	10/93	76r
Bride's wedding band	event	708	10/93	76r
Clergy	event	224	10/93	76r
Engagement ring	event	2756	10/93	76r
Flowers	event	863	10/93	76r
Formal wear for groom	event	106	10/93	76r
Groom's attendants' formal wear	event	530	10/93	76r
Groom's wedding band	event	402	10/93	76r
Music	event	600	10/93	76r
Photography	event	1088	10/93	76r
Shoes for bride	event	50	10/93	76r
Videography	event	483	10/93	76r
Wedding invitations and announcements	event	342	10/93	76r
Wedding reception	event	7000	10/93	76r

Jersey City, NJ

Item	Per	Value	Date	Ref.
Appliances				
Appliances (major), expenditures	year	145	91	81r
Average annual exp.				
Food, health care, personal goods, services	year	29496	91	81r
Charity				
Cash contributions, expenditures	year	708	91	81r
Clothing				
Apparel, men and boys, total expenditures	year	416	91	81r
Apparel, women and girls, total expenditures	year	744	91	81r
Footwear, expenditures	year	305	91	81r
Communications				
Long-distance telephone rate, day, addl. min., 1-10 mi.	min.	0.03	12/93	9s
Long-distance telephone rate, day, initial min., 1-10 mi.	min.	0.09	12/93	9s
Phone line, single, business, field visit	inst	98.50	12/93	9s
Phone line, single, business, no field visit	inst	79.50	12/93	9s
Phone line, single, residence, field visit	inst	56.50	12/93	9s
Phone line, single, residence, no field visit	inst	42.00	12/93	9s
Telephone service, expenditures	year	589	91	81r
Education				
Board, 4-year private college/university	year	2841	8/94	80s
Board, 4-year public college/university	year	1956	8/94	80s
Education, total expenditures	year	593	91	81r
Room, 4-year private college/university	year	2999	8/94	80s
Room, 4-year public college/university	year	2778	8/94	80s
Total cost, 4-year private college/university	year	18264	8/94	80s
Total cost, 4-year public college/university	year	8252	8/94	80s
Tuition, 2-year public college/university, in-state	year	1539	8/94	80s
Tuition, 4-year private college/university, in-state	year	12423	8/94	80s
Tuition, 4-year public college/university, in-state	year	3518	8/94	80s
Energy and Fuels				
Fuel oil and other fuels, expenditures	year	257	91	81r
Gas, natural, expenditures	year	285	91	81r
Gasoline and motor oil purchased	year	867	91	81r
Gasoline, unleaded midgrade	gallon	1.32	4/93	82r
Gasoline, unleaded premium	gallon	1.40	4/93	82r
Gasoline, unleaded regular	gallon	1.19	4/93	82r
Entertainment				
Entertainment, total expenditures	year	1331	91	81r
Fees and admissions, expenditures	year	398	91	81r
Pets, toys, playground equipment, expenditures	year	270	91	81r
Reading, expenditures	year	171	91	81r

Jersey City, NJ - continued

Item	Per	Value	Date	Ref.
Entertainment - continued				
Televisions, radios, and sound equipment, expenditures	year	429	91	81r
Funerals				
Burial, immediate, container provided by funeral home		1370.36	1/95	54r
Cards, acknowledgment		17.72	1/95	54r
Casket, minimum alternative		192.52	1/95	54r
Cosmetology, hair care, etc.		139.56	1/95	54r
Cremation, direct, container provided by funeral home		1049.24	1/95	54r
Embalming		387.57	1/95	54r
Funeral, funeral home		278.77	1/95	54r
Funeral, other facility		275.85	1/95	54r
Graveside service		213.08	1/95	54r
Hearse, local		157.27	1/95	54r
Limousine, local		146.45	1/95	54r
Memorial service		271.02	1/95	54r
Service charge, professional, nondeclinable		943.58	1/95	54r
Visitation and viewing		322.86	1/95	54r
Groceries				
Apples, Red Delicious	lb.	0.78	12/94	82r
Bacon, sliced	lb.	2.24	12/94	82r
Bananas	lb.	0.49	12/94	82r
Beef purchases	year	226	91	81r
Beverage purchases, alcoholic	year	332	91	81r
Beverage purchases, nonalcoholic	year	213	91	81r
Bread, white, pan	lb.	0.80	12/94	82r
Butter, salted, Grade AA, stick	lb.	1.67	12/94	82r
Carrots, short trimmed and topped	lb.	0.51	12/94	82r
Cereals and bakery products purchases	year	407	91	81r
Cereals and cereals products purchases	year	132	91	81r
Chicken breast, bone-in	lb.	2.22	12/94	82r
Chicken, fresh, whole	lb.	1.05	12/94	82r
Chuck roast, USDA choice, boneless	lb.	2.74	12/94	82r
Coffee, 100%, ground roast, all sizes	lb.	4.61	12/94	82r
Dairy products (other) purchases	year	161	91	81r
Eggs, Grade A large	dozen	1.12	12/94	82r
Fish and seafood purchases	year	112	91	81r
Food purchases, food eaten at home	year	2599	91	81r
Foods purchased away from home, not prepared by consumer	year	2024	91	81r
Fruits and vegetables purchases	year	444	91	81r
Grapefruit	lb.	0.44	12/94	82r
Grapes, Thompson seedless	lb.	2.24	12/94	82r
Ground chuck, 100% beef	lb.	1.67	12/94	82r
Ice cream, prepackaged, bulk, regular	1/2 gal.	2.93	12/94	82r
Lemons	lb.	1.06	12/94	82r
Lettuce, iceberg	lb.	0.92	12/94	82r
Meats, poultry, fish, and eggs purchases	year	751	91	81r
Milk and cream (fresh) purchases	year	152	91	81r
Orange juice, frozen concentrate 12-oz. can	16 oz.	1.92	12/94	82r
Oranges, Navel	lb.	0.56	12/94	82r
Pork chops, center cut, bone-in	lb.	3.09	12/94	82r
Pork purchases	year	130	91	81r
Potatoes, white	lb.	0.37	12/94	82r
Rib roast, USDA choice, bone-in	lb.	4.98	12/94	82r
Round roast, USDA choice, boneless	lb.	2.93	12/94	82r
Shortening, vegetable oil blends	lb.	1.03	12/94	82r
Spaghetti and macaroni	lb.	0.84	12/94	82r
Steak, round, USDA choice, boneless	lb.	3.48	12/94	82r
Steak, sirloin, USDA choice, bone-in	lb.	3.38	12/94	82r
Steak, sirloin, USDA choice, boneless	lb.	4.81	12/94	82r
Sugar and other sweets, eaten at home, expenditures	year	89	91	81r
Sugar, white, all sizes	lb.	0.46	12/94	82r
Tobacco products and smoking supplies, total expenditures	year	279	91	81r
Tomatoes, field grown	lb.	1.56	12/94	82r
Tuna, chunk, light	lb.	2.09	12/94	82r

Values are in dollars or fractions of dollars. In the column headed *Ref*, references are shown to sources. Each reference is followed by a letter. These refer to the geographical level for which data were reported: s=State, r=Region, and c=City or metro. The abbreviation *ex* is used to mean *except* or *excluding*; *exp* stands for expenditures. For other abbreviations and further explanations, please see the Introduction.

Jersey City, NJ - continued

Item	Per	Value	Date	Ref.
Health Care				
Childbirth, Cesarean delivery, hospital charge	birth	6334.00	12/91	69r
Childbirth, Cesarean delivery, physician charge	birth	2234.00	12/91	69r
Childbirth, normal delivery, hospital charge	birth	3225.00	12/91	69r
Childbirth, normal delivery, physician charge	birth	1623.00	12/91	69r
Drugs, expenditures	year	205	91	81r
Health care, total expenditures	year	1396	91	81r
Health insurance expenditures	year	553	91	81r
Insurance premium, family medical care	month	396.06	1/95	41s
Medical services expenditures	year	559	91	81r
Medical supplies expenditures	year	80	91	81r
Household Goods				
Floor coverings, expenditures	year	158	91	81r
Furniture, expenditures	year	341	91	81r
Household equipment, misc. expenditures	year	363	91	81r
Household expenditures, miscellaneous	year	194	91	81r
Household furnishings and equipment, expenditures	year	1158	91	81r
Household operations expenditures	year	378	91	81r
Household textiles, expenditures	year	88	91	81r
Housekeeping supplies, expenditures	year	426	91	81r
Laundry and cleaning supplies, expenditures	year	122	91	81r
Postage and stationery, expenditures	year	134	91	81r
Housing				
Add garage/carport		11,614	3/95	74r
Add room(s)		16,816	3/95	74r
Apartment condominium or co-op, median	unit	96700	12/94	62r
Dwellings (owned), expenditures	year	3305	91	81r
Enclose porch/patio/breezeway		2,980	3/95	74r
Finish room in basement/attic		4,330	3/95	74r
Home, existing, single-family, median	unit	161600	12/94	62r
Maintenance, repairs, insurance, and other housing expenditures	year	569	91	81r
Mortgage interest and charges expenditures	year	1852	91	81r
Princ. & int., mortgage, median-price exist. sing.-family home	mo.	765	12/94	62r
Property taxes expenditures	year	884	91	81r
Redesign, restructure more than half of home's interior		2,750	3/95	74r
Rental units expenditures	year	1832	91	81r
Insurance and Pensions				
Auto insurance, private passenger	year	1094.56	12/94	71s
Insurance and pensions, personal, expenditures	year	2690	91	81r
Insurance, life and other personal, expenditures	year	341	91	81r
Pensions and Social Security, expenditures	year	2349	91	81r
Legal Assistance				
Estate planning, law-firm partner	hr.	375.00	10/93	12r
Legal work, law firm associate	hour	78		10r
Legal work, law firm partner	hour	183		10r
Personal Services				
Personal services expenditures	year	184	91	81r
Restaurant Food				
Dining expenditures, family	week	34.26	94	73r
Taxes				
Taxes, Federal income, expenditures	year	2409	91	81r
Taxes, personal, expenditures	year	3094	91	81r
Taxes, State and local income, expenditures	year	620	91	81r
Transportation				
Cars and trucks purchased, new	year	1170	91	81r
Cars and trucks purchased, used	year	739	91	81r
Driver's learning permit fee	perm	5.00	1/94	84s
Driver's license fee	orig	16.00	1/94	84s
Driver's license fee, duplicate	lic	3.00	1/94	84s
Driver's license reinstatement fee, min.	susp	30.00	1/94	85s

Jersey City, NJ - continued

Item	Per	Value	Date	Ref.
Transportation - continued				
Driver's license renewal fee	renew	16.00	1/94	84s
Identification card, nondriver	card	5.50	1/94	83s
Motorcycle learning permit fee	perm	5.00	1/94	84s
Motorcycle license fee	orig	8.00	1/94	84s
Motorcycle license fee, duplicate	lic	3.00	1/94	84s
Motorcycle license renewal fee	renew	8.00	1/94	84s
Public transportation expenditures	year	430	91	81r
Transportation expenditures, total	year	4810	91	81r
Vehicle finance charges	year	238	91	81r
Vehicle insurance expenditures	year	630	91	81r
Vehicle maintenance and repairs expenditures	year	532	91	81r
Vehicle purchases	year	1920	91	81r
Vehicle rental, leases, licenses, etc. expenditures	year	193	91	81r
Vehicles purchased, other than cars and trucks	year	11	91	81r
Utilities				
Electricity expenditures	year	695	91	81r
Utilities, fuels, and public services, total expenditures	year	1981	91	81r
Water and other public services, expenditures	year	154	91	81r
Weddings				
Bridal attendants' gowns	event	750	10/93	76r
Bridal gown	event	852	10/93	76r
Bridal headpiece and veil	event	167	10/93	76r
Bride's wedding band	event	708	10/93	76r
Clergy	event	224	10/93	76r
Engagement ring	event	2756	10/93	76r
Flowers	event	863	10/93	76r
Formal wear for groom	event	106	10/93	76r
Groom's attendants' formal wear	event	530	10/93	76r
Groom's wedding band	event	402	10/93	76r
Music	event	600	10/93	76r
Photography	event	1088	10/93	76r
Shoes for bride	event	50	10/93	76r
Videography	event	483	10/93	76r
Wedding invitations and announcements	event	342	10/93	76r
Wedding reception	event	7000	10/93	76r

Johnson City, TN

Item	Per	Value	Date	Ref.
Composite, ACCRA index		91.80	12/94	2c
Alcoholic Beverages				
Beer, Miller Lite, Bud, 12-oz., ex deposit	6	3.65	12/94	2c
J & B Scotch	750-ml.	20.58	12/94	2c
Wine, Gallo Chablis blanc	1.5-lit	6.36	12/94	2c
Appliances				
Appliances (major), expenditures	year	153	91	81r
Average annual exp.				
Food, health care, personal goods, services	year	27020	91	81r
Charity				
Cash contributions, expenditures	year	839	91	81r
Clothing				
Apparel, men and boys, total expenditures	year	380	91	81r
Apparel, women and girls, total expenditures	year	660	91	81r
Footwear, expenditures	year	193	91	81r
Jeans, man's denim		28.99	12/94	2c
Shirt, man's dress shirt		31.00	12/94	2c
Undervest, boy's size 10-14, cotton	3	5.24	12/94	2c
Communications				
Long-distance telephone rate, day, addl. min., 1-10 mi.	min.	0.10	12/93	9s
Long-distance telephone rate, day, initial min., 1-10 mi.	min.	0.10	12/93	9s

Values are in dollars or fractions of dollars. In the column headed *Ref*, references are shown to sources. Each reference is followed by a letter. These refer to the geographical level for which data were reported: s=State, r=Region, and c=City or metro. The abbreviation *ex* is used to mean *except* or *excluding*; *exp* stands for expenditures. For other abbreviations and further explanations, please see the Introduction.

Johnson City, TN - continued

Item	Per	Value	Date	Ref.
Communications				
Newspaper subscription, dly. and Sun. delivery	month	8.25	12/94	2c
Phone line, single, business, field visit	inst	58.50	12/93	9s
Phone line, single, business, no field visit	inst	58.50	12/93	9s
Phone line, single, residence, field visit	inst	41.50	12/93	9s
Phone line, single, residence, no field visit	inst	41.50	12/93	9s
Telephone bill, family of four	month	21.60	12/94	2c
Telephone service, expenditures	year	616	91	81r
Education				
Board, 4-year private college/university	year	1846	8/94	80s
Board, 4-year public college/university	year	1700	8/94	80s
Education, total expenditures	year	319	91	81r
Room, 4-year private college/university	year	1553	8/94	80s
Room, 4-year public college/university	year	1524	8/94	80s
Total cost, 4-year private college/university	year	12025	8/94	80s
Total cost, 4-year public college/university	year	5021	8/94	80s
Tuition, 2-year public college/university, in-state	year	950	8/94	80s
Tuition, 4-year private college/university, in-state	year	8627	8/94	80s
Tuition, 4-year public college/university, in-state	year	1797	8/94	80s
Energy and Fuels				
Energy, combined forms, 1800 sq. ft.	mo.	102.12	12/94	2c
Energy, exc. electricity, 1800 sq. ft.	mo.	44.87	12/94	2c
Fuel oil and other fuels, expenditures	year	56	91	81r
Gas, natural, expenditures	year	150	91	81r
Gas, reg unlead, taxes inc., cash, self-service	gal	1.03	12/94	2c
Gasoline and motor oil purchased	year	1152	91	81r
Gasoline, unleaded midgrade	gallon	1.21	4/93	82r
Gasoline, unleaded premium	gallon	1.30	4/93	82r
Gasoline, unleaded regular	gallon	1.10	4/93	82r
Entertainment				
Bowling, evening rate	game	2.20	12/94	2c
Concert ticket, Pearl Jam group	perf	20.00	94	50r
Entertainment, total expenditures	year	1266	91	81r
Fees and admissions, expenditures	year	306	91	81r
Monopoly game, Parker Brothers', No. 9	game	9.72	12/94	2c
Movie	adm	5.50	12/94	2c
Pets, toys, playground equipment, expenditures	year	271	91	81r
Reading, expenditures	year	131	91	81r
Televisions, radios, and sound equipment, expenditures	year	439	91	81r
Tennis balls, yellow, Wilson or Penn, 3	can	2.10	12/94	2c
Funerals				
Burial, immediate, container provided by funeral home		1298.96	1/95	54r
Cards, acknowledgment		21.26	1/95	54r
Casket, minimum alternative		204.95	1/95	54r
Cosmetology, hair care, etc.		85.40	1/95	54r
Cremation, direct, container provided by funeral home		1054.77	1/95	54r
Embalming		287.71	1/95	54r
Funeral, funeral home		269.18	1/95	54r
Funeral, other facility		272.88	1/95	54r
Graveside service		302.54	1/95	54r
Hearse, local		122.08	1/95	54r
Limousine, local		80.31	1/95	54r
Memorial service		277.66	1/95	54r
Service charge, professional, nondeclinable		896.65	1/95	54r
Visitation and viewing		232.39	1/95	54r
Groceries				
Groceries, ACCRA Index		97.50	12/94	2c
Apples, Red Delicious	lb.	0.73	12/94	82r
Baby food, strained vegetables, lowest price	4-4.5 oz.	0.35	12/94	2c
Bacon, sliced	lb.	1.67	12/94	82r

Johnson City, TN - continued

Item	Per	Value	Date	Ref.
Groceries - continued				
Bananas	lb.	0.55	12/94	2c
Bananas	lb.	0.42	12/94	82r
Beef or hamburger, ground	lb.	1.65	12/94	2c
Beef purchases	year	213	91	81r
Beverage purchases, alcoholic	year	249	91	81r
Beverage purchases, nonalcoholic	year	207	91	81r
Bologna, all beef or mixed	lb.	2.27	12/94	82r
Bread, white	24-oz.	0.73	12/94	2c
Bread, white, pan	lb.	0.68	12/94	82r
Cabbage	lb.	0.42	12/94	82r
Carrots, short trimmed and topped	lb.	0.53	12/94	82r
Cereals and bakery products purchases	year	345	91	81r
Cereals and cereals products purchases	year	127	91	81r
Cheddar cheese, natural	lb.	3.58	12/94	82r
Cheese, Kraft grated Parmesan	8-oz.	3.29	12/94	2c
Chicken breast, bone-in	lb.	1.71	12/94	82r
Chicken, fresh, whole	lb.	0.78	12/94	82r
Chicken, whole fryer	lb.	0.90	12/94	2c
Chuck roast, USDA choice, boneless	lb.	2.26	12/94	82r
Cigarettes, Winston, Kings	carton	14.11	12/94	2c
Coffee, vacuum-packed	13 oz.	3.35	12/94	2c
Corn Flakes, Kellogg's or Post Toasties	18 oz.	2.34	12/94	2c
Corn, frozen, whole kernel, lowest price	10 oz.	0.62	12/94	2c
Crackers, soda, salted	lb.	1.27	12/94	82r
Cucumbers	lb.	0.65	12/94	82r
Dairy products (other) purchases	year	141	91	81r
Eggs, Grade A large	dozen	0.81	12/94	2c
Eggs, Grade A large	dozen	0.87	12/94	82r
Fish and seafood purchases	year	72	91	81r
Flour, white, all purpose	lb.	0.23	12/94	82r
Food purchases, food eaten at home	year	2381	91	81r
Foods purchased away from home, not prepared by consumer	year	1696	91	81r
Frankfurters, all meat or all beef	lb.	1.74	12/94	82r
Fruits and vegetables purchases	year	380	91	81r
Grapefruit	lb.	0.45	12/94	82r
Grapes, Thompson seedless	lb.	2.30	12/94	82r
Ground beef, 100% beef	lb.	1.37	12/94	82r
Ground chuck, 100% beef	lb.	1.97	12/94	82r
Ham, boneless, exc. canned	lb.	2.54	12/94	82r
Ice cream, prepackaged, bulk, regular	1/2 gal.	2.47	12/94	82r
Lemons	lb.	1.02	12/94	82r
Lettuce, iceberg	lb.	0.96	12/94	82r
Lettuce, iceberg	head	0.99	12/94	2c
Margarine, Blue Bonnet or Parkay cubes	lb.	0.52	12/94	2c
Margarine, stick	lb.	0.77	12/94	82r
Meats, poultry, fish, and eggs purchases	year	655	91	81r
Milk and cream (fresh) purchases	year	130	91	81r
Milk, whole	1/2 gal.	1.31	12/94	2c
Orange juice, frozen concentrate 12-oz. can	16 oz.	1.36	12/94	82r
Orange juice, Minute Maid frozen	12-oz.	1.11	12/94	2c
Oranges, Navel	lb.	0.54	12/94	82r
Peaches, halves or slices, Hunt's, Del Monte, or Libby's	29-oz.	1.19	12/94	2c
Pears, Anjou	lb.	0.81	12/94	82r
Peas, sweet, Del Monte or Green Giant	15-17 oz.	0.43	12/94	2c
Pork chops, center cut, bone-in	lb.	3.07	12/94	82r
Pork purchases	year	142	91	81r
Potato chips	16-oz.	3.15	12/94	82r
Potatoes, frozen, French fried	lb.	0.82	12/94	82r
Potatoes, white	lb.	0.34	12/94	82r
Potatoes, white or red	10-lb. sack	2.71	12/94	2c
Rice, white, long grain, uncooked	lb.	0.48	12/94	82r
Round roast, USDA choice, boneless	lb.	2.91	12/94	82r
Sausage, fresh	lb.	1.82	12/94	82r
Sausage, Jimmy Dean, 100% pork	lb.	2.41	12/94	2c
Shortening, vegetable oil blends	lb.	0.75	12/94	82r
Shortening, vegetable, Crisco	3-lb.	2.45	12/94	2c

Values are in dollars or fractions of dollars. In the column headed *Ref*, references are shown to sources. Each reference is followed by a letter. These refer to the geographical level for which data were reported: s = State, r = Region, and c = City or metro. The abbreviation *ex* is used to mean *except* or *excluding*; *exp* stands for expenditures. For other abbreviations and further explanations, please see the Introduction.

Johnson City, TN - continued

Item	Per	Value	Date	Ref.
Groceries				
Soft drink, Coca Cola, ex deposit	2 lit	0.95	12/94	2c
Spaghetti and macaroni	lb.	0.87	12/94	82r
Steak, rib eye, USDA choice, boneless	lb.	6.85	12/94	82r
Steak, round, graded & ungraded, exc. USDA prime & choice	lb.	2.96	12/94	82r
Steak, round, USDA choice, boneless	lb.	3.17	12/94	82r
Steak, sirloin, USDA choice, boneless	lb.	4.12	12/94	82r
Steak, t-bone	lb.	5.09	12/94	2c
Steak, T-bone, USDA choice, bone-in	lb.	5.63	12/94	82r
Sugar and other sweets, eaten at home, expenditures	year	93	91	81r
Sugar, cane or beet	4 lbs.	1.44	12/94	2c
Sugar, white, all sizes	lb.	0.39	12/94	82r
Tobacco products and smoking supplies, total expenditures	year	286	91	81r
Tomatoes, field grown	lb.	1.36	12/94	82r
Tomatoes, Hunt's or Del Monte	14.5 oz.	0.49	12/94	2c
Tuna, chunk, light	lb.	1.94	12/94	82r
Tuna, chunk, light, oil-packed	6.125-6.5 oz.	0.66	12/94	2c
Turkey, frozen, whole	lb.	0.96	12/94	82r
Yogurt, natural, fruit flavored	8 oz.	0.58	12/94	82r
Goods and Services				
Miscellaneous goods and services, ACCRA Index		90.60	12/94	2c
Health Care				
Health care, ACCRA Index		88.40	12/94	2c
Adenosine, emergency room	treat	100.00	95	23r
Antibiotic ointment, Polysporin	1.5 oz.	3.89	12/94	2c
Bladder tap, superpubic, infant, emergency room	treat	119.00	95	23r
Blood analysis, emergency room	treat	25.00	95	23r
Blood tests, abdominal pain, emergency room	treat	25.00	95	23r
Burn dressing, emergency room	treat	266.00	95	23r
Cardiology interpretation, emergency room	treat	26.00	95	23r
Chest X-ray, emergency room	treat	78.00	95	23r
Childbirth, Cesarean delivery, hospital charge	birth	5462.00	12/91	69r
Childbirth, Cesarean delivery, physician charge	birth	2228.00	12/91	69r
Childbirth, normal delivery, hospital charge	birth	2943.00	12/91	69r
Childbirth, normal delivery, physician charge	birth	1619.00	12/91	69r
Defibrillation pads, emergency room	treat	6.00	95	23r
Dentist's fee, adult teeth cleaning and periodic oral exam	visit	38.00	12/94	2c
Doctor's fee, routine exam, established patient	visit	46.00	12/94	2c
Drugs, expenditures	year	297	91	81r
Gastric tube insertion, nasal, emergency room	treat	25.00	95	23r
Health care, total expenditures	year	1600	91	81r
Health insurance expenditures	year	637	91	81r
Heart monitor, emergency room	treat	40.00	95	23r
Hospital care, semiprivate room	day	261.33	12/94	2c
Insurance premium, family medical care	month	344.21	1/95	41s
Intravenous fluids, emergency room	treat	130.00	95	23r
Intravenous fluids, emergency room	liter	26.00	95	23r
Intravenous line, central, emergency room	treat	342.00	95	23r
Liver function tests, abdominal pain, emergency room	treat	26.00	95	23r
Medical care charges, total, emergency room, third-degree burns	treat	2101.00	95	23r
Medical care charges, total, emergency, infant with fever	treat	628.00	95	23r
Medical services expenditures	year	573	91	81r
Medical supplies expenditures	year	93	91	81r
Morphine, emergency room	treat	34.00	95	23r
Nursing care and facilities charges, emergency room	treat	252.00	95	23r

Johnson City, TN - continued

Item	Per	Value	Date	Ref.
Health Care - continued				
Nursing care and facilities charges, emergency, infant with fever	treat	252.00	95	23r
Nursing care and facilities charges, emergency, third-degree burns	treat	861.00	95	23r
Physician's charges, emergency, infant with fever	treat	212.00	95	23r
Physician's charges, emergency, third-degree burns	treat	372.00	95	23r
Physician's fee, emergency room	treat	372.00	95	23r
Physician's fee, general practitioner	visit	51.20	12/93	60r
Surgery, open-heart	proc	42374.00	1/93	14r
Ultrasound, abdominal, emergency room	treat	276.00	95	23r
Urinalysis, emergency room	treat	20.00	95	23r
Urinalysis, infant, emergency room	treat	20.00	95	23r
X-rays, emergency room	treat	78.00	95	23r
Household Goods				
Appl. repair, service call, wash mach	min. lab. chg.	42.50	12/94	2c
Floor coverings, expenditures	year	48	91	81r
Furniture, expenditures	year	280	91	81r
Household equipment, misc. expenditures	year	342	91	81r
Household expenditures, miscellaneous	year	256	91	81r
Household furnishings and equipment, expenditures	year	988	91	81r
Household operations expenditures	year	468	91	81r
Household textiles, expenditures	year	95	91	81r
Housekeeping supplies, expenditures	year	380	91	81r
Laundry and cleaning supplies, expenditures	year	109	91	81r
Laundry detergent, Tide Ultra, Bold, or Cheer	42 oz.	2.69	12/94	2c
Postage and stationery, expenditures	year	105	91	81r
Tissues, facial, Kleenex brand	175	0.99	12/94	2c
Housing				
Housing, ACCRA Index		90.30	12/94	2c
Add garage/carport		6,980	3/95	74r
Add room(s)		11,403	3/95	74r
Apartment condominium or co-op, median	unit	68600	12/94	62r
Dwellings (owned), expenditures	year	2428	91	81r
Enclose porch/patio/breezeway		4,572	3/95	74r
Finish room in basement/attic		3,794	3/95	74r
Home, existing, single-family, median	unit	120200	12/94	62r
House payment, principal and interest, 25% down payment	mo.	681	12/94	2c
House, 1800 sq ft, 8000 sq ft lot, new, urban, utilities	total	112467	12/94	2c
Maintenance, repairs, insurance, and other housing expenditures	year	531	91	81r
Mortgage interest and charges expenditures	year	1506	91	81r
Mtge. rate, incl. points and orig. fee, 30-year conv. fixed or ARM	mo.	9.03	12/94	2c
Princ. & int., mortgage, median-price exist. sing.-family home	mo.	540	12/94	62r
Property taxes expenditures	year	391	91	81r
Redesign, restructure more than half of home's interior		17,641	3/95	74r
Rent, apartment, 2 br., 1 1/2-2 baths, unfurnished, 950 sq ft, water	mo.	510	12/94	2c
Rental units expenditures	year	1264	91	81r
Insurance and Pensions				
Auto insurance, private passenger	year	574.08	12/94	71s
Insurance and pensions, personal, expenditures	year	2395	91	81r
Insurance, life and other personal, expenditures	year	368	91	81r
Pensions and Social Security, expenditures	year	2027	91	81r
Personal Goods				
Shampoo, Alberto VO5	15-oz.	1.03	12/94	2c
Toothpaste, Crest or Colgate	6-7 oz.	1.82	12/94	2c

Values are in dollars or fractions of dollars. In the column headed *Ref*, references are shown to sources. Each reference is followed by a letter. These refer to the geographical level for which data were reported: s=State, r=Region, and c=City or metro. The abbreviation *ex* is used to mean *except* or *excluding*; *exp* stands for *expenditures*. For other abbreviations and further explanations, please see the Introduction.

Johnson City, TN - continued

Item	Per	Value	Date	Ref.
Personal Services				
Dry cleaning, man's 2-pc. suit		5.94	12/94	2c
Haircut, man's barbershop, no styling		8.60	12/94	2c
Haircut, woman's shampoo, trim, blow-dry		18.60	12/94	2c
Personal services expenditures	year	212	91	81r
Restaurant Food				
Chicken, fried, thigh and drumstick		1.60	12/94	2c
Dining expenditures, family	week	33.83	94	73r
Hamburger with cheese	1/4 lb.	0.99	12/94	2c
Pizza, Pizza Hut or Pizza Inn	12-13 in.	6.12	12/94	2c
Taxes				
Tax, cigarettes	year	379.00	10/93	43s
Taxes, Federal income, expenditures	year	2275	91	81r
Taxes, personal, expenditures	year	2715	91	81r
Taxes, State and local income, expenditures	year	365	91	81r
Transportation				
Transportation, ACCRA Index		91.30	12/94	2c
Cars and trucks purchased, new	year	1306	91	81r
Cars and trucks purchased, used	year	942	91	81r
Driver's learning permit fee	perm	5.50	1/94	84s
Driver's license fee	orig	16.00	1/94	84s
Driver's license fee, duplicate	lic	8.00	1/94	84s
Driver's license reinstatement fee, min.	susp	65.00	1/94	85s
Driver's license renewal fee	renew	14.00	1/94	84s
Identification card, nondriver	card	7.50	1/94	83s
Motorcycle learning permit fee	perm	6.50	1/94	84s
Motorcycle license fee	orig	17.00	1/94	84s
Motorcycle license fee, duplicate	lic	8.00	1/94	84s
Motorcycle license renewal fee	renew	15.00	1/94	84s
Public transportation expenditures	year	249	91	81r
Tire balance, computer or spin bal., front	wheel	6.10	12/94	2c
Transportation expenditures, total	year	5307	91	81r
Vehicle finance charges	year	346	91	81r
Vehicle insurance expenditures	year	544	91	81r
Vehicle maintenance and repairs expenditures	year	600	91	81r
Vehicle purchases	year	2275	91	81r
Vehicle rental, leases, licenses, etc. expenditures	year	141	91	81r
Vehicles purchased, other than cars and trucks	year	27	91	81r
Utilities				
Utilities, ACCRA Index		93.70	12/94	2c
Electricity expenditures	year	950	91	81r
Electricity, (part.), other, 1800 sq. ft., new home	mo.	57.25	12/94	2c
Utilities, fuels, and public services, total expenditures	year	2000	91	81r
Water and other public services, expenditures	year	227	91	81r
Weddings				
Bridal attendants' gowns	event	750	10/93	76r
Bridal gown	event	852	10/93	76r
Bridal headpiece and veil	event	167	10/93	76r
Bride's wedding band	event	708	10/93	76r
Clergy	event	224	10/93	76r
Engagement ring	event	2756	10/93	76r
Flowers	event	863	10/93	76r
Formal wear for groom	event	106	10/93	76r
Groom's attendants' formal wear	event	530	10/93	76r
Groom's wedding band	event	402	10/93	76r
Music	event	600	10/93	76r
Photography	event	1088	10/93	76r
Shoes for bride	event	50	10/93	76r
Videography	event	483	10/93	76r
Wedding invitations and announcements	event	342	10/93	76r
Wedding reception	event	7000	10/93	76r

Johnstown, PA

Item	Per	Value	Date	Ref.
Appliances				
Appliances (major), expenditures	year	145	91	81r
Average annual exp.				
Food, health care, personal goods, services	year	29496	91	81r
Charity				
Cash contributions, expenditures	year	708	91	81r
Clothing				
Apparel, men and boys, total expenditures	year	416	91	81r
Apparel, women and girls, total expenditures	year	744	91	81r
Footwear, expenditures	year	305	91	81r
Communications				
Long-distance telephone rate, day, addl. min., 1-10 mi.	min.	0.08	12/93	9s
Long-distance telephone rate, day, initial min., 1-10 mi.	min.	0.15	12/93	9s
Phone line, single, business, field visit	inst	75.00	12/93	9s
Phone line, single, business, no field visit	inst	75.00	12/93	9s
Phone line, single, residence, field visit	inst	40.00	12/93	9s
Phone line, single, residence, no field visit	inst	40.00	12/93	9s
Telephone service, expenditures	year	589	91	81r
Education				
Board, 4-year private college/university	year	2714	8/94	80s
Board, 4-year public college/university	year	1899	8/94	80s
Education, total expenditures	year	593	91	81r
Room, 4-year private college/university	year	2720	8/94	80s
Room, 4-year public college/university	year	2063	8/94	80s
Total cost, 4-year private college/university	year	18118	8/94	80s
Total cost, 4-year public college/university	year	8278	8/94	80s
Tuition, 2-year public college/university, in-state	year	1671	8/94	80s
Tuition, 4-year private college/university, in-state	year	12684	8/94	80s
Tuition, 4-year public college/university, in-state	year	4316	8/94	80s
Energy and Fuels				
Fuel oil and other fuels, expenditures	year	257	91	81r
Gas, natural, expenditures	year	285	91	81r
Gasoline and motor oil purchased	year	867	91	81r
Gasoline, unleaded midgrade	gallon	1.32	4/93	82r
Gasoline, unleaded premium	gallon	1.40	4/93	82r
Gasoline, unleaded regular	gallon	1.19	4/93	82r
Entertainment				
Entertainment, total expenditures	year	1331	91	81r
Fees and admissions, expenditures	year	398	91	81r
Pets, toys, playground equipment, expenditures	year	270	91	81r
Reading, expenditures	year	171	91	81r
Televisions, radios, and sound equipment, expenditures	year	429	91	81r
Funerals				
Burial, immediate, container provided by funeral home		1370.36	1/95	54r
Cards, acknowledgment		17.72	1/95	54r
Casket, minimum alternative		192.52	1/95	54r
Cosmetology, hair care, etc.		139.56	1/95	54r
Cremation, direct, container provided by funeral home		1049.24	1/95	54r
Embalming		387.57	1/95	54r
Funeral, funeral home		278.77	1/95	54r
Funeral, other facility		275.85	1/95	54r
Graveside service		213.08	1/95	54r
Hearse, local		157.27	1/95	54r
Limousine, local		146.45	1/95	54r
Memorial service		271.02	1/95	54r
Service charge, professional, nondeclinable		943.58	1/95	54r
Visitation and viewing		322.86	1/95	54r

Values are in dollars or fractions of dollars. In the column headed *Ref*, references are shown to sources. Each reference is followed by a letter. These refer to the geographical level for which data were reported: s=State, r=Region, and c=City or metro. The abbreviation *ex* is used to mean *except* or *excluding*; *exp* stands for expenditures. For other abbreviations and further explanations, please see the Introduction.

Johnstown, PA - continued

Item	Per	Value	Date	Ref.
Groceries				
Apples, Red Delicious	lb.	0.78	12/94	82r
Bacon, sliced	lb.	2.24	12/94	82r
Bananas	lb.	0.49	12/94	82r
Beef purchases	year	226	91	81r
Beverage purchases, alcoholic	year	332	91	81r
Beverage purchases, nonalcoholic	year	213	91	81r
Bread, white, pan	lb.	0.80	12/94	82r
Butter, salted, Grade AA, stick	lb.	1.67	12/94	82r
Carrots, short trimmed and topped	lb.	0.51	12/94	82r
Cereals and bakery products purchases	year	407	91	81r
Cereals and cereals products purchases	year	132	91	81r
Chicken breast, bone-in	lb.	2.22	12/94	82r
Chicken, fresh, whole	lb.	1.05	12/94	82r
Chuck roast, USDA choice, boneless	lb.	2.74	12/94	82r
Coffee, 100%, ground roast, all sizes	lb.	4.61	12/94	82r
Dairy products (other) purchases	year	161	91	81r
Eggs, Grade A large	dozen	1.12	12/94	82r
Fish and seafood purchases	year	112	91	81r
Food purchases, food eaten at home	year	2599	91	81r
Foods purchased away from home, not prepared by consumer	year	2024	91	81r
Fruits and vegetables purchases	year	444	91	81r
Grapefruit	lb.	0.44	12/94	82r
Grapes, Thompson seedless	lb.	2.24	12/94	82r
Ground chuck, 100% beef	lb.	1.67	12/94	82r
Ice cream, prepackaged, bulk, regular	1/2 gal.	2.93	12/94	82r
Lemons	lb.	1.06	12/94	82r
Lettuce, iceberg	lb.	0.92	12/94	82r
Meats, poultry, fish, and eggs purchases	year	751	91	81r
Milk and cream (fresh) purchases	year	152	91	81r
Orange juice, frozen concentrate 12-oz. can	16 oz.	1.92	12/94	82r
Oranges, Navel	lb.	0.56	12/94	82r
Pork chops, center cut, bone-in	lb.	3.09	12/94	82r
Pork purchases	year	130	91	81r
Potatoes, white	lb.	0.37	12/94	82r
Rib roast, USDA choice, bone-in	lb.	4.98	12/94	82r
Round roast, USDA choice, boneless	lb.	2.93	12/94	82r
Shortening, vegetable oil blends	lb.	1.03	12/94	82r
Spaghetti and macaroni	lb.	0.84	12/94	82r
Steak, round, USDA choice, boneless	lb.	3.48	12/94	82r
Steak, sirloin, USDA choice, bone-in	lb.	3.38	12/94	82r
Steak, sirloin, USDA choice, boneless	lb.	4.81	12/94	82r
Sugar and other sweets, eaten at home, expenditures	year	89	91	81r
Sugar, white, all sizes	lb.	0.46	12/94	82r
Tobacco products and smoking supplies, total expenditures	year	279	91	81r
Tomatoes, field grown	lb.	1.56	12/94	82r
Tuna, chunk, light	lb.	2.09	12/94	82r
Health Care				
Childbirth, Cesarean delivery, hospital charge	birth	6334.00	12/91	69r
Childbirth, Cesarean delivery, physician charge	birth	2234.00	12/91	69r
Childbirth, normal delivery, hospital charge	birth	3225.00	12/91	69r
Childbirth, normal delivery, physician charge	birth	1623.00	12/91	69r
Drugs, expenditures	year	205	91	81r
Health care, total expenditures	year	1396	91	81r
Health insurance expenditures	year	553	91	81r
Insurance premium, family medical care	month	349.05	1/95	41s
Medical services expenditures	year	559	91	81r
Medical supplies expenditures	year	80	91	81r
Household Goods				
Floor coverings, expenditures	year	158	91	81r
Furniture, expenditures	year	341	91	81r
Household equipment, misc. expenditures	year	363	91	81r
Household expenditures, miscellaneous	year	194	91	81r
Household furnishings and equipment, expenditures	year	1158	91	81r
Household operations expenditures	year	378	91	81r

Johnstown, PA - continued

Item	Per	Value	Date	Ref.
Household Goods - continued				
Household textiles, expenditures	year	88	91	81r
Housekeeping supplies, expenditures	year	426	91	81r
Laundry and cleaning supplies, expenditures	year	122	91	81r
Postage and stationery, expenditures	year	134	91	81r
Housing				
Add garage/carport		11,614	3/95	74r
Add room(s)		16,816	3/95	74r
Apartment condominium or co-op, median	unit	96700	12/94	62r
Dwellings (owned), expenditures	year	3305	91	81r
Enclose porch/patio/breezeway		2,980	3/95	74r
Finish room in basement/attic		4,330	3/95	74r
Home, existing, single-family, median	unit	161600	12/94	62r
Maintenance, repairs, insurance, and other housing expenditures	year	569	91	81r
Mortgage interest and charges expenditures	year	1852	91	81r
Princ. & int., mortgage, median-price exist. sing.-family home	mo.	765	12/94	62r
Property taxes expenditures	year	884	91	81r
Redesign, restructure more than half of home's interior		2,750	3/95	74r
Rental units expenditures	year	1832	91	81r
Insurance and Pensions				
Auto insurance, private passenger	year	721.50	12/94	71s
Insurance and pensions, personal, expenditures	year	2690	91	81r
Insurance, life and other personal, expenditures	year	341	91	81r
Pensions and Social Security, expenditures	year	2349	91	81r
Legal Assistance				
Estate planning, law-firm partner	hr.	375.00	10/93	12r
Legal work, law firm associate	hour	78		10r
Legal work, law firm partner	hour	183		10r
Personal Services				
Personal services expenditures	year	184	91	81r
Restaurant Food				
Dining expenditures, family	week	34.26	94	73r
Taxes				
Taxes, Federal income, expenditures	year	2409	91	81r
Taxes, personal, expenditures	year	3094	91	81r
Taxes, State and local income, expenditures	year	620	91	81r
Transportation				
Cars and trucks purchased, new	year	1170	91	81r
Cars and trucks purchased, used	year	739	91	81r
Driver's learning permit fee	perm	27.00	1/94	84s
Driver's license fee	orig	0.00	1/94	84s
Driver's license fee, duplicate	lic	7.00	1/94	84s
Driver's license reinstatement fee, min.	susp	25.00	1/94	85s
Driver's license renewal fee	renew	0.00	1/94	84s
Identification card, nondriver	card	5.00	1/94	83s
Motorcycle learning permit fee	perm	27.00	1/94	84s
Motorcycle license fee	orig	0.00	1/94	84s
Motorcycle license fee, duplicate	lic	7.00	1/94	84s
Motorcycle license renewal fee	renew	0.00	1/94	84s
Public transportation expenditures	year	430	91	81r
Transportation expenditures, total	year	4810	91	81r
Vehicle finance charges	year	238	91	81r
Vehicle insurance expenditures	year	630	91	81r
Vehicle maintenance and repairs expenditures	year	532	91	81r
Vehicle purchases	year	1920	91	81r
Vehicle rental, leases, licenses, etc. expenditures	year	193	91	81r
Vehicles purchased, other than cars and trucks	year	11	91	81r
Utilities				
Electricity expenditures	year	695	91	81r

Values are in dollars or fractions of dollars. In the column headed *Ref*, references are shown to sources. Each reference is followed by a letter. These refer to the geographical level for which data were reported: s=State, r=Region, and c=City or metro. The abbreviation *ex* is used to mean *except* or *excluding*; *exp* stands for expenditures. For other abbreviations and further explanations, please see the Introduction.

Johnstown, PA - continued

Item	Per	Value	Date	Ref.
Utilities				
Utilities, fuels, and public services, total expenditures	year	1981	91	81r
Water and other public services, expenditures	year	154	91	81r
Weddings				
Bridal attendants' gowns	event	750	10/93	76r
Bridal gown	event	852	10/93	76r
Bridal headpiece and veil	event	167	10/93	76r
Bride's wedding band	event	708	10/93	76r
Clergy	event	224	10/93	76r
Engagement ring	event	2756	10/93	76r
Flowers	event	863	10/93	76r
Formal wear for groom	event	106	10/93	76r
Groom's attendants' formal wear	event	530	10/93	76r
Groom's wedding band	event	402	10/93	76r
Music	event	600	10/93	76r
Photography	event	1088	10/93	76r
Shoes for bride	event	50	10/93	76r
Videography	event	483	10/93	76r
Wedding invitations and announcements	event	342	10/93	76r
Wedding reception	event	7000	10/93	76r

Joliet, IL

Item	Per	Value	Date	Ref.
Appliances				
Appliances (major), expenditures	year	131	91	81r
Average annual exp.				
Food, health care, personal goods, services	year	25935	91	81r
Charity				
Cash contributions, expenditures	year	745	91	81r
Clothing				
Apparel, men and boys, total expenditures	year	332	91	81r
Apparel, women and girls, total expenditures	year	578	91	81r
Footwear, expenditures	year	164	91	81r
Communications				
Long-distance telephone rate, day, addl. min., 1-10 mi.	min.	0.04	12/93	9s
Long-distance telephone rate, day, initial min., 1-10 mi.	min.	0.10	12/93	9s
Phone line, single, business, field visit	inst	84.50	12/93	9s
Phone line, single, business, no field visit	inst	84.50	12/93	9s
Phone line, single, residence, field visit	inst	55.00	12/93	9s
Phone line, single, residence, no field visit	inst	55.00	12/93	9s
Telephone service, expenditures	year	547	91	81r
Education				
Board, 4-year private college/university	year	2078	8/94	80s
Board, 4-year public college/university	year	2139	8/94	80s
Education, total expenditures	year	394	91	81r
Room, 4-year private college/university	year	2696	8/94	80s
Room, 4-year public college/university	year	1796	8/94	80s
Total cost, 4-year private college/university	year	15249	8/94	80s
Total cost, 4-year public college/university	year	6964	8/94	80s
Tuition, 2-year public college/university, in-state	year	1135	8/94	80s
Tuition, 4-year private college/university, in-state	year	10474	8/94	80s
Tuition, 4-year public college/university, in-state	year	3029	8/94	80s
Energy and Fuels				
Fuel oil and other fuels, expenditures	year	83	91	81r
Gas, natural, expenditures	year	373	91	81r
Gasoline and motor oil purchased	year	1000	91	81r
Gasoline, unleaded midgrade	gallon	1.15	4/93	82r
Gasoline, unleaded premium	gallon	1.23	4/93	82r
Gasoline, unleaded regular	gallon	1.07	4/93	82r

Joliet, IL - continued

Item	Per	Value	Date	Ref.
Entertainment				
Entertainment, total expenditures	year	1356	91	81r
Fees and admissions, expenditures	year	347	91	81r
Pets, toys, playground equipment, expenditures	year	270	91	81r
Reading, expenditures	year	160	91	81r
Televisions, radios, and sound equipment, expenditures	year	433	91	81r
Funerals				
Burial, immediate, container provided by funeral home		1268.31	1/95	54r
Cards, acknowledgment		26.12	1/95	54r
Casket, minimum alternative		198.03	1/95	54r
Cosmetology, hair care, etc.		122.19	1/95	54r
Cremation, direct, container provided by funeral home		977.81	1/95	54r
Embalming		334.00	1/95	54r
Funeral, funeral home		321.16	1/95	54r
Funeral, other facility		317.73	1/95	54r
Graveside service		292.48	1/95	54r
Hearse, local		153.20	1/95	54r
Limousine, local		123.52	1/95	54r
Memorial service		356.30	1/95	54r
Service charge, professional, nondeclinable		968.24	1/95	54r
Visitation and viewing		332.66	1/95	54r
Groceries				
Apples, Red Delicious	lb.	0.68	12/94	82r
Bacon, sliced	lb.	1.88	12/94	82r
Bananas	lb.	0.41	12/94	82r
Beef purchases	year	197	91	81r
Beef, stew, boneless	lb.	2.52	12/94	82r
Beverage purchases, alcoholic	year	293	91	81r
Beverage purchases, nonalcoholic	year	203	91	81r
Bologna, all beef or mixed	lb.	2.12	12/94	82r
Bread, white, pan	lb.	0.76	12/94	82r
Cabbage	lb.	0.44	12/94	82r
Carrots, short trimmed and topped	lb.	0.44	12/94	82r
Cereals and bakery products purchases	year	347	91	81r
Cereals and cereals products purchases	year	119	91	81r
Cheddar cheese, natural	lb.	3.28	12/94	82r
Chicken breast, bone-in	lb.	1.61	12/94	82r
Chicken, fresh, whole	lb.	0.89	12/94	82r
Chuck roast, USDA choice, boneless	lb.	2.33	12/94	82r
Coffee, 100%, ground roast, all sizes	lb.	4.28	12/94	82r
Cookies, chocolate chip	lb.	2.72	12/94	82r
Dairy products (other) purchases	year	148	91	81r
Eggs, Grade A large	dozen	0.76	12/94	82r
Fish and seafood purchases	year	61	91	81r
Flour, white, all purpose	lb.	0.22	12/94	82r
Food purchases, food eaten at home	year	2313	91	81r
Foods purchased away from home, not prepared by consumer	year	1709	91	81r
Fruits and vegetables purchases	year	372	91	81r
Grapefruit	lb.	0.47	12/94	82r
Grapes, Thompson seedless	lb.	2.15	12/94	82r
Ground beef, 100% beef	lb.	1.37	12/94	82r
Ground chuck, 100% beef	lb.	1.81	12/94	82r
Ham, boneless, exc. canned	lb.	2.16	12/94	82r
Ice cream, prepackaged, bulk, regular	1/2 gal.	2.48	12/94	82r
Lemons	lb.	1.08	12/94	82r
Lettuce, iceberg	lb.	0.81	12/94	82r
Margarine, stick	lb.	0.81	12/94	82r
Meats, poultry, fish, and eggs purchases	year	591	91	81r
Milk and cream (fresh) purchases	year	132	91	81r
Orange juice, frozen concentrate 12-oz. can	16 oz.	1.41	12/94	82r
Oranges, Navel	lb.	0.56	12/94	82r
Peanut butter, creamy, all sizes	lb.	1.81	12/94	82r
Pork chops, center cut, bone-in	lb.	2.76	12/94	82r
Pork purchases	year	130	91	81r
Potato chips	16-oz.	2.81	12/94	82r
Potatoes, frozen, French fried	lb.	0.83	12/94	82r

Values are in dollars or fractions of dollars. In the column headed *Ref*, references are shown to sources. Each reference is followed by a letter. These refer to the geographical level for which data were reported: s = State, r = Region, and c = City or metro. The abbreviation *ex* is used to mean *except* or *excluding*; *exp* stands for expenditures. For other abbreviations and further explanations, please see the Introduction.

Joliet, IL - continued

Item	Per	Value	Date	Ref.
Groceries				
Potatoes, white	lb.	0.28	12/94	82r
Round roast, USDA choice, boneless	lb.	2.90	12/94	82r
Shortening, vegetable oil blends	lb.	0.88	12/94	82r
Spaghetti and macaroni	lb.	0.78	12/94	82r
Steak, rib eye, USDA choice, boneless	lb.	6.15	12/94	82r
Steak, round, graded & ungraded, exc. USDA prime & choice	lb.	2.72	12/94	82r
Steak, round, USDA choice, boneless	lb.	3.02	12/94	82r
Steak, sirloin, USDA choice, boneless	lb.	3.85	12/94	82r
Steak, T-bone, USDA choice, bone-in	lb.	5.38	12/94	82r
Sugar and other sweets, eaten at home, expenditures	year	91	91	81r
Sugar, white, all sizes	lb.	0.36	12/94	82r
Tobacco products and smoking supplies, total expenditures	year	298	91	81r
Tomatoes, field grown	lb.	1.36	12/94	82r
Tuna, chunk, light	lb.	1.94	12/94	82r
Turkey, frozen, whole	lb.	0.96	12/94	82r
Yogurt, natural, fruit flavored	8 oz.	0.62	12/94	82r
Health Care				
Childbirth, Cesarean delivery, hospital charge	birth	5101.00	12/91	69r
Childbirth, Cesarean delivery, physician charge	birth	2234.00	12/91	69r
Childbirth, normal delivery, hospital charge	birth	2891.00	12/91	69r
Childbirth, normal delivery, physician charge	birth	1623.00	12/91	69r
Drugs, expenditures	year	248	91	81r
Health care, total expenditures	year	1336	91	81r
Health insurance expenditures	year	550	91	81r
Insurance premium, family medical care	month	363.57	1/95	41s
Medical services expenditures	year	457	91	81r
Medical supplies expenditures	year	82	91	81r
Household Goods				
Floor coverings, expenditures	year	105	91	81r
Furniture, expenditures	year	291	91	81r
Household equipment, misc. expenditures	year	341	91	81r
Household expenditures, miscellaneous	year	162	91	81r
Household furnishings and equipment, expenditures	year	1042	91	81r
Household operations expenditures	year	365	91	81r
Household textiles, expenditures	year	101	91	81r
Housekeeping supplies, expenditures	year	390	91	81r
Laundry and cleaning supplies, expenditures	year	110	91	81r
Postage and stationery, expenditures	year	115	91	81r
Housing				
Add garage/carport		8,479	3/95	74r
Add room(s)		21,347	3/95	74r
Apartment condominium or co-op, median	unit	87100	12/94	62r
Bathroom addition, average cost	add	9734.00	3/95	13r
Bathroom remodeling, average cost	remod	6414.00	3/95	13r
Bedroom, master suite addition, average cost	add	27122.00	3/95	13r
Deck addition, average cost	add	6665.00	3/95	13r
Dwellings (owned), expenditures	year	2566	91	81r
Enclose porch/patio/breezeway		4,556	3/95	74r
Exterior remodeling, average cost	remod	15395.00	3/95	13r
Family room addition, average cost	add	27658.00	3/95	13r
Finish room in basement/attic		5,074	3/95	74r
Home, existing, single-family, median	unit	106500	12/94	62r
Kitchen remodeling, major, average cost	remod	17084.00	3/95	13r
Kitchen remodeling, minor, average cost	remod	5804.00	3/95	13r
Maintenance, repairs, insurance, and other housing expenditures	year	484	91	81r
Mortgage interest and charges expenditures	year	1443	91	81r
Office, home addition, average cost	add	8121.00	3/95	13r
Princ. & int., mortgage, median-price exist. sing.-family home	mo.	515	12/94	62r
Property taxes expenditures	year	639	91	81r
Redesign, restructure more than half of home's interior		9,114	3/95	74r

Joliet, IL - continued

Item	Per	Value	Date	Ref.
Housing - continued				
Rental units expenditures	year	1200	91	81r
Sun-space addition, average cost	add	23768.00	3/95	13r
Wing addition, two-story, average cost	add	50410.00	3/95	13r
Insurance and Pensions				
Auto insurance, private passenger	year	679.48	12/94	71s
Insurance and pensions, personal, expenditures	year	2408	91	81r
Insurance, life and other personal, expenditures	year	355	91	81r
Pensions and Social Security, expenditures	year	2053	91	81r
Legal Assistance				
Legal work, law firm associate	hour	90		10r
Legal work, law firm partner	hour	139		10r
Personal Services				
Personal services expenditures	year	203	91	81r
Restaurant Food				
Dining expenditures, family	week	30.03	94	73r
Taxes				
Taxes, Federal income, expenditures	year	1756	91	81r
Taxes, personal, expenditures	year	2426	91	81r
Taxes, State and local income, expenditures	year	568	91	81r
Transportation				
Cars and trucks purchased, new	year	891	91	81r
Cars and trucks purchased, used	year	1155	91	81r
Driver's learning permit fee	perm	20.00	1/94	84s
Driver's license fee	orig	10.00	1/94	84s
Driver's license fee, duplicate	lic	5.00	1/94	84s
Driver's license reinstatement fee, min.	susp	30.00	1/94	85s
Driver's license renewal fee	renew	10.00	1/94	84s
Identification card, nondriver	card	4.00	1/94	83s
Motorcycle learning permit fee	perm	20.00	1/94	84s
Motorcycle license fee	orig	10.00	1/94	84s
Motorcycle license fee, duplicate	lic	5.00	1/94	84s
Motorcycle license renewal fee	renew	10.00	1/94	84s
Public transportation expenditures	year	209	91	81r
Transportation expenditures, total	year	4792	91	81r
Vehicle finance charges	year	300	91	81r
Vehicle insurance expenditures	year	485	91	81r
Vehicle maintenance and repairs expenditures	year	534	91	81r
Vehicle purchases	year	2068	91	81r
Vehicle rental, leases, licenses, etc. expenditures	year	197	91	81r
Vehicles purchased, other than cars and trucks	year	22	91	81r
Utilities				
Electricity expenditures	year	668	91	81r
Utilities, fuels, and public services, total expenditures	year	1838	91	81r
Water and other public services, expenditures	year	167	91	81r
Weddings				
Bridal attendants' gowns	event	750	10/93	76r
Bridal gown	event	852	10/93	76r
Bridal headpiece and veil	event	167	10/93	76r
Bride's wedding band	event	708	10/93	76r
Clergy	event	224	10/93	76r
Engagement ring	event	2756	10/93	76r
Flowers	event	863	10/93	76r
Formal wear for groom	event	106	10/93	76r
Groom's attendants' formal wear	event	530	10/93	76r
Groom's wedding band	event	402	10/93	76r
Music	event	600	10/93	76r
Photography	event	1088	10/93	76r
Shoes for bride	event	50	10/93	76r
Videography	event	483	10/93	76r
Wedding invitations and announcements	event	342	10/93	76r
Wedding reception	event	7000	10/93	76r

Values are in dollars or fractions of dollars. In the column headed *Ref*, references are shown to sources. Each reference is followed by a letter. These refer to the geographical level for which data were reported: s=State, r=Region, and c=City or metro. The abbreviation *ex* is used to mean *except* or *excluding*; *exp* stands for expenditures. For other abbreviations and further explanations, please see the Introduction.

Jonesboro, AR

Item	Per	Value	Date	Ref.
Composite, ACCRA index		89.50	12/94	2c
Alcoholic Beverages				
Beer, Miller Lite, Bud, 12-oz., ex deposit	6	4.60	12/94	2c
J & B Scotch	750-ml.	17.25	12/94	2c
Wine, Gallo Chablis blanc	1.5-lit	5.50	12/94	2c
Clothing				
Jeans, man's denim		35.00	12/94	2c
Shirt, man's dress shirt		28.50	12/94	2c
Undervest, boy's size 10-14, cotton	3	3.24	12/94	2c
Communications				
Newspaper subscription, dly. and Sun. delivery	month	7.50	12/94	2c
Telephone bill, family of four	month	21.19	12/94	2c
Telephone, residential, flat rate	mo.	13.91	12/93	8c
Energy and Fuels				
Energy, combined forms, 1800 sq. ft.	mo.	111.03	12/94	2c
Energy, exc. electricity, 1800 sq. ft.	mo.	45.67	12/94	2c
Gas, reg unlead, taxes inc., cash, self-service	gal	1.06	12/94	2c
Entertainment				
Bowling, evening rate	game	1.95	12/94	2c
Monopoly game, Parker Brothers', No. 9	game	11.61	12/94	2c
Movie	adm	5.50	12/94	2c
Tennis balls, yellow, Wilson or Penn, 3	can	1.97	12/94	2c
Groceries				
Groceries, ACCRA Index		95.50	12/94	2c
Baby food, strained vegetables, lowest price	4-4.5 oz.	0.33	12/94	2c
Bananas	lb.	0.42	12/94	2c
Beef or hamburger, ground	lb.	1.42	12/94	2c
Bread, white	24-oz.	0.70	12/94	2c
Cheese, Kraft grated Parmesan	8-oz.	3.66	12/94	2c
Chicken, whole fryer	lb.	0.76	12/94	2c
Cigarettes, Winston, Kings	carton	16.30	12/94	2c
Coffee, vacuum-packed	13 oz.	3.34	12/94	2c
Corn Flakes, Kellogg's or Post Toasties	18 oz.	1.74	12/94	2c
Corn, frozen, whole kernel, lowest price	10 oz.	0.78	12/94	2c
Eggs, Grade A large	dozen	0.66	12/94	2c
Lettuce, iceberg	head	0.88	12/94	2c
Margarine, Blue Bonnet or Parkay cubes	lb.	0.60	12/94	2c
Milk, whole	1/2 gal.	1.26	12/94	2c
Orange juice, Minute Maid frozen	12-oz.	1.18	12/94	2c
Peaches, halves or slices, Hunt's, Del Monte, or Libby's	29-oz.	1.44	12/94	2c
Peas, sweet, Del Monte or Green Giant	15-17 oz.	0.62	12/94	2c
Potatoes, white or red	10-lb. sack	1.82	12/94	2c
Sausage, Jimmy Dean, 100% pork	lb.	2.51	12/94	2c
Shortening, vegetable, Crisco	3-lb.	2.60	12/94	2c
Soft drink, Coca Cola, ex deposit	2 lit	1.01	12/94	2c
Steak, t-bone	lb.	4.89	12/94	2c
Sugar, cane or beet	4 lbs.	1.36	12/94	2c
Tomatoes, Hunt's or Del Monte	14.5 oz.	0.72	12/94	2c
Tuna, chunk, light, oil-packed	6.125-6.5 oz.	0.71	12/94	2c
Goods and Services				
Miscellaneous goods and services, ACCRA Index		95.50	12/94	2c
Health Care				
Health care, ACCRA Index		82.50	12/94	2c
Antibiotic ointment, Polysporin	1.5 oz.	3.84	12/94	2c
Dentist's fee, adult teeth cleaning and periodic oral exam	visit	46.00	12/94	2c
Doctor's fee, routine exam, established patient	visit	36.50	12/94	2c

Jonesboro, AR - continued

Item	Per	Value	Date	Ref.
Health Care - continued				
Hospital care, semiprivate room	day	202.50	12/94	2c
Household Goods				
Appl. repair, service call, wash mach	min. lab. chg.	30.32	12/94	2c
Laundry detergent, Tide Ultra, Bold, or Cheer	42 oz.	3.28	12/94	2c
Tissues, facial, Kleenex brand	175	1.01	12/94	2c
Housing				
Housing, ACCRA Index		78.90	12/94	2c
House payment, principal and interest, 25% down payment	mo.	600	12/94	2c
House, 1800 sq ft, 8000 sq ft lot, new, urban, utilities	total	96667	12/94	2c
Mtge. rate, incl. points and orig. fee, 30-year conv. fixed or ARM	mo.	9.32	12/94	2c
Rent, apartment, 2 br., 1 1/2-2 baths, unfurnished, 950 sq ft, water	mo.	429	12/94	2c
Personal Goods				
Shampoo, Alberto VO5	15-oz.	1.06	12/94	2c
Toothpaste, Crest or Colgate	6-7 oz.	1.91	12/94	2c
Personal Services				
Dry cleaning, man's 2-pc. suit		6.25	12/94	2c
Haircut, man's barbershop, no styling		6.00	12/94	2c
Haircut, woman's shampoo, trim, blow-dry		16.33	12/94	2c
Restaurant Food				
Chicken, fried, thigh and drumstick		2.05	12/94	2c
Hamburger with cheese	1/4 lb.	1.89	12/94	2c
Pizza, Pizza Hut or Pizza Inn	12-13 in.	7.62	12/94	2c
Transportation				
Transportation, ACCRA Index		85.50	12/94	2c
Tire balance, computer or spin bal., front	wheel	5.00	12/94	2c
Utilities				
Utilities, ACCRA Index		100.20	12/94	2c
Electricity, (part.), other, 1800 sq. ft., new home	mo.	65.36	12/94	2c

Joplin, MO

Item	Per	Value	Date	Ref.
Composite, ACCRA index		88.90	12/94	2c
Alcoholic Beverages				
Beer, Miller Lite, Bud, 12-oz., ex deposit	6	3.93	12/94	2c
J & B Scotch	750-ml.	16.50	12/94	2c
Wine, Gallo Chablis blanc	1.5-lit	4.96	12/94	2c
Appliances				
Appliances (major), expenditures	year	131	91	81r
Average annual exp.				
Food, health care, personal goods, services	year	25935	91	81r
Charity				
Cash contributions, expenditures	year	745	91	81r
Clothing				
Apparel, men and boys, total expenditures	year	332	91	81r
Apparel, women and girls, total expenditures	year	578	91	81r
Footwear, expenditures	year	164	91	81r
Jeans, man's denim		30.59	12/94	2c
Shirt, man's dress shirt		33.67	12/94	2c
Undervest, boy's size 10-14, cotton	3	3.31	12/94	2c
Communications				
Long-distance telephone rate, day, addl. min., 1-10 mi.	min.	0.08	12/93	9s
Long-distance telephone rate, day, initial min., 1-10 mi.	min.	0.10	12/93	9s

Values are in dollars or fractions of dollars. In the column headed *Ref*, references are shown to sources. Each reference is followed by a letter. These refer to the geographical level for which data were reported: s = State, r = Region, and c = City or metro. The abbreviation *ex* is used to mean *except* or *excluding*; *exp* stands for expenditures. For other abbreviations and further explanations, please see the Introduction.

Joplin, MO - continued

Item	Per	Value	Date	Ref.
Communications				
Newspaper subscription, dly. and Sun. delivery	month	10.80	12/94	2c
Phone line, single, business, field visit	inst	52.25	12/93	9s
Phone line, single, business, no field visit	inst	52.25	12/93	9s
Phone line, single, residence, field visit	inst	36.50	12/93	9s
Phone line, single, residence, no field visit	inst	36.50	12/93	9s
Telephone bill, family of four	month	15.56	12/94	2c
Telephone service, expenditures	year	547	91	81r
Telephone, residential, flat rate	mo.	9.10	12/93	8c
Education				
Board, 4-year private college/university	year	2296	8/94	80s
Board, 4-year public college/university	year	1544	8/94	80s
Education, total expenditures	year	394	91	81r
Room, 4-year private college/university	year	2012	8/94	80s
Room, 4-year public college/university	year	1817	8/94	80s
Total cost, 4-year private college/university	year	13053	8/94	80s
Total cost, 4-year public college/university	year	5836	8/94	80s
Tuition, 2-year public college/university, in-state	year	1152	8/94	80s
Tuition, 4-year private college/university, in-state	year	8745	8/94	80s
Tuition, 4-year public college/university, in-state	year	2475	8/94	80s
Energy and Fuels				
Energy, combined forms, 1800 sq. ft.	mo.	87.73	12/94	2c
Fuel oil and other fuels, expenditures	year	83	91	81r
Gas, natural, expenditures	year	373	91	81r
Gas, reg unlead, taxes inc., cash, self-service	gal	0.94	12/94	2c
Gasoline and motor oil purchased	year	1000	91	81r
Gasoline, unleaded midgrade	gallon	1.15	4/93	82r
Gasoline, unleaded premium	gallon	1.23	4/93	82r
Gasoline, unleaded regular	gallon	1.07	4/93	82r
Entertainment				
Bowling, evening rate	game	1.88	12/94	2c
Entertainment, total expenditures	year	1356	91	81r
Fees and admissions, expenditures	year	347	91	81r
Monopoly game, Parker Brothers', No. 9	game	10.21	12/94	2c
Movie	adm	4.92	12/94	2c
Pets, toys, playground equipment, expenditures	year	270	91	81r
Reading, expenditures	year	160	91	81r
Televisions, radios, and sound equipment, expenditures	year	433	91	81r
Tennis balls, yellow, Wilson or Penn, 3	can	1.99	12/94	2c
Funerals				
Burial, immediate, container provided by funeral home		1348.78	1/95	54r
Cards, acknowledgment		21.20	1/95	54r
Casket, minimum alternative		182.83	1/95	54r
Cosmetology, hair care, etc.		133.11	1/95	54r
Cremation, direct, container provided by funeral home		1101.95	1/95	54r
Embalming		314.45	1/95	54r
Funeral, funeral home		304.88	1/95	54r
Funeral, other facility		301.37	1/95	54r
Graveside service		290.59	1/95	54r
Hearse, local		137.37	1/95	54r
Limousine, local		82.84	1/95	54r
Memorial service		316.57	1/95	54r
Service charge, professional, nondeclinable		1099.00	1/95	54r
Visitation and viewing		209.25	1/95	54r
Groceries				
Groceries, ACCRA Index		92.80	12/94	2c
Apples, Red Delicious	lb.	0.68	12/94	82r
Baby food, strained vegetables, lowest price	4-4.5 oz.	0.39	12/94	2c
Bacon, sliced	lb.	1.88	12/94	82r
Bananas	lb.	0.42	12/94	2c

Joplin, MO - continued

Item	Per	Value	Date	Ref.
Groceries - continued				
Bananas	lb.	0.41	12/94	82r
Beef or hamburger, ground	lb.	0.94	12/94	2c
Beef purchases	year	197	91	81r
Beef, stew, boneless	lb.	2.52	12/94	82r
Beverage purchases, alcoholic	year	293	91	81r
Beverage purchases, nonalcoholic	year	203	91	81r
Bologna, all beef or mixed	lb.	2.12	12/94	82r
Bread, white	24-oz.	0.53	12/94	2c
Bread, white, pan	lb.	0.76	12/94	82r
Cabbage	lb.	0.44	12/94	82r
Carrots, short trimmed and topped	lb.	0.44	12/94	82r
Cereals and bakery products purchases	year	347	91	81r
Cereals and cereals products purchases	year	119	91	81r
Cheddar cheese, natural	lb.	3.28	12/94	82r
Cheese, Kraft grated Parmesan	8-oz.	3.27	12/94	2c
Chicken breast, bone-in	lb.	1.61	12/94	82r
Chicken, fresh, whole	lb.	0.89	12/94	82r
Chicken, whole fryer	lb.	0.68	12/94	2c
Chuck roast, USDA choice, boneless	lb.	2.33	12/94	82r
Cigarettes, Winston, Kings	carton	13.56	12/94	2c
Coffee, 100%, ground roast, all sizes	lb.	4.28	12/94	82r
Coffee, vacuum-packed	13 oz.	3.37	12/94	2c
Cookies, chocolate chip	lb.	2.72	12/94	82r
Corn Flakes, Kellogg's or Post Toasties	18 oz.	2.00	12/94	2c
Corn, frozen, whole kernel, lowest price	10 oz.	0.81	12/94	2c
Dairy products (other) purchases	year	148	91	81r
Eggs, Grade A large	dozen	0.81	12/94	2c
Eggs, Grade A large	dozen	0.76	12/94	82r
Fish and seafood purchases	year	61	91	81r
Flour, white, all purpose	lb.	0.22	12/94	82r
Food purchases, food eaten at home	year	2313	91	81r
Foods purchased away from home, not prepared by consumer	year	1709	91	81r
Fruits and vegetables purchases	year	372	91	81r
Grapefruit	lb.	0.47	12/94	82r
Grapes, Thompson seedless	lb.	2.15	12/94	82r
Ground beef, 100% beef	lb.	1.37	12/94	82r
Ground chuck, 100% beef	lb.	1.81	12/94	82r
Ham, boneless, exc. canned	lb.	2.16	12/94	82r
Ice cream, prepackaged, bulk, regular	1/2 gal.	2.48	12/94	82r
Lemons	lb.	1.08	12/94	82r
Lettuce, iceberg	lb.	0.81	12/94	82r
Lettuce, iceberg	head	0.73	12/94	2c
Margarine, Blue Bonnet or Parkay cubes	lb.	0.63	12/94	2c
Margarine, stick	lb.	0.81	12/94	82r
Meats, poultry, fish, and eggs purchases	year	591	91	81r
Milk and cream (fresh) purchases	year	132	91	81r
Milk, whole	1/2 gal.	1.29	12/94	2c
Orange juice, frozen concentrate 12-oz. can	16 oz.	1.41	12/94	82r
Orange juice, Minute Maid frozen	12-oz.	1.39	12/94	2c
Oranges, Navel	lb.	0.56	12/94	82r
Peaches, halves or slices, Hunt's, Del Monte, or Libby's	29-oz.	1.36	12/94	2c
Peanut butter, creamy, all sizes	lb.	1.81	12/94	82r
Peas, sweet, Del Monte or Green Giant	15-17 oz.	0.63	12/94	2c
Pork chops, center cut, bone-in	lb.	2.76	12/94	82r
Pork purchases	year	130	91	81r
Potato chips	16-oz.	2.81	12/94	82r
Potatoes, frozen, French fried	lb.	0.83	12/94	82r
Potatoes, white	lb.	0.28	12/94	82r
Potatoes, white or red	10-lb. sack	1.53	12/94	2c
Round roast, USDA choice, boneless	lb.	2.90	12/94	82r
Sausage, Jimmy Dean, 100% pork	lb.	2.85	12/94	2c
Shortening, vegetable oil blends	lb.	0.88	12/94	82r
Shortening, vegetable, Crisco	3-lb.	2.30	12/94	2c
Soft drink, Coca Cola, ex deposit	2 lit	0.94	12/94	2c
Spaghetti and macaroni	lb.	0.78	12/94	82r
Steak, rib eye, USDA choice, boneless	lb.	6.15	12/94	82r

Values are in dollars or fractions of dollars. In the column headed *Ref*, references are shown to sources. Each reference is followed by a letter. These refer to the geographical level for which data were reported: s = State, r = Region, and c = City or metro. The abbreviation *ex* is used to mean *except* or *excluding*; *exp* stands for expenditures. For other abbreviations and further explanations, please see the Introduction.

Joplin, MO - continued

Item	Per	Value	Date	Ref.
Groceries				
Steak, round, graded & ungraded, exc. USDA prime & choice	lb.	2.72	12/94	82r
Steak, round, USDA choice, boneless	lb.	3.02	12/94	82r
Steak, sirloin, USDA choice, boneless	lb.	3.85	12/94	82r
Steak, t-bone	lb.	4.61	12/94	2c
Steak, T-bone, USDA choice, bone-in	lb.	5.38	12/94	82r
Sugar and other sweets, eaten at home, expenditures	year	91	91	81r
Sugar, cane or beet	4 lbs.	1.23	12/94	2c
Sugar, white, all sizes	lb.	0.36	12/94	82r
Tobacco products and smoking supplies, total expenditures	year	298	91	81r
Tomatoes, field grown	lb.	1.36	12/94	82r
Tomatoes, Hunt's or Del Monte	14.5 oz.	0.82	12/94	2c
Tuna, chunk, light	lb.	1.94	12/94	82r
Tuna, chunk, light, oil-packed	6.125-6.5 oz.	0.79	12/94	2c
Turkey, frozen, whole	lb.	0.96	12/94	82r
Yogurt, natural, fruit flavored	8 oz.	0.62	12/94	82r
Goods and Services				
Miscellaneous goods and services, ACCRA Index		96.90	12/94	2c
Health Care				
Health care, ACCRA Index		92.20	12/94	2c
Antibiotic ointment, Polysporin	1.5 oz.	4.02	12/94	2c
Childbirth, Cesarean delivery, hospital charge	birth	5101.00	12/91	69r
Childbirth, Cesarean delivery, physician charge	birth	2234.00	12/91	69r
Childbirth, normal delivery, hospital charge	birth	2891.00	12/91	69r
Childbirth, normal delivery, physician charge	birth	1623.00	12/91	69r
Dentist's fee, adult teeth cleaning and periodic oral exam	visit	49.17	12/94	2c
Doctor's fee, routine exam, established patient	visit	35.60	12/94	2c
Drugs, expenditures	year	248	91	81r
Health care, total expenditures	year	1336	91	81r
Health insurance expenditures	year	550	91	81r
Hospital care, semiprivate room	day	358.00	12/94	2c
Insurance premium, family medical care	month	390.73	1/95	41s
Medical services expenditures	year	457	91	81r
Medical supplies expenditures	year	82	91	81r
Household Goods				
Appl. repair, service call, wash mach	min. lab. chg.	22.60	12/94	2c
Floor coverings, expenditures	year	105	91	81r
Furniture, expenditures	year	291	91	81r
Household equipment, misc. expenditures	year	341	91	81r
Household expenditures, miscellaneous	year	162	91	81r
Household furnishings and equipment, expenditures	year	1042	91	81r
Household operations expenditures	year	365	91	81r
Household textiles, expenditures	year	101	91	81r
Housekeeping supplies, expenditures	year	390	91	81r
Laundry and cleaning supplies, expenditures	year	110	91	81r
Laundry detergent, Tide Ultra, Bold, or Cheer	42 oz.	3.60	12/94	2c
Postage and stationery, expenditures	year	115	91	81r
Tissues, facial, Kleenex brand	175	0.96	12/94	2c
Housing				
Housing, ACCRA Index		81.70	12/94	2c
Add garage/carport		8,479	3/95	74r
Add room(s)		21,347	3/95	74r
Apartment condominium or co-op, median	unit	87100	12/94	62r
Bathroom addition, average cost	add	9734.00	3/95	13r
Bathroom remodeling, average cost	remod	6414.00	3/95	13r

Joplin, MO - continued

Item	Per	Value	Date	Ref.
Housing - continued				
Bedroom, master suite addition, average cost	add	27122.00	3/95	13r
Deck addition, average cost	add	6665.00	3/95	13r
Dwellings (owned), expenditures	year	2566	81r	
Enclose porch/patio/breezeway		4,556	3/95	74r
Exterior remodeling, average cost	remod	15395.00	3/95	13r
Family room addition, average cost	add	27658.00	3/95	13r
Finish room in basement/attic		5,074	3/95	74r
Home, existing, single-family, median	unit	106500	12/94	62r
House payment, principal and interest, 25% down payment	mo.	639	12/94	2c
House, 1800 sq ft, 8000 sq ft lot, new, urban, utilities	total	102250	12/94	2c
Kitchen remodeling, major, average cost	remod	17084.00	3/95	13r
Kitchen remodeling, minor, average cost	remod	5804.00	3/95	13r
Maintenance, repairs, insurance, and other housing expenditures	year	484	91	81r
Mortgage interest and charges expenditures	year	1443	91	81r
Mtge. rate, incl. points and orig. fee, 30-year conv. fixed or ARM	mo.	9.40	12/94	2c
Office, home addition, average cost	add	8121.00	3/95	13r
Princ. & int., mortgage, median-price exist. sing.-family home	mo.	515	12/94	62r
Property taxes expenditures	year	639	91	81r
Redesign, restructure more than half of home's interior		9,114	3/95	74r
Rent, apartment, 2 br., 1 1/2-2 baths, unfurnished, 950 sq ft, water	mo.	395	12/94	2c
Rental units expenditures	year	1200	91	81r
Sun-space addition, average cost	add	23768.00	3/95	13r
Wing addition, two-story, average cost	add	50410.00	3/95	13r
Insurance and Pensions				
Auto insurance, private passenger	year	600.64	12/94	71s
Insurance and pensions, personal, expenditures	year	2408	91	81r
Insurance, life and other personal, expenditures	year	355	91	81r
Pensions and Social Security, expenditures	year	2053	91	81r
Legal Assistance				
Legal work, law firm associate	hour	90		10r
Legal work, law firm partner	hour	139		10r
Personal Goods				
Shampoo, Alberto VO5	15-oz.	1.26	12/94	2c
Toothpaste, Crest or Colgate	6-7 oz.	1.86	12/94	2c
Personal Services				
Dry cleaning, man's 2-pc. suit		5.89	12/94	2c
Haircut, man's barbershop, no styling		5.75	12/94	2c
Haircut, woman's shampoo, trim, blow-dry		16.35	12/94	2c
Personal services expenditures	year	203	91	81r
Restaurant Food				
Chicken, fried, thigh and drumstick		2.59	12/94	2c
Dining expenditures, family	week	30.03	94	73r
Hamburger with cheese	1/4 lb.	1.89	12/94	2c
Pizza, Pizza Hut or Pizza Inn	12-13 in.	7.99	12/94	2c
Taxes				
Taxes, Federal income, expenditures	year	1756	91	81r
Taxes, personal, expenditures	year	2426	91	81r
Taxes, State and local income, expenditures	year	568	91	81r
Transportation				
Transportation, ACCRA Index		82.40	12/94	2c
Cars and trucks purchased, new	year	891	91	81r
Cars and trucks purchased, used	year	1155	91	81r
Driver's learning permit fee	perm	1.00	1/94	84s
Driver's license fee	orig	7.50	1/94	84s
Driver's license fee, duplicate	lic	7.50	1/94	84s
Driver's license reinstatement fee, min.	susp	20.00	1/94	85s
Driver's license renewal fee	renew	7.50	1/94	84s

Values are in dollars or fractions of dollars. In the column headed *Ref*, references are shown to sources. Each reference is followed by a letter. These refer to the geographical level for which data were reported: s = State, r = Region, and c = City or metro. The abbreviation *ex* is used to mean *except* or *excluding*; *exp* stands for *expenditures*. For other abbreviations and further explanations, please see the Introduction.

Joplin, MO - continued

Item	Per	Value	Date	Ref.
Transportation				
Identification card, nondriver	card	7.50	1/94	83s
Motorcycle license fee	orig	7.50	1/94	84s
Motorcycle license fee, duplicate	lic	7.50	1/94	84s
Motorcycle license renewal fee	renew	7.50	1/94	84s
Public transportation expenditures	year	209	91	81r
Tire balance, computer or spin bal., front	wheel	5.50	12/94	2c
Transportation expenditures, total	year	4792	91	81r
Vehicle finance charges	year	300	91	81r
Vehicle insurance expenditures	year	485	91	81r
Vehicle maintenance and repairs expenditures	year	534	91	81r
Vehicle purchases	year	2068	91	81r
Vehicle rental, leases, licenses, etc. expenditures	year	197	91	81r
Vehicles purchased, other than cars and trucks	year	22	91	81r
Utilities				
Utilities, ACCRA Index		78.40	12/94	2c
Electricity expenditures	year	668	91	81r
Electricity, 1800 sq. ft., new home	mo.	87.73	12/94	2c
Electricity, summer, 250 KWh	month	18.96	8/93	64c
Electricity, summer, 500 KWh	month	35.20	8/93	64c
Electricity, summer, 750 KWh	month	49.68	8/93	64c
Electricity, summer, 1000 KWh	month	62.98	8/93	64c
Utilities, fuels, and public services, total expenditures	year	1838	91	81r
Water and other public services, expenditures	year	167	91	81r
Weddings				
Bridal attendants' gowns	event	750	10/93	76r
Bridal gown	event	852	10/93	76r
Bridal headpiece and veil	event	167	10/93	76r
Bride's wedding band	event	708	10/93	76r
Clergy	event	224	10/93	76r
Engagement ring	event	2756	10/93	76r
Flowers	event	863	10/93	76r
Formal wear for groom	event	106	10/93	76r
Groom's attendants' formal wear	event	530	10/93	76r
Groom's wedding band	event	402	10/93	76r
Music	event	600	10/93	76r
Photography	event	1088	10/93	76r
Shoes for bride	event	50	10/93	76r
Videography	event	483	10/93	76r
Wedding invitations and announcements	event	342	10/93	76r
Wedding reception	event	7000	10/93	76r

Juneau, AK

Item	Per	Value	Date	Ref.
Composite, ACCRA index		135.80	12/94	2c
Alcoholic Beverages				
Beer, Miller Lite, Bud, 12-oz., ex deposit	6	4.90	12/94	2c
J & B Scotch	750-ml.	20.80	12/94	2c
Wine, Gallo Chablis blanc	1.5-lit	6.62	12/94	2c
Clothing				
Jeans, man's denim		29.49	12/94	2c
Shirt, man's dress shirt		36.50	12/94	2c
Undervest, boy's size 10-14, cotton	3	4.65	12/94	2c
Communications				
Newspaper subscription, dly. and Sun. delivery	month	17.73	12/94	2c
Telephone bill, family of four	month	14.86	12/94	2c
Energy and Fuels				
Energy, combined forms, 1800 sq. ft.	mo.	171.47	12/94	2c
Gas, reg unlead, taxes inc., cash, self-service	gal	1.31	12/94	2c

Juneau, AK - continued

Item	Per	Value	Date	Ref.
Entertainment				
Bowling, evening rate	game	2.25	12/94	2c
Monopoly game, Parker Brothers', No. 9	game	11.71	12/94	2c
Movie	adm	7.50	12/94	2c
Tennis balls, yellow, Wilson or Penn, 3	can	3.04	12/94	2c
Groceries				
Groceries, ACCRA Index		135.10	12/94	2c
Baby food, strained vegetables, lowest price	4-4.5 oz.	0.41	12/94	2c
Bananas	lb.	0.78	12/94	2c
Beef or hamburger, ground	lb.	1.77	12/94	2c
Bread, white	24-oz.	0.85	12/94	2c
Cheese, Kraft grated Parmesan	8-oz.	4.60	12/94	2c
Chicken, whole fryer	lb.	1.25	12/94	2c
Cigarettes, Winston, Kings	carton	17.68	12/94	2c
Coffee, vacuum-packed	13 oz.	4.57	12/94	2c
Corn Flakes, Kellogg's or Post Toasties	18 oz.	3.05	12/94	2c
Corn, frozen, whole kernel, lowest price	10 oz.	0.94	12/94	2c
Eggs, Grade A large	dozen	1.02	12/94	2c
Lettuce, iceberg	head	1.47	12/94	2c
Margarine, Blue Bonnet or Parkay cubes	lb.	0.95	12/94	2c
Milk, whole	1/2 gal.	1.96	12/94	2c
Orange juice, Minute Maid frozen	12-oz.	1.88	12/94	2c
Peaches, halves or slices, Hunt's, Del Monte, or Libby's	29-oz.	1.98	12/94	2c
Peas, sweet, Del Monte or Green Giant	15-17 oz.	0.90	12/94	2c
Potatoes, white or red	10-lb. sack	3.82	12/94	2c
Sausage, Jimmy Dean, 100% pork	lb.	3.63	12/94	2c
Shortening, vegetable, Crisco	3-lb.	3.20	12/94	2c
Soft drink, Coca Cola, ex deposit	2 lit	1.66	12/94	2c
Steak, t-bone	lb.	6.42	12/94	2c
Sugar, cane or beet	4 lbs.	2.00	12/94	2c
Tomatoes, Hunt's or Del Monte	14.5 oz.	0.96	12/94	2c
Tuna, chunk, light, oil-packed	6.125-6.5 oz.	0.98	12/94	2c
Goods and Services				
Miscellaneous goods and services, ACCRA Index		120.50	12/94	2c
Health Care				
Health care, ACCRA Index		170.30	12/94	2c
Antibiotic ointment, Polysporin	1.5 oz.	4.45	12/94	2c
Dentist's fee, adult teeth cleaning and periodic oral exam	visit	130.80	12/94	2c
Doctor's fee, routine exam, established patient	visit	60.00	12/94	2c
Hospital care, semiprivate room	day	390.00	12/94	2c
Household Goods				
Appl. repair, service call, wash mach	min. lab. chg.	53.17	12/94	2c
Laundry detergent, Tide Ultra, Bold, or Cheer	42 oz.	4.05	12/94	2c
Tissues, facial, Kleenex brand	175	1.41	12/94	2c
Housing				
Housing, ACCRA Index		154.00	12/94	2c
House payment, principal and interest, 25% down payment	mo.	1117	12/94	2c
House, 1800 sq ft, 8000 sq ft lot, new, urban, utilities	total	182300	12/94	2c
Mtge. rate, incl. points and orig. fee, 30-year conv. fixed or ARM	mo.	9.18	12/94	2c
Rent, apartment, 2 br., 1 1/2-2 baths, unfurnished, 950 sq ft, water	mo.	992	12/94	2c
Personal Goods				
Shampoo, Alberto VO5	15-oz.	1.47	12/94	2c
Toothpaste, Crest or Colgate	6-7 oz.	2.89	12/94	2c

Values are in dollars or fractions of dollars. In the column headed *Ref*, references are shown to sources. Each reference is followed by a letter. These refer to the geographical level for which data were reported: s=State, r=Region, and c=City or metro. The abbreviation *ex* is used to mean *except* or *excluding*; *exp* stands for *expenditures*. For other abbreviations and further explanations, please see the Introduction.

Juneau, AK - continued

Item	Per	Value	Date	Ref.
Personal Services				
Dry cleaning, man's 2-pc. suit		8.82	12/94	2c
Haircut, man's barbershop, no styling		15.33	12/94	2c
Haircut, woman's shampoo, trim, blow-dry		24.20	12/94	2c
Restaurant Food				
Chicken, fried, thigh and drumstick		2.36	12/94	2c
Hamburger with cheese	1/4 lb.	2.60	12/94	2c
Pizza, Pizza Hut or Pizza Inn	12-13 in.	8.00	12/94	2c
Transportation				
Transportation, ACCRA Index		107.10	12/94	2c
Bus fare, up to 10 miles	one-way	1.25	12/94	2c
Tire balance, computer or spin bal., front	wheel	5.88	12/94	2c
Utilities				
Utilities, ACCRA Index		142.50	12/94	2c
Electricity, 1800 sq. ft., new home	mo.	171.47	12/94	2c
Electricity, summer, 250 KWh	month	25.83	8/93	64c
Electricity, summer, 500 KWh	month	43.15	8/93	64c
Electricity, summer, 750 KWh	month	60.48	8/93	64c
Electricity, summer, 1000 KWh	month	77.80	8/93	64c

Kalamazoo, MI

Item	Per	Value	Date	Ref.
Appliances				
Appliances (major), expenditures	year	131	91	81r
Average annual exp.				
Food, health care, personal goods, services	year	25935	91	81r
Charity				
Cash contributions, expenditures	year	745	91	81r
Clothing				
Apparel, men and boys, total expenditures	year	332	91	81r
Apparel, women and girls, total expenditures	year	578	91	81r
Footwear, expenditures	year	164	91	81r
Communications				
Long-distance telephone rate, day, addl. min., 1-10 mi.	min.	0.08	12/93	9s
Long-distance telephone rate, day, initial min., 1-10 mi.	min.	0.14	12/93	9s
Phone line, single, business, field visit	inst	42.00	12/93	9s
Phone line, single, business, no field visit	inst	42.00	12/93	9s
Phone line, single, residence, field visit	inst	42.00	12/93	9s
Phone line, single, residence, no field visit	inst	42.00	12/93	9s
Telephone service, expenditures	year	547	91	81r
Telephone, residential, flat rate	mo.	10.42	12/93	8c
Education				
Board, 4-year private college/university	year	2064	8/94	80s
Board, 4-year public college/university	year	2304	8/94	80s
Education, total expenditures	year	394	91	81r
Room, 4-year private college/university	year	1814	8/94	80s
Room, 4-year public college/university	year	1856	8/94	80s
Total cost, 4-year private college/university	year	12178	8/94	80s
Total cost, 4-year public college/university	year	7642	8/94	80s
Tuition, 2-year public college/university, in-state	year	1358	8/94	80s
Tuition, 4-year private college/university, in-state	year	8300	8/94	80s
Tuition, 4-year public college/university, in-state	year	3481	8/94	80s
Energy and Fuels				
Fuel oil and other fuels, expenditures	year	83	91	81r
Gas, cooking, 10 therms	month	9.71	2/94	65c
Gas, cooking, 30 therms	month	18.63	2/94	65c
Gas, cooking, 50 therms	month	27.55	2/94	65c
Gas, heating, winter, 100 therms	month	49.85	2/94	65c
Gas, heating, winter, average use	month	91.96	2/94	65c
Gas, natural, expenditures	year	373	91	81r

Kalamazoo, MI - continued

Item	Per	Value	Date	Ref.
Energy and Fuels - continued				
Gasoline and motor oil purchased	year	1000	91	81r
Gasoline, unleaded midgrade	gallon	1.15	4/93	82r
Gasoline, unleaded premium	gallon	1.23	4/93	82r
Gasoline, unleaded regular	gallon	1.07	4/93	82r
Entertainment				
Entertainment, total expenditures	year	1356	91	81r
Fees and admissions, expenditures	year	347	91	81r
Pets, toys, playground equipment, expenditures	year	270	91	81r
Reading, expenditures	year	160	91	81r
Televisions, radios, and sound equipment, expenditures	year	433	91	81r
Funerals				
Burial, immediate, container provided by funeral home		1268.31	1/95	54r
Cards, acknowledgment		26.12	1/95	54r
Casket, minimum alternative		198.03	1/95	54r
Cosmetology, hair care, etc.		122.19	1/95	54r
Cremation, direct, container provided by funeral home		977.81	1/95	54r
Embalming		334.00	1/95	54r
Funeral, funeral home		321.16	1/95	54r
Funeral, other facility		317.73	1/95	54r
Graveside service		292.48	1/95	54r
Hearse, local		153.20	1/95	54r
Limousine, local		123.52	1/95	54r
Memorial service		356.30	1/95	54r
Service charge, professional, nondeclinable		968.24	1/95	54r
Visitation and viewing		332.66	1/95	54r
Groceries				
Apples, Red Delicious	lb.	0.68	12/94	82r
Bacon, sliced	lb.	1.88	12/94	82r
Bananas	lb.	0.41	12/94	82r
Beef purchases	year	197	91	81r
Beef, stew, boneless	lb.	2.52	12/94	82r
Beverage purchases, alcoholic	year	293	91	81r
Beverage purchases, nonalcoholic	year	203	91	81r
Bologna, all beef or mixed	lb.	2.12	12/94	82r
Bread, white, pan	lb.	0.76	12/94	82r
Cabbage	lb.	0.44	12/94	82r
Carrots, short trimmed and topped	lb.	0.44	12/94	82r
Cereals and bakery products purchases	year	347	91	81r
Cereals and cereals products purchases	year	119	91	81r
Cheddar cheese, natural	lb.	3.28	12/94	82r
Chicken breast, bone-in	lb.	1.61	12/94	82r
Chicken, fresh, whole	lb.	0.89	12/94	82r
Chuck roast, USDA choice, boneless	lb.	2.33	12/94	82r
Coffee, 100%, ground roast, all sizes	lb.	4.28	12/94	82r
Cookies, chocolate chip	lb.	2.72	12/94	82r
Dairy products (other) purchases	year	148	91	81r
Eggs, Grade A large	dozen	0.76	12/94	82r
Fish and seafood purchases	year	61	91	81r
Flour, white, all purpose	lb.	0.22	12/94	82r
Food purchases, food eaten at home	year	2313	91	81r
Foods purchased away from home, not prepared by consumer	year	1709	91	81r
Fruits and vegetables purchases	year	372	91	81r
Grapefruit	lb.	0.47	12/94	82r
Grapes, Thompson seedless	lb.	2.15	12/94	82r
Ground beef, 100% beef	lb.	1.37	12/94	82r
Ground chuck, 100% beef	lb.	1.81	12/94	82r
Ham, boneless, exc. canned	lb.	2.16	12/94	82r
Ice cream, prepackaged, bulk, regular	1/2 gal.	2.48	12/94	82r
Lemons	lb.	1.08	12/94	82r
Lettuce, iceberg	lb.	0.81	12/94	82r
Margarine, stick	lb.	0.81	12/94	82r
Meats, poultry, fish, and eggs purchases	year	591	91	81r
Milk and cream (fresh) purchases	year	132	91	81r
Orange juice, frozen concentrate 12-oz. can	16 oz.	1.41	12/94	82r
Oranges, Navel	lb.	0.56	12/94	82r

Values are in dollars or fractions of dollars. In the column headed *Ref*, references are shown to sources. Each reference is followed by a letter. These refer to the geographical level for which data were reported: s=State, r=Region, and c=City or metro. The abbreviation *ex* is used to mean *except* or *excluding*; *exp* stands for *expenditures*. For other abbreviations and further explanations, please see the Introduction.

Kalamazoo, MI - continued

Item	Per	Value	Date	Ref.
Groceries				
Peanut butter, creamy, all sizes	lb.	1.81	12/94	82r
Pork chops, center cut, bone-in	lb.	2.76	12/94	82r
Pork purchases	year	130	91	81r
Potato chips	16-oz.	2.81	12/94	82r
Potatoes, frozen, French fried	lb.	0.83	12/94	82r
Potatoes, white	lb.	0.28	12/94	82r
Round roast, USDA choice, boneless	lb.	2.90	12/94	82r
Shortening, vegetable oil blends	lb.	0.88	12/94	82r
Spaghetti and macaroni	lb.	0.78	12/94	82r
Steak, rib eye, USDA choice, boneless	lb.	6.15	12/94	82r
Steak, round, graded & ungraded, exc. USDA prime & choice	lb.	2.72	12/94	82r
Steak, round, USDA choice, boneless	lb.	3.02	12/94	82r
Steak, sirloin, USDA choice, boneless	lb.	3.85	12/94	82r
Steak, T-bone, USDA choice, bone-in	lb.	5.38	12/94	82r
Sugar and other sweets, eaten at home, expenditures	year	91	91	81r
Sugar, white, all sizes	lb.	0.36	12/94	82r
Tobacco products and smoking supplies, total expenditures	year	298	91	81r
Tomatoes, field grown	lb.	1.36	12/94	82r
Tuna, chunk, light	lb.	1.94	12/94	82r
Turkey, frozen, whole	lb.	0.96	12/94	82r
Yogurt, natural, fruit flavored	8 oz.	0.62	12/94	82r
Health Care				
Childbirth, Cesarean delivery, hospital charge	birth	5101.00	12/91	69r
Childbirth, Cesarean delivery, physician charge	birth	2234.00	12/91	69r
Childbirth, normal delivery, hospital charge	birth	2891.00	12/91	69r
Childbirth, normal delivery, physician charge	birth	1623.00	12/91	69r
Drugs, expenditures	year	248	91	81r
Health care, total expenditures	year	1336	91	81r
Health insurance expenditures	year	550	91	81r
Insurance premium, family medical care	month	369.41	1/95	41s
Medical services expenditures	year	457	91	81r
Medical supplies expenditures	year	82	91	81r
Household Goods				
Floor coverings, expenditures	year	105	91	81r
Furniture, expenditures	year	291	91	81r
Household equipment, misc. expenditures	year	341	91	81r
Household expenditures, miscellaneous	year	162	91	81r
Household furnishings and equipment, expenditures	year	1042	91	81r
Household operations expenditures	year	365	91	81r
Household textiles, expenditures	year	101	91	81r
Housekeeping supplies, expenditures	year	390	91	81r
Laundry and cleaning supplies, expenditures	year	110	91	81r
Postage and stationery, expenditures	year	115	91	81r
Housing				
Add garage/carport		8,479	3/95	74r
Add room(s)		21,347	3/95	74r
Apartment condominium or co-op, median	unit	87100	12/94	62r
Bathroom addition, average cost	add	9734.00	3/95	13r
Bathroom remodeling, average cost	remod	6414.00	3/95	13r
Bedroom, master suite addition, average cost	add	27122.00	3/95	13r
Deck addition, average cost	add	6665.00	3/95	13r
Dwellings (owned), expenditures	year	2566	91	81r
Enclose porch/patio/breezeway		4,556	3/95	74r
Exterior remodeling, average cost	remod	15395.00	3/95	13r
Family room addition, average cost	add	27658.00	3/95	13r
Finish room in basement/attic		5,074	3/95	74r
Home, existing, single-family, median	unit	106500	12/94	62r
Home, existing, single-family, median	unit	73.90	12/94	62c
Kitchen remodeling, major, average cost	remod	17084.00	3/95	13r
Kitchen remodeling, minor, average cost	remod	5804.00	3/95	13r
Maintenance, repairs, insurance, and other housing expenditures	year	484	91	81r
Mortgage interest and charges expenditures	year	1443	91	81r

Kalamazoo, MI - continued

Item	Per	Value	Date	Ref.
Housing - continued				
Office, home addition, average cost	add	8121.00	3/95	13r
Princ. & int., mortgage, median-price exist. sing.-family home	mo.	515	12/94	62r
Property taxes expenditures	year	639	91	81r
Redesign, restructure more than half of home's interior		9,114	3/95	74r
Rental units expenditures	year	1200	91	81r
Sun-space addition, average cost	add	23768.00	3/95	13r
Wing addition, two-story, average cost	add	50410.00	3/95	13r
Insurance and Pensions				
Auto insurance, private passenger	year	788.26	12/94	71s
Insurance and pensions, personal, expenditures	year	2408	91	81r
Insurance, life and other personal, expenditures	year	355	91	81r
Pensions and Social Security, expenditures	year	2053	91	81r
Legal Assistance				
Legal work, law firm associate	hour	90		10r
Legal work, law firm partner	hour	139		10r
Personal Services				
Personal services expenditures	year	203	91	81r
Restaurant Food				
Dining expenditures, family	week	30.03	94	73r
Taxes				
Taxes, Federal income, expenditures	year	1756	91	81r
Taxes, personal, expenditures	year	2426	91	81r
Taxes, State and local income, expenditures	year	568	91	81r
Transportation				
Bus fare, one-way	trip	1.00	12/95	1c
Cars and trucks purchased, new	year	891	91	81r
Cars and trucks purchased, used	year	1155	91	81r
Driver's learning permit fee	perm	12.00	1/94	84s
Driver's license fee	orig	12.00	1/94	84s
Driver's license fee, duplicate	lic	6.00	1/94	84s
Driver's license reinstatement fee, min.	susp	125.00	1/94	85s
Driver's license renewal fee	renew	12.00	1/94	84s
Identification card, nondriver	card	6.00	1/94	83s
Motorcycle license fee	orig	7.50	1/94	84s
Motorcycle license renewal fee	renew	4.00	1/94	84s
Public transportation expenditures	year	209	91	81r
Transportation expenditures, total	year	4792	91	81r
Vehicle finance charges	year	300	91	81r
Vehicle insurance expenditures	year	485	91	81r
Vehicle maintenance and repairs expenditures	year	534	91	81r
Vehicle purchases	year	2068	91	81r
Vehicle rental, leases, licenses, etc. expenditures	year	197	91	81r
Vehicles purchased, other than cars and trucks	year	22	91	81r
Utilities				
Electricity expenditures	year	668	91	81r
Utilities, fuels, and public services, total expenditures	year	1838	91	81r
Water and other public services, expenditures	year	167	91	81r
Weddings				
Bridal attendants' gowns	event	750	10/93	76r
Bridal gown	event	852	10/93	76r
Bridal headpiece and veil	event	167	10/93	76r
Bride's wedding band	event	708	10/93	76r
Clergy	event	224	10/93	76r
Engagement ring	event	2756	10/93	76r
Flowers	event	863	10/93	76r
Formal wear for groom	event	106	10/93	76r
Groom's attendants' formal wear	event	530	10/93	76r
Groom's wedding band	event	402	10/93	76r
Music	event	600	10/93	76r

Values are in dollars or fractions of dollars. In the column headed *Ref*, references are shown to sources. Each reference is followed by a letter. These refer to the geographical level for which data were reported: s=State, r=Region, and c=City or metro. The abbreviation *ex* is used to mean *except* or *excluding*; *exp* stands for expenditures. For other abbreviations and further explanations, please see the Introduction.

Kalamazoo, MI - continued

Item	Per	Value	Date	Ref.
Weddings				
Photography	event	1088	10/93	76r
Shoes for bride	event	50	10/93	76r
Videography	event	483	10/93	76r
Wedding invitations and announcements	event	342	10/93	76r
Wedding reception	event	7000	10/93	76r

Kankakee, IL

Item	Per	Value	Date	Ref.
Appliances				
Appliances (major), expenditures	year	131	91	81r
Average annual exp.				
Food, health care, personal goods, services	year	25935	91	81r
Charity				
Cash contributions, expenditures	year	745	91	81r
Clothing				
Apparel, men and boys, total expenditures	year	332	91	81r
Apparel, women and girls, total expenditures	year	578	91	81r
Footwear, expenditures	year	164	91	81r
Communications				
Long-distance telephone rate, day, addl. min., 1-10 mi.	min.	0.04	12/93	9s
Long-distance telephone rate, day, initial min., 1-10 mi.	min.	0.10	12/93	9s
Phone line, single, business, field visit	inst	84.50	12/93	9s
Phone line, single, business, no field visit	inst	84.50	12/93	9s
Phone line, single, residence, field visit	inst	55.00	12/93	9s
Phone line, single, residence, no field visit	inst	55.00	12/93	9s
Telephone service, expenditures	year	547	91	81r
Education				
Board, 4-year private college/university	year	2078	8/94	80s
Board, 4-year public college/university	year	2139	8/94	80s
Education, total expenditures	year	394	91	81r
Room, 4-year private college/university	year	2696	8/94	80s
Room, 4-year public college/university	year	1796	8/94	80s
Total cost, 4-year private college/university	year	15249	8/94	80s
Total cost, 4-year public college/university	year	6964	8/94	80s
Tuition, 2-year public college/university, in-state	year	1135	8/94	80s
Tuition, 4-year private college/university, in-state	year	10474	8/94	80s
Tuition, 4-year public college/university, in-state	year	3029	8/94	80s
Energy and Fuels				
Fuel oil and other fuels, expenditures	year	83	91	81r
Gas, natural, expenditures	year	373	91	81r
Gasoline and motor oil purchased	year	1000	91	81r
Gasoline, unleaded midgrade	gallon	1.15	4/93	82r
Gasoline, unleaded premium	gallon	1.23	4/93	82r
Gasoline, unleaded regular	gallon	1.07	4/93	82r
Entertainment				
Entertainment, total expenditures	year	1356	91	81r
Fees and admissions, expenditures	year	347	91	81r
Pets, toys, playground equipment, expenditures	year	270	91	81r
Reading, expenditures	year	160	91	81r
Televisions, radios, and sound equipment, expenditures	year	433	91	81r
Funerals				
Burial, immediate, container provided by funeral home		1268.31	1/95	54r
Cards, acknowledgment		26.12	1/95	54r
Casket, minimum alternative		198.03	1/95	54r
Cosmetology, hair care, etc.		122.19	1/95	54r
Cremation, direct, container provided by funeral home		977.81	1/95	54r
Embalming		334.00	1/95	54r
Funeral, funeral home		321.16	1/95	54r

Kankakee, IL - continued

Item	Per	Value	Date	Ref.
Funerals - continued				
Funeral, other facility		317.73	1/95	54r
Graveside service		292.48	1/95	54r
Hearse, local		153.20	1/95	54r
Limousine, local		123.52	1/95	54r
Memorial service		356.30	1/95	54r
Service charge, professional, nondeclinable		968.24	1/95	54r
Visitation and viewing		332.66	1/95	54r
Groceries				
Apples, Red Delicious	lb.	0.68	12/94	82r
Bacon, sliced	lb.	1.88	12/94	82r
Bananas	lb.	0.41	12/94	82r
Beef purchases	year	197	91	81r
Beef, stew, boneless	lb.	2.52	12/94	82r
Beverage purchases, alcoholic	year	293	91	81r
Beverage purchases, nonalcoholic	year	203	91	81r
Bologna, all beef or mixed	lb.	2.12	12/94	82r
Bread, white, pan	lb.	0.76	12/94	82r
Cabbage	lb.	0.44	12/94	82r
Carrots, short trimmed and topped	lb.	0.44	12/94	82r
Cereals and bakery products purchases	year	347	91	81r
Cereals and cereals products purchases	year	119	91	81r
Cheddar cheese, natural	lb.	3.28	12/94	82r
Chicken breast, bone-in	lb.	1.61	12/94	82r
Chicken, fresh, whole	lb.	0.89	12/94	82r
Chuck roast, USDA choice, boneless	lb.	2.33	12/94	82r
Coffee, 100%, ground roast, all sizes	lb.	4.28	12/94	82r
Cookies, chocolate chip	lb.	2.72	12/94	82r
Dairy products (other) purchases	year	148	91	81r
Eggs, Grade A large	dozen	0.76	12/94	82r
Fish and seafood purchases	year	61	91	81r
Flour, white, all purpose	lb.	0.22	12/94	82r
Food purchases, food eaten at home	year	2313	91	81r
Foods purchased away from home, not prepared by consumer	year	1709	91	81r
Fruits and vegetables purchases	year	372	91	81r
Grapefruit	lb.	0.47	12/94	82r
Grapes, Thompson seedless	lb.	2.15	12/94	82r
Ground beef, 100% beef	lb.	1.37	12/94	82r
Ground chuck, 100% beef	lb.	1.81	12/94	82r
Ham, boneless, exc. canned	lb.	2.16	12/94	82r
Ice cream, prepackaged, bulk, regular	1/2 gal.	2.48	12/94	82r
Lemons	lb.	1.08	12/94	82r
Lettuce, iceberg	lb.	0.81	12/94	82r
Margarine, stick	lb.	0.81	12/94	82r
Meats, poultry, fish, and eggs purchases	year	591	91	81r
Milk and cream (fresh) purchases	year	132	91	81r
Orange juice, frozen concentrate 12-oz. can	16 oz.	1.41	12/94	82r
Oranges, Navel	lb.	0.56	12/94	82r
Peanut butter, creamy, all sizes	lb.	1.81	12/94	82r
Pork chops, center cut, bone-in	lb.	2.76	12/94	82r
Pork purchases	year	130	91	81r
Potato chips	16-oz.	2.81	12/94	82r
Potatoes, frozen, French fried	lb.	0.83	12/94	82r
Potatoes, white	lb.	0.28	12/94	82r
Round roast, USDA choice, boneless	lb.	2.90	12/94	82r
Shortening, vegetable oil blends	lb.	0.88	12/94	82r
Spaghetti and macaroni	lb.	0.78	12/94	82r
Steak, rib eye, USDA choice, boneless	lb.	6.15	12/94	82r
Steak, round, graded & ungraded, exc. USDA prime & choice	lb.	2.72	12/94	82r
Steak, round, USDA choice, boneless	lb.	3.02	12/94	82r
Steak, sirloin, USDA choice, boneless	lb.	3.85	12/94	82r
Steak, T-bone, USDA choice, bone-in	lb.	5.38	12/94	82r
Sugar and other sweets, eaten at home, expenditures	year	91	91	81r
Sugar, white, all sizes	lb.	0.36	12/94	82r
Tobacco products and smoking supplies, total expenditures	year	298	91	81r
Tomatoes, field grown	lb.	1.36	12/94	82r
Tuna, chunk, light	lb.	1.94	12/94	82r
Turkey, frozen, whole	lb.	0.96	12/94	82r

Values are in dollars or fractions of dollars. In the column headed *Ref*, references are shown to sources. Each reference is followed by a letter. These refer to the geographical level for which data were reported: s=State, r=Region, and c=City or metro. The abbreviation *ex* is used to mean *except* or *excluding*; *exp* stands for expenditures. For other abbreviations and further explanations, please see the Introduction.

Kankakee, IL - continued

Item	Per	Value	Date	Ref.
Groceries				
Yogurt, natural, fruit flavored	8 oz.	0.62	12/94	82r
Health Care				
Childbirth, Cesarean delivery, hospital charge	birth	5101.00	12/91	69r
Childbirth, Cesarean delivery, physician charge	birth	2234.00	12/91	69r
Childbirth, normal delivery, hospital charge	birth	2891.00	12/91	69r
Childbirth, normal delivery, physician charge	birth	1623.00	12/91	69r
Drugs, expenditures	year	248	91	81r
Health care, total expenditures	year	1336	91	81r
Health insurance expenditures	year	550	91	81r
Insurance premium, family medical care	month	363.57	1/95	41s
Medical services expenditures	year	457	91	81r
Medical supplies expenditures	year	82	91	81r
Household Goods				
Floor coverings, expenditures	year	105	91	81r
Furniture, expenditures	year	291	91	81r
Household equipment, misc. expenditures	year	341	91	81r
Household expenditures, miscellaneous	year	162	91	81r
Household furnishings and equipment, expenditures	year	1042	91	81r
Household operations expenditures	year	365	91	81r
Household textiles, expenditures	year	101	91	81r
Housekeeping supplies, expenditures	year	390	91	81r
Laundry and cleaning supplies, expenditures	year	110	91	81r
Postage and stationery, expenditures	year	115	91	81r
Housing				
Add garage/carport		8,479	3/95	74r
Add room(s)		21,347	3/95	74r
Apartment condominium or co-op, median	unit	87100	12/94	62r
Bathroom addition, average cost	add	9734.00	3/95	13r
Bathroom remodeling, average cost	remod	6414.00	3/95	13r
Bedroom, master suite addition, average cost	add	27122.00	3/95	13r
Deck addition, average cost	add	6665.00	3/95	13r
Dwellings (owned), expenditures	year	2566	91	81r
Enclose porch/patio/breezeway		4,556	3/95	74r
Exterior remodeling, average cost	remod	15395.00	3/95	13r
Family room addition, average cost	add	27658.00	3/95	13r
Finish room in basement/attic		5,074	3/95	74r
Home, existing, single-family, median	unit	106500	12/94	62r
Kitchen remodeling, major, average cost	remod	17084.00	3/95	13r
Kitchen remodeling, minor, average cost	remod	5804.00	3/95	13r
Maintenance, repairs, insurance, and other housing expenditures	year	484	91	81r
Mortgage interest and charges expenditures	year	1443	91	81r
Office, home addition, average cost	add	8121.00	3/95	13r
Princ. & int., mortgage, median-price exist. sing.-family home	mo.	515	12/94	62r
Property taxes expenditures	year	639	91	81r
Redesign, restructure more than half of home's interior		9,114	3/95	74r
Rental units expenditures	year	1200	91	81r
Sun-space addition, average cost	add	23768.00	3/95	13r
Wing addition, two-story, average cost	add	50410.00	3/95	13r
Insurance and Pensions				
Auto insurance, private passenger	year	679.48	12/94	71s
Insurance and pensions, personal, expenditures	year	2408	91	81r
Insurance, life and other personal, expenditures	year	355	91	81r
Pensions and Social Security, expenditures	year	2053	91	81r
Legal Assistance				
Legal work, law firm associate	hour	90		10r
Legal work, law firm partner	hour	139		10r
Personal Services				
Personal services expenditures	year	203	91	81r

Kankakee, IL - continued

Item	Per	Value	Date	Ref.
Restaurant Food				
Dining expenditures, family	week	30.03	94	73r
Taxes				
Taxes, Federal income, expenditures	year	1756	91	81r
Taxes, personal, expenditures	year	2426	91	81r
Taxes, State and local income, expenditures	year	568	91	81r
Transportation				
Cars and trucks purchased, new	year	891	91	81r
Cars and trucks purchased, used	year	1155	91	81r
Driver's learning permit fee	perm	20.00	1/94	84s
Driver's license fee	orig	10.00	1/94	84s
Driver's license fee, duplicate	lic	5.00	1/94	84s
Driver's license reinstatement fee, min.	susp	30.00	1/94	85s
Driver's license renewal fee	renew	10.00	1/94	84s
Identification card, nondriver	card	4.00	1/94	83s
Motorcycle learning permit fee	perm	20.00	1/94	84s
Motorcycle license fee	orig	10.00	1/94	84s
Motorcycle license fee, duplicate	lic	5.00	1/94	84s
Motorcycle license renewal fee	renew	10.00	1/94	84s
Public transportation expenditures	year	209	91	81r
Transportation expenditures, total	year	4792	91	81r
Vehicle finance charges	year	300	91	81r
Vehicle insurance expenditures	year	485	91	81r
Vehicle maintenance and repairs expenditures	year	534	91	81r
Vehicle purchases	year	2068	91	81r
Vehicle rental, leases, licenses, etc. expenditures	year	197	91	81r
Vehicles purchased, other than cars and trucks	year	22	91	81r
Utilities				
Electricity expenditures	year	668	91	81r
Utilities, fuels, and public services, total expenditures	year	1838	91	81r
Water and other public services, expenditures	year	167	91	81r
Weddings				
Bridal attendants' gowns	event	750	10/93	76r
Bridal gown	event	852	10/93	76r
Bridal headpiece and veil	event	167	10/93	76r
Bride's wedding band	event	708	10/93	76r
Clergy	event	224	10/93	76r
Engagement ring	event	2756	10/93	76r
Flowers	event	863	10/93	76r
Formal wear for groom	event	106	10/93	76r
Groom's attendants' formal wear	event	530	10/93	76r
Groom's wedding band	event	402	10/93	76r
Music	event	600	10/93	76r
Photography	event	1088	10/93	76r
Shoes for bride	event	50	10/93	76r
Videography	event	483	10/93	76r
Wedding invitations and announcements	event	342	10/93	76r
Wedding reception	event	7000	10/93	76r

Kansas City, MO, KS

Item	Per	Value	Date	Ref.
Composite, ACCRA index		95.00	12/94	2c
Alcoholic Beverages				
Beer, Miller Lite, Bud, 12-oz., ex deposit	6	3.95	12/94	2c
J & B Scotch	750-ml.	16.54	12/94	2c
Wine, Gallo Chablis blanc	1.5-lit	4.72	12/94	2c
Appliances				
Appliances (major), expenditures	year	127	91	81c
Appliances (major), expenditures	year	131	91	81r
Average annual exp.				
Food, health care, personal goods, services	year	28189	91	81c
Food, health care, personal goods, services	year	25935	91	81r

Values are in dollars or fractions of dollars. In the column headed *Ref*, references are shown to sources. Each reference is followed by a letter. These refer to the geographical level for which data were reported: s = State, r = Region, and c = City or metro. The abbreviation *ex* is used to mean *except* or *excluding*; *exp* stands for expenditures. For other abbreviations and further explanations, please see the Introduction.

Kansas City, MO, KS - continued

Item	Per	Value	Date	Ref.
Business				
Dinner and tip, hotel, corporate rate	night	30.00	2/94	15c
Hotel room, corporate rate	night	77.00	2/94	15c
Charity				
Cash contributions, expenditures	year	1453	91	81c
Cash contributions, expenditures	year	745	91	81r
Clothing				
Apparel, men and boys, total expenditures	year	287	91	81c
Apparel, men and boys, total expenditures	year	332	91	81r
Apparel, women and girls, total expenditures	year	730	91	81c
Apparel, women and girls, total expenditures	year	578	91	81r
Footwear, expenditures	year	153	91	81c
Footwear, expenditures	year	164	91	81r
Jeans, man's denim		28.20	12/94	2c
Shirt, man's dress shirt		26.38	12/94	2c
Undervest, boy's size 10-14, cotton	3	4.13	12/94	2c
Communications				
Long-distance telephone rate, day, addl. min., 1-10 mi.	min.	0.08	12/93	9s
Long-distance telephone rate, day, initial min., 1-10 mi.	min.	0.10	12/93	9s
Newspaper subscription, dly. and Sun. delivery	month	13.26	12/94	2c
Phone line, single, business, field visit	inst	52.25	12/93	9s
Phone line, single, business, no field visit	inst	52.25	12/93	9s
Phone line, single, residence, field visit	inst	36.50	12/93	9s
Phone line, single, residence, no field visit	inst	36.50	12/93	9s
Telephone bill, family of four	month	19.45	12/94	2c
Telephone service, expenditures	year	564	91	81c
Telephone service, expenditures	year	547	91	81r
Telephone, residential, flat rate	mo.	12.05	12/93	8c
Telephone, residential, flat rate	mo.	11.35	12/93	8c
Education				
Board, 4-year private college/university	year	2296	8/94	80s
Board, 4-year public college/university	year	1544	8/94	80s
Education, total expenditures	year	332	91	81c
Education, total expenditures	year	394	91	81r
Room, 4-year private college/university	year	2012	8/94	80s
Room, 4-year public college/university	year	1817	8/94	80s
Total cost, 4-year private college/university	year	13053	8/94	80s
Total cost, 4-year public college/university	year	5836	8/94	80s
Tuition, 2-year public college/university, in-state	year	1152	8/94	80s
Tuition, 4-year private college/university, in-state	year	8745	8/94	80s
Tuition, 4-year public college/university, in-state	year	2475	8/94	80s
Energy and Fuels				
Energy, combined forms, 1800 sq. ft.	mo.	117.58	12/94	2c
Energy, exc. electricity, 1800 sq. ft.	mo.	42.80	12/94	2c
Fuel oil and other fuels, expenditures	year	20	91	81c
Fuel oil and other fuels, expenditures	year	83	91	81r
Gas, cooking, 10 therms	month	13.23	2/94	65c
Gas, cooking, 30 therms	month	21.60	2/94	65c
Gas, cooking, 50 therms	month	29.97	2/94	65c
Gas, heating, winter, 100 therms	month	50.90	2/94	65c
Gas, heating, winter, average use	month	92.73	2/94	65c
Gas, natural, expenditures	year	460	91	81c
Gas, natural, expenditures	year	373	91	81r
Gas, reg unlead, taxes inc., cash, self-service	gal	0.99	12/94	2c
Gasoline and motor oil purchased	year	987	91	81c
Gasoline and motor oil purchased	year	1000	91	81r
Gasoline, unleaded midgrade	gallon	1.15	4/93	82r
Gasoline, unleaded premium	gallon	1.23	4/93	82r
Gasoline, unleaded regular	gallon	1.07	4/93	82r
Entertainment				
Bowling, evening rate	game	2.20	12/94	2c
Entertainment supplies, equipment, and services, misc. expenditures	year	241	91	81c

Kansas City, MO, KS - continued

Item	Per	Value	Date	Ref.
Entertainment - continued				
Entertainment, total expenditures	year	1344	91	81c
Entertainment, total expenditures	year	1356	91	81r
Fees and admissions, expenditures	year	420	91	81c
Fees and admissions, expenditures	year	347	91	81r
Monopoly game, Parker Brothers', No. 9	game	10.91	12/94	2c
Movie	adm	5.65	12/94	2c
Pets, toys, playground equipment, expenditures	year	262	91	81c
Pets, toys, playground equipment, expenditures	year	270	91	81r
Reading, expenditures	year	165	91	81c
Reading, expenditures	year	160	91	81r
Televisions, radios, and sound equipment, expenditures	year	421	91	81c
Televisions, radios, and sound equipment, expenditures	year	433	91	81r
Tennis balls, yellow, Wilson or Penn, 3	can	1.93	12/94	2c
Funerals				
Burial, immediate, container provided by funeral home		1348.78	1/95	54r
Cards, acknowledgment		21.20	1/95	54r
Casket, minimum alternative		182.83	1/95	54r
Cosmetology, hair care, etc.		133.11	1/95	54r
Cremation, direct, container provided by funeral home		1101.95	1/95	54r
Embalming		314.45	1/95	54r
Funeral, funeral home		304.88	1/95	54r
Funeral, other facility		301.37	1/95	54r
Graveside service		290.59	1/95	54r
Hearse, local		137.37	1/95	54r
Limousine, local		82.84	1/95	54r
Memorial service		316.57	1/95	54r
Service charge, professional, nondeclinable		1099.00	1/95	54r
Visitation and viewing		209.25	1/95	54r
Groceries				
Groceries, ACCRA Index		97.00	12/94	2c
Apples, Red Delicious	lb.	0.68	12/94	82r
Baby food, strained vegetables, lowest price	4-4.5 oz.	0.30	12/94	2c
Bacon, sliced	lb.	1.88	12/94	82r
Bananas	lb.	0.43	12/94	2c
Bananas	lb.	0.41	12/94	82r
Beef or hamburger, ground	lb.	1.25	12/94	2c
Beef purchases	year	232	91	81c
Beef purchases	year	197	91	81r
Beef, stew, boneless	lb.	2.52	12/94	82r
Beverage purchases, alcoholic	year	126	91	81c
Beverage purchases, alcoholic	year	293	91	81r
Beverage purchases, nonalcoholic	year	258	91	81c
Beverage purchases, nonalcoholic	year	203	91	81r
Bologna, all beef or mixed	lb.	2.12	12/94	82r
Bread, white	24-oz.	0.78	12/94	2c
Bread, white, pan	lb.	0.76	12/94	82r
Cabbage	lb.	0.44	12/94	82r
Carrots, short trimmed and topped	lb.	0.44	12/94	82r
Cereals and bakery products purchases	year	454	91	81c
Cereals and bakery products purchases	year	347	91	81r
Cereals and cereal products purchases	year	157	91	81c
Cereals and cereals products purchases	year	119	91	81r
Cheddar cheese, natural	lb.	3.28	12/94	82r
Cheese, Kraft grated Parmesan	8-oz.	3.23	12/94	2c
Chicken breast, bone-in	lb.	1.61	12/94	82r
Chicken, fresh, whole	lb.	0.89	12/94	82r
Chicken, whole fryer	lb.	0.78	12/94	2c
Chuck roast, USDA choice, boneless	lb.	2.33	12/94	82r
Cigarettes, Winston, Kings	carton	16.22	12/94	2c
Coffee, 100%, ground roast, all sizes	lb.	4.28	12/94	82r
Coffee, vacuum-packed	13 oz.	3.60	12/94	2c
Cookies, chocolate chip	lb.	2.72	12/94	82r
Corn Flakes, Kellogg's or Post Toasties	18 oz.	2.34	12/94	2c
Corn, frozen, whole kernel, lowest price	10 oz.	0.64	12/94	2c

Values are in dollars or fractions of dollars. In the column headed *Ref*, references are shown to sources. Each reference is followed by a letter. These refer to the geographical level for which data were reported: s = State, r = Region, and c = City or metro. The abbreviation *ex* is used to mean *except* or *excluding*; *exp* stands for expenditures. For other abbreviations and further explanations, please see the Introduction.

Kansas City, MO, KS - continued

Item	Per	Value	Date	Ref.
Groceries				
Dairy products (other) purchases	year	184	91	81c
Dairy products (other) purchases	year	148	91	81r
Eggs, Grade A large	dozen	0.65	12/94	2c
Eggs, Grade A large	dozen	0.76	12/94	82r
Fish and seafood purchases	year	90	91	81c
Fish and seafood purchases	year	61	91	81r
Flour, white, all purpose	lb.	0.22	12/94	82r
Food purchases, food eaten at home	year	2929	91	81c
Food purchases, food eaten at home	year	2313	91	81r
Foods purchased away from home, not prepared by consumer	year	1498	91	81c
Foods purchased away from home, not prepared by consumer	year	1709	91	81r
Fruits and vegetables purchases	year	455	91	81c
Fruits and vegetables purchases	year	372	91	81r
Grapefruit	lb.	0.47	12/94	82r
Grapes, Thompson seedless	lb.	2.15	12/94	82r
Ground beef, 100% beef	lb.	1.37	12/94	82r
Ground chuck, 100% beef	lb.	1.81	12/94	82r
Ham, boneless, exc. canned	lb.	2.16	12/94	82r
Ice cream, prepackaged, bulk, regular	1/2 gal.	2.48	12/94	82r
Lemons	lb.	1.08	12/94	82r
Lettuce, iceberg	lb.	0.81	12/94	82r
Lettuce, iceberg	head	0.81	12/94	2c
Margarine, Blue Bonnet or Parkay cubes	lb.	0.66	12/94	2c
Margarine, stick	lb.	0.81	12/94	82r
Meats, poultry, fish, and eggs purchases	year	722	91	81c
Meats, poultry, fish, and eggs purchases	year	591	91	81r
Milk and cream (fresh) purchases	year	128	91	81c
Milk and cream (fresh) purchases	year	132	91	81r
Milk, whole	1/2 gal.	1.35	12/94	2c
Orange juice, frozen concentrate 12-oz. can	16 oz.	1.41	12/94	82r
Orange juice, Minute Maid frozen	12-oz.	1.24	12/94	2c
Oranges, Navel	lb.	0.56	12/94	82r
Peaches, halves or slices, Hunt's, Del Monte, or Libby's	29-oz.	1.29	12/94	2c
Peanut butter, creamy, all sizes	lb.	1.81	12/94	82r
Peas, sweet, Del Monte or Green Giant	15-17 oz.	0.57	12/94	2c
Pork chops, center cut, bone-in	lb.	2.76	12/94	82r
Pork purchases	year	165	91	81c
Pork purchases	year	130	91	81r
Potato chips	16-oz.	2.81	12/94	82r
Potatoes, frozen, French fried	lb.	0.83	12/94	82r
Potatoes, white	lb.	0.28	12/94	82r
Potatoes, white or red	10-lb. sack	2.03	12/94	2c
Round roast, USDA choice, boneless	lb.	2.90	12/94	82r
Sausage, Jimmy Dean, 100% pork	lb.	2.54	12/94	2c
Shortening, vegetable oil blends	lb.	0.88	12/94	82r
Shortening, vegetable, Crisco	3-lb.	2.14	12/94	2c
Soft drink, Coca Cola, ex deposit	2 lit	1.13	12/94	2c
Spaghetti and macaroni	lb.	0.78	12/94	82r
Steak, rib eye, USDA choice, boneless	lb.	6.15	12/94	82r
Steak, round, graded & ungraded, exc. USDA prime & choice	lb.	2.72	12/94	82r
Steak, round, USDA choice, boneless	lb.	3.02	12/94	82r
Steak, sirloin, USDA choice, boneless	lb.	3.85	12/94	82r
Steak, t-bone	lb.	5.34	12/94	2c
Steak, T-bone, USDA choice, bone-in	lb.	5.38	12/94	82r
Sugar and other sweets, eaten at home, expenditures	year	91	91	81r
Sugar and other sweets, eaten at home, purchases	year	129	91	81c
Sugar, cane or beet	4 lbs.	1.38	12/94	2c
Sugar, white, all sizes	lb.	0.36	12/94	82r
Tobacco products and smoking supplies, total expenditures	year	220	91	81c
Tobacco products and smoking supplies, total expenditures	year	298	91	81r

Kansas City, MO, KS - continued

Item	Per	Value	Date	Ref.
Groceries - continued				
Tomatoes, field grown	lb.	1.36	12/94	82r
Tomatoes, Hunt's or Del Monte	14.5 oz.	0.66	12/94	2c
Tuna, chunk, light	lb.	1.94	12/94	82r
Tuna, chunk, light, oil-packed	6.125-6.5 oz.	0.62	12/94	2c
Turkey, frozen, whole	lb.	0.96	12/94	82r
Yogurt, natural, fruit flavored	8 oz.	0.62	12/94	82r
Goods and Services				
Miscellaneous goods and services, ACCRA Index		96.10	12/94	2c
Health Care				
Health care, ACCRA Index		101.00	12/94	2c
Antibiotic ointment, Polysporin	1.5 oz.	3.64	12/94	2c
Childbirth, Cesarean delivery, hospital charge	birth	5101.00	12/91	69r
Childbirth, Cesarean delivery, physician charge	birth	2234.00	12/91	69r
Childbirth, normal delivery, hospital charge	birth	2891.00	12/91	69r
Childbirth, normal delivery, physician charge	birth	1623.00	12/91	69r
Dentist's fee, adult teeth cleaning and periodic oral exam	visit	53.29	12/94	2c
Doctor's fee, routine exam, established patient	visit	38.00	12/94	2c
Drugs, expenditures	year	252	91	81c
Drugs, expenditures	year	248	91	81r
Health care, total expenditures	year	1964	91	81c
Health care, total expenditures	year	1336	91	81r
Health insurance expenditures	year	873	91	81c
Health insurance expenditures	year	550	91	81r
Hospital care, semiprivate room	day	456.50	12/94	2c
Insurance premium, family medical care	month	390.73	1/95	41s
Medical services expenditures	year	773	91	81c
Medical services expenditures	year	457	91	81r
Medical supplies expenditures	year	66	91	81c
Medical supplies expenditures	year	82	91	81r
Household Goods				
Appl. repair, service call, wash mach	min. lab. chg.	34.04	12/94	2c
Floor coverings, expenditures	year	80	91	81c
Floor coverings, expenditures	year	105	91	81r
Furniture, expenditures	year	303	91	81c
Furniture, expenditures	year	291	91	81r
Household equipment, misc. expenditures	year	341	91	81r
Household equipment, misc., expenditures	year	293	91	81c
Household expenditures, miscellaneous	year	176	91	81c
Household expenditures, miscellaneous	year	162	91	81r
Household furnishings and equipment, expenditures	year	904	91	81c
Household furnishings and equipment, expenditures	year	1042	91	81r
Household operations expenditures	year	542	91	81c
Household operations expenditures	year	365	91	81r
Household textiles, expenditures	year	55	91	81c
Household textiles, expenditures	year	101	91	81r
Housekeeping supplies, expenditures	year	306	91	81c
Housekeeping supplies, expenditures	year	390	91	81r
Laundry and cleaning supplies, expenditures	year	68	91	81c
Laundry and cleaning supplies, expenditures	year	110	91	81r
Laundry detergent, Tide Ultra, Bold, or Cheer	42 oz.	3.07	12/94	2c
Postage and stationery, expenditures	year	108	91	81c
Postage and stationery, expenditures	year	115	91	81r
Tissues, facial, Kleenex brand	175	1.03	12/94	2c
Housing				
Housing, ACCRA Index		90.00	12/94	2c
Add garage/carport		8,479	3/95	74r

Values are in dollars or fractions of dollars. In the column headed *Ref*, references are shown to sources. Each reference is followed by a letter. These refer to the geographical level for which data were reported: s = State, r = Region, and c = City or metro. The abbreviation *ex* is used to mean *except* or *excluding*; *exp* stands for *expenditures*. For other abbreviations and further explanations, please see the Introduction.

Kansas City, MO, KS - continued

Item	Per	Value	Date	Ref.
Housing				
Add room(s)		21,347	3/95	74r
Apartment condominium or co-op, median	unit	87100	12/94	62r
Bathroom addition, average cost	add	9734.00	3/95	13r
Bathroom remodeling, average cost	remod	6414.00	3/95	13r
Bedroom, master suite addition, average cost	add	27122.00	3/95	13r
Deck addition, average cost	add	6665.00	3/95	13r
Dwellings (owned), expenditures	year	3357	91	81c
Dwellings (owned), expenditures	year	2566	91	81r
Enclose porch/patio/breezeway		4,556	3/95	74r
Exterior remodeling, average cost	remod	15395.00	3/95	13r
Family room addition, average cost	add	27658.00	3/95	13r
Finish room in basement/attic		5,074	3/95	74r
Home, existing, single-family, median	unit	106500	12/94	62r
Home, existing, single-family, median	unit	87.70	12/94	62c
Home, purchase price	unit	112.10	3/93	26c
House payment, principal and interest, 25% down payment	mo.	639	12/94	2c
House, 1800 sq ft, 8000 sq ft lot, new, urban, utilities	total	104000	12/94	2c
Kitchen remodeling, major, average cost	remod	17084.00	3/95	13r
Kitchen remodeling, minor, average cost	remod	5804.00	3/95	13r
Maintenance, repairs, insurance, and other housing expenditures	year	415	91	81c
Maintenance, repairs, insurance, and other housing expenditures	year	484	91	81r
Mortgage interest and charges expenditures	year	2460	91	81c
Mortgage interest and charges expenditures	year	1443	91	81r
Mtge. rate, incl. points and orig. fee, 30-year conv. fixed or ARM	mo.	9.20	12/94	2c
Office, home addition, average cost	add	8121.00	3/95	13r
Princ. & int., mortgage, median-price exist. sing.-family home	mo.	515	12/94	62r
Property taxes expenditures	year	483	91	81c
Property taxes expenditures	year	639	91	81r
Redesign, restructure more than half of home's interior		9,114	3/95	74r
Rent, apartment, 2 br., 1 1/2-2 baths, unfurnished, 950 sq ft, water	mo.	622	12/94	2c
Rental units expenditures	year	1214	900/00/ 91	81c
Rental units expenditures	year	1200	91	81r
Sun-space addition, average cost	add	23768.00	3/95	13r
Wing addition, two-story, average cost	add	50410.00	3/95	13r
Insurance and Pensions				
Auto insurance, private passenger	year	600.64	12/94	71s
Insurance and pensions, personal, expenditures	year	2464	91	81c
Insurance and pensions, personal, expenditures	year	2408	91	81r
Insurance, life and other personal, expenditures	year	387	91	81c
Insurance, life and other personal, expenditures	year	355	91	81r
Pensions and Social Security, expenditures	year	2077	91	81c
Pensions and Social Security, expenditures	year	2053	91	81r
Legal Assistance				
Lawyer's consultation fee	hour	125.00	93	45c
Legal work, law firm associate	hour	90		10r
Legal work, law firm partner	hour	139		10r
Personal Goods				
Personal care products and services, total expenditures	year	288	91	81c
Shampoo, Alberto VO5	15-oz.	1.34	12/94	2c
Toothpaste, Crest or Colgate	6-7 oz.	2.01	12/94	2c
Personal Services				
Dry cleaning, man's 2-pc. suit		6.61	12/94	2c
Haircut, man's barbershop, no styling		8.80	12/94	2c
Haircut, woman's shampoo, trim, blow-dry		20.10	12/94	2c
Personal services expenditures	year	366	91	81c

Kansas City, MO, KS - continued

Item	Per	Value	Date	Ref.
Personal Services - continued				
Personal services expenditures	year	203	91	81r
Restaurant Food				
Chicken, fried, thigh and drumstick		2.08	12/94	2c
Dining expenditures, family	week	30.03	94	73r
Hamburger with cheese	1/4 lb.	1.83	12/94	2c
Pizza, Pizza Hut or Pizza Inn	12-13 in.	7.99	12/94	2c
Taxes				
Tax rate, residential property, month	$100	1.15	1/92	79c
Taxes, Federal income, expenditures	year	884	91	81c
Taxes, Federal income, expenditures	year	1756	91	81r
Taxes, personal, expenditures	year	1348	91	81c
Taxes, personal, expenditures	year	2426	91	81r
Taxes, State and local income, expenditures	year	248	91	81c
Taxes, State and local income, expenditures	year	568	91	81r
Transportation				
Transportation, ACCRA Index		90.60	12/94	2c
Bus fare, one-way	trip	0.90	12/95	1c
Bus fare, up to 10 miles	one-way	0.90	12/94	2c
Cars and trucks purchased, new	year	460	91	81c
Cars and trucks purchased, new	year	891	91	81r
Cars and trucks purchased, used	year	1124	91	81c
Cars and trucks purchased, used	year	1155	91	81r
Driver's learning permit fee	perm	1.00	1/94	84s
Driver's license fee	orig	7.50	1/94	84s
Driver's license fee, duplicate	lic	7.50	1/94	84s
Driver's license reinstatement fee, min.	susp	20.00	1/94	85s
Driver's license renewal fee	renew	7.50	1/94	84s
Identification card, nondriver	card	7.50	1/94	83s
Motorcycle license fee	orig	7.50	1/94	84s
Motorcycle license fee, duplicate	lic	7.50	1/94	84s
Motorcycle license renewal fee	renew	7.50	1/94	84s
Public transportation expenditures	year	211	91	81c
Public transportation expenditures	year	209	91	81r
Rental car, economy size, unlim. mileage	wk.	134.99	5/95	70c
Shuttle, airport-to-downtown hotel	trip	10.00-15.00	5/95	70c
Tire balance, computer or spin bal., front	wheel	6.27	12/94	2c
Transportation expenditures, total	year	4661	91	81c
Transportation expenditures, total	year	4792	91	81r
Trolley bus, downtown-to-plaza	trip	4.00	5/95	70c
Vehicle expenses, miscellaneous	year	1876	91	81c
Vehicle finance charges	year	340	91	81c
Vehicle finance charges	year	300	91	81r
Vehicle insurance expenditures	year	582	91	81c
Vehicle insurance expenditures	year	485	91	81r
Vehicle maintenance and repairs expenditures	year	566	91	81c
Vehicle maintenance and repairs expenditures	year	534	91	81r
Vehicle purchases	year	1588	91	81c
Vehicle purchases	year	2068	91	81r
Vehicle rental, leases, licenses, etc. expenditures	year	388	91	81c
Vehicle rental, leases, licenses, etc. expenditures	year	197	91	81r
Vehicles purchased, other than cars and trucks	year	4	91	81c
Vehicles purchased, other than cars and trucks	year	22	91	81r
Travel				
Lodging, hotel suite, with continental breakfast	day	69.00-180.00	95	70c
Utilities				
Utilities, ACCRA Index		104.10	12/94	2c
Electricity expenditures	year	839	91	81c
Electricity expenditures	year	668	91	81r

Values are in dollars or fractions of dollars. In the column headed *Ref*, references are shown to sources. Each reference is followed by a letter. These refer to the geographical level for which data were reported: s = State, r = Region, and c = City or metro. The abbreviation *ex* is used to mean *except* or *excluding*; *exp* stands for *expenditures*. For other abbreviations and further explanations, please see the Introduction.

Kansas City, MO, KS - continued

Item	Per	Value	Date	Ref.
Utilities				
Electricity, (part.), other, 1800 sq. ft., new home	mo.	74.78	12/94	2c
Electricity, summer, 250 KWh	month	27.77	8/93	64c
Electricity, summer, 500 KWh	month	49.51	8/93	64c
Electricity, summer, 750 KWh	month	69.45	8/93	64c
Electricity, summer, 1000 KWh	month	89.40	8/93	64c
Utilities, fuels, and public services, total expenditures	year	2151	91	81c
Utilities, fuels, and public services, total expenditures	year	1838	91	81r
Water and other public services, expenditures	year	267	91	81c
Water and other public services, expenditures	year	167	91	81r
Weddings				
Bridal attendants' gowns	event	750	10/93	76r
Bridal gown	event	852	10/93	76r
Bridal headpiece and veil	event	167	10/93	76r
Bride's wedding band	event	708	10/93	76r
Clergy	event	224	10/93	76r
Engagement ring	event	2756	10/93	76r
Flowers	event	863	10/93	76r
Formal wear for groom	event	106	10/93	76r
Groom's attendants' formal wear	event	530	10/93	76r
Groom's wedding band	event	402	10/93	76r
Music	event	600	10/93	76r
Photography	event	1088	10/93	76r
Shoes for bride	event	50	10/93	76r
Videography	event	483	10/93	76r
Wedding invitations and announcements	event	342	10/93	76r
Wedding reception	event	7000	10/93	76r

Kearney, NE

Item	Per	Value	Date	Ref.
Composite, ACCRA index		96.70	12/94	2c
Alcoholic Beverages				
Beer, Miller Lite, Bud, 12-oz., ex deposit	6	4.39	12/94	2c
J & B Scotch	750-ml.	18.45	12/94	2c
Wine, Gallo Chablis blanc	1.5-lit	4.84	12/94	2c
Clothing				
Jeans, man's denim		29.46	12/94	2c
Shirt, man's dress shirt		38.67	12/94	2c
Undervest, boy's size 10-14, cotton	3	4.54	12/94	2c
Communications				
Newspaper subscription, dly. and Sun. delivery	month	8.78	12/94	2c
Telephone bill, family of four	month	15.44	12/94	2c
Energy and Fuels				
Energy, combined forms, 1800 sq. ft.	mo.	102.48	12/94	2c
Energy, exc. electricity, 1800 sq. ft.	mo.	40.40	12/94	2c
Gas, reg unlead, taxes inc., cash, self-service	gal	1.27	12/94	2c
Entertainment				
Bowling, evening rate	game	2.10	12/94	2c
Monopoly game, Parker Brothers', No. 9	game	9.94	12/94	2c
Movie	adm	4.88	12/94	2c
Tennis balls, yellow, Wilson or Penn, 3	can	2.15	12/94	2c
Groceries				
Groceries, ACCRA Index		108.20	12/94	2c
Baby food, strained vegetables, lowest price	4-4.5 oz.	0.42	12/94	2c
Bananas	lb.	0.37	12/94	2c
Beef or hamburger, ground	lb.	1.20	12/94	2c
Bread, white	24-oz.	0.97	12/94	2c
Cheese, Kraft grated Parmesan	8-oz.	3.53	12/94	2c
Chicken, whole fryer	lb.	0.87	12/94	2c
Cigarettes, Winston, Kings	carton	17.36	12/94	2c

Kearney, NE - continued

Item	Per	Value	Date	Ref.
Groceries - continued				
Coffee, vacuum-packed	13 oz.	3.61	12/94	2c
Corn Flakes, Kellogg's or Post Toasties	18 oz.	2.51	12/94	2c
Corn, frozen, whole kernel, lowest price	10 oz.	0.76	12/94	2c
Eggs, Grade A large	dozen	0.73	12/94	2c
Lettuce, iceberg	head	0.88	12/94	2c
Margarine, Blue Bonnet or Parkay cubes	lb.	0.69	12/94	2c
Milk, whole	1/2 gal.	1.38	12/94	2c
Orange juice, Minute Maid frozen	12-oz.	1.43	12/94	2c
Peaches, halves or slices, Hunt's, Del Monte, or Libby's	29-oz.	1.44	12/94	2c
Peas, sweet, Del Monte or Green Giant	15-17 oz.	0.62	12/94	2c
Potatoes, white or red	10-lb. sack	1.64	12/94	2c
Sausage, Jimmy Dean, 100% pork	lb.	3.23	12/94	2c
Shortening, vegetable, Crisco	3-lb.	2.79	12/94	2c
Soft drink, Coca Cola, ex deposit	2 lit	1.64	12/94	2c
Steak, t-bone	lb.	4.69	12/94	2c
Sugar, cane or beet	4 lbs.	1.44	12/94	2c
Tomatoes, Hunt's or Del Monte	14.5 oz.	0.81	12/94	2c
Tuna, chunk, light, oil-packed	6.125-6.5 oz.	0.71	12/94	2c
Goods and Services				
Miscellaneous goods and services, ACCRA Index		97.10	12/94	2c
Health Care				
Health care, ACCRA Index		89.00	12/94	2c
Antibiotic ointment, Polysporin	1.5 oz.	4.10	12/94	2c
Dentist's fee, adult teeth cleaning and periodic oral exam	visit	48.60	12/94	2c
Doctor's fee, routine exam, established patient	visit	35.67	12/94	2c
Hospital care, semiprivate room	day	297.00	12/94	2c
Household Goods				
Appl. repair, service call, wash mach	min. lab. chg.	24.98	12/94	2c
Laundry detergent, Tide Ultra, Bold, or Cheer	42 oz.	3.33	12/94	2c
Tissues, facial, Kleenex brand	175	1.11	12/94	2c
Housing				
Housing, ACCRA Index		91.40	12/94	2c
House payment, principal and interest, 25% down payment	mo.	717	12/94	2c
House, 1800 sq ft, 8000 sq ft lot, new, urban, utilities	total	114800	12/94	2c
Mtge. rate, incl. points and orig. fee, 30-year conv. fixed or ARM	mo.	9.42	12/94	2c
Rent, apartment, 2 br., 1 1/2-2 baths, unfurnished, 950 sq ft, water	mo.	435	12/94	2c
Personal Goods				
Shampoo, Alberto VO5	15-oz.	1.08	12/94	2c
Toothpaste, Crest or Colgate	6-7 oz.	2.28	12/94	2c
Personal Services				
Dry cleaning, man's 2-pc. suit		7.39	12/94	2c
Haircut, man's barbershop, no styling		7.50	12/94	2c
Haircut, woman's shampoo, trim, blow-dry		15.25	12/94	2c
Restaurant Food				
Chicken, fried, thigh and drumstick		1.80	12/94	2c
Hamburger with cheese	1/4 lb.	1.80	12/94	2c
Pizza, Pizza Hut or Pizza Inn	12-13 in.	7.49	12/94	2c
Transportation				
Transportation, ACCRA Index		102.70	12/94	2c
Tire balance, computer or spin bal., front	wheel	6.02	12/94	2c

Values are in dollars or fractions of dollars. In the column headed *Ref*, references are shown to sources. Each reference is followed by a letter. These refer to the geographical level for which data were reported: s=State, r=Region, and c=City or metro. The abbreviation *ex* is used to mean *except* or *excluding*; *exp* stands for expenditures. For other abbreviations and further explanations, please see the Introduction.

Kearney, NE - continued

Item	Per	Value	Date	Ref.
Utilities				
Utilities, ACCRA Index		89.70	12/94	2c
Electricity, (part.), other, 1800 sq. ft., new home	mo.	62.08	12/94	2c

Kennett, MO

Item	Per	Value	Date	Ref.
Composite, ACCRA index		85.20	12/94	2c
Alcoholic Beverages				
Beer, Miller Lite, Bud, 12-oz., ex deposit	6	3.92	12/94	2c
J & B Scotch	750-ml.	16.99	12/94	
Wine, Gallo Chablis blanc	1.5-lit	5.25	12/94	2c
Clothing				
Jeans, man's denim		26.50	12/94	2c
Shirt, man's dress shirt		32.00	12/94	2c
Undervest, boy's size 10-14, cotton	3	3.12	12/94	2c
Communications				
Newspaper subscription, dly. and Sun. delivery	month	12.86	12/94	2c
Telephone bill, family of four	month	16.45	12/94	2c
Telephone, residential, flat rate	mo.	9.10	12/93	8c
Energy and Fuels				
Energy, combined forms, 1800 sq. ft.	mo.	78.10	12/94	2c
Energy, exc. electricity, 1800 sq. ft.	mo.	44.70	12/94	2c
Gas, reg unlead, taxes inc., cash, self-service	gal	1.10	12/94	2c
Entertainment				
Bowling, evening rate	game	1.60	12/94	2c
Monopoly game, Parker Brothers', No. 9	game	10.22	12/94	2c
Movie	adm	4.00	12/94	2c
Tennis balls, yellow, Wilson or Penn, 3	can	1.93	12/94	2c
Groceries				
Groceries, ACCRA Index		99.30	12/94	2c
Baby food, strained vegetables, lowest price	4-4.5 oz.	0.41	12/94	2c
Bananas	lb.	0.49	12/94	2c
Beef or hamburger, ground	lb.	0.99	12/94	2c
Bread, white	24-oz.	0.65	12/94	2c
Cheese, Kraft grated Parmesan	8-oz.	3.86	12/94	2c
Chicken, whole fryer	lb.	0.84	12/94	2c
Cigarettes, Winston, Kings	carton	14.39	12/94	2c
Coffee, vacuum-packed	13 oz.	3.41	12/94	2c
Corn Flakes, Kellogg's or Post Toasties	18 oz.	2.64	12/94	2c
Corn, frozen, whole kernel, lowest price	10 oz.	0.73	12/94	2c
Eggs, Grade A large	dozen	0.75	12/94	2c
Lettuce, iceberg	head	0.69	12/94	2c
Margarine, Blue Bonnet or Parkay cubes	lb.	0.74	12/94	2c
Milk, whole	1/2 gal.	1.47	12/94	2c
Orange juice, Minute Maid frozen	12-oz.	1.50	12/94	2c
Peaches, halves or slices, Hunt's, Del Monte, or Libby's	29-oz.	1.49	12/94	2c
Peas, sweet, Del Monte or Green Giant	15-17 oz.	0.74	12/94	2c
Potatoes, white or red	10-lb. sack	1.34	12/94	2c
Sausage, Jimmy Dean, 100% pork	lb.	2.26	12/94	2c
Shortening, vegetable, Crisco	3-lb.	2.64	12/94	2c
Soft drink, Coca Cola, ex deposit	2 lit	0.99	12/94	2c
Steak, t-bone	lb.	4.19	12/94	2c
Sugar, cane or beet	4 lbs.	1.47	12/94	2c
Tomatoes, Hunt's or Del Monte	14.5 oz.	0.78	12/94	2c
Tuna, chunk, light, oil-packed	6.125-6.5 oz.	0.64	12/94	2c
Goods and Services				
Miscellaneous goods and services, ACCRA Index		93.90	12/94	2c

Kennett, MO - continued

Item	Per	Value	Date	Ref.
Health Care				
Health care, ACCRA Index		81.00	12/94	2c
Antibiotic ointment, Polysporin	1.5 oz.	3.57	12/94	2c
Dentist's fee, adult teeth cleaning and periodic oral exam	visit	46.50	12/94	2c
Doctor's fee, routine exam, established patient	visit	27.67	12/94	2c
Hospital care, semiprivate room	day	330.00	12/94	2c
Household Goods				
Appl. repair, service call, wash mach	min. lab. chg.	22.50	12/94	2c
Laundry detergent, Tide Ultra, Bold, or Cheer	42 oz.	3.54	12/94	2c
Tissues, facial, Kleenex brand	175	1.11	12/94	2c
Housing				
Housing, ACCRA Index		72.70	12/94	2c
House payment, principal and interest, 25% down payment	mo.	558	12/94	2c
House, 1800 sq ft, 8000 sq ft lot, new, urban, utilities	total	88350	12/94	2c
Mtge. rate, incl. points and orig. fee, 30-year conv. fixed or ARM	mo.	9.51	12/94	2c
Personal Goods				
Shampoo, Alberto VO5	15-oz.	0.97	12/94	2c
Toothpaste, Crest or Colgate	6-7 oz.	1.87	12/94	2c
Personal Services				
Dry cleaning, man's 2-pc. suit		6.00	12/94	2c
Haircut, man's barbershop, no styling		7.00	12/94	2c
Haircut, woman's shampoo, trim, blow-dry		14.00	12/94	2c
Restaurant Food				
Chicken, fried, thigh and drumstick		2.59	12/94	2c
Hamburger with cheese	1/4 lb.	1.79	12/94	2c
Pizza, Pizza Hut or Pizza Inn	12-13 in.	8.99	12/94	2c
Transportation				
Transportation, ACCRA Index		82.50	12/94	2c
Tire balance, computer or spin bal., front	wheel	4.17	12/94	2c
Utilities				
Utilities, ACCRA Index		71.60	12/94	2c
Electricity, (part.), other, 1800 sq. ft., new home	mo.	33.40	12/94	2c

Kenosha, WI

Item	Per	Value	Date	Ref.
Appliances				
Appliances (major), expenditures	year	131	91	81r
Average annual exp.				
Food, health care, personal goods, services	year	25935	91	81r
Charity				
Cash contributions, expenditures	year	745	91	81r
Clothing				
Apparel, men and boys, total expenditures	year	332	91	81r
Apparel, women and girls, total expenditures	year	578	91	81r
Footwear, expenditures	year	164	91	81r
Communications				
Long-distance telephone rate, day, addl. min., 1-10 mi.	min.	0.10	12/93	9s
Long-distance telephone rate, day, initial min., 1-10 mi.	min.	0.15	12/93	9s
Phone line, single, business, field visit	inst	64.65	12/93	9s
Phone line, single, business, no field visit	inst	64.65	12/93	9s
Phone line, single, residence, field visit	inst	33.05	12/93	9s
Phone line, single, residence, no field visit	inst	33.05	12/93	9s
Telephone service, expenditures	year	547	91	81r

Values are in dollars or fractions of dollars. In the column headed *Ref*, references are shown to sources. Each reference is followed by a letter. These refer to the geographical level for which data were reported: s = State, r = Region, and c = City or metro. The abbreviation *ex* is used to mean *except* or *excluding*; *exp* stands for expenditures. For other abbreviations and further explanations, please see the Introduction.

Kenosha, WI - continued

Item	Per	Value	Date	Ref.
Education				
Board, 4-year private college/university	year	2145	8/94	80s
Board, 4-year public college/university	year	1303	8/94	80s
Education, total expenditures	year	394	91	81r
Room, 4-year private college/university	year	1576	8/94	80s
Room, 4-year public college/university	year	1631	8/94	80s
Total cost, 4-year private college/university	year	13902	8/94	80s
Total cost, 4-year public college/university	year	5252	8/94	80s
Tuition, 2-year public college/university, in-state	year	1557	8/94	80s
Tuition, 4-year private college/university, in-state	year	10181	8/94	80s
Tuition, 4-year public college/university, in-state	year	2318	8/94	80s
Energy and Fuels				
Fuel oil and other fuels, expenditures	year	83	91	81r
Gas, natural, expenditures	year	373	91	81r
Gasoline and motor oil purchased	year	1000	91	81r
Gasoline, unleaded midgrade	gallon	1.15	4/93	82r
Gasoline, unleaded premium	gallon	1.23	4/93	82r
Gasoline, unleaded regular	gallon	1.07	4/93	82r
Entertainment				
Entertainment, total expenditures	year	1356	91	81r
Fees and admissions, expenditures	year	347	91	81r
Pets, toys, playground equipment, expenditures	year	270	91	81r
Reading, expenditures	year	160	91	81r
Televisions, radios, and sound equipment, expenditures	year	433	91	81r
Funerals				
Burial, immediate, container provided by funeral home		1268.31	1/95	54r
Cards, acknowledgment		26.12	1/95	54r
Casket, minimum alternative		198.03	1/95	54r
Cosmetology, hair care, etc.		122.19	1/95	54r
Cremation, direct, container provided by funeral home		977.81	1/95	54r
Embalming		334.00	1/95	54r
Funeral, funeral home		321.16	1/95	54r
Funeral, other facility		317.73	1/95	54r
Graveside service		292.48	1/95	54r
Hearse, local		153.20	1/95	54r
Limousine, local		123.52	1/95	54r
Memorial service		356.30	1/95	54r
Service charge, professional, nondeclinable		968.24	1/95	54r
Visitation and viewing		332.66	1/95	54r
Groceries				
Apples, Red Delicious	lb.	0.68	12/94	82r
Bacon, sliced	lb.	1.88	12/94	82r
Bananas	lb.	0.41	12/94	82r
Beef purchases	year	197	91	81r
Beef, stew, boneless	lb.	2.52	12/94	82r
Beverage purchases, alcoholic	year	293	91	81r
Beverage purchases, nonalcoholic	year	203	91	81r
Bologna, all beef or mixed	lb.	2.12	12/94	82r
Bread, white, pan	lb.	0.76	12/94	82r
Cabbage	lb.	0.44	12/94	82r
Carrots, short trimmed and topped	lb.	0.44	12/94	82r
Cereals and bakery products purchases	year	347	91	81r
Cereals and cereals products purchases	year	119	91	81r
Cheddar cheese, natural	lb.	3.28	12/94	82r
Chicken breast, bone-in	lb.	1.61	12/94	82r
Chicken, fresh, whole	lb.	0.89	12/94	82r
Chuck roast, USDA choice, boneless	lb.	2.33	12/94	82r
Coffee, 100%, ground roast, all sizes	lb.	4.28	12/94	82r
Cookies, chocolate chip	lb.	2.72	12/94	82r
Dairy products (other) purchases	year	148	91	81r
Eggs, Grade A large	dozen	0.76	12/94	82r
Fish and seafood purchases	year	61	91	81r
Flour, white, all purpose	lb.	0.22	12/94	82r
Food purchases, food eaten at home	year	2313	91	81r

Kenosha, WI - continued

Item	Per	Value	Date	Ref.
Groceries - continued				
Foods purchased away from home, not prepared by consumer	year	1709	91	81r
Fruits and vegetables purchases	year	372	91	81r
Grapefruit	lb.	0.47	12/94	82r
Grapes, Thompson seedless	lb.	2.15	12/94	82r
Ground beef, 100% beef	lb.	1.37	12/94	82r
Ground chuck, 100% beef	lb.	1.81	12/94	82r
Ham, boneless, exc. canned	lb.	2.16	12/94	82r
Ice cream, prepackaged, bulk, regular	1/2 gal.	2.48	12/94	82r
Lemons	lb.	1.08	12/94	82r
Lettuce, iceberg	lb.	0.81	12/94	82r
Margarine, stick	lb.	0.81	12/94	82r
Meats, poultry, fish, and eggs purchases	year	591	91	81r
Milk and cream (fresh) purchases	year	132	91	81r
Orange juice, frozen concentrate 12-oz. can	16 oz.	1.41	12/94	82r
Oranges, Navel	lb.	0.56	12/94	82r
Peanut butter, creamy, all sizes	lb.	1.81	12/94	82r
Pork chops, center cut, bone-in	lb.	2.76	12/94	82r
Pork purchases	year	130	91	81r
Potato chips	16-oz.	2.81	12/94	82r
Potatoes, frozen, French fried	lb.	0.83	12/94	82r
Potatoes, white	lb.	0.28	12/94	82r
Round roast, USDA choice, boneless	lb.	2.90	12/94	82r
Shortening, vegetable oil blends	lb.	0.88	12/94	82r
Spaghetti and macaroni	lb.	0.78	12/94	82r
Steak, rib eye, USDA choice, boneless	lb.	6.15	12/94	82r
Steak, round, graded & ungraded, exc. USDA prime & choice	lb.	2.72	12/94	82r
Steak, round, USDA choice, boneless	lb.	3.02	12/94	82r
Steak, sirloin, USDA choice, boneless	lb.	3.85	12/94	82r
Steak, T-bone, USDA choice, bone-in	lb.	5.38	12/94	82r
Sugar and other sweets, eaten at home, expenditures	year	91	91	81r
Sugar, white, all sizes	lb.	0.36	12/94	82r
Tobacco products and smoking supplies, total expenditures	year	298	91	81r
Tomatoes, field grown	lb.	1.36	12/94	82r
Tuna, chunk, light	lb.	1.94	12/94	82r
Turkey, frozen, whole	lb.	0.96	12/94	82r
Yogurt, natural, fruit flavored	8 oz.	0.62	12/94	82r
Health Care				
Childbirth, Cesarean delivery, hospital charge	birth	5101.00	12/91	69r
Childbirth, Cesarean delivery, physician charge	birth	2234.00	12/91	69r
Childbirth, normal delivery, hospital charge	birth	2891.00	12/91	69r
Childbirth, normal delivery, physician charge	birth	1623.00	12/91	69r
Drugs, expenditures	year	248	91	81r
Health care, total expenditures	year	1336	91	81r
Health insurance expenditures	year	550	91	81r
Insurance premium, family medical care	month	378.79	1/95	41s
Medical services expenditures	year	457	91	81r
Medical supplies expenditures	year	82	91	81r
Household Goods				
Floor coverings, expenditures	year	105	91	81r
Furniture, expenditures	year	291	91	81r
Household equipment, misc. expenditures	year	341	91	81r
Household expenditures, miscellaneous	year	162	91	81r
Household furnishings and equipment, expenditures	year	1042	91	81r
Household operations expenditures	year	365	91	81r
Household textiles, expenditures	year	101	91	81r
Housekeeping supplies, expenditures	year	390	91	81r
Laundry and cleaning supplies, expenditures	year	110	91	81r
Postage and stationery, expenditures	year	115	91	81r
Housing				
Add garage/carport		8,479	3/95	74r
Add room(s)		21,347	3/95	74r
Apartment condominium or co-op, median	unit	87100	12/94	62r

Values are in dollars or fractions of dollars. In the column headed *Ref*, references are shown to sources. Each reference is followed by a letter. These refer to the geographical level for which data were reported: s=State, r=Region, and c=City or metro. The abbreviation *ex* is used to mean *except* or *excluding*; *exp* stands for *expenditures*. For other abbreviations and further explanations, please see the Introduction.

Kenosha, WI - continued

Item	Per	Value	Date	Ref.
Housing				
Bathroom addition, average cost	add	9734.00	3/95	13r
Bathroom remodeling, average cost	remod	6414.00	3/95	13r
Bedroom, master suite addition, average cost	add	27122.00	3/95	13r
Deck addition, average cost	add	6665.00	3/95	13r
Dwellings (owned), expenditures	year	2566	91	81r
Enclose porch/patio/breezeway		4,556	3/95	74r
Exterior remodeling, average cost	remod	15395.00	3/95	13r
Family room addition, average cost	add	27658.00	3/95	13r
Finish room in basement/attic		5,074	3/95	74r
Home, existing, single-family, median	unit	106500	12/94	62r
Kitchen remodeling, major, average cost	remod	17084.00	3/95	13r
Kitchen remodeling, minor, average cost	remod	5804.00	3/95	13r
Maintenance, repairs, insurance, and other housing expenditures	year	484	91	81r
Mortgage interest and charges expenditures	year	1443	91	81r
Office, home addition, average cost	add	8121.00	3/95	13r
Princ. & int., mortgage, median-price exist. sing.-family home	mo.	515	12/94	62r
Property taxes expenditures	year	639	91	81r
Redesign, restructure more than half of home's interior		9,114	3/95	74r
Rental units expenditures	year	1200	91	81r
Sun-space addition, average cost	add	23768.00	3/95	13r
Wing addition, two-story, average cost	add	50410.00	3/95	13r
Insurance and Pensions				
Auto insurance, private passenger	year	554.10	12/94	71s
Insurance and pensions, personal, expenditures	year	2408	91	81r
Insurance, life and other personal, expenditures	year	355	91	81r
Pensions and Social Security, expenditures	year	2053	91	81r
Legal Assistance				
Legal work, law firm associate	hour	90		10r
Legal work, law firm partner	hour	139		10r
Personal Services				
Personal services expenditures	year	203	91	81r
Restaurant Food				
Dining expenditures, family	week	30.03	94	73r
Taxes				
Taxes, Federal income, expenditures	year	1756	91	81r
Taxes, personal, expenditures	year	2426	91	81r
Taxes, State and local income, expenditures	year	568	91	81r
Transportation				
Cars and trucks purchased, new	year	891	91	81r
Cars and trucks purchased, used	year	1155	91	81r
Driver's learning permit fee	perm	20.00	1/94	84s
Driver's license fee	orig	10.00	1/94	84s
Driver's license fee, duplicate	lic	4.00	1/94	84s
Driver's license reinstatement fee, min.	susp	50.00	1/94	85s
Driver's license renewal fee	renew	10.00	1/94	84s
Identification card, nondriver	card	4.00	1/94	83s
Motorcycle license fee	orig	4.00	1/94	84s
Motorcycle license fee, duplicate	lic	4.00	1/94	84s
Motorcycle license renewal fee	renew	4.00	1/94	84s
Public transportation expenditures	year	209	91	81r
Transportation expenditures, total	year	4792	91	81r
Vehicle finance charges	year	300	91	81r
Vehicle insurance expenditures	year	485	91	81r
Vehicle maintenance and repairs expenditures	year	534	91	81r
Vehicle purchases	year	2068	91	81r
Vehicle rental, leases, licenses, etc. expenditures	year	197	91	81r
Vehicles purchased, other than cars and trucks	year	22	91	81r

Kenosha, WI - continued

Item	Per	Value	Date	Ref.
Utilities				
Electricity expenditures	year	668	91	81r
Utilities, fuels, and public services, total expenditures	year	1838	91	81r
Water and other public services, expenditures	year	167	91	81r
Weddings				
Bridal attendants' gowns	event	750	10/93	76r
Bridal gown	event	852	10/93	76r
Bridal headpiece and veil	event	167	10/93	76r
Bride's wedding band	event	708	10/93	76r
Clergy	event	224	10/93	76r
Engagement ring	event	2756	10/93	76r
Flowers	event	863	10/93	76r
Formal wear for groom	event	106	10/93	76r
Groom's attendants' formal wear	event	530	10/93	76r
Groom's wedding band	event	402	10/93	76r
Music	event	600	10/93	76r
Photography	event	1088	10/93	76r
Shoes for bride	event	50	10/93	76r
Videography	event	483	10/93	76r
Wedding invitations and announcements	event	342	10/93	76r
Wedding reception	event	7000	10/93	76r

Killeen-Harker Heights, TX

Item	Per	Value	Date	Ref.
Composite, ACCRA index		94.00	12/94	2c
Alcoholic Beverages				
Beer, Miller Lite, Bud, 12-oz., ex deposit	6	3.68	12/94	2c
J & B Scotch	750-ml.	19.75	12/94	2c
Wine, Gallo Chablis blanc	1.5-lit	5.59	12/94	2c
Appliances				
Appliances (major), expenditures	year	153	91	81r
Average annual exp.				
Food, health care, personal goods, services	year	27020	91	81r
Charity				
Cash contributions, expenditures	year	839	91	81r
Clothing				
Apparel, men and boys, total expenditures	year	380	91	81r
Apparel, women and girls, total expenditures	year	660	91	81r
Footwear, expenditures	year	193	91	81r
Jeans, man's denim		28.25	12/94	2c
Shirt, man's dress shirt		30.00	12/94	2c
Undervest, boy's size 10-14, cotton	3	4.78	12/94	2c
Communications				
Long-distance telephone rate, day, addl. min., 1-10 mi.	min.	0.08	12/93	9s
Long-distance telephone rate, day, initial min., 1-10 mi.	min.	0.10	12/93	9s
Newspaper subscription, dly. and Sun. delivery	month	8.00	12/94	2c
Phone line, single, business, field visit	inst	71.90	12/93	9s
Phone line, single, business, no field visit	inst	57.30	12/93	9s
Phone line, single, residence, field visit	inst	52.95	12/93	9s
Phone line, single, residence, no field visit	inst	38.35	12/93	9s
Telephone bill, family of four	month	18.25	12/94	2c
Telephone service, expenditures	year	616	91	81r
Education				
Board, 4-year private college/university	year	2084	8/94	80s
Board, 4-year public college/university	year	1675	8/94	80s
Education, total expenditures	year	319	91	81r
Room, 4-year private college/university	year	1840	8/94	80s
Room, 4-year public college/university	year	1756	8/94	80s
Total cost, 4-year private college/university	year	11876	8/94	80s
Total cost, 4-year public college/university	year	4935	8/94	80s
Tuition, 2-year public college/university, in-state	year	625	8/94	80s

Values are in dollars or fractions of dollars. In the column headed *Ref*, references are shown to sources. Each reference is followed by a letter. These refer to the geographical level for which data were reported: s=State, r=Region, and c=City or metro. The abbreviation *ex* is used to mean *except* or *excluding*; *exp* stands for expenditures. For other abbreviations and further explanations, please see the Introduction.

Killeen-Harker Heights, TX - continued

Item	Per	Value	Date	Ref.
Education				
Tuition, 4-year private college/university, in-state	year	7952	8/94	80s
Tuition, 4-year public college/university, in-state	year	1503	8/94	80s
Energy and Fuels				
Energy, combined forms, 1800 sq. ft.	mo.	123.30	12/94	2c
Energy, exc. electricity, 1800 sq. ft.	mo.	25.43	12/94	2c
Fuel oil and other fuels, expenditures	year	56	91	81r
Gas, natural, expenditures	year	150	91	81r
Gas, reg unlead, taxes inc., cash, self-service	gal	1.08	12/94	2c
Gasoline and motor oil purchased	year	1152	91	81r
Gasoline, unleaded midgrade	gallon	1.21	4/93	82r
Gasoline, unleaded premium	gallon	1.30	4/93	82r
Gasoline, unleaded regular	gallon	1.10	4/93	82r
Entertainment				
Bowling, evening rate	game	2.23	12/94	2c
Concert ticket, Pearl Jam group	perf	20.00	94	50r
Entertainment, total expenditures	year	1266	91	81r
Fees and admissions, expenditures	year	306	91	81r
Monopoly game, Parker Brothers', No. 9	game	11.42	12/94	2c
Movie	adm	5.33	12/94	2c
Pets, toys, playground equipment, expenditures	year	271	91	81r
Reading, expenditures	year	131	91	81r
Televisions, radios, and sound equipment, expenditures	year	439	91	81r
Tennis balls, yellow, Wilson or Penn, 3	can	1.94	12/94	2c
Funerals				
Burial, immediate, container provided by funeral home		1574.60	1/95	54r
Cards, acknowledgment		22.24	1/95	54r
Casket, minimum alternative		239.41	1/95	54r
Cosmetology, hair care, etc.		91.04	1/95	54r
Cremation, direct, container provided by funeral home		1085.15	1/95	54r
Embalming		281.30	1/95	54r
Funeral, funeral home		323.04	1/95	54r
Funeral, other facility		327.58	1/95	54r
Graveside service		355.19	1/95	54r
Hearse, local		141.89	1/95	54r
Limousine, local		99.40	1/95	54r
Memorial service		284.67	1/95	54r
Service charge, professional, nondeclinable		904.06	1/95	54r
Visitation and viewing		187.04	1/95	54r
Groceries				
Groceries, ACCRA Index		95.30	12/94	2c
Apples, Red Delicious	lb.	0.73	12/94	82r
Baby food, strained vegetables, lowest price	4-4.5 oz.	0.27	12/94	2c
Bacon, sliced	lb.	1.67	12/94	82r
Bananas	lb.	0.38	12/94	2c
Bananas	lb.	0.42	12/94	82r
Beef or hamburger, ground	lb.	1.77	12/94	2c
Beef purchases	year	213	91	81r
Beverage purchases, alcoholic	year	249	91	81r
Beverage purchases, nonalcoholic	year	207	91	81r
Bologna, all beef or mixed	lb.	2.27	12/94	82r
Bread, white	24-oz.	0.69	12/94	2c
Bread, white, pan	lb.	0.68	12/94	82r
Cabbage	lb.	0.42	12/94	82r
Carrots, short trimmed and topped	lb.	0.53	12/94	82r
Cereals and bakery products purchases	year	345	91	81r
Cereals and cereals products purchases	year	127	91	81r
Cheddar cheese, natural	lb.	3.58	12/94	82r
Cheese, Kraft grated Parmesan	8-oz.	3.22	12/94	2c
Chicken breast, bone-in	lb.	1.71	12/94	82r
Chicken, fresh, whole	lb.	0.78	12/94	82r
Chicken, whole fryer	lb.	0.73	12/94	2c
Chuck roast, USDA choice, boneless	lb.	2.26	12/94	82r

Killeen-Harker Heights, TX - continued

Item	Per	Value	Date	Ref.
Groceries - continued				
Cigarettes, Winston, Kings	carton	16.14	12/94	2c
Coffee, vacuum-packed	13 oz.	3.55	12/94	2c
Corn Flakes, Kellogg's or Post Toasties	18 oz.	2.15	12/94	2c
Corn, frozen, whole kernel, lowest price	10 oz.	0.71	12/94	2c
Crackers, soda, salted	lb.	1.27	12/94	82r
Cucumbers	lb.	0.65	12/94	82r
Dairy products (other) purchases	year	141	91	81r
Eggs, Grade A large	dozen	0.71	12/94	2c
Eggs, Grade A large	dozen	0.87	12/94	82r
Fish and seafood purchases	year	72	91	81r
Flour, white, all purpose	lb.	0.23	12/94	82r
Food purchases, food eaten at home	year	2381	91	81r
Foods purchased away from home, not prepared by consumer	year	1696	91	81r
Frankfurters, all meat or all beef	lb.	1.74	12/94	82r
Fruits and vegetables purchases	year	380	91	81r
Grapefruit	lb.	0.45	12/94	82r
Grapes, Thompson seedless	lb.	2.30	12/94	82r
Ground beef, 100% beef	lb.	1.37	12/94	82r
Ground chuck, 100% beef	lb.	1.97	12/94	82r
Ham, boneless, exc. canned	lb.	2.54	12/94	82r
Ice cream, prepackaged, bulk, regular	1/2 gal.	2.47	12/94	82r
Lemons	lb.	1.02	12/94	82r
Lettuce, iceberg	lb.	0.96	12/94	82r
Lettuce, iceberg	head	0.97	12/94	2c
Margarine, Blue Bonnet or Parkay cubes	lb.	0.57	12/94	2c
Margarine, stick	lb.	0.77	12/94	82r
Meats, poultry, fish, and eggs purchases	year	655	91	81r
Milk and cream (fresh) purchases	year	130	91	81r
Milk, whole	1/2 gal.	1.39	12/94	2c
Orange juice, frozen concentrate 12-oz. can	16 oz.	1.36	12/94	82r
Orange juice, Minute Maid frozen	12-oz.	1.16	12/94	2c
Oranges, Navel	lb.	0.54	12/94	82r
Peaches, halves or slices, Hunt's, Del Monte, or Libby's	29-oz.	1.35	12/94	2c
Pears, Anjou	lb.	0.81	12/94	82r
Peas, sweet, Del Monte or Green Giant	15-17 oz.	0.47	12/94	2c
Pork chops, center cut, bone-in	lb.	3.07	12/94	82r
Pork purchases	year	142	91	81r
Potato chips	16-oz.	3.15	12/94	82r
Potatoes, frozen, French fried	lb.	0.82	12/94	82r
Potatoes, white	lb.	0.34	12/94	82r
Potatoes, white or red	10-lb. sack	2.74	12/94	2c
Rice, white, long grain, uncooked	lb.	0.48	12/94	82r
Round roast, USDA choice, boneless	lb.	2.91	12/94	82r
Sausage, fresh	lb.	1.82	12/94	82r
Sausage, Jimmy Dean, 100% pork	lb.	2.35	12/94	2c
Shortening, vegetable oil blends	lb.	0.75	12/94	82r
Shortening, vegetable, Crisco	3-lb.	2.28	12/94	2c
Soft drink, Coca Cola, ex deposit	2 lit	1.11	12/94	2c
Spaghetti and macaroni	lb.	0.87	12/94	82r
Steak, rib eye, USDA choice, boneless	lb.	6.85	12/94	82r
Steak, round, graded & ungraded, exc. USDA prime & choice	lb.	2.96	12/94	82r
Steak, round, USDA choice, boneless	lb.	3.17	12/94	82r
Steak, sirloin, USDA choice, boneless	lb.	4.12	12/94	82r
Steak, t-bone	lb.	4.56	12/94	2c
Steak, T-bone, USDA choice, bone-in	lb.	5.63	12/94	82r
Sugar and other sweets, eaten at home, expenditures	year	93	91	81r
Sugar, cane or beet	4 lbs.	1.48	12/94	2c
Sugar, white, all sizes	lb.	0.39	12/94	82r
Tobacco products and smoking supplies, total expenditures	year	286	91	81r
Tomatoes, field grown	lb.	1.36	12/94	82r
Tomatoes, Hunt's or Del Monte	14.5 oz.	0.63	12/94	2c
Tuna, chunk, light	lb.	1.94	12/94	82r

Values are in dollars or fractions of dollars. In the column headed *Ref*, references are shown to sources. Each reference is followed by a letter. These refer to the geographical level for which data were reported: s=State, r=Region, and c=City or metro. The abbreviation *ex* is used to mean *except* or *excluding*; *exp* stands for *expenditures*. For other abbreviations and further explanations, please see the Introduction.

Killeen-Harker Heights, TX - continued

Item	Per	Value	Date	Ref.
Groceries				
Tuna, chunk, light, oil-packed	6.125-6.5 oz.	0.65	12/94	2c
Turkey, frozen, whole	lb.	0.96	12/94	82r
Yogurt, natural, fruit flavored	8 oz.	0.58	12/94	82r
Goods and Services				
Miscellaneous goods and services, ACCRA Index		96.50	12/94	2c
Health Care				
Health care, ACCRA Index		88.60	12/94	2c
Adenosine, emergency room	treat	100.00	95	23r
Antibiotic ointment, Polysporin	1.5 oz.	3.99	12/94	2c
Bladder tap, superpubic, infant, emergency room	treat	119.00	95	23r
Blood analysis, emergency room	treat	25.00	95	23r
Blood tests, abdominal pain, emergency room	treat	25.00	95	23r
Burn dressing, emergency room	treat	266.00	95	23r
Cardiology interpretation, emergency room	treat	26.00	95	23r
Chest X-ray, emergency room	treat	78.00	95	23r
Childbirth, Cesarean delivery, hospital charge	birth	5462.00	12/91	69r
Childbirth, Cesarean delivery, physician charge	birth	2228.00	12/91	69r
Childbirth, normal delivery, hospital charge	birth	2943.00	12/91	69r
Childbirth, normal delivery, physician charge	birth	1619.00	12/91	69r
Defibrillation pads, emergency room	treat	6.00	95	23r
Dentist's fee, adult teeth cleaning and periodic oral exam	visit	43.40	12/94	2c
Doctor's fee, routine exam, established patient	visit	36.80	12/94	2c
Drugs, expenditures	year	297	91	81r
Gastric tube insertion, nasal, emergency room	treat	25.00	95	23r
Health care, total expenditures	year	1600	91	81r
Health insurance expenditures	year	637	91	81r
Heart monitor, emergency room	treat	40.00	95	23r
Hospital care, semiprivate room	day	344.00	12/94	2c
Insurance premium, family medical care	month	389.25	1/95	41s
Intravenous fluids, emergency room	treat	130.00	95	23r
Intravenous fluids, emergency room	liter	26.00	95	23r
Intravenous line, central, emergency room	treat	342.00	95	23r
Liver function tests, abdominal pain, emergency room	treat	26.00	95	23r
Medical care charges, total, emergency room, third-degree burns	treat	2101.00	95	23r
Medical care charges, total, emergency, infant with fever	treat	628.00	95	23r
Medical services expenditures	year	573	91	81r
Medical supplies expenditures	year	93	91	81r
Morphine, emergency room	treat	34.00	95	23r
Nursing care and facilities charges, emergency room	treat	252.00	95	23r
Nursing care and facilities charges, emergency, infant with fever	treat	252.00	95	23r
Nursing care and facilities charges, emergency, third-degree burns	treat	861.00	95	23r
Physician's charges, emergency, infant with fever	treat	212.00	95	23r
Physician's charges, emergency, third-degree burns	treat	372.00	95	23r
Physician's fee, emergency room	treat	372.00	95	23r
Physician's fee, general practitioner	visit	51.20	12/93	60r
Surgery, open-heart	proc	42374.00	1/93	14r
Ultrasound, abdominal, emergency room	treat	276.00	95	23r
Urinalysis, emergency room	treat	20.00	95	23r
Urinalysis, infant, emergency room	treat	20.00	95	23r
X-rays, emergency room	treat	78.00	95	23r
Household Goods				
Appl. repair, service call, wash mach	min. lab. chg.	32.50	12/94	2c

Killeen-Harker Heights, TX - continued

Item	Per	Value	Date	Ref.
Household Goods - continued				
Floor coverings, expenditures	year	48	91	81r
Furniture, expenditures	year	280	91	81r
Household equipment, misc. expenditures	year	342	91	81r
Household expenditures, miscellaneous	year	256	91	81r
Household furnishings and equipment, expenditures	year	988	91	81r
Household operations expenditures	year	468	91	81r
Household textiles, expenditures	year	95	91	81r
Housekeeping supplies, expenditures	year	380	91	81r
Laundry and cleaning supplies, expenditures	year	109	91	81r
Laundry detergent, Tide Ultra, Bold, or Cheer	42 oz.	2.96	12/94	2c
Postage and stationery, expenditures	year	105	91	81r
Tissues, facial, Kleenex brand	175	1.03	12/94	2c
Housing				
Housing, ACCRA Index		87.90	12/94	2c
Add garage/carport		6,980	3/95	74r
Add room(s)		11,403	3/95	74r
Apartment condominium or co-op, median	unit	68600	12/94	62r
Dwellings (owned), expenditures	year	2428	91	81r
Enclose porch/patio/breezeway		4,572	3/95	74r
Finish room in basement/attic		3,794	3/95	74r
Home, existing, single-family, median	unit	120200	12/94	62r
House payment, principal and interest, 25% down payment	mo.	628	12/94	2c
House, 1800 sq ft, 8000 sq ft lot, new, urban, utilities	total	99881	12/94	2c
Maintenance, repairs, insurance, and other housing expenditures	year	531	91	81r
Mortgage interest and charges expenditures	year	1506	91	81r
Mtge. rate, incl. points and orig. fee, 30-year conv. fixed or ARM	mo.	9.47	12/94	2c
Princ. & int., mortgage, median-price exist. sing.-family home	mo.	540	12/94	62r
Property taxes expenditures	year	391	91	81r
Redesign, restructure more than half of home's interior		17,641	3/95	74r
Rent, apartment, 2 br., 1 1/2-2 baths, unfurnished, 950 sq ft, water	mo.	594	12/94	2c
Rental units expenditures	year	1264	91	81r
Insurance and Pensions				
Auto insurance, private passenger	year	785.78	12/94	71s
Insurance and pensions, personal, expenditures	year	2395	91	81r
Insurance, life and other personal, expenditures	year	368	91	81r
Pensions and Social Security, expenditures	year	2027	91	81r
Personal Goods				
Shampoo, Alberto VO5	15-oz.	0.99	12/94	2c
Toothpaste, Crest or Colgate	6-7 oz.	1.70	12/94	2c
Personal Services				
Dry cleaning, man's 2-pc. suit		5.15	12/94	2c
Haircut, man's barbershop, no styling		8.79	12/94	2c
Haircut, woman's shampoo, trim, blow-dry		16.79	12/94	2c
Personal services expenditures	year	212	91	81r
Restaurant Food				
Chicken, fried, thigh and drumstick		2.18	12/94	2c
Dining expenditures, family	week	33.83	94	73r
Hamburger with cheese	1/4 lb.	1.89	12/94	2c
Pizza, Pizza Hut or Pizza Inn	12-13 in.	7.99	12/94	2c
Taxes				
Tax, cigarettes	year	584.00	10/93	43s
Taxes, Federal income, expenditures	year	2275	91	81r
Taxes, personal, expenditures	year	2715	91	81r
Taxes, State and local income, expenditures	year	365	91	81r

Values are in dollars or fractions of dollars. In the column headed *Ref*, references are shown to sources. Each reference is followed by a letter. These refer to the geographical level for which data were reported: s=State, r=Region, and c=City or metro. The abbreviation *ex* is used to mean *except* or *excluding*; *exp* stands for *expenditures*. For other abbreviations and further explanations, please see the Introduction.

Killeen-Harker Heights, TX - continued

Item	Per	Value	Date	Ref.
Transportation				
Transportation, ACCRA Index		92.40	12/94	2c
Cars and trucks purchased, new	year	1306	91	81r
Cars and trucks purchased, used	year	942	91	81r
Driver's learning permit fee	perm	5.00	1/94	84s
Driver's license fee	orig	16.00	1/94	84s
Driver's license fee, duplicate	lic	10.00	1/94	84s
Driver's license reinstatement fee, min.	susp	50.00	1/94	85s
Driver's license renewal fee	renew	16.00	1/94	84s
Identification card, nondriver	card	10.00	1/94	83s
Motorcycle learning permit fee	perm	5.00	1/94	84s
Motorcycle license fee	orig	16.00	1/94	84s
Motorcycle license fee, duplicate	lic	10.00	1/94	84s
Motorcycle license renewal fee	renew	21.00	1/94	84s
Public transportation expenditures	year	249	91	81r
Tire balance, computer or spin bal., front	wheel	5.89	12/94	2c
Transportation expenditures, total	year	5307	91	81r
Vehicle finance charges	year	346	91	81r
Vehicle insurance expenditures	year	544	91	81r
Vehicle maintenance and repairs expenditures	year	600	91	81r
Vehicle purchases	year	2275	91	81r
Vehicle rental, leases, licenses, etc. expenditures	year	141	91	81r
Vehicles purchased, other than cars and trucks	year	27	91	81r
Utilities				
Utilities, ACCRA Index		107.70	12/94	2c
Electricity expenditures	year	950	91	81r
Electricity, (part.), other, 1800 sq. ft., new home	mo.	97.87	12/94	2c
Utilities, fuels, and public services, total expenditures	year	2000	91	81r
Water and other public services, expenditures	year	227	91	81r
Weddings				
Bridal attendants' gowns	event	750	10/93	76r
Bridal gown	event	852	10/93	76r
Bridal headpiece and veil	event	167	10/93	76r
Bride's wedding band	event	708	10/93	76r
Clergy	event	224	10/93	76r
Engagement ring	event	2756	10/93	76r
Flowers	event	863	10/93	76r
Formal wear for groom	event	106	10/93	76r
Groom's attendants' formal wear	event	530	10/93	76r
Groom's wedding band	event	402	10/93	76r
Music	event	600	10/93	76r
Photography	event	1088	10/93	76r
Shoes for bride	event	50	10/93	76r
Videography	event	483	10/93	76r
Wedding invitations and announcements	event	342	10/93	76r
Wedding reception	event	7000	10/93	76r

Kingsport, TN

Item	Per	Value	Date	Ref.
Composite, ACCRA index		94.50	12/94	2c
Alcoholic Beverages				
Beer, Miller Lite, Bud, 12-oz., ex deposit	6	3.92	12/94	2c
J & B Scotch	750-ml.	19.86	12/94	2c
Wine, Gallo Chablis blanc	1.5-lit	6.72	12/94	2c
Clothing				
Jeans, man's denim		32.29	12/94	2c
Shirt, man's dress shirt		34.33	12/94	2c
Undervest, boy's size 10-14, cotton	3	6.31	12/94	2c
Communications				
Newspaper subscription, dly. and Sun. delivery	month	9.95	12/94	2c
Telephone bill, family of four	month	19.61	12/94	2c

Item	Per	Value	Date	Ref.
Energy and Fuels				
Energy, combined forms, 1800 sq. ft.	mo.	83.99	12/94	2c
Gas, reg unlead, taxes inc., cash, self-service	gal	1.00	12/94	2c
Entertainment				
Bowling, evening rate	game	1.72	12/94	2c
Monopoly game, Parker Brothers', No. 9	game	9.85	12/94	2c
Movie	adm	5.50	12/94	2c
Tennis balls, yellow, Wilson or Penn, 3	can	2.88	12/94	2c
Groceries				
Groceries, ACCRA Index		96.40	12/94	2c
Baby food, strained vegetables, lowest price	4-4.5 oz.	0.38	12/94	2c
Bananas	lb.	0.52	12/94	2c
Beef or hamburger, ground	lb.	1.48	12/94	2c
Bread, white	24-oz.	0.75	12/94	2c
Cheese, Kraft grated Parmesan	8-oz.	3.24	12/94	2c
Chicken, whole fryer	lb.	0.90	12/94	2c
Cigarettes, Winston, Kings	carton	14.00	12/94	2c
Coffee, vacuum-packed	13 oz.	3.29	12/94	2c
Corn Flakes, Kellogg's or Post Toasties	18 oz.	2.02	12/94	2c
Corn, frozen, whole kernel, lowest price	10 oz.	0.64	12/94	2c
Eggs, Grade A large	dozen	0.76	12/94	2c
Lettuce, iceberg	head	0.99	12/94	2c
Margarine, Blue Bonnet or Parkay cubes	lb.	0.53	12/94	2c
Milk, whole	1/2 gal.	1.30	12/94	2c
Orange juice, Minute Maid frozen	12-oz.	0.99	12/94	2c
Peaches, halves or slices, Hunt's, Del Monte, or Libby's	29-oz.	1.29	12/94	2c
Peas, sweet, Del Monte or Green Giant	15-17 oz.	0.47	12/94	2c
Potatoes, white or red	10-lb. sack	2.51	12/94	2c
Sausage, Jimmy Dean, 100% pork	lb.	2.34	12/94	2c
Shortening, vegetable, Crisco	3-lb.	2.42	12/94	2c
Soft drink, Coca Cola, ex deposit	2 lit	1.02	12/94	2c
Steak, t-bone	lb.	5.42	12/94	2c
Sugar, cane or beet	4 lbs.	1.42	12/94	2c
Tomatoes, Hunt's or Del Monte	14.5 oz.	0.56	12/94	2c
Tuna, chunk, light, oil-packed	6.125-6.5 oz.	0.64	12/94	2c
Goods and Services				
Miscellaneous goods and services, ACCRA Index		100.60	12/94	2c
Health Care				
Health care, ACCRA Index		84.50	12/94	2c
Antibiotic ointment, Polysporin	1.5 oz.	3.74	12/94	2c
Dentist's fee, adult teeth cleaning and periodic oral exam	visit	39.25	12/94	2c
Doctor's fee, routine exam, established patient	visit	40.00	12/94	2c
Hospital care, semiprivate room	day	276.50	12/94	2c
Household Goods				
Appl. repair, service call, wash mach	min. lab. chg.	31.13	12/94	2c
Laundry detergent, Tide Ultra, Bold, or Cheer	42 oz.	2.62	12/94	2c
Tissues, facial, Kleenex brand	175	0.99	12/94	2c
Housing				
Housing, ACCRA Index		91.80	12/94	2c
House payment, principal and interest, 25% down payment	mo.	722	12/94	2c
House, 1800 sq ft, 8000 sq ft lot, new, urban, utilities	total	118021	12/94	2c
Mtge. rate, incl. points and orig. fee, 30-year conv. fixed or ARM	mo.	9.16	12/94	2c

Values are in dollars or fractions of dollars. In the column headed *Ref*, references are shown to sources. Each reference is followed by a letter. These refer to the geographical level for which data were reported: s=State, r=Region, and c=City or metro. The abbreviation *ex* is used to mean *except* or *excluding*; *exp* stands for *expenditures*. For other abbreviations and further explanations, please see the Introduction.

Kingsport, TN - continued

Item	Per	Value	Date	Ref.
Housing				
Rent, apartment, 2 br., 1 1/2-2 baths, unfurnished, 950 sq ft, water	mo.	430	12/94	2c
Personal Goods				
Shampoo, Alberto VO5	15-oz.	1.12	12/94	2c
Toothpaste, Crest or Colgate	6-7 oz.	2.05	12/94	2c
Personal Services				
Dry cleaning, man's 2-pc. suit		5.58	12/94	2c
Haircut, man's barbershop, no styling		6.00	12/94	2c
Haircut, woman's shampoo, trim, blow-dry		19.50	12/94	2c
Restaurant Food				
Chicken, fried, thigh and drumstick		1.60	12/94	2c
Hamburger with cheese	1/4 lb.	1.79	12/94	2c
Pizza, Pizza Hut or Pizza Inn	12-13 in.	7.87	12/94	2c
Transportation				
Transportation, ACCRA Index		98.40	12/94	2c
Tire balance, computer or spin bal., front	wheel	7.57	12/94	2c
Utilities				
Utilities, ACCRA Index		78.30	12/94	2c
Electricity, 1800 sq. ft., new home	mo.	83.99	12/94	2c
Electricity, summer, 250 KWh	month	18.96	8/93	64c
Electricity, summer, 500 KWh	month	30.72	8/93	64c
Electricity, summer, 750 KWh	month	42.49	8/93	64c
Electricity, summer, 1000 KWh	month	54.26	8/93	64c

Kirksville, MO

Item	Per	Value	Date	Ref.
Composite, ACCRA index		97.40	12/94	2c
Alcoholic Beverages				
Beer, Miller Lite, Bud, 12-oz., ex deposit	6	3.69	12/94	2c
J & B Scotch	750-ml.	16.33	12/94	2c
Wine, Gallo Chablis blanc	1.5-lit	4.80	12/94	2c
Clothing				
Jeans, man's denim		31.95	12/94	2c
Shirt, man's dress shirt		34.25	12/94	2c
Undervest, boy's size 10-14, cotton	3	3.93	12/94	2c
Communications				
Newspaper subscription, dly. and Sun. delivery	month	17.83	12/94	2c
Telephone bill, family of four	month	15.43	12/94	2c
Telephone, residential, flat rate	mo.	9.10	12/93	8c
Energy and Fuels				
Energy, combined forms, 1800 sq. ft.	mo.	109.06	12/94	2c
Energy, exc. electricity, 1800 sq. ft.	mo.	44.14	12/94	2c
Gas, cooking, 10 therms	month	11.95	2/94	65c
Gas, cooking, 30 therms	month	21.84	2/94	65c
Gas, cooking, 50 therms	month	31.74	2/94	65c
Gas, heating, winter, 100 therms	month	56.48	2/94	65c
Gas, heating, winter, average use	month	84.69	2/94	65c
Gas, reg unlead, taxes inc., cash, self-service	gal	1.10	12/94	2c
Entertainment				
Bowling, evening rate	game	1.90	12/94	2c
Monopoly game, Parker Brothers', No. 9	game	10.74	12/94	2c
Movie	adm	4.50	12/94	2c
Tennis balls, yellow, Wilson or Penn, 3	can	2.14	12/94	2c
Groceries				
Groceries, ACCRA Index		91.50	12/94	2c
Baby food, strained vegetables, lowest price	4-4.5 oz.	0.31	12/94	2c
Bananas	lb.	0.39	12/94	2c
Beef or hamburger, ground	lb.	1.05	12/94	2c
Bread, white	24-oz.	0.63	12/94	2c
Cheese, Kraft grated Parmesan	8-oz.	3.35	12/94	2c
Chicken, whole fryer	lb.	0.68	12/94	2c

Kirksville, MO - continued

Item	Per	Value	Date	Ref.
Groceries - continued				
Cigarettes, Winston, Kings	carton	14.48	12/94	2c
Coffee, vacuum-packed	13 oz.	3.30	12/94	2c
Corn Flakes, Kellogg's or Post Toasties	18 oz.	1.93	12/94	2c
Corn, frozen, whole kernel, lowest price	10 oz.	0.63	12/94	2c
Eggs, Grade A large	dozen	0.67	12/94	2c
Lettuce, iceberg	head	0.71	12/94	2c
Margarine, Blue Bonnet or Parkay cubes	lb.	0.55	12/94	2c
Milk, whole	1/2 gal.	1.23	12/94	2c
Orange juice, Minute Maid frozen	12-oz.	1.13	12/94	2c
Peaches, halves or slices, Hunt's, Del Monte, or Libby's	29-oz.	1.33	12/94	2c
Peas, sweet, Del Monte or Green Giant	15-17 oz.	0.49	12/94	2c
Potatoes, white or red	10-lb. sack	1.95	12/94	2c
Sausage, Jimmy Dean, 100% pork	lb.	2.66	12/94	2c
Shortening, vegetable, Crisco	3-lb.	2.52	12/94	2c
Soft drink, Coca Cola, ex deposit	2 lit	1.12	12/94	2c
Steak, t-bone	lb.	5.15	12/94	2c
Sugar, cane or beet	4 lbs.	1.50	12/94	2c
Tomatoes, Hunt's or Del Monte	14.5 oz.	0.71	12/94	2c
Tuna, chunk, light, oil-packed	6.125-6.5 oz.	0.72	12/94	2c
Goods and Services				
Miscellaneous goods and services, ACCRA Index		100.50	12/94	2c
Health Care				
Health care, ACCRA Index		87.60	12/94	2c
Antibiotic ointment, Polysporin	1.5 oz.	3.84	12/94	2c
Dentist's fee, adult teeth cleaning and periodic oral exam	visit	49.75	12/94	2c
Doctor's fee, routine exam, established patient	visit	30.50	12/94	2c
Hospital care, semiprivate room	day	355.00	12/94	2c
Household Goods				
Appl. repair, service call, wash mach	min. lab. chg.	31.17	12/94	2c
Laundry detergent, Tide Ultra, Bold, or Cheer	42 oz.	3.78	12/94	2c
Tissues, facial, Kleenex brand	175	0.89	12/94	2c
Housing				
Housing, ACCRA Index		103.00	12/94	2c
House payment, principal and interest, 25% down payment	mo.	832	12/94	2c
House, 1800 sq ft, 8000 sq ft lot, new, urban, utilities	total	131667	12/94	2c
Mtge. rate, incl. points and orig. fee, 30-year conv. fixed or ARM	mo.	9.53	12/94	2c
Rent, apartment, 2 br., 1 1/2-2 baths, unfurnished, 950 sq ft, water	mo.	420	12/94	2c
Personal Goods				
Shampoo, Alberto VO5	15-oz.	1.18	12/94	2c
Toothpaste, Crest or Colgate	6-7 oz.	1.28	12/94	2c
Personal Services				
Dry cleaning, man's 2-pc. suit		5.40	12/94	2c
Haircut, man's barbershop, no styling		5.67	12/94	2c
Haircut, woman's shampoo, trim, blow-dry		16.67	12/94	2c
Restaurant Food				
Chicken, fried, thigh and drumstick		2.58	12/94	2c
Hamburger with cheese	1/4 lb.	1.89	12/94	2c
Pizza, Pizza Hut or Pizza Inn	12-13 in.	7.79	12/94	2c
Transportation				
Transportation, ACCRA Index		88.50	12/94	2c
Tire balance, computer or spin bal., front	wheel	5.13	12/94	2c

Values are in dollars or fractions of dollars. In the column headed *Ref*, references are shown to sources. Each reference is followed by a letter. These refer to the geographical level for which data were reported: s = State, r = Region, and c = City or metro. The abbreviation *ex* is used to mean *except* or *excluding*; *exp* stands for *expenditures*. For other abbreviations and further explanations, please see the Introduction.

Kirksville, MO - continued

Item	Per	Value	Date	Ref.
Utilities				
Utilities, ACCRA Index		94.70	12/94	2c
Electricity, (part.), other, 1800 sq. ft., new home	mo.	64.92	12/94	2c

Klamath Falls, OR

Item	Per	Value	Date	Ref.
Composite, ACCRA index		98.10	12/94	2c
Alcoholic Beverages				
Beer, Miller Lite, Bud, 12-oz., ex deposit	6	3.71	12/94	2c
J & B Scotch	750-ml.	20.95	12/94	2c
Wine, Gallo Chablis blanc	1.5-lit	4.22	12/94	2c
Clothing				
Jeans, man's denim		31.99	12/94	2c
Shirt, man's dress shirt		28.75	12/94	2c
Undervest, boy's size 10-14, cotton	3	4.19	12/94	2c
Communications				
Newspaper subscription, dly. and Sun. delivery	month	9.67	12/94	2c
Telephone bill, family of four	month	16.30	12/94	2c
Telephone, residential, flat rate	mo.	12.80	12/93	8c
Energy and Fuels				
Energy, combined forms, 1800 sq. ft.	mo.	82.83	12/94	2c
Gas, reg unlead, taxes inc., cash, self-service	gal	1.26	12/94	2c
Entertainment				
Bowling, evening rate	game	2.00	12/94	2c
Monopoly game, Parker Brothers', No. 9	game	9.22	12/94	2c
Movie	adm	5.00	12/94	2c
Tennis balls, yellow, Wilson or Penn, 3	can	2.12	12/94	2c
Groceries				
Groceries, ACCRA Index		94.30	12/94	2c
Baby food, strained vegetables, lowest price	4-4.5 oz.	0.24	12/94	2c
Bananas	lb.	0.44	12/94	2c
Beef or hamburger, ground	lb.	1.38	12/94	2c
Bread, white	24-oz.	0.57	12/94	2c
Cheese, Kraft grated Parmesan	8-oz.	3.59	12/94	2c
Chicken, whole fryer	lb.	0.83	12/94	2c
Cigarettes, Winston, Kings	carton	16.94	12/94	2c
Coffee, vacuum-packed	13 oz.	3.84	12/94	2c
Corn Flakes, Kellogg's or Post Toasties	18 oz.	1.97	12/94	2c
Corn, frozen, whole kernel, lowest price	10 oz.	0.68	12/94	2c
Eggs, Grade A large	dozen	0.88	12/94	2c
Lettuce, iceberg	head	0.76	12/94	2c
Margarine, Blue Bonnet or Parkay cubes	lb.	0.57	12/94	2c
Milk, whole	1/2 gal.	1.44	12/94	2c
Orange juice, Minute Maid frozen	12-oz.	1.05	12/94	2c
Peaches, halves or slices, Hunt's, Del Monte, or Libby's	29-oz.	1.74	12/94	2c
Peas, sweet, Del Monte or Green Giant	15-17 oz.	0.68	12/94	2c
Potatoes, white or red	10-lb. sack	1.37	12/94	2c
Sausage, Jimmy Dean, 100% pork	lb.	3.42	12/94	2c
Shortening, vegetable, Crisco	3-lb.	2.03	12/94	2c
Soft drink, Coca Cola, ex deposit	2 lit	1.21	12/94	2c
Steak, t-bone	lb.	3.87	12/94	2c
Sugar, cane or beet	4 lbs.	1.07	12/94	2c
Tomatoes, Hunt's or Del Monte	14.5 oz.	0.84	12/94	2c
Tuna, chunk, light, oil-packed	6.125-6.5 oz.	0.66	12/94	2c
Goods and Services				
Miscellaneous goods and services, ACCRA Index		99.60	12/94	2c

Klamath Falls, OR - continued

Item	Per	Value	Date	Ref.
Health Care				
Health care, ACCRA Index		121.10	12/94	2c
Antibiotic ointment, Polysporin	1.5 oz.	3.64	12/94	2c
Dentist's fee, adult teeth cleaning and periodic oral exam	visit	73.80	12/94	2c
Doctor's fee, routine exam, established patient	visit	47.12	12/94	2c
Hospital care, semiprivate room	day	430.00	12/94	2c
Household Goods				
Appl. repair, service call, wash mach	min. lab. chg.	35.00	12/94	2c
Laundry detergent, Tide Ultra, Bold, or Cheer	42 oz.	3.46	12/94	2c
Tissues, facial, Kleenex brand	175	1.08	12/94	2c
Housing				
Housing, ACCRA Index		97.20	12/94	2c
House payment, principal and interest, 25% down payment	mo.	748	12/94	2c
House, 1800 sq ft, 8000 sq ft lot, new, urban, utilities	total	122308	12/94	2c
Mtge. rate, incl. points and orig. fee, 30-year conv. fixed or ARM	mo.	9.15	12/94	2c
Rent, apartment, 2 br., 1 1/2-2 baths, unfurnished, 950 sq ft, water	mo.	505	12/94	2c
Personal Goods				
Shampoo, Alberto VO5	15-oz.	0.97	12/94	2c
Toothpaste, Crest or Colgate	6-7 oz.	1.71	12/94	2c
Personal Services				
Dry cleaning, man's 2-pc. suit		6.95	12/94	2c
Haircut, man's barbershop, no styling		7.25	12/94	2c
Haircut, woman's shampoo, trim, blow-dry		17.60	12/94	2c
Restaurant Food				
Chicken, fried, thigh and drumstick		2.69	12/94	2c
Hamburger with cheese	1/4 lb.	1.89	12/94	2c
Pizza, Pizza Hut or Pizza Inn	12-13 in.	8.75	12/94	2c
Transportation				
Transportation, ACCRA Index		107.60	12/94	2c
Bus fare, one-way	trip	0.70	12/95	1c
Tire balance, computer or spin bal., front	wheel	6.90	12/94	2c
Utilities				
Utilities, ACCRA Index		75.10	12/94	2c
Electricity, 1800 sq. ft., new home	mo.	82.83	12/94	2c

Knoxville, TN

Item	Per	Value	Date	Ref.
Appliances				
Appliances (major), expenditures	year	153	91	81r
Average annual exp.				
Food, health care, personal goods, services	year	27020	91	81r
Charity				
Cash contributions, expenditures	year	839	91	81r
Clothing				
Apparel, men and boys, total expenditures	year	380	91	81r
Apparel, women and girls, total expenditures	year	660	91	81r
Footwear, expenditures	year	193	91	81r
Communications				
Long-distance telephone rate, day, addl. min., 1-10 mi.	min.	0.10	12/93	9s
Long-distance telephone rate, day, initial min., 1-10 mi.	min.	0.10	12/93	9s
Phone line, single, business, field visit	inst	58.50	12/93	9s
Phone line, single, business, no field visit	inst	58.50	12/93	9s
Phone line, single, residence, field visit	inst	41.50	12/93	9s
Phone line, single, residence, no field visit	inst	41.50	12/93	9s

Values are in dollars or fractions of dollars. In the column headed *Ref*, references are shown to sources. Each reference is followed by a letter. These refer to the geographical level for which data were reported: s=State, r=Region, and c=City or metro. The abbreviation *ex* is used to mean *except* or *excluding*; *exp* stands for expenditures. For other abbreviations and further explanations, please see the Introduction.

Knoxville, TN - continued

Item	Per	Value	Date	Ref.
Communications				
Telephone service, expenditures	year	616	91	81r
Education				
Board, 4-year private college/university	year	1846	8/94	80s
Board, 4-year public college/university	year	1700	8/94	80s
Education, total expenditures	year	319	91	81r
Room, 4-year private college/university	year	1553	8/94	80s
Room, 4-year public college/university	year	1524	8/94	80s
Total cost, 4-year private college/university	year	12025	8/94	80s
Total cost, 4-year public college/university	year	5021	8/94	80s
Tuition, 2-year public college/university, in-state	year	950	8/94	80s
Tuition, 4-year private college/university, in-state	year	8627	8/94	80s
Tuition, 4-year public college/university, in-state	year	1797	8/94	80s
Energy and Fuels				
Fuel oil and other fuels, expenditures	year	56	91	81r
Gas, natural, expenditures	year	150	91	81r
Gasoline and motor oil purchased	year	1152	91	81r
Gasoline, unleaded midgrade	gallon	1.21	4/93	82r
Gasoline, unleaded premium	gallon	1.30	4/93	82r
Gasoline, unleaded regular	gallon	1.10	4/93	82r
Entertainment				
Concert ticket, Pearl Jam group	perf	20.00	94	50r
Entertainment, total expenditures	year	1266	91	81r
Fees and admissions, expenditures	year	306	91	81r
Pets, toys, playground equipment, expenditures	year	271	91	81r
Reading, expenditures	year	131	91	81r
Televisions, radios, and sound equipment, expenditures	year	439	91	81r
Funerals				
Burial, immediate, container provided by funeral home		1298.96	1/95	54r
Cards, acknowledgment		21.26	1/95	54r
Casket, minimum alternative		204.95	1/95	54r
Cosmetology, hair care, etc.		85.40	1/95	54r
Cremation, direct, container provided by funeral home		1054.77	1/95	54r
Embalming		287.71	1/95	54r
Funeral, funeral home		269.18	1/95	54r
Funeral, other facility		272.88	1/95	54r
Graveside service		302.54	1/95	54r
Hearse, local		122.08	1/95	54r
Limousine, local		80.31	1/95	54r
Memorial service		277.66	1/95	54r
Service charge, professional, nondeclinable		896.65	1/95	54r
Visitation and viewing		232.39	1/95	54r
Groceries				
Apples, Red Delicious	lb.	0.73	12/94	82r
Bacon, sliced	lb.	1.67	12/94	82r
Bananas	lb.	0.42	12/94	82r
Beef purchases	year	213	91	81r
Beverage purchases, alcoholic	year	249	91	81r
Beverage purchases, nonalcoholic	year	207	91	81r
Bologna, all beef or mixed	lb.	2.27	12/94	82r
Bread, white, pan	lb.	0.68	12/94	82r
Cabbage	lb.	0.42	12/94	82r
Carrots, short trimmed and topped	lb.	0.53	12/94	82r
Cereals and bakery products purchases	year	345	91	81r
Cereals and cereals products purchases	year	127	91	81r
Cheddar cheese, natural	lb.	3.58	12/94	82r
Chicken breast, bone-in	lb.	1.71	12/94	82r
Chicken, fresh, whole	lb.	0.78	12/94	82r
Chuck roast, USDA choice, boneless	lb.	2.26	12/94	82r
Crackers, soda, salted	lb.	1.27	12/94	82r
Cucumbers	lb.	0.65	12/94	82r
Dairy products (other) purchases	year	141	91	81r
Eggs, Grade A large	dozen	0.87	12/94	82r

Knoxville, TN - continued

Item	Per	Value	Date	Ref.
Groceries - continued				
Fish and seafood purchases	year	72	91	81r
Flour, white, all purpose	lb.	0.23	12/94	82r
Food purchases, food eaten at home	year	2381	91	81r
Foods purchased away from home, not prepared by consumer	year	1696	91	81r
Frankfurters, all meat or all beef	lb.	1.74	12/94	82r
Fruits and vegetables purchases	year	380	91	81r
Grapefruit	lb.	0.45	12/94	82r
Grapes, Thompson seedless	lb.	2.30	12/94	82r
Ground beef, 100% beef	lb.	1.37	12/94	82r
Ground chuck, 100% beef	lb.	1.97	12/94	82r
Ham, boneless, exc. canned	lb.	2.54	12/94	82r
Ice cream, prepackaged, bulk, regular	1/2 gal.	2.47	12/94	82r
Lemons	lb.	1.02	12/94	82r
Lettuce, iceberg	lb.	0.96	12/94	82r
Margarine, stick	lb.	0.77	12/94	82r
Meats, poultry, fish, and eggs purchases	year	655	91	81r
Milk and cream (fresh) purchases	year	130	91	81r
Orange juice, frozen concentrate 12-oz. can	16 oz.	1.36	12/94	82r
Oranges, Navel	lb.	0.54	12/94	82r
Pears, Anjou	lb.	0.81	12/94	82r
Pork chops, center cut, bone-in	lb.	3.07	12/94	82r
Pork purchases	year	142	91	81r
Potato chips	16-oz.	3.15	12/94	82r
Potatoes, frozen, French fried	lb.	0.82	12/94	82r
Potatoes, white	lb.	0.34	12/94	82r
Rice, white, long grain, uncooked	lb.	0.48	12/94	82r
Round roast, USDA choice, boneless	lb.	2.91	12/94	82r
Sausage, fresh	lb.	1.82	12/94	82r
Shortening, vegetable oil blends	lb.	0.75	12/94	82r
Spaghetti and macaroni	lb.	0.87	12/94	82r
Steak, rib eye, USDA choice, boneless	lb.	6.85	12/94	82r
Steak, round, graded & ungraded, exc. USDA prime & choice	lb.	2.96	12/94	82r
Steak, round, USDA choice, boneless	lb.	3.17	12/94	82r
Steak, sirloin, USDA choice, boneless	lb.	4.12	12/94	82r
Steak, T-bone, USDA choice, bone-in	lb.	5.63	12/94	82r
Sugar and other sweets, eaten at home, expenditures	year	93	91	81r
Sugar, white, all sizes	lb.	0.39	12/94	82r
Tobacco products and smoking supplies, total expenditures	year	286	91	81r
Tomatoes, field grown	lb.	1.36	12/94	82r
Tuna, chunk, light	lb.	1.94	12/94	82r
Turkey, frozen, whole	lb.	0.96	12/94	82r
Yogurt, natural, fruit flavored	8 oz.	0.58	12/94	82r
Health Care				
Adenosine, emergency room	treat	100.00	95	23r
Bladder tap, superpubic, infant, emergency room	treat	119.00	95	23r
Blood analysis, emergency room	treat	25.00	95	23r
Blood tests, abdominal pain, emergency room	treat	25.00	95	23r
Burn dressing, emergency room	treat	266.00	95	23r
Cardiology interpretation, emergency room	treat	26.00	95	23r
Chest X-ray, emergency room	treat	78.00	95	23r
Childbirth, Cesarean delivery, hospital charge	birth	5462.00	12/91	69r
Childbirth, Cesarean delivery, physician charge	birth	2228.00	12/91	69r
Childbirth, normal delivery, hospital charge	birth	2943.00	12/91	69r
Childbirth, normal delivery, physician charge	birth	1619.00	12/91	69r
Defibrillation pads, emergency room	treat	6.00	95	23r
Drugs, expenditures	year	297	91	81r
Gastric tube insertion, nasal, emergency room	treat	25.00	95	23r
Health care, total expenditures	year	1600	91	81r
Health insurance expenditures	year	637	91	81r
Heart monitor, emergency room	treat	40.00	95	23r
Insurance premium, family medical care	month	344.21	1/95	41s
Intravenous fluids, emergency room	treat	130.00	95	23r

Values are in dollars or fractions of dollars. In the column headed *Ref*, references are shown to sources. Each reference is followed by a letter. These refer to the geographical level for which data were reported: s=State, r=Region, and c=City or metro. The abbreviation *ex* is used to mean *except* or *excluding*; *exp* stands for *expenditures*. For other abbreviations and further explanations, please see the Introduction.

Knoxville, TN - continued

Item	Per	Value	Date	Ref.
Health Care				
Intravenous fluids, emergency room	liter	26.00	95	23r
Intravenous line, central, emergency room	treat	342.00	95	23r
Liver function tests, abdominal pain, emergency room	treat	26.00	95	23r
Medical care charges, total, emergency room, third-degree burns	treat	2101.00	95	23r
Medical care charges, total, emergency, infant with fever	treat	628.00	95	23r
Medical services expenditures	year	573	91	81r
Medical supplies expenditures	year	93	91	81r
Morphine, emergency room	treat	34.00	95	23r
Nursing care and facilities charges, emergency room	treat	252.00	95	23r
Nursing care and facilities charges, emergency, infant with fever	treat	252.00	95	23r
Nursing care and facilities charges, emergency, third-degree burns	treat	861.00	95	23r
Physician's charges, emergency, infant with fever	treat	212.00	95	23r
Physician's charges, emergency, third-degree burns	treat	372.00	95	23r
Physician's fee, emergency room	treat	372.00	95	23r
Physician's fee, general practitioner	visit	51.20	12/93	60r
Surgery, open-heart	proc	42374.00	1/93	14r
Ultrasound, abdominal, emergency room	treat	276.00 .	95	23r
Urinalysis, emergency room	treat	20.00	95	23r
Urinalysis, infant, emergency room	treat	20.00	95	23r
X-rays, emergency room	treat	78.00	95	23r
Household Goods				
Floor coverings, expenditures	year	48	91	81r
Furniture, expenditures	year	280	91	81r
Household equipment, misc. expenditures	year	342	91	81r
Household expenditures, miscellaneous	year	256	91	81r
Household furnishings and equipment, expenditures	year	988	91	81r
Household operations expenditures	year	468	91	81r
Household textiles, expenditures	year	95	91	81r
Housekeeping supplies, expenditures	year	380	91	81r
Laundry and cleaning supplies, expenditures	year	109	91	81r
Postage and stationery, expenditures	year	105	91	81r
Housing				
Add garage/carport		6,980	3/95	74r
Add room(s)		11,403	3/95	74r
Apartment condominium or co-op, median	unit	68600	12/94	62r
Dwellings (owned), expenditures	year	2428	91	81r
Enclose porch/patio/breezeway		4,572	3/95	74r
Finish room in basement/attic		3,794	3/95	74r
Home, existing, single-family, median	unit	120200	12/94	62r
Maintenance, repairs, insurance, and other housing expenditures	year	531	91	81r
Mortgage interest and charges expenditures	year	1506	91	81r
Princ. & int., mortgage, median-price exist. sing.-family home	mo.	540	12/94	62r
Property taxes expenditures	year	391	91	81r
Redesign, restructure more than half of home's interior		17,641	3/95	74r
Rental units expenditures	year	1264	91	81r
Insurance and Pensions				
Auto insurance, private passenger	year	574.08	12/94	71s
Insurance and pensions, personal, expenditures	year	2395	91	81r
Insurance, life and other personal, expenditures	year	368	91	81r
Pensions and Social Security, expenditures	year	2027	91	81r
Personal Services				
Personal services expenditures	year	212	91	81r
Restaurant Food				
Dining expenditures, family	week	33.83	94	73r

Knoxville, TN - continued

Item	Per	Value	Date	Ref.
Taxes				
Tax, cigarettes	year	379.00	10/93	43s
Taxes, Federal income, expenditures	year	2275	91	81r
Taxes, personal, expenditures	year	2715	91	81r
Taxes, State and local income, expenditures	year	365	91	81r
Transportation				
Cars and trucks purchased, new	year	1306	91	81r
Cars and trucks purchased, used	year	942	91	81r
Driver's learning permit fee	perm	5.50	1/94	84s
Driver's license fee	orig	16.00	1/94	84s
Driver's license fee, duplicate	lic	8.00	1/94	84s
Driver's license reinstatement fee, min.	susp	65.00	1/94	85s
Driver's license renewal fee	renew	14.00	1/94	84s
Identification card, nondriver	card	7.50	1/94	83s
Motorcycle learning permit fee	perm	6.50	1/94	84s
Motorcycle license fee	orig	17.00	1/94	84s
Motorcycle license fee, duplicate	lic	8.00	1/94	84s
Motorcycle license renewal fee	renew	15.00	1/94	84s
Public transportation expenditures	year	249	91	81r
Transportation expenditures, total	year	5307	91	81r
Vehicle finance charges	year	346	91	81r
Vehicle insurance expenditures	year	544	91	81r
Vehicle maintenance and repairs expenditures	year	600	91	81r
Vehicle purchases	year	2275	91	81r
Vehicle rental, leases, licenses, etc. expenditures	year	141	91	81r
Vehicles purchased, other than cars and trucks	year	27	91	81r
Utilities				
Electricity expenditures	year	950	91	81r
Utilities, fuels, and public services, total expenditures	year	2000	91	81r
Water and other public services, expenditures	year	227	91	81r
Weddings				
Bridal attendants' gowns	event	750	10/93	76r
Bridal gown	event	852	10/93	76r
Bridal headpiece and veil	event	167	10/93	76r
Bride's wedding band	event	708	10/93	76r
Clergy	event	224	10/93	76r
Engagement ring	event	2756	10/93	76r
Flowers	event	863	10/93	76r
Formal wear for groom	event	106	10/93	76r
Groom's attendants' formal wear	event	530	10/93	76r
Groom's wedding band	event	402	10/93	76r
Music	event	600	10/93	76r
Photography	event	1088	10/93	76r
Shoes for bride	event	50	10/93	76r
Videography	event	483	10/93	76r
Wedding invitations and announcements	event	342	10/93	76r
Wedding reception	event	7000	10/93	76r

Kodiak, AK

Item	Per	Value	Date	Ref.
Composite, ACCRA index		157.00	12/94	2c
Alcoholic Beverages				
Beer, Miller Lite, Bud, 12-oz., ex deposit	6	5.78	12/94	2c
J & B Scotch	750-ml.	23.15	12/94	2c
Wine, Gallo Chablis blanc	1.5-lit	7.76	12/94	2c
Clothing				
Jeans, man's denim		39.97	12/94	2c
Shirt, man's dress shirt		35.85	12/94	2c
Undervest, boy's size 10-14, cotton	3	6.23	12/94	2c
Communications				
Newspaper subscription, dly. and Sun. delivery	month	18.87	12/94	2c
Telephone bill, family of four	month	22.05	12/94	2c

Values are in dollars or fractions of dollars. In the column headed *Ref*, references are shown to sources. Each reference is followed by a letter. These refer to the geographical level for which data were reported: s = State, r = Region, and c = City or metro. The abbreviation *ex* is used to mean *except* or *excluding*; *exp* stands for *expenditures*. For other abbreviations and further explanations, please see the Introduction.

Kodiak, AK - continued

Item	Per	Value	Date	Ref.
Energy and Fuels				
Energy, combined forms, 1800 sq. ft.	mo.	222.78	12/94	2c
Energy, exc. electricity, 1800 sq. ft.	mo.	111.00	12/94	2c
Gas, reg unlead, taxes inc., cash, self-service	gal	1.56	12/94	2c
Entertainment				
Bowling, evening rate	game	2.00	12/94	2c
Monopoly game, Parker Brothers', No. 9	game	18.39	12/94	2c
Movie	adm	4.50	12/94	2c
Tennis balls, yellow, Wilson or Penn, 3	can	4.58	12/94	2c
Groceries				
Groceries, ACCRA Index		156.50	12/94	2c
Baby food, strained vegetables, lowest price	4-4.5 oz.	0.46	12/94	2c
Bananas	lb.	0.98	12/94	2c
Beef or hamburger, ground	lb.	1.92	12/94	2c
Bread, white	24-oz.	1.00	12/94	2c
Cheese, Kraft grated Parmesan	8-oz.	4.88	12/94	2c
Chicken, whole fryer	lb.	1.42	12/94	2c
Cigarettes, Winston, Kings	carton	19.66	12/94	2c
Coffee, vacuum-packed	13 oz.	5.35	12/94	2c
Corn Flakes, Kellogg's or Post Toasties	18 oz.	3.36	12/94	2c
Corn, frozen, whole kernel, lowest price	10 oz.	1.10	12/94	2c
Eggs, Grade A large	dozen	1.42	12/94	2c
Lettuce, iceberg	head	1.29	12/94	2c
Margarine, Blue Bonnet or Parkay cubes	lb.	1.26	12/94	2c
Milk, whole	1/2 gal.	2.40	12/94	2c
Orange juice, Minute Maid frozen	12-oz.	1.62	12/94	2c
Peaches, halves or slices, Hunt's, Del Monte, or Libby's	29-oz.	2.18	12/94	2c
Peas, sweet, Del Monte or Green Giant	15-17 oz.	1.18	12/94	2c
Potatoes, white or red	10-lb. sack	4.52	12/94	2c
Sausage, Jimmy Dean, 100% pork	lb.	4.12	12/94	2c
Shortening, vegetable, Crisco	3-lb.	3.54	12/94	2c
Soft drink, Coca Cola, ex deposit	2 lit	2.36	12/94	2c
Steak, t-bone	lb.	6.16	12/94	2c
Sugar, cane or beet	4 lbs.	2.15	12/94	2c
Tomatoes, Hunt's or Del Monte	14.5 oz.	1.01	12/94	2c
Tuna, chunk, light, oil-packed	6.125-6.5 oz.	1.21	12/94	2c
Goods and Services				
Miscellaneous goods and services, ACCRA Index		147.20	12/94	2c
Health Care				
Health care, ACCRA Index		174.80	12/94	2c
Antibiotic ointment, Polysporin	1.5 oz.	5.58	12/94	2c
Dentist's fee, adult teeth cleaning and periodic oral exam	visit	118.67	12/94	2c
Doctor's fee, routine exam, established patient	visit	61.50	12/94	2c
Hospital care, semiprivate room	day	553.70	12/94	2c
Household Goods				
Appl. repair, service call, wash mach	min. lab. chg.	68.00	12/94	2c
Laundry detergent, Tide Ultra, Bold, or Cheer	42 oz.	5.93	12/94	2c
Tissues, facial, Kleenex brand	175	1.96	12/94	2c
Housing				
Housing, ACCRA Index		171.20	12/94	2c
House payment, principal and interest, 25% down payment	mo.	1287	12/94	2c
House, 1800 sq ft, 8000 sq ft lot, new, urban, utilities	total	205000	12/94	2c
Mtge. rate, incl. points and orig. fee, 30-year conv. fixed or ARM	mo.	9.45	12/94	2c

Kodiak, AK - continued

Item	Per	Value	Date	Ref.
Housing - continued				
Rent, apartment, 2 br., 1 1/2-2 baths, unfurnished, 950 sq ft, water	mo.	975	12/94	2c
Personal Goods				
Shampoo, Alberto VO5	15-oz.	1.99	12/94	2c
Toothpaste, Crest or Colgate	6-7 oz.	3.46	12/94	2c
Personal Services				
Dry cleaning, man's 2-pc. suit		16.15	12/94	2c
Haircut, man's barbershop, no styling		10.50	12/94	2c
Haircut, woman's shampoo, trim, blow-dry		27.50	12/94	2c
Restaurant Food				
Chicken, fried, thigh and drumstick		3.69	12/94	2c
Hamburger with cheese	1/4 lb.	2.59	12/94	2c
Pizza, Pizza Hut or Pizza Inn	12-13 in.	11.99	12/94	2c
Transportation				
Transportation, ACCRA Index		111.30	12/94	2c
Tire balance, computer or spin bal., front	wheel	5.00	12/94	2c
Utilities				
Utilities, ACCRA Index		187.00	12/94	2c
Electricity, (part.), other, 1800 sq. ft., new home	mo.	111.78	12/94	2c

Kokomo, IN

Item	Per	Value	Date	Ref.
Appliances				
Appliances (major), expenditures	year	131	91	81r
Average annual exp.				
Food, health care, personal goods, services	year	25935	91	81r
Charity				
Cash contributions, expenditures	year	745	91	81r
Clothing				
Apparel, men and boys, total expenditures	year	332	91	81r
Apparel, women and girls, total expenditures	year	578	91	81r
Footwear, expenditures	year	164	91	81r
Communications				
Long-distance telephone rate, day, addl. min., 1-10 mi.	min.	0.10	12/93	9s
Long-distance telephone rate, day, initial min., 1-10 mi.	min.	0.18	12/93	9s
Phone line, single, business, field visit	inst	59.00	12/93	9s
Phone line, single, business, no field visit	inst	59.00	12/93	9s
Phone line, single, residence, field visit	inst	47.00	12/93	9s
Phone line, single, residence, no field visit	inst	47.00	12/93	9s
Telephone service, expenditures	year	547	91	81r
Education				
Board, 4-year private college/university	year	2095	8/94	80s
Board, 4-year public college/university	year	2300	8/94	80s
Education, total expenditures	year	394	91	81r
Room, 4-year private college/university	year	1784	8/94	80s
Room, 4-year public college/university	year	1718	8/94	80s
Total cost, 4-year private college/university	year	15045	8/94	80s
Total cost, 4-year public college/university	year	6639	8/94	80s
Tuition, 2-year public college/university, in-state	year	1737	8/94	80s
Tuition, 4-year private college/university, in-state	year	11165	8/94	80s
Tuition, 4-year public college/university, in-state	year	2621	8/94	80s
Energy and Fuels				
Fuel oil and other fuels, expenditures	year	83	91	81r
Gas, natural, expenditures	year	373	91	81r
Gasoline and motor oil purchased	year	1000	91	81r
Gasoline, unleaded midgrade	gallon	1.15	4/93	82r
Gasoline, unleaded premium	gallon	1.23	4/93	82r
Gasoline, unleaded regular	gallon	1.07	4/93	82r

Values are in dollars or fractions of dollars. In the column headed *Ref*, references are shown to sources. Each reference is followed by a letter. These refer to the geographical level for which data were reported: s=State, r=Region, and c=City or metro. The abbreviation *ex* is used to mean *except* or *excluding*; *exp* stands for expenditures. For other abbreviations and further explanations, please see the Introduction.

Kokomo, IN - continued

Item	Per	Value	Date	Ref.
Entertainment				
Entertainment, total expenditures	year	1356	91	81r
Fees and admissions, expenditures	year	347	91	81r
Pets, toys, playground equipment, expenditures	year	270	91	81r
Reading, expenditures	year	160	91	81r
Televisions, radios, and sound equipment, expenditures	year	433	91	81r
Funerals				
Burial, immediate, container provided by funeral home		1268.31	1/95	54r
Cards, acknowledgment		26.12	1/95	54r
Casket, minimum alternative		198.03	1/95	54r
Cosmetology, hair care, etc.		122.19	1/95	54r
Cremation, direct, container provided by funeral home		977.81	1/95	54r
Embalming		334.00	1/95	54r
Funeral, funeral home		321.16	1/95	54r
Funeral, other facility		317.73	1/95	54r
Graveside service		292.48	1/95	54r
Hearse, local		153.20	1/95	54r
Limousine, local		123.52	1/95	54r
Memorial service		356.30	1/95	54r
Service charge, professional, nondeclinable		968.24	1/95	54r
Visitation and viewing		332.66	1/95	54r
Groceries				
Apples, Red Delicious	lb.	0.68	12/94	82r
Bacon, sliced	lb.	1.88	12/94	82r
Bananas	lb.	0.41	12/94	82r
Beef purchases	year	197	91	81r
Beef, stew, boneless	lb.	2.52	12/94	82r
Beverage purchases, alcoholic	year	293	91	81r
Beverage purchases, nonalcoholic	year	203	91	81r
Bologna, all beef or mixed	lb.	2.12	12/94	82r
Bread, white, pan	lb.	0.76	12/94	82r
Cabbage	lb.	0.44	12/94	82r
Carrots, short trimmed and topped	lb.	0.44	12/94	82r
Cereals and bakery products purchases	year	347	91	81r
Cereals and cereals products purchases	year	119	91	81r
Cheddar cheese, natural	lb.	3.28	12/94	82r
Chicken breast, bone-in	lb.	1.61	12/94	82r
Chicken, fresh, whole	lb.	0.89	12/94	82r
Chuck roast, USDA choice, boneless	lb.	2.33	12/94	82r
Coffee, 100%, ground roast, all sizes	lb.	4.28	12/94	82r
Cookies, chocolate chip	lb.	2.72	12/94	82r
Dairy products (other) purchases	year	148	91	81r
Eggs, Grade A large	dozen	0.76	12/94	82r
Fish and seafood purchases	year	61	91	81r
Flour, white, all purpose	lb.	0.22	12/94	82r
Food purchases, food eaten at home	year	2313	91	81r
Foods purchased away from home, not prepared by consumer	year	1709	91	81r
Fruits and vegetables purchases	year	372	91	81r
Grapefruit	lb.	0.47	12/94	82r
Grapes, Thompson seedless	lb.	2.15	12/94	82r
Ground beef, 100% beef	lb.	1.37	12/94	82r
Ground chuck, 100% beef	lb.	1.81	12/94	82r
Ham, boneless, exc. canned	lb.	2.16	12/94	82r
Ice cream, prepackaged, bulk, regular	1/2 gal.	2.48	12/94	82r
Lemons	lb.	1.08	12/94	82r
Lettuce, iceberg	lb.	0.81	12/94	82r
Margarine, stick	lb.	0.81	12/94	82r
Meats, poultry, fish, and eggs purchases	year	591	91	81r
Milk and cream (fresh) purchases	year	132	91	81r
Orange juice, frozen concentrate 12-oz. can	16 oz.	1.41	12/94	82r
Oranges, Navel	lb.	0.56	12/94	82r
Peanut butter, creamy, all sizes	lb.	1.81	12/94	82r
Pork chops, center cut, bone-in	lb.	2.76	12/94	82r
Pork purchases	year	130	91	81r
Potato chips	16-oz.	2.81	12/94	82r
Potatoes, frozen, French fried	lb.	0.83	12/94	82r

Kokomo, IN - continued

Item	Per	Value	Date	Ref.
Groceries - continued				
Potatoes, white	lb.	0.28	12/94	82r
Round roast, USDA choice, boneless	lb.	2.90	12/94	82r
Shortening, vegetable oil blends	lb.	0.88	12/94	82r
Spaghetti and macaroni	lb.	0.78	12/94	82r
Steak, rib eye, USDA choice, boneless	lb.	6.15	12/94	82r
Steak, round, graded & ungraded, exc. USDA prime & choice	lb.	2.72	12/94	82r
Steak, round, USDA choice, boneless	lb.	3.02	12/94	82r
Steak, sirloin, USDA choice, boneless	lb.	3.85	12/94	82r
Steak, T-bone, USDA choice, bone-in	lb.	5.38	12/94	82r
Sugar and other sweets, eaten at home, expenditures	year	91	91	81r
Sugar, white, all sizes	lb.	0.36	12/94	82r
Tobacco products and smoking supplies, total expenditures	year	298	91	81r
Tomatoes, field grown	lb.	1.36	12/94	82r
Tuna, chunk, light	lb.	1.94	12/94	82r
Turkey, frozen, whole	lb.	0.96	12/94	82r
Yogurt, natural, fruit flavored	8 oz.	0.62	12/94	82r
Health Care				
Childbirth, Cesarean delivery, hospital charge	birth	5101.00	12/91	69r
Childbirth, Cesarean delivery, physician charge	birth	2234.00	12/91	69r
Childbirth, normal delivery, hospital charge	birth	2891.00	12/91	69r
Childbirth, normal delivery, physician charge	birth	1623.00	12/91	69r
Drugs, expenditures	year	248	91	81r
Health care, total expenditures	year	1336	91	81r
Health insurance expenditures	year	550	91	81r
Insurance premium, family medical care	month	353.94	1/95	41s
Medical services expenditures	year	457	91	81r
Medical supplies expenditures	year	82	91	81r
Household Goods				
Floor coverings, expenditures	year	105	91	81r
Furniture, expenditures	year	291	91	81r
Household equipment, misc. expenditures	year	341	91	81r
Household expenditures, miscellaneous	year	162	91	81r
Household furnishings and equipment, expenditures	year	1042	91	81r
Household operations expenditures	year	365	91	81r
Household textiles, expenditures	year	101	91	81r
Housekeeping supplies, expenditures	year	390	91	81r
Laundry and cleaning supplies, expenditures	year	110	91	81r
Postage and stationery, expenditures	year	115	91	81r
Housing				
Add garage/carport		8,479	3/95	74r
Add room(s)		21,347	3/95	74r
Apartment condominium or co-op, median	unit	87100	12/94	62r
Bathroom addition, average cost	add	9734.00	3/95	13r
Bathroom remodeling, average cost	remod	6414.00	3/95	13r
Bedroom, master suite addition, average cost	add	27122.00	3/95	13r
Deck addition, average cost	add	6665.00	3/95	13r
Dwellings (owned), expenditures	year	2566	91	81r
Enclose porch/patio/breezeway		4,556	3/95	74r
Exterior remodeling, average cost	remod	15395.00	3/95	13r
Family room addition, average cost	add	27658.00	3/95	13r
Finish room in basement/attic		5,074	3/95	74r
Home, existing, single-family, median	unit	106500	12/94	62r
Kitchen remodeling, major, average cost	remod	17084.00	3/95	13r
Kitchen remodeling, minor, average cost	remod	5804.00	3/95	13r
Maintenance, repairs, insurance, and other housing expenditures	year	484	91	81r
Mortgage interest and charges expenditures	year	1443	91	81r
Office, home addition, average cost	add	8121.00	3/95	13r
Princ. & int., mortgage, median-price exist. sing.-family home	mo.	515	12/94	62r
Property taxes expenditures	year	639	91	81r
Redesign, restructure more than half of home's interior		9,114	3/95	74r

Values are in dollars or fractions of dollars. In the column headed *Ref*, references are shown to sources. Each reference is followed by a letter. These refer to the geographical level for which data were reported: s=State, r=Region, and c=City or metro. The abbreviation *ex* is used to mean *except* or *excluding*; *exp* stands for expenditures. For other abbreviations and further explanations, please see the Introduction.

Kokomo, IN - continued

Item	Per	Value	Date	Ref.
Housing				
Rental units expenditures	year	1200	91	81r
Sun-space addition, average cost	add	23768.00	3/95	13r
Wing addition, two-story, average cost	add	50410.00	3/95	13r
Insurance and Pensions				
Auto insurance, private passenger	year	586.58	12/94	71s
Insurance and pensions, personal, expenditures	year	2408	91	81r
Insurance, life and other personal, expenditures	year	355	91	81r
Pensions and Social Security, expenditures	year	2053	91	81r
Legal Assistance				
Legal work, law firm associate	hour	90		10r
Legal work, law firm partner	hour	139		10r
Personal Services				
Personal services expenditures	year	203	91	81r
Restaurant Food				
Dining expenditures, family	week	30.03	94	73r
Taxes				
Taxes, Federal income, expenditures	year	1756	91	81r
Taxes, personal, expenditures	year	2426	91	81r
Taxes, State and local income, expenditures	year	568	91	81r
Transportation				
Cars and trucks purchased, new	year	891	91	81r
Cars and trucks purchased, used	year	1155	91	81r
Driver's learning permit fee	perm	2.00	1/94	84s
Driver's license fee	orig	6.00	1/94	84s
Driver's license fee, duplicate	lic	3.00	1/94	84s
Driver's license renewal fee	renew	6.00	1/94	84s
Identification card, nondriver	card	4.00	1/94	83s
Motorcycle learning permit fee	perm	2.00	1/94	84s
Motorcycle license fee	orig	6.00	1/94	84s
Motorcycle license fee, duplicate	lic	3.00	1/94	84s
Motorcycle license renewal fee	renew	6.00	1/94	84s
Public transportation expenditures	year	209	91	81r
Transportation expenditures, total	year	4792	91	81r
Vehicle finance charges	year	300	91	81r
Vehicle insurance expenditures	year	485	91	81r
Vehicle maintenance and repairs expenditures	year	534	91	81r
Vehicle purchases	year	2068	91	81r
Vehicle rental, leases, licenses, etc. expenditures	year	197	91	81r
Vehicles purchased, other than cars and trucks	year	22	91	81r
Utilities				
Electricity expenditures	year	668	91	81r
Utilities, fuels, and public services, total expenditures	year	1838	91	81r
Water and other public services, expenditures	year	167	91	81r
Weddings				
Bridal attendants' gowns	event	750	10/93	76r
Bridal gown	event	852	10/93	76r
Bridal headpiece and veil	event	167	10/93	76r
Bride's wedding band	event	708	10/93	76r
Clergy	event	224	10/93	76r
Engagement ring	event	2756	10/93	76r
Flowers	event	863	10/93	76r
Formal wear for groom	event	106	10/93	76r
Groom's attendants' formal wear	event	530	10/93	76r
Groom's wedding band	event	402	10/93	76r
Music	event	600	10/93	76r
Photography	event	1088	10/93	76r
Shoes for bride	event	50	10/93	76r
Videography	event	483	10/93	76r
Wedding invitations and announcements	event	342	10/93	76r
Wedding reception	event	7000	10/93	76r

La Crosse, WI

Item	Per	Value	Date	Ref.
Appliances				
Appliances (major), expenditures	year	131	91	81r
Average annual exp.				
Food, health care, personal goods, services	year	25935	91	81r
Charity				
Cash contributions, expenditures	year	745	91	81r
Clothing				
Apparel, men and boys, total expenditures	year	332	91	81r
Apparel, women and girls, total expenditures	year	578	91	81r
Footwear, expenditures	year	164	91	81r
Communications				
Long-distance telephone rate, day, addl. min., 1-10 mi.	min.	0.10	12/93	9s
Long-distance telephone rate, day, initial min., 1-10 mi.	min.	0.15	12/93	9s
Phone line, single, business, field visit	inst	64.65	12/93	9s
Phone line, single, business, no field visit	inst	64.65	12/93	9s
Phone line, single, residence, field visit	inst	33.05	12/93	9s
Phone line, single, residence, no field visit	inst	33.05	12/93	9s
Telephone service, expenditures	year	547	91	81r
Education				
Board, 4-year private college/university	year	2145	8/94	80s
Board, 4-year public college/university	year	1303	8/94	80s
Education, total expenditures	year	394	91	81r
Room, 4-year private college/university	year	1576	8/94	80s
Room, 4-year public college/university	year	1631	8/94	80s
Total cost, 4-year private college/university	year	13902	8/94	80s
Total cost, 4-year public college/university	year	5252	8/94	80s
Tuition, 2-year public college/university, in-state	year	1557	8/94	80s
Tuition, 4-year private college/university, in-state	year	10181	8/94	80s
Tuition, 4-year public college/university, in-state	year	2318	8/94	80s
Energy and Fuels				
Fuel oil and other fuels, expenditures	year	83	91	81r
Gas, natural, expenditures	year	373	91	81r
Gasoline and motor oil purchased	year	1000	91	81r
Gasoline, unleaded midgrade	gallon	1.15	4/93	82r
Gasoline, unleaded premium	gallon	1.23	4/93	82r
Gasoline, unleaded regular	gallon	1.07	4/93	82r
Entertainment				
Entertainment, total expenditures	year	1356	91	81r
Fees and admissions, expenditures	year	347	91	81r
Pets, toys, playground equipment, expenditures	year	270	91	81r
Reading, expenditures	year	160	91	81r
Televisions, radios, and sound equipment, expenditures	year	433	91	81r
Funerals				
Burial, immediate, container provided by funeral home		1268.31	1/95	54r
Cards, acknowledgment		26.12	1/95	54r
Casket, minimum alternative		198.03	1/95	54r
Cosmetology, hair care, etc.		122.19	1/95	54r
Cremation, direct, container provided by funeral home		977.81	1/95	54r
Embalming		334.00	1/95	54r
Funeral, funeral home		321.16	1/95	54r
Funeral, other facility		317.73	1/95	54r
Graveside service		292.48	1/95	54r
Hearse, local		153.20	1/95	54r
Limousine, local		123.52	1/95	54r
Memorial service		356.30	1/95	54r
Service charge, professional, nondeclinable		968.24	1/95	54r
Visitation and viewing		332.66	1/95	54r

Values are in dollars or fractions of dollars. In the column headed *Ref*, references are shown to sources. Each reference is followed by a letter. These refer to the geographical level for which data were reported: s=State, r=Region, and c=City or metro. The abbreviation *ex* is used to mean *except* or *excluding*; *exp* stands for expenditures. For other abbreviations and further explanations, please see the Introduction.

La Crosse, WI - continued

Item	Per	Value	Date	Ref.
Groceries				
Apples, Red Delicious	lb.	0.68	12/94	82r
Bacon, sliced	lb.	1.88	12/94	82r
Bananas	lb.	0.41	12/94	82r
Beef purchases	year	197	91	81r
Beef, stew, boneless	lb.	2.52	12/94	82r
Beverage purchases, alcoholic	year	293	91	81r
Beverage purchases, nonalcoholic	year	203	91	81r
Bologna, all beef or mixed	lb.	2.12	12/94	82r
Bread, white, pan	lb.	0.76	12/94	82r
Cabbage	lb.	0.44	12/94	82r
Carrots, short trimmed and topped	lb.	0.44	12/94	82r
Cereals and bakery products purchases	year	347	91	81r
Cereals and cereals products purchases	year	119	91	81r
Cheddar cheese, natural	lb.	3.28	12/94	82r
Chicken breast, bone-in	lb.	1.61	12/94	82r
Chicken, fresh, whole	lb.	0.89	12/94	82r
Chuck roast, USDA choice, boneless	lb.	2.33	12/94	82r
Coffee, 100%, ground roast, all sizes	lb.	4.28	12/94	82r
Cookies, chocolate chip	lb.	2.72	12/94	82r
Dairy products (other) purchases	year	148	91	81r
Eggs, Grade A large	dozen	0.76	12/94	82r
Fish and seafood purchases	year	61	91	81r
Flour, white, all purpose	lb.	0.22	12/94	82r
Food purchases, food eaten at home	year	2313	91	81r
Foods purchased away from home, not prepared by consumer	year	1709	91	81r
Fruits and vegetables purchases	year	372	91	81r
Grapefruit	lb.	0.47	12/94	82r
Grapes, Thompson seedless	lb.	2.15	12/94	82r
Ground beef, 100% beef	lb.	1.37	12/94	82r
Ground chuck, 100% beef	lb.	1.81	12/94	82r
Ham, boneless, exc. canned	lb.	2.16	12/94	82r
Ice cream, prepackaged, bulk, regular	1/2 gal.	2.48	12/94	82r
Lemons	lb.	1.08	12/94	82r
Lettuce, iceberg	lb.	0.81	12/94	82r
Margarine, stick	lb.	0.81	12/94	82r
Meats, poultry, fish, and eggs purchases	year	591	91	81r
Milk and cream (fresh) purchases	year	132	91	81r
Orange juice, frozen concentrate 12-oz. can	16 oz.	1.41	12/94	82r
Oranges, Navel	lb.	0.56	12/94	82r
Peanut butter, creamy, all sizes	lb.	1.81	12/94	82r
Pork chops, center cut, bone-in	lb.	2.76	12/94	82r
Pork purchases	year	130	91	81r
Potato chips	16-oz.	2.81	12/94	82r
Potatoes, frozen, French fried	lb.	0.83	12/94	82r
Potatoes, white	lb.	0.28	12/94	82r
Round roast, USDA choice, boneless	lb.	2.90	12/94	82r
Shortening, vegetable oil blends	lb.	0.88	12/94	82r
Spaghetti and macaroni	lb.	0.78	12/94	82r
Steak, rib eye, USDA choice, boneless	lb.	6.15	12/94	82r
Steak, round, graded & ungraded, exc. USDA prime & choice	lb.	2.72	12/94	82r
Steak, round, USDA choice, boneless	lb.	3.02	12/94	82r
Steak, sirloin, USDA choice, boneless	lb.	3.85	12/94	82r
Steak, T-bone, USDA choice, bone-in	lb.	5.38	12/94	82r
Sugar and other sweets, eaten at home, expenditures	year	91	91	81r
Sugar, white, all sizes	lb.	0.36	12/94	82r
Tobacco products and smoking supplies, total expenditures	year	298	91	81r
Tomatoes, field grown	lb.	1.36	12/94	82r
Tuna, chunk, light	lb.	1.94	12/94	82r
Turkey, frozen, whole	lb.	0.96	12/94	82r
Yogurt, natural, fruit flavored	8 oz.	0.62	12/94	82r
Health Care				
Childbirth, Cesarean delivery, hospital charge	birth	5101.00	12/91	69r
Childbirth, Cesarean delivery, physician charge	birth	2234.00	12/91	69r
Childbirth, normal delivery, hospital charge	birth	2891.00	12/91	69r
Childbirth, normal delivery, physician charge	birth	1623.00	12/91	69r

La Crosse, WI - continued

Item	Per	Value	Date	Ref.
Health Care - continued				
Drugs, expenditures	year	248	91	81r
Health care, total expenditures	year	1336	91	81r
Health insurance expenditures	year	550	91	81r
Insurance premium, family medical care	month	378.79	1/95	41s
Medical services expenditures	year	457	91	81r
Medical supplies expenditures	year	82	91	81r
Household Goods				
Floor coverings, expenditures	year	105	91	81r
Furniture, expenditures	year	291	91	81r
Household equipment, misc. expenditures	year	341	91	81r
Household expenditures, miscellaneous	year	162	91	81r
Household furnishings and equipment, expenditures	year	1042	91	81r
Household operations expenditures	year	365	91	81r
Household textiles, expenditures	year	101	91	81r
Housekeeping supplies, expenditures	year	390	91	81r
Laundry and cleaning supplies, expenditures	year	110	91	81r
Postage and stationery, expenditures	year	115	91	81r
Housing				
Add garage/carport		8,479	3/95	74r
Add room(s)		21,347	3/95	74r
Apartment condominium or co-op, median	unit	87100	12/94	62r
Bathroom addition, average cost	add	9734.00	3/95	13r
Bathroom remodeling, average cost	remod	6414.00	3/95	13r
Bedroom, master suite addition, average cost	add	27122.00	3/95	13r
Deck addition, average cost	add	6665.00	3/95	13r
Dwellings (owned), expenditures	year	2566	91	81r
Enclose porch/patio/breezeway		4,556	3/95	74r
Exterior remodeling, average cost	remod	15395.00	3/95	13r
Family room addition, average cost	add	27658.00	3/95	13r
Finish room in basement/attic		5,074	3/95	74r
Home, existing, single-family, median	unit	106500	12/94	62r
Kitchen remodeling, major, average cost	remod	17084.00	3/95	13r
Kitchen remodeling, minor, average cost	remod	5804.00	3/95	13r
Maintenance, repairs, insurance, and other housing expenditures	year	484	91	81r
Mortgage interest and charges expenditures	year	1443	91	81r
Office, home addition, average cost	add	8121.00	3/95	13r
Princ. & int., mortgage, median-price exist. sing.-family home	mo.	515	12/94	62r
Property taxes expenditures	year	639	91	81r
Redesign, restructure more than half of home's interior		9,114	3/95	74r
Rental units expenditures	year	1200	91	81r
Sun-space addition, average cost	add	23768.00	3/95	13r
Wing addition, two-story, average cost	add	50410.00	3/95	13r
Insurance and Pensions				
Auto insurance, private passenger	year	554.10	12/94	71s
Insurance and pensions, personal, expenditures	year	2408	91	81r
Insurance, life and other personal, expenditures	year	355	91	81r
Pensions and Social Security, expenditures	year	2053	91	81r
Legal Assistance				
Legal work, law firm associate	hour	90		10r
Legal work, law firm partner	hour	139		10r
Personal Services				
Personal services expenditures	year	203	91	81r
Restaurant Food				
Dining expenditures, family	week	30.03	94	73r
Taxes				
Taxes, Federal income, expenditures	year	1756	91	81r
Taxes, personal, expenditures	year	2426	91	81r
Taxes, State and local income, expenditures	year	568	91	81r

Values are in dollars or fractions of dollars. In the column headed *Ref*, references are shown to sources. Each reference is followed by a letter. These refer to the geographical level for which data were reported: s=State, r=Region, and c=City or metro. The abbreviation *ex* is used to mean *except* or *excluding*; *exp* stands for expenditures. For other abbreviations and further explanations, please see the Introduction.

La Crosse, WI - continued

Item	Per	Value	Date	Ref.
Transportation				
Cars and trucks purchased, new	year	891	91	81r
Cars and trucks purchased, used	year	1155	91	81r
Driver's learning permit fee	perm	20.00	1/94	84s
Driver's license fee	orig	10.00	1/94	84s
Driver's license fee, duplicate	lic	4.00	1/94	84s
Driver's license reinstatement fee, min.	susp	50.00	1/94	85s
Driver's license renewal fee	renew	10.00	1/94	84s
Identification card, nondriver	card	4.00	1/94	83s
Motorcycle license fee	orig	4.00	1/94	84s
Motorcycle license fee, duplicate	lic	4.00	1/94	84s
Motorcycle license renewal fee	renew	4.00	1/94	84s
Public transportation expenditures	year	209	91	81r
Transportation expenditures, total	year	4792	91	81r
Vehicle finance charges	year	300	91	81r
Vehicle insurance expenditures	year	485	91	81r
Vehicle maintenance and repairs expenditures	year	534	91	81r
Vehicle purchases	year	2068	91	81r
Vehicle rental, leases, licenses, etc. expenditures	year	197	91	81r
Vehicles purchased, other than cars and trucks	year	22	91	81r
Utilities				
Electricity expenditures	year	668	91	81r
Utilities, fuels, and public services, total expenditures	year	1838	91	81r
Water and other public services, expenditures	year	167	91	81r
Weddings				
Bridal attendants' gowns	event	750	10/93	76r
Bridal gown	event	852	10/93	76r
Bridal headpiece and veil	event	167	10/93	76r
Bride's wedding band	event	708	10/93	76r
Clergy	event	224	10/93	76r
Engagement ring	event	2756	10/93	76r
Flowers	event	863	10/93	76r
Formal wear for groom	event	106	10/93	76r
Groom's attendants' formal wear	event	530	10/93	76r
Groom's wedding band	event	402	10/93	76r
Music	event	600	10/93	76r
Photography	event	1088	10/93	76r
Shoes for bride	event	50	10/93	76r
Videography	event	483	10/93	76r
Wedding invitations and announcements	event	342	10/93	76r
Wedding reception	event	7000	10/93	76r

LaPorte-Michigan City, IN

Item	Per	Value	Date	Ref.
Composite, ACCRA index		95.60	12/94	2c
Alcoholic Beverages				
Beer, Miller Lite, Bud, 12-oz., ex deposit	6	3.75	12/94	2c
J & B Scotch	750-ml.	15.79	12/94	2c
Wine, Gallo Chablis blanc	1.5-lit	3.95	12/94	2c
Clothing				
Jeans, man's denim		30.19	12/94	2c
Shirt, man's dress shirt		29.00	12/94	2c
Undervest, boy's size 10-14, cotton	3	3.99	12/94	2c
Communications				
Newspaper subscription, dly. and Sun. delivery	month	10.00	12/94	2c
Telephone bill, family of four	month	20.42	12/94	2c
Energy and Fuels				
Energy, combined forms, 1800 sq. ft.	mo.	121.76	12/94	2c
Energy, exc. electricity, 1800 sq. ft.	mo.	52.64	12/94	2c
Gas, reg unlead, taxes inc., cash, self-service	gal	0.99	12/94	2c

LaPorte-Michigan City, IN - continued

Item	Per	Value	Date	Ref.
Entertainment				
Bowling, evening rate	game	1.80	12/94	2c
Monopoly game, Parker Brothers', No. 9	game	11.67	12/94	2c
Movie	adm	4.00	12/94	2c
Tennis balls, yellow, Wilson or Penn, 3	can	2.69	12/94	2c
Groceries				
Groceries, ACCRA Index		101.90	12/94	2c
Baby food, strained vegetables, lowest price	4-4.5 oz.	0.41	12/94	2c
Bananas	lb.	0.40	12/94	2c
Beef or hamburger, ground	lb.	1.15	12/94	2c
Bread, white	24-oz.	0.60	12/94	2c
Cheese, Kraft grated Parmesan	8-oz.	3.49	12/94	2c
Chicken, whole fryer	lb.	0.89	12/94	2c
Cigarettes, Winston, Kings	carton	14.47	12/94	2c
Coffee, vacuum-packed	13 oz.	3.54	12/94	2c
Corn Flakes, Kellogg's or Post Toasties	18 oz.	2.67	12/94	2c
Corn, frozen, whole kernel, lowest price	10 oz.	0.78	12/94	2c
Eggs, Grade A large	dozen	0.77	12/94	2c
Lettuce, iceberg	head	0.99	12/94	2c
Margarine, Blue Bonnet or Parkay cubes	lb.	0.64	12/94	2c
Milk, whole	1/2 gal.	1.56	12/94	2c
Orange juice, Minute Maid frozen	12-oz.	1.38	12/94	2c
Peaches, halves or slices, Hunt's, Del Monte, or Libby's	29-oz.	1.24	12/94	2c
Peas, sweet, Del Monte or Green Giant	15-17 oz.	0.58	12/94	2c
Potatoes, white or red	10-lb. sack	2.49	12/94	2c
Sausage, Jimmy Dean, 100% pork	lb.	2.85	12/94	2c
Shortening, vegetable, Crisco	3-lb.	2.52	12/94	2c
Soft drink, Coca Cola, ex deposit	2 lit	1.17	12/94	2c
Steak, t-bone	lb.	5.11	12/94	2c
Sugar, cane or beet	4 lbs.	1.61	12/94	2c
Tomatoes, Hunt's or Del Monte	14.5 oz.	0.78	12/94	2c
Tuna, chunk, light, oil-packed	6.125-6.5 oz.	0.78	12/94	2c
Goods and Services				
Miscellaneous goods and services, ACCRA Index		93.90	12/94	2c
Health Care				
Health care, ACCRA Index		96.20	12/94	2c
Antibiotic ointment, Polysporin	1.5 oz.	4.02	12/94	2c
Dentist's fee, adult teeth cleaning and periodic oral exam	visit	53.30	12/94	2c
Doctor's fee, routine exam, established patient	visit	38.25	12/94	2c
Hospital care, semiprivate room	day	337.50	12/94	2c
Household Goods				
Appl. repair, service call, wash mach	min. lab. chg.	24.73	12/94	2c
Laundry detergent, Tide Ultra, Bold, or Cheer	42 oz.	3.26	12/94	2c
Tissues, facial, Kleenex brand	175	1.07	12/94	2c
Housing				
Housing, ACCRA Index		92.20	12/94	2c
House payment, principal and interest, 25% down payment	mo.	722	12/94	2c
House, 1800 sq ft, 8000 sq ft lot, new, urban, utilities	total	115825	12/94	2c
Mtge. rate, incl. points and orig. fee, 30-year conv. fixed or ARM	mo.	9.36	12/94	2c
Rent, apartment, 2 br., 1 1/2-2 baths, unfurnished, 950 sq ft, water	mo.	442	12/94	2c
Personal Goods				
Shampoo, Alberto VO5	15-oz.	1.15	12/94	2c
Toothpaste, Crest or Colgate	6-7 oz.	2.27	12/94	2c

Values are in dollars or fractions of dollars. In the column headed *Ref*, references are shown to sources. Each reference is followed by a letter. These refer to the geographical level for which data were reported: s = State, r = Region, and c = City or metro. The abbreviation *ex* is used to mean *except* or *excluding*; *exp* stands for expenditures. For other abbreviations and further explanations, please see the Introduction.

LaPorte-Michigan City, IN - continued

Item	Per	Value	Date	Ref.
Personal Services				
Dry cleaning, man's 2-pc. suit		5.50	12/94	2c
Haircut, man's barbershop, no styling		6.90	12/94	2c
Haircut, woman's shampoo, trim, blow-dry		15.00	12/94	2c
Restaurant Food				
Chicken, fried, thigh and drumstick		1.96	12/94	2c
Hamburger with cheese	1/4 lb.	1.79	12/94	2c
Pizza, Pizza Hut or Pizza Inn	12-13 in.	7.99	12/94	2c
Transportation				
Transportation, ACCRA Index		89.60	12/94	2c
Tire balance, computer or spin bal., front	wheel	6.20	12/94	2c
Utilities				
Utilities, ACCRA Index		108.00	12/94	2c
Electricity, (part.), other, 1800 sq. ft., new home	mo.	69.12	12/94	2c

Lafayette, IN

Item	Per	Value	Date	Ref.
Composite, ACCRA index		101.30	12/94	2c
Alcoholic Beverages				
Beer, Miller Lite, Bud, 12-oz., ex deposit	6	3.66	12/94	2c
J & B Scotch	750-ml.	16.09	12/94	2c
Wine, Gallo Chablis blanc	1.5-lit	4.32	12/94	2c
Clothing				
Jeans, man's denim		31.59	12/94	2c
Shirt, man's dress shirt		33.87	12/94	2c
Undervest, boy's size 10-14, cotton	3	4.39	12/94	2c
Communications				
Newspaper subscription, dly. and Sun. delivery	month	14.13	12/94	2c
Telephone bill, family of four	month	25.46	12/94	2c
Energy and Fuels				
Energy, combined forms, 1800 sq. ft.	mo.	124.45	12/94	2c
Energy, exc. electricity, 1800 sq. ft.	mo.	69.97	12/94	2c
Gas, reg unlead, taxes inc., cash, self-service	gal	0.99	12/94	2c
Entertainment				
Bowling, evening rate	game	2.05	12/94	2c
Monopoly game, Parker Brothers', No. 9	game	11.90	12/94	2c
Movie	adm	6.00	12/94	2c
Tennis balls, yellow, Wilson or Penn, 3	can	3.34	12/94	2c
Groceries				
Groceries, ACCRA Index		108.10	12/94	2c
Baby food, strained vegetables, lowest price	4-4.5 oz.	0.34	12/94	2c
Bananas	lb.	0.44	12/94	2c
Beef or hamburger, ground	lb.	1.58	12/94	2c
Bread, white	24-oz.	0.94	12/94	2c
Cheese, Kraft grated Parmesan	8-oz.	3.43	12/94	2c
Chicken, whole fryer	lb.	0.86	12/94	2c
Cigarettes, Winston, Kings	carton	14.56	12/94	2c
Coffee, vacuum-packed	13 oz.	4.22	12/94	2c
Corn Flakes, Kellogg's or Post Toasties	18 oz.	2.45	12/94	2c
Corn, frozen, whole kernel, lowest price	10 oz.	0.77	12/94	2c
Eggs, Grade A large	dozen	0.63	12/94	2c
Lettuce, iceberg	head	0.96	12/94	2c
Margarine, Blue Bonnet or Parkay cubes	lb.	0.79	12/94	2c
Milk, whole	1/2 gal.	1.51	12/94	2c
Orange juice, Minute Maid frozen	12-oz.	1.22	12/94	2c
Peaches, halves or slices, Hunt's, Del Monte, or Libby's	29-oz.	1.20	12/94	2c
Peas, sweet, Del Monte or Green Giant	15-17 oz.	0.57	12/94	2c
Potatoes, white or red	10-lb. sack	2.99	12/94	2c

Lafayette, IN - continued

Item	Per	Value	Date	Ref.
Groceries - continued				
Sausage, Jimmy Dean, 100% pork	lb.	3.25	12/94	2c
Shortening, vegetable, Crisco	3-lb.	2.38	12/94	2c
Soft drink, Coca Cola, ex deposit	2 lit	1.22	12/94	2c
Steak, t-bone	lb.	5.72	12/94	2c
Sugar, cane or beet	4 lbs.	1.33	12/94	2c
Tomatoes, Hunt's or Del Monte	14.5 oz.	0.74	12/94	2c
Tuna, chunk, light, oil-packed	6.125-6.5 oz.	0.72	12/94	2c
Goods and Services				
Miscellaneous goods and services, ACCRA Index		104.60	12/94	2c
Health Care				
Health care, ACCRA Index		100.10	12/94	2c
Antibiotic ointment, Polysporin	1.5 oz.	4.18	12/94	2c
Dentist's fee, adult teeth cleaning and periodic oral exam	visit	52.40	12/94	2c
Doctor's fee, routine exam, established patient	visit	41.50	12/94	2c
Hospital care, semiprivate room	day	362.50	12/94	2c
Household Goods				
Appl. repair, service call, wash mach	min. lab. chg.	38.86	12/94	2c
Laundry detergent, Tide Ultra, Bold, or Cheer	42 oz.	3.99	12/94	2c
Tissues, facial, Kleenex brand	175	1.06	12/94	2c
Housing				
Housing, ACCRA Index		94.50	12/94	2c
House payment, principal and interest, 25% down payment	mo.	715	12/94	2c
House, 1800 sq ft, 8000 sq ft lot, new, urban, utilities	total	114431	12/94	2c
Mtge. rate, incl. points and orig. fee, 30-year conv. fixed or ARM	mo.	9.40	12/94	2c
Rent, apartment, 2 br., 1 1/2-2 baths, unfurnished, 950 sq ft, water	mo.	524	12/94	2c
Personal Goods				
Shampoo, Alberto VO5	15-oz.	1.36	12/94	2c
Toothpaste, Crest or Colgate	6-7 oz.	2.24	12/94	2c
Personal Services				
Dry cleaning, man's 2-pc. suit		7.76	12/94	2c
Haircut, man's barbershop, no styling		6.90	12/94	2c
Haircut, woman's shampoo, trim, blow-dry		15.79	12/94	2c
Restaurant Food				
Chicken, fried, thigh and drumstick		2.18	12/94	2c
Hamburger with cheese	1/4 lb.	1.70	12/94	2c
Pizza, Pizza Hut or Pizza Inn	12-13 in.	7.14	12/94	2c
Transportation				
Transportation, ACCRA Index		88.30	12/94	2c
Bus fare, one-way	trip	0.50	12/95	1c
Bus fare, up to 10 miles	one-way	0.50	12/94	2c
Tire balance, computer or spin bal., front	wheel	6.70	12/94	2c
Utilities				
Utilities, ACCRA Index		113.50	12/94	2c
Electricity, (part.), other, 1800 sq. ft., new home	mo.	54.48	12/94	2c

Lafayette, LA

Item	Per	Value	Date	Ref.
Composite, ACCRA index		98.60	12/94	2c
Alcoholic Beverages				
Beer, Miller Lite, Bud, 12-oz., ex deposit	6	3.75	12/94	2c

Values are in dollars or fractions of dollars. In the column headed *Ref*, references are shown to sources. Each reference is followed by a letter. These refer to the geographical level for which data were reported: s=State, r=Region, and c=City or metro. The abbreviation *ex* is used to mean *except* or *excluding*; *exp* stands for *expenditures*. For other abbreviations and further explanations, please see the Introduction.

Lafayette, LA - continued

Item	Per	Value	Date	Ref.
Alcoholic Beverages				
J & B Scotch	750-ml.	15.20	12/94	2c
Wine, Gallo Chablis blanc	1.5-lit	4.46	12/94	2c
Appliances				
Appliances (major), expenditures	year	153	91	81r
Average annual exp.				
Food, health care, personal goods, services	year	27020	91	81r
Charity				
Cash contributions, expenditures	year	839	91	81r
Clothing				
Apparel, men and boys, total expenditures	year	380	91	81r
Apparel, women and girls, total expenditures	year	660	91	81r
Footwear, expenditures	year	193	91	81r
Jeans, man's denim		29.00	12/94	2c
Shirt, man's dress shirt		34.25	12/94	2c
Undervest, boy's size 10-14, cotton	3	4.77	12/94	2c
Communications				
Long-distance telephone rate, day, addl. min., 1-10 mi.	min.	0.29	12/93	9s
Long-distance telephone rate, day, initial min., 1-10 mi.	min.	0.41	12/93	9s
Newspaper subscription, dly. and Sun. delivery	month	9.75	12/94	2c
Phone line, single, business, field visit	inst	85.00	12/93	9s
Phone line, single, business, no field visit	inst	85.00	12/93	9s
Phone line, single, residence, field visit	inst	50.00	12/93	9s
Phone line, single, residence, no field visit	inst	50.00	12/93	9s
Telephone bill, family of four	month	19.56	12/94	2c
Telephone service, expenditures	year	616	91	81r
Telephone, residential, flat rate	mo.	12.85	12/93	8c
Education				
Board, 4-year private college/university	year	2436	8/94	80s
Board, 4-year public college/university	year	1638	8/94	80s
Education, total expenditures	year	319	91	81r
Room, 4-year private college/university	year	2558	8/94	80s
Room, 4-year public college/university	year	1405	8/94	80s
Total cost, 4-year private college/university	year	16467	8/94	80s
Total cost, 4-year public college/university	year	5225	8/94	80s
Tuition, 2-year public college/university, in-state	year	956	8/94	80s
Tuition, 4-year private college/university, in-state	year	11473	8/94	80s
Tuition, 4-year public college/university, in-state	year	2182	8/94	80s
Energy and Fuels				
Energy, combined forms, 1800 sq. ft.	mo.	132.20	12/94	2c
Fuel oil and other fuels, expenditures	year	56	91	81r
Gas, cooking, 10 therms	month	11.70	2/94	65c
Gas, cooking, 30 therms	month	23.10	2/94	65c
Gas, cooking, 50 therms	month	34.51	2/94	65c
Gas, heating, winter, 100 therms	month	63.03	2/94	65c
Gas, heating, winter, average use	month	51.63	2/94	65c
Gas, natural, expenditures	year	150	91	81r
Gas, reg unlead, taxes inc., cash, self-service	gal	1.13	12/94	2c
Gasoline and motor oil purchased	year	1152	91	81r
Gasoline, unleaded midgrade	gallon	1.21	4/93	82r
Gasoline, unleaded premium	gallon	1.30	4/93	82r
Gasoline, unleaded regular	gallon	1.10	4/93	82r
Entertainment				
Bowling, evening rate	game	2.50	12/94	2c
Concert ticket, Pearl Jam group	perf	20.00	94	50r
Entertainment, total expenditures	year	1266	91	81r
Fees and admissions, expenditures	year	306	91	81r
Monopoly game, Parker Brothers', No. 9	game	10.50	12/94	2c
Movie	adm	5.50	12/94	2c
Pets, toys, playground equipment, expenditures	year	271	91	81r

Lafayette, LA - continued

Item	Per	Value	Date	Ref.
Entertainment - continued				
Reading, expenditures	year	131	91	81r
Televisions, radios, and sound equipment, expenditures	year	439	91	81r
Tennis balls, yellow, Wilson or Penn, 3	can	2.19	12/94	2c
Funerals				
Burial, immediate, container provided by funeral home		1574.60	1/95	54r
Cards, acknowledgment		22.24	1/95	54r
Casket, minimum alternative		239.41	1/95	54r
Cosmetology, hair care, etc.		91.04	1/95	54r
Cremation, direct, container provided by funeral home		1085.15	1/95	54r
Embalming		281.30	1/95	54r
Funeral, funeral home		323.04	1/95	54r
Funeral, other facility		327.58	1/95	54r
Graveside service		355.19	1/95	54r
Hearse, local		141.89	1/95	54r
Limousine, local		99.40	1/95	54r
Memorial service		284.67	1/95	54r
Service charge, professional, nondeclinable		904.06	1/95	54r
Visitation and viewing		187.04	1/95	54r
Groceries				
Groceries, ACCRA Index		97.60	12/94	2c
Apples, Red Delicious	lb.	0.73	12/94	82r
Baby food, strained vegetables, lowest price	4-4.5 oz.	0.32	12/94	2c
Bacon, sliced	lb.	1.67	12/94	82r
Bananas	lb.	0.47	12/94	2c
Bananas	lb.	0.42	12/94	82r
Beef or hamburger, ground	lb.	1.49	12/94	2c
Beef purchases	year	213	91	81r
Beverage purchases, alcoholic	year	249	91	81r
Beverage purchases, nonalcoholic	year	207	91	81r
Bologna, all beef or mixed	lb.	2.27	12/94	82r
Bread, white	24-oz.	0.78	12/94	2c
Bread, white, pan	lb.	0.68	12/94	82r
Cabbage	lb.	0.42	12/94	82r
Carrots, short trimmed and topped	lb.	0.53	12/94	82r
Cereals and bakery products purchases	year	345	91	81r
Cereals and cereals products purchases	year	127	91	81r
Cheddar cheese, natural	lb.	3.58	12/94	82r
Cheese, Kraft grated Parmesan	8-oz.	3.23	12/94	2c
Chicken breast, bone-in	lb.	1.71	12/94	82r
Chicken, fresh, whole	lb.	0.78	12/94	82r
Chicken, whole fryer	lb.	0.75	12/94	2c
Chuck roast, USDA choice, boneless	lb.	2.26	12/94	82r
Cigarettes, Winston, Kings	carton	14.66	12/94	2c
Coffee, vacuum-packed	13 oz.	3.51	12/94	2c
Corn Flakes, Kellogg's or Post Toasties	18 oz.	2.42	12/94	2c
Corn, frozen, whole kernel, lowest price	10 oz.	0.73	12/94	2c
Crackers, soda, salted	lb.	1.27	12/94	82r
Cucumbers	lb.	0.65	12/94	82r
Dairy products (other) purchases	year	141	91	81r
Eggs, Grade A large	dozen	0.80	12/94	2c
Eggs, Grade A large	dozen	0.87	12/94	82r
Fish and seafood purchases	year	72	91	81r
Flour, white, all purpose	lb.	0.23	12/94	82r
Food purchases, food eaten at home	year	2381	91	81r
Foods purchased away from home, not prepared by consumer	year	1696	91	81r
Frankfurters, all meat or all beef	lb.	1.74	12/94	82r
Fruits and vegetables purchases	year	380	91	81r
Grapefruit	lb.	0.45	12/94	82r
Grapes, Thompson seedless	lb.	2.30	12/94	82r
Ground beef, 100% beef	lb.	1.37	12/94	82r
Ground chuck, 100% beef	lb.	1.97	12/94	82r
Ham, boneless, exc. canned	lb.	2.54	12/94	82r
Ice cream, prepackaged, bulk, regular	1/2 gal.	2.47	12/94	82r
Lemons	lb.	1.02	12/94	82r
Lettuce, iceberg	lb.	0.96	12/94	82r

Values are in dollars or fractions of dollars. In the column headed *Ref*, references are shown to sources. Each reference is followed by a letter. These refer to the geographical level for which data were reported: s=State, r=Region, and c=City or metro. The abbreviation *ex* is used to mean *except* or *excluding*; *exp* stands for *expenditures*. For other abbreviations and further explanations, please see the Introduction.

Lafayette, LA - continued

Item	Per	Value	Date	Ref.
Groceries				
Lettuce, iceberg	head	0.75	12/94	2c
Margarine, Blue Bonnet or Parkay cubes	lb.	0.53	12/94	2c
Margarine, stick	lb.	0.77	12/94	82r
Meats, poultry, fish, and eggs purchases	year	655	91	81r
Milk and cream (fresh) purchases	year	130	91	81r
Milk, whole	1/2 gal.	1.38	12/94	2c
Orange juice, frozen concentrate 12-oz. can	16 oz.	1.36	12/94	82r
Orange juice, Minute Maid frozen	12-oz.	1.15	12/94	2c
Oranges, Navel	lb.	0.54	12/94	82r
Peaches, halves or slices, Hunt's, Del Monte, or Libby's	29-oz.	1.35	12/94	2c
Pears, Anjou	lb.	0.81	12/94	82r
Peas, sweet, Del Monte or Green Giant	15-17 oz.	0.58	12/94	2c
Pork chops, center cut, bone-in	lb.	3.07	12/94	82r
Pork purchases	year	142	91	81r
Potato chips	16-oz.	3.15	12/94	82r
Potatoes, frozen, French fried	lb.	0.82	12/94	82r
Potatoes, white	lb.	0.34	12/94	82r
Potatoes, white or red	10-lb. sack	2.21	12/94	2c
Rice, white, long grain, uncooked	lb.	0.48	12/94	82r
Round roast, USDA choice, boneless	lb.	2.91	12/94	82r
Sausage, fresh	lb.	1.82	12/94	82r
Sausage, Jimmy Dean, 100% pork	lb.	2.51	12/94	2c
Shortening, vegetable oil blends	lb.	0.75	12/94	82r
Shortening, vegetable, Crisco	3-lb.	2.48	12/94	2c
Soft drink, Coca Cola, ex deposit	2 lit	1.17	12/94	2c
Spaghetti and macaroni	lb.	0.87	12/94	82r
Steak, rib eye, USDA choice, boneless	lb.	6.85	12/94	82r
Steak, round, graded & ungraded, exc. USDA prime & choice	lb.	2.96	12/94	82r
Steak, round, USDA choice, boneless	lb.	3.17	12/94	82r
Steak, sirloin, USDA choice, boneless	lb.	4.12	12/94	82r
Steak, t-bone	lb.	4.96	12/94	2c
Steak, T-bone, USDA choice, bone-in	lb.	5.63	12/94	82r
Sugar and other sweets, eaten at home, expenditures	year	93	91	81r
Sugar, cane or beet	4 lbs.	1.51	12/94	2c
Sugar, white, all sizes	lb.	0.39	12/94	82r
Tobacco products and smoking supplies, total expenditures	year	286	91	81r
Tomatoes, field grown	lb.	1.36	12/94	82r
Tomatoes, Hunt's or Del Monte	14.5 oz.	0.76	12/94	2c
Tuna, chunk, light	lb.	1.94	12/94	82r
Tuna, chunk, light, oil-packed	6.125-6.5 oz.	0.66	12/94	2c
Turkey, frozen, whole	lb.	0.96	12/94	82r
Yogurt, natural, fruit flavored	8 oz.	0.58	12/94	82r
Goods and Services				
Miscellaneous goods and services, ACCRA Index		100.90	12/94	2c
Health Care				
Health care, ACCRA Index		89.60	12/94	2c
Adenosine, emergency room	treat	100.00	95	23r
Antibiotic ointment, Polysporin	1.5 oz.	4.01	12/94	2c
Bladder tap, superpubic, infant, emergency room	treat	119.00	95	23r
Blood analysis, emergency room	treat	25.00	95	23r
Blood tests, abdominal pain, emergency room	treat	25.00	95	23r
Burn dressing, emergency room	treat	266.00	95	23r
Cardiology interpretation, emergency room	treat	26.00	95	23r
Chest X-ray, emergency room	treat	78.00	95	23r
Childbirth, Cesarean delivery, hospital charge	birth	5462.00	12/91	69r
Childbirth, Cesarean delivery, physician charge	birth	2228.00	12/91	69r
Childbirth, normal delivery, hospital charge	birth	2943.00	12/91	69r

Lafayette, LA - continued

Item	Per	Value	Date	Ref.
Health Care - continued				
Childbirth, normal delivery, physician charge	birth	1619.00	12/91	69r
Defibrillation pads, emergency room	treat	6.00	95	23r
Dentist's fee, adult teeth cleaning and periodic oral exam	visit	49.20	12/94	2c
Doctor's fee, routine exam, established patient	visit	40.00	12/94	2c
Drugs, expenditures	year	297	91	81r
Gastric tube insertion, nasal, emergency room	treat	25.00	95	23r
Health care, total expenditures	year	1600	91	81r
Health insurance expenditures	year	637	91	81r
Heart monitor, emergency room	treat	40.00	95	23r
Hospital care, semiprivate room	day	232.00	12/94	2c
Insurance premium, family medical care	month	394.31	1/95	41s
Intravenous fluids, emergency room	treat	130.00	95	23r
Intravenous fluids, emergency room	liter	26.00	95	23r
Intravenous line, central, emergency room	treat	342.00	95	23r
Liver function tests, abdominal pain, emergency room	treat	26.00	95	23r
Medical care charges, total, emergency room, third-degree burns	treat	2101.00	95	23r
Medical care charges, total, emergency, infant with fever	treat	628.00	95	23r
Medical services expenditures	year	573	91	81r
Medical supplies expenditures	year	93	91	81r
Morphine, emergency room	treat	34.00	95	23r
Nursing care and facilities charges, emergency room	treat	252.00	95	23r
Nursing care and facilities charges, emergency, infant with fever	treat	252.00	95	23r
Nursing care and facilities charges, emergency, third-degree burns	treat	861.00	95	23r
Physician's charges, emergency, infant with fever	treat	212.00	95	23r
Physician's charges, emergency, third-degree burns	treat	372.00	95	23r
Physician's fee, emergency room	treat	372.00	95	23r
Physician's fee, general practitioner	visit	51.20	12/93	60r
Surgery, open-heart	proc	42374.00	1/93	14r
Ultrasound, abdominal, emergency room	treat	276.00	95	23r
Urinalysis, emergency room	treat	20.00	95	23r
Urinalysis, infant, emergency room	treat	20.00	95	23r
X-rays, emergency room	treat	78.00	95	23r
Household Goods				
Appl. repair, service call, wash mach	min. lab. chg.	38.00	12/94	2c
Floor coverings, expenditures	year	48	91	81r
Furniture, expenditures	year	280	91	81r
Household equipment, misc. expenditures	year	342	91	81r
Household expenditures, miscellaneous	year	256	91	81r
Household furnishings and equipment, expenditures	year	988	91	81r
Household operations expenditures	year	468	91	81r
Household textiles, expenditures	year	95	91	81r
Housekeeping supplies, expenditures	year	380	91	81r
Laundry and cleaning supplies, expenditures	year	109	91	81r
Laundry detergent, Tide Ultra, Bold, or Cheer	42 oz.	3.45	12/94	2c
Postage and stationery, expenditures	year	105	91	81r
Tissues, facial, Kleenex brand	175	0.88	12/94	2c
Housing				
Housing, ACCRA Index		92.50	12/94	2c
Add garage/carport		6,980	3/95	74r
Add room(s)		11,403	3/95	74r
Apartment condominium or co-op, median	unit	68600	12/94	62r
Dwellings (owned), expenditures	year	2428	91	81r
Enclose porch/patio/breezeway		4,572	3/95	74r
Finish room in basement/attic		3,794	3/95	74r
Home, existing, single-family, median	unit	120200	12/94	62r

Values are in dollars or fractions of dollars. In the column headed *Ref*, references are shown to sources. Each reference is followed by a letter. These refer to the geographical level for which data were reported: s=State, r=Region, and c=City or metro. The abbreviation *ex* is used to mean *except* or *excluding*; *exp* stands for expenditures. For other abbreviations and further explanations, please see the Introduction.

Lafayette, LA - continued

Item	Per	Value	Date	Ref.
Housing				
House payment, principal and interest, 25% down payment	mo.	690	12/94	2c
House, 1800 sq ft, 8000 sq ft lot, new, urban, utilities	total	111962	12/94	2c
Maintenance, repairs, insurance, and other housing expenditures	year	531	91	81r
Mortgage interest and charges expenditures	year	1506	91	81r
Mtge. rate, incl. points and orig. fee, 30-year conv. fixed or ARM	mo.	9.24	12/94	2c
Princ. & int., mortgage, median-price exist. sing.-family home	mo.	540	12/94	62r
Property taxes expenditures	year	391	91	81r
Redesign, restructure more than half of home's interior		17,641	3/95	74r
Rent, apartment, 2 br., 1 1/2-2 baths, unfurnished, 950 sq ft, water	mo.	542	12/94	2c
Rental units expenditures	year	1264	91	81r
Insurance and Pensions				
Auto insurance, private passenger	year	862.62	12/94	71s
Insurance and pensions, personal, expenditures	year	2395	91	81r
Insurance, life and other personal, expenditures	year	368	91	81r
Pensions and Social Security, expenditures	year	2027	91	81r
Personal Goods				
Shampoo, Alberto VO5	15-oz.	1.01	12/94	2c
Toothpaste, Crest or Colgate	6-7 oz.	2.25	12/94	2c
Personal Services				
Dry cleaning, man's 2-pc. suit		6.40	12/94	2c
Haircut, man's barbershop, no styling		9.20	12/94	2c
Haircut, woman's shampoo, trim, blow-dry		24.40	12/94	2c
Personal services expenditures	year	212	91	81r
Restaurant Food				
Chicken, fried, thigh and drumstick		1.99	12/94	2c
Dining expenditures, family	week	33.83	94	73r
Hamburger with cheese	1/4 lb.	1.89	12/94	2c
Pizza, Pizza Hut or Pizza Inn	12-13 in.	7.99	12/94	2c
Taxes				
Taxes, Federal income, expenditures	year	2275	91	81r
Taxes, personal, expenditures	year	2715	91	81r
Taxes, State and local income, expenditures	year	365	91	81r
Transportation				
Transportation, ACCRA Index		102.40	12/94	2c
Cars and trucks purchased, new	year	1306	91	81r
Cars and trucks purchased, used	year	942	91	81r
Driver's learning permit fee	perm	12.50	1/94	84s
Driver's license fee	orig	12.50	1/94	84s
Driver's license fee, duplicate	lic	5.00	1/94	84s
Driver's license reinstatement fee, min.	susp	60.00	1/94	85s
Driver's license renewal fee	renew	12.50	1/94	84s
Identification card, nondriver	card	7.00	1/94	83s
Motorcycle license fee	orig	8.00	1/94	84s
Motorcycle license renewal fee	renew	8.00	1/94	84s
Public transportation expenditures	year	249	91	81r
Tire balance, computer or spin bal., front	wheel	7.09	12/94	2c
Transportation expenditures, total	year	5307	91	81r
Vehicle finance charges	year	346	91	81r
Vehicle insurance expenditures	year	544	91	81r
Vehicle maintenance and repairs expenditures	year	600	91	81r
Vehicle purchases	year	2275	91	81r
Vehicle rental, leases, licenses, etc.	year	141	91	81r
Vehicles purchased, other than cars and trucks	year	27	91	81r

Lafayette, LA - continued

Item	Per	Value	Date	Ref.
Utilities				
Utilities, ACCRA Index		115.40	12/94	2c
Electricity expenditures	year	950	91	81r
Electricity, 1800 sq. ft., new home	mo.	132.20	12/94	2c
Utilities, fuels, and public services, total expenditures	year	2000	91	81r
Water and other public services, expenditures	year	227	91	81r
Weddings				
Bridal attendants' gowns	event	750	10/93	76r
Bridal gown	event	852	10/93	76r
Bridal headpiece and veil	event	167	10/93	76r
Bride's wedding band	event	708	10/93	76r
Clergy	event	224	10/93	76r
Engagement ring	event	2756	10/93	76r
Flowers	event	863	10/93	76r
Formal wear for groom	event	106	10/93	76r
Groom's attendants' formal wear	event	530	10/93	76r
Groom's wedding band	event	402	10/93	76r
Music	event	600	10/93	76r
Photography	event	1088	10/93	76r
Shoes for bride	event	50	10/93	76r
Videography	event	483	10/93	76r
Wedding invitations and announcements	event	342	10/93	76r
Wedding reception	event	7000	10/93	76r

Lake Charles, LA

Item	Per	Value	Date	Ref.
Composite, ACCRA index		96.30	12/94	2c
Alcoholic Beverages				
Beer, Miller Lite, Bud, 12-oz., ex deposit	6	4.04	12/94	2c
J & B Scotch	750-ml.	15.49	12/94	2c
Wine, Gallo Chablis blanc	1.5-lit	5.25	12/94	2c
Appliances				
Appliances (major), expenditures	year	153	91	81r
Average annual exp.				
Food, health care, personal goods, services	year	27020	91	81r
Charity				
Cash contributions, expenditures	year	839	91	81r
Clothing				
Apparel, men and boys, total expenditures	year	380	91	81r
Apparel, women and girls, total expenditures	year	660	91	81r
Footwear, expenditures	year	193	91	81r
Jeans, man's denim		37.30	12/94	2c
Shirt, man's dress shirt		34.73	12/94	2c
Undervest, boy's size 10-14, cotton	3	4.45	12/94	2c
Communications				
Long-distance telephone rate, day, addl. min., 1-10 mi.	min.	0.29	12/93	9s
Long-distance telephone rate, day, initial min., 1-10 mi.	min.	0.41	12/93	9s
Newspaper subscription, dly. and Sun. delivery	month	9.50	12/94	2c
Phone line, single, business, field visit	inst	85.00	12/93	9s
Phone line, single, business, no field visit	inst	85.00	12/93	9s
Phone line, single, residence, field visit	inst	50.00	12/93	9s
Phone line, single, residence, no field visit	inst	50.00	12/93	9s
Telephone bill, family of four	month	19.90	12/94	2c
Telephone service, expenditures	year	616	91	81r
Telephone, residential, flat rate	mo.	12.85	12/93	8c
Education				
Board, 4-year private college/university	year	2436	8/94	80s
Board, 4-year public college/university	year	1638	8/94	80s
Education, total expenditures	year	319	91	81r
Room, 4-year private college/university	year	2558	8/94	80s
Room, 4-year public college/university	year	1405	8/94	80s
Total cost, 4-year private college/university	year	16467	8/94	80s

Values are in dollars or fractions of dollars. In the column headed *Ref*, references are shown to sources. Each reference is followed by a letter. These refer to the geographical level for which data were reported: s = State, r = Region, and c = City or metro. The abbreviation *ex* is used to mean *except* or *excluding*; *exp* stands for *expenditures*. For other abbreviations and further explanations, please see the Introduction.

Lake Charles, LA - continued

Item	Per	Value	Date	Ref.
Education				
Total cost, 4-year public college/university	year	5225	8/94	80s
Tuition, 2-year public college/university, in-state	year	956	8/94	80s
Tuition, 4-year private college/university, in-state	year	11473	8/94	80s
Tuition, 4-year public college/university, in-state	year	2182	8/94	80s
Energy and Fuels				
Energy, combined forms, 1800 sq. ft.	mo.	118.94	12/94	2c
Fuel oil and other fuels, expenditures	year	56	91	81r
Gas, cooking, 10 therms	month	13.97	2/94	65c
Gas, cooking, 30 therms	month	22.91	2/94	65c
Gas, cooking, 50 therms	month	31.85	2/94	65c
Gas, heating, winter, 100 therms	month	64.47	2/94	65c
Gas, heating, winter, average use	month	45.26	2/94	65c
Gas, natural, expenditures	year	150	91	81r
Gas, reg unlead, taxes inc., cash, self-service	gal	1.14	12/94	2c
Gasoline and motor oil purchased	year	1152	91	81r
Gasoline, unleaded midgrade	gallon	1.21	4/93	82r
Gasoline, unleaded premium	gallon	1.30	4/93	82r
Gasoline, unleaded regular	gallon	1.10	4/93	82r
Entertainment				
Bowling, evening rate	game	2.04	12/94	2c
Concert ticket, Pearl Jam group	perf	20.00	94	50r
Entertainment, total expenditures	year	1266	91	81r
Fees and admissions, expenditures	year	306	91	81r
Monopoly game, Parker Brothers', No. 9	game	13.01	12/94	2c
Movie	adm	5.50	12/94	2c
Pets, toys, playground equipment, expenditures	year	271	91	81r
Reading, expenditures	year	131	91	81r
Televisions, radios, and sound equipment, expenditures	year	439	91	81r
Tennis balls, yellow, Wilson or Penn, 3	can	1.98	12/94	2c
Funerals				
Burial, immediate, container provided by funeral home		1574.60	1/95	54r
Cards, acknowledgment		22.24	1/95	54r
Casket, minimum alternative		239.41	1/95	54r
Cosmetology, hair care, etc.		91.04	1/95	54r
Cremation, direct, container provided by funeral home		1085.15	1/95	54r
Embalming		281.30	1/95	54r
Funeral, funeral home		323.04	1/95	54r
Funeral, other facility		327.58	1/95	54r
Graveside service		355.19	1/95	54r
Hearse, local		141.89	1/95	54r
Limousine, local		99.40	1/95	54r
Memorial service		284.67	1/95	54r
Service charge, professional, nondeclinable		904.06	1/95	54r
Visitation and viewing		187.04	1/95	54r
Groceries				
Groceries, ACCRA Index		93.80	12/94	2c
Apples, Red Delicious	lb.	0.73	12/94	82r
Baby food, strained vegetables, lowest price	4-4.5 oz.	0.24	12/94	2c
Bacon, sliced	lb.	1.67	12/94	82r
Bananas	lb.	0.38	12/94	2c
Bananas	lb.	0.42	12/94	82r
Beef or hamburger, ground	lb.	1.51	12/94	2c
Beef purchases	year	213	91	81r
Beverage purchases, alcoholic	year	249	91	81r
Beverage purchases, nonalcoholic	year	207	91	81r
Bologna, all beef or mixed	lb.	2.27	12/94	82r
Bread, white	24-oz.	0.68	12/94	2c
Bread, white, pan	lb.	0.68	12/94	82r
Cabbage	lb.	0.42	12/94	82r
Carrots, short trimmed and topped	lb.	0.53	12/94	82r
Cereals and bakery products purchases	year	345	91	81r

Lake Charles, LA - continued

Item	Per	Value	Date	Ref.
Groceries - continued				
Cereals and cereals products purchases	year	127	91	81r
Cheddar cheese, natural	lb.	3.58	12/94	82r
Cheese, Kraft grated Parmesan	8-oz.	2.95	12/94	2c
Chicken breast, bone-in	lb.	1.71	12/94	82r
Chicken, fresh, whole	lb.	0.78	12/94	82r
Chicken, whole fryer	lb.	0.64	12/94	2c
Chuck roast, USDA choice, boneless	lb.	2.26	12/94	82r
Cigarettes, Winston, Kings	carton	13.83	12/94	2c
Coffee, vacuum-packed	13 oz.	3.31	12/94	2c
Corn Flakes, Kellogg's or Post Toasties	18 oz.	2.33	12/94	2c
Corn, frozen, whole kernel, lowest price	10 oz.	0.77	12/94	2c
Crackers, soda, salted	lb.	1.27	12/94	82r
Cucumbers	lb.	0.65	12/94	82r
Dairy products (other) purchases	year	141	91	81r
Eggs, Grade A large	dozen	9.73	12/94	2c
Eggs, Grade A large	dozen	0.87	12/94	82r
Fish and seafood purchases	year	72	91	81r
Flour, white, all purpose	lb.	0.23	12/94	82r
Food purchases, food eaten at home	year	2381	91	81r
Foods purchased away from home, not prepared by consumer	year	1696	91	81r
Frankfurters, all meat or all beef	lb.	1.74	12/94	82r
Fruits and vegetables purchases	year	380	91	81r
Grapefruit	lb.	0.45	12/94	82r
Grapes, Thompson seedless	lb.	2.30	12/94	82r
Ground beef, 100% beef	lb.	1.37	12/94	82r
Ground chuck, 100% beef	lb.	1.97	12/94	82r
Ham, boneless, exc. canned	lb.	2.54	12/94	82r
Ice cream, prepackaged, bulk, regular	1/2 gal.	2.47	12/94	82r
Lemons	lb.	1.02	12/94	82r
Lettuce, iceberg	lb.	0.96	12/94	82r
Lettuce, iceberg	head	0.77	12/94	2c
Margarine, Blue Bonnet or Parkay cubes	lb.	0.60	12/94	2c
Margarine, stick	lb.	0.77	12/94	82r
Meats, poultry, fish, and eggs purchases	year	655	91	81r
Milk and cream (fresh) purchases	year	130	91	81r
Milk, whole	1/2 gal.	1.43	12/94	2c
Orange juice, frozen concentrate 12-oz. can	16 oz.	1.36	12/94	82r
Orange juice, Minute Maid frozen	12-oz.	1.25	12/94	2c
Oranges, Navel	lb.	0.54	12/94	82r
Peaches, halves or slices, Hunt's, Del Monte, or Libby's	29-oz.	1.42	12/94	2c
Pears, Anjou	lb.	0.81	12/94	82r
Peas, sweet, Del Monte or Green Giant	15-17 oz.	0.51	12/94	2c
Pork chops, center cut, bone-in	lb.	3.07	12/94	82r
Pork purchases	year	142	91	81r
Potato chips	16-oz.	3.15	12/94	82r
Potatoes, frozen, French fried	lb.	0.82	12/94	82r
Potatoes, white	lb.	0.34	12/94	82r
Potatoes, white or red	10-lb. sack	2.46	12/94	2c
Rice, white, long grain, uncooked	lb.	0.48	12/94	82r
Round roast, USDA choice, boneless	lb.	2.91	12/94	82r
Sausage, fresh	lb.	1.82	12/94	82r
Sausage, Jimmy Dean, 100% pork	lb.	2.58	12/94	2c
Shortening, vegetable oil blends	lb.	0.75	12/94	82r
Shortening, vegetable, Crisco	3-lb.	2.31	12/94	2c
Soft drink, Coca Cola, ex deposit	2 lit	1.24	12/94	2c
Spaghetti and macaroni	lb.	0.87	12/94	82r
Steak, rib eye, USDA choice, boneless	lb.	6.85	12/94	82r
Steak, round, graded & ungraded, exc. USDA prime & choice	lb.	2.96	12/94	82r
Steak, round, USDA choice, boneless	lb.	3.17	12/94	82r
Steak, sirloin, USDA choice, boneless	lb.	4.12	12/94	82r
Steak, t-bone	lb.	5.23	12/94	2c
Steak, T-bone, USDA choice, bone-in	lb.	5.63	12/94	82r
Sugar and other sweets, eaten at home, expenditures	year	93	91	81r
Sugar, cane or beet	4 lbs.	1.41	12/94	2c

Values are in dollars or fractions of dollars. In the column headed *Ref*, references are shown to sources. Each reference is followed by a letter. These refer to the geographical level for which data were reported: s=State, r=Region, and c=City or metro. The abbreviation *ex* is used to mean *except* or *excluding*; *exp* stands for expenditures. For other abbreviations and further explanations, please see the Introduction.

Lake Charles, LA - continued

Item	Per	Value	Date	Ref.
Groceries				
Sugar, white, all sizes	lb.	0.39	12/94	82r
Tobacco products and smoking supplies, total expenditures	year	286	91	81r
Tomatoes, field grown	lb.	1.36	12/94	82r
Tomatoes, Hunt's or Del Monte	14.5 oz.	0.72	12/94	2c
Tuna, chunk, light	lb.	1.94	12/94	82r
Tuna, chunk, light, oil-packed	6.125-6.5 oz.	0.70	12/94	2c
Turkey, frozen, whole	lb.	0.96	12/94	82r
Yogurt, natural, fruit flavored	8 oz.	0.58	12/94	82r
Goods and Services				
Miscellaneous goods and services, ACCRA Index		99.90	12/94	2c
Health Care				
Health care, ACCRA Index		88.90	12/94	2c
Adenosine, emergency room	treat	100.00	95	23r
Antibiotic ointment, Polysporin	1.5 oz.	4.42	12/94	2c
Bladder tap, superpubic, infant, emergency room	treat	119.00	95	23r
Blood analysis, emergency room	treat	25.00	95	23r
Blood tests, abdominal pain, emergency room	treat	25.00	95	23r
Burn dressing, emergency room	treat	266.00	95	23r
Cardiology interpretation, emergency room	treat	26.00	95	23r
Chest X-ray, emergency room	treat	78.00	95	23r
Childbirth, Cesarean delivery, hospital charge	birth	5462.00	12/91	69r
Childbirth, Cesarean delivery, physician charge	birth	2228.00	12/91	69r
Childbirth, normal delivery, hospital charge	birth	2943.00	12/91	69r
Childbirth, normal delivery, physician charge	birth	1619.00	12/91	69r
Defibrillation pads, emergency room	treat	6.00	95	23r
Dentist's fee, adult teeth cleaning and periodic oral exam	visit	46.20	12/94	2c
Doctor's fee, routine exam, established patient	visit	35.43	12/94	2c
Drugs, expenditures	year	297	91	81r
Gastric tube insertion, nasal, emergency room	treat	25.00	95	23r
Health care, total expenditures	year	1600	91	81r
Health insurance expenditures	year	637	91	81r
Heart monitor, emergency room	treat	40.00	95	23r
Hospital care, semiprivate room	day	312.50	12/94	2c
Insurance premium, family medical care	month	394.31	1/95	41s
Intravenous fluids, emergency room	treat	130.00	95	23r
Intravenous fluids, emergency room	liter	26.00	95	23r
Intravenous line, central, emergency room	treat	342.00	95	23r
Liver function tests, abdominal pain, emergency room	treat	26.00	95	23r
Medical care charges, total, emergency room, third-degree burns	treat	2101.00	95	23r
Medical care charges, total, emergency, infant with fever	treat	628.00	95	23r
Medical services expenditures	year	573	91	81r
Medical supplies expenditures	year	93	91	81r
Morphine, emergency room	treat	34.00	95	23r
Nursing care and facilities charges, emergency room	treat	252.00	95	23r
Nursing care and facilities charges, emergency, infant with fever	treat	252.00	95	23r
Nursing care and facilities charges, emergency, third-degree burns	treat	861.00	95	23r
Physician's charges, emergency, infant with fever	treat	212.00	95	23r
Physician's charges, emergency, third-degree burns	treat	372.00	95	23r
Physician's fee, emergency room	treat	372.00	95	23r
Physician's fee, general practitioner	visit	51.20	12/93	60r
Surgery, open-heart	proc	42374.00	1/93	14r
Ultrasound, abdominal, emergency room	treat	276.00	95	23r

Lake Charles, LA - continued

Item	Per	Value	Date	Ref.
Health Care - continued				
Urinalysis, emergency room	treat	20.00	95	23r
Urinalysis, infant, emergency room	treat	20.00	95	23r
X-rays, emergency room	treat	78.00	95	23r
Household Goods				
Appl. repair, service call, wash mach	min. lab. chg.	35.66	12/94	2c
Floor coverings, expenditures	year	48	91	81r
Furniture, expenditures	year	280	91	81r
Household equipment, misc. expenditures	year	342	91	81r
Household expenditures, miscellaneous	year	256	91	81r
Household furnishings and equipment, expenditures	year	988	91	81r
Household operations expenditures	year	468	91	81r
Household textiles, expenditures	year	95	91	81r
Housekeeping supplies, expenditures	year	380	91	81r
Laundry and cleaning supplies, expenditures	year	109	91	81r
Laundry detergent, Tide Ultra, Bold, or Cheer	42 oz.	3.20	12/94	2c
Postage and stationery, expenditures	year	105	91	81r
Tissues, facial, Kleenex brand	175	1.02	12/94	2c
Housing				
Housing, ACCRA Index		91.90	12/94	2c
Add garage/carport		6,980	3/95	74r
Add room(s)		11,403	3/95	74r
Apartment condominium or co-op, median	unit	68600	12/94	62r
Dwellings (owned), expenditures	year	2428	91	81r
Enclose porch/patio/breezeway		4,572	3/95	74r
Finish room in basement/attic		3,794	3/95	74r
Home, existing, single-family, median	unit	120200	12/94	62r
House payment, principal and interest, 25% down payment	mo.	716	12/94	2c
House, 1800 sq ft, 8000 sq ft lot, new, urban, utilities	total	114342	12/94	2c
Maintenance, repairs, insurance, and other housing expenditures	year	531	91	81r
Mortgage interest and charges expenditures	year	1506	91	81r
Mtge. rate, incl. points and orig. fee, 30-year conv. fixed or ARM	mo.	9.32	12/94	2c
Princ. & int., mortgage, median-price exist. sing.-family home	mo.	540	12/94	62r
Property taxes expenditures	year	391	91	81r
Redesign, restructure more than half of home's interior		17,641	3/95	74r
Rent, apartment, 2 br., 1 1/2-2 baths, unfurnished, 950 sq ft, water	mo.	449	12/94	2c
Rental units expenditures·	year	1264	91	81r
Insurance and Pensions				
Auto insurance, private passenger	year	862.62	12/94	71s
Insurance and pensions, personal, expenditures	year	2395	91	81r
Insurance, life and other personal, expenditures	year	368	91	81r
Pensions and Social Security, expenditures	year	2027	91	81r
Personal Goods				
Shampoo, Alberto VO5	15-oz.	1.02	12/94	2c
Toothpaste, Crest or Colgate	6-7 oz.	2.19	12/94	2c
Personal Services				
Dry cleaning, man's 2-pc. suit		6.64	12/94	2c
Haircut, man's barbershop, no styling		7.80	12/94	2c
Haircut, woman's shampoo, trim, blow-dry		19.30	12/94	2c
Personal services expenditures	year	212	91	81r
Restaurant Food				
Chicken, fried, thigh and drumstick		1.89	12/94	2c
Dining expenditures, family	week	33.83	94	73r
Hamburger with cheese	1/4 lb.	1.81	12/94	2c
Pizza, Pizza Hut or Pizza Inn	12-13 in.	5.98	12/94	2c

Values are in dollars or fractions of dollars. In the column headed *Ref*, references are shown to sources. Each reference is followed by a letter. These refer to the geographical level for which data were reported: s=State, r=Region, and c=City or metro. The abbreviation *ex* is used to mean *except* or *excluding*; *exp* stands for expenditures. For other abbreviations and further explanations, please see the Introduction.

Lake Charles, LA - continued

Item	Per	Value	Date	Ref.
Taxes				
Taxes, Federal income, expenditures	year	2275	91	81r
Taxes, personal, expenditures	year	2715	91	81r
Taxes, State and local income, expenditures	year	365	91	81r
Transportation				
Transportation, ACCRA Index		98.00	12/94	2c
Cars and trucks purchased, new	year	1306	91	81r
Cars and trucks purchased, used	year	942	91	81r
Driver's learning permit fee	perm	12.50	1/94	84s
Driver's license fee	orig	12.50	1/94	84s
Driver's license fee, duplicate	lic	5.00	1/94	84s
Driver's license reinstatement fee, min.	susp	60.00	1/94	85s
Driver's license renewal fee	renew	12.50	1/94	84s
Identification card, nondriver	card	7.00	1/94	83s
Motorcycle license fee	orig	8.00	1/94	84s
Motorcycle license renewal fee	renew	8.00	1/94	84s
Public transportation expenditures	year	249	91	81r
Tire balance, computer or spin bal., front	wheel	6.36	12/94	2c
Transportation expenditures, total	year	5307	91	81r
Vehicle finance charges	year	346	91	81r
Vehicle insurance expenditures	year	544	91	81r
Vehicle maintenance and repairs expenditures	year	600	91	81r
Vehicle purchases	year	2275	91	81r
Vehicle rental, leases, licenses, etc. expenditures	year	141	91	81r
Vehicles purchased, other than cars and trucks	year	27	91	81r
Utilities				
Utilities, ACCRA Index		105.50	12/94	2c
Electricity expenditures	year	950	91	81r
Electricity, 1800 sq. ft., new home	mo.	118.94	12/94	2c
Utilities, fuels, and public services, total expenditures	year	2000	91	81r
Water and other public services, expenditures	year	227	91	81r
Weddings				
Bridal attendants' gowns	event	750	10/93	76r
Bridal gown	event	852	10/93	76r
Bridal headpiece and veil	event	167	10/93	76r
Bride's wedding band	event	708	10/93	76r
Clergy	event	224	10/93	76r
Engagement ring	event	2756	10/93	76r
Flowers	event	863	10/93	76r
Formal wear for groom	event	106	10/93	76r
Groom's attendants' formal wear	event	530	10/93	76r
Groom's wedding band	event	402	10/93	76r
Music	event	600	10/93	76r
Photography	event	1088	10/93	76r
Shoes for bride	event	50	10/93	76r
Videography	event	483	10/93	76r
Wedding invitations and announcements	event	342	10/93	76r
Wedding reception	event	7000	10/93	76r

Lake Havasu City, AZ

Item	Per	Value	Date	Ref.
Composite, ACCRA index		100.90	12/94	2c
Alcoholic Beverages				
Beer, Miller Lite, Bud, 12-oz., ex deposit	6	3.65	12/94	2c
J & B Scotch	750-ml.	15.53	12/94	2c
Wine, Gallo Chablis blanc	1.5-lit	4.85	12/94	2c
Clothing				
Jeans, man's denim		41.00	12/94	2c
Shirt, man's dress shirt		26.50	12/94	2c
Undervest, boy's size 10-14, cotton	3	4.08	12/94	2c
Communications				
Newspaper subscription, dly. and Sun. delivery	month	13.70	12/94	2c

Lake Havasu City, AZ - continued

Item	Per	Value	Date	Ref.
Communications - continued				
Telephone bill, family of four	month	21.80	12/94	2c
Energy and Fuels				
Energy, combined forms, 1800 sq. ft.	mo.	121.18	12/94	2c
Gas, reg unlead, taxes inc., cash, self-service	gal	1.23	12/94	2c
Entertainment				
Bowling, evening rate	game	1.75	12/94	2c
Monopoly game, Parker Brothers', No. 9	game	10.21	12/94	2c
Movie	adm	5.00	12/94	2c
Tennis balls, yellow, Wilson or Penn, 3	can	2.62	12/94	2c
Groceries				
Groceries, ACCRA Index		107.80	12/94	2c
Baby food, strained vegetables, lowest price	4-4.5 oz.	0.32	12/94	2c
Bananas	lb.	0.47	12/94	2c
Beef or hamburger, ground	lb.	1.73	12/94	2c
Bread, white	24-oz.	0.92	12/94	2c
Cheese, Kraft grated Parmesan	8-oz.	3.39	12/94	2c
Chicken, whole fryer	lb.	0.97	12/94	2c
Cigarettes, Winston, Kings	carton	14.19	12/94	2c
Coffee, vacuum-packed	13 oz.	3.85	12/94	2c
Corn Flakes, Kellogg's or Post Toasties	18 oz.	2.44	12/94	2c
Corn, frozen, whole kernel, lowest price	10 oz.	0.70	12/94	2c
Eggs, Grade A large	dozen	0.76	12/94	2c
Lettuce, iceberg	head	0.62	12/94	2c
Margarine, Blue Bonnet or Parkay cubes	lb.	0.82	12/94	2c
Milk, whole	1/2 gal.	1.60	12/94	2c
Orange juice, Minute Maid frozen	12-oz.	1.37	12/94	2c
Peaches, halves or slices, Hunt's, Del Monte, or Libby's	29-oz.	1.40	12/94	2c
Peas, sweet, Del Monte or Green Giant	15-17 oz.	0.58	12/94	2c
Potatoes, white or red	10-lb. sack	1.86	12/94	2c
Sausage, Jimmy Dean, 100% pork	lb.	3.10	12/94	2c
Shortening, vegetable, Crisco	3-lb.	2.84	12/94	2c
Soft drink, Coca Cola, ex deposit	2 lit	1.25	12/94	2c
Steak, t-bone	lb.	4.91	12/94	2c
Sugar, cane or beet	4 lbs.	1.55	12/94	2c
Tomatoes, Hunt's or Del Monte	14.5 oz.	0.79	12/94	2c
Tuna, chunk, light, oil-packed	6.125-6.5 oz.	0.89	12/94	2c
Goods and Services				
Miscellaneous goods and services, ACCRA Index		102.60	12/94	2c
Health Care				
Health care, ACCRA Index		108.50	12/94	2c
Antibiotic ointment, Polysporin	1.5 oz.	3.92	12/94	2c
Dentist's fee, adult teeth cleaning and periodic oral exam	visit	57.60	12/94	2c
Doctor's fee, routine exam, established patient	visit	48.33	12/94	2c
Hospital care, semiprivate room	day	360.00	12/94	2c
Household Goods				
Appl. repair, service call, wash mach	min. lab. chg.	30.50	12/94	2c
Laundry detergent, Tide Ultra, Bold, or Cheer	42 oz.	3.27	12/94	2c
Tissues, facial, Kleenex brand	175	1.10	12/94	2c
Housing				
Housing, ACCRA Index		92.80	12/94	2c
House payment, principal and interest, 25% down payment	mo.	692	12/94	2c
House, 1800 sq ft, 8000 sq ft lot, new, urban, utilities	total	111000	12/94	2c

Values are in dollars or fractions of dollars. In the column headed *Ref*, references are shown to sources. Each reference is followed by a letter. These refer to the geographical level for which data were reported: s=State, r=Region, and c=City or metro. The abbreviation *ex* is used to mean *except* or *excluding*; *exp* stands for expenditures. For other abbreviations and further explanations, please see the Introduction.

Lake Havasu City, AZ - continued

Item	Per	Value	Date	Ref.
Housing				
Mtge. rate, incl. points and orig. fee, 30-year conv. fixed or ARM	mo.	9.37	12/94	2c
Rent, apartment, 2 br., 1 1/2-2 baths, unfurnished, 950 sq ft, water	mo.	545	12/94	2c
Personal Goods				
Shampoo, Alberto VO5	15-oz.	1.14	12/94	2c
Toothpaste, Crest or Colgate	6-7 oz.	1.94	12/94	2c
Personal Services				
Dry cleaning, man's 2-pc. suit		6.75	12/94	2c
Haircut, man's barbershop, no styling		7.40	12/94	2c
Haircut, woman's shampoo, trim, blow-dry		19.50	12/94	2c
Restaurant Food				
Chicken, fried, thigh and drumstick		2.49	12/94	2c
Hamburger with cheese	1/4 lb.	1.99	12/94	2c
Pizza, Pizza Hut or Pizza Inn	12-13 in.	7.50	12/94	2c
Transportation				
Transportation, ACCRA Index		96.30	12/94	2c
Tire balance, computer or spin bal., front	wheel	5.33	12/94	2c
Utilities				
Utilities, ACCRA Index		108.50	12/94	2c
Electricity, 1800 sq. ft., new home	mo.	121.18	12/94	2c
Electricity, summer, 250 KWh	month	24.23	8/93	64c
Electricity, summer, 500 KWh	month	42.05	8/93	64c
Electricity, summer, 750 KWh	month	59.87	8/93	64c
Electricity, summer, 1000 KWh	month	77.69	8/93	64c

Lakeland-Winter Haven, FL

Item	Per	Value	Date	Ref.
Appliances				
Appliances (major), expenditures	year	153	91	81r
Average annual exp.				
Food, health care, personal goods, services	year	27020	91	81r
Charity				
Cash contributions, expenditures	year	839	91	81r
Clothing				
Apparel, men and boys, total expenditures	year	380	91	81r
Apparel, women and girls, total expenditures	year	660	91	81r
Footwear, expenditures	year	193	91	81r
Communications				
Long-distance telephone rate, day, addl. min., 1-10 mi.	min.	0.08	12/93	9s
Long-distance telephone rate, day, initial min., 1-10 mi.	min.	0.15	12/93	9s
Phone line, single, business, field visit	inst	86.00	12/93	9s
Phone line, single, business, no field visit	inst	54.50	12/93	9s
Phone line, single, residence, field visit	inst	76.00	12/93	9s
Phone line, single, residence, no field visit	inst	44.50	12/93	9s
Telephone service, expenditures	year	616	91	81r
Education				
Bar examinination preparatory course	course	500.00-100	94	17s
Board, 4-year private college/university	year	2123	8/94	80s
Board, 4-year public college/university	year	2101	8/94	80s
Education, total expenditures	year	319	91	81r
Room, 4-year private college/university	year	2242	8/94	80s
Room, 4-year public college/university	year	1970	8/94	80s
Total cost, 4-year private college/university	year	13853	8/94	80s
Total cost, 4-year public college/university	year	5855	8/94	80s
Tuition, 2-year public college/university, in-state	year	1076	8/94	80s
Tuition, 4-year private college/university, in-state	year	9287	8/94	80s
Tuition, 4-year public college/university, in-state	year	1784	8/94	80s

Lakeland-Winter Haven, FL - continued

Item	Per	Value	Date	Ref.
Energy and Fuels				
Fuel oil and other fuels, expenditures	year	56	91	81r
Gas, natural, expenditures	year	150	91	81r
Gasoline and motor oil purchased	year	1152	91	81r
Gasoline, unleaded midgrade	gallon	1.21	4/93	82r
Gasoline, unleaded premium	gallon	1.30	4/93	82r
Gasoline, unleaded regular	gallon	1.10	4/93	82r
Entertainment				
Concert ticket, Pearl Jam group	perf	20.00	94	50r
Entertainment, total expenditures	year	1266	91	81r
Fees and admissions, expenditures	year	306	91	81r
Pets, toys, playground equipment, expenditures	year	271	91	81r
Reading, expenditures	year	131	91	81r
Televisions, radios, and sound equipment, expenditures	year	439	91	81r
Funerals				
Burial, immediate, container provided by funeral home		1370.36	1/95	54r
Cards, acknowledgment		14.83	1/95	54r
Casket, minimum alternative		192.52	1/95	54r
Cosmetology, hair care, etc.		102.27	1/95	54r
Cremation, direct, container provided by funeral home		1065.64	1/95	54r
Embalming		304.29	1/95	54r
Funeral, funeral home		287.83	1/95	54r
Funeral, other facility		284.14	1/95	54r
Graveside service		349.13	1/95	54r
Hearse, local		132.27	1/95	54r
Limousine, local		98.45	1/95	54r
Memorial service		270.59	1/95	54r
Service charge, professional, nondeclinable		933.59	1/95	54r
Visitation and viewing		225.83	1/95	54r
Groceries				
Apples, Red Delicious	lb.	0.73	12/94	82r
Bacon, sliced	lb.	1.67	12/94	82r
Bananas	lb.	0.42	12/94	82r
Beef purchases	year	213	91	81r
Beverage purchases, alcoholic	year	249	91	81r
Beverage purchases, nonalcoholic	year	207	91	81r
Bologna, all beef or mixed	lb.	2.27	12/94	82r
Bread, white, pan	lb.	0.68	12/94	82r
Cabbage	lb.	0.42	12/94	82r
Carrots, short trimmed and topped	lb.	0.53	12/94	82r
Cereals and bakery products purchases	year	345	91	81r
Cereals and cereals products purchases	year	127	91	81r
Cheddar cheese, natural	lb.	3.58	12/94	82r
Chicken breast, bone-in	lb.	1.71	12/94	82r
Chicken, fresh, whole	lb.	0.78	12/94	82r
Chuck roast, USDA choice, boneless	lb.	2.26	12/94	82r
Crackers, soda, salted	lb.	1.27	12/94	82r
Cucumbers	lb.	0.65	12/94	82r
Dairy products (other) purchases	year	141	91	81r
Eggs, Grade A large	dozen	0.87	12/94	82r
Fish and seafood purchases	year	72	91	81r
Flour, white, all purpose	lb.	0.23	12/94	82r
Food purchases, food eaten at home	year	2381	91	81r
Foods purchased away from home, not prepared by consumer	year	1696	91	81r
Frankfurters, all meat or all beef	lb.	1.74	12/94	82r
Fruits and vegetables purchases	year	380	91	81r
Grapefruit	lb.	0.45	12/94	82r
Grapes, Thompson seedless	lb.	2.30	12/94	82r
Ground beef, 100% beef	lb.	1.37	12/94	82r
Ground chuck, 100% beef	lb.	1.97	12/94	82r
Ham, boneless, exc. canned	lb.	2.54	12/94	82r
Ice cream, prepackaged, bulk, regular	1/2 gal.	2.47	12/94	82r
Lemons	lb.	1.02	12/94	82r
Lettuce, iceberg	lb.	0.96	12/94	82r
Margarine, stick	lb.	0.77	12/94	82r
Meats, poultry, fish, and eggs purchases	year	655	91	81r

Values are in dollars or fractions of dollars. In the column headed *Ref*, references are shown to sources. Each reference is followed by a letter. These refer to the geographical level for which data were reported: s = State, r = Region, and c = City or metro. The abbreviation *ex* is used to mean *except* or *excluding*; *exp* stands for expenditures. For other abbreviations and further explanations, please see the Introduction.

Lakeland-Winter Haven, FL - continued

Item	Per	Value	Date	Ref.
Groceries				
Milk and cream (fresh) purchases	year	130	91	81r
Orange juice, frozen concentrate 12-oz. can	16 oz.	1.36	12/94	82r
Oranges, Navel	lb.	0.54	12/94	82r
Pears, Anjou	lb.	0.81	12/94	82r
Pork chops, center cut, bone-in	lb.	3.07	12/94	82r
Pork purchases	year	142	91	81r
Potato chips	16-oz.	3.15	12/94	82r
Potatoes, frozen, French fried	lb.	0.82	12/94	82r
Potatoes, white	lb.	0.34	12/94	82r
Rice, white, long grain, uncooked	lb.	0.48	12/94	82r
Round roast, USDA choice, boneless	lb.	2.91	12/94	82r
Sausage, fresh	lb.	1.82	12/94	82r
Shortening, vegetable oil blends	lb.	0.75	12/94	82r
Spaghetti and macaroni	lb.	0.87	12/94	82r
Steak, rib eye, USDA choice, boneless	lb.	6.85	12/94	82r
Steak, round, graded & ungraded, exc. USDA prime & choice	lb.	2.96	12/94	82r
Steak, round, USDA choice, boneless	lb.	3.17	12/94	82r
Steak, sirloin, USDA choice, boneless	lb.	4.12	12/94	82r
Steak, T-bone, USDA choice, bone-in	lb.	5.63	12/94	82r
Sugar and other sweets, eaten at home, expenditures	year	93	91	81r
Sugar, white, all sizes	lb.	0.39	12/94	82r
Tobacco products and smoking supplies, total expenditures	year	286	91	81r
Tomatoes, field grown	lb.	1.36	12/94	82r
Tuna, chunk, light	lb.	1.94	12/94	82r
Turkey, frozen, whole	lb.	0.96	12/94	82r
Yogurt, natural, fruit flavored	8 oz.	0.58	12/94	82r
Health Care				
Adenosine, emergency room	treat	100.00	95	23r
Bladder tap, superpubic, infant, emergency room	treat	119.00	95	23r
Blood analysis, emergency room	treat	25.00	95	23r
Blood tests, abdominal pain, emergency room	treat	25.00	95	23r
Burn dressing, emergency room	treat	266.00	95	23r
Cardiology interpretation, emergency room	treat	26.00	95	23r
Chest X-ray, emergency room	treat	78.00	95	23r
Childbirth, Cesarean delivery, hospital charge	birth	5462.00	12/91	69r
Childbirth, Cesarean delivery, physician charge	birth	2228.00	12/91	69r
Childbirth, normal delivery, hospital charge	birth	2943.00	12/91	69r
Childbirth, normal delivery, physician charge	birth	1619.00	12/91	69r
Defibrillation pads, emergency room	treat	6.00	95	23r
Drugs, expenditures	year	297	91	81r
Gastric tube insertion, nasal, emergency room	treat	25.00	95	23r
Health care, total expenditures	year	1600	91	81r
Health insurance expenditures	year	637	91	81r
Heart monitor, emergency room	treat	40.00	95	23r
Insurance premium, family medical care	month	301.92	1/95	41s
Intravenous fluids, emergency room	treat	130.00	95	23r
Intravenous fluids, emergency room	liter	26.00	95	23r
Intravenous line, central, emergency room	treat	342.00	95	23r
Liver function tests, abdominal pain, emergency room	treat	26.00	95	23r
Medical care charges, total, emergency room, third-degree burns	treat	2101.00	95	23r
Medical care charges, total, emergency, infant with fever	treat	628.00	95	23r
Medical services expenditures	year	573	91	81r
Medical supplies expenditures	year	93	91	81r
Morphine, emergency room	treat	34.00	95	23r
Nursing care and facilities charges, emergency room	treat	252.00	95	23r
Nursing care and facilities charges, emergency, infant with fever	treat	252.00	95	23r
Nursing care and facilities charges, emergency, third-degree burns	treat	861.00	95	23r

Lakeland-Winter Haven, FL - continued

Item	Per	Value	Date	Ref.
Health Care - continued				
Physician's charges, emergency, infant with fever	treat	212.00	95	23r
Physician's charges, emergency, third-degree burns	treat	372.00	95	23r
Physician's fee, emergency room	treat	372.00	95	23r
Physician's fee, general practitioner	visit	51.20	12/93	60r
Surgery, open-heart	proc	42374.00	1/93	14r
Ultrasound, abdominal, emergency room	treat	276.00	95	23r
Urinalysis, emergency room	treat	20.00	95	23r
Urinalysis, infant, emergency room	treat	20.00	95	23r
X-rays, emergency room	treat	78.00	95	23r
Household Goods				
Floor coverings, expenditures	year	48	91	81r
Furniture, expenditures	year	280	91	81r
Household equipment, misc. expenditures	year	342	91	81r
Household expenditures, miscellaneous	year	256	91	81r
Household furnishings and equipment, expenditures	year	988	91	81r
Household operations expenditures	year	468	91	81r
Household textiles, expenditures	year	95	91	81r
Housekeeping supplies, expenditures	year	380	91	81r
Laundry and cleaning supplies, expenditures	year	109	91	81r
Postage and stationery, expenditures	year	105	91	81r
Housing				
Add garage/carport		6,980	3/95	74r
Add room(s)		11,403	3/95	74r
Apartment condominium or co-op, median	unit	68600	12/94	62r
Dwellings (owned), expenditures	year	2428	91	81r
Enclose porch/patio/breezeway		4,572	3/95	74r
Finish room in basement/attic		3,794	3/95	74r
Home, existing, single-family, median	unit	120200	12/94	62r
Maintenance, repairs, insurance, and other housing expenditures	year	531	91	81r
Mortgage interest and charges expenditures	year	1506	91	81r
Princ. & int., mortgage, median-price exist. sing.-family home	mo.	540	12/94	62r
Property taxes expenditures	year	391	91	81r
Redesign, restructure more than half of home's interior		17,641	3/95	74r
Rental units expenditures	year	1264	91	81r
Insurance and Pensions				
Auto insurance, private passenger	year	753.93	12/94	71s
Insurance and pensions, personal, expenditures	year	2395	91	81r
Insurance, life and other personal, expenditures	year	368	91	81r
Pensions and Social Security, expenditures	year	2027	91	81r
Personal Services				
Personal services expenditures	year	212	91	81r
Restaurant Food				
Dining expenditures, family	week	33.83	94	73r
Taxes				
Taxes, Federal income, expenditures	year	2275	91	81r
Taxes, personal, expenditures	year	2715	91	81r
Taxes, State and local income, expenditures	year	365	91	81r
Transportation				
Cars and trucks purchased, new	year	1306	91	81r
Cars and trucks purchased, used	year	942	91	81r
Driver's learning permit fee	perm	20.00	1/94	84s
Driver's license fee	orig	20.00	1/94	84s
Driver's license fee, duplicate	lic	10.00	1/94	84s
Driver's license reinstatement fee, min.	susp	25.00	1/94	85s
Driver's license renewal fee	renew	15.00	1/94	84s
Identification card, nondriver	card	3.00	1/94	83s
Motorcycle learning permit fee	perm	20.00	1/94	84s
Motorcycle license fee	orig	20.00	1/94	84s
Motorcycle license fee, duplicate	lic	10.00	1/94	84s

Values are in dollars or fractions of dollars. In the column headed *Ref*, references are shown to sources. Each reference is followed by a letter. These refer to the geographical level for which data were reported: s=State, r=Region, and c=City or metro. The abbreviation *ex* is used to mean *except* or *excluding*; *exp* stands for expenditures. For other abbreviations and further explanations, please see the Introduction.

Lakeland-Winter Haven, FL - continued

Item	Per	Value	Date	Ref.
Transportation				
Motorcycle license renewal fee	renew	15.00	1/94	84s
Public transportation expenditures	year	249	91	81r
Transportation expenditures, total	year	5307	91	81r
Vehicle finance charges	year	346	91	81r
Vehicle insurance expenditures	year	544	91	81r
Vehicle maintenance and repairs expenditures	year	600	91	81r
Vehicle purchases	year	2275	91	81r
Vehicle rental, leases, licenses, etc. expenditures	year	141	91	81r
Vehicles purchased, other than cars and trucks	year	27	91	81r
Utilities				
Electricity expenditures	year	950	91	81r
Utilities, fuels, and public services, total expenditures	year	2000	91	81r
Water and other public services, expenditures	year	227	91	81r
Weddings				
Bridal attendants' gowns	event	750	10/93	76r
Bridal gown	event	852	10/93	76r
Bridal headpiece and veil	event	167	10/93	76r
Bride's wedding band	event	708	10/93	76r
Clergy	event	224	10/93	76r
Engagement ring	event	2756	10/93	76r
Flowers	event	863	10/93	76r
Formal wear for groom	event	106	10/93	76r
Groom's attendants' formal wear	event	530	10/93	76r
Groom's wedding band	event	402	10/93	76r
Music	event	600	10/93	76r
Photography	event	1088	10/93	76r
Shoes for bride	event	50	10/93	76r
Videography	event	483	10/93	76r
Wedding invitations and announcements	event	342	10/93	76r
Wedding reception	event	7000	10/93	76r

Lakewood, CO

Item	Per	Value	Date	Ref.
Composite, ACCRA index		113.90	12/94	2c
Alcoholic Beverages				
Beer, Miller Lite, Bud, 12-oz., ex deposit	6	4.28	12/94	2c
J & B Scotch	750-ml.	18.11	12/94	2c
Wine, Gallo Chablis blanc	1.5-lit	4.53	12/94	2c
Clothing				
Jeans, man's denim		32.24	12/94	2c
Shirt, man's dress shirt		29.75	12/94	2c
Undervest, boy's size 10-14, cotton	3	3.86	12/94	2c
Communications				
Newspaper subscription, dly. and Sun. delivery	month	8.61	12/94	2c
Telephone bill, family of four	month	20.18	12/94	2c
Energy and Fuels				
Energy, combined forms, 1800 sq. ft.	mo.	101.91	12/94	2c
Energy, exc. electricity, 1800 sq. ft.	mo.	40.87	12/94	2c
Gas, reg unlead, taxes inc., cash, self-service	gal	1.16	12/94	2c
Entertainment				
Bowling, evening rate	game	2.00	12/94	2c
Monopoly game, Parker Brothers', No. 9	game	10.99	12/94	2c
Movie	adm	6.06	12/94	2c
Tennis balls, yellow, Wilson or Penn, 3	can	2.77	12/94	2c
Groceries				
Groceries, ACCRA Index		103.00	12/94	2c
Baby food, strained vegetables, lowest price	4-4.5 oz.	0.36	12/94	2c
Bananas	lb.	0.59	12/94	2c

Lakewood, CO - continued

Item	Per	Value	Date	Ref.
Groceries - continued				
Beef or hamburger, ground	lb.	1.61	12/94	2c
Beverage, Coca Cola	2 lit	0.92	4/95	30c
Beverage, Pepsi	2 lit	0.94	4/95	30c
Bread, white	24-oz.	0.65	12/94	2c
Cereal, Corn Flakes, Kellogg's	18 oz.	2.87	4/95	30c
Cereal, Corn Flakes, local brand	18 oz.	1.72	4/95	30c
Cheese, Kraft grated Parmesan	8-oz.	2.99	12/94	2c
Chicken, whole fryer	lb.	0.75	12/94	2c
Cigarettes, Winston, Kings	carton	13.79	12/94	2c
Coffee, vacuum-packed	13 oz.	3.93	12/94	2c
Corn Flakes, Kellogg's or Post Toasties	18 oz.	2.10	12/94	2c
Corn, frozen, whole kernel, lowest price	10 oz.	0.89	12/94	2c
Dishwashing detergent, Dawn brand	22 oz.	1.39	4/95	30c
Eggs, Grade A large	dozen	0.85	12/94	2c
Frozen dinner, Stouffer's Lean Cuisine brand, glazed chicken	pkg.	2.91	4/95	30c
Lettuce, iceberg	head	0.91	12/94	2c
Margarine, Blue Bonnet or Parkay cubes	lb.	0.57	12/94	2c
Milk, whole	1/2 gal.	1.68	12/94	2c
Orange juice, Minute Maid frozen	12-oz.	1.35	12/94	2c
Peaches, halves or slices, Hunt's, Del Monte, or Libby's	29-oz.	1.61	12/94	2c
Peas, canned, Le Sueur brand	8.5 oz.	0.60	4/95	30c
Peas, sweet, Del Monte or Green Giant	15-17 oz.	0.80	12/94	2c
Potatoes, white or red	10-lb. sack	2.29	12/94	2c
Sausage, Jimmy Dean, 100% pork	lb.	3.56	12/94	2c
Shortening, vegetable, Crisco	3-lb.	2.97	12/94	2c
Soft drink, Coca Cola, ex deposit	2 lit	0.82	12/94	2c
Steak, t-bone	lb.	5.19	12/94	2c
Sugar, cane or beet	4 lbs.	1.19	12/94	2c
Tomatoes, Hunt's or Del Monte	14.5 oz.	0.91	12/94	2c
Tuna, chunk, light, oil-packed	6.125-6.5 oz.	0.83	12/94	2c
Goods and Services				
Miscellaneous goods and services, ACCRA Index		100.70	12/94	2c
Health Care				
Health care, ACCRA Index		128.20	12/94	2c
Antibiotic ointment, Polysporin	1.5 oz.	4.18	12/94	2c
Dentist's fee, adult teeth cleaning and periodic oral exam	visit	67.86	12/94	2c
Doctor's fee, routine exam, established patient	visit	58.29	12/94	2c
Hospital care, semiprivate room	day	432.00	12/94	2c
Household Goods				
Appl. repair, service call, wash mach	min. lab. chg.	35.50	12/94	2c
Laundry detergent, Tide Ultra, Bold, or Cheer	42 oz.	3.65	12/94	2c
Tissues, facial, Kleenex brand	175	0.89	12/94	2c
Housing				
Housing, ACCRA Index		138.90	12/94	2c
House payment, principal and interest, 25% down payment	mo.	1078	12/94	2c
House, 1800 sq ft, 8000 sq ft lot, new, urban, utilities	total	173950	12/94	2c
Mtge. rate, incl. points and orig. fee, 30-year conv. fixed or ARM	mo.	9.30	12/94	2c
Rent, apartment, 2 br., 1 1/2-2 baths, unfurnished, 950 sq ft, water	mo.	693	12/94	2c
Personal Goods				
Shampoo, Alberto VO5	15-oz.	1.23	12/94	2c
Toothpaste, Crest or Colgate	6-7 oz.	1.87	12/94	2c

Values are in dollars or fractions of dollars. In the column headed *Ref*, references are shown to sources. Each reference is followed by a letter. These refer to the geographical level for which data were reported: s=State, r=Region, and c=City or metro. The abbreviation *ex* is used to mean *except* or *excluding*; *exp* stands for expenditures. For other abbreviations and further explanations, please see the Introduction.

Lakewood, CO - continued

Item	Per	Value	Date	Ref.
Personal Services				
Dry cleaning, man's 2-pc. suit		7.00	12/94	2c
Haircut, man's barbershop, no styling		9.90	12/94	2c
Haircut, woman's shampoo, trim, blow-dry		20.70	12/94	2c
Restaurant Food				
Chicken, fried, thigh and drumstick		1.99	12/94	2c
Hamburger with cheese	1/4 lb.	2.01	12/94	2c
Pizza, Pizza Hut or Pizza Inn	12-13 in.	7.49	12/94	2c
Transportation				
Transportation, ACCRA Index		113.00	12/94	2c
Bus fare, up to 10 miles	one-way	1.25	12/94	2c
Tire balance, computer or spin bal., front	wheel	8.18	12/94	2c
Utilities				
Utilities, ACCRA Index		92.50	12/94	2c
Electricity, (part.), other, 1800 sq. ft., new home	mo.	61.04	12/94	2c

Lancaster, PA

Item	Per	Value	Date	Ref.
Composite, ACCRA index		104.30	12/94	2c
Alcoholic Beverages				
Beer, Miller Lite, Bud, 12-oz., ex deposit	6	5.35	12/94	2c
J & B Scotch	750-ml.	16.99	12/94	2c
Wine, Gallo Chablis blanc	1.5-lit	5.99	12/94	2c
Appliances				
Appliances (major), expenditures	year	145	91	81r
Average annual exp.				
Food, health care, personal goods, services	year	29496	91	81r
Charity				
Cash contributions, expenditures	year	708	91	81r
Clothing				
Apparel, men and boys, total expenditures	year	416	91	81r
Apparel, women and girls, total expenditures	year	744	91	81r
Footwear, expenditures	year	305	91	81r
Jeans, man's denim		33.59	12/94	2c
Shirt, man's dress shirt		32.19	12/94	2c
Undervest, boy's size 10-14, cotton	3	3.97	12/94	2c
Communications				
Long-distance telephone rate, day, addl. min., 1-10 mi.	min.	0.08	12/93	9s
Long-distance telephone rate, day, initial min., 1-10 mi.	min.	0.15	12/93	9s
Newspaper subscription, dly. and Sun. delivery	month	15.65	12/94	2c
Phone line, single, business, field visit	inst	75.00	12/93	9s
Phone line, single, business, no field visit	inst	75.00	12/93	9s
Phone line, single, residence, field visit	inst	40.00	12/93	9s
Phone line, single, residence, no field visit	inst	40.00	12/93	9s
Telephone bill, family of four	month	17.69	12/94	2c
Telephone service, expenditures	year	589	91	81r
Telephone, residential, flat rate	mo.	21.00	12/93	8c
Education				
Board, 4-year private college/university	year	2714	8/94	80s
Board, 4-year public college/university	year	1899	8/94	80s
Education, total expenditures	year	593	91	81r
Room, 4-year private college/university	year	2720	8/94	80s
Room, 4-year public college/university	year	2063	8/94	80s
Total cost, 4-year private college/university	year	18118	8/94	80s
Total cost, 4-year public college/university	year	8278	8/94	80s
Tuition, 2-year public college/university, in-state	year	1671	8/94	80s
Tuition, 4-year private college/university, in-state	year	12684	8/94	80s

Lancaster, PA - continued

Item	Per	Value	Date	Ref.
Education - continued				
Tuition, 4-year public college/university, in-state	year	4316	8/94	80s
Energy and Fuels				
Energy, combined forms, 1800 sq. ft.	mo.	110.24	12/94	2c
Fuel oil and other fuels, expenditures	year	257	91	81r
Gas, natural, expenditures	year	285	91	81r
Gas, reg unlead, taxes inc., cash, self-service	gal	1.13	12/94	2c
Gasoline and motor oil purchased	year	867	91	81r
Gasoline, unleaded midgrade	gallon	1.32	4/93	82r
Gasoline, unleaded premium	gallon	1.40	4/93	82r
Gasoline, unleaded regular	gallon	1.19	4/93	82r
Entertainment				
Bowling, evening rate	game	2.40	12/94	2c
Entertainment, total expenditures	year	1331	91	81r
Fees and admissions, expenditures	year	398	91	81r
Monopoly game, Parker Brothers', No. 9	game	12.54	12/94	2c
Movie	adm	5.60	12/94	2c
Pets, toys, playground equipment, expenditures	year	270	91	81r
Reading, expenditures	year	171	91	81r
Televisions, radios, and sound equipment, expenditures	year	429	91	81r
Tennis balls, yellow, Wilson or Penn, 3	can	2.72	12/94	2c
Funerals				
Burial, immediate, container provided by funeral home		1370.36	1/95	54r
Cards, acknowledgment		17.72	1/95	54r
Casket, minimum alternative		192.52	1/95	54r
Cosmetology, hair care, etc.		139.56	1/95	54r
Cremation, direct, container provided by funeral home		1049.24	1/95	54r
Embalming		387.57	1/95	54r
Funeral, funeral home		278.77	1/95	54r
Funeral, other facility		275.85	1/95	54r
Graveside service		213.08	1/95	54r
Hearse, local		157.27	1/95	54r
Limousine, local		146.45	1/95	54r
Memorial service		271.02	1/95	54r
Service charge, professional, nondeclinable		943.58	1/95	54r
Visitation and viewing		322.86	1/95	54r
Groceries				
Groceries, ACCRA Index		99.70	12/94	2c
Apples, Red Delicious	lb.	0.78	12/94	82r
Baby food, strained vegetables, lowest price	4-4.5 oz.	0.39	12/94	2c
Bacon, sliced	lb.	2.24	12/94	82r
Bananas	lb.	0.36	12/94	2c
Bananas	lb.	0.49	12/94	82r
Beef or hamburger, ground	lb.	1.56	12/94	2c
Beef purchases	year	226	91	81r
Beverage purchases, alcoholic	year	332	91	81r
Beverage purchases, nonalcoholic	year	213	91	81r
Bread, white	24-oz.	0.75	12/94	2c
Bread, white, pan	lb.	0.80	12/94	82r
Butter, salted, Grade AA, stick	lb.	1.67	12/94	82r
Carrots, short trimmed and topped	lb.	0.51	12/94	82r
Cereals and bakery products purchases	year	407	91	81r
Cereals and cereals products purchases	year	132	91	81r
Cheese, Kraft grated Parmesan	8-oz.	3.34	12/94	2c
Chicken breast, bone-in	lb.	2.22	12/94	82r
Chicken, fresh, whole	lb.	1.05	12/94	82r
Chicken, whole fryer	lb.	0.85	12/94	2c
Chuck roast, USDA choice, boneless	lb.	2.74	12/94	82r
Cigarettes, Winston, Kings	carton	15.76	12/94	2c
Coffee, 100%, ground roast, all sizes	lb.	4.61	12/94	82r
Coffee, vacuum-packed	13 oz.	3.24	12/94	2c
Corn Flakes, Kellogg's or Post Toasties	18 oz.	2.36	12/94	2c
Corn, frozen, whole kernel, lowest price	10 oz.	0.64	12/94	2c
Dairy products (other) purchases	year	161	91	81r

Values are in dollars or fractions of dollars. In the column headed *Ref*, references are shown to sources. Each reference is followed by a letter. These refer to the geographical level for which data were reported: s = State, r = Region, and c = City or metro. The abbreviation *ex* is used to mean *except* or *excluding*; *exp* stands for expenditures. For other abbreviations and further explanations, please see the Introduction.

Lancaster, PA - continued

Item	Per	Value	Date	Ref.
Groceries				
Eggs, Grade A large	dozen	0.83	12/94	2c
Eggs, Grade A large	dozen	1.12	12/94	82r
Fish and seafood purchases	year	112	91	81r
Food purchases, food eaten at home	year	2599	91	81r
Foods purchased away from home, not prepared by consumer	year	2024	91	81r
Fruits and vegetables purchases	year	444	91	81r
Grapefruit	lb.	0.44	12/94	82r
Grapes, Thompson seedless	lb.	2.24	12/94	82r
Ground chuck, 100% beef	lb.	1.67	12/94	82r
Ice cream, prepackaged, bulk, regular	1/2 gal.	2.93	12/94	82r
Lemons	lb.	1.06	12/94	82r
Lettuce, iceberg	lb.	0.92	12/94	82r
Lettuce, iceberg	head	0.91	12/94	2c
Margarine, Blue Bonnet or Parkay cubes	lb.	0.72	12/94	2c
Meats, poultry, fish, and eggs purchases	year	751	91	81r
Milk and cream (fresh) purchases	year	152	91	81r
Milk, whole	1/2 gal.	1.21	12/94	2c
Orange juice, frozen concentrate 12-oz. can	16 oz.	1.92	12/94	82r
Orange juice, Minute Maid frozen	12-oz.	1.25	12/94	2c
Oranges, Navel	lb.	0.56	12/94	82r
Peaches, halves or slices, Hunt's, Del Monte, or Libby's	29-oz.	1.30	12/94	2c
Peas, sweet, Del Monte or Green Giant	15-17 oz.	0.44	12/94	2c
Pork chops, center cut, bone-in	lb.	3.09	12/94	82r
Pork purchases	year	130	91	81r
Potatoes, white	lb.	0.37	12/94	82r
Potatoes, white or red	10-lb. sack	2.65	12/94	2c
Rib roast, USDA choice, bone-in	lb.	4.98	12/94	82r
Round roast, USDA choice, boneless	lb.	2.93	12/94	82r
Sausage, Jimmy Dean, 100% pork	lb.	2.64	12/94	2c
Shortening, vegetable oil blends	lb.	1.03	12/94	82r
Shortening, vegetable, Crisco	3-lb.	2.57	12/94	2c
Soft drink, Coca Cola, ex deposit	2 lit	1.09	12/94	2c
Spaghetti and macaroni	lb.	0.84	12/94	82r
Steak, round, USDA choice, boneless	lb.	3.48	12/94	82r
Steak, sirloin, USDA choice, bone-in	lb.	3.38	12/94	82r
Steak, sirloin, USDA choice, boneless	lb.	4.81	12/94	82r
Steak, t-bone	lb.	5.01	12/94	2c
Sugar and other sweets, eaten at home, expenditures	year	89	91	81r
Sugar, cane or beet	4 lbs.	1.29	12/94	2c
Sugar, white, all sizes	lb.	0.46	12/94	82r
Tobacco products and smoking supplies, total expenditures	year	279	91	81r
Tomatoes, field grown	lb.	1.56	12/94	82r
Tomatoes, Hunt's or Del Monte	14.5 oz.	0.73	12/94	2c
Tuna, chunk, light	lb.	2.09	12/94	82r
Tuna, chunk, light, oil-packed	6.125-6.5 oz.	0.65	12/94	2c
Goods and Services				
Miscellaneous goods and services, ACCRA Index		106.40	12/94	2c
Health Care				
Health care, ACCRA Index		90.50	12/94	2c
Antibiotic ointment, Polysporin	1.5 oz.	4.23	12/94	2c
Childbirth, Cesarean delivery, hospital charge	birth	6334.00	12/91	69r
Childbirth, Cesarean delivery, physician charge	birth	2234.00	12/91	69r
Childbirth, normal delivery, hospital charge	birth	3225.00	12/91	69r
Childbirth, normal delivery, physician charge	birth	1623.00	12/91	69r
Dentist's fee, adult teeth cleaning and periodic oral exam	visit	52.40	12/94	2c
Doctor's fee, routine exam, established patient	visit	34.00	12/94	2c

Lancaster, PA - continued

Item	Per	Value	Date	Ref.
Health Care - continued				
Drugs, expenditures	year	205	91	81r
Health care, total expenditures	year	1396	91	81r
Health insurance expenditures	year	553	91	81r
Hospital care, semiprivate room	day	297.25	12/94	2c
Insurance premium, family medical care	month	349.05	1/95	41s
Medical services expenditures	year	559	91	81r
Medical supplies expenditures	year	80	91	81r
Household Goods				
Appl. repair, service call, wash mach	min. lab. chg.	30.89	12/94	2c
Floor coverings, expenditures	year	158	91	81r
Furniture, expenditures	year	341	91	81r
Household equipment, misc. expenditures	year	363	91	81r
Household expenditures, miscellaneous	year	194	91	81r
Household furnishings and equipment, expenditures	year	1158	91	81r
Household operations expenditures	year	378	91	81r
Household textiles, expenditures	year	88	91	81r
Housekeeping supplies, expenditures	year	426	91	81r
Laundry and cleaning supplies, expenditures	year	122	91	81r
Laundry detergent, Tide Ultra, Bold, or Cheer	42 oz.	3.54	12/94	2c
Postage and stationery, expenditures	year	134	91	81r
Tissues, facial, Kleenex brand	175	1.02	12/94	2c
Housing				
Housing, ACCRA Index		106.70	12/94	2c
Add garage/carport		11,614	3/95	74r
Add room(s)		16,816	3/95	74r
Apartment condominium or co-op, median	unit	96700	12/94	62r
Dwellings (owned), expenditures	year	3305	91	81r
Enclose porch/patio/breezeway		2,980	3/95	74r
Finish room in basement/attic		4,330	3/95	74r
Home, existing, single-family, median	unit	161600	12/94	62r
House payment, principal and interest, 25% down payment	mo.	818	12/94	2c
House, 1800 sq ft, 8000 sq ft lot, new, urban, utilities	total	133917	12/94	2c
Maintenance, repairs, insurance, and other housing expenditures	year	569	91	81r
Mortgage interest and charges expenditures	year	1852	91	81r
Mtge. rate, incl. points and orig. fee, 30-year conv. fixed or ARM	mo.	9.14	12/94	2c
Princ. & int., mortgage, median-price exist. sing.-family home	mo.	765	12/94	62r
Property taxes expenditures	year	884	91	81r
Redesign, restructure more than half of home's interior		2,750	3/95	74r
Rent, apartment, 2 br., 1 1/2-2 baths, unfurnished, 950 sq ft, water	mo.	563	12/94	2c
Rental units expenditures	year	1832	91	81r
Insurance and Pensions				
Auto insurance, private passenger	year	721.50	12/94	71s
Insurance and pensions, personal, expenditures	year	2690	91	81r
Insurance, life and other personal, expenditures	year	341	91	81r
Pensions and Social Security, expenditures	year	2349	91	81r
Legal Assistance				
Estate planning, law-firm partner	hr.	375.00	10/93	12r
Legal work, law firm associate	hour	78		10r
Legal work, law firm partner	hour	183		10r
Personal Goods				
Shampoo, Alberto VO5	15-oz.	1.17	12/94	2c
Toothpaste, Crest or Colgate	6-7 oz.	2.10	12/94	2c
Personal Services				
Dry cleaning, man's 2-pc. suit		7.11	12/94	2c
Haircut, man's barbershop, no styling		7.89	12/94	2c

Values are in dollars or fractions of dollars. In the column headed *Ref*, references are shown to sources. Each reference is followed by a letter. These refer to the geographical level for which data were reported: s = State, r = Region, and c = City or metro. The abbreviation *ex* is used to mean *except* or *excluding*; *exp* stands for expenditures. For other abbreviations and further explanations, please see the Introduction.

Lancaster, PA - continued

Item	Per	Value	Date	Ref.
Personal Services				
Haircut, woman's shampoo, trim, blow-dry		22.60	12/94	2c
Personal services expenditures	year	184	91	81r
Restaurant Food				
Chicken, fried, thigh and drumstick		2.29	12/94	2c
Dining expenditures, family	week	34.26	94	73r
Hamburger with cheese	1/4 lb.	1.89	12/94	2c
Pizza, Pizza Hut or Pizza Inn	12-13 in.	7.99	12/94	2c
Taxes				
Taxes, Federal income, expenditures	year	2409	91	81r
Taxes, personal, expenditures	year	3094	91	81r
Taxes, State and local income, expenditures	year	620	91	81r
Transportation				
Transportation, ACCRA Index		112.70	12/94	2c
Bus fare, one-way	trip	1.00	12/95	1c
Bus fare, up to 10 miles	one-way	1.65	12/94	2c
Cars and trucks purchased, new	year	1170	91	81r
Cars and trucks purchased, used	year	739	91	81r
Driver's learning permit fee	perm	27.00	1/94	84s
Driver's license fee	orig	0.00	1/94	84s
Driver's license fee, duplicate	lic	7.00	1/94	84s
Driver's license reinstatement fee, min.	susp	25.00	1/94	85s
Driver's license renewal fee	renew	0.00	1/94	84s
Identification card, nondriver	card	5.00	1/94	83s
Motorcycle learning permit fee	perm	27.00	1/94	84s
Motorcycle license fee	orig	0.00	1/94	84s
Motorcycle license fee, duplicate	lic	7.00	1/94	84s
Motorcycle license renewal fee	renew	0.00	1/94	84s
Public transportation expenditures	year	430	91	81r
Tire balance, computer or spin bal., front	wheel	7.60	12/94	2c
Transportation expenditures, total	year	4810	91	81r
Vehicle finance charges	year	238	91	81r
Vehicle insurance expenditures	year	630	91	81r
Vehicle maintenance and repairs expenditures	year	532	91	81r
Vehicle purchases	year	1920	91	81r
Vehicle rental, leases, licenses, etc. expenditures	year	193	91	81r
Vehicles purchased, other than cars and trucks	year	11	91	81r
Utilities				
Utilities, ACCRA Index		97.20	12/94	2c
Electricity expenditures	year	695	91	81r
Electricity, 1800 sq. ft., new home	mo.	110.24	12/94	2c
Utilities, fuels, and public services, total expenditures	year	1981	91	81r
Water and other public services, expenditures	year	154	91	81r
Weddings				
Bridal attendants' gowns	event	750	10/93	76r
Bridal gown	event	852	10/93	76r
Bridal headpiece and veil	event	167	10/93	76r
Bride's wedding band	event	708	10/93	76r
Clergy	event	224	10/93	76r
Engagement ring	event	2756	10/93	76r
Flowers	event	863	10/93	76r
Formal wear for groom	event	106	10/93	76r
Groom's attendants' formal wear	event	530	10/93	76r
Groom's wedding band	event	402	10/93	76r
Music	event	600	10/93	76r
Photography	event	1088	10/93	76r
Shoes for bride	event	50	10/93	76r
Videography	event	483	10/93	76r
Wedding invitations and announcements	event	342	10/93	76r
Wedding reception	event	7000	10/93	76r

Lansing, MI

Item	Per	Value	Date	Ref.
Composite, ACCRA index		104.20	12/94	2c
Alcoholic Beverages				
Beer, Miller Lite, Bud, 12-oz., ex deposit	6	4.09	12/94	2c
J & B Scotch	750-ml.	20.32	12/94	2c
Wine, Gallo Chablis blanc	1.5-lit	5.42	12/94	2c
Appliances				
Appliances (major), expenditures	year	131	91	81r
Average annual exp.				
Food, health care, personal goods, services	year	25935	91	81r
Charity				
Cash contributions, expenditures	year	745	91	81r
Clothing				
Apparel, men and boys, total expenditures	year	332	91	81r
Apparel, women and girls, total expenditures	year	578	91	81r
Footwear, expenditures	year	164	91	81r
Jeans, man's denim		28.66	12/94	2c
Shirt, man's dress shirt		27.25	12/94	2c
Undervest, boy's size 10-14, cotton	3	3.88	12/94	2c
Communications				
Long-distance telephone rate, day, addl. min., 1-10 mi.	min.	0.08	12/93	9s
Long-distance telephone rate, day, initial min., 1-10 mi.	min.	0.14	12/93	9s
Newspaper subscription, dly. and Sun. delivery	month	13.04	12/94	2c
Phone line, single, business, field visit	inst	42.00	12/93	9s
Phone line, single, business, no field visit	inst	42.00	12/93	9s
Phone line, single, residence, field visit	inst	42.00	12/93	9s
Phone line, single, residence, no field visit	inst	42.00	12/93	9s
Telephone bill, family of four	month	18.00	12/94	2c
Telephone service, expenditures	year	547	91	81r
Telephone, residential, flat rate	mo.	10.42	12/93	8c
Education				
Board, 4-year private college/university	year	2064	8/94	80s
Board, 4-year public college/university	year	2304	8/94	80s
Clothing, university student	year	270.00	5/96	22c
Education, total expenditures	year	394	91	81r
Living expenses, personal miscellaneous, university student	year	1100.00	5/96	22c
Living expenses, personal miscellaneous, university student	year	96.00	5/96	22c
Personal grooming expenses, university student	year	173.00	5/96	22c
Phone bills, university student	year	113.00	5/96	22c
Recreation and entertainment, university student	year	173.00	5/96	22c
Room, 4-year private college/university	year	1814	8/94	80s
Room, 4-year public college/university	year	1856	8/94	80s
Total cost, 4-year private college/university	year	12178	8/94	80s
Total cost, 4-year public college/university	year	7642	8/94	80s
Transportation (campus bus passes; one trip home) university student	year	269.00	5/96	22c
Tuition, 2-year public college/university, in-state	year	1358	8/94	80s
Tuition, 4-year private college/university, in-state	year	8300	8/94	80s
Tuition, 4-year public college/university, in-state	year	3481	8/94	80s
Energy and Fuels				
Energy, combined forms, 1800 sq. ft.	mo.	104.03	12/94	2c
Energy, exc. electricity, 1800 sq. ft.	mo.	53.70	12/94	2c
Fuel oil and other fuels, expenditures	year	83	91	81r
Gas, natural, expenditures	year	373	91	81r
Gas, reg unlead, taxes inc., cash, self-service	gal	1.08	12/94	2c
Gasoline and motor oil purchased	year	1000	91	81r
Gasoline, unleaded midgrade	gallon	1.15	4/93	82r
Gasoline, unleaded premium	gallon	1.23	4/93	82r

Values are in dollars or fractions of dollars. In the column headed *Ref*, references are shown to sources. Each reference is followed by a letter. These refer to the geographical level for which data were reported: s=State, r=Region, and c=City or metro. The abbreviation *ex* is used to mean *except* or *excluding*; *exp* stands for expenditures. For other abbreviations and further explanations, please see the Introduction.

Lansing, MI - continued

Item	Per	Value	Date	Ref.
Energy and Fuels				
Gasoline, unleaded regular	gallon	1.07	4/93	82r
Entertainment				
Bowling, evening rate	game	2.11	12/94	2c
Entertainment, total expenditures	year	1356	91	81r
Fees and admissions, expenditures	year	347	91	81r
Monopoly game, Parker Brothers', No. 9	game	9.99	12/94	2c
Movie	adm	5.83	12/94	2c
Pets, toys, playground equipment, expenditures	year	270	91	81r
Reading, expenditures	year	160	91	81r
Televisions, radios, and sound equipment, expenditures	year	433	91	81r
Tennis balls, yellow, Wilson or Penn, 3	can	2.24	12/94	2c
Funerals				
Burial, immediate, container provided by funeral home		1268.31	1/95	54r
Cards, acknowledgment		26.12	1/95	54r
Casket, minimum alternative		198.03	1/95	54r
Cosmetology, hair care, etc.		122.19	1/95	54r
Cremation, direct, container provided by funeral home		977.81	1/95	54r
Embalming		334.00	1/95	54r
Funeral, funeral home		321.16	1/95	54r
Funeral, other facility		317.73	1/95	54r
Graveside service		292.48	1/95	54r
Hearse, local		153.20	1/95	54r
Limousine, local		123.52	1/95	54r
Memorial service		356.30	1/95	54r
Service charge, professional, nondeclinable		968.24	1/95	54r
Visitation and viewing		332.66	1/95	54r
Groceries				
Groceries, ACCRA Index		105.90	12/94	2c
Apples, Red Delicious	lb.	0.68	12/94	82r
Baby food, strained vegetables, lowest price	4-4.5 oz.	0.34	12/94	2c
Bacon, sliced	lb.	1.88	12/94	82r
Bananas	lb.	0.38	12/94	2c
Bananas	lb.	0.41	12/94	82r
Beef or hamburger, ground	lb.	1.29	12/94	2c
Beef purchases	year	197	91	81r
Beef, stew, boneless	lb.	2.52	12/94	82r
Beverage purchases, alcoholic	year	293	91	81r
Beverage purchases, nonalcoholic	year	203	91	81r
Bologna, all beef or mixed	lb.	2.12	12/94	82r
Bread, white	24-oz.	0.69	12/94	2c
Bread, white, pan	lb.	0.76	12/94	82r
Cabbage	lb.	0.44	12/94	82r
Carrots, short trimmed and topped	lb.	0.44	12/94	82r
Cereals and bakery products purchases	year	347	91	81r
Cereals and cereals products purchases	year	119	91	81r
Cheddar cheese, natural	lb.	3.28	12/94	82r
Cheese, Kraft grated Parmesan	8-oz.	3.05	12/94	2c
Chicken breast, bone-in	lb.	1.61	12/94	82r
Chicken, fresh, whole	lb.	0.89	12/94	82r
Chicken, whole fryer	lb.	0.89	12/94	2c
Chuck roast, USDA choice, boneless	lb.	2.33	12/94	82r
Cigarettes, Winston, Kings	carton	21.29	12/94	2c
Coffee, 100%, ground roast, all sizes	lb.	4.28	12/94	82r
Coffee, vacuum-packed	13 oz.	4.17	12/94	2c
Cookies, chocolate chip	lb.	2.72	12/94	82r
Corn Flakes, Kellogg's or Post Toasties	18 oz.	2.41	12/94	2c
Corn, frozen, whole kernel, lowest price	10 oz.	0.74	12/94	2c
Dairy products (other) purchases	year	148	91	81r
Eggs, Grade A large	dozen	0.68	12/94	2c
Eggs, Grade A large	dozen	0.76	12/94	82r
Fish and seafood purchases	year	61	91	81r
Flour, white, all purpose	lb.	0.22	12/94	82r
Food purchases, food eaten at home	year	2313	91	81r
Foods purchased away from home, not prepared by consumer	year	1709	91	81r
Fruits and vegetables purchases	year	372	91	81r

Lansing, MI - continued

Item	Per	Value	Date	Ref.
Groceries - continued				
Grapefruit	lb.	0.47	12/94	82r
Grapes, Thompson seedless	lb.	2.15	12/94	82r
Ground beef, 100% beef	lb.	1.37	12/94	82r
Ground chuck, 100% beef	lb.	1.81	12/94	82r
Ham, boneless, exc. canned	lb.	2.16	12/94	82r
Ice cream, prepackaged, bulk, regular	1/2 gal.	2.48	12/94	82r
Lemons	lb.	1.08	12/94	82r
Lettuce, iceberg	lb.	0.81	12/94	82r
Lettuce, iceberg	head	0.89	12/94	2c
Margarine, Blue Bonnet or Parkay cubes	lb.	0.81	12/94	2c
Margarine, stick	lb.	0.81	12/94	82r
Meats, poultry, fish, and eggs purchases	year	591	91	81r
Milk and cream (fresh) purchases	year	132	91	81r
Milk, whole	1/2 gal.	1.52	12/94	2c
Orange juice, frozen concentrate 12-oz. can	16 oz.	1.41	12/94	82r
Orange juice, Minute Maid frozen	12-oz.	1.36	12/94	2c
Oranges, Navel	lb.	0.56	12/94	82r
Peaches, halves or slices, Hunt's, Del Monte, or Libby's	29-oz.	1.55	12/94	2c
Peanut butter, creamy, all sizes	lb.	1.81	12/94	82r
Peas, sweet, Del Monte or Green Giant	15-17 oz.	0.62	12/94	2c
Pork chops, center cut, bone-in	lb.	2.76	12/94	82r
Pork purchases	year	130	91	81r
Potato chips	16-oz.	2.81	12/94	82r
Potatoes, frozen, French fried	lb.	0.83	12/94	82r
Potatoes, white	lb.	0.28	12/94	82r
Potatoes, white or red	10-lb. sack	1.75	12/94	2c
Round roast, USDA choice, boneless	lb.	2.90	12/94	82r
Sausage, Jimmy Dean, 100% pork	lb.	2.71	12/94	2c
Shortening, vegetable oil blends	lb.	0.88	12/94	82r
Shortening, vegetable, Crisco	3-lb.	3.01	12/94	2c
Soft drink, Coca Cola, ex deposit	2 lit	1.35	12/94	2c
Spaghetti and macaroni	lb.	0.78	12/94	82r
Steak, rib eye, USDA choice, boneless	lb.	6.15	12/94	82r
Steak, round, graded & ungraded, exc. USDA prime & choice	lb.	2.72	12/94	82r
Steak, round, USDA choice, boneless	lb.	3.02	12/94	82r
Steak, sirloin, USDA choice, boneless	lb.	3.85	12/94	82r
Steak, t-bone	lb.	4.41	12/94	2c
Steak, T-bone, USDA choice, bone-in	lb.	5.38	12/94	82r
Sugar and other sweets, eaten at home, expenditures	year	91	91	81r
Sugar, cane or beet	4 lbs.	1.12	12/94	2c
Sugar, white, all sizes	lb.	0.36	12/94	82r
Tobacco products and smoking supplies, total expenditures	year	298	91	81r
Tomatoes, field grown	lb.	1.36	12/94	82r
Tomatoes, Hunt's or Del Monte	14.5 oz.	0.86	12/94	2c
Tuna, chunk, light	lb.	1.94	12/94	82r
Tuna, chunk, light, oil-packed	6.125-6.5 oz.	0.88	12/94	2c
Turkey, frozen, whole	lb.	0.96	12/94	82r
Yogurt, natural, fruit flavored	8 oz.	0.62	12/94	82r
Goods and Services				
Miscellaneous goods and services, ACCRA Index		96.20	12/94	2c
Health Care				
Health care, ACCRA Index		111.50	12/94	2c
Antibiotic ointment, Polysporin	1.5 oz.	4.53	12/94	2c
Childbirth, Cesarean delivery, hospital charge	birth	5101.00	12/91	69r
Childbirth, Cesarean delivery, physician charge	birth	2234.00	12/91	69r
Childbirth, normal delivery, hospital charge	birth	2891.00	12/91	69r
Childbirth, normal delivery, physician charge	birth	1623.00	12/91	69r

Values are in dollars or fractions of dollars. In the column headed *Ref*, references are shown to sources. Each reference is followed by a letter. These refer to the geographical level for which data were reported: s=State, r=Region, and c=City or metro. The abbreviation *ex* is used to mean *except* or *excluding*; *exp* stands for *expenditures*. For other abbreviations and further explanations, please see the Introduction.

Lansing, MI - continued

Item	Per	Value	Date	Ref.
Health Care				
Dentist's fee, adult teeth cleaning and periodic oral exam	visit	63.50	12/94	2c
Doctor's fee, routine exam, established patient	visit	40.58	12/94	2c
Drugs, expenditures	year	248	91	81r
Health care, total expenditures	year	1336	91	81r
Health insurance expenditures	year	550	91	81r
Hospital care, semiprivate room	day	438.50	12/94	2c
Insurance premium, family medical care	month	369.41	1/95	41s
Medical services expenditures	year	457	91	81r
Medical supplies expenditures	year	82	91	81r
Household Goods				
Appl. repair, service call, wash mach	min. lab. chg.	29.98	12/94	2c
Floor coverings, expenditures	year	105	91	81r
Furniture, expenditures	year	291	91	81r
Household equipment, misc. expenditures	year	341	91	81r
Household expenditures, miscellaneous	year	162	91	81r
Household furnishings and equipment, expenditures	year	1042	91	81r
Household operations expenditures	year	365	91	81r
Household textiles, expenditures	year	101	91	81r
Housekeeping supplies, expenditures	year	390	91	81r
Laundry and cleaning supplies, expenditures	year	110	91	81r
Laundry detergent, Tide Ultra, Bold, or Cheer	42 oz.	4.17	12/94	2c
Postage and stationery, expenditures	year	115	91	81r
Tissues, facial, Kleenex brand	175	1.13	12/94	2c
Housing				
Housing, ACCRA Index		116.80	12/94	2c
Add garage/carport		8,479	3/95	74r
Add room(s)		21,347	3/95	74r
Apartment condominium or co-op, median	unit	87100	12/94	62r
Bathroom addition, average cost	add	9734.00	3/95	13r
Bathroom remodeling, average cost	remod	6414.00	3/95	13r
Bedroom, master suite addition, average cost	add	27122.00	3/95	13r
Deck addition, average cost	add	6665.00	3/95	13r
Dwellings (owned), expenditures	year	2566	91	81r
Enclose porch/patio/breezeway		4,556	3/95	74r
Exterior remodeling, average cost	remod	15395.00	3/95	13r
Family room addition, average cost	add	27658.00	3/95	13r
Finish room in basement/attic		5,074	3/95	74r
Home, existing, single-family, median	unit	106500	12/94	62r
Home, existing, single-family, median	unit	77.10	12/94	62c
House payment, principal and interest, 25% down payment	mo.	922	12/94	2c
House, 1800 sq ft, 8000 sq ft lot, new, urban, utilities	total	151349	12/94	2c
Kitchen remodeling, major, average cost	remod	17084.00	3/95	13r
Kitchen remodeling, minor, average cost	remod	5804.00	3/95	13r
Maintenance, repairs, insurance, and other housing expenditures	year	484	91	81r
Mortgage interest and charges expenditures	year	1443	91	81r
Mtge. rate, incl. points and orig. fee, 30-year conv. fixed or ARM	mo.	9.11	12/94	2c
Office, home addition, average cost	add	8121.00	3/95	13r
Princ. & int., mortgage, median-price exist. sing.-family home	mo.	515	12/94	62r
Property taxes expenditures	year	639	91	81r
Redesign, restructure more than half of home's interior		9,114	3/95	74r
Rent, apartment, 2 br., 1 1/2-2 baths, unfurnished, 950 sq ft, water	mo.	537	12/94	2c
Rental units expenditures	year	1200	91	81r
Sun-space addition, average cost	add	23768.00	3/95	13r
Wing addition, two-story, average cost	add	50410.00	3/95	13r

Lansing, MI - continued

Item	Per	Value	Date	Ref.
Insurance and Pensions				
Auto insurance, private passenger	year	788.26	12/94	71s
Insurance and pensions, personal, expenditures	year	2408	91	81r
Insurance, life and other personal, expenditures	year	355	91	81r
Pensions and Social Security, expenditures	year	2053	91	81r
Legal Assistance				
Legal work, law firm associate	hour	90		10r
Legal work, law firm partner	hour	139		10r
Personal Goods				
Shampoo, Alberto VO5	15-oz.	0.99	12/94	2c
Toothpaste, Crest or Colgate	6-7 oz.	1.89	12/94	2c
Personal Services				
Dry cleaning, man's 2-pc. suit		5.81	12/94	2c
Haircut, man's barbershop, no styling		8.88	12/94	2c
Haircut, woman's shampoo, trim, blow-dry		16.50	12/94	2c
Personal services expenditures	year	203	91	81r
Restaurant Food				
Chicken, fried, thigh and drumstick		2.09	12/94	2c
Dining expenditures, family	week	30.03	94	73r
Hamburger with cheese	1/4 lb.	1.69	12/94	2c
Pizza, Pizza Hut or Pizza Inn	12-13 in.	9.00	12/94	2c
Taxes				
Taxes, Federal income, expenditures	year	1756	91	81r
Taxes, personal, expenditures	year	2426	91	81r
Taxes, State and local income, expenditures	year	568	91	81r
Transportation				
Transportation, ACCRA Index		97.20	12/94	2c
Bus fare, one-way	trip	0.85	12/95	1c
Bus fare, up to 10 miles	one-way	1.00	12/94	2c
Cars and trucks purchased, new	year	891	91	81r
Cars and trucks purchased, used	year	1155	91	81r
Driver's learning permit fee	perm	12.00	1/94	84s
Driver's license fee	orig	12.00	1/94	84s
Driver's license fee, duplicate	lic	6.00	1/94	84s
Driver's license reinstatement fee, min.	susp	125.00	1/94	85s
Driver's license renewal fee	renew	12.00	1/94	84s
Identification card, nondriver	card	6.00	1/94	83s
Motorcycle license fee	orig	7.50	1/94	84s
Motorcycle license renewal fee	renew	4.00	1/94	84s
Public transportation expenditures	year	209	91	81r
Tire balance, computer or spin bal., front	wheel	6.50	12/94	2c
Transportation expenditures, total	year	4792	91	81r
Vehicle finance charges	year	300	91	81r
Vehicle insurance expenditures	year	485	91	81r
Vehicle maintenance and repairs expenditures	year	534	91	81r
Vehicle purchases	year	2068	91	81r
Vehicle rental, leases, licenses, etc. expenditures	year	197	91	81r
Vehicles purchased, other than cars and trucks	year	22	91	81r
Utilities				
Utilities, ACCRA Index		92.60	12/94	2c
Electricity expenditures	year	668	91	81r
Electricity, (part.), other, 1800 sq. ft., new home	mo.	50.33	12/94	2c
Utilities, fuels, and public services, total expenditures	year	1838	91	81r
Water and other public services, expenditures	year	167	91	81r
Weddings				
Bridal attendants' gowns	event	750	10/93	76r
Bridal gown	event	852	10/93	76r
Bridal headpiece and veil	event	167	10/93	76r
Bride's wedding band	event	708	10/93	76r

Values are in dollars or fractions of dollars. In the column headed *Ref*, references are shown to sources. Each reference is followed by a letter. These refer to the geographical level for which data were reported: s = State, r = Region, and c = City or metro. The abbreviation *ex* is used to mean *except* or *excluding*; *exp* stands for expenditures. For other abbreviations and further explanations, please see the Introduction.

Lansing, MI - continued

Item	Per	Value	Date	Ref.
Weddings				
Clergy	event	224	10/93	76r
Engagement ring	event	2756	10/93	76r
Flowers	event	863	10/93	76r
Formal wear for groom	event	106	10/93	76r
Groom's attendants' formal wear	event	530	10/93	76r
Groom's wedding band	event	402	10/93	76r
Music	event	600	10/93	76r
Photography	event	1088	10/93	76r
Shoes for bride	event	50	10/93	76r
Videography	event	483	10/93	76r
Wedding invitations and announcements	event	342	10/93	76r
Wedding reception	event	7000	10/93	76r

Laramie, WY

Item	Per	Value	Date	Ref.
Composite, ACCRA index		98.70	12/94	2c
Alcoholic Beverages				
Beer, Miller Lite, Bud, 12-oz., ex deposit	6	4.20	12/94	2c
J & B Scotch	750-ml.	17.81	12/94	2c
Wine, Gallo Chablis blanc	1.5-lit	5.92	12/94	2c
Appliances				
Appliances (major), expenditures	year	160	91	81r
Average annual exp.				
Food, health care, personal goods, services	year	32461	91	81r
Charity				
Cash contributions, expenditures	year	975	91	81r
Clothing				
Apparel, men and boys, total expenditures	year	467	91	81r
Apparel, women and girls, total expenditures	year	737	91	81r
Footwear, expenditures	year	270	91	81r
Jeans, man's denim		34.97	12/94	2c
Shirt, man's dress shirt		28.73	12/94	2c
Undervest, boy's size 10-14, cotton	3	3.76	12/94	2c
Communications				
Long-distance telephone rate, day, addl. min., 1-10 mi.	min.	0.09	12/93	9s
Long-distance telephone rate, day, initial min., 1-10 mi.	min.	0.19	12/93	9s
Newspaper subscription, dly. and Sun. delivery	month	10.44	12/94	2c
Phone line, single, business, field visit	inst	86.25	12/93	9s
Phone line, single, business, no field visit	inst	86.25	12/93	9s
Phone line, single, residence, field visit	inst	41.25	12/93	9s
Phone line, single, residence, no field visit	inst	41.25	12/93	9s
Telephone bill, family of four	month	18.67	12/94	2c
Telephone service, expenditures	year	611	91	81r
Telephone, residential, flat rate	mo.	11.22	12/93	8c
Education				
Board, 4-year public college/university	year	1830	8/94	80s
Education, total expenditures	year	375	91	81r
Room, 4-year public college/university	year	1422	8/94	80s
Total cost, 4-year public college/university	year	4900	8/94	80s
Tuition, 4-year public college/university, in-state	year	1648	8/94	80s
Energy and Fuels				
Energy, combined forms, 1800 sq. ft.	mo.	82.77	12/94	2c
Energy, exc. electricity, 1800 sq. ft.	mo.	40.70	12/94	2c
Fuel oil and other fuels, expenditures	year	33	91	81r
Gas, natural, expenditures	year	212	91	81r
Gas, reg unlead, taxes inc., cash, self-service	gal	1.19	12/94	2c
Gasoline and motor oil purchased	year	1115	91	81r
Gasoline, unleaded midgrade	gallon	1.36	4/93	82r
Gasoline, unleaded premium	gallon	1.43	4/93	82r
Gasoline, unleaded regular	gallon	1.23	4/93	82r

Laramie, WY - continued

Item	Per	Value	Date	Ref.
Entertainment				
Bowling, evening rate	game	2.00	12/94	2c
Concert ticket, Pearl Jam group	perf	20.00	94	50r
Entertainment, total expenditures	year	1853	91	81r
Fees and admissions, expenditures	year	482	91	81r
Monopoly game, Parker Brothers', No. 9	game	11.50	12/94	2c
Movie	adm	5.00	12/94	2c
Pets, toys, playground equipment, expenditures	year	299	91	81r
Reading, expenditures	year	164	91	81r
Televisions, radios, and sound equipment, expenditures	year	528	91	81r
Tennis balls, yellow, Wilson or Penn, 3	can	2.33	12/94	2c
Funerals				
Burial, immediate, container provided by funeral home		1360.49	1/95	54r
Cards, acknowledgment		11.24	1/95	54r
Casket, minimum alternative		232.73	1/95	54r
Cosmetology, hair care, etc.		114.13	1/95	54r
Cremation, direct, container provided by funeral home		1027.08	1/95	54r
Embalming		286.24	1/95	54r
Funeral, funeral home		315.60	1/95	54r
Funeral, other facility		303.08	1/95	54r
Graveside service		423.83	1/95	54r
Hearse, local		133.12	1/95	54r
Limousine, local		99.10	1/95	54r
Memorial service		442.57	1/95	54r
Service charge, professional, nondeclinable		840.16	1/95	54r
Visitation and viewing		168.50	1/95	54r
Groceries				
Groceries, ACCRA Index		105.00	12/94	2c
Apples, Red Delicious	lb.	0.72	12/94	82r
Baby food, strained vegetables, lowest price	4-4.5 oz.	0.33	12/94	2c
Bacon, sliced	lb.	1.73	12/94	82r
Bananas	lb.	0.59	12/94	2c
Bananas	lb.	0.52	12/94	82r
Beef or hamburger, ground	lb.	0.94	12/94	2c
Beef purchases	year	241	91	81r
Beverage purchases, alcoholic	year	328	91	81r
Beverage purchases, nonalcoholic	year	234	91	81r
Bologna, all beef or mixed	lb.	2.33	12/94	82r
Bread, white	24-oz.	0.87	12/94	2c
Bread, white, pan	lb.	0.81	12/94	82r
Carrots, short trimmed and topped	lb.	0.43	12/94	82r
Cereals and bakery products purchases	year	392	91	81r
Cereals and cereals products purchases	year	139	91	81r
Cheese, Kraft grated Parmesan	8-oz.	3.17	12/94	2c
Chicken breast, bone-in	lb.	2.04	12/94	82r
Chicken, fresh, whole	lb.	0.95	12/94	82r
Chicken, whole fryer	lb.	0.79	12/94	2c
Cigarettes, Winston, Kings	carton	15.69	12/94	2c
Coffee, 100%, ground roast, all sizes	lb.	4.48	12/94	82r
Coffee, vacuum-packed	13 oz.	3.22	12/94	2c
Corn Flakes, Kellogg's or Post Toasties	18 oz.	2.55	12/94	2c
Corn, frozen, whole kernel, lowest price	10 oz.	0.61	12/94	2c
Dairy products (other) purchases	year	182	91	81r
Eggs, Grade A large	dozen	0.77	12/94	2c
Fish and seafood purchases	year	94	91	81r
Flour, white, all purpose	lb.	0.21	12/94	82r
Food purchases, food eaten at home	year	2749	91	81r
Foods purchased away from home, not prepared by consumer	year	1909	91	81r
Fruits and vegetables purchases	year	459	91	81r
Grapefruit	lb.	0.56	12/94	82r
Ground beef, 100% beef	lb.	1.31	12/94	82r
Ham, boneless, exc. canned	lb.	2.46	12/94	82r
Ice cream, prepackaged, bulk, regular	1/2 gal.	2.57	12/94	82r
Lemons	lb.	1.00	12/94	82r
Lettuce, iceberg	lb.	0.93	12/94	82r

Values are in dollars or fractions of dollars. In the column headed *Ref*, references are shown to sources. Each reference is followed by a letter. These refer to the geographical level for which data were reported: s = State, r = Region, and c = City or metro. The abbreviation *ex* is used to mean *except* or *excluding*; *exp* stands for expenditures. For other abbreviations and further explanations, please see the Introduction.

Laramie, WY - continued

Item	Per	Value	Date	Ref.
Groceries				
Lettuce, iceberg	head	0.77	12/94	2c
Margarine, Blue Bonnet or Parkay cubes	lb.	0.64	12/94	2c
Meats, poultry, fish, and eggs purchases	year	700	91	81r
Milk and cream (fresh) purchases	year	155	91	81r
Milk, whole	1/2 gal.	1.46	12/94	2c
Orange juice, frozen concentrate 12-oz. can	16 oz.	1.52	12/94	82r
Orange juice, Minute Maid frozen	12-oz.	1.30	12/94	2c
Oranges, Navel	lb.	0.56	12/94	82r
Peaches, halves or slices, Hunt's, Del Monte, or Libby's	29-oz.	1.49	12/94	2c
Peas, sweet, Del Monte or Green Giant	15-17 oz.	0.65	12/94	2c
Pork chops, center cut, bone-in	lb.	3.30	12/94	82r
Pork purchases	year	122	91	81r
Potato chips	16-oz.	3.03	12/94	82r
Potatoes, frozen, French fried	lb.	0.77	12/94	82r
Potatoes, white	lb.	0.35	12/94	82r
Potatoes, white or red	10-lb. sack	2.27	12/94	2c
Rice, white, long grain, uncooked	lb.	0.54	12/94	82r
Round roast, USDA choice, boneless	lb.	2.92	12/94	82r
Sausage, Jimmy Dean, 100% pork	lb.	3.42	12/94	2c
Shortening, vegetable oil blends	lb.	0.80	12/94	82r
Shortening, vegetable, Crisco	3-lb.	2.49	12/94	2c
Soft drink, Coca Cola, ex deposit	2 lit	1.77	12/94	2c
Spaghetti and macaroni	lb.	1.02	12/94	82r
Steak, round, graded & ungraded, exc. USDA prime & choice	lb.	3.13	12/94	82r
Steak, sirloin, USDA choice, boneless	lb.	4.07	12/94	82r
Steak, t-bone	lb.	4.92	12/94	2c
Sugar and other sweets, eaten at home, expenditures	year	105	91	81r
Sugar, cane or beet	4 lbs.	1.29	12/94	2c
Sugar, white, all sizes	lb.	0.38	12/94	82r
Tobacco products and smoking supplies, total expenditures	year	221	91	81r
Tomatoes, field grown	lb.	1.45	12/94	82r
Tomatoes, Hunt's or Del Monte	14.5 oz.	0.77	12/94	2c
Tuna, chunk, light	lb.	2.18	12/94	82r
Tuna, chunk, light, oil-packed	6.125-6.5 oz.	0.89	12/94	2c
Goods and Services				
Miscellaneous goods and services, ACCRA Index		102.20	12/94	2c
Health Care				
Health care, ACCRA Index		105.70	12/94	2c
Antibiotic ointment, Polysporin	1.5 oz.	3.94	12/94	2c
Childbirth, Cesarean delivery, hospital charge	birth	6059.00	12/91	69r
Childbirth, Cesarean delivery, physician charge	birth	2248.00	12/91	69r
Childbirth, normal delivery, hospital charge	birth	3006.00	12/91	69r
Childbirth, normal delivery, physician charge	birth	1634.00	12/91	69r
Dentist's fee, adult teeth cleaning and periodic oral exam	visit	53.11	12/94	2c
Doctor's fee, routine exam, established patient	visit	43.67	12/94	2c
Drugs, expenditures	year	230	91	81r
Health care, total expenditures	year	1544	91	81r
Health insurance expenditures	year	558	91	81r
Hospital care, semiprivate room	day	440.00	12/94	2c
Medical services expenditures	year	676	91	81r
Medical supplies expenditures	year	80	91	81r
Surgery, open-heart	proc	37818.00	1/93	14r
Household Goods				
Appl. repair, service call, wash mach	min. lab. chg.	31.00	12/94	2c
Floor coverings, expenditures	year	79	91	81r

Laramie, WY - continued

Item	Per	Value	Date	Ref.
Household Goods - continued				
Furniture, expenditures	year	352	91	81r
Household equipment, misc. expenditures	year	614	91	81r
Household expenditures, miscellaneous	year	294	91	81r
Household furnishings and equipment, expenditures	year	1416	91	81r
Household operations expenditures	year	580	91	81r
Household textiles, expenditures	year	113	91	81r
Housekeeping supplies, expenditures	year	447	91	81r
Laundry and cleaning supplies, expenditures	year	114	91	81r
Laundry detergent, Tide Ultra, Bold, or Cheer	42 oz.	3.23	12/94	2c
Postage and stationery, expenditures	year	145	91	81r
Tissues, facial, Kleenex brand	175	1.09	12/94	2c
Housing				
Housing, ACCRA Index		95.20	12/94	2c
Add garage/carport		6,422	3/95	74r
Add room(s)		26,583	3/95	74r
Apartment condominium or co-op, median	unit	105300	12/94	62r
Dwellings (owned), expenditures	year	3932	91	81r
Enclose porch/patio/breezeway		5,382	3/95	74r
Finish room in basement/attic		3,911	3/95	74r
Home, existing, single-family, median	unit	178600	12/94	62r
House payment, principal and interest, 25% down payment	mo.	730	12/94	2c
House, 1800 sq ft, 8000 sq ft lot, new, urban, utilities	total	120000	12/94	2c
Maintenance, repairs, insurance, and other housing expenditures	year	591	91	81r
Mortgage interest and charges expenditures	year	2747	91	81r
Mtge. rate, incl. points and orig. fee, 30-year conv. fixed or ARM	mo.	9.09	12/94	2c
Princ. & int., mortgage, median-price exist. sing.-family home	mo.	845	12/94	62r
Property taxes expenditures	year	594	91	81r
Redesign, restructure more than half of home's interior		5,467	3/95	74r
Rental units expenditures	year	2077	91	81r
Insurance and Pensions				
Auto insurance, private passenger	year	531.91	12/94	71s
Insurance and pensions, personal, expenditures	year	3042	91	81r
Insurance, life and other personal, expenditures	year	298	91	81r
Pensions and Social Security, expenditures	year	2744	91	81r
Legal Assistance				
Legal work, law firm associate	hour	91		10r
Legal work, law firm partner	hour	151		10r
Personal Goods				
Shampoo, Alberto VO5	15-oz.	0.95	12/94	2c
Toothpaste, Crest or Colgate	6-7 oz.	1.79	12/94	2c
Personal Services				
Dry cleaning, man's 2-pc. suit		7.00	12/94	2c
Haircut, man's barbershop, no styling		8.50	12/94	2c
Haircut, woman's shampoo, trim, blow-dry		15.88	12/94	2c
Personal services expenditures	year	286	91	81r
Restaurant Food				
Chicken, fried, thigh and drumstick		2.49	12/94	2c
Dining expenditures, family	week	32.25	94	73r
Hamburger with cheese	1/4 lb.	1.99	12/94	2c
Pizza, Pizza Hut or Pizza Inn	12-13 in.	9.00	12/94	2c
Taxes				
Tax, cigarettes	year	609.00	10/93	43s
Taxes, Federal income, expenditures	year	2946	91	81r
Taxes, personal, expenditures	year	3791	91	81r
Taxes, State and local income, expenditures	year	791	91	81r

Values are in dollars or fractions of dollars. In the column headed *Ref*, references are shown to sources. Each reference is followed by a letter. These refer to the geographical level for which data were reported: s=State, r=Region, and c=City or metro. The abbreviation *ex* is used to mean *except* or *excluding*; *exp* stands for expenditures. For other abbreviations and further explanations, please see the Introduction.

Laramie, WY - continued

Item	Per	Value	Date	Ref.
Transportation				
Transportation, ACCRA Index		100.50	12/94	2c
Cars and trucks purchased, new	year	1231	91	81r
Cars and trucks purchased, used	year	915	91	81r
Driver's learning permit fee	perm	10.00	1/94	84s
Driver's license fee	orig	20.00	1/94	84s
Driver's license fee, duplicate	lic	15.00	1/94	84s
Driver's license reinstatement fee, min.	susp	50.00	1/94	85s
Driver's license renewal fee	renew	15.00	1/94	84s
Identification card, nondriver	card	10.00	1/94	83s
Motorcycle learning permit fee	perm	10.00	1/94	84s
Motorcycle license fee	orig	20.00	1/94	84s
Motorcycle license fee, duplicate	lic	15.00	1/94	84s
Motorcycle license renewal fee	renew	15.00	1/94	84s
Public transportation expenditures	year	375	91	81r
Tire balance, computer or spin bal., front	wheel	6.30	12/94	2c
Transportation expenditures, total	year	5527	91	81r
Vehicle finance charges	year	287	91	81r
Vehicle insurance expenditures	year	624	91	81r
Vehicle maintenance and repairs expenditures	year	695	91	81r
Vehicle purchases	year	2174	91	81r
Vehicle rental, leases, licenses, etc. expenditures	year	257	91	81r
Vehicles purchased, other than cars and trucks	year	28	91	81r
Utilities				
Utilities, ACCRA Index		76.70	12/94	2c
Electricity expenditures	year	616	91	81r
Electricity, (part.), other, 1800 sq. ft., new home	mo.	42.07	12/94	2c
Utilities, fuels, and public services, total expenditures	year	1681	91	81r
Water and other public services, expenditures	year	209	91	81r
Weddings				
Bridal attendants' gowns	event	750	10/93	76r
Bridal gown	event	852	10/93	76r
Bridal headpiece and veil	event	167	10/93	76r
Bride's wedding band	event	708	10/93	76r
Clergy	event	224	10/93	76r
Engagement ring	event	2756	10/93	76r
Flowers	event	863	10/93	76r
Formal wear for groom	event	106	10/93	76r
Groom's attendants' formal wear	event	530	10/93	76r
Groom's wedding band	event	402	10/93	76r
Music	event	600	10/93	76r
Photography	event	1088	10/93	76r
Shoes for bride	event	50	10/93	76r
Videography	event	483	10/93	76r
Wedding invitations and announcements	event	342	10/93	76r
Wedding reception	event	7000	10/93	76r

Laredo, TX

Item	Per	Value	Date	Ref.
Appliances				
Appliances (major), expenditures	year	153	91	81r
Average annual exp.				
Food, health care, personal goods, services	year	27020	91	81r
Charity				
Cash contributions, expenditures	year	839	91	81r
Clothing				
Apparel, men and boys, total expenditures	year	380	91	81r
Apparel, women and girls, total expenditures	year	660	91	81r
Footwear, expenditures	year	193	91	81r
Communications				
Long-distance telephone rate, day, addl. min., 1-10 mi.	min.	0.08	12/93	9s

Laredo, TX - continued

Item	Per	Value	Date	Ref.
Communications - continued				
Long-distance telephone rate, day, initial min., 1-10 mi.	min.	0.10	12/93	9s
Phone line, single, business, field visit	inst	71.90	12/93	9s
Phone line, single, business, no field visit	inst	57.30	12/93	9s
Phone line, single, residence, field visit	inst	52.95	12/93	9s
Phone line, single, residence, no field visit	inst	38.35	12/93	9s
Telephone service, expenditures	year	616	91	81r
Education				
Board, 4-year private college/university	year	2084	8/94	80s
Board, 4-year public college/university	year	1675	8/94	80s
Education, total expenditures	year	319	91	81r
Room, 4-year private college/university	year	1840	8/94	80s
Room, 4-year public college/university	year	1756	8/94	80s
Total cost, 4-year private college/university	year	11876	8/94	80s
Total cost, 4-year public college/university	year	4935	8/94	80s
Tuition, 2-year public college/university, in-state	year	625	8/94	80s
Tuition, 4-year private college/university, in-state	year	7952	8/94	80s
Tuition, 4-year public college/university, in-state	year	1503	8/94	80s
Energy and Fuels				
Fuel oil and other fuels, expenditures	year	56	91	81r
Gas, natural, expenditures	year	150	91	81r
Gasoline and motor oil purchased	year	1152	91	81r
Gasoline, unleaded midgrade	gallon	1.21	4/93	82r
Gasoline, unleaded premium	gallon	1.30	4/93	82r
Gasoline, unleaded regular	gallon	1.10	4/93	82r
Entertainment				
Concert ticket, Pearl Jam group	perf	20.00	94	50r
Entertainment, total expenditures	year	1266	91	81r
Fees and admissions, expenditures	year	306	91	81r
Pets, toys, playground equipment, expenditures	year	271	91	81r
Reading, expenditures	year	131	91	81r
Televisions, radios, and sound equipment, expenditures	year	439	91	81r
Funerals				
Burial, immediate, container provided by funeral home		1574.60	1/95	54r
Cards, acknowledgment		22.24	1/95	54r
Casket, minimum alternative		239.41	1/95	54r
Cosmetology, hair care, etc.		91.04	1/95	54r
Cremation, direct, container provided by funeral home		1085.15	1/95	54r
Embalming		281.30	1/95	54r
Funeral, funeral home		323.04	1/95	54r
Funeral, other facility		327.58	1/95	54r
Graveside service		355.19	1/95	54r
Hearse, local		141.89	1/95	54r
Limousine, local		99.40	1/95	54r
Memorial service		284.67	1/95	54r
Service charge, professional, nondeclinable		904.06	1/95	54r
Visitation and viewing		187.04	1/95	54r
Groceries				
Apples, Red Delicious	lb.	0.73	12/94	82r
Bacon, sliced	lb.	1.67	12/94	82r
Bananas	lb.	0.42	12/94	82r
Beef purchases	year	213	91	81r
Beverage purchases, alcoholic	year	249	91	81r
Beverage purchases, nonalcoholic	year	207	91	81r
Bologna, all beef or mixed	lb.	2.27	12/94	82r
Bread, white, pan	lb.	0.68	12/94	82r
Cabbage	lb.	0.42	12/94	82r
Carrots, short trimmed and topped	lb.	0.53	12/94	82r
Cereals and bakery products purchases	year	345	91	81r
Cereals and cereals products purchases	year	127	91	81r
Cheddar cheese, natural	lb.	3.58	12/94	82r
Chicken breast, bone-in	lb.	1.71	12/94	82r

Values are in dollars or fractions of dollars. In the column headed *Ref*, references are shown to sources. Each reference is followed by a letter. These refer to the geographical level for which data were reported: s=State, r=Region, and c=City or metro. The abbreviation *ex* is used to mean *except* or *excluding*; *exp* stands for expenditures. For other abbreviations and further explanations, please see the Introduction.

Laredo, TX - continued

Item	Per	Value	Date	Ref.
Groceries				
Chicken, fresh, whole	lb.	0.78	12/94	82r
Chuck roast, USDA choice, boneless	lb.	2.26	12/94	82r
Crackers, soda, salted	lb.	1.27	12/94	82r
Cucumbers	lb.	0.65	12/94	82r
Dairy products (other) purchases	year	141	91	81r
Eggs, Grade A large	dozen	0.87	12/94	82r
Fish and seafood purchases	year	72	91	81r
Flour, white, all purpose	lb.	0.23	12/94	82r
Food purchases, food eaten at home	year	2381	91	81r
Foods purchased away from home, not prepared by consumer	year	1696	91	81r
Frankfurters, all meat or all beef	lb.	1.74	12/94	82r
Fruits and vegetables purchases	year	380	91	81r
Grapefruit	lb.	0.45	12/94	82r
Grapes, Thompson seedless	lb.	2.30	12/94	82r
Ground beef, 100% beef	lb.	1.37	12/94	82r
Ground chuck, 100% beef	lb.	1.97	12/94	82r
Ham, boneless, exc. canned	lb.	2.54	12/94	82r
Ice cream, prepackaged, bulk, regular	1/2 gal.	2.47	12/94	82r
Lemons	lb.	1.02	12/94	82r
Lettuce, iceberg	lb.	0.96	12/94	82r
Margarine, stick	lb.	0.77	12/94	82r
Meats, poultry, fish, and eggs purchases	year	655	91	81r
Milk and cream (fresh) purchases	year	130	91	81r
Orange juice, frozen concentrate 12-oz. can	16 oz.	1.36	12/94	82r
Oranges, Navel	lb.	0.54	12/94	82r
Pears, Anjou	lb.	0.81	12/94	82r
Pork chops, center cut, bone-in	lb.	3.07	12/94	82r
Pork purchases	year	142	91	81r
Potato chips	16-oz.	3.15	12/94	82r
Potatoes, frozen, French fried	lb.	0.82	12/94	82r
Potatoes, white	lb.	0.34	12/94	82r
Rice, white, long grain, uncooked	lb.	0.48	12/94	82r
Round roast, USDA choice, boneless	lb.	2.91	12/94	82r
Sausage, fresh	lb.	1.82	12/94	82r
Shortening, vegetable oil blends	lb.	0.75	12/94	82r
Spaghetti and macaroni	lb.	0.87	12/94	82r
Steak, rib eye, USDA choice, boneless	lb.	6.85	12/94	82r
Steak, round, graded & ungraded, exc. USDA prime & choice	lb.	2.96	12/94	82r
Steak, round, USDA choice, boneless	lb.	3.17	12/94	82r
Steak, sirloin, USDA choice, boneless	lb.	4.12	12/94	82r
Steak, T-bone, USDA choice, bone-in	lb.	5.63	12/94	82r
Sugar and other sweets, eaten at home, expenditures	year	93	91	81r
Sugar, white, all sizes	lb.	0.39	12/94	82r
Tobacco products and smoking supplies, total expenditures	year	286	91	81r
Tomatoes, field grown	lb.	1.36	12/94	82r
Tuna, chunk, light	lb.	1.94	12/94	82r
Turkey, frozen, whole	lb.	0.96	12/94	82r
Yogurt, natural, fruit flavored	8 oz.	0.58	12/94	82r
Health Care				
Adenosine, emergency room	treat	100.00	95	23r
Bladder tap, superpubic, infant, emergency room	treat	119.00	95	23r
Blood analysis, emergency room	treat	25.00	95	23r
Blood tests, abdominal pain, emergency room	treat	25.00	95	23r
Burn dressing, emergency room	treat	266.00	95	23r
Cardiology interpretation, emergency room	treat	26.00	95	23r
Chest X-ray, emergency room	treat	78.00	95	23r
Childbirth, Cesarean delivery, hospital charge	birth	5462.00	12/91	69r
Childbirth, Cesarean delivery, physician charge	birth	2228.00	12/91	69r
Childbirth, normal delivery, hospital charge	birth	2943.00	12/91	69r
Childbirth, normal delivery, physician charge	birth	1619.00	12/91	69r
Defibrillation pads, emergency room	treat	6.00	95	23r
Drugs, expenditures	year	297	91	81r

Laredo, TX - continued

Item	Per	Value	Date	Ref.
Health Care - continued				
Gastric tube insertion, nasal, emergency room	treat	25.00	95	23r
Health care, total expenditures	year	1600	91	81r
Health insurance expenditures	year	637	91	81r
Heart monitor, emergency room	treat	40.00	95	23r
Insurance premium, family medical care	month	389.25	1/95	41s
Intravenous fluids, emergency room	treat	130.00	95	23r
Intravenous fluids, emergency room	liter	26.00	95	23r
Intravenous line, central, emergency room	treat	342.00	95	23r
Liver function tests, abdominal pain, emergency room	treat	26.00	95	23r
Medical care charges, total, emergency room, third-degree burns	treat	2101.00	95	23r
Medical care charges, total, emergency, infant with fever	treat	628.00	95	23r
Medical services expenditures	year	573	91	81r
Medical supplies expenditures	year	93	91	81r
Morphine, emergency room	treat	34.00	95	23r
Nursing care and facilities charges, emergency room	treat	252.00	95	23r
Nursing care and facilities charges, emergency, infant with fever	treat	252.00	95	23r
Nursing care and facilities charges, emergency, third-degree burns	treat	861.00	95	23r
Physician's charges, emergency, infant with fever	treat	212.00	95	23r
Physician's charges, emergency, third-degree burns	treat	372.00	95	23r
Physician's fee, emergency room	treat	372.00	95	23r
Physician's fee, general practitioner	visit	51.20	12/93	60r
Surgery, open-heart	proc	42374.00	1/93	14r
Ultrasound, abdominal, emergency room	treat	276.00	95	23r
Urinalysis, emergency room	treat	20.00	95	23r
Urinalysis, infant, emergency room	treat	20.00	95	23r
X-rays, emergency room	treat	78.00	95	23r
Household Goods				
Floor coverings, expenditures	year	48	91	81r
Furniture, expenditures	year	280	91	81r
Household equipment, misc. expenditures	year	342	91	81r
Household expenditures, miscellaneous	year	256	91	81r
Household furnishings and equipment, expenditures	year	988	91	81r
Household operations expenditures	year	468	91	81r
Household textiles, expenditures	year	95	91	81r
Housekeeping supplies, expenditures	year	380	91	81r
Laundry and cleaning supplies, expenditures	year	109	91	81r
Postage and stationery, expenditures	year	105	91	81r
Housing				
Add garage/carport		6,980	3/95	74r
Add room(s)		11,403	3/95	74r
Apartment condominium or co-op, median	unit	68600	12/94	62r
Dwellings (owned), expenditures	year	2428	91	81r
Enclose porch/patio/breezeway		4,572	3/95	74r
Finish room in basement/attic		3,794	3/95	74r
Home, existing, single-family, median	unit	120200	12/94	62r
Maintenance, repairs, insurance, and other housing expenditures	year	531	91	81r
Mortgage interest and charges expenditures	year	1506	91	81r
Princ. & int., mortgage, median-price exist. sing.-family home	mo.	540	12/94	62r
Property taxes expenditures	year	391	91	81r
Redesign, restructure more than half of home's interior		17,641	3/95	74r
Rental units expenditures	year	1264	91	81r
Insurance and Pensions				
Auto insurance, private passenger	year	785.78	12/94	71s
Insurance and pensions, personal, expenditures	year	2395	91	81r
Insurance, life and other personal, expenditures	year	368	91	81r

Values are in dollars or fractions of dollars. In the column headed *Ref*, references are shown to sources. Each reference is followed by a letter. These refer to the geographical level for which data were reported: s = State, r = Region, and c = City or metro. The abbreviation *ex* is used to mean *except* or *excluding*; *exp* stands for expenditures. For other abbreviations and further explanations, please see the Introduction.

Laredo, TX - continued

Item	Per	Value	Date	Ref.
Insurance and Pensions				
Pensions and Social Security, expenditures	year	2027	91	81r
Personal Services				
Personal services expenditures	year	212	91	81r
Restaurant Food				
Dining expenditures, family	week	33.83	94	73r
Taxes				
Tax, cigarettes	year	584.00	10/93	43s
Taxes, Federal income, expenditures	year	2275	91	81r
Taxes, personal, expenditures	year	2715	91	81r
Taxes, State and local income, expenditures	year	365	91	81r
Transportation				
Cars and trucks purchased, new	year	1306	91	81r
Cars and trucks purchased, used	year	942	91	81r
Driver's learning permit fee	perm	5.00	1/94	84s
Driver's license fee	orig	16.00	1/94	84s
Driver's license fee, duplicate	lic	10.00	1/94	84s
Driver's license reinstatement fee, min.	susp	50.00	1/94	85s
Driver's license renewal fee	renew	16.00	1/94	84s
Identification card, nondriver	card	10.00	1/94	83s
Motorcycle learning permit fee	perm	5.00	1/94	84s
Motorcycle license fee	orig	16.00	1/94	84s
Motorcycle license fee, duplicate	lic	10.00	1/94	84s
Motorcycle license renewal fee	renew	21.00	1/94	84s
Public transportation expenditures	year	249	91	81r
Transportation expenditures, total	year	5307	91	81r
Vehicle finance charges	year	346	91	81r
Vehicle insurance expenditures	year	544	91	81r
Vehicle maintenance and repairs expenditures	year	600	91	81r
Vehicle purchases	year	2275	91	81r
Vehicle rental, leases, licenses, etc. expenditures	year	141	91	81r
Vehicles purchased, other than cars and trucks	year	27	91	81r
Utilities				
Electricity expenditures	year	950	91	81r
Utilities, fuels, and public services, total expenditures	year	2000	91	81r
Water and other public services, expenditures	year	227	91	81r
Weddings				
Bridal attendants' gowns	event	750	10/93	76r
Bridal gown	event	852	10/93	76r
Bridal headpiece and veil	event	167	10/93	76r
Bride's wedding band	event	708	10/93	76r
Clergy	event	224	10/93	76r
Engagement ring	event	2756	10/93	76r
Flowers	event	863	10/93	76r
Formal wear for groom	event	106	10/93	76r
Groom's attendants' formal wear	event	530	10/93	76r
Groom's wedding band	event	402	10/93	76r
Music	event	600	10/93	76r
Photography	event	1088	10/93	76r
Shoes for bride	event	50	10/93	76r
Videography	event	483	10/93	76r
Wedding invitations and announcements	event	342	10/93	76r
Wedding reception	event	7000	10/93	76r

Las Cruces, NM

Item	Per	Value	Date	Ref.
Composite, ACCRA index		97.70	12/94	2c
Alcoholic Beverages				
Beer, Miller Lite, Bud, 12-oz., ex deposit	6	4.01	12/94	2c
J & B Scotch	750-ml.	16.71	12/94	2c
Wine, Gallo Chablis blanc	1.5-lit	5.27	12/94	2c

Las Cruces, NM - continued

Item	Per	Value	Date	Ref.
Appliances				
Appliances (major), expenditures	year	160	91	81r
Average annual exp.				
Food, health care, personal goods, services	year	32461	91	81r
Charity				
Cash contributions, expenditures	year	975	91	81r
Clothing				
Apparel, men and boys, total expenditures	year	467	91	81r
Apparel, women and girls, total expenditures	year	737	91	81r
Footwear, expenditures	year	270	91	81r
Jeans, man's denim		29.66	12/94	2c
Shirt, man's dress shirt		33.00	12/94	2c
Undervest, boy's size 10-14, cotton	3	5.33	12/94	2c
Communications				
Long-distance telephone rate, day, addl. min., 1-10 mi.	min.	0.11	12/93	9s
Long-distance telephone rate, day, initial min., 1-10 mi.	min.	0.19	12/93	9s
Newspaper subscription, dly. and Sun. delivery	month	9.17	12/94	2c
Phone line, single, business, field visit	inst	53.95	12/93	9s
Phone line, single, business, no field visit	inst	53.95	12/93	9s
Phone line, single, residence, field visit	inst	30.00	12/93	9s
Phone line, single, residence, no field visit	inst	30.00	12/93	9s
Telephone bill, family of four	month	20.04	12/94	2c
Telephone service, expenditures	year	611	91	81r
Telephone, residential, flat rate	mo.	13.91	12/93	8c
Education				
Board, 4-year private college/university	year	2285	8/94	80s
Board, 4-year public college/university	year	1798	8/94	80s
Education, total expenditures	year	375	91	81r
Room, 4-year private college/university	year	2091	8/94	80s
Room, 4-year public college/university	year	1565	8/94	80s
Total cost, 4-year private college/university	year	14552	8/94	80s
Total cost, 4-year public college/university	year	5094	8/94	80s
Tuition, 2-year public college/university, in-state	year	625	8/94	80s
Tuition, 4-year private college/university, in-state	year	10176	8/94	80s
Tuition, 4-year public college/university, in-state	year	1731	8/94	80s
Energy and Fuels				
Energy, combined forms, 1800 sq. ft.	mo.	101.45	12/94	2c
Energy, exc. electricity, 1800 sq. ft.	mo.	21.12	12/94	2c
Fuel oil and other fuels, expenditures	year	33	91	81r
Gas, natural, expenditures	year	212	91	81r
Gas, reg unlead, taxes inc., cash, self-service	gal	1.21	12/94	2c
Gasoline and motor oil purchased	year	1115	91	81r
Gasoline, unleaded midgrade	gallon	1.36	4/93	82r
Gasoline, unleaded premium	gallon	1.43	4/93	82r
Gasoline, unleaded regular	gallon	1.23	4/93	82r
Entertainment				
Bowling, evening rate	game	2.45	12/94	2c
Concert ticket, Pearl Jam group	perf	20.00	94	50r
Entertainment, total expenditures	year	1853	91	81r
Fees and admissions, expenditures	year	482	91	81r
Monopoly game, Parker Brothers', No. 9	game	10.95	12/94	2c
Movie	adm	5.50	12/94	2c
Pets, toys, playground equipment, expenditures	year	299	91	81r
Reading, expenditures	year	164	91	81r
Televisions, radios, and sound equipment, expenditures	year	528	91	81r
Tennis balls, yellow, Wilson or Penn, 3	can	2.16	12/94	2c
Funerals				
Burial, immediate, container provided by funeral home		1360.49	1/95	54r
Cards, acknowledgment		11.24	1/95	54r

Values are in dollars or fractions of dollars. In the column headed *Ref*, references are shown to sources. Each reference is followed by a letter. These refer to the geographical level for which data were reported: s = State, r = Region, and c = City or metro. The abbreviation *ex* is used to mean *except* or *excluding*; *exp* stands for expenditures. For other abbreviations and further explanations, please see the Introduction.

Las Cruces, NM - continued

Item	Per	Value	Date	Ref.
Funerals				
Casket, minimum alternative		232.73	1/95	54r
Cosmetology, hair care, etc.		114.13	1/95	54r
Cremation, direct, container provided by funeral home		1027.08	1/95	54r
Embalming		286.24	1/95	54r
Funeral, funeral home		315.60	1/95	54r
Funeral, other facility		303.08	1/95	54r
Graveside service		423.83	1/95	54r
Hearse, local		133.12	1/95	54r
Limousine, local		99.10	1/95	54r
Memorial service		442.57	1/95	54r
Service charge, professional, nondeclinable		840.16	1/95	54r
Visitation and viewing		168.50	1/95	54r
Groceries				
Groceries, ACCRA Index		98.10	12/94	2c
Apples, Red Delicious	lb.	0.72	12/94	82r
Baby food, strained vegetables, lowest price	4-4.5 oz.	0.31	12/94	2c
Bacon, sliced	lb.	1.73	12/94	82r
Bananas	lb.	0.43	12/94	2c
Bananas	lb.	0.52	12/94	82r
Beef or hamburger, ground	lb.	1.02	12/94	2c
Beef purchases	year	241	91	81r
Beverage purchases, alcoholic	year	328	91	81r
Beverage purchases, nonalcoholic	year	234	91	81r
Bologna, all beef or mixed	lb.	2.33	12/94	82r
Bread, white	24-oz.	0.67		2c
Bread, white, pan	lb.	0.81	12/94	82r
Carrots, short trimmed and topped	lb.	0.43	12/94	82r
Cereals and bakery products purchases	year	392	91	81r
Cereals and cereals products purchases	year	139	91	81r
Cheese, Kraft grated Parmesan	8-oz.	3.67	12/94	2c
Chicken breast, bone-in	lb.	2.04	12/94	82r
Chicken, fresh, whole	lb.	0.95	12/94	82r
Chicken, whole fryer	lb.	0.67	12/94	2c
Cigarettes, Winston, Kings	carton	14.98	12/94	2c
Coffee, 100%, ground roast, all sizes	lb.	4.48	12/94	82r
Coffee, vacuum-packed	13 oz.	3.51	12/94	2c
Corn Flakes, Kellogg's or Post Toasties	18 oz.	2.49	12/94	2c
Corn, frozen, whole kernel, lowest price	10 oz.	0.73	12/94	2c
Dairy products (other) purchases	year	182	91	81r
Eggs, Grade A large	dozen	0.74	12/94	2c
Fish and seafood purchases	year	94	91	81r
Flour, white, all purpose	lb.	0.21	12/94	82r
Food purchases, food eaten at home	year	2749	91	81r
Foods purchased away from home, not prepared by consumer	year	1909	91	81r
Fruits and vegetables purchases	year	459	91	81r
Grapefruit	lb.	0.56	12/94	82r
Ground beef, 100% beef	lb.	1.31	12/94	82r
Ham, boneless, exc. canned	lb.	2.46	12/94	82r
Ice cream, prepackaged, bulk, regular	1/2 gal.	2.57	12/94	82r
Lemons	lb.	1.00	12/94	82r
Lettuce, iceberg	lb.	0.93	12/94	82r
Lettuce, iceberg	head	0.76	12/94	2c
Margarine, Blue Bonnet or Parkay cubes	lb.	0.73	12/94	2c
Meats, poultry, fish, and eggs purchases	year	700	91	81r
Milk and cream (fresh) purchases	year	155	91	81r
Milk, whole	1/2	1.39	12/94	2c
Orange juice, frozen concentrate 12-oz. can	16 oz.	1.52	12/94	82r
Orange juice, Minute Maid frozen	12-oz.	1.35	12/94	2c
Oranges, Navel	lb.	0.56	12/94	82r
Peaches, halves or slices, Hunt's, Del Monte, or Libby's	29-oz.	1.39	12/94	2c
Peas, sweet, Del Monte or Green Giant	15-17 oz.	0.70	12/94	2c
Pork chops, center cut, bone-in	lb.	3.30	12/94	82r
Pork purchases	year	122	91	81r
Potato chips	16-oz.	3.03	12/94	82r
Potatoes, frozen, French fried	lb.	0.77	12/94	82r

Las Cruces, NM - continued

Item	Per	Value	Date	Ref.
Groceries - continued				
Potatoes, white	lb.	0.35	12/94	82r
Potatoes, white or red	10-lb. sack	2.09	12/94	2c
Rice, white, long grain, uncooked	lb.	0.54	12/94	82r
Round roast, USDA choice, boneless	lb.	2.92	12/94	82r
Sausage, Jimmy Dean, 100% pork	lb.	2.31	12/94	2c
Shortening, vegetable oil blends	lb.	0.80	12/94	82r
Shortening, vegetable, Crisco	3-lb.	2.82	12/94	2c
Soft drink, Coca Cola, ex deposit	2 lit	1.23	12/94	2c
Spaghetti and macaroni	lb.	1.02	12/94	82r
Steak, round, graded & ungraded, exc. USDA prime & choice	lb.	3.13	12/94	82r
Steak, sirloin, USDA choice, boneless	lb.	4.07	12/94	82r
Steak, t-bone	lb.	4.50	12/94	2c
Sugar and other sweets, eaten at home, expenditures	year	105	91	81r
Sugar, cane or beet	4 lbs.	1.54	12/94	2c
Sugar, white, all sizes	lb.	0.38	12/94	82r
Tobacco products and smoking supplies, total expenditures	year	221	91	81r
Tomatoes, field grown	lb.	1.45	12/94	82r
Tomatoes, Hunt's or Del Monte	14.5 oz.	0.75	12/94	2c
Tuna, chunk, light	lb.	2.18	12/94	82r
Tuna, chunk, light, oil-packed	6.125-6.5 oz.	0.83	12/94	2c
Goods and Services				
Miscellaneous goods and services, ACCRA Index		95.10	12/94	2c
Health Care				
Health care, ACCRA Index		91.00	12/94	2c
Antibiotic ointment, Polysporin	1.5 oz.	4.22	12/94	2c
Childbirth, Cesarean delivery, hospital charge	birth	6059.00	12/91	69r
Childbirth, Cesarean delivery, physician charge	birth	2248.00	12/91	69r
Childbirth, normal delivery, hospital charge	birth	3006.00	12/91	69r
Childbirth, normal delivery, physician charge	birth	1634.00	12/91	69r
Dentist's fee, adult teeth cleaning and periodic oral exam	visit	57.34	12/94	2c
Doctor's fee, routine exam, established patient	visit	29.36	12/94	2c
Drugs, expenditures	year	230	91	81r
Health care, total expenditures	year	1544	91	81r
Health insurance expenditures	year	558	91	81r
Hospital care, semiprivate room	day	321.00	12/94	2c
Insurance premium, family medical care	month	331.96	1/95	41s
Medical services expenditures	year	676	91	81r
Medical supplies expenditures	year	80	91	81r
Surgery, open-heart	proc	37818.00	1/93	14r
Household Goods				
Appl. repair, service call, wash mach	min. lab. chg.	34.98	12/94	2c
Floor coverings, expenditures	year	79	91	81r
Furniture, expenditures	year	352	91	81r
Household equipment, misc. expenditures	year	614	91	81r
Household expenditures, miscellaneous	year	294	91	81r
Household furnishings and equipment, expenditures	year	1416	91	81r
Household operations expenditures	year	580	91	81r
Household textiles, expenditures	year	113	91	81r
Housekeeping supplies, expenditures	year	447	91	81r
Laundry and cleaning supplies, expenditures	year	114	91	81r
Laundry detergent, Tide Ultra, Bold, or Cheer	42 oz.	3.47	12/94	2c
Postage and stationery, expenditures	year	145	91	81r
Tissues, facial, Kleenex brand	175	1.14	12/94	2c

Values are in dollars or fractions of dollars. In the column headed *Ref*, references are shown to sources. Each reference is followed by a letter. These refer to the geographical level for which data were reported: s=State, r=Region, and c=City or metro. The abbreviation *ex* is used to mean *except* or *excluding*; *exp* stands for *expenditures*. For other abbreviations and further explanations, please see the Introduction.

Las Cruces, NM - continued

Item	Per	Value	Date	Ref.
Housing				
Housing, ACCRA Index		102.40	12/94	2c
Add garage/carport		6,422	3/95	74r
Add room(s)		26,583	3/95	74r
Apartment condominium or co-op, median	unit	105300	12/94	62r
Dwellings (owned), expenditures	year	3932	91	81r
Enclose porch/patio/breezeway		5,382	3/95	74r
Finish room in basement/attic		3,911	3/95	74r
Home, existing, single-family, median	unit	178600	12/94	62r
House payment, principal and interest, 25% down payment	mo.	803	12/94	2c
House, 1800 sq ft, 8000 sq ft lot, new, urban, utilities	total	127667	12/94	2c
Maintenance, repairs, insurance, and other housing expenditures	year	591	91	81r
Mortgage interest and charges expenditures	year	2747	91	81r
Mtge. rate, incl. points and orig. fee, 30-year conv. fixed or ARM	mo.	9.47	12/94	2c
Princ. & int., mortgage, median-price exist. sing.-family home	mo.	845	12/94	62r
Property taxes expenditures	year	594	91	81r
Redesign, restructure more than half of home's interior		5,467	3/95	74r
Rent, apartment, 2 br., 1 1/2-2 baths, unfurnished, 950 sq ft, water	mo.	487	12/94	2c
Rental units expenditures	year	2077	91	81r
Insurance and Pensions				
Auto insurance, private passenger	year	727.43	12/94	71s
Insurance and pensions, personal, expenditures	year	3042	91	81r
Insurance, life and other personal, expenditures	year	298	91	81r
Pensions and Social Security, expenditures	year	2744	91	81r
Legal Assistance				
Legal work, law firm associate	hour	91		10r
Legal work, law firm partner	hour	151		10r
Personal Goods				
Shampoo, Alberto VO5	15-oz.	1.24	12/94	2c
Toothpaste, Crest or Colgate	6-7 oz.	2.34	12/94	2c
Personal Services				
Dry cleaning, man's 2-pc. suit		6.42	12/94	2c
Haircut, man's barbershop, no styling		6.37	12/94	2c
Haircut, woman's shampoo, trim, blow-dry		20.43	12/94	2c
Personal services expenditures	year	286	91	81r
Restaurant Food				
Chicken, fried, thigh and drumstick		1.82	12/94	2c
Dining expenditures, family	week	32.25	94	73r
Hamburger with cheese	1/4 lb.	0.88	12/94	2c
Pizza, Pizza Hut or Pizza Inn	12-13 in.	8.25	12/94	2c
Taxes				
Taxes, Federal income, expenditures	year	2946	91	81r
Taxes, personal, expenditures	year	3791	91	81r
Taxes, State and local income, expenditures	year	791	91	81r
Transportation				
Transportation, ACCRA Index		101.50	12/94	2c
Bus fare, up to 10 miles	one-way	0.50	12/94	2c
Cars and trucks purchased, new	year	1231	91	81r
Cars and trucks purchased, used	year	915	91	81r
Driver's learning permit fee	perm	2.00	1/94	84s
Driver's license fee	orig	10.00	1/94	84s
Driver's license fee, duplicate	lic	10.00	1/94	84s
Driver's license reinstatement fee, min.	susp	25.00	1/94	85s
Driver's license renewal fee	renew	10.00	1/94	84s
Identification card, nondriver	card	5.00	1/94	83s
Motorcycle learning permit fee	perm	2.00	1/94	84s
Motorcycle license fee	orig	10.00	1/94	84s
Motorcycle license fee, duplicate	lic	10.00	1/94	84s

Las Cruces, NM - continued

Item	Per	Value	Date	Ref.
Transportation - continued				
Motorcycle license renewal fee	renew	10.00	1/94	84s
Public transportation expenditures	year	375	91	81r
Tire balance, computer or spin bal., front	wheel	7.27	12/94	2c
Transportation expenditures, total	year	5527	91	81r
Vehicle finance charges	year	287	91	81r
Vehicle insurance expenditures	year	624	91	81r
Vehicle maintenance and repairs expenditures	year	695	91	81r
Vehicle purchases	year	2174	91	81r
Vehicle rental, leases, licenses, etc. expenditures	year	257	91	81r
Vehicles purchased, other than cars and trucks	year	28	91	81r
Utilities				
Utilities, ACCRA Index		92.10	12/94	2c
Electricity expenditures	year	616	91	81r
Electricity, (part.), other, 1800 sq. ft., new home	mo.	80.33	12/94	2c
Electricity, summer, 250 KWh	month	30.24	8/93	64c
Electricity, summer, 500 KWh	month	54.49	8/93	64c
Electricity, summer, 750 KWh	month	78.72	8/93	64c
Electricity, summer, 1000 KWh	month	102.96	8/93	64c
Utilities, fuels, and public services, total expenditures	year	1681	91	81r
Water and other public services, expenditures	year	209	91	81r
Weddings				
Bridal attendants' gowns	event	750	10/93	76r
Bridal gown	event	852	10/93	76r
Bridal headpiece and veil	event	167	10/93	76r
Bride's wedding band	event	708	10/93	76r
Clergy	event	224	10/93	76r
Engagement ring	event	2756	10/93	76r
Flowers	event	863	10/93	76r
Formal wear for groom	event	106	10/93	76r
Groom's attendants' formal wear	event	530	10/93	76r
Groom's wedding band	event	402	10/93	76r
Music	event	600	10/93	76r
Photography	event	1088	10/93	76r
Shoes for bride	event	50	10/93	76r
Videography	event	483	10/93	76r
Wedding invitations and announcements	event	342	10/93	76r
Wedding reception	event	7000	10/93	76r

Las Vegas, NV

Item	Per	Value	Date	Ref.
Composite, ACCRA index		109.00	12/94	2c
Alcoholic Beverages				
Beer	bottle	2.00	94	35c
Beer, Miller Lite, Bud, 12-oz., ex deposit	6	3.72	12/94	2c
J & B Scotch	750-ml.	17.28	12/94	2c
Wine, Gallo Chablis blanc	1.5-lit	4.50	12/94	2c
Appliances				
Appliances (major), expenditures	year	160	91	81r
Average annual exp.				
Food, health care, personal goods, services	year	32461	91	81r
Charity				
Cash contributions, expenditures	year	975	91	81r
Clothing				
Apparel, men and boys, total expenditures	year	467	91	81r
Apparel, women and girls, total expenditures	year	737	91	81r
Footwear, expenditures	year	270	91	81r
Jeans, man's denim		32.17	12/94	2c
Shirt, dress, men's	shirt	29.30	1/92	44c
Shirt, man's dress shirt		37.90	12/94	2c
Undervest, boy's size 10-14, cotton	3	6.10	12/94	2c

Values are in dollars or fractions of dollars. In the column headed *Ref*, references are shown to sources. Each reference is followed by a letter. These refer to the geographical level for which data were reported: s = State, r = Region, and c = City or metro. The abbreviation *ex* is used to mean *except* or *excluding*; *exp* stands for expenditures. For other abbreviations and further explanations, please see the Introduction.

Las Vegas, NV - continued

Item	Per	Value	Date	Ref.
Communications				
Long-distance telephone rate, day, addl. min., 1-10 mi.	min.	0.06	12/93	9s
Long-distance telephone rate, day, initial min., 1-10 mi.	min.	0.16	12/93	9s
Newspaper subscription, dly. and Sun. delivery	month	10.87	12/94	2c
Phone line, single, business, field visit	inst	135.00	12/93	9s
Phone line, single, business, no field visit	inst	74.00	12/93	9s
Phone line, single, residence, field visit	inst	98.00	12/93	9s
Phone line, single, residence, no field visit	inst	45.00	12/93	9s
Telephone bill, family of four	month	11.05	12/94	2c
Telephone service, expenditures	year	611	91	81r
Telephone, residential, flat rate	mo.	10.50	12/93	8c
Education				
Board, 4-year public college/university	year	1862	8/94	80s
Education, total expenditures	year	375	91	81r
Room, 4-year private college/university	year	2600	8/94	80s
Room, 4-year public college/university	year	3003	8/94	80s
Total cost, 4-year public college/university	year	6403	8/94	80s
Tuition, 2-year public college/university, in-state	year	822	8/94	80s
Tuition, 4-year private college/university, in-state	year	7259	8/94	80s
Tuition, 4-year public college/university, in-state	year	1538	8/94	80s
Energy and Fuels				
Energy, combined forms, 1800 sq. ft.	mo.	115.09	12/94	2c
Energy, exc. electricity, 1800 sq. ft.	mo.	28.50	12/94	2c
Fuel oil and other fuels, expenditures	year	33	91	81r
Gas	gal.	1.12	1/92	44c
Gas, cooking, winter, 10 therms	month	10.87	2/94	65c
Gas, cooking, winter, 30 therms	month	21.39	2/94	65c
Gas, cooking, winter, 50 therms	month	31.91	2/94	65c
Gas, heating, winter, 100 therms	month	58.22	2/94	65c
Gas, heating, winter, average use	month	57.70	2/94	65c
Gas, natural, expenditures	year	212	91	81r
Gas, reg unlead, taxes inc., cash, self-service	gal	1.34	12/94	2c
Gasoline and motor oil purchased	year	1115	91	81r
Gasoline, unleaded midgrade	gallon	1.36	4/93	82r
Gasoline, unleaded premium	gallon	1.43	4/93	82r
Gasoline, unleaded regular	gallon	1.23	4/93	82r
Entertainment				
Bowling, evening rate	game	1.81	12/94	2c
Concert ticket, Pearl Jam group	perf	20.00	94	50r
Entertainment, total expenditures	year	1853	91	81r
Fees and admissions, expenditures	year	482	91	81r
Monopoly game, Parker Brothers', No. 9	game	11.42	12/94	2c
Movie	adm	6.75	12/94	2c
Movie ticket, adult	ticket	6.75	1/92	44c
Pets, toys, playground equipment, expenditures	year	299	91	81r
Reading, expenditures	year	164	91	81r
Televisions, radios, and sound equipment, expenditures	year	528	91	81r
Tennis balls, yellow, Wilson or Penn, 3	can	2.39	12/94	2c
Funerals				
Burial, immediate, container provided by funeral home		1360.49	1/95	54r
Cards, acknowledgment		11.24	1/95	54r
Casket, minimum alternative		232.73	1/95	54r
Cosmetology, hair care, etc.		114.13	1/95	54r
Cremation, direct, container provided by funeral home		1027.08	1/95	54r
Embalming		286.24	1/95	54r
Funeral, funeral home		315.60	1/95	54r
Funeral, other facility		303.08	1/95	54r
Graveside service		423.83	1/95	54r
Hearse, local		133.12	1/95	54r
Limousine, local		99.10	1/95	54r

Las Vegas, NV - continued

Item	Per	Value	Date	Ref.
Funerals - continued				
Memorial service		442.57	1/95	54r
Service charge, professional, nondeclinable		840.16	1/95	54r
Visitation and viewing		168.50	1/95	54r
Groceries				
Groceries, ACCRA Index		101.70	12/94	2c
Apples, Red Delicious	lb.	0.72	12/94	82r
Baby food, strained vegetables, lowest price	4-4.5 oz.	0.35	12/94	2c
Bacon, sliced	lb.	1.73	12/94	82r
Bananas	lb.	0.44	12/94	2c
Bananas	lb.	0.52	12/94	82r
Beef or hamburger, ground	lb.	1.29	12/94	2c
Beef purchases	year	241	91	81r
Beverage purchases, alcoholic	year	328	91	81r
Beverage purchases, nonalcoholic	year	234	91	81r
Big Mac hamburger	burger	1.92	94	35c
Bologna, all beef or mixed	lb.	2.33	12/94	82r
Bread, white	24-oz.	0.86	12/94	2c
Bread, white, pan	lb.	0.81	12/94	82r
Carrots, short trimmed and topped	lb.	0.43	12/94	82r
Cereals and bakery products purchases	year	392	91	81r
Cereals and cereals products purchases	year	139	91	81r
Cheese, Kraft grated Parmesan	8-oz.	3.23	12/94	2c
Chicken breast, bone-in	lb.	2.04	12/94	82r
Chicken, fresh, whole	lb.	0.95	12/94	82r
Chicken, whole fryer	lb.	0.70	12/94	2c
Cigarettes, Winston, Kings	carton	15.89	12/94	2c
Coffee, 100%, ground roast, all sizes	lb.	4.48	12/94	82r
Coffee, vacuum-packed	13 oz.	3.64	12/94	2c
Corn Flakes, Kellogg's or Post Toasties	18 oz.	2.41	12/94	2c
Corn, frozen, whole kernel, lowest price	10 oz.	0.78	12/94	2c
Dairy products (other) purchases	year	182	91	81r
Eggs, Grade A large	dozen	1.30	12/94	2c
Fish and seafood purchases	year	94	91	81r
Flour, white, all purpose	lb.	0.21	12/94	82r
Food purchases, food eaten at home	year	2749	91	81r
Foods purchased away from home, not prepared by consumer	year	1909	91	81r
Fruits and vegetables purchases	year	459	91	81r
Grapefruit	lb.	0.56	12/94	82r
Ground beef, 100% beef	lb.	1.31	12/94	82r
Ham, boneless, exc. canned	lb.	2.46	12/94	82r
Ice cream, prepackaged, bulk, regular	1/2 gal.	2.57	12/94	82r
Lemons	lb.	1.00	12/94	82r
Lettuce, iceberg	lb.	0.93	12/94	82r
Lettuce, iceberg	head	0.66	12/94	2c
Margarine, Blue Bonnet or Parkay cubes	lb.	0.58	12/94	2c
Meats, poultry, fish, and eggs purchases	year	700	91	81r
Milk and cream (fresh) purchases	year	155	91	81r
Milk, 2%	gal.	2.33	1/92	44c
Milk, whole	1/2 gal.	1.55	12/94	2c
Orange juice, frozen concentrate 12-oz. can	16 oz.	1.52	12/94	82r
Orange juice, Minute Maid frozen	12-oz.	1.31	12/94	2c
Oranges, Navel	lb.	0.56	12/94	82r
Peaches, halves or slices, Hunt's, Del Monte, or Libby's	29-oz.	1.16	12/94	2c
Peas, sweet, Del Monte or Green Giant	15-17 oz.	0.57	12/94	2c
Pork chops, center cut, bone-in	lb.	3.30	12/94	82r
Pork purchases	year	122	91	81r
Potato chips	16-oz.	3.03	12/94	82r
Potatoes, frozen, French fried	lb.	0.77	12/94	82r
Potatoes, white	lb.	0.35	12/94	82r
Potatoes, white or red	10-lb. sack	1.73	12/94	2c
Rental rate, 2-bedroom apartment	month	566.00	1/92	44c
Rice, white, long grain, uncooked	lb.	0.54	12/94	82r
Round roast, USDA choice, boneless	lb.	2.92	12/94	82r
Sausage, Jimmy Dean, 100% pork	lb.	3.15	12/94	2c
Shortening, vegetable oil blends	lb.	0.80	12/94	82r

Values are in dollars or fractions of dollars. In the column headed *Ref*, references are shown to sources. Each reference is followed by a letter. These refer to the geographical level for which data were reported: s=State, r=Region, and c=City or metro. The abbreviation *ex* is used to mean *except* or *excluding*; *exp* stands for expenditures. For other abbreviations and further explanations, please see the Introduction.

Las Vegas, NV - continued

Item	Per	Value	Date	Ref.
Groceries				
Shortening, vegetable, Crisco	3-lb.	2.92	12/94	2c
Soft drink, Coca Cola, ex deposit	2 lit	1.13	12/94	2c
Spaghetti and macaroni	lb.	1.02	12/94	82r
Steak, round, graded & ungraded, exc. USDA prime & choice	lb.	3.13	12/94	82r
Steak, sirloin, USDA choice, boneless	lb.	4.07	12/94	82r
Steak, t-bone	lb.	4.08	12/94	2c
Sugar and other sweets, eaten at home, expenditures	year	105	91	81r
Sugar, cane or beet	4 lbs.	1.23	12/94	2c
Sugar, white, all sizes	lb.	0.38	12/94	82r
Tobacco products and smoking supplies, total expenditures	year	221	91	81r
Tomatoes, field grown	lb.	1.45	12/94	82r
Tomatoes, Hunt's or Del Monte	14.5 oz.	0.70	12/94	2c
Tuna, chunk, light	lb.	2.18	12/94	82r
Tuna, chunk, light, oil-packed	6.125-6.5 oz.	0.97	12/94	2c
Goods and Services				
Miscellaneous goods and services, ACCRA Index		105.90	12/94	2c
Health Care				
Health care, ACCRA Index		116.80	12/94	2c
Antibiotic ointment, Polysporin	1.5 oz.	4.33	12/94	2c
Childbirth, Cesarean delivery, hospital charge	birth	6059.00	12/91	69r
Childbirth, Cesarean delivery, physician charge	birth	2248.00	12/91	69r
Childbirth, normal delivery, hospital charge	birth	3006.00	12/91	69r
Childbirth, normal delivery, physician charge	birth	1634.00	12/91	69r
Dentist's fee, adult teeth cleaning and periodic oral exam	visit	69.40	12/94	2c
Doctor's fee, routine exam, established patient	visit	49.80	12/94	2c
Drugs, expenditures	year	230	91	81r
Health care, total expenditures	year	1544	91	81r
Health insurance expenditures	year	558	91	81r
Hospital care, semiprivate room	day	321.50	12/94	2c
Insurance premium, family medical care	month	383.60	1/95	41s
Medical services expenditures	year	676	91	81r
Medical supplies expenditures	year	80	91	81r
Surgery, open-heart	proc	37818.00	1/93	14r
Household Goods				
Appl. repair, service call, wash mach	min. lab. chg.	30.88	12/94	2c
Floor coverings, expenditures	year	79	91	81r
Furniture, expenditures	year	352	91	81r
Household equipment, misc. expenditures	year	614	91	81r
Household expenditures, miscellaneous	year	294	91	81r
Household furnishings and equipment, expenditures	year	1416	91	81r
Household operations expenditures	year	580	91	81r
Household textiles, expenditures	year	113	91	81r
Housekeeping supplies, expenditures	year	447	91	81r
Laundry and cleaning supplies, expenditures	year	114	91	81r
Laundry detergent, Tide Ultra, Bold, or Cheer	42 oz.	3.52	12/94	2c
Postage and stationery, expenditures	year	145	91	81r
Tissues, facial, Kleenex brand	175	0.91	12/94	2c
Housing				
Housing, ACCRA Index		115.20	12/94	2c
Add garage/carport		6,422	3/95	74r
Add room(s)		26,583	3/95	74r
Apartment condominium or co-op, median	unit	105300	12/94	62r
Dwellings (owned), expenditures	year	3932	91	81r
Enclose porch/patio/breezeway		5,382	3/95	74r
Finish room in basement/attic		3,911	3/95	74r

Las Vegas, NV - continued

Item	Per	Value	Date	Ref.
Housing - continued				
Home, existing, single-family, median	unit	178600	12/94	62r
Home, existing, single-family, median	unit	111.00	12/94	62c
House payment, principal and interest, 25% down payment	mo.	884	12/94	2c
House, 1800 sq ft, 8000 sq ft lot, new, urban, utilities	total	143913	12/94	2c
Maintenance, repairs, insurance, and other housing expenditures	year	591	91	81r
Mortgage interest and charges expenditures	year	2747	91	81r
Mtge. rate, incl. points and orig. fee, 30-year conv. fixed or ARM	mo.	9.20	12/94	2c
Princ. & int., mortgage, median-price exist. sing.-family home	mo.	845	12/94	62r
Property taxes expenditures	year	594	91	81r
Redesign, restructure more than half of home's interior		5,467	3/95	74r
Rent, apartment, 2 br., 1 1/2-2 baths, unfurnished, 950 sq ft, water	mo.	606	12/94	2c
Rental units expenditures	year	2077	91	81r
Insurance and Pensions				
Auto insurance, private passenger	year	853.93	12/94	71s
Insurance and pensions, personal, expenditures	year	3042	91	81r
Insurance, life and other personal, expenditures	year	298	91	81r
Pensions and Social Security, expenditures	year	2744	91	81r
Legal Assistance				
Legal work, law firm associate	hour	91		10r
Legal work, law firm partner	hour	151		10r
Personal Goods				
Shampoo, Alberto VO5	15-oz.	1.28	12/94	2c
Toothpaste, Crest or Colgate	6-7 oz.	2.59	12/94	2c
Personal Services				
Dry cleaning, man's 2-pc. suit		6.45	12/94	2c
Dry cleaning, woman's dress	dress	6.95	1/92	44c
Haircut, man's barbershop, no styling		9.40	12/94	2c
Haircut, woman's shampoo, trim, blow-dry		18.40	12/94	2c
Personal services expenditures	year	286	91	81r
Restaurant Food				
Big Mac, small fries, medium drink	meal	3.53	1/92	44c
Chicken, fried, thigh and drumstick		2.30	12/94	2c
Dining expenditures, family	week	32.25	94	73r
Hamburger with cheese	1/4 lb.	1.85	12/94	2c
Pizza, Pizza Hut or Pizza Inn	12-13 in.	7.53	12/94	2c
Taxes				
Tax rate, residential property, month	$100	1.02	1/92	79c
Taxes, Federal income, expenditures	year	2946	91	81r
Taxes, personal, expenditures	year	3791	91	81r
Taxes, State and local income, expenditures	year	791	91	81r
Transportation				
Transportation, ACCRA Index		120.20	12/94	2c
Bus fare, one-way	trip	1.00	12/95	1c
Bus fare, up to 10 miles	one-way	1.00	12/94	2c
Cars and trucks purchased, new	year	1231	91	81r
Cars and trucks purchased, used	year	915	91	81r
Driver's learning permit fee	perm	10.00	1/94	84s
Driver's license fee	orig	6.00	1/94	84s
Driver's license reinstatement fee, min.	susp	40.00	1/94	85s
Driver's license renewal fee	renew	6.00	1/94	84s
Identification card, nondriver	card	10.00	1/94	83s
Motorcycle license fee	orig	6.00	1/94	84s
Motorcycle license renewal fee	renew	6.00	1/94	84s
parking, long-term lot, airport	3 days	12.00	1/92	44c
Public transportation expenditures	year	375	91	81r
Tire balance, computer or spin bal., front	wheel	8.55	12/94	2c
Transportation expenditures, total	year	5527	91	81r

Values are in dollars or fractions of dollars. In the column headed *Ref*, references are shown to sources. Each reference is followed by a letter. These refer to the geographical level for which data were reported: s=State, r=Region, and c=City or metro. The abbreviation *ex* is used to mean *except* or *excluding*; *exp* stands for expenditures. For other abbreviations and further explanations, please see the Introduction.

Las Vegas, NV - continued

Item	Per	Value	Date	Ref.
Transportation				
Vehicle finance charges	year	287	91	81r
Vehicle insurance expenditures	year	624	91	81r
Vehicle maintenance and repairs expenditures	year	695	91	81r
Vehicle purchases	year	2174	91	81r
Vehicle rental, leases, licenses, etc. expenditures	year	257	91	81r
Vehicles purchased, other than cars and trucks	year	28	91	81r
Utilities				
Utilities, ACCRA Index		96.40	12/94	2c
Electricity expenditures	year	616	91	81r
Electricity, (part.), other, 1800 sq. ft., new home	mo.	86.59	12/94	2c
Electricity, summer, 250 KWh	month	18.03	8/93	64c
Electricity, summer, 500 KWh	month	31.05	8/93	64c
Electricity, summer, 750 KWh	month	44.05	8/93	64c
Electricity, summer, 1000 KWh	month	57.06	8/93	64c
Utilities, fuels, and public services, total expenditures	year	1681	91	81r
Water and other public services, expenditures	year	209	91	81r
Weddings				
Bridal attendants' gowns	event	750	10/93	76r
Bridal gown	event	852	10/93	76r
Bridal headpiece and veil	event	167	10/93	76r
Bride's wedding band	event	708	10/93	76r
Clergy	event	224	10/93	76r
Engagement ring	event	2756	10/93	76r
Flowers	event	863	10/93	76r
Formal wear for groom	event	106	10/93	76r
Groom's attendants' formal wear	event	530	10/93	76r
Groom's wedding band	event	402	10/93	76r
Music	event	600	10/93	76r
Photography	event	1088	10/93	76r
Shoes for bride	event	50	10/93	76r
Videography	event	483	10/93	76r
Wedding invitations and announcements	event	342	10/93	76r
Wedding reception	event	7000	10/93	76r

Laurel-Jones County, MS

Item	Per	Value	Date	Ref.
Composite, ACCRA index		89.90	12/94	2c
Alcoholic Beverages				
Beer, Miller Lite, Bud, 12-oz., ex deposit	6	3.98	12/94	2c
J & B Scotch	750-ml.	16.84	12/94	2c
Wine, Gallo Chablis blanc	1.5-lit	5.43	12/94	2c
Clothing				
Jeans, man's denim		42.50	12/94	2c
Shirt, man's dress shirt		26.75	12/94	2c
Undervest, boy's size 10-14, cotton	3	3.18	12/94	2c
Communications				
Newspaper subscription, dly. and Sun. delivery	month	13.50	12/94	2c
Telephone bill, family of four	month	25.35	12/94	2c
Telephone, residential, flat rate	mo.	16.55	12/93	8c
Energy and Fuels				
Energy, combined forms, 1800 sq. ft.	mo.	92.67	12/94	2c
Gas, reg unlead, taxes inc., cash, self-service	gal	1.09	12/94	2c
Entertainment				
Bowling, evening rate	game	2.00	12/94	2c
Monopoly game, Parker Brothers', No. 9	game	10.91	12/94	2c
Movie	adm	5.00	12/94	2c
Tennis balls, yellow, Wilson or Penn, 3	can	1.88	12/94	2c

Laurel-Jones County, MS - continued

Item	Per	Value	Date	Ref.
Groceries				
Groceries, ACCRA Index		101.70	12/94	2c
Baby food, strained vegetables, lowest price	4-4.5 oz.	0.30	12/94	2c
Bananas	lb.	0.47	12/94	2c
Beef or hamburger, ground	lb.	1.76	12/94	2c
Bread, white	24-oz.	0.63	12/94	2c
Cheese, Kraft grated Parmesan	8-oz.	3.50	12/94	2c
Chicken, whole fryer	lb.	0.88	12/94	2c
Cigarettes, Winston, Kings	carton	14.61	12/94	2c
Coffee, vacuum-packed	13 oz.	3.48	12/94	2c
Corn Flakes, Kellogg's or Post Toasties	18 oz.	2.67	12/94	2c
Corn, frozen, whole kernel, lowest price	10 oz.	0.85	12/94	2c
Eggs, Grade A large	dozen	0.77	12/94	2c
Lettuce, iceberg	head	0.99	12/94	2c
Margarine, Blue Bonnet or Parkay cubes	lb.	0.57	12/94	2c
Milk, whole	1/2 gal.	1.42	12/94	2c
Orange juice, Minute Maid frozen	12-oz.	1.40	12/94	2c
Peaches, halves or slices, Hunt's, Del Monte, or Libby's	29-oz.	1.48	12/94	2c
Peas, sweet, Del Monte or Green Giant	15-17 oz.	0.62	12/94	2c
Potatoes, white or red	10-lb. sack	3.29	12/94	2c
Sausage, Jimmy Dean, 100% pork	lb.	2.62	12/94	2c
Shortening, vegetable, Crisco	3-lb.	2.65	12/94	2c
Soft drink, Coca Cola, ex deposit	2 lit	1.11	12/94	2c
Steak, t-bone	lb.	5.64	12/94	2c
Sugar, cane or beet	4 lbs.	1.50	12/94	2c
Tomatoes, Hunt's or Del Monte	14.5 oz.	0.83	12/94	2c
Tuna, chunk, light, oil-packed	6.125-6.5 oz.	0.63	12/94	2c
Goods and Services				
Miscellaneous goods and services, ACCRA Index		98.40	12/94	2c
Health Care				
Health care, ACCRA Index		87.70	12/94	2c
Antibiotic ointment, Polysporin	1.5 oz.	3.77	12/94	2c
Dentist's fee, adult teeth cleaning and periodic oral exam	visit	54.00	12/94	2c
Doctor's fee, routine exam, established patient	visit	37.67	12/94	2c
Hospital care, semiprivate room	day	185.00	12/94	2c
Household Goods				
Appl. repair, service call, wash mach	min. lab. chg.	32.50	12/94	2c
Laundry detergent, Tide Ultra, Bold, or Cheer	42 oz.	2.94	12/94	2c
Tissues, facial, Kleenex brand	175	1.16	12/94	2c
Housing				
Housing, ACCRA Index		72.00	12/94	2c
House payment, principal and interest, 25% down payment	mo.	550	12/94	2c
House, 1800 sq ft, 8000 sq ft lot, new, urban, utilities	total	88200	12/94	2c
Mtge. rate, incl. points and orig. fee, 30-year conv. fixed or ARM	mo.	9.37	12/94	2c
Rent, apartment, 2 br., 1 1/2-2 baths, unfurnished, 950 sq ft, water	mo.	385	12/94	2c
Personal Goods				
Shampoo, Alberto VO5	15-oz.	0.95	12/94	2c
Toothpaste, Crest or Colgate	6-7 oz.	1.78	12/94	2c
Personal Services				
Dry cleaning, man's 2-pc. suit		5.54	12/94	2c
Haircut, man's barbershop, no styling		6.33	12/94	2c
Haircut, woman's shampoo, trim, blow-dry		17.33	12/94	2c

Values are in dollars or fractions of dollars. In the column headed *Ref*, references are shown to sources. Each reference is followed by a letter. These refer to the geographical level for which data were reported: s=State, r=Region, and c=City or metro. The abbreviation *ex* is used to mean *except* or *excluding*; *exp* stands for *expenditures*. For other abbreviations and further explanations, please see the Introduction.

Laurel-Jones County, MS - continued

Item	Per	Value	Date	Ref.
Restaurant Food				
Chicken, fried, thigh and drumstick		1.96	12/94	2c
Hamburger with cheese	1/4 lb.	1.92	12/94	2c
Pizza, Pizza Hut or Pizza Inn	12-13 in.	7.95	12/94	2c
Transportation				
Transportation, ACCRA Index		95.60	12/94	2c
Tire balance, computer or spin bal., front	wheel	6.33	12/94	2c
Utilities				
Utilities, ACCRA Index		89.00	12/94	2c
Electricity, 1800 sq. ft., new home	mo.	92.67	12/94	2c

Lawrence, KS

Item	Per	Value	Date	Ref.
Composite, ACCRA index		93.80	12/94	2c
Alcoholic Beverages				
Beer, Miller Lite, Bud, 12-oz., ex deposit	6	4.24	12/94	2c
J & B Scotch	750-ml.	17.75	12/94	2c
Wine, Gallo Chablis blanc	1.5-lit	4.82	12/94	2c
Appliances				
Appliances (major), expenditures	year	131	91	81r
Average annual exp.				
Food, health care, personal goods, services	year	25935	91	81r
Charity				
Cash contributions, expenditures	year	745	91	81r
Clothing				
Apparel, men and boys, total expenditures	year	332	91	81r
Apparel, women and girls, total expenditures	year	578	91	81r
Footwear, expenditures	year	164	91	81r
Jeans, man's denim		27.63	12/94	2c
Shirt, man's dress shirt		27.41	12/94	2c
Undervest, boy's size 10-14, cotton	3	4.60	12/94	2c
Communications				
Long-distance telephone rate, day, addl. min., 1-10 mi.	min.	0.09	12/93	9s
Long-distance telephone rate, day, initial min., 1-10 mi.	min.	0.18	12/93	9s
Newspaper subscription, dly. and Sun. delivery	month	13.95	12/94	2c
Phone line, single, business, field visit	inst	57.40	12/93	9s
Phone line, single, business, no field visit	inst	57.40	12/93	9s
Phone line, single, residence, field visit	inst	39.00	12/93	9s
Phone line, single, residence, no field visit	inst	39.00	12/93	9s
Telephone bill, family of four	month	17.62	12/94	2c
Telephone service, expenditures	year	547	91	81r
Telephone, residential, flat rate	mo.	10.70	12/93	8c
Education				
Board, 4-year private college/university	year	2084	8/94	80s
Board, 4-year public college/university	year	1709	8/94	80s
Education, total expenditures	year	394	91	81r
Room, 4-year private college/university	year	1458	8/94	80s
Room, 4-year public college/university	year	1605	8/94	80s
Total cost, 4-year private college/university	year	11145	8/94	80s
Total cost, 4-year public college/university	year	5236	8/94	80s
Tuition, 2-year public college/university, in-state	year	960	8/94	80s
Tuition, 4-year private college/university, in-state	year	7602	8/94	80s
Tuition, 4-year public college/university, in-state	year	1921	8/94	80s
Energy and Fuels				
Energy, combined forms, 1800 sq. ft.	mo.	88.20	12/94	2c
Energy, exc. electricity, 1800 sq. ft.	mo.	39.28	12/94	2c
Fuel oil and other fuels, expenditures	year	83	91	81r
Gas, cooking, 10 therms	month	8.67	2/94	65c
Gas, cooking, 30 therms	month	17.71	2/94	65c

Lawrence, KS - continued

Item	Per	Value	Date	Ref.
Energy and Fuels - continued				
Gas, cooking, 50 therms	month	26.75	2/94	65c
Gas, heating, winter, 100 therms	month	49.35	2/94	65c
Gas, heating, winter, average use	month	84.15	2/94	65c
Gas, natural, expenditures	year	373	91	81r
Gas, reg unlead, taxes inc., cash, self-service	gal	1.06	12/94	2c
Gasoline and motor oil purchased	year	1000	91	81r
Gasoline, unleaded midgrade	gallon	1.15	4/93	82r
Gasoline, unleaded premium	gallon	1.23	4/93	82r
Gasoline, unleaded regular	gallon	1.07	4/93	82r
Entertainment				
Bowling, evening rate	game	1.75	12/94	2c
Entertainment, total expenditures	year	1356	91	81r
Fees and admissions, expenditures	year	347	91	81r
Monopoly game, Parker Brothers', No. 9	game	13.08	12/94	2c
Movie	adm	5.00	12/94	2c
Pets, toys, playground equipment, expenditures	year	270	91	81r
Reading, expenditures	year	160	91	81r
Televisions, radios, and sound equipment, expenditures	year	433	91	81r
Tennis balls, yellow, Wilson or Penn, 3	can	3.18	12/94	2c
Funerals				
Burial, immediate, container provided by funeral home		1348.78	1/95	54r
Cards, acknowledgment		21.20	1/95	54r
Casket, minimum alternative		182.83	1/95	54r
Cosmetology, hair care, etc.		133.11	1/95	54r
Cremation, direct, container provided by funeral home		1101.95	1/95	54r
Embalming		314.45	1/95	54r
Funeral, funeral home		304.88	1/95	54r
Funeral, other facility		301.37	1/95	54r
Graveside service		290.59	1/95	54r
Hearse, local		137.37	1/95	54r
Limousine, local		82.84	1/95	54r
Memorial service		316.57	1/95	54r
Service charge, professional, nondeclinable		1099.00	1/95	54r
Visitation and viewing		209.25	1/95	54r
Groceries				
Groceries, ACCRA Index		88.00	12/94	2c
Apples, Red Delicious	lb.	0.68	12/94	82r
Baby food, strained vegetables, lowest price	4-4.5 oz.	0.38	12/94	2c
Bacon, sliced	lb.	1.88	12/94	82r
Bananas	lb.	0.29	12/94	2c
Bananas	lb.	0.41	12/94	82r
Beef or hamburger, ground	lb.	1.06	12/94	2c
Beef purchases	year	197	91	81r
Beef, stew, boneless	lb.	2.52	12/94	82r
Beverage purchases, alcoholic	year	293	91	81r
Beverage purchases, nonalcoholic	year	203	91	81r
Bologna, all beef or mixed	lb.	2.12	12/94	82r
Bread, white	24-oz.	0.59	12/94	2c
Bread, white, pan	lb.	0.76	12/94	82r
Cabbage	lb.	0.44	12/94	82r
Carrots, short trimmed and topped	lb.	0.44	12/94	82r
Cereals and bakery products purchases	year	347	91	81r
Cereals and cereals products purchases	year	119	91	81r
Cheddar cheese, natural	lb.	3.28	12/94	82r
Cheese, Kraft grated Parmesan	8-oz.	3.18	12/94	2c
Chicken breast, bone-in	lb.	1.61	12/94	82r
Chicken, fresh, whole	lb.	0.89	12/94	82r
Chicken, whole fryer	lb.	0.75	12/94	2c
Chuck roast, USDA choice, boneless	lb.	2.33	12/94	82r
Cigarettes, Winston, Kings	carton	14.52	12/94	2c
Coffee, 100%, ground roast, all sizes	lb.	4.28	12/94	82r
Coffee, vacuum-packed	13 oz.	2.94	12/94	2c
Cookies, chocolate chip	lb.	2.72	12/94	82r
Corn Flakes, Kellogg's or Post Toasties	18 oz.	2.02	12/94	2c
Corn, frozen, whole kernel, lowest price	10 oz.	0.64	12/94	2c

Values are in dollars or fractions of dollars. In the column headed *Ref*, references are shown to sources. Each reference is followed by a letter. These refer to the geographical level for which data were reported: s = State, r = Region, and c = City or metro. The abbreviation *ex* is used to mean *except* or *excluding*; *exp* stands for *expenditures*. For other abbreviations and further explanations, please see the Introduction.

Lawrence, KS - continued

Item	Per	Value	Date	Ref.
Groceries				
Dairy products (other) purchases	year	148	91	81r
Eggs, Grade A large	dozen	0.66	12/94	2c
Eggs, Grade A large	dozen	0.76	12/94	82r
Fish and seafood purchases	year	61	91	81r
Flour, white, all purpose	lb.	0.22	12/94	82r
Food purchases, food eaten at home	year	2313	91	81r
Foods purchased away from home, not prepared by consumer	year	1709	91	81r
Fruits and vegetables purchases	year	372	91	81r
Grapefruit	lb.	0.47	12/94	82r
Grapes, Thompson seedless	lb.	2.15	12/94	82r
Ground beef, 100% beef	lb.	1.37	12/94	82r
Ground chuck, 100% beef	lb.	1.81	12/94	82r
Ham, boneless, exc. canned	lb.	2.16	12/94	82r
Ice cream, prepackaged, bulk, regular	1/2 gal.	2.48	12/94	82r
Lemons	lb.	1.08	12/94	82r
Lettuce, iceberg	lb.	0.81	12/94	82r
Lettuce, iceberg	head	0.56	12/94	2c
Margarine, Blue Bonnet or Parkay cubes	lb.	0.46	12/94	2c
Margarine, stick	lb.	0.81	12/94	82r
Meats, poultry, fish, and eggs purchases	year	591	91	81r
Milk and cream (fresh) purchases	year	132	91	81r
Milk, whole	1/2 gal.	1.46	12/94	2c
Orange juice, frozen concentrate 12-oz. can	16 oz.	1.41	12/94	82r
Orange juice, Minute Maid frozen	12-oz.	1.16	12/94	2c
Oranges, Navel	lb.	0.56	12/94	82r
Peaches, halves or slices, Hunt's, Del Monte, or Libby's	29-oz.	1.36	12/94	2c
Peanut butter, creamy, all sizes	lb.	1.81	12/94	82r
Peas, sweet, Del Monte or Green Giant	15-17 oz.	0.47	12/94	2c
Pork chops, center cut, bone-in	lb.	2.76	12/94	82r
Pork purchases	year	130	91	81r
Potato chips	16-oz.	2.81	12/94	82r
Potatoes, frozen, French fried	lb.	0.83	12/94	82r
Potatoes, white	lb.	0.28	12/94	82r
Potatoes, white or red	10-lb. sack	1.46	12/94	2c
Round roast, USDA choice, boneless	lb.	2.90	12/94	82r
Sausage, Jimmy Dean, 100% pork	lb.	2.78	12/94	2c
Shortening, vegetable oil blends	lb.	0.88	12/94	82r
Shortening, vegetable, Crisco	3-lb.	2.07	12/94	2c
Soft drink, Coca Cola, ex deposit	2 lit	1.11	12/94	2c
Spaghetti and macaroni	lb.	0.78	12/94	82r
Steak, rib eye, USDA choice, boneless	lb.	6.15	12/94	82r
Steak, round, graded & ungraded, exc. USDA prime & choice	lb.	2.72	12/94	82r
Steak, round, USDA choice, boneless	lb.	3.02	12/94	82r
Steak, sirloin, USDA choice, boneless	lb.	3.85	12/94	82r
Steak, t-bone	lb.	5.54	12/94	2c
Steak, T-bone, USDA choice, bone-in	lb.	5.38	12/94	82r
Sugar and other sweets, eaten at home, expenditures	year	91	91	81r
Sugar, cane or beet	4 lbs.	1.05	12/94	2c
Sugar, white, all sizes	lb.	0.36	12/94	82r
Tobacco products and smoking supplies, total expenditures	year	298	91	81r
Tomatoes, field grown	lb.	1.36	12/94	82r
Tomatoes, Hunt's or Del Monte	14.5 oz.	0.73	12/94	2c
Tuna, chunk, light	lb.	1.94	12/94	82r
Tuna, chunk, light, oil-packed	6.125-6.5 oz.	0.45	12/94	2c
Turkey, frozen, whole	lb.	0.96	12/94	82r
Yogurt, natural, fruit flavored	8 oz.	0.62	12/94	82r
Goods and Services				
Miscellaneous goods and services, ACCRA Index		97.30	12/94	2c

Lawrence, KS - continued

Item	Per	Value	Date	Ref.
Health Care				
Health care, ACCRA Index		89.60	12/94	2c
Antibiotic ointment, Polysporin	1.5 oz.	3.77	12/94	2c
Childbirth, Cesarean delivery, hospital charge	birth	5101.00	12/91	69r
Childbirth, Cesarean delivery, physician charge	birth	2234.00	12/91	69r
Childbirth, normal delivery, hospital charge	birth	2891.00	12/91	69r
Childbirth, normal delivery, physician charge	birth	1623.00	12/91	69r
Dentist's fee, adult teeth cleaning and periodic oral exam	visit	50.00	12/94	2c
Doctor's fee, routine exam, established patient	visit	36.75	12/94	2c
Drugs, expenditures	year	248	91	81r
Health care, total expenditures	year	1336	91	81r
Health insurance expenditures	year	550	91	81r
Hospital care, semiprivate room	day	290.00	12/94	2c
Insurance premium, family medical care	month	370.49	1/95	41s
Medical services expenditures	year	457	91	81r
Medical supplies expenditures	year	82	91	81r
Household Goods				
Appl. repair, service call, wash mach	min. lab. chg.	32.71	12/94	2c
Floor coverings, expenditures	year	105	91	81r
Furniture, expenditures	year	291	91	81r
Household equipment, misc. expenditures	year	341	91	81r
Household expenditures, miscellaneous	year	162	91	81r
Household furnishings and equipment, expenditures	year	1042	91	81r
Household operations expenditures	year	365	91	81r
Household textiles, expenditures	year	101	91	81r
Housekeeping supplies, expenditures	year	390	91	81r
Laundry and cleaning supplies, expenditures	year	110	91	81r
Laundry detergent, Tide Ultra, Bold, or Cheer	42 oz.	3.08	12/94	2c
Postage and stationery, expenditures	year	115	91	81r
Tissues, facial, Kleenex brand	175	1.01	12/94	2c
Housing				
Housing, ACCRA Index		97.80	12/94	2c
Add garage/carport		8,479	3/95	74r
Add room(s)		21,347	3/95	74r
Apartment condominium or co-op, median	unit	87100	12/94	62r
Bathroom addition, average cost	add	9734.00	3/95	13r
Bathroom remodeling, average cost	remod	6414.00	3/95	13r
Bedroom, master suite addition, average cost	add	27122.00	3/95	13r
Deck addition, average cost	add	6665.00	3/95	13r
Dwellings (owned), expenditures	year	2566	91	81r
Enclose porch/patio/breezeway		4,556	3/95	74r
Exterior remodeling, average cost	remod	15395.00	3/95	13r
Family room addition, average cost	add	27658.00	3/95	13r
Finish room in basement/attic		5,074	3/95	74r
Home, existing, single-family, median	unit	106500	12/94	62r
House payment, principal and interest, 25% down payment	mo.	748	12/94	2c
House, 1800 sq ft, 8000 sq ft lot, new, urban, utilities	total	122485	12/94	2c
Kitchen remodeling, major, average cost	remod	17084.00	3/95	13r
Kitchen remodeling, minor, average cost	remod	5804.00	3/95	13r
Maintenance, repairs, insurance, and other housing expenditures	year	484	91	81r
Mortgage interest and charges expenditures	year	1443	91	81r
Mtge. rate, incl. points and orig. fee, 30-year conv. fixed or ARM	mo.	9.13	12/94	2c
Office, home addition, average cost	add	8121.00	3/95	13r
Princ. & int., mortgage, median-price exist. sing.-family home	mo.	515	12/94	62r
Property taxes expenditures	year	639	91	81r
Redesign, restructure more than half of home's interior		9,114	3/95	74r

Values are in dollars or fractions of dollars. In the column headed *Ref*, references are shown to sources. Each reference is followed by a letter. These refer to the geographical level for which data were reported: s=State, r=Region, and c=City or metro. The abbreviation *ex* is used to mean *except* or *excluding*; *exp* stands for expenditures. For other abbreviations and further explanations, please see the Introduction.

Lawrence, KS - continued

Item	Per	Value	Date	Ref.
Housing				
Rent, apartment, 2 br., 1 1/2-2 baths, unfurnished, 950 sq ft, water	mo.	521	12/94	2c
Rental units expenditures	year	1200	91	81r
Sun-space addition, average cost	add	23768.00	3/95	13r
Wing addition, two-story, average cost	add	50410.00	3/95	13r
Insurance and Pensions				
Auto insurance, private passenger	year	526.96	12/94	71s
Insurance and pensions, personal, expenditures	year	2408	91	81r
Insurance, life and other personal, expenditures	year	355	91	81r
Pensions and Social Security, expenditures	year	2053	91	81r
Legal Assistance				
Legal work, law firm associate	hour	90		10r
Legal work, law firm partner	hour	139		10r
Personal Goods				
Shampoo, Alberto VO5	15-oz.	1.10	12/94	2c
Toothpaste, Crest or Colgate	6-7 oz.	1.52	12/94	2c
Personal Services				
Dry cleaning, man's 2-pc. suit		6.93	12/94	2c
Haircut, man's barbershop, no styling		7.38	12/94	2c
Haircut, woman's shampoo, trim, blow-dry		16.00	12/94	2c
Personal services expenditures	year	203	91	81r
Restaurant Food				
Chicken, fried, thigh and drumstick		2.09	12/94	2c
Dining expenditures, family	week	30.03	94	73r
Hamburger with cheese	1/4 lb.	1.89	12/94	2c
Pizza, Pizza Hut or Pizza Inn	12-13 in.	6.49	12/94	2c
Taxes				
Taxes, Federal income, expenditures	year	1756	91	81r
Taxes, personal, expenditures	year	2426	91	81r
Taxes, State and local income, expenditures	year	568	91	81r
Transportation				
Transportation, ACCRA Index		94.00	12/94	2c
Cars and trucks purchased, new	year	891	91	81r
Cars and trucks purchased, used	year	1155	91	81r
Driver's learning permit fee	perm	3.00	1/94	84s
Driver's license fee	orig	12.00	1/94	84s
Driver's license fee, duplicate	lic	5.00	1/94	84s
Driver's license reinstatement fee, min.	susp	25.00	1/94	85s
Driver's license renewal fee	renew	9.00	1/94	84s
Identification card, nondriver	card	6.00	1/94	83s
Motorcycle license fee	orig	9.00	1/94	84s
Motorcycle license fee, duplicate	lic	5.00	1/94	84s
Motorcycle license renewal fee	renew	6.00	1/94	84s
Public transportation expenditures	year	209	91	81r
Tire balance, computer or spin bal., front	wheel	6.31	12/94	2c
Transportation expenditures, total	year	4792	91	81r
Vehicle finance charges	year	300	91	81r
Vehicle insurance expenditures	year	485	91	81r
Vehicle maintenance and repairs expenditures	year	534	91	81r
Vehicle purchases	year	2068	91	81r
Vehicle rental, leases, licenses, etc. expenditures	year	197	91	81r
Vehicles purchased, other than cars and trucks	year	22	91	81r
Utilities				
Utilities, ACCRA Index		80.20	12/94	2c
Electricity expenditures	year	668	91	81r
Electricity, (part.), other, 1800 sq. ft., new home	mo.	48.92	12/94	2c
Utilities, fuels, and public services, total expenditures	year	1838	91	81r
Water and other public services, expenditures	year	167	91	81r

Lawrence, KS - continued

Item	Per	Value	Date	Ref.
Weddings				
Bridal attendants' gowns	event	750	10/93	76r
Bridal gown	event	852	10/93	76r
Bridal headpiece and veil	event	167	10/93	76r
Bride's wedding band	event	708	10/93	76r
Clergy	event	224	10/93	76r
Engagement ring	event	2756	10/93	76r
Flowers	event	863	10/93	76r
Formal wear for groom	event	106	10/93	76r
Groom's attendants' formal wear	event	530	10/93	76r
Groom's wedding band	event	402	10/93	76r
Music	event	600	10/93	76r
Photography	event	1088	10/93	76r
Shoes for bride	event	50	10/93	76r
Videography	event	483	10/93	76r
Wedding invitations and announcements	event	342	10/93	76r
Wedding reception	event	7000	10/93	76r

Lawrence-Haverhill, MA

Item	Per	Value	Date	Ref.
Appliances				
Appliances (major), expenditures	year	145	91	81r
Average annual exp.				
Food, health care, personal goods, services	year	29496	91	81r
Charity				
Cash contributions, expenditures	year	708	91	81r
Clothing				
Apparel, men and boys, total expenditures	year	416	91	81r
Apparel, women and girls, total expenditures	year	744	91	81r
Footwear, expenditures	year	305	91	81r
Communications				
Long-distance telephone rate, day, addl. min., 1-10 mi.	min.	0.09	12/93	9s
Long-distance telephone rate, day, initial min., 1-10 mi.	min.	0.19	12/93	9s
Phone line, single, business, field visit	inst	27.50	12/93	9s
Phone line, single, business, no field visit	inst	93.02	12/93	9s
Phone line, single, residence, field visit	inst	27.50	12/93	9s
Phone line, single, residence, no field visit	inst	37.07	12/93	9s
Telephone service, expenditures	year	589	91	81r
Education				
Board, 4-year private college/university	year	3179	8/94	80s
Board, 4-year public college/university	year	2035	8/94	80s
Education, total expenditures	year	593	91	81r
Room, 4-year private college/university	year	3369	8/94	80s
Room, 4-year public college/university	year	2290	8/94	80s
Total cost, 4-year private college/university	year	21346	8/94	80s
Total cost, 4-year public college/university	year	8467	8/94	80s
Tuition, 2-year public college/university, in-state	year	2361	8/94	80s
Tuition, 4-year private college/university, in-state	year	14797	8/94	80s
Tuition, 4-year public college/university, in-state	year	4142	8/94	80s
Energy and Fuels				
Fuel oil and other fuels, expenditures	year	257	91	81r
Gas, natural, expenditures	year	285	91	81r
Gasoline and motor oil purchased	year	867	91	81r
Gasoline, unleaded midgrade	gallon	1.32	4/93	82r
Gasoline, unleaded premium	gallon	1.40	4/93	82r
Gasoline, unleaded regular	gallon	1.19	4/93	82r
Entertainment				
Entertainment, total expenditures	year	1331	91	81r
Fees and admissions, expenditures	year	398	91	81r
Pets, toys, playground equipment, expenditures	year	270	91	81r
Reading, expenditures	year	171	91	81r

Values are in dollars or fractions of dollars. In the column headed *Ref*, references are shown to sources. Each reference is followed by a letter. These refer to the geographical level for which data were reported: s=State, r=Region, and c=City or metro. The abbreviation *ex* is used to mean *except* or *excluding*; *exp* stands for expenditures. For other abbreviations and further explanations, please see the Introduction.

Lawrence-Haverhill, MA - continued

Item	Per	Value	Date	Ref.
Entertainment				
Televisions, radios, and sound equipment, expenditures	year	429	91	81r
Funerals				
Burial, immediate, container provided by funeral home		1507.89	1/95	54r
Cards, acknowledgment		18.10	1/95	54r
Casket, minimum alternative		133.03	1/95	54r
Cosmetology, hair care, etc.		114.12	1/95	54r
Cremation, direct, container provided by funeral home		1309.19	1/95	54r
Embalming		320.97	1/95	54r
Funeral, funeral home		327.61	1/95	54r
Funeral, other facility		314.81	1/95	54r
Graveside service		286.11	1/95	54r
Hearse, local		158.95	1/95	54r
Limousine, local		149.45	1/95	54r
Memorial service		315.94	1/95	54r
Service charge, professional, nondeclinable		1148.43	1/95	54r
Visitation and viewing		249.66	1/95	54r
Groceries				
Apples, Red Delicious	lb.	0.78	12/94	82r
Bacon, sliced	lb.	2.24	12/94	82r
Bananas	lb.	0.49	12/94	82r
Beef purchases	year	226	91	81r
Beverage purchases, alcoholic	year	332	91	81r
Beverage purchases, nonalcoholic	year	213	91	81r
Bread, white, pan	lb.	0.80	12/94	82r
Butter, salted, Grade AA, stick	lb.	1.67	12/94	82r
Carrots, short trimmed and topped	lb.	0.51	12/94	82r
Cereals and bakery products purchases	year	407	91	81r
Cereals and cereals products purchases	year	132	91	81r
Chicken breast, bone-in	lb.	2.22	12/94	82r
Chicken, fresh, whole	lb.	1.05	12/94	82r
Chuck roast, USDA choice, boneless	lb.	2.74	12/94	82r
Coffee, 100%, ground roast, all sizes	lb.	4.61	12/94	82r
Dairy products (other) purchases	year	161	91	81r
Eggs, Grade A large	dozen	1.12	12/94	82r
Fish and seafood purchases	year	112	91	81r
Food purchases, food eaten at home	year	2599	91	81r
Foods purchased away from home, not prepared by consumer	year	2024	91	81r
Fruits and vegetables purchases	year	444	91	81r
Grapefruit	lb.	0.44	12/94	82r
Grapes, Thompson seedless	lb.	2.24	12/94	82r
Ground chuck, 100% beef	lb.	1.67	12/94	82r
Ice cream, prepackaged, bulk, regular	1/2 gal.	2.93	12/94	82r
Lemons	lb.	1.06	12/94	82r
Lettuce, iceberg	lb.	0.92	12/94	82r
Meats, poultry, fish, and eggs purchases	year	751	91	81r
Milk and cream (fresh) purchases	year	152	91	81r
Orange juice, frozen concentrate 12-oz. can	16 oz.	1.92	12/94	82r
Oranges, Navel	lb.	0.56	12/94	82r
Pork chops, center cut, bone-in	lb.	3.09	12/94	82r
Pork purchases	year	130	91	81r
Potatoes, white	lb.	0.37	12/94	82r
Rib roast, USDA choice, bone-in	lb.	4.98	12/94	82r
Round roast, USDA choice, boneless	lb.	2.93	12/94	82r
Shortening, vegetable oil blends	lb.	1.03	12/94	82r
Spaghetti and macaroni	lb.	0.84	12/94	82r
Steak, round, USDA choice, boneless	lb.	3.48	12/94	82r
Steak, sirloin, USDA choice, bone-in	lb.	3.38	12/94	82r
Steak, sirloin, USDA choice, boneless	lb.	4.81	12/94	82r
Sugar and other sweets, eaten at home, expenditures	year	89	91	81r
Sugar, white, all sizes	lb.	0.46	12/94	82r
Tobacco products and smoking supplies, total expenditures	year	279	91	81r
Tomatoes, field grown	lb.	1.56	12/94	82r
Tuna, chunk, light	lb.	2.09	12/94	82r

Lawrence-Haverhill, MA - continued

Item	Per	Value	Date	Ref.
Health Care				
Childbirth, Cesarean delivery, hospital charge	birth	6334.00	12/91	69r
Childbirth, Cesarean delivery, physician charge	birth	2234.00	12/91	69r
Childbirth, normal delivery, hospital charge	birth	3225.00	12/91	69r
Childbirth, normal delivery, physician charge	birth	1623.00	12/91	69r
Drugs, expenditures	year	205	91	81r
Health care, total expenditures	year	1396	91	81r
Health insurance expenditures	year	553	91	81r
Insurance premium, family medical care	month	457.38	1/95	41s
Medical services expenditures	year	559	91	81r
Medical supplies expenditures	year	80	91	81r
Household Goods				
Floor coverings, expenditures	year	158	91	81r
Furniture, expenditures	year	341	91	81r
Household equipment, misc. expenditures	year	363	91	81r
Household expenditures, miscellaneous	year	194	91	81r
Household furnishings and equipment, expenditures	year	1158	91	81r
Household operations expenditures	year	378	91	81r
Household textiles, expenditures	year	88	91	81r
Housekeeping supplies, expenditures	year	426	91	81r
Laundry and cleaning supplies, expenditures	year	122	91	81r
Postage and stationery, expenditures	year	134	91	81r
Housing				
Add garage/carport		11,614	3/95	74r
Add room(s)		16,816	3/95	74r
Apartment condominium or co-op, median	unit	96700	12/94	62r
Dwellings (owned), expenditures	year	3305	91	81r
Enclose porch/patio/breezeway		2,980	3/95	74r
Finish room in basement/attic		4,330	3/95	74r
Home, existing, single-family, median	unit	161600	12/94	62r
Maintenance, repairs, insurance, and other housing expenditures	year	569	91	81r
Mortgage interest and charges expenditures	year	1852	91	81r
Princ. & int., mortgage, median-price exist. sing.-family home	mo.	765	12/94	62r
Property taxes expenditures	year	884	91	81r
Redesign, restructure more than half of home's interior		2,750	3/95	74r
Rental units expenditures	year	1832	91	81r
Insurance and Pensions				
Auto insurance, private passenger	year	1009.56	12/94	71s
Insurance and pensions, personal, expenditures	year	2690	91	81r
Insurance, life and other personal, expenditures	year	341	91	81r
Pensions and Social Security, expenditures	year	2349	91	81r
Legal Assistance				
Estate planning, law-firm partner	hr.	375.00	10/93	12r
Legal work, law firm associate	hour	78		10r
Legal work, law firm partner	hour	183		10r
Personal Services				
Personal services expenditures	year	184	91	81r
Restaurant Food				
Dining expenditures, family	week	34.26	94	73r
Taxes				
Taxes, Federal income, expenditures	year	2409	91	81r
Taxes, personal, expenditures	year	3094	91	81r
Taxes, State and local income, expenditures	year	620	91	81r
Transportation				
Cars and trucks purchased, new	year	1170	91	81r
Cars and trucks purchased, used	year	739	91	81r
Driver's learning permit fee	perm	15.00	1/94	84s
Driver's license fee	orig	50.00	1/94	84s
Driver's license fee, duplicate	lic	15.00	1/94	84s
Driver's license renewal fee	renew	43.75	1/94	84s

Values are in dollars or fractions of dollars. In the column headed *Ref*, references are shown to sources. Each reference is followed by a letter. These refer to the geographical level for which data were reported: s=State, r=Region, and c=City or metro. The abbreviation *ex* is used to mean *except* or *excluding*; *exp* stands for *expenditures*. For other abbreviations and further explanations, please see the Introduction.

Lawrence-Haverhill, MA - continued

Item	Per	Value	Date	Ref.
Transportation				
Identification card, nondriver	card	15.00	1/94	83s
Motorcycle license fee	orig	50.00	1/94	84s
Motorcycle license fee, duplicate	lic	15.00	1/94	84s
Motorcycle license renewal fee	renew	43.75	1/94	84s
Public transportation expenditures	year	430	91	81r
Transportation expenditures, total	year	4810	91	81r
Vehicle finance charges	year	238	91	81r
Vehicle insurance expenditures	year	630	91	81r
Vehicle maintenance and repairs expenditures	year	532	91	81r
Vehicle purchases	year	1920	91	81r
Vehicle rental, leases, licenses, etc. expenditures	year	193	91	81r
Vehicles purchased, other than cars and trucks	year	11	91	81r
Utilities				
Electricity expenditures	year	695	91	81r
Utilities, fuels, and public services, total expenditures	year	1981	91	81r
Water and other public services, expenditures	year	154	91	81r
Weddings				
Bridal attendants' gowns	event	750	10/93	76r
Bridal gown	event	852	10/93	76r
Bridal headpiece and veil	event	167	10/93	76r
Bride's wedding band	event	708	10/93	76r
Clergy	event	224	10/93	76r
Engagement ring	event	2756	10/93	76r
Flowers	event	863	10/93	76r
Formal wear for groom	event	106	10/93	76r
Groom's attendants' formal wear	event	530	10/93	76r
Groom's wedding band	event	402	10/93	76r
Music	event	600	10/93	76r
Photography	event	1088	10/93	76r
Shoes for bride	event	50	10/93	76r
Videography	event	483	10/93	76r
Wedding invitations and announcements	event	342	10/93	76r
Wedding reception	event	7000	10/93	76r

Lawton, OK

Item	Per	Value	Date	Ref.
Appliances				
Appliances (major), expenditures	year	153	91	81r
Average annual exp.				
Food, health care, personal goods, services	year	27020	91	81r
Charity				
Cash contributions, expenditures	year	839	91	81r
Clothing				
Apparel, men and boys, total expenditures	year	380	91	81r
Apparel, women and girls, total expenditures	year	660	91	81r
Footwear, expenditures	year	193	91	81r
Communications				
Long-distance telephone rate, day, addl. min., 1-10 mi.	min.	0.07	12/93	9s
Long-distance telephone rate, day, initial min., 1-10 mi.	min.	0.12	12/93	9s
Phone line, single, business, field visit	inst	82.75	12/93	9s
Phone line, single, business, no field visit	inst	82.75	12/93	9s
Phone line, single, residence, field visit	inst	44.45	12/93	9s
Phone line, single, residence, no field visit	inst	44.45	12/93	9s
Telephone service, expenditures	year	616	91	81r
Education				
Board, 4-year private college/university	year	1974	8/94	80s
Board, 4-year public college/university	year	1502	8/94	80s
Education, total expenditures	year	319	91	81r
Room, 4-year private college/university	year	1618	8/94	80s
Room, 4-year public college/university	year	876	8/94	80s

Lawton, OK - continued

Item	Per	Value	Date	Ref.
Education - continued				
Total cost, 4-year private college/university	year	10801	8/94	80s
Total cost, 4-year public college/university	year	4023	8/94	80s
Tuition, 2-year public college/university, in-state	year	1095	8/94	80s
Tuition, 4-year private college/university, in-state	year	7210	8/94	80s
Tuition, 4-year public college/university, in-state	year	1645	8/94	80s
Energy and Fuels				
Fuel oil and other fuels, expenditures	year	56	91	81r
Gas, natural, expenditures	year	150	91	81r
Gasoline and motor oil purchased	year	1152	91	81r
Gasoline, unleaded midgrade	gallon	1.21	4/93	82r
Gasoline, unleaded premium	gallon	1.30	4/93	82r
Gasoline, unleaded regular	gallon	1.10	4/93	82r
Entertainment				
Concert ticket, Pearl Jam group	perf	20.00	94	50r
Entertainment, total expenditures	year	1266	91	81r
Fees and admissions, expenditures	year	306	91	81r
Pets, toys, playground equipment, expenditures	year	271	91	81r
Reading, expenditures	year	131	91	81r
Televisions, radios, and sound equipment, expenditures	year	439	91	81r
Funerals				
Burial, immediate, container provided by funeral home		1574.60	1/95	54r
Cards, acknowledgment		22.24	1/95	54r
Casket, minimum alternative		239.41	1/95	54r
Cosmetology, hair care, etc.		91.04	1/95	54r
Cremation, direct, container provided by funeral home		1085.15	1/95	54r
Embalming		281.30	1/95	54r
Funeral, funeral home		323.04	1/95	54r
Funeral, other facility		327.58	1/95	54r
Graveside service		355.19	1/95	54r
Hearse, local		141.89	1/95	54r
Limousine, local		99.40	1/95	54r
Memorial service		284.67	1/95	54r
Service charge, professional, nondeclinable		904.06	1/95	54r
Visitation and viewing		187.04	1/95	54r
Groceries				
Apples, Red Delicious	lb.	0.73	12/94	82r
Bacon, sliced	lb.	1.67	12/94	82r
Bananas	lb.	0.42	12/94	82r
Beef purchases	year	213	91	81r
Beverage purchases, alcoholic	year	249	91	81r
Beverage purchases, nonalcoholic	year	207	91	81r
Bologna, all beef or mixed	lb.	2.27	12/94	82r
Bread, white, pan	lb.	0.68	12/94	82r
Cabbage	lb.	0.42	12/94	82r
Carrots, short trimmed and topped	lb.	0.53	12/94	82r
Cereals and bakery products purchases	year	345	91	81r
Cereals and cereals products purchases	year	127	91	81r
Cheddar cheese, natural	lb.	3.58	12/94	82r
Chicken breast, bone-in	lb.	1.71	12/94	82r
Chicken, fresh, whole	lb.	0.78	12/94	82r
Chuck roast, USDA choice, boneless	lb.	2.26	12/94	82r
Crackers, soda, salted	lb.	1.27	12/94	82r
Cucumbers	lb.	0.65	12/94	82r
Dairy products (other) purchases	year	141	91	81r
Eggs, Grade A large	dozen	0.87	12/94	82r
Fish and seafood purchases	year	72	91	81r
Flour, white, all purpose	lb.	0.23	12/94	82r
Food purchases, food eaten at home	year	2381	91	81r
Foods purchased away from home, not prepared by consumer	year	1696	91	81r
Frankfurters, all meat or all beef	lb.	1.74	12/94	82r
Fruits and vegetables purchases	year	380	91	81r
Grapefruit	lb.	0.45	12/94	82r

Values are in dollars or fractions of dollars. In the column headed *Ref*, references are shown to sources. Each reference is followed by a letter. These refer to the geographical level for which data were reported: s=State, r=Region, and c=City or metro. The abbreviation *ex* is used to mean *except* or *excluding*; *exp* stands for expenditures. For other abbreviations and further explanations, please see the Introduction.

Lawton, OK - continued

Item	Per	Value	Date	Ref.
Groceries				
Grapes, Thompson seedless	lb.	2.30	12/94	82r
Ground beef, 100% beef	lb.	1.37	12/94	82r
Ground chuck, 100% beef	lb.	1.97	12/94	82r
Ham, boneless, exc. canned	lb.	2.54	12/94	82r
Ice cream, prepackaged, bulk, regular	1/2 gal.	2.47	12/94	82r
Lemons	lb.	1.02	12/94	82r
Lettuce, iceberg	lb.	0.96	12/94	82r
Margarine, stick	lb.	0.77	12/94	82r
Meats, poultry, fish, and eggs purchases	year	655	91	81r
Milk and cream (fresh) purchases	year	130	91	81r
Orange juice, frozen concentrate 12-oz. can	16 oz.	1.36	12/94	82r
Oranges, Navel	lb.	0.54	12/94	82r
Pears, Anjou	lb.	0.81	12/94	82r
Pork chops, center cut, bone-in	lb.	3.07	12/94	82r
Pork purchases	year	142	91	81r
Potato chips	16-oz.	3.15	12/94	82r
Potatoes, frozen, French fried	lb.	0.82	12/94	82r
Potatoes, white	lb.	0.34	12/94	82r
Rice, white, long grain, uncooked	lb.	0.48	12/94	82r
Round roast, USDA choice, boneless	lb.	2.91	12/94	82r
Sausage, fresh	lb.	1.82	12/94	82r
Shortening, vegetable oil blends	lb.	0.75	12/94	82r
Spaghetti and macaroni	lb.	0.87	12/94	82r
Steak, rib eye, USDA choice, boneless	lb.	6.85	12/94	82r
Steak, round, graded & ungraded, exc. USDA prime & choice	lb.	2.96	12/94	82r
Steak, round, USDA choice, boneless	lb.	3.17	12/94	82r
Steak, sirloin, USDA choice, boneless	lb.	4.12	12/94	82r
Steak, T-bone, USDA choice, bone-in	lb.	5.63	12/94	82r
Sugar and other sweets, eaten at home, expenditures	year	93	91	81r
Sugar, white, all sizes	lb.	0.39	12/94	82r
Tobacco products and smoking supplies, total expenditures	year	286	91	81r
Tomatoes, field grown	lb.	1.36	12/94	82r
Tuna, chunk, light	lb.	1.94	12/94	82r
Turkey, frozen, whole	lb.	0.96	12/94	82r
Yogurt, natural, fruit flavored	8 oz.	0.58	12/94	82r
Health Care				
Adenosine, emergency room	treat	100.00	95	23r
Bladder tap, superpubic, infant, emergency room	treat	119.00	95	23r
Blood analysis, emergency room	treat	25.00	95	23r
Blood tests, abdominal pain, emergency room	treat	25.00	95	23r
Burn dressing, emergency room	treat	266.00	95	23r
Cardiology interpretation, emergency room	treat	26.00	95	23r
Chest X-ray, emergency room	treat	78.00	95	23r
Childbirth, Cesarean delivery, hospital charge	birth	5462.00	12/91	69r
Childbirth, Cesarean delivery, physician charge	birth	2228.00	12/91	69r
Childbirth, normal delivery, hospital charge	birth	2943.00	12/91	69r
Childbirth, normal delivery, physician charge	birth	1619.00	12/91	69r
Defibrillation pads, emergency room	treat	6.00	95	23r
Drugs, expenditures	year	297	91	81r
Gastric tube insertion, nasal, emergency room	treat	25.00	95	23r
Health care, total expenditures	year	1600	91	81r
Health insurance expenditures	year	637	91	81r
Heart monitor, emergency room	treat	40.00	95	23r
Insurance premium, family medical care	month	373.98	1/95	41s
Intravenous fluids, emergency room	treat	130.00	95	23r
Intravenous fluids, emergency room	liter	26.00	95	23r
Intravenous line, central, emergency room	treat	342.00	95	23r
Liver function tests, abdominal pain, emergency room	treat	26.00	95	23r
Medical care charges, total, emergency room, third-degree burns	treat	2101.00	95	23r
Medical care charges, total, emergency, infant with fever	treat	628.00	95	23r

Lawton, OK - continued

Item	Per	Value	Date	Ref.
Health Care - continued				
Medical services expenditures	year	573	91	81r
Medical supplies expenditures	year	93	91	81r
Morphine, emergency room	treat	34.00	95	23r
Nursing care and facilities charges, emergency room	treat	252.00	95	23r
Nursing care and facilities charges, emergency, infant with fever	treat	252.00	95	23r
Nursing care and facilities charges, emergency, third-degree burns	treat	861.00	95	23r
Physician's charges, emergency, infant with fever	treat	212.00	95	23r
Physician's charges, emergency, third-degree burns	treat	372.00	95	23r
Physician's fee, emergency room	treat	372.00	95	23r
Physician's fee, general practitioner	visit	51.20	12/93	60r
Surgery, open-heart	proc	42374.00	1/93	14r
Ultrasound, abdominal, emergency room	treat	276.00	95	23r
Urinalysis, emergency room	treat	20.00	95	23r
Urinalysis, infant, emergency room	treat	20.00	95	23r
X-rays, emergency room	treat	78.00	95	23r
Household Goods				
Floor coverings, expenditures	year	48	91	81r
Furniture, expenditures	year	280	91	81r
Household equipment, misc. expenditures	year	342	91	81r
Household expenditures, miscellaneous	year	256	91	81r
Household furnishings and equipment, expenditures	year	988	91	81r
Household operations expenditures	year	468	91	81r
Household textiles, expenditures	year	95	91	81r
Housekeeping supplies, expenditures	year	380	91	81r
Laundry and cleaning supplies, expenditures	year	109	91	81r
Postage and stationery, expenditures	year	105	91	81r
Housing				
Add garage/carport		6,980	3/95	74r
Add room(s)		11,403	3/95	74r
Apartment condominium or co-op, median	unit	68600	12/94	62r
Dwellings (owned), expenditures	year	2428	91	81r
Enclose porch/patio/breezeway		4,572	3/95	74r
Finish room in basement/attic		3,794	3/95	74r
Home, existing, single-family, median	unit	120200	12/94	62r
Maintenance, repairs, insurance, and other housing expenditures	year	531	91	81r
Mortgage interest and charges expenditures	year	1506	91	81r
Princ. & int., mortgage, median-price exist. sing.-family home	mo.	540	12/94	62r
Property taxes expenditures	year	391	91	81r
Redesign, restructure more than half of home's interior		17,641	3/95	74r
Rental units expenditures	year	1264	91	81r
Insurance and Pensions				
Auto insurance, private passenger	year	604.38	12/94	71s
Insurance and pensions, personal, expenditures	year	2395	91	81r
Insurance, life and other personal, expenditures	year	368	91	81r
Pensions and Social Security, expenditures	year	2027	91	81r
Personal Services				
Personal services expenditures	year	212	91	81r
Restaurant Food				
Dining expenditures, family	week	33.83	94	73r
Taxes				
Tax, cigarettes	year	382.00	10/93	43s
Taxes, Federal income, expenditures	year	2275	91	81r
Taxes, personal, expenditures	year	2715	91	81r
Taxes, State and local income, expenditures	year	365	91	81r

Values are in dollars or fractions of dollars. In the column headed *Ref*, references are shown to sources. Each reference is followed by a letter. These refer to the geographical level for which data were reported: s=State, r=Region, and c=City or metro. The abbreviation *ex* is used to mean *except* or *excluding*; *exp* stands for expenditures. For other abbreviations and further explanations, please see the Introduction.

Lawton, OK - continued

Item	Per	Value	Date	Ref.
Transportation				
Cars and trucks purchased, new	year	1306	91	81r
Cars and trucks purchased, used	year	942	91	81r
Driver's learning permit fee	perm	19.00	1/94	84s
Driver's license fee	orig	19.00	1/94	84s
Driver's license fee, duplicate	lic	5.00	1/94	84s
Driver's license reinstatement fee, min.	susp	75.00	1/94	85s
Driver's license renewal fee	renew	15.00	1/94	84s
Identification card, nondriver	card	7.00	1/94	83s
Motorcycle license fee	orig	19.00	1/94	84s
Motorcycle license fee, duplicate	lic	5.00	1/94	84s
Motorcycle license renewal fee	renew	15.00	1/94	84s
Public transportation expenditures	year	249	91	81r
Transportation expenditures, total	year	5307	91	81r
Vehicle finance charges	year	346	91	81r
Vehicle insurance expenditures	year	544	91	81r
Vehicle maintenance and repairs expenditures	year	600	91	81r
Vehicle purchases	year	2275	91	81r
Vehicle rental, leases, licenses, etc. expenditures	year	141	91	81r
Vehicles purchased, other than cars and trucks	year	27	91	81r
Utilities				
Electricity expenditures	year	950	91	81r
Utilities, fuels, and public services, total expenditures	year	2000	91	81r
Water and other public services, expenditures	year	227	91	81r
Weddings				
Bridal attendants' gowns	event	750	10/93	76r
Bridal gown	event	852	10/93	76r
Bridal headpiece and veil	event	167	10/93	76r
Bride's wedding band	event	708	10/93	76r
Clergy	event	224	10/93	76r
Engagement ring	event	2756	10/93	76r
Flowers	event	863	10/93	76r
Formal wear for groom	event	106	10/93	76r
Groom's attendants' formal wear	event	530	10/93	76r
Groom's wedding band	event	402	10/93	76r
Music	event	600	10/93	76r
Photography	event	1088	10/93	76r
Shoes for bride	event	50	10/93	76r
Videography	event	483	10/93	76r
Wedding invitations and announcements	event	342	10/93	76r
Wedding reception	event	7000	10/93	76r

Lee's Summit, MO

Item	Per	Value	Date	Ref.
Composite, ACCRA index		97.80	12/94	2c
Alcoholic Beverages				
Beer, Miller Lite, Bud, 12-oz., ex deposit	6	4.07	12/94	2c
J & B Scotch	750-ml.	16.26	12/94	2c
Wine, Gallo Chablis blanc	1.5-lit	5.24	12/94	2c
Clothing				
Jeans, man's denim		28.74	12/94	2c
Shirt, man's dress shirt		26.50	12/94	2c
Undervest, boy's size 10-14, cotton	3	3.57	12/94	2c
Communications				
Newspaper subscription, dly. and Sun. delivery	month	14.09	12/94	2c
Telephone bill, family of four	month	23.83	12/94	2c
Energy and Fuels				
Energy, combined forms, 1800 sq. ft.	mo.	121.49	12/94	2c
Energy, exc. electricity, 1800 sq. ft.	mo.	43.87	12/94	2c
Gas, reg unlead, taxes inc., cash, self-service	gal	1.00	12/94	2c

Lee's Summit, MO - continued

Item	Per	Value	Date	Ref.
Entertainment				
Bowling, evening rate	game	2.45	12/94	2c
Monopoly game, Parker Brothers', No. 9	game	10.80	12/94	2c
Movie	adm	5.75	12/94	2c
Tennis balls, yellow, Wilson or Penn, 3	can	1.96	12/94	2c
Groceries				
Groceries, ACCRA Index		98.00	12/94	2c
Baby food, strained vegetables, lowest price	4-4.5 oz.	0.31	12/94	2c
Bananas	lb.	0.49	12/94	2c
Beef or hamburger, ground	lb.	1.26	12/94	2c
Bread, white	24-oz.	0.75	12/94	2c
Cheese, Kraft grated Parmesan	8-oz.	3.14	12/94	2c
Chicken, whole fryer	lb.	0.89	12/94	2c
Cigarettes, Winston, Kings	carton	16.97	12/94	2c
Coffee, vacuum-packed	13 oz.	3.12	12/94	2c
Corn Flakes, Kellogg's or Post Toasties	18 oz.	2.27	12/94	2c
Corn, frozen, whole kernel, lowest price	10 oz.	0.65	12/94	2c
Eggs, Grade A large	dozen	0.65	12/94	2c
Lettuce, iceberg	head	0.79	12/94	2c
Margarine, Blue Bonnet or Parkay cubes	lb.	0.62	12/94	2c
Milk, whole	1/2 gal.	1.39	12/94	2c
Orange juice, Minute Maid frozen	12-oz.	1.25	12/94	2c
Peaches, halves or slices, Hunt's, Del Monte, or Libby's	29-oz.	1.29	12/94	2c
Peas, sweet, Del Monte or Green Giant	15-17 oz.	0.66	12/94	2c
Potatoes, white or red	10-lb. sack	1.41	12/94	2c
Sausage, Jimmy Dean, 100% pork	lb.	2.87	12/94	2c
Shortening, vegetable, Crisco	3-lb.	2.21	12/94	2c
Soft drink, Coca Cola, ex deposit	2 lit	1.34	12/94	2c
Steak, t-bone	lb.	5.19	12/94	2c
Sugar, cane or beet	4 lbs.	1.35	12/94	2c
Tomatoes, Hunt's or Del Monte	14.5 oz.	0.74	12/94	2c
Tuna, chunk, light, oil-packed	6.125-6.5 oz.	0.66	12/94	2c
Goods and Services				
Miscellaneous goods and services, ACCRA Index		95.80	12/94	2c
Health Care				
Health care, ACCRA Index		101.90	12/94	2c
Antibiotic ointment, Polysporin	1.5 oz.	3.68	12/94	2c
Dentist's fee, adult teeth cleaning and periodic oral exam	visit	46.80	12/94	2c
Doctor's fee, routine exam, established patient	visit	44.40	12/94	2c
Hospital care, semiprivate room	day	450.50	12/94	2c
Household Goods				
Appl. repair, service call, wash mach	min. lab. chg.	33.63	12/94	2c
Laundry detergent, Tide Ultra, Bold, or Cheer	42 oz.	2.90	12/94	2c
Tissues, facial, Kleenex brand	175	1.10	12/94	2c
Housing				
Housing, ACCRA Index		96.50	12/94	2c
House payment, principal and interest, 25% down payment	mo.	742	12/94	2c
House, 1800 sq ft, 8000 sq ft lot, new, urban, utilities	total	122333	12/94	2c
Mtge. rate, incl. points and orig. fee, 30-year conv. fixed or ARM	mo.	9.06	12/94	2c
Rent, apartment, 2 br., 1 1/2-2 baths, unfurnished, 950 sq ft, water	mo.	501	12/94	2c
Personal Goods				
Shampoo, Alberto VO5	15-oz.	1.09	12/94	2c
Toothpaste, Crest or Colgate	6-7 oz.	1.67	12/94	2c

Values are in dollars or fractions of dollars. In the column headed *Ref*, references are shown to sources. Each reference is followed by a letter. These refer to the geographical level for which data were reported: s=State, r=Region, and c=City or metro. The abbreviation *ex* is used to mean *except* or *excluding*; *exp* stands for expenditures. For other abbreviations and further explanations, please see the Introduction.

Lee's Summit, MO - continued

Item	Per	Value	Date	Ref.
Personal Services				
Dry cleaning, man's 2-pc. suit		5.84	12/94	2c
Haircut, man's barbershop, no styling		9.75	12/94	2c
Haircut, woman's shampoo, trim, blow-dry		18.60	12/94	2c
Restaurant Food				
Chicken, fried, thigh and drumstick		2.09	12/94	2c
Hamburger with cheese	1/4 lb.	1.80	12/94	2c
Pizza, Pizza Hut or Pizza Inn	12-13 in.	7.99	12/94	2c
Transportation				
Transportation, ACCRA Index		95.00	12/94	2c
Tire balance, computer or spin bal., front	wheel	6.99	12/94	2c
Utilities				
Utilities, ACCRA Index		110.10	12/94	2c
Electricity, (part.), other, 1800 sq. ft., new home	mo.	77.62	12/94	2c

Lewiston-Auburn, ME

Item	Per	Value	Date	Ref.
Appliances				
Appliances (major), expenditures	year	145	91	81r
Average annual exp.				
Food, health care, personal goods, services	year	29496	91	81r
Charity				
Cash contributions, expenditures	year	708	91	81r
Clothing				
Apparel, men and boys, total expenditures	year	416	91	81r
Apparel, women and girls, total expenditures	year	744	91	81r
Footwear, expenditures	year	305	91	81r
Communications				
Long-distance telephone rate, day, addl. min., 1-10 mi.	min.	0.15	12/93	9s
Long-distance telephone rate, day, initial min., 1-10 mi.	min.	0.19	12/93	9s
Phone line, single, business, field visit	inst	35.00	12/93	9s
Phone line, single, business, no field visit	inst	56.00	12/93	9s
Phone line, single, residence, field visit	inst	26.00	12/93	9s
Phone line, single, residence, no field visit	inst	44.75	12/93	9s
Telephone service, expenditures	year	589	91	81r
Education				
Board, 4-year private college/university	year	2772	8/94	80s
Board, 4-year public college/university	year	2178	8/94	80s
Education, total expenditures	year	593	91	81r
Room, 4-year private college/university	year	2620	8/94	80s
Room, 4-year public college/university	year	2204	8/94	80s
Total cost, 4-year private college/university	year	19658	8/94	80s
Total cost, 4-year public college/university	year	7521	8/94	80s
Tuition, 2-year public college/university, in-state	year	1913	8/94	80s
Tuition, 4-year private college/university, in-state	year	14265	8/94	80s
Tuition, 4-year public college/university, in-state	year	3139	8/94	80s
Energy and Fuels				
Fuel oil and other fuels, expenditures	year	257	91	81r
Gas, natural, expenditures	year	285	91	81r
Gasoline and motor oil purchased	year	867	91	81r
Gasoline, unleaded midgrade	gallon	1.32	4/93	82r
Gasoline, unleaded premium	gallon	1.40	4/93	82r
Gasoline, unleaded regular	gallon	1.19	4/93	82r
Entertainment				
Entertainment, total expenditures	year	1331	91	81r
Fees and admissions, expenditures	year	398	91	81r
Pets, toys, playground equipment, expenditures	year	270	91	81r
Reading, expenditures	year	171	91	81r

Lewiston-Auburn, ME - continued

Item	Per	Value	Date	Ref.
Entertainment - continued				
Televisions, radios, and sound equipment, expenditures	year	429	91	81r
Funerals				
Burial, immediate, container provided by funeral home		1507.89	1/95	54r
Cards, acknowledgment		18.10	1/95	54r
Casket, minimum alternative		133.03	1/95	54r
Cosmetology, hair care, etc.		114.12	1/95	54r
Cremation, direct, container provided by funeral home		1309.19	1/95	54r
Embalming		320.97	1/95	54r
Funeral, funeral home		327.61	1/95	54r
Funeral, other facility		314.81	1/95	54r
Graveside service		286.11	1/95	54r
Hearse, local		158.95	1/95	54r
Limousine, local		149.45	1/95	54r
Memorial service		315.94	1/95	54r
Service charge, professional, nondeclinable		1148.43	1/95	54r
Visitation and viewing		249.66	1/95	54r
Groceries				
Apples, Red Delicious	lb.	0.78	12/94	82r
Bacon, sliced	lb.	2.24	12/94	82r
Bananas	lb.	0.49	12/94	82r
Beef purchases	year	226	91	81r
Beverage purchases, alcoholic	year	332	91	81r
Beverage purchases, nonalcoholic	year	213	91	81r
Bread, white, pan	lb.	0.80	12/94	82r
Butter, salted, Grade AA, stick	lb.	1.67	12/94	82r
Carrots, short trimmed and topped	lb.	0.51	12/94	82r
Cereals and bakery products purchases	year	407	91	81r
Cereals and cereals products purchases	year	132	91	81r
Chicken breast, bone-in	lb.	2.22	12/94	82r
Chicken, fresh, whole	lb.	1.05	12/94	82r
Chuck roast, USDA choice, boneless	lb.	2.74	12/94	82r
Coffee, 100%, ground roast, all sizes	lb.	4.61	12/94	82r
Dairy products (other) purchases	year	161	91	81r
Eggs, Grade A large	dozen	1.12	12/94	82r
Fish and seafood purchases	year	112	91	81r
Food purchases, food eaten at home	year	2599	91	81r
Foods purchased away from home, not prepared by consumer	year	2024	91	81r
Fruits and vegetables purchases	year	444	91	81r
Grapefruit	lb.	0.44	12/94	82r
Grapes, Thompson seedless	lb.	2.24	12/94	82r
Ground chuck, 100% beef	lb.	1.67	12/94	82r
Ice cream, prepackaged, bulk, regular	1/2 gal.	2.93	12/94	82r
Lemons	lb.	1.06	12/94	82r
Lettuce, iceberg	lb.	0.92	12/94	82r
Meats, poultry, fish, and eggs purchases	year	751	91	81r
Milk and cream (fresh) purchases	year	152	91	81r
Orange juice, frozen concentrate 12-oz. can	16 oz.	1.92	12/94	82r
Oranges, Navel	lb.	0.56	12/94	82r
Pork chops, center cut, bone-in	lb.	3.09	12/94	82r
Pork purchases	year	130	91	81r
Potatoes, white	lb.	0.37	12/94	82r
Rib roast, USDA choice, bone-in	lb.	4.98	12/94	82r
Round roast, USDA choice, boneless	lb.	2.93	12/94	82r
Shortening, vegetable oil blends	lb.	1.03	12/94	82r
Spaghetti and macaroni	lb.	0.84	12/94	82r
Steak, round, USDA choice, boneless	lb.	3.48	12/94	82r
Steak, sirloin, USDA choice, bone-in	lb.	3.38	12/94	82r
Steak, sirloin, USDA choice, boneless	lb.	4.81	12/94	82r
Sugar and other sweets, eaten at home, expenditures	year	89	91	81r
Sugar, white, all sizes	lb.	0.46	12/94	82r
Tobacco products and smoking supplies, total expenditures	year	279	91	81r
Tomatoes, field grown	lb.	1.56	12/94	82r
Tuna, chunk, light	lb.	2.09	12/94	82r

Values are in dollars or fractions of dollars. In the column headed *Ref*, references are shown to sources. Each reference is followed by a letter. These refer to the geographical level for which data were reported: s = State, r = Region, and c = City or metro. The abbreviation *ex* is used to mean *except* or *excluding*; *exp* stands for *expenditures*. For other abbreviations and further explanations, please see the Introduction.

Lewiston-Auburn, ME - continued

Item	Per	Value	Date	Ref.
Health Care				
Childbirth, Cesarean delivery, hospital charge	birth	6334.00	12/91	69r
Childbirth, Cesarean delivery, physician charge	birth	2234.00	12/91	69r
Childbirth, normal delivery, hospital charge	birth	3225.00	12/91	69r
Childbirth, normal delivery, physician charge	birth	1623.00	12/91	69r
Drugs, expenditures	year	205	91	81r
Health care, total expenditures	year	1396	91	81r
Health insurance expenditures	year	553	91	81r
Insurance premium, family medical care	month	473.31	1/95	41s
Medical services expenditures	year	559	91	81r
Medical supplies expenditures	year	80	91	81r
Household Goods				
Floor coverings, expenditures	year	158	91	81r
Furniture, expenditures	year	341	91	81r
Household equipment, misc. expenditures	year	363	91	81r
Household expenditures, miscellaneous	year	194	91	81r
Household furnishings and equipment, expenditures	year	1158	91	81r
Household operations expenditures	year	378	91	81r
Household textiles, expenditures	year	88	91	81r
Housekeeping supplies, expenditures	year	426	91	81r
Laundry and cleaning supplies, expenditures	year	122	91	81r
Postage and stationery, expenditures	year	134	91	81r
Housing				
Add garage/carport		11,614	3/95	74r
Add room(s)		16,816	3/95	74r
Apartment condominium or co-op, median	unit	96700	12/94	62r
Dwellings (owned), expenditures	year	3305	91	81r
Enclose porch/patio/breezeway		2,980	3/95	74r
Finish room in basement/attic		4,330	3/95	74r
Home, existing, single-family, median	unit	161600	12/94	62r
Maintenance, repairs, insurance, and other housing expenditures	year	569	91	81r
Mortgage interest and charges expenditures	year	1852	91	81r
Princ. & int., mortgage, median-price exist. sing.-family home	mo.	765	12/94	62r
Property taxes expenditures	year	884	91	81r
Redesign, restructure more than half of home's interior		2,750	3/95	74r
Rental units expenditures	year	1832	91	81r
Insurance and Pensions				
Auto insurance, private passenger	year	556.67	12/94	71s
Insurance and pensions, personal, expenditures	year	2690	91	81r
Insurance, life and other personal, expenditures	year	341	91	81r
Pensions and Social Security, expenditures	year	2349	91	81r
Legal Assistance				
Estate planning, law-firm partner	hr.	375.00	10/93	12r
Legal work, law firm associate	hour	78		10r
Legal work, law firm partner	hour	183		10r
Personal Services				
Personal services expenditures	year	184	91	81r
Restaurant Food				
Dining expenditures, family	week	34.26	94	73r
Taxes				
Taxes, Federal income, expenditures	year	2409	91	81r
Taxes, personal, expenditures	year	3094	91	81r
Taxes, State and local income, expenditures	year	620	91	81r
Transportation				
Cars and trucks purchased, new	year	1170	91	81r
Cars and trucks purchased, used	year	739	91	81r
Driver's learning permit fee	perm	10.00	1/94	84s
Driver's license fee	orig	29.00	1/94	84s
Driver's license fee, duplicate	lic	4.00	1/94	84s
Driver's license reinstatement fee, min.	susp	25.00	1/94	85s

Lewiston-Auburn, ME - continued

Item	Per	Value	Date	Ref.
Transportation - continued				
Driver's license renewal fee	renew	29.00	1/94	84s
Identification card, nondriver	card	5.00	1/94	83s
Motorcycle learning permit fee	perm	10.00	1/94	84s
Motorcycle license fee	orig	29.00	1/94	84s
Motorcycle license fee, duplicate	lic	4.00	1/94	84s
Motorcycle license renewal fee	renew	29.00	1/94	84s
Public transportation expenditures	year	430	91	81r
Transportation expenditures, total	year	4810	91	81r
Vehicle finance charges	year	238	91	81r
Vehicle insurance expenditures	year	630	91	81r
Vehicle maintenance and repairs expenditures	year	532	91	81r
Vehicle purchases	year	1920	91	81r
Vehicle rental, leases, licenses, etc. expenditures	year	193	91	81r
Vehicles purchased, other than cars and trucks	year	11	91	81r
Utilities				
Electricity expenditures	year	695	91	81r
Utilities, fuels, and public services, total expenditures	year	1981	91	81r
Water and other public services, expenditures	year	154	91	81r
Weddings				
Bridal attendants' gowns	event	750	10/93	76r
Bridal gown	event	852	10/93	76r
Bridal headpiece and veil	event	167	10/93	76r
Bride's wedding band	event	708	10/93	76r
Clergy	event	224	10/93	76r
Engagement ring	event	2756	10/93	76r
Flowers	event	863	10/93	76r
Formal wear for groom	event	106	10/93	76r
Groom's attendants' formal wear	event	530	10/93	76r
Groom's wedding band	event	402	10/93	76r
Music	event	600	10/93	76r
Photography	event	1088	10/93	76r
Shoes for bride	event	50	10/93	76r
Videography	event	483	10/93	76r
Wedding invitations and announcements	event	342	10/93	76r
Wedding reception	event	7000	10/93	76r

Lexington-Fayette, KY

Item	Per	Value	Date	Ref.
Composite, ACCRA index		99.20	12/94	2c
Alcoholic Beverages				
Beer, Miller Lite, Bud, 12-oz., ex deposit	6	4.04	12/94	2c
J & B Scotch	750-ml.	18.59	12/94	2c
Wine, Gallo Chablis blanc	1.5-lit	5.81	12/94	2c
Appliances				
Appliances (major), expenditures	year	153	91	81r
Average annual exp.				
Food, health care, personal goods, services	year	27020	91	81r
Charity				
Cash contributions, expenditures	year	839	91	81r
Clothing				
Apparel, men and boys, total expenditures	year	380	91	81r
Apparel, women and girls, total expenditures	year	660	91	81r
Footwear, expenditures	year	193	91	81r
Jeans, man's denim		35.59	12/94	2c
Shirt, man's dress shirt		31.60	12/94	2c
Undervest, boy's size 10-14, cotton	3	4.39	12/94	2c
Communications				
Long-distance telephone rate, day, addl. min., 1-10 mi.	min.	0.14	12/93	9s
Long-distance telephone rate, day, initial min., 1-10 mi.	min.	0.18	12/93	9s

Values are in dollars or fractions of dollars. In the column headed *Ref*, references are shown to sources. Each reference is followed by a letter. These refer to the geographical level for which data were reported: s=State, r=Region, and c=City or metro. The abbreviation *ex* is used to mean *except* or *excluding*; *exp* stands for expenditures. For other abbreviations and further explanations, please see the Introduction.

Lexington-Fayette, KY - continued

Item	Per	Value	Date	Ref.
Communications				
Newspaper subscription, dly. and Sun. delivery	month	18.20	12/94	2c
Phone line, single, business, field visit	inst	64.00	12/93	9s
Phone line, single, business, no field visit	inst	85.25	12/93	9s
Phone line, single, residence, field visit	inst	43.63	12/93	9s
Phone line, single, residence, no field visit	inst	29.38	12/93	9s
Telephone bill, family of four	month	26.92	12/94	2c
Telephone service, expenditures	year	616	91	81r
Education				
Board, 4-year private college/university	year	1897	8/94	80s
Board, 4-year public college/university	year	1744	8/94	80s
Education, total expenditures	year	319	91	81r
Room, 4-year private college/university	year	1644	8/94	80s
Room, 4-year public college/university	year	1370	8/94	80s
Total cost, 4-year private college/university	year	10097	8/94	80s
Total cost, 4-year public college/university	year	5027	8/94	80s
Tuition, 2-year public college/university, in-state	year	962	8/94	80s
Tuition, 4-year private college/university, in-state	year	6556	8/94	80s
Tuition, 4-year public college/university, in-state	year	1913	8/94	80s
Energy and Fuels				
Energy, combined forms, 1800 sq. ft.	mo.	92.37	12/94	2c
Energy, exc. electricity, 1800 sq. ft.	mo.	57.30	12/94	2c
Fuel oil and other fuels, expenditures	year	56	91	81r
Gas, cooking, 10 therms	month	11.44	2/94	65c
Gas, cooking, 30 therms	month	22.79	2/94	65c
Gas, cooking, 50 therms	month	34.14	2/94	65c
Gas, heating, winter, 100 therms	month	62.46	2/94	65c
Gas, heating, winter, average use	month	119.29	2/94	65c
Gas, natural, expenditures	year	150	91	81r
Gas, reg unlead, taxes inc., cash, self-service	gal	1.08	12/94	2c
Gasoline and motor oil purchased	year	1152	91	81r
Gasoline, unleaded midgrade	gallon	1.21	4/93	82r
Gasoline, unleaded premium	gallon	1.30	4/93	82r
Gasoline, unleaded regular	gallon	1.10	4/93	82r
Entertainment				
Bowling, evening rate	game	2.15	12/94	2c
Concert ticket, Pearl Jam group	perf	20.00	94	50r
Entertainment, total expenditures	year	1266	91	81r
Fees and admissions, expenditures	year	306	91	81r
Monopoly game, Parker Brothers', No. 9	game	8.41	12/94	2c
Movie	adm	5.05	12/94	2c
Pets, toys, playground equipment, expenditures	year	271	91	81r
Reading, expenditures	year	131	91	81r
Televisions, radios, and sound equipment, expenditures	year	439	91	81r
Tennis balls, yellow, Wilson or Penn, 3	can	1.97	12/94	2c
Funerals				
Burial, immediate, container provided by funeral home		1298.96	1/95	54r
Cards, acknowledgment		21.26	1/95	54r
Casket, minimum alternative		204.95	1/95	54r
Cosmetology, hair care, etc.		85.40	1/95	54r
Cremation, direct, container provided by funeral home		1054.77	1/95	54r
Embalming		287.71	1/95	54r
Funeral, funeral home		269.18	1/95	54r
Funeral, other facility		272.88	1/95	54r
Graveside service		302.54	1/95	54r
Hearse, local		122.08	1/95	54r
Limousine, local		80.31	1/95	54r
Memorial service		277.66	1/95	54r
Service charge, professional, nondeclinable		896.65	1/95	54r
Visitation and viewing		232.39	1/95	54r

Lexington-Fayette, KY - continued

Item	Per	Value	Date	Ref.
Groceries				
Groceries, ACCRA Index		101.40	12/94	2c
Apples, Red Delicious	lb.	0.73	12/94	82r
Baby food, strained vegetables, lowest price	4-4.5 oz.	0.30	12/94	2c
Bacon, sliced	lb.	1.67	12/94	82r
Bananas	lb.	0.50	12/94	2c
Bananas	lb.	0.42	12/94	82r
Beef or hamburger, ground	lb.	1.55	12/94	2c
Beef purchases	year	213	91	81r
Beverage purchases, alcoholic	year	249	91	81r
Beverage purchases, nonalcoholic	year	207	91	81r
Bologna, all beef or mixed	lb.	2.27	12/94	82r
Bread, white	24-oz.	0.86	12/94	2c
Bread, white, pan	lb.	0.68	12/94	82r
Cabbage	lb.	0.42	12/94	82r
Carrots, short trimmed and topped	lb.	0.53	12/94	82r
Cereals and bakery products purchases	year	345	91	81r
Cereals and cereals products purchases	year	127	91	81r
Cheddar cheese, natural	lb.	3.58	12/94	82r
Cheese, Kraft grated Parmesan	8-oz.	3.34	12/94	2c
Chicken breast, bone-in	lb.	1.71	12/94	82r
Chicken, fresh, whole	lb.	0.78	12/94	82r
Chicken, whole fryer	lb.	0.95	12/94	2c
Chuck roast, USDA choice, boneless	lb.	2.26	12/94	82r
Cigarettes, Winston, Kings	carton	13.48	12/94	2c
Coffee, vacuum-packed	13 oz.	3.27	12/94	2c
Corn Flakes, Kellogg's or Post Toasties	18 oz.	2.70	12/94	2c
Corn, frozen, whole kernel, lowest price	10 oz.	0.71	12/94	2c
Crackers, soda, salted	lb.	1.27	12/94	82r
Cucumbers	lb.	0.65	12/94	82r
Dairy products (other) purchases	year	141	91	81r
Eggs, Grade A large	dozen	0.70	12/94	2c
Eggs, Grade A large	dozen	0.87	12/94	82r
Fish and seafood purchases	year	72	91	81r
Flour, white, all purpose	lb.	0.23	12/94	82r
Food purchases, food eaten at home	year	2381	91	81r
Foods purchased away from home, not prepared by consumer	year	1696	91	81r
Frankfurters, all meat or all beef	lb.	1.74	12/94	82r
Fruits and vegetables purchases	year	380	91	81r
Grapefruit	lb.	0.45	12/94	82r
Grapes, Thompson seedless	lb.	2.30	12/94	82r
Ground beef, 100% beef	lb.	1.37	12/94	82r
Ground chuck, 100% beef	lb.	1.97	12/94	82r
Ham, boneless, exc. canned	lb.	2.54	12/94	82r
Ice cream, prepackaged, bulk, regular	1/2 gal.	2.47	12/94	82r
Lemons	lb.	1.02	12/94	82r
Lettuce, iceberg	lb.	0.96	12/94	82r
Lettuce, iceberg	head	0.84	12/94	2c
Margarine, Blue Bonnet or Parkay cubes	lb.	0.50	12/94	2c
Margarine, stick	lb.	0.77	12/94	82r
Meats, poultry, fish, and eggs purchases	year	655	91	81r
Milk and cream (fresh) purchases	year	130	91	81r
Milk, whole	1/2 gal.	1.48	12/94	2c
Orange juice, frozen concentrate 12-oz. can	16 oz.	1.36	12/94	82r
Orange juice, Minute Maid frozen	12-oz.	1.34	12/94	2c
Oranges, Navel	lb.	0.54	12/94	82r
Peaches, halves or slices, Hunt's, Del Monte, or Libby's	29-oz.	1.50	12/94	2c
Pears, Anjou	lb.	0.81	12/94	82r
Peas, sweet, Del Monte or Green Giant	15-17 oz.	0.53	12/94	2c
Pork chops, center cut, bone-in	lb.	3.07	12/94	82r
Pork purchases	year	142	91	81r
Potato chips	16-oz.	3.15	12/94	82r
Potatoes, frozen, French fried	lb.	0.82	12/94	82r
Potatoes, white	lb.	0.34	12/94	82r
Potatoes, white or red	10-lb. sack	2.49	12/94	2c
Rice, white, long grain, uncooked	lb.	0.48	12/94	82r

Values are in dollars or fractions of dollars. In the column headed *Ref*, references are shown to sources. Each reference is followed by a letter. These refer to the geographical level for which data were reported: s=State, r=Region, and c=City or metro. The abbreviation *ex* is used to mean *except* or *excluding*; *exp* stands for *expenditures*. For other abbreviations and further explanations, please see the Introduction.

Lexington-Fayette, KY - continued

Item	Per	Value	Date	Ref.
Groceries				
Round roast, USDA choice, boneless	lb.	2.91	12/94	82r
Sausage, fresh	lb.	1.82	12/94	82r
Sausage, Jimmy Dean, 100% pork	lb.	2.47	12/94	2c
Shortening, vegetable oil blends	lb.	0.75	12/94	82r
Shortening, vegetable, Crisco	3-lb.	2.18	12/94	2c
Soft drink, Coca Cola, ex deposit	2 lit	1.07	12/94	2c
Spaghetti and macaroni	lb.	0.87	12/94	82r
Steak, rib eye, USDA choice, boneless	lb.	6.85	12/94	82r
Steak, round, graded & ungraded, exc. USDA prime & choice	lb.	2.96	12/94	82r
Steak, round, USDA choice, boneless	lb.	3.17	12/94	82r
Steak, sirloin, USDA choice, boneless	lb.	4.12	12/94	82r
Steak, t-bone	lb.	5.91	12/94	2c
Steak, T-bone, USDA choice, bone-in	lb.	5.63	12/94	82r
Sugar and other sweets, eaten at home, expenditures	year	93	91	81r
Sugar, cane or beet	4 lbs.	1.44	12/94	2c
Sugar, white, all sizes	lb.	0.39	12/94	82r
Tobacco products and smoking supplies, total expenditures	year	286	91	81r
Tomatoes, field grown	lb.	1.36	12/94	82r
Tomatoes, Hunt's or Del Monte	14.5 oz.	0.71	12/94	2c
Tuna, chunk, light	lb.	1.94	12/94	82r
Tuna, chunk, light, oil-packed	6.125-6.5 oz.	0.79	12/94	2c
Turkey, frozen, whole	lb.	0.96	12/94	82r
Yogurt, natural, fruit flavored	8 oz.	0.58	12/94	82r
Goods and Services				
Miscellaneous goods and services, ACCRA Index		102.10	12/94	2c
Health Care				
Health care, ACCRA Index		114.10	12/94	2c
Adenosine, emergency room	treat	100.00	95	23r
Antibiotic ointment, Polysporin	1.5 oz.	5.08	12/94	2c
Bladder tap, superpubic, infant, emergency room	treat	119.00	95	23r
Blood analysis, emergency room	treat	25.00	95	23r
Blood tests, abdominal pain, emergency room	treat	25.00	95	23r
Burn dressing, emergency room	treat	266.00	95	23r
Cardiology interpretation, emergency room	treat	26.00	95	23r
Chest X-ray, emergency room	treat	78.00	95	23r
Childbirth, Cesarean delivery, hospital charge	birth	5462.00	12/91	69r
Childbirth, Cesarean delivery, physician charge	birth	2228.00	12/91	69r
Childbirth, normal delivery, hospital charge	birth	2943.00	12/91	69r
Childbirth, normal delivery, physician charge	birth	1619.00	12/91	69r
Defibrillation pads, emergency room	treat	6.00	95	23r
Dentist's fee, adult teeth cleaning and periodic oral exam	visit	54.80	12/94	2c
Doctor's fee, routine exam, established patient	visit	52.00	12/94	2c
Drugs, expenditures	year	297	91	81r
Gastric tube insertion, nasal, emergency room	treat	25.00	95	23r
Health care, total expenditures	year	1600	91	81r
Health insurance expenditures	year	637	91	81r
Heart monitor, emergency room	treat	40.00	95	23r
Hospital care, semiprivate room	day	382.80	12/94	2c
Insurance premium, family medical care	month	332.39	1/95	41s
Intravenous fluids, emergency room	treat	130.00	95	23r
Intravenous fluids, emergency room	liter	26.00	95	23r
Intravenous line, central, emergency room	treat	342.00	95	23r
Liver function tests, abdominal pain, emergency room	treat	26.00	95	23r
Medical care charges, total, emergency room, third-degree burns	treat	2101.00	95	23r
Medical care charges, total, emergency, infant with fever	treat	628.00	95	23r

Lexington-Fayette, KY - continued

Item	Per	Value	Date	Ref.
Health Care - continued				
Medical services expenditures	year	573	91	81r
Medical supplies expenditures	year	93	91	81r
Morphine, emergency room	treat	34.00	95	23r
Nursing care and facilities charges, emergency room	treat	252.00	95	23r
Nursing care and facilities charges, emergency, infant with fever	treat	252.00	95	23r
Nursing care and facilities charges, emergency, third-degree burns	treat	861.00	95	23r
Physician's charges, emergency, infant with fever	treat	212.00	95	23r
Physician's charges, emergency, third-degree burns	treat	372.00	95	23r
Physician's fee, emergency room	treat	372.00	95	23r
Physician's fee, general practitioner	visit	51.20	12/93	60r
Surgery, open-heart	proc	42374.00	1/93	14r
Ultrasound, abdominal, emergency room	treat	276.00	95	23r
Urinalysis, emergency room	treat	20.00	95	23r
Urinalysis, infant, emergency room	treat	20.00	95	23r
X-rays, emergency room	treat	78.00	95	23r
Household Goods				
Appl. repair, service call, wash mach	min. lab. chg.	36.75	12/94	2c
Floor coverings, expenditures	year	48	91	81r
Furniture, expenditures	year	280	91	81r
Household equipment, misc. expenditures	year	342	91	81r
Household expenditures, miscellaneous	year	256	91	81r
Household furnishings and equipment, expenditures	year	988	91	81r
Household operations expenditures	year	468	91	81r
Household textiles, expenditures	year	95	91	81r
Housekeeping supplies, expenditures	year	380	91	81r
Laundry and cleaning supplies, expenditures	year	109	91	81r
Laundry detergent, Tide Ultra, Bold, or Cheer	42 oz.	3.10	12/94	2c
Postage and stationery, expenditures	year	105	91	81r
Tissues, facial, Kleenex brand	175	0.99	12/94	2c
Housing				
Housing, ACCRA Index		96.90	12/94	2c
Add garage/carport		6,980	3/95	74r
Add room(s)		11,403	3/95	74r
Apartment condominium or co-op, median	unit	68600	12/94	62r
Dwellings (owned), expenditures	year	2428	91	81r
Enclose porch/patio/breezeway		4,572	3/95	74r
Finish room in basement/attic		3,794	3/95	74r
Home, existing, single-family, median	unit	120200	12/94	62r
Home, existing, single-family, median	unit	88.60	12/94	62c
House payment, principal and interest, 25% down payment	mo.	728	12/94	2c
House, 1800 sq ft, 8000 sq ft lot, new, urban, utilities	total	117500	12/94	2c
Maintenance, repairs, insurance, and other housing expenditures	year	531	91	81r
Mortgage interest and charges expenditures	year	1506	91	81r
Mtge. rate, incl. points and orig. fee, 30-year conv. fixed or ARM	mo.	9.29	12/94	2c
Princ. & int., mortgage, median-price exist. sing.-family home	mo.	540	12/94	62r
Property taxes expenditures	year	391	91	81r
Redesign, restructure more than half of home's interior		17,641	3/95	74r
Rent, apartment, 2 br., 1 1/2-2 baths, unfurnished, 950 sq ft, water	mo.	554	12/94	2c
Rental units expenditures	year	1264	91	81r
Insurance and Pensions				
Auto insurance, private passenger	year	616.22	12/94	71s
Insurance and pensions, personal, expenditures	year	2395	91	81r

Values are in dollars or fractions of dollars. In the column headed *Ref*, references are shown to sources. Each reference is followed by a letter. These refer to the geographical level for which data were reported: s = State, r = Region, and c = City or metro. The abbreviation *ex* is used to mean *except* or *excluding*; *exp* stands for *expenditures*. For other abbreviations and further explanations, please see the Introduction.

Lexington-Fayette, KY - continued

Item	Per	Value	Date	Ref.
Insurance and Pensions				
Insurance, life and other personal, expenditures	year	368	91	81r
Pensions and Social Security, expenditures	year	2027	91	81r
Personal Goods				
Shampoo, Alberto VO5	15-oz.	0.97	12/94	2c
Toothpaste, Crest or Colgate	6-7 oz.	1.60	12/94	2c
Personal Services				
Dry cleaning, man's 2-pc. suit		6.25	12/94	2c
Haircut, man's barbershop, no styling		8.10	12/94	2c
Haircut, woman's shampoo, trim, blow-dry		23.60	12/94	2c
Personal services expenditures	year	212	91	81r
Restaurant Food				
Chicken, fried, thigh and drumstick		2.20	12/94	2c
Dining expenditures, family	week	33.83	94	73r
Hamburger with cheese	1/4 lb.	1.94	12/94	2c
Pizza, Pizza Hut or Pizza Inn	12-13 in.	7.58	12/94	2c
Taxes				
Taxes, Federal income, expenditures	year	2275	91	81r
Taxes, personal, expenditures	year	2715	91	81r
Taxes, State and local income, expenditures	year	365	91	81r
Transportation				
Transportation, ACCRA Index		90.40	12/94	2c
Cars and trucks purchased, new	year	1306	91	81r
Cars and trucks purchased, used	year	942	91	81r
Driver's learning permit fee	perm	2.00	1/94	84s
Driver's license fee	orig	8.00	1/94	84s
Driver's license fee, duplicate	lic	2.00	1/94	84s
Driver's license reinstatement fee, min.	susp	30.00	1/94	85s
Driver's license renewal fee	renew	8.00	1/94	84s
Identification card, nondriver	card	4.00	1/94	83s
Motorcycle learning permit fee	perm	2.00	1/94	84s
Motorcycle license fee	orig	8.00	1/94	84s
Motorcycle license fee, duplicate	lic	2.00	1/94	84s
Motorcycle license renewal fee	renew	8.00	1/94	84s
Public transportation expenditures	year	249	91	81r
Tire balance, computer or spin bal., front	wheel	5.59	12/94	2c
Transportation expenditures, total	year	5307	91	81r
Vehicle finance charges	year	346	91	81r
Vehicle insurance expenditures	year	544	91	81r
Vehicle maintenance and repairs expenditures	year	600	91	81r
Vehicle purchases	year	2275	91	81r
Vehicle rental, leases, licenses, etc. expenditures	year	141	91	81r
Vehicles purchased, other than cars and trucks	year	27	91	81r
Utilities				
Utilities, ACCRA Index		89.90	12/94	2c
Electricity expenditures	year	950	91	81r
Electricity, (part.), other, 1800 sq. ft., new home	mo.	35.07	12/94	2c
Electricity, summer, 250 KWh	month	14.96	8/93	64c
Electricity, summer, 500 KWh	month	26.29	8/93	64c
Electricity, summer, 750 KWh	month	37.01	8/93	64c
Electricity, summer, 1000 KWh	month	47.72	8/93	64c
Utilities, fuels, and public services, total expenditures	year	2000	91	81r
Water and other public services, expenditures	year	227	91	81r
Weddings				
Bridal attendants' gowns	event	750	10/93	76r
Bridal gown	event	852	10/93	76r
Bridal headpiece and veil	event	167	10/93	76r
Bride's wedding band	event	708	10/93	76r
Clergy	event	224	10/93	76r
Engagement ring	event	2756	10/93	76r
Flowers	event	863	10/93	76r

Lexington-Fayette, KY - continued

Item	Per	Value	Date	Ref.
Weddings - continued				
Formal wear for groom	event	106	10/93	76r
Groom's attendants' formal wear	event	530	10/93	76r
Groom's wedding band	event	402	10/93	76r
Music	event	600	10/93	76r
Photography	event	1088	10/93	76r
Shoes for bride	event	50	10/93	76r
Videography	event	483	10/93	76r
Wedding invitations and announcements	event	342	10/93	76r
Wedding reception	event	7000	10/93	76r

Lima, OH

Item	Per	Value	Date	Ref.
Appliances				
Appliances (major), expenditures	year	131	91	81r
Average annual exp.				
Food, health care, personal goods, services	year	25935	91	81r
Charity				
Cash contributions, expenditures	year	745	91	81r
Clothing				
Apparel, men and boys, total expenditures	year	332	91	81r
Apparel, women and girls, total expenditures	year	578	91	81r
Footwear, expenditures	year	164	91	81r
Communications				
Long-distance telephone rate, day, addl. min., 1-10 mi.	min.	0.16	12/93	9s
Long-distance telephone rate, day, initial min., 1-10 mi.	min.	0.32	12/93	9s
Phone line, single, business, field visit	inst	55.42	12/93	9s
Phone line, single, business, no field visit	inst	55.42	12/93	9s
Phone line, single, residence, field visit	inst	30.38	12/93	9s
Phone line, single, residence, no field visit	inst	30.38	12/93	9s
Telephone service, expenditures	year	547	91	81r
Education				
Board, 4-year private college/university	year	2241	8/94	80s
Board, 4-year public college/university	year	1625	8/94	80s
Education, total expenditures	year	394	91	81r
Room, 4-year private college/university	year	2118	8/94	80s
Room, 4-year public college/university	year	2103	8/94	80s
Total cost, 4-year private college/university	year	15444	8/94	80s
Total cost, 4-year public college/university	year	6987	8/94	80s
Tuition, 2-year public college/university, in-state	year	2076	8/94	80s
Tuition, 4-year private college/university, in-state	year	11085	8/94	80s
Tuition, 4-year public college/university, in-state	year	3259	8/94	80s
Energy and Fuels				
Fuel oil and other fuels, expenditures	year	83	91	81r
Gas, natural, expenditures	year	373	91	81r
Gasoline and motor oil purchased	year	1000	91	81r
Gasoline, unleaded midgrade	gallon	1.15	4/93	82r
Gasoline, unleaded premium	gallon	1.23	4/93	82r
Gasoline, unleaded regular	gallon	1.07	4/93	82r
Entertainment				
Entertainment, total expenditures	year	1356	91	81r
Fees and admissions, expenditures	year	347	91	81r
Pets, toys, playground equipment, expenditures	year	270	91	81r
Reading, expenditures	year	160	91	81r
Televisions, radios, and sound equipment, expenditures	year	433	91	81r
Funerals				
Burial, immediate, container provided by funeral home		1268.31	1/95	54r
Cards, acknowledgment		26.12	1/95	54r
Casket, minimum alternative		198.03	1/95	54r
Cosmetology, hair care, etc.		122.19	1/95	54r

Values are in dollars or fractions of dollars. In the column headed *Ref*, references are shown to sources. Each reference is followed by a letter. These refer to the geographical level for which data were reported: s=State, r=Region, and c=City or metro. The abbreviation *ex* is used to mean *except* or *excluding*; *exp* stands for *expenditures*. For other abbreviations and further explanations, please see the Introduction.

Lima, OH - continued

Item	Per	Value	Date	Ref.
Funerals				
Cremation, direct, container provided by funeral home		977.81	1/95	54r
Embalming		334.00	1/95	54r
Funeral, funeral home		321.16	1/95	54r
Funeral, other facility		317.73	1/95	54r
Graveside service		292.48	1/95	54r
Hearse, local		153.20	1/95	54r
Limousine, local		123.52	1/95	54r
Memorial service		356.30	1/95	54r
Service charge, professional, nondeclinable		968.24	1/95	54r
Visitation and viewing		332.66	1/95	54r
Groceries				
Apples, Red Delicious	lb.	0.68	12/94	82r
Bacon, sliced	lb.	1.88	12/94	82r
Bananas	lb.	0.41	12/94	82r
Beef purchases	year	197	91	81r
Beef, stew, boneless	lb.	2.52	12/94	82r
Beverage purchases, alcoholic	year	293	91	81r
Beverage purchases, nonalcoholic	year	203	91	81r
Bologna, all beef or mixed	lb.	2.12	12/94	82r
Bread, white, pan	lb.	0.76	12/94	82r
Cabbage	lb.	0.44	12/94	82r
Carrots, short trimmed and topped	lb.	0.44	12/94	82r
Cereals and bakery products purchases	year	347	91	81r
Cereals and cereals products purchases	year	119	91	81r
Cheddar cheese, natural	lb.	3.28	12/94	82r
Chicken breast, bone-in	lb.	1.61	12/94	82r
Chicken, fresh, whole	lb.	0.89	12/94	82r
Chuck roast, USDA choice, boneless	lb.	2.33	12/94	82r
Coffee, 100%, ground roast, all sizes	lb.	4.28	12/94	82r
Cookies, chocolate chip	lb.	2.72	12/94	82r
Dairy products (other) purchases	year	148	91	81r
Eggs, Grade A large	dozen	0.76	12/94	82r
Fish and seafood purchases	year	61	91	81r
Flour, white, all purpose	lb.	0.22	12/94	82r
Food purchases, food eaten at home	year	2313	91	81r
Foods purchased away from home, not prepared by consumer	year	1709	91	81r
Fruits and vegetables purchases	year	372	91	81r
Grapefruit	lb.	0.47	12/94	82r
Grapes, Thompson seedless	lb.	2.15	12/94	82r
Ground beef, 100% beef	lb.	1.37	12/94	82r
Ground chuck, 100% beef	lb.	1.81	12/94	82r
Ham, boneless, exc. canned	lb.	2.16	12/94	82r
Ice cream, prepackaged, bulk, regular	1/2 gal.	2.48		82r
Lemons	lb.	1.08	12/94	82r
Lettuce, iceberg	lb.	0.81	12/94	82r
Margarine, stick	lb.	0.81	12/94	82r
Meats, poultry, fish, and eggs purchases	year	591	91	81r
Milk and cream (fresh) purchases	year	132	91	81r
Orange juice, frozen concentrate 12-oz. can	16 oz.	1.41	12/94	82r
Oranges, Navel	lb.	0.56	12/94	82r
Peanut butter, creamy, all sizes	lb.	1.81	12/94	82r
Pork chops, center cut, bone-in	lb.	2.76	12/94	82r
Pork purchases	year	130	91	81r
Potato chips	16-oz.	2.81	12/94	82r
Potatoes, frozen, French fried	lb.	0.83	12/94	82r
Potatoes, white	lb.	0.28	12/94	82r
Round roast, USDA choice, boneless	lb.	2.90	12/94	82r
Shortening, vegetable oil blends	lb.	0.88	12/94	82r
Spaghetti and macaroni	lb.	0.78	12/94	82r
Steak, rib eye, USDA choice, boneless	lb.	6.15	12/94	82r
Steak, round, graded & ungraded, exc. USDA prime & choice	lb.	2.72	12/94	82r
Steak, round, USDA choice, boneless	lb.	3.02	12/94	82r
Steak, sirloin, USDA choice, boneless	lb.	3.85	12/94	82r
Steak, T-bone, USDA choice, bone-in	lb.	5.38	12/94	82r
Sugar and other sweets, eaten at home, expenditures	year	91	91	81r
Sugar, white, all sizes	lb.	0.36	12/94	82r

Lima, OH - continued

Item	Per	Value	Date	Ref.
Groceries - continued				
Tobacco products and smoking supplies, total expenditures	year	298	91	81r
Tomatoes, field grown	lb.	1.36	12/94	82r
Tuna, chunk, light	lb.	1.94	12/94	82r
Turkey, frozen, whole	lb.	0.96	12/94	82r
Yogurt, natural, fruit flavored	8 oz.	0.62	12/94	82r
Health Care				
Childbirth, Cesarean delivery, hospital charge	birth	5101.00	12/91	69r
Childbirth, Cesarean delivery, physician charge	birth	2234.00	12/91	69r
Childbirth, normal delivery, hospital charge	birth	2891.00	12/91	69r
Childbirth, normal delivery, physician charge	birth	1623.00	12/91	69r
Drugs, expenditures	year	248	91	81r
Health care, total expenditures	year	1336	91	81r
Health insurance expenditures	year	550	91	81r
Insurance premium, family medical care	month	350.73	1/95	41s
Medical services expenditures	year	457	91	81r
Medical supplies expenditures	year	82	91	81r
Household Goods				
Floor coverings, expenditures	year	105	91	81r
Furniture, expenditures	year	291	91	81r
Household equipment, misc. expenditures	year	341	91	81r
Household expenditures, miscellaneous	year	162	91	81r
Household furnishings and equipment, expenditures	year	1042	91	81r
Household operations expenditures	year	365	91	81r
Household textiles, expenditures	year	101	91	81r
Housekeeping supplies, expenditures	year	390	91	81r
Laundry and cleaning supplies, expenditures	year	110	91	81r
Postage and stationery, expenditures	year	115	91	81r
Housing				
Add garage/carport		8,479	3/95	74r
Add room(s)		21,347	3/95	74r
Apartment condominium or co-op, median	unit	87100	12/94	62r
Bathroom addition, average cost	add	9734.00	3/95	13r
Bathroom remodeling, average cost	remod	6414.00	3/95	13r
Bedroom, master suite addition, average cost	add	27122.00	3/95	13r
Deck addition, average cost	add	6665.00	3/95	13r
Dwellings (owned), expenditures	year	2566	91	81r
Enclose porch/patio/breezeway		4,556	3/95	74r
Exterior remodeling, average cost	remod	15395.00	3/95	13r
Family room addition, average cost	add	27658.00	3/95	13r
Finish room in basement/attic		5,074	3/95	74r
Home, existing, single-family, median	unit	106500	12/94	62r
Kitchen remodeling, major, average cost	remod	17084.00	3/95	13r
Kitchen remodeling, minor, average cost	remod	5804.00	3/95	13r
Maintenance, repairs, insurance, and other housing expenditures	year	484	91	81r
Mortgage interest and charges expenditures	year	1443	91	81r
Office, home addition, average cost	add	8121.00	3/95	13r
Princ. & int., mortgage, median-price exist. sing.-family home	mo.	515	12/94	62r
Property taxes expenditures	year	639	91	81r
Redesign, restructure more than half of home's interior		9,114	3/95	74r
Rental units expenditures	year	1200	91	81r
Sun-space addition, average cost	add	23768.00	3/95	13r
Wing addition, two-story, average cost	add	50410.00	3/95	13r
Insurance and Pensions				
Auto insurance, private passenger	year	550.52	12/94	71s
Insurance and pensions, personal, expenditures	year	2408	91	81r
Insurance, life and other personal, expenditures	year	355	91	81r
Pensions and Social Security, expenditures	year	2053	91	81r

Values are in dollars or fractions of dollars. In the column headed *Ref*, references are shown to sources. Each reference is followed by a letter. These refer to the geographical level for which data were reported: s = State, r = Region, and c = City or metro. The abbreviation *ex* is used to mean *except* or *excluding*; *exp* stands for expenditures. For other abbreviations and further explanations, please see the Introduction.

Lima, OH - continued

Item	Per	Value	Date	Ref.
Legal Assistance				
Legal work, law firm associate	hour	90		10r
Legal work, law firm partner	hour	139		10r
Personal Services				
Personal services expenditures	year	203	91	81r
Restaurant Food				
Dining expenditures, family	week	30.03	94	73r
Taxes				
Taxes, Federal income, expenditures	year	1756	91	81r
Taxes, personal, expenditures	year	2426	91	81r
Taxes, State and local income, expenditures	year	568	91	81r
Transportation				
Cars and trucks purchased, new	year	891	91	81r
Cars and trucks purchased, used	year	1155	91	81r
Driver's learning permit fee	perm	3.00	1/94	84s
Driver's license fee	orig	5.00	1/94	84s
Driver's license fee, duplicate	lic	1.50	1/94	84s
Driver's license reinstatement fee, min.	susp	12.50-100.00	1/94	85s
Driver's license renewal fee	renew	5.00	1/94	84s
Identification card, nondriver	card	2.50	1/94	83s
Motorcycle learning permit fee	perm	3.00	1/94	84s
Motorcycle license fee	orig	5.00	1/94	84s
Motorcycle license fee, duplicate	lic	1.50	1/94	84s
Motorcycle license renewal fee	renew	5.00	1/94	84s
Public transportation expenditures	year	209	91	81r
Transportation expenditures, total	year	4792	91	81r
Vehicle finance charges	year	300	91	81r
Vehicle insurance expenditures	year	485	91	81r
Vehicle maintenance and repairs expenditures	year	534	91	81r
Vehicle purchases	year	2068	91	81r
Vehicle rental, leases, licenses, etc. expenditures	year	197	91	81r
Vehicles purchased, other than cars and trucks	year	22	91	81r
Utilities				
Electricity expenditures	year	668	91	81r
Utilities, fuels, and public services, total expenditures	year	1838	91	81r
Water and other public services, expenditures	year	167	91	81r
Weddings				
Bridal attendants' gowns	event	750	10/93	76r
Bridal gown	event	852	10/93	76r
Bridal headpiece and veil	event	167	10/93	76r
Bride's wedding band	event	708	10/93	76r
Clergy	event	224	10/93	76r
Engagement ring	event	2756	10/93	76r
Flowers	event	863	10/93	76r
Formal wear for groom	event	106	10/93	76r
Groom's attendants' formal wear	event	530	10/93	76r
Groom's wedding band	event	402	10/93	76r
Music	event	600	10/93	76r
Photography	event	1088	10/93	76r
Shoes for bride	event	50	10/93	76r
Videography	event	483	10/93	76r
Wedding invitations and announcements	event	342	10/93	76r
Wedding reception	event	7000	10/93	76r

Lincoln, NE

Item	Per	Value	Date	Ref.
Composite, ACCRA index		90.50	12/94	2c
Alcoholic Beverages				
Beer, Miller Lite, Bud, 12-oz., ex deposit	6	3.95	12/94	2c
J & B Scotch	750-ml.	15.79	12/94	2c
Wine, Gallo Chablis blanc	1.5-lit	4.55	12/94	2c

Lincoln, NE - continued

Item	Per	Value	Date	Ref.
Appliances				
Appliances (major), expenditures	year	131	91	81r
Average annual exp.				
Food, health care, personal goods, services	year	25935	91	81r
Charity				
Cash contributions, expenditures	year	745	91	81r
Clothing				
Apparel, men and boys, total expenditures	year	332	91	81r
Apparel, women and girls, total expenditures	year	578	91	81r
Footwear, expenditures	year	164	91	81r
Jeans, man's denim		24.59	12/94	2c
Shirt, man's dress shirt		25.83	12/94	2c
Undervest, boy's size 10-14, cotton	3	3.61	12/94	2c
Communications				
Long-distance telephone rate, day, addl. min., 1-10 mi.	min.	0.16	12/93	9s
Long-distance telephone rate, day, initial min., 1-10 mi.	min.	0.30	12/93	9s
Newspaper subscription, dly. and Sun. delivery	month	9.35	12/94	2c
Phone line, single, business, field visit	inst	45.00	12/93	9s
Phone line, single, business, no field visit	inst	45.00	12/93	9s
Phone line, single, residence, field visit	inst	28.00	12/93	9s
Phone line, single, residence, no field visit	inst	28.00	12/93	9s
Telephone bill, family of four	month	16.56	12/94	2c
Telephone service, expenditures	year	547	91	81r
Education				
Board, 4-year private college/university	year	1816	8/94	80s
Board, 4-year public college/university	year	1711	8/94	80s
Education, total expenditures	year	394	91	81r
Room, 4-year private college/university	year	1684	8/94	80s
Room, 4-year public college/university	year	1276	8/94	80s
Total cost, 4-year private college/university	year	11899	8/94	80s
Total cost, 4-year public college/university	year	4927	8/94	80s
Tuition, 2-year public college/university, in-state	year	1091	8/94	80s
Tuition, 4-year private college/university, in-state	year	8400	8/94	80s
Tuition, 4-year public college/university, in-state	year	1939	8/94	80s
Energy and Fuels				
Energy, combined forms, 1800 sq. ft.	mo.	104.52	12/94	2c
Energy, exc. electricity, 1800 sq. ft.	mo.	36.04	12/94	2c
Fuel oil and other fuels, expenditures	year	83	91	81r
Gas, natural, expenditures	year	373	91	81r
Gas, reg unlead, taxes inc., cash, self-service	gal	1.09	12/94	2c
Gasoline and motor oil purchased	year	1000	91	81r
Gasoline, unleaded midgrade	gallon	1.15	4/93	82r
Gasoline, unleaded premium	gallon	1.23	4/93	82r
Gasoline, unleaded regular	gallon	1.07	4/93	82r
Entertainment				
Bowling, evening rate	game	2.00	12/94	2c
Entertainment, total expenditures	year	1356	91	81r
Fees and admissions, expenditures	year	347	91	81r
Monopoly game, Parker Brothers', No. 9	game	9.46	12/94	2c
Movie	adm	5.00	12/94	2c
Pets, toys, playground equipment, expenditures	year	270	91	81r
Reading, expenditures	year	160	91	81r
Televisions, radios, and sound equipment, expenditures	year	433	91	81r
Tennis balls, yellow, Wilson or Penn, 3	can	3.09	12/94	2c
Funerals				
Burial, immediate, container provided by funeral home		1348.78	1/95	54r
Cards, acknowledgment		21.20	1/95	54r
Casket, minimum alternative		182.83	1/95	54r
Cosmetology, hair care, etc.		133.11	1/95	54r

Values are in dollars or fractions of dollars. In the column headed *Ref*, references are shown to sources. Each reference is followed by a letter. These refer to the geographical level for which data were reported: s = State, r = Region, and c = City or metro. The abbreviation *ex* is used to mean *except* or *excluding*; *exp* stands for expenditures. For other abbreviations and further explanations, please see the Introduction.

Lincoln, NE - continued

Item	Per	Value	Date	Ref.
Funerals				
Cremation, direct, container provided by funeral home		1101.95	1/95	54r
Embalming		314.45	1/95	54r
Funeral, funeral home		304.88	1/95	54r
Funeral, other facility		301.37	1/95	54r
Graveside service		290.59	1/95	54r
Hearse, local		137.37	1/95	54r
Limousine, local		82.84	1/95	54r
Memorial service		316.57	1/95	54r
Service charge, professional, nondeclinable		1099.00	1/95	54r
Visitation and viewing		209.25	1/95	54r
Groceries				
Groceries, ACCRA Index		97.50	12/94	2c
Apples, Red Delicious	lb.	0.68	12/94	82r
Baby food, strained vegetables, lowest price	4-4.5 oz.	0.39	12/94	2c
Bacon, sliced	lb.	1.88	12/94	82r
Bananas	lb.	0.35	12/94	2c
Bananas	lb.	0.41	12/94	82r
Beef or hamburger, ground	lb.	1.19	12/94	2c
Beef purchases	year	197	91	81r
Beef, stew, boneless	lb.	2.52	12/94	82r
Beverage purchases, alcoholic	year	293	91	81r
Beverage purchases, nonalcoholic	year	203	91	81r
Bologna, all beef or mixed	lb.	2.12	12/94	82r
Bread, white	24-oz.	0.95	12/94	2c
Bread, white, pan	lb.	0.76	12/94	82r
Cabbage	lb.	0.44	12/94	82r
Carrots, short trimmed and topped	lb.	0.44	12/94	82r
Cereals and bakery products purchases	year	347	91	81r
Cereals and cereals products purchases	year	119	91	81r
Cheddar cheese, natural	lb.	3.28	12/94	82r
Cheese, Kraft grated Parmesan	8-oz.	3.26	12/94	2c
Chicken breast, bone-in	lb.	1.61	12/94	82r
Chicken, fresh, whole	lb.	0.89	12/94	82r
Chicken, whole fryer	lb.	0.76	12/94	2c
Chuck roast, USDA choice, boneless	lb.	2.33	12/94	82r
Cigarettes, Winston, Kings	carton	18.85	12/94	2c
Coffee, 100%, ground roast, all sizes	lb.	4.28	12/94	82r
Coffee, vacuum-packed	13 oz.	2.93	12/94	2c
Cookies, chocolate chip	lb.	2.72	12/94	82r
Corn Flakes, Kellogg's or Post Toasties	18 oz.	2.18	12/94	2c
Corn, frozen, whole kernel, lowest price	10 oz.	0.70	12/94	2c
Dairy products (other) purchases	year	148	91	81r
Eggs, Grade A large	dozen	0.64	12/94	2c
Eggs, Grade A large	dozen	0.76	12/94	82r
Fish and seafood purchases	year	61	91	81r
Flour, white, all purpose	lb.	0.22	12/94	82r
Food purchases, food eaten at home	year	2313	91	81r
Foods purchased away from home, not prepared by consumer	year	1709	91	81r
Fruits and vegetables purchases	year	372	91	81r
Grapefruit	lb.	0.47	12/94	82r
Grapes, Thompson seedless	lb.	2.15	12/94	82r
Ground beef, 100% beef	lb.	1.37	12/94	82r
Ground chuck, 100% beef	lb.	1.81	12/94	82r
Ham, boneless, exc. canned	lb.	2.16	12/94	82r
Ice cream, prepackaged, bulk, regular	1/2 gal.	2.48	12/94	82r
Lemons	lb.	1.08	12/94	82r
Lettuce, iceberg	lb.	0.81	12/94	82r
Lettuce, iceberg	head	0.58	12/94	2c
Margarine, Blue Bonnet or Parkay cubes	lb.	0.51	12/94	2c
Margarine, stick	lb.	0.81	12/94	82r
Meats, poultry, fish, and eggs purchases	year	591	91	81r
Milk and cream (fresh) purchases	year	132	91	81r
Milk, whole	1/2 gal.	1.25	12/94	2c
Orange juice, frozen concentrate 12-oz. can	16 oz.	1.41	12/94	82r
Orange juice, Minute Maid frozen	12-oz.	0.98	12/94	2c
Oranges, Navel	lb.	0.56	12/94	82r

Lincoln, NE - continued

Item	Per	Value	Date	Ref.
Groceries - continued				
Peaches, halves or slices, Hunt's, Del Monte, or Libby's	29-oz.	1.32	12/94	2c
Peanut butter, creamy, all sizes	lb.	1.81	12/94	82r
Peas, sweet, Del Monte or Green Giant	15-17 oz.	0.56	12/94	2c
Pork chops, center cut, bone-in	lb.	2.76	12/94	82r
Pork purchases	year	130	91	81r
Potato chips	16-oz.	2.81	12/94	82r
Potatoes, frozen, French fried	lb.	0.83	12/94	82r
Potatoes, white	lb.	0.28	12/94	82r
Potatoes, white or red	10-lb. sack	2.10	12/94	2c
Round roast, USDA choice, boneless	lb.	2.90	12/94	82r
Sausage, Jimmy Dean, 100% pork	lb.	2.96	12/94	2c
Shortening, vegetable oil blends	lb.	0.88	12/94	82r
Shortening, vegetable, Crisco	3-lb.	2.49	12/94	2c
Soft drink, Coca Cola, ex deposit	2 lit	1.10	12/94	2c
Spaghetti and macaroni	lb.	0.78	12/94	82r
Steak, rib eye, USDA choice, boneless	lb.	6.15	12/94	82r
Steak, round, graded & ungraded, exc. USDA prime & choice	lb.	2.72	12/94	82r
Steak, round, USDA choice, boneless	lb.	3.02	12/94	82r
Steak, sirloin, USDA choice, boneless	lb.	3.85	12/94	82r
Steak, t-bone	lb.	4.48	12/94	2c
Steak, T-bone, USDA choice, bone-in	lb.	5.38	12/94	82r
Sugar and other sweets, eaten at home, expenditures	year	91	91	81r
Sugar, cane or beet	4 lbs.	1.41	12/94	2c
Sugar, white, all sizes	lb.	0.36	12/94	82r
Tobacco products and smoking supplies, total expenditures	year	298	91	81r
Tomatoes, field grown	lb.	1.36	12/94	82r
Tomatoes, Hunt's or Del Monte	14.5 oz.	0.65	12/94	2c
Tuna, chunk, light	lb.	1.94	12/94	82r
Tuna, chunk, light, oil-packed	6.125-6.5 oz.	0.59	12/94	2c
Turkey, frozen, whole	lb.	0.96	12/94	82r
Yogurt, natural, fruit flavored	8 oz.	0.62	12/94	82r
Goods and Services				
Miscellaneous goods and services, ACCRA Index		95.80	12/94	2c
Health Care				
Health care, ACCRA Index		86.50	12/94	2c
Antibiotic ointment, Polysporin	1.5 oz.	4.48	12/94	2c
Childbirth, Cesarean delivery, hospital charge	birth	5101.00	12/91	69r
Childbirth, Cesarean delivery, physician charge	birth	2234.00	12/91	69r
Childbirth, normal delivery, hospital charge	birth	2891.00	12/91	69r
Childbirth, normal delivery, physician charge	birth	1623.00	12/91	69r
Dentist's fee, adult teeth cleaning and periodic oral exam	visit	44.30	12/94	2c
Doctor's fee, routine exam, established patient	visit	33.20	12/94	2c
Drugs, expenditures	year	248	91	81r
Health care, total expenditures	year	1336	91	81r
Health insurance expenditures	year	550	91	81r
Hospital care, semiprivate room	day	325.67	12/94	2c
Insurance premium, family medical care	month	382.63	1/95	41s
Medical services expenditures	year	457	91	81r
Medical supplies expenditures	year	82	91	81r
Household Goods				
Appl. repair, service call, wash mach	min. lab. chg.	29.60	12/94	2c
Floor coverings, expenditures	year	105	91	81r
Furniture, expenditures	year	291	91	81r
Household equipment, misc. expenditures	year	341	91	81r
Household expenditures, miscellaneous	year	162	91	81r

Values are in dollars or fractions of dollars. In the column headed *Ref*, references are shown to sources. Each reference is followed by a letter. These refer to the geographical level for which data were reported: s = State, r = Region, and c = City or metro. The abbreviation *ex* is used to mean *except* or *excluding*; *exp* stands for *expenditures*. For other abbreviations and further explanations, please see the Introduction.

Lincoln, NE - continued

Item	Per	Value	Date	Ref.
Household Goods				
Household furnishings and equipment, expenditures	year	1042	91	81r
Household operations expenditures	year	365	91	81r
Household textiles, expenditures	year	101	91	81r
Housekeeping supplies, expenditures	year	390	91	81r
Laundry and cleaning supplies, expenditures	year	110	91	81r
Laundry detergent, Tide Ultra, Bold, or Cheer	42 oz.	3.50	12/94	2c
Postage and stationery, expenditures	year	115	91	81r
Tissues, facial, Kleenex brand	175	0.95	12/94	2c
Housing				
Housing, ACCRA Index		78.50	12/94	2c
Add garage/carport		8,479	3/95	74r
Add room(s)		21,347	3/95	74r
Apartment condominium or co-op, median	unit	87100	12/94	62r
Bathroom addition, average cost	add	9734.00	3/95	13r
Bathroom remodeling, average cost	remod	6414.00	3/95	13r
Bedroom, master suite addition, average cost	add	27122.00	3/95	13r
Deck addition, average cost	add	6665.00	3/95	13r
Dwellings (owned), expenditures	year	2566	91	81r
Enclose porch/patio/breezeway		4,556	3/95	74r
Exterior remodeling, average cost	remod	15395.00	3/95	13r
Family room addition, average cost	add	27658.00	3/95	13r
Finish room in basement/attic		5,074	3/95	74r
Home, existing, single-family, median	unit	106500	12/94	62r
Home, existing, single-family, median	unit	77.60	12/94	62c
House payment, principal and interest, 25% down payment	mo.	592	12/94	2c
House, 1800 sq ft, 8000 sq ft lot, new, urban, utilities	total	96137	12/94	2c
Kitchen remodeling, major, average cost	remod	17084.00	3/95	13r
Kitchen remodeling, minor, average cost	remod	5804.00	3/95	13r
Maintenance, repairs, insurance, and other housing expenditures	year	484	91	81r
Mortgage interest and charges expenditures	year	1443	91	81r
Mtge. rate, incl. points and orig. fee, 30-year conv. fixed or ARM	mo.	9.23	12/94	2c
Office, home addition, average cost	add	8121.00	3/95	13r
Princ. & int., mortgage, median-price exist. sing.-family home	mo.	515	12/94	62r
Property taxes expenditures	year	639	91	81r
Redesign, restructure more than half of home's interior		9,114	3/95	74r
Rent, apartment, 2 br., 1 1/2-2 baths, unfurnished, 950 sq ft, water	mo.	442	12/94	2c
Rental units expenditures	year	1200	91	81r
Sun-space addition, average cost	add	23768.00	3/95	13r
Wing addition, two-story, average cost	add	50410.00	3/95	13r
Insurance and Pensions				
Auto insurance, private passenger	year	494.85	12/94	71s
Insurance and pensions, personal, expenditures	year	2408	91	81r
Insurance, life and other personal, expenditures	year	355	91	81r
Pensions and Social Security, expenditures	year	2053	91	81r
Legal Assistance				
Legal work, law firm associate	hour	90		10r
Legal work, law firm partner	hour	139		10r
Personal Goods				
Shampoo, Alberto VO5	15-oz.	1.15	12/94	2c
Toothpaste, Crest or Colgate	6-7 oz.	2.01	12/94	2c
Personal Services				
Dry cleaning, man's 2-pc. suit		6.16	12/94	2c
Haircut, man's barbershop, no styling		8.90	12/94	2c
Haircut, woman's shampoo, trim, blow-dry		22.80	12/94	2c
Personal services expenditures	year	203	91	81r

Lincoln, NE - continued

Item	Per	Value	Date	Ref.
Restaurant Food				
Chicken, fried, thigh and drumstick		2.49	12/94	2c
Dining expenditures, family	week	30.03	94	73r
Hamburger with cheese	1/4 lb.	1.98	12/94	2c
Pizza, Pizza Hut or Pizza Inn	12-13 in.	7.49	12/94	2c
Taxes				
Taxes, Federal income, expenditures	year	1756	91	81r
Taxes, personal, expenditures	year	2426	91	81r
Taxes, State and local income, expenditures	year	568	91	81r
Transportation				
Transportation, ACCRA Index		96.80	12/94	2c
Bus fare, up to 10 miles	one-way	0.79	12/94	2c
Cars and trucks purchased, new	year	891	91	81r
Cars and trucks purchased, used	year	1155	91	81r
Driver's learning permit fee	perm	3.00	1/94	84s
Driver's license fee	orig	15.00	1/94	84s
Driver's license fee, duplicate	lic	5.00	1/94	84s
Driver's license reinstatement fee, min.	susp	95.00	1/94	85s
Driver's license renewal fee	renew	15.00	1/94	84s
Identification card, nondriver	card	10.00	1/94	83s
Motorcycle learning permit fee	perm	3.00	1/94	84s
Motorcycle license fee	orig	15.00	1/94	84s
Motorcycle license fee, duplicate	lic	5.00	1/94	84s
Motorcycle license renewal fee	renew	15.00	1/94	84s
Public transportation expenditures	year	209	91	81r
Tire balance, computer or spin bal., front	wheel	6.82	12/94	2c
Transportation expenditures, total	year	4792	91	81r
Vehicle finance charges	year	300	91	81r
Vehicle insurance expenditures	year	485	91	81r
Vehicle maintenance and repairs expenditures	year	534	91	81r
Vehicle purchases	year	2068	91	81r
Vehicle rental, leases, licenses, etc. expenditures	year	197	91	81r
Vehicles purchased, other than cars and trucks	year	22	91	81r
Utilities				
Utilities, ACCRA Index		92.00	12/94	2c
Electricity expenditures	year	668	91	81r
Electricity, (part.), other, 1800 sq. ft., new home	mo.	68.48	12/94	2c
Utilities, fuels, and public services, total expenditures	year	1838	91	81r
Water and other public services, expenditures	year	167	91	81r
Weddings				
Bridal attendants' gowns	event	750	10/93	76r
Bridal gown	event	852	10/93	76r
Bridal headpiece and veil	event	167	10/93	76r
Bride's wedding band	event	708	10/93	76r
Clergy	event	224	10/93	76r
Engagement ring	event	2756	10/93	76r
Flowers	event	863	10/93	76r
Formal wear for groom	event	106	10/93	76r
Groom's attendants' formal wear	event	530	10/93	76r
Groom's wedding band	event	402	10/93	76r
Music	event	600	10/93	76r
Photography	event	1088	10/93	76r
Shoes for bride	event	50	10/93	76r
Videography	event	483	10/93	76r
Wedding invitations and announcements	event	342	10/93	76r
Wedding reception	event	7000	10/93	76r

Values are in dollars or fractions of dollars. In the column headed *Ref*, references are shown to sources. Each reference is followed by a letter. These refer to the geographical level for which data were reported: s=State, r=Region, and c=City or metro. The abbreviation *ex* is used to mean *except* or *excluding*; *exp* stands for expenditures. For other abbreviations and further explanations, please see the Introduction.

Lincoln County, OR

Item	Per	Value	Date	Ref.
Composite, ACCRA index		107.10	12/94	2c
Alcoholic Beverages				
Beer, Miller Lite, Bud, 12-oz., ex deposit	6	4.13	12/94	2c
J & B Scotch	750-ml.	20.95	12/94	2c
Wine, Gallo Chablis blanc	1.5-lit	4.49	12/94	2c
Clothing				
Jeans, man's denim		28.66	12/94	2c
Shirt, man's dress shirt		31.99	12/94	2c
Undervest, boy's size 10-14, cotton	3	4.98	12/94	2c
Communications				
Newspaper subscription, dly. and Sun. delivery	month	11.50	12/94	2c
Telephone bill, family of four	month	18.82	12/94	2c
Energy and Fuels				
Energy, combined forms, 1800 sq. ft.	mo.	86.69	12/94	2c
Energy, exc. electricity, 1800 sq. ft.	mo.	37.41	12/94	2c
Gas, reg unlead, taxes inc., cash, self-service	gal	1.34	12/94	2c
Entertainment				
Bowling, evening rate	game	2.10	12/94	2c
Monopoly game, Parker Brothers', No. 9	game	11.92	12/94	2c
Movie	adm	5.00	12/94	2c
Tennis balls, yellow, Wilson or Penn, 3	can	2.39	12/94	2c
Groceries				
Groceries, ACCRA Index		107.20	12/94	2c
Baby food, strained vegetables, lowest price	4-4.5 oz.	0.34	12/94	2c
Bananas	lb.	0.44	12/94	2c
Beef or hamburger, ground	lb.	1.42	12/94	2c
Bread, white	24-oz.	0.67	12/94	2c
Cheese, Kraft grated Parmesan	8-oz.	3.66	12/94	2c
Chicken, whole fryer	lb.	0.91	12/94	2c
Cigarettes, Winston, Kings	carton	17.80	12/94	2c
Coffee, vacuum-packed	13 oz.	3.92	12/94	2c
Corn Flakes, Kellogg's or Post Toasties	18 oz.	2.68	12/94	2c
Corn, frozen, whole kernel, lowest price	10 oz.	0.76	12/94	2c
Eggs, Grade A large	dozen	0.98	12/94	2c
Lettuce, iceberg	head	0.69	12/94	2c
Margarine, Blue Bonnet or Parkay cubes	lb.	0.86	12/94	2c
Milk, whole	1/2 gal.	1.40	12/94	2c
Orange juice, Minute Maid frozen	12-oz.	1.35	12/94	2c
Peaches, halves or slices, Hunt's, Del Monte, or Libby's	29-oz.	1.65	12/94	2c
Peas, sweet, Del Monte or Green Giant	15-17 oz.	0.74	12/94	2c
Potatoes, white or red	10-lb. sack	1.72	12/94	2c
Sausage, Jimmy Dean, 100% pork	lb.	3.62	12/94	2c
Shortening, vegetable, Crisco	3-lb.	2.53	12/94	2c
Soft drink, Coca Cola, ex deposit	2 lit	1.45	12/94	2c
Steak, t-bone	lb.	3.99	12/94	2c
Sugar, cane or beet	4 lbs.	1.19	12/94	2c
Tomatoes, Hunt's or Del Monte	14.5 oz.	0.83	12/94	2c
Tuna, chunk, light, oil-packed	6.125-6.5 oz.	0.86	12/94	2c
Goods and Services				
Miscellaneous goods and services, ACCRA Index		100.50	12/94	2c
Health Care				
Health care, ACCRA Index		116.80	12/94	2c
Antibiotic ointment, Polysporin	1.5 oz.	3.96	12/94	2c
Dentist's fee, adult teeth cleaning and periodic oral exam	visit	71.80	12/94	2c
Doctor's fee, routine exam, established patient	visit	40.10	12/94	2c
Hospital care, semiprivate room	day	472.00	12/94	2c

Lincoln County, OR - continued

Item	Per	Value	Date	Ref.
Household Goods				
Appl. repair, service call, wash mach	min. lab. chg.	35.67	12/94	2c
Laundry detergent, Tide Ultra, Bold, or Cheer	42 oz.	4.01	12/94	2c
Tissues, facial, Kleenex brand	175	1.29	12/94	2c
Housing				
Housing, ACCRA Index		119.70	12/94	2c
House payment, principal and interest, 25% down payment	mo.	951	12/94	2c
House, 1800 sq ft, 8000 sq ft lot, new, urban, utilities	total	155833	12/94	2c
Mtge. rate, incl. points and orig. fee, 30-year conv. fixed or ARM	mo.	9.13	12/94	2c
Rent, apartment, 2 br., 1 1/2-2 baths, unfurnished, 950 sq ft, water	mo.	534	12/94	2c
Personal Goods				
Shampoo, Alberto VO5	15-oz.	1.34	12/94	2c
Toothpaste, Crest or Colgate	6-7 oz.	2.29	12/94	2c
Personal Services				
Dry cleaning, man's 2-pc. suit		7.33	12/94	2c
Haircut, man's barbershop, no styling		10.57	12/94	2c
Haircut, woman's shampoo, trim, blow-dry		17.33	12/94	2c
Restaurant Food				
Chicken, fried, thigh and drumstick		2.30	12/94	2c
Hamburger with cheese	1/4 lb.	1.74	12/94	2c
Pizza, Pizza Hut or Pizza Inn	12-13 in.	6.75	12/94	2c
Transportation				
Transportation, ACCRA Index		109.20	12/94	2c
Tire balance, computer or spin bal., front	wheel	6.45	12/94	2c
Utilities				
Utilities, ACCRA Index		79.80	12/94	2c
Electricity, (part.), other, 1800 sq. ft., new home	mo.	49.28	12/94	2c

Little Rock, AR

Item	Per	Value	Date	Ref.
Composite, ACCRA index		87.20	12/94	2c
Alcoholic Beverages				
Beer, Miller Lite, Bud, 12-oz., ex deposit	6	3.81	12/94	2c
J & B Scotch	750-ml.	15.88	12/94	2c
Wine, Gallo Chablis blanc	1.5-lit	4.95	12/94	2c
Appliances				
Appliances (major), expenditures	year	153	91	81r
Average annual exp.				
Food, health care, personal goods, services	year	27020	91	81r
Charity				
Cash contributions, expenditures	year	839	91	81r
Clothing				
Apparel, men and boys, total expenditures	year	380	91	81r
Apparel, women and girls, total expenditures	year	660	91	81r
Footwear, expenditures	year	193	91	81r
Jeans, man's denim		26.79	12/94	2c
Shirt, man's dress shirt		27.63	12/94	2c
Undervest, boy's size 10-14, cotton	3	3.43	12/94	2c
Communications				
Long-distance telephone rate, day, addl. min., 1-10 mi.	min.	0.08	12/93	9s
Long-distance telephone rate, day, initial min., 1-10 mi.	min.	0.10	12/93	9s
Newspaper subscription, dly. and Sun. delivery	month	8.25	12/94	2c
Phone line, single, business, field visit	inst	84.00	12/93	9s

Values are in dollars or fractions of dollars. In the column headed Ref, references are shown to sources. Each reference is followed by a letter. These refer to the geographical level for which data were reported: s=State, r=Region, and c=City or metro. The abbreviation ex is used to mean except or excluding; exp stands for expenditures. For other abbreviations and further explanations, please see the Introduction.

Little Rock, AR - continued

Item	Per	Value	Date	Ref.
Communications				
Phone line, single, business, no field visit	inst	84.00	12/93	9s
Phone line, single, residence, field visit	inst	39.70	12/93	9s
Phone line, single, residence, no field visit	inst	39.70	12/93	9s
Telephone bill, family of four	month	23.63	12/94	2c
Telephone service, expenditures	year	616	91	81r
Telephone, residential, flat rate	mo.	15.31	12/93	8c
Credit Cards				
Fee, conventional credit card, bal. carried	year	31.66	1/95	96c
Education				
Board, 4-year private college/university	year	1801	8/94	80s
Board, 4-year public college/university	year	1774	8/94	80s
Education, total expenditures	year	319	91	81r
Room, 4-year private college/university	year	1349	8/94	80s
Room, 4-year public college/university	year	1752	8/94	80s
Total cost, 4-year private college/university	year	8866	8/94	80s
Total cost, 4-year public college/university	year	5334	8/94	80s
Tuition, 2-year public college/university, in-state	year	833	8/94	80s
Tuition, 4-year private college/university, in-state	year	5716	8/94	80s
Tuition, 4-year public college/university, in-state	year	1808	8/94	80s
Energy and Fuels				
Energy, combined forms, 1800 sq. ft.	mo.	139.61	12/94	2c
Energy, exc. electricity, 1800 sq. ft.	mo.	42.57	12/94	2c
Fuel oil and other fuels, expenditures	year	56	91	81r
Gas, cooking, 10 therms	month	10.05	2/94	65c
Gas, cooking, 30 therms	month	19.64	2/94	65c
Gas, cooking, 50 therms	month	29.24	2/94	65c
Gas, heating, winter, 100 therms	month	53.23	2/94	65c
Gas, heating, winter, average use	month	79.14	2/94	65c
Gas, natural, expenditures	year	150	91	81r
Gas, reg unlead, taxes inc., cash, self-service	gal	1.10	12/94	2c
Gasoline and motor oil purchased	year	1152	91	81r
Gasoline, unleaded midgrade	gallon	1.21	4/93	82r
Gasoline, unleaded premium	gallon	1.30	4/93	82r
Gasoline, unleaded regular	gallon	1.10	4/93	82r
Entertainment				
Bowling, evening rate	game	2.15	12/94	2c
Concert ticket, Pearl Jam group	perf	20.00	94	50r
Entertainment, total expenditures	year	1266	91	81r
Fees and admissions, expenditures	year	306	91	81r
Monopoly game, Parker Brothers', No. 9	game	8.37	12/94	2c
Movie	adm	5.20	12/94	2c
Pets, toys, playground equipment, expenditures	year	271	91	81r
Reading, expenditures	year	131	91	81r
Televisions, radios, and sound equipment, expenditures	year	439	91	81r
Tennis balls, yellow, Wilson or Penn, 3	can	1.98	12/94	2c
Funerals				
Burial, immediate, container provided by funeral home		1574.60	1/95	54r
Cards, acknowledgment		22.24	1/95	54r
Casket, minimum alternative		239.41	1/95	54r
Cosmetology, hair care, etc.		91.04	1/95	54r
Cremation, direct, container provided by funeral home		1085.15	1/95	54r
Embalming		281.30	1/95	54r
Funeral, funeral home		323.04	1/95	54r
Funeral, other facility		327.58	1/95	54r
Graveside service		355.19	1/95	54r
Hearse, local		141.89	1/95	54r
Limousine, local		99.40	1/95	54r
Memorial service		284.67	1/95	54r
Service charge, professional, nondeclinable		904.06	1/95	54r
Visitation and viewing		187.04	1/95	54r

Little Rock, AR - continued

Item	Per	Value	Date	Ref.
Groceries				
Groceries, ACCRA Index		91.20	12/94	2c
Apples, Red Delicious	lb.	0.73	12/94	82r
Baby food, strained vegetables, lowest price	4-4.5 oz.	0.23	12/94	2c
Bacon, sliced	lb.	1.67	12/94	82r
Bananas	lb.	0.49	12/94	2c
Bananas	lb.	0.42	12/94	82r
Beef or hamburger, ground	lb.	0.90	12/94	2c
Beef purchases	year	213	91	81r
Beverage purchases, alcoholic	year	249	91	81r
Beverage purchases, nonalcoholic	year	207	91	81r
Bologna, all beef or mixed	lb.	2.27	12/94	82r
Bread, white	24-oz.	0.51	12/94	2c
Bread, white, pan	lb.	0.68	12/94	82r
Cabbage	lb.	0.42	12/94	82r
Carrots, short trimmed and topped	lb.	0.53	12/94	82r
Cereals and bakery products purchases	year	345	91	81r
Cereals and cereals products purchases	year	127	91	81r
Cheddar cheese, natural	lb.	3.58	12/94	82r
Cheese, Kraft grated Parmesan	8-oz.	3.61	12/94	2c
Chicken breast, bone-in	lb.	1.71	12/94	82r
Chicken, fresh, whole	lb.	0.78	12/94	82r
Chicken, whole fryer	lb.	0.70	12/94	2c
Chuck roast, USDA choice, boneless	lb.	2.26	12/94	82r
Cigarettes, Winston, Kings	carton	17.75	12/94	2c
Coffee, vacuum-packed	13 oz.	2.39	12/94	2c
Corn Flakes, Kellogg's or Post Toasties	18 oz.	2.51	12/94	2c
Corn, frozen, whole kernel, lowest price	10 oz.	0.86	12/94	2c
Crackers, soda, salted	lb.	1.27	12/94	82r
Cucumbers	lb.	0.65	12/94	82r
Dairy products (other) purchases	year	141	91	81r
Eggs, Grade A large	dozen	0.75	12/94	2c
Eggs, Grade A large	dozen	0.87	12/94	82r
Fish and seafood purchases	year	72	91	81r
Flour, white, all purpose	lb.	0.23	12/94	82r
Food purchases, food eaten at home	year	2381	91	81r
Foods purchased away from home, not prepared by consumer	year	1696	91	81r
Frankfurters, all meat or all beef	lb.	1.74	12/94	82r
Fruits and vegetables purchases	year	380	91	81r
Grapefruit	lb.	0.45	12/94	82r
Grapes, Thompson seedless	lb.	2.30	12/94	82r
Ground beef, 100% beef	lb.	1.37	12/94	82r
Ground chuck, 100% beef	lb.	1.97	12/94	82r
Ham, boneless, exc. canned	lb.	2.54	12/94	82r
Ice cream, prepackaged, bulk, regular	1/2 gal.	2.47	12/94	82r
Lemons	lb.	1.02	12/94	82r
Lettuce, iceberg	lb.	0.96	12/94	82r
Lettuce, iceberg	head	0.76	12/94	2c
Margarine, Blue Bonnet or Parkay cubes	lb.	0.55	12/94	2c
Margarine, stick	lb.	0.77	12/94	82r
Meats, poultry, fish, and eggs purchases	year	655	91	81r
Milk and cream (fresh) purchases	year	130	91	81r
Milk, whole	1/2 gal.	1.52	12/94	2c
Orange juice, frozen concentrate 12-oz. can	16 oz.	1.36	12/94	82r
Orange juice, Minute Maid frozen	12-oz.	1.28	12/94	2c
Oranges, Navel	lb.	0.54	12/94	82r
Peaches, halves or slices, Hunt's, Del Monte, or Libby's	29-oz.	1.17	12/94	2c
Pears, Anjou	lb.	0.81	12/94	82r
Peas, sweet, Del Monte or Green Giant	15-17 oz.	0.68	12/94	2c
Pork chops, center cut, bone-in	lb.	3.07	12/94	82r
Pork purchases	year	142	91	81r
Potato chips	16-oz.	3.15	12/94	82r
Potatoes, frozen, French fried	lb.	0.82	12/94	82r
Potatoes, white	lb.	0.34	12/94	82r
Potatoes, white or red	10-lb. sack	2.46	12/94	2c
Rice, white, long grain, uncooked	lb.	0.48	12/94	82r

Values are in dollars or fractions of dollars. In the column headed *Ref*, references are shown to sources. Each reference is followed by a letter. These refer to the geographical level for which data were reported: s = State, r = Region, and c = City or metro. The abbreviation *ex* is used to mean *except* or *excluding*; *exp* stands for *expenditures*. For other abbreviations and further explanations, please see the Introduction.

Little Rock, AR - continued

Item	Per	Value	Date	Ref.
Groceries				
Round roast, USDA choice, boneless	lb.	2.91	12/94	82r
Sausage, fresh	lb.	1.82	12/94	82r
Sausage, Jimmy Dean, 100% pork	lb.	2.13	12/94	2c
Shortening, vegetable oil blends	lb.	0.75	12/94	82r
Shortening, vegetable, Crisco	3-lb.	2.54	12/94	2c
Soft drink, Coca Cola, ex deposit	2 lit	1.03	12/94	2c
Spaghetti and macaroni	lb.	0.87	12/94	82r
Steak, rib eye, USDA choice, boneless	lb.	6.85	12/94	82r
Steak, round, graded & ungraded, exc. USDA prime & choice	lb.	2.96	12/94	82r
Steak, round, USDA choice, boneless	lb.	3.17	12/94	82r
Steak, sirloin, USDA choice, boneless	lb.	4.12	12/94	82r
Steak, t-bone	lb.	5.75	12/94	2c
Steak, T-bone, USDA choice, bone-in	lb.	5.63	12/94	82r
Sugar and other sweets, eaten at home, expenditures	year	93	91	81r
Sugar, cane or beet	4 lbs.	1.30	12/94	2c
Sugar, white, all sizes	lb.	0.39	12/94	82r
Tobacco products and smoking supplies, total expenditures	year	286	91	81r
Tomatoes, field grown	lb.	1.36	12/94	82r
Tomatoes, Hunt's or Del Monte	14.5 oz.	0.49	12/94	2c
Tuna, chunk, light	lb.	1.94	12/94	82r
Tuna, chunk, light, oil-packed	6.125-6.5 oz.	0.62	12/94	2c
Turkey, frozen, whole	lb.	0.96	12/94	82r
Yogurt, natural, fruit flavored	8 oz.	0.58	12/94	82r
Goods and Services				
Miscellaneous goods and services, ACCRA Index		84.60	12/94	2c
Health Care				
Health care, ACCRA Index		78.40	12/94	2c
Adenosine, emergency room	treat	100.00	95	23r
Antibiotic ointment, Polysporin	1.5 oz.	4.35	12/94	2c
Bladder tap, superpubic, infant, emergency room	treat	119.00	95	23r
Blood analysis, emergency room	treat	25.00	95	23r
Blood tests, abdominal pain, emergency room	treat	25.00	95	23r
Burn dressing, emergency room	treat	266.00	95	23r
Cardiology interpretation, emergency room	treat	26.00	95	23r
Chest X-ray, emergency room	treat	78.00	95	23r
Childbirth, Cesarean delivery, hospital charge	birth	5462.00	12/91	69r
Childbirth, Cesarean delivery, physician charge	birth	2228.00	12/91	69r
Childbirth, normal delivery, hospital charge	birth	2943.00	12/91	69r
Childbirth, normal delivery, physician charge	birth	1619.00	12/91	69r
Defibrillation pads, emergency room	treat	6.00	95	23r
Dentist's fee, adult teeth cleaning and periodic oral exam	visit	39.20	12/94	2c
Doctor's fee, routine exam, established patient	visit	34.20	12/94	2c
Drugs, expenditures	year	297	91	81r
Gastric tube insertion, nasal, emergency room	treat	25.00	95	23r
Health care, total expenditures	year	1600	91	81r
Health insurance expenditures	year	637	91	81r
Heart monitor, emergency room	treat	40.00	95	23r
Hospital care, semiprivate room	day	221.80	12/94	2c
Insurance premium, family medical care	month	326.03	1/95	41s
Intravenous fluids, emergency room	treat	130.00	95	23r
Intravenous fluids, emergency room	liter	26.00	95	23r
Intravenous line, central, emergency room	treat	342.00	95	23r
Liver function tests, abdominal pain, emergency room	treat	26.00	95	23r
Medical care charges, total, emergency room, third-degree burns	treat	2101.00	95	23r
Medical care charges, total, emergency, infant with fever	treat	628.00	95	23r

Little Rock, AR - continued

Item	Per	Value	Date	Ref.
Health Care - continued				
Medical services expenditures	year	573	91	81r
Medical supplies expenditures	year	93	91	81r
Morphine, emergency room	treat	34.00	95	23r
Nursing care and facilities charges, emergency room	treat	252.00	95	23r
Nursing care and facilities charges, emergency, infant with fever	treat	252.00	95	23r
Nursing care and facilities charges, emergency, third-degree burns	treat	861.00	95	23r
Physician's charges, emergency, infant with fever	treat	212.00	95	23r
Physician's charges, emergency, third-degree burns	treat	372.00	95	23r
Physician's fee, emergency room	treat	372.00	95	23r
Physician's fee, general practitioner	visit	51.20	12/93	60r
Surgery, open-heart	proc	42374.00	1/93	14r
Ultrasound, abdominal, emergency room	treat	276.00	95	23r
Urinalysis, emergency room	treat	20.00	95	23r
Urinalysis, infant, emergency room	treat	20.00	95	23r
X-rays, emergency room	treat	78.00	95	23r
Household Goods				
Appl. repair, service call, wash mach	min. lab. chg.	27.20	12/94	2c
Floor coverings, expenditures	year	48	91	81r
Furniture, expenditures	year	280	91	81r
Household equipment, misc. expenditures	year	342	91	81r
Household expenditures, miscellaneous	year	256	91	81r
Household furnishings and equipment, expenditures	year	988	91	81r
Household operations expenditures	year	468	91	81r
Household textiles, expenditures	year	95	91	81r
Housekeeping supplies, expenditures	year	380	91	81r
Laundry and cleaning supplies, expenditures	year	109	91	81r
Laundry detergent, Tide Ultra, Bold, or Cheer	42 oz.	3.55	12/94	2c
Postage and stationery, expenditures	year	105	91	81r
Tissues, facial, Kleenex brand	175	1.06	12/94	2c
Housing				
Housing, ACCRA Index		76.10	12/94	2c
Add garage/carport		6,980	3/95	74r
Add room(s)		11,403	3/95	74r
Apartment condominium or co-op, median	unit	68600	12/94	62r
Dwellings (owned), expenditures	year	2428	91	81r
Enclose porch/patio/breezeway		4,572	3/95	74r
Finish room in basement/attic		3,794	3/95	74r
Home, existing, single-family, median	unit	120200	12/94	62r
Home, existing, single-family, median	unit	76.80	12/94	62c
Home, single family, median	home	91,000	4/94	11c
House payment, principal and interest, 25% down payment	mo.	575	12/94	2c
House, 1800 sq ft, 8000 sq ft lot, new, urban, utilities	total	93500	12/94	2c
Maintenance, repairs, insurance, and other housing expenditures	year	531	91	81r
Mortgage interest and charges expenditures	year	1506	91	81r
Mtge. rate, incl. points and orig. fee, 30-year conv. fixed or ARM	mo.	9.21	12/94	2c
Princ. & int., mortgage, median-price exist. sing.-family home	mo.	540	12/94	62r
Property taxes expenditures	year	391	91	81r
Redesign, restructure more than half of home's interior		17,641	3/95	74r
Rent, apartment, 2 br., 1 1/2-2 baths, unfurnished, 950 sq ft, water	mo.	425	12/94	2c
Rental units expenditures	year	1264	91	81r
Insurance and Pensions				
Auto insurance, private passenger	year	565.35	12/94	71s
Insurance and pensions, personal, expenditures	year	2395	91	81r

Values are in dollars or fractions of dollars. In the column headed *Ref*, references are shown to sources. Each reference is followed by a letter. These refer to the geographical level for which data were reported: s=State, r=Region, and c=City or metro. The abbreviation *ex* is used to mean *except* or *excluding*; *exp* stands for expenditures. For other abbreviations and further explanations, please see the Introduction.

Little Rock, AR - continued

Item	Per	Value	Date	Ref.
Insurance and Pensions				
Insurance, life and other personal, expenditures	year	368	91	81r
Pensions and Social Security, expenditures	year	2027	91	81r
Personal Goods				
Shampoo, Alberto VO5	15-oz.	1.15	12/94	2c
Toothpaste, Crest or Colgate	6-7 oz.	2.03	12/94	2c
Personal Services				
Dry cleaning, man's 2-pc. suit		5.20	12/94	2c
Haircut, man's barbershop, no styling		9.30	12/94	2c
Haircut, woman's shampoo, trim, blow-dry		19.80	12/94	2c
Personal services expenditures	year	212	91	81r
Restaurant Food				
Chicken, fried, thigh and drumstick		1.99	12/94	2c
Dining expenditures, family	week	33.83	94	73r
Hamburger with cheese	1/4 lb.	1.00	12/94	2c
Pizza, Pizza Hut or Pizza Inn	12-13 in.	6.29	12/94	2c
Taxes				
Tax rate, residential property, month	$100	0.97	1/92	79c
Taxes, Federal income, expenditures	year	2275	91	81r
Taxes, personal, expenditures	year	2715	91	81r
Taxes, State and local income, expenditures	year	365	91	81r
Transportation				
Transportation, ACCRA Index		97.10	12/94	2c
Cars and trucks purchased, new	year	1306	91	81r
Cars and trucks purchased, used	year	942	91	81r
Driver's license fee	orig	14.00	1/94	84s
Driver's license fee, duplicate	lic	5.00	1/94	84s
Driver's license renewal fee	renew	14.00	1/94	84s
Identification card, nondriver	card	5.00	1/94	83s
Motorcycle license fee	orig	4.00	1/94	84s
Motorcycle license fee, duplicate	lic	5.00	1/94	84s
Public transportation expenditures	year	249	91	81r
Tire balance, computer or spin bal., front	wheel	6.47	12/94	2c
Transportation expenditures, total	year	5307	91	81r
Vehicle finance charges	year	346	91	81r
Vehicle insurance expenditures	year	544	91	81r
Vehicle maintenance and repairs expenditures	year	600	91	81r
Vehicle purchases	year	2275	91	81r
Vehicle rental, leases, licenses, etc. expenditures	year	141	91	81r
Vehicles purchased, other than cars and trucks	year	27	91	81r
Utilities				
Utilities, ACCRA Index		124.00	12/94	2c
Electricity expenditures	year	950	91	81r
Electricity, (part.), other, 1800 sq. ft., new home	mo.	97.04	12/94	2c
Electricity, summer, 250 KWh	month	32.56	8/93	64c
Electricity, summer, 500 KWh	month	57.83	8/93	64c
Electricity, summer, 750 KWh	month	83.08	8/93	64c
Electricity, summer, 1000 KWh	month	108.35	8/93	64c
Utilities, fuels, and public services, total expenditures	year	2000	91	81r
Water and other public services, expenditures	year	227	91	81r
Weddings				
Bridal attendants' gowns	event	750	10/93	76r
Bridal gown	event	852	10/93	76r
Bridal headpiece and veil	event	167	10/93	76r
Bride's wedding band	event	708	10/93	76r
Clergy	event	224	10/93	76r
Engagement ring	event	2756	10/93	76r
Flowers	event	863	10/93	76r
Formal wear for groom	event	106	10/93	76r
Groom's attendants' formal wear	event	530	10/93	76r
Groom's wedding band	event	402	10/93	76r

Little Rock, AR - continued

Item	Per	Value	Date	Ref.
Weddings - continued				
Music	event	600	10/93	76r
Photography	event	1088	10/93	76r
Shoes for bride	event	50	10/93	76r
Videography	event	483	10/93	76r
Wedding invitations and announcements	event	342	10/93	76r
Wedding reception	event	7000	10/93	76r

Logan, UT

Item	Per	Value	Date	Ref.
Composite, ACCRA index		101.80	12/94	2c
Alcoholic Beverages				
Beer, Miller Lite, Bud, 12-oz., ex deposit	6	4.09	12/94	2c
J & B Scotch	750-ml.	19.95	12/94	2c
Wine, Gallo Chablis blanc	1.5-lit	4.95	12/94	2c
Clothing				
Jeans, man's denim		34.19	12/94	2c
Shirt, man's dress shirt		34.12	12/94	2c
Undervest, boy's size 10-14, cotton	3	3.36	12/94	2c
Communications				
Newspaper subscription, dly. and Sun. delivery	month	10.50	12/94	2c
Telephone bill, family of four	month	16.11	12/94	2c
Telephone, business, connection charges, touch tone	inst	53.13	10/91	25c
Telephone, business, key system line, touch tone	month	32.79	10/91	25c
Telephone, business, PBX line, touch tone	month	33.27	10/91	25c
Telephone, business, single ln., touch tone	month	28.51	10/91	25c
Telephone, business, touch tone, inside wiring maintenance plan	month	0.79	10/91	25c
Telephone, residential, flat rate	mo.	7.98	12/93	8c
Energy and Fuels				
Energy, combined forms, 1800 sq. ft.	mo.	96.08	12/94	2c
Energy, exc. electricity, 1800 sq. ft.	mo.	44.43	12/94	2c
Gas, reg unlead, taxes inc., cash, self-service	gal	1.20	12/94	2c
Entertainment				
Bowling, evening rate	game	1.95	12/94	2c
Monopoly game, Parker Brothers', No. 9	game	11.34	12/94	2c
Movie	adm	5.08	12/94	2c
Tennis balls, yellow, Wilson or Penn, 3	can	1.98	12/94	2c
Groceries				
Groceries, ACCRA Index		103.10	12/94	2c
Baby food, strained vegetables, lowest price	4-4.5 oz.	0.36	12/94	2c
Bananas	lb.	0.41	12/94	2c
Beef or hamburger, ground	lb.	1.33	12/94	2c
Bread, white	24-oz.	0.89	12/94	2c
Cheese, Kraft grated Parmesan	8-oz.	3.74	12/94	2c
Chicken, whole fryer	lb.	0.86	12/94	2c
Cigarettes, Winston, Kings	carton	16.99	12/94	2c
Coffee, vacuum-packed	13 oz.	3.82	12/94	2c
Corn Flakes, Kellogg's or Post Toasties	18 oz.	2.42	12/94	2c
Corn, frozen, whole kernel, lowest price	10 oz.	0.66	12/94	2c
Eggs, Grade A large	dozen	0.79	12/94	2c
Lettuce, iceberg	head	0.44	12/94	2c
Margarine, Blue Bonnet or Parkay cubes	lb.	0.58	12/94	2c
Milk, whole	1/2 gal.	1.38	12/94	2c
Orange juice, Minute Maid frozen	12-oz.	1.26	12/94	2c
Peaches, halves or slices, Hunt's, Del Monte, or Libby's	29-oz.	1.40	12/94	2c
Peas, sweet, Del Monte or Green Giant	15-17 oz.	0.61	12/94	2c
Potatoes, white or red	10-lb. sack	1.47	12/94	2c
Sausage, Jimmy Dean, 100% pork	lb.	3.13	12/94	2c

Values are in dollars or fractions of dollars. In the column headed *Ref*, references are shown to sources. Each reference is followed by a letter. These refer to the geographical level for which data were reported: s=State, r=Region, and c=City or metro. The abbreviation *ex* is used to mean *except* or *excluding*; *exp* stands for expenditures. For other abbreviations and further explanations, please see the Introduction.

Logan, UT - continued

Item	Per	Value	Date	Ref.
Groceries				
Shortening, vegetable, Crisco	3-lb.	2.57	12/94	2c
Soft drink, Coca Cola, ex deposit	2 lit	1.29	12/94	2c
Steak, t-bone	lb.	4.23	12/94	2c
Sugar, cane or beet	4 lbs.	1.43	12/94	2c
Tomatoes, Hunt's or Del Monte	14.5 oz.	0.69	12/94	2c
Tuna, chunk, light, oil-packed	6.125-6.5 oz.	0.81	12/94	2c
Goods and Services				
Miscellaneous goods and services, ACCRA Index		100.80	12/94	2c
Health Care				
Health care, ACCRA Index		98.30	12/94	2c
Antibiotic ointment, Polysporin	1.5 oz.	4.02	12/94	2c
Dentist's fee, adult teeth cleaning and periodic oral exam	visit	50.60	12/94	2c
Doctor's fee, routine exam, established patient	visit	38.50	12/94	2c
Hospital care, semiprivate room	day	411.00	12/94	2c
Household Goods				
Appl. repair, service call, wash mach	min. lab. chg.	37.39	12/94	2c
Laundry detergent, Tide Ultra, Bold, or Cheer	42 oz.	3.92	12/94	2c
Tissues, facial, Kleenex brand	175	0.98	12/94	2c
Housing				
Housing, ACCRA Index		107.70	12/94	2c
House payment, principal and interest, 25% down payment	mo.	856	12/94	2c
House, 1800 sq ft, 8000 sq ft lot, new, urban, utilities	total	137880	12/94	2c
Mtge. rate, incl. points and orig. fee, 30-year conv. fixed or ARM	mo.	9.33	12/94	2c
Rent, apartment, 2 br., 1 1/2-2 baths, unfurnished, 950 sq ft, water	mo.	479	12/94	2c
Personal Goods				
Shampoo, Alberto VO5	15-oz.	1.37	12/94	2c
Toothpaste, Crest or Colgate	6-7 oz.	2.23	12/94	2c
Personal Services				
Dry cleaning, man's 2-pc. suit		7.15	12/94	2c
Haircut, man's barbershop, no styling		9.20	12/94	2c
Haircut, woman's shampoo, trim, blow-dry		16.25	12/94	2c
Restaurant Food				
Chicken, fried, thigh and drumstick		1.99	12/94	2c
Hamburger with cheese	1/4 lb.	1.99	12/94	2c
Pizza, Pizza Hut or Pizza Inn	12-13 in.	7.49	12/94	2c
Transportation				
Transportation, ACCRA Index		102.20	12/94	2c
Bus fare, one-way	trip	Free	12/95	1c
Tire balance, computer or spin bal., front	wheel	6.50	12/94	2c
Utilities				
Utilities, ACCRA Index		85.20	12/94	2c
Electricity, (part.), other, 1800 sq. ft., new home	mo.	51.65	12/94	2c

Longmont, CO

Item	Per	Value	Date	Ref.
Composite, ACCRA index		108.30	12/94	2c
Alcoholic Beverages				
Beer, Miller Lite, Bud, 12-oz., ex deposit	6	4.16	12/94	2c
J & B Scotch	750-ml.	17.99	12/94	2c
Wine, Gallo Chablis blanc	1.5-lit	4.16	12/94	2c

Longmont, CO - continued

Item	Per	Value	Date	Ref.
Clothing				
Jeans, man's denim		29.99	12/94	2c
Shirt, man's dress shirt		29.50	12/94	2c
Undervest, boy's size 10-14, cotton	3	4.09	12/94	2c
Communications				
Newspaper subscription, dly. and Sun. delivery	month	8.00	12/94	2c
Telephone bill, family of four	month	21.21	12/94	2c
Telephone, residential, flat rate	mo.	14.68	12/93	8c
Energy and Fuels				
Energy, combined forms, 1800 sq. ft.	mo.	73.84	12/94	2c
Energy, exc. electricity, 1800 sq. ft.	mo.	37.33	12/94	2c
Gas, reg unlead, taxes inc., cash, self-service	gal	1.12	12/94	2c
Entertainment				
Bowling, evening rate	game	2.23	12/94	2c
Monopoly game, Parker Brothers', No. 9	game	11.24	12/94	2c
Movie	adm	5.50	12/94	2c
Tennis balls, yellow, Wilson or Penn, 3	can	2.46	12/94	2c
Groceries				
Groceries, ACCRA Index		101.10	12/94	2c
Baby food, strained vegetables, lowest price	4-4.5 oz.	0.29	12/94	2c
Bananas	lb.	0.56	12/94	2c
Beef or hamburger, ground	lb.	1.09	12/94	2c
Bread, white	24-oz.	0.59	12/94	2c
Cheese, Kraft grated Parmesan	8-oz.	2.98	12/94	2c
Chicken, whole fryer	lb.	0.76	12/94	2c
Cigarettes, Winston, Kings	carton	14.99	12/94	2c
Coffee, vacuum-packed	13 oz.	3.89	12/94	2c
Corn Flakes, Kellogg's or Post Toasties	18 oz.	2.70	12/94	2c
Corn, frozen, whole kernel, lowest price	10 oz.	0.81	12/94	2c
Eggs, Grade A large	dozen	0.89	12/94	2c
Lettuce, iceberg	head	0.93	12/94	2c
Margarine, Blue Bonnet or Parkay cubes	lb.	0.65	12/94	2c
Milk, whole	1/2 gal.	1.78	12/94	2c
Orange juice, Minute Maid frozen	12-oz.	1.26	12/94	2c
Peaches, halves or slices, Hunt's, Del Monte, or Libby's	29-oz.	1.48	12/94	2c
Peas, sweet, Del Monte or Green Giant	15-17 oz.	0.70	12/94	2c
Potatoes, white or red	10-lb. sack	2.12	12/94	2c
Sausage, Jimmy Dean, 100% pork	lb.	3.54	12/94	2c
Shortening, vegetable, Crisco	3-lb.	2.80	12/94	2c
Soft drink, Coca Cola, ex deposit	2 lit	0.86	12/94	2c
Steak, t-bone	lb.	5.22	12/94	2c
Sugar, cane or beet	4 lbs.	1.61	12/94	2c
Tomatoes, Hunt's or Del Monte	14.5 oz.	0.84	12/94	2c
Tuna, chunk, light, oil-packed	6.125-6.5 oz.	0.80	12/94	2c
Goods and Services				
Miscellaneous goods and services, ACCRA Index		98.60	12/94	2c
Health Care				
Health care, ACCRA Index		116.10	12/94	2c
Antibiotic ointment, Polysporin	1.5 oz.	3.86	12/94	2c
Dentist's fee, adult teeth cleaning and periodic oral exam	visit	68.33	12/94	2c
Doctor's fee, routine exam, established patient	visit	42.76	12/94	2c
Hospital care, semiprivate room	day	465.00	12/94	2c
Household Goods				
Appl. repair, service call, wash mach	min. lab. chg.	34.33	12/94	2c

Values are in dollars or fractions of dollars. In the column headed *Ref*, references are shown to sources. Each reference is followed by a letter. These refer to the geographical level for which data were reported: s = State, r = Region, and c = City or metro. The abbreviation *ex* is used to mean *except* or *excluding*; *exp* stands for expenditures. For other abbreviations and further explanations, please see the Introduction.

Longmont, CO - continued

Item	Per	Value	Date	Ref.
Household Goods				
Laundry detergent, Tide Ultra, Bold, or Cheer	42 oz.	3.30	12/94	2c
Tissues, facial, Kleenex brand	175	0.96	12/94	2c
Housing				
Housing, ACCRA Index		135.40	12/94	2c
House payment, principal and interest, 25% down payment	mo.	1044	12/94	2c
House, 1800 sq ft, 8000 sq ft lot, new, urban, utilities	total	171250	12/94	2c
Mtge. rate, incl. points and orig. fee, 30-year conv. fixed or ARM	mo.	9.11	12/94	2c
Rent, apartment, 2 br., 1 1/2-2 baths, unfurnished, 950 sq ft, water	mo.	697	12/94	2c
Personal Goods				
Shampoo, Alberto VO5	15-oz.	1.27	12/94	2c
Toothpaste, Crest or Colgate	6-7 oz.	2.09	12/94	2c
Personal Services				
Dry cleaning, man's 2-pc. suit		7.21	12/94	2c
Haircut, man's barbershop, no styling		9.25	12/94	2c
Haircut, woman's shampoo, trim, blow-dry		19.50	12/94	2c
Restaurant Food				
Chicken, fried, thigh and drumstick		1.99	12/94	2c
Hamburger with cheese	1/4 lb.	1.99	12/94	2c
Pizza, Pizza Hut or Pizza Inn	12-13 in.	7.48	12/94	2c
Transportation				
Transportation, ACCRA Index		100.20	12/94	2c
Bus fare, one-way	trip	0.35	12/95	1c
Tire balance, computer or spin bal., front	wheel	6.79	12/94	2c
Utilities				
Utilities, ACCRA Index		71.60	12/94	2c
Electricity, (part.), other, 1800 sq. ft., new home	mo.	36.51	12/94	2c

Longview, TX

Item	Per	Value	Date	Ref.
Composite, ACCRA index		90.70	12/94	2c
Alcoholic Beverages				
Beer, Miller Lite, Bud, 12-oz., ex deposit	6	3.92	12/94	2c
J & B Scotch	750-ml.	16.29	12/94	2c
Wine, Gallo Chablis blanc	1.5-lit	5.29	12/94	2c
Appliances				
Appliances (major), expenditures	year	153	91	81r
Average annual exp.				
Food, health care, personal goods, services	year	27020	91	81r
Charity				
Cash contributions, expenditures	year	839	91	81r
Clothing				
Apparel, men and boys, total expenditures	year	380	91	81r
Apparel, women and girls, total expenditures	year	660	91	81r
Footwear, expenditures	year	193	91	81r
Jeans, man's denim		31.59	12/94	2c
Shirt, man's dress shirt		28.62	12/94	2c
Undervest, boy's size 10-14, cotton	3	3.10	12/94	2c
Communications				
Long-distance telephone rate, day, addl. min., 1-10 mi.	min.	0.08	12/93	9s
Long-distance telephone rate, day, initial min., 1-10 mi.	min.	0.10	12/93	9s
Newspaper subscription, dly. and Sun. delivery	month	8.25	12/94	2c
Phone line, single, business, field visit	inst	71.90	12/93	9s
Phone line, single, business, no field visit	inst	57.30	12/93	9s
Phone line, single, residence, field visit	inst	52.95	12/93	9s

Longview, TX - continued

Item	Per	Value	Date	Ref.
Communications - continued				
Phone line, single, residence, no field visit	inst	38.35	12/93	9s
Telephone bill, family of four	month	17.51	12/94	2c
Telephone service, expenditures	year	616	91	81r
Telephone, residential, flat rate	mo.	8.80	12/93	8c
Education				
Board, 4-year private college/university	year	2084	8/94	80s
Board, 4-year public college/university	year	1675	8/94	80s
Education, total expenditures	year	319	91	81r
Room, 4-year private college/university	year	1840	8/94	80s
Room, 4-year public college/university	year	1756	8/94	80s
Total cost, 4-year private college/university	year	11876	8/94	80s
Total cost, 4-year public college/university	year	4935	8/94	80s
Tuition, 2-year public college/university, in-state	year	625	8/94	80s
Tuition, 4-year private college/university, in-state	year	7952	8/94	80s
Tuition, 4-year public college/university, in-state	year	1503	8/94	80s
Energy and Fuels				
Energy, combined forms, 1800 sq. ft.	mo.	93.68	12/94	2c
Energy, exc. electricity, 1800 sq. ft.	mo.	29.36	12/94	2c
Fuel oil and other fuels, expenditures	year	56	91	81r
Gas, natural, expenditures	year	150	91	81r
Gas, reg unlead, taxes inc., cash, self-service	gal	1.12	12/94	2c
Gasoline and motor oil purchased	year	1152	91	81r
Gasoline, unleaded midgrade	gallon	1.21	4/93	82r
Gasoline, unleaded premium	gallon	1.30	4/93	82r
Gasoline, unleaded regular	gallon	1.10	4/93	82r
Entertainment				
Bowling, evening rate	game	2.25	12/94	2c
Concert ticket, Pearl Jam group	perf	20.00	94	50r
Entertainment, total expenditures	year	1266	91	81r
Fees and admissions, expenditures	year	306	91	81r
Monopoly game, Parker Brothers', No. 9	game	11.00	12/94	2c
Movie	adm	5.67	12/94	2c
Pets, toys, playground equipment, expenditures	year	271	91	81r
Reading, expenditures	year	131	91	81r
Televisions, radios, and sound equipment, expenditures	year	439	91	81r
Tennis balls, yellow, Wilson or Penn, 3	can	2.27	12/94	2c
Funerals				
Burial, immediate, container provided by funeral home		1574.60	1/95	54r
Cards, acknowledgment		22.24	1/95	54r
Casket, minimum alternative		239.41	1/95	54r
Cosmetology, hair care, etc.		91.04	1/95	54r
Cremation, direct, container provided by funeral home		1085.15	1/95	54r
Embalming		281.30	1/95	54r
Funeral, funeral home		323.04	1/95	54r
Funeral, other facility		327.58	1/95	54r
Graveside service		355.19	1/95	54r
Hearse, local		141.89	1/95	54r
Limousine, local		99.40	1/95	54r
Memorial service		284.67	1/95	54r
Service charge, professional, nondeclinable		904.06	1/95	54r
Visitation and viewing		187.04	1/95	54r
Groceries				
Groceries, ACCRA Index		96.80	12/94	2c
Apples, Red Delicious	lb.	0.73	12/94	82r
Baby food, strained vegetables, lowest price	4-4.5 oz.	0.26	12/94	2c
Bacon, sliced	lb.	1.67	12/94	82r
Bananas	lb.	0.36	12/94	2c
Bananas	lb.	0.42	12/94	82r
Beef or hamburger, ground	lb.	1.77	12/94	2c
Beef purchases	year	213	91	81r

Values are in dollars or fractions of dollars. In the column headed *Ref*, references are shown to sources. Each reference is followed by a letter. These refer to the geographical level for which data were reported: s = State, r = Region, and c = City or metro. The abbreviation *ex* is used to mean *except* or *excluding*; *exp* stands for *expenditures*. For other abbreviations and further explanations, please see the Introduction.

Longview, TX - continued

Item	Per	Value	Date	Ref.
Groceries				
Beverage purchases, alcoholic	year	249	91	81r
Beverage purchases, nonalcoholic	year	207	91	81r
Bologna, all beef or mixed	lb.	2.27	12/94	82r
Bread, white	24-oz.	0.74		2c
Bread, white, pan	lb.	0.68	12/94	82r
Cabbage	lb.	0.42	12/94	82r
Carrots, short trimmed and topped	lb.	0.53	12/94	82r
Cereals and bakery products purchases	year	345	91	81r
Cereals and cereals products purchases	year	127	91	81r
Cheddar cheese, natural	lb.	3.58	12/94	82r
Cheese, Kraft grated Parmesan	8-oz.	3.30		2c
Chicken breast, bone-in	lb.	1.71	12/94	82r
Chicken, fresh, whole	lb.	0.78	12/94	82r
Chicken, whole fryer	lb.	0.71	12/94	2c
Chuck roast, USDA choice, boneless	lb.	2.26	12/94	82r
Cigarettes, Winston, Kings	carton	17.11	12/94	2c
Coffee, vacuum-packed	13 oz.	3.34	12/94	2c
Corn Flakes, Kellogg's or Post Toasties	18 oz.	2.51	12/94	2c
Corn, frozen, whole kernel, lowest price	10 oz.	0.70	12/94	2c
Crackers, soda, salted	lb.	1.27	12/94	2c
Cucumbers	lb.	0.65	12/94	82r
Dairy products (other) purchases	year	141	91	81r
Eggs, Grade A large	dozen	0.79	12/94	2c
Eggs, Grade A large	dozen	0.87	12/94	82r
Fish and seafood purchases	year	72	91	81r
Flour, white, all purpose	lb.	0.23	12/94	82r
Food purchases, food eaten at home	year	2381	91	81r
Foods purchased away from home, not prepared by consumer	year	1696	91	81r
Frankfurters, all meat or all beef	lb.	1.74	12/94	82r
Fruits and vegetables purchases	year	380	91	81r
Grapefruit	lb.	0.45	12/94	82r
Grapes, Thompson seedless	lb.	2.30	12/94	82r
Ground beef, 100% beef	lb.	1.37	12/94	82r
Ground chuck, 100% beef	lb.	1.97	12/94	82r
Ham, boneless, exc. canned	lb.	2.54	12/94	82r
Ice cream, prepackaged, bulk, regular	1/2 gal.	2.47	12/94	82r
Lemons	lb.	1.02	12/94	82r
Lettuce, iceberg	lb.	0.96	12/94	82r
Lettuce, iceberg	head	0.87	12/94	2c
Margarine, Blue Bonnet or Parkay cubes	lb.	0.61	12/94	2c
Margarine, stick	lb.	0.77	12/94	82r
Meats, poultry, fish, and eggs purchases	year	655	91	81r
Milk and cream (fresh) purchases	year	130	91	81r
Milk, whole	1/2 gal.	1.41	12/94	2c
Orange juice, frozen concentrate 12-oz. can	16 oz.	1.36	12/94	82r
Orange juice, Minute Maid frozen	12-oz.	1.16	12/94	2c
Oranges, Navel	lb.	0.54	12/94	82r
Peaches, halves or slices, Hunt's, Del Monte, or Libby's	29-oz.	1.34	12/94	2c
Pears, Anjou	lb.	0.81	12/94	82r
Peas, sweet, Del Monte or Green Giant	15-17 oz.	0.56	12/94	2c
Pork chops, center cut, bone-in	lb.	3.07	12/94	82r
Pork purchases	year	142	91	81r
Potato chips	16-oz.	3.15	12/94	82r
Potatoes, frozen, French fried	lb.	0.82	12/94	82r
Potatoes, white	lb.	0.34	12/94	82r
Potatoes, white or red	10-lb. sack	1.87	12/94	2c
Rice, white, long grain, uncooked	lb.	0.48	12/94	82r
Round roast, USDA choice, boneless	lb.	2.91	12/94	82r
Sausage, fresh	lb.	1.82	12/94	82r
Sausage, Jimmy Dean, 100% pork	lb.	2.35	12/94	2c
Shortening, vegetable oil blends	lb.	0.75	12/94	82r
Shortening, vegetable, Crisco	3-lb.	2.13	12/94	2c
Soft drink, Coca Cola, ex deposit	2 lit	1.08	12/94	2c
Spaghetti and macaroni	lb.	0.87	12/94	82r
Steak, rib eye, USDA choice, boneless	lb.	6.85	12/94	82r

Longview, TX - continued

Item	Per	Value	Date	Ref.
Groceries - continued				
Steak, round, graded & ungraded, exc. USDA prime & choice	lb.	2.96	12/94	82r
Steak, round, USDA choice, boneless	lb.	3.17	12/94	82r
Steak, sirloin, USDA choice, boneless	lb.	4.12	12/94	82r
Steak, t-bone	lb.	5.15	12/94	2c
Steak, T-bone, USDA choice, bone-in	lb.	5.63	12/94	82r
Sugar and other sweets, eaten at home, expenditures	year	93	91	81r
Sugar, cane or beet	4 lbs.	1.53	12/94	2c
Sugar, white, all sizes	lb.	0.39	12/94	82r
Tobacco products and smoking supplies, total expenditures	year	286	91	81r
Tomatoes, field grown	lb.	1.36	12/94	82r
Tomatoes, Hunt's or Del Monte	14.5 oz.	0.70	12/94	2c
Tuna, chunk, light	lb.	1.94	12/94	82r
Tuna, chunk, light, oil-packed	6.125-6.5 oz.	0.66	12/94	2c
Turkey, frozen, whole	lb.	0.96	12/94	82r
Yogurt, natural, fruit flavored	8 oz.	0.58	12/94	82r
Goods and Services				
Miscellaneous goods and services, ACCRA Index		97.50	12/94	2c
Health Care				
Health care, ACCRA Index		91.30	12/94	2c
Adenosine, emergency room	treat	100.00	95	23r
Antibiotic ointment, Polysporin	1.5 oz.	3.22	12/94	2c
Bladder tap, superpubic, infant, emergency room	treat	119.00	95	23r
Blood analysis, emergency room	treat	25.00	95	23r
Blood tests, abdominal pain, emergency room	treat	25.00	95	23r
Burn dressing, emergency room	treat	266.00	95	23r
Cardiology interpretation, emergency room	treat	26.00	95	23r
Chest X-ray, emergency room	treat	78.00	95	23r
Childbirth, Cesarean delivery, hospital charge	birth	5462.00	12/91	69r
Childbirth, Cesarean delivery, physician charge	birth	2228.00	12/91	69r
Childbirth, normal delivery, hospital charge	birth	2943.00	12/91	69r
Childbirth, normal delivery, physician charge	birth	1619.00	12/91	69r
Defibrillation pads, emergency room	treat	6.00	95	23r
Dentist's fee, adult teeth cleaning and periodic oral exam	visit	40.80	12/94	2c
Doctor's fee, routine exam, established patient	visit	49.00	12/94	2c
Drugs, expenditures	year	297	91	81r
Gastric tube insertion, nasal, emergency room	treat	25.00	95	23r
Health care, total expenditures	year	1600	91	81r
Health insurance expenditures	year	637	91	81r
Heart monitor, emergency room	treat	40.00	95	23r
Hospital care, semiprivate room	day	268.00	12/94	2c
Insurance premium, family medical care	month	389.25	1/95	41s
Intravenous fluids, emergency room	treat	130.00	95	23r
Intravenous fluids, emergency room	liter	26.00	95	23r
Intravenous line, central, emergency room	treat	342.00	95	23r
Liver function tests, abdominal pain, emergency room	treat	26.00	95	23r
Medical care charges, total, emergency room, third-degree burns	treat	2101.00	95	23r
Medical care charges, total, emergency, infant with fever	treat	628.00	95	23r
Medical services expenditures	year	573	91	81r
Medical supplies expenditures	year	93	91	81r
Morphine, emergency room	treat	34.00	95	23r
Nursing care and facilities charges, emergency room	treat	252.00	95	23r
Nursing care and facilities charges, emergency, infant with fever	treat	252.00	95	23r

Values are in dollars or fractions of dollars. In the column headed *Ref*, references are shown to sources. Each reference is followed by a letter. These refer to the geographical level for which data were reported: s = State, r = Region, and c = City or metro. The abbreviation *ex* is used to mean *except* or *excluding*; *exp* stands for *expenditures*. For other abbreviations and further explanations, please see the Introduction.

Longview, TX - continued

Item	Per	Value	Date	Ref.
Health Care				
Nursing care and facilities charges, emergency, third-degree burns	treat	861.00	95	23r
Physician's charges, emergency, infant with fever	treat	212.00	95	23r
Physician's charges, emergency, third-degree burns	treat	372.00	95	23r
Physician's fee, emergency room	treat	372.00	95	23r
Physician's fee, general practitioner	visit	51.20	12/93	60r
Surgery, open-heart	proc	42374.00	1/93	14r
Ultrasound, abdominal, emergency room	treat	276.00	95	23r
Urinalysis, emergency room	treat	20.00	95	23r
Urinalysis, infant, emergency room	treat	20.00	95	23r
X-rays, emergency room	treat	78.00	95	23r
Household Goods				
Appl. repair, service call, wash mach	min. lab. chg.	36.15	12/94	2c
Floor coverings, expenditures	year	48	91	81r
Furniture, expenditures	year	280	91	81r
Household equipment, misc. expenditures	year	342	91	81r
Household expenditures, miscellaneous	year	256	91	81r
Household furnishings and equipment, expenditures	year	988	91	81r
Household operations expenditures	year	468	91	81r
Household textiles, expenditures	year	95	91	81r
Housekeeping supplies, expenditures	year	380	91	81r
Laundry and cleaning supplies, expenditures	year	109	91	81r
Laundry detergent, Tide Ultra, Bold, or Cheer	42 oz.	3.58	12/94	2c
Postage and stationery, expenditures	year	105	91	81r
Tissues, facial, Kleenex brand	175	1.07	12/94	2c
Housing				
Housing, ACCRA Index		80.00	12/94	2c
Add garage/carport		6,980	3/95	74r
Add room(s)		11,403	3/95	74r
Apartment condominium or co-op, median	unit	68600	12/94	62r
Dwellings (owned), expenditures	year	2428	91	81r
Enclose porch/patio/breezeway		4,572	3/95	74r
Finish room in basement/attic		3,794	3/95	74r
Home, existing, single-family, median	unit	120200	12/94	62r
House payment, principal and interest, 25% down payment	mo.	607	12/94	2c
House, 1800 sq ft, 8000 sq ft lot, new, urban, utilities	total	97500	12/94	2c
Maintenance, repairs, insurance, and other housing expenditures	year	531	91	81r
Mortgage interest and charges expenditures	year	1506	91	81r
Mtge. rate, incl. points and orig. fee, 30-year conv. fixed or ARM	mo.	9.35	12/94	2c
Princ. & int., mortgage, median-price exist. sing.-family home	mo.	540	12/94	62r
Property taxes expenditures	year	391	91	81r
Redesign, restructure more than half of home's interior		17,641	3/95	74r
Rent, apartment, 2 br., 1 1/2-2 baths, unfurnished, 950 sq ft, water	mo.	439	12/94	2c
Rental units expenditures	year	1264	91	81r
Insurance and Pensions				
Auto insurance, private passenger	year	785.78	12/94	71s
Insurance and pensions, personal, expenditures	year	2395	91	81r
Insurance, life and other personal, expenditures	year	368	91	81r
Pensions and Social Security, expenditures	year	2027	91	81r
Personal Goods				
Shampoo, Alberto VO5	15-oz.	0.98	12/94	2c
Toothpaste, Crest or Colgate	6-7 oz.	1.97	12/94	2c

Longview, TX - continued

Item	Per	Value	Date	Ref.
Personal Services				
Dry cleaning, man's 2-pc. suit		5.83	12/94	2c
Haircut, man's barbershop, no styling		8.20	12/94	2c
Haircut, woman's shampoo, trim, blow-dry		23.75	12/94	2c
Personal services expenditures	year	212	91	81r
Restaurant Food				
Chicken, fried, thigh and drumstick		2.07	12/94	2c
Dining expenditures, family	week	33.83	94	73r
Hamburger with cheese	1/4 lb.	1.75	12/94	2c
Pizza, Pizza Hut or Pizza Inn	12-13 in.	8.60	12/94	2c
Taxes				
Tax, cigarettes	year	584.00	10/93	43s
Taxes, Federal income, expenditures	year	2275	91	81r
Taxes, personal, expenditures	year	2715	91	81r
Taxes, State and local income, expenditures	year	365	91	81r
Transportation				
Transportation, ACCRA Index		93.70	12/94	2c
Cars and trucks purchased, new	year	1306	91	81r
Cars and trucks purchased, used	year	942	91	81r
Driver's learning permit fee	perm	5.00	1/94	84s
Driver's license fee	orig	16.00	1/94	84s
Driver's license fee, duplicate	lic	10.00	1/94	84s
Driver's license reinstatement fee, min.	susp	50.00	1/94	85s
Driver's license renewal fee	renew	16.00	1/94	84s
Identification card, nondriver	card	10.00	1/94	83s
Motorcycle learning permit fee	perm	5.00	1/94	84s
Motorcycle license fee	orig	16.00	1/94	84s
Motorcycle license fee, duplicate	lic	10.00	1/94	84s
Motorcycle license renewal fee	renew	21.00	1/94	84s
Public transportation expenditures	year	249	91	81r
Tire balance, computer or spin bal., front	wheel	5.80	12/94	2c
Transportation expenditures, total	year	5307	91	81r
Vehicle finance charges	year	346	91	81r
Vehicle insurance expenditures	year	544	91	81r
Vehicle maintenance and repairs expenditures	year	600	91	81r
Vehicle purchases	year	2275	91	81r
Vehicle rental, leases, licenses, etc. expenditures	year	141	91	81r
Vehicles purchased, other than cars and trucks	year	27	91	81r
Utilities				
Utilities, ACCRA Index		84.30	12/94	2c
Electricity expenditures	year	950	91	81r
Electricity, (part.), other, 1800 sq. ft., new home	mo.	64.32	12/94	2c
Electricity, summer, 250 KWh	month	24.04	8/93	64c
Electricity, summer, 500 KWh	month	41.05	8/93	64c
Electricity, summer, 750 KWh	month	58.09	8/93	64c
Electricity, summer, 1000 KWh	month	75.11	8/93	64c
Utilities, fuels, and public services, total expenditures	year	2000	91	81r
Water and other public services, expenditures	year	227	91	81r
Weddings				
Bridal attendants' gowns	event	750	10/93	76r
Bridal gown	event	852	10/93	76r
Bridal headpiece and veil	event	167	10/93	76r
Bride's wedding band	event	708	10/93	76r
Clergy	event	224	10/93	76r
Engagement ring	event	2756	10/93	76r
Flowers	event	863	10/93	76r
Formal wear for groom	event	106	10/93	76r
Groom's attendants' formal wear	event	530	10/93	76r
Groom's wedding band	event	402	10/93	76r
Music	event	600	10/93	76r
Photography	event	1088	10/93	76r
Shoes for bride	event	50	10/93	76r
Videography	event	483	10/93	76r

Values are in dollars or fractions of dollars. In the column headed *Ref*, references are shown to sources. Each reference is followed by a letter. These refer to the geographical level for which data were reported: s=State, r=Region, and c=City or metro. The abbreviation *ex* is used to mean *except* or *excluding*; *exp* stands for expenditures. For other abbreviations and further explanations, please see the Introduction.

Longview, TX - continued

Item	Per	Value	Date	Ref.
Weddings				
Wedding invitations and announcements	event	342	10/93	76r
Wedding reception	event	7000	10/93	76r

Lorain-Elyria, OH

Item	Per	Value	Date	Ref.
Appliances				
Appliances (major), expenditures	year	131	91	81r
Average annual exp.				
Food, health care, personal goods, services	year	25935	91	81r
Charity				
Cash contributions, expenditures	year	745	91	81r
Clothing				
Apparel, men and boys, total expenditures	year	332	91	81r
Apparel, women and girls, total expenditures	year	578	91	81r
Footwear, expenditures	year	164	91	81r
Communications				
Long-distance telephone rate, day, addl. min., 1-10 mi.	min.	0.16	12/93	9s
Long-distance telephone rate, day, initial min., 1-10 mi.	min.	0.32	12/93	9s
Phone line, single, business, field visit	inst	55.42	12/93	9s
Phone line, single, business, no field visit	inst	55.42	12/93	9s
Phone line, single, residence, field visit	inst	30.38	12/93	9s
Phone line, single, residence, no field visit	inst	30.38	12/93	9s
Telephone service, expenditures	year	547	91	81r
Education				
Board, 4-year private college/university	year	2241	8/94	80s
Board, 4-year public college/university	year	1625	8/94	80s
Education, total expenditures	year	394	91	81r
Room, 4-year private college/university	year	2118	8/94	80s
Room, 4-year public college/university	year	2103	8/94	80s
Total cost, 4-year private college/university	year	15444	8/94	80s
Total cost, 4-year public college/university	year	6987	8/94	80s
Tuition, 2-year public college/university, in-state	year	2076	8/94	80s
Tuition, 4-year private college/university, in-state	year	11085	8/94	80s
Tuition, 4-year public college/university, in-state	year	3259	8/94	80s
Energy and Fuels				
Fuel oil and other fuels, expenditures	year	83	91	81r
Gas, natural, expenditures	year	373	91	81r
Gasoline and motor oil purchased	year	1000	91	81r
Gasoline, unleaded midgrade	gallon	1.15	4/93	82r
Gasoline, unleaded premium	gallon	1.23	4/93	82r
Gasoline, unleaded regular	gallon	1.07	4/93	82r
Entertainment				
Entertainment, total expenditures	year	1356	91	81r
Fees and admissions, expenditures	year	347	91	81r
Pets, toys, playground equipment, expenditures	year	270	91	81r
Reading, expenditures	year	160	91	81r
Televisions, radios, and sound equipment, expenditures	year	433	91	81r
Funerals				
Burial, immediate, container provided by funeral home		1268.31	1/95	54r
Cards, acknowledgment		26.12	1/95	54r
Casket, minimum alternative		198.03	1/95	54r
Cosmetology, hair care, etc.		122.19	1/95	54r
Cremation, direct, container provided by funeral home		977.81	1/95	54r
Embalming		334.00	1/95	54r
Funeral, funeral home		321.16	1/95	54r
Funeral, other facility		317.73	1/95	54r
Graveside service		292.48	1/95	54r
Hearse, local		153.20	1/95	54r

Lorain-Elyria, OH - continued

Item	Per	Value	Date	Ref.
Funerals - continued				
Limousine, local		123.52	1/95	54r
Memorial service		356.30	1/95	54r
Service charge, professional, nondeclinable		968.24	1/95	54r
Visitation and viewing		332.66	1/95	54r
Groceries				
Apples, Red Delicious	lb.	0.68	12/94	82r
Bacon, sliced	lb.	1.88	12/94	82r
Bananas	lb.	0.41	12/94	82r
Beef purchases	year	197	91	81r
Beef, stew, boneless	lb.	2.52	12/94	82r
Beverage purchases, alcoholic	year	293	91	81r
Beverage purchases, nonalcoholic	year	203	91	81r
Bologna, all beef or mixed	lb.	2.12	12/94	82r
Bread, white, pan	lb.	0.76	12/94	82r
Cabbage	lb.	0.44	12/94	82r
Carrots, short trimmed and topped	lb.	0.44	12/94	82r
Cereals and bakery products purchases	year	347	91	81r
Cereals and cereals products purchases	year	119	91	81r
Cheddar cheese, natural	lb.	3.28	12/94	82r
Chicken breast, bone-in	lb.	1.61	12/94	82r
Chicken, fresh, whole	lb.	0.89	12/94	82r
Chuck roast, USDA choice, boneless	lb.	2.33	12/94	82r
Coffee, 100%, ground roast, all sizes	lb.	4.28	12/94	82r
Cookies, chocolate chip	lb.	2.72	12/94	82r
Dairy products (other) purchases	year	148	91	81r
Eggs, Grade A large	dozen	0.76	12/94	82r
Fish and seafood purchases	year	61	91	81r
Flour, white, all purpose	lb.	0.22	12/94	82r
Food purchases, food eaten at home	year	2313	91	81r
Foods purchased away from home, not prepared by consumer	year	1709	91	81r
Fruits and vegetables purchases	year	372	91	81r
Grapefruit	lb.	0.47	12/94	82r
Grapes, Thompson seedless	lb.	2.15	12/94	82r
Ground beef, 100% beef	lb.	1.37	12/94	82r
Ground chuck, 100% beef	lb.	1.81	12/94	82r
Ham, boneless, exc. canned	lb.	2.16	12/94	82r
Ice cream, prepackaged, bulk, regular	1/2 gal.	2.48	12/94	82r
Lemons	lb.	1.08	12/94	82r
Lettuce, iceberg	lb.	0.81	12/94	82r
Margarine, stick	lb.	0.81	12/94	82r
Meats, poultry, fish, and eggs purchases	year	591	91	81r
Milk and cream (fresh) purchases	year	132	91	81r
Orange juice, frozen concentrate 12-oz. can	16 oz.	1.41	12/94	82r
Oranges, Navel	lb.	0.56	12/94	82r
Peanut butter, creamy, all sizes	lb.	1.81	12/94	82r
Pork chops, center cut, bone-in	lb.	2.76	12/94	82r
Pork purchases	year	130	91	81r
Potato chips	16-oz.	2.81	12/94	82r
Potatoes, frozen, French fried	lb.	0.83	12/94	82r
Potatoes, white	lb.	0.28	12/94	82r
Round roast, USDA choice, boneless	lb.	2.90	12/94	82r
Shortening, vegetable oil blends	lb.	0.88	12/94	82r
Spaghetti and macaroni	lb.	0.78	12/94	82r
Steak, rib eye, USDA choice, boneless	lb.	6.15	12/94	82r
Steak, round, graded & ungraded, exc. USDA prime & choice	lb.	2.72	12/94	82r
Steak, round, USDA choice, boneless	lb.	3.02	12/94	82r
Steak, sirloin, USDA choice, boneless	lb.	3.85	12/94	82r
Steak, T-bone, USDA choice, bone-in	lb.	5.38	12/94	82r
Sugar and other sweets, eaten at home, expenditures	year	91	91	81r
Sugar, white, all sizes	lb.	0.36	12/94	82r
Tobacco products and smoking supplies, total expenditures	year	298	91	81r
Tomatoes, field grown	lb.	1.36	12/94	82r
Tuna, chunk, light	lb.	1.94	12/94	82r
Turkey, frozen, whole	lb.	0.96	12/94	82r
Yogurt, natural, fruit flavored	8 oz.	0.62	12/94	82r

Values are in dollars or fractions of dollars. In the column headed *Ref*, references are shown to sources. Each reference is followed by a letter. These refer to the geographical level for which data were reported: s=State, r=Region, and c=City or metro. The abbreviation *ex* is used to mean *except* or *excluding*; *exp* stands for expenditures. For other abbreviations and further explanations, please see the Introduction.

Lorain-Elyria, OH - continued

Item	Per	Value	Date	Ref.
Health Care				
Childbirth, Cesarean delivery, hospital charge	birth	5101.00	12/91	69r
Childbirth, Cesarean delivery, physician charge	birth	2234.00	12/91	69r
Childbirth, normal delivery, hospital charge	birth	2891.00	12/91	69r
Childbirth, normal delivery, physician charge	birth	1623.00	12/91	69r
Drugs, expenditures	year	248	91	81r
Health care, total expenditures	year	1336	91	81r
Health insurance expenditures	year	550	91	81r
Insurance premium, family medical care	month	350.73	1/95	41s
Medical services expenditures	year	457	91	81r
Medical supplies expenditures	year	82	91	81r
Household Goods				
Floor coverings, expenditures	year	105	91	81r
Furniture, expenditures	year	291	91	81r
Household equipment, misc. expenditures	year	341	91	81r
Household expenditures, miscellaneous	year	162	91	81r
Household furnishings and equipment, expenditures	year	1042	91	81r
Household operations expenditures	year	365	91	81r
Household textiles, expenditures	year	101	91	81r
Housekeeping supplies, expenditures	year	390	91	81r
Laundry and cleaning supplies, expenditures	year	110	91	81r
Postage and stationery, expenditures	year	115	91	81r
Housing				
Add garage/carport		8,479	3/95	74r
Add room(s)		21,347	3/95	74r
Apartment condominium or co-op, median	unit	87100	12/94	62r
Bathroom addition, average cost	add	9734.00	3/95	13r
Bathroom remodeling, average cost	remod	6414.00	3/95	13r
Bedroom, master suite addition, average cost	add	27122.00	3/95	13r
Deck addition, average cost	add	6665.00	3/95	13r
Dwellings (owned), expenditures	year	2566	91	81r
Enclose porch/patio/breezeway		4,556	3/95	74r
Exterior remodeling, average cost	remod	15395.00	3/95	13r
Family room addition, average cost	add	27658.00	3/95	13r
Finish room in basement/attic		5,074	3/95	74r
Home, existing, single-family, median	unit	106500	12/94	62r
Kitchen remodeling, major, average cost	remod	17084.00	3/95	13r
Kitchen remodeling, minor, average cost	remod	5804.00	3/95	13r
Maintenance, repairs, insurance, and other housing expenditures	year	484	91	81r
Mortgage interest and charges expenditures	year	1443	91	81r
Office, home addition, average cost	add	8121.00	3/95	13r
Princ. & int., mortgage, median-price exist. sing.-family home	mo.	515	12/94	62r
Property taxes expenditures	year	639	91	81r
Redesign, restructure more than half of home's interior		9,114	3/95	74r
Rental units expenditures	year	1200	91	81r
Sun-space addition, average cost	add	23768.00	3/95	13r
Wing addition, two-story, average cost	add	50410.00	3/95	13r
Insurance and Pensions				
Auto insurance, private passenger	year	550.52	12/94	71s
Insurance and pensions, personal, expenditures	year	2408	91	81r
Insurance, life and other personal, expenditures	year	355	91	81r
Pensions and Social Security, expenditures	year	2053	91	81r
Legal Assistance				
Legal work, law firm associate	hour	90		10r
Legal work, law firm partner	hour	139		10r
Personal Services				
Personal services expenditures	year	203	91	81r
Restaurant Food				
Dining expenditures, family	week	30.03	94	73r

Lorain-Elyria, OH - continued

Item	Per	Value	Date	Ref.
Taxes				
Taxes, Federal income, expenditures	year	1756	91	81r
Taxes, personal, expenditures	year	2426	91	81r
Taxes, State and local income, expenditures	year	568	91	81r
Transportation				
Cars and trucks purchased, new	year	891	91	81r
Cars and trucks purchased, used	year	1155	91	81r
Driver's learning permit fee	perm	3.00	1/94	84s
Driver's license fee	orig	5.00	1/94	84s
Driver's license fee, duplicate	lic	1.50	1/94	84s
Driver's license reinstatement fee, min.	susp	12.50-100.00	1/94	85s
Driver's license renewal fee	renew	5.00	1/94	84s
Identification card, nondriver	card	2.50	1/94	83s
Motorcycle learning permit fee	perm	3.00	1/94	84s
Motorcycle license fee	orig	5.00	1/94	84s
Motorcycle license fee, duplicate	lic	1.50	1/94	84s
Motorcycle license renewal fee	renew	5.00	1/94	84s
Public transportation expenditures	year	209	91	81r
Transportation expenditures, total	year	4792	91	81r
Vehicle finance charges	year	300	91	81r
Vehicle insurance expenditures	year	485	91	81r
Vehicle maintenance and repairs expenditures	year	534	91	81r
Vehicle purchases	year	2068	91	81r
Vehicle rental, leases, licenses, etc. expenditures	year	197	91	81r
Vehicles purchased, other than cars and trucks	year	22	91	81r
Utilities				
Electricity expenditures	year	668	91	81r
Utilities, fuels, and public services, total expenditures	year	1838	91	81r
Water and other public services, expenditures	year	167	91	81r
Weddings				
Bridal attendants' gowns	event	750	10/93	76r
Bridal gown	event	852	10/93	76r
Bridal headpiece and veil	event	167	10/93	76r
Bride's wedding band	event	708	10/93	76r
Clergy	event	224	10/93	76r
Engagement ring	event	2756	10/93	76r
Flowers	event	863	10/93	76r
Formal wear for groom	event	106	10/93	76r
Groom's attendants' formal wear	event	530	10/93	76r
Groom's wedding band	event	402	10/93	76r
Music	event	600	10/93	76r
Photography	event	1088	10/93	76r
Shoes for bride	event	50	10/93	76r
Videography	event	483	10/93	76r
Wedding invitations and announcements	event	342	10/93	76r
Wedding reception	event	7000	10/93	76r

Los Alamos, NM

Item	Per	Value	Date	Ref.
Composite, ACCRA index		122.00	12/94	2c
Alcoholic Beverages				
Beer, Miller Lite, Bud, 12-oz., ex deposit	6	3.94	12/94	2c
J & B Scotch	750-ml.	16.49	12/94	2c
Wine, Gallo Chablis blanc	1.5-lit	5.34	12/94	2c
Clothing				
Jeans, man's denim		28.98	12/94	2c
Shirt, man's dress shirt		32.98	12/94	2c
Undervest, boy's size 10-14, cotton	3	4.16	12/94	2c
Communications				
Newspaper subscription, dly. and Sun. delivery	month	10.25	12/94	2c
Telephone bill, family of four	month	19.78	12/94	2c

Values are in dollars or fractions of dollars. In the column headed *Ref*, references are shown to sources. Each reference is followed by a letter. These refer to the geographical level for which data were reported: s=State, r=Region, and c=City or metro. The abbreviation *ex* is used to mean *except* or *excluding*; *exp* stands for expenditures. For other abbreviations and further explanations, please see the Introduction.

Los Alamos, NM - continued

Item	Per	Value	Date	Ref.
Communications				
Telephone, residential, flat rate	mo.	13.91	12/93	8c
Energy and Fuels				
Energy, combined forms, 1800 sq. ft.	mo.	90.94	12/94	2c
Energy, exc. electricity, 1800 sq. ft.	mo.	34.38	12/94	2c
Gas, reg unlead, taxes inc., cash, self-service	gal	1.34	12/94	2c
Entertainment				
Bowling, evening rate	game	2.40	12/94	2c
Monopoly game, Parker Brothers', No. 9	game	12.99	12/94	2c
Movie	adm	5.75	12/94	2c
Tennis balls, yellow, Wilson or Penn, 3	can	3.58	12/94	2c
Groceries				
Groceries, ACCRA Index		109.50	12/94	2c
Baby food, strained vegetables, lowest price	4-4.5 oz.	0.34	12/94	2c
Bananas	lb.	0.59	12/94	2c
Beef or hamburger, ground	lb.	1.99	12/94	2c
Bread, white	24-oz.	0.69	12/94	2c
Cheese, Kraft grated Parmesan	8-oz.	4.02	12/94	2c
Chicken, whole fryer	lb.	0.78	12/94	2c
Cigarettes, Winston, Kings	carton	16.02	12/94	2c
Coffee, vacuum-packed	13 oz.	3.91	12/94	2c
Corn Flakes, Kellogg's or Post Toasties	18 oz.	2.68	12/94	2c
Corn, frozen, whole kernel, lowest price	10 oz.	0.82	12/94	2c
Eggs, Grade A large	dozen	1.16	12/94	2c
Lettuce, iceberg	head	0.99	12/94	2c
Margarine, Blue Bonnet or Parkay cubes	lb.	0.78	12/94	2c
Milk, whole	1/2 gal.	1.97	12/94	2c
Orange juice, Minute Maid frozen	12-oz.	1.28	12/94	2c
Peaches, halves or slices, Hunt's, Del Monte, or Libby's	29-oz.	1.36	12/94	2c
Peas, sweet, Del Monte or Green Giant	15-17 oz.	0.58	12/94	2c
Potatoes, white or red	10-lb. sack	1.99	12/94	2c
Sausage, Jimmy Dean, 100% pork	lb.	2.51	12/94	2c
Shortening, vegetable, Crisco	3-lb.	3.00	12/94	2c
Soft drink, Coca Cola, ex deposit	2 lit	1.25	12/94	2c
Steak, t-bone	lb.	4.39	12/94	2c
Sugar, cane or beet	4 lbs.	1.70	12/94	2c
Tomatoes, Hunt's or Del Monte	14.5 oz.	0.83	12/94	2c
Tuna, chunk, light, oil-packed	6.125-6.5 oz.	0.94	12/94	2c
Goods and Services				
Miscellaneous goods and services, ACCRA Index		107.50	12/94	2c
Health Care				
Health care, ACCRA Index		126.90	12/94	2c
Antibiotic ointment, Polysporin	1.5 oz.	4.84	12/94	2c
Dentist's fee, adult teeth cleaning and periodic oral exam	visit	66.50	12/94	2c
Doctor's fee, routine exam, established patient	visit	61.25	12/94	2c
Hospital care, semiprivate room	day	339.00	12/94	2c
Household Goods				
Appl. repair, service call, wash mach	min. lab. chg.	40.92	12/94	2c
Laundry detergent, Tide Ultra, Bold, or Cheer	42 oz.	3.40	12/94	2c
Tissues, facial, Kleenex brand	175	1.15	12/94	2c
Housing				
Housing, ACCRA Index		157.30	12/94	2c
House payment, principal and interest, 25% down payment	mo.	1250	12/94	2c

Los Alamos, NM - continued

Item	Per	Value	Date	Ref.
Housing - continued				
House, 1800 sq ft, 8000 sq ft lot, new, urban, utilities	total	204875	12/94	2c
Mtge. rate, incl. points and orig. fee, 30-year conv. fixed or ARM	mo.	9.12	12/94	2c
Rent, apartment, 2 br., 1 1/2-2 baths, unfurnished, 950 sq ft, water	mo.	702	12/94	2c
Personal Goods				
Shampoo, Alberto VO5	15-oz.	1.41	12/94	2c
Toothpaste, Crest or Colgate	6-7 oz.	2.47	12/94	2c
Personal Services				
Dry cleaning, man's 2-pc. suit		6.00	12/94	2c
Haircut, man's barbershop, no styling		8.33	12/94	2c
Haircut, woman's shampoo, trim, blow-dry		22.50	12/94	2c
Restaurant Food				
Chicken, fried, thigh and drumstick		2.09	12/94	2c
Hamburger with cheese	1/4 lb.	2.05	12/94	2c
Pizza, Pizza Hut or Pizza Inn	12-13 in.	7.99	12/94	2c
Transportation				
Transportation, ACCRA Index		118.30	12/94	2c
Tire balance, computer or spin bal., front	wheel	7.90	12/94	2c
Utilities				
Utilities, ACCRA Index		83.80	12/94	2c
Electricity, (part.), other, 1800 sq. ft., new home	mo.	56.56	12/94	2c

Los Angeles, CA

Item	Per	Value	Date	Ref.
Composite, ACCRA index		123.90	12/94	2c
Alcoholic Beverages				
Beer, Miller Lite, Bud, 12-oz., ex deposit	6	3.93	12/94	2c
J & B Scotch	750-ml.	16.44	12/94	2c
Wine, Gallo Chablis blanc	1.5-lit	4.37	12/94	2c
Appliances				
Appliances (major), expenditures	year	163	91	81c
Appliances (major), expenditures	year	160	91	81r
Average annual exp.				
Food, health care, personal goods, services	year	35673	91	81c
Food, health care, personal goods, services	year	32461	91	81r
Business				
Bank fee, bad check	check	11.05	12/93	5c
Dinner and tip, hotel, corporate rate	night	34.00	2/94	15c
Hotel room, corporate rate	night	104.00	2/94	15c
Charity				
Cash contributions, expenditures	year	827	91	81c
Cash contributions, expenditures	year	975	91	81r
Clothing				
Apparel, men and boys, total expenditures	year	618	91	81c
Apparel, men and boys, total expenditures	year	467	91	81r
Apparel, women and girls, total expenditures	year	970	91	81c
Apparel, women and girls, total expenditures	year	737	91	81r
Footwear, expenditures	year	419	91	81c
Footwear, expenditures	year	270	91	81r
Jeans, man's denim		32.99	12/94	2c
Shirt, man's dress shirt		36.90	12/94	2c
Undervest, boy's size 10-14, cotton	3	5.81	12/94	2c
Communications				
Long-distance telephone rate, day, addl. min., 1-10 mi.	min.	0.07	12/93	9s
Long-distance telephone rate, day, initial min., 1-10 mi.	min.	0.17	12/93	9s
Newspaper subscription, dly. and Sun. delivery	month	17.04	12/94	2c
Phone bill	month	62.33	93	37c

Values are in dollars or fractions of dollars. In the column headed *Ref*, references are shown to sources. Each reference is followed by a letter. These refer to the geographical level for which data were reported: s = State, r = Region, and c = City or metro. The abbreviation *ex* is used to mean *except* or *excluding*; *exp* stands for expenditures. For other abbreviations and further explanations, please see the Introduction.

Los Angeles, CA - continued

Item	Per	Value	Date	Ref.
Communications				
Phone line, single, business, field visit	inst	70.75	12/93	9s
Phone line, single, business, no field visit	inst	70.75	12/93	9s
Phone line, single, residence, field visit	inst	34.75	12/93	9s
Phone line, single, residence, no field visit	inst	34.75	12/93	9s
Telephone bill, family of four	month	12.59	12/94	2c
Telephone service, expenditures	year	748	91	81c
Telephone service, expenditures	year	611	91	81r
Telephone, residential, flat rate	mo.	8.35	12/93	8c
Education				
Board, 4-year private college/university	year	2945	8/94	80s
Board, 4-year public college/university	year	2321	8/94	80s
Education, total expenditures	year	547	91	81c
Education, total expenditures	year	375	91	81r
Room, 4-year private college/university	year	3094	8/94	80s
Room, 4-year public college/university	year	2812	8/94	80s
Student fee, university	year	21.00	93	18s
Total cost, 4-year private college/university	year	19321	8/94	80s
Total cost, 4-year public college/university	year	7511	8/94	80s
Tuition, 2-year public college/university, in-state	year	345	8/94	80s
Tuition, 4-year private college/university, in-state	year	13282	8/94	80s
Tuition, 4-year public college/university, in-state	year	2378	8/94	80s
Energy and Fuels				
Electricity	500 KWh	62.69	12/94	82c
Energy, combined forms, 1800 sq. ft.	mo.	95.24	12/94	2c
Energy, exc. electricity, 1800 sq. ft.	mo.	32.35	12/94	2c
Fuel oil and other fuels, expenditures	year	7	91	81c
Fuel oil and other fuels, expenditures	year	33	91	81r
Gas, cooking, 10 therms	month	8.38	2/94	65c
Gas, cooking, 30 therms	month	18.98	2/94	65c
Gas, cooking, 50 therms	month	29.61	2/94	65c
Gas, heating, winter, 100 therms	month	66.84	2/94	65c
Gas, heating, winter, average use	month	44.49	2/94	65c
Gas, natural, expenditures	year	291	91	81c
Gas, natural, expenditures	year	212	91	81r
Gas, piped	40 therms	24.71	12/94	82c
Gas, piped	100 therms	67.38	12/94	82c
Gas, piped	therm	0.68	12/94	82c
Gas, reg unlead, taxes inc., cash, self-service	gal	1.25	12/94	2c
Gasoline and motor oil purchased	year	1103	91	81c
Gasoline and motor oil purchased	year	1115	91	81r
Gasoline, unleaded midgrade	gallon	1.45	4/93	82c
Gasoline, unleaded midgrade	gallon	1.36	4/93	82r
Gasoline, unleaded premium	gallon	1.48	4/93	82c
Gasoline, unleaded premium	gallon	1.43	4/93	82r
Gasoline, unleaded regular	gallon	1.28	4/93	82c
Gasoline, unleaded regular	gallon	1.23	4/93	82r
Entertainment				
Bowling, evening rate	game	2.41	12/94	2c
Concert ticket, Pearl Jam group	perf	20.00	94	50r
Entertainment supplies, equipment, and services, misc. expenditures	year	715	91	81c
Entertainment, total expenditures	year	1896	91	81c
Entertainment, total expenditures	year	1853	91	81r
Fees and admissions, expenditures	year	410	91	81c
Fees and admissions, expenditures	year	482	91	81r
Monopoly game, Parker Brothers', No. 9	game	16.19	12/94	2c
Movie	adm	7.25	12/94	2c
Pets, toys, playground equipment, expenditures	year	282	91	81c
Pets, toys, playground equipment, expenditures	year	299	91	81r
Reading, expenditures	year	137	91	81c
Reading, expenditures	year	164	91	81r

Los Angeles, CA - continued

Item	Per	Value	Date	Ref.
Entertainment - continued				
Televisions, radios, and sound equipment, expenditures	year	488	91	81c
Televisions, radios, and sound equipment, expenditures	year	528	91	81r
Tennis balls, yellow, Wilson or Penn, 3	can	2.89	12/94	2c
Funerals				
Burial, immediate, container provided by funeral home		1382.70	1/95	54r
Cards, acknowledgment		21.87	1/95	54r
Casket, minimum alternative		128.54	1/95	54r
Cosmetology, hair care, etc.		119.69	1/95	54r
Cremation, direct, container provided by funeral home		1030.62	1/95	54r
Embalming		255.42	1/95	54r
Funeral, funeral home		437.38	1/95	54r
Funeral, other facility		444.46	1/95	54r
Graveside service		338.46	1/95	54r
Hearse, local		147.50	1/95	54r
Limousine, local		130.33	1/95	54r
Memorial service		553.16	1/95	54r
Service charge, professional, nondeclinable		859.15	1/95	54r
Visitation and viewing		93.23	1/95	54r
Groceries				
Groceries, ACCRA Index		114.30	12/94	2c
Apples, Red Delicious	lb.	0.72	12/94	82r
Baby food, strained vegetables, lowest price	4-4.5 oz.	0.37	12/94	2c
Bacon, sliced	lb.	1.73	12/94	82r
Bananas	lb.	0.53	12/94	2c
Bananas	lb.	0.52	12/94	82r
Bananas	pound	0.48	93	37c
Beef or hamburger, ground	lb.	1.55	12/94	2c
Beef purchases	year	260	91	81c
Beef purchases	year	241	91	81r
Beverage purchases, alcoholic	year	366	91	81c
Beverage purchases, alcoholic	year	328	91	81r
Beverage purchases, nonalcoholic	year	265	91	81c
Beverage purchases, nonalcoholic	year	234	91	81r
Bologna, all beef or mixed	lb.	2.33	12/94	82r
Bread, white	24-oz.	1.13	12/94	2c
Bread, white, pan	lb.	0.81	12/94	82r
Carrots, short trimmed and topped	lb.	0.43	12/94	82r
Cereals and bakery products purchases	year	438	91	81c
Cereals and bakery products purchases	year	392	91	81r
Cereals and cereal products purchases	year	155	91	81c
Cereals and cereals products purchases	year	139	91	81r
Cheese, Kraft grated Parmesan	8-oz.	3.31	12/94	2c
Chicken	pound	1.56	93	37c
Chicken breast, bone-in	lb.	2.04	12/94	82r
Chicken, fresh, whole	lb.	0.95	12/94	82r
Chicken, whole fryer	lb.	1.09	12/94	2c
Cigarettes, Winston, Kings	carton	16.59	12/94	2c
Coffee, 100%, ground roast, all sizes	lb.	4.48	12/94	82r
Coffee, vacuum-packed	13 oz.	4.20	12/94	2c
Corn Flakes, Kellogg's or Post Toasties	18 oz.	2.66	12/94	2c
Corn, frozen, whole kernel, lowest price	10 oz.	0.78	12/94	2c
Dairy products (other) purchases	year	182	91	81c
Dairy products (other) purchases	year	182	91	81r
Eggs, Grade A large	dozen	1.93	12/94	2c
Fish and seafood purchases	year	112	91	81c
Fish and seafood purchases	year	94	91	81r
Flour, white, all purpose	lb.	0.21	12/94	82r
Food purchases, food eaten at home	year	3018	91	81c
Food purchases, food eaten at home	year	2749	91	81r
Foods purchased away from home, not prepared by consumer	year	2026	91	81c
Foods purchased away from home, not prepared by consumer	year	1909	91	81r
Fruits and vegetables purchases	year	545	91	81c
Fruits and vegetables purchases	year	459	91	81r
Grapefruit	lb.	0.56	12/94	82r

Values are in dollars or fractions of dollars. In the column headed *Ref*, references are shown to sources. Each reference is followed by a letter. These refer to the geographical level for which data were reported: s=State, r=Region, and c=City or metro. The abbreviation *ex* is used to mean *except* or *excluding*; *exp* stands for *expenditures*. For other abbreviations and further explanations, please see the Introduction.

Los Angeles, CA - continued

Item	Per	Value	Date	Ref.
Groceries				
Ground beef, 100% beef	lb.	1.31	12/94	82r
Ham, boneless, exc. canned	lb.	2.46	12/94	82r
Ice cream, prepackaged, bulk, regular	1/2 gal.	2.57	12/94	82r
Lemons	lb.	1.00	12/94	82r
Lettuce, iceberg	lb.	0.93	12/94	82r
Lettuce, iceberg	head	0.77	12/94	2c
Margarine	pound	0.77	93	37c
Margarine, Blue Bonnet or Parkay cubes	lb.	0.82	12/94	2c
Meats, poultry, fish, and eggs purchases	year	790	91	81c
Meats, poultry, fish, and eggs purchases	year	700	91	81r
Milk	half-gallon	1.40	93	37c
Milk and cream (fresh) purchases	year	156	91	81c
Milk and cream (fresh) purchases	year	155	91	81r
Milk, whole	1/2 gal.	1.65	12/94	2c
Orange juice, frozen concentrate 12-oz. can	16 oz.	1.52	12/94	82r
Orange juice, Minute Maid frozen	12-oz.	1.08	12/94	2c
Oranges, Navel	lb.	0.56	12/94	82r
Parmesan	8-oz.	3.51	93	37c
Peaches, halves or slices, Hunt's, Del Monte, or Libby's	29-oz.	1.49	12/94	2c
Peas, sweet, Del Monte or Green Giant	15-17 oz.	0.70	12/94	2c
Pork chops, center cut, bone-in	lb.	3.30	12/94	82r
Pork purchases	year	128	91	81c
Pork purchases	year	122	91	81r
Potato chips	16-oz.	3.03	12/94	82r
Potatoes, frozen, French fried	lb.	0.77	12/94	82r
Potatoes, white	lb.	0.35	12/94	82r
Potatoes, white or red	10-lb. sack	1.99	12/94	2c
Rice, white, long grain, uncooked	lb.	0.54	12/94	82r
Round roast, USDA choice, boneless	lb.	2.92	12/94	82r
Sausage, Jimmy Dean, 100% pork	lb.	2.75	12/94	2c
Shortening, vegetable oil blends	lb.	0.80	12/94	82r
Shortening, vegetable, Crisco	3-lb.	2.94	12/94	2c
Soft drink	two-liter	1.11	93	37c
Soft drink, Coca Cola, ex deposit	2 lit	0.95	12/94	2c
Spaghetti and macaroni	lb.	1.02	12/94	82r
Steak, round, graded & ungraded, exc. USDA prime & choice	lb.	3.13	12/94	82r
Steak, sirloin, USDA choice, boneless	lb.	4.07	12/94	82r
Steak, T-bone	pound	4.09	93	37c
Steak, t-bone	lb.	5.62	12/94	2c
Sugar and other sweets, eaten at home, expenditures	year	105	91	81r
Sugar and other sweets, eaten at home, purchases	year	99	91	81c
Sugar, cane or beet	4 lbs.	1.43	12/94	2c
Sugar, white, all sizes	lb.	0.38	12/94	82r
Tobacco products and smoking supplies, total expenditures	year	184	91	81c
Tobacco products and smoking supplies, total expenditures	year	221	91	81r
Tomatoes, field grown	lb.	1.45	12/94	82r
Tomatoes, Hunt's or Del Monte	14.5 oz.	0.81	12/94	2c
Tuna	6.5-oz. can	0.64	93	37c
Tuna, chunk, light	lb.	2.18	12/94	82r
Tuna, chunk, light, oil-packed	6.125-6.5 oz.	0.87	12/94	2c
Goods and Services				
Miscellaneous goods and services, ACCRA Index		118.40	12/94	2c
Health Care				
Health care, ACCRA Index		142.10	12/94	2c
Antibiotic ointment, Polysporin	1.5 oz.	4.62	12/94	2c

Los Angeles, CA - continued

Item	Per	Value	Date	Ref.
Health Care - continued				
Appendectomy	proc	1430.00	12/92	69c
Birth, normal delivery	del	2,485	11/93	93c
Breast lesion excision (lumpectomy)	proc	802.00	12/92	69c
Broken arm treatment	treat	433	11/93	93c
Cesarean section delivery	proc	1465.00	12/92	69c
Childbirth, Cesarean delivery, hospital charge	birth	6059.00	12/91	69r
Childbirth, Cesarean delivery, physician charge	birth	2248.00	12/91	69r
Childbirth, normal delivery, hospital charge	birth	3006.00	12/91	69r
Childbirth, normal delivery, physician charge	birth	1634.00	12/91	69r
Cholecystectomy	proc	2258.00	12/92	69c
Coronary bypass, triple	proc	7071.00	12/92	69c
Dentist's fee, adult teeth cleaning and periodic oral exam	visit	57.80	12/94	2c
Doctor visit, routine	visit	32.00-110.00	1/94	88c
Doctor's fee, routine exam, established patient	visit	63.60	12/94	2c
Drugs, expenditures	year	189	91	81c
Drugs, expenditures	year	230	91	81r
Health care, total expenditures	year	1485	91	81c
Health care, total expenditures	year	1544	91	81r
Health insurance expenditures	year	535	91	81c
Health insurance expenditures	year	558	91	81r
Health insurance premium	month	41.99	7/93	94c
Hospital care, semiprivate room	day	723.80	12/94	2c
Hospital cost	adm	6,520	2/94	72c
Hysterectomy, abdominal	proc	2987.00	12/92	69c
Insurance premium, family medical care	month	380.27	1/95	41s
Medical services expenditures	year	677	91	81c
Medical services expenditures	year	676	91	81r
Medical supplies expenditures	year	85	91	81c
Medical supplies expenditures	year	80	91	81r
Oophorectomy	proc	1821.00	12/92	69c
Physical exam, well baby	check-up	58	11/93	93c
Physical, complete	phys	136	11/93	93c
Salpingo-oophorectomy	proc	1563.00	12/92	69c
Surgery, open-heart	proc	37818.00	1/93	14r
Surgery, open-heart	surg	7,086	11/93	93c
Household Goods				
Appl. repair, service call, wash mach	min. lab. chg.	47.45	12/94	2c
Floor coverings, expenditures	year	62	91	81c
Floor coverings, expenditures	year	79	91	81r
Furniture, expenditures	year	387	91	81c
Furniture, expenditures	year	352	91	81r
Household equipment, misc. expenditures	year	614	91	81r
Household equipment, misc., expenditures	year	945	91	81c
Household expenditures, miscellaneous	year	423	91	81c
Household expenditures, miscellaneous	year	294	91	81r
Household furnishings and equipment, expenditures	year	1805	91	81c
Household furnishings and equipment, expenditures	year	1416	91	81r
Household operations expenditures	year	832	91	81c
Household operations expenditures	year	580	91	81r
Household textiles, expenditures	year	154	91	81c
Household textiles, expenditures	year	113	91	81r
Housekeeping supplies, expenditures	year	468	91	81c
Housekeeping supplies, expenditures	year	447	91	81r
Laundry and cleaning supplies, expenditures	year	134	91	81c
Laundry and cleaning supplies, expenditures	year	114	91	81r
Laundry detergent, Tide Ultra, Bold, or Cheer	42 oz.	3.98	12/94	2c
Postage and stationery, expenditures	year	154	91	81c
Postage and stationery, expenditures	year	145	91	81r
Tissues, facial, Kleenex brand	175	1.03	12/94	2c

Values are in dollars or fractions of dollars. In the column headed *Ref*, references are shown to sources. Each reference is followed by a letter. These refer to the geographical level for which data were reported: s = State, r = Region, and c = City or metro. The abbreviation *ex* is used to mean *except* or *excluding*; *exp* stands for expenditures. For other abbreviations and further explanations, please see the Introduction.

Los Angeles, CA - continued

Item	Per	Value	Date	Ref.
Housing				
Housing, ACCRA Index		148.30	12/94	2c
Add garage/carport		6,422	3/95	74r
Add room(s)		26,583	3/95	74r
Apartment condominium or co-op, median	unit	105300	12/94	62r
Car rental	day	46.00	5/95	95c
Dwellings (owned), expenditures	year	4843	91	81c
Dwellings (owned), expenditures	year	3932	91	81r
Enclose porch/patio/breezeway		5,382	3/95	74r
Finish room in basement/attic		3,911	3/95	74r
Home repairs, maintenance, and insurance	year	650.00	93	37c
Home, existing, single-family, median	unit	178600	12/94	62r
Home, existing, single-family, median	unit	181.50	12/94	62c
Home, purchase price	unit	227.50	3/93	26c
Hotel room	day	153.00	5/95	95c
House payment, principal and interest, 25% down payment	mo.	1157	12/94	2c
House, 1800 sq ft, 8000 sq ft lot, new, urban, utilities	total	187490	12/94	2c
Maintenance, repairs, insurance, and other housing expenditures	year	650	91	81c
Maintenance, repairs, insurance, and other housing expenditures	year	591	91	81r
Mortgage	month	1206.00	93	37c
Mortgage interest and charges expenditures	year	3422	91	81c
Mortgage interest and charges expenditures	year	2747	91	81r
Mortgage payment	month	1335.00	1/94	78c
Mtge. rate, incl. points and orig. fee, 30-year conv. fixed or ARM	mo.	9.25	12/94	2c
Princ. & int., mortgage, median-price exist. sing.-family home	mo.	845	12/94	62r
Property taxes expenditures	year	770	91	81c
Property taxes expenditures	year	594	91	81r
Redesign, restructure more than half of home's interior		5,467	3/95	74r
Rent, apartment, 2 br., 1 1/2-2 baths, unfurnished, 950 sq ft, water	mo.	723	12/94	2c
Rental unit, two-bedroom	month	759.00	93	37c
Rental units expenditures	year	2786	900/00/ 91	81c
Rental units expenditures	year	2077	91	81r
Insurance and Pensions				
Auto insurance, private passenger	year	892.80	12/94	71s
Health insurance, HMO plan, cost to employer	year	3189	93	59c
Insurance and pensions, personal, expenditures	year	3035	91	81c
Insurance and pensions, personal, expenditures	year	3042	91	81r
Insurance, life and other personal, expenditures	year	208	91	81c
Insurance, life and other personal, expenditures	year	298	91	81r
Pensions and Social Security, expenditures	year	2826	91	81c
Pensions and Social Security, expenditures	year	2744	91	81r
Legal Assistance				
Legal work, law firm associate	hour	91		10r
Legal work, law firm partner	hour	151		10r
Personal Goods				
Personal care products and services, total expenditures	year	533	91	81c
Shampoo, Alberto VO5	15-oz.	1.41	12/94	2c
Toothpaste, Crest or Colgate	6-7 oz.	2.57	12/94	2c
Personal Services				
Dry cleaning, man's 2-pc. suit		6.91	12/94	2c
Haircut, man's barbershop, no styling		10.40	12/94	2c
Haircut, woman's shampoo, trim, blow-dry		21.60	12/94	2c
Personal services expenditures	year	409	91	81c
Personal services expenditures	year	286	91	81r

Los Angeles, CA - continued

Item	Per	Value	Date	Ref.
Restaurant Food				
Chicken, fried, thigh and drumstick		2.43	12/94	2c
Dining expenditures, family	week	32.25	94	73r
Hamburger with cheese	1/4 lb.	2.01	12/94	2c
Pizza, Pizza Hut or Pizza Inn	12-13 in.	9.05	12/94	2c
Taxes				
Tax rate, residential property, month	$100	0.63	1/92	79c
Taxes, Federal income, expenditures	year	2867	91	81c
Taxes, Federal income, expenditures	year	2946	91	81r
Taxes, personal, expenditures	year	3706	91	81c
Taxes, personal, expenditures	year	3791	91	81r
Taxes, State and local income, expenditures	year	817	91	81c
Taxes, State and local income, expenditures	year	791	91	81r
Transportation				
Transportation, ACCRA Index		110.60	12/94	2c
Bus fare, one-way	trip	0.83	12/95	1c
Bus fare, up to 10 miles	one-way	0.99	12/94	2c
Cars and trucks purchased, new	year	1079	91	81c
Cars and trucks purchased, new	year	1231	91	81r
Cars and trucks purchased, used	year	846	91	81c
Cars and trucks purchased, used	year	915	91	81r
Driver's learning permit fee	perm	12.00	1/94	84s
Driver's license fee	orig	12.00	1/94	84s
Driver's license fee, duplicate	lic	12.00	1/94	84s
Driver's license reinstatement fee, min.	susp	15.00	1/94	85s
Driver's license renewal fee	renew	12.00	1/94	84s
Driving expenses	mile	55.80	5/95	86c
Fine, illegal parking, handicapped zone	event	330.00	12/93	87c
Identification card, nondriver	card	6.00	1/94	83s
Mileage fee, mileage traveled over rental company limit	mile	0.25	95	7c
Motorcycle learning permit fee	perm	12.00	1/94	84s
Motorcycle license fee	orig	12.00	1/94	84s
Motorcycle license fee, duplicate	lic	12.00	1/94	84s
Motorcycle license renewal fee	renew	12.00	1/94	84s
Public transportation expenditures	year	309	91	81c
Public transportation expenditures	year	375	91	81r
Railway fare, commuter rail, one-way	trip	2.50	12/95	1c
Railway fare, heavy rail, one-way	trip	0.25	12/95	1c
Railway fare, light rail, one-way	trip	1.35	12/95	1c
Tire balance, computer or spin bal., front	wheel	7.60	12/94	2c
Transportation expenditures, total	year	5372	91	81c
Transportation expenditures, total	year	5527	91	81r
Vehicle expenses, miscellaneous	year	2016	91	81c
Vehicle finance charges	year	269	91	81c
Vehicle finance charges	year	287	91	81r
Vehicle insurance expenditures	year	724	91	81c
Vehicle insurance expenditures	year	624	91	81r
Vehicle maintenance and repairs expenditures	year	703	91	81c
Vehicle maintenance and repairs expenditures	year	695	91	81r
Vehicle purchases	year	1945	91	81c
Vehicle purchases	year	2174	91	81r
Vehicle rental, leases, licenses, etc. expenditures	year	320	91	81c
Vehicle rental, leases, licenses, etc. expenditures	year	257	91	81r
Vehicles purchased, other than cars and trucks	year	20	91	81c
Vehicles purchased, other than cars and trucks	year	28	91	81r
Travel				
Car rental, midsize car, unlimited mileage	day	42.00	6/95	55c
Dinner, restaurant, inc. tax and tips, no drink	one	25.80	6/95	55c
Hotel room, two persons, inc. tax	night	166.50	6/95	55c
Taxi fare, airport-to-hotel	one-way	27.00	6/95	55c

Values are in dollars or fractions of dollars. In the column headed *Ref*, references are shown to sources. Each reference is followed by a letter. These refer to the geographical level for which data were reported: s = State, r = Region, and c = City or metro. The abbreviation *ex* is used to mean *except* or *excluding*; *exp* stands for *expenditures*. For other abbreviations and further explanations, please see the Introduction.

Los Angeles, CA - continued

Item	Per	Value	Date	Ref.
Utilities				
Utilities, ACCRA Index		82.10	12/94	2c
Electricity	KWh	0.12	12/94	82c
Electricity expenditures	year	601	91	81c
Electricity expenditures	year	616	91	81r
Electricity, (part.), other, 1800 sq. ft., new home	mo.	62.89	12/94	2c
Electricity, summer, 250 KWh	month	27.79	8/93	64c
Electricity, summer, 500 KWh	month	62.38	8/93	64c
Electricity, summer, 750 KWh	month	97.48	8/93	64c
Electricity, summer, 1000 KWh	month	131.43	8/93	64c
Fee, water use, industrial	month	1183.97	1/95	16c
Utilities, fuels, and public services, total expenditures	year	1882	91	81c
Utilities, fuels, and public services, total expenditures	year	1681	91	81r
Water and other public services, expenditures	year	234	91	81c
Water and other public services, expenditures	year	209	91	81r
Weddings				
Bridal attendants' gowns	event	750	10/93	76r
Bridal gown	event	852	10/93	76r
Bridal headpiece and veil	event	167	10/93	76r
Bride's wedding band	event	708	10/93	76r
Clergy	event	224	10/93	76r
Engagement ring	event	2756	10/93	76r
Flowers	event	863	10/93	76r
Formal wear for groom	event	106	10/93	76r
Groom's attendants' formal wear	event	530	10/93	76r
Groom's wedding band	event	402	10/93	76r
Music	event	600	10/93	76r
Photography	event	1088	10/93	76r
Shoes for bride	event	50	10/93	76r
Videography	event	483	10/93	76r
Wedding invitations and announcements	event	342	10/93	76r
Wedding reception	event	7000	10/93	76r

Louisville, KY

Item	Per	Value	Date	Ref.
Composite, ACCRA index		91.50	12/94	2c
Alcoholic Beverages				
Beer, Miller Lite, Bud, 12-oz., ex deposit	6	3.89	12/94	2c
J & B Scotch	750-ml.	16.79	12/94	2c
Wine, Gallo Chablis blanc	1.5-lit	5.43	12/94	2c
Appliances				
Appliances (major), expenditures	year	153	91	81r
Average annual exp.				
Food, health care, personal goods, services	year	27020	91	81r
Charity				
Cash contributions, expenditures	year	839	91	81r
Clothing				
Apparel, men and boys, total expenditures	year	380	91	81r
Apparel, women and girls, total expenditures	year	660	91	81r
Footwear, expenditures	year	193	91	81r
Jeans, man's denim		31.79	12/94	2c
Shirt, dress, men's	shirt	22.00	1/92	44c
Shirt, man's dress shirt		27.40	12/94	2c
Undervest, boy's size 10-14, cotton	3	3.30	12/94	2c
Communications				
Long-distance telephone rate, day, addl. min., 1-10 mi.	min.	0.14	12/93	9s
Long-distance telephone rate, day, initial min., 1-10 mi.	min.	0.18	12/93	9s
Newspaper subscription, dly. and Sun. delivery	month	14.00	12/94	2c
Phone line, single, business, field visit	inst	64.00	12/93	9s
Phone line, single, business, no field visit	inst	85.25	12/93	9s

Louisville, KY - continued

Item	Per	Value	Date	Ref.
Communications - continued				
Phone line, single, residence, field visit	inst	43.63	12/93	9s
Phone line, single, residence, no field visit	inst	29.38	12/93	9s
Telephone bill, family of four	month	25.31	12/94	2c
Telephone service, expenditures	year	616	91	81r
Telephone, residential, flat rate	mo.	16.55	12/93	8c
Education				
Board, 4-year private college/university	year	1897	8/94	80s
Board, 4-year public college/university	year	1744	8/94	80s
Education, total expenditures	year	319	91	81r
Room, 4-year private college/university	year	1644	8/94	80s
Room, 4-year public college/university	year	1370	8/94	80s
Total cost, 4-year private college/university	year	10097	8/94	80s
Total cost, 4-year public college/university	year	5027	8/94	80s
Tuition, 2-year public college/university, in-state	year	962	8/94	80s
Tuition, 4-year private college/university, in-state	year	6556	8/94	80s
Tuition, 4-year public college/university, in-state	year	1913	8/94	80s
Energy and Fuels				
Energy, combined forms, 1800 sq. ft.	mo.	84.90	12/94	2c
Energy, exc. electricity, 1800 sq. ft.	mo.	45.11	12/94	2c
Fuel oil and other fuels, expenditures	year	56	91	81r
Gas	gal.	0.99	1/92	44c
Gas, cooking, 10 therms	month	8.41	2/94	65c
Gas, cooking, 30 therms	month	16.27	2/94	65c
Gas, cooking, 50 therms	month	24.15	2/94	65c
Gas, heating, winter, 100 therms	month	43.81	2/94	65c
Gas, heating, winter, average use	month	83.08	2/94	65c
Gas, natural, expenditures	year	150	91	81r
Gas, reg unlead, taxes inc., cash, self-service	gal	1.08	12/94	2c
Gasoline and motor oil purchased	year	1152	91	81r
Gasoline, unleaded midgrade	gallon	1.21	4/93	82r
Gasoline, unleaded premium	gallon	1.30	4/93	82r
Gasoline, unleaded regular	gallon	1.10	4/93	82r
Entertainment				
Bowling, evening rate	game	1.94	12/94	2c
Concert ticket, Pearl Jam group	perf	20.00	94	50r
Entertainment, total expenditures	year	1266	91	81r
Fees and admissions, expenditures	year	306	91	81r
Monopoly game, Parker Brothers', No. 9	game	9.76	12/94	2c
Movie	adm	7.50	12/94	2c
Movie ticket, adult	ticket	7.50	1/92	44c
Pets, toys, playground equipment, expenditures	year	271	91	81r
Reading, expenditures	year	131	91	81r
Televisions, radios, and sound equipment, expenditures	year	439	91	81r
Tennis balls, yellow, Wilson or Penn, 3	can	2.29	12/94	2c
Funerals				
Burial, immediate, container provided by funeral home		1298.96	1/95	54r
Cards, acknowledgment		21.26	1/95	54r
Casket, minimum alternative		204.95	1/95	54r
Cosmetology, hair care, etc.		85.40	1/95	54r
Cremation, direct, container provided by funeral home		1054.77	1/95	54r
Embalming		287.71	1/95	54r
Funeral, funeral home		269.18	1/95	54r
Funeral, other facility		272.88	1/95	54r
Graveside service		302.54	1/95	54r
Hearse, local		122.08	1/95	54r
Limousine, local		80.31	1/95	54r
Memorial service		277.66	1/95	54r
Service charge, professional, nondeclinable		896.65	1/95	54r
Visitation and viewing		232.39	1/95	54r
Groceries				
Groceries, ACCRA Index		96.40	12/94	2c

Values are in dollars or fractions of dollars. In the column headed *Ref*, references are shown to sources. Each reference is followed by a letter. These refer to the geographical level for which data were reported: s=State, r=Region, and c=City or metro. The abbreviation *ex* is used to mean *except* or *excluding*; *exp* stands for *expenditures*. For other abbreviations and further explanations, please see the Introduction.

Louisville, KY - continued

Item	Per	Value	Date	Ref.
Groceries				
Apples, Red Delicious	lb.	0.73	12/94	82r
Baby food, strained vegetables, lowest price	4-4.5 oz.	0.29	12/94	2c
Bacon, sliced	lb.	1.67	12/94	82r
Bananas	lb.	0.46	12/94	2c
Bananas	lb.	0.42	12/94	82r
Beef or hamburger, ground	lb.	1.50	12/94	2c
Beef purchases	year	213	91	81r
Beverage purchases, alcoholic	year	249	91	81r
Beverage purchases, nonalcoholic	year	207	91	81r
Bologna, all beef or mixed	lb.	2.27	12/94	82r
Bread, white	24-oz.	0.74	12/94	2c
Bread, white, pan	lb.	0.68	12/94	82r
Cabbage	lb.	0.42	12/94	82r
Carrots, short trimmed and topped	lb.	0.53	12/94	82r
Cereals and bakery products purchases	year	345	91	81r
Cereals and cereals products purchases	year	127	91	81r
Cheddar cheese, natural	lb.	3.58	12/94	82r
Cheese, Kraft grated Parmesan	8-oz.	3.50	12/94	2c
Chicken breast, bone-in	lb.	1.71	12/94	82r
Chicken, fresh, whole	lb.	0.78	12/94	82r
Chicken, whole fryer	lb.	0.49	12/94	2c
Chuck roast, USDA choice, boneless	lb.	2.26	12/94	82r
Cigarettes, Winston, Kings	carton	13.51	12/94	2c
Coffee, vacuum-packed	13 oz.	3.07	12/94	2c
Corn Flakes, Kellogg's or Post Toasties	18 oz.	3.05	12/94	2c
Corn, frozen, whole kernel, lowest price	10 oz.	0.67	12/94	2c
Crackers, soda, salted	lb.	1.27	12/94	82r
Cucumbers	lb.	0.65	12/94	82r
Dairy products (other) purchases	year	141	91	81r
Eggs, Grade A large	dozen	0.89	12/94	2c
Eggs, Grade A large	dozen	0.87	12/94	82r
Fish and seafood purchases	year	72	91	81r
Flour, white, all purpose	lb.	0.23	12/94	82r
Food purchases, food eaten at home	year	2381	91	81r
Foods purchased away from home, not prepared by consumer	year	1696	91	81r
Frankfurters, all meat or all beef	lb.	1.74	12/94	82r
Fruits and vegetables purchases	year	380	91	81r
Grapefruit	lb.	0.45	12/94	82r
Grapes, Thompson seedless	lb.	2.30	12/94	82r
Ground beef, 100% beef	lb.	1.37	12/94	82r
Ground chuck, 100% beef	lb.	1.97	12/94	82r
Ham, boneless, exc. canned	lb.	2.54	12/94	82r
Ice cream, prepackaged, bulk, regular	1/2 gal.	2.47	12/94	82r
Lemons	lb.	1.02	12/94	82r
Lettuce, iceberg	lb.	0.96	12/94	82r
Lettuce, iceberg	head	0.98	12/94	2c
Margarine, Blue Bonnet or Parkay cubes	lb.	0.61	12/94	2c
Margarine, stick	lb.	0.77	12/94	82r
Meats, poultry, fish, and eggs purchases	year	655	91	81r
Milk and cream (fresh) purchases	year	130	91	81r
Milk, 2%	gal.	2.09	1/92	44c
Milk, whole	1/2 gal.	1.47	12/94	2c
Orange juice, frozen concentrate 12-oz. can	16 oz.	1.36	12/94	82r
Orange juice, Minute Maid frozen	12-oz.	1.27	12/94	2c
Oranges, Navel	lb.	0.54	12/94	82r
Peaches, halves or slices, Hunt's, Del Monte, or Libby's	29-oz.	1.46	12/94	2c
Pears, Anjou	lb.	0.81	12/94	82r
Peas, sweet, Del Monte or Green Giant	15-17 oz.	0.57	12/94	2c
Pork chops, center cut, bone-in	lb.	3.07	12/94	82r
Pork purchases	year	142	91	81r
Potato chips	16-oz.	3.15	12/94	82r
Potatoes, frozen, French fried	lb.	0.82	12/94	82r
Potatoes, white	lb.	0.34	12/94	82r
Potatoes, white or red	10-lb. sack	2.59	12/94	2c
Rental rate, 2-bedroom apartment	month	400.00	1/92	44c

Louisville, KY - continued

Item	Per	Value	Date	Ref.
Groceries - continued				
Rice, white, long grain, uncooked	lb.	0.48	12/94	82r
Round roast, USDA choice, boneless	lb.	2.91	12/94	82r
Sausage, fresh	lb.	1.82	12/94	82r
Sausage, Jimmy Dean, 100% pork	lb.	2.37	12/94	2c
Shortening, vegetable oil blends	lb.	0.75	12/94	82r
Shortening, vegetable, Crisco	3-lb.	2.14	12/94	2c
Soft drink, Coca Cola, ex deposit	2 lit	1.09	12/94	2c
Spaghetti and macaroni	lb.	0.87	12/94	82r
Steak, rib eye, USDA choice, boneless	lb.	6.85	12/94	82r
Steak, round, graded & ungraded, exc. USDA prime & choice	lb.	2.96	12/94	82r
Steak, round, USDA choice, boneless	lb.	3.17	12/94	82r
Steak, sirloin, USDA choice, boneless	lb.	4.12	12/94	82r
Steak, t-bone	lb.	5.41	12/94	2c
Steak, T-bone, USDA choice, bone-in	lb.	5.63	12/94	82r
Sugar and other sweets, eaten at home, expenditures	year	93	91	81r
Sugar, cane or beet	4 lbs.	1.30	12/94	2c
Sugar, white, all sizes	lb.	0.39	12/94	82r
Tobacco products and smoking supplies, total expenditures	year	286	91	81r
Tomatoes, field grown	lb.	1.36	12/94	82r
Tomatoes, Hunt's or Del Monte	14.5 oz.	0.72	12/94	2c
Tuna, chunk, light	lb.	1.94	12/94	82r
Tuna, chunk, light, oil-packed	6.125-6.5 oz.	0.65	12/94	2c
Turkey, frozen, whole	lb.	0.96	12/94	82r
Yogurt, natural, fruit flavored	8 oz.	0.58	12/94	82r
Goods and Services				
Miscellaneous goods and services, ACCRA Index		95.80	12/94	2c
Health Care				
Health care, ACCRA Index		89.10	12/94	2c
Adenosine, emergency room	treat	100.00	95	23r
Antibiotic ointment, Polysporin	1.5 oz.	3.99	12/94	2c
Bladder tap, superpubic, infant, emergency room	treat	119.00	95	23r
Blood analysis, emergency room	treat	25.00	95	23r
Blood tests, abdominal pain, emergency room	treat	25.00	95	23r
Burn dressing, emergency room	treat	266.00	95	23r
Cardiology interpretation, emergency room	treat	26.00	95	23r
Chest X-ray, emergency room	treat	78.00	95	23r
Childbirth, Cesarean delivery, hospital charge	birth	5462.00	12/91	69r
Childbirth, Cesarean delivery, physician charge	birth	2228.00	12/91	69r
Childbirth, normal delivery, hospital charge	birth	2943.00	12/91	69r
Childbirth, normal delivery, physician charge	birth	1619.00	12/91	69r
Defibrillation pads, emergency room	treat	6.00	95	23r
Dentist's fee, adult teeth cleaning and periodic oral exam	visit	39.75	12/94	2c
Doctor's fee, routine exam, established patient	visit	40.20	12/94	2c
Drugs, expenditures	year	297	91	81r
Gastric tube insertion, nasal, emergency room	treat	25.00	95	23r
Health care, total expenditures	year	1600	91	81r
Health insurance expenditures	year	637	91	81r
Heart monitor, emergency room	treat	40.00	95	23r
Hospital care, semiprivate room	day	344.47	12/94	2c
Insurance premium, family medical care	month	332.39	1/95	41s
Intravenous fluids, emergency room	treat	130.00	95	23r
Intravenous fluids, emergency room	liter	26.00	95	23r
Intravenous line, central, emergency room	treat	342.00	95	23r
Liver function tests, abdominal pain, emergency room	treat	26.00	95	23r
Medical care charges, total, emergency room, third-degree burns	treat	2101.00	95	23r

Values are in dollars or fractions of dollars. In the column headed *Ref*, references are shown to sources. Each reference is followed by a letter. These refer to the geographical level for which data were reported: s = State, r = Region, and c = City or metro. The abbreviation *ex* is used to mean *except* or *excluding*; *exp* stands for expenditures. For other abbreviations and further explanations, please see the Introduction.

Louisville, KY - continued

Item	Per	Value	Date	Ref.
Health Care				
Medical care charges, total, emergency, infant with fever	treat	628.00	95	23r
Medical services expenditures	year	573	91	81r
Medical supplies expenditures	year	93	91	81r
Morphine, emergency room	treat	34.00	95	23r
Nursing care and facilities charges, emergency room	treat	252.00	95	23r
Nursing care and facilities charges, emergency, infant with fever	treat	252.00	95	23r
Nursing care and facilities charges, emergency, third-degree burns	treat	861.00	95	23r
Physician's charges, emergency, infant with fever	treat	212.00	95	23r
Physician's charges, emergency, third-degree burns	treat	372.00	95	23r
Physician's fee, emergency room	treat	372.00	95	23r
Physician's fee, general practitioner	visit	51.20	12/93	60r
Surgery, open-heart	proc	42374.00	1/93	14r
Ultrasound, abdominal, emergency room	treat	276.00	95	23r
Urinalysis, emergency room	treat	20.00	95	23r
Urinalysis, infant, emergency room	treat	20.00	95	23r
X-rays, emergency room	treat	78.00	95	23r
Household Goods				
Appl. repair, service call, wash mach	min. lab. chg.	32.62	12/94	2c
Floor coverings, expenditures	year	48	91	81r
Furniture, expenditures	year	280	91	81r
Household equipment, misc. expenditures	year	342	91	81r
Household expenditures, miscellaneous	year	256	91	81r
Household furnishings and equipment, expenditures	year	988	91	81r
Household operations expenditures	year	468	91	81r
Household textiles, expenditures	year	95	91	81r
Housekeeping supplies, expenditures	year	380	91	81r
Laundry and cleaning supplies, expenditures	year	109	91	81r
Laundry detergent, Tide Ultra, Bold, or Cheer	42 oz.	3.17	12/94	2c
Postage and stationery, expenditures	year	105	91	81r
Tissues, facial, Kleenex brand	175	1.01	12/94	2c
Housing				
Housing, ACCRA Index		84.60	12/94	2c
Add garage/carport		6,980	3/95	74r
Add room(s)		11,403	3/95	74r
Apartment condominium or co-op, median	unit	68600	12/94	62r
Dwellings (owned), expenditures	year	2428	91	81r
Enclose porch/patio/breezeway		4,572	3/95	74r
Finish room in basement/attic		3,794	3/95	74r
Home, existing, single-family, median	unit	120200	12/94	62r
Home, existing, single-family, median	unit	80.90	12/94	62c
Home, purchase price	unit	117.00	3/93	26c
Home, single family, median	home	79,000	4/94	11c
House payment, principal and interest, 25% down payment	mo.	636	12/94	2c
House, 1800 sq ft, 8000 sq ft lot, new, urban, utilities	total	104660	12/94	2c
Maintenance, repairs, insurance, and other housing expenditures	year	531	91	81r
Mortgage interest and charges expenditures	year	1506	91	81r
Mtge. rate, incl. points and orig. fee, 30-year conv. fixed or ARM	mo.	9.07	12/94	2c
Princ. & int., mortgage, median-price exist. sing.-family home	mo.	540	12/94	62r
Property taxes expenditures	year	391	91	81r
Redesign, restructure more than half of home's interior		17,641	3/95	74r
Rent, apartment, 2 br., 1 1/2-2 baths, unfurnished, 950 sq ft, water	mo.	482	12/94	2c
Rental units expenditures	year	1264	91	81r

Louisville, KY - continued

Item	Per	Value	Date	Ref.
Insurance and Pensions				
Auto insurance, private passenger	year	616.22	12/94	71s
Insurance and pensions, personal, expenditures	year	2395	91	81r
Insurance, life and other personal, expenditures	year	368	91	81r
Pensions and Social Security, expenditures	year	2027	91	81r
Personal Goods				
Shampoo, Alberto VO5	15-oz.	1.13	12/94	2c
Toothpaste, Crest or Colgate	6-7 oz.	1.61	12/94	2c
Personal Services				
Dry cleaning, man's 2-pc. suit		6.76	12/94	2c
Dry cleaning, woman's dress	dress	6.50	1/92	44c
Haircut, man's barbershop, no styling		7.20	12/94	2c
Haircut, woman's shampoo, trim, blow-dry		16.70	12/94	2c
Personal services expenditures	year	212	91	81r
Restaurant Food				
Big Mac, small fries, medium drink	meal	3.45	1/92	44c
Chicken, fried, thigh and drumstick		2.11	12/94	2c
Dining expenditures, family	week	33.83	94	73r
Hamburger with cheese	1/4 lb.	1.76	12/94	2c
Pizza, Pizza Hut or Pizza Inn	12-13 in.	6.69	12/94	2c
Taxes				
Tax rate, residential property, month	$100	0.95	1/92	79c
Taxes, Federal income, expenditures	year	2275	91	81r
Taxes, personal, expenditures	year	2715	91	81r
Taxes, State and local income, expenditures	year	365	91	81r
Transportation				
Transportation, ACCRA Index		97.70	12/94	2c
Bus fare, one-way	trip	0.75	12/95	1c
Bus fare, up to 10 miles	one-way	0.85	12/94	2c
Cars and trucks purchased, new	year	1306	91	81r
Cars and trucks purchased, used	year	942	91	81r
Driver's learning permit fee	perm	2.00	1/94	84s
Driver's license fee	orig	8.00	1/94	84s
Driver's license fee, duplicate	lic	2.00	1/94	84s
Driver's license reinstatement fee, min.	susp	30.00	1/94	85s
Driver's license renewal fee	renew	8.00	1/94	84s
Identification card, nondriver	card	4.00	1/94	83s
Motorcycle learning permit fee	perm	2.00	1/94	84s
Motorcycle license fee	orig	8.00	1/94	84s
Motorcycle license fee, duplicate	lic	2.00	1/94	84s
Motorcycle license renewal fee	renew	8.00	1/94	84s
parking, long-term lot, airport	3 days	12.00	1/92	44c
Public transportation expenditures	year	249	91	81r
Tire balance, computer or spin bal., front	wheel	6.90	12/94	2c
Transportation expenditures, total	year	5307	91	81r
Vehicle finance charges	year	346	91	81r
Vehicle insurance expenditures	year	544	91	81r
Vehicle maintenance and repairs expenditures	year	600	91	81r
Vehicle purchases	year	2275	91	81r
Vehicle rental, leases, licenses, etc. expenditures	year	141	91	81r
Vehicles purchased, other than cars and trucks	year	27	91	81r
Utilities				
Utilities, ACCRA Index		83.00	12/94	2c
Electricity expenditures	year	950	91	81r
Electricity, (part.), other, 1800 sq. ft., new home	mo.	39.79	12/94	2c
Electricity, summer, 250 KWh	month	18.83	8/93	64c
Electricity, summer, 500 KWh	month	34.37	8/93	64c
Electricity, summer, 750 KWh	month	49.91	8/93	64c
Electricity, summer, 1000 KWh	month	66.15	8/93	64c
Utilities, fuels, and public services, total expenditures	year	2000	91	81r

Values are in dollars or fractions of dollars. In the column headed *Ref*, references are shown to sources. Each reference is followed by a letter. These refer to the geographical level for which data were reported: s = State, r = Region, and c = City or metro. The abbreviation *ex* is used to mean *except* or *excluding*; *exp* stands for expenditures. For other abbreviations and further explanations, please see the Introduction.

Louisville, KY - continued

Item	Per	Value	Date	Ref.
Utilities				
Water and other public services, expenditures	year	227	91	81r
Weddings				
Bridal attendants' gowns	event	750	10/93	76r
Bridal gown	event	852	10/93	76r
Bridal headpiece and veil	event	167	10/93	76r
Bride's wedding band	event	708	10/93	76r
Clergy	event	224	10/93	76r
Engagement ring	event	2756	10/93	76r
Flowers	event	863	10/93	76r
Formal wear for groom	event	106	10/93	76r
Groom's attendants' formal wear	event	530	10/93	76r
Groom's wedding band	event	402	10/93	76r
Music	event	600	10/93	76r
Photography	event	1088	10/93	76r
Shoes for bride	event	50	10/93	76r
Videography	event	483	10/93	76r
Wedding invitations and announcements	event	342	10/93	76r
Wedding reception	event	7000	10/93	76r

Loveland, CO

Item	Per	Value	Date	Ref.
Composite, ACCRA index		97.10	12/94	2c
Alcoholic Beverages				
Beer, Miller Lite, Bud, 12-oz., ex deposit	6	4.36	12/94	2c
J & B Scotch	750-ml.	18.07	12/94	2c
Wine, Gallo Chablis blanc	1.5-lit	4.09	12/94	2c
Clothing				
Jeans, man's denim		28.59	12/94	2c
Shirt, man's dress shirt		27.60	12/94	2c
Undervest, boy's size 10-14, cotton	3	3.36	12/94	2c
Communications				
Newspaper subscription, dly. and Sun. delivery	month	12.25	12/94	2c
Telephone bill, family of four	month	20.53	12/94	2c
Telephone, residential, flat rate	mo.	14.68	12/93	8c
Energy and Fuels				
Energy, combined forms, 1800 sq. ft.	mo.	82.17	12/94	2c
Energy, exc. electricity, 1800 sq. ft.	mo.	42.35	12/94	2c
Gas, reg unlead, taxes inc., cash, self-service	gal	1.20	12/94	2c
Entertainment				
Bowling, evening rate	game	2.20	12/94	2c
Monopoly game, Parker Brothers', No. 9	game	8.44	12/94	2c
Movie	adm	5.83	12/94	2c
Tennis balls, yellow, Wilson or Penn, 3	can	2.06	12/94	2c
Groceries				
Groceries, ACCRA Index		101.90	12/94	2c
Baby food, strained vegetables, lowest price	4-4.5 oz.	0.35	12/94	2c
Bananas	lb.	0.57	12/94	2c
Beef or hamburger, ground	lb.	1.67	12/94	2c
Bread, white	24-oz.	0.67	12/94	2c
Cheese, Kraft grated Parmesan	8-oz.	2.96	12/94	2c
Chicken, whole fryer	lb.	0.79	12/94	2c
Cigarettes, Winston, Kings	carton	14.82	12/94	2c
Coffee, vacuum-packed	13 oz.	3.98	12/94	2c
Corn Flakes, Kellogg's or Post Toasties	18 oz.	2.93	12/94	2c
Corn, frozen, whole kernel, lowest price	10 oz.	0.86	12/94	2c
Eggs, Grade A large	dozen	0.79	12/94	2c
Lettuce, iceberg	head	0.72	12/94	2c
Margarine, Blue Bonnet or Parkay cubes	lb.	0.62	12/94	2c
Milk, whole	1/2 gal.	1.68	12/94	2c
Orange juice, Minute Maid frozen	12-oz.	1.25	12/94	2c
Peaches, halves or slices, Hunt's, Del Monte, or Libby's	29-oz.	1.51	12/94	2c

Loveland, CO - continued

Item	Per	Value	Date	Ref.
Groceries - continued				
Peas, sweet, Del Monte or Green Giant	15-17 oz.	0.78	12/94	2c
Potatoes, white or red	10-lb. sack	2.22	12/94	2c
Sausage, Jimmy Dean, 100% pork	lb.	3.13	12/94	2c
Shortening, vegetable, Crisco	3-lb.	2.80	12/94	2c
Soft drink, Coca Cola, ex deposit	2 lit	0.88	12/94	2c
Steak, t-bone	lb.	3.64	12/94	2c
Sugar, cane or beet	4 lbs.	1.50	12/94	2c
Tomatoes, Hunt's or Del Monte	14.5 oz.	0.79	12/94	2c
Tuna, chunk, light, oil-packed	6.125-6.5 oz.	0.70	12/94	2c
Goods and Services				
Miscellaneous goods and services, ACCRA Index		91.60	12/94	2c
Health Care				
Health care, ACCRA Index		101.80	12/94	2c
Antibiotic ointment, Polysporin	1.5 oz.	3.80	12/94	2c
Dentist's fee, adult teeth cleaning and periodic oral exam	visit	50.00	12/94	2c
Doctor's fee, routine exam, established patient	visit	42.76	12/94	2c
Hospital care, semiprivate room	day	426.30	12/94	2c
Household Goods				
Appl. repair, service call, wash mach	min. lab. chg.	23.50	12/94	2c
Laundry detergent, Tide Ultra, Bold, or Cheer	42 oz.	2.99	12/94	2c
Tissues, facial, Kleenex brand	175	0.95	12/94	2c
Housing				
Housing, ACCRA Index		104.10	12/94	2c
House payment, principal and interest, 25% down payment	mo.	813	12/94	2c
House, 1800 sq ft, 8000 sq ft lot, new, urban, utilities	total	130850	12/94	2c
Mtge. rate, incl. points and orig. fee, 30-year conv. fixed or ARM	mo.	9.33	12/94	2c
Rent, apartment, 2 br., 1 1/2-2 baths, unfurnished, 950 sq ft, water	mo.	503	12/94	2c
Personal Goods				
Shampoo, Alberto VO5	15-oz.	0.99	12/94	2c
Toothpaste, Crest or Colgate	6-7 oz.	1.86	12/94	2c
Personal Services				
Dry cleaning, man's 2-pc. suit		6.70	12/94	2c
Haircut, man's barbershop, no styling		6.59	12/94	2c
Haircut, woman's shampoo, trim, blow-dry		10.80	12/94	2c
Restaurant Food				
Chicken, fried, thigh and drumstick		1.99	12/94	2c
Hamburger with cheese	1/4 lb.	1.95	12/94	2c
Pizza, Pizza Hut or Pizza Inn	12-13 in.	7.69	12/94	2c
Transportation				
Transportation, ACCRA Index		101.10	12/94	2c
Tire balance, computer or spin bal., front	wheel	6.30	12/94	2c
Utilities				
Utilities, ACCRA Index		77.50	12/94	2c
Electricity, (part.), other, 1800 sq. ft., new home	mo.	39.82	12/94	2c

Values are in dollars or fractions of dollars. In the column headed *Ref*, references are shown to sources. Each reference is followed by a letter. These refer to the geographical level for which data were reported: s = State, r = Region, and c = City or metro. The abbreviation *ex* is used to mean *except* or *excluding*; *exp* stands for expenditures. For other abbreviations and further explanations, please see the Introduction.

Lowell, MA

Item	Per	Value	Date	Ref.
Appliances				
Appliances (major), expenditures	year	145	91	81r
Average annual exp.				
Food, health care, personal goods, services	year	29496	91	81r
Charity				
Cash contributions, expenditures	year	708	91	81r
Clothing				
Apparel, men and boys, total expenditures	year	416	91	81r
Apparel, women and girls, total expenditures	year	744	91	81r
Footwear, expenditures	year	305	91	81r
Communications				
Long-distance telephone rate, day, addl. min., 1-10 mi.	min.	0.09	12/93	9s
Long-distance telephone rate, day, initial min., 1-10 mi.	min.	0.19	12/93	9s
Phone line, single, business, field visit	inst	27.50	12/93	9s
Phone line, single, business, no field visit	inst	93.02	12/93	9s
Phone line, single, residence, field visit	inst	27.50	12/93	9s
Phone line, single, residence, no field visit	inst	37.07	12/93	9s
Telephone service, expenditures	year	589	91	81r
Education				
Board, 4-year private college/university	year	3179	8/94	80s
Board, 4-year public college/university	year	2035	8/94	80s
Education, total expenditures	year	593	91	81r
Room, 4-year private college/university	year	3369	8/94	80s
Room, 4-year public college/university	year	2290	8/94	80s
Total cost, 4-year private college/university	year	21346	8/94	80s
Total cost, 4-year public college/university	year	8467	8/94	80s
Tuition, 2-year public college/university, in-state	year	2361	8/94	80s
Tuition, 4-year private college/university, in-state	year	14797	8/94	80s
Tuition, 4-year public college/university, in-state	year	4142	8/94	80s
Energy and Fuels				
Fuel oil and other fuels, expenditures	year	257	91	81r
Gas, natural, expenditures	year	285	91	81r
Gasoline and motor oil purchased	year	867	91	81r
Gasoline, unleaded midgrade	gallon	1.32	4/93	82r
Gasoline, unleaded premium	gallon	1.40	4/93	82r
Gasoline, unleaded regular	gallon	1.19	4/93	82r
Entertainment				
Entertainment, total expenditures	year	1331	91	81r
Fees and admissions, expenditures	year	398	91	81r
Pets, toys, playground equipment, expenditures	year	270	91	81r
Reading, expenditures	year	171	91	81r
Televisions, radios, and sound equipment, expenditures	year	429	91	81r
Funerals				
Burial, immediate, container provided by funeral home		1507.89	1/95	54r
Cards, acknowledgment		18.10	1/95	54r
Casket, minimum alternative		133.03	1/95	54r
Cosmetology, hair care, etc.		114.12	1/95	54r
Cremation, direct, container provided by funeral home		1309.19	1/95	54r
Embalming		320.97	1/95	54r
Funeral, funeral home		327.61	1/95	54r
Funeral, other facility		314.81	1/95	54r
Graveside service		286.11	1/95	54r
Hearse, local		158.95	1/95	54r
Limousine, local		149.45	1/95	54r
Memorial service		315.94	1/95	54r
Service charge, professional, nondeclinable		1148.43	1/95	54r
Visitation and viewing		249.66	1/95	54r

Lowell, MA - continued

Item	Per	Value	Date	Ref.
Groceries				
Apples, Red Delicious	lb.	0.78	12/94	82r
Bacon, sliced	lb.	2.24	12/94	82r
Bananas	lb.	0.49	12/94	82r
Beef purchases	year	226	91	81r
Beverage purchases, alcoholic	year	332	91	81r
Beverage purchases, nonalcoholic	year	213	91	81r
Bread, white, pan	lb.	0.80	12/94	82r
Butter, salted, Grade AA, stick	lb.	1.67	12/94	82r
Carrots, short trimmed and topped	lb.	0.51	12/94	82r
Cereals and bakery products purchases	year	407	91	81r
Cereals and cereals products purchases	year	132	91	81r
Chicken breast, bone-in	lb.	2.22	12/94	82r
Chicken, fresh, whole	lb.	1.05	12/94	82r
Chuck roast, USDA choice, boneless	lb.	2.74	12/94	82r
Coffee, 100%, ground roast, all sizes	lb.	4.61	12/94	82r
Dairy products (other) purchases	year	161	91	81r
Eggs, Grade A large	dozen	1.12	12/94	82r
Fish and seafood purchases	year	112	91	81r
Food purchases, food eaten at home	year	2599	91	81r
Foods purchased away from home, not prepared by consumer	year	2024	91	81r
Fruits and vegetables purchases	year	444	91	81r
Grapefruit	lb.	0.44	12/94	82r
Grapes, Thompson seedless	lb.	2.24	12/94	82r
Ground chuck, 100% beef	lb.	1.67	12/94	82r
Ice cream, prepackaged, bulk, regular	1/2 gal.	2.93	12/94	82r
Lemons	lb.	1.06	12/94	82r
Lettuce, iceberg	lb.	0.92	12/94	82r
Meats, poultry, fish, and eggs purchases	year	751	91	81r
Milk and cream (fresh) purchases	year	152	91	81r
Orange juice, frozen concentrate 12-oz. can	16 oz.	1.92	12/94	82r
Oranges, Navel	lb.	0.56	12/94	82r
Pork chops, center cut, bone-in	lb.	3.09	12/94	82r
Pork purchases	year	130	91	81r
Potatoes, white	lb.	0.37	12/94	82r
Rib roast, USDA choice, bone-in	lb.	4.98	12/94	82r
Round roast, USDA choice, boneless	lb.	2.93	12/94	82r
Shortening, vegetable oil blends	lb.	1.03	12/94	82r
Spaghetti and macaroni	lb.	0.84	12/94	82r
Steak, round, USDA choice, boneless	lb.	3.48	12/94	82r
Steak, sirloin, USDA choice, bone-in	lb.	3.38	12/94	82r
Steak, sirloin, USDA choice, boneless	lb.	4.81	12/94	82r
Sugar and other sweets, eaten at home, expenditures	year	89	91	81r
Sugar, white, all sizes	lb.	0.46	12/94	82r
Tobacco products and smoking supplies, total expenditures	year	279	91	81r
Tomatoes, field grown	lb.	1.56	12/94	82r
Tuna, chunk, light	lb.	2.09	12/94	82r
Health Care				
Childbirth, Cesarean delivery, hospital charge	birth	6334.00	12/91	69r
Childbirth, Cesarean delivery, physician charge	birth	2234.00	12/91	69r
Childbirth, normal delivery, hospital charge	birth	3225.00	12/91	69r
Childbirth, normal delivery, physician charge	birth	1623.00	12/91	69r
Drugs, expenditures	year	205	91	81r
Health care, total expenditures	year	1396	91	81r
Health insurance expenditures	year	553	91	81r
Insurance premium, family medical care	month	457.38	1/95	41s
Medical services expenditures	year	559	91	81r
Medical supplies expenditures	year	80	91	81r
Household Goods				
Floor coverings, expenditures	year	158	91	81r
Furniture, expenditures	year	341	91	81r
Household equipment, misc. expenditures	year	363	91	81r
Household expenditures, miscellaneous	year	194	91	81r
Household furnishings and equipment, expenditures	year	1158	91	81r
Household operations expenditures	year	378	91	81r

Values are in dollars or fractions of dollars. In the column headed *Ref*, references are shown to sources. Each reference is followed by a letter. These refer to the geographical level for which data were reported: s=State, r=Region, and c=City or metro. The abbreviation *ex* is used to mean *except* or *excluding*; *exp* stands for expenditures. For other abbreviations and further explanations, please see the Introduction.

Lowell, MA - continued

Item	Per	Value	Date	Ref.
Household Goods				
Household textiles, expenditures	year	88	91	81r
Housekeeping supplies, expenditures	year	426	91	81r
Laundry and cleaning supplies, expenditures	year	122	91	81r
Postage and stationery, expenditures	year	134	91	81r
Housing				
Add garage/carport		11,614	3/95	74r
Add room(s)		16,816	3/95	74r
Apartment condominium or co-op, median	unit	96700	12/94	62r
Dwellings (owned), expenditures	year	3305	91	81r
Enclose porch/patio/breezeway		2,980	3/95	74r
Finish room in basement/attic		4,330	3/95	74r
Home, existing, single-family, median	unit	161600	12/94	62r
Maintenance, repairs, insurance, and other housing expenditures	year	569	91	81r
Mortgage interest and charges expenditures	year	1852	91	81r
Princ. & int., mortgage, median-price exist. sing.-family home	mo.	765	12/94	62r
Property taxes expenditures	year	884	91	81r
Redesign, restructure more than half of home's interior		2,750	3/95	74r
Rental units expenditures	year	1832	91	81r
Insurance and Pensions				
Auto insurance, private passenger	year	1009.56	12/94	71s
Insurance and pensions, personal, expenditures	year	2690	91	81r
Insurance, life and other personal, expenditures	year	341	91	81r
Pensions and Social Security, expenditures	year	2349	91	81r
Legal Assistance				
Estate planning, law-firm partner	hr.	375.00	10/93	12r
Legal work, law firm associate	hour	78		10r
Legal work, law firm partner	hour	183		10r
Personal Services				
Personal services expenditures	year	184	91	81r
Restaurant Food				
Dining expenditures, family	week	34.26	94	73r
Taxes				
Taxes, Federal income, expenditures	year	2409	91	81r
Taxes, personal, expenditures	year	3094	91	81r
Taxes, State and local income, expenditures	year	620	91	81r
Transportation				
Cars and trucks purchased, new	year	1170	91	81r
Cars and trucks purchased, used	year	739	91	81r
Driver's learning permit fee	perm	15.00	1/94	84s
Driver's license fee	orig	50.00	1/94	84s
Driver's license fee, duplicate	lic	15.00	1/94	84s
Driver's license renewal fee	renew	43.75	1/94	84s
Identification card, nondriver	card	15.00	1/94	83s
Motorcycle license fee	orig	50.00	1/94	84s
Motorcycle license fee, duplicate	lic	15.00	1/94	84s
Motorcycle license renewal fee	renew	43.75	1/94	84s
Public transportation expenditures	year	430	91	81r
Transportation expenditures, total	year	4810	91	81r
Vehicle finance charges	year	238	91	81r
Vehicle insurance expenditures	year	630	91	81r
Vehicle maintenance and repairs expenditures	year	532	91	81r
Vehicle purchases	year	1920	91	81r
Vehicle rental, leases, licenses, etc. expenditures	year	193	91	81r
Vehicles purchased, other than cars and trucks	year	11	91	81r
Utilities				
Electricity expenditures	year	695	91	81r
Utilities, fuels, and public services, total expenditures	year	1981	91	81r

Lowell, MA - continued

Item	Per	Value	Date	Ref.
Utilities - continued				
Water and other public services, expenditures	year	154	91	81r
Weddings				
Bridal attendants' gowns	event	750	10/93	76r
Bridal gown	event	852	10/93	76r
Bridal headpiece and veil	event	167	10/93	76r
Bride's wedding band	event	708	10/93	76r
Clergy	event	224	10/93	76r
Engagement ring	event	2756	10/93	76r
Flowers	event	863	10/93	76r
Formal wear for groom	event	106	10/93	76r
Groom's attendants' formal wear	event	530	10/93	76r
Groom's wedding band	event	402	10/93	76r
Music	event	600	10/93	76r
Photography	event	1088	10/93	76r
Shoes for bride	event	50	10/93	76r
Videography	event	483	10/93	76r
Wedding invitations and announcements	event	342	10/93	76r
Wedding reception	event	7000	10/93	76r

Lubbock, TX

Item	Per	Value	Date	Ref.
Composite, ACCRA index		92.30	12/94	2c
Alcoholic Beverages				
Beer, Miller Lite, Bud, 12-oz., ex deposit	6	4.93	12/94	2c
J & B Scotch	750-ml.	19.79	12/94	2c
Wine, Gallo Chablis blanc	1.5-lit	5.69	12/94	2c
Appliances				
Appliances (major), expenditures	year	153	91	81r
Average annual exp.				
Food, health care, personal goods, services	year	27020	91	81r
Charity				
Cash contributions, expenditures	year	839	91	81r
Clothing				
Apparel, men and boys, total expenditures	year	380	91	81r
Apparel, women and girls, total expenditures	year	660	91	81r
Footwear, expenditures	year	193	91	81r
Jeans, man's denim		28.00	12/94	2c
Shirt, man's dress shirt		30.20	12/94	2c
Undervest, boy's size 10-14, cotton	3	4.19	12/94	2c
Communications				
Long-distance telephone rate, day, addl. min., 1-10 mi.	min.	0.08	12/93	9s
Long-distance telephone rate, day, initial min., 1-10 mi.	min.	0.10	12/93	9s
Newspaper subscription, dly. and Sun. delivery	month	9.75	12/94	2c
Phone line, single, business, field visit	inst	71.90	12/93	9s
Phone line, single, business, no field visit	inst	57.30	12/93	9s
Phone line, single, residence, field visit	inst	52.95	12/93	9s
Phone line, single, residence, no field visit	inst	38.35	12/93	9s
Telephone bill, family of four	month	15.74	12/94	2c
Telephone service, expenditures	year	616	91	81r
Education				
Board, 4-year private college/university	year	2084	8/94	80s
Board, 4-year public college/university	year	1675	8/94	80s
Education, total expenditures	year	319	91	81r
Room, 4-year private college/university	year	1840	8/94	80s
Room, 4-year public college/university	year	1756	8/94	80s
Total cost, 4-year private college/university	year	11876	8/94	80s
Total cost, 4-year public college/university	year	4935	8/94	80s
Tuition, 2-year public college/university, in-state	year	625	8/94	80s
Tuition, 4-year private college/university, in-state	year	7952	8/94	80s

Lubbock, TX - continued

Item	Per	Value	Date	Ref.
Education				
Tuition, 4-year public college/university, in-state	year	1503	8/94	80s
Energy and Fuels				
Energy, combined forms, 1800 sq. ft.	mo.	80.36	12/94	2c
Energy, exc. electricity, 1800 sq. ft.	mo.	28.56	12/94	2c
Fuel oil and other fuels, expenditures	year	56	91	81r
Gas, natural, expenditures	year	150	91	81r
Gas, reg unlead, taxes inc., cash, self-service	gal	1.13	12/94	2c
Gasoline and motor oil purchased	year	1152	91	81r
Gasoline, unleaded midgrade	gallon	1.21	4/93	82r
Gasoline, unleaded premium	gallon	1.30	4/93	82r
Gasoline, unleaded regular	gallon	1.10	4/93	82r
Entertainment				
Bowling, evening rate	game	2.31	12/94	2c
Concert ticket, Pearl Jam group	perf	20.00	94	50r
Entertainment, total expenditures	year	1266	91	81r
Fees and admissions, expenditures	year	306	91	81r
Monopoly game, Parker Brothers', No. 9	game	11.94	12/94	2c
Movie	adm	5.50	12/94	2c
Pets, toys, playground equipment, expenditures	year	271	91	81r
Reading, expenditures	year	131	91	81r
Televisions, radios, and sound equipment, expenditures	year	439	91	81r
Tennis balls, yellow, Wilson or Penn, 3	can	2.26	12/94	2c
Funerals				
Burial, immediate, container provided by funeral home		1574.60	1/95	54r
Cards, acknowledgment		22.24	1/95	54r
Casket, minimum alternative		239.41	1/95	54r
Cosmetology, hair care, etc.		91.04	1/95	54r
Cremation, direct, container provided by funeral home		1085.15	1/95	54r
Embalming		281.30	1/95	54r
Funeral, funeral home		323.04	1/95	54r
Funeral, other facility		327.58	1/95	54r
Graveside service		355.19	1/95	54r
Hearse, local		141.89	1/95	54r
Limousine, local		99.40	1/95	54r
Memorial service		284.67	1/95	54r
Service charge, professional, nondeclinable		904.06	1/95	54r
Visitation and viewing		187.04	1/95	54r
Groceries				
Groceries, ACCRA Index		95.30	12/94	2c
Apples, Red Delicious	lb.	0.73	12/94	82r
Baby food, strained vegetables, lowest price	4-4.5 oz.	0.31	12/94	2c
Bacon, sliced	lb.	1.67	12/94	82r
Bananas	lb.	0.42	12/94	2c
Bananas	lb.	0.42	12/94	82r
Beef or hamburger, ground	lb.	1.25	12/94	2c
Beef purchases	year	213	91	81r
Beverage purchases, alcoholic	year	249	91	81r
Beverage purchases, nonalcoholic	year	207	91	81r
Bologna, all beef or mixed	lb.	2.27	12/94	82r
Bread, white	24-oz.	0.50	12/94	2c
Bread, white, pan	lb.	0.68	12/94	82r
Cabbage	lb.	0.42	12/94	82r
Carrots, short trimmed and topped	lb.	0.53	12/94	82r
Cereals and bakery products purchases	year	345	91	81r
Cereals and cereals products purchases	year	127	91	81r
Cheddar cheese, natural	lb.	3.58	12/94	82r
Cheese, Kraft grated Parmesan	8-oz.	3.82	12/94	2c
Chicken breast, bone-in	lb.	1.71	12/94	82r
Chicken, fresh, whole	lb.	0.78	12/94	82r
Chicken, whole fryer	lb.	0.75	12/94	2c
Chuck roast, USDA choice, boneless	lb.	2.26	12/94	82r
Cigarettes, Winston, Kings	carton	16.09	12/94	2c
Coffee, vacuum-packed	13 oz.	3.33	12/94	2c

Lubbock, TX - continued

Item	Per	Value	Date	Ref.
Groceries - continued				
Corn Flakes, Kellogg's or Post Toasties	18 oz.	2.56	12/94	2c
Corn, frozen, whole kernel, lowest price	10 oz.	0.74	12/94	2c
Crackers, soda, salted	lb.	1.27	12/94	82r
Cucumbers	lb.	0.65	12/94	82r
Dairy products (other) purchases	year	141	91	81r
Eggs, Grade A large	dozen	0.65	12/94	2c
Eggs, Grade A large	dozen	0.87	12/94	82r
Fish and seafood purchases	year	72	91	81r
Flour, white, all purpose	lb.	0.23	12/94	82r
Food purchases, food eaten at home	year	2381	91	81r
Foods purchased away from home, not prepared by consumer	year	1696	91	81r
Frankfurters, all meat or all beef	lb.	1.74	12/94	82r
Fruits and vegetables purchases	year	380	91	81r
Grapefruit	lb.	0.45	12/94	82r
Grapes, Thompson seedless	lb.	2.30	12/94	82r
Ground beef, 100% beef	lb.	1.37	12/94	82r
Ground chuck, 100% beef	lb.	1.97	12/94	82r
Ham, boneless, exc. canned	lb.	2.54	12/94	82r
Ice cream, prepackaged, bulk, regular	1/2 gal.	2.47	12/94	82r
Lemons	lb.	1.02	12/94	82r
Lettuce, iceberg	lb.	0.96	12/94	82r
Lettuce, iceberg	head	0.73	12/94	2c
Margarine, Blue Bonnet or Parkay cubes	lb.	0.69	12/94	2c
Margarine, stick	lb.	0.77	12/94	82r
Meats, poultry, fish, and eggs purchases	year	655	91	81r
Milk and cream (fresh) purchases	year	130	91	81r
Milk, whole	1/2 gal.	1.35	12/94	2c
Orange juice, frozen concentrate 12-oz. can	16 oz.	1.36	12/94	82r
Orange juice, Minute Maid frozen	12-oz.	1.29	12/94	2c
Oranges, Navel	lb.	0.54	12/94	82r
Peaches, halves or slices, Hunt's, Del Monte, or Libby's	29-oz.	1.46	12/94	2c
Pears, Anjou	lb.	0.81	12/94	82r
Peas, sweet, Del Monte or Green Giant	15-17 oz.	0.50	12/94	2c
Pork chops, center cut, bone-in	lb.	3.07	12/94	82r
Pork purchases	year	142	91	81r
Potato chips	16-oz.	3.15	12/94	82r
Potatoes, frozen, French fried	lb.	0.82	12/94	82r
Potatoes, white	lb.	0.34	12/94	82r
Potatoes, white or red	10-lb. sack	1.93	12/94	2c
Rice, white, long grain, uncooked	lb.	0.48	12/94	82r
Round roast, USDA choice, boneless	lb.	2.91	12/94	82r
Sausage, fresh	lb.	1.82	12/94	82r
Sausage, Jimmy Dean, 100% pork	lb.	2.49	12/94	2c
Shortening, vegetable oil blends	lb.	0.75	12/94	82r
Shortening, vegetable, Crisco	3-lb.	2.10	12/94	2c
Soft drink, Coca Cola, ex deposit	2 lit	1.65	12/94	2c
Spaghetti and macaroni	lb.	0.87	12/94	82r
Steak, rib eye, USDA choice, boneless	lb.	6.85	12/94	82r
Steak, round, graded & ungraded, exc. USDA prime & choice	lb.	2.96	12/94	82r
Steak, round, USDA choice, boneless	lb.	3.17	12/94	82r
Steak, sirloin, USDA choice, boneless	lb.	4.12	12/94	82r
Steak, t-bone	lb.	5.01	12/94	2c
Steak, T-bone, USDA choice, bone-in	lb.	5.63	12/94	82r
Sugar and other sweets, eaten at home, expenditures	year	93	91	81r
Sugar, cane or beet	4 lbs.	1.38	12/94	2c
Sugar, white, all sizes	lb.	0.39	12/94	82r
Tobacco products and smoking supplies, total expenditures	year	286	91	81r
Tomatoes, field grown	lb.	1.36	12/94	82r
Tomatoes, Hunt's or Del Monte	14.5 oz.	0.78	12/94	2c
Tuna, chunk, light	lb.	1.94	12/94	82r
Tuna, chunk, light, oil-packed	6.125-6.5 oz.	0.67	12/94	2c

Values are in dollars or fractions of dollars. In the column headed *Ref*, references are shown to sources. Each reference is followed by a letter. These refer to the geographical level for which data were reported: s=State, r=Region, and c=City or metro. The abbreviation *ex* is used to mean *except* or *excluding*; *exp* stands for *expenditures*. For other abbreviations and further explanations, please see the Introduction.

Lubbock, TX - continued

Item	Per	Value	Date	Ref.
Groceries				
Turkey, frozen, whole	lb.	0.96	12/94	82r
Yogurt, natural, fruit flavored	8 oz.	0.58	12/94	82r
Goods and Services				
Miscellaneous goods and services, ACCRA Index		98.60	12/94	2c
Health Care				
Health care, ACCRA Index		91.80	12/94	2c
Adenosine, emergency room	treat	100.00	95	23r
Antibiotic ointment, Polysporin	1.5 oz.	4.09	12/94	2c
Bladder tap, superpubic, infant, emergency room	treat	119.00	95	23r
Blood analysis, emergency room	treat	25.00	95	23r
Blood tests, abdominal pain, emergency room	treat	25.00	95	23r
Burn dressing, emergency room	treat	266.00	95	23r
Cardiology interpretation, emergency room	treat	26.00	95	23r
Chest X-ray, emergency room	treat	78.00	95	23r
Childbirth, Cesarean delivery, hospital charge	birth	5462.00	12/91	69r
Childbirth, Cesarean delivery, physician charge	birth	2228.00	12/91	69r
Childbirth, normal delivery, hospital charge	birth	2943.00	12/91	69r
Childbirth, normal delivery, physician charge	birth	1619.00	12/91	69r
Defibrillation pads, emergency room	treat	6.00	95	23r
Dentist's fee, adult teeth cleaning and periodic oral exam	visit	54.63	12/94	2c
Doctor's fee, routine exam, established patient	visit	32.44	12/94	2c
Drugs, expenditures	year	297	91	81r
Gastric tube insertion, nasal, emergency room	treat	25.00	95	23r
Health care, total expenditures	year	1600	91	81r
Health insurance expenditures	year	637	91	81r
Heart monitor, emergency room	treat	40.00	95	23r
Hospital care, semiprivate room	day	327.00	12/94	2c
Insurance premium, family medical care	month	389.25	1/95	41s
Intravenous fluids, emergency room	treat	130.00	95	23r
Intravenous fluids, emergency room	liter	26.00	95	23r
Intravenous line, central, emergency room	treat	342.00	95	23r
Liver function tests, abdominal pain, emergency room	treat	26.00	95	23r
Medical care charges, total, emergency room, third-degree burns	treat	2101.00	95	23r
Medical care charges, total, emergency, infant with fever	treat	628.00	95	23r
Medical services expenditures	year	573	91	81r
Medical supplies expenditures	year	93	91	81r
Morphine, emergency room	treat	34.00	95	23r
Nursing care and facilities charges, emergency room	treat	252.00	95	23r
Nursing care and facilities charges, emergency, infant with fever	treat	252.00	95	23r
Nursing care and facilities charges, emergency, third-degree burns	treat	861.00	95	23r
Physician's charges, emergency, infant with fever	treat	212.00	95	23r
Physician's charges, emergency, third-degree burns	treat	372.00	95	23r
Physician's fee, emergency room	treat	372.00	95	23r
Physician's fee, general practitioner	visit	51.20	12/93	60r
Surgery, open-heart	proc	42374.00	1/93	14r
Ultrasound, abdominal, emergency room	treat	276.00	95	23r
Urinalysis, emergency room	treat	20.00	95	23r
Urinalysis, infant, emergency room	treat	20.00	95	23r
X-rays, emergency room	treat	78.00	95	23r
Household Goods				
Appl. repair, service call, wash mach	min. lab. chg.	33.70	12/94	2c
Floor coverings, expenditures	year	48	91	81r
Furniture, expenditures	year	280	91	81r

Lubbock, TX - continued

Item	Per	Value	Date	Ref.
Household Goods - continued				
Household equipment, misc. expenditures	year	342	91	81r
Household expenditures, miscellaneous	year	256	91	81r
Household furnishings and equipment, expenditures	year	988	91	81r
Household operations expenditures	year	468	91	81r
Household textiles, expenditures	year	95	91	81r
Housekeeping supplies, expenditures	year	380	91	81r
Laundry and cleaning supplies, expenditures	year	109	91	81r
Laundry detergent, Tide Ultra, Bold, or Cheer	42 oz.	3.05	12/94	2c
Postage and stationery, expenditures	year	105	91	81r
Tissues, facial, Kleenex brand	175	0.94	12/94	2c
Housing				
Housing, ACCRA Index		88.10	12/94	2c
Add garage/carport		6,980	3/95	74r
Add room(s)		11,403	3/95	74r
Apartment condominium or co-op, median	unit	68600	12/94	62r
Dwellings (owned), expenditures	year	2428	91	81r
Enclose porch/patio/breezeway		4,572	3/95	74r
Finish room in basement/attic		3,794	3/95	74r
Home, existing, single-family, median	unit	120200	12/94	62r
House payment, principal and interest, 25% down payment	mo.	673	12/94	2c
House, 1800 sq ft, 8000 sq ft lot, new, urban, utilities	total	108020	12/94	2c
Maintenance, repairs, insurance, and other housing expenditures	year	531	91	81r
Mortgage interest and charges expenditures	year	1506	91	81r
Mtge. rate, incl. points and orig. fee, 30-year conv. fixed or ARM	mo.	9.37	12/94	2c
Princ. & int., mortgage, median-price exist. sing.-family home	mo.	540	12/94	62r
Property taxes expenditures	year	391	91	81r
Redesign, restructure more than half of home's interior		17,641	3/95	74r
Rent, apartment, 2 br., 1 1/2-2 baths, unfurnished, 950 sq ft, water	mo.	469	12/94	2c
Rental units expenditures	year	1264	91	81r
Insurance and Pensions				
Auto insurance, private passenger	year	785.78	12/94	71s
Insurance and pensions, personal, expenditures	year	2395	91	81r
Insurance, life and other personal, expenditures	year	368	91	81r
Pensions and Social Security, expenditures	year	2027	91	81r
Personal Goods				
Shampoo, Alberto VO5	15-oz.	1.06	12/94	2c
Toothpaste, Crest or Colgate	6-7 oz.	2.27	12/94	2c
Personal Services				
Dry cleaning, man's 2-pc. suit		5.68	12/94	2c
Haircut, man's barbershop, no styling		7.40	12/94	2c
Haircut, woman's shampoo, trim, blow-dry		17.50	12/94	2c
Personal services expenditures	year	212	91	81r
Restaurant Food				
Chicken, fried, thigh and drumstick		2.24	12/94	2c
Dining expenditures, family	week	33.83	94	73r
Hamburger with cheese	1/4 lb.	1.75	12/94	2c
Pizza, Pizza Hut or Pizza Inn	12-13 in.	7.99	12/94	2c
Taxes				
Tax, cigarettes	year	584.00	10/93	43s
Taxes, Federal income, expenditures	year	2275	91	81r
Taxes, personal, expenditures	year	2715	91	81r
Taxes, State and local income, expenditures	year	365	91	81r
Transportation				
Transportation, ACCRA Index		94.50	12/94	2c
Bus fare, one-way	trip	0.75	12/95	1c

Values are in dollars or fractions of dollars. In the column headed *Ref*, references are shown to sources. Each reference is followed by a letter. These refer to the geographical level for which data were reported: s = State, r = Region, and c = City or metro. The abbreviation *ex* is used to mean *except* or *excluding*; *exp* stands for expenditures. For other abbreviations and further explanations, please see the Introduction.

Lubbock, TX - continued

Item	Per	Value	Date	Ref.
Transportation				
Cars and trucks purchased, new	year	1306	91	81r
Cars and trucks purchased, used	year	942	91	81r
Driver's learning permit fee	perm	5.00	1/94	84s
Driver's license fee	orig	16.00	1/94	84s
Driver's license fee, duplicate	lic	10.00	1/94	84s
Driver's license reinstatement fee, min.	susp	50.00	1/94	85s
Driver's license renewal fee	renew	16.00	1/94	84s
Identification card, nondriver	card	10.00	1/94	83s
Motorcycle learning permit fee	perm	5.00	1/94	84s
Motorcycle license fee	orig	16.00	1/94	84s
Motorcycle license fee, duplicate	lic	10.00	1/94	84s
Motorcycle license renewal fee	renew	21.00	1/94	84s
Public transportation expenditures	year	249	91	81r
Tire balance, computer or spin bal., front	wheel	5.80	12/94	2c
Transportation expenditures, total	year	5307	91	81r
Vehicle finance charges	year	346	91	81r
Vehicle insurance expenditures	year	544	91	81r
Vehicle maintenance and repairs expenditures	year	600	91	81r
Vehicle purchases	year	2275	91	81r
Vehicle rental, leases, licenses, etc. expenditures	year	141	91	81r
Vehicles purchased, other than cars and trucks	year	27	91	81r
Utilities				
Utilities, ACCRA Index		72.80	12/94	2c
Electricity expenditures	year	950	91	81r
Electricity, (part.), other, 1800 sq. ft., new home	mo.	51.80	12/94	2c
Utilities, fuels, and public services, total expenditures	year	2000	91	81r
Water and other public services, expenditures	year	227	91	81r
Weddings				
Bridal attendants' gowns	event	750	10/93	76r
Bridal gown	event	852	10/93	76r
Bridal headpiece and veil	event	167	10/93	76r
Bride's wedding band	event	708	10/93	76r
Clergy	event	224	10/93	76r
Engagement ring	event	2756	10/93	76r
Flowers	event	863	10/93	76r
Formal wear for groom	event	106	10/93	76r
Groom's attendants' formal wear	event	530	10/93	76r
Groom's wedding band	event	402	10/93	76r
Music	event	600	10/93	76r
Photography	event	1088	10/93	76r
Shoes for bride	event	50	10/93	76r
Videography	event	483	10/93	76r
Wedding invitations and announcements	event	342	10/93	76r
Wedding reception	event	7000	10/93	76r

Lynchburg, VA

Item	Per	Value	Date	Ref.
Composite, ACCRA index		91.60	12/94	2c
Alcoholic Beverages				
Beer, Miller Lite, Bud, 12-oz., ex deposit	6	3.61	12/94	2c
J & B Scotch	750-ml.	18.45	12/94	2c
Wine, Gallo Chablis blanc	1.5-lit	4.79	12/94	2c
Appliances				
Appliances (major), expenditures	year	153	91	81r
Average annual exp.				
Food, health care, personal goods, services	year	27020	91	81r
Charity				
Cash contributions, expenditures	year	839	91	81r
Clothing				
Apparel, men and boys, total expenditures	year	380	91	81r
Apparel, women and girls, total expenditures	year	660	91	81r

Lynchburg, VA - continued

Item	Per	Value	Date	Ref.
Clothing - continued				
Footwear, expenditures	year	193	91	81r
Jeans, man's denim		31.96	12/94	2c
Shirt, man's dress shirt		26.70	12/94	2c
Undervest, boy's size 10-14, cotton	3	3.49	12/94	2c
Communications				
Long-distance telephone rate, day, addl. min., 1-10 mi.	min.	0.12	12/93	9s
Long-distance telephone rate, day, initial min., 1-10 mi.	min.	0.21	12/93	9s
Newspaper subscription, dly. and Sun. delivery	month	11.09	12/94	2c
Phone line, single, business, field visit	inst	0.00	12/93	9s
Phone line, single, business, no field visit	inst	64.00	12/93	9s
Phone line, single, residence, field visit	inst	0.00	12/93	9s
Phone line, single, residence, no field visit	inst	38.50	12/93	9s
Telephone bill, family of four	month	17.30	12/94	2c
Telephone service, expenditures	year	616	91	81r
Education				
Board, 4-year private college/university	year	2242	8/94	80s
Board, 4-year public college/university	year	1901	8/94	80s
Education, total expenditures	year	319	91	81r
Room, 4-year private college/university	year	2022	8/94	80s
Room, 4-year public college/university	year	2186	8/94	80s
Total cost, 4-year private college/university	year	14043	8/94	80s
Total cost, 4-year public college/university	year	7726	8/94	80s
Tuition, 2-year public college/university, in-state	year	1332	8/94	80s
Tuition, 4-year private college/university, in-state	year	9778	8/94	80s
Tuition, 4-year public college/university, in-state	year	3639	8/94	80s
Energy and Fuels				
Energy, combined forms, 1800 sq. ft.	mo.	94.75	12/94	2c
Fuel oil and other fuels, expenditures	year	56	91	81r
Gas, natural, expenditures	year	150	91	81r
Gas, reg unlead, taxes inc., cash, self-service	gal	1.03	12/94	2c
Gasoline and motor oil purchased	year	1152	91	81r
Gasoline, unleaded midgrade	gallon	1.21	4/93	82r
Gasoline, unleaded premium	gallon	1.30	4/93	82r
Gasoline, unleaded regular	gallon	1.10	4/93	82r
Entertainment				
Bowling, evening rate	game	2.37	12/94	2c
Concert ticket, Pearl Jam group	perf	20.00	94	50r
Entertainment, total expenditures	year	1266	91	81r
Fees and admissions, expenditures	year	306	91	81r
Monopoly game, Parker Brothers', No. 9	game	11.04	12/94	2c
Movie	adm	5.75	12/94	2c
Pets, toys, playground equipment, expenditures	year	271	91	81r
Reading, expenditures	year	131	91	81r
Televisions, radios, and sound equipment, expenditures	year	439	91	81r
Tennis balls, yellow, Wilson or Penn, 3	can	2.16	12/94	2c
Funerals				
Burial, immediate, container provided by funeral home		1370.36	1/95	54r
Cards, acknowledgment		14.83	1/95	54r
Casket, minimum alternative		192.52	1/95	54r
Cosmetology, hair care, etc.		102.27	1/95	54r
Cremation, direct, container provided by funeral home		1065.64	1/95	54r
Embalming		304.29	1/95	54r
Funeral, funeral home		287.83	1/95	54r
Funeral, other facility		284.14	1/95	54r
Graveside service		349.13	1/95	54r
Hearse, local		132.27	1/95	54r
Limousine, local		98.45	1/95	54r
Memorial service		270.59	1/95	54r

Values are in dollars or fractions of dollars. In the column headed *Ref*, references are shown to sources. Each reference is followed by a letter. These refer to the geographical level for which data were reported: s = State, r = Region, and c = City or metro. The abbreviation *ex* is used to mean *except* or *excluding*; *exp* stands for expenditures. For other abbreviations and further explanations, please see the Introduction.

Lynchburg, VA - continued

Item	Per	Value	Date	Ref.
Funerals				
Service charge, professional, nondeclinable		933.59	1/95	54r
Visitation and viewing		225.83	1/95	54r
Groceries				
Groceries, ACCRA Index		97.60	12/94	2c
Apples, Red Delicious	lb.	0.73	12/94	82r
Baby food, strained vegetables, lowest price	4-4.5 oz.	0.34	12/94	2c
Bacon, sliced	lb.	1.67	12/94	82r
Bananas	lb.	0.46	12/94	2c
Bananas	lb.	0.42	12/94	82r
Beef or hamburger, ground	lb.	1.51	12/94	2c
Beef purchases	year	213	91	81r
Beverage purchases, alcoholic	year	249	91	81r
Beverage purchases, nonalcoholic	year	207	91	81r
Bologna, all beef or mixed	lb.	2.27	12/94	82r
Bread, white	24-oz.	0.77	12/94	2c
Bread, white, pan	lb.	0.68	12/94	82r
Cabbage	lb.	0.42	12/94	82r
Carrots, short trimmed and topped	lb.	0.53	12/94	82r
Cereals and bakery products purchases	year	345	91	81r
Cereals and cereals products purchases	year	127	91	81r
Cheddar cheese, natural	lb.	3.58	12/94	82r
Cheese, Kraft grated Parmesan	8-oz.	3.18	12/94	2c
Chicken breast, bone-in	lb.	1.71	12/94	82r
Chicken, fresh, whole	lb.	0.78	12/94	82r
Chicken, whole fryer	lb.	0.81	12/94	2c
Chuck roast, USDA choice, boneless	lb.	2.26	12/94	82r
Cigarettes, Winston, Kings	carton	12.94	12/94	2c
Coffee, vacuum-packed	13 oz.	3.14	12/94	2c
Corn Flakes, Kellogg's or Post Toasties	18 oz.	2.45	12/94	2c
Corn, frozen, whole kernel, lowest price	10 oz.	0.62	12/94	2c
Crackers, soda, salted	lb.	1.27	12/94	82r
Cucumbers	lb.	0.65	12/94	82r
Dairy products (other) purchases	year	141	91	81r
Eggs, Grade A large	dozen	0.85	12/94	2c
Eggs, Grade A large	dozen	0.87	12/94	82r
Fish and seafood purchases	year	72	91	81r
Flour, white, all purpose	lb.	0.23	12/94	82r
Food purchases, food eaten at home	year	2381	91	81r
Foods purchased away from home, not prepared by consumer	year	1696	91	81r
Frankfurters, all meat or all beef	lb.	1.74	12/94	82r
Fruits and vegetables purchases	year	380	91	81r
Grapefruit	lb.	0.45	12/94	82r
Grapes, Thompson seedless	lb.	2.30	12/94	82r
Ground beef, 100% beef	lb.	1.37	12/94	82r
Ground chuck, 100% beef	lb.	1.97	12/94	82r
Ham, boneless, exc. canned	lb.	2.54	12/94	82r
Ice cream, prepackaged, bulk, regular	1/2 gal.	2.47	12/94	82r
Lemons	lb.	1.02	12/94	82r
Lettuce, iceberg	lb.	0.96	12/94	82r
Lettuce, iceberg	head	0.99	12/94	2c
Margarine, Blue Bonnet or Parkay cubes	lb.	0.56	12/94	2c
Margarine, stick	lb.	0.77	12/94	82r
Meats, poultry, fish, and eggs purchases	year	655	91	81r
Milk and cream (fresh) purchases	year	130	91	81r
Milk, whole	1/2 gal.	1.40	12/94	2c
Orange juice, frozen concentrate 12-oz. can	16 oz.	1.36	12/94	82r
Orange juice, Minute Maid frozen	12-oz.	1.21	12/94	2c
Oranges, Navel	lb.	0.54	12/94	82r
Peaches, halves or slices, Hunt's, Del Monte, or Libby's	29-oz.	1.26	12/94	2c
Pears, Anjou	lb.	0.81	12/94	82r
Peas, sweet, Del Monte or Green Giant	15-17 oz.	0.43	12/94	2c
Pork chops, center cut, bone-in	lb.	3.07	12/94	82r
Pork purchases	year	142	91	81r
Potato chips	16-oz.	3.15	12/94	82r
Potatoes, frozen, French fried	lb.	0.82	12/94	82r
Potatoes, white	lb.	0.34	12/94	82r

Lynchburg, VA - continued

Item	Per	Value	Date	Ref.
Groceries - continued				
Potatoes, white or red	10-lb. sack	2.74	12/94	2c
Rice, white, long grain, uncooked	lb.	0.48	12/94	82r
Round roast, USDA choice, boneless	lb.	2.91	12/94	82r
Sausage, fresh	lb.	1.82	12/94	82r
Sausage, Jimmy Dean, 100% pork	lb.	2.26	12/94	2c
Shortening, vegetable oil blends	lb.	0.75	12/94	82r
Shortening, vegetable, Crisco	3-lb.	2.50	12/94	2c
Soft drink, Coca Cola, ex deposit	2 lit	1.13	12/94	2c
Spaghetti and macaroni	lb.	0.87	12/94	82r
Steak, rib eye, USDA choice, boneless	lb.	6.85	12/94	82r
Steak, round, graded & ungraded, exc. USDA prime & choice	lb.	2.96	12/94	82r
Steak, round, USDA choice, boneless	lb.	3.17	12/94	82r
Steak, sirloin, USDA choice, boneless	lb.	4.12	12/94	82r
Steak, t-bone	lb.	5.91	12/94	2c
Steak, T-bone, USDA choice, bone-in	lb.	5.63	12/94	82r
Sugar and other sweets, eaten at home, expenditures	year	93	91	81r
Sugar, cane or beet	4 lbs.	1.50	12/94	2c
Sugar, white, all sizes	lb.	0.39	12/94	82r
Tobacco products and smoking supplies, total expenditures	year	286	91	81r
Tomatoes, field grown	lb.	1.36	12/94	82r
Tomatoes, Hunt's or Del Monte	14.5 oz.	0.53	12/94	2c
Tuna, chunk, light	lb.	1.94	12/94	82r
Tuna, chunk, light, oil-packed	6.125-6.5 oz.	0.66	12/94	2c
Turkey, frozen, whole	lb.	0.96	12/94	82r
Yogurt, natural, fruit flavored	8 oz.	0.58	12/94	82r
Goods and Services				
Miscellaneous goods and services, ACCRA Index		92.60	12/94	2c
Health Care				
Health care, ACCRA Index		88.60	12/94	2c
Adenosine, emergency room	treat	100.00	95	23r
Antibiotic ointment, Polysporin	1.5 oz.	3.85	12/94	2c
Bladder tap, superpubic, infant, emergency room	treat	119.00	95	23r
Blood analysis, emergency room	treat	25.00	95	23r
Blood tests, abdominal pain, emergency room	treat	25.00	95	23r
Burn dressing, emergency room	treat	266.00	95	23r
Cardiology interpretation, emergency room	treat	26.00	95	23r
Chest X-ray, emergency room	treat	78.00	95	23r
Childbirth, Cesarean delivery, hospital charge	birth	5462.00	12/91	69r
Childbirth, Cesarean delivery, physician charge	birth	2228.00	12/91	69r
Childbirth, normal delivery, hospital charge	birth	2943.00	12/91	69r
Childbirth, normal delivery, physician charge	birth	1619.00	12/91	69r
Defibrillation pads, emergency room	treat	6.00	95	23r
Delivery, uncomplicated, total charge	birth	6180	1/93	24s
Delivery, uncomplicated, vaginal, hospital charge	birth	3380	1/93	24s
Delivery, uncomplicated, vaginal, physician's charge	birth	2800	1/93	24s
Dentist's fee, adult teeth cleaning and periodic oral exam	visit	46.62	12/94	2c
Doctor's fee, routine exam, established patient	visit	37.60	12/94	2c
Drugs, expenditures	year	297	91	81r
Gastric tube insertion, nasal, emergency room	treat	25.00	95	23r
Health care, total expenditures	year	1600	91	81r
Health insurance expenditures	year	637	91	81r
Heart monitor, emergency room	treat	40.00	95	23r
Hospital care, semiprivate room	day	295.00	12/94	2c
Insurance premium, family medical care	month	386.57	1/95	41s
Intravenous fluids, emergency room	treat	130.00	95	23r

Values are in dollars or fractions of dollars. In the column headed *Ref*, references are shown to sources. Each reference is followed by a letter. These refer to the geographical level for which data were reported: s=State, r=Region, and c=City or metro. The abbreviation *ex* is used to mean *except* or *excluding*; *exp* stands for expenditures. For other abbreviations and further explanations, please see the Introduction.

Lynchburg, VA - continued

Item	Per	Value	Date	Ref.
Health Care				
Intravenous fluids, emergency room	liter	26.00	95	23r
Intravenous line, central, emergency room	treat	342.00	95	23r
Liver function tests, abdominal pain, emergency room	treat	26.00	95	23r
Medical care charges, total, emergency room, third-degree burns	treat	2101.00	95	23r
Medical care charges, total, emergency, infant with fever	treat	628.00	95	23r
Medical services expenditures	year	573	91	81r
Medical supplies expenditures	year	93	91	81r
Morphine, emergency room	treat	34.00	95	23r
Nursing care and facilities charges, emergency room	treat	252.00	95	23r
Nursing care and facilities charges, emergency, infant with fever	treat	252.00	95	23r
Nursing care and facilities charges, emergency, third-degree burns	treat	861.00	95	23r
Physician's charges, emergency, infant with fever	treat	212.00	95	23r
Physician's charges, emergency, third-degree burns	treat	372.00	95	23r
Physician's fee, emergency room	treat	372.00	95	23r
Physician's fee, general practitioner	visit	51.20	12/93	60r
Surgery, open-heart	proc	42374.00	1/93	14r
Ultrasound, abdominal, emergency room	treat	276.00	95	23r
Urinalysis, emergency room	treat	20.00	95	23r
Urinalysis, infant, emergency room	treat	20.00	95	23r
X-rays, emergency room	treat	78.00	95	23r
Household Goods				
Appl. repair, service call, wash mach	min. lab. chg.	32.11	12/94	2c
Floor coverings, expenditures	year	48	91	81r
Furniture, expenditures	year	280	91	81r
Household equipment, misc. expenditures	year	342	91	81r
Household expenditures, miscellaneous	year	256	91	81r
Household furnishings and equipment, expenditures	year	988	91	81r
Household operations expenditures	year	468	91	81r
Household textiles, expenditures	year	95	91	81r
Housekeeping supplies, expenditures	year	380	91	81r
Laundry and cleaning supplies, expenditures	year	109	91	81r
Laundry detergent, Tide Ultra, Bold, or Cheer	42 oz.	2.68	12/94	2c
Postage and stationery, expenditures	year	105	91	81r
Tissues, facial, Kleenex brand	175	1.00	12/94	2c
Housing				
Housing, ACCRA Index		91.90	12/94	2c
Add garage/carport		6,980	3/95	74r
Add room(s)		11,403	3/95	74r
Apartment condominium or co-op, median	unit	68600	12/94	62r
Dwellings (owned), expenditures	year	2428	91	81r
Enclose porch/patio/breezeway		4,572	3/95	74r
Finish room in basement/attic		3,794	3/95	74r
Home, existing, single-family, median	unit	120200	12/94	62r
House payment, principal and interest, 25% down payment	mo.	686	12/94	2c
House, 1800 sq ft, 8000 sq ft lot, new, urban, utilities	total	109700	12/94	2c
Maintenance, repairs, insurance, and other housing expenditures	year	531	91	81r
Mortgage interest and charges expenditures	year	1506	91	81r
Mtge. rate, incl. points and orig. fee, 30-year conv. fixed or ARM	mo.	9.40	12/94	2c
Princ. & int., mortgage, median-price exist. sing.-family home	mo.	540	12/94	62r
Property taxes expenditures	year	391	91	81r
Redesign, restructure more than half of home's interior		17,641	3/95	74r

Lynchburg, VA - continued

Item	Per	Value	Date	Ref.
Housing - continued				
Rent, apartment, 2 br., 1 1/2-2 baths, unfurnished, 950 sq ft, water	mo.	448	12/94	2c
Rental units expenditures	year	1264	91	81r
Insurance and Pensions				
Auto insurance, private passenger	year	564.07	12/94	71s
Insurance and pensions, personal, expenditures	year	2395	91	81r
Insurance, life and other personal, expenditures	year	368	91	81r
Pensions and Social Security, expenditures	year	2027	91	81r
Personal Goods				
Shampoo, Alberto VO5	15-oz.	0.98	12/94	2c
Toothpaste, Crest or Colgate	6-7 oz.	1.88	12/94	2c
Personal Services				
Dry cleaning, man's 2-pc. suit		6.92	12/94	2c
Haircut, man's barbershop, no styling		8.09	12/94	2c
Haircut, woman's shampoo, trim, blow-dry		20.82	12/94	2c
Personal services expenditures	year	212	91	81r
Restaurant Food				
Chicken, fried, thigh and drumstick		2.19	12/94	2c
Dining expenditures, family	week	33.83	94	73r
Hamburger with cheese	1/4 lb.	0.99	12/94	2c
Pizza, Pizza Hut or Pizza Inn	12-13 in.	7.50	12/94	2c
Taxes				
Taxes, Federal income, expenditures	year	2275	91	81r
Taxes, personal, expenditures	year	2715	91	81r
Taxes, State and local income, expenditures	year	365	91	81r
Transportation				
Transportation, ACCRA Index		84.60	12/94	2c
Bus fare, one-way	trip	0.75	12/95	1c
Cars and trucks purchased, new	year	1306	91	81r
Cars and trucks purchased, used	year	942	91	81r
Driver's learning permit fee	perm	3.00	1/94	84s
Driver's license fee	orig	12.00	1/94	84s
Driver's license fee, duplicate	lic	5.00	1/94	84s
Driver's license reinstatement fee, min.	susp	30.00	1/94	85s
Driver's license renewal fee	renew	12.00	1/94	84s
Identification card, nondriver	card	5.00	1/94	83s
Motorcycle license fee	orig	5.00	1/94	84s
Motorcycle license renewal fee	renew	5.00	1/94	84s
Public transportation expenditures	year	249	91	81r
Tire balance, computer or spin bal., front	wheel	5.10	12/94	2c
Transportation expenditures, total	year	5307	91	81r
Vehicle finance charges	year	346	91	81r
Vehicle insurance expenditures	year	544	91	81r
Vehicle maintenance and repairs expenditures	year	600	91	81r
Vehicle purchases	year	2275	91	81r
Vehicle rental, leases, licenses, etc. expenditures	year	141	91	81r
Vehicles purchased, other than cars and trucks	year	27	91	81r
Utilities				
Utilities, ACCRA Index		85.00	12/94	2c
Electricity expenditures	year	950	91	81r
Electricity, 1800 sq. ft., new home	mo.	94.75	12/94	2c
Utilities, fuels, and public services, total expenditures	year	2000	91	81r
Water and other public services, expenditures	year	227	91	81r
Weddings				
Bridal attendants' gowns	event	750	10/93	76r
Bridal gown	event	852	10/93	76r
Bridal headpiece and veil	event	167	10/93	76r
Bride's wedding band	event	708	10/93	76r
Clergy	event	224	10/93	76r
Engagement ring	event	2756	10/93	76r

Values are in dollars or fractions of dollars. In the column headed *Ref*, references are shown to sources. Each reference is followed by a letter. These refer to the geographical level for which data were reported: s = State, r = Region, and c = City or metro. The abbreviation *ex* is used to mean *except* or *excluding*; *exp* stands for *expenditures*. For other abbreviations and further explanations, please see the Introduction.

Lynchburg, VA - continued

Item	Per	Value	Date	Ref.
Weddings				
Flowers	event	863	10/93	76r
Formal wear for groom	event	106	10/93	76r
Groom's attendants' formal wear	event	530	10/93	76r
Groom's wedding band	event	402	10/93	76r
Music	event	600	10/93	76r
Photography	event	1088	10/93	76r
Shoes for bride	event	50	10/93	76r
Videography	event	483	10/93	76r
Wedding invitations and announcements	event	342	10/93	76r
Wedding reception	event	7000	10/93	76r

Macon, GA

Item	Per	Value	Date	Ref.
Appliances				
Appliances (major), expenditures	year	153	91	81r
Average annual exp.				
Food, health care, personal goods, services	year	27020	91	81r
Charity				
Cash contributions, expenditures	year	839	91	81r
Clothing				
Apparel, men and boys, total expenditures	year	380	91	81r
Apparel, women and girls, total expenditures	year	660	91	81r
Footwear, expenditures	year	193	91	81r
Communications				
Long-distance telephone rate, day, addl. min., 1-10 mi.	min.	0.04	12/93	9s
Long-distance telephone rate, day, initial min., 1-10 mi.	min.	0.08	12/93	9s
Phone line, single, business, field visit	inst	58.25	12/93	9s
Phone line, single, business, no field visit	inst	52.25	12/93	9s
Phone line, single, residence, field visit	inst	47.50	12/93	9s
Phone line, single, residence, no field visit	inst	42.50	12/93	9s
Telephone service, expenditures	year	616	91	81r
Education				
Board, 4-year private college/university	year	2288	8/94	80s
Board, 4-year public college/university	year	1723	8/94	80s
Education, total expenditures	year	319	91	81r
Room, 4-year private college/university	year	2409	8/94	80s
Room, 4-year public college/university	year	1459	8/94	80s
Total cost, 4-year private college/university	year	13950	8/94	80s
Total cost, 4-year public college/university	year	5075	8/94	80s
Tuition, 2-year public college/university, in-state	year	972	8/94	80s
Tuition, 4-year private college/university, in-state	year	9253	8/94	80s
Tuition, 4-year public college/university, in-state	year	1894	8/94	80s
Energy and Fuels				
Fuel oil and other fuels, expenditures	year	56	91	81r
Gas, natural, expenditures	year	150	91	81r
Gasoline and motor oil purchased	year	1152	91	81r
Gasoline, unleaded midgrade	gallon	1.21	4/93	82r
Gasoline, unleaded premium	gallon	1.30	4/93	82r
Gasoline, unleaded regular	gallon	1.10	4/93	82r
Entertainment				
Concert ticket, Pearl Jam group	perf	20.00	94	50r
Entertainment, total expenditures	year	1266	91	81r
Fees and admissions, expenditures	year	306	91	81r
Pets, toys, playground equipment, expenditures	year	271	91	81r
Reading, expenditures	year	131	91	81r
Televisions, radios, and sound equipment, expenditures	year	439	91	81r
Funerals				
Burial, immediate, container provided by funeral home		1370.36	1/95	54r
Cards, acknowledgment		14.83	1/95	54r

Macon, GA - continued

Item	Per	Value	Date	Ref.
Funerals - continued				
Casket, minimum alternative		192.52	1/95	54r
Cosmetology, hair care, etc.		102.27	1/95	54r
Cremation, direct, container provided by funeral home		1065.64	1/95	54r
Embalming		304.29	1/95	54r
Funeral, funeral home		287.83	1/95	54r
Funeral, other facility		284.14	1/95	54r
Graveside service		349.13	1/95	54r
Hearse, local		132.27	1/95	54r
Limousine, local		98.45	1/95	54r
Memorial service		270.59	1/95	54r
Service charge, professional, nondeclinable		933.59	1/95	54r
Visitation and viewing		225.83	1/95	54r
Groceries				
Apples, Red Delicious	lb.	0.73	12/94	82r
Bacon, sliced	lb.	1.67	12/94	82r
Bananas	lb.	0.42	12/94	82r
Beef purchases	year	213	91	81r
Beverage purchases, alcoholic	year	249	91	81r
Beverage purchases, nonalcoholic	year	207	91	81r
Bologna, all beef or mixed	lb.	2.27	12/94	82r
Bread, white, pan	lb.	0.68	12/94	82r
Cabbage	lb.	0.42	12/94	82r
Carrots, short trimmed and topped	lb.	0.53	12/94	82r
Cereals and bakery products purchases	year	345	91	81r
Cereals and cereals products purchases	year	127	91	81r
Cheddar cheese, natural	lb.	3.58	12/94	82r
Chicken breast, bone-in	lb.	1.71	12/94	82r
Chicken, fresh, whole	lb.	0.78	12/94	82r
Chuck roast, USDA choice, boneless	lb.	2.26	12/94	82r
Crackers, soda, salted	lb.	1.27	12/94	82r
Cucumbers	lb.	0.65	12/94	82r
Dairy products (other) purchases	year	141	91	81r
Eggs, Grade A large	dozen	0.87	12/94	82r
Fish and seafood purchases	year	72	91	81r
Flour, white, all purpose	lb.	0.23	12/94	82r
Food purchases, food eaten at home	year	2381	91	81r
Foods purchased away from home, not prepared by consumer	year	1696	91	81r
Frankfurters, all meat or all beef	lb.	1.74	12/94	82r
Fruits and vegetables purchases	year	380	91	81r
Grapefruit	lb.	0.45	12/94	82r
Grapes, Thompson seedless	lb.	2.30	12/94	82r
Ground beef, 100% beef	lb.	1.37	12/94	82r
Ground chuck, 100% beef	lb.	1.97	12/94	82r
Ham, boneless, exc. canned	lb.	2.54	12/94	82r
Ice cream, prepackaged, bulk, regular	1/2 gal.	2.47	12/94	82r
Lemons	lb.	1.02	12/94	82r
Lettuce, iceberg	lb.	0.96	12/94	82r
Margarine, stick	lb.	0.77	12/94	82r
Meats, poultry, fish, and eggs purchases	year	655	91	81r
Milk and cream (fresh) purchases	year	130	91	81r
Orange juice, frozen concentrate 12-oz. can	16 oz.	1.36	12/94	82r
Oranges, Navel	lb.	0.54	12/94	82r
Pears, Anjou	lb.	0.81	12/94	82r
Pork chops, center cut, bone-in	lb.	3.07	12/94	82r
Pork purchases	year	142	91	81r
Potato chips	16-oz.	3.15	12/94	82r
Potatoes, frozen, French fried	lb.	0.82	12/94	82r
Potatoes, white	lb.	0.34	12/94	82r
Rice, white, long grain, uncooked	lb.	0.48	12/94	82r
Round roast, USDA choice, boneless	lb.	2.91	12/94	82r
Sausage, fresh	lb.	1.82	12/94	82r
Shortening, vegetable oil blends	lb.	0.75	12/94	82r
Spaghetti and macaroni	lb.	0.87	12/94	82r
Steak, rib eye, USDA choice, boneless	lb.	6.85	12/94	82r
Steak, round, graded & ungraded, exc. USDA prime & choice	lb.	2.96	12/94	82r
Steak, round, USDA choice, boneless	lb.	3.17	12/94	82r
Steak, sirloin, USDA choice, boneless	lb.	4.12	12/94	82r
Steak, T-bone, USDA choice, bone-in	lb.	5.63	12/94	82r

Values are in dollars or fractions of dollars. In the column headed *Ref*, references are shown to sources. Each reference is followed by a letter. These refer to the geographical level for which data were reported: s = State, r = Region, and c = City or metro. The abbreviation *ex* is used to mean *except* or *excluding*; *exp* stands for expenditures. For other abbreviations and further explanations, please see the Introduction.

Macon, GA - continued

Item	Per	Value	Date	Ref.
Groceries				
Sugar and other sweets, eaten at home, expenditures	year	93	91	81r
Sugar, white, all sizes	lb.	0.39	12/94	82r
Tobacco products and smoking supplies, total expenditures	year	286	91	81r
Tomatoes, field grown	lb.	1.36	12/94	82r
Tuna, chunk, light	lb.	1.94	12/94	82r
Turkey, frozen, whole	lb.	0.96	12/94	82r
Yogurt, natural, fruit flavored	8 oz.	0.58	12/94	82r
Health Care				
Adenosine, emergency room	treat	100.00	95	23r
Bladder tap, superpubic, infant, emergency room	treat	119.00	95	23r
Blood analysis, emergency room	treat	25.00	95	23r
Blood tests, abdominal pain, emergency room	treat	25.00	95	23r
Burn dressing, emergency room	treat	266.00	95	23r
Cardiology interpretation, emergency room	treat	26.00	95	23r
Chest X-ray, emergency room	treat	78.00	95	23r
Childbirth, Cesarean delivery, hospital charge	birth	5462.00	12/91	69r
Childbirth, Cesarean delivery, physician charge	birth	2228.00	12/91	69r
Childbirth, normal delivery, hospital charge	birth	2943.00	12/91	69r
Childbirth, normal delivery, physician charge	birth	1619.00	12/91	69r
Defibrillation pads, emergency room	treat	6.00	95	23r
Drugs, expenditures	year	297	91	81r
Gastric tube insertion, nasal, emergency room	treat	25.00	95	23r
Health care, total expenditures	year	1600	91	81r
Health insurance expenditures	year	637	91	81r
Heart monitor, emergency room	treat	40.00	95	23r
Insurance premium, family medical care	month	320.13	1/95	41s
Intravenous fluids, emergency room	treat	130.00	95	23r
Intravenous fluids, emergency room	liter	26.00	95	23r
Intravenous line, central, emergency room	treat	342.00	95	23r
Liver function tests, abdominal pain, emergency room	treat	26.00	95	23r
Medical care charges, total, emergency room, third-degree burns	treat	2101.00	95	23r
Medical care charges, total, emergency, infant with fever	treat	628.00	95	23r
Medical services expenditures	year	573	91	81r
Medical supplies expenditures	year	93	91	81r
Morphine, emergency room	treat	34.00	95	23r
Nursing care and facilities charges, emergency room	treat	252.00	95	23r
Nursing care and facilities charges, emergency, infant with fever	treat	252.00	95	23r
Nursing care and facilities charges, emergency, third-degree burns	treat	861.00	95	23r
Physician's charges, emergency, infant with fever	treat	212.00	95	23r
Physician's charges, emergency, third-degree burns	treat	372.00	95	23r
Physician's fee, emergency room	treat	372.00	95	23r
Physician's fee, general practitioner	visit	51.20	12/93	60r
Surgery, open-heart	proc	42374.00	1/93	14r
Ultrasound, abdominal, emergency room	treat	276.00	95	23r
Urinalysis, emergency room	treat	20.00	95	23r
Urinalysis, infant, emergency room	treat	20.00	95	23r
X-rays, emergency room	treat	78.00	95	23r
Household Goods				
Floor coverings, expenditures	year	48	91	81r
Furniture, expenditures	year	280	91	81r
Household equipment, misc. expenditures	year	342	91	81r
Household expenditures, miscellaneous	year	256	91	81r
Household furnishings and equipment, expenditures	year	988	91	81r
Household operations expenditures	year	468	91	81r
Household textiles, expenditures	year	95	91	81r

Macon, GA - continued

Item	Per	Value	Date	Ref.
Household Goods - continued				
Housekeeping supplies, expenditures	year	380	91	81r
Laundry and cleaning supplies, expenditures	year	109	91	81r
Postage and stationery, expenditures	year	105	91	81r
Housing				
Add garage/carport		6,980	3/95	74r
Add room(s)		11,403	3/95	74r
Apartment condominium or co-op, median	unit	68600	12/94	62r
Dwellings (owned), expenditures	year	2428	91	81r
Enclose porch/patio/breezeway		4,572	3/95	74r
Finish room in basement/attic		3,794	3/95	74r
Home, existing, single-family, median	unit	120200	12/94	62r
Maintenance, repairs, insurance, and other housing expenditures	year	531	91	81r
Mortgage interest and charges expenditures	year	1506	91	81r
Princ. & int., mortgage, median-price exist. sing.-family home	mo.	540	12/94	62r
Property taxes expenditures	year	391	91	81r
Redesign, restructure more than half of home's interior		17,641	3/95	74r
Rental units expenditures	year	1264	91	81r
Insurance and Pensions				
Auto insurance, private passenger	year	664.85	12/94	71s
Insurance and pensions, personal, expenditures	year	2395	91	81r
Insurance, life and other personal, expenditures	year	368	91	81r
Pensions and Social Security, expenditures	year	2027	91	81r
Personal Services				
Personal services expenditures	year	212	91	81r
Restaurant Food				
Dining expenditures, family	week	33.83	94	73r
Taxes				
Taxes, Federal income, expenditures	year	2275	91	81r
Taxes, personal, expenditures	year	2715	91	81r
Taxes, State and local income, expenditures	year	365	91	81r
Transportation				
Cars and trucks purchased, new	year	1306	91	81r
Cars and trucks purchased, used	year	942	91	81r
Driver's learning permit fee	perm	10.00	1/94	84s
Driver's license fee	orig	15.00	1/94	84s
Driver's license fee, duplicate	lic	10.00	1/94	84s
Driver's license reinstatement fee, min.	susp	25.00	1/94	85s
Driver's license renewal fee	renew	15.00	1/94	84s
Identification card, nondriver	card	3.00	1/94	83s
Motorcycle learning permit fee	perm	10.00	1/94	84s
Motorcycle license fee	orig	15.00	1/94	84s
Motorcycle license fee, duplicate	lic	10.00	1/94	84s
Motorcycle license renewal fee	renew	15.00	1/94	84s
Public transportation expenditures	year	249	91	81r
Transportation expenditures, total	year	5307	91	81r
Vehicle finance charges	year	346	91	81r
Vehicle insurance expenditures	year	544	91	81r
Vehicle maintenance and repairs expenditures	year	600	91	81r
Vehicle purchases	year	2275	91	81r
Vehicle rental, leases, licenses, etc. expenditures	year	141	91	81r
Vehicles purchased, other than cars and trucks	year	27	91	81r
Utilities				
Electricity expenditures	year	950	91	81r
Utilities, fuels, and public services, total expenditures	year	2000	91	81r
Water and other public services, expenditures	year	227	91	81r

Values are in dollars or fractions of dollars. In the column headed *Ref*, references are shown to sources. Each reference is followed by a letter. These refer to the geographical level for which data were reported: s = State, r = Region, and c = City or metro. The abbreviation *ex* is used to mean *except* or *excluding*; *exp* stands for *expenditures*. For other abbreviations and further explanations, please see the Introduction.

Macon, GA - continued

Item	Per	Value	Date	Ref.
Weddings				
Bridal attendants' gowns	event	750	10/93	76r
Bridal gown	event	852	10/93	76r
Bridal headpiece and veil	event	167	10/93	76r
Bride's wedding band	event	708	10/93	76r
Clergy	event	224	10/93	76r
Engagement ring	event	2756	10/93	76r
Flowers	event	863	10/93	76r
Formal wear for groom	event	106	10/93	76r
Groom's attendants' formal wear	event	530	10/93	76r
Groom's wedding band	event	402	10/93	76r
Music	event	600	10/93	76r
Photography	event	1088	10/93	76r
Shoes for bride	event	50	10/93	76r
Videography	event	483	10/93	76r
Wedding invitations and announcements	event	342	10/93	76r
Wedding reception	event	7000	10/93	76r

Madison, WI

Item	Per	Value	Date	Ref.
Appliances				
Appliances (major), expenditures	year	131	91	81r
Average annual exp.				
Food, health care, personal goods, services	year	25935	91	81r
Charity				
Cash contributions, expenditures	year	745	91	81r
Clothing				
Apparel, men and boys, total expenditures	year	332	91	81r
Apparel, women and girls, total expenditures	year	578	91	81r
Footwear, expenditures	year	164	91	81r
Communications				
Long-distance telephone rate, day, addl. min., 1-10 mi.	min.	0.10	12/93	9s
Long-distance telephone rate, day, initial min., 1-10 mi.	min.	0.15	12/93	9s
Phone line, single, business, field visit	inst	64.65	12/93	9s
Phone line, single, business, no field visit	inst	64.65	12/93	9s
Phone line, single, residence, field visit	inst	33.05	12/93	9s
Phone line, single, residence, no field visit	inst	33.05	12/93	9s
Telephone service, expenditures	year	547	91	81r
Education				
Board, 4-year private college/university	year	2145	8/94	80s
Board, 4-year public college/university	year	1303	8/94	80s
Education, total expenditures	year	394	91	81r
Room, 4-year private college/university	year	1576	8/94	80s
Room, 4-year public college/university	year	1631	8/94	80s
Total cost, 4-year private college/university	year	13902	8/94	80s
Total cost, 4-year public college/university	year	5252	8/94	80s
Tuition, 2-year public college/university, in-state	year	1557	8/94	80s
Tuition, 4-year private college/university, in-state	year	10181	8/94	80s
Tuition, 4-year public college/university, in-state	year	2318	8/94	80s
Energy and Fuels				
Fuel oil and other fuels, expenditures	year	83	91	81r
Gas, natural, expenditures	year	373	91	81r
Gasoline and motor oil purchased	year	1000	91	81r
Gasoline, unleaded midgrade	gallon	1.15	4/93	82r
Gasoline, unleaded premium	gallon	1.23	4/93	82r
Gasoline, unleaded regular	gallon	1.07	4/93	82r
Entertainment				
Entertainment, total expenditures	year	1356	91	81r
Fees and admissions, expenditures	year	347	91	81r
Pets, toys, playground equipment, expenditures	year	270	91	81r
Reading, expenditures	year	160	91	81r

Madison, WI - continued

Item	Per	Value	Date	Ref.
Entertainment - continued				
Televisions, radios, and sound equipment, expenditures	year	433	91	81r
Funerals				
Burial, immediate, container provided by funeral home		1268.31	1/95	54r
Cards, acknowledgment		26.12	1/95	54r
Casket, minimum alternative		198.03	1/95	54r
Cosmetology, hair care, etc.		122.19	1/95	54r
Cremation, direct, container provided by funeral home		977.81	1/95	54r
Embalming		334.00	1/95	54r
Funeral, funeral home		321.16	1/95	54r
Funeral, other facility		317.73	1/95	54r
Graveside service		292.48	1/95	54r
Hearse, local		153.20	1/95	54r
Limousine, local		123.52	1/95	54r
Memorial service		356.30	1/95	54r
Service charge, professional, nondeclinable		968.24	1/95	54r
Visitation and viewing		332.66	1/95	54r
Groceries				
Apples, Red Delicious	lb.	0.68	12/94	82r
Bacon, sliced	lb.	1.88	12/94	82r
Bananas	lb.	0.41	12/94	82r
Beef purchases	year	197	91	81r
Beef, stew, boneless	lb.	2.52	12/94	82r
Beverage purchases, alcoholic	year	293	91	81r
Beverage purchases, nonalcoholic	year	203	91	81r
Bologna, all beef or mixed	lb.	2.12	12/94	82r
Bread, white, pan	lb.	0.76	12/94	82r
Cabbage	lb.	0.44	12/94	82r
Carrots, short trimmed and topped	lb.	0.44	12/94	82r
Cereals and bakery products purchases	year	347	91	81r
Cereals and cereals products purchases	year	119	91	81r
Cheddar cheese, natural	lb.	3.28	12/94	82r
Chicken breast, bone-in	lb.	1.61	12/94	82r
Chicken, fresh, whole	lb.	0.89	12/94	82r
Chuck roast, USDA choice, boneless	lb.	2.33	12/94	82r
Coffee, 100%, ground roast, all sizes	lb.	4.28	12/94	82r
Cookies, chocolate chip	lb.	2.72	12/94	82r
Dairy products (other) purchases	year	148	91	81r
Eggs, Grade A large	dozen	0.76	12/94	82r
Fish and seafood purchases	year	61	91	81r
Flour, white, all purpose	lb.	0.22	12/94	82r
Food purchases, food eaten at home	year	2313	91	81r
Foods purchased away from home, not prepared by consumer	year	1709	91	81r
Fruits and vegetables purchases	year	372	91	81r
Grapefruit	lb.	0.47	12/94	82r
Grapes, Thompson seedless	lb.	2.15	12/94	82r
Ground beef, 100% beef	lb.	1.37	12/94	82r
Ground chuck, 100% beef	lb.	1.81	12/94	82r
Ham, boneless, exc. canned	lb.	2.16	12/94	82r
Ice cream, prepackaged, bulk, regular	1/2 gal.	2.48	12/94	82r
Lemons	lb.	1.08	12/94	82r
Lettuce, iceberg	lb.	0.81	12/94	82r
Margarine, stick	lb.	0.81	12/94	82r
Meats, poultry, fish, and eggs purchases	year	591	91	81r
Milk and cream (fresh) purchases	year	132	91	81r
Orange juice, frozen concentrate 12-oz. can	16 oz.	1.41	12/94	82r
Oranges, Navel	lb.	0.56	12/94	82r
Peanut butter, creamy, all sizes	lb.	1.81	12/94	82r
Pork chops, center cut, bone-in	lb.	2.76	12/94	82r
Pork purchases	year	130	91	81r
Potato chips	16-oz.	2.81	12/94	82r
Potatoes, frozen, French fried	lb.	0.83	12/94	82r
Potatoes, white	lb.	0.28	12/94	82r
Round roast, USDA choice, boneless	lb.	2.90	12/94	82r
Shortening, vegetable oil blends	lb.	0.88	12/94	82r
Spaghetti and macaroni	lb.	0.78	12/94	82r
Steak, rib eye, USDA choice, boneless	lb.	6.15	12/94	82r

Values are in dollars or fractions of dollars. In the column headed *Ref*, references are shown to sources. Each reference is followed by a letter. These refer to the geographical level for which data were reported: s = State, r = Region, and c = City or metro. The abbreviation *ex* is used to mean *except* or *excluding*; *exp* stands for expenditures. For other abbreviations and further explanations, please see the Introduction.

Madison, WI - continued

Item	Per	Value	Date	Ref.
Groceries				
Steak, round, graded & ungraded, exc. USDA prime & choice	lb.	2.72	12/94	82r
Steak, round, USDA choice, boneless	lb.	3.02	12/94	82r
Steak, sirloin, USDA choice, boneless	lb.	3.85	12/94	82r
Steak, T-bone, USDA choice, bone-in	lb.	5.38	12/94	82r
Sugar and other sweets, eaten at home, expenditures	year	91	91	81r
Sugar, white, all sizes	lb.	0.36	12/94	82r
Tobacco products and smoking supplies, total expenditures	year	298	91	81r
Tomatoes, field grown	lb.	1.36	12/94	82r
Tuna, chunk, light	lb.	1.94	12/94	82r
Turkey, frozen, whole	lb.	0.96	12/94	82r
Yogurt, natural, fruit flavored	8 oz.	0.62	12/94	82r
Health Care				
Childbirth, Cesarean delivery, hospital charge	birth	5101.00	12/91	69r
Childbirth, Cesarean delivery, physician charge	birth	2234.00	12/91	69r
Childbirth, normal delivery, hospital charge	birth	2891.00	12/91	69r
Childbirth, normal delivery, physician charge	birth	1623.00	12/91	69r
Drugs, expenditures	year	248	91	81r
Health care, total expenditures	year	1336	91	81r
Health insurance expenditures	year	550	91	81r
Insurance premium, family medical care	month	378.79	1/95	41s
Medical services expenditures	year	457	91	81r
Medical supplies expenditures	year	82	91	81r
Household Goods				
Floor coverings, expenditures	year	105	91	81r
Furniture, expenditures	year	291	91	81r
Household equipment, misc. expenditures	year	341	91	81r
Household expenditures, miscellaneous	year	162	91	81r
Household furnishings and equipment, expenditures	year	1042	91	81r
Household operations expenditures	year	365	91	81r
Household textiles, expenditures	year	101	91	81r
Housekeeping supplies, expenditures	year	390	91	81r
Laundry and cleaning supplies, expenditures	year	110	91	81r
Postage and stationery, expenditures	year	115	91	81r
Housing				
Add garage/carport		8,479	3/95	74r
Add room(s)		21,347	3/95	74r
Apartment condominium or co-op, median	unit	87100	12/94	62r
Bathroom addition, average cost	add	9734.00	3/95	13r
Bathroom remodeling, average cost	remod	6414.00	3/95	13r
Bedroom, master suite addition, average cost	add	27122.00	3/95	13r
Deck addition, average cost	add	6665.00	3/95	13r
Dwellings (owned), expenditures	year	2566	91	81r
Enclose porch/patio/breezeway		4,556	3/95	74r
Exterior remodeling, average cost	remod	15395.00	3/95	13r
Family room addition, average cost	add	27658.00	3/95	13r
Finish room in basement/attic		5,074	3/95	74r
Home, existing, single-family, median	unit	106500	12/94	62r
Kitchen remodeling, major, average cost	remod	17084.00	3/95	13r
Kitchen remodeling, minor, average cost	remod	5804.00	3/95	13r
Maintenance, repairs, insurance, and other housing expenditures	year	484	91	81r
Mortgage interest and charges expenditures	year	1443	91	81r
Office, home addition, average cost	add	8121.00	3/95	13r
Princ. & int., mortgage, median-price exist. sing.-family home	mo.	515	12/94	62r
Property taxes expenditures	year	639	91	81r
Redesign, restructure more than half of home's interior		9,114	3/95	74r
Rental units expenditures	year	1200	91	81r
Sun-space addition, average cost	add	23768.00	3/95	13r
Wing addition, two-story, average cost	add	50410.00	3/95	13r

Madison, WI - continued

Item	Per	Value	Date	Ref.
Insurance and Pensions				
Auto insurance, private passenger	year	554.10	12/94	71s
Insurance and pensions, personal, expenditures	year	2408	91	81r
Insurance, life and other personal, expenditures	year	355	91	81r
Pensions and Social Security, expenditures	year	2053	91	81r
Legal Assistance				
Legal work, law firm associate	hour	90		10r
Legal work, law firm partner	hour	139		10r
Personal Services				
Personal services expenditures	year	203	91	81r
Restaurant Food				
Dining expenditures, family	week	30.03	94	73r
Taxes				
Taxes, Federal income, expenditures	year	1756	91	81r
Taxes, personal, expenditures	year	2426	91	81r
Taxes, State and local income, expenditures	year	568	91	81r
Transportation				
Cars and trucks purchased, new	year	891	91	81r
Cars and trucks purchased, used	year	1155	91	81r
Driver's learning permit fee	perm	20.00	1/94	84s
Driver's license fee	orig	10.00	1/94	84s
Driver's license fee, duplicate	lic	4.00	1/94	84s
Driver's license reinstatement fee, min.	susp	50.00	1/94	85s
Driver's license renewal fee	renew	10.00	1/94	84s
Identification card, nondriver	card	4.00	1/94	83s
Motorcycle license fee	orig	4.00	1/94	84s
Motorcycle license fee, duplicate	lic	4.00	1/94	84s
Motorcycle license renewal fee	renew	4.00	1/94	84s
Public transportation expenditures	year	209	91	81r
Transportation expenditures, total	year	4792	91	81r
Vehicle finance charges	year	300	91	81r
Vehicle insurance expenditures	year	485	91	81r
Vehicle maintenance and repairs expenditures	year	534	91	81r
Vehicle purchases	year	2068	91	81r
Vehicle rental, leases, licenses, etc. expenditures	year	197	91	81r
Vehicles purchased, other than cars and trucks	year	22	91	81r
Utilities				
Electricity expenditures	year	668	91	81r
Utilities, fuels, and public services, total expenditures	year	1838	91	81r
Water and other public services, expenditures	year	167	91	81r
Weddings				
Bridal attendants' gowns	event	750	10/93	76r
Bridal gown	event	852	10/93	76r
Bridal headpiece and veil	event	167	10/93	76r
Bride's wedding band	event	708	10/93	76r
Clergy	event	224	10/93	76r
Engagement ring	event	2756	10/93	76r
Flowers	event	863	10/93	76r
Formal wear for groom	event	106	10/93	76r
Groom's attendants' formal wear	event	530	10/93	76r
Groom's wedding band	event	402	10/93	76r
Music	event	600	10/93	76r
Photography	event	1088	10/93	76r
Shoes for bride	event	50	10/93	76r
Videography	event	483	10/93	76r
Wedding invitations and announcements	event	342	10/93	76r
Wedding reception	event	7000	10/93	76r

Values are in dollars or fractions of dollars. In the column headed *Ref*, references are shown to sources. Each reference is followed by a letter. These refer to the geographical level for which data were reported: s = State, r = Region, and c = City or metro. The abbreviation *ex* is used to mean *except* or *excluding*; *exp* stands for *expenditures*. For other abbreviations and further explanations, please see the Introduction.

Manchester, NH

Item	Per	Value	Date	Ref.
Composite, ACCRA index		111.60	12/94	2c
Alcoholic Beverages				
Beer, Miller Lite, Bud, 12-oz., ex deposit	6	3.92	12/94	2c
J & B Scotch	750-ml.	14.80	12/94	2c
Wine, Gallo Chablis blanc	1.5-lit	4.99	12/94	2c
Child Care				
Child care, for-profit daycare center	week	103.00	12/94	28c
Clothing				
Jeans, man's denim		31.99	12/94	2c
Shirt, man's dress shirt		23.99	12/94	2c
Undervest, boy's size 10-14, cotton	3	4.14	12/94	2c
Communications				
Newspaper subscription, dly. and Sun. delivery	month	14.57	12/94	2c
Telephone bill, family of four	month	20.06	12/94	2c
Telephone, residential, flat rate	mo.	16.56	12/93	8c
Energy and Fuels				
Energy, combined forms, 1800 sq. ft.	mo.	178.77	12/94	2c
Energy, exc. electricity, 1800 sq. ft.	mo.	81.23	12/94	2c
Gas, cooking, winter, 10 therms	month	13.68	2/94	65c
Gas, cooking, winter, 30 therms	month	29.18	2/94	65c
Gas, cooking, winter, 50 therms	month	44.17	2/94	65c
Gas, heating, winter, 100 therms	month	86.79	2/94	65c
Gas, heating, winter, average use	month	151.25	2/94	65c
Gas, reg unlead, taxes inc., cash, self-service	gal	1.08	12/94	2c
Entertainment				
Bowling, evening rate	game	1.86	12/94	2c
Monopoly game, Parker Brothers', No. 9	game	13.99	12/94	2c
Movie	adm	6.50	12/94	2c
Tennis balls, yellow, Wilson or Penn, 3	can	2.49	12/94	2c
Groceries				
Groceries, ACCRA Index		101.70	12/94	2c
Baby food, strained vegetables, lowest price	4-4.5 oz.	0.40	12/94	2c
Bananas	lb.	0.40	12/94	2c
Beef or hamburger, ground	lb.	1.62	12/94	2c
Bread, white	24-oz.	0.75	12/94	2c
Cheese, Kraft grated Parmesan	8-oz.	3.16	12/94	2c
Chicken, whole fryer	lb.	0.92	12/94	2c
Cigarettes, Winston, Kings	carton	14.86	12/94	2c
Coffee, vacuum-packed	13 oz.	3.56	12/94	2c
Corn Flakes, Kellogg's or Post Toasties	18 oz.	2.16	12/94	2c
Corn, frozen, whole kernel, lowest price	10 oz.	0.66	12/94	2c
Eggs, Grade A large	dozen	0.88	12/94	2c
Lettuce, iceberg	head	1.12	12/94	2c
Margarine, Blue Bonnet or Parkay cubes	lb.	0.59	12/94	2c
Milk, whole	1/2 gal.	1.19	12/94	2c
Orange juice, Minute Maid frozen	12-oz.	1.09	12/94	2c
Peaches, halves or slices, Hunt's, Del Monte, or Libby's	29-oz.	1.55	12/94	2c
Peas, sweet, Del Monte or Green Giant	15-17 oz.	0.47	12/94	2c
Potatoes, white or red	10-lb. sack	1.99	12/94	2c
Sausage, Jimmy Dean, 100% pork	lb.	3.21	12/94	2c
Shortening, vegetable, Crisco	3-lb.	2.66	12/94	2c
Soft drink, Coca Cola, ex deposit	2 lit	0.96	12/94	2c
Steak, t-bone	lb.	5.79	12/94	2c
Sugar, cane or beet	4 lbs.	1.26	12/94	2c
Tomatoes, Hunt's or Del Monte	14.5 oz.	0.74	12/94	2c
Tuna, chunk, light, oil-packed	6.125-6.5 oz.	0.77	12/94	2c
Goods and Services				
Miscellaneous goods and services, ACCRA Index		105.20	12/94	2c

Manchester, NH - continued

Item	Per	Value	Date	Ref.
Health Care				
Health care, ACCRA Index		106.90	12/94	2c
Antibiotic ointment, Polysporin	1.5 oz.	4.21	12/94	2c
Dentist's fee, adult teeth cleaning and periodic oral exam	visit	49.40	12/94	2c
Doctor's fee, routine exam, established patient	visit	47.00	12/94	2c
Hospital care, semiprivate room	day	443.00	12/94	2c
Household Goods				
Appl. repair, service call, wash mach	min. lab. chg.	43.25	12/94	2c
Laundry detergent, Tide Ultra, Bold, or Cheer	42 oz.	3.59	12/94	2c
Tissues, facial, Kleenex brand	175	1.06	12/94	2c
Housing				
Housing, ACCRA Index		117.50	12/94	2c
House payment, principal and interest, 25% down payment	mo.	886	12/94	2c
House, 1800 sq ft, 8000 sq ft lot, new, urban, utilities	total	146000	12/94	2c
Mtge. rate, incl. points and orig. fee, 30-year conv. fixed or ARM	mo.	9.07	12/94	2c
Rent, apartment, 2 br., 1 1/2-2 baths, unfurnished, 950 sq ft, water	mo.	660	12/94	2c
Personal Goods				
Shampoo, Alberto VO5	15-oz.	1.09	12/94	2c
Toothpaste, Crest or Colgate	6-7 oz.	2.21	12/94	2c
Personal Services				
Dry cleaning, man's 2-pc. suit		7.73	12/94	2c
Haircut, man's barbershop, no styling		9.20	12/94	2c
Haircut, woman's shampoo, trim, blow-dry		16.00	12/94	2c
Restaurant Food				
Chicken, fried, thigh and drumstick		2.89	12/94	2c
Hamburger with cheese	1/4 lb.	1.99	12/94	2c
Pizza, Pizza Hut or Pizza Inn	12-13 in.	7.99	12/94	2c
Taxes				
Tax rate, residential property, month	$100	2.75	1/92	79c
Transportation				
Transportation, ACCRA Index		101.40	12/94	2c
Bus fare, up to 10 miles	one-way	0.90	12/94	2c
Tire balance, computer or spin bal., front	wheel	7.50	12/94	2c
Utilities				
Utilities, ACCRA Index		151.70	12/94	2c
Electricity, (part.), other, 1800 sq. ft., new home	mo.	97.54	12/94	2c
Electricity, summer, 250 KWh	month	32.63	8/93	64c
Electricity, summer, 500 KWh	month	66.37	8/93	64c
Electricity, summer, 750 KWh	month	100.11	8/93	64c
Electricity, summer, 1000 KWh	month	131.03	8/93	64c

Manhattan, KS

Item	Per	Value	Date	Ref.
Composite, ACCRA index		95.00	12/94	2c
Alcoholic Beverages				
Beer, Miller Lite, Bud, 12-oz., ex deposit	6	4.07	12/94	2c
J & B Scotch	750-ml.	17.99	12/94	2c
Wine, Gallo Chablis blanc	1.5-lit	4.32	12/94	2c
Clothing				
Jeans, man's denim		27.32	12/94	2c
Shirt, man's dress shirt		28.17	12/94	2c
Undervest, boy's size 10-14, cotton	3	3.24	12/94	2c

Values are in dollars or fractions of dollars. In the column headed *Ref*, references are shown as sources. Each reference is followed by a letter. These refer to the geographical level for which data were reported: s=State, r=Region, and c=City or metro. The abbreviation *ex* is used to mean *except* or *excluding*; *exp* stands for expenditures. For other abbreviations and further explanations, please see the Introduction.

Manhattan, KS - continued

Item	Per	Value	Date	Ref.
Communications				
Newspaper subscription, dly. and Sun. delivery	month	11.50	12/94	2c
Telephone bill, family of four	month	17.34	12/94	2c
Telephone, residential, flat rate	mo.	10.70	12/93	8c
Energy and Fuels				
Energy, combined forms, 1800 sq. ft.	mo.	90.96	12/94	2c
Energy, exc. electricity, 1800 sq. ft.	mo.	42.59	12/94	2c
Gas, reg unlead, taxes inc., cash, self-service	gal	1.00	12/94	2c
Entertainment				
Bowling, evening rate	game	1.65	12/94	2c
Monopoly game, Parker Brothers', No. 9	game	11.23	12/94	2c
Movie	adm	5.50	12/94	2c
Tennis balls, yellow, Wilson or Penn, 3	can	2.11	12/94	2c
Groceries				
Groceries, ACCRA Index		97.10	12/94	2c
Baby food, strained vegetables, lowest price	4-4.5 oz.	0.38	12/94	2c
Bananas	lb.	0.39	12/94	2c
Beef or hamburger, ground	lb.	0.99	12/94	2c
Bread, white	24-oz.	0.60	12/94	2c
Cheese, Kraft grated Parmesan	8-oz.	3.47	12/94	2c
Chicken, whole fryer	lb.	0.78	12/94	2c
Cigarettes, Winston, Kings	carton	16.00	12/94	2c
Coffee, vacuum-packed	13 oz.	3.33	12/94	2c
Corn Flakes, Kellogg's or Post Toasties	18 oz.	2.58	12/94	2c
Corn, frozen, whole kernel, lowest price	10 oz.	0.71	12/94	2c
Eggs, Grade A large	dozen	0.67	12/94	2c
Lettuce, iceberg	head	0.75	12/94	2c
Margarine, Blue Bonnet or Parkay cubes	lb.	0.56	12/94	2c
Milk, whole	1/2 gal.	1.44	12/94	2c
Orange juice, Minute Maid frozen	12-oz.	1.41	12/94	2c
Peaches, halves or slices, Hunt's, Del Monte, or Libby's	29-oz.	1.40	12/94	2c
Peas, sweet, Del Monte or Green Giant	15-17 oz.	0.52	12/94	2c
Potatoes, white or red	10-lb. sack	1.59	12/94	2c
Sausage, Jimmy Dean, 100% pork	lb.	2.87	12/94	2c
Shortening, vegetable, Crisco	3-lb.	2.97	12/94	2c
Soft drink, Coca Cola, ex deposit	2 lit	1.22	12/94	2c
Steak, t-bone	lb.	5.05	12/94	2c
Sugar, cane or beet	4 lbs.	1.39	12/94	2c
Tomatoes, Hunt's or Del Monte	14.5 oz.	0.68	12/94	2c
Tuna, chunk, light, oil-packed	6.125-6.5 oz.	0.62	12/94	2c
Goods and Services				
Miscellaneous goods and services, ACCRA Index		93.00	12/94	2c
Health Care				
Health care, ACCRA Index		96.90	12/94	2c
Antibiotic ointment, Polysporin	1.5 oz.	3.77	12/94	2c
Dentist's fee, adult teeth cleaning and periodic oral exam	visit	46.33	12/94	2c
Doctor's fee, routine exam, established patient	visit	40.50	12/94	2c
Hospital care, semiprivate room	day	419.00	12/94	2c
Household Goods				
Appl. repair, service call, wash mach	min. lab. chg.	28.16	12/94	2c
Laundry detergent, Tide Ultra, Bold, or Cheer	42 oz.	3.27	12/94	2c
Tissues, facial, Kleenex brand	175	1.01	12/94	2c

Manhattan, KS - continued

Item	Per	Value	Date	Ref.
Housing				
Housing, ACCRA Index		100.60	12/94	2c
House payment, principal and interest, 25% down payment	mo.	773	12/94	2c
House, 1800 sq ft, 8000 sq ft lot, new, urban, utilities	total	123500	12/94	2c
Mtge. rate, incl. points and orig. fee, 30-year conv. fixed or ARM	mo.	9.42	12/94	2c
Rent, apartment, 2 br., 1 1/2-2 baths, unfurnished, 950 sq ft, water	mo.	523	12/94	2c
Personal Goods				
Shampoo, Alberto VO5	15-oz.	1.04	12/94	2c
Toothpaste, Crest or Colgate	6-7 oz.	1.74	12/94	2c
Personal Services				
Dry cleaning, man's 2-pc. suit		6.23	12/94	2c
Haircut, man's barbershop, no styling		6.82	12/94	2c
Haircut, woman's shampoo, trim, blow-dry		14.97	12/94	2c
Restaurant Food				
Chicken, fried, thigh and drumstick		2.20	12/94	2c
Hamburger with cheese	1/4 lb.	1.95	12/94	2c
Pizza, Pizza Hut or Pizza Inn	12-13 in.	7.80	12/94	2c
Transportation				
Transportation, ACCRA Index		91.90	12/94	2c
Tire balance, computer or spin bal., front	wheel	6.49	12/94	2c
Utilities				
Utilities, ACCRA Index		82.10	12/94	2c
Electricity, (part.), other, 1800 sq. ft., new home	mo.	48.37	12/94	2c

Mansfield, OH

Item	Per	Value	Date	Ref.
Composite, ACCRA index		97.50	12/94	2c
Alcoholic Beverages				
Beer, Miller Lite, Bud, 12-oz., ex deposit	6	4.05	12/94	2c
J & B Scotch	750-ml.	18.85	12/94	2c
Wine, Gallo Chablis blanc	1.5-lit	5.31	12/94	2c
Appliances				
Appliances (major), expenditures	year	131	91	81r
Average annual exp.				
Food, health care, personal goods, services	year	25935	91	81r
Charity				
Cash contributions, expenditures	year	745	91	81r
Clothing				
Apparel, men and boys, total expenditures	year	332	91	81r
Apparel, women and girls, total expenditures	year	578	91	81r
Footwear, expenditures	year	164	91	81r
Jeans, man's denim		31.16	12/94	2c
Shirt, man's dress shirt		34.95	12/94	2c
Undervest, boy's size 10-14, cotton	3	3.37	12/94	2c
Communications				
Long-distance telephone rate, day, addl. min., 1-10 mi.	min.	0.16	12/93	9s
Long-distance telephone rate, day, initial min., 1-10 mi.	min.	0.32	12/93	9s
Newspaper subscription, dly. and Sun. delivery	month	11.96	12/94	2c
Phone line, single, business, field visit	inst	55.42	12/93	9s
Phone line, single, business, no field visit	inst	55.42	12/93	9s
Phone line, single, residence, field visit	inst	30.38	12/93	9s
Phone line, single, residence, no field visit	inst	30.38	12/93	9s
Telephone bill, family of four	month	22.74	12/94	2c
Telephone service, expenditures	year	547	91	81r
Telephone, residential, flat rate	mo.	15.25	12/93	8c

Values are in dollars or fractions of dollars. In the column headed *Ref*, references are shown to sources. Each reference is followed by a letter. These refer to the geographical level for which data were reported: s = State, r = Region, and c = City or metro. The abbreviation *ex* is used to mean *except* or *excluding*; *exp* stands for expenditures. For other abbreviations and further explanations, please see the Introduction.

Mansfield, OH - continued

Item	Per	Value	Date	Ref.
Education				
Board, 4-year private college/university	year	2241	8/94	80s
Board, 4-year public college/university	year	1625	8/94	80s
Education, total expenditures	year	394	91	81r
Room, 4-year private college/university	year	2118	8/94	80s
Room, 4-year public college/university	year	2103	8/94	80s
Total cost, 4-year private college/university	year	15444	8/94	80s
Total cost, 4-year public college/university	year	6987	8/94	80s
Tuition, 2-year public college/university, in-state	year	2076	8/94	80s
Tuition, 4-year private college/university, in-state	year	11085	8/94	80s
Tuition, 4-year public college/university, in-state	year	3259	8/94	80s
Energy and Fuels				
Energy, combined forms, 1800 sq. ft.	mo.	137.00	12/94	2c
Energy, exc. electricity, 1800 sq. ft.	mo.	53.66	12/94	2c
Fuel oil and other fuels, expenditures	year	83	91	81r
Gas, natural, expenditures	year	373	91	81r
Gas, reg unlead, taxes inc., cash, self-service	gal	1.11	12/94	2c
Gasoline and motor oil purchased	year	1000	91	81r
Gasoline, unleaded midgrade	gallon	1.15	4/93	82r
Gasoline, unleaded premium	gallon	1.23	4/93	82r
Gasoline, unleaded regular	gallon	1.07	4/93	82r
Entertainment				
Bowling, evening rate	game	2.30	12/94	2c
Entertainment, total expenditures	year	1356	91	81r
Fees and admissions, expenditures	year	347	91	81r
Monopoly game, Parker Brothers', No. 9	game	10.34	12/94	2c
Movie	adm	5.12	12/94	2c
Pets, toys, playground equipment, expenditures	year	270	91	81r
Reading, expenditures	year	160	91	81r
Televisions, radios, and sound equipment, expenditures	year	433	91	81r
Tennis balls, yellow, Wilson or Penn, 3	can	2.26	12/94	2c
Funerals				
Burial, immediate, container provided by funeral home		1268.31	1/95	54r
Cards, acknowledgment		26.12	1/95	54r
Casket, minimum alternative		198.03	1/95	54r
Cosmetology, hair care, etc.		122.19	1/95	54r
Cremation, direct, container provided by funeral home		977.81	1/95	54r
Embalming		334.00	1/95	54r
Funeral, funeral home		321.16	1/95	54r
Funeral, other facility		317.73	1/95	54r
Graveside service		292.48	1/95	54r
Hearse, local		153.20	1/95	54r
Limousine, local		123.52	1/95	54r
Memorial service		356.30	1/95	54r
Service charge, professional, nondeclinable		968.24	1/95	54r
Visitation and viewing		332.66	1/95	54r
Groceries				
Groceries, ACCRA Index		90.10	12/94	2c
Apples, Red Delicious	lb.	0.68	12/94	82r
Baby food, strained vegetables, lowest price	4-4.5 oz.	0.26	12/94	2c
Bacon, sliced	lb.	1.88	12/94	82r
Bananas	lb.	0.34	12/94	2c
Bananas	lb.	0.41	12/94	82r
Bananas, brand name	lb.	0.39	3/94	58c
Beef or hamburger, ground	lb.	1.53	12/94	2c
Beef purchases	year	197	91	81r
Beef, stew, boneless	lb.	2.52	12/94	82r
Beverage purchases, alcoholic	year	293	91	81r
Beverage purchases, nonalcoholic	year	203	91	81r
Bologna, all beef or mixed	lb.	2.12	12/94	82r
Bread, Pepperidge Farm white	lb.	1.77	3/94	58c
Bread, white	24-oz.	0.54	12/94	2c

Mansfield, OH - continued

Item	Per	Value	Date	Ref.
Groceries - continued				
Bread, white, pan	lb.	0.76	12/94	82r
Butter, Land O'Lakes brand	lb.	1.49	3/94	58c
Butter, private label	lb.	0.48	3/94	58c
Cabbage	lb.	0.44	12/94	82r
Carrots, short trimmed and topped	lb.	0.44	12/94	82r
Cereal, Corn Flakes, Kellogg's	18 oz.	1.69	3/94	58c
Cereal, Fruit Loops	15 oz.	3.32	3/94	58c
Cereal, Rice Krispies	15 oz.	2.84	3/94	58c
Cereals and bakery products purchases	year	347	91	81r
Cereals and cereals products purchases	year	119	91	81r
Cheddar cheese, natural	lb.	3.28	12/94	82r
Cheese, Kraft grated Parmesan	8-oz.	2.93	12/94	2c
Chicken breast, bone-in	lb.	1.61	12/94	82r
Chicken, fresh, whole	lb.	0.89	12/94	82r
Chicken, whole fryer	lb.	0.89	12/94	2c
Chuck roast, USDA choice, boneless	lb.	2.33	12/94	82r
Cigarettes, Winston, Kings	carton	15.11	12/94	2c
Coffee, 100%, ground roast, all sizes	lb.	4.28	12/94	82r
Coffee, vacuum-packed	13 oz.	3.58	12/94	2c
Cookies, chocolate chip	lb.	2.72	12/94	82r
Corn Flakes, Kellogg's or Post Toasties	18 oz.	2.04	12/94	2c
Corn, frozen, whole kernel, lowest price	10 oz.	0.64	12/94	2c
Dairy products (other) purchases	year	148	91	81r
Detergent, powder, Tide Ultra brand	42 oz.	3.39	3/94	58c
Eggs, Grade A large	dozen	0.61	12/94	2c
Eggs, Grade A large	dozen	0.76	12/94	82r
Fish and seafood purchases	year	61	91	81r
Flour, white, all purpose	lb.	0.22	12/94	82r
Food purchases, food eaten at home	year	2313	91	81r
Foods purchased away from home, not prepared by consumer	year	1709	91	81r
Fruits and vegetables purchases	year	372	91	81r
Grapefruit	lb.	0.47	12/94	82r
Grapes, Thompson seedless	lb.	2.15	12/94	82r
Ground beef, 100% beef	lb.	1.37	12/94	82r
Ground chuck, 100% beef	lb.	1.81	12/94	82r
Ham, boneless, exc. canned	lb.	2.16	12/94	82r
Ice cream, prepackaged, bulk, regular	1/2 gal.	2.48	12/94	82r
Iceberg lettuce	head	0.76	3/94	58c
Jelly, Welch's brand, grape	48 oz.	2.22	3/94	58c
Ketchup, Heinz brand	12 oz.	1.23	3/94	58c
Lemons	lb.	1.08	12/94	82r
Lettuce, iceberg	lb.	0.81	12/94	82r
Lettuce, iceberg	head	0.85	12/94	2c
Margarine sticks, Parkay brand	lb.	0.56	3/94	58c
Margarine, Blue Bonnet or Parkay cubes	lb.	0.55	12/94	2c
Margarine, stick	lb.	0.81	12/94	82r
Mayonnaise, Hellmann's brand	1 quart	2.09	3/94	58c
Meats, poultry, fish, and eggs purchases	year	591	91	81r
Milk and cream (fresh) purchases	year	132	91	81r
Milk, whole	1/2 gal.	1.06	12/94	2c
Milk, whole, private label	gallon	1.49	3/94	58c
Orange juice, frozen concentrate 12-oz. can	16 oz.	1.41	12/94	82r
Orange juice, Minute Maid frozen	12-oz.	1.20	12/94	2c
Oranges, Navel	lb.	0.56	12/94	82r
Paper towels, Bounty brand	60 ft.	0.83	3/94	58c
Peaches, halves or slices, Hunt's, Del Monte, or Libby's	29-oz.	1.47	12/94	2c
Peanut butter, creamy, all sizes	lb.	1.81	12/94	82r
Peas, sweet, Del Monte or Green Giant	15-17 oz.	0.62	12/94	2c
Plastic wrap, Saran brand	50 sq. ft.	1.52	3/94	58c
Pork chops, center cut, bone-in	lb.	2.76	12/94	82r
Pork purchases	year	130	91	81r
Potato chips	16-oz.	2.81	12/94	82r
Potatoes, frozen, French fried	lb.	0.83	12/94	82r
Potatoes, white	lb.	0.28	12/94	82r
Potatoes, white or red	10-lb. sack	1.87	12/94	2c

Values are in dollars or fractions of dollars. In the column headed *Ref*, references are shown to sources. Each reference is followed by a letter. These refer to the geographical level for which data were reported: s=State, r=Region, and c=City or metro. The abbreviation *ex* is used to mean *except* or *excluding*; *exp* stands for *expenditures*. For other abbreviations and further explanations, please see the Introduction.

Mansfield, OH - continued

Item	Per	Value	Date	Ref.
Groceries				
Round roast, USDA choice, boneless	lb.	2.90	12/94	82r
Sausage, Jimmy Dean, 100% pork	lb.	2.49	12/94	2c
Shave cream, Barbasol brand	11 oz.	1.07	3/94	58c
Shortening, vegetable oil blends	lb.	0.88	12/94	82r
Shortening, vegetable, Crisco	3-lb.	2.31	12/94	2c
Soft drink, Coca Cola, ex deposit	2 lit	1.05	12/94	2c
Spaghetti and macaroni	lb.	0.78	12/94	82r
Spaghetti sauce, Prego brand	30 oz.	1.63	3/94	58c
Spaghetti, Mueller brand	16 oz.	0.54	3/94	58c
Steak, rib eye, USDA choice, boneless	lb.	6.15	12/94	82r
Steak, round, graded & ungraded, exc. USDA prime & choice	lb.	2.72	12/94	82r
Steak, round, USDA choice, boneless	lb.	3.02	12/94	82r
Steak, sirloin, USDA choice, boneless	lb.	3.85	12/94	82r
Steak, t-bone	lb.	4.97	12/94	2c
Steak, T-bone, USDA choice, bone-in	lb.	5.38	12/94	82r
Sugar and other sweets, eaten at home, expenditures	year	91	91	81r
Sugar, cane or beet	4 lbs.	1.16	12/94	2c
Sugar, Domino brand	5 lbs.	1.79	3/94	58c
Sugar, white, all sizes	lb.	0.36	12/94	82r
Tea, Lipton brand	100 bags	1.99	3/94	58c
Tobacco products and smoking supplies, total expenditures	year	298	91	81r
Tomatoes, field grown	lb.	1.36	12/94	82r
Tomatoes, Hunt's or Del Monte	14.5 oz.	0.73	12/94	2c
Tuna, chunk, light	lb.	1.94	12/94	82r
Tuna, chunk, light, oil-packed	6.125-6.5 oz.	0.66	12/94	2c
Turkey, frozen, whole	lb.	0.96	12/94	82r
Yogurt, natural, fruit flavored	8 oz.	0.62	12/94	82r
Goods and Services				
Miscellaneous goods and services, ACCRA Index		98.30	12/94	2c
Health Care				
Health care, ACCRA Index		90.30	12/94	2c
Antibiotic ointment, Polysporin	1.5 oz.	3.79	12/94	2c
Childbirth, Cesarean delivery, hospital charge	birth	5101.00	12/91	69r
Childbirth, Cesarean delivery, physician charge	birth	2234.00	12/91	69r
Childbirth, normal delivery, hospital charge	birth	2891.00	12/91	69r
Childbirth, normal delivery, physician charge	birth	1623.00	12/91	69r
Dentist's fee, adult teeth cleaning and periodic oral exam	visit	45.50	12/94	2c
Doctor's fee, routine exam, established patient	visit	35.75	12/94	2c
Drugs, expenditures	year	248	91	81r
Health care, total expenditures	year	1336	91	81r
Health insurance expenditures	year	550	91	81r
Hospital care, semiprivate room	day	378.00	12/94	2c
Insurance premium, family medical care	month	350.73	1/95	41s
Medical services expenditures	year	457	91	81r
Medical supplies expenditures	year	82	91	81r
Household Goods				
Appl. repair, service call, wash mach	min. lab. chg.	31.79	12/94	2c
Floor coverings, expenditures	year	105	91	81r
Furniture, expenditures	year	291	91	81r
Household equipment, misc. expenditures	year	341	91	81r
Household expenditures, miscellaneous	year	162	91	81r
Household furnishings and equipment, expenditures	year	1042	91	81r
Household operations expenditures	year	365	91	81r
Household textiles, expenditures	year	101	91	81r
Housekeeping supplies, expenditures	year	390	91	81r
Laundry and cleaning supplies, expenditures	year	110	91	81r

Mansfield, OH - continued

Item	Per	Value	Date	Ref.
Household Goods - continued				
Laundry detergent, Tide Ultra, Bold, or Cheer	42 oz.	3.13	12/94	2c
Postage and stationery, expenditures	year	115	91	81r
Tissues, facial, Kleenex brand	175	0.97	12/94	2c
Housing				
Housing, ACCRA Index		95.50	12/94	2c
Add garage/carport		8,479	3/95	74r
Add room(s)		21,347	3/95	74r
Apartment condominium or co-op, median	unit	87100	12/94	62r
Bathroom addition, average cost	add	9734.00	3/95	13r
Bathroom remodeling, average cost	remod	6414.00	3/95	13r
Bedroom, master suite addition, average cost	add	27122.00	3/95	13r
Deck addition, average cost	add	6665.00	3/95	13r
Dwellings (owned), expenditures	year	2566	91	81r
Enclose porch/patio/breezeway		4,556	3/95	74r
Exterior remodeling, average cost	remod	15395.00	3/95	13r
Family room addition, average cost	add	27658.00	3/95	13r
Finish room in basement/attic		5,074	3/95	74r
Home, existing, single-family, median	unit	106500	12/94	62r
House payment, principal and interest, 25% down payment	mo.	779	12/94	2c
House, 1800 sq ft, 8000 sq ft lot, new, urban, utilities	total	126788	12/94	2c
Kitchen remodeling, major, average cost	remod	17084.00	3/95	13r
Kitchen remodeling, minor, average cost	remod	5804.00	3/95	13r
Maintenance, repairs, insurance, and other housing expenditures	year	484	91	81r
Mortgage interest and charges expenditures	year	1443	91	81r
Mtge. rate, incl. points and orig. fee, 30-year conv. fixed or ARM	mo.	9.20	12/94	2c
Office, home addition, average cost	add	8121.00	3/95	13r
Princ. & int., mortgage, median-price exist. sing.-family home	mo.	515	12/94	62r
Property taxes expenditures	year	639	91	81r
Redesign, restructure more than half of home's interior		9,114	3/95	74r
Rent, apartment, 2 br., 1 1/2-2 baths, unfurnished, 950 sq ft, water	mo.	369	12/94	2c
Rental units expenditures	year	1200	91	81r
Sun-space addition, average cost	add	23768.00	3/95	13r
Wing addition, two-story, average cost	add	50410.00	3/95	13r
Insurance and Pensions				
Auto insurance, private passenger	year	550.52	12/94	71s
Insurance and pensions, personal, expenditures	year	2408	91	81r
Insurance, life and other personal, expenditures	year	355	91	81r
Pensions and Social Security, expenditures	year	2053	91	81r
Legal Assistance				
Legal work, law firm associate	hour	90		10r
Legal work, law firm partner	hour	139		10r
Personal Goods				
Shampoo, Alberto VO5	15-oz.	0.89	12/94	2c
Toothpaste, Crest or Colgate	6-7 oz.	1.59	12/94	2c
Personal Services				
Dry cleaning, man's 2-pc. suit		6.51	12/94	2c
Haircut, man's barbershop, no styling		7.20	12/94	2c
Haircut, woman's shampoo, trim, blow-dry		18.70	12/94	2c
Personal services expenditures	year	203	91	81r
Restaurant Food				
Chicken, fried, thigh and drumstick		1.89	12/94	2c
Dining expenditures, family	week	30.03	94	73r
Hamburger with cheese	1/4 lb.	1.88	12/94	2c
Pizza, Pizza Hut or Pizza Inn	12-13 in.	7.95	12/94	2c

Values are in dollars or fractions of dollars. In the column headed *Ref*, references are shown to sources. Each reference is followed by a letter. These refer to the geographical level for which data were reported: s = State, r = Region, and c = City or metro. The abbreviation *ex* is used to mean *except* or *excluding*; *exp* stands for *expenditures*. For other abbreviations and further explanations, please see the Introduction.

Mansfield, OH - continued

Item	Per	Value	Date	Ref.
Taxes				
Taxes, Federal income, expenditures	year	1756	91	81r
Taxes, personal, expenditures	year	2426	91	81r
Taxes, State and local income, expenditures	year	568	91	81r
Transportation				
Transportation, ACCRA Index		97.70	12/94	2c
Cars and trucks purchased, new	year	891	91	81r
Cars and trucks purchased, used	year	1155	91	81r
Driver's learning permit fee	perm	3.00	1/94	84s
Driver's license fee	orig	5.00	1/94	84s
Driver's license fee, duplicate	lic	1.50	1/94	84s
Driver's license reinstatement fee, min.	susp	12.50-100.00	1/94	85s
Driver's license renewal fee	renew	5.00	1/94	84s
Identification card, nondriver	card	2.50	1/94	83s
Motorcycle learning permit fee	perm	3.00	1/94	84s
Motorcycle license fee	orig	5.00	1/94	84s
Motorcycle license fee, duplicate	lic	1.50	1/94	84s
Motorcycle license renewal fee	renew	5.00	1/94	84s
Public transportation expenditures	year	209	91	81r
Tire balance, computer or spin bal., front	wheel	6.50	12/94	2c
Transportation expenditures, total	year	4792	91	81r
Vehicle finance charges	year	300	91	81r
Vehicle insurance expenditures	year	485	91	81r
Vehicle maintenance and repairs expenditures	year	534	91	81r
Vehicle purchases	year	2068	91	81r
Vehicle rental, leases, licenses, etc. expenditures	year	197	91	81r
Vehicles purchased, other than cars and trucks	year	22	91	81r
Utilities				
Utilities, ACCRA Index		121.30	12/94	2c
Electricity expenditures	year	668	91	81r
Electricity, (part.), other, 1800 sq. ft., new home	mo.	83.34	12/94	2c
Utilities, fuels, and public services, total expenditures	year	1838	91	81r
Water and other public services, expenditures	year	167	91	81r
Weddings				
Bridal attendants' gowns	event	750	10/93	76r
Bridal gown	event	852	10/93	76r
Bridal headpiece and veil	event	167	10/93	76r
Bride's wedding band	event	708	10/93	76r
Clergy	event	224	10/93	76r
Engagement ring	event	2756	10/93	76r
Flowers	event	863	10/93	76r
Formal wear for groom	event	106	10/93	76r
Groom's attendants' formal wear	event	530	10/93	76r
Groom's wedding band	event	402	10/93	76r
Music	event	600	10/93	76r
Photography	event	1088	10/93	76r
Shoes for bride	event	50	10/93	76r
Videography	event	483	10/93	76r
Wedding invitations and announcements	event	342	10/93	76r
Wedding reception	event	7000	10/93	76r

Marinette, WI

Item	Per	Value	Date	Ref.
Composite, ACCRA index		98.40	12/94	2c
Alcoholic Beverages				
Beer, Miller Lite, Bud, 12-oz., ex deposit	6	3.40	12/94	2c
J & B Scotch	750-ml.	16.66	12/94	2c
Wine, Gallo Chablis blanc	1.5-lit	4.59	12/94	2c
Clothing				
Jeans, man's denim		45.00	12/94	2c
Shirt, man's dress shirt		26.00	12/94	2c
Undervest, boy's size 10-14, cotton	3	3.25	12/94	2c

Marinette, WI - continued

Item	Per	Value	Date	Ref.
Communications				
Newspaper subscription, dly. and Sun. delivery	month	12.83	12/94	2c
Telephone bill, family of four	month	16.31	12/94	2c
Telephone, residential, flat rate	mo.	6.00	12/93	8c
Energy and Fuels				
Energy, combined forms, 1800 sq. ft.	mo.	82.76	12/94	2c
Energy, exc. electricity, 1800 sq. ft.	mo.	41.94	12/94	2c
Gas, reg unlead, taxes inc., cash, self-service	gal	1.23	12/94	2c
Entertainment				
Bowling, evening rate	game	1.85	12/94	2c
Monopoly game, Parker Brothers', No. 9	game	10.99	12/94	2c
Movie	adm	4.00	12/94	2c
Tennis balls, yellow, Wilson or Penn, 3	can	1.99	12/94	2c
Groceries				
Groceries, ACCRA Index		101.60	12/94	2c
Baby food, strained vegetables, lowest price	4-4.5 oz.	0.38	12/94	2c
Bananas	lb.	0.28	12/94	2c
Beef or hamburger, ground	lb.	1.62	12/94	2c
Bread, white	24-oz.	0.64	12/94	2c
Cheese, Kraft grated Parmesan	8-oz.	2.99	12/94	2c
Chicken, whole fryer	lb.	1.00	12/94	2c
Cigarettes, Winston, Kings	carton	17.82	12/94	2c
Coffee, vacuum-packed	13 oz.	3.56	12/94	2c
Corn Flakes, Kellogg's or Post Toasties	18 oz.	2.36	12/94	2c
Corn, frozen, whole kernel, lowest price	10 oz.	0.70	12/94	2c
Eggs, Grade A large	dozen	0.70	12/94	2c
Lettuce, iceberg	head	0.92	12/94	2c
Margarine, Blue Bonnet or Parkay cubes	lb.	0.55	12/94	2c
Milk, whole	1/2 gal.	1.51	12/94	2c
Orange juice, Minute Maid frozen	12-oz.	1.43	12/94	2c
Peaches, halves or slices, Hunt's, Del Monte, or Libby's	29-oz.	1.50	12/94	2c
Peas, sweet, Del Monte or Green Giant	15-17 oz.	0.61	12/94	2c
Potatoes, white or red	10-lb. sack	1.81	12/94	2c
Sausage, Jimmy Dean, 100% pork	lb.	2.59	12/94	2c
Shortening, vegetable, Crisco	3-lb.	2.46	12/94	2c
Soft drink, Coca Cola, ex deposit	2 lit	1.19	12/94	2c
Steak, t-bone	lb.	5.42	12/94	2c
Sugar, cane or beet	4 lbs.	1.58	12/94	2c
Tomatoes, Hunt's or Del Monte	14.5 oz.	0.74	12/94	2c
Tuna, chunk, light, oil-packed	6.125-6.5 oz.	0.66	12/94	2c
Goods and Services				
Miscellaneous goods and services, ACCRA Index		101.10	12/94	2c
Health Care				
Health care, ACCRA Index		93.00	12/94	2c
Antibiotic ointment, Polysporin	1.5 oz.	4.64	12/94	2c
Dentist's fee, adult teeth cleaning and periodic oral exam	visit	46.67	12/94	2c
Doctor's fee, routine exam, established patient	visit	45.00	12/94	2c
Hospital care, semiprivate room	day	215.00	12/94	2c
Household Goods				
Appl. repair, service call, wash mach	min. lab. chg.	36.33	12/94	2c
Laundry detergent, Tide Ultra, Bold, or Cheer	42 oz.	3.82	12/94	2c
Tissues, facial, Kleenex brand	175	1.05	12/94	2c

Values are in dollars or fractions of dollars. In the column headed *Ref*, references are shown to sources. Each reference is followed by a letter. These refer to the geographical level for which data were reported: s=State, r=Region, and c=City or metro. The abbreviation *ex* is used to mean *except* or *excluding*; *exp* stands for expenditures. For other abbreviations and further explanations, please see the Introduction.

Marinette, WI - continued

Item	Per	Value	Date	Ref.
Housing				
Housing, ACCRA Index		99.60	12/94	2c
House payment, principal and interest, 25% down payment	mo.	765	12/94	2c
House, 1800 sq ft, 8000 sq ft lot, new, urban, utilities	total	124000	12/94	2c
Mtge. rate, incl. points and orig. fee, 30-year conv. fixed or ARM	mo.	9.24	12/94	2c
Personal Goods				
Shampoo, Alberto VO5	15-oz.	1.32	12/94	2c
Toothpaste, Crest or Colgate	6-7 oz.	1.86	12/94	2c
Personal Services				
Dry cleaning, man's 2-pc. suit		6.76	12/94	2c
Haircut, man's barbershop, no styling		9.17	12/94	2c
Haircut, woman's shampoo, trim, blow-dry		14.58	12/94	2c
Restaurant Food				
Chicken, fried, thigh and drumstick		2.18	12/94	2c
Hamburger with cheese	1/4 lb.	1.88	12/94	2c
Pizza, Pizza Hut or Pizza Inn	12-13 in.	8.49	12/94	2c
Transportation				
Transportation, ACCRA Index		103.80	12/94	2c
Tire balance, computer or spin bal., front	wheel	6.50	12/94	2c
Utilities				
Utilities, ACCRA Index		75.10	12/94	2c
Electricity, (part.), other, 1800 sq. ft., new home	mo.	40.82	12/94	2c

Marion-McDowell County, NC

Item	Per	Value	Date	Ref.
Composite, ACCRA index		89.90	12/94	2c
Alcoholic Beverages				
Beer, Miller Lite, Bud, 12-oz., ex deposit	6	3.50	12/94	2c
J & B Scotch	750-ml.	18.60	12/94	2c
Wine, Gallo Chablis blanc	1.5-lit	4.39	12/94	2c
Clothing				
Jeans, man's denim		25.44	12/94	2c
Shirt, man's dress shirt		33.00	12/94	2c
Undervest, boy's size 10-14, cotton	3	3.24	12/94	2c
Communications				
Newspaper subscription, dly. and Sun. delivery	month	12.17	12/94	2c
Telephone bill, family of four	month	22.95	12/94	2c
Energy and Fuels				
Energy, combined forms, 1800 sq. ft.	mo.	112.27	12/94	2c
Gas, reg unlead, taxes inc., cash, self-service	gal	1.10	12/94	2c
Entertainment				
Bowling, evening rate	game	2.00	12/94	2c
Monopoly game, Parker Brothers', No. 9	game	11.48	12/94	2c
Movie	adm	5.50	12/94	2c
Tennis balls, yellow, Wilson or Penn, 3	can	1.98	12/94	2c
Groceries				
Groceries, ACCRA Index		93.50	12/94	2c
Baby food, strained vegetables, lowest price	4-4.5 oz.	0.34	12/94	2c
Bananas	lb.	0.43	12/94	2c
Beef or hamburger, ground	lb.	1.69	12/94	2c
Bread, white	24-oz.	0.68	12/94	2c
Cheese, Kraft grated Parmesan	8-oz.	3.16	12/94	2c
Chicken, whole fryer	lb.	0.91	12/94	2c
Cigarettes, Winston, Kings	carton	12.16	12/94	2c
Coffee, vacuum-packed	13 oz.	3.16	12/94	2c
Corn Flakes, Kellogg's or Post Toasties	18 oz.	2.08	12/94	2c
Corn, frozen, whole kernel, lowest price	10 oz.	0.62	12/94	2c
Eggs, Grade A large	dozen	0.84	12/94	2c

Marion-McDowell County, NC - continued

Item	Per	Value	Date	Ref.
Groceries - continued				
Lettuce, iceberg	head	0.99	12/94	2c
Margarine, Blue Bonnet or Parkay cubes	lb.	0.53	12/94	2c
Milk, whole	1/2 gal.	1.38	12/94	2c
Orange juice, Minute Maid frozen	12-oz.	1.09	12/94	2c
Peaches, halves or slices, Hunt's, Del Monte, or Libby's	29-oz.	1.27	12/94	2c
Peas, sweet, Del Monte or Green Giant	15-17 oz.	0.48	12/94	2c
Potatoes, white or red	10-lb. sack	2.16	12/94	2c
Sausage, Jimmy Dean, 100% pork	lb.	2.33	12/94	2c
Shortening, vegetable, Crisco	3-lb.	2.47	12/94	2c
Soft drink, Coca Cola, ex deposit	2 lit	1.12	12/94	2c
Steak, t-bone	lb.	4.64	12/94	2c
Sugar, cane or beet	4 lbs.	1.47	12/94	2c
Tomatoes, Hunt's or Del Monte	14.5 oz.	0.55	12/94	2c
Tuna, chunk, light, oil-packed	6.125-6.5 oz.	0.62	12/94	2c
Goods and Services				
Miscellaneous goods and services, ACCRA Index		95.30	12/94	2c
Health Care				
Health care, ACCRA Index		76.10	12/94	2c
Antibiotic ointment, Polysporin	1.5 oz.	4.03	12/94	2c
Dentist's fee, adult teeth cleaning and periodic oral exam	visit	35.67	12/94	2c
Doctor's fee, routine exam, established patient	visit	32.50	12/94	2c
Hospital care, semiprivate room	day	270.00	12/94	2c
Household Goods				
Appl. repair, service call, wash mach	min. lab. chg.	32.50	12/94	2c
Laundry detergent, Tide Ultra, Bold, or Cheer	42 oz.	2.60	12/94	2c
Tissues, facial, Kleenex brand	175	0.99	12/94	2c
Housing				
Housing, ACCRA Index		83.80	12/94	2c
House payment, principal and interest, 25% down payment	mo.	683	12/94	2c
House, 1800 sq ft, 8000 sq ft lot, new, urban, utilities	total	112500	12/94	2c
Mtge. rate, incl. points and orig. fee, 30-year conv. fixed or ARM	mo.	9.07	12/94	2c
Rent, apartment, 2 br., 1 1/2-2 baths, unfurnished, 950 sq ft, water	mo.	325	12/94	2c
Personal Goods				
Shampoo, Alberto VO5	15-oz.	0.95	12/94	2c
Toothpaste, Crest or Colgate	6-7 oz.	1.88	12/94	2c
Personal Services				
Dry cleaning, man's 2-pc. suit		5.55	12/94	2c
Haircut, man's barbershop, no styling		6.50	12/94	2c
Haircut, woman's shampoo, trim, blow-dry		15.00	12/94	2c
Restaurant Food				
Chicken, fried, thigh and drumstick		2.29	12/94	2c
Hamburger with cheese	1/4 lb.	1.90	12/94	2c
Pizza, Pizza Hut or Pizza Inn	12-13 in.	7.95	12/94	2c
Transportation				
Transportation, ACCRA Index		80.80	12/94	2c
Tire balance, computer or spin bal., front	wheel	3.90	12/94	2c
Utilities				
Utilities, ACCRA Index		102.40	12/94	2c
Electricity, 1800 sq. ft., new home	mo.	112.27	12/94	2c

Values are in dollars or fractions of dollars. In the column headed *Ref*, references are shown to sources. Each reference is followed by a letter. These refer to the geographical level for which data were reported: s = State, r = Region, and c = City or metro. The abbreviation *ex* is used to mean *except* or *excluding*; *exp* stands for expenditures. For other abbreviations and further explanations, please see the Introduction.

Marshfield, WI

Item	Per	Value	Date	Ref.
Composite, ACCRA index		101.00	12/94	2c
Alcoholic Beverages				
Beer, Miller Lite, Bud, 12-oz., ex deposit	6	3.44	12/94	2c
J & B Scotch	750-ml.	16.99	12/94	2c
Wine, Gallo Chablis blanc	1.5-lit	4.48	12/94	2c
Clothing				
Jeans, man's denim		45.00	12/94	2c
Shirt, man's dress shirt		29.50	12/94	2c
Undervest, boy's size 10-14, cotton	3	3.09	12/94	2c
Communications				
Newspaper subscription, dly. and Sun. delivery	month	14.19	12/94	2c
Telephone bill, family of four	month	29.90	12/94	2c
Telephone, residential, flat rate	mo.	6.00	12/93	8c
Energy and Fuels				
Energy, combined forms, 1800 sq. ft.	mo.	95.00	12/94	2c
Energy, exc. electricity, 1800 sq. ft.	mo.	64.48	12/94	2c
Gas, reg unlead, taxes inc., cash, self-service	gal	1.16	12/94	2c
Entertainment				
Bowling, evening rate	game	1.95	12/94	2c
Monopoly game, Parker Brothers', No. 9	game	9.98	12/94	2c
Movie	adm	5.25	12/94	2c
Tennis balls, yellow, Wilson or Penn, 3	can	2.13	12/94	2c
Groceries				
Groceries, ACCRA Index		99.10	12/94	2c
Baby food, strained vegetables, lowest price	4-4.5 oz.	0.47	12/94	2c
Bananas	lb.	0.35	12/94	2c
Beef or hamburger, ground	lb.	1.46	12/94	2c
Bread, white	24-oz.	0.65	12/94	2c
Cheese, Kraft grated Parmesan	8-oz.	2.99	12/94	2c
Chicken, whole fryer	lb.	0.96	12/94	2c
Cigarettes, Winston, Kings	carton	16.60	12/94	2c
Coffee, vacuum-packed	13 oz.	3.44	12/94	2c
Corn Flakes, Kellogg's or Post Toasties	18 oz.	2.49	12/94	2c
Corn, frozen, whole kernel, lowest price	10 oz.	0.56	12/94	2c
Eggs, Grade A large	dozen	0.67	12/94	2c
Lettuce, iceberg	head	0.69	12/94	2c
Margarine, Blue Bonnet or Parkay cubes	lb.	0.56	12/94	2c
Milk, whole	1/2 gal.	1.29	12/94	2c
Orange juice, Minute Maid frozen	12-oz.	1.26	12/94	2c
Peaches, halves or slices, Hunt's, Del Monte, or Libby's	29-oz.	1.40	12/94	2c
Peas, sweet, Del Monte or Green Giant	15-17 oz.	0.52	12/94	2c
Potatoes, white or red	10-lb. sack	1.72	12/94	2c
Sausage, Jimmy Dean, 100% pork	lb.	2.72	12/94	2c
Shortening, vegetable, Crisco	3-lb.	2.49	12/94	2c
Soft drink, Coca Cola, ex deposit	2 lit	1.09	12/94	2c
Steak, t-bone	lb.	5.09	12/94	2c
Sugar, cane or beet	4 lbs.	1.33	12/94	2c
Tomatoes, Hunt's or Del Monte	14.5 oz.	0.76	12/94	2c
Tuna, chunk, light, oil-packed	6.125-6.5 oz.	0.65	12/94	2c
Goods and Services				
Miscellaneous goods and services, ACCRA Index		102.70	12/94	2c
Health Care				
Health care, ACCRA Index		107.70	12/94	2c
Antibiotic ointment, Polysporin	1.5 oz.	3.50	12/94	2c
Dentist's fee, adult teeth cleaning and periodic oral exam	visit	51.25	12/94	2c
Doctor's fee, routine exam, established patient	visit	59.25	12/94	2c

Marshfield, WI - continued

Item	Per	Value	Date	Ref.
Health Care - continued				
Hospital care, semiprivate room	day	267.00	12/94	2c
Household Goods				
Appl. repair, service call, wash mach	min. lab. chg.	32.00	12/94	2c
Laundry detergent, Tide Ultra, Bold, or Cheer	42 oz.	3.58	12/94	2c
Tissues, facial, Kleenex brand	175	0.94	12/94	2c
Housing				
Housing, ACCRA Index		102.00	12/94	2c
House payment, principal and interest, 25% down payment	mo.	793	12/94	2c
House, 1800 sq ft, 8000 sq ft lot, new, urban, utilities	total	130000	12/94	2c
Mtge. rate, incl. points and orig. fee, 30-year conv. fixed or ARM	mo.	9.13	12/94	2c
Rent, apartment, 2 br., 1 1/2-2 baths, unfurnished, 950 sq ft, water	mo.	504	12/94	2c
Personal Goods				
Shampoo, Alberto VO5	15-oz.	1.18	12/94	2c
Toothpaste, Crest or Colgate	6-7 oz.	2.14	12/94	2c
Personal Services				
Dry cleaning, man's 2-pc. suit		6.08	12/94	2c
Haircut, man's barbershop, no styling		9.12	12/94	2c
Haircut, woman's shampoo, trim, blow-dry		15.25	12/94	2c
Restaurant Food				
Chicken, fried, thigh and drumstick		2.09	12/94	2c
Hamburger with cheese	1/4 lb.	1.77	12/94	2c
Pizza, Pizza Hut or Pizza Inn	12-13 in.	8.91	12/94	2c
Transportation				
Transportation, ACCRA Index		96.90	12/94	2c
Tire balance, computer or spin bal., front	wheel	5.98	12/94	2c
Utilities				
Utilities, ACCRA Index		93.90	12/94	2c
Electricity, (part.), other, 1800 sq. ft., new home	mo.	30.52	12/94	2c

Martinsburg-Berkeley County, WV

Item	Per	Value	Date	Ref.
Composite, ACCRA index		91.80	12/94	2c
Alcoholic Beverages				
Beer, Miller Lite, Bud, 12-oz., ex deposit	6	3.98	12/94	2c
J & B Scotch	750-ml.	16.81	12/94	2c
Wine, Gallo Chablis blanc	1.5-lit	5.41	12/94	2c
Clothing				
Jeans, man's denim		25.99	12/94	2c
Shirt, man's dress shirt		21.79	12/94	2c
Undervest, boy's size 10-14, cotton	3	3.99	12/94	2c
Communications				
Newspaper subscription, dly. and Sun. delivery	month	8.00	12/94	2c
Telephone bill, family of four	month	22.17	12/94	2c
Telephone, residential, flat rate	mo.	6.00	12/93	8c
Energy and Fuels				
Energy, combined forms, 1800 sq. ft.	mo.	124.89	12/94	2c
Gas, reg unlead, taxes inc., cash, self-service	gal	1.09	12/94	2c
Entertainment				
Bowling, evening rate	game	2.00	12/94	2c
Monopoly game, Parker Brothers', No. 9	game	11.32	12/94	2c
Movie	adm	5.00	12/94	2c
Tennis balls, yellow, Wilson or Penn, 3	can	2.22	12/94	2c

Values are in dollars or fractions of dollars. In the column headed *Ref*, references are shown to sources. Each reference is followed by a letter. These refer to the geographical level for which data were reported: s=State, r=Region, and c=City or metro. The abbreviation *ex* is used to mean *except* or *excluding*; *exp* stands for expenditures. For other abbreviations and further explanations, please see the Introduction.

Martinsburg-Berkeley County, WV - continued

Item	Per	Value	Date	Ref.
Groceries				
Groceries, ACCRA Index		94.20	12/94	2c
Baby food, strained vegetables, lowest price	4-4.5 oz.	0.38	12/94	2c
Bananas	lb.	0.37	12/94	2c
Beef or hamburger, ground	lb.	1.52	12/94	2c
Bread, white	24-oz.	0.63	12/94	2c
Cheese, Kraft grated Parmesan	8-oz.	3.29	12/94	2c
Chicken, whole fryer	lb.	0.77	12/94	2c
Cigarettes, Winston, Kings	carton	14.73	12/94	2c
Coffee, vacuum-packed	13 oz.	3.23	12/94	2c
Corn Flakes, Kellogg's or Post Toasties	18 oz.	2.34	12/94	2c
Corn, frozen, whole kernel, lowest price	10 oz.	0.61	12/94	2c
Eggs, Grade A large	dozen	0.81	12/94	2c
Lettuce, iceberg	head	0.93	12/94	2c
Margarine, Blue Bonnet or Parkay cubes	lb.	0.57	12/94	2c
Milk, whole	1/2 gal.	1.14	12/94	2c
Orange juice, Minute Maid frozen	12-oz.	1.19	12/94	2c
Peaches, halves or slices, Hunt's, Del Monte, or Libby's	29-oz.	1.23	12/94	2c
Peas, sweet, Del Monte or Green Giant	15-17 oz.	0.48	12/94	2c
Potatoes, white or red	10-lb. sack	2.29	12/94	2c
Sausage, Jimmy Dean, 100% pork	lb.	2.12	12/94	2c
Shortening, vegetable, Crisco	3-lb.	2.56	12/94	2c
Soft drink, Coca Cola, ex deposit	2 lit	1.07	12/94	2c
Steak, t-bone	lb.	5.36	12/94	2c
Sugar, cane or beet	4 lbs.	1.43	12/94	2c
Tomatoes, Hunt's or Del Monte	14.5 oz.	0.75	12/94	2c
Tuna, chunk, light, oil-packed	6.125-6.5 oz.	0.67	12/94	2c
Goods and Services				
Miscellaneous goods and services, ACCRA Index		90.10	12/94	2c
Health Care				
Health care, ACCRA Index		79.00	12/94	2c
Antibiotic ointment, Polysporin	1.5 oz.	3.55	12/94	2c
Dentist's fee, adult teeth cleaning and periodic oral exam	visit	41.20	12/94	2c
Doctor's fee, routine exam, established patient	visit	35.43	12/94	2c
Hospital care, semiprivate room	day	231.00	12/94	2c
Household Goods				
Appl. repair, service call, wash mach	min. lab. chg.	29.67	12/94	2c
Laundry detergent, Tide Ultra, Bold, or Cheer	42 oz.	2.73	12/94	2c
Tissues, facial, Kleenex brand	175	1.00	12/94	2c
Housing				
Housing, ACCRA Index		90.60	12/94	2c
House payment, principal and interest, 25% down payment	mo.	701	12/94	2c
House, 1800 sq ft, 8000 sq ft lot, new, urban, utilities	total	113667	12/94	2c
Mtge. rate, incl. points and orig. fee, 30-year conv. fixed or ARM	mo.	9.24	12/94	2c
Rent, apartment, 2 br., 1 1/2-2 baths, unfurnished, 950 sq ft, water	mo.	450	12/94	2c
Personal Goods				
Shampoo, Alberto VO5	15-oz.	1.11	12/94	2c
Toothpaste, Crest or Colgate	6-7 oz.	2.02	12/94	2c
Personal Services				
Dry cleaning, man's 2-pc. suit		5.80	12/94	2c
Haircut, man's barbershop, no styling		5.05	12/94	2c
Haircut, woman's shampoo, trim, blow-dry		12.83	12/94	2c

Martinsburg-Berkeley County, WV - continued

Item	Per	Value	Date	Ref.
Restaurant Food				
Chicken, fried, thigh and drumstick		2.36	12/94	2c
Hamburger with cheese	1/4 lb.	1.80	12/94	2c
Pizza, Pizza Hut or Pizza Inn	12-13 in.	7.69	12/94	2c
Transportation				
Transportation, ACCRA Index		88.90	12/94	2c
Tire balance, computer or spin bal., front	wheel	5.22	12/94	2c
Utilities				
Utilities, ACCRA Index		111.60	12/94	2c
Electricity, 1800 sq. ft., new home	mo.	124.89	12/94	2c

Mason City, IA

Item	Per	Value	Date	Ref.
Composite, ACCRA index		94.80	12/94	2c
Alcoholic Beverages				
Beer, Miller Lite, Bud, 12-oz., ex deposit	6	3.59	12/94	2c
J & B Scotch	750-ml.	18.20	12/94	2c
Wine, Gallo Chablis blanc	1.5-lit	5.60	12/94	2c
Clothing				
Jeans, man's denim		27.99	12/94	2c
Shirt, man's dress shirt		39.75	12/94	2c
Undervest, boy's size 10-14, cotton	3	3.74	12/94	2c
Communications				
Newspaper subscription, dly. and Sun. delivery	month	16.31	12/94	2c
Telephone bill, family of four	month	18.85	12/94	2c
Telephone, residential, flat rate	mo.	13.45	12/93	8c
Energy and Fuels				
Energy, combined forms, 1800 sq. ft.	mo.	96.60	12/94	2c
Energy, exc. electricity, 1800 sq. ft.	mo.	44.26	12/94	2c
Gas, cooking, 10 therms	month	12.09	2/94	65c
Gas, cooking, 30 therms	month	21.36	2/94	65c
Gas, cooking, 50 therms	month	30.64	2/94	65c
Gas, reg unlead, taxes inc., cash, self-service	gal	1.16	12/94	2c
Entertainment				
Bowling, evening rate	game	1.66	12/94	2c
Monopoly game, Parker Brothers', No. 9	game	10.42	12/94	2c
Movie	adm	4.50	12/94	2c
Tennis balls, yellow, Wilson or Penn, 3	can	2.31	12/94	2c
Groceries				
Groceries, ACCRA Index		94.50	12/94	2c
Baby food, strained vegetables, lowest price	4-4.5 oz.	0.34	12/94	2c
Bananas	lb.	0.31	12/94	2c
Beef or hamburger, ground	lb.	1.29	12/94	2c
Bread, white	24-oz.	0.65	12/94	2c
Cheese, Kraft grated Parmesan	8-oz.	3.32	12/94	2c
Chicken, whole fryer	lb.	0.75	12/94	2c
Cigarettes, Winston, Kings	carton	17.27	12/94	2c
Coffee, vacuum-packed	13 oz.	3.58	12/94	2c
Corn Flakes, Kellogg's or Post Toasties	18 oz.	2.58	12/94	2c
Corn, frozen, whole kernel, lowest price	10 oz.	0.72	12/94	2c
Eggs, Grade A large	dozen	0.68	12/94	2c
Lettuce, iceberg	head	0.68	12/94	2c
Margarine, Blue Bonnet or Parkay cubes	lb.	0.54	12/94	2c
Milk, whole	1/2 gal.	1.17	12/94	2c
Orange juice, Minute Maid frozen	12-oz.	1.09	12/94	2c
Peaches, halves or slices, Hunt's, Del Monte, or Libby's	29-oz.	1.37	12/94	2c
Peas, sweet, Del Monte or Green Giant	15-17 oz.	0.59	12/94	2c
Potatoes, white or red	10-lb. sack	2.05	12/94	2c
Sausage, Jimmy Dean, 100% pork	lb.	2.42	12/94	2c

Values are in dollars or fractions of dollars. In the column headed *Ref*, references are shown to sources. Each reference is followed by a letter. These refer to the geographical level for which data were reported: s=State, r=Region, and c=City or metro. The abbreviation *ex* is used to mean *except* or *excluding*; *exp* stands for expenditures. For other abbreviations and further explanations, please see the Introduction.

Mason City, IA - continued

Item	Per	Value	Date	Ref.
Groceries				
Shortening, vegetable, Crisco	3-lb.	2.27	12/94	2c
Soft drink, Coca Cola, ex deposit	2 lit	1.19	12/94	2c
Steak, t-bone	lb.	4.67	12/94	2c
Sugar, cane or beet	4 lbs.	1.42	12/94	2c
Tomatoes, Hunt's or Del Monte	14.5 oz.	0.77	12/94	2c
Tuna, chunk, light, oil-packed	6.125-6.5 oz.	0.66	12/94	2c
Goods and Services				
Miscellaneous goods and services, ACCRA Index		99.30	12/94	2c
Health Care				
Health care, ACCRA Index		96.70	12/94	2c
Antibiotic ointment, Polysporin	1.5 oz.	3.91	12/94	2c
Dentist's fee, adult teeth cleaning and periodic oral exam	visit	48.42	12/94	2c
Doctor's fee, routine exam, established patient	visit	43.00	12/94	2c
Hospital care, semiprivate room	day	337.00	12/94	2c
Household Goods				
Appl. repair, service call, wash mach	min. lab. chg.	32.32	12/94	2c
Laundry detergent, Tide Ultra, Bold, or Cheer	42 oz.	3.76	12/94	2c
Tissues, facial, Kleenex brand	175	0.89	12/94	2c
Housing				
Housing, ACCRA Index		89.20	12/94	2c
House payment, principal and interest, 25% down payment	mo.	710	12/94	2c
House, 1800 sq ft, 8000 sq ft lot, new, urban, utilities	total	116500	12/94	2c
Mtge. rate, incl. points and orig. fee, 30-year conv. fixed or ARM	mo.	9.11	12/94	2c
Rent, apartment, 2 br., 1 1/2-2 baths, unfurnished, 950 sq ft, water	mo.	396	12/94	2c
Personal Goods				
Shampoo, Alberto VO5	15-oz.	1.15	12/94	2c
Toothpaste, Crest or Colgate	6-7 oz.	2.03	12/94	2c
Personal Services				
Dry cleaning, man's 2-pc. suit		6.25	12/94	2c
Haircut, man's barbershop, no styling		8.33	12/94	2c
Haircut, woman's shampoo, trim, blow-dry		16.00	12/94	2c
Restaurant Food				
Chicken, fried, thigh and drumstick		2.17	12/94	2c
Hamburger with cheese	1/4 lb.	1.94	12/94	2c
Pizza, Pizza Hut or Pizza Inn	12-13 in.	7.49	12/94	2c
Transportation				
Transportation, ACCRA Index		101.40	12/94	2c
Tire balance, computer or spin bal., front	wheel	6.70	12/94	2c
Utilities				
Utilities, ACCRA Index		87.50	12/94	2c
Electricity, (part.), other, 1800 sq. ft., new home	mo.	52.34	12/94	2c

Mcallen-Edinburg-Mission, TX

Item	Per	Value	Date	Ref.
Composite, ACCRA index		92.60	12/94	2c
Alcoholic Beverages				
Beer, Miller Lite, Bud, 12-oz., ex deposit	6	3.74	12/94	2c
J & B Scotch	750-ml.	18.49	12/94	2c
Wine, Gallo Chablis blanc	1.5-lit	4.76	12/94	2c

Mcallen-Edinburg-Mission, TX - continued

Item	Per	Value	Date	Ref.
Appliances				
Appliances (major), expenditures	year	153	91	81r
Average annual exp.				
Food, health care, personal goods, services	year	27020	91	81r
Charity				
Cash contributions, expenditures	year	839	91	81r
Clothing				
Apparel, men and boys, total expenditures	year	380	91	81r
Apparel, women and girls, total expenditures	year	660	91	81r
Footwear, expenditures	year	193	91	81r
Jeans, man's denim		26.21	12/94	2c
Shirt, man's dress shirt		33.84	12/94	2c
Undervest, boy's size 10-14, cotton	3	4.55	12/94	2c
Communications				
Long-distance telephone rate, day, addl. min., 1-10 mi.	min.	0.08	12/93	9s
Long-distance telephone rate, day, initial min., 1-10 mi.	min.	0.10	12/93	9s
Newspaper subscription, dly. and Sun. delivery	month	8.25	12/94	2c
Phone line, single, business, field visit	inst	71.90	12/93	9s
Phone line, single, business, no field visit	inst	57.30	12/93	9s
Phone line, single, residence, field visit	inst	52.95	12/93	9s
Phone line, single, residence, no field visit	inst	38.35	12/93	9s
Telephone bill, family of four	month	15.14	12/94	2c
Telephone service, expenditures	year	616	91	81r
Telephone, residential, flat rate	mo.	9.10	12/93	8c
Education				
Board, 4-year private college/university	year	2084	8/94	80s
Board, 4-year public college/university	year	1675	8/94	80s
Education, total expenditures	year	319	91	81r
Room, 4-year private college/university	year	1840	8/94	80s
Room, 4-year public college/university	year	1756	8/94	80s
Total cost, 4-year private college/university	year	11876	8/94	80s
Total cost, 4-year public college/university	year	4935	8/94	80s
Tuition, 2-year public college/university, in-state	year	625	8/94	80s
Tuition, 4-year private college/university, in-state	year	7952	8/94	80s
Tuition, 4-year public college/university, in-state	year	1503	8/94	80s
Energy and Fuels				
Energy, combined forms, 1800 sq. ft.	mo.	124.31	12/94	2c
Energy, exc. electricity, 1800 sq. ft.	mo.	21.46	12/94	2c
Fuel oil and other fuels, expenditures	year	56	91	81r
Gas, natural, expenditures	year	150	91	81r
Gas, reg unlead, taxes inc., cash, self-service	gal	1.01	12/94	2c
Gasoline and motor oil purchased	year	1152	91	81r
Gasoline, unleaded midgrade	gallon	1.21	4/93	82r
Gasoline, unleaded premium	gallon	1.30	4/93	82r
Gasoline, unleaded regular	gallon	1.10	4/93	82r
Entertainment				
Bowling, evening rate	game	2.19	12/94	2c
Concert ticket, Pearl Jam group	perf	20.00	94	50r
Entertainment, total expenditures	year	1266	91	81r
Fees and admissions, expenditures	year	306	91	81r
Monopoly game, Parker Brothers', No. 9	game	10.60	12/94	2c
Movie	adm	5.25	12/94	2c
Pets, toys, playground equipment, expenditures	year	271	91	81r
Reading, expenditures	year	131	91	81r
Televisions, radios, and sound equipment, expenditures	year	439	91	81r
Tennis balls, yellow, Wilson or Penn, 3	can	2.36	12/94	2c
Funerals				
Burial, immediate, container provided by funeral home		1574.60	1/95	54r
Cards, acknowledgment		22.24	1/95	54r

Values are in dollars or fractions of dollars. In the column headed *Ref*, references are shown to sources. Each reference is followed by a letter. These refer to the geographical level for which data were reported: s=State, r=Region, and c=City or metro. The abbreviation *ex* is used to mean *except* or *excluding*; *exp* stands for expenditures. For other abbreviations and further explanations, please see the Introduction.

Mcallen-Edinburg-Mission, TX - continued

Item	Per	Value	Date	Ref.
Funerals				
Casket, minimum alternative		239.41	1/95	54r
Cosmetology, hair care, etc.		91.04	1/95	54r
Cremation, direct, container provided by funeral home		1085.15	1/95	54r
Embalming		281.30	1/95	54r
Funeral, funeral home		323.04	1/95	54r
Funeral, other facility		327.58	1/95	54r
Graveside service		355.19	1/95	54r
Hearse, local		141.89	1/95	54r
Limousine, local		99.40	1/95	54r
Memorial service		284.67	1/95	54r
Service charge, professional, nondeclinable		904.06	1/95	54r
Visitation and viewing		187.04	1/95	54r
Groceries				
Groceries, ACCRA Index		92.70	12/94	2c
Apples, Red Delicious	lb.	0.73	12/94	82r
Baby food, strained vegetables, lowest price	4-4.5 oz.	0.28	12/94	2c
Bacon, sliced	lb.	1.67	12/94	82r
Bananas	lb.	0.32	12/94	2c
Bananas	lb.	0.42	12/94	82r
Beef or hamburger, ground	lb.	1.44	12/94	2c
Beef purchases	year	213	91	81r
Beverage purchases, alcoholic	year	249	91	81r
Beverage purchases, nonalcoholic	year	207	91	81r
Bologna, all beef or mixed	lb.	2.27	12/94	82r
Bread, white	24-oz.	0.51	12/94	2c
Bread, white, pan	lb.	0.68	12/94	82r
Cabbage	lb.	0.42	12/94	82r
Carrots, short trimmed and topped	lb.	0.53	12/94	82r
Cereals and bakery products purchases	year	345	91	81r
Cereals and cereals products purchases	year	127	91	81r
Cheddar cheese, natural	lb.	3.58	12/94	82r
Cheese, Kraft grated Parmesan	8-oz.	3.13	12/94	2c
Chicken breast, bone-in	lb.	1.71	12/94	82r
Chicken, fresh, whole	lb.	0.78	12/94	82r
Chicken, whole fryer	lb.	0.81	12/94	2c
Chuck roast, USDA choice, boneless	lb.	2.26	12/94	82r
Cigarettes, Winston, Kings	carton	17.00	12/94	2c
Coffee, vacuum-packed	13 oz.	3.23	12/94	2c
Corn Flakes, Kellogg's or Post Toasties	18 oz.	2.43	12/94	2c
Corn, frozen, whole kernel, lowest price	10 oz.	0.64	12/94	2c
Crackers, soda, salted	lb.	1.27	12/94	82r
Cucumbers	lb.	0.65	12/94	82r
Dairy products (other) purchases	year	141	91	81r
Eggs, Grade A large	dozen	0.71	12/94	2c
Eggs, Grade A large	dozen	0.87	12/94	82r
Fish and seafood purchases	year	72	91	81r
Flour, white, all purpose	lb.	0.23	12/94	82r
Food purchases, food eaten at home	year	2381	91	81r
Foods purchased away from home, not prepared by consumer	year	1696	91	81r
Frankfurters, all meat or all beef	lb.	1.74	12/94	82r
Fruits and vegetables purchases	year	380	91	81r
Grapefruit	lb.	0.45	12/94	82r
Grapes, Thompson seedless	lb.	2.30	12/94	82r
Ground beef, 100% beef	lb.	1.37	12/94	82r
Ground chuck, 100% beef	lb.	1.97	12/94	82r
Ham, boneless, exc. canned	lb.	2.54	12/94	82r
Ice cream, prepackaged, bulk, regular	1/2 gal.	2.47	12/94	82r
Lemons	lb.	1.02	12/94	82r
Lettuce, iceberg	lb.	0.96	12/94	82r
Lettuce, iceberg	head	0.83	12/94	2c
Margarine, Blue Bonnet or Parkay cubes	lb.	0.59	12/94	2c
Margarine, stick	lb.	0.77	12/94	82r
Meats, poultry, fish, and eggs purchases	year	655	91	81r
Milk and cream (fresh) purchases	year	130	91	81r
Milk, whole	1/2 gal.	1.18	12/94	2c
Orange juice, frozen concentrate 12-oz. can	16 oz.	1.36	12/94	82r
Orange juice, Minute Maid frozen	12-oz.	1.25	12/94	2c

Mcallen-Edinburg-Mission, TX - continued

Item	Per	Value	Date	Ref.
Groceries - continued				
Oranges, Navel	lb.	0.54	12/94	82r
Peaches, halves or slices, Hunt's, Del Monte, or Libby's	29-oz.	1.27	12/94	2c
Pears, Anjou	lb.	0.81	12/94	82r
Peas, sweet, Del Monte or Green Giant	15-17 oz.	0.41	12/94	2c
Pork chops, center cut, bone-in	lb.	3.07	12/94	82r
Pork purchases	year	142	91	81r
Potato chips	16-oz.	3.15	12/94	82r
Potatoes, frozen, French fried	lb.	0.82	12/94	82r
Potatoes, white	lb.	0.34	12/94	82r
Potatoes, white or red	10-lb. sack	1.96	12/94	2c
Rice, white, long grain, uncooked	lb.	0.48	12/94	82r
Round roast, USDA choice, boneless	lb.	2.91	12/94	82r
Sausage, fresh	lb.	1.82	12/94	82r
Sausage, Jimmy Dean, 100% pork	lb.	2.24	12/94	2c
Shortening, vegetable oil blends	lb.	0.75	12/94	82r
Shortening, vegetable, Crisco	3-lb.	2.38	12/94	2c
Soft drink, Coca Cola, ex deposit	2 lit	1.37	12/94	2c
Spaghetti and macaroni	lb.	0.87	12/94	82r
Steak, rib eye, USDA choice, boneless	lb.	6.85	12/94	82r
Steak, round, graded & ungraded, exc. USDA prime & choice	lb.	2.96	12/94	82r
Steak, round, USDA choice, boneless	lb.	3.17	12/94	82r
Steak, sirloin, USDA choice, boneless	lb.	4.12	12/94	82r
Steak, t-bone	lb.	6.25	12/94	2c
Steak, T-bone, USDA choice, bone-in	lb.	5.63	12/94	82r
Sugar and other sweets, eaten at home, expenditures	year	93	91	81r
Sugar, cane or beet	4 lbs.	1.39	12/94	2c
Sugar, white, all sizes	lb.	0.39	12/94	82r
Tobacco products and smoking supplies, total expenditures	year	286	91	81r
Tomatoes, field grown	lb.	1.36	12/94	82r
Tomatoes, Hunt's or Del Monte	14.5 oz.	0.57	12/94	2c
Tuna, chunk, light	lb.	1.94	12/94	82r
Tuna, chunk, light, oil-packed	6.125-6.5 oz.	0.67	12/94	2c
Turkey, frozen, whole	lb.	0.96	12/94	82r
Yogurt, natural, fruit flavored	8 oz.	0.58	12/94	82r
Goods and Services				
Miscellaneous goods and services, ACCRA Index		98.60	12/94	2c
Health Care				
Health care, ACCRA Index		94.10	12/94	2c
Adenosine, emergency room	treat	100.00	95	23r
Antibiotic ointment, Polysporin	1.5 oz.	4.21	12/94	2c
Bladder tap, superpubic, infant, emergency room	treat	119.00	95	23r
Blood analysis, emergency room	treat	25.00	95	23r
Blood tests, abdominal pain, emergency room	treat	25.00	95	23r
Burn dressing, emergency room	treat	266.00	95	23r
Cardiology interpretation, emergency room	treat	26.00	95	23r
Chest X-ray, emergency room	treat	78.00	95	23r
Childbirth, Cesarean delivery, hospital charge	birth	5462.00	12/91	69r
Childbirth, Cesarean delivery, physician charge	birth	2228.00	12/91	69r
Childbirth, normal delivery, hospital charge	birth	2943.00	12/91	69r
Childbirth, normal delivery, physician charge	birth	1619.00	12/91	69r
Defibrillation pads, emergency room	treat	6.00	95	23r
Dentist's fee, adult teeth cleaning and periodic oral exam	visit	51.78	12/94	2c
Doctor's fee, routine exam, established patient	visit	39.80	12/94	2c
Drugs, expenditures	year	297	91	81r
Gastric tube insertion, nasal, emergency room	treat	25.00	95	23r

Values are in dollars or fractions of dollars. In the column headed *Ref*, references are shown to sources. Each reference is followed by a letter. These refer to the geographical level for which data were reported: s=State, r=Region, and c=City or metro. The abbreviation *ex* is used to mean *except* or *excluding*; *exp* stands for expenditures. For other abbreviations and further explanations, please see the Introduction.

Mcallen-Edinburg-Mission, TX - continued

Item	Per	Value	Date	Ref.
Health Care				
Health care, total expenditures	year	1600	91	81r
Health insurance expenditures	year	637	91	81r
Heart monitor, emergency room	treat	40.00	95	23r
Hospital care, semiprivate room	day	280.75	12/94	2c
Insurance premium, family medical care	month	389.25	1/95	41s
Intravenous fluids, emergency room	treat	130.00	95	23r
Intravenous fluids, emergency room	liter	26.00	95	23r
Intravenous line, central, emergency room	treat	342.00	95	23r
Liver function tests, abdominal pain, emergency room	treat	26.00	95	23r
Medical care charges, total, emergency room, third-degree burns	treat	2101.00	95	23r
Medical care charges, total, emergency, infant with fever	treat	628.00	95	23r
Medical services expenditures	year	573	91	81r
Medical supplies expenditures	year	93	91	81r
Morphine, emergency room	treat	34.00	95	23r
Nursing care and facilities charges, emergency room	treat	252.00	95	23r
Nursing care and facilities charges, emergency, infant with fever	treat	252.00	95	23r
Nursing care and facilities charges, emergency, third-degree burns	treat	861.00	95	23r
Physician's charges, emergency, infant with fever	treat	212.00	95	23r
Physician's charges, emergency, third-degree burns	treat	372.00	95	23r
Physician's fee, emergency room	treat	372.00	95	23r
Physician's fee, general practitioner	visit	51.20	12/93	60r
Surgery, open-heart	proc	42374.00	1/93	14r
Ultrasound, abdominal, emergency room	treat	276.00	95	23r
Urinalysis, emergency room	treat	20.00	95	23r
Urinalysis, infant, emergency room	treat	20.00	95	23r
X-rays, emergency room	treat	78.00	95	23r
Household Goods				
Appl. repair, service call, wash mach	min. lab. chg.	21.60	12/94	2c
Floor coverings, expenditures	year	48	91	81r
Furniture, expenditures	year	280	91	81r
Household equipment, misc. expenditures	year	342	91	81r
Household expenditures, miscellaneous	year	256	91	81r
Household furnishings and equipment, expenditures	year	988	91	81r
Household operations expenditures	year	468	91	81r
Household textiles, expenditures	year	95	91	81r
Housekeeping supplies, expenditures	year	380	91	81r
Laundry and cleaning supplies, expenditures	year	109	91	81r
Laundry detergent, Tide Ultra, Bold, or Cheer	42 oz.	3.58	12/94	2c
Postage and stationery, expenditures	year	105	91	81r
Tissues, facial, Kleenex brand	175	0.82	12/94	2c
Housing				
Housing, ACCRA Index		82.10	12/94	2c
Add garage/carport		6,980	3/95	74r
Add room(s)		11,403	3/95	74r
Apartment condominium or co-op, median	unit	68600	12/94	62r
Dwellings (owned), expenditures	year	2428	91	81r
Enclose porch/patio/breezeway		4,572	3/95	74r
Finish room in basement/attic		3,794	3/95	74r
Home, existing, single-family, median	unit	120200	12/94	62r
House payment, principal and interest, 25% down payment	mo.	617	12/94	2c
House, 1800 sq ft, 8000 sq ft lot, new, urban, utilities	total	100800	12/94	2c
Maintenance, repairs, insurance, and other housing expenditures	year	531	91	81r
Mortgage interest and charges expenditures	year	1506	91	81r
Mtge. rate, incl. points and orig. fee, 30-year conv. fixed or ARM	mo.	9.17	12/94	2c

Item	Per	Value	Date	Ref.
Housing - continued				
Princ. & int., mortgage, median-price exist. sing.-family home	mo.	540	12/94	62r
Property taxes expenditures	year	391	91	81r
Redesign, restructure more than half of home's interior		17,641	3/95	74r
Rent, apartment, 2 br., 1 1/2-2 baths, unfurnished, 950 sq ft, water	mo.	467	12/94	2c
Rental units expenditures	year	1264	91	81r
Insurance and Pensions				
Auto insurance, private passenger	year	785.78	12/94	71s
Insurance and pensions, personal, expenditures	year	2395	91	81r
Insurance, life and other personal, expenditures	year	368	91	81r
Pensions and Social Security, expenditures	year	2027	91	81r
Personal Goods				
Shampoo, Alberto VO5	15-oz.	1.07	12/94	2c
Toothpaste, Crest or Colgate	6-7 oz.	2.09	12/94	2c
Personal Services				
Dry cleaning, man's 2-pc. suit		6.47	12/94	2c
Haircut, man's barbershop, no styling		7.80	12/94	2c
Haircut, woman's shampoo, trim, blow-dry		22.50	12/94	2c
Personal services expenditures	year	212	91	81r
Restaurant Food				
Chicken, fried, thigh and drumstick		2.13	12/94	2c
Dining expenditures, family	week	33.83	94	73r
Hamburger with cheese	1/4 lb.	2.03	12/94	2c
Pizza, Pizza Hut or Pizza Inn	12-13 in.	8.83	12/94	2c
Taxes				
Tax, cigarettes	year	584.00	10/93	43s
Taxes, Federal income, expenditures	year	2275	91	81r
Taxes, personal, expenditures	year	2715	91	81r
Taxes, State and local income, expenditures	year	365	91	81r
Transportation				
Transportation, ACCRA Index		89.90	12/94	2c
Cars and trucks purchased, new	year	1306	91	81r
Cars and trucks purchased, used	year	942	91	81r
Driver's learning permit fee	perm	5.00	1/94	84s
Driver's license fee	orig	16.00	1/94	84s
Driver's license fee, duplicate	lic	10.00	1/94	84s
Driver's license reinstatement fee, min.	susp	50.00	1/94	85s
Driver's license renewal fee	renew	16.00	1/94	84s
Identification card, nondriver	card	10.00	1/94	83s
Motorcycle learning permit fee	perm	5.00	1/94	84s
Motorcycle license fee	orig	16.00	1/94	84s
Motorcycle license fee, duplicate	lic	10.00	1/94	84s
Motorcycle license renewal fee	renew	21.00	1/94	84s
Public transportation expenditures	year	249	91	81r
Tire balance, computer or spin bal., front	wheel	6.09	12/94	2c
Transportation expenditures, total	year	5307	91	81r
Vehicle finance charges	year	346	91	81r
Vehicle insurance expenditures	year	544	91	81r
Vehicle maintenance and repairs expenditures	year	600	91	81r
Vehicle purchases	year	2275	91	81r
Vehicle rental, leases, licenses, etc. expenditures	year	141	91	81r
Vehicles purchased, other than cars and trucks	year	27	91	81r
Utilities				
Utilities, ACCRA Index		106.30	12/94	2c
Electricity expenditures	year	950	91	81r
Electricity, (part.), other, 1800 sq. ft., new home	mo.	102.85	12/94	2c
Utilities, fuels, and public services, total expenditures	year	2000	91	81r

Values are in dollars or fractions of dollars. In the column headed *Ref*, references are shown to sources. Each reference is followed by a letter. These refer to the geographical level for which data were reported: s=State, r=Region, and c=City or metro. The abbreviation *ex* is used to mean *except* or *excluding*; *exp* stands for *expenditures*. For other abbreviations and further explanations, please see the Introduction.

Mcallen-Edinburg-Mission, TX - continued

Item	Per	Value	Date	Ref.
Utilities				
Water and other public services, expenditures	year	227	91	81r
Weddings				
Bridal attendants' gowns	event	750	10/93	76r
Bridal gown	event	852	10/93	76r
Bridal headpiece and veil	event	167	10/93	76r
Bride's wedding band	event	708	10/93	76r
Clergy	event	224	10/93	76r
Engagement ring	event	2756	10/93	76r
Flowers	event	863	10/93	76r
Formal wear for groom	event	106	10/93	76r
Groom's attendants' formal wear	event	530	10/93	76r
Groom's wedding band	event	402	10/93	76r
Music	event	600	10/93	76r
Photography	event	1088	10/93	76r
Shoes for bride	event	50	10/93	76r
Videography	event	483	10/93	76r
Wedding invitations and announcements	event	342	10/93	76r
Wedding reception	event	7000	10/93	76r

Medford, OR

Item	Per	Value	Date	Ref.
Composite, ACCRA index		102.80	12/94	2c
Alcoholic Beverages				
Beer, Miller Lite, Bud, 12-oz., ex deposit	6	3.79	12/94	2c
J & B Scotch	750-ml.	20.95	12/94	2c
Wine, Gallo Chablis blanc	1.5-lit	4.18	12/94	2c
Appliances				
Appliances (major), expenditures	year	160	91	81r
Average annual exp.				
Food, health care, personal goods, services	year	32461	91	81r
Charity				
Cash contributions, expenditures	year	975	91	81r
Clothing				
Apparel, men and boys, total expenditures	year	467	91	81r
Apparel, women and girls, total expenditures	year	737	91	81r
Footwear, expenditures	year	270	91	81r
Jeans, man's denim		35.99	12/94	2c
Shirt, man's dress shirt		29.83	12/94	2c
Undervest, boy's size 10-14, cotton	3	3.42	12/94	2c
Communications				
Long-distance telephone rate, day, addl. min., 1-10 mi.	min.	0.10	12/93	9s
Long-distance telephone rate, day, initial min., 1-10 mi.	min.	0.13	12/93	9s
Newspaper subscription, dly. and Sun. delivery	month	9.25	12/94	2c
Phone line, single, business, field visit	inst	31.00	12/93	9s
Phone line, single, business, no field visit	inst	31.00	12/93	9s
Phone line, single, residence, field visit	inst	12.00	12/93	9s
Phone line, single, residence, no field visit	inst	12.00	12/93	9s
Telephone bill, family of four	month	19.50	12/94	2c
Telephone service, expenditures	year	611	91	81r
Telephone, residential, flat rate	mo.	12.80	12/93	8c
Education				
Board, 4-year private college/university	year	2338	8/94	80s
Board, 4-year public college/university	year	2211	8/94	80s
Education, total expenditures	year	375	91	81r
Room, 4-year private college/university	year	1959	8/94	80s
Room, 4-year public college/university	year	1604	8/94	80s
Total cost, 4-year private college/university	year	16622	8/94	80s
Total cost, 4-year public college/university	year	6648	8/94	80s
Tuition, 2-year public college/university, in-state	year	1186	8/94	80s
Tuition, 4-year private college/university, in-state	year	12325	8/94	80s

Medford, OR - continued

Item	Per	Value	Date	Ref.
Education - continued				
Tuition, 4-year public college/university, in-state	year	2833	8/94	80s
Energy and Fuels				
Energy, combined forms, 1800 sq. ft.	mo.	83.49	12/94	2c
Energy, exc. electricity, 1800 sq. ft.	mo.	41.76	12/94	2c
Fuel oil and other fuels, expenditures	year	33	91	81r
Gas, cooking, winter, 10 therms	month	8.94	2/94	65c
Gas, cooking, winter, 30 therms	month	19.82	2/94	65c
Gas, cooking, winter, 50 therms	month	30.70	2/94	65c
Gas, heating, winter, 100 therms	month	57.89	2/94	65c
Gas, heating, winter, average use	month	60.61	2/94	65c
Gas, natural, expenditures	year	212	91	81r
Gas, reg unlead, taxes inc., cash, self-service	gal	1.31	12/94	2c
Gasoline and motor oil purchased	year	1115	91	81r
Gasoline, unleaded midgrade	gallon	1.36	4/93	82r
Gasoline, unleaded premium	gallon	1.43	4/93	82r
Gasoline, unleaded regular	gallon	1.23	4/93	82r
Entertainment				
Bowling, evening rate	game	1.82	12/94	2c
Concert ticket, Pearl Jam group	perf	20.00	94	50r
Entertainment, total expenditures	year	1853	91	81r
Fees and admissions, expenditures	year	482	91	81r
Monopoly game, Parker Brothers', No. 9	game	11.32	12/94	2c
Movie	adm	5.00	12/94	2c
Pets, toys, playground equipment, expenditures	year	299	91	81r
Reading, expenditures	year	164	91	81r
Televisions, radios, and sound equipment, expenditures	year	528	91	81r
Tennis balls, yellow, Wilson or Penn, 3	can	1.81	12/94	2c
Funerals				
Burial, immediate, container provided by funeral home		1382.70	1/95	54r
Cards, acknowledgment		21.87	1/95	54r
Casket, minimum alternative		128.54	1/95	54r
Cosmetology, hair care, etc.		119.69	1/95	54r
Cremation, direct, container provided by funeral home		1030.62	1/95	54r
Embalming		255.42	1/95	54r
Funeral, funeral home		437.38	1/95	54r
Funeral, other facility		444.46	1/95	54r
Graveside service		338.46	1/95	54r
Hearse, local		147.50	1/95	54r
Limousine, local		130.33	1/95	54r
Memorial service		553.16	1/95	54r
Service charge, professional, nondeclinable		859.15	1/95	54r
Visitation and viewing		93.23	1/95	54r
Groceries				
Groceries, ACCRA Index		92.00	12/94	2c
Apples, Red Delicious	lb.	0.72	12/94	82r
Baby food, strained vegetables, lowest price	4-4.5 oz.	0.22	12/94	2c
Bacon, sliced	lb.	1.73	12/94	82r
Bananas	lb.	0.40	12/94	2c
Bananas	lb.	0.52	12/94	82r
Beef or hamburger, ground	lb.	1.12	12/94	2c
Beef purchases	year	241	91	81r
Beverage purchases, alcoholic	year	328	91	81r
Beverage purchases, nonalcoholic	year	234	91	81r
Bologna, all beef or mixed	lb.	2.33	12/94	82r
Bread, white	24-oz.	0.65	12/94	2c
Bread, white, pan	lb.	0.81	12/94	82r
Carrots, short trimmed and topped	lb.	0.43	12/94	82r
Cereals and bakery products purchases	year	392	91	81r
Cereals and cereals products purchases	year	139	91	81r
Cheese, Kraft grated Parmesan	8-oz.	3.49	12/94	2c
Chicken breast, bone-in	lb.	2.04	12/94	82r
Chicken, fresh, whole	lb.	0.95	12/94	82r
Chicken, whole fryer	lb.	0.82	12/94	2c

Values are in dollars or fractions of dollars. In the column headed *Ref*, references are shown to sources. Each reference is followed by a letter. These refer to the geographical level for which data were reported: s=State, r=Region, and c=City or metro. The abbreviation *ex* is used to mean *except* or *excluding*; *exp* stands for expenditures. For other abbreviations and further explanations, please see the Introduction.

Medford, OR - continued

Item	Per	Value	Date	Ref.
Groceries				
Cigarettes, Winston, Kings	carton	15.71	12/94	2c
Coffee, 100%, ground roast, all sizes	lb.	4.48	12/94	82r
Coffee, vacuum-packed	13 oz.	3.85	12/94	2c
Corn Flakes, Kellogg's or Post Toasties	18 oz.	1.74	12/94	2c
Corn, frozen, whole kernel, lowest price	10 oz.	0.70	12/94	2c
Dairy products (other) purchases	year	182	91	81r
Eggs, Grade A large	dozen	0.88	12/94	2c
Fish and seafood purchases	year	94	91	81r
Flour, white, all purpose	lb.	0.21	12/94	82r
Food purchases, food eaten at home	year	2749	91	81r
Foods purchased away from home, not prepared by consumer	year	1909	91	81r
Fruits and vegetables purchases	year	459	91	81r
Grapefruit	lb.	0.56	12/94	82r
Ground beef, 100% beef	lb.	1.31	12/94	82r
Ham, boneless, exc. canned	lb.	2.46	12/94	82r
Ice cream, prepackaged, bulk, regular	1/2 gal.	2.57	12/94	82r
Lemons	lb.	1.00	12/94	82r
Lettuce, iceberg	lb.	0.93	12/94	82r
Lettuce, iceberg	head	0.78	12/94	2c
Margarine, Blue Bonnet or Parkay cubes	lb.	0.50	12/94	2c
Meats, poultry, fish, and eggs purchases	year	700	91	81r
Milk and cream (fresh) purchases	year	155	91	81r
Milk, whole	1/2 gal.	1.43	12/94	2c
Orange juice, frozen concentrate 12-oz. can	16 oz.	1.52	12/94	82r
Orange juice, Minute Maid frozen	12-oz.	0.98	12/94	2c
Oranges, Navel	lb.	0.56	12/94	82r
Peaches, halves or slices, Hunt's, Del Monte, or Libby's	29-oz.	1.66	12/94	2c
Peas, sweet, Del Monte or Green Giant	15-17 oz.	0.56	12/94	2c
Pork chops, center cut, bone-in	lb.	3.30	12/94	82r
Pork purchases	year	122	91	81r
Potato chips	16-oz.	3.03	12/94	82r
Potatoes, frozen, French fried	lb.	0.77	12/94	82r
Potatoes, white	lb.	0.35	12/94	82r
Potatoes, white or red	10-lb. sack	1.53	12/94	2c
Rice, white, long grain, uncooked	lb.	0.54	12/94	82r
Round roast, USDA choice, boneless	lb.	2.92	12/94	82r
Sausage, Jimmy Dean, 100% pork	lb.	3.27	12/94	2c
Shortening, vegetable oil blends	lb.	0.80	12/94	82r
Shortening, vegetable, Crisco	3-lb.	1.90	12/94	2c
Soft drink, Coca Cola, ex deposit	2 lit	1.13	12/94	2c
Spaghetti and macaroni	lb.	1.02	12/94	82r
Steak, round, graded & ungraded, exc. USDA prime & choice	lb.	3.13	12/94	82r
Steak, sirloin, USDA choice, boneless	lb.	4.07	12/94	82r
Steak, t-bone	lb.	4.65	12/94	2c
Sugar and other sweets, eaten at home, expenditures	year	105	91	81r
Sugar, cane or beet	4 lbs.	0.98	12/94	2c
Sugar, white, all sizes	lb.	0.38	12/94	82r
Tobacco products and smoking supplies, total expenditures	year	221	91	81r
Tomatoes, field grown	lb.	1.45	12/94	82r
Tomatoes, Hunt's or Del Monte	14.5 oz.	0.68	12/94	2c
Tuna, chunk, light	lb.	2.18	12/94	82r
Tuna, chunk, light, oil-packed	6.125-6.5 oz.	0.76	12/94	2c
Goods and Services				
Miscellaneous goods and services, ACCRA Index		99.80	12/94	2c
Health Care				
Health care, ACCRA Index		123.90	12/94	2c
Antibiotic ointment, Polysporin	1.5 oz.	3.89	12/94	2c
Childbirth, Cesarean delivery, hospital charge	birth	6059.00	12/91	69r

Medford, OR - continued

Item	Per	Value	Date	Ref.
Health Care - continued				
Childbirth, Cesarean delivery, physician charge	birth	2248.00	12/91	69r
Childbirth, normal delivery, hospital charge	birth	3006.00	12/91	69r
Childbirth, normal delivery, physician charge	birth	1634.00	12/91	69r
Dentist's fee, adult teeth cleaning and periodic oral exam	visit	73.00	12/94	2c
Doctor's fee, routine exam, established patient	visit	47.70	12/94	2c
Drugs, expenditures	year	230	91	81r
Health care, total expenditures	year	1544	91	81r
Health insurance expenditures	year	558	91	81r
Hospital care, semiprivate room	day	472.00	12/94	2c
Insurance premium, family medical care	month	331.06	1/95	41s
Medical services expenditures	year	676	91	81r
Medical supplies expenditures	year	80	91	81r
Surgery, open-heart	proc	37818.00	1/93	14r
Household Goods				
Appl. repair, service call, wash mach	min. lab. chg.	33.59	12/94	2c
Floor coverings, expenditures	year	79	91	81r
Furniture, expenditures	year	352	91	81r
Household equipment, misc. expenditures	year	614	91	81r
Household expenditures, miscellaneous	year	294	91	81r
Household furnishings and equipment, expenditures	year	1416	91	81r
Household operations expenditures	year	580	91	81r
Household textiles, expenditures	year	113	91	81r
Housekeeping supplies, expenditures	year	447	91	81r
Laundry and cleaning supplies, expenditures	year	114	91	81r
Laundry detergent, Tide Ultra, Bold, or Cheer	42 oz.	3.15	12/94	2c
Postage and stationery, expenditures	year	145	91	81r
Tissues, facial, Kleenex brand	175	1.13	12/94	2c
Housing				
Housing, ACCRA Index		113.00	12/94	2c
Add garage/carport		6,422	3/95	74r
Add room(s)		26,583	3/95	74r
Apartment condominium or co-op, median	unit	105300	12/94	62r
Dwellings (owned), expenditures	year	3932	91	81r
Enclose porch/patio/breezeway		5,382	3/95	74r
Finish room in basement/attic		3,911	3/95	74r
Home, existing, single-family, median	unit	178600	12/94	62r
House payment, principal and interest, 25% down payment	mo.	869	12/94	2c
House, 1800 sq ft, 8000 sq ft lot, new, urban, utilities	total	140308	12/94	2c
Maintenance, repairs, insurance, and other housing expenditures	year	591	91	81r
Mortgage interest and charges expenditures	year	2747	91	81r
Mtge. rate, incl. points and orig. fee, 30-year conv. fixed or ARM	mo.	9.29	12/94	2c
Princ. & int., mortgage, median-price exist. sing.-family home	mo.	845	12/94	62r
Property taxes expenditures	year	594	91	81r
Redesign, restructure more than half of home's interior		5,467	3/95	74r
Rent, apartment, 2 br., 1 1/2-2 baths, unfurnished, 950 sq ft, water	mo.	588	12/94	2c
Rental units expenditures	year	2077	91	81r
Insurance and Pensions				
Auto insurance, private passenger	year	632.21	12/94	71s
Insurance and pensions, personal, expenditures	year	3042	91	81r
Insurance, life and other personal, expenditures	year	298	91	81r
Pensions and Social Security, expenditures	year	2744	91	81r

Values are in dollars or fractions of dollars. In the column headed *Ref*, references are shown to sources. Each reference is followed by a letter. These refer to the geographical level for which data were reported: s = State, r = Region, and c = City or metro. The abbreviation *ex* is used to mean *except* or *excluding*; *exp* stands for *expenditures*. For other abbreviations and further explanations, please see the Introduction.

Medford, OR - continued

Item	Per	Value	Date	Ref.
Legal Assistance				
Legal work, law firm associate	hour	91		10r
Legal work, law firm partner	hour	151		10r
Personal Goods				
Shampoo, Alberto VO5	15-oz.	1.00	12/94	2c
Toothpaste, Crest or Colgate	6-7 oz.	1.76	12/94	2c
Personal Services				
Dry cleaning, man's 2-pc. suit		7.06	12/94	2c
Haircut, man's barbershop, no styling		7.60	12/94	2c
Haircut, woman's shampoo, trim, blow-dry		17.40	12/94	2c
Personal services expenditures	year	286	91	81r
Restaurant Food				
Chicken, fried, thigh and drumstick		2.50	12/94	2c
Dining expenditures, family	week	32.25	94	73r
Hamburger with cheese	1/4 lb.	1.89	12/94	2c
Pizza, Pizza Hut or Pizza Inn	12-13 in.	8.83	12/94	2c
Taxes				
Taxes, Federal income, expenditures	year	2946	91	81r
Taxes, personal, expenditures	year	3791	91	81r
Taxes, State and local income, expenditures	year	791	91	81r
Transportation				
Transportation, ACCRA Index		109.60	12/94	2c
Cars and trucks purchased, new	year	1231	91	81r
Cars and trucks purchased, used	year	915	91	81r
Driver's learning permit fee	perm	13.00	1/94	84s
Driver's license fee	orig	26.25	1/94	84s
Driver's license fee, duplicate	lic	11.00	1/94	84s
Driver's license reinstatement fee, min.	susp	53.00	1/94	85s
Driver's license renewal fee	renew	16.25	1/94	84s
Identification card, nondriver	card	13.00	1/94	83s
Motorcycle learning permit fee	perm	13.00	1/94	84s
Motorcycle license fee	orig	30.00	1/94	84s
Motorcycle license fee, duplicate	lic	11.00	1/94	84s
Motorcycle license renewal fee	renew	7.00	1/94	84s
Public transportation expenditures	year	375	91	81r
Tire balance, computer or spin bal., front	wheel	6.75	12/94	2c
Transportation expenditures, total	year	5527	91	81r
Vehicle finance charges	year	287	91	81r
Vehicle insurance expenditures	year	624	91	81r
Vehicle maintenance and repairs expenditures	year	695	91	81r
Vehicle purchases	year	2174	91	81r
Vehicle rental, leases, licenses, etc. expenditures	year	257	91	81r
Vehicles purchased, other than cars and trucks	year	28	91	81r
Utilities				
Utilities, ACCRA Index		77.80	12/94	2c
Electricity expenditures	year	616	91	81r
Electricity, (part.), other, 1800 sq. ft., new home	mo.	41.73	12/94	2c
Electricity, summer, 250 KWh	month	15.86	8/93	64c
Electricity, summer, 500 KWh	month	27.69	8/93	64c
Electricity, summer, 750 KWh	month	39.76	8/93	64c
Electricity, summer, 1000 KWh	month	51.83	8/93	64c
Utilities, fuels, and public services, total expenditures	year	1681	91	81r
Water and other public services, expenditures	year	209	91	81r
Weddings				
Bridal attendants' gowns	event	750	10/93	76r
Bridal gown	event	852	10/93	76r
Bridal headpiece and veil	event	167	10/93	76r
Bride's wedding band	event	708	10/93	76r
Clergy	event	224	10/93	76r
Engagement ring	event	2756	10/93	76r
Flowers	event	863	10/93	76r
Formal wear for groom	event	106	10/93	76r

Medford, OR - continued

Item	Per	Value	Date	Ref.
Weddings - continued				
Groom's attendants' formal wear	event	530	10/93	76r
Groom's wedding band	event	402	10/93	76r
Music	event	600	10/93	76r
Photography	event	1088	10/93	76r
Shoes for bride	event	50	10/93	76r
Videography	event	483	10/93	76r
Wedding invitations and announcements	event	342	10/93	76r
Wedding reception	event	7000	10/93	76r

Melbourne-Titusville-Palm Bay, FL

Item	Per	Value	Date	Ref.
Appliances				
Appliances (major), expenditures	year	153	91	81r
Average annual exp.				
Food, health care, personal goods, services	year	27020	91	81r
Charity				
Cash contributions, expenditures	year	839	91	81r
Clothing				
Apparel, men and boys, total expenditures	year	380	91	81r
Apparel, women and girls, total expenditures	year	660	91	81r
Footwear, expenditures	year	193	91	81r
Communications				
Long-distance telephone rate, day, addl. min., 1-10 mi.	min.	0.08	12/93	9s
Long-distance telephone rate, day, initial min., 1-10 mi.	min.	0.15	12/93	9s
Phone line, single, business, field visit	inst	86.00	12/93	9s
Phone line, single, business, no field visit	inst	54.50	12/93	9s
Phone line, single, residence, field visit	inst	76.00	12/93	9s
Phone line, single, residence, no field visit	inst	44.50	12/93	9s
Telephone service, expenditures	year	616	91	81r
Education				
Bar examination preparatory course	course	500.00-100	94	17s
Board, 4-year private college/university	year	2123	8/94	80s
Board, 4-year public college/university	year	2101	8/94	80s
Education, total expenditures	year	319	91	81r
Room, 4-year private college/university	year	2242	8/94	80s
Room, 4-year public college/university	year	1970	8/94	80s
Total cost, 4-year private college/university	year	13853	8/94	80s
Total cost, 4-year public college/university	year	5855	8/94	80s
Tuition, 2-year public college/university, in-state	year	1076	8/94	80s
Tuition, 4-year private college/university, in-state	year	9287	8/94	80s
Tuition, 4-year public college/university, in-state	year	1784	8/94	80s
Energy and Fuels				
Fuel oil and other fuels, expenditures	year	56	91	81r
Gas, natural, expenditures	year	150	91	81r
Gasoline and motor oil purchased	year	1152	91	81r
Gasoline, unleaded midgrade	gallon	1.21	4/93	82r
Gasoline, unleaded premium	gallon	1.30	4/93	82r
Gasoline, unleaded regular	gallon	1.10	4/93	82r
Entertainment				
Concert ticket, Pearl Jam group	perf	20.00	94	50r
Entertainment, total expenditures	year	1266	91	81r
Fees and admissions, expenditures	year	306	91	81r
Pets, toys, playground equipment, expenditures	year	271	91	81r
Reading, expenditures	year	131	91	81r
Televisions, radios, and sound equipment, expenditures	year	439	91	81r
Funerals				
Burial, immediate, container provided by funeral home		1370.36	1/95	54r
Cards, acknowledgment		14.83	1/95	54r

Values are in dollars or fractions of dollars. In the column headed *Ref*, references are shown to sources. Each reference is followed by a letter. These refer to the geographical level for which data were reported: s = State, r = Region, and c = City or metro. The abbreviation *ex* is used to mean *except* or *excluding*; *exp* stands for expenditures. For other abbreviations and further explanations, please see the Introduction.

Melbourne-Titusville-Palm Bay, FL - continued

Item	Per	Value	Date	Ref.
Funerals				
Casket, minimum alternative		192.52	1/95	54r
Cosmetology, hair care, etc.		102.27	1/95	54r
Cremation, direct, container provided by funeral home		1065.64	1/95	54r
Embalming		304.29	1/95	54r
Funeral, funeral home		287.83	1/95	54r
Funeral, other facility		284.14	1/95	54r
Graveside service		349.13	1/95	54r
Hearse, local		132.27	1/95	54r
Limousine, local		98.45	1/95	54r
Memorial service		270.59	1/95	54r
Service charge, professional, nondeclinable		933.59	1/95	54r
Visitation and viewing		225.83	1/95	54r
Groceries				
Apples, Red Delicious	lb.	0.73	12/94	82r
Bacon, sliced	lb.	1.67	12/94	82r
Bananas	lb.	0.42	12/94	82r
Beef purchases	year	213	91	81r
Beverage purchases, alcoholic	year	249	91	81r
Beverage purchases, nonalcoholic	year	207	91	81r
Bologna, all beef or mixed	lb.	2.27	12/94	82r
Bread, white, pan	lb.	0.68	12/94	82r
Cabbage	lb.	0.42	12/94	82r
Carrots, short trimmed and topped	lb.	0.53	12/94	82r
Cereals and bakery products purchases	year	345	91	81r
Cereals and cereals products purchases	year	127	91	81r
Cheddar cheese, natural	lb.	3.58	12/94	82r
Chicken breast, bone-in	lb.	1.71	12/94	82r
Chicken, fresh, whole	lb.	0.78	12/94	82r
Chuck roast, USDA choice, boneless	lb.	2.26	12/94	82r
Crackers, soda, salted	lb.	1.27	12/94	82r
Cucumbers	lb.	0.65	12/94	82r
Dairy products (other) purchases	year	141	91	81r
Eggs, Grade A large	dozen	0.87	12/94	82r
Fish and seafood purchases	year	72	91	81r
Flour, white, all purpose	lb.	0.23	12/94	82r
Food purchases, food eaten at home	year	2381	91	81r
Foods purchased away from home, not prepared by consumer	year	1696	91	81r
Frankfurters, all meat or all beef	lb.	1.74	12/94	82r
Fruits and vegetables purchases	year	380	91	81r
Grapefruit	lb.	0.45	12/94	82r
Grapes, Thompson seedless	lb.	2.30	12/94	82r
Ground beef, 100% beef	lb.	1.37	12/94	82r
Ground chuck, 100% beef	lb.	1.97	12/94	82r
Ham, boneless, exc. canned	lb.	2.54	12/94	82r
Ice cream, prepackaged, bulk, regular	1/2 gal.	2.47	12/94	82r
Lemons	lb.	1.02	12/94	82r
Lettuce, iceberg	lb.	0.96	12/94	82r
Margarine, stick	lb.	0.77	12/94	82r
Meats, poultry, fish, and eggs purchases	year	655	91	81r
Milk and cream (fresh) purchases	year	130	91	81r
Orange juice, frozen concentrate 12-oz. can	16 oz.	1.36	12/94	82r
Oranges, Navel	lb.	0.54	12/94	82r
Pears, Anjou	lb.	0.81	12/94	82r
Pork chops, center cut, bone-in	lb.	3.07	12/94	82r
Pork purchases	year	142	91	81r
Potato chips	16-oz.	3.15	12/94	82r
Potatoes, frozen, French fried	lb.	0.82	12/94	82r
Potatoes, white	lb.	0.34	12/94	82r
Rice, white, long grain, uncooked	lb.	0.48	12/94	82r
Round roast, USDA choice, boneless	lb.	2.91	12/94	82r
Sausage, fresh	lb.	1.82	12/94	82r
Shortening, vegetable oil blends	lb.	0.75	12/94	82r
Spaghetti and macaroni	lb.	0.87	12/94	82r
Steak, rib eye, USDA choice, boneless	lb.	6.85	12/94	82r
Steak, round, graded & ungraded, exc. USDA prime & choice	lb.	2.96	12/94	82r
Steak, round, USDA choice, boneless	lb.	3.17	12/94	82r
Steak, sirloin, USDA choice, boneless	lb.	4.12	12/94	82r
Steak, T-bone, USDA choice, bone-in	lb.	5.63	12/94	82r

Melbourne-Titusville-Palm Bay, FL - continued

Item	Per	Value	Date	Ref.
Groceries - continued				
Sugar and other sweets, eaten at home, expenditures	year	93	91	81r
Sugar, white, all sizes	lb.	0.39	12/94	82r
Tobacco products and smoking supplies, total expenditures	year	286	91	81r
Tomatoes, field grown	lb.	1.36	12/94	82r
Tuna, chunk, light	lb.	1.94	12/94	82r
Turkey, frozen, whole	lb.	0.96	12/94	82r
Yogurt, natural, fruit flavored	8 oz.	0.58	12/94	82r
Health Care				
Adenosine, emergency room	treat	100.00	95	23r
Bladder tap, superpubic, infant, emergency room	treat	119.00	95	23r
Blood analysis, emergency room	treat	25.00	95	23r
Blood tests, abdominal pain, emergency room	treat	25.00	95	23r
Burn dressing, emergency room	treat	266.00	95	23r
Cardiology interpretation, emergency room	treat	26.00	95	23r
Chest X-ray, emergency room	treat	78.00	95	23r
Childbirth, Cesarean delivery, hospital charge	birth	5462.00	12/91	69r
Childbirth, Cesarean delivery, physician charge	birth	2228.00	12/91	69r
Childbirth, normal delivery, hospital charge	birth	2943.00	12/91	69r
Childbirth, normal delivery, physician charge	birth	1619.00	12/91	69r
Defibrillation pads, emergency room	treat	6.00	95	23r
Drugs, expenditures	year	297	91	81r
Gastric tube insertion, nasal, emergency room	treat	25.00	95	23r
Health care, total expenditures	year	1600	91	81r
Health insurance expenditures	year	637	91	81r
Heart monitor, emergency room	treat	40.00	95	23r
Insurance premium, family medical care	month	301.92	1/95	41s
Intravenous fluids, emergency room	treat	130.00	95	23r
Intravenous fluids, emergency room	liter	26.00	95	23r
Intravenous line, central, emergency room	treat	342.00	95	23r
Liver function tests, abdominal pain, emergency room	treat	26.00	95	23r
Medical care charges, total, emergency room, third-degree burns	treat	2101.00	95	23r
Medical care charges, total, emergency, infant with fever	treat	628.00	95	23r
Medical services expenditures	year	573	91	81r
Medical supplies expenditures	year	93	91	81r
Morphine, emergency room	treat	34.00	95	23r
Nursing care and facilities charges, emergency room	treat	252.00	95	23r
Nursing care and facilities charges, emergency, infant with fever	treat	252.00	95	23r
Nursing care and facilities charges, emergency, third-degree burns	treat	861.00	95	23r
Physician's charges, emergency, infant with fever	treat	212.00	95	23r
Physician's charges, emergency, third-degree burns	treat	372.00	95	23r
Physician's fee, emergency room	treat	372.00	95	23r
Physician's fee, general practitioner	visit	51.20	12/93	60r
Surgery, open-heart	proc	42374.00	1/93	14r
Ultrasound, abdominal, emergency room	treat	276.00	95	23r
Urinalysis, emergency room	treat	20.00	95	23r
Urinalysis, infant, emergency room	treat	20.00	95	23r
X-rays, emergency room	treat	78.00	95	23r
Household Goods				
Floor coverings, expenditures	year	48	91	81r
Furniture, expenditures	year	280	91	81r
Household equipment, misc. expenditures	year	342	91	81r
Household expenditures, miscellaneous	year	256	91	81r
Household furnishings and equipment, expenditures	year	988	91	81r
Household operations expenditures	year	468	91	81r
Household textiles, expenditures	year	95	91	81r

Values are in dollars or fractions of dollars. In the column headed *Ref*, references are shown to sources. Each reference is followed by a letter. These refer to the geographical level for which data were reported: s=State, r=Region, and c=City or metro. The abbreviation *ex* is used to mean *except* or *excluding*; *exp* stands for *expenditures*. For other abbreviations and further explanations, please see the Introduction.

Melbourne-Titusville-Palm Bay, FL - continued

Item	Per	Value	Date	Ref.
Household Goods				
Housekeeping supplies, expenditures	year	380	91	81r
Laundry and cleaning supplies, expenditures	year	109	91	81r
Postage and stationery, expenditures	year	105	91	81r
Housing				
Add garage/carport		6,980	3/95	74r
Add room(s)		11,403	3/95	74r
Apartment condominium or co-op, median	unit	68600	12/94	62r
Dwellings (owned), expenditures	year	2428	91	81r
Enclose porch/patio/breezeway		4,572	3/95	74r
Finish room in basement/attic		3,794	3/95	74r
Home, existing, single-family, median	unit	120200	12/94	62r
Maintenance, repairs, insurance, and other housing expenditures	year	531	91	81r
Mortgage interest and charges expenditures	year	1506	91	81r
Princ. & int., mortgage, median-price exist. sing.-family home	mo.	540	12/94	62r
Property taxes expenditures	year	391	91	81r
Redesign, restructure more than half of home's interior		17,641	3/95	74r
Rental units expenditures	year	1264	91	81r
Insurance and Pensions				
Auto insurance, private passenger	year	753.93	12/94	71s
Insurance and pensions, personal, expenditures	year	2395	91	81r
Insurance, life and other personal, expenditures	year	368	91	81r
Pensions and Social Security, expenditures	year	2027	91	81r
Personal Services				
Personal services expenditures	year	212	91	81r
Restaurant Food				
Dining expenditures, family	week	33.83	94	73r
Taxes				
Taxes, Federal income, expenditures	year	2275	91	81r
Taxes, personal, expenditures	year	2715	91	81r
Taxes, State and local income, expenditures	year	365	91	81r
Transportation				
Cars and trucks purchased, new	year	1306	91	81r
Cars and trucks purchased, used	year	942	91	81r
Driver's learning permit fee	perm	20.00	1/94	84s
Driver's license fee	orig	20.00	1/94	84s
Driver's license fee, duplicate	lic	10.00	1/94	84s
Driver's license reinstatement fee, min.	susp	25.00	1/94	85s
Driver's license renewal fee	renew	15.00	1/94	84s
Identification card, nondriver	card	3.00	1/94	83s
Motorcycle learning permit fee	perm	20.00	1/94	84s
Motorcycle license fee	orig	20.00	1/94	84s
Motorcycle license fee, duplicate	lic	10.00	1/94	84s
Motorcycle license renewal fee	renew	15.00	1/94	84s
Public transportation expenditures	year	249	91	81r
Transportation expenditures, total	year	5307	91	81r
Vehicle finance charges	year	346	91	81r
Vehicle insurance expenditures	year	544	91	81r
Vehicle maintenance and repairs expenditures	year	600	91	81r
Vehicle purchases	year	2275	91	81r
Vehicle rental, leases, licenses, etc. expenditures	year	141	91	81r
Vehicles purchased, other than cars and trucks	year	27	91	81r
Utilities				
Electricity expenditures	year	950	91	81r
Utilities, fuels, and public services, total expenditures	year	2000	91	81r
Water and other public services, expenditures	year	227	91	81r

Melbourne-Titusville-Palm Bay, FL - continued

Item	Per	Value	Date	Ref.
Weddings				
Bridal attendants' gowns	event	750	10/93	76r
Bridal gown	event	852	10/93	76r
Bridal headpiece and veil	event	167	10/93	76r
Bride's wedding band	event	708	10/93	76r
Clergy	event	224	10/93	76r
Engagement ring	event	2756	10/93	76r
Flowers	event	863	10/93	76r
Formal wear for groom	event	106	10/93	76r
Groom's attendants' formal wear	event	530	10/93	76r
Groom's wedding band	event	402	10/93	76r
Music	event	600	10/93	76r
Photography	event	1088	10/93	76r
Shoes for bride	event	50	10/93	76r
Videography	event	483	10/93	76r
Wedding invitations and announcements	event	342	10/93	76r
Wedding reception	event	7000	10/93	76r

Memphis, TN

Item	Per	Value	Date	Ref.
Composite, ACCRA index		96.10	12/94	2c
Alcoholic Beverages				
Beer, Miller Lite, Bud, 12-oz., ex deposit	6	3.95	12/94	2c
J & B Scotch	750-ml.	18.34	12/94	2c
Wine, Gallo Chablis blanc	1.5-lit	5.49	12/94	2c
Appliances				
Appliances (major), expenditures	year	153	91	81r
Average annual exp.				
Food, health care, personal goods, services	year	27020	91	81r
Charity				
Cash contributions, expenditures	year	839	91	81r
Clothing				
Apparel, men and boys, total expenditures	year	380	91	81r
Apparel, women and girls, total expenditures	year	660	91	81r
Footwear, expenditures	year	193	91	81r
Jeans, man's denim		31.19	12/94	2c
Shirt, man's dress shirt		28.60	12/94	2c
Undervest, boy's size 10-14, cotton	3	3.04	12/94	2c
Communications				
Long-distance telephone rate, day, addl. min., 1-10 mi.	min.	0.10	12/93	9s
Long-distance telephone rate, day, initial min., 1-10 mi.	min.	0.10	12/93	9s
Newspaper subscription, dly. and Sun. delivery	month	14.50	12/94	2c
Phone line, single, business, field visit	inst	58.50	12/93	9s
Phone line, single, business, no field visit	inst	58.50	12/93	9s
Phone line, single, residence, field visit	inst	41.50	12/93	9s
Phone line, single, residence, no field visit	inst	41.50	12/93	9s
Telephone bill, family of four	month	20.14	12/94	2c
Telephone service, expenditures	year	616	91	81r
Telephone, business, addl. line, touch tone	month	3.00	10/91	25c
Telephone, business, connection charges, touch tone	inst	66.05	10/91	25c
Telephone, business, key system line, touch tone	month	80.94	10/91	25c
Telephone, business, PBX line, touch tone	month	86.14	10/91	25c
Telephone, business, single ln., touch tone	month	51.16	10/91	25c
Telephone, business, touch tone, inside wiring maintenance plan	month	1.25	10/91	25c
Telephone, residential, flat rate	mo.	12.15	12/93	8c
Education				
Board, 4-year private college/university	year	1846	8/94	80s
Board, 4-year public college/university	year	1700	8/94	80s
Education, total expenditures	year	319	91	81r
Room, 4-year private college/university	year	1553	8/94	80s
Room, 4-year public college/university	year	1524	8/94	80s
Total cost, 4-year private college/university	year	12025	8/94	80s

Values are in dollars or fractions of dollars. In the column headed *Ref*, references are shown to sources. Each reference is followed by a letter. These refer to the geographical level for which data were reported: s=State, r=Region, and c=City or metro. The abbreviation *ex* is used to mean *except* or *excluding*; *exp* stands for expenditures. For other abbreviations and further explanations, please see the Introduction.

Memphis, TN - continued

Item	Per	Value	Date	Ref.
Education				
Total cost, 4-year public college/university	year	5021	8/94	80s
Tuition, 2-year public college/university, in-state	year	950	8/94	80s
Tuition, 4-year private college/university, in-state	year	8627	8/94	80s
Tuition, 4-year public college/university, in-state	year	1797	8/94	80s
Energy and Fuels				
Energy, combined forms, 1800 sq. ft.	mo.	100.24	12/94	2c
Energy, exc. electricity, 1800 sq. ft.	mo.	24.86	12/94	2c
Fuel oil and other fuels, expenditures	year	56	91	81r
Gas, natural, expenditures	year	150	91	81r
Gas, reg unlead, taxes inc., cash, self-service	gal	1.15	12/94	2c
Gasoline and motor oil purchased	year	1152	91	81r
Gasoline, unleaded midgrade	gallon	1.21	4/93	82r
Gasoline, unleaded premium	gallon	1.30	4/93	82r
Gasoline, unleaded regular	gallon	1.10	4/93	82r
Entertainment				
Bowling, evening rate	game	2.37	12/94	2c
Concert ticket, Pearl Jam group	perf	20.00	94	50r
Entertainment, total expenditures	year	1266	91	81r
Fees and admissions, expenditures	year	306	91	81r
Monopoly game, Parker Brothers', No. 9	game	9.59	12/94	2c
Movie	adm	6.00	12/94	2c
Pets, toys, playground equipment, expenditures	year	271	91	81r
Reading, expenditures	year	131	91	81r
Televisions, radios, and sound equipment, expenditures	year	439	91	81r
Tennis balls, yellow, Wilson or Penn, 3	can	2.04	12/94	2c
Funerals				
Burial, immediate, container provided by funeral home		1298.96	1/95	54r
Cards, acknowledgment		21.26	1/95	54r
Casket, minimum alternative		204.95	1/95	54r
Cosmetology, hair care, etc.		85.40	1/95	54r
Cremation, direct, container provided by funeral home		1054.77	1/95	54r
Embalming		287.71	1/95	54r
Funeral, funeral home		269.18	1/95	54r.
Funeral, other facility		272.88	1/95	54r
Graveside service		302.54	1/95	54r
Hearse, local		122.08	1/95	54r
Limousine, local		80.31	1/95	54r
Memorial service		277.66	1/95	54r
Service charge, professional, nondeclinable		896.65	1/95	54r
Visitation and viewing		232.39	1/95	54r
Groceries				
Groceries, ACCRA Index		101.80	12/94	2c
Apples, Red Delicious	lb.	0.73	12/94	82r
Baby food, strained vegetables, lowest price	4-4.5 oz.	0.31	12/94	2c
Bacon, sliced	lb.	1.67	12/94	82r
Bananas	lb.	0.47	12/94	2c
Bananas	lb.	0.42	12/94	82r
Beef or hamburger, ground	lb.	1.45	12/94	2c
Beef purchases	year	213	91	81r
Beverage purchases, alcoholic	year	249	91	81r
Beverage purchases, nonalcoholic	year	207	91	81r
Bologna, all beef or mixed	lb.	2.27	12/94	82r
Bread, white	24-oz.	0.72	12/94	2c
Bread, white, pan	lb.	0.68	12/94	82r
Cabbage	lb.	0.42	12/94	82r
Carrots, short trimmed and topped	lb.	0.53	12/94	82r
Cereals and bakery products purchases	year	345	91	81r
Cereals and cereals products purchases	year	127	91	81r
Cheddar cheese, natural	lb.	3.58	12/94	82r
Cheese, Kraft grated Parmesan	8-oz.	3.54	12/94	2c
Chicken breast, bone-in	lb.	1.71	12/94	82r

Memphis, TN - continued

Item	Per	Value	Date	Ref.
Groceries - continued				
Chicken, fresh, whole	lb.	0.78	12/94	82r
Chicken, whole fryer	lb.	0.88	12/94	2c
Chuck roast, USDA choice, boneless	lb.	2.26	12/94	82r
Cigarettes, Winston, Kings	carton	14.66	12/94	2c
Coffee, vacuum-packed	13 oz.	4.09	12/94	2c
Corn Flakes, Kellogg's or Post Toasties	18 oz.	3.05	12/94	2c
Corn, frozen, whole kernel, lowest price	10 oz.	0.78	12/94	2c
Crackers, soda, salted	lb.	1.27	12/94	82r
Cucumbers	lb.	0.65	12/94	82r
Dairy products (other) purchases	year	141	91	81r
Eggs, Grade A large	dozen	0.62	12/94	2c
Eggs, Grade A large	dozen	0.87	12/94	82r
Fish and seafood purchases	year	72	91	81r
Flour, white, all purpose	lb.	0.23	12/94	82r
Food purchases, food eaten at home	year	2381	91	81r
Foods purchased away from home, not prepared by consumer	year	1696	91	81r
Frankfurters, all meat or all beef	lb.	1.74	12/94	82r
Fruits and vegetables purchases	year	380	91	81r
Grapefruit	lb.	0.45	12/94	82r
Grapes, Thompson seedless	lb.	2.30	12/94	82r
Ground beef, 100% beef	lb.	1.37	12/94	82r
Ground chuck, 100% beef	lb.	1.97	12/94	82r
Ham, boneless, exc. canned	lb.	2.54	12/94	82r
Ice cream, prepackaged, bulk, regular	1/2 gal.	2.47	12/94	82r
Lemons	lb.	1.02	12/94	82r
Lettuce, iceberg	lb.	0.96	12/94	82r
Lettuce, iceberg	head	0.70	12/94	2c
Margarine, Blue Bonnet or Parkay cubes	lb.	0.55	12/94	2c
Margarine, stick	lb.	0.77	12/94	82r
Meats, poultry, fish, and eggs purchases	year	655	91	81r
Milk and cream (fresh) purchases	year	130	91	81r
Milk, whole	1/2 gal.	1.53	12/94	2c
Orange juice, frozen concentrate 12-oz. can	16 oz.	1.36	12/94	82r
Orange juice, Minute Maid frozen	12-oz.	1.38	12/94	2c
Oranges, Navel	lb.	0.54	12/94	82r
Peaches, halves or slices, Hunt's, Del Monte, or Libby's	29-oz.	1.64	12/94	2c
Pears, Anjou	lb.	0.81	12/94	82r
Peas, sweet, Del Monte or Green Giant	15-17 oz.	0.62	12/94	2c
Pork chops, center cut, bone-in	lb.	3.07	12/94	82r
Pork purchases	year	142	91	81r
Potato chips	16-oz.	3.15	12/94	82r
Potatoes, frozen, French fried	lb.	0.82	12/94	82r
Potatoes, white	lb.	0.34	12/94	82r
Potatoes, white or red	10-lb. sack	2.65	12/94	2c
Rice, white, long grain, uncooked	lb.	0.48	12/94	82r
Round roast, USDA choice, boneless	lb.	2.91	12/94	82r
Sausage, fresh	lb.	1.82	12/94	82r
Sausage, Jimmy Dean, 100% pork	lb.	2.21	12/94	2c
Shortening, vegetable oil blends	lb.	0.75	12/94	82r
Shortening, vegetable, Crisco	3-lb.	2.65	12/94	2c
Soft drink, Coca Cola, ex deposit	2 lit	0.96	12/94	2c
Spaghetti and macaroni	lb.	0.87	12/94	82r
Steak, rib eye, USDA choice, boneless	lb.	6.85	12/94	82r
Steak, round, graded & ungraded, exc. USDA prime & choice	lb.	2.96	12/94	82r
Steak, round, USDA choice, boneless	lb.	3.17	12/94	82r
Steak, sirloin, USDA choice, boneless	lb.	4.12	12/94	82r
Steak, t-bone	lb.	5.12	12/94	2c
Steak, T-bone, USDA choice, bone-in	lb.	5.63	12/94	82r
Sugar and other sweets, eaten at home, expenditures	year	93	91	81r
Sugar, cane or beet	4 lbs.	1.73	12/94	2c
Sugar, white, all sizes	lb.	0.39	12/94	82r
Tobacco products and smoking supplies, total expenditures	year	286	91	81r
Tomatoes, field grown	lb.	1.36	12/94	82r

Values are in dollars or fractions of dollars. In the column headed *Ref*, references are shown to sources. Each reference is followed by a letter. These refer to the geographical level for which data were reported: s = State, r = Region, and c = City or metro. The abbreviation *ex* is used to mean *except* or *excluding*; *exp* stands for expenditures. For other abbreviations and further explanations, please see the Introduction.

Memphis, TN - continued

Item	Per	Value	Date	Ref.
Groceries				
Tomatoes, Hunt's or Del Monte	14.5 oz.	0.75	12/94	2c
Tuna, chunk, light	lb.	1.94	12/94	82r
Tuna, chunk, light, oil-packed	6.125-6.5 oz.	0.60	12/94	2c
Turkey, frozen, whole	lb.	0.96	12/94	82r
Yogurt, natural, fruit flavored	8 oz.	0.58	12/94	82r
Goods and Services				
Miscellaneous goods and services, ACCRA Index		97.60	12/94	2c
Health Care				
Health care, ACCRA Index		99.40	12/94	2c
Adenosine, emergency room	treat	100.00	95	23r
Antibiotic ointment, Polysporin	1.5 oz.	3.99	12/94	2c
Bladder tap, superpubic, infant, emergency room	treat	119.00	95	23r
Blood analysis, emergency room	treat	25.00	95	23r
Blood tests, abdominal pain, emergency room	treat	25.00	95	23r
Burn dressing, emergency room	treat	266.00	95	23r
Cardiology interpretation, emergency room	treat	26.00	95	23r
Chest X-ray, emergency room	treat	78.00	95	23r
Childbirth, Cesarean delivery, hospital charge	birth	5462.00	12/91	69r
Childbirth, Cesarean delivery, physician charge	birth	2228.00	12/91	69r
Childbirth, normal delivery, hospital charge	birth	2943.00	12/91	69r
Childbirth, normal delivery, physician charge	birth	1619.00	12/91	69r
Defibrillation pads, emergency room	treat	6.00	95	23r
Dentist's fee, adult teeth cleaning and periodic oral exam	visit	56.00	12/94	2c
Doctor's fee, routine exam, established patient	visit	44.40	12/94	2c
Drugs, expenditures	year	297	91	81r
Gastric tube insertion, nasal, emergency room	treat	25.00	95	23r
Health care, total expenditures	year	1600	91	81r
Health insurance expenditures	year	637	91	81r
Heart monitor, emergency room	treat	40.00	95	23r
Hospital care, semiprivate room	day	263.00	12/94	2c
Insurance premium, family medical care	month	344.21	1/95	41s
Intravenous fluids, emergency room	treat	130.00	95	23r
Intravenous fluids, emergency room	liter	26.00	95	23r
Intravenous line, central, emergency room	treat	342.00	95	23r
Liver function tests, abdominal pain, emergency room	treat	26.00	95	23r
Medical care charges, total, emergency room, third-degree burns	treat	2101.00	95	23r
Medical care charges, total, emergency, infant with fever	treat	628.00	95	23r
Medical services expenditures	year	573	91	81r
Medical supplies expenditures	year	93	91	81r
Morphine, emergency room	treat	34.00	95	23r
Nursing care and facilities charges, emergency room	treat	252.00	95	23r
Nursing care and facilities charges, emergency, infant with fever	treat	252.00	95	23r
Nursing care and facilities charges, emergency, third-degree burns	treat	861.00	95	23r
Physician's charges, emergency, infant with fever	treat	212.00	95	23r
Physician's charges, emergency, third-degree burns	treat	372.00	95	23r
Physician's fee, emergency room	treat	372.00	95	23r
Physician's fee, general practitioner	visit	51.20	12/93	60r
Surgery, open-heart	proc	42374.00	1/93	14r
Ultrasound, abdominal, emergency room	treat	276.00	95	23r
Urinalysis, emergency room	treat	20.00	95	23r
Urinalysis, infant, emergency room	treat	20.00	95	23r
X-rays, emergency room	treat	78.00	95	23r

Memphis, TN - continued

Item	Per	Value	Date	Ref.
Household Goods				
Appl. repair, service call, wash mach	min. lab. chg.	28.29	12/94	2c
Floor coverings, expenditures	year	48	91	81r
Furniture, expenditures	year	280	91	81r
Household equipment, misc. expenditures	year	342	91	81r
Household expenditures, miscellaneous	year	256	91	81r
Household furnishings and equipment, expenditures	year	988	91	81r
Household operations expenditures	year	468	91	81r
Household textiles, expenditures	year	95	91	81r
Housekeeping supplies, expenditures	year	380	91	81r
Laundry and cleaning supplies, expenditures	year	109	91	81r
Laundry detergent, Tide Ultra, Bold, or Cheer	42 oz.	3.43	12/94	2c
Postage and stationery, expenditures	year	105	91	81r
Tissues, facial, Kleenex brand	175	1.02	12/94	2c
Housing				
Housing, ACCRA Index		88.40	12/94	2c
Add garage/carport		6,980	3/95	74r
Add room(s)		11,403	3/95	74r
Apartment condominium or co-op, median	unit	68600	12/94	62r
Dwellings (owned), expenditures	year	2428	91	81r
Enclose porch/patio/breezeway		4,572	3/95	74r
Finish room in basement/attic		3,794	3/95	74r
Home, existing, single-family, median	unit	120200	12/94	62r
Home, existing, single-family, median	unit	85.10	12/94	62c
Home, single family, median	home	100000	4/94	11c
Home, three-bedrooms, one-and-a-half baths	home	105000	93	92c
House payment, principal and interest, 25% down payment	mo.	635	12/94	2c
House, 1800 sq ft, 8000 sq ft lot, new, urban, utilities	total	102066	12/94	2c
Maintenance, repairs, insurance, and other housing expenditures	year	531	91	81r
Mortgage interest and charges expenditures	year	1506	91	81r
Mtge. rate, incl. points and orig. fee, 30-year conv. fixed or ARM	mo.	9.35	12/94	2c
Princ. & int., mortgage, median-price exist. sing.-family home	mo.	540	12/94	62r
Property taxes expenditures	year	391	91	81r
Redesign, restructure more than half of home's interior		17,641	3/95	74r
Rent, apartment, 2 br., 1 1/2-2 baths, unfurnished, 950 sq ft, water	mo.	587	12/94	2c
Rental units expenditures	year	1264	91	81r
Insurance and Pensions				
Auto insurance, private passenger	year	574.08	12/94	71s
Insurance and pensions, personal, expenditures	year	2395	91	81r
Insurance, life and other personal, expenditures	year	368	91	81r
Pensions and Social Security, expenditures	year	2027	91	81r
Legal Assistance				
Lawyer's fee, apartment complex mortgage closing	closing	15,000	93	92c
Personal Goods				
Shampoo, Alberto VO5	15-oz.	1.20	12/94	2c
Toothpaste, Crest or Colgate	6-7 oz.	2.21	12/94	2c
Personal Services				
Dry cleaning, man's 2-pc. suit		6.89	12/94	2c
Haircut, man's barbershop, no styling		9.40	12/94	2c
Haircut, woman's shampoo, trim, blow-dry		17.79	12/94	2c
Personal services expenditures	year	212	91	81r
Restaurant Food				
Chicken, fried, thigh and drumstick		2.11	12/94	2c
Dining expenditures, family	week	33.83	94	73r

Values are in dollars or fractions of dollars. In the column headed *Ref*, references are shown to sources. Each reference is followed by a letter. These refer to the geographical level for which data were reported: s=State, r=Region, and c=City or metro. The abbreviation *ex* is used to mean *except* or *excluding*; *exp* stands for expenditures. For other abbreviations and further explanations, please see the Introduction.

Memphis, TN - continued

Item	Per	Value	Date	Ref.
Restaurant Food				
Hamburger with cheese	1/4 lb.	1.85	12/94	2c
Pizza, Pizza Hut or Pizza Inn	12-13 in.	7.89	12/94	2c
Taxes				
Tax rate, residential property, month	$100	0.67	1/92	79c
Tax, cigarettes	year	379.00	10/93	43s
Taxes, Federal income, expenditures	year	2275	91	81r
Taxes, personal, expenditures	year	2715	91	81r
Taxes, State and local income, expenditures	year	365	91	81r
Transportation				
Transportation, ACCRA Index		106.20	12/94	2c
Bus fare, one-way	trip	1.10	12/95	1c
Bus fare, up to 10 miles	one-way	1.10	12/94	2c
Cars and trucks purchased, new	year	1306	91	81r
Cars and trucks purchased, used	year	942	91	81r
Driver's learning permit fee	perm	5.50	1/94	84s
Driver's license fee	orig	16.00	1/94	84s
Driver's license fee, duplicate	lic	8.00	1/94	84s
Driver's license reinstatement fee, min.	susp	65.00	1/94	85s
Driver's license renewal fee	renew	14.00	1/94	84s
Identification card, nondriver	card	7.50	1/94	83s
Motorcycle learning permit fee	perm	6.50	1/94	84s
Motorcycle license fee	orig	17.00	1/94	84s
Motorcycle license fee, duplicate	lic	8.00	1/94	84s
Motorcycle license renewal fee	renew	15.00	1/94	84s
Public transportation expenditures	year	249	91	81r
Railway fare, light rail, one-way	trip	0.50	12/95	1c
Tire balance, computer or spin bal., front	wheel	7.39	12/94	2c
Transportation expenditures, total	year	5307	91	81r
Vehicle finance charges	year	346	91	81r
Vehicle insurance expenditures	year	544	91	81r
Vehicle maintenance and repairs expenditures	year	600	91	81r
Vehicle purchases	year	2275	91	81r
Vehicle rental, leases, licenses, etc. expenditures	year	141	91	81r
Vehicles purchased, other than cars and trucks	year	27	91	81r
Utilities				
Utilities, ACCRA Index		91.20	12/94	2c
Electricity expenditures	year	950	91	81r
Electricity, (part.), other, 1800 sq. ft., new home	mo.	75.38	12/94	2c
Utilities, fuels, and public services, total expenditures	year	2000	91	81r
Water and other public services, expenditures	year	227	91	81r
Weddings				
Bridal attendants' gowns	event	750	10/93	76r
Bridal gown	event	852	10/93	76r
Bridal headpiece and veil	event	167	10/93	76r
Bride's wedding band	event	708	10/93	76r
Clergy	event	224	10/93	76r
Engagement ring	event	2756	10/93	76r
Flowers	event	863	10/93	76r
Formal wear for groom	event	106	10/93	76r
Groom's attendants' formal wear	event	530	10/93	76r
Groom's wedding band	event	402	10/93	76r
Music	event	600	10/93	76r
Photography	event	1088	10/93	76r
Shoes for bride	event	50	10/93	76r
Videography	event	483	10/93	76r
Wedding invitations and announcements	event	342	10/93	76r
Wedding reception	event	7000	10/93	76r

Merced, CA

Item	Per	Value	Date	Ref.
Appliances				
Appliances (major), expenditures	year	160	91	81r
Average annual exp.				
Food, health care, personal goods, services	year	32461	91	81r
Charity				
Cash contributions, expenditures	year	975	91	81r
Clothing				
Apparel, men and boys, total expenditures	year	467	91	81r
Apparel, women and girls, total expenditures	year	737	91	81r
Footwear, expenditures	year	270	91	81r
Communications				
Long-distance telephone rate, day, addl. min., 1-10 mi.	min.	0.07	12/93	9s
Long-distance telephone rate, day, initial min., 1-10 mi.	min.	0.17	12/93	9s
Phone line, single, business, field visit	inst	70.75	12/93	9s
Phone line, single, business, no field visit	inst	70.75	12/93	9s
Phone line, single, residence, field visit	inst	34.75	12/93	9s
Phone line, single, residence, no field visit	inst	34.75	12/93	9s
Telephone service, expenditures	year	611	91	81r
Education				
Board, 4-year private college/university	year	2945	8/94	80s
Board, 4-year public college/university	year	2321	8/94	80s
Education, total expenditures	year	375	91	81r
Room, 4-year private college/university	year	3094	8/94	80s
Room, 4-year public college/university	year	2812	8/94	80s
Student fee, university	year	21.00	93	18s
Total cost, 4-year private college/university	year	19321	8/94	80s
Total cost, 4-year public college/university	year	7511	8/94	80s
Tuition, 2-year public college/university, in-state	year	345	8/94	80s
Tuition, 4-year private college/university, in-state	year	13282	8/94	80s
Tuition, 4-year public college/university, in-state	year	2378	8/94	80s
Energy and Fuels				
Fuel oil and other fuels, expenditures	year	33	91	81r
Gas, natural, expenditures	year	212	91	81r
Gasoline and motor oil purchased	year	1115	91	81r
Gasoline, unleaded midgrade	gallon	1.36	4/93	82r
Gasoline, unleaded premium	gallon	1.43	4/93	82r
Gasoline, unleaded regular	gallon	1.23	4/93	82r
Entertainment				
Concert ticket, Pearl Jam group	perf	20.00	94	50r
Entertainment, total expenditures	year	1853	91	81r
Fees and admissions, expenditures	year	482	91	81r
Pets, toys, playground equipment, expenditures	year	299	91	81r
Reading, expenditures	year	164	91	81r
Televisions, radios, and sound equipment, expenditures	year	528	91	81r
Funerals				
Burial, immediate, container provided by funeral home		1382.70	1/95	54r
Cards, acknowledgment		21.87	1/95	54r
Casket, minimum alternative		128.54	1/95	54r
Cosmetology, hair care, etc.		119.69	1/95	54r
Cremation, direct, container provided by funeral home		1030.62	1/95	54r
Embalming		255.42	1/95	54r
Funeral, funeral home		437.38	1/95	54r
Funeral, other facility		444.46	1/95	54r
Graveside service		338.46	1/95	54r
Hearse, local		147.50	1/95	54r
Limousine, local		130.33	1/95	54r
Memorial service		553.16	1/95	54r
Service charge, professional, nondeclinable		859.15	1/95	54r
Visitation and viewing		93.23	1/95	54r

Values are in dollars or fractions of dollars. In the column headed *Ref*, references are shown to sources. Each reference is followed by a letter. These refer to the geographical level for which data were reported: s=State, r=Region, and c=City or metro. The abbreviation *ex* is used to mean *except* or *excluding*; *exp* stands for expenditures. For other abbreviations and further explanations, please see the Introduction.

Merced, CA - continued

Item	Per	Value	Date	Ref.
Groceries				
Apples, Red Delicious	lb.	0.72	12/94	82r
Bacon, sliced	lb.	1.73	12/94	82r
Bananas	lb.	0.52	12/94	82r
Beef purchases	year	241	91	81r
Beverage purchases, alcoholic	year	328	91	81r
Beverage purchases, nonalcoholic	year	234	91	81r
Bologna, all beef or mixed	lb.	2.33	12/94	82r
Bread, white, pan	lb.	0.81	12/94	82r
Carrots, short trimmed and topped	lb.	0.43	12/94	82r
Cereals and bakery products purchases	year	392	91	81r
Cereals and cereals products purchases	year	139	91	81r
Chicken breast, bone-in	lb.	2.04	12/94	82r
Chicken, fresh, whole	lb.	0.95	12/94	82r
Coffee, 100%, ground roast, all sizes	lb.	4.48	12/94	82r
Dairy products (other) purchases	year	182	91	81r
Fish and seafood purchases	year	94	91	81r
Flour, white, all purpose	lb.	0.21	12/94	82r
Food purchases, food eaten at home	year	2749	91	81r
Foods purchased away from home, not prepared by consumer	year	1909	91	81r
Fruits and vegetables purchases	year	459	91	81r
Grapefruit	lb.	0.56	12/94	82r
Ground beef, 100% beef	lb.	1.31	12/94	82r
Ham, boneless, exc. canned	lb.	2.46	12/94	82r
Ice cream, prepackaged, bulk, regular	1/2 gal.	2.57	12/94	82r
Lemons	lb.	1.00	12/94	82r
Lettuce, iceberg	lb.	0.93	12/94	82r
Meats, poultry, fish, and eggs purchases	year	700	91	81r
Milk and cream (fresh) purchases	year	155	91	81r
Orange juice, frozen concentrate 12-oz. can	16 oz.	1.52	12/94	82r
Oranges, Navel	lb.	0.56	12/94	82r
Pork chops, center cut, bone-in	lb.	3.30	12/94	82r
Pork purchases	year	122	91	81r
Potato chips	16-oz.	3.03	12/94	82r
Potatoes, frozen, French fried	lb.	0.77	12/94	82r
Potatoes, white	lb.	0.35	12/94	82r
Rice, white, long grain, uncooked	lb.	0.54	12/94	82r
Round roast, USDA choice, boneless	lb.	2.92	12/94	82r
Shortening, vegetable oil blends	lb.	0.80	12/94	82r
Spaghetti and macaroni	lb.	1.02	12/94	82r
Steak, round, graded & ungraded, exc. USDA prime & choice	lb.	3.13	12/94	82r
Steak, sirloin, USDA choice, boneless	lb.	4.07	12/94	82r
Sugar and other sweets, eaten at home, expenditures	year	105	91	81r
Sugar, white, all sizes	lb.	0.38	12/94	82r
Tobacco products and smoking supplies, total expenditures	year	221	91	81r
Tomatoes, field grown	lb.	1.45	12/94	82r
Tuna, chunk, light	lb.	2.18	12/94	82r
Health Care				
Childbirth, Cesarean delivery, hospital charge	birth	6059.00	12/91	69r
Childbirth, Cesarean delivery, physician charge	birth	2248.00	12/91	69r
Childbirth, normal delivery, hospital charge	birth	3006.00	12/91	69r
Childbirth, normal delivery, physician charge	birth	1634.00	12/91	69r
Drugs, expenditures	year	230	91	81r
Health care, total expenditures	year	1544	91	81r
Health insurance expenditures	year	558	91	81r
Insurance premium, family medical care	month	380.27	1/95	41s
Medical services expenditures	year	676	91	81r
Medical supplies expenditures	year	80	91	81r
Surgery, open-heart	proc	37818.00	1/93	14r
Household Goods				
Floor coverings, expenditures	year	79	91	81r
Furniture, expenditures	year	352	91	81r
Household equipment, misc. expenditures	year	614	91	81r
Household expenditures, miscellaneous	year	294	91	81r

Merced, CA - continued

Item	Per	Value	Date	Ref.
Household Goods - continued				
Household furnishings and equipment, expenditures	year	1416	91	81r
Household operations expenditures	year	580	91	81r
Household textiles, expenditures	year	113	91	81r
Housekeeping supplies, expenditures	year	447	91	81r
Laundry and cleaning supplies, expenditures	year	114	91	81r
Postage and stationery, expenditures	year	145	91	81r
Housing				
Add garage/carport		6,422	3/95	74r
Add room(s)		26,583	3/95	74r
Apartment condominium or co-op, median	unit	105300	12/94	62r
Dwellings (owned), expenditures	year	3932	91	81r
Enclose porch/patio/breezeway		5,382	3/95	74r
Finish room in basement/attic		3,911	3/95	74r
Home, existing, single-family, median	unit	178600	12/94	62r
Maintenance, repairs, insurance, and other housing expenditures	year	591	91	81r
Mortgage interest and charges expenditures	year	2747	91	81r
Princ. & int., mortgage, median-price exist. sing.-family home	mo.	845	12/94	62r
Property taxes expenditures	year	594	91	81r
Redesign, restructure more than half of home's interior		5,467	3/95	74r
Rental units expenditures	year	2077	91	81r
Insurance and Pensions				
Auto insurance, private passenger	year	892.80	12/94	71s
Insurance and pensions, personal, expenditures	year	3042	91	81r
Insurance, life and other personal, expenditures	year	298	91	81r
Pensions and Social Security, expenditures	year	2744	91	81r
Legal Assistance				
Legal work, law firm associate	hour	91		10r
Legal work, law firm partner	hour	151		10r
Personal Services				
Personal services expenditures	year	286	91	81r
Restaurant Food				
Dining expenditures, family	week	32.25	94	73r
Taxes				
Taxes, Federal income, expenditures	year	2946	91	81r
Taxes, personal, expenditures	year	3791	91	81r
Taxes, State and local income, expenditures	year	791	91	81r
Transportation				
Cars and trucks purchased, new	year	1231	91	81r
Cars and trucks purchased, used	year	915	91	81r
Driver's learning permit fee	perm	12.00	1/94	84s
Driver's license fee	orig	12.00	1/94	84s
Driver's license fee, duplicate	lic	12.00	1/94	84s
Driver's license reinstatement fee, min.	susp	15.00	1/94	85s
Driver's license renewal fee	renew	12.00	1/94	84s
Identification card, nondriver	card	6.00	1/94	83s
Motorcycle learning permit fee	perm	12.00	1/94	84s
Motorcycle license fee	orig	12.00	1/94	84s
Motorcycle license fee, duplicate	lic	12.00	1/94	84s
Motorcycle license renewal fee	renew	12.00	1/94	84s
Public transportation expenditures	year	375	91	81r
Transportation expenditures, total	year	5527	91	81r
Vehicle finance charges	year	287	91	81r
Vehicle insurance expenditures	year	624	91	81r
Vehicle maintenance and repairs expenditures	year	695	91	81r
Vehicle purchases	year	2174	91	81r
Vehicle rental, leases, licenses, etc. expenditures	year	257	91	81r
Vehicles purchased, other than cars and trucks	year	28	91	81r

Values are in dollars or fractions of dollars. In the column headed *Ref*, references are shown to sources. Each reference is followed by a letter. These refer to the geographical level for which data were reported: s = State, r = Region, and c = City or metro. The abbreviation *ex* is used to mean *except* or *excluding*; *exp* stands for *expenditures*. For other abbreviations and further explanations, please see the Introduction.

Merced, CA - continued

Item	Per	Value	Date	Ref.
Utilities				
Electricity expenditures	year	616	91	81r
Utilities, fuels, and public services, total expenditures	year	1681	91	81r
Water and other public services, expenditures	year	209	91	81r
Weddings				
Bridal attendants' gowns	event	750	10/93	76r
Bridal gown	event	852	10/93	76r
Bridal headpiece and veil	event	167	10/93	76r
Bride's wedding band	event	708	10/93	76r
Clergy	event	224	10/93	76r
Engagement ring	event	2756	10/93	76r
Flowers	event	863	10/93	76r
Formal wear for groom	event	106	10/93	76r
Groom's attendants' formal wear	event	530	10/93	76r
Groom's wedding band	event	402	10/93	76r
Music	event	600	10/93	76r
Photography	event	1088	10/93	76r
Shoes for bride	event	50	10/93	76r
Videography	event	483	10/93	76r
Wedding invitations and announcements	event	342	10/93	76r
Wedding reception	event	7000	10/93	76r

Miami, FL

Item	Per	Value	Date	Ref.
Composite, ACCRA index		107.80	12/94	2c
Alcoholic Beverages				
Beer, Miller Lite, Bud, 12-oz., ex deposit	6	3.91	12/94	2c
J & B Scotch	750-ml.	17.94	12/94	2c
Wine, Gallo Chablis blanc	1.5-lit	4.99	12/94	2c
Appliances				
Appliances (major), expenditures	year	125	91	81c
Appliances (major), expenditures	year	153	91	81r
Average annual exp.				
Food, health care, personal goods, services	year	32053	91	81c
Food, health care, personal goods, services	year	27020	91	81r
Business				
Bank fee, bad check	check	25.20	12/93	5c
Dinner and tip, hotel, corporate rate	night	33.00	2/94	15c
Hotel room, corporate rate	night	97.00	2/94	15c
Business Expenses				
Car rental, midsized car	day	33.99	92	52c
Continental breakfast, room service	meal	7.25	92	52c
Lunch, convention center	meal	7.59	92	52c
Restaurant meal	meal	41.00	92	52c
Room rate, hotel	day	89.14	92	52c
Taxicab fare, airport to convention center	trip	20.00	92	52c
Charity				
Cash contributions, expenditures	year	798	91	81c
Cash contributions, expenditures	year	839	91	81r
Clothing				
Apparel, men and boys, total expenditures	year	505	91	81c
Apparel, men and boys, total expenditures	year	380	91	81r
Apparel, women and girls, total expenditures	year	667	91	81c
Apparel, women and girls, total expenditures	year	660	91	81r
Footwear, expenditures	year	307	91	81c
Footwear, expenditures	year	193	91	81r
Formal wear rental, tuxedo, downtown store	rental	45.00	92	52c
Jeans, man's denim		30.79	12/94	2c
Shirt, man's dress shirt		34.50	12/94	2c
Undervest, boy's size 10-14, cotton	3	3.89	12/94	2c
Communications				
Long-distance telephone rate, day, addl. min., 1-10 mi.	min.	0.08	12/93	9s
Long-distance telephone rate, day, initial min., 1-10 mi.	min.	0.15	12/93	9s

Miami, FL - continued

Item	Per	Value	Date	Ref.
Communications - continued				
Newspaper cost, major daily	1	0.35	92	52c
Newspaper subscription, dly. and Sun. delivery	month	11.81	12/94	2c
Phone line, single, business, field visit	inst	86.00	12/93	9s
Phone line, single, business, no field visit	inst	54.50	12/93	9s
Phone line, single, residence, field visit	inst	76.00	12/93	9s
Phone line, single, residence, no field visit	inst	44.50	12/93	9s
Telephone bill, family of four	month	16.27	12/94	2c
Telephone service, expenditures	year	778	91	81c
Telephone service, expenditures	year	616	91	81r
Telephone, residential, flat rate	mo.	10.65	12/93	8c
Education				
Bar examination preparatory course	course	500.00-100	94	17s
Board, 4-year private college/university	year	2123	8/94	80s
Board, 4-year public college/university	year	2101	8/94	80s
Education, total expenditures	year	173	91	81c
Education, total expenditures	year	319	91	81r
Room, 4-year private college/university	year	2242	8/94	80s
Room, 4-year public college/university	year	1970	8/94	80s
Total cost, 4-year private college/university	year	13853	8/94	80s
Total cost, 4-year public college/university	year	5855	8/94	80s
Tuition, 2-year public college/university, in-state	year	1076	8/94	80s
Tuition, 4-year private college/university, in-state	year	9287	8/94	80s
Tuition, 4-year public college/university, in-state	year	1784	8/94	80s
Energy and Fuels				
Electricity	500 KWh	42.18	12/94	82c
Energy, combined forms, 1800 sq. ft.	mo.	141.66	12/94	2c
Fuel oil and other fuels, expenditures	year	5	91	81c
Fuel oil and other fuels, expenditures	year	56	91	81r
Gas, cooking, 10 therms	month	12.75	2/94	65c
Gas, cooking, 30 therms	month	26.25	2/94	65c
Gas, cooking, 50 therms	month	39.76	2/94	65c
Gas, heating, winter, 100 therms	month	73.52	2/94	65c
Gas, heating, winter, average use	month	23.55	2/94	65c
Gas, natural, expenditures	year	32	91	81c
Gas, natural, expenditures	year	150	91	81r
Gas, piped	40 therms	40.51	12/94	82c
Gas, piped	100 therms	89.88	12/94	82c
Gas, piped	therm	1.06	12/94	82c
Gas, reg unlead, taxes inc., cash, self-service	gal	1.26	12/94	2c
Gasoline and motor oil purchased	year	950	91	81c
Gasoline and motor oil purchased	year	1152	91	81r
Gasoline, unleaded midgrade	gallon	1.32	4/93	82c
Gasoline, unleaded midgrade	gallon	1.21	4/93	82r
Gasoline, unleaded premium	gallon	1.39	4/93	82c
Gasoline, unleaded premium	gallon	1.30	4/93	82r
Gasoline, unleaded regular	gallon	1.17	4/93	82c
Gasoline, unleaded regular	gallon	1.10	4/93	82r
Entertainment				
Admission fee, museum	visit	5.00	92	52c
Admission fee, seating, symphony performance		25.00	92	52c
Bowling, evening rate	game	3.00	12/94	2c
Concert ticket, Pearl Jam group	perf	20.00	94	50r
Entertainment supplies, equipment, and services, misc. expenditures	year	324	91	81c
Entertainment, total expenditures	year	1451	91	81c
Entertainment, total expenditures	year	1266	91	81r
Fees and admissions, expenditures	year	431	91	81c
Fees and admissions, expenditures	year	306	91	81r
Monopoly game, Parker Brothers', No. 9	game	12.59	12/94	2c
Movie	adm	6.60	12/94	2c

Values are in dollars or fractions of dollars. In the column headed *Ref*, references are shown to sources. Each reference is followed by a letter. These refer to the geographical level for which data were reported: s=State, r=Region, and c=City or metro. The abbreviation *ex* is used to mean *except* or *excluding*; *exp* stands for *expenditures*. For other abbreviations and further explanations, please see the Introduction.

Miami, FL - continued

Item	Per	Value	Date	Ref.
Entertainment				
Pets, toys, playground equipment, expenditures	year	307	91	81c
Pets, toys, playground equipment, expenditures	year	271	91	81r
Reading, expenditures	year	120	91	81c
Reading, expenditures	year	131	91	81r
Televisions, radios, and sound equipment, expenditures	year	389	91	81c
Televisions, radios, and sound equipment, expenditures	year	439	91	81r
Tennis balls, yellow, Wilson or Penn, 3	can	2.57	12/94	2c
Ticket, basketball game		9.00-29.00	92	52c
Funerals				
Burial, immediate, container provided by funeral home		1370.36	1/95	54r
Cards, acknowledgment		14.83	1/95	54r
Casket, minimum alternative		192.52	1/95	54r
Cosmetology, hair care, etc.		102.27	1/95	54r
Cremation, direct, container provided by funeral home		1065.64	1/95	54r
Embalming		304.29	1/95	54r
Funeral, funeral home		287.83	1/95	54r
Funeral, other facility		284.14	1/95	54r
Graveside service		349.13	1/95	54r
Hearse, local		132.27	1/95	54r
Limousine, local		98.45	1/95	54r
Memorial service		270.59	1/95	54r
Service charge, professional, nondeclinable		933.59	1/95	54r
Visitation and viewing		225.83	1/95	54r
Groceries				
Groceries, ACCRA Index		101.40	12/94	2c
Apples, Red Delicious	lb.	0.73	12/94	82r
Baby food, strained vegetables, lowest price	4-4.5 oz.	0.35	12/94	2c
Bacon, sliced	lb.	1.67	12/94	82r
Bananas	lb.	0.39	12/94	2c
Bananas	lb.	0.42	12/94	82r
Beef or hamburger, ground	lb.	1.73	12/94	2c
Beef purchases	year	209	91	81c
Beef purchases	year	213	91	81r
Beverage purchases, alcoholic	year	457	91	81c
Beverage purchases, alcoholic	year	249	91	81r
Beverage purchases, nonalcoholic	year	205	91	81c
Beverage purchases, nonalcoholic	year	207	91	81r
Bologna, all beef or mixed	lb.	2.27	12/94	82r
Bread, white	24-oz.	0.75	12/94	2c
Bread, white, pan	lb.	0.68	12/94	82r
Cabbage	lb.	0.42	12/94	2c
Carrots, short trimmed and topped	lb.	0.53	12/94	82r
Cereals and bakery products purchases	year	340	91	81c
Cereals and bakery products purchases	year	345	91	81r
Cereals and cereal products purchases	year	124	91	81c
Cereals and cereals products purchases	year	127	91	81r
Cheddar cheese, natural	lb.	3.58	12/94	82r
Cheese, Kraft grated Parmesan	8-oz.	3.05	12/94	2c
Chicken breast, bone-in	lb.	1.71	12/94	82r
Chicken, fresh, whole	lb.	0.78	12/94	2c
Chicken, whole fryer	lb.	0.87	12/94	2c
Chuck roast, USDA choice, boneless	lb.	2.26	12/94	82r
Cigarettes, Winston, Kings	carton	17.07	12/94	2c
Coffee, vacuum-packed	13 oz.	3.27	12/94	2c
Corn Flakes, Kellogg's or Post Toasties	18 oz.	2.09	12/94	2c
Corn, frozen, whole kernel, lowest price	10 oz.	0.66	12/94	2c
Crackers, soda, salted	lb.	1.27	12/94	82r
Cucumbers	lb.	0.65	12/94	82r
Dairy products (other) purchases	year	153	91	81c
Dairy products (other) purchases	year	141	91	81r
Eggs, Grade A large	dozen	0.77	12/94	2c
Eggs, Grade A large	dozen	0.87	12/94	82r
Fish and seafood purchases	year	112	91	81c

Miami, FL - continued

Item	Per	Value	Date	Ref.
Groceries - continued				
Fish and seafood purchases	year	72	91	81r
Flour, white, all purpose	lb.	0.23	12/94	82r
Food purchases, food eaten at home	year	2434	91	81c
Food purchases, food eaten at home	year	2381	91	81r
Foods purchased away from home, not prepared by consumer	year	2759	91	81c
Foods purchased away from home, not prepared by consumer	year	1696	91	81r
Frankfurters, all meat or all beef	lb.	1.74	12/94	82r
Fruits and vegetables purchases	year	442	91	81c
Fruits and vegetables purchases	year	380	91	81r
Grapefruit	lb.	0.45	12/94	82r
Grapes, Thompson seedless	lb.	2.30	12/94	82r
Ground beef, 100% beef	lb.	1.37	12/94	82r
Ground chuck, 100% beef	lb.	1.97	12/94	82r
Ham, boneless, exc. canned	lb.	2.54	12/94	82r
Ice cream, prepackaged, bulk, regular	1/2 gal.	2.47	12/94	82r
Lemons	lb.	1.02	12/94	82r
Lettuce, iceberg	lb.	0.96	12/94	82r
Lettuce, iceberg	head	0.81	12/94	2c
Margarine, Blue Bonnet or Parkay cubes	lb.	0.57	12/94	2c
Margarine, stick	lb.	0.77	12/94	82r
Meats, poultry, fish, and eggs purchases	year	697	91	81c
Meats, poultry, fish, and eggs purchases	year	655	91	81r
Milk and cream (fresh) purchases	year	143	91	81c
Milk and cream (fresh) purchases	year	130	91	81r
Milk, whole	1/2 gal.	1.49	12/94	2c
Orange juice, frozen concentrate 12-oz. can	16 oz.	1.36	12/94	82r
Orange juice, Minute Maid frozen	12-oz.	1.13	12/94	2c
Oranges, Navel	lb.	0.54	12/94	82r
Peaches, halves or slices, Hunt's, Del Monte, or Libby's	29-oz.	1.20	12/94	2c
Pears, Anjou	lb.	0.81	12/94	82r
Peas, sweet, Del Monte or Green Giant	15-17 oz.	0.50	12/94	2c
Pork chops, center cut, bone-in	lb.	3.07	12/94	82r
Pork purchases	year	126	91	81c
Pork purchases	year	142	91	81r
Potato chips	16-oz.	3.15	12/94	82r
Potatoes, frozen, French fried	lb.	0.82	12/94	82r
Potatoes, white	lb.	0.34	12/94	82r
Potatoes, white or red	10-lb. sack	3.18	12/94	2c
Rice, white, long grain, uncooked	lb.	0.48	12/94	82r
Round roast, USDA choice, boneless	lb.	2.91	12/94	82r
Sausage, fresh	lb.	1.82	12/94	82r
Sausage, Jimmy Dean, 100% pork	lb.	2.55	12/94	2c
Shortening, vegetable oil blends	lb.	0.75	12/94	82r
Shortening, vegetable, Crisco	3-lb.	2.62	12/94	2c
Soft drink, Coca Cola, ex deposit	2 lit	1.04	12/94	2c
Spaghetti and macaroni	lb.	0.87	12/94	82r
Steak, rib eye, USDA choice, boneless	lb.	6.85	12/94	82r
Steak, round, graded & ungraded, exc. USDA prime & choice	lb.	2.96	12/94	82r
Steak, round, USDA choice, boneless	lb.	3.17	12/94	82r
Steak, sirloin, USDA choice, boneless	lb.	4.12	12/94	82r
Steak, t-bone	lb.	6.29	12/94	2c
Steak, T-bone, USDA choice, bone-in	lb.	5.63	12/94	82r
Sugar and other sweets, eaten at home, expenditures	year	93	91	81r
Sugar and other sweets, eaten at home, purchases	year	74	91	81c
Sugar, cane or beet	4 lbs.	1.50	12/94	2c
Sugar, white, all sizes	lb.	0.39	12/94	82r
Tobacco products and smoking supplies, total expenditures	year	228	91	81c
Tobacco products and smoking supplies, total expenditures	year	286	91	81r
Tomatoes, field grown	lb.	1.36	12/94	82r

Values are in dollars or fractions of dollars. In the column headed *Ref*, references are shown to sources. Each reference is followed by a letter. These refer to the geographical level for which data were reported: s = State, r = Region, and c = City or metro. The abbreviation *ex* is used to mean *except* or *excluding*; *exp* stands for expenditures. For other abbreviations and further explanations, please see the Introduction.

Miami, FL - continued

Item	Per	Value	Date	Ref.
Groceries				
Tomatoes, Hunt's or Del Monte	14.5 oz.	0.71	12/94	2c
Tuna, chunk, light	lb.	1.94	12/94	82r
Tuna, chunk, light, oil-packed	6.125-6.5 oz.	0.90	12/94	2c
Turkey, frozen, whole	lb.	0.96	12/94	82r
Yogurt, natural, fruit flavored	8 oz.	0.58	12/94	82r
Goods and Services				
Miscellaneous goods and services, ACCRA Index		107.00	12/94	2c
Health Care				
Health care, ACCRA Index		120.20	12/94	2c
Adenosine, emergency room	treat	100.00	95	23r
Antibiotic ointment, Polysporin	1.5 oz.	4.33	12/94	2c
Bladder tap, superpubic, infant, emergency room	treat	119.00	95	23r
Blood analysis, emergency room	treat	25.00	95	23r
Blood tests, abdominal pain, emergency room	treat	25.00	95	23r
Burn dressing, emergency room	treat	266.00	95	23r
Cardiology interpretation, emergency room	treat	26.00	95	23r
Chest X-ray, emergency room	treat	78.00	95	23r
Childbirth, Cesarean delivery, hospital charge	birth	5462.00	12/91	69r
Childbirth, Cesarean delivery, physician charge	birth	2228.00	12/91	69r
Childbirth, normal delivery, hospital charge	birth	2943.00	12/91	69r
Childbirth, normal delivery, physician charge	birth	1619.00	12/91	69r
Defibrillation pads, emergency room	treat	6.00	95	23r
Dentist's fee, adult teeth cleaning and periodic oral exam	visit	52.00	12/94	2c
Doctor's fee, routine exam, established patient	visit	63.00	12/94	2c
Drugs, expenditures	year	224	91	81c
Drugs, expenditures	year	297	91	81r
Gastric tube insertion, nasal, emergency room	treat	25.00	95	23r
Health care, total expenditures	year	1686	91	81c
Health care, total expenditures	year	1600	91	81r
Health insurance expenditures	year	765	91	81c
Health insurance expenditures	year	637	91	81r
Heart monitor, emergency room	treat	40.00	95	23r
Hospital care, semiprivate room	day	395.60	12/94	2c
Hospital cost	adm	7,035	2/94	72c
Insurance premium, family medical care	month	301.92	1/95	41s
Intravenous fluids, emergency room	treat	130.00	95	23r
Intravenous fluids, emergency room	liter	26.00	95	23r
Intravenous line, central, emergency room	treat	342.00	95	23r
Liver function tests, abdominal pain, emergency room	treat	26.00	95	23r
Medical care charges, total, emergency room, third-degree burns	treat	2101.00	95	23r
Medical care charges, total, emergency, infant with fever	treat	628.00	95	23r
Medical services expenditures	year	630	91	81c
Medical services expenditures	year	573	91	81r
Medical supplies expenditures	year	68	91	81c
Medical supplies expenditures	year	93	91	81r
Morphine, emergency room	treat	34.00	95	23r
Nursing care and facilities charges, emergency room	treat	252.00	95	23r
Nursing care and facilities charges, emergency, infant with fever	treat	252.00	95	23r
Nursing care and facilities charges, emergency, third-degree burns	treat	861.00	95	23r
Physician's charges, emergency, infant with fever	treat	212.00	95	23r
Physician's charges, emergency, third-degree burns	treat	372.00	95	23r
Physician's fee, emergency room	treat	372.00	95	23r
Physician's fee, general practitioner	visit	51.20	12/93	60r

Miami, FL - continued

Item	Per	Value	Date	Ref.
Health Care - continued				
Surgery, open-heart	proc	42374.00	1/93	14r
Ultrasound, abdominal, emergency room	treat	276.00	95	23r
Urinalysis, emergency room	treat	20.00	95	23r
Urinalysis, infant, emergency room	treat	20.00	95	23r
X-rays, emergency room	treat	78.00	95	23r
Household Goods				
Appl. repair, service call, wash mach	min. lab. chg.	52.00	12/94	2c
Floor coverings, expenditures	year	20	91	81c
Floor coverings, expenditures	year	48	91	81r
Furniture, expenditures	year	424	91	81c
Furniture, expenditures	year	280	91	81r
Household equipment, misc. expenditures	year	342	91	81r
Household equipment, misc., expenditures	year	440	91	81c
Household expenditures, miscellaneous	year	404	91	81c
Household expenditures, miscellaneous	year	256	91	81r
Household furnishings and equipment, expenditures	year	1120	91	81c
Household furnishings and equipment, expenditures	year	988	91	81r
Household operations expenditures	year	572	91	81c
Household operations expenditures	year	468	91	81r
Household textiles, expenditures	year	65	91	81c
Household textiles, expenditures	year	95	91	81r
Housekeeping supplies, expenditures	year	445	91	81c
Housekeeping supplies, expenditures	year	380	91	81r
Laundry and cleaning supplies, expenditures	year	122	91	81c
Laundry and cleaning supplies, expenditures	year	109	91	81r
Laundry detergent, Tide Ultra, Bold, or Cheer	42 oz.	3.39	12/94	2c
Postage and stationery, expenditures	year	144	91	81c
Postage and stationery, expenditures	year	105	91	81r
Tissues, facial, Kleenex brand	175	0.98	12/94	2c
Housing				
Housing, ACCRA Index		104.00	12/94	2c
Add garage/carport		6,980	3/95	74r
Add room(s)		11,403	3/95	74r
Apartment condominium or co-op, median	unit	68600	12/94	62r
Car rental	day	29.00	5/95	95c
Dwellings (owned), expenditures	year	3415	91	81c
Dwellings (owned), expenditures	year	2428	91	81r
Enclose porch/patio/breezeway		4,572	3/95	74r
Finish room in basement/attic		3,794	3/95	74r
Home, existing, single-family, median	unit	120200	12/94	62r
Home, existing, single-family, median	unit	103.30	12/94	62c
Home, purchase price	unit	125.40	3/93	26c
Hotel room	day	118.00	5/95	95c
House payment, principal and interest, 25% down payment	mo.	753	12/94	2c
House, 1800 sq ft, 8000 sq ft lot, new, urban, utilities	total	121829	12/94	2c
Maintenance, repairs, insurance, and other housing expenditures	year	598	91	81c
Maintenance, repairs, insurance, and other housing expenditures	year	531	91	81r
Mortgage interest and charges expenditures	year	2090	91	81c
Mortgage interest and charges expenditures	year	1506	91	81r
Mtge. rate, incl. points and orig. fee, 30-year conv. fixed or ARM	mo.	9.27	12/94	2c
Princ. & int., mortgage, median-price exist. sing.-family home	mo.	540	12/94	62r
Property taxes expenditures	year	727	91	81c
Property taxes expenditures	year	391	91	81r
Redesign, restructure more than half of home's interior		17,641	3/95	74r
Rent, apartment, 2 br., 1 1/2-2 baths, unfurnished, 950 sq ft, water	mo.	676	12/94	2c

Values are in dollars or fractions of dollars. In the column headed *Ref*, references are shown to sources. Each reference is followed by a letter. These refer to the geographical level for which data were reported: s = State, r = Region, and c = City or metro. The abbreviation *ex* is used to mean *except* or *excluding*; *exp* stands for expenditures. For other abbreviations and further explanations, please see the Introduction.

Miami, FL - continued

Item	Per	Value	Date	Ref.
Housing				
Rental units expenditures	year	2179	900/00/ 91	81c
Rental units expenditures	year	1264	91	81r
Insurance and Pensions				
Auto insurance, private passenger	year	753.93	12/94	71s
Insurance and pensions, personal, expenditures	year	2511	91	81c
Insurance and pensions, personal, expenditures	year	2395	91	81r
Insurance, life and other personal, expenditures	year	273	91	81c
Insurance, life and other personal, expenditures	year	368	91	81r
Pensions and Social Security, expenditures	year	2238	91	81c
Pensions and Social Security, expenditures	year	2027	91	81r
Personal Goods				
Personal care products and services, total expenditures	year	455	91	81c
Shampoo, Alberto VO5	15-oz.	0.93	12/94	2c
Toothpaste, Crest or Colgate	6-7 oz.	1.59	12/94	2c
Personal Services				
Dry cleaning	serv	7.50	92	52c
Dry cleaning, man's 2-pc. suit		6.96	12/94	2c
Haircut, man's barbershop, no styling		10.20	12/94	2c
Haircut, woman's shampoo, trim, blow-dry		23.40	12/94	2c
Manicure		20.00	92	52c
Personal services expenditures	year	168	91	81c
Personal services expenditures	year	212	91	81r
Restaurant Food				
Chicken, fried, thigh and drumstick		1.96	12/94	2c
Dining expenditures, family	week	33.83	94	73r
Hamburger with cheese	1/4 lb.	1.89	12/94	2c
Pizza, Pizza Hut or Pizza Inn	12-13 in.	7.99	12/94	2c
Taxes				
Taxes, Federal income, expenditures	year	2504	91	81c
Taxes, Federal income, expenditures	year	2275	91	81r
Taxes, personal, expenditures	year	2620	91	81c
Taxes, personal, expenditures	year	2715	91	81r
Taxes, State and local income, expenditures	year	365	91	81r
Transportation				
Transportation, ACCRA Index		114.10	12/94	2c
Bus fare, one-way	trip	1.25	12/95	1c
Bus fare, up to 10 miles	one-way	1.25	12/94	2c
Cars and trucks purchased, new	year	1042	91	81c
Cars and trucks purchased, new	year	1306	91	81r
Cars and trucks purchased, used	year	976	91	81c
Cars and trucks purchased, used	year	942	91	81r
Commuter rail fare (automated guideway), one-way	trip	0.25	12/95	1c
Driver's learning permit fee	perm	20.00	1/94	84s
Driver's license fee	orig	20.00	1/94	84s
Driver's license fee, duplicate	lic	10.00	1/94	84s
Driver's license reinstatement fee, min.	susp	25.00	1/94	85s
Driver's license renewal fee	renew	15.00	1/94	84s
Fine, illegal parking, handicapped zone	event	125.00	12/93	87c
Identification card, nondriver	card	3.00	1/94	83s
Motorcycle learning permit fee	perm	20.00	1/94	84s
Motorcycle license fee	orig	20.00	1/94	84s
Motorcycle license fee, duplicate	lic	10.00	1/94	84s
Motorcycle license renewal fee	renew	15.00	1/94	84s
Public transportation expenditures	year	936	91	81c
Public transportation expenditures	year	249	91	81r
Railway fare, commuter rail, one-way	trip	3.00	12/95	1c
Railway fare, heavy rail, one-way	trip	1.25	12/95	1c
Tire balance, computer or spin bal., front	wheel	7.59	12/94	2c
Transportation expenditures, total	year	5788	91	81c
Transportation expenditures, total	year	5307	91	81r

Miami, FL - continued

Item	Per	Value	Date	Ref.
Transportation - continued				
Vehicle expenses, miscellaneous	year	1884	91	81c
Vehicle finance charges	year	323	91	81c
Vehicle finance charges	year	346	91	81r
Vehicle insurance expenditures	year	704	91	81c
Vehicle insurance expenditures	year	544	91	81r
Vehicle maintenance and repairs expenditures	year	631	91	81c
Vehicle maintenance and repairs expenditures	year	600	91	81r
Vehicle purchases	year	2018	91	81c
Vehicle purchases	year	2275	91	81r
Vehicle rental, leases, licenses, etc. expenditures	year	227	91	81c
Vehicle rental, leases, licenses, etc. expenditures	year	141	91	81r
Vehicles purchased, other than cars and trucks	year	27	91	81r
Utilities				
Utilities, ACCRA Index		120.50	12/94	2c
Electricity	KWh	0.08	12/94	82c
Electricity expenditures	year	1043	91	81c
Electricity expenditures	year	950	91	81r
Electricity, 1800 sq. ft., new home	mo.	141.66	12/94	2c
Electricity, summer, 250 KWh	month	22.78	8/93	64c
Electricity, summer, 500 KWh	month	39.89	8/93	64c
Electricity, summer, 750 KWh	month	57.02	8/93	64c
Electricity, summer, 1000 KWh	month	76.63	8/93	64c
Utilities, fuels, and public services, total expenditures	year	2050	91	81c
Utilities, fuels, and public services, total expenditures	year	2000	91	81r
Water and other public services, expenditures	year	192	91	81c
Water and other public services, expenditures	year	227	91	81r
Weddings				
Bridal attendants' gowns	event	750	10/93	76r
Bridal gown	event	852	10/93	76r
Bridal headpiece and veil	event	167	10/93	76r
Bride's wedding band	event	708	10/93	76r
Clergy	event	224	10/93	76r
Engagement ring	event	2756	10/93	76r
Flowers	event	863	10/93	76r
Formal wear for groom	event	106	10/93	76r
Groom's attendants' formal wear	event	530	10/93	76r
Groom's wedding band	event	402	10/93	76r
Music	event	600	10/93	76r
Photography	event	1088	10/93	76r
Shoes for bride	event	50	10/93	76r
Videography	event	483	10/93	76r
Wedding invitations and announcements	event	342	10/93	76r
Wedding reception	event	7000	10/93	76r

Middlesex-Somerset-Hunterdon, NJ

Item	Per	Value	Date	Ref.
Appliances				
Appliances (major), expenditures	year	145	91	81r
Average annual exp.				
Food, health care, personal goods, services	year	29496	91	81r
Charity				
Cash contributions, expenditures	year	708	91	81r
Clothing				
Apparel, men and boys, total expenditures	year	416	91	81r
Apparel, women and girls, total expenditures	year	744	91	81r
Footwear, expenditures	year	305	91	81r
Communications				
Long-distance telephone rate, day, addl. min., 1-10 mi.	min.	0.03	12/93	9s

Values are in dollars or fractions of dollars. In the column headed *Ref*, references are shown to sources. Each reference is followed by a letter. These refer to the geographical level for which data were reported: s=State, r=Region, and c=City or metro. The abbreviation *ex* is used to mean *except* or *excluding*; *exp* stands for expenditures. For other abbreviations and further explanations, please see the Introduction.

Middlesex-Somerset-Hunterdon, NJ - continued

Item	Per	Value	Date	Ref.
Communications				
Long-distance telephone rate, day, initial min., 1-10 mi.	min.	0.09	12/93	9s
Phone line, single, business, field visit	inst	98.50	12/93	9s
Phone line, single, business, no field visit	inst	79.50	12/93	9s
Phone line, single, residence, field visit	inst	56.50	12/93	9s
Phone line, single, residence, no field visit	inst	42.00	12/93	9s
Telephone service, expenditures	year	589	91	81r
Education				
Board, 4-year private college/university	year	2841	8/94	80s
Board, 4-year public college/university	year	1956	8/94	80s
Education, total expenditures	year	593	91	81r
Room, 4-year private college/university	year	2999	8/94	80s
Room, 4-year public college/university	year	2778	8/94	80s
Total cost, 4-year private college/university	year	18264	8/94	80s
Total cost, 4-year public college/university	year	8252	8/94	80s
Tuition, 2-year public college/university, in-state	year	1539	8/94	80s
Tuition, 4-year private college/university, in-state	year	12423	8/94	80s
Tuition, 4-year public college/university, in-state	year	3518	8/94	80s
Energy and Fuels				
Fuel oil and other fuels, expenditures	year	257	91	81r
Gas, natural, expenditures	year	285	91	81r
Gasoline and motor oil purchased	year	867	91	81r
Gasoline, unleaded midgrade	gallon	1.32	4/93	82r
Gasoline, unleaded premium	gallon	1.40	4/93	82r
Gasoline, unleaded regular	gallon	1.19	4/93	82r
Entertainment				
Entertainment, total expenditures	year	1331	91	81r
Fees and admissions, expenditures	year	398	91	81r
Pets, toys, playground equipment, expenditures	year	270	91	81r
Reading, expenditures	year	171	91	81r
Televisions, radios, and sound equipment, expenditures	year	429	91	81r
Funerals				
Burial, immediate, container provided by funeral home		1370.36	1/95	54r
Cards, acknowledgment		17.72	1/95	54r
Casket, minimum alternative		192.52	1/95	54r
Cosmetology, hair care, etc.		139.56	1/95	54r
Cremation, direct, container provided by funeral home		1049.24	1/95	54r
Embalming		387.57	1/95	54r
Funeral, funeral home		278.77	1/95	54r
Funeral, other facility		275.85	1/95	54r
Graveside service		213.08	1/95	54r
Hearse, local		157.27	1/95	54r
Limousine, local		146.45	1/95	54r
Memorial service		271.02	1/95	54r
Service charge, professional, nondeclinable		943.58	1/95	54r
Visitation and viewing		322.86	1/95	54r
Groceries				
Apples, Red Delicious	lb.	0.78	12/94	82r
Bacon, sliced	lb.	2.24	12/94	82r
Bananas	lb.	0.49	12/94	82r
Beef purchases	year	226	91	81r
Beverage purchases, alcoholic	year	332	91	81r
Beverage purchases, nonalcoholic	year	213	91	81r
Bread, white, pan	lb.	0.80	12/94	82r
Butter, salted, Grade AA, stick	lb.	1.67	12/94	82r
Carrots, short trimmed and topped	lb.	0.51	12/94	82r
Cereals and bakery products purchases	year	407	91	81r
Cereals and cereals products purchases	year	132	91	81r
Chicken breast, bone-in	lb.	2.22	12/94	82r
Chicken, fresh, whole	lb.	1.05	12/94	82r
Chuck roast, USDA choice, boneless	lb.	2.74	12/94	82s
Coffee, 100%, ground roast, all sizes	lb.	4.61	12/94	82r

Middlesex-Somerset-Hunterdon, NJ - continued

Item	Per	Value	Date	Ref.
Groceries - continued				
Dairy products (other) purchases	year	161	91	81r
Eggs, Grade A large	dozen	1.12	12/94	82r
Fish and seafood purchases	year	112	91	81r
Food purchases, food eaten at home	year	2599	91	81r
Foods purchased away from home, not prepared by consumer	year	2024	91	81r
Fruits and vegetables purchases	year	444	91	81r
Grapefruit	lb.	0.44	12/94	82r
Grapes, Thompson seedless	lb.	2.24	12/94	82r
Ground chuck, 100% beef	lb.	1.67	12/94	82r
Ice cream, prepackaged, bulk, regular	1/2 gal.	2.93	12/94	82r
Lemons	lb.	1.06	12/94	82r
Lettuce, iceberg	lb.	0.92	12/94	82r
Meats, poultry, fish, and eggs purchases	year	751	91	81r
Milk and cream (fresh) purchases	year	152	91	81r
Orange juice, frozen concentrate 12-oz. can	16 oz.	1.92	12/94	82r
Oranges, Navel	lb.	0.56	12/94	82r
Pork chops, center cut, bone-in	lb.	3.09	12/94	82r
Pork purchases	year	130	91	81r
Potatoes, white	lb.	0.37	12/94	82r
Rib roast, USDA choice, bone-in	lb.	4.98	12/94	82r
Round roast, USDA choice, boneless	lb.	2.93	12/94	82r
Shortening, vegetable oil blends	lb.	1.03	12/94	82r
Spaghetti and macaroni	lb.	0.84	12/94	82r
Steak, round, USDA choice, boneless	lb.	3.48	12/94	82r
Steak, sirloin, USDA choice, bone-in	lb.	3.38	12/94	82r
Steak, sirloin, USDA choice, boneless	lb.	4.81	12/94	82r
Sugar and other sweets, eaten at home, expenditures	year	89	91	81r
Sugar, white, all sizes	lb.	0.46	12/94	82r
Tobacco products and smoking supplies, total expenditures	year	279	91	81r
Tomatoes, field grown	lb.	1.56	12/94	82r
Tuna, chunk, light	lb.	2.09	12/94	82r
Health Care				
Childbirth, Cesarean delivery, hospital charge	birth	6334.00	12/91	69r
Childbirth, Cesarean delivery, physician charge	birth	2234.00	12/91	69r
Childbirth, normal delivery, hospital charge	birth	3225.00	12/91	69r
Childbirth, normal delivery, physician charge	birth	1623.00	12/91	69r
Drugs, expenditures	year	205	91	81r
Health care, total expenditures	year	1396	91	81r
Health insurance expenditures	year	553	91	81r
Insurance premium, family medical care	month	396.06	1/95	41s
Medical services expenditures	year	559	91	81r
Medical supplies expenditures	year	80	91	81r
Household Goods				
Floor coverings, expenditures	year	158	91	81r
Furniture, expenditures	year	341	91	81r
Household equipment, misc. expenditures	year	363	91	81r
Household expenditures, miscellaneous	year	194	91	81r
Household furnishings and equipment, expenditures	year	1158	91	81r
Household operations expenditures	year	378	91	81r
Household textiles, expenditures	year	88	91	81r
Housekeeping supplies, expenditures	year	426	91	81r
Laundry and cleaning supplies, expenditures	year	122	91	81r
Postage and stationery, expenditures	year	134	91	81r
Housing				
Add garage/carport		11,614	3/95	74r
Add room(s)		16,816	3/95	74r
Apartment condominium or co-op, median	unit	96700	12/94	62r
Dwellings (owned), expenditures	year	3305	91	81r
Enclose porch/patio/breezeway		2,980	3/95	74r
Finish room in basement/attic		4,330	3/95	74r
Home, existing, single-family, median	unit	161600	12/94	62r
Maintenance, repairs, insurance, and other housing expenditures	year	569	91	81r

Values are in dollars or fractions of dollars. In the column headed *Ref*, references are shown to sources. Each reference is followed by a letter. These refer to the geographical level for which data were reported: s = State, r = Region, and c = City or metro. The abbreviation *ex* is used to mean *except* or *excluding*; *exp* stands for *expenditures*. For other abbreviations and further explanations, please see the Introduction.

Middlesex-Somerset-Hunterdon, NJ - continued

Item	Per	Value	Date	Ref.
Housing				
Mortgage interest and charges expenditures	year	1852	91	81r
Princ. & int., mortgage, median-price exist. sing.-family home	mo.	765	12/94	62r
Property taxes expenditures	year	884	91	81r
Redesign, restructure more than half of home's interior		2,750	3/95	74r
Rental units expenditures	year	1832	91	81r
Insurance and Pensions				
Auto insurance, private passenger	year	1094.56	12/94	71s
Insurance and pensions, personal, expenditures	year	2690	91	81r
Insurance, life and other personal, expenditures	year	341	91	81r
Pensions and Social Security, expenditures	year	2349	91	81r
Legal Assistance				
Estate planning, law-firm partner	hr.	375.00	10/93	12r
Legal work, law firm associate	hour	78		10r
Legal work, law firm partner	hour	183		10r
Personal Services				
Personal services expenditures	year	184	91	81r
Restaurant Food				
Dining expenditures, family	week	34.26	94	73r
Taxes				
Taxes, Federal income, expenditures	year	2409	91	81r
Taxes, personal, expenditures	year	3094	91	81r
Taxes, State and local income, expenditures	year	620	91	81r
Transportation				
Cars and trucks purchased, new	year	1170	91	81r
Cars and trucks purchased, used	year	739	91	81r
Driver's learning permit fee	perm	5.00	1/94	84s
Driver's license fee	orig	16.00	1/94	84s
Driver's license fee, duplicate	lic	3.00	1/94	84s
Driver's license reinstatement fee, min.	susp	30.00	1/94	85s
Driver's license renewal fee	renew	16.00	1/94	84s
Identification card, nondriver	card	5.50	1/94	83s
Motorcycle learning permit fee	perm	5.00	1/94	84s
Motorcycle license fee	orig	8.00	1/94	84s
Motorcycle license fee, duplicate	lic	3.00	1/94	84s
Motorcycle license renewal fee	renew	8.00	1/94	84s
Public transportation expenditures	year	430	91	81r
Transportation expenditures, total	year	4810	91	81r
Vehicle finance charges	year	238	91	81r
Vehicle insurance expenditures	year	630	91	81r
Vehicle maintenance and repairs expenditures	year	532	91	81r
Vehicle purchases	year	1920	91	81r
Vehicle rental, leases, licenses, etc. expenditures	year	193	91	81r
Vehicles purchased, other than cars and trucks	year	11	91	81r
Utilities				
Electricity expenditures	year	695	91	81r
Utilities, fuels, and public services, total expenditures	year	1981	91	81r
Water and other public services, expenditures	year	154	91	81r
Weddings				
Bridal attendants' gowns	event	750	10/93	76r
Bridal gown	event	852	10/93	76r
Bridal headpiece and veil	event	167	10/93	76r
Bride's wedding band	event	708	10/93	76r
Clergy	event	224	10/93	76r
Engagement ring	event	2756	10/93	76r
Flowers	event	863	10/93	76r
Formal wear for groom	event	106	10/93	76r
Groom's attendants' formal wear	event	530	10/93	76r
Groom's wedding band	event	402	10/93	76r
Music	event	600	10/93	76r

Middlesex-Somerset-Hunterdon, NJ - continued

Item	Per	Value	Date	Ref.
Weddings - continued				
Photography	event	1088	10/93	76r
Shoes for bride	event	50	10/93	76r
Videography	event	483	10/93	76r
Wedding invitations and announcements	event	342	10/93	76r
Wedding reception	event	7000	10/93	76r

Middletown, CT

Item	Per	Value	Date	Ref.
Appliances				
Appliances (major), expenditures	year	145	91	81r
Average annual exp.				
Food, health care, personal goods, services	year	29496	91	81r
Charity				
Cash contributions, expenditures	year	708	91	81r
Clothing				
Apparel, men and boys, total expenditures	year	416	91	81r
Apparel, women and girls, total expenditures	year	744	91	81r
Footwear, expenditures	year	305	91	81r
Communications				
Long-distance telephone rate, day, addl. min., 1-10 mi.	min.	0.09	12/93	9s
Long-distance telephone rate, day, initial min., 1-10 mi.	min.	0.09	12/93	9s
Phone line, single, business, field visit	inst	127.44	12/93	9s
Phone line, single, business, no field visit	inst	95.58	12/93	9s
Phone line, single, residence, field visit	inst	64.85	12/93	9s
Phone line, single, residence, no field visit	inst	38.27	12/93	9s
Telephone service, expenditures	year	589	91	81r
Education				
Board, 4-year private college/university	year	2664	8/94	80s
Board, 4-year public college/university	year	2137	8/94	80s
Education, total expenditures	year	593	91	81r
Room, 4-year private college/university	year	3287	8/94	80s
Room, 4-year public college/university	year	2310	8/94	80s
Total cost, 4-year private college/university	year	20726	8/94	80s
Total cost, 4-year public college/university	year	7926	8/94	80s
Tuition, 2-year public college/university, in-state	year	1398	8/94	80s
Tuition, 4-year private college/university, in-state	year	14775	8/94	80s
Tuition, 4-year public college/university, in-state	year	3479	8/94	80s
Energy and Fuels				
Fuel oil and other fuels, expenditures	year	257	91	81r
Gas, natural, expenditures	year	285	91	81r
Gasoline and motor oil purchased	year	867	91	81r
Gasoline, unleaded midgrade	gallon	1.32	4/93	82r
Gasoline, unleaded premium	gallon	1.40	4/93	82r
Gasoline, unleaded regular	gallon	1.19	4/93	82r
Entertainment				
Entertainment, total expenditures	year	1331	91	81r
Fees and admissions, expenditures	year	398	91	81r
Pets, toys, playground equipment, expenditures	year	270	91	81r
Reading, expenditures	year	171	91	81r
Televisions, radios, and sound equipment, expenditures	year	429	91	81r
Funerals				
Burial, immediate, container provided by funeral home		1507.89	1/95	54r
Cards, acknowledgment		18.10	1/95	54r
Casket, minimum alternative		133.03	1/95	54r
Cosmetology, hair care, etc.		114.12	1/95	54r
Cremation, direct, container provided by funeral home		1309.19	1/95	54r
Embalming		320.97	1/95	54r
Funeral, funeral home		327.61	1/95	54r

Values are in dollars or fractions of dollars. In the column headed *Ref*, references are shown to sources. Each reference is followed by a letter. These refer to the geographical level for which data were reported: s = State, r = Region, and c = City or metro. The abbreviation *ex* is used to mean *except* or *excluding*; *exp* stands for *expenditures*. For other abbreviations and further explanations, please see the Introduction.

Middletown, CT - continued

Item	Per	Value	Date	Ref.
Funerals				
Funeral, other facility		314.81	1/95	54r
Graveside service		286.11	1/95	54r
Hearse, local		158.95	1/95	54r
Limousine, local		149.45	1/95	54r
Memorial service		315.94	1/95	54r
Service charge, professional, nondeclinable		1148.43	1/95	54r
Visitation and viewing		249.66	1/95	54r
Groceries				
Apples, Red Delicious	lb.	0.78	12/94	82r
Bacon, sliced	lb.	2.24	12/94	82r
Bananas	lb.	0.49	12/94	82r
Beef purchases	year	226	91	81r
Beverage purchases, alcoholic	year	332	91	81r
Beverage purchases, nonalcoholic	year	213	91	81r
Bread, white, pan	lb.	0.80	12/94	82r
Butter, salted, Grade AA, stick	lb.	1.67	12/94	82r
Carrots, short trimmed and topped	lb.	0.51	12/94	82r
Cereals and bakery products purchases	year	407	91	81r
Cereals and cereals products purchases	year	132	91	81r
Chicken breast, bone-in	lb.	2.22	12/94	82r
Chicken, fresh, whole	lb.	1.05	12/94	82r
Chuck roast, USDA choice, boneless	lb.	2.74	12/94	82r
Coffee, 100%, ground roast, all sizes	lb.	4.61	12/94	82r
Dairy products (other) purchases	year	161	91	81r
Eggs, Grade A large	dozen	1.12	12/94	82r
Fish and seafood purchases	year	112	91	81r
Food purchases, food eaten at home	year	2599	91	81r
Foods purchased away from home, not prepared by consumer	year	2024	91	81r
Fruits and vegetables purchases	year	444	91	81r
Grapefruit	lb.	0.44	12/94	82r
Grapes, Thompson seedless	lb.	2.24	12/94	82r
Ground chuck, 100% beef	lb.	1.67	12/94	82r
Ice cream, prepackaged, bulk, regular	1/2 gal.	2.93	12/94	82r
Lemons	lb.	1.06	12/94	82r
Lettuce, iceberg	lb.	0.92	12/94	82r
Meats, poultry, fish, and eggs purchases	year	751	91	81r
Milk and cream (fresh) purchases	year	152	91	81r
Orange juice, frozen concentrate 12-oz. can	16 oz.	1.92	12/94	82r
Oranges, Navel	lb.	0.56	12/94	82r
Pork chops, center cut, bone-in	lb.	3.09	12/94	82r
Pork purchases	year	130	91	81r
Potatoes, white	lb.	0.37	12/94	82r
Rib roast, USDA choice, bone-in	lb.	4.98	12/94	82r
Round roast, USDA choice, boneless	lb.	2.93	12/94	82r
Shortening, vegetable oil blends	lb.	1.03	12/94	82r
Spaghetti and macaroni	lb.	0.84	12/94	82r
Steak, round, USDA choice, boneless	lb.	3.48	12/94	82r
Steak, sirloin, USDA choice, bone-in	lb.	3.38	12/94	82r
Steak, sirloin, USDA choice, boneless	lb.	4.81	12/94	82r
Sugar and other sweets, eaten at home, expenditures	year	89	91	81r
Sugar, white, all sizes	lb.	0.46	12/94	82r
Tobacco products and smoking supplies, total expenditures	year	279	91	81r
Tomatoes, field grown	lb.	1.56	12/94	82r
Tuna, chunk, light	lb.	2.09	12/94	82r
Health Care				
Childbirth, Cesarean delivery, hospital charge	birth	6334.00	12/91	69r
Childbirth, Cesarean delivery, physician charge	birth	2234.00	12/91	69r
Childbirth, normal delivery, hospital charge	birth	3225.00	12/91	69r
Childbirth, normal delivery, physician charge	birth	1623.00	12/91	69r
Drugs, expenditures	year	205	91	81r
Health care, total expenditures	year	1396	91	81r
Health insurance expenditures	year	553	91	81r
Insurance premium, family medical care	month	500.40	1/95	41s
Medical services expenditures	year	559	91	81r
Medical supplies expenditures	year	80	91	81r

Middletown, CT - continued

Item	Per	Value	Date	Ref.
Household Goods				
Floor coverings, expenditures	year	158	91	81r
Furniture, expenditures	year	341	91	81r
Household equipment, misc. expenditures	year	363	91	81r
Household expenditures, miscellaneous	year	194	91	81r
Household furnishings and equipment, expenditures	year	1158	91	81r
Household operations expenditures	year	378	91	81r
Household textiles, expenditures	year	88	91	81r
Housekeeping supplies, expenditures	year	426	91	81r
Laundry and cleaning supplies, expenditures	year	122	91	81r
Postage and stationery, expenditures	year	134	91	81r
Housing				
Add garage/carport		11,614	3/95	74r
Add room(s)		16,816	3/95	74r
Apartment condominium or co-op, median	unit	96700	12/94	62r
Dwellings (owned), expenditures	year	3305	91	81r
Enclose porch/patio/breezeway		2,980	3/95	74r
Finish room in basement/attic		4,330	3/95	74r
Home, existing, single-family, median	unit	161600	12/94	62r
Maintenance, repairs, insurance, and other housing expenditures	year	569	91	81r
Mortgage interest and charges expenditures	year	1852	91	81r
Princ. & int., mortgage, median-price exist. sing.-family home	mo.	765	12/94	62r
Property taxes expenditures	year	884	91	81r
Redesign, restructure more than half of home's interior		2,750	3/95	74r
Rental units expenditures	year	1832	91	81r
Insurance and Pensions				
Auto insurance, private passenger	year	1002.84	12/94	71s
Insurance and pensions, personal, expenditures	year	2690	91	81r
Insurance, life and other personal, expenditures	year	341	91	81r
Pensions and Social Security, expenditures	year	2349	91	81r
Legal Assistance				
Estate planning, law-firm partner	hr.	375.00	10/93	12r
Legal work, law firm associate	hour	78		10r
Legal work, law firm partner	hour	183		10r
Personal Services				
Personal services expenditures	year	184	91	81r
Restaurant Food				
Dining expenditures, family	week	34.26	94	73r
Taxes				
Taxes, Federal income, expenditures	year	2409	91	81r
Taxes, personal, expenditures	year	3094	91	81r
Taxes, State and local income, expenditures	year	620	91	81r
Transportation				
Cars and trucks purchased, new	year	1170	91	81r
Cars and trucks purchased, used	year	739	91	81r
Driver's learning permit fee	perm	3.50	1/94	84s
Driver's license fee	orig	38.00	1/94	84s
Driver's license fee, duplicate	lic	5.00	1/94	84s
Driver's license reinstatement fee, min.	susp	30.00	1/94	85s
Driver's license renewal fee	renew	31.00	1/94	84s
Identification card, nondriver	card	4.00	1/94	83s
Motorcycle learning permit fee	perm	3.50	1/94	84s
Motorcycle license fee	orig	38.00	1/94	84s
Motorcycle license fee, duplicate	lic	5.00	1/94	84s
Motorcycle license renewal fee	renew	31.00	1/94	84s
Public transportation expenditures	year	430	91	81r
Transportation expenditures, total	year	4810	91	81r
Vehicle finance charges	year	238	91	81r
Vehicle insurance expenditures	year	630	91	81r
Vehicle maintenance and repairs expenditures	year	532	91	81r
Vehicle purchases	year	1920	91	81r

Values are in dollars or fractions of dollars. In the column headed *Ref*, references are shown to sources. Each reference is followed by a letter. These refer to the geographical level for which data were reported: s=State, r=Region, and c=City or metro. The abbreviation *ex* is used to mean *except* or *excluding*; *exp* stands for expenditures. For other abbreviations and further explanations, please see the Introduction.

Middletown, CT - continued

Item	Per	Value	Date	Ref.
Transportation				
Vehicle rental, leases, licenses, etc. expenditures	year	193	91	81r
Vehicles purchased, other than cars and trucks	year	11	91	81r
Utilities				
Electricity expenditures	year	695	91	81r
Utilities, fuels, and public services, total expenditures	year	1981	91	81r
Water and other public services, expenditures	year	154	91	81r
Weddings				
Bridal attendants' gowns	event	750	10/93	76r
Bridal gown	event	852	10/93	76r
Bridal headpiece and veil	event	167	10/93	76r
Bride's wedding band	event	708	10/93	76r
Clergy	event	224	10/93	76r
Engagement ring	event	2756	10/93	76r
Flowers	event	863	10/93	76r
Formal wear for groom	event	106	10/93	76r
Groom's attendants' formal wear	event	530	10/93	76r
Groom's wedding band	event	402	10/93	76r
Music	event	600	10/93	76r
Photography	event	1088	10/93	76r
Shoes for bride	event	50	10/93	76r
Videography	event	483	10/93	76r
Wedding invitations and announcements	event	342	10/93	76r
Wedding reception	event	7000	10/93	76r

Midland, TX

Item	Per	Value	Date	Ref.
Composite, ACCRA index		94.40	12/94	2c
Alcoholic Beverages				
Beer, Miller Lite, Bud, 12-oz., ex deposit	6	3.99	12/94	2c
J & B Scotch	750-ml.	18.62	12/94	2c
Wine, Gallo Chablis blanc	1.5-lit	4.75	12/94	2c
Appliances				
Appliances (major), expenditures	year	153	91	81r
Average annual exp.				
Food, health care, personal goods, services	year	27020	91	81r
Charity				
Cash contributions, expenditures	year	839	91	81r
Clothing				
Apparel, men and boys, total expenditures	year	380	91	81r
Apparel, women and girls, total expenditures	year	660	91	81r
Footwear, expenditures	year	193	91	81r
Jeans, man's denim		24.79	12/94	2c
Shirt, man's dress shirt		28.17	12/94	2c
Undervest, boy's size 10-14, cotton	3	4.90	12/94	2c
Communications				
Long-distance telephone rate, day, addl. min., 1-10 mi.	min.	0.08	12/93	9s
Long-distance telephone rate, day, initial min., 1-10 mi.	min.	0.10	12/93	9s
Newspaper subscription, dly. and Sun. delivery	month	10.00	12/94	2c
Phone line, single, business, field visit	inst	71.90	12/93	9s
Phone line, single, business, no field visit	inst	57.30	12/93	9s
Phone line, single, residence, field visit	inst	52.95	12/93	9s
Phone line, single, residence, no field visit	inst	38.35	12/93	9s
Telephone bill, family of four	month	15.83	12/94	2c
Telephone service, expenditures	year	616	91	81r
Telephone, residential, flat rate	mo.	9.10	12/93	8c
Education				
Board, 4-year private college/university	year	2084	8/94	80s
Board, 4-year public college/university	year	1675	8/94	80s
Education, total expenditures	year	319	91	81r

Midland, TX - continued

Item	Per	Value	Date	Ref.
Education - continued				
Room, 4-year private college/university	year	1840	8/94	80s
Room, 4-year public college/university	year	1756	8/94	80s
Total cost, 4-year private college/university	year	11876	8/94	80s
Total cost, 4-year public college/university	year	4935	8/94	80s
Tuition, 2-year public college/university, in-state	year	625	8/94	80s
Tuition, 4-year private college/university, in-state	year	7952	8/94	80s
Tuition, 4-year public college/university, in-state	year	1503	8/94	80s
Energy and Fuels				
Energy, combined forms, 1800 sq. ft.	mo.	150.02	12/94	2c
Energy, exc. electricity, 1800 sq. ft.	mo.	38.12	12/94	2c
Fuel oil and other fuels, expenditures	year	56	91	81r
Gas, natural, expenditures	year	150	91	81r
Gas, reg unlead, taxes inc., cash, self-service	gal	1.22	12/94	2c
Gasoline and motor oil purchased	year	1152	91	81r
Gasoline, unleaded midgrade	gallon	1.21	4/93	82r
Gasoline, unleaded premium	gallon	1.30	4/93	82r
Gasoline, unleaded regular	gallon	1.10	4/93	82r
Entertainment				
Bowling, evening rate	game	2.10	12/94	2c
Concert ticket, Pearl Jam group	perf	20.00	94	50r
Entertainment, total expenditures	year	1266	91	81r
Fees and admissions, expenditures	year	306	91	81r
Monopoly game, Parker Brothers', No. 9	game	11.25	12/94	2c
Movie	adm	5.67	12/94	2c
Pets, toys, playground equipment, expenditures	year	271	91	81r
Reading, expenditures	year	131	91	81r
Televisions, radios, and sound equipment, expenditures	year	439	91	81r
Tennis balls, yellow, Wilson or Penn, 3	can	2.56	12/94	2c
Funerals				
Burial, immediate, container provided by funeral home		1574.60	1/95	54r
Cards, acknowledgment		22.24	1/95	54r
Casket, minimum alternative		239.41	1/95	54r
Cosmetology, hair care, etc.		91.04	1/95	54r
Cremation, direct, container provided by funeral home		1085.15	1/95	54r
Embalming		281.30	1/95	54r
Funeral, funeral home		323.04	1/95	54r
Funeral, other facility		327.58	1/95	54r
Graveside service		355.19	1/95	54r
Hearse, local		141.89	1/95	54r
Limousine, local		99.40	1/95	54r
Memorial service		284.67	1/95	54r
Service charge, professional, nondeclinable		904.06	1/95	54r
Visitation and viewing		187.04	1/95	54r
Groceries				
Groceries, ACCRA Index		87.80	12/94	2c
Apples, Red Delicious	lb.	0.73	12/94	82r
Baby food, strained vegetables, lowest price	4-4.5 oz.	0.23	12/94	2c
Bacon, sliced	lb.	1.67	12/94	82r
Bananas	lb.	0.34	12/94	2c
Bananas	lb.	0.42	12/94	82r
Beef or hamburger, ground	lb.	1.25	12/94	2c
Beef purchases	year	213	91	81r
Beverage purchases, alcoholic	year	249	91	81r
Beverage purchases, nonalcoholic	year	207	91	81r
Bologna, all beef or mixed	lb.	2.27	12/94	82r
Bread, white	24-oz.	0.53	12/94	2c
Bread, white, pan	lb.	0.68	12/94	82r
Cabbage	lb.	0.42	12/94	82r
Carrots, short trimmed and topped	lb.	0.53	12/94	82r
Cereals and bakery products purchases	year	345	91	81r
Cereals and cereals products purchases	year	127	91	81r

Values are in dollars or fractions of dollars. In the column headed *Ref*, references are shown to sources. Each reference is followed by a letter. These refer to the geographical level for which data were reported: s=State, r=Region, and c=City or metro. The abbreviation *ex* is used to mean *except* or *excluding*; *exp* stands for expenditures. For other abbreviations and further explanations, please see the Introduction.

Midland, TX - continued

Item	Per	Value	Date	Ref.
Groceries				
Cheddar cheese, natural	lb.	3.58	12/94	82r
Cheese, Kraft grated Parmesan	8-oz.	3.19	12/94	2c
Chicken breast, bone-in	lb.	1.71	12/94	82r
Chicken, fresh, whole	lb.	0.78	12/94	82r
Chicken, whole fryer	lb.	0.57	12/94	2c
Chuck roast, USDA choice, boneless	lb.	2.26	12/94	82r
Cigarettes, Winston, Kings	carton	16.08	12/94	2c
Coffee, vacuum-packed	13 oz.	3.45	12/94	2c
Corn Flakes, Kellogg's or Post Toasties	18 oz.	2.43	12/94	2c
Corn, frozen, whole kernel, lowest price	10 oz.	0.74	12/94	2c
Crackers, soda, salted	lb.	1.27	12/94	82r
Cucumbers	lb.	0.65	12/94	82r
Dairy products (other) purchases	year	141	91	81r
Eggs, Grade A large	dozen	0.64	12/94	2c
Eggs, Grade A large	dozen	0.87	12/94	82r
Fish and seafood purchases	year	72	91	81r
Flour, white, all purpose	lb.	0.23	12/94	82r
Food purchases, food eaten at home	year	2381	91	81r
Foods purchased away from home, not prepared by consumer	year	1696	91	81r
Frankfurters, all meat or all beef	lb.	1.74	12/94	82r
Fruits and vegetables purchases	year	380	91	81r
Grapefruit	lb.	0.45	12/94	82r
Grapes, Thompson seedless	lb.	2.30	12/94	82r
Ground beef, 100% beef	lb.	1.37	12/94	82r
Ground chuck, 100% beef	lb.	1.97	12/94	82r
Ham, boneless, exc. canned	lb.	2.54	12/94	82r
Ice cream, prepackaged, bulk, regular	1/2 gal.	2.47	12/94	82r
Lemons	lb.	1.02	12/94	82r
Lettuce, iceberg	lb.	0.96	12/94	82r
Lettuce, iceberg	head	0.63	12/94	2c
Margarine, Blue Bonnet or Parkay cubes	lb.	0.55	12/94	2c
Margarine, stick	lb.	0.77	12/94	82r
Meats, poultry, fish, and eggs purchases	year	655	91	81r
Milk and cream (fresh) purchases	year	130	91	81r
Milk, whole	1/2 gal.	1.47	12/94	2c
Orange juice, frozen concentrate 12-oz. can	16 oz.	1.36	12/94	82r
Orange juice, Minute Maid frozen	12-oz.	1.09	12/94	2c
Oranges, Navel	lb.	0.54	12/94	82r
Peaches, halves or slices, Hunt's, Del Monte, or Libby's	29-oz.	1.36	12/94	2c
Pears, Anjou	lb.	0.81	12/94	82r
Peas, sweet, Del Monte or Green Giant	15-17 oz.	0.41	12/94	2c
Pork chops, center cut, bone-in	lb.	3.07	12/94	82r
Pork purchases	year	142	91	81r
Potato chips	16-oz.	3.15	12/94	82r
Potatoes, frozen, French fried	lb.	0.82	12/94	82r
Potatoes, white	lb.	0.34	12/94	82r
Potatoes, white or red	10-lb. sack	1.99	12/94	2c
Rice, white, long grain, uncooked	lb.	0.48	12/94	82r
Round roast, USDA choice, boneless	lb.	2.91	12/94	82r
Sausage, fresh	lb.	1.82	12/94	82r
Sausage, Jimmy Dean, 100% pork	lb.	2.19	12/94	2c
Shortening, vegetable oil blends	lb.	0.75	12/94	82r
Shortening, vegetable, Crisco	3-lb.	2.09	12/94	2c
Soft drink, Coca Cola, ex deposit	2 lit	1.59	12/94	2c
Spaghetti and macaroni	lb.	0.87	12/94	82r
Steak, rib eye, USDA choice, boneless	lb.	6.85	12/94	82r
Steak, round, graded & ungraded, exc. USDA prime & choice	lb.	2.96	12/94	82r
Steak, round, USDA choice, boneless	lb.	3.17	12/94	82r
Steak, sirloin, USDA choice, boneless	lb.	4.12	12/94	82r
Steak, t-bone	lb.	4.26	12/94	2c
Steak, T-bone, USDA choice, bone-in	lb.	5.63	12/94	82r
Sugar and other sweets, eaten at home, expenditures	year	93	91	81r
Sugar, cane or beet	4 lbs.	1.13	12/94	2c
Sugar, white, all sizes	lb.	0.39	12/94	82r

Midland, TX - continued

Item	Per	Value	Date	Ref.
Groceries - continued				
Tobacco products and smoking supplies, total expenditures	year	286	91	81r
Tomatoes, field grown	lb.	1.36	12/94	82r
Tomatoes, Hunt's or Del Monte	14.5 oz.	0.78	12/94	2c
Tuna, chunk, light	lb.	1.94	12/94	82r
Tuna, chunk, light, oil-packed	6.125-6.5 oz.	0.65	12/94	2c
Turkey, frozen, whole	lb.	0.96	12/94	82r
Yogurt, natural, fruit flavored	8 oz.	0.58	12/94	82r
Goods and Services				
Miscellaneous goods and services, ACCRA Index		99.00	12/94	2c
Health Care				
Health care, ACCRA Index		101.40	12/94	2c
Adenosine, emergency room	treat	100.00	95	23r
Antibiotic ointment, Polysporin	1.5 oz.	4.07	12/94	2c
Bladder tap, superpubic, infant, emergency room	treat	119.00	95	23r
Blood analysis, emergency room	treat	25.00	95	23r
Blood tests, abdominal pain, emergency room	treat	25.00	95	23r
Burn dressing, emergency room	treat	266.00	95	23r
Cardiology interpretation, emergency room	treat	26.00	95	23r
Chest X-ray, emergency room	treat	78.00	95	23r
Childbirth, Cesarean delivery, hospital charge	birth	5462.00	12/91	69r
Childbirth, Cesarean delivery, physician charge	birth	2228.00	12/91	69r
Childbirth, normal delivery, hospital charge	birth	2943.00	12/91	69r
Childbirth, normal delivery, physician charge	birth	1619.00	12/91	69r
Defibrillation pads, emergency room	treat	6.00	95	23r
Dentist's fee, adult teeth cleaning and periodic oral exam	visit	58.44	12/94	2c
Doctor's fee, routine exam, established patient	visit	42.77	12/94	2c
Drugs, expenditures	year	297	91	81r
Gastric tube insertion, nasal, emergency room	treat	25.00	95	23r
Health care, total expenditures	year	1600	91	81r
Health insurance expenditures	year	637	91	81r
Heart monitor, emergency room	treat	40.00	95	23r
Hospital care, semiprivate room	day	294.50	12/94	2c
Insurance premium, family medical care	month	389.25	1/95	41s
Intravenous fluids, emergency room	treat	130.00	95	23r
Intravenous fluids, emergency room	liter	26.00	95	23r
Intravenous line, central, emergency room	treat	342.00	95	23r
Liver function tests, abdominal pain, emergency room	treat	26.00	95	23r
Medical care charges, total, emergency room, third-degree burns	treat	2101.00	95	23r
Medical care charges, total, emergency, infant with fever	treat	628.00	95	23r
Medical services expenditures	year	573	91	81r
Medical supplies expenditures	year	93	91	81r
Morphine, emergency room	treat	34.00	95	23r
Nursing care and facilities charges, emergency room	treat	252.00	95	23r
Nursing care and facilities charges, emergency, infant with fever	treat	252.00	95	23r
Nursing care and facilities charges, emergency, third-degree burns	treat	861.00	95	23r
Physician's charges, emergency, infant with fever	treat	212.00	95	23r
Physician's charges, emergency, third-degree burns	treat	372.00	95	23r
Physician's fee, emergency room	treat	372.00	95	23r
Physician's fee, general practitioner	visit	51.20	12/93	60r
Surgery, open-heart	proc	42374.00	1/93	14r
Ultrasound, abdominal, emergency room	treat	276.00	95	23r
Urinalysis, emergency room	treat	20.00	95	23r

Values are in dollars or fractions of dollars. In the column headed *Ref*, references are shown to sources. Each reference is followed by a letter. These refer to the geographical level for which data were reported: s=State, r=Region, and c=City or metro. The abbreviation *ex* is used to mean *except* or *excluding*; *exp* stands for *expenditures*. For other abbreviations and further explanations, please see the Introduction.

Midland, TX - continued

Item	Per	Value	Date	Ref.
Health Care				
Urinalysis, infant, emergency room	treat	20.00	95	23r
X-rays, emergency room	treat	78.00	95	23r
Household Goods				
Appl. repair, service call, wash mach	min. lab. chg.	35.00	12/94	2c
Floor coverings, expenditures	year	48	91	81r
Furniture, expenditures	year	280	91	81r
Household equipment, misc. expenditures	year	342	91	81r
Household expenditures, miscellaneous	year	256	91	81r
Household furnishings and equipment, expenditures	year	988	91	81r
Household operations expenditures	year	468	91	81r
Household textiles, expenditures	year	95	91	81r
Housekeeping supplies, expenditures	year	380	91	81r
Laundry and cleaning supplies, expenditures	year	109	91	81r
Laundry detergent, Tide Ultra, Bold, or Cheer	42 oz.	2.89	12/94	2c
Postage and stationery, expenditures	year	105	91	81r
Tissues, facial, Kleenex brand	175	0.91	12/94	2c
Housing				
Housing, ACCRA Index		79.80	12/94	2c
Add garage/carport		6,980	3/95	74r
Add room(s)		11,403	3/95	74r
Apartment condominium or co-op, median	unit	68600	12/94	62r
Dwellings (owned), expenditures	year	2428	91	81r
Enclose porch/patio/breezeway		4,572	3/95	74r
Finish room in basement/attic		3,794	3/95	74r
Home, existing, single-family, median	unit	120200	12/94	62r
House payment, principal and interest, 25% down payment	mo.	598	12/94	2c
House, 1800 sq ft, 8000 sq ft lot, new, urban, utilities	total	96667	12/94	2c
Maintenance, repairs, insurance, and other housing expenditures	year	531	91	81r
Mortgage interest and charges expenditures	year	1506	91	81r
Mtge. rate, incl. points and orig. fee, 30-year conv. fixed or ARM	mo.	9.27	12/94	2c
Princ. & int., mortgage, median-price exist. sing.-family home	mo.	540	12/94	62r
Property taxes expenditures	year	391	91	81r
Redesign, restructure more than half of home's interior		17,641	3/95	74r
Rent, apartment, 2 br., 1 1/2-2 baths, unfurnished, 950 sq ft, water	mo.	461	12/94	2c
Rental units expenditures	year	1264	91	81r
Insurance and Pensions				
Auto insurance, private passenger	year	785.78	12/94	71s
Insurance and pensions, personal, expenditures	year	2395	91	81r
Insurance, life and other personal, expenditures	year	368	91	81r
Pensions and Social Security, expenditures	year	2027	91	81r
Personal Goods				
Shampoo, Alberto VO5	15-oz.	0.98	12/94	2c
Toothpaste, Crest or Colgate	6-7 oz.	2.45	12/94	2c
Personal Services				
Dry cleaning, man's 2-pc. suit		6.31	12/94	2c
Haircut, man's barbershop, no styling		7.39	12/94	2c
Haircut, woman's shampoo, trim, blow-dry		23.75	12/94	2c
Personal services expenditures	year	212	91	81r
Restaurant Food				
Chicken, fried, thigh and drumstick		2.13	12/94	2c
Dining expenditures, family	week	33.83	94	73r
Hamburger with cheese	1/4 lb.	1.94	12/94	2c
Pizza, Pizza Hut or Pizza Inn	12-13 in.	8.79	12/94	2c

Midland, TX - continued

Item	Per	Value	Date	Ref.
Taxes				
Tax, cigarettes	year	584.00	10/93	43s
Taxes, Federal income, expenditures	year	2275	91	81r
Taxes, personal, expenditures	year	2715	91	81r
Taxes, State and local income, expenditures	year	365	91	81r
Transportation				
Transportation, ACCRA Index		101.60	12/94	2c
Cars and trucks purchased, new	year	1306	91	81r
Cars and trucks purchased, used	year	942	91	81r
Driver's learning permit fee	perm	5.00	1/94	84s
Driver's license fee	orig	16.00	1/94	84s
Driver's license fee, duplicate	lic	10.00	1/94	84s
Driver's license reinstatement fee, min.	susp	50.00	1/94	85s
Driver's license renewal fee	renew	16.00	1/94	84s
Identification card, nondriver	card	10.00	1/94	83s
Motorcycle learning permit fee	perm	5.00	1/94	84s
Motorcycle license fee	orig	16.00	1/94	84s
Motorcycle license fee, duplicate	lic	10.00	1/94	84s
Motorcycle license renewal fee	renew	21.00	1/94	84s
Public transportation expenditures	year	249	91	81r
Tire balance, computer or spin bal., front	wheel	6.24	12/94	2c
Transportation expenditures, total	year	5307	91	81r
Vehicle finance charges	year	346	91	81r
Vehicle insurance expenditures	year	544	91	81r
Vehicle maintenance and repairs expenditures	year	600	91	81r
Vehicle purchases	year	2275	91	81r
Vehicle rental, leases, licenses, etc. expenditures	year	141	91	81r
Vehicles purchased, other than cars and trucks	year	27	91	81r
Utilities				
Utilities, ACCRA Index		126.60	12/94	2c
Electricity expenditures	year	950	91	81r
Electricity, (part.), other, 1800 sq. ft., new home	mo.	111.90	12/94	2c
Utilities, fuels, and public services, total expenditures	year	2000	91	81r
Water and other public services, expenditures	year	227	91	81r
Weddings				
Bridal attendants' gowns	event	750	10/93	76r
Bridal gown	event	852	10/93	76r
Bridal headpiece and veil	event	167	10/93	76r
Bride's wedding band	event	708	10/93	76r
Clergy	event	224	10/93	76r
Engagement ring	event	2756	10/93	76r
Flowers	event	863	10/93	76r
Formal wear for groom	event	106	10/93	76r
Groom's attendants' formal wear	event	530	10/93	76r
Groom's wedding band	event	402	10/93	76r
Music	event	600	10/93	76r
Photography	event	1088	10/93	76r
Shoes for bride	event	50	10/93	76r
Videography	event	483	10/93	76r
Wedding invitations and announcements	event	342	10/93	76r
Wedding reception	event	7000	10/93	76r

Milwaukee, WI

Item	Per	Value	Date	Ref.
Appliances				
Appliances (major), expenditures	year	162	91	81c
Appliances (major), expenditures	year	131	91	81r
Average annual exp.				
Food, health care, personal goods, services	year	27843	91	81c
Food, health care, personal goods, services	year	25935	91	81r
Charity				
Cash contributions, expenditures	year	673	91	81c
Cash contributions, expenditures	year	745	91	81r

Values are in dollars or fractions of dollars. In the column headed *Ref*, references are shown to sources. Each reference is followed by a letter. These refer to the geographical level for which data were reported: s = State, r = Region, and c = City or metro. The abbreviation *ex* is used to mean *except* or *excluding*; *exp* stands for expenditures. For other abbreviations and further explanations, please see the Introduction.

Milwaukee, WI - continued

Item	Per	Value	Date	Ref.
Clothing				
Apparel, men and boys, total expenditures	year	393	91	81c
Apparel, men and boys, total expenditures	year	332	91	81r
Apparel, women and girls, total expenditures	year	704	91	81c
Apparel, women and girls, total expenditures	year	578	91	81r
Footwear, expenditures	year	219	91	81c
Footwear, expenditures	year	164	91	81r
Shirt, dress, men's	shirt	25.00	1/92	44c
Communications				
Long-distance telephone rate, day, addl. min., 1-10 mi.	min.	0.10	12/93	9s
Long-distance telephone rate, day, initial min., 1-10 mi.	min.	0.15	12/93	9s
Phone line, single, business, field visit	inst	64.65	12/93	9s
Phone line, single, business, no field visit	inst	64.65	12/93	9s
Phone line, single, residence, field visit	inst	33.05	12/93	9s
Phone line, single, residence, no field visit	inst	33.05	12/93	9s
Telephone service, expenditures	year	538	91	81c
Telephone service, expenditures	year	547	91	81r
Telephone, business, addl. line, touch tone	month	1.00	10/91	25c
Telephone, business, connection charges, touch tone	inst	72.28	10/91	25c
Telephone, business, key system line, touch tone	month	41.67	10/91	25c
Telephone, business, PBX line, touch tone	month	41.73	10/91	25c
Telephone, business, single ln., touch tone	month	41.67	10/91	25c
Telephone, business, touch tone, inside wiring maintenance plan	month	1.00	10/91	25c
Telephone, residential, flat rate	mo.	6.00	12/93	8c
Education				
Board, 4-year private college/university	year	2145	8/94	80s
Board, 4-year public college/university	year	1303	8/94	80s
Education, total expenditures	year	613	91	81c
Education, total expenditures	year	394	91	81r
Room, 4-year private college/university	year	1576	8/94	80s
Room, 4-year public college/university	year	1631	8/94	80s
Total cost, 4-year private college/university	year	13902	8/94	80s
Total cost, 4-year public college/university	year	5252	8/94	80s
Tuition, 2-year public college/university, in-state	year	1557	8/94	80s
Tuition, 4-year private college/university, in-state	year	10181	8/94	80s
Tuition, 4-year public college/university, in-state	year	2318	8/94	80s
Energy and Fuels				
Fuel oil and other fuels, expenditures	year	64	91	81c
Fuel oil and other fuels, expenditures	year	83	91	81r
Gas	gal.	1.09	1/92	44c
Gas, cooking, winter, 10 therms	month	10.56	2/94	65c
Gas, cooking, winter, 30 therms	month	22.23	2/94	65c
Gas, cooking, winter, 50 therms	month	29.64	2/94	65c
Gas, heating, winter, 100 therms	month	67.35	2/94	65c
Gas, heating, winter, average use	month	122.55	2/94	65c
Gas, natural, expenditures	year	447	91	81c
Gas, natural, expenditures	year	373	91	81r
Gasoline and motor oil purchased	year	867	91	81c
Gasoline and motor oil purchased	year	1000	91	81r
Gasoline, unleaded midgrade	gallon	1.15	4/93	82r
Gasoline, unleaded premium	gallon	1.23	4/93	82r
Gasoline, unleaded regular	gallon	1.07	4/93	82r
Entertainment				
Entertainment supplies, equipment, and services, misc. expenditures	year	467	91	81c
Entertainment, total expenditures	year	1702	91	81c
Entertainment, total expenditures	year	1356	91	81r
Fees and admissions, expenditures	year	471	91	81c
Fees and admissions, expenditures	year	347	91	81r
Movie ticket, adult	ticket	6.00	1/92	44c
Pets, toys, playground equipment, expenditures	year	340	91	81c

Milwaukee, WI - continued

Item	Per	Value	Date	Ref.
Entertainment - continued				
Pets, toys, playground equipment, expenditures	year	270	91	81r
Reading, expenditures	year	171	91	81c
Reading, expenditures	year	160	91	81r
Televisions, radios, and sound equipment, expenditures	year	424	91	81c
Televisions, radios, and sound equipment, expenditures	year	433	91	81r
Funerals				
Burial, immediate, container provided by funeral home		1268.31	1/95	54r
Cards, acknowledgment		26.12	1/95	54r
Casket, minimum alternative		198.03	1/95	54r
Cosmetology, hair care, etc.		122.19	1/95	54r
Cremation, direct, container provided by funeral home		977.81	1/95	54r
Embalming		334.00	1/95	54r
Funeral, funeral home		321.16	1/95	54r
Funeral, other facility		317.73	1/95	54r
Graveside service		292.48	1/95	54r
Hearse, local		153.20	1/95	54r
Limousine, local		123.52	1/95	54r
Memorial service		356.30	1/95	54r
Service charge, professional, nondeclinable		968.24	1/95	54r
Visitation and viewing		332.66	1/95	54r
Groceries				
Apples, Red Delicious	lb.	0.68	12/94	82r
Bacon, sliced	lb.	1.88	12/94	82r
Bananas	lb.	0.41	12/94	82r
Beef purchases	year	188	91	81c
Beef purchases	year	197	91	81r
Beef, stew, boneless	lb.	2.52	12/94	82r
Beverage purchases, alcoholic	year	373	91	81c
Beverage purchases, alcoholic	year	293	91	81r
Beverage purchases, nonalcoholic	year	234	91	81c
Beverage purchases, nonalcoholic	year	203	91	81r
Bologna, all beef or mixed	lb.	2.12	12/94	82r
Bread, white, pan	lb.	0.76	12/94	82r
Cabbage	lb.	0.44	12/94	82r
Carrots, short trimmed and topped	lb.	0.44	12/94	82r
Cereals and bakery products purchases	year	400	91	81c
Cereals and bakery products purchases	year	347	91	81r
Cereals and cereal products purchases	year	141	91	81c
Cereals and cereals products purchases	year	119	91	81r
Cheddar cheese, natural	lb.	3.28	12/94	82r
Chicken breast, bone-in	lb.	1.61	12/94	82r
Chicken, fresh, whole	lb.	0.89	12/94	82r
Chuck roast, USDA choice, boneless	lb.	2.33	12/94	82r
Coffee, 100%, ground roast, all sizes	lb.	4.28	12/94	82r
Cookies, chocolate chip	lb.	2.72	12/94	82r
Dairy products (other) purchases	year	163	91	81c
Dairy products (other) purchases	year	148	91	81r
Eggs, Grade A large	dozen	0.76	12/94	82r
Fish and seafood purchases	year	57	91	81c
Fish and seafood purchases	year	61	91	81r
Flour, white, all purpose	lb.	0.22	12/94	82r
Food purchases, food eaten at home	year	2518	91	81c
Food purchases, food eaten at home	year	2313	91	81r
Foods purchased away from home, not prepared by consumer	year	1573	91	81c
Foods purchased away from home, not prepared by consumer	year	1709	91	81r
Fruits and vegetables purchases	year	385	91	81c
Fruits and vegetables purchases	year	372	91	81r
Grapefruit	lb.	0.47	12/94	82r
Grapes, Thompson seedless	lb.	2.15	12/94	82r
Ground beef, 100% beef	lb.	1.37	12/94	82r
Ground chuck, 100% beef	lb.	1.81	12/94	82r
Ham, boneless, exc. canned	lb.	2.16	12/94	82r
Ice cream, prepackaged, bulk, regular	1/2 gal.	2.48	12/94	82r

Values are in dollars or fractions of dollars. In the column headed *Ref*, references are shown to sources. Each reference is followed by a letter. These refer to the geographical level for which data were reported: s=State, r=Region, and c=City or metro. The abbreviation *ex* is used to mean *except* or *excluding*; *exp* stands for expenditures. For other abbreviations and further explanations, please see the Introduction.

Milwaukee, WI - continued

Item	Per	Value	Date	Ref.
Groceries				
Lemons	lb.	1.08	12/94	82r
Lettuce, iceberg	lb.	0.81	12/94	82r
Margarine, stick	lb.	0.81	12/94	82r
Meats, poultry, fish, and eggs purchases	year	610	91	81c
Meats, poultry, fish, and eggs purchases	year	591	91	81r
Milk and cream (fresh) purchases	year	140	91	81c
Milk and cream (fresh) purchases	year	132	91	81r
Milk, 2%	gal.	2.10	1/92	44c
Orange juice, frozen concentrate 12-oz. can	16 oz.	1.41	12/94	82r
Oranges, Navel	lb.	0.56	12/94	82r
Peanut butter, creamy, all sizes	lb.	1.81	12/94	82r
Pork chops, center cut, bone-in	lb.	2.76	12/94	82r
Pork purchases	year	128	91	81c
Pork purchases	year	130	91	81r
Potato chips	16-oz.	2.81	12/94	82r
Potatoes, frozen, French fried	lb.	0.83	12/94	82r
Potatoes, white	lb.	0.28	12/94	82r
Rental rate, 2-bedroom apartment	month	600.00	1/92	44c
Round roast, USDA choice, boneless	lb.	2.90	12/94	82r
Shortening, vegetable oil blends	lb.	0.88	12/94	82r
Spaghetti and macaroni	lb.	0.78	12/94	82r
Steak, rib eye, USDA choice, boneless	lb.	6.15	12/94	82r
Steak, round, graded & ungraded, exc. USDA prime & choice	lb.	2.72	12/94	82r
Steak, round, USDA choice, boneless	lb.	3.02	12/94	82r
Steak, sirloin, USDA choice, boneless	lb.	3.85	12/94	82r
Steak, T-bone, USDA choice, bone-in	lb.	5.38	12/94	82r
Sugar and other sweets, eaten at home, expenditures	year	91	91	81r
Sugar and other sweets, eaten at home, purchases	year	97	91	81c
Sugar, white, all sizes	lb.	0.36	12/94	82r
Tobacco products and smoking supplies, total expenditures	year	230	91	81c
Tobacco products and smoking supplies, total expenditures	year	298	91	81r
Tomatoes, field grown	lb.	1.36	12/94	82r
Tuna, chunk, light	lb.	1.94	12/94	82r
Turkey, frozen, whole	lb.	0.96	12/94	82r
Yogurt, natural, fruit flavored	8 oz.	0.62	12/94	82r
Health Care				
Childbirth, Cesarean delivery, hospital charge	birth	5101.00	12/91	69r
Childbirth, Cesarean delivery, physician charge	birth	2234.00	12/91	69r
Childbirth, normal delivery, hospital charge	birth	2891.00	12/91	69r
Childbirth, normal delivery, physician charge	birth	1623.00	12/91	69r
Drugs, expenditures	year	181	91	81c
Drugs, expenditures	year	248	91	81r
Health care, total expenditures	year	1228	91	81c
Health care, total expenditures	year	1336	91	81r
Health insurance expenditures	year	553	91	81c
Health insurance expenditures	year	550	91	81r
Insurance premium, family medical care	month	378.79	1/95	41s
Medical services expenditures	year	414	91	81c
Medical services expenditures	year	457	91	81r
Medical supplies expenditures	year	80	91	81c
Medical supplies expenditures	year	82	91	81r
Household Goods				
Floor coverings, expenditures	year	53	91	81c
Floor coverings, expenditures	year	105	91	81r
Furniture, expenditures	year	364	91	81c
Furniture, expenditures	year	291	91	81r
Household equipment, misc. expenditures	year	341	91	81r
Household equipment, misc., expenditures	year	435	91	81c
Household expenditures, miscellaneous	year	130	91	81c
Household expenditures, miscellaneous	year	162	91	81r
Household furnishings and equipment, expenditures	year	1189	91	81c
Household furnishings and equipment, expenditures	year	1042	91	81r

Milwaukee, WI - continued

Item	Per	Value	Date	Ref.
Household Goods - continued				
Household operations expenditures	year	251	91	81c
Household operations expenditures	year	365	91	81r
Household textiles, expenditures	year	77	91	81c
Household textiles, expenditures	year	101	91	81r
Housekeeping supplies, expenditures	year	479	91	81c
Housekeeping supplies, expenditures	year	390	91	81r
Laundry and cleaning supplies, expenditures	year	140	91	81c
Laundry and cleaning supplies, expenditures	year	110	91	81r
Postage and stationery, expenditures	year	134	91	81c
Postage and stationery, expenditures	year	115	91	81r
Housing				
Add garage/carport		8,479	3/95	74r
Add room(s)		21,347	3/95	74r
Apartment condominium or co-op, median	unit	87100	12/94	62r
Bathroom addition, average cost	add	9734.00	3/95	13r
Bathroom remodeling, average cost	remod	6414.00	3/95	13r
Bedroom, master suite addition, average cost	add	27122.00	3/95	13r
Deck addition, average cost	add	6665.00	3/95	13r
Dwellings (owned), expenditures	year	3471	91	81c
Dwellings (owned), expenditures	year	2566	91	81r
Enclose porch/patio/breezeway		4,556	3/95	74r
Exterior remodeling, average cost	remod	15395.00	3/95	13r
Family room addition, average cost	add	27658.00	3/95	13r
Finish room in basement/attic		5,074	3/95	74r
Home, existing, single-family, median	unit	106500	12/94	62r
Home, existing, single-family, median	unit	106.60	12/94	62c
Home, purchase price	unit	129.50	3/93	26c
Kitchen remodeling, major, average cost	remod	17084.00	3/95	13r
Kitchen remodeling, minor, average cost	remod	5804.00	3/95	13r
Maintenance, repairs, insurance, and other housing expenditures	year	532	91	81c
Maintenance, repairs, insurance, and other housing expenditures	year	484	91	81r
Mortgage interest and charges expenditures	year	1522	91	81c
Mortgage interest and charges expenditures	year	1443	91	81r
Office, home addition, average cost	add	8121.00	3/95	13r
Princ. & int., mortgage, median-price exist. sing.-family home	mo.	515	12/94	62r
Property taxes expenditures	year	1417	91	81c
Property taxes expenditures	year	639	91	81r
Redesign, restructure more than half of home's interior		9,114	3/95	74r
Rental units expenditures	year	1737	900/00/ 91	81c
Rental units expenditures	year	1200	91	81r
Sun-space addition, average cost	add	23768.00	3/95	13r
Wing addition, two-story, average cost	add	50410.00	3/95	13r
Insurance and Pensions				
Auto insurance, private passenger	year	554.10	12/94	71s
Insurance and pensions, personal, expenditures	year	2358	91	81c
Insurance and pensions, personal, expenditures	year	2408	91	81r
Insurance, life and other personal, expenditures	year	245	91	81c
Insurance, life and other personal, expenditures	year	355	91	81r
Pensions and Social Security, expenditures	year	2112	91	81c
Pensions and Social Security, expenditures	year	2053	91	81r
Legal Assistance				
Legal work, law firm associate	hour	90		10r
Legal work, law firm partner	hour	139		10r
Personal Goods				
Personal care products and services, total expenditures	year	379	91	81c

Values are in dollars or fractions of dollars. In the column headed *Ref*, references are shown to sources. Each reference is followed by a letter. These refer to the geographical level for which data were reported: s=State, r=Region, and c=City or metro. The abbreviation *ex* is used to mean *except* or *excluding*; *exp* stands for expenditures. For other abbreviations and further explanations, please see the Introduction.

Milwaukee, WI - continued

Item	Per	Value	Date	Ref.
Personal Services				
Dry cleaning, woman's dress	dress	7.50	1/92	44c
Personal services expenditures	year	121	91	81c
Personal services expenditures	year	203	91	81r
Restaurant Food				
Big Mac, small fries, medium drink	meal	3.00	1/92	44c
Dining expenditures, family	week	30.03	94	73r
Taxes				
Tax rate, residential property, month	$100	3.83	1/92	79c
Taxes, Federal income, expenditures	year	1232	91	81c
Taxes, Federal income, expenditures	year	1756	91	81r
Taxes, personal, expenditures	year	1764	91	81c
Taxes, personal, expenditures	year	2426	91	81r
Taxes, State and local income, expenditures	year	510	91	81c
Taxes, State and local income, expenditures	year	568	91	81r
Transportation				
Bus fare, one-way	trip	1.03	12/95	1c
Cars and trucks purchased, new	year	1076	91	81c
Cars and trucks purchased, new	year	891	91	81r
Cars and trucks purchased, used	year	833	91	81c
Cars and trucks purchased, used	year	1155	91	81r
Driver's learning permit fee	perm	20.00	1/94	84s
Driver's license fee	orig	10.00	1/94	84s
Driver's license fee, duplicate	lic	4.00	1/94	84s
Driver's license reinstatement fee, min.	susp	50.00	1/94	85s
Driver's license renewal fee	renew	10.00	1/94	84s
Identification card, nondriver	card	4.00	1/94	83s
Motorcycle license fee	orig	4.00	1/94	84s
Motorcycle license fee, duplicate	lic	4.00	1/94	84s
Motorcycle license renewal fee	renew	4.00	1/94	84s
parking, long-term lot, airport	3 days	9.00	1/92	44c
Public transportation expenditures	year	288	91	81c
Public transportation expenditures	year	209	91	81r
Transportation expenditures, total	year	4622	91	81c
Transportation expenditures, total	year	4792	91	81r
Vehicle expenses, miscellaneous	year	1529	91	81c
Vehicle finance charges	year	259	91	81c
Vehicle finance charges	year	300	91	81r
Vehicle insurance expenditures	year	439	91	81c
Vehicle insurance expenditures	year	485	91	81r
Vehicle maintenance and repairs expenditures	year	603	91	81c
Vehicle maintenance and repairs expenditures	year	534	91	81r
Vehicle purchases	year	1937	91	81c
Vehicle purchases	year	2068	91	81r
Vehicle rental, leases, licenses, etc. expenditures	year	228	91	81c
Vehicle rental, leases, licenses, etc. expenditures	year	197	91	81r
Vehicles purchased, other than cars and trucks	year	28	91	81c
Vehicles purchased, other than cars and trucks	year	22	91	81r
Utilities				
Electricity expenditures	year	502	91	81c
Electricity expenditures	year	668	91	81r
Electricity, summer, 250 KWh	month	20.73	8/93	64c
Electricity, summer, 500 KWh	month	37.95	8/93	64c
Electricity, summer, 750 KWh	month	55.18	8/93	64c
Electricity, summer, 1000 KWh	month	59.93	8/93	64c
Utilities, fuels, and public services, total expenditures	year	1658	91	81c
Utilities, fuels, and public services, total expenditures	year	1838	91	81r
Water and other public services, expenditures	year	106	91	81c
Water and other public services, expenditures	year	167	91	81r

Milwaukee, WI - continued

Item	Per	Value	Date	Ref.
Weddings				
Bridal attendants' gowns	event	750	10/93	76r
Bridal gown	event	852	10/93	76r
Bridal headpiece and veil	event	167	10/93	76r
Bride's wedding band	event	708	10/93	76r
Clergy	event	224	10/93	76r
Engagement ring	event	2756	10/93	76r
Flowers	event	863	10/93	76r
Formal wear for groom	event	106	10/93	76r
Groom's attendants' formal wear	event	530	10/93	76r
Groom's wedding band	event	402	10/93	76r
Music	event	600	10/93	76r
Photography	event	1088	10/93	76r
Shoes for bride	event	50	10/93	76r
Videography	event	483	10/93	76r
Wedding invitations and announcements	event	342	10/93	76r
Wedding reception	event	7000	10/93	76r

Minneapolis-Saint Paul, MN

Item	Per	Value	Date	Ref.
Composite, ACCRA index		101.50	12/94	2c
Alcoholic Beverages				
Beer, Miller Lite, Bud, 12-oz., ex deposit	6	3.91	12/94	2c
J & B Scotch	750-ml.	16.39	12/94	2c
Wine, Gallo Chablis blanc	1.5-lit	6.59	12/94	2c
Appliances				
Appliances (major), expenditures	year	118	91	81c
Appliances (major), expenditures	year	131	91	81r
Average annual exp.				
Food, health care, personal goods, services	year	34801	91	81c
Food, health care, personal goods, services	year	25935	91	81r
Business				
Dinner and tip, hotel, corporate rate	night	31.00	2/94	15c
Hotel room, corporate rate	night	78.00	2/94	15c
Charity				
Cash contributions, expenditures	year	1194	91	81c
Cash contributions, expenditures	year	745	91	81r
Child Care				
Child care, for-profit daycare center	week	120.00	12/94	28c
Clothing				
Apparel, men and boys, total expenditures	year	453	91	81c
Apparel, men and boys, total expenditures	year	332	91	81r
Apparel, women and girls, total expenditures	year	872	91	81c
Apparel, women and girls, total expenditures	year	578	91	81r
Footwear, expenditures	year	221	91	81c
Footwear, expenditures	year	164	91	81r
Jeans, man's denim		28.99	12/94	2c
Shirt, man's dress shirt		34.79	12/94	2c
Undervest, boy's size 10-14, cotton	3	4.69	12/94	2c
Communications				
Long-distance telephone rate, day, addl. min., 1-10 mi.	min.	0.05	12/93	9s
Long-distance telephone rate, day, initial min., 1-10 mi.	min.	0.14	12/93	9s
Newspaper subscription, dly. and Sun. delivery	month	14.35	12/94	2c
Phone line, single, business, field visit	inst	45.00	12/93	9s
Phone line, single, business, no field visit	inst	45.00	12/93	9s
Phone line, single, residence, field visit	inst	16.25	12/93	9s
Phone line, single, residence, no field visit	inst	16.25	12/93	9s
Telephone bill, family of four	month	20.74	12/94	2c
Telephone service, expenditures	year	524	91	81c
Telephone service, expenditures	year	547	91	81r
Education				
Board, 4-year private college/university	year	2070	8/94	80s
Board, 4-year public college/university	year	1545	8/94	80s
Education, total expenditures	year	602	91	81c

Values are in dollars or fractions of dollars. In the column headed *Ref*, references are shown to sources. Each reference is followed by a letter. These refer to the geographical level for which data were reported: s=State, r=Region, and c=City or metro. The abbreviation *ex* is used to mean *except* or *excluding*; *exp* stands for expenditures. For other abbreviations and further explanations, please see the Introduction.

Minneapolis-Saint Paul, MN - continued

Item	Per	Value	Date	Ref.
Education				
Education, total expenditures	year	394	91	81r
Living expenses, personal miscellaneous, university student	year	4200.00	5/96	22s
Room, 4-year private college/university	year	1894	8/94	80s
Room, 4-year public college/university	year	1580	8/94	80s
Total cost, 4-year private college/university	year	15556	8/94	80s
Total cost, 4-year public college/university	year	5904	8/94	80s
Tuition, 2-year public college/university, in-state	year	1858	8/94	80s
Tuition, 4-year private college/university, in-state	year	11592	8/94	80s
Tuition, 4-year public college/university, in-state	year	2780	8/94	80s
Energy and Fuels				
Energy, combined forms, 1800 sq. ft.	mo.	97.42	12/94	2c
Energy, exc. electricity, 1800 sq. ft.	mo.	48.14	12/94	2c
Fuel oil and other fuels, expenditures	year	64	91	81c
Fuel oil and other fuels, expenditures	year	83	91	81r
Gas, cooking, 10 therms	month	9.92	2/94	65c
Gas, cooking, 30 therms	month	19.52	2/94	65c
Gas, cooking, 50 therms	month	29.12	2/94	65c
Gas, heating, winter, 100 therms	month	53.12	2/94	65c
Gas, heating, winter, average use	month	84.02	2/94	65c
Gas, natural, expenditures	year	363	91	81c
Gas, natural, expenditures	year	373	91	81r
Gas, reg unlead, taxes inc., cash, self-service	gal	1.15	12/94	2c
Gasoline and motor oil purchased	year	1146	91	81c
Gasoline and motor oil purchased	year	1000	91	81r
Gasoline, unleaded midgrade	gallon	1.15	4/93	82r
Gasoline, unleaded premium	gallon	1.23	4/93	82r
Gasoline, unleaded regular	gallon	1.07	4/93	82r
Entertainment				
Bowling, evening rate	game	2.04	12/94	2c
Entertainment supplies, equipment, and services, misc. expenditures	year	392	91	81c
Entertainment, total expenditures	year	1605	91	81c
Entertainment, total expenditures	year	1356	91	81r
Fees and admissions, expenditures	year	493	91	81c
Fees and admissions, expenditures	year	347	91	81r
Monopoly game, Parker Brothers', No. 9	game	11.19	12/94	2c
Movie	adm	6.30	12/94	2c
Pets, toys, playground equipment, expenditures	year	269	91	81c
Pets, toys, playground equipment, expenditures	year	270	91	81r
Reading, expenditures	year	232	91	81c
Reading, expenditures	year	160	91	81r
Televisions, radios, and sound equipment, expenditures	year	450	91	81c
Televisions, radios, and sound equipment, expenditures	year	433	91	81r
Tennis balls, yellow, Wilson or Penn, 3	can	2.63	12/94	2c
Funerals				
Burial, immediate, container provided by funeral home		1348.78	1/95	54r
Cards, acknowledgment		21.20	1/95	54r
Casket, minimum alternative		182.83	1/95	54r
Cosmetology, hair care, etc.		133.11	1/95	54r
Cremation, direct, container provided by funeral home		1101.95	1/95	54r
Embalming		314.45	1/95	54r
Funeral, funeral home		304.88	1/95	54r
Funeral, other facility		301.37	1/95	54r
Graveside service		290.59	1/95	54r
Hearse, local		137.37	1/95	54r
Limousine, local		82.84	1/95	54r
Memorial service		316.57	1/95	54r
Service charge, professional, nondeclinable		1099.00	1/95	54r
Visitation and viewing		209.25	1/95	54r

Minneapolis-Saint Paul, MN - continued

Item	Per	Value	Date	Ref.
Groceries				
Groceries, ACCRA Index		99.20	12/94	2c
Apples, Red Delicious	lb.	0.68	12/94	82r
Baby food, strained vegetables, lowest price	4-4.5 oz.	0.39	12/94	2c
Bacon, sliced	lb.	1.88	12/94	82r
Bananas	lb.	0.41	12/94	2c
Bananas	lb.	0.41	12/94	82r
Beef or hamburger, ground	lb.	1.19	12/94	2c
Beef purchases	year	232	91	81c
Beef purchases	year	197	91	81r
Beef, stew, boneless	lb.	2.52	12/94	82r
Beverage purchases, alcoholic	year	529	91	81c
Beverage purchases, alcoholic	year	293	91	81r
Beverage purchases, nonalcoholic	year	261	91	81c
Beverage purchases, nonalcoholic	year	203	91	81r
Bologna, all beef or mixed	lb.	2.12	12/94	82r
Bread, white	24-oz.	0.69	12/94	2c
Bread, white, pan	lb.	0.76	12/94	82r
Cabbage	lb.	0.44	12/94	82r
Carrots, short trimmed and topped	lb.	0.44	12/94	82r
Cereals and bakery products purchases	year	434	91	81c
Cereals and bakery products purchases	year	347	91	81r
Cereals and cereal products purchases	year	152	91	81c
Cereals and cereals products purchases	year	119	91	81r
Cheddar cheese, natural	lb.	3.28	12/94	82r
Cheese, Kraft grated Parmesan	8-oz.	3.19	12/94	2c
Chicken breast, bone-in	lb.	1.61	12/94	82r
Chicken, fresh, whole	lb.	0.89	12/94	82r
Chicken, whole fryer	lb.	0.86	12/94	2c
Chuck roast, USDA choice, boneless	lb.	2.33	12/94	82r
Cigarettes, Winston, Kings	carton	20.38	12/94	2c
Coffee, 100%, ground roast, all sizes	lb.	4.28	12/94	82r
Coffee, vacuum-packed	13 oz.	3.32	12/94	2c
Cookies, chocolate chip	lb.	2.72	12/94	82r
Corn Flakes, Kellogg's or Post Toasties	18 oz.	1.89	12/94	2c
Corn, frozen, whole kernel, lowest price	10 oz.	0.64	12/94	2c
Dairy products (other) purchases	year	188	91	81c
Dairy products (other) purchases	year	148	91	81r
Eggs, Grade A large	dozen	0.68	12/94	2c
Eggs, Grade A large	dozen	0.76	12/94	82r
Fish and seafood purchases	year	72	91	81c
Fish and seafood purchases	year	61	91	81r
Flour, white, all purpose	lb.	0.22	12/94	82r
Food purchases, food eaten at home	year	2849	91	81c
Food purchases, food eaten at home	year	2313	91	81r
Foods purchased away from home, not prepared by consumer	year	2034	91	81c
Foods purchased away from home, not prepared by consumer	year	1709	91	81r
Fruits and vegetables purchases	year	444	91	81c
Fruits and vegetables purchases	year	372	91	81r
Grapefruit	lb.	0.47	12/94	82r
Grapes, Thompson seedless	lb.	2.15	12/94	82r
Ground beef, 100% beef	lb.	1.37	12/94	82r
Ground chuck, 100% beef	lb.	1.81	12/94	82r
Ham, boneless, exc. canned	lb.	2.16	12/94	82r
Ice cream, prepackaged, bulk, regular	1/2 gal.	2.48	12/94	82r
Lemons	lb.	1.08	12/94	82r
Lettuce, iceberg	lb.	0.81	12/94	82r
Lettuce, iceberg	head	0.85	12/94	2c
Margarine, Blue Bonnet or Parkay cubes	lb.	0.64	12/94	2c
Margarine, stick	lb.	0.81	12/94	82r
Meats, poultry, fish, and eggs purchases	year	653	91	81c
Meats, poultry, fish, and eggs purchases	year	591	91	81r
Milk and cream (fresh) purchases	year	156	91	81c
Milk and cream (fresh) purchases	year	132	91	81r
Milk, whole	1/2 gal.	1.42	12/94	2c
Orange juice, frozen concentrate 12-oz. can	16 oz.	1.41	12/94	82r
Orange juice, Minute Maid frozen	12-oz.	1.24	12/94	2c
Oranges, Navel	lb.	0.56	12/94	82r

Values are in dollars or fractions of dollars. In the column headed *Ref*, references are shown to sources. Each reference is followed by a letter. These refer to the geographical level for which data were reported: s=State, r=Region, and c=City or metro. The abbreviation *ex* is used to mean *except* or *excluding*; *exp* stands for *expenditures*. For other abbreviations and further explanations, please see the Introduction.

Minneapolis-Saint Paul, MN - continued

Item	Per	Value	Date	Ref.
Groceries				
Peaches, halves or slices, Hunt's, Del Monte, or Libby's	29-oz.	1.28	12/94	2c
Peanut butter, creamy, all sizes	lb.	1.81	12/94	82r
Peas, sweet, Del Monte or Green Giant	15-17 oz.	0.48	12/94	2c
Pork chops, center cut, bone-in	lb.	2.76	12/94	82r
Pork purchases	year	134	91	81c
Pork purchases	year	130	91	81r
Potato chips	16-oz.	2.81	12/94	82r
Potatoes, frozen, French fried	lb.	0.83	12/94	82r
Potatoes, white	lb.	0.28	12/94	82r
Potatoes, white or red	10-lb. sack	2.66	12/94	2c
Round roast, USDA choice, boneless	lb.	2.90	12/94	82r
Sausage, Jimmy Dean, 100% pork	lb.	2.92	12/94	2c
Shortening, vegetable oil blends	lb.	0.88	12/94	82r
Shortening, vegetable, Crisco	3-lb.	2.71	12/94	2c
Soft drink, Coca Cola, ex deposit	2 lit	1.03	12/94	2c
Spaghetti and macaroni	lb.	0.78	12/94	82r
Steak, rib eye, USDA choice, boneless	lb.	6.15	12/94	82r
Steak, round, graded & ungraded, exc. USDA prime & choice	lb.	2.72	12/94	82r
Steak, round, USDA choice, boneless	lb.	3.02	12/94	82r
Steak, sirloin, USDA choice, boneless	lb.	3.85	12/94	82r
Steak, t-bone	lb.	5.17	12/94	2c
Steak, T-bone, USDA choice, bone-in	lb.	5.38	12/94	82r
Sugar and other sweets, eaten at home, expenditures	year	91	91	81r
Sugar and other sweets, eaten at home, purchases	year	129	91	81c
Sugar, cane or beet	4 lbs.	1.40	12/94	2c
Sugar, white, all sizes	lb.	0.36	12/94	82r
Tobacco products and smoking supplies, total expenditures	year	357	91	81c
Tobacco products and smoking supplies, total expenditures	year	298	91	81r
Tomatoes, field grown	lb.	1.36	12/94	82r
Tomatoes, Hunt's or Del Monte	14.5 oz.	0.78	12/94	2c
Tuna, chunk, light	lb.	1.94	12/94	82r
Tuna, chunk, light, oil-packed	6.125-6.5 oz.	0.61	12/94	2c
Turkey, frozen, whole	lb.	0.96	12/94	82r
Yogurt, natural, fruit flavored	8 oz.	0.62	12/94	82r
Goods and Services				
Miscellaneous goods and services, ACCRA Index		104.00	12/94	2c
Health Care				
Health care, ACCRA Index		126.20	12/94	2c
Antibiotic ointment, Polysporin	1.5 oz.	3.97	12/94	2c
Childbirth, Cesarean delivery, hospital charge	birth	5101.00	12/91	69r
Childbirth, Cesarean delivery, physician charge	birth	2234.00	12/91	69r
Childbirth, normal delivery, hospital charge	birth	2891.00	12/91	69r
Childbirth, normal delivery, physician charge	birth	1623.00	12/91	69r
Dentist's fee, adult teeth cleaning and periodic oral exam	visit	66.00	12/94	2c
Doctor's fee, routine exam, established patient	visit	50.20	12/94	2c
Drugs, expenditures	year	217	91	81c
Drugs, expenditures	year	248	91	81r
Health care, total expenditures	year	1438	91	81c
Health care, total expenditures	year	1336	91	81r
Health insurance expenditures	year	756	91	81c
Health insurance expenditures	year	550	91	81r
Health insurance premium	month	363.00	7/93	94c
Hospital care, semiprivate room	day	564.10	12/94	2c
Insurance premium, family medical care	month	375.35	1/95	41s
Medical services expenditures	year	336	91	81c
Medical services expenditures	year	457	91	81r

Minneapolis-Saint Paul, MN - continued

Item	Per	Value	Date	Ref.
Health Care - continued				
Medical supplies expenditures	year	129	91	81c
Medical supplies expenditures	year	82	91	81r
Household Goods				
Appl. repair, service call, wash mach	min. lab. chg.	36.66	12/94	2c
Floor coverings, expenditures	year	69	91	81c
Floor coverings, expenditures	year	105	91	81r
Furniture, expenditures	year	271	91	81c
Furniture, expenditures	year	291	91	81r
Household equipment, misc. expenditures	year	341	91	81r
Household equipment, misc., expenditures	year	630	91	81c
Household expenditures, miscellaneous	year	206	91	81c
Household expenditures, miscellaneous	year	162	91	81r
Household furnishings and equipment, expenditures	year	1292	91	81c
Household furnishings and equipment, expenditures	year	1042	91	81r
Household operations expenditures	year	501	91	81c
Household operations expenditures	year	365	91	81r
Household textiles, expenditures	year	109	91	81c
Household textiles, expenditures	year	101	91	81r
Housekeeping supplies, expenditures	year	579	91	81c
Housekeeping supplies, expenditures	year	390	91	81r
Laundry and cleaning supplies, expenditures	year	145	91	81c
Laundry and cleaning supplies, expenditures	year	110	91	81r
Laundry detergent, Tide Ultra, Bold, or Cheer	42 oz.	2.73	12/94	2c
Postage and stationery, expenditures	year	185	91	81c
Postage and stationery, expenditures	year	115	91	81r
Tissues, facial, Kleenex brand	175	0.99	12/94	2c
Housing				
Housing, ACCRA Index		96.40	12/94	2c
Add garage/carport		8,479	3/95	74r
Add room(s)		21,347	3/95	74r
Apartment condominium or co-op, median	unit	87100	12/94	62r
Bathroom addition, average cost	add	9734.00	3/95	13r
Bathroom remodeling, average cost	remod	6414.00	3/95	13r
Bedroom, master suite addition, average cost	add	27122.00	3/95	13r
Car rental	day	52.00	5/95	95c
Deck addition, average cost	add	6665.00	3/95	13r
Dwellings (owned), expenditures	year	4236	91	81c
Dwellings (owned), expenditures	year	2566	91	81r
Enclose porch/patio/breezeway		4,556	3/95	74r
Exterior remodeling, average cost	remod	15395.00	3/95	13r
Family room addition, average cost	add	27658.00	3/95	13r
Finish room in basement/attic		5,074	3/95	74r
Home, existing, single-family, median	unit	106500	12/94	62r
Home, existing, single-family, median	unit	101.40	12/94	62c
Home, purchase price	unit	125.30	3/93	26c
Hotel room	day	128.00	5/95	95c
House payment, principal and interest, 25% down payment	mo.	717	12/94	2c
House, 1800 sq ft, 8000 sq ft lot, new, urban, utilities	total	118987	12/94	2c
Kitchen remodeling, major, average cost	remod	17084.00	3/95	13r
Kitchen remodeling, minor, average cost	remod	5804.00	3/95	13r
Maintenance, repairs, insurance, and other housing expenditures	year	523	91	81c
Maintenance, repairs, insurance, and other housing expenditures	year	484	91	81r
Mortgage interest and charges expenditures	year	2895	91	81c
Mortgage interest and charges expenditures	year	1443	91	81r
Mtge. rate, incl. points and orig. fee, 30-year conv. fixed or ARM	mo.	8.99	12/94	2c
Office, home addition, average cost	add	8121.00	3/95	13r
Princ. & int., mortgage, median-price exist. sing.-family home	mo.	515	12/94	62r

Values are in dollars or fractions of dollars. In the column headed *Ref*, references are shown to sources. Each reference is followed by a letter. These refer to the geographical level for which data were reported: s=State, r=Region, and c=City or metro. The abbreviation *ex* is used to mean *except* or *excluding*; *exp* stands for *expenditures*. For other abbreviations and further explanations, please see the Introduction.

Minneapolis-Saint Paul, MN - continued

Item	Per	Value	Date	Ref.
Housing				
Property taxes expenditures	year	817	91	81c
Property taxes expenditures	year	639	91	81r
Redesign, restructure more than half of home's interior		9,114	3/95	74r
Rent, apartment, 2 br., 1 1/2-2 baths, unfurnished, 950 sq ft, water	mo.	571	12/94	2c
Rental units expenditures	year	1737	900/00/ 91	81c
Rental units expenditures	year	1200	91	81r
Sun-space addition, average cost	add	23768.00	3/95	13r
Wing addition, two-story, average cost	add	50410.00	3/95	13r
Insurance and Pensions				
Auto insurance, private passenger	year	656.87	12/94	71s
Health insurance, HMO plan, cost to employer	year	2969	93	59c
Insurance and pensions, personal, expenditures	year	4374	91	81c
Insurance and pensions, personal, expenditures	year	2408	91	81r
Insurance, life and other personal, expenditures	year	363	91	81c
Insurance, life and other personal, expenditures	year	355	91	81r
Pensions and Social Security, expenditures	year	4011	91	81c
Pensions and Social Security, expenditures	year	2053	91	81r
Legal Assistance				
Legal work, law firm associate	hour	90		10r
Legal work, law firm partner	hour	139		10r
Personal Goods				
Personal care products and services, total expenditures	year	462	91	81c
Shampoo, Alberto VO5	15-oz.	1.27	12/94	2c
Toothpaste, Crest or Colgate	6-7 oz.	1.82	12/94	2c
Personal Services				
Dry cleaning, man's 2-pc. suit		6.84	12/94	2c
Haircut, man's barbershop, no styling		8.59	12/94	2c
Haircut, woman's shampoo, trim, blow-dry		19.80	12/94	2c
Personal services expenditures	year	295	91	81c
Personal services expenditures	year	203	91	81r
Restaurant Food				
Chicken, fried, thigh and drumstick		2.15	12/94	2c
Dining expenditures, family	week	30.03	94	73r
Hamburger with cheese	1/4 lb.	1.89	12/94	2c
Pizza, Pizza Hut or Pizza Inn	12-13 in.	7.59	12/94	2c
Taxes				
Tax rate, residential property, month	$100	1.39	1/92	79c
Tax, cigarettes	year	400.00	10/93	43s
Taxes, Federal income, expenditures	year	3133	91	81c
Taxes, Federal income, expenditures	year	1756	91	81r
Taxes, personal, expenditures	year	4476	91	81c
Taxes, personal, expenditures	year	2426	91	81r
Taxes, State and local income, expenditures	year	1361	91	81c
Taxes, State and local income, expenditures	year	568	91	81r
Transportation				
Transportation, ACCRA Index		106.20	12/94	2c
Bus fare, one-way	trip	1.00	12/95	1c
Bus fare, up to 10 miles	one-way	1.25	12/94	2c
Cars and trucks purchased, new	year	993	91	81c
Cars and trucks purchased, new	year	891	91	81r
Cars and trucks purchased, used	year	1060	91	81c
Cars and trucks purchased, used	year	1155	91	81r
Driver's learning permit fee	perm	6.00	1/94	84s
Driver's license fee	orig	15.00	1/94	84s
Driver's license fee, duplicate	lic	4.50	1/94	84s
Driver's license reinstatement fee, min.	susp	20.00	1/94	85s
Driver's license renewal fee	renew	15.00	1/94	84s

Minneapolis-Saint Paul, MN - continued

Item	Per	Value	Date	Ref.
Transportation - continued				
Fine, illegal parking, handicapped zone	event	100.00	12/93	87c
Identification card, nondriver	card	9.00	1/94	83s
Public transportation expenditures	year	314	91	81c
Public transportation expenditures	year	209	91	81r
Tire balance, computer or spin bal., front	wheel	7.10	12/94	2c
Transportation expenditures, total	year	5665	91	81c
Transportation expenditures, total	year	4792	91	81r
Vehicle expenses, miscellaneous	year	2151	91	81c
Vehicle finance charges	year	336	91	81c
Vehicle finance charges	year	300	91	81r
Vehicle insurance expenditures	year	700	91	81c
Vehicle insurance expenditures	year	485	91	81r
Vehicle maintenance and repairs expenditures	year	804	91	81c
Vehicle maintenance and repairs expenditures	year	534	91	81r
Vehicle purchases	year	2053	91	81c
Vehicle purchases	year	2068	91	81r
Vehicle rental, leases, licenses, etc. expenditures	year	311	91	81c
Vehicle rental, leases, licenses, etc. expenditures	year	197	91	81r
Vehicles purchased, other than cars and trucks	year	22	91	81r
Utilities				
Utilities, ACCRA Index		89.40	12/94	2c
Electricity expenditures	year	579	91	81c
Electricity expenditures	year	668	91	81r
Electricity, (part.), other, 1800 sq. ft., new home	mo.	49.28	12/94	2c
Electricity, summer, 250 KWh	month	21.26	8/93	64c
Electricity, summer, 500 KWh	month	43.07	8/93	64c
Electricity, summer, 750 KWh	month	62.11	8/93	64c
Electricity, summer, 1000 KWh	month	81.16	8/93	64c
Utilities, fuels, and public services, total expenditures	year	1778	91	81c
Utilities, fuels, and public services, total expenditures	year	1838	91	81r
Water and other public services, expenditures	year	249	91	81c
Water and other public services, expenditures	year	167	91	81r
Weddings				
Bridal attendants' gowns	event	750	10/93	76r
Bridal gown	event	852	10/93	76r
Bridal headpiece and veil	event	167	10/93	76r
Bride's wedding band	event	708	10/93	76r
Clergy	event	224	10/93	76r
Engagement ring	event	2756	10/93	76r
Flowers	event	863	10/93	76r
Formal wear for groom	event	106	10/93	76r
Groom's attendants' formal wear	event	530	10/93	76r
Groom's wedding band	event	402	10/93	76r
Music	event	600	10/93	76r
Photography	event	1088	10/93	76r
Shoes for bride	event	50	10/93	76r
Videography	event	483	10/93	76r
Wedding invitations and announcements	event	342	10/93	76r
Wedding reception	event	7000	10/93	76r

Minot, ND

Item	Per	Value	Date	Ref.
Composite, ACCRA index		94.50	12/94	2c
Alcoholic Beverages				
Beer, Miller Lite, Bud, 12-oz., ex deposit	6	4.00	12/94	2c
J & B Scotch	750-ml.	17.31	12/94	2c
Wine, Gallo Chablis blanc	1.5-lit	5.10	12/94	2c

Values are in dollars or fractions of dollars. In the column headed *Ref*, references are shown to sources. Each reference is followed by a letter. These refer to the geographical level for which data were reported: s = State, r = Region, and c = City or metro. The abbreviation *ex* is used to mean *except* or *excluding*; *exp* stands for expenditures. For other abbreviations and further explanations, please see the Introduction.

Minot, ND - continued

Item	Per	Value	Date	Ref.
Clothing				
Jeans, man's denim		38.00	12/94	2c
Shirt, man's dress shirt		25.33	12/94	2c
Undervest, boy's size 10-14, cotton	3	4.70	12/94	2c
Communications				
Newspaper subscription, dly. and Sun. delivery	month	9.25	12/94	2c
Telephone bill, family of four	month	9.57	12/94	2c
Telephone, residential, flat rate	mo.	10.42	12/93	8c
Energy and Fuels				
Energy, combined forms, 1800 sq. ft.	mo.	93.78	12/94	2c
Energy, exc. electricity, 1800 sq. ft.	mo.	45.48	12/94	2c
Gas, reg unlead, taxes inc., cash, self-service	gal	1.25	12/94	2c
Entertainment				
Bowling, evening rate	game	1.75	12/94	2c
Monopoly game, Parker Brothers', No. 9	game	10.94	12/94	2c
Movie	adm	5.50	12/94	2c
Tennis balls, yellow, Wilson or Penn, 3	can	2.12	12/94	2c
Groceries				
Groceries, ACCRA Index		101.40	12/94	2c
Baby food, strained vegetables, lowest price	4-4.5 oz.	0.32	12/94	2c
Bananas	lb.	0.35	12/94	2c
Beef or hamburger, ground	lb.	1.42	12/94	2c
Bread, white	24-oz.	0.69	12/94	2c
Cheese, Kraft grated Parmesan	8-oz.	3.65	12/94	2c
Chicken, whole fryer	lb.	0.84	12/94	2c
Cigarettes, Winston, Kings	carton	18.09	12/94	2c
Coffee, vacuum-packed	13 oz.	3.66	12/94	2c
Corn Flakes, Kellogg's or Post Toasties	18 oz.	2.37	12/94	2c
Corn, frozen, whole kernel, lowest price	10 oz.	0.79	12/94	2c
Eggs, Grade A large	dozen	0.78	12/94	2c
Lettuce, iceberg	head	0.92	12/94	2c
Margarine, Blue Bonnet or Parkay cubes	lb.	0.50	12/94	2c
Milk, whole	1/2 gal.	1.46	12/94	2c
Orange juice, Minute Maid frozen	12-oz.	1.44	12/94	2c
Peaches, halves or slices, Hunt's, Del Monte, or Libby's	29-oz.	1.51	12/94	2c
Peas, sweet, Del Monte or Green Giant	15-17 oz.	0.61	12/94	2c
Potatoes, white or red	10-lb. sack	2.18	12/94	2c
Sausage, Jimmy Dean, 100% pork	lb.	3.29	12/94	2c
Shortening, vegetable, Crisco	3-lb.	2.63	12/94	2c
Soft drink, Coca Cola, ex deposit	2 lit	0.89	12/94	2c
Steak, t-bone	lb.	5.32	12/94	2c
Sugar, cane or beet	4 lbs.	1.50	12/94	2c
Tomatoes, Hunt's or Del Monte	14.5 oz.	0.71	12/94	2c
Tuna, chunk, light, oil-packed	6.125-6.5 oz.	0.68	12/94	2c
Goods and Services				
Miscellaneous goods and services, ACCRA Index		97.60	12/94	2c
Health Care				
Health care, ACCRA Index		81.30	12/94	2c
Antibiotic ointment, Polysporin	1.5 oz.	3.92	12/94	2c
Dentist's fee, adult teeth cleaning and periodic oral exam	visit	39.00	12/94	2c
Doctor's fee, routine exam, established patient	visit	33.67	12/94	2c
Hospital care, semiprivate room	day	315.00	12/94	2c
Household Goods				
Appl. repair, service call, wash mach	min. lab. chg.	23.33	12/94	2c

Minot, ND - continued

Item	Per	Value	Date	Ref.
Household Goods - continued				
Laundry detergent, Tide Ultra, Bold, or Cheer	42 oz.	3.76	12/94	2c
Tissues, facial, Kleenex brand	175	0.99	12/94	2c
Housing				
Housing, ACCRA Index		94.50	12/94	2c
House payment, principal and interest, 25% down payment	mo.	763	12/94	2c
House, 1800 sq ft, 8000 sq ft lot, new, urban, utilities	total	123750	12/94	2c
Mtge. rate, incl. points and orig. fee, 30-year conv. fixed or ARM	mo.	9.24	12/94	2c
Rent, apartment, 2 br., 1 1/2-2 baths, unfurnished, 950 sq ft, water	mo.	387	12/94	2c
Personal Goods				
Shampoo, Alberto VO5	15-oz.	1.52	12/94	2c
Toothpaste, Crest or Colgate	6-7 oz.	2.30	12/94	2c
Personal Services				
Dry cleaning, man's 2-pc. suit		5.62	12/94	2c
Haircut, man's barbershop, no styling		7.63	12/94	2c
Haircut, woman's shampoo, trim, blow-dry		15.50	12/94	2c
Restaurant Food				
Chicken, fried, thigh and drumstick		1.96	12/94	2c
Hamburger with cheese	1/4 lb.	1.89	12/94	2c
Pizza, Pizza Hut or Pizza Inn	12-13 in.	8.49	12/94	2c
Transportation				
Transportation, ACCRA Index		93.90	12/94	2c
Tire balance, computer or spin bal., front	wheel	4.75	12/94	2c
Utilities				
Utilities, ACCRA Index		78.90	12/94	2c
Electricity, (part.), other, 1800 sq. ft., new home	mo.	48.30	12/94	2c

Missoula, MT

Item	Per	Value	Date	Ref.
Composite, ACCRA index		104.00	12/94	2c
Alcoholic Beverages				
Beer, Miller Lite, Bud, 12-oz., ex deposit	6	4.19	12/94	2c
J & B Scotch	750-ml.	18.85	12/94	2c
Wine, Gallo Chablis blanc	1.5-lit	4.84	12/94	2c
Clothing				
Jeans, man's denim		33.21	12/94	2c
Shirt, man's dress shirt		37.50	12/94	2c
Undervest, boy's size 10-14, cotton	3	5.49	12/94	2c
Communications				
Newspaper subscription, dly. and Sun. delivery	month	13.70	12/94	2c
Telephone bill, family of four	month	18.22	12/94	2c
Energy and Fuels				
Energy, combined forms, 1800 sq. ft.	mo.	97.77	12/94	2c
Energy, exc. electricity, 1800 sq. ft.	mo.	53.80	12/94	2c
Gas, cooking, 10 therms	month	8.26	2/94	65c
Gas, cooking, 30 therms	month	16.37	2/94	65c
Gas, cooking, 50 therms	month	24.47	2/94	65c
Gas, heating, winter, 100 therms	month	44.74	2/94	65c
Gas, heating, winter, average use	month	70.05	2/94	65c
Gas, reg unlead, taxes inc., cash, self-service	gal	1.34	12/94	2c
Entertainment				
Bowling, evening rate	game	1.58	12/94	2c
Monopoly game, Parker Brothers', No. 9	game	11.66	12/94	2c
Movie	adm	5.42	12/94	2c
Tennis balls, yellow, Wilson or Penn, 3	can	2.49	12/94	2c

Values are in dollars or fractions of dollars. In the column headed *Ref*, references are shown to sources. Each reference is followed by a letter. These refer to the geographical level for which data were reported: s = State, r = Region, and c = City or metro. The abbreviation *ex* is used to mean *except* or *excluding*; *exp* stands for *expenditures*. For other abbreviations and further explanations, please see the Introduction.

Missoula, MT - continued

Item	Per	Value	Date	Ref.
Groceries				
Groceries, ACCRA Index		107.80	12/94	2c
Baby food, strained vegetables, lowest price	4-4.5 oz.	0.34	12/94	2c
Bananas	lb.	0.61	12/94	2c
Beef or hamburger, ground	lb.	1.58	12/94	2c
Bread, white	24-oz.	0.73	12/94	2c
Cheese, Kraft grated Parmesan	8-oz.	3.83	12/94	2c
Chicken, whole fryer	lb.	1.00	12/94	2c
Cigarettes, Winston, Kings	carton	15.31	12/94	2c
Coffee, vacuum-packed	13 oz.	3.85	12/94	2c
Corn Flakes, Kellogg's or Post Toasties	18 oz.	2.44	12/94	2c
Corn, frozen, whole kernel, lowest price	10 oz.	0.72	12/94	2c
Eggs, Grade A large	dozen	0.91	12/94	2c
Lettuce, iceberg	head	0.98	12/94	2c
Margarine, Blue Bonnet or Parkay cubes	lb.	0.73	12/94	2c
Milk, whole	1/2 gal.	1.45	12/94	2c
Orange juice, Minute Maid frozen	12-oz.	1.40	12/94	2c
Peaches, halves or slices, Hunt's, Del Monte, or Libby's	29-oz.	1.40	12/94	2c
Peas, sweet, Del Monte or Green Giant	15-17 oz.	0.62	12/94	2c
Potatoes, white or red	10-lb. sack	1.99	12/94	2c
Sausage, Jimmy Dean, 100% pork	lb.	3.67	12/94	2c
Shortening, vegetable, Crisco	3-lb.	2.11	12/94	2c
Soft drink, Coca Cola, ex deposit	2 lit	1.24	12/94	2c
Steak, t-bone	lb.	4.89	12/94	2c
Sugar, cane or beet	4 lbs.	1.50	12/94	2c
Tomatoes, Hunt's or Del Monte	14.5 oz.	0.74	12/94	2c
Tuna, chunk, light, oil-packed	6.125-6.5 oz.	0.85	12/94	2c
Goods and Services				
Miscellaneous goods and services, ACCRA Index		106.40	12/94	2c
Health Care				
Health care, ACCRA Index		104.30	12/94	2c
Antibiotic ointment, Polysporin	1.5 oz.	4.23	12/94	2c
Dentist's fee, adult teeth cleaning and periodic oral exam	visit	61.80	12/94	2c
Doctor's fee, routine exam, established patient	visit	37.70	12/94	2c
Hospital care, semiprivate room	day	384.00	12/94	2c
Household Goods				
Appl. repair, service call, wash mach	min. lab. chg.	32.25	12/94	2c
Laundry detergent, Tide Ultra, Bold, or Cheer	42 oz.	3.11	12/94	2c
Tissues, facial, Kleenex brand	175	1.09	12/94	2c
Housing				
Housing, ACCRA Index		103.10	12/94	2c
House payment, principal and interest, 25% down payment	mo.	772	12/94	2c
House, 1800 sq ft, 8000 sq ft lot, new, urban, utilities	total	122588	12/94	2c
Mtge. rate, incl. points and orig. fee, 30-year conv. fixed or ARM	mo.	9.49	12/94	2c
Rent, apartment, 2 br., 1 1/2-2 baths, unfurnished, 950 sq ft, water	mo.	595	12/94	2c
Personal Goods				
Shampoo, Alberto VO5	15-oz.	1.24	12/94	2c
Toothpaste, Crest or Colgate	6-7 oz.	2.53	12/94	2c
Personal Services				
Dry cleaning, man's 2-pc. suit		7.37	12/94	2c
Haircut, man's barbershop, no styling		7.70	12/94	2c
Haircut, woman's shampoo, trim, blow-dry		20.00	12/94	2c

Missoula, MT - continued

Item	Per	Value	Date	Ref.
Restaurant Food				
Chicken, fried, thigh and drumstick		1.98	12/94	2c
Hamburger with cheese	1/4 lb.	1.89	12/94	2c
Pizza, Pizza Hut or Pizza Inn	12-13 in.	9.00	12/94	2c
Transportation				
Transportation, ACCRA Index		105.30	12/94	2c
Bus fare, up to 10 miles	one-way	0.65	12/94	2c
Tire balance, computer or spin bal., front	wheel	6.56	12/94	2c
Utilities				
Utilities, ACCRA Index		88.00	12/94	2c
Electricity, (part.), other, 1800 sq. ft., new home	mo.	43.97	12/94	2c

Mobile, AL

Item	Per	Value	Date	Ref.
Composite, ACCRA index		92.60	12/94	2c
Alcoholic Beverages				
Beer, Miller Lite, Bud, 12-oz., ex deposit	6	4.20	12/94	2c
J & B Scotch	750-ml.	20.99	12/94	2c
Wine, Gallo Chablis blanc	1.5-lit	5.05	12/94	2c
Appliances				
Appliances (major), expenditures	year	153	91	81r
Average annual exp.				
Food, health care, personal goods, services	year	27020	91	81r
Charity				
Cash contributions, expenditures	year	839	91	81r
Clothing				
Apparel, men and boys, total expenditures	year	380	91	81r
Apparel, women and girls, total expenditures	year	660	91	81r
Footwear, expenditures	year	193	91	81r
Jeans, man's denim		27.18	12/94	2c
Shirt, man's dress shirt		28.89	12/94	2c
Undervest, boy's size 10-14, cotton	3	3.78	12/94	2c
Communications				
Long-distance telephone rate, day, addl. min., 1-10 mi.	min.	0.09	12/93	9s
Long-distance telephone rate, day, initial min., 1-10 mi.	min.	0.11	12/93	9s
Newspaper subscription, dly. and Sun. delivery	month	9.05	12/94	2c
Phone line, single, business, field visit	inst	69.00	12/93	9s
Phone line, single, business, no field visit	inst	69.00	12/93	9s
Phone line, single, residence, field visit	inst	40.00	12/93	9s
Phone line, single, residence, no field visit	inst	40.00	12/93	9s
Telephone bill, family of four	month	24.74	12/94	2c
Telephone service, expenditures	year	616	91	81r
Telephone, residential, flat rate	mo.	18.40	12/93	8c
Education				
Board, 4-year private college/university	year	2072	8/94	80s
Board, 4-year public college/university	year	1706	8/94	80s
Education, total expenditures	year	319	91	81r
Room, 4-year private college/university	year	1607	8/94	80s
Room, 4-year public college/university	year	1598	8/94	80s
Total cost, 4-year private college/university	year	10664	8/94	80s
Total cost, 4-year public college/university	year	5287	8/94	80s
Tuition, 2-year public college/university, in-state	year	1110	8/94	80s
Tuition, 4-year private college/university, in-state	year	6985	8/94	80s
Tuition, 4-year public college/university, in-state	year	1983	8/94	80s
Energy and Fuels				
Energy, combined forms, 1800 sq. ft.	mo.	125.96	12/94	2c
Energy, exc. electricity, 1800 sq. ft.	mo.	36.81	12/94	2c

Values are in dollars or fractions of dollars. In the column headed *Ref*, references are shown to sources. Each reference is followed by a letter. These refer to the geographical level for which data were reported: s=State, r=Region, and c=City or metro. The abbreviation *ex* is used to mean *except* or *excluding*; *exp* stands for expenditures. For other abbreviations and further explanations, please see the Introduction.

Mobile, AL - continued

Item	Per	Value	Date	Ref.
Energy and Fuels				
Fuel oil and other fuels, expenditures	year	56	91	81r
Gas, cooking, 10 therms	month	13.38	2/94	65c
Gas, cooking, 30 therms	month	26.04	2/94	65c
Gas, cooking, 50 therms	month	36.97	2/94	65c
Gas, heating, winter, 100 therms	month	64.27	2/94	65c
Gas, heating, winter, average use	month	62.20	2/94	65c
Gas, natural, expenditures	year	150	91	81r
Gas, reg unlead, taxes inc., cash, self-service	gal	1.11	12/94	2c
Gasoline and motor oil purchased	year	1152	91	81r
Gasoline, unleaded midgrade	gallon	1.21	4/93	82r
Gasoline, unleaded premium	gallon	1.30	4/93	82r
Gasoline, unleaded regular	gallon	1.10	4/93	82r
Entertainment				
Bowling, evening rate	game	2.50	12/94	2c
Concert ticket, Pearl Jam group	perf	20.00	94	50r
Entertainment, total expenditures	year	1266	91	81r
Fees and admissions, expenditures	year	306	91	81r
Monopoly game, Parker Brothers', No. 9	game	11.90	12/94	2c
Movie	adm	5.75	12/94	2c
Pets, toys, playground equipment, expenditures	year	271	91	81r
Reading, expenditures	year	131	91	81r
Televisions, radios, and sound equipment, expenditures	year	439	91	81r
Tennis balls, yellow, Wilson or Penn, 3	can	2.26	12/94	2c
Funerals				
Burial, immediate, container provided by funeral home		1298.96	1/95	54r
Cards, acknowledgment		21.26	1/95	54r
Casket, minimum alternative		204.95	1/95	54r
Cosmetology, hair care, etc.		85.40	1/95	54r
Cremation, direct, container provided by funeral home		1054.77	1/95	54r
Embalming		287.71	1/95	54r
Funeral, funeral home		269.18	1/95	54r
Funeral, other facility		272.88	1/95	54r
Graveside service		302.54	1/95	54r
Hearse, local		122.08	1/95	54r
Limousine, local		80.31	1/95	54r
Memorial service		277.66	1/95	54r
Service charge, professional, nondeclinable		896.65	1/95	54r
Visitation and viewing		232.39	1/95	54r
Groceries				
Groceries, ACCRA Index		99.30	12/94	2c
Apples, Red Delicious	lb.	0.73	12/94	82r
Baby food, strained vegetables, lowest price	4-4.5 oz.	0.32	12/94	2c
Bacon, sliced	lb.	1.67	12/94	82r
Bananas	lb.	0.44	12/94	2c
Bananas	lb.	0.42	12/94	82r
Beef or hamburger, ground	lb.	1.77	12/94	2c
Beef purchases	year	213	91	81r
Beverage purchases, alcoholic	year	249	91	81r
Beverage purchases, nonalcoholic	year	207	91	81r
Bologna, all beef or mixed	lb.	2.27	12/94	82r
Bread, white	24-oz.	0.89	12/94	2c
Bread, white, pan	lb.	0.68	12/94	82r
Cabbage	lb.	0.42	12/94	82r
Carrots, short trimmed and topped	lb.	0.53	12/94	82r
Cereals and bakery products purchases	year	345	91	81r
Cereals and cereals products purchases	year	127	91	81r
Cheddar cheese, natural	lb.	3.58	12/94	82r
Cheese, Kraft grated Parmesan	8-oz.	3.29	12/94	2c
Chicken breast, bone-in	lb.	1.71	12/94	82r
Chicken, fresh, whole	lb.	0.78	12/94	82r
Chicken, whole fryer	lb.	0.79	12/94	2c
Chuck roast, USDA choice, boneless	lb.	2.26	12/94	82r
Cigarettes, Winston, Kings	carton	15.72	12/94	2c
Coffee, vacuum-packed	13 oz.	3.29	12/94	2c
Corn Flakes, Kellogg's or Post Toasties	18 oz.	1.82	12/94	2c

Mobile, AL - continued

Item	Per	Value	Date	Ref.
Groceries - continued				
Corn, frozen, whole kernel, lowest price	10 oz.	0.68	12/94	2c
Crackers, soda, salted	lb.	1.27	12/94	82r
Cucumbers	lb.	0.65	12/94	82r
Dairy products (other) purchases	year	141	91	81r
Eggs, Grade A large	dozen	0.81	12/94	2c
Eggs, Grade A large	dozen	0.87	12/94	82r
Fish and seafood purchases	year	72	91	81r
Flour, white, all purpose	lb.	0.23	12/94	82r
Food purchases, food eaten at home	year	2381	91	81r
Foods purchased away from home, not prepared by consumer	year	1696	91	81r
Frankfurters, all meat or all beef	lb.	1.74	12/94	82r
Fruits and vegetables purchases	year	380	91	81r
Grapefruit	lb.	0.45	12/94	82r
Grapes, Thompson seedless	lb.	2.30	12/94	82r
Ground beef, 100% beef	lb.	1.37	12/94	82r
Ground chuck, 100% beef	lb.	1.97	12/94	82r
Ham, boneless, exc. canned	lb.	2.54	12/94	82r
Ice cream, prepackaged, bulk, regular	1/2 gal.	2.47	12/94	82r
Lemons	lb.	1.02	12/94	82r
Lettuce, iceberg	lb.	0.96	12/94	82r
Lettuce, iceberg	head	0.82	12/94	2c
Margarine, Blue Bonnet or Parkay cubes	lb.	0.55	12/94	2c
Margarine, stick	lb.	0.77	12/94	82r
Meats, poultry, fish, and eggs purchases	year	655	91	81r
Milk and cream (fresh) purchases	year	130	91	81r
Milk, whole	1/2 gal.	1.35	12/94	2c
Orange juice, frozen concentrate 12-oz. can	16 oz.	1.36	12/94	82r
Orange juice, Minute Maid frozen	12-oz.	1.15	12/94	2c
Oranges, Navel	lb.	0.54	12/94	82r
Peaches, halves or slices, Hunt's, Del Monte, or Libby's	29-oz.	1.29	12/94	2c
Pears, Anjou	lb.	0.81	12/94	82r
Peas, sweet, Del Monte or Green Giant	15-17 oz.	0.61	12/94	2c
Pork chops, center cut, bone-in	lb.	3.07	12/94	82r
Pork purchases	year	142	91	81r
Potato chips	16-oz.	3.15	12/94	82r
Potatoes, frozen, French fried	lb.	0.82	12/94	82r
Potatoes, white	lb.	0.34	12/94	82r
Potatoes, white or red	10-lb. sack	3.11	12/94	2c
Rice, white, long grain, uncooked	lb.	0.48	12/94	82r
Round roast, USDA choice, boneless	lb.	2.91	12/94	82r
Sausage, fresh	lb.	1.82	12/94	82r
Sausage, Jimmy Dean, 100% pork	lb.	2.09	12/94	2c
Shortening, vegetable oil blends	lb.	0.75	12/94	82r
Shortening, vegetable, Crisco	3-lb.	2.49	12/94	2c
Soft drink, Coca Cola, ex deposit	2 lit	1.07	12/94	2c
Spaghetti and macaroni	lb.	0.87	12/94	82r
Steak, rib eye, USDA choice, boneless	lb.	6.85	12/94	82r
Steak, round, graded & ungraded, exc. USDA prime & choice	lb.	2.96	12/94	82r
Steak, round, USDA choice, boneless	lb.	3.17	12/94	82r
Steak, sirloin, USDA choice, boneless	lb.	4.12	12/94	82r
Steak, t-bone	lb.	5.85	12/94	2c
Steak, T-bone, USDA choice, bone-in	lb.	5.63	12/94	82r
Sugar and other sweets, eaten at home, expenditures	year	93	91	81r
Sugar, cane or beet	4 lbs.	1.39	12/94	2c
Sugar, white, all sizes	lb.	0.39	12/94	82r
Tobacco products and smoking supplies, total expenditures	year	286	91	81r
Tomatoes, field grown	lb.	1.36	12/94	82r
Tomatoes, Hunt's or Del Monte	14.5 oz.	0.65	12/94	2c
Tuna, chunk, light	lb.	1.94	12/94	82r
Tuna, chunk, light, oil-packed	6.125-6.5 oz.	0.64	12/94	2c
Turkey, frozen, whole	lb.	0.96	12/94	82r

Values are in dollars or fractions of dollars. In the column headed *Ref*, references are shown to sources. Each reference is followed by a letter. These refer to the geographical level for which data were reported: s=State, r=Region, and c=City or metro. The abbreviation *ex* is used to mean *except* or *excluding*; *exp* stands for expenditures. For other abbreviations and further explanations, please see the Introduction.

Mobile, AL - continued

Item	Per	Value	Date	Ref.
Groceries				
Yogurt, natural, fruit flavored	8 oz.	0.58	12/94	82r
Goods and Services				
Miscellaneous goods and services, ACCRA Index		93.60	12/94	2c
Health Care				
Health care, ACCRA Index		89.40	12/94	2c
Adenosine, emergency room	treat	100.00	95	23r
Antibiotic ointment, Polysporin	1.5 oz.	4.06	12/94	2c
Bladder tap, superpubic, infant, emergency room	treat	119.00	95	23r
Blood analysis, emergency room	treat	25.00	95	23r
Blood tests, abdominal pain, emergency room	treat	25.00	95	23r
Burn dressing, emergency room	treat	266.00	95	23r
Cardiology interpretation, emergency room	treat	26.00	95	23r
Chest X-ray, emergency room	treat	78.00	95	23r
Childbirth, Cesarean delivery, hospital charge	birth	5462.00	12/91	69r
Childbirth, Cesarean delivery, physician charge	birth	2228.00	12/91	69r
Childbirth, normal delivery, hospital charge	birth	2943.00	12/91	69r
Childbirth, normal delivery, physician charge	birth	1619.00	12/91	69r
Defibrillation pads, emergency room	treat	6.00	95	23r
Dentist's fee, adult teeth cleaning and periodic oral exam	visit	41.00	12/94	2c
Doctor's fee, routine exam, established patient	visit	47.40	12/94	2c
Drugs, expenditures	year	297	91	81r
Gastric tube insertion, nasal, emergency room	treat	25.00	95	23r
Health care, total expenditures	year	1600	91	81r
Health insurance expenditures	year	637	91	81r
Heart monitor, emergency room	treat	40.00	95	23r
Hospital care, semiprivate room	day	210.60	12/94	2c
Insurance premium, family medical care	month	360.67	1/95	41s
Intravenous fluids, emergency room	treat	130.00	95	23r
Intravenous fluids, emergency room	liter	26.00	95	23r
Intravenous line, central, emergency room	treat	342.00	95	23r
Liver function tests, abdominal pain, emergency room	treat	26.00	95	23r
Medical care charges, total, emergency room, third-degree burns	treat	2101.00	95	23r
Medical care charges, total, emergency, infant with fever	treat	628.00	95	23r
Medical services expenditures	year	573	91	81r
Medical supplies expenditures	year	93	91	81r
Morphine, emergency room	treat	34.00	95	23r
Nursing care and facilities charges, emergency room	treat	252.00	95	23r
Nursing care and facilities charges, emergency, infant with fever	treat	252.00	95	23r
Nursing care and facilities charges, emergency, third-degree burns	treat	861.00	95	23r
Physician's charges, emergency, infant with fever	treat	212.00	95	23r
Physician's charges, emergency, third-degree burns	treat	372.00	95	23r
Physician's fee, emergency room	treat	372.00	95	23r
Physician's fee, general practitioner	visit	51.20	12/93	60r
Surgery, open-heart	proc	42374.00	1/93	14r
Ultrasound, abdominal, emergency room	treat	276.00	95	23r
Urinalysis, emergency room	treat	20.00	95	23r
Urinalysis, infant, emergency room	treat	20.00	95	23r
X-rays, emergency room	treat	78.00	95	23r
Household Goods				
Appl. repair, service call, wash mach	min. lab. chg.	35.33	12/94	2c
Floor coverings, expenditures	year	48	91	81r
Furniture, expenditures	year	280	91	81r
Household equipment, misc. expenditures	year	342	91	81r

Mobile, AL - continued

Item	Per	Value	Date	Ref.
Household Goods - continued				
Household expenditures, miscellaneous	year	256	91	81r
Household furnishings and equipment, expenditures	year	988	91	81r
Household operations expenditures	year	468	91	81r
Household textiles, expenditures	year	95	91	81r
Housekeeping supplies, expenditures	year	380	91	81r
Laundry and cleaning supplies, expenditures	year	109	91	81r
Laundry detergent, Tide Ultra, Bold, or Cheer	42 oz.	3.47	12/94	2c
Postage and stationery, expenditures	year	105	91	81r
Tissues, facial, Kleenex brand	175	1.04	12/94	2c
Housing				
Housing, ACCRA Index		76.70	12/94	2c
Add garage/carport		6,980	3/95	74r
Add room(s)		11,403	3/95	74r
Apartment condominium or co-op, median	unit	68600	12/94	62r
Dwellings (owned), expenditures	year	2428	91	81r
Enclose porch/patio/breezeway		4,572	3/95	74r
Finish room in basement/attic		3,794	3/95	74r
Home, existing, single-family, median	unit	120200	12/94	62r
Home, existing, single-family, median	unit	69.60	12/94	62c
House payment, principal and interest, 25% down payment	mo.	595	12/94	2c
House, 1800 sq ft, 8000 sq ft lot, new, urban, utilities	total	96710	12/94	2c
Maintenance, repairs, insurance, and other housing expenditures	year	531	91	81r
Mortgage interest and charges expenditures	year	1506	91	81r
Mtge. rate, incl. points and orig. fee, 30-year conv. fixed or ARM	mo.	9.21	12/94	2c
Princ. & int., mortgage, median-price exist. sing.-family home	mo.	540	12/94	62r
Property taxes expenditures	year	391	91	81r
Redesign, restructure more than half of home's interior		17,641	3/95	74r
Rent, apartment, 2 br., 1 1/2-2 baths, unfurnished, 950 sq ft, water	mo.	385	12/94	2c
Rental units expenditures	year	1264	91	81r
Insurance and Pensions				
Auto insurance, private passenger	year	604.07	12/94	71s
Insurance and pensions, personal, expenditures	year	2395	91	81r
Insurance, life and other personal, expenditures	year	368	91	81r
Pensions and Social Security, expenditures	year	2027	91	81r
Personal Goods				
Shampoo, Alberto VO5	15-oz.	1.18	12/94	2c
Toothpaste, Crest or Colgate	6-7 oz.	2.11	12/94	2c
Personal Services				
Dry cleaning, man's 2-pc. suit		5.50	12/94	2c
Haircut, man's barbershop, no styling		8.60	12/94	2c
Haircut, woman's shampoo, trim, blow-dry		21.20	12/94	2c
Personal services expenditures	year	212	91	81r
Restaurant Food				
Chicken, fried, thigh and drumstick		1.22	12/94	2c
Dining expenditures, family	week	33.83	94	73r
Hamburger with cheese	1/4 lb.	1.73	12/94	2c
Pizza, Pizza Hut or Pizza Inn	12-13 in.	7.99	12/94	2c
Taxes				
Taxes, Federal income, expenditures	year	2275	91	81r
Taxes, personal, expenditures	year	2715	91	81r
Taxes, State and local income, expenditures	year	365	91	81r
Transportation				
Transportation, ACCRA Index		109.40	12/94	2c
Bus fare, one-way	trip	1.00	12/95	1c
Cars and trucks purchased, new	year	1306	91	81r

Values are in dollars or fractions of dollars. In the column headed *Ref*, references are shown to sources. Each reference is followed by a letter. These refer to the geographical level for which data were reported: s=State, r=Region, and c=City or metro. The abbreviation *ex* is used to mean *except* or *excluding*; *exp* stands for expenditures. For other abbreviations and further explanations, please see the Introduction.

Mobile, AL - continued

Item	Per	Value	Date	Ref.
Transportation				
Cars and trucks purchased, used	year	942	91	81r
Driver's learning permit fee	perm	20.00	1/94	84s
Driver's license fee	orig	20.00	1/94	84s
Driver's license fee, duplicate	lic	5.00	1/94	84s
Driver's license reinstatement fee, min.	susp	50.00	1/94	85s
Driver's license renewal fee	renew	20.00	1/94	84s
Identification card, nondriver	card	20.00	1/94	83s
Motorcycle license fee	orig	20.00	1/94	84s
Motorcycle license fee, duplicate	lic	5.00	1/94	84s
Motorcycle license renewal fee	renew	20.00	1/94	84s
Public transportation expenditures	year	249	91	81r
Tire balance, computer or spin bal., front	wheel	8.35	12/94	2c
Transportation expenditures, total	year	5307	91	81r
Vehicle finance charges	year	346	91	81r
Vehicle insurance expenditures	year	544	91	81r
Vehicle maintenance and repairs expenditures	year	600	91	81r
Vehicle purchases	year	2275	91	81r
Vehicle rental, leases, licenses, etc. expenditures	year	141	91	81r
Vehicles purchased, other than cars and trucks	year	27	91	81r
Utilities				
Utilities, ACCRA Index		114.20	12/94	2c
Electricity expenditures	year	950	91	81r
Electricity, (part.), other, 1800 sq. ft., new home	mo.	89.15	12/94	2c
Utilities, fuels, and public services, total expenditures	year	2000	91	81r
Water and other public services, expenditures	year	227	91	81r
Weddings				
Bridal attendants' gowns	event	750	10/93	76r
Bridal gown	event	852	10/93	76r
Bridal headpiece and veil	event	167	10/93	76r
Bride's wedding band	event	708	10/93	76r
Clergy	event	224	10/93	76r
Engagement ring	event	2756	10/93	76r
Flowers	event	863	10/93	76r
Formal wear for groom	event	106	10/93	76r
Groom's attendants' formal wear	event	530	10/93	76r
Groom's wedding band	event	402	10/93	76r
Music	event	600	10/93	76r
Photography	event	1088	10/93	76r
Shoes for bride	event	50	10/93	76r
Videography	event	483	10/93	76r
Wedding invitations and announcements	event	342	10/93	76r
Wedding reception	event	7000	10/93	76r

Modesto, CA

Item	Per	Value	Date	Ref.
Appliances				
Appliances (major), expenditures	year	160	91	81r
Average annual exp.				
Food, health care, personal goods, services	year	32461	91	81r
Charity				
Cash contributions, expenditures	year	975	91	81r
Clothing				
Apparel, men and boys, total expenditures	year	467	91	81r
Apparel, women and girls, total expenditures	year	737	91	81r
Footwear, expenditures	year	270	91	81r
Communications				
Long-distance telephone rate, day, addl. min., 1-10 mi.	min.	0.07	12/93	9s
Long-distance telephone rate, day, initial min., 1-10 mi.	min.	0.17	12/93	9s
Phone line, single, business, field visit	inst	70.75	12/93	9s
Phone line, single, business, no field visit	inst	70.75	12/93	9s

Modesto, CA - continued

Item	Per	Value	Date	Ref.
Communications - continued				
Phone line, single, residence, field visit	inst	34.75	12/93	9s
Phone line, single, residence, no field visit	inst	34.75	12/93	9s
Telephone service, expenditures	year	611	91	81r
Education				
Board, 4-year private college/university	year	2945	8/94	80s
Board, 4-year public college/university	year	2321	8/94	80s
Education, total expenditures	year	375	91	81r
Room, 4-year private college/university	year	3094	8/94	80s
Room, 4-year public college/university	year	2812	8/94	80s
Student fee, university	year	21.00	93	18s
Total cost, 4-year private college/university	year	19321	8/94	80s
Total cost, 4-year public college/university	year	7511	8/94	80s
Tuition, 2-year public college/university, in-state	year	345	8/94	80s
Tuition, 4-year private college/university, in-state	year	13282	8/94	80s
Tuition, 4-year public college/university, in-state	year	2378	8/94	80s
Energy and Fuels				
Fuel oil and other fuels, expenditures	year	33	91	81r
Gas, natural, expenditures	year	212	91	81r
Gasoline and motor oil purchased	year	1115	91	81r
Gasoline, unleaded midgrade	gallon	1.36	4/93	82r
Gasoline, unleaded premium	gallon	1.43	4/93	82r
Gasoline, unleaded regular	gallon	1.23	4/93	82r
Entertainment				
Concert ticket, Pearl Jam group	perf	20.00	94	50r
Entertainment, total expenditures	year	1853	91	81r
Fees and admissions, expenditures	year	482	91	81r
Pets, toys, playground equipment, expenditures	year	299	91	81r
Reading, expenditures	year	164	91	81r
Televisions, radios, and sound equipment, expenditures	year	528	91	81r
Funerals				
Burial, immediate, container provided by funeral home		1382.70	1/95	54r
Cards, acknowledgment		21.87	1/95	54r
Casket, minimum alternative		128.54	1/95	54r
Cosmetology, hair care, etc.		119.69	1/95	54r
Cremation, direct, container provided by funeral home		1030.62	1/95	54r
Embalming		255.42	1/95	54r
Funeral, funeral home		437.38	1/95	54r
Funeral, other facility		444.46	1/95	54r
Graveside service		338.46	1/95	54r
Hearse, local		147.50	1/95	54r
Limousine, local		130.33	1/95	54r
Memorial service		553.16	1/95	54r
Service charge, professional, nondeclinable		859.15	1/95	54r
Visitation and viewing		93.23	1/95	54r
Groceries				
Apples, Red Delicious	lb.	0.72	12/94	82r
Bacon, sliced	lb.	1.73	12/94	82r
Bananas	lb.	0.52	12/94	82r
Beef purchases	year	241	91	81r
Beverage purchases, alcoholic	year	328	91	81r
Beverage purchases, nonalcoholic	year	234	91	81r
Bologna, all beef or mixed	lb.	2.33	12/94	82r
Bread, white, pan	lb.	0.81	12/94	82r
Carrots, short trimmed and topped	lb.	0.43	12/94	82r
Cereals and bakery products purchases	year	392	91	81r
Cereals and cereals products purchases	year	139	91	81r
Chicken breast, bone-in	lb.	2.04	12/94	82r
Chicken, fresh, whole	lb.	0.95	12/94	82r
Coffee, 100%, ground roast, all sizes	lb.	4.48	12/94	82r
Dairy products (other) purchases	year	182	91	81r
Fish and seafood purchases	year	94	91	81r
Flour, white, all purpose	lb.	0.21	12/94	82r

Values are in dollars or fractions of dollars. In the column headed *Ref*, references are shown to sources. Each reference is followed by a letter. These refer to the geographical level for which data were reported: s=State, r=Region, and c=City or metro. The abbreviation *ex* is used to mean *except* or *excluding*; *exp* stands for expenditures. For other abbreviations and further explanations, please see the Introduction.

Modesto, CA - continued

Item	Per	Value	Date	Ref.
Groceries				
Food purchases, food eaten at home	year	2749	91	81r
Foods purchased away from home, not prepared by consumer	year	1909	91	81r
Fruits and vegetables purchases	year	459	91	81r
Grapefruit	lb.	0.56	12/94	82r
Ground beef, 100% beef	lb.	1.31	12/94	82r
Ham, boneless, exc. canned	lb.	2.46	12/94	82r
Ice cream, prepackaged, bulk, regular	1/2 gal.	2.57	12/94	82r
Lemons	lb.	1.00	12/94	82r
Lettuce, iceberg	lb.	0.93	12/94	82r
Meats, poultry, fish, and eggs purchases	year	700	91	81r
Milk and cream (fresh) purchases	year	155	91	81r
Orange juice, frozen concentrate 12-oz. can	16 oz.	1.52	12/94	82r
Oranges, Navel	lb.	0.56	12/94	82r
Pork chops, center cut, bone-in	lb.	3.30	12/94	82r
Pork purchases	year	122	91	81r
Potato chips	16-oz.	3.03	12/94	82r
Potatoes, frozen, French fried	lb.	0.77	12/94	82r
Potatoes, white	lb.	0.35	12/94	82r
Rice, white, long grain, uncooked	lb.	0.54	12/94	82r
Round roast, USDA choice, boneless	lb.	2.92	12/94	82r
Shortening, vegetable oil blends	lb.	0.80	12/94	82r
Spaghetti and macaroni	lb.	1.02	12/94	82r
Steak, round, graded & ungraded, exc. USDA prime & choice	lb.	3.13	12/94	82r
Steak, sirloin, USDA choice, boneless	lb.	4.07	12/94	82r
Sugar and other sweets, eaten at home, expenditures	year	105	91	81r
Sugar, white, all sizes	lb.	0.38	12/94	82r
Tobacco products and smoking supplies, total expenditures	year	221	91	81r
Tomatoes, field grown	lb.	1.45	12/94	82r
Tuna, chunk, light	lb.	2.18	12/94	82r
Health Care				
Childbirth, Cesarean delivery, hospital charge	birth	6059.00	12/91	69r
Childbirth, Cesarean delivery, physician charge	birth	2248.00	12/91	69r
Childbirth, normal delivery, hospital charge	birth	3006.00	12/91	69r
Childbirth, normal delivery, physician charge	birth	1634.00	12/91	69r
Drugs, expenditures	year	230	91	81r
Health care, total expenditures	year	1544	91	81r
Health insurance expenditures	year	558	91	81r
Insurance premium, family medical care	month	380.27	1/95	41s
Medical services expenditures	year	676	91	81r
Medical supplies expenditures	year	80	91	81r
Surgery, open-heart	proc	37818.00	1/93	14r
Household Goods				
Floor coverings, expenditures	year	79	91	81r
Furniture, expenditures	year	352	91	81r
Household equipment, misc. expenditures	year	614	91	81r
Household expenditures, miscellaneous	year	294	91	81r
Household furnishings and equipment, expenditures	year	1416	91	81r
Household operations expenditures	year	580	91	81r
Household textiles, expenditures	year	113	91	81r
Housekeeping supplies, expenditures	year	447	91	81r
Laundry and cleaning supplies, expenditures	year	114	91	81r
Postage and stationery, expenditures	year	145	91	81r
Housing				
Add garage/carport		6,422	3/95	74r
Add room(s)		26,583	3/95	74r
Apartment condominium or co-op, median	unit	105300	12/94	62r
Dwellings (owned), expenditures	year	3932	91	81r
Enclose porch/patio/breezeway		5,382	3/95	74r
Finish room in basement/attic		3,911	3/95	74r
Home, existing, single-family, median	unit	178600	12/94	62r
Maintenance, repairs, insurance, and other housing expenditures	year	591	91	81r

Modesto, CA - continued

Item	Per	Value	Date	Ref.
Housing - continued				
Mortgage interest and charges expenditures	year	2747	91	81r
Princ. & int., mortgage, median-price exist. sing.-family home	mo.	845	12/94	62r
Property taxes expenditures	year	594	91	81r
Redesign, restructure more than half of home's interior		5,467	3/95	74r
Rental units expenditures	year	2077	91	81r
Insurance and Pensions				
Auto insurance, private passenger	year	892.80	12/94	71s
Insurance and pensions, personal, expenditures	year	3042	91	81r
Insurance, life and other personal, expenditures	year	298	91	81r
Pensions and Social Security, expenditures	year	2744	91	81r
Legal Assistance				
Legal work, law firm associate	hour	91		10r
Legal work, law firm partner	hour	151		10r
Personal Services				
Personal services expenditures	year	286	91	81r
Restaurant Food				
Dining expenditures, family	week	32.25	94	73r
Taxes				
Taxes, Federal income, expenditures	year	2946	91	81r
Taxes, personal, expenditures	year	3791	91	81r
Taxes, State and local income, expenditures	year	791	91	81r
Transportation				
Cars and trucks purchased, new	year	1231	91	81r
Cars and trucks purchased, used	year	915	91	81r
Driver's learning permit fee	perm	12.00	1/94	84s
Driver's license fee	orig	12.00	1/94	84s
Driver's license fee, duplicate	lic	12.00	1/94	84s
Driver's license reinstatement fee, min.	susp	15.00	1/94	85s
Driver's license renewal fee	renew	12.00	1/94	84s
Identification card, nondriver	card	6.00	1/94	83s
Motorcycle learning permit fee	perm	12.00	1/94	84s
Motorcycle license fee	orig	12.00	1/94	84s
Motorcycle license fee, duplicate	lic	12.00	1/94	84s
Motorcycle license renewal fee	renew	12.00	1/94	84s
Public transportation expenditures	year	375	91	81r
Transportation expenditures, total	year	5527	91	81r
Vehicle finance charges	year	287	91	81r
Vehicle insurance expenditures	year	624	91	81r
Vehicle maintenance and repairs expenditures	year	695	91	81r
Vehicle purchases	year	2174	91	81r
Vehicle rental, leases, licenses, etc. expenditures	year	257	91	81r
Vehicles purchased, other than cars and trucks	year	28	91	81r
Utilities				
Electricity expenditures	year	616	91	81r
Utilities, fuels, and public services, total expenditures	year	1681	91	81r
Water and other public services, expenditures	year	209	91	81r
Weddings				
Bridal attendants' gowns	event	750	10/93	76r
Bridal gown	event	852	10/93	76r
Bridal headpiece and veil	event	167	10/93	76r
Bride's wedding band	event	708	10/93	76r
Clergy	event	224	10/93	76r
Engagement ring	event	2756	10/93	76r
Flowers	event	863	10/93	76r
Formal wear for groom	event	106	10/93	76r
Groom's attendants' formal wear	event	530	10/93	76r
Groom's wedding band	event	402	10/93	76r
Music	event	600	10/93	76r
Photography	event	1088	10/93	76r

Values are in dollars or fractions of dollars. In the column headed *Ref*, references are shown to sources. Each reference is followed by a letter. These refer to the geographical level for which data were reported: s=State, r=Region, and c=City or metro. The abbreviation *ex* is used to mean *except* or *excluding*; *exp* stands for expenditures. For other abbreviations and further explanations, please see the Introduction.

Modesto, CA - continued

Item	Per	Value	Date	Ref.
Weddings				
Shoes for bride	event	50	10/93	76r
Videography	event	483	10/93	76r
Wedding invitations and announcements	event	342	10/93	76r
Wedding reception	event	7000	10/93	76r

Monmouth-Ocean, NJ

Item	Per	Value	Date	Ref.
Appliances				
Appliances (major), expenditures	year	145	91	81r
Average annual exp.				
Food, health care, personal goods, services	year	29496	91	81r
Charity				
Cash contributions, expenditures	year	708	91	81r
Clothing				
Apparel, men and boys, total expenditures	year	416	91	81r
Apparel, women and girls, total expenditures	year	744	91	81r
Footwear, expenditures	year	305	91	81r
Communications				
Long-distance telephone rate, day, addl. min., 1-10 mi.	min.	0.03	12/93	9s
Long-distance telephone rate, day, initial min., 1-10 mi.	min.	0.09	12/93	9s
Phone line, single, business, field visit	inst	98.50	12/93	9s
Phone line, single, business, no field visit	inst	79.50	12/93	9s
Phone line, single, residence, field visit	inst	56.50	12/93	9s
Phone line, single, residence, no field visit	inst	42.00	12/93	9s
Telephone service, expenditures	year	589	91	81r
Education				
Board, 4-year private college/university	year	2841	8/94	80s
Board, 4-year public college/university	year	1956	8/94	80s
Education, total expenditures	year	593	91	81r
Room, 4-year private college/university	year	2999	8/94	80s
Room, 4-year public college/university	year	2778	8/94	80s
Total cost, 4-year private college/university	year	18264	8/94	80s
Total cost, 4-year public college/university	year	8252	8/94	80s
Tuition, 2-year public college/university, in-state	year	1539	8/94	80s
Tuition, 4-year private college/university, in-state	year	12423	8/94	80s
Tuition, 4-year public college/university, in-state	year	3518	8/94	80s
Energy and Fuels				
Fuel oil and other fuels, expenditures	year	257	91	81r
Gas, natural, expenditures	year	285	91	81r
Gasoline and motor oil purchased	year	867	91	81r
Gasoline, unleaded midgrade	gallon	1.32	4/93	82r
Gasoline, unleaded premium	gallon	1.40	4/93	82r
Gasoline, unleaded regular	gallon	1.19	4/93	82r
Entertainment				
Entertainment, total expenditures	year	1331	91	81r
Fees and admissions, expenditures	year	398	91	81r
Pets, toys, playground equipment, expenditures	year	270	91	81r
Reading, expenditures	year	171	91	81r
Televisions, radios, and sound equipment, expenditures	year	429	91	81r
Funerals				
Burial, immediate, container provided by funeral home		1370.36	1/95	54r
Cards, acknowledgment		17.72	1/95	54r
Casket, minimum alternative		192.52	1/95	54r
Cosmetology, hair care, etc.		139.56	1/95	54r
Cremation, direct, container provided by funeral home		1049.24	1/95	54r
Embalming		387.57	1/95	54r
Funeral, funeral home		278.77	1/95	54r
Funeral, other facility		275.85	1/95	54r

Item	Per	Value	Date	Ref.
Funerals - continued				
Graveside service		213.08	1/95	54r
Hearse, local		157.27	1/95	54r
Limousine, local		146.45	1/95	54r
Memorial service		271.02	1/95	54r
Service charge, professional, nondeclinable		943.58	1/95	54r
Visitation and viewing		322.86	1/95	54r
Groceries				
Apples, Red Delicious	lb.	0.78	12/94	82r
Bacon, sliced	lb.	2.24	12/94	82r
Bananas	lb.	0.49	12/94	82r
Beef purchases	year	226	91	81r
Beverage purchases, alcoholic	year	332	91	81r
Beverage purchases, nonalcoholic	year	213	91	81r
Bread, white, pan	lb.	0.80	12/94	82r
Butter, salted, Grade AA, stick	lb.	1.67	12/94	82r
Carrots, short trimmed and topped	lb.	0.51	12/94	82r
Cereals and bakery products purchases	year	407	91	81r
Cereals and cereals products purchases	year	132	91	81r
Chicken breast, bone-in	lb.	2.22	12/94	82r
Chicken, fresh, whole	lb.	1.05	12/94	82r
Chuck roast, USDA choice, boneless	lb.	2.74	12/94	82r
Coffee, 100%, ground roast, all sizes	lb.	4.61	12/94	82r
Dairy products (other) purchases	year	161	91	81r
Eggs, Grade A large	dozen	1.12	12/94	82r
Fish and seafood purchases	year	112	91	81r
Food purchases, food eaten at home	year	2599	91	81r
Foods purchased away from home, not prepared by consumer	year	2024	91	81r
Fruits and vegetables purchases	year	444	91	81r
Grapefruit	lb.	0.44	12/94	82r
Grapes, Thompson seedless	lb.	2.24	12/94	82r
Ground chuck, 100% beef	lb.	1.67	12/94	82r
Ice cream, prepackaged, bulk, regular	1/2 gal.	2.93	12/94	82r
Lemons	lb.	1.06	12/94	82r
Lettuce, iceberg	lb.	0.92	12/94	82r
Meats, poultry, fish, and eggs purchases	year	751	91	81r
Milk and cream (fresh) purchases	year	152	91	81r
Orange juice, frozen concentrate 12-oz. can	16 oz.	1.92	12/94	82r
Oranges, Navel	lb.	0.56	12/94	82r
Pork chops, center cut, bone-in	lb.	3.09	12/94	82r
Pork purchases	year	130	91	81r
Potatoes, white	lb.	0.37	12/94	82r
Rib roast, USDA choice, bone-in	lb.	4.98	12/94	82r
Round roast, USDA choice, boneless	lb.	2.93	12/94	82r
Shortening, vegetable oil blends	lb.	1.03	12/94	82r
Spaghetti and macaroni	lb.	0.84	12/94	82r
Steak, round, USDA choice, boneless	lb.	3.48	12/94	82r
Steak, sirloin, USDA choice, bone-in	lb.	3.38	12/94	82r
Steak, sirloin, USDA choice, boneless	lb.	4.81	12/94	82r
Sugar and other sweets, eaten at home, expenditures	year	89	91	81r
Sugar, white, all sizes	lb.	0.46	12/94	82r
Tobacco products and smoking supplies, total expenditures	year	279	91	81r
Tomatoes, field grown	lb.	1.56	12/94	82r
Tuna, chunk, light	lb.	2.09	12/94	82r
Health Care				
Childbirth, Cesarean delivery, hospital charge	birth	6334.00	12/91	69r
Childbirth, Cesarean delivery, physician charge	birth	2234.00	12/91	69r
Childbirth, normal delivery, hospital charge	birth	3225.00	12/91	69r
Childbirth, normal delivery, physician charge	birth	1623.00	12/91	69r
Drugs, expenditures	year	205	91	81r
Health care, total expenditures	year	1396	91	81r
Health insurance expenditures	year	553	91	81r
Insurance premium, family medical care	month	396.06	1/95	41s
Medical services expenditures	year	559	91	81r
Medical supplies expenditures	year	80	91	81r

Values are in dollars or fractions of dollars. In the column headed *Ref*, references are shown to sources. Each reference is followed by a letter. These refer to the geographical level for which data were reported: s = State, r = Region, and c = City or metro. The abbreviation *ex* is used to mean *except* or *excluding*; *exp* stands for expenditures. For other abbreviations and further explanations, please see the Introduction.

Monmouth-Ocean, NJ - continued

Item	Per	Value	Date	Ref.
Household Goods				
Floor coverings, expenditures	year	158	91	81r
Furniture, expenditures	year	341	91	81r
Household equipment, misc. expenditures	year	363	91	81r
Household expenditures, miscellaneous	year	194	91	81r
Household furnishings and equipment, expenditures	year	1158	91	81r
Household operations expenditures	year	378	91	81r
Household textiles, expenditures	year	88	91	81r
Housekeeping supplies, expenditures	year	426	91	81r
Laundry and cleaning supplies, expenditures	year	122	91	81r
Postage and stationery, expenditures	year	134	91	81r
Housing				
Add garage/carport		11,614	3/95	74r
Add room(s)		16,816	3/95	74r
Apartment condominium or co-op, median	unit	96700	12/94	62r
Dwellings (owned), expenditures	year	3305	91	81r
Enclose porch/patio/breezeway		2,980	3/95	74r
Finish room in basement/attic		4,330	3/95	74r
Home, existing, single-family, median	unit	161600	12/94	62r
Maintenance, repairs, insurance, and other housing expenditures	year	569	91	81r
Mortgage interest and charges expenditures	year	1852	91	81r
Princ. & int., mortgage, median-price exist. sing.-family home	mo.	765	12/94	62r
Property taxes expenditures	year	884	91	81r
Redesign, restructure more than half of home's interior		2,750	3/95	74r
Rental units expenditures	year	1832	91	81r
Insurance and Pensions				
Auto insurance, private passenger	year	1094.56	12/94	71s
Insurance and pensions, personal, expenditures	year	2690	91	81r
Insurance, life and other personal, expenditures	year	341	91	81r
Pensions and Social Security, expenditures	year	2349	91	81r
Legal Assistance				
Estate planning, law-firm partner	hr.	375.00	10/93	12r
Legal work, law firm associate	hour	78		10r
Legal work, law firm partner	hour	183		10r
Personal Services				
Personal services expenditures	year	184	91	81r
Restaurant Food				
Dining expenditures, family	week	34.26	94	73r
Taxes				
Taxes, Federal income, expenditures	year	2409	91	81r
Taxes, personal, expenditures	year	3094	91	81r
Taxes, State and local income, expenditures	year	620	91	81r
Transportation				
Cars and trucks purchased, new	year	1170	91	81r
Cars and trucks purchased, used	year	739	91	81r
Driver's learning permit fee	perm	5.00	1/94	84s
Driver's license fee	orig	16.00	1/94	84s
Driver's license fee, duplicate	lic	3.00	1/94	84s
Driver's license reinstatement fee, min.	susp	30.00	1/94	85s
Driver's license renewal fee	renew	16.00	1/94	84s
Identification card, nondriver	card	5.50	1/94	83s
Motorcycle learning permit fee	perm	5.00	1/94	84s
Motorcycle license fee	orig	8.00	1/94	84s
Motorcycle license fee, duplicate	lic	3.00	1/94	84s
Motorcycle license renewal fee	renew	8.00	1/94	84s
Public transportation expenditures	year	430	91	81r
Transportation expenditures, total	year	4810	91	81r
Vehicle finance charges	year	238	91	81r
Vehicle insurance expenditures	year	630	91	81r
Vehicle maintenance and repairs expenditures	year	532	91	81r
Vehicle purchases	year	1920	91	81r

Monmouth-Ocean, NJ - continued

Item	Per	Value	Date	Ref.
Transportation - continued				
Vehicle rental, leases, licenses, etc. expenditures	year	193	91	81r
Vehicles purchased, other than cars and trucks	year	11	91	81r
Utilities				
Electricity expenditures	year	695	91	81r
Utilities, fuels, and public services, total expenditures	year	1981	91	81r
Water and other public services, expenditures	year	154	91	81r
Weddings				
Bridal attendants' gowns	event	750	10/93	76r
Bridal gown	event	852	10/93	76r
Bridal headpiece and veil	event	167	10/93	76r
Bride's wedding band	event	708	10/93	76r
Clergy	event	224	10/93	76r
Engagement ring	event	2756	10/93	76r
Flowers	event	863	10/93	76r
Formal wear for groom	event	106	10/93	76r
Groom's attendants' formal wear	event	530	10/93	76r
Groom's wedding band	event	402	10/93	76r
Music	event	600	10/93	76r
Photography	event	1088	10/93	76r
Shoes for bride	event	50	10/93	76r
Videography	event	483	10/93	76r
Wedding invitations and announcements	event	342	10/93	76r
Wedding reception	event	7000	10/93	76r

Monroe, LA

Item	Per	Value	Date	Ref.
Composite, ACCRA index		94.40	12/94	2c
Alcoholic Beverages				
Beer, Miller Lite, Bud, 12-oz., ex deposit	6	4.12	12/94	2c
J & B Scotch	750-ml.	16.39	12/94	2c
Wine, Gallo Chablis blanc	1.5-lit	4.36	12/94	2c
Appliances				
Appliances (major), expenditures	year	153	91	81r
Average annual exp.				
Food, health care, personal goods, services	year	27020	91	81r
Charity				
Cash contributions, expenditures	year	839	91	81r
Clothing				
Apparel, men and boys, total expenditures	year	380	91	81r
Apparel, women and girls, total expenditures	year	660	91	81r
Footwear, expenditures	year	193	91	81r
Jeans, man's denim		31.99	12/94	2c
Shirt, man's dress shirt		31.33	12/94	2c
Undervest, boy's size 10-14, cotton	3	6.27	12/94	2c
Communications				
Long-distance telephone rate, day, addl. min., 1-10 mi.	min.	0.29	12/93	9s
Long-distance telephone rate, day, initial min., 1-10 mi.	min.	0.41	12/93	9s
Newspaper subscription, dly. and Sun. delivery	month	12.00	12/94	2c
Phone line, single, business, field visit	inst	85.00	12/93	9s
Phone line, single, business, no field visit	inst	85.00	12/93	9s
Phone line, single, residence, field visit	inst	50.00	12/93	9s
Phone line, single, residence, no field visit	inst	50.00	12/93	9s
Telephone bill, family of four	month	19.27	12/94	2c
Telephone service, expenditures	year	616	91	81r
Telephone, residential, flat rate	mo.	12.64	12/93	8c
Education				
Board, 4-year private college/university	year	2436	8/94	80s
Board, 4-year public college/university	year	1638	8/94	80s
Education, total expenditures	year	319	91	81r

Values are in dollars or fractions of dollars. In the column headed *Ref*, references are shown to sources. Each reference is followed by a letter. These refer to the geographical level for which data were reported: s=State, r=Region, and c=City or metro. The abbreviation *ex* is used to mean *except* or *excluding*; *exp* stands for expenditures. For other abbreviations and further explanations, please see the Introduction.

Monroe, LA - continued

Item	Per	Value	Date	Ref.
Education				
Room, 4-year private college/university	year	2558	8/94	80s
Room, 4-year public college/university	year	1405	8/94	80s
Total cost, 4-year private college/university	year	16467	8/94	80s
Total cost, 4-year public college/university	year	5225	8/94	80s
Tuition, 2-year public college/university, in-state	year	956	8/94	80s
Tuition, 4-year private college/university, in-state	year	11473	8/94	80s
Tuition, 4-year public college/university, in-state	year	2182	8/94	80s
Energy and Fuels				
Energy, combined forms, 1800 sq. ft.	mo.	126.54	12/94	2c
Fuel oil and other fuels, expenditures	year	56	91	81r
Gas, natural, expenditures	year	150	91	81r
Gas, reg unlead, taxes inc., cash, self-service	gal.	1.09	12/94	2c
Gasoline and motor oil purchased	year	1152	91	81r
Gasoline, unleaded midgrade	gallon	1.21	4/93	82r
Gasoline, unleaded premium	gallon	1.30	4/93	82r
Gasoline, unleaded regular	gallon	1.10	4/93	82r
Entertainment				
Bowling, evening rate	game	2.50	12/94	2c
Concert ticket, Pearl Jam group	perf	20.00	94	50r
Entertainment, total expenditures	year	1266	91	81r
Fees and admissions, expenditures	year	306	91	81r
Monopoly game, Parker Brothers', No. 9	game	12.28	12/94	2c
Movie	adm	5.00	12/94	2c
Pets, toys, playground equipment, expenditures	year	271	91	81r
Reading, expenditures	year	131	91	81r
Televisions, radios, and sound equipment, expenditures	year	439	91	81r
Tennis balls, yellow, Wilson or Penn, 3	can	2.55	12/94	2c
Funerals				
Burial, immediate, container provided by funeral home		1574.60	1/95	54r
Cards, acknowledgment		22.24	1/95	54r
Casket, minimum alternative		239.41	1/95	54r
Cosmetology, hair care, etc.		91.04	1/95	54r
Cremation, direct, container provided by funeral home		1085.15	1/95	54r
Embalming		281.30	1/95	54r
Funeral, funeral home		323.04	1/95	54r
Funeral, other facility		327.58	1/95	54r
Graveside service		355.19	1/95	54r
Hearse, local		141.89	1/95	54r
Limousine, local		99.40	1/95	54r
Memorial service		284.67	1/95	54r
Service charge, professional, nondeclinable		904.06	1/95	54r
Visitation and viewing		187.04	1/95	54r
Groceries				
Groceries, ACCRA Index		95.70	12/94	2c
Apples, Red Delicious	lb.	0.73	12/94	82r
Baby food, strained vegetables, lowest price	4-4.5 oz.	0.28	12/94	2c
Bacon, sliced	lb.	1.67	12/94	82r
Bananas	lb.	0.44	12/94	2c
Bananas	lb.	0.42	12/94	82r
Beef or hamburger, ground	lb.	1.54	12/94	2c
Beef purchases	year	213	91	81r
Beverage purchases, alcoholic	year	249	91	81r
Beverage purchases, nonalcoholic	year	207	91	81r
Bologna, all beef or mixed	lb.	2.27	12/94	82r
Bread, white	24-oz.	0.73	12/94	2c
Bread, white, pan	lb.	0.68	12/94	82r
Cabbage	lb.	0.42	12/94	82r
Carrots, short trimmed and topped	lb.	0.53	12/94	82r
Cereals and bakery products purchases	year	345	91	81r
Cereals and cereals products purchases	year	127	91	81r
Cheddar cheese, natural	lb.	3.58	12/94	82r

Monroe, LA - continued

Item	Per	Value	Date	Ref.
Groceries - continued				
Cheese, Kraft grated Parmesan	8-oz.	3.42	12/94	2c
Chicken breast, bone-in	lb.	1.71	12/94	82r
Chicken, fresh, whole	lb.	0.78	12/94	82r
Chicken, whole fryer	lb.	0.68	12/94	2c
Chuck roast, USDA choice, boneless	lb.	2.26	12/94	82r
Cigarettes, Winston, Kings	carton	14.61	12/94	2c
Coffee, vacuum-packed	13 oz.	3.42	12/94	2c
Corn Flakes, Kellogg's or Post Toasties	18 oz.	1.89	12/94	2c
Corn, frozen, whole kernel, lowest price	10 oz.	0.78	12/94	2c
Crackers, soda, salted	lb.	1.27	12/94	82r
Cucumbers	lb.	0.65	12/94	82r
Dairy products (other) purchases	year	141	91	81r
Eggs, Grade A large	dozen	0.71	12/94	2c
Eggs, Grade A large	dozen	0.87	12/94	82r
Fish and seafood purchases	year	72	91	81r
Flour, white, all purpose	lb.	0.23	12/94	82r
Food purchases, food eaten at home	year	2381	91	81r
Foods purchased away from home, not prepared by consumer	year	1696	91	81r
Frankfurters, all meat or all beef	lb.	1.74	12/94	82r
Fruits and vegetables purchases	year	380	91	81r
Grapefruit	lb.	0.45	12/94	82r
Grapes, Thompson seedless	lb.	2.30	12/94	82r
Ground beef, 100% beef	lb.	1.37	12/94	82r
Ground chuck, 100% beef	lb.	1.97	12/94	82r
Ham, boneless, exc. canned	lb.	2.54	12/94	82r
Ice cream, prepackaged, bulk, regular	1/2 gal.	2.47	12/94	82r
Lemons	lb.	1.02	12/94	82r
Lettuce, iceberg	lb.	0.96	12/94	82r
Lettuce, iceberg	head	0.83	12/94	2c
Margarine, Blue Bonnet or Parkay cubes	lb.	0.57	12/94	2c
Margarine, stick	lb.	0.77	12/94	82r
Meats, poultry, fish, and eggs purchases	year	655	91	81r
Milk and cream (fresh) purchases	year	130	91	81r
Milk, whole	1/2 gal.	1.34	12/94	2c
Orange juice, frozen concentrate 12-oz. can	16 oz.	1.36	12/94	82r
Orange juice, Minute Maid frozen	12-oz.	1.25	12/94	2c
Oranges, Navel	lb.	0.54	12/94	82r
Peaches, halves or slices, Hunt's, Del Monte, or Libby's	29-oz.	1.33	12/94	2c
Pears, Anjou	lb.	0.81	12/94	82r
Peas, sweet, Del Monte or Green Giant	15-17 oz.	0.54	12/94	2c
Pork chops, center cut, bone-in	lb.	3.07	12/94	82r
Pork purchases	year	142	91	81r
Potato chips	16-oz.	3.15	12/94	82r
Potatoes, frozen, French fried	lb.	0.82	12/94	82r
Potatoes, white	lb.	0.34	12/94	82r
Potatoes, white or red	10-lb. sack	2.18	12/94	2c
Rice, white, long grain, uncooked	lb.	0.48	12/94	82r
Round roast, USDA choice, boneless	lb.	2.91	12/94	82r
Sausage, fresh	lb.	1.82	12/94	82r
Sausage, Jimmy Dean, 100% pork	lb.	2.51	12/94	2c
Shortening, vegetable oil blends	lb.	0.75	12/94	82r
Shortening, vegetable, Crisco	3-lb.	2.40	12/94	2c
Soft drink, Coca Cola, ex deposit	2 lit	1.04	12/94	2c
Spaghetti and macaroni	lb.	0.87	12/94	82r
Steak, rib eye, USDA choice, boneless	lb.	6.85	12/94	82r
Steak, round, graded & ungraded, exc. USDA prime & choice	lb.	2.96	12/94	82r
Steak, round, USDA choice, boneless	lb.	3.17	12/94	82r
Steak, sirloin, USDA choice, boneless	lb.	4.12	12/94	82r
Steak, t-bone	lb.	5.69	12/94	2c
Steak, T-bone, USDA choice, bone-in	lb.	5.63	12/94	82r
Sugar and other sweets, eaten at home, expenditures	year	93	91	81r
Sugar, cane or beet	4 lbs.	1.50	12/94	2c
Sugar, white, all sizes	lb.	0.39	12/94	82r

Values are in dollars or fractions of dollars. In the column headed *Ref*, references are shown to sources. Each reference is followed by a letter. These refer to the geographical level for which data were reported: s=State, r=Region, and c=City or metro. The abbreviation *ex* is used to mean *except* or *excluding*; *exp* stands for *expenditures*. For other abbreviations and further explanations, please see the Introduction.

Monroe, LA - continued

Item	Per	Value	Date	Ref.
Groceries				
Tobacco products and smoking supplies, total expenditures	year	286	91	81r
Tomatoes, field grown	lb.	1.36	12/94	82r
Tomatoes, Hunt's or Del Monte	14.5 oz.	0.67	12/94	2c
Tuna, chunk, light	lb.	1.94	12/94	82r
Tuna, chunk, light, oil-packed	6.125-6.5 oz.	0.70	12/94	2c
Turkey, frozen, whole	lb.	0.96	12/94	82r
Yogurt, natural, fruit flavored	8 oz.	0.58	12/94	82r
Goods and Services				
Miscellaneous goods and services, ACCRA Index		102.70	12/94	2c
Health Care				
Health care, ACCRA Index		89.00	12/94	2c
Adenosine, emergency room	treat	100.00	95	23r
Antibiotic ointment, Polysporin	1.5 oz.	4.09	12/94	2c
Bladder tap, superpubic, infant, emergency room	treat	119.00	95	23r
Blood analysis, emergency room	treat	25.00	95	23r
Blood tests, abdominal pain, emergency room	treat	25.00	95	23r
Burn dressing, emergency room	treat	266.00	95	23r
Cardiology interpretation, emergency room	treat	26.00	95	23r
Chest X-ray, emergency room	treat	78.00	95	23r
Childbirth, Cesarean delivery, hospital charge	birth	5462.00	12/91	69r
Childbirth, Cesarean delivery, physician charge	birth	2228.00	12/91	69r
Childbirth, normal delivery, hospital charge	birth	2943.00	12/91	69r
Childbirth, normal delivery, physician charge	birth	1619.00	12/91	69r
Defibrillation pads, emergency room	treat	6.00	95	23r
Dentist's fee, adult teeth cleaning and periodic oral exam	visit	48.17	12/94	2c
Doctor's fee, routine exam, established patient	visit	40.17	12/94	2c
Drugs, expenditures	year	297	91	81r
Gastric tube insertion, nasal, emergency room	treat	25.00	95	23r
Health care, total expenditures	year	1600	91	81r
Health insurance expenditures	year	637	91	81r
Heart monitor, emergency room	treat	40.00	95	23r
Hospital care, semiprivate room	day	228.25	12/94	2c
Insurance premium, family medical care	month	394.31	1/95	41s
Intravenous fluids, emergency room	treat	130.00	95	23r
Intravenous fluids, emergency room	liter	26.00	95	23r
Intravenous line, central, emergency room	treat	342.00	95	23r
Liver function tests, abdominal pain, emergency room	treat	26.00	95	23r
Medical care charges, total, emergency room, third-degree burns	treat	2101.00	95	23r
Medical care charges, total, emergency, infant with fever	treat	628.00	95	23r
Medical services expenditures	year	573	91	81r
Medical supplies expenditures	year	93	91	81r
Morphine, emergency room	treat	34.00	95	23r
Nursing care and facilities charges, emergency room	treat	252.00	95	23r
Nursing care and facilities charges, emergency, infant with fever	treat	252.00	95	23r
Nursing care and facilities charges, emergency, third-degree burns	treat	861.00	95	23r
Physician's charges, emergency, infant with fever	treat	212.00	95	23r
Physician's charges, emergency, third-degree burns	treat	372.00	95	23r
Physician's fee, emergency room	treat	372.00	95	23r
Physician's fee, general practitioner	visit	51.20	12/93	60r
Surgery, open-heart	proc	42374.00	1/93	14r
Ultrasound, abdominal, emergency room	treat	276.00	95	23r
Urinalysis, emergency room	treat	20.00	95	23r

Monroe, LA - continued

Item	Per	Value	Date	Ref.
Health Care - continued				
Urinalysis, infant, emergency room	treat	20.00	95	23r
X-rays, emergency room	treat	78.00	95	23r
Household Goods				
Appl. repair, service call, wash mach	min. lab. chg.	39.18	12/94	2c
Floor coverings, expenditures	year	48	91	81r
Furniture, expenditures	year	280	91	81r
Household equipment, misc. expenditures	year	342	91	81r
Household expenditures, miscellaneous	year	256	91	81r
Household furnishings and equipment, expenditures	year	988	91	81r
Household operations expenditures	year	468	91	81r
Household textiles, expenditures	year	95	91	81r
Housekeeping supplies, expenditures	year	380	91	81r
Laundry and cleaning supplies, expenditures	year	109	91	81r
Laundry detergent, Tide Ultra, Bold, or Cheer	42 oz.	3.16	12/94	2c
Postage and stationery, expenditures	year	105	91	81r
Tissues, facial, Kleenex brand	175	1.07	12/94	2c
Housing				
Housing, ACCRA Index		79.60	12/94	2c
Add garage/carport		6,980	3/95	74r
Add room(s)		11,403	3/95	74r
Apartment condominium or co-op, median	unit	68600	12/94	62r
Dwellings (owned), expenditures	year	2428	91	81r
Enclose porch/patio/breezeway		4,572	3/95	74r
Finish room in basement/attic		3,794	3/95	74r
Home, existing, single-family, median	unit	120200	12/94	62r
House payment, principal and interest, 25% down payment	mo.	594	12/94	2c
House, 1800 sq ft, 8000 sq ft lot, new, urban, utilities	total	96160	12/94	2c
Maintenance, repairs, insurance, and other housing expenditures	year	531	91	81r
Mortgage interest and charges expenditures	year	1506	91	81r
Mtge. rate, incl. points and orig. fee, 30-year conv. fixed or ARM	mo.	9.27	12/94	2c
Princ. & int., mortgage, median-price exist. sing.-family home	mo.	540	12/94	62r
Property taxes expenditures	year	391	91	81r
Redesign, restructure more than half of home's interior		17,641	3/95	74r
Rent, apartment, 2 br., 1 1/2-2 baths, unfurnished, 950 sq ft, water	mo.	465	12/94	2c
Rental units expenditures	year	1264	91	81r
Insurance and Pensions				
Auto insurance, private passenger	year	862.62	12/94	71s
Insurance and pensions, personal, expenditures	year	2395	91	81r
Insurance, life and other personal, expenditures	year	368	91	81r
Pensions and Social Security, expenditures	year	2027	91	81r
Personal Goods				
Shampoo, Alberto VO5	15-oz.	1.16	12/94	2c
Toothpaste, Crest or Colgate	6-7 oz.	1.88	12/94	2c
Personal Services				
Dry cleaning, man's 2-pc. suit		6.90	12/94	2c
Haircut, man's barbershop, no styling		10.33	12/94	2c
Haircut, woman's shampoo, trim, blow-dry		16.00	12/94	2c
Personal services expenditures	year	212	91	81r
Restaurant Food				
Chicken, fried, thigh and drumstick		1.78	12/94	2c
Dining expenditures, family	week	33.83	94	73r
Hamburger with cheese	1/4 lb.	1.76	12/94	2c
Pizza, Pizza Hut or Pizza Inn	12-13 in.	7.99	12/94	2c

Values are in dollars or fractions of dollars. In the column headed *Ref*, references are shown to sources. Each reference is followed by a letter. These refer to the geographical level for which data were reported: s = State, r = Region, and c = City or metro. The abbreviation *ex* is used to mean *except* or *excluding*; *exp* stands for *expenditures*. For other abbreviations and further explanations, please see the Introduction.

Monroe, LA - continued

Item	Per	Value	Date	Ref.
Taxes				
Taxes, Federal income, expenditures	year	2275	91	81r
Taxes, personal, expenditures	year	2715	91	81r
Taxes, State and local income, expenditures	year	365	91	81r
Transportation				
Transportation, ACCRA Index		97.00	12/94	2c
Bus fare, one-way	trip	0.80	12/95	1c
Cars and trucks purchased, new	year	1306	91	81r
Cars and trucks purchased, used	year	942	91	81r
Driver's learning permit fee	perm	12.50	1/94	84s
Driver's license fee	orig	12.50	1/94	84s
Driver's license fee, duplicate	lic	5.00	1/94	84s
Driver's license reinstatement fee, min.	susp	60.00	1/94	85s
Driver's license renewal fee	renew	12.50	1/94	84s
Identification card, nondriver	card	7.00	1/94	83s
Motorcycle license fee	orig	8.00	1/94	84s
Motorcycle license renewal fee	renew	8.00	1/94	84s
Public transportation expenditures	year	249	91	81r
Tire balance, computer or spin bal., front	wheel	6.57	12/94	2c
Transportation expenditures, total	year	5307	91	81r
Vehicle finance charges	year	346	91	81r
Vehicle insurance expenditures	year	544	91	81r
Vehicle maintenance and repairs expenditures	year	600	91	81r
Vehicle purchases	year	2275	91	81r
Vehicle rental, leases, licenses, etc. expenditures	year	141	91	81r
Vehicles purchased, other than cars and trucks	year	27	91	81r
Utilities				
Utilities, ACCRA Index		110.90	12/94	2c
Electricity expenditures	year	950	91	81r
Electricity, 1800 sq. ft., new home	mo.	126.54	12/94	2c
Utilities, fuels, and public services, total expenditures	year	2000	91	81r
Water and other public services, expenditures	year	227	91	81r
Weddings				
Bridal attendants' gowns	event	750	10/93	76r
Bridal gown	event	852	10/93	76r
Bridal headpiece and veil	event	167	10/93	76r
Bride's wedding band	event	708	10/93	76r
Clergy	event	224	10/93	76r
Engagement ring	event	2756	10/93	76r
Flowers	event	863	10/93	76r
Formal wear for groom	event	106	10/93	76r
Groom's attendants' formal wear	event	530	10/93	76r
Groom's wedding band	event	402	10/93	76r
Music	event	600	10/93	76r
Photography	event	1088	10/93	76r
Shoes for bride	event	50	10/93	76r
Videography	event	483	10/93	76r
Wedding invitations and announcements	event	342	10/93	76r
Wedding reception	event	7000	10/93	76r

Montgomery, AL

Item	Per	Value	Date	Ref.
Appliances				
Appliances (major), expenditures	year	153	91	81r
Average annual exp.				
Food, health care, personal goods, services	year	27020	91	81r
Charity				
Cash contributions, expenditures	year	839	91	81r
Clothing				
Apparel, men and boys, total expenditures	year	380	91	81r
Apparel, women and girls, total expenditures	year	660	91	81r
Footwear, expenditures	year	193	91	81r

Montgomery, AL - continued

Item	Per	Value	Date	Ref.
Communications				
Long-distance telephone rate, day, addl. min., 1-10 mi.	min.	0.09	12/93	9s
Long-distance telephone rate, day, initial min., 1-10 mi.	min.	0.11	12/93	9s
Phone line, single, business, field visit	inst	69.00	12/93	9s
Phone line, single, business, no field visit	inst	69.00	12/93	9s
Phone line, single, residence, field visit	inst	40.00	12/93	9s
Phone line, single, residence, no field visit	inst	40.00	12/93	9s
Telephone service, expenditures	year	616	91	81r
Education				
Board, 4-year private college/university	year	2072	8/94	80s
Board, 4-year public college/university	year	1706	8/94	80s
Education, total expenditures	year	319	91	81r
Room, 4-year private college/university	year	1607	8/94	80s
Room, 4-year public college/university	year	1598	8/94	80s
Total cost, 4-year private college/university	year	10664	8/94	80s
Total cost, 4-year public college/university	year	5287	8/94	80s
Tuition, 2-year public college/university, in-state	year	1110	8/94	80s
Tuition, 4-year private college/university, in-state	year	6985	8/94	80s
Tuition, 4-year public college/university, in-state	year	1983	8/94	80s
Energy and Fuels				
Fuel oil and other fuels, expenditures	year	56	91	81r
Gas, natural, expenditures	year	150	91	81r
Gasoline and motor oil purchased	year	1152	91	81r
Gasoline, unleaded midgrade	gallon	1.21	4/93	82r
Gasoline, unleaded premium	gallon	1.30	4/93	82r
Gasoline, unleaded regular	gallon	1.10	4/93	82r
Entertainment				
Concert ticket, Pearl Jam group	perf	20.00	94	50r
Entertainment, total expenditures	year	1266	91	81r
Fees and admissions, expenditures	year	306	91	81r
Pets, toys, playground equipment, expenditures	year	271	91	81r
Reading, expenditures	year	131	91	81r
Televisions, radios, and sound equipment, expenditures	year	439	91	81r
Funerals				
Burial, immediate, container provided by funeral home		1298.96	1/95	54r
Cards, acknowledgment		21.26	1/95	54r
Casket, minimum alternative		204.95	1/95	54r
Cosmetology, hair care, etc.		85.40	1/95	54r
Cremation, direct, container provided by funeral home		1054.77	1/95	54r
Embalming		287.71	1/95	54r
Funeral, funeral home		269.18	1/95	54r
Funeral, other facility		272.88	1/95	54r
Graveside service		302.54	1/95	54r
Hearse, local		122.08	1/95	54r
Limousine, local		80.31	1/95	54r
Memorial service		277.66	1/95	54r
Service charge, professional, nondeclinable		896.65	1/95	54r
Visitation and viewing		232.39	1/95	54r
Groceries				
Apples, Red Delicious	lb.	0.73	12/94	82r
Bacon, sliced	lb.	1.67	12/94	82r
Bananas	lb.	0.42	12/94	82r
Beef purchases	year	213	91	81r
Beverage purchases, alcoholic	year	249	91	81r
Beverage purchases, nonalcoholic	year	207	91	81r
Bologna, all beef or mixed	lb.	2.27	12/94	82r
Bread, white, pan	lb.	0.68	12/94	82r
Cabbage	lb.	0.42	12/94	82r
Carrots, short trimmed and topped	lb.	0.53	12/94	82r
Cereals and bakery products purchases	year	345	91	81r
Cereals and cereals products purchases	year	127	91	81r

Values are in dollars or fractions of dollars. In the column headed *Ref*, references are shown to sources. Each reference is followed by a letter. These refer to the geographical level for which data were reported: s = State, r = Region, and c = City or metro. The abbreviation *ex* is used to mean *except* or *excluding*; *exp* stands for expenditures. For other abbreviations and further explanations, please see the Introduction.

Montgomery, AL - continued

Item	Per	Value	Date	Ref.
Groceries				
Cheddar cheese, natural	lb.	3.58	12/94	82r
Chicken breast, bone-in	lb.	1.71	12/94	82r
Chicken, fresh, whole	lb.	0.78	12/94	82r
Chuck roast, USDA choice, boneless	lb.	2.26	12/94	82r
Crackers, soda, salted	lb.	1.27	12/94	82r
Cucumbers	lb.	0.65	12/94	82r
Dairy products (other) purchases	year	141	91	81r
Eggs, Grade A large	dozen	0.87	12/94	82r
Fish and seafood purchases	year	72	91	81r
Flour, white, all purpose	lb.	0.23	12/94	82r
Food purchases, food eaten at home	year	2381	91	81r
Foods purchased away from home, not prepared by consumer	year	1696	91	81r
Frankfurters, all meat or all beef	lb.	1.74	12/94	82r
Fruits and vegetables purchases	year	380	91	81r
Grapefruit	lb.	0.45	12/94	82r
Grapes, Thompson seedless	lb.	2.30	12/94	82r
Ground beef, 100% beef	lb.	1.37	12/94	82r
Ground chuck, 100% beef	lb.	1.97	12/94	82r
Ham, boneless, exc. canned	lb.	2.54	12/94	82r
Ice cream, prepackaged, bulk, regular	1/2 gal.	2.47	12/94	82r
Lemons	lb.	1.02	12/94	82r
Lettuce, iceberg	lb.	0.96	12/94	82r
Margarine, stick	lb.	0.77	12/94	82r
Meats, poultry, fish, and eggs purchases	year	655	91	81r
Milk and cream (fresh) purchases	year	130	91	81r
Orange juice, frozen concentrate 12-oz. can	16 oz.	1.36	12/94	82r
Oranges, Navel	lb.	0.54	12/94	82r
Pears, Anjou	lb.	0.81	12/94	82r
Pork chops, center cut, bone-in	lb.	3.07	12/94	82r
Pork purchases	year	142	91	81r
Potato chips	16-oz.	3.15	12/94	82r
Potatoes, frozen, French fried	lb.	0.82	12/94	82r
Potatoes, white	lb.	0.34	12/94	82r
Rice, white, long grain, uncooked	lb.	0.48	12/94	82r
Round roast, USDA choice, boneless	lb.	2.91	12/94	82r
Sausage, fresh	lb.	1.82	12/94	82r
Shortening, vegetable oil blends	lb.	0.75	12/94	82r
Spaghetti and macaroni	lb.	0.87	12/94	82r
Steak, rib eye, USDA choice, boneless	lb.	6.85	12/94	82r
Steak, round, graded & ungraded, exc. USDA prime & choice	lb.	2.96	12/94	82r
Steak, round, USDA choice, boneless	lb.	3.17	12/94	82r
Steak, sirloin, USDA choice, boneless	lb.	4.12	12/94	82r
Steak, T-bone, USDA choice, bone-in	lb.	5.63	12/94	82r
Sugar and other sweets, eaten at home, expenditures	year	93	91	81r
Sugar, white, all sizes	lb.	0.39	12/94	82r
Tobacco products and smoking supplies, total expenditures	year	286	91	81r
Tomatoes, field grown	lb.	1.36	12/94	82r
Tuna, chunk, light	lb.	1.94	12/94	82r
Turkey, frozen, whole	lb.	0.96	12/94	82r
Yogurt, natural, fruit flavored	8 oz.	0.58	12/94	82r
Health Care				
Adenosine, emergency room	treat	100.00	95	23r
Bladder tap, superpubic, infant, emergency room	treat	119.00	95	23r
Blood analysis, emergency room	treat	25.00	95	23r
Blood tests, abdominal pain, emergency room	treat	25.00	95	23r
Burn dressing, emergency room	treat	266.00	95	23r
Cardiology interpretation, emergency room	treat	26.00	95	23r
Chest X-ray, emergency room	treat	78.00	95	23r
Childbirth, Cesarean delivery, hospital charge	birth	5462.00	12/91	69r
Childbirth, Cesarean delivery, physician charge	birth	2228.00	12/91	69r
Childbirth, normal delivery, hospital charge	birth	2943.00	12/91	69r
Childbirth, normal delivery, physician charge	birth	1619.00	12/91	69r
Defibrillation pads, emergency room	treat	6.00	95	23r

Montgomery, AL - continued

Item	Per	Value	Date	Ref.
Health Care - continued				
Drugs, expenditures	year	297	91	81r
Gastric tube insertion, nasal, emergency room	treat	25.00	95	23r
Health care, total expenditures	year	1600	91	81r
Health insurance expenditures	year	637	91	81r
Heart monitor, emergency room	treat	40.00	95	23r
Insurance premium, family medical care	month	360.67	1/95	41s
Intravenous fluids, emergency room	treat	130.00	95	23r
Intravenous fluids, emergency room	liter	26.00	95	23r
Intravenous line, central, emergency room	treat	342.00	95	23r
Liver function tests, abdominal pain, emergency room	treat	26.00	95	23r
Medical care charges, total, emergency room, third-degree burns	treat	2101.00	95	23r
Medical care charges, total, emergency, infant with fever	treat	628.00	95	23r
Medical services expenditures	year	573	91	81r
Medical supplies expenditures	year	93	91	81r
Morphine, emergency room	treat	34.00	95	23r
Nursing care and facilities charges, emergency room	treat	252.00	95	23r
Nursing care and facilities charges, emergency, infant with fever	treat	252.00	95	23r
Nursing care and facilities charges, emergency, third-degree burns	treat	861.00	95	23r
Physician's charges, emergency, infant with fever	treat	212.00	95	23r
Physician's charges, emergency, third-degree burns	treat	372.00	95	23r
Physician's fee, emergency room	treat	372.00	95	23r
Physician's fee, general practitioner	visit	51.20	12/93	60r
Surgery, open-heart	proc	42374.00	1/93	14r
Ultrasound, abdominal, emergency room	treat	276.00	95	23r
Urinalysis, emergency room	treat	20.00	95	23r
Urinalysis, infant, emergency room	treat	20.00	95	23r
X-rays, emergency room	treat	78.00	95	23r
Household Goods				
Floor coverings, expenditures	year	48	91	81r
Furniture, expenditures	year	280	91	81r
Household equipment, misc. expenditures	year	342	91	81r
Household expenditures, miscellaneous	year	256	91	81r
Household furnishings and equipment, expenditures	year	988	91	81r
Household operations expenditures	year	468	91	81r
Household textiles, expenditures	year	95	91	81r
Housekeeping supplies, expenditures	year	380	91	81r
Laundry and cleaning supplies, expenditures	year	109	91	81r
Postage and stationery, expenditures	year	105	91	81r
Housing				
Add garage/carport		6,980	3/95	74r
Add room(s)		11,403	3/95	74r
Apartment condominium or co-op, median	unit	68600	12/94	62r
Dwellings (owned), expenditures	year	2428	91	81r
Enclose porch/patio/breezeway		4,572	3/95	74r
Finish room in basement/attic		3,794	3/95	74r
Home, existing, single-family, median	unit	120200	12/94	62r
Maintenance, repairs, insurance, and other housing expenditures	year	531	91	81r
Mortgage interest and charges expenditures	year	1506	91	81r
Princ. & int., mortgage, median-price exist. sing.-family home	mo.	540	12/94	62r
Property taxes expenditures	year	391	91	81r
Redesign, restructure more than half of home's interior		17,641	3/95	74r
Rental units expenditures	year	1264	91	81r
Insurance and Pensions				
Auto insurance, private passenger	year	604.07	12/94	71s
Insurance and pensions, personal, expenditures	year	2395	91	81r

Values are in dollars or fractions of dollars. In the column headed *Ref*, references are shown to sources. Each reference is followed by a letter. These refer to the geographical level for which data were reported: s = State, r = Region, and c = City or metro. The abbreviation *ex* is used to mean *except* or *excluding*; *exp* stands for expenditures. For other abbreviations and further explanations, please see the Introduction.

Montgomery, AL - continued

Item	Per	Value	Date	Ref.
Insurance and Pensions				
Insurance, life and other personal, expenditures	year	368	91	81r
Pensions and Social Security, expenditures	year	2027	91	81r
Personal Services				
Personal services expenditures	year	212	91	81r
Restaurant Food				
Dining expenditures, family	week	33.83	94	73r
Taxes				
Taxes, Federal income, expenditures	year	2275	91	81r
Taxes, personal, expenditures	year	2715	91	81r
Taxes, State and local income, expenditures	year	365	91	81r
Transportation				
Cars and trucks purchased, new	year	1306	91	81r
Cars and trucks purchased, used	year	942	91	81r
Driver's learning permit fee	perm	20.00	1/94	84s
Driver's license fee	orig	20.00	1/94	84s
Driver's license fee, duplicate	lic	5.00	1/94	84s
Driver's license reinstatement fee, min.	susp	50.00	1/94	85s
Driver's license renewal fee	renew	20.00	1/94	84s
Identification card, nondriver	card	20.00	1/94	83s
Motorcycle license fee	orig	20.00	1/94	84s
Motorcycle license fee, duplicate	lic	5.00	1/94	84s
Motorcycle license renewal fee	renew	20.00	1/94	84s
Public transportation expenditures	year	249	91	81r
Transportation expenditures, total	year	5307	91	81r
Vehicle finance charges	year	346	91	81r
Vehicle insurance expenditures	year	544	91	81r
Vehicle maintenance and repairs expenditures	year	600	91	81r
Vehicle purchases	year	2275	91	81r
Vehicle rental, leases, licenses, etc. expenditures	year	141	91	81r
Vehicles purchased, other than cars and trucks	year	27	91	81r
Utilities				
Electricity expenditures	year	950	91	81r
Utilities, fuels, and public services, total expenditures	year	2000	91	81r
Water and other public services, expenditures	year	227	91	81r
Weddings				
Bridal attendants' gowns	event	750	10/93	76r
Bridal gown	event	852	10/93	76r
Bridal headpiece and veil	event	167	10/93	76r
Bride's wedding band	event	708	10/93	76r
Clergy	event	224	10/93	76r
Engagement ring	event	2756	10/93	76r
Flowers	event	863	10/93	76r
Formal wear for groom	event	106	10/93	76r
Groom's attendants' formal wear	event	530	10/93	76r
Groom's wedding band	event	402	10/93	76r
Music	event	600	10/93	76r
Photography	event	1088	10/93	76r
Shoes for bride	event	50	10/93	76r
Videography	event	483	10/93	76r
Wedding invitations and announcements	event	342	10/93	76r
Wedding reception	event	7000	10/93	76r

Morristown, TN

Item	Per	Value	Date	Ref.
Composite, ACCRA index		94.60	12/94	2c
Alcoholic Beverages				
Beer, Miller Lite, Bud, 12-oz., ex deposit	6	4.01	12/94	2c
J & B Scotch	750-ml.	20.53	12/94	2c
Wine, Gallo Chablis blanc	1.5-lit	6.37	12/94	2c

Morristown, TN - continued

Item	Per	Value	Date	Ref.
Clothing				
Jeans, man's denim		29.99	12/94	2c
Shirt, man's dress shirt		38.17	12/94	2c
Undervest, boy's size 10-14, cotton	3	3.18	12/94	2c
Communications				
Newspaper subscription, dly. and Sun. delivery	month	8.25	12/94	2c
Telephone bill, family of four	month	17.96	12/94	2c
Telephone, residential, flat rate	mo.	8.50	12/93	8c
Energy and Fuels				
Energy, combined forms, 1800 sq. ft.	mo.	104.77	12/94	2c
Gas, reg unlead, taxes inc., cash, self-service	gal	1.09	12/94	2c
Entertainment				
Bowling, evening rate	game	2.00	12/94	2c
Monopoly game, Parker Brothers', No. 9	game	11.16	12/94	2c
Movie	adm	5.25	12/94	2c
Tennis balls, yellow, Wilson or Penn, 3	can	2.12	12/94	2c
Groceries				
Groceries, ACCRA Index		96.40	12/94	2c
Baby food, strained vegetables, lowest price	4-4.5 oz.	0.33	12/94	2c
Bananas	lb.	0.46	12/94	2c
Beef or hamburger, ground	lb.	1.51	12/94	2c
Bread, white	24-oz.	0.68	12/94	2c
Cheese, Kraft grated Parmesan	8-oz.	2.97	12/94	2c
Chicken, whole fryer	lb.	0.93	12/94	2c
Cigarettes, Winston, Kings	carton	13.93	12/94	2c
Coffee, vacuum-packed	13 oz.	3.17	12/94	2c
Corn Flakes, Kellogg's or Post Toasties	18 oz.	2.24	12/94	2c
Corn, frozen, whole kernel, lowest price	10 oz.	0.61	12/94	2c
Eggs, Grade A large	dozen	0.83	12/94	2c
Lettuce, iceberg	head	0.96	12/94	2c
Margarine, Blue Bonnet or Parkay cubes	lb.	0.61	12/94	2c
Milk, whole	1/2 gal.	1.35	12/94	2c
Orange juice, Minute Maid frozen	12-oz.	1.17	12/94	2c
Peaches, halves or slices, Hunt's, Del Monte, or Libby's	29-oz.	1.32	12/94	2c
Peas, sweet, Del Monte or Green Giant	15-17 oz.	0.50	12/94	2c
Potatoes, white or red	10-lb. sack	2.39	12/94	2c
Sausage, Jimmy Dean, 100% pork	lb.	2.43	12/94	2c
Shortening, vegetable, Crisco	3-lb.	2.45	12/94	2c
Soft drink, Coca Cola, ex deposit	2 lit	1.03	12/94	2c
Steak, t-bone	lb.	5.69	12/94	2c
Sugar, cane or beet	4 lbs.	1.43	12/94	2c
Tomatoes, Hunt's or Del Monte	14.5 oz.	0.61	12/94	2c
Tuna, chunk, light, oil-packed	6.125-6.5 oz.	0.65	12/94	2c
Goods and Services				
Miscellaneous goods and services, ACCRA Index		99.90	12/94	2c
Health Care				
Health care, ACCRA Index		81.60	12/94	2c
Antibiotic ointment, Polysporin	1.5 oz.	3.77	12/94	2c
Dentist's fee, adult teeth cleaning and periodic oral exam	visit	45.60	12/94	2c
Doctor's fee, routine exam, established patient	visit	35.50	12/94	2c
Hospital care, semiprivate room	day	210.00	12/94	2c
Household Goods				
Appl. repair, service call, wash mach	min. lab. chg.	35.00	12/94	2c
Laundry detergent, Tide Ultra, Bold, or Cheer	42 oz.	3.25	12/94	2c

Values are in dollars or fractions of dollars. In the column headed *Ref*, references are shown to sources. Each reference is followed by a letter. These refer to the geographical level for which data were reported: s=State, r=Region, and c=City or metro. The abbreviation *ex* is used to mean *except* or *excluding*; *exp* stands for expenditures. For other abbreviations and further explanations, please see the Introduction.

Morristown, TN - continued

Item	Per	Value	Date	Ref.
Household Goods				
Tissues, facial, Kleenex brand	175	0.95	12/94	2c
Housing				
Housing, ACCRA Index		89.40	12/94	2c
House payment, principal and interest, 25% down payment	mo.	699	12/94	2c
House, 1800 sq ft, 8000 sq ft lot, new, urban, utilities	total	110633	12/94	2c
Mtge. rate, incl. points and orig. fee, 30-year conv. fixed or ARM	mo.	9.52	12/94	2c
Rent, apartment, 2 br., 1 1/2-2 baths, unfurnished, 950 sq ft, water	mo.	430	12/94	2c
Personal Goods				
Shampoo, Alberto VO5	15-oz.	1.04	12/94	2c
Toothpaste, Crest or Colgate	6-7 oz.	1.92	12/94	2c
Personal Services				
Dry cleaning, man's 2-pc. suit		5.79	12/94	2c
Haircut, man's barbershop, no styling		6.00	12/94	2c
Haircut, woman's shampoo, trim, blow-dry		14.75	12/94	2c
Restaurant Food				
Chicken, fried, thigh and drumstick		2.30	12/94	2c
Hamburger with cheese	1/4 lb.	1.85	12/94	2c
Pizza, Pizza Hut or Pizza Inn	12-13 in.	7.99	12/94	2c
Transportation				
Transportation, ACCRA Index		97.60	12/94	2c
Tire balance, computer or spin bal., front	wheel	6.67	12/94	2c
Utilities				
Utilities, ACCRA Index		93.20	12/94	2c
Electricity, 1800 sq. ft., new home	mo.	104.77	12/94	2c

Mount Vernon-Knox County, OH

Item	Per	Value	Date	Ref.
Composite, ACCRA index		96.20	12/94	2c
Alcoholic Beverages				
Beer, Miller Lite, Bud, 12-oz., ex deposit	6	4.09	12/94	2c
J & B Scotch	750-ml.	18.60	12/94	2c
Wine, Gallo Chablis blanc	1.5-lit	5.49	12/94	2c
Clothing				
Jeans, man's denim		30.99	12/94	2c
Shirt, man's dress shirt		31.50	12/94	2c
Undervest, boy's size 10-14, cotton	3	3.82	12/94	2c
Communications				
Newspaper subscription, dly. and Sun. delivery	month	11.30	12/94	2c
Telephone bill, family of four	month	21.68	12/94	2c
Telephone, residential, flat rate	mo.	15.25	12/93	8c
Energy and Fuels				
Energy, combined forms, 1800 sq. ft.	mo.	103.31	12/94	2c
Energy, exc. electricity, 1800 sq. ft.	mo.	55.37	12/94	2c
Gas, reg unlead, taxes inc., cash, self-service	gal	1.13	12/94	2c
Entertainment				
Bowling, evening rate	game	1.90	12/94	2c
Monopoly game, Parker Brothers', No. 9	game	10.99	12/94	2c
Movie	adm	5.00	12/94	2c
Tennis balls, yellow, Wilson or Penn, 3	can	2.62	12/94	2c
Groceries				
Groceries, ACCRA Index		99.80	12/94	2c
Baby food, strained vegetables, lowest price	4-4.5 oz.	0.17	12/94	2c
Bananas	lb.	0.56	12/94	2c
Beef or hamburger, ground	lb.	1.39	12/94	2c
Bread, white	24-oz.	0.57	12/94	2c
Cheese, Kraft grated Parmesan	8-oz.	2.99	12/94	2c

Mount Vernon-Knox County, OH - continued

Item	Per	Value	Date	Ref.
Groceries - continued				
Chicken, whole fryer	lb.	0.96	12/94	2c
Cigarettes, Winston, Kings	carton	15.79	12/94	2c
Coffee, vacuum-packed	13 oz.	3.96	12/94	2c
Corn Flakes, Kellogg's or Post Toasties	18 oz.	2.29	12/94	2c
Corn, frozen, whole kernel, lowest price	10 oz.	0.71	12/94	2c
Eggs, Grade A large	dozen	0.79	12/94	2c
Lettuce, iceberg	head	0.98	12/94	2c
Margarine, Blue Bonnet or Parkay cubes	lb.	0.72	12/94	2c
Milk, whole	1/2 gal.	1.32	12/94	2c
Orange juice, Minute Maid frozen	12-oz.	1.29	12/94	2c
Peaches, halves or slices, Hunt's, Del Monte, or Libby's	29-oz.	1.64	12/94	2c
Peas, sweet, Del Monte or Green Giant	15-17 oz.	0.64	12/94	2c
Potatoes, white or red	10-lb. sack	2.22	12/94	2c
Sausage, Jimmy Dean, 100% pork	lb.	2.66	12/94	2c
Shortening, vegetable, Crisco	3-lb.	2.12	12/94	2c
Soft drink, Coca Cola, ex deposit	2 lit	1.19	12/94	2c
Steak, t-bone	lb.	6.02	12/94	2c
Sugar, cane or beet	4 lbs.	1.25	12/94	2c
Tomatoes, Hunt's or Del Monte	14.5 oz.	0.77	12/94	2c
Tuna, chunk, light, oil-packed	6.125-6.5 oz.	0.82	12/94	2c
Goods and Services				
Miscellaneous goods and services, ACCRA Index		95.40	12/94	2c
Health Care				
Health care, ACCRA Index		88.90	12/94	2c
Antibiotic ointment, Polysporin	1.5 oz.	3.69	12/94	2c
Dentist's fee, adult teeth cleaning and periodic oral exam	visit	44.67	12/94	2c
Doctor's fee, routine exam, established patient	visit	38.00	12/94	2c
Hospital care, semiprivate room	day	329.00	12/94	2c
Household Goods				
Appl. repair, service call, wash mach	min. lab. chg.	25.97	12/94	2c
Laundry detergent, Tide Ultra, Bold, or Cheer	42 oz.	4.24	12/94	2c
Tissues, facial, Kleenex brand	175	1.16	12/94	2c
Housing				
Housing, ACCRA Index		94.70	12/94	2c
House payment, principal and interest, 25% down payment	mo.	760	12/94	2c
House, 1800 sq ft, 8000 sq ft lot, new, urban, utilities	total	122333	12/94	2c
Mtge. rate, incl. points and orig. fee, 30-year conv. fixed or ARM	mo.	9.32	12/94	2c
Rent, apartment, 2 br., 1 1/2-2 baths, unfurnished, 950 sq ft, water	mo.	403	12/94	2c
Personal Goods				
Shampoo, Alberto VO5	15-oz.	1.09	12/94	2c
Toothpaste, Crest or Colgate	6-7 oz.	1.82	12/94	2c
Personal Services				
Dry cleaning, man's 2-pc. suit		6.75	12/94	2c
Haircut, man's barbershop, no styling		6.00	12/94	2c
Haircut, woman's shampoo, trim, blow-dry		15.00	12/94	2c
Restaurant Food				
Chicken, fried, thigh and drumstick		1.89	12/94	2c
Hamburger with cheese	1/4 lb.	1.79	12/94	2c
Pizza, Pizza Hut or Pizza Inn	12-13 in.	7.20	12/94	2c

Values are in dollars or fractions of dollars. In the column headed *Ref*, references are shown to sources. Each reference is followed by a letter. These refer to the geographical level for which data were reported: s = State, r = Region, and c = City or metro. The abbreviation *ex* is used to mean *except* or *excluding*; *exp* stands for expenditures. For other abbreviations and further explanations, please see the Introduction.

Mount Vernon-Knox County, OH - continued

Item	Per	Value	Date	Ref.
Transportation				
Transportation, ACCRA Index		103.80	12/94	2c
Tire balance, computer or spin bal., front	wheel	7.33	12/94	2c
Utilities				
Utilities, ACCRA Index		94.60	12/94	2c
Electricity, (part.), other, 1800 sq. ft., new home	mo.	47.94	12/94	2c

Muncie, IN

Item	Per	Value	Date	Ref.
Composite, ACCRA index		98.90	12/94	2c
Alcoholic Beverages				
Beer, Miller Lite, Bud, 12-oz., ex deposit	6	3.85	12/94	2c
J & B Scotch	750-ml.	16.99	12/94	2c
Wine, Gallo Chablis blanc	1.5-lit	4.56	12/94	2c
Appliances				
Appliances (major), expenditures	year	131	91	81r
Average annual exp.				
Food, health care, personal goods, services	year	25935	91	81r
Charity				
Cash contributions, expenditures	year	745	91	81r
Clothing				
Apparel, men and boys, total expenditures	year	332	91	81r
Apparel, women and girls, total expenditures	year	578	91	81r
Footwear, expenditures	year	164	91	81r
Jeans, man's denim		29.98	12/94	2c
Shirt, man's dress shirt		34.00	12/94	2c
Undervest, boy's size 10-14, cotton	3	3.90	12/94	2c
Communications				
Long-distance telephone rate, day, addl. min., 1-10 mi.	min.	0.10	12/93	9s
Long-distance telephone rate, day, initial min., 1-10 mi.	min.	0.18	12/93	9s
Newspaper subscription, dly. and Sun. delivery	month	11.52	12/94	2c
Phone line, single, business, field visit	inst	59.00	12/93	9s
Phone line, single, business, no field visit	inst	59.00	12/93	9s
Phone line, single, residence, field visit	inst	47.00	12/93	9s
Phone line, single, residence, no field visit	inst	47.00	12/93	9s
Telephone bill, family of four	month	18.17	12/94	2c
Telephone service, expenditures	year	547	91	81r
Telephone, residential, flat rate	mo.	11.11	12/93	8c
Education				
Board, 4-year private college/university	year	2095	8/94	80s
Board, 4-year public college/university	year	2300	8/94	80s
Education, total expenditures	year	394	91	81r
Room, 4-year private college/university	year	1784	8/94	80s
Room, 4-year public college/university	year	1718	8/94	80s
Total cost, 4-year private college/university	year	15045	8/94	80s
Total cost, 4-year public college/university	year	6639	8/94	80s
Tuition, 2-year public college/university, in-state	year	1737	8/94	80s
Tuition, 4-year private college/university, in-state	year	11165	8/94	80s
Tuition, 4-year public college/university, in-state	year	2621	8/94	80s
Energy and Fuels				
Energy, combined forms, 1800 sq. ft.	mo.	104.43	12/94	2c
Energy, exc. electricity, 1800 sq. ft.	mo.	44.50	12/94	2c
Fuel oil and other fuels, expenditures	year	83	91	81r
Gas, cooking, 10 therms	month	15.41	2/94	65c
Gas, cooking, 30 therms	month	28.21	2/94	65c
Gas, cooking, 50 therms	month	40.68	2/94	65c
Gas, heating, winter, 100 therms	month	69.21	2/94	65c
Gas, heating, winter, average use	month	127.99	2/94	65c
Gas, natural, expenditures	year	373	91	81r

Muncie, IN - continued

Item	Per	Value	Date	Ref.
Energy and Fuels - continued				
Gas, reg unlead, taxes inc., cash, self-service	gal	1.00	12/94	2c
Gasoline and motor oil purchased	year	1000	91	81r
Gasoline, unleaded midgrade	gallon	1.15	4/93	82r
Gasoline, unleaded premium	gallon	1.23	4/93	82r
Gasoline, unleaded regular	gallon	1.07	4/93	82r
Entertainment				
Bowling, evening rate	game	1.92	12/94	2c
Entertainment, total expenditures	year	1356	91	81r
Fees and admissions, expenditures	year	347	91	81r
Monopoly game, Parker Brothers', No. 9	game	9.78	12/94	2c
Movie	adm	5.00	12/94	2c
Pets, toys, playground equipment, expenditures	year	270	91	81r
Reading, expenditures	year	160	91	81r
Televisions, radios, and sound equipment, expenditures	year	433	91	81r
Tennis balls, yellow, Wilson or Penn, 3	can	1.90	12/94	2c
Funerals				
Burial, immediate, container provided by funeral home		1268.31	1/95	54r
Cards, acknowledgment		26.12	1/95	54r
Casket, minimum alternative		198.03	1/95	54r
Cosmetology, hair care, etc.		122.19	1/95	54r
Cremation, direct, container provided by funeral home		977.81	1/95	54r
Embalming		334.00	1/95	54r
Funeral, funeral home		321.16	1/95	54r
Funeral, other facility		317.73	1/95	54r
Graveside service		292.48	1/95	54r
Hearse, local		153.20	1/95	54r
Limousine, local		123.52	1/95	54r
Memorial service		356.30	1/95	54r
Service charge, professional, nondeclinable		968.24	1/95	54r
Visitation and viewing		332.66	1/95	54r
Groceries				
Groceries, ACCRA Index		98.90	12/94	2c
Apples, Red Delicious	lb.	0.68	12/94	82r
Baby food, strained vegetables, lowest price	4-4.5 oz.	0.39	12/94	2c
Bacon, sliced	lb.	1.88	12/94	82r
Bananas	lb.	0.29	12/94	2c
Bananas	lb.	0.41	12/94	82r
Beef or hamburger, ground	lb.	1.07	12/94	2c
Beef purchases	year	197	91	81r
Beef, stew, boneless	lb.	2.52	12/94	82r
Beverage purchases, alcoholic	year	293	91	81r
Beverage purchases, nonalcoholic	year	203	91	81r
Bologna, all beef or mixed	lb.	2.12	12/94	82r
Bread, white	24-oz.	0.78	12/94	2c
Bread, white, pan	lb.	0.76	12/94	82r
Cabbage	lb.	0.44	12/94	82r
Carrots, short trimmed and topped	lb.	0.44	12/94	82r
Cereals and bakery products purchases	year	347	91	81r
Cereals and cereals products purchases	year	119	91	81r
Cheddar cheese, natural	lb.	3.28	12/94	82r
Cheese, Kraft grated Parmesan	8-oz.	2.99	12/94	2c
Chicken breast, bone-in	lb.	1.61	12/94	82r
Chicken, fresh, whole	lb.	0.89	12/94	82r
Chicken, whole fryer	lb.	0.89	12/94	2c
Chuck roast, USDA choice, boneless	lb.	2.33	12/94	82r
Cigarettes, Winston, Kings	carton	14.58	12/94	2c
Coffee, 100%, ground roast, all sizes	lb.	4.28	12/94	82r
Coffee, vacuum-packed	13 oz.	3.54	12/94	2c
Cookies, chocolate chip	lb.	2.72	12/94	82r
Corn Flakes, Kellogg's or Post Toasties	18 oz.	2.34	12/94	2c
Corn, frozen, whole kernel, lowest price	10 oz.	0.75	12/94	2c
Dairy products (other) purchases	year	148	91	81r
Eggs, Grade A large	dozen	0.70	12/94	2c
Eggs, Grade A large	dozen	0.76	12/94	82r
Fish and seafood purchases	year	61	91	81r

Values are in dollars or fractions of dollars. In the column headed *Ref*, references are shown to sources. Each reference is followed by a letter. These refer to the geographical level for which data were reported: s=State, r=Region, and c=City or metro. The abbreviation *ex* is used to mean *except* or *excluding*; *exp* stands for expenditures. For other abbreviations and further explanations, please see the Introduction.

Muncie, IN - continued

Item	Per	Value	Date	Ref.
Groceries				
Flour, white, all purpose	lb.	0.22	12/94	82r
Food purchases, food eaten at home	year	2313	91	81r
Foods purchased away from home, not prepared by consumer	year	1709	91	81r
Fruits and vegetables purchases	year	372	91	81r
Grapefruit	lb.	0.47	12/94	82r
Grapes, Thompson seedless	lb.	2.15	12/94	82r
Ground beef, 100% beef	lb.	1.37	12/94	82r
Ground chuck, 100% beef	lb.	1.81	12/94	82r
Ham, boneless, exc. canned	lb.	2.16	12/94	82r
Ice cream, prepackaged, bulk, regular	1/2 gal.	2.48	12/94	82r
Lemons	lb.	1.08	12/94	82r
Lettuce, iceberg	lb.	0.81	12/94	82r
Lettuce, iceberg	head	0.85	12/94	2c
Margarine, Blue Bonnet or Parkay cubes	lb.	0.59	12/94	2c
Margarine, stick	lb.	0.81	12/94	82r
Meats, poultry, fish, and eggs purchases	year	591	91	81r
Milk and cream (fresh) purchases	year	132	91	81r
Milk, whole	1/2 gal.	1.31	12/94	2c
Orange juice, frozen concentrate 12-oz. can	16 oz.	1.41	12/94	82r
Orange juice, Minute Maid frozen	12-oz.	1.31	12/94	2c
Oranges, Navel	lb.	0.56	12/94	82r
Peaches, halves or slices, Hunt's, Del Monte, or Libby's	29-oz.	1.20	12/94	2c
Peanut butter, creamy, all sizes	lb.	1.81	12/94	82r
Peas, sweet, Del Monte or Green Giant	15-17 oz.	0.59	12/94	2c
Pork chops, center cut, bone-in	lb.	2.76	12/94	82r
Pork purchases	year	130	91	81r
Potato chips	16-oz.	2.81	12/94	82r
Potatoes, frozen, French fried	lb.	0.83	12/94	82r
Potatoes, white	lb.	0.28	12/94	82r
Potatoes, white or red	10-lb. sack	1.76	12/94	2c
Round roast, USDA choice, boneless	lb.	2.90	12/94	82r
Sausage, Jimmy Dean, 100% pork	lb.	3.07	12/94	2c
Shortening, vegetable oil blends	lb.	0.88	12/94	82r
Shortening, vegetable, Crisco	3-lb.	2.33	12/94	2c
Soft drink, Coca Cola, ex deposit	2 lit	1.24	12/94	2c
Spaghetti and macaroni	lb.	0.78	12/94	82r
Steak, rib eye, USDA choice, boneless	lb.	6.15	12/94	82r
Steak, round, graded & ungraded, exc. USDA prime & choice	lb.	2.72	12/94	82r
Steak, round, USDA choice, boneless	lb.	3.02	12/94	82r
Steak, sirloin, USDA choice, boneless	lb.	3.85	12/94	82r
Steak, t-bone	lb.	4.75	12/94	2c
Steak, T-bone, USDA choice, bone-in	lb.	5.38	12/94	82r
Sugar and other sweets, eaten at home, expenditures	year	91	91	81r
Sugar, cane or beet	4 lbs.	1.45	12/94	2c
Sugar, white, all sizes	lb.	0.36	12/94	82r
Tobacco products and smoking supplies, total expenditures	year	298	91	81r
Tomatoes, field grown	lb.	1.36	12/94	82r
Tomatoes, Hunt's or Del Monte	14.5 oz.	0.86	12/94	2c
Tuna, chunk, light	lb.	1.94	12/94	82r
Tuna, chunk, light, oil-packed	6.125-6.5 oz.	0.77	12/94	2c
Turkey, frozen, whole	lb.	0.96	12/94	82r
Yogurt, natural, fruit flavored	8 oz.	0.62	12/94	82r
Goods and Services				
Miscellaneous goods and services, ACCRA Index		95.80	12/94	2c
Health Care				
Health care, ACCRA Index		87.80	12/94	2c
Antibiotic ointment, Polysporin	1.5 oz.	3.70	12/94	2c
Childbirth, Cesarean delivery, hospital charge	birth	5101.00	12/91	69r

Muncie, IN - continued

Item	Per	Value	Date	Ref.
Health Care - continued				
Childbirth, Cesarean delivery, physician charge	birth	2234.00	12/91	69r
Childbirth, normal delivery, hospital charge	birth	2891.00	12/91	69r
Childbirth, normal delivery, physician charge	birth	1623.00	12/91	69r
Dentist's fee, adult teeth cleaning and periodic oral exam	visit	45.00	12/94	2c
Doctor's fee, routine exam, established patient	visit	37.40	12/94	2c
Drugs, expenditures	year	248	91	81r
Health care, total expenditures	year	1336	91	81r
Health insurance expenditures	year	550	91	81r
Hospital care, semiprivate room	day	321.00	12/94	2c
Insurance premium, family medical care	month	353.94	1/95	41s
Medical services expenditures	year	457	91	81r
Medical supplies expenditures	year	82	91	81r
Household Goods				
Appl. repair, service call, wash mach	min. lab. chg.	36.00	12/94	2c
Floor coverings, expenditures	year	105	91	81r
Furniture, expenditures	year	291	91	81r
Household equipment, misc. expenditures	year	341	91	81r
Household expenditures, miscellaneous	year	162	91	81r
Household furnishings and equipment, expenditures	year	1042	91	81r
Household operations expenditures	year	365	91	81r
Household textiles, expenditures	year	101	91	81r
Housekeeping supplies, expenditures	year	390	91	81r
Laundry and cleaning supplies, expenditures	year	110	91	81r
Laundry detergent, Tide Ultra, Bold, or Cheer	42 oz.	3.66	12/94	2c
Postage and stationery, expenditures	year	115	91	81r
Tissues, facial, Kleenex brand	175	0.89	12/94	2c
Housing				
Housing, ACCRA Index		106.30	12/94	2c
Add garage/carport		8,479	3/95	74r
Add room(s)		21,347	3/95	74r
Apartment condominium or co-op, median	unit	87100	12/94	62r
Bathroom addition, average cost	add	9734.00	3/95	13r
Bathroom remodeling, average cost	remod	6414.00	3/95	13r
Bedroom, master suite addition, average cost	add	27122.00	3/95	13r
Deck addition, average cost	add	6665.00	3/95	13r
Dwellings (owned), expenditures	year	2566	91	81r
Enclose porch/patio/breezeway		4,556	3/95	74r
Exterior remodeling, average cost	remod	15395.00	3/95	13r
Family room addition, average cost	add	27658.00	3/95	13r
Finish room in basement/attic		5,074	3/95	74r
Home, existing, single-family, median	unit	106500	12/94	62r
House payment, principal and interest, 25% down payment	mo.	817	12/94	2c
House, 1800 sq ft, 8000 sq ft lot, new, urban, utilities	total	129967	12/94	2c
Kitchen remodeling, major, average cost	remod	17084.00	3/95	13r
Kitchen remodeling, minor, average cost	remod	5804.00	3/95	13r
Maintenance, repairs, insurance, and other housing expenditures	year	484	91	81r
Mortgage interest and charges expenditures	year	1443	91	81r
Mtge. rate, incl. points and orig. fee, 30-year conv. fixed or ARM	mo.	9.49	12/94	2c
Office, home addition, average cost	add	8121.00	3/95	13r
Princ. & int., mortgage, median-price exist. sing.-family home	mo.	515	12/94	62r
Property taxes expenditures	year	639	91	81r
Redesign, restructure more than half of home's interior		9,114	3/95	74r
Rent, apartment, 2 br., 1 1/2-2 baths, unfurnished, 950 sq ft, water	mo.	555	12/94	2c
Rental units expenditures	year	1200	91	81r
Sun-space addition, average cost	add	23768.00	3/95	13r

Values are in dollars or fractions of dollars. In the column headed *Ref*, references are shown to sources. Each reference is followed by a letter. These refer to the geographical level for which data were reported: s = State, r = Region, and c = City or metro. The abbreviation *ex* is used to mean *except* or *excluding*; *exp* stands for *expenditures*. For other abbreviations and further explanations, please see the Introduction.

Muncie, IN - continued

Item	Per	Value	Date	Ref.
Housing				
Wing addition, two-story, average cost	add	50410.00	3/95	13r
Insurance and Pensions				
Auto insurance, private passenger	year	586.58	12/94	71s
Insurance and pensions, personal, expenditures	year	2408	91	81r
Insurance, life and other personal, expenditures	year	355	91	81r
Pensions and Social Security, expenditures	year	2053	91	81r
Legal Assistance				
Legal work, law firm associate	hour	90		10r
Legal work, law firm partner	hour	139		10r
Personal Goods				
Shampoo, Alberto VO5	15-oz.	1.26	12/94	2c
Toothpaste, Crest or Colgate	6-7 oz.	1.99	12/94	2c
Personal Services				
Dry cleaning, man's 2-pc. suit		6.08	12/94	2c
Haircut, man's barbershop, no styling		7.50	12/94	2c
Haircut, woman's shampoo, trim, blow-dry		19.60	12/94	2c
Personal services expenditures	year	203	91	81r
Restaurant Food				
Chicken, fried, thigh and drumstick		1.99	12/94	2c
Dining expenditures, family	week	30.03	94	73r
Hamburger with cheese	1/4 lb.	1.69	12/94	2c
Pizza, Pizza Hut or Pizza Inn	12-13 in.	7.50	12/94	2c
Taxes				
Taxes, Federal income, expenditures	year	1756	91	81r
Taxes, personal, expenditures	year	2426	91	81r
Taxes, State and local income, expenditures	year	568	91	81r
Transportation				
Transportation, ACCRA Index		99.70	12/94	2c
Bus fare, one-way	trip	0.50	12/95	1c
Cars and trucks purchased, new	year	891	91	81r
Cars and trucks purchased, used	year	1155	91	81r
Driver's learning permit fee	perm	2.00	1/94	84s
Driver's license fee	orig	6.00	1/94	84s
Driver's license fee, duplicate	lic	3.00	1/94	84s
Driver's license renewal fee	renew	6.00	1/94	84s
Identification card, nondriver	card	4.00	1/94	83s
Motorcycle learning permit fee	perm	2.00	1/94	84s
Motorcycle license fee	orig	6.00	1/94	84s
Motorcycle license fee, duplicate	lic	3.00	1/94	84s
Motorcycle license renewal fee	renew	6.00	1/94	84s
Public transportation expenditures	year	209	91	81r
Tire balance, computer or spin bal., front	wheel	7.75	12/94	2c
Transportation expenditures, total	year	4792	91	81r
Vehicle finance charges	year	300	91	81r
Vehicle insurance expenditures	year	485	91	81r
Vehicle maintenance and repairs expenditures	year	534	91	81r
Vehicle purchases	year	2068	91	81r
Vehicle rental, leases, licenses, etc. expenditures	year	197	91	81r
Vehicles purchased, other than cars and trucks	year	22	91	81r
Utilities				
Utilities, ACCRA Index		93.10	12/94	2c
Electricity expenditures	year	668	91	81r
Electricity, (part.), other, 1800 sq. ft., new home	mo.	59.93	12/94	2c
Utilities, fuels, and public services, total expenditures	year	1838	91	81r
Water and other public services, expenditures	year	167	91	81r
Weddings				
Bridal attendants' gowns	event	750	10/93	76r
Bridal gown	event	852	10/93	76r

Muncie, IN - continued

Item	Per	Value	Date	Ref.
Weddings - continued				
Bridal headpiece and veil	event	167	10/93	76r
Bride's wedding band	event	708	10/93	76r
Clergy	event	224	10/93	76r
Engagement ring	event	2756	10/93	76r
Flowers	event	863	10/93	76r
Formal wear for groom	event	106	10/93	76r
Groom's attendants' formal wear	event	530	10/93	76r
Groom's wedding band	event	402	10/93	76r
Music	event	600	10/93	76r
Photography	event	1088	10/93	76r
Shoes for bride	event	50	10/93	76r
Videography	event	483	10/93	76r
Wedding invitations and announcements	event	342	10/93	76r
Wedding reception	event	7000	10/93	76r

Murfreesboro-Smyrna, TN

Item	Per	Value	Date	Ref.
Composite, ACCRA index		94.60	12/94	2c
Alcoholic Beverages				
Beer, Miller Lite, Bud, 12-oz., ex deposit	6	3.86	12/94	2c
J & B Scotch	750-ml.	18.85	12/94	2c
Wine, Gallo Chablis blanc	1.5-lit	5.79	12/94	2c
Clothing				
Jeans, man's denim		29.59	12/94	2c
Shirt, man's dress shirt		39.90	12/94	2c
Undervest, boy's size 10-14, cotton	3	3.15	12/94	2c
Communications				
Newspaper subscription, dly. and Sun. delivery	month	13.86	12/94	2c
Telephone bill, family of four	month	19.27	12/94	2c
Telephone, residential, flat rate	mo.	12.15	12/93	8c
Energy and Fuels				
Energy, combined forms, 1800 sq. ft.	mo.	101.12	12/94	2c
Energy, exc. electricity, 1800 sq. ft.	mo.	40.61	12/94	2c
Gas, reg unlead, taxes inc., cash, self-service	gal	1.07	12/94	2c
Entertainment				
Bowling, evening rate	game	2.65	12/94	2c
Monopoly game, Parker Brothers', No. 9	game	10.38	12/94	2c
Movie	adm	5.00	12/94	2c
Tennis balls, yellow, Wilson or Penn, 3	can	2.06	12/94	2c
Groceries				
Groceries, ACCRA Index		94.80	12/94	2c
Baby food, strained vegetables, lowest price	4-4.5 oz.	0.35	12/94	2c
Bananas	lb.	0.45	12/94	2c
Beef or hamburger, ground	lb.	1.75	12/94	2c
Bread, white	24-oz.	0.70	12/94	2c
Cheese, Kraft grated Parmesan	8-oz.	3.09	12/94	2c
Chicken, whole fryer	lb.	0.65	12/94	2c
Cigarettes, Winston, Kings	carton	13.38	12/94	2c
Coffee, vacuum-packed	13 oz.	3.05	12/94	2c
Corn Flakes, Kellogg's or Post Toasties	18 oz.	2.22	12/94	2c
Corn, frozen, whole kernel, lowest price	10 oz.	0.67	12/94	2c
Eggs, Grade A large	dozen	0.73	12/94	2c
Lettuce, iceberg	head	0.95	12/94	2c
Margarine, Blue Bonnet or Parkay cubes	lb.	0.55	12/94	2c
Milk, whole	1/2 gal.	1.29	12/94	2c
Orange juice, Minute Maid frozen	12-oz.	1.17	12/94	2c
Peaches, halves or slices, Hunt's, Del Monte, or Libby's	29-oz.	1.15	12/94	2c
Peas, sweet, Del Monte or Green Giant	15-17 oz.	0.48	12/94	2c
Potatoes, white or red	10-lb. sack	2.95	12/94	2c
Sausage, Jimmy Dean, 100% pork	lb.	1.87	12/94	2c

Values are in dollars or fractions of dollars. In the column headed *Ref*, references are shown to sources. Each reference is followed by a letter. These refer to the geographical level for which data were reported: s=State, r=Region, and c=City or metro. The abbreviation *ex* is used to mean *except* or *excluding*; *exp* stands for expenditures. For other abbreviations and further explanations, please see the Introduction.

Murfreesboro-Smyrna, TN - continued

Item	Per	Value	Date	Ref.
Groceries				
Shortening, vegetable, Crisco	3-lb.	2.25	12/94	2c
Soft drink, Coca Cola, ex deposit	2 lit	1.17	12/94	2c
Steak, t-bone	lb.	5.13	12/94	2c
Sugar, cane or beet	4 lbs.	1.63	12/94	2c
Tomatoes, Hunt's or Del Monte	14.5 oz.	0.57	12/94	2c
Tuna, chunk, light, oil-packed	6.125-6.5 oz.	0.67	12/94	2c
Goods and Services				
Miscellaneous goods and services, ACCRA Index		101.40	12/94	2c
Health Care				
Health care, ACCRA Index		87.10	12/94	2c
Antibiotic ointment, Polysporin	1.5 oz.	3.96	12/94	2c
Dentist's fee, adult teeth cleaning and periodic oral exam	visit	46.40	12/94	2c
Doctor's fee, routine exam, established patient	visit	38.50	12/94	2c
Hospital care, semiprivate room	day	248.00	12/94	2c
Household Goods				
Appl. repair, service call, wash mach	min. lab. chg.	33.11	12/94	2c
Laundry detergent, Tide Ultra, Bold, or Cheer	42 oz.	2.92	12/94	2c
Tissues, facial, Kleenex brand	175	1.05	12/94	2c
Housing				
Housing, ACCRA Index		88.00	12/94	2c
House payment, principal and interest, 25% down payment	mo.	657	12/94	2c
House, 1800 sq ft, 8000 sq ft lot, new, urban, utilities	total	105756	12/94	2c
Mtge. rate, incl. points and orig. fee, 30-year conv. fixed or ARM	mo.	9.33	12/94	2c
Rent, apartment, 2 br., 1 1/2-2 baths, unfurnished, 950 sq ft, water	mo.	515	12/94	2c
Personal Goods				
Shampoo, Alberto VO5	15-oz.	1.04	12/94	2c
Toothpaste, Crest or Colgate	6-7 oz.	1.24	12/94	2c
Personal Services				
Dry cleaning, man's 2-pc. suit		5.97	12/94	2c
Haircut, man's barbershop, no styling		8.00	12/94	2c
Haircut, woman's shampoo, trim, blow-dry		15.67	12/94	2c
Restaurant Food				
Chicken, fried, thigh and drumstick		2.13	12/94	2c
Hamburger with cheese	1/4 lb.	1.86	12/94	2c
Pizza, Pizza Hut or Pizza Inn	12-13 in.	8.33	12/94	2c
Transportation				
Transportation, ACCRA Index		97.60	12/94	2c
Tire balance, computer or spin bal., front	wheel	6.80	12/94	2c
Utilities				
Utilities, ACCRA Index		91.30	12/94	2c
Electricity, (part.), other, 1800 sq. ft., new home	mo.	60.51	12/94	2c

Murray, KY

Item	Per	Value	Date	Ref.
Composite, ACCRA index		90.90	12/94	2c
Alcoholic Beverages				
Beer, Miller Lite, Bud, 12-oz., ex deposit	6	4.19	12/94	2c
J & B Scotch	750-ml.	17.08	12/94	2c
Wine, Gallo Chablis blanc	1.5-lit	4.77	12/94	2c

Murray, KY - continued

Item	Per	Value	Date	Ref.
Clothing				
Jeans, man's denim		35.99	12/94	2c
Shirt, man's dress shirt		31.25	12/94	2c
Undervest, boy's size 10-14, cotton	3	3.66	12/94	2c
Communications				
Newspaper subscription, dly. and Sun. delivery	month	11.44	12/94	2c
Telephone bill, family of four	month	22.49	12/94	2c
Telephone, residential, flat rate	mo.	12.02	12/93	8c
Energy and Fuels				
Energy, combined forms, 1800 sq. ft.	mo.	111.35	12/94	2c
Energy, exc. electricity, 1800 sq. ft.	mo.	35.68	12/94	2c
Gas, reg unlead, taxes inc., cash, self-service	gal	1.11	12/94	2c
Entertainment				
Bowling, evening rate	game	1.85	12/94	2c
Monopoly game, Parker Brothers', No. 9	game	10.86	12/94	2c
Movie	adm	4.50	12/94	2c
Tennis balls, yellow, Wilson or Penn, 3	can	1.92	12/94	2c
Groceries				
Groceries, ACCRA Index		100.50	12/94	2c
Baby food, strained vegetables, lowest price	4-4.5 oz.	0.36	12/94	2c
Bananas	lb.	0.50	12/94	2c
Beef or hamburger, ground	lb.	1.21	12/94	2c
Bread, white	24-oz.	0.76	12/94	2c
Cheese, Kraft grated Parmesan	8-oz.	3.44	12/94	2c
Chicken, whole fryer	lb.	0.86	12/94	2c
Cigarettes, Winston, Kings	carton	12.20	12/94	2c
Coffee, vacuum-packed	13 oz.	3.70	12/94	2c
Corn Flakes, Kellogg's or Post Toasties	18 oz.	2.72	12/94	2c
Corn, frozen, whole kernel, lowest price	10 oz.	0.87	12/94	2c
Eggs, Grade A large	dozen	0.71	12/94	2c
Lettuce, iceberg	head	0.69	12/94	2c
Margarine, Blue Bonnet or Parkay cubes	lb.	0.64	12/94	2c
Milk, whole	1/2 gal.	1.62	12/94	2c
Orange juice, Minute Maid frozen	12-oz.	1.42	12/94	2c
Peaches, halves or slices, Hunt's, Del Monte, or Libby's	29-oz.	1.22	12/94	2c
Peas, sweet, Del Monte or Green Giant	15-17 oz.	0.60	12/94	2c
Potatoes, white or red	10-lb. sack	2.22	12/94	2c
Sausage, Jimmy Dean, 100% pork	lb.	2.02	12/94	2c
Shortening, vegetable, Crisco	3-lb.	2.72	12/94	2c
Soft drink, Coca Cola, ex deposit	2 lit	1.09	12/94	2c
Steak, t-bone	lb.	4.49	12/94	2c
Sugar, cane or beet	4 lbs.	1.47	12/94	2c
Tomatoes, Hunt's or Del Monte	14.5 oz.	0.82	12/94	2c
Tuna, chunk, light, oil-packed	6.125-6.5 oz.	0.68	12/94	2c
Goods and Services				
Miscellaneous goods and services, ACCRA Index		101.10	12/94	2c
Health Care				
Health care, ACCRA Index		83.80	12/94	2c
Antibiotic ointment, Polysporin	1.5 oz.	3.57	12/94	2c
Dentist's fee, adult teeth cleaning and periodic oral exam	visit	46.00	12/94	2c
Doctor's fee, routine exam, established patient	visit	35.50	12/94	2c
Hospital care, semiprivate room	day	260.00	12/94	2c
Household Goods				
Appl. repair, service call, wash mach	min. lab. chg.	33.33	12/94	2c

Values are in dollars or fractions of dollars. In the column headed *Ref*, references are shown to sources. Each reference is followed by a letter. These refer to the geographical level for which data were reported: s=State, r=Region, and c=City or metro. The abbreviation *ex* is used to mean *except* or *excluding*; *exp* stands for expenditures. For other abbreviations and further explanations, please see the Introduction.

Murray, KY - continued

Item	Per	Value	Date	Ref.
Household Goods				
Laundry detergent, Tide Ultra, Bold, or Cheer	42 oz.	3.72	12/94	2c
Tissues, facial, Kleenex brand	175	1.08	12/94	2c
Housing				
Housing, ACCRA Index		74.10	12/94	2c
House payment, principal and interest, 25% down payment	mo.	569	12/94	2c
House, 1800 sq ft, 8000 sq ft lot, new, urban, utilities	total	90833	12/94	2c
Mtge. rate, incl. points and orig. fee, 30-year conv. fixed or ARM	mo.	9.43	12/94	2c
Personal Goods				
Shampoo, Alberto VO5	15-oz.	1.14	12/94	2c
Toothpaste, Crest or Colgate	6-7 oz.	2.21	12/94	2c
Personal Services				
Dry cleaning, man's 2-pc. suit		5.53	12/94	2c
Haircut, man's barbershop, no styling		9.00	12/94	2c
Haircut, woman's shampoo, trim, blow-dry		17.00	12/94	2c
Restaurant Food				
Chicken, fried, thigh and drumstick		2.39	12/94	2c
Hamburger with cheese	1/4 lb.	2.00	12/94	2c
Pizza, Pizza Hut or Pizza Inn	12-13 in.	8.49	12/94	2c
Transportation				
Transportation, ACCRA Index		84.40	12/94	2c
Tire balance, computer or spin bal., front	wheel	4.38	12/94	2c
Utilities				
Utilities, ACCRA Index		101.40	12/94	2c
Electricity, (part.), other, 1800 sq. ft., new home	mo.	75.67	12/94	2c

Muskegon, MI

Item	Per	Value	Date	Ref.
Appliances				
Appliances (major), expenditures	year	131	91	81r
Average annual exp.				
Food, health care, personal goods, services	year	25935	91	81r
Charity				
Cash contributions, expenditures	year	745	91	81r
Clothing				
Apparel, men and boys, total expenditures	year	332	91	81r
Apparel, women and girls, total expenditures	year	578	91	81r
Footwear, expenditures	year	164	91	81r
Communications				
Long-distance telephone rate, day, addl. min., 1-10 mi.	min.	0.08	12/93	9s
Long-distance telephone rate, day, initial min., 1-10 mi.	min.	0.14	12/93	9s
Phone line, single, business, field visit	inst	42.00	12/93	9s
Phone line, single, business, no field visit	inst	42.00	12/93	9s
Phone line, single, residence, field visit	inst	42.00	12/93	9s
Phone line, single, residence, no field visit	inst	42.00	12/93	9s
Telephone service, expenditures	year	547	91	81r
Education				
Board, 4-year private college/university	year	2064	8/94	80s
Board, 4-year public college/university	year	2304	8/94	80s
Education, total expenditures	year	394	91	81r
Room, 4-year private college/university	year	1814	8/94	80s
Room, 4-year public college/university	year	1856	8/94	80s
Total cost, 4-year private college/university	year	12178	8/94	80s
Total cost, 4-year public college/university	year	7642	8/94	80s
Tuition, 2-year public college/university, in-state	year	1358	8/94	80s
Tuition, 4-year private college/university, in-state	year	8300	8/94	80s

Muskegon, MI - continued

Item	Per	Value	Date	Ref.
Education - continued				
Tuition, 4-year public college/university, in-state	year	3481	8/94	80s
Energy and Fuels				
Fuel oil and other fuels, expenditures	year	83	91	81r
Gas, natural, expenditures	year	373	91	81r
Gasoline and motor oil purchased	year	1000	91	81r
Gasoline, unleaded midgrade	gallon	1.15	4/93	82r
Gasoline, unleaded premium	gallon	1.23	4/93	82r
Gasoline, unleaded regular	gallon	1.07	4/93	82r
Entertainment				
Entertainment, total expenditures	year	1356	91	81r
Fees and admissions, expenditures	year	347	91	81r
Pets, toys, playground equipment, expenditures	year	270	91	81r
Reading, expenditures	year	160	91	81r
Televisions, radios, and sound equipment, expenditures	year	433	91	81r
Funerals				
Burial, immediate, container provided by funeral home		1268.31	1/95	54r
Cards, acknowledgment		26.12	1/95	54r
Casket, minimum alternative		198.03	1/95	54r
Cosmetology, hair care, etc.		122.19	1/95	54r
Cremation, direct, container provided by funeral home		977.81	1/95	54r
Embalming		334.00	1/95	54r
Funeral, funeral home		321.16	1/95	54r
Funeral, other facility		317.73	1/95	54r
Graveside service		292.48	1/95	54r
Hearse, local		153.20	1/95	54r
Limousine, local		123.52	1/95	54r
Memorial service		356.30	1/95	54r
Service charge, professional, nondeclinable		968.24	1/95	54r
Visitation and viewing		332.66	1/95	54r
Groceries				
Apples, Red Delicious	lb.	0.68	12/94	82r
Bacon, sliced	lb.	1.88	12/94	82r
Bananas	lb.	0.41	12/94	82r
Beef purchases	year	197	91	81r
Beef, stew, boneless	lb.	2.52	12/94	82r
Beverage purchases, alcoholic	year	293	91	81r
Beverage purchases, nonalcoholic	year	203	91	81r
Bologna, all beef or mixed	lb.	2.12	12/94	82r
Bread, white, pan	lb.	0.76	12/94	82r
Cabbage	lb.	0.44	12/94	82r
Carrots, short trimmed and topped	lb.	0.44	12/94	82r
Cereals and bakery products purchases	year	347	91	81r
Cereals and cereals products purchases	year	119	91	81r
Cheddar cheese, natural	lb.	3.28	12/94	82r
Chicken breast, bone-in	lb.	1.61	12/94	82r
Chicken, fresh, whole	lb.	0.89	12/94	82r
Chuck roast, USDA choice, boneless	lb.	2.33	12/94	82r
Coffee, 100%, ground roast, all sizes	lb.	4.28	12/94	82r
Cookies, chocolate chip	lb.	2.72	12/94	82r
Dairy products (other) purchases	year	148	91	81r
Eggs, Grade A large	dozen	0.76	12/94	82r
Fish and seafood purchases	year	61	91	81r
Flour, white, all purpose	lb.	0.22	12/94	82r
Food purchases, food eaten at home	year	2313	91	81r
Foods purchased away from home, not prepared by consumer	year	1709	91	81r
Fruits and vegetables purchases	year	372	91	81r
Grapefruit	lb.	0.47	12/94	82r
Grapes, Thompson seedless	lb.	2.15	12/94	82r
Ground beef, 100% beef	lb.	1.37	12/94	82r
Ground chuck, 100% beef	lb.	1.81	12/94	82r
Ham, boneless, exc. canned	lb.	2.16	12/94	82r
Ice cream, prepackaged, bulk, regular	1/2 gal.	2.48	12/94	82r
Lemons	lb.	1.08	12/94	82r

Values are in dollars or fractions of dollars. In the column headed *Ref*, references are shown to sources. Each reference is followed by a letter. These refer to the geographical level for which data were reported: s=State, r=Region, and c=City or metro. The abbreviation *ex* is used to mean *except* or *excluding*; *exp* stands for *expenditures*. For other abbreviations and further explanations, please see the Introduction.

Muskegon, MI - continued

Item	Per	Value	Date	Ref.
Groceries				
Lettuce, iceberg	lb.	0.81	12/94	82r
Margarine, stick	lb.	0.81	12/94	82r
Meats, poultry, fish, and eggs purchases	year	591	91	81r
Milk and cream (fresh) purchases	year	132	91	81r
Orange juice, frozen concentrate 12-oz. can	16 oz.	1.41	12/94	82r
Oranges, Navel	lb.	0.56	12/94	82r
Peanut butter, creamy, all sizes	lb.	1.81	12/94	82r
Pork chops, center cut, bone-in	lb.	2.76	12/94	82r
Pork purchases	year	130	91	81r
Potato chips	16-oz.	2.81	12/94	82r
Potatoes, frozen, French fried	lb.	0.83	12/94	82r
Potatoes, white	lb.	0.28	12/94	82r
Round roast, USDA choice, boneless	lb.	2.90	12/94	82r
Shortening, vegetable oil blends	lb.	0.88	12/94	82r
Spaghetti and macaroni	lb.	0.78	12/94	82r
Steak, rib eye, USDA choice, boneless	lb.	6.15	12/94	82r
Steak, round, graded & ungraded, exc. USDA prime & choice	lb.	2.72	12/94	82r
Steak, round, USDA choice, boneless	lb.	3.02	12/94	82r
Steak, sirloin, USDA choice, boneless	lb.	3.85	12/94	82r
Steak, T-bone, USDA choice, bone-in	lb.	5.38	12/94	82r
Sugar and other sweets, eaten at home, expenditures	year	91	91	81r
Sugar, white, all sizes	lb.	0.36	12/94	82r
Tobacco products and smoking supplies, total expenditures	year	298	91	81r
Tomatoes, field grown	lb.	1.36	12/94	82r
Tuna, chunk, light	lb.	1.94	12/94	82r
Turkey, frozen, whole	lb.	0.96	12/94	82r
Yogurt, natural, fruit flavored	8 oz.	0.62	12/94	82r
Health Care				
Childbirth, Cesarean delivery, hospital charge	birth	5101.00	12/91	69r
Childbirth, Cesarean delivery, physician charge	birth	2234.00	12/91	69r
Childbirth, normal delivery, hospital charge	birth	2891.00	12/91	69r
Childbirth, normal delivery, physician charge	birth	1623.00	12/91	69r
Drugs, expenditures	year	248	91	81r
Health care, total expenditures	year	1336	91	81r
Health insurance expenditures	year	550	91	81r
Insurance premium, family medical care	month	369.41	1/95	41s
Medical services expenditures	year	457	91	81r
Medical supplies expenditures	year	82	91	81r
Household Goods				
Floor coverings, expenditures	year	105	91	81r
Furniture, expenditures	year	291	91	81r
Household equipment, misc. expenditures	year	341	91	81r
Household expenditures, miscellaneous	year	162	91	81r
Household furnishings and equipment, expenditures	year	1042	91	81r
Household operations expenditures	year	365	91	81r
Household textiles, expenditures	year	101	91	81r
Housekeeping supplies, expenditures	year	390	91	81r
Laundry and cleaning supplies, expenditures	year	110	91	81r
Postage and stationery, expenditures	year	115	91	81r
Housing				
Add garage/carport		8,479	3/95	74r
Add room(s)		21,347	3/95	74r
Apartment condominium or co-op, median	unit	87100	12/94	62r
Bathroom addition, average cost	add	9734.00	3/95	13r
Bathroom remodeling, average cost	remod	6414.00	3/95	13r
Bedroom, master suite addition, average cost	add	27122.00	3/95	13r
Deck addition, average cost	add	6665.00	3/95	13r
Dwellings (owned), expenditures	year	2566	91	81r
Enclose porch/patio/breezeway		4,556	3/95	74r
Exterior remodeling, average cost	remod	15395.00	3/95	13r
Family room addition, average cost	add	27658.00	3/95	13r
Finish room in basement/attic		5,074	3/95	74r
Home, existing, single-family, median	unit	106500	12/94	62r

Muskegon, MI - continued

Item	Per	Value	Date	Ref.
Housing - continued				
Kitchen remodeling, major, average cost	remod	17084.00	3/95	13r
Kitchen remodeling, minor, average cost	remod	5804.00	3/95	13r
Maintenance, repairs, insurance, and other housing expenditures	year	484	91	81r
Mortgage interest and charges expenditures	year	1443	91	81r
Office, home addition, average cost	add	8121.00	3/95	13r
Princ. & int., mortgage, median-price exist. sing.-family home	mo.	515	12/94	62r
Property taxes expenditures	year	639	91	81r
Redesign, restructure more than half of home's interior		9,114	3/95	74r
Rental units expenditures	year	1200	91	81r
Sun-space addition, average cost	add	23768.00	3/95	13r
Wing addition, two-story, average cost	add	50410.00	3/95	13r
Insurance and Pensions				
Auto insurance, private passenger	year	788.26	12/94	71s
Insurance and pensions, personal, expenditures	year	2408	91	81r
Insurance, life and other personal, expenditures	year	355	91	81r
Pensions and Social Security, expenditures	year	2053	91	81r
Legal Assistance				
Legal work, law firm associate	hour	90		10r
Legal work, law firm partner	hour	139		10r
Personal Services				
Personal services expenditures	year	203	91	81r
Restaurant Food				
Dining expenditures, family	week	30.03	94	73r
Taxes				
Taxes, Federal income, expenditures	year	1756	91	81r
Taxes, personal, expenditures	year	2426	91	81r
Taxes, State and local income, expenditures	year	568	91	81r
Transportation				
Cars and trucks purchased, new	year	891	91	81r
Cars and trucks purchased, used	year	1155	91	81r
Driver's learning permit fee	perm	12.00	1/94	84s
Driver's license fee	orig	12.00	1/94	84s
Driver's license fee, duplicate	lic	6.00	1/94	84s
Driver's license reinstatement fee, min.	susp	125.00	1/94	85s
Driver's license renewal fee	renew	12.00	1/94	84s
Identification card, nondriver	card	6.00	1/94	83s
Motorcycle license fee	orig	7.50	1/94	84s
Motorcycle license renewal fee	renew	4.00	1/94	84s
Public transportation expenditures	year	209	91	81r
Transportation expenditures, total	year	4792	91	81r
Vehicle finance charges	year	300	91	81r
Vehicle insurance expenditures	year	485	91	81r
Vehicle maintenance and repairs expenditures	year	534	91	81r
Vehicle purchases	year	2068	91	81r
Vehicle rental, leases, licenses, etc. expenditures	year	197	91	81r
Vehicles purchased, other than cars and trucks	year	22	91	81r
Utilities				
Electricity expenditures	year	668	91	81r
Utilities, fuels, and public services, total expenditures	year	1838	91	81r
Water and other public services, expenditures	year	167	91	81r
Weddings				
Bridal attendants' gowns	event	750	10/93	76r
Bridal gown	event	852	10/93	76r
Bridal headpiece and veil	event	167	10/93	76r
Bride's wedding band	event	708	10/93	76r
Clergy	event	224	10/93	76r
Engagement ring	event	2756	10/93	76r
Flowers	event	863	10/93	76r

Values are in dollars or fractions of dollars. In the column headed *Ref*, references are shown to sources. Each reference is followed by a letter. These refer to the geographical level for which data were reported: s = State, r = Region, and c = City or metro. The abbreviation *ex* is used to mean *except* or *excluding*; *exp* stands for expenditures. For other abbreviations and further explanations, please see the Introduction.

Muskegon, MI - continued

Weddings

Item	Per	Value	Date	Ref.
Formal wear for groom	event	106	10/93	76r
Groom's attendants' formal wear	event	530	10/93	76r
Groom's wedding band	event	402	10/93	76r
Music	event	600	10/93	76r
Photography	event	1088	10/93	76r
Shoes for bride	event	50	10/93	76r
Videography	event	483	10/93	76r
Wedding invitations and announcements	event	342	10/93	76r
Wedding reception	event	7000	10/93	76r

Muskogee, OK

Item	Per	Value	Date	Ref.
Composite, ACCRA index		89.10	12/94	2c

Alcoholic Beverages

Item	Per	Value	Date	Ref.
Beer, Miller Lite, Bud, 12-oz., ex deposit	6	4.00	12/94	2c
J & B Scotch	750-ml.	16.60	12/94	2c
Wine, Gallo Chablis blanc	1.5-lit	5.82	12/94	2c

Clothing

Item	Per	Value	Date	Ref.
Jeans, man's denim		26.49	12/94	2c
Shirt, man's dress shirt		34.12	12/94	2c
Undervest, boy's size 10-14, cotton	3	4.53	12/94	2c

Communications

Item	Per	Value	Date	Ref.
Newspaper subscription, dly. and Sun. delivery	month	10.75	12/94	2c
Telephone bill, family of four	month	18.96	12/94	2c
Telephone, residential, flat rate	mo.	11.32	12/93	8c

Energy and Fuels

Item	Per	Value	Date	Ref.
Energy, combined forms, 1800 sq. ft.	mo.	124.02	12/94	2c
Energy, exc. electricity, 1800 sq. ft.	mo.	40.77	12/94	2c
Gas, reg unlead, taxes inc., cash, self-service	gal	0.95	12/94	2c

Entertainment

Item	Per	Value	Date	Ref.
Bowling, evening rate	game	1.75	12/94	2c
Monopoly game, Parker Brothers', No. 9	game	11.65	12/94	2c
Movie	adm	5.25	12/94	2c
Tennis balls, yellow, Wilson or Penn, 3	can	2.01	12/94	2c

Groceries

Item	Per	Value	Date	Ref.
Groceries, ACCRA Index		105.60	12/94	2c
Baby food, strained vegetables, lowest price	4-4.5 oz.	0.43	12/94	2c
Bananas	lb.	0.48	12/94	2c
Beef or hamburger, ground	lb.	1.20	12/94	2c
Bread, white	24-oz.	0.92	12/94	2c
Cheese, Kraft grated Parmesan	8-oz.	3.48	12/94	2c
Chicken, whole fryer	lb.	0.80	12/94	2c
Cigarettes, Winston, Kings	carton	14.74	12/94	2c
Coffee, vacuum-packed	13 oz.	3.87	12/94	2c
Corn Flakes, Kellogg's or Post Toasties	18 oz.	2.54	12/94	2c
Corn, frozen, whole kernel, lowest price	10 oz.	0.77	12/94	2c
Eggs, Grade A large	dozen	0.72	12/94	2c
Lettuce, iceberg	head	0.73	12/94	2c
Margarine, Blue Bonnet or Parkay cubes	lb.	0.65	12/94	2c
Milk, whole	1/2 gal.	1.44	12/94	2c
Orange juice, Minute Maid frozen	12-oz.	1.40	12/94	2c
Peaches, halves or slices, Hunt's, Del Monte, or Libby's	29-oz.	1.19	12/94	2c
Peas, sweet, Del Monte or Green Giant	15-17 oz.	0.65	12/94	2c
Potatoes, white or red	10-lb. sack	1.76	12/94	2c
Sausage, Jimmy Dean, 100% pork	lb.	2.46	12/94	2c
Shortening, vegetable, Crisco	3-lb.	2.89	12/94	2c
Soft drink, Coca Cola, ex deposit	2 lit	1.13	12/94	2c
Steak, t-bone	lb.	5.06	12/94	2c
Sugar, cane or beet	4 lbs.	1.52	12/94	2c

Muskogee, OK - continued

Groceries - continued

Item	Per	Value	Date	Ref.
Tomatoes, Hunt's or Del Monte	14.5 oz.	0.82	12/94	2c
Tuna, chunk, light, oil-packed	6.125-6.5 oz.	0.72	12/94	2c

Goods and Services

Item	Per	Value	Date	Ref.
Miscellaneous goods and services, ACCRA Index		92.70	12/94	

Health Care

Item	Per	Value	Date	Ref.
Health care, ACCRA Index		83.20	12/94	2c
Antibiotic ointment, Polysporin	1.5 oz.	3.68	12/94	2c
Dentist's fee, adult teeth cleaning and periodic oral exam	visit	44.40	12/94	2c
Doctor's fee, routine exam, established patient	visit	37.80	12/94	2c
Hospital care, semiprivate room	day	225.00	12/94	2c

Household Goods

Item	Per	Value	Date	Ref.
Appl. repair, service call, wash mach	min. lab. chg.	30.86	12/94	2c
Laundry detergent, Tide Ultra, Bold, or Cheer	42 oz.	3.88	12/94	2c
Tissues, facial, Kleenex brand	175	1.12	12/94	2c

Housing

Item	Per	Value	Date	Ref.
Housing, ACCRA Index		74.50	12/94	2c
House payment, principal and interest, 25% down payment	mo.	576	12/94	2c
House, 1800 sq ft, 8000 sq ft lot, new, urban, utilities	total	91800	12/94	2c
Mtge. rate, incl. points and orig. fee, 30-year conv. fixed or ARM	mo.	9.45	12/94	2c
Rent, apartment, 2 br., 1 1/2-2 baths, unfurnished, 950 sq ft, water	mo.	377	12/94	2c

Personal Goods

Item	Per	Value	Date	Ref.
Shampoo, Alberto VO5	15-oz.	0.98	12/94	2c
Toothpaste, Crest or Colgate	6-7 oz.	1.84	12/94	2c

Personal Services

Item	Per	Value	Date	Ref.
Dry cleaning, man's 2-pc. suit		6.42	12/94	2c
Haircut, man's barbershop, no styling		7.62	12/94	2c
Haircut, woman's shampoo, trim, blow-dry		14.00	12/94	2c

Restaurant Food

Item	Per	Value	Date	Ref.
Chicken, fried, thigh and drumstick		1.78	12/94	2c
Hamburger with cheese	1/4 lb.	1.99	12/94	2c
Pizza, Pizza Hut or Pizza Inn	12-13 in.	5.50	12/94	2c

Transportation

Item	Per	Value	Date	Ref.
Transportation, ACCRA Index		78.70	12/94	2c
Tire balance, computer or spin bal., front	wheel	4.75	12/94	2c

Utilities

Item	Per	Value	Date	Ref.
Utilities, ACCRA Index		108.70	12/94	2c
Electricity, (part.), other, 1800 sq. ft., new home	mo.	83.25	12/94	2c

Myrtle Beach, SC

Item	Per	Value	Date	Ref.
Composite, ACCRA index		97.80	12/94	2c

Alcoholic Beverages

Item	Per	Value	Date	Ref.
Beer, Miller Lite, Bud, 12-oz., ex deposit	6	3.92	12/94	2c
J & B Scotch	750-ml.	18.54	12/94	2c
Wine, Gallo Chablis blanc	1.5-lit	4.69	12/94	2c

Clothing

Item	Per	Value	Date	Ref.
Jeans, man's denim		34.59	12/94	2c
Shirt, man's dress shirt		29.99	12/94	2c
Undervest, boy's size 10-14, cotton	3	3.74	12/94	2c

Values are in dollars or fractions of dollars. In the column headed *Ref*, references are shown to sources. Each reference is followed by a letter. These refer to the geographical level for which data were reported: s = State, r = Region, and c = City or metro. The abbreviation *ex* is used to mean *except* or *excluding*; *exp* stands for expenditures. For other abbreviations and further explanations, please see the Introduction.

Myrtle Beach, SC - continued

Item	Per	Value	Date	Ref.
Communications				
Newspaper subscription, dly. and Sun. delivery	month	9.36	12/94	2c
Telephone bill, family of four	month	20.07	12/94	2c
Energy and Fuels				
Energy, combined forms, 1800 sq. ft.	mo.	105.27	12/94	2c
Gas, reg unlead, taxes inc., cash, self-service	gal	1.06	12/94	2c
Entertainment				
Bowling, evening rate	game	2.19	12/94	2c
Monopoly game, Parker Brothers', No. 9	game	12.14	12/94	2c
Movie	adm	5.88	12/94	2c
Tennis balls, yellow, Wilson or Penn, 3	can	2.32	12/94	2c
Groceries				
Groceries, ACCRA Index		94.90	12/94	2c
Baby food, strained vegetables, lowest price	4-4.5 oz.	0.33	12/94	2c
Bananas	lb.	0.52	12/94	2c
Beef or hamburger, ground	lb.	1.38	12/94	2c
Bread, white	24-oz.	0.69	12/94	2c
Cheese, Kraft grated Parmesan	8-oz.	3.17	12/94	2c
Chicken, whole fryer	lb.	0.79	12/94	2c
Cigarettes, Winston, Kings	carton	13.25	12/94	2c
Coffee, vacuum-packed	13 oz.	3.35	12/94	2c
Corn Flakes, Kellogg's or Post Toasties	18 oz.	2.32	12/94	2c
Corn, frozen, whole kernel, lowest price	10 oz.	0.64	12/94	2c
Eggs, Grade A large	dozen	0.83	12/94	2c
Lettuce, iceberg	head	0.99	12/94	2c
Margarine, Blue Bonnet or Parkay cubes	lb.	0.58	12/94	2c
Milk, whole	1/2 gal.	1.38	12/94	2c
Orange juice, Minute Maid frozen	12-oz.	1.14	12/94	2c
Peaches, halves or slices, Hunt's, Del Monte, or Libby's	29-oz.	1.32	12/94	2c
Peas, sweet, Del Monte or Green Giant	15-17 oz.	0.44	12/94	2c
Potatoes, white or red	10-lb. sack	2.17	12/94	2c
Sausage, Jimmy Dean, 100% pork	lb.	2.19	12/94	2c
Shortening, vegetable, Crisco	3-lb.	2.61	12/94	2c
Soft drink, Coca Cola, ex deposit	2 lit	1.13	12/94	2c
Steak, t-bone	lb.	4.27	12/94	2c
Sugar, cane or beet	4 lbs.	1.49	12/94	2c
Tomatoes, Hunt's or Del Monte	14.5 oz.	0.58	12/94	2c
Tuna, chunk, light, oil-packed	6.125-6.5 oz.	0.67	12/94	2c
Goods and Services				
Miscellaneous goods and services, ACCRA Index		99.40	12/94	2c
Health Care				
Health care, ACCRA Index		90.80	12/94	2c
Antibiotic ointment, Polysporin	1.5 oz.	3.75	12/94	2c
Dentist's fee, adult teeth cleaning and periodic oral exam	visit	43.00	12/94	2c
Doctor's fee, routine exam, established patient	visit	39.20	12/94	2c
Hospital care, semiprivate room	day	359.50	12/94	2c
Household Goods				
Appl. repair, service call, wash mach	min. lab. chg.	35.60	12/94	2c
Laundry detergent, Tide Ultra, Bold, or Cheer	42 oz.	2.82	12/94	2c
Tissues, facial, Kleenex brand	175	0.99	12/94	2c
Housing				
Housing, ACCRA Index		101.60	12/94	2c
House payment, principal and interest, 25% down payment	mo.	779	12/94	2c

Myrtle Beach, SC - continued

Item	Per	Value	Date	Ref.
Housing - continued				
House, 1800 sq ft, 8000 sq ft lot, new, urban, utilities	total	125000	12/94	2c
Mtge. rate, incl. points and orig. fee, 30-year conv. fixed or ARM	mo.	9.36	12/94	2c
Rent, apartment, 2 br., 1 1/2-2 baths, unfurnished, 950 sq ft, water	mo.	536	12/94	2c
Personal Goods				
Shampoo, Alberto VO5	15-oz.	1.12	12/94	2c
Toothpaste, Crest or Colgate	6-7 oz.	1.84	12/94	2c
Personal Services				
Dry cleaning, man's 2-pc. suit		5.80	12/94	2c
Haircut, man's barbershop, no styling		7.75	12/94	2c
Haircut, woman's shampoo, trim, blow-dry		21.10	12/94	2c
Restaurant Food				
Chicken, fried, thigh and drumstick		2.15	12/94	2c
Hamburger with cheese	1/4 lb.	1.94	12/94	2c
Pizza, Pizza Hut or Pizza Inn	12-13 in.	6.50	12/94	2c
Transportation				
Transportation, ACCRA Index		92.50	12/94	2c
Tire balance, computer or spin bal., front	wheel	6.10	12/94	2c
Utilities				
Utilities, ACCRA Index		95.00	12/94	2c
Electricity, 1800 sq. ft., new home	mo.	105.27	12/94	2c

Naples, FL

Item	Per	Value	Date	Ref.
Appliances				
Appliances (major), expenditures	year	153	91	81r
Average annual exp.				
Food, health care, personal goods, services	year	27020	91	81r
Charity				
Cash contributions, expenditures	year	839	91	81r
Clothing				
Apparel, men and boys, total expenditures	year	380	91	81r
Apparel, women and girls, total expenditures	year	660	91	81r
Footwear, expenditures	year	193	91	81r
Communications				
Long-distance telephone rate, day, addl. min., 1-10 mi.	min.	0.08	12/93	9s
Long-distance telephone rate, day, initial min., 1-10 mi.	min.	0.15	12/93	9s
Phone line, single, business, field visit	inst	86.00	12/93	9s
Phone line, single, business, no field visit	inst	54.50	12/93	9s
Phone line, single, residence, field visit	inst	76.00	12/93	9s
Phone line, single, residence, no field visit	inst	44.50	12/93	9s
Telephone service, expenditures	year	616	91	81r
Education				
Bar examination preparatory course	course	500.00-100	94	17s
Board, 4-year private college/university	year	2123	8/94	80s
Board, 4-year public college/university	year	2101	8/94	80s
Education, total expenditures	year	319	91	81r
Room, 4-year private college/university	year	2242	8/94	80s
Room, 4-year public college/university	year	1970	8/94	80s
Total cost, 4-year private college/university	year	13853	8/94	80s
Total cost, 4-year public college/university	year	5855	8/94	80s
Tuition, 2-year public college/university, in-state	year	1076	8/94	80s
Tuition, 4-year private college/university, in-state	year	9287	8/94	80s
Tuition, 4-year public college/university, in-state	year	1784	8/94	80s

Values are in dollars or fractions of dollars. In the column headed *Ref*, references are shown to sources. Each reference is followed by a letter. These refer to the geographical level for which data were reported: s = State, r = Region, and c = City or metro. The abbreviation *ex* is used to mean *except* or *excluding*; *exp* stands for expenditures. For other abbreviations and further explanations, please see the Introduction.

Naples, FL - continued

Item	Per	Value	Date	Ref.
Energy and Fuels				
Fuel oil and other fuels, expenditures	year	56	91	81r
Gas, natural, expenditures	year	150	91	81r
Gasoline and motor oil purchased	year	1152	91	81r
Gasoline, unleaded midgrade	gallon	1.21	4/93	82r
Gasoline, unleaded premium	gallon	1.30	4/93	82r
Gasoline, unleaded regular	gallon	1.10	4/93	82r
Entertainment				
Concert ticket, Pearl Jam group	perf	20.00	94	50r
Entertainment, total expenditures	year	1266	91	81r
Fees and admissions, expenditures	year	306	91	81r
Pets, toys, playground equipment, expenditures	year	271	91	81r
Reading, expenditures	year	131	91	81r
Televisions, radios, and sound equipment, expenditures	year	439	91	81r
Funerals				
Burial, immediate, container provided by funeral home		1370.36	1/95	54r
Cards, acknowledgment		14.83	1/95	54r
Casket, minimum alternative		192.52	1/95	54r
Cosmetology, hair care, etc.		102.27	1/95	54r
Cremation, direct, container provided by funeral home		1065.64	1/95	54r
Embalming		304.29	1/95	54r
Funeral, funeral home		287.83	1/95	54r
Funeral, other facility		284.14	1/95	54r
Graveside service		349.13	1/95	54r
Hearse, local		132.27	1/95	54r
Limousine, local		98.45	1/95	54r
Memorial service		270.59	1/95	54r
Service charge, professional, nondeclinable		933.59	1/95	54r
Visitation and viewing		225.83	1/95	54r
Groceries				
Apples, Red Delicious	lb.	0.73	12/94	82r
Bacon, sliced	lb.	1.67	12/94	82r
Bananas	lb.	0.42	12/94	82r
Beef purchases	year	213	91	81r
Beverage purchases, alcoholic	year	249	91	81r
Beverage purchases, nonalcoholic	year	207	91	81r
Bologna, all beef or mixed	lb.	2.27	12/94	82r
Bread, white, pan	lb.	0.68	12/94	82r
Cabbage	lb.	0.42	12/94	82r
Carrots, short trimmed and topped	lb.	0.53	12/94	82r
Cereals and bakery products purchases	year	345	91	81r
Cereals and cereals products purchases	year	127	91	81r
Cheddar cheese, natural	lb.	3.58	12/94	82r
Chicken breast, bone-in	lb.	1.71	12/94	82r
Chicken, fresh, whole	lb.	0.78	12/94	82r
Chuck roast, USDA choice, boneless	lb.	2.26	12/94	82r
Crackers, soda, salted	lb.	1.27	12/94	82r
Cucumbers	lb.	0.65	12/94	82r
Dairy products (other) purchases	year	141	91	81r
Eggs, Grade A large	dozen	0.87	12/94	82r
Fish and seafood purchases	year	72	91	81r
Flour, white, all purpose	lb.	0.23	12/94	82r
Food purchases, food eaten at home	year	2381	91	81r
Foods purchased away from home, not prepared by consumer	year	1696	91	81r
Frankfurters, all meat or all beef	lb.	1.74	12/94	82r
Fruits and vegetables purchases	year	380	91	81r
Grapefruit	lb.	0.45	12/94	82r
Grapes, Thompson seedless	lb.	2.30	12/94	82r
Ground beef, 100% beef	lb.	1.37	12/94	82r
Ground chuck, 100% beef	lb.	1.97	12/94	82r
Ham, boneless, exc. canned	lb.	2.54	12/94	82r
Ice cream, prepackaged, bulk, regular	1/2 gal.	2.47	12/94	82r
Lemons	lb.	1.02	12/94	82r
Lettuce, iceberg	lb.	0.96	12/94	82r
Margarine, stick	lb.	0.77	12/94	82r
Meats, poultry, fish, and eggs purchases	year	655	91	81r

Naples, FL - continued

Item	Per	Value	Date	Ref.
Groceries - continued				
Milk and cream (fresh) purchases	year	130	91	81r
Orange juice, frozen concentrate 12-oz. can	16 oz.	1.36	12/94	82r
Oranges, Navel	lb.	0.54	12/94	82r
Pears, Anjou	lb.	0.81	12/94	82r
Pork chops, center cut, bone-in	lb.	3.07	12/94	82r
Pork purchases	year	142	91	81r
Potato chips	16-oz.	3.15	12/94	82r
Potatoes, frozen, French fried	lb.	0.82	12/94	82r
Potatoes, white	lb.	0.34	12/94	82r
Rice, white, long grain, uncooked	lb.	0.48	12/94	82r
Round roast, USDA choice, boneless	lb.	2.91	12/94	82r
Sausage, fresh	lb.	1.82	12/94	82r
Shortening, vegetable oil blends	lb.	0.75	12/94	82r
Spaghetti and macaroni	lb.	0.87	12/94	82r
Steak, rib eye, USDA choice, boneless	lb.	6.85	12/94	82r
Steak, round, graded & ungraded, exc. USDA prime & choice	lb.	2.96	12/94	82r
Steak, round, USDA choice, boneless	lb.	3.17	12/94	82r
Steak, sirloin, USDA choice, boneless	lb.	4.12	12/94	82r
Steak, T-bone, USDA choice, bone-in	lb.	5.63	12/94	82r
Sugar and other sweets, eaten at home, expenditures	year	93	91	81r
Sugar, white, all sizes	lb.	0.39	12/94	82r
Tobacco products and smoking supplies, total expenditures	year	286	91	81r
Tomatoes, field grown	lb.	1.36	12/94	82r
Tuna, chunk, light	lb.	1.94	12/94	82r
Turkey, frozen, whole	lb.	0.96	12/94	82r
Yogurt, natural, fruit flavored	8 oz.	0.58	12/94	82r
Health Care				
Adenosine, emergency room	treat	100.00	95	23r
Bladder tap, superpubic, infant, emergency room	treat	119.00	95	23r
Blood analysis, emergency room	treat	25.00	95	23r
Blood tests, abdominal pain, emergency room	treat	25.00	95	23r
Burn dressing, emergency room	treat	266.00	95	23r
Cardiology interpretation, emergency room	treat	26.00	95	23r
Chest X-ray, emergency room	treat	78.00	95	23r
Childbirth, Cesarean delivery, hospital charge	birth	5462.00	12/91	69r
Childbirth, Cesarean delivery, physician charge	birth	2228.00	12/91	69r
Childbirth, normal delivery, hospital charge	birth	2943.00	12/91	69r
Childbirth, normal delivery, physician charge	birth	1619.00	12/91	69r
Defibrillation pads, emergency room	treat	6.00	95	23r
Drugs, expenditures	year	297	91	81r
Gastric tube insertion, nasal, emergency room	treat	25.00	95	23r
Health care, total expenditures	year	1600	91	81r
Health insurance expenditures	year	637	91	81r
Heart monitor, emergency room	treat	40.00	95	23r
Insurance premium, family medical care	month	301.92	1/95	41s
Intravenous fluids, emergency room	treat	130.00	95	23r
Intravenous fluids, emergency room	liter	26.00	95	23r
Intravenous line, central, emergency room	treat	342.00	95	23r
Liver function tests, abdominal pain, emergency room	treat	26.00	95	23r
Medical care charges, total, emergency room, third-degree burns	treat	2101.00	95	23r
Medical care charges, total, emergency, infant with fever	treat	628.00	95	23r
Medical services expenditures	year	573	91	81r
Medical supplies expenditures	year	93	91	81r
Morphine, emergency room	treat	34.00	95	23r
Nursing care and facilities charges, emergency room	treat	252.00	95	23r
Nursing care and facilities charges, emergency, infant with fever	treat	252.00	95	23r
Nursing care and facilities charges, emergency, third-degree burns	treat	861.00	95	23r

Values are in dollars or fractions of dollars. In the column headed *Ref*, references are shown to sources. Each reference is followed by a letter. These refer to the geographical level for which data were reported: s = State, r = Region, and c = City or metro. The abbreviation *ex* is used to mean *except* or *excluding*; *exp* stands for expenditures. For other abbreviations and further explanations, please see the Introduction.

Naples, FL - continued

Item	Per	Value	Date	Ref.
Health Care				
Physician's charges, emergency, infant with fever	treat	212.00	95	23r
Physician's charges, emergency, third-degree burns	treat	372.00	95	23r
Physician's fee, emergency room	treat	372.00	95	23r
Physician's fee, general practitioner	visit	51.20	12/93	60r
Surgery, open-heart	proc	42374.00	1/93	14r
Ultrasound, abdominal, emergency room	treat	276.00	95	23r
Urinalysis, emergency room	treat	20.00	95	23r
Urinalysis, infant, emergency room	treat	20.00	95	23r
X-rays, emergency room	treat	78.00	95	23r
Household Goods				
Floor coverings, expenditures	year	48	91	81r
Furniture, expenditures	year	280	91	81r
Household equipment, misc. expenditures	year	342	91	81r
Household expenditures, miscellaneous	year	256	91	81r
Household furnishings and equipment, expenditures	year	988	91	81r
Household operations expenditures	year	468	91	81r
Household textiles, expenditures	year	95	91	81r
Housekeeping supplies, expenditures	year	380	91	81r
Laundry and cleaning supplies, expenditures	year	109	91	81r
Postage and stationery, expenditures	year	105	91	81r
Housing				
Add garage/carport		6,980	3/95	74r
Add room(s)		11,403	3/95	74r
Apartment condominium or co-op, median	unit	68600	12/94	62r
Dwellings (owned), expenditures	year	2428	91	81r
Enclose porch/patio/breezeway		4,572	3/95	74r
Finish room in basement/attic		3,794	3/95	74r
Home, existing, single-family, median	unit	120200	12/94	62r
Maintenance, repairs, insurance, and other housing expenditures	year	531	91	81r
Mortgage interest and charges expenditures	year	1506	91	81r
Princ. & int., mortgage, median-price exist. sing.-family home	mo.	540	12/94	62r
Property taxes expenditures	year	391	91	81r
Redesign, restructure more than half of home's interior		17,641	3/95	74r
Rental units expenditures	year	1264	91	81r
Insurance and Pensions				
Auto insurance, private passenger	year	753.93	12/94	71s
Insurance and pensions, personal, expenditures	year	2395	91	81r
Insurance, life and other personal, expenditures	year	368	91	81r
Pensions and Social Security, expenditures	year	2027	91	81r
Personal Services				
Personal services expenditures	year	212	91	81r
Restaurant Food				
Dining expenditures, family	week	33.83	94	73r
Taxes				
Taxes, Federal income, expenditures	year	2275	91	81r
Taxes, personal, expenditures	year	2715	91	81r
Taxes, State and local income, expenditures	year	365	91	81r
Transportation				
Cars and trucks purchased, new	year	1306	91	81r
Cars and trucks purchased, used	year	942	91	81r
Driver's learning permit fee	perm	20.00	1/94	84s
Driver's license fee	orig	20.00	1/94	84s
Driver's license fee, duplicate	lic	10.00	1/94	84s
Driver's license reinstatement fee, min.	susp	25.00	1/94	85s
Driver's license renewal fee	renew	15.00	1/94	84s
Identification card, nondriver	card	3.00	1/94	83s
Motorcycle learning permit fee	perm	20.00	1/94	84s
Motorcycle license fee	orig	20.00	1/94	84s
Motorcycle license fee, duplicate	lic	10.00	1/94	84s

Naples, FL - continued

Item	Per	Value	Date	Ref.
Transportation - continued				
Motorcycle license renewal fee	renew	15.00	1/94	84s
Public transportation expenditures	year	249	91	81r
Transportation expenditures, total	year	5307	91	81r
Vehicle finance charges	year	346	91	81r
Vehicle insurance expenditures	year	544	91	81r
Vehicle maintenance and repairs expenditures	year	600	91	81r
Vehicle purchases	year	2275	91	81r
Vehicle rental, leases, licenses, etc. expenditures	year	141	91	81r
Vehicles purchased, other than cars and trucks	year	27	91	81r
Utilities				
Electricity expenditures	year	950	91	81r
Utilities, fuels, and public services, total expenditures	year	2000	91	81r
Water and other public services, expenditures	year	227	91	81r
Weddings				
Bridal attendants' gowns	event	750	10/93	76r
Bridal gown	event	852	10/93	76r
Bridal headpiece and veil	event	167	10/93	76r
Bride's wedding band	event	708	10/93	76r
Clergy	event	224	10/93	76r
Engagement ring	event	2756	10/93	76r
Flowers	event	863	10/93	76r
Formal wear for groom	event	106	10/93	76r
Groom's attendants' formal wear	event	530	10/93	76r
Groom's wedding band	event	402	10/93	76r
Music	event	600	10/93	76r
Photography	event	1088	10/93	76r
Shoes for bride	event	50	10/93	76r
Videography	event	483	10/93	76r
Wedding invitations and announcements	event	342	10/93	76r
Wedding reception	event	7000	10/93	76r

Nashville-Franklin, TN

Item	Per	Value	Date	Ref.
Composite, ACCRA index		90.70	12/94	2c
Alcoholic Beverages				
Beer, Miller Lite, Bud, 12-oz., ex deposit	6	4.19	12/94	2c
J & B Scotch	750-ml.	19.32	12/94	2c
Wine, Gallo Chablis blanc	1.5-lit	5.57	12/94	2c
Appliances				
Appliances (major), expenditures	year	153	91	81r
Average annual exp.				
Food, health care, personal goods, services	year	27020	91	81r
Charity				
Cash contributions, expenditures	year	839	91	81r
Clothing				
Apparel, men and boys, total expenditures	year	380	91	81r
Apparel, women and girls, total expenditures	year	660	91	81r
Footwear, expenditures	year	193	91	81r
Jeans, man's denim		30.99	12/94	2c
Shirt, man's dress shirt		31.30	12/94	2c
Undervest, boy's size 10-14, cotton	3	3.13	12/94	2c
Communications				
Long-distance telephone rate, day, addl. min., 1-10 mi.	min.	0.10	12/93	9s
Long-distance telephone rate, day, initial min., 1-10 mi.	min.	0.10	12/93	9s
Newspaper subscription, dly. and Sun. delivery	month	13.04	12/94	2c
Phone line, single, business, field visit	inst	58.50	12/93	9s
Phone line, single, business, no field visit	inst	58.50	12/93	9s
Phone line, single, residence, field visit	inst	41.50	12/93	9s

Values are in dollars or fractions of dollars. In the column headed *Ref*, references are shown to sources. Each reference is followed by a letter. These refer to the geographical level for which data were reported: s=State, r=Region, and c=City or metro. The abbreviation *ex* is used to mean *except* or *excluding*; *exp* stands for expenditures. For other abbreviations and further explanations, please see the Introduction.

Nashville-Franklin, TN - continued

Item	Per	Value	Date	Ref.
Communications				
Phone line, single, residence, no field visit	inst	41.50	12/93	9s
Telephone bill, family of four	month	18.99	12/94	2c
Telephone service, expenditures	year	616	91	81r
Telephone, business, addl. line, touch tone	month	3.00	10/91	25c
Telephone, business, connection charges, touch tone	inst	63.12	10/91	25c
Telephone, business, key system line, touch tone	month	78.57	10/91	25c
Telephone, business, PBX line, touch tone	month	82.12	10/91	25c
Telephone, business, single ln., touch tone	month	48.79	10/91	25c
Telephone, business, touch tone, inside wiring maintenance plan	month	1.25	10/91	25c
Telephone, residential, flat rate	mo.	12.15	12/93	8c
Education				
Board, 4-year private college/university	year	1846	8/94	80s
Board, 4-year public college/university	year	1700	8/94	80s
Education, total expenditures	year	319	91	81r
Room, 4-year private college/university	year	1553	8/94	80s
Room, 4-year public college/university	year	1524	8/94	80s
Total cost, 4-year private college/university	year	12025	8/94	80s
Total cost, 4-year public college/university	year	5021	8/94	80s
Tuition, 2-year public college/university, in-state	year	950	8/94	80s
Tuition, 4-year private college/university, in-state	year	8627	8/94	80s
Tuition, 4-year public college/university, in-state	year	1797	8/94	80s
Energy and Fuels				
Energy, combined forms, 1800 sq. ft.	mo.	98.67	12/94	2c
Fuel oil and other fuels, expenditures	year	56	91	81r
Gas, heating, winter, 100 therms	month	64.29	2/94	65c
Gas, heating, winter, average use	month	123.09	2/94	65c
Gas, natural, expenditures	year	150	91	81r
Gas, reg unlead, taxes inc., cash, self-service	gal	1.07	12/94	2c
Gasoline and motor oil purchased	year	1152	91	81r
Gasoline, unleaded midgrade	gallon	1.21	4/93	82r
Gasoline, unleaded premium	gallon	1.30	4/93	82r
Gasoline, unleaded regular	gallon	1.10	4/93	82r
Entertainment				
Bowling, evening rate	game	2.08	12/94	2c
Concert ticket, Pearl Jam group	perf	20.00	94	50r
Entertainment, total expenditures	year	1266	91	81r
Fees and admissions, expenditures	year	306	91	81r
Monopoly game, Parker Brothers', No. 9	game	10.56	12/94	2c
Movie	adm	5.35	12/94	2c
Pets, toys, playground equipment, expenditures	year	271	91	81r
Reading, expenditures	year	131	91	81r
Televisions, radios, and sound equipment, expenditures	year	439	91	81r
Tennis balls, yellow, Wilson or Penn, 3	can	1.96	12/94	2c
Funerals				
Burial, immediate, container provided by funeral home		1298.96	1/95	54r
Cards, acknowledgment		21.26	1/95	54r
Casket, minimum alternative		204.95	1/95	54r
Cosmetology, hair care, etc.		85.40	1/95	54r
Cremation, direct, container provided by funeral home		1054.77	1/95	54r
Embalming		287.71	1/95	54r
Funeral, funeral home		269.18	1/95	54r
Funeral, other facility		272.88	1/95	54r
Graveside service		302.54	1/95	54r
Hearse, local		122.08	1/95	54r
Limousine, local		80.31	1/95	54r
Memorial service		277.66	1/95	54r
Service charge, professional, nondeclinable		896.65	1/95	54r
Visitation and viewing		232.39	1/95	54r

Nashville-Franklin, TN - continued

Item	Per	Value	Date	Ref.
Groceries				
Groceries, ACCRA Index		96.90	12/94	2c
Apples, Red Delicious	lb.	0.73	12/94	82r
Baby food, strained vegetables, lowest price	4-4.5 oz.	0.37	12/94	2c
Bacon, sliced	lb.	1.67	12/94	82r
Bananas	lb.	0.40	12/94	2c
Bananas	lb.	0.42	12/94	82r
Beef or hamburger, ground	lb.	1.50	12/94	2c
Beef purchases	year	213	91	81r
Beverage purchases, alcoholic	year	249	91	81r
Beverage purchases, nonalcoholic	year	207	91	81r
Bologna, all beef or mixed	lb.	2.27	12/94	82r
Bread, white	24-oz.	0.84	12/94	2c
Bread, white, pan	lb.	0.68	12/94	82r
Cabbage	lb.	0.42	12/94	82r
Carrots, short trimmed and topped	lb.	0.53	12/94	82r
Cereals and bakery products purchases	year	345	91	81r
Cereals and cereals products purchases	year	127	91	81r
Cheddar cheese, natural	lb.	3.58	12/94	82r
Cheese, Kraft grated Parmesan	8-oz.	3.20	12/94	2c
Chicken breast, bone-in	lb.	1.71	12/94	82r
Chicken, fresh, whole	lb.	0.78	12/94	82r
Chicken, whole fryer	lb.	0.59	12/94	2c
Chuck roast, USDA choice, boneless	lb.	2.26	12/94	82r
Cigarettes, Winston, Kings	carton	14.21	12/94	2c
Coffee, vacuum-packed	13 oz.	3.34	12/94	2c
Corn Flakes, Kellogg's or Post Toasties	18 oz.	2.62	12/94	2c
Corn, frozen, whole kernel, lowest price	10 oz.	0.66	12/94	2c
Crackers, soda, salted	lb.	1.27	12/94	82r
Cucumbers	lb.	0.65	12/94	82r
Dairy products (other) purchases	year	141	91	81r
Eggs, Grade A large	dozen	0.68	12/94	2c
Eggs, Grade A large	dozen	0.87	12/94	82r
Fish and seafood purchases	year	72	91	81r
Flour, white, all purpose	lb.	0.23	12/94	82r
Food purchases, food eaten at home	year	2381	91	81r
Foods purchased away from home, not prepared by consumer	year	1696	91	81r
Frankfurters, all meat or all beef	lb.	1.74	12/94	82r
Fruits and vegetables purchases	year	380	91	81r
Grapefruit	lb.	0.45	12/94	82r
Grapes, Thompson seedless	lb.	2.30	12/94	82r
Ground beef, 100% beef	lb.	1.37	12/94	82r
Ground chuck, 100% beef	lb.	1.97	12/94	82r
Ham, boneless, exc. canned	lb.	2.54	12/94	82r
Ice cream, prepackaged, bulk, regular	1/2 gal.	2.47	12/94	82r
Lemons	lb.	1.02	12/94	82r
Lettuce, iceberg	lb.	0.96	12/94	82r
Lettuce, iceberg	head	0.83	12/94	2c
Margarine, Blue Bonnet or Parkay cubes	lb.	0.60	12/94	2c
Margarine, stick	lb.	0.77	12/94	82r
Meats, poultry, fish, and eggs purchases	year	655	91	81r
Milk and cream (fresh) purchases	year	130	91	81r
Milk, whole	1/2 gal.	1.33	12/94	2c
Orange juice, frozen concentrate 12-oz. can	16 oz.	1.36	12/94	82r
Orange juice, Minute Maid frozen	12-oz.	1.18	12/94	2c
Oranges, Navel	lb.	0.54	12/94	82r
Peaches, halves or slices, Hunt's, Del Monte, or Libby's	29-oz.	1.23	12/94	2c
Pears, Anjou	lb.	0.81	12/94	82r
Peas, sweet, Del Monte or Green Giant	15-17 oz.	0.44	12/94	2c
Pork chops, center cut, bone-in	lb.	3.07	12/94	82r
Pork purchases	year	142	91	81r
Potato chips	16-oz.	3.15	12/94	82r
Potatoes, frozen, French fried	lb.	0.82	12/94	82r
Potatoes, white	lb.	0.34	12/94	82r
Potatoes, white or red	10-lb. sack	2.61	12/94	2c
Rice, white, long grain, uncooked	lb.	0.48	12/94	82r

Values are in dollars or fractions of dollars. In the column headed *Ref*, references are shown to sources. Each reference is followed by a letter. These refer to the geographical level for which data were reported: s=State, r=Region, and c=City or metro. The abbreviation *ex* is used to mean *except* or *excluding*; *exp* stands for expenditures. For other abbreviations and further explanations, please see the Introduction.

Nashville-Franklin, TN - continued

Item	Per	Value	Date	Ref.
Groceries				
Round roast, USDA choice, boneless	lb.	2.91	12/94	82r
Sausage, fresh	lb.	1.82	12/94	82r
Sausage, Jimmy Dean, 100% pork	lb.	2.35	12/94	2c
Shortening, vegetable oil blends	lb.	0.75	12/94	82r
Shortening, vegetable, Crisco	3-lb.	2.45	12/94	2c
Soft drink, Coca Cola, ex deposit	2 lit	1.01	12/94	2c
Spaghetti and macaroni	lb.	0.87	12/94	82r
Steak, rib eye, USDA choice, boneless	lb.	6.85	12/94	82r
Steak, round, graded & ungraded, exc. USDA prime & choice	lb.	2.96	12/94	82r
Steak, round, USDA choice, boneless	lb.	3.17	12/94	82r
Steak, sirloin, USDA choice, boneless	lb.	4.12	12/94	82r
Steak, t-bone	lb.	4.77	12/94	2c
Steak, T-bone, USDA choice, bone-in	lb.	5.63	12/94	82r
Sugar and other sweets, eaten at home, expenditures	year	93	91	81r
Sugar, cane or beet	4 lbs.	1.38	12/94	2c
Sugar, white, all sizes	lb.	0.39	12/94	82r
Tobacco products and smoking supplies, total expenditures	year	286	91	81r
Tomatoes, field grown	lb.	1.36	12/94	82r
Tomatoes, Hunt's or Del Monte	14.5 oz.	0.63	12/94	2c
Tuna, chunk, light	lb.	1.94	12/94	82r
Tuna, chunk, light, oil-packed	6.125-6.5 oz.	0.68	12/94	2c
Turkey, frozen, whole	lb.	0.96	12/94	82r
Yogurt, natural, fruit flavored	8 oz.	0.58	12/94	82r
Goods and Services				
Miscellaneous goods and services, ACCRA Index		95.70	12/94	2c
Health Care				
Health care, ACCRA Index		81.50	12/94	2c
Adenosine, emergency room	treat	100.00	95	23r
Antibiotic ointment, Polysporin	1.5 oz.	4.19	12/94	2c
Bladder tap, superpubic, infant, emergency room	treat	119.00	95	23r
Blood analysis, emergency room	treat	25.00	95	23r
Blood tests, abdominal pain, emergency room	treat	25.00	95	23r
Burn dressing, emergency room	treat	266.00	95	23r
Cardiology interpretation, emergency room	treat	26.00	95	23r
Chest X-ray, emergency room	treat	78.00	95	23r
Childbirth, Cesarean delivery, hospital charge	birth	5462.00	12/91	69r
Childbirth, Cesarean delivery, physician charge	birth	2228.00	12/91	69r
Childbirth, normal delivery, hospital charge	birth	2943.00	12/91	69r
Childbirth, normal delivery, physician charge	birth	1619.00	12/91	69r
Defibrillation pads, emergency room	treat	6.00	95	23r
Dentist's fee, adult teeth cleaning and periodic oral exam	visit	41.00	12/94	2c
Doctor's fee, routine exam, established patient	visit	34.80	12/94	2c
Drugs, expenditures	year	297	91	81r
Gastric tube insertion, nasal, emergency room	treat	25.00	95	23r
Health care, total expenditures	year	1600	91	81r
Health insurance expenditures	year	637	91	81r
Heart monitor, emergency room	treat	40.00	95	23r
Hospital care, semiprivate room	day	259.14	12/94	2c
Insurance premium, family medical care	month	344.21	1/95	41s
Intravenous fluids, emergency room	treat	130.00	95	23r
Intravenous fluids, emergency room	liter	26.00	95	23r
Intravenous line, central, emergency room	treat	342.00	95	23r
Liver function tests, abdominal pain, emergency room	treat	26.00	95	23r
Medical care charges, total, emergency room, third-degree burns	treat	2101.00	95	23r
Medical care charges, total, emergency, infant with fever	treat	628.00	95	23r

Nashville-Franklin, TN - continued

Item	Per	Value	Date	Ref.
Health Care - continued				
Medical services expenditures	year	573	91	81r
Medical supplies expenditures	year	93	91	81r
Morphine, emergency room	treat	34.00	95	23r
Nursing care and facilities charges, emergency room	treat	252.00	95	23r
Nursing care and facilities charges, emergency, infant with fever	treat	252.00	95	23r
Nursing care and facilities charges, emergency, third-degree burns	treat	861.00	95	23r
Physician's charges, emergency, infant with fever	treat	212.00	95	23r
Physician's charges, emergency, third-degree burns	treat	372.00	95	23r
Physician's fee, emergency room	treat	372.00	95	23r
Physician's fee, general practitioner	visit	51.20	12/93	60r
Surgery, open-heart	proc	42374.00	1/93	14r
Ultrasound, abdominal, emergency room	treat	276.00	95	23r
Urinalysis, emergency room	treat	20.00	95	23r
Urinalysis, infant, emergency room	treat	20.00	95	23r
X-rays, emergency room	treat	78.00	95	23r
Household Goods				
Appl. repair, service call, wash mach	min. lab. chg.	32.17	12/94	2c
Floor coverings, expenditures	year	48	91	81r
Furniture, expenditures	year	280	91	81r
Household equipment, misc. expenditures	year	342	91	81r
Household expenditures, miscellaneous	year	256	91	81r
Household furnishings and equipment, expenditures	year	988	91	81r
Household operations expenditures	year	468	91	81r
Household textiles, expenditures	year	95	91	81r
Housekeeping supplies, expenditures	year	380	91	81r
Laundry and cleaning supplies, expenditures	year	109	91	81r
Laundry detergent, Tide Ultra, Bold, or Cheer	42 oz.	3.18	12/94	2c
Postage and stationery, expenditures	year	105	91	81r
Tissues, facial, Kleenex brand	175	0.99	12/94	2c
Housing				
Housing, ACCRA Index		83.30	12/94	2c
Add garage/carport		6,980	3/95	74r
Add room(s)		11,403	3/95	74r
Apartment condominium or co-op, median	unit	68600	12/94	62r
Dwellings (owned), expenditures	year	2428	91	81r
Enclose porch/patio/breezeway		4,572	3/95	74r
Finish room in basement/attic		3,794	3/95	74r
Home, existing, single-family, median	unit	120200	12/94	62r
Home, existing, single-family, median	unit	99.50	12/94	62c
Home, three-bedrooms, one-and-a-half baths	home	105000	93	92c
House payment, principal and interest, 25% down payment	mo.	615	12/94	2c
House, 1800 sq ft, 8000 sq ft lot, new, urban, utilities	total	101265	12/94	2c
Maintenance, repairs, insurance, and other housing expenditures	year	531	91	81r
Mortgage interest and charges expenditures	year	1506	91	81r
Mtge. rate, incl. points and orig. fee, 30-year conv. fixed or ARM	mo.	9.08	12/94	2c
Princ. & int., mortgage, median-price exist. sing.-family home	mo.	540		62r
Property taxes expenditures	year	391	91	81r
Redesign, restructure more than half of home's interior		17,641	3/95	74r
Rent, apartment, 2 br., 1 1/2-2 baths, unfurnished, 950 sq ft, water	mo.	507	12/94	2c
Rental units expenditures	year	1264	91	81r
Insurance and Pensions				
Auto insurance, private passenger	year	574.08	12/94	71s

Values are in dollars or fractions of dollars. In the column headed *Ref*, references are shown to sources. Each reference is followed by a letter. These refer to the geographical level for which data were reported: s=State, r=Region, and c=City or metro. The abbreviation *ex* is used to mean *except* or *excluding*; *exp* stands for expenditures. For other abbreviations and further explanations, please see the Introduction.

Nashville-Franklin, TN - continued

Item	Per	Value	Date	Ref.
Insurance and Pensions				
Insurance and pensions, personal, expenditures	year	2395	91	81r
Insurance, life and other personal, expenditures	year	368	91	81r
Pensions and Social Security, expenditures	year	2027	91	81r
Personal Goods				
Shampoo, Alberto VO5	15-oz.	1.07	12/94	2c
Toothpaste, Crest or Colgate	6-7 oz.	1.91	12/94	2c
Personal Services				
Dry cleaning, man's 2-pc. suit		5.30	12/94	2c
Haircut, man's barbershop, no styling		6.10	12/94	2c
Haircut, woman's shampoo, trim, blow-dry		18.00	12/94	2c
Personal services expenditures	year	212	91	81r
Restaurant Food				
Chicken, fried, thigh and drumstick		1.99	12/94	2c
Dining expenditures, family	week	33.83	94	73r
Hamburger with cheese	1/4 lb.	1.78	12/94	2c
Pizza, Pizza Hut or Pizza Inn	12-13 in.	7.89	12/94	2c
Taxes				
Tax, cigarettes	year	379.00	10/93	43s
Taxes, Federal income, expenditures	year	2275	91	81r
Taxes, personal, expenditures	year	2715	91	81r
Taxes, State and local income, expenditures	year	365	91	81r
Transportation				
Transportation, ACCRA Index		92.00	12/94	2c
Bus fare, one-way	trip	1.15	12/95	1c
Bus fare, up to 10 miles	one-way	1.15	12/94	2c
Cars and trucks purchased, new	year	1306	91	81r
Cars and trucks purchased, used	year	942	91	81r
Driver's learning permit fee	perm	5.50	1/94	84s
Driver's license fee	orig	16.00	1/94	84s
Driver's license fee, duplicate	lic	8.00	1/94	84s
Driver's license reinstatement fee, min.	susp	65.00	1/94	85s
Driver's license renewal fee	renew	14.00	1/94	84s
Driving expenses	mile	37.10	5/95	89c
Identification card, nondriver	card	7.50	1/94	83s
Motorcycle learning permit fee	perm	6.50	1/94	84s
Motorcycle license fee	orig	17.00	1/94	84s
Motorcycle license fee, duplicate	lic	8.00	1/94	84s
Motorcycle license renewal fee	renew	15.00	1/94	84s
Public transportation expenditures	year	249	91	81r
Tire balance, computer or spin bal., front	wheel	5.35	12/94	2c
Transportation expenditures, total	year	5307	91	81r
Vehicle finance charges	year	346	91	81r
Vehicle insurance expenditures	year	544	91	81r
Vehicle maintenance and repairs expenditures	year	600	91	81r
Vehicle purchases	year	2275	91	81r
Vehicle rental, leases, licenses, etc. expenditures	year	141	91	81r
Vehicles purchased, other than cars and trucks	year	27	91	81r
Utilities				
Utilities, ACCRA Index		89.20	12/94	2c
Electricity expenditures	year	950	91	81r
Electricity, 1800 sq. ft., new home	mo.	98.67	12/94	2c
Fee, water use, industrial	month	1819.98	1/95	16c
Utilities, fuels, and public services, total expenditures	year	2000	91	81r
Water and other public services, expenditures	year	227	91	81r
Weddings				
Bridal attendants' gowns	event	750	10/93	76r
Bridal gown	event	852	10/93	76r
Bridal headpiece and veil	event	167	10/93	76r
Bride's wedding band	event	708	10/93	76r

Nashville-Franklin, TN - continued

Item	Per	Value	Date	Ref.
Weddings - continued				
Clergy	event	224	10/93	76r
Engagement ring	event	2756	10/93	76r
Flowers	event	863	10/93	76r
Formal wear for groom	event	106	10/93	76r
Groom's attendants' formal wear	event	530	10/93	76r
Groom's wedding band	event	402	10/93	76r
Music	event	600	10/93	76r
Photography	event	1088	10/93	76r
Shoes for bride	event	50	10/93	76r
Videography	event	483	10/93	76r
Wedding invitations and announcements	event	342	10/93	76r
Wedding reception	event	7000	10/93	76r

Nassau-Suffolk, NY

Item	Per	Value	Date	Ref.
Appliances				
Appliances (major), expenditures	year	145	91	81r
Average annual exp.				
Food, health care, personal goods, services	year	29496	91	81r
Charity				
Cash contributions, expenditures	year	708	91	81r
Clothing				
Apparel, men and boys, total expenditures	year	416	91	81r
Apparel, women and girls, total expenditures	year	744	91	81r
Footwear, expenditures	year	305	91	81r
Communications				
Long-distance telephone rate, day, addl. min., 1-10 mi.	min.	4.00	12/93	9s
Long-distance telephone rate, day, initial min., 1-10 mi.	min.	14.90	12/93	9s
Phone line, single, business, field visit	inst	143.26	12/93	9s
Phone line, single, business, no field visit	inst	106.05	12/93	9s
Phone line, single, residence, field visit	inst	85.46	12/93	9s
Phone line, single, residence, no field visit	inst	55.00	12/93	9s
Telephone service, expenditures	year	589	91	81r
Education				
Board, 4-year private college/university	year	2918	8/94	80s
Board, 4-year public college/university	year	2177	8/94	80s
Education, total expenditures	year	593	91	81r
Room, 4-year private college/university	year	3302	8/94	80s
Room, 4-year public college/university	year	2624	8/94	80s
Total cost, 4-year private college/university	year	18451	8/94	80s
Total cost, 4-year public college/university	year	7723	8/94	80s
Tuition, 2-year public college/university, in-state	year	2112	8/94	80s
Tuition, 4-year private college/university, in-state	year	12231	8/94	80s
Tuition, 4-year public college/university, in-state	year	2921	8/94	80s
Energy and Fuels				
Fuel oil and other fuels, expenditures	year	257	91	81r
Gas, natural, expenditures	year	285	91	81r
Gasoline and motor oil purchased	year	867	91	81r
Gasoline, unleaded midgrade	gallon	1.32	4/93	82r
Gasoline, unleaded premium	gallon	1.40	4/93	82r
Gasoline, unleaded regular	gallon	1.19	4/93	82r
Entertainment				
Entertainment, total expenditures	year	1331	91	81r
Fees and admissions, expenditures	year	398	91	81r
Pets, toys, playground equipment, expenditures	year	270	91	81r
Reading, expenditures	year	171	91	81r
Televisions, radios, and sound equipment, expenditures	year	429	91	81r
Funerals				
Burial, immediate, container provided by funeral home		1370.36	1/95	54r

Values are in dollars or fractions of dollars. In the column headed *Ref*, references are shown to sources. Each reference is followed by a letter. These refer to the geographical level for which data were reported: s = State, r = Region, and c = City or metro. The abbreviation *ex* is used to mean *except* or *excluding*; *exp* stands for *expenditures*. For other abbreviations and further explanations, please see the Introduction.

Nassau-Suffolk, NY - continued

Item	Per	Value	Date	Ref.
Funerals				
Cards, acknowledgment		17.72	1/95	54r
Casket, minimum alternative		192.52	1/95	54r
Cosmetology, hair care, etc.		139.56	1/95	54r
Cremation, direct, container provided by funeral home		1049.24	1/95	54r
Embalming		387.57	1/95	54r
Funeral, funeral home		278.77	1/95	54r
Funeral, other facility		275.85	1/95	54r
Graveside service		213.08	1/95	54r
Hearse, local		157.27	1/95	54r
Limousine, local		146.45	1/95	54r
Memorial service		271.02	1/95	54r
Service charge, professional, nondeclinable		943.58	1/95	54r
Visitation and viewing		322.86	1/95	54r
Groceries				
Apples, Red Delicious	lb.	0.78	12/94	82r
Bacon, sliced	lb.	2.24	12/94	82r
Bananas	lb.	0.49	12/94	82r
Beef purchases	year	226	91	81r
Beverage purchases, alcoholic	year	332	91	81r
Beverage purchases, nonalcoholic	year	213	91	81r
Bread, white, pan	lb.	0.80	12/94	82r
Butter, salted, Grade AA, stick	lb.	1.67	12/94	82r
Carrots, short trimmed and topped	lb.	0.51	12/94	82r
Cereals and bakery products purchases	year	407	91	81r
Cereals and cereals products purchases	year	132	91	81r
Chicken breast, bone-in	lb.	2.22	12/94	82r
Chicken, fresh, whole	lb.	1.05	12/94	82r
Chuck roast, USDA choice, boneless	lb.	2.74	12/94	82r
Coffee, 100%, ground roast, all sizes	lb.	4.61	12/94	82r
Dairy products (other) purchases	year	161	91	81r
Eggs, Grade A large	dozen	1.12	12/94	82r
Fish and seafood purchases	year	112	91	81r
Food purchases, food eaten at home	year	2599	91	81r
Foods purchased away from home, not prepared by consumer	year	2024	91	81r
Fruits and vegetables purchases	year	444	91	81r
Grapefruit	lb.	0.44	12/94	82r
Grapes, Thompson seedless	lb.	2.24	12/94	82r
Ground chuck, 100% beef	lb.	1.67	12/94	82r
Ice cream, prepackaged, bulk, regular	1/2 gal.	2.93	12/94	82r
Lemons	lb.	1.06	12/94	82r
Lettuce, iceberg	lb.	0.92	12/94	82r
Meats, poultry, fish, and eggs purchases	year	751	91	81r
Milk and cream (fresh) purchases	year	152	91	81r
Orange juice, frozen concentrate 12-oz. can	16 oz.	1.92	12/94	82r
Oranges, Navel	lb.	0.56	12/94	82r
Pork chops, center cut, bone-in	lb.	3.09	12/94	82r
Pork purchases	year	130	91	81r
Potatoes, white	lb.	0.37	12/94	82r
Rib roast, USDA choice, bone-in	lb.	4.98	12/94	82r
Round roast, USDA choice, boneless	lb.	2.93	12/94	82r
Shortening, vegetable oil blends	lb.	1.03	12/94	82r
Spaghetti and macaroni	lb.	0.84	12/94	82r
Steak, round, USDA choice, boneless	lb.	3.48	12/94	82r
Steak, sirloin, USDA choice, bone-in	lb.	3.38	12/94	82r
Steak, sirloin, USDA choice, boneless	lb.	4.81	12/94	82r
Sugar and other sweets, eaten at home, expenditures	year	89	91	81r
Sugar, white, all sizes	lb.	0.46	12/94	82r
Tobacco products and smoking supplies, total expenditures	year	279	91	81r
Tomatoes, field grown	lb.	1.56	12/94	82r
Tuna, chunk, light	lb.	2.09	12/94	82r
Health Care				
Childbirth, Cesarean delivery, hospital charge	birth	6334.00	12/91	69r
Childbirth, Cesarean delivery, physician charge	birth	2234.00	12/91	69r
Childbirth, normal delivery, hospital charge	birth	3225.00	12/91	69r

Nassau-Suffolk, NY - continued

Item	Per	Value	Date	Ref.
Health Care - continued				
Childbirth, normal delivery, physician charge	birth	1623.00	12/91	69r
Drugs, expenditures	year	205	91	81r
Health care, total expenditures	year	1396	91	81r
Health insurance expenditures	year	553	91	81r
Insurance premium, family medical care	month	384.24	1/95	41s
Medical services expenditures	year	559	91	81r
Medical supplies expenditures	year	80	91	81r
Household Goods				
Floor coverings, expenditures	year	158	91	81r
Furniture, expenditures	year	341	91	81r
Household equipment, misc. expenditures	year	363	91	81r
Household expenditures, miscellaneous	year	194	91	81r
Household furnishings and equipment, expenditures	year	1158	91	81r
Household operations expenditures	year	378	91	81r
Household textiles, expenditures	year	88	91	81r
Housekeeping supplies, expenditures	year	426	91	81r
Laundry and cleaning supplies, expenditures	year	122	91	81r
Postage and stationery, expenditures	year	134	91	81r
Housing				
Add garage/carport		11,614	3/95	74r
Add room(s)		16,816	3/95	74r
Apartment condominium or co-op, median	unit	96700	12/94	62r
Dwellings (owned), expenditures	year	3305	91	81r
Enclose porch/patio/breezeway		2,980	3/95	74r
Finish room in basement/attic		4,330	3/95	74r
Home, existing, single-family, median	unit	161600	12/94	62r
Maintenance, repairs, insurance, and other housing expenditures	year	569	91	81r
Mortgage interest and charges expenditures	year	1852	91	81r
Princ. & int., mortgage, median-price exist. sing.-family home	mo.	765	12/94	62r
Property taxes expenditures	year	884	91	81r
Redesign, restructure more than half of home's interior		2,750	3/95	74r
Rental units expenditures	year	1832	91	81r
Insurance and Pensions				
Auto insurance, private passenger	year	985.07	12/94	71s
Insurance and pensions, personal, expenditures	year	2690	91	81r
Insurance, life and other personal, expenditures	year	341	91	81r
Pensions and Social Security, expenditures	year	2349	91	81r
Legal Assistance				
Estate planning, law-firm partner	hr.	375.00	10/93	12r
Legal work, law firm associate	hour	78		10r
Legal work, law firm partner	hour	183		10r
Personal Services				
Personal services expenditures	year	184	91	81r
Restaurant Food				
Dining expenditures, family	week	34.26	94	73r
Taxes				
Taxes, Federal income, expenditures	year	2409	91	81r
Taxes, personal, expenditures	year	3094	91	81r
Taxes, State and local income, expenditures	year	620	91	81r
Transportation				
Cars and trucks purchased, new	year	1170	91	81r
Cars and trucks purchased, used	year	739	91	81r
Driver's learning permit fee	perm	10.00	1/94	84s
Driver's license fee	orig	32.00-37.00	1/94	84s
Driver's license fee, duplicate	lic	7.25	1/94	84s
Driver's license reinstatement fee, min.	susp	25.00	1/94	85s
Driver's license renewal fee	renew	22.25	1/94	84s
Identification card, nondriver	card	6.25	1/94	83s
Motorcycle license fee	orig	32.00-37.00	1/94	84s

Values are in dollars or fractions of dollars. In the column headed *Ref*, references are shown to sources. Each reference is followed by a letter. These refer to the geographical level for which data were reported: s=State, r=Region, and c=City or metro. The abbreviation *ex* is used to mean *except* or *excluding*; *exp* stands for expenditures. For other abbreviations and further explanations, please see the Introduction.

Nassau-Suffolk, NY - continued

Item	Per	Value	Date	Ref.
Transportation				
Motorcycle license fee, duplicate	lic	7.25	1/94	84s
Motorcycle license renewal fee	renew	22.25	1/94	84s
Public transportation expenditures	year	430	91	81r
Transportation expenditures, total	year	4810	91	81r
Vehicle finance charges	year	238	91	81r
Vehicle insurance expenditures	year	630	91	81r
Vehicle maintenance and repairs expenditures	year	532	91	81r
Vehicle purchases	year	1920	91	81r
Vehicle rental, leases, licenses, etc. expenditures	year	193	91	81r
Vehicles purchased, other than cars and trucks	year	11	91	81r
Utilities				
Electricity expenditures	year	695	91	81r
Utilities, fuels, and public services, total expenditures	year	1981	91	81r
Water and other public services, expenditures	year	154	91	81r
Weddings				
Bridal attendants' gowns	event	750	10/93	76r
Bridal gown	event	852	10/93	76r
Bridal headpiece and veil	event	167	10/93	76r
Bride's wedding band	event	708	10/93	76r
Clergy	event	224	10/93	76r
Engagement ring	event	2756	10/93	76r
Flowers	event	863	10/93	76r
Formal wear for groom	event	106	10/93	76r
Groom's attendants' formal wear	event	530	10/93	76r
Groom's wedding band	event	402	10/93	76r
Music	event	600	10/93	76r
Photography	event	1088	10/93	76r
Shoes for bride	event	50	10/93	76r
Videography	event	483	10/93	76r
Wedding invitations and announcements	event	342	10/93	76r
Wedding reception	event	7000	10/93	76r

Nevada, MO

Item	Per	Value	Date	Ref.
Composite, ACCRA index		92.00	12/94	2c
Alcoholic Beverages				
Beer, Miller Lite, Bud, 12-oz., ex deposit	6	3.98	12/94	2c
J & B Scotch	750-ml.	18.00	12/94	2c
Wine, Gallo Chablis blanc	1.5-lit	7.00	12/94	2c
Clothing				
Jeans, man's denim		34.00	12/94	2c
Shirt, man's dress shirt		29.00	12/94	2c
Undervest, boy's size 10-14, cotton	3	3.95	12/94	2c
Communications				
Newspaper subscription, dly. and Sun. delivery	month	10.40	12/94	2c
Telephone bill, family of four	month	16.74	12/94	2c
Telephone, residential, flat rate	mo.	9.10	12/93	8c
Energy and Fuels				
Energy, combined forms, 1800 sq. ft.	mo.	109.96	12/94	2c
Gas, reg unlead, taxes inc., cash, self-service	gal	0.92	12/94	2c
Entertainment				
Bowling, evening rate	game	1.75	12/94	2c
Monopoly game, Parker Brothers', No. 9	game	12.31	12/94	2c
Movie	adm	4.00	12/94	2c
Tennis balls, yellow, Wilson or Penn, 3	can	3.21	12/94	2c
Groceries				
Groceries, ACCRA Index		92.80	12/94	2c
Baby food, strained vegetables, lowest price	4-4.5 oz.	0.40	12/94	2c

Nevada, MO - continued

Item	Per	Value	Date	Ref.
Groceries - continued				
Bananas	lb.	0.40	12/94	2c
Beef or hamburger, ground	lb.	1.25	12/94	2c
Bread, white	24-oz.	0.53	12/94	2c
Cheese, Kraft grated Parmesan	8-oz.	3.75	12/94	2c
Chicken, whole fryer	lb.	0.74	12/94	2c
Cigarettes, Winston, Kings	carton	13.64	12/94	2c
Coffee, vacuum-packed	13 oz.	3.45	12/94	2c
Corn Flakes, Kellogg's or Post Toasties	18 oz.	2.52	12/94	2c
Corn, frozen, whole kernel, lowest price	10 oz.	0.68	12/94	2c
Eggs, Grade A large	dozen	0.62	12/94	2c
Lettuce, iceberg	head	0.56	12/94	2c
Margarine, Blue Bonnet or Parkay cubes	lb.	0.69	12/94	2c
Milk, whole	1/2 gal.	1.33	12/94	2c
Orange juice, Minute Maid frozen	12-oz.	1.58	12/94	2c
Peaches, halves or slices, Hunt's, Del Monte, or Libby's	29-oz.	1.28	12/94	2c
Peas, sweet, Del Monte or Green Giant	15-17 oz.	0.61	12/94	2c
Potatoes, white or red	10-lb. sack	0.99	12/94	2c
Sausage, Jimmy Dean, 100% pork	lb.	2.64	12/94	2c
Shortening, vegetable, Crisco	3-lb.	2.24	12/94	2c
Soft drink, Coca Cola, ex deposit	2 lit	1.04	12/94	2c
Steak, t-bone	lb.	3.65	12/94	2c
Sugar, cane or beet	4 lbs.	0.76	12/94	2c
Tomatoes, Hunt's or Del Monte	14.5 oz.	0.79	12/94	2c
Tuna, chunk, light, oil-packed	6.125-6.5 oz.	0.78	12/94	2c
Goods and Services				
Miscellaneous goods and services, ACCRA Index		100.00	12/94	2c
Health Care				
Health care, ACCRA Index		71.40	12/94	2c
Antibiotic ointment, Polysporin	1.5 oz.	3.86	12/94	2c
Dentist's fee, adult teeth cleaning and periodic oral exam	visit	33.25	12/94	2c
Doctor's fee, routine exam, established patient	visit	26.00	12/94	2c
Hospital care, semiprivate room	day	327.00	12/94	2c
Household Goods				
Appl. repair, service call, wash mach	min. lab. chg.	23.25	12/94	2c
Laundry detergent, Tide Ultra, Bold, or Cheer	42 oz.	3.64	12/94	2c
Tissues, facial, Kleenex brand	175	0.93	12/94	2c
Housing				
Housing, ACCRA Index		87.70	12/94	2c
House payment, principal and interest, 25% down payment	mo.	673	12/94	2c
House, 1800 sq ft, 8000 sq ft lot, new, urban, utilities	total	108000	12/94	2c
Mtge. rate, incl. points and orig. fee, 30-year conv. fixed or ARM	mo.	9.37	12/94	2c
Personal Goods				
Shampoo, Alberto VO5	15-oz.	1.11	12/94	2c
Toothpaste, Crest or Colgate	6-7 oz.	2.07	12/94	2c
Personal Services				
Dry cleaning, man's 2-pc. suit		5.78	12/94	2c
Haircut, man's barbershop, no styling		3.08	12/94	2c
Haircut, woman's shampoo, trim, blow-dry		14.50	12/94	2c
Restaurant Food				
Chicken, fried, thigh and drumstick		2.59	12/94	2c
Hamburger with cheese	1/4 lb.	1.80	12/94	2c
Pizza, Pizza Hut or Pizza Inn	12-13 in.	7.99	12/94	2c

Values are in dollars or fractions of dollars. In the column headed *Ref*, references are shown to sources. Each reference is followed by a letter. These refer to the geographical level for which data were reported: s=State, r=Region, and c=City or metro. The abbreviation *ex* is used to mean *except* or *excluding*; *exp* stands for expenditures. For other abbreviations and further explanations, please see the Introduction.

Nevada, MO - continued

Item	Per	Value	Date	Ref.
Transportation				
Transportation, ACCRA Index		84.70	12/94	2c
Tire balance, computer or spin bal., front	wheel	6.00	12/94	2c
Utilities				
Utilities, ACCRA Index		96.30	12/94	2c
Electricity, 1800 sq. ft., new home	mo.	109.96	12/94	2c

New Bedford, MA

Item	Per	Value	Date	Ref.
Appliances				
Appliances (major), expenditures	year	145	91	81r
Average annual exp.				
Food, health care, personal goods, services	year	29496	91	81r
Charity				
Cash contributions, expenditures	year	708	91	81r
Clothing				
Apparel, men and boys, total expenditures	year	416	91	81r
Apparel, women and girls, total expenditures	year	744	91	81r
Footwear, expenditures	year	305	91	81r
Communications				
Long-distance telephone rate, day, addl. min., 1-10 mi.	min.	0.09	12/93	9s
Long-distance telephone rate, day, initial min., 1-10 mi.	min.	0.19	12/93	9s
Phone line, single, business, field visit	inst	27.50	12/93	9s
Phone line, single, business, no field visit	inst	93.02	12/93	9s
Phone line, single, residence, field visit	inst	27.50	12/93	9s
Phone line, single, residence, no field visit	inst	37.07	12/93	9s
Telephone service, expenditures	year	589	91	81r
Education				
Board, 4-year private college/university	year	3179	8/94	80s
Board, 4-year public college/university	year	2035	8/94	80s
Education, total expenditures	year	593	91	81r
Room, 4-year private college/university	year	3369	8/94	80s
Room, 4-year public college/university	year	2290	8/94	80s
Total cost, 4-year private college/university	year	21346	8/94	80s
Total cost, 4-year public college/university	year	8467	8/94	80s
Tuition, 2-year public college/university, in-state	year	2361	8/94	80s
Tuition, 4-year private college/university, in-state	year	14797	8/94	80s
Tuition, 4-year public college/university, in-state	year	4142	8/94	80s
Energy and Fuels				
Fuel oil and other fuels, expenditures	year	257	91	81r
Gas, natural, expenditures	year	285	91	81r
Gasoline and motor oil purchased	year	867	91	81r
Gasoline, unleaded midgrade	gallon	1.32	4/93	82r
Gasoline, unleaded premium	gallon	1.40	4/93	82r
Gasoline, unleaded regular	gallon	1.19	4/93	82r
Entertainment				
Entertainment, total expenditures	year	1331	91	81r
Fees and admissions, expenditures	year	398	91	81r
Pets, toys, playground equipment, expenditures	year	270	91	81r
Reading, expenditures	year	171	91	81r
Televisions, radios, and sound equipment, expenditures	year	429	91	81r
Funerals				
Burial, immediate, container provided by funeral home		1507.89	1/95	54r
Cards, acknowledgment		18.10	1/95	54r
Casket, minimum alternative		133.03	1/95	54r
Cosmetology, hair care, etc.		114.12	1/95	54r
Cremation, direct, container provided by funeral home		1309.19	1/95	54r
Embalming		320.97	1/95	54r

New Bedford, MA - continued

Item	Per	Value	Date	Ref.
Funerals - continued				
Funeral, funeral home		327.61	1/95	54r
Funeral, other facility		314.81	1/95	54r
Graveside service		286.11	1/95	54r
Hearse, local		158.95	1/95	54r
Limousine, local		149.45	1/95	54r
Memorial service		315.94	1/95	54r
Service charge, professional, nondeclinable		1148.43	1/95	54r
Visitation and viewing		249.66	1/95	54r
Groceries				
Apples, Red Delicious	lb.	0.78	12/94	82r
Bacon, sliced	lb.	2.24	12/94	82r
Bananas	lb.	0.49	12/94	82r
Beef purchases	year	226	91	81r
Beverage purchases, alcoholic	year	332	91	81r
Beverage purchases, nonalcoholic	year	213	91	81r
Bread, white, pan	lb.	0.80	12/94	82r
Butter, salted, Grade AA, stick	lb.	1.67	12/94	82r
Carrots, short trimmed and topped	lb.	0.51	12/94	82r
Cereals and bakery products purchases	year	407	91	81r
Cereals and cereals products purchases	year	132	91	81r
Chicken breast, bone-in	lb.	2.22	12/94	82r
Chicken, fresh, whole	lb.	1.05	12/94	82r
Chuck roast, USDA choice, boneless	lb.	2.74	12/94	82r
Coffee, 100%, ground roast, all sizes	lb.	4.61	12/94	82r
Dairy products (other) purchases	year	161	91	81r
Eggs, Grade A large	dozen	1.12	12/94	82r
Fish and seafood purchases	year	112	91	81r
Food purchases, food eaten at home	year	2599	91	81r
Foods purchased away from home, not prepared by consumer	year	2024	91	81r
Fruits and vegetables purchases	year	444	91	81r
Grapefruit	lb.	0.44	12/94	82r
Grapes, Thompson seedless	lb.	2.24	12/94	82r
Ground chuck, 100% beef	lb.	1.67	12/94	82r
Ice cream, prepackaged, bulk, regular	1/2 gal.	2.93	12/94	82r
Lemons	lb.	1.06	12/94	82r
Lettuce, iceberg	lb.	0.92	12/94	82r
Meats, poultry, fish, and eggs purchases	year	751	91	81r
Milk and cream (fresh) purchases	year	152	91	81r
Orange juice, frozen concentrate 12-oz. can	16 oz.	1.92	12/94	82r
Oranges, Navel	lb.	0.56	12/94	82r
Pork chops, center cut, bone-in	lb.	3.09	12/94	82r
Pork purchases	year	130	91	81r
Potatoes, white	lb.	0.37	12/94	82r
Rib roast, USDA choice, bone-in	lb.	4.98	12/94	82r
Round roast, USDA choice, boneless	lb.	2.93	12/94	82r
Shortening, vegetable oil blends	lb.	1.03	12/94	82r
Spaghetti and macaroni	lb.	0.84	12/94	82r
Steak, round, USDA choice, boneless	lb.	3.48	12/94	82r
Steak, sirloin, USDA choice, bone-in	lb.	3.38	12/94	82r
Steak, sirloin, USDA choice, boneless	lb.	4.81	12/94	82r
Sugar and other sweets, eaten at home, expenditures	year	89	91	81r
Sugar, white, all sizes	lb.	0.46	12/94	82r
Tobacco products and smoking supplies, total expenditures	year	279	91	81r
Tomatoes, field grown	lb.	1.56	12/94	82r
Tuna, chunk, light	lb.	2.09	12/94	82r
Health Care				
Childbirth, Cesarean delivery, hospital charge	birth	6334.00	12/91	69r
Childbirth, Cesarean delivery, physician charge	birth	2234.00	12/91	69r
Childbirth, normal delivery, hospital charge	birth	3225.00	12/91	69r
Childbirth, normal delivery, physician charge	birth	1623.00	12/91	69r
Drugs, expenditures	year	205	91	81r
Health care, total expenditures	year	1396	91	81r
Health insurance expenditures	year	553	91	81r
Insurance premium, family medical care	month	457.38	1/95	41s
Medical services expenditures	year	559	91	81r

Values are in dollars or fractions of dollars. In the column headed *Ref*, references are shown to sources. Each reference is followed by a letter. These refer to the geographical level for which data were reported: s=State, r=Region, and c=City or metro. The abbreviation *ex* is used to mean *except* or *excluding*; *exp* stands for expenditures. For other abbreviations and further explanations, please see the Introduction.

New Bedford, MA - continued

Item	Per	Value	Date	Ref.
Health Care				
Medical supplies expenditures	year	80	91	81r
Household Goods				
Floor coverings, expenditures	year	158	91	81r
Furniture, expenditures	year	341	91	81r
Household equipment, misc. expenditures	year	363	91	81r
Household expenditures, miscellaneous	year	194	91	81r
Household furnishings and equipment, expenditures	year	1158	91	81r
Household operations expenditures	year	378	91	81r
Household textiles, expenditures	year	88	91	81r
Housekeeping supplies, expenditures	year	426	91	81r
Laundry and cleaning supplies, expenditures	year	122	91	81r
Postage and stationery, expenditures	year	134	91	81r
Housing				
Add garage/carport		11,614	3/95	74r
Add room(s)		16,816	3/95	74r
Apartment condominium or co-op, median	unit	96700	12/94	62r
Dwellings (owned), expenditures	year	3305	91	81r
Enclose porch/patio/breezeway		2,980	3/95	74r
Finish room in basement/attic		4,330	3/95	74r
Home, existing, single-family, median	unit	161600	12/94	62r
Maintenance, repairs, insurance, and other housing expenditures	year	569	91	81r
Mortgage interest and charges expenditures	year	1852	91	81r
Princ. & int., mortgage, median-price exist. sing.-family home	mo.	765	12/94	62r
Property taxes expenditures	year	884	91	81r
Redesign, restructure more than half of home's interior		2,750	3/95	74r
Rental units expenditures	year	1832	91	81r
Insurance and Pensions				
Auto insurance, private passenger	year	1009.56	12/94	71s
Insurance and pensions, personal, expenditures	year	2690	91	81r
Insurance, life and other personal, expenditures	year	341	91	81r
Pensions and Social Security, expenditures	year	2349	91	81r
Legal Assistance				
Estate planning, law-firm partner	hr.	375.00	10/93	12r
Legal work, law firm associate	hour	78		10r
Legal work, law firm partner	hour	183		10r
Personal Services				
Personal services expenditures	year	184	91	81r
Restaurant Food				
Dining expenditures, family	week	34.26	94	73r
Taxes				
Taxes, Federal income, expenditures	year	2409	91	81r
Taxes, personal, expenditures	year	3094	91	81r
Taxes, State and local income, expenditures	year	620	91	81r
Transportation				
Cars and trucks purchased, new	year	1170	91	81r
Cars and trucks purchased, used	year	739	91	81r
Driver's learning permit fee	perm	15.00	1/94	84s
Driver's license fee	orig	50.00	1/94	84s
Driver's license fee, duplicate	lic	15.00	1/94	84s
Driver's license renewal fee	renew	43.75	1/94	84s
Identification card, nondriver	card	15.00	1/94	83s
Motorcycle license fee	orig	50.00	1/94	84s
Motorcycle license fee, duplicate	lic	15.00	1/94	84s
Motorcycle license renewal fee	renew	43.75	1/94	84s
Public transportation expenditures	year	430	91	81r
Transportation expenditures, total	year	4810	91	81r
Vehicle finance charges	year	238	91	81r
Vehicle insurance expenditures	year	630	91	81r
Vehicle maintenance and repairs expenditures	year	532	91	81r
Vehicle purchases	year	1920	91	81r

New Bedford, MA - continued

Item	Per	Value	Date	Ref.
Transportation - continued				
Vehicle rental, leases, licenses, etc. expenditures	year	193	91	81r
Vehicles purchased, other than cars and trucks	year	11	91	81r
Utilities				
Electricity expenditures	year	695	91	81r
Utilities, fuels, and public services, total expenditures	year	1981	91	81r
Water and other public services, expenditures	year	154	91	81r
Weddings				
Bridal attendants' gowns	event	750	10/93	76r
Bridal gown	event	852	10/93	76r
Bridal headpiece and veil	event	167	10/93	76r
Bride's wedding band	event	708	10/93	76r
Clergy	event	224	10/93	76r
Engagement ring	event	2756	10/93	76r
Flowers	event	863	10/93	76r
Formal wear for groom	event	106	10/93	76r
Groom's attendants' formal wear	event	530	10/93	76r
Groom's wedding band	event	402	10/93	76r
Music	event	600	10/93	76r
Photography	event	1088	10/93	76r
Shoes for bride	event	50	10/93	76r
Videography	event	483	10/93	76r
Wedding invitations and announcements	event	342	10/93	76r
Wedding reception	event	7000	10/93	76r

New Britain, CT

Item	Per	Value	Date	Ref.
Appliances				
Appliances (major), expenditures	year	145	91	81r
Average annual exp.				
Food, health care, personal goods, services	year	29496	91	81r
Charity				
Cash contributions, expenditures	year	708	91	81r
Clothing				
Apparel, men and boys, total expenditures	year	416	91	81r
Apparel, women and girls, total expenditures	year	744	91	81r
Footwear, expenditures	year	305	91	81r
Communications				
Long-distance telephone rate, day, addl. min., 1-10 mi.	min.	0.09	12/93	9s
Long-distance telephone rate, day, initial min., 1-10 mi.	min.	0.09	12/93	9s
Phone line, single, business, field visit	inst	127.44	12/93	9s
Phone line, single, business, no field visit	inst	95.58	12/93	9s
Phone line, single, residence, field visit	inst	64.85	12/93	9s
Phone line, single, residence, no field visit	inst	38.27	12/93	9s
Telephone service, expenditures	year	589	91	81r
Education				
Board, 4-year private college/university	year	2664	8/94	80s
Board, 4-year public college/university	year	2137	8/94	80s
Education, total expenditures	year	593	91	81r
Room, 4-year private college/university	year	3287	8/94	80s
Room, 4-year public college/university	year	2310	8/94	80s
Total cost, 4-year private college/university	year	20726	8/94	80s
Total cost, 4-year public college/university	year	7926	8/94	80s
Tuition, 2-year public college/university, in-state	year	1398	8/94	80s
Tuition, 4-year private college/university, in-state	year	14775	8/94	80s
Tuition, 4-year public college/university, in-state	year	3479	8/94	80s
Energy and Fuels				
Fuel oil and other fuels, expenditures	year	257	91	81r
Gas, natural, expenditures	year	285	91	81r

Values are in dollars or fractions of dollars. In the column headed *Ref*, references are shown to sources. Each reference is followed by a letter. These refer to the geographical level for which data were reported: s=State, r=Region, and c=City or metro. The abbreviation *ex* is used to mean *except* or *excluding*; *exp* stands for expenditures. For other abbreviations and further explanations, please see the Introduction.

New Britain, CT - continued

Item	Per	Value	Date	Ref.
Energy and Fuels				
Gasoline and motor oil purchased	year	867	91	81r
Gasoline, unleaded midgrade	gallon	1.32	4/93	82r
Gasoline, unleaded premium	gallon	1.40	4/93	82r
Gasoline, unleaded regular	gallon	1.19	4/93	82r
Entertainment				
Entertainment, total expenditures	year	1331	91	81r
Fees and admissions, expenditures	year	398	91	81r
Pets, toys, playground equipment, expenditures	year	270	91	81r
Reading, expenditures	year	171	91	81r
Televisions, radios, and sound equipment, expenditures	year	429	91	81r
Funerals				
Burial, immediate, container provided by funeral home		1507.89	1/95	54r
Cards, acknowledgment		18.10	1/95	54r
Casket, minimum alternative		133.03	1/95	54r
Cosmetology, hair care, etc.		114.12	1/95	54r
Cremation, direct, container provided by funeral home		1309.19	1/95	54r
Embalming		320.97	1/95	54r
Funeral, funeral home		327.61	1/95	54r
Funeral, other facility		314.81	1/95	54r
Graveside service		286.11	1/95	54r
Hearse, local		158.95	1/95	54r
Limousine, local		149.45	1/95	54r
Memorial service		315.94	1/95	54r
Service charge, professional, nondeclinable		1148.43	1/95	54r
Visitation and viewing		249.66	1/95	54r
Groceries				
Apples, Red Delicious	lb.	0.78	12/94	82r
Bacon, sliced	lb.	2.24	12/94	82r
Bananas	lb.	0.49	12/94	82r
Beef purchases	year	226	91	81r
Beverage purchases, alcoholic	year	332	91	81r
Beverage purchases, nonalcoholic	year	213	91	81r
Bread, white, pan	lb.	0.80	12/94	82r
Butter, salted, Grade AA, stick	lb.	1.67	12/94	82r
Carrots, short trimmed and topped	lb.	0.51	12/94	82r
Cereals and bakery products purchases	year	407	91	81r
Cereals and cereals products purchases	year	132	91	81r
Chicken breast, bone-in	lb.	2.22	12/94	82r
Chicken, fresh, whole	lb.	1.05	12/94	82r
Chuck roast, USDA choice, boneless	lb.	2.74	12/94	82r
Coffee, 100%, ground roast, all sizes	lb.	4.61	12/94	82r
Dairy products (other) purchases	year	161	91	81r
Eggs, Grade A large	dozen	1.12	12/94	82r
Fish and seafood purchases	year	112	91	81r
Food purchases, food eaten at home	year	2599	91	81r
Foods purchased away from home, not prepared by consumer	year	2024	91	81r
Fruits and vegetables purchases	year	444	91	81r
Grapefruit	lb.	0.44	12/94	82r
Grapes, Thompson seedless	lb.	2.24	12/94	82r
Ground chuck, 100% beef	lb.	1.67	12/94	82r
Ice cream, prepackaged, bulk, regular	1/2 gal.	2.93	12/94	82r
Lemons	lb.	1.06	12/94	82r
Lettuce, iceberg	lb.	0.92	12/94	82r
Meats, poultry, fish, and eggs purchases	year	751	91	81r
Milk and cream (fresh) purchases	year	152	91	81r
Orange juice, frozen concentrate 12-oz. can	16 oz.	1.92	12/94	82r
Oranges, Navel	lb.	0.56	12/94	82r
Pork chops, center cut, bone-in	lb.	3.09	12/94	82r
Pork purchases	year	130	91	81r
Potatoes, white	lb.	0.37	12/94	82r
Rib roast, USDA choice, bone-in	lb.	4.98	12/94	82r
Round roast, USDA choice, boneless	lb.	2.93	12/94	82r
Shortening, vegetable oil blends	lb.	1.03	12/94	82r
Spaghetti and macaroni	lb.	0.84	12/94	82r
Steak, round, USDA choice, boneless	lb.	3.48	12/94	82r

New Britain, CT - continued

Item	Per	Value	Date	Ref.
Groceries - continued				
Steak, sirloin, USDA choice, bone-in	lb.	3.38	12/94	82r
Steak, sirloin, USDA choice, boneless	lb.	4.81	12/94	82r
Sugar and other sweets, eaten at home, expenditures	year	89	91	81r
Sugar, white, all sizes	lb.	0.46	12/94	82r
Tobacco products and smoking supplies, total expenditures	year	279	91	81r
Tomatoes, field grown	lb.	1.56	12/94	82r
Tuna, chunk, light	lb.	2.09	12/94	82r
Health Care				
Childbirth, Cesarean delivery, hospital charge	birth	6334.00	12/91	69r
Childbirth, Cesarean delivery, physician charge	birth	2234.00	12/91	69r
Childbirth, normal delivery, hospital charge	birth	3225.00	12/91	69r
Childbirth, normal delivery, physician charge	birth	1623.00	12/91	69r
Drugs, expenditures	year	205	91	81r
Health care, total expenditures	year	1396	91	81r
Health insurance expenditures	year	553	91	81r
Insurance premium, family medical care	month	500.40	1/95	41s
Medical services expenditures	year	559	91	81r
Medical supplies expenditures	year	80	91	81r
Household Goods				
Floor coverings, expenditures	year	158	91	81r
Furniture, expenditures	year	341	91	81r
Household equipment, misc. expenditures	year	363	91	81r
Household expenditures, miscellaneous	year	194	91	81r
Household furnishings and equipment, expenditures	year	1158	91	81r
Household operations expenditures	year	378	91	81r
Household textiles, expenditures	year	88	91	81r
Housekeeping supplies, expenditures	year	426	91	81r
Laundry and cleaning supplies, expenditures	year	122	91	81r
Postage and stationery, expenditures	year	134	91	81r
Housing				
Add garage/carport		11,614	3/95	74r
Add room(s)		16,816	3/95	74r
Apartment condominium or co-op, median	unit	96700	12/94	62r
Dwellings (owned), expenditures	year	3305	91	81r
Enclose porch/patio/breezeway		2,980	3/95	74r
Finish room in basement/attic		4,330	3/95	74r
Home, existing, single-family, median	unit	161600	12/94	62r
Maintenance, repairs, insurance, and other housing expenditures	year	569	91	81r
Mortgage interest and charges expenditures	year	1852	91	81r
Princ. & int., mortgage, median-price exist. sing.-family home	mo.	765	12/94	62r
Property taxes expenditures	year	884	91	81r
Redesign, restructure more than half of home's interior		2,750	3/95	74r
Rental units expenditures	year	1832	91	81r
Insurance and Pensions				
Auto insurance, private passenger	year	1002.84	12/94	71s
Insurance and pensions, personal, expenditures	year	2690	91	81r
Insurance, life and other personal, expenditures	year	341	91	81r
Pensions and Social Security, expenditures	year	2349	91	81r
Legal Assistance				
Estate planning, law-firm partner	hr.	375.00	10/93	12r
Legal work, law firm associate	hour	78		10r
Legal work, law firm partner	hour	183		10r
Personal Services				
Personal services expenditures	year	184	91	81r
Restaurant Food				
Dining expenditures, family	week	34.26	94	73r

Values are in dollars or fractions of dollars. In the column headed *Ref*, references are shown to sources. Each reference is followed by a letter. These refer to the geographical level for which data were reported: s = State, r = Region, and c = City or metro. The abbreviation *ex* is used to mean *except* or *excluding*; *exp* stands for *expenditures*. For other abbreviations and further explanations, please see the Introduction.

New Britain, CT - continued

Item	Per	Value	Date	Ref.
Taxes				
Taxes, Federal income, expenditures	year	2409	91	81r
Taxes, personal, expenditures	year	3094	91	81r
Taxes, State and local income, expenditures	year	620	91	81r
Transportation				
Cars and trucks purchased, new	year	1170	91	81r
Cars and trucks purchased, used	year	739	91	81r
Driver's learning permit fee	perm	3.50	1/94	84s
Driver's license fee	orig	38.00	1/94	84s
Driver's license fee, duplicate	lic	5.00	1/94	84s
Driver's license reinstatement fee, min.	susp	30.00	1/94	85s
Driver's license renewal fee	renew	31.00	1/94	84s
Identification card, nondriver	card	4.00	1/94	83s
Motorcycle learning permit fee	perm	3.50	1/94	84s
Motorcycle license fee	orig	38.00	1/94	84s
Motorcycle license fee, duplicate	lic	5.00	1/94	84s
Motorcycle license renewal fee	renew	31.00	1/94	84s
Public transportation expenditures	year	430	91	81r
Transportation expenditures, total	year	4810	91	81r
Vehicle finance charges	year	238	91	81r
Vehicle insurance expenditures	year	630	91	81r
Vehicle maintenance and repairs expenditures	year	532	91	81r
Vehicle purchases	year	1920	91	81r
Vehicle rental, leases, licenses, etc. expenditures	year	193	91	81r
Vehicles purchased, other than cars and trucks	year	11	91	81r
Utilities				
Electricity expenditures	year	695	91	81r
Utilities, fuels, and public services, total expenditures	year	1981	91	81r
Water and other public services, expenditures	year	154	91	81r
Weddings				
Bridal attendants' gowns	event	750	10/93	76r
Bridal gown	event	852	10/93	76r
Bridal headpiece and veil	event	167	10/93	76r
Bride's wedding band	event	708	10/93	76r
Clergy	event	224	10/93	76r
Engagement ring	event	2756	10/93	76r
Flowers	event	863	10/93	76r
Formal wear for groom	event	106	10/93	76r
Groom's attendants' formal wear	event	530	10/93	76r
Groom's wedding band	event	402	10/93	76r
Music	event	600	10/93	76r
Photography	event	1088	10/93	76r
Shoes for bride	event	50	10/93	76r
Videography	event	483	10/93	76r
Wedding invitations and announcements	event	342	10/93	76r
Wedding reception	event	7000	10/93	76r

New Haven, CT

Item	Per	Value	Date	Ref.
Appliances				
Appliances (major), expenditures	year	145	91	81r
Average annual exp.				
Food, health care, personal goods, services	year	29496	91	81r
Charity				
Cash contributions, expenditures	year	708	91	81r
Clothing				
Apparel, men and boys, total expenditures	year	416	91	81r
Apparel, women and girls, total expenditures	year	744	91	81r
Footwear, expenditures	year	305	91	81r
Communications				
Long-distance telephone rate, day, addl. min., 1-10 mi.	min.	0.09	12/93	9s

New Haven, CT - continued

Item	Per	Value	Date	Ref.
Communications - continued				
Long-distance telephone rate, day, initial min., 1-10 mi.	min.	0.09	12/93	9s
Phone line, single, business, field visit	inst	127.44	12/93	9s
Phone line, single, business, no field visit	inst	95.58	12/93	9s
Phone line, single, residence, field visit	inst	64.85	12/93	9s
Phone line, single, residence, no field visit	inst	38.27	12/93	9s
Telephone service, expenditures	year	589	91	81r
Education				
Board, 4-year private college/university	year	2664	8/94	80s
Board, 4-year public college/university	year	2137	8/94	80s
Education, total expenditures	year	593	91	81r
Room, 4-year private college/university	year	3287	8/94	80s
Room, 4-year public college/university	year	2310	8/94	80s
Total cost, 4-year private college/university	year	20726	8/94	80s
Total cost, 4-year public college/university	year	7926	8/94	80s
Tuition, 2-year public college/university, in-state	year	1398	8/94	80s
Tuition, 4-year private college/university, in-state	year	14775	8/94	80s
Tuition, 4-year public college/university, in-state	year	3479	8/94	80s
Energy and Fuels				
Fuel oil and other fuels, expenditures	year	257	91	81r
Gas, natural, expenditures	year	285	91	81r
Gasoline and motor oil purchased	year	867	91	81r
Gasoline, unleaded midgrade	gallon	1.32	4/93	82r
Gasoline, unleaded premium	gallon	1.40	4/93	82r
Gasoline, unleaded regular	gallon	1.19	4/93	82r
Entertainment				
Entertainment, total expenditures	year	1331	91	81r
Fees and admissions, expenditures	year	398	91	81r
Pets, toys, playground equipment, expenditures	year	270	91	81r
Reading, expenditures	year	171	91	81r
Televisions, radios, and sound equipment, expenditures	year	429	91	81r
Funerals				
Burial, immediate, container provided by funeral home		1507.89	1/95	54r
Cards, acknowledgment		18.10	1/95	54r
Casket, minimum alternative		133.03	1/95	54r
Cosmetology, hair care, etc.		114.12	1/95	54r
Cremation, direct, container provided by funeral home		1309.19	1/95	54r
Embalming		320.97	1/95	54r
Funeral, funeral home		327.61	1/95	54r
Funeral, other facility		314.81	1/95	54r
Graveside service		286.11	1/95	54r
Hearse, local		158.95	1/95	54r
Limousine, local		149.45	1/95	54r
Memorial service		315.94	1/95	54r
Service charge, professional, nondeclinable		1148.43	1/95	54r
Visitation and viewing		249.66	1/95	54r
Groceries				
Apples, Red Delicious	lb.	0.78	12/94	82r
Bacon, sliced	lb.	2.24	12/94	82r
Bananas	lb.	0.49	12/94	82r
Beef purchases	year	226	91	81r
Beverage purchases, alcoholic	year	332	91	81r
Beverage purchases, nonalcoholic	year	213	91	81r
Bread, white, pan	lb.	0.80	12/94	82r
Butter, salted, Grade AA, stick	lb.	1.67	12/94	82r
Carrots, short trimmed and topped	lb.	0.51	12/94	82r
Cereals and bakery products purchases	year	407	91	81r
Cereals and cereals products purchases	year	132	91	81r
Chicken breast, bone-in	lb.	2.22	12/94	82r
Chicken, fresh, whole	lb.	1.05	12/94	82r
Chuck roast, USDA choice, boneless	lb.	2.74	12/94	82r
Coffee, 100%, ground roast, all sizes	lb.	4.61	12/94	82r

Values are in dollars or fractions of dollars. In the column headed *Ref*, references are shown to sources. Each reference is followed by a letter. These refer to the geographical level for which data were reported: s=State, r=Region, and c=City or metro. The abbreviation *ex* is used to mean *except* or *excluding*; *exp* stands for expenditures. For other abbreviations and further explanations, please see the Introduction.

New Haven, CT - continued

Item	Per	Value	Date	Ref.
Groceries				
Dairy products (other) purchases	year	161	91	81r
Eggs, Grade A large	dozen	1.12	12/94	82r
Fish and seafood purchases	year	112	91	81r
Food purchases, food eaten at home	year	2599	91	81r
Foods purchased away from home, not prepared by consumer	year	2024	91	81r
Fruits and vegetables purchases	year	444	91	81r
Grapefruit	lb.	0.44	12/94	82r
Grapes, Thompson seedless	lb.	2.24	12/94	82r
Ground chuck, 100% beef	lb.	1.67	12/94	82r
Ice cream, prepackaged, bulk, regular	1/2 gal.	2.93	12/94	82r
Lemons	lb.	1.06	12/94	82r
Lettuce, iceberg	lb.	0.92	12/94	82r
Meats, poultry, fish, and eggs purchases	year	751	91	81r
Milk and cream (fresh) purchases	year	152	91	81r
Orange juice, frozen concentrate 12-oz. can	16 oz.	1.92	12/94	82r
Oranges, Navel	lb.	0.56	12/94	82r
Pork chops, center cut, bone-in	lb.	3.09	12/94	82r
Pork purchases	year	130	91	81r
Potatoes, white	lb.	0.37	12/94	82r
Rib roast, USDA choice, bone-in	lb.	4.98	12/94	82r
Round roast, USDA choice, boneless	lb.	2.93	12/94	82r
Shortening, vegetable oil blends	lb.	1.03	12/94	82r
Spaghetti and macaroni	lb.	0.84	12/94	82r
Steak, round, USDA choice, boneless	lb.	3.48	12/94	82r
Steak, sirloin, USDA choice, bone-in	lb.	3.38	12/94	82r
Steak, sirloin, USDA choice, boneless	lb.	4.81	12/94	82r
Sugar and other sweets, eaten at home, expenditures	year	89	91	81r
Sugar, white, all sizes	lb.	0.46	12/94	82r
Tobacco products and smoking supplies, total expenditures	year	279	91	81r
Tomatoes, field grown	lb.	1.56	12/94	82r
Tuna, chunk, light	lb.	2.09	12/94	82r
Health Care				
Childbirth, Cesarean delivery, hospital charge	birth	6334.00	12/91	69r
Childbirth, Cesarean delivery, physician charge	birth	2234.00	12/91	69r
Childbirth, normal delivery, hospital charge	birth	3225.00	12/91	69r
Childbirth, normal delivery, physician charge	birth	1623.00	12/91	69r
Drugs, expenditures	year	205	91	81r
Health care, total expenditures	year	1396	91	81r
Health insurance expenditures	year	553	91	81r
Insurance premium, family medical care	month	500.40	1/95	41s
Medical services expenditures	year	559	91	81r
Medical supplies expenditures	year	80	91	81r
Household Goods				
Floor coverings, expenditures	year	158	91	81r
Furniture, expenditures	year	341	91	81r
Household equipment, misc. expenditures	year	363	91	81r
Household expenditures, miscellaneous	year	194	91	81r
Household furnishings and equipment, expenditures	year	1158	91	81r
Household operations expenditures	year	378	91	81r
Household textiles, expenditures	year	88	91	81r
Housekeeping supplies, expenditures	year	426	91	81r
Laundry and cleaning supplies, expenditures	year	122	91	81r
Postage and stationery, expenditures	year	134	91	81r
Housing				
Add garage/carport		11,614	3/95	74r
Add room(s)		16,816	3/95	74r
Apartment condominium or co-op, median	unit	96700	12/94	62r
Dwellings (owned), expenditures	year	3305	91	81r
Enclose porch/patio/breezeway		2,980	3/95	74r
Finish room in basement/attic		4,330	3/95	74r
Home, existing, single-family, median	unit	161600	12/94	62r
Maintenance, repairs, insurance, and other housing expenditures	year	569	91	81r

New Haven, CT - continued

Item	Per	Value	Date	Ref.
Housing - continued				
Mortgage interest and charges expenditures	year	1852	91	81r
Princ. & int., mortgage, median-price exist. sing.-family home	mo.	765	12/94	62r
Property taxes expenditures	year	884	91	81r
Redesign, restructure more than half of home's interior		2,750	3/95	74r
Rental units expenditures	year	1832	91	81r
Insurance and Pensions				
Auto insurance, private passenger	year	1002.84	12/94	71s
Insurance and pensions, personal, expenditures	year	2690	91	81r
Insurance, life and other personal, expenditures	year	341	91	81r
Pensions and Social Security, expenditures	year	2349	91	81r
Legal Assistance				
Estate planning, law-firm partner	hr.	375.00	10/93	12r
Legal work, law firm associate	hour	78		10r
Legal work, law firm partner	hour	183		10r
Personal Services				
Personal services expenditures	year	184	91	81r
Restaurant Food				
Dining expenditures, family	week	34.26	94	73r
Taxes				
Taxes, Federal income, expenditures	year	2409	91	81r
Taxes, personal, expenditures	year	3094	91	81r
Taxes, State and local income, expenditures	year	620	91	81r
Transportation				
Cars and trucks purchased, new	year	1170	91	81r
Cars and trucks purchased, used	year	739	91	81r
Driver's learning permit fee	perm	3.50	1/94	84s
Driver's license fee	orig	38.00	1/94	84s
Driver's license fee, duplicate	lic	5.00	1/94	84s
Driver's license reinstatement fee, min.	susp	30.00	1/94	85s
Driver's license renewal fee	renew	31.00	1/94	84s
Identification card, nondriver	card	4.00	1/94	83s
Motorcycle learning permit fee	perm	3.50	1/94	84s
Motorcycle license fee	orig	38.00	1/94	84s
Motorcycle license fee, duplicate	lic	5.00	1/94	84s
Motorcycle license renewal fee	renew	31.00	1/94	84s
Public transportation expenditures	year	430	91	81r
Transportation expenditures, total	year	4810	91	81r
Vehicle finance charges	year	238	91	81r
Vehicle insurance expenditures	year	630	91	81r
Vehicle maintenance and repairs expenditures	year	532	91	81r
Vehicle purchases	year	1920	91	81r
Vehicle rental, leases, licenses, etc. expenditures	year	193	91	81r
Vehicles purchased, other than cars and trucks	year	11	91	81r
Utilities				
Electricity expenditures	year	695	91	81r
Utilities, fuels, and public services, total expenditures	year	1981	91	81r
Water and other public services, expenditures	year	154	91	81r
Weddings				
Bridal attendants' gowns	event	750	10/93	76r
Bridal gown	event	852	10/93	76r
Bridal headpiece and veil	event	167	10/93	76r
Bride's wedding band	event	708	10/93	76r
Clergy	event	224	10/93	76r
Engagement ring	event	2756	10/93	76r
Flowers	event	863	10/93	76r
Formal wear for groom	event	106	10/93	76r
Groom's attendants' formal wear	event	530	10/93	76r
Groom's wedding band	event	402	10/93	76r
Music	event	600	10/93	76r

Values are in dollars or fractions of dollars. In the column headed *Ref*, references are shown to sources. Each reference is followed by a letter. These refer to the geographical level for which data were reported: s=State, r=Region, and c=City or metro. The abbreviation *ex* is used to mean *except* or *excluding*; *exp* stands for expenditures. For other abbreviations and further explanations, please see the Introduction.

New Haven, CT - continued

Item	Per	Value	Date	Ref.
Weddings				
Photography	event	1088	10/93	76r
Shoes for bride	event	50	10/93	76r
Videography	event	483	10/93	76r
Wedding invitations and announcements	event	342	10/93	76r
Wedding reception	event	7000	10/93	76r

New London, CT

Item	Per	Value	Date	Ref.
Appliances				
Appliances (major), expenditures	year	145	91	81r
Average annual exp.				
Food, health care, personal goods, services	year	29496	91	81r
Charity				
Cash contributions, expenditures	year	708	91	81r
Clothing				
Apparel, men and boys, total expenditures	year	416	91	81r
Apparel, women and girls, total expenditures	year	744	91	81r
Footwear, expenditures	year	305	91	81r
Communications				
Long-distance telephone rate, day, addl. min., 1-10 mi.	min.	0.09	12/93	9s
Long-distance telephone rate, day, initial min., 1-10 mi.	min.	0.09	12/93	9s
Phone line, single, business, field visit	inst	127.44	12/93	9s
Phone line, single, business, no field visit	inst	95.58	12/93	9s
Phone line, single, residence, field visit	inst	64.85	12/93	9s
Phone line, single, residence, no field visit	inst	38.27	12/93	9s
Telephone service, expenditures	year	589	91	81r
Education				
Board, 4-year private college/university	year	2664	8/94	80s
Board, 4-year public college/university	year	2137	8/94	80s
Education, total expenditures	year	593	91	81r
Room, 4-year private college/university	year	3287	8/94	80s
Room, 4-year public college/university	year	2310	8/94	80s
Total cost, 4-year private college/university	year	20726	8/94	80s
Total cost, 4-year public college/university	year	7926	8/94	80s
Tuition, 2-year public college/university, in-state	year	1398	8/94	80s
Tuition, 4-year private college/university, in-state	year	14775	8/94	80s
Tuition, 4-year public college/university, in-state	year	3479	8/94	80s
Energy and Fuels				
Fuel oil and other fuels, expenditures	year	257	91	81r
Gas, natural, expenditures	year	285	91	81r
Gasoline and motor oil purchased	year	867	91	81r
Gasoline, unleaded midgrade	gallon	1.32	4/93	82r
Gasoline, unleaded premium	gallon	1.40	4/93	82r
Gasoline, unleaded regular	gallon	1.19	4/93	82r
Entertainment				
Entertainment, total expenditures	year	1331	91	81r
Fees and admissions, expenditures	year	398	91	81r
Pets, toys, playground equipment, expenditures	year	270	91	81r
Reading, expenditures	year	171	91	81r
Televisions, radios, and sound equipment, expenditures	year	429	91	81r
Funerals				
Burial, immediate, container provided by funeral home		1507.89	1/95	54r
Cards, acknowledgment		18.10	1/95	54r
Casket, minimum alternative		133.03	1/95	54r
Cosmetology, hair care, etc.		114.12	1/95	54r
Cremation, direct, container provided by funeral home		1309.19	1/95	54r
Embalming		320.97	1/95	54r
Funeral, funeral home		327.61	1/95	54r

New London, CT - continued

Item	Per	Value	Date	Ref.
Funerals - continued				
Funeral, other facility		314.81	1/95	54r
Graveside service		286.11	1/95	54r
Hearse, local		158.95	1/95	54r
Limousine, local		149.45	1/95	54r
Memorial service		315.94	1/95	54r
Service charge, professional, nondeclinable		1148.43	1/95	54r
Visitation and viewing		249.66	1/95	54r
Groceries				
Apples, Red Delicious	lb.	0.78	12/94	82r
Bacon, sliced	lb.	2.24	12/94	82r
Bananas	lb.	0.49	12/94	82r
Beef purchases	year	226	91	81r
Beverage purchases, alcoholic	year	332	91	81r
Beverage purchases, nonalcoholic	year	213	91	81r
Bread, white, pan	lb.	0.80	12/94	82r
Butter, salted, Grade AA, stick	lb.	1.67	12/94	82r
Carrots, short trimmed and topped	lb.	0.51	12/94	82r
Cereals and bakery products purchases	year	407	91	81r
Cereals and cereals products purchases	year	132	91	81r
Chicken breast, bone-in	lb.	2.22	12/94	82r
Chicken, fresh, whole	lb.	1.05	12/94	82r
Chuck roast, USDA choice, boneless	lb.	2.74	12/94	82r
Coffee, 100%, ground roast, all sizes	lb.	4.61	12/94	82r
Dairy products (other) purchases	year	161	91	81r
Eggs, Grade A large	dozen	1.12	12/94	82r
Fish and seafood purchases	year	112	91	81r
Food purchases, food eaten at home	year	2599	91	81r
Foods purchased away from home, not prepared by consumer	year	2024	91	81r
Fruits and vegetables purchases	year	444	91	81r
Grapefruit	lb.	0.44	12/94	82r
Grapes, Thompson seedless	lb.	2.24	12/94	82r
Ground chuck, 100% beef	lb.	1.67	12/94	82r
Ice cream, prepackaged, bulk, regular	1/2 gal.	2.93	12/94	82r
Lemons	lb.	1.06	12/94	82r
Lettuce, iceberg	lb.	0.92	12/94	82r
Meats, poultry, fish, and eggs purchases	year	751	91	81r
Milk and cream (fresh) purchases	year	152	91	81r
Orange juice, frozen concentrate 12-oz. can	16 oz.	1.92	12/94	82r
Oranges, Navel	lb.	0.56	12/94	82r
Pork chops, center cut, bone-in	lb.	3.09	12/94	82r
Pork purchases	year	130	91	81r
Potatoes, white	lb.	0.37	12/94	82r
Rib roast, USDA choice, bone-in	lb.	4.98	12/94	82r
Round roast, USDA choice, boneless	lb.	2.93	12/94	82r
Shortening, vegetable oil blends	lb.	1.03	12/94	82r
Spaghetti and macaroni	lb.	0.84	12/94	82r
Steak, round, USDA choice, boneless	lb.	3.48	12/94	82r
Steak, sirloin, USDA choice, bone-in	lb.	3.38	12/94	82r
Steak, sirloin, USDA choice, boneless	lb.	4.81	12/94	82r
Sugar and other sweets, eaten at home, expenditures	year	89	91	81r
Sugar, white, all sizes	lb.	0.46	12/94	82r
Tobacco products and smoking supplies, total expenditures	year	279	91	81r
Tomatoes, field grown	lb.	1.56	12/94	82r
Tuna, chunk, light	lb.	2.09	12/94	82r
Health Care				
Childbirth, Cesarean delivery, hospital charge	birth	6334.00	12/91	69r
Childbirth, Cesarean delivery, physician charge	birth	2234.00	12/91	69r
Childbirth, normal delivery, hospital charge	birth	3225.00	12/91	69r
Childbirth, normal delivery, physician charge	birth	1623.00	12/91	69r
Drugs, expenditures	year	205	91	81r
Health care, total expenditures	year	1396	91	81r
Health insurance expenditures	year	553	91	81r
Insurance premium, family medical care	month	500.40	1/95	41s
Medical services expenditures	year	559	91	81r
Medical supplies expenditures	year	80	91	81r

Values are in dollars or fractions of dollars. In the column headed *Ref*, references are shown to sources. Each reference is followed by a letter. These refer to the geographical level for which data were reported: s=State, r=Region, and c=City or metro. The abbreviation *ex* is used to mean *except* or *excluding*; *exp* stands for expenditures. For other abbreviations and further explanations, please see the Introduction.

New London, CT - continued

Item	Per	Value	Date	Ref.
Household Goods				
Floor coverings, expenditures	year	158	91	81r
Furniture, expenditures	year	341	91	81r
Household equipment, misc. expenditures	year	363	91	81r
Household expenditures, miscellaneous	year	194	91	81r
Household furnishings and equipment, expenditures	year	1158	91	81r
Household operations expenditures	year	378	91	81r
Household textiles, expenditures	year	88	91	81r
Housekeeping supplies, expenditures	year	426	91	81r
Laundry and cleaning supplies, expenditures	year	122	91	81r
Postage and stationery, expenditures	year	134	91	81r
Housing				
Add garage/carport		11,614	3/95	74r
Add room(s)		16,816	3/95	74r
Apartment condominium or co-op, median	unit	96700	12/94	62r
Dwellings (owned), expenditures	year	3305	91	81r
Enclose porch/patio/breezeway		2,980	3/95	74r
Finish room in basement/attic		4,330	3/95	74r
Home, existing, single-family, median	unit	161600	12/94	62r
Maintenance, repairs, insurance, and other housing expenditures	year	569	91	81r
Mortgage interest and charges expenditures	year	1852	91	81r
Princ. & int., mortgage, median-price exist. sing.-family home	mo.	765	12/94	62r
Property taxes expenditures	year	884	91	81r
Redesign, restructure more than half of home's interior		2,750	3/95	74r
Rental units expenditures	year	1832	91	81r
Insurance and Pensions				
Auto insurance, private passenger	year	1002.84	12/94	71s
Insurance and pensions, personal, expenditures	year	2690	91	81r
Insurance, life and other personal, expenditures	year	341	91	81r
Pensions and Social Security, expenditures	year	2349	91	81r
Legal Assistance				
Estate planning, law-firm partner	hr.	375.00	10/93	12r
Legal work, law firm associate	hour	78		10r
Legal work, law firm partner	hour	183		10r
Personal Services				
Personal services expenditures	year	184	91	81r
Restaurant Food				
Dining expenditures, family	week	34.26	94	73r
Taxes				
Taxes, Federal income, expenditures	year	2409	91	81r
Taxes, personal, expenditures	year	3094	91	81r
Taxes, State and local income, expenditures	year	620	91	81r
Transportation				
Cars and trucks purchased, new	year	1170	91	81r
Cars and trucks purchased, used	year	739	91	81r
Driver's learning permit fee	perm	3.50	1/94	84s
Driver's license fee	orig	38.00	1/94	84s
Driver's license fee, duplicate	lic	5.00	1/94	84s
Driver's license reinstatement fee, min.	susp	30.00	1/94	85s
Driver's license renewal fee	renew	31.00	1/94	84s
Identification card, nondriver	card	4.00	1/94	83s
Motorcycle learning permit fee	perm	3.50	1/94	84s
Motorcycle license fee	orig	38.00	1/94	84s
Motorcycle license fee, duplicate	lic	5.00	1/94	84s
Motorcycle license renewal fee	renew	31.00	1/94	84s
Public transportation expenditures	year	430	91	81r
Transportation expenditures, total	year	4810	91	81r
Vehicle finance charges	year	238	91	81r
Vehicle insurance expenditures	year	630	91	81r
Vehicle maintenance and repairs expenditures	year	532	91	81r
Vehicle purchases	year	1920	91	81r

New London, CT - continued

Item	Per	Value	Date	Ref.
Transportation - continued				
Vehicle rental, leases, licenses, etc. expenditures	year	193	91	81r
Vehicles purchased, other than cars and trucks	year	11	91	81r
Utilities				
Electricity expenditures	year	695	91	81r
Utilities, fuels, and public services, total expenditures	year	1981	91	81r
Water and other public services, expenditures	year	154	91	81r
Weddings				
Bridal attendants' gowns	event	750	10/93	76r
Bridal gown	event	852	10/93	76r
Bridal headpiece and veil	event	167	10/93	76r
Bride's wedding band	event	708	10/93	76r
Clergy	event	224	10/93	76r
Engagement ring	event	2756	10/93	76r
Flowers	event	863	10/93	76r
Formal wear for groom	event	106	10/93	76r
Groom's attendants' formal wear	event	530	10/93	76r
Groom's wedding band	event	402	10/93	76r
Music	event	600	10/93	76r
Photography	event	1088	10/93	76r
Shoes for bride	event	50	10/93	76r
Videography	event	483	10/93	76r
Wedding invitations and announcements	event	342	10/93	76r
Wedding reception	event	7000	10/93	76r

New Orleans, LA

Item	Per	Value	Date	Ref.
Composite, ACCRA index		95.80	12/94	2c
Alcoholic Beverages				
Beer, Miller Lite, Bud, 12-oz., ex deposit	6	3.60	12/94	2c
J & B Scotch	750-ml.	14.87	12/94	2c
Wine, Gallo Chablis blanc	1.5-lit	4.17	12/94	2c
Appliances				
Appliances (major), expenditures	year	153	91	81r
Average annual exp.				
Food, health care, personal goods, services	year	27020	91	81r
Business				
Dinner and tip, hotel, corporate rate	night	31.00	2/94	15c
Hotel room, corporate rate	night	96.00	2/94	15c
Charity				
Cash contributions, expenditures	year	839	91	81r
Clothing				
Apparel, men and boys, total expenditures	year	380	91	81r
Apparel, women and girls, total expenditures	year	660	91	81r
Footwear, expenditures	year	193	91	81r
Jeans, man's denim		28.19	12/94	2c
Shirt, dress, men's	shirt	30.00	1/92	44c
Shirt, man's dress shirt		24.39	12/94	2c
Undervest, boy's size 10-14, cotton	3	3.89	12/94	2c
Communications				
Long-distance telephone rate, day, addl. min., 1-10 mi.	min.	0.29	12/93	9s
Long-distance telephone rate, day, initial min., 1-10 mi.	min.	0.41	12/93	9s
Newspaper subscription, dly. and Sun. delivery	month	9.50	12/94	2c
Phone line, single, business, field visit	inst	85.00	12/93	9s
Phone line, single, business, no field visit	inst	85.00	12/93	9s
Phone line, single, residence, field visit	inst	50.00	12/93	9s
Phone line, single, residence, no field visit	inst	50.00	12/93	9s
Telephone bill, family of four	month	23.23	12/94	2c
Telephone service, expenditures	year	616	91	81r
Telephone, residential, flat rate	mo.	14.42	12/93	8c

Values are in dollars or fractions of dollars. In the column headed *Ref*, references are shown to sources. Each reference is followed by a letter. These refer to the geographical level for which data were reported: s=State, r=Region, and c=City or metro. The abbreviation *ex* is used to mean *except* or *excluding*; *exp* stands for expenditures. For other abbreviations and further explanations, please see the Introduction.

New Orleans, LA - continued

Item	Per	Value	Date	Ref.
Education				
Board, 4-year private college/university	year	2436	8/94	80s
Board, 4-year public college/university	year	1638	8/94	80s
Education, total expenditures	year	319	91	81r
Room, 4-year private college/university	year	2558	8/94	80s
Room, 4-year public college/university	year	1405	8/94	80s
Total cost, 4-year private college/university	year	16467	8/94	80s
Total cost, 4-year public college/university	year	5225	8/94	80s
Tuition, 2-year public college/university, in-state	year	956	8/94	80s
Tuition, 4-year private college/university, in-state	year	11473	8/94	80s
Tuition, 4-year public college/university, in-state	year	2182	8/94	80s
Energy and Fuels				
Energy, combined forms, 1800 sq. ft.	mo.	142.06	12/94	2c
Energy, exc. electricity, 1800 sq. ft.	mo.	29.25	12/94	2c
Fuel oil and other fuels, expenditures	year	56	91	81r
Gas	gal.	1.15	1/92	44c
Gas, natural, expenditures	year	150	91	81r
Gas, reg unlead, taxes inc., cash, self-service	gal	1.12	12/94	2c
Gasoline and motor oil purchased	year	1152	91	81r
Gasoline, unleaded midgrade	gallon	1.21	4/93	82r
Gasoline, unleaded premium	gallon	1.30	4/93	82r
Gasoline, unleaded regular	gallon	1.10	4/93	82r
Entertainment				
Bowling, evening rate	game	2.15	12/94	2c
Concert ticket, Pearl Jam group	perf	20.00	94	50r
Entertainment, total expenditures	year	1266	91	81r
Fees and admissions, expenditures	year	306	91	81r
Monopoly game, Parker Brothers', No. 9	game	10.79	12/94	2c
Movie	adm	5.65	12/94	2c
Movie ticket, adult	ticket	6.00	1/92	44c
Pets, toys, playground equipment, expenditures	year	271	91	81r
Reading, expenditures	year	131	91	81r
Televisions, radios, and sound equipment, expenditures	year	439	91	81r
Tennis balls, yellow, Wilson or Penn, 3	can	2.11	12/94	2c
Funerals				
Burial, immediate, container provided by funeral home		1574.60	1/95	54r
Cards, acknowledgment		22.24	1/95	54r
Casket, minimum alternative		239.41	1/95	54r
Cosmetology, hair care, etc.		91.04	1/95	54r
Cremation, direct, container provided by funeral home		1085.15	1/95	54r
Embalming		281.30	1/95	54r
Funeral, funeral home		323.04	1/95	54r
Funeral, other facility		327.58	1/95	54r
Graveside service		355.19	1/95	54r
Hearse, local		141.89	1/95	54r
Limousine, local		99.40	1/95	54r
Memorial service		284.67	1/95	54r
Service charge, professional, nondeclinable		904.06	1/95	54r
Visitation and viewing		187.04	1/95	54r
Groceries				
Groceries, ACCRA Index		94.90	12/94	2c
Apples, Red Delicious	lb.	0.73	12/94	82r
Baby food, strained vegetables, lowest price	4-4.5 oz.	0.26	12/94	2c
Bacon, sliced	lb.	1.67	12/94	82r
Bananas	lb.	0.42	12/94	2c
Bananas	lb.	0.42	12/94	82r
Beef or hamburger, ground	lb.	1.34	12/94	2c
Beef purchases	year	213	91	81r
Beverage purchases, alcoholic	year	249	91	81r
Beverage purchases, nonalcoholic	year	207	91	81r
Bologna, all beef or mixed	lb.	2.27	12/94	82r
Bread, white	24-oz.	0.71	12/94	2c

New Orleans, LA - continued

Item	Per	Value	Date	Ref.
Groceries - continued				
Bread, white, pan	lb.	0.68	12/94	82r
Cabbage	lb.	0.42	12/94	82r
Carrots, short trimmed and topped	lb.	0.53	12/94	82r
Cereals and bakery products purchases	year	345	91	81r
Cereals and cereals products purchases	year	127	91	81r
Cheddar cheese, natural	lb.	3.58	12/94	82r
Cheese, Kraft grated Parmesan	8-oz.	3.11	12/94	2c
Chicken breast, bone-in	lb.	1.71	12/94	82r
Chicken, fresh, whole	lb.	0.78	12/94	82r
Chicken, whole fryer	lb.	0.82	12/94	2c
Chuck roast, USDA choice, boneless	lb.	2.26	12/94	82r
Cigarettes, Winston, Kings	carton	14.83	12/94	2c
Coffee, vacuum-packed	13 oz.	3.20	12/94	2c
Corn Flakes, Kellogg's or Post Toasties	18 oz.	2.09	12/94	2c
Corn, frozen, whole kernel, lowest price	10 oz.	0.67	12/94	2c
Crackers, soda, salted	lb.	1.27	12/94	82r
Cucumbers	lb.	0.65	12/94	82r
Dairy products (other) purchases	year	141	91	81r
Eggs, Grade A large	dozen	0.76	12/94	2c
Eggs, Grade A large	dozen	0.87	12/94	82r
Fish and seafood purchases	year	72	91	81r
Flour, white, all purpose	lb.	0.23	12/94	82r
Food purchases, food eaten at home	year	2381	91	81r
Foods purchased away from home, not prepared by consumer	year	1696	91	81r
Frankfurters, all meat or all beef	lb,	1.74	12/94	82r
Fruits and vegetables purchases	year	380	91	81r
Grapefruit	lb.	0.45	12/94	82r
Grapes, Thompson seedless	lb.	2.30	12/94	82r
Ground beef, 100% beef	lb.	1.37	12/94	82r
Ground chuck, 100% beef	lb.	1.97	12/94	82r
Ham, boneless, exc. canned	lb.	2.54	12/94	82r
Ice cream, prepackaged, bulk, regular	1/2 gal.	2.47	12/94	82r
Lemons	lb.	1.02	12/94	82r
Lettuce, iceberg	lb.	0.96	12/94	82r
Lettuce, iceberg	head	0.99	12/94	2c
Margarine, Blue Bonnet or Parkay cubes	lb.	0.58	12/94	2c
Margarine, stick	lb.	0.77	12/94	82r
Meats, poultry, fish, and eggs purchases	year	655	91	81r
Milk and cream (fresh) purchases	year	130	91	81r
Milk, 2%	gal.	2.59	1/92	44c
Milk, whole	1/2 gal.	1.31	12/94	2c
Orange juice, frozen concentrate 12-oz. can	16 oz.	1.36	12/94	82r
Orange juice, Minute Maid frozen	12-oz.	1.20	12/94	2c
Oranges, Navel	lb.	0.54	12/94	82r
Peaches, halves or slices, Hunt's, Del Monte, or Libby's	29-oz.	1.21	12/94	2c
Pears, Anjou	lb.	0.81	12/94	82r
Peas, sweet, Del Monte or Green Giant	15-17 oz.	0.58	12/94	2c
Pork chops, center cut, bone-in	lb.	3.07	12/94	82r
Pork purchases	year	142	91	81r
Potato chips	16-oz.	3.15	12/94	82r
Potatoes, frozen, French fried	lb.	0.82	12/94	82r
Potatoes, white	lb.	0.34	12/94	82r
Potatoes, white or red	10-lb. sack	2.15	12/94	2c
Rice, white, long grain, uncooked	lb.	0.48	12/94	82r
Round roast, USDA choice, boneless	lb.	2.91	12/94	82r
Sausage, fresh	lb.	1.82	12/94	82r
Sausage, Jimmy Dean, 100% pork	lb.	2.52	12/94	2c
Shortening, vegetable oil blends	lb.	0.75	12/94	82r
Shortening, vegetable, Crisco	3-lb.	2.48	12/94	2c
Soft drink, Coca Cola, ex deposit	2 lit	1.10	12/94	2c
Spaghetti and macaroni	lb.	0.87	12/94	82r
Steak, rib eye, USDA choice, boneless	lb.	6.85	12/94	82r
Steak, round, graded & ungraded, exc. USDA prime & choice	lb.	2.96	12/94	82r
Steak, round, USDA choice, boneless	lb.	3.17	12/94	82r

Values are in dollars or fractions of dollars. In the column headed *Ref*, references are shown to sources. Each reference is followed by a letter. These refer to the geographical level for which data were reported: s = State, r = Region, and c = City or metro. The abbreviation *ex* is used to mean *except* or *excluding*; *exp* stands for *expenditures*. For other abbreviations and further explanations, please see the Introduction.

New Orleans, LA - continued

Item	Per	Value	Date	Ref.
Groceries				
Steak, sirloin, USDA choice, boneless	lb.	4.12	12/94	82r
Steak, t-bone	lb.	6.71	12/94	2c
Steak, T-bone, USDA choice, bone-in	lb.	5.63	12/94	82r
Sugar and other sweets, eaten at home, expenditures	year	93	91	81r
Sugar, cane or beet	4 lbs.	1.67	12/94	2c
Sugar, white, all sizes	lb.	0.39	12/94	82r
Tobacco products and smoking supplies, total expenditures	year	286	91	81r
Tomatoes, field grown	lb.	1.36	12/94	82r
Tomatoes, Hunt's or Del Monte	14.5 oz.	0.61	12/94	2c
Tuna, chunk, light	lb.	1.94	12/94	82r
Tuna, chunk, light, oil-packed	6.125-6.5 oz.	0.62	12/94	2c
Turkey, frozen, whole	lb.	0.96	12/94	82r
Yogurt, natural, fruit flavored	8 oz.	0.58	12/94	82r
Goods and Services				
Miscellaneous goods and services, ACCRA Index		91.60	12/94	2c
Health Care				
Health care, ACCRA Index		94.70	12/94	2c
Adenosine, emergency room	treat	100.00	95	23r
Antibiotic ointment, Polysporin	1.5 oz.	5.11	12/94	2c
Bladder tap, superpubic, infant, emergency room	treat	119.00	95	23r
Blood analysis, emergency room	treat	25.00	95	23r
Blood tests, abdominal pain, emergency room	treat	25.00	95	23r
Burn dressing, emergency room	treat	266.00	95	23r
Cardiology interpretation, emergency room	treat	26.00	95	23r
Chest X-ray, emergency room	treat	78.00	95	23r
Childbirth, Cesarean delivery, hospital charge	birth	5462.00	12/91	69r
Childbirth, Cesarean delivery, physician charge	birth	2228.00	12/91	69r
Childbirth, normal delivery, hospital charge	birth	2943.00	12/91	69r
Childbirth, normal delivery, physician charge	birth	1619.00	12/91	69r
Defibrillation pads, emergency room	treat	6.00	95	23r
Dentist's fee, adult teeth cleaning and periodic oral exam	visit	44.20	12/94	2c
Doctor's fee, routine exam, established patient	visit	38.20	12/94	2c
Drugs, expenditures	year	297	91	81r
Gastric tube insertion, nasal, emergency room	treat	25.00	95	23r
Health care, total expenditures	year	1600	91	81r
Health insurance expenditures	year	637	91	81r
Heart monitor, emergency room	treat	40.00	95	23r
Hospital care, semiprivate room	day	370.60	12/94	2c
Insurance premium, family medical care	month	394.31	1/95	41s
Intravenous fluids, emergency room	treat	130.00	95	23r
Intravenous fluids, emergency room	liter	26.00	95	23r
Intravenous line, central, emergency room	treat	342.00	95	23r
Liver function tests, abdominal pain, emergency room	treat	26.00	95	23r
Medical care charges, total, emergency room, third-degree burns	treat	2101.00	95	23r
Medical care charges, total, emergency, infant with fever	treat	628.00	95	23r
Medical services expenditures	year	573	91	81r
Medical supplies expenditures	year	93	91	81r
Morphine, emergency room	treat	34.00	95	23r
Nursing care and facilities charges, emergency room	treat	252.00	95	23r
Nursing care and facilities charges, emergency, infant with fever	treat	252.00	95	23r
Nursing care and facilities charges, emergency, third-degree burns	treat	861.00	95	23r
Physician's charges, emergency, infant with fever	treat	212.00	95	23r

New Orleans, LA - continued

Item	Per	Value	Date	Ref.
Health Care - continued				
Physician's charges, emergency, third-degree burns	treat	372.00	95	23r
Physician's fee, emergency room	treat	372.00	95	23r
Physician's fee, general practitioner	visit	51.20	12/93	60r
Surgery, open-heart	proc	42374.00	1/93	14r
Ultrasound, abdominal, emergency room	treat	276.00	95	23r
Urinalysis, emergency room	treat	20.00	95	23r
Urinalysis, infant, emergency room	treat	20.00	95	23r
X-rays, emergency room	treat	78.00	95	23r
Household Goods				
Appl. repair, service call, wash mach	min. lab. chg.	25.80	12/94	2c
Floor coverings, expenditures	year	48	91	81r
Furniture, expenditures	year	280	91	81r
Household equipment, misc. expenditures	year	342	91	81r
Household expenditures, miscellaneous	year	256	91	81r
Household furnishings and equipment, expenditures	year	988	91	81r
Household operations expenditures	year	468	91	81r
Household textiles, expenditures	year	95	91	81r
Housekeeping supplies, expenditures	year	380	91	81r
Laundry and cleaning supplies, expenditures	year	109	91	81r
Laundry detergent, Tide Ultra, Bold, or Cheer	42 oz.	2.80	12/94	2c
Postage and stationery, expenditures	year	105	91	81r
Tissues, facial, Kleenex brand	175	0.96	12/94	2c
Housing				
Housing, ACCRA Index		90.50	12/94	2c
Add garage/carport		6,980	3/95	74r
Add room(s)		11,403	3/95	74r
Apartment condominium or co-op, median	unit	68600	12/94	62r
Car rental	day	42.00	5/95	95c
Dwellings (owned), expenditures	year	2428	91	81r
Enclose porch/patio/breezeway		4,572	3/95	74r
Finish room in basement/attic		3,794	3/95	74r
Home, existing, single-family, median	unit	120200	12/94	62r
Home, existing, single-family, median	unit	77.80	12/94	62c
Hotel room	day	120.00	5/95	95c
House payment, principal and interest, 25% down payment	mo.	669	12/94	2c
House, 1800 sq ft, 8000 sq ft lot, new, urban, utilities	total	108360	12/94	2c
Maintenance, repairs, insurance, and other housing expenditures	year	531	91	81r
Mortgage interest and charges expenditures	year	1506	91	81r
Mtge. rate, incl. points and orig. fee, 30-year conv. fixed or ARM	mo.	9.26	12/94	2c
Princ. & int., mortgage, median-price exist. sing.-family home	mo.	540	12/94	62r
Property taxes expenditures	year	391	91	81r
Redesign, restructure more than half of home's interior		17,641	3/95	74r
Rent, apartment, 2 br., 1 1/2-2 baths, unfurnished, 950 sq ft, water	mo.	548	12/94	2c
Rental units expenditures	year	1264	91	81r
Insurance and Pensions				
Auto insurance, private passenger	year	862.62	12/94	71s
Insurance and pensions, personal, expenditures	year	2395	91	81r
Insurance, life and other personal, expenditures	year	368	91	81r
Pensions and Social Security, expenditures	year	2027	91	81r
Personal Goods				
Shampoo, Alberto VO5	15-oz.	0.97	12/94	2c
Toothpaste, Crest or Colgate	6-7 oz.	1.80	12/94	2c
Personal Services				
Dry cleaning, man's 2-pc. suit		5.65	12/94	2c

Values are in dollars or fractions of dollars. In the column headed *Ref*, references are shown to sources. Each reference is followed by a letter. These refer to the geographical level for which data were reported: s = State, r = Region, and c = City or metro. The abbreviation *ex* is used to mean *except* or *excluding*; *exp* stands for *expenditures*. For other abbreviations and further explanations, please see the Introduction.

New Orleans, LA - continued

Item	Per	Value	Date	Ref.
Personal Services				
Dry cleaning, woman's dress	dress	10.00	1/92	44c
Haircut, man's barbershop, no styling		7.80	12/94	2c
Haircut, woman's shampoo, trim, blow-dry		19.09	12/94	2c
Personal services expenditures	year	212	91	81r
Restaurant Food				
Big Mac, small fries, medium drink	meal	2.37	1/92	44c
Chicken, fried, thigh and drumstick		1.83	12/94	2c
Dining expenditures, family	week	33.83	94	73r
Hamburger with cheese	1/4 lb.	1.91	12/94	2c
Pizza, Pizza Hut or Pizza Inn	12-13 in.	8.78	12/94	2c
Taxes				
Tax rate, residential property, month	$100	1.61	1/92	79c
Taxes, Federal income, expenditures	year	2275	91	81r
Taxes, personal, expenditures	year	2715	91	81r
Taxes, State and local income, expenditures	year	365	91	81r
Transportation				
Transportation, ACCRA Index		103.40	12/94	2c
Bus fare, one-way	trip	1.00	12/95	1c
Bus fare, up to 10 miles	one-way	1.25	12/94	2c
Cars and trucks purchased, new	year	1306	91	81r
Cars and trucks purchased, used	year	942	91	81r
Driver's learning permit fee	perm	12.50	1/94	84s
Driver's license fee	orig	12.50	1/94	84s
Driver's license fee, duplicate	lic	5.00	1/94	84s
Driver's license reinstatement fee, min.	susp	60.00	1/94	85s
Driver's license renewal fee	renew	12.50	1/94	84s
Identification card, nondriver	card	7.00	1/94	83s
Motorcycle license fee	orig	8.00	1/94	84s
Motorcycle license renewal fee	renew	8.00	1/94	84s
parking, long-term lot, airport	3 days	36.00	1/92	44c
Public transportation expenditures	year	249	91	81r
Railway fare, light rail, one-way	trip	1.00	12/95	1c
Tire balance, computer or spin bal., front	wheel	6.80	12/94	2c
Transportation expenditures, total	year	5307	91	81r
Vehicle finance charges	year	346	91	81r
Vehicle insurance expenditures	year	544	91	81r
Vehicle maintenance and repairs expenditures	year	600	91	81r
Vehicle purchases	year	2275	91	81r
Vehicle rental, leases, licenses, etc. expenditures	year	141	91	81r
Vehicles purchased, other than cars and trucks	year	27	91	81r
Utilities				
Utilities, ACCRA Index		125.60	12/94	2c
Electricity expenditures	year	950	91	81r
Electricity, (part.), other, 1800 sq. ft., new home	mo.	112.81	12/94	2c
Utilities, fuels, and public services, total expenditures	year	2000	91	81r
Water and other public services, expenditures	year	227	91	81r
Weddings				
Bridal attendants' gowns	event	750	10/93	76r
Bridal gown	event	852	10/93	76r
Bridal headpiece and veil	event	167	10/93	76r
Bride's wedding band	event	708	10/93	76r
Clergy	event	224	10/93	76r
Engagement ring	event	2756	10/93	76r
Flowers	event	863	10/93	76r
Formal wear for groom	event	106	10/93	76r
Groom's attendants' formal wear	event	530	10/93	76r
Groom's wedding band	event	402	10/93	76r
Music	event	600	10/93	76r
Photography	event	1088	10/93	76r
Shoes for bride	event	50	10/93	76r
Videography	event	483	10/93	76r

New Orleans, LA - continued

Item	Per	Value	Date	Ref.
Weddings - continued				
Wedding invitations and announcements	event	342	10/93	76r
Wedding reception	event	7000	10/93	76r

New York, NY

Item	Per	Value	Date	Ref.
Composite, ACCRA index		228.30	12/94	2c
Alcoholic Beverages				
Beer	bottle	4.00	94	35c
Beer, Miller Lite, Bud, 12-oz., ex deposit	6	4.56	12/94	2c
J & B Scotch	750-ml.	17.88	12/94	2c
Wine, Gallo Chablis blanc	1.5-lit	6.24	12/94	2c
Appliances				
Appliances (major), expenditures	year	122	91	81c
Appliances (major), expenditures	year	145	91	81r
Average annual exp.				
Food, health care, personal goods, services	year	34583	91	81c
Food, health care, personal goods, services	year	29496	91	81r
Banking				
Bank fee, ATM, different bank	trans	1.06	6/95	39c
Bank fee, ATM, same bank	trans	0.31	6/95	39c
Bank fee, banking by personal computer, individuals	mo.	4.74	6/95	39c
Bank fee, banking by personal computer, low balance	trans	Free	6/95	39c
Bank fee, banking by personal computer, small businesses	mo.	18.13	6/95	39c
Bank fee, bill paying, phone or ATM	mo.	0.63	6/95	39c
Bank fee, bill paying, phone or ATM, low balance	trans	Free	6/95	39c
Business				
Dinner and tip, hotel, corporate rate	night	53.00	2/94	15c
Hotel room, corporate rate	night	164.00	2/94	15c
Photocopies, copy shop	10 copies	1.00	7/95	4c
Photocopies, copy shop	100 copies	10.00	7/95	4c
Photocopies, copy shop	500 copies	50.00	7/95	4c
Photocopies, copy shop	1000 copies	80.00	7/95	4c
Photocopies, copy shop	5000 copies	260.00	7/95	4c
Charity				
Cash contributions, expenditures	year	950	91	81c
Cash contributions, expenditures	year	708	91	81r
Clothing				
Apparel, men and boys, total expenditures	year	521	91	81c
Apparel, men and boys, total expenditures	year	416	91	81r
Apparel, women and girls, total expenditures	year	922	91	81c
Apparel, women and girls, total expenditures	year	744	91	81r
Footwear, expenditures	year	427	91	81c
Footwear, expenditures	year	305	91	81r
Jeans, man's denim		33.16	12/94	2c
Shirt, man's dress shirt		49.69	12/94	2c
Undervest, boy's size 10-14, cotton	3	7.56	12/94	2c
Communications				
Long-distance telephone rate, day, addl. min., 1-10 mi.	min.	4.00	12/93	9s
Long-distance telephone rate, day, initial min., 1-10 mi.	min.	14.90	12/93	9s
Newspaper subscription, dly. and Sun. delivery	month	17.17	12/94	2c
Phone bill	month	64.16	93	37c
Phone bill, AT & T Direct Dial plan	mo.	52.12	1/95	3c
Phone bill, MCI Direct Dial plan	mo.	52.02	1/95	3c
Phone bill, Sprint Direct Dian plan	mo.	52.12	1/95	3c

Values are in dollars or fractions of dollars. In the column headed *Ref*, references are shown to sources. Each reference is followed by a letter. These refer to the geographical level for which data were reported: s=State, r=Region, and c=City or metro. The abbreviation *ex* is used to mean *except* or *excluding*; *exp* stands for expenditures. For other abbreviations and further explanations, please see the Introduction.

New York, NY - continued

Item	Per	Value	Date	Ref.
Communications				
Phone line, single, business, field visit	inst	143.26	12/93	9s
Phone line, single, business, no field visit	inst	106.05	12/93	9s
Phone line, single, residence, field visit	inst	85.46	12/93	9s
Phone line, single, residence, no field visit	inst	55.00	12/93	9s
Telephone bill, family of four	month	24.06	12/94	2c
Telephone service, expenditures	year	770	91	81c
Telephone service, expenditures	year	589	91	81r
Telephone, business, addl. line, touch tone	month	4.84	10/91	25c
Telephone, business, connection charges, touch tone	inst	151.53	10/91	25c
Telephone, business, key system line, touch tone	month	50.67	10/91	25c
Telephone, business, PBX line, touch tone	month	50.78	10/91	25c
Telephone, business, single ln., touch tone	month	51.93	10/91	25c
Telephone, business, touch tone, inside wiring maintenance plan	month	5.97	10/91	25c
Telephone, residential, flat rate	mo.	22.27	12/93	8c
Education				
Board, 4-year private college/university	year	2918	8/94	80s
Board, 4-year public college/university	year	2177	8/94	80s
Education, total expenditures	year	601	91	81c
Education, total expenditures	year	593	91	81r
Room, 4-year private college/university	year	3302	8/94	80s
Room, 4-year public college/university	year	2624	8/94	80s
Total cost, 4-year private college/university	year	18451	8/94	80s
Total cost, 4-year public college/university	year	7723	8/94	80s
Tuition, 2-year public college/university, in-state	year	2112	8/94	80s
Tuition, 4-year private college/university, in-state	year	12231	8/94	80s
Tuition, 4-year public college/university, in-state	year	2921	8/94	80s
Energy and Fuels				
Electricity	500 KWh	73.05	12/94	82c
Energy, combined forms, 1800 sq. ft.	mo.	166.88	12/94	2c
Energy, exc. electricity, 1800 sq. ft.	mo.	49.21	12/94	2c
Fuel oil #2	gallon	1.01	12/94	82c
Fuel oil and other fuels, expenditures	year	242	91	81c
Fuel oil and other fuels, expenditures	year	257	91	81r
Gas, cooking, winter, 10 therms	month	17.96	2/94	65c
Gas, cooking, winter, 30 therms	month	35.05	2/94	65c
Gas, cooking, winter, 50 therms	month	52.16	2/94	65c
Gas, heating, winter, 100 therms	month	86.14	2/94	65c
Gas, heating, winter, average use	month	284.99	2/94	65c
Gas, natural, expenditures	year	368	91	81c
Gas, natural, expenditures	year	285	91	81r
Gas, piped	40 therms	45.40	12/94	82c
Gas, piped	100 therms	90.52	12/94	82c
Gas, piped	therm	0.94	12/94	82c
Gas, reg unlead, taxes inc., cash, self-service	gal	1.38	12/94	2c
Gasoline and motor oil purchased	year	784	91	81c
Gasoline and motor oil purchased	year	867	91	81r
Gasoline, unleaded midgrade	gallon	1.36	4/93	82c
Gasoline, unleaded midgrade	gallon	1.32	4/93	82r
Gasoline, unleaded premium	gallon	1.44	4/93	82c
Gasoline, unleaded premium	gallon	1.40	4/93	82r
Gasoline, unleaded regular	gallon	1.21	4/93	82c
Gasoline, unleaded regular	gallon	1.19	4/93	82r
Entertainment				
Baseball game, four-person family	game	115.25	4/94	47c
Bowling, evening rate	game	3.37	12/94	2c
Entertainment supplies, equipment, and services, misc. expenditures	year	340	91	81c
Entertainment, total expenditures	year	1560	91	81c
Entertainment, total expenditures	year	1331	91	81r
Fees and admissions, expenditures	year	508	91	81c
Fees and admissions, expenditures	year	398	91	81r

New York, NY - continued

Item	Per	Value	Date	Ref.
Entertainment - continued				
Monopoly game, Parker Brothers', No. 9	game	16.99	12/94	2c
Movie	adm	8.00	12/94	2c
Pets, toys, playground equipment, expenditures	year	254	91	81c
Pets, toys, playground equipment, expenditures	year	270	91	81r
Reading, expenditures	year	178	91	81c
Reading, expenditures	year	171	91	81r
Televisions, radios, and sound equipment, expenditures	year	458	91	81c
Televisions, radios, and sound equipment, expenditures	year	429	91	81r
Tennis balls, yellow, Wilson or Penn, 3	can	2.31	12/94	2c
Funerals				
Burial, immediate, container provided by funeral home		1370.36	1/95	54r
Cards, acknowledgment		17.72	1/95	54r
Casket, minimum alternative		192.52	1/95	54r
Cosmetology, hair care, etc.		139.56	1/95	54r
Cremation, direct, container provided by funeral home		1049.24	1/95	54r
Embalming		387.57	1/95	54r
Funeral, funeral home		278.77	1/95	54r
Funeral, other facility		275.85	1/95	54r
Graveside service		213.08	1/95	54r
Hearse, local		157.27	1/95	54r
Limousine, local		146.45	1/95	54r
Memorial service		271.02	1/95	54r
Service charge, professional, nondeclinable		943.58	1/95	54r
Visitation and viewing		322.86	1/95	54r
Groceries				
Groceries, ACCRA Index		150.30	12/94	2c
Apples, Red Delicious	lb.	0.78	12/94	82r
Baby food, strained vegetables, lowest price	4-4.5 oz.	0.52	12/94	2c
Bacon, sliced	lb.	2.24	12/94	82r
Bananas	lb.	0.67	12/94	2c
Bananas	lb.	0.49	12/94	82r
Beef or hamburger, ground	lb.	2.03	12/94	2c
Beef purchases	year	243	91	81c
Beef purchases	year	226	91	81r
Beverage purchases, alcoholic	year	412	91	81c
Beverage purchases, alcoholic	year	332	91	81r
Beverage purchases, nonalcoholic	year	208	91	81c
Beverage purchases, nonalcoholic	year	213	91	81r
Big Mac hamburger	burger	2.81	94	35c
Bread, white	24-oz.	1.38	12/94	2c
Bread, white, pan	lb.	0.80	12/94	82r
Butter, salted, Grade AA, stick	lb.	1.67	12/94	82r
Carrots, short trimmed and topped	lb.	0.51	12/94	82r
Cereals and bakery products purchases	year	438	91	81c
Cereals and bakery products purchases	year	407	91	81r
Cereals and cereal products purchases	year	141	91	81c
Cereals and cereals products purchases	year	132	91	81r
Cheese, Kraft grated Parmesan	8-oz.	4.46	12/94	2c
Chicken breast, bone-in	lb.	2.22	12/94	82r
Chicken, fresh, whole	lb.	1.05	12/94	82r
Chicken, whole fryer	lb.	1.43	12/94	2c
Chuck roast, USDA choice, boneless	lb.	2.74	12/94	82r
Cigarettes, Winston, Kings	carton	22.50	12/94	2c
Coffee, 100%, ground roast, all sizes	lb.	4.61	12/94	82r
Coffee, vacuum-packed	13 oz.	4.43	12/94	2c
Corn Flakes, Kellogg's or Post Toasties	18 oz.	3.13	12/94	2c
Corn, frozen, whole kernel, lowest price	10 oz.	0.87	12/94	2c
Dairy products (other) purchases	year	163	91	81c
Dairy products (other) purchases	year	161	91	81r
Eggs, Grade A large	dozen	1.39	12/94	2c
Eggs, Grade A large	dozen	1.12	12/94	82r
Fish and seafood purchases	year	143	91	81c
Fish and seafood purchases	year	112	91	81r
Food purchases, food eaten at home	year	2725	91	81c

Values are in dollars or fractions of dollars. In the column headed *Ref*, references are shown to sources. Each reference is followed by a letter. These refer to the geographical level for which data were reported: s = State, r = Region, and c = City or metro. The abbreviation *ex* is used to mean *except* or *excluding*; *exp* stands for *expenditures*. For other abbreviations and further explanations, please see the Introduction.

New York, NY - continued

Item	Per	Value	Date	Ref.
Groceries				
Food purchases, food eaten at home	year	2599	91	81r
Foods purchased away from home, not prepared by consumer	year	2406	91	81c
Foods purchased away from home, not prepared by consumer	year	2024	91	81r
Fruits and vegetables purchases	year	490	91	81c
Fruits and vegetables purchases	year	444	91	81r
Grapefruit	lb.	0.44	12/94	82r
Grapes, Thompson seedless	lb.	2.24	12/94	82r
Ground chuck, 100% beef	lb.	1.67	12/94	82r
Ice cream, prepackaged, bulk, regular	1/2 gal.	2.93	12/94	82r
Lemons	lb.	1.06	12/94	82r
Lettuce, iceberg	lb.	0.92	12/94	82r
Lettuce, iceberg	head	1.43	12/94	2c
Margarine, Blue Bonnet or Parkay cubes	lb.	1.25	12/94	2c
Meats, poultry, fish, and eggs purchases	year	850	91	81c
Meats, poultry, fish, and eggs purchases	year	751	91	81r
Milk	quart	0.73	12/93	60c
Milk and cream (fresh) purchases	year	145	91	81c
Milk and cream (fresh) purchases	year	152	91	81r
Milk, whole	1/2 gal.	1.73	12/94	2c
Orange juice, frozen concentrate 12-oz. can	12-oz.	1.92	12/94	82r
Orange juice, Minute Maid frozen	12-oz.	1.60	12/94	2c
Oranges, Navel	lb.	0.56	12/94	82r
Peaches, halves or slices, Hunt's, Del Monte, or Libby's	29-oz.	1.86	12/94	2c
Peas, sweet, Del Monte or Green Giant	15-17 oz.	0.84	12/94	2c
Pork chops, center cut, bone-in	lb.	3.09	12/94	82r
Pork purchases	year	131	91	81c
Pork purchases	year	130	91	81r
Potatoes, white	lb.	0.37	12/94	82r
Potatoes, white or red	10-lb. sack	2.36	12/94	2c
Rib roast, USDA choice, bone-in	lb.	4.98	12/94	82r
Round roast, USDA choice, boneless	lb.	2.93	12/94	82r
Sausage, Jimmy Dean, 100% pork	lb.	3.30	12/94	2c
Shortening, vegetable oil blends	lb.	1.03	12/94	82r
Shortening, vegetable, Crisco	3-lb.	4.52	12/94	2c
Soft drink, Coca Cola, ex deposit	2 lit	1.57	12/94	2c
Spaghetti and macaroni	lb.	0.84	12/94	82r
Steak, round, USDA choice, boneless	lb.	3.48	12/94	82r
Steak, sirloin, USDA choice, bone-in	lb.	3.38	12/94	82r
Steak, sirloin, USDA choice, boneless	lb.	4.81	12/94	82r
Steak, t-bone	lb.	8.49	12/94	2c
Sugar and other sweets, eaten at home, expenditures	year	89	91	81r
Sugar and other sweets, eaten at home, purchases	year	80	91	81c
Sugar, cane or beet	4 lbs.	1.90	12/94	2c
Sugar, white, all sizes	lb.	0.46	12/94	82r
Tobacco products and smoking supplies, total expenditures	year	299	91	81c
Tobacco products and smoking supplies, total expenditures	year	279	91	81r
Tomatoes, field grown	lb.	1.56	12/94	82r
Tomatoes, Hunt's or Del Monte	14.5 oz.	1.20	12/94	2c
Tuna, chunk, light	lb.	2.09	12/94	82r
Tuna, chunk, light, oil-packed	6.125-6.5 oz.	1.38	12/94	2c
Goods and Services				
Miscellaneous goods and services, ACCRA Index		137.60	12/94	2c
Health Care				
Health care, ACCRA Index		205.30	12/94	2c
Antibiotic ointment, Polysporin	1.5 oz.	4.92	12/94	2c
Appendectomy	proc	1850.00	12/92	69c
Birth, normal delivery	del	4,275	11/93	93c

New York, NY - continued

Item	Per	Value	Date	Ref.
Health Care - continued				
Breast lesion excision (lumpectomy)	proc	1365.00	12/92	69c
Broken arm treatment	treat	675	11/93	93c
Cesarean section delivery	proc	4994.00	12/92	69c
Childbirth, Cesarean delivery, hospital charge	birth	6334.00	12/91	69r
Childbirth, Cesarean delivery, physician charge	birth	2234.00	12/91	69r
Childbirth, normal delivery, hospital charge	birth	3225.00	12/91	69r
Childbirth, normal delivery, physician charge	birth	1623.00	12/91	69r
Cholecystectomy	proc	2980.00	12/92	69c
Coronary bypass, triple	proc	8500.00	12/92	69c
Dentist's fee, adult teeth cleaning and periodic oral exam	visit	90.80	12/94	2c
Doctor's fee, routine exam, established patient	visit	86.10	12/94	2c
Drugs, expenditures	year	196	91	81c
Drugs, expenditures	year	205	91	81r
Health care, total expenditures	year	1533	91	81c
Health care, total expenditures	year	1396	91	81r
Health insurance expenditures	year	531	91	81c
Health insurance expenditures	year	553	91	81r
Hospital care, semiprivate room	day	1142.22	12/94	2c
Hospital cost	adm	8,093	2/94	72c
Hysterectomy, abdominal	proc	1234.00	12/92	69c
Insurance premium, family medical care	month	384.24	1/95	41s
Medical services expenditures	year	737	91	81c
Medical services expenditures	year	559	91	81r
Medical supplies expenditures	year	70	91	81c
Medical supplies expenditures	year	80	91	81r
Oophorectomy	proc	2513.00	12/92	69c
Physical exam, well baby	check-up	76	11/93	93c
Physical, complete	phys	204	11/93	93c
Salpingo-oophorectomy	proc	3099.00	12/92	69c
Surgery, open-heart	surg	8,113	11/93	93c
Household Goods				
Appl. repair, service call, wash mach	min. lab. chg.	57.72	12/94	2c
Floor coverings, expenditures	year	68	91	81c
Floor coverings, expenditures	year	158	91	81r
Furniture, expenditures	year	313	91	81c
Furniture, expenditures	year	341	91	81r
Household equipment, misc. expenditures	year	363	91	81r
Household equipment, misc., expenditures	year	470	91	81c
Household expenditures, miscellaneous	year	311	91	81c
Household expenditures, miscellaneous	year	194	91	81r
Household furnishings and equipment, expenditures	year	1172	91	81c
Household furnishings and equipment, expenditures	year	1158	91	81r
Household operations expenditures	year	526	91	81c
Household operations expenditures	year	378	91	81r
Household textiles, expenditures	year	122	91	81c
Household textiles, expenditures	year	88	91	81r
Housekeeping supplies, expenditures	year	413	91	81c
Housekeeping supplies, expenditures	year	426	91	81r
Laundry and cleaning supplies, expenditures	year	113	91	81c
Laundry and cleaning supplies, expenditures	year	122	91	81r
Laundry detergent, Tide Ultra, Bold, or Cheer	42 oz.	5.45	12/94	2c
Postage and stationery, expenditures	year	137	91	81c
Postage and stationery, expenditures	year	134	91	81r
Tissues, facial, Kleenex brand	175	1.50	12/94	2c
Housing				
Housing, ACCRA Index		439.50	12/94	2c
Add garage/carport		11,614	3/95	74r
Add room(s)		16,816	3/95	74r
Apartment condominium or co-op, median	unit	96700	12/94	62r

Values are in dollars or fractions of dollars. In the column headed *Ref*, references are shown to sources. Each reference is followed by a letter. These refer to the geographical level for which data were reported: s = State, r = Region, and c = City or metro. The abbreviation *ex* is used to mean *except* or *excluding*; *exp* stands for expenditures. For other abbreviations and further explanations, please see the Introduction.

New York, NY - continued

Item	Per	Value	Date	Ref.
Housing				
Car rental	day	58.00	5/95	95c
Dwellings (owned), expenditures	year	4522	91	81c
Dwellings (owned), expenditures	year	3305	91	81r
Enclose porch/patio/breezeway		2,980	3/95	74r
Finish room in basement/attic		4,330	3/95	74r
Home repairs, maintenance, and insurance	year	706.00	93	37c
Home, existing, single-family, median	unit	161600	12/94	62r
Home, existing, single-family, median	unit	168.70	12/94	62c
Home, purchase price	unit	189.00	3/93	26c
Hotel room	day	204.00	5/95	95c
House payment, principal and interest, 25% down payment	mo.	3324	12/94	2c
House, 1800 sq ft, 8000 sq ft lot, new, urban, utilities	total	540400	12/94	2c
Maintenance, repairs, insurance, and other housing expenditures	year	706	91	81c
Maintenance, repairs, insurance, and other housing expenditures	year	569	91	81r
Mortgage interest and charges expenditures	year	2573	91	81c
Mortgage interest and charges expenditures	year	1852	91	81r
Mtge. rate, incl. points and orig. fee, 30-year conv. fixed or ARM	mo.	9.22	12/94	2c
Princ. & int., mortgage, median-price exist. sing.-family home	mo.	765	12/94	62r
Property taxes expenditures	year	1243	91	81c
Property taxes expenditures	year	884	91	81r
Redesign, restructure more than half of home's interior		2,750	3/95	74r
Rent, apartment, 2 br., 1 1/2-2 baths, unfurnished, 950 sq ft, water	mo.	2443	12/94	2c
Rental units expenditures	year	2613	900/00/91	81c
Rental units expenditures	year	1832	91	81r
Insurance and Pensions				
Auto insurance, private passenger	year	985.07	12/94	71s
Health insurance, HMO plan, cost to employer	year	3448	93	59c
Insurance and pensions, personal, expenditures	year	3108	91	81c
Insurance and pensions, personal, expenditures	year	2690	91	81r
Insurance, life and other personal, expenditures	year	422	91	81c
Insurance, life and other personal, expenditures	year	341	91	81r
Pensions and Social Security, expenditures	year	2686	91	81c
Pensions and Social Security, expenditures	year	2349	91	81r
Legal Assistance				
Estate planning, law-firm partner	hr.	375.00	10/93	12r
Legal work, law firm associate	hour	78		10r
Legal work, law firm partner	hour	183		10r
Legal Fees				
Legal fee, private attorney for Legal Aid Society indigent client	hr.	25.00-40.00	10/94	6c
Personal Goods				
Personal care products and services, total expenditures	year	482	91	81c
Shampoo, Alberto VO5	15-oz.	1.79	12/94	2c
Toothpaste, Crest or Colgate	6-7 oz.	2.80	12/94	2c
Personal Services				
Dry cleaning, man's 2-pc. suit		7.95	12/94	2c
Haircut, man's barbershop, no styling		16.60	12/94	2c
Haircut, styling, blow dry	visit	85.00	12/93	60c
Haircut, woman's shampoo, trim, blow-dry		40.75	12/94	2c
Personal services expenditures	year	215	91	81c
Personal services expenditures	year	184	91	81r
Restaurant Food				
Chicken, fried, thigh and drumstick		2.54	12/94	2c
Dining expenditures, family	week	34.26	94	73r

New York, NY - continued

Item	Per	Value	Date	Ref.
Restaurant Food - continued				
Hamburger with cheese	1/4 lb.	2.78	12/94	2c
Pizza, Pizza Hut or Pizza Inn	12-13 in.	8.69	12/94	2c
Taxes				
Tax rate, residential property, month	$100	0.87	1/92	79c
Taxes, Federal income, expenditures	year	2787	91	81c
Taxes, Federal income, expenditures	year	2409	91	81r
Taxes, personal, expenditures	year	3590	91	81c
Taxes, personal, expenditures	year	3094	91	81r
Taxes, State and local income, expenditures	year	771	91	81c
Taxes, State and local income, expenditures	year	620	91	81r
Transportation				
Transportation, ACCRA Index		132.10	12/94	2c
Bus fare, one-way	trip	1.13	12/95	1c
Bus fare, up to 10 miles	one-way	1.25	12/94	2c
Cars and trucks purchased, new	year	998	91	81c
Cars and trucks purchased, new	year	1170	91	81r
Cars and trucks purchased, used	year	561	91	81c
Cars and trucks purchased, used	year	739	91	81r
Driver's learning permit fee	perm	10.00	1/94	84s
Driver's license fee	orig	32.00-37.00	1/94	84s
Driver's license fee, duplicate	lic	7.25	1/94	84s
Driver's license reinstatement fee, min.	susp	25.00	1/94	85s
Driver's license renewal fee	renew	22.25	1/94	84s
Ferry boat fare, one-way	trip	1.13	12/95	1c
Fine, illegal parking, handicapped zone	event	50.00	12/93	87c
Identification card, nondriver	card	6.25	1/94	83s
Mileage fee, mileage traveled over rental company limit	mile	0.29	95	7c
Motorcycle license fee	orig	32.00-37.00	1/94	84s
Motorcycle license fee, duplicate	lic	7.25	1/94	84s
Motorcycle license renewal fee	renew	22.25	1/94	84s
Public transportation expenditures	year	841	91	81c
Public transportation expenditures	year	430	91	81r
Railway fare, commuter rail, one-way	trip	2.40	12/95	1c
Railway fare, heavy rail, one-way	trip	0.75	12/95	1c
Railway fare, light rail, one-way	trip	1.00	12/95	1c
Taxi fare	init charge	1.50	4/94	61c
Tire balance, computer or spin bal., front	wheel	9.85	12/94	2c
Transportation expenditures, total	year	4873	91	81c
Transportation expenditures, total	year	4810	91	81r
Vehicle expenses, miscellaneous	year	1688	91	81c
Vehicle finance charges	year	177	91	81c
Vehicle finance charges	year	238	91	81r
Vehicle insurance expenditures	year	726	91	81c
Vehicle insurance expenditures	year	630	91	81r
Vehicle maintenance and repairs expenditures	year	513	91	81c
Vehicle maintenance and repairs expenditures	year	532	91	81r
Vehicle purchases	year	1560	91	81c
Vehicle purchases	year	1920	91	81r
Vehicle rental, leases, licenses, etc. expenditures	year	272	91	81c
Vehicle rental, leases, licenses, etc. expenditures	year	193	91	81r
Vehicles purchased, other than cars and trucks	year	1	91	81c
Vehicles purchased, other than cars and trucks	year	11	91	81r
Utilities				
Utilities, ACCRA Index		145.30	12/94	2c
Electricity	KWh	0.14	12/94	82c
Electricity expenditures	year	720	91	81c
Electricity expenditures	year	695	91	81r
Electricity, (part.), other, 1800 sq. ft., new home	mo.	117.36	12/94	2c

Values are in dollars or fractions of dollars. In the column headed *Ref*, references are shown to sources. Each reference is followed by a letter. These refer to the geographical level for which data were reported: s = State, r = Region, and c = City or metro. The abbreviation *ex* is used to mean *except* or *excluding*; *exp* stands for *expenditures*. For other abbreviations and further explanations, please see the Introduction.

New York, NY - continued

Item	Per	Value	Date	Ref.
Utilities				
Electricity, summer, 250 KWh	month	41.82	8/93	64c
Electricity, summer, 500 KWh	month	80.63	8/93	64c
Electricity, summer, 750 KWh	month	119.44	8/93	64c
Electricity, summer, 1000 KWh	month	158.24	8/93	64c
Utilities, fuels, and public services, total expenditures	year	2240	91	81c
Utilities, fuels, and public services, total expenditures	year	1981	91	81r
Water and other public services, expenditures	year	139	91	81c
Water and other public services, expenditures	year	154	91	81r
Weddings				
Bridal attendants' gowns	event	750	10/93	76r
Bridal gown	event	852	10/93	76r
Bridal headpiece and veil	event	167	10/93	76r
Bride's wedding band	event	708	10/93	76r
Clergy	event	224	10/93	76r
Engagement ring	event	2756	10/93	76r
Flowers	event	863	10/93	76r
Formal wear for groom	event	106	10/93	76r
Groom's attendants' formal wear	event	530	10/93	76r
Groom's wedding band	event	402	10/93	76r
Music	event	600	10/93	76r
Photography	event	1088	10/93	76r
Shoes for bride	event	50	10/93	76r
Videography	event	483	10/93	76r
Wedding invitations and announcements	event	342	10/93	76r
Wedding reception	event	7000	10/93	76r

Newark, NJ

Item	Per	Value	Date	Ref.
Appliances				
Appliances (major), expenditures	year	145	91	81r
Average annual exp.				
Food, health care, personal goods, services	year	29496	91	81r
Charity				
Cash contributions, expenditures	year	708	91	81r
Clothing				
Apparel, men and boys, total expenditures	year	416	91	81r
Apparel, women and girls, total expenditures	year	744	91	81r
Footwear, expenditures	year	305	91	81r
Communications				
Long-distance telephone rate, day, addl. min., 1-10 mi.	min.	0.03	12/93	9s
Long-distance telephone rate, day, initial min., 1-10 mi.	min.	0.09	12/93	9s
Phone line, single, business, field visit	inst	98.50	12/93	9s
Phone line, single, business, no field visit	inst	79.50	12/93	9s
Phone line, single, residence, field visit	inst	56.50	12/93	9s
Phone line, single, residence, no field visit	inst	42.00	12/93	9s
Telephone service, expenditures	year	589	91	81r
Education				
Board, 4-year private college/university	year	2841	8/94	80s
Board, 4-year public college/university	year	1956	8/94	80s
Education, total expenditures	year	593	91	81r
Room, 4-year private college/university	year	2999	8/94	80s
Room, 4-year public college/university	year	2778	8/94	80s
Total cost, 4-year private college/university	year	18264	8/94	80s
Total cost, 4-year public college/university	year	8252	8/94	80s
Tuition, 2-year public college/university, in-state	year	1539	8/94	80s
Tuition, 4-year private college/university, in-state	year	12423	8/94	80s
Tuition, 4-year public college/university, in-state	year	3518	8/94	80s

Newark, NJ - continued

Item	Per	Value	Date	Ref.
Energy and Fuels				
Fuel oil and other fuels, expenditures	year	257	91	81r
Gas, natural, expenditures	year	285	91	81r
Gasoline and motor oil purchased	year	867	91	81r
Gasoline, unleaded midgrade	gallon	1.32	4/93	82r
Gasoline, unleaded premium	gallon	1.40	4/93	82r
Gasoline, unleaded regular	gallon	1.19	4/93	82r
Entertainment				
Entertainment, total expenditures	year	1331	91	81r
Fees and admissions, expenditures	year	398	91	81r
Pets, toys, playground equipment, expenditures	year	270	91	81r
Reading, expenditures	year	171	91	81r
Televisions, radios, and sound equipment, expenditures	year	429	91	81r
Funerals				
Burial, immediate, container provided by funeral home		1370.36	1/95	54r
Cards, acknowledgment		17.72	1/95	54r
Casket, minimum alternative		192.52	1/95	54r
Cosmetology, hair care, etc.		139.56	1/95	54r
Cremation, direct, container provided by funeral home		1049.24	1/95	54r
Embalming		387.57	1/95	54r
Funeral, funeral home		278.77	1/95	54r
Funeral, other facility		275.85	1/95	54r
Graveside service		213.08	1/95	54r
Hearse, local		157.21	1/95	54r
Limousine, local		146.45	1/95	54r
Memorial service		271.02	1/95	54r
Service charge, professional, nondeclinable		943.58	1/95	54r
Visitation and viewing		322.86	1/95	54r
Groceries				
Apples, Red Delicious	lb.	0.78	12/94	82r
Bacon, sliced	lb.	2.24	12/94	82r
Bananas	lb.	0.49	12/94	82r
Beef purchases	year	226	91	81r
Beverage purchases, alcoholic	year	332	91	81r
Beverage purchases, nonalcoholic	year	213	91	81r
Bread, white, pan	lb.	0.80	12/94	82r
Butter, salted, Grade AA, stick	lb.	1.67	12/94	82r
Carrots, short trimmed and topped	lb.	0.51	12/94	82r
Cereals and bakery products purchases	year	407	91	81r
Cereals and cereals products purchases	year	132	91	81r
Chicken breast, bone-in	lb.	2.22	12/94	82r
Chicken, fresh, whole	lb.	1.05	12/94	82r
Chuck roast, USDA choice, boneless	lb.	2.74	12/94	82r
Coffee, 100%, ground roast, all sizes	lb.	4.61	12/94	82r
Dairy products (other) purchases	year	161	91	81r
Eggs, Grade A large	dozen	1.12	12/94	82r
Fish and seafood purchases	year	112	91	81r
Food purchases, food eaten at home	year	2599	91	81r
Foods purchased away from home, not prepared by consumer	year	2024	91	81r
Fruits and vegetables purchases	year	444	91	81r
Grapefruit	lb.	0.44	12/94	82r
Grapes, Thompson seedless	lb.	2.24	12/94	82r
Ground chuck, 100% beef	lb.	1.67	12/94	82r
Ice cream, prepackaged, bulk, regular	1/2 gal.	2.93	12/94	82r
Lemons	lb.	1.06	12/94	82r
Lettuce, iceberg	lb.	0.92	12/94	82r
Meats, poultry, fish, and eggs purchases	year	751	91	81r
Milk and cream (fresh) purchases	year	152	91	81r
Orange juice, frozen concentrate 12-oz. can	16 oz.	1.92	12/94	82r
Oranges, Navel	lb.	0.56	12/94	82r
Pork chops, center cut, bone-in	lb.	3.09	12/94	82r
Pork purchases	year	130	91	81r
Potatoes, white	lb.	0.37	12/94	82r
Rib roast, USDA choice, bone-in	lb.	4.98	12/94	82r
Round roast, USDA choice, boneless	lb.	2.93	12/94	82r
Shortening, vegetable oil blends	lb.	1.03	12/94	82r

Values are in dollars or fractions of dollars. In the column headed *Ref*, references are shown to sources. Each reference is followed by a letter. These refer to the geographical level for which data were reported: s=State, r=Region, and c=City or metro. The abbreviation *ex* is used to mean *except* or *excluding*; *exp* stands for *expenditures*. For other abbreviations and further explanations, please see the Introduction.

Newark, NJ - continued

Item	Per	Value	Date	Ref.
Groceries				
Spaghetti and macaroni	lb.	0.84	12/94	82r
Steak, round, USDA choice, boneless	lb.	3.48	12/94	82r
Steak, sirloin, USDA choice, bone-in	lb.	3.38	12/94	82r
Steak, sirloin, USDA choice, boneless	lb.	4.81	12/94	82r
Sugar and other sweets, eaten at home, expenditures	year	89	91	81r
Sugar, white, all sizes	lb.	0.46	12/94	82r
Tobacco products and smoking supplies, total expenditures	year	279	91	81r
Tomatoes, field grown	lb.	1.56	12/94	82r
Tuna, chunk, light	lb.	2.09	12/94	82r
Health Care				
Childbirth, Cesarean delivery, hospital charge	birth	6334.00	12/91	69r
Childbirth, Cesarean delivery, physician charge	birth	2234.00	12/91	69r
Childbirth, normal delivery, hospital charge	birth	3225.00	12/91	69r
Childbirth, normal delivery, physician charge	birth	1623.00	12/91	69r
Drugs, expenditures	year	205	91	81r
Health care, total expenditures	year	1396	91	81r
Health insurance expenditures	year	553	91	81r
Insurance premium, family medical care	month	396.06	1/95	41s
Medical services expenditures	year	559	91	81r
Medical supplies expenditures	year	80	91	81r
Household Goods				
Floor coverings, expenditures	year	158	91	81r
Furniture, expenditures	year	341	91	81r
Household equipment, misc. expenditures	year	363	91	81r
Household expenditures, miscellaneous	year	194	91	81r
Household furnishings and equipment, expenditures	year	1158	91	81r
Household operations expenditures	year	378	91	81r
Household textiles, expenditures	year	88	91	81r
Housekeeping supplies, expenditures	year	426	91	81r
Laundry and cleaning supplies, expenditures	year	122	91	81r
Postage and stationery, expenditures	year	134	91	81r
Housing				
Add garage/carport		11,614	3/95	74r
Add room(s)		16,816	3/95	74r
Apartment condominium or co-op, median	unit	96700	12/94	62r
Dwellings (owned), expenditures	year	3305	91	81r
Enclose porch/patio/breezeway		2,980	3/95	74r
Finish room in basement/attic		4,330	3/95	74r
Home, existing, single-family, median	unit	161600	12/94	62r
Maintenance, repairs, insurance, and other housing expenditures	year	569	91	81r
Mortgage interest and charges expenditures	year	1852	91	81r
Princ. & int., mortgage, median-price exist. sing.-family home	mo.	765	12/94	62r
Property taxes expenditures	year	884	91	81r
Redesign, restructure more than half of home's interior		2,750	3/95	74r
Rental units expenditures	year	1832	91	81r
Insurance and Pensions				
Auto insurance, private passenger	year	1094.56	12/94	71s
Insurance and pensions, personal, expenditures	year	2690	91	81r
Insurance, life and other personal, expenditures	year	341	91	81r
Pensions and Social Security, expenditures	year	2349	91	81r
Legal Assistance				
Estate planning, law-firm partner	hr.	375.00	10/93	12r
Legal work, law firm associate	hour	78		10r
Legal work, law firm partner	hour	183		10r
Personal Services				
Personal services expenditures	year	184	91	81r

Newark, NJ - continued

Item	Per	Value	Date	Ref.
Restaurant Food				
Dining expenditures, family	week	34.26	94	73r
Taxes				
Taxes, Federal income, expenditures	year	2409	91	81r
Taxes, personal, expenditures	year	3094	91	81r
Taxes, State and local income, expenditures	year	620	91	81r
Transportation				
Cars and trucks purchased, new	year	1170	91	81r
Cars and trucks purchased, used	year	739	91	81r
Driver's learning permit fee	perm	5.00	1/94	84s
Driver's license fee	orig	16.00	1/94	84s
Driver's license fee, duplicate	lic	3.00	1/94	84s
Driver's license reinstatement fee, min.	susp	30.00	1/94	85s
Driver's license renewal fee	renew	16.00	1/94	84s
Identification card, nondriver	card	5.50	1/94	83s
Motorcycle learning permit fee	perm	5.00	1/94	84s
Motorcycle license fee	orig	8.00	1/94	84s
Motorcycle license fee, duplicate	lic	3.00	1/94	84s
Motorcycle license renewal fee	renew	8.00	1/94	84s
Public transportation expenditures	year	430	91	81r
Transportation expenditures, total	year	4810	91	81r
Vehicle finance charges	year	238	91	81r
Vehicle insurance expenditures	year	630	91	81r
Vehicle maintenance and repairs expenditures	year	532	91	81r
Vehicle purchases	year	1920	91	81r
Vehicle rental, leases, licenses, etc. expenditures	year	193	91	81r
Vehicles purchased, other than cars and trucks	year	11	91	81r
Utilities				
Electricity expenditures	year	695	91	81r
Utilities, fuels, and public services, total expenditures	year	1981	91	81r
Water and other public services, expenditures	year	154	91	81r
Weddings				
Bridal attendants' gowns	event	750	10/93	76r
Bridal gown	event	852	10/93	76r
Bridal headpiece and veil	event	167	10/93	76r
Bride's wedding band	event	708	10/93	76r
Clergy	event	224	10/93	76r
Engagement ring	event	2756	10/93	76r
Flowers	event	863	10/93	76r
Formal wear for groom	event	106	10/93	76r
Groom's attendants' formal wear	event	530	10/93	76r
Groom's wedding band	event	402	10/93	76r
Music	event	600	10/93	76r
Photography	event	1088	10/93	76r
Shoes for bride	event	50	10/93	76r
Videography	event	483	10/93	76r
Wedding invitations and announcements	event	342	10/93	76r
Wedding reception	event	7000	10/93	76r

Newark-Licking County, OH

Item	Per	Value	Date	Ref.
Composite, ACCRA index		97.70	12/94	2c
Alcoholic Beverages				
Beer, Miller Lite, Bud, 12-oz., ex deposit	6	4.09	12/94	2c
J & B Scotch	750-ml.	18.60	12/94	2c
Wine, Gallo Chablis blanc	1.5-lit	5.16	12/94	2c
Clothing				
Jeans, man's denim		29.99	12/94	2c
Shirt, man's dress shirt		32.00	12/94	2c
Undervest, boy's size 10-14, cotton	3	2.99	12/94	2c
Communications				
Newspaper subscription, dly. and Sun. delivery	month	9.35	12/94	2c

Values are in dollars or fractions of dollars. In the column headed *Ref*, references are shown to sources. Each reference is followed by a letter. These refer to the geographical level for which data were reported: s = State, r = Region, and c = City or metro. The abbreviation *ex* is used to mean *except* or *excluding*; *exp* stands for expenditures. For other abbreviations and further explanations, please see the Introduction.

Newark-Licking County, OH - continued

Item	Per	Value	Date	Ref.
Communications				
Telephone bill, family of four	month	17.24	12/94	2c
Telephone, residential, flat rate	mo.	15.25	12/93	8c
Energy and Fuels				
Energy, combined forms, 1800 sq. ft.	mo.	146.72	12/94	2c
Energy, exc. electricity, 1800 sq. ft.	mo.	61.72	12/94	2c
Gas, reg unlead, taxes inc., cash, self-service	gal	1.00	12/94	2c
Entertainment				
Bowling, evening rate	game	2.42	12/94	2c
Monopoly game, Parker Brothers', No. 9	game	10.36	12/94	2c
Movie	adm	5.00	12/94	2c
Tennis balls, yellow, Wilson or Penn, 3	can	1.92	12/94	2c
Groceries				
Groceries, ACCRA Index		100.10	12/94	2c
Baby food, strained vegetables, lowest price	4-4.5 oz.	0.31	12/94	2c
Bananas	lb.	0.42	12/94	2c
Beef or hamburger, ground	lb.	1.47	12/94	2c
Bread, white	24-oz.	0.50	12/94	2c
Cheese, Kraft grated Parmesan	8-oz.	3.05	12/94	2c
Chicken, whole fryer	lb.	0.87	12/94	2c
Cigarettes, Winston, Kings	carton	15.70	12/94	2c
Coffee, vacuum-packed	13 oz.	4.36	12/94	2c
Corn Flakes, Kellogg's or Post Toasties	18 oz.	2.20	12/94	2c
Corn, frozen, whole kernel, lowest price	10 oz.	0.77	12/94	2c
Eggs, Grade A large	dozen	0.92	12/94	2c
Lettuce, iceberg	head	0.96	12/94	2c
Margarine, Blue Bonnet or Parkay cubes	lb.	0.64	12/94	2c
Milk, whole	1/2 gal.	1.38	12/94	2c
Orange juice, Minute Maid frozen	12-oz.	1.25	12/94	2c
Peaches, halves or slices, Hunt's, Del Monte, or Libby's	29-oz.	1.44	12/94	2c
Peas, sweet, Del Monte or Green Giant	15-17 oz.	0.65	12/94	2c
Potatoes, white or red	10-lb. sack	2.60	12/94	2c
Sausage, Jimmy Dean, 100% pork	lb.	2.69	12/94	2c
Shortening, vegetable, Crisco	3-lb.	2.34	12/94	2c
Soft drink, Coca Cola, ex deposit	2 lit	1.19	12/94	2c
Steak, t-bone	lb.	6.08	12/94	2c
Sugar, cane or beet	4 lbs.	1.29	12/94	2c
Tomatoes, Hunt's or Del Monte	14.5 oz.	0.89	12/94	2c
Tuna, chunk, light, oil-packed	6.125-6.5 oz.	0.73	12/94	2c
Goods and Services				
Miscellaneous goods and services, ACCRA Index		93.60	12/94	2c
Health Care				
Health care, ACCRA Index		94.80	12/94	2c
Antibiotic ointment, Polysporin	1.5 oz.	3.99	12/94	2c
Dentist's fee, adult teeth cleaning and periodic oral exam	visit	56.25	12/94	2c
Doctor's fee, routine exam, established patient	visit	35.00	12/94	2c
Hospital care, semiprivate room	day	328.00	12/94	2c
Household Goods				
Appl. repair, service call, wash mach	min. lab. chg.	26.25	12/94	2c
Laundry detergent, Tide Ultra, Bold, or Cheer	42 oz.	4.20	12/94	2c
Tissues, facial, Kleenex brand	175	1.00	12/94	2c
Housing				
Housing, ACCRA Index		92.60	12/94	2c
House payment, principal and interest, 25% down payment	mo.	702	12/94	2c

Newark-Licking County, OH - continued

Item	Per	Value	Date	Ref.
Housing - continued				
House, 1800 sq ft, 8000 sq ft lot, new, urban, utilities	total	113300	12/94	2c
Mtge. rate, incl. points and orig. fee, 30-year conv. fixed or ARM	mo.	9.30	12/94	2c
Rent, apartment, 2 br., 1 1/2-2 baths, unfurnished, 950 sq ft, water	mo.	509	12/94	2c
Personal Goods				
Shampoo, Alberto VO5	15-oz.	1.06	12/94	2c
Toothpaste, Crest or Colgate	6-7 oz.	1.64	12/94	2c
Personal Services				
Dry cleaning, man's 2-pc. suit		7.34	12/94	2c
Haircut, man's barbershop, no styling		7.50	12/94	2c
Haircut, woman's shampoo, trim, blow-dry		14.74	12/94	2c
Restaurant Food				
Chicken, fried, thigh and drumstick		1.94	12/94	2c
Hamburger with cheese	1/4 lb.	1.79	12/94	2c
Pizza, Pizza Hut or Pizza Inn	12-13 in.	7.69	12/94	2c
Transportation				
Transportation, ACCRA Index		102.20	12/94	2c
Tire balance, computer or spin bal., front	wheel	8.15	12/94	2c
Utilities				
Utilities, ACCRA Index		125.00	12/94	2c
Electricity, (part.), other, 1800 sq. ft., new home	mo.	85.00	12/94	2c

Niagara Falls, NY

Item	Per	Value	Date	Ref.
Appliances				
Appliances (major), expenditures	year	145	91	81r
Average annual exp.				
Food, health care, personal goods, services	year	29496	91	81r
Charity				
Cash contributions, expenditures	year	708	91	81r
Clothing				
Apparel, men and boys, total expenditures	year	416	91	81r
Apparel, women and girls, total expenditures	year	744	91	81r
Footwear, expenditures	year	305	91	81r
Communications				
Long-distance telephone rate, day, addl. min., 1-10 mi.	min.	4.00	12/93	9s
Long-distance telephone rate, day, initial min., 1-10 mi.	min.	14.90	12/93	9s
Phone line, single, business, field visit	inst	143.26	12/93	9s
Phone line, single, business, no field visit	inst	106.05	12/93	9s
Phone line, single, residence, field visit	inst	85.46	12/93	9s
Phone line, single, residence, no field visit	inst	55.00	12/93	9s
Telephone service, expenditures	year	589	91	81r
Education				
Board, 4-year private college/university	year	2918	8/94	80s
Board, 4-year public college/university	year	2177	8/94	80s
Education, total expenditures	year	593	91	81r
Room, 4-year private college/university	year	3302	8/94	80s
Room, 4-year public college/university	year	2624	8/94	80s
Total cost, 4-year private college/university	year	18451	8/94	80s
Total cost, 4-year public college/university	year	7723	8/94	80s
Tuition, 2-year public college/university, in-state	year	2112	8/94	80s
Tuition, 4-year private college/university, in-state	year	12231	8/94	80s
Tuition, 4-year public college/university, in-state	year	2921	8/94	80s
Energy and Fuels				
Fuel oil and other fuels, expenditures	year	257	91	81r
Gas, natural, expenditures	year	285	91	81r

Values are in dollars or fractions of dollars. In the column headed *Ref*, references are shown to sources. Each reference is followed by a letter. These refer to the geographical level for which data were reported: s=State, r=Region, and c=City or metro. The abbreviation *ex* is used to mean *except* or *excluding*; *exp* stands for expenditures. For other abbreviations and further explanations, please see the Introduction.

Niagara Falls, NY - continued

Item	Per	Value	Date	Ref.
Energy and Fuels				
Gasoline and motor oil purchased	year	867	91	81r
Gasoline, unleaded midgrade	gallon	1.32	4/93	82r
Gasoline, unleaded premium	gallon	1.40	4/93	82r
Gasoline, unleaded regular	gallon	1.19	4/93	82r
Entertainment				
Entertainment, total expenditures	year	1331	91	81r
Fees and admissions, expenditures	year	398	91	81r
Pets, toys, playground equipment, expenditures	year	270	91	81r
Reading, expenditures	year	171	91	81r
Televisions, radios, and sound equipment, expenditures	year	429	91	81r
Funerals				
Burial, immediate, container provided by funeral home		1370.36	1/95	54r
Cards, acknowledgment		17.72	1/95	54r
Casket, minimum alternative		192.52	1/95	54r
Cosmetology, hair care, etc.		139.56	1/95	54r
Cremation, direct, container provided by funeral home		1049.24	1/95	54r
Embalming		387.57	1/95	54r
Funeral, funeral home		278.77	1/95	54r
Funeral, other facility		275.85	1/95	54r
Graveside service		213.08	1/95	54r
Hearse, local		157.27	1/95	54r
Limousine, local		146.45	1/95	54r
Memorial service		271.02	1/95	54r
Service charge, professional, nondeclinable		943.58	1/95	54r
Visitation and viewing		322.86	1/95	54r
Groceries				
Apples, Red Delicious	lb.	0.78	12/94	82r
Bacon, sliced	lb.	2.24	12/94	82r
Bananas	lb.	0.49	12/94	82r
Beef purchases	year	226	91	81r
Beverage purchases, alcoholic	year	332	91	81r
Beverage purchases, nonalcoholic	year	213	91	81r
Bread, white, pan	lb.	0.80	12/94	82r
Butter, salted, Grade AA, stick	lb.	1.67	12/94	82r
Carrots, short trimmed and topped	lb.	0.51	12/94	82r
Cereals and bakery products purchases	year	407	91	81r
Cereals and cereals products purchases	year	132	91	81r
Chicken breast, bone-in	lb.	2.22	12/94	82r
Chicken, fresh, whole	lb.	1.05	12/94	82r
Chuck roast, USDA choice, boneless	lb.	2.74	12/94	82r
Coffee, 100%, ground roast, all sizes	lb.	4.61	12/94	82r
Dairy products (other) purchases	year	161	91	81r
Eggs, Grade A large	dozen	1.12	12/94	82r
Fish and seafood purchases	year	112	91	81r
Food purchases, food eaten at home	year	2599	91	81r
Foods purchased away from home, not prepared by consumer	year	2024	91	81r
Fruits and vegetables purchases	year	444	91	81r
Grapefruit	lb.	0.44	12/94	82r
Grapes, Thompson seedless	lb.	2.24	12/94	82r
Ground chuck, 100% beef	lb.	1.67	12/94	82r
Ice cream, prepackaged, bulk, regular	1/2 gal.	2.93	12/94	82r
Lemons	lb.	1.06	12/94	82r
Lettuce, iceberg	lb.	0.92	12/94	82r
Meats, poultry, fish, and eggs purchases	year	751	91	81r
Milk and cream (fresh) purchases	year	152	91	81r
Orange juice, frozen concentrate 12-oz. can	16 oz.	1.92	12/94	82r
Oranges, Navel	lb.	0.56	12/94	82r
Pork chops, center cut, bone-in	lb.	3.09	12/94	82r
Pork purchases	year	130	91	81r
Potatoes, white	lb.	0.37	12/94	82r
Rib roast, USDA choice, bone-in	lb.	4.98	12/94	82r
Round roast, USDA choice, boneless	lb.	2.93	12/94	82r
Shortening, vegetable oil blends	lb.	1.03	12/94	82r
Spaghetti and macaroni	lb.	0.84	12/94	82r
Steak, round, USDA choice, boneless	lb.	3.48	12/94	82r

Niagara Falls, NY - continued

Item	Per	Value	Date	Ref.
Groceries - continued				
Steak, sirloin, USDA choice, bone-in	lb.	3.38	12/94	82r
Steak, sirloin, USDA choice, boneless	lb.	4.81	12/94	82r
Sugar and other sweets, eaten at home, expenditures	year	89	91	81r
Sugar, white, all sizes	lb.	0.46	12/94	82r
Tobacco products and smoking supplies, total expenditures	year	279	91	81r
Tomatoes, field grown	lb.	1.56	12/94	82r
Tuna, chunk, light	lb.	2.09	12/94	82r
Health Care				
Childbirth, Cesarean delivery, hospital charge	birth	6334.00	12/91	69r
Childbirth, Cesarean delivery, physician charge	birth	2234.00	12/91	69r
Childbirth, normal delivery, hospital charge	birth	3225.00	12/91	69r
Childbirth, normal delivery, physician charge	birth	1623.00	12/91	69r
Drugs, expenditures	year	205	91	81r
Health care, total expenditures	year	1396	91	81r
Health insurance expenditures	year	553	91	81r
Insurance premium, family medical care	month	384.24	1/95	41s
Medical services expenditures	year	559	91	81r
Medical supplies expenditures	year	80	91	81r
Household Goods				
Floor coverings, expenditures	year	158	91	81r
Furniture, expenditures	year	341	91	81r
Household equipment, misc. expenditures	year	363	91	81r
Household expenditures, miscellaneous	year	194	91	81r
Household furnishings and equipment, expenditures	year	1158	91	81r
Household operations expenditures	year	378	91	81r
Household textiles, expenditures	year	88	91	81r
Housekeeping supplies, expenditures	year	426	91	81r
Laundry and cleaning supplies, expenditures	year	122	91	81r
Postage and stationery, expenditures	year	134	91	81r
Housing				
Add garage/carport		11,614	3/95	74r
Add room(s)		16,816	3/95	74r
Apartment condominium or co-op, median	unit	96700	12/94	62r
Dwellings (owned), expenditures	year	3305	91	81r
Enclose porch/patio/breezeway		2,980	3/95	74r
Finish room in basement/attic		4,330	3/95	74r
Home, existing, single-family, median	unit	161600	12/94	62r
Maintenance, repairs, insurance, and other housing expenditures	year	569	91	81r
Mortgage interest and charges expenditures	year	1852	91	81r
Princ. & int., mortgage, median-price exist. sing.-family home	mo.	765	12/94	62r
Property taxes expenditures	year	884	91	81r
Redesign, restructure more than half of home's interior		2,750	3/95	74r
Rental units expenditures	year	1832	91	81r
Insurance and Pensions				
Auto insurance, private passenger	year	985.07	12/94	71s
Insurance and pensions, personal, expenditures	year	2690	91	81r
Insurance, life and other personal, expenditures	year	341	91	81r
Pensions and Social Security, expenditures	year	2349	91	81r
Legal Assistance				
Estate planning, law-firm partner	hr.	375.00	10/93	12r
Legal work, law firm associate	hour	78		10r
Legal work, law firm partner	hour	183		10r
Personal Services				
Personal services expenditures	year	184	91	81r
Restaurant Food				
Dining expenditures, family	week	34.26	94	73r

Values are in dollars or fractions of dollars. In the column headed *Ref*, references are shown to sources. Each reference is followed by a letter. These refer to the geographical level for which data were reported: s=State, r=Region, and c=City or metro. The abbreviation *ex* is used to mean *except* or *excluding*; *exp* stands for expenditures. For other abbreviations and further explanations, please see the Introduction.

Niagara Falls, NY - continued

Item	Per	Value	Date	Ref.
Taxes				
Taxes, Federal income, expenditures	year	2409	91	81r
Taxes, personal, expenditures	year	3094	91	81r
Taxes, State and local income, expenditures	year	620	91	81r
Transportation				
Cars and trucks purchased, new	year	1170	91	81r
Cars and trucks purchased, used	year	739	91	81r
Driver's learning permit fee	perm	10.00	1/94	84s
Driver's license fee	orig	32.00-37.00	1/94	84s
Driver's license fee, duplicate	lic	7.25	1/94	84s
Driver's license reinstatement fee, min.	susp	25.00	1/94	85s
Driver's license renewal fee	renew	22.25	1/94	84s
Identification card, nondriver	card	6.25	1/94	83s
Motorcycle license fee	orig	32.00-37.00	1/94	84s
Motorcycle license fee, duplicate	lic	7.25	1/94	84s
Motorcycle license renewal fee	renew	22.25	1/94	84s
Public transportation expenditures	year	430	91	81r
Transportation expenditures, total	year	4810	91	81r
Vehicle finance charges	year	238	91	81r
Vehicle insurance expenditures	year	630	91	81r
Vehicle maintenance and repairs expenditures	year	532	91	81r
Vehicle purchases	year	1920	91	81r
Vehicle rental, leases, licenses, etc. expenditures	year	193	91	81r
Vehicles purchased, other than cars and trucks	year	11	91	81r
Utilities				
Electricity expenditures	year	695	91	81r
Utilities, fuels, and public services, total expenditures	year	1981	91	81r
Water and other public services, expenditures	year	154	91	81r
Weddings				
Bridal attendants' gowns	event	750	10/93	76r
Bridal gown	event	852	10/93	76r
Bridal headpiece and veil	event	167	10/93	76r
Bride's wedding band	event	708	10/93	76r
Clergy	event	224	10/93	76r
Engagement ring	event	2756	10/93	76r
Flowers	event	863	10/93	76r
Formal wear for groom	event	106	10/93	76r
Groom's attendants' formal wear	event	530	10/93	76r
Groom's wedding band	event	402	10/93	76r
Music	event	600	10/93	76r
Photography	event	1088	10/93	76r
Shoes for bride	event	50	10/93	76r
Videography	event	483	10/93	76r
Wedding invitations and announcements	event	342	10/93	76r
Wedding reception	event	7000	10/93	76r

Norfolk, VA

Item	Per	Value	Date	Ref.
Appliances				
Appliances (major), expenditures	year	153	91	81r
Average annual exp.				
Food, health care, personal goods, services	year	27020	91	81r
Charity				
Cash contributions, expenditures	year	839	91	81r
Clothing				
Apparel, men and boys, total expenditures	year	380	91	81r
Apparel, women and girls, total expenditures	year	660	91	81r
Footwear, expenditures	year	193	91	81r
Communications				
Long-distance telephone rate, day, addl. min., 1-10 mi.	min.	0.12	12/93	9s

Norfolk, VA - continued

Item	Per	Value	Date	Ref.
Communications - continued				
Long-distance telephone rate, day, initial min., 1-10 mi.	min.	0.21	12/93	9s
Phone line, single, business, field visit	inst	0.00	12/93	9s
Phone line, single, business, no field visit	inst	64.00	12/93	9s
Phone line, single, residence, field visit	inst	0.00	12/93	9s
Phone line, single, residence, no field visit	inst	38.50	12/93	9s
Telephone service, expenditures	year	616	91	81r
Education				
Board, 4-year private college/university	year	2242	8/94	80s
Board, 4-year public college/university	year	1901	8/94	80s
Education, total expenditures	year	319	91	81r
Room, 4-year private college/university	year	2022	8/94	80s
Room, 4-year public college/university	year	2186	8/94	80s
Total cost, 4-year private college/university	year	14043	8/94	80s
Total cost, 4-year public college/university	year	7726	8/94	80s
Tuition, 2-year public college/university, in-state	year	1332	8/94	80s
Tuition, 4-year private college/university, in-state	year	9778	8/94	80s
Tuition, 4-year public college/university, in-state	year	3639	8/94	80s
Energy and Fuels				
Fuel oil and other fuels, expenditures	year	56	91	81r
Gas, natural, expenditures	year	150	91	81r
Gasoline and motor oil purchased	year	1152	91	81r
Gasoline, unleaded midgrade	gallon	1.21	4/93	82r
Gasoline, unleaded premium	gallon	1.30	4/93	82r
Gasoline, unleaded regular	gallon	1.10	4/93	82r
Entertainment				
Concert ticket, Pearl Jam group	perf	20.00	94	50r
Entertainment, total expenditures	year	1266	91	81r
Fees and admissions, expenditures	year	306	91	81r
Pets, toys, playground equipment, expenditures	year	271	91	81r
Reading, expenditures	year	131	91	81r
Televisions, radios, and sound equipment, expenditures	year	439	91	81r
Funerals				
Burial, immediate, container provided by funeral home		1370.36	1/95	54r
Cards, acknowledgment		14.83	1/95	54r
Casket, minimum alternative		192.52	1/95	54r
Cosmetology, hair care, etc.		102.27	1/95	54r
Cremation, direct, container provided by funeral home		1065.64	1/95	54r
Embalming		304.29	1/95	54r
Funeral, funeral home		287.83	1/95	54r
Funeral, other facility		284.14	1/95	54r
Graveside service		349.13	1/95	54r
Hearse, local		132.27	1/95	54r
Limousine, local		98.45	1/95	54r
Memorial service		270.59	1/95	54r
Service charge, professional, nondeclinable		933.59	1/95	54r
Visitation and viewing		225.83	1/95	54r
Groceries				
Apples, Red Delicious	lb.	0.73	12/94	82r
Bacon, sliced	lb.	1.67	12/94	82r
Bananas	lb.	0.42	12/94	82r
Beef purchases	year	213	91	81r
Beverage purchases, alcoholic	year	249	91	81r
Beverage purchases, nonalcoholic	year	207	91	81r
Bologna, all beef or mixed	lb.	2.27	12/94	82r
Bread, white, pan	lb.	0.68	12/94	82r
Cabbage	lb.	0.42	12/94	82r
Carrots, short trimmed and topped	lb.	0.53	12/94	82r
Cereals and bakery products purchases	year	345	91	81r
Cereals and cereals products purchases	year	127	91	81r
Cheddar cheese, natural	lb.	3.58	12/94	82r
Chicken breast, bone-in	lb.	1.71	12/94	82r

Values are in dollars or fractions of dollars. In the column headed *Ref*, references are shown to sources. Each reference is followed by a letter. These refer to the geographical level for which data were reported: s = State, r = Region, and c = City or metro. The abbreviation *ex* is used to mean *except* or *excluding*; *exp* stands for expenditures. For other abbreviations and further explanations, please see the Introduction.

Norfolk, VA - continued

Item	Per	Value	Date	Ref.
Groceries				
Chicken, fresh, whole	lb.	0.78	12/94	82r
Chuck roast, USDA choice, boneless	lb.	2.26	12/94	82r
Crackers, soda, salted	lb.	1.27	12/94	82r
Cucumbers	lb.	0.65	12/94	82r
Dairy products (other) purchases	year	141	91	81r
Eggs, Grade A large	dozen	0.87	12/94	82r
Fish and seafood purchases	year	72	91	81r
Flour, white, all purpose	lb.	0.23	12/94	82r
Food purchases, food eaten at home	year	2381	91	81r
Foods purchased away from home, not prepared by consumer	year	1696	91	81r
Frankfurters, all meat or all beef	lb.	1.74	12/94	82r
Fruits and vegetables purchases	year	380	91	81r
Grapefruit	lb.	0.45	12/94	82r
Grapes, Thompson seedless	lb.	2.30	12/94	82r
Ground beef, 100% beef	lb.	1.37	12/94	82r
Ground chuck, 100% beef	lb.	1.97	12/94	82r
Ham, boneless, exc. canned	lb.	2.54	12/94	82r
Ice cream, prepackaged, bulk, regular	1/2 gal.	2.47	12/94	82r
Lemons	lb.	1.02	12/94	82r
Lettuce, iceberg	lb.	0.96	12/94	82r
Margarine, stick	lb.	0.77	12/94	82r
Meats, poultry, fish, and eggs purchases	year	655	91	81r
Milk and cream (fresh) purchases	year	130	91	81r
Orange juice, frozen concentrate 12-oz. can	16 oz.	1.36	12/94	82r
Oranges, Navel	lb.	0.54	12/94	82r
Pears, Anjou	lb.	0.81	12/94	82r
Pork chops, center cut, bone-in	lb.	3.07	12/94	82r
Pork purchases	year	142	91	81r
Potato chips	16-oz.	3.15	12/94	82r
Potatoes, frozen, French fried	lb.	0.82	12/94	82r
Potatoes, white	lb.	0.34	12/94	82r
Rice, white, long grain, uncooked	lb.	0.48	12/94	82r
Round roast, USDA choice, boneless	lb.	2.91	12/94	82r
Sausage, fresh	lb.	1.82	12/94	82r
Shortening, vegetable oil blends	lb.	0.75	12/94	82r
Spaghetti and macaroni	lb.	0.87	12/94	82r
Steak, rib eye, USDA choice, boneless	lb.	6.85	12/94	82r
Steak, round, graded & ungraded, exc. USDA prime & choice	lb.	2.96	12/94	82r
Steak, round, USDA choice, boneless	lb.	3.17	12/94	82r
Steak, sirloin, USDA choice, boneless	lb.	4.12	12/94	82r
Steak, T-bone, USDA choice, bone-in	lb.	5.63	12/94	82r
Sugar and other sweets, eaten at home, expenditures	year	93	91	81r
Sugar, white, all sizes	lb.	0.39	12/94	82r
Tobacco products and smoking supplies, total expenditures	year	286	91	81r
Tomatoes, field grown	lb.	1.36	12/94	82r
Tuna, chunk, light	lb.	1.94	12/94	82r
Turkey, frozen, whole	lb.	0.96	12/94	82r
Yogurt, natural, fruit flavored	8 oz.	0.58	12/94	82r
Health Care				
Adenosine, emergency room	treat	100.00	95	23r
Bladder tap, superpubic, infant, emergency room	treat	119.00	95	23r
Blood analysis, emergency room	treat	25.00	95	23r
Blood tests, abdominal pain, emergency room	treat	25.00	95	23r
Burn dressing, emergency room	treat	266.00	95	23r
Cardiology interpretation, emergency room	treat	26.00	95	23r
Chest X-ray, emergency room	treat	78.00	95	23r
Childbirth, Cesarean delivery, hospital charge	birth	5462.00	12/91	69r
Childbirth, Cesarean delivery, physician charge	birth	2228.00	12/91	69r
Childbirth, normal delivery, hospital charge	birth	2943.00	12/91	69r
Childbirth, normal delivery, physician charge	birth	1619.00	12/91	69r
Defibrillation pads, emergency room	treat	6.00	95	23r
Delivery, uncomplicated, total charge	birth	6180	1/93	24s

Norfolk, VA - continued

Item	Per	Value	Date	Ref.
Health Care - continued				
Delivery, uncomplicated, vaginal, hospital charge	birth	3380	1/93	24s
Delivery, uncomplicated, vaginal, physician's charge	birth	2800	1/93	24s
Drugs, expenditures	year	297	91	81r
Gastric tube insertion, nasal, emergency room	treat	25.00	95	23r
Health care, total expenditures	year	1600	91	81r
Health insurance expenditures	year	637	91	81r
Heart monitor, emergency room	treat	40.00	95	23r
Insurance premium, family medical care	month	386.57	1/95	41s
Intravenous fluids, emergency room	treat	130.00	95	23r
Intravenous fluids, emergency room	liter	26.00	95	23r
Intravenous line, central, emergency room	treat	342.00	95	23r
Liver function tests, abdominal pain, emergency room	treat	26.00	95	23r
Medical care charges, total, emergency room, third-degree burns	treat	2101.00	95	23r
Medical care charges, total, emergency, infant with fever	treat	628.00	95	23r
Medical services expenditures	year	573	91	81r
Medical supplies expenditures	year	93	91	81r
Morphine, emergency room	treat	34.00	95	23r
Nursing care and facilities charges, emergency room	treat	252.00	95	23r
Nursing care and facilities charges, emergency, infant with fever	treat	252.00	95	23r
Nursing care and facilities charges, emergency, third-degree burns	treat	861.00	95	23r
Physician's charges, emergency, infant with fever	treat	212.00	95	23r
Physician's charges, emergency, third-degree burns	treat	372.00	95	23r
Physician's fee, emergency room	treat	372.00	95	23r
Physician's fee, general practitioner	visit	51.20	12/93	60r
Surgery, open-heart	proc	42374.00	1/93	14r
Ultrasound, abdominal, emergency room	treat	276.00	95	23r
Urinalysis, emergency room	treat	20.00	95	23r
Urinalysis, infant, emergency room	treat	20.00	95	23r
X-rays, emergency room	treat	78.00	95	23r
Household Goods				
Floor coverings, expenditures	year	48	91	81r
Furniture, expenditures	year	280	91	81r
Household equipment, misc. expenditures	year	342	91	81r
Household expenditures, miscellaneous	year	256	91	81r
Household furnishings and equipment, expenditures	year	988	91	81r
Household operations expenditures	year	468	91	81r
Household textiles, expenditures	year	95	91	81r
Housekeeping supplies, expenditures	year	380	91	81r
Laundry and cleaning supplies, expenditures	year	109	91	81r
Postage and stationery, expenditures	year	105	91	81r
Housing				
Add garage/carport		6,980	3/95	74r
Add room(s)		11,403	3/95	74r
Apartment condominium or co-op, median	unit	68600	12/94	62r
Dwellings (owned), expenditures	year	2428	91	81r
Enclose porch/patio/breezeway		4,572	3/95	74r
Finish room in basement/attic		3,794	3/95	74r
Home, existing, single-family, median	unit	120200	12/94	62r
Maintenance, repairs, insurance, and other housing expenditures	year	531	91	81r
Mortgage interest and charges expenditures	year	1506	91	81r
Princ. & int., mortgage, median-price exist. sing.-family home	mo.	540	12/94	62r
Property taxes expenditures	year	391	91	81r
Redesign, restructure more than half of home's interior		17,641	3/95	74r
Rental units expenditures	year	1264	91	81r

Values are in dollars or fractions of dollars. In the column headed *Ref*, references are shown to sources. Each reference is followed by a letter. These refer to the geographical level for which data were reported: s=State, r=Region, and c=City or metro. The abbreviation *ex* is used to mean *except* or *excluding*; *exp* stands for expenditures. For other abbreviations and further explanations, please see the Introduction.

Norfolk, VA - continued

Item	Per	Value	Date	Ref.
Insurance and Pensions				
Auto insurance, private passenger	year	564.07	12/94	71s
Insurance and pensions, personal, expenditures	year	2395	91	81r
Insurance, life and other personal, expenditures	year	368	91	81r
Pensions and Social Security, expenditures	year	2027	91	81r
Personal Services				
Personal services expenditures	year	212	91	81r
Restaurant Food				
Dining expenditures, family	week	33.83	94	73r
Taxes				
Taxes, Federal income, expenditures	year	2275	91	81r
Taxes, personal, expenditures	year	2715	91	81r
Taxes, State and local income, expenditures	year	365	91	81r
Transportation				
Cars and trucks purchased, new	year	1306	91	81r
Cars and trucks purchased, used	year	942	91	81r
Driver's learning permit fee	perm	3.00	1/94	84s
Driver's license fee	orig	12.00	1/94	84s
Driver's license fee, duplicate	lic	5.00	1/94	84s
Driver's license reinstatement fee, min.	susp	30.00	1/94	85s
Driver's license renewal fee	renew	12.00	1/94	84s
Identification card, nondriver	card	5.00	1/94	83s
Motorcycle license fee	orig	5.00	1/94	84s
Motorcycle license renewal fee	renew	5.00	1/94	84s
Public transportation expenditures	year	249	91	81r
Transportation expenditures, total	year	5307	91	81r
Vehicle finance charges	year	346	91	81r
Vehicle insurance expenditures	year	544	91	81r
Vehicle maintenance and repairs expenditures	year	600	91	81r
Vehicle purchases	year	2275	91	81r
Vehicle rental, leases, licenses, etc. expenditures	year	141	91	81r
Vehicles purchased, other than cars and trucks	year	27	91	81r
Utilities				
Electricity expenditures	year	950	91	81r
Utilities, fuels, and public services, total expenditures	year	2000	91	81r
Water and other public services, expenditures	year	227	91	81r
Weddings				
Bridal attendants' gowns	event	750	10/93	76r
Bridal gown	event	852	10/93	76r
Bridal headpiece and veil	event	167	10/93	76r
Bride's wedding band	event	708	10/93	76r
Clergy	event	224	10/93	76r
Engagement ring	event	2756	10/93	76r
Flowers	event	863	10/93	76r
Formal wear for groom	event	106	10/93	76r
Groom's attendants' formal wear	event	530	10/93	76r
Groom's wedding band	event	402	10/93	76r
Music	event	600	10/93	76r
Photography	event	1088	10/93	76r
Shoes for bride	event	50	10/93	76r
Videography	event	483	10/93	76r
Wedding invitations and announcements	event	342	10/93	76r
Wedding reception	event	7000	10/93	76r

Norwalk, CT

Item	Per	Value	Date	Ref.
Appliances				
Appliances (major), expenditures	year	145	91	81r
Average annual exp.				
Food, health care, personal goods, services	year	29496	91	81r

Norwalk, CT - continued

Item	Per	Value	Date	Ref.
Charity				
Cash contributions, expenditures	year	708	91	81r
Clothing				
Apparel, men and boys, total expenditures	year	416	91	81r
Apparel, women and girls, total expenditures	year	744	91	81r
Footwear, expenditures	year	305	91	81r
Communications				
Long-distance telephone rate, day, addl. min., 1-10 mi.	min.	0.09	12/93	9s
Long-distance telephone rate, day, initial min., 1-10 mi.	min.	0.09	12/93	9s
Phone line, single, business, field visit	inst	127.44	12/93	9s
Phone line, single, business, no field visit	inst	95.58	12/93	9s
Phone line, single, residence, field visit	inst	64.85	12/93	9s
Phone line, single, residence, no field visit	inst	38.27	12/93	9s
Telephone service, expenditures	year	589	91	81r
Education				
Board, 4-year private college/university	year	2664	8/94	80s
Board, 4-year public college/university	year	2137	8/94	80s
Education, total expenditures	year	593	91	81r
Room, 4-year private college/university	year	3287	8/94	80s
Room, 4-year public college/university	year	2310	8/94	80s
Total cost, 4-year private college/university	year	20726	8/94	80s
Total cost, 4-year public college/university	year	7926	8/94	80s
Tuition, 2-year public college/university, in-state	year	1398	8/94	80s
Tuition, 4-year private college/university, in-state	year	14775	8/94	80s
Tuition, 4-year public college/university, in-state	year	3479	8/94	80s
Energy and Fuels				
Fuel oil and other fuels, expenditures	year	257	91	81r
Gas, natural, expenditures	year	285	91	81r
Gasoline and motor oil purchased	year	867	91	81r
Gasoline, unleaded midgrade	gallon	1.32	4/93	82r
Gasoline, unleaded premium	gallon	1.40	4/93	82r
Gasoline, unleaded regular	gallon	1.19	4/93	82r
Entertainment				
Entertainment, total expenditures	year	1331	91	81r
Fees and admissions, expenditures	year	398	91	81r
Pets, toys, playground equipment, expenditures	year	270	91	81r
Reading, expenditures	year	171	91	81r
Televisions, radios, and sound equipment, expenditures	year	429	91	81r
Funerals				
Burial, immediate, container provided by funeral home		1507.89	1/95	54r
Cards, acknowledgment		18.10	1/95	54r
Casket, minimum alternative		133.03	1/95	54r
Cosmetology, hair care, etc.		114.12	1/95	54r
Cremation, direct, container provided by funeral home		1309.19	1/95	54r
Embalming		320.97	1/95	54r
Funeral, funeral home		327.61	1/95	54r
Funeral, other facility		314.81	1/95	54r
Graveside service		286.11	1/95	54r
Hearse, local		158.95	1/95	54r
Limousine, local		149.45	1/95	54r
Memorial service		315.94	1/95	54r
Service charge, professional, nondeclinable		1148.43	1/95	54r
Visitation and viewing		249.66	1/95	54r
Groceries				
Apples, Red Delicious	lb.	0.78	12/94	82r
Bacon, sliced	lb.	2.24	12/94	82r
Bananas	lb.	0.49	12/94	82r
Beef purchases	year	226	91	81r
Beverage purchases, alcoholic	year	332	91	81r
Beverage purchases, nonalcoholic	year	213	91	81r

Values are in dollars or fractions of dollars. In the column headed *Ref*, references are shown to sources. Each reference is followed by a letter. These refer to the geographical level for which data were reported: s = State, r = Region, and c = City or metro. The abbreviation *ex* is used to mean *except* or *excluding*; *exp* stands for *expenditures*. For other abbreviations and further explanations, please see the Introduction.

Norwalk, CT - continued

Item	Per	Value	Date	Ref.
Groceries				
Bread, white, pan	lb.	0.80	12/94	82r
Butter, salted, Grade AA, stick	lb.	1.67	12/94	82r
Carrots, short trimmed and topped	lb.	0.51	12/94	82r
Cereals and bakery products purchases	year	407	91	81r
Cereals and cereals products purchases	year	132	91	81r
Chicken breast, bone-in	lb.	2.22	12/94	82r
Chicken, fresh, whole	lb.	1.05	12/94	82r
Chuck roast, USDA choice, boneless	lb.	2.74	12/94	82r
Coffee, 100%, ground roast, all sizes	lb.	4.61	12/94	82r
Dairy products (other) purchases	year	161	91	81r
Eggs, Grade A large	dozen	1.12	12/94	82r
Fish and seafood purchases	year	112	91	81r
Food purchases, food eaten at home	year	2599	91	81r
Foods purchased away from home, not prepared by consumer	year	2024	91	81r
Fruits and vegetables purchases	year	444	91	81r
Grapefruit	lb.	0.44	12/94	82r
Grapes, Thompson seedless	lb.	2.24	12/94	82r
Ground chuck, 100% beef	lb.	1.67	12/94	82r
Ice cream, prepackaged, bulk, regular	1/2 gal.	2.93	12/94	82r
Lemons	lb.	1.06	12/94	82r
Lettuce, iceberg	lb.	0.92	12/94	82r
Meats, poultry, fish, and eggs purchases	year	751	91	81r
Milk and cream (fresh) purchases	year	152	91	81r
Orange juice, frozen concentrate 12-oz. can	16 oz.	1.92	12/94	82r
Oranges, Navel	lb.	0.56	12/94	82r
Pork chops, center cut, bone-in	lb.	3.09	12/94	82r
Pork purchases	year	130	91	81r
Potatoes, white	lb.	0.37	12/94	82r
Rib roast, USDA choice, bone-in	lb.	4.98	12/94	82r
Round roast, USDA choice, boneless	lb.	2.93	12/94	82r
Shortening, vegetable oil blends	lb.	1.03	12/94	82r
Spaghetti and macaroni	lb.	0.84	12/94	82r
Steak, round, USDA choice, boneless	lb.	3.48	12/94	82r
Steak, sirloin, USDA choice, bone-in	lb.	3.38	12/94	82r
Steak, sirloin, USDA choice, boneless	lb.	4.81	12/94	82r
Sugar and other sweets, eaten at home, expenditures	year	89	91	81r
Sugar, white, all sizes	lb.	0.46	12/94	82r
Tobacco products and smoking supplies, total expenditures	year	279	91	81r
Tomatoes, field grown	lb.	1.56	12/94	82r
Tuna, chunk, light	lb.	2.09	12/94	82r
Health Care				
Childbirth, Cesarean delivery, hospital charge	birth	6334.00	12/91	69r
Childbirth, Cesarean delivery, physician charge	birth	2234.00	12/91	69r
Childbirth, normal delivery, hospital charge	birth	3225.00	12/91	69r
Childbirth, normal delivery, physician charge	birth	1623.00	12/91	69r
Drugs, expenditures	year	205	91	81r
Health care, total expenditures	year	1396	91	81r
Health insurance expenditures	year	553	91	81r
Insurance premium, family medical care	month	500.40	1/95	41s
Medical services expenditures	year	559	91	81r
Medical supplies expenditures	year	80	91	81r
Household Goods				
Floor coverings, expenditures	year	158	91	81r
Furniture, expenditures	year	341	91	81r
Household equipment, misc. expenditures	year	363	91	81r
Household expenditures, miscellaneous	year	194	91	81r
Household furnishings and equipment, expenditures	year	1158	91	81r
Household operations expenditures	year	378	91	81r
Household textiles, expenditures	year	88	91	81r
Housekeeping supplies, expenditures	year	426	91	81r
Laundry and cleaning supplies, expenditures	year	122	91	81r
Postage and stationery, expenditures	year	134	91	81r

Norwalk, CT - continued

Item	Per	Value	Date	Ref.
Housing				
Add garage/carport		11,614	3/95	74r
Add room(s)		16,816	3/95	74r
Apartment condominium or co-op, median	unit	96700	12/94	62r
Dwellings (owned), expenditures	year	3305	91	81r
Enclose porch/patio/breezeway		2,980	3/95	74r
Finish room in basement/attic		4,330	3/95	74r
Home, existing, single-family, median	unit	161600	12/94	62r
Maintenance, repairs, insurance, and other housing expenditures	year	569	91	81r
Mortgage interest and charges expenditures	year	1852	91	81r
Princ. & int., mortgage, median-price exist. sing.-family home	mo.	765	12/94	62r
Property taxes expenditures	year	884	91	81r
Redesign, restructure more than half of home's interior		2,750	3/95	74r
Rental units expenditures	year	1832	91	81r
Insurance and Pensions				
Auto insurance, private passenger	year	1002.84	12/94	71s
Insurance and pensions, personal, expenditures	year	2690	91	81r
Insurance, life and other personal, expenditures	year	341	91	81r
Pensions and Social Security, expenditures	year	2349	91	81r
Legal Assistance				
Estate planning, law-firm partner	hr.	375.00	10/93	12r
Legal work, law firm associate	hour	78		10r
Legal work, law firm partner	hour	183		10r
Personal Services				
Personal services expenditures	year	184	91	81r
Restaurant Food				
Dining expenditures, family	week	34.26	94	73r
Taxes				
Taxes, Federal income, expenditures	year	2409	91	81r
Taxes, personal, expenditures	year	3094	91	81r
Taxes, State and local income, expenditures	year	620	91	81r
Transportation				
Cars and trucks purchased, new	year	1170	91	81r
Cars and trucks purchased, used	year	739	91	81r
Driver's learning permit fee	perm	3.50	1/94	84s
Driver's license fee	orig	38.00	1/94	84s
Driver's license fee, duplicate	lic	5.00	1/94	84s
Driver's license reinstatement fee, min.	susp	30.00	1/94	85s
Driver's license renewal fee	renew	31.00	1/94	84s
Identification card, nondriver	card	4.00	1/94	83s
Motorcycle learning permit fee	perm	3.50	1/94	84s
Motorcycle license fee	orig	38.00	1/94	84s
Motorcycle license fee, duplicate	lic	5.00	1/94	84s
Motorcycle license renewal fee	renew	31.00	1/94	84s
Public transportation expenditures	year	430	91	81r
Transportation expenditures, total	year	4810	91	81r
Vehicle finance charges	year	238	91	81r
Vehicle insurance expenditures	year	630	91	81r
Vehicle maintenance and repairs expenditures	year	532	91	81r
Vehicle purchases	year	1920	91	81r
Vehicle rental, leases, licenses, etc. expenditures	year	193	91	81r
Vehicles purchased, other than cars and trucks	year	11	91	81r
Utilities				
Electricity expenditures	year	695	91	81r
Utilities, fuels, and public services, total expenditures	year	1981	91	81r
Water and other public services, expenditures	year	154	91	81r
Weddings				
Bridal attendants' gowns	event	750	10/93	76r
Bridal gown	event	852	10/93	76r

Values are in dollars or fractions of dollars. In the column headed *Ref*, references are shown to sources. Each reference is followed by a letter. These refer to the geographical level for which data were reported: s=State, r=Region, and c=City or metro. The abbreviation *ex* is used to mean *except* or *excluding*; *exp* stands for *expenditures*. For other abbreviations and further explanations, please see the Introduction.

Norwalk, CT - continued

Item	Per	Value	Date	Ref.
Weddings				
Bridal headpiece and veil	event	167	10/93	76r
Bride's wedding band	event	708	10/93	76r
Clergy	event	224	10/93	76r
Engagement ring	event	2756	10/93	76r
Flowers	event	863	10/93	76r
Formal wear for groom	event	106	10/93	76r
Groom's attendants' formal wear	event	530	10/93	76r
Groom's wedding band	event	402	10/93	76r
Music	event	600	10/93	76r
Photography	event	1088	10/93	76r
Shoes for bride	event	50	10/93	76r
Videography	event	483	10/93	76r
Wedding invitations and announcements	event	342	10/93	76r
Wedding reception	event	7000	10/93	76r

Oakland, CA

Item	Per	Value	Date	Ref.
Appliances				
Appliances (major), expenditures	year	160	91	81r
Average annual exp.				
Food, health care, personal goods, services	year	32461	91	81r
Charity				
Cash contributions, expenditures	year	975	91	81r
Clothing				
Apparel, men and boys, total expenditures	year	467	91	81r
Apparel, women and girls, total expenditures	year	737	91	81r
Footwear, expenditures	year	270	91	81r
Communications				
Long-distance telephone rate, day, addl. min., 1-10 mi.	min.	0.07	12/93	9s
Long-distance telephone rate, day, initial min., 1-10 mi.	min.	0.17	12/93	9s
Phone line, single, business, field visit	inst	70.75	12/93	9s
Phone line, single, business, no field visit	inst	70.75	12/93	9s
Phone line, single, residence, field visit	inst	34.75	12/93	9s
Phone line, single, residence, no field visit	inst	34.75	12/93	9s
Telephone service, expenditures	year	611	91	81r
Education				
Board, 4-year private college/university	year	2945	8/94	80s
Board, 4-year public college/university	year	2321	8/94	80s
Education, total expenditures	year	375	91	81r
Room, 4-year private college/university	year	3094	8/94	80s
Room, 4-year public college/university	year	2812	8/94	80s
Student fee, university	year	21.00	93	18s
Total cost, 4-year private college/university	year	19321	8/94	80s
Total cost, 4-year public college/university	year	7511	8/94	80s
Tuition, 2-year public college/university, in-state	year	345	8/94	80s
Tuition, 4-year private college/university, in-state	year	13282	8/94	80s
Tuition, 4-year public college/university, in-state	year	2378	8/94	80s
Energy and Fuels				
Fuel oil and other fuels, expenditures	year	33	91	81r
Gas, natural, expenditures	year	212	91	81r
Gasoline and motor oil purchased	year	1115	91	81r
Gasoline, unleaded midgrade	gallon	1.36	4/93	82r
Gasoline, unleaded premium	gallon	1.43	4/93	82r
Gasoline, unleaded regular	gallon	1.23	4/93	82r
Entertainment				
Concert ticket, Pearl Jam group	perf	20.00	94	50r
Entertainment, total expenditures	year	1853	91	81r
Fees and admissions, expenditures	year	482	91	81r
Pets, toys, playground equipment, expenditures	year	299	91	81r
Reading, expenditures	year	164	91	81r

Oakland, CA - continued

Item	Per	Value	Date	Ref.
Entertainment - continued				
Televisions, radios, and sound equipment, expenditures	year	528	91	81r
Funerals				
Burial, immediate, container provided by funeral home		1382.70	1/95	54r
Cards, acknowledgment		21.87	1/95	54r
Casket, minimum alternative		128.54	1/95	54r
Cosmetology, hair care, etc.		119.69	1/95	54r
Cremation, direct, container provided by funeral home		1030.62	1/95	54r
Embalming		255.42	1/95	54r
Funeral, funeral home		437.38	1/95	54r
Funeral, other facility		444.46	1/95	54r
Graveside service		338.46	1/95	54r
Hearse, local		147.50	1/95	54r
Limousine, local		130.33	1/95	54r
Memorial service		553.16	1/95	54r
Service charge, professional, nondeclinable		859.15	1/95	54r
Visitation and viewing		93.23	1/95	54r
Groceries				
Apples, Red Delicious	lb.	0.72	12/94	82r
Bacon, sliced	lb.	1.73	12/94	82r
Bananas	lb.	0.52	12/94	82r
Beef purchases	year	241	91	81r
Beverage purchases, alcoholic	year	328	91	81r
Beverage purchases, nonalcoholic	year	234	91	81r
Bologna, all beef or mixed	lb.	2.33	12/94	82r
Bread, white, pan	lb.	0.81	12/94	82r
Carrots, short trimmed and topped	lb.	0.43	12/94	82r
Cereals and bakery products purchases	year	392	91	81r
Cereals and cereals products purchases	year	139	91	81r
Chicken breast, bone-in	lb.	2.04	12/94	82r
Chicken, fresh, whole	lb.	0.95	12/94	82r
Coffee, 100%, ground roast, all sizes	lb.	4.48	12/94	82r
Dairy products (other) purchases	year	182	91	81r
Fish and seafood purchases	year	94	91	81r
Flour, white, all purpose	lb.	0.21	12/94	82r
Food purchases, food eaten at home	year	2749	91	81r
Foods purchased away from home, not prepared by consumer	year	1909	91	81r
Fruits and vegetables purchases	year	459	91	81r
Grapefruit	lb.	0.56	12/94	82r
Ground beef, 100% beef	lb.	1.31	12/94	82r
Ham, boneless, exc. canned	lb.	2.46	12/94	82r
Ice cream, prepackaged, bulk, regular	1/2 gal.	2.57	12/94	82r
Lemons	lb.	1.00	12/94	82r
Lettuce, iceberg	lb.	0.93	12/94	82r
Meats, poultry, fish, and eggs purchases	year	700	91	81r
Milk and cream (fresh) purchases	year	155	91	81r
Orange juice, frozen concentrate 12-oz. can	16 oz.	1.52	12/94	82r
Oranges, Navel	lb.	0.56	12/94	82r
Pork chops, center cut, bone-in	lb.	3.30	12/94	82r
Pork purchases	year	122	91	81r
Potato chips	16-oz.	3.03	12/94	82r
Potatoes, frozen, French fried	lb.	0.77	12/94	82r
Potatoes, white	lb.	0.35	12/94	82r
Rice, white, long grain, uncooked	lb.	0.54	12/94	82r
Round roast, USDA choice, boneless	lb.	2.92	12/94	82r
Shortening, vegetable oil blends	lb.	0.80	12/94	82r
Spaghetti and macaroni	lb.	1.02	12/94	82r
Steak, round, graded & ungraded, exc. USDA prime & choice	lb.	3.13	12/94	82r
Steak, sirloin, USDA choice, boneless	lb.	4.07	12/94	82r
Sugar and other sweets, eaten at home, expenditures	year	105	91	81r
Sugar, white, all sizes	lb.	0.38	12/94	82r
Tobacco products and smoking supplies, total expenditures	year	221	91	81r
Tomatoes, field grown	lb.	1.45	12/94	82r
Tuna, chunk, light	lb.	2.18	12/94	82r

Values are in dollars or fractions of dollars. In the column headed *Ref*, references are shown to sources. Each reference is followed by a letter. These refer to the geographical level for which data were reported: s=State, r=Region, and c=City or metro. The abbreviation *ex* is used to mean *except* or *excluding*; *exp* stands for expenditures. For other abbreviations and further explanations, please see the Introduction.

Oakland, CA - continued

Item	Per	Value	Date	Ref.
Health Care				
Childbirth, Cesarean delivery, hospital charge	birth	6059.00	12/91	69r
Childbirth, Cesarean delivery, physician charge	birth	2248.00	12/91	69r
Childbirth, normal delivery, hospital charge	birth	3006.00	12/91	69r
Childbirth, normal delivery, physician charge	birth	1634.00	12/91	69r
Drugs, expenditures	year	230	91	81r
Health care, total expenditures	year	1544	91	81r
Health insurance expenditures	year	558	91	81r
Insurance premium, family medical care	month	380.27	1/95	41s
Medical services expenditures	year	676	91	81r
Medical supplies expenditures	year	80	91	81r
Surgery, open-heart	proc	37818.00	1/93	14r
Household Goods				
Floor coverings, expenditures	year	79	91	81r
Furniture, expenditures	year	352	91	81r
Household equipment, misc. expenditures	year	614	91	81r
Household expenditures, miscellaneous	year	294	91	81r
Household furnishings and equipment, expenditures	year	1416	91	81r
Household operations expenditures	year	580	91	81r
Household textiles, expenditures	year	113	91	81r
Housekeeping supplies, expenditures	year	447	91	81r
Laundry and cleaning supplies, expenditures	year	114	91	81r
Postage and stationery, expenditures	year	145	91	81r
Housing				
Add garage/carport		6,422	3/95	74r
Add room(s)		26,583	3/95	74r
Apartment condominium or co-op, median	unit	105300	12/94	62r
Dwellings (owned), expenditures	year	3932	91	81r
Enclose porch/patio/breezeway		5,382	3/95	74r
Finish room in basement/attic		3,911	3/95	74r
Home, existing, single-family, median	unit	178600	12/94	62r
Maintenance, repairs, insurance, and other housing expenditures	year	591	91	81r
Mortgage interest and charges expenditures	year	2747	91	81r
Princ. & int., mortgage, median-price exist. sing.-family home	mo.	845	12/94	62r
Property taxes expenditures	year	594	91	81r
Redesign, restructure more than half of home's interior		5,467	3/95	74r
Rental units expenditures	year	2077	91	81r
Insurance and Pensions				
Auto insurance, private passenger	year	892.80	12/94	71s
Insurance and pensions, personal, expenditures	year	3042	91	81r
Insurance, life and other personal, expenditures	year	298	91	81r
Pensions and Social Security, expenditures	year	2744	91	81r
Legal Assistance				
Legal work, law firm associate	hour	91		10r
Legal work, law firm partner	hour	151		10r
Personal Services				
Personal services expenditures	year	286	91	81r
Restaurant Food				
Dining expenditures, family	week	32.25	94	73r
Taxes				
Taxes, Federal income, expenditures	year	2946	91	81r
Taxes, personal, expenditures	year	3791	91	81r
Taxes, State and local income, expenditures	year	791	91	81r
Transportation				
Cars and trucks purchased, new	year	1231	91	81r
Cars and trucks purchased, used	year	915	91	81r
Driver's learning permit fee	perm	12.00	1/94	84s
Driver's license fee	orig	12.00	1/94	84s
Driver's license fee, duplicate	lic	12.00	1/94	84s
Driver's license reinstatement fee, min.	susp	15.00	1/94	85s

Oakland, CA - continued

Item	Per	Value	Date	Ref.
Transportation - continued				
Driver's license renewal fee	renew	12.00	1/94	84s
Identification card, nondriver	card	6.00	1/94	83s
Motorcycle learning permit fee	perm	12.00	1/94	84s
Motorcycle license fee	orig	12.00	1/94	84s
Motorcycle license fee, duplicate	lic	12.00	1/94	84s
Motorcycle license renewal fee	renew	12.00	1/94	84s
Public transportation expenditures	year	375	91	81r
Transportation expenditures, total	year	5527	91	81r
Vehicle finance charges	year	287	91	81r
Vehicle insurance expenditures	year	624	91	81r
Vehicle maintenance and repairs expenditures	year	695	91	81r
Vehicle purchases	year	2174	91	81r
Vehicle rental, leases, licenses, etc. expenditures	year	257	91	81r
Vehicles purchased, other than cars and trucks	year	28	91	81r
Utilities				
Electricity expenditures	year	616	91	81r
Utilities, fuels, and public services, total expenditures	year	1681	91	81r
Water and other public services, expenditures	year	209	91	81r
Weddings				
Bridal attendants' gowns	event	750	10/93	76r
Bridal gown	event	852	10/93	76r
Bridal headpiece and veil	event	167	10/93	76r
Bride's wedding band	event	708	10/93	76r
Clergy	event	224	10/93	76r
Engagement ring	event	2756	10/93	76r
Flowers	event	863	10/93	76r
Formal wear for groom	event	106	10/93	76r
Groom's attendants' formal wear	event	530	10/93	76r
Groom's wedding band	event	402	10/93	76r
Music	event	600	10/93	76r
Photography	event	1088	10/93	76r
Shoes for bride	event	50	10/93	76r
Videography	event	483	10/93	76r
Wedding invitations and announcements	event	342	10/93	76r
Wedding reception	event	7000	10/93	76r

Ocala, FL

Item	Per	Value	Date	Ref.
Composite, ACCRA index		95.40	12/94	2c
Alcoholic Beverages				
Beer, Miller Lite, Bud, 12-oz., ex deposit	6	3.70	12/94	2c
J & B Scotch	750-ml.	17.19	12/94	2c
Wine, Gallo Chablis blanc	1.5-lit	4.87	12/94	2c
Appliances				
Appliances (major), expenditures	year	153	91	81r
Average annual exp.				
Food, health care, personal goods, services	year	27020	91	81r
Charity				
Cash contributions, expenditures	year	839	91	81r
Clothing				
Apparel, men and boys, total expenditures	year	380	91	81r
Apparel, women and girls, total expenditures	year	660	91	81r
Footwear, expenditures	year	193	91	81r
Jeans, man's denim		30.19	12/94	2c
Shirt, man's dress shirt		33.70	12/94	2c
Undervest, boy's size 10-14, cotton	3	5.27	12/94	2c
Communications				
Long-distance telephone rate, day, addl. min., 1-10 mi.	min.	0.08	12/93	9s
Long-distance telephone rate, day, initial min., 1-10 mi.	min.	0.15	12/93	9s

Values are in dollars or fractions of dollars. In the column headed *Ref*, references are shown to sources. Each reference is followed by a letter. These refer to the geographical level for which data were reported: s = State, r = Region, and c = City or metro. The abbreviation *ex* is used to mean *except* or *excluding*; *exp* stands for expenditures. For other abbreviations and further explanations, please see the Introduction.

Ocala, FL - continued

Item	Per	Value	Date	Ref.
Communications				
Newspaper subscription, dly. and Sun. delivery	month	13.00	12/94	2c
Phone line, single, business, field visit	inst	86.00	12/93	9s
Phone line, single, business, no field visit	inst	54.50	12/93	9s
Phone line, single, residence, field visit	inst	76.00	12/93	9s
Phone line, single, residence, no field visit	inst	44.50	12/93	9s
Telephone bill, family of four	month	14.75	12/94	2c
Telephone service, expenditures	year	616	91	81r
Education				
Bar examinination preparatory course	course	500.00-100	94	17s
Board, 4-year private college/university	year	2123	8/94	80s
Board, 4-year public college/university	year	2101	8/94	80s
Education, total expenditures	year	319	91	81r
Room, 4-year private college/university	year	2242	8/94	80s
Room, 4-year public college/university	year	1970	8/94	80s
Total cost, 4-year private college/university	year	13853	8/94	80s
Total cost, 4-year public college/university	year	5855	8/94	80s
Tuition, 2-year public college/university, in-state	year	1076	8/94	80s
Tuition, 4-year private college/university, in-state	year	9287	8/94	80s
Tuition, 4-year public college/university, in-state	year	1784	8/94	80s
Energy and Fuels				
Energy, combined forms, 1800 sq. ft.	mo.	121.08	12/94	2c
Fuel oil and other fuels, expenditures	year	56	91	81r
Gas, natural, expenditures	year	150	91	81r
Gas, reg unlead, taxes inc., cash, self-service	gal	1.12	12/94	2c
Gasoline and motor oil purchased	year	1152	91	81r
Gasoline, unleaded midgrade	gallon	1.21	4/93	82r
Gasoline, unleaded premium	gallon	1.30	4/93	82r
Gasoline, unleaded regular	gallon	1.10	4/93	82r
Entertainment				
Bowling, evening rate	game	2.38	12/94	2c
Concert ticket, Pearl Jam group	perf	20.00	94	50r
Entertainment, total expenditures	year	1266	91	81r
Fees and admissions, expenditures	year	306	91	81r
Monopoly game, Parker Brothers', No. 9	game	12.78	12/94	2c
Movie	adm	5.75	12/94	2c
Pets, toys, playground equipment, expenditures	year	271	91	81r
Reading, expenditures	year	131	91	81r
Televisions, radios, and sound equipment, expenditures	year	439	91	81r
Tennis balls, yellow, Wilson or Penn, 3	can	2.22	12/94	2c
Funerals				
Burial, immediate, container provided by funeral home		1370.36	1/95	54r
Cards, acknowledgment		14.83	1/95	54r
Casket, minimum alternative		192.52	1/95	54r
Cosmetology, hair care, etc.		102.27	1/95	54r
Cremation, direct, container provided by funeral home		1065.64	1/95	54r
Embalming		304.29	1/95	54r
Funeral, funeral home		287.83	1/95	54r
Funeral, other facility		284.14	1/95	54r
Graveside service		349.13	1/95	54r
Hearse, local		132.27	1/95	54r
Limousine, local		98.45	1/95	54r
Memorial service		270.59	1/95	54r
Service charge, professional, nondeclinable		933.59	1/95	54r
Visitation and viewing		225.83	1/95	54r
Groceries				
Groceries, ACCRA Index		96.60	12/94	2c
Apples, Red Delicious	lb.	0.73	12/94	82r
Baby food, strained vegetables, lowest price	4-4.5 oz.	0.36	12/94	2c

Ocala, FL - continued

Item	Per	Value	Date	Ref.
Groceries - continued				
Bacon, sliced	lb.	1.67	12/94	82r
Bananas	lb.	0.34	12/94	2c
Bananas	lb.	0.42	12/94	82r
Beef or hamburger, ground	lb.	1.21	12/94	2c
Beef purchases	year	213	91	81r
Beverage purchases, alcoholic	year	249	91	81r
Beverage purchases, nonalcoholic	year	207	91	81r
Bologna, all beef or mixed	lb.	2.27	12/94	82r
Bread, white	24-oz.	0.79	12/94	2c
Bread, white, pan	lb.	0.68	12/94	82r
Cabbage	lb.	0.42	12/94	82r
Carrots, short trimmed and topped	lb.	0.53	12/94	82r
Cereals and bakery products purchases	year	345	91	81r
Cereals and cereals products purchases	year	127	91	81r
Cheddar cheese, natural	lb.	3.58	12/94	82r
Cheese, Kraft grated Parmesan	8-oz.	3.15	12/94	2c
Chicken breast, bone-in	lb.	1.71	12/94	82r
Chicken, fresh, whole	lb.	0.78	12/94	82r
Chicken, whole fryer	lb.	0.83	12/94	2c
Chuck roast, USDA choice, boneless	lb.	2.26	12/94	82r
Cigarettes, Winston, Kings	carton	16.38	12/94	2c
Coffee, vacuum-packed	13 oz.	3.17	12/94	2c
Corn Flakes, Kellogg's or Post Toasties	18 oz.	2.16	12/94	2c
Corn, frozen, whole kernel, lowest price	10 oz.	0.61	12/94	2c
Crackers, soda, salted	lb.	1.27	12/94	82r
Cucumbers	lb.	0.65	12/94	82r
Dairy products (other) purchases	year	141	91	81r
Eggs, Grade A large	dozen	0.74	12/94	2c
Eggs, Grade A large	dozen	0.87	12/94	82r
Fish and seafood purchases	year	72	91	81r
Flour, white, all purpose	lb.	0.23	12/94	82r
Food purchases, food eaten at home	year	2381	91	81r
Foods purchased away from home, not prepared by consumer	year	1696	91	81r
Frankfurters, all meat or all beef	lb.	1.74	12/94	82r
Fruits and vegetables purchases	year	380	91	81r
Grapefruit	lb.	0.45	12/94	82r
Grapes, Thompson seedless	lb.	2.30	12/94	82r
Ground beef, 100% beef	lb.	1.37	12/94	82r
Ground chuck, 100% beef	lb.	1.97	12/94	82r
Ham, boneless, exc. canned	lb.	2.54	12/94	82r
Ice cream, prepackaged, bulk, regular	1/2 gal.	2.47	12/94	82r
Lemons	lb.	1.02	12/94	82r
Lettuce, iceberg	lb.	0.96	12/94	82r
Lettuce, iceberg	head	0.95	12/94	2c
Margarine, Blue Bonnet or Parkay cubes	lb.	0.57	12/94	2c
Margarine, stick	lb.	0.77	12/94	82r
Meats, poultry, fish, and eggs purchases	year	655	91	81r
Milk and cream (fresh) purchases	year	130	91	81r
Milk, whole	1/2 gal.	1.39	12/94	2c
Orange juice, frozen concentrate 12-oz. can	16 oz.	1.36	12/94	82r
Orange juice, Minute Maid frozen	12-oz.	1.10	12/94	2c
Oranges, Navel	lb.	0.54	12/94	82r
Peaches, halves or slices, Hunt's, Del Monte, or Libby's	29-oz.	1.33	12/94	2c
Pears, Anjou	lb.	0.81	12/94	82r
Peas, sweet, Del Monte or Green Giant	15-17 oz.	0.50	12/94	2c
Pork chops, center cut, bone-in	lb.	3.07	12/94	82r
Pork purchases	year	142	91	81r
Potato chips	16-oz.	3.15	12/94	82r
Potatoes, frozen, French fried	lb.	0.82	12/94	82r
Potatoes, white	lb.	0.34	12/94	82r
Potatoes, white or red	10-lb. sack	3.29	12/94	2c
Rice, white, long grain, uncooked	lb.	0.48	12/94	82r
Round roast, USDA choice, boneless	lb.	2.91	12/94	82r
Sausage, fresh	lb.	1.82	12/94	82r
Sausage, Jimmy Dean, 100% pork	lb.	2.43	12/94	2c
Shortening, vegetable oil blends	lb.	0.75	12/94	82r

Values are in dollars or fractions of dollars. In the column headed *Ref*, references are shown to sources. Each reference is followed by a letter. These refer to the geographical level for which data were reported: s=State, r=Region, and c=City or metro. The abbreviation *ex* is used to mean *except* or *excluding*; *exp* stands for expenditures. For other abbreviations and further explanations, please see the Introduction.

Ocala, FL - continued

Item	Per	Value	Date	Ref.
Groceries				
Shortening, vegetable, Crisco	3-lb.	2.33	12/94	2c
Soft drink, Coca Cola, ex deposit	2 lit	1.12	12/94	2c
Spaghetti and macaroni	lb.	0.87	12/94	82r
Steak, rib eye, USDA choice, boneless	lb.	6.85	12/94	82r
Steak, round, graded & ungraded, exc. USDA prime & choice	lb.	2.96	12/94	82r
Steak, round, USDA choice, boneless	lb.	3.17	12/94	82r
Steak, sirloin, USDA choice, boneless	lb.	4.12	12/94	82r
Steak, t-bone	lb.	5.54	12/94	2c
Steak, T-bone, USDA choice, bone-in	lb.	5.63	12/94	82r
Sugar and other sweets, eaten at home, expenditures	year	93	91	81r
Sugar, cane or beet	4 lbs.	1.41	12/94	2c
Sugar, white, all sizes	lb.	0.39	12/94	82r
Tobacco products and smoking supplies, total expenditures	year	286	91	81r
Tomatoes, field grown	lb.	1.36	12/94	82r
Tomatoes, Hunt's or Del Monte	14.5 oz.	0.71	12/94	2c
Tuna, chunk, light	lb.	1.94	12/94	82r
Tuna, chunk, light, oil-packed	6.125-6.5 oz.	0.65	12/94	2c
Turkey, frozen, whole	lb.	0.96	12/94	82r
Yogurt, natural, fruit flavored	8 oz.	0.58	12/94	82r
Goods and Services				
Miscellaneous goods and services, ACCRA Index		102.50	12/94	2c
Health Care				
Health care, ACCRA Index		90.20	12/94	2c
Adenosine, emergency room	treat	100.00	95	23r
Antibiotic ointment, Polysporin	1.5 oz.	3.82	12/94	2c
Bladder tap, superpubic, infant, emergency room	treat	119.00	95	23r
Blood analysis, emergency room	treat	25.00	95	23r
Blood tests, abdominal pain, emergency room	treat	25.00	95	23r
Burn dressing, emergency room	treat	266.00	95	23r
Cardiology interpretation, emergency room	treat	26.00	95	23r
Chest X-ray, emergency room	treat	78.00	95	23r
Childbirth, Cesarean delivery, hospital charge	birth	5462.00	12/91	69r
Childbirth, Cesarean delivery, physician charge	birth	2228.00	12/91	69r
Childbirth, normal delivery, hospital charge	birth	2943.00	12/91	69r
Childbirth, normal delivery, physician charge	birth	1619.00	12/91	69r
Defibrillation pads, emergency room	treat	6.00	95	23r
Dentist's fee, adult teeth cleaning and periodic oral exam	visit	40.60	12/94	2c
Doctor's fee, routine exam, established patient	visit	43.00	12/94	2c
Drugs, expenditures	year	297	91	81r
Gastric tube insertion, nasal, emergency room	treat	25.00	95	23r
Health care, total expenditures	year	1600	91	81r
Health insurance expenditures	year	637	91	81r
Heart monitor, emergency room	treat	40.00	95	23r
Hospital care, semiprivate room	day	316.50	12/94	2c
Insurance premium, family medical care	month	301.92	1/95	41s
Intravenous fluids, emergency room	treat	130.00	95	23r
Intravenous fluids, emergency room	liter	26.00	95	23r
Intravenous line, central, emergency room	treat	342.00	95	23r
Liver function tests, abdominal pain, emergency room	treat	26.00	95	23r
Medical care charges, total, emergency room, third-degree burns	treat	2101.00	95	23r
Medical care charges, total, emergency, infant with fever	treat	628.00	95	23r
Medical services expenditures	year	573	91	81r
Medical supplies expenditures	year	93	91	81r
Morphine, emergency room	treat	34.00	95	23r

Item	Per	Value	Date	Ref.
Health Care - continued				
Nursing care and facilities charges, emergency room	treat	252.00	95	23r
Nursing care and facilities charges, emergency, infant with fever	treat	252.00	95	23r
Nursing care and facilities charges, emergency, third-degree burns	treat	861.00	95	23r
Physician's charges, emergency, infant with fever	treat	212.00	95	23r
Physician's charges, emergency, third-degree burns	treat	372.00	95	23r
Physician's fee, emergency room	treat	372.00	95	23r
Physician's fee, general practitioner	visit	51.20	12/93	60r
Surgery, open-heart	proc	42374.00	1/93	14r
Ultrasound, abdominal, emergency room	treat	276.00	95	23r
Urinalysis, emergency room	treat	20.00	95	23r
Urinalysis, infant, emergency room	treat	20.00	95	23r
X-rays, emergency room	treat	78.00	95	23r
Household Goods				
Appl. repair, service call, wash mach	min. lab. chg.	31.78	12/94	2c
Floor coverings, expenditures	year	48	91	81r
Furniture, expenditures	year	280	91	81r
Household equipment, misc. expenditures	year	342	91	81r
Household expenditures, miscellaneous	year	256	91	81r
Household furnishings and equipment, expenditures	year	988	91	81r
Household operations expenditures	year	468	91	81r
Household textiles, expenditures	year	95	91	81r
Housekeeping supplies, expenditures	year	380	91	81r
Laundry and cleaning supplies, expenditures	year	109	91	81r
Laundry detergent, Tide Ultra, Bold, or Cheer	42 oz.	2.64	12/94	2c
Postage and stationery, expenditures	year	105	91	81r
Tissues, facial, Kleenex brand	175	0.97	12/94	2c
Housing				
Housing, ACCRA Index		84.60	12/94	2c
Add garage/carport		6,980	3/95	74r
Add room(s)		11,403	3/95	74r
Apartment condominium or co-op, median	unit	68600	12/94	62r
Dwellings (owned), expenditures	year	2428	91	81r
Enclose porch/patio/breezeway		4,572	3/95	74r
Finish room in basement/attic		3,794	3/95	74r
Home, existing, single-family, median	unit	120200	12/94	62r
Home, existing, single-family, median	unit	59.60	12/94	62c
House payment, principal and interest, 25% down payment	mo.	650	12/94	2c
House, 1800 sq ft, 8000 sq ft lot, new, urban, utilities	total	103925	12/94	2c
Maintenance, repairs, insurance, and other housing expenditures	year	531	91	81r
Mortgage interest and charges expenditures	year	1506	91	81r
Mtge. rate, incl. points and orig. fee, 30-year conv. fixed or ARM	mo.	9.41	12/94	2c
Princ. & int., mortgage, median-price exist. sing.-family home	mo.	540	12/94	62r
Property taxes expenditures	year	391	91	81r
Redesign, restructure more than half of home's interior		17,641	3/95	74r
Rent, apartment, 2 br., 1 1/2-2 baths, unfurnished, 950 sq ft, water	mo.	440	12/94	2c
Rental units expenditures	year	1264	91	81r
Insurance and Pensions				
Auto insurance, private passenger	year	753.93	12/94	71s
Insurance and pensions, personal, expenditures	year	2395	91	81r
Insurance, life and other personal, expenditures	year	368	91	81r
Pensions and Social Security, expenditures	year	2027	91	81r

Values are in dollars or fractions of dollars. In the column headed *Ref*, references are shown to sources. Each reference is followed by a letter. These refer to the geographical level for which data were reported: s = State, r = Region, and c = City or metro. The abbreviation *ex* is used to mean *except* or *excluding*; *exp* stands for *expenditures*. For other abbreviations and further explanations, please see the Introduction.

Ocala, FL - continued

Item	Per	Value	Date	Ref.
Personal Goods				
Shampoo, Alberto VO5	15-oz.	1.03	12/94	2c
Toothpaste, Crest or Colgate	6-7 oz.	1.65	12/94	2c
Personal Services				
Dry cleaning, man's 2-pc. suit		5.94	12/94	2c
Haircut, man's barbershop, no styling		5.10	12/94	2c
Haircut, woman's shampoo, trim, blow-dry		16.99	12/94	2c
Personal services expenditures	year	212	91	81r
Restaurant Food				
Chicken, fried, thigh and drumstick		2.26	12/94	2c
Dining expenditures, family	week	33.83	94	73r
Hamburger with cheese	1/4 lb.	2.05	12/94	2c
Pizza, Pizza Hut or Pizza Inn	12-13 in.	7.99	12/94	2c
Taxes				
Taxes, Federal income, expenditures	year	2275	91	81r
Taxes, personal, expenditures	year	2715	91	81r
Taxes, State and local income, expenditures	year	365	91	81r
Transportation				
Transportation, ACCRA Index		97.10	12/94	2c
Cars and trucks purchased, new	year	1306	91	81r
Cars and trucks purchased, used	year	942	91	81r
Driver's learning permit fee	perm	20.00	1/94	84s
Driver's license fee	orig	20.00	1/94	84s
Driver's license fee, duplicate	lic	10.00	1/94	84s
Driver's license reinstatement fee, min.	susp	25.00	1/94	85s
Driver's license renewal fee	renew	15.00	1/94	84s
Identification card, nondriver	card	3.00	1/94	83s
Motorcycle learning permit fee	perm	20.00	1/94	84s
Motorcycle license fee	orig	20.00	1/94	84s
Motorcycle license fee, duplicate	lic	10.00	1/94	84s
Motorcycle license renewal fee	renew	15.00	1/94	84s
Public transportation expenditures	year	249	91	81r
Tire balance, computer or spin bal., front	wheel	6.30	12/94	2c
Transportation expenditures, total	year	5307	91	81r
Vehicle finance charges	year	346	91	81r
Vehicle insurance expenditures	year	544	91	81r
Vehicle maintenance and repairs expenditures	year	600	91	81r
Vehicle purchases	year	2275	91	81r
Vehicle rental, leases, licenses, etc. expenditures	year	141	91	81r
Vehicles purchased, other than cars and trucks	year	27	91	81r
Utilities				
Utilities, ACCRA Index		103.50	12/94	2c
Electricity expenditures	year	950	91	81r
Electricity, 1800 sq. ft., new home	mo.	121.08	12/94	2c
Utilities, fuels, and public services, total expenditures	year	2000	91	81r
Water and other public services, expenditures	year	227	91	81r
Weddings				
Bridal attendants' gowns	event	750	10/93	76r
Bridal gown	event	852	10/93	76r
Bridal headpiece and veil	event	167	10/93	76r
Bride's wedding band	event	708	10/93	76r
Clergy	event	224	10/93	76r
Engagement ring	event	2756	10/93	76r
Flowers	event	863	10/93	76r
Formal wear for groom	event	106	10/93	76r
Groom's attendants' formal wear	event	530	10/93	76r
Groom's wedding band	event	402	10/93	76r
Music	event	600	10/93	76r
Photography	event	1088	10/93	76r
Shoes for bride	event	50	10/93	76r
Videography	event	483	10/93	76r
Wedding invitations and announcements	event	342	10/93	76r
Wedding reception	event	7000	10/93	76r

Odessa, TX

Item	Per	Value	Date	Ref.
Composite, ACCRA index		95.90	12/94	2c
Alcoholic Beverages				
Beer, Miller Lite, Bud, 12-oz., ex deposit	6	3.95	12/94	2c
J & B Scotch	750-ml.	18.59	12/94	2c
Wine, Gallo Chablis blanc	1.5-lit	4.80	12/94	2c
Appliances				
Appliances (major), expenditures	year	153	91	81r
Average annual exp.				
Food, health care, personal goods, services	year	27020	91	81r
Charity				
Cash contributions, expenditures	year	839	91	81r
Clothing				
Apparel, men and boys, total expenditures	year	380	91	81r
Apparel, women and girls, total expenditures	year	660	91	81r
Footwear, expenditures	year	193	91	81r
Jeans, man's denim		27.79	12/94	2c
Shirt, man's dress shirt		29.00	12/94	2c
Undervest, boy's size 10-14, cotton	3	5.11	12/94	2c
Communications				
Long-distance telephone rate, day, addl. min., 1-10 mi.	min.	0.08	12/93	9s
Long-distance telephone rate, day, initial min., 1-10 mi.	min.	0.10	12/93	9s
Newspaper subscription, dly. and Sun. delivery	month	9.48	12/94	2c
Phone line, single, business, field visit	inst	71.90	12/93	9s
Phone line, single, business, no field visit	inst	57.30	12/93	9s
Phone line, single, residence, field visit	inst	52.95	12/93	9s
Phone line, single, residence, no field visit	inst	38.35	12/93	9s
Telephone bill, family of four	month	15.31	12/94	2c
Telephone service, expenditures	year	616	91	81r
Telephone, residential, flat rate	mo.	8.80	12/93	8c
Education				
Board, 4-year private college/university	year	2084	8/94	80s
Board, 4-year public college/university	year	1675	8/94	80s
Education, total expenditures	year	319	91	81r
Room, 4-year private college/university	year	1840	8/94	80s
Room, 4-year public college/university	year	1756	8/94	80s
Total cost, 4-year private college/university	year	11876	8/94	80s
Total cost, 4-year public college/university	year	4935	8/94	80s
Tuition, 2-year public college/university, in-state	year	625	8/94	80s
Tuition, 4-year private college/university, in-state	year	7952	8/94	80s
Tuition, 4-year public college/university, in-state	year	1503	8/94	80s
Energy and Fuels				
Energy, combined forms, 1800 sq. ft.	mo.	148.22	12/94	2c
Energy, exc. electricity, 1800 sq. ft.	mo.	39.24	12/94	2c
Fuel oil and other fuels, expenditures	year	56	91	81r
Gas, natural, expenditures	year	150	91	81r
Gas, reg unlead, taxes inc., cash, self-service	gal	1.21	12/94	2c
Gasoline and motor oil purchased	year	1152	91	81r
Gasoline, unleaded midgrade	gallon	1.21	4/93	82r
Gasoline, unleaded premium	gallon	1.30	4/93	82r
Gasoline, unleaded regular	gallon	1.10	4/93	82r
Entertainment				
Bowling, evening rate	game	1.60	12/94	2c
Concert ticket, Pearl Jam group	perf	20.00	94	50r
Entertainment, total expenditures	year	1266	91	81r
Fees and admissions, expenditures	year	306	91	81r
Monopoly game, Parker Brothers', No. 9	game	11.86	12/94	2c
Movie	adm	5.50	12/94	2c
Pets, toys, playground equipment, expenditures	year	271	91	81r
Reading, expenditures	year	131	91	81r

Values are in dollars or fractions of dollars. In the column headed *Ref*, references are shown to sources. Each reference is followed by a letter. These refer to the geographical level for which data were reported: s=State, r=Region, and c=City or metro. The abbreviation *ex* is used to mean *except* or *excluding*; *exp* stands for expenditures. For other abbreviations and further explanations, please see the Introduction.

Odessa, TX - continued

Item	Per	Value	Date	Ref.
Entertainment				
Televisions, radios, and sound equipment, expenditures	year	439	91	81r
Tennis balls, yellow, Wilson or Penn, 3	can	2.61	12/94	2c
Funerals				
Burial, immediate, container provided by funeral home		1574.60	1/95	54r
Cards, acknowledgment		22.24	1/95	54r
Casket, minimum alternative		239.41	1/95	54r
Cosmetology, hair care, etc.		91.04	1/95	54r
Cremation, direct, container provided by funeral home		1085.15	1/95	54r
Embalming		281.30	1/95	54r
Funeral, funeral home		323.04	1/95	54r
Funeral, other facility		327.58	1/95	54r
Graveside service		355.19	1/95	54r
Hearse, local		141.89	1/95	54r
Limousine, local		99.40	1/95	54r
Memorial service		284.67	1/95	54r
Service charge, professional, nondeclinable		904.06	1/95	54r
Visitation and viewing		187.04	1/95	54r
Groceries				
Groceries, ACCRA Index		95.30	12/94	2c
Apples, Red Delicious	lb.	0.73	12/94	82r
Baby food, strained vegetables, lowest price	4-4.5 oz.	0.24	12/94	2c
Bacon, sliced	lb.	1.67	12/94	82r
Bananas	lb.	0.41	12/94	2c
Bananas	lb.	0.42	12/94	82r
Beef or hamburger, ground	lb.	1.29	12/94	2c
Beef purchases	year	213	91	81r
Beverage purchases, alcoholic	year	249	91	81r
Beverage purchases, nonalcoholic	year	207	91	81r
Bologna, all beef or mixed	lb.	2.27	12/94	82r
Bread, white	24-oz.	0.73	12/94	2c
Bread, white, pan	lb.	0.68	12/94	82r
Cabbage	lb.	0.42	12/94	82r
Carrots, short trimmed and topped	lb.	0.53	12/94	82r
Cereals and bakery products purchases	year	345	91	81r
Cereals and cereals products purchases	year	127	91	81r
Cheddar cheese, natural	lb.	3.58	12/94	82r
Cheese, Kraft grated Parmesan	8-oz.	3.43	12/94	2c
Chicken breast, bone-in	lb.	1.71	12/94	82r
Chicken, fresh, whole	lb.	0.78	12/94	82r
Chicken, whole fryer	lb.	0.57	12/94	2c
Chuck roast, USDA choice, boneless	lb.	2.26	12/94	82r
Cigarettes, Winston, Kings	carton	15.79	12/94	2c
Coffee, vacuum-packed	13 oz.	3.60	12/94	2c
Corn Flakes, Kellogg's or Post Toasties	18 oz.	2.28	12/94	2c
Corn, frozen, whole kernel, lowest price	10 oz.	0.75	12/94	2c
Crackers, soda, salted	lb.	1.27	12/94	82r
Cucumbers	lb.	0.65	12/94	82r
Dairy products (other) purchases	year	141	91	81r
Eggs, Grade A large	dozen	0.81	12/94	2c
Eggs, Grade A large	dozen	0.87	12/94	82r
Fish and seafood purchases	year	72	91	81r
Flour, white, all purpose	lb.	0.23	12/94	82r
Food purchases, food eaten at home	year	2381	91	81r
Foods purchased away from home, not prepared by consumer	year	1696	91	81r
Frankfurters, all meat or all beef	lb.	1.74	12/94	82r
Fruits and vegetables purchases	year	380	91	81r
Grapefruit	lb.	0.45	12/94	82r
Grapes, Thompson seedless	lb.	2.30	12/94	82r
Ground beef, 100% beef	lb.	1.37	12/94	82r
Ground chuck, 100% beef	lb.	1.97	12/94	82r
Ham, boneless, exc. canned	lb.	2.54	12/94	82r
Ice cream, prepackaged, bulk, regular	1/2 gal.	2.47	12/94	82r
Lemons	lb.	1.02	12/94	82r
Lettuce, iceberg	lb.	0.96	12/94	82r
Lettuce, iceberg	head	0.83	12/94	2c

Odessa, TX - continued

Item	Per	Value	Date	Ref.
Groceries - continued				
Margarine, Blue Bonnet or Parkay cubes	lb.	0.68	12/94	2c
Margarine, stick	lb.	0.77	12/94	82r
Meats, poultry, fish, and eggs purchases	year	655	91	81r
Milk and cream (fresh) purchases	year	130	91	81r
Milk, whole	1/2 gal.	1.40	12/94	2c
Orange juice, frozen concentrate 12-oz. can	16 oz.	1.36	12/94	82r
Orange juice, Minute Maid frozen	12-oz.	1.08	12/94	2c
Oranges, Navel	lb.	0.54	12/94	82r
Peaches, halves or slices, Hunt's, Del Monte, or Libby's	29-oz.	1.47	12/94	2c
Pears, Anjou	lb.	0.81	12/94	82r
Peas, sweet, Del Monte or Green Giant	15-17 oz.	0.55	12/94	2c
Pork chops, center cut, bone-in	lb.	3.07	12/94	82r
Pork purchases	year	142	91	81r
Potato chips	16-oz.	3.15	12/94	82r
Potatoes, frozen, French fried	lb.	0.82	12/94	82r
Potatoes, white	lb.	0.34	12/94	82r
Potatoes, white or red	10-lb. sack	2.01	12/94	2c
Rice, white, long grain, uncooked	lb.	0.48	12/94	82r
Round roast, USDA choice, boneless	lb.	2.91	12/94	82r
Sausage, fresh	lb.	1.82	12/94	82r
Sausage, Jimmy Dean, 100% pork	lb.	2.38	12/94	2c
Shortening, vegetable oil blends	lb.	0.75	12/94	82r
Shortening, vegetable, Crisco	3-lb.	2.32	12/94	2c
Soft drink, Coca Cola, ex deposit	2 lit	1.51	12/94	2c
Spaghetti and macaroni	lb.	0.87	12/94	82r
Steak, rib eye, USDA choice, boneless	lb.	6.85	12/94	82r
Steak, round, graded & ungraded, exc. USDA prime & choice	lb.	2.96	12/94	82r
Steak, round, USDA choice, boneless	lb.	3.17	12/94	82r
Steak, sirloin, USDA choice, boneless	lb.	4.12	12/94	82r
Steak, t-bone	lb.	4.75	12/94	2c
Steak, T-bone, USDA choice, bone-in	lb.	5.63	12/94	82r
Sugar and other sweets, eaten at home, expenditures	year	93	91	81r
Sugar, cane or beet	4 lbs.	1.39	12/94	2c
Sugar, white, all sizes	lb.	0.39	12/94	82r
Tobacco products and smoking supplies, total expenditures	year	286	91	81r
Tomatoes, field grown	lb.	1.36	12/94	82r
Tomatoes, Hunt's or Del Monte	14.5 oz.	0.75	12/94	2c
Tuna, chunk, light	lb.	1.94	12/94	82r
Tuna, chunk, light, oil-packed	6.125-6.5 oz.	0.70	12/94	2c
Turkey, frozen, whole	lb.	0.96	12/94	82r
Yogurt, natural, fruit flavored	8 oz.	0.58	12/94	82r
Goods and Services				
Miscellaneous goods and services, ACCRA Index		98.70	12/94	2c
Health Care				
Health care, ACCRA Index		101.70	12/94	2c
Adenosine, emergency room	treat	100.00	95	23r
Antibiotic ointment, Polysporin	1.5 oz.	3.99	12/94	2c
Bladder tap, superpubic, infant, emergency room	treat	119.00	95	23r
Blood analysis, emergency room	treat	25.00	95	23r
Blood tests, abdominal pain, emergency room	treat	25.00	95	23r
Burn dressing, emergency room	treat	266.00	95	23r
Cardiology interpretation, emergency room	treat	26.00	95	23r
Chest X-ray, emergency room	treat	78.00	95	23r
Childbirth, Cesarean delivery, hospital charge	birth	5462.00	12/91	69r
Childbirth, Cesarean delivery, physician charge	birth	2228.00	12/91	69r
Childbirth, normal delivery, hospital charge	birth	2943.00	12/91	69r
Childbirth, normal delivery, physician charge	birth	1619.00	12/91	69r

Values are in dollars or fractions of dollars. In the column headed *Ref*, references are shown to sources. Each reference is followed by a letter. These refer to the geographical level for which data were reported: s=State, r=Region, and c=City or metro. The abbreviation *ex* is used to mean *except* or *excluding*; *exp* stands for *expenditures*. For other abbreviations and further explanations, please see the Introduction.

Odessa, TX - continued

Item	Per	Value	Date	Ref.
Health Care				
Defibrillation pads, emergency room	treat	6.00	95	23r
Dentist's fee, adult teeth cleaning and periodic oral exam	visit	52.40	12/94	2c
Doctor's fee, routine exam, established patient	visit	51.00	12/94	2c
Drugs, expenditures	year	297	91	81r
Gastric tube insertion, nasal, emergency room	treat	25.00	95	23r
Health care, total expenditures	year	1600	91	81r
Health insurance expenditures	year	637	91	81r
Heart monitor, emergency room	treat	40.00	95	23r
Hospital care, semiprivate room	day	245.00	12/94	2c
Insurance premium, family medical care	month	389.25	1/95	41s
Intravenous fluids, emergency room	treat	130.00	95	23r
Intravenous fluids, emergency room	liter	26.00	95	23r
Intravenous line, central, emergency room	treat	342.00	95	23r
Liver function tests, abdominal pain, emergency room	treat	26.00	95	23r
Medical care charges, total, emergency room, third-degree burns	treat	2101.00	95	23r
Medical care charges, total, emergency, infant with fever	treat	628.00	95	23r
Medical services expenditures	year	573	91	81r
Medical supplies expenditures	year	93	91	81r
Morphine, emergency room	treat	34.00	95	23r
Nursing care and facilities charges, emergency room	treat	252.00	95	23r
Nursing care and facilities charges, emergency, infant with fever	treat	252.00	95	23r
Nursing care and facilities charges, emergency, third-degree burns	treat	861.00	95	23r
Physician's charges, emergency, infant with fever	treat	212.00	95	23r
Physician's charges, emergency, third-degree burns	treat	372.00	95	23r
Physician's fee, emergency room	treat	372.00	95	23r
Physician's fee, general practitioner	visit	51.20	12/93	60r
Surgery, open-heart	proc	42374.00	1/93	14r
Ultrasound, abdominal, emergency room	treat	276.00	95	23r
Urinalysis, emergency room	treat	20.00	95	23r
Urinalysis, infant, emergency room	treat	20.00	95	23r
X-rays, emergency room	treat	78.00	95	23r
Household Goods				
Appl. repair, service call, wash mach	min. lab. chg.	33.99	12/94	2c
Floor coverings, expenditures	year	48	91	81r
Furniture, expenditures	year	280	91	81r
Household equipment, misc. expenditures	year	342	91	81r
Household expenditures, miscellaneous	year	256	91	81r
Household furnishings and equipment, expenditures	year	988	91	81r
Household operations expenditures	year	468	91	81r
Household textiles, expenditures	year	95	91	81r
Housekeeping supplies, expenditures	year	380	91	81r
Laundry and cleaning supplies, expenditures	year	109	91	81r
Laundry detergent, Tide Ultra, Bold, or Cheer	42 oz.	3.72	12/94	2c
Postage and stationery, expenditures	year	105	91	81r
Tissues, facial, Kleenex brand	175	0.93	12/94	2c
Housing				
Housing, ACCRA Index		81.00	12/94	2c
Add garage/carport		6,980	3/95	74r
Add room(s)		11,403	3/95	74r
Apartment condominium or co-op, median	unit	68600	12/94	62r
Dwellings (owned), expenditures	year	2428	91	81r
Enclose porch/patio/breezeway		4,572	3/95	74r
Finish room in basement/attic		3,794	3/95	74r
Home, existing, single-family, median	unit	120200	12/94	62r

Odessa, TX - continued

Item	Per	Value	Date	Ref.
Housing - continued				
House payment, principal and interest, 25% down payment	mo.	633	12/94	2c
House, 1800 sq ft, 8000 sq ft lot, new, urban, utilities	total	102350	12/94	2c
Maintenance, repairs, insurance, and other housing expenditures	year	531	91	81r
Mortgage interest and charges expenditures	year	1506	91	81r
Mtge. rate, incl. points and orig. fee, 30-year conv. fixed or ARM	mo.	9.27	12/94	2c
Princ. & int., mortgage, median-price exist. sing.-family home	mo.	540	12/94	62r
Property taxes expenditures	year	391	91	81r
Redesign, restructure more than half of home's interior		17,641	3/95	74r
Rent, apartment, 2 br., 1 1/2-2 baths, unfurnished, 950 sq ft, water	mo.	392	12/94	2c
Rental units expenditures	year	1264	91	81r
Insurance and Pensions				
Auto insurance, private passenger	year	785.78	12/94	71s
Insurance and pensions, personal, expenditures	year	2395	91	81r
Insurance, life and other personal, expenditures	year	368	91	81r
Pensions and Social Security, expenditures	year	2027	91	81r
Personal Goods				
Shampoo, Alberto VO5	15-oz.	1.08	12/94	2c
Toothpaste, Crest or Colgate	6-7 oz.	2.00	12/94	2c
Personal Services				
Dry cleaning, man's 2-pc. suit		5.70	12/94	2c
Haircut, man's barbershop, no styling		8.00	12/94	2c
Haircut, woman's shampoo, trim, blow-dry		17.00	12/94	2c
Personal services expenditures	year	212	91	81r
Restaurant Food				
Chicken, fried, thigh and drumstick		2.03	12/94	2c
Dining expenditures, family	week	33.83	94	73r
Hamburger with cheese	1/4 lb.	1.99	12/94	2c
Pizza, Pizza Hut or Pizza Inn	12-13 in.	8.73	12/94	2c
Taxes				
Tax, cigarettes	year	584.00	10/93	43s
Taxes, Federal income, expenditures	year	2275	91	81r
Taxes, personal, expenditures	year	2715	91	81r
Taxes, State and local income, expenditures	year	365	91	81r
Transportation				
Transportation, ACCRA Index		102.90	12/94	2c
Cars and trucks purchased, new	year	1306	91	81r
Cars and trucks purchased, used	year	942	91	81r
Driver's learning permit fee	perm	5.00	1/94	84s
Driver's license fee	orig	16.00	1/94	84s
Driver's license fee, duplicate	lic	10.00	1/94	84s
Driver's license reinstatement fee, min.	susp	50.00	1/94	85s
Driver's license renewal fee	renew	16.00	1/94	84s
Identification card, nondriver	card	10.00	1/94	83s
Motorcycle learning permit fee	perm	5.00	1/94	84s
Motorcycle license fee	orig	16.00	1/94	84s
Motorcycle license fee, duplicate	lic	10.00	1/94	84s
Motorcycle license renewal fee	renew	21.00	1/94	84s
Public transportation expenditures	year	249	91	81r
Tire balance, computer or spin bal., front	wheel	6.50	12/94	2c
Transportation expenditures, total	year	5307	91	81r
Vehicle finance charges	year	346	91	81r
Vehicle insurance expenditures	year	544	91	81r
Vehicle maintenance and repairs expenditures	year	600	91	81r
Vehicle purchases	year	2275	91	81r
Vehicle rental, leases, licenses, etc. expenditures	year	141	91	81r
Vehicles purchased, other than cars and trucks	year	27	91	81r

Values are in dollars or fractions of dollars. In the column headed *Ref*, references are shown to sources. Each reference is followed by a letter. These refer to the geographical level for which data were reported: s=State, r=Region, and c=City or metro. The abbreviation *ex* is used to mean *except* or *excluding*; *exp* stands for expenditures. For other abbreviations and further explanations, please see the Introduction.

Odessa, TX - continued

Item	Per	Value	Date	Ref.
Utilities				
Utilities, ACCRA Index		124.90	12/94	2c
Electricity expenditures	year	950	91	81r
Electricity, (part.), other, 1800 sq. ft., new home	mo.	108.98	12/94	2c
Utilities, fuels, and public services, total expenditures	year	2000	91	81r
Water and other public services, expenditures	year	227	91	81r
Weddings				
Bridal attendants' gowns	event	750	10/93	76r
Bridal gown	event	852	10/93	76r
Bridal headpiece and veil	event	167	10/93	76r
Bride's wedding band	event	708	10/93	76r
Clergy	event	224	10/93	76r
Engagement ring	event	2756	10/93	76r
Flowers	event	863	10/93	76r
Formal wear for groom	event	106	10/93	76r
Groom's attendants' formal wear	event	530	10/93	76r
Groom's wedding band	event	402	10/93	76r
Music	event	600	10/93	76r
Photography	event	1088	10/93	76r
Shoes for bride	event	50	10/93	76r
Videography	event	483	10/93	76r
Wedding invitations and announcements	event	342	10/93	76r
Wedding reception	event	7000	10/93	76r

Oklahoma City, OK

Item	Per	Value	Date	Ref.
Composite, ACCRA index		92.90	12/94	2c
Alcoholic Beverages				
Beer, Miller Lite, Bud, 12-oz., ex deposit	6	3.67	12/94	2c
J & B Scotch	750-ml.	15.15	12/94	2c
Wine, Gallo Chablis blanc	1.5-lit	5.66	12/94	2c
Appliances				
Appliances (major), expenditures	year	153	91	81r
Average annual exp.				
Food, health care, personal goods, services	year	27020	91	81r
Charity				
Cash contributions, expenditures	year	839	91	81r
Clothing				
Apparel, men and boys, total expenditures	year	380	91	81r
Apparel, women and girls, total expenditures	year	660	91	81r
Footwear, expenditures	year	193	91	81r
Jeans, man's denim		29.69	12/94	2c
Shirt, dress, men's	shirt	20.00	1/92	44c
Shirt, man's dress shirt		30.10	12/94	2c
Undervest, boy's size 10-14, cotton	3	4.49	12/94	2c
Communications				
Long-distance telephone rate, day, addl. min., 1-10 mi.	min.	0.07	12/93	9s
Long-distance telephone rate, day, initial min., 1-10 mi.	min.	0.12	12/93	9s
Newspaper subscription, dly. and Sun. delivery	month	12.85	12/94	2c
Phone line, single, business, field visit	inst	82.75	12/93	9s
Phone line, single, business, no field visit	inst	82.75	12/93	9s
Phone line, single, residence, field visit	inst	44.45	12/93	9s
Phone line, single, residence, no field visit	inst	44.45	12/93	9s
Telephone bill, family of four	month	20.58	12/94	2c
Telephone service, expenditures	year	616	91	81r
Telephone, residential, flat rate	mo.	12.97	12/93	8c
Education				
Board, 4-year private college/university	year	1974	8/94	80s
Board, 4-year public college/university	year	1502	8/94	80s
Education, total expenditures	year	319	91	81r
Room, 4-year private college/university	year	1618	8/94	80s

Oklahoma City, OK - continued

Item	Per	Value	Date	Ref.
Education - continued				
Room, 4-year public college/university	year	876	8/94	80s
Total cost, 4-year private college/university	year	10801	8/94	80s
Total cost, 4-year public college/university	year	4023	8/94	80s
Tuition, 2-year public college/university, in-state	year	1095	8/94	80s
Tuition, 4-year private college/university, in-state	year	7210	8/94	80s
Tuition, 4-year public college/university, in-state	year	1645	8/94	80s
Energy and Fuels				
Energy, combined forms, 1800 sq. ft.	mo.	120.16	12/94	2c
Energy, exc. electricity, 1800 sq. ft.	mo.	39.23	12/94	2c
Fuel oil and other fuels, expenditures	year	56	91	81r
Gas	gal.	1.13	1/92	44c
Gas, cooking, winter, 10 therms	month	10.44	2/94	65c
Gas, cooking, winter, 30 therms	month	21.97	2/94	65c
Gas, cooking, winter, 50 therms	month	29.79	2/94	65c
Gas, heating, winter, average use	month	70.11	2/94	65c
Gas, natural, expenditures	year	150	91	81r
Gas, reg unlead, taxes inc., cash, self-service	gal	1.05	12/94	2c
Gasoline and motor oil purchased	year	1152	91	81r
Gasoline, unleaded midgrade	gallon	1.21	4/93	82r
Gasoline, unleaded premium	gallon	1.30	4/93	82r
Gasoline, unleaded regular	gallon	1.10	4/93	82r
Entertainment				
Bowling, evening rate	game	2.18	12/94	2c
Concert ticket, Pearl Jam group	perf	20.00	94	50r
Entertainment, total expenditures	year	1266	91	81r
Fees and admissions, expenditures	year	306	91	81r
Monopoly game, Parker Brothers', No. 9	game	11.62	12/94	2c
Movie	adm	5.88	12/94	2c
Movie ticket, adult	ticket	7.00	1/92	44c
Pets, toys, playground equipment, expenditures	year	271	91	81r
Reading, expenditures	year	131	91	81r
Televisions, radios, and sound equipment, expenditures	year	439	91	81r
Tennis balls, yellow, Wilson or Penn, 3	can	2.64	12/94	2c
Funerals				
Burial, immediate, container provided by funeral home		1574.60	1/95	54r
Cards, acknowledgment		22.24	1/95	54r
Casket, minimum alternative		239.41	1/95	54r
Cosmetology, hair care, etc.		91.04	1/95	54r
Cremation, direct, container provided by funeral home		1085.15	1/95	54r
Embalming		281.30	1/95	54r
Funeral, funeral home		323.04	1/95	54r
Funeral, other facility		327.58	1/95	54r
Graveside service		355.19	1/95	54r
Hearse, local		141.89	1/95	54r
Limousine, local		99.40	1/95	54r
Memorial service		284.67	1/95	54r
Service charge, professional, nondeclinable		904.06	1/95	54r
Visitation and viewing		187.04	1/95	54r
Groceries				
Groceries, ACCRA Index		93.50	12/94	2c
Apples, Red Delicious	lb.	0.73	12/94	82r
Baby food, strained vegetables, lowest price	4-4.5 oz.	0.29	12/94	2c
Bacon, sliced	lb.	1.67	12/94	82r
Bananas	lb.	0.39	12/94	2c
Bananas	lb.	0.42	12/94	82r
Beef or hamburger, ground	lb.	1.13	12/94	2c
Beef purchases	year	213	91	81r
Beverage purchases, alcoholic	year	249	91	81r
Beverage purchases, nonalcoholic	year	207	91	81r
Bologna, all beef or mixed	lb.	2.27	12/94	82r
Bread, white	24-oz.	0.70	12/94	2c

Values are in dollars or fractions of dollars. In the column headed *Ref*, references are shown to sources. Each reference is followed by a letter. These refer to the geographical level for which data were reported: s=State, r=Region, and c=City or metro. The abbreviation *ex* is used to mean *except* or *excluding*; *exp* stands for *expenditures*. For other abbreviations and further explanations, please see the Introduction.

Oklahoma City, OK - continued

Item	Per	Value	Date	Ref.
Groceries				
Bread, white, pan	lb.	0.68	12/94	82r
Cabbage	lb.	0.42	12/94	82r
Carrots, short trimmed and topped	lb.	0.53	12/94	82r
Cereals and bakery products purchases	year	345	91	81r
Cereals and cereals products purchases	year	127	91	81r
Cheddar cheese, natural	lb.	3.58	12/94	82r
Cheese, Kraft grated Parmesan	8-oz.	3.14	12/94	2c
Chicken breast, bone-in	lb.	1.71	12/94	82r
Chicken, fresh, whole	lb.	0.78	12/94	82r
Chicken, whole fryer	lb.	0.71	12/94	2c
Chuck roast, USDA choice, boneless	lb.	2.26	12/94	82r
Cigarettes, Winston, Kings	carton	15.17	12/94	2c
Coffee, vacuum-packed	13 oz.	3.47	12/94	2c
Corn Flakes, Kellogg's or Post Toasties	18 oz.	2.40	12/94	2c
Corn, frozen, whole kernel, lowest price	10 oz.	0.71	12/94	2c
Crackers, soda, salted	lb.	1.27	12/94	82r
Cucumbers	lb.	0.65	12/94	82r
Dairy products (other) purchases	year	141	91	81r
Eggs, Grade A large	dozen	0.74	12/94	2c
Eggs, Grade A large	dozen	0.87	12/94	82r
Fish and seafood purchases	year	72	91	81r
Flour, white, all purpose	lb.	0.23	12/94	82r
Food purchases, food eaten at home	year	2381	91	81r
Foods purchased away from home, not prepared by consumer	year	1696	91	81r
Frankfurters, all meat or all beef	lb.	1.74	12/94	82r
Fruits and vegetables purchases	year	380	91	81r
Grapefruit	lb.	0.45	12/94	82r
Grapes, Thompson seedless	lb.	2.30	12/94	82r
Ground beef, 100% beef	lb.	1.37	12/94	82r
Ground chuck, 100% beef	lb.	1.97	12/94	82r
Ham, boneless, exc. canned	lb.	2.54	12/94	82r
Ice cream, prepackaged, bulk, regular	1/2 gal.	2.47	12/94	82r
Lemons	lb.	1.02	12/94	82r
Lettuce, iceberg	lb.	0.96	12/94	82r
Lettuce, iceberg	head	0.76	12/94	2c
Margarine, Blue Bonnet or Parkay cubes	lb.	0.57	12/94	2c
Margarine, stick	lb.	0.77	12/94	82r
Meats, poultry, fish, and eggs purchases	year	655	91	81r
Milk and cream (fresh) purchases	year	130	91	81r
Milk, 2%	gal.	1.89	1/92	44c
Milk, whole	1/2 gal.	1.26	12/94	2c
Orange juice, frozen concentrate 12-oz. can	16 oz.	1.36	12/94	82r
Orange juice, Minute Maid frozen	12-oz.	1.19	12/94	2c
Oranges, Navel	lb.	0.54	12/94	82r
Peaches, halves or slices, Hunt's, Del Monte, or Libby's	29-oz.	1.32	12/94	2c
Pears, Anjou	lb.	0.81	12/94	82r
Peas, sweet, Del Monte or Green Giant	15-17 oz.	0.50	12/94	2c
Pork chops, center cut, bone-in	lb.	3.07	12/94	82r
Pork purchases	year	142	91	81r
Potato chips	16-oz.	3.15	12/94	82r
Potatoes, frozen, French fried	lb.	0.82	12/94	82r
Potatoes, white	lb.	0.34	12/94	82r
Potatoes, white or red	10-lb. sack	2.06	12/94	2c
Rental rate, 2-bedroom apartment	month	345.00	1/92	44c
Rice, white, long grain, uncooked	lb.	0.48	12/94	82r
Round roast, USDA choice, boneless	lb.	2.91	12/94	82r
Sausage, fresh	lb.	1.82	12/94	82r
Sausage, Jimmy Dean, 100% pork	lb.	2.46	12/94	2c
Shortening, vegetable oil blends	lb.	0.75	12/94	82r
Shortening, vegetable, Crisco	3-lb.	2.09	12/94	2c
Soft drink, Coca Cola, ex deposit	2 lit	1.04	12/94	2c
Spaghetti and macaroni	lb.	0.87	12/94	82r
Steak, rib eye, USDA choice, boneless	lb.	6.85	12/94	82r
Steak, round, graded & ungraded, exc. USDA prime & choice	lb.	2.96	12/94	82r
Steak, round, USDA choice, boneless	lb.	3.17	12/94	82r

Oklahoma City, OK - continued

Item	Per	Value	Date	Ref.
Groceries - continued				
Steak, sirloin, USDA choice, boneless	lb.	4.12	12/94	82r
Steak, t-bone	lb.	5.15	12/94	2c
Steak, T-bone, USDA choice, bone-in	lb.	5.63	12/94	82r
Sugar and other sweets, eaten at home, expenditures	year	93	91	81r
Sugar, cane or beet	4 lbs.	1.35	12/94	2c
Sugar, white, all sizes	lb.	0.39	12/94	82r
Tobacco products and smoking supplies, total expenditures	year	286	91	81r
Tomatoes, field grown	lb.	1.36	12/94	82r
Tomatoes, Hunt's or Del Monte	14.5 oz.	0.69	12/94	2c
Tuna, chunk, light	lb.	1.94	12/94	82r
Tuna, chunk, light, oil-packed	6.125-6.5 oz.	0.72	12/94	2c
Turkey, frozen, whole	lb.	0.96	12/94	82r
Yogurt, natural, fruit flavored	8 oz.	0.58	12/94	82r
Goods and Services				
Miscellaneous goods and services, ACCRA Index		99.50	12/94	2c
Health Care				
Health care, ACCRA Index		96.90	12/94	2c
Adenosine, emergency room	treat	100.00	95	23r
Antibiotic ointment, Polysporin	1.5 oz.	4.07	12/94	2c
Bladder tap, superpubic, infant, emergency room	treat	119.00	95	23r
Blood analysis, emergency room	treat	25.00	95	23r
Blood tests, abdominal pain, emergency room	treat	25.00	95	23r
Burn dressing, emergency room	treat	266.00	95	23r
Cardiology interpretation, emergency room	treat	26.00	95	23r
Chest X-ray, emergency room	treat	78.00	95	23r
Childbirth, Cesarean delivery, hospital charge	birth	5462.00	12/91	69r
Childbirth, Cesarean delivery, physician charge	birth	2228.00	12/91	69r
Childbirth, normal delivery, hospital charge	birth	2943.00	12/91	69r
Childbirth, normal delivery, physician charge	birth	1619.00	12/91	69r
Defibrillation pads, emergency room	treat	6.00	95	23r
Dentist's fee, adult teeth cleaning and periodic oral exam	visit	58.10	12/94	2c
Doctor's fee, routine exam, established patient	visit	40.00	12/94	2c
Drugs, expenditures	year	297	91	81r
Gastric tube insertion, nasal, emergency room	treat	25.00	95	23r
Health care, total expenditures	year	1600	91	81r
Health insurance expenditures	year	637	91	81r
Heart monitor, emergency room	treat	40.00	95	23r
Hospital care, semiprivate room	day	256.30	12/94	2c
Insurance premium, family medical care	month	373.98	1/95	41s
Intravenous fluids, emergency room	treat	130.00	95	23r
Intravenous fluids, emergency room	liter	26.00	95	23r
Intravenous line, central, emergency room	treat	342.00	95	23r
Liver function tests, abdominal pain, emergency room	treat	26.00	95	23r
Medical care charges, total, emergency room, third-degree burns	treat	2101.00	95	23r
Medical care charges, total, emergency, infant with fever	treat	628.00	95	23r
Medical services expenditures	year	573	91	81r
Medical supplies expenditures	year	93	91	81r
Morphine, emergency room	treat	34.00	95	23r
Nursing care and facilities charges, emergency room	treat	252.00	95	23r
Nursing care and facilities charges, emergency, infant with fever	treat	252.00	95	23r
Nursing care and facilities charges, emergency, third-degree burns	treat	861.00	95	23r
Physician's charges, emergency, infant with fever	treat	212.00	95	23r

Values are in dollars or fractions of dollars. In the column headed *Ref*, references are shown to sources. Each reference is followed by a letter. These refer to the geographical level for which data were reported: s = State, r = Region, and c = City or metro. The abbreviation *ex* is used to mean *except* or *excluding*; *exp* stands for expenditures. For other abbreviations and further explanations, please see the Introduction.

Oklahoma City, OK - continued

Item	Per	Value	Date	Ref.
Health Care				
Physician's charges, emergency, third-degree burns	treat	372.00	95	23r
Physician's fee, emergency room	treat	372.00	95	23r
Physician's fee, general practitioner	visit	51.20	12/93	60r
Surgery, open-heart	proc	42374.00	1/93	14r
Ultrasound, abdominal, emergency room	treat	276.00	95	23r
Urinalysis, emergency room	treat	20.00	95	23r
Urinalysis, infant, emergency room	treat	20.00	95	23r
X-rays, emergency room	treat	78.00	95	23r
Household Goods				
Appl. repair, service call, wash mach	min. lab. chg.	28.22	12/94	2c
Floor coverings, expenditures	year	48	91	81r
Furniture, expenditures	year	280	91	81r
Household equipment, misc. expenditures	year	342	91	81r
Household expenditures, miscellaneous	year	256	91	81r
Household furnishings and equipment, expenditures	year	988	91	81r
Household operations expenditures	year	468	91	81r
Household textiles, expenditures	year	95	91	81r
Housekeeping supplies, expenditures	year	380	91	81r
Laundry and cleaning supplies, expenditures	year	109	91	81r
Laundry detergent, Tide Ultra, Bold, or Cheer	42 oz.	3.45	12/94	2c
Postage and stationery, expenditures	year	105	91	81r
Tissues, facial, Kleenex brand	175	1.03	12/94	2c
Housing				
Housing, ACCRA Index		79.60	12/94	2c
Add garage/carport		6,980	3/95	74r
Add room(s)		11,403	3/95	74r
Apartment condominium or co-op, median	unit	68600	12/94	62r
Dwellings (owned), expenditures	year	2428	91	81r
Enclose porch/patio/breezeway		4,572	3/95	74r
Finish room in basement/attic		3,794	3/95	74r
Home, existing, single-family, median	unit	120200	12/94	62r
Home, existing, single-family, median	unit	65.70	12/94	62c
House payment, principal and interest, 25% down payment	mo.	588	12/94	2c
House, 1800 sq ft, 8000 sq ft lot, new, urban, utilities	total	96597	12/94	2c
Maintenance, repairs, insurance, and other housing expenditures	year	531	91	81r
Mortgage interest and charges expenditures	year	1506	91	81r
Mtge. rate, incl. points and orig. fee, 30-year conv. fixed or ARM	mo.	9.10	12/94	2c
Princ. & int., mortgage, median-price exist. sing.-family home	mo.	540	12/94	62r
Property taxes expenditures	year	391	91	81r
Redesign, restructure more than half of home's interior		17,641	3/95	74r
Rent, apartment, 2 br., 1 1/2-2 baths, unfurnished, 950 sq ft, water	mo.	483	12/94	2c
Rental units expenditures	year	1264	91	81r
Insurance and Pensions				
Auto insurance, private passenger	year	604.38	12/94	71s
Insurance and pensions, personal, expenditures	year	2395	91	81r
Insurance, life and other personal, expenditures	year	368	91	81r
Pensions and Social Security, expenditures	year	2027	91	81r
Personal Goods				
Shampoo, Alberto VO5	15-oz.	1.22	12/94	2c
Toothpaste, Crest or Colgate	6-7 oz.	2.19	12/94	2c
Personal Services				
Dry cleaning, man's 2-pc. suit		6.04	12/94	2c
Dry cleaning, woman's dress	dress	8.43	1/92	44c
Haircut, man's barbershop, no styling		7.05	12/94	2c

Oklahoma City, OK - continued

Item	Per	Value	Date	Ref.
Personal Services - continued				
Haircut, woman's shampoo, trim, blow-dry		21.00	12/94	2c
Personal services expenditures	year	212	91	81r
Restaurant Food				
Big Mac, small fries, medium drink	meal	3.35	1/92	44c
Chicken, fried, thigh and drumstick		1.99	12/94	2c
Dining expenditures, family	week	33.83	94	73r
Hamburger with cheese	1/4 lb.	1.75	12/94	2c
Pizza, Pizza Hut or Pizza Inn	12-13 in.	8.39	12/94	2c
Taxes				
Tax rate, residential property, month	$100	1.04	1/92	79c
Tax, cigarettes	year	382.00	10/93	43s
Taxes, Federal income, expenditures	year	2275	91	81r
Taxes, personal, expenditures	year	2715	91	81r
Taxes, State and local income, expenditures	year	365	91	81r
Transportation				
Transportation, ACCRA Index		94.00	12/94	2c
Bus fare, one-way	trip	0.75	12/95	1c
Bus fare, up to 10 miles	one-way	0.75	12/94	2c
Cars and trucks purchased, new	year	1306	91	81r
Cars and trucks purchased, used	year	942	91	81r
Driver's learning permit fee	perm	19.00	1/94	84s
Driver's license fee	orig	19.00	1/94	84s
Driver's license fee, duplicate	lic	5.00	1/94	84s
Driver's license reinstatement fee, min.	susp	75.00	1/94	85s
Driver's license renewal fee	renew	15.00	1/94	84s
Identification card, nondriver	card	7.00	1/94	83s
Motorcycle license fee	orig	19.00	1/94	84s
Motorcycle license fee, duplicate	lic	5.00	1/94	84s
Motorcycle license renewal fee	renew	15.00	1/94	84s
parking, long-term lot, airport	3 days	72.00	1/92	44c
Public transportation expenditures	year	249	91	81r
Tire balance, computer or spin bal., front	wheel	6.70	12/94	2c
Transportation expenditures, total	year	5307	91	81r
Vehicle finance charges	year	346	91	81r
Vehicle insurance expenditures	year	544	91	81r
Vehicle maintenance and repairs expenditures	year	600	91	81r
Vehicle purchases	year	2275	91	81r
Vehicle rental, leases, licenses, etc. expenditures	year	141	91	81r
Vehicles purchased, other than cars and trucks	year	27	91	81r
Utilities				
Utilities, ACCRA Index		106.90	12/94	2c
Electricity expenditures	year	950	91	81r
Electricity, (part.), other, 1800 sq. ft., new home	mo.	80.93	12/94	2c
Electricity, summer, 250 KWh	month	26.18	8/93	64c
Electricity, summer, 500 KWh	month	45.73	8/93	64c
Electricity, summer, 750 KWh	month	65.28	8/93	64c
Electricity, summer, 1000 KWh	month	84.83	8/93	64c
Utilities, fuels, and public services, total expenditures	year	2000	91	81r
Water and other public services, expenditures	year	227	91	81r
Weddings				
Bridal attendants' gowns	event	750	10/93	76r
Bridal gown	event	852	10/93	76r
Bridal headpiece and veil	event	167	10/93	76r
Bride's wedding band	event	708	10/93	76r
Clergy	event	224	10/93	76r
Engagement ring	event	2756	10/93	76r
Flowers	event	863	10/93	76r
Formal wear for groom	event	106	10/93	76r
Groom's attendants' formal wear	event	530	10/93	76r
Groom's wedding band	event	402	10/93	76r
Music	event	600	10/93	76r

Values are in dollars or fractions of dollars. In the column headed *Ref*, references are shown to sources. Each reference is followed by a letter. These refer to the geographical level for which data were reported: s=State, r=Region, and c=City or metro. The abbreviation *ex* is used to mean *except* or *excluding*; *exp* stands for expenditures. For other abbreviations and further explanations, please see the Introduction.

Oklahoma City, OK - continued

Item	Per	Value	Date	Ref.
Weddings				
Photography	event	1088	10/93	76r
Shoes for bride	event	50	10/93	76r
Videography	event	483	10/93	76r
Wedding invitations and announcements	event	342	10/93	76r
Wedding reception	event	7000	10/93	76r

Olympia, WA

Item	Per	Value	Date	Ref.
Appliances				
Appliances (major), expenditures	year	160	91	81r
Average annual exp.				
Food, health care, personal goods, services	year	32461	91	81r
Charity				
Cash contributions, expenditures	year	975	91	81r
Clothing				
Apparel, men and boys, total expenditures	year	467	91	81r
Apparel, women and girls, total expenditures	year	737	91	81r
Footwear, expenditures	year	270	91	81r
Communications				
Long-distance telephone rate, day, addl. min., 1-10 mi.	min.	0.01	12/93	9s
Long-distance telephone rate, day, initial min., 1-10 mi.	min.	0.15	12/93	9s
Phone line, single, business, field visit	inst	48.00	12/93	9s
Phone line, single, business, no field visit	inst	48.00	12/93	9s
Phone line, single, residence, field visit	inst	31.00	12/93	9s
Phone line, single, residence, no field visit	inst	31.00	12/93	9s
Telephone service, expenditures	year	611	91	81r
Education				
Board, 4-year private college/university	year	1928	8/94	80s
Board, 4-year public college/university	year	2194	8/94	80s
Education, total expenditures	year	375	91	81r
Room, 4-year private college/university	year	2455	8/94	80s
Room, 4-year public college/university	year	1952	8/94	80s
Total cost, 4-year private college/university	year	16332	8/94	80s
Total cost, 4-year public college/university	year	6483	8/94	80s
Tuition, 2-year public college/university, in-state	year	1141	8/94	80s
Tuition, 4-year private college/university, in-state	year	11949	8/94	80s
Tuition, 4-year public college/university, in-state	year	2337	8/94	80s
Energy and Fuels				
Fuel oil and other fuels, expenditures	year	33	91	81r
Gas, natural, expenditures	year	212	91	81r
Gasoline and motor oil purchased	year	1115	91	81r
Gasoline, unleaded midgrade	gallon	1.36	4/93	82r
Gasoline, unleaded premium	gallon	1.43	4/93	82r
Gasoline, unleaded regular	gallon	1.23	4/93	82r
Entertainment				
Concert ticket, Pearl Jam group	perf	20.00	94	50r
Entertainment, total expenditures	year	1853	91	81r
Fees and admissions, expenditures	year	482	91	81r
Pets, toys, playground equipment, expenditures	year	299	91	81r
Reading, expenditures	year	164	91	81r
Televisions, radios, and sound equipment, expenditures	year	528	91	81r
Funerals				
Burial, immediate, container provided by funeral home		1382.70	1/95	54r
Cards, acknowledgment		21.87	1/95	54r
Casket, minimum alternative		128.54	1/95	54r
Cosmetology, hair care, etc.		119.69	1/95	54r
Cremation, direct, container provided by funeral home		1030.62	1/95	54r
Embalming		255.42	1/95	54r

Olympia, WA - continued

Item	Per	Value	Date	Ref.
Funerals - continued				
Funeral, funeral home		437.38	1/95	54r
Funeral, other facility		444.46	1/95	54r
Graveside service		338.46	1/95	54r
Hearse, local		147.50	1/95	54r
Limousine, local		130.33	1/95	54r
Memorial service		553.16	1/95	54r
Service charge, professional, nondeclinable		859.15	1/95	54r
Visitation and viewing		93.23	1/95	54r
Groceries				
Apples, Red Delicious	lb.	0.72	12/94	82r
Bacon, sliced	lb.	1.73	12/94	82r
Bananas	lb.	0.52	12/94	82r
Beef purchases	year	241	91	81r
Beverage purchases, alcoholic	year	328	91	81r
Beverage purchases, nonalcoholic	year	234	91	81r
Bologna, all beef or mixed	lb.	2.33	12/94	82r
Bread, white, pan	lb.	0.81	12/94	82r
Carrots, short trimmed and topped	lb.	0.43	12/94	82r
Cereals and bakery products purchases	year	392	91	81r
Cereals and cereals products purchases	year	139	91	81r
Chicken breast, bone-in	lb.	2.04	12/94	82r
Chicken, fresh, whole	lb.	0.95	12/94	82r
Coffee, 100%, ground roast, all sizes	lb.	4.48	12/94	82r
Dairy products (other) purchases	year	182	91	81r
Fish and seafood purchases	year	94	91	81r
Flour, white, all purpose	lb.	0.21	12/94	82r
Food purchases, food eaten at home	year	2749	91	81r
Foods purchased away from home, not prepared by consumer	year	1909	91	81r
Fruits and vegetables purchases	year	459	91	81r
Grapefruit	lb.	0.56	12/94	82r
Ground beef, 100% beef	lb.	1.31	12/94	82r
Ham, boneless, exc. canned	lb.	2.46	12/94	82r
Ice cream, prepackaged, bulk, regular	1/2 gal.	2.57	12/94	82r
Lemons	lb.	1.00	12/94	82r
Lettuce, iceberg	lb.	0.93	12/94	82r
Meats, poultry, fish, and eggs purchases	year	700	91	81r
Milk and cream (fresh) purchases	year	155	91	81r
Orange juice, frozen concentrate 12-oz. can	16 oz.	1.52	12/94	82r
Oranges, Navel	lb.	0.56	12/94	82r
Pork chops, center cut, bone-in	lb.	3.30	12/94	82r
Pork purchases	year	122	91	81r
Potato chips	16-oz.	3.03	12/94	82r
Potatoes, frozen, French fried	lb.	0.77	12/94	82r
Potatoes, white	lb.	0.35	12/94	82r
Rice, white, long grain, uncooked	lb.	0.54	12/94	82r
Round roast, USDA choice, boneless	lb.	2.92	12/94	82r
Shortening, vegetable oil blends	lb.	0.80	12/94	82r
Spaghetti and macaroni	lb.	1.02	12/94	82r
Steak, round, graded & ungraded, exc. USDA prime & choice	lb.	3.13	12/94	82r
Steak, sirloin, USDA choice, boneless	lb.	4.07	12/94	82r
Sugar and other sweets, eaten at home, expenditures	year	105	91	81r
Sugar, white, all sizes	lb.	0.38	12/94	82r
Tobacco products and smoking supplies, total expenditures	year	221	91	81r
Tomatoes, field grown	lb.	1.45	12/94	82r
Tuna, chunk, light	lb.	2.18	12/94	82r
Health Care				
Childbirth, Cesarean delivery, hospital charge	birth	6059.00	12/91	69r
Childbirth, Cesarean delivery, physician charge	birth	2248.00	12/91	69r
Childbirth, normal delivery, hospital charge	birth	3006.00	12/91	69r
Childbirth, normal delivery, physician charge	birth	1634.00	12/91	69r
Drugs, expenditures	year	230	91	81r
Health care, total expenditures	year	1544	91	81r
Health insurance expenditures	year	558	91	81r
Insurance premium, family medical care	month	382.32	1/95	41s

Values are in dollars or fractions of dollars. In the column headed *Ref,* references are shown to sources. Each reference is followed by a letter. These refer to the geographical level for which data were reported: s = State, r = Region, and c = City or metro. The abbreviation *ex* is used to mean *except* or *excluding; exp* stands for expenditures. For other abbreviations and further explanations, please see the Introduction.

Olympia, WA - continued

Item	Per	Value	Date	Ref.
Health Care				
Medical services expenditures	year	676	91	81r
Medical supplies expenditures	year	80	91	81r
Surgery, open-heart	proc	37818.00	1/93	14r
Household Goods				
Floor coverings, expenditures	year	79	91	81r
Furniture, expenditures	year	352	91	81r
Household equipment, misc. expenditures	year	614	91	81r
Household expenditures, miscellaneous	year	294	91	81r
Household furnishings and equipment, expenditures	year	1416	91	81r
Household operations expenditures	year	580	91	81r
Household textiles, expenditures	year	113	91	81r
Housekeeping supplies, expenditures	year	447	91	81r
Laundry and cleaning supplies, expenditures	year	114	91	81r
Postage and stationery, expenditures	year	145	91	81r
Housing				
Add garage/carport		6,422	3/95	74r
Add room(s)		26,583	3/95	74r
Apartment condominium or co-op, median	unit	105300	12/94	62r
Dwellings (owned), expenditures	year	3932	91	81r
Enclose porch/patio/breezeway		5,382	3/95	74r
Finish room in basement/attic		3,911	3/95	74r
Home, existing, single-family, median	unit	178600	12/94	62r
Maintenance, repairs, insurance, and other housing expenditures	year	591	91	81r
Mortgage interest and charges expenditures	year	2747	91	81r
Princ. & int., mortgage, median-price exist. sing.-family home	mo.	845	12/94	62r
Property taxes expenditures	year	594	91	81r
Redesign, restructure more than half of home's interior		5,467	3/95	74r
Rental units expenditures	year	2077	91	81r
Insurance and Pensions				
Auto insurance, private passenger	year	711.57	12/94	71s
Insurance and pensions, personal, expenditures	year	3042	91	81r
Insurance, life and other personal, expenditures	year	298	91	81r
Pensions and Social Security, expenditures	year	2744	91	81r
Legal Assistance				
Legal work, law firm associate	hour	91		10r
Legal work, law firm partner	hour	151		10r
Personal Services				
Personal services expenditures	year	286	91	81r
Restaurant Food				
Dining expenditures, family	week	32.25	94	73r
Taxes				
Taxes, Federal income, expenditures	year	2946	91	81r
Taxes, personal, expenditures	year	3791	91	81r
Taxes, State and local income, expenditures	year	791	91	81r
Transportation				
Cars and trucks purchased, new	year	1231	91	81r
Cars and trucks purchased, used	year	915	91	81r
Driver's learning permit fee	perm	4.00	1/94	84s
Driver's license fee	orig	21.00	1/94	84s
Driver's license fee, duplicate	lic	5.00	1/94	84s
Driver's license reinstatement fee, min.	susp	20.00-50.00	1/94	85s
Driver's license renewal fee	renew	14.00	1/94	84s
Identification card, nondriver	card	4.00	1/94	83s
Motorcycle license fee	orig	8.00	1/94	84s
Motorcycle license renewal fee	renew	7.50	1/94	84s
Public transportation expenditures	year	375	91	81r
Transportation expenditures, total	year	5527	91	81r
Vehicle finance charges	year	287	91	81r
Vehicle insurance expenditures	year	624	91	81r

Olympia, WA - continued

Item	Per	Value	Date	Ref.
Transportation - continued				
Vehicle maintenance and repairs expenditures	year	695	91	81r
Vehicle purchases	year	2174	91	81r
Vehicle rental, leases, licenses, etc. expenditures	year	257	91	81r
Vehicles purchased, other than cars and trucks	year	28	91	81r
Utilities				
Electricity expenditures	year	616	91	81r
Utilities, fuels, and public services, total expenditures	year	1681	91	81r
Water and other public services, expenditures	year	209	91	81r
Weddings				
Bridal attendants' gowns	event	750	10/93	76r
Bridal gown	event	852	10/93	76r
Bridal headpiece and veil	event	167	10/93	76r
Bride's wedding band	event	708	10/93	76r
Clergy	event	224	10/93	76r
Engagement ring	event	2756	10/93	76r
Flowers	event	863	10/93	76r
Formal wear for groom	event	106	10/93	76r
Groom's attendants' formal wear	event	530	10/93	76r
Groom's wedding band	event	402	10/93	76r
Music	event	600	10/93	76r
Photography	event	1088	10/93	76r
Shoes for bride	event	50	10/93	76r
Videography	event	483	10/93	76r
Wedding invitations and announcements	event	342	10/93	76r
Wedding reception	event	7000	10/93	76r

Omaha, NE

Item	Per	Value	Date	Ref.
Composite, ACCRA index		92.10	12/94	2c
Alcoholic Beverages				
Beer, Miller Lite, Bud, 12-oz., ex deposit	6	4.07	12/94	2c
J & B Scotch	750-ml.	16.29	12/94	2c
Wine, Gallo Chablis blanc	1.5-lit	4.59	12/94	2c
Appliances				
Appliances (major), expenditures	year	131	91	81r
Average annual exp.				
Food, health care, personal goods, services	year	25935	91	81r
Business				
Dinner and tip, hotel, corporate rate	night	28.00	2/94	15c
Hotel room, corporate rate	night	67.00	2/94	15c
Charity				
Cash contributions, expenditures	year	745	91	81r
Clothing				
Apparel, men and boys, total expenditures	year	332	91	81r
Apparel, women and girls, total expenditures	year	578	91	81r
Footwear, expenditures	year	164	91	81r
Jeans, man's denim		29.78	12/94	2c
Shirt, man's dress shirt		20.49	12/94	2c
Undervest, boy's size 10-14, cotton	3	4.08	12/94	2c
Communications				
Long-distance telephone rate, day, addl. min., 1-10 mi.	min.	0.16	12/93	9s
Long-distance telephone rate, day, initial min., 1-10 mi.	min.	0.30	12/93	9s
Newspaper subscription, dly. and Sun. delivery	month	8.70	12/94	2c
Phone line, single, business, field visit	inst	45.00	12/93	9s
Phone line, single, business, no field visit	inst	45.00	12/93	9s
Phone line, single, residence, field visit	inst	28.00	12/93	9s
Phone line, single, residence, no field visit	inst	28.00	12/93	9s
Telephone bill, family of four	month	21.02	12/94	2c

Values are in dollars or fractions of dollars. In the column headed *Ref*, references are shown to sources. Each reference is followed by a letter. These refer to the geographical level for which data were reported: s = State, r = Region, and c = City or metro. The abbreviation *ex* is used to mean *except* or *excluding*; *exp* stands for expenditures. For other abbreviations and further explanations, please see the Introduction.

Omaha, NE - continued

Item	Per	Value	Date	Ref.
Communications				
Telephone service, expenditures	year	547	91	81r
Telephone, residential, flat rate	mo.	14.90	12/93	8c
Education				
Board, 4-year private college/university	year	1816	8/94	80s
Board, 4-year public college/university	year	1711	8/94	80s
Education, total expenditures	year	394	91	81r
Room, 4-year private college/university	year	1684	8/94	80s
Room, 4-year public college/university	year	1276	8/94	80s
Total cost, 4-year private college/university	year	11899	8/94	80s
Total cost, 4-year public college/university	year	4927	8/94	80s
Tuition, 2-year public college/university, in-state	year	1091	8/94	80s
Tuition, 4-year private college/university, in-state	year	8400	8/94	80s
Tuition, 4-year public college/university, in-state	year	1939	8/94	80s
Energy and Fuels				
Energy, combined forms, 1800 sq. ft.	mo.	106.49	12/94	2c
Energy, exc. electricity, 1800 sq. ft.	mo.	38.28	12/94	2c
Fuel oil and other fuels, expenditures	year	83	91	81r
Gas, natural, expenditures	year	373	91	81r
Gas, reg unlead, taxes inc., cash, self-service	gal	1.15	12/94	2c
Gasoline and motor oil purchased	year	1000	91	81r
Gasoline, unleaded midgrade	gallon	1.15	4/93	82r
Gasoline, unleaded premium	gallon	1.23	4/93	82r
Gasoline, unleaded regular	gallon	1.07	4/93	82r
Entertainment				
Bowling, evening rate	game	1.63	12/94	2c
Entertainment, total expenditures	year	1356	91	81r
Fees and admissions, expenditures	year	347	91	81r
Monopoly game, Parker Brothers', No. 9	game	10.55	12/94	2c
Movie	adm	5.05	12/94	2c
Pets, toys, playground equipment, expenditures	year	270	91	81r
Reading, expenditures	year	160	91	81r
Televisions, radios, and sound equipment, expenditures	year	433	91	81r
Tennis balls, yellow, Wilson or Penn, 3	can	2.22	12/94	2c
Funerals				
Burial, immediate, container provided by funeral home		1348.78	1/95	54r
Cards, acknowledgment		21.20	1/95	54r
Casket, minimum alternative		182.83	1/95	54r
Cosmetology, hair care, etc.		133.11	1/95	54r
Cremation, direct, container provided by funeral home		1101.95	1/95	54r
Embalming		314.45	1/95	54r
Funeral, funeral home		304.88	1/95	54r
Funeral, other facility		301.37	1/95	54r
Graveside service		290.59	1/95	54r
Hearse, local		137.37	1/95	54r
Limousine, local		82.84	1/95	54r
Memorial service		316.57	1/95	54r
Service charge, professional, nondeclinable		1099.00	1/95	54r
Visitation and viewing		209.25	1/95	54r
Groceries				
Groceries, ACCRA Index		95.80	12/94	2c
Apples, Red Delicious	lb.	0.68	12/94	82r
Baby food, strained vegetables, lowest price	4-4.5 oz.	0.25	12/94	2c
Bacon, sliced	lb.	1.88	12/94	82r
Bananas	lb.	0.47	12/94	2c
Bananas	lb.	0.41	12/94	82r
Beef or hamburger, ground	lb.	1.21	12/94	2c
Beef purchases	year	197	91	81r
Beef, stew, boneless	lb.	2.52	12/94	82r
Beverage purchases, alcoholic	year	293	91	81r
Beverage purchases, nonalcoholic	year	203	91	81r

Omaha, NE - continued

Item	Per	Value	Date	Ref.
Groceries - continued				
Bologna, all beef or mixed	lb.	2.12	12/94	82r
Bread, white	24-oz.	0.87	12/94	2c
Bread, white, pan	lb.	0.76	12/94	82r
Cabbage	lb.	0.44	12/94	82r
Carrots, short trimmed and topped	lb.	0.44	12/94	82r
Cereals and bakery products purchases	year	347	91	81r
Cereals and cereals products purchases	year	119	91	81r
Cheddar cheese, natural	lb.	3.28	12/94	82r
Cheese, Kraft grated Parmesan	8-oz.	3.12	12/94	2c
Chicken breast, bone-in	lb.	1.61	12/94	82r
Chicken, fresh, whole	lb.	0.89	12/94	82r
Chicken, whole fryer	lb.	0.78	12/94	2c
Chuck roast, USDA choice, boneless	lb.	2.33	12/94	82r
Cigarettes, Winston, Kings	carton	16.06	12/94	2c
Coffee, 100%, ground roast, all sizes	lb.	4.28	12/94	82r
Coffee, vacuum-packed	13 oz.	3.37	12/94	2c
Cookies, chocolate chip	lb.	2.72	12/94	82r
Corn Flakes, Kellogg's or Post Toasties	18 oz.	2.30	12/94	2c
Corn, frozen, whole kernel, lowest price	10 oz.	0.69	12/94	2c
Dairy products (other) purchases	year	148	91	81r
Eggs, Grade A large	dozen	0.68	12/94	2c
Eggs, Grade A large	dozen	0.76	12/94	82r
Fish and seafood purchases	year	61	91	81r
Flour, white, all purpose	lb.	0.22	12/94	82r
Food purchases, food eaten at home	year	2313	91	81r
Foods purchased away from home, not prepared by consumer	year	1709	91	81r
Fruits and vegetables purchases	year	372	91	81r
Grapefruit	lb.	0.47	12/94	82r
Grapes, Thompson seedless	lb.	2.15	12/94	82r
Ground beef, 100% beef	lb.	1.37	12/94	82r
Ground chuck, 100% beef	lb.	1.81	12/94	82r
Ham, boneless, exc. canned	lb.	2.16	12/94	82r
Ice cream, prepackaged, bulk, regular	1/2 gal.	2.48	12/94	82r
Lemons	lb.	1.08	12/94	82r
Lettuce, iceberg	lb.	0.81	12/94	82r
Lettuce, iceberg	head	0.74	12/94	2c
Margarine, Blue Bonnet or Parkay cubes	lb.	0.44	12/94	2c
Margarine, stick	lb.	0.81	12/94	82r
Meats, poultry, fish, and eggs purchases	year	591	91	81r
Milk and cream (fresh) purchases	year	132	91	81r
Milk, whole	1/2 gal.	1.41	12/94	2c
Orange juice, frozen concentrate 12-oz. can	16 oz.	1.41	12/94	82r
Orange juice, Minute Maid frozen	12-oz.	1.23	12/94	2c
Oranges, Navel	lb.	0.56	12/94	82r
Peaches, halves or slices, Hunt's, Del Monte, or Libby's	29-oz.	1.32	12/94	2c
Peanut butter, creamy, all sizes	lb.	1.81	12/94	82r
Peas, sweet, Del Monte or Green Giant	15-17 oz.	0.50	12/94	2c
Pork chops, center cut, bone-in	lb.	2.76	12/94	82r
Pork purchases	year	130	91	81r
Potato chips	16-oz.	2.81	12/94	82r
Potatoes, frozen, French fried	lb.	0.83	12/94	82r
Potatoes, white	lb.	0.28	12/94	82r
Potatoes, white or red	10-lb. sack	1.96	12/94	2c
Round roast, USDA choice, boneless	lb.	2.90	12/94	82r
Sausage, Jimmy Dean, 100% pork	lb.	3.17	12/94	2c
Shortening, vegetable oil blends	lb.	0.88	12/94	82r
Shortening, vegetable, Crisco	3-lb.	2.21	12/94	2c
Soft drink, Coca Cola, ex deposit	2 lit	1.02	12/94	2c
Spaghetti and macaroni	lb.	0.78	12/94	82r
Steak, rib eye, USDA choice, boneless	lb.	6.15	12/94	82r
Steak, round, graded & ungraded, exc. USDA prime & choice	lb.	2.72	12/94	82r
Steak, round, USDA choice, boneless	lb.	3.02	12/94	82r
Steak, sirloin, USDA choice, boneless	lb.	3.85	12/94	82r
Steak, t-bone	lb.	5.21	12/94	2c
Steak, T-bone, USDA choice, bone-in	lb.	5.38	12/94	82r

Values are in dollars or fractions of dollars. In the column headed *Ref*, references are shown to sources. Each reference is followed by a letter. These refer to the geographical level for which data were reported: s=State, r=Region, and c=City or metro. The abbreviation *ex* is used to mean *except* or *excluding*; *exp* stands for expenditures. For other abbreviations and further explanations, please see the Introduction.

Omaha, NE - continued

Item	Per	Value	Date	Ref.
Groceries				
Sugar and other sweets, eaten at home, expenditures	year	91	91	81r
Sugar, cane or beet	4 lbs.	1.31	12/94	2c
Sugar, white, all sizes	lb.	0.36	12/94	82r
Tobacco products and smoking supplies, total expenditures	year	298	91	81r
Tomatoes, field grown	lb.	1.36	12/94	82r
Tomatoes, Hunt's or Del Monte	14.5 oz.	0.71	12/94	2c
Tuna, chunk, light	lb.	1.94	12/94	82r
Tuna, chunk, light, oil-packed	6.125-6.5 oz.	0.64	12/94	2c
Turkey, frozen, whole	lb.	0.96	12/94	82r
Yogurt, natural, fruit flavored	8 oz.	0.62	12/94	82r
Goods and Services				
Miscellaneous goods and services, ACCRA Index		90.30	12/94	2c
Health Care				
Health care, ACCRA Index		89.00	12/94	2c
Antibiotic ointment, Polysporin	1.5 oz.	4.10	12/94	2c
Childbirth, Cesarean delivery, hospital charge	birth	5101.00	12/91	69r
Childbirth, Cesarean delivery, physician charge	birth	2234.00	12/91	69r
Childbirth, normal delivery, hospital charge	birth	2891.00	12/91	69r
Childbirth, normal delivery, physician charge	birth	1623.00	12/91	69r
Dentist's fee, adult teeth cleaning and periodic oral exam	visit	53.00	12/94	2c
Doctor's fee, routine exam, established patient	visit	33.40	12/94	2c
Drugs, expenditures	year	248	91	81r
Health care, total expenditures	year	1336	91	81r
Health insurance expenditures	year	550	91	81r
Hospital care, semiprivate room	day	277.80	12/94	2c
Insurance premium, family medical care	month	382.63	1/95	41s
Medical services expenditures	year	457	91	81r
Medical supplies expenditures	year	82	91	81r
Household Goods				
Appl. repair, service call, wash mach	min. lab. chg.	27.17	12/94	2c
Floor coverings, expenditures	year	105	91	81r
Furniture, expenditures	year	291	91	81r
Household equipment, misc. expenditures	year	341	91	81r
Household expenditures, miscellaneous	year	162	91	81r
Household furnishings and equipment, expenditures	year	1042	91	81r
Household operations expenditures	year	365	91	81r
Household textiles, expenditures	year	101	91	81r
Housekeeping supplies, expenditures	year	390	91	81r
Laundry and cleaning supplies, expenditures	year	110	91	81r
Laundry detergent, Tide Ultra, Bold, or Cheer	42 oz.	2.83	12/94	2c
Postage and stationery, expenditures	year	115	91	81r
Tissues, facial, Kleenex brand	175	0.98	12/94	2c
Housing				
Housing, ACCRA Index		88.00	12/94	2c
Add garage/carport		8,479	3/95	74r
Add room(s)		21,347	3/95	74r
Apartment condominium or co-op, median	unit	87100	12/94	62r
Bathroom addition, average cost	add	9734.00	3/95	13r
Bathroom remodeling, average cost	remod	6414.00	3/95	13r
Bedroom, master suite addition, average cost	add	27122.00	3/95	13r
Deck addition, average cost	add	6665.00	3/95	13r
Dwellings (owned), expenditures	year	2566	91	81r
Enclose porch/patio/breezeway		4,556	3/95	74r
Exterior remodeling, average cost	remod	15395.00	3/95	13r
Family room addition, average cost	add	27658.00	3/95	13r

Omaha, NE - continued

Item	Per	Value	Date	Ref.
Housing - continued				
Finish room in basement/attic		5,074	3/95	74r
Home, existing, single-family, median	unit	106500	12/94	62r
Home, existing, single-family, median	unit	75.80	12/94	62c
House payment, principal and interest, 25% down payment	mo.	681	12/94	2c
House, 1800 sq ft, 8000 sq ft lot, new, urban, utilities	total	109400	12/94	2c
Kitchen remodeling, major, average cost	remod	17084.00	3/95	13r
Kitchen remodeling, minor, average cost	remod	5804.00	3/95	13r
Maintenance, repairs, insurance, and other housing expenditures	year	484	91	81r
Mortgage interest and charges expenditures	year	1443	91	81r
Mtge. rate, incl. points and orig. fee, 30-year conv. fixed or ARM	mo.	9.35	12/94	2c
Office, home addition, average cost	add	8121.00	3/95	13r
Princ. & int., mortgage, median-price exist. sing.-family home	mo.	515	12/94	62r
Property taxes expenditures	year	639	91	81r
Redesign, restructure more than half of home's interior		9,114	3/95	74r
Rent, apartment, 2 br., 1 1/2-2 baths, unfurnished, 950 sq ft, water	mo.	446	12/94	2c
Rental units expenditures	year	1200	91	81r
Sun-space addition, average cost	add	23768.00	3/95	13r
Wing addition, two-story, average cost	add	50410.00	3/95	13r
Insurance and Pensions				
Auto insurance, private passenger	year	494.85	12/94	71s
Insurance and pensions, personal, expenditures	year	2408	91	81r
Insurance, life and other personal, expenditures	year	355	91	81r
Pensions and Social Security, expenditures	year	2053	91	81r
Legal Assistance				
Legal work, law firm associate	hour	90		10r
Legal work, law firm partner	hour	139		10r
Personal Goods				
Shampoo, Alberto VO5	15-oz.	0.99	12/94	2c
Toothpaste, Crest or Colgate	6-7 oz.	1.57	12/94	2c
Personal Services				
Dry cleaning, man's 2-pc. suit		6.14	12/94	2c
Haircut, man's barbershop, no styling		9.20	12/94	2c
Haircut, woman's shampoo, trim, blow-dry		18.70	12/94	2c
Personal services expenditures	year	203	91	81r
Restaurant Food				
Chicken, fried, thigh and drumstick		2.10	12/94	2c
Dining expenditures, family	week	30.03	94	73r
Hamburger with cheese	1/4 lb.	1.79	12/94	2c
Pizza, Pizza Hut or Pizza Inn	12-13 in.	8.29	12/94	2c
Taxes				
Tax rate, residential property, month	$100	2.29	1/92	79c
Taxes, Federal income, expenditures	year	1756	91	81r
Taxes, personal, expenditures	year	2426	91	81r
Taxes, State and local income, expenditures	year	568	91	81r
Transportation				
Transportation, ACCRA Index		103.00	12/94	2c
Bus fare, one-way	trip	0.90	12/95	1c
Bus fare, up to 10 miles	one-way	0.90	12/94	2c
Cars and trucks purchased, new	year	891	91	81r
Cars and trucks purchased, used	year	1155	91	81r
Driver's learning permit fee	perm	3.00	1/94	84s
Driver's license fee	orig	15.00	1/94	84s
Driver's license fee, duplicate	lic	5.00	1/94	84s
Driver's license reinstatement fee, min.	susp	95.00	1/94	85s
Driver's license renewal fee	renew	15.00	1/94	84s
Identification card, nondriver	card	10.00	1/94	83s
Motorcycle learning permit fee	perm	3.00	1/94	84s

Values are in dollars or fractions of dollars. In the column headed *Ref*, references are shown to sources. Each reference is followed by a letter. These refer to the geographical level for which data were reported: s=State, r=Region, and c=City or metro. The abbreviation *ex* is used to mean *except* or *excluding*; *exp* stands for expenditures. For other abbreviations and further explanations, please see the Introduction.

Omaha, NE - continued

Item	Per	Value	Date	Ref.
Transportation				
Motorcycle license fee	orig	15.00	1/94	84s
Motorcycle license fee, duplicate	lic	5.00	1/94	84s
Motorcycle license renewal fee	renew	15.00	1/94	84s
Public transportation expenditures	year	209	91	81r
Tire balance, computer or spin bal., front	wheel	7.19	12/94	2c
Transportation expenditures, total	year	4792	91	81r
Vehicle finance charges	year	300	91	81r
Vehicle insurance expenditures	year	485	91	81r
Vehicle maintenance and repairs expenditures	year	534	91	81r
Vehicle purchases	year	2068	91	81r
Vehicle rental, leases, licenses, etc. expenditures	year	197	91	81r
Vehicles purchased, other than cars and trucks	year	22	91	81r
Utilities				
Utilities, ACCRA Index		96.60	12/94	2c
Electricity expenditures	year	668	91	81r
Electricity, (part.), other, 1800 sq. ft., new home	mo.	68.21	12/94	2c
Utilities, fuels, and public services, total expenditures	year	1838	91	81r
Water and other public services, expenditures	year	167	91	81r
Weddings				
Bridal attendants' gowns	event	750	10/93	76r
Bridal gown	event	852	10/93	76r
Bridal headpiece and veil	event	167	10/93	76r
Bride's wedding band	event	708	10/93	76r
Clergy	event	224	10/93	76r
Engagement ring	event	2756	10/93	76r
Flowers	event	863	10/93	76r
Formal wear for groom	event	106	10/93	76r
Groom's attendants' formal wear	event	530	10/93	76r
Groom's wedding band	event	402	10/93	76r
Music	event	600	10/93	76r
Photography	event	1088	10/93	76r
Shoes for bride	event	50	10/93	76r
Videography	event	483	10/93	76r
Wedding invitations and announcements	event	342	10/93	76r
Wedding reception	event	7000	10/93	76r

Orlando, FL

Item	Per	Value	Date	Ref.
Composite, ACCRA index		98.50	12/94	2c
Alcoholic Beverages				
Beer, Miller Lite, Bud, 12-oz., ex deposit	6	3.60	12/94	2c
J & B Scotch	750-ml.	17.44	12/94	2c
Wine, Gallo Chablis blanc	1.5-lit	4.80	12/94	2c
Appliances				
Appliances (major), expenditures	year	153	91	81r
Average annual exp.				
Food, health care, personal goods, services	year	27020	91	81r
Charity				
Cash contributions, expenditures	year	839	91	81r
Clothing				
Apparel, men and boys, total expenditures	year	380	91	81r
Apparel, women and girls, total expenditures	year	660	91	81r
Footwear, expenditures	year	193	91	81r
Jeans, man's denim		28.39	12/94	2c
Shirt, man's dress shirt		33.90	12/94	2c
Undervest, boy's size 10-14, cotton	3	4.34	12/94	2c
Communications				
Long-distance telephone rate, day, addl. min., 1-10 mi.	min.	0.08	12/93	9s

Orlando, FL - continued

Item	Per	Value	Date	Ref.
Communications - continued				
Long-distance telephone rate, day, initial min., 1-10 mi.	min.	0.15	12/93	9s
Newspaper subscription, dly. and Sun. delivery	month	17.28	12/94	2c
Phone line, single, business, field visit	inst	86.00	12/93	9s
Phone line, single, business, no field visit	inst	54.50	12/93	9s
Phone line, single, residence, field visit	inst	76.00	12/93	9s
Phone line, single, residence, no field visit	inst	44.50	12/93	9s
Telephone bill, family of four	month	19.32	12/94	2c
Telephone service, expenditures	year	616	91	81r
Telephone, residential, flat rate	mo.	10.45	12/93	8c
Education				
Bar examination preparatory course	course	500.00-100	94	17s
Board, 4-year private college/university	year	2123	8/94	80s
Board, 4-year public college/university	year	2101	8/94	80s
Education, total expenditures	year	319	91	81r
Room, 4-year private college/university	year	2242	8/94	80s
Room, 4-year public college/university	year	1970	8/94	80s
Total cost, 4-year private college/university	year	13853	8/94	80s
Total cost, 4-year public college/university	year	5855	8/94	80s
Tuition, 2-year public college/university, in-state	year	1076	8/94	80s
Tuition, 4-year private college/university, in-state	year	9287	8/94	80s
Tuition, 4-year public college/university, in-state	year	1784	8/94	80s
Energy and Fuels				
Energy, combined forms, 1800 sq. ft.	mo.	125.04	12/94	2c
Fuel oil and other fuels, expenditures	year	56	91	81r
Gas, natural, expenditures	year	150	91	81r
Gas, reg unlead, taxes inc., cash, self-service	gal	1.15	12/94	2c
Gasoline and motor oil purchased	year	1152	91	81r
Gasoline, unleaded midgrade	gallon	1.21	4/93	82r
Gasoline, unleaded premium	gallon	1.30	4/93	82r
Gasoline, unleaded regular	gallon	1.10	4/93	82r
Entertainment				
Bowling, evening rate	game	2.62	12/94	2c
Concert ticket, Pearl Jam group	perf	20.00	94	50r
Entertainment, total expenditures	year	1266	91	81r
Fees and admissions, expenditures	year	306	91	81r
Monopoly game, Parker Brothers', No. 9	game	10.23	12/94	2c
Movie	adm	6.13	12/94	2c
Pets, toys, playground equipment, expenditures	year	271	91	81r
Reading, expenditures	year	131	91	81r
Televisions, radios, and sound equipment, expenditures	year	439	91	81r
Tennis balls, yellow, Wilson or Penn, 3	can	2.51	12/94	2c
Funerals				
Burial, immediate, container provided by funeral home		1370.36	1/95	54r
Cards, acknowledgment		14.83	1/95	54r
Casket, minimum alternative		192.52	1/95	54r
Cosmetology, hair care, etc.		102.27	1/95	54r
Cremation, direct, container provided by funeral home		1065.64	1/95	54r
Embalming		304.29	1/95	54r
Funeral, funeral home		287.83	1/95	54r
Funeral, other facility		284.14	1/95	54r
Graveside service		349.13	1/95	54r
Hearse, local		132.27	1/95	54r
Limousine, local		98.45	1/95	54r
Memorial service		270.59	1/95	54r
Service charge, professional, nondeclinable		933.59	1/95	54r
Visitation and viewing		225.83	1/95	54r
Groceries				
Groceries, ACCRA Index		96.90	12/94	2c

Values are in dollars or fractions of dollars. In the column headed *Ref*, references are shown to sources. Each reference is followed by a letter. These refer to the geographical level for which data were reported: s=State, r=Region, and c=City or metro. The abbreviation *ex* is used to mean *except* or *excluding*; *exp* stands for expenditures. For other abbreviations and further explanations, please see the Introduction.

Orlando, FL - continued

Item	Per	Value	Date	Ref.
Groceries				
Apples, Red Delicious	lb.	0.73	12/94	82r
Baby food, strained vegetables, lowest price	4-4.5 oz.	0.36	12/94	2c
Bacon, sliced	lb.	1.67	12/94	82r
Bananas	lb.	0.36	12/94	2c
Bananas	lb.	0.42	12/94	82r
Beef or hamburger, ground	lb.	1.00	12/94	2c
Beef purchases	year	213	91	81r
Beverage purchases, alcoholic	year	249	91	81r
Beverage purchases, nonalcoholic	year	207	91	81r
Bologna, all beef or mixed	lb.	2.27	12/94	82r
Bread, white	24-oz.	0.79	12/94	2c
Bread, white, pan	lb.	0.68	12/94	82r
Cabbage	lb.	0.42	12/94	82r
Carrots, short trimmed and topped	lb.	0.53	12/94	82r
Cereals and bakery products purchases	year	345	91	81r
Cereals and cereals products purchases	year	127	91	81r
Cheddar cheese, natural	lb.	3.58	12/94	82r
Cheese, Kraft grated Parmesan	8-oz.	2.99	12/94	2c
Chicken breast, bone-in	lb.	1.71	12/94	82r
Chicken, fresh, whole	lb.	0.78	12/94	82r
Chicken, whole fryer	lb.	0.92	12/94	2c
Chuck roast, USDA choice, boneless	lb.	2.26	12/94	82r
Cigarettes, Winston, Kings	carton	16.69	12/94	2c
Coffee, vacuum-packed	13 oz.	3.23	12/94	2c
Corn Flakes, Kellogg's or Post Toasties	18 oz.	2.17	12/94	2c
Corn, frozen, whole kernel, lowest price	10 oz.	0.63	12/94	2c
Crackers, soda, salted	lb.	1.27	12/94	82r
Cucumbers	lb.	0.65	12/94	82r
Dairy products (other) purchases	year	141	91	81r
Eggs, Grade A large	dozen	0.79	12/94	2c
Eggs, Grade A large	dozen	0.87	12/94	82r
Fish and seafood purchases	year	72	91	81r
Flour, white, all purpose	lb.	0.23	12/94	82r
Food purchases, food eaten at home	year	2381	91	81r
Foods purchased away from home, not prepared by consumer	year	1696	91	81r
Frankfurters, all meat or all beef	lb.	1.74	12/94	82r
Fruits and vegetables purchases	year	380	91	81r
Grapefruit	lb.	0.45	12/94	82r
Grapes, Thompson seedless	lb.	2.30	12/94	82r
Ground beef, 100% beef	lb.	1.37	12/94	82r
Ground chuck, 100% beef	lb.	1.97	12/94	82r
Ham, boneless, exc. canned	lb.	2.54	12/94	82r
Ice cream, prepackaged, bulk, regular	1/2 gal.	2.47	12/94	82r
Lemons	lb.	1.02	12/94	82r
Lettuce, iceberg	lb.	0.96	12/94	82r
Lettuce, iceberg	head	0.96	12/94	2c
Margarine, Blue Bonnet or Parkay cubes	lb.	0.58	12/94	2c
Margarine, stick	lb.	0.77	12/94	82r
Meats, poultry, fish, and eggs purchases	year	655	91	81r
Milk and cream (fresh) purchases	year	130	91	81r
Milk, whole	1/2 gal.	1.38	12/94	2c
Orange juice, frozen concentrate 12-oz. can	16 oz.	1.36	12/94	82r
Orange juice, Minute Maid frozen	12-oz.	1.08	12/94	2c
Oranges, Navel	lb.	0.54	12/94	82r
Peaches, halves or slices, Hunt's, Del Monte, or Libby's	29-oz.	1.35	12/94	2c
Pears, Anjou	lb.	0.81	12/94	82r
Peas, sweet, Del Monte or Green Giant	15-17 oz.	0.55	12/94	2c
Pork chops, center cut, bone-in	lb.	3.07	12/94	82r
Pork purchases	year	142	91	81r
Potato chips	16-oz.	3.15	12/94	82r
Potatoes, frozen, French fried	lb.	0.82	12/94	82r
Potatoes, white	lb.	0.34	12/94	82r
Potatoes, white or red	10-lb. sack	2.46	12/94	2c
Rice, white, long grain, uncooked	lb.	0.48	12/94	82r
Round roast, USDA choice, boneless	lb.	2.91	12/94	82r

Orlando, FL - continued

Item	Per	Value	Date	Ref.
Groceries - continued				
Sausage, fresh	lb.	1.82	12/94	82r
Sausage, Jimmy Dean, 100% pork	lb.	2.16	12/94	2c
Shortening, vegetable oil blends	lb.	0.75	12/94	82r
Shortening, vegetable, Crisco	3-lb.	2.69	12/94	2c
Soft drink, Coca Cola, ex deposit	2 lit	1.09	12/94	2c
Spaghetti and macaroni	lb.	0.87	12/94	82r
Steak, rib eye, USDA choice, boneless	lb.	6.85	12/94	82r
Steak, round, graded & ungraded, exc. USDA prime & choice	lb.	2.96	12/94	82r
Steak, round, USDA choice, boneless	lb.	3.17	12/94	82r
Steak, sirloin, USDA choice, boneless	lb.	4.12	12/94	82r
Steak, t-bone	lb.	5.89	12/94	2c
Steak, T-bone, USDA choice, bone-in	lb.	5.63	12/94	82r
Sugar and other sweets, eaten at home, expenditures	year	93	91	81r
Sugar, cane or beet	4 lbs.	1.56	12/94	2c
Sugar, white, all sizes	lb.	0.39	12/94	82r
Tobacco products and smoking supplies, total expenditures	year	286	91	81r
Tomatoes, field grown	lb.	1.36	12/94	82r
Tomatoes, Hunt's or Del Monte	14.5 oz.	0.67	12/94	2c
Tuna, chunk, light	lb.	1.94	12/94	82r
Tuna, chunk, light, oil-packed	6.125-6.5 oz.	0.66	12/94	2c
Turkey, frozen, whole	lb.	0.96	12/94	82r
Yogurt, natural, fruit flavored	8 oz.	0.58	12/94	82r
Goods and Services				
Miscellaneous goods and services, ACCRA Index		102.20	12/94	2c
Health Care				
Health care, ACCRA Index		111.50	12/94	2c
Adenosine, emergency room	treat	100.00	95	23r
Antibiotic ointment, Polysporin	1.5 oz.	3.91	12/94	2c
Bladder tap, superpubic, infant, emergency room	treat	119.00	95	23r
Blood analysis, emergency room	treat	25.00	95	23r
Blood tests, abdominal pain, emergency room	treat	25.00	95	23r
Burn dressing, emergency room	treat	266.00	95	23r
Cardiology interpretation, emergency room	treat	26.00	95	23r
Chest X-ray, emergency room	treat	78.00	95	23r
Childbirth, Cesarean delivery, hospital charge	birth	5462.00	12/91	69r
Childbirth, Cesarean delivery, physician charge	birth	2228.00	12/91	69r
Childbirth, normal delivery, hospital charge	birth	2943.00	12/91	69r
Childbirth, normal delivery, physician charge	birth	1619.00	12/91	69r
Defibrillation pads, emergency room	treat	6.00	95	23r
Dentist's fee, adult teeth cleaning and periodic oral exam	visit	59.60	12/94	2c
Doctor's fee, routine exam, established patient	visit	45.00	12/94	2c
Drugs, expenditures	year	297	91	81r
Gastric tube insertion, nasal, emergency room	treat	25.00	95	23r
Health care, total expenditures	year	1600	91	81r
Health insurance expenditures	year	637	91	81r
Heart monitor, emergency room	treat	40.00	95	23r
Hospital care, semiprivate room	day	449.00	12/94	2c
Insurance premium, family medical care	month	301.92	1/95	41s
Intravenous fluids, emergency room	treat	130.00	95	23r
Intravenous fluids, emergency room	liter	26.00	95	23r
Intravenous line, central, emergency room	treat	342.00	95	23r
Liver function tests, abdominal pain, emergency room	treat	26.00	95	23r
Medical care charges, total, emergency room, third-degree burns	treat	2101.00	95	23r
Medical care charges, total, emergency, infant with fever	treat	628.00	95	23r
Medical services expenditures	year	573	91	81r

Values are in dollars or fractions of dollars. In the column headed *Ref*, references are shown to sources. Each reference is followed by a letter. These refer to the geographical level for which data were reported: s=State, r=Region, and c=City or metro. The abbreviation *ex* is used to mean *except* or *excluding*; *exp* stands for expenditures. For other abbreviations and further explanations, please see the Introduction.

Orlando, FL - continued

Item	Per	Value	Date	Ref.
Health Care				
Medical supplies expenditures	year	93	91	81r
Morphine, emergency room	treat	34.00	95	23r
Nursing care and facilities charges, emergency room	treat	252.00	95	23r
Nursing care and facilities charges, emergency, infant with fever	treat	252.00	95	23r
Nursing care and facilities charges, emergency, third-degree burns	treat	861.00	95	23r
Physician's charges, emergency, infant with fever	treat	212.00	95	23r
Physician's charges, emergency, third-degree burns	treat	372.00	95	23r
Physician's fee, emergency room	treat	372.00	95	23r
Physician's fee, general practitioner	visit	51.20	12/93	60r
Surgery, open-heart	proc	42374.00	1/93	14r
Ultrasound, abdominal, emergency room	treat	276.00	95	23r
Urinalysis, emergency room	treat	20.00	95	23r
Urinalysis, infant, emergency room	treat	20.00	95	23r
X-rays, emergency room	treat	78.00	95	23r
Household Goods				
Appl. repair, service call, wash mach	min. lab. chg.	33.30	12/94	2c
Floor coverings, expenditures	year	48	91	81r
Furniture, expenditures	year	280	91	81r
Household equipment, misc. expenditures	year	342	91	81r
Household expenditures, miscellaneous	year	256	91	81r
Household furnishings and equipment, expenditures	year	988	91	81r
Household operations expenditures	year	468	91	81r
Household textiles, expenditures	year	95	91	81r
Housekeeping supplies, expenditures	year	380	91	81r
Laundry and cleaning supplies, expenditures	year	109	91	81r
Laundry detergent, Tide Ultra, Bold, or Cheer	42 oz.	2.84	12/94	2c
Postage and stationery, expenditures	year	105	91	81r
Tissues, facial, Kleenex brand	175	0.94	12/94	2c
Housing				
Housing, ACCRA Index		89.10	12/94	2c
Add garage/carport		6,980	3/95	74r
Add room(s)		11,403	3/95	74r
Apartment condominium or co-op, median	unit	68600	12/94	62r
Car rental	day	31.00	5/95	95c
Dwellings (owned), expenditures	year	2428	91	81r
Enclose porch/patio/breezeway		4,572	3/95	74r
Finish room in basement/attic		3,794	3/95	74r
Home, existing, single-family, median	unit	120200	12/94	62r
Home, existing, single-family, median	unit	89.20	12/94	62c
Hotel room	day	98.00	5/95	95c
House payment, principal and interest, 25% down payment	mo.	642	12/94	2c
House, 1800 sq ft, 8000 sq ft lot, new, urban, utilities	total	105156	12/94	2c
Maintenance, repairs, insurance, and other housing expenditures	year	531	91	81r
Mortgage interest and charges expenditures	year	1506	91	81r
Mtge. rate, incl. points and orig. fee, 30-year conv. fixed or ARM	mo.	9.13	12/94	2c
Princ. & int., mortgage, median-price exist. sing.-family home	mo.	540	12/94	62r
Property taxes expenditures	year	391	91	81r
Redesign, restructure more than half of home's interior		17,641	3/95	74r
Rent, apartment, 2 br., 1 1/2-2 baths, unfurnished, 950 sq ft, water	mo.	589	12/94	2c
Rental units expenditures	year	1264	91	81r
Insurance and Pensions				
Auto insurance, private passenger	year	753.93	12/94	71s
Insurance and pensions, personal, expenditures	year	2395	91	81r

Orlando, FL - continued

Item	Per	Value	Date	Ref.
Insurance and Pensions - continued				
Insurance, life and other personal, expenditures	year	368	91	81r
Pensions and Social Security, expenditures	year	2027	91	81r
Personal Goods				
Shampoo, Alberto VO5	15-oz.	0.97	12/94	2c
Toothpaste, Crest or Colgate	6-7 oz.	1.68	12/94	2c
Personal Services				
Dry cleaning, man's 2-pc. suit		6.31	12/94	2c
Haircut, man's barbershop, no styling		6.70	12/94	2c
Haircut, woman's shampoo, trim, blow-dry		25.00	12/94	2c
Personal services expenditures	year	212	91	81r
Restaurant Food				
Chicken, fried, thigh and drumstick		2.08	12/94	2c
Dining expenditures, family	week	33.83	94	73r
Hamburger with cheese	1/4 lb.	1.86	12/94	2c
Pizza, Pizza Hut or Pizza Inn	12-13 in.	7.99	12/94	2c
Taxes				
Taxes, Federal income, expenditures	year	2275	91	81r
Taxes, personal, expenditures	year	2715	91	81r
Taxes, State and local income, expenditures	year	365	91	81r
Transportation				
Transportation, ACCRA Index		97.80	12/94	2c
Bus fare, one-way	trip	0.75	12/95	1c
Bus fare, up to 10 miles	one-way	0.75	12/94	2c
Cars and trucks purchased, new	year	1306	91	81r
Cars and trucks purchased, used	year	942	91	81r
Driver's learning permit fee	perm	20.00	1/94	84s
Driver's license fee	orig	20.00	1/94	84s
Driver's license fee, duplicate	lic	10.00	1/94	84s
Driver's license reinstatement fee, min.	susp	25.00	1/94	85s
Driver's license renewal fee	renew	15.00	1/94	84s
Identification card, nondriver	card	3.00	1/94	83s
Motorcycle learning permit fee	perm	20.00	1/94	84s
Motorcycle license fee	orig	20.00	1/94	84s
Motorcycle license fee, duplicate	lic	10.00	1/94	84s
Motorcycle license renewal fee	renew	15.00	1/94	84s
Public transportation expenditures	year	249	91	81r
Tire balance, computer or spin bal., front	wheel	6.59	12/94	2c
Transportation expenditures, total	year	5307	91	81r
Vehicle finance charges	year	346	91	81r
Vehicle insurance expenditures	year	544	91	81r
Vehicle maintenance and repairs expenditures	year	600	91	81r
Vehicle purchases	year	2275	91	81r
Vehicle rental, leases, licenses, etc. expenditures	year	141	91	81r
Vehicles purchased, other than cars and trucks	year	27	91	81r
Travel				
Car rental	day	33.99	1/93	49c
Car rental	week	144.99	1/93	49c
Utilities				
Utilities, ACCRA Index		109.80	12/94	2c
Electricity expenditures	year	950	91	81r
Electricity, 1800 sq. ft., new home	mo.	125.04	12/94	2c
Utilities, fuels, and public services, total expenditures	year	2000	91	81r
Water and other public services, expenditures	year	227	91	81r
Weddings				
Bridal attendants' gowns	event	750	10/93	76r
Bridal gown	event	852	10/93	76r
Bridal headpiece and veil	event	167	10/93	76r
Bride's wedding band	event	708	10/93	76r
Clergy	event	224	10/93	76r
Engagement ring	event	2756	10/93	76r

Values are in dollars or fractions of dollars. In the column headed *Ref*, references are shown to sources. Each reference is followed by a letter. These refer to the geographical level for which data were reported: s=State, r=Region, and c=City or metro. The abbreviation *ex* is used to mean *except* or *excluding*; *exp* stands for *expenditures*. For other abbreviations and further explanations, please see the Introduction.

Orlando, FL - continued

Item	Per	Value	Date	Ref.
Weddings				
Flowers	event	863	10/93	76r
Formal wear for groom	event	106	10/93	76r
Groom's attendants' formal wear	event	530	10/93	76r
Groom's wedding band	event	402	10/93	76r
Music	event	600	10/93	76r
Photography	event	1088	10/93	76r
Shoes for bride	event	50	10/93	76r
Videography	event	483	10/93	76r
Wedding invitations and announcements	event	342	10/93	76r
Wedding reception	event	7000	10/93	76r

Owensboro, KY

Item	Per	Value	Date	Ref.
Composite, ACCRA index		94.10	12/94	2c
Alcoholic Beverages				
Beer, Miller Lite, Bud, 12-oz., ex deposit	6	3.92	12/94	2c
J & B Scotch	750-ml.	15.96	12/94	2c
Wine, Gallo Chablis blanc	1.5-lit	5.16	12/94	2c
Appliances				
Appliances (major), expenditures	year	153	91	81r
Average annual exp.				
Food, health care, personal goods, services	year	27020	91	81r
Charity				
Cash contributions, expenditures	year	839	91	81r
Clothing				
Apparel, men and boys, total expenditures	year	380	91	81r
Apparel, women and girls, total expenditures	year	660	91	81r
Footwear, expenditures	year	193	91	81r
Jeans, man's denim		32.59	12/94	2c
Shirt, man's dress shirt		28.74	12/94	2c
Undervest, boy's size 10-14, cotton	3	4.19	12/94	2c
Communications				
Long-distance telephone rate, day, addl. min., 1-10 mi.	min.	0.14	12/93	9s
Long-distance telephone rate, day, initial min., 1-10 mi.	min.	0.18	12/93	9s
Newspaper subscription, dly. and Sun. delivery	month	10.95	12/94	2c
Phone line, single, business, field visit	inst	64.00	12/93	9s
Phone line, single, business, no field visit	inst	85.25	12/93	9s
Phone line, single, residence, field visit	inst	43.63	12/93	9s
Phone line, single, residence, no field visit	inst	29.38	12/93	9s
Telephone bill, family of four	month	19.95	12/94	2c
Telephone service, expenditures	year	616	91	81r
Telephone, residential, flat rate	mo.	12.69	12/93	8c
Education				
Board, 4-year private college/university	year	1897	8/94	80s
Board, 4-year public college/university	year	1744	8/94	80s
Education, total expenditures	year	319	91	81r
Room, 4-year private college/university	year	1644	8/94	80s
Room, 4-year public college/university	year	1370	8/94	80s
Total cost, 4-year private college/university	year	10097	8/94	80s
Total cost, 4-year public college/university	year	5027	8/94	80s
Tuition, 2-year public college/university, in-state	year	962	8/94	80s
Tuition, 4-year private college/university, in-state	year	6556	8/94	80s
Tuition, 4-year public college/university, in-state	year	1913	8/94	80s
Energy and Fuels				
Energy, combined forms, 1800 sq. ft.	mo.	88.00	12/94	2c
Energy, exc. electricity, 1800 sq. ft.	mo.	37.17	12/94	2c
Fuel oil and other fuels, expenditures	year	56	91	81r
Gas, cooking, 10 therms	month	8.56	2/94	65c
Gas, cooking, 30 therms	month	16.98	2/94	65c
Gas, cooking, 50 therms	month	25.39	2/94	65c

Owensboro, KY - continued

Item	Per	Value	Date	Ref.
Energy and Fuels - continued				
Gas, heating, winter, 100 therms	month	46.43	2/94	65c
Gas, heating, winter, average use	month	80.17	2/94	65c
Gas, natural, expenditures	year	150	91	81r
Gas, reg unlead, taxes inc., cash, self-service	gal	1.11	12/94	2c
Gasoline and motor oil purchased	year	1152	91	81r
Gasoline, unleaded midgrade	gallon	1.21	4/93	82r
Gasoline, unleaded premium	gallon	1.30	4/93	82r
Gasoline, unleaded regular	gallon	1.10	4/93	82r
Entertainment				
Bowling, evening rate	game	2.13	12/94	2c
Concert ticket, Pearl Jam group	perf	20.00	94	50r
Entertainment, total expenditures	year	1266	91	81r
Fees and admissions, expenditures	year	306	91	81r
Monopoly game, Parker Brothers', No. 9	game	11.20	12/94	2c
Movie	adm	5.50	12/94	2c
Pets, toys, playground equipment, expenditures	year	271	91	81r
Reading, expenditures	year	131	91	81r
Televisions, radios, and sound equipment, expenditures	year	439	91	81r
Tennis balls, yellow, Wilson or Penn, 3	can	2.13	12/94	2c
Funerals				
Burial, immediate, container provided by funeral home		1298.96	1/95	54r
Cards, acknowledgment		21.26	1/95	54r
Casket, minimum alternative		204.95	1/95	54r
Cosmetology, hair care, etc.		85.40	1/95	54r
Cremation, direct, container provided by funeral home		1054.77	1/95	54r
Embalming		287.71	1/95	54r
Funeral, funeral home		269.18	1/95	54r
Funeral, other facility		272.88	1/95	54r
Graveside service		302.54	1/95	54r
Hearse, local		122.08	1/95	54r
Limousine, local		80.31	1/95	54r
Memorial service		277.66	1/95	54r
Service charge, professional, nondeclinable		896.65	1/95	54r
Visitation and viewing		232.39	1/95	54r
Groceries				
Groceries, ACCRA Index		100.30	12/94	2c
Apples, Red Delicious	lb.	0.73	12/94	82r
Baby food, strained vegetables, lowest price	4-4.5 oz.	0.31	12/94	2c
Bacon, sliced	lb.	1.67	12/94	82r
Bananas	lb.	0.51	12/94	2c
Bananas	lb.	0.42	12/94	82r
Beef or hamburger, ground	lb.	1.23	12/94	2c
Beef purchases	year	213	91	81r
Beverage purchases, alcoholic	year	249	91	81r
Beverage purchases, nonalcoholic	year	207	91	81r
Bologna, all beef or mixed	lb.	2.27	12/94	82r
Bread, white	24-oz.	0.83	12/94	2c
Bread, white, pan	lb.	0.68	12/94	82r
Cabbage	lb.	0.42	12/94	82r
Carrots, short trimmed and topped	lb.	0.53	12/94	82r
Cereals and bakery products purchases	year	345	91	81r
Cereals and cereals products purchases	year	127	91	81r
Cheddar cheese, natural	lb.	3.58	12/94	82r
Cheese, Kraft grated Parmesan	8-oz.	3.19	12/94	2c
Chicken breast, bone-in	lb.	1.71	12/94	82r
Chicken, fresh, whole	lb.	0.78	12/94	82r
Chicken, whole fryer	lb.	0.84	12/94	2c
Chuck roast, USDA choice, boneless	lb.	2.26	12/94	82r
Cigarettes, Winston, Kings	carton	13.45	12/94	2c
Coffee, vacuum-packed	13 oz.	3.19	12/94	2c
Corn Flakes, Kellogg's or Post Toasties	18 oz.	2.96	12/94	2c
Corn, frozen, whole kernel, lowest price	10 oz.	0.78	12/94	2c
Crackers, soda, salted	lb.	1.27	12/94	82r
Cucumbers	lb.	0.65	12/94	82r
Dairy products (other) purchases	year	141	91	81r

Values are in dollars or fractions of dollars. In the column headed *Ref*, references are shown to sources. Each reference is followed by a letter. These refer to the geographical level for which data were reported: s = State, r = Region, and c = City or metro. The abbreviation *ex* is used to mean *except* or *excluding*; *exp* stands for *expenditures*. For other abbreviations and further explanations, please see the Introduction.

Owensboro, KY - continued

Item	Per	Value	Date	Ref.
Groceries				
Eggs, Grade A large	dozen	0.76	12/94	2c
Eggs, Grade A large	dozen	0.87	12/94	82r
Fish and seafood purchases	year	72	91	81r
Flour, white, all purpose	lb.	0.23	12/94	82r
Food purchases, food eaten at home	year	2381	91	81r
Foods purchased away from home, not prepared by consumer	year	1696	91	81r
Frankfurters, all meat or all beef	lb.	1.74	12/94	82r
Fruits and vegetables purchases	year	380	91	81r
Grapefruit	lb.	0.45	12/94	82r
Grapes, Thompson seedless	lb.	2.30	12/94	82r
Ground beef, 100% beef	lb.	1.37	12/94	82r
Ground chuck, 100% beef	lb.	1.97	12/94	82r
Ham, boneless, exc. canned	lb.	2.54	12/94	82r
Ice cream, prepackaged, bulk, regular	1/2 gal.	2.47	12/94	82r
Lemons	lb.	1.02	12/94	82r
Lettuce, iceberg	lb.	0.96	12/94	82r
Lettuce, iceberg	head	0.96	12/94	2c
Margarine, Blue Bonnet or Parkay cubes	lb.	0.53	12/94	2c
Margarine, stick	lb.	0.77	12/94	82r
Meats, poultry, fish, and eggs purchases	year	655	91	81r
Milk and cream (fresh) purchases	year	130	91	81r
Milk, whole	1/2 gal.	1.58	12/94	2c
Orange juice, frozen concentrate 12-oz. can	16 oz.	1.36	12/94	82r
Orange juice, Minute Maid frozen	12-oz.	1.22	12/94	2c
Oranges, Navel	lb.	0.54	12/94	82r
Peaches, halves or slices, Hunt's, Del Monte, or Libby's	29-oz.	1.44	12/94	2c
Pears, Anjou	lb.	0.81	12/94	82r
Peas, sweet, Del Monte or Green Giant	15-17 oz.	0.54	12/94	2c
Pork chops, center cut, bone-in	lb.	3.07	12/94	82r
Pork purchases	year	142	91	81r
Potato chips	16-oz.	3.15	12/94	82r
Potatoes, frozen, French fried	lb.	0.82	12/94	82r
Potatoes, white	lb.	0.34	12/94	82r
Potatoes, white or red	10-lb. sack	2.71	12/94	2c
Rice, white, long grain, uncooked	lb.	0.48	12/94	82r
Round roast, USDA choice, boneless	lb.	2.91	12/94	82r
Sausage, fresh	lb.	1.82	12/94	82r
Sausage, Jimmy Dean, 100% pork	lb.	2.21	12/94	2c
Shortening, vegetable oil blends	lb.	0.75	12/94	82r
Shortening, vegetable, Crisco	3-lb.	2.12	12/94	2c
Soft drink, Coca Cola, ex deposit	2 lit	1.14	12/94	2c
Spaghetti and macaroni	lb.	0.87	12/94	82r
Steak, rib eye, USDA choice, boneless	lb.	6.85	12/94	82r
Steak, round, graded & ungraded, exc. USDA prime & choice	lb.	2.96	12/94	82r
Steak, round, USDA choice, boneless	lb.	3.17	12/94	82r
Steak, sirloin, USDA choice, boneless	lb.	4.12	12/94	82r
Steak, t-bone	lb.	5.24	12/94	2c
Steak, T-bone, USDA choice, bone-in	lb.	5.63	12/94	82r
Sugar and other sweets, eaten at home, expenditures	year	93	91	81r
Sugar, cane or beet	4 lbs.	1.48	12/94	2c
Sugar, white, all sizes	lb.	0.39	12/94	82r
Tobacco products and smoking supplies, total expenditures	year	286	91	81r
Tomatoes, field grown	lb.	1.36	12/94	82r
Tomatoes, Hunt's or Del Monte	14.5 oz.	0.73	12/94	2c
Tuna, chunk, light	lb.	1.94	12/94	82r
Tuna, chunk, light, oil-packed	6.125-6.5 oz.	0.71	12/94	2c
Turkey, frozen, whole	lb.	0.96	12/94	82r
Yogurt, natural, fruit flavored	8 oz.	0.58	12/94	82r
Goods and Services				
Miscellaneous goods and services, ACCRA Index		97.50	12/94	2c

Owensboro, KY - continued

Item	Per	Value	Date	Ref.
Health Care				
Health care, ACCRA Index		90.70	12/94	2c
Adenosine, emergency room	treat	100.00	95	23r
Antibiotic ointment, Polysporin	1.5 oz.	3.93	12/94	2c
Bladder tap, superpubic, infant, emergency room	treat	119.00	95	23r
Blood analysis, emergency room	treat	25.00	95	23r
Blood tests, abdominal pain, emergency room	treat	25.00	95	23r
Burn dressing, emergency room	treat	266.00	95	23r
Cardiology interpretation, emergency room	treat	26.00	95	23r
Chest X-ray, emergency room	treat	78.00	95	23r
Childbirth, Cesarean delivery, hospital charge	birth	5462.00	12/91	69r
Childbirth, Cesarean delivery, physician charge	birth	2228.00	12/91	69r
Childbirth, normal delivery, hospital charge	birth	2943.00	12/91	69r
Childbirth, normal delivery, physician charge	birth	1619.00	12/91	69r
Defibrillation pads, emergency room	treat	6.00	95	23r
Dentist's fee, adult teeth cleaning and periodic oral exam	visit	48.40	12/94	2c
Doctor's fee, routine exam, established patient	visit	33.60	12/94	2c
Drugs, expenditures	year	297	91	81r
Gastric tube insertion, nasal, emergency room	treat	25.00	95	23r
Health care, total expenditures	year	1600	91	81r
Health insurance expenditures	year	637	91	81r
Heart monitor, emergency room	treat	40.00	95	23r
Hospital care, semiprivate room	day	377.00	12/94	2c
Insurance premium, family medical care	month	332.39	1/95	41s
Intravenous fluids, emergency room	treat	130.00	95	23r
Intravenous fluids, emergency room	liter	26.00	95	23r
Intravenous line, central, emergency room	treat	342.00	95	23r
Liver function tests, abdominal pain, emergency room	treat	26.00	95	23r
Medical care charges, total, emergency room, third-degree burns	treat	2101.00	95	23r
Medical care charges, total, emergency, infant with fever	treat	628.00	95	23r
Medical services expenditures	year	573	91	81r
Medical supplies expenditures	year	93	91	81r
Morphine, emergency room	treat	34.00	95	23r
Nursing care and facilities charges, emergency room	treat	252.00	95	23r
Nursing care and facilities charges, emergency, infant with fever	treat	252.00	95	23r
Nursing care and facilities charges, emergency, third-degree burns	treat	861.00	95	23r
Physician's charges, emergency, infant with fever	treat	212.00	95	23r
Physician's charges, emergency, third-degree burns	treat	372.00	95	23r
Physician's fee, emergency room	treat	372.00	95	23r
Physician's fee, general practitioner	visit	51.20	12/93	60r
Surgery, open-heart	proc	42374.00	1/93	14r
Ultrasound, abdominal, emergency room	treat	276.00	95	23r
Urinalysis, emergency room	treat	20.00	95	23r
Urinalysis, infant, emergency room	treat	20.00	95	23r
X-rays, emergency room	treat	78.00	95	23r
Household Goods				
Appl. repair, service call, wash mach	min. lab. chg.	28.80	12/94	2c
Floor coverings, expenditures	year	48	91	81r
Furniture, expenditures	year	280	91	81r
Household equipment, misc. expenditures	year	342	91	81r
Household expenditures, miscellaneous	year	256	91	81r
Household furnishings and equipment, expenditures	year	988	91	81r
Household operations expenditures	year	468	91	81r
Household textiles, expenditures	year	95	91	81r
Housekeeping supplies, expenditures	year	380	91	81r

Values are in dollars or fractions of dollars. In the column headed *Ref*, references are shown to sources. Each reference is followed by a letter. These refer to the geographical level for which data were reported: s=State, r=Region, and c=City or metro. The abbreviation *ex* is used to mean *except* or *excluding*; *exp* stands for *expenditures*. For other abbreviations and further explanations, please see the Introduction.

Owensboro, KY - continued

Item	Per	Value	Date	Ref.
Household Goods				
Laundry and cleaning supplies, expenditures	year	109	91	81r
Laundry detergent, Tide Ultra, Bold, or Cheer	42 oz.	3.56	12/94	2c
Postage and stationery, expenditures	year	105	91	81r
Tissues, facial, Kleenex brand	175	1.04	12/94	2c
Housing				
Housing, ACCRA Index		90.50	12/94	2c
Add garage/carport		6,980	3/95	74r
Add room(s)		11,403	3/95	74r
Apartment condominium or co-op, median	unit	68600	12/94	62r
Dwellings (owned), expenditures	year	2428	91	81r
Enclose porch/patio/breezeway		4,572	3/95	74r
Finish room in basement/attic		3,794	3/95	74r
Home, existing, single-family, median	unit	120200	12/94	62r
House payment, principal and interest, 25% down payment	mo.	717	12/94	2c
House, 1800 sq ft, 8000 sq ft lot, new, urban, utilities	total	116333	12/94	2c
Maintenance, repairs, insurance, and other housing expenditures	year	531	91	81r
Mortgage interest and charges expenditures	year	1506	91	81r
Mtge. rate, incl. points and orig. fee, 30-year conv. fixed or ARM	mo.	9.24	12/94	2c
Princ. & int., mortgage, median-price exist. sing.-family home	mo.	540	12/94	62r
Property taxes expenditures	year	391	91	81r
Redesign, restructure more than half of home's interior		17,641	3/95	74r
Rent, apartment, 2 br., 1 1/2-2 baths, unfurnished, 950 sq ft, water	mo.	408	12/94	2c
Rental units expenditures	year	1264	91	81r
Insurance and Pensions				
Auto insurance, private passenger	year	616.22	12/94	71s
Insurance and pensions, personal, expenditures	year	2395	91	81r
Insurance, life and other personal, expenditures	year	368	91	81r
Pensions and Social Security, expenditures	year	2027	91	81r
Personal Goods				
Shampoo, Alberto VO5	15-oz.	1.25	12/94	2c
Toothpaste, Crest or Colgate	6-7 oz.	1.94	12/94	2c
Personal Services				
Dry cleaning, man's 2-pc. suit		5.48	12/94	2c
Haircut, man's barbershop, no styling		8.75	12/94	2c
Haircut, woman's shampoo, trim, blow-dry		18.90	12/94	2c
Personal services expenditures	year	212	91	81r
Restaurant Food				
Chicken, fried, thigh and drumstick		2.29	12/94	2c
Dining expenditures, family	week	33.83	94	73r
Hamburger with cheese	1/4 lb.	1.75	12/94	2c
Pizza, Pizza Hut or Pizza Inn	12-13 in.	7.50	12/94	2c
Taxes				
Taxes, Federal income, expenditures	year	2275	91	81r
Taxes, personal, expenditures	year	2715	91	81r
Taxes, State and local income, expenditures	year	365	91	81r
Transportation				
Transportation, ACCRA Index		94.70	12/94	2c
Bus fare, one-way	trip	1.00	12/95	1c
Cars and trucks purchased, new	year	1306	91	81r
Cars and trucks purchased, used	year	942	91	81r
Driver's learning permit fee	perm	2.00	1/94	84s
Driver's license fee	orig	8.00	1/94	84s
Driver's license fee, duplicate	lic	2.00	1/94	84s
Driver's license reinstatement fee, min.	susp	30.00	1/94	85s
Driver's license renewal fee	renew	8.00	1/94	84s
Identification card, nondriver	card	4.00	1/94	83s

Owensboro, KY - continued

Item	Per	Value	Date	Ref.
Transportation - continued				
Motorcycle learning permit fee	perm	2.00	1/94	84s
Motorcycle license fee	orig	8.00	1/94	84s
Motorcycle license fee, duplicate	lic	2.00	1/94	84s
Motorcycle license renewal fee	renew	8.00	1/94	84s
Public transportation expenditures	year	249	91	81r
Tire balance, computer or spin bal., front	wheel	6.00	12/94	2c
Transportation expenditures, total	year	5307	91	81r
Vehicle finance charges	year	346	91	81r
Vehicle insurance expenditures	year	544	91	81r
Vehicle maintenance and repairs expenditures	year	600	91	81r
Vehicle purchases	year	2275	91	81r
Vehicle rental, leases, licenses, etc. expenditures	year	141	91	81r
Vehicles purchased, other than cars and trucks	year	27	91	81r
Utilities				
Utilities, ACCRA Index		81.60	12/94	2c
Electricity expenditures	year	950	91	81r
Electricity, (part.), other, 1800 sq. ft., new home	mo.	50.83	12/94	2c
Utilities, fuels, and public services, total expenditures	year	2000	91	81r
Water and other public services, expenditures	year	227	91	81r
Weddings				
Bridal attendants' gowns	event	750	10/93	76r
Bridal gown	event	852	10/93	76r
Bridal headpiece and veil	event	167	10/93	76r
Bride's wedding band	event	708	10/93	76r
Clergy	event	224	10/93	76r
Engagement ring	event	2756	10/93	76r
Flowers	event	863	10/93	76r
Formal wear for groom	event	106	10/93	76r
Groom's attendants' formal wear	event	530	10/93	76r
Groom's wedding band	event	402	10/93	76r
Music	event	600	10/93	76r
Photography	event	1088	10/93	76r
Shoes for bride	event	50	10/93	76r
Videography	event	483	10/93	76r
Wedding invitations and announcements	event	342	10/93	76r
Wedding reception	event	7000	10/93	76r

Oxnard-Ventura, CA

Item	Per	Value	Date	Ref.
Appliances				
Appliances (major), expenditures	year	160	91	81r
Average annual exp.				
Food, health care, personal goods, services	year	32461	91	81r
Charity				
Cash contributions, expenditures	year	975	91	81r
Clothing				
Apparel, men and boys, total expenditures	year	467	91	81r
Apparel, women and girls, total expenditures	year	737	91	81r
Footwear, expenditures	year	270	91	81r
Communications				
Long-distance telephone rate, day, addl. min., 1-10 mi.	min.	0.07	12/93	9s
Long-distance telephone rate, day, initial min., 1-10 mi.	min.	0.17	12/93	9s
Phone line, single, business, field visit	inst	70.75	12/93	9s
Phone line, single, business, no field visit	inst	70.75	12/93	9s
Phone line, single, residence, field visit	inst	34.75	12/93	9s
Phone line, single, residence, no field visit	inst	34.75	12/93	9s
Telephone service, expenditures	year	611	91	81r

Values are in dollars or fractions of dollars. In the column headed *Ref*, references are shown to sources. Each reference is followed by a letter. These refer to the geographical level for which data were reported: s = State, r = Region, and c = City or metro. The abbreviation *ex* is used to mean *except* or *excluding*; *exp* stands for expenditures. For other abbreviations and further explanations, please see the Introduction.

Oxnard-Ventura, CA - continued

Item	Per	Value	Date	Ref.
Education				
Board, 4-year private college/university	year	2945	8/94	80s
Board, 4-year public college/university	year	2321	8/94	80s
Education, total expenditures	year	375	91	81r
Room, 4-year private college/university	year	3094	8/94	80s
Room, 4-year public college/university	year	2812	8/94	80s
Student fee, university	year	21.00	93	18s
Total cost, 4-year private college/university	year	19321	8/94	80s
Total cost, 4-year public college/university	year	7511	8/94	80s
Tuition, 2-year public college/university, in-state	year	345	8/94	80s
Tuition, 4-year private college/university, in-state	year	13282	8/94	80s
Tuition, 4-year public college/university, in-state	year	2378	8/94	80s
Energy and Fuels				
Fuel oil and other fuels, expenditures	year	33	91	81r
Gas, natural, expenditures	year	212	91	81r
Gasoline and motor oil purchased	year	1115	91	81r
Gasoline, unleaded midgrade	gallon	1.36	4/93	82r
Gasoline, unleaded premium	gallon	1.43	4/93	82r
Gasoline, unleaded regular	gallon	1.23	4/93	82r
Entertainment				
Concert ticket, Pearl Jam group	perf	20.00	94	50r
Entertainment, total expenditures	year	1853	91	81r
Fees and admissions, expenditures	year	482	91	81r
Pets, toys, playground equipment, expenditures	year	299	91	81r
Reading, expenditures	year	164	91	81r
Televisions, radios, and sound equipment, expenditures	year	528	91	81r
Funerals				
Burial, immediate, container provided by funeral home		1382.70	1/95	54r
Cards, acknowledgment		21.87	1/95	54r
Casket, minimum alternative		128.54	1/95	54r
Cosmetology, hair care, etc.		119.69	1/95	54r
Cremation, direct, container provided by funeral home		1030.62	1/95	54r
Embalming		255.42	1/95	54r
Funeral, funeral home		437.38	1/95	54r
Funeral, other facility		444.46	1/95	54r
Graveside service		338.46	1/95	54r
Hearse, local		147.50	1/95	54r
Limousine, local		130.33	1/95	54r
Memorial service		553.16	1/95	54r
Service charge, professional, nondeclinable		859.15	1/95	54r
Visitation and viewing		93.23	1/95	54r
Groceries				
Apples, Red Delicious	lb.	0.72	12/94	82r
Bacon, sliced	lb.	1.73	12/94	82r
Bananas	lb.	0.52	12/94	82r
Beef purchases	year	241	91	81r
Beverage purchases, alcoholic	year	328	91	81r
Beverage purchases, nonalcoholic	year	234	91	81r
Bologna, all beef or mixed	lb.	2.33	12/94	82r
Bread, white, pan	lb.	0.81	12/94	82r
Carrots, short trimmed and topped	lb.	0.43	12/94	82r
Cereals and bakery products purchases	year	392	91	81r
Cereals and cereals products purchases	year	139	91	81r
Chicken breast, bone-in	lb.	2.04	12/94	82r
Chicken, fresh, whole	lb.	0.95	12/94	82r
Coffee, 100%, ground roast, all sizes	lb.	4.48	12/94	82r
Dairy products (other) purchases	year	182	91	81r
Fish and seafood purchases	year	94	91	81r
Flour, white, all purpose	lb.	0.21	12/94	82r
Food purchases, food eaten at home	year	2749	91	81r
Foods purchased away from home, not prepared by consumer	year	1909	91	81r
Fruits and vegetables purchases	year	459	91	81r
Grapefruit	lb.	0.56	12/94	82r

Oxnard-Ventura, CA - continued

Item	Per	Value	Date	Ref.
Groceries - continued				
Ground beef, 100% beef	lb.	1.31	12/94	82r
Ham, boneless, exc. canned	lb.	2.46	12/94	82r
Ice cream, prepackaged, bulk, regular	1/2 gal.	2.57	12/94	82r
Lemons	lb.	1.00	12/94	82r
Lettuce, iceberg	lb.	0.93	12/94	82r
Meats, poultry, fish, and eggs purchases	year	700	91	81r
Milk and cream (fresh) purchases	year	155	91	81r
Orange juice, frozen concentrate 12-oz. can	16 oz.	1.52	12/94	82r
Oranges, Navel	lb.	0.56	12/94	82r
Pork chops, center cut, bone-in	lb.	3.30	12/94	82r
Pork purchases	year	122	91	81r
Potato chips	16-oz.	3.03	12/94	82r
Potatoes, frozen, French fried	lb.	0.77	12/94	82r
Potatoes, white	lb.	0.35	12/94	82r
Rice, white, long grain, uncooked	lb.	0.54	12/94	82r
Round roast, USDA choice, boneless	lb.	2.92	12/94	82r
Shortening, vegetable oil blends	lb.	0.80	12/94	82r
Spaghetti and macaroni	lb.	1.02	12/94	82r
Steak, round, graded & ungraded, exc. USDA prime & choice	lb.	3.13	12/94	82r
Steak, sirloin, USDA choice, boneless	lb.	4.07	12/94	82r
Sugar and other sweets, eaten at home, expenditures	year	105	91	81r
Sugar, white, all sizes	lb.	0.38	12/94	82r
Tobacco products and smoking supplies, total expenditures	year	221	91	81r
Tomatoes, field grown	lb.	1.45	12/94	82r
Tuna, chunk, light	lb.	2.18	12/94	82r
Health Care				
Childbirth, Cesarean delivery, hospital charge	birth	6059.00	12/91	69r
Childbirth, Cesarean delivery, physician charge	birth	2248.00	12/91	69r
Childbirth, normal delivery, hospital charge	birth	3006.00	12/91	69r
Childbirth, normal delivery, physician charge	birth	1634.00	12/91	69r
Drugs, expenditures	year	230	91	81r
Health care, total expenditures	year	1544	91	81r
Health insurance expenditures	year	558	91	81r
Insurance premium, family medical care	month	380.27	1/95	41s
Medical services expenditures	year	676	91	81r
Medical supplies expenditures	year	80	91	81r
Surgery, open-heart	proc	37818.00	1/93	14r
Household Goods				
Floor coverings, expenditures	year	79	91	81r
Furniture, expenditures	year	352	91	81r
Household equipment, misc. expenditures	year	614	91	81r
Household expenditures, miscellaneous	year	294	91	81r
Household furnishings and equipment, expenditures	year	1416	91	81r
Household operations expenditures	year	580	91	81r
Household textiles, expenditures	year	113	91	81r
Housekeeping supplies, expenditures	year	447	91	81r
Laundry and cleaning supplies, expenditures	year	114	91	81r
Postage and stationery, expenditures	year	145	91	81r
Housing				
Add garage/carport		6,422	3/95	74r
Add room(s)		26,583	3/95	74r
Apartment condominium or co-op, median	unit	105300	12/94	62r
Dwellings (owned), expenditures	year	3932	91	81r
Enclose porch/patio/breezeway		5,382	3/95	74r
Finish room in basement/attic		3,911	3/95	74r
Home, existing, single-family, median	unit	178600	12/94	62r
Maintenance, repairs, insurance, and other housing expenditures	year	591	91	81r
Mortgage interest and charges expenditures	year	2747	91	81r
Princ. & int., mortgage, median-price exist. sing.-family home	mo.	845	12/94	62r
Property taxes expenditures	year	594	91	81r

Values are in dollars or fractions of dollars. In the column headed *Ref*, references are shown to sources. Each reference is followed by a letter. These refer to the geographical level for which data were reported: s=State, r=Region, and c=City or metro. The abbreviation *ex* is used to mean *except* or *excluding*; *exp* stands for expenditures. For other abbreviations and further explanations, please see the Introduction.

Oxnard-Ventura, CA - continued

Item	Per	Value	Date	Ref.
Housing				
Redesign, restructure more than half of home's interior		5,467	3/95	74r
Rental units expenditures	year	2077	91	81r
Insurance and Pensions				
Auto insurance, private passenger	year	892.80	12/94	71s
Insurance and pensions, personal, expenditures	year	3042	91	81r
Insurance, life and other personal, expenditures	year	298	91	81r
Pensions and Social Security, expenditures	year	2744	91	81r
Legal Assistance				
Legal work, law firm associate	hour	91		10r
Legal work, law firm partner	hour	151		10r
Personal Services				
Personal services expenditures	year	286	91	81r
Restaurant Food				
Dining expenditures, family	week	32.25	94	73r
Taxes				
Taxes, Federal income, expenditures	year	2946	91	81r
Taxes, personal, expenditures	year	3791	91	81r
Taxes, State and local income, expenditures	year	791	91	81r
Transportation				
Cars and trucks purchased, new	year	1231	91	81r
Cars and trucks purchased, used	year	915	91	81r
Driver's learning permit fee	perm	12.00	1/94	84s
Driver's license fee	orig	12.00	1/94	84s
Driver's license fee, duplicate	lic	12.00	1/94	84s
Driver's license reinstatement fee, min.	susp	15.00	1/94	85s
Driver's license renewal fee	renew	12.00	1/94	84s
Identification card, nondriver	card	6.00	1/94	83s
Motorcycle learning permit fee	perm	12.00	1/94	84s
Motorcycle license fee	orig	12.00	1/94	84s
Motorcycle license fee, duplicate	lic	12.00	1/94	84s
Motorcycle license renewal fee	renew	12.00	1/94	84s
Public transportation expenditures	year	375	91	81r
Transportation expenditures, total	year	5527	91	81r
Vehicle finance charges	year	287	91	81r
Vehicle insurance expenditures	year	624	91	81r
Vehicle maintenance and repairs expenditures	year	695	91	81r
Vehicle purchases	year	2174	91	81r
Vehicle rental, leases, licenses, etc. expenditures	year	257	91	81r
Vehicles purchased, other than cars and trucks	year	28	91	81r
Utilities				
Electricity expenditures	year	616	91	81r
Utilities, fuels, and public services, total expenditures	year	1681	91	81r
Water and other public services, expenditures	year	209	91	81r
Weddings				
Bridal attendants' gowns	event	750	10/93	76r
Bridal gown	event	852	10/93	76r
Bridal headpiece and veil	event	167	10/93	76r
Bride's wedding band	event	708	10/93	76r
Clergy	event	224	10/93	76r
Engagement ring	event	2756	10/93	76r
Flowers	event	863	10/93	76r
Formal wear for groom	event	106	10/93	76r
Groom's attendants' formal wear	event	530	10/93	76r
Groom's wedding band	event	402	10/93	76r
Music	event	600	10/93	76r
Photography	event	1088	10/93	76r
Shoes for bride	event	50	10/93	76r
Videography	event	483	10/93	76r
Wedding invitations and announcements	event	342	10/93	76r
Wedding reception	event	7000	10/93	76r

Paducah, KY

Item	Per	Value	Date	Ref.
Composite, ACCRA index		93.40	12/94	2c
Alcoholic Beverages				
Beer, Miller Lite, Bud, 12-oz., ex deposit	6	4.19	12/94	2c
J & B Scotch	750-ml.	17.08	12/94	2c
Wine, Gallo Chablis blanc	1.5-lit	4.77	12/94	2c
Clothing				
Jeans, man's denim		28.00	12/94	2c
Shirt, man's dress shirt		27.47	12/94	2c
Undervest, boy's size 10-14, cotton	3	4.36	12/94	2c
Communications				
Newspaper subscription, dly. and Sun. delivery	month	10.30	12/94	2c
Telephone bill, family of four	month	20.43	12/94	2c
Telephone, residential, flat rate	mo.	12.69	12/93	8c
Energy and Fuels				
Energy, combined forms, 1800 sq. ft.	mo.	94.86	12/94	2c
Energy, exc. electricity, 1800 sq. ft.	mo.	37.90	12/94	2c
Gas, reg unlead, taxes inc., cash, self-service	gal	1.10	12/94	2c
Entertainment				
Bowling, evening rate	game	1.95	12/94	2c
Monopoly game, Parker Brothers', No. 9	game	13.66	12/94	2c
Movie	adm	5.25	12/94	2c
Tennis balls, yellow, Wilson or Penn, 3	can	1.92	12/94	2c
Groceries				
Groceries, ACCRA Index		100.30	12/94	2c
Baby food, strained vegetables, lowest price	4-4.5 oz.	0.34	12/94	2c
Bananas	lb.	0.38	12/94	2c
Beef or hamburger, ground	lb.	1.38	12/94	2c
Bread, white	24-oz.	0.66	12/94	2c
Cheese, Kraft grated Parmesan	8-oz.	3.44	12/94	2c
Chicken, whole fryer	lb.	0.76	12/94	2c
Cigarettes, Winston, Kings	carton	12.82	12/94	2c
Coffee, vacuum-packed	13 oz.	4.04	12/94	2c
Corn Flakes, Kellogg's or Post Toasties	18 oz.	2.50	12/94	2c
Corn, frozen, whole kernel, lowest price	10 oz.	0.75	12/94	2c
Eggs, Grade A large	dozen	0.65	12/94	2c
Lettuce, iceberg	head	0.89	12/94	2c
Margarine, Blue Bonnet or Parkay cubes	lb.	0.66	12/94	2c
Milk, whole	1/2 gal.	1.52	12/94	2c
Orange juice, Minute Maid frozen	12-oz.	1.42	12/94	2c
Peaches, halves or slices, Hunt's, Del Monte, or Libby's	29-oz.	1.46	12/94	2c
Peas, sweet, Del Monte or Green Giant	15-17 oz.	0.72	12/94	2c
Potatoes, white or red	10-lb. sack	2.68	12/94	2c
Sausage, Jimmy Dean, 100% pork	lb.	2.48	12/94	2c
Shortening, vegetable, Crisco	3-lb.	2.68	12/94	2c
Soft drink, Coca Cola, ex deposit	2 lit	1.19	12/94	2c
Steak, t-bone	lb.	5.66	12/94	2c
Sugar, cane or beet	4 lbs.	1.48	12/94	2c
Tomatoes, Hunt's or Del Monte	14.5 oz.	0.77	12/94	2c
Tuna, chunk, light, oil-packed	6.125-6.5 oz.	0.68	12/94	2c
Goods and Services				
Miscellaneous goods and services, ACCRA Index		96.80	12/94	2c
Health Care				
Health care, ACCRA Index		79.90	12/94	2c
Antibiotic ointment, Polysporin	1.5 oz.	4.36	12/94	2c
Dentist's fee, adult teeth cleaning and periodic oral exam	visit	41.50	12/94	2c
Doctor's fee, routine exam, established patient	visit	32.00	12/94	2c

Values are in dollars or fractions of dollars. In the column headed *Ref*, references are shown to sources. Each reference is followed by a letter. These refer to the geographical level for which data were reported: s=State, r=Region, and c=City or metro. The abbreviation *ex* is used to mean *except* or *excluding*; *exp* stands for expenditures. For other abbreviations and further explanations, please see the Introduction.

Paducah, KY - continued

Item	Per	Value	Date	Ref.
Health Care				
Hospital care, semiprivate room	day	257.50	12/94	2c
Household Goods				
Appl. repair, service call, wash mach	min. lab. chg.	31.25	12/94	2c
Laundry detergent, Tide Ultra, Bold, or Cheer	42 oz.	3.30	12/94	2c
Tissues, facial, Kleenex brand	175	1.05	12/94	2c
Housing				
Housing, ACCRA Index		91.10	12/94	2c
House payment, principal and interest, 25% down payment	mo.	731	12/94	2c
House, 1800 sq ft, 8000 sq ft lot, new, urban, utilities	total	119135	12/94	2c
Mtge. rate, incl. points and orig. fee, 30-year conv. fixed or ARM	mo.	9.19	12/94	2c
Rent, apartment, 2 br., 1 1/2-2 baths, unfurnished, 950 sq ft, water	mo.	385	12/94	2c
Personal Goods				
Shampoo, Alberto VO5	15-oz.	1.46	12/94	2c
Toothpaste, Crest or Colgate	6-7 oz.	2.39	12/94	2c
Personal Services				
Dry cleaning, man's 2-pc. suit		5.72	12/94	2c
Haircut, man's barbershop, no styling		6.60	12/94	2c
Haircut, woman's shampoo, trim, blow-dry		18.40	12/94	2c
Restaurant Food				
Chicken, fried, thigh and drumstick		2.26	12/94	2c
Hamburger with cheese	1/4 lb.	1.89	12/94	2c
Pizza, Pizza Hut or Pizza Inn	12-13 in.	7.97	12/94	2c
Transportation				
Transportation, ACCRA Index		90.20	12/94	2c
Tire balance, computer or spin bal., front	wheel	5.40	12/94	2c
Utilities				
Utilities, ACCRA Index		87.30	12/94	2c
Electricity, (part.), other, 1800 sq. ft., new home	mo.	56.96	12/94	2c

Palm Springs, CA

Item	Per	Value	Date	Ref.
Composite, ACCRA index		116.00	12/94	2c
Alcoholic Beverages				
Beer	bottle	2.75	94	34c
Beer, Miller Lite, Bud, 12-oz., ex deposit	6	3.85	12/94	2c
J & B Scotch	750-ml.	15.05	12/94	2c
Wine, Gallo Chablis blanc	1.5-lit	3.91	12/94	2c
Clothing				
Jeans, man's denim		32.99	12/94	2c
Shirt, man's dress shirt		35.00	12/94	2c
Undervest, boy's size 10-14, cotton	3	6.28	12/94	2c
Communications				
Newspaper subscription, dly. and Sun. delivery	month	9.19	12/94	2c
Telephone bill, family of four	month	15.75	12/94	2c
Energy and Fuels				
Energy, combined forms, 1800 sq. ft.	mo.	138.83	12/94	2c
Energy, exc. electricity, 1800 sq. ft.	mo.	22.72	12/94	2c
Gas, reg unlead, taxes inc., cash, self-service	gal	1.27	12/94	2c
Entertainment				
Bowling, evening rate	game	2.75	12/94	2c
Monopoly game, Parker Brothers', No. 9	game	15.34	12/94	2c
Movie	adm	7.00	12/94	2c
Tennis balls, yellow, Wilson or Penn, 3	can	2.79	12/94	2c

Palm Springs, CA - continued

Item	Per	Value	Date	Ref.
Groceries				
Groceries, ACCRA Index		111.00	12/94	2c
Baby food, strained vegetables, lowest price	4-4.5 oz.	0.36	12/94	2c
Bananas	lb.	0.58	12/94	2c
Beef or hamburger, ground	lb.	1.50	12/94	2c
Big Mac hamburger	burger	1.99	94	34c
Bread, white	24-oz.	0.89	12/94	2c
Cheese, Kraft grated Parmesan	8-oz.	3.31	12/94	2c
Chicken, whole fryer	lb.	1.09	12/94	2c
Cigarettes, Winston, Kings	carton	16.67	12/94	2c
Coffee, vacuum-packed	13 oz.	3.59	12/94	2c
Corn Flakes, Kellogg's or Post Toasties	18 oz.	2.61	12/94	2c
Corn, frozen, whole kernel, lowest price	10 oz.	0.93	12/94	2c
Eggs, Grade A large	dozen	1.93	12/94	2c
Lettuce, iceberg	head	0.89	12/94	2c
Margarine, Blue Bonnet or Parkay cubes	lb.	0.75	12/94	2c
Milk, whole	1/2 gal.	1.64	12/94	2c
Orange juice, Minute Maid frozen	12-oz.	1.47	12/94	2c
Peaches, halves or slices, Hunt's, Del Monte, or Libby's	29-oz.	1.24	12/94	2c
Peas, sweet, Del Monte or Green Giant	15-17 oz.	0.57	12/94	2c
Potatoes, white or red	10-lb. sack	1.79	12/94	2c
Sausage, Jimmy Dean, 100% pork	lb.	3.13	12/94	2c
Shortening, vegetable, Crisco	3-lb.	2.91	12/94	2c
Soft drink, Coca Cola, ex deposit	2 lit	1.07	12/94	2c
Steak, t-bone	lb.	5.52	12/94	2c
Sugar, cane or beet	4 lbs.	1.42	12/94	2c
Tomatoes, Hunt's or Del Monte	14.5 oz.	0.75	12/94	2c
Tuna, chunk, light, oil-packed	6.125-6.5 oz.	0.69	12/94	2c
Goods and Services				
Miscellaneous goods and services, ACCRA Index		113.90	12/94	2c
Health Care				
Health care, ACCRA Index		143.60	12/94	2c
Antibiotic ointment, Polysporin	1.5 oz.	4.79	12/94	2c
Dentist's fee, adult teeth cleaning and periodic oral exam	visit	79.40	12/94	2c
Doctor's fee, routine exam, established patient	visit	55.00	12/94	2c
Hospital care, semiprivate room	day	605.00	12/94	2c
Household Goods				
Appl. repair, service call, wash mach	min. lab. chg.	37.46	12/94	2c
Laundry detergent, Tide Ultra, Bold, or Cheer	42 oz.	3.67	12/94	2c
Tissues, facial, Kleenex brand	175	1.01	12/94	2c
Housing				
Housing, ACCRA Index		117.00	12/94	2c
House payment, principal and interest, 25% down payment	mo.	886	12/94	2c
House, 1800 sq ft, 8000 sq ft lot, new, urban, utilities	total	145250	12/94	2c
Mtge. rate, incl. points and orig. fee, 30-year conv. fixed or ARM	mo.	9.12	12/94	2c
Rent, apartment, 2 br., 1 1/2-2 baths, unfurnished, 950 sq ft, water	mo.	648	12/94	2c
Personal Goods				
Shampoo, Alberto VO5	15-oz.	1.37	12/94	2c
Toothpaste, Crest or Colgate	6-7 oz.	2.37	12/94	2c
Personal Services				
Dry cleaning, man's 2-pc. suit		7.25	12/94	2c
Haircut, man's barbershop, no styling		12.00	12/94	2c
Haircut, woman's shampoo, trim, blow-dry		31.25	12/94	2c

Values are in dollars or fractions of dollars. In the column headed *Ref*, references are shown to sources. Each reference is followed by a letter. These refer to the geographical level for which data were reported: s = State, r = Region, and c = City or metro. The abbreviation *ex* is used to mean *except* or *excluding*; *exp* stands for expenditures. For other abbreviations and further explanations, please see the Introduction.

Palm Springs, CA - continued

Item	Per	Value	Date	Ref.
Restaurant Food				
Chicken, fried, thigh and drumstick		2.15	12/94	2c
Hamburger with cheese	1/4 lb.	1.99	12/94	2c
Pizza, Pizza Hut or Pizza Inn	12-13 in.	8.90	12/94	2c
Transportation				
Transportation, ACCRA Index		109.60	12/94	2c
Bus fare, up to 10 miles	one-way	0.75	12/94	2c
Tire balance, computer or spin bal., front	wheel	7.69	12/94	2c
Utilities				
Utilities, ACCRA Index		117.90	12/94	2c
Electricity, (part.), other, 1800 sq. ft., new home	mo.	116.11	12/94	2c

Panama City, FL

Item	Per	Value	Date	Ref.
Appliances				
Appliances (major), expenditures	year	153	91	81r
Average annual exp.				
Food, health care, personal goods, services	year	27020	91	81r
Charity				
Cash contributions, expenditures	year	839	91	81r
Clothing				
Apparel, men and boys, total expenditures	year	380	91	81r
Apparel, women and girls, total expenditures	year	660	91	81r
Footwear, expenditures	year	193	91	81r
Communications				
Long-distance telephone rate, day, addl. min., 1-10 mi.	min.	0.08	12/93	9s
Long-distance telephone rate, day, initial min., 1-10 mi.	min.	0.15	12/93	9s
Phone line, single, business, field visit	inst	86.00	12/93	9s
Phone line, single, business, no field visit	inst	54.50	12/93	9s
Phone line, single, residence, field visit	inst	76.00	12/93	9s
Phone line, single, residence, no field visit	inst	44.50	12/93	9s
Telephone service, expenditures	year	616	91	81r
Education				
Bar examination preparatory course	course	500.00-100	94	17s
Board, 4-year private college/university	year	2123	8/94	80s
Board, 4-year public college/university	year	2101	8/94	80s
Education, total expenditures	year	319	91	81r
Room, 4-year private college/university	year	2242	8/94	80s
Room, 4-year public college/university	year	1970	8/94	80s
Total cost, 4-year private college/university	year	13853	8/94	80s
Total cost, 4-year public college/university	year	5855	8/94	80s
Tuition, 2-year public college/university, in-state	year	1076	8/94	80s
Tuition, 4-year private college/university, in-state	year	9287	8/94	80s
Tuition, 4-year public college/university, in-state	year	1784	8/94	80s
Energy and Fuels				
Fuel oil and other fuels, expenditures	year	56	91	81r
Gas, natural, expenditures	year	150	91	81r
Gasoline and motor oil purchased	year	1152	91	81r
Gasoline, unleaded midgrade	gallon	1.21	4/93	82r
Gasoline, unleaded premium	gallon	1.30	4/93	82r
Gasoline, unleaded regular	gallon	1.10	4/93	82r
Entertainment				
Concert ticket, Pearl Jam group	perf	20.00	94	50r
Entertainment, total expenditures	year	1266	91	81r
Fees and admissions, expenditures	year	306	91	81r
Pets, toys, playground equipment, expenditures	year	271	91	81r
Reading, expenditures	year	131	91	81r

Panama City, FL - continued

Item	Per	Value	Date	Ref.
Entertainment - continued				
Televisions, radios, and sound equipment, expenditures	year	439	91	81r
Funerals				
Burial, immediate, container provided by funeral home		1370.36	1/95	54r
Cards, acknowledgment		14.83	1/95	54r
Casket, minimum alternative		192.52	1/95	54r
Cosmetology, hair care, etc.		102.27	1/95	54r
Cremation, direct, container provided by funeral home		1065.64	1/95	54r
Embalming		304.29	1/95	54r
Funeral, funeral home		287.83	1/95	54r
Funeral, other facility		284.14	1/95	54r
Graveside service		349.13	1/95	54r
Hearse, local		132.27	1/95	54r
Limousine, local		98.45	1/95	54r
Memorial service		270.59	1/95	54r
Service charge, professional, nondeclinable		933.59	1/95	54r
Visitation and viewing		225.83	1/95	54r
Groceries				
Apples, Red Delicious	lb.	0.73	12/94	82r
Bacon, sliced	lb.	1.67	12/94	82r
Bananas	lb.	0.42	12/94	82r
Beef purchases	year	213	91	81r
Beverage purchases, alcoholic	year	249	91	81r
Beverage purchases, nonalcoholic	year	207	91	81r
Bologna, all beef or mixed	lb.	2.27	12/94	82r
Bread, white, pan	lb.	0.68	12/94	82r
Cabbage	lb.	0.42	12/94	82r
Carrots, short trimmed and topped	lb.	0.53	12/94	82r
Cereals and bakery products purchases	year	345	91	81r
Cereals and cereals products purchases	year	127	91	81r
Cheddar cheese, natural	lb.	3.58	12/94	82r
Chicken breast, bone-in	lb.	1.71	12/94	82r
Chicken, fresh, whole	lb.	0.78	12/94	82r
Chuck roast, USDA choice, boneless	lb.	2.26	12/94	82r
Crackers, soda, salted	lb.	1.27	12/94	82r
Cucumbers	lb.	0.65	12/94	82r
Dairy products (other) purchases	year	141	91	81r
Eggs, Grade A large	dozen	0.87	12/94	82r
Fish and seafood purchases	year	72	91	81r
Flour, white, all purpose	lb.	0.23	12/94	82r
Food purchases, food eaten at home	year	2381	91	81r
Foods purchased away from home, not prepared by consumer	year	1696	91	81r
Frankfurters, all meat or all beef	lb.	1.74	12/94	82r
Fruits and vegetables purchases	year	380	91	81r
Grapefruit	lb.	0.45	12/94	82r
Grapes, Thompson seedless	lb.	2.30	12/94	82r
Ground beef, 100% beef	lb.	1.37	12/94	82r
Ground chuck, 100% beef	lb.	1.97	12/94	82r
Ham, boneless, exc. canned	lb.	2.54	12/94	82r
Ice cream, prepackaged, bulk, regular	1/2 gal.	2.47	12/94	82r
Lemons	lb.	1.02	12/94	82r
Lettuce, iceberg	lb.	0.96	12/94	82r
Margarine, stick	lb.	0.77	12/94	82r
Meats, poultry, fish, and eggs purchases	year	655	91	81r
Milk and cream (fresh) purchases	year	130	91	81r
Orange juice, frozen concentrate 12-oz. can	16 oz.	1.36	12/94	82r
Oranges, Navel	lb.	0.54	12/94	82r
Pears, Anjou	lb.	0.81	12/94	82r
Pork chops, center cut, bone-in	lb.	3.07	12/94	82r
Pork purchases	year	142	91	81r
Potato chips	16-oz.	3.15	12/94	82r
Potatoes, frozen, French fried	lb.	0.82	12/94	82r
Potatoes, white	lb.	0.34	12/94	82r
Rice, white, long grain, uncooked	lb.	0.48	12/94	82r
Round roast, USDA choice, boneless	lb.	2.91	12/94	82r
Sausage, fresh	lb.	1.82	12/94	82r
Shortening, vegetable oil blends	lb.	0.75	12/94	82r

Values are in dollars or fractions of dollars. In the column headed *Ref*, references are shown to sources. Each reference is followed by a letter. These refer to the geographical level for which data were reported: s = State, r = Region, and c = City or metro. The abbreviation *ex* is used to mean *except* or *excluding*; *exp* stands for *expenditures*. For other abbreviations and further explanations, please see the Introduction.

Panama City, FL - continued

Item	Per	Value	Date	Ref.
Groceries				
Spaghetti and macaroni	lb.	0.87	12/94	82r
Steak, rib eye, USDA choice, boneless	lb.	6.85	12/94	82r
Steak, round, graded & ungraded, exc. USDA prime & choice	lb.	2.96	12/94	82r
Steak, round, USDA choice, boneless	lb.	3.17	12/94	82r
Steak, sirloin, USDA choice, boneless	lb.	4.12	12/94	82r
Steak, T-bone, USDA choice, bone-in	lb.	5.63	12/94	82r
Sugar and other sweets, eaten at home, expenditures	year	93	91	81r
Sugar, white, all sizes	lb.	0.39	12/94	82r
Tobacco products and smoking supplies, total expenditures	year	286	91	81r
Tomatoes, field grown	lb.	1.36	12/94	82r
Tuna, chunk, light	lb.	1.94	12/94	82r
Turkey, frozen, whole	lb.	0.96	12/94	82r
Yogurt, natural, fruit flavored	8 oz.	0.58	12/94	82r
Health Care				
Adenosine, emergency room	treat	100.00	95	23r
Bladder tap, superpubic, infant, emergency room	treat	119.00	95	23r
Blood analysis, emergency room	treat	25.00	95	23r
Blood tests, abdominal pain, emergency room	treat	25.00	95	23r
Burn dressing, emergency room	treat	266.00	95	23r
Cardiology interpretation, emergency room	treat	26.00	95	23r
Chest X-ray, emergency room	treat	78.00	95	23r
Childbirth, Cesarean delivery, hospital charge	birth	5462.00	12/91	69r
Childbirth, Cesarean delivery, physician charge	birth	2228.00	12/91	69r
Childbirth, normal delivery, hospital charge	birth	2943.00	12/91	69r
Childbirth, normal delivery, physician charge	birth	1619.00	12/91	69r
Defibrillation pads, emergency room	treat	6.00	95	23r
Drugs, expenditures	year	297	91	81r
Gastric tube insertion, nasal, emergency room	treat	25.00	95	23r
Health care, total expenditures	year	1600	91	81r
Health insurance expenditures	year	637	91	81r
Heart monitor, emergency room	treat	40.00	95	23r
Insurance premium, family medical care	month	301.92	1/95	41s
Intravenous fluids, emergency room	treat	130.00	95	23r
Intravenous fluids, emergency room	liter	26.00	95	23r
Intravenous line, central, emergency room	treat	342.00	95	23r
Liver function tests, abdominal pain, emergency room	treat	26.00	95	23r
Medical care charges, total, emergency room, third-degree burns	treat	2101.00	95	23r
Medical care charges, total, emergency, infant with fever	treat	628.00	95	23r
Medical services expenditures	year	573	91	81r
Medical supplies expenditures	year	93	91	81r
Morphine, emergency room	treat	34.00	95	23r
Nursing care and facilities charges, emergency room	treat	252.00	95	23r
Nursing care and facilities charges, emergency, infant with fever	treat	252.00	95	23r
Nursing care and facilities charges, emergency, third-degree burns	treat	861.00	95	23r
Physician's charges, emergency, infant with fever	treat	212.00	95	23r
Physician's charges, emergency, third-degree burns	treat	372.00	95	23r
Physician's fee, emergency room	treat	372.00	95	23r
Physician's fee, general practitioner	visit	51.20	12/93	60r
Surgery, open-heart	proc	42374.00	1/93	14r
Ultrasound, abdominal, emergency room	treat	276.00	95	23r
Urinalysis, emergency room	treat	20.00	95	23r
Urinalysis, infant, emergency room	treat	20.00	95	23r
X-rays, emergency room	treat	78.00	95	23r

Panama City, FL - continued

Item	Per	Value	Date	Ref.
Household Goods				
Floor coverings, expenditures	year	48	91	81r
Furniture, expenditures	year	280	91	81r
Household equipment, misc. expenditures	year	342	91	81r
Household expenditures, miscellaneous	year	256	91	81r
Household furnishings and equipment, expenditures	year	988	91	81r
Household operations expenditures	year	468	91	81r
Household textiles, expenditures	year	95	91	81r
Housekeeping supplies, expenditures	year	380	91	81r
Laundry and cleaning supplies, expenditures	year	109	91	81r
Postage and stationery, expenditures	year	105	91	81r
Housing				
Add garage/carport		6,980	3/95	74r
Add room(s)		11,403	3/95	74r
Apartment condominium or co-op, median	unit	68600	12/94	62r
Dwellings (owned), expenditures	year	2428	91	81r
Enclose porch/patio/breezeway		4,572	3/95	74r
Finish room in basement/attic		3,794	3/95	74r
Home, existing, single-family, median	unit	120200	12/94	62r
Maintenance, repairs, insurance, and other housing expenditures	year	531	91	81r
Mortgage interest and charges expenditures	year	1506	91	81r
Princ. & int., mortgage, median-price exist. sing.-family home	mo.	540	12/94	62r
Property taxes expenditures	year	391	91	81r
Redesign, restructure more than half of home's interior		17,641	3/95	74r
Rental units expenditures	year	1264	91	81r
Insurance and Pensions				
Auto insurance, private passenger	year	753.93	12/94	71s
Insurance and pensions, personal, expenditures	year	2395	91	81r
Insurance, life and other personal, expenditures	year	368	91	81r
Pensions and Social Security, expenditures	year	2027	91	81r
Personal Services				
Personal services expenditures	year	212	91	81r
Restaurant Food				
Dining expenditures, family	week	33.83	94	73r
Taxes				
Taxes, Federal income, expenditures	year	2275	91	81r
Taxes, personal, expenditures	year	2715	91	81r
Taxes, State and local income, expenditures	year	365	91	81r
Transportation				
Cars and trucks purchased, new	year	1306	91	81r
Cars and trucks purchased, used	year	942	91	81r
Driver's learning permit fee	perm	20.00	1/94	84s
Driver's license fee	orig	20.00	1/94	84s
Driver's license fee, duplicate	lic	10.00	1/94	84s
Driver's license reinstatement fee, min.	susp	25.00	1/94	85s
Driver's license renewal fee	renew	15.00	1/94	84s
Identification card, nondriver	card	3.00	1/94	83s
Motorcycle learning permit fee	perm	20.00	1/94	84s
Motorcycle license fee	orig	20.00	1/94	84s
Motorcycle license fee, duplicate	lic	10.00	1/94	84s
Motorcycle license renewal fee	renew	15.00	1/94	84s
Public transportation expenditures	year	249	91	81r
Transportation expenditures, total	year	5307	91	81r
Vehicle finance charges	year	346	91	81r
Vehicle insurance expenditures	year	544	91	81r
Vehicle maintenance and repairs expenditures	year	600	91	81r
Vehicle purchases	year	2275	91	81r
Vehicle rental, leases, licenses, etc. expenditures	year	141	91	81r
Vehicles purchased, other than cars and trucks	year	27	91	81r

Values are in dollars or fractions of dollars. In the column headed *Ref*, references are shown to sources. Each reference is followed by a letter. These refer to the geographical level for which data were reported: s=State, r=Region, and c=City or metro. The abbreviation *ex* is used to mean *except* or *excluding*; *exp* stands for expenditures. For other abbreviations and further explanations, please see the Introduction.

Panama City, FL - continued

Item	Per	Value	Date	Ref.
Utilities				
Electricity expenditures	year	950	91	81r
Utilities, fuels, and public services, total expenditures	year	2000	91	81r
Water and other public services, expenditures	year	227	91	81r
Weddings				
Bridal attendants' gowns	event	750	10/93	76r
Bridal gown	event	852	10/93	76r
Bridal headpiece and veil	event	167	10/93	76r
Bride's wedding band	event	708	10/93	76r
Clergy	event	224	10/93	76r
Engagement ring	event	2756	10/93	76r
Flowers	event	863	10/93	76r
Formal wear for groom	event	106	10/93	76r
Groom's attendants' formal wear	event	530	10/93	76r
Groom's wedding band	event	402	10/93	76r
Music	event	600	10/93	76r
Photography	event	1088	10/93	76r
Shoes for bride	event	50	10/93	76r
Videography	event	483	10/93	76r
Wedding invitations and announcements	event	342	10/93	76r
Wedding reception	event	7000	10/93	76r

Parkersburg-Marietta, WV, OH

Item	Per	Value	Date	Ref.
Composite, ACCRA index		99.00	12/94	2c
Alcoholic Beverages				
Beer, Miller Lite, Bud, 12-oz., ex deposit	6	3.97	12/94	2c
J & B Scotch	750-ml.	18.65	12/94	2c
Wine, Gallo Chablis blanc	1.5-lit	5.29	12/94	2c
Appliances				
Appliances (major), expenditures	year	153	91	81r
Average annual exp.				
Food, health care, personal goods, services	year	27020	91	81r
Charity				
Cash contributions, expenditures	year	839	91	81r
Clothing				
Apparel, men and boys, total expenditures	year	380	91	81r
Apparel, women and girls, total expenditures	year	660	91	81r
Footwear, expenditures	year	193	91	81r
Jeans, man's denim		38.98	12/94	2c
Shirt, man's dress shirt		44.00	12/94	2c
Undervest, boy's size 10-14, cotton	3	4.14	12/94	2c
Communications				
Long-distance telephone rate, day, addl. min., 1-10 mi.	min.	0.13	12/93	9s
Long-distance telephone rate, day, initial min., 1-10 mi.	min.	0.26	12/93	9s
Newspaper subscription, dly. and Sun. delivery	month	10.65	12/94	2c
Phone line, single, business, field visit	inst	0.00	12/93	9s
Phone line, single, business, no field visit	inst	96.90	12/93	9s
Phone line, single, residence, field visit	inst	0.00	12/93	9s
Phone line, single, residence, no field visit	inst	42.00	12/93	9s
Telephone bill, family of four	month	25.77	12/94	2c
Telephone service, expenditures	year	616	91	81r
Telephone, residential, flat rate	mo.	15.25	12/93	8c
Telephone, residential, flat rate	mo.	6.00	12/93	8c
Education				
Board, 4-year private college/university	year	2166	8/94	80s
Board, 4-year public college/university	year	1968	8/94	80s
Education, total expenditures	year	319	91	81r
Room, 4-year private college/university	year	1745	8/94	80s
Room, 4-year public college/university	year	1847	8/94	80s
Total cost, 4-year private college/university	year	13220	8/94	80s
Total cost, 4-year public college/university	year	5691	8/94	80s

Parkersburg-Marietta, WV, OH - continued

Item	Per	Value	Date	Ref.
Education - continued				
Tuition, 2-year public college/university, in-state	year	1247	8/94	80s
Tuition, 4-year private college/university, in-state	year	9310	8/94	80s
Tuition, 4-year public college/university, in-state	year	1875	8/94	80s
Energy and Fuels				
Energy, combined forms, 1800 sq. ft.	mo.	104.08	12/94	2c
Energy, exc. electricity, 1800 sq. ft.	mo.	49.78	12/94	2c
Fuel oil and other fuels, expenditures	year	56	91	81r
Gas, cooking, winter, 10 therms	month	11.81	2/94	65c
Gas, cooking, winter, 10 therms	month	13.84	2/94	65c
Gas, cooking, winter, 30 therms	month	23.62	2/94	65c
Gas, cooking, winter, 30 therms	month	26.53	2/94	65c
Gas, cooking, winter, 50 therms	month	35.44	2/94	65c
Gas, cooking, winter, 50 therms	month	39.22	2/94	65c
Gas, heating, winter, 100 therms	month	64.98	2/94	65c
Gas, heating, winter, 100 therms	month	70.93	2/94	65c
Gas, heating, winter, average use	month	101.61	2/94	65c
Gas, heating, winter, average use	month	122.94	2/94	65c
Gas, natural, expenditures	year	150	91	81r
Gas, reg unlead, taxes inc., cash, self-service	gal	1.16	12/94	2c
Gasoline and motor oil purchased	year	1152	91	81r
Gasoline, unleaded midgrade	gallon	1.21	4/93	82r
Gasoline, unleaded premium	gallon	1.30	4/93	82r
Gasoline, unleaded regular	gallon	1.10	4/93	82r
Entertainment				
Bowling, evening rate	game	2.12	12/94	2c
Concert ticket, Pearl Jam group	perf	20.00	94	50r
Entertainment, total expenditures	year	1266	91	81r
Fees and admissions, expenditures	year	306	91	81r
Monopoly game, Parker Brothers', No. 9	game	9.60	12/94	2c
Movie	adm	5.00	12/94	2c
Pets, toys, playground equipment, expenditures	year	271	91	81r
Reading, expenditures	year	131	91	81r
Televisions, radios, and sound equipment, expenditures	year	439	91	81r
Tennis balls, yellow, Wilson or Penn, 3	can	2.02	12/94	2c
Funerals				
Burial, immediate, container provided by funeral home		1370.36	1/95	54r
Cards, acknowledgment		14.83	1/95	54r
Casket, minimum alternative		192.52	1/95	54r
Cosmetology, hair care, etc.		102.27	1/95	54r
Cremation, direct, container provided by funeral home		1065.64	1/95	54r
Embalming		304.29	1/95	54r
Funeral, funeral home		287.83	1/95	54r
Funeral, other facility		284.14	1/95	54r
Graveside service		349.13	1/95	54r
Hearse, local		132.27	1/95	54r
Limousine, local		98.45	1/95	54r
Memorial service		270.59	1/95	54r
Service charge, professional, nondeclinable		933.59	1/95	54r
Visitation and viewing		225.83	1/95	54r
Groceries				
Groceries, ACCRA Index		95.30	12/94	2c
Apples, Red Delicious	lb.	0.73	12/94	82r
Baby food, strained vegetables, lowest price	4-4.5 oz.	0.21	12/94	2c
Bacon, sliced	lb.	1.67	12/94	82r
Bananas	lb.	0.51	12/94	2c
Bananas	lb.	0.42	12/94	82r
Beef or hamburger, ground	lb.	1.09	12/94	2c
Beef purchases	year	213	91	81r
Beverage purchases, alcoholic	year	249	91	81r
Beverage purchases, nonalcoholic	year	207	91	81r
Bologna, all beef or mixed	lb.	2.27	12/94	82r

Values are in dollars or fractions of dollars. In the column headed *Ref*, references are shown to sources. Each reference is followed by a letter. These refer to the geographical level for which data were reported: s = State, r = Region, and c = City or metro. The abbreviation *ex* is used to mean *except* or *excluding*; *exp* stands for expenditures. For other abbreviations and further explanations, please see the Introduction.

Item	Per	Value	Date	Ref.
Groceries				
Bread, white	24-oz.	0.55	12/94	2c
Bread, white, pan	lb.	0.68	12/94	82r
Cabbage	lb.	0.42	12/94	82r
Carrots, short trimmed and topped	lb.	0.53	12/94	82r
Cereals and bakery products purchases	year	345	91	81r
Cereals and cereals products purchases	year	127	91	81r
Cheddar cheese, natural	lb.	3.58	12/94	82r
Cheese, Kraft grated Parmesan	8-oz.	3.19	12/94	2c
Chicken breast, bone-in	lb.	1.71	12/94	82r
Chicken, fresh, whole	lb.	0.78	12/94	82r
Chicken, whole fryer	lb.	0.87	12/94	2c
Chuck roast, USDA choice, boneless	lb.	2.26	12/94	82r
Cigarettes, Winston, Kings	carton	15.38	12/94	2c
Coffee, vacuum-packed	13 oz.	3.64	12/94	2c
Corn Flakes, Kellogg's or Post Toasties	18 oz.	2.58	12/94	2c
Corn, frozen, whole kernel, lowest price	10 oz.	0.77	12/94	2c
Crackers, soda, salted	lb.	1.27	12/94	82r
Cucumbers	lb.	0.65	12/94	82r
Dairy products (other) purchases	year	141	91	81r
Eggs, Grade A large	dozen	0.79	12/94	2c
Eggs, Grade A large	dozen	0.87	12/94	82r
Fish and seafood purchases	year	72	91	81r
Flour, white, all purpose	lb.	0.23	12/94	82r
Food purchases, food eaten at home	year	2381	91	81r
Foods purchased away from home, not prepared by consumer	year	1696	91	81r
Frankfurters, all meat or all beef	lb.	1.74	12/94	82r
Fruits and vegetables purchases	year	380	91	81r
Grapefruit	lb.	0.45	12/94	82r
Grapes, Thompson seedless	lb.	2.30	12/94	82r
Ground beef, 100% beef	lb.	1.37	12/94	82r
Ground chuck, 100% beef	lb.	1.97	12/94	82r
Ham, boneless, exc. canned	lb.	2.54	12/94	82r
Ice cream, prepackaged, bulk, regular	1/2 gal.	2.47	12/94	82r
Lemons	lb.	1.02	12/94	82r
Lettuce, iceberg	lb.	0.96	12/94	82r
Lettuce, iceberg	head	0.99	12/94	2c
Margarine, Blue Bonnet or Parkay cubes	lb.	0.66	12/94	2c
Margarine, stick	lb.	0.77	12/94	82r
Meats, poultry, fish, and eggs purchases	year	655	91	81r
Milk and cream (fresh) purchases	year	130	91	81r
Milk, whole	1/2 gal.	1.51	12/94	2c
Orange juice, frozen concentrate 12-oz. can	16 oz.	1.36	12/94	82r
Orange juice, Minute Maid frozen	12-oz.	1.30	12/94	2c
Oranges, Navel	lb.	0.54	12/94	82r
Peaches, halves or slices, Hunt's, Del Monte, or Libby's	29-oz.	1.46	12/94	2c
Pears, Anjou	lb.	0.81	12/94	82r
Peas, sweet, Del Monte or Green Giant	15-17 oz.	0.48	12/94	2c
Pork chops, center cut, bone-in	lb.	3.07	12/94	82r
Pork purchases	year	142	91	81r
Potato chips	16-oz.	3.15	12/94	82r
Potatoes, frozen, French fried	lb.	0.82	12/94	82r
Potatoes, white	lb.	0.34	12/94	82r
Potatoes, white or red	10-lb. sack	1.87	12/94	2c
Rice, white, long grain, uncooked	lb.	0.48	12/94	82r
Round roast, USDA choice, boneless	lb.	2.91	12/94	82r
Sausage, fresh	lb.	1.82	12/94	82r
Sausage, Jimmy Dean, 100% pork	lb.	2.67	12/94	2c
Shortening, vegetable oil blends	lb.	0.75	12/94	82r
Shortening, vegetable, Crisco	3-lb.	2.24	12/94	2c
Soft drink, Coca Cola, ex deposit	2 lit	1.17	12/94	2c
Spaghetti and macaroni	lb.	0.87	12/94	82r
Steak, rib eye, USDA choice, boneless	lb.	6.85	12/94	82r
Steak, round, graded & ungraded, exc. USDA prime & choice	lb.	2.96	12/94	82r
Steak, round, USDA choice, boneless	lb.	3.17	12/94	82r
Steak, sirloin, USDA choice, boneless	lb.	4.12	12/94	82r

Item	Per	Value	Date	Ref.
Groceries - continued				
Steak, t-bone	lb.	5.01	12/94	2c
Steak, T-bone, USDA choice, bone-in	lb.	5.63	12/94	82r
Sugar and other sweets, eaten at home, expenditures	year	93	91	81r
Sugar, cane or beet	4 lbs.	1.29	12/94	2c
Sugar, white, all sizes	lb.	0.39	12/94	82r
Tobacco products and smoking supplies, total expenditures	year	286	91	81r
Tomatoes, field grown	lb.	1.36	12/94	82r
Tomatoes, Hunt's or Del Monte	14.5 oz.	0.81	12/94	2c
Tuna, chunk, light	lb.	1.94	12/94	82r
Tuna, chunk, light, oil-packed	6.125-6.5 oz.	0.70	12/94	2c
Turkey, frozen, whole	lb.	0.96	12/94	82r
Yogurt, natural, fruit flavored	8 oz.	0.58	12/94	82r
Goods and Services				
Miscellaneous goods and services, ACCRA Index		105.20	12/94	2c
Health Care				
Health care, ACCRA Index		83.50	12/94	2c
Adenosine, emergency room	treat	100.00	95	23r
Antibiotic ointment, Polysporin	1.5 oz.	4.05	12/94	2c
Bladder tap, superpubic, infant, emergency room	treat	119.00	95	23r
Blood analysis, emergency room	treat	25.00	95	23r
Blood tests, abdominal pain, emergency room	treat	25.00	95	23r
Burn dressing, emergency room	treat	266.00	95	23r
Cardiology interpretation, emergency room	treat	26.00	95	23r
Chest X-ray, emergency room	treat	78.00	95	23r
Childbirth, Cesarean delivery, hospital charge	birth	5462.00	12/91	69r
Childbirth, Cesarean delivery, physician charge	birth	2228.00	12/91	69r
Childbirth, normal delivery, hospital charge	birth	2943.00	12/91	69r
Childbirth, normal delivery, physician charge	birth	1619.00	12/91	69r
Defibrillation pads, emergency room	treat	6.00	95	23r
Dentist's fee, adult teeth cleaning and periodic oral exam	visit	39.29	12/94	2c
Doctor's fee, routine exam, established patient	visit	34.29	12/94	2c
Drugs, expenditures	year	297	91	81r
Gastric tube insertion, nasal, emergency room	treat	25.00	95	23r
Health care, total expenditures	year	1600	91	81r
Health insurance expenditures	year	637	91	81r
Heart monitor, emergency room	treat	40.00	95	23r
Hospital care, semiprivate room	day	336.00	12/94	2c
Intravenous fluids, emergency room	treat	130.00	95	23r
Intravenous fluids, emergency room	liter	26.00	95	23r
Intravenous line, central, emergency room	treat	342.00	95	23r
Liver function tests, abdominal pain, emergency room	treat	26.00	95	23r
Medical care charges, total, emergency room, third-degree burns	treat	2101.00	95	23r
Medical care charges, total, emergency, infant with fever	treat	628.00	95	23r
Medical services expenditures	year	573	91	81r
Medical supplies expenditures	year	93	91	81r
Morphine, emergency room	treat	34.00	95	23r
Nursing care and facilities charges, emergency room	treat	252.00	95	23r
Nursing care and facilities charges, emergency, infant with fever	treat	252.00	95	23r
Nursing care and facilities charges, emergency, third-degree burns	treat	861.00	95	23r
Physician's charges, emergency, infant with fever	treat	212.00	95	23r
Physician's charges, emergency, third-degree burns	treat	372.00	95	23r

Values are in dollars or fractions of dollars. In the column headed *Ref*, references are shown to sources. Each reference is followed by a letter. These refer to the geographical level for which data were reported: s=State, r=Region, and c=City or metro. The abbreviation *ex* is used to mean *except* or *excluding*; *exp* stands for *expenditures*. For other abbreviations and further explanations, please see the Introduction.

Parkersburg-Marietta, WV, OH - continued

Item	Per	Value	Date	Ref.
Health Care				
Physician's fee, emergency room	treat	372.00	95	23r
Physician's fee, general practitioner	visit	51.20	12/93	60r
Surgery, open-heart	proc	42374.00	1/93	14r
Ultrasound, abdominal, emergency room	treat	276.00	95	23r
Urinalysis, emergency room	treat	20.00	95	23r
Urinalysis, infant, emergency room	treat	20.00	95	23r
X-rays, emergency room	treat	78.00	95	23r
Household Goods				
Appl. repair, service call, wash mach	min. lab. chg.	36.32	12/94	2c
Floor coverings, expenditures	year	48	91	81r
Furniture, expenditures	year	280	91	81r
Household equipment, misc. expenditures	year	342	91	81r
Household expenditures, miscellaneous	year	256	91	81r
Household furnishings and equipment, expenditures	year	988	91	81r
Household operations expenditures	year	468	91	81r
Household textiles, expenditures	year	95	91	81r
Housekeeping supplies, expenditures	year	380	91	81r
Laundry and cleaning supplies, expenditures	year	109	91	81r
Laundry detergent, Tide Ultra, Bold, or Cheer	42 oz.	3.10	12/94	2c
Postage and stationery, expenditures	year	105	91	81r
Tissues, facial, Kleenex brand	175	1.03	12/94	2c
Housing				
Housing, ACCRA Index		99.20	12/94	2c
Add garage/carport		6,980	3/95	74r
Add room(s)		11,403	3/95	74r
Apartment condominium or co-op, median	unit	68600	12/94	62r
Dwellings (owned), expenditures	year	2428	91	81r
Enclose porch/patio/breezeway		4,572	3/95	74r
Finish room in basement/attic		3,794	3/95	74r
Home, existing, single-family, median	unit	120200	12/94	62r
House payment, principal and interest, 25% down payment	mo.	803	12/94	2c
House, 1800 sq ft, 8000 sq ft lot, new, urban, utilities	total	131500	12/94	2c
Maintenance, repairs, insurance, and other housing expenditures	year	531	91	81r
Mortgage interest and charges expenditures	year	1506	91	81r
Mtge. rate, incl. points and orig. fee, 30-year conv. fixed or ARM	mo.	9.13	12/94	2c
Princ. & int., mortgage, median-price exist. sing.-family home	mo.	540	12/94	62r
Property taxes expenditures	year	391	91	81r
Redesign, restructure more than half of home's interior		17,641	3/95	74r
Rent, apartment, 2 br., 1 1/2-2 baths, unfurnished, 950 sq ft, water	mo.	400	12/94	2c
Rental units expenditures	year	1264	91	81r
Insurance and Pensions				
Auto insurance, private passenger	year	696.89	12/94	71s
Insurance and pensions, personal, expenditures	year	2395	91	81r
Insurance, life and other personal, expenditures	year	368	91	81r
Pensions and Social Security, expenditures	year	2027	91	81r
Personal Goods				
Shampoo, Alberto VO5	15-oz.	1.05	12/94	2c
Toothpaste, Crest or Colgate	6-7 oz.	1.78	12/94	2c
Personal Services				
Dry cleaning, man's 2-pc. suit		6.25	12/94	2c
Haircut, man's barbershop, no styling		6.80	12/94	2c
Haircut, woman's shampoo, trim, blow-dry		18.30	12/94	2c
Personal services expenditures	year	212	91	81r

Parkersburg-Marietta, WV, OH - continued

Item	Per	Value	Date	Ref.
Restaurant Food				
Chicken, fried, thigh and drumstick		2.30	12/94	2c
Dining expenditures, family	week	33.83	94	73r
Hamburger with cheese	1/4 lb.	1.75	12/94	2c
Pizza, Pizza Hut or Pizza Inn	12-13 in.	6.89	12/94	2c
Taxes				
Taxes, Federal income, expenditures	year	2275	91	81r
Taxes, personal, expenditures	year	2715	91	81r
Taxes, State and local income, expenditures	year	365	91	81r
Transportation				
Transportation, ACCRA Index		93.70	12/94	2c
Bus fare, one-way	trip	0.50	12/95	1c
Cars and trucks purchased, new	year	1306	91	81r
Cars and trucks purchased, used	year	942	91	81r
Driver's learning permit fee	perm	4.00	1/94	84s
Driver's license fee	orig	10.50	1/94	84s
Driver's license fee, duplicate	lic	5.00	1/94	84s
Driver's license renewal fee	renew	10.50	1/94	84s
Identification card, nondriver	card	5.00	1/94	83s
Motorcycle learning permit fee	perm	5.00	1/94	84s
Motorcycle license fee	orig	10.00	1/94	84s
Motorcycle license fee, duplicate	lic	5.00	1/94	84s
Motorcycle license renewal fee	renew	10.00	1/94	84s
Public transportation expenditures	year	249	91	81r
Tire balance, computer or spin bal., front	wheel	5.50	12/94	2c
Transportation expenditures, total	year	5307	91	81r
Vehicle finance charges	year	346	91	81r
Vehicle insurance expenditures	year	544	91	81r
Vehicle maintenance and repairs expenditures	year	600	91	81r
Vehicle purchases	year	2275	91	81r
Vehicle rental, leases, licenses, etc. expenditures	year	141	91	81r
Vehicles purchased, other than cars and trucks	year	27	91	81r
Utilities				
Utilities, ACCRA Index		98.10	12/94	2c
Electricity expenditures	year	950	91	81r
Electricity, (part.), other, 1800 sq. ft., new home	mo.	54.30	12/94	2c
Electricity, summer, 250 KWh	month	18.00	8/93	64c
Electricity, summer, 250 KWh	month	27.23	8/93	64s
Electricity, summer, 500 KWh	month	32.69	8/93	64c
Electricity, summer, 500 KWh	month	36.96	8/93	64s
Electricity, summer, 750 KWh	month	47.39	8/93	64c
Electricity, summer, 750 KWh	month	52.76	8/93	64s
Electricity, summer, 1000 KWh	month	62.08	8/93	64c
Electricity, summer, 1000 KWh	month	68.52	8/93	64s
Utilities, fuels, and public services, total expenditures	year	2000	91	81r
Water and other public services, expenditures	year	227	91	81r
Weddings				
Bridal attendants' gowns	event	750	10/93	76r
Bridal gown	event	852	10/93	76r
Bridal headpiece and veil	event	167	10/93	76r
Bride's wedding band	event	708	10/93	76r
Clergy	event	224	10/93	76r
Engagement ring	event	2756	10/93	76r
Flowers	event	863	10/93	76r
Formal wear for groom	event	106	10/93	76r
Groom's attendants' formal wear	event	530	10/93	76r
Groom's wedding band	event	402	10/93	76r
Music	event	600	10/93	76r
Photography	event	1088	10/93	76r
Shoes for bride	event	50	10/93	76r
Videography	event	483	10/93	76r
Wedding invitations and announcements	event	342	10/93	76r
Wedding reception	event	7000	10/93	76r

Values are in dollars or fractions of dollars. In the column headed *Ref*, references are shown to sources. Each reference is followed by a letter. These refer to the geographical level for which data were reported: s=State, r=Region, and c=City or metro. The abbreviation *ex* is used to mean *except* or *excluding*; *exp* stands for *expenditures*. For other abbreviations and further explanations, please see the Introduction.

Pascagoula, MS

Item	Per	Value	Date	Ref.
Appliances				
Appliances (major), expenditures	year	153	91	81r
Average annual exp.				
Food, health care, personal goods, services	year	27020	91	81r
Charity				
Cash contributions, expenditures	year	839	91	81r
Clothing				
Apparel, men and boys, total expenditures	year	380	91	81r
Apparel, women and girls, total expenditures	year	660	91	81r
Footwear, expenditures	year	193	91	81r
Communications				
Long-distance telephone rate, day, addl. min., 1-10 mi.	min.	0.11	12/93	9s
Long-distance telephone rate, day, initial min., 1-10 mi.	min.	0.19	12/93	9s
Phone line, single, business, field visit	inst	67.00	12/93	9s
Phone line, single, business, no field visit	inst	67.00	12/93	9s
Phone line, single, residence, field visit	inst	46.00	12/93	9s
Phone line, single, residence, no field visit	inst	46.00	12/93	9s
Telephone service, expenditures	year	616	91	81r
Education				
Board, 4-year private college/university	year	1394	8/94	80s
Board, 4-year public college/university	year	1380	8/94	80s
Education, total expenditures	year	319	91	81r
Room, 4-year private college/university	year	1400	8/94	80s
Room, 4-year public college/university	year	1343	8/94	80s
Total cost, 4-year private college/university	year	8754	8/94	80s
Total cost, 4-year public college/university	year	5093	8/94	80s
Tuition, 2-year public college/university, in-state	year	939	8/94	80s
Tuition, 4-year private college/university, in-state	year	5959	8/94	80s
Tuition, 4-year public college/university, in-state	year	2370	8/94	80s
Energy and Fuels				
Fuel oil and other fuels, expenditures	year	56	91	81r
Gas, natural, expenditures	year	150	91	81r
Gasoline and motor oil purchased	year	1152	91	81r
Gasoline, unleaded midgrade	gallon	1.21	4/93	82r
Gasoline, unleaded premium	gallon	1.30	4/93	82r
Gasoline, unleaded regular	gallon	1.10	4/93	82r
Entertainment				
Concert ticket, Pearl Jam group	perf	20.00	94	50r
Entertainment, total expenditures	year	1266	91	81r
Fees and admissions, expenditures	year	306	91	81r
Pets, toys, playground equipment, expenditures	year	271	91	81r
Reading, expenditures	year	131	91	81r
Televisions, radios, and sound equipment, expenditures	year	439	91	81r
Funerals				
Burial, immediate, container provided by funeral home		1298.96	1/95	54r
Cards, acknowledgment		21.26	1/95	54r
Casket, minimum alternative		204.95	1/95	54r
Cosmetology, hair care, etc.		85.40	1/95	54r
Cremation, direct, container provided by funeral home		1054.77	1/95	54r
Embalming		287.71	1/95	54r
Funeral, funeral home		269.18	1/95	54r
Funeral, other facility		272.88	1/95	54r
Graveside service		302.54	1/95	54r
Hearse, local		122.08	1/95	54r
Limousine, local		80.31	1/95	54r
Memorial service		277.66	1/95	54r
Service charge, professional, nondeclinable		896.65	1/95	54r
Visitation and viewing		232.39	1/95	54r

Item	Per	Value	Date	Ref.
Groceries				
Apples, Red Delicious	lb.	0.73	12/94	82r
Bacon, sliced	lb.	1.67	12/94	82r
Bananas	lb.	0.42	12/94	82r
Beef purchases	year	213	91	81r
Beverage purchases, alcoholic	year	249	91	81r
Beverage purchases, nonalcoholic	year	207	91	81r
Bologna, all beef or mixed	lb.	2.27	12/94	82r
Bread, white, pan	lb.	0.68	12/94	82r
Cabbage	lb.	0.42	12/94	82r
Carrots, short trimmed and topped	lb.	0.53	12/94	82r
Cereals and bakery products purchases	year	345	91	81r
Cereals and cereals products purchases	year	127	91	81r
Cheddar cheese, natural	lb.	3.58	12/94	82r
Chicken breast, bone-in	lb.	1.71	12/94	82r
Chicken, fresh, whole	lb.	0.78	12/94	82r
Chuck roast, USDA choice, boneless	lb.	2.26	12/94	82r
Crackers, soda, salted	lb.	1.27	12/94	82r
Cucumbers	lb.	0.65	12/94	82r
Dairy products (other) purchases	year	141	91	81r
Eggs, Grade A large	dozen	0.87	12/94	82r
Fish and seafood purchases	year	72	91	81r
Flour, white, all purpose	lb.	0.23	12/94	82r
Food purchases, food eaten at home	year	2381	91	81r
Foods purchased away from home, not prepared by consumer	year	1696	91	81r
Frankfurters, all meat or all beef	lb.	1.74	12/94	82r
Fruits and vegetables purchases	year	380	91	81r
Grapefruit	lb.	0.45	12/94	82r
Grapes, Thompson seedless	lb.	2.30	12/94	82r
Ground beef, 100% beef	lb.	1.37	12/94	82r
Ground chuck, 100% beef	lb.	1.97	12/94	82r
Ham, boneless, exc. canned	lb.	2.54	12/94	82r
Ice cream, prepackaged, bulk, regular	1/2 gal.	2.47	12/94	82r
Lemons	lb.	1.02	12/94	82r
Lettuce, iceberg	lb.	0.96	12/94	82r
Margarine, stick	lb.	0.77	12/94	82r
Meats, poultry, fish, and eggs purchases	year	655	91	81r
Milk and cream (fresh) purchases	year	130	91	81r
Orange juice, frozen concentrate 12-oz. can	16 oz.	1.36	12/94	82r
Oranges, Navel	lb.	0.54	12/94	82r
Pears, Anjou	lb.	0.81	12/94	82r
Pork chops, center cut, bone-in	lb.	3.07	12/94	82r
Pork purchases	year	142	91	81r
Potato chips	16-oz.	3.15	12/94	82r
Potatoes, frozen, French fried	lb.	0.82	12/94	82r
Potatoes, white	lb.	0.34	12/94	82r
Rice, white, long grain, uncooked	lb.	0.48	12/94	82r
Round roast, USDA choice, boneless	lb.	2.91	12/94	82r
Sausage, fresh	lb.	1.82	12/94	82r
Shortening, vegetable oil blends	lb.	0.75	12/94	82r
Spaghetti and macaroni	lb.	0.87	12/94	82r
Steak, rib eye, USDA choice, boneless	lb.	6.85	12/94	82r
Steak, round, graded & ungraded, exc. USDA prime & choice	lb.	2.96	12/94	82r
Steak, round, USDA choice, boneless	lb.	3.17	12/94	82r
Steak, sirloin, USDA choice, boneless	lb.	4.12	12/94	82r
Steak, T-bone, USDA choice, bone-in	lb.	5.63	12/94	82r
Sugar and other sweets, eaten at home, expenditures	year	93	91	81r
Sugar, white, all sizes	lb.	0.39	12/94	82r
Tobacco products and smoking supplies, total expenditures	year	286	91	81r
Tomatoes, field grown	lb.	1.36	12/94	82r
Tuna, chunk, light	lb.	1.94	12/94	82r
Turkey, frozen, whole	lb.	0.96	12/94	82r
Yogurt, natural, fruit flavored	8 oz.	0.58	12/94	82r
Health Care				
Adenosine, emergency room	treat	100.00	95	23r
Bladder tap, superpubic, infant, emergency room	treat	119.00	95	23r
Blood analysis, emergency room	treat	25.00	95	23r

Values are in dollars or fractions of dollars. In the column headed *Ref*, references are shown to sources. Each reference is followed by a letter. These refer to the geographical level for which data were reported: s = State, r = Region, and c = City or metro. The abbreviation *ex* is used to mean *except* or *excluding*; *exp* stands for expenditures. For other abbreviations and further explanations, please see the Introduction.

Pascagoula, MS - continued

Item	Per	Value	Date	Ref.
Health Care				
Blood tests, abdominal pain, emergency room	treat	25.00	95	23r
Burn dressing, emergency room	treat	266.00	95	23r
Cardiology interpretation, emergency room	treat	26.00	95	23r
Chest X-ray, emergency room	treat	78.00	95	23r
Childbirth, Cesarean delivery, hospital charge	birth	5462.00	12/91	69r
Childbirth, Cesarean delivery, physician charge	birth	2228.00	12/91	69r
Childbirth, normal delivery, hospital charge	birth	2943.00	12/91	69r
Childbirth, normal delivery, physician charge	birth	1619.00	12/91	69r
Defibrillation pads, emergency room	treat	6.00	95	23r
Drugs, expenditures	year	297	91	81r
Gastric tube insertion, nasal, emergency room	treat	25.00	95	23r
Health care, total expenditures	year	1600	91	81r
Health insurance expenditures	year	637	91	81r
Heart monitor, emergency room	treat	40.00	95	23r
Intravenous fluids, emergency room	treat	130.00	95	23r
Intravenous fluids, emergency room	liter	26.00	95	23r
Intravenous line, central, emergency room	treat	342.00	95	23r
Liver function tests, abdominal pain, emergency room	treat	26.00	95	23r
Medical care charges, total, emergency room, third-degree burns	treat	2101.00	95	23r
Medical care charges, total, emergency, infant with fever	treat	628.00	95	23r
Medical services expenditures	year	573	91	81r
Medical supplies expenditures	year	93	91	81r
Morphine, emergency room	treat	34.00	95	23r
Nursing care and facilities charges, emergency room	treat	252.00	95	23r
Nursing care and facilities charges, emergency, infant with fever	treat	252.00	95	23r
Nursing care and facilities charges, emergency, third-degree burns	treat	861.00	95	23r
Physician's charges, emergency, infant with fever	treat	212.00	95	23r
Physician's charges, emergency, third-degree burns	treat	372.00	95	23r
Physician's fee, emergency room	treat	372.00	95	23r
Physician's fee, general practitioner	visit	51.20	12/93	60r
Surgery, open-heart	proc	42374.00	1/93	14r
Ultrasound, abdominal, emergency room	treat	276.00	95	23r
Urinalysis, emergency room	treat	20.00	95	23r
Urinalysis, infant, emergency room	treat	20.00	95	23r
X-rays, emergency room	treat	78.00	95	23r
Household Goods				
Floor coverings, expenditures	year	48	91	81r
Furniture, expenditures	year	280	91	81r
Household equipment, misc. expenditures	year	342	91	81r
Household expenditures, miscellaneous	year	256	91	81r
Household furnishings and equipment, expenditures	year	988	91	81r
Household operations expenditures	year	468	91	81r
Household textiles, expenditures	year	95	91	81r
Housekeeping supplies, expenditures	year	380	91	81r
Laundry and cleaning supplies, expenditures	year	109	91	81r
Postage and stationery, expenditures	year	105	91	81r
Housing				
Add garage/carport		6,980	3/95	74r
Add room(s)		11,403	3/95	74r
Apartment condominium or co-op, median	unit	68600	12/94	62r
Dwellings (owned), expenditures	year	2428	91	81r
Enclose porch/patio/breezeway		4,572	3/95	74r
Finish room in basement/attic		3,794	3/95	74r
Home, existing, single-family, median	unit	120200	12/94	62r
Maintenance, repairs, insurance, and other housing expenditures	year	531	91	81r
Mortgage interest and charges expenditures	year	1506	91	81r

Pascagoula, MS - continued

Item	Per	Value	Date	Ref.
Housing - continued				
Princ. & int., mortgage, median-price exist. sing.-family home	mo.	540	12/94	62r
Property taxes expenditures	year	391	91	81r
Redesign, restructure more than half of home's interior		17,641	3/95	74r
Rental units expenditures	year	1264	91	81r
Insurance and Pensions				
Auto insurance, private passenger	year	643.74	12/94	71s
Insurance and pensions, personal, expenditures	year	2395	91	81r
Insurance, life and other personal, expenditures	year	368	91	81r
Pensions and Social Security, expenditures	year	2027	91	81r
Personal Services				
Personal services expenditures	year	212	91	81r
Restaurant Food				
Dining expenditures, family	week	33.83	94	73r
Taxes				
Taxes, Federal income, expenditures	year	2275	91	81r
Taxes, personal, expenditures	year	2715	91	81r
Taxes, State and local income, expenditures	year	365	91	81r
Transportation				
Cars and trucks purchased, new	year	1306	91	81r
Cars and trucks purchased, used	year	942	91	81r
Driver's learning permit fee	perm	1.00	1/94	84s
Driver's license fee	orig	20.00	1/94	84s
Driver's license fee, duplicate	lic	5.00	1/94	84s
Driver's license renewal fee	renew	20.00	1/94	84s
Identification card, nondriver	card	13.00	1/94	83s
Motorcycle license fee	orig	5.00	1/94	84s
Public transportation expenditures	year	249	91	81r
Transportation expenditures, total	year	5307	91	81r
Vehicle finance charges	year	346	91	81r
Vehicle insurance expenditures	year	544	91	81r
Vehicle maintenance and repairs expenditures	year	600	91	81r
Vehicle purchases	year	2275	91	81r
Vehicle rental, leases, licenses, etc. expenditures	year	141	91	81r
Vehicles purchased, other than cars and trucks	year	27	91	81r
Utilities				
Electricity expenditures	year	950	91	81r
Utilities, fuels, and public services, total expenditures	year	2000	91	81r
Water and other public services, expenditures	year	227	91	81r
Weddings				
Bridal attendants' gowns	event	750	10/93	76r
Bridal gown	event	852	10/93	76r
Bridal headpiece and veil	event	167	10/93	76r
Bride's wedding band	event	708	10/93	76r
Clergy	event	224	10/93	76r
Engagement ring	event	2756	10/93	76r
Flowers	event	863	10/93	76r
Formal wear for groom	event	106	10/93	76r
Groom's attendants' formal wear	event	530	10/93	76r
Groom's wedding band	event	402	10/93	76r
Music	event	600	10/93	76r
Photography	event	1088	10/93	76r
Shoes for bride	event	50	10/93	76r
Videography	event	483	10/93	76r
Wedding invitations and announcements	event	342	10/93	76r
Wedding reception	event	7000	10/93	76r

Values are in dollars or fractions of dollars. In the column headed *Ref*, references are shown to sources. Each reference is followed by a letter. These refer to the geographical level for which data were reported: s=State, r=Region, and c=City or metro. The abbreviation *ex* is used to mean *except* or *excluding*; *exp* stands for *expenditures*. For other abbreviations and further explanations, please see the Introduction.

Pawtucket-Woonsocket-Attleboro, RI, MA

Item	Per	Value	Date	Ref.
Appliances				
Appliances (major), expenditures	year	145	91	81r
Average annual exp.				
Food, health care, personal goods, services	year	29496	91	81r
Charity				
Cash contributions, expenditures	year	708	91	81r
Clothing				
Apparel, men and boys, total expenditures	year	416	91	81r
Apparel, women and girls, total expenditures	year	744	91	81r
Footwear, expenditures	year	305	91	81r
Communications				
Long-distance telephone rate, day, addl. min., 1-10 mi.	min.	0.14	12/93	9s
Long-distance telephone rate, day, initial min., 1-10 mi.	min.	0.31	12/93	9s
Phone line, single, business, field visit	inst	22.81	12/93	9s
Phone line, single, business, no field visit	inst	44.61	12/93	9s
Phone line, single, residence, field visit	inst	15.30	12/93	9s
Phone line, single, residence, no field visit	inst	33.83	12/93	9s
Telephone service, expenditures	year	589	91	81r
Education				
Board, 4-year private college/university	year	2821	8/94	80s
Board, 4-year public college/university	year	2482	8/94	80s
Education, total expenditures	year	593	91	81r
Room, 4-year private college/university	year	3262	8/94	80s
Room, 4-year public college/university	year	2719	8/94	80s
Total cost, 4-year private college/university	year	19518	8/94	80s
Total cost, 4-year public college/university	year	8603	8/94	80s
Tuition, 2-year public college/university, in-state	year	1546	8/94	80s
Tuition, 4-year private college/university, in-state	year	13434	8/94	80s
Tuition, 4-year public college/university, in-state	year	3402	8/94	80s
Energy and Fuels				
Fuel oil and other fuels, expenditures	year	257	91	81r
Gas, natural, expenditures	year	285	91	81r
Gasoline and motor oil purchased	year	867	91	81r
Gasoline, unleaded midgrade	gallon	1.32	4/93	82r
Gasoline, unleaded premium	gallon	1.40	4/93	82r
Gasoline, unleaded regular	gallon	1.19	4/93	82r
Entertainment				
Entertainment, total expenditures	year	1331	91	81r
Fees and admissions, expenditures	year	398	91	81r
Pets, toys, playground equipment, expenditures	year	270	91	81r
Reading, expenditures	year	171	91	81r
Televisions, radios, and sound equipment, expenditures	year	429	91	81r
Funerals				
Burial, immediate, container provided by funeral home		1507.89	1/95	54r
Cards, acknowledgment		18.10	1/95	54r
Casket, minimum alternative		133.03	1/95	54r
Cosmetology, hair care, etc.		114.12	1/95	54r
Cremation, direct, container provided by funeral home		1309.19	1/95	54r
Embalming		320.97	1/95	54r
Funeral, funeral home		327.61	1/95	54r
Funeral, other facility		314.81	1/95	54r
Graveside service		286.11	1/95	54r
Hearse, local		158.95	1/95	54r
Limousine, local		149.45	1/95	54r
Memorial service		315.94	1/95	54r
Service charge, professional, nondeclinable		1148.43	1/95	54r
Visitation and viewing		249.66	1/95	54r

Pawtucket-Woonsocket-Attleboro, RI, MA - continued

Item	Per	Value	Date	Ref.
Groceries				
Apples, Red Delicious	lb.	0.78	12/94	82r
Bacon, sliced	lb.	2.24	12/94	82r
Bananas	lb.	0.49	12/94	82r
Beef purchases	year	226	91	81r
Beverage purchases, alcoholic	year	332	91	81r
Beverage purchases, nonalcoholic	year	213	91	81r
Bread, white, pan	lb.	0.80	12/94	82r
Butter, salted, Grade AA, stick	lb.	1.67	12/94	82r
Carrots, short trimmed and topped	lb.	0.51	12/94	82r
Cereals and bakery products purchases	year	407	91	81r
Cereals and cereals products purchases	year	132	91	81r
Chicken breast, bone-in	lb.	2.22	12/94	82r
Chicken, fresh, whole	lb.	1.05	12/94	82r
Chuck roast, USDA choice, boneless	lb.	2.74	12/94	82r
Coffee, 100%, ground roast, all sizes	lb.	4.61	12/94	82r
Dairy products (other) purchases	year	161	91	81r
Eggs, Grade A large	dozen	1.12	12/94	82r
Fish and seafood purchases	year	112	91	81r
Food purchases, food eaten at home	year	2599	91	81r
Foods purchased away from home, not prepared by consumer	year	2024	91	81r
Fruits and vegetables purchases	year	444	91	81r
Grapefruit	lb.	0.44	12/94	82r
Grapes, Thompson seedless	lb.	2.24	12/94	82r
Ground chuck, 100% beef	lb.	1.67	12/94	82r
Ice cream, prepackaged, bulk, regular	1/2 gal.	2.93	12/94	82r
Lemons	lb.	1.06	12/94	82r
Lettuce, iceberg	lb.	0.92	12/94	82r
Meats, poultry, fish, and eggs purchases	year	751	91	81r
Milk and cream (fresh) purchases	year	152	91	81r
Orange juice, frozen concentrate 12-oz. can	16 oz.	1.92	12/94	82r
Oranges, Navel	lb.	0.56	12/94	82r
Pork chops, center cut, bone-in	lb.	3.09	12/94	82r
Pork purchases	year	130	91	81r
Potatoes, white	lb.	0.37	12/94	82r
Rib roast, USDA choice, bone-in	lb.	4.98	12/94	82r
Round roast, USDA choice, boneless	lb.	2.93	12/94	82r
Shortening, vegetable oil blends	lb.	1.03	12/94	82r
Spaghetti and macaroni	lb.	0.84	12/94	82r
Steak, round, USDA choice, boneless	lb.	3.48	12/94	82r
Steak, sirloin, USDA choice, bone-in	lb.	3.38	12/94	82r
Steak, sirloin, USDA choice, boneless	lb.	4.81	12/94	82r
Sugar and other sweets, eaten at home, expenditures	year	89	91	81r
Sugar, white, all sizes	lb.	0.46	12/94	82r
Tobacco products and smoking supplies, total expenditures	year	279	91	81r
Tomatoes, field grown	lb.	1.56	12/94	82r
Tuna, chunk, light	lb.	2.09	12/94	82r
Health Care				
Childbirth, Cesarean delivery, hospital charge	birth	6334.00	12/91	69r
Childbirth, Cesarean delivery, physician charge	birth	2234.00	12/91	69r
Childbirth, normal delivery, hospital charge	birth	3225.00	12/91	69r
Childbirth, normal delivery, physician charge	birth	1623.00	12/91	69r
Drugs, expenditures	year	205	91	81r
Health care, total expenditures	year	1396	91	81r
Health insurance expenditures	year	553	91	81r
Insurance premium, family medical care	month	365.49	1/95	41s
Medical services expenditures	year	559	91	81r
Medical supplies expenditures	year	80	91	81r
Household Goods				
Floor coverings, expenditures	year	158	91	81r
Furniture, expenditures	year	341	91	81r
Household equipment, misc. expenditures	year	363	91	81r
Household expenditures, miscellaneous	year	194	91	81r
Household furnishings and equipment, expenditures	year	1158	91	81r
Household operations expenditures	year	378	91	81r

Values are in dollars or fractions of dollars. In the column headed *Ref*, references are shown to sources. Each reference is followed by a letter. These refer to the geographical level for which data were reported: s=State, r=Region, and c=City or metro. The abbreviation *ex* is used to mean *except* or *excluding*; *exp* stands for expenditures. For other abbreviations and further explanations, please see the Introduction.

Pawtucket-Woonsocket-Attleboro, RI, MA - continued

Item	Per	Value	Date	Ref.
Household Goods				
Household textiles, expenditures	year	88	91	81r
Housekeeping supplies, expenditures	year	426	91	81r
Laundry and cleaning supplies, expenditures	year	122	91	81r
Postage and stationery, expenditures	year	134	91	81r
Housing				
Add garage/carport		11,614	3/95	74r
Add room(s)		16,816	3/95	74r
Apartment condominium or co-op, median	unit	96700	12/94	62r
Dwellings (owned), expenditures	year	3305	91	81r
Enclose porch/patio/breezeway		2,980	3/95	74r
Finish room in basement/attic		4,330	3/95	74r
Home, existing, single-family, median	unit	161600	12/94	62r
Maintenance, repairs, insurance, and other housing expenditures	year	569	91	81r
Mortgage interest and charges expenditures	year	1852	91	81r
Princ. & int., mortgage, median-price exist. sing.-family home	mo.	765	12/94	62r
Property taxes expenditures	year	884	91	81r
Redesign, restructure more than half of home's interior		2,750	3/95	74r
Rental units expenditures	year	1832	91	81r
Insurance and Pensions				
Auto insurance, private passenger	year	1034.46	12/94	71s
Insurance and pensions, personal, expenditures	year	2690	91	81r
Insurance, life and other personal, expenditures	year	341	91	81r
Pensions and Social Security, expenditures	year	2349	91	81r
Legal Assistance				
Estate planning, law-firm partner	hr.	375.00	10/93	12r
Legal work, law firm associate	hour	78		10r
Legal work, law firm partner	hour	183		10r
Personal Services				
Personal services expenditures	year	184	91	81r
Restaurant Food				
Dining expenditures, family	week	34.26	94	73r
Taxes				
Taxes, Federal income, expenditures	year	2409	91	81r
Taxes, personal, expenditures	year	3094	91	81r
Taxes, State and local income, expenditures	year	620	91	81r
Transportation				
Cars and trucks purchased, new	year	1170	91	81r
Cars and trucks purchased, used	year	739	91	81r
Driver's learning permit fee	perm	5.00	1/94	84s
Driver's license fee	orig	12.00	1/94	84s
Driver's license reinstatement fee, min.	susp	25.00	1/94	85s
Driver's license renewal fee	renew	30.00	1/94	84s
Identification card, nondriver	card	1.00	1/94	83s
Motorcycle learning permit fee	perm	5.00	1/94	84s
Motorcycle license fee	orig	12.00	1/94	84s
Motorcycle license renewal fee	renew	30.00	1/94	84s
Public transportation expenditures	year	430	91	81r
Transportation expenditures, total	year	4810	91	81r
Vehicle finance charges	year	238	91	81r
Vehicle insurance expenditures	year	630	91	81r
Vehicle maintenance and repairs expenditures	year	532	91	81r
Vehicle purchases	year	1920	91	81r
Vehicle rental, leases, licenses, etc. expenditures	year	193	91	81r
Vehicles purchased, other than cars and trucks	year	11	91	81r
Utilities				
Electricity expenditures	year	695	91	81r
Utilities, fuels, and public services, total expenditures	year	1981	91	81r

Pawtucket-Woonsocket-Attleboro, RI, MA - continued

Item	Per	Value	Date	Ref.
Utilities - continued				
Water and other public services, expenditures	year	154	91	81r
Weddings				
Bridal attendants' gowns	event	750	10/93	76r
Bridal gown	event	852	10/93	76r
Bridal headpiece and veil	event	167	10/93	76r
Bride's wedding band	event	708	10/93	76r
Clergy	event	224	10/93	76r
Engagement ring	event	2756	10/93	76r
Flowers	event	863	10/93	76r
Formal wear for groom	event	106	10/93	76r
Groom's attendants' formal wear	event	530	10/93	76r
Groom's wedding band	event	402	10/93	76r
Music	event	600	10/93	76r
Photography	event	1088	10/93	76r
Shoes for bride	event	50	10/93	76r
Videography	event	483	10/93	76r
Wedding invitations and announcements	event	342	10/93	76r
Wedding reception	event	7000	10/93	76r

Pensacola, FL

Item	Per	Value	Date	Ref.
Composite, ACCRA index		94.80	12/94	2c
Alcoholic Beverages				
Beer, Miller Lite, Bud, 12-oz., ex deposit	6	3.57	12/94	2c
J & B Scotch	750-ml.	18.02	12/94	2c
Wine, Gallo Chablis blanc	1.5-lit	5.03	12/94	2c
Appliances				
Appliances (major), expenditures	year	153	91	81r
Average annual exp.				
Food, health care, personal goods, services	year	27020	91	81r
Charity				
Cash contributions, expenditures	year	839	91	81r
Clothing				
Apparel, men and boys, total expenditures	year	380	91	81r
Apparel, women and girls, total expenditures	year	660	91	81r
Footwear, expenditures	year	193	91	81r
Jeans, man's denim		30.00	12/94	2c
Shirt, man's dress shirt		29.83	12/94	2c
Undervest, boy's size 10-14, cotton	3	6.96	12/94	2c
Communications				
Long-distance telephone rate, day, addl. min., 1-10 mi.	min.	0.08	12/93	9s
Long-distance telephone rate, day, initial min., 1-10 mi.	min.	0.15	12/93	9s
Newspaper subscription, dly. and Sun. delivery	month	13.91	12/94	2c
Phone line, single, business, field visit	inst	86.00	12/93	9s
Phone line, single, business, no field visit	inst	54.50	12/93	9s
Phone line, single, residence, field visit	inst	76.00	12/93	9s
Phone line, single, residence, no field visit	inst	44.50	12/93	9s
Telephone bill, family of four	month	14.86	12/94	2c
Telephone service, expenditures	year	616	91	81r
Telephone, residential, flat rate	mo.	9.15	12/93	8c
Education				
Bar examination preparatory course	course	500.00-100	94	17s
Board, 4-year private college/university	year	2123	8/94	80s
Board, 4-year public college/university	year	2101	8/94	80s
Education, total expenditures	year	319	91	81r
Room, 4-year private college/university	year	2242	8/94	80s
Room, 4-year public college/university	year	1970	8/94	80s
Total cost, 4-year private college/university	year	13853	8/94	80s
Total cost, 4-year public college/university	year	5855	8/94	80s
Tuition, 2-year public college/university, in-state	year	1076	8/94	80s

Values are in dollars or fractions of dollars. In the column headed *Ref*, references are shown to sources. Each reference is followed by a letter. These refer to the geographical level for which data were reported: s = State, r = Region, and c = City or metro. The abbreviation *ex* is used to mean *except* or *excluding*; *exp* stands for *expenditures*. For other abbreviations and further explanations, please see the Introduction.

Pensacola, FL - continued

Item	Per	Value	Date	Ref.
Education				
Tuition, 4-year private college/university, in-state	year	9287	8/94	80s
Tuition, 4-year public college/university, in-state	year	1784	8/94	80s
Energy and Fuels				
Energy, combined forms, 1800 sq. ft.	mo.	106.31	12/94	2c
Energy, exc. electricity, 1800 sq. ft.	mo.	30.29	12/94	2c
Fuel oil and other fuels, expenditures	year	56	91	81r
Gas, natural, expenditures	year	150	91	81r
Gas, reg unlead, taxes inc., cash, self-service	gal	1.10	12/94	2c
Gasoline and motor oil purchased	year	1152	91	81r
Gasoline, unleaded midgrade	gallon	1.21	4/93	82r
Gasoline, unleaded premium	gallon	1.30	4/93	82r
Gasoline, unleaded regular	gallon	1.10	4/93	82r
Entertainment				
Bowling, evening rate	game	1.38	12/94	2c
Concert ticket, Pearl Jam group	perf	20.00	94	50r
Entertainment, total expenditures	year	1266	91	81r
Fees and admissions, expenditures	year	306	91	81r
Monopoly game, Parker Brothers', No. 9	game	12.24	12/94	2c
Movie	adm	5.50	12/94	2c
Pets, toys, playground equipment, expenditures	year	271	91	81r
Reading, expenditures	year	131	91	81r
Televisions, radios, and sound equipment, expenditures	year	439	91	81r
Tennis balls, yellow, Wilson or Penn, 3	can	1.99	12/94	2c
Funerals				
Burial, immediate, container provided by funeral home		1370.36	1/95	54r
Cards, acknowledgment		14.83	1/95	54r
Casket, minimum alternative		192.52	1/95	54r
Cosmetology, hair care, etc.		102.27	1/95	54r
Cremation, direct, container provided by funeral home		1065.64	1/95	54r
Embalming		304.29	1/95	54r
Funeral, funeral home		287.83	1/95	54r
Funeral, other facility		284.14	1/95	54r
Graveside service		349.13	1/95	54r
Hearse, local		132.27	1/95	54r
Limousine, local		98.45	1/95	54r
Memorial service		270.59	1/95	54r
Service charge, professional, nondeclinable		933.59	1/95	54r
Visitation and viewing		225.83	1/95	54r
Groceries				
Groceries, ACCRA Index		96.80	12/94	2c
Apples, Red Delicious	lb.	0.73	12/94	82r
Baby food, strained vegetables, lowest price	4-4.5 oz.	0.27	12/94	2c
Bacon, sliced	lb.	1.67	12/94	82r
Bananas	lb.	0.43	12/94	2c
Bananas	lb.	0.42	12/94	82r
Beef or hamburger, ground	lb.	1.63	12/94	2c
Beef purchases	year	213	91	81r
Beverage purchases, alcoholic	year	249	91	81r
Beverage purchases, nonalcoholic	year	207	91	81r
Bologna, all beef or mixed	lb.	2.27	12/94	82r
Bread, white	24-oz.	0.85	12/94	2c
Bread, white, pan	lb.	0.68	12/94	82r
Cabbage	lb.	0.42	12/94	82r
Carrots, short trimmed and topped	lb.	0.53	12/94	82r
Cereals and bakery products purchases	year	345	91	81r
Cereals and cereals products purchases	year	127	91	81r
Cheddar cheese, natural	lb.	3.58	12/94	82r
Cheese, Kraft grated Parmesan	8-oz.	3.29	12/94	2c
Chicken breast, bone-in	lb.	1.71	12/94	82r
Chicken, fresh, whole	lb.	0.78	12/94	82r
Chicken, whole fryer	lb.	0.77	12/94	2c
Chuck roast, USDA choice, boneless	lb.	2.26	12/94	82r

Pensacola, FL - continued

Item	Per	Value	Date	Ref.
Groceries - continued				
Cigarettes, Winston, Kings	carton	16.50	12/94	2c
Coffee, vacuum-packed	13 oz.	3.13	12/94	2c
Corn Flakes, Kellogg's or Post Toasties	18 oz.	1.99	12/94	2c
Corn, frozen, whole kernel, lowest price	10 oz.	0.63	12/94	2c
Crackers, soda, salted	lb.	1.27	12/94	82r
Cucumbers	lb.	0.65	12/94	82r
Dairy products (other) purchases	year	141	91	81r
Eggs, Grade A large	dozen	0.73	12/94	2c
Eggs, Grade A large	dozen	0.87	12/94	82r
Fish and seafood purchases	year	72	91	81r
Flour, white, all purpose	lb.	0.23	12/94	82r
Food purchases, food eaten at home	year	2381	91	81r
Foods purchased away from home, not prepared by consumer	year	1696	91	81r
Frankfurters, all meat or all beef	lb.	1.74	12/94	82r
Fruits and vegetables purchases	year	380	91	81r
Grapefruit	lb.	0.45	12/94	82r
Grapes, Thompson seedless	lb.	2.30	12/94	82r
Ground beef, 100% beef	lb.	1.37	12/94	82r
Ground chuck, 100% beef	lb.	1.97	12/94	82r
Ham, boneless, exc. canned	lb.	2.54	12/94	82r
Ice cream, prepackaged, bulk, regular	1/2 gal.	2.47	12/94	82r
Lemons	lb.	1.02	12/94	82r
Lettuce, iceberg	lb.	0.96	12/94	82r
Lettuce, iceberg	head	0.90	12/94	2c
Margarine, Blue Bonnet or Parkay cubes	lb.	0.58	12/94	2c
Margarine, stick	lb.	0.77	12/94	82r
Meats, poultry, fish, and eggs purchases	year	655	91	81r
Milk and cream (fresh) purchases	year	130	91	81r
Milk, whole	1/2 gal.	1.31	12/94	2c
Orange juice, frozen concentrate 12-oz. can	16 oz.	1.36	12/94	82r
Orange juice, Minute Maid frozen	12-oz.	1.12	12/94	2c
Oranges, Navel	lb.	0.54	12/94	82r
Peaches, halves or slices, Hunt's, Del Monte, or Libby's	29-oz.	1.24	12/94	2c
Pears, Anjou	lb.	0.81	12/94	82r
Peas, sweet, Del Monte or Green Giant	15-17 oz.	0.55	12/94	2c
Pork chops, center cut, bone-in	lb.	3.07	12/94	82r
Pork purchases	year	142	91	81r
Potato chips	16-oz.	3.15	12/94	82r
Potatoes, frozen, French fried	lb.	0.82	12/94	82r
Potatoes, white	lb.	0.34	12/94	82r
Potatoes, white or red	10-lb. sack	2.93	12/94	2c
Rice, white, long grain, uncooked	lb.	0.48	12/94	82r
Round roast, USDA choice, boneless	lb.	2.91	12/94	82r
Sausage, fresh	lb.	1.82	12/94	82r
Sausage, Jimmy Dean, 100% pork	lb.	2.22	12/94	2c
Shortening, vegetable oil blends	lb.	0.75	12/94	82r
Shortening, vegetable, Crisco	3-lb.	2.49	12/94	2c
Soft drink, Coca Cola, ex deposit	2 lit	1.09	12/94	2c
Spaghetti and macaroni	lb.	0.87	12/94	82r
Steak, rib eye, USDA choice, boneless	lb.	6.85	12/94	82r
Steak, round, graded & ungraded, exc. USDA prime & choice	lb.	2.96	12/94	82r
Steak, round, USDA choice, boneless	lb.	3.17	12/94	82r
Steak, sirloin, USDA choice, boneless	lb.	4.12	12/94	82r
Steak, t-bone	lb.	5.14	12/94	2c
Steak, T-bone, USDA choice, bone-in	lb.	5.63	12/94	82r
Sugar and other sweets, eaten at home, expenditures	year	93	91	81r
Sugar, cane or beet	4 lbs.	1.48	12/94	2c
Sugar, white, all sizes	lb.	0.39	12/94	82r
Tobacco products and smoking supplies, total expenditures	year	286	91	81r
Tomatoes, field grown	lb.	1.36	12/94	82r
Tomatoes, Hunt's or Del Monte	14.5 oz.	0.62	12/94	2c
Tuna, chunk, light	lb.	1.94	12/94	82r

Values are in dollars or fractions of dollars. In the column headed *Ref*, references are shown to sources. Each reference is followed by a letter. These refer to the geographical level for which data were reported: s=State, r=Region, and c=City or metro. The abbreviation *ex* is used to mean *except* or *excluding*; *exp* stands for expenditures. For other abbreviations and further explanations, please see the Introduction.

Pensacola, FL

Pensacola, FL - continued

Item	Per	Value	Date	Ref.
Groceries				
Tuna, chunk, light, oil-packed	6.125-6.5 oz.	0.64	12/94	2c
Turkey, frozen, whole	lb.	0.96	12/94	82r
Yogurt, natural, fruit flavored	8 oz.	0.58	12/94	82r
Goods and Services				
Miscellaneous goods and services, ACCRA Index		97.90	12/94	2c
Health Care				
Health care, ACCRA Index		104.20	12/94	2c
Adenosine, emergency room	treat	100.00	95	23r
Antibiotic ointment, Polysporin	1.5 oz.	3.94	12/94	2c
Bladder tap, superpubic, infant, emergency room	treat	119.00	95	23r
Blood analysis, emergency room	treat	25.00	95	23r
Blood tests, abdominal pain, emergency room	treat	25.00	95	23r
Burn dressing, emergency room	treat	266.00	95	23r
Cardiology interpretation, emergency room	treat	26.00	95	23r
Chest X-ray, emergency room	treat	78.00	95	23r
Childbirth, Cesarean delivery, hospital charge	birth	5462.00	12/91	69r
Childbirth, Cesarean delivery, physician charge	birth	2228.00	12/91	69r
Childbirth, normal delivery, hospital charge	birth	2943.00	12/91	69r
Childbirth, normal delivery, physician charge	birth	1619.00	12/91	69r
Defibrillation pads, emergency room	treat	6.00	95	23r
Dentist's fee, adult teeth cleaning and periodic oral exam	visit	56.86	12/94	2c
Doctor's fee, routine exam, established patient	visit	42.18	12/94	2c
Drugs, expenditures	year	297	91	81r
Gastric tube insertion, nasal, emergency room	treat	25.00	95	23r
Health care, total expenditures	year	1600	91	81r
Health insurance expenditures	year	637	91	81r
Heart monitor, emergency room	treat	40.00	95	23r
Hospital care, semiprivate room	day	386.67	12/94	2c
Insurance premium, family medical care	month	301.92	1/95	41s
Intravenous fluids, emergency room	treat	130.00	95	23r
Intravenous fluids, emergency room	liter	26.00	95	23r
Intravenous line, central, emergency room	treat	342.00	95	23r
Liver function tests, abdominal pain, emergency room	treat	26.00	95	23r
Medical care charges, total, emergency room, third-degree burns	treat	2101.00	95	23r
Medical care charges, total, emergency, infant with fever	treat	628.00	95	23r
Medical services expenditures	year	573	91	81r
Medical supplies expenditures	year	93	91	81r
Morphine, emergency room	treat	34.00	95	23r
Nursing care and facilities charges, emergency room	treat	252.00	95	23r
Nursing care and facilities charges, emergency, infant with fever	treat	252.00	95	23r
Nursing care and facilities charges, emergency, third-degree burns	treat	861.00	95	23r
Physician's charges, emergency, infant with fever	treat	212.00	95	23r
Physician's charges, emergency, third-degree burns	treat	372.00	95	23r
Physician's fee, emergency room	treat	372.00	95	23r
Physician's fee, general practitioner	visit	51.20	12/93	60r
Surgery, open-heart	proc	42374.00	1/93	14r
Ultrasound, abdominal, emergency room	treat	276.00	95	23r
Urinalysis, emergency room	treat	20.00	95	23r
Urinalysis, infant, emergency room	treat	20.00	95	23r
X-rays, emergency room	treat	78.00	95	23r
Household Goods				
Appl. repair, service call, wash mach	min. lab. chg.	26.10	12/94	2c

Pensacola, FL - continued

Item	Per	Value	Date	Ref.
Household Goods - continued				
Floor coverings, expenditures	year	48	91	81r
Furniture, expenditures	year	280	91	81r
Household equipment, misc. expenditures	year	342	91	81r
Household expenditures, miscellaneous	year	256	91	81r
Household furnishings and equipment, expenditures	year	988	91	81r
Household operations expenditures	year	468	91	81r
Household textiles, expenditures	year	95	91	81r
Housekeeping supplies, expenditures	year	380	91	81r
Laundry and cleaning supplies, expenditures	year	109	91	81r
Laundry detergent, Tide Ultra, Bold, or Cheer	42 oz.	3.20	12/94	2c
Postage and stationery, expenditures	year	105	91	81r
Tissues, facial, Kleenex brand	175	1.03	12/94	2c
Housing				
Housing, ACCRA Index		89.80	12/94	2c
Add garage/carport		6,980	3/95	74r
Add room(s)		11,403	3/95	74r
Apartment condominium or co-op, median	unit	68600	12/94	62r
Dwellings (owned), expenditures	year	2428	91	81r
Enclose porch/patio/breezeway		4,572	3/95	74r
Finish room in basement/attic		3,794	3/95	74r
Home, existing, single-family, median	unit	120200		62r
Home, existing, single-family, median	unit	74.60	12/94	62c
House payment, principal and interest, 25% down payment	mo.	684	12/94	2c
House, 1800 sq ft, 8000 sq ft lot, new, urban, utilities	total	100667	12/94	2c
Maintenance, repairs, insurance, and other housing expenditures	year	531	91	81r
Mortgage interest and charges expenditures	year	1506	91	81r
Mtge. rate, incl. points and orig. fee, 30-year conv. fixed or ARM	mo.	9.27	12/94	2c
Princ. & int., mortgage, median-price exist. sing.-family home	mo.	540	12/94	62r
Property taxes expenditures	year	391	91	81r
Redesign, restructure more than half of home's interior		17,641	3/95	74r
Rent, apartment, 2 br., 1 1/2-2 baths, unfurnished, 950 sq ft, water	mo.	486	12/94	2c
Rental units expenditures	year	1264	91	81r
Insurance and Pensions				
Auto insurance, private passenger	year	753.93	12/94	71s
Insurance and pensions, personal, expenditures	year	2395	91	81r
Insurance, life and other personal, expenditures	year	368	91	81r
Pensions and Social Security, expenditures	year	2027	91	81r
Personal Goods				
Shampoo, Alberto VO5	15-oz.	0.92	12/94	2c
Toothpaste, Crest or Colgate	6-7 oz.	1.92	12/94	2c
Personal Services				
Dry cleaning, man's 2-pc. suit		6.42	12/94	2c
Haircut, man's barbershop, no styling		5.67	12/94	2c
Haircut, woman's shampoo, trim, blow-dry		21.86	12/94	2c
Personal services expenditures	year	212	91	81r
Restaurant Food				
Chicken, fried, thigh and drumstick		2.13	12/94	2c
Dining expenditures, family	week	33.83	94	73r
Hamburger with cheese	1/4 lb.	1.79	12/94	2c
Pizza, Pizza Hut or Pizza Inn	12-13 in.	7.99	12/94	2c
Taxes				
Taxes, Federal income, expenditures	year	2275	91	81r
Taxes, personal, expenditures	year	2715	91	81r
Taxes, State and local income, expenditures	year	365	91	81r

Values are in dollars or fractions of dollars. In the column headed *Ref*, references are shown to sources. Each reference is followed by a letter. These refer to the geographical level for which data were reported: s=State, r=Region, and c=City or metro. The abbreviation *ex* is used to mean *except* or *excluding*; *exp* stands for expenditures. For other abbreviations and further explanations, please see the Introduction.

Pensacola, FL - continued

Item	Per	Value	Date	Ref.
Transportation				
Transportation, ACCRA Index		91.10	12/94	2c
Bus fare, one-way	trip	1.00	12/95	1c
Cars and trucks purchased, new	year	1306	91	81r
Cars and trucks purchased, used	year	942	91	81r
Driver's learning permit fee	perm	20.00	1/94	84s
Driver's license fee	orig	20.00	1/94	84s
Driver's license fee, duplicate	lic	10.00	1/94	84s
Driver's license reinstatement fee, min.	susp	25.00	1/94	85s
Driver's license renewal fee	renew	15.00	1/94	84s
Identification card, nondriver	card	3.00	1/94	83s
Motorcycle learning permit fee	perm	20.00	1/94	84s
Motorcycle license fee	orig	20.00	1/94	84s
Motorcycle license fee, duplicate	lic	10.00	1/94	84s
Motorcycle license renewal fee	renew	15.00	1/94	84s
Public transportation expenditures	year	249	91	81r
Tire balance, computer or spin bal., front	wheel	5.49	12/94	2c
Transportation expenditures, total	year	5307	91	81r
Vehicle finance charges	year	346	91	81r
Vehicle insurance expenditures	year	544	91	81r
Vehicle maintenance and repairs expenditures	year	600	91	81r
Vehicle purchases	year	2275	91	81r
Vehicle rental, leases, licenses, etc. expenditures	year	141	91	81r
Vehicles purchased, other than cars and trucks	year	27	91	81r
Utilities				
Utilities, ACCRA Index		92.20	12/94	2c
Electricity expenditures	year	950	91	81r
Electricity, (part.), other, 1800 sq. ft., new home	mo.	76.02	12/94	2c
Electricity, summer, 250 KWh	month	22.64	8/93	64c
Electricity, summer, 500 KWh	month	37.20	8/93	64c
Electricity, summer, 750 KWh	month	51.75	8/93	64c
Electricity, summer, 1000 KWh	month	66.31	8/93	64c
Utilities, fuels, and public services, total expenditures	year	2000	91	81r
Water and other public services, expenditures	year	227	91	81r
Weddings				
Bridal attendants' gowns	event	750	10/93	76r
Bridal gown	event	852	10/93	76r
Bridal headpiece and veil	event	167	10/93	76r
Bride's wedding band	event	708	10/93	76r
Clergy	event	224	10/93	76r
Engagement ring	event	2756	10/93	76r
Flowers	event	863	10/93	76r
Formal wear for groom	event	106	10/93	76r
Groom's attendants' formal wear	event	530	10/93	76r
Groom's wedding band	event	402	10/93	76r
Music	event	600	10/93	76r
Photography	event	1088	10/93	76r
Shoes for bride	event	50	10/93	76r
Videography	event	483	10/93	76r
Wedding invitations and announcements	event	342	10/93	76r
Wedding reception	event	7000	10/93	76r

Peoria, IL

Item	Per	Value	Date	Ref.
Composite, ACCRA index		97.00	12/94	2c
Alcoholic Beverages				
Beer, Miller Lite, Bud, 12-oz., ex deposit	6	3.59	12/94	2c
J & B Scotch	750-ml.	15.23	12/94	2c
Wine, Gallo Chablis blanc	1.5-lit	3.43	12/94	2c
Appliances				
Appliances (major), expenditures	year	131	91	81r

Peoria, IL - continued

Item	Per	Value	Date	Ref.
Average annual exp.				
Food, health care, personal goods, services	year	25935	91	81r
Charity				
Cash contributions, expenditures	year	745	91	81r
Clothing				
Apparel, men and boys, total expenditures	year	332	91	81r
Apparel, women and girls, total expenditures	year	578	91	81r
Footwear, expenditures	year	164	91	81r
Jeans, man's denim		27.99	12/94	2c
Shirt, man's dress shirt		24.50	12/94	2c
Undervest, boy's size 10-14, cotton	3	4.99	12/94	2c
Communications				
Long-distance telephone rate, day, addl. min., 1-10 mi.	min.	0.04	12/93	9s
Long-distance telephone rate, day, initial min., 1-10 mi.	min.	0.10	12/93	9s
Newspaper subscription, dly. and Sun. delivery	month	16.09	12/94	2c
Phone line, single, business, field visit	inst	84.50	12/93	9s
Phone line, single, business, no field visit	inst	84.50	12/93	9s
Phone line, single, residence, field visit	inst	55.00	12/93	9s
Phone line, single, residence, no field visit	inst	55.00	12/93	9s
Telephone bill, family of four	month	23.88	12/94	2c
Telephone service, expenditures	year	547	91	81r
Education				
Board, 4-year private college/university	year	2078	8/94	80s
Board, 4-year public college/university	year	2139	8/94	80s
Education, total expenditures	year	394	91	81r
Room, 4-year private college/university	year	2696	8/94	80s
Room, 4-year public college/university	year	1796	8/94	80s
Total cost, 4-year private college/university	year	15249	8/94	80s
Total cost, 4-year public college/university	year	6964	8/94	80s
Tuition, 2-year public college/university, in-state	year	1135	8/94	80s
Tuition, 4-year private college/university, in-state	year	10474	8/94	80s
Tuition, 4-year public college/university, in-state	year	3029	8/94	80s
Energy and Fuels				
Energy, combined forms, 1800 sq. ft.	mo.	103.41	12/94	2c
Energy, exc. electricity, 1800 sq. ft.	mo.	45.98	12/94	2c
Fuel oil and other fuels, expenditures	year	83	91	81r
Gas, natural, expenditures	year	373	91	81r
Gas, reg unlead, taxes inc., cash, self-service	gal	1.15	12/94	2c
Gasoline and motor oil purchased	year	1000	91	81r
Gasoline, unleaded midgrade	gallon	1.15	4/93	82r
Gasoline, unleaded premium	gallon	1.23	4/93	82r
Gasoline, unleaded regular	gallon	1.07	4/93	82r
Entertainment				
Bowling, evening rate	game	1.75	12/94	2c
Entertainment, total expenditures	year	1356	91	81r
Fees and admissions, expenditures	year	347	91	81r
Monopoly game, Parker Brothers', No. 9	game	11.49	12/94	2c
Movie	adm	5.50	12/94	2c
Pets, toys, playground equipment, expenditures	year	270	91	81r
Reading, expenditures	year	160	91	81r
Televisions, radios, and sound equipment, expenditures	year	433	91	81r
Tennis balls, yellow, Wilson or Penn, 3	can	2.29	12/94	2c
Funerals				
Burial, immediate, container provided by funeral home		1268.31	1/95	54r
Cards, acknowledgment		26.12	1/95	54r
Casket, minimum alternative		198.03	1/95	54r
Cosmetology, hair care, etc.		122.19	1/95	54r
Cremation, direct, container provided by funeral home		977.81	1/95	54r

Values are in dollars or fractions of dollars. In the column headed *Ref*, references are shown to sources. Each reference is followed by a letter. These refer to the geographical level for which data were reported: s=State, r=Region, and c=City or metro. The abbreviation *ex* is used to mean *except* or *excluding*; *exp* stands for *expenditures*. For other abbreviations and further explanations, please see the Introduction.

Peoria, IL - continued

Item	Per	Value	Date	Ref.
Funerals				
Embalming		334.00	1/95	54r
Funeral, funeral home		321.16	1/95	54r
Funeral, other facility		317.73	1/95	54r
Graveside service		292.48	1/95	54r
Hearse, local		153.20	1/95	54r
Limousine, local		123.52	1/95	54r
Memorial service		356.30	1/95	54r
Service charge, professional, nondeclinable		968.24	1/95	54r
Visitation and viewing		332.66	1/95	54r
Groceries				
Groceries, ACCRA Index		94.30	12/94	2c
Apples, Red Delicious	lb.	0.68	12/94	82r
Baby food, strained vegetables, lowest price	4-4.5 oz.	0.28	12/94	2c
Bacon, sliced	lb.	1.88	12/94	82r
Bananas	lb.	0.42	12/94	2c
Bananas	lb.	0.41	12/94	82r
Beef or hamburger, ground	lb.	1.11	12/94	2c
Beef purchases	year	197	91	81r
Beef, stew, boneless	lb.	2.52	12/94	82r
Beverage purchases, alcoholic	year	293	91	81r
Beverage purchases, nonalcoholic	year	203	91	81r
Bologna, all beef or mixed	lb.	2.12	12/94	82r
Bread, white	24-oz.	0.46	12/94	2c
Bread, white, pan	lb.	0.76	12/94	82r
Cabbage	lb.	0.44	12/94	82r
Carrots, short trimmed and topped	lb.	0.44	12/94	82r
Cereals and bakery products purchases	year	347	91	81r
Cereals and cereals products purchases	year	119	91	81r
Cheddar cheese, natural	lb.	3.28	12/94	82r
Cheese, Kraft grated Parmesan	8-oz.	3.25	12/94	2c
Chicken breast, bone-in	lb.	1.61	12/94	82r
Chicken, fresh, whole	lb.	0.89	12/94	82r
Chicken, whole fryer	lb.	0.75	12/94	2c
Chuck roast, USDA choice, boneless	lb.	2.33	12/94	82r
Cigarettes, Winston, Kings	carton	17.06	12/94	2c
Coffee, 100%, ground roast, all sizes	lb.	4.28	12/94	82r
Coffee, vacuum-packed	13 oz.	3.58	12/94	2c
Cookies, chocolate chip	lb.	2.72	12/94	82r
Corn Flakes, Kellogg's or Post Toasties	18 oz.	2.44	12/94	2c
Corn, frozen, whole kernel, lowest price	10 oz.	0.70	12/94	2c
Dairy products (other) purchases	year	148	91	81r
Eggs, Grade A large	dozen	0.74	12/94	2c
Eggs, Grade A large	dozen	0.76	12/94	82r
Fish and seafood purchases	year	61	91	81r
Flour, white, all purpose	lb.	0.22	12/94	82r
Food purchases, food eaten at home	year	2313	91	81r
Foods purchased away from home, not prepared by consumer	year	1709	91	81r
Fruits and vegetables purchases	year	372	91	81r
Grapefruit	lb.	0.47	12/94	82r
Grapes, Thompson seedless	lb.	2.15	12/94	82r
Ground beef, 100% beef	lb.	1.37	12/94	82r
Ground chuck, 100% beef	lb.	1.81	12/94	82r
Ham, boneless, exc. canned	lb.	2.16	12/94	82r
Ice cream, prepackaged, bulk, regular	1/2 gal.	2.48	12/94	82r
Lemons	lb.	1.08	12/94	82r
Lettuce, iceberg	lb.	0.81	12/94	82r
Lettuce, iceberg	head	0.93	12/94	2c
Margarine, Blue Bonnet or Parkay cubes	lb.	0.60	12/94	2c
Margarine, stick	lb.	0.81	12/94	82r
Meats, poultry, fish, and eggs purchases	year	591	91	81r
Milk and cream (fresh) purchases	year	132	91	81r
Milk, whole	1/2 gal.	1.71	12/94	2c
Orange juice, frozen concentrate 12-oz. can	16 oz.	1.41	12/94	82r
Orange juice, Minute Maid frozen	12-oz.	1.41	12/94	2c
Oranges, Navel	lb.	0.56	12/94	82r
Peaches, halves or slices, Hunt's, Del Monte, or Libby's	29-oz.	1.35	12/94	2c
Peanut butter, creamy, all sizes	lb.	1.81	12/94	82r

Peoria, IL - continued

Item	Per	Value	Date	Ref.
Groceries - continued				
Peas, sweet, Del Monte or Green Giant	15-17 oz.	0.59	12/94	2c
Pork chops, center cut, bone-in	lb.	2.76	12/94	82r
Pork purchases	year	130	91	81r
Potato chips	16-oz.	2.81	12/94	82r
Potatoes, frozen, French fried	lb.	0.83	12/94	82r
Potatoes, white	lb.	0.28	12/94	82r
Potatoes, white or red	10-lb. sack	2.31	12/94	2c
Round roast, USDA choice, boneless	lb.	2.90	12/94	82r
Sausage, Jimmy Dean, 100% pork	lb.	2.75	12/94	2c
Shortening, vegetable oil blends	lb.	0.88	12/94	82r
Shortening, vegetable, Crisco	3-lb.	2.29	12/94	2c
Soft drink, Coca Cola, ex deposit	2 lit	1.03	12/94	2c
Spaghetti and macaroni	lb.	0.78	12/94	82r
Steak, rib eye, USDA choice, boneless	lb.	6.15	12/94	82r
Steak, round, graded & ungraded, exc. USDA prime & choice	lb.	2.72	12/94	82r
Steak, round, USDA choice, boneless	lb.	3.02	12/94	82r
Steak, sirloin, USDA choice, boneless	lb.	3.85	12/94	82r
Steak, t-bone	lb.	5.51	12/94	2c
Steak, T-bone, USDA choice, bone-in	lb.	5.38	12/94	82r
Sugar and other sweets, eaten at home, expenditures	year	91	91	81r
Sugar, cane or beet	4 lbs.	1.26	12/94	2c
Sugar, white, all sizes	lb.	0.36	12/94	82r
Tobacco products and smoking supplies, total expenditures	year	298	91	81r
Tomatoes, field grown	lb.	1.36	12/94	82r
Tomatoes, Hunt's or Del Monte	14.5 oz.	0.80	12/94	2c
Tuna, chunk, light	lb.	1.94	12/94	82r
Tuna, chunk, light, oil-packed	6.125-6.5 oz.	0.60	12/94	2c
Turkey, frozen, whole	lb.	0.96	12/94	82r
Yogurt, natural, fruit flavored	8 oz.	0.62	12/94	82r
Goods and Services				
Miscellaneous goods and services, ACCRA Index		97.90	12/94	2c
Health Care				
Health care, ACCRA Index		88.80	12/94	2c
Antibiotic ointment, Polysporin	1.5 oz.	3.47	12/94	2c
Childbirth, Cesarean delivery, hospital charge	birth	5101.00	12/91	69r
Childbirth, Cesarean delivery, physician charge	birth	2234.00	12/91	69r
Childbirth, normal delivery, hospital charge	birth	2891.00	12/91	69r
Childbirth, normal delivery, physician charge	birth	1623.00	12/91	69r
Dentist's fee, adult teeth cleaning and periodic oral exam	visit	52.20	12/94	2c
Doctor's fee, routine exam, established patient	visit	34.40	12/94	2c
Drugs, expenditures	year	248	91	81r
Health care, total expenditures	year	1336	91	81r
Health insurance expenditures	year	550	91	81r
Hospital care, semiprivate room	day	300.00	12/94	2c
Insurance premium, family medical care	month	363.57	1/95	41s
Medical services expenditures	year	457	91	81r
Medical supplies expenditures	year	82	91	81r
Household Goods				
Appl. repair, service call, wash mach	min. lab. chg.	30.69	12/94	2c
Floor coverings, expenditures	year	105	91	81r
Furniture, expenditures	year	291	91	81r
Household equipment, misc. expenditures	year	341	91	81r
Household expenditures, miscellaneous	year	162	91	81r
Household furnishings and equipment, expenditures	year	1042	91	81r
Household operations expenditures	year	365	91	81r
Household textiles, expenditures	year	101	91	81r

Values are in dollars or fractions of dollars. In the column headed *Ref*, references are shown to sources. Each reference is followed by a letter. These refer to the geographical level for which data were reported: s=State, r=Region, and c=City or metro. The abbreviation *ex* is used to mean *except* or *excluding*; *exp* stands for expenditures. For other abbreviations and further explanations, please see the Introduction.

Peoria, IL - continued

Item	Per	Value	Date	Ref.
Household Goods				
Housekeeping supplies, expenditures	year	390	91	81r
Laundry and cleaning supplies, expenditures	year	110	91	81r
Laundry detergent, Tide Ultra, Bold, or Cheer	42 oz.	3.10	12/94	2c
Postage and stationery, expenditures	year	115	91	81r
Tissues, facial, Kleenex brand	175	0.88	12/94	2c
Housing				
Housing, ACCRA Index		98.10	12/94	2c
Add garage/carport		8,479	3/95	74r
Add room(s)		21,347	3/95	74r
Apartment condominium or co-op, median	unit	87100	12/94	62r
Bathroom addition, average cost	add	9734.00	3/95	13r
Bathroom remodeling, average cost	remod	6414.00	3/95	13r
Bedroom, master suite addition, average cost	add	27122.00	3/95	13r
Deck addition, average cost	add	6665.00	3/95	13r
Dwellings (owned), expenditures	year	2566	91	81r
Enclose porch/patio/breezeway		4,556	3/95	74r
Exterior remodeling, average cost	remod	15395.00	3/95	13r
Family room addition, average cost	add	27658.00	3/95	13r
Finish room in basement/attic		5,074	3/95	74r
Home, existing, single-family, median	unit	106500	12/94	62r
Home, existing, single-family, median	unit	66.60	12/94	62c
House payment, principal and interest, 25% down payment	mo.	764	12/94	2c
House, 1800 sq ft, 8000 sq ft lot, new, urban, utilities	total	124550	12/94	2c
Kitchen remodeling, major, average cost	remod	17084.00	3/95	13r
Kitchen remodeling, minor, average cost	remod	5804.00	3/95	13r
Maintenance, repairs, insurance, and other housing expenditures	year	484	91	81r
Mortgage interest and charges expenditures	year	1443	91	81r
Mtge. rate, incl. points and orig. fee, 30-year conv. fixed or ARM	mo.	9.18	12/94	2c
Office, home addition, average cost	add	8121.00	3/95	13r
Princ. & int., mortgage, median-price exist. sing.-family home	mo.	515	12/94	62r
Property taxes expenditures	year	639	91	81r
Redesign, restructure more than half of home's interior		9,114	3/95	74r
Rent, apartment, 2 br., 1 1/2-2 baths, unfurnished, 950 sq ft, water	mo.	484	12/94	2c
Rental units expenditures	year	1200	91	81r
Sun-space addition, average cost	add	23768.00	3/95	13r
Wing addition, two-story, average cost	add	50410.00	3/95	13r
Insurance and Pensions				
Auto insurance, private passenger	year	679.48	12/94	71s
Insurance and pensions, personal, expenditures	year	2408	91	81r
Insurance, life and other personal, expenditures	year	355	91	81r
Pensions and Social Security, expenditures	year	2053	91	81r
Legal Assistance				
Legal work, law firm associate	hour	90		10r
Legal work, law firm partner	hour	139		10r
Personal Goods				
Shampoo, Alberto VO5	15-oz.	1.19	12/94	2c
Toothpaste, Crest or Colgate	6-7 oz.	2.23	12/94	2c
Personal Services				
Dry cleaning, man's 2-pc. suit		6.93	12/94	2c
Haircut, man's barbershop, no styling		9.00	12/94	2c
Haircut, woman's shampoo, trim, blow-dry		26.90	12/94	2c
Personal services expenditures	year	203	91	81r
Restaurant Food				
Chicken, fried, thigh and drumstick		2.20	12/94	2c
Dining expenditures, family	week	30.03	94	73r
Hamburger with cheese	1/4 lb.	1.84	12/94	2c

Peoria, IL - continued

Item	Per	Value	Date	Ref.
Restaurant Food - continued				
Pizza, Pizza Hut or Pizza Inn	12-13 in.	7.97	12/94	2c
Taxes				
Taxes, Federal income, expenditures	year	1756	91	81r
Taxes, personal, expenditures	year	2426	91	81r
Taxes, State and local income, expenditures	year	568	91	81r
Transportation				
Transportation, ACCRA Index		101.40	12/94	2c
Bus fare, one-way	trip	0.75	12/95	1c
Bus fare, up to 10 miles	one-way	0.75	12/94	2c
Cars and trucks purchased, new	year	891	91	81r
Cars and trucks purchased, used	year	1155	91	81r
Driver's learning permit fee	perm	20.00	1/94	84s
Driver's license fee	orig	10.00	1/94	84s
Driver's license fee, duplicate	lic	5.00	1/94	84s
Driver's license reinstatement fee, min.	susp	30.00	1/94	85s
Driver's license renewal fee	renew	10.00	1/94	84s
Identification card, nondriver	card	4.00	1/94	83s
Motorcycle learning permit fee	perm	20.00	1/94	84s
Motorcycle license fee	orig	10.00	1/94	84s
Motorcycle license fee, duplicate	lic	5.00	1/94	84s
Motorcycle license renewal fee	renew	10.00	1/94	84s
Public transportation expenditures	year	209	91	81r
Tire balance, computer or spin bal., front	wheel	7.20	12/94	2c
Transportation expenditures, total	year	4792	91	81r
Vehicle finance charges	year	300	91	81r
Vehicle insurance expenditures	year	485	91	81r
Vehicle maintenance and repairs expenditures	year	534	91	81r
Vehicle purchases	year	2068	91	81r
Vehicle rental, leases, licenses, etc. expenditures	year	197	91	81r
Vehicles purchased, other than cars and trucks	year	22	91	81r
Utilities				
Utilities, ACCRA Index		96.20	12/94	2c
Electricity expenditures	year	668	91	81r
Electricity, (part.), other, 1800 sq. ft., new home	mo.	57.43	12/94	2c
Electricity, summer, 250 KWh	month	22.41	8/93	64c
Electricity, summer, 500 KWh	month	41.13	8/93	64c
Electricity, summer, 750 KWh	month	59.84	8/93	64c
Electricity, summer, 1000 KWh	month	78.55	8/93	64c
Utilities, fuels, and public services, total expenditures	year	1838	91	81r
Water and other public services, expenditures	year	167	91	81r
Weddings				
Bridal attendants' gowns	event	750	10/93	76r
Bridal gown	event	852	10/93	76r
Bridal headpiece and veil	event	167	10/93	76r
Bride's wedding band	event	708	10/93	76r
Clergy	event	224	10/93	76r
Engagement ring	event	2756	10/93	76r
Flowers	event	863	10/93	76r
Formal wear for groom	event	106	10/93	76r
Groom's attendants' formal wear	event	530	10/93	76r
Groom's wedding band	event	402	10/93	76r
Music	event	600	10/93	76r
Photography	event	1088	10/93	76r
Shoes for bride	event	50	10/93	76r
Videography	event	483	10/93	76r
Wedding invitations and announcements	event	342	10/93	76r
Wedding reception	event	7000	10/93	76r

Values are in dollars or fractions of dollars. In the column headed *Ref*, references are shown to sources. Each reference is followed by a letter. These refer to the geographical level for which data were reported: s = State, r = Region, and c = City or metro. The abbreviation *ex* is used to mean *except* or *excluding*; *exp* stands for expenditures. For other abbreviations and further explanations, please see the Introduction.

Philadelphia, PA

Item	Per	Value	Date	Ref.
Composite, ACCRA index		127.80	12/94	2c
Alcoholic Beverages				
Beer, Miller Lite, Bud, 12-oz., ex deposit	6	5.55	12/94	2c
J & B Scotch	750-ml.	16.99	12/94	2c
Wine, Gallo Chablis blanc	1.5-lit	5.99	12/94	2c
Appliances				
Appliances (major), expenditures	year	202	91	81c
Appliances (major), expenditures	year	145	91	81r
Average annual exp.				
Food, health care, personal goods, services	year	31795	91	81c
Food, health care, personal goods, services	year	29496	91	81r
Business				
Bank fee, bad check	check	28.90	12/93	5c
Charity				
Cash contributions, expenditures	year	905	91	81c
Cash contributions, expenditures	year	708	91	81r
Child Care				
Child care, for-profit daycare center	week	105.00	12/94	28c
Clothing				
Apparel, men and boys, total expenditures	year	550	91	81c
Apparel, men and boys, total expenditures	year	416	91	81r
Apparel, women and girls, total expenditures	year	934	91	81c
Apparel, women and girls, total expenditures	year	744	91	81r
Footwear, expenditures	year	203	91	81c
Footwear, expenditures	year	305	91	81r
Jeans, man's denim		35.37	12/94	2c
Shirt, man's dress shirt		26.00	12/94	2c
Suit, two-piece, medium weight wool, man's, Armani name	suit	1495.00	12/93	60c
Undervest, boy's size 10-14, cotton	3	6.16	12/94	2c
Communications				
Long-distance telephone rate, day, addl. min., 1-10 mi.	min.	0.08	12/93	9s
Long-distance telephone rate, day, initial min., 1-10 mi.	min.	0.15	12/93	9s
Newspaper subscription, dly. and Sun. delivery	month	14.25	12/94	2c
Phone line, single, business, field visit	inst	75.00	12/93	9s
Phone line, single, business, no field visit	inst	75.00	12/93	9s
Phone line, single, residence, field visit	inst	40.00	12/93	9s
Phone line, single, residence, no field visit	inst	40.00	12/93	9s
Telephone bill, family of four	month	14.92	12/94	2c
Telephone service, expenditures	year	622	91	81c
Telephone service, expenditures	year	589	91	81r
Telephone, business, addl. line, touch tone	month	1.90	10/91	25c
Telephone, business, connection charges, touch tone	inst	79.50	10/91	25c
Telephone, business, key system line, touch tone	month	26.18	10/91	25c
Telephone, business, PBX line, touch tone	month	26.12	10/91	25c
Telephone, business, single ln., touch tone	month	26.98	10/91	25c
Telephone, business, touch tone, inside wiring maintenance plan	month	0.95	10/91	25c
Telephone, residential, flat rate	mo.	21.00	12/93	8c
Credit Cards				
Fee, conventional credit card, secured	year	15.00	1/95	96c
Education				
Board, 4-year private college/university	year	2714	8/94	80s
Board, 4-year public college/university	year	1899	8/94	80s
Education, total expenditures	year	650	91	81c
Education, total expenditures	year	593	91	81r
Room, 4-year private college/university	year	2720	8/94	80s
Room, 4-year public college/university	year	2063	8/94	80s
Total cost, 4-year private college/university	year	18118	8/94	80s
Total cost, 4-year public college/university	year	8278	8/94	80s
Tuition, 2-year public college/university, in-state	year	1671	8/94	80s

Philadelphia, PA - continued

Item	Per	Value	Date	Ref.
Education - continued				
Tuition, 4-year private college/university, in-state	year	12684	8/94	80s
Tuition, 4-year public college/university, in-state	year	4316	8/94	80s
Energy and Fuels				
Electricity	500 KWh	62.09	12/94	82c
Energy, combined forms, 1800 sq. ft.	mo.	225.74	12/94	2c
Fuel oil #2	gallon	0.84	12/94	82c
Fuel oil and other fuels, expenditures	year	170	91	81c
Fuel oil and other fuels, expenditures	year	257	91	81r
Gas, natural, expenditures	year	340	91	81c
Gas, natural, expenditures	year	285	91	81r
Gas, piped	40 therms	34.03	12/94	82c
Gas, piped	100 therms	75.68	12/94	82c
Gas, piped	therm	0.77	12/94	82c
Gas, reg unlead, taxes inc., cash, self-service	gal	1.16	12/94	2c
Gasoline and motor oil purchased	year	863	91	81c
Gasoline and motor oil purchased	year	867	91	81r
Gasoline, unleaded midgrade	gallon	1.30	4/93	82c
Gasoline, unleaded midgrade	gallon	1.32	4/93	82r
Gasoline, unleaded premium	gallon	1.38	4/93	82c
Gasoline, unleaded premium	gallon	1.40	4/93	82r
Gasoline, unleaded regular	gallon	1.17	4/93	82c
Gasoline, unleaded regular	gallon	1.19	4/93	82r
Entertainment				
Bowling, evening rate	game	2.43	12/94	2c
Entertainment supplies, equipment, and services, misc. expenditures	year	345	91	81c
Entertainment, total expenditures	year	1452	91	81c
Entertainment, total expenditures	year	1331	91	81r
Fees and admissions, expenditures	year	404	91	81c
Fees and admissions, expenditures	year	398	91	81r
Monopoly game, Parker Brothers', No. 9	game	12.44	12/94	2c
Movie	adm	6.50	12/94	2c
Pets, toys, playground equipment, expenditures	year	237	91	81c
Pets, toys, playground equipment, expenditures	year	270	91	81r
Reading, expenditures	year	200	91	81c
Reading, expenditures	year	171	91	81r
Televisions, radios, and sound equipment, expenditures	year	466	91	81c
Televisions, radios, and sound equipment, expenditures	year	429	91	81r
Tennis balls, yellow, Wilson or Penn, 3	can	2.89	12/94	2c
Funerals				
Burial, immediate, container provided by funeral home		1370.36	1/95	54r
Cards, acknowledgment		17.72	1/95	54r
Casket, minimum alternative		192.52	1/95	54r
Cosmetology, hair care, etc.		139.56	1/95	54r
Cremation, direct, container provided by funeral home		1049.24	1/95	54r
Embalming		387.57	1/95	54r
Funeral, funeral home		278.77	1/95	54r
Funeral, other facility		275.85	1/95	54r
Graveside service		213.08	1/95	54r
Hearse, local		157.27	1/95	54r
Limousine, local		146.45	1/95	54r
Memorial service		271.02	1/95	54r
Service charge, professional, nondeclinable		943.58	1/95	54r
Visitation and viewing		322.86	1/95	54r
Groceries				
Groceries, ACCRA Index		120.60	12/94	2c
Apples, Red Delicious	lb.	0.78	12/94	82r

Values are in dollars or fractions of dollars. In the column headed *Ref*, references are shown to sources. Each reference is followed by a letter. These refer to the geographical level for which data were reported: s=State, r=Region, and c=City or metro. The abbreviation *ex* is used to mean *except* or *excluding*; *exp* stands for expenditures. For other abbreviations and further explanations, please see the Introduction.

Philadelphia, PA - continued

Item	Per	Value	Date	Ref.
Groceries				
Baby food, strained vegetables, lowest price	4-4.5 oz.	0.41	12/94	2c
Bacon, sliced	lb.	2.24	12/94	82r
Bananas	lb.	0.64	12/94	2c
Bananas	lb.	0.49	12/94	82r
Beef or hamburger, ground	lb.	2.11	12/94	2c
Beef purchases	year	232	91	81c
Beef purchases	year	226	91	81r
Beverage purchases, alcoholic	year	338	91	81c
Beverage purchases, alcoholic	year	332	91	81r
Beverage purchases, nonalcoholic	year	194	91	81c
Beverage purchases, nonalcoholic	year	213	91	81r
Bread, white	24-oz.	1.18	12/94	2c
Bread, white, pan	lb.	0.80	12/94	82r
Butter, salted, Grade AA, stick	lb.	1.67	12/94	82r
Carrots, short trimmed and topped	lb.	0.51	12/94	82r
Cereals and bakery products purchases	year	416	91	81c
Cereals and bakery products purchases	year	407	91	81r
Cereals and cereal products purchases	year	140	91	81c
Cereals and cereals products purchases	year	132	91	81r
Cheese, Kraft grated Parmesan	8-oz.	3.76	12/94	2c
Chicken breast, bone-in	lb.	2.22	12/94	82r
Chicken, fresh, whole	lb.	1.05	12/94	82r
Chicken, whole fryer	lb.	0.99	12/94	2c
Chuck roast, USDA choice, boneless	lb.	2.74	12/94	82r
Cigarettes, Winston, Kings	carton	16.76	12/94	2c
Coffee, 100%, ground roast, all sizes	lb.	4.61	12/94	82r
Coffee, vacuum-packed	13 oz.	2.72	12/94	2c
Corn Flakes, Kellogg's or Post Toasties	18 oz.	2.54	12/94	2c
Corn, frozen, whole kernel, lowest price	10 oz.	0.74	12/94	2c
Dairy products (other) purchases	year	176	91	81c
Dairy products (other) purchases	year	161	91	81r
Eggs, Grade A large	dozen	1.06	12/94	2c
Eggs, Grade A large	dozen	1.12	12/94	82r
Fish and seafood purchases	year	93	91	81c
Fish and seafood purchases	year	112	91	81r
Food purchases, food eaten at home	year	2586	91	81c
Food purchases, food eaten at home	year	2599	91	81r
Foods purchased away from home, not prepared by consumer	year	1941	91	81c
Foods purchased away from home, not prepared by consumer	year	2024	91	81r
Fruits and vegetables purchases	year	430	91	81c
Fruits and vegetables purchases	year	444	91	81r
Grapefruit	lb.	0.44	12/94	82r
Grapes, Thompson seedless	lb.	2.24	12/94	82r
Ground chuck, 100% beef	lb.	1.67	12/94	82r
Ice cream, prepackaged, bulk, regular	1/2 gal.	2.93	12/94	82r
Lemons	lb.	1.06	12/94	82r
Lettuce, iceberg	lb.	0.92	12/94	82r
Lettuce, iceberg	head	0.91	12/94	2c
Margarine, Blue Bonnet or Parkay cubes	lb.	1.00	12/94	2c
Meats, poultry, fish, and eggs purchases	year	759	91	81c
Meats, poultry, fish, and eggs purchases	year	751	91	81r
Milk and cream (fresh) purchases	year	138	91	81c
Milk and cream (fresh) purchases	year	152	91	81r
Milk, whole	1/2 gal.	1.30	12/94	2c
Orange juice, frozen concentrate 12-oz. can	16 oz.	1.92	12/94	82r
Orange juice, Minute Maid frozen	12-oz.	1.54	12/94	2c
Oranges, Navel	lb.	0.56	12/94	82r
Peaches, halves or slices, Hunt's, Del Monte, or Libby's	29-oz.	1.48	12/94	2c
Peas, sweet, Del Monte or Green Giant	15-17 oz.	0.71	12/94	2c
Pork chops, center cut, bone-in	lb.	3.09	12/94	82r
Pork purchases	year	131	91	81c
Pork purchases	year	130	91	81r
Potatoes, white	lb.	0.37	12/94	82r
Potatoes, white or red	10-lb. sack	2.41	12/94	2c

Philadelphia, PA - continued

Item	Per	Value	Date	Ref.
Groceries - continued				
Rib roast, USDA choice, bone-in	lb.	4.98	12/94	82r
Round roast, USDA choice, boneless	lb.	2.93	12/94	82r
Sausage, Jimmy Dean, 100% pork	lb.	3.21	12/94	2c
Shortening, vegetable oil blends	lb.	1.03	12/94	82r
Shortening, vegetable, Crisco	3-lb.	2.83	12/94	2c
Soft drink, Coca Cola, ex deposit	2 lit	1.34	12/94	2c
Spaghetti and macaroni	lb.	0.84	12/94	82r
Steak, round, USDA choice, boneless	lb.	3.48	12/94	82r
Steak, sirloin, USDA choice, bone-in	lb.	3.38	12/94	82r
Steak, sirloin, USDA choice, boneless	lb.	4.81	12/94	82r
Steak, t-bone	lb.	5.99	12/94	2c
Sugar and other sweets, eaten at home, expenditures	year	89	91	81r
Sugar and other sweets, eaten at home, purchases	year	93	91	81c
Sugar, cane or beet	4 lbs.	1.82	12/94	2c
Sugar, white, all sizes	lb.	0.46	12/94	82r
Tobacco products and smoking supplies, total expenditures	year	256	91	81c
Tobacco products and smoking supplies, total expenditures	year	279	91	81r
Tomatoes, field grown	lb.	1.56	12/94	82r
Tomatoes, Hunt's or Del Monte	14.5 oz.	0.90	12/94	2c
Tuna, chunk, light	lb.	2.09	12/94	82r
Tuna, chunk, light, oil-packed	6.125-6.5 oz.	0.90	12/94	2c
Goods and Services				
Miscellaneous goods and services, ACCRA Index		111.50	12/94	2c
Health Care				
Health care, ACCRA Index		106.40	12/94	2c
Antibiotic ointment, Polysporin	1.5 oz.	3.74	12/94	2c
Appendectomy	proc	1111.00	12/92	69c
Breast lesion excision (lumpectomy)	proc	674.00	12/92	69c
Cesarean section delivery	proc	2587.00	12/92	69c
Childbirth, Cesarean delivery, hospital charge	birth	6334.00	12/91	69r
Childbirth, Cesarean delivery, physician charge	birth	2234.00	12/91	69r
Childbirth, normal delivery, hospital charge	birth	3225.00	12/91	69r
Childbirth, normal delivery, physician charge	birth	1623.00	12/91	69r
Cholecystectomy	proc	1685.00	12/92	69c
Coronary bypass, triple	proc	6414.00	12/92	69c
Dentist's fee, adult teeth cleaning and periodic oral exam	visit	58.75	12/94	2c
Doctor's fee, routine exam, established patient	visit	40.00	12/94	2c
Drugs, expenditures	year	202	91	81c
Drugs, expenditures	year	205	91	81r
Health care, total expenditures	year	1648	91	81c
Health care, total expenditures	year	1396	91	81r
Health insurance expenditures	year	753	91	81c
Health insurance expenditures	year	553	91	81r
Health insurance premium	month	402.00	7/93	94c
Hospital care, semiprivate room	day	453.25	12/94	2c
Hospital cost	adm	6,709	2/94	72c
Hysterectomy, abdominal	proc	2615.00	12/92	69c
Insurance premium, family medical care	month	349.05	1/95	41s
Medical services expenditures	year	594	91	81c
Medical services expenditures	year	559	91	81r
Medical supplies expenditures	year	98	91	81c
Medical supplies expenditures	year	80	91	81r
Oophorectomy	proc	1822.00	12/92	69c
Salpingo-oophorectomy	proc	1996.00	12/92	69c
Household Goods				
Appl. repair, service call, wash mach	min. lab. chg.	37.21	12/94	2c
Floor coverings, expenditures	year	72	91	81c
Floor coverings, expenditures	year	158	91	81r

Values are in dollars or fractions of dollars. In the column headed *Ref*, references are shown to sources. Each reference is followed by a letter. These refer to the geographical level for which data were reported: s = State, r = Region, and c = City or metro. The abbreviation *ex* is used to mean *except* or *excluding*; *exp* stands for expenditures. For other abbreviations and further explanations, please see the Introduction.

Philadelphia, PA - continued

Item	Per	Value	Date	Ref.
Household Goods				
Furniture, expenditures	year	564	91	81c
Furniture, expenditures	year	341	91	81r
Household equipment, misc. expenditures	year	363	91	81r
Household equipment, misc., expenditures	year	448	91	81c
Household expenditures, miscellaneous	year	183	91	81c
Household expenditures, miscellaneous	year	194	91	81r
Household furnishings and equipment, expenditures	year	1474	91	81c
Household furnishings and equipment, expenditures	year	1158	91	81r
Household operations expenditures	year	423	91	81c
Household operations expenditures	year	378	91	81r
Household textiles, expenditures	year	108	91	81c
Household textiles, expenditures	year	88	91	81r
Housekeeping supplies, expenditures	year	518	91	81c
Housekeeping supplies, expenditures	year	426	91	81r
Laundry and cleaning supplies, expenditures	year	147	91	81c
Laundry and cleaning supplies, expenditures	year	122	91	81r
Laundry detergent, Tide Ultra, Bold, or Cheer	42 oz.	3.95	12/94	2c
Postage and stationery, expenditures	year	109	91	81c
Postage and stationery, expenditures	year	134	91	81r
Tissues, facial, Kleenex brand	175	1.16	12/94	2c
Housing				
Housing, ACCRA Index		143.50	12/94	2c
Add garage/carport		11,614	3/95	74r
Add room(s)		16,816	3/95	74r
Apartment condominium or co-op, median	unit	96700	12/94	62r
Dwellings (owned), expenditures	year	3697	91	81c
Dwellings (owned), expenditures	year	3305	91	81r
Enclose porch/patio/breezeway		2,980	3/95	74r
Finish room in basement/attic		4,330	3/95	74r
Home, existing, single-family, median	unit	161600	12/94	62r
Home, existing, single-family, median	unit	115.40	12/94	62c
Home, purchase price	unit	161.20	3/93	26c
House payment, principal and interest, 25% down payment	mo.	1114	12/94	2c
House, 1800 sq ft, 8000 sq ft lot, new, urban, utilities	total	185974	12/94	2c
Maintenance, repairs, insurance, and other housing expenditures	year	707	91	81c
Maintenance, repairs, insurance, and other housing expenditures	year	569	91	81r
Mortgage interest and charges expenditures	year	1855	91	81c
Mortgage interest and charges expenditures	year	1852	91	81r
Mtge. rate, incl. points and orig. fee, 30-year conv. fixed or ARM	mo.	8.92	12/94	2c
Princ. & int., mortgage, median-price exist. sing.-family home	mo.	765	12/94	62r
Property taxes expenditures	year	1135	91	81c
Property taxes expenditures	year	884	91	81r
Redesign, restructure more than half of home's interior		2,750	3/95	74r
Rent, apartment, 2 br., 1 1/2-2 baths, unfurnished, 950 sq ft, water	mo.	717	12/94	2c
Rent, office space	sq. ft.	7.82	93	57c
Rental units expenditures	year	1705	900/00/91	81c
Rental units expenditures	year	1832	91	81r
Insurance and Pensions				
Auto insurance, private passenger	year	721.50	12/94	71s
Health insurance, HMO plan, cost to employer	year	3319	93	59c
Insurance and pensions, personal, expenditures	year	3119	91	81c
Insurance and pensions, personal, expenditures	year	2690	91	81r
Insurance, life and other personal, expenditures	year	398	91	81c

Philadelphia, PA - continued

Item	Per	Value	Date	Ref.
Insurance and Pensions - continued				
Insurance, life and other personal, expenditures	year	341	91	81r
Pensions and Social Security, expenditures	year	2721	91	81c
Pensions and Social Security, expenditures	year	2349	91	81r
Legal Assistance				
Estate planning, law-firm partner	hr.	375.00	10/93	12r
Legal work, law firm associate	hour	78		10r
Legal work, law firm partner	hour	183		10r
Personal Goods				
Personal care products and services, total expenditures	year	422	91	81c
Shampoo, Alberto VO5	15-oz.	1.66	12/94	2c
Toothpaste, Crest or Colgate	6-7 oz.	2.29	12/94	2c
Personal Services				
Dry cleaning, man's 2-pc. suit		7.11	12/94	2c
Haircut, man's barbershop, no styling		11.45	12/94	2c
Haircut, woman's shampoo, trim, blow-dry		24.70	12/94	2c
Personal services expenditures	year	240	91	81c
Personal services expenditures	year	184	91	81r
Restaurant Food				
Chicken, fried, thigh and drumstick		2.43	12/94	2c
Dining expenditures, family	week	34.26	94	73r
Hamburger with cheese	1/4 lb.	1.98	12/94	2c
Pizza, Pizza Hut or Pizza Inn	12-13 in.	7.93	12/94	2c
Taxes				
Tax rate, residential property, month	$100	8.26	1/92	79c
Taxes, Federal income, expenditures	year	3634	91	81c
Taxes, Federal income, expenditures	year	2409	91	81r
Taxes, personal, expenditures	year	4858	91	81c
Taxes, personal, expenditures	year	3094	91	81r
Taxes, State and local income, expenditures	year	1014	91	81c
Taxes, State and local income, expenditures	year	620	91	81r
Transportation				
Transportation, ACCRA Index		115.40	12/94	2c
Bus fare, one-way	trip	1.30	12/95	1c
Bus fare, up to 10 miles	one-way	1.45	12/94	2c
Cars and trucks purchased, new	year	1341	91	81c
Cars and trucks purchased, new	year	1170	91	81r
Cars and trucks purchased, used	year	404	91	81c
Cars and trucks purchased, used	year	739	91	81r
Driver's learning permit fee	perm	27.00	1/94	84s
Driver's license fee	orig	0.00	1/94	84s
Driver's license fee, duplicate	lic	7.00	1/94	84s
Driver's license reinstatement fee, min.	susp	25.00	1/94	85s
Driver's license renewal fee	renew	0.00	1/94	84s
Driving expenses	mile	49.00	5/95	86c
Identification card, nondriver	card	5.00	1/94	83s
Motorcycle learning permit fee	perm	27.00	1/94	84s
Motorcycle license fee	orig	0.00	1/94	84s
Motorcycle license fee, duplicate	lic	7.00	1/94	84s
Motorcycle license renewal fee	renew	0.00	1/94	84s
Public transportation expenditures	year	299	91	81c
Public transportation expenditures	year	430	91	81r
Railway fare, commuter rail, one-way	trip	3.25	12/95	1c
Railway fare, heavy rail, one-way	trip	0.68	12/95	1c
Railway fare, light rail, one-way	trip	1.60	12/95	1c
Tire balance, computer or spin bal., front	wheel	8.24	12/94	2c
Transportation expenditures, total	year	4832	91	81c
Transportation expenditures, total	year	4810	91	81r
Trolley fare, one-way	trip	1.60	12/95	1c
Vehicle expenses, miscellaneous	year	1922	91	81c
Vehicle finance charges	year	160	91	81c
Vehicle finance charges	year	238	91	81r
Vehicle insurance expenditures	year	794	91	81c
Vehicle insurance expenditures	year	630	91	81r
Vehicle maintenance and repairs expenditures	year	718	91	81c

Values are in dollars or fractions of dollars. In the column headed *Ref*, references are shown to sources. Each reference is followed by a letter. These refer to the geographical level for which data were reported: s=State, r=Region, and c=City or metro. The abbreviation *ex* is used to mean *except* or *excluding*; *exp* stands for *expenditures*. For other abbreviations and further explanations, please see the Introduction.

Philadelphia, PA - continued

Item	Per	Value	Date	Ref.
Transportation				
Vehicle maintenance and repairs expenditures	year	532	91	81r
Vehicle purchases	year	1747	91	81c
Vehicle purchases	year	1920	91	81r
Vehicle rental, leases, licenses, etc. expenditures	year	250	91	81c
Vehicle rental, leases, licenses, etc. expenditures	year	193	91	81r
Vehicles purchased, other than cars and trucks	year	2	91	81c
Vehicles purchased, other than cars and trucks	year	11	91	81r
Utilities				
Utilities, ACCRA Index		184.30	12/94	2c
Electricity	KWh	0.12	12/94	82c
Electricity expenditures	year	850	91	81c
Electricity expenditures	year	695	91	81r
Electricity, 1800 sq. ft., new home	mo.	225.74	12/94	2c
Electricity, summer, 250 KWh	month	36.74	8/93	64c
Electricity, summer, 500 KWh	month	68.39	8/93	64c
Electricity, summer, 750 KWh	month	104.67	8/93	64c
Electricity, summer, 1000 KWh	month	140.95	8/93	64c
Utilities, fuels, and public services, total expenditures	year	2224	91	81c
Utilities, fuels, and public services, total expenditures	year	1981	91	81r
Water and other public services, expenditures	year	242	91	81c
Water and other public services, expenditures	year	154	91	81r
Weddings				
Bridal attendants' gowns	event	750	10/93	76r
Bridal gown	event	852	10/93	76r
Bridal headpiece and veil	event	167	10/93	76r
Bride's wedding band	event	708	10/93	76r
Clergy	event	224	10/93	76r
Engagement ring	event	2756	10/93	76r
Flowers	event	863	10/93	76r
Formal wear for groom	event	106	10/93	76r
Groom's attendants' formal wear	event	530	10/93	76r
Groom's wedding band	event	402	10/93	76r
Music	event	600	10/93	76r
Photography	event	1088	10/93	76r
Shoes for bride	event	50	10/93	76r
Videography	event	483	10/93	76r
Wedding invitations and announcements	event	342	10/93	76r
Wedding reception	event	7000	10/93	76r

Phoenix, AZ

Item	Per	Value	Date	Ref.
Composite, ACCRA index		101.20	12/94	2c
Alcoholic Beverages				
Beer, Miller Lite, Bud, 12-oz., ex deposit	6	3.69	12/94	2c
J & B Scotch	750-ml.	15.78	12/94	2c
Wine, Gallo Chablis blanc	1.5-lit	4.78	12/94	2c
Appliances				
Appliances (major), expenditures	year	160	91	81r
Average annual exp.				
Food, health care, personal goods, services	year	32461	91	81r
Business				
Dinner and tip, hotel, corporate rate	night	31.00	2/94	15c
Hotel room, corporate rate	night	74.00	2/94	15c
Business Expenses				
Car rental, midsized car	day	38.99	92	52c
Continental breakfast, room service	meal	5.25	92	52c
Lunch, convention center	meal	6.25	92	52c
Restaurant meal	meal	36.00	92	52c

Phoenix, AZ - continued

Item	Per	Value	Date	Ref.
Business Expenses - continued				
Room rate, hotel	day	83.16	92	52c
Taxicab fare, airport to convention center	trip	6.00-8.00	92	52c
Charity				
Cash contributions, expenditures	year	975	91	81r
Clothing				
Apparel, men and boys, total expenditures	year	467	91	81r
Apparel, women and girls, total expenditures	year	737	91	81r
Footwear, expenditures	year	270	91	81r
Formal wear rental, tuxedo, downtown store	rental	42.00	92	52c
Jeans, man's denim		29.49	12/94	2c
Shirt, dress, men's	shirt	50.00	1/92	44c
Shirt, man's dress shirt		32.50	12/94	2c
Undervest, boy's size 10-14, cotton	3	5.49	12/94	2c
Communications				
Long-distance telephone rate, day, addl. min., 1-10 mi.	min.	0.10	12/93	9s
Long-distance telephone rate, day, initial min., 1-10 mi.	min.	0.24	12/93	9s
Newspaper cost, major daily	1	0.50	92	52c
Newspaper subscription, dly. and Sun. delivery	month	13.70	12/94	2c
Phone line, single, business, field visit	inst	56.00	12/93	9s
Phone line, single, business, no field visit	inst	56.00	12/93	9s
Phone line, single, residence, field visit	inst	46.50	12/93	9s
Phone line, single, residence, no field visit	inst	46.50	12/93	9s
Telephone bill, family of four	month	17.82	12/94	2c
Telephone service, expenditures	year	611	91	81r
Telephone, residential, flat rate	mo.	12.40	12/93	8c
Education				
Board, 4-year private college/university	year	2044	8/94	80s
Board, 4-year public college/university	year	1904	8/94	80s
Education, total expenditures	year	375	91	81r
Room, 4-year private college/university	year	1617	8/94	80s
Room, 4-year public college/university	year	1739	8/94	80s
Total cost, 4-year private college/university	year	9542	8/94	80s
Total cost, 4-year public college/university	year	5462	8/94	80s
Tuition, 2-year public college/university, in-state	year	729	8/94	80s
Tuition, 4-year private college/university, in-state	year	5881	8/94	80s
Tuition, 4-year public college/university, in-state	year	1819	8/94	80s
Energy and Fuels				
Energy, combined forms, 1800 sq. ft.	mo.	116.76	12/94	2c
Fuel oil and other fuels, expenditures	year	33	91	81r
Gas	gal.	1.05	1/92	44c
Gas, cooking, 10 therms	month	11.70	2/94	65c
Gas, cooking, 30 therms	month	24.09	2/94	65c
Gas, cooking, 50 therms	month	36.49	2/94	65c
Gas, heating, winter, 100 therms	month	67.48	2/94	65c
Gas, heating, winter, average use	month	53.84	2/94	65c
Gas, natural, expenditures	year	212	91	81r
Gas, reg unlead, taxes inc., cash, self-service	gal	1.18	12/94	2c
Gasoline and motor oil purchased	year	1115	91	81r
Gasoline, unleaded midgrade	gallon	1.36	4/93	82r
Gasoline, unleaded premium	gallon	1.43	4/93	82r
Gasoline, unleaded regular	gallon	1.23	4/93	82r
Entertainment				
Admission fee, museum	visit	5.00	92	52c
Admission fee, seating, symphony performance		35.00	92	52c
Bowling, evening rate	game	2.00	12/94	2c
Concert ticket, Pearl Jam group	perf	20.00	94	50r
Entertainment, total expenditures	year	1853	91	81r
Fees and admissions, expenditures	year	482	91	81r
Monopoly game, Parker Brothers', No. 9	game	10.85	12/94	2c
Movie	adm	5.67	12/94	2c
Movie ticket, adult	ticket	5.00	1/92	44c

Values are in dollars or fractions of dollars. In the column headed *Ref*, references are shown to sources. Each reference is followed by a letter. These refer to the geographical level for which data were reported: s = State, r = Region, and c = City or metro. The abbreviation *ex* is used to mean *except* or *excluding*; *exp* stands for expenditures. For other abbreviations and further explanations, please see the Introduction.

Phoenix, AZ - continued

Item	Per	Value	Date	Ref.
Entertainment				
Pets, toys, playground equipment, expenditures	year	299	91	81r
Reading, expenditures	year	164	91	81r
Televisions, radios, and sound equipment, expenditures	year	528	91	81r
Tennis balls, yellow, Wilson or Penn, 3	can	2.57	12/94	2c
Ticket, basketball game		9.00-70.00	92	52c
Funerals				
Burial, immediate, container provided by funeral home		1360.49	1/95	54r
Cards, acknowledgment		11.24	1/95	54r
Casket, minimum alternative		232.73	1/95	54r
Cosmetology, hair care, etc.		114.13	1/95	54r
Cremation, direct, container provided by funeral home		1027.08	1/95	54r
Embalming		286.24	1/95	54r
Funeral, funeral home		315.60	1/95	54r
Funeral, other facility		303.08	1/95	54r
Graveside service		423.83	1/95	54r
Hearse, local		133.12	1/95	54r
Limousine, local		99.10	1/95	54r
Memorial service		442.57	1/95	54r
Service charge, professional, nondeclinable		840.16	1/95	54r
Visitation and viewing		168.50	1/95	54r
Groceries				
Groceries, ACCRA Index		105.00	12/94	2c
Apples, Red Delicious	lb.	0.72	12/94	82r
Baby food, strained vegetables, lowest price	4-4.5 oz.	0.30	12/94	2c
Bacon, sliced	lb.	1.73	12/94	82r
Bananas	lb.	0.45	12/94	2c
Bananas	lb.	0.52	12/94	82r
Beef or hamburger, ground	lb.	1.50	12/94	2c
Beef purchases	year	241	91	81r
Beverage purchases, alcoholic	year	328	91	81r
Beverage purchases, nonalcoholic	year	234	91	81r
Bologna, all beef or mixed	lb.	2.33	12/94	82r
Bread, white	24-oz.	0.82	12/94	2c
Bread, white, pan	lb.	0.81	12/94	82r
Carrots, short trimmed and topped	lb.	0.43	12/94	82r
Cereals and bakery products purchases	year	392	91	81r
Cereals and cereals products purchases	year	139	91	81r
Cheese, Kraft grated Parmesan	8-oz.	3.62	12/94	2c
Chicken breast, bone-in	lb.	2.04	12/94	82r
Chicken, fresh, whole	lb.	0.95	12/94	82r
Chicken, whole fryer	lb.	0.90	12/94	2c
Cigarettes, Winston, Kings	carton	14.99	12/94	2c
Coffee, 100%, ground roast, all sizes	lb.	4.48	12/94	82r
Coffee, vacuum-packed	13 oz.	3.88	12/94	2c
Corn Flakes, Kellogg's or Post Toasties	18 oz.	2.85	12/94	2c
Corn, frozen, whole kernel, lowest price	10 oz.	0.67	12/94	2c
Dairy products (other) purchases	year	182	91	81r
Eggs, Grade A large	dozen	0.76	12/94	2c
Fish and seafood purchases	year	94	91	81r
Flour, white, all purpose	lb.	0.21	12/94	82r
Food purchases, food eaten at home	year	2749	91	81r
Foods purchased away from home, not prepared by consumer	year	1909	91	81r
Fruits and vegetables purchases	year	459	91	81r
Grapefruit	lb.	0.56	12/94	82r
Ground beef, 100% beef	lb.	1.31	12/94	82r
Ham, boneless, exc. canned	lb.	2.46	12/94	82r
Ice cream, prepackaged, bulk, regular	1/2 gal.	2.57	12/94	82r
Lemons	lb.	1.00	12/94	82r
Lettuce, iceberg	lb.	0.93	12/94	82r
Lettuce, iceberg	head	0.72	12/94	2c
Margarine, Blue Bonnet or Parkay cubes	lb.	0.77	12/94	2c
Meats, poultry, fish, and eggs purchases	year	700	91	81r
Milk and cream (fresh) purchases	year	155	91	81r

Phoenix, AZ - continued

Item	Per	Value	Date	Ref.
Groceries - continued				
Milk, 2%	gal.	2.35	1/92	44c
Milk, whole	1/2 gal.	1.51	12/94	2c
Orange juice, frozen concentrate 12-oz. can	16 oz.	1.52	12/94	82r
Orange juice, Minute Maid frozen	12-oz.	1.28	12/94	2c
Oranges, Navel	lb.	0.56	12/94	82r
Peaches, halves or slices, Hunt's, Del Monte, or Libby's	29-oz.	1.47	12/94	2c
Peas, sweet, Del Monte or Green Giant	15-17 oz.	0.62	12/94	2c
Pork chops, center cut, bone-in	lb.	3.30	12/94	82r
Pork purchases	year	122	91	81r
Potato chips	16-oz.	3.03	12/94	82r
Potatoes, frozen, French fried	lb.	0.77	12/94	82r
Potatoes, white	lb.	0.35	12/94	82r
Potatoes, white or red	10-lb. sack	1.39	12/94	2c
Rental rate, 2-bedroom apartment	month	495.00	1/92	44c
Rice, white, long grain, uncooked	lb.	0.54	12/94	82r
Round roast, USDA choice, boneless	lb.	2.92	12/94	82r
Sausage, Jimmy Dean, 100% pork	lb.	3.16	12/94	2c
Shortening, vegetable oil blends	lb.	0.80	12/94	82r
Shortening, vegetable, Crisco	3-lb.	2.95	12/94	2c
Soft drink, Coca Cola, ex deposit	2 lit	1.25	12/94	2c
Spaghetti and macaroni	lb.	1.02	12/94	82r
Steak, round, graded & ungraded, exc. USDA prime & choice	lb.	3.13	12/94	82r
Steak, sirloin, USDA choice, boneless	lb.	4.07	12/94	82r
Steak, t-bone	lb.	4.94	12/94	2c
Sugar and other sweets, eaten at home, expenditures	year	105	91	81r
Sugar, cane or beet	4 lbs.	1.36	12/94	2c
Sugar, white, all sizes	lb.	0.38	12/94	82r
Tobacco products and smoking supplies, total expenditures	year	221	91	81r
Tomatoes, field grown	lb.	1.45	12/94	82r
Tomatoes, Hunt's or Del Monte	14.5 oz.	0.76	12/94	2c
Tuna, chunk, light	lb.	2.18	12/94	82r
Tuna, chunk, light, oil-packed	6.125-6.5 oz.	0.79	12/94	2c
Goods and Services				
Miscellaneous goods and services, ACCRA Index		101.10	12/94	2c
Health Care				
Health care, ACCRA Index		109.50	12/94	2c
Antibiotic ointment, Polysporin	1.5 oz.	4.07	12/94	2c
Childbirth, Cesarean delivery, hospital charge	birth	6059.00	12/91	69r
Childbirth, Cesarean delivery, physician charge	birth	2248.00	12/91	69r
Childbirth, normal delivery, hospital charge	birth	3006.00	12/91	69r
Childbirth, normal delivery, physician charge	birth	1634.00	12/91	69r
Dentist's fee, adult teeth cleaning and periodic oral exam	visit	56.25	12/94	2c
Doctor's fee, routine exam, established patient	visit	44.75	12/94	2c
Drugs, expenditures	year	230	91	81r
Health care, total expenditures	year	1544	91	81r
Health insurance expenditures	year	558	91	81r
Hospital care, semiprivate room	day	449.84	12/94	2c
Insurance premium, family medical care	month	364.71	1/95	41s
Medical services expenditures	year	676	91	81r
Medical supplies expenditures	year	80	91	81r
Surgery, open-heart	proc	37818.00	1/93	14r
Household Goods				
Appl. repair, service call, wash mach	min. lab. chg.	30.39	12/94	2c
Floor coverings, expenditures	year	79	91	81r
Furniture, expenditures	year	352	91	81r

Values are in dollars or fractions of dollars. In the column headed *Ref*, references are shown to sources. Each reference is followed by a letter. These refer to the geographical level for which data were reported: s=State, r=Region, and c=City or metro. The abbreviation *ex* is used to mean *except* or *excluding*; *exp* stands for expenditures. For other abbreviations and further explanations, please see the Introduction.

Phoenix, AZ - continued

Item	Per	Value	Date	Ref.
Household Goods				
Household equipment, misc. expenditures	year	614	91	81r
Household expenditures, miscellaneous	year	294	91	81r
Household furnishings and equipment, expenditures	year	1416	91	81r
Household operations expenditures	year	580	91	81r
Household textiles, expenditures	year	113	91	81r
Housekeeping supplies, expenditures	year	447	91	81r
Laundry and cleaning supplies, expenditures	year	114	91	81r
Laundry detergent, Tide Ultra, Bold, or Cheer	42 oz.	3.69	12/94	2c
Postage and stationery, expenditures	year	145	91	81r
Tissues, facial, Kleenex brand	175	1.15	12/94	2c
Housing				
Housing, ACCRA Index		94.20	12/94	2c
Add garage/carport		6,422	3/95	74r
Add room(s)		26,583	3/95	74r
Apartment condominium or co-op, median	unit	105300	12/94	62r
Car rental	day	36.00	5/95	95c
Dwellings (owned), expenditures	year	3932	91	81r
Enclose porch/patio/breezeway		5,382	3/95	74r
Finish room in basement/attic		3,911	3/95	74r
Home, existing, single-family, median	unit	178600	12/94	62r
Home, existing, single-family, median	unit	92.00	12/94	62c
Home, purchase price	unit	117.50	3/93	26c
Hotel room	day	149.00	5/95	95c
House payment, principal and interest, 25% down payment	mo.	693	12/94	2c
House, 1800 sq ft, 8000 sq ft lot, new, urban, utilities	total	112885	12/94	2c
Maintenance, repairs, insurance, and other housing expenditures	year	591	91	81r
Mortgage interest and charges expenditures	year	2747	91	81r
Mtge. rate, incl. points and orig. fee, 30-year conv. fixed or ARM	mo.	9.20	12/94	2c
Princ. & int., mortgage, median-price exist. sing.-family home	mo.	845	12/94	62r
Property taxes expenditures	year	594	91	81r
Redesign, restructure more than half of home's interior		5,467	3/95	74r
Rent, apartment, 2 br., 1 1/2-2 baths, unfurnished, 950 sq ft, water	mo.	578	12/94	2c
Rental units expenditures	year	2077	91	81r
Insurance and Pensions				
Auto insurance, private passenger	year	782.68	12/94	71s
Insurance and pensions, personal, expenditures	year	3042	91	81r
Insurance, life and other personal, expenditures	year	298	91	81r
Pensions and Social Security, expenditures	year	2744	91	81r
Legal Assistance				
Legal work, law firm associate	hour	91		10r
Legal work, law firm partner	hour	151		10r
Personal Goods				
Shampoo, Alberto VO5	15-oz.	1.23	12/94	2c
Toothpaste, Crest or Colgate	6-7 oz.	2.17	12/94	2c
Personal Services				
Dry cleaning	serv	5.25	92	52c
Dry cleaning, man's 2-pc. suit		7.88	12/94	2c
Dry cleaning, woman's dress	dress	5.00	1/92	44c
Haircut, man's barbershop, no styling		8.37	12/94	2c
Haircut, woman's shampoo, trim, blow-dry		20.81	12/94	2c
Manicure		15.00	92	52c
Personal services expenditures	year	286	91	81r
Restaurant Food				
Big Mac, small fries, medium drink	meal	2.57	1/92	44c
Chicken, fried, thigh and drumstick		1.89	12/94	2c
Dining expenditures, family	week	32.25	94	73r
Hamburger with cheese	1/4 lb.	2.04	12/94	2c

Phoenix, AZ - continued

Item	Per	Value	Date	Ref.
Restaurant Food - continued				
Pizza, Pizza Hut or Pizza Inn	12-13 in.	7.23	12/94	2c
Taxes				
Tax rate, residential property, month	$100	1.53	1/92	79c
Tax, cigarettes	year	368.00	10/93	43s
Taxes, Federal income, expenditures	year	2946	91	81r
Taxes, personal, expenditures	year	3791	91	81r
Taxes, State and local income, expenditures	year	791	91	81r
Transportation				
Transportation, ACCRA Index		110.60	12/94	2c
Bus fare, one-way	trip	1.00	12/95	1c
Bus fare, up to 10 miles	one-way	1.00	12/94	2c
Cars and trucks purchased, new	year	1231	91	81r
Cars and trucks purchased, used	year	915	91	81r
Driver's learning permit fee	perm	7.00	1/94	84s
Driver's license fee	orig	7.00	1/94	84s
Driver's license fee, duplicate	lic	4.00	1/94	84s
Driver's license reinstatement fee, min.	susp	10.00	1/94	85s
Driver's license renewal fee	renew	7.00	1/94	84s
Identification card, nondriver	card	5.00	1/94	83s
Motorcycle learning permit fee	perm	7.00	1/94	84s
Motorcycle license fee	orig	7.00	1/94	84s
Motorcycle license fee, duplicate	lic	4.00	1/94	84s
Motorcycle license renewal fee	renew	7.00	1/94	84s
parking, long-term lot, airport	3 days	30.00	1/92	44c
Public transportation expenditures	year	375	91	81r
Tire balance, computer or spin bal., front	wheel	8.12	12/94	2c
Transportation expenditures, total	year	5527	91	81r
Vehicle finance charges	year	287	91	81r
Vehicle insurance expenditures	year	624	91	81r
Vehicle maintenance and repairs expenditures	year	695	91	81r
Vehicle purchases	year	2174	91	81r
Vehicle rental, leases, licenses, etc. expenditures	year	257	91	81r
Vehicles purchased, other than cars and trucks	year	28	91	81r
Utilities				
Utilities, ACCRA Index		102.30	12/94	2c
Electricity expenditures	year	616	91	81r
Electricity, 1800 sq. ft., new home	mo.	116.76	12/94	2c
Electricity, summer, 250 KWh	month	27.46	8/93	64c
Electricity, summer, 500 KWh	month	50.30	8/93	64c
Electricity, summer, 750 KWh	month	77.49	8/93	64c
Electricity, summer, 1000 KWh	month	105.25	8/93	64c
Utilities, fuels, and public services, total expenditures	year	1681	91	81r
Water and other public services, expenditures	year	209	91	81r
Weddings				
Bridal attendants' gowns	event	750	10/93	76r
Bridal gown	event	852	10/93	76r
Bridal headpiece and veil	event	167	10/93	76r
Bride's wedding band	event	708	10/93	76r
Clergy	event	224	10/93	76r
Engagement ring	event	2756	10/93	76r
Flowers	event	863	10/93	76r
Formal wear for groom	event	106	10/93	76r
Groom's attendants' formal wear	event	530	10/93	76r
Groom's wedding band	event	402	10/93	76r
Music	event	600	10/93	76r
Photography	event	1088	10/93	76r
Shoes for bride	event	50	10/93	76r
Videography	event	483	10/93	76r
Wedding invitations and announcements	event	342	10/93	76r
Wedding reception	event	7000	10/93	76r

Values are in dollars or fractions of dollars. In the column headed *Ref*, references are shown to sources. Each reference is followed by a letter. These refer to the geographical level for which data were reported: s = State, r = Region, and c = City or metro. The abbreviation *ex* is used to mean *except* or *excluding*; *exp* stands for expenditures. For other abbreviations and further explanations, please see the Introduction.

Pikeville, KY

Item	Per	Value	Date	Ref.
Composite, ACCRA index		99.80	12/94	2c
Alcoholic Beverages				
Beer, Miller Lite, Bud, 12-oz., ex deposit	6	4.05	12/94	2c
J & B Scotch	750-ml.	19.56	12/94	2c
Wine, Gallo Chablis blanc	1.5-lit	6.13	12/94	2c
Clothing				
Jeans, man's denim		30.32	12/94	2c
Shirt, man's dress shirt		26.49	12/94	2c
Undervest, boy's size 10-14, cotton	3	3.21	12/94	2c
Communications				
Newspaper subscription, dly. and Sun. delivery	month	18.20	12/94	2c
Telephone bill, family of four	month	20.43	12/94	2c
Telephone, residential, flat rate	mo.	12.02	12/93	8c
Energy and Fuels				
Energy, combined forms, 1800 sq. ft.	mo.	95.32	12/94	2c
Gas, reg unlead, taxes inc., cash, self-service	gal	1.25	12/94	2c
Entertainment				
Bowling, evening rate	game	2.00	12/94	2c
Monopoly game, Parker Brothers', No. 9	game	10.91	12/94	2c
Movie	adm	5.00	12/94	2c
Tennis balls, yellow, Wilson or Penn, 3	can	1.97	12/94	2c
Groceries				
Groceries, ACCRA Index		96.50	12/94	2c
Baby food, strained vegetables, lowest price	4-4.5 oz.	0.28	12/94	2c
Bananas	lb.	0.42	12/94	2c
Beef or hamburger, ground	lb.	1.41	12/94	2c
Bread, white	24-oz.	0.81	12/94	2c
Cheese, Kraft grated Parmesan	8-oz.	3.23	12/94	2c
Chicken, whole fryer	lb.	0.94	12/94	2c
Cigarettes, Winston, Kings	carton	12.68	12/94	2c
Coffee, vacuum-packed	13 oz.	3.41	12/94	2c
Corn Flakes, Kellogg's or Post Toasties	18 oz.	2.38	12/94	2c
Corn, frozen, whole kernel, lowest price	10 oz.	0.77	12/94	2c
Eggs, Grade A large	dozen	0.80	12/94	2c
Lettuce, iceberg	head	0.99	12/94	2c
Margarine, Blue Bonnet or Parkay cubes	lb.	0.49	12/94	2c
Milk, whole	1/2 gal.	1.53	12/94	2c
Orange juice, Minute Maid frozen	12-oz.	1.16	12/94	2c
Peaches, halves or slices, Hunt's, Del Monte, or Libby's	29-oz.	1.30	12/94	2c
Peas, sweet, Del Monte or Green Giant	15-17 oz.	0.54	12/94	2c
Potatoes, white or red	10-lb. sack	2.41	12/94	2c
Sausage, Jimmy Dean, 100% pork	lb.	2.49	12/94	2c
Shortening, vegetable, Crisco	3-lb.	2.34	12/94	2c
Soft drink, Coca Cola, ex deposit	2 lit	1.07	12/94	2c
Steak, t-bone	lb.	4.59	12/94	2c
Sugar, cane or beet	4 lbs.	1.36	12/94	2c
Tomatoes, Hunt's or Del Monte	14.5 oz.	0.68	12/94	2c
Tuna, chunk, light, oil-packed	6.125-6.5 oz.	0.66	12/94	2c
Goods and Services				
Miscellaneous goods and services, ACCRA Index		96.20	12/94	2c
Health Care				
Health care, ACCRA Index		102.10	12/94	2c
Antibiotic ointment, Polysporin	1.5 oz.	3.85	12/94	2c
Dentist's fee, adult teeth cleaning and periodic oral exam	visit	51.17	12/94	2c
Doctor's fee, routine exam, established patient	visit	45.00	12/94	2c
Hospital care, semiprivate room	day	378.00	12/94	2c

Pikeville, KY - continued

Item	Per	Value	Date	Ref.
Household Goods				
Appl. repair, service call, wash mach	min. lab. chg.	40.00	12/94	2c
Laundry detergent, Tide Ultra, Bold, or Cheer	42 oz.	3.18	12/94	2c
Tissues, facial, Kleenex brand	175	1.00	12/94	2c
Housing				
Housing, ACCRA Index		109.30	12/94	2c
House payment, principal and interest, 25% down payment	mo.	873	12/94	2c
House, 1800 sq ft, 8000 sq ft lot, new, urban, utilities	total	138485	12/94	2c
Mtge. rate, incl. points and orig. fee, 30-year conv. fixed or ARM	mo.	9.50	12/94	2c
Rent, apartment, 2 br., 1 1/2-2 baths, unfurnished, 950 sq ft, water	mo.	475	12/94	2c
Personal Goods				
Shampoo, Alberto VO5	15-oz.	1.12	12/94	2c
Toothpaste, Crest or Colgate	6-7 oz.	2.08	12/94	2c
Personal Services				
Dry cleaning, man's 2-pc. suit		5.29	12/94	2c
Haircut, man's barbershop, no styling		7.99	12/94	2c
Haircut, woman's shampoo, trim, blow-dry		14.49	12/94	2c
Restaurant Food				
Chicken, fried, thigh and drumstick		2.00	12/94	2c
Hamburger with cheese	1/4 lb.	1.75	12/94	2c
Pizza, Pizza Hut or Pizza Inn	12-13 in.	7.99	12/94	2c
Transportation				
Transportation, ACCRA Index		99.10	12/94	2c
Tire balance, computer or spin bal., front	wheel	5.59	12/94	2c
Utilities				
Utilities, ACCRA Index		87.60	12/94	2c
Electricity, 1800 sq. ft., new home	mo.	95.32	12/94	2c

Pine Bluff, AR

Item	Per	Value	Date	Ref.
Appliances				
Appliances (major), expenditures	year	153	91	81r
Average annual exp.				
Food, health care, personal goods, services	year	27020	91	81r
Charity				
Cash contributions, expenditures	year	839	91	81r
Clothing				
Apparel, men and boys, total expenditures	year	380	91	81r
Apparel, women and girls, total expenditures	year	660	91	81r
Footwear, expenditures	year	193	91	81r
Communications				
Long-distance telephone rate, day, addl. min., 1-10 mi.	min.	0.08	12/93	9s
Long-distance telephone rate, day, initial min., 1-10 mi.	min.	0.10	12/93	9s
Phone line, single, business, field visit	inst	84.00	12/93	9s
Phone line, single, business, no field visit	inst	84.00	12/93	9s
Phone line, single, residence, field visit	inst	39.70	12/93	9s
Phone line, single, residence, no field visit	inst	39.70	12/93	9s
Telephone service, expenditures	year	616	91	81r
Credit Cards				
Fee, conventional credit card, bal. carried	year	35.00	1/95	96c
Education				
Board, 4-year private college/university	year	1801	8/94	80s
Board, 4-year public college/university	year	1774	8/94	80s
Education, total expenditures	year	319	91	81r
Room, 4-year private college/university	year	1349	8/94	80s

Values are in dollars or fractions of dollars. In the column headed *Ref*, references are shown to sources. Each reference is followed by a letter. These refer to the geographical level for which data were reported: s=State, r=Region, and c=City or metro. The abbreviation *ex* is used to mean *except* or *excluding*; *exp* stands for expenditures. For other abbreviations and further explanations, please see the Introduction.

Pine Bluff, AR - continued

Item	Per	Value	Date	Ref.
Education				
Room, 4-year public college/university	year	1752	8/94	80s
Total cost, 4-year private college/university	year	8866	8/94	80s
Total cost, 4-year public college/university	year	5334	8/94	80s
Tuition, 2-year public college/university, in-state	year	833	8/94	80s
Tuition, 4-year private college/university, in-state	year	5716	8/94	80s
Tuition, 4-year public college/university, in-state	year	1808	8/94	80s
Energy and Fuels				
Fuel oil and other fuels, expenditures	year	56	91	81r
Gas, natural, expenditures	year	150	91	81r
Gasoline and motor oil purchased	year	1152	91	81r
Gasoline, unleaded midgrade	gallon	1.21	4/93	82r
Gasoline, unleaded premium	gallon	1.30	4/93	82r
Gasoline, unleaded regular	gallon	1.10	4/93	82r
Entertainment				
Concert ticket, Pearl Jam group	perf	20.00	94	50r
Entertainment, total expenditures	year	1266	91	81r
Fees and admissions, expenditures	year	306	91	81r
Pets, toys, playground equipment, expenditures	year	271	91	81r
Reading, expenditures	year	131	91	81r
Televisions, radios, and sound equipment, expenditures	year	439	91	81r
Funerals				
Burial, immediate, container provided by funeral home		1574.60	1/95	54r
Cards, acknowledgment		22.24	1/95	54r
Casket, minimum alternative		239.41	1/95	54r
Cosmetology, hair care, etc.		91.04	1/95	54r
Cremation, direct, container provided by funeral home		1085.15	1/95	54r
Embalming		281.30	1/95	54r
Funeral, funeral home		323.04	1/95	54r
Funeral, other facility		327.58	1/95	54r
Graveside service		355.19	1/95	54r
Hearse, local		141.89	1/95	54r
Limousine, local		99.40	1/95	54r
Memorial service		284.67	1/95	54r
Service charge, professional, nondeclinable		904.06	1/95	54r
Visitation and viewing		187.04	1/95	54r
Groceries				
Apples, Red Delicious	lb.	0.73	12/94	82r
Bacon, sliced	lb.	1.67	12/94	82r
Bananas	lb.	0.42	12/94	82r
Beef purchases	year	213	91	81r
Beverage purchases, alcoholic	year	249	91	81r
Beverage purchases, nonalcoholic	year	207	91	81r
Bologna, all beef or mixed	lb.	2.27	12/94	82r
Bread, white, pan	lb.	0.68	12/94	82r
Cabbage	lb.	0.42	12/94	82r
Carrots, short trimmed and topped	lb.	0.53	12/94	82r
Cereals and bakery products purchases	year	345	91	81r
Cereals and cereals products purchases	year	127	91	81r
Cheddar cheese, natural	lb.	3.58	12/94	82r
Chicken breast, bone-in	lb.	1.71	12/94	82r
Chicken, fresh, whole	lb.	0.78	12/94	82r
Chuck roast, USDA choice, boneless	lb.	2.26	12/94	82r
Crackers, soda, salted	lb.	1.27	12/94	82r
Cucumbers	lb.	0.65	12/94	82r
Dairy products (other) purchases	year	141	91	81r
Eggs, Grade A large	dozen	0.87	12/94	82r
Fish and seafood purchases	year	72	91	81r
Flour, white, all purpose	lb.	0.23	12/94	82r
Food purchases, food eaten at home	year	2381	91	81r
Foods purchased away from home, not prepared by consumer	year	1696	91	81r
Frankfurters, all meat or all beef	lb.	1.74	12/94	82r
Fruits and vegetables purchases	year	380	91	81r

Pine Bluff, AR - continued

Item	Per	Value	Date	Ref.
Groceries - continued				
Grapefruit	lb.	0.45	12/94	82r
Grapes, Thompson seedless	lb.	2.30	12/94	82r
Ground beef, 100% beef	lb.	1.37	12/94	82r
Ground chuck, 100% beef	lb.	1.97	12/94	82r
Ham, boneless, exc. canned	lb.	2.54	12/94	82r
Ice cream, prepackaged, bulk, regular	1/2 gal.	2.47	12/94	82r
Lemons	lb.	1.02	12/94	82r
Lettuce, iceberg	lb.	0.96	12/94	82r
Margarine, stick	lb.	0.77	12/94	82r
Meats, poultry, fish, and eggs purchases	year	655	91	81r
Milk and cream (fresh) purchases	year	130	91	81r
Orange juice, frozen concentrate 12-oz. can	16 oz.	1.36	12/94	82r
Oranges, Navel	lb.	0.54	12/94	82r
Pears, Anjou	lb.	0.81	12/94	82r
Pork chops, center cut, bone-in	lb.	3.07	12/94	82r
Pork purchases	year	142	91	81r
Potato chips	16-oz.	3.15	12/94	82r
Potatoes, frozen, French fried	lb.	0.82	12/94	82r
Potatoes, white	lb.	0.34	12/94	82r
Rice, white, long grain, uncooked	lb.	0.48	12/94	82r
Round roast, USDA choice, boneless	lb.	2.91	12/94	82r
Sausage, fresh	lb.	1.82	12/94	82r
Shortening, vegetable oil blends	lb.	0.75	12/94	82r
Spaghetti and macaroni	lb.	0.87	12/94	82r
Steak, rib eye, USDA choice, boneless	lb.	6.85	12/94	82r
Steak, round, graded & ungraded, exc. USDA prime & choice	lb.	2.96	12/94	82r
Steak, round, USDA choice, boneless	lb.	3.17	12/94	82r
Steak, sirloin, USDA choice, boneless	lb.	4.12	12/94	82r
Steak, T-bone, USDA choice, bone-in	lb.	5.63	12/94	82r
Sugar and other sweets, eaten at home, expenditures	year	93	91	81r
Sugar, white, all sizes	lb.	0.39	12/94	82r
Tobacco products and smoking supplies, total expenditures	year	286	91	81r
Tomatoes, field grown	lb.	1.36	12/94	82r
Tuna, chunk, light	lb.	1.94	12/94	82r
Turkey, frozen, whole	lb.	0.96	12/94	82r
Yogurt, natural, fruit flavored	8 oz.	0.58	12/94	82r
Health Care				
Adenosine, emergency room	treat	100.00	95	23r
Bladder tap, superpubic, infant, emergency room	treat	119.00	95	23r
Blood analysis, emergency room	treat	25.00	95	23r
Blood tests, abdominal pain, emergency room	treat	25.00	95	23r
Burn dressing, emergency room	treat	266.00	95	23r
Cardiology interpretation, emergency room	treat	26.00	95	23r
Chest X-ray, emergency room	treat	78.00	95	23r
Childbirth, Cesarean delivery, hospital charge	birth	5462.00	12/91	69r
Childbirth, Cesarean delivery, physician charge	birth	2228.00	12/91	69r
Childbirth, normal delivery, hospital charge	birth	2943.00	12/91	69r
Childbirth, normal delivery, physician charge	birth	1619.00	12/91	69r
Defibrillation pads, emergency room	treat	6.00	95	23r
Drugs, expenditures	year	297	91	81r
Gastric tube insertion, nasal, emergency room	treat	25.00	95	23r
Health care, total expenditures	year	1600	91	81r
Health insurance expenditures	year	637	91	81r
Heart monitor, emergency room	treat	40.00	95	23r
Insurance premium, family medical care	month	326.03	1/95	41s
Intravenous fluids, emergency room	treat	130.00	95	23r
Intravenous fluids, emergency room	liter	26.00	95	23r
Intravenous line, central, emergency room	treat	342.00	95	23r
Liver function tests, abdominal pain, emergency room	treat	26.00	95	23r
Medical care charges, total, emergency room, third-degree burns	treat	2101.00	95	23r

Values are in dollars or fractions of dollars. In the column headed *Ref*, references are shown to sources. Each reference is followed by a letter. These refer to the geographical level for which data were reported: s = State, r = Region, and c = City or metro. The abbreviation *ex* is used to mean *except* or *excluding*; *exp* stands for expenditures. For other abbreviations and further explanations, please see the Introduction.

Pine Bluff, AR - continued

Item	Per	Value	Date	Ref.
Health Care				
Medical care charges, total, emergency, infant with fever	treat	628.00	95	23r
Medical services expenditures	year	573	91	81r
Medical supplies expenditures	year	93	91	81r
Morphine, emergency room	treat	34.00	95	23r
Nursing care and facilities charges, emergency room	treat	252.00	95	23r
Nursing care and facilities charges, emergency, infant with fever	treat	252.00	95	23r
Nursing care and facilities charges, emergency, third-degree burns	treat	861.00	95	23r
Physician's charges, emergency, infant with fever	treat	212.00	95	23r
Physician's charges, emergency, third-degree burns	treat	372.00	95	23r
Physician's fee, emergency room	treat	372.00	95	23r
Physician's fee, general practitioner	visit	51.20	12/93	60r
Surgery, open-heart	proc	42374.00	1/93	14r
Ultrasound, abdominal, emergency room	treat	276.00	95	23r
Urinalysis, emergency room	treat	20.00	95	23r
Urinalysis, infant, emergency room	treat	20.00	95	23r
X-rays, emergency room	treat	78.00	95	23r
Household Goods				
Floor coverings, expenditures	year	48	91	81r
Furniture, expenditures	year	280	91	81r
Household equipment, misc. expenditures	year	342	91	81r
Household expenditures, miscellaneous	year	256	91	81r
Household furnishings and equipment, expenditures	year	988	91	81r
Household operations expenditures	year	468	91	81r
Household textiles, expenditures	year	95	91	81r
Housekeeping supplies, expenditures	year	380	91	81r
Laundry and cleaning supplies, expenditures	year	109	91	81r
Postage and stationery, expenditures	year	105	91	81r
Housing				
Add garage/carport		6,980	3/95	74r
Add room(s)		11,403	3/95	74r
Apartment condominium or co-op, median	unit	68600	12/94	62r
Dwellings (owned), expenditures	year	2428	91	81r
Enclose porch/patio/breezeway		4,572	3/95	74r
Finish room in basement/attic		3,794	3/95	74r
Home, existing, single-family, median	unit	120200	12/94	62r
Maintenance, repairs, insurance, and other housing expenditures	year	531	91	81r
Mortgage interest and charges expenditures	year	1506	91	81r
Princ. & int., mortgage, median-price exist. sing.-family home	mo.	540	12/94	62r
Property taxes expenditures	year	391	91	81r
Redesign, restructure more than half of home's interior		17,641	3/95	74r
Rental units expenditures	year	1264	91	81r
Insurance and Pensions				
Auto insurance, private passenger	year	565.35	12/94	71s
Insurance and pensions, personal, expenditures	year	2395	91	81r
Insurance, life and other personal, expenditures	year	368	91	81r
Pensions and Social Security, expenditures	year	2027	91	81r
Personal Services				
Personal services expenditures	year	212	91	81r
Restaurant Food				
Dining expenditures, family	week	33.83	94	73r
Taxes				
Taxes, Federal income, expenditures	year	2275	91	81r
Taxes, personal, expenditures	year	2715	91	81r
Taxes, State and local income, expenditures	year	365	91	81r

Pine Bluff, AR - continued

Item	Per	Value	Date	Ref.
Transportation				
Cars and trucks purchased, new	year	1306	91	81r
Cars and trucks purchased, used	year	942	91	81r
Driver's license fee	orig	14.00	1/94	84s
Driver's license fee, duplicate	lic	5.00	1/94	84s
Driver's license renewal fee	renew	14.00	1/94	84s
Identification card, nondriver	card	5.00	1/94	83s
Motorcycle license fee	orig	4.00	1/94	84s
Motorcycle license fee, duplicate	lic	5.00	1/94	84s
Public transportation expenditures	year	249	91	81r
Transportation expenditures, total	year	5307	91	81r
Vehicle finance charges	year	346	91	81r
Vehicle insurance expenditures	year	544	91	81r
Vehicle maintenance and repairs expenditures	year	600	91	81r
Vehicle purchases	year	2275	91	81r
Vehicle rental, leases, licenses, etc. expenditures	year	141	91	81r
Vehicles purchased, other than cars and trucks	year	27	91	81r
Utilities				
Electricity expenditures	year	950	91	81r
Utilities, fuels, and public services, total expenditures	year	2000	91	81r
Water and other public services, expenditures	year	227	91	81r
Weddings				
Bridal attendants' gowns	event	750	10/93	76r
Bridal gown	event	852	10/93	76r
Bridal headpiece and veil	event	167	10/93	76r
Bride's wedding band	event	708	10/93	76r
Clergy	event	224	10/93	76r
Engagement ring	event	2756	10/93	76r
Flowers	event	863	10/93	76r
Formal wear for groom	event	106	10/93	76r
Groom's attendants' formal wear	event	530	10/93	76r
Groom's wedding band	event	402	10/93	76r
Music	event	600	10/93	76r
Photography	event	1088	10/93	76r
Shoes for bride	event	50	10/93	76r
Videography	event	483	10/93	76r
Wedding invitations and announcements	event	342	10/93	76r
Wedding reception	event	7000	10/93	76r

Pittsburgh, PA

Item	Per	Value	Date	Ref.
Appliances				
Appliances (major), expenditures	year	141	91	81c
Appliances (major), expenditures	year	145	91	81r
Average annual exp.				
Food, health care, personal goods, services	year	28626	91	81c
Food, health care, personal goods, services	year	29496	91	81r
Charity				
Cash contributions, expenditures	year	545	91	81c
Cash contributions, expenditures	year	708	91	81r
Clothing				
Apparel, men and boys, total expenditures	year	362	91	81c
Apparel, men and boys, total expenditures	year	416	91	81r
Apparel, women and girls, total expenditures	year	929	91	81c
Apparel, women and girls, total expenditures	year	744	91	81r
Footwear, expenditures	year	275	91	81c
Footwear, expenditures	year	305	91	81r
Communications				
Long-distance telephone rate, day, addl. min., 1-10 mi.	min.	0.08	12/93	9s
Long-distance telephone rate, day, initial min., 1-10 mi.	min.	0.15	12/93	9s
Phone line, single, business, field visit	inst	75.00	12/93	9s
Phone line, single, business, no field visit	inst	75.00	12/93	9s

Values are in dollars or fractions of dollars. In the column headed *Ref*, references are shown to sources. Each reference is followed by a letter. These refer to the geographical level for which data were reported: s=State, r=Region, and c=City or metro. The abbreviation *ex* is used to mean *except* or *excluding*; *exp* stands for expenditures. For other abbreviations and further explanations, please see the Introduction.

Pittsburgh, PA - continued

Item	Per	Value	Date	Ref.
Communications				
Phone line, single, residence, field visit	inst	40.00	12/93	9s
Phone line, single, residence, no field visit	inst	40.00	12/93	9s
Telephone service, expenditures	year	500	91	81c
Telephone service, expenditures	year	589	91	81r
Telephone, business, addl. line, touch tone	month	1.90	10/91	25c
Telephone, business, connection charges, touch tone	inst	79.50	10/91	25c
Telephone, business, key system line, touch tone	month	26.18	10/91	25c
Telephone, business, PBX line, touch tone	month	26.12	10/91	25c
Telephone, business, single ln., touch tone	month	26.98	10/91	25c
Telephone, business, touch tone, inside wiring maintenance plan	month	0.95	10/91	25c
Education				
Board, 4-year private college/university	year	2714	8/94	80s
Board, 4-year public college/university	year	1899	8/94	80s
Education, total expenditures	year	752	91	81c
Education, total expenditures	year	593	91	81r
Room, 4-year private college/university	year	2720	8/94	80s
Room, 4-year public college/university	year	2063	8/94	80s
Total cost, 4-year private college/university	year	18118	8/94	80s
Total cost, 4-year public college/university	year	8278	8/94	80s
Tuition, 2-year public college/university, in-state	year	1671	8/94	80s
Tuition, 4-year private college/university, in-state	year	12684	8/94	80s
Tuition, 4-year public college/university, in-state	year	4316	8/94	80s
Energy and Fuels				
Electricity	500 KWh	51.22	12/94	82c
Fuel oil and other fuels, expenditures	year	39	91	81c
Fuel oil and other fuels, expenditures	year	257	91	81r
Gas, cooking, winter, 10 therms	month	15.25	2/94	65c
Gas, cooking, winter, 30 therms	month	27.42	2/94	65c
Gas, cooking, winter, 50 therms	month	39.59	2/94	65c
Gas, heating, winter, average use	month	124.88	2/94	65c
Gas, natural, expenditures	year	599	91	81c
Gas, natural, expenditures	year	285	91	81r
Gas, piped	40 therms	39.51	12/94	82c
Gas, piped	100 therms	72.60	12/94	82c
Gas, piped	therm	0.76	12/94	82c
Gasoline and motor oil purchased	year	819	91	81c
Gasoline and motor oil purchased	year	867	91	81r
Gasoline, unleaded midgrade	gallon	1.28	4/93	82c
Gasoline, unleaded midgrade	gallon	1.32	4/93	82r
Gasoline, unleaded premium	gallon	1.38	4/93	82c
Gasoline, unleaded premium	gallon	1.40	4/93	82r
Gasoline, unleaded regular	gallon	1.16	4/93	82c
Gasoline, unleaded regular	gallon	1.19	4/93	82r
Entertainment				
Entertainment supplies, equipment, and services, misc. expenditures	year	213	91	81c
Entertainment, total expenditures	year	1482	91	81c
Entertainment, total expenditures	year	1331	91	81r
Fees and admissions, expenditures	year	517	91	81c
Fees and admissions, expenditures	year	398	91	81r
Pets, toys, playground equipment, expenditures	year	333	91	81c
Pets, toys, playground equipment, expenditures	year	270	91	81r
Reading, expenditures	year	164	91	81c
Reading, expenditures	year	171	91	81r
Televisions, radios, and sound equipment, expenditures	year	419	91	81c
Televisions, radios, and sound equipment, expenditures	year	429	91	81r

Pittsburgh, PA - continued

Item	Per	Value	Date	Ref.
Funerals				
Burial, immediate, container provided by funeral home		1370.36	1/95	54r
Cards, acknowledgment		17.72	1/95	54r
Casket, minimum alternative		192.52	1/95	54r
Cosmetology, hair care, etc.		139.56	1/95	54r
Cremation, direct, container provided by funeral home		1049.24	1/95	54r
Embalming		387.57	1/95	54r
Funeral, funeral home		278.77	1/95	54r
Funeral, other facility		275.85	1/95	54r
Graveside service		213.08	1/95	54r
Hearse, local		157.27	1/95	54r
Limousine, local		146.45	1/95	54r
Memorial service		271.02	1/95	54r
Service charge, professional, nondeclinable		943.58	1/95	54r
Visitation and viewing		322.86	1/95	54r
Groceries				
Apples, Red Delicious	lb.	0.78	12/94	82r
Bacon, sliced	lb.	2.24	12/94	82r
Bananas	lb.	0.49	12/94	82r
Beef purchases	year	214	91	81c
Beef purchases	year	226	91	81r
Beverage purchases, alcoholic	year	220	91	81c
Beverage purchases, alcoholic	year	332	91	81r
Beverage purchases, nonalcoholic	year	236	91	81c
Beverage purchases, nonalcoholic	year	213	91	81r
Bread, white, pan	lb.	0.80	12/94	82r
Butter, salted, Grade AA, stick	lb.	1.67	12/94	82r
Carrots, short trimmed and topped	lb.	0.51	12/94	82r
Cereals and bakery products purchases	year	422	91	81c
Cereals and bakery products purchases	year	407	91	81r
Cereals and cereal products purchases	year	139	91	81c
Cereals and cereals products purchases	year	132	91	81r
Chicken breast, bone-in	lb.	2.22	12/94	82r
Chicken, fresh, whole	lb.	1.05	12/94	82r
Chuck roast, USDA choice, boneless	lb.	2.74	12/94	82r
Coffee, 100%, ground roast, all sizes	lb.	4.61	12/94	82r
Dairy products (other) purchases	year	179	91	81c
Dairy products (other) purchases	year	161	91	81r
Eggs, Grade A large	dozen	1.12	12/94	82r
Fish and seafood purchases	year	87	91	81c
Fish and seafood purchases	year	112	91	81r
Food purchases, food eaten at home	year	2783	91	81c
Food purchases, food eaten at home	year	2599	91	81r
Foods purchased away from home, not prepared by consumer	year	1674	91	81c
Foods purchased away from home, not prepared by consumer	year	2024	91	81r
Fruits and vegetables purchases	year	432	91	81c
Fruits and vegetables purchases	year	444	91	81r
Grapefruit	lb.	0.44	12/94	82r
Grapes, Thompson seedless	lb.	2.24	12/94	82r
Ground chuck, 100% beef	lb.	1.67	12/94	82r
Ice cream, prepackaged, bulk, regular	1/2 gal.	2.93	12/94	82r
Lemons	lb.	1.06	12/94	82r
Lettuce, iceberg	lb.	0.92	12/94	82r
Meats, poultry, fish, and eggs purchases	year	740	91	81c
Meats, poultry, fish, and eggs purchases	year	751	91	81r
Milk and cream (fresh) purchases	year	143	91	81c
Milk and cream (fresh) purchases	year	152	91	81r
Orange juice, frozen concentrate 12-oz. can	16 oz.	1.92	12/94	82r
Oranges, Navel	lb.	0.56	12/94	82r
Pork chops, center cut, bone-in	lb.	3.09	12/94	82r
Pork purchases	year	166	91	81c
Pork purchases	year	130	91	81r
Potatoes, white	lb.	0.37	12/94	82r
Rib roast, USDA choice, bone-in	lb.	4.98	12/94	82r
Round roast, USDA choice, boneless	lb.	2.93	12/94	82r
Shortening, vegetable oil blends	lb.	1.03	12/94	82r
Spaghetti and macaroni	lb.	0.84	12/94	82r
Steak, round, USDA choice, boneless	lb.	3.48	12/94	82r

Values are in dollars or fractions of dollars. In the column headed *Ref*, references are shown to sources. Each reference is followed by a letter. These refer to the geographical level for which data were reported: s = State, r = Region, and c = City or metro. The abbreviation *ex* is used to mean *except* or *excluding*; *exp* stands for expenditures. For other abbreviations and further explanations, please see the Introduction.

Pittsburgh, PA - continued

Item	Per	Value	Date	Ref.
Groceries				
Steak, sirloin, USDA choice, bone-in	lb.	3.38	12/94	82r
Steak, sirloin, USDA choice, boneless	lb.	4.81	12/94	82r
Sugar and other sweets, eaten at home, expenditures	year	89	91	81r
Sugar and other sweets, eaten at home, purchases	year	108	91	81c
Sugar, white, all sizes	lb.	0.46	12/94	82r
Tobacco products and smoking supplies, total expenditures	year	229	91	81c
Tobacco products and smoking supplies, total expenditures	year	279	91	81r
Tomatoes, field grown	lb.	1.56	12/94	82r
Tuna, chunk, light	lb.	2.09	12/94	82r
Health Care				
Childbirth, Cesarean delivery, hospital charge	birth	6334.00	12/91	69r
Childbirth, Cesarean delivery, physician charge	birth	2234.00	12/91	69r
Childbirth, normal delivery, hospital charge	birth	3225.00	12/91	69r
Childbirth, normal delivery, physician charge	birth	1623.00	12/91	69r
Drugs, expenditures	year	265	91	81c
Drugs, expenditures	year	205	91	81r
Health care, total expenditures	year	1290	91	81c
Health care, total expenditures	year	1396	91	81r
Health insurance expenditures	year	552	91	81c
Health insurance expenditures	year	553	91	81r
Insurance premium, family medical care	month	349.05	1/95	41s
Medical services expenditures	year	389	91	81c
Medical services expenditures	year	559	91	81r
Medical supplies expenditures	year	84	91	81c
Medical supplies expenditures	year	80	91	81r
Household Goods				
Floor coverings, expenditures	year	886	91	81c
Floor coverings, expenditures	year	158	91	81r
Furniture, expenditures	year	353	91	81c
Furniture, expenditures	year	341	91	81r
Household equipment, misc. expenditures	year	363	91	81r
Household equipment, misc., expenditures	year	312	91	81c
Household expenditures, miscellaneous	year	309	91	81c
Household expenditures, miscellaneous	year	194	91	81r
Household furnishings and equipment, expenditures	year	1842	91	81c
Household furnishings and equipment, expenditures	year	1158	91	81r
Household operations expenditures	year	487	91	81c
Household operations expenditures	year	378	91	81r
Household textiles, expenditures	year	87	91	81c
Household textiles, expenditures	year	88	91	81r
Housekeeping supplies, expenditures	year	391	91	81c
Housekeeping supplies, expenditures	year	426	91	81r
Laundry and cleaning supplies, expenditures	year	110	91	81c
Laundry and cleaning supplies, expenditures	year	122	91	81r
Postage and stationery, expenditures	year	135	91	81c
Postage and stationery, expenditures	year	134	91	81r
Housing				
Add garage/carport		11,614	3/95	74r
Add room(s)		16,816	3/95	74r
Apartment condominium or co-op, median	unit	96700	12/94	62r
Car rental	day	46.00	5/95	95c
Dwellings (owned), expenditures	year	2775	91	81c
Dwellings (owned), expenditures	year	3305	91	81r
Enclose porch/patio/breezeway		2,980	3/95	74r
Finish room in basement/attic		4,330	3/95	74r
Home, existing, single-family, median	unit	161600	12/94	62r
Home, purchase price	unit	115.80	3/93	26c
Hotel room	day	117.00	5/95	95c
Maintenance, repairs, insurance, and other housing expenditures	year	648	91	81c

Pittsburgh, PA - continued

Item	Per	Value	Date	Ref.
Housing - continued				
Maintenance, repairs, insurance, and other housing expenditures	year	569	91	81r
Mortgage interest and charges expenditures	year	1267	91	81c
Mortgage interest and charges expenditures	year	1852	91	81r
Princ. & int., mortgage, median-price exist. sing.-family home	mo.	765	12/94	62r
Property taxes expenditures	year	860	91	81c
Property taxes expenditures	year	884	91	81r
Redesign, restructure more than half of home's interior		2,750	3/95	74r
Rental units expenditures	year	1032	900/00/ 91	81c
Rental units expenditures	year	1832	91	81r
Insurance and Pensions				
Auto insurance, private passenger	year	721.50	12/94	71s
Insurance and pensions, personal, expenditures	year	2563	91	81c
Insurance and pensions, personal, expenditures	year	2690	91	81r
Insurance, life and other personal, expenditures	year	396	91	81c
Insurance, life and other personal, expenditures	year	341	91	81r
Pensions and Social Security, expenditures	year	2167	91	81c
Pensions and Social Security, expenditures	year	2349	91	81r
Legal Assistance				
Estate planning, law-firm partner	hr.	375.00	10/93	12r
Legal work, law firm associate	hour	78		10r
Legal work, law firm partner	hour	183		10r
Personal Goods				
Personal care products and services, total expenditures	year	355	91	81c
Personal Services				
Personal services expenditures	year	178	91	81c
Personal services expenditures	year	184	91	81r
Restaurant Food				
Dining expenditures, family	week	34.26	94	73r
Taxes				
Taxes, Federal income, expenditures	year	5811	91	81c
Taxes, Federal income, expenditures	year	2409	91	81r
Taxes, personal, expenditures	year	6755	91	81c
Taxes, personal, expenditures	year	3094	91	81r
Taxes, State and local income, expenditures	year	924	91	81c
Taxes, State and local income, expenditures	year	620	91	81r
Transportation				
Bus fare, one-way	trip	1.23	12/95	1c
Cars and trucks purchased, new	year	1168	91	81c
Cars and trucks purchased, new	year	1170	91	81r
Cars and trucks purchased, used	year	757	91	81c
Cars and trucks purchased, used	year	739	91	81r
Commuter rail (inclined plane) fare, one-way	trip	1.00	12/95	1c
Driver's learning permit fee	perm	27.00	1/94	84s
Driver's license fee	orig	0.00	1/94	84s
Driver's license fee, duplicate	lic	7.00	1/94	84s
Driver's license reinstatement fee, min.	susp	25.00	1/94	85s
Driver's license renewal fee	renew	0.00	1/94	84s
Identification card, nondriver	card	5.00	1/94	83s
Motorcycle learning permit fee	perm	27.00	1/94	84s
Motorcycle license fee	orig	0.00	1/94	84s
Motorcycle license fee, duplicate	lic	7.00	1/94	84s
Motorcycle license renewal fee	renew	0.00	1/94	84s
Public transportation expenditures	year	282	91	81c
Public transportation expenditures	year	430	91	81r
Railway fare, light rail, one-way	trip	1.25	12/95	1c
Transportation expenditures, total	year	4699	91	81c
Transportation expenditures, total	year	4810	91	81r
Vehicle expenses, miscellaneous	year	1656	91	81c
Vehicle finance charges	year	241	91	81c

Values are in dollars or fractions of dollars. In the column headed *Ref*, references are shown to sources. Each reference is followed by a letter. These refer to the geographical level for which data were reported: s = State, r = Region, and c = City or metro. The abbreviation *ex* is used to mean *except* or *excluding*; *exp* stands for expenditures. For other abbreviations and further explanations, please see the Introduction.

Pittsburgh, PA - continued

Item	Per	Value	Date	Ref.
Transportation				
Vehicle finance charges	year	238	91	81r
Vehicle insurance expenditures	year	572	91	81c
Vehicle insurance expenditures	year	630	91	81r
Vehicle maintenance and repairs expenditures	year	545	91	81c
Vehicle maintenance and repairs expenditures	year	532	91	81r
Vehicle purchases	year	1941	91	81c
Vehicle purchases	year	1920	91	81r
Vehicle rental, leases, licenses, etc. expenditures	year	299	91	81c
Vehicle rental, leases, licenses, etc. expenditures	year	193	91	81r
Vehicles purchased, other than cars and trucks	year	17	91	81c
Vehicles purchased, other than cars and trucks	year	11	91	81r
Utilities				
Electricity	KWh	0.09	12/94	82c
Electricity expenditures	year	727	91	81c
Electricity expenditures	year	695	91	81r
Electricity, summer, 250 KWh	month	38.29	8/93	64c
Electricity, summer, 500 KWh	month	69.65	8/93	64c
Electricity, summer, 750 KWh	month	101.03	8/93	64c
Electricity, summer, 1000 KWh	month	132.39	8/93	64c
Utilities, fuels, and public services, total expenditures	year	2130	91	81c
Utilities, fuels, and public services, total expenditures	year	1981	91	81r
Water and other public services, expenditures	year	265	91	81c
Water and other public services, expenditures	year	154	91	81r
Weddings				
Bridal attendants' gowns	event	750	10/93	76r
Bridal gown	event	852	10/93	76r
Bridal headpiece and veil	event	167	10/93	76r
Bride's wedding band	event	708	10/93	76r
Clergy	event	224	10/93	76r
Engagement ring	event	2756	10/93	76r
Flowers	event	863	10/93	76r
Formal wear for groom	event	106	10/93	76r
Groom's attendants' formal wear	event	530	10/93	76r
Groom's wedding band	event	402	10/93	76r
Music	event	600	10/93	76r
Photography	event	1088	10/93	76r
Shoes for bride	event	50	10/93	76r
Videography	event	483	10/93	76r
Wedding invitations and announcements	event	342	10/93	76r
Wedding reception	event	7000	10/93	76r

Pittsfield, MA

Item	Per	Value	Date	Ref.
Appliances				
Appliances (major), expenditures	year	145	91	81r
Average annual exp.				
Food, health care, personal goods, services	year	29496	91	81r
Charity				
Cash contributions, expenditures	year	708	91	81r
Clothing				
Apparel, men and boys, total expenditures	year	416	91	81r
Apparel, women and girls, total expenditures	year	744	91	81r
Footwear, expenditures	year	305	91	81r
Communications				
Long-distance telephone rate, day, addl. min., 1-10 mi.	min.	0.09	12/93	9s
Long-distance telephone rate, day, initial min., 1-10 mi.	min.	0.19	12/93	9s

Pittsfield, MA - continued

Item	Per	Value	Date	Ref.
Communications - continued				
Phone line, single, business, field visit	inst	27.50	12/93	9s
Phone line, single, business, no field visit	inst	93.02	12/93	9s
Phone line, single, residence, field visit	inst	27.50	12/93	9s
Phone line, single, residence, no field visit	inst	37.07	12/93	9s
Telephone service, expenditures	year	589	91	81r
Education				
Board, 4-year private college/university	year	3179	8/94	80s
Board, 4-year public college/university	year	2035	8/94	80s
Education, total expenditures	year	593	91	81r
Room, 4-year private college/university	year	3369	8/94	80s
Room, 4-year public college/university	year	2290	8/94	80s
Total cost, 4-year private college/university	year	21346	8/94	80s
Total cost, 4-year public college/university	year	8467	8/94	80s
Tuition, 2-year public college/university, in-state	year	2361	8/94	80s
Tuition, 4-year private college/university, in-state	year	14797	8/94	80s
Tuition, 4-year public college/university, in-state	year	4142	8/94	80s
Energy and Fuels				
Fuel oil and other fuels, expenditures	year	257	91	81r
Gas, natural, expenditures	year	285	91	81r
Gasoline and motor oil purchased	year	867	91	81r
Gasoline, unleaded midgrade	gallon	1.32	4/93	82r
Gasoline, unleaded premium	gallon	1.40	4/93	82r
Gasoline, unleaded regular	gallon	1.19	4/93	82r
Entertainment				
Entertainment, total expenditures	year	1331	91	81r
Fees and admissions, expenditures	year	398	91	81r
Pets, toys, playground equipment, expenditures	year	270	91	81r
Reading, expenditures	year	171	91	81r
Televisions, radios, and sound equipment, expenditures	year	429	91	81r
Funerals				
Burial, immediate, container provided by funeral home		1507.89	1/95	54r
Cards, acknowledgment		18.10	1/95	54r
Casket, minimum alternative		133.03	1/95	54r
Cosmetology, hair care, etc.		114.12	1/95	54r
Cremation, direct, container provided by funeral home		1309.19	1/95	54r
Embalming		320.97	1/95	54r
Funeral, funeral home		327.61	1/95	54r
Funeral, other facility		314.81	1/95	54r
Graveside service		286.11	1/95	54r
Hearse, local		158.95	1/95	54r
Limousine, local		149.45	1/95	54r
Memorial service		315.94	1/95	54r
Service charge, professional, nondeclinable		1148.43	1/95	54r
Visitation and viewing		249.66	1/95	54r
Groceries				
Apples, Red Delicious	lb.	0.78	12/94	82r
Bacon, sliced	lb.	2.24	12/94	82r
Bananas	lb.	0.49	12/94	82r
Beef purchases	year	226	91	81r
Beverage purchases, alcoholic	year	332	91	81r
Beverage purchases, nonalcoholic	year	213	91	81r
Bread, white, pan	lb.	0.80	12/94	82r
Butter, salted, Grade AA, stick	lb.	1.67	12/94	82r
Carrots, short trimmed and topped	lb.	0.51	12/94	82r
Cereals and bakery products purchases	year	407	91	81r
Cereals and cereals products purchases	year	132	91	81r
Chicken breast, bone-in	lb.	2.22	12/94	82r
Chicken, fresh, whole	lb.	1.05	12/94	82r
Chuck roast, USDA choice, boneless	lb.	2.74	12/94	82r
Coffee, 100%, ground roast, all sizes	lb.	4.61	12/94	82r
Dairy products (other) purchases	year	161	91	81r
Eggs, Grade A large	dozen	1.12	12/94	82r

Values are in dollars or fractions of dollars. In the column headed *Ref*, references are shown to sources. Each reference is followed by a letter. These refer to the geographical level for which data were reported: s=State, r=Region, and c=City or metro. The abbreviation *ex* is used to mean *except* or *excluding*; *exp* stands for expenditures. For other abbreviations and further explanations, please see the Introduction.

Pittsfield, MA - continued

Item	Per	Value	Date	Ref.
Groceries				
Fish and seafood purchases	year	112	91	81r
Food purchases, food eaten at home	year	2599	91	81r
Foods purchased away from home, not prepared by consumer	year	2024	91	81r
Fruits and vegetables purchases	year	444	91	81r
Grapefruit	lb.	0.44	12/94	82r
Grapes, Thompson seedless	lb.	2.24	12/94	82r
Ground chuck, 100% beef	lb.	1.67	12/94	82r
Ice cream, prepackaged, bulk, regular	1/2 gal.	2.93	12/94	82r
Lemons	lb.	1.06	12/94	82r
Lettuce, iceberg	lb.	0.92	12/94	82r
Meats, poultry, fish, and eggs purchases	year	751	91	81r
Milk and cream (fresh) purchases	year	152	91	81r
Orange juice, frozen concentrate 12-oz. can	16 oz.	1.92	12/94	82r
Oranges, Navel	lb.	0.56	12/94	82r
Pork chops, center cut, bone-in	lb.	3.09	12/94	82r
Pork purchases	year	130	91	81r
Potatoes, white	lb.	0.37	12/94	82r
Rib roast, USDA choice, bone-in	lb.	4.98	12/94	82r
Round roast, USDA choice, boneless	lb.	2.93	12/94	82r
Shortening, vegetable oil blends	lb.	1.03	12/94	82r
Spaghetti and macaroni	lb.	0.84	12/94	82r
Steak, round, USDA choice, boneless	lb.	3.48	12/94	82r
Steak, sirloin, USDA choice, bone-in	lb.	3.38	12/94	82r
Steak, sirloin, USDA choice, boneless	lb.	4.81	12/94	82r
Sugar and other sweets, eaten at home, expenditures	year	89	91	81r
Sugar, white, all sizes	lb.	0.46	12/94	82r
Tobacco products and smoking supplies, total expenditures	year	279	91	81r
Tomatoes, field grown	lb.	1.56	12/94	82r
Tuna, chunk, light	lb.	2.09	12/94	82r
Health Care				
Childbirth, Cesarean delivery, hospital charge	birth	6334.00	12/91	69r
Childbirth, Cesarean delivery, physician charge	birth	2234.00	12/91	69r
Childbirth, normal delivery, hospital charge	birth	3225.00	12/91	69r
Childbirth, normal delivery, physician charge	birth	1623.00	12/91	69r
Drugs, expenditures	year	205	91	81r
Health care, total expenditures	year	1396	91	81r
Health insurance expenditures	year	553	91	81r
Insurance premium, family medical care	month	457.38	1/95	41s
Medical services expenditures	year	559	91	81r
Medical supplies expenditures	year	80	91	81r
Household Goods				
Floor coverings, expenditures	year	158	91	81r
Furniture, expenditures	year	341	91	81r
Household equipment, misc. expenditures	year	363	91	81r
Household expenditures, miscellaneous	year	194	91	81r
Household furnishings and equipment, expenditures	year	1158	91	81r
Household operations expenditures	year	378	91	81r
Household textiles, expenditures	year	88	91	81r
Housekeeping supplies, expenditures	year	426	91	81r
Laundry and cleaning supplies, expenditures	year	122	91	81r
Postage and stationery, expenditures	year	134	91	81r
Housing				
Add garage/carport		11,614	3/95	74r
Add room(s)		16,816	3/95	74r
Apartment condominium or co-op, median	unit	96700	12/94	62r
Dwellings (owned), expenditures	year	3305	91	81r
Enclose porch/patio/breezeway		2,980	3/95	74r
Finish room in basement/attic		4,330	3/95	74r
Home, existing, single-family, median	unit	161600	12/94	62r
Maintenance, repairs, insurance, and other housing expenditures	year	569	91	81r
Mortgage interest and charges expenditures	year	1852	91	81r

Item	Per	Value	Date	Ref.
Housing - continued				
Princ. & int., mortgage, median-price exist. sing.-family home	mo.	765	12/94	62r
Property taxes expenditures	year	884	91	81r
Redesign, restructure more than half of home's interior		2,750	3/95	74r
Rental units expenditures	year	1832	91	81r
Insurance and Pensions				
Auto insurance, private passenger	year	1009.56	12/94	71s
Insurance and pensions, personal, expenditures	year	2690	91	81r
Insurance, life and other personal, expenditures	year	341	91	81r
Pensions and Social Security, expenditures	year	2349	91	81r
Legal Assistance				
Estate planning, law-firm partner	hr.	375.00	10/93	12r
Legal work, law firm associate	hour	78		10r
Legal work, law firm partner	hour	183		10r
Personal Services				
Personal services expenditures	year	184	91	81r
Restaurant Food				
Dining expenditures, family	week	34.26	94	73r
Taxes				
Taxes, Federal income, expenditures	year	2409	91	81r
Taxes, personal, expenditures	year	3094	91	81r
Taxes, State and local income, expenditures	year	620	91	81r
Transportation				
Cars and trucks purchased, new	year	1170	91	81r
Cars and trucks purchased, used	year	739	91	81r
Driver's learning permit fee	perm	15.00	1/94	84s
Driver's license fee	orig	50.00	1/94	84s
Driver's license fee, duplicate	lic	15.00	1/94	84s
Driver's license renewal fee	renew	43.75	1/94	84s
Identification card, nondriver	card	15.00	1/94	83s
Motorcycle license fee	orig	50.00	1/94	84s
Motorcycle license fee, duplicate	lic	15.00	1/94	84s
Motorcycle license renewal fee	renew	43.75	1/94	84s
Public transportation expenditures	year	430	91	81r
Transportation expenditures, total	year	4810	91	81r
Vehicle finance charges	year	238	91	81r
Vehicle insurance expenditures	year	630	91	81r
Vehicle maintenance and repairs expenditures	year	532	91	81r
Vehicle purchases	year	1920	91	81r
Vehicle rental, leases, licenses, etc. expenditures	year	193	91	81r
Vehicles purchased, other than cars and trucks	year	11	91	81r
Utilities				
Electricity expenditures	year	695	91	81r
Utilities, fuels, and public services, total expenditures	year	1981	91	81r
Water and other public services, expenditures	year	154	91	81r
Weddings				
Bridal attendants' gowns	event	750	10/93	76r
Bridal gown	event	852	10/93	76r
Bridal headpiece and veil	event	167	10/93	76r
Bride's wedding band	event	708	10/93	76r
Clergy	event	224	10/93	76r
Engagement ring	event	2756	10/93	76r
Flowers	event	863	10/93	76r
Formal wear for groom	event	106	10/93	76r
Groom's attendants' formal wear	event	530	10/93	76r
Groom's wedding band	event	402	10/93	76r
Music	event	600	10/93	76r
Photography	event	1088	10/93	76r
Shoes for bride	event	50	10/93	76r
Videography	event	483	10/93	76r

Values are in dollars or fractions of dollars. In the column headed *Ref*, references are shown to sources. Each reference is followed by a letter. These refer to the geographical level for which data were reported: s=State, r=Region, and c=City or metro. The abbreviation *ex* is used to mean *except* or *excluding*; *exp* stands for *expenditures*. For other abbreviations and further explanations, please see the Introduction.

Pittsfield, MA - continued

Item	Per	Value	Date	Ref.
Weddings				
Wedding invitations and announcements	event	342	10/93	76r
Wedding reception	event	7000	10/93	76r

Pocatello, ID

Item	Per	Value	Date	Ref.
Composite, ACCRA index		102.90	12/94	2c
Alcoholic Beverages				
Beer, Miller Lite, Bud, 12-oz., ex deposit	6	3.96	12/94	2c
J & B Scotch	750-ml.	18.85	12/94	2c
Wine, Gallo Chablis blanc	1.5-lit	4.97	12/94	2c
Clothing				
Jeans, man's denim		31.94	12/94	2c
Shirt, man's dress shirt		24.29	12/94	2c
Undervest, boy's size 10-14, cotton	3	5.61	12/94	2c
Communications				
Newspaper subscription, dly. and Sun. delivery	month	11.17	12/94	2c
Telephone bill, family of four	month	17.00	12/94	2c
Telephone, residential, flat rate	mo.	12.03	12/93	8c
Energy and Fuels				
Energy, combined forms, 1800 sq. ft.	mo.	96.45	12/94	2c
Gas, reg unlead, taxes inc., cash, self-service	gal	1.21	12/94	2c
Entertainment				
Bowling, evening rate	game	1.83	12/94	2c
Monopoly game, Parker Brothers', No. 9	game	11.69	12/94	2c
Movie	adm	5.00	12/94	2c
Tennis balls, yellow, Wilson or Penn, 3	can	3.24	12/94	2c
Groceries				
Groceries, ACCRA Index		101.90	12/94	2c
Baby food, strained vegetables, lowest price	4-4.5 oz.	0.33	12/94	2c
Bananas	lb.	0.57	12/94	2c
Beef or hamburger, ground	lb.	1.29	12/94	2c
Bread, white	24-oz.	0.78	12/94	2c
Cheese, Kraft grated Parmesan	8-oz.	3.76	12/94	2c
Chicken, whole fryer	lb.	0.85	12/94	2c
Cigarettes, Winston, Kings	carton	17.09	12/94	2c
Coffee, vacuum-packed	13 oz.	3.68	12/94	2c
Corn Flakes, Kellogg's or Post Toasties	18 oz.	2.22	12/94	2c
Corn, frozen, whole kernel, lowest price	10 oz.	0.70	12/94	2c
Eggs, Grade A large	dozen	0.69	12/94	2c
Lettuce, iceberg	head	0.70	12/94	2c
Margarine, Blue Bonnet or Parkay cubes	lb.	0.59	12/94	2c
Milk, whole	1/2 gal.	1.45	12/94	2c
Orange juice, Minute Maid frozen	12-oz.	1.31	12/94	2c
Peaches, halves or slices, Hunt's, Del Monte, or Libby's	29-oz.	1.37	12/94	2c
Peas, sweet, Del Monte or Green Giant	15-17 oz.	0.51	12/94	2c
Potatoes, white or red	10-lb. sack	1.89	12/94	2c
Sausage, Jimmy Dean, 100% pork	lb.	3.17	12/94	2c
Shortening, vegetable, Crisco	3-lb.	2.60	12/94	2c
Soft drink, Coca Cola, ex deposit	2 lit	1.11	12/94	2c
Steak, t-bone	lb.	4.82	12/94	2c
Sugar, cane or beet	4 lbs.	1.37	12/94	2c
Tomatoes, Hunt's or Del Monte	14.5 oz.	0.76	12/94	2c
Tuna, chunk, light, oil-packed	6.125-6.5 oz.	0.77	12/94	2c
Goods and Services				
Miscellaneous goods and services, ACCRA Index		105.00	12/94	2c

Pocatello, ID - continued

Item	Per	Value	Date	Ref.
Health Care				
Health care, ACCRA Index		96.40	12/94	2c
Antibiotic ointment, Polysporin	1.5 oz.	4.34	12/94	2c
Dentist's fee, adult teeth cleaning and periodic oral exam	visit	53.80	12/94	2c
Doctor's fee, routine exam, established patient	visit	34.20	12/94	2c
Hospital care, semiprivate room	day	385.00	12/94	2c
Household Goods				
Appl. repair, service call, wash mach	min. lab. chg.	37.68	12/94	2c
Laundry detergent, Tide Ultra, Bold, or Cheer	42 oz.	3.06	12/94	2c
Tissues, facial, Kleenex brand	175	0.97	12/94	2c
Housing				
Housing, ACCRA Index		108.80	12/94	2c
House payment, principal and interest, 25% down payment	mo.	835	12/94	2c
House, 1800 sq ft, 8000 sq ft lot, new, urban, utilities	total	132050	12/94	2c
Mtge. rate, incl. points and orig. fee, 30-year conv. fixed or ARM	mo.	9.53	12/94	2c
Personal Goods				
Shampoo, Alberto VO5	15-oz.	1.35	12/94	2c
Toothpaste, Crest or Colgate	6-7 oz.	2.18	12/94	2c
Personal Services				
Dry cleaning, man's 2-pc. suit		5.97	12/94	2c
Haircut, man's barbershop, no styling		9.00	12/94	2c
Haircut, woman's shampoo, trim, blow-dry		18.10	12/94	2c
Restaurant Food				
Chicken, fried, thigh and drumstick		2.20	12/94	2c
Hamburger with cheese	1/4 lb.	1.99	12/94	2c
Pizza, Pizza Hut or Pizza Inn	12-13 in.	10.00	12/94	2c
Transportation				
Transportation, ACCRA Index		98.00	12/94	2c
Tire balance, computer or spin bal., front	wheel	5.75	12/94	2c
Utilities				
Utilities, ACCRA Index		86.10	12/94	2c
Electricity, 1800 sq. ft., new home	mo.	96.45	12/94	2c

Poplar Bluff, MO

Item	Per	Value	Date	Ref.
Composite, ACCRA index		89.00	12/94	2c
Alcoholic Beverages				
Beer, Miller Lite, Bud, 12-oz., ex deposit	6	3.76	12/94	2c
J & B Scotch	750-ml.	15.27	12/94	2c
Wine, Gallo Chablis blanc	1.5-lit	5.17	12/94	2c
Clothing				
Jeans, man's denim		29.31	12/94	2c
Shirt, man's dress shirt		29.32	12/94	2c
Undervest, boy's size 10-14, cotton	3	3.28	12/94	2c
Communications				
Newspaper subscription, dly. and Sun. delivery	month	13.70	12/94	2c
Telephone bill, family of four	month	16.78	12/94	2c
Telephone, residential, flat rate	mo.	9.10	12/93	8c
Energy and Fuels				
Energy, combined forms, 1800 sq. ft.	mo.	99.26	12/94	2c
Gas, reg unlead, taxes inc., cash, self-service	gal	1.10	12/94	2c
Entertainment				
Bowling, evening rate	game	1.90	12/94	2c
Monopoly game, Parker Brothers', No. 9	game	10.57	12/94	2c

Values are in dollars or fractions of dollars. In the column headed *Ref*, references are shown to sources. Each reference is followed by a letter. These refer to the geographical level for which data were reported: s = State, r = Region, and c = City or metro. The abbreviation *ex* is used to mean *except* or *excluding*; *exp* stands for *expenditures*. For other abbreviations and further explanations, please see the Introduction.

Poplar Bluff, MO - continued

Item	Per	Value	Date	Ref.
Entertainment				
Movie	adm	1.75	12/94	2c
Tennis balls, yellow, Wilson or Penn, 3	can	2.04	12/94	2c
Groceries				
Groceries, ACCRA Index		101.80	12/94	2c
Baby food, strained vegetables, lowest price	4-4.5 oz.	0.42	12/94	2c
Bananas	lb.	0.42	12/94	2c
Beef or hamburger, ground	lb.	1.32	12/94	2c
Bread, white	24-oz.	0.64	12/94	2c
Cheese, Kraft grated Parmesan	8-oz.	3.45	12/94	2c
Chicken, whole fryer	lb.	0.82	12/94	2c
Cigarettes, Winston, Kings	carton	14.19	12/94	2c
Coffee, vacuum-packed	13 oz.	3.71	12/94	2c
Corn Flakes, Kellogg's or Post Toasties	18 oz.	3.00	12/94	2c
Corn, frozen, whole kernel, lowest price	10 oz.	0.88	12/94	2c
Eggs, Grade A large	dozen	0.71	12/94	2c
Lettuce, iceberg	head	0.76	12/94	2c
Margarine, Blue Bonnet or Parkay cubes	lb.	0.59	12/94	2c
Milk, whole	1/2 gal.	1.52	12/94	2c
Orange juice, Minute Maid frozen	12-oz.	1.58	12/94	2c
Peaches, halves or slices, Hunt's, Del Monte, or Libby's	29-oz.	1.52	12/94	2c
Peas, sweet, Del Monte or Green Giant	15-17 oz.	0.72	12/94	2c
Potatoes, white or red	10-lb. sack	2.29	12/94	2c
Sausage, Jimmy Dean, 100% pork	lb.	2.21	12/94	2c
Shortening, vegetable, Crisco	3-lb.	2.60	12/94	2c
Soft drink, Coca Cola, ex deposit	2 lit	1.02	12/94	2c
Steak, t-bone	lb.	5.29	12/94	2c
Sugar, cane or beet	4 lbs.	1.51	12/94	2c
Tomatoes, Hunt's or Del Monte	14.5 oz.	0.85	12/94	2c
Tuna, chunk, light, oil-packed	6.125-6.5 oz.	0.65	12/94	2c
Goods and Services				
Miscellaneous goods and services, ACCRA Index		93.60	12/94	2c
Health Care				
Health care, ACCRA Index		82.20	12/94	2c
Antibiotic ointment, Polysporin	1.5 oz.	4.34	12/94	2c
Dentist's fee, adult teeth cleaning and periodic oral exam	visit	41.33	12/94	2c
Doctor's fee, routine exam, established patient	visit	34.00	12/94	2c
Hospital care, semiprivate room	day	273.50	12/94	2c
Household Goods				
Appl. repair, service call, wash mach	min. lab. chg.	29.33	12/94	2c
Laundry detergent, Tide Ultra, Bold, or Cheer	42 oz.	3.06	12/94	2c
Tissues, facial, Kleenex brand	175	1.12	12/94	2c
Housing				
Housing, ACCRA Index		75.60	12/94	2c
House payment, principal and interest, 25% down payment	mo.	580	12/94	2c
House, 1800 sq ft, 8000 sq ft lot, new, urban, utilities	total	94000	12/94	2c
Mtge. rate, incl. points and orig. fee, 30-year conv. fixed or ARM	mo.	9.25	12/94	2c
Personal Goods				
Shampoo, Alberto VO5	15-oz.	0.95	12/94	2c
Toothpaste, Crest or Colgate	6-7 oz.	1.94	12/94	2c
Personal Services				
Dry cleaning, man's 2-pc. suit		5.92	12/94	2c
Haircut, man's barbershop, no styling		8.65	12/94	2c

Poplar Bluff, MO - continued

Item	Per	Value	Date	Ref.
Personal Services - continued				
Haircut, woman's shampoo, trim, blow-dry		16.48	12/94	2c
Restaurant Food				
Chicken, fried, thigh and drumstick		2.59	12/94	2c
Hamburger with cheese	1/4 lb.	1.99	12/94	2c
Pizza, Pizza Hut or Pizza Inn	12-13 in.	6.88	12/94	2c
Transportation				
Transportation, ACCRA Index		96.90	12/94	2c
Tire balance, computer or spin bal., front	wheel	6.50	12/94	2c
Utilities				
Utilities, ACCRA Index		88.10	12/94	2c
Electricity, 1800 sq. ft., new home	mo.	99.26	12/94	2c

Portland, ME

Item	Per	Value	Date	Ref.
Appliances				
Appliances (major), expenditures	year	145	91	81r
Average annual exp.				
Food, health care, personal goods, services	year	29496	91	81r
Charity				
Cash contributions, expenditures	year	708	91	81r
Clothing				
Apparel, men and boys, total expenditures	year	416	91	81r
Apparel, women and girls, total expenditures	year	744	91	81r
Footwear, expenditures	year	305	91	81r
Communications				
Long-distance telephone rate, day, addl. min., 1-10 mi.	min.	0.15	12/93	9s
Long-distance telephone rate, day, initial min., 1-10 mi.	min.	0.19	12/93	9s
Phone line, single, business, field visit	inst	35.00	12/93	9s
Phone line, single, business, no field visit	inst	56.00	12/93	9s
Phone line, single, residence, field visit	inst	26.00	12/93	9s
Phone line, single, residence, no field visit	inst	44.75	12/93	9s
Telephone service, expenditures	year	589	91	81r
Education				
Board, 4-year private college/university	year	2772	8/94	80s
Board, 4-year public college/university	year	2178	8/94	80s
Education, total expenditures	year	593	91	81r
Room, 4-year private college/university	year	2620	8/94	80s
Room, 4-year public college/university	year	2204	8/94	80s
Total cost, 4-year private college/university	year	19658	8/94	80s
Total cost, 4-year public college/university	year	7521	8/94	80s
Tuition, 2-year public college/university, in-state	year	1913	8/94	80s
Tuition, 4-year private college/university, in-state	year	14265	8/94	80s
Tuition, 4-year public college/university, in-state	year	3139	8/94	80s
Energy and Fuels				
Fuel oil and other fuels, expenditures	year	257	91	81r
Gas, natural, expenditures	year	285	91	81r
Gasoline and motor oil purchased	year	867	91	81r
Gasoline, unleaded midgrade	gallon	1.32	4/93	82r
Gasoline, unleaded premium	gallon	1.40	4/93	82r
Gasoline, unleaded regular	gallon	1.19	4/93	82r
Entertainment				
Entertainment, total expenditures	year	1331	91	81r
Fees and admissions, expenditures	year	398	91	81r
Pets, toys, playground equipment, expenditures	year	270	91	81r
Reading, expenditures	year	171	91	81r
Televisions, radios, and sound equipment, expenditures	year	429	91	81r

Values are in dollars or fractions of dollars. In the column headed *Ref*, references are shown to sources. Each reference is followed by a letter. These refer to the geographical level for which data were reported: s = State, r = Region, and c = City or metro. The abbreviation *ex* is used to mean *except* or *excluding*; *exp* stands for expenditures. For other abbreviations and further explanations, please see the Introduction.

Portland, ME - continued

Item	Per	Value	Date	Ref.
Funerals				
Burial, immediate, container provided by funeral home		1507.89	1/95	54r
Cards, acknowledgment		18.10	1/95	54r
Casket, minimum alternative		133.03	1/95	54r
Cosmetology, hair care, etc.		114.12	1/95	54r
Cremation, direct, container provided by funeral home		1309.19	1/95	54r
Embalming		320.97	1/95	54r
Funeral, funeral home		327.61	1/95	54r
Funeral, other facility		314.81	1/95	54r
Graveside service		286.11	1/95	54r
Hearse, local		158.95	1/95	54r
Limousine, local		149.45	1/95	54r
Memorial service		315.94	1/95	54r
Service charge, professional, nondeclinable		1148.43	1/95	54r
Visitation and viewing		249.66	1/95	54r
Groceries				
Apples, Red Delicious	lb.	0.78	12/94	82r
Bacon, sliced	lb.	2.24	12/94	82r
Bananas	lb.	0.49	12/94	82r
Beef purchases	year	226	91	81r
Beverage purchases, alcoholic	year	332	91	81r
Beverage purchases, nonalcoholic	year	213	91	81r
Bread, white, pan	lb.	0.80	12/94	82r
Butter, salted, Grade AA, stick	lb.	1.67	12/94	82r
Carrots, short trimmed and topped	lb.	0.51	12/94	82r
Cereals and bakery products purchases	year	407	91	81r
Cereals and cereals products purchases	year	132	91	81r
Chicken breast, bone-in	lb.	2.22	12/94	82r
Chicken, fresh, whole	lb.	1.05	12/94	82r
Chuck roast, USDA choice, boneless	lb.	2.74	12/94	82r
Coffee, 100%, ground roast, all sizes	lb.	4.61	12/94	82r
Dairy products (other) purchases	year	161	91	81r
Eggs, Grade A large	dozen	1.12	12/94	82r
Fish and seafood purchases	year	112	91	81r
Food purchases, food eaten at home	year	2599	91	81r
Foods purchased away from home, not prepared by consumer	year	2024	91	81r
Fruits and vegetables purchases	year	444	91	81r
Grapefruit	lb.	0.44	12/94	82r
Grapes, Thompson seedless	lb.	2.24	12/94	82r
Ground chuck, 100% beef	lb.	1.67	12/94	82r
Ice cream, prepackaged, bulk, regular	1/2 gal.	2.93	12/94	82r
Lemons	lb.	1.06	12/94	82r
Lettuce, iceberg	lb.	0.92	12/94	82r
Meats, poultry, fish, and eggs purchases	year	751	91	81r
Milk and cream (fresh) purchases	year	152	91	81r
Orange juice, frozen concentrate 12-oz. can	16 oz.	1.92	12/94	82r
Oranges, Navel	lb.	0.56	12/94	82r
Pork chops, center cut, bone-in	lb.	3.09	12/94	82r
Pork purchases	year	130	91	81r
Potatoes, white	lb.	0.37	12/94	82r
Rib roast, USDA choice, bone-in	lb.	4.98	12/94	82r
Round roast, USDA choice, boneless	lb.	2.93	12/94	82r
Shortening, vegetable oil blends	lb.	1.03	12/94	82r
Spaghetti and macaroni	lb.	0.84	12/94	82r
Steak, round, USDA choice, boneless	lb.	3.48	12/94	82r
Steak, sirloin, USDA choice, bone-in	lb.	3.38	12/94	82r
Steak, sirloin, USDA choice, boneless	lb.	4.81	12/94	82r
Sugar and other sweets, eaten at home, expenditures	year	89	91	81r
Sugar, white, all sizes	lb.	0.46	12/94	82r
Tobacco products and smoking supplies, total expenditures	year	279	91	81r
Tomatoes, field grown	lb.	1.56	12/94	82r
Tuna, chunk, light	lb.	2.09	12/94	82r
Health Care				
Childbirth, Cesarean delivery, hospital charge	birth	6334.00	12/91	69r

Portland, ME - continued

Item	Per	Value	Date	Ref.
Health Care - continued				
Childbirth, Cesarean delivery, physician charge	birth	2234.00	12/91	69r
Childbirth, normal delivery, hospital charge	birth	3225.00	12/91	69r
Childbirth, normal delivery, physician charge	birth	1623.00	12/91	69r
Drugs, expenditures	year	205	91	81r
Health care, total expenditures	year	1396	91	81r
Health insurance expenditures	year	553	91	81r
Insurance premium, family medical care	month	473.31	1/95	41s
Medical services expenditures	year	559	91	81r
Medical supplies expenditures	year	80	91	81r
Household Goods				
Floor coverings, expenditures	year	158	91	81r
Furniture, expenditures	year	341	91	81r
Household equipment, misc. expenditures	year	363	91	81r
Household expenditures, miscellaneous	year	194	91	81r
Household furnishings and equipment, expenditures	year	1158	91	81r
Household operations expenditures	year	378	91	81r
Household textiles, expenditures	year	88	91	81r
Housekeeping supplies, expenditures	year	426	91	81r
Laundry and cleaning supplies, expenditures	year	122	91	81r
Postage and stationery, expenditures	year	134	91	81r
Housing				
Add garage/carport		11,614	3/95	74r
Add room(s)		16,816	3/95	74r
Apartment condominium or co-op, median	unit	96700	12/94	62r
Dwellings (owned), expenditures	year	3305	91	81r
Enclose porch/patio/breezeway		2,980	3/95	74r
Finish room in basement/attic		4,330	3/95	74r
Home, existing, single-family, median	unit	161600	12/94	62r
Maintenance, repairs, insurance, and other housing expenditures	year	569	91	81r
Mortgage interest and charges expenditures	year	1852	91	81r
Princ. & int., mortgage, median-price exist. sing.-family home	mo.	765	12/94	62r
Property taxes expenditures	year	884	91	81r
Redesign, restructure more than half of home's interior		2,750	3/95	74r
Rental units expenditures	year	1832	91	81r
Insurance and Pensions				
Auto insurance, private passenger	year	556.67	12/94	71s
Insurance and pensions, personal, expenditures	year	2690	91	81r
Insurance, life and other personal, expenditures	year	341	91	81r
Pensions and Social Security, expenditures	year	2349	91	81r
Legal Assistance				
Estate planning, law-firm partner	hr.	375.00	10/93	12r
Legal work, law firm associate	hour	78		10r
Legal work, law firm partner	hour	183		10r
Personal Services				
Personal services expenditures	year	184	91	81r
Restaurant Food				
Dining expenditures, family	week	34.26	94	73r
Taxes				
Taxes, Federal income, expenditures	year	2409	91	81r
Taxes, personal, expenditures	year	3094	91	81r
Taxes, State and local income, expenditures	year	620	91	81r
Transportation				
Cars and trucks purchased, new	year	1170	91	81r
Cars and trucks purchased, used	year	739	91	81r
Driver's learning permit fee	perm	10.00	1/94	84s
Driver's license fee	orig	29.00	1/94	84s
Driver's license fee, duplicate	lic	4.00	1/94	84s
Driver's license reinstatement fee, min.	susp	25.00	1/94	85s
Driver's license renewal fee	renew	29.00	1/94	84s
Identification card, nondriver	card	5.00	1/94	83s

Values are in dollars or fractions of dollars. In the column headed *Ref*, references are shown to sources. Each reference is followed by a letter. These refer to the geographical level for which data were reported: s=State, r=Region, and c=City or metro. The abbreviation *ex* is used to mean *except* or *excluding*; *exp* stands for expenditures. For other abbreviations and further explanations, please see the Introduction.

Portland, ME - continued

Item	Per	Value	Date	Ref.
Transportation				
Motorcycle learning permit fee	perm	10.00	1/94	84s
Motorcycle license fee	orig	29.00	1/94	84s
Motorcycle license fee, duplicate	lic	4.00	1/94	84s
Motorcycle license renewal fee	renew	29.00	1/94	84s
Public transportation expenditures	year	430	91	81r
Transportation expenditures, total	year	4810	91	81r
Vehicle finance charges	year	238	91	81r
Vehicle insurance expenditures	year	630	91	81r
Vehicle maintenance and repairs expenditures	year	532	91	81r
Vehicle purchases	year	1920	91	81r
Vehicle rental, leases, licenses, etc. expenditures	year	193	91	81r
Vehicles purchased, other than cars and trucks	year	11	91	81r
Utilities				
Electricity expenditures	year	695	91	81r
Utilities, fuels, and public services, total expenditures	year	1981	91	81r
Water and other public services, expenditures	year	154	91	81r
Weddings				
Bridal attendants' gowns	event	750	10/93	76r
Bridal gown	event	852	10/93	76r
Bridal headpiece and veil	event	167	10/93	76r
Bride's wedding band	event	708	10/93	76r
Clergy	event	224	10/93	76r
Engagement ring	event	2756	10/93	76r
Flowers	event	863	10/93	76r
Formal wear for groom	event	106	10/93	76r
Groom's attendants' formal wear	event	530	10/93	76r
Groom's wedding band	event	402	10/93	76r
Music	event	600	10/93	76r
Photography	event	1088	10/93	76r
Shoes for bride	event	50	10/93	76r
Videography	event	483	10/93	76r
Wedding invitations and announcements	event	342	10/93	76r
Wedding reception	event	7000	10/93	76r

Portland, OR

Item	Per	Value	Date	Ref.
Composite, ACCRA index		109.70	12/94	2c
Alcoholic Beverages				
Beer, Miller Lite, Bud, 12-oz., ex deposit	6	4.02	12/94	2c
J & B Scotch	750-ml.	20.95	12/94	2c
Wine, Gallo Chablis blanc	1.5-lit	4.23	12/94	2c
Appliances				
Appliances (major), expenditures	year	136	91	81c
Appliances (major), expenditures	year	160	91	81r
Average annual exp.				
Food, health care, personal goods, services	year	29228	91	81c
Food, health care, personal goods, services	year	32461	91	81r
Business				
Dinner and tip, hotel, corporate rate	night	27.00	2/94	15c
Hotel room, corporate rate	night	86.00	2/94	15c
Charity				
Cash contributions, expenditures	year	822	91	81c
Cash contributions, expenditures	year	975	91	81r
Clothing				
Apparel, men and boys, total expenditures	year	505	91	81c
Apparel, men and boys, total expenditures	year	467	91	81r
Apparel, women and girls, total expenditures	year	473	91	81c
Apparel, women and girls, total expenditures	year	737	91	81r
Footwear, expenditures	year	150	91	81c
Footwear, expenditures	year	270	91	81r
Jeans, man's denim		30.37	12/94	2c

Portland, OR - continued

Item	Per	Value	Date	Ref.
Clothing - continued				
Shirt, dress, men's	shirt	25.00	1/92	44c
Shirt, man's dress shirt		32.90	12/94	2c
Undervest, boy's size 10-14, cotton	3	4.19	12/94	2c
Communications				
Long-distance telephone rate, day, addl. min., 1-10 mi.	min.	0.10	12/93	9s
Long-distance telephone rate, day, initial min., 1-10 mi.	min.	0.13	12/93	9s
Newspaper subscription, dly. and Sun. delivery	month	11.96	12/94	2c
Phone line, single, business, field visit	inst	31.00	12/93	9s
Phone line, single, business, no field visit	inst	31.00	12/93	9s
Phone line, single, residence, field visit	inst	12.00	12/93	9s
Phone line, single, residence, no field visit	inst	12.00	12/93	9s
Telephone bill, family of four	month	20.58	12/94	2c
Telephone service, expenditures	year	585	91	81c
Telephone service, expenditures	year	611	91	81r
Telephone, business, connection charges, touch tone	inst	31.15	10/91	25c
Telephone, business, key system line, touch tone	month	46.40	10/91	25c
Telephone, business, PBX line, touch tone	month	46.65	10/91	25c
Telephone, business, single ln., touch tone	month	44.28	10/91	25c
Telephone, business, touch tone, inside wiring maintenance plan	month	2.00	10/91	25c
Credit Cards				
Fee, conventional credit card, secured	year	45.00	1/95	96c
Education				
Board, 4-year private college/university	year	2338	8/94	80s
Board, 4-year public college/university	year	2211	8/94	80s
Education, total expenditures	year	349	91	81c
Education, total expenditures	year	375	91	81r
Room, 4-year private college/university	year	1959	8/94	80s
Room, 4-year public college/university	year	1604	8/94	80s
Total cost, 4-year private college/university	year	16622	8/94	80s
Total cost, 4-year public college/university	year	6648	8/94	80s
Tuition, 2-year public college/university, in-state	year	1186	8/94	80s
Tuition, 4-year private college/university, in-state	year	12325	8/94	80s
Tuition, 4-year public college/university, in-state	year	2833	8/94	80s
Energy and Fuels				
Energy, combined forms, 1800 sq. ft.	mo.	81.99	12/94	2c
Energy, exc. electricity, 1800 sq. ft.	mo.	43.07	12/94	2c
Fuel oil and other fuels, expenditures	year	62	91	81c
Fuel oil and other fuels, expenditures	year	33	91	81r
Gas	gal.	1.13	1/92	44c
Gas, cooking, winter, 10 therms	month	9.87	2/94	65c
Gas, cooking, winter, 30 therms	month	22.60	2/94	65c
Gas, cooking, winter, 50 therms	month	35.34	2/94	65c
Gas, heating, winter, 100 therms	month	67.18	2/94	65c
Gas, heating, winter, average use	month	79.91	2/94	65c
Gas, natural, expenditures	year	161	91	81c
Gas, natural, expenditures	year	212	91	81r
Gas, reg unlead, taxes inc., cash, self-service	gal	1.30	12/94	2c
Gasoline and motor oil purchased	year	1033	91	81c
Gasoline and motor oil purchased	year	1115	91	81r
Gasoline, unleaded midgrade	gallon	1.36	4/93	82r
Gasoline, unleaded premium	gallon	1.43	4/93	82r
Gasoline, unleaded regular	gallon	1.23	4/93	82r
Entertainment				
Bowling, evening rate	game	2.13	12/94	2c
Concert ticket, Pearl Jam group	perf	20.00	94	50r
Entertainment supplies, equipment, and services, misc. expenditures	year	381	91	81c
Entertainment, total expenditures	year	1608	91	81c
Entertainment, total expenditures	year	1853	91	81r

Values are in dollars or fractions of dollars. In the column headed *Ref*, references are shown to sources. Each reference is followed by a letter. These refer to the geographical level for which data were reported: s=State, r=Region, and c=City or metro. The abbreviation *ex* is used to mean *except* or *excluding*; *exp* stands for *expenditures*. For other abbreviations and further explanations, please see the Introduction.

Portland, OR - continued

Item	Per	Value	Date	Ref.
Entertainment				
Fees and admissions, expenditures	year	431	91	81c
Fees and admissions, expenditures	year	482	91	81r
Monopoly game, Parker Brothers', No. 9	game	10.59	12/94	2c
Movie	adm	6.12	12/94	2c
Movie ticket, adult	ticket	6.00	1/92	44c
Pets, toys, playground equipment, expenditures	year	287	91	81c
Pets, toys, playground equipment, expenditures	year	299	91	81r
Reading, expenditures	year	185	91	81c
Reading, expenditures	year	164	91	81r
Televisions, radios, and sound equipment, expenditures	year	509	91	81c
Televisions, radios, and sound equipment, expenditures	year	528	91	81r
Tennis balls, yellow, Wilson or Penn, 3	can	2.77	12/94	2c
Funerals				
Burial, immediate, container provided by funeral home		1382.70	1/95	54r
Cards, acknowledgment		21.87	1/95	54r
Casket, minimum alternative		128.54	1/95	54r
Cosmetology, hair care, etc.		119.69	1/95	54r
Cremation, direct, container provided by funeral home		1030.62	1/95	54r
Embalming		255.42	1/95	54r
Funeral, funeral home		437.38	1/95	54r
Funeral, other facility		444.46	1/95	54r
Graveside service		338.46	1/95	54r
Hearse, local		147.50	1/95	54r
Limousine, local		130.33	1/95	54r
Memorial service		553.16	1/95	54r
Service charge, professional, nondeclinable		859.15	1/95	54r
Visitation and viewing		93.23	1/95	54r
Groceries				
Groceries, ACCRA Index		99.90	12/94	2c
Apples, Red Delicious	lb.	0.72	12/94	82r
Baby food, strained vegetables, lowest price	4-4.5 oz.	0.28	12/94	2c
Bacon, sliced	lb.	1.73	12/94	82r
Bananas	lb.	0.45	12/94	2c
Bananas	lb.	0.52	12/94	82r
Beef or hamburger, ground	lb.	1.59	12/94	2c
Beef purchases	year	211	91	81c
Beef purchases	year	241	91	81r
Beverage purchases, alcoholic	year	244	91	81c
Beverage purchases, alcoholic	year	328	91	81r
Beverage purchases, nonalcoholic	year	218	91	81c
Beverage purchases, nonalcoholic	year	234	91	81r
Bologna, all beef or mixed	lb.	2.33	12/94	82r
Bread, white	24-oz.	0.61	12/94	2c
Bread, white, pan	lb.	0.81	12/94	82r
Carrots, short trimmed and topped	lb.	0.43	12/94	82r
Cereals and bakery products purchases	year	360	91	81c
Cereals and bakery products purchases	year	392	91	81r
Cereals and cereal products purchases	year	128	91	81c
Cereals and cereals products purchases	year	139	91	81r
Cheese, Kraft grated Parmesan	8-oz.	3.59	12/94	2c
Chicken breast, bone-in	lb.	2.04	12/94	82r
Chicken, fresh, whole	lb.	0.95	12/94	82r
Chicken, whole fryer	lb.	0.87	12/94	2c
Cigarettes, Winston, Kings	carton	18.79	12/94	2c
Coffee, 100%, ground roast, all sizes	lb.	4.48	12/94	82r
Coffee, vacuum-packed	13 oz.	3.99	12/94	2c
Corn Flakes, Kellogg's or Post Toasties	18 oz.	2.25	12/94	2c
Corn, frozen, whole kernel, lowest price	10 oz.	0.75	12/94	2c
Dairy products (other) purchases	year	173	91	81c
Dairy products (other) purchases	year	182	91	81r
Eggs, Grade A large	dozen	0.89	12/94	2c
Fish and seafood purchases	year	78	91	81c
Fish and seafood purchases	year	94	91	81r
Flour, white, all purpose	lb.	0.21	12/94	82r

Portland, OR - continued

Item	Per	Value	Date	Ref.
Groceries - continued				
Food purchases, food eaten at home	year	2535	91	81c
Food purchases, food eaten at home	year	2749	91	81r
Foods purchased away from home, not prepared by consumer	year	1546	91	81c
Foods purchased away from home, not prepared by consumer	year	1909	91	81r
Fruits and vegetables purchases	year	405	91	81c
Fruits and vegetables purchases	year	459	91	81r
Grapefruit	lb.	0.56	12/94	82r
Ground beef, 100% beef	lb.	1.31	12/94	82r
Ham, boneless, exc. canned	lb.	2.46	12/94	82r
Ice cream, prepackaged, bulk, regular	1/2 gal.	2.57	12/94	82r
Lemons	lb.	1.00	12/94	82r
Lettuce, iceberg	lb.	0.93	12/94	82r
Lettuce, iceberg	head	0.74	12/94	2c
Margarine, Blue Bonnet or Parkay cubes	lb.	0.56	12/94	2c
Meats, poultry, fish, and eggs purchases	year	626	91	81c
Meats, poultry, fish, and eggs purchases	year	700	91	81r
Milk and cream (fresh) purchases	year	145	91	81c
Milk and cream (fresh) purchases	year	155	91	81r
Milk, 2%	gal.	1.99	1/92	44c
Milk, whole	1/2 gal.	1.42	12/94	2c
Orange juice, frozen concentrate 12-oz. can	16 oz.	1.52	12/94	82r
Orange juice, Minute Maid frozen	12-oz.	1.07	12/94	2c
Oranges, Navel	lb.	0.56	12/94	82r
Peaches, halves or slices, Hunt's, Del Monte, or Libby's	29-oz.	1.67	12/94	2c
Peas, sweet, Del Monte or Green Giant	15-17 oz.	0.67	12/94	2c
Pork chops, center cut, bone-in	lb.	3.30	12/94	82r
Pork purchases	year	111	91	81c
Pork purchases	year	122	91	81r
Potato chips	16-oz.	3.03	12/94	82r
Potatoes, frozen, French fried	lb.	0.77	12/94	82r
Potatoes, white	lb.	0.35	12/94	82r
Potatoes, white or red	10-lb. sack	1.56	12/94	2c
Rental rate, 2-bedroom apartment	month	425.00	1/92	44c
Rice, white, long grain, uncooked	lb.	0.54	12/94	82r
Round roast, USDA choice, boneless	lb.	2.92	12/94	82r
Sausage, Jimmy Dean, 100% pork	lb.	3.43	12/94	2c
Shortening, vegetable oil blends	lb.	0.80	12/94	82r
Shortening, vegetable, Crisco	3-lb.	2.07	12/94	2c
Soft drink, Coca Cola, ex deposit	2 lit	1.12	12/94	2c
Spaghetti and macaroni	lb.	1.02	12/94	82r
Steak, round, graded & ungraded, exc. USDA prime & choice	lb.	3.13	12/94	82r
Steak, sirloin, USDA choice, boneless	lb.	4.07	12/94	82r
Steak, t-bone	lb.	5.05	12/94	2c
Sugar and other sweets, eaten at home, expenditures	year	105	91	81r
Sugar and other sweets, eaten at home, purchases	year	94	91	81c
Sugar, cane or beet	4 lbs.	1.26	12/94	2c
Sugar, white, all sizes	lb.	0.38	12/94	82r
Tobacco products and smoking supplies, total expenditures	year	252	91	81c
Tobacco products and smoking supplies, total expenditures	year	221	91	81r
Tomatoes, field grown	lb.	1.45	12/94	82r
Tomatoes, Hunt's or Del Monte	14.5 oz.	0.76	12/94	2c
Tuna, chunk, light	lb.	2.18	12/94	82r
Tuna, chunk, light, oil-packed	6.125-6.5 oz.	0.74	12/94	2c
Goods and Services				
Miscellaneous goods and services, ACCRA Index		106.70	12/94	2c

Values are in dollars or fractions of dollars. In the column headed *Ref*, references are shown to sources. Each reference is followed by a letter. These refer to the geographical level for which data were reported: s=State, r=Region, and c=City or metro. The abbreviation *ex* is used to mean *except* or *excluding*; *exp* stands for expenditures. For other abbreviations and further explanations, please see the Introduction.

Portland, OR - continued

Item	Per	Value	Date	Ref.
Health Care				
Health care, ACCRA Index		127.30	12/94	2c
Antibiotic ointment, Polysporin	1.5 oz.	3.92	12/94	2c
Childbirth, Cesarean delivery, hospital charge	birth	6059.00	12/91	69r
Childbirth, Cesarean delivery, physician charge	birth	2248.00	12/91	69r
Childbirth, normal delivery, hospital charge	birth	3006.00	12/91	69r
Childbirth, normal delivery, physician charge	birth	1634.00	12/91	69r
Dentist's fee, adult teeth cleaning and periodic oral exam	visit	75.80	12/94	2c
Doctor's fee, routine exam, established patient	visit	49.44	12/94	2c
Drugs, expenditures	year	234	91	81c
Drugs, expenditures	year	230	91	81r
Health care, total expenditures	year	1318	91	81c
Health care, total expenditures	year	1544	91	81r
Health insurance expenditures	year	570	91	81c
Health insurance expenditures	year	558	91	81r
Hospital care, semiprivate room	day	471.20	12/94	2c
Insurance premium, family medical care	month	331.06	1/95	41s
Medical services expenditures	year	436	91	81c
Medical services expenditures	year	676	91	81r
Medical supplies expenditures	year	78	91	81c
Medical supplies expenditures	year	80	91	81r
Surgery, open-heart	proc	37818.00	1/93	14r
Household Goods				
Appl. repair, service call, wash mach	min. lab. chg.	36.58	12/94	2c
Floor coverings, expenditures	year	36	91	81c
Floor coverings, expenditures	year	79	91	81r
Furniture, expenditures	year	310	91	81c
Furniture, expenditures	year	352	91	81r
Household equipment, misc. expenditures	year	614	91	81r
Household equipment, misc., expenditures	year	321	91	81c
Household expenditures, miscellaneous	year	232	91	81c
Household expenditures, miscellaneous	year	294	91	81r
Household furnishings and equipment, expenditures	year	985	91	81c
Household furnishings and equipment, expenditures	year	1416	91	81r
Household operations expenditures	year	552	91	81c
Household operations expenditures	year	580	91	81r
Household textiles, expenditures	year	87	91	81c
Household textiles, expenditures	year	113	91	81r
Housekeeping supplies, expenditures	year	314	91	81c
Housekeeping supplies, expenditures	year	447	91	81r
Laundry and cleaning supplies, expenditures	year	65	91	81c
Laundry and cleaning supplies, expenditures	year	114	91	81r
Laundry detergent, Tide Ultra, Bold, or Cheer	42 oz.	3.29	12/94	2c
Postage and stationery, expenditures	year	109	91	81c
Postage and stationery, expenditures	year	145	91	81r
Tissues, facial, Kleenex brand	175	1.20	12/94	2c
Housing				
Housing, ACCRA Index		124.20	12/94	2c
Add garage/carport		6,422	3/95	74r
Add room(s)		26,583	3/95	74r
Apartment condominium or co-op, median	unit	105300	12/94	62r
Dwellings (owned), expenditures	year	3288	91	81c
Dwellings (owned), expenditures	year	3932	91	81r
Enclose porch/patio/breezeway		5,382	3/95	74r
Finish room in basement/attic		3,911	3/95	74r
Home, existing, single-family, median	unit	178600	12/94	62r
Home, existing, single-family, median	unit	120.00	12/94	62c
Home, purchase price	unit	136.90	3/93	26c
House payment, principal and interest, 25% down payment	mo.	936	12/94	2c

Portland, OR - continued

Item	Per	Value	Date	Ref.
Housing - continued				
House, 1800 sq ft, 8000 sq ft lot, new, urban, utilities	total	153000	12/94	2c
Maintenance, repairs, insurance, and other housing expenditures	year	422	91	81c
Maintenance, repairs, insurance, and other housing expenditures	year	591	91	81r
Mortgage interest and charges expenditures	year	1790	91	81c
Mortgage interest and charges expenditures	year	2747	91	81r
Mtge. rate, incl. points and orig. fee, 30-year conv. fixed or ARM	mo.	9.15	12/94	2c
Princ. & int., mortgage, median-price exist. sing.-family home	mo.	845	12/94	62r
Property taxes expenditures	year	1077	91	81c
Property taxes expenditures	year	594	91	81r
Redesign, restructure more than half of home's interior		5,467	3/95	74r
Rent, apartment, 2 br., 1 1/2-2 baths, unfurnished, 950 sq ft, water	mo.	700	12/94	2c
Rental units expenditures	year	1898	900/00/ 91	81c
Rental units expenditures	year	2077	91	81r
Insurance and Pensions				
Auto insurance, private passenger	year	632.21	12/94	71s
Insurance and pensions, personal, expenditures	year	3431	91	81c
Insurance and pensions, personal, expenditures	year	3042	91	81r
Insurance, life and other personal, expenditures	year	320	91	81c
Insurance, life and other personal, expenditures	year	298	91	81r
Pensions and Social Security, expenditures	year	3111	91	81c
Pensions and Social Security, expenditures	year	2744	91	81r
Legal Assistance				
Legal work, law firm associate	hour	91		10r
Legal work, law firm partner	hour	151		10r
Personal Goods				
Personal care products and services, total expenditures	year	322	91	81c
Shampoo, Alberto VO5	15-oz.	1.20	12/94	2c
Toothpaste, Crest or Colgate	6-7 oz.	2.06	12/94	2c
Personal Services				
Dry cleaning, man's 2-pc. suit		7.98	12/94	2c
Dry cleaning, woman's dress	dress	5.50	1/92	44c
Haircut, man's barbershop, no styling		8.70	12/94	2c
Haircut, woman's shampoo, trim, blow-dry		25.20	12/94	2c
Personal services expenditures	year	320	91	81c
Personal services expenditures	year	286	91	81r
Restaurant Food				
Big Mac, small fries, medium drink	meal	3.98	1/92	44c
Chicken, fried, thigh and drumstick		2.40	12/94	2c
Dining expenditures, family	week	32.25	94	73r
Hamburger with cheese	1/4 lb.	1.97	12/94	2c
Pizza, Pizza Hut or Pizza Inn	12-13 in.	8.99	12/94	2c
Taxes				
Tax rate, residential property, month	$100	2.32	1/92	79c
Taxes, Federal income, expenditures	year	2734	91	81c
Taxes, Federal income, expenditures	year	2946	91	81r
Taxes, personal, expenditures	year	4149	91	81c
Taxes, personal, expenditures	year	3791	91	81r
Taxes, State and local income, expenditures	year	1286	91	81c
Taxes, State and local income, expenditures	year	791	91	81r
Transportation				
Transportation, ACCRA Index		110.30	12/94	2c
Bus fare, one-way	trip	0.80	12/95	1c
Bus fare, up to 10 miles	one-way	1.30	12/94	2c

Values are in dollars or fractions of dollars. In the column headed *Ref*, references are shown to sources. Each reference is followed by a letter. These refer to the geographical level for which data were reported: s = State, r = Region, and c = City or metro. The abbreviation *ex* is used to mean *except* or *excluding*; *exp* stands for *expenditures*. For other abbreviations and further explanations, please see the Introduction.

Portland, OR - continued

Item	Per	Value	Date	Ref.
Transportation				
Cars and trucks purchased, new	year	683	91	81c
Cars and trucks purchased, new	year	1231	91	81r
Cars and trucks purchased, used	year	1413	91	81c
Cars and trucks purchased, used	year	915	91	81r
Driver's learning permit fee	perm	13.00	1/94	84s
Driver's license fee	orig	26.25	1/94	84s
Driver's license fee, duplicate	lic	11.00	1/94	84s
Driver's license reinstatement fee, min.	susp	53.00	1/94	85s
Driver's license renewal fee	renew	16.25	1/94	84s
Identification card, nondriver	card	13.00	1/94	83s
Motorcycle learning permit fee	perm	13.00	1/94	84s
Motorcycle license fee	orig	30.00	1/94	84s
Motorcycle license fee, duplicate	lic	11.00	1/94	84s
Motorcycle license renewal fee	renew	7.00	1/94	84s
parking, long-term lot, airport	3 days	18.00	1/92	44c
Public transportation expenditures	year	306	91	81c
Public transportation expenditures	year	375	91	81r
Railway fare, light rail, one-way	trip	1.00	12/95	1c
Tire balance, computer or spin bal., front	wheel	6.45	12/94	2c
Transportation expenditures, total	year	5275	91	81c
Transportation expenditures, total	year	5527	91	81r
Vehicle expenses, miscellaneous	year	1759	91	81c
Vehicle finance charges	year	348	91	81c
Vehicle finance charges	year	287	91	81r
Vehicle insurance expenditures	year	638	91	81c
Vehicle insurance expenditures	year	624	91	81r
Vehicle maintenance and repairs expenditures	year	614	91	81c
Vehicle maintenance and repairs expenditures	year	695	91	81r
Vehicle purchases	year	2177	91	81c
Vehicle purchases	year	2174	91	81r
Vehicle rental, leases, licenses, etc. expenditures	year	159	91	81c
Vehicle rental, leases, licenses, etc. expenditures	year	257	91	81r
Vehicles purchased, other than cars and trucks	year	81	91	81c
Vehicles purchased, other than cars and trucks	year	28	91	81r
Utilities				
Utilities, ACCRA Index		77.40	12/94	2c
Electricity expenditures	year	601	91	81c
Electricity expenditures	year	616	91	81r
Electricity, (part.), other, 1800 sq. ft., new home	mo.	38.92	12/94	2c
Electricity, summer, 250 KWh	month	14.67	8/93	64c
Electricity, summer, 500 KWh	month	25.94	8/93	64c
Electricity, summer, 750 KWh	month	37.60	8/93	64c
Electricity, summer, 1000 KWh	month	49.27	8/93	64c
Utilities, fuels, and public services, total expenditures	year	1655	91	81c
Utilities, fuels, and public services, total expenditures	year	1681	91	81r
Water and other public services, expenditures	year	247	91	81c
Water and other public services, expenditures	year	209	91	81r
Weddings				
Bridal attendants' gowns	event	750	10/93	76r
Bridal gown	event	852	10/93	76r
Bridal headpiece and veil	event	167	10/93	76r
Bride's wedding band	event	708	10/93	76r
Clergy	event	224	10/93	76r
Engagement ring	event	2756	10/93	76r
Flowers	event	863	10/93	76r
Formal wear for groom	event	106	10/93	76r
Groom's attendants' formal wear	event	530	10/93	76r
Groom's wedding band	event	402	10/93	76r
Music	event	600	10/93	76r
Photography	event	1088	10/93	76r

Portland, OR - continued

Item	Per	Value	Date	Ref.
Weddings - continued				
Shoes for bride	event	50	10/93	76r
Videography	event	483	10/93	76r
Wedding invitations and announcements	event	342	10/93	76r
Wedding reception	event	7000	10/93	76r

Poughkeepsie, NY

Item	Per	Value	Date	Ref.
Appliances				
Appliances (major), expenditures	year	145	91	81r
Average annual exp.				
Food, health care, personal goods, services	year	29496	91	81r
Charity				
Cash contributions, expenditures	year	708	91	81r
Clothing				
Apparel, men and boys, total expenditures	year	416	91	81r
Apparel, women and girls, total expenditures	year	744	91	81r
Footwear, expenditures	year	305	91	81r
Communications				
Long-distance telephone rate, day, addl. min., 1-10 mi.	min.	4.00	12/93	9s
Long-distance telephone rate, day, initial min., 1-10 mi.	min.	14.90	12/93	9s
Phone line, single, business, field visit	inst	143.26	12/93	9s
Phone line, single, business, no field visit	inst	106.05	12/93	9s
Phone line, single, residence, field visit	inst	85.46	12/93	9s
Phone line, single, residence, no field visit	inst	55.00	12/93	9s
Telephone service, expenditures	year	589	91	81r
Education				
Board, 4-year private college/university	year	2918	8/94	80s
Board, 4-year public college/university	year	2177	8/94	80s
Education, total expenditures	year	593	91	81r
Room, 4-year private college/university	year	3302	8/94	80s
Room, 4-year public college/university	year	2624	8/94	80s
Total cost, 4-year private college/university	year	18451	8/94	80s
Total cost, 4-year public college/university	year	7723	8/94	80s
Tuition, 2-year public college/university, in-state	year	2112	8/94	80s
Tuition, 4-year private college/university, in-state	year	12231	8/94	80s
Tuition, 4-year public college/university, in-state	year	2921	8/94	80s
Energy and Fuels				
Fuel oil and other fuels, expenditures	year	257	91	81r
Gas, natural, expenditures	year	285	91	81r
Gasoline and motor oil purchased	year	867	91	81r
Gasoline, unleaded midgrade	gallon	1.32	4/93	82r
Gasoline, unleaded premium	gallon	1.40	4/93	82r
Gasoline, unleaded regular	gallon	1.19	4/93	82r
Entertainment				
Entertainment, total expenditures	year	1331	91	81r
Fees and admissions, expenditures	year	398	91	81r
Pets, toys, playground equipment, expenditures	year	270	91	81r
Reading, expenditures	year	171	91	81r
Televisions, radios, and sound equipment, expenditures	year	429	91	81r
Funerals				
Burial, immediate, container provided by funeral home		1370.36	1/95	54r
Cards, acknowledgment		17.72	1/95	54r
Casket, minimum alternative		192.52	1/95	54r
Cosmetology, hair care, etc.		139.56	1/95	54r
Cremation, direct, container provided by funeral home		1049.24	1/95	54r
Embalming		387.57	1/95	54r
Funeral, funeral home		278.77	1/95	54r
Funeral, other facility		275.85	1/95	54r

Values are in dollars or fractions of dollars. In the column headed *Ref*, references are shown to sources. Each reference is followed by a letter. These refer to the geographical level for which data were reported: s=State, r=Region, and c=City or metro. The abbreviation *ex* is used to mean *except* or *excluding*; *exp* stands for *expenditures*. For other abbreviations and further explanations, please see the Introduction.

Poughkeepsie, NY - continued

Item	Per	Value	Date	Ref.
Funerals				
Graveside service		213.08	1/95	54r
Hearse, local		157.27	1/95	54r
Limousine, local		146.45	1/95	54r
Memorial service		271.02	1/95	54r
Service charge, professional, nondeclinable		943.58	1/95	54r
Visitation and viewing		322.86	1/95	54r
Groceries				
Apples, Red Delicious	lb.	0.78	12/94	82r
Bacon, sliced	lb.	2.24	12/94	82r
Bananas	lb.	0.49	12/94	82r
Beef purchases	year	226	91	81r
Beverage purchases, alcoholic	year	332	91	81r
Beverage purchases, nonalcoholic	year	213	91	81r
Bread, white, pan	lb.	0.80	12/94	82r
Butter, salted, Grade AA, stick	lb.	1.67	12/94	82r
Carrots, short trimmed and topped	lb.	0.51	12/94	82r
Cereals and bakery products purchases	year	407	91	81r
Cereals and cereals products purchases	year	132	91	81r
Chicken breast, bone-in	lb.	2.22	12/94	82r
Chicken, fresh, whole	lb.	1.05	12/94	82r
Chuck roast, USDA choice, boneless	lb.	2.74	12/94	82r
Coffee, 100%, ground roast, all sizes	lb.	4.61	12/94	82r
Dairy products (other) purchases	year	161	91	81r
Eggs, Grade A large	dozen	1.12	12/94	82r
Fish and seafood purchases	year	112	91	81r
Food purchases, food eaten at home	year	2599	91	81r
Foods purchased away from home, not prepared by consumer	year	2024	91	81r
Fruits and vegetables purchases	year	444	91	81r
Grapefruit	lb.	0.44	12/94	82r
Grapes, Thompson seedless	lb.	2.24	12/94	82r
Ground chuck, 100% beef	lb.	1.67	12/94	82r
Ice cream, prepackaged, bulk, regular	1/2 gal.	2.93	12/94	82r
Lemons	lb.	1.06	12/94	82r
Lettuce, iceberg	lb.	0.92	12/94	82r
Meats, poultry, fish, and eggs purchases	year	751	91	81r
Milk and cream (fresh) purchases	year	152	91	81r
Orange juice, frozen concentrate 12-oz. can	16 oz.	1.92	12/94	82r
Oranges, Navel	lb.	0.56	12/94	82r
Pork chops, center cut, bone-in	lb.	3.09	12/94	82r
Pork purchases	year	130	91	81r
Potatoes, white	lb.	0.37	12/94	82r
Rib roast, USDA choice, bone-in	lb.	4.98	12/94	82r
Round roast, USDA choice, boneless	lb.	2.93	12/94	82r
Shortening, vegetable oil blends	lb.	1.03	12/94	82r
Spaghetti and macaroni	lb.	0.84	12/94	82r
Steak, round, USDA choice, boneless	lb.	3.48	12/94	82r
Steak, sirloin, USDA choice, bone-in	lb.	3.38	12/94	82r
Steak, sirloin, USDA choice, boneless	lb.	4.81	12/94	82r
Sugar and other sweets, eaten at home, expenditures	year	89	91	81r
Sugar, white, all sizes	lb.	0.46	12/94	82r
Tobacco products and smoking supplies, total expenditures	year	279	91	81r
Tomatoes, field grown	lb.	1.56	12/94	82r
Tuna, chunk, light	lb.	2.09	12/94	82r
Health Care				
Childbirth, Cesarean delivery, hospital charge	birth	6334.00	12/91	69r
Childbirth, Cesarean delivery, physician charge	birth	2234.00	12/91	69r
Childbirth, normal delivery, hospital charge	birth	3225.00	12/91	69r
Childbirth, normal delivery, physician charge	birth	1623.00	12/91	69r
Drugs, expenditures	year	205	91	81r
Health care, total expenditures	year	1396	91	81r
Health insurance expenditures	year	553	91	81r
Insurance premium, family medical care	month	384.24	1/95	41s
Medical services expenditures	year	559	91	81r
Medical supplies expenditures	year	80	91	81r

Poughkeepsie, NY - continued

Item	Per	Value	Date	Ref.
Household Goods				
Floor coverings, expenditures	year	158	91	81r
Furniture, expenditures	year	341	91	81r
Household equipment, misc. expenditures	year	363	91	81r
Household expenditures, miscellaneous	year	194	91	81r
Household furnishings and equipment, expenditures	year	1158	91	81r
Household operations expenditures	year	378	91	81r
Household textiles, expenditures	year	88	91	81r
Housekeeping supplies, expenditures	year	426	91	81r
Laundry and cleaning supplies, expenditures	year	122	91	81r
Postage and stationery, expenditures	year	134	91	81r
Housing				
Add garage/carport		11,614	3/95	74r
Add room(s)		16,816	3/95	74r
Apartment condominium or co-op, median	unit	96700	12/94	62r
Dwellings (owned), expenditures	year	3305	91	81r
Enclose porch/patio/breezeway		2,980	3/95	74r
Finish room in basement/attic		4,330	3/95	74r
Home, existing, single-family, median	unit	161600	12/94	62r
Maintenance, repairs, insurance, and other housing expenditures	year	569	91	81r
Mortgage interest and charges expenditures	year	1852	91	81r
Princ. & int., mortgage, median-price exist. sing.-family home	mo.	765	12/94	62r
Property taxes expenditures	year	884	91	81r
Redesign, restructure more than half of home's interior		2,750	3/95	74r
Rental units expenditures	year	1832	91	81r
Insurance and Pensions				
Auto insurance, private passenger	year	985.07	12/94	71s
Insurance and pensions, personal, expenditures	year	2690	91	81r
Insurance, life and other personal, expenditures	year	341	91	81r
Pensions and Social Security, expenditures	year	2349	91	81r
Legal Assistance				
Estate planning, law-firm partner	hr.	375.00	10/93	12r
Legal work, law firm associate	hour	78		10r
Legal work, law firm partner	hour	183		10r
Personal Services				
Personal services expenditures	year	184	91	81r
Restaurant Food				
Dining expenditures, family	week	34.26	94	73r
Taxes				
Taxes, Federal income, expenditures	year	2409	91	81r
Taxes, personal, expenditures	year	3094	91	81r
Taxes, State and local income, expenditures	year	620	91	81r
Transportation				
Cars and trucks purchased, new	year	1170	91	81r
Cars and trucks purchased, used	year	739	91	81r
Driver's learning permit fee	perm	10.00	1/94	84s
Driver's license fee	orig	32.00-37.00	1/94	84s
Driver's license fee, duplicate	lic	7.25	1/94	84s
Driver's license reinstatement fee, min.	susp	25.00	1/94	85s
Driver's license renewal fee	renew	22.25	1/94	84s
Identification card, nondriver	card	6.25	1/94	83s
Motorcycle license fee	orig	32.00-37.00	1/94	84s
Motorcycle license fee, duplicate	lic	7.25	1/94	84s
Motorcycle license renewal fee	renew	22.25	1/94	84s
Public transportation expenditures	year	430	91	81r
Transportation expenditures, total	year	4810	91	81r
Vehicle finance charges	year	238	91	81r
Vehicle insurance expenditures	year	630	91	81r
Vehicle maintenance and repairs expenditures	year	532	91	81r

Values are in dollars or fractions of dollars. In the column headed *Ref*, references are shown to sources. Each reference is followed by a letter. These refer to the geographical level for which data were reported: s=State, r=Region, and c=City or metro. The abbreviation *ex* is used to mean *except* or *excluding*; *exp* stands for *expenditures*. For other abbreviations and further explanations, please see the Introduction.

Poughkeepsie, NY - continued

Item	Per	Value	Date	Ref.
Transportation				
Vehicle purchases	year	1920	91	81r
Vehicle rental, leases, licenses, etc. expenditures	year	193	91	81r
Vehicles purchased, other than cars and trucks	year	11	91	81r
Utilities				
Electricity expenditures	year	695	91	81r
Utilities, fuels, and public services, total expenditures	year	1981	91	81r
Water and other public services, expenditures	year	154	91	81r
Weddings				
Bridal attendants' gowns	event	750	10/93	76r
Bridal gown	event	852	10/93	76r
Bridal headpiece and veil	event	167	10/93	76r
Bride's wedding band	event	708	10/93	76r
Clergy	event	224	10/93	76r
Engagement ring	event	2756	10/93	76r
Flowers	event	863	10/93	76r
Formal wear for groom	event	106	10/93	76r
Groom's attendants' formal wear	event	530	10/93	76r
Groom's wedding band	event	402	10/93	76r
Music	event	600	10/93	76r
Photography	event	1088	10/93	76r
Shoes for bride	event	50	10/93	76r
Videography	event	483	10/93	76r
Wedding invitations and announcements	event	342	10/93	76r
Wedding reception	event	7000	10/93	76r

Prescott-Prescott Valley, AZ

Item	Per	Value	Date	Ref.
Composite, ACCRA index		109.20	12/94	2c
Alcoholic Beverages				
Beer, Miller Lite, Bud, 12-oz., ex deposit	6	3.72	12/94	2c
J & B Scotch	750-ml.	15.95	12/94	2c
Wine, Gallo Chablis blanc	1.5-lit	4.79	12/94	2c
Clothing				
Jeans, man's denim		29.95	12/94	2c
Shirt, man's dress shirt		29.50	12/94	2c
Undervest, boy's size 10-14, cotton	3	3.24	12/94	2c
Communications				
Newspaper subscription, dly. and Sun. delivery	month	12.61	12/94	2c
Telephone bill, family of four	month	19.44	12/94	2c
Telephone, residential, flat rate	mo.	12.40	12/93	8c
Energy and Fuels				
Energy, combined forms, 1800 sq. ft.	mo.	95.05	12/94	2c
Energy, exc. electricity, 1800 sq. ft.	mo.	44.15	12/94	2c
Gas, reg unlead, taxes inc., cash, self-service	gal	1.19	12/94	2c
Entertainment				
Bowling, evening rate	game	2.25	12/94	2c
Monopoly game, Parker Brothers', No. 9	game	10.74	12/94	2c
Movie	adm	4.75	12/94	2c
Tennis balls, yellow, Wilson or Penn, 3	can	1.97	12/94	2c
Groceries				
Groceries, ACCRA Index		104.00	12/94	2c
Baby food, strained vegetables, lowest price	4-4.5 oz.	0.31	12/94	2c
Bananas	lb.	0.40	12/94	2c
Beef or hamburger, ground	lb.	1.27	12/94	2c
Bread, white	24-oz.	0.80	12/94	2c
Cheese, Kraft grated Parmesan	8-oz.	3.73	12/94	2c
Chicken, whole fryer	lb.	0.86	12/94	2c
Cigarettes, Winston, Kings	carton	14.99	12/94	2c
Coffee, vacuum-packed	13 oz.	3.90	12/94	2c

Prescott-Prescott Valley, AZ - continued

Item	Per	Value	Date	Ref.
Groceries - continued				
Corn Flakes, Kellogg's or Post Toasties	18 oz.	2.68	12/94	2c
Corn, frozen, whole kernel, lowest price	10 oz.	0.66	12/94	2c
Eggs, Grade A large	dozen	0.69	12/94	2c
Lettuce, iceberg	head	0.61	12/94	2c
Margarine, Blue Bonnet or Parkay cubes	lb.	0.72	12/94	2c
Milk, whole	1/2 gal.	1.39	12/94	2c
Orange juice, Minute Maid frozen	12-oz.	1.31	12/94	2c
Peaches, halves or slices, Hunt's, Del Monte, or Libby's	29-oz.	1.46	12/94	2c
Peas, sweet, Del Monte or Green Giant	15-17 oz.	0.49	12/94	2c
Potatoes, white or red	10-lb. sack	1.91	12/94	2c
Sausage, Jimmy Dean, 100% pork	lb.	3.24	12/94	2c
Shortening, vegetable, Crisco	3-lb.	2.90	12/94	2c
Soft drink, Coca Cola, ex deposit	2 lit	1.25	12/94	2c
Steak, t-bone	lb.	4.79	12/94	2c
Sugar, cane or beet	4 lbs.	1.75	12/94	2c
Tomatoes, Hunt's or Del Monte	14.5 oz.	0.75	12/94	2c
Tuna, chunk, light, oil-packed	6.125-6.5 oz.	0.78	12/94	2c
Goods and Services				
Miscellaneous goods and services, ACCRA Index		97.70	12/94	2c
Health Care				
Health care, ACCRA Index		104.10	12/94	2c
Antibiotic ointment, Polysporin	1.5 oz.	4.03	12/94	2c
Dentist's fee, adult teeth cleaning and periodic oral exam	visit	54.50	12/94	2c
Doctor's fee, routine exam, established patient	visit	40.41	12/94	2c
Hospital care, semiprivate room	day	440.00	12/94	2c
Household Goods				
Appl. repair, service call, wash mach	min. lab. chg.	37.33	12/94	2c
Laundry detergent, Tide Ultra, Bold, or Cheer	42 oz.	4.02	12/94	2c
Tissues, facial, Kleenex brand	175	1.12	12/94	2c
Housing				
Housing, ACCRA Index		135.50	12/94	2c
House payment, principal and interest, 25% down payment	mo.	1094	12/94	2c
House, 1800 sq ft, 8000 sq ft lot, new, urban, utilities	total	117250	12/94	2c
Mtge. rate, incl. points and orig. fee, 30-year conv. fixed or ARM	mo.	9.26	12/94	2c
Rent, apartment, 2 br., 1 1/2-2 baths, unfurnished, 950 sq ft, water	mo.	552	12/94	2c
Personal Goods				
Shampoo, Alberto VO5	15-oz.	1.37	12/94	2c
Toothpaste, Crest or Colgate	6-7 oz.	1.95	12/94	2c
Personal Services				
Dry cleaning, man's 2-pc. suit		6.39	12/94	2c
Haircut, man's barbershop, no styling		8.00	12/94	2c
Haircut, woman's shampoo, trim, blow-dry		27.20	12/94	2c
Restaurant Food				
Chicken, fried, thigh and drumstick		2.00	12/94	2c
Hamburger with cheese	1/4 lb.	1.99	12/94	2c
Pizza, Pizza Hut or Pizza Inn	12-13 in.	7.80	12/94	2c
Transportation				
Transportation, ACCRA Index		102.60	12/94	2c
Tire balance, computer or spin bal., front	wheel	6.62	12/94	2c

Values are in dollars or fractions of dollars. In the column headed *Ref*, references are shown to sources. Each reference is followed by a letter. These refer to the geographical level for which data were reported: s = State, r = Region, and c = City or metro. The abbreviation *ex* is used to mean *except* or *excluding*; *exp* stands for expenditures. For other abbreviations and further explanations, please see the Introduction.

Prescott-Prescott Valley, AZ - continued

Item	Per	Value	Date	Ref.
Utilities				
Utilities, ACCRA Index		86.70	12/94	2c
Electricity, (part.), other, 1800 sq. ft., new home	mo.	50.90	12/94	2c

Prince William, VA

Item	Per	Value	Date	Ref.
Composite, ACCRA index		112.80	12/94	2c
Alcoholic Beverages				
Beer, Miller Lite, Bud, 12-oz., ex deposit	6	3.95	12/94	2c
J & B Scotch	750-ml.	18.45	12/94	2c
Wine, Gallo Chablis blanc	1.5-lit	5.69	12/94	2c
Clothing				
Jeans, man's denim		27.99	12/94	2c
Shirt, man's dress shirt		26.16	12/94	2c
Undervest, boy's size 10-14, cotton	3	3.88	12/94	2c
Communications				
Newspaper subscription, dly. and Sun. delivery	month	10.00	12/94	2c
Telephone bill, family of four	month	21.89	12/94	2c
Energy and Fuels				
Energy, combined forms, 1800 sq. ft.	mo.	130.75	12/94	2c
Gas, reg unlead, taxes inc., cash, self-service	gal	1.10	12/94	2c
Entertainment				
Bowling, evening rate	game	3.01	12/94	2c
Monopoly game, Parker Brothers', No. 9	game	10.54	12/94	2c
Movie	adm	5.82	12/94	2c
Tennis balls, yellow, Wilson or Penn, 3	can	2.22	12/94	2c
Groceries				
Groceries, ACCRA Index		106.10	12/94	2c
Baby food, strained vegetables, lowest price	4-4.5 oz.	0.41	12/94	2c
Bananas	lb.	0.46	12/94	2c
Beef or hamburger, ground	lb.	1.70	12/94	2c
Bread, white	24-oz.	0.66	12/94	2c
Cheese, Kraft grated Parmesan	8-oz.	3.53	12/94	2c
Chicken, whole fryer	lb.	1.03	12/94	2c
Cigarettes, Winston, Kings	carton	12.35	12/94	2c
Coffee, vacuum-packed	13 oz.	3.74	12/94	2c
Corn Flakes, Kellogg's or Post Toasties	18 oz.	2.53	12/94	2c
Corn, frozen, whole kernel, lowest price	10 oz.	0.81	12/94	2c
Eggs, Grade A large	dozen	0.88	12/94	2c
Lettuce, iceberg	head	0.89	12/94	2c
Margarine, Blue Bonnet or Parkay cubes	lb.	0.86	12/94	2c
Milk, whole	1/2 gal.	1.29	12/94	2c
Orange juice, Minute Maid frozen	12-oz.	1.17	12/94	2c
Peaches, halves or slices, Hunt's, Del Monte, or Libby's	29-oz.	1.43	12/94	2c
Peas, sweet, Del Monte or Green Giant	15-17 oz.	0.53	12/94	2c
Potatoes, white or red	10-lb. sack	2.97	12/94	2c
Sausage, Jimmy Dean, 100% pork	lb.	2.75	12/94	2c
Shortening, vegetable, Crisco	3-lb.	2.85	12/94	2c
Soft drink, Coca Cola, ex deposit	2 lit	1.00	12/94	2c
Steak, t-bone	lb.	6.27	12/94	2c
Sugar, cane or beet	4 lbs.	1.51	12/94	2c
Tomatoes, Hunt's or Del Monte	14.5 oz.	0.76	12/94	2c
Tuna, chunk, light, oil-packed	6.125-6.5 oz.	0.86	12/94	2c
Goods and Services				
Miscellaneous goods and services, ACCRA Index		98.20	12/94	2c

Item	Per	Value	Date	Ref.
Health Care				
Health care, ACCRA Index		105.80	12/94	2c
Antibiotic ointment, Polysporin	1.5 oz.	3.47	12/94	2c
Dentist's fee, adult teeth cleaning and periodic oral exam	visit	62.33	12/94	2c
Doctor's fee, routine exam, established patient	visit	48.67	12/94	2c
Hospital care, semiprivate room	day	263.00	12/94	2c
Household Goods				
Appl. repair, service call, wash mach	min. lab. chg.	30.59	12/94	2c
Laundry detergent, Tide Ultra, Bold, or Cheer	42 oz.	3.69	12/94	2c
Tissues, facial, Kleenex brand	175	1.12	12/94	2c
Housing				
Housing, ACCRA Index		136.20	12/94	2c
House payment, principal and interest, 25% down payment	mo.	727	12/94	2c
House, 1800 sq ft, 8000 sq ft lot, new, urban, utilities	total	119438	12/94	2c
Mtge. rate, incl. points and orig. fee, 30-year conv. fixed or ARM	mo.	9.10	12/94	2c
Rent, apartment, 2 br., 1 1/2-2 baths, unfurnished, 950 sq ft, water	mo.	419	12/94	2c
Personal Goods				
Shampoo, Alberto VO5	15-oz.	1.29	12/94	2c
Toothpaste, Crest or Colgate	6-7 oz.	2.27	12/94	2c
Personal Services				
Dry cleaning, man's 2-pc. suit		6.22	12/94	2c
Haircut, man's barbershop, no styling		7.60	12/94	2c
Haircut, woman's shampoo, trim, blow-dry		19.00	12/94	2c
Restaurant Food				
Chicken, fried, thigh and drumstick		2.29	12/94	2c
Hamburger with cheese	1/4 lb.	1.99	12/94	2c
Pizza, Pizza Hut or Pizza Inn	12-13 in.	7.59	12/94	2c
Transportation				
Transportation, ACCRA Index		107.30	12/94	2c
Tire balance, computer or spin bal., front	wheel	8.15	12/94	2c
Utilities				
Utilities, ACCRA Index		115.90	12/94	2c
Electricity, 1800 sq. ft., new home	mo.	130.75	12/94	2c

Providence, RI

Item	Per	Value	Date	Ref.
Appliances				
Appliances (major), expenditures	year	145	91	81r
Average annual exp.				
Food, health care, personal goods, services	year	29496	91	81r
Charity				
Cash contributions, expenditures	year	708	91	81r
Clothing				
Apparel, men and boys, total expenditures	year	416	91	81r
Apparel, women and girls, total expenditures	year	744	91	81r
Footwear, expenditures	year	305	91	81r
Communications				
Long-distance telephone rate, day, addl. min., 1-10 mi.	min.	0.14	12/93	9s
Long-distance telephone rate, day, initial min., 1-10 mi.	min.	0.31	12/93	9s
Phone line, single, business, field visit	inst	22.81	12/93	9s
Phone line, single, business, no field visit	inst	44.61	12/93	9s
Phone line, single, residence, field visit	inst	15.30	12/93	9s
Phone line, single, residence, no field visit	inst	33.83	12/93	9s
Telephone service, expenditures	year	589	91	81r

Values are in dollars or fractions of dollars. In the column headed *Ref*, references are shown to sources. Each reference is followed by a letter. These refer to the geographical level for which data were reported: s=State, r=Region, and c=City or metro. The abbreviation *ex* is used to mean *except* or *excluding*; *exp* stands for expenditures. For other abbreviations and further explanations, please see the Introduction.

Providence, RI - continued

Item	Per	Value	Date	Ref.
Communications				
Telephone, business, addl. line, touch tone	month	2.02	10/91	25c
Telephone, business, connection charges, touch tone	inst	38.84	10/91	25c
Telephone, business, key system line, touch tone	month	40.30	10/91	25c
Telephone, business, PBX line, touch tone	month	40.33	10/91	25c
Telephone, business, single In., touch tone	month	40.30	10/91	25c
Telephone, business, touch tone, inside wiring maintenance plan	month	0.60	10/91	25c
Telephone, residential, flat rate	mo.	17.26	12/93	8c
Education				
Board, 4-year private college/university	year	2821	8/94	80s
Board, 4-year public college/university	year	2482	8/94	80s
Education, total expenditures	year	593	91	81r
Room, 4-year private college/university	year	3262	8/94	80s
Room, 4-year public college/university	year	2719	8/94	80s
Total cost, 4-year private college/university	year	19518	8/94	80s
Total cost, 4-year public college/university	year	8603	8/94	80s
Tuition, 2-year public college/university, in-state	year	1546	8/94	80s
Tuition, 4-year private college/university, in-state	year	13434	8/94	80s
Tuition, 4-year public college/university, in-state	year	3402	8/94	80s
Energy and Fuels				
Fuel oil and other fuels, expenditures	year	257	91	81r
Gas, cooking, winter, 10 therms	month	15.58	2/94	65c
Gas, cooking, winter, 30 therms	month	32.73	2/94	65c
Gas, cooking, winter, 50 therms	month	49.37	2/94	65c
Gas, heating, winter, 100 therms	month	94.22	2/94	65c
Gas, heating, winter, average use	month	184.18	2/94	65c
Gas, natural, expenditures	year	285	91	81r
Gasoline and motor oil purchased	year	867	91	81r
Gasoline, unleaded midgrade	gallon	1.32	4/93	82r
Gasoline, unleaded premium	gallon	1.40	4/93	82r
Gasoline, unleaded regular	gallon	1.19	4/93	82r
Entertainment				
Entertainment, total expenditures	year	1331	91	81r
Fees and admissions, expenditures	year	398	91	81r
Pets, toys, playground equipment, expenditures	year	270	91	81r
Reading, expenditures	year	171	91	81r
Televisions, radios, and sound equipment, expenditures	year	429	91	81r
Funerals				
Burial, immediate, container provided by funeral home		1507.89	1/95	54r
Cards, acknowledgment		18.10	1/95	54r
Casket, minimum alternative		133.03	1/95	54r
Cosmetology, hair care, etc.		114.12	1/95	54r
Cremation, direct, container provided by funeral home		1309.19	1/95	54r
Embalming		320.97	1/95	54r
Funeral, funeral home		327.61	1/95	54r
Funeral, other facility		314.81	1/95	54r
Graveside service		286.11	1/95	54r
Hearse, local		158.95	1/95	54r
Limousine, local		149.45	1/95	54r
Memorial service		315.94	1/95	54r
Service charge, professional, nondeclinable		1148.43	1/95	54r
Visitation and viewing		249.66	1/95	54r
Groceries				
Apples, Red Delicious	lb.	0.78	12/94	82r
Bacon, sliced	lb.	2.24	12/94	82r
Bananas	lb.	0.49	12/94	82r
Beef purchases	year	226	91	81r
Beverage purchases, alcoholic	year	332	91	81r
Beverage purchases, nonalcoholic	year	213	91	81r
Bread, white, pan	lb.	0.80	12/94	82r

Providence, RI - continued

Item	Per	Value	Date	Ref.
Groceries - continued				
Butter, salted, Grade AA, stick	lb.	1.67	12/94	82r
Carrots, short trimmed and topped	lb.	0.51	12/94	82r
Cereals and bakery products purchases	year	407	91	81r
Cereals and cereals products purchases	year	132	91	81r
Chicken breast, bone-in	lb.	2.22	12/94	82r
Chicken, fresh, whole	lb.	1.05	12/94	82r
Chuck roast, USDA choice, boneless	lb.	2.74	12/94	82r
Coffee, 100%, ground roast, all sizes	lb.	4.61	12/94	82r
Dairy products (other) purchases	year	161	91	81r
Eggs, Grade A large	dozen	1.12	12/94	82r
Fish and seafood purchases	year	112	91	81r
Food purchases, food eaten at home	year	2599	91	81r
Foods purchased away from home, not prepared by consumer	year	2024	91	81r
Fruits and vegetables purchases	year	444	91	81r
Grapefruit	lb.	0.44	12/94	82r
Grapes, Thompson seedless	lb.	2.24	12/94	82r
Ground chuck, 100% beef	lb.	1.67	12/94	82r
Ice cream, prepackaged, bulk, regular	1/2 gal.	2.93	12/94	82r
Lemons	lb.	1.06	12/94	82r
Lettuce, iceberg	lb.	0.92	12/94	82r
Meats, poultry, fish, and eggs purchases	year	751	91	81r
Milk and cream (fresh) purchases	year	152	91	81r
Orange juice, frozen concentrate 12-oz. can	16 oz.	1.92	12/94	82r
Oranges, Navel	lb.	0.56	12/94	82r
Pork chops, center cut, bone-in	lb.	3.09	12/94	82r
Pork purchases	year	130	91	81r
Potatoes, white	lb.	0.37	12/94	82r
Rib roast, USDA choice, bone-in	lb.	4.98	12/94	82r
Round roast, USDA choice, boneless	lb.	2.93	12/94	82r
Shortening, vegetable oil blends	lb.	1.03	12/94	82r
Spaghetti and macaroni	lb.	0.84	12/94	82r
Steak, round, USDA choice, boneless	lb.	3.48	12/94	82r
Steak, sirloin, USDA choice, bone-in	lb.	3.38	12/94	82r
Steak, sirloin, USDA choice, boneless	lb.	4.81	12/94	82r
Sugar and other sweets, eaten at home, expenditures	year	89	91	81r
Sugar, white, all sizes	lb.	0.46	12/94	82r
Tobacco products and smoking supplies, total expenditures	year	279	91	81r
Tomatoes, field grown	lb.	1.56	12/94	82r
Tuna, chunk, light	lb.	2.09	12/94	82r
Health Care				
Childbirth, Cesarean delivery, hospital charge	birth	6334.00	12/91	69r
Childbirth, Cesarean delivery, physician charge	birth	2234.00	12/91	69r
Childbirth, normal delivery, hospital charge	birth	3225.00	12/91	69r
Childbirth, normal delivery, physician charge	birth	1623.00	12/91	69r
Drugs, expenditures	year	205	91	81r
Health care, total expenditures	year	1396	91	81r
Health insurance expenditures	year	553	91	81r
Insurance premium, family medical care	month	365.49	1/95	41s
Medical services expenditures	year	559	91	81r
Medical supplies expenditures	year	80	91	81r
Household Goods				
Floor coverings, expenditures	year	158	91	81r
Furniture, expenditures	year	341	91	81r
Household equipment, misc. expenditures	year	363	91	81r
Household expenditures, miscellaneous	year	194	91	81r
Household furnishings and equipment, expenditures	year	1158	91	81r
Household operations expenditures	year	378	91	81r
Household textiles, expenditures	year	88	91	81r
Housekeeping supplies, expenditures	year	426	91	81r
Laundry and cleaning supplies, expenditures	year	122	91	81r
Postage and stationery, expenditures	year	134	91	81r

Values are in dollars or fractions of dollars. In the column headed *Ref*, references are shown to sources. Each reference is followed by a letter. These refer to the geographical level for which data were reported: s = State, r = Region, and c = City or metro. The abbreviation *ex* is used to mean *except* or *excluding*; *exp* stands for expenditures. For other abbreviations and further explanations, please see the Introduction.

Providence, RI - continued

Item	Per	Value	Date	Ref.
Housing				
Add garage/carport		11,614	3/95	74r
Add room(s)		16,816	3/95	74r
Apartment condominium or co-op, median	unit	96700	12/94	62r
Dwellings (owned), expenditures	year	3305	91	81r
Enclose porch/patio/breezeway		2,980	3/95	74r
Finish room in basement/attic		4,330	3/95	74r
Home, existing, single-family, median	unit	161600	12/94	62r
Home, existing, single-family, median	unit	115.20	12/94	62c
Maintenance, repairs, insurance, and other housing expenditures	year	569	91	81r
Mortgage interest and charges expenditures	year	1852	91	81r
Princ. & int., mortgage, median-price exist. sing.-family home	mo.	765	12/94	62r
Property taxes expenditures	year	884	91	81r
Redesign, restructure more than half of home's interior		2,750	3/95	74r
Rental units expenditures	year	1832	91	81r
Insurance and Pensions				
Auto insurance, private passenger	year	1034.46	12/94	71s
Insurance and pensions, personal, expenditures	year	2690	91	81r
Insurance, life and other personal, expenditures	year	341	91	81r
Pensions and Social Security, expenditures	year	2349	91	81r
Legal Assistance				
Estate planning, law-firm partner	hr.	375.00	10/93	12r
Legal work, law firm associate	hour	78		10r
Legal work, law firm partner	hour	183		10r
Personal Services				
Personal services expenditures	year	184	91	81r
Restaurant Food				
Dining expenditures, family	week	34.26	94	73r
Taxes				
Tax rate, residential property, month	$100	2.55	1/92	79c
Taxes, Federal income, expenditures	year	2409	91	81r
Taxes, personal, expenditures	year	3094	91	81r
Taxes, State and local income, expenditures	year	620	91	81r
Transportation				
Bus fare, one-way	trip	0.85	12/95	1c
Cars and trucks purchased, new	year	1170	91	81r
Cars and trucks purchased, used	year	739	91	81r
Driver's learning permit fee	perm	5.00	1/94	84s
Driver's license fee	orig	12.00	1/94	84s
Driver's license reinstatement fee, min.	susp	25.00	1/94	85s
Driver's license renewal fee	renew	30.00	1/94	84s
Driving expenses	mile	48.50	5/95	86c
Identification card, nondriver	card	1.00	1/94	83s
Motorcycle learning permit fee	perm	5.00	1/94	84s
Motorcycle license fee	orig	12.00	1/94	84s
Motorcycle license renewal fee	renew	30.00	1/94	84s
Public transportation expenditures	year	430	91	81r
Transportation expenditures, total	year	4810	91	81r
Vehicle finance charges	year	238	91	81r
Vehicle insurance expenditures	year	630	91	81r
Vehicle maintenance and repairs expenditures	year	532	91	81r
Vehicle purchases	year	1920	91	81r
Vehicle rental, leases, licenses, etc. expenditures	year	193	91	81r
Vehicles purchased, other than cars and trucks	year	11	91	81r
Utilities				
Electricity expenditures	year	695	91	81r
Electricity, summer, 250 KWh	month	30.23	8/93	64c
Electricity, summer, 500 KWh	month	57.95	8/93	64c
Electricity, summer, 750 KWh	month	85.68	8/93	64c
Electricity, summer, 1000 KWh	month	113.40	8/93	64c

Providence, RI - continued

Item	Per	Value	Date	Ref.
Utilities - continued				
Utilities, fuels, and public services, total expenditures	year	1981	91	81r
Water and other public services, expenditures	year	154	91	81r
Weddings				
Bridal attendants' gowns	event	750	10/93	76r
Bridal gown	event	852	10/93	76r
Bridal headpiece and veil	event	167	10/93	76r
Bride's wedding band	event	708	10/93	76r
Clergy	event	224	10/93	76r
Engagement ring	event	2756	10/93	76r
Flowers	event	863	10/93	76r
Formal wear for groom	event	106	10/93	76r
Groom's attendants' formal wear	event	530	10/93	76r
Groom's wedding band	event	402	10/93	76r
Music	event	600	10/93	76r
Photography	event	1088	10/93	76r
Shoes for bride	event	50	10/93	76r
Videography	event	483	10/93	76r
Wedding invitations and announcements	event	342	10/93	76r
Wedding reception	event	7000	10/93	76r

Provo-Orem, UT

Item	Per	Value	Date	Ref.
Composite, ACCRA index		96.80	12/94	2c
Alcoholic Beverages				
Beer, Miller Lite, Bud, 12-oz., ex deposit	6	3.93	12/94	2c
J & B Scotch	750-ml.	19.95	12/94	2c
Wine, Gallo Chablis blanc	1.5-lit	4.95	12/94	2c
Appliances				
Appliances (major), expenditures	year	160	91	81r
Average annual exp.				
Food, health care, personal goods, services	year	32461	91	81r
Charity				
Cash contributions, expenditures	year	975	91	81r
Clothing				
Apparel, men and boys, total expenditures	year	467	91	81r
Apparel, women and girls, total expenditures	year	737	91	81r
Footwear, expenditures	year	270	91	81r
Jeans, man's denim		27.49	12/94	2c
Shirt, man's dress shirt		29.23	12/94	2c
Undervest, boy's size 10-14, cotton	3	3.84	12/94	2c
Communications				
Long-distance telephone rate, day, addl. min., 1-10 mi.	min.	0.08	12/93	9s
Long-distance telephone rate, day, initial min., 1-10 mi.	min.	0.11	12/93	9s
Newspaper subscription, dly. and Sun. delivery	month	8.25	12/94	2c
Phone line, single, business, field visit	inst	50.00	12/93	9s
Phone line, single, business, no field visit	inst	50.00	12/93	9s
Phone line, single, residence, field visit	inst	18.75	12/93	9s
Phone line, single, residence, no field visit	inst	18.75	12/93	9s
Telephone bill, family of four	month	17.20	12/94	2c
Telephone service, expenditures	year	611	91	81r
Telephone, residential, flat rate	mo.	7.98	12/93	8c
Education				
Board, 4-year private college/university	year	2817	8/94	80s
Board, 4-year public college/university	year	1981	8/94	80s
Education, total expenditures	year	375	91	81r
Room, 4-year private college/university	year	1300	8/94	80s
Room, 4-year public college/university	year	1282	8/94	80s
Total cost, 4-year private college/university	year	6661	8/94	80s
Total cost, 4-year public college/university	year	5227	8/94	80s
Tuition, 2-year public college/university, in-state	year	1315	8/94	80s

Values are in dollars or fractions of dollars. In the column headed *Ref*, references are shown to sources. Each reference is followed by a letter. These refer to the geographical level for which data were reported: s=State, r=Region, and c=City or metro. The abbreviation *ex* is used to mean *except* or *excluding*; *exp* stands for expenditures. For other abbreviations and further explanations, please see the Introduction.

Provo-Orem, UT - continued

Item	Per	Value	Date	Ref.
Education				
Tuition, 4-year private college/university, in-state	year	2545	8/94	80s
Tuition, 4-year public college/university, in-state	year	1964	8/94	80s
Energy and Fuels				
Energy, combined forms, 1800 sq. ft.	mo.	89.48	12/94	2c
Energy, exc. electricity, 1800 sq. ft.	mo.	42.97	12/94	2c
Fuel oil and other fuels, expenditures	year	33	91	81r
Gas, natural, expenditures	year	212	91	81r
Gas, reg unlead, taxes inc., cash, self-service	gal	1.18	12/94	2c
Gasoline and motor oil purchased	year	1115	91	81r
Gasoline, unleaded midgrade	gallon	1.36	4/93	82r
Gasoline, unleaded premium	gallon	1.43	4/93	82r
Gasoline, unleaded regular	gallon	1.23	4/93	82r
Entertainment				
Bowling, evening rate	game	2.05	12/94	2c
Concert ticket, Pearl Jam group	perf	20.00	94	50r
Entertainment, total expenditures	year	1853	91	81r
Fees and admissions, expenditures	year	482	91	81r
Monopoly game, Parker Brothers', No. 9	game	10.24	12/94	2c
Movie	adm	5.33	12/94	2c
Pets, toys, playground equipment, expenditures	year	299	91	81r
Reading, expenditures	year	164	91	81r
Televisions, radios, and sound equipment, expenditures	year	528	91	81r
Tennis balls, yellow, Wilson or Penn, 3	can	2.63	12/94	2c
Funerals				
Burial, immediate, container provided by funeral home		1360.49	1/95	54r
Cards, acknowledgment		11.24	1/95	54r
Casket, minimum alternative		232.73	1/95	54r
Cosmetology, hair care, etc.		114.13	1/95	54r
Cremation, direct, container provided by funeral home		1027.08	1/95	54r
Embalming		286.24	1/95	54r
Funeral, funeral home		315.60	1/95	54r
Funeral, other facility		303.08	1/95	54r
Graveside service		423.83	1/95	54r
Hearse, local		133.12	1/95	54r
Limousine, local		99.10	1/95	54r
Memorial service		442.57	1/95	54r
Service charge, professional, nondeclinable		840.16	1/95	54r
Visitation and viewing		168.50	1/95	54r
Groceries				
Groceries, ACCRA Index		95.10	12/94	2c
Apples, Red Delicious	lb.	0.72	12/94	82r
Baby food, strained vegetables, lowest price	4-4.5 oz.	0.37	12/94	2c
Bacon, sliced	lb.	1.73	12/94	82r
Bananas	lb.	0.33	12/94	2c
Bananas	lb.	0.52	12/94	82r
Beef or hamburger, ground	lb.	1.21	12/94	2c
Beef purchases	year	241	91	81r
Beverage purchases, alcoholic	year	328	91	81r
Beverage purchases, nonalcoholic	year	234	91	81r
Bologna, all beef or mixed	lb.	2.33	12/94	82r
Bread, white	24-oz.	0.72	12/94	2c
Bread, white, pan	lb.	0.81	12/94	82r
Carrots, short trimmed and topped	lb.	0.43	12/94	82r
Cereals and bakery products purchases	year	392	91	81r
Cereals and cereals products purchases	year	139	91	81r
Cheese, Kraft grated Parmesan	8-oz.	3.44	12/94	2c
Chicken breast, bone-in	lb.	2.04	12/94	82r
Chicken, fresh, whole	lb.	0.95	12/94	82r
Chicken, whole fryer	lb.	0.83	12/94	2c
Cigarettes, Winston, Kings	carton	15.89	12/94	2c
Coffee, 100%, ground roast, all sizes	lb.	4.48	12/94	82r
Coffee, vacuum-packed	13 oz.	3.71	12/94	2c

Provo-Orem, UT - continued

Item	Per	Value	Date	Ref.
Groceries - continued				
Corn Flakes, Kellogg's or Post Toasties	18 oz.	2.25	12/94	2c
Corn, frozen, whole kernel, lowest price	10 oz.	0.73	12/94	2c
Dairy products (other) purchases	year	182	91	81r
Eggs, Grade A large	dozen	0.70	12/94	2c
Fish and seafood purchases	year	94	91	81r
Flour, white, all purpose	lb.	0.21	12/94	82r
Food purchases, food eaten at home	year	2749	91	81r
Foods purchased away from home, not prepared by consumer	year	1909	91	81r
Fruits and vegetables purchases	year	459	91	81r
Grapefruit	lb.	0.56	12/94	82r
Ground beef, 100% beef	lb.	1.31	12/94	82r
Ham, boneless, exc. canned	lb.	2.46	12/94	82r
Ice cream, prepackaged, bulk, regular	1/2 gal.	2.57	12/94	82r
Lemons	lb.	1.00	12/94	82r
Lettuce, iceberg	lb.	0.93	12/94	82r
Lettuce, iceberg	head	0.60	12/94	2c
Margarine, Blue Bonnet or Parkay cubes	lb.	0.52	12/94	2c
Meats, poultry, fish, and eggs purchases	year	700	91	81r
Milk and cream (fresh) purchases	year	155	91	81r
Milk, whole	1/2 gal.	1.35	12/94	2c
Orange juice, frozen concentrate 12-oz. can	16 oz.	1.52	12/94	82r
Orange juice, Minute Maid frozen	12-oz.	1.22	12/94	2c
Oranges, Navel	lb.	0.56	12/94	82r
Peaches, halves or slices, Hunt's, Del Monte, or Libby's	29-oz.	1.29	12/94	2c
Peas, sweet, Del Monte or Green Giant	15-17 oz.	0.51	12/94	2c
Pork chops, center cut, bone-in	lb.	3.30	12/94	82r
Pork purchases	year	122	91	81r
Potato chips	16-oz.	3.03	12/94	82r
Potatoes, frozen, French fried	lb.	0.77	12/94	82r
Potatoes, white	lb.	0.35	12/94	82r
Potatoes, white or red	10-lb. sack	1.14	12/94	2c
Rice, white, long grain, uncooked	lb.	0.54	12/94	82r
Round roast, USDA choice, boneless	lb.	2.92	12/94	82r
Sausage, Jimmy Dean, 100% pork	lb.	2.89	12/94	2c
Shortening, vegetable oil blends	lb.	0.80	12/94	82r
Shortening, vegetable, Crisco	3-lb.	2.19	12/94	2c
Soft drink, Coca Cola, ex deposit	2 lit	1.04	12/94	2c
Spaghetti and macaroni	lb.	1.02	12/94	82r
Steak, round, graded & ungraded, exc. USDA prime & choice	lb.	3.13	12/94	82r
Steak, sirloin, USDA choice, boneless	lb.	4.07	12/94	82r
Steak, t-bone	lb.	3.91	12/94	2c
Sugar and other sweets, eaten at home, expenditures	year	105	91	81r
Sugar, cane or beet	4 lbs.	1.29	12/94	2c
Sugar, white, all sizes	lb.	0.38	12/94	82r
Tobacco products and smoking supplies, total expenditures	year	221	91	81r
Tomatoes, field grown	lb.	1.45	12/94	82r
Tomatoes, Hunt's or Del Monte	14.5 oz.	0.65	12/94	2c
Tuna, chunk, light	lb.	2.18	12/94	82r
Tuna, chunk, light, oil-packed	6.125-6.5 oz.	0.69	12/94	2c
Goods and Services				
Miscellaneous goods and services, ACCRA Index		96.00	12/94	2c
Health Care				
Health care, ACCRA Index		102.10	12/94	2c
Antibiotic ointment, Polysporin	1.5 oz.	4.49	12/94	2c
Childbirth, Cesarean delivery, hospital charge	birth	6059.00	12/91	69r
Childbirth, Cesarean delivery, physician charge	birth	2248.00	12/91	69r
Childbirth, normal delivery, hospital charge	birth	3006.00	12/91	69r

Values are in dollars or fractions of dollars. In the column headed *Ref*, references are shown to sources. Each reference is followed by a letter. These refer to the geographical level for which data were reported: s=State, r=Region, and c=City or metro. The abbreviation *ex* is used to mean *except* or *excluding*; *exp* stands for *expenditures*. For other abbreviations and further explanations, please see the Introduction.

Provo-Orem, UT - continued

Item	Per	Value	Date	Ref.
Health Care				
Childbirth, normal delivery, physician charge	birth	1634.00	12/91	69r
Dentist's fee, adult teeth cleaning and periodic oral exam	visit	48.00	12/94	2c
Doctor's fee, routine exam, established patient	visit	42.00	12/94	2c
Drugs, expenditures	year	230	91	81r
Health care, total expenditures	year	1544	91	81r
Health insurance expenditures	year	558	91	81r
Hospital care, semiprivate room	day	435.80	12/94	2c
Insurance premium, family medical care	month	378.32	1/95	41s
Medical services expenditures	year	676	91	81r
Medical supplies expenditures	year	80	91	81r
Surgery, open-heart	proc	37818.00	1/93	14r
Household Goods				
Appl. repair, service call, wash mach	min. lab. chg.	32.50	12/94	2c
Floor coverings, expenditures	year	79	91	81r
Furniture, expenditures	year	352	91	81r
Household equipment, misc. expenditures	year	614	91	81r
Household expenditures, miscellaneous	year	294	91	81r
Household furnishings and equipment, expenditures	year	1416	91	81r
Household operations expenditures	year	580	91	81r
Household textiles, expenditures	year	113	91	81r
Housekeeping supplies, expenditures	year	447	91	81r
Laundry and cleaning supplies, expenditures	year	114	91	81r
Laundry detergent, Tide Ultra, Bold, or Cheer	42 oz.	3.64	12/94	2c
Postage and stationery, expenditures	year	145	91	81r
Tissues, facial, Kleenex brand	175	1.02	12/94	2c
Housing				
Housing, ACCRA Index		98.90	12/94	2c
Add garage/carport		6,422	3/95	74r
Add room(s)		26,583	3/95	74r
Apartment condominium or co-op, median	unit	105300	12/94	62r
Dwellings (owned), expenditures	year	3932	91	81r
Enclose porch/patio/breezeway		5,382	3/95	74r
Finish room in basement/attic		3,911	3/95	74r
Home, existing, single-family, median	unit	178600	12/94	62r
House payment, principal and interest, 25% down payment	mo.	762	12/94	2c
House, 1800 sq ft, 8000 sq ft lot, new, urban, utilities	total	121000	12/94	2c
Maintenance, repairs, insurance, and other housing expenditures	year	591	91	81r
Mortgage interest and charges expenditures	year	2747	91	81r
Mtge. rate, incl. points and orig. fee, 30-year conv. fixed or ARM	mo.	9.48	12/94	2c
Princ. & int., mortgage, median-price exist. sing.-family home	mo.	845	12/94	62r
Property taxes expenditures	year	594	91	81r
Redesign, restructure more than half of home's interior		5,467	3/95	74r
Rent, apartment, 2 br., 1 1/2-2 baths, unfurnished, 950 sq ft, water	mo.	512	12/94	2c
Rental units expenditures	year	2077	91	81r
Insurance and Pensions				
Auto insurance, private passenger	year	607.42	12/94	71s
Insurance and pensions, personal, expenditures	year	3042	91	81r
Insurance, life and other personal, expenditures	year	298	91	81r
Pensions and Social Security, expenditures	year	2744	91	81r
Legal Assistance				
Legal work, law firm associate	hour	91		10r
Legal work, law firm partner	hour	151		10r

Provo-Orem, UT - continued

Item	Per	Value	Date	Ref.
Personal Goods				
Shampoo, Alberto VO5	15-oz.	1.22	12/94	2c
Toothpaste, Crest or Colgate	6-7 oz.	2.22	12/94	2c
Personal Services				
Dry cleaning, man's 2-pc. suit		5.83	12/94	2c
Haircut, man's barbershop, no styling		8.33	12/94	2c
Haircut, woman's shampoo, trim, blow-dry		15.00	12/94	2c
Personal services expenditures	year	286	91	81r
Restaurant Food				
Chicken, fried, thigh and drumstick		2.00	12/94	2c
Dining expenditures, family	week	32.25	94	73r
Hamburger with cheese	1/4 lb.	1.99	12/94	2c
Pizza, Pizza Hut or Pizza Inn	12-13 in.	7.49	12/94	2c
Taxes				
Taxes, Federal income, expenditures	year	2946	91	81r
Taxes, personal, expenditures	year	3791	91	81r
Taxes, State and local income, expenditures	year	791	91	81r
Transportation				
Transportation, ACCRA Index		106.80	12/94	2c
Bus fare, one-way	trip	0.65	12/95	1c
Cars and trucks purchased, new	year	1231	91	81r
Cars and trucks purchased, used	year	915	91	81r
Driver's learning permit fee	perm	20.00	1/94	84s
Driver's license fee	orig	0.00	1/94	84s
Driver's license fee, duplicate	lic	10.00	1/94	84s
Driver's license renewal fee	renew	15.00	1/94	84s
Identification card, nondriver	card	5.00	1/94	83s
Motorcycle license fee	orig	0.00	1/94	84s
Public transportation expenditures	year	375	91	81r
Tire balance, computer or spin bal., front	wheel	7.42	12/94	2c
Transportation expenditures, total	year	5527	91	81r
Vehicle finance charges	year	287	91	81r
Vehicle insurance expenditures	year	624	91	81r
Vehicle maintenance and repairs expenditures	year	695	91	81r
Vehicle purchases	year	2174	91	81r
Vehicle rental, leases, licenses, etc. expenditures	year	257	91	81r
Vehicles purchased, other than cars and trucks	year	28	91	81r
Utilities				
Utilities, ACCRA Index		80.90	12/94	2c
Electricity expenditures	year	616	91	81r
Electricity, (part.), other, 1800 sq. ft., new home	mo.	46.51	12/94	2c
Utilities, fuels, and public services, total expenditures	year	1681	91	81r
Water and other public services, expenditures	year	209	91	81r
Weddings				
Bridal attendants' gowns	event	750	10/93	76r
Bridal gown	event	852	10/93	76r
Bridal headpiece and veil	event	167	10/93	76r
Bride's wedding band	event	708	10/93	76r
Clergy	event	224	10/93	76r
Engagement ring	event	2756	10/93	76r
Flowers	event	863	10/93	76r
Formal wear for groom	event	106	10/93	76r
Groom's attendants' formal wear	event	530	10/93	76r
Groom's wedding band	event	402	10/93	76r
Music	event	600	10/93	76r
Photography	event	1088	10/93	76r
Shoes for bride	event	50	10/93	76r
Videography	event	483	10/93	76r
Wedding invitations and announcements	event	342	10/93	76r
Wedding reception	event	7000	10/93	76r

Values are in dollars or fractions of dollars. In the column headed *Ref*, references are shown to sources. Each reference is followed by a letter. These refer to the geographical level for which data were reported: s=State, r=Region, and c=City or metro. The abbreviation *ex* is used to mean *except* or *excluding*; *exp* stands for expenditures. For other abbreviations and further explanations, please see the Introduction.

Pryor Creek, OK

Item	Per	Value	Date	Ref.
Composite, ACCRA index		89.90	12/94	2c
Alcoholic Beverages				
Beer, Miller Lite, Bud, 12-oz., ex deposit	6	4.18	12/94	2c
J & B Scotch	750-ml.	15.42	12/94	2c
Wine, Gallo Chablis blanc	1.5-lit	5.78	12/94	2c
Clothing				
Jeans, man's denim		23.99	12/94	2c
Shirt, man's dress shirt		27.99	12/94	2c
Undervest, boy's size 10-14, cotton	3	3.56	12/94	2c
Communications				
Newspaper subscription, dly. and Sun. delivery	month	8.25	12/94	2c
Telephone bill, family of four	month	19.91	12/94	2c
Telephone, residential, flat rate	mo.	10.87	12/93	8c
Energy and Fuels				
Energy, combined forms, 1800 sq. ft.	mo.	89.39	12/94	2c
Energy, exc. electricity, 1800 sq. ft.	mo.	30.62	12/94	2c
Gas, reg unlead, taxes inc., cash, self-service	gal	1.01	12/94	2c
Entertainment				
Bowling, evening rate	game	2.25	12/94	2c
Monopoly game, Parker Brothers', No. 9	game	10.74	12/94	2c
Movie	adm	5.96	12/94	2c
Tennis balls, yellow, Wilson or Penn, 3	can	1.88	12/94	2c
Groceries				
Groceries, ACCRA Index		96.80	12/94	2c
Baby food, strained vegetables, lowest price	4-4.5 oz.	0.39	12/94	2c
Bananas	lb.	0.39	12/94	2c
Beef or hamburger, ground	lb.	1.35	12/94	2c
Bread, white	24-oz.	0.57	12/94	2c
Cheese, Kraft grated Parmesan	8-oz.	3.65	12/94	2c
Chicken, whole fryer	lb.	0.78	12/94	2c
Cigarettes, Winston, Kings	carton	14.84	12/94	2c
Coffee, vacuum-packed	13 oz.	3.52	12/94	2c
Corn Flakes, Kellogg's or Post Toasties	18 oz.	2.44	12/94	2c
Corn, frozen, whole kernel, lowest price	10 oz.	0.76	12/94	2c
Eggs, Grade A large	dozen	0.69	12/94	2c
Lettuce, iceberg	head	0.85	12/94	2c
Margarine, Blue Bonnet or Parkay cubes	lb.	0.63	12/94	2c
Milk, whole	1/2 gal.	1.23	12/94	2c
Orange juice, Minute Maid frozen	12-oz.	1.21	12/94	2c
Peaches, halves or slices, Hunt's, Del Monte, or Libby's	29-oz.	1.35	12/94	2c
Peas, sweet, Del Monte or Green Giant	15-17 oz.	0.54	12/94	2c
Potatoes, white or red	10-lb. sack	2.12	12/94	2c
Sausage, Jimmy Dean, 100% pork	lb.	2.56	12/94	2c
Shortening, vegetable, Crisco	3-lb.	2.65	12/94	2c
Soft drink, Coca Cola, ex deposit	2 lit	1.03	12/94	2c
Steak, t-bone	lb.	5.15	12/94	2c
Sugar, cane or beet	4 lbs.	1.55	12/94	2c
Tomatoes, Hunt's or Del Monte	14.5 oz.	0.78	12/94	2c
Tuna, chunk, light, oil-packed	6.125-6.5 oz.	0.74	12/94	2c
Goods and Services				
Miscellaneous goods and services, ACCRA Index		95.30	12/94	2c
Health Care				
Health care, ACCRA Index		88.90	12/94	2c
Antibiotic ointment, Polysporin	1.5 oz.	3.93	12/94	2c
Dentist's fee, adult teeth cleaning and periodic oral exam	visit	53.20	12/94	2c
Doctor's fee, routine exam, established patient	visit	34.40	12/94	2c

Pryor Creek, OK - continued

Item	Per	Value	Date	Ref.
Health Care - continued				
Hospital care, semiprivate room	day	265.00	12/94	2c
Household Goods				
Appl. repair, service call, wash mach	min. lab. chg.	32.00	12/94	2c
Laundry detergent, Tide Ultra, Bold, or Cheer	42 oz.	3.01	12/94	2c
Tissues, facial, Kleenex brand	175	1.04	12/94	2c
Housing				
Housing, ACCRA Index		83.40	12/94	2c
House payment, principal and interest, 25% down payment	mo.	640	12/94	2c
House, 1800 sq ft, 8000 sq ft lot, new, urban, utilities	total	101525	12/94	2c
Mtge. rate, incl. points and orig. fee, 30-year conv. fixed or ARM	mo.	9.49	12/94	2c
Personal Goods				
Shampoo, Alberto VO5	15-oz.	1.38	12/94	2c
Toothpaste, Crest or Colgate	6-7 oz.	1.90	12/94	2c
Personal Services				
Dry cleaning, man's 2-pc. suit		5.67	12/94	2c
Haircut, man's barbershop, no styling		6.65	12/94	2c
Haircut, woman's shampoo, trim, blow-dry		18.80	12/94	2c
Restaurant Food				
Chicken, fried, thigh and drumstick		2.59	12/94	2c
Hamburger with cheese	1/4 lb.	1.99	12/94	2c
Pizza, Pizza Hut or Pizza Inn	12-13 in.	7.90	12/94	2c
Transportation				
Transportation, ACCRA Index		85.40	12/94	2c
Tire balance, computer or spin bal., front	wheel	5.40	12/94	2c
Utilities				
Utilities, ACCRA Index		82.70	12/94	2c
Electricity, (part.), other, 1800 sq. ft., new home	mo.	58.77	12/94	2c

Pueblo, CO

Item	Per	Value	Date	Ref.
Composite, ACCRA index		91.40	12/94	2c
Alcoholic Beverages				
Beer, Miller Lite, Bud, 12-oz., ex deposit	6	4.03	12/94	2c
J & B Scotch	750-ml.	17.07	12/94	2c
Wine, Gallo Chablis blanc	1.5-lit	4.18	12/94	2c
Appliances				
Appliances (major), expenditures	year	160	91	81r
Average annual exp.				
Food, health care, personal goods, services	year	32461	91	81r
Charity				
Cash contributions, expenditures	year	975	91	81r
Clothing				
Apparel, men and boys, total expenditures	year	467	91	81r
Apparel, women and girls, total expenditures	year	737	91	81r
Footwear, expenditures	year	270	91	81r
Jeans, man's denim		27.99	12/94	2c
Shirt, man's dress shirt		19.99	12/94	2c
Undervest, boy's size 10-14, cotton	3	4.61	12/94	2c
Communications				
Long-distance telephone rate, day, addl. min., 1-10 mi.	min.	0.13	12/93	9s
Long-distance telephone rate, day, initial min., 1-10 mi.	min.	0.17	12/93	9s
Newspaper subscription, dly. and Sun. delivery	month	8.00	12/94	2c

Values are in dollars or fractions of dollars. In the column headed *Ref*, references are shown to sources. Each reference is followed by a letter. These refer to the geographical level for which data were reported: s = State, r = Region, and c = City or metro. The abbreviation *ex* is used to mean *except* or *excluding*; *exp* stands for expenditures. For other abbreviations and further explanations, please see the Introduction.

Pueblo, CO - continued

Item	Per	Value	Date	Ref.
Communications				
Phone line, single, business, field visit	inst	70.00	12/93	9s
Phone line, single, business, no field visit	inst	70.00	12/93	9s
Phone line, single, residence, field visit	inst	35.00	12/93	9s
Phone line, single, residence, no field visit	inst	35.00	12/93	9s
Telephone bill, family of four	month	17.35	12/94	2c
Telephone service, expenditures	year	611	91	81r
Telephone, residential, flat rate	mo.	14.68	12/93	8c
Education				
Board, 4-year private college/university	year	2468	8/94	80s
Board, 4-year public college/university	year	2148	8/94	80s
Education, total expenditures	year	375	91	81r
Room, 4-year private college/university	year	2492	8/94	80s
Room, 4-year public college/university	year	1772	8/94	80s
Total cost, 4-year private college/university	year	16064	8/94	80s
Total cost, 4-year public college/university	year	6183	8/94	80s
Tuition, 2-year public college/university, in-state	year	1193	8/94	80s
Tuition, 4-year private college/university, in-state	year	11104	8/94	80s
Tuition, 4-year public college/university, in-state	year	2262	8/94	80s
Energy and Fuels				
Energy, combined forms, 1800 sq. ft.	mo.	84.41	12/94	2c
Energy, exc. electricity, 1800 sq. ft.	mo.	35.28	12/94	2c
Fuel oil and other fuels, expenditures	year	33	91	81r
Gas, natural, expenditures	year	212	91	81r
Gas, reg unlead, taxes inc., cash, self-service	gal	1.16	12/94	2c
Gasoline and motor oil purchased	year	1115	91	81r
Gasoline, unleaded midgrade	gallon	1.36	4/93	82r
Gasoline, unleaded premium	gallon	1.43	4/93	82r
Gasoline, unleaded regular	gallon	1.23	4/93	82r
Entertainment				
Bowling, evening rate	game	1.75	12/94	2c
Concert ticket, Pearl Jam group	perf	20.00	94	50r
Entertainment, total expenditures	year	1853	91	81r
Fees and admissions, expenditures	year	482	91	81r
Monopoly game, Parker Brothers', No. 9	game	11.69	12/94	2c
Movie	adm	5.25	12/94	2c
Pets, toys, playground equipment, expenditures	year	299	91	81r
Reading, expenditures	year	164	91	81r
Televisions, radios, and sound equipment, expenditures	year	528	91	81r
Tennis balls, yellow, Wilson or Penn, 3	can	2.18	12/94	2c
Funerals				
Burial, immediate, container provided by funeral home		1360.49	1/95	54r
Cards, acknowledgment		11.24	1/95	54r
Casket, minimum alternative		232.73	1/95	54r
Cosmetology, hair care, etc.		114.13	1/95	54r
Cremation, direct, container provided by funeral home		1027.08	1/95	54r
Embalming		286.24	1/95	54r
Funeral, funeral home		315.60	1/95	54r
Funeral, other facility		303.08	1/95	54r
Graveside service		423.83	1/95	54r
Hearse, local		133.12	1/95	54r
Limousine, local		99.10	1/95	54r
Memorial service		442.57	1/95	54r
Service charge, professional, nondeclinable		840.16	1/95	54r
Visitation and viewing		168.50	1/95	54r
Groceries				
Groceries, ACCRA Index		108.90	12/94	2c
Apples, Red Delicious	lb.	0.72	12/94	82r
Baby food, strained vegetables, lowest price	4-4.5 oz.	0.37	12/94	2c
Bacon, sliced	lb.	1.73	12/94	82r
Bananas	lb.	0.55	12/94	2c

Pueblo, CO - continued

Item	Per	Value	Date	Ref.
Groceries - continued				
Bananas	lb.	0.52	12/94	82r
Beef or hamburger, ground	lb.	1.21	12/94	2c
Beef purchases	year	241	91	81r
Beverage purchases, alcoholic	year	328	91	81r
Beverage purchases, nonalcoholic	year	234	91	81r
Bologna, all beef or mixed	lb.	2.33	12/94	82r
Bread, white	24-oz.	0.80	12/94	2c
Bread, white, pan	lb.	0.81	12/94	82r
Carrots, short trimmed and topped	lb.	0.43	12/94	82r
Cereals and bakery products purchases	year	392	91	81r
Cereals and cereals products purchases	year	139	91	81r
Cheese, Kraft grated Parmesan	8-oz.	3.29	12/94	2c
Chicken breast, bone-in	lb.	2.04	12/94	82r
Chicken, fresh, whole	lb.	0.95	12/94	82r
Chicken, whole fryer	lb.	0.83	12/94	2c
Cigarettes, Winston, Kings	carton	14.97	12/94	2c
Coffee, 100%, ground roast, all sizes	lb.	4.48	12/94	82r
Coffee, vacuum-packed	13 oz.	3.85	12/94	2c
Corn Flakes, Kellogg's or Post Toasties	18 oz.	2.81	12/94	2c
Corn, frozen, whole kernel, lowest price	10 oz.	0.84	12/94	2c
Dairy products (other) purchases	year	182	91	81r
Eggs, Grade A large	dozen	0.87	12/94	2c
Fish and seafood purchases	year	94	91	81r
Flour, white, all purpose	lb.	0.21	12/94	82r
Food purchases, food eaten at home	year	2749	91	81r
Foods purchased away from home, not prepared by consumer	year	1909	91	81r
Fruits and vegetables purchases	year	459	91	81r
Grapefruit	lb.	0.56	12/94	82r
Ground beef, 100% beef	lb.	1.31	12/94	82r
Ham, boneless, exc. canned	lb.	2.46	12/94	82r
Ice cream, prepackaged, bulk, regular	1/2 gal.	2.57	12/94	82r
Lemons	lb.	1.00	12/94	82r
Lettuce, iceberg	lb.	0.93	12/94	82r
Lettuce, iceberg	head	0.78	12/94	2c
Margarine, Blue Bonnet or Parkay cubes	lb.	0.73	12/94	2c
Meats, poultry, fish, and eggs purchases	year	700	91	81r
Milk and cream (fresh) purchases	year	155	91	81r
Milk, whole	1/2 gal.	1.68	12/94	2c
Orange juice, frozen concentrate 12-oz. can	16 oz.	1.52	12/94	82r
Orange juice, Minute Maid frozen	12-oz.	1.47	12/94	2c
Oranges, Navel	lb.	0.56	12/94	82r
Peaches, halves or slices, Hunt's, Del Monte, or Libby's	29-oz.	1.56	12/94	2c
Peas, sweet, Del Monte or Green Giant	15-17 oz.	0.78	12/94	2c
Pork chops, center cut, bone-in	lb.	3.30	12/94	82r
Pork purchases	year	122	91	81r
Potato chips	16-oz.	3.03	12/94	82r
Potatoes, frozen, French fried	lb.	0.77	12/94	82r
Potatoes, white	lb.	0.35	12/94	82r
Potatoes, white or red	10-lb. sack	2.45	12/94	2c
Rice, white, long grain, uncooked	lb.	0.54	12/94	82r
Round roast, USDA choice, boneless	lb.	2.92	12/94	82r
Sausage, Jimmy Dean, 100% pork	lb.	3.56	12/94	2c
Shortening, vegetable oil blends	lb.	0.80	12/94	82r
Shortening, vegetable, Crisco	3-lb.	2.82	12/94	2c
Soft drink, Coca Cola, ex deposit	2 lit	1.28	12/94	2c
Spaghetti and macaroni	lb.	1.02	12/94	82r
Steak, round, graded & ungraded, exc. USDA prime & choice	lb.	3.13	12/94	82r
Steak, sirloin, USDA choice, boneless	lb.	4.07	12/94	82r
Steak, t-bone	lb.	4.87	12/94	2c
Sugar and other sweets, eaten at home, expenditures	year	105	91	81r
Sugar, cane or beet	4 lbs.	1.26	12/94	2c
Sugar, white, all sizes	lb.	0.38	12/94	82r
Tobacco products and smoking supplies, total expenditures	year	221	91	81r

Values are in dollars or fractions of dollars. In the column headed *Ref*, references are shown to sources. Each reference is followed by a letter. These refer to the geographical level for which data were reported: s = State, r = Region, and c = City or metro. The abbreviation *ex* is used to mean *except* or *excluding*; *exp* stands for *expenditures*. For other abbreviations and further explanations, please see the Introduction.

Pueblo, CO - continued

Item	Per	Value	Date	Ref.
Groceries				
Tomatoes, field grown	lb.	1.45	12/94	82r
Tomatoes, Hunt's or Del Monte	14.5 oz.	0.82	12/94	2c
Tuna, chunk, light	lb.	2.18	12/94	82r
Tuna, chunk, light, oil-packed	6.125-6.5 oz.	0.90	12/94	2c
Goods and Services				
Miscellaneous goods and services, ACCRA Index		89.30	12/94	2c
Health Care				
Health care, ACCRA Index		115.10	12/94	2c
Antibiotic ointment, Polysporin	1.5 oz.	4.04	12/94	2c
Childbirth, Cesarean delivery, hospital charge	birth	6059.00	12/91	69r
Childbirth, Cesarean delivery, physician charge	birth	2248.00	12/91	69r
Childbirth, normal delivery, hospital charge	birth	3006.00	12/91	69r
Childbirth, normal delivery, physician charge	birth	1634.00	12/91	69r
Dentist's fee, adult teeth cleaning and periodic oral exam	visit	62.00	12/94	2c
Doctor's fee, routine exam, established patient	visit	55.20	12/94	2c
Drugs, expenditures	year	230	91	81r
Health care, total expenditures	year	1544	91	81r
Health insurance expenditures	year	558	91	81r
Hospital care, semiprivate room	day	310.00	12/94	2c
Insurance premium, family medical care	month	362.55	1/95	41s
Medical services expenditures	year	676	91	81r
Medical supplies expenditures	year	80	91	81r
Surgery, open-heart	proc	37818.00	1/93	14r
Household Goods				
Appl. repair, service call, wash mach	min. lab. chg.	26.24	12/94	2c
Floor coverings, expenditures	year	79	91	81r
Furniture, expenditures	year	352	91	81r
Household equipment, misc. expenditures	year	614	91	81r
Household expenditures, miscellaneous	year	294	91	81r
Household furnishings and equipment, expenditures	year	1416	91	81r
Household operations expenditures	year	580	91	81r
Household textiles, expenditures	year	113	91	81r
Housekeeping supplies, expenditures	year	447	91	81r
Laundry and cleaning supplies, expenditures	year	114	91	81r
Laundry detergent, Tide Ultra, Bold, or Cheer	42 oz.	3.45	12/94	2c
Postage and stationery, expenditures	year	145	91	81r
Tissues, facial, Kleenex brand	175	1.08	12/94	2c
Housing				
Housing, ACCRA Index		81.90	12/94	2c
Add garage/carport		6,422	3/95	74r
Add room(s)		26,583	3/95	74r
Apartment condominium or co-op, median	unit	105300	12/94	62r
Dwellings (owned), expenditures	year	3932	91	81r
Enclose porch/patio/breezeway		5,382	3/95	74r
Finish room in basement/attic		3,911	3/95	74r
Home, existing, single-family, median	unit	178600	12/94	62r
House payment, principal and interest, 25% down payment	mo.	632	12/94	2c
House, 1800 sq ft, 8000 sq ft lot, new, urban, utilities	total	101372	12/94	2c
Maintenance, repairs, insurance, and other housing expenditures	year	591	91	81r
Mortgage interest and charges expenditures	year	2747	91	81r
Mtge. rate, incl. points and orig. fee, 30-year conv. fixed or ARM	mo.	9.36	12/94	2c
Princ. & int., mortgage, median-price exist. sing.-family home	mo.	845	12/94	62r
Property taxes expenditures	year	594	91	81r

Pueblo, CO - continued

Item	Per	Value	Date	Ref.
Housing - continued				
Redesign, restructure more than half of home's interior		5,467	3/95	74r
Rent, apartment, 2 br., 1 1/2-2 baths, unfurnished, 950 sq ft, water	mo.	419	12/94	2c
Rental units expenditures	year	2077	91	81r
Insurance and Pensions				
Auto insurance, private passenger	year	804.17	12/94	71s
Insurance and pensions, personal, expenditures	year	3042	91	81r
Insurance, life and other personal, expenditures	year	298	91	81r
Pensions and Social Security, expenditures	year	2744	91	81r
Legal Assistance				
Legal work, law firm associate	hour	91		10r
Legal work, law firm partner	hour	151		10r
Personal Goods				
Shampoo, Alberto VO5	15-oz.	1.25	12/94	2c
Toothpaste, Crest or Colgate	6-7 oz.	2.34	12/94	2c
Personal Services				
Dry cleaning, man's 2-pc. suit		6.30	12/94	2c
Haircut, man's barbershop, no styling		7.05	12/94	2c
Haircut, woman's shampoo, trim, blow-dry		16.00	12/94	2c
Personal services expenditures	year	286	91	81r
Restaurant Food				
Chicken, fried, thigh and drumstick		1.95	12/94	2c
Dining expenditures, family	week	32.25	94	73r
Hamburger with cheese	1/4 lb.	1.95	12/94	2c
Pizza, Pizza Hut or Pizza Inn	12-13 in.	6.99	12/94	2c
Taxes				
Taxes, Federal income, expenditures	year	2946	91	81r
Taxes, personal, expenditures	year	3791	91	81r
Taxes, State and local income, expenditures	year	791	91	81r
Transportation				
Transportation, ACCRA Index		94.70	12/94	2c
Bus fare, up to 10 miles	one-way	0.50	12/94	2c
Cars and trucks purchased, new	year	1231	91	81r
Cars and trucks purchased, used	year	915	91	81r
Driver's learning permit fee	perm	10.00	1/94	84s
Driver's license fee	orig	15.00	1/94	84s
Driver's license fee, duplicate	lic	5.00	1/94	84s
Driver's license reinstatement fee, min.	susp	40.00	1/94	85s
Driver's license renewal fee	renew	15.00	1/94	84s
Identification card, nondriver	card	3.50	1/94	83s
Motorcycle license fee	orig	16.00	1/94	84s
Public transportation expenditures	year	375	91	81r
Tire balance, computer or spin bal., front	wheel	6.40	12/94	2c
Transportation expenditures, total	year	5527	91	81r
Vehicle finance charges	year	287	91	81r
Vehicle insurance expenditures	year	624	91	81r
Vehicle maintenance and repairs expenditures	year	695	91	81r
Vehicle purchases	year	2174	91	81r
Vehicle rental, leases, licenses, etc. expenditures	year	257	91	81r
Vehicles purchased, other than cars and trucks	year	28	91	81r
Utilities				
Utilities, ACCRA Index		77.10	12/94	2c
Electricity expenditures	year	616	91	81r
Electricity, (part.), other, 1800 sq. ft., new home	mo.	49.13	12/94	2c
Electricity, summer, 250 KWh	month	20.83	8/93	64c
Electricity, summer, 500 KWh	month	36.06	8/93	64c
Electricity, summer, 750 KWh	month	51.29	8/93	64c
Electricity, summer, 1000 KWh	month	66.52	8/93	64c

Values are in dollars or fractions of dollars. In the column headed *Ref*, references are shown to sources. Each reference is followed by a letter. These refer to the geographical level for which data were reported: s = State, r = Region, and c = City or metro. The abbreviation *ex* is used to mean *except* or *excluding*; *exp* stands for *expenditures*. For other abbreviations and further explanations, please see the Introduction.

Pueblo, CO - continued

Item	Per	Value	Date	Ref.
Utilities				
Utilities, fuels, and public services, total expenditures	year	1681	91	81r
Water and other public services, expenditures	year	209	91	81r
Weddings				
Bridal attendants' gowns	event	750	10/93	76r
Bridal gown	event	852	10/93	76r
Bridal headpiece and veil	event	167	10/93	76r
Bride's wedding band	event	708	10/93	76r
Clergy	event	224	10/93	76r
Engagement ring	event	2756	10/93	76r
Flowers	event	863	10/93	76r
Formal wear for groom	event	106	10/93	76r
Groom's attendants' formal wear	event	530	10/93	76r
Groom's wedding band	event	402	10/93	76r
Music	event	600	10/93	76r
Photography	event	1088	10/93	76r
Shoes for bride	event	50	10/93	76r
Videography	event	483	10/93	76r
Wedding invitations and announcements	event	342	10/93	76r
Wedding reception	event	7000	10/93	76r

Pullman, WA

Item	Per	Value	Date	Ref.
Composite, ACCRA index		105.90	12/94	2c
Alcoholic Beverages				
Beer, Miller Lite, Bud, 12-oz., ex deposit	6	3.96	12/94	2c
J & B Scotch	750-ml.	18.95	12/94	2c
Wine, Gallo Chablis blanc	1.5-lit	4.64	12/94	2c
Clothing				
Jeans, man's denim		33.16	12/94	2c
Shirt, man's dress shirt		25.70	12/94	2c
Undervest, boy's size 10-14, cotton	3	4.84	12/94	2c
Communications				
Newspaper subscription, dly. and Sun. delivery	month	12.50	12/94	2c
Telephone bill, family of four	month	15.71	12/94	2c
Energy and Fuels				
Energy, combined forms, 1800 sq. ft.	mo.	69.41	12/94	2c
Energy, exc. electricity, 1800 sq. ft.	mo.	32.00	12/94	2c
Gas, reg unlead, taxes inc., cash, self-service	gal	1.33	12/94	2c
Entertainment				
Bowling, evening rate	game	1.40	12/94	2c
Monopoly game, Parker Brothers', No. 9	game	11.87	12/94	2c
Movie	adm	5.25	12/94	2c
Tennis balls, yellow, Wilson or Penn, 3	can	2.72	12/94	2c
Groceries				
Groceries, ACCRA Index		110.80	12/94	2c
Baby food, strained vegetables, lowest price	4-4.5 oz.	0.42	12/94	2c
Bananas	lb.	0.59	12/94	2c
Beef or hamburger, ground	lb.	1.45	12/94	2c
Bread, white	24-oz.	0.69	12/94	2c
Cheese, Kraft grated Parmesan	8-oz.	3.85	12/94	2c
Chicken, whole fryer	lb.	0.99	12/94	2c
Cigarettes, Winston, Kings	carton	20.75	12/94	2c
Coffee, vacuum-packed	13 oz.	3.80	12/94	2c
Corn Flakes, Kellogg's or Post Toasties	18 oz.	2.72	12/94	2c
Corn, frozen, whole kernel, lowest price	10 oz.	0.86	12/94	2c
Eggs, Grade A large	dozen	1.01	12/94	2c
Lettuce, iceberg	head	0.87	12/94	2c
Margarine, Blue Bonnet or Parkay cubes	lb.	0.69	12/94	2c
Milk, whole	1/2 gal.	1.55	12/94	2c
Orange juice, Minute Maid frozen	12-oz.	1.33	12/94	2c

Pullman, WA - continued

Item	Per	Value	Date	Ref.
Groceries - continued				
Peaches, halves or slices, Hunt's, Del Monte, or Libby's	29-oz.	1.54	12/94	2c
Peas, sweet, Del Monte or Green Giant	15-17 oz.	0.63	12/94	2c
Potatoes, white or red	10-lb. sack	1.81	12/94	2c
Sausage, Jimmy Dean, 100% pork	lb.	3.10	12/94	2c
Shortening, vegetable, Crisco	3-lb.	2.73	12/94	2c
Soft drink, Coca Cola, ex deposit	2 lit	1.42	12/94	2c
Steak, t-bone	lb.	4.50	12/94	2c
Sugar, cane or beet	4 lbs.	1.51	12/94	2c
Tomatoes, Hunt's or Del Monte	14.5 oz.	0.76	12/94	2c
Tuna, chunk, light, oil-packed	6.125-6.5 oz.	0.75	12/94	2c
Goods and Services				
Miscellaneous goods and services, ACCRA Index		100.20	12/94	2c
Health Care				
Health care, ACCRA Index		116.40	12/94	2c
Antibiotic ointment, Polysporin	1.5 oz.	3.87	12/94	2c
Dentist's fee, adult teeth cleaning and periodic oral exam	visit	74.00	12/94	2c
Doctor's fee, routine exam, established patient	visit	41.60	12/94	2c
Hospital care, semiprivate room	day	414.67	12/94	2c
Household Goods				
Appl. repair, service call, wash mach	min. lab. chg.	25.00	12/94	2c
Laundry detergent, Tide Ultra, Bold, or Cheer	42 oz.	3.61	12/94	2c
Tissues, facial, Kleenex brand	175	1.04	12/94	2c
Housing				
Housing, ACCRA Index		119.80	12/94	2c
House payment, principal and interest, 25% down payment	mo.	837	12/94	2c
House, 1800 sq ft, 8000 sq ft lot, new, urban, utilities	total	138000	12/94	2c
Mtge. rate, incl. points and orig. fee, 30-year conv. fixed or ARM	mo.	9.05	12/94	2c
Rent, apartment, 2 br., 1 1/2-2 baths, unfurnished, 950 sq ft, water	mo.	595	12/94	2c
Personal Goods				
Shampoo, Alberto VO5	15-oz.	1.30	12/94	2c
Toothpaste, Crest or Colgate	6-7 oz.	2.23	12/94	2c
Personal Services				
Dry cleaning, man's 2-pc. suit		7.65	12/94	2c
Haircut, man's barbershop, no styling		7.80	12/94	2c
Haircut, woman's shampoo, trim, blow-dry		17.00	12/94	2c
Restaurant Food				
Chicken, fried, thigh and drumstick		1.87	12/94	2c
Hamburger with cheese	1/4 lb.	2.10	12/94	2c
Pizza, Pizza Hut or Pizza Inn	12-13 in.	9.35	12/94	2c
Transportation				
Transportation, ACCRA Index		104.50	12/94	2c
Tire balance, computer or spin bal., front	wheel	5.80	12/94	2c
Utilities				
Utilities, ACCRA Index		64.40	12/94	2c
Electricity, (part.), other, 1800 sq. ft., new home	mo.	37.41	12/94	2c

Values are in dollars or fractions of dollars. In the column headed *Ref*, references are shown to sources. Each reference is followed by a letter. These refer to the geographical level for which data were reported: s = State, r = Region, and c = City or metro. The abbreviation *ex* is used to mean *except* or *excluding*; *exp* stands for *expenditures*. For other abbreviations and further explanations, please see the Introduction.

Quad-Cities, IL,IA

Item	Per	Value	Date	Ref.
Composite, ACCRA index		95.60	12/94	2c
Alcoholic Beverages				
Beer, Miller Lite, Bud, 12-oz., ex deposit	6	3.93	12/94	2c
J & B Scotch	750-ml.	16.15	12/94	2c
Wine, Gallo Chablis blanc	1.5-lit	3.71	12/94	2c
Clothing				
Jeans, man's denim		28.10	12/94	2c
Shirt, man's dress shirt		30.12	12/94	2c
Undervest, boy's size 10-14, cotton	3	3.62	12/94	2c
Communications				
Newspaper subscription, dly. and Sun. delivery	month	15.22	12/94	2c
Telephone bill, family of four	month	22.07	12/94	2c
Energy and Fuels				
Energy, combined forms, 1800 sq. ft.	mo.	99.99	12/94	2c
Energy, exc. electricity, 1800 sq. ft.	mo.	35.02	12/94	2c
Gas, reg unlead, taxes inc., cash, self-service	gal	1.12	12/94	2c
Entertainment				
Bowling, evening rate	game	1.79	12/94	2c
Monopoly game, Parker Brothers', No. 9	game	11.62	12/94	2c
Movie	adm	6.25	12/94	2c
Tennis balls, yellow, Wilson or Penn, 3	can	1.99	12/94	2c
Groceries				
Groceries, ACCRA Index		96.70	12/94	2c
Baby food, strained vegetables, lowest price	4-4.5 oz.	0.39	12/94	2c
Bananas	lb.	0.41	12/94	2c
Beef or hamburger, ground	lb.	1.45	12/94	2c
Bread, white	24-oz.	0.62	12/94	2c
Cheese, Kraft grated Parmesan	8-oz.	3.33	12/94	2c
Chicken, whole fryer	lb.	0.63	12/94	2c
Cigarettes, Winston, Kings	carton	16.72	12/94	2c
Coffee, vacuum-packed	13 oz.	3.35	12/94	2c
Corn Flakes, Kellogg's or Post Toasties	18 oz.	2.19	12/94	2c
Corn, frozen, whole kernel, lowest price	10 oz.	0.70	12/94	2c
Eggs, Grade A large	dozen	0.71	12/94	2c
Lettuce, iceberg	head	0.86	12/94	2c
Margarine, Blue Bonnet or Parkay cubes	lb.	0.63	12/94	2c
Milk, whole	1/2 gal.	1.43	12/94	2c
Orange juice, Minute Maid frozen	12-oz.	1.27	12/94	2c
Peaches, halves or slices, Hunt's, Del Monte, or Libby's	29-oz.	1.42	12/94	2c
Peas, sweet, Del Monte or Green Giant	15-17 oz.	0.53	12/94	2c
Potatoes, white or red	10-lb. sack	2.30	12/94	2c
Sausage, Jimmy Dean, 100% pork	lb.	2.53	12/94	2c
Shortening, vegetable, Crisco	3-lb.	2.54	12/94	2c
Soft drink, Coca Cola, ex deposit	2 lit	1.20	12/94	2c
Steak, t-bone	lb.	5.40	12/94	2c
Sugar, cane or beet	4 lbs.	1.15	12/94	2c
Tomatoes, Hunt's or Del Monte	14.5 oz.	0.72	12/94	2c
Tuna, chunk, light, oil-packed	6.125-6.5 oz.	0.66	12/94	2c
Goods and Services				
Miscellaneous goods and services, ACCRA Index		96.00	12/94	2c
Health Care				
Health care, ACCRA Index		94.30	12/94	2c
Antibiotic ointment, Polysporin	1.5 oz.	4.05	12/94	2c
Dentist's fee, adult teeth cleaning and periodic oral exam	visit	50.80	12/94	2c
Doctor's fee, routine exam, established patient	visit	40.40	12/94	2c
Hospital care, semiprivate room	day	295.00	12/94	2c

Quad-Cities, IL,IA - continued

Item	Per	Value	Date	Ref.
Household Goods				
Appl. repair, service call, wash mach	min. lab. chg.	39.33	12/94	2c
Laundry detergent, Tide Ultra, Bold, or Cheer	42 oz.	3.10	12/94	2c
Tissues, facial, Kleenex brand	175	0.95	12/94	2c
Housing				
Housing, ACCRA Index		94.30	12/94	2c
House payment, principal and interest, 25% down payment	mo.	748	12/94	2c
House, 1800 sq ft, 8000 sq ft lot, new, urban, utilities	total	120704	12/94	2c
Mtge. rate, incl. points and orig. fee, 30-year conv. fixed or ARM	mo.	9.30	12/94	2c
Rent, apartment, 2 br., 1 1/2-2 baths, unfurnished, 950 sq ft, water	mo.	423	12/94	2c
Personal Goods				
Shampoo, Alberto VO5	15-oz.	0.99	12/94	2c
Toothpaste, Crest or Colgate	6-7 oz.	1.46	12/94	2c
Personal Services				
Dry cleaning, man's 2-pc. suit		6.20	12/94	2c
Haircut, man's barbershop, no styling		7.70	12/94	2c
Haircut, woman's shampoo, trim, blow-dry		16.20	12/94	2c
Restaurant Food				
Chicken, fried, thigh and drumstick		2.19	12/94	2c
Hamburger with cheese	1/4 lb.	1.89	12/94	2c
Pizza, Pizza Hut or Pizza Inn	12-13 in.	7.29	12/94	2c
Transportation				
Transportation, ACCRA Index		99.50	12/94	2c
Bus fare, up to 10 miles	one-way	0.70	12/94	2c
Tire balance, computer or spin bal., front	wheel	7.20	12/94	2c
Utilities				
Utilities, ACCRA Index		92.30	12/94	2c
Electricity, (part.), other, 1800 sq. ft., new home	mo.	64.97	12/94	2c

Quincy, IL

Item	Per	Value	Date	Ref.
Composite, ACCRA index		99.80	12/94	2c
Alcoholic Beverages				
Beer, Miller Lite, Bud, 12-oz., ex deposit	6	3.76	12/94	2c
J & B Scotch	750-ml.	16.12	12/94	2c
Wine, Gallo Chablis blanc	1.5-lit	4.38	12/94	2c
Clothing				
Jeans, man's denim		32.70	12/94	2c
Shirt, man's dress shirt		26.63	12/94	2c
Undervest, boy's size 10-14, cotton	3	4.91	12/94	2c
Communications				
Newspaper subscription, dly. and Sun. delivery	month	9.62	12/94	2c
Telephone bill, family of four	month	19.95	12/94	2c
Telephone, residential, flat rate	mo.	13.55	12/93	8c
Energy and Fuels				
Energy, combined forms, 1800 sq. ft.	mo.	128.71	12/94	2c
Gas, cooking, 10 therms	month	12.04	2/94	65c
Gas, cooking, 30 therms	month	22.13	2/94	65c
Gas, cooking, 50 therms	month	32.33	2/94	65c
Gas, heating, winter, 100 therms	month	54.97	2/94	65c
Gas, heating, winter, average use	month	105.02	2/94	65c
Gas, reg unlead, taxes inc., cash, self-service	gal	1.15	12/94	2c

Values are in dollars or fractions of dollars. In the column headed *Ref*, references are shown to sources. Each reference is followed by a letter. These refer to the geographical level for which data were reported: s=State, r=Region, and c=City or metro. The abbreviation *ex* is used to mean *except* or *excluding*; *exp* stands for *expenditures*. For other abbreviations and further explanations, please see the Introduction.

Quincy, IL - continued

Item	Per	Value	Date	Ref.
Entertainment				
Bowling, evening rate	game	1.25	12/94	2c
Monopoly game, Parker Brothers', No. 9	game	10.82	12/94	2c
Movie	adm	5.00	12/94	2c
Tennis balls, yellow, Wilson or Penn, 3	can	2.27	12/94	2c
Groceries				
Groceries, ACCRA Index		94.30	12/94	2c
Baby food, strained vegetables, lowest price	4-4.5 oz.	0.27	12/94	2c
Bananas	lb.	0.39	12/94	2c
Beef or hamburger, ground	lb.	1.84	12/94	2c
Bread, white	24-oz.	0.41	12/94	2c
Cheese, Kraft grated Parmesan	8-oz.	3.07	12/94	2c
Chicken, whole fryer	lb.	0.79	12/94	2c
Cigarettes, Winston, Kings	carton	17.33	12/94	2c
Coffee, vacuum-packed	13 oz.	4.00	12/94	2c
Corn Flakes, Kellogg's or Post Toasties	18 oz.	2.24	12/94	2c
Corn, frozen, whole kernel, lowest price	10 oz.	0.74	12/94	2c
Eggs, Grade A large	dozen	0.69	12/94	2c
Lettuce, iceberg	head	0.83	12/94	2c
Margarine, Blue Bonnet or Parkay cubes	lb.	0.54	12/94	2c
Milk, whole	1/2 gal.	1.46	12/94	2c
Orange juice, Minute Maid frozen	12-oz.	1.28	12/94	2c
Peaches, halves or slices, Hunt's, Del Monte, or Libby's	29-oz.	1.20	12/94	2c
Peas, sweet, Del Monte or Green Giant	15-17 oz.	0.53	12/94	2c
Potatoes, white or red	10-lb. sack	1.95	12/94	2c
Sausage, Jimmy Dean, 100% pork	lb.	3.00	12/94	2c
Shortening, vegetable, Crisco	3-lb.	1.93	12/94	2c
Soft drink, Coca Cola, ex deposit	2 lit	1.15	12/94	2c
Steak, t-bone	lb.	5.51	12/94	2c
Sugar, cane or beet	4 lbs.	1.24	12/94	2c
Tomatoes, Hunt's or Del Monte	14.5 oz.	0.73	12/94	2c
Tuna, chunk, light, oil-packed	6.125-6.5 oz.	0.58	12/94	2c
Goods and Services				
Miscellaneous goods and services, ACCRA Index		95.90	12/94	2c
Health Care				
Health care, ACCRA Index		91.90	12/94	2c
Antibiotic ointment, Polysporin	1.5 oz.	4.53	12/94	2c
Dentist's fee, adult teeth cleaning and periodic oral exam	visit	51.40	12/94	2c
Doctor's fee, routine exam, established patient	visit	36.20	12/94	2c
Hospital care, semiprivate room	day	285.00	12/94	2c
Household Goods				
Appl. repair, service call, wash mach	min. lab. chg.	28.20	12/94	2c
Laundry detergent, Tide Ultra, Bold, or Cheer	42 oz.	3.33	12/94	2c
Tissues, facial, Kleenex brand	175	0.99	12/94	2c
Housing				
Housing, ACCRA Index		105.80	12/94	2c
House payment, principal and interest, 25% down payment	mo.	854	12/94	2c
House, 1800 sq ft, 8000 sq ft lot, new, urban, utilities	total	135540	12/94	2c
Mtge. rate, incl. points and orig. fee, 30-year conv. fixed or ARM	mo.	9.49	12/94	2c
Rent, apartment, 2 br., 1 1/2-2 baths, unfurnished, 950 sq ft, water	mo.	435	12/94	2c
Personal Goods				
Shampoo, Alberto VO5	15-oz.	1.23	12/94	2c
Toothpaste, Crest or Colgate	6-7 oz.	1.86	12/94	2c

Quincy, IL - continued

Item	Per	Value	Date	Ref.
Personal Services				
Dry cleaning, man's 2-pc. suit		6.91	12/94	2c
Haircut, man's barbershop, no styling		6.50	12/94	2c
Haircut, woman's shampoo, trim, blow-dry		18.30	12/94	2c
Restaurant Food				
Chicken, fried, thigh and drumstick		2.59	12/94	2c
Hamburger with cheese	1/4 lb.	1.89	12/94	2c
Pizza, Pizza Hut or Pizza Inn	12-13 in.	7.10	12/94	2c
Transportation				
Transportation, ACCRA Index		98.30	12/94	2c
Tire balance, computer or spin bal., front	wheel	6.30	12/94	2c
Utilities				
Utilities, ACCRA Index		113.00	12/94	2c
Electricity, 1800 sq. ft., new home	mo.	128.71	12/94	2c
Electricity, summer, 250 KWh	month	26.09	8/93	64c
Electricity, summer, 500 KWh	month	47.18	8/93	64c
Electricity, summer, 750 KWh	month	68.26	8/93	64c
Electricity, summer, 1000 KWh	month	89.35	8/93	64c

Racine, WI

Item	Per	Value	Date	Ref.
Appliances				
Appliances (major), expenditures	year	131	91	81r
Average annual exp.				
Food, health care, personal goods, services	year	25935	91	81r
Charity				
Cash contributions, expenditures	year	745	91	81r
Clothing				
Apparel, men and boys, total expenditures	year	332	91	81r
Apparel, women and girls, total expenditures	year	578	91	81r
Footwear, expenditures	year	164	91	81r
Communications				
Long-distance telephone rate, day, addl. min., 1-10 mi.	min.	0.10	12/93	9s
Long-distance telephone rate, day, initial min., 1-10 mi.	min.	0.15	12/93	9s
Phone line, single, business, field visit	inst	64.65	12/93	9s
Phone line, single, business, no field visit	inst	64.65	12/93	9s
Phone line, single, residence, field visit	inst	33.05	12/93	9s
Phone line, single, residence, no field visit	inst	33.05	12/93	9s
Telephone service, expenditures	year	547	91	81r
Education				
Board, 4-year private college/university	year	2145	8/94	80s
Board, 4-year public college/university	year	1303	8/94	80s
Education, total expenditures	year	394	91	81r
Room, 4-year private college/university	year	1576	8/94	80s
Room, 4-year public college/university	year	1631	8/94	80s
Total cost, 4-year private college/university	year	13902	8/94	80s
Total cost, 4-year public college/university	year	5252	8/94	80s
Tuition, 2-year public college/university, in-state	year	1557	8/94	80s
Tuition, 4-year private college/university, in-state	year	10181	8/94	80s
Tuition, 4-year public college/university, in-state	year	2318	8/94	80s
Energy and Fuels				
Fuel oil and other fuels, expenditures	year	83	91	81r
Gas, natural, expenditures	year	373	91	81r
Gasoline and motor oil purchased	year	1000	91	81r
Gasoline, unleaded midgrade	gallon	1.15	4/93	82r
Gasoline, unleaded premium	gallon	1.23	4/93	82r
Gasoline, unleaded regular	gallon	1.07	4/93	82r
Entertainment				
Entertainment, total expenditures	year	1356	91	81r
Fees and admissions, expenditures	year	347	91	81r

Values are in dollars or fractions of dollars. In the column headed *Ref*, references are shown to sources. Each reference is followed by a letter. These refer to the geographical level for which data were reported: s=State, r=Region, and c=City or metro. The abbreviation *ex* is used to mean *except* or *excluding*; *exp* stands for expenditures. For other abbreviations and further explanations, please see the Introduction.

Racine, WI - continued

Item	Per	Value	Date	Ref.
Entertainment				
Pets, toys, playground equipment, expenditures	year	270	91	81r
Reading, expenditures	year	160	91	81r
Televisions, radios, and sound equipment, expenditures	year	433	91	81r
Funerals				
Burial, immediate, container provided by funeral home		1268.31	1/95	54r
Cards, acknowledgment		26.12	1/95	54r
Casket, minimum alternative		198.03	1/95	54r
Cosmetology, hair care, etc.		122.19	1/95	54r
Cremation, direct, container provided by funeral home		977.81	1/95	54r
Embalming		334.00	1/95	54r
Funeral, funeral home		321.16	1/95	54r
Funeral, other facility		317.73	1/95	54r
Graveside service		292.48	1/95	54r
Hearse, local		153.20	1/95	54r
Limousine, local		123.52	1/95	54r
Memorial service		356.30	1/95	54r
Service charge, professional, nondeclinable		968.24	1/95	54r
Visitation and viewing		332.66	1/95	54r
Groceries				
Apples, Red Delicious	lb.	0.68	12/94	82r
Bacon, sliced	lb.	1.88	12/94	82r
Bananas	lb.	0.41	12/94	82r
Beef purchases	year	197	91	81r
Beef, stew, boneless	lb.	2.52	12/94	82r
Beverage purchases, alcoholic	year	293	91	81r
Beverage purchases, nonalcoholic	year	203	91	81r
Bologna, all beef or mixed	lb.	2.12	12/94	82r
Bread, white, pan	lb.	0.76	12/94	82r
Cabbage	lb.	0.44	12/94	82r
Carrots, short trimmed and topped	lb.	0.44	12/94	82r
Cereals and bakery products purchases	year	347	91	81r
Cereals and cereals products purchases	year	119	91	81r
Cheddar cheese, natural	lb.	3.28	12/94	82r
Chicken breast, bone-in	lb.	1.61	12/94	82r
Chicken, fresh, whole	lb.	0.89	12/94	82r
Chuck roast, USDA choice, boneless	lb.	2.33	12/94	82r
Coffee, 100%, ground roast, all sizes	lb.	4.28	12/94	82r
Cookies, chocolate chip	lb.	2.72	12/94	82r
Dairy products (other) purchases	year	148	91	81r
Eggs, Grade A large	dozen	0.76	12/94	82r
Fish and seafood purchases	year	61	91	81r
Flour, white, all purpose	lb.	0.22	12/94	82r
Food purchases, food eaten at home	year	2313	91	81r
Foods purchased away from home, not prepared by consumer	year	1709	91	81r
Fruits and vegetables purchases	year	372	91	81r
Grapefruit	lb.	0.47	12/94	82r
Grapes, Thompson seedless	lb.	2.15	12/94	82r
Ground beef, 100% beef	lb.	1.37	12/94	82r
Ground chuck, 100% beef	lb.	1.81	12/94	82r
Ham, boneless, exc. canned	lb.	2.16	12/94	82r
Ice cream, prepackaged, bulk, regular	1/2 gal.	2.48	12/94	82r
Lemons	lb.	1.08	12/94	82r
Lettuce, iceberg	lb.	0.81	12/94	82r
Margarine, stick	lb.	0.81	12/94	82r
Meats, poultry, fish, and eggs purchases	year	591	91	81r
Milk and cream (fresh) purchases	year	132	91	81r
Orange juice, frozen concentrate 12-oz. can	16 oz.	1.41	12/94	82r
Oranges, Navel	lb.	0.56	12/94	82r
Peanut butter, creamy, all sizes	lb.	1.81	12/94	82r
Pork chops, center cut, bone-in	lb.	2.76	12/94	82r
Pork purchases	year	130	91	81r
Potato chips	16-oz.	2.81	12/94	82r
Potatoes, frozen, French fried	lb.	0.83	12/94	82r
Potatoes, white	lb.	0.28	12/94	82r
Round roast, USDA choice, boneless	lb.	2.90	12/94	82r

Racine, WI - continued

Item	Per	Value	Date	Ref.
Groceries - continued				
Shortening, vegetable oil blends	lb.	0.88	12/94	82r
Spaghetti and macaroni	lb.	0.78	12/94	82r
Steak, rib eye, USDA choice, boneless	lb.	6.15	12/94	82r
Steak, round, graded & ungraded, exc. USDA prime & choice	lb.	2.72	12/94	82r
Steak, round, USDA choice, boneless	lb.	3.02	12/94	82r
Steak, sirloin, USDA choice, boneless	lb.	3.85	12/94	82r
Steak, T-bone, USDA choice, bone-in	lb.	5.38	12/94	82r
Sugar and other sweets, eaten at home, expenditures	year	91	91	81r
Sugar, white, all sizes	lb.	0.36	12/94	82r
Tobacco products and smoking supplies, total expenditures	year	298	91	81r
Tomatoes, field grown	lb.	1.36	12/94	82r
Tuna, chunk, light	lb.	1.94	12/94	82r
Turkey, frozen, whole	lb.	0.96	12/94	82r
Yogurt, natural, fruit flavored	8 oz.	0.62	12/94	82r
Health Care				
Childbirth, Cesarean delivery, hospital charge	birth	5101.00	12/91	69r
Childbirth, Cesarean delivery, physician charge	birth	2234.00	12/91	69r
Childbirth, normal delivery, hospital charge	birth	2891.00	12/91	69r
Childbirth, normal delivery, physician charge	birth	1623.00	12/91	69r
Drugs, expenditures	year	248	91	81r
Health care, total expenditures	year	1336	91	81r
Health insurance expenditures	year	550	91	81r
Insurance premium, family medical care	month	378.79	1/95	41s
Medical services expenditures	year	457	91	81r
Medical supplies expenditures	year	82	91	81r
Household Goods				
Floor coverings, expenditures	year	105	91	81r
Furniture, expenditures	year	291	91	81r
Household equipment, misc. expenditures	year	341	91	81r
Household expenditures, miscellaneous	year	162	91	81r
Household furnishings and equipment, expenditures	year	1042	91	81r
Household operations expenditures	year	365	91	81r
Household textiles, expenditures	year	101	91	81r
Housekeeping supplies, expenditures	year	390	91	81r
Laundry and cleaning supplies, expenditures	year	110	91	81r
Postage and stationery, expenditures	year	115	91	81r
Housing				
Add garage/carport		8,479	3/95	74r
Add room(s)		21,347	3/95	74r
Apartment condominium or co-op, median	unit	87100	12/94	62r
Bathroom addition, average cost	add	9734.00	3/95	13r
Bathroom remodeling, average cost	remod	6414.00	3/95	13r
Bedroom, master suite addition, average cost	add	27122.00	3/95	13r
Deck addition, average cost	add	6665.00	3/95	13r
Dwellings (owned), expenditures	year	2566	91	81r
Enclose porch/patio/breezeway		4,556	3/95	74r
Exterior remodeling, average cost	remod	15395.00	3/95	13r
Family room addition, average cost	add	27658.00	3/95	13r
Finish room in basement/attic		5,074	3/95	74r
Home, existing, single-family, median	unit	106500	12/94	62r
Kitchen remodeling, major, average cost	remod	17084.00	3/95	13r
Kitchen remodeling, minor, average cost	remod	5804.00	3/95	13r
Maintenance, repairs, insurance, and other housing expenditures	year	484	91	81r
Mortgage interest and charges expenditures	year	1443	91	81r
Office, home addition, average cost	add	8121.00	3/95	13r
Princ. & int., mortgage, median-price exist. sing.-family home	mo.	515	12/94	62r
Property taxes expenditures	year	639	91	81r
Redesign, restructure more than half of home's interior		9,114	3/95	74r
Rental units expenditures	year	1200	91	81r
Sun-space addition, average cost	add	23768.00	3/95	13r

Values are in dollars or fractions of dollars. In the column headed *Ref*, references are shown to sources. Each reference is followed by a letter. These refer to the geographical level for which data were reported: s = State, r = Region, and c = City or metro. The abbreviation *ex* is used to mean *except* or *excluding*; *exp* stands for *expenditures*. For other abbreviations and further explanations, please see the Introduction.

Racine, WI - continued

Item	Per	Value	Date	Ref.
Housing				
Wing addition, two-story, average cost	add	50410.00	3/95	13r
Insurance and Pensions				
Auto insurance, private passenger	year	554.10	12/94	71s
Insurance and pensions, personal, expenditures	year	2408	91	81r
Insurance, life and other personal, expenditures	year	355	91	81r
Pensions and Social Security, expenditures	year	2053	91	81r
Legal Assistance				
Legal work, law firm associate	hour	90		10r
Legal work, law firm partner	hour	139		10r
Personal Services				
Personal services expenditures	year	203	91	81r
Restaurant Food				
Dining expenditures, family	week	30.03	94	73r
Taxes				
Taxes, Federal income, expenditures	year	1756	91	81r
Taxes, personal, expenditures	year	2426	91	81r
Taxes, State and local income, expenditures	year	568	91	81r
Transportation				
Cars and trucks purchased, new	year	891	91	81r
Cars and trucks purchased, used	year	1155	91	81r
Driver's learning permit fee	perm	20.00	1/94	84s
Driver's license fee	orig	10.00	1/94	84s
Driver's license fee, duplicate	lic	4.00	1/94	84s
Driver's license reinstatement fee, min.	susp	50.00	1/94	85s
Driver's license renewal fee	renew	10.00	1/94	84s
Identification card, nondriver	card	4.00	1/94	83s
Motorcycle license fee	orig	4.00	1/94	84s
Motorcycle license fee, duplicate	lic	4.00	1/94	84s
Motorcycle license renewal fee	renew	4.00	1/94	84s
Public transportation expenditures	year	209	91	81r
Transportation expenditures, total	year	4792	91	81r
Vehicle finance charges	year	300	91	81r
Vehicle insurance expenditures	year	485	91	81r
Vehicle maintenance and repairs expenditures	year	534	91	81r
Vehicle purchases	year	2068	91	81r
Vehicle rental, leases, licenses, etc. expenditures	year	197	91	81r
Vehicles purchased, other than cars and trucks	year	22	91	81r
Utilities				
Electricity expenditures	year	668	91	81r
Utilities, fuels, and public services, total expenditures	year	1838	91	81r
Water and other public services, expenditures	year	167	91	81r
Weddings				
Bridal attendants' gowns	event	750	10/93	76r
Bridal gown	event	852	10/93	76r
Bridal headpiece and veil	event	167	10/93	76r
Bride's wedding band	event	708	10/93	76r
Clergy	event	224	10/93	76r
Engagement ring	event	2756	10/93	76r
Flowers	event	863	10/93	76r
Formal wear for groom	event	106	10/93	76r
Groom's attendants' formal wear	event	530	10/93	76r
Groom's wedding band	event	402	10/93	76r
Music	event	600	10/93	76r
Photography	event	1088	10/93	76r
Shoes for bride	event	50	10/93	76r
Videography	event	483	10/93	76r
Wedding invitations and announcements	event	342	10/93	76r
Wedding reception	event	7000	10/93	76r

Raleigh-Durham, NC

Item	Per	Value	Date	Ref.
Composite, ACCRA index		98.00	12/94	2c
Alcoholic Beverages				
Beer, Miller Lite, Bud, 12-oz., ex deposit	6	3.56	12/94	2c
J & B Scotch	750-ml.	18.60	12/94	2c
Wine, Gallo Chablis blanc	1.5-lit	4.31	12/94	2c
Appliances				
Appliances (major), expenditures	year	153	91	81r
Average annual exp.				
Food, health care, personal goods, services	year	27020	91	81r
Business				
Dinner and tip, hotel, corporate rate	night	30.00	2/94	15c
Hotel room, corporate rate	night	69.00	2/94	15c
Charity				
Cash contributions, expenditures	year	839	91	81r
Clothing				
Apparel, men and boys, total expenditures	year	380	91	81r
Apparel, women and girls, total expenditures	year	660	91	81r
Footwear, expenditures	year	193	91	81r
Jeans, man's denim		29.85	12/94	2c
Shirt, man's dress shirt		35.82	12/94	2c
Undervest, boy's size 10-14, cotton	3	3.52	12/94	2c
Communications				
Long-distance telephone rate, day, addl. min., 1-10 mi.	min.	0.10	12/93	9s
Long-distance telephone rate, day, initial min., 1-10 mi.	min.	0.16	12/93	9s
Newspaper subscription, dly. and Sun. delivery	month	11.96	12/94	2c
Phone line, single, business, field visit	inst	62.50	12/93	9s
Phone line, single, business, no field visit	inst	62.50	12/93	9s
Phone line, single, residence, field visit	inst	42.75	12/93	9s
Phone line, single, residence, no field visit	inst	42.75	12/93	9s
Telephone bill, family of four	month	18.93	12/94	2c
Telephone service, expenditures	year	616	91	81r
Telephone, business, addl. line, touch tone	month	1.95	10/91	25c
Telephone, business, connection charges, touch tone	inst	62.50	10/91	25c
Telephone, business, key system line, touch tone	month	59.20	10/91	25c
Telephone, business, PBX line, touch tone	month	61.69	10/91	25c
Telephone, business, single ln., touch tone	month	41.43	10/91	25c
Telephone, business, touch tone, inside wiring maintenance plan	month	2.00	10/91	25c
Education				
Board, 4-year private college/university	year	2069	8/94	80s
Board, 4-year public college/university	year	1627	8/94	80s
Education, total expenditures	year	319	91	81r
Room, 4-year private college/university	year	1824	8/94	80s
Room, 4-year public college/university	year	1669	8/94	80s
Total cost, 4-year private college/university	year	13505	8/94	80s
Total cost, 4-year public college/university	year	4704	8/94	80s
Tuition, 2-year public college/university, in-state	year	577	8/94	80s
Tuition, 4-year private college/university, in-state	year	9612	8/94	80s
Tuition, 4-year public college/university, in-state	year	1409	8/94	80s
Energy and Fuels				
Energy, combined forms, 1800 sq. ft.	mo.	117.78	12/94	2c
Fuel oil and other fuels, expenditures	year	56	91	81r
Gas, cooking, winter, 10 therms	month	13.35	2/94	65c
Gas, cooking, winter, 30 therms	month	62.04	2/94	65c
Gas, cooking, winter, 50 therms	month	38.73	2/94	65c
Gas, heating, winter, 100 therms	month	70.45	2/94	65c
Gas, heating, winter, average use	month	92.02	2/94	65c
Gas, natural, expenditures	year	150	91	81r

Values are in dollars or fractions of dollars. In the column headed *Ref*, references are shown as sources. Each reference is followed by a letter. These refer to the geographical level for which data were reported: s=State, r=Region, and c=City or metro. The abbreviation *ex* is used to mean *except* or *excluding*; *exp* stands for *expenditures*. For other abbreviations and further explanations, please see the Introduction.

Raleigh-Durham, NC - continued

Item	Per	Value	Date	Ref.
Energy and Fuels				
Gas, reg unlead, taxes inc., cash, self-service	gal	1.07	12/94	2c
Gasoline and motor oil purchased	year	1152	91	81r
Gasoline, unleaded midgrade	gallon	1.21	4/93	82r
Gasoline, unleaded premium	gallon	1.30	4/93	82r
Gasoline, unleaded regular	gallon	1.10	4/93	82r
Entertainment				
Bowling, evening rate	game	2.27	12/94	2c
Concert ticket, Pearl Jam group	perf	20.00	94	50r
Entertainment, total expenditures	year	1266	91	81r
Fees and admissions, expenditures	year	306	91	81r
Monopoly game, Parker Brothers', No. 9	game	10.76	12/94	2c
Movie	adm	5.75	12/94	2c
Pets, toys, playground equipment, expenditures	year	271	91	81r
Reading, expenditures	year	131	91	81r
Televisions, radios, and sound equipment, expenditures	year	439	91	81r
Tennis balls, yellow, Wilson or Penn, 3	can	2.07	12/94	2c
Funerals				
Burial, immediate, container provided by funeral home		1370.36	1/95	54r
Cards, acknowledgment		14.83	1/95	54r
Casket, minimum alternative		192.52	1/95	54r
Cosmetology, hair care, etc.		102.27	1/95	54r
Cremation, direct, container provided by funeral home		1065.64	1/95	54r
Embalming		304.29	1/95	54r
Funeral, funeral home		287.83	1/95	54r
Funeral, other facility		284.14	1/95	54r
Graveside service		349.13	1/95	54r
Hearse, local		132.27	1/95	54r
Limousine, local		98.45	1/95	54r
Memorial service		270.59	1/95	54r
Service charge, professional, nondeclinable		933.59	1/95	54r
Visitation and viewing		225.83	1/95	54r
Groceries				
Groceries, ACCRA Index		94.50	12/94	2c
Apples, Red Delicious	lb.	0.73	12/94	82r
Baby food, strained vegetables, lowest price	4-4.5 oz.	0.33	12/94	2c
Bacon, sliced	lb.	1.67	12/94	82r
Bananas	lb.	0.48	12/94	2c
Bananas	lb.	0.42	12/94	82r
Beef or hamburger, ground	lb.	1.22	12/94	2c
Beef purchases	year	213	91	81r
Beverage purchases, alcoholic	year	249	91	81r
Beverage purchases, nonalcoholic	year	207	91	81r
Bologna, all beef or mixed	lb.	2.27	12/94	82r
Bread, white	24-oz.	0.71	12/94	2c
Bread, white, pan	lb.	0.68	12/94	82r
Cabbage	lb.	0.42	12/94	82r
Carrots, short trimmed and topped	lb.	0.53	12/94	82r
Cereals and bakery products purchases	year	345	91	81r
Cereals and cereals products purchases	year	127	91	81r
Cheddar cheese, natural	lb.	3.58	12/94	82r
Cheese, Kraft grated Parmesan	8-oz.	2.93	12/94	2c
Chicken breast, bone-in	lb.	1.71	12/94	82r
Chicken, fresh, whole	lb.	0.78	12/94	82r
Chicken, whole fryer	lb.	0.77	12/94	2c
Chuck roast, USDA choice, boneless	lb.	2.26	12/94	82r
Cigarettes, Winston, Kings	carton	12.91	12/94	2c
Coffee, vacuum-packed	13 oz.	3.39	12/94	2c
Corn Flakes, Kellogg's or Post Toasties	18 oz.	2.28	12/94	2c
Corn, frozen, whole kernel, lowest price	10 oz.	0.63	12/94	2c
Crackers, soda, salted	lb.	1.27	12/94	82r
Cucumbers	lb.	0.65	12/94	82r
Dairy products (other) purchases	year	141	91	81r
Eggs, Grade A large	dozen	0.85	12/94	2c
Eggs, Grade A large	dozen	0.87	12/94	82r
Fish and seafood purchases	year	72	91	81r

Raleigh-Durham, NC - continued

Item	Per	Value	Date	Ref.
Groceries - continued				
Flour, white, all purpose	lb.	0.23	12/94	82r
Food purchases, food eaten at home	year	2381	91	81r
Foods purchased away from home, not prepared by consumer	year	1696	91	81r
Frankfurters, all meat or all beef	lb.	1.74	12/94	82r
Fruits and vegetables purchases	year	380	91	81r
Grapefruit	lb.	0.45	12/94	82r
Grapes, Thompson seedless	lb.	2.30	12/94	82r
Ground beef, 100% beef	lb.	1.37	12/94	82r
Ground chuck, 100% beef	lb.	1.97	12/94	82r
Ham, boneless, exc. canned	lb.	2.54	12/94	82r
Ice cream, prepackaged, bulk, regular	1/2 gal.	2.47	12/94	82r
Lemons	lb.	1.02	12/94	82r
Lettuce, iceberg	lb.	0.96	12/94	82r
Lettuce, iceberg	head	1.16	12/94	2c
Margarine, Blue Bonnet or Parkay cubes	lb.	0.56	12/94	2c
Margarine, stick	lb.	0.77	12/94	82r
Meats, poultry, fish, and eggs purchases	year	655	91	81r
Milk and cream (fresh) purchases	year	130	91	81r
Milk, whole	1/2 gal.	1.40	12/94	2c
Orange juice, frozen concentrate 12-oz. can	16 oz.	1.36	12/94	82r
Orange juice, Minute Maid frozen	12-oz.	1.20	12/94	2c
Oranges, Navel	lb.	0.54	12/94	82r
Peaches, halves or slices, Hunt's, Del Monte, or Libby's	29-oz.	1.28	12/94	2c
Pears, Anjou	lb.	0.81	12/94	82r
Peas, sweet, Del Monte or Green Giant	15-17 oz.	0.50	12/94	2c
Pork chops, center cut, bone-in	lb.	3.07	12/94	82r
Pork purchases	year	142	91	81r
Potato chips	16-oz.	3.15	12/94	82r
Potatoes, frozen, French fried	lb.	0.82	12/94	82r
Potatoes, white	lb.	0.34	12/94	82r
Potatoes, white or red	10-lb. sack	2.54	12/94	2c
Rice, white, long grain, uncooked	lb.	0.48	12/94	82r
Round roast, USDA choice, boneless	lb.	2.91	12/94	82r
Sausage, fresh	lb.	1.82	12/94	82r
Sausage, Jimmy Dean, 100% pork	lb.	2.18	12/94	2c
Shortening, vegetable oil blends	lb.	0.75	12/94	82r
Shortening, vegetable, Crisco	3-lb.	2.52	12/94	2c
Soft drink, Coca Cola, ex deposit	2 lit	1.06	12/94	2c
Spaghetti and macaroni	lb.	0.87	12/94	82r
Steak, rib eye, USDA choice, boneless	lb.	6.85	12/94	82r
Steak, round, graded & ungraded, exc. USDA prime & choice	lb.	2.96	12/94	82r
Steak, round, USDA choice, boneless	lb.	3.17	12/94	82r
Steak, sirloin, USDA choice, boneless	lb.	4.12	12/94	82r
Steak, t-bone	lb.	4.94	12/94	2c
Steak, T-bone, USDA choice, bone-in	lb.	5.63	12/94	82r
Sugar and other sweets, eaten at home, expenditures	year	93	91	81r
Sugar, cane or beet	4 lbs.	1.52	12/94	2c
Sugar, white, all sizes	lb.	0.39	12/94	82r
Tobacco products and smoking supplies, total expenditures	year	286	91	81r
Tomatoes, field grown	lb.	1.36	12/94	82r
Tomatoes, Hunt's or Del Monte	14.5 oz.	0.56	12/94	2c
Tuna, chunk, light	lb.	1.94	12/94	82r
Tuna, chunk, light, oil-packed	6.125-6.5 oz.	0.66	12/94	2c
Turkey, frozen, whole	lb.	0.96	12/94	82r
Yogurt, natural, fruit flavored	8 oz.	0.58	12/94	82r
Goods and Services				
Miscellaneous goods and services, ACCRA Index		96.80	12/94	2c

Values are in dollars or fractions of dollars. In the column headed *Ref*, references are shown to sources. Each reference is followed by a letter. These refer to the geographical level for which data were reported: s=State, r=Region, and c=City or metro. The abbreviation *ex* is used to mean *except* or *excluding*; *exp* stands for expenditures. For other abbreviations and further explanations, please see the Introduction.

Raleigh-Durham, NC - continued

Item	Per	Value	Date	Ref.
Health Care				
Health care, ACCRA Index		105.00	12/94	2c
Adenosine, emergency room	treat	100.00	95	23r
Antibiotic ointment, Polysporin	1.5 oz.	3.69	12/94	2c
Bladder tap, superpubic, infant, emergency room	treat	119.00	95	23r
Blood analysis, emergency room	treat	25.00	95	23r
Blood tests, abdominal pain, emergency room	treat	25.00	95	23r
Burn dressing, emergency room	treat	266.00	95	23r
Cardiology interpretation, emergency room	treat	26.00	95	23r
Chest X-ray, emergency room	treat	78.00	95	23r
Childbirth, Cesarean delivery, hospital charge	birth	5462.00	12/91	69r
Childbirth, Cesarean delivery, physician charge	birth	2228.00	12/91	69r
Childbirth, normal delivery, hospital charge	birth	2943.00	12/91	69r
Childbirth, normal delivery, physician charge	birth	1619.00	12/91	69r
Defibrillation pads, emergency room	treat	6.00	95	23r
Dentist's fee, adult teeth cleaning and periodic oral exam	visit	53.33	12/94	2c
Doctor's fee, routine exam, established patient	visit	53.00	12/94	2c
Drugs, expenditures	year	297	91	81r
Gastric tube insertion, nasal, emergency room	treat	25.00	95	23r
Health care, total expenditures	year	1600	91	81r
Health insurance expenditures	year	637	91	81r
Heart monitor, emergency room	treat	40.00	95	23r
Hospital care, semiprivate room	day	280.12	12/94	2c
Insurance premium, family medical care	month	405.45	1/95	41s
Intravenous fluids, emergency room	treat	130.00	95	23r
Intravenous fluids, emergency room	liter	26.00	95	23r
Intravenous line, central, emergency room	treat	342.00	95	23r
Liver function tests, abdominal pain, emergency room	treat	26.00	95	23r
Medical care charges, total, emergency room, third-degree burns	treat	2101.00	95	23r
Medical care charges, total, emergency, infant with fever	treat	628.00	95	23r
Medical services expenditures	year	573	91	81r
Medical supplies expenditures	year	93	91	81r
Morphine, emergency room	treat	34.00	95	23r
Nursing care and facilities charges, emergency room	treat	252.00	95	23r
Nursing care and facilities charges, emergency, infant with fever	treat	252.00	95	23r
Nursing care and facilities charges, emergency, third-degree burns	treat	861.00	95	23r
Physician's charges, emergency, infant with fever	treat	212.00	95	23r
Physician's charges, emergency, third-degree burns	treat	372.00	95	23r
Physician's fee, emergency room	treat	372.00	95	23r
Physician's fee, general practitioner	visit	51.20	12/93	60r
Surgery, open-heart	proc	42374.00	1/93	14r
Ultrasound, abdominal, emergency room	treat	276.00	95	23r
Urinalysis, emergency room	treat	20.00	95	23r
Urinalysis, infant, emergency room	treat	20.00	95	23r
X-rays, emergency room	treat	78.00	95	23r
Household Goods				
Appl. repair, service call, wash mach	min. lab. chg.	30.02	12/94	2c
Floor coverings, expenditures	year	48	91	81r
Furniture, expenditures	year	280	91	81r
Household equipment, misc. expenditures	year	342	91	81r
Household expenditures, miscellaneous	year	256	91	81r
Household furnishings and equipment, expenditures	year	988	91	81r
Household operations expenditures	year	468	91	81r
Household textiles, expenditures	year	95	91	81r
Housekeeping supplies, expenditures	year	380	91	81r

Item	Per	Value	Date	Ref.
Household Goods - continued				
Laundry and cleaning supplies, expenditures	year	109	91	81r
Laundry detergent, Tide Ultra, Bold, or Cheer	42 oz.	2.65	12/94	2c
Postage and stationery, expenditures	year	105	91	81r
Tissues, facial, Kleenex brand	175	0.89	12/94	2c
Housing				
Housing, ACCRA Index		100.10	12/94	2c
Add garage/carport		6,980	3/95	74r
Add room(s)		11,403	3/95	74r
Apartment condominium or co-op, median	unit	68600	12/94	62r
Dwellings (owned), expenditures	year	2428	91	81r
Enclose porch/patio/breezeway		4,572	3/95	74r
Finish room in basement/attic		3,794	3/95	74r
Home, existing, single-family, median	unit	120200	12/94	62r
Home, existing, single-family, median	unit	124.50	12/94	62c
House payment, principal and interest, 25% down payment	mo.	773	12/94	2c
House, 1800 sq ft, 8000 sq ft lot, new, urban, utilities	total	125083	12/94	2c
Maintenance, repairs, insurance, and other housing expenditures	year	531	91	81r
Mortgage interest and charges expenditures	year	1506	91	81r
Mtge. rate, incl. points and orig. fee, 30-year conv. fixed or ARM	mo.	9.27	12/94	2c
Princ. & int., mortgage, median-price exist. sing.-family home	mo.	540	12/94	62r
Property taxes expenditures	year	391	91	81r
Redesign, restructure more than half of home's interior		17,641	3/95	74r
Rent, apartment, 2 br., 1 1/2-2 baths, unfurnished, 950 sq ft, water	mo.	511	12/94	2c
Rental units expenditures	year	1264	91	81r
Insurance and Pensions				
Auto insurance, private passenger	year	528.43	12/94	71s
Insurance and pensions, personal, expenditures	year	2395	91	81r
Insurance, life and other personal, expenditures	year	368	91	81r
Pensions and Social Security, expenditures	year	2027	91	81r
Personal Goods				
Shampoo, Alberto VO5	15-oz.	1.02	12/94	2c
Toothpaste, Crest or Colgate	6-7 oz.	1.73	12/94	2c
Personal Services				
Dry cleaning, man's 2-pc. suit		6.00	12/94	2c
Haircut, man's barbershop, no styling		7.80	12/94	2c
Haircut, woman's shampoo, trim, blow-dry		19.82	12/94	2c
Personal services expenditures	year	212	91	81r
Restaurant Food				
Chicken, fried, thigh and drumstick		2.09	12/94	2c
Dining expenditures, family	week	33.83	94	73r
Hamburger with cheese	1/4 lb.	1.83	12/94	2c
Pizza, Pizza Hut or Pizza Inn	12-13 in.	6.43	12/94	2c
Taxes				
Taxes, Federal income, expenditures	year	2275	91	81r
Taxes, personal, expenditures	year	2715	91	81r
Taxes, State and local income, expenditures	year	365	91	81r
Transportation				
Transportation, ACCRA Index		92.70	12/94	2c
Bus fare, one-way	trip	0.55	12/95	1c
Bus fare, one-way	trip	1.00	12/95	1c
Bus fare, up to 10 miles	one-way	0.50	12/94	2c
Cars and trucks purchased, new	year	1306	91	81r
Cars and trucks purchased, used	year	942	91	81r
Driver's learning permit fee	perm	10.00	1/94	84s
Driver's license fee	orig	10.00	1/94	84s

Values are in dollars or fractions of dollars. In the column headed *Ref*, references are shown to sources. Each reference is followed by a letter. These refer to the geographical level for which data were reported: s=State, r=Region, and c=City or metro. The abbreviation *ex* is used to mean *except* or *excluding*; *exp* stands for expenditures. For other abbreviations and further explanations, please see the Introduction.

Raleigh-Durham, NC - continued

Item	Per	Value	Date	Ref.
Transportation				
Driver's license fee, duplicate	lic	5.00	1/94	84s
Driver's license reinstatement fee, min.	susp	25.00	1/94	85s
Driver's license renewal fee	renew	10.00	1/94	84s
Driving expenses	mile	37.10	5/95	89c
Fine, safety belt violation	ticket	25.00	95	56s
Identification card, nondriver	card	10.00	1/94	83s
Motorcycle license fee	orig	5.00	1/94	84s
Public transportation expenditures	year	249	91	81r
Tire balance, computer or spin bal., front	wheel	6.83	12/94	2c
Transportation expenditures, total	year	5307	91	81r
Vehicle finance charges	year	346	91	81r
Vehicle insurance expenditures	year	544	91	81r
Vehicle maintenance and repairs expenditures	year	600	91	81r
Vehicle purchases	year	2275	91	81r
Vehicle rental, leases, licenses, etc. expenditures	year	141	91	81r
Vehicles purchased, other than cars and trucks	year	27	91	81r
Utilities				
Utilities, ACCRA Index		103.90	12/94	2c
Electricity expenditures	year	950	91	81r
Electricity, 1800 sq. ft., new home	mo.	117.78	12/94	2c
Electricity, summer, 250 KWh	month	27.99	8/93	64c
Electricity, summer, 500 KWh	month	49.23	8/93	64c
Electricity, summer, 750 KWh	month	70.47	8/93	64c
Electricity, summer, 1000 KWh	month	91.71	8/93	64c
Utilities, fuels, and public services, total expenditures	year	2000	91	81r
Water and other public services, expenditures	year	227	91	81r
Weddings				
Bridal attendants' gowns	event	750	10/93	76r
Bridal gown	event	852	10/93	76r
Bridal headpiece and veil	event	167	10/93	76r
Bride's wedding band	event	708	10/93	76r
Clergy	event	224	10/93	76r
Engagement ring	event	2756	10/93	76r
Flowers	event	863	10/93	76r
Formal wear for groom	event	106	10/93	76r
Groom's attendants' formal wear	event	530	10/93	76r
Groom's wedding band	event	402	10/93	76r
Music	event	600	10/93	76r
Photography	event	1088	10/93	76r
Shoes for bride	event	50	10/93	76r
Videography	event	483	10/93	76r
Wedding invitations and announcements	event	342	10/93	76r
Wedding reception	event	7000	10/93	76r

Rapid City, SD

Item	Per	Value	Date	Ref.
Composite, ACCRA index		97.40	12/94	2c
Alcoholic Beverages				
Beer, Miller Lite, Bud, 12-oz., ex deposit	6	3.78	12/94	2c
J & B Scotch	750-ml.	18.35	12/94	2c
Wine, Gallo Chablis blanc	1.5-lit	5.45	12/94	2c
Appliances				
Appliances (major), expenditures	year	131	91	81r
Average annual exp.				
Food, health care, personal goods, services	year	25935	91	81r
Charity				
Cash contributions, expenditures	year	745	91	81r
Clothing				
Apparel, men and boys, total expenditures	year	332	91	81r
Apparel, women and girls, total expenditures	year	578	91	81r
Footwear, expenditures	year	164	91	81r
Jeans, man's denim		29.79	12/94	2c

Rapid City, SD - continued

Item	Per	Value	Date	Ref.
Clothing - continued				
Shirt, man's dress shirt		36.67	12/94	2c
Undervest, boy's size 10-14, cotton	3	3.26	12/94	2c
Communications				
Long-distance telephone rate, day, addl. min., 1-10 mi.	min.	0.15	12/93	9s
Long-distance telephone rate, day, initial min., 1-10 mi.	min.	0.21	12/93	9s
Newspaper subscription, dly. and Sun. delivery	month	11.75	12/94	2c
Phone line, single, business, field visit	inst	47.00	12/93	9s
Phone line, single, business, no field visit	inst	47.00	12/93	9s
Phone line, single, residence, field visit	inst	25.00	12/93	9s
Phone line, single, residence, no field visit	inst	25.00	12/93	9s
Telephone bill, family of four	month	22.46	12/94	2c
Telephone service, expenditures	year	547	91	81r
Telephone, residential, flat rate	mo.	14.70	12/93	8c
Education				
Board, 4-year private college/university	year	2219	8/94	80s
Board, 4-year public college/university	year	1526	8/94	80s
Education, total expenditures	year	394	91	81r
Room, 4-year private college/university	year	1445	8/94	80s
Room, 4-year public college/university	year	1060	8/94	80s
Total cost, 4-year private college/university	year	11387	8/94	80s
Total cost, 4-year public college/university	year	4874	8/94	80s
Tuition, 2-year public college/university, in-state	year	2640	8/94	80s
Tuition, 4-year private college/university, in-state	year	7722	8/94	80s
Tuition, 4-year public college/university, in-state	year	2288	8/94	80s
Energy and Fuels				
Energy, combined forms, 1800 sq. ft.	mo.	117.38	12/94	2c
Energy, exc. electricity, 1800 sq. ft.	mo.	56.00	12/94	2c
Fuel oil and other fuels, expenditures	year	83	91	81r
Gas, cooking, winter, 10 therms	month	11.50	2/94	65c
Gas, cooking, winter, 30 therms	month	20.50	2/94	65c
Gas, cooking, winter, 50 therms	month	29.50	2/94	65c
Gas, heating, winter, 100 therms	month	51.50	2/94	65c
Gas, heating, winter, average use	month	82.54	2/94	65c
Gas, natural, expenditures	year	373	91	81r
Gas, reg unlead, taxes inc., cash, self-service	gal	1.22	12/94	2c
Gasoline and motor oil purchased	year	1000	91	81r
Gasoline, unleaded midgrade	gallon	1.15	4/93	82r
Gasoline, unleaded premium	gallon	1.23	4/93	82r
Gasoline, unleaded regular	gallon	1.07	4/93	82r
Entertainment				
Bowling, evening rate	game	2.00	12/94	2c
Entertainment, total expenditures	year	1356	91	81r
Fees and admissions, expenditures	year	347	91	81r
Monopoly game, Parker Brothers', No. 9	game	10.37	12/94	2c
Movie	adm	5.50	12/94	2c
Pets, toys, playground equipment, expenditures	year	270	91	81r
Reading, expenditures	year	160	91	81r
Televisions, radios, and sound equipment, expenditures	year	433	91	81r
Tennis balls, yellow, Wilson or Penn, 3	can	2.41	12/94	2c
Funerals				
Burial, immediate, container provided by funeral home		1348.78	1/95	54r
Cards, acknowledgment		21.20	1/95	54r
Casket, minimum alternative		182.83	1/95	54r
Cosmetology, hair care, etc.		133.11	1/95	54r
Cremation, direct, container provided by funeral home		1101.95	1/95	54r
Embalming		314.45	1/95	54r
Funeral, funeral home		304.88	1/95	54r
Funeral, other facility		301.37	1/95	54r

Values are in dollars or fractions of dollars. In the column headed *Ref*, references are shown to sources. Each reference is followed by a letter. These refer to the geographical level for which data were reported: s = State, r = Region, and c = City or metro. The abbreviation *ex* is used to mean *except* or *excluding*; *exp* stands for expenditures. For other abbreviations and further explanations, please see the Introduction.

Rapid City, SD - continued

Item	Per	Value	Date	Ref.
Funerals				
Graveside service		290.59	1/95	54r
Hearse, local		137.37	1/95	54r
Limousine, local		82.84	1/95	54r
Memorial service		316.57	1/95	54r
Service charge, professional, nondeclinable		1099.00	1/95	54r
Visitation and viewing		209.25	1/95	54r
Groceries				
Groceries, ACCRA Index		97.40	12/94	2c
Apples, Red Delicious	lb.	0.68	12/94	82r
Baby food, strained vegetables, lowest price	4-4.5 oz.	0.34	12/94	2c
Bacon, sliced	lb.	1.88	12/94	82r
Bananas	lb.	0.57	12/94	2c
Bananas	lb.	0.41	12/94	82r
Beef or hamburger, ground	lb.	1.24	12/94	2c
Beef purchases	year	197	91	81r
Beef, stew, boneless	lb.	2.52	12/94	82r
Beverage purchases, alcoholic	year	293	91	81r
Beverage purchases, nonalcoholic	year	203	91	81r
Bologna, all beef or mixed	lb.	2.12	12/94	82r
Bread, white	24-oz.	0.57	12/94	2c
Bread, white, pan	lb.	0.76	12/94	82r
Cabbage	lb.	0.44	12/94	82r
Carrots, short trimmed and topped	lb.	0.44	12/94	82r
Cereals and bakery products purchases	year	347	91	81r
Cereals and cereals products purchases	year	119	91	81r
Cheddar cheese, natural	lb.	3.28	12/94	82r
Cheese, Kraft grated Parmesan	8-oz.	3.27	12/94	2c
Chicken breast, bone-in	lb.	1.61	12/94	82r
Chicken, fresh, whole	lb.	0.89	12/94	82r
Chicken, whole fryer	lb.	0.79	12/94	2c
Chuck roast, USDA choice, boneless	lb.	2.33	12/94	82r
Cigarettes, Winston, Kings	carton	14.68	12/94	2c
Coffee, 100%, ground roast, all sizes	lb.	4.28	12/94	82r
Coffee, vacuum-packed	13 oz.	3.41	12/94	2c
Cookies, chocolate chip	lb.	2.72	12/94	82r
Corn Flakes, Kellogg's or Post Toasties	18 oz.	2.00	12/94	2c
Corn, frozen, whole kernel, lowest price	10 oz.	0.67	12/94	2c
Dairy products (other) purchases	year	148	91	81r
Eggs, Grade A large	dozen	0.74	12/94	2c
Eggs, Grade A large	dozen	0.76	12/94	82r
Fish and seafood purchases	year	61	91	81r
Flour, white, all purpose	lb.	0.22	12/94	82r
Food purchases, food eaten at home	year	2313	91	81r
Foods purchased away from home, not prepared by consumer	year	1709	91	81r
Fruits and vegetables purchases	year	372	91	81r
Grapefruit	lb.	0.47	12/94	82r
Grapes, Thompson seedless	lb.	2.15	12/94	82r
Ground beef, 100% beef	lb.	1.37	12/94	82r
Ground chuck, 100% beef	lb.	1.81	12/94	82r
Ham, boneless, exc. canned	lb.	2.16	12/94	82r
Ice cream, prepackaged, bulk, regular	1/2 gal.	2.48	12/94	82r
Lemons	lb.	1.08	12/94	82r
Lettuce, iceberg	lb.	0.81	12/94	82r
Lettuce, iceberg	head	0.72	12/94	2c
Margarine, Blue Bonnet or Parkay cubes	lb.	0.66	12/94	2c
Margarine, stick	lb.	0.81	12/94	82r
Meats, poultry, fish, and eggs purchases	year	591	91	81r
Milk and cream (fresh) purchases	year	132	91	81r
Milk, whole	1/2 gal.	1.47	12/94	2c
Orange juice, frozen concentrate 12-oz. can	16 oz.	1.41	12/94	82r
Orange juice, Minute Maid frozen	12-oz.	1.27	12/94	2c
Oranges, Navel	lb.	0.56	12/94	82r
Peaches, halves or slices, Hunt's, Del Monte, or Libby's	29-oz.	1.41	12/94	2c
Peanut butter, creamy, all sizes	lb.	1.81	12/94	82r
Peas, sweet, Del Monte or Green Giant	15-17 oz.	0.60	12/94	2c
Pork chops, center cut, bone-in	lb.	2.76	12/94	82r

Rapid City, SD - continued

Item	Per	Value	Date	Ref.
Groceries - continued				
Pork purchases	year	130	91	81r
Potato chips	16-oz.	2.81	12/94	82r
Potatoes, frozen, French fried	lb.	0.83	12/94	82r
Potatoes, white	lb.	0.28	12/94	82r
Potatoes, white or red	10-lb. sack	1.31	12/94	2c
Round roast, USDA choice, boneless	lb.	2.90	12/94	82r
Sausage, Jimmy Dean, 100% pork	lb.	3.59	12/94	2c
Shortening, vegetable oil blends	lb.	0.88	12/94	82r
Shortening, vegetable, Crisco	3-lb.	2.49	12/94	2c
Soft drink, Coca Cola, ex deposit	2 lit	1.37	12/94	2c
Spaghetti and macaroni	lb.	0.78	12/94	82r
Steak, rib eye, USDA choice, boneless	lb.	6.15	12/94	82r
Steak, round, graded & ungraded, exc. USDA prime & choice	lb.	2.72	12/94	82r
Steak, round, USDA choice, boneless	lb.	3.02	12/94	82r
Steak, sirloin, USDA choice, boneless	lb.	3.85	12/94	82r
Steak, t-bone	lb.	4.92	12/94	2c
Steak, T-bone, USDA choice, bone-in	lb.	5.38	12/94	82r
Sugar and other sweets, eaten at home, expenditures	year	91	91	81r
Sugar, cane or beet	4 lbs.	1.35	12/94	2c
Sugar, white, all sizes	lb.	0.36	12/94	82r
Tobacco products and smoking supplies, total expenditures	year	298	91	81r
Tomatoes, field grown	lb.	1.36	12/94	82r
Tomatoes, Hunt's or Del Monte	14.5 oz.	0.76	12/94	2c
Tuna, chunk, light	lb.	1.94	12/94	82r
Tuna, chunk, light, oil-packed	6.125-6.5 oz.	0.66	12/94	2c
Turkey, frozen, whole	lb.	0.96	12/94	82r
Yogurt, natural, fruit flavored	8 oz.	0.62	12/94	82r
Goods and Services				
Miscellaneous goods and services, ACCRA Index		96.20	12/94	2c
Health Care				
Health care, ACCRA Index		93.00	12/94	2c
Antibiotic ointment, Polysporin	1.5 oz.	4.21	12/94	2c
Childbirth, Cesarean delivery, hospital charge	birth	5101.00	12/91	69r
Childbirth, Cesarean delivery, physician charge	birth	2234.00	12/91	69r
Childbirth, normal delivery, hospital charge	birth	2891.00	12/91	69r
Childbirth, normal delivery, physician charge	birth	1623.00	12/91	69r
Dentist's fee, adult teeth cleaning and periodic oral exam	visit	55.80	12/94	2c
Doctor's fee, routine exam, established patient	visit	34.20	12/94	2c
Drugs, expenditures	year	248	91	81r
Health care, total expenditures	year	1336	91	81r
Health insurance expenditures	year	550	91	81r
Hospital care, semiprivate room	day	300.00	12/94	2c
Insurance premium, family medical care	month	337.90	1/95	41s
Medical services expenditures	year	457	91	81r
Medical supplies expenditures	year	82	91	81r
Household Goods				
Appl. repair, service call, wash mach	min. lab. chg.	31.19	12/94	2c
Floor coverings, expenditures	year	105	91	81r
Furniture, expenditures	year	291	91	81r
Household equipment, misc. expenditures	year	341	91	81r
Household expenditures, miscellaneous	year	162	91	81r
Household furnishings and equipment, expenditures	year	1042	91	81r
Household operations expenditures	year	365	91	81r
Household textiles, expenditures	year	101	91	81r
Housekeeping supplies, expenditures	year	390	91	81r
Laundry and cleaning supplies, expenditures	year	110	91	81r

Values are in dollars or fractions of dollars. In the column headed *Ref*, references are shown to sources. Each reference is followed by a letter. These refer to the geographical level for which data were reported: s=State, r=Region, and c=City or metro. The abbreviation *ex* is used to mean *except* or *excluding*; *exp* stands for *expenditures*. For other abbreviations and further explanations, please see the Introduction.

Rapid City, SD - continued

Item	Per	Value	Date	Ref.
Household Goods				
Laundry detergent, Tide Ultra, Bold, or Cheer	42 oz.	3.21	12/94	2c
Postage and stationery, expenditures	year	115	91	81r
Tissues, facial, Kleenex brand	175	0.94	12/94	2c
Housing				
Housing, ACCRA Index		97.50	12/94	2c
Add garage/carport		8,479	3/95	74r
Add room(s)		21,347	3/95	74r
Apartment condominium or co-op, median	unit	87100	12/94	62r
Bathroom addition, average cost	add	9734.00	3/95	13r
Bathroom remodeling, average cost	remod	6414.00	3/95	13r
Bedroom, master suite addition, average cost	add	27122.00	3/95	13r
Deck addition, average cost	add	6665.00	3/95	13r
Dwellings (owned), expenditures	year	2566	91	81r
Enclose porch/patio/breezeway		4,556	3/95	74r
Exterior remodeling, average cost	remod	15395.00	3/95	13r
Family room addition, average cost	add	27658.00	3/95	13r
Finish room in basement/attic		5,074	3/95	74r
Home, existing, single-family, median	unit	106500	12/94	62r
House payment, principal and interest, 25% down payment	mo.	728	12/94	2c
House, 1800 sq ft, 8000 sq ft lot, new, urban, utilities	total	115860	12/94	2c
Kitchen remodeling, major, average cost	remod	17084.00	3/95	13r
Kitchen remodeling, minor, average cost	remod	5804.00	3/95	13r
Maintenance, repairs, insurance, and other housing expenditures	year	484	91	81r
Mortgage interest and charges expenditures	year	1443	91	81r
Mtge. rate, incl. points and orig. fee, 30-year conv. fixed or ARM	mo.	9.46	12/94	2c
Office, home addition, average cost	add	8121.00	3/95	13r
Princ. & int., mortgage, median-price exist. sing.-family home	mo.	515	12/94	62r
Property taxes expenditures	year	639	91	81r
Redesign, restructure more than half of home's interior		9,114	3/95	74r
Rent, apartment, 2 br., 1 1/2-2 baths, unfurnished, 950 sq ft, water	mo.	569	12/94	2c
Rental units expenditures	year	1200	91	81r
Sun-space addition, average cost	add	23768.00	3/95	13r
Wing addition, two-story, average cost	add	50410.00	3/95	13r
Insurance and Pensions				
Auto insurance, private passenger	year	484.96	12/94	71s
Insurance and pensions, personal, expenditures	year	2408	91	81r
Insurance, life and other personal, expenditures	year	355	91	81r
Pensions and Social Security, expenditures	year	2053	91	81r
Legal Assistance				
Legal work, law firm associate	hour	90		10r
Legal work, law firm partner	hour	139		10r
Personal Goods				
Shampoo, Alberto VO5	15-oz.	1.16	12/94	2c
Toothpaste, Crest or Colgate	6-7 oz.	1.81	12/94	2c
Personal Services				
Dry cleaning, man's 2-pc. suit		6.71	12/94	2c
Haircut, man's barbershop, no styling		9.09	12/94	2c
Haircut, woman's shampoo, trim, blow-dry		12.70	12/94	2c
Personal services expenditures	year	203	91	81r
Restaurant Food				
Chicken, fried, thigh and drumstick		2.18	12/94	2c
Dining expenditures, family	week	30.03	94	73r
Hamburger with cheese	1/4 lb.	1.80	12/94	2c
Pizza, Pizza Hut or Pizza Inn	12-13 in.	4.99	12/94	2c

Rapid City, SD - continued

Item	Per	Value	Date	Ref.
Taxes				
Tax, cigarettes	year	459.00	10/93	43s
Taxes, Federal income, expenditures	year	1756	91	81r
Taxes, personal, expenditures	year	2426	91	81r
Taxes, State and local income, expenditures	year	568	91	81r
Transportation				
Transportation, ACCRA Index		96.90	12/94	2c
Cars and trucks purchased, new	year	891	91	81r
Cars and trucks purchased, used	year	1155	91	81r
Driver's learning permit fee	perm	8.00	1/94	84s
Driver's license fee	orig	8.00	1/94	84s
Driver's license fee, duplicate	lic	6.00	1/94	84s
Driver's license reinstatement fee, min.	susp	50.00	1/94	85s
Driver's license renewal fee	renew	8.00	1/94	84s
Identification card, nondriver	card	6.00	1/94	83s
Motorcycle learning permit fee	perm	8.00	1/94	84s
Motorcycle license fee	orig	8.00	1/94	84s
Motorcycle license fee, duplicate	lic	6.00	1/94	84s
Motorcycle license renewal fee	renew	8.00	1/94	84s
Public transportation expenditures	year	209	91	81r
Tire balance, computer or spin bal., front	wheel	5.49	12/94	2c
Transportation expenditures, total	year	4792	91	81r
Vehicle finance charges	year	300	91	81r
Vehicle insurance expenditures	year	485	91	81r
Vehicle maintenance and repairs expenditures	year	534	91	81r
Vehicle purchases	year	2068	91	81r
Vehicle rental, leases, licenses, etc. expenditures	year	197	91	81r
Vehicles purchased, other than cars and trucks	year	22	91	81r
Utilities				
Utilities, ACCRA Index		106.00	12/94	2c
Electricity expenditures	year	668	91	81r
Electricity, (part.), other, 1800 sq. ft., new home	mo.	61.38	12/94	2c
Electricity, summer, 250 KWh	month	24.19	8/93	64c
Electricity, summer, 500 KWh	month	41.38	8/93	64c
Electricity, summer, 750 KWh	month	58.56	8/93	64c
Electricity, summer, 1000 KWh	month	75.75	8/93	64c
Utilities, fuels, and public services, total expenditures	year	1838	91	81r
Water and other public services, expenditures	year	167	91	81r
Weddings				
Bridal attendants' gowns	event	750	10/93	76r
Bridal gown	event	852	10/93	76r
Bridal headpiece and veil	event	167	10/93	76r
Bride's wedding band	event	708	10/93	76r
Clergy	event	224	10/93	76r
Engagement ring	event	2756	10/93	76r
Flowers	event	863	10/93	76r
Formal wear for groom	event	106	10/93	76r
Groom's attendants' formal wear	event	530	10/93	76r
Groom's wedding band	event	402	10/93	76r
Music	event	600	10/93	76r
Photography	event	1088	10/93	76r
Shoes for bride	event	50	10/93	76r
Videography	event	483	10/93	76r
Wedding invitations and announcements	event	342	10/93	76r
Wedding reception	event	7000	10/93	76r

Reading, PA

Item	Per	Value	Date	Ref.
Appliances				
Appliances (major), expenditures	year	145	91	81r
Average annual exp.				
Food, health care, personal goods, services	year	29496	91	81r

Values are in dollars or fractions of dollars. In the column headed *Ref*, references are shown to sources. Each reference is followed by a letter. These refer to the geographical level for which data were reported: s=State, r=Region, and c=City or metro. The abbreviation *ex* is used to mean *except* or *excluding*; *exp* stands for expenditures. For other abbreviations and further explanations, please see the Introduction.

Reading, PA - continued

Item	Per	Value	Date	Ref.
Charity				
Cash contributions, expenditures	year	708	91	81r
Clothing				
Apparel, men and boys, total expenditures	year	416	91	81r
Apparel, women and girls, total expenditures	year	744	91	81r
Footwear, expenditures	year	305	91	81r
Communications				
Long-distance telephone rate, day, addl. min., 1-10 mi.	min.	0.08	12/93	9s
Long-distance telephone rate, day, initial min., 1-10 mi.	min.	0.15	12/93	9s
Phone line, single, business, field visit	inst	75.00	12/93	9s
Phone line, single, business, no field visit	inst	75.00	12/93	9s
Phone line, single, residence, field visit	inst	40.00	12/93	9s
Phone line, single, residence, no field visit	inst	40.00	12/93	9s
Telephone service, expenditures	year	589	91	81r
Education				
Board, 4-year private college/university	year	2714	8/94	80s
Board, 4-year public college/university	year	1899	8/94	80s
Education, total expenditures	year	593	91	81r
Room, 4-year private college/university	year	2720	8/94	80s
Room, 4-year public college/university	year	2063	8/94	80s
Total cost, 4-year private college/university	year	18118	8/94	80s
Total cost, 4-year public college/university	year	8278	8/94	80s
Tuition, 2-year public college/university, in-state	year	1671	8/94	80s
Tuition, 4-year private college/university, in-state	year	12684	8/94	80s
Tuition, 4-year public college/university, in-state	year	4316	8/94	80s
Energy and Fuels				
Fuel oil and other fuels, expenditures	year	257	91	81r
Gas, natural, expenditures	year	285	91	81r
Gasoline and motor oil purchased	year	867	91	81r
Gasoline, unleaded midgrade	gallon	1.32	4/93	82r
Gasoline, unleaded premium	gallon	1.40	4/93	82r
Gasoline, unleaded regular	gallon	1.19	4/93	82r
Entertainment				
Entertainment, total expenditures	year	1331	91	81r
Fees and admissions, expenditures	year	398	91	81r
Pets, toys, playground equipment, expenditures	year	270	91	81r
Reading, expenditures	year	171	91	81r
Televisions, radios, and sound equipment, expenditures	year	429	91	81r
Funerals				
Burial, immediate, container provided by funeral home		1370.36	1/95	54r
Cards, acknowledgment		17.72	1/95	54r
Casket, minimum alternative		192.52	1/95	54r
Cosmetology, hair care, etc.		139.56	1/95	54r
Cremation, direct, container provided by funeral home		1049.24	1/95	54r
Embalming		387.57	1/95	54r
Funeral, funeral home		278.77	1/95	54r
Funeral, other facility		275.85	1/95	54r
Graveside service		213.08	1/95	54r
Hearse, local		157.27	1/95	54r
Limousine, local		146.45	1/95	54r
Memorial service		271.02	1/95	54r
Service charge, professional, nondeclinable		943.58	1/95	54r
Visitation and viewing		322.86	1/95	54r
Groceries				
Apples, Red Delicious	lb.	0.78	12/94	82r
Bacon, sliced	lb.	2.24	12/94	82r
Bananas	lb.	0.49	12/94	82r
Beef purchases	year	226	91	81r
Beverage purchases, alcoholic	year	332	91	81r
Beverage purchases, nonalcoholic	year	213	91	81r

Reading, PA - continued

Item	Per	Value	Date	Ref.
Groceries - continued				
Bread, white, pan	lb.	0.80	12/94	82r
Butter, salted, Grade AA, stick	lb.	1.67	12/94	82r
Carrots, short trimmed and topped	lb.	0.51	12/94	82r
Cereals and bakery products purchases	year	407	91	81r
Cereals and cereals products purchases	year	132	91	81r
Chicken breast, bone-in	lb.	2.22	12/94	82r
Chicken, fresh, whole	lb.	1.05	12/94	82r
Chuck roast, USDA choice, boneless	lb.	2.74	12/94	82r
Coffee, 100%, ground roast, all sizes	lb.	4.61	12/94	82r
Dairy products (other) purchases	year	161	91	81r
Eggs, Grade A large	dozen	1.12	12/94	82r
Fish and seafood purchases	year	112	91	81r
Food purchases, food eaten at home	year	2599	91	81r
Foods purchased away from home, not prepared by consumer	year	2024	91	81r
Fruits and vegetables purchases	year	444	91	81r
Grapefruit	lb.	0.44	12/94	82r
Grapes, Thompson seedless	lb.	2.24	12/94	82r
Ground chuck, 100% beef	lb.	1.67	12/94	82r
Ice cream, prepackaged, bulk, regular	1/2 gal.	2.93	12/94	82r
Lemons	lb.	1.06	12/94	82r
Lettuce, iceberg	lb.	0.92	12/94	82r
Meats, poultry, fish, and eggs purchases	year	751	91	81r
Milk and cream (fresh) purchases	year	152	91	81r
Orange juice, frozen concentrate 12-oz. can	16 oz.	1.92	12/94	82r
Oranges, Navel	lb.	0.56	12/94	82r
Pork chops, center cut, bone-in	lb.	3.09	12/94	82r
Pork purchases	year	130	91	81r
Potatoes, white	lb.	0.37	12/94	82r
Rib roast, USDA choice, bone-in	lb.	4.98	12/94	82r
Round roast, USDA choice, boneless	lb.	2.93	12/94	82r
Shortening, vegetable oil blends	lb.	1.03	12/94	82r
Spaghetti and macaroni	lb.	0.84	12/94	82r
Steak, round, USDA choice, boneless	lb.	3.48	12/94	82r
Steak, sirloin, USDA choice, bone-in	lb.	3.38	12/94	82r
Steak, sirloin, USDA choice, boneless	lb.	4.81	12/94	82r
Sugar and other sweets, eaten at home, expenditures	year	89	91	81r
Sugar, white, all sizes	lb.	0.46	12/94	82r
Tobacco products and smoking supplies, total expenditures	year	279	91	81r
Tomatoes, field grown	lb.	1.56	12/94	82r
Tuna, chunk, light	lb.	2.09	12/94	82r
Health Care				
Childbirth, Cesarean delivery, hospital charge	birth	6334.00	12/91	69r
Childbirth, Cesarean delivery, physician charge	birth	2234.00	12/91	69r
Childbirth, normal delivery, hospital charge	birth	3225.00	12/91	69r
Childbirth, normal delivery, physician charge	birth	1623.00	12/91	69r
Drugs, expenditures	year	205	91	81r
Health care, total expenditures	year	1396	91	81r
Health insurance expenditures	year	553	91	81r
Insurance premium, family medical care	month	349.05	1/95	41s
Medical services expenditures	year	559	91	81r
Medical supplies expenditures	year	80	91	81r
Household Goods				
Floor coverings, expenditures	year	158	91	81r
Furniture, expenditures	year	341	91	81r
Household equipment, misc. expenditures	year	363	91	81r
Household expenditures, miscellaneous	year	194	91	81r
Household furnishings and equipment, expenditures	year	1158	91	81r
Household operations expenditures	year	378	91	81r
Household textiles, expenditures	year	88	91	81r
Housekeeping supplies, expenditures	year	426	91	81r
Laundry and cleaning supplies, expenditures	year	122	91	81r
Postage and stationery, expenditures	year	134	91	81r

Values are in dollars or fractions of dollars. In the column headed *Ref*, references are shown to sources. Each reference is followed by a letter. These refer to the geographical level for which data were reported: s = State, r = Region, and c = City or metro. The abbreviation *ex* is used to mean *except* or *excluding*; *exp* stands for expenditures. For other abbreviations and further explanations, please see the Introduction.

Reading, PA - continued

Item	Per	Value	Date	Ref.
Housing				
Add garage/carport		11,614	3/95	74r
Add room(s)		16,816	3/95	74r
Apartment condominium or co-op, median	unit	96700	12/94	62r
Dwellings (owned), expenditures	year	3305	91	81r
Enclose porch/patio/breezeway		2,980	3/95	74r
Finish room in basement/attic		4,330	3/95	74r
Home, existing, single-family, median	unit	161600	12/94	62r
Maintenance, repairs, insurance, and other housing expenditures	year	569	91	81r
Mortgage interest and charges expenditures	year	1852	91	81r
Princ. & int., mortgage, median-price exist. sing.-family home	mo.	765	12/94	62r
Property taxes expenditures	year	884	91	81r
Redesign, restructure more than half of home's interior		2,750	3/95	74r
Rental units expenditures	year	1832	91	81r
Insurance and Pensions				
Auto insurance, private passenger	year	721.50	12/94	71s
Insurance and pensions, personal, expenditures	year	2690	91	81r
Insurance, life and other personal, expenditures	year	341	91	81r
Pensions and Social Security, expenditures	year	2349	91	81r
Legal Assistance				
Estate planning, law-firm partner	hr.	375.00	10/93	12r
Legal work, law firm associate	hour	78		10r
Legal work, law firm partner	hour	183		10r
Personal Services				
Personal services expenditures	year	184	91	81r
Restaurant Food				
Dining expenditures, family	week	34.26	94	73r
Taxes				
Taxes, Federal income, expenditures	year	2409	91	81r
Taxes, personal, expenditures	year	3094	91	81r
Taxes, State and local income, expenditures	year	620	91	81r
Transportation				
Cars and trucks purchased, new	year	1170	91	81r
Cars and trucks purchased, used	year	739	91	81r
Driver's learning permit fee	perm	27.00	1/94	84s
Driver's license fee	orig	0.00	1/94	84s
Driver's license fee, duplicate	lic	7.00	1/94	84s
Driver's license reinstatement fee, min.	susp	25.00	1/94	85s
Driver's license renewal fee	renew	0.00	1/94	84s
Identification card, nondriver	card	5.00	1/94	83s
Motorcycle learning permit fee	perm	27.00	1/94	84s
Motorcycle license fee	orig	0.00	1/94	84s
Motorcycle license fee, duplicate	lic	7.00	1/94	84s
Motorcycle license renewal fee	renew	0.00	1/94	84s
Public transportation expenditures	year	430	91	81r
Transportation expenditures, total	year	4810	91	81r
Vehicle finance charges	year	238	91	81r
Vehicle insurance expenditures	year	630	91	81r
Vehicle maintenance and repairs expenditures	year	532	91	81r
Vehicle purchases	year	1920	91	81r
Vehicle rental, leases, licenses, etc. expenditures	year	193	91	81r
Vehicles purchased, other than cars and trucks	year	11	91	81r
Utilities				
Electricity expenditures	year	695	91	81r
Utilities, fuels, and public services, total expenditures	year	1981	91	81r
Water and other public services, expenditures	year	154	91	81r
Weddings				
Bridal attendants' gowns	event	750	10/93	76r
Bridal gown	event	852	10/93	76r

Reading, PA - continued

Item	Per	Value	Date	Ref.
Weddings - continued				
Bridal headpiece and veil	event	167	10/93	76r
Bride's wedding band	event	708	10/93	76r
Clergy	event	224	10/93	76r
Engagement ring	event	2756	10/93	76r
Flowers	event	863	10/93	76r
Formal wear for groom	event	106	10/93	76r
Groom's attendants' formal wear	event	530	10/93	76r
Groom's wedding band	event	402	10/93	76r
Music	event	600	10/93	76r
Photography	event	1088	10/93	76r
Shoes for bride	event	50	10/93	76r
Videography	event	483	10/93	76r
Wedding invitations and announcements	event	342	10/93	76r
Wedding reception	event	7000	10/93	76r

Redding, CA

Item	Per	Value	Date	Ref.
Appliances				
Appliances (major), expenditures	year	160	91	81r
Average annual exp.				
Food, health care, personal goods, services	year	32461	91	81r
Charity				
Cash contributions, expenditures	year	975	91	81r
Clothing				
Apparel, men and boys, total expenditures	year	467	91	81r
Apparel, women and girls, total expenditures	year	737	91	81r
Footwear, expenditures	year	270	91	81r
Communications				
Long-distance telephone rate, day, addl. min., 1-10 mi.	min.	0.07	12/93	9s
Long-distance telephone rate, day, initial min., 1-10 mi.	min.	0.17	12/93	9s
Phone line, single, business, field visit	inst	70.75	12/93	9s
Phone line, single, business, no field visit	inst	70.75	12/93	9s
Phone line, single, residence, field visit	inst	34.75	12/93	9s
Phone line, single, residence, no field visit	inst	34.75	12/93	9s
Telephone service, expenditures	year	611	91	81r
Education				
Board, 4-year private college/university	year	2945	8/94	80s
Board, 4-year public college/university	year	2321	8/94	80s
Education, total expenditures	year	375	91	81r
Room, 4-year private college/university	year	3094	8/94	80s
Room, 4-year public college/university	year	2812	8/94	80s
Student fee, university	year	21.00	93	18s
Total cost, 4-year private college/university	year	19321	8/94	80s
Total cost, 4-year public college/university	year	7511	8/94	80s
Tuition, 2-year public college/university, in-state	year	345	8/94	80s
Tuition, 4-year private college/university, in-state	year	13282	8/94	80s
Tuition, 4-year public college/university, in-state	year	2378	8/94	80s
Energy and Fuels				
Fuel oil and other fuels, expenditures	year	33	91	81r
Gas, natural, expenditures	year	212	91	81r
Gasoline and motor oil purchased	year	1115	91	81r
Gasoline, unleaded midgrade	gallon	1.36	4/93	82r
Gasoline, unleaded premium	gallon	1.43	4/93	82r
Gasoline, unleaded regular	gallon	1.23	4/93	82r
Entertainment				
Concert ticket, Pearl Jam group	perf	20.00	94	50r
Entertainment, total expenditures	year	1853	91	81r
Fees and admissions, expenditures	year	482	91	81r
Pets, toys, playground equipment, expenditures	year	299	91	81r
Reading, expenditures	year	164	91	81r

Values are in dollars or fractions of dollars. In the column headed *Ref*, references are shown to sources. Each reference is followed by a letter. These refer to the geographical level for which data were reported: s=State, r=Region, and c=City or metro. The abbreviation *ex* is used to mean *except* or *excluding*; *exp* stands for expenditures. For other abbreviations and further explanations, please see the Introduction.

Redding, CA - continued

Item	Per	Value	Date	Ref.
Entertainment				
Televisions, radios, and sound equipment, expenditures	year	528	91	81r
Funerals				
Burial, immediate, container provided by funeral home		1382.70	1/95	54r
Cards, acknowledgment		21.87	1/95	54r
Casket, minimum alternative		128.54	1/95	54r
Cosmetology, hair care, etc.		119.69	1/95	54r
Cremation, direct, container provided by funeral home		1030.62	1/95	54r
Embalming		255.42	1/95	54r
Funeral, funeral home		437.38	1/95	54r
Funeral, other facility		444.46	1/95	54r
Graveside service		338.46	1/95	54r
Hearse, local		147.50	1/95	54r
Limousine, local		130.33	1/95	54r
Memorial service		553.16	1/95	54r
Service charge, professional, nondeclinable		859.15	1/95	54r
Visitation and viewing		93.23	1/95	54r
Groceries				
Apples, Red Delicious	lb.	0.72	12/94	82r
Bacon, sliced	lb.	1.73	12/94	82r
Bananas	lb.	0.52	12/94	82r
Beef purchases	year	241	91	81r
Beverage purchases, alcoholic	year	328	91	81r
Beverage purchases, nonalcoholic	year	234	91	81r
Bologna, all beef or mixed	lb.	2.33	12/94	82r
Bread, white, pan	lb.	0.81	12/94	82r
Carrots, short trimmed and topped	lb.	0.43	12/94	82r
Cereals and bakery products purchases	year	392	91	81r
Cereals and cereals products purchases	year	139	91	81r
Chicken breast, bone-in	lb.	2.04	12/94	82r
Chicken, fresh, whole	lb.	0.95	12/94	82r
Coffee, 100%, ground roast, all sizes	lb.	4.48	12/94	82r
Dairy products (other) purchases	year	182	91	81r
Fish and seafood purchases	year	94	91	81r
Flour, white, all purpose	lb.	0.21	12/94	82r
Food purchases, food eaten at home	year	2749	91	81r
Foods purchased away from home, not prepared by consumer	year	1909	91	81r
Fruits and vegetables purchases	year	459	91	81r
Grapefruit	lb.	0.56	12/94	82r
Ground beef, 100% beef	lb.	1.31	12/94	82r
Ham, boneless, exc. canned	lb.	2.46	12/94	82r
Ice cream, prepackaged, bulk, regular	1/2 gal.	2.57	12/94	82r
Lemons	lb.	1.00	12/94	82r
Lettuce, iceberg	lb.	0.93	12/94	82r
Meats, poultry, fish, and eggs purchases	year	700	91	81r
Milk and cream (fresh) purchases	year	155	91	81r
Orange juice, frozen concentrate 12-oz. can	16 oz.	1.52	12/94	82r
Oranges, Navel	lb.	0.56	12/94	82r
Pork chops, center cut, bone-in	lb.	3.30	12/94	82r
Pork purchases	year	122	91	81r
Potato chips	16-oz.	3.03	12/94	82r
Potatoes, frozen, French fried	lb.	0.77	12/94	82r
Potatoes, white	lb.	0.35	12/94	82r
Rice, white, long grain, uncooked	lb.	0.54	12/94	82r
Round roast, USDA choice, boneless	lb.	2.92	12/94	82r
Shortening, vegetable oil blends	lb.	0.80	12/94	82r
Spaghetti and macaroni	lb.	1.02	12/94	82r
Steak, round, graded & ungraded, exc. USDA prime & choice	lb.	3.13	12/94	82r
Steak, sirloin, USDA choice, boneless	lb.	4.07	12/94	82r
Sugar and other sweets, eaten at home, expenditures	year	105	91	81r
Sugar, white, all sizes	lb.	0.38	12/94	82r
Tobacco products and smoking supplies, total expenditures	year	221	91	81r
Tomatoes, field grown	lb.	1.45	12/94	82r
Tuna, chunk, light	lb.	2.18	12/94	82r

Redding, CA - continued

Item	Per	Value	Date	Ref.
Health Care				
Childbirth, Cesarean delivery, hospital charge	birth	6059.00	12/91	69r
Childbirth, Cesarean delivery, physician charge	birth	2248.00	12/91	69r
Childbirth, normal delivery, hospital charge	birth	3006.00	12/91	69r
Childbirth, normal delivery, physician charge	birth	1634.00	12/91	69r
Drugs, expenditures	year	230	91	81r
Health care, total expenditures	year	1544	91	81r
Health insurance expenditures	year	558	91	81r
Insurance premium, family medical care	month	380.27	1/95	41s
Medical services expenditures	year	676	91	81r
Medical supplies expenditures	year	80	91	81r
Surgery, open-heart	proc	37818.00	1/93	14r
Household Goods				
Floor coverings, expenditures	year	79	91	81r
Furniture, expenditures	year	352	91	81r
Household equipment, misc. expenditures	year	614	91	81r
Household expenditures, miscellaneous	year	294	91	81r
Household furnishings and equipment, expenditures	year	1416	91	81r
Household operations expenditures	year	580	91	81r
Household textiles, expenditures	year	113	91	81r
Housekeeping supplies, expenditures	year	447	91	81r
Laundry and cleaning supplies, expenditures	year	114	91	81r
Postage and stationery, expenditures	year	145	91	81r
Housing				
Add garage/carport		6,422	3/95	74r
Add room(s)		26,583	3/95	74r
Apartment condominium or co-op, median	unit	105300	12/94	62r
Dwellings (owned), expenditures	year	3932	91	81r
Enclose porch/patio/breezeway		5,382	3/95	74r
Finish room in basement/attic		3,911	3/95	74r
Home, existing, single-family, median	unit	178600	12/94	62r
Maintenance, repairs, insurance, and other housing expenditures	year	591	91	81r
Mortgage interest and charges expenditures	year	2747	91	81r
Princ. & int., mortgage, median-price exist. sing.-family home	mo.	845	12/94	62r
Property taxes expenditures	year	594	91	81r
Redesign, restructure more than half of home's interior		5,467	3/95	74r
Rental units expenditures	year	2077	91	81r
Insurance and Pensions				
Auto insurance, private passenger	year	892.80	12/94	71s
Insurance and pensions, personal, expenditures	year	3042	91	81r
Insurance, life and other personal, expenditures	year	298	91	81r
Pensions and Social Security, expenditures	year	2744	91	81r
Legal Assistance				
Legal work, law firm associate	hour	91		10r
Legal work, law firm partner	hour	151		10r
Personal Services				
Personal services expenditures	year	286	91	81r
Restaurant Food				
Dining expenditures, family	week	32.25	94	73r
Taxes				
Taxes, Federal income, expenditures	year	2946	91	81r
Taxes, personal, expenditures	year	3791	91	81r
Taxes, State and local income, expenditures	year	791	91	81r
Transportation				
Cars and trucks purchased, new	year	1231	91	81r
Cars and trucks purchased, used	year	915	91	81r
Driver's learning permit fee	perm	12.00	1/94	84s
Driver's license fee	orig	12.00	1/94	84s
Driver's license fee, duplicate	lic	12.00	1/94	84s
Driver's license reinstatement fee, min.	susp	15.00	1/94	85s

Values are in dollars or fractions of dollars. In the column headed *Ref*, references are shown to sources. Each reference is followed by a letter. These refer to the geographical level for which data were reported: s=State, r=Region, and c=City or metro. The abbreviation *ex* is used to mean *except* or *excluding*; *exp* stands for expenditures. For other abbreviations and further explanations, please see the Introduction.

Redding, CA - continued

Item	Per	Value	Date	Ref.
Transportation				
Driver's license renewal fee	renew	12.00	1/94	84s
Identification card, nondriver	card	6.00	1/94	83s
Motorcycle learning permit fee	perm	12.00	1/94	84s
Motorcycle license fee	orig	12.00	1/94	84s
Motorcycle license fee, duplicate	lic	12.00	1/94	84s
Motorcycle license renewal fee	renew	12.00	1/94	84s
Public transportation expenditures	year	375	91	81r
Transportation expenditures, total	year	5527	91	81r
Vehicle finance charges	year	287	91	81r
Vehicle insurance expenditures	year	624	91	81r
Vehicle maintenance and repairs expenditures	year	695	91	81r
Vehicle purchases	year	2174	91	81r
Vehicle rental, leases, licenses, etc. expenditures	year	257	91	81r
Vehicles purchased, other than cars and trucks	year	28	91	81r
Utilities				
Electricity expenditures	year	616	91	81r
Utilities, fuels, and public services, total expenditures	year	1681	91	81r
Water and other public services, expenditures	year	209	91	81r
Weddings				
Bridal attendants' gowns	event	750	10/93	76r
Bridal gown	event	852	10/93	76r
Bridal headpiece and veil	event	167	10/93	76r
Bride's wedding band	event	708	10/93	76r
Clergy	event	224	10/93	76r
Engagement ring	event	2756	10/93	76r
Flowers	event	863	10/93	76r
Formal wear for groom	event	106	10/93	76r
Groom's attendants' formal wear	event	530	10/93	76r
Groom's wedding band	event	402	10/93	76r
Music	event	600	10/93	76r
Photography	event	1088	10/93	76r
Shoes for bride	event	50	10/93	76r
Videography	event	483	10/93	76r
Wedding invitations and announcements	event	342	10/93	76r
Wedding reception	event	7000	10/93	76r

Reno, NV

Item	Per	Value	Date	Ref.
Composite, ACCRA index		111.90	12/94	2c
Alcoholic Beverages				
Beer, Miller Lite, Bud, 12-oz., ex deposit	6	4.15	12/94	2c
J & B Scotch	750-ml.	17.39	12/94	2c
Wine, Gallo Chablis blanc	1.5-lit	4.77	12/94	2c
Appliances				
Appliances (major), expenditures	year	160	91	81r
Average annual exp.				
Food, health care, personal goods, services	year	32461	91	81r
Charity				
Cash contributions, expenditures	year	975	91	81r
Clothing				
Apparel, men and boys, total expenditures	year	467	91	81r
Apparel, women and girls, total expenditures	year	737	91	81r
Footwear, expenditures	year	270	91	81r
Jeans, man's denim		35.80	12/94	2c
Shirt, man's dress shirt		31.90	12/94	2c
Undervest, boy's size 10-14, cotton	3	5.46	12/94	2c
Communications				
Long-distance telephone rate, day, addl. min., 1-10 mi.	min.	0.06	12/93	9s
Long-distance telephone rate, day, initial min., 1-10 mi.	min.	0.16	12/93	9s

Reno, NV - continued

Item	Per	Value	Date	Ref.
Communications - continued				
Newspaper subscription, dly. and Sun. delivery	month	14.13	12/94	2c
Phone line, single, business, field visit	inst	135.00	12/93	9s
Phone line, single, business, no field visit	inst	74.00	12/93	9s
Phone line, single, residence, field visit	inst	98.00	12/93	9s
Phone line, single, residence, no field visit	inst	45.00	12/93	9s
Telephone bill, family of four	month	13.58	12/94	2c
Telephone service, expenditures	year	611	91	81r
Telephone, residential, flat rate	mo.	10.50	12/93	8c
Education				
Board, 4-year public college/university	year	1862	8/94	80s
Education, total expenditures	year	375	91	81r
Room, 4-year private college/university	year	2600	8/94	80s
Room, 4-year public college/university	year	3003	8/94	80s
Total cost, 4-year public college/university	year	6403	8/94	80s
Tuition, 2-year public college/university, in-state	year	822	8/94	80s
Tuition, 4-year private college/university, in-state	year	7259	8/94	80s
Tuition, 4-year public college/university, in-state	year	1538	8/94	80s
Energy and Fuels				
Energy, combined forms, 1800 sq. ft.	mo.	104.85	12/94	2c
Energy, exc. electricity, 1800 sq. ft.	mo.	45.11	12/94	2c
Fuel oil and other fuels, expenditures	year	33	91	81r
Gas, cooking, winter, 10 therms	month	8.74	2/94	65c
Gas, cooking, winter, 30 therms	month	19.72	2/94	65c
Gas, cooking, winter, 50 therms	month	30.71	2/94	65c
Gas, heating, winter, 100 therms	month	58.17	2/94	65c
Gas, heating, winter, average use	month	63.66	2/94	65c
Gas, natural, expenditures	year	212	91	81r
Gas, reg unlead, taxes inc., cash, self-service	gal	1.31	12/94	2c
Gasoline and motor oil purchased	year	1115	91	81r
Gasoline, unleaded midgrade	gallon	1.36	4/93	82r
Gasoline, unleaded premium	gallon	1.43	4/93	82r
Gasoline, unleaded regular	gallon	1.23	4/93	82r
Entertainment				
Bowling, evening rate	game	1.82	12/94	2c
Concert ticket, Pearl Jam group	perf	20.00	94	50r
Entertainment, total expenditures	year	1853	91	81r
Fees and admissions, expenditures	year	482	91	81r
Monopoly game, Parker Brothers', No. 9	game	10.59	12/94	2c
Movie	adm	6.75	12/94	2c
Pets, toys, playground equipment, expenditures	year	299	91	81r
Reading, expenditures	year	164	91	81r
Televisions, radios, and sound equipment, expenditures	year	528	91	81r
Tennis balls, yellow, Wilson or Penn, 3	can	2.65	12/94	2c
Funerals				
Burial, immediate, container provided by funeral home		1360.49	1/95	54r
Cards, acknowledgment		11.24	1/95	54r
Casket, minimum alternative		232.73	1/95	54r
Cosmetology, hair care, etc.		114.13	1/95	54r
Cremation, direct, container provided by funeral home		1027.08	1/95	54r
Embalming		286.24	1/95	54r
Funeral, funeral home		315.60	1/95	54r
Funeral, other facility		303.08	1/95	54r
Graveside service		423.83	1/95	54r
Hearse, local		133.12	1/95	54r
Limousine, local		99.10	1/95	54r
Memorial service		442.57	1/95	54r
Service charge, professional, nondeclinable		840.16	1/95	54r
Visitation and viewing		168.50	1/95	54r
Groceries				
Groceries, ACCRA Index		104.10	12/94	2c

Values are in dollars or fractions of dollars. In the column headed *Ref*, references are shown to sources. Each reference is followed by a letter. These refer to the geographical level for which data were reported: s = State, r = Region, and c = City or metro. The abbreviation *ex* is used to mean *except* or *excluding*; *exp* stands for *expenditures*. For other abbreviations and further explanations, please see the Introduction.

Reno, NV - continued

Item	Per	Value	Date	Ref.
Groceries				
Apples, Red Delicious	lb.	0.72	12/94	82r
Baby food, strained vegetables, lowest price	4-4.5 oz.	0.35	12/94	2c
Bacon, sliced	lb.	1.73	12/94	82r
Bananas	lb.	0.45	12/94	2c
Bananas	lb.	0.52	12/94	82r
Beef or hamburger, ground	lb.	1.29	12/94	2c
Beef purchases	year	241	91	81r
Beverage purchases, alcoholic	year	328	91	81r
Beverage purchases, nonalcoholic	year	234	91	81r
Bologna, all beef or mixed	lb.	2.33	12/94	82r
Bread, white	24-oz.	0.85	12/94	2c
Bread, white, pan	lb.	0.81	12/94	82r
Carrots, short trimmed and topped	lb.	0.43	12/94	82r
Cereals and bakery products purchases	year	392	91	81r
Cereals and cereals products purchases	year	139	91	81r
Cheese, Kraft grated Parmesan	8-oz.	3.79	12/94	2c
Chicken breast, bone-in	lb.	2.04	12/94	82r
Chicken, fresh, whole	lb.	0.95	12/94	82r
Chicken, whole fryer	lb.	0.76	12/94	2c
Cigarettes, Winston, Kings	carton	17.49	12/94	2c
Coffee, 100%, ground roast, all sizes	lb.	4.48	12/94	82r
Coffee, vacuum-packed	13 oz.	3.83	12/94	2c
Corn Flakes, Kellogg's or Post Toasties	18 oz.	2.56	12/94	2c
Corn, frozen, whole kernel, lowest price	10 oz.	0.68	12/94	2c
Dairy products (other) purchases	year	182	91	81r
Eggs, Grade A large	dozen	0.79	12/94	2c
Fish and seafood purchases	year	94	91	81r
Flour, white, all purpose	lb.	0.21	12/94	82r
Food purchases, food eaten at home	year	2749	91	81r
Foods purchased away from home, not prepared by consumer	year	1909	91	81r
Fruits and vegetables purchases	year	459	91	81r
Grapefruit	lb.	0.56	12/94	82r
Ground beef, 100% beef	lb.	1.31	12/94	82r
Ham, boneless, exc. canned	lb.	2.46	12/94	82r
Ice cream, prepackaged, bulk, regular	1/2 gal.	2.57	12/94	82r
Lemons	lb.	1.00	12/94	82r
Lettuce, iceberg	lb.	0.93	12/94	82r
Lettuce, iceberg	head	0.59	12/94	2c
Margarine, Blue Bonnet or Parkay cubes	lb.	0.70	12/94	2c
Meats, poultry, fish, and eggs purchases	year	700	91	81r
Milk and cream (fresh) purchases	year	155	91	81r
Milk, whole	1/2 gal.	1.26	12/94	2c
Orange juice, frozen concentrate 12-oz. can	16 oz.	1.52	12/94	82r
Orange juice, Minute Maid frozen	12-oz.	1.30	12/94	2c
Oranges, Navel	lb.	0.56	12/94	82r
Peaches, halves or slices, Hunt's, Del Monte, or Libby's	29-oz.	1.37	12/94	2c
Peas, sweet, Del Monte or Green Giant	15-17 oz.	0.61	12/94	2c
Pork chops, center cut, bone-in	lb.	3.30	12/94	82r
Pork purchases	year	122	91	81r
Potato chips	16-oz.	3.03	12/94	82r
Potatoes, frozen, French fried	lb.	0.77	12/94	82r
Potatoes, white	lb.	0.35	12/94	82r
Potatoes, white or red	10-lb. sack	1.75	12/94	2c
Rice, white, long grain, uncooked	lb.	0.54	12/94	82r
Round roast, USDA choice, boneless	lb.	2.92	12/94	82r
Sausage, Jimmy Dean, 100% pork	lb.	3.23	12/94	2c
Shortening, vegetable oil blends	lb.	0.80	12/94	82r
Shortening, vegetable, Crisco	3-lb.	2.84	12/94	2c
Soft drink, Coca Cola, ex deposit	2 lit	1.21	12/94	2c
Spaghetti and macaroni	lb.	1.02	12/94	82r
Steak, round, graded & ungraded, exc. USDA prime & choice	lb.	3.13	12/94	82r
Steak, sirloin, USDA choice, boneless	lb.	4.07	12/94	82r
Steak, t-bone	lb.	4.99	12/94	2c

Reno, NV - continued

Item	Per	Value	Date	Ref.
Groceries - continued				
Sugar and other sweets, eaten at home, expenditures	year	105	91	81r
Sugar, cane or beet	4 lbs.	1.55	12/94	2c
Sugar, white, all sizes	lb.	0.38	12/94	82r
Tobacco products and smoking supplies, total expenditures	year	221	91	81r
Tomatoes, field grown	lb.	1.45	12/94	82r
Tomatoes, Hunt's or Del Monte	14.5 oz.	0.71	12/94	2c
Tuna, chunk, light	lb.	2.18	12/94	82r
Tuna, chunk, light, oil-packed	6.125-6.5 oz.	0.78	12/94	2c
Goods and Services				
Miscellaneous goods and services, ACCRA Index		108.40	12/94	2c
Health Care				
Health care, ACCRA Index		125.50	12/94	2c
Antibiotic ointment, Polysporin	1.5 oz.	4.35	12/94	2c
Childbirth, Cesarean delivery, hospital charge	birth	6059.00	12/91	69r
Childbirth, Cesarean delivery, physician charge	birth	2248.00	12/91	69r
Childbirth, normal delivery, hospital charge	birth	3006.00	12/91	69r
Childbirth, normal delivery, physician charge	birth	1634.00	12/91	69r
Dentist's fee, adult teeth cleaning and periodic oral exam	visit	71.17	12/94	2c
Doctor's fee, routine exam, established patient	visit	47.20	12/94	2c
Drugs, expenditures	year	230	91	81r
Health care, total expenditures	year	1544	91	81r
Health insurance expenditures	year	558	91	81r
Hospital care, semiprivate room	day	512.33	12/94	2c
Insurance premium, family medical care	month	383.60	1/95	41s
Medical services expenditures	year	676	91	81r
Medical supplies expenditures	year	80	91	81r
Surgery, open-heart	proc	37818.00	1/93	14r
Household Goods				
Appl. repair, service call, wash mach	min. lab. chg.	39.19	12/94	2c
Floor coverings, expenditures	year	79	91	81r
Furniture, expenditures	year	352	91	81r
Household equipment, misc. expenditures	year	614	91	81r
Household expenditures, miscellaneous	year	294	91	81r
Household furnishings and equipment, expenditures	year	1416	91	81r
Household operations expenditures	year	580	91	81r
Household textiles, expenditures	year	113	91	81r
Housekeeping supplies, expenditures	year	447	91	81r
Laundry and cleaning supplies, expenditures	year	114	91	81r
Laundry detergent, Tide Ultra, Bold, or Cheer	42 oz.	3.41	12/94	2c
Postage and stationery, expenditures	year	145	91	81r
Tissues, facial, Kleenex brand	175	1.01	12/94	2c
Housing				
Housing, ACCRA Index		124.30	12/94	2c
Add garage/carport		6,422	3/95	74r
Add room(s)		26,583	3/95	74r
Apartment condominium or co-op, median	unit	105300	12/94	62r
Dwellings (owned), expenditures	year	3932	91	81r
Enclose porch/patio/breezeway		5,382	3/95	74r
Finish room in basement/attic		3,911	3/95	74r
Home, existing, single-family, median	unit	178600	12/94	62r
Home, existing, single-family, median	unit	133.50	12/94	62c
House payment, principal and interest, 25% down payment	mo.	950	12/94	2c
House, 1800 sq ft, 8000 sq ft lot, new, urban, utilities	total	155375	12/94	2c

Values are in dollars or fractions of dollars. In the column headed *Ref*, references are shown to sources. Each reference is followed by a letter. These refer to the geographical level for which data were reported: s = State, r = Region, and c = City or metro. The abbreviation *ex* is used to mean *except* or *excluding*; *exp* stands for expenditures. For other abbreviations and further explanations, please see the Introduction.

Reno, NV - continued

Item	Per	Value	Date	Ref.
Housing				
Maintenance, repairs, insurance, and other housing expenditures	year	591	91	81r
Mortgage interest and charges expenditures	year	2747	91	81r
Mtge. rate, incl. points and orig. fee, 30-year conv. fixed or ARM	mo.	9.14	12/94	2c
Princ. & int., mortgage, median-price exist. sing.-family home	mo.	845	12/94	62r
Property taxes expenditures	year	594	91	81r
Redesign, restructure more than half of home's interior		5,467	3/95	74r
Rent, apartment, 2 br., 1 1/2-2 baths, unfurnished, 950 sq ft, water	mo.	664	12/94	2c
Rental units expenditures	year	2077	91	81r
Insurance and Pensions				
Auto insurance, private passenger	year	853.93	12/94	71s
Insurance and pensions, personal, expenditures	year	3042	91	81r
Insurance, life and other personal, expenditures	year	298	91	81r
Pensions and Social Security, expenditures	year	2744	91	81r
Legal Assistance				
Legal work, law firm associate	hour	91		10r
Legal work, law firm partner	hour	151		10r
Personal Goods				
Shampoo, Alberto VO5	15-oz.	1.35	12/94	2c
Toothpaste, Crest or Colgate	6-7 oz.	1.97	12/94	2c
Personal Services				
Dry cleaning, man's 2-pc. suit		7.39	12/94	2c
Haircut, man's barbershop, no styling		9.59	12/94	2c
Haircut, woman's shampoo, trim, blow-dry		23.20	12/94	2c
Personal services expenditures	year	286	91	81r
Restaurant Food				
Chicken, fried, thigh and drumstick		2.13	12/94	2c
Dining expenditures, family	week	32.25	94	73r
Hamburger with cheese	1/4 lb.	1.93	12/94	2c
Pizza, Pizza Hut or Pizza Inn	12-13 in.	8.75	12/94	2c
Taxes				
Taxes, Federal income, expenditures	year	2946	91	81r
Taxes, personal, expenditures	year	3791	91	81r
Taxes, State and local income, expenditures	year	791	91	81r
Transportation				
Transportation, ACCRA Index		110.80	12/94	2c
Bus fare, one-way	trip	1.00	12/95	1c
Bus fare, up to 10 miles	one-way	1.00	12/94	2c
Cars and trucks purchased, new	year	1231	91	81r
Cars and trucks purchased, used	year	915	91	81r
Driver's learning permit fee	perm	10.00	1/94	84s
Driver's license fee	orig	6.00	1/94	84s
Driver's license reinstatement fee, min.	susp	40.00	1/94	85s
Driver's license renewal fee	renew	6.00	1/94	84s
Identification card, nondriver	card	10.00	1/94	83s
Motorcycle license fee	orig	6.00	1/94	84s
Motorcycle license renewal fee	renew	6.00	1/94	84s
Public transportation expenditures	year	375	91	81r
Tire balance, computer or spin bal., front	wheel	7.09	12/94	2c
Transportation expenditures, total	year	5527	91	81r
Vehicle finance charges	year	287	91	81r
Vehicle insurance expenditures	year	624	91	81r
Vehicle maintenance and repairs expenditures	year	695	91	81r
Vehicle purchases	year	2174	91	81r
Vehicle rental, leases, licenses, etc. expenditures	year	257	91	81r
Vehicles purchased, other than cars and trucks	year	28	91	81r

Reno, NV - continued

Item	Per	Value	Date	Ref.
Utilities				
Utilities, ACCRA Index		90.20	12/94	2c
Electricity expenditures	year	616	91	81r
Electricity, (part.), other, 1800 sq. ft., new home	mo.	59.74	12/94	2c
Electricity, summer, 250 KWh	month	23.81	8/93	64c
Electricity, summer, 500 KWh	month	44.55	8/93	64c
Electricity, summer, 750 KWh	month	65.28	8/93	64c
Electricity, summer, 1000 KWh	month	86.03	8/93	64c
Utilities, fuels, and public services, total expenditures	year	1681	91	81r
Water and other public services, expenditures	year	209	91	81r
Weddings				
Bridal attendants' gowns	event	750	10/93	76r
Bridal gown	event	852	10/93	76r
Bridal headpiece and veil	event	167	10/93	76r
Bride's wedding band	event	708	10/93	76r
Clergy	event	224	10/93	76r
Engagement ring	event	2756	10/93	76r
Flowers	event	863	10/93	76r
Formal wear for groom	event	106	10/93	76r
Groom's attendants' formal wear	event	530	10/93	76r
Groom's wedding band	event	402	10/93	76r
Music	event	600	10/93	76r
Photography	event	1088	10/93	76r
Shoes for bride	event	50	10/93	76r
Videography	event	483	10/93	76r
Wedding invitations and announcements	event	342	10/93	76r
Wedding reception	event	7000	10/93	76r

Richland-Kennewick-Pasco, WA

Item	Per	Value	Date	Ref.
Composite, ACCRA index		108.10	12/94	2c
Alcoholic Beverages				
Beer, Miller Lite, Bud, 12-oz., ex deposit	6	3.64	12/94	2c
J & B Scotch	750-ml.	18.95	12/94	2c
Wine, Gallo Chablis blanc	1.5-lit	4.07	12/94	2c
Appliances				
Appliances (major), expenditures	year	160	91	81r
Average annual exp.				
Food, health care, personal goods, services	year	32461	91	81r
Charity				
Cash contributions, expenditures	year	975	91	81r
Clothing				
Apparel, men and boys, total expenditures	year	467	91	81r
Apparel, women and girls, total expenditures	year	737	91	81r
Footwear, expenditures	year	270	91	81r
Jeans, man's denim		29.91	12/94	2c
Shirt, man's dress shirt		36.11	12/94	2c
Undervest, boy's size 10-14, cotton	3	4.55	12/94	2c
Communications				
Long-distance telephone rate, day, addl. min., 1-10 mi.	min.	0.01	12/93	9s
Long-distance telephone rate, day, initial min., 1-10 mi.	min.	0.15	12/93	9s
Newspaper subscription, dly. and Sun. delivery	month	10.00	12/94	2c
Phone line, single, business, field visit	inst	48.00	12/93	9s
Phone line, single, business, no field visit	inst	48.00	12/93	9s
Phone line, single, residence, field visit	inst	31.00	12/93	9s
Phone line, single, residence, no field visit	inst	31.00	12/93	9s
Telephone bill, family of four	month	17.68	12/94	2c
Telephone service, expenditures	year	611	91	81r
Education				
Board, 4-year private college/university	year	1928	8/94	80s
Board, 4-year public college/university	year	2194	8/94	80s

Values are in dollars or fractions of dollars. In the column headed *Ref*, references are shown to sources. Each reference is followed by a letter. These refer to the geographical level for which data were reported: s = State, r = Region, and c = City or metro. The abbreviation *ex* is used to mean *except* or *excluding*; *exp* stands for expenditures. For other abbreviations and further explanations, please see the Introduction.

Richland-Kennewick-Pasco, WA - continued

Item	Per	Value	Date	Ref.
Education				
Education, total expenditures	year	375	91	81r
Room, 4-year private college/university	year	2455	8/94	80s
Room, 4-year public college/university	year	1952	8/94	80s
Total cost, 4-year private college/university	year	16332	8/94	80s
Total cost, 4-year public college/university	year	6483	8/94	80s
Tuition, 2-year public college/university, in-state	year	1141	8/94	80s
Tuition, 4-year private college/university, in-state	year	11949	8/94	80s
Tuition, 4-year public college/university, in-state	year	2337	8/94	80s
Energy and Fuels				
Energy, combined forms, 1800 sq. ft.	mo.	93.32	12/94	2c
Fuel oil and other fuels, expenditures	year	33	91	81r
Gas, natural, expenditures	year	212	91	81r
Gas, reg unlead, taxes inc., cash, self-service	gal	1.25	12/94	2c
Gasoline and motor oil purchased	year	1115	91	81r
Gasoline, unleaded midgrade	gallon	1.36	4/93	82r
Gasoline, unleaded premium	gallon	1.43	4/93	82r
Gasoline, unleaded regular	gallon	1.23	4/93	82r
Entertainment				
Bowling, evening rate	game	1.91	12/94	2c
Concert ticket, Pearl Jam group	perf	20.00	94	50r
Entertainment, total expenditures	year	1853	91	81r
Fees and admissions, expenditures	year	482	91	81r
Monopoly game, Parker Brothers', No. 9	game	11.94	12/94	2c
Movie	adm	5.50	12/94	2c
Pets, toys, playground equipment, expenditures	year	299	91	81r
Reading, expenditures	year	164	91	81r
Televisions, radios, and sound equipment, expenditures	year	528	91	81r
Tennis balls, yellow, Wilson or Penn, 3	can	2.65	12/94	2c
Funerals				
Burial, immediate, container provided by funeral home		1382.70	1/95	54r
Cards, acknowledgment		21.87	1/95	54r
Casket, minimum alternative		128.54	1/95	54r
Cosmetology, hair care, etc.		119.69	1/95	54r
Cremation, direct, container provided by funeral home		1030.62	1/95	54r
Embalming		255.42	1/95	54r
Funeral, funeral home		437.38	1/95	54r
Funeral, other facility		444.46	1/95	54r
Graveside service		338.46	1/95	54r
Hearse, local		147.50	1/95	54r
Limousine, local		130.33	1/95	54r
Memorial service		553.16	1/95	54r
Service charge, professional, nondeclinable		859.15	1/95	54r
Visitation and viewing		93.23	1/95	54r
Groceries				
Groceries, ACCRA Index		102.10	12/94	2c
Apples, Red Delicious	lb.	0.72	12/94	82r
Baby food, strained vegetables, lowest price	4-4.5 oz.	0.34	12/94	2c
Bacon, sliced	lb.	1.73	12/94	82r
Bananas	lb.	0.38	12/94	2c
Bananas	lb.	0.52	12/94	82r
Beef or hamburger, ground	lb.	1.28	12/94	2c
Beef purchases	year	241	91	81r
Beverage purchases, alcoholic	year	328	91	81r
Beverage purchases, nonalcoholic	year	234	91	81r
Bologna, all beef or mixed	lb.	2.33	12/94	82r
Bread, white	24-oz.	0.58	12/94	2c
Bread, white, pan	lb.	0.81	12/94	82r
Carrots, short trimmed and topped	lb.	0.43	12/94	82r
Cereals and bakery products purchases	year	392	91	81r
Cereals and cereals products purchases	year	139	91	81r
Cheese, Kraft grated Parmesan	8-oz.	3.56	12/94	2c

Richland-Kennewick-Pasco, WA - continued

Item	Per	Value	Date	Ref.
Groceries - continued				
Chicken breast, bone-in	lb.	2.04	12/94	82r
Chicken, fresh, whole	lb.	0.95	12/94	82r
Chicken, whole fryer	lb.	0.98	12/94	2c
Cigarettes, Winston, Kings	carton	19.21	12/94	2c
Coffee, 100%, ground roast, all sizes	lb.	4.48	12/94	82r
Coffee, vacuum-packed	13 oz.	3.95	12/94	2c
Corn Flakes, Kellogg's or Post Toasties	18 oz.	2.34	12/94	2c
Corn, frozen, whole kernel, lowest price	10 oz.	0.65	12/94	2c
Dairy products (other) purchases	year	182	91	81r
Eggs, Grade A large	dozen	0.80	12/94	2c
Fish and seafood purchases	year	94	91	81r
Flour, white, all purpose	lb.	0.21	12/94	82r
Food purchases, food eaten at home	year	2749	91	81r
Foods purchased away from home, not prepared by consumer	year	1909	91	81r
Fruits and vegetables purchases	year	459	91	81r
Grapefruit	lb.	0.56	12/94	82r
Ground beef, 100% beef	lb.	1.31	12/94	82r
Ham, boneless, exc. canned	lb.	2.46	12/94	82r
Ice cream, prepackaged, bulk, regular	1/2 gal.	2.57	12/94	82r
Lemons	lb.	1.00	12/94	82r
Lettuce, iceberg	lb.	0.93	12/94	82r
Lettuce, iceberg	head	0.75	12/94	2c
Margarine, Blue Bonnet or Parkay cubes	lb.	0.74	12/94	2c
Meats, poultry, fish, and eggs purchases	year	700	91	81r
Milk and cream (fresh) purchases	year	155	91	81r
Milk, whole	1/2 gal.	1.23	12/94	2c
Orange juice, frozen concentrate 12-oz. can	16 oz.	1.52	12/94	82r
Orange juice, Minute Maid frozen	12-oz.	1.40	12/94	2c
Oranges, Navel	lb.	0.56	12/94	82r
Peaches, halves or slices, Hunt's, Del Monte, or Libby's	29-oz.	1.43	12/94	2c
Peas, sweet, Del Monte or Green Giant	15-17 oz.	0.57	12/94	2c
Pork chops, center cut, bone-in	lb.	3.30	12/94	82r
Pork purchases	year	122	91	81r
Potato chips	16-oz.	3.03	12/94	82r
Potatoes, frozen, French fried	lb.	0.77	12/94	82r
Potatoes, white	lb.	0.35	12/94	82r
Potatoes, white or red	10-lb. sack	1.63	12/94	2c
Rice, white, long grain, uncooked	lb.	0.54	12/94	82r
Round roast, USDA choice, boneless	lb.	2.92	12/94	82r
Sausage, Jimmy Dean, 100% pork	lb.	3.50	12/94	2c
Shortening, vegetable oil blends	lb.	0.80	12/94	82r
Shortening, vegetable, Crisco	3-lb.	2.24	12/94	2c
Soft drink, Coca Cola, ex deposit	2 lit	1.16	12/94	2c
Spaghetti and macaroni	lb.	1.02	12/94	82r
Steak, round, graded & ungraded, exc. USDA prime & choice	lb.	3.13	12/94	82r
Steak, sirloin, USDA choice, boneless	lb.	4.07	12/94	82r
Steak, t-bone	lb.	4.74	12/94	2c
Sugar and other sweets, eaten at home, expenditures	year	105	91	81r
Sugar, cane or beet	4 lbs.	1.14	12/94	2c
Sugar, white, all sizes	lb.	0.38	12/94	82r
Tobacco products and smoking supplies, total expenditures	year	221	91	81r
Tomatoes, field grown	lb.	1.45	12/94	82r
Tomatoes, Hunt's or Del Monte	14.5 oz.	0.76	12/94	2c
Tuna, chunk, light	lb.	2.18	12/94	82r
Tuna, chunk, light, oil-packed	6.125-6.5 oz.	0.79	12/94	2c
Goods and Services				
Miscellaneous goods and services, ACCRA Index		105.90	12/94	2c

Values are in dollars or fractions of dollars. In the column headed *Ref*, references are shown to sources. Each reference is followed by a letter. These refer to the geographical level for which data were reported: s=State, r=Region, and c=City or metro. The abbreviation *ex* is used to mean *except* or *excluding*; *exp* stands for expenditures. For other abbreviations and further explanations, please see the Introduction.

Richland-Kennewick-Pasco, WA - continued

Item	Per	Value	Date	Ref.
Health Care				
Health care, ACCRA Index		132.20	12/94	2c
Antibiotic ointment, Polysporin	1.5 oz.	4.14	12/94	2c
Childbirth, Cesarean delivery, hospital charge	birth	6059.00	12/91	69r
Childbirth, Cesarean delivery, physician charge	birth	2248.00	12/91	69r
Childbirth, normal delivery, hospital charge	birth	3006.00	12/91	69r
Childbirth, normal delivery, physician charge	birth	1634.00	12/91	69r
Dentist's fee, adult teeth cleaning and periodic oral exam	visit	81.25	12/94	2c
Doctor's fee, routine exam, established patient	visit	49.83	12/94	2c
Drugs, expenditures	year	230	91	81r
Health care, total expenditures	year	1544	91	81r
Health insurance expenditures	year	558	91	81r
Hospital care, semiprivate room	day	478.33	12/94	2c
Insurance premium, family medical care	month	382.32	1/95	41s
Medical services expenditures	year	676	91	81r
Medical supplies expenditures	year	80	91	81r
Surgery, open-heart	proc	37818.00	1/93	14r
Household Goods				
Appl. repair, service call, wash mach	min. lab. chg.	38.00	12/94	2c
Floor coverings, expenditures	year	79	91	81r
Furniture, expenditures	year	352	91	81r
Household equipment, misc. expenditures	year	614	91	81r
Household expenditures, miscellaneous	year	294	91	81r
Household furnishings and equipment, expenditures	year	1416	91	81r
Household operations expenditures	year	580	91	81r
Household textiles, expenditures	year	113	91	81r
Housekeeping supplies, expenditures	year	447	91	81r
Laundry and cleaning supplies, expenditures	year	114	91	81r
Laundry detergent, Tide Ultra, Bold, or Cheer	42 oz.	3.95	12/94	2c
Postage and stationery, expenditures	year	145	91	81r
Tissues, facial, Kleenex brand	175	1.15	12/94	2c
Housing				
Housing, ACCRA Index		118.00	12/94	2c
Add garage/carport		6,422	3/95	74r
Add room(s)		26,583	3/95	74r
Apartment condominium or co-op, median	unit	105300	12/94	62r
Dwellings (owned), expenditures	year	3932	91	81r
Enclose porch/patio/breezeway		5,382	3/95	74r
Finish room in basement/attic		3,911	3/95	74r
Home, existing, single-family, median	unit	178600	12/94	62r
Home, existing, single-family, median	unit	108.10	12/94	62c
House payment, principal and interest, 25% down payment	mo.	947	12/94	2c
House, 1800 sq ft, 8000 sq ft lot, new, urban, utilities	total	153380	12/94	2c
Maintenance, repairs, insurance, and other housing expenditures	year	591	91	81r
Mortgage interest and charges expenditures	year	2747	91	81r
Mtge. rate, incl. points and orig. fee, 30-year conv. fixed or ARM	mo.	9.26	12/94	2c
Princ. & int., mortgage, median-price exist. sing.-family home	mo.	845	12/94	62c
Property taxes expenditures	year	594	91	81r
Redesign, restructure more than half of home's interior		5,467	3/95	74r
Rent, apartment, 2 br., 1 1/2-2 baths, unfurnished, 950 sq ft, water	mo.	547	12/94	2c
Rental units expenditures	year	2077	91	81r
Insurance and Pensions				
Auto insurance, private passenger	year	711.57	12/94	71s
Insurance and pensions, personal, expenditures	year	3042	91	81r

Richland-Kennewick-Pasco, WA - continued

Item	Per	Value	Date	Ref.
Insurance and Pensions - continued				
Insurance, life and other personal, expenditures	year	298	91	81r
Pensions and Social Security, expenditures	year	2744	91	81r
Legal Assistance				
Legal work, law firm associate	hour	91		10r
Legal work, law firm partner	hour	151		10r
Personal Goods				
Shampoo, Alberto VO5	15-oz.	1.13	12/94	2c
Toothpaste, Crest or Colgate	6-7 oz.	1.98	12/94	2c
Personal Services				
Dry cleaning, man's 2-pc. suit		8.15	12/94	2c
Haircut, man's barbershop, no styling		8.50	12/94	2c
Haircut, woman's shampoo, trim, blow-dry		26.00	12/94	2c
Personal services expenditures	year	286	91	81r
Restaurant Food				
Chicken, fried, thigh and drumstick		21.90	12/94	2c
Dining expenditures, family	week	32.25	94	73r
Hamburger with cheese	1/4 lb.	1.99	12/94	2c
Pizza, Pizza Hut or Pizza Inn	12-13 in.	8.99	12/94	2c
Taxes				
Taxes, Federal income, expenditures	year	2946	91	81r
Taxes, personal, expenditures	year	3791	91	81r
Taxes, State and local income, expenditures	year	791	91	81r
Transportation				
Transportation, ACCRA Index		101.30	12/94	2c
Bus fare, one-way	trip	0.40	12/95	1c
Cars and trucks purchased, new	year	1231	91	81r
Cars and trucks purchased, used	year	915	91	81r
Driver's learning permit fee	perm	4.00	1/94	84s
Driver's license fee	orig	21.00	1/94	84s
Driver's license fee, duplicate	lic	5.00	1/94	84s
Driver's license reinstatement fee, min.	susp	20.00-50.00	1/94	85s
Driver's license renewal fee	renew	14.00	1/94	84s
Identification card, nondriver	card	4.00	1/94	83s
Motorcycle license fee	orig	8.00	1/94	84s
Motorcycle license renewal fee	renew	7.50	1/94	84s
Public transportation expenditures	year	375	91	81r
Tire balance, computer or spin bal., front	wheel	5.97	12/94	2c
Transportation expenditures, total	year	5527	91	81r
Vehicle finance charges	year	287	91	81r
Vehicle insurance expenditures	year	624	91	81r
Vehicle maintenance and repairs expenditures	year	695	91	81r
Vehicle purchases	year	2174	91	81r
Vehicle rental, leases, licenses, etc. expenditures	year	257	91	81r
Vehicles purchased, other than cars and trucks	year	28	91	81r
Utilities				
Utilities, ACCRA Index		84.20	12/94	2c
Electricity expenditures	year	616	91	81r
Electricity, 1800 sq. ft., new home	mo.	93.32	12/94	2c
Utilities, fuels, and public services, total expenditures	year	1681	91	81r
Water and other public services, expenditures	year	209	91	81r
Weddings				
Bridal attendants' gowns	event	750	10/93	76r
Bridal gown	event	852	10/93	76r
Bridal headpiece and veil	event	167	10/93	76r
Bride's wedding band	event	708	10/93	76r
Clergy	event	224	10/93	76r
Engagement ring	event	2756	10/93	76r
Flowers	event	863	10/93	76r
Formal wear for groom	event	106	10/93	76r
Groom's attendants' formal wear	event	530	10/93	76r

Values are in dollars or fractions of dollars. In the column headed *Ref*, references are shown to sources. Each reference is followed by a letter. These refer to the geographical level for which data were reported: s = State, r = Region, and c = City or metro. The abbreviation *ex* is used to mean *except* or *excluding*; *exp* stands for expenditures. For other abbreviations and further explanations, please see the Introduction.

Richland-Kennewick-Pasco, WA - continued

Item	Per	Value	Date	Ref.
Weddings				
Groom's wedding band	event	402	10/93	76r
Music	event	600	10/93	76r
Photography	event	1088	10/93	76r
Shoes for bride	event	50	10/93	76r
Videography	event	483	10/93	76r
Wedding invitations and announcements	event	342	10/93	76r
Wedding reception	event	7000	10/93	76r

Richmond, VA

Item	Per	Value	Date	Ref.
Composite, ACCRA index		100.90	12/94	2c
Alcoholic Beverages				
Beer, Miller Lite, Bud, 12-oz., ex deposit	6	3.67	12/94	2c
J & B Scotch	750-ml.	18.45	12/94	2c
Wine, Gallo Chablis blanc	1.5-lit	4.79	12/94	2c
Appliances				
Appliances (major), expenditures	year	153	91	81r
Average annual exp.				
Food, health care, personal goods, services	year	27020	91	81r
Charity				
Cash contributions, expenditures	year	839	91	81r
Clothing				
Apparel, men and boys, total expenditures	year	380	91	81r
Apparel, women and girls, total expenditures	year	660	91	81r
Footwear, expenditures	year	193	91	81r
Jeans, man's denim		37.39	12/94	2c
Shirt, man's dress shirt		35.99	12/94	2c
Undervest, boy's size 10-14, cotton	3	4.18	12/94	2c
Communications				
Long-distance telephone rate, day, addl. min., 1-10 mi.	min.	0.12	12/93	9s
Long-distance telephone rate, day, initial min., 1-10 mi.	min.	0.21	12/93	9s
Newspaper subscription, dly. and Sun. delivery	month	12.92	12/94	2c
Phone line, single, business, field visit	inst	0.00	12/93	9s
Phone line, single, business, no field visit	inst	64.00	12/93	9s
Phone line, single, residence, field visit	inst	0.00	12/93	9s
Phone line, single, residence, no field visit	inst	38.50	12/93	9s
Telephone bill, family of four	month	19.86	12/94	2c
Telephone service, expenditures	year	616	91	81r
Telephone, business, addl. line, touch tone	month	1.85	10/91	25c
Telephone, business, connection charges, touch tone	inst	64.00	10/91	25c
Telephone, business, key system line, touch tone	month	69.96	10/91	25c
Telephone, business, PBX line, touch tone	month	70.81	10/91	25c
Telephone, business, single ln., touch tone	month	69.08	10/91	25c
Telephone, business, touch tone, inside wiring maintenance plan	month	3.00	10/91	25c
Education				
Board, 4-year private college/university	year	2242	8/94	80s
Board, 4-year public college/university	year	1901	8/94	80s
Education, total expenditures	year	319	91	81r
Room, 4-year private college/university	year	2022	8/94	80s
Room, 4-year public college/university	year	2186	8/94	80s
Total cost, 4-year private college/university	year	14043	8/94	80s
Total cost, 4-year public college/university	year	7726	8/94	80s
Tuition, 2-year public college/university, in-state	year	1332	8/94	80s
Tuition, 4-year private college/university, in-state	year	9778	8/94	80s
Tuition, 4-year public college/university, in-state	year	3639	8/94	80s

Richmond, VA - continued

Item	Per	Value	Date	Ref.
Energy and Fuels				
Energy, combined forms, 1800 sq. ft.	mo.	115.45	12/94	2c
Fuel oil and other fuels, expenditures	year	56	91	81r
Gas, natural, expenditures	year	150	91	81r
Gas, reg unlead, taxes inc., cash, self-service	gal	1.08	12/94	2c
Gasoline and motor oil purchased	year	1152	91	81r
Gasoline, unleaded midgrade	gallon	1.21	4/93	82r
Gasoline, unleaded premium	gallon	1.30	4/93	82r
Gasoline, unleaded regular	gallon	1.10	4/93	82r
Entertainment				
Bowling, evening rate	game	2.92	12/94	2c
Concert ticket, Pearl Jam group	perf	20.00	94	50r
Entertainment, total expenditures	year	1266	91	81r
Fees and admissions, expenditures	year	306	91	81r
Monopoly game, Parker Brothers', No. 9	game	11.33	12/94	2c
Movie	adm	5.75	12/94	2c
Pets, toys, playground equipment, expenditures	year	271	91	81r
Reading, expenditures	year	131	91	81r
Televisions, radios, and sound equipment, expenditures	year	439	91	81r
Tennis balls, yellow, Wilson or Penn, 3	can	2.08	12/94	2c
Funerals				
Burial, immediate, container provided by funeral home		1370.36	1/95	54r
Cards, acknowledgment		14.83	1/95	54r
Casket, minimum alternative		192.52	1/95	54r
Cosmetology, hair care, etc.		102.27	1/95	54r
Cremation, direct, container provided by funeral home		1065.64	1/95	54r
Embalming		304.29	1/95	54r
Funeral, funeral home		287.83	1/95	54r
Funeral, other facility		284.14	1/95	54r
Graveside service		349.13	1/95	54r
Hearse, local		132.27	1/95	54r
Limousine, local		98.45	1/95	54r
Memorial service		270.59	1/95	54r
Service charge, professional, nondeclinable		933.59	1/95	54r
Visitation and viewing		225.83	1/95	54r
Groceries				
Groceries, ACCRA Index		98.80	12/94	2c
Apples, Red Delicious	lb.	0.73	12/94	82r
Baby food, strained vegetables, lowest price	4-4.5 oz.	0.37	12/94	2c
Bacon, sliced	lb.	1.67	12/94	82r
Bananas	lb.	0.49	12/94	2c
Bananas	lb.	0.42	12/94	82r
Beef or hamburger, ground	lb.	1.67	12/94	2c
Beef purchases	year	213	91	81r
Beverage purchases, alcoholic	year	249	91	81r
Beverage purchases, nonalcoholic	year	207	91	81r
Bologna, all beef or mixed	lb.	2.27	12/94	82r
Bread, white	24-oz.	0.77	12/94	2c
Bread, white, pan	lb.	0.68	12/94	82r
Cabbage	lb.	0.42	12/94	82r
Carrots, short trimmed and topped	lb.	0.53	12/94	82r
Cereals and bakery products purchases	year	345	91	81r
Cereals and cereals products purchases	year	127	91	81r
Cheddar cheese, natural	lb.	3.58	12/94	82r
Cheese, Kraft grated Parmesan	8-oz.	3.33	12/94	2c
Chicken breast, bone-in	lb.	1.71	12/94	82r
Chicken, fresh, whole	lb.	0.78	12/94	82r
Chicken, whole fryer	lb.	0.81	12/94	2c
Chuck roast, USDA choice, boneless	lb.	2.26	12/94	82r
Cigarettes, Winston, Kings	carton	12.54	12/94	2c
Coffee, vacuum-packed	13 oz.	3.21	12/94	2c
Corn Flakes, Kellogg's or Post Toasties	18 oz.	2.45	12/94	2c
Corn, frozen, whole kernel, lowest price	10 oz.	0.66	12/94	2c
Crackers, soda, salted	lb.	1.27	12/94	82r
Cucumbers	lb.	0.65	12/94	82r
Dairy products (other) purchases	year	141	91	81r

Values are in dollars or fractions of dollars. In the column headed *Ref*, references are shown to sources. Each reference is followed by a letter. These refer to the geographical level for which data were reported: s = State, r = Region, and c = City or metro. The abbreviation *ex* is used to mean *except* or *excluding*; *exp* stands for *expenditures*. For other abbreviations and further explanations, please see the Introduction.

Richmond, VA - continued

Item	Per	Value	Date	Ref.
Groceries				
Eggs, Grade A large	dozen	0.82	12/94	2c
Eggs, Grade A large	dozen	0.87	12/94	82r
Fish and seafood purchases	year	72	91	81r
Flour, white, all purpose	lb.	0.23	12/94	82r
Food purchases, food eaten at home	year	2381	91	81r
Foods purchased away from home, not prepared by consumer	year	1696	91	81r
Frankfurters, all meat or all beef	lb.	1.74	12/94	82r
Fruits and vegetables purchases	year	380	91	81r
Grapefruit	lb.	0.45	12/94	82r
Grapes, Thompson seedless	lb.	2.30	12/94	82r
Ground beef, 100% beef	lb.	1.37	12/94	82r
Ground chuck, 100% beef	lb.	1.97	12/94	82r
Ham, boneless, exc. canned	lb.	2.54	12/94	82r
Ice cream, prepackaged, bulk, regular	1/2 gal.	2.47	12/94	82r
Lemons	lb.	1.02	12/94	82r
Lettuce, iceberg	lb.	0.96	12/94	82r
Lettuce, iceberg	head	1.05	12/94	2c
Margarine, Blue Bonnet or Parkay cubes	lb.	0.60	12/94	2c
Margarine, stick	lb.	0.77	12/94	82r
Meats, poultry, fish, and eggs purchases	year	655	91	81r
Milk and cream (fresh) purchases	year	130	91	81r
Milk, whole	1/2 gal.	1.41	12/94	2c
Orange juice, frozen concentrate 12-oz. can	16 oz.	1.36	12/94	82r
Orange juice, Minute Maid frozen	12-oz.	1.22	12/94	2c
Oranges, Navel	lb.	0.54	12/94	82r
Peaches, halves or slices, Hunt's, Del Monte, or Libby's	29-oz.	1.37	12/94	2c
Pears, Anjou	lb.	0.81	12/94	82r
Peas, sweet, Del Monte or Green Giant	15-17 oz.	0.50	12/94	2c
Pork chops, center cut, bone-in	lb.	3.07	12/94	82r
Pork purchases	year	142	91	81r
Potato chips	16-oz.	3.15	12/94	82r
Potatoes, frozen, French fried	lb.	0.82	12/94	82r
Potatoes, white	lb.	0.34	12/94	82r
Potatoes, white or red	10-lb. sack	2.31	12/94	2c
Rice, white, long grain, uncooked	lb.	0.48	12/94	82r
Round roast, USDA choice, boneless	lb.	2.91	12/94	82r
Sausage, fresh	lb.	1.82	12/94	82r
Sausage, Jimmy Dean, 100% pork	lb.	2.17	12/94	2c
Shortening, vegetable oil blends	lb.	0.75	12/94	82r
Shortening, vegetable, Crisco	3-lb.	2.55	12/94	2c
Soft drink, Coca Cola, ex deposit	2 lit	0.97	12/94	2c
Spaghetti and macaroni	lb.	0.87	12/94	82r
Steak, rib eye, USDA choice, boneless	lb.	6.85	12/94	82r
Steak, round, graded & ungraded, exc. USDA prime & choice	lb.	2.96	12/94	82r
Steak, round, USDA choice, boneless	lb.	3.17	12/94	82r
Steak, sirloin, USDA choice, boneless	lb.	4.12	12/94	82r
Steak, t-bone	lb.	5.15	12/94	2c
Steak, T-bone, USDA choice, bone-in	lb.	5.63	12/94	82r
Sugar and other sweets, eaten at home, expenditures	year	93	91	81r
Sugar, cane or beet	4 lbs.	1.51	12/94	2c
Sugar, white, all sizes	lb.	0.39	12/94	82r
Tobacco products and smoking supplies, total expenditures	year	286	91	81r
Tomatoes, field grown	lb.	1.36	12/94	82r
Tomatoes, Hunt's or Del Monte	14.5 oz.	0.60	12/94	2c
Tuna, chunk, light	lb.	1.94	12/94	82r
Tuna, chunk, light, oil-packed	6.125-6.5 oz.	0.65	12/94	2c
Turkey, frozen, whole	lb.	0.96	12/94	82r
Yogurt, natural, fruit flavored	8 oz.	0.58	12/94	82r
Goods and Services				
Miscellaneous goods and services, ACCRA Index		100.70	12/94	2c

Richmond, VA - continued

Item	Per	Value	Date	Ref.
Health Care				
Health care, ACCRA Index		102.90	12/94	2c
Adenosine, emergency room	treat	100.00	95	23r
Antibiotic ointment, Polysporin	1.5 oz.	4.10	12/94	2c
Bladder tap, superpubic, infant, emergency room	treat	119.00	95	23r
Blood analysis, emergency room	treat	25.00	95	23r
Blood tests, abdominal pain, emergency room	treat	25.00	95	23r
Burn dressing, emergency room	treat	266.00	95	23r
Cardiology interpretation, emergency room	treat	26.00	95	23r
Chest X-ray, emergency room	treat	78.00	95	23r
Childbirth, Cesarean delivery, hospital charge	birth	5462.00	12/91	69r
Childbirth, Cesarean delivery, physician charge	birth	2228.00	12/91	69r
Childbirth, normal delivery, hospital charge	birth	2943.00	12/91	69r
Childbirth, normal delivery, physician charge	birth	1619.00	12/91	69r
Defibrillation pads, emergency room	treat	6.00	95	23r
Delivery, uncomplicated, total charge	birth	6180	1/93	24s
Delivery, uncomplicated, vaginal, hospital charge	birth	3380	1/93	24s
Delivery, uncomplicated, vaginal, physician's charge	birth	2800	1/93	24s
Dentist's fee, adult teeth cleaning and periodic oral exam	visit	56.50	12/94	2c
Doctor's fee, routine exam, established patient	visit	41.50	12/94	2c
Drugs, expenditures	year	297	91	81r
Gastric tube insertion, nasal, emergency room	treat	25.00	95	23r
Health care, total expenditures	year	1600	91	81r
Health insurance expenditures	year	637	91	81r
Heart monitor, emergency room	treat	40.00	95	23r
Hospital care, semiprivate room	day	368.00	12/94	2c
Insurance premium, family medical care	month	386.57	1/95	41s
Intravenous fluids, emergency room	treat	130.00	95	23r
Intravenous fluids, emergency room	liter	26.00	95	23r
Intravenous line, central, emergency room	treat	342.00	95	23r
Liver function tests, abdominal pain, emergency room	treat	26.00	95	23r
Medical care charges, total, emergency room, third-degree burns	treat	2101.00	95	23r
Medical care charges, total, emergency, infant with fever	treat	628.00	95	23r
Medical services expenditures	year	573	91	81r
Medical supplies expenditures	year	93	91	81r
Morphine, emergency room	treat	34.00	95	23r
Nursing care and facilities charges, emergency room	treat	252.00	95	23r
Nursing care and facilities charges, emergency, infant with fever	treat	252.00	95	23r
Nursing care and facilities charges, emergency, third-degree burns	treat	861.00	95	23r
Physician's charges, emergency, infant with fever	treat	212.00	95	23r
Physician's charges, emergency, third-degree burns	treat	372.00	95	23r
Physician's fee, emergency room	treat	372.00	95	23r
Physician's fee, general practitioner	visit	51.20	12/93	60r
Surgery, open-heart	proc	42374.00	1/93	14r
Ultrasound, abdominal, emergency room	treat	276.00	95	23r
Urinalysis, emergency room	treat	20.00	95	23r
Urinalysis, infant, emergency room	treat	20.00	95	23r
X-rays, emergency room	treat	78.00	95	23r
Household Goods				
Appl. repair, service call, wash mach	min. lab. chg.	37.60	12/94	2c
Floor coverings, expenditures	year	48	91	81r
Furniture, expenditures	year	280	91	81r
Household equipment, misc. expenditures	year	342	91	81r
Household expenditures, miscellaneous	year	256	91	81r

Values are in dollars or fractions of dollars. In the column headed *Ref*, references are shown to sources. Each reference is followed by a letter. These refer to the geographical level for which data were reported: s=State, r=Region, and c=City or metro. The abbreviation *ex* is used to mean *except* or *excluding*; *exp* stands for *expenditures*. For other abbreviations and further explanations, please see the Introduction.

Richmond, VA - continued

Item	Per	Value	Date	Ref.
Household Goods				
Household furnishings and equipment, expenditures	year	988	91	81r
Household operations expenditures	year	468	91	81r
Household textiles, expenditures	year	95	91	81r
Housekeeping supplies, expenditures	year	380	91	81r
Laundry and cleaning supplies, expenditures	year	109	91	81r
Laundry detergent, Tide Ultra, Bold, or Cheer	42 oz.	3.39	12/94	2c
Postage and stationery, expenditures	year	105	91	81r
Tissues, facial, Kleenex brand	175	1.00	12/94	2c
Housing				
Housing, ACCRA Index		100.90	12/94	2c
Add garage/carport		6,980	3/95	74r
Add room(s)		11,403	3/95	74r
Apartment condominium or co-op, median	unit	68600	12/94	62r
Dwellings (owned), expenditures	year	2428	91	81r
Enclose porch/patio/breezeway		4,572	3/95	74r
Finish room in basement/attic		3,794	3/95	74r
Home, existing, single-family, median	unit	120200	12/94	62r
Home, existing, single-family, median	unit	99.20	12/94	62c
House payment, principal and interest, 25% down payment	mo.	1088	12/94	2c
House, 1800 sq ft, 8000 sq ft lot, new, urban, utilities	total	176200	12/94	2c
Maintenance, repairs, insurance, and other housing expenditures	year	531	91	81r
Mortgage interest and charges expenditures	year	1506	91	81r
Mtge. rate, incl. points and orig. fee, 30-year conv. fixed or ARM	mo.	9.26	12/94	2c
Princ. & int., mortgage, median-price exist. sing.-family home	mo.	540	12/94	62r
Property taxes expenditures	year	391	91	81r
Redesign, restructure more than half of home's interior		17,641	3/95	74r
Rent, apartment, 2 br., 1 1/2-2 baths, unfurnished, 950 sq ft, water	mo.	590	12/94	2c
Rental units expenditures	year	1264	91	81r
Insurance and Pensions				
Auto insurance, private passenger	year	564.07	12/94	71s
Health insurance, HMO plan, cost to employer	year	3074	93	59c
Insurance and pensions, personal, expenditures	year	2395	91	81r
Insurance, life and other personal, expenditures	year	368	91	81r
Pensions and Social Security, expenditures	year	2027	91	81r
Personal Goods				
Shampoo, Alberto VO5	15-oz.	1.08	12/94	2c
Toothpaste, Crest or Colgate	6-7 oz.	1.92	12/94	2c
Personal Services				
Dry cleaning, man's 2-pc. suit		7.06	12/94	2c
Haircut, man's barbershop, no styling		8.00	12/94	2c
Haircut, woman's shampoo, trim, blow-dry		20.60	12/94	2c
Personal services expenditures	year	212	91	81r
Restaurant Food				
Chicken, fried, thigh and drumstick		2.09	12/94	2c
Dining expenditures, family	week	33.83	94	73r
Hamburger with cheese	1/4 lb.	0.99	12/94	2c
Pizza, Pizza Hut or Pizza Inn	12-13 in.	6.88	12/94	2c
Taxes				
Taxes, Federal income, expenditures	year	2275	91	81r
Taxes, personal, expenditures	year	2715	91	81r
Taxes, State and local income, expenditures	year	365	91	81r
Transportation				
Transportation, ACCRA Index		102.30	12/94	2c
Bus fare, one-way	trip	1.25	12/95	1c

Richmond, VA - continued

Item	Per	Value	Date	Ref.
Transportation - continued				
Bus fare, up to 10 miles	one-way	1.25	12/94	2c
Cars and trucks purchased, new	year	1306	91	81r
Cars and trucks purchased, used	year	942	91	81r
Driver's learning permit fee	perm	3.00	1/94	84s
Driver's license fee	orig	12.00	1/94	84s
Driver's license fee, duplicate	lic	5.00	1/94	84s
Driver's license reinstatement fee, min.	susp	30.00	1/94	85s
Driver's license renewal fee	renew	12.00	1/94	84s
Identification card, nondriver	card	5.00	1/94	83s
Motorcycle license fee	orig	5.00	1/94	84s
Motorcycle license renewal fee	renew	5.00	1/94	84s
Public transportation expenditures	year	249	91	81r
Tire balance, computer or spin bal., front	wheel	6.99	12/94	2c
Transportation expenditures, total	year	5307	91	81r
Vehicle finance charges	year	346	91	81r
Vehicle insurance expenditures	year	544	91	81r
Vehicle maintenance and repairs expenditures	year	600	91	81r
Vehicle purchases	year	2275	91	81r
Vehicle rental, leases, licenses, etc. expenditures	year	141	91	81r
Vehicles purchased, other than cars and trucks	year	27	91	81r
Utilities				
Utilities, ACCRA Index		102.70	12/94	2c
Electricity expenditures	year	950	91	81r
Electricity, 1800 sq. ft., new home	mo.	115.45	12/94	2c
Utilities, fuels, and public services, total expenditures	year	2000	91	81r
Water and other public services, expenditures	year	227	91	81r
Weddings				
Bridal attendants' gowns	event	750	10/93	76r
Bridal gown	event	852	10/93	76r
Bridal headpiece and veil	event	167	10/93	76r
Bride's wedding band	event	708	10/93	76r
Clergy	event	224	10/93	76r
Engagement ring	event	2756	10/93	76r
Flowers	event	863	10/93	76r
Formal wear for groom	event	106	10/93	76r
Groom's attendants' formal wear	event	530	10/93	76r
Groom's wedding band	event	402	10/93	76r
Music	event	600	10/93	76r
Photography	event	1088	10/93	76r
Shoes for bride	event	50	10/93	76r
Videography	event	483	10/93	76r
Wedding invitations and announcements	event	342	10/93	76r
Wedding reception	event	7000	10/93	76r

Riverside, CA

Item	Per	Value	Date	Ref.
Composite, ACCRA index		110.50	12/94	2c
Alcoholic Beverages				
Beer, Miller Lite, Bud, 12-oz., ex deposit	6	3.61	12/94	2c
J & B Scotch	750-ml.	14.77	12/94	2c
Wine, Gallo Chablis blanc	1.5-lit	3.77	12/94	2c
Appliances				
Appliances (major), expenditures	year	160	91	81r
Average annual exp.				
Food, health care, personal goods, services	year	32461	91	81r
Charity				
Cash contributions, expenditures	year	975	91	81r
Clothing				
Apparel, men and boys, total expenditures	year	467	91	81r
Apparel, women and girls, total expenditures	year	737	91	81r
Footwear, expenditures	year	270	91	81r

Values are in dollars or fractions of dollars. In the column headed *Ref*, references are shown to sources. Each reference is followed by a letter. These refer to the geographical level for which data were reported: s=State, r=Region, and c=City or metro. The abbreviation *ex* is used to mean *except* or *excluding*; *exp* stands for expenditures. For other abbreviations and further explanations, please see the Introduction.

Riverside, CA - continued

Item	Per	Value	Date	Ref.
Clothing				
Jeans, man's denim		37.50	12/94	2c
Shirt, man's dress shirt		27.00	12/94	2c
Undervest, boy's size 10-14, cotton	3	6.62	12/94	2c
Communications				
Long-distance telephone rate, day, addl. min., 1-10 mi.	min.	0.07	12/93	9s
Long-distance telephone rate, day, initial min., 1-10 mi.	min.	0.17	12/93	9s
Newspaper subscription, dly. and Sun. delivery	month	8.00	12/94	2c
Phone line, single, business, field visit	inst	70.75	12/93	9s
Phone line, single, business, no field visit	inst	70.75	12/93	9s
Phone line, single, residence, field visit	inst	34.75	12/93	9s
Phone line, single, residence, no field visit	inst	34.75	12/93	9s
Telephone bill, family of four	month	14.49	12/94	2c
Telephone service, expenditures	year	611	91	81r
Telephone, residential, flat rate	mo.	8.35	12/93	8c
Education				
Board, 4-year private college/university	year	2945	8/94	80s
Board, 4-year public college/university	year	2321	8/94	80s
Education, total expenditures	year	375	91	81r
Room, 4-year private college/university	year	3094	8/94	80s
Room, 4-year public college/university	year	2812	8/94	80s
Student fee, university	year	21.00	93	18s
Total cost, 4-year private college/university	year	19321	8/94	80s
Total cost, 4-year public college/university	year	7511	8/94	80s
Tuition, 2-year public college/university, in-state	year	345	8/94	80s
Tuition, 4-year private college/university, in-state	year	13282	8/94	80s
Tuition, 4-year public college/university, in-state	year	2378	8/94	80s
Energy and Fuels				
Energy, combined forms, 1800 sq. ft.	mo.	106.80	12/94	2c
Energy, exc. electricity, 1800 sq. ft.	mo.	29.10	12/94	2c
Fuel oil and other fuels, expenditures	year	33	91	81r
Gas, natural, expenditures	year	212	91	81r
Gas, reg unlead, taxes inc., cash, self-service	gal	1.26	12/94	2c
Gasoline and motor oil purchased	year	1115	91	81r
Gasoline, unleaded midgrade	gallon	1.36	4/93	82r
Gasoline, unleaded premium	gallon	1.43	4/93	82r
Gasoline, unleaded regular	gallon	1.23	4/93	82r
Entertainment				
Bowling, evening rate	game	3.02	12/94	2c
Concert ticket, Pearl Jam group	perf	20.00	94	50r
Entertainment, total expenditures	year	1853	91	81r
Fees and admissions, expenditures	year	482	91	81r
Monopoly game, Parker Brothers', No. 9	game	13.03	12/94	2c
Movie	adm	6.33	12/94	2c
Pets, toys, playground equipment, expenditures	year	299	91	81r
Reading, expenditures	year	164	91	81r
Televisions, radios, and sound equipment, expenditures	year	528	91	81r
Tennis balls, yellow, Wilson or Penn, 3	can	2.58	12/94	2c
Funerals				
Burial, immediate, container provided by funeral home		1382.70	1/95	54r
Cards, acknowledgment		21.87	1/95	54r
Casket, minimum alternative		128.54	1/95	54r
Cosmetology, hair care, etc.		119.69	1/95	54r
Cremation, direct, container provided by funeral home		1030.62	1/95	54r
Embalming		255.42	1/95	54r
Funeral, funeral home		437.38	1/95	54r
Funeral, other facility		444.46	1/95	54r
Graveside service		338.46	1/95	54r
Hearse, local		147.50	1/95	54r

Riverside, CA - continued

Item	Per	Value	Date	Ref.
Funerals - continued				
Limousine, local		130.33	1/95	54r
Memorial service		553.16	1/95	54r
Service charge, professional, nondeclinable		859.15	1/95	54r
Visitation and viewing		93.23	1/95	54r
Groceries				
Groceries, ACCRA Index		106.90	12/94	2c
Apples, Red Delicious	lb.	0.72	12/94	82r
Baby food, strained vegetables, lowest price	4-4.5 oz.	0.36	12/94	2c
Bacon, sliced	lb.	1.73	12/94	82r
Bananas	lb.	0.55	12/94	2c
Bananas	lb.	0.52	12/94	82r
Beef or hamburger, ground	lb.	1.48	12/94	2c
Beef purchases	year	241	91	81r
Beverage purchases, alcoholic	year	328	91	81r
Beverage purchases, nonalcoholic	year	234	91	81r
Bologna, all beef or mixed	lb.	2.33	12/94	82r
Bread, white	24-oz.	0.91	12/94	2c
Bread, white, pan	lb.	0.81	12/94	82r
Carrots, short trimmed and topped	lb.	0.43	12/94	82r
Cereals and bakery products purchases	year	392	91	81r
Cereals and cereals products purchases	year	139	91	81r
Cheese, Kraft grated Parmesan	8-oz.	2.91	12/94	2c
Chicken breast, bone-in	lb.	2.04	12/94	82r
Chicken, fresh, whole	lb.	0.95	12/94	82r
Chicken, whole fryer	lb.	0.96	12/94	2c
Cigarettes, Winston, Kings	carton	16.65	12/94	2c
Coffee, 100%, ground roast, all sizes	lb.	4.48	12/94	82r
Coffee, vacuum-packed	13 oz.	3.72	12/94	2c
Corn Flakes, Kellogg's or Post Toasties	18 oz.	2.30	12/94	2c
Corn, frozen, whole kernel, lowest price	10 oz.	0.86	12/94	2c
Dairy products (other) purchases	year	182	91	81r
Eggs, Grade A large	dozen	1.94	12/94	2c
Fish and seafood purchases	year	94	91	81r
Flour, white, all purpose	lb.	0.21	12/94	82r
Food purchases, food eaten at home	year	2749	91	81r
Foods purchased away from home, not prepared by consumer	year	1909	91	81r
Fruits and vegetables purchases	year	459	91	81r
Grapefruit	lb.	0.56	12/94	82r
Ground beef, 100% beef	lb.	1.31	12/94	82r
Ham, boneless, exc. canned	lb.	2.46	12/94	82r
Ice cream, prepackaged, bulk, regular	1/2 gal.	2.57	12/94	82r
Lemons	lb.	1.00	12/94	82r
Lettuce, iceberg	lb.	0.93	12/94	82r
Lettuce, iceberg	head	0.83	12/94	2c
Margarine, Blue Bonnet or Parkay cubes	lb.	0.72	12/94	2c
Meats, poultry, fish, and eggs purchases	year	700	91	81r
Milk and cream (fresh) purchases	year	155	91	81r
Milk, whole	1/2 gal.	1.58	12/94	2c
Orange juice, frozen concentrate 12-oz. can	16 oz.	1.52	12/94	82r
Orange juice, Minute Maid frozen	12-oz.	1.29	12/94	2c
Oranges, Navel	lb.	0.56	12/94	82r
Peaches, halves or slices, Hunt's, Del Monte, or Libby's	29-oz.	1.17	12/94	2c
Peas, sweet, Del Monte or Green Giant	15-17 oz.	0.58	12/94	2c
Pork chops, center cut, bone-in	lb.	3.30	12/94	82r
Pork purchases	year	122	91	81r
Potato chips	16-oz.	3.03	12/94	82r
Potatoes, frozen, French fried	lb.	0.77	12/94	82r
Potatoes, white	lb.	0.35	12/94	82r
Potatoes, white or red	10-lb. sack	1.79	12/94	2c
Rice, white, long grain, uncooked	lb.	0.54	12/94	82r
Round roast, USDA choice, boneless	lb.	2.92	12/94	82r
Sausage, Jimmy Dean, 100% pork	lb.	3.03	12/94	2c
Shortening, vegetable oil blends	lb.	0.80	12/94	82r
Shortening, vegetable, Crisco	3-lb.	2.72	12/94	2c
Soft drink, Coca Cola, ex deposit	2 lit	1.03	12/94	2c

Values are in dollars or fractions of dollars. In the column headed *Ref*, references are shown to sources. Each reference is followed by a letter. These refer to the geographical level for which data were reported: s=State, r=Region, and c=City or metro. The abbreviation *ex* is used to mean *except* or *excluding*; *exp* stands for expenditures. For other abbreviations and further explanations, please see the Introduction.

Riverside, CA - continued

Item	Per	Value	Date	Ref.
Groceries				
Spaghetti and macaroni	lb.	1.02	12/94	82r
Steak, round, graded & ungraded, exc. USDA prime & choice	lb.	3.13	12/94	82r
Steak, sirloin, USDA choice, boneless	lb.	4.07	12/94	82r
Steak, t-bone	lb.	4.76	12/94	2c
Sugar and other sweets, eaten at home, expenditures	year	105	91	81r
Sugar, cane or beet	4 lbs.	1.36	12/94	2c
Sugar, white, all sizes	lb.	0.38	12/94	82r
Tobacco products and smoking supplies, total expenditures	year	221	91	81r
Tomatoes, field grown	lb.	1.45	12/94	82r
Tomatoes, Hunt's or Del Monte	14.5 oz.	0.86	12/94	2c
Tuna, chunk, light	lb.	2.18	12/94	82r
Tuna, chunk, light, oil-packed	6.125-6.5 oz.	0.69	12/94	2c
Goods and Services				
Miscellaneous goods and services, ACCRA Index		108.30	12/94	2c
Health Care				
Health care, ACCRA Index		131.10	12/94	2c
Antibiotic ointment, Polysporin	1.5 oz.	4.26	12/94	2c
Childbirth, Cesarean delivery, hospital charge	birth	6059.00	12/91	69r
Childbirth, Cesarean delivery, physician charge	birth	2248.00	12/91	69r
Childbirth, normal delivery, hospital charge	birth	3006.00	12/91	69r
Childbirth, normal delivery, physician charge	birth	1634.00	12/91	69r
Dentist's fee, adult teeth cleaning and periodic oral exam	visit	80.50	12/94	2c
Doctor's fee, routine exam, established patient	visit	44.50	12/94	2c
Drugs, expenditures	year	230	91	81r
Health care, total expenditures	year	1544	91	81r
Health insurance expenditures	year	558	91	81r
Hospital care, semiprivate room	day	549.00	12/94	2c
Insurance premium, family medical care	month	380.27	1/95	41s
Medical services expenditures	year	676	91	81r
Medical supplies expenditures	year	80	91	81r
Surgery, open-heart	proc	37818.00	1/93	14r
Household Goods				
Appl. repair, service call, wash mach	min. lab. chg.	36.59	12/94	2c
Floor coverings, expenditures	year	79	91	81r
Furniture, expenditures	year	352	91	81r
Household equipment, misc. expenditures	year	614	91	81r
Household expenditures, miscellaneous	year	294	91	81r
Household furnishings and equipment, expenditures	year	1416	91	81r
Household operations expenditures	year	580	91	81r
Household textiles, expenditures	year	113	91	81r
Housekeeping supplies, expenditures	year	447	91	81r
Laundry and cleaning supplies, expenditures	year	114	91	81r
Laundry detergent, Tide Ultra, Bold, or Cheer	42 oz.	3.60	12/94	2c
Postage and stationery, expenditures	year	145	91	81r
Tissues, facial, Kleenex brand	175	1.03	12/94	2c
Housing				
Housing, ACCRA Index		115.00	12/94	2c
Add garage/carport		6,422	3/95	74r
Add room(s)		26,583	3/95	74r
Apartment condominium or co-op, median	unit	105300	12/94	62r
Dwellings (owned), expenditures	year	3932	91	81r
Enclose porch/patio/breezeway		5,382	3/95	74r
Finish room in basement/attic		3,911	3/95	74r
Home, existing, single-family, median	unit	178600	12/94	62r
Home, existing, single-family, median	unit	127.20	12/94	62c

Riverside, CA - continued

Item	Per	Value	Date	Ref.
Housing - continued				
House payment, principal and interest, 25% down payment	mo.	889	12/94	2c
House, 1800 sq ft, 8000 sq ft lot, new, urban, utilities	total	144663	12/94	2c
Maintenance, repairs, insurance, and other housing expenditures	year	591	91	81r
Mortgage interest and charges expenditures	year	2747	91	81r
Mtge. rate, incl. points and orig. fee, 30-year conv. fixed or ARM	mo.	9.21	12/94	2c
Princ. & int., mortgage, median-price exist. sing.-family home	mo.	845	12/94	62r
Property taxes expenditures	year	594	91	81r
Redesign, restructure more than half of home's interior		5,467	3/95	74r
Rent, apartment, 2 br., 1 1/2-2 baths, unfurnished, 950 sq ft, water	mo.	583	12/94	2c
Rental units expenditures	year	2077	91	81r
Insurance and Pensions				
Auto insurance, private passenger	year	892.80	12/94	71s
Insurance and pensions, personal, expenditures	year	3042	91	81r
Insurance, life and other personal, expenditures	year	298	91	81r
Pensions and Social Security, expenditures	year	2744	91	81r
Legal Assistance				
Legal work, law firm associate	hour	91		10r
Legal work, law firm partner	hour	151		10r
Personal Goods				
Shampoo, Alberto VO5	15-oz.	1.23	12/94	2c
Toothpaste, Crest or Colgate	6-7 oz.	2.39	12/94	2c
Personal Services				
Dry cleaning, man's 2-pc. suit		6.81	12/94	2c
Haircut, man's barbershop, no styling		9.00	12/94	2c
Haircut, woman's shampoo, trim, blow-dry		23.38	12/94	2c
Personal services expenditures	year	286	91	81r
Restaurant Food				
Chicken, fried, thigh and drumstick		2.15	12/94	2c
Dining expenditures, family	week	32.25	94	73r
Hamburger with cheese	1/4 lb.	1.92	12/94	2c
Pizza, Pizza Hut or Pizza Inn	12-13 in.	8.79	12/94	2c
Taxes				
Taxes, Federal income, expenditures	year	2946	91	81r
Taxes, personal, expenditures	year	3791	91	81r
Taxes, State and local income, expenditures	year	791	91	81r
Transportation				
Transportation, ACCRA Index		113.60	12/94	2c
Bus fare, one-way	trip	0.75	12/95	1c
Bus fare, up to 10 miles	one-way	0.75	12/94	2c
Cars and trucks purchased, new	year	1231	91	81r
Cars and trucks purchased, used	year	915	91	81r
Driver's learning permit fee	perm	12.00	1/94	84s
Driver's license fee	orig	12.00	1/94	84s
Driver's license fee, duplicate	lic	12.00	1/94	84s
Driver's license reinstatement fee, min.	susp	15.00	1/94	85s
Driver's license renewal fee	renew	12.00	1/94	84s
Identification card, nondriver	card	6.00	1/94	83s
Motorcycle learning permit fee	perm	12.00	1/94	84s
Motorcycle license fee	orig	12.00	1/94	84s
Motorcycle license fee, duplicate	lic	12.00	1/94	84s
Motorcycle license renewal fee	renew	12.00	1/94	84s
Public transportation expenditures	year	375	91	81r
Tire balance, computer or spin bal., front	wheel	8.48	12/94	2c
Transportation expenditures, total	year	5527	91	81r
Vehicle finance charges	year	287	91	81r
Vehicle insurance expenditures	year	624	91	81r

Values are in dollars or fractions of dollars. In the column headed *Ref*, references are shown to sources. Each reference is followed by a letter. These refer to the geographical level for which data were reported: s = State, r = Region, and c = City or metro. The abbreviation *ex* is used to mean *except* or *excluding*; *exp* stands for expenditures. For other abbreviations and further explanations, please see the Introduction.

Riverside, CA - continued

Item	Per	Value	Date	Ref.
Transportation				
Vehicle maintenance and repairs expenditures	year	695	91	81r
Vehicle purchases	year	2174	91	81r
Vehicle rental, leases, licenses, etc. expenditures	year	257	91	81r
Vehicles purchased, other than cars and trucks	year	28	91	81r
Utilities				
Utilities, ACCRA Index		92.40	12/94	2c
Electricity expenditures	year	616	91	81r
Electricity, (part.), other, 1800 sq. ft., new home	mo.	77.70	12/94	2c
Utilities, fuels, and public services, total expenditures	year	1681	91	81r
Water and other public services, expenditures	year	209	91	81r
Weddings				
Bridal attendants' gowns	event	750	10/93	76r
Bridal gown	event	852	10/93	76r
Bridal headpiece and veil	event	167	10/93	76r
Bride's wedding band	event	708	10/93	76r
Clergy	event	224	10/93	76r
Engagement ring	event	2756	10/93	76r
Flowers	event	863	10/93	76r
Formal wear for groom	event	106	10/93	76r
Groom's attendants' formal wear	event	530	10/93	76r
Groom's wedding band	event	402	10/93	76r
Music	event	600	10/93	76r
Photography	event	1088	10/93	76r
Shoes for bride	event	50	10/93	76r
Videography	event	483	10/93	76r
Wedding invitations and announcements	event	342	10/93	76r
Wedding reception	event	7000	10/93	76r

Roanoke, VA

Item	Per	Value	Date	Ref.
Composite, ACCRA index		91.30	12/94	2c
Alcoholic Beverages				
Beer, Miller Lite, Bud, 12-oz., ex deposit	6	3.61	12/94	2c
J & B Scotch	750-ml.	18.45	12/94	2c
Wine, Gallo Chablis blanc	1.5-lit	4.76	12/94	2c
Appliances				
Appliances (major), expenditures	year	153	91	81r
Average annual exp.				
Food, health care, personal goods, services	year	27020	91	81r
Charity				
Cash contributions, expenditures	year	839	91	81r
Clothing				
Apparel, men and boys, total expenditures	year	380	91	81r
Apparel, women and girls, total expenditures	year	660	91	81r
Footwear, expenditures	year	193	91	81r
Jeans, man's denim		26.69	12/94	2c
Shirt, man's dress shirt		30.08	12/94	2c
Undervest, boy's size 10-14, cotton	3	4.54	12/94	2c
Communications				
Long-distance telephone rate, day, addl. min., 1-10 mi.	min.	0.12	12/93	9s
Long-distance telephone rate, day, initial min., 1-10 mi.	min.	0.21	12/93	9s
Newspaper subscription, dly. and Sun. delivery	month	10.40	12/94	2c
Phone line, single, business, field visit	inst	0.00	12/93	9s
Phone line, single, business, no field visit	inst	64.00	12/93	9s
Phone line, single, residence, field visit	inst	0.00	12/93	9s
Phone line, single, residence, no field visit	inst	38.50	12/93	9s
Telephone bill, family of four	month	19.37	12/94	2c

Roanoke, VA - continued

Item	Per	Value	Date	Ref.
Communications - continued				
Telephone service, expenditures	year	616	91	81r
Education				
Board, 4-year private college/university	year	2242	8/94	80s
Board, 4-year public college/university	year	1901	8/94	80s
Education, total expenditures	year	319	91	81r
Room, 4-year private college/university	year	2022	8/94	80s
Room, 4-year public college/university	year	2186	8/94	80s
Total cost, 4-year private college/university	year	14043	8/94	80s
Total cost, 4-year public college/university	year	7726	8/94	80s
Tuition, 2-year public college/university, in-state	year	1332	8/94	80s
Tuition, 4-year private college/university, in-state	year	9778	8/94	80s
Tuition, 4-year public college/university, in-state	year	3639	8/94	80s
Energy and Fuels				
Energy, combined forms, 1800 sq. ft.	mo.	94.75	12/94	2c
Fuel oil and other fuels, expenditures	year	56	91	81r
Gas, cooking, winter, 10 therms	month	13.71	2/94	65c
Gas, cooking, winter, 30 therms	month	26.62	2/94	65c
Gas, cooking, winter, 50 therms	month	39.54	2/94	65c
Gas, heating, winter, 100 therms	month	69.32	2/94	65c
Gas, heating, winter, average use	month	119.13	2/94	65c
Gas, natural, expenditures	year	150	91	81r
Gas, reg unlead, taxes inc., cash, self-service	gal	1.08	12/94	2c
Gasoline and motor oil purchased	year	1152	91	81r
Gasoline, unleaded midgrade	gallon	1.21	4/93	82r
Gasoline, unleaded premium	gallon	1.30	4/93	82r
Gasoline, unleaded regular	gallon	1.10	4/93	82r
Entertainment				
Bowling, evening rate	game	1.73	12/94	2c
Concert ticket, Pearl Jam group	perf	20.00	94	50r
Entertainment, total expenditures	year	1266	91	81r
Fees and admissions, expenditures	year	306	91	81r
Monopoly game, Parker Brothers', No. 9	game	10.42	12/94	2c
Movie	adm	5.69	12/94	2c
Pets, toys, playground equipment, expenditures	year	271	91	81r
Reading, expenditures	year	131	91	81r
Televisions, radios, and sound equipment, expenditures	year	439	91	81r
Tennis balls, yellow, Wilson or Penn, 3	can	2.17	12/94	2c
Funerals				
Burial, immediate, container provided by funeral home		1370.36	1/95	54r
Cards, acknowledgment		14.83	1/95	54r
Casket, minimum alternative		192.52	1/95	54r
Cosmetology, hair care, etc.		102.27	1/95	54r
Cremation, direct, container provided by funeral home		1065.64	1/95	54r
Embalming		304.29	1/95	54r
Funeral, funeral home		287.83	1/95	54r
Funeral, other facility		284.14	1/95	54r
Graveside service		349.13	1/95	54r
Hearse, local		132.27	1/95	54r
Limousine, local		98.45	1/95	54r
Memorial service		270.59	1/95	54r
Service charge, professional, nondeclinable		933.59	1/95	54r
Visitation and viewing		225.83	1/95	54r
Groceries				
Groceries, ACCRA Index		96.40	12/94	2c
Apples, Red Delicious	lb.	0.73	12/94	82r
Baby food, strained vegetables, lowest price	4-4.5 oz.	0.33	12/94	2c
Bacon, sliced	lb.	1.67	12/94	82r
Bananas	lb.	0.53	12/94	2c
Bananas	lb.	0.42	12/94	82r
Beef or hamburger, ground	lb.	1.29	12/94	2c

Values are in dollars or fractions of dollars. In the column headed *Ref*, references are shown to sources. Each reference is followed by a letter. These refer to the geographical level for which data were reported: s=State, r=Region, and c=City or metro. The abbreviation *ex* is used to mean *except* or *excluding*; *exp* stands for expenditures. For other abbreviations and further explanations, please see the Introduction.

Roanoke, VA - continued

Item	Per	Value	Date	Ref.
Groceries				
Beef purchases	year	213	91	81r
Beverage purchases, alcoholic	year	249	91	81r
Beverage purchases, nonalcoholic	year	207	91	81r
Bologna, all beef or mixed	lb.	2.27	12/94	82r
Bread, white	24-oz.	0.78	12/94	2c
Bread, white, pan	lb.	0.68	12/94	82r
Cabbage	lb.	0.42	12/94	82r
Carrots, short trimmed and topped	lb.	0.53	12/94	82r
Cereals and bakery products purchases	year	345	91	81r
Cereals and cereals products purchases	year	127	91	81r
Cheddar cheese, natural	lb.	3.58	12/94	82r
Cheese, Kraft grated Parmesan	8-oz.	3.25	12/94	2c
Chicken breast, bone-in	lb.	1.71	12/94	82r
Chicken, fresh, whole	lb.	0.78	12/94	82r
Chicken, whole fryer	lb.	0.82	12/94	2c
Chuck roast, USDA choice, boneless	lb.	2.26	12/94	82r
Cigarettes, Winston, Kings	carton	13.52	12/94	2c
Coffee, vacuum-packed	13 oz.	3.22	12/94	2c
Corn Flakes, Kellogg's or Post Toasties	18 oz.	2.44	12/94	2c
Corn, frozen, whole kernel, lowest price	10 oz.	0.63	12/94	2c
Crackers, soda, salted	lb.	1.27	12/94	82r
Cucumbers	lb.	0.65	12/94	82r
Dairy products (other) purchases	year	141	91	81r
Eggs, Grade A large	dozen	0.88	12/94	2c
Eggs, Grade A large	dozen	0.87	12/94	82r
Fish and seafood purchases	year	72	91	81r
Flour, white, all purpose	lb.	0.23	12/94	82r
Food purchases, food eaten at home	year	2381	91	81r
Foods purchased away from home, not prepared by consumer	year	1696	91	81r
Frankfurters, all meat or all beef	lb.	1.74	12/94	82r
Fruits and vegetables purchases	year	380	91	81r
Grapefruit	lb.	0.45	12/94	82r
Grapes, Thompson seedless	lb.	2.30	12/94	82r
Ground beef, 100% beef	lb.	1.37	12/94	82r
Ground chuck, 100% beef	lb.	1.97	12/94	82r
Ham, boneless, exc. canned	lb.	2.54	12/94	82r
Ice cream, prepackaged, bulk, regular	1/2 gal.	2.47	12/94	82r
Lemons	lb.	1.02	12/94	82r
Lettuce, iceberg	lb.	0.96	12/94	82r
Lettuce, iceberg	head	1.02	12/94	2c
Margarine, Blue Bonnet or Parkay cubes	lb.	0.53	12/94	2c
Margarine, stick	lb.	0.77	12/94	82r
Meats, poultry, fish, and eggs purchases	year	655	91	81r
Milk and cream (fresh) purchases	year	130	91	81r
Milk, whole	1/2 gal.	1.41	12/94	2c
Orange juice, frozen concentrate 12-oz. can	16 oz.	1.36	12/94	82r
Orange juice, Minute Maid frozen	12-oz.	1.13	12/94	2c
Oranges, Navel	lb.	0.54	12/94	82r
Peaches, halves or slices, Hunt's, Del Monte, or Libby's	29-oz.	1.26	12/94	2c
Pears, Anjou	lb.	0.81	12/94	82r
Peas, sweet, Del Monte or Green Giant	15-17 oz.	0.40	12/94	2c
Pork chops, center cut, bone-in	lb.	3.07	12/94	82r
Pork purchases	year	142	91	81r
Potato chips	16-oz.	3.15	12/94	82r
Potatoes, frozen, French fried	lb.	0.82	12/94	82r
Potatoes, white	lb.	0.34	12/94	82r
Potatoes, white or red	10-lb. sack	2.47	12/94	2c
Rice, white, long grain, uncooked	lb.	0.48	12/94	82r
Round roast, USDA choice, boneless	lb.	2.91	12/94	82r
Sausage, fresh	lb.	1.82	12/94	82r
Sausage, Jimmy Dean, 100% pork	lb.	2.27	12/94	2c
Shortening, vegetable oil blends	lb.	0.75	12/94	82r
Shortening, vegetable, Crisco	3-lb.	2.50	12/94	2c
Soft drink, Coca Cola, ex deposit	2 lit	1.01	12/94	2c
Spaghetti and macaroni	lb.	0.87	12/94	82r
Steak, rib eye, USDA choice, boneless	lb.	6.85	12/94	82r

Roanoke, VA - continued

Item	Per	Value	Date	Ref.
Groceries - continued				
Steak, round, graded & ungraded, exc. USDA prime & choice	lb.	2.96	12/94	82r
Steak, round, USDA choice, boneless	lb.	3.17	12/94	82r
Steak, sirloin, USDA choice, boneless	lb.	4.12	12/94	82r
Steak, t-bone	lb.	5.24	12/94	2c
Steak, T-bone, USDA choice, bone-in	lb.	5.63	12/94	82r
Sugar and other sweets, eaten at home, expenditures	year	93	91	81r
Sugar, cane or beet	4 lbs.	1.48	12/94	2c
Sugar, white, all sizes	lb.	0.39	12/94	82r
Tobacco products and smoking supplies, total expenditures	year	286	91	81r
Tomatoes, field grown	lb.	1.36	12/94	82r
Tomatoes, Hunt's or Del Monte	14.5 oz.	0.55	12/94	2c
Tuna, chunk, light	lb.	1.94	12/94	82r
Tuna, chunk, light, oil-packed	6.125-6.5 oz.	0.66	12/94	2c
Turkey, frozen, whole	lb.	0.96	12/94	82r
Yogurt, natural, fruit flavored	8 oz.	0.58	12/94	82r
Goods and Services				
Miscellaneous goods and services, ACCRA Index		90.20	12/94	2c
Health Care				
Health care, ACCRA Index		91.60	12/94	2c
Adenosine, emergency room	treat	100.00	95	23r
Antibiotic ointment, Polysporin	1.5 oz.	3.99	12/94	2c
Bladder tap, superpubic, infant, emergency room	treat	119.00	95	23r
Blood analysis, emergency room	treat	25.00	95	23r
Blood tests, abdominal pain, emergency room	treat	25.00	95	23r
Burn dressing, emergency room	treat	266.00	95	23r
Cardiology interpretation, emergency room	treat	26.00	95	23r
Chest X-ray, emergency room	treat	78.00	95	23r
Childbirth, Cesarean delivery, hospital charge	birth	5462.00	12/91	69r
Childbirth, Cesarean delivery, physician charge	birth	2228.00	12/91	69r
Childbirth, normal delivery, hospital charge	birth	2943.00	12/91	69r
Childbirth, normal delivery, physician charge	birth	1619.00	12/91	69r
Defibrillation pads, emergency room	treat	6.00	95	23r
Delivery, uncomplicated, total charge	birth	6180	1/93	24s
Delivery, uncomplicated, vaginal, hospital charge	birth	3380	1/93	24s
Delivery, uncomplicated, vaginal, physician's charge	birth	2800	1/93	24s
Dentist's fee, adult teeth cleaning and periodic oral exam	visit	45.20	12/94	2c
Doctor's fee, routine exam, established patient	visit	40.75	12/94	2c
Drugs, expenditures	year	297	91	81r
Gastric tube insertion, nasal, emergency room	treat	25.00	95	23r
Health care, total expenditures	year	1600	91	81r
Health insurance expenditures	year	637	91	81r
Heart monitor, emergency room	treat	40.00	95	23r
Hospital care, semiprivate room	day	314.00	12/94	2c
Insurance premium, family medical care	month	386.57	1/95	41s
Intravenous fluids, emergency room	treat	130.00	95	23r
Intravenous fluids, emergency room	liter	26.00	95	23r
Intravenous line, central, emergency room	treat	342.00	95	23r
Liver function tests, abdominal pain, emergency room	treat	26.00	95	23r
Medical care charges, total, emergency room, third-degree burns	treat	2101.00	95	23r
Medical care charges, total, emergency, infant with fever	treat	628.00	95	23r
Medical services expenditures	year	573	91	81r
Medical supplies expenditures	year	93	91	81r
Morphine, emergency room	treat	34.00	95	23r

Values are in dollars or fractions of dollars. In the column headed *Ref*, references are shown to sources. Each reference is followed by a letter. These refer to the geographical level for which data were reported: s=State, r=Region, and c=City or metro. The abbreviation *ex* is used to mean *except* or *excluding*; *exp* stands for *expenditures*. For other abbreviations and further explanations, please see the Introduction.

Roanoke, VA - continued

Item	Per	Value	Date	Ref.
Health Care				
Nursing care and facilities charges, emergency room	treat	252.00	95	23r
Nursing care and facilities charges, emergency, infant with fever	treat	252.00	95	23r
Nursing care and facilities charges, emergency, third-degree burns	treat	861.00	95	23r
Physician's charges, emergency, infant with fever	treat	212.00	95	23r
Physician's charges, emergency, third-degree burns	treat	372.00	95	23r
Physician's fee, emergency room	treat	372.00	95	23r
Physician's fee, general practitioner	visit	51.20	12/93	60r
Surgery, open-heart	proc	42374.00	1/93	14r
Ultrasound, abdominal, emergency room	treat	276.00	95	23r
Urinalysis, emergency room	treat	20.00	95	23r
Urinalysis, infant, emergency room	treat	20.00	95	23r
X-rays, emergency room	treat	78.00	95	23r
Household Goods				
Appl. repair, service call, wash mach	min. lab. chg.	34.00	12/94	2c
Floor coverings, expenditures	year	48	91	81r
Furniture, expenditures	year	280	91	81r
Household equipment, misc. expenditures	year	342	91	81r
Household expenditures, miscellaneous	year	256	91	81r
Household furnishings and equipment, expenditures	year	988	91	81r
Household operations expenditures	year	468	91	81r
Household textiles, expenditures	year	95	91	81r
Housekeeping supplies, expenditures	year	380	91	81r
Laundry and cleaning supplies, expenditures	year	109	91	81r
Laundry detergent, Tide Ultra, Bold, or Cheer	42 oz.	2.70	12/94	2c
Postage and stationery, expenditures	year	105	91	81r
Tissues, facial, Kleenex brand	175	0.97	12/94	2c
Housing				
Housing, ACCRA Index		89.70	12/94	2c
Add garage/carport		6,980	3/95	74r
Add room(s)		11,403	3/95	74r
Apartment condominium or co-op, median	unit	68600	12/94	62r
Dwellings (owned), expenditures	year	2428	91	81r
Enclose porch/patio/breezeway		4,572	3/95	74r
Finish room in basement/attic		3,794	3/95	74r
Home, existing, single-family, median	unit	120200	12/94	62r
House payment, principal and interest, 25% down payment	mo.	775	12/94	2c
House, 1800 sq ft, 8000 sq ft lot, new, urban, utilities	total	128000	12/94	2c
Maintenance, repairs, insurance, and other housing expenditures	year	531	91	81r
Mortgage interest and charges expenditures	year	1506	91	81r
Mtge. rate, incl. points and orig. fee, 30-year conv. fixed or ARM	mo.	9.03	12/94	2c
Princ. & int., mortgage, median-price exist. sing.-family home	mo.	540	12/94	62r
Property taxes expenditures	year	391	91	81r
Redesign, restructure more than half of home's interior		17,641	3/95	74r
Rent, apartment, 2 br., 1 1/2-2 baths, unfurnished, 950 sq ft, water	mo.	528	12/94	2c
Rental units expenditures	year	1264	91	81r
Insurance and Pensions				
Auto insurance, private passenger	year	564.07	12/94	71s
Insurance and pensions, personal, expenditures	year	2395	91	81r
Insurance, life and other personal, expenditures	year	368	91	81r
Pensions and Social Security, expenditures	year	2027	91	81r

Roanoke, VA - continued

Item	Per	Value	Date	Ref.
Personal Goods				
Shampoo, Alberto VO5	15-oz.	0.96	12/94	2c
Toothpaste, Crest or Colgate	6-7 oz.	1.84	12/94	2c
Personal Services				
Dry cleaning, man's 2-pc. suit		6.41	12/94	2c
Haircut, man's barbershop, no styling		8.43	12/94	2c
Haircut, woman's shampoo, trim, blow-dry		16.67	12/94	2c
Personal services expenditures	year	212	91	81r
Restaurant Food				
Chicken, fried, thigh and drumstick		1.74	12/94	2c
Dining expenditures, family	week	33.83	94	73r
Hamburger with cheese	1/4 lb.	0.99	12/94	2c
Pizza, Pizza Hut or Pizza Inn	12-13 in.	7.49	12/94	2c
Taxes				
Taxes, Federal income, expenditures	year	2275	91	81r
Taxes, personal, expenditures	year	2715	91	81r
Taxes, State and local income, expenditures	year	365	91	81r
Transportation				
Transportation, ACCRA Index		95.30	12/94	2c
Bus fare, up to 10 miles	one-way	1.25	12/94	2c
Cars and trucks purchased, new	year	1306	91	81r
Cars and trucks purchased, used	year	942	91	81r
Driver's learning permit fee	perm	3.00	1/94	84s
Driver's license fee	orig	12.00	1/94	84s
Driver's license fee, duplicate	lic	5.00	1/94	84s
Driver's license reinstatement fee, min.	susp	30.00	1/94	85s
Driver's license renewal fee	renew	12.00	1/94	84s
Identification card, nondriver	card	5.00	1/94	83s
Motorcycle license fee	orig	5.00	1/94	84s
Motorcycle license renewal fee	renew	5.00	1/94	84s
Public transportation expenditures	year	249	91	81r
Tire balance, computer or spin bal., front	wheel	5.72	12/94	2c
Transportation expenditures, total	year	5307	91	81r
Vehicle finance charges	year	346	91	81r
Vehicle insurance expenditures	year	544	91	81r
Vehicle maintenance and repairs expenditures	year	600	91	81r
Vehicle purchases	year	2275	91	81r
Vehicle rental, leases, licenses, etc. expenditures	year	141	91	81r
Vehicles purchased, other than cars and trucks	year	27	91	81r
Utilities				
Utilities, ACCRA Index		86.40	12/94	2c
Electricity expenditures	year	950	91	81r
Electricity, 1800 sq. ft., new home	mo.	94.75	12/94	2c
Electricity, summer, 250 KWh	month	20.67	8/93	64c
Electricity, summer, 500 KWh	month	35.15	8/93	64c
Electricity, summer, 750 KWh	month	49.63	8/93	64c
Electricity, summer, 1000 KWh	month	63.04	8/93	64c
Utilities, fuels, and public services, total expenditures	year	2000	91	81r
Water and other public services, expenditures	year	227	91	81r
Weddings				
Bridal attendants' gowns	event	750	10/93	76r
Bridal gown	event	852	10/93	76r
Bridal headpiece and veil	event	167	10/93	76r
Bride's wedding band	event	708	10/93	76r
Clergy	event	224	10/93	76r
Engagement ring	event	2756	10/93	76r
Flowers	event	863	10/93	76r
Formal wear for groom	event	106	10/93	76r
Groom's attendants' formal wear	event	530	10/93	76r
Groom's wedding band	event	402	10/93	76r
Music	event	600	10/93	76r
Photography	event	1088	10/93	76r
Shoes for bride	event	50	10/93	76r

Values are in dollars or fractions of dollars. In the column headed *Ref*, references are shown to sources. Each reference is followed by a letter. These refer to the geographical level for which data were reported: s=State, r=Region, and c=City or metro. The abbreviation *ex* is used to mean *except* or *excluding*; *exp* stands for expenditures. For other abbreviations and further explanations, please see the Introduction.

Roanoke, VA - continued

Item	Per	Value	Date	Ref.
Weddings				
Videography	event	483	10/93	76r
Wedding invitations and announcements	event	342	10/93	76r
Wedding reception	event	7000	10/93	76r

Rochester, MN

Item	Per	Value	Date	Ref.
Composite, ACCRA index		99.50	12/94	2c
Alcoholic Beverages				
Beer, Miller Lite, Bud, 12-oz., ex deposit	6	3.94	12/94	2c
J & B Scotch	750-ml.	18.81	12/94	2c
Wine, Gallo Chablis blanc	1.5-lit	5.03	12/94	2c
Appliances				
Appliances (major), expenditures	year	131	91	81r
Average annual exp.				
Food, health care, personal goods, services	year	25935	91	81r
Charity				
Cash contributions, expenditures	year	745	91	81r
Clothing				
Apparel, men and boys, total expenditures	year	332	91	81r
Apparel, women and girls, total expenditures	year	578	91	81r
Footwear, expenditures	year	164	91	81r
Jeans, man's denim		35.20	12/94	2c
Shirt, man's dress shirt		31.50	12/94	2c
Undervest, boy's size 10-14, cotton	3	3.83	12/94	2c
Communications				
Long-distance telephone rate, day, addl. min., 1-10 mi.	min.	0.05	12/93	9s
Long-distance telephone rate, day, initial min., 1-10 mi.	min.	0.14	12/93	9s
Newspaper subscription, dly. and Sun. delivery	month	10.77	12/94	2c
Phone line, single, business, field visit	inst	45.00	12/93	9s
Phone line, single, business, no field visit	inst	45.00	12/93	9s
Phone line, single, residence, field visit	inst	16.25	12/93	9s
Phone line, single, residence, no field visit	inst	16.25	12/93	9s
Telephone bill, family of four	month	23.88	12/94	2c
Telephone service, expenditures	year	547	91	81r
Telephone, residential, flat rate	mo.	14.58	12/93	8c
Education				
Board, 4-year private college/university	year	2070	8/94	80s
Board, 4-year public college/university	year	1545	8/94	80s
Education, total expenditures	year	394	91	81r
Living expenses, personal miscellaneous, university student	year	4200.00	5/96	22s
Room, 4-year private college/university	year	1894	8/94	80s
Room, 4-year public college/university	year	1580	8/94	80s
Total cost, 4-year private college/university	year	15556	8/94	80s
Total cost, 4-year public college/university	year	5904	8/94	80s
Tuition, 2-year public college/university, in-state	year	1858	8/94	80s
Tuition, 4-year private college/university, in-state	year	11592	8/94	80s
Tuition, 4-year public college/university, in-state	year	2780	8/94	80s
Energy and Fuels				
Energy, combined forms, 1800 sq. ft.	mo.	109.40	12/94	2c
Energy, exc. electricity, 1800 sq. ft.	mo.	56.20	12/94	2c
Fuel oil and other fuels, expenditures	year	83	91	81r
Gas, cooking, 10 therms	month	10.44	2/94	65c
Gas, cooking, 30 therms	month	19.32	2/94	65c
Gas, cooking, 50 therms	month	28.20	2/94	65c
Gas, heating, winter, 100 therms	month	50.39	2/94	65c
Gas, heating, winter, average use	month	84.54	2/94	65c
Gas, natural, expenditures	year	373	91	81r
Gas, reg unlead, taxes inc., cash, self-service	gal	1.13	12/94	2c

Rochester, MN - continued

Item	Per	Value	Date	Ref.
Energy and Fuels - continued				
Gasoline and motor oil purchased	year	1000	91	81r
Gasoline, unleaded midgrade	gallon	1.15	4/93	82r
Gasoline, unleaded premium	gallon	1.23	4/93	82r
Gasoline, unleaded regular	gallon	1.07	4/93	82r
Entertainment				
Bowling, evening rate	game	1.76	12/94	2c
Entertainment, total expenditures	year	1356	91	81r
Fees and admissions, expenditures	year	347	91	81r
Monopoly game, Parker Brothers', No. 9	game	10.53	12/94	2c
Movie	adm	5.50	12/94	2c
Pets, toys, playground equipment, expenditures	year	270	91	81r
Reading, expenditures	year	160	91	81r
Televisions, radios, and sound equipment, expenditures	year	433	91	81r
Tennis balls, yellow, Wilson or Penn, 3	can	2.97	12/94	2c
Funerals				
Burial, immediate, container provided by funeral home		1348.78	1/95	54r
Cards, acknowledgment		21.20	1/95	54r
Casket, minimum alternative		182.83	1/95	54r
Cosmetology, hair care, etc.		133.11	1/95	54r
Cremation, direct, container provided by funeral home		1101.95	1/95	54r
Embalming		314.45	1/95	54r
Funeral, funeral home		304.88	1/95	54r
Funeral, other facility		301.37	1/95	54r
Graveside service		290.59	1/95	54r
Hearse, local		137.37	1/95	54r
Limousine, local		82.84	1/95	54r
Memorial service		316.57	1/95	54r
Service charge, professional, nondeclinable		1099.00	1/95	54r
Visitation and viewing		209.25	1/95	54r
Groceries				
Groceries, ACCRA Index		99.50	12/94	2c
Apples, Red Delicious	lb.	0.68	12/94	82r
Baby food, strained vegetables, lowest price	4-4.5 oz.	0.36	12/94	2c
Bacon, sliced	lb.	1.88	12/94	82r
Bananas	lb.	0.37	12/94	2c
Bananas	lb.	0.41	12/94	82r
Beef or hamburger, ground	lb.	1.61	12/94	2c
Beef purchases	year	197	91	81r
Beef, stew, boneless	lb.	2.52	12/94	82r
Beverage purchases, alcoholic	year	293	91	81r
Beverage purchases, nonalcoholic	year	203	91	81r
Bologna, all beef or mixed	lb.	2.12	12/94	82r
Bread, white	24-oz.	0.61	12/94	2c
Bread, white, pan	lb.	0.76	12/94	82r
Cabbage	lb.	0.44	12/94	82r
Carrots, short trimmed and topped	lb.	0.44	12/94	82r
Cereals and bakery products purchases	year	347	91	81r
Cereals and cereals products purchases	year	119	91	81r
Cheddar cheese, natural	lb.	3.28	12/94	82r
Cheese, Kraft grated Parmesan	8-oz.	3.02	12/94	2c
Chicken breast, bone-in	lb.	1.61	12/94	82r
Chicken, fresh, whole	lb.	0.89	12/94	2c
Chicken, whole fryer	lb.	0.83	12/94	2c
Chuck roast, USDA choice, boneless	lb.	2.33	12/94	82r
Cigarettes, Winston, Kings	carton	21.09	12/94	2c
Coffee, 100%, ground roast, all sizes	lb.	4.28	12/94	82r
Coffee, vacuum-packed	13 oz.	3.57	12/94	2c
Cookies, chocolate chip	lb.	2.72	12/94	82r
Corn Flakes, Kellogg's or Post Toasties	18 oz.	2.10	12/94	2c
Corn, frozen, whole kernel, lowest price	10 oz.	0.63	12/94	2c
Dairy products (other) purchases	year	148	91	81r
Eggs, Grade A large	dozen	0.64	12/94	2c
Eggs, Grade A large	dozen	0.76	12/94	82r
Fish and seafood purchases	year	61	91	81r
Flour, white, all purpose	lb.	0.22	12/94	82r
Food purchases, food eaten at home	year	2313	91	81r

Values are in dollars or fractions of dollars. In the column headed *Ref*, references are shown to sources. Each reference is followed by a letter. These refer to the geographical level for which data were reported: s=State, r=Region, and c=City or metro. The abbreviation *ex* is used to mean *except* or *excluding*; *exp* stands for expenditures. For other abbreviations and further explanations, please see the Introduction.

674

Rochester, MN - continued

Item	Per	Value	Date	Ref.
Groceries				
Foods purchased away from home, not prepared by consumer	year	1709	91	81r
Fruits and vegetables purchases	year	372	91	81r
Grapefruit	lb.	0.47	12/94	82r
Grapes, Thompson seedless	lb.	2.15	12/94	82r
Ground beef, 100% beef	lb.	1.37	12/94	82r
Ground chuck, 100% beef	lb.	1.81	12/94	82r
Ham, boneless, exc. canned	lb.	2.16	12/94	82r
Ice cream, prepackaged, bulk, regular	1/2 gal.	2.48	12/94	82r
Lemons	lb.	1.08	12/94	82r
Lettuce, iceberg	lb.	0.81	12/94	82r
Lettuce, iceberg	head	0.70	12/94	2c
Margarine, Blue Bonnet or Parkay cubes	lb.	0.67	12/94	2c
Margarine, stick	lb.	0.81	12/94	82r
Meats, poultry, fish, and eggs purchases	year	591	91	81r
Milk and cream (fresh) purchases	year	132	91	81r
Milk, whole	1/2 gal.	1.23	12/94	2c
Orange juice, frozen concentrate 12-oz. can	16 oz.	1.41	12/94	82r
Orange juice, Minute Maid frozen	12-oz.	1.31	12/94	2c
Oranges, Navel	lb.	0.56	12/94	82r
Peaches, halves or slices, Hunt's, Del Monte, or Libby's	29-oz.	1.12	12/94	2c
Peanut butter, creamy, all sizes	lb.	1.81	12/94	82r
Peas, sweet, Del Monte or Green Giant	15-17 oz.	0.59	12/94	2c
Pork chops, center cut, bone-in	lb.	2.76	12/94	82r
Pork purchases	year	130	91	81r
Potato chips	16-oz.	2.81	12/94	82r
Potatoes, frozen, French fried	lb.	0.83	12/94	82r
Potatoes, white	lb.	0.28	12/94	82r
Potatoes, white or red	10-lb. sack	1.76	12/94	2c
Round roast, USDA choice, boneless	lb.	2.90	12/94	82r
Sausage, Jimmy Dean, 100% pork	lb.	2.96	12/94	2c
Shortening, vegetable oil blends	lb.	0.88	12/94	82r
Shortening, vegetable, Crisco	3-lb.	2.28	12/94	2c
Soft drink, Coca Cola, ex deposit	2 lit	1.22	12/94	2c
Spaghetti and macaroni	lb.	0.78	12/94	82r
Steak, rib eye, USDA choice, boneless	lb.	6.15	12/94	82r
Steak, round, graded & ungraded, exc. USDA prime & choice	lb.	2.72	12/94	82r
Steak, round, USDA choice, boneless	lb.	3.02	12/94	82r
Steak, sirloin, USDA choice, boneless	lb.	3.85	12/94	82r
Steak, t-bone, USDA choice	lb.	4.67	12/94	2c
Steak, T-bone, USDA choice, bone-in	lb.	5.38	12/94	82r
Sugar and other sweets, eaten at home, expenditures	year	91	91	81r
Sugar, cane or beet	4 lbs.	1.50	12/94	2c
Sugar, white, all sizes	lb.	0.36	12/94	82r
Tobacco products and smoking supplies, total expenditures	year	298	91	81r
Tomatoes, field grown	lb.	1.36	12/94	82r
Tomatoes, Hunt's or Del Monte	14.5 oz.	0.75	12/94	2c
Tuna, chunk, light	lb.	1.94	12/94	82r
Tuna, chunk, light, oil-packed	6.125-6.5 oz.	0.68	12/94	2c
Turkey, frozen, whole	lb.	0.96	12/94	82r
Yogurt, natural, fruit flavored	8 oz.	0.62	12/94	82r
Goods and Services				
Miscellaneous goods and services, ACCRA Index		102.70	12/94	2c
Health Care				
Health care, ACCRA Index		100.90	12/94	2c
Antibiotic ointment, Polysporin	1.5 oz.	4.74	12/94	2c
Childbirth, Cesarean delivery, hospital charge	birth	5101.00	12/91	69r
Childbirth, Cesarean delivery, physician charge	birth	2234.00	12/91	69r

Rochester, MN - continued

Item	Per	Value	Date	Ref.
Health Care - continued				
Childbirth, normal delivery, hospital charge	birth	2891.00	12/91	69r
Childbirth, normal delivery, physician charge	birth	1623.00	12/91	69r
Dentist's fee, adult teeth cleaning and periodic oral exam	visit	46.72	12/94	2c
Doctor's fee, routine exam, established patient	visit	41.84	12/94	2c
Drugs, expenditures	year	248	91	81r
Health care, total expenditures	year	1336	91	81r
Health insurance expenditures	year	550	91	81r
Hospital care, semiprivate room	day	418.33	12/94	2c
Insurance premium, family medical care	month	375.35	1/95	41s
Medical services expenditures	year	457	91	81r
Medical supplies expenditures	year	82	91	81r
Household Goods				
Appl. repair, service call, wash mach	min. lab. chg.	33.47	12/94	2c
Floor coverings, expenditures	year	105	91	81r
Furniture, expenditures	year	291	91	81r
Household equipment, misc. expenditures	year	341	91	81r
Household expenditures, miscellaneous	year	162	91	81r
Household furnishings and equipment, expenditures	year	1042	91	81r
Household operations expenditures	year	365	91	81r
Household textiles, expenditures	year	101	91	81r
Housekeeping supplies, expenditures	year	390	91	81r
Laundry and cleaning supplies, expenditures	year	110	91	81r
Laundry detergent, Tide Ultra, Bold, or Cheer	42 oz.	3.66	12/94	2c
Postage and stationery, expenditures	year	115	91	81r
Tissues, facial, Kleenex brand	175	1.08	12/94	2c
Housing				
Housing, ACCRA Index		92.00	12/94	2c
Add garage/carport		8,479	3/95	74r
Add room(s)		21,347	3/95	74r
Apartment condominium or co-op, median	unit	87100	12/94	62r
Bathroom addition, average cost	add	9734.00	3/95	13r
Bathroom remodeling, average cost	remod	6414.00	3/95	13r
Bedroom, master suite addition, average cost	add	27122.00	3/95	13r
Deck addition, average cost	add	6665.00	3/95	13r
Dwellings (owned), expenditures	year	2566	91	81r
Enclose porch/patio/breezeway		4,556	3/95	74r
Exterior remodeling, average cost	remod	15395.00	3/95	13r
Family room addition, average cost	add	27658.00	3/95	13r
Finish room in basement/attic		5,074	3/95	74r
Home, existing, single-family, median	unit	106500	12/94	62r
House payment, principal and interest, 25% down payment	mo.	666	12/94	2c
House, 1800 sq ft, 8000 sq ft lot, new, urban, utilities	total	109908	12/94	2c
Kitchen remodeling, major, average cost	remod	17084.00	3/95	13r
Kitchen remodeling, minor, average cost	remod	5804.00	3/95	13r
Maintenance, repairs, insurance, and other housing expenditures	year	484	91	81r
Mortgage interest and charges expenditures	year	1443	91	81r
Mtge. rate, incl. points and orig. fee, 30-year conv. fixed or ARM	mo.	9.04	12/94	2c
Office, home addition, average cost	add	8121.00	3/95	13r
Princ. & int., mortgage, median-price exist. sing.-family home	mo.	515	12/94	62r
Property taxes expenditures	year	639	91	81r
Redesign, restructure more than half of home's interior		9,114	3/95	74r
Rent, apartment, 2 br., 1 1/2-2 baths, unfurnished, 950 sq ft, water	mo.	599	12/94	2c
Rental units expenditures	year	1200	91	81r
Sun-space addition, average cost	add	23768.00	3/95	13r
Wing addition, two-story, average cost	add	50410.00	3/95	13r

Values are in dollars or fractions of dollars. In the column headed *Ref*, references are shown to sources. Each reference is followed by a letter. These refer to the geographical level for which data were reported: s=State, r=Region, and c=City or metro. The abbreviation *ex* is used to mean *except* or *excluding*; *exp* stands for *expenditures*. For other abbreviations and further explanations, please see the Introduction.

Rochester, MN - continued

Item	Per	Value	Date	Ref.
Insurance and Pensions				
Auto insurance, private passenger	year	656.87	12/94	71s
Insurance and pensions, personal, expenditures	year	2408	91	81r
Insurance, life and other personal, expenditures	year	355	91	81r
Pensions and Social Security, expenditures	year	2053	91	81r
Legal Assistance				
Legal work, law firm associate	hour	90		10r
Legal work, law firm partner	hour	139		10r
Personal Goods				
Shampoo, Alberto VO5	15-oz.	1.19	12/94	2c
Toothpaste, Crest or Colgate	6-7 oz.	1.79	12/94	2c
Personal Services				
Dry cleaning, man's 2-pc. suit		6.82	12/94	2c
Haircut, man's barbershop, no styling		8.98	12/94	2c
Haircut, woman's shampoo, trim, blow-dry		16.89	12/94	2c
Personal services expenditures	year	203	91	81r
Restaurant Food				
Chicken, fried, thigh and drumstick		2.17	12/94	2c
Dining expenditures, family	week	30.03	94	73r
Hamburger with cheese	1/4 lb.	1.85	12/94	2c
Pizza, Pizza Hut or Pizza Inn	12-13 in.	8.35	12/94	2c
Taxes				
Tax, cigarettes	year	400.00	10/93	43s
Taxes, Federal income, expenditures	year	1756	91	81r
Taxes, personal, expenditures	year	2426	91	81r
Taxes, State and local income, expenditures	year	568	91	81r
Transportation				
Transportation, ACCRA Index		108.40	12/94	2c
Cars and trucks purchased, new	year	891	91	81r
Cars and trucks purchased, used	year	1155	91	81r
Driver's learning permit fee	perm	6.00	1/94	84s
Driver's license fee	orig	15.00	1/94	84s
Driver's license fee, duplicate	lic	4.50	1/94	84s
Driver's license reinstatement fee, min.	susp	20.00	1/94	85s
Driver's license renewal fee	renew	15.00	1/94	84s
Identification card, nondriver	card	9.00	1/94	83s
Public transportation expenditures	year	209	91	81r
Tire balance, computer or spin bal., front	wheel	8.07	12/94	2c
Transportation expenditures, total	year	4792	91	81r
Vehicle finance charges	year	300	91	81r
Vehicle insurance expenditures	year	485	91	81r
Vehicle maintenance and repairs expenditures	year	534	91	81r
Vehicle purchases	year	2068	91	81r
Vehicle rental, leases, licenses, etc. expenditures	year	197	91	81r
Vehicles purchased, other than cars and trucks	year	22	91	81r
Utilities				
Utilities, ACCRA Index		100.90	12/94	2c
Electricity expenditures	year	668	91	81r
Electricity, (part.), other, 1800 sq. ft., new home	mo.	53.20	12/94	2c
Utilities, fuels, and public services, total expenditures	year	1838	91	81r
Water and other public services, expenditures	year	167	91	81r
Weddings				
Bridal attendants' gowns	event	750	10/93	76r
Bridal gown	event	852	10/93	76r
Bridal headpiece and veil	event	167	10/93	76r
Bride's wedding band	event	708	10/93	76r
Clergy	event	224	10/93	76r
Engagement ring	event	2756	10/93	76r
Flowers	event	863	10/93	76r
Formal wear for groom	event	106	10/93	76r

Rochester, MN - continued

Item	Per	Value	Date	Ref.
Weddings - continued				
Groom's attendants' formal wear	event	530	10/93	76r
Groom's wedding band	event	402	10/93	76r
Music	event	600	10/93	76r
Photography	event	1088	10/93	76r
Shoes for bride	event	50	10/93	76r
Videography	event	483	10/93	76r
Wedding invitations and announcements	event	342	10/93	76r
Wedding reception	event	7000	10/93	76r

Rochester, NY

Item	Per	Value	Date	Ref.
Appliances				
Appliances (major), expenditures	year	145	91	81r
Average annual exp.				
Food, health care, personal goods, services	year	29496	91	81r
Charity				
Cash contributions, expenditures	year	708	91	81r
Clothing				
Apparel, men and boys, total expenditures	year	416	91	81r
Apparel, women and girls, total expenditures	year	744	91	81r
Footwear, expenditures	year	305	91	81r
Shirt, dress, men's	shirt	24.00	1/92	44c
Communications				
Long-distance telephone rate, day, addl. min., 1-10 mi.	min.	4.00	12/93	9s
Long-distance telephone rate, day, initial min., 1-10 mi.	min.	14.90	12/93	9s
Phone line, single, business, field visit	inst	143.26	12/93	9s
Phone line, single, business, no field visit	inst	106.05	12/93	9s
Phone line, single, residence, field visit	inst	85.46	12/93	9s
Phone line, single, residence, no field visit	inst	55.00	12/93	9s
Telephone service, expenditures	year	589	91	81r
Telephone, business, addl. line, touch tone	month	4.12	10/91	25c
Telephone, business, connection charges, touch tone	inst	59.61	10/91	25c
Telephone, business, key system line, touch tone	month	48.54	10/91	25c
Telephone, business, PBX line, touch tone	month	48.78	10/91	25c
Telephone, business, single ln., touch tone	month	46.44	10/91	25c
Telephone, business, touch tone, inside wiring maintenance plan	month	2.08	10/91	25c
Education				
Board, 4-year private college/university	year	2918	8/94	80s
Board, 4-year public college/university	year	2177	8/94	80s
Education, total expenditures	year	593	91	81r
Room, 4-year private college/university	year	3302	8/94	80s
Room, 4-year public college/university	year	2624	8/94	80s
Total cost, 4-year private college/university	year	18451	8/94	80s
Total cost, 4-year public college/university	year	7723	8/94	80s
Tuition, 2-year public college/university, in-state	year	2112	8/94	80s
Tuition, 4-year private college/university, in-state	year	12231	8/94	80s
Tuition, 4-year public college/university, in-state	year	2921	8/94	80s
Energy and Fuels				
Fuel oil and other fuels, expenditures	year	257	91	81r
Gas	gal.	1.17	1/92	44c
Gas, cooking, winter, 10 therms	month	12.46	2/94	65c
Gas, cooking, winter, 30 therms	month	26.75	2/94	65c
Gas, cooking, winter, 50 therms	month	41.02	2/94	65c
Gas, heating, winter, 100 therms	month	76.72	2/94	65c
Gas, heating, winter, average use	month	173.78	2/94	65c
Gas, natural, expenditures	year	285	91	81r
Gasoline and motor oil purchased	year	867	91	81r
Gasoline, unleaded midgrade	gallon	1.32	4/93	82r
Gasoline, unleaded premium	gallon	1.40	4/93	82r
Gasoline, unleaded regular	gallon	1.19	4/93	82r

Values are in dollars or fractions of dollars. In the column headed *Ref*, references are shown to sources. Each reference is followed by a letter. These refer to the geographical level for which data were reported: s=State, r=Region, and c=City or metro. The abbreviation *ex* is used to mean *except* or *excluding*; *exp* stands for *expenditures*. For other abbreviations and further explanations, please see the Introduction.

Rochester, NY - continued

Item	Per	Value	Date	Ref.
Entertainment				
Entertainment, total expenditures	year	1331	91	81r
Fees and admissions, expenditures	year	398	91	81r
Movie ticket, adult	ticket	7.00	1/92	44c
Pets, toys, playground equipment, expenditures	year	270	91	81r
Reading, expenditures	year	171	91	81r
Televisions, radios, and sound equipment, expenditures	year	429	91	81r
Funerals				
Burial, immediate, container provided by funeral home		1370.36	1/95	54r
Cards, acknowledgment		17.72	1/95	54r
Casket, minimum alternative		192.52	1/95	54r
Cosmetology, hair care, etc.		139.56	1/95	54r
Cremation, direct, container provided by funeral home		1049.24	1/95	54r
Embalming		387.57	1/95	54r
Funeral, funeral home		278.77	1/95	54r
Funeral, other facility		275.85	1/95	54r
Graveside service		213.08	1/95	54r
Hearse, local		157.27	1/95	54r
Limousine, local		146.45	1/95	54r
Memorial service		271.02	1/95	54r
Service charge, professional, nondeclinable		943.58	1/95	54r
Visitation and viewing		322.86	1/95	54r
Groceries				
Apples, Red Delicious	lb.	0.78	12/94	82r
Bacon, sliced	lb.	2.24	12/94	82r
Bananas	lb.	0.49	12/94	82r
Beef purchases	year	226	91	81r
Beverage purchases, alcoholic	year	332	91	81r
Beverage purchases, nonalcoholic	year	213	91	81r
Bread, white, pan	lb.	0.80	12/94	82r
Butter, salted, Grade AA, stick	lb.	1.67	12/94	82r
Carrots, short trimmed and topped	lb.	0.51	12/94	82r
Cereals and bakery products purchases	year	407	91	81r
Cereals and cereals products purchases	year	132	91	81r
Chicken breast, bone-in	lb.	2.22	12/94	82r
Chicken, fresh, whole	lb.	1.05	12/94	82r
Chuck roast, USDA choice, boneless	lb.	2.74	12/94	82r
Coffee, 100%, ground roast, all sizes	lb.	4.61	12/94	82r
Dairy products (other) purchases	year	161	91	81r
Eggs, Grade A large	dozen	1.12	12/94	82r
Fish and seafood purchases	year	112	91	81r
Food purchases, food eaten at home	year	2599	91	81r
Foods purchased away from home, not prepared by consumer	year	2024	91	81r
Fruits and vegetables purchases	year	444	91	81r
Grapefruit	lb.	0.44	12/94	82r
Grapes, Thompson seedless	lb.	2.24	12/94	82r
Ground chuck, 100% beef	lb.	1.67	12/94	82r
Ice cream, prepackaged, bulk, regular	1/2 gal.	2.93	12/94	82r
Lemons	lb.	1.06	12/94	82r
Lettuce, iceberg	lb.	0.92	12/94	82r
Meats, poultry, fish, and eggs purchases	year	751	91	81r
Milk and cream (fresh) purchases	year	152	91	81r
Milk, 2%	gal.	1.89	1/92	44c
Orange juice, frozen concentrate 12-oz. can	16 oz.	1.92	12/94	82r
Oranges, Navel	lb.	0.56	12/94	82r
Pork chops, center cut, bone-in	lb.	3.09	12/94	82r
Pork purchases	year	130	91	81r
Potatoes, white	lb.	0.37	12/94	82r
Rental rate, 2-bedroom apartment	month	600.00	1/92	44c
Rib roast, USDA choice, bone-in	lb.	4.98	12/94	82r
Round roast, USDA choice, boneless	lb.	2.93	12/94	82r
Shortening, vegetable oil blends	lb.	1.03	12/94	82r
Spaghetti and macaroni	lb.	0.84	12/94	82r
Steak, round, USDA choice, boneless	lb.	3.48	12/94	82r
Steak, sirloin, USDA choice, bone-in	lb.	3.38	12/94	82r
Steak, sirloin, USDA choice, boneless	lb.	4.81	12/94	82r

Rochester, NY - continued

Item	Per	Value	Date	Ref.
Groceries - continued				
Sugar and other sweets, eaten at home, expenditures	year	89	91	81r
Sugar, white, all sizes	lb.	0.46	12/94	82r
Tobacco products and smoking supplies, total expenditures	year	279	91	81r
Tomatoes, field grown	lb.	1.56	12/94	82r
Tuna, chunk, light	lb.	2.09	12/94	82r
Health Care				
Childbirth, Cesarean delivery, hospital charge	birth	6334.00	12/91	69r
Childbirth, Cesarean delivery, physician charge	birth	2234.00	12/91	69r
Childbirth, normal delivery, hospital charge	birth	3225.00	12/91	69r
Childbirth, normal delivery, physician charge	birth	1623.00	12/91	69r
Drugs, expenditures	year	205	91	81r
Health care, total expenditures	year	1396	91	81r
Health insurance expenditures	year	553	91	81r
Insurance premium, family medical care	month	384.24	1/95	41s
Medical services expenditures	year	559	91	81r
Medical supplies expenditures	year	80	91	81r
Household Goods				
Floor coverings, expenditures	year	158	91	81r
Furniture, expenditures	year	341	91	81r
Household equipment, misc. expenditures	year	363	91	81r
Household expenditures, miscellaneous	year	194	91	81r
Household furnishings and equipment, expenditures	year	1158	91	81r
Household operations expenditures	year	378	91	81r
Household textiles, expenditures	year	88	91	81r
Housekeeping supplies, expenditures	year	426	91	81r
Laundry and cleaning supplies, expenditures	year	122	91	81r
Postage and stationery, expenditures	year	134	91	81r
Housing				
Add garage/carport		11,614	3/95	74r
Add room(s)		16,816	3/95	74r
Apartment condominium or co-op, median	unit	96700	12/94	62r
Dwellings (owned), expenditures	year	3305	91	81r
Enclose porch/patio/breezeway		2,980	3/95	74r
Finish room in basement/attic		4,330	3/95	74r
Home, existing, single-family, median	unit	161600	12/94	62r
Home, existing, single-family, median	unit	84.80	12/94	62c
Home, purchase price	unit	128.80	3/93	26c
Maintenance, repairs, insurance, and other housing expenditures	year	569	91	81r
Mortgage interest and charges expenditures	year	1852	91	81r
Princ. & int., mortgage, median-price exist. sing.-family home	mo.	765	12/94	62r
Property taxes expenditures	year	884	91	81r
Redesign, restructure more than half of home's interior		2,750	3/95	74r
Rental units expenditures	year	1832	91	81r
Insurance and Pensions				
Auto insurance, private passenger	year	985.07	12/94	71s
Insurance and pensions, personal, expenditures	year	2690	91	81r
Insurance, life and other personal, expenditures	year	341	91	81r
Pensions and Social Security, expenditures	year	2349	91	81r
Legal Assistance				
Estate planning, law-firm partner	hr.	375.00	10/93	12r
Legal work, law firm associate	hour	78		10r
Legal work, law firm partner	hour	183		10r
Personal Services				
Dry cleaning, woman's dress	dress	7.50	1/92	44c
Personal services expenditures	year	184	91	81r

Values are in dollars or fractions of dollars. In the column headed *Ref*, references are shown to sources. Each reference is followed by a letter. These refer to the geographical level for which data were reported: s = State, r = Region, and c = City or metro. The abbreviation *ex* is used to mean *except* or *excluding*; *exp* stands for expenditures. For other abbreviations and further explanations, please see the Introduction.

Rochester, NY - continued

Item	Per	Value	Date	Ref.
Restaurant Food				
Big Mac, small fries, medium drink	meal	3.50	1/92	44c
Dining expenditures, family	week	34.26	94	73r
Taxes				
Taxes, Federal income, expenditures	year	2409	91	81r
Taxes, personal, expenditures	year	3094	91	81r
Taxes, State and local income, expenditures	year	620	91	81r
Transportation				
Bus fare, one-way	trip	1.00	12/95	1c
Cars and trucks purchased, new	year	1170	91	81r
Cars and trucks purchased, used	year	739	91	81r
Driver's learning permit fee	perm	10.00	1/94	84s
Driver's license fee	orig	32.00-37.00	1/94	84s
Driver's license fee, duplicate	lic	7.25	1/94	84s
Driver's license reinstatement fee, min.	susp	25.00	1/94	85s
Driver's license renewal fee	renew	22.25	1/94	84s
Identification card, nondriver	card	6.25	1/94	83s
Motorcycle license fee	orig	32.00-37.00	1/94	84s
Motorcycle license fee, duplicate	lic	7.25	1/94	84s
Motorcycle license renewal fee	renew	22.25	1/94	84s
parking, long-term lot, airport	3 days	13.50	1/92	44c
Public transportation expenditures	year	430	91	81r
Transportation expenditures, total	year	4810	91	81r
Vehicle finance charges	year	238	91	81r
Vehicle insurance expenditures	year	630	91	81r
Vehicle maintenance and repairs expenditures	year	532	91	81r
Vehicle purchases	year	1920	91	81r
Vehicle rental, leases, licenses, etc. expenditures	year	193	91	81r
Vehicles purchased, other than cars and trucks	year	11	91	81r
Utilities				
Electricity expenditures	year	695	91	81r
Electricity, summer, 250 KWh	month	32.83	8/93	64c
Electricity, summer, 500 KWh	month	57.51	8/93	64c
Electricity, summer, 750 KWh	month	82.17	8/93	64c
Electricity, summer, 1000 KWh	month	106.84	8/93	64c
Utilities, fuels, and public services, total expenditures	year	1981	91	81r
Water and other public services, expenditures	year	154	91	81r
Weddings				
Bridal attendants' gowns	event	750	10/93	76r
Bridal gown	event	852	10/93	76r
Bridal headpiece and veil	event	167	10/93	76r
Bride's wedding band	event	708	10/93	76r
Clergy	event	224	10/93	76r
Engagement ring	event	2756	10/93	76r
Flowers	event	863	10/93	76r
Formal wear for groom	event	106	10/93	76r
Groom's attendants' formal wear	event	530	10/93	76r
Groom's wedding band	event	402	10/93	76r
Music	event	600	10/93	76r
Photography	event	1088	10/93	76r
Shoes for bride	event	50	10/93	76r
Videography	event	483	10/93	76r
Wedding invitations and announcements	event	342	10/93	76r
Wedding reception	event	7000	10/93	76r

Rockford, IL

Item	Per	Value	Date	Ref.
Composite, ACCRA index		105.30	12/94	2c
Alcoholic Beverages				
Beer, Miller Lite, Bud, 12-oz., ex deposit	6	3.97	12/94	2c
J & B Scotch	750-ml.	14.37	12/94	2c
Wine, Gallo Chablis blanc	1.5-lit	4.47	12/94	2c

Rockford, IL - continued

Item	Per	Value	Date	Ref.
Appliances				
Appliances (major), expenditures	year	131	91	81r
Average annual exp.				
Food, health care, personal goods, services	year	25935	91	81r
Charity				
Cash contributions, expenditures	year	745	91	81r
Clothing				
Apparel, men and boys, total expenditures	year	332	91	81r
Apparel, women and girls, total expenditures	year	578	91	81r
Footwear, expenditures	year	164	91	81r
Jeans, man's denim		35.32	12/94	2c
Shirt, man's dress shirt		37.42	12/94	2c
Undervest, boy's size 10-14, cotton	3	5.83	12/94	2c
Communications				
Long-distance telephone rate, day, addl. min., 1-10 mi.	min.	0.04	12/93	9s
Long-distance telephone rate, day, initial min., 1-10 mi.	min.	0.10	12/93	9s
Newspaper subscription, dly. and Sun. delivery	month	14.13	12/94	2c
Phone line, single, business, field visit	inst	84.50	12/93	9s
Phone line, single, business, no field visit	inst	84.50	12/93	9s
Phone line, single, residence, field visit	inst	55.00	12/93	9s
Phone line, single, residence, no field visit	inst	55.00	12/93	9s
Telephone bill, family of four	month	22.52	12/94	2c
Telephone service, expenditures	year	547	91	81r
Education				
Board, 4-year private college/university	year	2078	8/94	80s
Board, 4-year public college/university	year	2139	8/94	80s
Education, total expenditures	year	394	91	81r
Room, 4-year private college/university	year	2696	8/94	80s
Room, 4-year public college/university	year	1796	8/94	80s
Total cost, 4-year private college/university	year	15249	8/94	80s
Total cost, 4-year public college/university	year	6964	8/94	80s
Tuition, 2-year public college/university, in-state	year	1135	8/94	80s
Tuition, 4-year private college/university, in-state	year	10474	8/94	80s
Tuition, 4-year public college/university, in-state	year	3029	8/94	80s
Energy and Fuels				
Energy, combined forms, 1800 sq. ft.	mo.	114.16	12/94	2c
Energy, exc. electricity, 1800 sq. ft.	mo.	51.32	12/94	2c
Fuel oil and other fuels, expenditures	year	83	91	81r
Gas, cooking, 10 therms	month	8.84	2/94	65c
Gas, cooking, 30 therms	month	18.51	2/94	65c
Gas, cooking, 50 therms	month	28.18	2/94	65c
Gas, heating, winter, 100 therms	month	48.08	2/94	65c
Gas, heating, winter, average use	month	98.22	2/94	65c
Gas, natural, expenditures	year	373	91	81r
Gas, reg unlead, taxes inc., cash, self-service	gal	1.21	12/94	2c
Gasoline and motor oil purchased	year	1000	91	81r
Gasoline, unleaded midgrade	gallon	1.15	4/93	82r
Gasoline, unleaded premium	gallon	1.23	4/93	82r
Gasoline, unleaded regular	gallon	1.07	4/93	82r
Entertainment				
Bowling, evening rate	game	1.80	12/94	2c
Entertainment, total expenditures	year	1356	91	81r
Fees and admissions, expenditures	year	347	91	81r
Monopoly game, Parker Brothers', No. 9	game	12.68	12/94	2c
Movie	adm	5.75	12/94	2c
Pets, toys, playground equipment, expenditures	year	270	91	81r
Reading, expenditures	year	160	91	81r
Televisions, radios, and sound equipment, expenditures	year	433	91	81r
Tennis balls, yellow, Wilson or Penn, 3	can	2.13	12/94	2c

Values are in dollars or fractions of dollars. In the column headed *Ref*, references are shown to sources. Each reference is followed by a letter. These refer to the geographical level for which data were reported: s = State, r = Region, and c = City or metro. The abbreviation *ex* is used to mean *except* or *excluding*; *exp* stands for expenditures. For other abbreviations and further explanations, please see the Introduction.

Rockford, IL - continued

Item	Per	Value	Date	Ref.
Funerals				
Burial, immediate, container provided by funeral home		1268.31	1/95	54r
Cards, acknowledgment		26.12	1/95	54r
Casket, minimum alternative		198.03	1/95	54r
Cosmetology, hair care, etc.		122.19	1/95	54r
Cremation, direct, container provided by funeral home		977.81	1/95	54r
Embalming		334.00	1/95	54r
Funeral, funeral home		321.16	1/95	54r
Funeral, other facility		317.73	1/95	54r
Graveside service		292.48	1/95	54r
Hearse, local		153.20	1/95	54r
Limousine, local		123.52	1/95	54r
Memorial service		356.30	1/95	54r
Service charge, professional, nondeclinable		968.24	1/95	54r
Visitation and viewing		332.66	1/95	54r
Groceries				
Groceries, ACCRA Index		101.60	12/94	2c
Apples, Red Delicious	lb.	0.68	12/94	82r
Baby food, strained vegetables, lowest price	4-4.5 oz.	0.41	12/94	2c
Bacon, sliced	lb.	1.88	12/94	82r
Bananas	lb.	0.41	12/94	2c
Bananas	lb.	0.41	12/94	82r
Beef or hamburger, ground	lb.	1.70	12/94	2c
Beef purchases	year	197	91	81r
Beef, stew, boneless	lb.	2.52	12/94	82r
Beverage purchases, alcoholic	year	293	91	81r
Beverage purchases, nonalcoholic	year	203	91	81r
Bologna, all beef or mixed	lb.	2.12	12/94	82r
Bread, white	24-oz.	0.63	12/94	2c
Bread, white, pan	lb.	0.76	12/94	82r
Cabbage	lb.	0.44	12/94	82r
Carrots, short trimmed and topped	lb.	0.44	12/94	82r
Cereals and bakery products purchases	year	347	91	81r
Cereals and cereals products purchases	year	119	91	81r
Cheddar cheese, natural	lb.	3.28	12/94	82r
Cheese, Kraft grated Parmesan	8-oz.	3.22	12/94	2c
Chicken breast, bone-in	lb.	1.61	12/94	82r
Chicken, fresh, whole	lb.	0.89	12/94	82r
Chicken, whole fryer	lb.	0.90	12/94	2c
Chuck roast, USDA choice, boneless	lb.	2.33	12/94	82r
Cigarettes, Winston, Kings	carton	17.28	12/94	2c
Coffee, 100%, ground roast, all sizes	lb.	4.28	12/94	82r
Coffee, vacuum-packed	13 oz.	3.65	12/94	2c
Cookies, chocolate chip	lb.	2.72	12/94	82r
Corn Flakes, Kellogg's or Post Toasties	18 oz.	2.45	12/94	2c
Corn, frozen, whole kernel, lowest price	10 oz.	0.70	12/94	2c
Dairy products (other) purchases	year	148	91	81r
Eggs, Grade A large	dozen	0.58	12/94	2c
Eggs, Grade A large	dozen	0.76	12/94	82r
Fish and seafood purchases	year	61	91	81r
Flour, white, all purpose	lb.	0.22	12/94	82r
Food purchases, food eaten at home	year	2313	91	81r
Foods purchased away from home, not prepared by consumer	year	1709	91	81r
Fruits and vegetables purchases	year	372	91	81r
Grapefruit	lb.	0.47	12/94	82r
Grapes, Thompson seedless	lb.	2.15	12/94	82r
Ground beef, 100% beef	lb.	1.37	12/94	82r
Ground chuck, 100% beef	lb.	1.81	12/94	82r
Ham, boneless, exc. canned	lb.	2.16	12/94	82r
Ice cream, prepackaged, bulk, regular	1/2 gal.	2.48	12/94	82r
Lemons	lb.	1.08	12/94	82r
Lettuce, iceberg	lb.	0.81	12/94	82r
Lettuce, iceberg	head	0.80	12/94	2c
Margarine, Blue Bonnet or Parkay cubes	lb.	0.69	12/94	2c
Margarine, stick	lb.	0.81	12/94	82r
Meats, poultry, fish, and eggs purchases	year	591	91	81r
Milk and cream (fresh) purchases	year	132	91	81r

Rockford, IL - continued

Item	Per	Value	Date	Ref.
Groceries - continued				
Milk, whole	1/2 gal.	1.44	12/94	2c
Orange juice, frozen concentrate 12-oz. can	16 oz.	1.41	12/94	82r
Orange juice, Minute Maid frozen	12-oz.	1.13	12/94	2c
Oranges, Navel	lb.	0.56	12/94	82r
Peaches, halves or slices, Hunt's, Del Monte, or Libby's	29-oz.	1.45	12/94	2c
Peanut butter, creamy, all sizes	lb.	1.81	12/94	82r
Peas, sweet, Del Monte or Green Giant	15-17 oz.	0.57	12/94	2c
Pork chops, center cut, bone-in	lb.	2.76	12/94	82r
Pork purchases	year	130	91	81r
Potato chips	16-oz.	2.81	12/94	82r
Potatoes, frozen, French fried	lb.	0.83	12/94	82r
Potatoes, white	lb.	0.28	12/94	82r
Potatoes, white or red	10-lb. sack	2.51	12/94	2c
Round roast, USDA choice, boneless	lb.	2.90	12/94	82r
Sausage, Jimmy Dean, 100% pork	lb.	2.75	12/94	2c
Shortening, vegetable oil blends	lb.	0.88	12/94	82r
Shortening, vegetable, Crisco	3-lb.	2.60	12/94	2c
Soft drink, Coca Cola, ex deposit	2 lit	1.27	12/94	2c
Spaghetti and macaroni	lb.	0.78	12/94	82r
Steak, rib eye, USDA choice, boneless	lb.	6.15	12/94	82r
Steak, round, graded & ungraded, exc. USDA prime & choice	lb.	2.72	12/94	82r
Steak, round, USDA choice, boneless	lb.	3.02	12/94	82r
Steak, sirloin, USDA choice, boneless	lb.	3.85	12/94	82r
Steak, t-bone	lb.	5.06	12/94	2c
Steak, T-bone, USDA choice, bone-in	lb.	5.38	12/94	82r
Sugar and other sweets, eaten at home, expenditures	year	91	91	81r
Sugar, cane or beet	4 lbs.	1.19	12/94	2c
Sugar, white, all sizes	lb.	0.36	12/94	82r
Tobacco products and smoking supplies, total expenditures	year	298	91	81r
Tomatoes, field grown	lb.	1.36	12/94	82r
Tomatoes, Hunt's or Del Monte	14.5 oz.	0.72	12/94	2c
Tuna, chunk, light	lb.	1.94	12/94	82r
Tuna, chunk, light, oil-packed	6.125-6.5 oz.	0.70	12/94	2c
Turkey, frozen, whole	lb.	0.96	12/94	82r
Yogurt, natural, fruit flavored	8 oz.	0.62	12/94	82r
Goods and Services				
Miscellaneous goods and services, ACCRA Index		105.20	12/94	2c
Health Care				
Health care, ACCRA Index		103.80	12/94	2c
Antibiotic ointment, Polysporin	1.5 oz.	3.93	12/94	2c
Childbirth, Cesarean delivery, hospital charge	birth	5101.00	12/91	69r
Childbirth, Cesarean delivery, physician charge	birth	2234.00	12/91	69r
Childbirth, normal delivery, hospital charge	birth	2891.00	12/91	69r
Childbirth, normal delivery, physician charge	birth	1623.00	12/91	69r
Dentist's fee, adult teeth cleaning and periodic oral exam	visit	55.86	12/94	2c
Doctor's fee, routine exam, established patient	visit	43.35	12/94	2c
Drugs, expenditures	year	248	91	81r
Health care, total expenditures	year	1336	91	81r
Health insurance expenditures	year	550	91	81r
Hospital care, semiprivate room	day	372.60	12/94	2c
Insurance premium, family medical care	month	363.57	1/95	41s
Medical services expenditures	year	457	91	81r
Medical supplies expenditures	year	82	91	81r
Household Goods				
Appl. repair, service call, wash mach	min. lab. chg.	38.13	12/94	2c

Values are in dollars or fractions of dollars. In the column headed *Ref*, references are shown to sources. Each reference is followed by a letter. These refer to the geographical level for which data were reported: s=State, r=Region, and c=City or metro. The abbreviation *ex* is used to mean *except* or *excluding*; *exp* stands for *expenditures*. For other abbreviations and further explanations, please see the Introduction.

Rockford, IL - continued

Item	Per	Value	Date	Ref.
Household Goods				
Floor coverings, expenditures	year	105	91	81r
Furniture, expenditures	year	291	91	81r
Household equipment, misc. expenditures	year	341	91	81r
Household expenditures, miscellaneous	year	162	91	81r
Household furnishings and equipment, expenditures	year	1042	91	81r
Household operations expenditures	year	365	91	81r
Household textiles, expenditures	year	101	91	81r
Housekeeping supplies, expenditures	year	390	91	81r
Laundry and cleaning supplies, expenditures	year	110	91	81r
Laundry detergent, Tide Ultra, Bold, or Cheer	42 oz.	3.44	12/94	2c
Postage and stationery, expenditures	year	115	91	81r
Tissues, facial, Kleenex brand	175	0.96	12/94	2c
Housing				
Housing, ACCRA Index		108.00	12/94	2c
Add garage/carport		8,479	3/95	74r
Add room(s)		21,347	3/95	74r
Apartment condominium or co-op, median	unit	87100	12/94	62r
Bathroom addition, average cost	add	9734.00	3/95	13r
Bathroom remodeling, average cost	remod	6414.00	3/95	13r
Bedroom, master suite addition, average cost	add	27122.00	3/95	13r
Deck addition, average cost	add	6665.00	3/95	13r
Dwellings (owned), expenditures	year	2566	91	81r
Enclose porch/patio/breezeway		4,556	3/95	74r
Exterior remodeling, average cost	remod	15395.00	3/95	13r
Family room addition, average cost	add	27658.00	3/95	13r
Finish room in basement/attic		5,074	3/95	74r
Home, existing, single-family, median	unit	106500	12/94	62r
Home, existing, single-family, median	unit	85.80	12/94	62c
House payment, principal and interest, 25% down payment	mo.	836	12/94	2c
House, 1800 sq ft, 8000 sq ft lot, new, urban, utilities	total	134280	12/94	2c
Kitchen remodeling, major, average cost	remod	17084.00	3/95	13r
Kitchen remodeling, minor, average cost	remod	5804.00	3/95	13r
Maintenance, repairs, insurance, and other housing expenditures	year	484	91	81r
Mortgage interest and charges expenditures	year	1443	91	81r
Mtge. rate, incl. points and orig. fee, 30-year conv. fixed or ARM	mo.	9.35	12/94	2c
Office, home addition, average cost	add	8121.00	3/95	13r
Princ. & int., mortgage, median-price exist. sing.-family home	mo.	515	12/94	62r
Property taxes expenditures	year	639	91	81r
Redesign, restructure more than half of home's interior		9,114	3/95	74r
Rent, apartment, 2 br., 1 1/2-2 baths, unfurnished, 950 sq ft, water	mo.	545	12/94	2c
Rental units expenditures	year	1200	91	81r
Sun-space addition, average cost	add	23768.00	3/95	13r
Wing addition, two-story, average cost	add	50410.00	3/95	13r
Insurance and Pensions				
Auto insurance, private passenger	year	679.48	12/94	71s
Insurance and pensions, personal, expenditures	year	2408	91	81r
Insurance, life and other personal, expenditures	year	355	91	81r
Pensions and Social Security, expenditures	year	2053	91	81r
Legal Assistance				
Legal work, law firm associate	hour	90		10r
Legal work, law firm partner	hour	139		10r
Personal Goods				
Shampoo, Alberto VO5	15-oz.	1.11	12/94	2c
Toothpaste, Crest or Colgate	6-7 oz.	1.85	12/94	2c
Personal Services				
Dry cleaning, man's 2-pc. suit		6.11	12/94	2c

Rockford, IL - continued

Item	Per	Value	Date	Ref.
Personal Services - continued				
Haircut, man's barbershop, no styling		7.50	12/94	2c
Haircut, woman's shampoo, trim, blow-dry		19.65	12/94	2c
Personal services expenditures	year	203	91	81r
Restaurant Food				
Chicken, fried, thigh and drumstick		2.29	12/94	2c
Dining expenditures, family	week	30.03	94	73r
Hamburger with cheese	1/4 lb.	1.69	12/94	2c
Pizza, Pizza Hut or Pizza Inn	12-13 in.	7.59	12/94	2c
Taxes				
Taxes, Federal income, expenditures	year	1756	91	81r
Taxes, personal, expenditures	year	2426	91	81r
Taxes, State and local income, expenditures	year	568	91	81r
Transportation				
Transportation, ACCRA Index		106.50	12/94	2c
Bus fare, one-way	trip	0.80	12/95	1c
Bus fare, up to 10 miles	one-way	0.80	12/94	2c
Cars and trucks purchased, new	year	891	91	81r
Cars and trucks purchased, used	year	1155	91	81r
Driver's learning permit fee	perm	20.00	1/94	84s
Driver's license fee	orig	10.00	1/94	84s
Driver's license fee, duplicate	lic	5.00	1/94	84s
Driver's license reinstatement fee, min.	susp	30.00	1/94	85s
Driver's license renewal fee	renew	10.00	1/94	84s
Identification card, nondriver	card	4.00	1/94	83s
Motorcycle learning permit fee	perm	20.00	1/94	84s
Motorcycle license fee	orig	10.00	1/94	84s
Motorcycle license fee, duplicate	lic	5.00	1/94	84s
Motorcycle license renewal fee	renew	10.00	1/94	84s
Public transportation expenditures	year	209	91	81r
Tire balance, computer or spin bal., front	wheel	7.57	12/94	2c
Transportation expenditures, total	year	4792	91	81r
Vehicle finance charges	year	300	91	81r
Vehicle insurance expenditures	year	485	91	81r
Vehicle maintenance and repairs expenditures	year	534	91	81r
Vehicle purchases	year	2068	91	81r
Vehicle rental, leases, licenses, etc. expenditures	year	197	91	81r
Vehicles purchased, other than cars and trucks	year	22	91	81r
Utilities				
Utilities, ACCRA Index		103.60	12/94	2c
Electricity expenditures	year	668	91	81r
Electricity, (part.), other, 1800 sq. ft., new home	mo.	62.84	12/94	2c
Utilities, fuels, and public services, total expenditures	year	1838	91	81r
Water and other public services, expenditures	year	167	91	81r
Weddings				
Bridal attendants' gowns	event	750	10/93	76r
Bridal gown	event	852	10/93	76r
Bridal headpiece and veil	event	167	10/93	76r
Bride's wedding band	event	708	10/93	76r
Clergy	event	224	10/93	76r
Engagement ring	event	2756	10/93	76r
Flowers	event	863	10/93	76r
Formal wear for groom	event	106	10/93	76r
Groom's attendants' formal wear	event	530	10/93	76r
Groom's wedding band	event	402	10/93	76r
Music	event	600	10/93	76r
Photography	event	1088	10/93	76r
Shoes for bride	event	50	10/93	76r
Videography	event	483	10/93	76r
Wedding invitations and announcements	event	342	10/93	76r
Wedding reception	event	7000	10/93	76r

Values are in dollars or fractions of dollars. In the column headed *Ref*, references are shown to sources. Each reference is followed by a letter. These refer to the geographical level for which data were reported: s=State, r=Region, and c=City or metro. The abbreviation *ex* is used to mean *except* or *excluding*; *exp* stands for *expenditures*. For other abbreviations and further explanations, please see the Introduction.

Roswell, NM

Item	Per	Value	Date	Ref.
Composite, ACCRA index		90.70	12/94	2c
Alcoholic Beverages				
Beer, Miller Lite, Bud, 12-oz., ex deposit	6	4.08	12/94	2c
J & B Scotch	750-ml.	16.32	12/94	2c
Wine, Gallo Chablis blanc	1.5-lit	5.66	12/94	2c
Clothing				
Jeans, man's denim		28.19	12/94	2c
Shirt, man's dress shirt		26.00	12/94	2c
Undervest, boy's size 10-14, cotton	3	3.12	12/94	2c
Communications				
Newspaper subscription, dly. and Sun. delivery	month	13.00	12/94	2c
Telephone bill, family of four	month	22.58	12/94	2c
Telephone, residential, flat rate	mo.	13.91	12/93	8c
Energy and Fuels				
Energy, combined forms, 1800 sq. ft.	mo.	85.49	12/94	2c
Energy, exc. electricity, 1800 sq. ft.	mo.	41.48	12/94	2c
Gas, reg unlead, taxes inc., cash, self-service	gal	1.31	12/94	2c
Entertainment				
Bowling, evening rate	game	2.25	12/94	2c
Monopoly game, Parker Brothers', No. 9	game	11.32	12/94	2c
Movie	adm	5.00	12/94	2c
Tennis balls, yellow, Wilson or Penn, 3	can	2.39	12/94	2c
Groceries				
Groceries, ACCRA index		98.50	12/94	2c
Baby food, strained vegetables, lowest price	4-4.5 oz.	0.25	12/94	2c
Bananas	lb.	0.36	12/94	2c
Beef or hamburger, ground	lb.	0.80	12/94	2c
Bread, white	24-oz.	0.86	12/94	2c
Cheese, Kraft grated Parmesan	8-oz.	3.92	12/94	2c
Chicken, whole fryer	lb.	0.58	12/94	2c
Cigarettes, Winston, Kings	carton	14.82	12/94	2c
Coffee, vacuum-packed	13 oz.	3.72	12/94	2c
Corn Flakes, Kellogg's or Post Toasties	18 oz.	2.46	12/94	2c
Corn, frozen, whole kernel, lowest price	10 oz.	0.80	12/94	2c
Eggs, Grade A large	dozen	0.78	12/94	2c
Lettuce, iceberg	head	0.83	12/94	2c
Margarine, Blue Bonnet or Parkay cubes	lb.	0.78	12/94	2c
Milk, whole	1/2 gal.	1.34	12/94	2c
Orange juice, Minute Maid frozen	12-oz.	1.42	12/94	2c
Peaches, halves or slices, Hunt's, Del Monte, or Libby's	29-oz.	1.52	12/94	2c
Peas, sweet, Del Monte or Green Giant	15-17 oz.	0.56	12/94	2c
Potatoes, white or red	10-lb. sack	2.06	12/94	2c
Sausage, Jimmy Dean, 100% pork	lb.	2.28	12/94	2c
Shortening, vegetable, Crisco	3-lb.	2.71	12/94	2c
Soft drink, Coca Cola, ex deposit	2 lit	1.52	12/94	2c
Steak, t-bone	lb.	4.66	12/94	2c
Sugar, cane or beet	4 lbs.	1.53	12/94	2c
Tomatoes, Hunt's or Del Monte	14.5 oz.	0.78	12/94	2c
Tuna, chunk, light, oil-packed	6.125-6.5 oz.	0.78	12/94	2c
Goods and Services				
Miscellaneous goods and services, ACCRA Index		97.40	12/94	2c
Health Care				
Health care, ACCRA Index		80.70	12/94	2c
Antibiotic ointment, Polysporin	1.5 oz.	4.08	12/94	2c
Dentist's fee, adult teeth cleaning and periodic oral exam	visit	40.40	12/94	2c
Doctor's fee, routine exam, established patient	visit	32.20	12/94	2c

Roswell, NM - continued

Item	Per	Value	Date	Ref.
Health Care - continued				
Hospital care, semiprivate room	day	300.00	12/94	2c
Household Goods				
Appl. repair, service call, wash mach	min. lab. chg.	35.86	12/94	2c
Laundry detergent, Tide Ultra, Bold, or Cheer	42 oz.	3.38	12/94	2c
Tissues, facial, Kleenex brand	175	0.96	12/94	2c
Housing				
Housing, ACCRA Index		79.70	12/94	2c
House payment, principal and interest, 25% down payment	mo.	620	12/94	2c
House, 1800 sq ft, 8000 sq ft lot, new, urban, utilities	total	100180	12/94	2c
Mtge. rate, incl. points and orig. fee, 30-year conv. fixed or ARM	mo.	9.29	12/94	2c
Rent, apartment, 2 br., 1 1/2-2 baths, unfurnished, 950 sq ft, water	mo.	394	12/94	2c
Personal Goods				
Shampoo, Alberto VO5	15-oz.	1.17	12/94	2c
Toothpaste, Crest or Colgate	6-7 oz.	2.12	12/94	2c
Personal Services				
Dry cleaning, man's 2-pc. suit		6.27	12/94	2c
Haircut, man's barbershop, no styling		6.78	12/94	2c
Haircut, woman's shampoo, trim, blow-dry		15.60	12/94	2c
Restaurant Food				
Chicken, fried, thigh and drumstick		2.19	12/94	2c
Hamburger with cheese	1/4 lb.	1.89	12/94	2c
Pizza, Pizza Hut or Pizza Inn	12-13 in.	8.99	12/94	2c
Transportation				
Transportation, ACCRA Index		100.90	12/94	2c
Bus fare, up to 10 miles	one-way	0.75	12/94	2c
Tire balance, computer or spin bal., front	wheel	5.85	12/94	2c
Utilities				
Utilities, ACCRA Index		81.50	12/94	2c
Electricity, (part.), other, 1800 sq. ft., new home	mo.	44.01	12/94	2c .
Electricity, summer, 250 KWh	month	19.45	8/93	64c
Electricity, summer, 500 KWh	month	33.89	8/93	64c
Electricity, summer, 750 KWh	month	48.34	8/93	64c
Electricity, summer, 1000 KWh	month	62.79	8/93	64c

Sacramento, CA

Item	Per	Value	Date	Ref.
Appliances				
Appliances (major), expenditures	year	160	91	81r
Average annual exp.				
Food, health care, personal goods, services	year	32461	91	81r
Charity				
Cash contributions, expenditures	year	975	91	81r
Clothing				
Apparel, men and boys, total expenditures	year	467	91	81r
Apparel, women and girls, total expenditures	year	737	91	81r
Footwear, expenditures	year	270	91	81r
Communications				
Long-distance telephone rate, day, addl. min., 1-10 mi.	min.	0.07	12/93	9s
Long-distance telephone rate, day, initial min., 1-10 mi.	min.	0.17	12/93	9s
Phone line, single, business, field visit	inst	70.75	12/93	9s
Phone line, single, business, no field visit	inst	70.75	12/93	9s
Phone line, single, residence, field visit	inst	34.75	12/93	9s
Phone line, single, residence, no field visit	inst	34.75	12/93	9s

Values are in dollars or fractions of dollars. In the column headed *Ref*, references are shown to sources. Each reference is followed by a letter. These refer to the geographical level for which data were reported: s=State, r=Region, and c=City or metro. The abbreviation *ex* is used to mean *except* or *excluding*; *exp* stands for *expenditures*. For other abbreviations and further explanations, please see the Introduction.

Sacramento, CA - continued

Item	Per	Value	Date	Ref.
Communications				
Telephone service, expenditures	year	611	91	81r
Education				
Board, 4-year private college/university	year	2945	8/94	80s
Board, 4-year public college/university	year	2321	8/94	80s
Education, total expenditures	year	375	91	81r
Room, 4-year private college/university	year	3094	8/94	80s
Room, 4-year public college/university	year	2812	8/94	80s
Student fee, university	year	21.00	93	18s
Total cost, 4-year private college/university	year	19321	8/94	80s
Total cost, 4-year public college/university	year	7511	8/94	80s
Tuition, 2-year public college/university, in-state	year	345	8/94	80s
Tuition, 4-year private college/university, in-state	year	13282	8/94	80s
Tuition, 4-year public college/university, in-state	year	2378	8/94	80s
Energy and Fuels				
Fuel oil and other fuels, expenditures	year	33	91	81r
Gas, natural, expenditures	year	212	91	81r
Gasoline and motor oil purchased	year	1115	91	81r
Gasoline, unleaded midgrade	gallon	1.36	4/93	82r
Gasoline, unleaded premium	gallon	1.43	4/93	82r
Gasoline, unleaded regular	gallon	1.23	4/93	82r
Entertainment				
Concert ticket, Pearl Jam group	perf	20.00	94	50r
Entertainment, total expenditures	year	1853	91	81r
Fees and admissions, expenditures	year	482	91	81r
Pets, toys, playground equipment, expenditures	year	299	91	81r
Reading, expenditures	year	164	91	81r
Televisions, radios, and sound equipment, expenditures	year	528	91	81r
Funerals				
Burial, immediate, container provided by funeral home		1382.70	1/95	54r
Cards, acknowledgment		21.87	1/95	54r
Casket, minimum alternative		128.54	1/95	54r
Cosmetology, hair care, etc.		119.69	1/95	54r
Cremation, direct, container provided by funeral home		1030.62	1/95	54r
Embalming		255.42	1/95	54r
Funeral, funeral home		437.38	1/95	54r
Funeral, other facility		444.46	1/95	54r
Graveside service		338.46	1/95	54r
Hearse, local		147.50	1/95	54r
Limousine, local		130.33	1/95	54r
Memorial service		553.16	1/95	54r
Service charge, professional, nondeclinable		859.15	1/95	54r
Visitation and viewing		93.23	1/95	54r
Groceries				
Apples, Red Delicious	lb.	0.72	12/94	82r
Bacon, sliced	lb.	1.73	12/94	82r
Bananas	lb.	0.52	12/94	82r
Beef purchases	year	241	91	81r
Beverage purchases, alcoholic	year	328	91	81r
Beverage purchases, nonalcoholic	year	234	91	81r
Bologna, all beef or mixed	lb.	2.33	12/94	82r
Bread, white, pan	lb.	0.81	12/94	82r
Carrots, short trimmed and topped	lb.	0.43	12/94	82r
Cereals and bakery products purchases	year	392	91	81r
Cereals and cereals products purchases	year	139	91	81r
Chicken breast, bone-in	lb.	2.04	12/94	82r
Chicken, fresh, whole	lb.	0.95	12/94	82r
Coffee, 100%, ground roast, all sizes	lb.	4.48	12/94	82r
Dairy products (other) purchases	year	182	91	81r
Fish and seafood purchases	year	94	91	81r
Flour, white, all purpose	lb.	0.21	12/94	82r
Food purchases, food eaten at home	year	2749	91	81r

Sacramento, CA - continued

Item	Per	Value	Date	Ref.
Groceries - continued				
Foods purchased away from home, not prepared by consumer	year	1909	91	81r
Fruits and vegetables purchases	year	459	91	81r
Grapefruit	lb.	0.56	12/94	82r
Ground beef, 100% beef	lb.	1.31	12/94	82r
Ham, boneless, exc. canned	lb.	2.46	12/94	82r
Ice cream, prepackaged, bulk, regular	1/2 gal.	2.57	12/94	82r
Lemons	lb.	1.00	12/94	82r
Lettuce, iceberg	lb.	0.93	12/94	82r
Meats, poultry, fish, and eggs purchases	year	700	91	81r
Milk and cream (fresh) purchases	year	155	91	81r
Orange juice, frozen concentrate 12-oz. can	16 oz.	1.52	12/94	82r
Oranges, Navel	lb.	0.56	12/94	82r
Pork chops, center cut, bone-in	lb.	3.30	12/94	82r
Pork purchases	year	122	91	81r
Potato chips	16-oz.	3.03	12/94	82r
Potatoes, frozen, French fried	lb.	0.77	12/94	82r
Potatoes, white	lb.	0.35	12/94	82r
Rice, white, long grain, uncooked	lb.	0.54	12/94	82r
Round roast, USDA choice, boneless	lb.	2.92	12/94	82r
Shortening, vegetable oil blends	lb.	0.80	12/94	82r
Spaghetti and macaroni	lb.	1.02	12/94	82r
Steak, round, graded & ungraded, exc. USDA prime & choice	lb.	3.13	12/94	82r
Steak, sirloin, USDA choice, boneless	lb.	4.07	12/94	82r
Sugar and other sweets, eaten at home, expenditures	year	105	91	81r
Sugar, white, all sizes	lb.	0.38	12/94	82r
Tobacco products and smoking supplies, total expenditures	year	221	91	81r
Tomatoes, field grown	lb.	1.45	12/94	82r
Tuna, chunk, light	lb.	2.18	12/94	82r
Health Care				
Childbirth, Cesarean delivery, hospital charge	birth	6059.00	12/91	69r
Childbirth, Cesarean delivery, physician charge	birth	2248.00	12/91	69r
Childbirth, normal delivery, hospital charge	birth	3006.00	12/91	69r
Childbirth, normal delivery, physician charge	birth	1634.00	12/91	69r
Drugs, expenditures	year	230	91	81r
Health care, total expenditures	year	1544	91	81r
Health insurance expenditures	year	558	91	81r
Insurance premium, family medical care	month	380.27	1/95	41s
Medical services expenditures	year	676	91	81r
Medical supplies expenditures	year	80	91	81r
Surgery, open-heart	proc	37818.00	1/93	14r
Household Goods				
Floor coverings, expenditures	year	79	91	81r
Furniture, expenditures	year	352	91	81r
Household equipment, misc. expenditures	year	614	91	81r
Household expenditures, miscellaneous	year	294	91	81r
Household furnishings and equipment, expenditures	year	1416	91	81r
Household operations expenditures	year	580	91	81r
Household textiles, expenditures	year	113	91	81r
Housekeeping supplies, expenditures	year	447	91	81r
Laundry and cleaning supplies, expenditures	year	114	91	81r
Postage and stationery, expenditures	year	145	91	81r
Housing				
Add garage/carport		6,422	3/95	74r
Add room(s)		26,583	3/95	74r
Apartment condominium or co-op, median	unit	105300	12/94	62r
Dwellings (owned), expenditures	year	3932	91	81r
Enclose porch/patio/breezeway		5,382	3/95	74r
Finish room in basement/attic		3,911	3/95	74r
Home, existing, single-family, median	unit	178600	12/94	62r
Maintenance, repairs, insurance, and other housing expenditures	year	591	91	81r
Mortgage interest and charges expenditures	year	2747	91	81r

Values are in dollars or fractions of dollars. In the column headed *Ref*, references are shown to sources. Each reference is followed by a letter. These refer to the geographical level for which data were reported: s = State, r = Region, and c = City or metro. The abbreviation *ex* is used to mean *except* or *excluding*; *exp* stands for expenditures. For other abbreviations and further explanations, please see the Introduction.

Sacramento, CA - continued

Item	Per	Value	Date	Ref.
Housing				
Princ. & int., mortgage, median-price exist. sing.-family home	mo.	845	12/94	62r
Property taxes expenditures	year	594	91	81r
Redesign, restructure more than half of home's interior		5,467	3/95	74r
Rental units expenditures	year	2077	91	81r
Insurance and Pensions				
Auto insurance, private passenger	year	892.80	12/94	71s
Insurance and pensions, personal, expenditures	year	3042	91	81r
Insurance, life and other personal, expenditures	year	298	91	81r
Pensions and Social Security, expenditures	year	2744	91	81r
Legal Assistance				
Legal work, law firm associate	hour	91		10r
Legal work, law firm partner	hour	151		10r
Personal Services				
Personal services expenditures	year	286	91	81r
Restaurant Food				
Dining expenditures, family	week	32.25	94	73r
Taxes				
Taxes, Federal income, expenditures	year	2946	91	81r
Taxes, personal, expenditures	year	3791	91	81r
Taxes, State and local income, expenditures	year	791	91	81r
Transportation				
Cars and trucks purchased, new	year	1231	91	81r
Cars and trucks purchased, used	year	915	91	81r
Driver's learning permit fee	perm	12.00	1/94	84s
Driver's license fee	orig	12.00	1/94	84s
Driver's license fee, duplicate	lic	12.00	1/94	84s
Driver's license reinstatement fee, min.	susp	15.00	1/94	85s
Driver's license renewal fee	renew	12.00	1/94	84s
Identification card, nondriver	card	6.00	1/94	83s
Motorcycle learning permit fee	perm	12.00	1/94	84s
Motorcycle license fee	orig	12.00	1/94	84s
Motorcycle license fee, duplicate	lic	12.00	1/94	84s
Motorcycle license renewal fee	renew	12.00	1/94	84s
Public transportation expenditures	year	375	91	81r
Transportation expenditures, total	year	5527	91	81r
Vehicle finance charges	year	287	91	81r
Vehicle insurance expenditures	year	624	91	81r
Vehicle maintenance and repairs expenditures	year	695	91	81r
Vehicle purchases	year	2174	91	81r
Vehicle rental, leases, licenses, etc. expenditures	year	257	91	81r
Vehicles purchased, other than cars and trucks	year	28	91	81r
Utilities				
Electricity expenditures	year	616	91	81r
Utilities, fuels, and public services, total expenditures	year	1681	91	81r
Water and other public services, expenditures	year	209	91	81r
Weddings				
Bridal attendants' gowns	event	750	10/93	76r
Bridal gown	event	852	10/93	76r
Bridal headpiece and veil	event	167	10/93	76r
Bride's wedding band	event	708	10/93	76r
Clergy	event	224	10/93	76r
Engagement ring	event	2756	10/93	76r
Flowers	event	863	10/93	76r
Formal wear for groom	event	106	10/93	76r
Groom's attendants' formal wear	event	530	10/93	76r
Groom's wedding band	event	402	10/93	76r
Music	event	600	10/93	76r
Photography	event	1088	10/93	76r
Shoes for bride	event	50	10/93	76r

Sacramento, CA - continued

Item	Per	Value	Date	Ref.
Weddings - continued				
Videography	event	483	10/93	76r
Wedding invitations and announcements	event	342	10/93	76r
Wedding reception	event	7000	10/93	76r

Saginaw-Bay City-Midland, MI

Item	Per	Value	Date	Ref.
Appliances				
Appliances (major), expenditures	year	131	91	81r
Average annual exp.				
Food, health care, personal goods, services	year	25935	91	81r
Charity				
Cash contributions, expenditures	year	745	91	81r
Clothing				
Apparel, men and boys, total expenditures	year	332	91	81r
Apparel, women and girls, total expenditures	year	578	91	81r
Footwear, expenditures	year	164	91	81r
Communications				
Long-distance telephone rate, day, addl. min., 1-10 mi.	min.	0.08	12/93	9s
Long-distance telephone rate, day, initial min., 1-10 mi.	min.	0.14	12/93	9s
Phone line, single, business, field visit	inst	42.00	12/93	9s
Phone line, single, business, no field visit	inst	42.00	12/93	9s
Phone line, single, residence, field visit	inst	42.00	12/93	9s
Phone line, single, residence, no field visit	inst	42.00	12/93	9s
Telephone service, expenditures	year	547	91	81r
Education				
Board, 4-year private college/university	year	2064	8/94	80s
Board, 4-year public college/university	year	2304	8/94	80s
Education, total expenditures	year	394	91	81r
Room, 4-year private college/university	year	1814	8/94	80s
Room, 4-year public college/university	year	1856	8/94	80s
Total cost, 4-year private college/university	year	12178	8/94	80s
Total cost, 4-year public college/university	year	7642	8/94	80s
Tuition, 2-year public college/university, in-state	year	1358	8/94	80s
Tuition, 4-year private college/university, in-state	year	8300	8/94	80s
Tuition, 4-year public college/university, in-state	year	3481	8/94	80s
Energy and Fuels				
Fuel oil and other fuels, expenditures	year	83	91	81r
Gas, natural, expenditures	year	373	91	81r
Gasoline and motor oil purchased	year	1000	91	81r
Gasoline, unleaded midgrade	gallon	1.15	4/93	82r
Gasoline, unleaded premium	gallon	1.23	4/93	82r
Gasoline, unleaded regular	gallon	1.07	4/93	82r
Entertainment				
Entertainment, total expenditures	year	1356	91	81r
Fees and admissions, expenditures	year	347	91	81r
Pets, toys, playground equipment, expenditures	year	270	91	81r
Reading, expenditures	year	160	91	81r
Televisions, radios, and sound equipment, expenditures	year	433	91	81r
Funerals				
Burial, immediate, container provided by funeral home		1268.31	1/95	54r
Cards, acknowledgment		26.12	1/95	54r
Casket, minimum alternative		198.03	1/95	54r
Cosmetology, hair care, etc.		122.19	1/95	54r
Cremation, direct, container provided by funeral home		977.81	1/95	54r
Embalming		334.00	1/95	54r
Funeral, funeral home		321.16	1/95	54r
Funeral, other facility		317.73	1/95	54r
Graveside service		292.48	1/95	54r

Values are in dollars or fractions of dollars. In the column headed *Ref*, references are shown to sources. Each reference is followed by a letter. These refer to the geographical level for which data were reported: s=State, r=Region, and c=City or metro. The abbreviation *ex* is used to mean *except* or *excluding; exp* stands for expenditures. For other abbreviations and further explanations, please see the Introduction.

Saginaw-Bay City-Midland, MI - continued

Item	Per	Value	Date	Ref.
Funerals				
Hearse, local		153.20	1/95	54r
Limousine, local		123.52	1/95	54r
Memorial service		356.30	1/95	54r
Service charge, professional, nondeclinable		968.24	1/95	54r
Visitation and viewing		332.66	1/95	54r
Groceries				
Apples, Red Delicious	lb.	0.68	12/94	82r
Bacon, sliced	lb.	1.88	12/94	82r
Bananas	lb.	0.41	12/94	82r
Beef purchases	year	197	91	81r
Beef, stew, boneless	lb.	2.52	12/94	82r
Beverage purchases, alcoholic	year	293	91	81r
Beverage purchases, nonalcoholic	year	203	91	81r
Bologna, all beef or mixed	lb.	2.12	12/94	82r
Bread, white, pan	lb.	0.76	12/94	82r
Cabbage	lb.	0.44	12/94	82r
Carrots, short trimmed and topped	lb.	0.44	12/94	82r
Cereals and bakery products purchases	year	347	91	81r
Cereals and cereals products purchases	year	119	91	81r
Cheddar cheese, natural	lb.	3.28	12/94	82r
Chicken breast, bone-in	lb.	1.61	12/94	82r
Chicken, fresh, whole	lb.	0.89	12/94	82r
Chuck roast, USDA choice, boneless	lb.	2.33	12/94	82r
Coffee, 100%, ground roast, all sizes	lb.	4.28	12/94	82r
Cookies, chocolate chip	lb.	2.72	12/94	82r
Dairy products (other) purchases	year	148	91	81r
Eggs, Grade A large	dozen	0.76	12/94	82r
Fish and seafood purchases	year	61	91	81r
Flour, white, all purpose	lb.	0.22	12/94	82r
Food purchases, food eaten at home	year	2313	91	81r
Foods purchased away from home, not prepared by consumer	year	1709	91	81r
Fruits and vegetables purchases	year	372	91	81r
Grapefruit	lb.	0.47	12/94	82r
Grapes, Thompson seedless	lb.	2.15	12/94	82r
Ground beef, 100% beef	lb.	1.37	12/94	82r
Ground chuck, 100% beef	lb.	1.81	12/94	82r
Ham, boneless, exc. canned	lb.	2.16	12/94	82r
Ice cream, prepackaged, bulk, regular	1/2 gal.	2.48	12/94	82r
Lemons	lb.	1.08	12/94	82r
Lettuce, iceberg	lb.	0.81	12/94	82r
Margarine, stick	lb.	0.81	12/94	82r
Meats, poultry, fish, and eggs purchases	year	591	91	81r
Milk and cream (fresh) purchases	year	132	91	81r
Orange juice, frozen concentrate 12-oz. can	16 oz.	1.41	12/94	82r
Oranges, Navel	lb.	0.56	12/94	82r
Peanut butter, creamy, all sizes	lb.	1.81	12/94	82r
Pork chops, center cut, bone-in	lb.	2.76	12/94	82r
Pork purchases	year	130	91	81r
Potato chips	16-oz.	2.81	12/94	82r
Potatoes, frozen, French fried	lb.	0.83	12/94	82r
Potatoes, white	lb.	0.28	12/94	82r
Round roast, USDA choice, boneless	lb.	2.90	12/94	82r
Shortening, vegetable oil blends	lb.	0.88	12/94	82r
Spaghetti and macaroni	lb.	0.78	12/94	82r
Steak, rib eye, USDA choice, boneless	lb.	6.15	12/94	82r
Steak, round, graded & ungraded, exc. USDA prime & choice	lb.	2.72	12/94	82r
Steak, round, USDA choice, boneless	lb.	3.02	12/94	82r
Steak, sirloin, USDA choice, boneless	lb.	3.85	12/94	82r
Steak, T-bone, USDA choice, bone-in	lb.	5.38	12/94	82r
Sugar and other sweets, eaten at home, expenditures	year	91	91	81r
Sugar, white, all sizes	lb.	0.36	12/94	82r
Tobacco products and smoking supplies, total expenditures	year	298	91	81r
Tomatoes, field grown	lb.	1.36	12/94	82r
Tuna, chunk, light	lb.	1.94	12/94	82r
Turkey, frozen, whole	lb.	0.96	12/94	82r
Yogurt, natural, fruit flavored	8 oz.	0.62	12/94	82r

Item	Per	Value	Date	Ref.
Health Care				
Childbirth, Cesarean delivery, hospital charge	birth	5101.00	12/91	69r
Childbirth, Cesarean delivery, physician charge	birth	2234.00	12/91	69r
Childbirth, normal delivery, hospital charge	birth	2891.00	12/91	69r
Childbirth, normal delivery, physician charge	birth	1623.00	12/91	69r
Drugs, expenditures	year	248	91	81r
Health care, total expenditures	year	1336	91	81r
Health insurance expenditures	year	550	91	81r
Insurance premium, family medical care	month	369.41	1/95	41s
Medical services expenditures	year	457	91	81r
Medical supplies expenditures	year	82	91	81r
Household Goods				
Floor coverings, expenditures	year	105	91	81r
Furniture, expenditures	year	291	91	81r
Household equipment, misc. expenditures	year	341	91	81r
Household expenditures, miscellaneous	year	162	91	81r
Household furnishings and equipment, expenditures	year	1042	91	81r
Household operations expenditures	year	365	91	81r
Household textiles, expenditures	year	101	91	81r
Housekeeping supplies, expenditures	year	390	91	81r
Laundry and cleaning supplies, expenditures	year	110	91	81r
Postage and stationery, expenditures	year	115	91	81r
Housing				
Add garage/carport		8,479	3/95	74r
Add room(s)		21,347	3/95	74r
Apartment condominium or co-op, median	unit	87100	12/94	62r
Bathroom addition, average cost	add	9734.00	3/95	13r
Bathroom remodeling, average cost	remod	6414.00	3/95	13r
Bedroom, master suite addition, average cost	add	27122.00	3/95	13r
Deck addition, average cost	add	6665.00	3/95	13r
Dwellings (owned), expenditures	year	2566	91	81r
Enclose porch/patio/breezeway		4,556	3/95	74r
Exterior remodeling, average cost	remod	15395.00	3/95	13r
Family room addition, average cost	add	27658.00	3/95	13r
Finish room in basement/attic		5,074	3/95	74r
Home, existing, single-family, median	unit	106500	12/94	62r
Kitchen remodeling, major, average cost	remod	17084.00	3/95	13r
Kitchen remodeling, minor, average cost	remod	5804.00	3/95	13r
Maintenance, repairs, insurance, and other housing expenditures	year	484	91	81r
Mortgage interest and charges expenditures	year	1443	91	81r
Office, home addition, average cost	add	8121.00	3/95	13r
Princ. & int., mortgage, median-price exist. sing.-family home	mo.	515	12/94	62r
Property taxes expenditures	year	639	91	81r
Redesign, restructure more than half of home's interior		9,114	3/95	74r
Rental units expenditures	year	1200	91	81r
Sun-space addition, average cost	add	23768.00	3/95	13r
Wing addition, two-story, average cost	add	50410.00	3/95	13r
Insurance and Pensions				
Auto insurance, private passenger	year	788.26	12/94	71s
Insurance and pensions, personal, expenditures	year	2408	91	81r
Insurance, life and other personal, expenditures	year	355	91	81r
Pensions and Social Security, expenditures	year	2053	91	81r
Legal Assistance				
Legal work, law firm associate	hour	90		10r
Legal work, law firm partner	hour	139		10r
Personal Services				
Personal services expenditures	year	203	91	81r
Restaurant Food				
Dining expenditures, family	week	30.03	94	73r

Values are in dollars or fractions of dollars. In the column headed *Ref*, references are shown to sources. Each reference is followed by a letter. These refer to the geographical level for which data were reported: s=State, r=Region, and c=City or metro. The abbreviation *ex* is used to mean *except* or *excluding*; *exp* stands for *expenditures*. For other abbreviations and further explanations, please see the Introduction.

Saginaw-Bay City-Midland, MI - continued

Item	Per	Value	Date	Ref.
Taxes				
Taxes, Federal income, expenditures	year	1756	91	81r
Taxes, personal, expenditures	year	2426	91	81r
Taxes, State and local income, expenditures	year	568	91	81r
Transportation				
Cars and trucks purchased, new	year	891	91	81r
Cars and trucks purchased, used	year	1155	91	81r
Driver's learning permit fee	perm	12.00	1/94	84s
Driver's license fee	orig	12.00	1/94	84s
Driver's license fee, duplicate	lic	6.00	1/94	84s
Driver's license reinstatement fee, min.	susp	125.00	1/94	85s
Driver's license renewal fee	renew	12.00	1/94	84s
Identification card, nondriver	card	6.00	1/94	83s
Motorcycle license fee	orig	7.50	1/94	84s
Motorcycle license renewal fee	renew	4.00	1/94	84s
Public transportation expenditures	year	209	91	81r
Transportation expenditures, total	year	4792	91	81r
Vehicle finance charges	year	300	91	81r
Vehicle insurance expenditures	year	485	91	81r
Vehicle maintenance and repairs expenditures	year	534	91	81r
Vehicle purchases	year	2068	91	81r
Vehicle rental, leases, licenses, etc. expenditures	year	197	91	81r
Vehicles purchased, other than cars and trucks	year	22	91	81r
Utilities				
Electricity expenditures	year	668	91	81r
Utilities, fuels, and public services, total expenditures	year	1838	91	81r
Water and other public services, expenditures	year	167	91	81r
Weddings				
Bridal attendants' gowns	event	750	10/93	76r
Bridal gown	event	852	10/93	76r
Bridal headpiece and veil	event	167	10/93	76r
Bride's wedding band	event	708	10/93	76r
Clergy	event	224	10/93	76r
Engagement ring	event	2756	10/93	76r
Flowers	event	863	10/93	76r
Formal wear for groom	event	106	10/93	76r
Groom's attendants' formal wear	event	530	10/93	76r
Groom's wedding band	event	402	10/93	76r
Music	event	600	10/93	76r
Photography	event	1088	10/93	76r
Shoes for bride	event	50	10/93	76r
Videography	event	483	10/93	76r
Wedding invitations and announcements	event	342	10/93	76r
Wedding reception	event	7000	10/93	76r

Saint Charles, MO

Item	Per	Value	Date	Ref.
Composite, ACCRA index		101.90	12/94	2c
Alcoholic Beverages				
Beer, Miller Lite, Bud, 12-oz., ex deposit	6	4.02	12/94	2c
J & B Scotch	750-ml.	16.14	12/94	2c
Wine, Gallo Chablis blanc	1.5-lit	7.16	12/94	2c
Clothing				
Jeans, man's denim		29.99	12/94	2c
Shirt, man's dress shirt		33.17	12/94	2c
Undervest, boy's size 10-14, cotton	3	7.66	12/94	2c
Communications				
Newspaper subscription, dly. and Sun. delivery	month	14.50	12/94	2c
Telephone bill, family of four	month	18.58	12/94	2c
Energy and Fuels				
Energy, combined forms, 1800 sq. ft.	mo.	122.18	12/94	2c
Energy, exc. electricity, 1800 sq. ft.	mo.	53.78	12/94	2c

Saint Charles, MO - continued

Item	Per	Value	Date	Ref.
Energy and Fuels - continued				
Gas, reg unlead, taxes inc., cash, self-service	gal	1.07	12/94	2c
Entertainment				
Bowling, evening rate	game	2.10	12/94	2c
Monopoly game, Parker Brothers', No. 9	game	9.62	12/94	2c
Movie	adm	5.88	12/94	2c
Tennis balls, yellow, Wilson or Penn, 3	can	2.28	12/94	2c
Groceries				
Groceries, ACCRA Index		111.20	12/94	2c
Baby food, strained vegetables, lowest price	4-4.5 oz.	0.38	12/94	2c
Bananas	lb.	0.58	12/94	2c
Beef or hamburger, ground	lb.	1.49	12/94	2c
Bread, white	24-oz.	0.93	12/94	2c
Cheese, Kraft grated Parmesan	8-oz.	3.26	12/94	2c
Chicken, whole fryer	lb.	0.78	12/94	2c
Cigarettes, Winston, Kings	carton	14.82	12/94	2c
Coffee, vacuum-packed	13 oz.	4.04	12/94	2c
Corn Flakes, Kellogg's or Post Toasties	18 oz.	2.57	12/94	2c
Corn, frozen, whole kernel, lowest price	10 oz.	0.73	12/94	2c
Eggs, Grade A large	dozen	0.82	12/94	2c
Lettuce, iceberg	head	0.88	12/94	2c
Margarine, Blue Bonnet or Parkay cubes	lb.	0.76	12/94	2c
Milk, whole	1/2 gal.	1.74	12/94	2c
Orange juice, Minute Maid frozen	12-oz.	1.64	12/94	2c
Peaches, halves or slices, Hunt's, Del Monte, or Libby's	29-oz.	1.44	12/94	2c
Peas, sweet, Del Monte or Green Giant	15-17 oz.	0.69	12/94	2c
Potatoes, white or red	10-lb. sack	1.94	12/94	2c
Sausage, Jimmy Dean, 100% pork	lb.	2.72	12/94	2c
Shortening, vegetable, Crisco	3-lb.	2.99	12/94	2c
Soft drink, Coca Cola, ex deposit	2 lit	0.96	12/94	2c
Steak, t-bone	lb.	5.37	12/94	2c
Sugar, cane or beet	4 lbs.	1.47	12/94	2c
Tomatoes, Hunt's or Del Monte	14.5 oz.	0.84	12/94	2c
Tuna, chunk, light, oil-packed	6.125-6.5 oz.	0.93	12/94	2c
Goods and Services				
Miscellaneous goods and services, ACCRA Index		100.40	12/94	2c
Health Care				
Health care, ACCRA Index		105.60	12/94	2c
Antibiotic ointment, Polysporin	1.5 oz.	5.19	12/94	2c
Dentist's fee, adult teeth cleaning and periodic oral exam	visit	53.00	12/94	2c
Doctor's fee, routine exam, established patient	visit	43.00	12/94	2c
Hospital care, semiprivate room	day	383.80	12/94	2c
Household Goods				
Appl. repair, service call, wash mach	min. lab. chg.	20.65	12/94	2c
Laundry detergent, Tide Ultra, Bold, or Cheer	42 oz.	3.86	12/94	2c
Tissues, facial, Kleenex brand	175	1.17	12/94	2c
Housing				
Housing, ACCRA Index		97.90	12/94	2c
House payment, principal and interest, 25% down payment	mo.	749	12/94	2c
House, 1800 sq ft, 8000 sq ft lot, new, urban, utilities	total	120400	12/94	2c
Mtge. rate, incl. points and orig. fee, 30-year conv. fixed or ARM	mo.	9.35	12/94	2c
Rent, apartment, 2 br., 1 1/2-2 baths, unfurnished, 950 sq ft, water	mo.	519	12/94	2c

Values are in dollars or fractions of dollars. In the column headed *Ref*, references are shown to sources. Each reference is followed by a letter. These refer to the geographical level for which data were reported: s = State, r = Region, and c = City or metro. The abbreviation *ex* is used to mean *except* or *excluding*; *exp* stands for *expenditures*. For other abbreviations and further explanations, please see the Introduction.

Saint Charles, MO - continued

Item	Per	Value	Date	Ref.
Personal Goods				
Shampoo, Alberto VO5	15-oz.	0.93	12/94	2c
Toothpaste, Crest or Colgate	6-7 oz.	1.24	12/94	2c
Personal Services				
Dry cleaning, man's 2-pc. suit		6.98	12/94	2c
Haircut, man's barbershop, no styling		8.00	12/94	2c
Haircut, woman's shampoo, trim, blow-dry		19.17	12/94	2c
Restaurant Food				
Chicken, fried, thigh and drumstick		1.95	12/94	2c
Hamburger with cheese	1/4 lb.	1.88	12/94	2c
Pizza, Pizza Hut or Pizza Inn	12-13 in.	7.49	12/94	2c
Transportation				
Transportation, ACCRA Index		96.60	12/94	2c
Tire balance, computer or spin bal., front	wheel	6.67	12/94	2c
Utilities				
Utilities, ACCRA Index		107.00	12/94	2c
Electricity, (part.), other, 1800 sq. ft., new home	mo.	68.40	12/94	2c

Saint Cloud, MN

Item	Per	Value	Date	Ref.
Composite, ACCRA index		96.60	12/94	2c
Alcoholic Beverages				
Beer, Miller Lite, Bud, 12-oz., ex deposit	6	3.99	12/94	2c
J & B Scotch	750-ml.	15.49	12/94	2c
Wine, Gallo Chablis blanc	1.5-lit	4.09	12/94	2c
Appliances				
Appliances (major), expenditures	year	131	91	81r
Average annual exp.				
Food, health care, personal goods, services	year	25935	91	81r
Charity				
Cash contributions, expenditures	year	745	91	81r
Clothing				
Apparel, men and boys, total expenditures	year	332	91	81r
Apparel, women and girls, total expenditures	year	578	91	81r
Footwear, expenditures	year	164	91	81r
Jeans, man's denim		32.99	12/94	2c
Shirt, man's dress shirt		36.38	12/94	2c
Undervest, boy's size 10-14, cotton	3	3.73	12/94	2c
Communications				
Long-distance telephone rate, day, addl. min., 1-10 mi.	min.	0.05	12/93	9s
Long-distance telephone rate, day, initial min., 1-10 mi.	min.	0.14	12/93	9s
Newspaper subscription, dly. and Sun. delivery	month	13.04	12/94	2c
Phone line, single, business, field visit	inst	45.00	12/93	9s
Phone line, single, business, no field visit	inst	45.00	12/93	9s
Phone line, single, residence, field visit	inst	16.25	12/93	9s
Phone line, single, residence, no field visit	inst	16.25	12/93	9s
Telephone bill, family of four	month	22.35	12/94	2c
Telephone service, expenditures	year	547	91	81r
Telephone, residential, flat rate	mo.	14.58	12/93	8c
Education				
Board, 4-year private college/university	year	2070	8/94	80s
Board, 4-year public college/university	year	1545	8/94	80s
Education, total expenditures	year	394	91	81r
Living expenses, personal miscellaneous, university student	year	4200.00	5/96	22s
Room, 4-year private college/university	year	1894	8/94	80s
Room, 4-year public college/university	year	1580	8/94	80s
Total cost, 4-year private college/university	year	15556	8/94	80s
Total cost, 4-year public college/university	year	5904	8/94	80s
Tuition, 2-year public college/university, in-state	year	1858	8/94	80s

Saint Cloud, MN - continued

Item	Per	Value	Date	Ref.
Education - continued				
Tuition, 4-year private college/university, in-state	year	11592	8/94	80s
Tuition, 4-year public college/university, in-state	year	2780	8/94	80s
Energy and Fuels				
Energy, combined forms, 1800 sq. ft.	mo.	105.41	12/94	2c
Energy, exc. electricity, 1800 sq. ft.	mo.	49.33	12/94	2c
Fuel oil and other fuels, expenditures	year	83	91	81r
Gas, natural, expenditures	year	373	91	81r
Gas, reg unlead, taxes inc., cash, self-service	gal	1.18	12/94	2c
Gasoline and motor oil purchased	year	1000	91	81r
Gasoline, unleaded midgrade	gallon	1.15	4/93	82r
Gasoline, unleaded premium	gallon	1.23	4/93	82r
Gasoline, unleaded regular	gallon	1.07	4/93	82r
Entertainment				
Bowling, evening rate	game	1.86	12/94	2c
Entertainment, total expenditures	year	1356	91	81r
Fees and admissions, expenditures	year	347	91	81r
Monopoly game, Parker Brothers', No. 9	game	8.99	12/94	2c
Movie	adm	5.50	12/94	2c
Pets, toys, playground equipment, expenditures	year	270	91	81r
Reading, expenditures	year	160	91	81r
Televisions, radios, and sound equipment, expenditures	year	433	91	81r
Tennis balls, yellow, Wilson or Penn, 3	can	2.76	12/94	2c
Funerals				
Burial, immediate, container provided by funeral home		1348.78	1/95	54r
Cards, acknowledgment		21.20	1/95	54r
Casket, minimum alternative		182.83	1/95	54r
Cosmetology, hair care, etc.		133.11	1/95	54r
Cremation, direct, container provided by funeral home		1101.95	1/95	54r
Embalming		314.45	1/95	54r
Funeral, funeral home		304.88	1/95	54r
Funeral, other facility		301.37	1/95	54r
Graveside service		290.59	1/95	54r
Hearse, local		137.37	1/95	54r
Limousine, local		82.84	1/95	54r
Memorial service		316.57	1/95	54r
Service charge, professional, nondeclinable		1099.00	1/95	54r
Visitation and viewing		209.25	1/95	54r
Groceries				
Groceries, ACCRA Index		102.30	12/94	2c
Apples, Red Delicious	lb.	0.68	12/94	82r
Baby food, strained vegetables, lowest price	4-4.5 oz.	0.36	12/94	2c
Bacon, sliced	lb.	1.88	12/94	82r
Bananas	lb.	0.42	12/94	2c
Bananas	lb.	0.41	12/94	82r
Beef or hamburger, ground	lb.	1.71	12/94	2c
Beef purchases	year	197	91	81r
Beef, stew, boneless	lb.	2.52	12/94	82r
Beverage purchases, alcoholic	year	293	91	81r
Beverage purchases, nonalcoholic	year	203	91	81r
Bologna, all beef or mixed	lb.	2.12	12/94	82r
Bread, white	24-oz.	0.73	12/94	2c
Bread, white, pan	lb.	0.76	12/94	82r
Cabbage	lb.	0.44	12/94	82r
Carrots, short trimmed and topped	lb.	0.44	12/94	82r
Cereals and bakery products purchases	year	347	91	81r
Cereals and cereals products purchases	year	119	91	81r
Cheddar cheese, natural	lb.	3.28	12/94	82r
Cheese, Kraft grated Parmesan	8-oz.	2.97	12/94	2c
Chicken breast, bone-in	lb.	1.61	12/94	82r
Chicken, fresh, whole	lb.	0.89	12/94	82r
Chicken, whole fryer	lb.	0.93	12/94	2c
Chuck roast, USDA choice, boneless	lb.	2.33	12/94	82r

Values are in dollars or fractions of dollars. In the column headed *Ref*, references are shown to sources. Each reference is followed by a letter. These refer to the geographical level for which data were reported: s=State, r=Region, and c=City or metro. The abbreviation *ex* is used to mean *except* or *excluding*; *exp* stands for expenditures. For other abbreviations and further explanations, please see the Introduction.

Saint Cloud, MN - continued

Item	Per	Value	Date	Ref.
Groceries				
Cigarettes, Winston, Kings	carton	19.02	12/94	2c
Coffee, 100%, ground roast, all sizes	lb.	4.28	12/94	82r
Coffee, vacuum-packed	13 oz.	3.65	12/94	2c
Cookies, chocolate chip	lb.	2.72	12/94	82r
Corn Flakes, Kellogg's or Post Toasties	18 oz.	2.01	12/94	2c
Corn, frozen, whole kernel, lowest price	10 oz.	0.72	12/94	2c
Dairy products (other) purchases	year	148	91	81r
Eggs, Grade A large	dozen	0.68	12/94	2c
Eggs, Grade A large	dozen	0.76	12/94	82r
Fish and seafood purchases	year	61	91	81r
Flour, white, all purpose	lb.	0.22	12/94	82r
Food purchases, food eaten at home	year	2313	91	81r
Foods purchased away from home, not prepared by consumer	year	1709	91	81r
Fruits and vegetables purchases	year	372	91	81r
Grapefruit	lb.	0.47	12/94	82r
Grapes, Thompson seedless	lb.	2.15	12/94	82r
Ground beef, 100% beef	lb.	1.37	12/94	82r
Ground chuck, 100% beef	lb.	1.81	12/94	82r
Ham, boneless, exc. canned	lb.	2.16	12/94	82r
Ice cream, prepackaged, bulk, regular	1/2 gal.	2.48	12/94	82r
Lemons	lb.	1.08	12/94	82r
Lettuce, iceberg	lb.	0.81	12/94	82r
Lettuce, iceberg	head	0.74	12/94	2c
Margarine, Blue Bonnet or Parkay cubes	lb.	0.65	12/94	2c
Margarine, stick	lb.	0.81	12/94	82r
Meats, poultry, fish, and eggs purchases	year	591	91	81r
Milk and cream (fresh) purchases	year	132	91	81r
Milk, whole	1/2 gal.	1.46	12/94	2c
Orange juice, frozen concentrate 12-oz. can	16 oz.	1.41	12/94	82r
Orange juice, Minute Maid frozen	12-oz.	1.30	12/94	2c
Oranges, Navel	lb.	0.56	12/94	82r
Peaches, halves or slices, Hunt's, Del Monte, or Libby's	29-oz.	1.20	12/94	2c
Peanut butter, creamy, all sizes	lb.	1.81	12/94	82r
Peas, sweet, Del Monte or Green Giant	15-17 oz.	0.56	12/94	2c
Pork chops, center cut, bone-in	lb.	2.76	12/94	82r
Pork purchases	year	130	91	81r
Potato chips	16-oz.	2.81	12/94	82r
Potatoes, frozen, French fried	lb.	0.83	12/94	82r
Potatoes, white	lb.	0.28	12/94	82r
Potatoes, white or red	10-lb. sack	2.06	12/94	2c
Round roast, USDA choice, boneless	lb.	2.90	12/94	82r
Sausage, Jimmy Dean, 100% pork	lb.	3.14	12/94	2c
Shortening, vegetable oil blends	lb.	0.88	12/94	82r
Shortening, vegetable, Crisco	3-lb.	2.55	12/94	2c
Soft drink, Coca Cola, ex deposit	2 lit	1.06	12/94	2c
Spaghetti and macaroni	lb.	0.78	12/94	82r
Steak, rib eye, USDA choice, boneless	lb.	6.15	12/94	82r
Steak, round, graded & ungraded, exc. USDA prime & choice	lb.	2.72	12/94	82r
Steak, round, USDA choice, boneless	lb.	3.02	12/94	82r
Steak, sirloin, USDA choice, boneless	lb.	3.85	12/94	82r
Steak, t-bone	lb.	5.47	12/94	2c
Steak, T-bone, USDA choice, bone-in	lb.	5.38	12/94	82r
Sugar and other sweets, eaten at home, expenditures	year	91	91	81r
Sugar, cane or beet	4 lbs.	1.51	12/94	2c
Sugar, white, all sizes	lb.	0.36	12/94	82r
Tobacco products and smoking supplies, total expenditures	year	298	91	81r
Tomatoes, field grown	lb.	1.36	12/94	82r
Tomatoes, Hunt's or Del Monte	14.5 oz.	0.74	12/94	2c
Tuna, chunk, light	lb.	1.94	12/94	82r
Tuna, chunk, light, oil-packed	6.125-6.5 oz.	0.62	12/94	2c
Turkey, frozen, whole	lb.	0.96	12/94	82r

Saint Cloud, MN - continued

Item	Per	Value	Date	Ref.
Groceries - continued				
Yogurt, natural, fruit flavored	8 oz.	0.62	12/94	82r
Goods and Services				
Miscellaneous goods and services, ACCRA Index		103.10	12/94	2c
Health Care				
Health care, ACCRA Index		95.50	12/94	2c
Antibiotic ointment, Polysporin	1.5 oz.	4.11	12/94	2c
Childbirth, Cesarean delivery, hospital charge	birth	5101.00	12/91	69r
Childbirth, Cesarean delivery, physician charge	birth	2234.00	12/91	69r
Childbirth, normal delivery, hospital charge	birth	2891.00	12/91	69r
Childbirth, normal delivery, physician charge	birth	1623.00	12/91	69r
Dentist's fee, adult teeth cleaning and periodic oral exam	visit	49.80	12/94	2c
Doctor's fee, routine exam, established patient	visit	39.25	12/94	2c
Drugs, expenditures	year	248	91	81r
Health care, total expenditures	year	1336	91	81r
Health insurance expenditures	year	550	91	81r
Hospital care, semiprivate room	day	349.00	12/94	2c
Insurance premium, family medical care	month	375.35	1/95	41s
Medical services expenditures	year	457	91	81r
Medical supplies expenditures	year	82	91	81r
Household Goods				
Appl. repair, service call, wash mach	min. lab. chg.	31.61	12/94	2c
Floor coverings, expenditures	year	105	91	81r
Furniture, expenditures	year	291	91	81r
Household equipment, misc. expenditures	year	341	91	81r
Household expenditures, miscellaneous	year	162	91	81r
Household furnishings and equipment, expenditures	year	1042	91	81r
Household operations expenditures	year	365	91	81r
Household textiles, expenditures	year	101	91	81r
Housekeeping supplies, expenditures	year	390	91	81r
Laundry and cleaning supplies, expenditures	year	110	91	81r
Laundry detergent, Tide Ultra, Bold, or Cheer	42 oz.	3.56	12/94	2c
Postage and stationery, expenditures	year	115	91	81r
Tissues, facial, Kleenex brand	175	0.95	12/94	2c
Housing				
Housing, ACCRA Index		82.40	12/94	2c
Add garage/carport		8,479	3/95	74r
Add room(s)		21,347	3/95	74r
Apartment condominium or co-op, median	unit	87100	12/94	62r
Bathroom addition, average cost	add	9734.00	3/95	13r
Bathroom remodeling, average cost	remod	6414.00	3/95	13r
Bedroom, master suite addition, average cost	add	27122.00	3/95	13r
Deck addition, average cost	add	6665.00	3/95	13r
Dwellings (owned), expenditures	year	2566	91	81r
Enclose porch/patio/breezeway		4,556	3/95	74r
Exterior remodeling, average cost	remod	15395.00	3/95	13r
Family room addition, average cost	add	27658.00	3/95	13r
Finish room in basement/attic		5,074	3/95	74r
Home, existing, single-family, median	unit	106500	12/94	62r
House payment, principal and interest, 25% down payment	mo.	624	12/94	2c
House, 1800 sq ft, 8000 sq ft lot, new, urban, utilities	total	100155	12/94	2c
Kitchen remodeling, major, average cost	remod	17084.00	3/95	13r
Kitchen remodeling, minor, average cost	remod	5804.00	3/95	13r
Maintenance, repairs, insurance, and other housing expenditures	year	484	91	81r
Mortgage interest and charges expenditures	year	1443	91	81r
Mtge. rate, incl. points and orig. fee, 30-year conv. fixed or ARM	mo.	9.36	12/94	2c

Values are in dollars or fractions of dollars. In the column headed *Ref*, references are shown to sources. Each reference is followed by a letter. These refer to the geographical level for which data were reported: s = State, r = Region, and c = City or metro. The abbreviation *ex* is used to mean *except* or *excluding*; *exp* stands for *expenditures*. For other abbreviations and further explanations, please see the Introduction.

Saint Cloud, MN - continued

Item	Per	Value	Date	Ref.
Housing				
Office, home addition, average cost	add	8121.00	3/95	13r
Princ. & int., mortgage, median-price exist. sing.-family home	mo.	515	12/94	62r
Property taxes expenditures	year	639	91	81r
Redesign, restructure more than half of home's interior		9,114	3/95	74r
Rent, apartment, 2 br., 1 1/2-2 baths, unfurnished, 950 sq ft, water	mo.	456	12/94	2c
Rental units expenditures	year	1200	91	81r
Sun-space addition, average cost	add	23768.00	3/95	13r
Wing addition, two-story, average cost	add	50410.00	3/95	13r
Insurance and Pensions				
Auto insurance, private passenger	year	656.87	12/94	71s
Insurance and pensions, personal, expenditures	year	2408	91	81r
Insurance, life and other personal, expenditures	year	355	91	81r
Pensions and Social Security, expenditures	year	2053	91	81r
Legal Assistance				
Legal work, law firm associate	hour	90		10r
Legal work, law firm partner	hour	139		10r
Personal Goods				
Shampoo, Alberto VO5	15-oz.	1.07	12/94	2c
Toothpaste, Crest or Colgate	6-7 oz.	1.78	12/94	2c
Personal Services				
Dry cleaning, man's 2-pc. suit		6.48	12/94	2c
Haircut, man's barbershop, no styling		9.24	12/94	2c
Haircut, woman's shampoo, trim, blow-dry		16.94	12/94	2c
Personal services expenditures	year	203	91	81r
Restaurant Food				
Chicken, fried, thigh and drumstick		2.38	12/94	2c
Dining expenditures, family	week	30.03	94	73r
Hamburger with cheese	1/4 lb.	1.80	12/94	2c
Pizza, Pizza Hut or Pizza Inn	12-13 in.	8.59	12/94	2c
Taxes				
Tax, cigarettes	year	400.00	10/93	43s
Taxes, Federal income, expenditures	year	1756	91	81r
Taxes, personal, expenditures	year	2426	91	81r
Taxes, State and local income, expenditures	year	568	91	81r
Transportation				
Transportation, ACCRA Index		107.40	12/94	2c
Bus fare, one-way	trip	0.35	12/95	1c
Cars and trucks purchased, new	year	891	91	81r
Cars and trucks purchased, used	year	1155	91	81r
Driver's learning permit fee	perm	6.00	1/94	84s
Driver's license fee	orig	15.00	1/94	84s
Driver's license fee, duplicate	lic	4.50	1/94	84s
Driver's license reinstatement fee, min.	susp	20.00	1/94	85s
Driver's license renewal fee	renew	15.00	1/94	84s
Identification card, nondriver	card	9.00	1/94	83s
Public transportation expenditures	year	209	91	81r
Tire balance, computer or spin bal., front	wheel	7.50	12/94	2c
Transportation expenditures, total	year	4792	91	81r
Vehicle finance charges	year	300	91	81r
Vehicle insurance expenditures	year	485	91	81r
Vehicle maintenance and repairs expenditures	year	534	91	81r
Vehicle purchases	year	2068	91	81r
Vehicle rental, leases, licenses, etc. expenditures	year	197	91	81r
Vehicles purchased, other than cars and trucks	year	22	91	81r
Utilities				
Utilities, ACCRA Index		96.70	12/94	2c
Electricity expenditures	year	668	91	81r
Electricity, (part.), other, 1800 sq. ft., new home	mo.	56.08	12/94	2c

Saint Cloud, MN - continued

Item	Per	Value	Date	Ref.
Utilities - continued				
Utilities, fuels, and public services, total expenditures	year	1838	91	81r
Water and other public services, expenditures	year	167	91	81r
Weddings				
Bridal attendants' gowns	event	750	10/93	76r
Bridal gown	event	852	10/93	76r
Bridal headpiece and veil	event	167	10/93	76r
Bride's wedding band	event	708	10/93	76r
Clergy	event	224	10/93	76r
Engagement ring	event	2756	10/93	76r
Flowers	event	863	10/93	76r
Formal wear for groom	event	106	10/93	76r
Groom's attendants' formal wear	event	530	10/93	76r
Groom's wedding band	event	402	10/93	76r
Music	event	600	10/93	76r
Photography	event	1088	10/93	76r
Shoes for bride	event	50	10/93	76r
Videography	event	483	10/93	76r
Wedding invitations and announcements	event	342	10/93	76r
Wedding reception	event	7000	10/93	76r

Saint George, UT

Item	Per	Value	Date	Ref.
Composite, ACCRA index		102.20	12/94	2c
Alcoholic Beverages				
Beer, Miller Lite, Bud, 12-oz., ex deposit	6	4.11	12/94	2c
J & B Scotch	750-ml.	19.95	12/94	2c
Wine, Gallo Chablis blanc	1.5-lit	4.95	12/94	2c
Clothing				
Jeans, man's denim		33.65	12/94	2c
Shirt, man's dress shirt		26.83	12/94	2c
Undervest, boy's size 10-14, cotton	3	3.96	12/94	2c
Communications				
Newspaper subscription, dly. and Sun. delivery	month	11.00	12/94	2c
Telephone bill, family of four	month	13.67	12/94	2c
Telephone, residential, flat rate	mo.	7.98	12/93	8c
Energy and Fuels				
Energy, combined forms, 1800 sq. ft.	mo.	90.85	12/94	2c
Gas, reg unlead, taxes inc., cash, self-service	gal	1.19	12/94	2c
Entertainment				
Bowling, evening rate	game	2.00	12/94	2c
Monopoly game, Parker Brothers', No. 9	game	12.98	12/94	2c
Movie	adm	5.00	12/94	2c
Tennis balls, yellow, Wilson or Penn, 3	can	2.98	12/94	2c
Groceries				
Groceries, ACCRA Index		101.10	12/94	2c
Baby food, strained vegetables, lowest price	4-4.5 oz.	0.41	12/94	2c
Bananas	lb.	0.54	12/94	2c
Beef or hamburger, ground	lb.	1.32	12/94	2c
Bread, white	24-oz.	0.68	12/94	2c
Cheese, Kraft grated Parmesan	8-oz.	3.19	12/94	2c
Chicken, whole fryer	lb.	0.79	12/94	2c
Cigarettes, Winston, Kings	carton	16.32	12/94	2c
Coffee, vacuum-packed	13 oz.	3.89	12/94	2c
Corn Flakes, Kellogg's or Post Toasties	18 oz.	2.66	12/94	2c
Corn, frozen, whole kernel, lowest price	10 oz.	0.63	12/94	2c
Eggs, Grade A large	dozen	0.76	12/94	2c
Lettuce, iceberg	head	0.59	12/94	2c
Margarine, Blue Bonnet or Parkay cubes	lb.	0.57	12/94	2c
Milk, whole	1/2 gal.	1.28	12/94	2c
Orange juice, Minute Maid frozen	12-oz.	1.32	12/94	2c

Values are in dollars or fractions of dollars. In the column headed *Ref*, references are shown to sources. Each reference is followed by a letter. These refer to the geographical level for which data were reported: s=State, r=Region, and c=City or metro. The abbreviation *ex* is used to mean *except* or *excluding*; *exp* stands for *expenditures*. For other abbreviations and further explanations, please see the Introduction.

Saint George, UT - continued

Item	Per	Value	Date	Ref.
Groceries				
Peaches, halves or slices, Hunt's, Del Monte, or Libby's	29-oz.	1.55	12/94	2c
Peas, sweet, Del Monte or Green Giant	15-17 oz.	0.56	12/94	2c
Potatoes, white or red	10-lb. sack	1.52	12/94	2c
Sausage, Jimmy Dean, 100% pork	lb.	2.90	12/94	2c
Shortening, vegetable, Crisco	3-lb.	2.60	12/94	2c
Soft drink, Coca Cola, ex deposit	2 lit	1.18	12/94	2c
Steak, t-bone	lb.	4.69	12/94	2c
Sugar, cane or beet	4 lbs.	1.35	12/94	2c
Tomatoes, Hunt's or Del Monte	14.5 oz.	0.74	12/94	2c
Tuna, chunk, light, oil-packed	6.125-6.5 oz.	0.78	12/94	2c
Goods and Services				
Miscellaneous goods and services, ACCRA Index		101.40	12/94	2c
Health Care				
Health care, ACCRA Index		96.90	12/94	2c
Antibiotic ointment, Polysporin	1.5 oz.	4.66	12/94	2c
Dentist's fee, adult teeth cleaning and periodic oral exam	visit	50.60	12/94	2c
Doctor's fee, routine exam, established patient	visit	37.40	12/94	2c
Hospital care, semiprivate room	day	367.50	12/94	2c
Household Goods				
Appl. repair, service call, wash mach	min. lab. chg.	23.35	12/94	2c
Laundry detergent, Tide Ultra, Bold, or Cheer	42 oz.	3.01	12/94	2c
Tissues, facial, Kleenex brand	175	1.06	12/94	2c
Housing				
Housing, ACCRA Index		111.30	12/94	2c
House payment, principal and interest, 25% down payment	mo.	870	12/94	2c
House, 1800 sq ft, 8000 sq ft lot, new, urban, utilities	total	139250	12/94	2c
Mtge. rate, incl. points and orig. fee, 30-year conv. fixed or ARM	mo.	9.40	12/94	2c
Rent, apartment, 2 br., 1 1/2-2 baths, unfurnished, 950 sq ft, water	mo.	538	12/94	2c
Personal Goods				
Shampoo, Alberto VO5	15-oz.	1.36	12/94	2c
Toothpaste, Crest or Colgate	6-7 oz.	2.29	12/94	2c
Personal Services				
Dry cleaning, man's 2-pc. suit		7.85	12/94	2c
Haircut, man's barbershop, no styling		6.00	12/94	2c
Haircut, woman's shampoo, trim, blow-dry		19.67	12/94	2c
Restaurant Food				
Chicken, fried, thigh and drumstick		2.00	12/94	2c
Hamburger with cheese	1/4 lb.	2.09	12/94	2c
Pizza, Pizza Hut or Pizza Inn	12-13 in.	8.49	12/94	2c
Transportation				
Transportation, ACCRA Index		102.50	12/94	2c
Tire balance, computer or spin bal., front	wheel	6.63	12/94	2c
Utilities				
Utilities, ACCRA Index		79.50	12/94	2c
Electricity, 1800 sq. ft., new home	mo.	90.85	12/94	2c

Saint Joseph, MO

Item	Per	Value	Date	Ref.
Composite, ACCRA index		96.50	12/94	2c
Alcoholic Beverages				
Beer, Miller Lite, Bud, 12-oz., ex deposit	6	3.79	12/94	2c
J & B Scotch	750-ml.	16.69	12/94	2c
Wine, Gallo Chablis blanc	1.5-lit	6.74	12/94	2c
Clothing				
Jeans, man's denim		27.37	12/94	2c
Shirt, man's dress shirt		34.37	12/94	2c
Undervest, boy's size 10-14, cotton	3	4.61	12/94	2c
Communications				
Newspaper subscription, dly. and Sun. delivery	month	10.03	12/94	2c
Telephone bill, family of four	month	20.12	12/94	2c
Telephone, residential, flat rate	mo.	9.10	12/93	8c
Energy and Fuels				
Energy, combined forms, 1800 sq. ft.	mo.	101.40	12/94	2c
Energy, exc. electricity, 1800 sq. ft.	mo.	37.07	12/94	2c
Gas, reg unlead, taxes inc., cash, self-service	gal	0.99	12/94	2c
Entertainment				
Bowling, evening rate	game	1.62	12/94	2c
Monopoly game, Parker Brothers', No. 9	game	12.37	12/94	2c
Movie	adm	4.50	12/94	2c
Tennis balls, yellow, Wilson or Penn, 3	can	2.25	12/94	2c
Groceries				
Groceries, ACCRA Index		96.40	12/94	2c
Baby food, strained vegetables, lowest price	4-4.5 oz.	0.41	12/94	2c
Bananas	lb.	0.47	12/94	2c
Beef or hamburger, ground	lb.	0.99	12/94	2c
Bread, white	24-oz.	0.49	12/94	2c
Cheese, Kraft grated Parmesan	8-oz.	3.20	12/94	2c
Chicken, whole fryer	lb.	0.79	12/94	2c
Cigarettes, Winston, Kings	carton	13.21	12/94	2c
Coffee, vacuum-packed	13 oz.	3.80	12/94	2c
Corn Flakes, Kellogg's or Post Toasties	18 oz.	2.56	12/94	2c
Corn, frozen, whole kernel, lowest price	10 oz.	0.64	12/94	2c
Eggs, Grade A large	dozen	0.66	12/94	2c
Lettuce, iceberg	head	0.78	12/94	2c
Margarine, Blue Bonnet or Parkay cubes	lb.	0.69	12/94	2c
Milk, whole	1/2 gal.	1.43	12/94	2c
Orange juice, Minute Maid frozen	12-oz.	1.40	12/94	2c
Peaches, halves or slices, Hunt's, Del Monte, or Libby's	29-oz.	1.22	12/94	2c
Peas, sweet, Del Monte or Green Giant	15-17 oz.	0.61	12/94	2c
Potatoes, white or red	10-lb. sack	1.49	12/94	2c
Sausage, Jimmy Dean, 100% pork	lb.	2.82	12/94	2c
Shortening, vegetable, Crisco	3-lb.	2.69	12/94	2c
Soft drink, Coca Cola, ex deposit	2 lit	1.15	12/94	2c
Steak, t-bone	lb.	4.79	12/94	2c
Sugar, cane or beet	4 lbs.	1.34	12/94	2c
Tomatoes, Hunt's or Del Monte	14.5 oz.	0.73	12/94	2c
Tuna, chunk, light, oil-packed	6.125-6.5 oz.	0.72	12/94	2c
Goods and Services				
Miscellaneous goods and services, ACCRA Index		96.50	12/94	2c
Health Care				
Health care, ACCRA Index		95.30	12/94	2c
Antibiotic ointment, Polysporin	1.5 oz.	4.23	12/94	2c
Dentist's fee, adult teeth cleaning and periodic oral exam	visit	45.33	12/94	2c
Doctor's fee, routine exam, established patient	visit	39.60	12/94	2c

Values are in dollars or fractions of dollars. In the column headed *Ref*, references are shown to sources. Each reference is followed by a letter. These refer to the geographical level for which data were reported: s=State, r=Region, and c=City or metro. The abbreviation *ex* is used to mean *except* or *excluding*; *exp* stands for expenditures. For other abbreviations and further explanations, please see the Introduction.

Saint Joseph, MO - continued

Item	Per	Value	Date	Ref.
Health Care				
Hospital care, semiprivate room	day	390.00	12/94	2c
Household Goods				
Appl. repair, service call, wash mach	min. lab. chg.	27.49	12/94	2c
Laundry detergent, Tide Ultra, Bold, or Cheer	42 oz.	2.83	12/94	2c
Tissues, facial, Kleenex brand	175	1.10	12/94	2c
Housing				
Housing, ACCRA Index		99.90	12/94	2c
House payment, principal and interest, 25% down payment	mo.	777	12/94	2c
House, 1800 sq ft, 8000 sq ft lot, new, urban, utilities	total	125033	12/94	2c
Mtge. rate, incl. points and orig. fee, 30-year conv. fixed or ARM	mo.	9.33	12/94	2c
Rent, apartment, 2 br., 1 1/2-2 baths, unfurnished, 950 sq ft, water	mo.	494	12/94	2c
Personal Goods				
Shampoo, Alberto VO5	15-oz.	1.24	12/94	2c
Toothpaste, Crest or Colgate	6-7 oz.	1.93	12/94	2c
Personal Services				
Dry cleaning, man's 2-pc. suit		5.05	12/94	2c
Haircut, man's barbershop, no styling		6.13	12/94	2c
Haircut, woman's shampoo, trim, blow-dry		15.42	12/94	2c
Restaurant Food				
Chicken, fried, thigh and drumstick		2.05	12/94	2c
Hamburger with cheese	1/4 lb.	1.89	12/94	2c
Pizza, Pizza Hut or Pizza Inn	12-13 in.	7.99	12/94	2c
Transportation				
Transportation, ACCRA Index		91.30	12/94	2c
Tire balance, computer or spin bal., front	wheel	6.44	12/94	2c
Utilities				
Utilities, ACCRA Index		92.10	12/94	2c
Electricity, (part.), other, 1800 sq. ft., new home	mo.	64.33	12/94	2c
Electricity, summer, 250 KWh	month	18.87	8/93	64c
Electricity, summer, 500 KWh	month	35.03	8/93	64c
Electricity, summer, 750 KWh	month	50.49	8/93	64c
Electricity, summer, 1000 KWh	month	64.88	8/93	64c

Saint Louis, MO

Item	Per	Value	Date	Ref.
Composite, ACCRA index		97.80	12/94	2c
Alcoholic Beverages				
Beer, Miller Lite, Bud, 12-oz., ex deposit	6	3.70	12/94	2c
J & B Scotch	750-ml.	16.38	12/94	2c
Wine, Gallo Chablis blanc	1.5-lit	4.93	12/94	2c
Appliances				
Appliances (major), expenditures	year	208	91	81c
Appliances (major), expenditures	year	131	91	81r
Average annual exp.				
Food, health care, personal goods, services	year	27743	91	81c
Food, health care, personal goods, services	year	25935	91	81r
Business				
Dinner and tip, hotel, corporate rate	night	31.00	2/94	15c
Hotel room, corporate rate	night	79.00	2/94	15c
Charity				
Cash contributions, expenditures	year	790	91	81c
Cash contributions, expenditures	year	745	91	81r
Clothing				
Apparel, men and boys, total expenditures	year	361	91	81c

Saint Louis, MO - continued

Item	Per	Value	Date	Ref.
Clothing - continued				
Apparel, men and boys, total expenditures	year	332	91	81r
Apparel, women and girls, total expenditures	year	539	91	81c
Apparel, women and girls, total expenditures	year	578	91	81r
Footwear, expenditures	year	149	91	81c
Footwear, expenditures	year	164	91	81r
Jeans, man's denim		27.60	12/94	2c
Shirt, man's dress shirt		29.08	12/94	2c
Undervest, boy's size 10-14, cotton	3	3.13	12/94	2c
Communications				
Long-distance telephone rate, day, addl. min., 1-10 mi.	min.	0.08	12/93	9s
Long-distance telephone rate, day, initial min., 1-10 mi.	min.	0.10	12/93	9s
Newspaper subscription, dly. and Sun. delivery	month	14.83	12/94	2c
Phone line, single, business, field visit	inst	52.25	12/93	9s
Phone line, single, business, no field visit	inst	52.25	12/93	9s
Phone line, single, residence, field visit	inst	36.50	12/93	9s
Phone line, single, residence, no field visit	inst	36.50	12/93	9s
Telephone bill, family of four	month	18.38	12/94	2c
Telephone service, expenditures	year	592	91	81c
Telephone service, expenditures	year	547	91	81r
Telephone, residential, flat rate	mo.	11.35	12/93	8c
Education				
Board, 4-year private college/university	year	2296	8/94	80s
Board, 4-year public college/university	year	1544	8/94	80s
Education, total expenditures	year	607	91	81c
Education, total expenditures	year	394	91	81r
Room, 4-year private college/university	year	2012	8/94	80s
Room, 4-year public college/university	year	1817	8/94	80s
Total cost, 4-year private college/university	year	13053	8/94	80s
Total cost, 4-year public college/university	year	5836	8/94	80s
Tuition, 2-year public college/university, in-state	year	1152	8/94	80s
Tuition, 4-year private college/university, in-state	year	8745	8/94	80s
Tuition, 4-year public college/university, in-state	year	2475	8/94	80s
Energy and Fuels				
Electricity	500 KWh	41.26	12/94	82c
Energy, combined forms, 1800 sq. ft.	mo.	120.91	12/94	2c
Energy, exc. electricity, 1800 sq. ft.	mo.	53.78	12/94	2c
Fuel oil and other fuels, expenditures	year	32	91	81c
Fuel oil and other fuels, expenditures	year	83	91	81r
Gas, cooking, 10 therms	month	14.13	2/94	65c
Gas, cooking, 30 therms	month	23.40	2/94	65c
Gas, cooking, 50 therms	month	32.67	2/94	65c
Gas, heating, winter, 100 therms	month	55.14	2/94	65c
Gas, heating, winter, average use	month	85.74	2/94	65c
Gas, natural, expenditures	year	380	91	81c
Gas, natural, expenditures	year	373	91	81r
Gas, piped	40 therms	28.35	12/94	82c
Gas, piped	100 therms	51.38	12/94	82c
Gas, piped	therm	0.50	12/94	82c
Gas, reg unlead, taxes inc., cash, self-service	gal	1.01	12/94	2c
Gasoline and motor oil purchased	year	1037	91	81c
Gasoline and motor oil purchased	year	1000	91	81r
Gasoline, unleaded midgrade	gallon	1.12	4/93	82c
Gasoline, unleaded midgrade	gallon	1.15	4/93	82r
Gasoline, unleaded premium	gallon	1.18	4/93	82c
Gasoline, unleaded premium	gallon	1.23	4/93	82r
Gasoline, unleaded regular	gallon	0.97	4/93	82c
Gasoline, unleaded regular	gallon	1.07	4/93	82r
Entertainment				
Bowling, evening rate	game	2.04	12/94	2c

Values are in dollars or fractions of dollars. In the column headed *Ref*, references are shown to sources. Each reference is followed by a letter. These refer to the geographical level for which data were reported: s = State, r = Region, and c = City or metro. The abbreviation *ex* is used to mean *except* or *excluding*; *exp* stands for expenditures. For other abbreviations and further explanations, please see the Introduction.

Saint Louis, MO - continued

Item	Per	Value	Date	Ref.
Entertainment				
Entertainment supplies, equipment, and services, misc. expenditures	year	810	91	81c
Entertainment, total expenditures	year	1935	91	81c
Entertainment, total expenditures	year	1356	91	81r
Fees and admissions, expenditures	year	405	91	81c
Fees and admissions, expenditures	year	347	91	81r
Monopoly game, Parker Brothers', No. 9	game	10.10	12/94	2c
Movie	adm	5.85	12/94	2c
Pets, toys, playground equipment, expenditures	year	280	91	81c
Pets, toys, playground equipment, expenditures	year	270	91	81r
Reading, expenditures	year	156	91	81c
Reading, expenditures	year	160	91	81r
Televisions, radios, and sound equipment, expenditures	year	441	91	81c
Televisions, radios, and sound equipment, expenditures	year	433	91	81r
Tennis balls, yellow, Wilson or Penn, 3	can	2.11	12/94	2c
Funerals				
Burial, immediate, container provided by funeral home		1348.78	1/95	54r
Cards, acknowledgment		21.20	1/95	54r
Casket, minimum alternative		182.83	1/95	54r
Cosmetology, hair care, etc.		133.11	1/95	54r
Cremation, direct, container provided by funeral home		1101.95	1/95	54r
Embalming		314.45	1/95	54r
Funeral, funeral home		304.88	1/95	54r
Funeral, other facility		301.37	1/95	54r
Graveside service		290.59	1/95	54r
Hearse, local		137.37	1/95	54r
Limousine, local		82.84	1/95	54r
Memorial service		316.57	1/95	54r
Service charge, professional, nondeclinable		1099.00	1/95	54r
Visitation and viewing		209.25	1/95	54r
Groceries				
Groceries, ACCRA Index		102.60	12/94	2c
Apples, Red Delicious	lb.	0.68	12/94	82r
Baby food, strained vegetables, lowest price	4-4.5 oz.	0.35	12/94	2c
Bacon, sliced	lb.	1.88	12/94	82r
Bananas	lb.	0.52	12/94	2c
Bananas	lb.	0.41	12/94	82r
Beef or hamburger, ground	lb.	1.45	12/94	2c
Beef purchases	year	159	91	81c
Beef purchases	year	197	91	81r
Beef, stew, boneless	lb.	2.52	12/94	82r
Beverage purchases, alcoholic	year	267	91	81c
Beverage purchases, alcoholic	year	293	91	81r
Beverage purchases, nonalcoholic	year	181	91	81c
Beverage purchases, nonalcoholic	year	203	91	81r
Bologna, all beef or mixed	lb.	2.12	12/94	82r
Bread, white	24-oz.	0.83	12/94	2c
Bread, white, pan	lb.	0.76	12/94	82r
Cabbage	lb.	0.44	12/94	82r
Carrots, short trimmed and topped	lb.	0.44	12/94	82r
Cereals and bakery products purchases	year	362	91	81c
Cereals and bakery products purchases	year	347	91	81r
Cereals and cereal products purchases	year	124	91	81c
Cereals and cereals products purchases	year	119	91	81r
Cheddar cheese, natural	lb.	3.28	12/94	82r
Cheese, Kraft grated Parmesan	8-oz.	3.31	12/94	2c
Chicken breast, bone-in	lb.	1.61	12/94	82r
Chicken, fresh, whole	lb.	0.89	12/94	82r
Chicken, whole fryer	lb.	0.69	12/94	2c
Chuck roast, USDA choice, boneless	lb.	2.33	12/94	82r
Cigarettes, Winston, Kings	carton	15.31	12/94	2c
Coffee, 100%, ground roast, all sizes	lb.	4.28	12/94	82r
Coffee, vacuum-packed	13 oz.	3.70	12/94	2c
Cookies, chocolate chip	lb.	2.72	12/94	82r

Saint Louis, MO - continued

Item	Per	Value	Date	Ref.
Groceries - continued				
Corn Flakes, Kellogg's or Post Toasties	18 oz.	2.41	12/94	2c
Corn, frozen, whole kernel, lowest price	10 oz.	0.68	12/94	2c
Dairy products (other) purchases	year	150	91	81c
Dairy products (other) purchases	year	148	91	81r
Eggs, Grade A large	dozen	0.82	12/94	2c
Eggs, Grade A large	dozen	0.76	12/94	82r
Fish and seafood purchases	year	59	91	81c
Fish and seafood purchases	year	61	91	81r
Flour, white, all purpose	lb.	0.22	12/94	82r
Food purchases, food eaten at home	year	2233	91	81c
Food purchases, food eaten at home	year	2313	91	81r
Foods purchased away from home, not prepared by consumer	year	1459	91	81c
Foods purchased away from home, not prepared by consumer	year	1709	91	81r
Fruits and vegetables purchases	year	324	91	81c
Fruits and vegetables purchases	year	372	91	81r
Grapefruit	lb.	0.47	12/94	82r
Grapes, Thompson seedless	lb.	2.15	12/94	82r
Ground beef, 100% beef	lb.	1.37	12/94	82r
Ground chuck, 100% beef	lb.	1.81	12/94	82r
Ham, boneless, exc. canned	lb.	2.16	12/94	82r
Ice cream, prepackaged, bulk, regular	1/2 gal.	2.48	12/94	82r
Lemons	lb.	1.08	12/94	82r
Lettuce, iceberg	lb.	0.81	12/94	82r
Lettuce, iceberg	head	0.84	12/94	2c
Margarine, Blue Bonnet or Parkay cubes	lb.	0.72	12/94	2c
Margarine, stick	lb.	0.81	12/94	82r
Meats, poultry, fish, and eggs purchases	year	547	91	81c
Meats, poultry, fish, and eggs purchases	year	591	91	81r
Milk and cream (fresh) purchases	year	123	91	81c
Milk and cream (fresh) purchases	year	132	91	81r
Milk, whole	1/2 gal.	1.60	12/94	2c
Orange juice, frozen concentrate 12-oz. can	16 oz.	1.41	12/94	82r
Orange juice, Minute Maid frozen	12-oz.	1.30	12/94	2c
Oranges, Navel	lb.	0.56	12/94	82r
Peaches, halves or slices, Hunt's, Del Monte, or Libby's	29-oz.	1.32	12/94	2c
Peanut butter, creamy, all sizes	lb.	1.81	12/94	82r
Peas, sweet, Del Monte or Green Giant	15-17 oz.	0.58	12/94	2c
Pork chops, center cut, bone-in	lb.	2.76	12/94	82r
Pork purchases	year	131	91	81c
Pork purchases	year	130	91	81r
Potato chips	16-oz.	2.81	12/94	82r
Potatoes, frozen, French fried	lb.	0.83	12/94	82r
Potatoes, white	lb.	0.28	12/94	82r
Potatoes, white or red	10-lb. sack	1.97	12/94	2c
Round roast, USDA choice, boneless	lb.	2.90	12/94	82r
Sausage, Jimmy Dean, 100% pork	lb.	2.50	12/94	2c
Shortening, vegetable oil blends	lb.	0.88	12/94	82r
Shortening, vegetable, Crisco	3-lb.	2.69	12/94	2c
Soft drink, Coca Cola, ex deposit	2 lit	0.97	12/94	2c
Spaghetti and macaroni	lb.	0.78	12/94	82r
Steak, rib eye, USDA choice, boneless	lb.	6.15	12/94	82r
Steak, round, graded & ungraded, exc. USDA prime & choice	lb.	2.72	12/94	82r
Steak, round, USDA choice, boneless	lb.	3.02	12/94	82r
Steak, sirloin, USDA choice, boneless	lb.	3.85	12/94	82r
Steak, t-bone	lb.	5.50	12/94	2c
Steak, T-bone, USDA choice, bone-in	lb.	5.38	12/94	82r
Sugar and other sweets, eaten at home, expenditures	year	91	91	81r
Sugar and other sweets, eaten at home, purchases	year	85	91	81c
Sugar, cane or beet	4 lbs.	1.41	12/94	2c
Sugar, white, all sizes	lb.	0.36	12/94	82r
Tobacco products and smoking supplies, total expenditures	year	274	91	81c

Values are in dollars or fractions of dollars. In the column headed *Ref*, references are shown to sources. Each reference is followed by a letter. These refer to the geographical level for which data were reported: s = State, r = Region, and c = City or metro. The abbreviation *ex* is used to mean *except* or *excluding*; *exp* stands for *expenditures*. For other abbreviations and further explanations, please see the Introduction.

Saint Louis, MO

American Cost of Living Survey, 2nd Edition

Saint Louis, MO - continued

Item	Per	Value	Date	Ref.
Groceries				
Tobacco products and smoking supplies, total expenditures	year	298	91	81r
Tomatoes, field grown	lb.	1.36	12/94	82r
Tomatoes, Hunt's or Del Monte	14.5 oz.	0.72	12/94	2c
Tuna, chunk, light	lb.	1.94	12/94	82r
Tuna, chunk, light, oil-packed	6.125-6.5 oz.	0.79	12/94	2c
Turkey, frozen, whole	lb.	0.96	12/94	82r
Yogurt, natural, fruit flavored	8 oz.	0.62	12/94	82r
Goods and Services				
Miscellaneous goods and services, ACCRA Index		96.10	12/94	2c
Health Care				
Health care, ACCRA Index		109.30	12/94	2c
Antibiotic ointment, Polysporin	1.5 oz.	4.43	12/94	2c
Childbirth, Cesarean delivery, hospital charge	birth	5101.00	12/91	69r
Childbirth, Cesarean delivery, physician charge	birth	2234.00	12/91	69r
Childbirth, normal delivery, hospital charge	birth	2891.00	12/91	69r
Childbirth, normal delivery, physician charge	birth	1623.00	12/91	69r
Dentist's fee, adult teeth cleaning and periodic oral exam	visit	52.50	12/94	2c
Doctor visit, routine	visit	15.00-110.00	1/94	88c
Doctor's fee, routine exam, established patient	visit	48.70	12/94	2c
Drugs, expenditures	year	260	91	81c
Drugs, expenditures	year	248	91	81r
Health care, total expenditures	year	1416	91	81c
Health care, total expenditures	year	1336	91	81r
Health insurance expenditures	year	695	91	81c
Health insurance expenditures	year	550	91	81r
Hospital care, semiprivate room	day	408.00	12/94	2c
Insurance premium, family medical care	month	390.73	1/95	41s
Medical services expenditures	year	380	91	81c
Medical services expenditures	year	457	91	81r
Medical supplies expenditures	year	82	91	81c
Medical supplies expenditures	year	82	91	81r
Household Goods				
Appl. repair, service call, wash mach	min. lab. chg.	30.18	12/94	2c
Floor coverings, expenditures	year	98	91	81c
Floor coverings, expenditures	year	105	91	81r
Furniture, expenditures	year	303	91	81c
Furniture, expenditures	year	291	91	81r
Household equipment, misc. expenditures	year	341	91	81r
Household equipment, misc. expenditures	year	412	91	81c
Household expenditures, miscellaneous	year	181	91	81c
Household expenditures, miscellaneous	year	162	91	81r
Household furnishings and equipment, expenditures	year	1219	91	81c
Household furnishings and equipment, expenditures	year	1042	91	81r
Household operations expenditures	year	441	91	81c
Household operations expenditures	year	365	91	81r
Household textiles, expenditures	year	101	91	81c
Household textiles, expenditures	year	101	91	81r
Housekeeping supplies, expenditures	year	330	91	81c
Housekeeping supplies, expenditures	year	390	91	81r
Laundry and cleaning supplies, expenditures	year	91	91	81c
Laundry and cleaning supplies, expenditures	year	110	91	81r
Laundry detergent, Tide Ultra, Bold, or Cheer	42 oz.	3.37	12/94	2c
Postage and stationery, expenditures	year	116	91	81c
Postage and stationery, expenditures	year	115	91	81r
Tissues, facial, Kleenex brand	175	1.09	12/94	2c

Saint Louis, MO - continued

Item	Per	Value	Date	Ref.
Housing				
Housing, ACCRA Index		93.50	12/94	2c
Add garage/carport		8,479	3/95	74r
Add room(s)		21,347	3/95	74r
Apartment condominium or co-op, median	unit	87100	12/94	62r
Bathroom addition, average cost	add	9734.00	3/95	13r
Bathroom remodeling, average cost	remod	6414.00	3/95	13r
Bedroom, master suite addition, average cost	add	27122.00	3/95	13r
Car rental	day	64.00	5/95	95c
Deck addition, average cost	add	6665.00	3/95	13r
Dwellings (owned), expenditures	year	2841	91	81c
Dwellings (owned), expenditures	year	2566	91	81r
Enclose porch/patio/breezeway		4,556	3/95	74r
Exterior remodeling, average cost	remod	15395.00	3/95	13r
Family room addition, average cost	add	27658.00	3/95	13r
Finish room in basement/attic		5,074	3/95	74r
Home, existing, single-family, median	unit	106500	12/94	62r
Home, existing, single-family, median	unit	82.90	12/94	62c
Home, purchase price	unit	133.80	3/93	26c
Home, single family, median	home	100,000	4/94	11c
Hotel room	day	103.00	5/95	95c
House payment, principal and interest, 25% down payment	mo.	675	12/94	2c
House, 1800 sq ft, 8000 sq ft lot, new, urban, utilities	total	111500	12/94	2c
Kitchen remodeling, major, average cost	remod	17084.00	3/95	13r
Kitchen remodeling, minor, average cost	remod	5804.00	3/95	13r
Maintenance, repairs, insurance, and other housing expenditures	year	496	91	81c
Maintenance, repairs, insurance, and other housing expenditures	year	484	91	81r
Mortgage interest and charges expenditures	year	1798	91	81c
Mortgage interest and charges expenditures	year	1443	91	81r
Mtge. rate, incl. points and orig. fee, 30-year conv. fixed or ARM	mo.	9.03	12/94	2c
Office, home addition, average cost	add	8121.00	3/95	13r
Princ. & int., mortgage, median-price exist. sing.-family home	mo.	515	12/94	62r
Property taxes expenditures	year	547	91	81c
Property taxes expenditures	year	639	91	81r
Redesign, restructure more than half of home's interior		9,114	3/95	74r
Rent, apartment, 2 br., 1 1/2-2 baths, unfurnished, 950 sq ft, water	mo.	611	12/94	2c
Rental units expenditures	year	1171	900/00/91	81c
Rental units expenditures	year	1200	91	81r
Sun-space addition, average cost	add	23768.00	3/95	13r
Wing addition, two-story, average cost	add	50410.00	3/95	13r
Insurance and Pensions				
Auto insurance, private passenger	year	600.64	12/94	71s
Insurance and pensions, personal, expenditures	year	2710	91	81c
Insurance and pensions, personal, expenditures	year	2408	91	81r
Insurance, life and other personal, expenditures	year	333	91	81c
Insurance, life and other personal, expenditures	year	355	91	81r
Pensions and Social Security, expenditures	year	2377	91	81c
Pensions and Social Security, expenditures	year	2053	91	81r
Legal Assistance				
Legal work, law firm associate	hour	90		10r
Legal work, law firm partner	hour	139		10r
Personal Goods				
Personal care products and services, total expenditures	year	333	91	81c
Shampoo, Alberto VO5	15-oz.	1.12	12/94	2c
Toothpaste, Crest or Colgate	6-7 oz.	1.65	12/94	2c

Values are in dollars or fractions of dollars. In the column headed *Ref*, references are shown to sources. Each reference is followed by a letter. These refer to the geographical level for which data were reported: s = State, r = Region, and c = City or metro. The abbreviation *ex* is used to mean *except* or *excluding*; *exp* stands for *expenditures*. For other abbreviations and further explanations, please see the Introduction.

Saint Louis, MO - continued

Item	Per	Value	Date	Ref.
Personal Services				
Dry cleaning, man's 2-pc. suit		6.64	12/94	2c
Haircut, man's barbershop, no styling		10.40	12/94	2c
Haircut, woman's shampoo, trim, blow-dry		21.75	12/94	2c
Personal services expenditures	year	260	91	81c
Personal services expenditures	year	203	91	81r
Restaurant Food				
Chicken, fried, thigh and drumstick		2.12	12/94	2c
Dining expenditures, family	week	30.03	94	73r
Hamburger with cheese	1/4 lb.	1.93	12/94	2c
Pizza, Pizza Hut or Pizza Inn	12-13 in.	7.73	12/94	2c
Taxes				
Taxes, Federal income, expenditures	year	1818	91	81c
Taxes, Federal income, expenditures	year	1756	91	81r
Taxes, personal, expenditures	year	2710	91	81c
Taxes, personal, expenditures	year	2426	91	81r
Taxes, State and local income, expenditures	year	509	91	81c
Taxes, State and local income, expenditures	year	568	91	81r
Transportation				
Transportation, ACCRA Index		93.60	12/94	2c
Bus fare, one-way	trip	1.00	12/95	1c
Bus fare, up to 10 miles	one-way	1.00	12/94	2c
Cars and trucks purchased, new	year	689	91	81c
Cars and trucks purchased, new	year	891	91	81r
Cars and trucks purchased, used	year	980	91	81c
Cars and trucks purchased, used	year	1155	91	81r
Driver's learning permit fee	perm	1.00	1/94	84s
Driver's license fee	orig	7.50	1/94	84s
Driver's license fee, duplicate	lic	7.50	1/94	84s
Driver's license reinstatement fee, min.	susp	20.00	1/94	85s
Driver's license renewal fee	renew	7.50	1/94	84s
Fine, illegal parking, handicapped zone	event	50.00	12/93	87c
Identification card, nondriver	card	7.50	1/94	83s
Motorcycle license fee	orig	7.50	1/94	84s
Motorcycle license fee, duplicate	lic	7.50	1/94	84s
Motorcycle license renewal fee	renew	7.50	1/94	84s
Public transportation expenditures	year	266	91	81c
Public transportation expenditures	year	209	91	81r
Railway fare, light rail, one-way	trip	1.00	12/95	1c
Tire balance, computer or spin bal., front	wheel	6.45	12/94	2c
Transportation expenditures, total	year	4822	91	81c
Transportation expenditures, total	year	4792	91	81r
Vehicle expenses, miscellaneous	year	1823	91	81c
Vehicle finance charges	year	315	91	81c
Vehicle finance charges	year	300	91	81r
Vehicle insurance expenditures	year	579	91	81c
Vehicle insurance expenditures	year	485	91	81r
Vehicle maintenance and repairs expenditures	year	770	91	81c
Vehicle maintenance and repairs expenditures	year	534	91	81r
Vehicle purchases	year	1696	91	81c
Vehicle purchases	year	2068	91	81r
Vehicle rental, leases, licenses, etc. expenditures	year	160	91	81c
Vehicle rental, leases, licenses, etc. expenditures	year	197	91	81r
Vehicles purchased, other than cars and trucks	year	27	91	81c
Vehicles purchased, other than cars and trucks	year	22	91	81r
Utilities				
Utilities, ACCRA Index		105.90	12/94	2c
Electricity	KWh	0.07	12/94	82c
Electricity expenditures	year	972	91	81c
Electricity expenditures	year	668	91	81r
Electricity, (part.), other, 1800 sq. ft., new home	mo.	67.13	12/94	2c
Electricity, summer, 250 KWh	month	28.27	8/93	64c

Saint Louis, MO - continued

Item	Per	Value	Date	Ref.
Utilities - continued				
Electricity, summer, 500 KWh	month	50.49	8/93	64c
Electricity, summer, 750 KWh	month	72.70	8/93	64c
Electricity, summer, 1000 KWh	month	94.92	8/93	64c
Utilities, fuels, and public services, total expenditures	year	2228	91	81c
Utilities, fuels, and public services, total expenditures	year	1838	91	81r
Water and other public services, expenditures	year	251	91	81c
Water and other public services, expenditures	year	167	91	81r
Weddings				
Bridal attendants' gowns	event	750	10/93	76r
Bridal gown	event	852	10/93	76r
Bridal headpiece and veil	event	167	10/93	76r
Bride's wedding band	event	708	10/93	76r
Clergy	event	224	10/93	76r
Engagement ring	event	2756	10/93	76r
Flowers	event	863	10/93	76r
Formal wear for groom	event	106	10/93	76r
Groom's attendants' formal wear	event	530	10/93	76r
Groom's wedding band	event	402	10/93	76r
Music	event	600	10/93	76r
Photography	event	1088	10/93	76r
Shoes for bride	event	50	10/93	76r
Videography	event	483	10/93	76r
Wedding invitations and announcements	event	342	10/93	76r
Wedding reception	event	7000	10/93	76r

Salem, OR

Item	Per	Value	Date	Ref.
Composite, ACCRA index		103.20	12/94	2c
Alcoholic Beverages				
Beer, Miller Lite, Bud, 12-oz., ex deposit	6	3.94	12/94	2c
J & B Scotch	750-ml.	20.95	12/94	2c
Wine, Gallo Chablis blanc	1.5-lit	4.26	12/94	2c
Appliances				
Appliances (major), expenditures	year	160	91	81r
Average annual exp.				
Food, health care, personal goods, services	year	32461	91	81r
Charity				
Cash contributions, expenditures	year	975	91	81r
Clothing				
Apparel, men and boys, total expenditures	year	467	91	81r
Apparel, women and girls, total expenditures	year	737	91	81r
Footwear, expenditures	year	270	91	81r
Jeans, man's denim		33.55	12/94	2c
Shirt, man's dress shirt		31.19	12/94	2c
Undervest, boy's size 10-14, cotton	3	4.13	12/94	2c
Communications				
Long-distance telephone rate, day, addl. min., 1-10 mi.	min.	0.10	12/93	9s
Long-distance telephone rate, day, initial min., 1-10 mi.	min.	0.13	12/93	9s
Newspaper subscription, dly. and Sun. delivery	month	11.50	12/94	2c
Phone line, single, business, field visit	inst	31.00	12/93	9s
Phone line, single, business, no field visit	inst	31.00	12/93	9s
Phone line, single, residence, field visit	inst	12.00	12/93	9s
Phone line, single, residence, no field visit	inst	12.00	12/93	9s
Telephone bill, family of four	month	18.53	12/94	2c
Telephone service, expenditures	year	611	91	81r
Education				
Board, 4-year private college/university	year	2338	8/94	80s
Board, 4-year public college/university	year	2211	8/94	80s
Education, total expenditures	year	375	91	81r

Values are in dollars or fractions of dollars. In the column headed *Ref*, references are shown to sources. Each reference is followed by a letter. These refer to the geographical level for which data were reported: s = State, r = Region, and c = City or metro. The abbreviation *ex* is used to mean *except* or *excluding*; *exp* stands for expenditures. For other abbreviations and further explanations, please see the Introduction.

Salem, OR - continued

Item	Per	Value	Date	Ref.
Education				
Room, 4-year private college/university	year	1959	8/94	80s
Room, 4-year public college/university	year	1604	8/94	80s
Total cost, 4-year private college/university	year	16622	8/94	80s
Total cost, 4-year public college/university	year	6648	8/94	80s
Tuition, 2-year public college/university, in-state	year	1186	8/94	80s
Tuition, 4-year private college/university, in-state	year	12325	8/94	80s
Tuition, 4-year public college/university, in-state	year	2833	8/94	80s
Energy and Fuels				
Energy, combined forms, 1800 sq. ft.	mo.	94.78	12/94	2c
Fuel oil and other fuels, expenditures	year	33	91	81r
Gas, natural, expenditures	year	212	91	81r
Gas, reg unlead, taxes inc., cash, self-service	gal	1.30	12/94	2c
Gasoline and motor oil purchased	year	1115	91	81r
Gasoline, unleaded midgrade	gallon	1.36	4/93	82r
Gasoline, unleaded premium	gallon	1.43	4/93	82r
Gasoline, unleaded regular	gallon	1.23	4/93	82r
Entertainment				
Bowling, evening rate	game	2.08	12/94	2c
Concert ticket, Pearl Jam group	perf	20.00	94	50r
Entertainment, total expenditures	year	1853	91	81r
Fees and admissions, expenditures	year	482	91	81r
Monopoly game, Parker Brothers', No. 9	game	10.07	12/94	2c
Movie	adm	6.00	12/94	2c
Pets, toys, playground equipment, expenditures	year	299	91	81r
Reading, expenditures	year	164	91	81r
Televisions, radios, and sound equipment, expenditures	year	528	91	81r
Tennis balls, yellow, Wilson or Penn, 3	can	2.31	12/94	2c
Funerals				
Burial, immediate, container provided by funeral home		1382.70	1/95	54r
Cards, acknowledgment		21.87	1/95	54r
Casket, minimum alternative		128.54	1/95	54r
Cosmetology, hair care, etc.		119.69	1/95	54r
Cremation, direct, container provided by funeral home		1030.62	1/95	54r
Embalming		255.42	1/95	54r
Funeral, funeral home		437.38	1/95	54r
Funeral, other facility		444.46	1/95	54r
Graveside service		338.46	1/95	54r
Hearse, local		147.50	1/95	54r
Limousine, local		130.33	1/95	54r
Memorial service		553.16	1/95	54r
Service charge, professional, nondeclinable		859.15	1/95	54r
Visitation and viewing		93.23	1/95	54r
Groceries				
Groceries, ACCRA Index		92.50	12/94	2c
Apples, Red Delicious	lb.	0.72	12/94	82r
Baby food, strained vegetables, lowest price	4-4.5 oz.	0.16	12/94	2c
Bacon, sliced	lb.	1.73	12/94	82r
Bananas	lb.	0.48	12/94	2c
Bananas	lb.	0.52	12/94	82r
Beef or hamburger, ground	lb.	1.47	12/94	2c
Beef purchases	year	241	91	81r
Beverage purchases, alcoholic	year	328	91	81r
Beverage purchases, nonalcoholic	year	234	91	81r
Bologna, all beef or mixed	lb.	2.33	12/94	82r
Bread, white	24-oz.	0.53	12/94	2c
Bread, white, pan	lb.	0.81	12/94	82r
Carrots, short trimmed and topped	lb.	0.43	12/94	82r
Cereals and bakery products purchases	year	392	91	81r
Cereals and cereals products purchases	year	139	91	81r
Cheese, Kraft grated Parmesan	8-oz.	3.41	12/94	2c
Chicken breast, bone-in	lb.	2.04	12/94	82r

Salem, OR - continued

Item	Per	Value	Date	Ref.
Groceries - continued				
Chicken, fresh, whole	lb.	0.95	12/94	82r
Chicken, whole fryer	lb.	0.90	12/94	2c
Cigarettes, Winston, Kings	carton	16.71	12/94	2c
Coffee, 100%, ground roast, all sizes	lb.	4.48	12/94	82r
Coffee, vacuum-packed	13 oz.	3.68	12/94	2c
Corn Flakes, Kellogg's or Post Toasties	18 oz.	1.54	12/94	2c
Corn, frozen, whole kernel, lowest price	10 oz.	0.74	12/94	2c
Dairy products (other) purchases	year	182	91	81r
Eggs, Grade A large	dozen	0.74	12/94	2c
Fish and seafood purchases	year	94	91	81r
Flour, white, all purpose	lb.	0.21	12/94	82r
Food purchases, food eaten at home	year	2749	91	81r
Foods purchased away from home, not prepared by consumer	year	1909	91	81r
Fruits and vegetables purchases	year	459	91	81r
Grapefruit	lb.	0.56	12/94	82r
Ground beef, 100% beef	lb.	1.31	12/94	82r
Ham, boneless, exc. canned	lb.	2.46	12/94	82r
Ice cream, prepackaged, bulk, regular	1/2 gal.	2.57	12/94	82r
Lemons	lb.	1.00	12/94	82r
Lettuce, iceberg	lb.	0.93	12/94	82r
Lettuce, iceberg	head	0.86	12/94	2c
Margarine, Blue Bonnet or Parkay cubes	lb.	0.54	12/94	2c
Meats, poultry, fish, and eggs purchases	year	700	91	81r
Milk and cream (fresh) purchases	year	155	91	81r
Milk, whole	1/2 gal.	1.37	12/94	2c
Orange juice, frozen concentrate 12-oz. can	16 oz.	1.52	12/94	82r
Orange juice, Minute Maid frozen	12-oz.	1.14	12/94	2c
Oranges, Navel	lb.	0.56	12/94	82r
Peaches, halves or slices, Hunt's, Del Monte, or Libby's	29-oz.	1.38	12/94	2c
Peas, sweet, Del Monte or Green Giant	15-17 oz.	0.60	12/94	2c
Pork chops, center cut, bone-in	lb.	3.30	12/94	82r
Pork purchases	year	122	91	81r
Potato chips	16-oz.	3.03	12/94	82r
Potatoes, frozen, French fried	lb.	0.77	12/94	82r
Potatoes, white	lb.	0.35	12/94	82r
Potatoes, white or red	10-lb. sack	1.42	12/94	2c
Rice, white, long grain, uncooked	lb.	0.54	12/94	82r
Round roast, USDA choice, boneless	lb.	2.92	12/94	82r
Sausage, Jimmy Dean, 100% pork	lb.	3.34	12/94	2c
Shortening, vegetable oil blends	lb.	0.80	12/94	82r
Shortening, vegetable, Crisco	3-lb.	1.89	12/94	2c
Soft drink, Coca Cola, ex deposit	2 lit	1.24	12/94	2c
Spaghetti and macaroni	lb.	1.02	12/94	82r
Steak, round, graded & ungraded, exc. USDA prime & choice	lb.	3.13	12/94	82r
Steak, sirloin, USDA choice, boneless	lb.	4.07	12/94	82r
Steak, t-bone	lb.	4.81	12/94	2c
Sugar and other sweets, eaten at home, expenditures	year	105	91	81r
Sugar, cane or beet	4 lbs.	0.98	12/94	2c
Sugar, white, all sizes	lb.	0.38	12/94	82r
Tobacco products and smoking supplies, total expenditures	year	221	91	81r
Tomatoes, field grown	lb.	1.45	12/94	82r
Tomatoes, Hunt's or Del Monte	14.5 oz.	0.79	12/94	2c
Tuna, chunk, light	lb.	2.18	12/94	82r
Tuna, chunk, light, oil-packed	6.125-6.5 oz.	0.72	12/94	2c
Goods and Services				
Miscellaneous goods and services, ACCRA Index		104.80	12/94	2c
Health Care				
Health care, ACCRA Index		116.40	12/94	2c
Antibiotic ointment, Polysporin	1.5 oz.	3.92	12/94	2c

Values are in dollars or fractions of dollars. In the column headed *Ref*, references are shown to sources. Each reference is followed by a letter. These refer to the geographical level for which data were reported: s=State, r=Region, and c=City or metro. The abbreviation *ex* is used to mean *except* or *excluding*; *exp* stands for expenditures. For other abbreviations and further explanations, please see the Introduction.

Salem, OR - continued

Item	Per	Value	Date	Ref.
Health Care				
Childbirth, Cesarean delivery, hospital charge	birth	6059.00	12/91	69r
Childbirth, Cesarean delivery, physician charge	birth	2248.00	12/91	69r
Childbirth, normal delivery, hospital charge	birth	3006.00	12/91	69r
Childbirth, normal delivery, physician charge	birth	1634.00	12/91	69r
Dentist's fee, adult teeth cleaning and periodic oral exam	visit	75.80	12/94	2c
Doctor's fee, routine exam, established patient	visit	44.55	12/94	2c
Drugs, expenditures	year	230	91	81r
Health care, total expenditures	year	1544	91	81r
Health insurance expenditures	year	558	91	81r
Hospital care, semiprivate room	day	340.00	12/94	2c
Insurance premium, family medical care	month	331.06	1/95	41s
Medical services expenditures	year	676	91	81r
Medical supplies expenditures	year	80	91	81r
Surgery, open-heart	proc	37818.00	1/93	14r
Household Goods				
Appl. repair, service call, wash mach	min. lab. chg.	34.48	12/94	2c
Floor coverings, expenditures	year	79	91	81r
Furniture, expenditures	year	352	91	81r
Household equipment, misc. expenditures	year	614	91	81r
Household expenditures, miscellaneous	year	294	91	81r
Household furnishings and equipment, expenditures	year	1416	91	81r
Household operations expenditures	year	580	91	81r
Household textiles, expenditures	year	113	91	81r
Housekeeping supplies, expenditures	year	447	91	81r
Laundry and cleaning supplies, expenditures	year	114	91	81r
Laundry detergent, Tide Ultra, Bold, or Cheer	42 oz.	3.69	12/94	2c
Postage and stationery, expenditures	year	145	91	81r
Tissues, facial, Kleenex brand	175	1.10	12/94	2c
Housing				
Housing, ACCRA Index		108.10	12/94	2c
Add garage/carport		6,422	3/95	74r
Add room(s)		26,583	3/95	74r
Apartment condominium or co-op, median	unit	105300	12/94	62r
Dwellings (owned), expenditures	year	3932	91	81r
Enclose porch/patio/breezeway		5,382	3/95	74r
Finish room in basement/attic		3,911	3/95	74r
Home, existing, single-family, median	unit	178600	12/94	62r
House payment, principal and interest, 25% down payment	mo.	854	12/94	2c
House, 1800 sq ft, 8000 sq ft lot, new, urban, utilities	total	138000	12/94	2c
Maintenance, repairs, insurance, and other housing expenditures	year	591	91	81r
Mortgage interest and charges expenditures	year	2747	91	81r
Mtge. rate, incl. points and orig. fee, 30-year conv. fixed or ARM	mo.	9.32	12/94	2c
Princ. & int., mortgage, median-price exist. sing.-family home	mo.	845	12/94	62r
Property taxes expenditures	year	594	91	81r
Redesign, restructure more than half of home's interior		5,467	3/95	74r
Rent, apartment, 2 br., 1 1/2-2 baths, unfurnished, 950 sq ft, water	mo.	495	12/94	2c
Rental units expenditures	year	2077	91	81r
Insurance and Pensions				
Auto insurance, private passenger	year	632.21	12/94	71s
Insurance and pensions, personal, expenditures	year	3042	91	81r
Insurance, life and other personal, expenditures	year	298	91	81r
Pensions and Social Security, expenditures	year	2744	91	81r

Salem, OR - continued

Item	Per	Value	Date	Ref.
Legal Assistance				
Legal work, law firm associate	hour	91		10r
Legal work, law firm partner	hour	151		10r
Personal Goods				
Shampoo, Alberto VO5	15-oz.	1.02	12/94	2c
Toothpaste, Crest or Colgate	6-7 oz.	2.05	12/94	2c
Personal Services				
Dry cleaning, man's 2-pc. suit		7.69	12/94	2c
Haircut, man's barbershop, no styling		8.30	12/94	2c
Haircut, woman's shampoo, trim, blow-dry		22.00	12/94	2c
Personal services expenditures	year	286	91	81r
Restaurant Food				
Chicken, fried, thigh and drumstick		2.74	12/94	2c
Dining expenditures, family	week	32.25	94	73r
Hamburger with cheese	1/4 lb.	1.82	12/94	2c
Pizza, Pizza Hut or Pizza Inn	12-13 in.	8.90	12/94	2c
Taxes				
Taxes, Federal income, expenditures	year	2946	91	81r
Taxes, personal, expenditures	year	3791	91	81r
Taxes, State and local income, expenditures	year	791	91	81r
Transportation				
Transportation, ACCRA Index		108.10	12/94	2c
Bus fare, one-way	trip	0.50	12/95	1c
Cars and trucks purchased, new	year	1231	91	81r
Cars and trucks purchased, used	year	915	91	81r
Driver's learning permit fee	perm	13.00	1/94	84s
Driver's license fee	orig	26.25	1/94	84s
Driver's license fee, duplicate	lic	11.00	1/94	84s
Driver's license reinstatement fee, min.	susp	53.00	1/94	85s
Driver's license renewal fee	renew	16.25	1/94	84s
Identification card, nondriver	card	13.00	1/94	83s
Motorcycle learning permit fee	perm	13.00	1/94	84s
Motorcycle license fee	orig	30.00	1/94	84s
Motorcycle license fee, duplicate	lic	11.00	1/94	84s
Motorcycle license renewal fee	renew	7.00	1/94	84s
Public transportation expenditures	year	375	91	81r
Tire balance, computer or spin bal., front	wheel	6.65	12/94	2c
Transportation expenditures, total	year	5527	91	81r
Vehicle finance charges	year	287	91	81r
Vehicle insurance expenditures	year	624	91	81r
Vehicle maintenance and repairs expenditures	year	695	91	81r
Vehicle purchases	year	2174	91	81r
Vehicle rental, leases, licenses, etc. expenditures	year	257	91	81r
Vehicles purchased, other than cars and trucks	year	28	91	81r
Utilities				
Utilities, ACCRA Index		85.90	12/94	2c
Electricity expenditures	year	616	91	81r
Electricity, 1800 sq. ft., new home	mo.	94.78	12/94	2c
Utilities, fuels, and public services, total expenditures	year	1681	91	81r
Water and other public services, expenditures	year	209	91	81r
Weddings				
Bridal attendants' gowns	event	750	10/93	76r
Bridal gown	event	852	10/93	76r
Bridal headpiece and veil	event	167	10/93	76r
Bride's wedding band	event	708	10/93	76r
Clergy	event	224	10/93	76r
Engagement ring	event	2756	10/93	76r
Flowers	event	863	10/93	76r
Formal wear for groom	event	106	10/93	76r
Groom's attendants' formal wear	event	530	10/93	76r
Groom's wedding band	event	402	10/93	76r
Music	event	600	10/93	76r
Photography	event	1088	10/93	76r

Values are in dollars or fractions of dollars. In the column headed *Ref*, references are shown to sources. Each reference is followed by a letter. These refer to the geographical level for which data were reported: s=State, r=Region, and c=City or metro. The abbreviation *ex* is used to mean *except* or *excluding*; *exp* stands for expenditures. For other abbreviations and further explanations, please see the Introduction.

Salem, OR - continued

Item	Per	Value	Date	Ref.
Weddings				
Shoes for bride	event	50	10/93	76r
Videography	event	483	10/93	76r
Wedding invitations and announcements	event	342	10/93	76r
Wedding reception	event	7000	10/93	76r

Salem-Gloucester, MA

Item	Per	Value	Date	Ref.
Appliances				
Appliances (major), expenditures	year	145	91	81r
Average annual exp.				
Food, health care, personal goods, services	year	29496	91	81r
Charity				
Cash contributions, expenditures	year	708	91	81r
Clothing				
Apparel, men and boys, total expenditures	year	416	91	81r
Apparel, women and girls, total expenditures	year	744	91	81r
Footwear, expenditures	year	305	91	81r
Communications				
Long-distance telephone rate, day, addl. min., 1-10 mi.	min.	0.09	12/93	9s
Long-distance telephone rate, day, initial min., 1-10 mi.	min.	0.19	12/93	9s
Phone line, single, business, field visit	inst	27.50	12/93	9s
Phone line, single, business, no field visit	inst	93.02	12/93	9s
Phone line, single, residence, field visit	inst	27.50	12/93	9s
Phone line, single, residence, no field visit	inst	37.07	12/93	9s
Telephone service, expenditures	year	589	91	81r
Education				
Board, 4-year private college/university	year	3179	8/94	80s
Board, 4-year public college/university	year	2035	8/94	80s
Education, total expenditures	year	593	91	81r
Room, 4-year private college/university	year	3369	8/94	80s
Room, 4-year public college/university	year	2290	8/94	80s
Total cost, 4-year private college/university	year	21346	8/94	80s
Total cost, 4-year public college/university	year	8467	8/94	80s
Tuition, 2-year public college/university, in-state	year	2361	8/94	80s
Tuition, 4-year private college/university, in-state	year	14797	8/94	80s
Tuition, 4-year public college/university, in-state	year	4142	8/94	80s
Energy and Fuels				
Fuel oil and other fuels, expenditures	year	257	91	81r
Gas, natural, expenditures	year	285	91	81r
Gasoline and motor oil purchased	year	867	91	81r
Gasoline, unleaded midgrade	gallon	1.32	4/93	82r
Gasoline, unleaded premium	gallon	1.40	4/93	82r
Gasoline, unleaded regular	gallon	1.19	4/93	82r
Entertainment				
Entertainment, total expenditures	year	1331	91	81r
Fees and admissions, expenditures	year	398	91	81r
Pets, toys, playground equipment, expenditures	year	270	91	81r
Reading, expenditures	year	171	91	81r
Televisions, radios, and sound equipment, expenditures	year	429	91	81r
Funerals				
Burial, immediate, container provided by funeral home		1507.89	1/95	54r
Cards, acknowledgment		18.10	1/95	54r
Casket, minimum alternative		133.03	1/95	54r
Cosmetology, hair care, etc.		114.12	1/95	54r
Cremation, direct, container provided by funeral home		1309.19	1/95	54r
Embalming		320.97	1/95	54r
Funeral, funeral home		327.61	1/95	54r
Funeral, other facility		314.81	1/95	54r

Salem-Gloucester, MA - continued

Item	Per	Value	Date	Ref.
Funerals - continued				
Graveside service		286.11	1/95	54r
Hearse, local		158.95	1/95	54r
Limousine, local		149.45	1/95	54r
Memorial service		315.94	1/95	54r
Service charge, professional, nondeclinable		1148.43	1/95	54r
Visitation and viewing		249.66	1/95	54r
Groceries				
Apples, Red Delicious	lb.	0.78	12/94	82r
Bacon, sliced	lb.	2.24	12/94	82r
Bananas	lb.	0.49	12/94	82r
Beef purchases	year	226	91	81r
Beverage purchases, alcoholic	year	332	91	81r
Beverage purchases, nonalcoholic	year	213	91	81r
Bread, white, pan	lb.	0.80	12/94	82r
Butter, salted, Grade AA, stick	lb.	1.67	12/94	82r
Carrots, short trimmed and topped	lb.	0.51	12/94	82r
Cereals and bakery products purchases	year	407	91	81r
Cereals and cereals products purchases	year	132	91	81r
Chicken breast, bone-in	lb.	2.22	12/94	82r
Chicken, fresh, whole	lb.	1.05	12/94	82r
Chuck roast, USDA choice, boneless	lb.	2.74	12/94	82r
Coffee, 100%, ground roast, all sizes	lb.	4.61	12/94	82r
Dairy products (other) purchases	year	161	91	81r
Eggs, Grade A large	dozen	1.12	12/94	82r
Fish and seafood purchases	year	112	91	81r
Food purchases, food eaten at home	year	2599	91	81r
Foods purchased away from home, not prepared by consumer	year	2024	91	81r
Fruits and vegetables purchases	year	444	91	81r
Grapefruit	lb.	0.44	12/94	82r
Grapes, Thompson seedless	lb.	2.24	12/94	82r
Ground chuck, 100% beef	lb.	1.67	12/94	82r
Ice cream, prepackaged, bulk, regular	1/2 gal.	2.93	12/94	82r
Lemons	lb.	1.06	12/94	82r
Lettuce, iceberg	lb.	0.92	12/94	82r
Meats, poultry, fish, and eggs purchases	year	751	91	81r
Milk and cream (fresh) purchases	year	152	91	81r
Orange juice, frozen concentrate 12-oz. can	16 oz.	1.92	12/94	82r
Oranges, Navel	lb.	0.56	12/94	82r
Pork chops, center cut, bone-in	lb.	3.09	12/94	82r
Pork purchases	year	130	91	81r
Potatoes, white	lb.	0.37	12/94	82r
Rib roast, USDA choice, bone-in	lb.	4.98	12/94	82r
Round roast, USDA choice, boneless	lb.	2.93	12/94	82r
Shortening, vegetable oil blends	lb.	1.03	12/94	82r
Spaghetti and macaroni	lb.	0.84	12/94	82r
Steak, round, USDA choice, boneless	lb.	3.48	12/94	82r
Steak, sirloin, USDA choice, bone-in	lb.	3.38	12/94	82r
Steak, sirloin, USDA choice, boneless	lb.	4.81	12/94	82r
Sugar and other sweets, eaten at home, expenditures	year	89	91	81r
Sugar, white, all sizes	lb.	0.46	12/94	82r
Tobacco products and smoking supplies, total expenditures	year	279	91	81r
Tomatoes, field grown	lb.	1.56	12/94	82r
Tuna, chunk, light	lb.	2.09	12/94	82r
Health Care				
Childbirth, Cesarean delivery, hospital charge	birth	6334.00	12/91	69r
Childbirth, Cesarean delivery, physician charge	birth	2234.00	12/91	69r
Childbirth, normal delivery, hospital charge	birth	3225.00	12/91	69r
Childbirth, normal delivery, physician charge	birth	1623.00	12/91	69r
Drugs, expenditures	year	205	91	81r
Health care, total expenditures	year	1396	91	81r
Health insurance expenditures	year	553	91	81r
Insurance premium, family medical care	month	457.38	1/95	41s
Medical services expenditures	year	559	91	81r
Medical supplies expenditures	year	80	91	81r

Values are in dollars or fractions of dollars. In the column headed *Ref*, references are shown to sources. Each reference is followed by a letter. These refer to the geographical level for which data are reported: s=State, r=Region, and c=City or metro. The abbreviation *ex* is used to mean *except* or *excluding*; *exp* stands for *expenditures*. For other abbreviations and further explanations, please see the Introduction.

Salem-Gloucester, MA - continued

Item	Per	Value	Date	Ref.
Household Goods				
Floor coverings, expenditures	year	158	91	81r
Furniture, expenditures	year	341	91	81r
Household equipment, misc. expenditures	year	363	91	81r
Household expenditures, miscellaneous	year	194	91	81r
Household furnishings and equipment, expenditures	year	1158	91	81r
Household operations expenditures	year	378	91	81r
Household textiles, expenditures	year	88	91	81r
Housekeeping supplies, expenditures	year	426	91	81r
Laundry and cleaning supplies, expenditures	year	122	91	81r
Postage and stationery, expenditures	year	134	91	81r
Housing				
Add garage/carport		11,614	3/95	74r
Add room(s)		16,816	3/95	74r
Apartment condominium or co-op, median	unit	96700	12/94	62r
Dwellings (owned), expenditures	year	3305	91	81r
Enclose porch/patio/breezeway		2,980	3/95	74r
Finish room in basement/attic		4,330	3/95	74r
Home, existing, single-family, median	unit	161600	12/94	62r
Maintenance, repairs, insurance, and other housing expenditures	year	569	91	81r
Mortgage interest and charges expenditures	year	1852	91	81r
Princ. & int., mortgage, median-price exist. sing.-family home	mo.	765	12/94	62r
Property taxes expenditures	year	884	91	81r
Redesign, restructure more than half of home's interior		2,750	3/95	74r
Rental units expenditures	year	1832	91	81r
Insurance and Pensions				
Auto insurance, private passenger	year	1009.56	12/94	71s
Insurance and pensions, personal, expenditures	year	2690	91	81r
Insurance, life and other personal, expenditures	year	341	91	81r
Pensions and Social Security, expenditures	year	2349	91	81r
Legal Assistance				
Estate planning, law-firm partner	hr.	375.00	10/93	12r
Legal work, law firm associate	hour	78		10r
Legal work, law firm partner	hour	183		10r
Personal Services				
Personal services expenditures	year	184	91	81r
Restaurant Food				
Dining expenditures, family	week	34.26	94	73r
Taxes				
Taxes, Federal income, expenditures	year	2409	91	81r
Taxes, personal, expenditures	year	3094	91	81r
Taxes, State and local income, expenditures	year	620	91	81r
Transportation				
Cars and trucks purchased, new	year	1170	91	81r
Cars and trucks purchased, used	year	739	91	81r
Driver's learning permit fee	perm	15.00	1/94	84s
Driver's license fee	orig	50.00	1/94	84s
Driver's license fee, duplicate	lic	15.00	1/94	84s
Driver's license renewal fee	renew	43.75	1/94	84s
Identification card, nondriver	card	15.00	1/94	83s
Motorcycle license fee	orig	50.00	1/94	84s
Motorcycle license fee, duplicate	lic	15.00	1/94	84s
Motorcycle license renewal fee	renew	43.75	1/94	84s
Public transportation expenditures	year	430	91	81r
Transportation expenditures, total	year	4810	91	81r
Vehicle finance charges	year	238	91	81r
Vehicle insurance expenditures	year	630	91	81r
Vehicle maintenance and repairs expenditures	year	532	91	81r
Vehicle purchases	year	1920	91	81r
Vehicle rental, leases, licenses, etc. expenditures	year	193	91	81r

Salem-Gloucester, MA - continued

Item	Per	Value	Date	Ref.
Transportation - continued				
Vehicles purchased, other than cars and trucks	year	11	91	81r
Utilities				
Electricity expenditures	year	695	91	81r
Utilities, fuels, and public services, total expenditures	year	1981	91	81r
Water and other public services, expenditures	year	154	91	81r
Weddings				
Bridal attendants' gowns	event	750	10/93	76r
Bridal gown	event	852	10/93	76r
Bridal headpiece and veil	event	167	10/93	76r
Bride's wedding band	event	708	10/93	76r
Clergy	event	224	10/93	76r
Engagement ring	event	2756	10/93	76r
Flowers	event	863	10/93	76r
Formal wear for groom	event	106	10/93	76r
Groom's attendants' formal wear	event	530	10/93	76r
Groom's wedding band	event	402	10/93	76r
Music	event	600	10/93	76r
Photography	event	1088	10/93	76r
Shoes for bride	event	50	10/93	76r
Videography	event	483	10/93	76r
Wedding invitations and announcements	event	342	10/93	76r
Wedding reception	event	7000	10/93	76r

Salinas-Seaside-Monterey, CA

Item	Per	Value	Date	Ref.
Appliances				
Appliances (major), expenditures	year	160	91	81r
Average annual exp.				
Food, health care, personal goods, services	year	32461	91	81r
Charity				
Cash contributions, expenditures	year	975	91	81r
Clothing				
Apparel, men and boys, total expenditures	year	467	91	81r
Apparel, women and girls, total expenditures	year	737	91	81r
Footwear, expenditures	year	270	91	81r
Communications				
Long-distance telephone rate, day, addl. min., 1-10 mi.	min.	0.07	12/93	9s
Long-distance telephone rate, day, initial min., 1-10 mi.	min.	0.17	12/93	9s
Phone line, single, business, field visit	inst	70.75	12/93	9s
Phone line, single, business, no field visit	inst	70.75	12/93	9s
Phone line, single, residence, field visit	inst	34.75	12/93	9s
Phone line, single, residence, no field visit	inst	34.75	12/93	9s
Telephone service, expenditures	year	611	91	81r
Education				
Board, 4-year private college/university	year	2945	8/94	80s
Board, 4-year public college/university	year	2321	8/94	80s
Education, total expenditures	year	375	91	81r
Room, 4-year private college/university	year	3094	8/94	80s
Room, 4-year public college/university	year	2812	8/94	80s
Student fee, university	year	21.00	93	18s
Total cost, 4-year private college/university	year	19321	8/94	80s
Total cost, 4-year public college/university	year	7511	8/94	80s
Tuition, 2-year public college/university, in-state	year	345	8/94	80s
Tuition, 4-year private college/university, in-state	year	13282	8/94	80s
Tuition, 4-year public college/university, in-state	year	2378	8/94	80s
Energy and Fuels				
Fuel oil and other fuels, expenditures	year	33	91	81r
Gas, natural, expenditures	year	212	91	81r
Gasoline and motor oil purchased	year	1115	91	81r

Values are in dollars or fractions of dollars. In the column headed *Ref*, references are shown to sources. Each reference is followed by a letter. These refer to the geographical level for which data were reported: s=State, r=Region, and c=City or metro. The abbreviation *ex* is used to mean *except* or *excluding*; *exp* stands for expenditures. For other abbreviations and further explanations, please see the Introduction.

Salinas-Seaside-Monterey, CA - continued

Item	Per	Value	Date	Ref.
Energy and Fuels				
Gasoline, unleaded midgrade	gallon	1.36	4/93	82r
Gasoline, unleaded premium	gallon	1.43	4/93	82r
Gasoline, unleaded regular	gallon	1.23	4/93	82r
Entertainment				
Concert ticket, Pearl Jam group	perf	20.00	94	50r
Entertainment, total expenditures	year	1853	91	81r
Fees and admissions, expenditures	year	482	91	81r
Pets, toys, playground equipment, expenditures	year	299	91	81r
Reading, expenditures	year	164	91	81r
Televisions, radios, and sound equipment, expenditures	year	528	91	81r
Funerals				
Burial, immediate, container provided by funeral home		1382.70	1/95	54r
Cards, acknowledgment		21.87	1/95	54r
Casket, minimum alternative		128.54	1/95	54r
Cosmetology, hair care, etc.		119.69	1/95	54r
Cremation, direct, container provided by funeral home		1030.62	1/95	54r
Embalming		255.42	1/95	54r
Funeral, funeral home		437.38	1/95	54r
Funeral, other facility		444.46	1/95	54r
Graveside service		338.46	1/95	54r
Hearse, local		147.50	1/95	54r
Limousine, local		130.33	1/95	54r
Memorial service		553.16	1/95	54r
Service charge, professional, nondeclinable		859.15	1/95	54r
Visitation and viewing		93.23	1/95	54r
Groceries				
Apples, Red Delicious	lb.	0.72	12/94	82r
Bacon, sliced	lb.	1.73	12/94	82r
Bananas	lb.	0.52	12/94	82r
Beef purchases	year	241	91	81r
Beverage purchases, alcoholic	year	328	91	81r
Beverage purchases, nonalcoholic	year	234	91	81r
Bologna, all beef or mixed	lb.	2.33	12/94	82r
Bread, white, pan	lb.	0.81	12/94	82r
Carrots, short trimmed and topped	lb.	0.43	12/94	82r
Cereals and bakery products purchases	year	392	91	81r
Cereals and cereals products purchases	year	139	91	81r
Chicken breast, bone-in	lb.	2.04	12/94	82r
Chicken, fresh, whole	lb.	0.95	12/94	82r
Coffee, 100%, ground roast, all sizes	lb.	4.48	12/94	82r
Dairy products (other) purchases	year	182	91	81r
Fish and seafood purchases	year	94	91	81r
Flour, white, all purpose	lb.	0.21	12/94	82r
Food purchases, food eaten at home	year	2749	91	81r
Foods purchased away from home, not prepared by consumer	year	1909	91	81r
Fruits and vegetables purchases	year	459	91	81r
Grapefruit	lb.	0.56	12/94	82r
Ground beef, 100% beef	lb.	1.31	12/94	82r
Ham, boneless, exc. canned	lb.	2.46	12/94	82r
Ice cream, prepackaged, bulk, regular	1/2 gal.	2.57	12/94	82r
Lemons	lb.	1.00	12/94	82r
Lettuce, iceberg	lb.	0.93	12/94	82r
Meats, poultry, fish, and eggs purchases	year	700	91	81r
Milk and cream (fresh) purchases	year	155	91	81r
Orange juice, frozen concentrate 12-oz. can	16 oz.	1.52	12/94	82r
Oranges, Navel	lb.	0.56	12/94	82r
Pork chops, center cut, bone-in	lb.	3.30	12/94	82r
Pork purchases	year	122	91	81r
Potato chips	16-oz.	3.03	12/94	82r
Potatoes, frozen, French fried	lb.	0.77	12/94	82r
Potatoes, white	lb.	0.35	12/94	82r
Rice, white, long grain, uncooked	lb.	0.54	12/94	82r
Round roast, USDA choice, boneless	lb.	2.92	12/94	82r
Shortening, vegetable oil blends	lb.	0.80	12/94	82r
Spaghetti and macaroni	lb.	1.02	12/94	82r

Salinas-Seaside-Monterey, CA - continued

Item	Per	Value	Date	Ref.
Groceries - continued				
Steak, round, graded & ungraded, exc. USDA prime & choice	lb.	3.13	12/94	82r
Steak, sirloin, USDA choice, boneless	lb.	4.07	12/94	82r
Sugar and other sweets, eaten at home, expenditures	year	105	91	81r
Sugar, white, all sizes	lb.	0.38	12/94	82r
Tobacco products and smoking supplies, total expenditures	year	221	91	81r
Tomatoes, field grown	lb.	1.45	12/94	82r
Tuna, chunk, light	lb.	2.18	12/94	82r
Health Care				
Childbirth, Cesarean delivery, hospital charge	birth	6059.00	12/91	69r
Childbirth, Cesarean delivery, physician charge	birth	2248.00	12/91	69r
Childbirth, normal delivery, hospital charge	birth	3006.00	12/91	69r
Childbirth, normal delivery, physician charge	birth	1634.00	12/91	69r
Drugs, expenditures	year	230	91	81r
Health care, total expenditures	year	1544	91	81r
Health insurance expenditures	year	558	91	81r
Insurance premium, family medical care	month	380.27	1/95	41s
Medical services expenditures	year	676	91	81r
Medical supplies expenditures	year	80	91	81r
Surgery, open-heart	proc	37818.00	1/93	14r
Household Goods				
Floor coverings, expenditures	year	79	91	81r
Furniture, expenditures	year	352	91	81r
Household equipment, misc. expenditures	year	614	91	81r
Household expenditures, miscellaneous	year	294	91	81r
Household furnishings and equipment, expenditures	year	1416	91	81r
Household operations expenditures	year	580	91	81r
Household textiles, expenditures	year	113	91	81r
Housekeeping supplies, expenditures	year	447	91	81r
Laundry and cleaning supplies, expenditures	year	114	91	81r
Postage and stationery, expenditures	year	145	91	81r
Housing				
Add garage/carport		6,422	3/95	74r
Add room(s)		26,583	3/95	74r
Apartment condominium or co-op, median	unit	105300	12/94	62r
Dwellings (owned), expenditures	year	3932	91	81r
Enclose porch/patio/breezeway		5,382	3/95	74r
Finish room in basement/attic		3,911	3/95	74r
Home, existing, single-family, median	unit	178600	12/94	62r
Maintenance, repairs, insurance, and other housing expenditures	year	591	91	81r
Mortgage interest and charges expenditures	year	2747	91	81r
Princ. & int., mortgage, median-price exist. sing.-family home	mo.	845	12/94	62r
Property taxes expenditures	year	594	91	81r
Redesign, restructure more than half of home's interior		5,467	3/95	74r
Rental units expenditures	year	2077	91	81r
Insurance and Pensions				
Auto insurance, private passenger	year	892.80	12/94	71s
Insurance and pensions, personal, expenditures	year	3042	91	81r
Insurance, life and other personal, expenditures	year	298	91	81r
Pensions and Social Security, expenditures	year	2744	91	81r
Legal Assistance				
Legal work, law firm associate	hour	91		10r
Legal work, law firm partner	hour	151		10r
Personal Services				
Personal services expenditures	year	286	91	81r

Values are in dollars or fractions of dollars. In the column headed *Ref*, references are shown to sources. Each reference is followed by a letter. These refer to the geographical level for which data were reported: s = State, r = Region, and c = City or metro. The abbreviation *ex* is used to mean *except* or *excluding*; *exp* stands for expenditures. For other abbreviations and further explanations, please see the Introduction.

Salinas-Seaside-Monterey, CA - continued

Item	Per	Value	Date	Ref.
Restaurant Food				
Dining expenditures, family	week	32.25	94	73r
Taxes				
Taxes, Federal income, expenditures	year	2946	91	81r
Taxes, personal, expenditures	year	3791	91	81r
Taxes, State and local income, expenditures	year	791	91	81r
Transportation				
Cars and trucks purchased, new	year	1231	91	81r
Cars and trucks purchased, used	year	915	91	81r
Driver's learning permit fee	perm	12.00	1/94	84s
Driver's license fee	orig	12.00	1/94	84s
Driver's license fee, duplicate	lic	12.00	1/94	84s
Driver's license reinstatement fee, min.	susp	15.00	1/94	85s
Driver's license renewal fee	renew	12.00	1/94	84s
Identification card, nondriver	card	6.00	1/94	83s
Motorcycle learning permit fee	perm	12.00	1/94	84s
Motorcycle license fee	orig	12.00	1/94	84s
Motorcycle license fee, duplicate	lic	12.00	1/94	84s
Motorcycle license renewal fee	renew	12.00	1/94	84s
Public transportation expenditures	year	375	91	81r
Transportation expenditures, total	year	5527	91	81r
Vehicle finance charges	year	287	91	81r
Vehicle insurance expenditures	year	624	91	81r
Vehicle maintenance and repairs expenditures	year	695	91	81r
Vehicle purchases	year	2174	91	81r
Vehicle rental, leases, licenses, etc. expenditures	year	257	91	81r
Vehicles purchased, other than cars and trucks	year	28	91	81r
Utilities				
Electricity expenditures	year	616	91	81r
Utilities, fuels, and public services, total expenditures	year	1681	91	81r
Water and other public services, expenditures	year	209	91	81r
Weddings				
Bridal attendants' gowns	event	750	10/93	76r
Bridal gown	event	852	10/93	76r
Bridal headpiece and veil	event	167	10/93	76r
Bride's wedding band	event	708	10/93	76r
Clergy	event	224	10/93	76r
Engagement ring	event	2756	10/93	76r
Flowers	event	863	10/93	76r
Formal wear for groom	event	106	10/93	76r
Groom's attendants' formal wear	event	530	10/93	76r
Groom's wedding band	event	402	10/93	76r
Music	event	600	10/93	76r
Photography	event	1088	10/93	76r
Shoes for bride	event	50	10/93	76r
Videography	event	483	10/93	76r
Wedding invitations and announcements	event	342	10/93	76r
Wedding reception	event	7000	10/93	76r

Salt Lake City, UT

Item	Per	Value	Date	Ref.
Composite, ACCRA index		108.00	12/94	2c
Alcoholic Beverages				
Beer, Miller Lite, Bud, 12-oz., ex deposit	6	3.89	12/94	2c
J & B Scotch	750-ml.	19.95	12/94	2c
Wine, Gallo Chablis blanc	1.5-lit	5.95	12/94	2c
Appliances				
Appliances (major), expenditures	year	160	91	81r
Average annual exp.				
Food, health care, personal goods, services	year	32461	91	81r

Salt Lake City, UT - continued

Item	Per	Value	Date	Ref.
Business				
Dinner and tip, hotel, corporate rate	night	30.00	2/94	15c
Hotel room, corporate rate	night	75.00	2/94	15c
Charity				
Cash contributions, expenditures	year	975	91	81r
Clothing				
Apparel, men and boys, total expenditures	year	467	91	81r
Apparel, women and girls, total expenditures	year	737	91	81r
Footwear, expenditures	year	270	91	81r
Jeans, man's denim		26.78	12/94	2c
Shirt, man's dress shirt		30.14	12/94	2c
Undervest, boy's size 10-14, cotton	3	3.82	12/94	2c
Communications				
Long-distance telephone rate, day, addl. min., 1-10 mi.	min.	0.08	12/93	9s
Long-distance telephone rate, day, initial min., 1-10 mi.	min.	0.11	12/93	9s
Newspaper subscription, dly. and Sun. delivery	month	8.96	12/94	2c
Phone line, single, business, field visit	inst	50.00	12/93	9s
Phone line, single, business, no field visit	inst	50.00	12/93	9s
Phone line, single, residence, field visit	inst	18.75	12/93	9s
Phone line, single, residence, no field visit	inst	18.75	12/93	9s
Telephone bill, family of four	month	18.68	12/94	2c
Telephone service, expenditures	year	611	91	81r
Telephone, residential, flat rate	mo.	7.98	12/93	8c
Education				
Board, 4-year private college/university	year	2817	8/94	80s
Board, 4-year public college/university	year	1981	8/94	80s
Education, total expenditures	year	375	91	81r
Room, 4-year private college/university	year	1300	8/94	80s
Room, 4-year public college/university	year	1282	8/94	80s
Total cost, 4-year private college/university	year	6661	8/94	80s
Total cost, 4-year public college/university	year	5227	8/94	80s
Tuition, 2-year public college/university, in-state	year	1315	8/94	80s
Tuition, 4-year private college/university, in-state	year	2545	8/94	80s
Tuition, 4-year public college/university, in-state	year	1964	8/94	80s
Energy and Fuels				
Energy, combined forms, 1800 sq. ft.	mo.	103.49	12/94	2c
Energy, exc. electricity, 1800 sq. ft.	mo.	42.89	12/94	2c
Fuel oil and other fuels, expenditures	year	33	91	81r
Gas, cooking, winter, 10 therms	month	9.37	2/94	65c
Gas, cooking, winter, 30 therms	month	18.12	2/94	65c
Gas, cooking, winter, 50 therms	month	26.87	2/94	65c
Gas, heating, winter, 100 therms	month	48.75	2/94	65c
Gas, heating, winter, average use	month	77.18	2/94	65c
Gas, natural, expenditures	year	212	91	81r
Gas, reg unlead, taxes inc., cash, self-service	gal	1.19	12/94	2c
Gasoline and motor oil purchased	year	1115	91	81r
Gasoline, unleaded midgrade	gallon	1.36	4/93	82r
Gasoline, unleaded premium	gallon	1.43	4/93	82r
Gasoline, unleaded regular	gallon	1.23	4/93	82r
Entertainment				
Bowling, evening rate	game	2.04	12/94	2c
Concert ticket, Pearl Jam group	perf	20.00	94	50r
Entertainment, total expenditures	year	1853	91	81r
Fees and admissions, expenditures	year	482	91	81r
Monopoly game, Parker Brothers', No. 9	game	11.92	12/94	2c
Movie	adm	5.50	12/94	2c
Pets, toys, playground equipment, expenditures	year	299	91	81r
Reading, expenditures	year	164	91	81r
Televisions, radios, and sound equipment, expenditures	year	528	91	81r
Tennis balls, yellow, Wilson or Penn, 3	can	2.04	12/94	2c

Values are in dollars or fractions of dollars. In the column headed *Ref*, references are shown to sources. Each reference is followed by a letter. These refer to the geographical level for which data were reported: s=State, r=Region, and c=City or metro. The abbreviation *ex* is used to mean *except* or *excluding*; *exp* stands for expenditures. For other abbreviations and further explanations, please see the Introduction.

Salt Lake City, UT - continued

Item	Per	Value	Date	Ref.
Funerals				
Burial, immediate, container provided by funeral home		1360.49	1/95	54r
Cards, acknowledgment		11.24	1/95	54r
Casket, minimum alternative		232.73	1/95	54r
Cosmetology, hair care, etc.		114.13	1/95	54r
Cremation, direct, container provided by funeral home		1027.08	1/95	54r
Embalming		286.24	1/95	54r
Funeral, funeral home		315.60	1/95	54r
Funeral, other facility		303.08	1/95	54r
Graveside service		423.83	1/95	54r
Hearse, local		133.12	1/95	54r
Limousine, local		99.10	1/95	54r
Memorial service		442.57	1/95	54r
Service charge, professional, nondeclinable		840.16	1/95	54r
Visitation and viewing		168.50	1/95	54r
Groceries				
Groceries, ACCRA Index		99.80	12/94	2c
Apples, Red Delicious	lb.	0.72	12/94	82r
Baby food, strained vegetables, lowest price	4-4.5 oz.	0.38	12/94	2c
Bacon, sliced	lb.	1.73	12/94	82r
Bananas	lb.	0.36	12/94	2c
Bananas	lb.	0.52	12/94	82r
Beef or hamburger, ground	lb.	1.59	12/94	2c
Beef purchases	year	241	91	81r
Beverage purchases, alcoholic	year	328	91	81r
Beverage purchases, nonalcoholic	year	234	91	81r
Bologna, all beef or mixed	lb.	2.33	12/94	82r
Bread, white	24-oz.	0.76	12/94	2c
Bread, white, pan	lb.	0.81	12/94	82r
Carrots, short trimmed and topped	lb.	0.43	12/94	82r
Cereals and bakery products purchases	year	392	91	81r
Cereals and cereals products purchases	year	139	91	81r
Cheese, Kraft grated Parmesan	8-oz.	3.99	12/94	2c
Chicken breast, bone-in	lb.	2.04	12/94	82r
Chicken, fresh, whole	lb.	0.95	12/94	82r
Chicken, whole fryer	lb.	0.79	12/94	2c
Cigarettes, Winston, Kings	carton	16.99	12/94	2c
Coffee, 100%, ground roast, all sizes	lb.	4.48	12/94	82r
Coffee, vacuum-packed	13 oz.	3.61	12/94	2c
Corn Flakes, Kellogg's or Post Toasties	18 oz.	2.52	12/94	2c
Corn, frozen, whole kernel, lowest price	10 oz.	0.71	12/94	2c
Dairy products (other) purchases	year	182	91	81r
Eggs, Grade A large	dozen	0.72	12/94	2c
Fish and seafood purchases	year	94	91	81r
Flour, white, all purpose	lb.	0.21	12/94	82r
Food purchases, food eaten at home	year	2749	91	81r
Foods purchased away from home, not prepared by consumer	year	1909	91	81r
Fruits and vegetables purchases	year	459	91	81r
Grapefruit	lb.	0.56	12/94	82r
Ground beef, 100% beef	lb.	1.31	12/94	82r
Ham, boneless, exc. canned	lb.	2.46	12/94	82r
Ice cream, prepackaged, bulk, regular	1/2 gal.	2.57	12/94	82r
Lemons	lb.	1.00	12/94	82r
Lettuce, iceberg	lb.	0.93	12/94	82r
Lettuce, iceberg	head	0.72	12/94	2c
Margarine, Blue Bonnet or Parkay cubes	lb.	0.56	12/94	2c
Meats, poultry, fish, and eggs purchases	year	700	91	81r
Milk and cream (fresh) purchases	year	155	91	81r
Milk, whole	1/2 gal.	1.39	12/94	2c
Orange juice, frozen concentrate 12-oz. can	16 oz.	1.52	12/94	82r
Orange juice, Minute Maid frozen	12-oz.	1.23	12/94	2c
Oranges, Navel	lb.	0.56	12/94	82r
Peaches, halves or slices, Hunt's, Del Monte, or Libby's	29-oz.	1.42	12/94	2c
Peas, sweet, Del Monte or Green Giant	15-17 oz.	0.58	12/94	2c
Pork chops, center cut, bone-in	lb.	3.30	12/94	82r

Salt Lake City, UT - continued

Item	Per	Value	Date	Ref.
Groceries - continued				
Pork purchases	year	122	91	81r
Potato chips	16-oz.	3.03	12/94	82r
Potatoes, frozen, French fried	lb.	0.77	12/94	82r
Potatoes, white	lb.	0.35	12/94	82r
Potatoes, white or red	10-lb. sack	1.46	12/94	2c
Rice, white, long grain, uncooked	lb.	0.54	12/94	82r
Round roast, USDA choice, boneless	lb.	2.92	12/94	82r
Sausage, Jimmy Dean, 100% pork	lb.	2.90	12/94	2c
Shortening, vegetable oil blends	lb.	0.80	12/94	82r
Shortening, vegetable, Crisco	3-lb.	2.49	12/94	2c
Soft drink, Coca Cola, ex deposit	2 lit	1.14	12/94	2c
Spaghetti and macaroni	lb.	1.02	12/94	82r
Steak, round, graded & ungraded, exc. USDA prime & choice	lb.	3.13	12/94	82r
Steak, sirloin, USDA choice, boneless	lb.	4.07	12/94	82r
Steak, t-bone	lb.	3.95	12/94	2c
Sugar and other sweets, eaten at home, expenditures	year	105	91	81r
Sugar, cane or beet	4 lbs.	1.45	12/94	2c
Sugar, white, all sizes	lb.	0.38	12/94	82r
Tobacco products and smoking supplies, total expenditures	year	221	91	81r
Tomatoes, field grown	lb.	1.45	12/94	82r
Tomatoes, Hunt's or Del Monte	14.5 oz.	0.64	12/94	2c
Tuna, chunk, light	lb.	2.18	12/94	82r
Tuna, chunk, light, oil-packed	6.125-6.5 oz.	0.65	12/94	2c
Goods and Services				
Miscellaneous goods and services, ACCRA Index		96.10	12/94	2c
Health Care				
Health care, ACCRA Index		104.50	12/94	2c
Antibiotic ointment, Polysporin	1.5 oz.	3.89	12/94	2c
Childbirth, Cesarean delivery, hospital charge	birth	6059.00	12/91	69r
Childbirth, Cesarean delivery, physician charge	birth	2248.00	12/91	69r
Childbirth, normal delivery, hospital charge	birth	3006.00	12/91	69r
Childbirth, normal delivery, physician charge	birth	1634.00	12/91	69r
Dentist's fee, adult teeth cleaning and periodic oral exam	visit	55.40	12/94	2c
Doctor's fee, routine exam, established patient	visit	38.40	12/94	2c
Drugs, expenditures	year	230	91	81r
Health care, total expenditures	year	1544	91	81r
Health insurance expenditures	year	558	91	81r
Hospital care, semiprivate room	day	478.00	12/94	2c
Insurance premium, family medical care	month	378.32	1/95	41s
Medical services expenditures	year	676	91	81r
Medical supplies expenditures	year	80	91	81r
Surgery, open-heart	proc	37818.00	1/93	14r
Household Goods				
Appl. repair, service call, wash mach	min. lab. chg.	30.79	12/94	2c
Floor coverings, expenditures	year	79	91	81r
Furniture, expenditures	year	352	91	81r
Household equipment, misc. expenditures	year	614	91	81r
Household expenditures, miscellaneous	year	294	91	81r
Household furnishings and equipment, expenditures	year	1416	91	81r
Household operations expenditures	year	580	91	81r
Household textiles, expenditures	year	113	91	81r
Housekeeping supplies, expenditures	year	447	91	81r
Laundry and cleaning supplies, expenditures	year	114	91	81r
Laundry detergent, Tide Ultra, Bold, or Cheer	42 oz.	3.76	12/94	2c
Postage and stationery, expenditures	year	145	91	81r

Values are in dollars or fractions of dollars. In the column headed *Ref*, references are shown to sources. Each reference is followed by a letter. These refer to the geographical level for which data were reported: s=State, r=Region, and c=City or metro. The abbreviation *ex* is used to mean *except* or *excluding*; *exp* stands for expenditures. For other abbreviations and further explanations, please see the Introduction.

Salt Lake City, UT - continued

Item	Per	Value	Date	Ref.
Household Goods				
Tissues, facial, Kleenex brand	175	0.89	12/94	2c
Housing				
Housing, ACCRA Index		134.20	12/94	2c
Add garage/carport		6,422	3/95	74r
Add room(s)		26,583	3/95	74r
Apartment condominium or co-op, median	unit	105300	12/94	62r
Dwellings (owned), expenditures	year	3932	91	81r
Enclose porch/patio/breezeway		5,382	3/95	74r
Finish room in basement/attic		3,911	3/95	74r
Home, existing, single-family, median	unit	178600	12/94	62r
Home, existing, single-family, median	unit	102.20	12/94	62c
Home, purchase price	unit	122.40	3/93	26c
House payment, principal and interest, 25% down payment	mo.	1091	12/94	2c
House, 1800 sq ft, 8000 sq ft lot, new, urban, utilities	total	175775	12/94	2c
Maintenance, repairs, insurance, and other housing expenditures	year	591	91	81r
Mortgage interest and charges expenditures	year	2747	91	81r
Mtge. rate, incl. points and orig. fee, 30-year conv. fixed or ARM	mo.	9.31	12/94	2c
Princ. & int., mortgage, median-price exist. sing.-family home	mo.	845	12/94	62r
Property taxes expenditures	year	594	91	81r
Redesign, restructure more than half of home's interior		5,467	3/95	74r
Rent, apartment, 2 br., 1 1/2-2 baths, unfurnished, 950 sq ft, water	mo.	529	12/94	2c
Rental units expenditures	year	2077	91	81r
Insurance and Pensions				
Auto insurance, private passenger	year	607.42	12/94	71s
Insurance and pensions, personal, expenditures	year	3042	91	81r
Insurance, life and other personal, expenditures	year	298	91	81r
Pensions and Social Security, expenditures	year	2744	91	81r
Legal Assistance				
Legal work, law firm associate	hour	91		10r
Legal work, law firm partner	hour	151		10r
Personal Goods				
Shampoo, Alberto VO5	15-oz.	1.42	12/94	2c
Toothpaste, Crest or Colgate	6-7 oz.	2.22	12/94	2c
Personal Services				
Dry cleaning, man's 2-pc. suit		7.20	12/94	2c
Haircut, man's barbershop, no styling		7.20	12/94	2c
Haircut, woman's shampoo, trim, blow-dry		18.20	12/94	2c
Personal services expenditures	year	286	91	81r
Restaurant Food				
Chicken, fried, thigh and drumstick		1.99	12/94	2c
Dining expenditures, family	week	32.25	94	73r
Hamburger with cheese	1/4 lb.	1.99	12/94	2c
Pizza, Pizza Hut or Pizza Inn	12-13 in.	7.49	12/94	2c
Taxes				
Tax rate, residential property, month	$100	1.43	1/92	79c
Taxes, Federal income, expenditures	year	2946	91	81r
Taxes, personal, expenditures	year	3791	91	81r
Taxes, State and local income, expenditures	year	791	91	81r
Transportation				
Transportation, ACCRA Index		100.40	12/94	2c
Bus fare, one-way	trip	0.65	12/95	1c
Bus fare, up to 10 miles	one-way	0.65	12/94	2c
Cars and trucks purchased, new	year	1231	91	81r
Cars and trucks purchased, used	year	915	91	81r
Driver's learning permit fee	perm	20.00	1/94	84s
Driver's license fee	orig	0.00	1/94	84s
Driver's license fee, duplicate	lic	10.00	1/94	84s

Salt Lake City, UT - continued

Item	Per	Value	Date	Ref.
Transportation - continued				
Driver's license renewal fee	renew	15.00	1/94	84s
Identification card, nondriver	card	5.00	1/94	83s
Motorcycle license fee	orig	0.00	1/94	84s
Public transportation expenditures	year	375	91	81r
Tire balance, computer or spin bal., front	wheel	6.88	12/94	2c
Transportation expenditures, total	year	5527	91	81r
Vehicle finance charges	year	287	91	81r
Vehicle insurance expenditures	year	624	91	81r
Vehicle maintenance and repairs expenditures	year	695	91	81r
Vehicle purchases	year	2174	91	81r
Vehicle rental, leases, licenses, etc. expenditures	year	257	91	81r
Vehicles purchased, other than cars and trucks	year	28	91	81r
Utilities				
Utilities, ACCRA Index		92.70	12/94	2c
Electricity expenditures	year	616	91	81r
Electricity, (part.), other, 1800 sq. ft., new home	mo.	60.60	12/94	2c
Electricity, summer, 250 KWh	month	18.10	8/93	64c
Electricity, summer, 500 KWh	month	35.20	8/93	64c
Electricity, summer, 750 KWh	month	52.29	8/93	64c
Electricity, summer, 1000 KWh	month	69.39	8/93	64c
Utilities, fuels, and public services, total expenditures	year	1681	91	81r
Water and other public services, expenditures	year	209	91	81r
Weddings				
Bridal attendants' gowns	event	750	10/93	76r
Bridal gown	event	852	10/93	76r
Bridal headpiece and veil	event	167	10/93	76r
Bride's wedding band	event	708	10/93	76r
Clergy	event	224	10/93	76r
Engagement ring	event	2756	10/93	76r
Flowers	event	863	10/93	76r
Formal wear for groom	event	106	10/93	76r
Groom's attendants' formal wear	event	530	10/93	76r
Groom's wedding band	event	402	10/93	76r
Music	event	600	10/93	76r
Photography	event	1088	10/93	76r
Shoes for bride	event	50	10/93	76r
Videography	event	483	10/93	76r
Wedding invitations and announcements	event	342	10/93	76r
Wedding reception	event	7000	10/93	76r

San Angelo, TX

Item	Per	Value	Date	Ref.
Appliances				
Appliances (major), expenditures	year	153	91	81r
Average annual exp.				
Food, health care, personal goods, services	year	27020	91	81r
Charity				
Cash contributions, expenditures	year	839	91	81r
Clothing				
Apparel, men and boys, total expenditures	year	380	91	81r
Apparel, women and girls, total expenditures	year	660	91	81r
Footwear, expenditures	year	193	91	81r
Communications				
Long-distance telephone rate, day, addl. min., 1-10 mi.	min.	0.08	12/93	9s
Long-distance telephone rate, day, initial min., 1-10 mi.	min.	0.10	12/93	9s
Phone line, single, business, field visit	inst	71.90	12/93	9s
Phone line, single, business, no field visit	inst	57.30	12/93	9s
Phone line, single, residence, field visit	inst	52.95	12/93	9s
Phone line, single, residence, no field visit	inst	38.35	12/93	9s
Telephone service, expenditures	year	616	91	81r

Values are in dollars or fractions of dollars. In the column headed Ref, references are shown to sources. Each reference is followed by a letter. These refer to the geographical level for which data were reported: s = State, r = Region, and c = City or metro. The abbreviation ex is used to mean except or excluding; exp stands for expenditures. For other abbreviations and further explanations, please see the Introduction.

San Angelo, TX - continued

Item	Per	Value	Date	Ref.
Education				
Board, 4-year private college/university	year	2084	8/94	80s
Board, 4-year public college/university	year	1675	8/94	80s
Education, total expenditures	year	319	91	81r
Room, 4-year private college/university	year	1840	8/94	80s
Room, 4-year public college/university	year	1756	8/94	80s
Total cost, 4-year private college/university	year	11876	8/94	80s
Total cost, 4-year public college/university	year	4935	8/94	80s
Tuition, 2-year public college/university, in-state	year	625	8/94	80s
Tuition, 4-year private college/university, in-state	year	7952	8/94	80s
Tuition, 4-year public college/university, in-state	year	1503	8/94	80s
Energy and Fuels				
Fuel oil and other fuels, expenditures	year	56	91	81r
Gas, natural, expenditures	year	150	91	81r
Gasoline and motor oil purchased	year	1152	91	81r
Gasoline, unleaded midgrade	gallon	1.21	4/93	82r
Gasoline, unleaded premium	gallon	1.30	4/93	82r
Gasoline, unleaded regular	gallon	1.10	4/93	82r
Entertainment				
Concert ticket, Pearl Jam group	perf	20.00	94	50r
Entertainment, total expenditures	year	1266	91	81r
Fees and admissions, expenditures	year	306	91	81r
Pets, toys, playground equipment, expenditures	year	271	91	81r
Reading, expenditures	year	131	91	81r
Televisions, radios, and sound equipment, expenditures	year	439	91	81r
Funerals				
Burial, immediate, container provided by funeral home		1574.60	1/95	54r
Cards, acknowledgment		22.24	1/95	54r
Casket, minimum alternative		239.41	1/95	54r
Cosmetology, hair care, etc.		91.04	1/95	54r
Cremation, direct, container provided by funeral home		1085.15	1/95	54r
Embalming		281.30	1/95	54r
Funeral, funeral home		323.04	1/95	54r
Funeral, other facility		327.58	1/95	54r
Graveside service		355.19	1/95	54r
Hearse, local		141.89	1/95	54r
Limousine, local		99.40	1/95	54r
Memorial service		284.67	1/95	54r
Service charge, professional, nondeclinable		904.06	1/95	54r
Visitation and viewing		187.04	1/95	54r
Groceries				
Apples, Red Delicious	lb.	0.73	12/94	82r
Bacon, sliced	lb.	1.67	12/94	82r
Bananas	lb.	0.42	12/94	82r
Beef purchases	year	213	91	81r
Beverage purchases, alcoholic	year	249	91	81r
Beverage purchases, nonalcoholic	year	207	91	81r
Bologna, all beef or mixed	lb.	2.27	12/94	82r
Bread, white, pan	lb.	0.68	12/94	82r
Cabbage	lb.	0.42	12/94	82r
Carrots, short trimmed and topped	lb.	0.53	12/94	82r
Cereals and bakery products purchases	year	345	91	81r
Cereals and cereals products purchases	year	127	91	81r
Cheddar cheese, natural	lb.	3.58	12/94	82r
Chicken breast, bone-in	lb.	1.71	12/94	82r
Chicken, fresh, whole	lb.	0.78	12/94	82r
Chuck roast, USDA choice, boneless	lb.	2.26	12/94	82r
Crackers, soda, salted	lb.	1.27	12/94	82r
Cucumbers	lb.	0.65	12/94	82r
Dairy products (other) purchases	year	141	91	81r
Eggs, Grade A large	dozen	0.87	12/94	82r
Fish and seafood purchases	year	72	91	81r
Flour, white, all purpose	lb.	0.23	12/94	82r
Food purchases, food eaten at home	year	2381	91	81r

San Angelo, TX - continued

Item	Per	Value	Date	Ref.
Groceries - continued				
Foods purchased away from home, not prepared by consumer	year	1696	91	81r
Frankfurters, all meat or all beef	lb.	1.74	12/94	82r
Fruits and vegetables purchases	year	380	91	81r
Grapefruit	lb.	0.45	12/94	82r
Grapes, Thompson seedless	lb.	2.30	12/94	82r
Ground beef, 100% beef	lb.	1.37	12/94	82r
Ground chuck, 100% beef	lb.	1.97	12/94	82r
Ham, boneless, exc. canned	lb.	2.54	12/94	82r
Ice cream, prepackaged, bulk, regular	1/2 gal.	2.47	12/94	82r
Lemons	lb.	1.02	12/94	82r
Lettuce, iceberg	lb.	0.96	12/94	82r
Margarine, stick	lb.	0.77	12/94	82r
Meats, poultry, fish, and eggs purchases	year	655	91	81r
Milk and cream (fresh) purchases	year	130	91	81r
Orange juice, frozen concentrate 12-oz. can	16 oz.	1.36	12/94	82r
Oranges, Navel	lb.	0.54	12/94	82r
Pears, Anjou	lb.	0.81	12/94	82r
Pork chops, center cut, bone-in	lb.	3.07	12/94	82r
Pork purchases	year	142	91	81r
Potato chips	16-oz.	3.15	12/94	82r
Potatoes, frozen, French fried	lb.	0.82	12/94	82r
Potatoes, white	lb.	0.34	12/94	82r
Rice, white, long grain, uncooked	lb.	0.48	12/94	82r
Round roast, USDA choice, boneless	lb.	2.91	12/94	82r
Sausage, fresh	lb.	1.82	12/94	82r
Shortening, vegetable oil blends	lb.	0.75	12/94	82r
Spaghetti and macaroni	lb.	0.87	12/94	82r
Steak, rib eye, USDA choice, boneless	lb.	6.85	12/94	82r
Steak, round, graded & ungraded, exc. USDA prime & choice	lb.	2.96	12/94	82r
Steak, round, USDA choice, boneless	lb.	3.17	12/94	82r
Steak, sirloin, USDA choice, boneless	lb.	4.12	12/94	82r
Steak, T-bone, USDA choice, bone-in	lb.	5.63	12/94	82r
Sugar and other sweets, eaten at home, expenditures	year	93	91	81r
Sugar, white, all sizes	lb.	0.39	12/94	82r
Tobacco products and smoking supplies, total expenditures	year	286	91	81r
Tomatoes, field grown	lb.	1.36	12/94	82r
Tuna, chunk, light	lb.	1.94	12/94	82r
Turkey, frozen, whole	lb.	0.96	12/94	82r
Yogurt, natural, fruit flavored	8 oz.	0.58	12/94	82r
Health Care				
Adenosine, emergency room	treat	100.00	95	23r
Bladder tap, superpubic, infant, emergency room	treat	119.00	95	23r
Blood analysis, emergency room	treat	25.00	95	23r
Blood tests, abdominal pain, emergency room	treat	25.00	95	23r
Burn dressing, emergency room	treat	266.00	95	23r
Cardiology interpretation, emergency room	treat	26.00	95	23r
Chest X-ray, emergency room	treat	78.00	95	23r
Childbirth, Cesarean delivery, hospital charge	birth	5462.00	12/91	69r
Childbirth, Cesarean delivery, physician charge	birth	2228.00	12/91	69r
Childbirth, normal delivery, hospital charge	birth	2943.00	12/91	69r
Childbirth, normal delivery, physician charge	birth	1619.00	12/91	69r
Defibrillation pads, emergency room	treat	6.00	95	23r
Drugs, expenditures	year	297	91	81r
Gastric tube insertion, nasal, emergency room	treat	25.00	95	23r
Health care, total expenditures	year	1600	91	81r
Health insurance expenditures	year	637	91	81r
Heart monitor, emergency room	treat	40.00	95	23r
Insurance premium, family medical care	month	389.25	1/95	41s
Intravenous fluids, emergency room	treat	130.00	95	23r
Intravenous fluids, emergency room	liter	26.00	95	23r
Intravenous line, central, emergency room	treat	342.00	95	23r

Values are in dollars or fractions of dollars. In the column headed *Ref*, references are shown to sources. Each reference is followed by a letter. These refer to the geographical level for which data were reported: s = State, r = Region, and c = City or metro. The abbreviation *ex* is used to mean *except* or *excluding*; *exp* stands for expenditures. For other abbreviations and further explanations, please see the Introduction.

San Angelo, TX - continued

Item	Per	Value	Date	Ref.
Health Care				
Liver function tests, abdominal pain, emergency room	treat	26.00	95	23r
Medical care charges, total, emergency room, third-degree burns	treat	2101.00	95	23r
Medical care charges, total, emergency, infant with fever	treat	628.00	95	23r
Medical services expenditures	year	573	91	81r
Medical supplies expenditures	year	93	91	81r
Morphine, emergency room	treat	34.00	95	23r
Nursing care and facilities charges, emergency room	treat	252.00	95	23r
Nursing care and facilities charges, emergency, infant with fever	treat	252.00	95	23r
Nursing care and facilities charges, emergency, third-degree burns	treat	861.00	95	23r
Physician's charges, emergency, infant with fever	treat	212.00	95	23r
Physician's charges, emergency, third-degree burns	treat	372.00	95	23r
Physician's fee, emergency room	treat	372.00	95	23r
Physician's fee, general practitioner	visit	51.20	12/93	60r
Surgery, open-heart	proc	42374.00	1/93	14r
Ultrasound, abdominal, emergency room	treat	276.00	95	23r
Urinalysis, emergency room	treat	20.00	95	23r
Urinalysis, infant, emergency room	treat	20.00	95	23r
X-rays, emergency room	treat	78.00	95	23r
Household Goods				
Floor coverings, expenditures	year	48	91	81r
Furniture, expenditures	year	280	91	81r
Household equipment, misc. expenditures	year	342	91	81r
Household expenditures, miscellaneous	year	256	91	81r
Household furnishings and equipment, expenditures	year	988	91	81r
Household operations expenditures	year	468	91	81r
Household textiles, expenditures	year	95	91	81r
Housekeeping supplies, expenditures	year	380	91	81r
Laundry and cleaning supplies, expenditures	year	109	91	81r
Postage and stationery, expenditures	year	105	91	81r
Housing				
Add garage/carport		6,980	3/95	74r
Add room(s)		11,403	3/95	74r
Apartment condominium or co-op, median	unit	68600	12/94	62r
Dwellings (owned), expenditures	year	2428	91	81r
Enclose porch/patio/breezeway		4,572	3/95	74r
Finish room in basement/attic		3,794	3/95	74r
Home, existing, single-family, median	unit	120200	12/94	62r
Maintenance, repairs, insurance, and other housing expenditures	year	531	91	81r
Mortgage interest and charges expenditures	year	1506	91	81r
Princ. & int., mortgage, median-price exist. sing.-family home	mo.	540	12/94	62r
Property taxes expenditures	year	391	91	81r
Redesign, restructure more than half of home's interior		17,641	3/95	74r
Rental units expenditures	year	1264	91	81r
Insurance and Pensions				
Auto insurance, private passenger	year	785.78	12/94	71s
Insurance and pensions, personal, expenditures	year	2395	91	81r
Insurance, life and other personal, expenditures	year	368	91	81r
Pensions and Social Security, expenditures	year	2027	91	81r
Personal Services				
Personal services expenditures	year	212	91	81r
Restaurant Food				
Dining expenditures, family	week	33.83	94	73r

San Angelo, TX - continued

Item	Per	Value	Date	Ref.
Taxes				
Tax, cigarettes	year	584.00	10/93	43s
Taxes, Federal income, expenditures	year	2275	91	81r
Taxes, personal, expenditures	year	2715	91	81r
Taxes, State and local income, expenditures	year	365	91	81r
Transportation				
Cars and trucks purchased, new	year	1306	91	81r
Cars and trucks purchased, used	year	942	91	81r
Driver's learning permit fee	perm	5.00	1/94	84s
Driver's license fee	orig	16.00	1/94	84s
Driver's license fee, duplicate	lic	10.00	1/94	84s
Driver's license reinstatement fee, min.	susp	50.00	1/94	85s
Driver's license renewal fee	renew	16.00	1/94	84s
Identification card, nondriver	card	10.00	1/94	83s
Motorcycle learning permit fee	perm	5.00	1/94	84s
Motorcycle license fee	orig	16.00	1/94	84s
Motorcycle license fee, duplicate	lic	10.00	1/94	84s
Motorcycle license renewal fee	renew	21.00	1/94	84s
Public transportation expenditures	year	249	91	81r
Transportation expenditures, total	year	5307	91	81r
Vehicle finance charges	year	346	91	81r
Vehicle insurance expenditures	year	544	91	81r
Vehicle maintenance and repairs expenditures	year	600	91	81r
Vehicle purchases	year	2275	91	81r
Vehicle rental, leases, licenses, etc. expenditures	year	141	91	81r
Vehicles purchased, other than cars and trucks	year	27	91	81r
Utilities				
Electricity expenditures	year	950	91	81r
Utilities, fuels, and public services, total expenditures	year	2000	91	81r
Water and other public services, expenditures	year	227	91	81r
Weddings				
Bridal attendants' gowns	event	750	10/93	76r
Bridal gown	event	852	10/93	76r
Bridal headpiece and veil	event	167	10/93	76r
Bride's wedding band	event	708	10/93	76r
Clergy	event	224	10/93	76r
Engagement ring	event	2756	10/93	76r
Flowers	event	863	10/93	76r
Formal wear for groom	event	106	10/93	76r
Groom's attendants' formal wear	event	530	10/93	76r
Groom's wedding band	event	402	10/93	76r
Music	event	600	10/93	76r
Photography	event	1088	10/93	76r
Shoes for bride	event	50	10/93	76r
Videography	event	483	10/93	76r
Wedding invitations and announcements	event	342	10/93	76r
Wedding reception	event	7000	10/93	76r

San Antonio, TX

Item	Per	Value	Date	Ref.
Composite, ACCRA index		94.90	12/94	2c
Alcoholic Beverages				
Beer, Miller Lite, Bud, 12-oz., ex deposit	6	3.89	12/94	2c
J & B Scotch	750-ml.	19.99	12/94	2c
Wine, Gallo Chablis blanc	1.5-lit	4.80	12/94	2c
Appliances				
Appliances (major), expenditures	year	153	91	81r
Average annual exp.				
Food, health care, personal goods, services	year	27020	91	81r
Charity				
Cash contributions, expenditures	year	839	91	81r

Values are in dollars or fractions of dollars. In the column headed *Ref*, references are shown to sources. Each reference is followed by a letter. These refer to the geographical level for which data were reported: s = State, r = Region, and c = City or metro. The abbreviation *ex* is used to mean *except* or *excluding*; *exp* stands for *expenditures*. For other abbreviations and further explanations, please see the Introduction.

San Antonio, TX - continued

Item	Per	Value	Date	Ref.
Clothing				
Apparel, men and boys, total expenditures	year	380	91	81r
Apparel, women and girls, total expenditures	year	660	91	81r
Footwear, expenditures	year	193	91	81r
Jeans, man's denim		27.57	12/94	2c
Shirt, man's dress shirt		36.80	12/94	2c
Undervest, boy's size 10-14, cotton	3	5.02	12/94	2c
Communications				
Long-distance telephone rate, day, addl. min., 1-10 mi.	min.	0.08	12/93	9s
Long-distance telephone rate, day, initial min., 1-10 mi.	min.	0.10	12/93	9s
Newspaper subscription, dly. and Sun. delivery	month	8.75	12/94	2c
Phone line, single, business, field visit	inst	71.90	12/93	9s
Phone line, single, business, no field visit	inst	57.30	12/93	9s
Phone line, single, residence, field visit	inst	52.95	12/93	9s
Phone line, single, residence, no field visit	inst	38.35	12/93	9s
Telephone bill, family of four	month	17.33	12/94	2c
Telephone service, expenditures	year	616	91	81r
Telephone, business, addl. line, touch tone	month	1.75	10/91	25c
Telephone, business, connection charges, touch tone	inst	68.47	10/91	25c
Telephone, business, key system line, touch tone	month	33.86	10/91	25c
Telephone, business, PBX line, touch tone	month	34.79	10/91	25c
Telephone, business, single ln., touch tone	month	29.36	10/91	25c
Telephone, business, touch tone, inside wiring maintenance plan	month	2.25	10/91	25c
Telephone, residential, flat rate	mo.	9.85	12/93	8c
Education				
Board, 4-year private college/university	year	2084	8/94	80s
Board, 4-year public college/university	year	1675	8/94	80s
Education, total expenditures	year	319	91	81r
Room, 4-year private college/university	year	1840	8/94	80s
Room, 4-year public college/university	year	1756	8/94	80s
Total cost, 4-year private college/university	year	11876	8/94	80s
Total cost, 4-year public college/university	year	4935	8/94	80s
Tuition, 2-year public college/university, in-state	year	625	8/94	80s
Tuition, 4-year private college/university, in-state	year	7952	8/94	80s
Tuition, 4-year public college/university, in-state	year	1503	8/94	80s
Energy and Fuels				
Energy, combined forms, 1800 sq. ft.	mo.	88.85	12/94	2c
Energy, exc. electricity, 1800 sq. ft.	mo.	23.52	12/94	2c
Fuel oil and other fuels, expenditures	year	56	91	81r
Gas, natural, expenditures	year	150	91	81r
Gas, reg unlead, taxes inc., cash, self-service	gal	1.08	12/94	2c
Gasoline and motor oil purchased	year	1152	91	81r
Gasoline, unleaded midgrade	gallon	1.21	4/93	82r
Gasoline, unleaded premium	gallon	1.30	4/93	82r
Gasoline, unleaded regular	gallon	1.10	4/93	82r
Entertainment				
Bowling, evening rate	game	1.77	12/94	2c
Concert ticket, Pearl Jam group	perf	20.00	94	50r
Entertainment, total expenditures	year	1266	91	81r
Fees and admissions, expenditures	year	306	91	81r
Monopoly game, Parker Brothers', No. 9	game	10.58	12/94	2c
Movie	adm	6.06	12/94	2c
Pets, toys, playground equipment, expenditures	year	271	91	81r
Reading, expenditures	year	131	91	81r
Televisions, radios, and sound equipment, expenditures	year	439	91	81r
Tennis balls, yellow, Wilson or Penn, 3	can	2.38	12/94	2c

San Antonio, TX - continued

Item	Per	Value	Date	Ref.
Funerals				
Burial, immediate, container provided by funeral home		1574.60	1/95	54r
Cards, acknowledgment		22.24	1/95	54r
Casket, minimum alternative		239.41	1/95	54r
Cosmetology, hair care, etc.		91.04	1/95	54r
Cremation, direct, container provided by funeral home		1085.15	1/95	54r
Embalming		281.30	1/95	54r
Funeral, funeral home		323.04	1/95	54r
Funeral, other facility		327.58	1/95	54r
Graveside service		355.19	1/95	54r
Hearse, local		141.89	1/95	54r
Limousine, local		99.40	1/95	54r
Memorial service		284.67	1/95	54r
Service charge, professional, nondeclinable		904.06	1/95	54r
Visitation and viewing		187.04	1/95	54r
Groceries				
Groceries, ACCRA Index		93.80	12/94	2c
Apples, Red Delicious	lb.	0.73	12/94	82r
Baby food, strained vegetables, lowest price	4-4.5 oz.	0.25	12/94	2c
Bacon, sliced	lb.	1.67	12/94	82r
Bananas	lb.	0.33	12/94	2c
Bananas	lb.	0.42	12/94	82r
Beef or hamburger, ground	lb.	1.35	12/94	2c
Beef purchases	year	213	91	81r
Beverage purchases, alcoholic	year	249	91	81r
Beverage purchases, nonalcoholic	year	207	91	81r
Bologna, all beef or mixed	lb.	2.27	12/94	82r
Bread, white	24-oz.	0.57	12/94	2c
Bread, white, pan	lb.	0.68	12/94	82r
Cabbage	lb.	0.42	12/94	82r
Carrots, short trimmed and topped	lb.	0.53	12/94	82r
Cereals and bakery products purchases	year	345	91	81r
Cereals and cereals products purchases	year	127	91	81r
Cheddar cheese, natural	lb.	3.58	12/94	82r
Cheese, Kraft grated Parmesan	8-oz.	3.15	12/94	2c
Chicken breast, bone-in	lb.	1.71	12/94	82r
Chicken, fresh, whole	lb.	0.78	12/94	82r
Chicken, whole fryer	lb.	0.78	12/94	2c
Chuck roast, USDA choice, boneless	lb.	2.26	12/94	82r
Cigarettes, Winston, Kings	carton	17.38	12/94	2c
Coffee, vacuum-packed	13 oz.	3.45	12/94	2c
Corn Flakes, Kellogg's or Post Toasties	18 oz.	2.67	12/94	2c
Corn, frozen, whole kernel, lowest price	10 oz.	0.68	12/94	2c
Crackers, soda, salted	lb.	1.27	12/94	82r
Cucumbers	lb.	0.65	12/94	82r
Dairy products (other) purchases	year	141	91	81r
Eggs, Grade A large	dozen	0.73	12/94	2c
Eggs, Grade A large	dozen	0.87	12/94	82r
Fish and seafood purchases	year	72	91	81r
Flour, white, all purpose	lb.	0.23	12/94	82r
Food purchases, food eaten at home	year	2381	91	81r
Foods purchased away from home, not prepared by consumer	year	1696	91	81r
Frankfurters, all meat or all beef	lb.	1.74	12/94	82r
Fruits and vegetables purchases	year	380	91	81r
Grapefruit	lb.	0.45	12/94	82r
Grapes, Thompson seedless	lb.	2.30	12/94	82r
Ground beef, 100% beef	lb.	1.37	12/94	82r
Ground chuck, 100% beef	lb.	1.97	12/94	82r
Ham, boneless, exc. canned	lb.	2.54	12/94	82r
Ice cream, prepackaged, bulk, regular	1/2 gal.	2.47	12/94	82r
Lemons	lb.	1.02	12/94	82r
Lettuce, iceberg	lb.	0.96	12/94	82r
Lettuce, iceberg	head	0.89	12/94	2c
Margarine, Blue Bonnet or Parkay cubes	lb.	0.63	12/94	2c
Margarine, stick	lb.	0.77	12/94	82r
Meats, poultry, fish, and eggs purchases	year	655	91	81r
Milk and cream (fresh) purchases	year	130	91	81r

Values are in dollars or fractions of dollars. In the column headed *Ref*, references are shown to sources. Each reference is followed by a letter. These refer to the geographical level for which data were reported: s=State, r=Region, and c=City or metro. The abbreviation *ex* is used to mean *except* or *excluding*; *exp* stands for *expenditures*. For other abbreviations and further explanations, please see the Introduction.

San Antonio, TX - continued

Item	Per	Value	Date	Ref.
Groceries				
Milk, whole	1/2 gal.	1.62	12/94	2c
Orange juice, frozen concentrate 12-oz. can	16 oz.	1.36	12/94	82r
Orange juice, Minute Maid frozen	12-oz.	1.20	12/94	2c
Oranges, Navel	lb.	0.54	12/94	82r
Peaches, halves or slices, Hunt's, Del Monte, or Libby's	29-oz.	1.27	12/94	2c
Pears, Anjou	lb.	0.81	12/94	82r
Peas, sweet, Del Monte or Green Giant	15-17 oz.	0.51	12/94	2c
Pork chops, center cut, bone-in	lb.	3.07	12/94	82r
Pork purchases	year	142	91	81r
Potato chips	16-oz.	3.15	12/94	82r
Potatoes, frozen, French fried	lb.	0.82	12/94	82r
Potatoes, white	lb.	0.34	12/94	82r
Potatoes, white or red	10-lb. sack	2.02	12/94	2c
Rice, white, long grain, uncooked	lb.	0.48	12/94	82r
Round roast, USDA choice, boneless	lb.	2.91	12/94	82r
Sausage, fresh	lb.	1.82	12/94	82r
Sausage, Jimmy Dean, 100% pork	lb.	2.41	12/94	2c
Shortening, vegetable oil blends	lb.	0.75	12/94	82r
Shortening, vegetable, Crisco	3-lb.	2.35	12/94	2c
Soft drink, Coca Cola, ex deposit	2 lit	1.67	12/94	2c
Spaghetti and macaroni	lb.	0.87	12/94	82r
Steak, rib eye, USDA choice, boneless	lb.	6.85	12/94	82r
Steak, round, graded & ungraded, exc. USDA prime & choice	lb.	2.96	12/94	82r
Steak, round, USDA choice, boneless	lb.	3.17	12/94	82r
Steak, sirloin, USDA choice, boneless	lb.	4.12	12/94	82r
Steak, t-bone	lb.	3.63	12/94	2c
Steak, T-bone, USDA choice, bone-in	lb.	5.63	12/94	82r
Sugar and other sweets, eaten at home, expenditures	year	93	91	81r
Sugar, cane or beet	4 lbs.	1.39	12/94	2c
Sugar, white, all sizes	lb.	0.39	12/94	82r
Tobacco products and smoking supplies, total expenditures	year	286	91	81r
Tomatoes, field grown	lb.	1.36	12/94	82r
Tomatoes, Hunt's or Del Monte	14.5 oz.	0.65	12/94	2c
Tuna, chunk, light	lb.	1.94	12/94	82r
Tuna, chunk, light, oil-packed	6.125-6.5 oz.	0.62	12/94	2c
Turkey, frozen, whole	lb.	0.96	12/94	82r
Yogurt, natural, fruit flavored	8 oz.	0.58	12/94	82r
Goods and Services				
Miscellaneous goods and services, ACCRA Index		98.30	12/94	2c
Health Care				
Health care, ACCRA Index		96.30	12/94	2c
Adenosine, emergency room	treat	100.00	95	23r
Antibiotic ointment, Polysporin	1.5 oz.	3.87	12/94	2c
Bladder tap, superpubic, infant, emergency room	treat	119.00	95	23r
Blood analysis, emergency room	treat	25.00	95	23r
Blood tests, abdominal pain, emergency room	treat	25.00	95	23r
Burn dressing, emergency room	treat	266.00	95	23r
Cardiology interpretation, emergency room	treat	26.00	95	23r
Chest X-ray, emergency room	treat	78.00	95	23r
Childbirth, Cesarean delivery, hospital charge	birth	5462.00	12/91	69r
Childbirth, Cesarean delivery, physician charge	birth	2228.00	12/91	69r
Childbirth, normal delivery, hospital charge	birth	2943.00	12/91	69r
Childbirth, normal delivery, physician charge	birth	1619.00	12/91	69r
Defibrillation pads, emergency room	treat	6.00	95	23r
Dentist's fee, adult teeth cleaning and periodic oral exam	visit	49.80	12/94	2c

San Antonio, TX - continued

Item	Per	Value	Date	Ref.
Health Care - continued				
Doctor's fee, routine exam, established patient	visit	41.80	12/94	2c
Drugs, expenditures	year	297	91	81r
Gastric tube insertion, nasal, emergency room	treat	25.00	95	23r
Health care, total expenditures	year	1600	91	81r
Health insurance expenditures	year	637	91	81r
Heart monitor, emergency room	treat	40.00	95	23r
Hospital care, semiprivate room	day	334.80	12/94	2c
Insurance premium, family medical care	month	389.25	1/95	41s
Intravenous fluids, emergency room	treat	130.00	95	23r
Intravenous fluids, emergency room	liter	26.00	95	23r
Intravenous line, central, emergency room	treat	342.00	95	23r
Liver function tests, abdominal pain, emergency room	treat	26.00	95	23r
Medical care charges, total, emergency room, third-degree burns	treat	2101.00	95	23r
Medical care charges, total, emergency, infant with fever	treat	628.00	95	23r
Medical services expenditures	year	573	91	81r
Medical supplies expenditures	year	93	91	81r
Morphine, emergency room	treat	34.00	95	23r
Nursing care and facilities charges, emergency room	treat	252.00	95	23r
Nursing care and facilities charges, emergency, infant with fever	treat	252.00	95	23r
Nursing care and facilities charges, emergency, third-degree burns	treat	861.00	95	23r
Physician's charges, emergency, infant with fever	treat	212.00	95	23r
Physician's charges, emergency, third-degree burns	treat	372.00	95	23r
Physician's fee, emergency room	treat	372.00	95	23r
Physician's fee, general practitioner	visit	51.20	12/93	60r
Surgery, open-heart	proc	42374.00	1/93	14r
Ultrasound, abdominal, emergency room	treat	276.00	95	23r
Urinalysis, emergency room	treat	20.00	95	23r
Urinalysis, infant, emergency room	treat	20.00	95	23r
X-rays, emergency room	treat	78.00	95	23r
Household Goods				
Appl. repair, service call, wash mach	min. lab. chg.	30.85	12/94	2c
Floor coverings, expenditures	year	48	91	81r
Furniture, expenditures	year	280	91	81r
Household equipment, misc. expenditures	year	342	91	81r
Household expenditures, miscellaneous	year	256	91	81r
Household furnishings and equipment, expenditures	year	988	91	81r
Household operations expenditures	year	468	91	81r
Household textiles, expenditures	year	95	91	81r
Housekeeping supplies, expenditures	year	380	91	81r
Laundry and cleaning supplies, expenditures	year	109	91	81r
Laundry detergent, Tide Ultra, Bold, or Cheer	42 oz.	3.07	12/94	2c
Postage and stationery, expenditures	year	105	91	81r
Tissues, facial, Kleenex brand	175	0.87	12/94	2c
Housing				
Housing, ACCRA Index		90.70	12/94	2c
Add garage/carport		6,980	3/95	74r
Add room(s)		11,403	3/95	74r
Apartment condominium or co-op, median	unit	68600	12/94	62r
Dwellings (owned), expenditures	year	2428	91	81r
Enclose porch/patio/breezeway		4,572	3/95	74r
Finish room in basement/attic		3,794	3/95	74r
Home, existing, single-family, median	unit	120200	12/94	62r
Home, existing, single-family, median	unit	77.30	12/94	62c
House payment, principal and interest, 25% down payment	mo.	674	12/94	2c

Values are in dollars or fractions of dollars. In the column headed *Ref*, references are shown to sources. Each reference is followed by a letter. These refer to the geographical level for which data were reported: s = State, r = Region, and c = City or metro. The abbreviation *ex* is used to mean *except* or *excluding*; *exp* stands for expenditures. For other abbreviations and further explanations, please see the Introduction.

San Antonio, TX - continued

Item	Per	Value	Date	Ref.
Housing				
House, 1800 sq ft, 8000 sq ft lot, new, urban, utilities	total	111700	12/94	2c
Maintenance, repairs, insurance, and other housing expenditures	year	531	91	81r
Mortgage interest and charges expenditures	year	1506	91	81r
Mtge. rate, incl. points and orig. fee, 30-year conv. fixed or ARM	mo.	9.00	12/94	2c
Princ. & int., mortgage, median-price exist. sing.-family home	mo.	540	12/94	62r
Property taxes expenditures	year	391	91	81r
Redesign, restructure more than half of home's interior		17,641	3/95	74r
Rent, apartment, 2 br., 1 1/2-2 baths, unfurnished, 950 sq ft, water	mo.	539	12/94	2c
Rental units expenditures	year	1264	91	81r
Insurance and Pensions				
Auto insurance, private passenger	year	785.78	12/94	71s
Insurance and pensions, personal, expenditures	year	2395	91	81r
Insurance, life and other personal, expenditures	year	368	91	81r
Pensions and Social Security, expenditures	year	2027	91	81r
Personal Goods				
Shampoo, Alberto VO5	15-oz.	0.94	12/94	2c
Toothpaste, Crest or Colgate	6-7 oz.	2.00	12/94	2c
Personal Services				
Dry cleaning, man's 2-pc. suit		6.46	12/94	2c
Haircut, man's barbershop, no styling		7.60	12/94	2c
Haircut, woman's shampoo, trim, blow-dry		22.29	12/94	2c
Personal services expenditures	year	212	91	81r
Restaurant Food				
Chicken, fried, thigh and drumstick		1.59	12/94	2c
Dining expenditures, family	week	33.83	94	73r
Hamburger with cheese	1/4 lb.	1.95	12/94	2c
Pizza, Pizza Hut or Pizza Inn	12-13 in.	7.99	12/94	2c
Taxes				
Tax, cigarettes	year	584.00	10/93	43s
Taxes, Federal income, expenditures	year	2275	91	81r
Taxes, personal, expenditures	year	2715	91	81r
Taxes, State and local income, expenditures	year	365	91	81r
Transportation				
Transportation, ACCRA Index		108.90	12/94	2c
Bus fare, one-way	trip	0.40	12/95	1c
Bus fare, up to 10 miles	one-way	1.55	12/94	2c
Cars and trucks purchased, new	year	1306	91	81r
Cars and trucks purchased, used	year	942	91	81r
Driver's learning permit fee	perm	5.00	1/94	84s
Driver's license fee	orig	16.00	1/94	84s
Driver's license fee, duplicate	lic	10.00	1/94	84s
Driver's license reinstatement fee, min.	susp	50.00	1/94	85s
Driver's license renewal fee	renew	16.00	1/94	84s
Identification card, nondriver	card	10.00	1/94	83s
Motorcycle learning permit fee	perm	5.00	1/94	84s
Motorcycle license fee	orig	16.00	1/94	84s
Motorcycle license fee, duplicate	lic	10.00	1/94	84s
Motorcycle license renewal fee	renew	21.00	1/94	84s
Public transportation expenditures	year	249	91	81r
Tire balance, computer or spin bal., front	wheel	7.55	12/94	2c
Transportation expenditures, total	year	5307	91	81r
Vehicle finance charges	year	346	91	81r
Vehicle insurance expenditures	year	544	91	81r
Vehicle maintenance and repairs expenditures	year	600	91	81r
Vehicle purchases	year	2275	91	81r
Vehicle rental, leases, licenses, etc. expenditures	year	141	91	81r

San Antonio, TX - continued

Item	Per	Value	Date	Ref.
Transportation - continued				
Vehicles purchased, other than cars and trucks	year	27	91	81r
Utilities				
Utilities, ACCRA Index		80.50	12/94	2c
Electricity expenditures	year	950	91	81r
Electricity, (part.), other, 1800 sq. ft., new home	mo.	65.33	12/94	2c
Utilities, fuels, and public services, total expenditures	year	2000	91	81r
Water and other public services, expenditures	year	227	91	81r
Weddings				
Bridal attendants' gowns	event	750	10/93	76r
Bridal gown	event	852	10/93	76r
Bridal headpiece and veil	event	167	10/93	76r
Bride's wedding band	event	708	10/93	76r
Clergy	event	224	10/93	76r
Engagement ring	event	2756	10/93	76r
Flowers	event	863	10/93	76r
Formal wear for groom	event	106	10/93	76r
Groom's attendants' formal wear	event	530	10/93	76r
Groom's wedding band	event	402	10/93	76r
Music	event	600	10/93	76r
Photography	event	1088	10/93	76r
Shoes for bride	event	50	10/93	76r
Videography	event	483	10/93	76r
Wedding invitations and announcements	event	342	10/93	76r
Wedding reception	event	7000	10/93	76r

San Diego, CA

Item	Per	Value	Date	Ref.
Composite, ACCRA index		122.30	12/94	2c
Alcoholic Beverages				
Beer, Miller Lite, Bud, 12-oz., ex deposit	6	3.52	12/94	2c
J & B Scotch	750-ml.	15.94	12/94	2c
Wine, Gallo Chablis blanc	1.5-lit	5.13	12/94	2c
Appliances				
Appliances (major), expenditures	year	96	91	81c
Appliances (major), expenditures	year	160	91	81r
Average annual exp.				
Food, health care, personal goods, services	year	32983	91	81c
Food, health care, personal goods, services	year	32461	91	81r
Charity				
Cash contributions, expenditures	year	781	91	81c
Cash contributions, expenditures	year	975	91	81r
Clothing				
Apparel, men and boys, total expenditures	year	583	91	81c
Apparel, men and boys, total expenditures	year	467	91	81r
Apparel, women and girls, total expenditures	year	585	91	81c
Apparel, women and girls, total expenditures	year	737	91	81r
Footwear, expenditures	year	240	91	81c
Footwear, expenditures	year	270	91	81r
Jeans, man's denim		28.49	12/94	2c
Shirt, man's dress shirt		27.74	12/94	2c
Undervest, boy's size 10-14, cotton	3	4.31	12/94	2c
Communications				
Long-distance telephone rate, day, addl. min., 1-10 mi.	min.	0.07	12/93	9s
Long-distance telephone rate, day, initial min., 1-10 mi.	min.	0.17	12/93	9s
Newspaper subscription, dly. and Sun. delivery	month	10.50	12/94	2c
Phone line, single, business, field visit	inst	70.75	12/93	9s
Phone line, single, business, no field visit	inst	70.75	12/93	9s
Phone line, single, residence, field visit	inst	34.75	12/93	9s
Phone line, single, residence, no field visit	inst	34.75	12/93	9s

Values are in dollars or fractions of dollars. In the column headed *Ref*, references are shown to sources. Each reference is followed by a letter. These refer to the geographical level for which data were reported: s = State, r = Region, and c = City or metro. The abbreviation *ex* is used to mean *except* or *excluding*; *exp* stands for expenditures. For other abbreviations and further explanations, please see the Introduction.

San Diego, CA - continued

Item	Per	Value	Date	Ref.
Communications				
Telephone bill, family of four	month	14.18	12/94	2c
Telephone service, expenditures	year	608	91	81c
Telephone service, expenditures	year	611	91	81r
Telephone, residential, flat rate	mo.	8.35	12/93	8c
Education				
Board, 4-year private college/university	year	2945	8/94	80s
Board, 4-year public college/university	year	2321	8/94	80s
Education, total expenditures	year	447	91	81c
Education, total expenditures	year	375	91	81r
Room, 4-year private college/university	year	3094	8/94	80s
Room, 4-year public college/university	year	2812	8/94	80s
Student fee, university	year	21.00	93	18s
Total cost, 4-year private college/university	year	19321	8/94	80s
Total cost, 4-year public college/university	year	7511	8/94	80s
Tuition, 2-year public college/university, in-state	year	345	8/94	80s
Tuition, 4-year private college/university, in-state	year	13282	8/94	80s
Tuition, 4-year public college/university, in-state	year	2378	8/94	80s
Energy and Fuels				
Energy, combined forms, 1800 sq. ft.	mo.	107.23	12/94	2c
Energy, exc. electricity, 1800 sq. ft.	mo.	24.59	12/94	2c
Fuel oil and other fuels, expenditures	year	20	91	81c
Fuel oil and other fuels, expenditures	year	33	91	81r
Gas, cooking, 10 therms	month	6.09	2/94	65c
Gas, cooking, 30 therms	month	18.26	2/94	65c
Gas, cooking, 50 therms	month	31.93	2/94	65c
Gas, heating, winter, 100 therms	month	72.97	2/94	65c
Gas, heating, winter, average use	month	39.30	2/94	65c
Gas, natural, expenditures	year	48	91	81c
Gas, natural, expenditures	year	212	91	81r
Gas, reg unlead, taxes inc., cash, self-service	gal	1.26	12/94	2c
Gasoline and motor oil purchased	year	1184	91	81c
Gasoline and motor oil purchased	year	1115	91	81r
Gasoline, unleaded midgrade	gallon	1.36	4/93	82r
Gasoline, unleaded premium	gallon	1.43	4/93	82r
Gasoline, unleaded regular	gallon	1.23	4/93	82r
Entertainment				
Bowling, evening rate	game	2.24	12/94	2c
Concert ticket, Pearl Jam group	perf	20.00	94	50r
Entertainment supplies, equipment, and services, misc. expenditures	year	240	91	81c
Entertainment, total expenditures	year	1539	91	81c
Entertainment, total expenditures	year	1853	91	81r
Fees and admissions, expenditures	year	460	91	81c
Fees and admissions, expenditures	year	482	91	81r
Monopoly game, Parker Brothers', No. 9	game	11.84	12/94	2c
Movie	adm	6.83	12/94	2c
Pets, toys, playground equipment, expenditures	year	309	91	81c
Pets, toys, playground equipment, expenditures	year	299	91	81r
Reading, expenditures	year	165	91	81c
Reading, expenditures	year	164	91	81r
Televisions, radios, and sound equipment, expenditures	year	529	91	81c
Televisions, radios, and sound equipment, expenditures	year	528	91	81r
Tennis balls, yellow, Wilson or Penn, 3	can	2.47	12/94	2c
Funerals				
Burial, immediate, container provided by funeral home		1382.70	1/95	54r
Cards, acknowledgment		21.87	1/95	54r
Casket, minimum alternative		128.54	1/95	54r
Cosmetology, hair care, etc.		119.69	1/95	54r
Cremation, direct, container provided by funeral home		1030.62	1/95	54r
Embalming		255.42	1/95	54r

San Diego, CA - continued

Item	Per	Value	Date	Ref.
Funerals - continued				
Funeral, funeral home		437.38	1/95	54r
Funeral, other facility		444.46	1/95	54r
Graveside service		338.46	1/95	54r
Hearse, local		147.50	1/95	54r
Limousine, local		130.33	1/95	54r
Memorial service		553.16	1/95	54r
Service charge, professional, nondeclinable		859.15	1/95	54r
Visitation and viewing		93.23	1/95	54r
Groceries				
Groceries, ACCRA Index		112.20	12/94	2c
Apples, Red Delicious	lb.	0.72	12/94	82r
Baby food, strained vegetables, lowest price	4-4.5 oz.	0.38	12/94	2c
Bacon, sliced	lb.	1.73	12/94	82r
Bananas	lb.	0.59	12/94	2c
Bananas	lb.	0.52	12/94	82r
Beef or hamburger, ground	lb.	1.47	12/94	2c
Beef purchases	year	202	91	81c
Beef purchases	year	241	91	81r
Beverage purchases, alcoholic	year	349	91	81c
Beverage purchases, alcoholic	year	328	91	81r
Beverage purchases, nonalcoholic	year	272	91	81c
Beverage purchases, nonalcoholic	year	234	91	81r
Bologna, all beef or mixed	lb.	2.33	12/94	82r
Bread, white	24-oz.	0.84	12/94	2c
Bread, white, pan	lb.	0.81	12/94	82r
Carrots, short trimmed and topped	lb.	0.43	12/94	82r
Cereals and bakery products purchases	year	393	91	81c
Cereals and bakery products purchases	year	392	91	81r
Cereals and cereal products purchases	year	128	91	81c
Cereals and cereals products purchases	year	139	91	81r
Cheese, Kraft grated Parmesan	8-oz.	3.30	12/94	2c
Chicken breast, bone-in	lb.	2.04	12/94	82r
Chicken, fresh, whole	lb.	0.95	12/94	82r
Chicken, whole fryer	lb.	1.13	12/94	2c
Cigarettes, Winston, Kings	carton	16.84	12/94	2c
Coffee, 100%, ground roast, all sizes	lb.	4.48	12/94	82r
Coffee, vacuum-packed	13 oz.	3.80	12/94	2c
Corn Flakes, Kellogg's or Post Toasties	18 oz.	2.57	12/94	2c
Corn, frozen, whole kernel, lowest price	10 oz.	0.84	12/94	2c
Dairy products (other) purchases	year	186	91	81c
Dairy products (other) purchases	year	182	91	81r
Eggs, Grade A large	dozen	2.05	12/94	2c
Fish and seafood purchases	year	88	91	81c
Fish and seafood purchases	year	94	91	81r
Flour, white, all purpose	lb.	0.21	12/94	82r
Food purchases, food eaten at home	year	2748	91	81c
Food purchases, food eaten at home	year	2749	91	81r
Foods purchased away from home, not prepared by consumer	year	1709	91	81c
Foods purchased away from home, not prepared by consumer	year	1909	91	81r
Fruits and vegetables purchases	year	441	91	81c
Fruits and vegetables purchases	year	459	91	81r
Grapefruit	lb.	0.56	12/94	82r
Ground beef, 100% beef	lb.	1.31	12/94	82r
Ham, boneless, exc. canned	lb.	2.46	12/94	82r
Ice cream, prepackaged, bulk, regular	1/2 gal.	2.57	12/94	82r
Lemons	lb.	1.00	12/94	82r
Lettuce, iceberg	lb.	0.93	12/94	82r
Lettuce, iceberg	head	0.88	12/94	2c
Margarine, Blue Bonnet or Parkay cubes	lb.	0.87	12/94	2c
Meats, poultry, fish, and eggs purchases	year	679	91	81c
Meats, poultry, fish, and eggs purchases	year	700	91	81r
Milk and cream (fresh) purchases	year	140	91	81c
Milk and cream (fresh) purchases	year	155	91	81r
Milk, whole	1/2 gal.	1.68	12/94	2c
Orange juice, frozen concentrate 12-oz. can	16 oz.	1.52	12/94	82r
Orange juice, Minute Maid frozen	12-oz.	1.47	12/94	2c
Oranges, Navel	lb.	0.56	12/94	82r

Values are in dollars or fractions of dollars. In the column headed *Ref*, references are shown to sources. Each reference is followed by a letter. These refer to the geographical level for which data were reported: s = State, r = Region, and c = City or metro. The abbreviation *ex* is used to mean *except* or *excluding*; *exp* stands for expenditures. For other abbreviations and further explanations, please see the Introduction.

San Diego, CA - continued

Item	Per	Value	Date	Ref.
Groceries				
Peaches, halves or slices, Hunt's, Del Monte, or Libby's	29-oz.	1.26	12/94	2c
Peas, sweet, Del Monte or Green Giant	15-17 oz.	0.64	12/94	2c
Pork chops, center cut, bone-in	lb.	3.30	12/94	82r
Pork purchases	year	131	91	81c
Pork purchases	year	122	91	81r
Potato chips	16-oz.	3.03	12/94	82r
Potatoes, frozen, French fried	lb.	0.77	12/94	82r
Potatoes, white	lb.	0.35	12/94	82r
Potatoes, white or red	10-lb. sack	1.74	12/94	2c
Rice, white, long grain, uncooked	lb.	0.54	12/94	82r
Round roast, USDA choice, boneless	lb.	2.92	12/94	82r
Sausage, Jimmy Dean, 100% pork	lb.	2.82	12/94	2c
Shortening, vegetable oil blends	lb.	0.80	12/94	82r
Shortening, vegetable, Crisco	3-lb.	2.88	12/94	2c
Soft drink, Coca Cola, ex deposit	2 lit	1.06	12/94	2c
Spaghetti and macaroni	lb.	1.02	12/94	82r
Steak, round, graded & ungraded, exc. USDA prime & choice	lb.	3.13	12/94	82r
Steak, sirloin, USDA choice, boneless	lb.	4.07	12/94	82r
Steak, t-bone	lb.	4.79	12/94	2c
Sugar and other sweets, eaten at home, expenditures	year	105	91	81r
Sugar and other sweets, eaten at home, purchases	year	120	91	81c
Sugar, cane or beet	4 lbs.	1.47	12/94	2c
Sugar, white, all sizes	lb.	0.38	12/94	82r
Tobacco products and smoking supplies, total expenditures	year	216	91	81c
Tobacco products and smoking supplies, total expenditures	year	221	91	81r
Tomatoes, field grown	lb.	1.45	12/94	82r
Tomatoes, Hunt's or Del Monte	14.5 oz.	0.76	12/94	2c
Tuna, chunk, light	lb.	2.18	12/94	82r
Tuna, chunk, light, oil-packed	6.125-6.5 oz.	0.74	12/94	2c
Goods and Services				
Miscellaneous goods and services, ACCRA Index		101.80	12/94	2c
Health Care				
Health care, ACCRA Index		125.10	12/94	2c
Antibiotic ointment, Polysporin	1.5 oz.	4.59	12/94	2c
Childbirth, Cesarean delivery, hospital charge	birth	6059.00	12/91	69r
Childbirth, Cesarean delivery, physician charge	birth	2248.00	12/91	69r
Childbirth, normal delivery, hospital charge	birth	3006.00	12/91	69r
Childbirth, normal delivery, physician charge	birth	1634.00	12/91	69r
Dentist's fee, adult teeth cleaning and periodic oral exam	visit	65.10	12/94	2c
Doctor's fee, routine exam, established patient	visit	47.44	12/94	2c
Drugs, expenditures	year	171	91	81c
Drugs, expenditures	year	230	91	81r
Health care, total expenditures	year	1178	91	81c
Health care, total expenditures	year	1544	91	81r
Health insurance expenditures	year	465	91	81c
Health insurance expenditures	year	558	91	81r
Hospital care, semiprivate room	day	567.12	12/94	2c
Insurance premium, family medical care	month	380.27	1/95	41s
Medical services expenditures	year	473	91	81c
Medical services expenditures	year	676	91	81r
Medical supplies expenditures	year	69	91	81c
Medical supplies expenditures	year	80	91	81r
Surgery, open-heart	proc	37818.00	1/93	14r

San Diego, CA - continued

Item	Per	Value	Date	Ref.
Household Goods				
Appl. repair, service call, wash mach	min. lab. chg.	31.47	12/94	2c
Floor coverings, expenditures	year	16	91	81c
Floor coverings, expenditures	year	79	91	81r
Furniture, expenditures	year	276	91	81c
Furniture, expenditures	year	352	91	81r
Household equipment, misc. expenditures	year	614	91	81r
Household equipment, misc., expenditures	year	417	91	81c
Household expenditures, miscellaneous	year	374	91	81c
Household expenditures, miscellaneous	year	294	91	81r
Household furnishings and equipment, expenditures	year	1064	91	81c
Household furnishings and equipment, expenditures	year	1416	91	81r
Household operations expenditures	year	655	91	81c
Household operations expenditures	year	580	91	81r
Household textiles, expenditures	year	182	91	81c
Household textiles, expenditures	year	113	91	81r
Housekeeping supplies, expenditures	year	433	91	81c
Housekeeping supplies, expenditures	year	447	91	81r
Laundry and cleaning supplies, expenditures	year	96	91	81c
Laundry and cleaning supplies, expenditures	year	114	91	81r
Laundry detergent, Tide Ultra, Bold, or Cheer	42 oz.	4.06	12/94	2c
Postage and stationery, expenditures	year	152	91	81c
Postage and stationery, expenditures	year	145	91	81r
Tissues, facial, Kleenex brand	175	1.13	12/94	2c
Housing				
Housing, ACCRA Index		163.70	12/94	2c
Add garage/carport		6,422	3/95	74r
Add room(s)		26,583	3/95	74r
Apartment condominium or co-op, median	unit	105300	12/94	62r
Dwellings (owned), expenditures	year	4218	91	81c
Dwellings (owned), expenditures	year	3932	91	81r
Enclose porch/patio/breezeway		5,382	3/95	74r
Finish room in basement/attic		3,911	3/95	74r
Home, existing, single-family, median	unit	178600	12/94	62r
Home, existing, single-family, median	unit	170.40	12/94	62c
Home, purchase price	unit	179.90	3/93	26c
House payment, principal and interest, 25% down payment	mo.	1251	12/94	2c
House, 1800 sq ft, 8000 sq ft lot, new, urban, utilities	total	204900	12/94	2c
Maintenance, repairs, insurance, and other housing expenditures	year	493	91	81c
Maintenance, repairs, insurance, and other housing expenditures	year	591	91	81r
Mortgage interest and charges expenditures	year	3086	91	81c
Mortgage interest and charges expenditures	year	2747	91	81r
Mtge. rate, incl. points and orig. fee, 30-year conv. fixed or ARM	mo.	9.13	12/94	2c
Princ. & int., mortgage, median-price exist. sing.-family home	mo.	845	12/94	62r
Property taxes expenditures	year	639	91	81c
Property taxes expenditures	year	594	91	81r
Redesign, restructure more than half of home's interior		5,467	3/95	74r
Rent, apartment, 2 br., 1 1/2-2 baths, unfurnished, 950 sq ft, water	mo.	875	12/94	2c
Rental units expenditures	year	3189	900/00/91	81c
Rental units expenditures	year	2077	91	81r
Insurance and Pensions				
Auto insurance, private passenger	year	892.80	12/94	71s
Insurance and pensions, personal, expenditures	year	3127	91	81c
Insurance and pensions, personal, expenditures	year	3042	91	81r

Values are in dollars or fractions of dollars. In the column headed *Ref*, references are shown to sources. Each reference is followed by a letter. These refer to the geographical level for which data were reported: s=State, r=Region, and c=City or metro. The abbreviation *ex* is used to mean *except* or *excluding*; *exp* stands for expenditures. For other abbreviations and further explanations, please see the Introduction.

San Diego, CA - continued

Item	Per	Value	Date	Ref.
Insurance and Pensions				
Insurance, life and other personal, expenditures	year	222	91	81c
Insurance, life and other personal, expenditures	year	298	91	81r
Pensions and Social Security, expenditures	year	2905	91	81c
Pensions and Social Security, expenditures	year	2744	91	81r
Legal Assistance				
Legal work, law firm associate	hour	91		10r
Legal work, law firm partner	hour	151		10r
Personal Goods				
Personal care products and services, total expenditures	year	403	91	81c
Shampoo, Alberto VO5	15-oz.	1.47	12/94	2c
Toothpaste, Crest or Colgate	6-7 oz.	2.45	12/94	2c
Personal Services				
Dry cleaning, man's 2-pc. suit		6.47	12/94	2c
Haircut, man's barbershop, no styling		8.44	12/94	2c
Haircut, woman's shampoo, trim, blow-dry		25.95	12/94	2c
Personal services expenditures	year	280	91	81c
Personal services expenditures	year	286	91	81r
Restaurant Food				
Chicken, fried, thigh and drumstick		2.18	12/94	2c
Dining expenditures, family	week	32.25	94	73r
Hamburger with cheese	1/4 lb.	1.96	12/94	2c
Pizza, Pizza Hut or Pizza Inn	12-13 in.	8.80	12/94	2c
Taxes				
Taxes, Federal income, expenditures	year	2831	91	81c
Taxes, Federal income, expenditures	year	2946	91	81r
Taxes, personal, expenditures	year	3508	91	81c
Taxes, personal, expenditures	year	3791	91	81r
Taxes, State and local income, expenditures	year	645	91	81c
Taxes, State and local income, expenditures	year	791	91	81r
Transportation				
Transportation, ACCRA Index		127.90	12/94	2c
Bus fare, one-way	trip	1.28	12/95	1c
Bus fare, up to 10 miles	one-way	1.67	12/94	2c
Cars and trucks purchased, new	year	1358	91	81c
Cars and trucks purchased, new	year	1231	91	81r
Cars and trucks purchased, used	year	888	91	81c
Cars and trucks purchased, used	year	915	91	81r
Driver's learning permit fee	perm	12.00	1/94	84s
Driver's license fee	orig	12.00	1/94	84s
Driver's license fee, duplicate	lic	12.00	1/94	84s
Driver's license reinstatement fee, min.	susp	15.00	1/94	85s
Driver's license renewal fee	renew	12.00	1/94	84s
Identification card, nondriver	card	6.00	1/94	83s
Motorcycle learning permit fee	perm	12.00	1/94	84s
Motorcycle license fee	orig	12.00	1/94	84s
Motorcycle license fee, duplicate	lic	12.00	1/94	84s
Motorcycle license renewal fee	renew	12.00	1/94	84s
Public transportation expenditures	year	509	91	81c
Public transportation expenditures	year	375	91	81r
Railway fare, commuter rail, one-way	trip	2.50	12/95	1c
Railway fare, light rail, one-way	trip	1.00	12/95	1c
Tire balance, computer or spin bal., front	wheel	9.18	12/94	2c
Transportation expenditures, total	year	6076	91	81c
Transportation expenditures, total	year	5527	91	81r
Vehicle expenses, miscellaneous	year	2082	91	81c
Vehicle finance charges	year	252	91	81c
Vehicle finance charges	year	287	91	81r
Vehicle insurance expenditures	year	730	91	81c
Vehicle insurance expenditures	year	624	91	81r
Vehicle maintenance and repairs expenditures	year	743	91	81c
Vehicle maintenance and repairs expenditures	year	695	91	81r
Vehicle purchases	year	2301	91	81c

San Diego, CA - continued

Item	Per	Value	Date	Ref.
Transportation - continued				
Vehicle purchases	year	2174	91	81r
Vehicle rental, leases, licenses, etc. expenditures	year	357	91	81c
Vehicle rental, leases, licenses, etc. expenditures	year	257	91	81r
Vehicles purchased, other than cars and trucks	year	55	91	81c
Vehicles purchased, other than cars and trucks	year	28	91	81r
Utilities				
Utilities, ACCRA Index		74.10	12/94	2c
Electricity expenditures	year	615	91	81c
Electricity expenditures	year	616	91	81r
Electricity, (part.), other, 1800 sq. ft., new home	mo.	58.87	12/94	2c
Electricity, summer, 250 KWh	month	25.35	8/93	64c
Electricity, summer, 500 KWh	month	57.22	8/93	64c
Electricity, summer, 750 KWh	month	89.08	8/93	64c
Electricity, summer, 1000 KWh	month	120.94	8/93	64c
Utilities, fuels, and public services, total expenditures	year	1522	91	81c
Utilities, fuels, and public services, total expenditures	year	1681	91	81r
Water and other public services, expenditures	year	231	91	81c
Water and other public services, expenditures	year	209	91	81r
Weddings				
Bridal attendants' gowns	event	750	10/93	76r
Bridal gown	event	852	10/93	76r
Bridal headpiece and veil	event	167	10/93	76r
Bride's wedding band	event	708	10/93	76r
Clergy	event	224	10/93	76r
Engagement ring	event	2756	10/93	76r
Flowers	event	863	10/93	76r
Formal wear for groom	event	106	10/93	76r
Groom's attendants' formal wear	event	530	10/93	76r
Groom's wedding band	event	402	10/93	76r
Music	event	600	10/93	76r
Photography	event	1088	10/93	76r
Shoes for bride	event	50	10/93	76r
Videography	event	483	10/93	76r
Wedding invitations and announcements	event	342	10/93	76r
Wedding reception	event	7000	10/93	76r

San Francisco, CA

Item	Per	Value	Date	Ref.
Appliances				
Appliances (major), expenditures	year	166	91	81c
Appliances (major), expenditures	year	160	91	81r
Average annual exp.				
Food, health care, personal goods, services	year	39707	91	81c
Food, health care, personal goods, services	year	32461	91	81r
Business				
Dinner and tip, hotel, corporate rate	night	39.00	2/94	15c
Hotel room, corporate rate	night	119.00	2/94	15c
Photocopies, copy shop	10 copies	0.50	7/95	4c
Photocopies, copy shop	100 copies	2.00	7/95	4c
Photocopies, copy shop	500 copies	9.50	7/95	4c
Photocopies, copy shop	1000 copies	18.00	7/95	4c
Photocopies, copy shop	5000 copies	90.00	7/95	4c
Charity				
Cash contributions, expenditures	year	1433	91	81c

Values are in dollars or fractions of dollars. In the column headed *Ref*, references are shown to sources. Each reference is followed by a letter. These refer to the geographical level for which data were reported: s = State, r = Region, and c = City or metro. The abbreviation *ex* is used to mean *except* or *excluding*; *exp* stands for expenditures. For other abbreviations and further explanations, please see the Introduction.

San Francisco, CA - continued

Item	Per	Value	Date	Ref.
Charity				
Cash contributions, expenditures	year	975	91	81r
Clothing				
Apparel, men and boys, total expenditures	year	571	91	81c
Apparel, men and boys, total expenditures	year	467	91	81r
Apparel, women and girls, total expenditures	year	982	91	81c
Apparel, women and girls, total expenditures	year	737	91	81r
Footwear, expenditures	year	314	91	81c
Footwear, expenditures	year	270	91	81r
Communications				
Long-distance telephone rate, day, addl. min., 1-10 mi.	min.	0.07	12/93	9s
Long-distance telephone rate, day, initial min., 1-10 mi.	min.	0.17	12/93	9s
Phone line, single, business, field visit	inst	70.75	12/93	9s
Phone line, single, business, no field visit	inst	70.75	12/93	9s
Phone line, single, residence, field visit	inst	34.75	12/93	9s
Phone line, single, residence, no field visit	inst	34.75	12/93	9s
Telephone service, expenditures	year	608	91	81c
Telephone service, expenditures	year	611	91	81r
Education				
Board, 4-year private college/university	year	2945	8/94	80s
Board, 4-year public college/university	year	2321	8/94	80s
Education, total expenditures	year	452	91	81c
Education, total expenditures	year	375	91	81r
Room, 4-year private college/university	year	3094	8/94	80s
Room, 4-year public college/university	year	2812	8/94	80s
Student fee, university	year	21.00	93	18s
Total cost, 4-year private college/university	year	19321	8/94	80s
Total cost, 4-year public college/university	year	7511	8/94	80s
Tuition, 2-year public college/university, in-state	year	345	8/94	80s
Tuition, 4-year private college/university, in-state	year	13282	8/94	80s
Tuition, 4-year public college/university, in-state	year	2378	8/94	80s
Energy and Fuels				
Electricity	500 KWh	62.98	12/94	82c
Fuel oil and other fuels, expenditures	year	38	91	81c
Fuel oil and other fuels, expenditures	year	33	91	81r
Gas, natural, expenditures	year	258	91	81c
Gas, natural, expenditures	year	212	91	81r
Gas, piped	40 therms	22.65	12/94	82c
Gas, piped	100 therms	66.85	12/94	82c
Gas, piped	therm	0.64	12/94	82c
Gasoline and motor oil purchased	year	1029	91	81c
Gasoline and motor oil purchased	year	1115	91	81r
Gasoline, unleaded midgrade	gallon	1.37	4/93	82c
Gasoline, unleaded midgrade	gallon	1.36	4/93	82r
Gasoline, unleaded premium	gallon	1.47	4/93	82c
Gasoline, unleaded premium	gallon	1.43	4/93	82r
Gasoline, unleaded regular	gallon	1.23	4/93	82c
Gasoline, unleaded regular	gallon	1.23	4/93	82r
Entertainment				
Baseball game, four-person family	game	100.80	4/94	47c
Concert ticket, Pearl Jam group	perf	20.00	94	50r
Entertainment supplies, equipment, and services, misc. expenditures	year	520	91	81c
Entertainment, total expenditures	year	2145	91	81c
Entertainment, total expenditures	year	1853	91	81r
Fees and admissions, expenditures	year	636	91	81c
Fees and admissions, expenditures	year	482	91	81r
Pets, toys, playground equipment, expenditures	year	336	91	81c
Pets, toys, playground equipment, expenditures	year	299	91	81r
Reading, expenditures	year	204	91	81c

San Francisco, CA - continued

Item	Per	Value	Date	Ref.
Entertainment - continued				
Reading, expenditures	year	164	91	81r
Televisions, radios, and sound equipment, expenditures	year	653	91	81c
Televisions, radios, and sound equipment, expenditures	year	528	91	81r
Funerals				
Burial, immediate, container provided by funeral home		1382.70	1/95	54r
Cards, acknowledgment		21.87	1/95	54r
Casket, minimum alternative		128.54	1/95	54r
Cosmetology, hair care, etc.		119.69	1/95	54r
Cremation, direct, container provided by funeral home		1030.62	1/95	54r
Embalming		255.42	1/95	54r
Funeral, funeral home		437.38	1/95	54r
Funeral, other facility		444.46	1/95	54r
Graveside service		338.46	1/95	54r
Hearse, local		147.50	1/95	54r
Limousine, local		130.33	1/95	54r
Memorial service		553.16	1/95	54r
Service charge, professional, nondeclinable		859.15	1/95	54r
Visitation and viewing		93.23	1/95	54r
Groceries				
Apples, Red Delicious	lb.	0.72	12/94	82r
Bacon, sliced	lb.	1.73	12/94	82r
Bananas	lb.	0.52	12/94	82r
Beef purchases	year	218	91	81c
Beef purchases	year	241	91	81r
Beverage purchases, alcoholic	year	567	91	81c
Beverage purchases, alcoholic	year	328	91	81r
Beverage purchases, nonalcoholic	year	241	91	81c
Beverage purchases, nonalcoholic	year	234	91	81r
Bologna, all beef or mixed	lb.	2.33	12/94	82r
Bread, white, pan	lb.	0.81	12/94	82r
Carrots, short trimmed and topped	lb.	0.43	12/94	82r
Cereals and bakery products purchases	year	486	91	81c
Cereals and bakery products purchases	year	392	91	81r
Cereals and cereal products purchases	year	170	91	81c
Cereals and cereals products purchases	year	139	91	81r
Chicken breast, bone-in	lb.	2.04	12/94	82r
Chicken, fresh, whole	lb.	0.95	12/94	82r
Coffee, 100%, ground roast, all sizes	lb.	4.48	12/94	82r
Dairy products (other) purchases	year	207	91	81c
Dairy products (other) purchases	year	182	91	81r
Fish and seafood purchases	year	110	91	81c
Fish and seafood purchases	year	94	91	81r
Flour, white, all purpose	lb.	0.21	12/94	82r
Food purchases, food eaten at home	year	3032	91	81c
Food purchases, food eaten at home	year	2749	91	81r
Foods purchased away from home, not prepared by consumer	year	2252	91	81c
Foods purchased away from home, not prepared by consumer	year	1909	91	81r
Fruits and vegetables purchases	year	520	91	81c
Fruits and vegetables purchases	year	459	91	81r
Grapefruit	lb.	0.56	12/94	82r
Ground beef, 100% beef	lb.	1.31	12/94	82r
Ham, boneless, exc. canned	lb.	2.46	12/94	82r
Ice cream, prepackaged, bulk, regular	1/2 gal.	2.57	12/94	82r
Lemons	lb.	1.00	12/94	82r
Lettuce, iceberg	lb.	0.93	12/94	82r
Meats, poultry, fish, and eggs purchases	year	729	91	81c
Meats, poultry, fish, and eggs purchases	year	700	91	81r
Milk and cream (fresh) purchases	year	125	91	81c
Milk and cream (fresh) purchases	year	155	91	81r
Orange juice, frozen concentrate 12-oz. can	16 oz.	1.52	12/94	82r
Oranges, Navel	lb.	0.56	12/94	82r
Pork chops, center cut, bone-in	lb.	3.30	12/94	82r
Pork purchases	year	124	91	81c
Pork purchases	year	122	91	81r

Values are in dollars or fractions of dollars. In the column headed *Ref*, references are shown to sources. Each reference is followed by a letter. These refer to the geographical level for which data were reported: s=State, r=Region, and c=City or metro. The abbreviation *ex* is used to mean *except* or *excluding*; *exp* stands for expenditures. For other abbreviations and further explanations, please see the Introduction.

San Francisco, CA - continued

Item	Per	Value	Date	Ref.
Groceries				
Potato chips	16-oz.	3.03	12/94	82r
Potatoes, frozen, French fried	lb.	0.77	12/94	82r
Potatoes, white	lb.	0.35	12/94	82r
Rice, white, long grain, uncooked	lb.	0.54	12/94	82r
Round roast, USDA choice, boneless	lb.	2.92	12/94	82r
Shortening, vegetable oil blends	lb.	0.80	12/94	82r
Spaghetti and macaroni	lb.	1.02	12/94	82r
Steak, round, graded & ungraded, exc. USDA prime & choice	lb.	3.13	12/94	82r
Steak, sirloin, USDA choice, boneless	lb.	4.07	12/94	82r
Sugar and other sweets, eaten at home, expenditures	year	105	91	81r
Sugar and other sweets, eaten at home, purchases	year	124	91	81c
Sugar, white, all sizes	lb.	0.38	12/94	82r
Tobacco products and smoking supplies, total expenditures	year	218	91	81c
Tobacco products and smoking supplies, total expenditures	year	221	91	81r
Tomatoes, field grown	lb.	1.45	12/94	82r
Tuna, chunk, light	lb.	2.18	12/94	82r
Health Care				
Childbirth, Cesarean delivery, hospital charge	birth	6059.00	12/91	69r
Childbirth, Cesarean delivery, physician charge	birth	2248.00	12/91	69r
Childbirth, normal delivery, hospital charge	birth	3006.00	12/91	69r
Childbirth, normal delivery, physician charge	birth	1634.00	12/91	69r
Drugs, expenditures	year	198	91	81c
Drugs, expenditures	year	230	91	81r
Health care, total expenditures	year	1536	91	81c
Health care, total expenditures	year	1544	91	81r
Health insurance expenditures	year	656	91	81c
Health insurance expenditures	year	558	91	81r
Health insurance premium	month	417.00	7/93	94c
Hospital cost	adm	7,866	2/94	72c
Insurance premium, family medical care	month	380.27	1/95	41s
Medical services expenditures	year	582	91	81c
Medical services expenditures	year	676	91	81r
Medical supplies expenditures	year	100	91	81c
Medical supplies expenditures	year	80	91	81r
Surgery, open-heart	proc	37818.00	1/93	14r
Household Goods				
Floor coverings, expenditures	year	39	91	81c
Floor coverings, expenditures	year	79	91	81r
Furniture, expenditures	year	376	91	81c
Furniture, expenditures	year	352	91	81r
Household equipment, misc. expenditures	year	614	91	81r
Household equipment, misc., expenditures	year	484	91	81c
Household expenditures, miscellaneous	year	270	91	81c
Household expenditures, miscellaneous	year	294	91	81r
Household furnishings and equipment, expenditures	year	1400	91	81c
Household furnishings and equipment, expenditures	year	1416	91	81r
Household operations expenditures	year	731	91	81c
Household operations expenditures	year	580	91	81r
Household textiles, expenditures	year	182	91	81c
Household textiles, expenditures	year	113	91	81r
Housekeeping supplies, expenditures	year	618	91	81c
Housekeeping supplies, expenditures	year	447	91	81r
Laundry and cleaning supplies, expenditures	year	122	91	81c
Laundry and cleaning supplies, expenditures	year	114	91	81r
Postage and stationery, expenditures	year	266	91	81c
Postage and stationery, expenditures	year	145	91	81r
Housing				
Add garage/carport		6,422	3/95	74r
Add room(s)		26,583	3/95	74r
Apartment condominium or co-op, median	unit	105300	12/94	62r

San Francisco, CA - continued

Item	Per	Value	Date	Ref.
Housing - continued				
Car rental	day	43.00	5/95	95c
Dwellings (owned), expenditures	year	6113	91	81c
Dwellings (owned), expenditures	year	3932	91	81r
Enclose porch/patio/breezeway		5,382	3/95	74r
Finish room in basement/attic		3,911	3/95	74r
Home, existing, single-family, median	unit	178600	12/94	62r
Home, existing, single-family, median	unit	254.50	12/94	62c
Home, purchase price	unit	241.00	3/93	26c
Hotel room	day	165.00	5/95	95c
Maintenance, repairs, insurance, and other housing expenditures	year	742	91	81c
Maintenance, repairs, insurance, and other housing expenditures	year	591	91	81r
Mortgage interest and charges expenditures	year	4444	91	81c
Mortgage interest and charges expenditures	year	2747	91	81r
Princ. & int., mortgage, median-price exist. sing.-family home	mo.	845	12/94	62r
Property taxes expenditures	year	927	91	81c
Property taxes expenditures	year	594	91	81r
Redesign, restructure more than half of home's interior		5,467	3/95	74r
Rent, office space	sq. ft.	9.86	93	57c
Rental units expenditures	year	2852	900/00/ 91	81c
Rental units expenditures	year	2077	91	81r
Insurance and Pensions				
Auto insurance, private passenger	year	892.80	12/94	71s
Health insurance, HMO plan, cost to employer	year	3092	93	59c
Insurance and pensions, personal, expenditures	year	3624	91	81c
Insurance and pensions, personal, expenditures	year	3042	91	81r
Insurance, life and other personal, expenditures	year	286	91	81c
Insurance, life and other personal, expenditures	year	298	91	81r
Pensions and Social Security, expenditures	year	3338	91	81c
Pensions and Social Security, expenditures	year	2744	91	81r
Legal Assistance				
Legal work, law firm associate	hour	91		10r
Legal work, law firm partner	hour	151		10r
Personal Goods				
Personal care products and services, total expenditures	year	483	91	81c
Personal Services				
Personal services expenditures	year	461	91	81c
Personal services expenditures	year	286	91	81r
Restaurant Food				
Dining expenditures, family	week	32.25	94	73r
Taxes				
Taxes, Federal income, expenditures	year	4252	91	81c
Taxes, Federal income, expenditures	year	2946	91	81r
Taxes, personal, expenditures	year	5467	91	81c
Taxes, personal, expenditures	year	3791	91	81r
Taxes, State and local income, expenditures	year	1154	91	81c
Taxes, State and local income, expenditures	year	791	91	81r
Transportation				
Bus fare, one-way	trip	1.12	12/95	1c
Cable car fare, one-way	trip	2.00	12/95	1c
Cars and trucks purchased, new	year	1330	91	81c
Cars and trucks purchased, new	year	1231	91	81r
Cars and trucks purchased, used	year	956	91	81c
Cars and trucks purchased, used	year	915	91	81r
Driver's learning permit fee	perm	12.00	1/94	84s
Driver's license fee	orig	12.00	1/94	84s
Driver's license fee, duplicate	lic	12.00	1/94	84s
Driver's license reinstatement fee, min.	susp	15.00	1/94	85s

Values are in dollars or fractions of dollars. In the column headed *Ref*, references are shown to sources. Each reference is followed by a letter. These refer to the geographical level for which data were reported: s = State, r = Region, and c = City or metro. The abbreviation *ex* is used to mean *except* or *excluding*; *exp* stands for expenditures. For other abbreviations and further explanations, please see the Introduction.

San Francisco, CA - continued

Item	Per	Value	Date	Ref.
Transportation				
Driver's license renewal fee	renew	12.00	1/94	84s
Ferry boat fare, one-way	trip	4.25	12/95	1c
Identification card, nondriver	card	6.00	1/94	83s
Motorcycle learning permit fee	perm	12.00	1/94	84s
Motorcycle license fee	orig	12.00	1/94	84s
Motorcycle license fee, duplicate	lic	12.00	1/94	84s
Motorcycle license renewal fee	renew	12.00	1/94	84s
Public transportation expenditures	year	548	91	81c
Public transportation expenditures	year	375	91	81r
Railway fare, commuter rail, one-way	trip	1.00	12/95	1c
Railway fare, heavy rail, one-way	trip	0.90	12/95	1c
Railway fare, light rail, one-way	trip	1.00	12/95	1c
Transportation expenditures, total	year	6116	91	81c
Transportation expenditures, total	year	5527	91	81r
Trolley fare, one-way	trip	1.00	12/95	1c
Vehicle expenses, miscellaneous	year	2253	91	81c
Vehicle finance charges	year	273	91	81c
Vehicle finance charges	year	287	91	81r
Vehicle insurance expenditures	year	786	91	81c
Vehicle insurance expenditures	year	624	91	81r
Vehicle maintenance and repairs expenditures	year	768	91	81c
Vehicle maintenance and repairs expenditures	year	695	91	81r
Vehicle purchases	year	2286	91	81c
Vehicle purchases	year	2174	91	81r
Vehicle rental, leases, licenses, etc. expenditures	year	426	91	81c
Vehicle rental, leases, licenses, etc. expenditures	year	257	91	81r
Vehicles purchased, other than cars and trucks	year	28	91	81r
Travel				
Car rental	day	48.99	1/93	49c
Car rental	week	175.99	1/93	49c
Utilities				
Electricity	KWh	0.13	12/94	82c
Electricity expenditures	year	578	91	81c
Electricity expenditures	year	616	91	81r
Fee, water use, industrial	month	1730.34	1/95	16c
Utilities, fuels, and public services, total expenditures	year	1717	91	81c
Utilities, fuels, and public services, total expenditures	year	1681	91	81r
Water and other public services, expenditures	year	236	91	81c
Water and other public services, expenditures	year	209	91	81r
Weddings				
Bridal attendants' gowns	event	750	10/93	76r
Bridal gown	event	852	10/93	76r
Bridal headpiece and veil	event	167	10/93	76r
Bride's wedding band	event	708	10/93	76r
Clergy	event	224	10/93	76r
Engagement ring	event	2756	10/93	76r
Flowers	event	863	10/93	76r
Formal wear for groom	event	106	10/93	76r
Groom's attendants' formal wear	event	530	10/93	76r
Groom's wedding band	event	402	10/93	76r
Music	event	600	10/93	76r
Photography	event	1088	10/93	76r
Shoes for bride	event	50	10/93	76r
Videography	event	483	10/93	76r
Wedding invitations and announcements	event	342	10/93	76r
Wedding reception	event	7000	10/93	76r

San Jose, CA

Item	Per	Value	Date	Ref.
Appliances				
Appliances (major), expenditures	year	160	91	81r
Average annual exp.				
Food, health care, personal goods, services	year	32461	91	81r
Charity				
Cash contributions, expenditures	year	975	91	81r
Clothing				
Apparel, men and boys, total expenditures	year	467	91	81r
Apparel, women and girls, total expenditures	year	737	91	81r
Footwear, expenditures	year	270	91	81r
Communications				
Long-distance telephone rate, day, addl. min., 1-10 mi.	min.	0.07	12/93	9s
Long-distance telephone rate, day, initial min., 1-10 mi.	min.	0.17	12/93	9s
Phone line, single, business, field visit	inst	70.75	12/93	9s
Phone line, single, business, no field visit	inst	70.75	12/93	9s
Phone line, single, residence, field visit	inst	34.75	12/93	9s
Phone line, single, residence, no field visit	inst	34.75	12/93	9s
Telephone service, expenditures	year	611	91	81r
Education				
Board, 4-year private college/university	year	2945	8/94	80s
Board, 4-year public college/university	year	2321	8/94	80s
Education, total expenditures	year	375	91	81r
Room, 4-year private college/university	year	3094	8/94	80s
Room, 4-year public college/university	year	2812	8/94	80s
Student fee, university	year	21.00	93	18s
Total cost, 4-year private college/university	year	19321	8/94	80s
Total cost, 4-year public college/university	year	7511	8/94	80s
Tuition, 2-year public college/university, in-state	year	345	8/94	80s
Tuition, 4-year private college/university, in-state	year	13282	8/94	80s
Tuition, 4-year public college/university, in-state	year	2378	8/94	80s
Energy and Fuels				
Fuel oil and other fuels, expenditures	year	33	91	81r
Gas, natural, expenditures	year	212	91	81r
Gasoline and motor oil purchased	year	1115	91	81r
Gasoline, unleaded midgrade	gallon	1.36	4/93	82r
Gasoline, unleaded premium	gallon	1.43	4/93	82r
Gasoline, unleaded regular	gallon	1.23	4/93	82r
Entertainment				
Concert ticket, Pearl Jam group	perf	20.00	94	50r
Entertainment, total expenditures	year	1853	91	81r
Fees and admissions, expenditures	year	482	91	81r
Pets, toys, playground equipment, expenditures	year	299	91	81r
Reading, expenditures	year	164	91	81r
Televisions, radios, and sound equipment, expenditures	year	528	91	81r
Funerals				
Burial, immediate, container provided by funeral home		1382.70	1/95	54r
Cards, acknowledgment		21.87	1/95	54r
Casket, minimum alternative		128.54	1/95	54r
Cosmetology, hair care, etc.		119.69	1/95	54r
Cremation, direct, container provided by funeral home		1030.62	1/95	54r
Embalming		255.42	1/95	54r
Funeral, funeral home		437.38	1/95	54r
Funeral, other facility		444.46	1/95	54r
Graveside service		338.46	1/95	54r
Hearse, local		147.50	1/95	54r
Limousine, local		130.33	1/95	54r
Memorial service		553.16	1/95	54r
Service charge, professional, nondeclinable		859.15	1/95	54r
Visitation and viewing		93.23	1/95	54r

Values are in dollars or fractions of dollars. In the column headed *Ref*, references are shown to sources. Each reference is followed by a letter. These refer to the geographical level for which data were reported: s=State, r=Region, and c=City or metro. The abbreviation *ex* is used to mean *except* or *excluding*; *exp* stands for *expenditures*. For other abbreviations and further explanations, please see the Introduction.

San Jose, CA - continued

Item	Per	Value	Date	Ref.
Groceries				
Apples, Red Delicious	lb.	0.72	12/94	82r
Bacon, sliced	lb.	1.73	12/94	82r
Bananas	lb.	0.52	12/94	82r
Beef purchases	year	241	91	81r
Beverage purchases, alcoholic	year	328	91	81r
Beverage purchases, nonalcoholic	year	234	91	81r
Bologna, all beef or mixed	lb.	2.33	12/94	82r
Bread, white, pan	lb.	0.81	12/94	82r
Carrots, short trimmed and topped	lb.	0.43	12/94	82r
Cereals and bakery products purchases	year	392	91	81r
Cereals and cereals products purchases	year	139	91	81r
Chicken breast, bone-in	lb.	2.04	12/94	82r
Chicken, fresh, whole	lb.	0.95	12/94	82r
Coffee, 100%, ground roast, all sizes	lb.	4.48	12/94	82r
Dairy products (other) purchases	year	182	91	81r
Fish and seafood purchases	year	94	91	81r
Flour, white, all purpose	lb.	0.21	12/94	82r
Food purchases, food eaten at home	year	2749	91	81r
Foods purchased away from home, not prepared by consumer	year	1909	91	81r
Fruits and vegetables purchases	year	459	91	81r
Grapefruit	lb.	0.56	12/94	82r
Ground beef, 100% beef	lb.	1.31	12/94	82r
Ham, boneless, exc. canned	lb.	2.46	12/94	82r
Ice cream, prepackaged, bulk, regular	1/2 gal.	2.57	12/94	82r
Lemons	lb.	1.00	12/94	82r
Lettuce, iceberg	lb.	0.93	12/94	82r
Meats, poultry, fish, and eggs purchases	year	700	91	81r
Milk and cream (fresh) purchases	year	155	91	81r
Orange juice, frozen concentrate 12-oz. can	16 oz.	1.52	12/94	82r
Oranges, Navel	lb.	0.56	12/94	82r
Pork chops, center cut, bone-in	lb.	3.30	12/94	82r
Pork purchases	year	122	91	81r
Potato chips	16-oz.	3.03	12/94	82r
Potatoes, frozen, French fried	lb.	0.77	12/94	82r
Potatoes, white	lb.	0.35	12/94	82r
Rice, white, long grain, uncooked	lb.	0.54	12/94	82r
Round roast, USDA choice, boneless	lb.	2.92	12/94	82r
Shortening, vegetable oil blends	lb.	0.80	12/94	82r
Spaghetti and macaroni	lb.	1.02	12/94	82r
Steak, round, graded & ungraded, exc. USDA prime & choice	lb.	3.13	12/94	82r
Steak, sirloin, USDA choice, boneless	lb.	4.07	12/94	82r
Sugar and other sweets, eaten at home, expenditures	year	105	91	81r
Sugar, white, all sizes	lb.	0.38	12/94	82r
Tobacco products and smoking supplies, total expenditures	year	221	91	81r
Tomatoes, field grown	lb.	1.45	12/94	82r
Tuna, chunk, light	lb.	2.18	12/94	82r
Health Care				
Childbirth, Cesarean delivery, hospital charge	birth	6059.00	12/91	69r
Childbirth, Cesarean delivery, physician charge	birth	2248.00	12/91	69r
Childbirth, normal delivery, hospital charge	birth	3006.00	12/91	69r
Childbirth, normal delivery, physician charge	birth	1634.00	12/91	69r
Drugs, expenditures	year	230	91	81r
Health care, total expenditures	year	1544	91	81r
Health insurance expenditures	year	558	91	81r
Insurance premium, family medical care	month	380.27	1/95	41s
Medical services expenditures	year	676	91	81r
Medical supplies expenditures	year	80	91	81r
Surgery, open-heart	proc	37818.00	1/93	14r
Household Goods				
Floor coverings, expenditures	year	79	91	81r
Furniture, expenditures	year	352	91	81r
Household equipment, misc. expenditures	year	614	91	81r
Household expenditures, miscellaneous	year	294	91	81r

San Jose, CA - continued

Item	Per	Value	Date	Ref.
Household Goods - continued				
Household furnishings and equipment, expenditures	year	1416	91	81r
Household operations expenditures	year	580	91	81r
Household textiles, expenditures	year	113	91	81r
Housekeeping supplies, expenditures	year	447	91	81r
Laundry and cleaning supplies, expenditures	year	114	91	81r
Postage and stationery, expenditures	year	145	91	81r
Housing				
Add garage/carport		6,422	3/95	74r
Add room(s)		26,583	3/95	74r
Apartment condominium or co-op, median	unit	105300	12/94	62r
Dwellings (owned), expenditures	year	3932	91	81r
Enclose porch/patio/breezeway		5,382	3/95	74r
Finish room in basement/attic		3,911	3/95	74r
Home, existing, single-family, median	unit	178600	12/94	62r
Maintenance, repairs, insurance, and other housing expenditures	year	591	91	81r
Mortgage interest and charges expenditures	year	2747	91	81r
Princ. & int., mortgage, median-price exist. sing.-family home	mo.	845	12/94	62r
Property taxes expenditures	year	594	91	81r
Redesign, restructure more than half of home's interior		5,467	3/95	74r
Rental units expenditures	year	2077	91	81r
Insurance and Pensions				
Auto insurance, private passenger	year	892.80	12/94	71s
Insurance and pensions, personal, expenditures	year	3042	91	81r
Insurance, life and other personal, expenditures	year	298	91	81r
Pensions and Social Security, expenditures	year	2744	91	81r
Legal Assistance				
Legal work, law firm associate	hour	91		10r
Legal work, law firm partner	hour	151		10r
Personal Services				
Personal services expenditures	year	286	91	81r
Restaurant Food				
Dining expenditures, family	week	32.25	94	73r
Taxes				
Taxes, Federal income, expenditures	year	2946	91	81r
Taxes, personal, expenditures	year	3791	91	81r
Taxes, State and local income, expenditures	year	791	91	81r
Transportation				
Cars and trucks purchased, new	year	1231	91	81r
Cars and trucks purchased, used	year	915	91	81r
Driver's learning permit fee	perm	12.00	1/94	84s
Driver's license fee	orig	12.00	1/94	84s
Driver's license fee, duplicate	lic	12.00	1/94	84s
Driver's license reinstatement fee, min.	susp	15.00	1/94	85s
Driver's license renewal fee	renew	12.00	1/94	84s
Identification card, nondriver	card	6.00	1/94	83s
Motorcycle learning permit fee	perm	12.00	1/94	84s
Motorcycle license fee	orig	12.00	1/94	84s
Motorcycle license fee, duplicate	lic	12.00	1/94	84s
Motorcycle license renewal fee	renew	12.00	1/94	84s
Public transportation expenditures	year	375	91	81r
Transportation expenditures, total	year	5527	91	81r
Vehicle finance charges	year	287	91	81r
Vehicle insurance expenditures	year	624	91	81r
Vehicle maintenance and repairs expenditures	year	695	91	81r
Vehicle purchases	year	2174	91	81r
Vehicle rental, leases, licenses, etc. expenditures	year	257	91	81r
Vehicles purchased, other than cars and trucks	year	28	91	81r

Values are in dollars or fractions of dollars. In the column headed *Ref*, references are shown to sources. Each reference is followed by a letter. These refer to the geographical level for which data were reported: s=State, r=Region, and c=City or metro. The abbreviation *ex* is used to mean *except* or *excluding*; *exp* stands for *expenditures*. For other abbreviations and further explanations, please see the Introduction.

San Jose, CA - continued

Item	Per	Value	Date	Ref.
Utilities				
Electricity expenditures	year	616	91	81r
Utilities, fuels, and public services, total expenditures	year	1681	91	81r
Water and other public services, expenditures	year	209	91	81r
Weddings				
Bridal attendants' gowns	event	750	10/93	76r
Bridal gown	event	852	10/93	76r
Bridal headpiece and veil	event	167	10/93	76r
Bride's wedding band	event	708	10/93	76r
Clergy	event	224	10/93	76r
Engagement ring	event	2756	10/93	76r
Flowers	event	863	10/93	76r
Formal wear for groom	event	106	10/93	76r
Groom's attendants' formal wear	event	530	10/93	76r
Groom's wedding band	event	402	10/93	76r
Music	event	600	10/93	76r
Photography	event	1088	10/93	76r
Shoes for bride	event	50	10/93	76r
Videography	event	483	10/93	76r
Wedding invitations and announcements	event	342	10/93	76r
Wedding reception	event	7000	10/93	76r

San Marcos, TX

Item	Per	Value	Date	Ref.
Composite, ACCRA index		98.40	12/94	2c
Alcoholic Beverages				
Beer, Miller Lite, Bud, 12-oz., ex deposit	6	3.96	12/94	2c
J & B Scotch	750-ml.	19.16	12/94	2c
Wine, Gallo Chablis blanc	1.5-lit	4.99	12/94	2c
Clothing				
Jeans, man's denim		26.66	12/94	2c
Shirt, man's dress shirt		28.00	12/94	2c
Undervest, boy's size 10-14, cotton	3	4.82	12/94	2c
Communications				
Newspaper subscription, dly. and Sun. delivery	month	10.40	12/94	2c
Telephone bill, family of four	month	10.83	12/94	2c
Energy and Fuels				
Energy, combined forms, 1800 sq. ft.	mo.	102.87	12/94	2c
Gas, reg unlead, taxes inc., cash, self-service	gal	1.11	12/94	2c
Entertainment				
Bowling, evening rate	game	1.95	12/94	2c
Monopoly game, Parker Brothers', No. 9	game	10.74	12/94	2c
Movie	adm	5.00	12/94	2c
Tennis balls, yellow, Wilson or Penn, 3	can	2.15	12/94	2c
Groceries				
Groceries, ACCRA Index		95.70	12/94	2c
Baby food, strained vegetables, lowest price	4-4.5 oz.	0.24	12/94	2c
Bananas	lb.	0.32	12/94	2c
Beef or hamburger, ground	lb.	1.39	12/94	2c
Bread, white	24-oz.	0.56	12/94	2c
Cheese, Kraft grated Parmesan	8-oz.	3.28	12/94	2c
Chicken, whole fryer	lb.	0.79	12/94	2c
Cigarettes, Winston, Kings	carton	17.48	12/94	2c
Coffee, vacuum-packed	13 oz.	3.37	12/94	2c
Corn Flakes, Kellogg's or Post Toasties	18 oz.	2.51	12/94	2c
Corn, frozen, whole kernel, lowest price	10 oz.	0.70	12/94	2c
Eggs, Grade A large	dozen	0.75	12/94	2c
Lettuce, iceberg	head	0.96	12/94	2c
Margarine, Blue Bonnet or Parkay cubes	lb.	0.72	12/94	2c
Milk, whole	1/2 gal.	1.14	12/94	2c
Orange juice, Minute Maid frozen	12-oz.	1.16	12/94	2c

San Marcos, TX - continued

Item	Per	Value	Date	Ref.
Groceries - continued				
Peaches, halves or slices, Hunt's, Del Monte, or Libby's	29-oz.	1.42	12/94	2c
Peas, sweet, Del Monte or Green Giant	15-17 oz.	0.57	12/94	2c
Potatoes, white or red	10-lb. sack	2.71	12/94	2c
Sausage, Jimmy Dean, 100% pork	lb.	2.66	12/94	2c
Shortening, vegetable, Crisco	3-lb.	2.25	12/94	2c
Soft drink, Coca Cola, ex deposit	2 lit	1.52	12/94	2c
Steak, t-bone	lb.	4.14	12/94	2c
Sugar, cane or beet	4 lbs.	1.38	12/94	2c
Tomatoes, Hunt's or Del Monte	14.5 oz.	0.61	12/94	2c
Tuna, chunk, light, oil-packed	6.125-6.5 oz.	0.71	12/94	2c
Goods and Services				
Miscellaneous goods and services, ACCRA Index		95.10	12/94	2c
Health Care				
Health care, ACCRA Index		102.50	12/94	2c
Antibiotic ointment, Polysporin	1.5 oz.	4.01	12/94	2c
Dentist's fee, adult teeth cleaning and periodic oral exam	visit	57.00	12/94	2c
Doctor's fee, routine exam, established patient	visit	41.67	12/94	2c
Hospital care, semiprivate room	day	357.00	12/94	2c
Household Goods				
Appl. repair, service call, wash mach	min. lab. chg.	35.17	12/94	2c
Laundry detergent, Tide Ultra, Bold, or Cheer	42 oz.	3.60	12/94	2c
Tissues, facial, Kleenex brand	175	1.17	12/94	2c
Housing				
Housing, ACCRA Index		102.90	12/94	2c
House payment, principal and interest, 25% down payment	mo.	772	12/94	2c
House, 1800 sq ft, 8000 sq ft lot, new, urban, utilities	total	123967	12/94	2c
Mtge. rate, incl. points and orig. fee, 30-year conv. fixed or ARM	mo.	9.36	12/94	2c
Rent, apartment, 2 br., 1 1/2-2 baths, unfurnished, 950 sq ft, water	mo.	590	12/94	2c
Personal Goods				
Shampoo, Alberto VO5	15-oz.	1.05	12/94	2c
Toothpaste, Crest or Colgate	6-7 oz.	2.04	12/94	2c
Personal Services				
Dry cleaning, man's 2-pc. suit		5.58	12/94	2c
Haircut, man's barbershop, no styling		8.82	12/94	2c
Haircut, woman's shampoo, trim, blow-dry		14.67	12/94	2c
Restaurant Food				
Chicken, fried, thigh and drumstick		2.17	12/94	2c
Hamburger with cheese	1/4 lb.	1.95	12/94	2c
Pizza, Pizza Hut or Pizza Inn	12-13 in.	7.24	12/94	2c
Transportation				
Transportation, ACCRA Index		108.60	12/94	2c
Tire balance, computer or spin bal., front	wheel	8.25	12/94	2c
Utilities				
Utilities, ACCRA Index		86.80	12/94	2c
Electricity, 1800 sq. ft., new home	mo.	102.87	12/94	2c

Values are in dollars or fractions of dollars. In the column headed *Ref*, references are shown to sources. Each reference is followed by a letter. These refer to the geographical level for which data were reported: s=State, r=Region, and c=City or metro. The abbreviation *ex* is used to mean *except* or *excluding*; *exp* stands for *expenditures*. For other abbreviations and further explanations, please see the Introduction.

Santa Barbara-Santa Maria-Lompoc, CA

Item	Per	Value	Date	Ref.
Appliances				
Appliances (major), expenditures	year	160	91	81r
Average annual exp.				
Food, health care, personal goods, services	year	32461	91	81r
Charity				
Cash contributions, expenditures	year	975	91	81r
Clothing				
Apparel, men and boys, total expenditures	year	467	91	81r
Apparel, women and girls, total expenditures	year	737	91	81r
Footwear, expenditures	year	270	91	81r
Communications				
Long-distance telephone rate, day, addl. min., 1-10 mi.	min.	0.07	12/93	9s
Long-distance telephone rate, day, initial min., 1-10 mi.	min.	0.17	12/93	9s
Phone line, single, business, field visit	inst	70.75	12/93	9s
Phone line, single, business, no field visit	inst	70.75	12/93	9s
Phone line, single, residence, field visit	inst	34.75	12/93	9s
Phone line, single, residence, no field visit	inst	34.75	12/93	9s
Telephone service, expenditures	year	611	91	81r
Education				
Board, 4-year private college/university	year	2945	8/94	80s
Board, 4-year public college/university	year	2321	8/94	80s
Education, total expenditures	year	375	91	81r
Room, 4-year private college/university	year	3094	8/94	80s
Room, 4-year public college/university	year	2812	8/94	80s
Student fee, university	year	21.00	93	18s
Total cost, 4-year private college/university	year	19321	8/94	80s
Total cost, 4-year public college/university	year	7511	8/94	80s
Tuition, 2-year public college/university, in-state	year	345	8/94	80s
Tuition, 4-year private college/university, in-state	year	13282	8/94	80s
Tuition, 4-year public college/university, in-state	year	2378	8/94	80s
Energy and Fuels				
Fuel oil and other fuels, expenditures	year	33	91	81r
Gas, natural, expenditures	year	212	91	81r
Gasoline and motor oil purchased	year	1115	91	81r
Gasoline, unleaded midgrade	gallon	1.36	4/93	82r
Gasoline, unleaded premium	gallon	1.43	4/93	82r
Gasoline, unleaded regular	gallon	1.23	4/93	82r
Entertainment				
Concert ticket, Pearl Jam group	perf	20.00	94	50r
Entertainment, total expenditures	year	1853	91	81r
Fees and admissions, expenditures	year	482	91	81r
Pets, toys, playground equipment, expenditures	year	299	91	81r
Reading, expenditures	year	164	91	81r
Televisions, radios, and sound equipment, expenditures	year	528	91	81r
Funerals				
Burial, immediate, container provided by funeral home		1382.70	1/95	54r
Cards, acknowledgment		21.87	1/95	54r
Casket, minimum alternative		128.54	1/95	54r
Cosmetology, hair care, etc.		119.69	1/95	54r
Cremation, direct, container provided by funeral home		1030.62	1/95	54r
Embalming		255.42	1/95	54r
Funeral, funeral home		437.38	1/95	54r
Funeral, other facility		444.46	1/95	54r
Graveside service		338.46	1/95	54r
Hearse, local		147.50	1/95	54r
Limousine, local		130.33	1/95	54r
Memorial service		553.16	1/95	54r
Service charge, professional, nondeclinable		859.15	1/95	54r
Visitation and viewing		93.23	1/95	54r

Santa Barbara-Santa Maria-Lompoc, CA - continued

Item	Per	Value	Date	Ref.
Groceries				
Apples, Red Delicious	lb.	0.72	12/94	82r
Bacon, sliced	lb.	1.73	12/94	82r
Bananas	lb.	0.52	12/94	82r
Beef purchases	year	241	91	81r
Beverage purchases, alcoholic	year	328	91	81r
Beverage purchases, nonalcoholic	year	234	91	81r
Bologna, all beef or mixed	lb.	2.33	12/94	82r
Bread, white, pan	lb.	0.81	12/94	82r
Carrots, short trimmed and topped	lb.	0.43	12/94	82r
Cereals and bakery products purchases	year	392	91	81r
Cereals and cereals products purchases	year	139	91	81r
Chicken breast, bone-in	lb.	2.04	12/94	82r
Chicken, fresh, whole	lb.	0.95	12/94	82r
Coffee, 100%, ground roast, all sizes	lb.	4.48	12/94	82r
Dairy products (other) purchases	year	182	91	81r
Fish and seafood purchases	year	94	91	81r
Flour, white, all purpose	lb.	0.21	12/94	82r
Food purchases, food eaten at home	year	2749	91	81r
Foods purchased away from home, not prepared by consumer	year	1909	91	81r
Fruits and vegetables purchases	year	459	91	81r
Grapefruit	lb.	0.56	12/94	82r
Ground beef, 100% beef	lb.	1.31	12/94	82r
Ham, boneless, exc. canned	lb.	2.46	12/94	82r
Ice cream, prepackaged, bulk, regular	1/2 gal.	2.57	12/94	82r
Lemons	lb.	1.00	12/94	82r
Lettuce, iceberg	lb.	0.93	12/94	82r
Meats, poultry, fish, and eggs purchases	year	700	91	81r
Milk and cream (fresh) purchases	year	155	91	81r
Orange juice, frozen concentrate 12-oz. can	16 oz.	1.52	12/94	82r
Oranges, Navel	lb.	0.56	12/94	82r
Pork chops, center cut, bone-in	lb.	3.30	12/94	82r
Pork purchases	year	122	91	81r
Potato chips	16-oz.	3.03	12/94	82r
Potatoes, frozen, French fried	lb.	0.77	12/94	82r
Potatoes, white	lb.	0.35	12/94	82r
Rice, white, long grain, uncooked	lb.	0.54	12/94	82r
Round roast, USDA choice, boneless	lb.	2.92	12/94	82r
Shortening, vegetable oil blends	lb.	0.80	12/94	82r
Spaghetti and macaroni	lb.	1.02	12/94	82r
Steak, round, graded & ungraded, exc. USDA prime & choice	lb.	3.13	12/94	82r
Steak, sirloin, USDA choice, boneless	lb.	4.07	12/94	82r
Sugar and other sweets, eaten at home, expenditures	year	105	91	81r
Sugar, white, all sizes	lb.	0.38	12/94	82r
Tobacco products and smoking supplies, total expenditures	year	221	91	81r
Tomatoes, field grown	lb.	1.45	12/94	82r
Tuna, chunk, light	lb.	2.18	12/94	82r
Health Care				
Childbirth, Cesarean delivery, hospital charge	birth	6059.00	12/91	69r
Childbirth, Cesarean delivery, physician charge	birth	2248.00	12/91	69r
Childbirth, normal delivery, hospital charge	birth	3006.00	12/91	69r
Childbirth, normal delivery, physician charge	birth	1634.00	12/91	69r
Drugs, expenditures	year	230	91	81r
Health care, total expenditures	year	1544	91	81r
Health insurance expenditures	year	558	91	81r
Insurance premium, family medical care	month	380.27	1/95	41s
Medical services expenditures	year	676	91	81r
Medical supplies expenditures	year	80	91	81r
Surgery, open-heart	proc	37818.00	1/93	14r
Household Goods				
Floor coverings, expenditures	year	79	91	81r
Furniture, expenditures	year	352	91	81r
Household equipment, misc. expenditures	year	614	91	81r
Household expenditures, miscellaneous	year	294	91	81r

Values are in dollars or fractions of dollars. In the column headed *Ref*, references are shown to sources. Each reference is followed by a letter. These refer to the geographical level for which data were reported: s=State, r=Region, and c=City or metro. The abbreviation *ex* is used to mean *except* or *excluding*; *exp* stands for expenditures. For other abbreviations and further explanations, please see the Introduction.

Santa Barbara-Santa Maria-Lompoc, CA - continued

Item	Per	Value	Date	Ref.
Household Goods				
Household furnishings and equipment, expenditures	year	1416	91	81r
Household operations expenditures	year	580	91	81r
Household textiles, expenditures	year	113	91	81r
Housekeeping supplies, expenditures	year	447	91	81r
Laundry and cleaning supplies, expenditures	year	114	91	81r
Postage and stationery, expenditures	year	145	91	81r
Housing				
Add garage/carport		6,422	3/95	74r
Add room(s)		26,583	3/95	74r
Apartment condominium or co-op, median	unit	105300	12/94	62r
Dwellings (owned), expenditures	year	3932	91	81r
Enclose porch/patio/breezeway		5,382	3/95	74r
Finish room in basement/attic		3,911	3/95	74r
Home, existing, single-family, median	unit	178600	12/94	62r
Maintenance, repairs, insurance, and other housing expenditures	year	591	91	81r
Mortgage interest and charges expenditures	year	2747	91	81r
Princ. & int., mortgage, median-price exist. sing.-family home	mo.	845	12/94	62r
Property taxes expenditures	year	594	91	81r
Redesign, restructure more than half of home's interior		5,467	3/95	74r
Rental units expenditures	year	2077	91	81r
Insurance and Pensions				
Auto insurance, private passenger	year	892.80	12/94	71s
Insurance and pensions, personal, expenditures	year	3042	91	81r
Insurance, life and other personal, expenditures	year	298	91	81r
Pensions and Social Security, expenditures	year	2744	91	81r
Legal Assistance				
Legal work, law firm associate	hour	91		10r
Legal work, law firm partner	hour	151		10r
Personal Services				
Personal services expenditures	year	286	91	81r
Restaurant Food				
Dining expenditures, family	week	32.25	94	73r
Taxes				
Taxes, Federal income, expenditures	year	2946	91	81r
Taxes, personal, expenditures	year	3791	91	81r
Taxes, State and local income, expenditures	year	791	91	81r
Transportation				
Cars and trucks purchased, new	year	1231	91	81r
Cars and trucks purchased, used	year	915	91	81r
Driver's learning permit fee	perm	12.00	1/94	84s
Driver's license fee	orig	12.00	1/94	84s
Driver's license fee, duplicate	lic	12.00	1/94	84s
Driver's license reinstatement fee, min.	susp	15.00	1/94	85s
Driver's license renewal fee	renew	12.00	1/94	84s
Identification card, nondriver	card	6.00	1/94	83s
Motorcycle learning permit fee	perm	12.00	1/94	84s
Motorcycle license fee	orig	12.00	1/94	84s
Motorcycle license fee, duplicate	lic	12.00	1/94	84s
Motorcycle license renewal fee	renew	12.00	1/94	84s
Public transportation expenditures	year	375	91	81r
Transportation expenditures, total	year	5527	91	81r
Vehicle finance charges	year	287	91	81r
Vehicle insurance expenditures	year	624	91	81r
Vehicle maintenance and repairs expenditures	year	695	91	81r
Vehicle purchases	year	2174	91	81r
Vehicle rental, leases, licenses, etc. expenditures	year	257	91	81r
Vehicles purchased, other than cars and trucks	year	28	91	81r

Santa Barbara-Santa Maria-Lompoc, CA - continued

Item	Per	Value	Date	Ref.
Utilities				
Electricity expenditures	year	616	91	81r
Utilities, fuels, and public services, total expenditures	year	1681	91	81r
Water and other public services, expenditures	year	209	91	81r
Weddings				
Bridal attendants' gowns	event	750	10/93	76r
Bridal gown	event	852	10/93	76r
Bridal headpiece and veil	event	167	10/93	76r
Bride's wedding band	event	708	10/93	76r
Clergy	event	224	10/93	76r
Engagement ring	event	2756	10/93	76r
Flowers	event	863	10/93	76r
Formal wear for groom	event	106	10/93	76r
Groom's attendants' formal wear	event	530	10/93	76r
Groom's wedding band	event	402	10/93	76r
Music	event	600	10/93	76r
Photography	event	1088	10/93	76r
Shoes for bride	event	50	10/93	76r
Videography	event	483	10/93	76r
Wedding invitations and announcements	event	342	10/93	76r
Wedding reception	event	7000	10/93	76r

Santa Cruz, CA

Item	Per	Value	Date	Ref.
Appliances				
Appliances (major), expenditures	year	160	91	81r
Average annual exp.				
Food, health care, personal goods, services	year	32461	91	81r
Charity				
Cash contributions, expenditures	year	975	91	81r
Clothing				
Apparel, men and boys, total expenditures	year	467	91	81r
Apparel, women and girls, total expenditures	year	737	91	81r
Footwear, expenditures	year	270	91	81r
Communications				
Long-distance telephone rate, day, addl. min., 1-10 mi.	min.	0.07	12/93	9s
Long-distance telephone rate, day, initial min., 1-10 mi.	min.	0.17	12/93	9s
Phone line, single, business, field visit	inst	70.75	12/93	9s
Phone line, single, business, no field visit	inst	70.75	12/93	9s
Phone line, single, residence, field visit	inst	34.75	12/93	9s
Phone line, single, residence, no field visit	inst	34.75	12/93	9s
Telephone service, expenditures	year	611	91	81r
Education				
Board, 4-year private college/university	year	2945	8/94	80s
Board, 4-year public college/university	year	2321	8/94	80s
Education, total expenditures	year	375	91	81r
Room, 4-year private college/university	year	3094	8/94	80s
Room, 4-year public college/university	year	2812	8/94	80s
Student fee, university	year	21.00	93	18s
Total cost, 4-year private college/university	year	19321	8/94	80s
Total cost, 4-year public college/university	year	7511	8/94	80s
Tuition, 2-year public college/university, in-state	year	345	8/94	80s
Tuition, 4-year private college/university, in-state	year	13282	8/94	80s
Tuition, 4-year public college/university, in-state	year	2378	8/94	80s
Energy and Fuels				
Fuel oil and other fuels, expenditures	year	33	91	81r
Gas, natural, expenditures	year	212	91	81r
Gasoline and motor oil purchased	year	1115	91	81r
Gasoline, unleaded midgrade	gallon	1.36	4/93	82r
Gasoline, unleaded premium	gallon	1.43	4/93	82r
Gasoline, unleaded regular	gallon	1.23	4/93	82r

Values are in dollars or fractions of dollars. In the column headed *Ref*, references are shown to sources. Each reference is followed by a letter. These refer to the geographical level for which data were reported: s=State, r=Region, and c=City or metro. The abbreviation *ex* is used to mean *except* or *excluding*; *exp* stands for *expenditures*. For other abbreviations and further explanations, please see the Introduction.

Santa Cruz, CA - continued

Item	Per	Value	Date	Ref.
Entertainment				
Concert ticket, Pearl Jam group	perf	20.00	94	50r
Entertainment, total expenditures	year	1853	91	81r
Fees and admissions, expenditures	year	482	91	81r
Pets, toys, playground equipment, expenditures	year	299	91	81r
Reading, expenditures	year	164	91	81r
Televisions, radios, and sound equipment, expenditures	year	528	91	81r
Funerals				
Burial, immediate, container provided by funeral home		1382.70	1/95	54r
Cards, acknowledgment		21.87	1/95	54r
Casket, minimum alternative		128.54	1/95	54r
Cosmetology, hair care, etc.		119.69	1/95	54r
Cremation, direct, container provided by funeral home		1030.62	1/95	54r
Embalming		255.42	1/95	54r
Funeral, funeral home		437.38	1/95	54r
Funeral, other facility		444.46	1/95	54r
Graveside service		338.46	1/95	54r
Hearse, local		147.50	1/95	54r
Limousine, local		130.33	1/95	54r
Memorial service		553.16	1/95	54r
Service charge, professional, nondeclinable		859.15	1/95	54r
Visitation and viewing		93.23	1/95	54r
Groceries				
Apples, Red Delicious	lb.	0.72	12/94	82r
Bacon, sliced	lb.	1.73	12/94	82r
Bananas	lb.	0.52	12/94	82r
Beef purchases	year	241	91	81r
Beverage purchases, alcoholic	year	328	91	81r
Beverage purchases, nonalcoholic	year	234	91	81r
Bologna, all beef or mixed	lb.	2.33	12/94	82r
Bread, white, pan	lb.	0.81	12/94	82r
Carrots, short trimmed and topped	lb.	0.43	12/94	82r
Cereals and bakery products purchases	year	392	91	81r
Cereals and cereals products purchases	year	139	91	81r
Chicken breast, bone-in	lb.	2.04	12/94	82r
Chicken, fresh, whole	lb.	0.95	12/94	82r
Coffee, 100%, ground roast, all sizes	lb.	4.48	12/94	82r
Dairy products (other) purchases	year	182	91	81r
Fish and seafood purchases	year	94	91	81r
Flour, all purpose	lb.	0.21	12/94	82r
Food purchases, food eaten at home	year	2749	91	81r
Foods purchased away from home, not prepared by consumer	year	1909	91	81r
Fruits and vegetables purchases	year	459	91	81r
Grapefruit	lb.	0.56	12/94	82r
Ground beef, 100% beef	lb.	1.31	12/94	82r
Ham, boneless, exc. canned	lb.	2.46	12/94	82r
Ice cream, prepackaged, bulk, regular	1/2 gal.	2.57	12/94	82r
Lemons	lb.	1.00	12/94	82r
Lettuce, iceberg	lb.	0.93	12/94	82r
Meats, poultry, fish, and eggs purchases	year	700	91	81r
Milk and cream (fresh) purchases	year	155	91	81r
Orange juice, frozen concentrate 12-oz. can	16 oz.	1.52	12/94	82r
Oranges, Navel	lb.	0.56	12/94	82r
Pork chops, center cut, bone-in	lb.	3.30	12/94	82r
Pork purchases	year	122	91	81r
Potato chips	16-oz.	3.03	12/94	82r
Potatoes, frozen, French fried	lb.	0.77	12/94	82r
Potatoes, white	lb.	0.35	12/94	82r
Rice, white, long grain, uncooked	lb.	0.54	12/94	82r
Round roast, USDA choice, boneless	lb.	2.92	12/94	82r
Shortening, vegetable oil blends	lb.	0.80	12/94	82r
Spaghetti and macaroni	lb.	1.02	12/94	82r
Steak, round, graded & ungraded, exc. USDA prime & choice	lb.	3.13	12/94	82r
Steak, sirloin, USDA choice, boneless	lb.	4.07	12/94	82r

Santa Cruz, CA - continued

Item	Per	Value	Date	Ref.
Groceries - continued				
Sugar and other sweets, eaten at home, expenditures	year	105	91	81r
Sugar, white, all sizes	lb.	0.38	12/94	82r
Tobacco products and smoking supplies, total expenditures	year	221	91	81r
Tomatoes, field grown	lb.	1.45	12/94	82r
Tuna, chunk, light	lb.	2.18	12/94	82r
Health Care				
Childbirth, Cesarean delivery, hospital charge	birth	6059.00	12/91	69r
Childbirth, Cesarean delivery, physician charge	birth	2248.00	12/91	69r
Childbirth, normal delivery, hospital charge	birth	3006.00	12/91	69r
Childbirth, normal delivery, physician charge	birth	1634.00	12/91	69r
Drugs, expenditures	year	230	91	81r
Health care, total expenditures	year	1544	91	81r
Health insurance expenditures	year	558	91	81r
Insurance premium, family medical care	month	380.27	1/95	41s
Medical services expenditures	year	676	91	81r
Medical supplies expenditures	year	80	91	81r
Surgery, open-heart	proc	37818.00	1/93	14r
Household Goods				
Floor coverings, expenditures	year	79	91	81r
Furniture, expenditures	year	352	91	81r
Household equipment, misc. expenditures	year	614	91	81r
Household expenditures, miscellaneous	year	294	91	81r
Household furnishings and equipment, expenditures	year	1416	91	81r
Household operations expenditures	year	580	91	81r
Household textiles, expenditures	year	113	91	81r
Housekeeping supplies, expenditures	year	447	91	81r
Laundry and cleaning supplies, expenditures	year	114	91	81r
Postage and stationery, expenditures	year	145	91	81r
Housing				
Add garage/carport		6,422	3/95	74r
Add room(s)		26,583	3/95	74r
Apartment condominium or co-op, median	unit	105300	12/94	62r
Dwellings (owned), expenditures	year	3932	91	81r
Enclose porch/patio/breezeway		5,382	3/95	74r
Finish room in basement/attic		3,911	3/95	74r
Home, existing, single-family, median	unit	178600	12/94	62r
Maintenance, repairs, insurance, and other housing expenditures	year	591	91	81r
Mortgage interest and charges expenditures	year	2747	91	81r
Princ. & int., mortgage, median-price exist. sing.-family home	mo.	845	12/94	62r
Property taxes expenditures	year	594	91	81r
Redesign, restructure more than half of home's interior		5,467	3/95	74r
Rental units expenditures	year	2077	91	81r
Insurance and Pensions				
Auto insurance, private passenger	year	892.80	12/94	71s
Insurance and pensions, personal, expenditures	year	3042	91	81r
Insurance, life and other personal, expenditures	year	298	91	81r
Pensions and Social Security, expenditures	year	2744	91	81r
Legal Assistance				
Legal work, law firm associate	hour	91		10r
Legal work, law firm partner	hour	151		10r
Personal Services				
Personal services expenditures	year	286	91	81r
Restaurant Food				
Dining expenditures, family	week	32.25	94	73r
Taxes				
Taxes, Federal income, expenditures	year	2946	91	81r
Taxes, personal, expenditures	year	3791	91	81r

Values are in dollars or fractions of dollars. In the column headed *Ref*, references are shown in source. Each reference is followed by a letter. These refer to the geographical level for which data were reported: s=State, r=Region, and c=City or metro. The abbreviation *ex* is used to mean *except* or *excluding*; *exp* stands for expenditures. For other abbreviations and further explanations, please see the Introduction.

Santa Cruz, CA - continued

Item	Per	Value	Date	Ref.
Taxes				
Taxes, State and local income, expenditures	year	791	91	81r
Transportation				
Cars and trucks purchased, new	year	1231	91	81r
Cars and trucks purchased, used	year	915	91	81r
Driver's learning permit fee	perm	12.00	1/94	84s
Driver's license fee	orig	12.00	1/94	84s
Driver's license fee, duplicate	lic	12.00	1/94	84s
Driver's license reinstatement fee, min.	susp	15.00	1/94	85s
Driver's license renewal fee	renew	12.00	1/94	84s
Identification card, nondriver	card	6.00	1/94	83s
Motorcycle learning permit fee	perm	12.00	1/94	84s
Motorcycle license fee	orig	12.00	1/94	84s
Motorcycle license fee, duplicate	lic	12.00	1/94	84s
Motorcycle license renewal fee	renew	12.00	1/94	84s
Public transportation expenditures	year	375	91	81r
Transportation expenditures, total	year	5527	91	81r
Vehicle finance charges	year	287	91	81r
Vehicle insurance expenditures	year	624	91	81r
Vehicle maintenance and repairs expenditures	year	695	91	81r
Vehicle purchases	year	2174	91	81r
Vehicle rental, leases, licenses, etc. expenditures	year	257	91	81r
Vehicles purchased, other than cars and trucks	year	28	91	81r
Utilities				
Electricity expenditures	year	616	91	81r
Utilities, fuels, and public services, total expenditures	year	1681	91	81r
Water and other public services, expenditures	year	209	91	81r
Weddings				
Bridal attendants' gowns	event	750	10/93	76r
Bridal gown	event	852	10/93	76r
Bridal headpiece and veil	event	167	10/93	76r
Bride's wedding band	event	708	10/93	76r
Clergy	event	224	10/93	76r
Engagement ring	event	2756	10/93	76r
Flowers	event	863	10/93	76r
Formal wear for groom	event	106	10/93	76r
Groom's attendants' formal wear	event	530	10/93	76r
Groom's wedding band	event	402	10/93	76r
Music	event	600	10/93	76r
Photography	event	1088	10/93	76r
Shoes for bride	event	50	10/93	76r
Videography	event	483	10/93	76r
Wedding invitations and announcements	event	342	10/93	76r
Wedding reception	event	7000	10/93	76r

Santa Fe, NM

Item	Per	Value	Date	Ref.
Composite, ACCRA index		121.70	12/94	2c
Alcoholic Beverages				
Beer, Miller Lite, Bud, 12-oz., ex deposit	6	3.99	12/94	2c
J & B Scotch	750-ml.	15.32	12/94	2c
Wine, Gallo Chablis blanc	1.5-lit	5.49	12/94	2c
Appliances				
Appliances (major), expenditures	year	160	91	81r
Average annual exp.				
Food, health care, personal goods, services	year	32461	91	81r
Charity				
Cash contributions, expenditures	year	975	91	81r
Clothing				
Apparel, men and boys, total expenditures	year	467	91	81r
Apparel, women and girls, total expenditures	year	737	91	81r
Footwear, expenditures	year	270	91	81r

Santa Fe, NM - continued

Item	Per	Value	Date	Ref.
Clothing - continued				
Jeans, man's denim		30.97	12/94	2c
Shirt, man's dress shirt		28.00	12/94	2c
Undervest, boy's size 10-14, cotton	3	5.25	12/94	2c
Communications				
Long-distance telephone rate, day, addl. min., 1-10 mi.	min.	0.11	12/93	9s
Long-distance telephone rate, day, initial min., 1-10 mi.	min.	0.19	12/93	9s
Newspaper subscription, dly. and Sun. delivery	month	11.96	12/94	2c
Phone line, single, business, field visit	inst	53.95	12/93	9s
Phone line, single, business, no field visit	inst	53.95	12/93	9s
Phone line, single, residence, field visit	inst	30.00	12/93	9s
Phone line, single, residence, no field visit	inst	30.00	12/93	9s
Telephone bill, family of four	month	20.85	12/94	2c
Telephone service, expenditures	year	611	91	81r
Telephone, residential, flat rate	mo.	13.91	12/93	8c
Education				
Board, 4-year private college/university	year	2285	8/94	80s
Board, 4-year public college/university	year	1798	8/94	80s
Education, total expenditures	year	375	91	81r
Room, 4-year private college/university	year	2091	8/94	80s
Room, 4-year public college/university	year	1565	8/94	80s
Total cost, 4-year private college/university	year	14552	8/94	80s
Total cost, 4-year public college/university	year	5094	8/94	80s
Tuition, 2-year public college/university, in-state	year	625	8/94	80s
Tuition, 4-year private college/university, in-state	year	10176	8/94	80s
Tuition, 4-year public college/university, in-state	year	1731	8/94	80s
Energy and Fuels				
Energy, combined forms, 1800 sq. ft.	mo.	125.82	12/94	2c
Energy, exc. electricity, 1800 sq. ft.	mo.	41.92	12/94	2c
Fuel oil and other fuels, expenditures	year	33	91	81r
Gas, natural, expenditures	year	212	91	81r
Gas, reg unlead, taxes inc., cash, self-service	gal	1.34	12/94	2c
Gasoline and motor oil purchased	year	1115	91	81r
Gasoline, unleaded midgrade	gallon	1.36	4/93	82r
Gasoline, unleaded premium	gallon	1.43	4/93	82r
Gasoline, unleaded regular	gallon	1.23	4/93	82r
Entertainment				
Bowling, evening rate	game	2.40	12/94	2c
Concert ticket, Pearl Jam group	perf	20.00	94	50r
Entertainment, total expenditures	year	1853	91	81r
Fees and admissions, expenditures	year	482	91	81r
Monopoly game, Parker Brothers', No. 9	game	12.32	12/94	2c
Movie	adm	6.25	12/94	2c
Pets, toys, playground equipment, expenditures	year	299	91	81r
Reading, expenditures	year	164	91	81r
Televisions, radios, and sound equipment, expenditures	year	528	91	81r
Tennis balls, yellow, Wilson or Penn, 3	can	2.42	12/94	2c
Funerals				
Burial, immediate, container provided by funeral home		1360.49	1/95	54r
Cards, acknowledgment		11.24	1/95	54r
Casket, minimum alternative		232.73	1/95	54r
Cosmetology, hair care, etc.		114.13	1/95	54r
Cremation, direct, container provided by funeral home		1027.08	1/95	54r
Embalming		286.24	1/95	54r
Funeral, funeral home		315.60	1/95	54r
Funeral, other facility		303.08	1/95	54r
Graveside service		423.83	1/95	54r
Hearse, local		133.12	1/95	54r
Limousine, local		99.10	1/95	54r

Values are in dollars or fractions of dollars. In the column headed *Ref*, references are shown to sources. Each reference is followed by a letter. These refer to the geographical level for which data were reported: s = State, r = Region, and c = City or metro. The abbreviation *ex* is used to mean *except* or *excluding*; *exp* stands for *expenditures*. For other abbreviations and further explanations, please see the Introduction.

Santa Fe, NM - continued

Item	Per	Value	Date	Ref.
Funerals				
Memorial service		442.57	1/95	54r
Service charge, professional, nondeclinable		840.16	1/95	54r
Visitation and viewing		168.50	1/95	54r
Groceries				
Groceries, ACCRA Index		99.90	12/94	2c
Apples, Red Delicious	lb.	0.72	12/94	82r
Baby food, strained vegetables, lowest price	4-4.5 oz.	0.28	12/94	2c
Bacon, sliced	lb.	1.73	12/94	82r
Bananas	lb.	0.40	12/94	2c
Bananas	lb.	0.52	12/94	82r
Beef or hamburger, ground	lb.	0.89	12/94	2c
Beef purchases	year	241	91	81r
Beverage purchases, alcoholic	year	328	91	81r
Beverage purchases, nonalcoholic	year	234	91	81r
Bologna, all beef or mixed	lb.	2.33	12/94	82r
Bread, white	24-oz.	0.89	12/94	2c
Bread, white, pan	lb.	0.81	12/94	82r
Carrots, short trimmed and topped	lb.	0.43	12/94	82r
Cereals and bakery products purchases	year	392	91	81r
Cereals and cereals products purchases	year	139	91	81r
Cheese, Kraft grated Parmesan	8-oz.	3.99	12/94	2c
Chicken breast, bone-in	lb.	2.04	12/94	82r
Chicken, fresh, whole	lb.	0.95	12/94	82r
Chicken, whole fryer	lb.	0.84	12/94	2c
Cigarettes, Winston, Kings	carton	14.59	12/94	2c
Coffee, 100%, ground roast, all sizes	lb.	4.48	12/94	82r
Coffee, vacuum-packed	13 oz.	3.89	12/94	2c
Corn Flakes, Kellogg's or Post Toasties	18 oz.	2.22	12/94	2c
Corn, frozen, whole kernel, lowest price	10 oz.	0.68	12/94	2c
Dairy products (other) purchases	year	182	91	81r
Eggs, Grade A large	dozen	0.90	12/94	2c
Fish and seafood purchases	year	94	91	81r
Flour, white, all purpose	lb.	0.21	12/94	82r
Food purchases, food eaten at home	year	2749	91	81r
Foods purchased away from home, not prepared by consumer	year	1909	91	81r
Fruits and vegetables purchases	year	459	91	81r
Grapefruit	lb.	0.56	12/94	82r
Ground beef, 100% beef	lb.	1.31	12/94	82r
Ham, boneless, exc. canned	lb.	2.46	12/94	82r
Ice cream, prepackaged, bulk, regular	1/2 gal.	2.57	12/94	82r
Lemons	lb.	1.00	12/94	82r
Lettuce, iceberg	lb.	0.93	12/94	82r
Lettuce, iceberg	head	0.86	12/94	2c
Margarine, Blue Bonnet or Parkay cubes	lb.	0.79	12/94	2c
Meats, poultry, fish, and eggs purchases	year	700	91	81r
Milk and cream (fresh) purchases	year	155	91	81r
Milk, whole	1/2 gal.	1.45	12/94	2c
Orange juice, frozen concentrate 12-oz. can	16 oz.	1.52	12/94	82r
Orange juice, Minute Maid frozen	12-oz.	1.09	12/94	2c
Oranges, Navel	lb.	0.56	12/94	82r
Peaches, halves or slices, Hunt's, Del Monte, or Libby's	29-oz.	1.48	12/94	2c
Peas, sweet, Del Monte or Green Giant	15-17 oz.	0.55	12/94	2c
Pork chops, center cut, bone-in	lb.	3.30	12/94	82r
Pork purchases	year	122	91	81r
Potato chips	16-oz.	3.03	12/94	82r
Potatoes, frozen, French fried	lb.	0.77	12/94	82r
Potatoes, white	lb.	0.35	12/94	82r
Potatoes, white or red	10-lb. sack	2.26	12/94	2c
Rice, white, long grain, uncooked	lb.	0.54	12/94	82r
Round roast, USDA choice, boneless	lb.	2.92	12/94	82r
Sausage, Jimmy Dean, 100% pork	lb.	2.34	12/94	2c
Shortening, vegetable oil blends	lb.	0.80	12/94	82r
Shortening, vegetable, Crisco	3-lb.	3.02	12/94	2c
Soft drink, Coca Cola, ex deposit	2 lit	0.86	12/94	2c
Spaghetti and macaroni	lb.	1.02	12/94	82r

Santa Fe, NM - continued

Item	Per	Value	Date	Ref.
Groceries - continued				
Steak, round, graded & ungraded, exc. USDA prime & choice	lb.	3.13	12/94	82r
Steak, sirloin, USDA choice, boneless	lb.	4.07	12/94	82r
Steak, t-bone	lb.	4.86	12/94	2c
Sugar and other sweets, eaten at home, expenditures	year	105	91	81r
Sugar, cane or beet	4 lbs.	1.57	12/94	2c
Sugar, white, all sizes	lb.	0.38	12/94	82r
Tobacco products and smoking supplies, total expenditures	year	221	91	81r
Tomatoes, field grown	lb.	1.45	12/94	82r
Tomatoes, Hunt's or Del Monte	14.5 oz.	0.75	12/94	2c
Tuna, chunk, light	lb.	2.18	12/94	82r
Tuna, chunk, light, oil-packed	6.125-6.5 oz.	0.84	12/94	2c
Goods and Services				
Miscellaneous goods and services, ACCRA Index		103.40	12/94	2c
Health Care				
Health care, ACCRA Index		115.10	12/94	2c
Antibiotic ointment, Polysporin	1.5 oz.	4.39	12/94	2c
Childbirth, Cesarean delivery, hospital charge	birth	6059.00	12/91	69r
Childbirth, Cesarean delivery, physician charge	birth	2248.00	12/91	69r
Childbirth, normal delivery, hospital charge	birth	3006.00	12/91	69r
Childbirth, normal delivery, physician charge	birth	1634.00	12/91	69r
Dentist's fee, adult teeth cleaning and periodic oral exam	visit	75.80	12/94	2c
Doctor's fee, routine exam, established patient	visit	43.60	12/94	2c
Drugs, expenditures	year	230	91	81r
Health care, total expenditures	year	1544	91	81r
Health insurance expenditures	year	558	91	81r
Hospital care, semiprivate room	day	305.00	12/94	2c
Insurance premium, family medical care	month	331.96	1/95	41s
Medical services expenditures	year	676	91	81r
Medical supplies expenditures	year	80	91	81r
Surgery, open-heart	proc	37818.00	1/93	14r
Household Goods				
Appl. repair, service call, wash mach	min. lab. chg.	38.36	12/94	2c
Floor coverings, expenditures	year	79	91	81r
Furniture, expenditures	year	352	91	81r
Household equipment, misc. expenditures	year	614	91	81r
Household expenditures, miscellaneous	year	294	91	81r
Household furnishings and equipment, expenditures	year	1416	91	81r
Household operations expenditures	year	580	91	81r
Household textiles, expenditures	year	113	91	81r
Housekeeping supplies, expenditures	year	447	91	81r
Laundry and cleaning supplies, expenditures	year	114	91	81r
Laundry detergent, Tide Ultra, Bold, or Cheer	42 oz.	3.42	12/94	2c
Postage and stationery, expenditures	year	145	91	81r
Tissues, facial, Kleenex brand	175	1.06	12/94	2c
Housing				
Housing, ACCRA Index		161.10	12/94	2c
Add garage/carport		6,422	3/95	74r
Add room(s)		26,583	3/95	74r
Apartment condominium or co-op, median	unit	105300	12/94	62r
Dwellings (owned), expenditures	year	3932	91	81r
Enclose porch/patio/breezeway		5,382	3/95	74r
Finish room in basement/attic		3,911	3/95	74r
Home, existing, single-family, median	unit	178600	12/94	62r
House payment, principal and interest, 25% down payment	mo.	1272	12/94	2c

Values are in dollars or fractions of dollars. In the column headed *Ref*, references are shown to sources. Each reference is followed by a letter. These refer to the geographical level for which data were reported: s=State, r=Region, and c=City or metro. The abbreviation *ex* is used to mean *except* or *excluding*; *exp* stands for expenditures. For other abbreviations and further explanations, please see the Introduction.

Santa Fe, NM - continued

Item	Per	Value	Date	Ref.
Housing				
House, 1800 sq ft, 8000 sq ft lot, new, urban, utilities	total	208000	12/94	2c
Maintenance, repairs, insurance, and other housing expenditures	year	591	91	81r
Mortgage interest and charges expenditures	year	2747	91	81r
Mtge. rate, incl. points and orig. fee, 30-year conv. fixed or ARM	mo.	9.15	12/94	2c
Princ. & int., mortgage, median-price exist. sing.-family home	mo.	845	12/94	62r
Property taxes expenditures	year	594	91	81r
Redesign, restructure more than half of home's interior		5,467	3/95	74r
Rent, apartment, 2 br., 1 1/2-2 baths, unfurnished, 950 sq ft, water	mo.	740	12/94	2c
Rental units expenditures	year	2077	91	81r
Insurance and Pensions				
Auto insurance, private passenger	year	727.43	12/94	71s
Insurance and pensions, personal, expenditures	year	3042	91	81r
Insurance, life and other personal, expenditures	year	298	91	81r
Pensions and Social Security, expenditures	year	2744	91	81r
Legal Assistance				
Legal work, law firm associate	hour	91		10r
Legal work, law firm partner	hour	151		10r
Personal Goods				
Shampoo, Alberto VO5	15-oz.	1.29	12/94	2c
Toothpaste, Crest or Colgate	6-7 oz.	2.32	12/94	2c
Personal Services				
Dry cleaning, man's 2-pc. suit		8.33	12/94	2c
Haircut, man's barbershop, no styling		7.96	12/94	2c
Haircut, woman's shampoo, trim, blow-dry		21.00	12/94	2c
Personal services expenditures	year	286	91	81r
Restaurant Food				
Chicken, fried, thigh and drumstick		1.99	12/94	2c
Dining expenditures, family	week	32.25	94	73r
Hamburger with cheese	1/4 lb.	1.99	12/94	2c
Pizza, Pizza Hut or Pizza Inn	12-13 in.	7.99	12/94	2c
Taxes				
Taxes, Federal income, expenditures	year	2946	91	81r
Taxes, personal, expenditures	year	3791	91	81r
Taxes, State and local income, expenditures	year	791	91	81r
Transportation				
Transportation, ACCRA Index		118.70	12/94	2c
Cars and trucks purchased, new	year	1231	91	81r
Cars and trucks purchased, used	year	915	91	81r
Driver's learning permit fee	perm	2.00	1/94	84s
Driver's license fee	orig	10.00	1/94	84s
Driver's license fee, duplicate	lic	10.00	1/94	84s
Driver's license reinstatement fee, min.	susp	25.00	1/94	85s
Driver's license renewal fee	renew	10.00	1/94	84s
Identification card, nondriver	card	5.00	1/94	83s
Motorcycle learning permit fee	perm	2.00	1/94	84s
Motorcycle license fee	orig	10.00	1/94	84s
Motorcycle license fee, duplicate	lic	10.00	1/94	84s
Motorcycle license renewal fee	renew	10.00	1/94	84s
Public transportation expenditures	year	375	91	81r
Tire balance, computer or spin bal., front	wheel	7.99	12/94	2c
Transportation expenditures, total	year	5527	91	81r
Vehicle finance charges	year	287	91	81r
Vehicle insurance expenditures	year	624	91	81r
Vehicle maintenance and repairs expenditures	year	695	91	81r
Vehicle purchases	year	2174	91	81r
Vehicle rental, leases, licenses, etc. expenditures	year	257	91	81r

Santa Fe, NM - continued

Item	Per	Value	Date	Ref.
Transportation - continued				
Vehicles purchased, other than cars and trucks	year	28	91	81r
Utilities				
Utilities, ACCRA Index		111.40	12/94	2c
Electricity expenditures	year	616	91	81r
Electricity, (part.), other, 1800 sq. ft., new home	mo.	83.90	12/94	2c
Utilities, fuels, and public services, total expenditures	year	1681	91	81r
Water and other public services, expenditures	year	209	91	81r
Weddings				
Bridal attendants' gowns	event	750	10/93	76r
Bridal gown	event	852	10/93	76r
Bridal headpiece and veil	event	167	10/93	76r
Bride's wedding band	event	708	10/93	76r
Clergy	event	224	10/93	76r
Engagement ring	event	2756	10/93	76r
Flowers	event	863	10/93	76r
Formal wear for groom	event	106	10/93	76r
Groom's attendants' formal wear	event	530	10/93	76r
Groom's wedding band	event	402	10/93	76r
Music	event	600	10/93	76r
Photography	event	1088	10/93	76r
Shoes for bride	event	50	10/93	76r
Videography	event	483	10/93	76r
Wedding invitations and announcements	event	342	10/93	76r
Wedding reception	event	7000	10/93	76r

Santa Rosa-Petaluma, CA

Item	Per	Value	Date	Ref.
Composite, ACCRA index		122.40	12/94	2c
Alcoholic Beverages				
Beer, Miller Lite, Bud, 12-oz., ex deposit	6	3.99	12/94	2c
J & B Scotch	750-ml.	15.55	12/94	2c
Wine, Gallo Chablis blanc	1.5-lit	4.55	12/94	2c
Appliances				
Appliances (major), expenditures	year	160	91	81r
Average annual exp.				
Food, health care, personal goods, services	year	32461	91	81r
Charity				
Cash contributions, expenditures	year	975	91	81r
Clothing				
Apparel, men and boys, total expenditures	year	467	91	81r
Apparel, women and girls, total expenditures	year	737	91	81r
Footwear, expenditures	year	270	91	81r
Jeans, man's denim		29.48	12/94	2c
Shirt, man's dress shirt		26.30	12/94	2c
Undervest, boy's size 10-14, cotton	3	6.59	12/94	2c
Communications				
Long-distance telephone rate, day, addl. min., 1-10 mi.	min.	0.07	12/93	9s
Long-distance telephone rate, day, initial min., 1-10 mi.	min.	0.17	12/93	9s
Newspaper subscription, dly. and Sun. delivery	month	13.04	12/94	2c
Phone line, single, business, field visit	inst	70.75	12/93	9s
Phone line, single, business, no field visit	inst	70.75	12/93	9s
Phone line, single, residence, field visit	inst	34.75	12/93	9s
Phone line, single, residence, no field visit	inst	34.75	12/93	9s
Telephone bill, family of four	month	22.84	12/94	2c
Telephone service, expenditures	year	611	91	81r
Telephone, residential, flat rate	mo.	8.35	12/93	8c
Education				
Board, 4-year private college/university	year	2945	8/94	80s
Board, 4-year public college/university	year	2321	8/94	80s

Values are in dollars or fractions of dollars. In the column headed *Ref*, references are shown to sources. Each reference is followed by a letter. These refer to the geographical level for which data were reported: s=State, r=Region, and c=City or metro. The abbreviation *ex* is used to mean *except* or *excluding*; *exp* stands for expenditures. For other abbreviations and further explanations, please see the Introduction.

Santa Rosa-Petaluma, CA - continued

Item	Per	Value	Date	Ref.
Education				
Education, total expenditures	year	375	91	81r
Room, 4-year private college/university	year	3094	8/94	80s
Room, 4-year public college/university	year	2812	8/94	80s
Student fee, university	year	21.00	93	18s
Total cost, 4-year private college/university	year	19321	8/94	80s
Total cost, 4-year public college/university	year	7511	8/94	80s
Tuition, 2-year public college/university, in-state	year	345	8/94	80s
Tuition, 4-year private college/university, in-state	year	13282	8/94	80s
Tuition, 4-year public college/university, in-state	year	2378	8/94	80s
Energy and Fuels				
Energy, combined forms, 1800 sq. ft.	mo.	134.52	12/94	2c
Energy, exc. electricity, 1800 sq. ft.	mo.	38.36	12/94	2c
Fuel oil and other fuels, expenditures	year	33	91	81r
Gas, natural, expenditures	year	212	91	81r
Gas, reg unlead, taxes inc., cash, self-service	gal	1.34	12/94	2c
Gasoline and motor oil purchased	year	1115	91	81r
Gasoline, unleaded midgrade	gallon	1.36	4/93	82r
Gasoline, unleaded premium	gallon	1.43	4/93	82r
Gasoline, unleaded regular	gallon	1.23	4/93	82r
Entertainment				
Bowling, evening rate	game	2.75	12/94	2c
Concert ticket, Pearl Jam group	perf	20.00	94	50r
Entertainment, total expenditures	year	1853	91	81r
Fees and admissions, expenditures	year	482	91	81r
Monopoly game, Parker Brothers', No. 9	game	12.35	12/94	2c
Movie	adm	6.00	12/94	2c
Pets, toys, playground equipment, expenditures	year	299	91	81r
Reading, expenditures	year	164	91	81r
Televisions, radios, and sound equipment, expenditures	year	528	91	81r
Tennis balls, yellow, Wilson or Penn, 3	can	2.29	12/94	2c
Funerals				
Burial, immediate, container provided by funeral home		1382.70	1/95	54r
Cards, acknowledgment		21.87	1/95	54r
Casket, minimum alternative		128.54	1/95	54r
Cosmetology, hair care, etc.		119.69	1/95	54r
Cremation, direct, container provided by funeral home		1030.62	1/95	54r
Embalming		255.42	1/95	54r
Funeral, funeral home		437.38	1/95	54r
Funeral, other facility		444.46	1/95	54r
Graveside service		338.46	1/95	54r
Hearse, local		147.50	1/95	54r
Limousine, local		130.33	1/95	54r
Memorial service		553.16	1/95	54r
Service charge, professional, nondeclinable		859.15	1/95	54r
Visitation and viewing		93.23	1/95	54r
Groceries				
Groceries, ACCRA Index		107.90	12/94	2c
Apples, Red Delicious	lb.	0.72	12/94	82r
Baby food, strained vegetables, lowest price	4-4.5 oz.	0.38	12/94	2c
Bacon, sliced	lb.	1.73	12/94	82r
Bananas	lb.	0.42	12/94	2c
Bananas	lb.	0.52	12/94	82r
Beef or hamburger, ground	lb.	1.49	12/94	2c
Beef purchases	year	241	91	81r
Beverage purchases, alcoholic	year	328	91	81r
Beverage purchases, nonalcoholic	year	234	91	81r
Bologna, all beef or mixed	lb.	2.33	12/94	82r
Bread, white	24-oz.	0.99	12/94	2c
Bread, white, pan	lb.	0.81	12/94	82r
Carrots, short trimmed and topped	lb.	0.43	12/94	82r
Cereals and bakery products purchases	year	392	91	81r

Santa Rosa-Petaluma, CA - continued

Item	Per	Value	Date	Ref.
Groceries - continued				
Cereals and cereals products purchases	year	139	91	81r
Cheese, Kraft grated Parmesan	8-oz.	3.38	12/94	2c
Chicken breast, bone-in	lb.	2.04	12/94	82r
Chicken, fresh, whole	lb.	0.95	12/94	82r
Chicken, whole fryer	lb.	0.78	12/94	2c
Cigarettes, Winston, Kings	carton	19.61	12/94	2c
Coffee, 100%, ground roast, all sizes	lb.	4.48	12/94	82r
Coffee, vacuum-packed	13 oz.	3.53	12/94	2c
Corn Flakes, Kellogg's or Post Toasties	18 oz.	2.15	12/94	2c
Corn, frozen, whole kernel, lowest price	10 oz.	0.71	12/94	2c
Dairy products (other) purchases	year	182	91	81r
Eggs, Grade A large	dozen	1.89	12/94	2c
Fish and seafood purchases	year	94	91	81r
Flour, white, all purpose	lb.	0.21	12/94	82r
Food purchases, food eaten at home	year	2749	91	81r
Foods purchased away from home, not prepared by consumer	year	1909	91	81r
Fruits and vegetables purchases	year	459	91	81r
Grapefruit	lb.	0.56	12/94	82r
Ground beef, 100% beef	lb.	1.31	12/94	82r
Ham, boneless, exc. canned	lb.	2.46	12/94	82r
Ice cream, prepackaged, bulk, regular	1/2 gal.	2.57	12/94	82r
Lemons	lb.	1.00	12/94	82r
Lettuce, iceberg	lb.	0.93	12/94	82r
Lettuce, iceberg	head	0.73	12/94	2c
Margarine, Blue Bonnet or Parkay cubes	lb.	0.70	12/94	2c
Meats, poultry, fish, and eggs purchases	year	700	91	81r
Milk and cream (fresh) purchases	year	155	91	81r
Milk, whole	1/2 gal.	1.43	12/94	2c
Orange juice, frozen concentrate 12-oz. can	16 oz.	1.52	12/94	82r
Orange juice, Minute Maid frozen	12-oz.	1.37	12/94	2c
Oranges, Navel	lb.	0.56	12/94	82r
Peaches, halves or slices, Hunt's, Del Monte, or Libby's	29-oz.	1.53	12/94	2c
Peas, sweet, Del Monte or Green Giant	15-17 oz.	0.62	12/94	2c
Pork chops, center cut, bone-in	lb.	3.30	12/94	82r
Pork purchases	year	122	91	81r
Potato chips	16-oz.	3.03	12/94	82r
Potatoes, frozen, French fried	lb.	0.77	12/94	82r
Potatoes, white	lb.	0.35	12/94	82r
Potatoes, white or red	10-lb. sack	2.01	12/94	2c
Rice, white, long grain, uncooked	lb.	0.54	12/94	82r
Round roast, USDA choice, boneless	lb.	2.92	12/94	82r
Sausage, Jimmy Dean, 100% pork	lb.	3.35	12/94	2c
Shortening, vegetable oil blends	lb.	0.80	12/94	82r
Shortening, vegetable, Crisco	3-lb.	2.67	12/94	2c
Soft drink, Coca Cola, ex deposit	2 lit	1.29	12/94	2c
Spaghetti and macaroni	lb.	1.02	12/94	82r
Steak, round, graded & ungraded, exc. USDA prime & choice	lb.	3.13	12/94	82r
Steak, sirloin, USDA choice, boneless	lb.	4.07	12/94	82r
Steak, t-bone	lb.	4.59	12/94	2c
Sugar and other sweets, eaten at home, expenditures	year	105	91	81r
Sugar, cane or beet	4 lbs.	1.36	12/94	2c
Sugar, white, all sizes	lb.	0.38	12/94	82r
Tobacco products and smoking supplies, total expenditures	year	221	91	81r
Tomatoes, field grown	lb.	1.45	12/94	82r
Tomatoes, Hunt's or Del Monte	14.5 oz.	0.70	12/94	2c
Tuna, chunk, light	lb.	2.18	12/94	82r
Tuna, chunk, light, oil-packed	6.125-6.5 oz.	0.73	12/94	2c
Goods and Services				
Miscellaneous goods and services, ACCRA Index		100.70	12/94	2c

Values are in dollars or fractions of dollars. In the column headed *Ref*, references are shown to sources. Each reference is followed by a letter. These refer to the geographical level for which data were reported: s=State, r=Region, and c=City or metro. The abbreviation *ex* is used to mean *except* or *excluding*; *exp* stands for *expenditures*. For other abbreviations and further explanations, please see the Introduction.

Santa Rosa-Petaluma, CA - continued

Item	Per	Value	Date	Ref.
Health Care				
Health care, ACCRA Index		133.60	12/94	2c
Antibiotic ointment, Polysporin	1.5 oz.	3.90	12/94	2c
Childbirth, Cesarean delivery, hospital charge	birth	6059.00	12/91	69r
Childbirth, Cesarean delivery, physician charge	birth	2248.00	12/91	69r
Childbirth, normal delivery, hospital charge	birth	3006.00	12/91	69r
Childbirth, normal delivery, physician charge	birth	1634.00	12/91	69r
Dentist's fee, adult teeth cleaning and periodic oral exam	visit	75.75	12/94	2c
Doctor's fee, routine exam, established patient	visit	47.50	12/94	2c
Drugs, expenditures	year	230	91	81r
Health care, total expenditures	year	1544	91	81r
Health insurance expenditures	year	558	91	81r
Hospital care, semiprivate room	day	630.00	12/94	2c
Insurance premium, family medical care	month	380.27	1/95	41s
Medical services expenditures	year	676	91	81r
Medical supplies expenditures	year	80	91	81r
Surgery, open-heart	proc	37818.00	1/93	14r
Household Goods				
Appl. repair, service call, wash mach	min. lab. chg.	41.49	12/94	2c
Floor coverings, expenditures	year	79	91	81r
Furniture, expenditures	year	352	91	81r
Household equipment, misc. expenditures	year	614	91	81r
Household expenditures, miscellaneous	year	294	91	81r
Household furnishings and equipment, expenditures	year	1416	91	81r
Household operations expenditures	year	580	91	81r
Household textiles, expenditures	year	113	91	81r
Housekeeping supplies, expenditures	year	447	91	81r
Laundry and cleaning supplies, expenditures	year	114	91	81r
Laundry detergent, Tide Ultra, Bold, or Cheer	42 oz.	3.19	12/94	2c
Postage and stationery, expenditures	year	145	91	81r
Tissues, facial, Kleenex brand	175	1.05	12/94	2c
Housing				
Housing, ACCRA Index		160.80	12/94	2c
Add garage/carport		6,422	3/95	74r
Add room(s)		26,583	3/95	74r
Apartment condominium or co-op, median	unit	105300	12/94	62r
Dwellings (owned), expenditures	year	3932	91	81r
Enclose porch/patio/breezeway		5,382	3/95	74r
Finish room in basement/attic		3,911	3/95	74r
Home, existing, single-family, median	unit	178600	12/94	62r
House payment, principal and interest, 25% down payment	mo.	1288	12/94	2c
House, 1800 sq ft, 8000 sq ft lot, new, urban, utilities	total	209433	12/94	2c
Maintenance, repairs, insurance, and other housing expenditures	year	591	91	81r
Mortgage interest and charges expenditures	year	2747	91	81r
Mtge. rate, incl. points and orig. fee, 30-year conv. fixed or ARM	mo.	9.22	12/94	2c
Princ. & int., mortgage, median-price exist. sing.-family home	mo.	845	12/94	62r
Property taxes expenditures	year	594	91	81r
Redesign, restructure more than half of home's interior		5,467	3/95	74r
Rent, apartment, 2 br., 1 1/2-2 baths, unfurnished, 950 sq ft, water	mo.	688	12/94	2c
Rental units expenditures	year	2077	91	81r
Insurance and Pensions				
Auto insurance, private passenger	year	892.80	12/94	71s
Insurance and pensions, personal, expenditures	year	3042	91	81r
Insurance, life and other personal, expenditures	year	298	91	81r

Item	Per	Value	Date	Ref.
Insurance and Pensions - continued				
Pensions and Social Security, expenditures	year	2744	91	81r
Legal Assistance				
Legal work, law firm associate	hour	91		10r
Legal work, law firm partner	hour	151		10r
Personal Goods				
Shampoo, Alberto VO5	15-oz.	1.55	12/94	2c
Toothpaste, Crest or Colgate	6-7 oz.	2.03	12/94	2c
Personal Services				
Dry cleaning, man's 2-pc. suit		8.10	12/94	2c
Haircut, man's barbershop, no styling		8.25	12/94	2c
Haircut, woman's shampoo, trim, blow-dry		25.60	12/94	2c
Personal services expenditures	year	286	91	81r
Restaurant Food				
Chicken, fried, thigh and drumstick		2.04	12/94	2c
Dining expenditures, family	week	32.25	94	73r
Hamburger with cheese	1/4 lb.	2.02	12/94	2c
Pizza, Pizza Hut or Pizza Inn	12-13 in.	4.50	12/94	2c
Taxes				
Taxes, Federal income, expenditures	year	2946	91	81r
Taxes, personal, expenditures	year	3791	91	81r
Taxes, State and local income, expenditures	year	791	91	81r
Transportation				
Transportation, ACCRA Index		122.60	12/94	2c
Bus fare, one-way	trip	1.00	12/95	1c
Cars and trucks purchased, new	year	1231	91	81r
Cars and trucks purchased, used	year	915	91	81r
Driver's learning permit fee	perm	12.00	1/94	84s
Driver's license fee	orig	12.00	1/94	84s
Driver's license fee, duplicate	lic	12.00	1/94	84s
Driver's license reinstatement fee, min.	susp	15.00	1/94	85s
Driver's license renewal fee	renew	12.00	1/94	84s
Identification card, nondriver	card	6.00	1/94	83s
Motorcycle learning permit fee	perm	12.00	1/94	84s
Motorcycle license fee	orig	12.00	1/94	84s
Motorcycle license fee, duplicate	lic	12.00	1/94	84s
Motorcycle license renewal fee	renew	12.00	1/94	84s
Public transportation expenditures	year	375	91	81r
Tire balance, computer or spin bal., front	wheel	8.60	12/94	2c
Transportation expenditures, total	year	5527	91	81r
Vehicle finance charges	year	287	91	81r
Vehicle insurance expenditures	year	624	91	81r
Vehicle maintenance and repairs expenditures	year	695	91	81r
Vehicle purchases	year	2174	91	81r
Vehicle rental, leases, licenses, etc. expenditures	year	257	91	81r
Vehicles purchased, other than cars and trucks	year	28	91	81r
Utilities				
Utilities, ACCRA Index		98.50	12/94	2c
Electricity expenditures	year	616	91	81r
Electricity, (part.), other, 1800 sq. ft., new home	mo.	100.06	12/94	2c
Utilities, fuels, and public services, total expenditures	year	1681	91	81r
Water and other public services, expenditures	year	209	91	81r
Weddings				
Bridal attendants' gowns	event	750	10/93	76r
Bridal gown	event	852	10/93	76r
Bridal headpiece and veil	event	167	10/93	76r
Bride's wedding band	event	708	10/93	76r
Clergy	event	224	10/93	76r
Engagement ring	event	2756	10/93	76r
Flowers	event	863	10/93	76r
Formal wear for groom	event	106	10/93	76r
Groom's attendants' formal wear	event	530	10/93	76r

Values are in dollars or fractions of dollars. In the column headed *Ref*, references are shown to sources. Each reference is followed by a letter. These refer to the geographical level for which data were reported: s = State, r = Region, and c = City or metro. The abbreviation *ex* is used to mean *except* or *excluding*; *exp* stands for expenditures. For other abbreviations and further explanations, please see the Introduction.

Santa Rosa-Petaluma, CA - continued

Item	Per	Value	Date	Ref.
Weddings				
Groom's wedding band	event	402	10/93	76r
Music	event	600	10/93	76r
Photography	event	1088	10/93	76r
Shoes for bride	event	50	10/93	76r
Videography	event	483	10/93	76r
Wedding invitations and announcements	event	342	10/93	76r
Wedding reception	event	7000	10/93	76r

Sarasota, FL

Item	Per	Value	Date	Ref.
Composite, ACCRA index		104.20	12/94	2c
Alcoholic Beverages				
Beer	bottle	2.50	94	36c
Beer, Miller Lite, Bud, 12-oz., ex deposit	6	3.74	12/94	2c
J & B Scotch	750-ml.	18.24	12/94	2c
Wine, Gallo Chablis blanc	1.5-lit	4.74	12/94	2c
Appliances				
Appliances (major), expenditures	year	153	91	81r
Average annual exp.				
Food, health care, personal goods, services	year	27020	91	81r
Charity				
Cash contributions, expenditures	year	839	91	81r
Clothing				
Apparel, men and boys, total expenditures	year	380	91	81r
Apparel, women and girls, total expenditures	year	660	91	81r
Footwear, expenditures	year	193	91	81r
Jeans, man's denim		34.74	12/94	2c
Shirt, man's dress shirt		31.25	12/94	2c
Undervest, boy's size 10-14, cotton	3	3.94	12/94	2c
Communications				
Long-distance telephone rate, day, addl. min., 1-10 mi.	min.	0.08	12/93	9s
Long-distance telephone rate, day, initial min., 1-10 mi.	min.	0.15	12/93	9s
Newspaper subscription, dly. and Sun. delivery	month	11.27	12/94	2c
Phone line, single, business, field visit	inst	86.00	12/93	9s
Phone line, single, business, no field visit	inst	54.50	12/93	9s
Phone line, single, residence, field visit	inst	76.00	12/93	9s
Phone line, single, residence, no field visit	inst	44.50	12/93	9s
Telephone bill, family of four	month	19.13	12/94	2c
Telephone service, expenditures	year	616	91	81r
Education				
Bar examination preparatory course	course	500.00-100	94	17s
Board, 4-year private college/university	year	2123	8/94	80s
Board, 4-year public college/university	year	2101	8/94	80s
Education, total expenditures	year	319	91	81r
Room, 4-year private college/university	year	2242	8/94	80s
Room, 4-year public college/university	year	1970	8/94	80s
Total cost, 4-year private college/university	year	13853	8/94	80s
Total cost, 4-year public college/university	year	5855	8/94	80s
Tuition, 2-year public college/university, in-state	year	1076	8/94	80s
Tuition, 4-year private college/university, in-state	year	9287	8/94	80s
Tuition, 4-year public college/university, in-state	year	1784	8/94	80s
Energy and Fuels				
Energy, combined forms, 1800 sq. ft.	mo.	122.97	12/94	2c
Fuel oil and other fuels, expenditures	year	56	91	81r
Gas, natural, expenditures	year	150	91	81r
Gas, reg unlead, taxes inc., cash, self-service	gal	1.19	12/94	2c
Gasoline and motor oil purchased	year	1152	91	81r
Gasoline, unleaded midgrade	gallon	1.21	4/93	82r

Sarasota, FL - continued

Item	Per	Value	Date	Ref.
Energy and Fuels - continued				
Gasoline, unleaded premium	gallon	1.30	4/93	82r
Gasoline, unleaded regular	gallon	1.10	4/93	82r
Entertainment				
Bowling, evening rate	game	2.30	12/94	2c
Concert ticket, Pearl Jam group	perf	20.00	94	50r
Entertainment, total expenditures	year	1266	91	81r
Fees and admissions, expenditures	year	306	91	81r
Monopoly game, Parker Brothers', No. 9	game	9.81	12/94	2c
Movie	adm	5.94	12/94	2c
Pets, toys, playground equipment, expenditures	year	271	91	81r
Reading, expenditures	year	131	91	81r
Televisions, radios, and sound equipment, expenditures	year	439	91	81r
Tennis balls, yellow, Wilson or Penn, 3	can	2.43	12/94	2c
Funerals				
Burial, immediate, container provided by funeral home		1370.36	1/95	54r
Cards, acknowledgment		14.83	1/95	54r
Casket, minimum alternative		192.52	1/95	54r
Cosmetology, hair care, etc.		102.27	1/95	54r
Cremation, direct, container provided by funeral home		1065.64	1/95	54r
Embalming		304.29	1/95	54r
Funeral, funeral home		287.83	1/95	54r
Funeral, other facility		284.14	1/95	54r
Graveside service		349.13	1/95	54r
Hearse, local		132.27	1/95	54r
Limousine, local		98.45	1/95	54r
Memorial service		270.59	1/95	54r
Service charge, professional, nondeclinable		933.59	1/95	54r
Visitation and viewing		225.83	1/95	54r
Groceries				
Groceries, ACCRA Index		97.00	12/94	2c
Apples, Red Delicious	lb.	0.73	12/94	82r
Baby food, strained vegetables, lowest price	4-4.5 oz.	0.36	12/94	2c
Bacon, sliced	lb.	1.67	12/94	82r
Bananas	lb.	0.39	12/94	2c
Bananas	lb.	0.42	12/94	82r
Beef or hamburger, ground	lb.	1.14	12/94	2c
Beef purchases	year	213	91	81r
Beverage purchases, alcoholic	year	249	91	81r
Beverage purchases, nonalcoholic	year	207	91	81r
Big Mac hamburger	burger	2.03	94	36c
Bologna, all beef or mixed	lb.	2.27	12/94	82r
Bread, white	24-oz.	0.78	12/94	2c
Bread, white, pan	lb.	0.68	12/94	82r
Cabbage	lb.	0.42	12/94	82r
Carrots, short trimmed and topped	lb.	0.53	12/94	82r
Cereals and bakery products purchases	year	345	91	81r
Cereals and cereals products purchases	year	127	91	81r
Cheddar cheese, natural	lb.	3.58	12/94	82r
Cheese, Kraft grated Parmesan	8-oz.	3.19	12/94	2c
Chicken breast, bone-in	lb.	1.71	12/94	82r
Chicken, fresh, whole	lb.	0.78	12/94	2c
Chicken, whole fryer	lb.	0.83	12/94	2c
Chuck roast, USDA choice, boneless	lb.	2.26	12/94	82r
Cigarettes, Winston, Kings	carton	16.27	12/94	2c
Coffee, vacuum-packed	13 oz.	2.81	12/94	2c
Corn Flakes, Kellogg's or Post Toasties	18 oz.	2.12	12/94	2c
Corn, frozen, whole kernel, lowest price	10 oz.	0.63	12/94	2c
Crackers, soda, salted	lb.	1.27	12/94	82r
Cucumbers	lb.	0.65	12/94	82r
Dairy products (other) purchases	year	141	91	81r
Eggs, Grade A large	dozen	0.74	12/94	2c
Eggs, Grade A large	dozen	0.87	12/94	82r
Fish and seafood purchases	year	72	91	81r
Flour, white, all purpose	lb.	0.23	12/94	82r
Food purchases, food eaten at home	year	2381	91	81r

Values are in dollars or fractions of dollars. In the column headed *Ref*, references are shown to sources. Each reference is followed by a letter. These refer to the geographical level for which data were reported: s=State, r=Region, and c=City or metro. The abbreviation *ex* is used to mean *except* or *excluding*; *exp* stands for expenditures. For other abbreviations and further explanations, please see the Introduction.

Sarasota, FL - continued

Item	Per	Value	Date	Ref.
Groceries				
Foods purchased away from home, not prepared by consumer	year	1696	91	81r
Frankfurters, all meat or all beef	lb.	1.74	12/94	82r
Fruits and vegetables purchases	year	380	91	81r
Grapefruit	lb.	0.45	12/94	82r
Grapes, Thompson seedless	lb.	2.30	12/94	82r
Ground beef, 100% beef	lb.	1.37	12/94	82r
Ground chuck, 100% beef	lb.	1.97	12/94	82r
Ham, boneless, exc. canned	lb.	2.54	12/94	82r
Ice cream, prepackaged, bulk, regular	1/2 gal.	2.47	12/94	82r
Lemons	lb.	1.02	12/94	82r
Lettuce, iceberg	lb.	0.96	12/94	82r
Lettuce, iceberg	head	0.94	12/94	2c
Margarine, Blue Bonnet or Parkay cubes	lb.	0.61	12/94	2c
Margarine, stick	lb.	0.77	12/94	82r
Meats, poultry, fish, and eggs purchases	year	655	91	81r
Milk and cream (fresh) purchases	year	130	91	81r
Milk, whole	1/2 gal.	1.39	12/94	2c
Orange juice, frozen concentrate 12-oz. can	16 oz.	1.36	12/94	82r
Orange juice, Minute Maid frozen	12-oz.	1.18	12/94	2c
Oranges, Navel	lb.	0.54	12/94	82r
Peaches, halves or slices, Hunt's, Del Monte, or Libby's	29-oz.	1.52	12/94	2c
Pears, Anjou	lb.	0.81	12/94	82r
Peas, sweet, Del Monte or Green Giant	15-17 oz.	0.54	12/94	2c
Pork chops, center cut, bone-in	lb.	3.07	12/94	82r
Pork purchases	year	142	91	81r
Potato chips	16-oz.	3.15	12/94	82r
Potatoes, frozen, French fried	lb.	0.82	12/94	82r
Potatoes, white	lb.	0.34	12/94	82r
Potatoes, white or red	10-lb. sack	3.17	12/94	2c
Rice, white, long grain, uncooked	lb.	0.48	12/94	82r
Round roast, USDA choice, boneless	lb.	2.91	12/94	82r
Sausage, fresh	lb.	1.82	12/94	82r
Sausage, Jimmy Dean, 100% pork	lb.	2.29	12/94	2c
Shortening, vegetable oil blends	lb.	0.75	12/94	82r
Shortening, vegetable, Crisco	3-lb.	2.43	12/94	2c
Soft drink, Coca Cola, ex deposit	2 lit	0.97	12/94	2c
Spaghetti and macaroni	lb.	0.87	12/94	82r
Steak, rib eye, USDA choice, boneless	lb.	6.85	12/94	82r
Steak, round, graded & ungraded, exc. USDA prime & choice	lb.	2.96	12/94	82r
Steak, round, USDA choice, boneless	lb.	3.17	12/94	82r
Steak, sirloin, USDA choice, boneless	lb.	4.12	12/94	82r
Steak, t-bone	lb.	5.89	12/94	2c
Steak, T-bone, USDA choice, bone-in	lb.	5.63	12/94	82r
Sugar and other sweets, eaten at home, expenditures	year	93	91	81r
Sugar, cane or beet	4 lbs.	1.40	12/94	2c
Sugar, white, all sizes	lb.	0.39	12/94	82r
Tobacco products and smoking supplies, total expenditures	year	286	91	81r
Tomatoes, field grown	lb.	1.36	12/94	82r
Tomatoes, Hunt's or Del Monte	14.5 oz.	0.76	12/94	2c
Tuna, chunk, light	lb.	1.94	12/94	82r
Tuna, chunk, light, oil-packed	6.125-6.5 oz.	0.66	12/94	2c
Turkey, frozen, whole	lb.	0.96	12/94	82r
Yogurt, natural, fruit flavored	8 oz.	0.58	12/94	82r
Goods and Services				
Miscellaneous goods and services, ACCRA Index		104.70	12/94	2c
Health Care				
Health care, ACCRA Index		102.90	12/94	2c
Adenosine, emergency room	treat	100.00	95	23r
Antibiotic ointment, Polysporin	1.5 oz.	4.37	12/94	2c

Sarasota, FL - continued

Item	Per	Value	Date	Ref.
Health Care - continued				
Bladder tap, superpubic, infant, emergency room	treat	119.00	95	23r
Blood analysis, emergency room	treat	25.00	95	23r
Blood tests, abdominal pain, emergency room	treat	25.00	95	23r
Burn dressing, emergency room	treat	266.00	95	23r
Cardiology interpretation, emergency room	treat	26.00	95	23r
Chest X-ray, emergency room	treat	78.00	95	23r
Childbirth, Cesarean delivery, hospital charge	birth	5462.00	12/91	69r
Childbirth, Cesarean delivery, physician charge	birth	2228.00	12/91	69r
Childbirth, normal delivery, hospital charge	birth	2943.00	12/91	69r
Childbirth, normal delivery, physician charge	birth	1619.00	12/91	69r
Defibrillation pads, emergency room	treat	6.00	95	23r
Dentist's fee, adult teeth cleaning and periodic oral exam	visit	51.00	12/94	2c
Doctor's fee, routine exam, established patient	visit	44.00	12/94	2c
Drugs, expenditures	year	297	91	81r
Gastric tube insertion, nasal, emergency room	treat	25.00	95	23r
Health care, total expenditures	year	1600	91	81r
Health insurance expenditures	year	637	91	81r
Heart monitor, emergency room	treat	40.00	95	23r
Hospital care, semiprivate room	day	385.00	12/94	2c
Insurance premium, family medical care	month	301.92	1/95	41s
Intravenous fluids, emergency room	treat	130.00	95	23r
Intravenous fluids, emergency room	liter	26.00	95	23r
Intravenous line, central, emergency room	treat	342.00	95	23r
Liver function tests, abdominal pain, emergency room	treat	26.00	95	23r
Medical care charges, total, emergency room, third-degree burns	treat	2101.00	95	23r
Medical care charges, total, emergency, infant with fever	treat	628.00	95	23r
Medical services expenditures	year	573	91	81r
Medical supplies expenditures	year	93	91	81r
Morphine, emergency room	treat	34.00	95	23r
Nursing care and facilities charges, emergency room	treat	252.00	95	23r
Nursing care and facilities charges, emergency, infant with fever	treat	252.00	95	23r
Nursing care and facilities charges, emergency, third-degree burns	treat	861.00	95	23r
Physician's charges, emergency, infant with fever	treat	212.00	95	23r
Physician's charges, emergency, third-degree burns	treat	372.00	95	23r
Physician's fee, emergency room	treat	372.00	95	23r
Physician's fee, general practitioner	visit	51.20	12/93	60r
Surgery, open-heart	proc	42374.00	1/93	14r
Ultrasound, abdominal, emergency room	treat	276.00	95	23r
Urinalysis, emergency room	treat	20.00	95	23r
Urinalysis, infant, emergency room	treat	20.00	95	23r
X-rays, emergency room	treat	78.00	95	23r
Household Goods				
Appl. repair, service call, wash mach	min. lab. chg.	38.75	12/94	2c
Floor coverings, expenditures	year	48	91	81r
Furniture, expenditures	year	280	91	81r
Household equipment, misc. expenditures	year	342	91	81r
Household expenditures, miscellaneous	year	256	91	81r
Household furnishings and equipment, expenditures	year	988	91	81r
Household operations expenditures	year	468	91	81r
Household textiles, expenditures	year	95	91	81r
Housekeeping supplies, expenditures	year	380	91	81r
Laundry and cleaning supplies, expenditures	year	109	91	81r

Values are in dollars or fractions of dollars. In the column headed *Ref*, references are shown to sources. Each reference is followed by a letter. These refer to the geographical level for which data were reported: s=State, r=Region, and c=City or metro. The abbreviation *ex* is used to mean *except* or *excluding*; *exp* stands for expenditures. For other abbreviations and further explanations, please see the Introduction.

Sarasota, FL - continued

Item	Per	Value	Date	Ref.
Household Goods				
Laundry detergent, Tide Ultra, Bold, or Cheer	42 oz.	3.00	12/94	2c
Postage and stationery, expenditures	year	105	91	81r
Tissues, facial, Kleenex brand	175	0.97	12/94	2c
Housing				
Housing, ACCRA Index		112.20	12/94	2c
Add garage/carport		6,980	3/95	74r
Add room(s)		11,403	3/95	74r
Apartment condominium or co-op, median	unit	68600	12/94	62r
Dwellings (owned), expenditures	year	2428	91	81r
Enclose porch/patio/breezeway		4,572	3/95	74r
Finish room in basement/attic		3,794	3/95	74r
Home, existing, single-family, median	unit	120200	12/94	62r
Home, existing, single-family, median	unit	97.90	12/94	62c
House payment, principal and interest, 25% down payment	mo.	845	12/94	2c
House, 1800 sq ft, 8000 sq ft lot, new, urban, utilities	total	138733	12/94	2c
Maintenance, repairs, insurance, and other housing	year	531	91	81r
Mortgage interest and charges expenditures	year	1506	91	81r
Mtge. rate, incl. points and orig. fee, 30-year conv. fixed or ARM	mo.	9.21	12/94	2c
Princ. & int., mortgage, median-price exist. sing.-family home	mo.	540	12/94	62r
Property taxes expenditures	year	391	91	81r
Redesign, restructure more than half of home's interior		17,641	3/95	74r
Rent, apartment, 2 br., 1 1/2-2 baths, unfurnished, 950 sq ft, water	mo.	635	12/94	2c
Rental units expenditures	year	1264	91	81r
Insurance and Pensions				
Auto insurance, private passenger	year	753.93	12/94	71s
Insurance and pensions, personal, expenditures	year	2395	91	81r
Insurance, life and other personal, expenditures	year	368	91	81r
Pensions and Social Security, expenditures	year	2027	91	81r
Personal Goods				
Shampoo, Alberto VO5	15-oz.	1.08	12/94	2c
Toothpaste, Crest or Colgate	6-7 oz.	2.33	12/94	2c
Personal Services				
Dry cleaning, man's 2-pc. suit		7.49	12/94	2c
Haircut, man's barbershop, no styling		7.38	12/94	2c
Haircut, woman's shampoo, trim, blow-dry		19.75	12/94	2c
Personal services expenditures	year	212	91	81r
Restaurant Food				
Chicken, fried, thigh and drumstick		2.50	12/94	2c
Dining expenditures, family	week	33.83	94	73r
Hamburger with cheese	1/4 lb.	1.97	12/94	2c
Pizza, Pizza Hut or Pizza Inn	12-13 in.	7.99	12/94	2c
Taxes				
Taxes, Federal income, expenditures	year	2275	91	81r
Taxes, personal, expenditures	year	2715	91	81r
Taxes, State and local income, expenditures	year	365	91	81r
Transportation				
Transportation, ACCRA Index		87.60	12/94	2c
Bus fare, one-way	trip	0.25	12/95	1c
Bus fare, up to 10 miles	one-way	0.25	12/94	2c
Cars and trucks purchased, new	year	1306	91	81r
Cars and trucks purchased, used	year	942	91	81r
Driver's learning permit fee	perm	20.00	1/94	84s
Driver's license fee	orig	20.00	1/94	84s
Driver's license fee, duplicate	lic	10.00	1/94	84s
Driver's license reinstatement fee, min.	susp	25.00	1/94	85s
Driver's license renewal fee	renew	15.00	1/94	84s

Sarasota, FL - continued

Item	Per	Value	Date	Ref.
Transportation - continued				
Identification card, nondriver	card	3.00	1/94	83s
Motorcycle learning permit fee	perm	20.00	1/94	84s
Motorcycle license fee	orig	20.00	1/94	84s
Motorcycle license fee, duplicate	lic	10.00	1/94	84s
Motorcycle license renewal fee	renew	15.00	1/94	84s
Public transportation expenditures	year	249	91	81r
Tire balance, computer or spin bal., front	wheel	5.44	12/94	2c
Transportation expenditures, total	year	5307	91	81r
Vehicle finance charges	year	346	91	81r
Vehicle insurance expenditures	year	544	91	81r
Vehicle maintenance and repairs expenditures	year	600	91	81r
Vehicle purchases	year	2275	91	81r
Vehicle rental, leases, licenses, etc. expenditures	year	141	91	81r
Vehicles purchased, other than cars and trucks	year	27	91	81r
Utilities				
Utilities, ACCRA Index		108.00	12/94	2c
Electricity expenditures	year	950	91	81r
Electricity, 1800 sq. ft., new home	mo.	122.97	12/94	2c
Utilities, fuels, and public services, total expenditures	year	2000	91	81r
Water and other public services, expenditures	year	227	91	81r
Weddings				
Bridal attendants' gowns	event	750	10/93	76r
Bridal gown	event	852	10/93	76r
Bridal headpiece and veil	event	167	10/93	76r
Bride's wedding band	event	708	10/93	76r
Clergy	event	224	10/93	76r
Engagement ring	event	2756	10/93	76r
Flowers	event	863	10/93	76r
Formal wear for groom	event	106	10/93	76r
Groom's attendants' formal wear	event	530	10/93	76r
Groom's wedding band	event	402	10/93	76r
Music	event	600	10/93	76r
Photography	event	1088	10/93	76r
Shoes for bride	event	50	10/93	76r
Videography	event	483	10/93	76r
Wedding invitations and announcements	event	342	10/93	76r
Wedding reception	event	7000	10/93	76r

Saratoga, NY

Item	Per	Value	Date	Ref.
Travel				
Car rental, midsize car, 150 fee miles, Hertz	day	43.95	6/95	67c
Dinner, restaurant, inc. tax and tips, no drink	one	16.80	6/95	67c
Hotel room, two persons, inc. tax	night	100.00	6/95	67c
Taxi fare, to airport	one-way	41.00	6/95	67c

Savannah, GA

Item	Per	Value	Date	Ref.
Appliances				
Appliances (major), expenditures	year	153	91	81r
Average annual exp.				
Food, health care, personal goods, services	year	27020	91	81r
Charity				
Cash contributions, expenditures	year	839	91	81r
Clothing				
Apparel, men and boys, total expenditures	year	380	91	81r
Apparel, women and girls, total expenditures	year	660	91	81r
Footwear, expenditures	year	193	91	81r
Communications				
Long-distance telephone rate, day, addl. min., 1-10 mi.	min.	0.04	12/93	9s

Values are in dollars or fractions of dollars. In the column headed *Ref*, references are shown to sources. Each reference is followed by a letter. These refer to the geographical level for which data were reported: s = State, r = Region, and c = City or metro. The abbreviation *ex* is used to mean *except* or *excluding*; *exp* stands for expenditures. For other abbreviations and further explanations, please see the Introduction.

Savannah, GA - continued

Item	Per	Value	Date	Ref.
Communications				
Long-distance telephone rate, day, initial min., 1-10 mi.	min.	0.08	12/93	9s
Phone line, single, business, field visit	inst	58.25	12/93	9s
Phone line, single, business, no field visit	inst	52.25	12/93	9s
Phone line, single, residence, field visit	inst	47.50	12/93	9s
Phone line, single, residence, no field visit	inst	42.50	12/93	9s
Telephone service, expenditures	year	616	91	81r
Education				
Board, 4-year private college/university	year	2288	8/94	80s
Board, 4-year public college/university	year	1723	8/94	80s
Education, total expenditures	year	319	81	81r
Room, 4-year private college/university	year	2409	8/94	80s
Room, 4-year public college/university	year	1459	8/94	80s
Total cost, 4-year private college/university	year	13950	8/94	80s
Total cost, 4-year public college/university	year	5075	8/94	80s
Tuition, 2-year public college/university, in-state	year	972	8/94	80s
Tuition, 4-year private college/university, in-state	year	9253	8/94	80s
Tuition, 4-year public college/university, in-state	year	1894	8/94	80s
Energy and Fuels				
Fuel oil and other fuels, expenditures	year	56	91	81r
Gas, natural, expenditures	year	150	91	81r
Gasoline and motor oil purchased	year	1152	91	81r
Gasoline, unleaded midgrade	gallon	1.21	4/93	82r
Gasoline, unleaded premium	gallon	1.30	4/93	82r
Gasoline, unleaded regular	gallon	1.10	4/93	82r
Entertainment				
Concert ticket, Pearl Jam group	perf	20.00	94	50r
Entertainment, total expenditures	year	1266	91	81r
Fees and admissions, expenditures	year	306	91	81r
Pets, toys, playground equipment, expenditures	year	271	91	81r
Reading, expenditures	year	131	91	81r
Televisions, radios, and sound equipment, expenditures	year	439	91	81r
Funerals				
Burial, immediate, container provided by funeral home		1370.36	1/95	54r
Cards, acknowledgment		14.83	1/95	54r
Casket, minimum alternative		192.52	1/95	54r
Cosmetology, hair care, etc.		102.27	1/95	54r
Cremation, direct, container provided by funeral home		1065.64	1/95	54r
Embalming		304.29	1/95	54r
Funeral, funeral home		287.83	1/95	54r
Funeral, other facility		284.14	1/95	54r
Graveside service		349.13	1/95	54r
Hearse, local		132.27	1/95	54r
Limousine, local		98.45	1/95	54r
Memorial service		270.59	1/95	54r
Service charge, professional, nondeclinable		933.59	1/95	54r
Visitation and viewing		225.83	1/95	54r
Groceries				
Apples, Red Delicious	lb.	0.73	12/94	82r
Bacon, sliced	lb.	1.67	12/94	82r
Bananas	lb.	0.42	12/94	82r
Beef purchases	year	213	91	81r
Beverage purchases, alcoholic	year	249	91	81r
Beverage purchases, nonalcoholic	year	207	91	81r
Bologna, all beef or mixed	lb.	2.27	12/94	82r
Bread, white, pan	lb.	0.68	12/94	82r
Cabbage	lb.	0.42	12/94	82r
Carrots, short trimmed and topped	lb.	0.53	12/94	82r
Cereals and bakery products purchases	year	345	91	81r
Cereals and cereals products purchases	year	127	91	81r
Cheddar cheese, natural	lb.	3.58	12/94	82r
Chicken breast, bone-in	lb.	1.71	12/94	82r

Savannah, GA - continued

Item	Per	Value	Date	Ref.
Groceries - continued				
Chicken, fresh, whole	lb.	0.78	12/94	82r
Chuck roast, USDA choice, boneless	lb.	2.26	12/94	82r
Crackers, soda, salted	lb.	1.27	12/94	82r
Cucumbers	lb.	0.65	12/94	82r
Dairy products (other) purchases	year	141	91	81r
Eggs, Grade A large	dozen	0.87	12/94	82r
Fish and seafood purchases	year	72	91	81r
Flour, white, all purpose	lb.	0.23	12/94	82r
Food purchases, food eaten at home	year	2381	91	81r
Foods purchased away from home, not prepared by consumer	year	1696	91	81r
Frankfurters, all meat or all beef	lb.	1.74	12/94	82r
Fruits and vegetables purchases	year	380	91	81r
Grapefruit	lb.	0.45	12/94	82r
Grapes, Thompson seedless	lb.	2.30	12/94	82r
Ground beef, 100% beef	lb.	1.37	12/94	82r
Ground chuck, 100% beef	lb.	1.97	12/94	82r
Ham, boneless, exc. canned	lb.	2.54	12/94	82r
Ice cream, prepackaged, bulk, regular	1/2 gal.	2.47	12/94	82r
Lemons	lb.	1.02	12/94	82r
Lettuce, iceberg	lb.	0.96	12/94	82r
Margarine, stick	lb.	0.77	12/94	82r
Meats, poultry, fish, and eggs purchases	year	655	91	81r
Milk and cream (fresh) purchases	year	130	91	81r
Orange juice, frozen concentrate 12-oz. can	16 oz.	1.36	12/94	82r
Oranges, Navel	lb.	0.54	12/94	82r
Pears, Anjou	lb.	0.81	12/94	82r
Pork chops, center cut, bone-in	lb.	3.07	12/94	82r
Pork purchases	year	142	91	81r
Potato chips	16-oz.	3.15	12/94	82r
Potatoes, frozen, French fried	lb.	0.82	12/94	82r
Potatoes, white	lb.	0.34	12/94	82r
Rice, white, long grain, uncooked	lb.	0.48	12/94	82r
Round roast, USDA choice, boneless	lb.	2.91	12/94	82r
Sausage, fresh	lb.	1.82	12/94	82r
Shortening, vegetable oil blends	lb.	0.75	12/94	82r
Spaghetti and macaroni	lb.	0.87	12/94	82r
Steak, rib eye, USDA choice, boneless	lb.	6.85	12/94	82r
Steak, round, graded & ungraded, exc. USDA prime & choice	lb.	2.96	12/94	82r
Steak, round, USDA choice, boneless	lb.	3.17	12/94	82r
Steak, sirloin, USDA choice, boneless	lb.	4.12	12/94	82r
Steak, T-bone, USDA choice, bone-in	lb.	5.63	12/94	82r
Sugar and other sweets, eaten at home, expenditures	year	93	91	81r
Sugar, white, all sizes	lb.	0.39	12/94	82r
Tobacco products and smoking supplies, total expenditures	year	286	91	81r
Tomatoes, field grown	lb.	1.36	12/94	82r
Tuna, chunk, light	lb.	1.94	12/94	82r
Turkey, frozen, whole	lb.	0.96	12/94	82r
Yogurt, natural, fruit flavored	8 oz.	0.58	12/94	82r
Health Care				
Adenosine, emergency room	treat	100.00	95	23r
Bladder tap, superpubic, infant, emergency room	treat	119.00	95	23r
Blood analysis, emergency room	treat	25.00	95	23r
Blood tests, abdominal pain, emergency room	treat	25.00	95	23r
Burn dressing, emergency room	treat	266.00	95	23r
Cardiology interpretation, emergency room	treat	26.00	95	23r
Chest X-ray, emergency room	treat	78.00	95	23r
Childbirth, Cesarean delivery, hospital charge	birth	5462.00	12/91	69r
Childbirth, Cesarean delivery, physician charge	birth	2228.00	12/91	69r
Childbirth, normal delivery, hospital charge	birth	2943.00	12/91	69r
Childbirth, normal delivery, physician charge	birth	1619.00	12/91	69r
Defibrillation pads, emergency room	treat	6.00	95	23r
Drugs, expenditures	year	297	91	81r

Values are in dollars or fractions of dollars. In the column headed *Ref*, references are shown to sources. Each reference is followed by a letter. These refer to the geographical level for which data were reported: s = State, r = Region, and c = City or metro. The abbreviation *ex* is used to mean *except* or *excluding*; *exp* stands for expenditures. For other abbreviations and further explanations, please see the Introduction.

Savannah, GA - continued

Item	Per	Value	Date	Ref.
Health Care				
Gastric tube insertion, nasal, emergency room	treat	25.00	95	23r
Health care, total expenditures	year	1600	91	81r
Health insurance expenditures	year	637	91	81r
Heart monitor, emergency room	treat	40.00	95	23r
Insurance premium, family medical care	month	320.13	1/95	41s
Intravenous fluids, emergency room	treat	130.00	95	23r
Intravenous fluids, emergency room	liter	26.00	95	23r
Intravenous line, central, emergency room	treat	342.00	95	23r
Liver function tests, abdominal pain, emergency room	treat	26.00	95	23r
Medical care charges, total, emergency room, third-degree burns	treat	2101.00	95	23r
Medical care charges, total, emergency, infant with fever	treat	628.00	95	23r
Medical services expenditures	year	573	91	81r
Medical supplies expenditures	year	93	91	81r
Morphine, emergency room	treat	34.00	95	23r
Nursing care and facilities charges, emergency room	treat	252.00	95	23r
Nursing care and facilities charges, emergency, infant with fever	treat	252.00	95	23r
Nursing care and facilities charges, emergency, third-degree burns	treat	861.00	95	23r
Physician's charges, emergency, infant with fever	treat	212.00	95	23r
Physician's charges, emergency, third-degree burns	treat	372.00	95	23r
Physician's fee, emergency room	treat	372.00	95	23r
Physician's fee, general practitioner	visit	51.20	12/93	60r
Surgery, open-heart	proc	42374.00	1/93	14r
Ultrasound, abdominal, emergency room	treat	276.00	95	23r
Urinalysis, emergency room	treat	20.00	95	23r
Urinalysis, infant, emergency room	treat	20.00	95	23r
X-rays, emergency room	treat	78.00	95	23r
Household Goods				
Floor coverings, expenditures	year	48	91	81r
Furniture, expenditures	year	280	91	81r
Household equipment, misc. expenditures	year	342	91	81r
Household expenditures, miscellaneous	year	256	91	81r
Household furnishings and equipment, expenditures	year	988	91	81r
Household operations expenditures	year	468	91	81r
Household textiles, expenditures	year	95	91	81r
Housekeeping supplies, expenditures	year	380	91	81r
Laundry and cleaning supplies, expenditures	year	109	91	81r
Postage and stationery, expenditures	year	105	91	81r
Housing				
Add garage/carport		6,980	3/95	74r
Add room(s)		11,403	3/95	74r
Apartment condominium or co-op, median	unit	68600	12/94	62r
Dwellings (owned), expenditures	year	2428	91	81r
Enclose porch/patio/breezeway		4,572	3/95	74r
Finish room in basement/attic		3,794	3/95	74r
Home, existing, single-family, median	unit	120200	12/94	62r
Maintenance, repairs, insurance, and other housing expenditures	year	531	91	81r
Mortgage interest and charges expenditures	year	1506	91	81r
Princ. & int., mortgage, median-price exist. sing.-family home	mo.	540	12/94	62r
Property taxes expenditures	year	391	91	81r
Redesign, restructure more than half of home's interior		17,641	3/95	74r
Rental units expenditures	year	1264	91	81r
Insurance and Pensions				
Auto insurance, private passenger	year	664.85	12/94	71s
Insurance and pensions, personal, expenditures	year	2395	91	81r
Insurance, life and other personal, expenditures	year	368	91	81r

Savannah, GA - continued

Item	Per	Value	Date	Ref.
Insurance and Pensions - continued				
Pensions and Social Security, expenditures	year	2027	91	81r
Personal Services				
Personal services expenditures	year	212	91	81r
Restaurant Food				
Dining expenditures, family	week	33.83	94	73r
Taxes				
Taxes, Federal income, expenditures	year	2275	91	81r
Taxes, personal, expenditures	year	2715	91	81r
Taxes, State and local income, expenditures	year	365	91	81r
Transportation				
Cars and trucks purchased, new	year	1306	91	81r
Cars and trucks purchased, used	year	942	91	81r
Driver's learning permit fee	perm	10.00	1/94	84s
Driver's license fee	orig	15.00	1/94	84s
Driver's license fee, duplicate	lic	10.00	1/94	84s
Driver's license reinstatement fee, min.	susp	25.00	1/94	85s
Driver's license renewal fee	renew	15.00	1/94	84s
Identification card, nondriver	card	3.00	1/94	83s
Motorcycle learning permit fee	perm	10.00	1/94	84s
Motorcycle license fee	orig	15.00	1/94	84s
Motorcycle license fee, duplicate	lic	10.00	1/94	84s
Motorcycle license renewal fee	renew	15.00	1/94	84s
Public transportation expenditures	year	249	91	81r
Transportation expenditures, total	year	5307	91	81r
Vehicle finance charges	year	346	91	81r
Vehicle insurance expenditures	year	544	91	81r
Vehicle maintenance and repairs expenditures	year	600	91	81r
Vehicle purchases	year	2275	91	81r
Vehicle rental, leases, licenses, etc. expenditures	year	141	91	81r
Vehicles purchased, other than cars and trucks	year	27	91	81r
Utilities				
Electricity expenditures	year	950	91	81r
Utilities, fuels, and public services, total expenditures	year	2000	91	81r
Water and other public services, expenditures	year	227	91	81r
Weddings				
Bridal attendants' gowns	event	750	10/93	76r
Bridal gown	event	852	10/93	76r
Bridal headpiece and veil	event	167	10/93	76r
Bride's wedding band	event	708	10/93	76r
Clergy	event	224	10/93	76r
Engagement ring	event	2756	10/93	76r
Flowers	event	863	10/93	76r
Formal wear for groom	event	106	10/93	76r
Groom's attendants' formal wear	event	530	10/93	76r
Groom's wedding band	event	402	10/93	76r
Music	event	600	10/93	76r
Photography	event	1088	10/93	76r
Shoes for bride	event	50	10/93	76r
Videography	event	483	10/93	76r
Wedding invitations and announcements	event	342	10/93	76r
Wedding reception	event	7000	10/93	76r

Scottsdale, AZ

Item	Per	Value	Date	Ref.
Composite, ACCRA index		102.50	12/94	2c
Alcoholic Beverages				
Beer, Miller Lite, Bud, 12-oz., ex deposit	6	3.90	12/94	2c
J & B Scotch	750-ml.	15.42	12/94	2c
Wine, Gallo Chablis blanc	1.5-lit	4.98	12/94	2c

Values are in dollars or fractions of dollars. In the column headed *Ref*, references are shown to sources. Each reference is followed by a letter. These refer to the geographical level for which data were reported: s=State, r=Region, and c=City or metro. The abbreviation *ex* is used to mean *except* or *excluding*; *exp* stands for expenditures. For other abbreviations and further explanations, please see the Introduction.

Scottsdale, AZ - continued

Item	Per	Value	Date	Ref.
Clothing				
Jeans, man's denim		27.98	12/94	2c
Shirt, man's dress shirt		24.65	12/94	2c
Undervest, boy's size 10-14, cotton	3	3.39	12/94	2c
Communications				
Newspaper subscription, dly. and Sun. delivery	month	13.70	12/94	2c
Telephone bill, family of four	month	17.81	12/94	2c
Telephone, residential, flat rate	mo.	12.40	12/93	8c
Energy and Fuels				
Energy, combined forms, 1800 sq. ft.	mo.	116.76	12/94	2c
Gas, reg unlead, taxes inc., cash, self-service	gal	1.20	12/94	2c
Entertainment				
Bowling, evening rate	game	2.26	12/94	2c
Monopoly game, Parker Brothers', No. 9	game	10.19	12/94	2c
Movie	adm	5.92	12/94	2c
Tennis balls, yellow, Wilson or Penn, 3	can	2.04	12/94	2c
Groceries				
Groceries, ACCRA Index		97.20	12/94	2c
Baby food, strained vegetables, lowest price	4-4.5 oz.	0.28	12/94	2c
Bananas	lb.	0.43	12/94	2c
Beef or hamburger, ground	lb.	1.34	12/94	2c
Bread, white	24-oz.	0.66	12/94	2c
Cheese, Kraft grated Parmesan	8-oz.	3.74	12/94	2c
Chicken, whole fryer	lb.	0.65	12/94	2c
Cigarettes, Winston, Kings	carton	14.99	12/94	2c
Coffee, vacuum-packed	13 oz.	3.49	12/94	2c
Corn Flakes, Kellogg's or Post Toasties	18 oz.	2.86	12/94	2c
Corn, frozen, whole kernel, lowest price	10 oz.	0.65	12/94	2c
Eggs, Grade A large	dozen	0.71	12/94	2c
Lettuce, iceberg	head	0.72	12/94	2c
Margarine, Blue Bonnet or Parkay cubes	lb.	0.66	12/94	2c
Milk, whole	1/2 gal.	1.45	12/94	2c
Orange juice, Minute Maid frozen	12-oz.	1.26	12/94	2c
Peaches, halves or slices, Hunt's, Del Monte, or Libby's	29-oz.	1.53	12/94	2c
Peas, sweet, Del Monte or Green Giant	15-17 oz.	0.46	12/94	2c
Potatoes, white or red	10-lb. sack	1.39	12/94	2c
Sausage, Jimmy Dean, 100% pork	lb.	3.26	12/94	2c
Shortening, vegetable, Crisco	3-lb.	2.91	12/94	2c
Soft drink, Coca Cola, ex deposit	2 lit	1.22	12/94	2c
Steak, t-bone	lb.	4.44	12/94	2c
Sugar, cane or beet	4 lbs.	1.35	12/94	2c
Tomatoes, Hunt's or Del Monte	14.5 oz.	0.75	12/94	2c
Tuna, chunk, light, oil-packed	6.125-6.5 oz.	0.69	12/94	2c
Goods and Services				
Miscellaneous goods and services, ACCRA Index		93.20	12/94	2c
Health Care				
Health care, ACCRA Index		111.50	12/94	2c
Antibiotic ointment, Polysporin	1.5 oz.	4.19	12/94	2c
Dentist's fee, adult teeth cleaning and periodic oral exam	visit	56.40	12/94	2c
Doctor's fee, routine exam, established patient	visit	46.40	12/94	2c
Hospital care, semiprivate room	day	451.33	12/94	2c
Household Goods				
Appl. repair, service call, wash mach	min. lab. chg.	22.98	12/94	2c
Laundry detergent, Tide Ultra, Bold, or Cheer	42 oz.	3.14	12/94	2c

Scottsdale, AZ - continued

Item	Per	Value	Date	Ref.
Household Goods - continued				
Tissues, facial, Kleenex brand	175	1.06	12/94	2c
Housing				
Housing, ACCRA Index		113.40	12/94	2c
House payment, principal and interest, 25% down payment	mo.	857	12/94	2c
House, 1800 sq ft, 8000 sq ft lot, new, urban, utilities	total	139613	12/94	2c
Mtge. rate, incl. points and orig. fee, 30-year conv. fixed or ARM	mo.	9.19	12/94	2c
Rent, apartment, 2 br., 1 1/2-2 baths, unfurnished, 950 sq ft, water	mo.	633	12/94	2c
Personal Goods				
Shampoo, Alberto VO5	15-oz.	1.14	12/94	2c
Toothpaste, Crest or Colgate	6-7 oz.	1.92	12/94	2c
Personal Services				
Dry cleaning, man's 2-pc. suit		6.88	12/94	2c
Haircut, man's barbershop, no styling		8.90	12/94	2c
Haircut, woman's shampoo, trim, blow-dry		29.00	12/94	2c
Restaurant Food				
Chicken, fried, thigh and drumstick		1.99	12/94	2c
Hamburger with cheese	1/4 lb.	1.99	12/94	2c
Pizza, Pizza Hut or Pizza Inn	12-13 in.	6.99	12/94	2c
Transportation				
Transportation, ACCRA Index		105.90	12/94	2c
Bus fare, up to 10 miles	one-way	1.00	12/94	2c
Tire balance, computer or spin bal., front	wheel	7.09	12/94	2c
Utilities				
Utilities, ACCRA Index		102.30	12/94	2c
Electricity, 1800 sq. ft., new home	mo.	116.76	12/94	2c

Scranton, PA

Item	Per	Value	Date	Ref.
Appliances				
Appliances (major), expenditures	year	145	91	81r
Average annual exp.				
Food, health care, personal goods, services	year	29496	91	81r
Charity				
Cash contributions, expenditures	year	708	91	81r
Clothing				
Apparel, men and boys, total expenditures	year	416	91	81r
Apparel, women and girls, total expenditures	year	744	91	81r
Footwear, expenditures	year	305	91	81r
Communications				
Long-distance telephone rate, day, addl. min., 1-10 mi.	min.	0.08	12/93	9s
Long-distance telephone rate, day, initial min., 1-10 mi.	min.	0.15	12/93	9s
Phone line, single, business, field visit	inst	75.00	12/93	9s
Phone line, single, business, no field visit	inst	75.00	12/93	9s
Phone line, single, residence, field visit	inst	40.00	12/93	9s
Phone line, single, residence, no field visit	inst	40.00	12/93	9s
Telephone service, expenditures	year	589	91	81r
Education				
Board, 4-year private college/university	year	2714	8/94	80s
Board, 4-year public college/university	year	1899	8/94	80s
Education, total expenditures	year	593	91	81r
Room, 4-year private college/university	year	2720	8/94	80s
Room, 4-year public college/university	year	2063	8/94	80s
Total cost, 4-year private college/university	year	18118	8/94	80s
Total cost, 4-year public college/university	year	8278	8/94	80s
Tuition, 2-year public college/university, in-state	year	1671	8/94	80s

Values are in dollars or fractions of dollars. In the column headed *Ref*, references are shown to sources. Each reference is followed by a letter. These refer to the geographical level for which data were reported: s=State, r=Region, and c=City or metro. The abbreviation *ex* is used to mean *except* or *excluding*; *exp* stands for *expenditures*. For other abbreviations and further explanations, please see the Introduction.

Scranton, PA - continued

Item	Per	Value	Date	Ref.
Education				
Tuition, 4-year private college/university, in-state	year	12684	8/94	80s
Tuition, 4-year public college/university, in-state	year	4316	8/94	80s
Energy and Fuels				
Fuel oil and other fuels, expenditures	year	257	91	81r
Gas, natural, expenditures	year	285	91	81r
Gasoline and motor oil purchased	year	867	91	81r
Gasoline, unleaded midgrade	gallon	1.32	4/93	82r
Gasoline, unleaded premium	gallon	1.40	4/93	82r
Gasoline, unleaded regular	gallon	1.19	4/93	82r
Entertainment				
Entertainment, total expenditures	year	1331	91	81r
Fees and admissions, expenditures	year	398	91	81r
Pets, toys, playground equipment, expenditures	year	270	91	81r
Reading, expenditures	year	171	91	81r
Televisions, radios, and sound equipment, expenditures	year	429	91	81r
Funerals				
Burial, immediate, container provided by funeral home		1370.36	1/95	54r
Cards, acknowledgment		17.72	1/95	54r
Casket, minimum alternative		192.52	1/95	54r
Cosmetology, hair care, etc.		139.56	1/95	54r
Cremation, direct, container provided by funeral home		1049.24	1/95	54r
Embalming		387.57	1/95	54r
Funeral, funeral home		278.77	1/95	54r
Funeral, other facility		275.85	1/95	54r
Graveside service		213.08	1/95	54r
Hearse, local		157.27	1/95	54r
Limousine, local		146.45	1/95	54r
Memorial service		271.02	1/95	54r
Service charge, professional, nondeclinable		943.58	1/95	54r
Visitation and viewing		322.86	1/95	54r
Groceries				
Apples, Red Delicious	lb.	0.78	12/94	82r
Bacon, sliced	lb.	2.24	12/94	82r
Bananas	lb.	0.49	12/94	82r
Beef purchases	year	226	91	81r
Beverage purchases, alcoholic	year	332	91	81r
Beverage purchases, nonalcoholic	year	213	91	81r
Bread, white, pan	lb.	0.80	12/94	82r
Butter, salted, Grade AA, stick	lb.	1.67	12/94	82r
Carrots, short trimmed and topped	lb.	0.51	12/94	82r
Cereals and bakery products purchases	year	407	91	81r
Cereals and cereals products purchases	year	132	91	81r
Chicken breast, bone-in	lb.	2.22	12/94	82r
Chicken, fresh, whole	lb.	1.05	12/94	82r
Chuck roast, USDA choice, boneless	lb.	2.74	12/94	82r
Coffee, 100%, ground roast, all sizes	lb.	4.61	12/94	82r
Dairy products (other) purchases	year	161	91	81r
Eggs, Grade A large	dozen	1.12	12/94	82r
Fish and seafood purchases	year	112	91	81r
Food purchases, food eaten at home	year	2599	91	81r
Foods purchased away from home, not prepared by consumer	year	2024	91	81r
Fruits and vegetables purchases	year	444	91	81r
Grapefruit	lb.	0.44	12/94	82r
Grapes, Thompson seedless	lb.	2.24	12/94	82r
Ground chuck, 100% beef	lb.	1.67	12/94	82r
Ice cream, prepackaged, bulk, regular	1/2 gal.	2.93	12/94	82r
Lemons	lb.	1.06	12/94	82r
Lettuce, iceberg	lb.	0.92	12/94	82r
Meats, poultry, fish, and eggs purchases	year	751	91	81r
Milk and cream (fresh) purchases	year	152	91	81r
Orange juice, frozen concentrate 12-oz. can	16 oz.	1.92	12/94	82r
Oranges, Navel	lb.	0.56	12/94	82r

Scranton, PA - continued

Item	Per	Value	Date	Ref.
Groceries - continued				
Pork chops, center cut, bone-in	lb.	3.09	12/94	82r
Pork purchases	year	130	91	81r
Potatoes, white	lb.	0.37	12/94	82r
Rib roast, USDA choice, bone-in	lb.	4.98	12/94	82r
Round roast, USDA choice, boneless	lb.	2.93	12/94	82r
Shortening, vegetable oil blends	lb.	1.03	12/94	82r
Spaghetti and macaroni	lb.	0.84	12/94	82r
Steak, round, USDA choice, boneless	lb.	3.48	12/94	82r
Steak, sirloin, USDA choice, bone-in	lb.	3.38	12/94	82r
Steak, sirloin, USDA choice, boneless	lb.	4.81	12/94	82r
Sugar and other sweets, eaten at home, expenditures	year	89	91	81r
Sugar, white, all sizes	lb.	0.46	12/94	82r
Tobacco products and smoking supplies, total expenditures	year	279	91	81r
Tomatoes, field grown	lb.	1.56	12/94	82r
Tuna, chunk, light	lb.	2.09	12/94	82r
Health Care				
Childbirth, Cesarean delivery, hospital charge	birth	6334.00	12/91	69r
Childbirth, Cesarean delivery, physician charge	birth	2234.00	12/91	69r
Childbirth, normal delivery, hospital charge	birth	3225.00	12/91	69r
Childbirth, normal delivery, physician charge	birth	1623.00	12/91	69r
Drugs, expenditures	year	205	91	81r
Health care, total expenditures	year	1396	91	81r
Health insurance expenditures	year	553	91	81r
Insurance premium, family medical care	month	349.05	1/95	41s
Medical services expenditures	year	559	91	81r
Medical supplies expenditures	year	80	91	81r
Household Goods				
Floor coverings, expenditures	year	158	91	81r
Furniture, expenditures	year	341	91	81r
Household equipment, misc. expenditures	year	363	91	81r
Household expenditures, miscellaneous	year	194	91	81r
Household furnishings and equipment, expenditures	year	1158	91	81r
Household operations expenditures	year	378	91	81r
Household textiles, expenditures	year	88	91	81r
Housekeeping supplies, expenditures	year	426	91	81r
Laundry and cleaning supplies, expenditures	year	122	91	81r
Postage and stationery, expenditures	year	134	91	81r
Housing				
Add garage/carport		11,614	3/95	74r
Add room(s)		16,816	3/95	74r
Apartment condominium or co-op, median	unit	96700	12/94	62r
Dwellings (owned), expenditures	year	3305	91	81r
Enclose porch/patio/breezeway		2,980	3/95	74r
Finish room in basement/attic		4,330	3/95	74r
Home, existing, single-family, median	unit	161600	12/94	62r
Maintenance, repairs, insurance, and other housing expenditures	year	569	91	81r
Mortgage interest and charges expenditures	year	1852	91	81r
Princ. & int., mortgage, median-price exist. sing.-family home	mo.	765	12/94	62r
Property taxes expenditures	year	884	91	81r
Redesign, restructure more than half of home's interior		2,750	3/95	74r
Rental units expenditures	year	1832	91	81r
Insurance and Pensions				
Auto insurance, private passenger	year	721.50	12/94	71s
Insurance and pensions, personal, expenditures	year	2690	91	81r
Insurance, life and other personal, expenditures	year	341	91	81r
Pensions and Social Security, expenditures	year	2349	91	81r
Legal Assistance				
Estate planning, law-firm partner	hr.	375.00	10/93	12r

Values are in dollars or fractions of dollars. In the column headed *Ref*, references are shown to sources. Each reference is followed by a letter. These refer to the geographical level for which data were reported: s=State, r=Region, and c=City or metro. The abbreviation *ex* is used to mean *except* or *excluding*; *exp* stands for *expenditures*. For other abbreviations and further explanations, please see the Introduction.

Scranton, PA - continued

Item	Per	Value	Date	Ref.
Legal Assistance				
Legal work, law firm associate	hour	78		10r
Legal work, law firm partner	hour	183		10r
Personal Services				
Personal services expenditures	year	184	91	81r
Restaurant Food				
Dining expenditures, family	week	34.26	94	73r
Taxes				
Taxes, Federal income, expenditures	year	2409	91	81r
Taxes, personal, expenditures	year	3094	91	81r
Taxes, State and local income, expenditures	year	620	91	81r
Transportation				
Cars and trucks purchased, new	year	1170	91	81r
Cars and trucks purchased, used	year	739	91	81r
Driver's learning permit fee	perm	27.00	1/94	84s
Driver's license fee	orig	0.00	1/94	84s
Driver's license fee, duplicate	lic	7.00	1/94	84s
Driver's license reinstatement fee, min.	susp	25.00	1/94	85s
Driver's license renewal fee	renew	0.00	1/94	84s
Identification card, nondriver	card	5.00	1/94	83s
Motorcycle learning permit fee	perm	27.00	1/94	84s
Motorcycle license fee	orig	0.00	1/94	84s
Motorcycle license fee, duplicate	lic	7.00	1/94	84s
Motorcycle license renewal fee	renew	0.00	1/94	84s
Public transportation expenditures	year	430	91	81r
Transportation expenditures, total	year	4810	91	81r
Vehicle finance charges	year	238	91	81r
Vehicle insurance expenditures	year	630	91	81r
Vehicle maintenance and repairs expenditures	year	532	91	81r
Vehicle purchases	year	1920	91	81r
Vehicle rental, leases, licenses, etc. expenditures	year	193	91	81r
Vehicles purchased, other than cars and trucks	year	11	91	81r
Utilities				
Electricity expenditures	year	695	91	81r
Utilities, fuels, and public services, total expenditures	year	1981	91	81r
Water and other public services, expenditures	year	154	91	81r
Weddings				
Bridal attendants' gowns	event	750	10/93	76r
Bridal gown	event	852	10/93	76r
Bridal headpiece and veil	event	167	10/93	76r
Bride's wedding band	event	708	10/93	76r
Clergy	event	224	10/93	76r
Engagement ring	event	2756	10/93	76r
Flowers	event	863	10/93	76r
Formal wear for groom	event	106	10/93	76r
Groom's attendants' formal wear	event	530	10/93	76r
Groom's wedding band	event	402	10/93	76r
Music	event	600	10/93	76r
Photography	event	1088	10/93	76r
Shoes for bride	event	50	10/93	76r
Videography	event	483	10/93	76r
Wedding invitations and announcements	event	342	10/93	76r
Wedding reception	event	7000	10/93	76r

Seattle, WA

Item	Per	Value	Date	Ref.
Appliances				
Appliances (major), expenditures	year	189	91	81c
Appliances (major), expenditures	year	160	91	81r
Average annual exp.				
Food, health care, personal goods, services	year	35086	91	81c
Food, health care, personal goods, services	year	32461	91	81r

Seattle, WA - continued

Item	Per	Value	Date	Ref.
Business				
Dinner and tip, hotel, corporate rate	night	33.00	2/94	15c
Hotel room, corporate rate	night	88.00	2/94	15c
Charity				
Cash contributions, expenditures	year	886	91	81c
Cash contributions, expenditures	year	975	91	81r
Clothing				
Apparel, men and boys, total expenditures	year	509	91	81c
Apparel, men and boys, total expenditures	year	467	91	81r
Apparel, women and girls, total expenditures	year	719	91	81c
Apparel, women and girls, total expenditures	year	737	91	81r
Footwear, expenditures	year	189	91	81c
Footwear, expenditures	year	270	91	81r
Shirt, dress, men's	shirt	0.00	1/92	44c
Communications				
Long-distance telephone rate, day, addl. min., 1-10 mi.	min.	0.01	12/93	9s
Long-distance telephone rate, day, initial min., 1-10 mi.	min.	0.15	12/93	9s
Phone line, single, business, field visit	inst	48.00	12/93	9s
Phone line, single, business, no field visit	inst	48.00	12/93	9s
Phone line, single, residence, field visit	inst	31.00	12/93	9s
Phone line, single, residence, no field visit	inst	31.00	12/93	9s
Telephone service, expenditures	year	607	91	81c
Telephone service, expenditures	year	611	91	81r
Telephone, business, addl. line, touch tone	month	0.54	10/91	25c
Telephone, business, connection charges, touch tone	inst	56.16	10/91	25c
Telephone, business, key system line, touch tone	month	38.54	10/91	25c
Telephone, business, PBX line, touch tone	month	38.95	10/91	25c
Telephone, business, single In., touch tone	month	35.72	10/91	25c
Telephone, business, touch tone, inside wiring maintenance plan	month	1.00	10/91	25c
Telephone, residential, flat rate	mo.	10.75	12/93	8c
Education				
Board, 4-year private college/university	year	1928	8/94	80s
Board, 4-year public college/university	year	2194	8/94	80s
Education, total expenditures	year	395	91	81c
Education, total expenditures	year	375	91	81r
Room, 4-year private college/university	year	2455	8/94	80s
Room, 4-year public college/university	year	1952	8/94	80s
Total cost, 4-year private college/university	year	16332	8/94	80s
Total cost, 4-year public college/university	year	6483	8/94	80s
Tuition, 2-year public college/university, in-state	year	1141	8/94	80s
Tuition, 4-year private college/university, in-state	year	11949	8/94	80s
Tuition, 4-year public college/university, in-state	year	2337	8/94	80s
Energy and Fuels				
Fuel oil and other fuels, expenditures	year	67	91	81c
Fuel oil and other fuels, expenditures	year	33	91	81r
Gas	gal.	1.17	1/92	44c
Gas, cooking, winter, 10 therms	month	7.03	2/94	65c
Gas, cooking, winter, 30 therms	month	21.10	2/94	65c
Gas, cooking, winter, 50 therms	month	35.16	2/94	65c
Gas, heating, winter, 100 therms	month	54.90	2/94	65c
Gas, heating, winter, average use	month	64.84	2/94	65c
Gas, natural, expenditures	year	164	91	81c
Gas, natural, expenditures	year	212	91	81r
Gasoline and motor oil purchased	year	1090	91	81c
Gasoline and motor oil purchased	year	1115	91	81r
Gasoline, unleaded midgrade	gallon	1.36	4/93	82r
Gasoline, unleaded premium	gallon	1.43	4/93	82r
Gasoline, unleaded regular	gallon	1.23	4/93	82r
Entertainment				
Concert ticket, Pearl Jam group	perf	20.00	94	50r
Entertainment supplies, equipment, and services, misc. expenditures	year	505	91	81c

Values are in dollars or fractions of dollars. In the column headed *Ref*, references are shown to sources. Each reference is followed by a letter. These refer to the geographical level for which data were reported: s=State, r=Region, and c=City or metro. The abbreviation *ex* is used to mean *except* or *excluding*; *exp* stands for expenditures. For other abbreviations and further explanations, please see the Introduction.

Seattle, WA - continued

Item	Per	Value	Date	Ref.
Entertainment				
Entertainment, total expenditures	year	1940	91	81c
Entertainment, total expenditures	year	1853	91	81r
Fees and admissions, expenditures	year	580	91	81c
Fees and admissions, expenditures	year	482	91	81r
Movie ticket, adult	ticket	6.00	1/92	44c
Pets, toys, playground equipment, expenditures	year	300	91	81c
Pets, toys, playground equipment, expenditures	year	299	91	81r
Reading, expenditures	year	200	91	81c
Reading, expenditures	year	164	91	81r
Televisions, radios, and sound equipment, expenditures	year	555	91	81c
Televisions, radios, and sound equipment, expenditures	year	528	91	81r
Funerals				
Burial, immediate, container provided by funeral home		1382.70	1/95	54r
Cards, acknowledgment		21.87	1/95	54r
Casket, minimum alternative		128.54	1/95	54r
Cosmetology, hair care, etc.		119.69	1/95	54r
Cremation, direct, container provided by funeral home		1030.62	1/95	54r
Embalming		255.42	1/95	54r
Funeral, funeral home		437.38	1/95	54r
Funeral, other facility		444.46	1/95	54r
Graveside service		338.46	1/95	54r
Hearse, local		147.50	1/95	54r
Limousine, local		130.33	1/95	54r
Memorial service		553.16	1/95	54r
Service charge, professional, nondeclinable		859.15	1/95	54r
Visitation and viewing		93.23	1/95	54r
Groceries				
Apples, Red Delicious	lb.	0.72	12/94	82r
Bacon, sliced	lb.	1.73	12/94	82r
Bananas	lb.	0.52	12/94	82r
Beef purchases	year	186	91	81c
Beef purchases	year	241	91	81r
Beverage purchases, alcoholic	year	335	91	81c
Beverage purchases, alcoholic	year	328	91	81r
Beverage purchases, nonalcoholic	year	209	91	81c
Beverage purchases, nonalcoholic	year	234	91	81r
Bologna, all beef or mixed	lb.	2.33	12/94	82r
Bread, white, pan	lb.	0.81	12/94	82r
Carrots, short trimmed and topped	lb.	0.43	12/94	82r
Cereals and bakery products purchases	year	432	91	81c
Cereals and bakery products purchases	year	392	91	81r
Cereals and cereal products purchases	year	157	91	81c
Cereals and cereals products purchases	year	139	91	81r
Chicken breast, bone-in	lb.	2.04	12/94	82r
Chicken, fresh, whole	lb.	0.95	12/94	82r
Coffee, 100%, ground roast, all sizes	lb.	4.48	12/94	82r
Dairy products (other) purchases	year	203	91	81c
Dairy products (other) purchases	year	182	91	81r
Fish and seafood purchases	year	94	91	81c
Fish and seafood purchases	year	94	91	81r
Flour, white, all purpose	lb.	0.21	12/94	82r
Food purchases, food eaten at home	year	2810	91	81c
Food purchases, food eaten at home	year	2749	91	81r
Foods purchased away from home, not prepared by consumer	year	1789	91	81c
Foods purchased away from home, not prepared by consumer	year	1909	91	81r
Fruits and vegetables purchases	year	483	91	81c
Fruits and vegetables purchases	year	459	91	81r
Grapefruit	lb.	0.56	12/94	82r
Ground beef, 100% beef	lb.	1.31	12/94	82r
Ham, boneless, exc. canned	lb.	2.46	12/94	82r
Ice cream, prepackaged, bulk, regular	1/2 gal.	2.57	12/94	82r
Lemons	lb.	1.00	12/94	82r

Seattle, WA - continued

Item	Per	Value	Date	Ref.
Groceries - continued				
Lettuce, iceberg	lb.	0.93	12/94	82r
Meats, poultry, fish, and eggs purchases	year	648	91	81c
Meats, poultry, fish, and eggs purchases	year	700	91	81r
Milk and cream (fresh) purchases	year	147	91	81c
Milk and cream (fresh) purchases	year	155	91	81r
Milk, 2%	gal.	2.40	1/92	44c
Orange juice, frozen concentrate 12-oz. can	16 oz.	1.52	12/94	82r
Oranges, Navel	lb.	0.56	12/94	82r
Pork chops, center cut, bone-in	lb.	3.30	12/94	82r
Pork purchases	year	131	91	81c
Pork purchases	year	122	91	81r
Potato chips	16-oz.	3.03	12/94	82r
Potatoes, frozen, French fried	lb.	0.77	12/94	82r
Potatoes, white	lb.	0.35	12/94	82r
Rental rate, 2-bedroom apartment	month	550.00	1/92	44c
Rice, white, long grain, uncooked	lb.	0.54	12/94	82r
Round roast, USDA choice, boneless	lb.	2.92	12/94	82r
Shortening, vegetable oil blends	lb.	0.80	12/94	82r
Spaghetti and macaroni	lb.	1.02	12/94	82r
Steak, round, graded & ungraded, exc. USDA prime & choice	lb.	3.13	12/94	82r
Steak, sirloin, USDA choice, boneless	lb.	4.07	12/94	82r
Sugar and other sweets, eaten at home, expenditures	year	105	91	81r
Sugar and other sweets, eaten at home, purchases	year	111	91	81c
Sugar, white, all sizes	lb.	0.38	12/94	82r
Tobacco products and smoking supplies, total expenditures	year	253	91	81c
Tobacco products and smoking supplies, total expenditures	year	221	91	81r
Tomatoes, field grown	lb.	1.45	12/94	82r
Tuna, chunk, light	lb.	2.18	12/94	82r
Health Care				
Childbirth, Cesarean delivery, hospital charge	birth	6059.00	12/91	69r
Childbirth, Cesarean delivery, physician charge	birth	2248.00	12/91	69r
Childbirth, normal delivery, hospital charge	birth	3006.00	12/91	69r
Childbirth, normal delivery, physician charge	birth	1634.00	12/91	69r
Drugs, expenditures	year	239	91	81c
Drugs, expenditures	year	230	91	81r
Health care, total expenditures	year	1646	91	81c
Health care, total expenditures	year	1544	91	81r
Health insurance expenditures	year	509	91	81c
Health insurance expenditures	year	558	91	81r
Insurance premium, family medical care	month	382.32	1/95	41s
Medical services expenditures	year	811	91	81c
Medical services expenditures	year	676	91	81r
Medical supplies expenditures	year	87	91	81c
Medical supplies expenditures	year	80	91	81r
Surgery, open-heart	proc	37818.00	1/93	14r
Household Goods				
Floor coverings, expenditures	year	109	91	81c
Floor coverings, expenditures	year	79	91	81r
Furniture, expenditures	year	284	91	81c
Furniture, expenditures	year	352	91	81r
Household equipment, misc. expenditures	year	614	91	81r
Household equipment, misc., expenditures	year	727	91	81c
Household expenditures, miscellaneous	year	317	91	81c
Household expenditures, miscellaneous	year	294	91	81r
Household furnishings and equipment, expenditures	year	1545	91	81c
Household furnishings and equipment, expenditures	year	1416	91	81r
Household operations expenditures	year	606	91	81c
Household operations expenditures	year	580	91	81r
Household textiles, expenditures	year	93	91	81c
Household textiles, expenditures	year	113	91	81r
Housekeeping supplies, expenditures	year	545	91	81c
Housekeeping supplies, expenditures	year	447	91	81r

Values are in dollars or fractions of dollars. In the column headed *Ref*, references are shown to sources. Each reference is followed by a letter. These refer to the geographical level for which data were reported: s=State, r=Region, and c=City or metro. The abbreviation *ex* is used to mean *except* or *excluding*; *exp* stands for *expenditures*. For other abbreviations and further explanations, please see the Introduction.

Seattle, WA - continued

Item	Per	Value	Date	Ref.
Household Goods				
Laundry and cleaning supplies, expenditures	year	97	91	81c
Laundry and cleaning supplies, expenditures	year	114	91	81r
Postage and stationery, expenditures	year	142	91	81c
Postage and stationery, expenditures	year	145	91	81r
Housing				
Add garage/carport		6,422	3/95	74r
Add room(s)		26,583	3/95	74r
Apartment condominium or co-op, median	unit	105300	12/94	62r
Car rental	day	33.00	5/95	95c
Dwellings (owned), expenditures	year	4798	91	81c
Dwellings (owned), expenditures	year	3932	91	81r
Enclose porch/patio/breezeway		5,382	3/95	74r
Finish room in basement/attic		3,911	3/95	74r
Home, existing, single-family, median	unit	178600	12/94	62r
Home, existing, single-family, median	unit	156.40	12/94	62c
Home, purchase price	unit	172.00	3/93	26c
Hotel room	day	125.00	5/95	95c
Maintenance, repairs, insurance, and other housing expenditures	year	573	91	81c
Maintenance, repairs, insurance, and other housing expenditures	year	591	91	81r
Mortgage interest and charges expenditures	year	3445	91	81c
Mortgage interest and charges expenditures	year	2747	91	81r
Princ. & int., mortgage, median-price exist. sing.-family home	mo.	845	12/94	62r
Property taxes expenditures	year	780	91	81c
Property taxes expenditures	year	594	91	81r
Redesign, restructure more than half of home's interior		5,467	3/95	74r
Rental units expenditures	year	1917	900/00/ 91	81c
Rental units expenditures	year	2077	91	81r
Insurance and Pensions				
Auto insurance, private passenger	year	711.57	12/94	71s
Health insurance, HMO plan, cost to employer	year	3092	93	59c
Insurance and pensions, personal, expenditures	year	4103	91	81c
Insurance and pensions, personal, expenditures	year	3042	91	81r
Insurance, life and other personal, expenditures	year	430	91	81c
Insurance, life and other personal, expenditures	year	298	91	81r
Pensions and Social Security, expenditures	year	3673	91	81c
Pensions and Social Security, expenditures	year	2744	91	81r
Legal Assistance				
Legal work, law firm associate	hour	91		10r
Legal work, law firm partner	hour	151		10r
Personal Goods				
Personal care products and services, total expenditures	year	483	91	81c
Personal Services				
Dry cleaning, woman's dress	dress	9.25	1/92	44c
Personal services expenditures	year	289	91	81c
Personal services expenditures	year	286	91	81r
Restaurant Food				
Big Mac, small fries, medium drink	meal	3.61	1/92	44c
Dining expenditures, family	week	32.25	94	73r
Taxes				
Tax rate, residential property, month	$100	1.05	1/92	79c
Taxes, Federal income, expenditures	year	4843	91	81c
Taxes, Federal income, expenditures	year	2946	91	81r
Taxes, personal, expenditures	year	4819	91	81c
Taxes, personal, expenditures	year	3791	91	81r
Taxes, State and local income, expenditures	year	12	91	81c

Seattle, WA - continued

Item	Per	Value	Date	Ref.
Taxes - continued				
Taxes, State and local income, expenditures	year	791	91	81r
Transportation				
Bus fare, one-way	trip	0.62	12/95	1c
Cars and trucks purchased, new	year	980	91	81c
Cars and trucks purchased, new	year	1231	91	81r
Cars and trucks purchased, used	year	811	91	81c
Cars and trucks purchased, used	year	915	91	81r
Driver's learning permit fee	perm	4.00	1/94	84s
Driver's license fee	orig	21.00	1/94	84s
Driver's license fee, duplicate	lic	5.00	1/94	84s
Driver's license reinstatement fee, min.	susp	20.00- 50.00	1/94	85s
Driver's license renewal fee	renew	14.00	1/94	84s
Ferry boat fare, one-way	trip	3.50	12/95	1c
Identification card, nondriver	card	4.00	1/94	83s
Motorcycle license fee	orig	8.00	1/94	84s
Motorcycle license renewal fee	renew	7.50	1/94	84s
parking, long-term lot, airport	3 days	29.52	1/92	44c
Public transportation expenditures	year	510	91	81c
Public transportation expenditures	year	375	91	81r
Railway fare, light rail, one-way	trip	0.85	12/95	1c
Transportation expenditures, total	year	5701	91	81c
Transportation expenditures, total	year	5527	91	81r
Trolley fare, one-way	trip	0.85	12/95	1c
Vehicle expenses, miscellaneous	year	2285	91	81c
Vehicle finance charges	year	377	91	81c
Vehicle finance charges	year	287	91	81r
Vehicle insurance expenditures	year	675	91	81c
Vehicle insurance expenditures	year	624	91	81r
Vehicle maintenance and repairs expenditures	year	819	91	81c
Vehicle maintenance and repairs expenditures	year	695	91	81r
Vehicle purchases	year	1815	91	81c
Vehicle purchases	year	2174	91	81r
Vehicle rental, leases, licenses, etc. expenditures	year	413	91	81c
Vehicle rental, leases, licenses, etc. expenditures	year	257	91	81r
Vehicles purchased, other than cars and trucks	year	24	91	81c
Vehicles purchased, other than cars and trucks	year	28	91	81r
Utilities				
Electricity expenditures	year	486	91	81c
Electricity expenditures	year	616	91	81r
Fee, water use, industrial	month	1224.78	1/95	16c
Utilities, fuels, and public services, total expenditures	year	1592	91	81c
Utilities, fuels, and public services, total expenditures	year	1681	91	81r
Water and other public services, expenditures	year	268	91	81c
Water and other public services, expenditures	year	209	91	81r
Weddings				
Bridal attendants' gowns	event	750	10/93	76r
Bridal gown	event	852	10/93	76r
Bridal headpiece and veil	event	167	10/93	76r
Bride's wedding band	event	708	10/93	76r
Clergy	event	224	10/93	76r
Engagement ring	event	2756	10/93	76r
Flowers	event	863	10/93	76r
Formal wear for groom	event	106	10/93	76r
Groom's attendants' formal wear	event	530	10/93	76r
Groom's wedding band	event	402	10/93	76r
Music	event	600	10/93	76r
Photography	event	1088	10/93	76r
Shoes for bride	event	50	10/93	76r
Videography	event	483	10/93	76r
Wedding invitations and announcements	event	342	10/93	76r

Values are in dollars or fractions of dollars. In the column headed *Ref*, references are shown to sources. Each reference is followed by a letter. These refer to the geographical level for which data were reported: s=State, r=Region, and c=City or metro. The abbreviation *ex* is used to mean *except* or *excluding*; *exp* stands for expenditures. For other abbreviations and further explanations, please see the Introduction.

Seattle, WA - continued

Item	Per	Value	Date	Ref.
Weddings				
Wedding reception	event	7000	10/93	76r

Sharon, PA

Item	Per	Value	Date	Ref.
Appliances				
Appliances (major), expenditures	year	145	91	81r
Average annual exp.				
Food, health care, personal goods, services	year	29496	91	81r
Charity				
Cash contributions, expenditures	year	708	91	81r
Clothing				
Apparel, men and boys, total expenditures	year	416	91	81r
Apparel, women and girls, total expenditures	year	744	91	81r
Footwear, expenditures	year	305	91	81r
Communications				
Long-distance telephone rate, day, addl. min., 1-10 mi.	min.	0.08	12/93	9s
Long-distance telephone rate, day, initial min., 1-10 mi.	min.	0.15	12/93	9s
Phone line, single, business, field visit	inst	75.00	12/93	9s
Phone line, single, business, no field visit	inst	75.00	12/93	9s
Phone line, single, residence, field visit	inst	40.00	12/93	9s
Phone line, single, residence, no field visit	inst	40.00	12/93	9s
Telephone service, expenditures	year	589	91	81r
Education				
Board, 4-year private college/university	year	2714	8/94	80s
Board, 4-year public college/university	year	1899	8/94	80s
Education, total expenditures	year	593	91	81r
Room, 4-year private college/university	year	2720	8/94	80s
Room, 4-year public college/university	year	2063	8/94	80s
Total cost, 4-year private college/university	year	18118	8/94	80s
Total cost, 4-year public college/university	year	8278	8/94	80s
Tuition, 2-year public college/university, in-state	year	1671	8/94	80s
Tuition, 4-year private college/university, in-state	year	12684	8/94	80s
Tuition, 4-year public college/university, in-state	year	4316	8/94	80s
Energy and Fuels				
Fuel oil and other fuels, expenditures	year	257	91	81r
Gas, natural, expenditures	year	285	91	81r
Gasoline and motor oil purchased	year	867	91	81r
Gasoline, unleaded midgrade	gallon	1.32	4/93	82r
Gasoline, unleaded premium	gallon	1.40	4/93	82r
Gasoline, unleaded regular	gallon	1.19	4/93	82r
Entertainment				
Entertainment, total expenditures	year	1331	91	81r
Fees and admissions, expenditures	year	398	91	81r
Pets, toys, playground equipment, expenditures	year	270	91	81r
Reading, expenditures	year	171	91	81r
Televisions, radios, and sound equipment, expenditures	year	429	91	81r
Funerals				
Burial, immediate, container provided by funeral home		1370.36	1/95	54r
Cards, acknowledgment		17.72	1/95	54r
Casket, minimum alternative		192.52	1/95	54r
Cosmetology, hair care, etc.		139.56	1/95	54r
Cremation, direct, container provided by funeral home		1049.24	1/95	54r
Embalming		387.57	1/95	54r
Funeral, funeral home		278.77	1/95	54r
Funeral, other facility		275.85	1/95	54r
Graveside service		213.08	1/95	54r
Hearse, local		157.27	1/95	54r
Limousine, local		146.45	1/95	54r

Sharon, PA - continued

Item	Per	Value	Date	Ref.
Funerals - continued				
Memorial service		271.02	1/95	54r
Service charge, professional, nondeclinable		943.58	1/95	54r
Visitation and viewing		322.86	1/95	54r
Groceries				
Apples, Red Delicious	lb.	0.78	12/94	82r
Bacon, sliced	lb.	2.24	12/94	82r
Bananas	lb.	0.49	12/94	82r
Beef purchases	year	226	91	81r
Beverage purchases, alcoholic	year	332	91	81r
Beverage purchases, nonalcoholic	year	213	91	81r
Bread, white, pan	lb.	0.80	12/94	82r
Butter, salted, Grade AA, stick	lb.	1.67	12/94	82r
Carrots, short trimmed and topped	lb.	0.51	12/94	82r
Cereals and bakery products purchases	year	407	91	81r
Cereals and cereals products purchases	year	132	91	81r
Chicken breast, bone-in	lb.	2.22	12/94	82r
Chicken, fresh, whole	lb.	1.05	12/94	82r
Chuck roast, USDA choice, boneless	lb.	2.74	12/94	82r
Coffee, 100%, ground roast, all sizes	lb.	4.61	12/94	82r
Dairy products (other) purchases	year	161	91	81r
Eggs, Grade A large	dozen	1.12	12/94	82r
Fish and seafood purchases	year	112	91	81r
Food purchases, food eaten at home	year	2599	91	81r
Foods purchased away from home, not prepared by consumer	year	2024	91	81r
Fruits and vegetables purchases	year	444	91	81r
Grapefruit	lb.	0.44	12/94	82r
Grapes, Thompson seedless	lb.	2.24	12/94	82r
Ground chuck, 100% beef	lb.	1.67	12/94	82r
Ice cream, prepackaged, bulk, regular	1/2 gal.	2.93	12/94	82r
Lemons	lb.	1.06	12/94	82r
Lettuce, iceberg	lb.	0.92	12/94	82r
Meats, poultry, fish, and eggs purchases	year	751	91	81r
Milk and cream (fresh) purchases	year	152	91	81r
Orange juice, frozen concentrate 12-oz. can	16 oz.	1.92	12/94	82r
Oranges, Navel	lb.	0.56	12/94	82r
Pork chops, center cut, bone-in	lb.	3.09	12/94	82r
Pork purchases	year	130	91	81r
Potatoes, white	lb.	0.37	12/94	82r
Rib roast, USDA choice, bone-in	lb.	4.98	12/94	82r
Round roast, USDA choice, boneless	lb.	2.93	12/94	82r
Shortening, vegetable oil blends	lb.	1.03	12/94	82r
Spaghetti and macaroni	lb.	0.84	12/94	82r
Steak, round, USDA choice, boneless	lb.	3.48	12/94	82r
Steak, sirloin, USDA choice, bone-in	lb.	3.38	12/94	82r
Steak, sirloin, USDA choice, boneless	lb.	4.81	12/94	82r
Sugar and other sweets, eaten at home, expenditures	year	89	91	81r
Sugar, white, all sizes	lb.	0.46	12/94	82r
Tobacco products and smoking supplies, total expenditures	year	279	91	81r
Tomatoes, field grown	lb.	1.56	12/94	82r
Tuna, chunk, light	lb.	2.09	12/94	82r
Health Care				
Childbirth, Cesarean delivery, hospital charge	birth	6334.00	12/91	69r
Childbirth, Cesarean delivery, physician charge	birth	2234.00	12/91	69r
Childbirth, normal delivery, hospital charge	birth	3225.00	12/91	69r
Childbirth, normal delivery, physician charge	birth	1623.00	12/91	69r
Drugs, expenditures	year	205	91	81r
Health care, total expenditures	year	1396	91	81r
Health insurance expenditures	year	553	91	81r
Insurance premium, family medical care	month	349.05	1/95	41s
Medical services expenditures	year	559	91	81r
Medical supplies expenditures	year	80	91	81r
Household Goods				
Floor coverings, expenditures	year	158	91	81r
Furniture, expenditures	year	341	91	81r
Household equipment, misc. expenditures	year	363	91	81r

Values are in dollars or fractions of dollars. In the column headed *Ref*, references are shown to sources. Each reference is followed by a letter. These refer to the geographical level for which data were reported: s=State, r=Region, and c=City or metro. The abbreviation *ex* is used to mean *except* or *excluding*; *exp* stands for expenditures. For other abbreviations and further explanations, please see the Introduction.

Sharon, PA - continued

Item	Per	Value	Date	Ref.
Household Goods				
Household expenditures, miscellaneous	year	194	91	81r
Household furnishings and equipment, expenditures	year	1158	91	81r
Household operations expenditures	year	378	91	81r
Household textiles, expenditures	year	88	91	81r
Housekeeping supplies, expenditures	year	426	91	81r
Laundry and cleaning supplies, expenditures	year	122	91	81r
Postage and stationery, expenditures	year	134	91	81r
Housing				
Add garage/carport		11,614	3/95	74r
Add room(s)		16,816	3/95	74r
Apartment condominium or co-op, median	unit	96700	12/94	62r
Dwellings (owned), expenditures	year	3305	91	81r
Enclose porch/patio/breezeway		2,980	3/95	74r
Finish room in basement/attic		4,330	3/95	74r
Home, existing, single-family, median	unit	161600	12/94	62r
Maintenance, repairs, insurance, and other housing expenditures	year	569	91	81r
Mortgage interest and charges expenditures	year	1852	91	81r
Princ. & int., mortgage, median-price exist. sing.-family home	mo.	765	12/94	62r
Property taxes expenditures	year	884	91	81r
Redesign, restructure more than half of home's interior		2,750	3/95	74r
Rental units expenditures	year	1832	91	81r
Insurance and Pensions				
Auto insurance, private passenger	year	721.50	12/94	71s
Insurance and pensions, personal, expenditures	year	2690	91	81r
Insurance, life and other personal, expenditures	year	341	91	81r
Pensions and Social Security, expenditures	year	2349	91	81r
Legal Assistance				
Estate planning, law-firm partner	hr.	375.00	10/93	12r
Legal work, law firm associate	hour	78		10r
Legal work, law firm partner	hour	183		10r
Personal Services				
Personal services expenditures	year	184	91	81r
Restaurant Food				
Dining expenditures, family	week	34.26	94	73r
Taxes				
Taxes, Federal income, expenditures	year	2409	91	81r
Taxes, personal, expenditures	year	3094	91	81r
Taxes, State and local income, expenditures	year	620	91	81r
Transportation				
Cars and trucks purchased, new	year	1170	91	81r
Cars and trucks purchased, used	year	739	91	81r
Driver's learning permit fee	perm	27.00	1/94	84s
Driver's license fee	orig	0.00	1/94	84s
Driver's license fee, duplicate	lic	7.00	1/94	84s
Driver's license reinstatement fee, min.	susp	25.00	1/94	85s
Driver's license renewal fee	renew	0.00	1/94	84s
Identification card, nondriver	card	5.00	1/94	83s
Motorcycle learning permit fee	perm	27.00	1/94	84s
Motorcycle license fee	orig	0.00	1/94	84s
Motorcycle license fee, duplicate	lic	7.00	1/94	84s
Motorcycle license renewal fee	renew	0.00	1/94	84s
Public transportation expenditures	year	430	91	81r
Transportation expenditures, total	year	4810	91	81r
Vehicle finance charges	year	238	91	81r
Vehicle insurance expenditures	year	630	91	81r
Vehicle maintenance and repairs expenditures	year	532	91	81r
Vehicle purchases	year	1920	91	81r
Vehicle rental, leases, licenses, etc. expenditures	year	193	91	81r

Sharon, PA - continued

Item	Per	Value	Date	Ref.
Transportation - continued				
Vehicles purchased, other than cars and trucks	year	11	91	81r
Utilities				
Electricity expenditures	year	695	91	81r
Utilities, fuels, and public services, total expenditures	year	1981	91	81r
Water and other public services, expenditures	year	154	91	81r
Weddings				
Bridal attendants' gowns	event	750	10/93	76r
Bridal gown	event	852	10/93	76r
Bridal headpiece and veil	event	167	10/93	76r
Bride's wedding band	event	708	10/93	76r
Clergy	event	224	10/93	76r
Engagement ring	event	2756	10/93	76r
Flowers	event	863	10/93	76r
Formal wear for groom	event	106	10/93	76r
Groom's attendants' formal wear	event	530	10/93	76r
Groom's wedding band	event	402	10/93	76r
Music	event	600	10/93	76r
Photography	event	1088	10/93	76r
Shoes for bride	event	50	10/93	76r
Videography	event	483	10/93	76r
Wedding invitations and announcements	event	342	10/93	76r
Wedding reception	event	7000	10/93	76r

Sheboygan, WI

Item	Per	Value	Date	Ref.
Composite, ACCRA index		98.70	12/94	2c
Alcoholic Beverages				
Beer, Miller Lite, Bud, 12-oz., ex deposit	6	3.12	12/94	2c
J & B Scotch	750-ml.	14.98	12/94	2c
Wine, Gallo Chablis blanc	1.5-lit	4.20	12/94	2c
Appliances				
Appliances (major), expenditures	year	131	91	81r
Average annual exp.				
Food, health care, personal goods, services	year	25935	91	81r
Charity				
Cash contributions, expenditures	year	745	91	81r
Clothing				
Apparel, men and boys, total expenditures	year	332	91	81r
Apparel, women and girls, total expenditures	year	578	91	81r
Footwear, expenditures	year	164	91	81r
Jeans, man's denim		30.74	12/94	2c
Shirt, man's dress shirt		36.30	12/94	2c
Undervest, boy's size 10-14, cotton	3	3.62	12/94	2c
Communications				
Long-distance telephone rate, day, addl. min., 1-10 mi.	min.	0.10	12/93	9s
Long-distance telephone rate, day, initial min., 1-10 mi.	min.	0.15	12/93	9s
Newspaper subscription, dly. and Sun. delivery	month	12.12	12/94	2c
Phone line, single, business, field visit	inst	64.65	12/93	9s
Phone line, single, business, no field visit	inst	64.65	12/93	9s
Phone line, single, residence, field visit	inst	33.05	12/93	9s
Phone line, single, residence, no field visit	inst	33.05	12/93	9s
Telephone bill, family of four	month	15.95	12/94	2c
Telephone service, expenditures	year	547	91	81r
Telephone, residential, flat rate	mo.	6.00	12/93	8c
Education				
Board, 4-year private college/university	year	2145	8/94	80s
Board, 4-year public college/university	year	1303	8/94	80s
Education, total expenditures	year	394	91	81r
Room, 4-year private college/university	year	1576	8/94	80s
Room, 4-year public college/university	year	1631	8/94	80s

Values are in dollars or fractions of dollars. In the column headed *Ref*, references are shown to sources. Each reference is followed by a letter. These refer to the geographical level for which data were reported: s=State, r=Region, and c=City or metro. The abbreviation *ex* is used to mean *except* or *excluding*; *exp* stands for *expenditures*. For other abbreviations and further explanations, please see the Introduction.

Sheboygan, WI - continued

Item	Per	Value	Date	Ref.
Education				
Total cost, 4-year private college/university	year	13902	8/94	80s
Total cost, 4-year public college/university	year	5252	8/94	80s
Tuition, 2-year public college/university, in-state	year	1557	8/94	80s
Tuition, 4-year private college/university, in-state	year	10181	8/94	80s
Tuition, 4-year public college/university, in-state	year	2318	8/94	80s
Energy and Fuels				
Energy, combined forms, 1800 sq. ft.	mo.	93.20	12/94	2c
Energy, exc. electricity, 1800 sq. ft.	mo.	54.20	12/94	2c
Fuel oil and other fuels, expenditures	year	83	91	81r
Gas, natural, expenditures	year	373	91	81r
Gas, reg unlead, taxes inc., cash, self-service	gal	1.17	12/94	2c
Gasoline and motor oil purchased	year	1000	91	81r
Gasoline, unleaded midgrade	gallon	1.15	4/93	82r
Gasoline, unleaded premium	gallon	1.23	4/93	82r
Gasoline, unleaded regular	gallon	1.07	4/93	82r
Entertainment				
Bowling, evening rate	game	1.70	12/94	2c
Entertainment, total expenditures	year	1356	91	81r
Fees and admissions, expenditures	year	347	91	81r
Monopoly game, Parker Brothers', No. 9	game	10.64	12/94	2c
Movie	adm	6.00	12/94	2c
Pets, toys, playground equipment, expenditures	year	270	91	81r
Reading, expenditures	year	160	91	81r
Televisions, radios, and sound equipment, expenditures	year	433	91	81r
Tennis balls, yellow, Wilson or Penn, 3	can	1.98	12/94	2c
Funerals				
Burial, immediate, container provided by funeral home		1268.31	1/95	54r
Cards, acknowledgment		26.12	1/95	54r
Casket, minimum alternative		198.03	1/95	54r
Cosmetology, hair care, etc.		122.19	1/95	54r
Cremation, direct, container provided by funeral home		977.81	1/95	54r
Embalming		334.00	1/95	54r
Funeral, funeral home		321.16	1/95	54r
Funeral, other facility		317.73	1/95	54r
Graveside service		292.48	1/95	54r
Hearse, local		153.20	1/95	54r
Limousine, local		123.52	1/95	54r
Memorial service		356.30	1/95	54r
Service charge, professional, nondeclinable		968.24	1/95	54r
Visitation and viewing		332.66	1/95	54r
Groceries				
Groceries, ACCRA Index		99.10	12/94	2c
Apples, Red Delicious	lb.	0.68	12/94	82r
Baby food, strained vegetables, lowest price	4-4.5 oz.	0.42	12/94	2c
Bacon, sliced	lb.	1.88	12/94	82r
Bananas	lb.	0.29	12/94	2c
Bananas	lb.	0.41	12/94	82r
Beef or hamburger, ground	lb.	1.46	12/94	2c
Beef purchases	year	197	91	81r
Beef, stew, boneless	lb.	2.52	12/94	82r
Beverage purchases, alcoholic	year	293	91	81r
Beverage purchases, nonalcoholic	year	203	91	81r
Bologna, all beef or mixed	lb.	2.12	12/94	82r
Bread, white	24-oz.	0.68	12/94	2c
Bread, white, pan	lb.	0.76	12/94	82r
Cabbage	lb.	0.44	12/94	82r
Carrots, short trimmed and topped	lb.	0.44	12/94	82r
Cereals and bakery products purchases	year	347	91	81r
Cereals and cereals products purchases	year	119	91	81r
Cheddar cheese, natural	lb.	3.28	12/94	82r
Cheese, Kraft grated Parmesan	8-oz.	3.01	12/94	2c

Sheboygan, WI - continued

Item	Per	Value	Date	Ref.
Groceries - continued				
Chicken breast, bone-in	lb.	1.61	12/94	82r
Chicken, fresh, whole	lb.	0.89	12/94	82r
Chicken, whole fryer	lb.	0.96	12/94	2c
Chuck roast, USDA choice, boneless	lb.	2.33	12/94	82r
Cigarettes, Winston, Kings	carton	16.78	12/94	2c
Coffee, 100%, ground roast, all sizes	lb.	4.28	12/94	82r
Coffee, vacuum-packed	13 oz.	3.41	12/94	2c
Cookies, chocolate chip	lb.	2.72	12/94	82r
Corn Flakes, Kellogg's or Post Toasties	18 oz.	2.46	12/94	2c
Corn, frozen, whole kernel, lowest price	10 oz.	0.69	12/94	2c
Dairy products (other) purchases	year	148	91	81r
Eggs, Grade A large	dozen	0.59	12/94	2c
Eggs, Grade A large	dozen	0.76	12/94	82r
Fish and seafood purchases	year	61	91	81r
Flour, white, all purpose	lb.	0.22	12/94	82r
Food purchases, food eaten at home	year	2313	91	81r
Foods purchased away from home, not prepared by consumer	year	1709	91	81r
Fruits and vegetables purchases	year	372	91	81r
Grapefruit	lb.	0.47	12/94	82r
Grapes, Thompson seedless	lb.	2.15	12/94	82r
Ground beef, 100% beef	lb.	1.37	12/94	82r
Ground chuck, 100% beef	lb.	1.81	12/94	82r
Ham, boneless, exc. canned	lb.	2.16	12/94	82r
Ice cream, prepackaged, bulk, regular	1/2 gal.	2.48	12/94	82r
Lemons	lb.	1.08	12/94	82r
Lettuce, iceberg	lb.	0.81	12/94	82r
Lettuce, iceberg	head	0.92	12/94	2c
Margarine, Blue Bonnet or Parkay cubes	lb.	0.59	12/94	2c
Margarine, stick	lb.	0.81	12/94	82r
Meats, poultry, fish, and eggs purchases	year	591	91	81r
Milk and cream (fresh) purchases	year	132	91	81r
Milk, whole	1/2 gal.	1.51	12/94	2c
Orange juice, frozen concentrate 12-oz. can	16 oz.	1.41	12/94	82r
Orange juice, Minute Maid frozen	12-oz.	1.09	12/94	2c
Oranges, Navel	lb.	0.56	12/94	82r
Peaches, halves or slices, Hunt's, Del Monte, or Libby's	29-oz.	1.52	12/94	2c
Peanut butter, creamy, all sizes	lb.	1.81	12/94	82r
Peas, sweet, Del Monte or Green Giant	15-17 oz.	0.57	12/94	2c
Pork chops, center cut, bone-in	lb.	2.76	12/94	82r
Pork purchases	year	130	91	81r
Potato chips	16-oz.	2.81	12/94	82r
Potatoes, frozen, French fried	lb.	0.83	12/94	82r
Potatoes, white	lb.	0.28	12/94	82r
Potatoes, white or red	10-lb. sack	1.50	12/94	2c
Round roast, USDA choice, boneless	lb.	2.90	12/94	82r
Sausage, Jimmy Dean, 100% pork	lb.	2.75	12/94	2c
Shortening, vegetable oil blends	lb.	0.88	12/94	82r
Shortening, vegetable, Crisco	3-lb.	2.67	12/94	2c
Soft drink, Coca Cola, ex deposit	2 lit	1.03	12/94	2c
Spaghetti and macaroni	lb.	0.78	12/94	82r
Steak, rib eye, USDA choice, boneless	lb.	6.15	12/94	82r
Steak, round, graded & ungraded, exc. USDA prime & choice	lb.	2.72	12/94	82r
Steak, round, USDA choice, boneless	lb.	3.02	12/94	82r
Steak, sirloin, USDA choice, boneless	lb.	3.85	12/94	82r
Steak, t-bone	lb.	4.30	12/94	2c
Steak, T-bone, USDA choice, bone-in	lb.	5.38	12/94	82r
Sugar and other sweets, eaten at home, expenditures	year	91	91	81r
Sugar, cane or beet	4 lbs.	1.40	12/94	2c
Sugar, white, all sizes	lb.	0.36	12/94	82r
Tobacco products and smoking supplies, total expenditures	year	298	91	81r
Tomatoes, field grown	lb.	1.36	12/94	82r
Tomatoes, Hunt's or Del Monte	14.5 oz.	0.71	12/94	2c

Values are in dollars or fractions of dollars. In the column headed *Ref*, references are shown to sources. Each reference is followed by a letter. These refer to the geographical level for which data were reported: s=State, r=Region, and c=City or metro. The abbreviation *ex* is used to mean *except* or *excluding*; *exp* stands for *expenditures*. For other abbreviations and further explanations, please see the Introduction.

Sheboygan, WI - continued

Item	Per	Value	Date	Ref.
Groceries				
Tuna, chunk, light	lb.	1.94	12/94	82r
Tuna, chunk, light, oil-packed	6.125-6.5 oz.	0.71	12/94	2c
Turkey, frozen, whole	lb.	0.96	12/94	82r
Yogurt, natural, fruit flavored	8 oz.	0.62	12/94	82r
Goods and Services				
Miscellaneous goods and services, ACCRA Index		97.10	12/94	2c
Health Care				
Health care, ACCRA Index		97.10	12/94	2c
Antibiotic ointment, Polysporin	1.5 oz.	4.01	12/94	2c
Childbirth, Cesarean delivery, hospital charge	birth	5101.00	12/91	69r
Childbirth, Cesarean delivery, physician charge	birth	2234.00	12/91	69r
Childbirth, normal delivery, hospital charge	birth	2891.00	12/91	69r
Childbirth, normal delivery, physician charge	birth	1623.00	12/91	69r
Dentist's fee, adult teeth cleaning and periodic oral exam	visit	52.25	12/94	2c
Doctor's fee, routine exam, established patient	visit	44.50	12/94	2c
Drugs, expenditures	year	248	91	81r
Health care, total expenditures	year	1336	91	81r
Health insurance expenditures	year	550	91	81r
Hospital care, semiprivate room	day	291.10	12/94	2c
Insurance premium, family medical care	month	378.79	1/95	41s
Medical services expenditures	year	457	91	81r
Medical supplies expenditures	year	82	91	81r
Household Goods				
Appl. repair, service call, wash mach	min. lab. chg.	25.00	12/94	2c
Floor coverings, expenditures	year	105	91	81r
Furniture, expenditures	year	291	91	81r
Household equipment, misc. expenditures	year	341	91	81r
Household expenditures, miscellaneous	year	162	91	81r
Household furnishings and equipment, expenditures	year	1042	91	81r
Household operations expenditures	year	365	91	81r
Household textiles, expenditures	year	101	91	81r
Housekeeping supplies, expenditures	year	390	91	81r
Laundry and cleaning supplies, expenditures	year	110	91	81r
Laundry detergent, Tide Ultra, Bold, or Cheer	42 oz.	3.91	12/94	2c
Postage and stationery, expenditures	year	115	91	81r
Tissues, facial, Kleenex brand	175	1.01	12/94	2c
Housing				
Housing, ACCRA Index		104.50	12/94	2c
Add garage/carport		8,479	3/95	74r
Add room(s)		21,347	3/95	74r
Apartment condominium or co-op, median	unit	87100	12/94	62r
Bathroom addition, average cost	add	9734.00	3/95	13r
Bathroom remodeling, average cost	remod	6414.00	3/95	13r
Bedroom, master suite addition, average cost	add	27122.00	3/95	13r
Deck addition, average cost	add	6665.00	3/95	13r
Dwellings (owned), expenditures	year	2566	91	81r
Enclose porch/patio/breezeway		4,556	3/95	74r
Exterior remodeling, average cost	remod	15395.00	3/95	13r
Family room addition, average cost	add	27658.00	3/95	13r
Finish room in basement/attic		5,074	3/95	74r
Home, existing, single-family, median	unit	106500	12/94	62r
House payment, principal and interest, 25% down payment	mo.	781	12/94	2c
House, 1800 sq ft, 8000 sq ft lot, new, urban, utilities	total	125000	12/94	2c
Kitchen remodeling, major, average cost	remod	17084.00	3/95	13r
Kitchen remodeling, minor, average cost	remod	5804.00	3/95	13r

Sheboygan, WI - continued

Item	Per	Value	Date	Ref.
Housing - continued				
Maintenance, repairs, insurance, and other housing expenditures	year	484	91	81r
Mortgage interest and charges expenditures	year	1443	91	81r
Mtge. rate, incl. points and orig. fee, 30-year conv. fixed or ARM	mo.	9.40	12/94	2c
Office, home addition, average cost	add	8121.00	3/95	13r
Princ. & int., mortgage, median-price exist. sing.-family home	mo.	515	12/94	62r
Property taxes expenditures	year	639	91	81r
Redesign, restructure more than half of home's interior		9,114	3/95	74r
Rent, apartment, 2 br., 1 1/2-2 baths, unfurnished, 950 sq ft, water	mo.	607	12/94	2c
Rental units expenditures	year	1200	91	81r
Sun-space addition, average cost	add	23768.00	3/95	13r
Wing addition, two-story, average cost	add	50410.00	3/95	13r
Insurance and Pensions				
Auto insurance, private passenger	year	554.10	12/94	71s
Insurance and pensions, personal, expenditures	year	2408	91	81r
Insurance, life and other personal, expenditures	year	355	91	81r
Pensions and Social Security, expenditures	year	2053	91	81r
Legal Assistance				
Legal work, law firm associate	hour	90		10r
Legal work, law firm partner	hour	139		10r
Personal Goods				
Shampoo, Alberto VO5	15-oz.	1.02	12/94	2c
Toothpaste, Crest or Colgate	6-7 oz.	1.53	12/94	2c
Personal Services				
Dry cleaning, man's 2-pc. suit		7.49	12/94	2c
Haircut, man's barbershop, no styling		8.00	12/94	2c
Haircut, woman's shampoo, trim, blow-dry		17.10	12/94	2c
Personal services expenditures	year	203	91	81r
Restaurant Food				
Chicken, fried, thigh and drumstick		1.78	12/94	2c
Dining expenditures, family	week	30.03	94	73r
Hamburger with cheese	1/4 lb.	1.69	12/94	2c
Pizza, Pizza Hut or Pizza Inn	12-13 in.	10.00	12/94	2c
Taxes				
Taxes, Federal income, expenditures	year	1756	91	81r
Taxes, personal, expenditures	year	2426	91	81r
Taxes, State and local income, expenditures	year	568	91	81r
Transportation				
Transportation, ACCRA Index		100.70	12/94	2c
Cars and trucks purchased, new	year	891	91	81r
Cars and trucks purchased, used	year	1155	91	81r
Driver's learning permit fee	perm	20.00	1/94	84s
Driver's license fee	orig	10.00	1/94	84s
Driver's license fee, duplicate	lic	4.00	1/94	84s
Driver's license reinstatement fee, min.	susp	50.00	1/94	85s
Driver's license renewal fee	renew	10.00	1/94	84s
Identification card, nondriver	card	4.00	1/94	83s
Motorcycle license fee	orig	4.00	1/94	84s
Motorcycle license fee, duplicate	lic	4.00	1/94	84s
Motorcycle license renewal fee	renew	4.00	1/94	84s
Public transportation expenditures	year	209	91	81r
Tire balance, computer or spin bal., front	wheel	6.50	12/94	2c
Transportation expenditures, total	year	4792	91	81r
Vehicle finance charges	year	300	91	81r
Vehicle insurance expenditures	year	485	91	81r
Vehicle maintenance and repairs expenditures	year	534	91	81r
Vehicle purchases	year	2068	91	81r
Vehicle rental, leases, licenses, etc. expenditures	year	197	91	81r

Values are in dollars or fractions of dollars. In the column headed *Ref*, references are shown to sources. Each reference is followed by a letter. These refer to the geographical level for which data were reported: s=State, r=Region, and c=City or metro. The abbreviation *ex* is used to mean *except* or *excluding*; *exp* stands for *expenditures*. For other abbreviations and further explanations, please see the Introduction.

Sheboygan, WI - continued

Item	Per	Value	Date	Ref.
Transportation				
Vehicles purchased, other than cars and trucks	year	22	91	81r
Utilities				
Utilities, ACCRA Index		82.90	12/94	2c
Electricity expenditures	year	668	91	81r
Electricity, (part.), other, 1800 sq. ft., new home	mo.	39.00	12/94	2c
Utilities, fuels, and public services, total expenditures	year	1838	91	81r
Water and other public services, expenditures	year	167	91	81r
Weddings				
Bridal attendants' gowns	event	750	10/93	76r
Bridal gown	event	852	10/93	76r
Bridal headpiece and veil	event	167	10/93	76r
Bride's wedding band	event	708	10/93	76r
Clergy	event	224	10/93	76r
Engagement ring	event	2756	10/93	76r
Flowers	event	863	10/93	76r
Formal wear for groom	event	106	10/93	76r
Groom's attendants' formal wear	event	530	10/93	76r
Groom's wedding band	event	402	10/93	76r
Music	event	600	10/93	76r
Photography	event	1088	10/93	76r
Shoes for bride	event	50	10/93	76r
Videography	event	483	10/93	76r
Wedding invitations and announcements	event	342	10/93	76r
Wedding reception	event	7000	10/93	76r

Sherman-Denison, TX

Item	Per	Value	Date	Ref.
Appliances				
Appliances (major), expenditures	year	153	91	81r
Average annual exp.				
Food, health care, personal goods, services	year	27020	91	81r
Charity				
Cash contributions, expenditures	year	839	91	81r
Clothing				
Apparel, men and boys, total expenditures	year	380	91	81r
Apparel, women and girls, total expenditures	year	660	91	81r
Footwear, expenditures	year	193	91	81r
Communications				
Long-distance telephone rate, day, addl. min., 1-10 mi.	min.	0.08	12/93	9s
Long-distance telephone rate, day, initial min., 1-10 mi.	min.	0.10	12/93	9s
Phone line, single, business, field visit	inst	71.90	12/93	9s
Phone line, single, business, no field visit	inst	57.30	12/93	9s
Phone line, single, residence, field visit	inst	52.95	12/93	9s
Phone line, single, residence, no field visit	inst	38.35	12/93	9s
Telephone service, expenditures	year	616	91	81r
Education				
Board, 4-year private college/university	year	2084	8/94	80s
Board, 4-year public college/university	year	1675	8/94	80s
Education, total expenditures	year	319	91	81r
Room, 4-year private college/university	year	1840	8/94	80s
Room, 4-year public college/university	year	1756	8/94	80s
Total cost, 4-year private college/university	year	11876	8/94	80s
Total cost, 4-year public college/university	year	4935	8/94	80s
Tuition, 2-year public college/university, in-state	year	625	8/94	80s
Tuition, 4-year private college/university, in-state	year	7952	8/94	80s
Tuition, 4-year public college/university, in-state	year	1503	8/94	80s

Sherman-Denison, TX - continued

Item	Per	Value	Date	Ref.
Energy and Fuels				
Fuel oil and other fuels, expenditures	year	56	91	81r
Gas, natural, expenditures	year	150	91	81r
Gasoline and motor oil purchased	year	1152	91	81r
Gasoline, unleaded midgrade	gallon	1.21	4/93	82r
Gasoline, unleaded premium	gallon	1.30	4/93	82r
Gasoline, unleaded regular	gallon	1.10	4/93	82r
Entertainment				
Concert ticket, Pearl Jam group	perf	20.00	94	50r
Entertainment, total expenditures	year	1266	91	81r
Fees and admissions, expenditures	year	306	91	81r
Pets, toys, playground equipment, expenditures	year	271	91	81r
Reading, expenditures	year	131	91	81r
Televisions, radios, and sound equipment, expenditures	year	439	91	81r
Funerals				
Burial, immediate, container provided by funeral home		1574.60	1/95	54r
Cards, acknowledgment		22.24	1/95	54r
Casket, minimum alternative		239.41	1/95	54r
Cosmetology, hair care, etc.		91.04	1/95	54r
Cremation, direct, container provided by funeral home		1085.15	1/95	54r
Embalming		281.30	1/95	54r
Funeral, funeral home		323.04	1/95	54r
Funeral, other facility		327.58	1/95	54r
Graveside service		355.19	1/95	54r
Hearse, local		141.89	1/95	54r
Limousine, local		99.40	1/95	54r
Memorial service		284.67	1/95	54r
Service charge, professional, nondeclinable		904.06	1/95	54r
Visitation and viewing		187.04	1/95	54r
Groceries				
Apples, Red Delicious	lb.	0.73	12/94	82r
Bacon, sliced	lb.	1.67	12/94	82r
Bananas	lb.	0.42	12/94	82r
Beef purchases	year	213	91	81r
Beverage purchases, alcoholic	year	249	91	81r
Beverage purchases, nonalcoholic	year	207	91	81r
Bologna, all beef or mixed	lb.	2.27	12/94	82r
Bread, white, pan	lb.	0.68	12/94	82r
Cabbage	lb.	0.42	12/94	82r
Carrots, short trimmed and topped	lb.	0.53	12/94	82r
Cereals and bakery products purchases	year	345	91	81r
Cereals and cereals products purchases	year	127	91	81r
Cheddar cheese, natural	lb.	3.58	12/94	82r
Chicken breast, bone-in	lb.	1.71	12/94	82r
Chicken, fresh, whole	lb.	0.78	12/94	82r
Chuck roast, USDA choice, boneless	lb.	2.26	12/94	82r
Crackers, soda, salted	lb.	1.27	12/94	82r
Cucumbers	lb.	0.65	12/94	82r
Dairy products (other) purchases	year	141	91	81r
Eggs, Grade A large	dozen	0.87	12/94	82r
Fish and seafood purchases	year	72	91	81r
Flour, white, all purpose	lb.	0.23	12/94	82r
Food purchases, food eaten at home	year	2381	91	81r
Foods purchased away from home, not prepared by consumer	year	1696	91	81r
Frankfurters, all meat or all beef	lb.	1.74	12/94	82r
Fruits and vegetables purchases	year	380	91	81r
Grapefruit	lb.	0.45	12/94	82r
Grapes, Thompson seedless	lb.	2.30	12/94	82r
Ground beef, 100% beef	lb.	1.37	12/94	82r
Ground chuck, 100% beef	lb.	1.97	12/94	82r
Ham, boneless, exc. canned	lb.	2.54	12/94	82r
Ice cream, prepackaged, bulk, regular	1/2 gal.	2.47	12/94	82r
Lemons	lb.	1.02	12/94	82r
Lettuce, iceberg	lb.	0.96	12/94	82r
Margarine, stick	lb.	0.77	12/94	82r
Meats, poultry, fish, and eggs purchases	year	655	91	81r

Values are in dollars or fractions of dollars. In the column headed *Ref*, references are shown to sources. Each reference is followed by a letter. These refer to the geographical level for which data were reported: s = State, r = Region, and c = City or metro. The abbreviation *ex* is used to mean *except* or *excluding*; *exp* stands for expenditures. For other abbreviations and further explanations, please see the Introduction.

Sherman-Denison, TX - continued

Item	Per	Value	Date	Ref.
Groceries				
Milk and cream (fresh) purchases	year	130	91	81r
Orange juice, frozen concentrate 12-oz. can	16 oz.	1.36	12/94	82r
Oranges, Navel	lb.	0.54	12/94	82r
Pears, Anjou	lb.	0.81	12/94	82r
Pork chops, center cut, bone-in	lb.	3.07	12/94	82r
Pork purchases	year	142	91	81r
Potato chips	16-oz.	3.15	12/94	82r
Potatoes, frozen, French fried	lb.	0.82	12/94	82r
Potatoes, white	lb.	0.34	12/94	82r
Rice, white, long grain, uncooked	lb.	0.48	12/94	82r
Round roast, USDA choice, boneless	lb.	2.91	12/94	82r
Sausage, fresh	lb.	1.82	12/94	82r
Shortening, vegetable oil blends	lb.	0.75	12/94	82r
Spaghetti and macaroni	lb.	0.87	12/94	82r
Steak, rib eye, USDA choice, boneless	lb.	6.85	12/94	82r
Steak, round, graded & ungraded, exc. USDA prime & choice	lb.	2.96	12/94	82r
Steak, round, USDA choice, boneless	lb.	3.17	12/94	82r
Steak, sirloin, USDA choice, boneless	lb.	4.12	12/94	82r
Steak, T-bone, USDA choice, bone-in	lb.	5.63	12/94	82r
Sugar and other sweets, eaten at home, expenditures	year	93	91	81r
Sugar, white, all sizes	lb.	0.39	12/94	82r
Tobacco products and smoking supplies, total expenditures	year	286	91	81r
Tomatoes, field grown	lb.	1.36	12/94	82r
Tuna, chunk, light	lb.	1.94	12/94	82r
Turkey, frozen, whole	lb.	0.96	12/94	82r
Yogurt, natural, fruit flavored	8 oz.	0.58	12/94	82r
Health Care				
Adenosine, emergency room	treat	100.00	95	23r
Bladder tap, superpubic, infant, emergency room	treat	119.00	95	23r
Blood analysis, emergency room	treat	25.00	95	23r
Blood tests, abdominal pain, emergency room	treat	25.00	95	23r
Burn dressing, emergency room	treat	266.00	95	23r
Cardiology interpretation, emergency room	treat	26.00	95	23r
Chest X-ray, emergency room	treat	78.00	95	23r
Childbirth, Cesarean delivery, hospital charge	birth	5462.00	12/91	69r
Childbirth, Cesarean delivery, physician charge	birth	2228.00	12/91	69r
Childbirth, normal delivery, hospital charge	birth	2943.00	12/91	69r
Childbirth, normal delivery, physician charge	birth	1619.00	12/91	69r
Defibrillation pads, emergency room	treat	6.00	95	23r
Drugs, expenditures	year	297	91	81r
Gastric tube insertion, nasal, emergency room	treat	25.00	95	23r
Health care, total expenditures	year	1600	91	81r
Health insurance expenditures	year	637	91	81r
Heart monitor, emergency room	treat	40.00	95	23r
Insurance premium, family medical care	month	389.25	1/95	41s
Intravenous fluids, emergency room	treat	130.00	95	23r
Intravenous fluids, emergency room	liter	26.00	95	23r
Intravenous line, central, emergency room	treat	342.00	95	23r
Liver function tests, abdominal pain, emergency room	treat	26.00	95	23r
Medical care charges, total, emergency room, third-degree burns	treat	2101.00	95	23r
Medical care charges, total, emergency, infant with fever	treat	628.00	95	23r
Medical services expenditures	year	573	91	81r
Medical supplies expenditures	year	93	91	81r
Morphine, emergency room	treat	34.00	95	23r
Nursing care and facilities charges, emergency room	treat	252.00	95	23r
Nursing care and facilities charges, emergency, infant with fever	treat	252.00	95	23r
Nursing care and facilities charges, emergency, third-degree burns	treat	861.00	95	23r

Sherman-Denison, TX - continued

Item	Per	Value	Date	Ref.
Health Care - continued				
Physician's charges, emergency, infant with fever	treat	212.00	95	23r
Physician's charges, emergency, third-degree burns	treat	372.00	95	23r
Physician's fee, emergency room	treat	372.00	95	23r
Physician's fee, general practitioner	visit	51.20	12/93	60r
Surgery, open-heart	proc	42374.00	1/93	14r
Ultrasound, abdominal, emergency room	treat	276.00	95	23r
Urinalysis, emergency room	treat	20.00	95	23r
Urinalysis, infant, emergency room	treat	20.00	95	23r
X-rays, emergency room	treat	78.00	95	23r
Household Goods				
Floor coverings, expenditures	year	48	91	81r
Furniture, expenditures	year	280	91	81r
Household equipment, misc. expenditures	year	342	91	81r
Household expenditures, miscellaneous	year	256	91	81r
Household furnishings and equipment, expenditures	year	988	91	81r
Household operations expenditures	year	468	91	81r
Household textiles, expenditures	year	95	91	81r
Housekeeping supplies, expenditures	year	380	91	81r
Laundry and cleaning supplies, expenditures	year	109	91	81r
Postage and stationery, expenditures	year	105	91	81r
Housing				
Add garage/carport		6,980	3/95	74r
Add room(s)		11,403	3/95	74r
Apartment condominium or co-op, median	unit	68600	12/94	62r
Dwellings (owned), expenditures	year	2428	91	81r
Enclose porch/patio/breezeway		4,572	3/95	74r
Finish room in basement/attic		3,794	3/95	74r
Home, existing, single-family, median	unit	120200	12/94	62r
Maintenance, repairs, insurance, and other housing expenditures	year	531	91	81r
Mortgage interest and charges expenditures	year	1506	91	81r
Princ. & int., mortgage, median-price exist. sing.-family home	mo.	540	12/94	62r
Property taxes expenditures	year	391	91	81r
Redesign, restructure more than half of home's interior		17,641	3/95	74r
Rental units expenditures	year	1264	91	81r
Insurance and Pensions				
Auto insurance, private passenger	year	785.78	12/94	71s
Insurance and pensions, personal, expenditures	year	2395	91	81r
Insurance, life and other personal, expenditures	year	368	91	81r
Pensions and Social Security, expenditures	year	2027	91	81r
Personal Services				
Personal services expenditures	year	212	91	81r
Restaurant Food				
Dining expenditures, family	week	33.83	94	73r
Taxes				
Tax, cigarettes	year	584.00	10/93	43s
Taxes, Federal income, expenditures	year	2275	91	81r
Taxes, personal, expenditures	year	2715	91	81r
Taxes, State and local income, expenditures	year	365	91	81r
Transportation				
Cars and trucks purchased, new	year	1306	91	81r
Cars and trucks purchased, used	year	942	91	81r
Driver's learning permit fee	perm	5.00	1/94	84s
Driver's license fee	orig	16.00	1/94	84s
Driver's license fee, duplicate	lic	10.00	1/94	84s
Driver's license reinstatement fee, min.	susp	50.00	1/94	85s
Driver's license renewal fee	renew	16.00	1/94	84s
Identification card, nondriver	card	10.00	1/94	83s
Motorcycle learning permit fee	perm	5.00	1/94	84s
Motorcycle license fee	orig	16.00	1/94	84s

Values are in dollars or fractions of dollars. In the column headed *Ref*, references are shown to sources. Each reference is followed by a letter. These refer to the geographical level for which data were reported: s = State, r = Region, and c = City or metro. The abbreviation *ex* is used to mean *except* or *excluding*; *exp* stands for expenditures. For other abbreviations and further explanations, please see the Introduction.

Sherman-Denison, TX - continued

Item	Per	Value	Date	Ref.
Transportation				
Motorcycle license fee, duplicate	lic	10.00	1/94	84s
Motorcycle license renewal fee	renew	21.00	1/94	84s
Public transportation expenditures	year	249	91	81r
Transportation expenditures, total	year	5307	91	81r
Vehicle finance charges	year	346	91	81r
Vehicle insurance expenditures	year	544	91	81r
Vehicle maintenance and repairs expenditures	year	600	91	81r
Vehicle purchases	year	2275	91	81r
Vehicle rental, leases, licenses, etc. expenditures	year	141	91	81r
Vehicles purchased, other than cars and trucks	year	27	91	81r
Utilities				
Electricity expenditures	year	950	91	81r
Utilities, fuels, and public services, total expenditures	year	2000	91	81r
Water and other public services, expenditures	year	227	91	81r
Weddings				
Bridal attendants' gowns	event	750	10/93	76r
Bridal gown	event	852	10/93	76r
Bridal headpiece and veil	event	167	10/93	76r
Bride's wedding band	event	708	10/93	76r
Clergy	event	224	10/93	76r
Engagement ring	event	2756	10/93	76r
Flowers	event	863	10/93	76r
Formal wear for groom	event	106	10/93	76r
Groom's attendants' formal wear	event	530	10/93	76r
Groom's wedding band	event	402	10/93	76r
Music	event	600	10/93	76r
Photography	event	1088	10/93	76r
Shoes for bride	event	50	10/93	76r
Videography	event	483	10/93	76r
Wedding invitations and announcements	event	342	10/93	76r
Wedding reception	event	7000	10/93	76r

Shreveport, LA

Item	Per	Value	Date	Ref.
Appliances				
Appliances (major), expenditures	year	153	91	81r
Average annual exp.				
Food, health care, personal goods, services	year	27020	91	81r
Charity				
Cash contributions, expenditures	year	839	91	81r
Clothing				
Apparel, men and boys, total expenditures	year	380	91	81r
Apparel, women and girls, total expenditures	year	660	91	81r
Footwear, expenditures	year	193	91	81r
Communications				
Long-distance telephone rate, day, addl. min., 1-10 mi.	min.	0.29	12/93	9s
Long-distance telephone rate, day, initial min., 1-10 mi.	min.	0.41	12/93	9s
Phone line, single, business, field visit	inst	85.00	12/93	9s
Phone line, single, business, no field visit	inst	85.00	12/93	9s
Phone line, single, residence, field visit	inst	50.00	12/93	9s
Phone line, single, residence, no field visit	inst	50.00	12/93	9s
Telephone service, expenditures	year	616	91	81r
Education				
Board, 4-year private college/university	year	2436	8/94	80s
Board, 4-year public college/university	year	1638	8/94	80s
Education, total expenditures	year	319	91	81r
Room, 4-year private college/university	year	2558	8/94	80s
Room, 4-year public college/university	year	1405	8/94	80s
Total cost, 4-year private college/university	year	16467	8/94	80s
Total cost, 4-year public college/university	year	5225	8/94	80s

Shreveport, LA - continued

Item	Per	Value	Date	Ref.
Education - continued				
Tuition, 2-year public college/university, in-state	year	956	8/94	80s
Tuition, 4-year private college/university, in-state	year	11473	8/94	80s
Tuition, 4-year public college/university, in-state	year	2182	8/94	80s
Energy and Fuels				
Fuel oil and other fuels, expenditures	year	56	91	81r
Gas, natural, expenditures	year	150	91	81r
Gasoline and motor oil purchased	year	1152	91	81r
Gasoline, unleaded midgrade	gallon	1.21	4/93	82r
Gasoline, unleaded premium	gallon	1.30	4/93	82r
Gasoline, unleaded regular	gallon	1.10	4/93	82r
Entertainment				
Concert ticket, Pearl Jam group	perf	20.00	94	50r
Entertainment, total expenditures	year	1266	91	81r
Fees and admissions, expenditures	year	306	91	81r
Pets, toys, playground equipment, expenditures	year	271	91	81r
Reading, expenditures	year	131	91	81r
Televisions, radios, and sound equipment, expenditures	year	439	91	81r
Funerals				
Burial, immediate, container provided by funeral home		1574.60	1/95	54r
Cards, acknowledgment		22.24	1/95	54r
Casket, minimum alternative		239.41	1/95	54r
Cosmetology, hair care, etc.		91.04	1/95	54r
Cremation, direct, container provided by funeral home		1085.15	1/95	54r
Embalming		281.30	1/95	54r
Funeral, funeral home		323.04	1/95	54r
Funeral, other facility		327.58	1/95	54r
Graveside service		355.19	1/95	54r
Hearse, local		141.89	1/95	54r
Limousine, local		99.40	1/95	54r
Memorial service		284.67	1/95	54r
Service charge, professional, nondeclinable		904.06	1/95	54r
Visitation and viewing		187.04	1/95	54r
Groceries				
Apples, Red Delicious	lb.	0.73	12/94	82r
Bacon, sliced	lb.	1.67	12/94	82r
Bananas	lb.	0.42	12/94	82r
Beef purchases	year	213	91	81r
Beverage purchases, alcoholic	year	249	91	81r
Beverage purchases, nonalcoholic	year	207	91	81r
Bologna, all beef or mixed	lb.	2.27	12/94	82r
Bread, white, pan	lb.	0.68	12/94	82r
Cabbage	lb.	0.42	12/94	82r
Carrots, short trimmed and topped	lb.	0.53	12/94	82r
Cereals and bakery products purchases	year	345	91	81r
Cereals and cereals products purchases	year	127	91	81r
Cheddar cheese, natural	lb.	3.58	12/94	82r
Chicken breast, bone-in	lb.	1.71	12/94	82r
Chicken, fresh, whole	lb.	0.78	12/94	82r
Chuck roast, USDA choice, boneless	lb.	2.26	12/94	82r
Crackers, soda, salted	lb.	1.27	12/94	82r
Cucumbers	lb.	0.65	12/94	82r
Dairy products (other) purchases	year	141	91	81r
Eggs, Grade A large	dozen	0.87	12/94	82r
Fish and seafood purchases	year	72	91	81r
Flour, white, all purpose	lb.	0.23	12/94	82r
Food purchases, food eaten at home	year	2381	91	81r
Foods purchased away from home, not prepared by consumer	year	1696	91	81r
Frankfurters, all meat or all beef	lb.	1.74	12/94	82r
Fruits and vegetables purchases	year	380	91	81r
Grapefruit	lb.	0.45	12/94	82r
Grapes, Thompson seedless	lb.	2.30	12/94	82r
Ground beef, 100% beef	lb.	1.37	12/94	82r

Values are in dollars or fractions of dollars. In the column headed *Ref*, references are shown to sources. Each reference is followed by a letter. These refer to the geographical level for which data were reported: s = State, r = Region, and c = City or metro. The abbreviation *ex* is used to mean *except* or *excluding*; *exp* stands for expenditures. For other abbreviations and further explanations, please see the Introduction.

Shreveport, LA - continued

Item	Per	Value	Date	Ref.
Groceries				
Ground chuck, 100% beef	lb.	1.97	12/94	82r
Ham, boneless, exc. canned	lb.	2.54	12/94	82r
Ice cream, prepackaged, bulk, regular	1/2 gal.	2.47	12/94	82r
Lemons	lb.	1.02	12/94	82r
Lettuce, iceberg	lb.	0.96	12/94	82r
Margarine, stick	lb.	0.77	12/94	82r
Meats, poultry, fish, and eggs purchases	year	655	91	81r
Milk and cream (fresh) purchases	year	130	91	81r
Orange juice, frozen concentrate 12-oz. can	16 oz.	1.36	12/94	82r
Oranges, Navel	lb.	0.54	12/94	82r
Pears, Anjou	lb.	0.81	12/94	82r
Pork chops, center cut, bone-in	lb.	3.07	12/94	82r
Pork purchases	year	142	91	81r
Potato chips	16-oz.	3.15	12/94	82r
Potatoes, frozen, French fried	lb.	0.82	12/94	82r
Potatoes, white	lb.	0.34	12/94	82r
Rice, white, long grain, uncooked	lb.	0.48	12/94	82r
Round roast, USDA choice, boneless	lb.	2.91	12/94	82r
Sausage, fresh	lb.	1.82	12/94	82r
Shortening, vegetable oil blends	lb.	0.75	12/94	82r
Spaghetti and macaroni	lb.	0.87	12/94	82r
Steak, rib eye, USDA choice, boneless	lb.	6.85	12/94	82r
Steak, round, graded & ungraded, exc. USDA prime & choice	lb.	2.96	12/94	82r
Steak, round, USDA choice, boneless	lb.	3.17	12/94	82r
Steak, sirloin, USDA choice, boneless	lb.	4.12	12/94	82r
Steak, T-bone, USDA choice, bone-in	lb.	5.63	12/94	82r
Sugar and other sweets, eaten at home, expenditures	year	93	91	81r
Sugar, white, all sizes	lb.	0.39	12/94	82r
Tobacco products and smoking supplies, total expenditures	year	286	91	81r
Tomatoes, field grown	lb.	1.36	12/94	82r
Tuna, chunk, light	lb.	1.94	12/94	82r
Turkey, frozen, whole	lb.	0.96	12/94	82r
Yogurt, natural, fruit flavored	8 oz.	0.58	12/94	82r
Health Care				
Adenosine, emergency room	treat	100.00	95	23r
Bladder tap, superpubic, infant, emergency room	treat	119.00	95	23r
Blood analysis, emergency room	treat	25.00	95	23r
Blood tests, abdominal pain, emergency room	treat	25.00	95	23r
Burn dressing, emergency room	treat	266.00	95	23r
Cardiology interpretation, emergency room	treat	26.00	95	23r
Chest X-ray, emergency room	treat	78.00	95	23r
Childbirth, Cesarean delivery, hospital charge	birth	5462.00	12/91	69r
Childbirth, Cesarean delivery, physician charge	birth	2228.00	12/91	69r
Childbirth, normal delivery, hospital charge	birth	2943.00	12/91	69r
Childbirth, normal delivery, physician charge	birth	1619.00	12/91	69r
Defibrillation pads, emergency room	treat	6.00	95	23r
Drugs, expenditures	year	297	91	81r
Gastric tube insertion, nasal, emergency room	treat	25.00	95	23r
Health care, total expenditures	year	1600	91	81r
Health insurance expenditures	year	637	91	81r
Heart monitor, emergency room	treat	40.00	95	23r
Insurance premium, family medical care	month	394.31	1/95	41s
Intravenous fluids, emergency room	treat	130.00	95	23r
Intravenous fluids, emergency room	liter	26.00	95	23r
Intravenous line, central, emergency room	treat	342.00	95	23r
Liver function tests, abdominal pain, emergency room	treat	26.00	95	23r
Medical care charges, total, emergency room, third-degree burns	treat	2101.00	95	23r
Medical care charges, total, emergency, infant with fever	treat	628.00	95	23r
Medical services expenditures	year	573	91	81r
Medical supplies expenditures	year	93	91	81r

Shreveport, LA - continued

Item	Per	Value	Date	Ref.
Health Care - continued				
Morphine, emergency room	treat	34.00	95	23r
Nursing care and facilities charges, emergency room	treat	252.00	95	23r
Nursing care and facilities charges, emergency, infant with fever	treat	252.00	95	23r
Nursing care and facilities charges, emergency, third-degree burns	treat	861.00	95	23r
Physician's charges, emergency, infant with fever	treat	212.00	95	23r
Physician's charges, emergency, third-degree burns	treat	372.00	95	23r
Physician's fee, emergency room	treat	372.00	95	23r
Physician's fee, general practitioner	visit	51.20	12/93	60r
Surgery, open-heart	proc	42374.00	1/93	14r
Ultrasound, abdominal, emergency room	treat	276.00	95	23r
Urinalysis, emergency room	treat	20.00	95	23r
Urinalysis, infant, emergency room	treat	20.00	95	23r
X-rays, emergency room	treat	78.00	95	23r
Household Goods				
Floor coverings, expenditures	year	48	91	81r
Furniture, expenditures	year	280	91	81r
Household equipment, misc. expenditures	year	342	91	81r
Household expenditures, miscellaneous	year	256	91	81r
Household furnishings and equipment, expenditures	year	988	91	81r
Household operations expenditures	year	468	91	81r
Household textiles, expenditures	year	95	91	81r
Housekeeping supplies, expenditures	year	380	91	81r
Laundry and cleaning supplies, expenditures	year	109	91	81r
Postage and stationery, expenditures	year	105	91	81r
Housing				
Add garage/carport		6,980	3/95	74r
Add room(s)		11,403	3/95	74r
Apartment condominium or co-op, median	unit	68600	12/94	62r
Dwellings (owned), expenditures	year	2428	91	81r
Enclose porch/patio/breezeway		4,572	3/95	74r
Finish room in basement/attic		3,794	3/95	74r
Home, existing, single-family, median	unit	120200	12/94	62r
Maintenance, repairs, insurance, and other housing expenditures	year	531	91	81r
Mortgage interest and charges expenditures	year	1506	91	81r
Princ. & int., mortgage, median-price exist. sing.-family home	mo.	540	12/94	62r
Property taxes expenditures	year	391	91	81r
Redesign, restructure more than half of home's interior		17,641	3/95	74r
Rental units expenditures	year	1264	91	81r
Insurance and Pensions				
Auto insurance, private passenger	year	862.62	12/94	71s
Insurance and pensions, personal, expenditures	year	2395	91	81r
Insurance, life and other personal, expenditures	year	368	91	81r
Pensions and Social Security, expenditures	year	2027	91	81r
Personal Services				
Personal services expenditures	year	212	91	81r
Restaurant Food				
Dining expenditures, family	week	33.83	94	73r
Taxes				
Taxes, Federal income, expenditures	year	2275	91	81r
Taxes, personal, expenditures	year	2715	91	81r
Taxes, State and local income, expenditures	year	365	91	81r
Transportation				
Cars and trucks purchased, new	year	1306	91	81r
Cars and trucks purchased, used	year	942	91	81r
Driver's learning permit fee	perm	12.50	1/94	84s
Driver's license fee	orig	12.50	1/94	84s

Values are in dollars or fractions of dollars. In the column headed *Ref*, references are shown to sources. Each reference is followed by a letter. These refer to the geographical level for which data were reported: s = State, r = Region, and c = City or metro. The abbreviation *ex* is used to mean *except* or *excluding*; *exp* stands for expenditures. For other abbreviations and further explanations, please see the Introduction.

Shreveport, LA - continued

Item	Per	Value	Date	Ref.
Transportation				
Driver's license fee, duplicate	lic	5.00	1/94	84s
Driver's license reinstatement fee, min.	susp	60.00	1/94	85s
Driver's license renewal fee	renew	12.50	1/94	84s
Identification card, nondriver	card	7.00	1/94	83s
Motorcycle license fee	orig	8.00	1/94	84s
Motorcycle license renewal fee	renew	8.00	1/94	84s
Public transportation expenditures	year	249	91	81r
Transportation expenditures, total	year	5307	91	81r
Vehicle finance charges	year	346	91	81r
Vehicle insurance expenditures	year	544	91	81r
Vehicle maintenance and repairs expenditures	year	600	91	81r
Vehicle purchases	year	2275	91	81r
Vehicle rental, leases, licenses, etc. expenditures	year	141	91	81r
Vehicles purchased, other than cars and trucks	year	27	91	81r
Utilities				
Electricity expenditures	year	950	91	81r
Utilities, fuels, and public services, total expenditures	year	2000	91	81r
Water and other public services, expenditures	year	227	91	81r
Weddings				
Bridal attendants' gowns	event	750	10/93	76r
Bridal gown	event	852	10/93	76r
Bridal headpiece and veil	event	167	10/93	76r
Bride's wedding band	event	708	10/93	76r
Clergy	event	224	10/93	76r
Engagement ring	event	2756	10/93	76r
Flowers	event	863	10/93	76r
Formal wear for groom	event	106	10/93	76r
Groom's attendants' formal wear	event	530	10/93	76r
Groom's wedding band	event	402	10/93	76r
Music	event	600	10/93	76r
Photography	event	1088	10/93	76r
Shoes for bride	event	50	10/93	76r
Videography	event	483	10/93	76r
Wedding invitations and announcements	event	342	10/93	76r
Wedding reception	event	7000	10/93	76r

Sioux City, IA

Item	Per	Value	Date	Ref.
Appliances				
Appliances (major), expenditures	year	131	91	81r
Average annual exp.				
Food, health care, personal goods, services	year	25935	91	81r
Charity				
Cash contributions, expenditures	year	745	91	81r
Clothing				
Apparel, men and boys, total expenditures	year	332	91	81r
Apparel, women and girls, total expenditures	year	578	91	81r
Footwear, expenditures	year	164	91	81r
Communications				
Long-distance telephone rate, day, addl. min., 1-10 mi.	min.	0.11	12/93	9s
Long-distance telephone rate, day, initial min., 1-10 mi.	min.	0.21	12/93	9s
Phone line, single, business, field visit	inst	50.00	12/93	9s
Phone line, single, business, no field visit	inst	50.00	12/93	9s
Phone line, single, residence, field visit	inst	35.00	12/93	9s
Phone line, single, residence, no field visit	inst	35.00	12/93	9s
Telephone service, expenditures	year	547	91	81r
Education				
Board, 4-year private college/university	year	1971	8/94	80s
Board, 4-year public college/university	year	1562	8/94	80s
Education, total expenditures	year	394	91	81r

Sioux City, IA - continued

Item	Per	Value	Date	Ref.
Education - continued				
Room, 4-year private college/university	year	1707	8/94	80s
Room, 4-year public college/university	year	1526	8/94	80s
Total cost, 4-year private college/university	year	14510	8/94	80s
Total cost, 4-year public college/university	year	5440	8/94	80s
Tuition, 2-year public college/university, in-state	year	1612	8/94	80s
Tuition, 4-year private college/university, in-state	year	10832	8/94	80s
Tuition, 4-year public college/university, in-state	year	2352	8/94	80s
Energy and Fuels				
Fuel oil and other fuels, expenditures	year	83	91	81r
Gas, natural, expenditures	year	373	91	81r
Gasoline and motor oil purchased	year	1000	91	81r
Gasoline, unleaded midgrade	gallon	1.15	4/93	82r
Gasoline, unleaded premium	gallon	1.23	4/93	82r
Gasoline, unleaded regular	gallon	1.07	4/93	82r
Entertainment				
Entertainment, total expenditures	year	1356	91	81r
Fees and admissions, expenditures	year	347	91	81r
Pets, toys, playground equipment, expenditures	year	270	91	81r
Reading, expenditures	year	160	91	81r
Televisions, radios, and sound equipment, expenditures	year	433	91	81r
Funerals				
Burial, immediate, container provided by funeral home		1348.78	1/95	54r
Cards, acknowledgment		21.20	1/95	54r
Casket, minimum alternative		182.83	1/95	54r
Cosmetology, hair care, etc.		133.11	1/95	54r
Cremation, direct, container provided by funeral home		1101.95	1/95	54r
Embalming		314.45	1/95	54r
Funeral, funeral home		304.88	1/95	54r
Funeral, other facility		301.37	1/95	54r
Graveside service		290.59	1/95	54r
Hearse, local		137.37	1/95	54r
Limousine, local		82.84	1/95	54r
Memorial service		316.57	1/95	54r
Service charge, professional, nondeclinable		1099.00	1/95	54r
Visitation and viewing		209.25	1/95	54r
Groceries				
Apples, Red Delicious	lb.	0.68	12/94	82r
Bacon, sliced	lb.	1.88	12/94	82r
Bananas	lb.	0.41	12/94	82r
Beef purchases	year	197	91	81r
Beef, stew, boneless	lb.	2.52	12/94	82r
Beverage purchases, alcoholic	year	293	91	81r
Beverage purchases, nonalcoholic	year	203	91	81r
Bologna, all beef or mixed	lb.	2.12	12/94	82r
Bread, white, pan	lb.	0.76	12/94	82r
Cabbage	lb.	0.44	12/94	82r
Carrots, short trimmed and topped	lb.	0.44	12/94	82r
Cereals and bakery products purchases	year	347	91	81r
Cereals and cereals products purchases	year	119	91	81r
Cheddar cheese, natural	lb.	3.28	12/94	82r
Chicken breast, bone-in	lb.	1.61	12/94	82r
Chicken, fresh, whole	lb.	0.89	12/94	82r
Chuck roast, USDA choice, boneless	lb.	2.33	12/94	82r
Coffee, 100%, ground roast, all sizes	lb.	4.28	12/94	82r
Cookies, chocolate chip	lb.	2.72	12/94	82r
Dairy products (other) purchases	year	148	91	81r
Eggs, Grade A large	dozen	0.76	12/94	82r
Fish and seafood purchases	year	61	91	81r
Flour, white, all purpose	lb.	0.22	12/94	82r
Food purchases, food eaten at home	year	2313	91	81r
Foods purchased away from home, not prepared by consumer	year	1709	91	81r
Fruits and vegetables purchases	year	372	91	81r

Values are in dollars or fractions of dollars. In the column headed *Ref*, references are shown to sources. Each reference is followed by a letter. These refer to the geographical level for which data were reported: s=State, r=Region, and c=City or metro. The abbreviation *ex* is used to mean *except* or *excluding*; *exp* stands for expenditures. For other abbreviations and further explanations, please see the Introduction.

Sioux City, IA - continued

Item	Per	Value	Date	Ref.
Groceries				
Grapefruit	lb.	0.47	12/94	82r
Grapes, Thompson seedless	lb.	2.15	12/94	82r
Ground beef, 100% beef	lb.	1.37	12/94	82r
Ground chuck, 100% beef	lb.	1.81	12/94	82r
Ham, boneless, exc. canned	lb.	2.16	12/94	82r
Ice cream, prepackaged, bulk, regular	1/2 gal.	2.48	12/94	82r
Lemons	lb.	1.08	12/94	82r
Lettuce, iceberg	lb.	0.81	12/94	82r
Margarine, stick	lb.	0.81	12/94	82r
Meats, poultry, fish, and eggs purchases	year	591	91	81r
Milk and cream (fresh) purchases	year	132	91	81r
Orange juice, frozen concentrate 12-oz. can	16 oz.	1.41	12/94	82r
Oranges, Navel	lb.	0.56	12/94	82r
Peanut butter, creamy, all sizes	lb.	1.81	12/94	82r
Pork chops, center cut, bone-in	lb.	2.76	12/94	82r
Pork purchases	year	130	91	81r
Potato chips	16-oz.	2.81	12/94	82r
Potatoes, frozen, French fried	lb.	0.83	12/94	82r
Potatoes, white	lb.	0.28	12/94	82r
Round roast, USDA choice, boneless	lb.	2.90	12/94	82r
Shortening, vegetable oil blends	lb.	0.88	12/94	82r
Spaghetti and macaroni	lb.	0.78	12/94	82r
Steak, rib eye, USDA choice, boneless	lb.	6.15	12/94	82r
Steak, round, graded & ungraded, exc. USDA prime & choice	lb.	2.72	12/94	82r
Steak, round, USDA choice, boneless	lb.	3.02	12/94	82r
Steak, sirloin, USDA choice, boneless	lb.	3.85	12/94	82r
Steak, T-bone, USDA choice, bone-in	lb.	5.38	12/94	82r
Sugar and other sweets, eaten at home, expenditures	year	91	91	81r
Sugar, white, all sizes	lb.	0.36	12/94	82r
Tobacco products and smoking supplies, total expenditures	year	298	91	81r
Tomatoes, field grown	lb.	1.36	12/94	82r
Tuna, chunk, light	lb.	1.94	12/94	82r
Turkey, frozen, whole	lb.	0.96	12/94	82r
Yogurt, natural, fruit flavored	8 oz.	0.62	12/94	82r
Health Care				
Childbirth, Cesarean delivery, hospital charge	birth	5101.00	12/91	69r
Childbirth, Cesarean delivery, physician charge	birth	2234.00	12/91	69r
Childbirth, normal delivery, hospital charge	birth	2891.00	12/91	69r
Childbirth, normal delivery, physician charge	birth	1623.00	12/91	69r
Drugs, expenditures	year	248	91	81r
Health care, total expenditures	year	1336	91	81r
Health insurance expenditures	year	550	91	81r
Insurance premium, family medical care	month	395.98	1/95	41s
Medical services expenditures	year	457	91	81r
Medical supplies expenditures	year	82	91	81r
Household Goods				
Floor coverings, expenditures	year	105	91	81r
Furniture, expenditures	year	291	91	81r
Household equipment, misc. expenditures	year	341	91	81r
Household expenditures, miscellaneous	year	162	91	81r
Household furnishings and equipment, expenditures	year	1042	91	81r
Household operations expenditures	year	365	91	81r
Household textiles, expenditures	year	101	91	81r
Housekeeping supplies, expenditures	year	390	91	81r
Laundry and cleaning supplies, expenditures	year	110	91	81r
Postage and stationery, expenditures	year	115	91	81r
Housing				
Add garage/carport		8,479	3/95	74r
Add room(s)		21,347	3/95	74r
Apartment condominium or co-op, median	unit	87100	12/94	62r
Bathroom addition, average cost	add	9734.00	3/95	13r
Bathroom remodeling, average cost	remod	6414.00	3/95	13r

Sioux City, IA - continued

Item	Per	Value	Date	Ref.
Housing - continued				
Bedroom, master suite addition, average cost	add	27122.00	3/95	13r
Deck addition, average cost	add	6665.00	3/95	13r
Dwellings (owned), expenditures	year	2566	91	81r
Enclose porch/patio/breezeway		4,556	3/95	74r
Exterior remodeling, average cost	remod	15395.00	3/95	13r
Family room addition, average cost	add	27658.00	3/95	13r
Finish room in basement/attic		5,074	3/95	74r
Home, existing, single-family, median	unit	106500	12/94	62r
Kitchen remodeling, major, average cost	remod	17084.00	3/95	13r
Kitchen remodeling, minor, average cost	remod	5804.00	3/95	13r
Maintenance, repairs, insurance, and other housing expenditures	year	484	91	81r
Mortgage interest and charges expenditures	year	1443	91	81r
Office, home addition, average cost	add	8121.00	3/95	13r
Princ. & int., mortgage, median-price exist. sing.-family home	mo.	515	12/94	62r
Property taxes expenditures	year	639	91	81r
Redesign, restructure more than half of home's interior		9,114	3/95	74r
Rental units expenditures	year	1200	91	81r
Sun-space addition, average cost	add	23768.00	3/95	13r
Wing addition, two-story, average cost	add	50410.00	3/95	13r
Insurance and Pensions				
Auto insurance, private passenger	year	467.45	12/94	71s
Insurance and pensions, personal, expenditures	year	2408	91	81r
Insurance, life and other personal, expenditures	year	355	91	81r
Pensions and Social Security, expenditures	year	2053	91	81r
Legal Assistance				
Legal work, law firm associate	hour	90		10r
Legal work, law firm partner	hour	139		10r
Personal Services				
Personal services expenditures	year	203	91	81r
Restaurant Food				
Dining expenditures, family	week	30.03	94	73r
Taxes				
Taxes, Federal income, expenditures	year	1756	91	81r
Taxes, personal, expenditures	year	2426	91	81r
Taxes, State and local income, expenditures	year	568	91	81r
Transportation				
Cars and trucks purchased, new	year	891	91	81r
Cars and trucks purchased, used	year	1155	91	81r
Driver's learning permit fee	perm	6.00	1/94	84s
Driver's license fee	orig	0.00	1/94	84s
Driver's license fee, duplicate	lic	3.00	1/94	84s
Driver's license reinstatement fee, min.	susp	20.00	1/94	85s
Driver's license renewal fee	renew	0.00	1/94	84s
Identification card, nondriver	card	5.00	1/94	83s
Motorcycle learning permit fee	perm	8.00	1/94	84s
Motorcycle license fee	orig	8.00	1/94	84s
Motorcycle license fee, duplicate	lic	3.00	1/94	84s
Motorcycle license renewal fee	renew	8.00	1/94	84s
Public transportation expenditures	year	209	91	81r
Transportation expenditures, total	year	4792	91	81r
Vehicle finance charges	year	300	91	81r
Vehicle insurance expenditures	year	485	91	81r
Vehicle maintenance and repairs expenditures	year	534	91	81r
Vehicle purchases	year	2068	91	81r
Vehicle rental, leases, licenses, etc. expenditures	year	197	91	81r
Vehicles purchased, other than cars and trucks	year	22	91	81r
Utilities				
Electricity expenditures	year	668	91	81r

Values are in dollars or fractions of dollars. In the column headed *Ref*, references are shown to sources. Each reference is followed by a letter. These refer to the geographical level for which data were reported: s = State, r = Region, and c = City or metro. The abbreviation *ex* is used to mean *except* or *excluding*; *exp* stands for *expenditures*. For other abbreviations and further explanations, please see the Introduction.

Sioux City, IA - continued

Item	Per	Value	Date	Ref.
Utilities				
Utilities, fuels, and public services, total expenditures	year	1838	91	81r
Water and other public services, expenditures	year	167	91	81r
Weddings				
Bridal attendants' gowns	event	750	10/93	76r
Bridal gown	event	852	10/93	76r
Bridal headpiece and veil	event	167	10/93	76r
Bride's wedding band	event	708	10/93	76r
Clergy	event	224	10/93	76r
Engagement ring	event	2756	10/93	76r
Flowers	event	863	10/93	76r
Formal wear for groom	event	106	10/93	76r
Groom's attendants' formal wear	event	530	10/93	76r
Groom's wedding band	event	402	10/93	76r
Music	event	600	10/93	76r
Photography	event	1088	10/93	76r
Shoes for bride	event	50	10/93	76r
Videography	event	483	10/93	76r
Wedding invitations and announcements	event	342	10/93	76r
Wedding reception	event	7000	10/93	76r

Sioux Falls, SD

Item	Per	Value	Date	Ref.
Composite, ACCRA index		96.60	12/94	2c
Alcoholic Beverages				
Beer, Miller Lite, Bud, 12-oz., ex deposit	6	3.83	12/94	2c
J & B Scotch	750-ml.	16.35	12/94	2c
Wine, Gallo Chablis blanc	1.5-lit	5.11	12/94	2c
Appliances				
Appliances (major), expenditures	year	131	91	81r
Average annual exp.				
Food, health care, personal goods, services	year	25935	91	81r
Charity				
Cash contributions, expenditures	year	745	91	81r
Clothing				
Apparel, men and boys, total expenditures	year	332	91	81r
Apparel, women and girls, total expenditures	year	578	91	81r
Footwear, expenditures	year	164	91	81r
Jeans, man's denim		27.19	12/94	2c
Shirt, man's dress shirt		26.19	12/94	2c
Undervest, boy's size 10-14, cotton	3	3.45	12/94	2c
Communications				
Long-distance telephone rate, day, addl. min., 1-10 mi.	min.	0.15	12/93	9s
Long-distance telephone rate, day, initial min., 1-10 mi.	min.	0.21	12/93	9s
Newspaper subscription, dly. and Sun. delivery	month	13.00	12/94	2c
Phone line, single, business, field visit	inst	47.00	12/93	9s
Phone line, single, business, no field visit	inst	47.00	12/93	9s
Phone line, single, residence, field visit	inst	25.00	12/93	9s
Phone line, single, residence, no field visit	inst	25.00	12/93	9s
Telephone bill, family of four	month	23.00	12/94	2c
Telephone service, expenditures	year	547	91	81r
Telephone, residential, flat rate	mo.	15.20	12/93	8c
Credit Cards				
Fee, conventional credit card, secured	year	25.00	1/95	96c
Education				
Board, 4-year private college/university	year	2219	8/94	80s
Board, 4-year public college/university	year	1526	8/94	80s
Education, total expenditures	year	394	91	81r
Room, 4-year private college/university	year	1445	8/94	80s
Room, 4-year public college/university	year	1060	8/94	80s
Total cost, 4-year private college/university	year	11387	8/94	80s
Total cost, 4-year public college/university	year	4874	8/94	80s

Sioux Falls, SD - continued

Item	Per	Value	Date	Ref.
Education - continued				
Tuition, 2-year public college/university, in-state	year	2640	8/94	80s
Tuition, 4-year private college/university, in-state	year	7722	8/94	80s
Tuition, 4-year public college/university, in-state	year	2288	8/94	80s
Energy and Fuels				
Energy, combined forms, 1800 sq. ft.	mo.	96.66	12/94	2c
Energy, exc. electricity, 1800 sq. ft.	mo.	45.48	12/94	2c
Fuel oil and other fuels, expenditures	year	83	91	81r
Gas, cooking, winter, 10 therms	month	6.79	2/94	65c
Gas, cooking, winter, 30 therms	month	16.18	2/94	65c
Gas, cooking, winter, 50 therms	month	25.58	2/94	65c
Gas, heating, winter, 100 therms	month	49.06	2/94	65c
Gas, heating, winter, average use	month	92.42	2/94	65c
Gas, natural, expenditures	year	373	91	81r
Gas, reg unlead, taxes inc., cash, self-service	gal	1.15	12/94	2c
Gasoline and motor oil purchased	year	1000	91	81r
Gasoline, unleaded midgrade	gallon	1.15	4/93	82r
Gasoline, unleaded premium	gallon	1.23	4/93	82r
Gasoline, unleaded regular	gallon	1.07	4/93	82r
Entertainment				
Bowling, evening rate	game	2.18	12/94	2c
Entertainment, total expenditures	year	1356	91	81r
Fees and admissions, expenditures	year	347	91	81r
Monopoly game, Parker Brothers', No. 9	game	10.35	12/94	2c
Movie	adm	5.50	12/94	2c
Pets, toys, playground equipment, expenditures	year	270	91	81r
Reading, expenditures	year	160	91	81r
Televisions, radios, and sound equipment, expenditures	year	433	91	81r
Tennis balls, yellow, Wilson or Penn, 3	can	2.18	12/94	2c
Funerals				
Burial, immediate, container provided by funeral home		1348.78	1/95	54r
Cards, acknowledgment		21.20	1/95	54r
Casket, minimum alternative		182.83	1/95	54r
Cosmetology, hair care, etc.		133.11	1/95	54r
Cremation, direct, container provided by funeral home		1101.95	1/95	54r
Embalming		314.45	1/95	54r
Funeral, funeral home		304.88	1/95	54r
Funeral, other facility		301.37	1/95	54r
Graveside service		290.59	1/95	54r
Hearse, local		137.37	1/95	54r
Limousine, local		82.84	1/95	54r
Memorial service		316.57	1/95	54r
Service charge, professional, nondeclinable		1099.00	1/95	54r
Visitation and viewing		209.25	1/95	54r
Groceries				
Groceries, ACCRA Index		98.80	12/94	2c
Apples, Red Delicious	lb.	0.68	12/94	82r
Baby food, strained vegetables, lowest price	4-4.5 oz.	0.28	12/94	2c
Bacon, sliced	lb.	1.88	12/94	82r
Bananas	lb.	0.52	12/94	2c
Bananas	lb.	0.41	12/94	82r
Beef or hamburger, ground	lb.	1.31	12/94	2c
Beef purchases	year	197	91	81r
Beef, stew, boneless	lb.	2.52	12/94	82r
Beverage purchases, alcoholic	year	293	91	81r
Beverage purchases, nonalcoholic	year	203	91	81r
Bologna, all beef or mixed	lb.	2.12	12/94	82r
Bread, white	24-oz.	0.73	12/94	2c
Bread, white, pan	lb.	0.76	12/94	82r
Cabbage	lb.	0.44	12/94	82r
Carrots, short trimmed and topped	lb.	0.44	12/94	82r
Cereals and bakery products purchases	year	347	91	81r

Values are in dollars or fractions of dollars. In the column headed *Ref*, references are shown to sources. Each reference is followed by a letter. These refer to the geographical level for which data were reported: s=State, r=Region, and c=City or metro. The abbreviation *ex* is used to mean *except* or *excluding*; *exp* stands for *expenditures*. For other abbreviations and further explanations, please see the Introduction.

Sioux Falls, SD - continued

Item	Per	Value	Date	Ref.
Groceries				
Cereals and cereals products purchases	year	119	91	81r
Cheddar cheese, natural	lb.	3.28	12/94	82r
Cheese, Kraft grated Parmesan	8-oz.	3.49	12/94	2c
Chicken breast, bone-in	lb.	1.61	12/94	82r
Chicken, fresh, whole	lb.	0.89	12/94	82r
Chicken, whole fryer	lb.	0.81	12/94	2c
Chuck roast, USDA choice, boneless	lb.	2.33	12/94	82r
Cigarettes, Winston, Kings	carton	15.03	12/94	2c
Coffee, 100%, ground roast, all sizes	lb.	4.28	12/94	82r
Coffee, vacuum-packed	13 oz.	3.49	12/94	2c
Cookies, chocolate chip	lb.	2.72	12/94	82r
Corn Flakes, Kellogg's or Post Toasties	18 oz.	2.05	12/94	2c
Corn, frozen, whole kernel, lowest price	10 oz.	0.74	12/94	2c
Dairy products (other) purchases	year	148	91	81r
Eggs, Grade A large	dozen	0.63	12/94	2c
Eggs, Grade A large	dozen	0.76	12/94	82r
Fish and seafood purchases	year	61	91	81r
Flour, white, all purpose	lb.	0.22	12/94	82r
Food purchases, food eaten at home	year	2313	91	81r
Foods purchased away from home, not prepared by consumer	year	1709	91	81r
Fruits and vegetables purchases	year	372	91	81r
Grapefruit	lb.	0.47	12/94	82r
Grapes, Thompson seedless	lb.	2.15	12/94	82r
Ground beef, 100% beef	lb.	1.37	12/94	82r
Ground chuck, 100% beef	lb.	1.81	12/94	82r
Ham, boneless, exc. canned	lb.	2.16	12/94	82r
Ice cream, prepackaged, bulk, regular	1/2 gal.	2.48	12/94	82r
Lemons	lb.	1.08	12/94	82r
Lettuce, iceberg	lb.	0.81	12/94	82r
Lettuce, iceberg	head	0.89	12/94	2c
Margarine, Blue Bonnet or Parkay cubes	lb.	0.57	12/94	2c
Margarine, stick	lb.	0.81	12/94	82r
Meats, poultry, fish, and eggs purchases	year	591	91	81r
Milk and cream (fresh) purchases	year	132	91	81r
Milk, whole	1/2 gal.	1.25	12/94	2c
Orange juice, frozen concentrate 12-oz. can	16 oz.	1.41	12/94	82r
Orange juice, Minute Maid frozen	12-oz.	1.29	12/94	2c
Oranges, Navel	lb.	0.56	12/94	82r
Peaches, halves or slices, Hunt's, Del Monte, or Libby's	29-oz.	1.44	12/94	2c
Peanut butter, creamy, all sizes	lb.	1.81	12/94	82r
Peas, sweet, Del Monte or Green Giant	15-17 oz.	0.57	12/94	2c
Pork chops, center cut, bone-in	lb.	2.76	12/94	82r
Pork purchases	year	130	91	81r
Potato chips	16-oz.	2.81	12/94	82r
Potatoes, frozen, French fried	lb.	0.83	12/94	82r
Potatoes, white	lb.	0.28	12/94	82r
Potatoes, white or red	10-lb. sack	2.71	12/94	2c
Round roast, USDA choice, boneless	lb.	2.90	12/94	82r
Sausage, Jimmy Dean, 100% pork	lb.	3.35	12/94	2c
Shortening, vegetable oil blends	lb.	0.88	12/94	82r
Shortening, vegetable, Crisco	3-lb.	2.33	12/94	2c
Soft drink, Coca Cola, ex deposit	2 lit	1.21	12/94	2c
Spaghetti and macaroni	lb.	0.78	12/94	82r
Steak, rib eye, USDA choice, boneless	lb.	6.15	12/94	82r
Steak, round, graded & ungraded, exc. USDA prime & choice	lb.	2.72	12/94	82r
Steak, round, USDA choice, boneless	lb.	3.02	12/94	82r
Steak, sirloin, USDA choice, boneless	lb.	3.85	12/94	82r
Steak, t-bone	lb.	5.35	12/94	2c
Steak, T-bone, USDA choice, bone-in	lb.	5.38	12/94	82r
Sugar and other sweets, eaten at home, expenditures	year	91	91	81r
Sugar, cane or beet	4 lbs.	1.47	12/94	2c
Sugar, white, all sizes	lb.	0.36	12/94	82r
Tobacco products and smoking supplies, total expenditures	year	298	91	81r

Sioux Falls, SD - continued

Item	Per	Value	Date	Ref.
Groceries - continued				
Tomatoes, field grown	lb.	1.36	12/94	82r
Tomatoes, Hunt's or Del Monte	14.5 oz.	0.77	12/94	2c
Tuna, chunk, light	lb.	1.94	12/94	82r
Tuna, chunk, light, oil-packed	6.125-6.5 oz.	0.66	12/94	2c
Turkey, frozen, whole	lb.	0.96	12/94	82r
Yogurt, natural, fruit flavored	8 oz.	0.62	12/94	82r
Goods and Services				
Miscellaneous goods and services, ACCRA Index		95.10	12/94	2c
Health Care				
Health care, ACCRA Index		96.60	12/94	2c
Antibiotic ointment, Polysporin	1.5 oz.	3.82	12/94	2c
Childbirth, Cesarean delivery, hospital charge	birth	5101.00	12/91	69r
Childbirth, Cesarean delivery, physician charge	birth	2234.00	12/91	69r
Childbirth, normal delivery, hospital charge	birth	2891.00	12/91	69r
Childbirth, normal delivery, physician charge	birth	1623.00	12/91	69r
Dentist's fee, adult teeth cleaning and periodic oral exam	visit	55.25	12/94	2c
Doctor's fee, routine exam, established patient	visit	36.38	12/94	2c
Drugs, expenditures	year	248	91	81r
Health care, total expenditures	year	1336	91	81r
Health insurance expenditures	year	550	91	81r
Hospital care, semiprivate room	day	361.00	12/94	2c
Insurance premium, family medical care	month	337.90	1/95	41s
Medical services expenditures	year	457	91	81r
Medical supplies expenditures	year	82	91	81r
Household Goods				
Appl. repair, service call, wash mach	min. lab. chg.	34.00	12/94	2c
Floor coverings, expenditures	year	105	91	81r
Furniture, expenditures	year	291	91	81r
Household equipment, misc. expenditures	year	341	91	81r
Household expenditures, miscellaneous	year	162	91	81r
Household furnishings and equipment, expenditures	year	1042	91	81r
Household operations expenditures	year	365	91	81r
Household textiles, expenditures	year	101	91	81r
Housekeeping supplies, expenditures	year	390	91	81r
Laundry and cleaning supplies, expenditures	year	110	91	81r
Laundry detergent, Tide Ultra, Bold, or Cheer	42 oz.	3.01	12/94	2c
Postage and stationery, expenditures	year	115	91	81r
Tissues, facial, Kleenex brand	175	0.96	12/94	2c
Housing				
Housing, ACCRA Index		98.10	12/94	2c
Add garage/carport		8,479	3/95	74r
Add room(s)		21,347	3/95	74r
Apartment condominium or co-op, median	unit	87100	12/94	62r
Bathroom addition, average cost	add	9734.00	3/95	13r
Bathroom remodeling, average cost	remod	6414.00	3/95	13r
Bedroom, master suite addition, average cost	add	27122.00	3/95	13r
Deck addition, average cost	add	6665.00	3/95	13r
Dwellings (owned), expenditures	year	2566	91	81r
Enclose porch/patio/breezeway		4,556	3/95	74r
Exterior remodeling, average cost	remod	15395.00	3/95	13r
Family room addition, average cost	add	27658.00	3/95	13r
Finish room in basement/attic		5,074	3/95	74r
Home, existing, single-family, median	unit	106500	12/94	62r
Home, existing, single-family, median	unit	80.10	12/94	62c
House payment, principal and interest, 25% down payment	mo.	729	12/94	2c

Values are in dollars or fractions of dollars. In the column headed *Ref*, references are shown to sources. Each reference is followed by a letter. These refer to the geographical level for which data were reported: s=State, r=Region, and c=City or metro. The abbreviation *ex* is used to mean *except* or *excluding*; *exp* stands for *expenditures*. For other abbreviations and further explanations, please see the Introduction.

Sioux Falls, SD - continued

Item	Per	Value	Date	Ref.
Housing				
House, 1800 sq ft, 8000 sq ft lot, new, urban, utilities	total	116380	12/94	2c
Kitchen remodeling, major, average cost	remod	17084.00	3/95	13r
Kitchen remodeling, minor, average cost	remod	5804.00	3/95	13r
Maintenance, repairs, insurance, and other housing expenditures	year	484	91	81r
Mortgage interest and charges expenditures	year	1443	91	81r
Mtge. rate, incl. points and orig. fee, 30-year conv. fixed or ARM	mo.	9.43	12/94	2c
Office, home addition, average cost	add	8121.00	3/95	13r
Princ. & int., mortgage, median-price exist. sing.-family home	mo.	515	12/94	62r
Property taxes expenditures	year	639	91	81r
Redesign, restructure more than half of home's interior		9,114	3/95	74r
Rent, apartment, 2 br., 1 1/2-2 baths, unfurnished, 950 sq ft, water	mo.	581	12/94	2c
Rental units expenditures	year	1200	91	81r
Sun-space addition, average cost	add	23768.00	3/95	13r
Wing addition, two-story, average cost	add	50410.00	3/95	13r
Insurance and Pensions				
Auto insurance, private passenger	year	484.96	12/94	71s
Insurance and pensions, personal, expenditures	year	2408	91	81r
Insurance, life and other personal, expenditures	year	355	91	81r
Pensions and Social Security, expenditures	year	2053	91	81r
Legal Assistance				
Legal work, law firm associate	hour	90		10r
Legal work, law firm partner	hour	139		10r
Personal Goods				
Shampoo, Alberto VO5	15-oz.	1.29	12/94	2c
Toothpaste, Crest or Colgate	6-7 oz.	1.77	12/94	2c
Personal Services				
Dry cleaning, man's 2-pc. suit		6.16	12/94	2c
Haircut, man's barbershop, no styling		9.45	12/94	2c
Haircut, woman's shampoo, trim, blow-dry		16.10	12/94	2c
Personal services expenditures	year	203	91	81r
Restaurant Food				
Chicken, fried, thigh and drumstick		2.25	12/94	2c
Dining expenditures, family	week	30.03	94	73r
Hamburger with cheese	1/4 lb.	1.85	12/94	2c
Pizza, Pizza Hut or Pizza Inn	12-13 in.	7.69	12/94	2c
Taxes				
Tax rate, residential property, month	$100	2.36	1/92	79c
Tax, cigarettes	year	459.00	10/93	43s
Taxes, Federal income, expenditures	year	1756	91	81r
Taxes, personal, expenditures	year	2426	91	81r
Taxes, State and local income, expenditures	year	568	91	81r
Transportation				
Transportation, ACCRA Index		99.40	12/94	2c
Bus fare, one-way	trip	0.75	12/95	1c
Cars and trucks purchased, new	year	891	91	81r
Cars and trucks purchased, used	year	1155	91	81r
Driver's learning permit fee	perm	8.00	1/94	84s
Driver's license fee	orig	8.00	1/94	84s
Driver's license fee, duplicate	lic	6.00	1/94	84s
Driver's license reinstatement fee, min.	susp	50.00	1/94	85s
Driver's license renewal fee	renew	8.00	1/94	84s
Driving expenses	mile	35.80	5/95	89c
Identification card, nondriver	card	6.00	1/94	83s
Motorcycle learning permit fee	perm	8.00	1/94	84s
Motorcycle license fee	orig	8.00	1/94	84s
Motorcycle license fee, duplicate	lic	6.00	1/94	84s
Motorcycle license renewal fee	renew	8.00	1/94	84s
Public transportation expenditures	year	209	91	81r
Tire balance, computer or spin bal., front	wheel	6.50	12/94	2c

Sioux Falls, SD - continued

Item	Per	Value	Date	Ref.
Transportation - continued				
Transportation expenditures, total	year	4792	91	81r
Vehicle finance charges	year	300	91	81r
Vehicle insurance expenditures	year	485	91	81r
Vehicle maintenance and repairs expenditures	year	534	91	81r
Vehicle purchases	year	2068	91	81r
Vehicle rental, leases, licenses, etc. expenditures	year	197	91	81r
Vehicles purchased, other than cars and trucks	year	22	91	81r
Utilities				
Utilities, ACCRA Index		90.40	12/94	2c
Electricity expenditures	year	668	91	81r
Electricity, (part.), other, 1800 sq. ft., new home	mo.	51.18	12/94	2c
Electricity, summer, 250 KWh	month	24.58	8/93	64c
Electricity, summer, 500 KWh	month	42.62	8/93	64c
Electricity, summer, 750 KWh	month	60.65	8/93	64c
Electricity, summer, 1000 KWh	month	78.68	8/93	64c
Utilities, fuels, and public services, total expenditures	year	1838	91	81r
Water and other public services, expenditures	year	167	91	81r
Weddings				
Bridal attendants' gowns	event	750	10/93	76r
Bridal gown	event	852	10/93	76r
Bridal headpiece and veil	event	167	10/93	76r
Bride's wedding band	event	708	10/93	76r
Clergy	event	224	10/93	76r
Engagement ring	event	2756	10/93	76r
Flowers	event	863	10/93	76r
Formal wear for groom	event	106	10/93	76r
Groom's attendants' formal wear	event	530	10/93	76r
Groom's wedding band	event	402	10/93	76r
Music	event	600	10/93	76r
Photography	event	1088	10/93	76r
Shoes for bride	event	50	10/93	76r
Videography	event	483	10/93	76r
Wedding invitations and announcements	event	342	10/93	76r
Wedding reception	event	7000	10/93	76r

South Bend, IN

Item	Per	Value	Date	Ref.
Composite, ACCRA index		91.50	12/94	2c
Alcoholic Beverages				
Beer, Miller Lite, Bud, 12-oz., ex deposit	6	3.60	12/94	2c
J & B Scotch	750-ml.	15.49	12/94	2c
Wine, Gallo Chablis blanc	1.5-lit	3.89	12/94	2c
Appliances				
Appliances (major), expenditures	year	131	91	81r
Average annual exp.				
Food, health care, personal goods, services	year	25935	91	81r
Charity				
Cash contributions, expenditures	year	745	91	81r
Clothing				
Apparel, men and boys, total expenditures	year	332	91	81r
Apparel, women and girls, total expenditures	year	578	91	81r
Footwear, expenditures	year	164	91	81r
Jeans, man's denim		28.39	12/94	2c
Shirt, man's dress shirt		30.87	12/94	2c
Undervest, boy's size 10-14, cotton	3	3.49	12/94	2c
Communications				
Long-distance telephone rate, day, addl. min., 1-10 mi.	min.	0.10	12/93	9s
Long-distance telephone rate, day, initial min., 1-10 mi.	min.	0.18	12/93	9s

Values are in dollars or fractions of dollars. In the column headed *Ref*, references are shown to sources. Each reference is followed by a letter. These refer to the geographical level for which data were reported: s = State, r = Region, and c = City or metro. The abbreviation *ex* is used to mean *except* or *excluding*; *exp* stands for expenditures. For other abbreviations and further explanations, please see the Introduction.

South Bend, IN - continued

Item	Per	Value	Date	Ref.
Communications				
Newspaper subscription, dly. and Sun. delivery	month	10.00	12/94	2c
Phone line, single, business, field visit	inst	59.00	12/93	9s
Phone line, single, business, no field visit	inst	59.00	12/93	9s
Phone line, single, residence, field visit	inst	47.00	12/93	9s
Phone line, single, residence, no field visit	inst	47.00	12/93	9s
Telephone bill, family of four	month	19.06	12/94	2c
Telephone service, expenditures	year	547	91	81r
Telephone, residential, flat rate	mo.	11.11	12/93	8c
Education				
Board, 4-year private college/university	year	2095	8/94	80s
Board, 4-year public college/university	year	2300	8/94	80s
Education, total expenditures	year	394	91	81r
Room, 4-year private college/university	year	1784	8/94	80s
Room, 4-year public college/university	year	1718	8/94	80s
Total cost, 4-year private college/university	year	15045	8/94	80s
Total cost, 4-year public college/university	year	6639	8/94	80s
Tuition, 2-year public college/university, in-state	year	1737	8/94	80s
Tuition, 4-year private college/university, in-state	year	11165	8/94	80s
Tuition, 4-year public college/university, in-state	year	2621	8/94	80s
Energy and Fuels				
Energy, combined forms, 1800 sq. ft.	mo.	122.15	12/94	2c
Energy, exc. electricity, 1800 sq. ft.	mo.	62.05	12/94	2c
Fuel oil and other fuels, expenditures	year	83	91	81r
Gas, natural, expenditures	year	373	91	81r
Gas, reg unlead, taxes inc., cash, self-service	gal	0.98	12/94	2c
Gasoline and motor oil purchased	year	1000	91	81r
Gasoline, unleaded midgrade	gallon	1.15	4/93	82r
Gasoline, unleaded premium	gallon	1.23	4/93	82r
Gasoline, unleaded regular	gallon	1.07	4/93	82r
Entertainment				
Bowling, evening rate	game	2.16	12/94	2c
Entertainment, total expenditures	year	1356	91	81r
Fees and admissions, expenditures	year	347	91	81r
Monopoly game, Parker Brothers', No. 9	game	9.97	12/94	2c
Movie	adm	5.90	12/94	2c
Pets, toys, playground equipment, expenditures	year	270	91	81r
Reading, expenditures	year	160	91	81r
Televisions, radios, and sound equipment, expenditures	year	433	91	81r
Tennis balls, yellow, Wilson or Penn, 3	can	2.06	12/94	2c
Funerals				
Burial, immediate, container provided by funeral home		1268.31	1/95	54r
Cards, acknowledgment		26.12	1/95	54r
Casket, minimum alternative		198.03	1/95	54r
Cosmetology, hair care, etc.		122.19	1/95	54r
Cremation, direct, container provided by funeral home		977.81	1/95	54r
Embalming		334.00	1/95	54r
Funeral, funeral home		321.16	1/95	54r
Funeral, other facility		317.73	1/95	54r
Graveside service		292.48	1/95	54r
Hearse, local		153.20	1/95	54r
Limousine, local		123.52	1/95	54r
Memorial service		356.30	1/95	54r
Service charge, professional, nondeclinable		968.24	1/95	54r
Visitation and viewing		332.66	1/95	54r
Groceries				
Groceries, ACCRA Index		91.80	12/94	2c
Apples, Red Delicious	lb.	0.68	12/94	82r
Baby food, strained vegetables, lowest price	4-4.5 oz.	0.36	12/94	2c
Bacon, sliced	lb.	1.88	12/94	82r

South Bend, IN - continued

Item	Per	Value	Date	Ref.
Groceries - continued				
Bananas	lb.	0.39	12/94	2c
Bananas	lb.	0.41	12/94	82r
Beef or hamburger, ground	lb.	1.17	12/94	2c
Beef purchases	year	197	91	81r
Beef, stew, boneless	lb.	2.52	12/94	82r
Beverage purchases, alcoholic	year	293	91	81r
Beverage purchases, nonalcoholic	year	203	91	81r
Bologna, all beef or mixed	lb.	2.12	12/94	82r
Bread, white	24-oz.	0.63	12/94	2c
Bread, white, pan	lb.	0.76	12/94	82r
Cabbage	lb.	0.44	12/94	82r
Carrots, short trimmed and topped	lb.	0.44	12/94	82r
Cereals and bakery products purchases	year	347	91	81r
Cereals and cereals products purchases	year	119	91	81r
Cheddar cheese, natural	lb.	3.28	12/94	82r
Cheese, Kraft grated Parmesan	8-oz.	3.23	12/94	2c
Chicken breast, bone-in	lb.	1.61	12/94	82r
Chicken, fresh, whole	lb.	0.89	12/94	82r
Chicken, whole fryer	lb.	0.89	12/94	2c
Chuck roast, USDA choice, boneless	lb.	2.33	12/94	82r
Cigarettes, Winston, Kings	carton	14.11	12/94	2c
Coffee, 100%, ground roast, all sizes	lb.	4.28	12/94	82r
Coffee, vacuum-packed	13 oz.	3.44	12/94	2c
Cookies, chocolate chip	lb.	2.72	12/94	82r
Corn Flakes, Kellogg's or Post Toasties	18 oz.	2.01	12/94	2c
Corn, frozen, whole kernel, lowest price	10 oz.	0.71	12/94	2c
Dairy products (other) purchases	year	148	91	81r
Eggs, Grade A large	dozen	0.68	12/94	2c
Eggs, Grade A large	dozen	0.76	12/94	82r
Fish and seafood purchases	year	61	91	81r
Flour, white, all purpose	lb.	0.22	12/94	82r
Food purchases, food eaten at home	year	2313	91	81r
Foods purchased away from home, not prepared by consumer	year	1709	91	81r
Fruits and vegetables purchases	year	372	91	81r
Grapefruit	lb.	0.47	12/94	82r
Grapes, Thompson seedless	lb.	2.15	12/94	82r
Ground beef, 100% beef	lb.	1.37	12/94	82r
Ground chuck, 100% beef	lb.	1.81	12/94	82r
Ham, boneless, exc. canned	lb.	2.16	12/94	82r
Ice cream, prepackaged, bulk, regular	1/2 gal.	2.48	12/94	82r
Lemons	lb.	1.08	12/94	82r
Lettuce, iceberg	lb.	0.81	12/94	82r
Lettuce, iceberg	head	0.81	12/94	2c
Margarine, Blue Bonnet or Parkay cubes	lb.	0.56	12/94	2c
Margarine, stick	lb.	0.81	12/94	82r
Meats, poultry, fish, and eggs purchases	year	591	91	81r
Milk and cream (fresh) purchases	year	132	91	81r
Milk, whole	1/2 gal.	1.22	12/94	2c
Orange juice, frozen concentrate 12-oz. can	16 oz.	1.41	12/94	82r
Orange juice, Minute Maid frozen	12-oz.	1.17	12/94	2c
Oranges, Navel	lb.	0.56	12/94	82r
Peaches, halves or slices, Hunt's, Del Monte, or Libby's	29-oz.	1.21	12/94	2c
Peanut butter, creamy, all sizes	lb.	1.81	12/94	82r
Peas, sweet, Del Monte or Green Giant	15-17 oz.	0.52	12/94	2c
Pork chops, center cut, bone-in	lb.	2.76	12/94	82r
Pork purchases	year	130	91	81r
Potato chips	16-oz.	2.81	12/94	82r
Potatoes, frozen, French fried	lb.	0.83	12/94	82r
Potatoes, white	lb.	0.28	12/94	82r
Potatoes, white or red	10-lb. sack	1.97	12/94	2c
Round roast, USDA choice, boneless	lb.	2.90	12/94	82r
Sausage, Jimmy Dean, 100% pork	lb.	2.40	12/94	2c
Shortening, vegetable oil blends	lb.	0.88	12/94	82r
Shortening, vegetable, Crisco	3-lb.	2.03	12/94	2c
Soft drink, Coca Cola, ex deposit	2 lit	1.12	12/94	2c
Spaghetti and macaroni	lb.	0.78	12/94	82r

Values are in dollars or fractions of dollars. In the column headed *Ref*, references are shown to sources. Each reference is followed by a letter. These refer to the geographical level for which data were reported: s=State, r=Region, and c=City or metro. The abbreviation *ex* is used to mean *except* or *excluding*; *exp* stands for expenditures. For other abbreviations and further explanations, please see the Introduction.

South Bend, IN - continued

Item	Per	Value	Date	Ref.
Groceries				
Steak, rib eye, USDA choice, boneless	lb.	6.15	12/94	82r
Steak, round, graded & ungraded, exc. USDA prime & choice	lb.	2.72	12/94	82r
Steak, round, USDA choice, boneless	lb.	3.02	12/94	82r
Steak, sirloin, USDA choice, boneless	lb.	3.85	12/94	82r
Steak, t-bone	lb.	5.38	12/94	2c
Steak, T-bone, USDA choice, bone-in	lb.	5.38	12/94	82r
Sugar and other sweets, eaten at home, expenditures	year	91	91	81r
Sugar, cane or beet	4 lbs.	1.03	12/94	2c
Sugar, white, all sizes	lb.	0.36	12/94	82r
Tobacco products and smoking supplies, total expenditures	year	298	91	81r
Tomatoes, field grown	lb.	1.36	12/94	82r
Tomatoes, Hunt's or Del Monte	14.5 oz.	0.80	12/94	2c
Tuna, chunk, light	lb.	1.94	12/94	82r
Tuna, chunk, light, oil-packed	6.125-6.5 oz.	0.61	12/94	2c
Turkey, frozen, whole	lb.	0.96	12/94	82r
Yogurt, natural, fruit flavored	8 oz.	0.62	12/94	82r
Goods and Services				
Miscellaneous goods and services, ACCRA Index		93.00	12/94	2c
Health Care				
Health care, ACCRA Index		95.30	12/94	2c
Antibiotic ointment, Polysporin	1.5 oz.	4.07	12/94	2c
Childbirth, Cesarean delivery, hospital charge	birth	5101.00	12/91	69r
Childbirth, Cesarean delivery, physician charge	birth	2234.00	12/91	69r
Childbirth, normal delivery, hospital charge	birth	2891.00	12/91	69r
Childbirth, normal delivery, physician charge	birth	1623.00	12/91	69r
Dentist's fee, adult teeth cleaning and periodic oral exam	visit	42.60	12/94	2c
Doctor's fee, routine exam, established patient	visit	37.40	12/94	2c
Drugs, expenditures	year	248	91	81r
Health care, total expenditures	year	1336	91	81r
Health insurance expenditures	year	550	91	81r
Hospital care, semiprivate room	day	472.75	12/94	2c
Insurance premium, family medical care	month	353.94	1/95	41s
Medical services expenditures	year	457	91	81r
Medical supplies expenditures	year	82	91	81r
Household Goods				
Appl. repair, service call, wash mach	min. lab. chg.	28.12	12/94	2c
Floor coverings, expenditures	year	105	91	81r
Furniture, expenditures	year	291	91	81r
Household equipment, misc. expenditures	year	341	91	81r
Household expenditures, miscellaneous	year	162	91	81r
Household furnishings and equipment, expenditures	year	1042	91	81r
Household operations expenditures	year	365	91	81r
Household textiles, expenditures	year	101	91	81r
Housekeeping supplies, expenditures	year	390	91	81r
Laundry and cleaning supplies, expenditures	year	110	91	81r
Laundry detergent, Tide Ultra, Bold, or Cheer	42 oz.	2.92	12/94	2c
Postage and stationery, expenditures	year	115	91	81r
Tissues, facial, Kleenex brand	175	0.92	12/94	2c
Housing				
Housing, ACCRA Index		85.80	12/94	2c
Add garage/carport		8,479	3/95	74r
Add room(s)		21,347	3/95	74r
Apartment condominium or co-op, median	unit	87100	12/94	62r
Bathroom addition, average cost	add	9734.00	3/95	13r
Bathroom remodeling, average cost	remod	6414.00	3/95	13r

South Bend, IN - continued

Item	Per	Value	Date	Ref.
Housing - continued				
Bedroom, master suite addition, average cost	add	27122.00	3/95	13r
Deck addition, average cost	add	6665.00	3/95	13r
Dwellings (owned), expenditures	year	2566	91	81r
Enclose porch/patio/breezeway		4,556	3/95	74r
Exterior remodeling, average cost	remod	15395.00	3/95	13r
Family room addition, average cost	add	27658.00	3/95	13r
Finish room in basement/attic		5,074	3/95	74r
Home, existing, single-family, median	unit	106500	12/94	62r
Home, existing, single-family, median	unit	61.60	12/94	62c
House payment, principal and interest, 25% down payment	mo.	627	12/94	2c
House, 1800 sq ft, 8000 sq ft lot, new, urban, utilities	total	100780	12/94	2c
Kitchen remodeling, major, average cost	remod	17084.00	3/95	13r
Kitchen remodeling, minor, average cost	remod	5804.00	3/95	13r
Maintenance, repairs, insurance, and other housing expenditures	year	484	91	81r
Mortgage interest and charges expenditures	year	1443	91	81r
Mtge. rate, incl. points and orig. fee, 30-year conv. fixed or ARM	mo.	9.34	12/94	2c
Office, home addition, average cost	add	8121.00	3/95	13r
Princ. & int., mortgage, median-price exist. sing.-family home	mo.	515	12/94	62r
Property taxes expenditures	year	639	91	81r
Redesign, restructure more than half of home's interior		9,114	3/95	74r
Rent, apartment, 2 br., 1 1/2-2 baths, unfurnished, 950 sq ft, water	mo.	542	12/94	2c
Rental units expenditures	year	1200	91	81r
Sun-space addition, average cost	add	23768.00	3/95	13r
Wing addition, two-story, average cost	add	50410.00	3/95	13r
Insurance and Pensions				
Auto insurance, private passenger	year	586.58	12/94	71s
Insurance and pensions, personal, expenditures	year	2408	91	81r
Insurance, life and other personal, expenditures	year	355	91	81r
Pensions and Social Security, expenditures	year	2053	91	81r
Legal Assistance				
Legal work, law firm associate	hour	90		10r
Legal work, law firm partner	hour	139		10r
Personal Goods				
Shampoo, Alberto VO5	15-oz.	1.11	12/94	2c
Toothpaste, Crest or Colgate	6-7 oz.	1.28	12/94	2c
Personal Services				
Dry cleaning, man's 2-pc. suit		6.04	12/94	2c
Haircut, man's barbershop, no styling		9.10	12/94	2c
Haircut, woman's shampoo, trim, blow-dry		23.60	12/94	2c
Personal services expenditures	year	203	91	81r
Restaurant Food				
Chicken, fried, thigh and drumstick		2.18	12/94	2c
Dining expenditures, family	week	30.03	94	73r
Hamburger with cheese	1/4 lb.	1.78	12/94	2c
Pizza, Pizza Hut or Pizza Inn	12-13 in.	6.50	12/94	2c
Taxes				
Taxes, Federal income, expenditures	year	1756	91	81r
Taxes, personal, expenditures	year	2426	91	81r
Taxes, State and local income, expenditures	year	568	91	81r
Transportation				
Transportation, ACCRA Index		86.60	12/94	2c
Bus fare, one-way	trip	0.75	12/95	1c
Bus fare, up to 10 miles	one-way	0.75	12/94	2c
Cars and trucks purchased, new	year	891	91	81r
Cars and trucks purchased, used	year	1155	91	81r
Driver's learning permit fee	perm	2.00	1/94	84s

Values are in dollars or fractions of dollars. In the column headed *Ref*, references are shown to sources. Each reference is followed by a letter. These refer to the geographical level for which data were reported: s=State, r=Region, and c=City or metro. The abbreviation *ex* is used to mean *except* or *excluding*; *exp* stands for *expenditures*. For other abbreviations and further explanations, please see the Introduction.

South Bend, IN - continued

Item	Per	Value	Date	Ref.
Transportation				
Driver's license fee	orig	6.00	1/94	84s
Driver's license fee, duplicate	lic	3.00	1/94	84s
Driver's license renewal fee	renew	6.00	1/94	84s
Identification card, nondriver	card	4.00	1/94	83s
Motorcycle learning permit fee	perm	2.00	1/94	84s
Motorcycle license fee	orig	6.00	1/94	84s
Motorcycle license fee, duplicate	lic	3.00	1/94	84s
Motorcycle license renewal fee	renew	6.00	1/94	84s
Public transportation expenditures	year	209	91	81r
Tire balance, computer or spin bal., front	wheel	5.99	12/94	2c
Transportation expenditures, total	year	4792	91	81r
Vehicle finance charges	year	300	91	81r
Vehicle insurance expenditures	year	485	91	81r
Vehicle maintenance and repairs expenditures	year	534	91	81r
Vehicle purchases	year	2068	91	81r
Vehicle rental, leases, licenses, etc. expenditures	year	197	91	81r
Vehicles purchased, other than cars and trucks	year	22	91	81r
Utilities				
Utilities, ACCRA Index		107.30	12/94	2c
Electricity expenditures	year	668	91	81r
Electricity, (part.), other, 1800 sq. ft., new home	mo.	60.10	12/94	2c
Utilities, fuels, and public services, total expenditures	year	1838	91	81r
Water and other public services, expenditures	year	167	91	81r
Weddings				
Bridal attendants' gowns	event	750	10/93	76r
Bridal gown	event	852	10/93	76r
Bridal headpiece and veil	event	167	10/93	76r
Bride's wedding band	event	708	10/93	76r
Clergy	event	224	10/93	76r
Engagement ring	event	2756	10/93	76r
Flowers	event	863	10/93	76r
Formal wear for groom	event	106	10/93	76r
Groom's attendants' formal wear	event	530	10/93	76r
Groom's wedding band	event	402	10/93	76r
Music	event	600	10/93	76r
Photography	event	1088	10/93	76r
Shoes for bride	event	50	10/93	76r
Videography	event	483	10/93	76r
Wedding invitations and announcements	event	342	10/93	76r
Wedding reception	event	7000	10/93	76r

Spartanburg, SC

Item	Per	Value	Date	Ref.
Composite, ACCRA index		96.20	12/94	2c
Alcoholic Beverages				
Beer, Miller Lite, Bud, 12-oz., ex deposit	6	3.82	12/94	2c
J & B Scotch	750-ml.	18.20	12/94	2c
Wine, Gallo Chablis blanc	1.5-lit	4.71	12/94	2c
Appliances				
Appliances (major), expenditures	year	153	91	81r
Average annual exp.				
Food, health care, personal goods, services	year	27020	91	81r
Charity				
Cash contributions, expenditures	year	839	91	81r
Clothing				
Apparel, men and boys, total expenditures	year	380	91	81r
Apparel, women and girls, total expenditures	year	660	91	81r
Footwear, expenditures	year	193	91	81r
Jeans, man's denim		29.79	12/94	2c
Shirt, man's dress shirt		30.30	12/94	2c
Undervest, boy's size 10-14, cotton	3	4.98	12/94	2c

Spartanburg, SC - continued

Item	Per	Value	Date	Ref.
Communications				
Long-distance telephone rate, day, addl. min., 1-10 mi.	min.	0.13	12/93	9s
Long-distance telephone rate, day, initial min., 1-10 mi.	min.	0.24	12/93	9s
Newspaper subscription, dly. and Sun. delivery	month	9.10	12/94	2c
Phone line, single, business, field visit	inst	82.50	12/93	9s
Phone line, single, business, no field visit	inst	64.00	12/93	9s
Phone line, single, residence, field visit	inst	62.50	12/93	9s
Phone line, single, residence, no field visit	inst	44.00	12/93	9s
Telephone bill, family of four	month	22.35	12/94	2c
Telephone service, expenditures	year	616	91	81r
Education				
Board, 4-year private college/university	year	1831	8/94	80s
Board, 4-year public college/university	year	1462	8/94	80s
Education, total expenditures	year	319	91	81r
Room, 4-year private college/university	year	1744	8/94	80s
Room, 4-year public college/university	year	1851	8/94	80s
Total cost, 4-year private college/university	year	12082	8/94	80s
Total cost, 4-year public college/university	year	6203	8/94	80s
Tuition, 2-year public college/university, in-state	year	1061	8/94	80s
Tuition, 4-year private college/university, in-state	year	8507	8/94	80s
Tuition, 4-year public college/university, in-state	year	2891	8/94	80s
Energy and Fuels				
Energy, combined forms, 1800 sq. ft.	mo.	107.16	12/94	2c
Fuel oil and other fuels, expenditures	year	56	91	81r
Gas, natural, expenditures	year	150	91	81r
Gas, reg unlead, taxes inc., cash, self-service	gal	1.01	12/94	2c
Gasoline and motor oil purchased	year	1152	91	81r
Gasoline, unleaded midgrade	gallon	1.21	4/93	82r
Gasoline, unleaded premium	gallon	1.30	4/93	82r
Gasoline, unleaded regular	gallon	1.10	4/93	82r
Entertainment				
Bowling, evening rate	game	2.47	12/94	2c
Concert ticket, Pearl Jam group	perf	20.00	94	50r
Entertainment, total expenditures	year	1266	91	81r
Fees and admissions, expenditures	year	306	91	81r
Monopoly game, Parker Brothers', No. 9	game	10.40	12/94	2c
Movie	adm	5.50	12/94	2c
Pets, toys, playground equipment, expenditures	year	271	91	81r
Reading, expenditures	year	131	91	81r
Televisions, radios, and sound equipment, expenditures	year	439	91	81r
Tennis balls, yellow, Wilson or Penn, 3	can	2.22	12/94	2c
Funerals				
Burial, immediate, container provided by funeral home		1370.36	1/95	54r
Cards, acknowledgment		14.83	1/95	54r
Casket, minimum alternative		192.52	1/95	54r
Cosmetology, hair care, etc.		102.27	1/95	54r
Cremation, direct, container provided by funeral home		1065.64	1/95	54r
Embalming		304.29	1/95	54r
Funeral, funeral home		287.83	1/95	54r
Funeral, other facility		284.14	1/95	54r
Graveside service		349.13	1/95	54r
Hearse, local		132.27	1/95	54r
Limousine, local		98.45	1/95	54r
Memorial service		270.59	1/95	54r
Service charge, professional, nondeclinable		933.59	1/95	54r
Visitation and viewing		225.83	1/95	54r
Groceries				
Groceries, ACCRA Index		98.20	12/94	2c
Apples, Red Delicious	lb.	0.73	12/94	82r

Values are in dollars or fractions of dollars. In the column headed *Ref*, references are shown to sources. Each reference is followed by a letter. These refer to the geographical level for which data were reported: s = State, r = Region, and c = City or metro. The abbreviation *ex* is used to mean *except* or *excluding*; *exp* stands for *expenditures*. For other abbreviations and further explanations, please see the Introduction.

Spartanburg, SC - continued

Item	Per	Value	Date	Ref.
Groceries				
Baby food, strained vegetables, lowest price	4-4.5 oz.	0.34	12/94	2c
Bacon, sliced	lb.	1.67	12/94	82r
Bananas	lb.	0.49	12/94	2c
Bananas	lb.	0.42	12/94	82r
Beef or hamburger, ground	lb.	1.77	12/94	2c
Beef purchases	year	213	91	81r
Beverage purchases, alcoholic	year	249	91	81r
Beverage purchases, nonalcoholic	year	207	91	81r
Bologna, all beef or mixed	lb.	2.27	12/94	82r
Bread, white	24-oz.	0.68	12/94	2c
Bread, white, pan	lb.	0.68	12/94	82r
Cabbage	lb.	0.42	12/94	82r
Carrots, short trimmed and topped	lb.	0.53	12/94	82r
Cereals and bakery products purchases	year	345	91	81r
Cereals and cereals products purchases	year	127	91	81r
Cheddar cheese, natural	lb.	3.58	12/94	82r
Cheese, Kraft grated Parmesan	8-oz.	3.11	12/94	2c
Chicken breast, bone-in	lb.	1.71	12/94	82r
Chicken, fresh, whole	lb.	0.78	12/94	82r
Chicken, whole fryer	lb.	0.95	12/94	2c
Chuck roast, USDA choice, boneless	lb.	2.26	12/94	82r
Cigarettes, Winston, Kings	carton	13.31	12/94	2c
Coffee, vacuum-packed	13 oz.	3.17	12/94	2c
Corn Flakes, Kellogg's or Post Toasties	18 oz.	2.21	12/94	2c
Corn, frozen, whole kernel, lowest price	10 oz.	0.62	12/94	2c
Crackers, soda, salted	lb.	1.27	12/94	82r
Cucumbers	lb.	0.65	12/94	82r
Dairy products (other) purchases	year	141	91	81r
Eggs, Grade A large	dozen	0.87	12/94	2c
Eggs, Grade A large	dozen	0.87	12/94	82r
Fish and seafood purchases	year	72	91	81r
Flour, white, all purpose	lb.	0.23	12/94	82r
Food purchases, food eaten at home	year	2381	91	81r
Foods purchased away from home, not prepared by consumer	year	1696	91	81r
Frankfurters, all meat or all beef	lb.	1.74	12/94	82r
Fruits and vegetables purchases	year	380	91	81r
Grapefruit	lb.	0.45	12/94	82r
Grapes, Thompson seedless	lb.	2.30	12/94	82r
Ground beef, 100% beef	lb.	1.37	12/94	82r
Ground chuck, 100% beef	lb.	1.97	12/94	82r
Ham, boneless, exc. canned	lb.	2.54	12/94	82r
Ice cream, prepackaged, bulk, regular	1/2 gal.	2.47	12/94	82r
Lemons	lb.	1.02	12/94	82r
Lettuce, iceberg	lb.	0.96	12/94	82r
Lettuce, iceberg	head	1.03	12/94	2c
Margarine, Blue Bonnet or Parkay cubes	lb.	0.58	12/94	2c
Margarine, stick	lb.	0.77	12/94	82r
Meats, poultry, fish, and eggs purchases	year	655	91	81r
Milk and cream (fresh) purchases	year	130	91	81r
Milk, whole	1/2 gal.	1.47	12/94	2c
Orange juice, frozen concentrate 12-oz. can	16 oz.	1.36	12/94	82r
Orange juice, Minute Maid frozen	12-oz.	1.25	12/94	2c
Oranges, Navel	lb.	0.54	12/94	82r
Peaches, halves or slices; Hunt's, Del Monte, or Libby's	29-oz.	1.32	12/94	2c
Pears, Anjou	lb.	0.81	12/94	82r
Peas, sweet, Del Monte or Green Giant	15-17 oz.	0.50	12/94	2c
Pork chops, center cut, bone-in	lb.	3.07	12/94	82r
Pork purchases	year	142	91	81r
Potato chips	16-oz.	3.15	12/94	82r
Potatoes, frozen, French fried	lb.	0.82	12/94	82r
Potatoes, white	lb.	0.34	12/94	82r
Potatoes, white or red	10-lb. sack	2.65	12/94	2c
Rice, white, long grain, uncooked	lb.	0.48	12/94	82r
Round roast, USDA choice, boneless	lb.	2.91	12/94	82r
Sausage, fresh	lb.	1.82	12/94	82r

Spartanburg, SC - continued

Item	Per	Value	Date	Ref.
Groceries - continued				
Sausage, Jimmy Dean, 100% pork	lb.	2.51	12/94	2c
Shortening, vegetable oil blends	lb.	0.75	12/94	82r
Shortening, vegetable, Crisco	3-lb.	2.51	12/94	2c
Soft drink, Coca Cola, ex deposit	2 lit	1.11	12/94	2c
Spaghetti and macaroni	lb.	0.87	12/94	82r
Steak, rib eye, USDA choice, boneless	lb.	6.85	12/94	82r
Steak, round, graded & ungraded, exc. USDA prime & choice	lb.	2.96	12/94	82r
Steak, round, USDA choice, boneless	lb.	3.17	12/94	82r
Steak, sirloin, USDA choice, boneless	lb.	4.12	12/94	82r
Steak, t-bone	lb.	5.77	12/94	2c
Steak, T-bone, USDA choice, bone-in	lb.	5.63	12/94	82r
Sugar and other sweets, eaten at home, expenditures	year	93	91	81r
Sugar, cane or beet	4 lbs.	1.49	12/94	2c
Sugar, white, all sizes	lb.	0.39	12/94	82r
Tobacco products and smoking supplies, total expenditures	year	286	91	81r
Tomatoes, field grown	lb.	1.36	12/94	82r
Tomatoes, Hunt's or Del Monte	14.5 oz.	0.53	12/94	2c
Tuna, chunk, light	lb.	1.94	12/94	82r
Tuna, chunk, light, oil-packed	6.125-6.5 oz.	0.65	12/94	2c
Turkey, frozen, whole	lb.	0.96	12/94	82r
Yogurt, natural, fruit flavored	8 oz.	0.58	12/94	82r
Goods and Services				
Miscellaneous goods and services, ACCRA Index		96.20	12/94	2c
Health Care				
Health care, ACCRA Index		92.10	12/94	2c
Adenosine, emergency room	treat	100.00	95	23r
Antibiotic ointment, Polysporin	1.5 oz.	3.81	12/94	2c
Bladder tap, superpubic, infant, emergency room	treat	119.00	95	23r
Blood analysis, emergency room	treat	25.00	95	23r
Blood tests, abdominal pain, emergency room	treat	25.00	95	23r
Burn dressing, emergency room	treat	266.00	95	23r
Cardiology interpretation, emergency room	treat	26.00	95	23r
Chest X-ray, emergency room	treat	78.00	95	23r
Childbirth, Cesarean delivery, hospital charge	birth	5462.00	12/91	69r
Childbirth, Cesarean delivery, physician charge	birth	2228.00	12/91	69r
Childbirth, normal delivery, hospital charge	birth	2943.00	12/91	69r
Childbirth, normal delivery, physician charge	birth	1619.00	12/91	69r
Defibrillation pads, emergency room	treat	6.00	95	23r
Dentist's fee, adult teeth cleaning and periodic oral exam	visit	48.20	12/94	2c
Doctor's fee, routine exam, established patient	visit	42.00	12/94	2c
Drugs, expenditures	year	297	91	81r
Gastric tube insertion, nasal, emergency room	treat	25.00	95	23r
Health care, total expenditures	year	1600	91	81r
Health insurance expenditures	year	637	91	81r
Heart monitor, emergency room	treat	40.00	95	23r
Hospital care, semiprivate room	day	275.00	12/94	2c
Insurance premium, family medical care	month	414.49	1/95	41s
Intravenous fluids, emergency room	treat	130.00	95	23r
Intravenous fluids, emergency room	liter	26.00	95	23r
Intravenous line, central, emergency room	treat	342.00	95	23r
Liver function tests, abdominal pain, emergency room	treat	26.00	95	23r
Medical care charges, total, emergency room, third-degree burns	treat	2101.00	95	23r
Medical care charges, total, emergency, infant with fever	treat	628.00	95	23r
Medical services expenditures	year	573	91	81r
Medical supplies expenditures	year	93	91	81r

Values are in dollars or fractions of dollars. In the column headed *Ref*, references are shown to sources. Each reference is followed by a letter. These refer to the geographical level for which data were reported: s=State, r=Region, and c=City or metro. The abbreviation *ex* is used to mean *except* or *excluding*; *exp* stands for expenditures. For other abbreviations and further explanations, please see the Introduction.

Spartanburg, SC - continued

Item	Per	Value	Date	Ref.
Health Care				
Morphine, emergency room	treat	34.00	95	23r
Nursing care and facilities charges, emergency room	treat	252.00	95	23r
Nursing care and facilities charges, emergency, infant with fever	treat	252.00	95	23r
Nursing care and facilities charges, emergency, third-degree burns	treat	861.00	95	23r
Physician's charges, emergency, infant with fever	treat	212.00	95	23r
Physician's charges, emergency, third-degree burns	treat	372.00	95	23r
Physician's fee, emergency room	treat	372.00	95	23r
Physician's fee, general practitioner	visit	51.20	12/93	60r
Surgery, open-heart	proc	42374.00	1/93	14r
Ultrasound, abdominal, emergency room	treat	276.00	95	23r
Urinalysis, emergency room	treat	20.00	95	23r
Urinalysis, infant, emergency room	treat	20.00	95	23r
X-rays, emergency room	treat	78.00	95	23r
Household Goods				
Appl. repair, service call, wash mach	min. lab. chg.	30.90	12/94	2c
Floor coverings, expenditures	year	48	91	81r
Furniture, expenditures	year	280	91	81r
Household equipment, misc. expenditures	year	342	91	81r
Household expenditures, miscellaneous	year	256	91	81r
Household furnishings and equipment, expenditures	year	988	91	81r
Household operations expenditures	year	468	91	81r
Household textiles, expenditures	year	95	91	81r
Housekeeping supplies, expenditures	year	380	91	81r
Laundry and cleaning supplies, expenditures	year	109	91	81r
Laundry detergent, Tide Ultra, Bold, or Cheer	42 oz.	2.65	12/94	2c
Postage and stationery, expenditures	year	105	91	81r
Tissues, facial, Kleenex brand	175	0.91	12/94	2c
Housing				
Housing, ACCRA Index		95.10	12/94	2c
Add garage/carport		6,980	3/95	74r
Add room(s)		11,403	3/95	74r
Apartment condominium or co-op, median	unit	68600	12/94	62r
Dwellings (owned), expenditures	year	2428	91	81r
Enclose porch/patio/breezeway		4,572	3/95	74r
Finish room in basement/attic		3,794	3/95	74r
Home, existing, single-family, median	unit	120200	12/94	62r
House payment, principal and interest, 25% down payment	mo.	734	12/94	2c
House, 1800 sq ft, 8000 sq ft lot, new, urban, utilities	total	119300	12/94	2c
Maintenance, repairs, insurance, and other housing expenditures	year	531	91	81r
Mortgage interest and charges expenditures	year	1506	91	81r
Mtge. rate, incl. points and orig. fee, 30-year conv. fixed or ARM	mo.	9.21	12/94	2c
Princ. & int., mortgage, median-price exist. sing.-family home	mo.	540	12/94	62r
Property taxes expenditures	year	391	91	81r
Redesign, restructure more than half of home's interior		17,641	3/95	74r
Rent, apartment, 2 br., 1 1/2-2 baths, unfurnished, 950 sq ft, water	mo.	486	12/94	2c
Rental units expenditures	year	1264	91	81r
Insurance and Pensions				
Auto insurance, private passenger	year	684.10	12/94	71s
Insurance and pensions, personal, expenditures	year	2395	91	81r
Insurance, life and other personal, expenditures	year	368	91	81r
Pensions and Social Security, expenditures	year	2027	91	81r

Spartanburg, SC - continued

Item	Per	Value	Date	Ref.
Personal Goods				
Shampoo, Alberto VO5	15-oz.	0.97	12/94	2c
Toothpaste, Crest or Colgate	6-7 oz.	1.58	12/94	2c
Personal Services				
Dry cleaning, man's 2-pc. suit		6.71	12/94	2c
Haircut, man's barbershop, no styling		8.60	12/94	2c
Haircut, woman's shampoo, trim, blow-dry		20.20	12/94	2c
Personal services expenditures	year	212	91	81r
Restaurant Food				
Chicken, fried, thigh and drumstick		2.11	12/94	2c
Dining expenditures, family	week	33.83	94	73r
Hamburger with cheese	1/4 lb.	1.84	12/94	2c
Pizza, Pizza Hut or Pizza Inn	12-13 in.	6.38	12/94	2c
Taxes				
Taxes, Federal income, expenditures	year	2275	91	81r
Taxes, personal, expenditures	year	2715	91	81r
Taxes, State and local income, expenditures	year	365	91	81r
Transportation				
Transportation, ACCRA Index		96.80	12/94	2c
Cars and trucks purchased, new	year	1306	91	81r
Cars and trucks purchased, used	year	942	91	81r
Driver's learning permit fee	perm	2.00	1/94	84s
Driver's license fee	orig	10.00	1/94	84s
Driver's license fee, duplicate	lic	0.50	1/94	84s
Driver's license reinstatement fee, min.	susp	30.00	1/94	85s
Driver's license renewal fee	renew	10.00	1/94	84s
Identification card, nondriver	card	5.00	1/94	83s
Motorcycle learning permit fee	perm	2.00	1/94	84s
Motorcycle license fee	orig	10.00	1/94	84s
Motorcycle license fee, duplicate	lic	0.50	1/94	84s
Motorcycle license renewal fee	renew	10.00	1/94	84s
Public transportation expenditures	year	249	91	81r
Tire balance, computer or spin bal., front	wheel	7.20	12/94	2c
Transportation expenditures, total	year	5307	91	81r
Vehicle finance charges	year	346	91	81r
Vehicle insurance expenditures	year	544	91	81r
Vehicle maintenance and repairs expenditures	year	600	91	81r
Vehicle purchases	year	2275	91	81r
Vehicle rental, leases, licenses, etc. expenditures	year	141	91	81r
Vehicles purchased, other than cars and trucks	year	27	91	81r
Utilities				
Utilities, ACCRA Index		98.10	12/94	2c
Electricity expenditures	year	950	91	81r
Electricity, 1800 sq. ft., new home	mo.	107.16	12/94	2c
Utilities, fuels, and public services, total expenditures	year	2000	91	81r
Water and other public services, expenditures	year	227	91	81r
Weddings				
Bridal attendants' gowns	event	750	10/93	76r
Bridal gown	event	852	10/93	76r
Bridal headpiece and veil	event	167	10/93	76r
Bride's wedding band	event	708	10/93	76r
Clergy	event	224	10/93	76r
Engagement ring	event	2756	10/93	76r
Flowers	event	863	10/93	76r
Formal wear for groom	event	106	10/93	76r
Groom's attendants' formal wear	event	530	10/93	76r
Groom's wedding band	event	402	10/93	76r
Music	event	600	10/93	76r
Photography	event	1088	10/93	76r
Shoes for bride	event	50	10/93	76r
Videography	event	483	10/93	76r
Wedding invitations and announcements	event	342	10/93	76r
Wedding reception	event	7000	10/93	76r

Values are in dollars or fractions of dollars. In the column headed *Ref*, references are shown to sources. Each reference is followed by a letter. These refer to the geographical level for which data were reported: s = State, r = Region, and c = City or metro. The abbreviation *ex* is used to mean *except* or *excluding*; *exp* stands for *expenditures*. For other abbreviations and further explanations, please see the Introduction.

American Cost of Living Survey, 2nd Edition

Spokane, WA

Item	Per	Value	Date	Ref.
Appliances				
Appliances (major), expenditures	year	160	91	81r
Average annual exp.				
Food, health care, personal goods, services	year	32461	91	81r
Charity				
Cash contributions, expenditures	year	975	91	81r
Clothing				
Apparel, men and boys, total expenditures	year	467	91	81r
Apparel, women and girls, total expenditures	year	737	91	81r
Footwear, expenditures	year	270	91	81r
Communications				
Long-distance telephone rate, day, addl. min., 1-10 mi.	min.	0.01	12/93	9s
Long-distance telephone rate, day, initial 1-10 mi.	min.	0.15	12/93	9s
Phone line, single, business, field visit	inst	48.00	12/93	9s
Phone line, single, business, no field visit	inst	48.00	12/93	9s
Phone line, single, residence, field visit	inst	31.00	12/93	9s
Phone line, single, residence, no field visit	inst	31.00	12/93	9s
Telephone service, expenditures	year	611	91	81r
Education				
Board, 4-year private college/university	year	1928	8/94	80s
Board, 4-year public college/university	year	2194	8/94	80s
Education, total expenditures	year	375	91	81r
Room, 4-year private college/university	year	2455	8/94	80s
Room, 4-year public college/university	year	1952	8/94	80s
Total cost, 4-year private college/university	year	16332	8/94	80s
Total cost, 4-year public college/university	year	6483	8/94	80s
Tuition, 2-year public college/university, in-state	year	1141	8/94	80s
Tuition, 4-year private college/university, in-state	year	11949	8/94	80s
Tuition, 4-year public college/university, in-state	year	2337	8/94	80s
Energy and Fuels				
Fuel oil and other fuels, expenditures	year	33	91	81r
Gas, natural, expenditures	year	212	91	81r
Gasoline and motor oil purchased	year	1115	91	81r
Gasoline, unleaded midgrade	gallon	1.36	4/93	82r
Gasoline, unleaded premium	gallon	1.43	4/93	82r
Gasoline, unleaded regular	gallon	1.23	4/93	82r
Entertainment				
Concert ticket, Pearl Jam group	perf	20.00	94	50r
Entertainment, total expenditures	year	1853	91	81r
Fees and admissions, expenditures	year	482	91	81r
Pets, toys, playground equipment, expenditures	year	299	91	81r
Reading, expenditures	year	164	91	81r
Televisions, radios, and sound equipment, expenditures	year	528	91	81r
Funerals				
Burial, immediate, container provided by funeral home		1382.70	1/95	54r
Cards, acknowledgment		21.87	1/95	54r
Casket, minimum alternative		128.54	1/95	54r
Cosmetology, hair care, etc.		119.69	1/95	54r
Cremation, direct, container provided by funeral home		1030.62	1/95	54r
Embalming		255.42	1/95	54r
Funeral, funeral home		437.38	1/95	54r
Funeral, other facility		444.46	1/95	54r
Graveside service		338.46	1/95	54r
Hearse, local		147.50	1/95	54r
Limousine, local		130.33	1/95	54r
Memorial service		553.16	1/95	54r
Service charge, professional, nondeclinable		859.15	1/95	54r
Visitation and viewing		93.23	1/95	54r

Spokane, WA - continued

Item	Per	Value	Date	Ref.
Groceries				
Apples, Red Delicious	lb.	0.72	12/94	82r
Bacon, sliced	lb.	1.73	12/94	82r
Bananas	lb.	0.52	12/94	82r
Beef purchases	year	241	91	81r
Beverage purchases, alcoholic	year	328	91	81r
Beverage purchases, nonalcoholic	year	234	91	81r
Bologna, all beef or mixed	lb.	2.33	12/94	82r
Bread, white, pan	lb.	0.81	12/94	82r
Carrots, short trimmed and topped	lb.	0.43	12/94	82r
Cereals and bakery products purchases	year	392	91	81r
Cereals and cereals products purchases	year	139	91	81r
Chicken breast, bone-in	lb.	2.04	12/94	82r
Chicken, fresh, whole	lb.	0.95	12/94	82r
Coffee, 100%, ground roast, all sizes	lb.	4.48	12/94	82r
Dairy products (other) purchases	year	182	91	81r
Fish and seafood purchases	year	94	91	81r
Flour, white, all purpose	lb.	0.21	12/94	82r
Food purchases, food eaten at home	year	2749	91	81r
Foods purchased away from home, not prepared by consumer	year	1909	91	81r
Fruits and vegetables purchases	year	459	91	81r
Grapefruit	lb.	0.56	12/94	82r
Ground beef, 100% beef	lb.	1.31	12/94	82r
Ham, boneless, exc. canned	lb.	2.46	12/94	82r
Ice cream, prepackaged, bulk, regular	1/2 gal.	2.57	12/94	82r
Lemons	lb.	1.00	12/94	82r
Lettuce, iceberg	lb.	0.93	12/94	82r
Meats, poultry, fish, and eggs purchases	year	700	91	81r
Milk and cream (fresh) purchases	year	155	91	81r
Orange juice, frozen concentrate 12-oz. can	16 oz.	1.52	12/94	82r
Oranges, Navel	lb.	0.56	12/94	82r
Pork chops, center cut, bone-in	lb.	3.30	12/94	82r
Pork purchases	year	122	91	81r
Potato chips	16-oz.	3.03	12/94	82r
Potatoes, frozen, French fried	lb.	0.77	12/94	82r
Potatoes, white	lb.	0.35	12/94	82r
Rice, white, long grain, uncooked	lb.	0.54	12/94	82r
Round roast, USDA choice, boneless	lb.	2.92	12/94	82r
Shortening, vegetable oil blends	lb.	0.80	12/94	82r
Spaghetti and macaroni	lb.	1.02	12/94	82r
Steak, round, graded & ungraded, exc. USDA prime & choice	lb.	3.13	12/94	82r
Steak, sirloin, USDA choice, boneless	lb.	4.07	12/94	82r
Sugar and other sweets, eaten at home, expenditures	year	105	91	81r
Sugar, white, all sizes	lb.	0.38	12/94	82r
Tobacco products and smoking supplies, total expenditures	year	221	91	81r
Tomatoes, field grown	lb.	1.45	12/94	82r
Tuna, chunk, light	lb.	2.18	12/94	82r
Health Care				
Childbirth, Cesarean delivery, hospital charge	birth	6059.00	12/91	69r
Childbirth, Cesarean delivery, physician charge	birth	2248.00	12/91	69r
Childbirth, normal delivery, hospital charge	birth	3006.00	12/91	69r
Childbirth, normal delivery, physician charge	birth	1634.00	12/91	69r
Drugs, expenditures	year	230	91	81r
Health care, total expenditures	year	1544	91	81r
Health insurance expenditures	year	558	91	81r
Insurance premium, family medical care	month	382.32	1/95	41s
Medical services expenditures	year	676	91	81r
Medical supplies expenditures	year	80	91	81r
Surgery, open-heart	proc	37818.00	1/93	14r
Household Goods				
Floor coverings, expenditures	year	79	91	81r
Furniture, expenditures	year	352	91	81r
Household equipment, misc. expenditures	year	614	91	81r
Household expenditures, miscellaneous	year	294	91	81r

Values are in dollars or fractions of dollars. In the column headed *Ref*, references are shown to sources. Each reference is followed by a letter. These refer to the geographical level for which data were reported: s = State, r = Region, and c = City or metro. The abbreviation *ex* is used to mean *except* or *excluding*; *exp* stands for expenditures. For other abbreviations and further explanations, please see the Introduction.

751

Spokane, WA - continued

Item	Per	Value	Date	Ref.
Household Goods				
Household furnishings and equipment, expenditures	year	1416	91	81r
Household operations expenditures	year	580	91	81r
Household textiles, expenditures	year	113	91	81r
Housekeeping supplies, expenditures	year	447	91	81r
Laundry and cleaning supplies, expenditures	year	114	91	81r
Postage and stationery, expenditures	year	145	91	81r
Housing				
Add garage/carport		6,422	3/95	74r
Add room(s)		26,583	3/95	74r
Apartment condominium or co-op, median	unit	105300	12/94	62r
Dwellings (owned), expenditures	year	3932	91	81r
Enclose porch/patio/breezeway		5,382	3/95	74r
Finish room in basement/attic		3,911	3/95	74r
Home, existing, single-family, median	unit	178600	12/94	62r
Maintenance, repairs, insurance, and other housing expenditures	year	591	91	81r
Mortgage interest and charges expenditures	year	2747	91	81r
Princ. & int., mortgage, median-price exist. sing.-family home	mo.	845	12/94	62r
Property taxes expenditures	year	594	91	81r
Redesign, restructure more than half of home's interior		5,467	3/95	74r
Rental units expenditures	year	2077	91	81r
Insurance and Pensions				
Auto insurance, private passenger	year	711.57	12/94	71s
Insurance and pensions, personal, expenditures	year	3042	91	81r
Insurance, life and other personal, expenditures	year	298	91	81r
Pensions and Social Security, expenditures	year	2744	91	81r
Legal Assistance				
Legal work, law firm associate	hour	91		10r
Legal work, law firm partner	hour	151		10r
Personal Services				
Personal services expenditures	year	286	91	81r
Restaurant Food				
Dining expenditures, family	week	32.25	94	73r
Taxes				
Taxes, Federal income, expenditures	year	2946	91	81r
Taxes, personal, expenditures	year	3791	91	81r
Taxes, State and local income, expenditures	year	791	91	81r
Transportation				
Cars and trucks purchased, new	year	1231	91	81r
Cars and trucks purchased, used	year	915	91	81r
Driver's learning permit fee	perm	4.00	1/94	84s
Driver's license fee	orig	21.00	1/94	84s
Driver's license fee, duplicate	lic	5.00	1/94	84s
Driver's license reinstatement fee, min.	susp	20.00-50.00	1/94	85s
Driver's license renewal fee	renew	14.00	1/94	84s
Identification card, nondriver	card	4.00	1/94	83s
Motorcycle license fee	orig	8.00	1/94	84s
Motorcycle license renewal fee	renew	7.50	1/94	84s
Public transportation expenditures	year	375	91	81r
Transportation expenditures, total	year	5527	91	81r
Vehicle finance charges	year	287	91	81r
Vehicle insurance expenditures	year	624	91	81r
Vehicle maintenance and repairs expenditures	year	695	91	81r
Vehicle purchases	year	2174	91	81r
Vehicle rental, leases, licenses, etc. expenditures	year	257	91	81r
Vehicles purchased, other than cars and trucks	year	28	91	81r

Spokane, WA - continued

Item	Per	Value	Date	Ref.
Utilities				
Electricity expenditures	year	616	91	81r
Utilities, fuels, and public services, total expenditures	year	1681	91	81r
Water and other public services, expenditures	year	209	91	81r
Weddings				
Bridal attendants' gowns	event	750	10/93	76r
Bridal gown	event	852	10/93	76r
Bridal headpiece and veil	event	167	10/93	76r
Bride's wedding band	event	708	10/93	76r
Clergy	event	224	10/93	76r
Engagement ring	event	2756	10/93	76r
Flowers	event	863	10/93	76r
Formal wear for groom	event	106	10/93	76r
Groom's attendants' formal wear	event	530	10/93	76r
Groom's wedding band	event	402	10/93	76r
Music	event	600	10/93	76r
Photography	event	1088	10/93	76r
Shoes for bride	event	50	10/93	76r
Videography	event	483	10/93	76r
Wedding invitations and announcements	event	342	10/93	76r
Wedding reception	event	7000	10/93	76r

Springfield, IL

Item	Per	Value	Date	Ref.
Appliances				
Appliances (major), expenditures	year	131	91	81r
Average annual exp.				
Food, health care, personal goods, services	year	25935	91	81r
Charity				
Cash contributions, expenditures	year	745	91	81r
Clothing				
Apparel, men and boys, total expenditures	year	332	91	81r
Apparel, women and girls, total expenditures	year	578	91	81r
Footwear, expenditures	year	164	91	81r
Communications				
Long-distance telephone rate, day, addl. min., 1-10 mi.	min.	0.04	12/93	9s
Long-distance telephone rate, day, initial min., 1-10 mi.	min.	0.10	12/93	9s
Phone line, single, business, field visit	inst	84.50	12/93	9s
Phone line, single, business, no field visit	inst	84.50	12/93	9s
Phone line, single, residence, field visit	inst	55.00	12/93	9s
Phone line, single, residence, no field visit	inst	55.00	12/93	9s
Telephone service, expenditures	year	547	91	81r
Education				
Board, 4-year private college/university	year	2078	8/94	80s
Board, 4-year public college/university	year	2139	8/94	80s
Education, total expenditures	year	394	91	81r
Room, 4-year private college/university	year	2696	8/94	80s
Room, 4-year public college/university	year	1796	8/94	80s
Total cost, 4-year private college/university	year	15249	8/94	80s
Total cost, 4-year public college/university	year	6964	8/94	80s
Tuition, 2-year public college/university, in-state	year	1135	8/94	80s
Tuition, 4-year private college/university, in-state	year	10474	8/94	80s
Tuition, 4-year public college/university, in-state	year	3029	8/94	80s
Energy and Fuels				
Fuel oil and other fuels, expenditures	year	83	91	81r
Gas, natural, expenditures	year	373	91	81r
Gasoline and motor oil purchased	year	1000	91	81r
Gasoline, unleaded midgrade	gallon	1.15	4/93	82r
Gasoline, unleaded premium	gallon	1.23	4/93	82r
Gasoline, unleaded regular	gallon	1.07	4/93	82r

Values are in dollars or fractions of dollars. In the column headed *Ref*, references are shown to sources. Each reference is followed by a letter. These refer to the geographical level for which data were reported: s = State, r = Region, and c = City or metro. The abbreviation *ex* is used to mean *except* or *excluding*; *exp* stands for *expenditures*. For other abbreviations and further explanations, please see the Introduction.

Springfield, IL - continued

Item	Per	Value	Date	Ref.
Entertainment				
Entertainment, total expenditures	year	1356	91	81r
Fees and admissions, expenditures	year	347	91	81r
Pets, toys, playground equipment, expenditures	year	270	91	81r
Reading, expenditures	year	160	91	81r
Televisions, radios, and sound equipment, expenditures	year	433	91	81r
Funerals				
Burial, immediate, container provided by funeral home		1268.31	1/95	54r
Cards, acknowledgment		26.12	1/95	54r
Casket, minimum alternative		198.03	1/95	54r
Cosmetology, hair care, etc.		122.19	1/95	54r
Cremation, direct, container provided by funeral home		977.81	1/95	54r
Embalming		334.00	1/95	54r
Funeral, funeral home		321.16	1/95	54r
Funeral, other facility		317.73	1/95	54r
Graveside service		292.48	1/95	54r
Hearse, local		153.20	1/95	54r
Limousine, local		123.52	1/95	54r
Memorial service		356.30	1/95	54r
Service charge, professional, nondeclinable		968.24	1/95	54r
Visitation and viewing		332.66	1/95	54r
Groceries				
Apples, Red Delicious	lb.	0.68	12/94	82r
Bacon, sliced	lb.	1.88	12/94	82r
Bananas	lb.	0.41	12/94	82r
Beef purchases	year	197	91	81r
Beef, stew, boneless	lb.	2.52	12/94	82r
Beverage purchases, alcoholic	year	293	91	81r
Beverage purchases, nonalcoholic	year	203	91	81r
Bologna, all beef or mixed	lb.	2.12	12/94	82r
Bread, white, pan	lb.	0.76	12/94	82r
Cabbage	lb.	0.44	12/94	82r
Carrots, short trimmed and topped	lb.	0.44	12/94	82r
Cereals and bakery products purchases	year	347	91	81r
Cereals and cereals products purchases	year	119	91	81r
Cheddar cheese, natural	lb.	3.28	12/94	82r
Chicken breast, bone-in	lb.	1.61	12/94	82r
Chicken, fresh, whole	lb.	0.89	12/94	82r
Chuck roast, USDA choice, boneless	lb.	2.33	12/94	82r
Coffee, 100%, ground roast, all sizes	lb.	4.28	12/94	82r
Cookies, chocolate chip	lb.	2.72	12/94	82r
Dairy products (other) purchases	year	148	91	81r
Eggs, Grade A large	dozen	0.76	12/94	82r
Fish and seafood purchases	year	61	91	81r
Flour, white, all purpose	lb.	0.22	12/94	82r
Food purchases, food eaten at home	year	2313	91	81r
Foods purchased away from home, not prepared by consumer	year	1709	91	81r
Fruits and vegetables purchases	year	372	91	81r
Grapefruit	lb.	0.47	12/94	82r
Grapes, Thompson seedless	lb.	2.15	12/94	82r
Ground beef, 100% beef	lb.	1.37	12/94	82r
Ground chuck, 100% beef	lb.	1.81	12/94	82r
Ham, boneless, exc. canned	lb.	2.16	12/94	82r
Ice cream, prepackaged, bulk, regular	1/2 gal.	2.48	12/94	82r
Lemons	lb.	1.08	12/94	82r
Lettuce, iceberg	lb.	0.81	12/94	82r
Margarine, stick	lb.	0.81	12/94	82r
Meats, poultry, fish, and eggs purchases	year	591	91	81r
Milk and cream (fresh) purchases	year	132	91	81r
Orange juice, frozen concentrate 12-oz. can	16 oz.	1.41	12/94	82r
Oranges, Navel	lb.	0.56	12/94	82r
Peanut butter, creamy, all sizes	lb.	1.81	12/94	82r
Pork chops, center cut, bone-in	lb.	2.76	12/94	82r
Pork purchases	year	130	91	81r
Potato chips	16-oz.	2.81	12/94	82r
Potatoes, frozen, French fried	lb.	0.83	12/94	82r

Item	Per	Value	Date	Ref.
Groceries - continued				
Potatoes, white	lb.	0.28	12/94	82r
Round roast, USDA choice, boneless	lb.	2.90	12/94	82r
Shortening, vegetable oil blends	lb.	0.88	12/94	82r
Spaghetti and macaroni	lb.	0.78	12/94	82r
Steak, rib eye, USDA choice, boneless	lb.	6.15	12/94	82r
Steak, round, graded & ungraded, exc. USDA prime & choice	lb.	2.72	12/94	82r
Steak, round, USDA choice, boneless	lb.	3.02	12/94	82r
Steak, sirloin, USDA choice, boneless	lb.	3.85	12/94	82r
Steak, T-bone, USDA choice, bone-in	lb.	5.38	12/94	82r
Sugar and other sweets, eaten at home, expenditures	year	91	91	81r
Sugar, white, all sizes	lb.	0.36	12/94	82r
Tobacco products and smoking supplies, total expenditures	year	298	91	81r
Tomatoes, field grown	lb.	1.36	12/94	82r
Tuna, chunk, light	lb.	1.94	12/94	82r
Turkey, frozen, whole	lb.	0.96	12/94	82r
Yogurt, natural, fruit flavored	8 oz.	0.62	12/94	82r
Health Care				
Childbirth, Cesarean delivery, hospital charge	birth	5101.00	12/91	69r
Childbirth, Cesarean delivery, physician charge	birth	2234.00	12/91	69r
Childbirth, normal delivery, hospital charge	birth	2891.00	12/91	69r
Childbirth, normal delivery, physician charge	birth	1623.00	12/91	69r
Drugs, expenditures	year	248	91	81r
Health care, total expenditures	year	1336	91	81r
Health insurance expenditures	year	550	91	81r
Insurance premium, family medical care	month	363.57	1/95	41s
Medical services expenditures	year	457	91	81r
Medical supplies expenditures	year	82	91	81r
Household Goods				
Floor coverings, expenditures	year	105	91	81r
Furniture, expenditures	year	291	91	81r
Household equipment, misc. expenditures	year	341	91	81r
Household expenditures, miscellaneous	year	162	91	81r
Household furnishings and equipment, expenditures	year	1042	91	81r
Household operations expenditures	year	365	91	81r
Household textiles, expenditures	year	101	91	81r
Housekeeping supplies, expenditures	year	390	91	81r
Laundry and cleaning supplies, expenditures	year	110	91	81r
Postage and stationery, expenditures	year	115	91	81r
Housing				
Add garage/carport		8,479	3/95	74r
Add room(s)		21,347	3/95	74r
Apartment condominium or co-op, median	unit	87100	12/94	62r
Bathroom addition, average cost	add	9734.00	3/95	13r
Bathroom remodeling, average cost	remod	6414.00	3/95	13r
Bedroom, master suite addition, average cost	add	27122.00	3/95	13r
Deck addition, average cost	add	6665.00	3/95	13r
Dwellings (owned), expenditures	year	2566	91	81r
Enclose porch/patio/breezeway		4,556	3/95	74r
Exterior remodeling, average cost	remod	15395.00	3/95	13r
Family room addition, average cost	add	27658.00	3/95	13r
Finish room in basement/attic		5,074	3/95	74r
Home, existing, single-family, median	unit	106500	12/94	62r
Kitchen remodeling, major, average cost	remod	17084.00	3/95	13r
Kitchen remodeling, minor, average cost	remod	5804.00	3/95	13r
Maintenance, repairs, insurance, and other housing expenditures	year	484	91	81r
Mortgage interest and charges expenditures	year	1443	91	81r
Office, home addition, average cost	add	8121.00	3/95	13r
Princ. & int., mortgage, median-price exist. sing.-family home	mo.	515	12/94	62r
Property taxes expenditures	year	639	91	81r
Redesign, restructure more than half of home's interior		9,114	3/95	74r

Values are in dollars or fractions of dollars. In the column headed *Ref*, references are shown to sources. Each reference is followed by a letter. These refer to the geographical level for which data were reported: s = State, r = Region, and c = City or metro. The abbreviation *ex* is used to mean *except* or *excluding*; *exp* stands for *expenditures*. For other abbreviations and further explanations, please see the Introduction.

Springfield, IL - continued

Item	Per	Value	Date	Ref.
Housing				
Rental units expenditures	year	1200	91	81r
Sun-space addition, average cost	add	23768.00	3/95	13r
Wing addition, two-story, average cost	add	50410.00	3/95	13r
Insurance and Pensions				
Auto insurance, private passenger	year	679.48	12/94	71s
Insurance and pensions, personal, expenditures	year	2408	91	81r
Insurance, life and other personal, expenditures	year	355	91	81r
Pensions and Social Security, expenditures	year	2053	91	81r
Legal Assistance				
Legal work, law firm associate	hour	90		10r
Legal work, law firm partner	hour	139		10r
Personal Services				
Personal services expenditures	year	203	91	81r
Restaurant Food				
Dining expenditures, family	week	30.03	94	73r
Taxes				
Taxes, Federal income, expenditures	year	1756	91	81r
Taxes, personal, expenditures	year	2426	91	81r
Taxes, State and local income, expenditures	year	568	91	81r
Transportation				
Cars and trucks purchased, new	year	891	91	81r
Cars and trucks purchased, used	year	1155	91	81r
Driver's learning permit fee	perm	20.00	1/94	84s
Driver's license fee	orig	10.00	1/94	84s
Driver's license fee, duplicate	lic	5.00	1/94	84s
Driver's license reinstatement fee, min.	susp	30.00	1/94	85s
Driver's license renewal fee	renew	10.00	1/94	84s
Identification card, nondriver	card	4.00	1/94	83s
Motorcycle learning permit fee	perm	20.00	1/94	84s
Motorcycle license fee	orig	10.00	1/94	84s
Motorcycle license fee, duplicate	lic	5.00	1/94	84s
Motorcycle license renewal fee	renew	10.00	1/94	84s
Public transportation expenditures	year	209	91	81r
Transportation expenditures, total	year	4792	91	81r
Vehicle finance charges	year	300	91	81r
Vehicle insurance expenditures	year	485	91	81r
Vehicle maintenance and repairs expenditures	year	534	91	81r
Vehicle purchases	year	2068	91	81r
Vehicle rental, leases, licenses, etc. expenditures	year	197	91	81r
Vehicles purchased, other than cars and trucks	year	22	91	81r
Utilities				
Electricity expenditures	year	668	91	81r
Utilities, fuels, and public services, total expenditures	year	1838	91	81r
Water and other public services, expenditures	year	167	91	81r
Weddings				
Bridal attendants' gowns	event	750	10/93	76r
Bridal gown	event	852	10/93	76r
Bridal headpiece and veil	event	167	10/93	76r
Bride's wedding band	event	708	10/93	76r
Clergy	event	224	10/93	76r
Engagement ring	event	2756	10/93	76r
Flowers	event	863	10/93	76r
Formal wear for groom	event	106	10/93	76r
Groom's attendants' formal wear	event	530	10/93	76r
Groom's wedding band	event	402	10/93	76r
Music	event	600	10/93	76r
Photography	event	1088	10/93	76r
Shoes for bride	event	50	10/93	76r
Videography	event	483	10/93	76r
Wedding invitations and announcements	event	342	10/93	76r
Wedding reception	event	7000	10/93	76r

Springfield, MA

Item	Per	Value	Date	Ref.
Appliances				
Appliances (major), expenditures	year	145	91	81r
Average annual exp.				
Food, health care, personal goods, services	year	29496	91	81r
Charity				
Cash contributions, expenditures	year	708	91	81r
Clothing				
Apparel, men and boys, total expenditures	year	416	91	81r
Apparel, women and girls, total expenditures	year	744	91	81r
Footwear, expenditures	year	305	91	81r
Communications				
Long-distance telephone rate, day, addl. min., 1-10 mi.	min.	0.09	12/93	9s
Long-distance telephone rate, day, initial min., 1-10 mi.	min.	0.19	12/93	9s
Phone line, single, business, field visit	inst	27.50	12/93	9s
Phone line, single, business, no field visit	inst	93.02	12/93	9s
Phone line, single, residence, field visit	inst	27.50	12/93	9s
Phone line, single, residence, no field visit	inst	37.07	12/93	9s
Telephone service, expenditures	year	589	91	81r
Education				
Board, 4-year private college/university	year	3179	8/94	80s
Board, 4-year public college/university	year	2035	8/94	80s
Education, total expenditures	year	593	91	81r
Room, 4-year private college/university	year	3369	8/94	80s
Room, 4-year public college/university	year	2290	8/94	80s
Total cost, 4-year private college/university	year	21346	8/94	80s
Total cost, 4-year public college/university	year	8467	8/94	80s
Tuition, 2-year public college/university, in-state	year	2361	8/94	80s
Tuition, 4-year private college/university, in-state	year	14797	8/94	80s
Tuition, 4-year public college/university, in-state	year	4142	8/94	80s
Energy and Fuels				
Fuel oil and other fuels, expenditures	year	257	91	81r
Gas, natural, expenditures	year	285	91	81r
Gasoline and motor oil purchased	year	867	91	81r
Gasoline, unleaded midgrade	gallon	1.32	4/93	82r
Gasoline, unleaded premium	gallon	1.40	4/93	82r
Gasoline, unleaded regular	gallon	1.19	4/93	82r
Entertainment				
Entertainment, total expenditures	year	1331	91	81r
Fees and admissions, expenditures	year	398	91	81r
Pets, toys, playground equipment, expenditures	year	270	91	81r
Reading, expenditures	year	171	91	81r
Televisions, radios, and sound equipment, expenditures	year	429	91	81r
Funerals				
Burial, immediate, container provided by funeral home		1507.89	1/95	54r
Cards, acknowledgment		18.10	1/95	54r
Casket, minimum alternative		133.03	1/95	54r
Cosmetology, hair care, etc.		114.12	1/95	54r
Cremation, direct, container provided by funeral home		1309.19	1/95	54r
Embalming		320.97	1/95	54r
Funeral, funeral home		327.61	1/95	54r
Funeral, other facility		314.81	1/95	54r
Graveside service		286.11	1/95	54r
Hearse, local		158.95	1/95	54r
Limousine, local		149.45	1/95	54r
Memorial service		315.94	1/95	54r
Service charge, professional, nondeclinable		1148.43	1/95	54r
Visitation and viewing		249.66	1/95	54r

Values are in dollars or fractions of dollars. In the column headed *Ref*, references are shown to sources. Each reference is followed by a letter. These refer to the geographical level for which data were reported: s = State, r = Region, and c = City or metro. The abbreviation *ex* is used to mean *except* or *excluding*; *exp* stands for expenditures. For other abbreviations and further explanations, please see the Introduction.

Springfield, MA - continued

Item	Per	Value	Date	Ref.
Groceries				
Apples, Red Delicious	lb.	0.78	12/94	82r
Bacon, sliced	lb.	2.24	12/94	82r
Bananas	lb.	0.49	12/94	82r
Beef purchases	year	226	91	81r
Beverage purchases, alcoholic	year	332	91	81r
Beverage purchases, nonalcoholic	year	213	91	81r
Bread, white, pan	lb.	0.80	12/94	82r
Butter, salted, Grade AA, stick	lb.	1.67	12/94	82r
Carrots, short trimmed and topped	lb.	0.51	12/94	82r
Cereals and bakery products purchases	year	407	91	81r
Cereals and cereals products purchases	year	132	91	81r
Chicken breast, bone-in	lb.	2.22	12/94	82r
Chicken, fresh, whole	lb.	1.05	12/94	82r
Chuck roast, USDA choice, boneless	lb.	2.74	12/94	82r
Coffee, 100%, ground roast, all sizes	lb.	4.61	12/94	82r
Dairy products (other) purchases	year	161	91	81r
Eggs, Grade A large	dozen	1.12	12/94	82r
Fish and seafood purchases	year	112	91	81r
Food purchases, food eaten at home	year	2599	91	81r
Foods purchased away from home, not prepared by consumer	year	2024	91	81r
Fruits and vegetables purchases	year	444	91	81r
Grapefruit	lb.	0.44	12/94	82r
Grapes, Thompson seedless	lb.	2.24	12/94	82r
Ground chuck, 100% beef	lb.	1.67	12/94	82r
Ice cream, prepackaged, bulk, regular	1/2 gal.	2.93	12/94	82r
Lemons	lb.	1.06	12/94	82r
Lettuce, iceberg	lb.	0.92	12/94	82r
Meats, poultry, fish, and eggs purchases	year	751	91	81r
Milk and cream (fresh) purchases	year	152	91	81r
Orange juice, frozen concentrate 12-oz. can	16 oz.	1.92	12/94	82r
Oranges, Navel	lb.	0.56	12/94	82r
Pork chops, center cut, bone-in	lb.	3.09	12/94	82r
Pork purchases	year	130	91	81r
Potatoes, white	lb.	0.37	12/94	82r
Rib roast, USDA choice, bone-in	lb.	4.98	12/94	82r
Round roast, USDA choice, boneless	lb.	2.93	12/94	82r
Shortening, vegetable oil blends	lb.	1.03	12/94	82r
Spaghetti and macaroni	lb.	0.84	12/94	82r
Steak, round, USDA choice, boneless	lb.	3.48	12/94	82r
Steak, sirloin, USDA choice, bone-in	lb.	3.38	12/94	82r
Steak, sirloin, USDA choice, boneless	lb.	4.81	12/94	82r
Sugar and other sweets, eaten at home, expenditures	year	89	91	81r
Sugar, white, all sizes	lb.	0.46	12/94	82r
Tobacco products and smoking supplies, total expenditures	year	279	91	81r
Tomatoes, field grown	lb.	1.56	12/94	82r
Tuna, chunk, light	lb.	2.09	12/94	82r
Health Care				
Childbirth, Cesarean delivery, hospital charge	birth	6334.00	12/91	69r
Childbirth, Cesarean delivery, physician charge	birth	2234.00	12/91	69r
Childbirth, normal delivery, hospital charge	birth	3225.00	12/91	69r
Childbirth, normal delivery, physician charge	birth	1623.00	12/91	69r
Drugs, expenditures	year	205	91	81r
Health care, total expenditures	year	1396	91	81r
Health insurance expenditures	year	553	91	81r
Insurance premium, family medical care	month	457.38	1/95	41s
Medical services expenditures	year	559	91	81r
Medical supplies expenditures	year	80	91	81r
Household Goods				
Floor coverings, expenditures	year	158	91	81r
Furniture, expenditures	year	341	91	81r
Household equipment, misc. expenditures	year	363	91	81r
Household expenditures, miscellaneous	year	194	91	81r
Household furnishings and equipment, expenditures	year	1158	91	81r
Household operations expenditures	year	378	91	81r

Springfield, MA - continued

Item	Per	Value	Date	Ref.
Household Goods - continued				
Household textiles, expenditures	year	88	91	81r
Housekeeping supplies, expenditures	year	426	91	81r
Laundry and cleaning supplies, expenditures	year	122	91	81r
Postage and stationery, expenditures	year	134	91	81r
Housing				
Add garage/carport		11,614	3/95	74r
Add room(s)		16,816	3/95	74r
Apartment condominium or co-op, median	unit	96700	12/94	62r
Dwellings (owned), expenditures	year	3305	91	81r
Enclose porch/patio/breezeway		2,980	3/95	74r
Finish room in basement/attic		4,330	3/95	74r
Home, existing, single-family, median	unit	161600	12/94	62r
Maintenance, repairs, insurance, and other housing expenditures	year	569	91	81r
Mortgage interest and charges expenditures	year	1852	91	81r
Princ. & int., mortgage, median-price exist. sing.-family home	mo.	765	12/94	62r
Property taxes expenditures	year	884	91	81r
Redesign, restructure more than half of home's interior		2,750	3/95	74r
Rental units expenditures	year	1832	91	81r
Insurance and Pensions				
Auto insurance, private passenger	year	1009.56	12/94	71s
Insurance and pensions, personal, expenditures	year	2690	91	81r
Insurance, life and other personal, expenditures	year	341	91	81r
Pensions and Social Security, expenditures	year	2349	91	81r
Legal Assistance				
Estate planning, law-firm partner	hr.	375.00	10/93	12r
Legal work, law firm associate	hour	78		10r
Legal work, law firm partner	hour	183		10r
Personal Services				
Personal services expenditures	year	184	91	81r
Restaurant Food				
Dining expenditures, family	week	34.26	94	73r
Taxes				
Taxes, Federal income, expenditures	year	2409	91	81r
Taxes, personal, expenditures	year	3094	91	81r
Taxes, State and local income, expenditures	year	620	91	81r
Transportation				
Cars and trucks purchased, new	year	1170	91	81r
Cars and trucks purchased, used	year	739	91	81r
Driver's learning permit fee	perm	15.00	1/94	84s
Driver's license fee	orig	50.00	1/94	84s
Driver's license fee, duplicate	lic	15.00	1/94	84s
Driver's license renewal fee	renew	43.75	1/94	84s
Identification card, nondriver	card	15.00	1/94	83s
Motorcycle license fee	orig	50.00	1/94	84s
Motorcycle license fee, duplicate	lic	15.00	1/94	84s
Motorcycle license renewal fee	renew	43.75	1/94	84s
Public transportation expenditures	year	430	91	81r
Transportation expenditures, total	year	4810	91	81r
Vehicle finance charges	year	238	91	81r
Vehicle insurance expenditures	year	630	91	81r
Vehicle maintenance and repairs expenditures	year	532	91	81r
Vehicle purchases	year	1920	91	81r
Vehicle rental, leases, licenses, etc. expenditures	year	193	91	81r
Vehicles purchased, other than cars and trucks	year	11	91	81r
Utilities				
Electricity expenditures	year	695	91	81r
Utilities, fuels, and public services, total expenditures	year	1981	91	81r

Values are in dollars or fractions of dollars. In the column headed *Ref*, references are shown to sources. Each reference is followed by a letter. These refer to the geographical level for which data were reported: s=State, r=Region, and c=City or metro. The abbreviation *ex* is used to mean *except* or *excluding*; *exp* stands for *expenditures*. For other abbreviations and further explanations, please see the Introduction.

Springfield, MA - continued

Item	Per	Value	Date	Ref.
Utilities				
Water and other public services, expenditures	year	154	91	81r
Weddings				
Bridal attendants' gowns	event	750	10/93	76r
Bridal gown	event	852	10/93	76r
Bridal headpiece and veil	event	167	10/93	76r
Bride's wedding band	event	708	10/93	76r
Clergy	event	224	10/93	76r
Engagement ring	event	2756	10/93	76r
Flowers	event	863	10/93	76r
Formal wear for groom	event	106	10/93	76r
Groom's attendants' formal wear	event	530	10/93	76r
Groom's wedding band	event	402	10/93	76r
Music	event	600	10/93	76r
Photography	event	1088	10/93	76r
Shoes for bride	event	50	10/93	76r
Videography	event	483	10/93	76r
Wedding invitations and announcements	event	342	10/93	76r
Wedding reception	event	7000	10/93	76r

Springfield, MO

Item	Per	Value	Date	Ref.
Composite, ACCRA index		91.70	12/94	2c
Alcoholic Beverages				
Beer, Miller Lite, Bud, 12-oz., ex deposit	6	4.24	12/94	2c
J & B Scotch	750-ml.	16.33	12/94	2c
Wine, Gallo Chablis blanc	1.5-lit	4.87	12/94	2c
Appliances				
Appliances (major), expenditures	year	131	91	81r
Average annual exp.				
Food, health care, personal goods, services	year	25935	91	81r
Charity				
Cash contributions, expenditures	year	745	91	81r
Clothing				
Apparel, men and boys, total expenditures	year	332	91	81r
Apparel, women and girls, total expenditures	year	578	91	81r
Footwear, expenditures	year	164	91	81r
Jeans, man's denim		26.50	12/94	2c
Shirt, man's dress shirt		26.12	12/94	2c
Undervest, boy's size 10-14, cotton	3	4.36	12/94	2c
Communications				
Long-distance telephone rate, day, addl. min., 1-10 mi.	min.	0.08	12/93	9s
Long-distance telephone rate, day, initial min., 1-10 mi.	min.	0.10	12/93	9s
Newspaper subscription, dly. and Sun. delivery	month	11.95	12/94	2c
Phone line, single, business, field visit	inst	52.25	12/93	9s
Phone line, single, business, no field visit	inst	52.25	12/93	9s
Phone line, single, residence, field visit	inst	36.50	12/93	9s
Phone line, single, residence, no field visit	inst	36.50	12/93	9s
Telephone bill, family of four	month	18.51	12/94	2c
Telephone service, expenditures	year	547	91	81r
Telephone, residential, flat rate	mo.	10.10	12/93	8c
Education				
Board, 4-year private college/university	year	2296	8/94	80s
Board, 4-year public college/university	year	1544	8/94	80s
Education, total expenditures	year	394	91	81r
Room, 4-year private college/university	year	2012	8/94	80s
Room, 4-year public college/university	year	1817	8/94	80s
Total cost, 4-year private college/university	year	13053	8/94	80s
Total cost, 4-year public college/university	year	5836	8/94	80s
Tuition, 2-year public college/university, in-state	year	1152	8/94	80s
Tuition, 4-year private college/university, in-state	year	8745	8/94	80s

Springfield, MO - continued

Item	Per	Value	Date	Ref.
Education - continued				
Tuition, 4-year public college/university, in-state	year	2475	8/94	80s
Energy and Fuels				
Energy, combined forms, 1800 sq. ft.	mo.	93.83	12/94	2c
Energy, exc. electricity, 1800 sq. ft.	mo.	42.87	12/94	2c
Fuel oil and other fuels, expenditures	year	83	91	81r
Gas, natural, expenditures	year	373	91	81r
Gas, reg unlead, taxes inc., cash, self-service	gal	0.99	12/94	2c
Gasoline and motor oil purchased	year	1000	91	81r
Gasoline, unleaded midgrade	gallon	1.15	4/93	82r
Gasoline, unleaded premium	gallon	1.23	4/93	82r
Gasoline, unleaded regular	gallon	1.07	4/93	82r
Entertainment				
Bowling, evening rate	game	1.74	12/94	2c
Entertainment, total expenditures	year	1356	91	81r
Fees and admissions, expenditures	year	347	91	81r
Monopoly game, Parker Brothers', No. 9	game	8.94	12/94	2c
Movie	adm	5.25	12/94	2c
Pets, toys, playground equipment, expenditures	year	270	91	81r
Reading, expenditures	year	160	91	81r
Televisions, radios, and sound equipment, expenditures	year	433	91	81r
Tennis balls, yellow, Wilson or Penn, 3	can	2.03	12/94	2c
Funerals				
Burial, immediate, container provided by funeral home		1348.78	1/95	54r
Cards, acknowledgment		21.20	1/95	54r
Casket, minimum alternative		182.83	1/95	54r
Cosmetology, hair care, etc.		133.11	1/95	54r
Cremation, direct, container provided by funeral home		1101.95	1/95	54r
Embalming		314.45	1/95	54r
Funeral, funeral home		304.88	1/95	54r
Funeral, other facility		301.37	1/95	54r
Graveside service		290.59	1/95	54r
Hearse, local		137.37	1/95	54r
Limousine, local		82.84	1/95	54r
Memorial service		316.57	1/95	54r
Service charge, professional, nondeclinable		1099.00	1/95	54r
Visitation and viewing		209.25	1/95	54r
Groceries				
Groceries, ACCRA Index		90.00	12/94	2c
Apples, Red Delicious	lb.	0.68	12/94	82r
Baby food, strained vegetables, lowest price	4-4.5 oz.	0.34	12/94	2c
Bacon, sliced	lb.	1.88	12/94	82r
Bananas	lb.	0.35	12/94	2c
Bananas	lb.	0.41	12/94	82r
Beef or hamburger, ground	lb.	1.34	12/94	2c
Beef purchases	year	197	91	81r
Beef, stew, boneless	lb.	2.52	12/94	82r
Beverage purchases, alcoholic	year	293	91	81r
Beverage purchases, nonalcoholic	year	203	91	81r
Bologna, all beef or mixed	lb.	2.12	12/94	82r
Bread, white	24-oz.	0.59	12/94	2c
Bread, white, pan	lb.	0.76	12/94	82r
Cabbage	lb.	0.44	12/94	82r
Carrots, short trimmed and topped	lb.	0.44	12/94	82r
Cereals and bakery products purchases	year	347	91	81r
Cereals and cereals products purchases	year	119	91	81r
Cheddar cheese, natural	lb.	3.28	12/94	82r
Cheese, Kraft grated Parmesan	8-oz.	2.94	12/94	2c
Chicken breast, bone-in	lb.	1.61	12/94	82r
Chicken, fresh, whole	lb.	0.89	12/94	82r
Chicken, whole fryer	lb.	0.79	12/94	2c
Chuck roast, USDA choice, boneless	lb.	2.33	12/94	82r
Cigarettes, Winston, Kings	carton	14.34	12/94	2c
Coffee, 100%, ground roast, all sizes	lb.	4.28	12/94	82r

Values are in dollars or fractions of dollars. In the column headed *Ref*, references are shown to sources. Each reference is followed by a letter. These refer to the geographical level for which data were reported: s=State, r=Region, and c=City or metro. The abbreviation *ex* is used to mean *except* or *excluding*; *exp* stands for expenditures. For other abbreviations and further explanations, please see the Introduction.

Springfield, MO - continued

Item	Per	Value	Date	Ref.
Groceries				
Coffee, vacuum-packed	13 oz.	3.22	12/94	2c
Cookies, chocolate chip	lb.	2.72	12/94	82r
Corn Flakes, Kellogg's or Post Toasties	18 oz.	2.33	12/94	2c
Corn, frozen, whole kernel, lowest price	10 oz.	0.74	12/94	2c
Dairy products (other) purchases	year	148	91	81r
Eggs, Grade A large	dozen	0.75	12/94	2c
Eggs, Grade A large	dozen	0.76	12/94	82r
Fish and seafood purchases	year	61	91	81r
Flour, white, all purpose	lb.	0.22	12/94	82r
Food purchases, food eaten at home	year	2313	91	81r
Foods purchased away from home, not prepared by consumer	year	1709	91	81r
Fruits and vegetables purchases	year	372	91	81r
Grapefruit	lb.	0.47	12/94	82r
Grapes, Thompson seedless	lb.	2.15	12/94	82r
Ground beef, 100% beef	lb.	1.37	12/94	82r
Ground chuck, 100% beef	lb.	1.81	12/94	82r
Ham, boneless, exc. canned	lb.	2.16	12/94	82r
Ice cream, prepackaged, bulk, regular	1/2 gal.	2.48	12/94	82r
Lemons	lb.	1.08	12/94	82r
Lettuce, iceberg	lb.	0.81	12/94	82r
Lettuce, iceberg	head	0.61	12/94	2c
Margarine, Blue Bonnet or Parkay cubes	lb.	0.55	12/94	2c
Margarine, stick	lb.	0.81	12/94	82r
Meats, poultry, fish, and eggs purchases	year	591	91	81r
Milk and cream (fresh) purchases	year	132	91	81r
Milk, whole	1/2 gal.	1.16	12/94	2c
Orange juice, frozen concentrate 12-oz. can	16 oz.	1.41	12/94	82r
Orange juice, Minute Maid frozen	12-oz.	1.14	12/94	2c
Oranges, Navel	lb.	0.56	12/94	82r
Peaches, halves or slices, Hunt's, Del Monte, or Libby's	29-oz.	1.49	12/94	2c
Peanut butter, creamy, all sizes	lb.	1.81	12/94	82r
Peas, sweet, Del Monte or Green Giant	15-17 oz.	0.46	12/94	2c
Pork chops, center cut, bone-in	lb.	2.76	12/94	82r
Pork purchases	year	130	91	81r
Potato chips	16-oz.	2.81	12/94	82r
Potatoes, frozen, French fried	lb.	0.83	12/94	82r
Potatoes, white	lb.	0.28	12/94	82r
Potatoes, white or red	10-lb. sack	1.74	12/94	2c
Round roast, USDA choice, boneless	lb.	2.90	12/94	82r
Sausage, Jimmy Dean, 100% pork	lb.	2.51	12/94	2c
Shortening, vegetable oil blends	lb.	0.88	12/94	82r
Shortening, vegetable, Crisco	3-lb.	1.98	12/94	2c
Soft drink, Coca Cola, ex deposit	2 lit	0.87	12/94	2c
Spaghetti and macaroni	lb.	0.78	12/94	82r
Steak, rib eye, USDA choice, boneless	lb.	6.15	12/94	82r
Steak, round, graded & ungraded, exc. USDA prime & choice	lb.	2.72	12/94	82r
Steak, round, USDA choice, boneless	lb.	3.02	12/94	82r
Steak, sirloin, USDA choice, boneless	lb.	3.85	12/94	82r
Steak, t-bone	lb.	4.46	12/94	2c
Steak, T-bone, USDA choice, bone-in	lb.	5.38	12/94	82r
Sugar and other sweets, eaten at home, expenditures	year	91	91	81r
Sugar, cane or beet	4 lbs.	1.22	12/94	2c
Sugar, white, all sizes	lb.	0.36	12/94	82r
Tobacco products and smoking supplies, total expenditures	year	298	91	81r
Tomatoes, field grown	lb.	1.36	12/94	82r
Tomatoes, Hunt's or Del Monte	14.5 oz.	0.80	12/94	2c
Tuna, chunk, light	lb.	1.94	12/94	82r
Tuna, chunk, light, oil-packed	6.125-6.5 oz.	0.66	12/94	2c
Turkey, frozen, whole	lb.	0.96	12/94	82r
Yogurt, natural, fruit flavored	8 oz.	0.62	12/94	82r

Springfield, MO - continued

Item	Per	Value	Date	Ref.
Goods and Services				
Miscellaneous goods and services, ACCRA Index		92.20	12/94	2c
Health Care				
Health care, ACCRA Index		97.40	12/94	2c
Antibiotic ointment, Polysporin	1.5 oz.	4.05	12/94	2c
Childbirth, Cesarean delivery, hospital charge	birth	5101.00	12/91	69r
Childbirth, Cesarean delivery, physician charge	birth	2234.00	12/91	69r
Childbirth, normal delivery, hospital charge	birth	2891.00	12/91	69r
Childbirth, normal delivery, physician charge	birth	1623.00	12/91	69r
Dentist's fee, adult teeth cleaning and periodic oral exam	visit	49.50	12/94	2c
Doctor's fee, routine exam, established patient	visit	43.31	12/94	2c
Drugs, expenditures	year	248	91	81r
Health care, total expenditures	year	1336	91	81r
Health insurance expenditures	year	550	91	81r
Hospital care, semiprivate room	day	325.00	12/94	2c
Insurance premium, family medical care	month	390.73	1/95	41s
Medical services expenditures	year	457	91	81r
Medical supplies expenditures	year	82	91	81r
Household Goods				
Appl. repair, service call, wash mach	min. lab. chg.	33.21	12/94	2c
Floor coverings, expenditures	year	105	91	81r
Furniture, expenditures	year	291	91	81r
Household equipment, misc. expenditures	year	341	91	81r
Household expenditures, miscellaneous	year	162	91	81r
Household furnishings and equipment, expenditures	year	1042	91	81r
Household operations expenditures	year	365	91	81r
Household textiles, expenditures	year	101	91	81r
Housekeeping supplies, expenditures	year	390	91	81r
Laundry and cleaning supplies, expenditures	year	110	91	81r
Laundry detergent, Tide Ultra, Bold, or Cheer	42 oz.	3.71	12/94	2c
Postage and stationery, expenditures	year	115	91	81r
Tissues, facial, Kleenex brand	175	0.94	12/94	2c
Housing				
Housing, ACCRA Index		90.60	12/94	2c
Add garage/carport		8,479	3/95	74r
Add room(s)		21,347	3/95	74r
Apartment condominium or co-op, median	unit	87100	12/94	62r
Bathroom addition, average cost	add	9734.00	3/95	13r
Bathroom remodeling, average cost	remod	6414.00	3/95	13r
Bedroom, master suite addition, average cost	add	27122.00	3/95	13r
Deck addition, average cost	add	6665.00	3/95	13r
Dwellings (owned), expenditures	year	2566	91	81r
Enclose porch/patio/breezeway		4,556	3/95	74r
Exterior remodeling, average cost	remod	15395.00	3/95	13r
Family room addition, average cost	add	27658.00	3/95	13r
Finish room in basement/attic		5,074	3/95	74r
Home, existing, single-family, median	unit	106500	12/94	62r
Home, existing, single-family, median	unit	75.50	12/94	62c
House payment, principal and interest, 25% down payment	mo.	696	12/94	2c
House, 1800 sq ft, 8000 sq ft lot, new, urban, utilities	total	112500	12/94	2c
Kitchen remodeling, major, average cost	remod	17084.00	3/95	13r
Kitchen remodeling, minor, average cost	remod	5804.00	3/95	13r
Maintenance, repairs, insurance, and other housing expenditures	year	484	91	81r
Mortgage interest and charges expenditures	year	1443	91	81r
Mtge. rate, incl. points and orig. fee, 30-year conv. fixed or ARM	mo.	9.27	12/94	2c
Office, home addition, average cost	add	8121.00	3/95	13r

Values are in dollars or fractions of dollars. In the column headed *Ref*, references are shown to sources. Each reference is followed by a letter. These refer to the geographical level for which data were reported: s=State, r=Region, and c=City or metro. The abbreviation *ex* is used to mean *except* or *excluding*; *exp* stands for expenditures. For other abbreviations and further explanations, please see the Introduction.

Springfield, MO - continued

Item	Per	Value	Date	Ref.
Housing				
Princ. & int., mortgage, median-price exist. sing.-family home	mo.	515	12/94	62r
Property taxes expenditures	year	639	91	81r
Redesign, restructure more than half of home's interior		9,114	3/95	74r
Rent, apartment, 2 br., 1 1/2-2 baths, unfurnished, 950 sq ft, water	mo.	475	12/94	2c
Rental units expenditures	year	1200	91	81r
Sun-space addition, average cost	add	23768.00	3/95	13r
Wing addition, two-story, average cost	add	50410.00	3/95	13r
Insurance and Pensions				
Auto insurance, private passenger	year	600.64	12/94	71s
Insurance and pensions, personal, expenditures	year	2408	91	81r
Insurance, life and other personal, expenditures	year	355	91	81r
Pensions and Social Security, expenditures	year	2053	91	81r
Legal Assistance				
Legal work, law firm associate	hour	90		10r
Legal work, law firm partner	hour	139		10r
Personal Goods				
Shampoo, Alberto VO5	15-oz.	1.21	12/94	2c
Toothpaste, Crest or Colgate	6-7 oz.	2.04	12/94	2c
Personal Services				
Dry cleaning, man's 2-pc. suit		5.96	12/94	2c
Haircut, man's barbershop, no styling		7.13	12/94	2c
Haircut, woman's shampoo, trim, blow-dry		19.00	12/94	2c
Personal services expenditures	year	203	91	81r
Restaurant Food				
Chicken, fried, thigh and drumstick		1.80	12/94	2c
Dining expenditures, family	week	30.03	94	73r
Hamburger with cheese	1/4 lb.	1.79	12/94	2c
Pizza, Pizza Hut or Pizza Inn	12-13 in.	8.79	12/94	2c
Taxes				
Taxes, Federal income, expenditures	year	1756	91	81r
Taxes, personal, expenditures	year	2426	91	81r
Taxes, State and local income, expenditures	year	568	91	81r
Transportation				
Transportation, ACCRA Index		98.60	12/94	2c
Bus fare, one-way	trip	0.50	12/95	1c
Cars and trucks purchased, new	year	891	91	81r
Cars and trucks purchased, used	year	1155	91	81r
Driver's learning permit fee	perm	1.00	1/94	84s
Driver's license fee	orig	7.50	1/94	84s
Driver's license fee, duplicate	lic	7.50	1/94	84s
Driver's license reinstatement fee, min.	susp	20.00	1/94	85s
Driver's license renewal fee	renew	7.50	1/94	84s
Identification card, nondriver	card	7.50	1/94	83s
Motorcycle license fee	orig	7.50	1/94	84s
Motorcycle license fee, duplicate	lic	7.50	1/94	84s
Motorcycle license renewal fee	renew	7.50	1/94	84s
Public transportation expenditures	year	209	91	81r
Tire balance, computer or spin bal., front	wheel	7.63	12/94	2c
Transportation expenditures, total	year	4792	91	81r
Vehicle finance charges	year	300	91	81r
Vehicle insurance expenditures	year	485	91	81r
Vehicle maintenance and repairs expenditures	year	534	91	81r
Vehicle purchases	year	2068	91	81r
Vehicle rental, leases, licenses, etc. expenditures	year	197	91	81r
Vehicles purchased, other than cars and trucks	year	22	91	81r
Utilities				
Utilities, ACCRA Index		85.10	12/94	2c
Electricity expenditures	year	668	91	81r

Springfield, MO - continued

Item	Per	Value	Date	Ref.
Utilities - continued				
Electricity, (part.), other, 1800 sq. ft., new home	mo.	50.96	12/94	2c
Utilities, fuels, and public services, total expenditures	year	1838	91	81r
Water and other public services, expenditures	year	167	91	81r
Weddings				
Bridal attendants' gowns	event	750	10/93	76r
Bridal gown	event	852	10/93	76r
Bridal headpiece and veil	event	167	10/93	76r
Bride's wedding band	event	708	10/93	76r
Clergy	event	224	10/93	76r
Engagement ring	event	2756	10/93	76r
Flowers	event	863	10/93	76r
Formal wear for groom	event	106	10/93	76r
Groom's attendants' formal wear	event	530	10/93	76r
Groom's wedding band	event	402	10/93	76r
Music	event	600	10/93	76r
Photography	event	1088	10/93	76r
Shoes for bride	event	50	10/93	76r
Videography	event	483	10/93	76r
Wedding invitations and announcements	event	342	10/93	76r
Wedding reception	event	7000	10/93	76r

State College, PA

Item	Per	Value	Date	Ref.
Appliances				
Appliances (major), expenditures	year	145	91	81r
Average annual exp.				
Food, health care, personal goods, services	year	29496	91	81r
Charity				
Cash contributions, expenditures	year	708	91	81r
Clothing				
Apparel, men and boys, total expenditures	year	416	91	81r
Apparel, women and girls, total expenditures	year	744	91	81r
Footwear, expenditures	year	305	91	81r
Communications				
Long-distance telephone rate, day, addl. min., 1-10 mi.	min.	0.08	12/93	9s
Long-distance telephone rate, day, initial min., 1-10 mi.	min.	0.15	12/93	9s
Phone line, single, business, field visit	inst	75.00	12/93	9s
Phone line, single, business, no field visit	inst	75.00	12/93	9s
Phone line, single, residence, field visit	inst	40.00	12/93	9s
Phone line, single, residence, no field visit	inst	40.00	12/93	9s
Telephone service, expenditures	year	589	91	81r
Education				
Board, 4-year private college/university	year	2714	8/94	80s
Board, 4-year public college/university	year	1899	8/94	80s
Education, total expenditures	year	593	91	81r
Room, 4-year private college/university	year	2720	8/94	80s
Room, 4-year public college/university	year	2063	8/94	80s
Total cost, 4-year private college/university	year	18118	8/94	80s
Total cost, 4-year public college/university	year	8278	8/94	80s
Tuition, 2-year public college/university, in-state	year	1671	8/94	80s
Tuition, 4-year private college/university, in-state	year	12684	8/94	80s
Tuition, 4-year public college/university, in-state	year	4316	8/94	80s
Energy and Fuels				
Fuel oil and other fuels, expenditures	year	257	91	81r
Gas, natural, expenditures	year	285	91	81r
Gasoline and motor oil purchased	year	867	91	81r
Gasoline, unleaded midgrade	gallon	1.32	4/93	82r
Gasoline, unleaded premium	gallon	1.40	4/93	82r
Gasoline, unleaded regular	gallon	1.19	4/93	82r

Values are in dollars or fractions of dollars. In the column headed *Ref*, references are shown to sources. Each reference is followed by a letter. These refer to the geographical level for which data were reported: s=State, r=Region, and c=City or metro. The abbreviation *ex* is used to mean *except* or *excluding*; *exp* stands for expenditures. For other abbreviations and further explanations, please see the Introduction.

State College, PA - continued

Item	Per	Value	Date	Ref.
Entertainment				
Entertainment, total expenditures	year	1331	91	81r
Fees and admissions, expenditures	year	398	91	81r
Pets, toys, playground equipment, expenditures	year	270	91	81r
Reading, expenditures	year	171	91	81r
Televisions, radios, and sound equipment, expenditures	year	429	91	81r
Funerals				
Burial, immediate, container provided by funeral home		1370.36	1/95	54r
Cards, acknowledgment		17.72	1/95	54r
Casket, minimum alternative		192.52	1/95	54r
Cosmetology, hair care, etc.		139.56	1/95	54r
Cremation, direct, container provided by funeral home		1049.24	1/95	54r
Embalming		387.57	1/95	54r
Funeral, funeral home		278.77	1/95	54r
Funeral, other facility		275.85	1/95	54r
Graveside service		213.08	1/95	54r
Hearse, local		157.27	1/95	54r
Limousine, local		146.45	1/95	54r
Memorial service		271.02	1/95	54r
Service charge, professional, nondeclinable		943.58	1/95	54r
Visitation and viewing		322.86	1/95	54r
Groceries				
Apples, Red Delicious	lb.	0.78	12/94	82r
Bacon, sliced	lb.	2.24	12/94	82r
Bananas	lb.	0.49	12/94	82r
Beef purchases	year	226	91	81r
Beverage purchases, alcoholic	year	332	91	81r
Beverage purchases, nonalcoholic	year	213	91	81r
Bread, white, pan	lb.	0.80	12/94	82r
Butter, salted, Grade AA, stick	lb.	1.67	12/94	82r
Carrots, short trimmed and topped	lb.	0.51	12/94	82r
Cereals and bakery products purchases	year	407	91	81r
Cereals and cereals products purchases	year	132	91	81r
Chicken breast, bone-in	lb.	2.22	12/94	82r
Chicken, fresh, whole	lb.	1.05	12/94	82r
Chuck roast, USDA choice, boneless	lb.	2.74	12/94	82r
Coffee, 100%, ground roast, all sizes	lb.	4.61	12/94	82r
Dairy products (other) purchases	year	161	91	81r
Eggs, Grade A large	dozen	1.12	12/94	82r
Fish and seafood purchases	year	112	91	81r
Food purchases, food eaten at home	year	2599	91	81r
Foods purchased away from home, not prepared by consumer	year	2024	91	81r
Fruits and vegetables purchases	year	444	91	81r
Grapefruit	lb.	0.44	12/94	82r
Grapes, Thompson seedless	lb.	2.24	12/94	82r
Ground chuck, 100% beef	lb.	1.67	12/94	82r
Ice cream, prepackaged, bulk, regular	1/2 gal.	2.93	12/94	82r
Lemons	lb.	1.06	12/94	82r
Lettuce, iceberg	lb.	0.92	12/94	82r
Meats, poultry, fish, and eggs purchases	year	751	91	81r
Milk and cream (fresh) purchases	year	152	91	81r
Orange juice, frozen concentrate 12-oz. can	16 oz.	1.92	12/94	82r
Oranges, Navel	lb.	0.56	12/94	82r
Pork chops, center cut, bone-in	lb.	3.09	12/94	82r
Pork purchases	year	130	91	81r
Potatoes, white	lb.	0.37	12/94	82r
Rib roast, USDA choice, bone-in	lb.	4.98	12/94	82r
Round roast, USDA choice, boneless	lb.	2.93	12/94	82r
Shortening, vegetable oil blends	lb.	1.03	12/94	82r
Spaghetti and macaroni	lb.	0.84	12/94	82r
Steak, round, USDA choice, boneless	lb.	3.48	12/94	82r
Steak, sirloin, USDA choice, bone-in	lb.	3.38	12/94	82r
Steak, sirloin, USDA choice, boneless	lb.	4.81	12/94	82r
Sugar and other sweets, eaten at home, expenditures	year	89	91	81r
Sugar, white, all sizes	lb.	0.46	12/94	82r

State College, PA - continued

Item	Per	Value	Date	Ref.
Groceries - continued				
Tobacco products and smoking supplies, total expenditures	year	279	91	81r
Tomatoes, field grown	lb.	1.56	12/94	82r
Tuna, chunk, light	lb.	2.09	12/94	82r
Health Care				
Childbirth, Cesarean delivery, hospital charge	birth	6334.00	12/91	69r
Childbirth, Cesarean delivery, physician charge	birth	2234.00	12/91	69r
Childbirth, normal delivery, hospital charge	birth	3225.00	12/91	69r
Childbirth, normal delivery, physician charge	birth	1623.00	12/91	69r
Drugs, expenditures	year	205	91	81r
Health care, total expenditures	year	1396	91	81r
Health insurance expenditures	year	553	91	81r
Insurance premium, family medical care	month	349.05	1/95	41s
Medical services expenditures	year	559	91	81r
Medical supplies expenditures	year	80	91	81r
Household Goods				
Floor coverings, expenditures	year	158	91	81r
Furniture, expenditures	year	341	91	81r
Household equipment, misc. expenditures	year	363	91	81r
Household expenditures, miscellaneous	year	194	91	81r
Household furnishings and equipment, expenditures	year	1158	91	81r
Household operations expenditures	year	378	91	81r
Household textiles, expenditures	year	88	91	81r
Housekeeping supplies, expenditures	year	426	91	81r
Laundry and cleaning supplies, expenditures	year	122	91	81r
Postage and stationery, expenditures	year	134	91	81r
Housing				
Add garage/carport		11,614	3/95	74r
Add room(s)		16,816	3/95	74r
Apartment condominium or co-op, median	unit	96700	12/94	62r
Dwellings (owned), expenditures	year	3305	91	81r
Enclose porch/patio/breezeway		2,980	3/95	74r
Finish room in basement/attic		4,330	3/95	74r
Home, existing, single-family, median	unit	161600	12/94	62r
Maintenance, repairs, insurance, and other housing expenditures	year	569	91	81r
Mortgage interest and charges expenditures	year	1852	91	81r
Princ. & int., mortgage, median-price exist. sing.-family home	mo.	765	12/94	62r
Property taxes expenditures	year	884	91	81r
Redesign, restructure more than half of home's interior		2,750	3/95	74r
Rental units expenditures	year	1832	91	81r
Insurance and Pensions				
Auto insurance, private passenger	year	721.50	12/94	71s
Insurance and pensions, personal, expenditures	year	2690	91	81r
Insurance, life and other personal, expenditures	year	341	91	81r
Pensions and Social Security, expenditures	year	2349	91	81r
Legal Assistance				
Estate planning, law-firm partner	hr.	375.00	10/93	12r
Legal work, law firm associate	hour	78		10r
Legal work, law firm partner	hour	183		10r
Personal Services				
Personal services expenditures	year	184	91	81r
Restaurant Food				
Dining expenditures, family	week	34.26	94	73r
Taxes				
Taxes, Federal income, expenditures	year	2409	91	81r
Taxes, personal, expenditures	year	3094	91	81r
Taxes, State and local income, expenditures	year	620	91	81r

Values are in dollars or fractions of dollars. In the column headed *Ref*, references are shown to sources. Each reference is followed by a letter. These refer to the geographical level for which data were reported: s = State, r = Region, and c = City or metro. The abbreviation *ex* is used to mean *except* or *excluding*; *exp* stands for expenditures. For other abbreviations and further explanations, please see the Introduction.

State College, PA - continued

State College, PA - continued

Item	Per	Value	Date	Ref.
Transportation				
Cars and trucks purchased, new	year	1170	91	81r
Cars and trucks purchased, used	year	739	91	81r
Driver's learning permit fee	perm	27.00	1/94	84s
Driver's license fee	orig	0.00	1/94	84s
Driver's license fee, duplicate	lic	7.00	1/94	84s
Driver's license reinstatement fee, min.	susp	25.00	1/94	85s
Driver's license renewal fee	renew	0.00	1/94	84s
Identification card, nondriver	card	5.00	1/94	83s
Motorcycle learning permit fee	perm	27.00	1/94	84s
Motorcycle license fee	orig	0.00	1/94	84s
Motorcycle license fee, duplicate	lic	7.00	1/94	84s
Motorcycle license renewal fee	renew	0.00	1/94	84s
Public transportation expenditures	year	430	91	81r
Transportation expenditures, total	year	4810	91	81r
Vehicle finance charges	year	238	91	81r
Vehicle insurance expenditures	year	630	91	81r
Vehicle maintenance and repairs expenditures	year	532	91	81r
Vehicle purchases	year	1920	91	81r
Vehicle rental, leases, licenses, etc. expenditures	year	193	91	81r
Vehicles purchased, other than cars and trucks	year	11	91	81r
Utilities				
Electricity expenditures	year	695	91	81r
Utilities, fuels, and public services, total expenditures	year	1981	91	81r
Water and other public services, expenditures	year	154	91	81r
Weddings				
Bridal attendants' gowns	event	750	10/93	76r
Bridal gown	event	852	10/93	76r
Bridal headpiece and veil	event	167	10/93	76r
Bride's wedding band	event	708	10/93	76r
Clergy	event	224	10/93	76r
Engagement ring	event	2756	10/93	76r
Flowers	event	863	10/93	76r
Formal wear for groom	event	106	10/93	76r
Groom's attendants' formal wear	event	530	10/93	76r
Groom's wedding band	event	402	10/93	76r
Music	event	600	10/93	76r
Photography	event	1088	10/93	76r
Shoes for bride	event	50	10/93	76r
Videography	event	483	10/93	76r
Wedding invitations and announcements	event	342	10/93	76r
Wedding reception	event	7000	10/93	76r

Statesville, NC

Item	Per	Value	Date	Ref.
Composite, ACCRA index		97.60	12/94	2c
Alcoholic Beverages				
Beer, Miller Lite, Bud, 12-oz., ex deposit	6	3.39	12/94	2c
J & B Scotch	750-ml.	18.60	12/94	2c
Wine, Gallo Chablis blanc	1.5-lit	4.39	12/94	2c
Clothing				
Jeans, man's denim		34.74	12/94	2c
Shirt, man's dress shirt		29.50	12/94	2c
Undervest, boy's size 10-14, cotton	3	3.00	12/94	2c
Communications				
Newspaper subscription, dly. and Sun. delivery	month	9.75	12/94	2c
Telephone bill, family of four	month	16.40	12/94	2c
Energy and Fuels				
Energy, combined forms, 1800 sq. ft.	mo.	120.13	12/94	2c
Gas, reg unlead, taxes inc., cash, self-service	gal	1.08	12/94	2c

Statesville, NC - continued

Item	Per	Value	Date	Ref.
Entertainment				
Bowling, evening rate	game	2.25	12/94	2c
Monopoly game, Parker Brothers', No. 9	game	9.96	12/94	2c
Movie	adm	5.33	12/94	2c
Tennis balls, yellow, Wilson or Penn, 3	can	2.78	12/94	2c
Groceries				
Groceries, ACCRA Index		95.30	12/94	2c
Baby food, strained vegetables, lowest price	4-4.5 oz.	0.39	12/94	2c
Bananas	lb.	0.49	12/94	2c
Beef or hamburger, ground	lb.	1.62	12/94	2c
Bread, white	24-oz.	0.69	12/94	2c
Cheese, Kraft grated Parmesan	8-oz.	3.19	12/94	2c
Chicken, whole fryer	lb.	0.74	12/94	2c
Cigarettes, Winston, Kings	carton	12.89	12/94	2c
Coffee, vacuum-packed	13 oz.	3.32	12/94	2c
Corn Flakes, Kellogg's or Post Toasties	18 oz.	2.27	12/94	2c
Corn, frozen, whole kernel, lowest price	10 oz.	0.67	12/94	2c
Eggs, Grade A large	dozen	0.79	12/94	2c
Lettuce, iceberg	head	0.99	12/94	2c
Margarine, Blue Bonnet or Parkay cubes	lb.	0.59	12/94	2c
Milk, whole	1/2 gal.	1.41	12/94	2c
Orange juice, Minute Maid frozen	12-oz.	1.11	12/94	2c
Peaches, halves or slices, Hunt's, Del Monte, or Libby's	29-oz.	1.26	12/94	2c
Peas, sweet, Del Monte or Green Giant	15-17 oz.	0.51	12/94	2c
Potatoes, white or red	10-lb. sack	2.29	12/94	2c
Sausage, Jimmy Dean, 100% pork	lb.	2.15	12/94	2c
Shortening, vegetable, Crisco	3-lb.	2.52	12/94	2c
Soft drink, Coca Cola, ex deposit	2 lit	0.96	12/94	2c
Steak, t-bone	lb.	5.59	12/94	2c
Sugar, cane or beet	4 lbs.	1.47	12/94	2c
Tomatoes, Hunt's or Del Monte	14.5 oz.	0.54	12/94	2c
Tuna, chunk, light, oil-packed	6.125-6.5 oz.	0.66	12/94	2c
Goods and Services				
Miscellaneous goods and services, ACCRA Index		98.50	12/94	2c
Health Care				
Health care, ACCRA Index		81.40	12/94	2c
Antibiotic ointment, Polysporin	1.5 oz.	3.83	12/94	2c
Dentist's fee, adult teeth cleaning and periodic oral exam	visit	42.50	12/94	2c
Doctor's fee, routine exam, established patient	visit	37.00	12/94	2c
Hospital care, semiprivate room	day	219.67	12/94	2c
Household Goods				
Appl. repair, service call, wash mach	min. lab. chg.	33.10	12/94	2c
Laundry detergent, Tide Ultra, Bold, or Cheer	42 oz.	2.57	12/94	2c
Tissues, facial, Kleenex brand	175	0.85	12/94	2c
Housing				
Housing, ACCRA Index		97.60	12/94	2c
House payment, principal and interest, 25% down payment	mo.	761	12/94	2c
House, 1800 sq ft, 8000 sq ft lot, new, urban, utilities	total	123000	12/94	2c
Mtge. rate, incl. points and orig. fee, 30-year conv. fixed or ARM	mo.	9.28	12/94	2c
Rent, apartment, 2 br., 1 1/2-2 baths, unfurnished, 950 sq ft, water	mo.	477	12/94	2c
Personal Goods				
Shampoo, Alberto VO5	15-oz.	0.93	12/94	2c
Toothpaste, Crest or Colgate	6-7 oz.	1.64	12/94	2c

Values are in dollars or fractions of dollars. In the column headed *Ref*, references are shown to sources. Each reference is followed by a letter. These refer to the geographical level for which data were reported: s = State, r = Region, and c = City or metro. The abbreviation *ex* is used to mean *except* or *excluding*; *exp* stands for expenditures. For other abbreviations and further explanations, please see the Introduction.

Statesville, NC - continued

Item	Per	Value	Date	Ref.
Personal Services				
Dry cleaning, man's 2-pc. suit		6.23	12/94	2c
Haircut, man's barbershop, no styling		8.60	12/94	2c
Haircut, woman's shampoo, trim, blow-dry		15.67	12/94	2c
Restaurant Food				
Chicken, fried, thigh and drumstick		2.09	12/94	2c
Hamburger with cheese	1/4 lb.	1.86	12/94	2c
Pizza, Pizza Hut or Pizza Inn	12-13 in.	7.99	12/94	2c
Transportation				
Transportation, ACCRA Index		104.00	12/94	2c
Tire balance, computer or spin bal., front	wheel	7.75	12/94	2c
Utilities				
Utilities, ACCRA Index		104.00	12/94	2c
Electricity, 1800 sq. ft., new home	mo.	120.13	12/94	2c

Steubenville-Weirton, OH

Item	Per	Value	Date	Ref.
Appliances				
Appliances (major), expenditures	year	131	91	81r
Average annual exp.				
Food, health care, personal goods, services	year	25935	91	81r
Charity				
Cash contributions, expenditures	year	745	91	81r
Clothing				
Apparel, men and boys, total expenditures	year	332	91	81r
Apparel, women and girls, total expenditures	year	578	91	81r
Footwear, expenditures	year	164	91	81r
Communications				
Long-distance telephone rate, day, addl. min., 1-10 mi.	min.	0.16	12/93	9s
Long-distance telephone rate, day, initial min., 1-10 mi.	min.	0.32	12/93	9s
Phone line, single, business, field visit	inst	55.42	12/93	9s
Phone line, single, business, no field visit	inst	55.42	12/93	9s
Phone line, single, residence, field visit	inst	30.38	12/93	9s
Phone line, single, residence, no field visit	inst	30.38	12/93	9s
Telephone service, expenditures	year	547	91	81r
Education				
Board, 4-year private college/university	year	2241	8/94	80s
Board, 4-year public college/university	year	1625	8/94	80s
Education, total expenditures	year	394	91	81r
Room, 4-year private college/university	year	2118	8/94	80s
Room, 4-year public college/university	year	2103	8/94	80s
Total cost, 4-year private college/university	year	15444	8/94	80s
Total cost, 4-year public college/university	year	6987	8/94	80s
Tuition, 2-year public college/university, in-state	year	2076	8/94	80s
Tuition, 4-year private college/university, in-state	year	11085	8/94	80s
Tuition, 4-year public college/university, in-state	year	3259	8/94	80s
Energy and Fuels				
Fuel oil and other fuels, expenditures	year	83	91	81r
Gas, natural, expenditures	year	373	91	81r
Gasoline and motor oil purchased	year	1000	91	81r
Gasoline, unleaded midgrade	gallon	1.15	4/93	82r
Gasoline, unleaded premium	gallon	1.23	4/93	82r
Gasoline, unleaded regular	gallon	1.07	4/93	82r
Entertainment				
Entertainment, total expenditures	year	1356	91	81r
Fees and admissions, expenditures	year	347	91	81r
Pets, toys, playground equipment, expenditures	year	270	91	81r
Reading, expenditures	year	160	91	81r
Televisions, radios, and sound equipment, expenditures	year	433	91	81r

Steubenville-Weirton, OH - continued

Item	Per	Value	Date	Ref.
Funerals				
Burial, immediate, container provided by funeral home		1268.31	1/95	54r
Cards, acknowledgment		26.12	1/95	54r
Casket, minimum alternative		198.03	1/95	54r
Cosmetology, hair care, etc.		122.19	1/95	54r
Cremation, direct, container provided by funeral home		977.81	1/95	54r
Embalming		334.00	1/95	54r
Funeral, funeral home		321.16	1/95	54r
Funeral, other facility		317.73	1/95	54r
Graveside service		292.48	1/95	54r
Hearse, local		153.20	1/95	54r
Limousine, local		123.52	1/95	54r
Memorial service		356.30	1/95	54r
Service charge, professional, nondeclinable		968.24	1/95	54r
Visitation and viewing		332.66	1/95	54r
Groceries				
Apples, Red Delicious	lb.	0.68	12/94	82r
Bacon, sliced	lb.	1.88	12/94	82r
Bananas	lb.	0.41	12/94	82r
Beef purchases	year	197	91	81r
Beef, stew, boneless	lb.	2.52	12/94	82r
Beverage purchases, alcoholic	year	293	91	81r
Beverage purchases, nonalcoholic	year	203	91	81r
Bologna, all beef or mixed	lb.	2.12	12/94	82r
Bread, white, pan	lb.	0.76	12/94	82r
Cabbage	lb.	0.44	12/94	82r
Carrots, short trimmed and topped	lb.	0.44	12/94	82r
Cereals and bakery products purchases	year	347	91	81r
Cereals and cereals products purchases	year	119	91	81r
Cheddar cheese, natural	lb.	3.28	12/94	82r
Chicken breast, bone-in	lb.	1.61	12/94	82r
Chicken, fresh, whole	lb.	0.89	12/94	82r
Chuck roast, USDA choice, boneless	lb.	2.33	12/94	82r
Coffee, 100%, ground roast, all sizes	lb.	4.28	12/94	82r
Cookies, chocolate chip	lb.	2.72	12/94	82r
Dairy products (other) purchases	year	148	91	81r
Eggs, Grade A large	dozen	0.76	12/94	82r
Fish and seafood purchases	year	61	91	81r
Flour, white, all purpose	lb.	0.22	12/94	82r
Food purchases, food eaten at home	year	2313	91	81r
Foods purchased away from home, not prepared by consumer	year	1709	91	81r
Fruits and vegetables purchases	year	372	91	81r
Grapefruit	lb.	0.47	12/94	82r
Grapes, Thompson seedless	lb.	2.15	12/94	82r
Ground beef, 100% beef	lb.	1.37	12/94	82r
Ground chuck, 100% beef	lb.	1.81	12/94	82r
Ham, boneless, exc. canned	lb.	2.16	12/94	82r
Ice cream, prepackaged, bulk, regular	1/2 gal.	2.48	12/94	82r
Lemons	lb.	1.08	12/94	82r
Lettuce, iceberg	lb.	0.81	12/94	82r
Margarine, stick	lb.	0.81	12/94	82r
Meats, poultry, fish, and eggs purchases	year	591	91	81r
Milk and cream (fresh) purchases	year	132	91	81r
Orange juice, frozen concentrate 12-oz. can	16 oz.	1.41	12/94	82r
Oranges, Navel	lb.	0.56	12/94	82r
Peanut butter, creamy, all sizes	lb.	1.81	12/94	82r
Pork chops, center cut, bone-in	lb.	2.76	12/94	82r
Pork purchases	year	130	91	81r
Potato chips	16-oz.	2.81	12/94	82r
Potatoes, frozen, French fried	lb.	0.83	12/94	82r
Potatoes, white	lb.	0.28	12/94	82r
Round roast, USDA choice, boneless	lb.	2.90	12/94	82r
Shortening, vegetable oil blends	lb.	0.88	12/94	82r
Spaghetti and macaroni	lb.	0.78	12/94	82r
Steak, rib eye, USDA choice, boneless	lb.	6.15	12/94	82r
Steak, round, graded & ungraded, exc. USDA prime & choice	lb.	2.72	12/94	82r
Steak, round, USDA choice, boneless	lb.	3.02	12/94	82r
Steak, sirloin, USDA choice, boneless	lb.	3.85	12/94	82r

Values are in dollars or fractions of dollars. In the column headed *Ref*, references are shown to sources. Each reference is followed by a letter. These refer to the geographical level for which data were reported: s=State, r=Region, and c=City or metro. The abbreviation *ex* is used to mean *except* or *excluding*; *exp* stands for expenditures. For other abbreviations and further explanations, please see the Introduction.

Steubenville-Weirton, OH - continued

Item	Per	Value	Date	Ref.
Groceries				
Steak, T-bone, USDA choice, bone-in	lb.	5.38	12/94	82r
Sugar and other sweets, eaten at home, expenditures	year	91	91	81r
Sugar, white, all sizes	lb.	0.36	12/94	82r
Tobacco products and smoking supplies, total expenditures	year	298	91	81r
Tomatoes, field grown	lb.	1.36	12/94	82r
Tuna, chunk, light	lb.	1.94	12/94	82r
Turkey, frozen, whole	lb.	0.96	12/94	82r
Yogurt, natural, fruit flavored	8 oz.	0.62	12/94	82r
Health Care				
Childbirth, Cesarean delivery, hospital charge	birth	5101.00	12/91	69r
Childbirth, Cesarean delivery, physician charge	birth	2234.00	12/91	69r
Childbirth, normal delivery, hospital charge	birth	2891.00	12/91	69r
Childbirth, normal delivery, physician charge	birth	1623.00	12/91	69r
Drugs, expenditures	year	248	91	81r
Health care, total expenditures	year	1336	91	81r
Health insurance expenditures	year	550	91	81r
Insurance premium, family medical care	month	350.73	1/95	41s
Medical services expenditures	year	457	91	81r
Medical supplies expenditures	year	82	91	81r
Household Goods				
Floor coverings, expenditures	year	105	91	81r
Furniture, expenditures	year	291	91	81r
Household equipment, misc. expenditures	year	341	91	81r
Household expenditures, miscellaneous	year	162	91	81r
Household furnishings and equipment, expenditures	year	1042	91	81r
Household operations expenditures	year	365	91	81r
Household textiles, expenditures	year	101	91	81r
Housekeeping supplies, expenditures	year	390	91	81r
Laundry and cleaning supplies, expenditures	year	110	91	81r
Postage and stationery, expenditures	year	115	91	81r
Housing				
Add garage/carport		8,479	3/95	74r
Add room(s)		21,347	3/95	74r
Apartment condominium or co-op, median	unit	87100	12/94	62r
Bathroom addition, average cost	add	9734.00	3/95	13r
Bathroom remodeling, average cost	remod	6414.00	3/95	13r
Bedroom, master suite addition, average cost	add	27122.00	3/95	13r
Deck addition, average cost	add	6665.00	3/95	13r
Dwellings (owned), expenditures	year	2566	91	81r
Enclose porch/patio/breezeway		4,556	3/95	74r
Exterior remodeling, average cost	remod	15395.00	3/95	13r
Family room addition, average cost	add	27658.00	3/95	13r
Finish room in basement/attic		5,074	3/95	74r
Home, existing, single-family, median	unit	106500	12/94	62r
Kitchen remodeling, major, average cost	remod	17084.00	3/95	13r
Kitchen remodeling, minor, average cost	remod	5804.00	3/95	13r
Maintenance, repairs, insurance, and other housing expenditures	year	484	91	81r
Mortgage interest and charges expenditures	year	1443	91	81r
Office, home addition, average cost	add	8121.00	3/95	13r
Princ. & int., mortgage, median-price exist. sing.-family home	mo.	515	12/94	62r
Property taxes expenditures	year	639	91	81r
Redesign, restructure more than half of home's interior		9,114	3/95	74r
Rental units expenditures	year	1200	91	81r
Sun-space addition, average cost	add	23768.00	3/95	13r
Wing addition, two-story, average cost	add	50410.00	3/95	13r
Insurance and Pensions				
Auto insurance, private passenger	year	550.52	12/94	71s
Insurance and pensions, personal, expenditures	year	2408	91	81r

Steubenville-Weirton, OH - continued

Item	Per	Value	Date	Ref.
Insurance and Pensions - continued				
Insurance, life and other personal, expenditures	year	355	91	81r
Pensions and Social Security, expenditures	year	2053	91	81r
Legal Assistance				
Legal work, law firm associate	hour	90		10r
Legal work, law firm partner	hour	139		10r
Personal Services				
Personal services expenditures	year	203	91	81r
Restaurant Food				
Dining expenditures, family	week	30.03	94	73r
Taxes				
Taxes, Federal income, expenditures	year	1756	91	81r
Taxes, personal, expenditures	year	2426	91	81r
Taxes, State and local income, expenditures	year	568	91	81r
Transportation				
Cars and trucks purchased, new	year	891	91	81r
Cars and trucks purchased, used	year	1155	91	81r
Driver's learning permit fee	perm	3.00	1/94	84s
Driver's license fee	orig	5.00	1/94	84s
Driver's license fee, duplicate	lic	1.50	1/94	84s
Driver's license reinstatement fee, min.	susp	12.50-100.00	1/94	85s
Driver's license renewal fee	renew	5.00	1/94	84s
Identification card, nondriver	card	2.50	1/94	83s
Motorcycle learning permit fee	perm	3.00	1/94	84s
Motorcycle license fee	orig	5.00	1/94	84s
Motorcycle license fee, duplicate	lic	1.50	1/94	84s
Motorcycle license renewal fee	renew	5.00	1/94	84s
Public transportation expenditures	year	209	91	81r
Transportation expenditures, total	year	4792	91	81r
Vehicle finance charges	year	300	91	81r
Vehicle insurance expenditures	year	485	91	81r
Vehicle maintenance and repairs expenditures	year	534	91	81r
Vehicle purchases	year	2068	91	81r
Vehicle rental, leases, licenses, etc. expenditures	year	197	91	81r
Vehicles purchased, other than cars and trucks	year	22	91	81r
Utilities				
Electricity expenditures	year	668	91	81r
Utilities, fuels, and public services, total expenditures	year	1838	91	81r
Water and other public services, expenditures	year	167	91	81r
Weddings				
Bridal attendants' gowns	event	750	10/93	76r
Bridal gown	event	852	10/93	76r
Bridal headpiece and veil	event	167	10/93	76r
Bride's wedding band	event	708	10/93	76r
Clergy	event	224	10/93	76r
Engagement ring	event	2756	10/93	76r
Flowers	event	863	10/93	76r
Formal wear for groom	event	106	10/93	76r
Groom's attendants' formal wear	event	530	10/93	76r
Groom's wedding band	event	402	10/93	76r
Music	event	600	10/93	76r
Photography	event	1088	10/93	76r
Shoes for bride	event	50	10/93	76r
Videography	event	483	10/93	76r
Wedding invitations and announcements	event	342	10/93	76r
Wedding reception	event	7000	10/93	76r

Values are in dollars or fractions of dollars. In the column headed *Ref*, references are shown to sources. Each reference is followed by a letter. These refer to the geographical level for which data were reported: s=State, r=Region, and c=City or metro. The abbreviation *ex* is used to mean *except* or *excluding*; *exp* stands for expenditures. For other abbreviations and further explanations, please see the Introduction.

Stillwater, OK

Item	Per	Value	Date	Ref.
Composite, ACCRA index		96.70	12/94	2c
Alcoholic Beverages				
Beer, Miller Lite, Bud, 12-oz., ex deposit	6	4.01	12/94	2c
J & B Scotch	750-ml.	16.46	12/94	2c
Wine, Gallo Chablis blanc	1.5-lit	5.80	12/94	2c
Clothing				
Jeans, man's denim		28.48	12/94	2c
Shirt, man's dress shirt		39.83	12/94	2c
Undervest, boy's size 10-14, cotton	3	4.69	12/94	2c
Communications				
Newspaper subscription, dly. and Sun. delivery	month	9.00	12/94	2c
Telephone bill, family of four	month	18.84	12/94	2c
Telephone, residential, flat rate	mo.	11.32	12/93	8c
Energy and Fuels				
Energy, combined forms, 1800 sq. ft.	mo.	110.86	12/94	2c
Energy, exc. electricity, 1800 sq. ft.	mo.	43.32	12/94	2c
Gas, reg unlead, taxes inc., cash, self-service	gal	1.02	12/94	2c
Entertainment				
Bowling, evening rate	game	2.20	12/94	2c
Monopoly game, Parker Brothers', No. 9	game	12.56	12/94	2c
Movie	adm	5.50	12/94	2c
Tennis balls, yellow, Wilson or Penn, 3	can	2.84	12/94	2c
Groceries				
Groceries, ACCRA Index		95.30	12/94	2c
Baby food, strained vegetables, lowest price	4-4.5 oz.	0.33	12/94	2c
Bananas	lb.	0.39	12/94	2c
Beef or hamburger, ground	lb.	1.07	12/94	2c
Bread, white	24-oz.	0.70	12/94	2c
Cheese, Kraft grated Parmesan	8-oz.	3.08	12/94	2c
Chicken, whole fryer	lb.	0.76	12/94	2c
Cigarettes, Winston, Kings	carton	14.78	12/94	2c
Coffee, vacuum-packed	13 oz.	3.70	12/94	2c
Corn Flakes, Kellogg's or Post Toasties	18 oz.	2.71	12/94	2c
Corn, frozen, whole kernel, lowest price	10 oz.	0.67	12/94	2c
Eggs, Grade A large	dozen	0.74	12/94	2c
Lettuce, iceberg	head	0.69	12/94	2c
Margarine, Blue Bonnet or Parkay cubes	lb.	0.61	12/94	2c
Milk, whole	1/2 gal.	1.22	12/94	2c
Orange juice, Minute Maid frozen	12-oz.	1.22	12/94	2c
Peaches, halves or slices, Hunt's, Del Monte, or Libby's	29-oz.	1.36	12/94	2c
Peas, sweet, Del Monte or Green Giant	15-17 oz.	0.57	12/94	2c
Potatoes, white or red	10-lb. sack	1.25	12/94	2c
Sausage, Jimmy Dean, 100% pork	lb.	2.50	12/94	2c
Shortening, vegetable, Crisco	3-lb.	2.21	12/94	2c
Soft drink, Coca Cola, ex deposit	2 lit	1.03	12/94	2c
Steak, t-bone	lb.	5.12	12/94	2c
Sugar, cane or beet	4 lbs.	1.49	12/94	2c
Tomatoes, Hunt's or Del Monte	14.5 oz.	0.70	12/94	2c
Tuna, chunk, light, oil-packed	6.125-6.5 oz.	0.72	12/94	2c
Goods and Services				
Miscellaneous goods and services, ACCRA Index		105.50	12/94	2c
Health Care				
Health care, ACCRA Index		99.60	12/94	2c
Antibiotic ointment, Polysporin	1.5 oz.	3.86	12/94	2c
Dentist's fee, adult teeth cleaning and periodic oral exam	visit	56.50	12/94	2c
Doctor's fee, routine exam, established patient	visit	45.50	12/94	2c

Stillwater, OK - continued

Item	Per	Value	Date	Ref.
Health Care - continued				
Hospital care, semiprivate room	day	250.00	12/94	2c
Household Goods				
Appl. repair, service call, wash mach	min. lab. chg.	30.50	12/94	2c
Laundry detergent, Tide Ultra, Bold, or Cheer	42 oz.	3.55	12/94	2c
Tissues, facial, Kleenex brand	175	1.06	12/94	2c
Housing				
Housing, ACCRA Index		85.50	12/94	2c
House payment, principal and interest, 25% down payment	mo.	654	12/94	2c
House, 1800 sq ft, 8000 sq ft lot, new, urban, utilities	total	105126	12/94	2c
Mtge. rate, incl. points and orig. fee, 30-year conv. fixed or ARM	mo.	9.34	12/94	2c
Rent, apartment, 2 br., 1 1/2-2 baths, unfurnished, 950 sq ft, water	mo.	455	12/94	2c
Personal Goods				
Shampoo, Alberto VO5	15-oz.	1.23	12/94	2c
Toothpaste, Crest or Colgate	6-7 oz.	2.27	12/94	2c
Personal Services				
Dry cleaning, man's 2-pc. suit		6.37	12/94	2c
Haircut, man's barbershop, no styling		7.28	12/94	2c
Haircut, woman's shampoo, trim, blow-dry		17.56	12/94	2c
Restaurant Food				
Chicken, fried, thigh and drumstick		2.25	12/94	2c
Hamburger with cheese	1/4 lb.	1.99	12/94	2c
Pizza, Pizza Hut or Pizza Inn	12-13 in.	8.03	12/94	2c
Transportation				
Transportation, ACCRA Index		97.70	12/94	2c
Tire balance, computer or spin bal., front	wheel	7.25	12/94	2c
Utilities				
Utilities, ACCRA Index		98.50	12/94	2c
Electricity, (part.), other, 1800 sq. ft., new home	mo.	67.54	12/94	2c

Stockton, CA

Item	Per	Value	Date	Ref.
Appliances				
Appliances (major), expenditures	year	160	91	81r
Average annual exp.				
Food, health care, personal goods, services	year	32461	91	81r
Charity				
Cash contributions, expenditures	year	975	91	81r
Clothing				
Apparel, men and boys, total expenditures	year	467	91	81r
Apparel, women and girls, total expenditures	year	737	91	81r
Footwear, expenditures	year	270	91	81r
Communications				
Long-distance telephone rate, day, addl. min., 1-10 mi.	min.	0.07	12/93	9s
Long-distance telephone rate, day, initial min., 1-10 mi.	min.	0.17	12/93	9s
Phone line, single, business, field visit	inst	70.75	12/93	9s
Phone line, single, business, no field visit	inst	70.75	12/93	9s
Phone line, single, residence, field visit	inst	34.75	12/93	9s
Phone line, single, residence, no field visit	inst	34.75	12/93	9s
Telephone service, expenditures	year	611	91	81r
Education				
Board, 4-year private college/university	year	2945	8/94	80s
Board, 4-year public college/university	year	2321	8/94	80s
Education, total expenditures	year	375	91	81r

Values are in dollars or fractions of dollars. In the column headed *Ref*, references are shown to sources. Each reference is followed by a letter. These refer to the geographical level for which data were reported: s=State, r=Region, and c=City or metro. The abbreviation *ex* is used to mean *except* or *excluding*; *exp* stands for expenditures. For other abbreviations and further explanations, please see the Introduction.

Stockton, CA - continued

Item	Per	Value	Date	Ref.
Education				
Room, 4-year private college/university	year	3094	8/94	80s
Room, 4-year public college/university	year	2812	8/94	80s
Student fee, university	year	21.00	93	18s
Total cost, 4-year private college/university	year	19321	8/94	80s
Total cost, 4-year public college/university	year	7511	8/94	80s
Tuition, 2-year public college/university, in-state	year	345	8/94	80s
Tuition, 4-year private college/university, in-state	year	13282	8/94	80s
Tuition, 4-year public college/university, in-state	year	2378	8/94	80s
Energy and Fuels				
Fuel oil and other fuels, expenditures	year	33	91	81r
Gas, natural, expenditures	year	212	91	81r
Gasoline and motor oil purchased	year	1115	91	81r
Gasoline, unleaded midgrade	gallon	1.36	4/93	82r
Gasoline, unleaded premium	gallon	1.43	4/93	82r
Gasoline, unleaded regular	gallon	1.23	4/93	82r
Entertainment				
Concert ticket, Pearl Jam group	perf	20.00	94	50r
Entertainment, total expenditures	year	1853	91	81r
Fees and admissions, expenditures	year	482	91	81r
Pets, toys, playground equipment, expenditures	year	299	91	81r
Reading, expenditures	year	164	91	81r
Televisions, radios, and sound equipment, expenditures	year	528	91	81r
Funerals				
Burial, immediate, container provided by funeral home		1382.70	1/95	54r
Cards, acknowledgment		21.87	1/95	54r
Casket, minimum alternative		128.54	1/95	54r
Cosmetology, hair care, etc.		119.69	1/95	54r
Cremation, direct, container provided by funeral home		1030.62	1/95	54r
Embalming		255.42	1/95	54r
Funeral, funeral home		437.38	1/95	54r
Funeral, other facility		444.46	1/95	54r
Graveside service		338.46	1/95	54r
Hearse, local		147.50	1/95	54r
Limousine, local		130.33	1/95	54r
Memorial service		553.16	1/95	54r
Service charge, professional, nondeclinable		859.15	1/95	54r
Visitation and viewing		93.23	1/95	54r
Groceries				
Apples, Red Delicious	lb.	0.72	12/94	82r
Bacon, sliced	lb.	1.73	12/94	82r
Bananas	lb.	0.52	12/94	82r
Beef purchases	year	241	91	81r
Beverage purchases, alcoholic	year	328	91	81r
Beverage purchases, nonalcoholic	year	234	91	81r
Bologna, all beef or mixed	lb.	2.33	12/94	82r
Bread, white, pan	lb.	0.81	12/94	82r
Carrots, short trimmed and topped	lb.	0.43	12/94	82r
Cereals and bakery products purchases	year	392	91	81r
Cereals and cereals products purchases	year	139	91	81r
Chicken breast, bone-in	lb.	2.04	12/94	82r
Chicken, fresh, whole	lb.	0.95	12/94	82r
Coffee, 100%, ground roast, all sizes	lb.	4.48	12/94	82r
Dairy products (other) purchases	year	182	91	81r
Fish and seafood purchases	year	94	91	81r
Flour, white, all purpose	lb.	0.21	12/94	82r
Food purchases, food eaten at home	year	2749	91	81r
Foods purchased away from home, not prepared by consumer	year	1909	91	81r
Fruits and vegetables purchases	year	459	91	81r
Grapefruit	lb.	0.56	12/94	82r
Ground beef, 100% beef	lb.	1.31	12/94	82r
Ham, boneless, exc. canned	lb.	2.46	12/94	82r

Stockton, CA - continued

Item	Per	Value	Date	Ref.
Groceries - continued				
Ice cream, prepackaged, bulk, regular	1/2 gal.	2.57	12/94	82r
Lemons	lb.	1.00	12/94	82r
Lettuce, iceberg	lb.	0.93	12/94	82r
Meats, poultry, fish, and eggs purchases	year	700	91	81r
Milk and cream (fresh) purchases	year	155	91	81r
Orange juice, frozen concentrate 12-oz. can	16 oz.	1.52	12/94	82r
Oranges, Navel	lb.	0.56	12/94	82r
Pork chops, center cut, bone-in	lb.	3.30	12/94	82r
Pork purchases	year	122	91	81r
Potato chips	16-oz.	3.03	12/94	82r
Potatoes, frozen, French fried	lb.	0.77	12/94	82r
Potatoes, white	lb.	0.35	12/94	82r
Rice, white, long grain, uncooked	lb.	0.54	12/94	82r
Round roast, USDA choice, boneless	lb.	2.92	12/94	82r
Shortening, vegetable oil blends	lb.	0.80	12/94	82r
Spaghetti and macaroni	lb.	1.02	12/94	82r
Steak, round, graded & ungraded, exc. USDA prime & choice	lb.	3.13	12/94	82r
Steak, sirloin, USDA choice, boneless	lb.	4.07	12/94	82r
Sugar and other sweets, eaten at home, expenditures	year	105	91	81r
Sugar, white, all sizes	lb.	0.38	12/94	82r
Tobacco products and smoking supplies, total expenditures	year	221	91	81r
Tomatoes, field grown	lb.	1.45	12/94	82r
Tuna, chunk, light	lb.	2.18	12/94	82r
Health Care				
Childbirth, Cesarean delivery, hospital charge	birth	6059.00	12/91	69r
Childbirth, Cesarean delivery, physician charge	birth	2248.00	12/91	69r
Childbirth, normal delivery, hospital charge	birth	3006.00	12/91	69r
Childbirth, normal delivery, physician charge	birth	1634.00	12/91	69r
Drugs, expenditures	year	230	91	81r
Health care, total expenditures	year	1544	91	81r
Health insurance expenditures	year	558	91	81r
Insurance premium, family medical care	month	380.27	1/95	41s
Medical services expenditures	year	676	91	81r
Medical supplies expenditures	year	80	91	81r
Surgery, open-heart	proc	37818.00	1/93	14r
Household Goods				
Floor coverings, expenditures	year	79	91	81r
Furniture, expenditures	year	352	91	81r
Household equipment, misc. expenditures	year	614	91	81r
Household expenditures, miscellaneous	year	294	91	81r
Household furnishings and equipment, expenditures	year	1416	91	81r
Household operations expenditures	year	580	91	81r
Household textiles, expenditures	year	113	91	81r
Housekeeping supplies, expenditures	year	447	91	81r
Laundry and cleaning supplies, expenditures	year	114	91	81r
Postage and stationery, expenditures	year	145	91	81r
Housing				
Add garage/carport		6,422	3/95	74r
Add room(s)		26,583	3/95	74r
Apartment condominium or co-op, median	unit	105300	12/94	62r
Dwellings (owned), expenditures	year	3932	91	81r
Enclose porch/patio/breezeway		5,382	3/95	74r
Finish room in basement/attic		3,911	3/95	74r
Home, existing, single-family, median	unit	178600	12/94	62r
Maintenance, repairs, insurance, and other housing expenditures	year	591	91	81r
Mortgage interest and charges expenditures	year	2747	91	81r
Princ. & int., mortgage, median-price exist. sing.-family home	mo.	845	12/94	62r
Property taxes expenditures	year	594	91	81r
Redesign, restructure more than half of home's interior		5,467	3/95	74r
Rental units expenditures	year	2077	91	81r

Values are in dollars or fractions of dollars. In the column headed *Ref*, references are shown to sources. Each reference is followed by a letter. These refer to the geographical level for which data were reported: s=State, r=Region, and c=City or metro. The abbreviation *ex* is used to mean *except* or *excluding*; *exp* stands for expenditures. For other abbreviations and further explanations, please see the Introduction.

Stockton, CA - continued

Item	Per	Value	Date	Ref.
Insurance and Pensions				
Auto insurance, private passenger	year	892.80	12/94	71s
Insurance and pensions, personal, expenditures	year	3042	91	81r
Insurance, life and other personal, expenditures	year	298	91	81r
Pensions and Social Security, expenditures	year	2744	91	81r
Legal Assistance				
Legal work, law firm associate	hour	91		10r
Legal work, law firm partner	hour	151		10r
Personal Services				
Personal services expenditures	year	286	91	81r
Restaurant Food				
Dining expenditures, family	week	32.25	94	73r
Taxes				
Taxes, Federal income, expenditures	year	2946	91	81r
Taxes, personal, expenditures	year	3791	91	81r
Taxes, State and local income, expenditures	year	791	91	81r
Transportation				
Bus fare, one-way	trip	0.75	12/95	1c
Cars and trucks purchased, new	year	1231	91	81r
Cars and trucks purchased, used	year	915	91	81r
Driver's learning permit fee	perm	12.00	1/94	84s
Driver's license fee	orig	12.00	1/94	84s
Driver's license fee, duplicate	lic	12.00	1/94	84s
Driver's license reinstatement fee, min.	susp	15.00	1/94	85s
Driver's license renewal fee	renew	12.00	1/94	84s
Identification card, nondriver	card	6.00	1/94	83s
Motorcycle learning permit fee	perm	12.00	1/94	84s
Motorcycle license fee	orig	12.00	1/94	84s
Motorcycle license fee, duplicate	lic	12.00	1/94	84s
Motorcycle license renewal fee	renew	12.00	1/94	84s
Public transportation expenditures	year	375	91	81r
Transportation expenditures, total	year	5527	91	81r
Vehicle finance charges	year	287	91	81r
Vehicle insurance expenditures	year	624	91	81r
Vehicle maintenance and repairs expenditures	year	695	91	81r
Vehicle purchases	year	2174	91	81r
Vehicle rental, leases, licenses, etc. expenditures	year	257	91	81r
Vehicles purchased, other than cars and trucks	year	28	91	81r
Utilities				
Electricity expenditures	year	616	91	81r
Utilities, fuels, and public services, total expenditures	year	1681	91	81r
Water and other public services, expenditures	year	209	91	81r
Weddings				
Bridal attendants' gowns	event	750	10/93	76r
Bridal gown	event	852	10/93	76r
Bridal headpiece and veil	event	167	10/93	76r
Bride's wedding band	event	708	10/93	76r
Clergy	event	224	10/93	76r
Engagement ring	event	2756	10/93	76r
Flowers	event	863	10/93	76r
Formal wear for groom	event	106	10/93	76r
Groom's attendants' formal wear	event	530	10/93	76r
Groom's wedding band	event	402	10/93	76r
Music	event	600	10/93	76r
Photography	event	1088	10/93	76r
Shoes for bride	event	50	10/93	76r
Videography	event	483	10/93	76r
Wedding invitations and announcements	event	342	10/93	76r
Wedding reception	event	7000	10/93	76r

Sumter, SC

Item	Per	Value	Date	Ref.
Composite, ACCRA index		91.60	12/94	2c
Alcoholic Beverages				
Beer, Miller Lite, Bud, 12-oz., ex deposit	6	3.87	12/94	2c
J & B Scotch	750-ml.	18.41	12/94	2c
Wine, Gallo Chablis blanc	1.5-lit	4.43	12/94	2c
Clothing				
Jeans, man's denim		38.46	12/94	2c
Shirt, man's dress shirt		29.17	12/94	2c
Undervest, boy's size 10-14, cotton	3	3.98	12/94	2c
Communications				
Newspaper subscription, dly. and Sun. delivery	month	12.59	12/94	2c
Telephone bill, family of four	month	22.53	12/94	2c
Energy and Fuels				
Energy, combined forms, 1800 sq. ft.	mo.	119.15	12/94	2c
Gas, reg unlead, taxes inc., cash, self-service	gal	1.07	12/94	2c
Entertainment				
Bowling, evening rate	game	2.50	12/94	2c
Monopoly game, Parker Brothers', No. 9	game	10.92	12/94	2c
Movie	adm	5.25	12/94	2c
Tennis balls, yellow, Wilson or Penn, 3	can	2.43	12/94	2c
Groceries				
Groceries, ACCRA Index		96.80	12/94	2c
Baby food, strained vegetables, lowest price	4-4.5 oz.	0.34	12/94	2c
Bananas	lb.	0.51	12/94	2c
Beef or hamburger, ground	lb.	1.74	12/94	2c
Bread, white	24-oz.	0.70	12/94	2c
Cheese, Kraft grated Parmesan	8-oz.	3.13	12/94	2c
Chicken, whole fryer	lb.	0.87	12/94	2c
Cigarettes, Winston, Kings	carton	13.09	12/94	2c
Coffee, vacuum-packed	13 oz.	3.37	12/94	2c
Corn Flakes, Kellogg's or Post Toasties	18 oz.	2.35	12/94	2c
Corn, frozen, whole kernel, lowest price	10 oz.	0.64	12/94	2c
Eggs, Grade A large	dozen	0.86	12/94	2c
Lettuce, iceberg	head	0.99	12/94	2c
Margarine, Blue Bonnet or Parkay cubes	lb.	0.55	12/94	2c
Milk, whole	1/2 gal.	1.38	12/94	2c
Orange juice, Minute Maid frozen	12-oz.	1.09	12/94	2c
Peaches, halves or slices, Hunt's, Del Monte, or Libby's	29-oz.	1.23	12/94	2c
Peas, sweet, Del Monte or Green Giant	15-17 oz.	0.50	12/94	2c
Potatoes, white or red	10-lb. sack	1.97	12/94	2c
Sausage, Jimmy Dean, 100% pork	lb.	2.23	12/94	2c
Shortening, vegetable, Crisco	3-lb.	2.55	12/94	2c
Soft drink, Coca Cola, ex deposit	2 lit	1.15	12/94	2c
Steak, t-bone	lb.	4.97	12/94	2c
Sugar, cane or beet	4 lbs.	1.51	12/94	2c
Tomatoes, Hunt's or Del Monte	14.5 oz.	0.58	12/94	2c
Tuna, chunk, light, oil-packed	6.125-6.5 oz.	0.64	12/94	2c
Goods and Services				
Miscellaneous goods and services, ACCRA Index		97.10	12/94	2c
Health Care				
Health care, ACCRA Index		89.80	12/94	2c
Antibiotic ointment, Polysporin	1.5 oz.	4.21	12/94	2c
Dentist's fee, adult teeth cleaning and periodic oral exam	visit	51.80	12/94	2c
Doctor's fee, routine exam, established patient	visit	40.25	12/94	2c
Hospital care, semiprivate room	day	208.00	12/94	2c

Values are in dollars or fractions of dollars. In the column headed *Ref*, references are shown to sources. Each reference is followed by a letter. These refer to the geographical level for which data were reported: s = State, r = Region, and c = City or metro. The abbreviation *ex* is used to mean *except* or *excluding*; *exp* stands for expenditures. For other abbreviations and further explanations, please see the Introduction.

Sumter, SC - continued

Item	Per	Value	Date	Ref.
Household Goods				
Appl. repair, service call, wash mach	min. lab. chg.	35.42	12/94	2c
Laundry detergent, Tide Ultra, Bold, or Cheer	42 oz.	3.27	12/94	2c
Tissues, facial, Kleenex brand	175	0.95	12/94	2c
Housing				
Housing, ACCRA Index		75.60	12/94	2c
House payment, principal and interest, 25% down payment	mo.	572	12/94	2c
House, 1800 sq ft, 8000 sq ft lot, new, urban, utilities	total	94000	12/94	2c
Mtge. rate, incl. points and orig. fee, 30-year conv. fixed or ARM	mo.	9.09	12/94	2c
Rent, apartment, 2 br., 1 1/2-2 baths, unfurnished, 950 sq ft, water	mo.	421	12/94	2c
Personal Goods				
Shampoo, Alberto VO5	15-oz.	0.99	12/94	2c
Toothpaste, Crest or Colgate	6-7 oz.	1.90	12/94	2c
Personal Services				
Dry cleaning, man's 2-pc. suit		6.10	12/94	2c
Haircut, man's barbershop, no styling		7.40	12/94	2c
Haircut, woman's shampoo, trim, blow-dry		18.80	12/94	2c
Restaurant Food				
Chicken, fried, thigh and drumstick		2.04	12/94	2c
Hamburger with cheese	1/4 lb.	0.99	12/94	2c
Pizza, Pizza Hut or Pizza Inn	12-13 in.	7.52	12/94	2c
Transportation				
Transportation, ACCRA Index		99.20	12/94	2c
Tire balance, computer or spin bal., front	wheel	7.09	12/94	2c
Utilities				
Utilities, ACCRA Index		107.40	12/94	2c
Electricity, 1800 sq. ft., new home	mo.	119.15	12/94	2c

Syracuse, NY

Item	Per	Value	Date	Ref.
Composite, ACCRA index		104.60	12/94	2c
Alcoholic Beverages				
Beer, Miller Lite, Bud, 12-oz., ex deposit	6	4.37	12/94	2c
J & B Scotch	750-ml.	17.59	12/94	2c
Wine, Gallo Chablis blanc	1.5-lit	5.49	12/94	2c
Appliances				
Appliances (major), expenditures	year	145	91	81r
Average annual exp.				
Food, health care, personal goods, services	year	29496	91	81r
Charity				
Cash contributions, expenditures	year	708	91	81r
Clothing				
Apparel, men and boys, total expenditures	year	416	91	81r
Apparel, women and girls, total expenditures	year	744	91	81r
Footwear, expenditures	year	305	91	81r
Jeans, man's denim		36.79	12/94	2c
Shirt, man's dress shirt		28.60	12/94	2c
Undervest, boy's size 10-14, cotton	3	4.21	12/94	2c
Communications				
Long-distance telephone rate, day, addl. min., 1-10 mi.	min.	4.00	12/93	9s
Long-distance telephone rate, day, initial min., 1-10 mi.	min.	14.90	12/93	9s
Newspaper subscription, dly. and Sun. delivery	month	15.65	12/94	2c
Phone line, single, business, field visit	inst	143.26	12/93	9s
Phone line, single, business, no field visit	inst	106.05	12/93	9s

Syracuse, NY - continued

Item	Per	Value	Date	Ref.
Communications - continued				
Phone line, single, residence, field visit	inst	85.46	12/93	9s
Phone line, single, residence, no field visit	inst	55.00	12/93	9s
Telephone bill, family of four	month	34.75	12/94	2c
Telephone service, expenditures	year	589	91	81r
Telephone, residential, flat rate	mo.	20.16	12/93	8c
Education				
Board, 4-year private college/university	year	2918	8/94	80s
Board, 4-year public college/university	year	2177	8/94	80s
Education, total expenditures	year	593	91	81r
Room, 4-year private college/university	year	3302	8/94	80s
Room, 4-year public college/university	year	2624	8/94	80s
Total cost, 4-year private college/university	year	18451	8/94	80s
Total cost, 4-year public college/university	year	7723	8/94	80s
Tuition, 2-year public college/university, in-state	year	2112	8/94	80s
Tuition, 4-year private college/university, in-state	year	12231	8/94	80s
Tuition, 4-year public college/university, in-state	year	2921	8/94	80s
Energy and Fuels				
Energy, combined forms, 1800 sq. ft.	mo.	153.78	12/94	2c
Energy, exc. electricity, 1800 sq. ft.	mo.	67.42	12/94	2c
Fuel oil and other fuels, expenditures	year	257	91	81r
Gas, cooking, winter, 10 therms	month	12.51	2/94	65c
Gas, cooking, winter, 30 therms	month	28.80	2/94	65c
Gas, cooking, winter, 50 therms	month	42.93	2/94	65c
Gas, heating, winter, 100 therms	month	73.18	2/94	65c
Gas, heating, winter, average use	month	169.66	2/94	65c
Gas, natural, expenditures	year	285	91	81r
Gas, reg unlead, taxes inc., cash, self-service	gal	1.22	12/94	2c
Gasoline and motor oil purchased	year	867	91	81r
Gasoline, unleaded midgrade	gallon	1.32	4/93	82r
Gasoline, unleaded premium	gallon	1.40	4/93	82r
Gasoline, unleaded regular	gallon	1.19	4/93	82r
Entertainment				
Bowling, evening rate	game	2.13	12/94	2c
Entertainment, total expenditures	year	1331	91	81r
Fees and admissions, expenditures	year	398	91	81r
Monopoly game, Parker Brothers', No. 9	game	11.14	12/94	2c
Movie	adm	6.31	12/94	2c
Pets, toys, playground equipment, expenditures	year	270	91	81r
Reading, expenditures	year	171	91	81r
Televisions, radios, and sound equipment, expenditures	year	429	91	81r
Tennis balls, yellow, Wilson or Penn, 3	can	2.41	12/94	2c
Funerals				
Burial, immediate, container provided by funeral home		1370.36	1/95	54r
Cards, acknowledgment		17.72	1/95	54r
Casket, minimum alternative		192.52	1/95	54r
Cosmetology, hair care, etc.		139.56	1/95	54r
Cremation, direct, container provided by funeral home		1049.24	1/95	54r
Embalming		387.57	1/95	54r
Funeral, funeral home		278.77	1/95	54r
Funeral, other facility		275.85	1/95	54r
Graveside service		213.08	1/95	54r
Hearse, local		157.27	1/95	54r
Limousine, local		146.45	1/95	54r
Memorial service		271.02	1/95	54r
Service charge, professional, nondeclinable		943.58	1/95	54r
Visitation and viewing		322.86	1/95	54r
Groceries				
Groceries, ACCRA Index		107.50	12/94	2c
Apples, Red Delicious	lb.	0.78	12/94	82r
Baby food, strained vegetables, lowest price	4-4.5 oz.	0.42	12/94	2c

Values are in dollars or fractions of dollars. In the column headed *Ref*, references are shown to sources. Each reference is followed by a letter. These refer to the geographical level for which data were reported: s=State, r=Region, and c=City or metro. The abbreviation *ex* is used to mean *except* or *excluding*; *exp* stands for expenditures. For other abbreviations and further explanations, please see the Introduction.

Syracuse, NY - continued

Item	Per	Value	Date	Ref.
Groceries				
Bacon, sliced	lb.	2.24	12/94	82r
Bananas	lb.	0.52	12/94	2c
Bananas	lb.	0.49	12/94	82r
Beef or hamburger, ground	lb.	1.63	12/94	2c
Beef purchases	year	226	91	81r
Beverage purchases, alcoholic	year	332	91	81r
Beverage purchases, nonalcoholic	year	213	91	81r
Bread, white	24-oz.	0.81	12/94	2c
Bread, white, pan	lb.	0.80	12/94	82r
Butter, salted, Grade AA, stick	lb.	1.67	12/94	82r
Carrots, short trimmed and topped	lb.	0.51	12/94	82r
Cereals and bakery products purchases	year	407	91	81r
Cereals and cereals products purchases	year	132	91	81r
Cheese, Kraft grated Parmesan	8-oz.	3.13	12/94	2c
Chicken breast, bone-in	lb.	2.22	12/94	82r
Chicken, fresh, whole	lb.	1.05	12/94	82r
Chicken, whole fryer	lb.	0.93	12/94	2c
Chuck roast, USDA choice, boneless	lb.	2.74	12/94	82r
Cigarettes, Winston, Kings	carton	19.73	12/94	2c
Coffee, 100%, ground roast, all sizes	lb.	4.61	12/94	82r
Coffee, vacuum-packed	13 oz.	3.63	12/94	2c
Corn Flakes, Kellogg's or Post Toasties	18 oz.	2.29	12/94	2c
Corn, frozen, whole kernel, lowest price	10 oz.	0.69	12/94	2c
Dairy products (other) purchases	year	161	91	81r
Eggs, Grade A large	dozen	0.93	12/94	2c
Eggs, Grade A large	dozen	1.12	12/94	82r
Fish and seafood purchases	year	112	91	81r
Food purchases, food eaten at home	year	2599	91	81r
Foods purchased away from home, not prepared by consumer	year	2024	91	81r
Fruits and vegetables purchases	year	444	91	81r
Grapefruit	lb.	0.44	12/94	82r
Grapes, Thompson seedless	lb.	2.24	12/94	82r
Ground chuck, 100% beef	lb.	1.67	12/94	82r
Ice cream, prepackaged, bulk, regular	1/2 gal.	2.93	12/94	82r
Lemons	lb.	1.06	12/94	82r
Lettuce, iceberg	lb.	0.92	12/94	82r
Lettuce, iceberg	head	0.83	12/94	2c
Margarine, Blue Bonnet or Parkay cubes	lb.	0.71	12/94	2c
Meats, poultry, fish, and eggs purchases	year	751	91	81r
Milk and cream (fresh) purchases	year	152	91	81r
Milk, whole	1/2 gal.	1.13	12/94	2c
Orange juice, frozen concentrate 12-oz. can	16 oz.	1.92	12/94	82r
Orange juice, Minute Maid frozen	12-oz.	1.23	12/94	2c
Oranges, Navel	lb.	0.56	12/94	82r
Peaches, halves or slices, Hunt's, Del Monte, or Libby's	29-oz.	1.51	12/94	2c
Peas, sweet, Del Monte or Green Giant	15-17 oz.	0.69	12/94	2c
Pork chops, center cut, bone-in	lb.	3.09	12/94	82r
Pork purchases	year	130	91	81r
Potatoes, white	lb.	0.37	12/94	82r
Potatoes, white or red	10-lb. sack	1.99	12/94	2c
Rib roast, USDA choice, bone-in	lb.	4.98	12/94	82r
Round roast, USDA choice, boneless	lb.	2.93	12/94	82r
Sausage, Jimmy Dean, 100% pork	lb.	2.84	12/94	2c
Shortening, vegetable oil blends	lb.	1.03	12/94	82r
Shortening, vegetable, Crisco	3-lb.	2.55	12/94	2c
Soft drink, Coca Cola, ex deposit	2 lit	1.13	12/94	2c
Spaghetti and macaroni	lb.	0.84	12/94	82r
Steak, round, USDA choice, boneless	lb.	3.48	12/94	82r
Steak, sirloin, USDA choice, bone-in	lb.	3.38	12/94	82r
Steak, sirloin, USDA choice, boneless	lb.	4.81	12/94	82r
Steak, t-bone	lb.	5.51	12/94	2c
Sugar and other sweets, eaten at home, expenditures	year	89	91	81r
Sugar, cane or beet	4 lbs.	1.45	12/94	2c
Sugar, white, all sizes	lb.	0.46	12/94	82r

Syracuse, NY - continued

Item	Per	Value	Date	Ref.
Groceries - continued				
Tobacco products and smoking supplies, total expenditures	year	279	91	81r
Tomatoes, field grown	lb.	1.56	12/94	82r
Tomatoes, Hunt's or Del Monte	14.5 oz.	0.78	12/94	2c
Tuna, chunk, light	lb.	2.09	12/94	82r
Tuna, chunk, light, oil-packed	6.125-6.5 oz.	0.82	12/94	2c
Goods and Services				
Miscellaneous goods and services, ACCRA Index		104.20	12/94	2c
Health Care				
Health care, ACCRA Index		109.80	12/94	2c
Antibiotic ointment, Polysporin	1.5 oz.	3.99	12/94	2c
Childbirth, Cesarean delivery, hospital charge	birth	6334.00	12/91	69r
Childbirth, Cesarean delivery, physician charge	birth	2234.00	12/91	69r
Childbirth, normal delivery, hospital charge	birth	3225.00	12/91	69r
Childbirth, normal delivery, physician charge	birth	1623.00	12/91	69r
Dentist's fee, adult teeth cleaning and periodic oral exam	visit	55.17	12/94	2c
Doctor's fee, routine exam, established patient	visit	45.25	12/94	2c
Drugs, expenditures	year	205	91	81r
Health care, total expenditures	year	1396	91	81r
Health insurance expenditures	year	553	91	81r
Hospital care, semiprivate room	day	464.25	12/94	2c
Insurance premium, family medical care	month	384.24	1/95	41s
Medical services expenditures	year	559	91	81r
Medical supplies expenditures	year	80	91	81r
Household Goods				
Appl. repair, service call, wash mach	min. lab. chg.	30.39	12/94	2c
Floor coverings, expenditures	year	158	91	81r
Furniture, expenditures	year	341	91	81r
Household equipment, misc. expenditures	year	363	91	81r
Household expenditures, miscellaneous	year	194	91	81r
Household furnishings and equipment, expenditures	year	1158	91	81r
Household operations expenditures	year	378	91	81r
Household textiles, expenditures	year	88	91	81r
Housekeeping supplies, expenditures	year	426	91	81r
Laundry and cleaning supplies, expenditures	year	122	91	81r
Laundry detergent, Tide Ultra, Bold, or Cheer	42 oz.	3.63	12/94	2c
Postage and stationery, expenditures	year	134	91	81r
Tissues, facial, Kleenex brand	175	1.11	12/94	2c
Housing				
Housing, ACCRA Index		90.70	12/94	2c
Add garage/carport		11,614	3/95	74r
Add room(s)		16,816	3/95	74r
Apartment condominium or co-op, median	unit	96700	12/94	62r
Dwellings (owned), expenditures	year	3305	91	81r
Enclose porch/patio/breezeway		2,980	3/95	74r
Finish room in basement/attic		4,330	3/95	74r
Home, existing, single-family, median	unit	161600	12/94	62r
Home, existing, single-family, median	unit	81.40	12/94	62c
House payment, principal and interest, 25% down payment	mo.	684	12/94	2c
House, 1800 sq ft, 8000 sq ft lot, new, urban, utilities	total	111525	12/94	2c
Maintenance, repairs, insurance, and other housing expenditures	year	569	91	81r
Mortgage interest and charges expenditures	year	1852	91	81r
Mtge. rate, incl. points and orig. fee, 30-year conv. fixed or ARM	mo.	9.19	12/94	2c

Values are in dollars or fractions of dollars. In the column headed *Ref*, references are shown to sources. Each reference is followed by a letter. These refer to the geographical level for which data were reported: s=State, r=Region, and c=City or metro. The abbreviation *ex* is used to mean *except* or *excluding*; *exp* stands for expenditures. For other abbreviations and further explanations, please see the Introduction.

Syracuse, NY - continued

Item	Per	Value	Date	Ref.
Housing				
Princ. & int., mortgage, median-price exist. sing.-family home	mo.	765	12/94	62r
Property taxes expenditures	year	884	91	81r
Redesign, restructure more than half of home's interior		2,750	3/95	74r
Rent, apartment, 2 br., 1 1/2-2 baths, unfurnished, 950 sq ft, water	mo.	509	12/94	2c
Rental units expenditures	year	1832	91	81r
Insurance and Pensions				
Auto insurance, private passenger	year	985.07	12/94	71s
Insurance and pensions, personal, expenditures	year	2690	91	81r
Insurance, life and other personal, expenditures	year	341	91	81r
Pensions and Social Security, expenditures	year	2349	91	81r
Legal Assistance				
Estate planning, law-firm partner	hr.	375.00	10/93	12r
Legal work, law firm associate	hour	78		10r
Legal work, law firm partner	hour	183		10r
Personal Goods				
Shampoo, Alberto VO5	15-oz.	1.27	12/94	2c
Toothpaste, Crest or Colgate	6-7 oz.	2.11	12/94	2c
Personal Services				
Dry cleaning, man's 2-pc. suit		7.04	12/94	2c
Haircut, man's barbershop, no styling		7.17	12/94	2c
Haircut, woman's shampoo, trim, blow-dry		16.29	12/94	2c
Personal services expenditures	year	184	91	81r
Restaurant Food				
Chicken, fried, thigh and drumstick		2.51	12/94	2c
Dining expenditures, family	week	34.26	94	73r
Hamburger with cheese	1/4 lb.	1.91	12/94	2c
Pizza, Pizza Hut or Pizza Inn	12-13 in.	7.49	12/94	2c
Taxes				
Taxes, Federal income, expenditures	year	2409	91	81r
Taxes, personal, expenditures	year	3094	91	81r
Taxes, State and local income, expenditures	year	620	91	81r
Transportation				
Transportation, ACCRA Index		107.10	12/94	2c
Bus fare, one-way	trip	1.00	12/95	1c
Bus fare, up to 10 miles	one-way	1.00	12/94	2c
Cars and trucks purchased, new	year	1170	91	81r
Cars and trucks purchased, used	year	739	91	81r
Driver's learning permit fee	perm	10.00	1/94	84s
Driver's license fee	orig	32.00-37.00	1/94	84s
Driver's license fee, duplicate	lic	7.25	1/94	84s
Driver's license reinstatement fee, min.	susp	25.00	1/94	85s
Driver's license renewal fee	renew	22.25	1/94	84s
Identification card, nondriver	card	6.25	1/94	83s
Motorcycle license fee	orig	32.00-37.00	1/94	84s
Motorcycle license fee, duplicate	lic	7.25	1/94	84s
Motorcycle license renewal fee	renew	22.25	1/94	84s
Public transportation expenditures	year	430	91	81r
Tire balance, computer or spin bal., front	wheel	7.18	12/94	2c
Transportation expenditures, total	year	4810	91	81r
Vehicle finance charges	year	238	91	81r
Vehicle insurance expenditures	year	630	91	81r
Vehicle maintenance and repairs expenditures	year	532	91	81r
Vehicle purchases	year	1920	91	81r
Vehicle rental, leases, licenses, etc. expenditures	year	193	91	81r
Vehicles purchased, other than cars and trucks	year	11	91	81r

Syracuse, NY - continued

Item	Per	Value	Date	Ref.
Utilities				
Utilities, ACCRA Index		142.60	12/94	2c
Electricity expenditures	year	695	91	81r
Electricity, (part.), other, 1800 sq. ft., new home	mo.	86.36	12/94	2c
Utilities, fuels, and public services, total expenditures	year	1981	91	81r
Water and other public services, expenditures	year	154	91	81r
Weddings				
Bridal attendants' gowns	event	750	10/93	76r
Bridal gown	event	852	10/93	76r
Bridal headpiece and veil	event	167	10/93	76r
Bride's wedding band	event	708	10/93	76r
Clergy	event	224	10/93	76r
Engagement ring	event	2756	10/93	76r
Flowers	event	863	10/93	76r
Formal wear for groom	event	106	10/93	76r
Groom's attendants' formal wear	event	530	10/93	76r
Groom's wedding band	event	402	10/93	76r
Music	event	600	10/93	76r
Photography	event	1088	10/93	76r
Shoes for bride	event	50	10/93	76r
Videography	event	483	10/93	76r
Wedding invitations and announcements	event	342	10/93	76r
Wedding reception	event	7000	10/93	76r

Tacoma, WA

Item	Per	Value	Date	Ref.
Composite, ACCRA index		104.00	12/94	2c
Alcoholic Beverages				
Beer, Miller Lite, Bud, 12-oz., ex deposit	6	3.93	12/94	2c
J & B Scotch	750-ml.	18.95	12/94	2c
Wine, Gallo Chablis blanc	1.5-lit	4.62	12/94	2c
Appliances				
Appliances (major), expenditures	year	160	91	81r
Average annual exp.				
Food, health care, personal goods, services	year	32461	91	81r
Charity				
Cash contributions, expenditures	year	975	91	81r
Clothing				
Apparel, men and boys, total expenditures	year	467	91	81r
Apparel, women and girls, total expenditures	year	737	91	81r
Footwear, expenditures	year	270	91	81r
Jeans, man's denim		37.59	12/94	2c
Shirt, man's dress shirt		29.59	12/94	2c
Undervest, boy's size 10-14, cotton	3	4.45	12/94	2c
Communications				
Long-distance telephone rate, day, addl. min., 1-10 mi.	min.	0.01	12/93	9s
Long-distance telephone rate, day, initial min., 1-10 mi.	min.	0.15	12/93	9s
Newspaper subscription, dly. and Sun. delivery	month	10.00	12/94	2c
Phone line, single, business, field visit	inst	48.00	12/93	9s
Phone line, single, business, no field visit	inst	48.00	12/93	9s
Phone line, single, residence, field visit	inst	31.00	12/93	9s
Phone line, single, residence, no field visit	inst	31.00	12/93	9s
Telephone bill, family of four	month	17.23	12/94	2c
Telephone service, expenditures	year	611	91	81r
Telephone, residential, flat rate	mo.	10.75	12/93	8c
Education				
Board, 4-year private college/university	year	1928	8/94	80s
Board, 4-year public college/university	year	2194	8/94	80s
Education, total expenditures	year	375	91	81r
Room, 4-year private college/university	year	2455	8/94	80s
Room, 4-year public college/university	year	1952	8/94	80s

Values are in dollars or fractions of dollars. In the column headed *Ref*, references are shown to sources. Each reference is followed by a letter. These refer to the geographical level for which data were reported: s = State, r = Region, and c = City or metro. The abbreviation *ex* is used to mean *except* or *excluding*; *exp* stands for expenditures. For other abbreviations and further explanations, please see the Introduction.

Tacoma, WA - continued

Item	Per	Value	Date	Ref.
Education				
Total cost, 4-year private college/university	year	16332	8/94	80s
Total cost, 4-year public college/university	year	6483	8/94	80s
Tuition, 2-year public college/university, in-state	year	1141	8/94	80s
Tuition, 4-year private college/university, in-state	year	11949	8/94	80s
Tuition, 4-year public college/university, in-state	year	2337	8/94	80s
Energy and Fuels				
Energy, combined forms, 1800 sq. ft.	mo.	68.50	12/94	2c
Fuel oil and other fuels, expenditures	year	33	91	81r
Gas, natural, expenditures	year	212	91	81r
Gas, reg unlead, taxes inc., cash, self-service	gal	1.24	12/94	2c
Gasoline and motor oil purchased	year	1115	91	81r
Gasoline, unleaded midgrade	gallon	1.36	4/93	82r
Gasoline, unleaded premium	gallon	1.43	4/93	82r
Gasoline, unleaded regular	gallon	1.23	4/93	82r
Entertainment				
Bowling, evening rate	game	1.70	12/94	2c
Concert ticket, Pearl Jam group	perf	20.00	94	50r
Entertainment, total expenditures	year	1853	91	81r
Fees and admissions, expenditures	year	482	91	81r
Monopoly game, Parker Brothers', No. 9	game	9.99	12/94	2c
Movie	adm	6.65	12/94	2c
Pets, toys, playground equipment, expenditures	year	299	91	81r
Reading, expenditures	year	164	91	81r
Televisions, radios, and sound equipment, expenditures	year	528	91	81r
Tennis balls, yellow, Wilson or Penn, 3	can	2.15	12/94	2c
Funerals				
Burial, immediate, container provided by funeral home		1382.70	1/95	54r
Cards, acknowledgment		21.87	1/95	54r
Casket, minimum alternative		128.54	1/95	54r
Cosmetology, hair care, etc.		119.69	1/95	54r
Cremation, direct, container provided by funeral home		1030.62	1/95	54r
Embalming		255.42	1/95	54r
Funeral, funeral home		437.38	1/95	54r
Funeral, other facility		444.46	1/95	54r
Graveside service		338.46	1/95	54r
Hearse, local		147.50	1/95	54r
Limousine, local		130.33	1/95	54r
Memorial service		553.16	1/95	54r
Service charge, professional, nondeclinable		859.15	1/95	54r
Visitation and viewing		93.23	1/95	54r
Groceries				
Groceries, ACCRA Index		111.00	12/94	2c
Apples, Red Delicious	lb.	0.72	12/94	82r
Baby food, strained vegetables, lowest price	4-4.5 oz.	0.25	12/94	2c
Bacon, sliced	lb.	1.73	12/94	82r
Bananas	lb.	0.59	12/94	2c
Bananas	lb.	0.52	12/94	82r
Beef or hamburger, ground	lb.	1.69	12/94	2c
Beef purchases	year	241	91	81r
Beverage purchases, alcoholic	year	328	91	81r
Beverage purchases, nonalcoholic	year	234	91	81r
Bologna, all beef or mixed	lb.	2.33	12/94	82r
Bread, white	24-oz.	0.59	12/94	2c
Bread, white, pan	lb.	0.81	12/94	82r
Carrots, short trimmed and topped	lb.	0.43	12/94	82r
Cereals and bakery products purchases	year	392	91	81r
Cereals and cereals products purchases	year	139	91	81r
Cheese, Kraft grated Parmesan	8-oz.	3.88	12/94	2c
Chicken breast, bone-in	lb.	2.04	12/94	82r
Chicken, fresh, whole	lb.	0.95	12/94	82r
Chicken, whole fryer	lb.	1.11	12/94	2c

Tacoma, WA - continued

Item	Per	Value	Date	Ref.
Groceries - continued				
Cigarettes, Winston, Kings	carton	20.89	12/94	2c
Coffee, 100%, ground roast, all sizes	lb.	4.48	12/94	82r
Coffee, vacuum-packed	13 oz.	4.14	12/94	2c
Corn Flakes, Kellogg's or Post Toasties	18 oz.	2.99	12/94	2c
Corn, frozen, whole kernel, lowest price	10 oz.	0.79	12/94	2c
Dairy products (other) purchases	year	182	91	81r
Eggs, Grade A large	dozen	0.99	12/94	2c
Fish and seafood purchases	year	94	91	81r
Flour, white, all purpose	lb.	0.21	12/94	82r
Food purchases, food eaten at home	year	2749	91	81r
Foods purchased away from home, not prepared by consumer	year	1909	91	81r
Fruits and vegetables purchases	year	459	91	81r
Grapefruit	lb.	0.56	12/94	82r
Ground beef, 100% beef	lb.	1.31	12/94	82r
Ham, boneless, exc. canned	lb.	2.46	12/94	82r
Ice cream, prepackaged, bulk, regular	1/2 gal.	2.57	12/94	82r
Lemons	lb.	1.00	12/94	82r
Lettuce, iceberg	lb.	0.93	12/94	82r
Lettuce, iceberg	head	0.78	12/94	2c
Margarine, Blue Bonnet or Parkay cubes	lb.	0.85	12/94	2c
Meats, poultry, fish, and eggs purchases	year	700	91	81r
Milk and cream (fresh) purchases	year	155	91	81r
Milk, whole	1/2 gal.	1.49	12/94	2c
Orange juice, frozen concentrate 12-oz. can	16 oz.	1.52	12/94	82r
Orange juice, Minute Maid frozen	12-oz.	1.42	12/94	2c
Oranges, Navel	lb.	0.56	12/94	82r
Peaches, halves or slices, Hunt's, Del Monte, or Libby's	29-oz.	1.54	12/94	2c
Peas, sweet, Del Monte or Green Giant	15-17 oz.	0.69	12/94	2c
Pork chops, center cut, bone-in	lb.	3.30	12/94	82r
Pork purchases	year	122	91	81r
Potato chips	16-oz.	3.03	12/94	82r
Potatoes, frozen, French fried	lb.	0.77	12/94	82r
Potatoes, white	lb.	0.35	12/94	82r
Potatoes, white or red	10-lb. sack	1.85	12/94	2c
Rice, white, long grain, uncooked	lb.	0.54	12/94	82r
Round roast, USDA choice, boneless	lb.	2.92	12/94	82r
Sausage, Jimmy Dean, 100% pork	lb.	2.71	12/94	2c
Shortening, vegetable oil blends	lb.	0.80	12/94	82r
Shortening, vegetable, Crisco	3-lb.	2.79	12/94	2c
Soft drink, Coca Cola, ex deposit	2 lit	1.21	12/94	2c
Spaghetti and macaroni	lb.	1.02	12/94	82r
Steak, round, graded & ungraded, exc. USDA prime & choice	lb.	3.13	12/94	82r
Steak, sirloin, USDA choice, boneless	lb.	4.07	12/94	82r
Steak, t-bone	lb.	5.41	12/94	2c
Sugar and other sweets, eaten at home, expenditures	year	105	91	81r
Sugar, cane or beet	4 lbs.	1.42	12/94	2c
Sugar, white, all sizes	lb.	0.38	12/94	82r
Tobacco products and smoking supplies, total expenditures	year	221	91	81r
Tomatoes, field grown	lb.	1.45	12/94	82r
Tomatoes, Hunt's or Del Monte	14.5 oz.	0.77	12/94	2c
Tuna, chunk, light	lb.	2.18	12/94	82r
Tuna, chunk, light, oil-packed	6.125-6.5 oz.	1.06	12/94	2c
Goods and Services				
Miscellaneous goods and services, ACCRA Index		101.40	12/94	2c
Health Care				
Health care, ACCRA Index		144.60	12/94	2c
Antibiotic ointment, Polysporin	1.5 oz.	4.26	12/94	2c
Childbirth, Cesarean delivery, hospital charge	birth	6059.00	12/91	69r

Values are in dollars or fractions of dollars. In the column headed *Ref*, references are shown to sources. Each reference is followed by a letter. These refer to the geographical level for which data were reported: s = State, r = Region, and c = City or metro. The abbreviation *ex* is used to mean *except* or *excluding*; *exp* stands for *expenditures*. For other abbreviations and further explanations, please see the Introduction.

Tacoma, WA - continued

Item	Per	Value	Date	Ref.
Health Care				
Childbirth, Cesarean delivery, physician charge	birth	2248.00	12/91	69r
Childbirth, normal delivery, hospital charge	birth	3006.00	12/91	69r
Childbirth, normal delivery, physician charge	birth	1634.00	12/91	69r
Dentist's fee, adult teeth cleaning and periodic oral exam	visit	95.00	12/94	2c
Doctor's fee, routine exam, established patient	visit	55.00	12/94	2c
Drugs, expenditures	year	230	91	81r
Health care, total expenditures	year	1544	91	81r
Health insurance expenditures	year	558	91	81r
Hospital care, semiprivate room	day	448.33	12/94	2c
Insurance premium, family medical care	month	382.32	1/95	41s
Medical services expenditures	year	676	91	81r
Medical supplies expenditures	year	80	91	81r
Surgery, open-heart	proc	37818.00	1/93	14r
Household Goods				
Appl. repair, service call, wash mach	min. lab. chg.	29.07	12/94	2c
Floor coverings, expenditures	year	79	91	81r
Furniture, expenditures	year	352	91	81r
Household equipment, misc. expenditures	year	614	91	81r
Household expenditures, miscellaneous	year	294	91	81r
Household furnishings and equipment, expenditures	year	1416	91	81r
Household operations expenditures	year	580	91	81r
Household textiles, expenditures	year	113	91	81r
Housekeeping supplies, expenditures	year	447	91	81r
Laundry and cleaning supplies, expenditures	year	114	91	81r
Laundry detergent, Tide Ultra, Bold, or Cheer	42 oz.	4.09	12/94	2c
Postage and stationery, expenditures	year	145	91	81r
Tissues, facial, Kleenex brand	175	1.16	12/94	2c
Housing				
Housing, ACCRA Index		103.80	12/94	2c
Add garage/carport		6,422	3/95	74r
Add room(s)		26,583	3/95	74r
Apartment condominium or co-op, median	unit	105300	12/94	62r
Dwellings (owned), expenditures	year	3932	91	81r
Enclose porch/patio/breezeway		5,382	3/95	74r
Finish room in basement/attic		3,911	3/95	74r
Home, existing, single-family, median	unit	178600	12/94	62r
Home, existing, single-family, median	unit	119.40	12/94	62c
House payment, principal and interest, 25% down payment	mo.	870	12/94	2c
House, 1800 sq ft, 8000 sq ft lot, new, urban, utilities	total	139790	12/94	2c
Maintenance, repairs, insurance, and other housing expenditures	year	591	91	81r
Mortgage interest and charges expenditures	year	2747	91	81r
Mtge. rate, incl. points and orig. fee, 30-year conv. fixed or ARM	mo.	9.35	12/94	2c
Princ. & int., mortgage, median-price exist. sing.-family home	mo.	845	12/94	62r
Property taxes expenditures	year	594	91	81r
Redesign, restructure more than half of home's interior		5,467	3/95	74r
Rent, apartment, 2 br., 1 1/2-2 baths, unfurnished, 950 sq ft, water	mo.	721	12/94	2c
Rental units expenditures	year	2077	91	81r
Insurance and Pensions				
Auto insurance, private passenger	year	711.57	12/94	71s
Insurance and pensions, personal, expenditures	year	3042	91	81r
Insurance, life and other personal, expenditures	year	298	91	81r
Pensions and Social Security, expenditures	year	2744	91	81r

Tacoma, WA - continued

Item	Per	Value	Date	Ref.
Legal Assistance				
Legal work, law firm associate	hour	91		10r
Legal work, law firm partner	hour	151		10r
Personal Goods				
Shampoo, Alberto VO5	15-oz.	1.23	12/94	2c
Toothpaste, Crest or Colgate	6-7 oz.	2.47	12/94	2c
Personal Services				
Dry cleaning, man's 2-pc. suit		7.35	12/94	2c
Haircut, man's barbershop, no styling		7.10	12/94	2c
Haircut, woman's shampoo, trim, blow-dry		19.60	12/94	2c
Personal services expenditures	year	286	91	81r
Restaurant Food				
Chicken, fried, thigh and drumstick		2.17	12/94	2c
Dining expenditures, family	week	32.25	94	73r
Hamburger with cheese	1/4 lb.	1.89	12/94	2c
Pizza, Pizza Hut or Pizza Inn	12-13 in.	8.20	12/94	2c
Taxes				
Taxes, Federal income, expenditures	year	2946	91	81r
Taxes, personal, expenditures	year	3791	91	81r
Taxes, State and local income, expenditures	year	791	91	81r
Transportation				
Transportation, ACCRA Index		109.10	12/94	2c
Bus fare, one-way	trip	0.75	12/95	1c
Cars and trucks purchased, new	year	1231	91	81r
Cars and trucks purchased, used	year	915	91	81r
Driver's learning permit fee	perm	4.00	1/94	84s
Driver's license fee	orig	21.00	1/94	84s
Driver's license fee, duplicate	lic	5.00	1/94	84s
Driver's license reinstatement fee, min.	susp	20.00-50.00	1/94	85s
Driver's license renewal fee	renew	14.00	1/94	84s
Identification card, nondriver	card	4.00	1/94	83s
Motorcycle license fee	orig	8.00	1/94	84s
Motorcycle license renewal fee	renew	7.50	1/94	84s
Public transportation expenditures	year	375	91	81r
Tire balance, computer or spin bal., front	wheel	7.27	12/94	2c
Transportation expenditures, total	year	5527	91	81r
Vehicle finance charges	year	287	91	81r
Vehicle insurance expenditures	year	624	91	81r
Vehicle maintenance and repairs expenditures	year	695	91	81r
Vehicle purchases	year	2174	91	81r
Vehicle rental, leases, licenses, etc. expenditures	year	257	91	81r
Vehicles purchased, other than cars and trucks	year	28	91	81r
Utilities				
Utilities, ACCRA Index		64.70	12/94	2c
Electricity expenditures	year	616	91	81r
Electricity, 1800 sq. ft., new home	mo.	68.50	12/94	2c
Utilities, fuels, and public services, total expenditures	year	1681	91	81r
Water and other public services, expenditures	year	209	91	81r
Weddings				
Bridal attendants' gowns	event	750	10/93	76r
Bridal gown	event	852	10/93	76r
Bridal headpiece and veil	event	167	10/93	76r
Bride's wedding band	event	708	10/93	76r
Clergy	event	224	10/93	76r
Engagement ring	event	2756	10/93	76r
Flowers	event	863	10/93	76r
Formal wear for groom	event	106	10/93	76r
Groom's attendants' formal wear	event	530	10/93	76r
Groom's wedding band	event	402	10/93	76r
Music	event	600	10/93	76r
Photography	event	1088	10/93	76r
Shoes for bride	event	50	10/93	76r

Values are in dollars or fractions of dollars. In the column headed *Ref*, references are shown to sources. Each reference is followed by a letter. These refer to the geographical level for which data were reported: s = State, r = Region, and c = City or metro. The abbreviation *ex* is used to mean *except* or *excluding*; *exp* stands for expenditures. For other abbreviations and further explanations, please see the Introduction.

Tacoma, WA - continued

Item	Per	Value	Date	Ref.
Weddings				
Videography	event	483	10/93	76r
Wedding invitations and announcements	event	342	10/93	76r
Wedding reception	event	7000	10/93	76r

Tallahassee, FL

Item	Per	Value	Date	Ref.
Composite, ACCRA index		100.80	12/94	2c
Alcoholic Beverages				
Beer	bottle	2.40	94	34c
Beer, Miller Lite, Bud, 12-oz., ex deposit	6	3.73	12/94	2c
J & B Scotch	750-ml.	16.99	12/94	2c
Wine, Gallo Chablis blanc	1.5-lit	4.71	12/94	2c
Appliances				
Appliances (major), expenditures	year	153	91	81r
Average annual exp.				
Food, health care, personal goods, services	year	27020	91	81r
Charity				
Cash contributions, expenditures	year	839	91	81r
Clothing				
Apparel, men and boys, total expenditures	year	380	91	81r
Apparel, women and girls, total expenditures	year	660	91	81r
Footwear, expenditures	year	193	91	81r
Jeans, man's denim		29.99	12/94	2c
Shirt, man's dress shirt		27.87	12/94	2c
Undervest, boy's size 10-14, cotton	3	6.39	12/94	2c
Communications				
Long-distance telephone rate, day, addl. min., 1-10 mi.	min.	0.08	12/93	9s
Long-distance telephone rate, day, initial min., 1-10 mi.	min.	0.15	12/93	9s
Newspaper subscription, dly. and Sun. delivery	month	13.77	12/94	2c
Phone line, single, business, field visit	inst	86.00	12/93	9s
Phone line, single, business, no field visit	inst	54.50	12/93	9s
Phone line, single, residence, field visit	inst	76.00	12/93	9s
Phone line, single, residence, no field visit	inst	44.50	12/93	9s
Telephone bill, family of four	month	16.51	12/94	2c
Telephone service, expenditures	year	616	91	81r
Education				
Bar examinination preparatory course	course	500.00-100	94	17s
Board, 4-year private college/university	year	2123	8/94	80s
Board, 4-year public college/university	year	2101	8/94	80s
Education, total expenditures	year	319	91	81r
Room, 4-year private college/university	year	2242	8/94	80s
Room, 4-year public college/university	year	1970	8/94	80s
Total cost, 4-year private college/university	year	13853	8/94	80s
Total cost, 4-year public college/university	year	5855	8/94	80s
Tuition, 2-year public college/university, in-state	year	1076	8/94	80s
Tuition, 4-year private college/university, in-state	year	9287	8/94	80s
Tuition, 4-year public college/university, in-state	year	1784	8/94	80s
Energy and Fuels				
Energy, combined forms, 1800 sq. ft.	mo.	106.56	12/94	2c
Energy, exc. electricity, 1800 sq. ft.	mo.	10.19	12/94	2c
Fuel oil and other fuels, expenditures	year	56	91	81r
Gas, natural, expenditures	year	150	91	81r
Gas, reg unlead, taxes inc., cash, self-service	gal	1.15	12/94	2c
Gasoline and motor oil purchased	year	1152	91	81r
Gasoline, unleaded midgrade	gallon	1.21	4/93	82r
Gasoline, unleaded premium	gallon	1.30	4/93	82r
Gasoline, unleaded regular	gallon	1.10	4/93	82r

Tallahassee, FL - continued

Item	Per	Value	Date	Ref.
Entertainment				
Bowling, evening rate	game	2.45	12/94	2c
Concert ticket, Pearl Jam group	perf	20.00	94	50r
Entertainment, total expenditures	year	1266	91	81r
Fees and admissions, expenditures	year	306	91	81r
Monopoly game, Parker Brothers', No. 9	game	10.03	12/94	2c
Movie	adm	5.50	12/94	2c
Pets, toys, playground equipment, expenditures	year	271	91	81r
Reading, expenditures	year	131	91	81r
Televisions, radios, and sound equipment, expenditures	year	439	91	81r
Tennis balls, yellow, Wilson or Penn, 3	can	2.48	12/94	2c
Funerals				
Burial, immediate, container provided by funeral home		1370.36	1/95	54r
Cards, acknowledgment		14.83	1/95	54r
Casket, minimum alternative		192.52	1/95	54r
Cosmetology, hair care, etc.		102.27	1/95	54r
Cremation, direct, container provided by funeral home		1065.64	1/95	54r
Embalming		304.29	1/95	54r
Funeral, funeral home		287.83	1/95	54r
Funeral, other facility		284.14	1/95	54r
Graveside service		349.13	1/95	54r
Hearse, local		132.27	1/95	54r
Limousine, local		98.45	1/95	54r
Memorial service		270.59	1/95	54r
Service charge, professional, nondeclinable		933.59	1/95	54r
Visitation and viewing		225.83	1/95	54r
Groceries				
Groceries, ACCRA Index		97.20	12/94	2c
Apples, Red Delicious	lb.	0.73	12/94	82r
Baby food, strained vegetables, lowest price	4-4.5 oz.	0.35	12/94	2c
Bacon, sliced	lb.	1.67	12/94	82r
Bananas	lb.	0.32	12/94	2c
Bananas	lb.	0.42	12/94	82r
Beef or hamburger, ground	lb.	1.41	12/94	2c
Beef purchases	year	213	91	81r
Beverage purchases, alcoholic	year	249	91	81r
Beverage purchases, nonalcoholic	year	207	91	81r
Big Mac hamburger	burger	0.99	94	34c
Bologna, all beef or mixed	lb.	2.27	12/94	82r
Bread, white	24-oz.	0.79	12/94	2c
Bread, white, pan	lb.	0.68	12/94	82r
Cabbage	lb.	0.42	12/94	82r
Carrots, short trimmed and topped	lb.	0.53	12/94	82r
Cereals and bakery products purchases	year	345	91	81r
Cereals and cereals products purchases	year	127	91	81r
Cheddar cheese, natural	lb.	3.58	12/94	82r
Cheese, Kraft grated Parmesan	8-oz.	3.27	12/94	2c
Chicken breast, bone-in	lb.	1.71	12/94	82r
Chicken, fresh, whole	lb.	0.78	12/94	82r
Chicken, whole fryer	lb.	0.97	12/94	2c
Chuck roast, USDA choice, boneless	lb.	2.26	12/94	82r
Cigarettes, Winston, Kings	carton	16.25	12/94	2c
Coffee, vacuum-packed	13 oz.	3.13	12/94	2c
Corn Flakes, Kellogg's or Post Toasties	18 oz.	2.18	12/94	2c
Corn, frozen, whole kernel, lowest price	10 oz.	0.62	12/94	2c
Crackers, soda, salted	lb.	1.27	12/94	82r
Cucumbers	lb.	0.65	12/94	82r
Dairy products (other) purchases	year	141	91	81r
Eggs, Grade A large	dozen	0.78	12/94	2c
Eggs, Grade A large	dozen	0.87	12/94	82r
Fish and seafood purchases	year	72	91	81r
Flour, white, all purpose	lb.	0.23	12/94	82r
Food purchases, food eaten at home	year	2381	91	81r
Foods purchased away from home, not prepared by consumer	year	1696	91	81r
Frankfurters, all meat or all beef	lb.	1.74	12/94	82r
Fruits and vegetables purchases	year	380	91	81r

Tallahassee, FL - continued

Item	Per	Value	Date	Ref.
Groceries				
Grapefruit	lb.	0.45	12/94	82r
Grapes, Thompson seedless	lb.	2.30	12/94	82r
Ground beef, 100% beef	lb.	1.37	12/94	82r
Ground chuck, 100% beef	lb.	1.97	12/94	82r
Ham, boneless, exc. canned	lb.	2.54	12/94	82r
Ice cream, prepackaged, bulk, regular	1/2 gal.	2.47	12/94	82r
Lemons	lb.	1.02	12/94	82r
Lettuce, iceberg	lb.	0.96	12/94	82r
Lettuce, iceberg	head	0.91	12/94	2c
Margarine, Blue Bonnet or Parkay cubes	lb.	0.56	12/94	2c
Margarine, stick	lb.	0.77	12/94	82r
Meats, poultry, fish, and eggs purchases	year	655	91	81r
Milk and cream (fresh) purchases	year	130	91	81r
Milk, whole	1/2 gal.	1.35	12/94	2c
Orange juice, frozen concentrate 12-oz. can	16 oz.	1.36	12/94	82r
Orange juice, Minute Maid frozen	12-oz.	1.11	12/94	2c
Oranges, Navel	lb.	0.54	12/94	82r
Peaches, halves or slices, Hunt's, Del Monte, or Libby's	29-oz.	1.34	12/94	2c
Pears, Anjou	lb.	0.81	12/94	82r
Peas, sweet, Del Monte or Green Giant	15-17 oz.	0.48	12/94	2c
Pork chops, center cut, bone-in	lb.	3.07	12/94	82r
Pork purchases	year	142	91	81r
Potato chips	16-oz.	3.15	12/94	82r
Potatoes, frozen, French fried	lb.	0.82	12/94	82r
Potatoes, white	lb.	0.34	12/94	82r
Potatoes, white or red	10-lb. sack	2.42	12/94	2c
Rice, white, long grain, uncooked	lb.	0.48	12/94	82r
Round roast, USDA choice, boneless	lb.	2.91	12/94	82r
Sausage, fresh	lb.	1.82	12/94	82r
Sausage, Jimmy Dean, 100% pork	lb.	2.27	12/94	2c
Shortening, vegetable oil blends	lb.	0.75	12/94	82r
Shortening, vegetable, Crisco	3-lb.	2.57	12/94	2c
Soft drink, Coca Cola, ex deposit	2 lit	1.15	12/94	2c
Spaghetti and macaroni	lb.	0.87	12/94	82r
Steak, rib eye, USDA choice, boneless	lb.	6.85	12/94	82r
Steak, round, graded & ungraded, exc. USDA prime & choice	lb.	2.96	12/94	82r
Steak, round, USDA choice, boneless	lb.	3.17	12/94	82r
Steak, sirloin, USDA choice, boneless	lb.	4.12	12/94	82r
Steak, t-bone	lb.	5.95	12/94	2c
Steak, T-bone, USDA choice, bone-in	lb.	5.63	12/94	82r
Sugar and other sweets, eaten at home, expenditures	year	93	91	81r
Sugar, cane or beet	4 lbs.	1.53	12/94	2c
Sugar, white, all sizes	lb.	0.39	12/94	82r
Tobacco products and smoking supplies, total expenditures	year	286	91	81r
Tomatoes, field grown	lb.	1.36	12/94	82r
Tomatoes, Hunt's or Del Monte	14.5 oz.	0.69	12/94	2c
Tuna, chunk, light	lb.	1.94	12/94	82r
Tuna, chunk, light, oil-packed	6.125-6.5 oz.	0.64	12/94	2c
Turkey, frozen, whole	lb.	0.96	12/94	82r
Yogurt, natural, fruit flavored	8 oz.	0.58	12/94	82r
Goods and Services				
Miscellaneous goods and services, ACCRA Index		101.20	12/94	2c
Health Care				
Health care, ACCRA Index		105.30	12/94	2c
Adenosine, emergency room	treat	100.00	95	23r
Antibiotic ointment, Polysporin	1.5 oz.	3.46	12/94	2c
Bladder tap, superpubic, infant, emergency room	treat	119.00	95	23r
Blood analysis, emergency room	treat	25.00	95	23r

Tallahassee, FL - continued

Item	Per	Value	Date	Ref.
Health Care - continued				
Blood tests, abdominal pain, emergency room	treat	25.00	95	23r
Burn dressing, emergency room	treat	266.00	95	23r
Cardiology interpretation, emergency room	treat	26.00	95	23r
Chest X-ray, emergency room	treat	78.00	95	23r
Childbirth, Cesarean delivery, hospital charge	birth	5462.00	12/91	69r
Childbirth, Cesarean delivery, physician charge	birth	2228.00	12/91	69r
Childbirth, normal delivery, hospital charge	birth	2943.00	12/91	69r
Childbirth, normal delivery, physician charge	birth	1619.00	12/91	69r
Defibrillation pads, emergency room	treat	6.00	95	23r
Dentist's fee, adult teeth cleaning and periodic oral exam	visit	48.40	12/94	2c
Doctor's fee, routine exam, established patient	visit	49.00	12/94	2c
Drugs, expenditures	year	297	91	81r
Gastric tube insertion, nasal, emergency room	treat	25.00	95	23r
Health care, total expenditures	year	1600	91	81r
Health insurance expenditures	year	637	91	81r
Heart monitor, emergency room	treat	40.00	95	23r
Hospital care, semiprivate room	day	430.50	12/94	2c
Insurance premium, family medical care	month	301.92	1/95	41s
Intravenous fluids, emergency room	treat	130.00	95	23r
Intravenous fluids, emergency room	liter	26.00	95	23r
Intravenous line, central, emergency room	treat	342.00	95	23r
Liver function tests, abdominal pain, emergency room	treat	26.00	95	23r
Medical care charges, total, emergency room, third-degree burns	treat	2101.00	95	23r
Medical care charges, total, emergency, infant with fever	treat	628.00	95	23r
Medical services expenditures	year	573	91	81r
Medical supplies expenditures	year	93	91	81r
Morphine, emergency room	treat	34.00	95	23r
Nursing care and facilities charges, emergency room	treat	252.00	95	23r
Nursing care and facilities charges, emergency, infant with fever	treat	252.00	95	23r
Nursing care and facilities charges, emergency, third-degree burns	treat	861.00	95	23r
Physician's charges, emergency, infant with fever	treat	212.00	95	23r
Physician's charges, emergency, third-degree burns	treat	372.00	95	23r
Physician's fee, emergency room	treat	372.00	95	23r
Physician's fee, general practitioner	visit	51.20	12/93	60r
Surgery, open-heart	proc	42374.00	1/93	14r
Ultrasound, abdominal, emergency room	treat	276.00	95	23r
Urinalysis, emergency room	treat	20.00	95	23r
Urinalysis, infant, emergency room	treat	20.00	95	23r
X-rays, emergency room	treat	78.00	95	23r
Household Goods				
Appl. repair, service call, wash mach	min. lab. chg.	34.39	12/94	2c
Floor coverings, expenditures	year	48	91	81r
Furniture, expenditures	year	280	91	81r
Household equipment, misc. expenditures	year	342	91	81r
Household expenditures, miscellaneous	year	256	91	81r
Household furnishings and equipment, expenditures	year	988	91	81r
Household operations expenditures	year	468	91	81r
Household textiles, expenditures	year	95	91	81r
Housekeeping supplies, expenditures	year	380	91	81r
Laundry and cleaning supplies, expenditures	year	109	91	81r
Laundry detergent, Tide Ultra, Bold, or Cheer	42 oz.	2.73	12/94	2c
Postage and stationery, expenditures	year	105	91	81r
Tissues, facial, Kleenex brand	175	0.93	12/94	2c

Values are in dollars or fractions of dollars. In the column headed *Ref*, references are shown to sources. Each reference is followed by a letter. These refer to the geographical level for which data were reported: s=State, r=Region, and c=City or metro. The abbreviation *ex* is used to mean *except* or *excluding*; *exp* stands for *expenditures*. For other abbreviations and further explanations, please see the Introduction.

Tallahassee, FL - continued

Item	Per	Value	Date	Ref.
Housing				
Housing, ACCRA Index		103.80	12/94	2c
Add garage/carport		6,980	3/95	74r
Add room(s)		11,403	3/95	74r
Apartment condominium or co-op, median	unit	68600	12/94	62r
Dwellings (owned), expenditures	year	2428	91	81r
Enclose porch/patio/breezeway		4,572	3/95	74r
Finish room in basement/attic		3,794	3/95	74r
Home, existing, single-family, median	unit	120200	12/94	62r
Home, existing, single-family, median	unit	98.70	12/94	62c
House payment, principal and interest, 25% down payment	mo.	790	12/94	2c
House, 1800 sq ft, 8000 sq ft lot, new, urban, utilities	total	128690	12/94	2c
Maintenance, repairs, insurance, and other housing expenditures	year	531	91	81r
Mortgage interest and charges expenditures	year	1506	91	81r
Mtge. rate, incl. points and orig. fee, 30-year conv. fixed or ARM	mo.	9.19	12/94	2c
Princ. & int., mortgage, median-price exist. sing.-family home	mo.	540	12/94	62r
Property taxes expenditures	year	391	91	81r
Redesign, restructure more than half of home's interior		17,641	3/95	74r
Rent, apartment, 2 br., 1 1/2-2 baths, unfurnished, 950 sq ft, water	mo.	563	12/94	2c
Rental units expenditures	year	1264	91	81r
Insurance and Pensions				
Auto insurance, private passenger	year	753.93	12/94	71s
Insurance and pensions, personal, expenditures	year	2395	91	81r
Insurance, life and other personal, expenditures	year	368	91	81r
Pensions and Social Security, expenditures	year	2027	91	81r
Personal Goods				
Shampoo, Alberto VO5	15-oz.	0.97	12/94	2c
Toothpaste, Crest or Colgate	6-7 oz.	1.60	12/94	2c
Personal Services				
Dry cleaning, man's 2-pc. suit		6.59	12/94	2c
Haircut, man's barbershop, no styling		8.49	12/94	2c
Haircut, woman's shampoo, trim, blow-dry		18.18	12/94	2c
Personal services expenditures	year	212	91	81r
Restaurant Food				
Chicken, fried, thigh and drumstick		2.23	12/94	2c
Dining expenditures, family	week	33.83	94	73r
Hamburger with cheese	1/4 lb.	1.90	12/94	2c
Pizza, Pizza Hut or Pizza Inn	12-13 in.	7.99	12/94	2c
Taxes				
Taxes, Federal income, expenditures	year	2275	91	81r
Taxes, personal, expenditures	year	2715	91	81r
Taxes, State and local income, expenditures	year	365	91	81r
Transportation				
Transportation, ACCRA Index		100.30	12/94	2c
Bus fare, one-way	trip	0.75	12/95	1c
Bus fare, up to 10 miles	one-way	0.75	12/94	2c
Cars and trucks purchased, new	year	1306	91	81r
Cars and trucks purchased, used	year	942	91	81r
Driver's learning permit fee	perm	20.00	1/94	84s
Driver's license fee	orig	20.00	1/94	84s
Driver's license fee, duplicate	lic	10.00	1/94	84s
Driver's license reinstatement fee, min.	susp	25.00	1/94	85s
Driver's license renewal fee	renew	15.00	1/94	84s
Identification card, nondriver	card	3.00	1/94	83s
Motorcycle learning permit fee	perm	20.00	1/94	84s
Motorcycle license fee	orig	20.00	1/94	84s
Motorcycle license fee, duplicate	lic	10.00	1/94	84s
Motorcycle license renewal fee	renew	15.00	1/94	84s
Public transportation expenditures	year	249	91	81r

Tallahassee, FL - continued

Item	Per	Value	Date	Ref.
Transportation - continued				
Tire balance, computer or spin bal., front	wheel	7.00	12/94	2c
Transportation expenditures, total	year	5307	91	81r
Vehicle finance charges	year	346	91	81r
Vehicle insurance expenditures	year	544	91	81r
Vehicle maintenance and repairs expenditures	year	600	91	81r
Vehicle purchases	year	2275	91	81r
Vehicle rental, leases, licenses, etc. expenditures	year	141	91	81r
Vehicles purchased, other than cars and trucks	year	27	91	81r
Utilities				
Utilities, ACCRA Index		93.60	12/94	2c
Electricity expenditures	year	950	91	81r
Electricity, (part.), other, 1800 sq. ft., new home	mo.	96.37	12/94	2c
Utilities, fuels, and public services, total expenditures	year	2000	91	81r
Water and other public services, expenditures	year	227	91	81r
Weddings				
Bridal attendants' gowns	event	750	10/93	76r
Bridal gown	event	852	10/93	76r
Bridal headpiece and veil	event	167	10/93	76r
Bride's wedding band	event	708	10/93	76r
Clergy	event	224	10/93	76r
Engagement ring	event	2756	10/93	76r
Flowers	event	863	10/93	76r
Formal wear for groom	event	106	10/93	76r
Groom's attendants' formal wear	event	530	10/93	76r
Groom's wedding band	event	402	10/93	76r
Music	event	600	10/93	76r
Photography	event	1088	10/93	76r
Shoes for bride	event	50	10/93	76r
Videography	event	483	10/93	76r
Wedding invitations and announcements	event	342	10/93	76r
Wedding reception	event	7000	10/93	76r

Tampa, FL

Item	Per	Value	Date	Ref.
Composite, ACCRA index		94.90	12/94	2c
Alcoholic Beverages				
Beer, Miller Lite, Bud, 12-oz., ex deposit	6	3.64	12/94	2c
J & B Scotch	750-ml.	17.79	12/94	2c
Wine, Gallo Chablis blanc	1.5-lit	6.79	12/94	2c
Appliances				
Appliances (major), expenditures	year	153	91	81r
Average annual exp.				
Food, health care, personal goods, services	year	27020	91	81r
Charity				
Cash contributions, expenditures	year	839	91	81r
Clothing				
Apparel, men and boys, total expenditures	year	380	91	81r
Apparel, women and girls, total expenditures	year	660	91	81r
Footwear, expenditures	year	193	91	81r
Jeans, man's denim		31.60	12/94	2c
Shirt, dress, men's	shirt	35.00	1/92	44c
Shirt, man's dress shirt		26.90	12/94	2c
Undervest, boy's size 10-14, cotton	3	4.20	12/94	2c
Communications				
Long-distance telephone rate, day, addl. min., 1-10 mi.	min.	0.08	12/93	9s
Long-distance telephone rate, day, initial min., 1-10 mi.	min.	0.15	12/93	9s
Newspaper subscription, dly. and Sun. delivery	month	10.87	12/94	2c

Values are in dollars or fractions of dollars. In the column headed *Ref*, references are shown to sources. Each reference is followed by a letter. These refer to the geographical level for which data were reported: s=State, r=Region, and c=City or metro. The abbreviation *ex* is used to mean *except* or *excluding*; *exp* stands for expenditures. For other abbreviations and further explanations, please see the Introduction.

Tampa, FL - continued

Item	Per	Value	Date	Ref.
Communications				
Phone line, single, business, field visit	inst	86.00	12/93	9s
Phone line, single, business, no field visit	inst	54.50	12/93	9s
Phone line, single, residence, field visit	inst	76.00	12/93	9s
Phone line, single, residence, no field visit	inst	44.50	12/93	9s
Telephone bill, family of four	month	18.77	12/94	2c
Telephone service, expenditures	year	616	91	81r
Education				
Bar examinination preparatory course	course	500.00-100	94	17s
Board, 4-year private college/university	year	2123	8/94	80s
Board, 4-year public college/university	year	2101	8/94	80s
Education, total expenditures	year	319	91	81r
Room, 4-year private college/university	year	2242	8/94	80s
Room, 4-year public college/university	year	1970	8/94	80s
Total cost, 4-year private college/university	year	13853	8/94	80s
Total cost, 4-year public college/university	year	5855	8/94	80s
Tuition, 2-year public college/university, in-state	year	1076	8/94	80s
Tuition, 4-year private college/university, in-state	year	9287	8/94	80s
Tuition, 4-year public college/university, in-state	year	1784	8/94	80s
Energy and Fuels				
Energy, combined forms, 1800 sq. ft.	mo.	113.31	12/94	2c
Fuel oil and other fuels, expenditures	year	56	91	81r
Gas	gal.	1.10	1/92	44c
Gas, cooking, 10 therms	month	13.90	2/94	65c
Gas, cooking, 30 therms	month	27.71	2/94	65c
Gas, cooking, 50 therms	month	41.51	2/94	65c
Gas, heating, winter, 100 therms	month	76.02	2/94	65c
Gas, heating, winter, average use	month	29.09	2/94	65c
Gas, natural, expenditures	year	150	91	81r
Gas, reg unlead, taxes inc., cash, self-service	gal	1.15	12/94	2c
Gasoline and motor oil purchased	year	1152	91	81r
Gasoline, unleaded midgrade	gallon	1.21	4/93	82r
Gasoline, unleaded premium	gallon	1.30	4/93	82r
Gasoline, unleaded regular	gallon	1.10	4/93	82r
Entertainment				
Bowling, evening rate	game	2.31	12/94	2c
Concert ticket, Pearl Jam group	perf	20.00	94	50r
Entertainment, total expenditures	year	1266	91	81r
Fees and admissions, expenditures	year	306	91	81r
Monopoly game, Parker Brothers', No. 9	game	10.13	12/94	2c
Movie	adm	5.95	12/94	2c
Movie ticket, adult	ticket	5.50	1/92	44c
Pets, toys, playground equipment, expenditures	year	271	91	81r
Reading, expenditures	year	131	91	81r
Televisions, radios, and sound equipment, expenditures	year	439	91	81r
Tennis balls, yellow, Wilson or Penn, 3	can	1.65	12/94	2c
Funerals				
Burial, immediate, container provided by funeral home		1370.36	1/95	54r
Cards, acknowledgment		14.83	1/95	54r
Casket, minimum alternative		192.52	1/95	54r
Cosmetology, hair care, etc.		102.27	1/95	54r
Cremation, direct, container provided by funeral home		1065.64	1/95	54r
Embalming		304.29	1/95	54r
Funeral, funeral home		287.83	1/95	54r
Funeral, other facility		284.14	1/95	54r
Graveside service		349.13	1/95	54r
Hearse, local		132.27	1/95	54r
Limousine, local		98.45	1/95	54r
Memorial service		270.59	1/95	54r
Service charge, professional, nondeclinable		933.59	1/95	54r
Visitation and viewing		225.83	1/95	54r

Tampa, FL - continued

Item	Per	Value	Date	Ref.
Groceries				
Groceries, ACCRA Index		97.10	12/94	2c
Apples, Red Delicious	lb.	0.73	12/94	2c
Baby food, strained vegetables, lowest price	4-4.5 oz.	0.36	12/94	2c
Bacon, sliced	lb.	1.67	12/94	82r
Bananas	lb.	0.36	12/94	2c
Bananas	lb.	0.42	12/94	82r
Beef or hamburger, ground	lb.	1.25	12/94	2c
Beef purchases	year	213	91	81r
Beverage purchases, alcoholic	year	249	91	81r
Beverage purchases, nonalcoholic	year	207	91	81r
Bologna, all beef or mixed	lb.	2.27	12/94	82r
Bread, white	24-oz.	0.80	12/94	2c
Bread, white, pan	lb.	0.68	12/94	82r
Cabbage	lb.	0.42	12/94	82r
Carrots, short trimmed and topped	lb.	0.53	12/94	82r
Cereals and bakery products purchases	year	345	91	81r
Cereals and cereals products purchases	year	127	91	81r
Cheddar cheese, natural	lb.	3.58	12/94	82r
Cheese, Kraft grated Parmesan	8-oz.	3.05	12/94	2c
Chicken breast, bone-in	lb.	1.71	12/94	82r
Chicken, fresh, whole	lb.	0.78	12/94	82r
Chicken, whole fryer	lb.	0.89	12/94	2c
Chuck roast, USDA choice, boneless	lb.	2.26	12/94	82r
Cigarettes, Winston, Kings	carton	16.40	12/94	2c
Coffee, vacuum-packed	13 oz.	3.06	12/94	2c
Corn Flakes, Kellogg's or Post Toasties	18 oz.	2.10	12/94	2c
Corn, frozen, whole kernel, lowest price	10 oz.	0.58	12/94	2c
Crackers, soda, salted	lb.	1.27	12/94	82r
Cucumbers	lb.	0.65	12/94	82r
Dairy products (other) purchases	year	141	91	81r
Eggs, Grade A large	dozen	0.74	12/94	2c
Eggs, Grade A large	dozen	0.87	12/94	82r
Fish and seafood purchases	year	72	91	81r
Flour, white, all purpose	lb.	0.23	12/94	82r
Food purchases, food eaten at home	year	2381	91	81r
Foods purchased away from home, not prepared by consumer	year	1696	91	81r
Frankfurters, all meat or all beef	lb.	1.74	12/94	82r
Fruits and vegetables purchases	year	380	91	81r
Grapefruit	lb.	0.45	12/94	82r
Grapes, Thompson seedless	lb.	2.30	12/94	82r
Ground beef, 100% beef	lb.	1.37	12/94	82r
Ground chuck, 100% beef	lb.	1.97	12/94	82r
Ham, boneless, exc. canned	lb.	2.54	12/94	82r
Ice cream, prepackaged, bulk, regular	1/2 gal.	2.47	12/94	82r
Lemons	lb.	1.02	12/94	82r
Lettuce, iceberg	lb.	0.96	12/94	82r
Lettuce, iceberg	head	0.76	12/94	2c
Margarine, Blue Bonnet or Parkay cubes	lb.	0.56	12/94	2c
Margarine, stick	lb.	0.77	12/94	82r
Meats, poultry, fish, and eggs purchases	year	655	91	81r
Milk and cream (fresh) purchases	year	130	91	81r
Milk, 2%	gal.	2.20	1/92	44c
Milk, whole	1/2 gal.	1.39	12/94	2c
Orange juice, frozen concentrate 12-oz. can	16 oz.	1.36	12/94	82r
Orange juice, Minute Maid frozen	12-oz.	1.07	12/94	2c
Oranges, Navel	lb.	0.54	12/94	82r
Peaches, halves or slices, Hunt's, Del Monte, or Libby's	29-oz.	1.33	12/94	2c
Pears, Anjou	lb.	0.81	12/94	82r
Peas, sweet, Del Monte or Green Giant	15-17 oz.	0.53	12/94	2c
Pork chops, center cut, bone-in	lb.	3.07	12/94	82r
Pork purchases	year	142	91	81r
Potato chips	16-oz.	3.15	12/94	82r
Potatoes, frozen, French fried	lb.	0.82	12/94	82r
Potatoes, white	lb.	0.34	12/94	82r
Potatoes, white or red	10-lb. sack	3.71	12/94	2c

Values are in dollars or fractions of dollars. In the column headed *Ref*, references are shown to sources. Each reference is followed by a letter. These refer to the geographical level for which data were reported: s = State, r = Region, and c = City or metro. The abbreviation *ex* is used to mean *except* or *excluding*; *exp* stands for expenditures. For other abbreviations and further explanations, please see the Introduction.

Tampa, FL - continued

Item	Per	Value	Date	Ref.
Groceries				
Rental rate, 2-bedroom apartment	month	525.00-575	1/92	44c
Rice, white, long grain, uncooked	lb.	0.48	12/94	82r
Round roast, USDA choice, boneless	lb.	2.91	12/94	82r
Sausage, fresh	lb.	1.82	12/94	82r
Sausage, Jimmy Dean, 100% pork	lb.	2.36	12/94	2c
Shortening, vegetable oil blends	lb.	0.75	12/94	82r
Shortening, vegetable, Crisco	3-lb.	2.57	12/94	2c
Soft drink, Coca Cola, ex deposit	2 lit	1.09	12/94	2c
Spaghetti and macaroni	lb.	0.87	12/94	82r
Steak, rib eye, USDA choice, boneless	lb.	6.85	12/94	82r
Steak, round, graded & ungraded, exc. USDA prime & choice	lb.	2.96	12/94	82r
Steak, round, USDA choice, boneless	lb.	3.17	12/94	82r
Steak, sirloin, USDA choice, boneless	lb.	4.12	12/94	82r
Steak, t-bone	lb.	4.92	12/94	2c
Steak, T-bone, USDA choice, bone-in	lb.	5.63	12/94	82r
Sugar and other sweets, eaten at home, expenditures	year	93	91	81r
Sugar, cane or beet	4 lbs.	1.50	12/94	2c
Sugar, white, all sizes	lb.	0.39	12/94	82r
Tobacco products and smoking supplies, total expenditures	year	286	91	81r
Tomatoes, field grown	lb.	1.36	12/94	82r
Tomatoes, Hunt's or Del Monte	14.5 oz.	0.72	12/94	2c
Tuna, chunk, light	lb.	1.94	12/94	82r
Tuna, chunk, light, oil-packed	6.125-6.5 oz.	0.65	12/94	2c
Turkey, frozen, whole	lb.	0.96	12/94	82r
Yogurt, natural, fruit flavored	8 oz.	0.58	12/94	82r
Goods and Services				
Miscellaneous goods and services, ACCRA Index		90.70	12/94	2c
Health Care				
Health care, ACCRA Index		103.60	12/94	2c
Adenosine, emergency room	treat	100.00	95	23r
Antibiotic ointment, Polysporin	1.5 oz.	3.82	12/94	2c
Bladder tap, superpubic, infant, emergency room	treat	119.00	95	23r
Blood analysis, emergency room	treat	25.00	95	23r
Blood tests, abdominal pain, emergency room	treat	25.00	95	23r
Burn dressing, emergency room	treat	266.00	95	23r
Cardiology interpretation, emergency room	treat	26.00	95	23r
Chest X-ray, emergency room	treat	78.00	95	23r
Childbirth, Cesarean delivery, hospital charge	birth	5462.00	12/91	69r
Childbirth, Cesarean delivery, physician charge	birth	2228.00	12/91	69r
Childbirth, normal delivery, hospital charge	birth	2943.00	12/91	69r
Childbirth, normal delivery, physician charge	birth	1619.00	12/91	69r
Defibrillation pads, emergency room	treat	6.00	95	23r
Dentist's fee, adult teeth cleaning and periodic oral exam	visit	52.20	12/94	2c
Doctor's fee, routine exam, established patient	visit	45.50	12/94	2c
Drugs, expenditures	year	297	91	81r
Gastric tube insertion, nasal, emergency room	treat	25.00	95	23r
Health care, total expenditures	year	1600	91	81r
Health insurance expenditures	year	637	91	81r
Heart monitor, emergency room	treat	40.00	95	23r
Hospital care, semiprivate room	day	386.24	12/94	2c
Insurance premium, family medical care	month	301.92	1/95	41s
Intravenous fluids, emergency room	treat	130.00	95	23r
Intravenous fluids, emergency room	liter	26.00	95	23r
Intravenous line, central, emergency room	treat	342.00	95	23r
Liver function tests, abdominal pain, emergency room	treat	26.00	95	23r

Tampa, FL - continued

Item	Per	Value	Date	Ref.
Health Care - continued				
Medical care charges, total, emergency room, third-degree burns	treat	2101.00	95	23r
Medical care charges, total, emergency, infant with fever	treat	628.00	95	23r
Medical services expenditures	year	573	91	81r
Medical supplies expenditures	year	93	91	81r
Morphine, emergency room	treat	34.00	95	23r
Nursing care and facilities charges, emergency room	treat	252.00	95	23r
Nursing care and facilities charges, emergency, infant with fever	treat	252.00	95	23r
Nursing care and facilities charges, emergency, third-degree burns	treat	861.00	95	23r
Physician's charges, emergency, infant with fever	treat	212.00	95	23r
Physician's charges, emergency, third-degree burns	treat	372.00	95	23r
Physician's fee, emergency room	treat	372.00	95	23r
Physician's fee, general practitioner	visit	51.20	12/93	60r
Surgery, open-heart	proc	42374.00	1/93	14r
Ultrasound, abdominal, emergency room	treat	276.00	95	23r
Urinalysis, emergency room	treat	20.00	95	23r
Urinalysis, infant, emergency room	treat	20.00	95	23r
X-rays, emergency room	treat	78.00	95	23r
Household Goods				
Appl. repair, service call, wash mach	min. lab. chg.	24.39	12/94	2c
Floor coverings, expenditures	year	48	91	81r
Furniture, expenditures	year	280	91	81r
Household equipment, misc. expenditures	year	342	91	81r
Household expenditures, miscellaneous	year	256	91	81r
Household furnishings and equipment, expenditures	year	988	91	81r
Household operations expenditures	year	468	91	81r
Household textiles, expenditures	year	95	91	81r
Housekeeping supplies, expenditures	year	380	91	81r
Laundry and cleaning supplies, expenditures	year	109	91	81r
Laundry detergent, Tide Ultra, Bold, or Cheer	42 oz.	3.05	12/94	2c
Postage and stationery, expenditures	year	105	91	81r
Tissues, facial, Kleenex brand	175	0.96	12/94	2c
Housing				
Housing, ACCRA Index		94.60	12/94	2c
Add garage/carport		6,980	3/95	74r
Add room(s)		11,403	3/95	74r
Apartment condominium or co-op, median	unit	68600	12/94	62r
Dwellings (owned), expenditures	year	2428	91	81r
Enclose porch/patio/breezeway		4,572	3/95	74r
Finish room in basement/attic		3,794	3/95	74r
Home, existing, single-family, median	unit	120200	12/94	62r
Home, existing, single-family, median	unit	78.20	12/94	62c
Home, purchase price	unit	102.70	3/93	26c
House payment, principal and interest, 25% down payment	mo.	683	12/94	2c
House, 1800 sq ft, 8000 sq ft lot, new, urban, utilities	total	110500	12/94	2c
Maintenance, repairs, insurance, and other housing expenditures	year	531	91	81r
Mortgage interest and charges expenditures	year	1506	91	81r
Mtge. rate, incl. points and orig. fee, 30-year conv. fixed or ARM	mo.	9.28	12/94	2c
Princ. & int., mortgage, median-price exist. sing.-family home	mo.	540	12/94	62r
Property taxes expenditures	year	391	91	81r
Redesign, restructure more than half of home's interior		17,641	3/95	74r
Rent, apartment, 2 br., 1 1/2-2 baths, unfurnished, 950 sq ft, water	mo.	619	12/94	2c
Rental units expenditures	year	1264	91	81r

Values are in dollars or fractions of dollars. In the column headed *Ref*, references are shown to sources. Each reference is followed by a letter. These refer to the geographical level for which data were reported: s = State, r = Region, and c = City or metro. The abbreviation *ex* is used to mean *except* or *excluding*; *exp* stands for *expenditures*. For other abbreviations and further explanations, please see the Introduction.

Tampa, FL - continued

Item	Per	Value	Date	Ref.
Insurance and Pensions				
Auto insurance, private passenger	year	753.93	12/94	71s
Insurance and pensions, personal, expenditures	year	2395	91	81r
Insurance, life and other personal, expenditures	year	368	91	81r
Pensions and Social Security, expenditures	year	2027	91	81r
Personal Goods				
Shampoo, Alberto VO5	15-oz.	1.08	12/94	2c
Toothpaste, Crest or Colgate	6-7 oz.	2.03	12/94	2c
Personal Services				
Dry cleaning, man's 2-pc. suit		6.34	12/94	2c
Dry cleaning, woman's dress	dress	6.00	1/92	44c
Haircut, man's barbershop, no styling		8.50	12/94	2c
Haircut, woman's shampoo, trim, blow-dry		18.20	12/94	2c
Personal services expenditures	year	212	91	81r
Restaurant Food				
Big Mac, small fries, medium drink	meal	2.75	1/92	44c
Chicken, fried, thigh and drumstick		2.01	12/94	2c
Dining expenditures, family	week	33.83	94	73r
Hamburger with cheese	1/4 lb.	1.01	12/94	2c
Pizza, Pizza Hut or Pizza Inn	12-13 in.	7.99	12/94	2c
Taxes				
Taxes, Federal income, expenditures	year	2275	91	81r
Taxes, personal, expenditures	year	2715	91	81r
Taxes, State and local income, expenditures	year	365	91	81r
Transportation				
Transportation, ACCRA Index		96.50	12/94	2c
Bus fare, one-way	trip	0.95	12/95	1c
Bus fare, up to 10 miles	one-way	1.00	12/94	2c
Cars and trucks purchased, new	year	1306	91	81r
Cars and trucks purchased, used	year	942	91	81r
Driver's learning permit fee	perm	20.00	1/94	84s
Driver's license fee	orig	20.00	1/94	84s
Driver's license fee, duplicate	lic	10.00	1/94	84s
Driver's license reinstatement fee, min.	susp	25.00	1/94	85s
Driver's license renewal fee	renew	15.00	1/94	84s
Identification card, nondriver	card	3.00	1/94	83s
Motorcycle learning permit fee	perm	20.00	1/94	84s
Motorcycle license fee	orig	20.00	1/94	84s
Motorcycle license fee, duplicate	lic	10.00	1/94	84s
Motorcycle license renewal fee	renew	15.00	1/94	84s
parking, long-term lot, airport	3 days	15.00	1/92	44c
Public transportation expenditures	year	249	91	81r
Tire balance, computer or spin bal., front	wheel	5.86	12/94	2c
Transportation expenditures, total	year	5307	91	81r
Vehicle finance charges	year	346	91	81r
Vehicle insurance expenditures	year	544	91	81r
Vehicle maintenance and repairs expenditures	year	600	91	81r
Vehicle purchases	year	2275	91	81r
Vehicle rental, leases, licenses, etc. expenditures	year	141	91	81r
Vehicles purchased, other than cars and trucks	year	27	91	81r
Utilities				
Utilities, ACCRA Index		100.30	12/94	2c
Electricity expenditures	year	950	91	81r
Electricity, 1800 sq. ft., new home	mo.	113.31	12/94	2c
Electricity, summer, 250 KWh	month	26.17	8/93	64c
Electricity, summer, 500 KWh	month	43.82	8/93	64c
Electricity, summer, 750 KWh	month	61.49	8/93	64c
Electricity, summer, 1000 KWh	month	79.14	8/93	64c
Utilities, fuels, and public services, total expenditures	year	2000	91	81r
Water and other public services, expenditures	year	227	91	81r

Tampa, FL - continued

Item	Per	Value	Date	Ref.
Weddings				
Bridal attendants' gowns	event	750	10/93	76r
Bridal gown	event	852	10/93	76r
Bridal headpiece and veil	event	167	10/93	76r
Bride's wedding band	event	708	10/93	76r
Clergy	event	224	10/93	76r
Engagement ring	event	2756	10/93	76r
Flowers	event	863	10/93	76r
Formal wear for groom	event	106	10/93	76r
Groom's attendants' formal wear	event	530	10/93	76r
Groom's wedding band	event	402	10/93	76r
Music	event	600	10/93	76r
Photography	event	1088	10/93	76r
Shoes for bride	event	50	10/93	76r
Videography	event	483	10/93	76r
Wedding invitations and announcements	event	342	10/93	76r
Wedding reception	event	7000	10/93	76r

Terre Haute, IN

Item	Per	Value	Date	Ref.
Composite, ACCRA index		98.10	12/94	2c
Alcoholic Beverages				
Beer, Miller Lite, Bud, 12-oz., ex deposit	6	3.62	12/94	2c
J & B Scotch	750-ml.	17.75	12/94	2c
Wine, Gallo Chablis blanc	1.5-lit	4.64	12/94	2c
Appliances				
Appliances (major), expenditures	year	131	91	81r
Average annual exp.				
Food, health care, personal goods, services	year	25935	91	81r
Charity				
Cash contributions, expenditures	year	745	91	81r
Clothing				
Apparel, men and boys, total expenditures	year	332	91	81r
Apparel, women and girls, total expenditures	year	578	91	81r
Footwear, expenditures	year	164	91	81r
Jeans, man's denim		28.24	12/94	2c
Shirt, man's dress shirt		28.32	12/94	2c
Undervest, boy's size 10-14, cotton	3	4.34	12/94	2c
Communications				
Long-distance telephone rate, day, addl. min., 1-10 mi.	min.	0.10	12/93	9s
Long-distance telephone rate, day, initial min., 1-10 mi.	min.	0.18	12/93	9s
Newspaper subscription, dly. and Sun. delivery	month	13.04	12/94	2c
Phone line, single, business, field visit	inst	59.00	12/93	9s
Phone line, single, business, no field visit	inst	59.00	12/93	9s
Phone line, single, residence, field visit	inst	47.00	12/93	9s
Phone line, single, residence, no field visit	inst	47.00	12/93	9s
Telephone bill, family of four	month	21.90	12/94	2c
Telephone service, expenditures	year	547	91	81r
Education				
Board, 4-year private college/university	year	2095	8/94	80s
Board, 4-year public college/university	year	2300	8/94	80s
Education, total expenditures	year	394	91	81r
Room, 4-year private college/university	year	1784	8/94	80s
Room, 4-year public college/university	year	1718	8/94	80s
Total cost, 4-year private college/university	year	15045	8/94	80s
Total cost, 4-year public college/university	year	6639	8/94	80s
Tuition, 2-year public college/university, in-state	year	1737	8/94	80s
Tuition, 4-year private college/university, in-state	year	11165	8/94	80s
Tuition, 4-year public college/university, in-state	year	2621	8/94	80s

Values are in dollars or fractions of dollars. In the column headed *Ref*, references are shown to sources. Each reference is followed by a letter. These refer to the geographical level for which data were reported: s = State, r = Region, and c = City or metro. The abbreviation *ex* is used to mean *except* or *excluding*; *exp* stands for expenditures. For other abbreviations and further explanations, please see the Introduction.

Terre Haute, IN - continued

Item	Per	Value	Date	Ref.
Energy and Fuels				
Energy, combined forms, 1800 sq. ft.	mo.	103.24	12/94	2c
Energy, exc. electricity, 1800 sq. ft.	mo.	50.73	12/94	2c
Fuel oil and other fuels, expenditures	year	83	91	81r
Gas, natural, expenditures	year	373	91	81r
Gas, reg unlead, taxes inc., cash, self-service	gal	1.00	12/94	2c
Gasoline and motor oil purchased	year	1000	91	81r
Gasoline, unleaded midgrade	gallon	1.15	4/93	82r
Gasoline, unleaded premium	gallon	1.23	4/93	82r
Gasoline, unleaded regular	gallon	1.07	4/93	82r
Entertainment				
Bowling, evening rate	game	1.80	12/94	2c
Entertainment, total expenditures	year	1356	91	81r
Fees and admissions, expenditures	year	347	91	81r
Monopoly game, Parker Brothers', No. 9	game	9.11	12/94	2c
Movie	adm	5.50	12/94	2c
Pets, toys, playground equipment, expenditures	year	270	91	81r
Reading, expenditures	year	160	91	81r
Televisions, radios, and sound equipment, expenditures	year	433	91	81r
Tennis balls, yellow, Wilson or Penn, 3	can	2.56	12/94	2c
Funerals				
Burial, immediate, container provided by funeral home		1268.31	1/95	54r
Cards, acknowledgment		26.12	1/95	54r
Casket, minimum alternative		198.03	1/95	54r
Cosmetology, hair care, etc.		122.19	1/95	54r
Cremation, direct, container provided by funeral home		977.81	1/95	54r
Embalming		334.00	1/95	54r
Funeral, funeral home		321.16	1/95	54r
Funeral, other facility		317.73	1/95	54r
Graveside service		292.48	1/95	54r
Hearse, local		153.20	1/95	54r
Limousine, local		123.52	1/95	54r
Memorial service		356.30	1/95	54r
Service charge, professional, nondeclinable		968.24	1/95	54r
Visitation and viewing		332.66	1/95	54r
Groceries				
Groceries, ACCRA Index		96.10	12/94	2c
Apples, Red Delicious	lb.	0.68	12/94	82r
Baby food, strained vegetables, lowest price	4-4.5 oz.	0.36	12/94	2c
Bacon, sliced	lb.	1.88	12/94	82r
Bananas	lb.	0.39	12/94	2c
Bananas	lb.	0.41	12/94	82r
Beef or hamburger, ground	lb.	1.20	12/94	2c
Beef purchases	year	197	91	81r
Beef, stew, boneless	lb.	2.52	12/94	82r
Beverage purchases, alcoholic	year	293	91	81r
Beverage purchases, nonalcoholic	year	203	91	81r
Bologna, all beef or mixed	lb.	2.12	12/94	82r
Bread, white	24-oz.	0.55	12/94	2c
Bread, white, pan	lb.	0.76	12/94	82r
Cabbage	lb.	0.44	12/94	82r
Carrots, short trimmed and topped	lb.	0.44	12/94	82r
Cereals and bakery products purchases	year	347	91	81r
Cereals and cereals products purchases	year	119	91	81r
Cheddar cheese, natural	lb.	3.28	12/94	82r
Cheese, Kraft grated Parmesan	8-oz.	3.07	12/94	2c
Chicken breast, bone-in	lb.	1.61	12/94	82r
Chicken, fresh, whole	lb.	0.89	12/94	82r
Chicken, whole fryer	lb.	0.70	12/94	2c
Chuck roast, USDA choice, boneless	lb.	2.33	12/94	82r
Cigarettes, Winston, Kings	carton	14.49	12/94	2c
Coffee, 100%, ground roast, all sizes	lb.	4.28	12/94	82r
Coffee, vacuum-packed	13 oz.	3.51	12/94	2c
Cookies, chocolate chip	lb.	2.72	12/94	82r
Corn Flakes, Kellogg's or Post Toasties	18 oz.	2.10	12/94	2c
Corn, frozen, whole kernel, lowest price	10 oz.	0.70	12/94	2c

Terre Haute, IN - continued

Item	Per	Value	Date	Ref.
Groceries - continued				
Dairy products (other) purchases	year	148	91	81r
Eggs, Grade A large	dozen	0.78	12/94	2c
Eggs, Grade A large	dozen	0.76	12/94	82r
Fish and seafood purchases	year	61	91	81r
Flour, white, all purpose	lb.	0.22	12/94	82r
Food purchases, food eaten at home	year	2313	91	81r
Foods purchased away from home, not prepared by consumer	year	1709	91	81r
Fruits and vegetables purchases	year	372	91	81r
Grapefruit	lb.	0.47	12/94	82r
Grapes, Thompson seedless	lb.	2.15	12/94	82r
Ground beef, 100% beef	lb.	1.37	12/94	82r
Ground chuck, 100% beef	lb.	1.81	12/94	82r
Ham, boneless, exc. canned	lb.	2.16	12/94	82r
Ice cream, prepackaged, bulk, regular	1/2 gal.	2.48	12/94	82r
Lemons	lb.	1.08	12/94	82r
Lettuce, iceberg	lb.	0.81	12/94	82r
Lettuce, iceberg	head	0.82	12/94	2c
Margarine, Blue Bonnet or Parkay cubes	lb.	0.56	12/94	2c
Margarine, stick	lb.	0.81	12/94	82r
Meats, poultry, fish, and eggs purchases	year	591	91	81r
Milk and cream (fresh) purchases	year	132	91	81r
Milk, whole	1/2 gal.	1.68	12/94	2c
Orange juice, frozen concentrate 12-oz. can	16 oz.	1.41	12/94	82r
Orange juice, Minute Maid frozen	12-oz.	1.24	12/94	2c
Oranges, Navel	lb.	0.56	12/94	82r
Peaches, halves or slices, Hunt's, Del Monte, or Libby's	29-oz.	1.21	12/94	2c
Peanut butter, creamy, all sizes	lb.	1.81	12/94	82r
Peas, sweet, Del Monte or Green Giant	15-17 oz.	0.52	12/94	2c
Pork chops, center cut, bone-in	lb.	2.76	12/94	82r
Pork purchases	year	130	91	81r
Potato chips	16-oz.	2.81	12/94	82r
Potatoes, frozen, French fried	lb.	0.83	12/94	82r
Potatoes, white	lb.	0.28	12/94	82r
Potatoes, white or red	10-lb. sack	3.31	12/94	2c
Round roast, USDA choice, boneless	lb.	2.90	12/94	82r
Sausage, Jimmy Dean, 100% pork	lb.	2.56	12/94	2c
Shortening, vegetable oil blends	lb.	0.88	12/94	82r
Shortening, vegetable, Crisco	3-lb.	2.46	12/94	2c
Soft drink, Coca Cola, ex deposit	2 lit	1.23	12/94	2c
Spaghetti and macaroni	lb.	0.78	12/94	82r
Steak, rib eye, USDA choice, boneless	lb.	6.15	12/94	82r
Steak, round, graded & ungraded, exc. USDA prime & choice	lb.	2.72	12/94	82r
Steak, round, USDA choice, boneless	lb.	3.02	12/94	82r
Steak, sirloin, USDA choice, boneless	lb.	3.85	12/94	82r
Steak, t-bone	lb.	5.92	12/94	2c
Steak, T-bone, USDA choice, bone-in	lb.	5.38	12/94	82r
Sugar and other sweets, eaten at home, expenditures	year	91	91	81r
Sugar, cane or beet	4 lbs.	1.29	12/94	2c
Sugar, white, all sizes	lb.	0.36	12/94	82r
Tobacco products and smoking supplies, total expenditures	year	298	91	81r
Tomatoes, field grown	lb.	1.36	12/94	82r
Tomatoes, Hunt's or Del Monte	14.5 oz.	0.79	12/94	2c
Tuna, chunk, light	lb.	1.94	12/94	82r
Tuna, chunk, light, oil-packed	6.125-6.5 oz.	0.68	12/94	2c
Turkey, frozen, whole	lb.	0.96	12/94	82r
Yogurt, natural, fruit flavored	8 oz.	0.62	12/94	82r
Goods and Services				
Miscellaneous goods and services, ACCRA Index		95.30	12/94	2c

Values are in dollars or fractions of dollars. In the column headed *Ref*, references are shown to sources. Each reference is followed by a letter. These refer to the geographical level for which data were reported: s=State, r=Region, and c=City or metro. The abbreviation *ex* is used to mean *except* or *excluding*; *exp* stands for expenditures. For other abbreviations and further explanations, please see the Introduction.

Terre Haute, IN - continued

Item	Per	Value	Date	Ref.
Health Care				
Health care, ACCRA Index		93.00	12/94	2c
Antibiotic ointment, Polysporin	1.5 oz.	4.18	12/94	2c
Childbirth, Cesarean delivery, hospital charge	birth	5101.00	12/91	69r
Childbirth, Cesarean delivery, physician charge	birth	2234.00	12/91	69r
Childbirth, normal delivery, hospital charge	birth	2891.00	12/91	69r
Childbirth, normal delivery, physician charge	birth	1623.00	12/91	69r
Dentist's fee, adult teeth cleaning and periodic oral exam	visit	53.25	12/94	2c
Doctor's fee, routine exam, established patient	visit	33.33	12/94	2c
Drugs, expenditures	year	248	91	81r
Health care, total expenditures	year	1336	91	81r
Health insurance expenditures	year	550	91	81r
Hospital care, semiprivate room	day	350.00	12/94	2c
Insurance premium, family medical care	month	353.94	1/95	41s
Medical services expenditures	year	457	91	81r
Medical supplies expenditures	year	82	91	81r
Household Goods				
Appl. repair, service call, wash mach	min. lab. chg.	41.65	12/94	2c
Floor coverings, expenditures	year	105	91	81r
Furniture, expenditures	year	291	91	81r
Household equipment, misc. expenditures	year	341	91	81r
Household expenditures, miscellaneous	year	162	91	81r
Household furnishings and equipment, expenditures	year	1042	91	81r
Household operations expenditures	year	365	91	81r
Household textiles, expenditures	year	101	91	81r
Housekeeping supplies, expenditures	year	390	91	81r
Laundry and cleaning supplies, expenditures	year	110	91	81r
Laundry detergent, Tide Ultra, Bold, or Cheer	42 oz.	3.30	12/94	2c
Postage and stationery, expenditures	year	115	91	81r
Tissues, facial, Kleenex brand	175	1.02	12/94	2c
Housing				
Housing, ACCRA Index		104.90	12/94	2c
Add garage/carport		8,479	3/95	74r
Add room(s)		21,347	3/95	74r
Apartment condominium or co-op, median	unit	87100	12/94	62r
Bathroom addition, average cost	add	9734.00	3/95	13r
Bathroom remodeling, average cost	remod	6414.00	3/95	13r
Bedroom, master suite addition, average cost	add	27122.00	3/95	13r
Deck addition, average cost	add	6665.00	3/95	13r
Dwellings (owned), expenditures	year	2566	91	81r
Enclose porch/patio/breezeway		4,556	3/95	74r
Exterior remodeling, average cost	remod	15395.00	3/95	13r
Family room addition, average cost	add	27658.00	3/95	13r
Finish room in basement/attic		5,074	3/95	74r
Home, existing, single-family, median	unit	106500	12/94	62r
House payment, principal and interest, 25% down payment	mo.	817	12/94	2c
House, 1800 sq ft, 8000 sq ft lot, new, urban, utilities	total	130633	12/94	2c
Kitchen remodeling, major, average cost	remod	17084.00	3/95	13r
Kitchen remodeling, minor, average cost	remod	5804.00	3/95	13r
Maintenance, repairs, insurance, and other housing expenditures	year	484	91	81r
Mortgage interest and charges expenditures	year	1443	91	81r
Mtge. rate, incl. points and orig. fee, 30-year conv. fixed or ARM	mo.	9.41	12/94	2c
Office, home addition, average cost	add	8121.00	3/95	13r
Princ. & int., mortgage, median-price exist. sing.-family home	mo.	515	12/94	62r
Property taxes expenditures	year	639	91	81r
Redesign, restructure more than half of home's interior		9,114	3/95	74r

Terre Haute, IN - continued

Item	Per	Value	Date	Ref.
Housing - continued				
Rent, apartment, 2 br., 1 1/2-2 baths, unfurnished, 950 sq ft, water	mo.	515	12/94	2c
Rental units expenditures	year	1200	91	81r
Sun-space addition, average cost	add	23768.00	3/95	13r
Wing addition, two-story, average cost	add	50410.00	3/95	13r
Insurance and Pensions				
Auto insurance, private passenger	year	586.58	12/94	71s
Insurance and pensions, personal, expenditures	year	2408	91	81r
Insurance, life and other personal, expenditures	year	355	91	81r
Pensions and Social Security, expenditures	year	2053	91	81r
Legal Assistance				
Legal work, law firm associate	hour	90		10r
Legal work, law firm partner	hour	139		10r
Personal Goods				
Shampoo, Alberto VO5	15-oz.	1.27	12/94	2c
Toothpaste, Crest or Colgate	6-7 oz.	1.84	12/94	2c
Personal Services				
Dry cleaning, man's 2-pc. suit		6.60	12/94	2c
Haircut, man's barbershop, no styling		8.40	12/94	2c
Haircut, woman's shampoo, trim, blow-dry		16.39	12/94	2c
Personal services expenditures	year	203	91	81r
Restaurant Food				
Chicken, fried, thigh and drumstick		1.80	12/94	2c
Dining expenditures, family	week	30.03	94	73r
Hamburger with cheese	1/4 lb.	1.89	12/94	2c
Pizza, Pizza Hut or Pizza Inn	12-13 in.	6.75	12/94	2c
Taxes				
Taxes, Federal income, expenditures	year	1756	91	81r
Taxes, personal, expenditures	year	2426	91	81r
Taxes, State and local income, expenditures	year	568	91	81r
Transportation				
Transportation, ACCRA Index		97.70	12/94	2c
Cars and trucks purchased, new	year	891	91	81r
Cars and trucks purchased, used	year	1155	91	81r
Driver's learning permit fee	perm	2.00	1/94	84s
Driver's license fee	orig	6.00	1/94	84s
Driver's license fee, duplicate	lic	3.00	1/94	84s
Driver's license renewal fee	renew	6.00	1/94	84s
Identification card, nondriver	card	4.00	1/94	83s
Motorcycle learning permit fee	perm	2.00	1/94	84s
Motorcycle license fee	orig	6.00	1/94	84s
Motorcycle license fee, duplicate	lic	3.00	1/94	84s
Motorcycle license renewal fee	renew	6.00	1/94	84s
Public transportation expenditures	year	209	91	81r
Tire balance, computer or spin bal., front	wheel	7.38	12/94	2c
Transportation expenditures, total	year	4792	91	81r
Vehicle finance charges	year	300	91	81r
Vehicle insurance expenditures	year	485	91	81r
Vehicle maintenance and repairs expenditures	year	534	91	81r
Vehicle purchases	year	2068	91	81r
Vehicle rental, leases, licenses, etc. expenditures	year	197	91	81r
Vehicles purchased, other than cars and trucks	year	22	91	81r
Utilities				
Utilities, ACCRA Index		94.70	12/94	2c
Electricity expenditures	year	668	91	81r
Electricity, (part.), other, 1800 sq. ft., new home	mo.	52.51	12/94	2c
Electricity, summer, 250 KWh	month	25.30	8/93	64c
Electricity, summer, 500 KWh	month	38.26	8/93	64c
Electricity, summer, 750 KWh	month	49.84	8/93	64c
Electricity, summer, 1000 KWh	month	61.41	8/93	64c

Values are in dollars or fractions of dollars. In the column headed *Ref*, references are shown to sources. Each reference is followed by a letter. These refer to the geographical level for which data were reported: s=State, r=Region, and c=City or metro. The abbreviation *ex* is used to mean *except* or *excluding*; *exp* stands for *expenditures*. For other abbreviations and further explanations, please see the Introduction.

Terre Haute, IN - continued

Item	Per	Value	Date	Ref.
Utilities				
Utilities, fuels, and public services, total expenditures	year	1838	91	81r
Water and other public services, expenditures	year	167	91	81r
Weddings				
Bridal attendants' gowns	event	750	10/93	76r
Bridal gown	event	852	10/93	76r
Bridal headpiece and veil	event	167	10/93	76r
Bride's wedding band	event	708	10/93	76r
Clergy	event	224	10/93	76r
Engagement ring	event	2756	10/93	76r
Flowers	event	863	10/93	76r
Formal wear for groom	event	106	10/93	76r
Groom's attendants' formal wear	event	530	10/93	76r
Groom's wedding band	event	402	10/93	76r
Music	event	600	10/93	76r
Photography	event	1088	10/93	76r
Shoes for bride	event	50	10/93	76r
Videography	event	483	10/93	76r
Wedding invitations and announcements	event	342	10/93	76r
Wedding reception	event	7000	10/93	76r

Texarkana, TX, AR

Item	Per	Value	Date	Ref.
Composite, ACCRA index		92.10	12/94	2c
Alcoholic Beverages				
Beer, Miller Lite, Bud, 12-oz., ex deposit	6	4.56	12/94	2c
J & B Scotch	750-ml.	18.63	12/94	2c
Wine, Gallo Chablis blanc	1.5-lit	5.70	12/94	2c
Appliances				
Appliances (major), expenditures	year	153	91	81r
Average annual exp.				
Food, health care, personal goods, services	year	27020	91	81r
Charity				
Cash contributions, expenditures	year	839	91	81r
Clothing				
Apparel, men and boys, total expenditures	year	380	91	81r
Apparel, women and girls, total expenditures	year	660	91	81r
Footwear, expenditures	year	193	91	81r
Jeans, man's denim		30.39	12/94	2c
Shirt, man's dress shirt		31.00	12/94	2c
Undervest, boy's size 10-14, cotton	3	3.94	12/94	2c
Communications				
Long-distance telephone rate, day, addl. min., 1-10 mi.	min.	0.08	12/93	9s
Long-distance telephone rate, day, initial min., 1-10 mi.	min.	0.10	12/93	9s
Newspaper subscription, dly. and Sun. delivery	month	9.50	12/94	2c
Phone line, single, business, field visit	inst	71.90	12/93	9s
Phone line, single, business, no field visit	inst	57.30	12/93	9s
Phone line, single, residence, field visit	inst	52.95	12/93	9s
Phone line, single, residence, no field visit	inst	38.35	12/93	9s
Telephone bill, family of four	month	15.96	12/94	2c
Telephone service, expenditures	year	616	91	81r
Education				
Board, 4-year private college/university	year	2084	8/94	80s
Board, 4-year public college/university	year	1675	8/94	80s
Education, total expenditures	year	319	91	81r
Room, 4-year private college/university	year	1840	8/94	80s
Room, 4-year public college/university	year	1756	8/94	80s
Total cost, 4-year private college/university	year	11876	8/94	80s
Total cost, 4-year public college/university	year	4935	8/94	80s
Tuition, 2-year public college/university, in-state	year	625	8/94	80s

Texarkana, TX, AR - continued

Item	Per	Value	Date	Ref.
Education - continued				
Tuition, 4-year private college/university, in-state	year	7952	8/94	80s
Tuition, 4-year public college/university, in-state	year	1503	8/94	80s
Energy and Fuels				
Energy, combined forms, 1800 sq. ft.	mo.	112.48	12/94	2c
Energy, exc. electricity, 1800 sq. ft.	mo.	36.01	12/94	2c
Fuel oil and other fuels, expenditures	year	56	91	81r
Gas, cooking, winter, 10 therms	month	10.05	2/94	65c
Gas, cooking, winter, 30 therms	month	19.64	2/94	65c
Gas, cooking, winter, 50 therms	month	29.25	2/94	65c
Gas, heating, winter, 100 therms	month	53.23	2/94	65c
Gas, heating, winter, average use	month	64.26	2/94	65c
Gas, natural, expenditures	year	150	91	81r
Gas, reg unlead, taxes inc., cash, self-service	gal	1.12	12/94	2c
Gasoline and motor oil purchased	year	1152	91	81r
Gasoline, unleaded midgrade	gallon	1.21	4/93	82r
Gasoline, unleaded premium	gallon	1.30	4/93	82r
Gasoline, unleaded regular	gallon	1.10	4/93	82r
Entertainment				
Bowling, evening rate	game	1.95	12/94	2c
Concert ticket, Pearl Jam group	perf	20.00	94	50r
Entertainment, total expenditures	year	1266	91	81r
Fees and admissions, expenditures	year	306	91	81r
Monopoly game, Parker Brothers', No. 9	game	11.90	12/94	2c
Movie	adm	5.00	12/94	2c
Pets, toys, playground equipment, expenditures	year	271	91	81r
Reading, expenditures	year	131	91	81r
Televisions, radios, and sound equipment, expenditures	year	439	91	81r
Tennis balls, yellow, Wilson or Penn, 3	can	2.29	12/94	2c
Funerals				
Burial, immediate, container provided by funeral home		1574.60	1/95	54r
Cards, acknowledgment		22.24	1/95	54r
Casket, minimum alternative		239.41	1/95	54r
Cosmetology, hair care, etc.		91.04	1/95	54r
Cremation, direct, container provided by funeral home		1085.15	1/95	54r
Embalming		281.30	1/95	54r
Funeral, funeral home		323.04	1/95	54r
Funeral, other facility		327.58	1/95	54r
Graveside service		355.19	1/95	54r
Hearse, local		141.89	1/95	54r
Limousine, local		99.40	1/95	54r
Memorial service		284.67	1/95	54r
Service charge, professional, nondeclinable		904.06	1/95	54r
Visitation and viewing		187.04	1/95	54r
Groceries				
Groceries, ACCRA Index		92.30	12/94	2c
Apples, Red Delicious	lb.	0.73	12/94	82r
Baby food, strained vegetables, lowest price	4-4.5 oz.	0.25	12/94	2c
Bacon, sliced	lb.	1.67	12/94	82r
Bananas	lb.	0.39	12/94	2c
Bananas	lb.	0.42	12/94	82r
Beef or hamburger, ground	lb.	1.40	12/94	2c
Beef purchases	year	213	91	81r
Beverage purchases, alcoholic	year	249	91	81r
Beverage purchases, nonalcoholic	year	207	91	81r
Bologna, all beef or mixed	lb.	2.27	12/94	82r
Bread, white	24-oz.	0.58	12/94	2c
Bread, white, pan	lb.	0.68	12/94	82r
Cabbage	lb.	0.42	12/94	82r
Carrots, short trimmed and topped	lb.	0.53	12/94	82r
Cereals and bakery products purchases	year	345	91	81r
Cereals and cereals products purchases	year	127	91	81r
Cheddar cheese, natural	lb.	3.58	12/94	82r

Values are in dollars or fractions of dollars. In the column headed *Ref*, references are shown to sources. Each reference is followed by a letter. These refer to the geographical level for which data were reported: s = State, r = Region, and c = City or metro. The abbreviation *ex* is used to mean *except* or *excluding*; *exp* stands for expenditures. For other abbreviations and further explanations, please see the Introduction.

Texarkana, TX, AR - continued

Item	Per	Value	Date	Ref.
Groceries				
Cheese, Kraft grated Parmesan	8-oz.	3.44	12/94	2c
Chicken breast, bone-in	lb.	1.71	12/94	82r
Chicken, fresh, whole	lb.	0.78	12/94	82r
Chicken, whole fryer	lb.	0.76	12/94	2c
Chuck roast, USDA choice, boneless	lb.	2.26	12/94	82r
Cigarettes, Winston, Kings	carton	16.70	12/94	2c
Coffee, vacuum-packed	13 oz.	3.13	12/94	2c
Corn Flakes, Kellogg's or Post Toasties	18 oz.	2.30	12/94	2c
Corn, frozen, whole kernel, lowest price	10 oz.	0.69	12/94	2c
Crackers, soda, salted	lb.	1.27	12/94	82r
Cucumbers	lb.	0.65	12/94	82r
Dairy products (other) purchases	year	141	91	81r
Eggs, Grade A large	dozen	0.72	12/94	2c
Eggs, Grade A large	dozen	0.87	12/94	82r
Fish and seafood purchases	year	72	91	81r
Flour, white, all purpose	lb.	0.23	12/94	82r
Food purchases, food eaten at home	year	2381	91	81r
Foods purchased away from home, not prepared by consumer	year	1696	91	81r
Frankfurters, all meat or all beef	lb.	1.74	12/94	82r
Fruits and vegetables purchases	year	380	91	81r
Grapefruit	lb.	0.45	12/94	82r
Grapes, Thompson seedless	lb.	2.30	12/94	82r
Ground beef, 100% beef	lb.	1.37	12/94	82r
Ground chuck, 100% beef	lb.	1.97	12/94	82r
Ham, boneless, exc. canned	lb.	2.54	12/94	82r
Ice cream, prepackaged, bulk, regular	1/2 gal.	2.47	12/94	82r
Lemons	lb.	1.02	12/94	82r
Lettuce, iceberg	lb.	0.96	12/94	82r
Lettuce, iceberg	head	0.79	12/94	2c
Margarine, Blue Bonnet or Parkay cubes	lb.	0.58	12/94	2c
Margarine, stick	lb.	0.77	12/94	82r
Meats, poultry, fish, and eggs purchases	year	655	91	81r
Milk and cream (fresh) purchases	year	130	91	81r
Milk, whole	1/2 gal.	1.14	12/94	2c
Orange juice, frozen concentrate 12-oz. can	16 oz.	1.36	12/94	82r
Orange juice, Minute Maid frozen	12-oz.	1.07	12/94	2c
Oranges, Navel	lb.	0.54	12/94	82r
Peaches, halves or slices, Hunt's, Del Monte, or Libby's	29-oz.	1.48	12/94	2c
Pears, Anjou	lb.	0.81	12/94	82r
Peas, sweet, Del Monte or Green Giant	15-17 oz.	0.46	12/94	2c
Pork chops, center cut, bone-in	lb.	3.07	12/94	82r
Pork purchases	year	142	91	81r
Potato chips	16-oz.	3.15	12/94	82r
Potatoes, frozen, French fried	lb.	0.82	12/94	82r
Potatoes, white	lb.	0.34	12/94	82r
Potatoes, white or red	10-lb. sack	2.17	12/94	2c
Rice, white, long grain, uncooked	lb.	0.48	12/94	82r
Round roast, USDA choice, boneless	lb.	2.91	12/94	82r
Sausage, fresh	lb.	1.82	12/94	82r
Sausage, Jimmy Dean, 100% pork	lb.	2.43	12/94	2c
Shortening, vegetable oil blends	lb.	0.75	12/94	82r
Shortening, vegetable, Crisco	3-lb.	2.26	12/94	2c
Soft drink, Coca Cola, ex deposit	2 lit	1.37	12/94	2c
Spaghetti and macaroni	lb.	0.87	12/94	82r
Steak, rib eye, USDA choice, boneless	lb.	6.85	12/94	82r
Steak, round, graded & ungraded, exc. USDA prime & choice	lb.	2.96	12/94	82r
Steak, round, USDA choice, boneless	lb.	3.17	12/94	82r
Steak, sirloin, USDA choice, boneless	lb.	4.12	12/94	82r
Steak, t-bone	lb.	4.85	12/94	2c
Steak, T-bone, USDA choice, bone-in	lb.	5.63	12/94	82r
Sugar and other sweets, eaten at home, expenditures	year	93	91	81r
Sugar, cane or beet	4 lbs.	1.43	12/94	2c
Sugar, white, all sizes	lb.	0.39	12/94	82r

Texarkana, TX, AR - continued

Item	Per	Value	Date	Ref.
Groceries - continued				
Tobacco products and smoking supplies, total expenditures	year	286	91	81r
Tomatoes, field grown	lb.	1.36	12/94	82r
Tomatoes, Hunt's or Del Monte	14.5 oz.	0.64	12/94	2c
Tuna, chunk, light	lb.	1.94	12/94	82r
Tuna, chunk, light, oil-packed	6.125-6.5 oz.	0.61	12/94	2c
Turkey, frozen, whole	lb.	0.96	12/94	82r
Yogurt, natural, fruit flavored	8 oz.	0.58	12/94	82r
Goods and Services				
Miscellaneous goods and services, ACCRA Index		98.00	12/94	2c
Health Care				
Health care, ACCRA Index		96.40	12/94	2c
Adenosine, emergency room	treat	100.00	95	23r
Antibiotic ointment, Polysporin	1.5 oz.	3.92	12/94	2c
Bladder tap, superpubic, infant, emergency room	treat	119.00	95	23r
Blood analysis, emergency room	treat	25.00	95	23r
Blood tests, abdominal pain, emergency room	treat	25.00	95	23r
Burn dressing, emergency room	treat	266.00	95	23r
Cardiology interpretation, emergency room	treat	26.00	95	23r
Chest X-ray, emergency room	treat	78.00	95	23r
Childbirth, Cesarean delivery, hospital charge	birth	5462.00	12/91	69r
Childbirth, Cesarean delivery, physician charge	birth	2228.00	12/91	69r
Childbirth, normal delivery, hospital charge	birth	2943.00	12/91	69r
Childbirth, normal delivery, physician charge	birth	1619.00	12/91	69r
Defibrillation pads, emergency room	treat	6.00	95	23r
Dentist's fee, adult teeth cleaning and periodic oral exam	visit	37.20	12/94	2c
Doctor's fee, routine exam, established patient	visit	51.65	12/94	2c
Drugs, expenditures	year	297	91	81r
Gastric tube insertion, nasal, emergency room	treat	25.00	95	23r
Health care, total expenditures	year	1600	91	81r
Health insurance expenditures	year	637	91	81r
Heart monitor, emergency room	treat	40.00	95	23r
Hospital care, semiprivate room	day	333.00	12/94	2c
Insurance premium, family medical care	month	389.25	1/95	41s
Intravenous fluids, emergency room	treat	130.00	95	23r
Intravenous fluids, emergency room	liter	26.00	95	23r
Intravenous line, central, emergency room	treat	342.00	95	23r
Liver function tests, abdominal pain, emergency room	treat	26.00	95	23r
Medical care charges, total, emergency room, third-degree burns	treat	2101.00	95	23r
Medical care charges, total, emergency, infant with fever	treat	628.00	95	23r
Medical services expenditures	year	573	91	81r
Medical supplies expenditures	year	93	91	81r
Morphine, emergency room	treat	34.00	95	23r
Nursing care and facilities charges, emergency room	treat	252.00	95	23r
Nursing care and facilities charges, emergency, infant with fever	treat	252.00	95	23r
Nursing care and facilities charges, emergency, third-degree burns	treat	861.00	95	23r
Physician's charges, emergency, infant with fever	treat	212.00	95	23r
Physician's charges, emergency, third-degree burns	treat	372.00	95	23r
Physician's fee, emergency room	treat	372.00	95	23r
Physician's fee, general practitioner	visit	51.20	12/93	60r
Surgery, open-heart	proc	42374.00	1/93	14r
Ultrasound, abdominal, emergency room	treat	276.00	95	23r
Urinalysis, emergency room	treat	20.00	95	23r

Values are in dollars or fractions of dollars. In the column headed *Ref*, references are shown to sources. Each reference is followed by a letter. These refer to the geographical level for which data were reported: s = State, r = Region, and c = City or metro. The abbreviation *ex* is used to mean *except* or *excluding*; *exp* stands for expenditures. For other abbreviations and further explanations, please see the Introduction.

Texarkana, TX, AR - continued

Item	Per	Value	Date	Ref.
Health Care				
Urinalysis, infant, emergency room	treat	20.00	95	23r
X-rays, emergency room	treat	78.00	95	23r
Household Goods				
Appl. repair, service call, wash mach	min. lab. chg.	36.20	12/94	2c
Floor coverings, expenditures	year	48	91	81r
Furniture, expenditures	year	280	91	81r
Household equipment, misc. expenditures	year	342	91	81r
Household expenditures, miscellaneous	year	256	91	81r
Household furnishings and equipment, expenditures	year	988	91	81r
Household operations expenditures	year	468	91	81r
Household textiles, expenditures	year	95	91	81r
Housekeeping supplies, expenditures	year	380	91	81r
Laundry and cleaning supplies, expenditures	year	109	91	81r
Laundry detergent, Tide Ultra, Bold, or Cheer	42 oz.	3.72	12/94	2c
Postage and stationery, expenditures	year	105	91	81r
Tissues, facial, Kleenex brand	175	0.97	12/94	2c
Housing				
Housing, ACCRA Index		80.90	12/94	2c
Add garage/carport		6,980	3/95	74r
Add room(s)		11,403	3/95	74r
Apartment condominium or co-op, median	unit	68600	12/94	62r
Dwellings (owned), expenditures	year	2428	91	81r
Enclose porch/patio/breezeway		4,572	3/95	74r
Finish room in basement/attic		3,794	3/95	74r
Home, existing, single-family, median	unit	120200	12/94	62r
House payment, principal and interest, 25% down payment	mo.	611	12/94	2c
House, 1800 sq ft, 8000 sq ft lot, new, urban, utilities	total	97500	12/94	2c
Maintenance, repairs, insurance, and other housing expenditures	year	531	91	81r
Mortgage interest and charges expenditures	year	1506	91	81r
Mtge. rate, incl. points and orig. fee, 30-year conv. fixed or ARM	mo.	9.42	12/94	2c
Princ. & int., mortgage, median-price exist. sing.-family home	mo.	540	12/94	62r
Property taxes expenditures	year	391	91	81r
Redesign, restructure more than half of home's interior		17,641	3/95	74r
Rent, apartment, 2 br., 1 1/2-2 baths, unfurnished, 950 sq ft, water	mo.	455	12/94	2c
Rental units expenditures	year	1264	91	81r
Insurance and Pensions				
Auto insurance, private passenger	year	785.78	12/94	71s
Insurance and pensions, personal, expenditures	year	2395	91	81r
Insurance, life and other personal, expenditures	year	368	91	81r
Pensions and Social Security, expenditures	year	2027	91	81r
Personal Goods				
Shampoo, Alberto VO5	15-oz.	0.95	12/94	2c
Toothpaste, Crest or Colgate	6-7 oz.	2.03	12/94	2c
Personal Services				
Dry cleaning, man's 2-pc. suit		6.94	12/94	2c
Haircut, man's barbershop, no styling		8.20	12/94	2c
Haircut, woman's shampoo, trim, blow-dry		20.20	12/94	2c
Personal services expenditures	year	212	91	81r
Restaurant Food				
Chicken, fried, thigh and drumstick		1.94	12/94	2c
Dining expenditures, family	week	33.83	94	73r
Hamburger with cheese	1/4 lb.	1.85	12/94	2c
Pizza, Pizza Hut or Pizza Inn	12-13 in.	7.74	12/94	2c

Texarkana, TX, AR - continued

Item	Per	Value	Date	Ref.
Taxes				
Tax, cigarettes	year	584.00	10/93	43s
Taxes, Federal income, expenditures	year	2275	91	81r
Taxes, personal, expenditures	year	2715	91	81r
Taxes, State and local income, expenditures	year	365	91	81r
Transportation				
Transportation, ACCRA Index		97.40	12/94	2c
Cars and trucks purchased, new	year	1306	91	81r
Cars and trucks purchased, used	year	942	91	81r
Driver's learning permit fee	perm	5.00	1/94	84s
Driver's license fee	orig	16.00	1/94	84s
Driver's license fee, duplicate	lic	10.00	1/94	84s
Driver's license reinstatement fee, min.	susp	50.00	1/94	85s
Driver's license renewal fee	renew	16.00	1/94	84s
Identification card, nondriver	card	10.00	1/94	83s
Motorcycle learning permit fee	perm	5.00	1/94	84s
Motorcycle license fee	orig	16.00	1/94	84s
Motorcycle license fee, duplicate	lic	10.00	1/94	84s
Motorcycle license renewal fee	renew	21.00	1/94	84s
Public transportation expenditures	year	249	91	81r
Tire balance, computer or spin bal., front	wheel	6.40	12/94	2c
Transportation expenditures, total	year	5307	91	81r
Vehicle finance charges	year	346	91	81r
Vehicle insurance expenditures	year	544	91	81r
Vehicle maintenance and repairs expenditures	year	600	91	81r
Vehicle purchases	year	2275	91	81r
Vehicle rental, leases, licenses, etc. expenditures	year	141	91	81r
Vehicles purchased, other than cars and trucks	year	27	91	81r
Utilities				
Utilities, ACCRA Index		97.80	12/94	2c
Electricity expenditures	year	950	91	81r
Electricity, (part.), other, 1800 sq. ft., new home	mo.	76.47	12/94	2c
Utilities, fuels, and public services, total expenditures	year	2000	91	81r
Water and other public services, expenditures	year	227	91	81r
Weddings				
Bridal attendants' gowns	event	750	10/93	76r
Bridal gown	event	852	10/93	76r
Bridal headpiece and veil	event	167	10/93	76r
Bride's wedding band	event	708	10/93	76r
Clergy	event	224	10/93	76r
Engagement ring	event	2756	10/93	76r
Flowers	event	863	10/93	76r
Formal wear for groom	event	106	10/93	76r
Groom's attendants' formal wear	event	530	10/93	76r
Groom's wedding band	event	402	10/93	76r
Music	event	600	10/93	76r
Photography	event	1088	10/93	76r
Shoes for bride	event	50	10/93	76r
Videography	event	483	10/93	76r
Wedding invitations and announcements	event	342	10/93	76r
Wedding reception	event	7000	10/93	76r

Tifton, GA

Item	Per	Value	Date	Ref.
Composite, ACCRA index		96.30	12/94	2c
Alcoholic Beverages				
Beer, Miller Lite, Bud, 12-oz., ex deposit	6	4.38	12/94	2c
J & B Scotch	750-ml.	16.52	12/94	2c
Wine, Gallo Chablis blanc	1.5-lit	5.43	12/94	2c
Clothing				
Jeans, man's denim		36.83	12/94	2c
Shirt, man's dress shirt		38.98	12/94	2c
Undervest, boy's size 10-14, cotton	3	5.82	12/94	2c

Values are in dollars or fractions of dollars. In the column headed *Ref*, references are shown to sources. Each reference is followed by a letter. These refer to the geographical level for which data were reported: s=State, r=Region, and c=City or metro. The abbreviation *ex* is used to mean *except* or *excluding*; *exp* stands for expenditures. For other abbreviations and further explanations, please see the Introduction.

Tifton, GA - continued

Item	Per	Value	Date	Ref.
Communications				
Newspaper subscription, dly. and Sun. delivery	month	9.00	12/94	2c
Telephone bill, family of four	month	20.09	12/94	2c
Telephone, residential, flat rate	mo.	11.20	12/93	8c
Energy and Fuels				
Energy, combined forms, 1800 sq. ft.	mo.	124.18	12/94	2c
Gas, reg unlead, taxes inc., cash, self-service	gal	1.00	12/94	2c
Entertainment				
Bowling, evening rate	game	1.95	12/94	2c
Monopoly game, Parker Brothers', No. 9	game	10.56	12/94	2c
Movie	adm	4.83	12/94	2c
Tennis balls, yellow, Wilson or Penn, 3	can	2.81	12/94	2c
Groceries				
Groceries, ACCRA Index		96.80	12/94	2c
Baby food, strained vegetables, lowest price	4-4.5 oz.	0.27	12/94	2c
Bananas	lb.	0.40	12/94	2c
Beef or hamburger, ground	lb.	1.54	12/94	2c
Bread, white	24-oz.	0.74	12/94	2c
Cheese, Kraft grated Parmesan	8-oz.	3.26	12/94	2c
Chicken, whole fryer	lb.	0.79	12/94	2c
Cigarettes, Winston, Kings	carton	13.54	12/94	2c
Coffee, vacuum-packed	13 oz.	3.60	12/94	2c
Corn Flakes, Kellogg's or Post Toasties	18 oz.	2.46	12/94	2c
Corn, frozen, whole kernel, lowest price	10 oz.	0.60	12/94	2c
Eggs, Grade A large	dozen	0.80	12/94	2c
Lettuce, iceberg	head	0.93	12/94	2c
Margarine, Blue Bonnet or Parkay cubes	lb.	0.58	12/94	2c
Milk, whole	1/2 gal.	1.43	12/94	2c
Orange juice, Minute Maid frozen	12-oz.	1.24	12/94	2c
Peaches, halves or slices, Hunt's, Del Monte, or Libby's	29-oz.	1.20	12/94	2c
Peas, sweet, Del Monte or Green Giant	15-17 oz.	0.51	12/94	2c
Potatoes, white or red	10-lb. sack	2.54	12/94	2c
Sausage, Jimmy Dean, 100% pork	lb.	2.34	12/94	2c
Shortening, vegetable, Crisco	3-lb.	2.59	12/94	2c
Soft drink, Coca Cola, ex deposit	2 lit	1.21	12/94	2c
Steak, t-bone	lb.	5.98	12/94	2c
Sugar, cane or beet	4 lbs.	1.39	12/94	2c
Tomatoes, Hunt's or Del Monte	14.5 oz.	0.63	12/94	2c
Tuna, chunk, light, oil-packed	6.125-6.5 oz.	0.68	12/94	2c
Goods and Services				
Miscellaneous goods and services, ACCRA Index		107.80	12/94	2c
Health Care				
Health care, ACCRA Index		87.80	12/94	2c
Antibiotic ointment, Polysporin	1.5 oz.	3.79	12/94	2c
Dentist's fee, adult teeth cleaning and periodic oral exam	visit	51.20	12/94	2c
Doctor's fee, routine exam, established patient	visit	39.00	12/94	2c
Hospital care, semiprivate room	day	200.00	12/94	2c
Household Goods				
Appl. repair, service call, wash mach	min. lab. chg.	35.75	12/94	2c
Laundry detergent, Tide Ultra, Bold, or Cheer	42 oz.	3.06	12/94	2c
Tissues, facial, Kleenex brand	175	0.97	12/94	2c
Housing				
Housing, ACCRA Index		82.90	12/94	2c

Tifton, GA - continued

Item	Per	Value	Date	Ref.
Housing - continued				
House payment, principal and interest, 25% down payment	mo.	632	12/94	2c
House, 1800 sq ft, 8000 sq ft lot, new, urban, utilities	total	104310	12/94	2c
Mtge. rate, incl. points and orig. fee, 30-year conv. fixed or ARM	mo.	9.05	12/94	2c
Rent, apartment, 2 br., 1 1/2-2 baths, unfurnished, 950 sq ft, water	mo.	446	12/94	2c
Personal Goods				
Shampoo, Alberto VO5	15-oz.	1.00	12/94	2c
Toothpaste, Crest or Colgate	6-7 oz.	1.92	12/94	2c
Personal Services				
Dry cleaning, man's 2-pc. suit		5.38	12/94	2c
Haircut, man's barbershop, no styling		6.50	12/94	2c
Haircut, woman's shampoo, trim, blow-dry		19.00	12/94	2c
Restaurant Food				
Chicken, fried, thigh and drumstick		2.29	12/94	2c
Hamburger with cheese	1/4 lb.	1.99	12/94	2c
Pizza, Pizza Hut or Pizza Inn	12-13 in.	7.99	12/94	2c
Transportation				
Transportation, ACCRA Index		88.80	12/94	2c
Tire balance, computer or spin bal., front	wheel	6.00	12/94	2c
Utilities				
Utilities, ACCRA Index		109.70	12/94	2c
Electricity, 1800 sq. ft., new home	mo.	124.18	12/94	2c

Toledo, OH

Item	Per	Value	Date	Ref.
Composite, ACCRA index		98.80	12/94	2c
Alcoholic Beverages				
Beer, Miller Lite, Bud, 12-oz., ex deposit	6	3.99	12/94	2c
J & B Scotch	750-ml.	18.95	12/94	2c
Wine, Gallo Chablis blanc	1.5-lit	4.99	12/94	2c
Appliances				
Appliances (major), expenditures	year	131	91	81r
Average annual exp.				
Food, health care, personal goods, services	year	25935	91	81r
Charity				
Cash contributions, expenditures	year	745	91	81r
Clothing				
Apparel, men and boys, total expenditures	year	332	91	81r
Apparel, women and girls, total expenditures	year	578	91	81r
Footwear, expenditures	year	164	91	81r
Jeans, man's denim		27.98	12/94	2c
Shirt, man's dress shirt		29.87	12/94	2c
Undervest, boy's size 10-14, cotton	3	4.89	12/94	2c
Communications				
Long-distance telephone rate, day, addl. min., 1-10 mi.	min.	0.16	12/93	9s
Long-distance telephone rate, day, initial min., 1-10 mi.	min.	0.32	12/93	9s
Newspaper subscription, dly. and Sun. delivery	month	11.30	12/94	2c
Phone line, single, business, field visit	inst	55.42	12/93	9s
Phone line, single, business, no field visit	inst	55.42	12/93	9s
Phone line, single, residence, field visit	inst	30.38	12/93	9s
Phone line, single, residence, no field visit	inst	30.38	12/93	9s
Telephone bill, family of four	month	21.96	12/94	2c
Telephone service, expenditures	year	547	91	81r
Telephone, business, addl. line, touch tone	month	3.25	10/91	25c
Telephone, business, connection charges, touch tone	inst	72.15	10/91	25c
Telephone, business, key system line, touch tone	month	44.71	10/91	25c

Values are in dollars or fractions of dollars. In the column headed *Ref*, references are shown to sources. Each reference is followed by a letter. These refer to the geographical level for which data were reported: s = State, r = Region, and c = City or metro. The abbreviation *ex* is used to mean *except* or *excluding*; *exp* stands for expenditures. For other abbreviations and further explanations, please see the Introduction.

Toledo, OH - continued

Item	Per	Value	Date	Ref.
Communications				
Telephone, business, PBX line, touch tone	month	44.84	10/91	25c
Telephone, business, single ln., touch tone	month	41.01	10/91	25c
Telephone, business, touch tone, inside wiring maintenance plan	month	1.50	10/91	25c
Telephone, residential, flat rate	mo.	15.25	12/93	8c
Education				
Board, 4-year private college/university	year	2241	8/94	80s
Board, 4-year public college/university	year	1625	8/94	80s
Education, total expenditures	year	394	91	81r
Room, 4-year private college/university	year	2118	8/94	80s
Room, 4-year public college/university	year	2103	8/94	80s
Total cost, 4-year private college/university	year	15444	8/94	80s
Total cost, 4-year public college/university	year	6987	8/94	80s
Tuition, 2-year public college/university, in-state	year	2076	8/94	80s
Tuition, 4-year private college/university, in-state	year	11085	8/94	80s
Tuition, 4-year public college/university, in-state	year	3259	8/94	80s
Energy and Fuels				
Energy, combined forms, 1800 sq. ft.	mo.	134.55	12/94	2c
Energy, exc. electricity, 1800 sq. ft.	mo.	61.72	12/94	2c
Fuel oil and other fuels, expenditures	year	83	91	81r
Gas, natural, expenditures	year	373	91	81r
Gas, reg unlead, taxes inc., cash, self-service	gal	1.12	12/94	2c
Gasoline and motor oil purchased	year	1000	91	81r
Gasoline, unleaded midgrade	gallon	1.15	4/93	82r
Gasoline, unleaded premium	gallon	1.23	4/93	82r
Gasoline, unleaded regular	gallon	1.07	4/93	82r
Entertainment				
Bowling, evening rate	game	2.00	12/94	2c
Entertainment, total expenditures	year	1356	91	81r
Fees and admissions, expenditures	year	347	91	81r
Monopoly game, Parker Brothers', No. 9	game	10.15	12/94	2c
Movie	adm	6.25	12/94	2c
Pets, toys, playground equipment, expenditures	year	270	91	81r
Reading, expenditures	year	160	91	81r
Televisions, radios, and sound equipment, expenditures	year	433	91	81r
Tennis balls, yellow, Wilson or Penn, 3	can	2.49	12/94	2c
Funerals				
Burial, immediate, container provided by funeral home		1268.31	1/95	54r
Cards, acknowledgment		26.12	1/95	54r
Casket, minimum alternative		198.03	1/95	54r
Cosmetology, hair care, etc.		122.19	1/95	54r
Cremation, direct, container provided by funeral home		977.81	1/95	54r
Embalming		334.00	1/95	54r
Funeral, funeral home		321.16	1/95	54r
Funeral, other facility		317.73	1/95	54r
Graveside service		292.48	1/95	54r
Hearse, local		153.20	1/95	54r
Limousine, local		123.52	1/95	54r
Memorial service		356.30	1/95	54r
Service charge, professional, nondeclinable		968.24	1/95	54r
Visitation and viewing		332.66	1/95	54r
Groceries				
Groceries, ACCRA Index		97.10	12/94	2c
Apples, Red Delicious	lb.	0.68	12/94	82r
Baby food, strained vegetables, lowest price	4-4.5 oz.	0.24	12/94	2c
Bacon, sliced	lb.	1.88	12/94	82r
Bananas	lb.	0.42	12/94	2c
Bananas	lb.	0.41	12/94	82r
Beef or hamburger, ground	lb.	1.31	12/94	2c
Beef purchases	year	197	91	81r

Toledo, OH - continued

Item	Per	Value	Date	Ref.
Groceries - continued				
Beef, stew, boneless	lb.	2.52	12/94	82r
Beverage purchases, alcoholic	year	293	91	81r
Beverage purchases, nonalcoholic	year	203	91	81r
Bologna, all beef or mixed	lb.	2.12	12/94	82r
Bread, white	24-oz.	0.74	12/94	2c
Bread, white, pan	lb.	0.76	12/94	82r
Cabbage	lb.	0.44	12/94	82r
Carrots, short trimmed and topped	lb.	0.44	12/94	82r
Cereals and bakery products purchases	year	347	91	81r
Cereals and cereals products purchases	year	119	91	81r
Cheddar cheese, natural	lb.	3.28	12/94	82r
Cheese, Kraft grated Parmesan	8-oz.	3.17	12/94	2c
Chicken breast, bone-in	lb.	1.61	12/94	82r
Chicken, fresh, whole	lb.	0.89	12/94	82r
Chicken, whole fryer	lb.	0.81	12/94	2c
Chuck roast, USDA choice, boneless	lb.	2.33	12/94	82r
Cigarettes, Winston, Kings	carton	15.20	12/94	2c
Coffee, 100%, ground roast, all sizes	lb.	4.28	12/94	82r
Coffee, vacuum-packed	13 oz.	3.33	12/94	2c
Cookies, chocolate chip	lb.	2.72	12/94	82r
Corn Flakes, Kellogg's or Post Toasties	18 oz.	2.28	12/94	2c
Corn, frozen, whole kernel, lowest price	10 oz.	0.68	12/94	2c
Dairy products (other) purchases	year	148	91	81r
Eggs, Grade A large	dozen	0.85	12/94	2c
Eggs, Grade A large	dozen	0.76	12/94	82r
Fish and seafood purchases	year	61	91	81r
Flour, white, all purpose	lb.	0.22	12/94	82r
Food purchases, food eaten at home	year	2313	91	81r
Foods purchased away from home, not prepared by consumer	year	1709	91	81r
Fruits and vegetables purchases	year	372	91	81r
Grapefruit	lb.	0.47	12/94	82r
Grapes, Thompson seedless	lb.	2.15	12/94	82r
Ground beef, 100% beef	lb.	1.37	12/94	82r
Ground chuck, 100% beef	lb.	1.81	12/94	82r
Ham, boneless, exc. canned	lb.	2.16	12/94	82r
Ice cream, prepackaged, bulk, regular	1/2 gal.	2.48	12/94	82r
Lemons	lb.	1.08	12/94	82r
Lettuce, iceberg	lb.	0.81	12/94	82r
Lettuce, iceberg	head	0.85	12/94	2c
Margarine, Blue Bonnet or Parkay cubes	lb.	0.67	12/94	2c
Margarine, stick	lb.	0.81	12/94	82r
Meats, poultry, fish, and eggs purchases	year	591	91	81r
Milk and cream (fresh) purchases	year	132	91	81r
Milk, whole	1/2 gal.	1.34	12/94	2c
Orange juice, frozen concentrate 12-oz. can	16 oz.	1.41	12/94	82r
Orange juice, Minute Maid frozen	12-oz.	1.29	12/94	2c
Oranges, Navel	lb.	0.56	12/94	82r
Peaches, halves or slices, Hunt's, Del Monte, or Libby's	29-oz.	1.49	12/94	2c
Peanut butter, creamy, all sizes	lb.	1.81	12/94	82r
Peas, sweet, Del Monte or Green Giant	15-17 oz.	0.70	12/94	2c
Pork chops, center cut, bone-in	lb.	2.76	12/94	82r
Pork purchases	year	130	91	81r
Potato chips	16-oz.	2.81	12/94	82r
Potatoes, frozen, French fried	lb.	0.83	12/94	82r
Potatoes, white	lb.	0.28	12/94	82r
Potatoes, white or red	10-lb. sack	1.93	12/94	2c
Round roast, USDA choice, boneless	lb.	2.90	12/94	82r
Sausage, Jimmy Dean, 100% pork	lb.	2.71	12/94	2c
Shortening, vegetable oil blends	lb.	0.88	12/94	82r
Shortening, vegetable, Crisco	3-lb.	2.19	12/94	2c
Soft drink, Coca Cola, ex deposit	2 lit	0.97	12/94	2c
Spaghetti and macaroni	lb.	0.78	12/94	82r
Steak, rib eye, USDA choice, boneless	lb.	6.15	12/94	82r
Steak, round, graded & ungraded, exc. USDA prime & choice	lb.	2.72	12/94	82r
Steak, round, USDA choice, boneless	lb.	3.02	12/94	82r

Values are in dollars or fractions of dollars. In the column headed *Ref*, references are shown to sources. Each reference is followed by a letter. These refer to the geographical level for which data were reported: s=State, r=Region, and c=City or metro. The abbreviation *ex* is used to mean *except* or *excluding*; *exp* stands for *expenditures*. For other abbreviations and further explanations, please see the Introduction.

Toledo, OH - continued

Item	Per	Value	Date	Ref.
Groceries				
Steak, sirloin, USDA choice, boneless	lb.	3.85	12/94	82r
Steak, t-bone	lb.	6.09	12/94	2c
Steak, T-bone, USDA choice, bone-in	lb.	5.38	12/94	82r
Sugar and other sweets, eaten at home, expenditures	year	91	91	81r
Sugar, cane or beet	4 lbs.	1.37	12/94	2c
Sugar, white, all sizes	lb.	0.36	12/94	82r
Tobacco products and smoking supplies, total expenditures	year	298	91	81r
Tomatoes, field grown	lb.	1.36	12/94	82r
Tomatoes, Hunt's or Del Monte	14.5 oz.	0.78	12/94	2c
Tuna, chunk, light	lb.	1.94	12/94	82r
Tuna, chunk, light, oil-packed	6.125-6.5 oz.	0.68	12/94	2c
Turkey, frozen, whole	lb.	0.96	12/94	82r
Yogurt, natural, fruit flavored	8 oz.	0.62	12/94	82r
Goods and Services				
Miscellaneous goods and services, ACCRA Index		100.00	12/94	2c
Health Care				
Health care, ACCRA Index		94.70	12/94	2c
Antibiotic ointment, Polysporin	1.5 oz.	3.89	12/94	2c
Childbirth, Cesarean delivery, hospital charge	birth	5101.00	12/91	69r
Childbirth, Cesarean delivery, physician charge	birth	2234.00	12/91	69r
Childbirth, normal delivery, hospital charge	birth	2891.00	12/91	69r
Childbirth, normal delivery, physician charge	birth	1623.00	12/91	69r
Dentist's fee, adult teeth cleaning and periodic oral exam	visit	53.20	12/94	2c
Doctor's fee, routine exam, established patient	visit	40.40	12/94	2c
Drugs, expenditures	year	248	91	81r
Health care, total expenditures	year	1336	91	81r
Health insurance expenditures	year	550	91	81r
Hospital care, semiprivate room	day	279.60	12/94	2c
Immunization, DTP, measles, mumps, polio	inject	66.00	8/93	90c
Insurance premium, family medical care	month	350.73	1/95	41s
Medical services expenditures	year	457	91	81r
Medical supplies expenditures	year	82	91	81r
Household Goods				
Appl. repair, service call, wash mach	min. lab. chg.	37.36	12/94	2c
Floor coverings, expenditures	year	105	91	81r
Furniture, expenditures	year	291	91	81r
Household equipment, misc. expenditures	year	341	91	81r
Household expenditures, miscellaneous	year	162	91	81r
Household furnishings and equipment, expenditures	year	1042	91	81r
Household operations expenditures	year	365	91	81r
Household textiles, expenditures	year	101	91	81r
Housekeeping supplies, expenditures	year	390	91	81r
Laundry and cleaning supplies, expenditures	year	110	91	81r
Laundry detergent, Tide Ultra, Bold, or Cheer	42 oz.	3.91	12/94	2c
Postage and stationery, expenditures	year	115	91	81r
Tissues, facial, Kleenex brand	175	1.05	12/94	2c
Housing				
Housing, ACCRA Index		90.90	12/94	2c
Add garage/carport		8,479	3/95	74r
Add room(s)		21,347	3/95	74r
Apartment condominium or co-op, median	unit	87100	12/94	62r
Bathroom addition, average cost	add	9734.00	3/95	13r
Bathroom remodeling, average cost	remod	6414.00	3/95	13r
Bedroom, master suite addition, average cost	add	27122.00	3/95	13r

Toledo, OH - continued

Item	Per	Value	Date	Ref.
Housing - continued				
Deck addition, average cost	add	6665.00	3/95	13r
Dwellings (owned), expenditures	year	2566	91	81r
Enclose porch/patio/breezeway		4,556	3/95	74r
Exterior remodeling, average cost	remod	15395.00	3/95	13r
Family room addition, average cost	add	27658.00	3/95	13r
Finish room in basement/attic		5,074	3/95	74r
Home, existing, single-family, median	unit	106500	12/94	62r
Home, existing, single-family, median	unit	69.40	12/94	62c
House payment, principal and interest, 25% down payment	mo.	707	12/94	2c
House, 1800 sq ft, 8000 sq ft lot, new, urban, utilities	total	114375	12/94	2c
Kitchen remodeling, major, average cost	remod	17084.00	3/95	13r
Kitchen remodeling, minor, average cost	remod	5804.00	3/95	13r
Maintenance, repairs, insurance, and other housing expenditures	year	484	91	81r
Mortgage interest and charges expenditures	year	1443	91	81r
Mtge. rate, incl. points and orig. fee, 30-year conv. fixed or ARM	mo.	9.27	12/94	2c
Office, home addition, average cost	add	8121.00	3/95	13r
Princ. & int., mortgage, median-price exist. sing.-family home	mo.	515	12/94	62c
Property taxes expenditures	year	639	91	81r
Redesign, restructure more than half of home's interior		9,114	3/95	74r
Rent, apartment, 2 br., 1 1/2-2 baths, unfurnished, 950 sq ft, water	mo.	450	12/94	2c
Rental units expenditures	year	1200	91	81r
Sun-space addition, average cost	add	23768.00	3/95	13r
Wing addition, two-story, average cost	add	50410.00	3/95	13r
Insurance and Pensions				
Auto insurance, private passenger	year	550.52	12/94	71s
Insurance and pensions, personal, expenditures	year	2408	91	81r
Insurance, life and other personal, expenditures	year	355	91	81r
Pensions and Social Security, expenditures	year	2053	91	81r
Legal Assistance				
Legal work, law firm associate	hour	90		10r
Legal work, law firm partner	hour	139		10r
Personal Goods				
Shampoo, Alberto VO5	15-oz.	1.01	12/94	2c
Toothpaste, Crest or Colgate	6-7 oz.	1.86	12/94	2c
Personal Services				
Dry cleaning, man's 2-pc. suit		7.11	12/94	2c
Haircut, man's barbershop, no styling		8.35	12/94	2c
Haircut, woman's shampoo, trim, blow-dry		20.90	12/94	2c
Personal services expenditures	year	203	91	81r
Restaurant Food				
Chicken, fried, thigh and drumstick		2.30	12/94	2c
Dining expenditures, family	week	30.03	94	73r
Hamburger with cheese	1/4 lb.	1.85	12/94	2c
Pizza, Pizza Hut or Pizza Inn	12-13 in.	7.59	12/94	2c
Taxes				
Taxes, Federal income, expenditures	year	1756	91	81r
Taxes, personal, expenditures	year	2426	91	81r
Taxes, State and local income, expenditures	year	568	91	81r
Transportation				
Transportation, ACCRA Index		107.10	12/94	2c
Bus fare, one-way	trip	0.85	12/95	1c
Bus fare, up to 10 miles	one-way	0.85	12/94	2c
Cars and trucks purchased, new	year	891	91	81r
Cars and trucks purchased, used	year	1155	91	81r
Driver's learning permit fee	perm	3.00	1/94	84s
Driver's license fee	orig	5.00	1/94	84s
Driver's license fee, duplicate	lic	1.50	1/94	84s

Values are in dollars or fractions of dollars. In the column headed *Ref*, references are shown to sources. Each reference is followed by a letter. These refer to the geographical level for which data were reported: s=State, r=Region, and c=City or metro. The abbreviation *ex* is used to mean *except* or *excluding*; *exp* stands for expenditures. For other abbreviations and further explanations, please see the Introduction.

Toledo, OH - continued

Item	Per	Value	Date	Ref.
Transportation				
Driver's license reinstatement fee, min.	susp	12.50-100.00	1/94	85s
Driver's license renewal fee	renew	5.00	1/94	84s
Identification card, nondriver	card	2.50	1/94	83s
Motorcycle learning permit fee	perm	3.00	1/94	84s
Motorcycle license fee	orig	5.00	1/94	84s
Motorcycle license fee, duplicate	lic	1.50	1/94	84s
Motorcycle license renewal fee	renew	5.00	1/94	84s
Public transportation expenditures	year	209	91	81r
Tire balance, computer or spin bal., front	wheel	7.29	12/94	2c
Transportation expenditures, total	year	4792	91	81r
Vehicle finance charges	year	300	91	81r
Vehicle insurance expenditures	year	485	91	81r
Vehicle maintenance and repairs expenditures	year	534	91	81r
Vehicle purchases	year	2068	91	81r
Vehicle rental, leases, licenses, etc. expenditures	year	197	91	81r
Vehicles purchased, other than cars and trucks	year	22	91	81r
Utilities				
Utilities, ACCRA Index		118.90	12/94	2c
Electricity expenditures	year	668	91	81r
Electricity, (part.), other, 1800 sq. ft., new home	mo.	72.83	12/94	2c
Electricity, summer, 250 KWh	month	33.91	8/93	64c
Electricity, summer, 500 KWh	month	63.86	8/93	64c
Electricity, summer, 750 KWh	month	93.81	8/93	64c
Electricity, summer, 1000 KWh	month	123.76	8/93	64c
Utilities, fuels, and public services, total expenditures	year	1838	91	81r
Water and other public services, expenditures	year	167	91	81r
Weddings				
Bridal attendants' gowns	event	750	10/93	76r
Bridal gown	event	852	10/93	76r
Bridal headpiece and veil	event	167	10/93	76r
Bride's wedding band	event	708	10/93	76r
Clergy	event	224	10/93	76r
Engagement ring	event	2756	10/93	76r
Flowers	event	863	10/93	76r
Formal wear for groom	event	106	10/93	76r
Groom's attendants' formal wear	event	530	10/93	76r
Groom's wedding band	event	402	10/93	76r
Music	event	600	10/93	76r
Photography	event	1088	10/93	76r
Shoes for bride	event	50	10/93	76r
Videography	event	483	10/93	76r
Wedding invitations and announcements	event	342	10/93	76r
Wedding reception	event	7000	10/93	76r

Topeka, KS

Item	Per	Value	Date	Ref.
Appliances				
Appliances (major), expenditures	year	131	91	81r
Average annual exp.				
Food, health care, personal goods, services	year	25935	91	81r
Charity				
Cash contributions, expenditures	year	745	91	81r
Clothing				
Apparel, men and boys, total expenditures	year	332	91	81r
Apparel, women and girls, total expenditures	year	578	91	81r
Footwear, expenditures	year	164	91	81r
Communications				
Long-distance telephone rate, day, addl. min., 1-10 mi.	min.	0.09	12/93	9s
Long-distance telephone rate, day, initial min., 1-10 mi.	min.	0.18	12/93	9s

Topeka, KS - continued

Item	Per	Value	Date	Ref.
Communications - continued				
Phone line, single, business, field visit	inst	57.40	12/93	9s
Phone line, single, business, no field visit	inst	57.40	12/93	9s
Phone line, single, residence, field visit	inst	39.00	12/93	9s
Phone line, single, residence, no field visit	inst	39.00	12/93	9s
Telephone service, expenditures	year	547	91	81r
Education				
Board, 4-year private college/university	year	2084	8/94	80s
Board, 4-year public college/university	year	1709	8/94	80s
Education, total expenditures	year	394	91	81r
Room, 4-year private college/university	year	1458	8/94	80s
Room, 4-year public college/university	year	1605	8/94	80s
Total cost, 4-year private college/university	year	11145	8/94	80s
Total cost, 4-year public college/university	year	5236	8/94	80s
Tuition, 2-year public college/university, in-state	year	960	8/94	80s
Tuition, 4-year private college/university, in-state	year	7602	8/94	80s
Tuition, 4-year public college/university, in-state	year	1921	8/94	80s
Energy and Fuels				
Fuel oil and other fuels, expenditures	year	83	91	81r
Gas, natural, expenditures	year	373	91	81r
Gasoline and motor oil purchased	year	1000	91	81r
Gasoline, unleaded midgrade	gallon	1.15	4/93	82r
Gasoline, unleaded premium	gallon	1.23	4/93	82r
Gasoline, unleaded regular	gallon	1.07	4/93	82r
Entertainment				
Entertainment, total expenditures	year	1356	91	81r
Fees and admissions, expenditures	year	347	91	81r
Pets, toys, playground equipment, expenditures	year	270	91	81r
Reading, expenditures	year	160	91	81r
Televisions, radios, and sound equipment, expenditures	year	433	91	81r
Funerals				
Burial, immediate, container provided by funeral home		1348.78	1/95	54r
Cards, acknowledgment		21.20	1/95	54r
Casket, minimum alternative		182.83	1/95	54r
Cosmetology, hair care, etc.		133.11	1/95	54r
Cremation, direct, container provided by funeral home		1101.95	1/95	54r
Embalming		314.45	1/95	54r
Funeral, funeral home		304.88	1/95	54r
Funeral, other facility		301.37	1/95	54r
Graveside service		290.59	1/95	54r
Hearse, local		137.37	1/95	54r
Limousine, local		82.84	1/95	54r
Memorial service		316.57	1/95	54r
Service charge, professional, nondeclinable		1099.00	1/95	54r
Visitation and viewing		209.25	1/95	54r
Groceries				
Apples, Red Delicious	lb.	0.68	12/94	82r
Bacon, sliced	lb.	1.88	12/94	82r
Bananas	lb.	0.41	12/94	82r
Beef purchases	year	197	91	81r
Beef, stew, boneless	lb.	2.52	12/94	82r
Beverage purchases, alcoholic	year	293	91	81r
Beverage purchases, nonalcoholic	year	203	91	81r
Bologna, all beef or mixed	lb.	2.12	12/94	82r
Bread, white, pan	lb.	0.76	12/94	82r
Cabbage	lb.	0.44	12/94	82r
Carrots, short trimmed and topped	lb.	0.44	12/94	82r
Cereals and bakery products purchases	year	347	91	81r
Cereals and cereals products purchases	year	119	91	81r
Cheddar cheese, natural	lb.	3.28	12/94	82r
Chicken breast, bone-in	lb.	1.61	12/94	82r
Chicken, fresh, whole	lb.	0.89	12/94	82r
Chuck roast, USDA choice, boneless	lb.	2.33	12/94	82r

Values are in dollars or fractions of dollars. In the column headed *Ref*, references are shown to sources. Each reference is followed by a letter. These refer to the geographical level for which data were reported: s=State, r=Region, and c=City or metro. The abbreviation *ex* is used to mean *except* or *excluding*; *exp* stands for *expenditures*. For other abbreviations and further explanations, please see the Introduction.

Topeka, KS - continued

Item	Per	Value	Date	Ref.
Groceries				
Coffee, 100%, ground roast, all sizes	lb.	4.28	12/94	82r
Cookies, chocolate chip	lb.	2.72	12/94	82r
Dairy products (other) purchases	year	148	91	81r
Eggs, Grade A large	dozen	0.76	12/94	82r
Fish and seafood purchases	year	61	91	81r
Flour, white, all purpose	lb.	0.22	12/94	82r
Food purchases, food eaten at home	year	2313	91	81r
Foods purchased away from home, not prepared by consumer	year	1709	91	81r
Fruits and vegetables purchases	year	372	91	81r
Grapefruit	lb.	0.47	12/94	82r
Grapes, Thompson seedless	lb.	2.15	12/94	82r
Ground beef, 100% beef	lb.	1.37	12/94	82r
Ground chuck, 100% beef	lb.	1.81	12/94	82r
Ham, boneless, exc. canned	lb.	2.16	12/94	82r
Ice cream, prepackaged, bulk, regular	1/2 gal.	2.48	12/94	82r
Lemons	lb.	1.08	12/94	82r
Lettuce, iceberg	lb.	0.81	12/94	82r
Margarine, stick	lb.	0.81	12/94	82r
Meats, poultry, fish, and eggs purchases	year	591	91	81r
Milk and cream (fresh) purchases	year	132	91	81r
Orange juice, frozen concentrate 12-oz. can	16 oz.	1.41	12/94	82r
Oranges, Navel	lb.	0.56	12/94	82r
Peanut butter, creamy, all sizes	lb.	1.81	12/94	82r
Pork chops, center cut, bone-in	lb.	2.76	12/94	82r
Pork purchases	year	130	91	81r
Potato chips	16-oz.	2.81	12/94	82r
Potatoes, frozen, French fried	lb.	0.83	12/94	82r
Potatoes, white	lb.	0.28	12/94	82r
Round roast, USDA choice, boneless	lb.	2.90	12/94	82r
Shortening, vegetable oil blends	lb.	0.88	12/94	82r
Spaghetti and macaroni	lb.	0.78	12/94	82r
Steak, rib eye, USDA choice, boneless	lb.	6.15	12/94	82r
Steak, round, graded & ungraded, exc. USDA prime & choice	lb.	2.72	12/94	82r
Steak, round, USDA choice, boneless	lb.	3.02	12/94	82r
Steak, sirloin, USDA choice, boneless	lb.	3.85	12/94	82r
Steak, T-bone, USDA choice, bone-in	lb.	5.38	12/94	82r
Sugar and other sweets, eaten at home, expenditures	year	91	91	81r
Sugar, white, all sizes	lb.	0.36	12/94	82r
Tobacco products and smoking supplies, total expenditures	year	298	91	81r
Tomatoes, field grown	lb.	1.36	12/94	82r
Tuna, chunk, light	lb.	1.94	12/94	82r
Turkey, frozen, whole	lb.	0.96	12/94	82r
Yogurt, natural, fruit flavored	8 oz.	0.62	12/94	82r
Health Care				
Childbirth, Cesarean delivery, hospital charge	birth	5101.00	12/91	69r
Childbirth, Cesarean delivery, physician charge	birth	2234.00	12/91	69r
Childbirth, normal delivery, hospital charge	birth	2891.00	12/91	69r
Childbirth, normal delivery, physician charge	birth	1623.00	12/91	69r
Drugs, expenditures	year	248	91	81r
Health care, total expenditures	year	1336	91	81r
Health insurance expenditures	year	550	91	81r
Insurance premium, family medical care	month	370.49	1/95	41s
Medical services expenditures	year	457	91	81r
Medical supplies expenditures	year	82	91	81r
Household Goods				
Floor coverings, expenditures	year	105	91	81r
Furniture, expenditures	year	291	91	81r
Household equipment, misc. expenditures	year	341	91	81r
Household expenditures, miscellaneous	year	162	91	81r
Household furnishings and equipment, expenditures	year	1042	91	81r
Household operations expenditures	year	365	91	81r
Household textiles, expenditures	year	101	91	81r
Housekeeping supplies, expenditures	year	390	91	81r

Topeka, KS - continued

Item	Per	Value	Date	Ref.
Household Goods - continued				
Laundry and cleaning supplies, expenditures	year	110	91	81r
Postage and stationery, expenditures	year	115	91	81r
Housing				
Add garage/carport		8,479	3/95	74r
Add room(s)		21,347	3/95	74r
Apartment condominium or co-op, median	unit	87100	12/94	62r
Bathroom addition, average cost	add	9734.00	3/95	13r
Bathroom remodeling, average cost	remod	6414.00	3/95	13r
Bedroom, master suite addition, average cost	add	27122.00	3/95	13r
Deck addition, average cost	add	6665.00	3/95	13r
Dwellings (owned), expenditures	year	2566	91	81r
Enclose porch/patio/breezeway		4,556	3/95	74r
Exterior remodeling, average cost	remod	15395.00	3/95	13r
Family room addition, average cost	add	27658.00	3/95	13r
Finish room in basement/attic		5,074	3/95	74r
Home, existing, single-family, median	unit	106500	12/94	62r
Kitchen remodeling, major, average cost	remod	17084.00	3/95	13r
Kitchen remodeling, minor, average cost	remod	5804.00	3/95	13r
Maintenance, repairs, insurance, and other housing expenditures	year	484	91	81r
Mortgage interest and charges expenditures	year	1443	91	81r
Office, home addition, average cost	add	8121.00	3/95	13r
Princ. & int., mortgage, median-price exist. sing.-family home	mo.	515	12/94	62r
Property taxes expenditures	year	639	91	81r
Redesign, restructure more than half of home's interior		9,114	3/95	74r
Rental units expenditures	year	1200	91	81r
Sun-space addition, average cost	add	23768.00	3/95	13r
Wing addition, two-story, average cost	add	50410.00	3/95	13r
Insurance and Pensions				
Auto insurance, private passenger	year	526.96	12/94	71s
Insurance and pensions, personal, expenditures	year	2408	91	81r
Insurance, life and other personal, expenditures	year	355	91	81r
Pensions and Social Security, expenditures	year	2053	91	81r
Legal Assistance				
Legal work, law firm associate	hour	90		10r
Legal work, law firm partner	hour	139		10r
Personal Services				
Personal services expenditures	year	203	91	81r
Restaurant Food				
Dining expenditures, family	week	30.03	94	73r
Taxes				
Taxes, Federal income, expenditures	year	1756	91	81r
Taxes, personal, expenditures	year	2426	91	81r
Taxes, State and local income, expenditures	year	568	91	81r
Transportation				
Cars and trucks purchased, new	year	891	91	81r
Cars and trucks purchased, used	year	1155	91	81r
Driver's learning permit fee	perm	3.00	1/94	84s
Driver's license fee	orig	12.00	1/94	84s
Driver's license fee, duplicate	lic	5.00	1/94	84s
Driver's license reinstatement fee, min.	susp	25.00	1/94	85s
Driver's license renewal fee	renew	9.00	1/94	84s
Identification card, nondriver	card	6.00	1/94	83s
Motorcycle license fee	orig	9.00	1/94	84s
Motorcycle license fee, duplicate	lic	5.00	1/94	84s
Motorcycle license renewal fee	renew	6.00	1/94	84s
Public transportation expenditures	year	209	91	81r
Transportation expenditures, total	year	4792	91	81r
Vehicle finance charges	year	300	91	81r
Vehicle insurance expenditures	year	485	91	81r
Vehicle maintenance and repairs expenditures	year	534	91	81r

Values are in dollars or fractions of dollars. In the column headed *Ref*, references are shown to sources. Each reference is followed by a letter. These refer to the geographical level for which data were reported: s=State, r=Region, and c=City or metro. The abbreviation *ex* is used to mean *except* or *excluding*; *exp* stands for expenditures. For other abbreviations and further explanations, please see the Introduction.

Topeka, KS - continued

Item	Per	Value	Date	Ref.
Transportation				
Vehicle purchases	year	2068	91	81r
Vehicle rental, leases, licenses, etc. expenditures	year	197	91	81r
Vehicles purchased, other than cars and trucks	year	22	91	81r
Utilities				
Electricity expenditures	year	668	91	81r
Utilities, fuels, and public services, total expenditures	year	1838	91	81r
Water and other public services, expenditures	year	167	91	81r
Weddings				
Bridal attendants' gowns	event	750	10/93	76r
Bridal gown	event	852	10/93	76r
Bridal headpiece and veil	event	167	10/93	76r
Bride's wedding band	event	708	10/93	76r
Clergy	event	224	10/93	76r
Engagement ring	event	2756	10/93	76r
Flowers	event	863	10/93	76r
Formal wear for groom	event	106	10/93	76r
Groom's attendants' formal wear	event	530	10/93	76r
Groom's wedding band	event	402	10/93	76r
Music	event	600	10/93	76r
Photography	event	1088	10/93	76r
Shoes for bride	event	50	10/93	76r
Videography	event	483	10/93	76r
Wedding invitations and announcements	event	342	10/93	76r
Wedding reception	event	7000	10/93	76r

Trenton, NJ

Item	Per	Value	Date	Ref.
Appliances				
Appliances (major), expenditures	year	145	91	81r
Average annual exp.				
Food, health care, personal goods, services	year	29496	91	81r
Charity				
Cash contributions, expenditures	year	708	91	81r
Clothing				
Apparel, men and boys, total expenditures	year	416	91	81r
Apparel, women and girls, total expenditures	year	744	91	81r
Footwear, expenditures	year	305	91	81r
Communications				
Long-distance telephone rate, day, addl. min., 1-10 mi.	min.	0.03	12/93	9s
Long-distance telephone rate, day, initial min., 1-10 mi.	min.	0.09	12/93	9s
Phone line, single, business, field visit	inst	98.50	12/93	9s
Phone line, single, business, no field visit	inst	79.50	12/93	9s
Phone line, single, residence, field visit	inst	56.50	12/93	9s
Phone line, single, residence, no field visit	inst	42.00	12/93	9s
Telephone service, expenditures	year	589	91	81r
Education				
Board, 4-year private college/university	year	2841	8/94	80s
Board, 4-year public college/university	year	1956	8/94	80s
Education, total expenditures	year	593	91	81r
Room, 4-year private college/university	year	2999	8/94	80s
Room, 4-year public college/university	year	2778	8/94	80s
Total cost, 4-year private college/university	year	18264	8/94	80s
Total cost, 4-year public college/university	year	8252	8/94	80s
Tuition, 2-year public college/university, in-state	year	1539	8/94	80s
Tuition, 4-year private college/university, in-state	year	12423	8/94	80s
Tuition, 4-year public college/university, in-state	year	3518	8/94	80s

Trenton, NJ - continued

Item	Per	Value	Date	Ref.
Energy and Fuels				
Fuel oil and other fuels, expenditures	year	257	91	81r
Gas, natural, expenditures	year	285	91	81r
Gasoline and motor oil purchased	year	867	91	81r
Gasoline, unleaded midgrade	gallon	1.32	4/93	82r
Gasoline, unleaded premium	gallon	1.40	4/93	82r
Gasoline, unleaded regular	gallon	1.19	4/93	82r
Entertainment				
Entertainment, total expenditures	year	1331	91	81r
Fees and admissions, expenditures	year	398	91	81r
Pets, toys, playground equipment, expenditures	year	270	91	81r
Reading, expenditures	year	171	91	81r
Televisions, radios, and sound equipment, expenditures	year	429	91	81r
Funerals				
Burial, immediate, container provided by funeral home		1370.36	1/95	54r
Cards, acknowledgment		17.72	1/95	54r
Casket, minimum alternative		192.52	1/95	54r
Cosmetology, hair care, etc.		139.56	1/95	54r
Cremation, direct, container provided by funeral home		1049.24	1/95	54r
Embalming		387.57	1/95	54r
Funeral, funeral home		278.77	1/95	54r
Funeral, other facility		275.85	1/95	54r
Graveside service		213.08	1/95	54r
Hearse, local		157.27	1/95	54r
Limousine, local		146.45	1/95	54r
Memorial service		271.02	1/95	54r
Service charge, professional, nondeclinable		943.58	1/95	54r
Visitation and viewing		322.86	1/95	54r
Groceries				
Apples, Red Delicious	lb.	0.78	12/94	82r
Bacon, sliced	lb.	2.24	12/94	82r
Bananas	lb.	0.49	12/94	82r
Beef purchases	year	226	91	81r
Beverage purchases, alcoholic	year	332	91	81r
Beverage purchases, nonalcoholic	year	213	91	81r
Bread, white, pan	lb.	0.80	12/94	82r
Butter, salted, Grade AA, stick	lb.	1.67	12/94	82r
Carrots, short trimmed and topped	lb.	0.51	12/94	82r
Cereals and bakery products purchases	year	407	91	81r
Cereals and cereals products purchases	year	132	91	81r
Chicken breast, bone-in	lb.	2.22	12/94	82r
Chicken, fresh, whole	lb.	1.05	12/94	82r
Chuck roast, USDA choice, boneless	lb.	2.74	12/94	82r
Coffee, 100%, ground roast, all sizes	lb.	4.61	12/94	82r
Dairy products (other) purchases	year	161	91	81r
Eggs, Grade A large	dozen	1.12	12/94	82r
Fish and seafood purchases	year	112	91	81r
Food purchases, food eaten at home	year	2599	91	81r
Foods purchased away from home, not prepared by consumer	year	2024	91	81r
Fruits and vegetables purchases	year	444	91	81r
Grapefruit	lb.	0.44	12/94	82r
Grapes, Thompson seedless	lb.	2.24	12/94	82r
Ground chuck, 100% beef	lb.	1.67	12/94	82r
Ice cream, prepackaged, bulk, regular	1/2 gal.	2.93	12/94	82r
Lemons	lb.	1.06	12/94	82r
Lettuce, iceberg	lb.	0.92	12/94	82r
Meats, poultry, fish, and eggs purchases	year	751	91	81r
Milk and cream (fresh) purchases	year	152	91	81r
Orange juice, frozen concentrate 12-oz. can	16 oz.	1.92	12/94	82r
Oranges, Navel	lb.	0.56	12/94	82r
Pork chops, center cut, bone-in	lb.	3.09	12/94	82r
Pork purchases	year	130	91	81r
Potatoes, white	lb.	0.37	12/94	82r
Rib roast, USDA choice, bone-in	lb.	4.98	12/94	82r
Round roast, USDA choice, boneless	lb.	2.93	12/94	82r
Shortening, vegetable oil blends	lb.	1.03	12/94	82r

Values are in dollars or fractions of dollars. In the column headed *Ref*, references are shown to sources. Each reference is followed by a letter. These refer to the geographical level for which data were reported: s = State, r = Region, and c = City or metro. The abbreviation *ex* is used to mean *except* or *excluding*; *exp* stands for expenditures. For other abbreviations and further explanations, please see the Introduction.

Trenton, NJ - continued

Item	Per	Value	Date	Ref.
Groceries				
Spaghetti and macaroni	lb.	0.84	12/94	82r
Steak, round, USDA choice, boneless	lb.	3.48	12/94	82r
Steak, sirloin, USDA choice, bone-in	lb.	3.38	12/94	82r
Steak, sirloin, USDA choice, boneless	lb.	4.81	12/94	82r
Sugar and other sweets, eaten at home, expenditures	year	89	91	81r
Sugar, white, all sizes	lb.	0.46	12/94	82r
Tobacco products and smoking supplies, total expenditures	year	279	91	81r
Tomatoes, field grown	lb.	1.56	12/94	82r
Tuna, chunk, light	lb.	2.09	12/94	82r
Health Care				
Childbirth, Cesarean delivery, hospital charge	birth	6334.00	12/91	69r
Childbirth, Cesarean delivery, physician charge	birth	2234.00	12/91	69r
Childbirth, normal delivery, hospital charge	birth	3225.00	12/91	69r
Childbirth, normal delivery, physician charge	birth	1623.00	12/91	69r
Drugs, expenditures	year	205	91	81r
Health care, total expenditures	year	1396	91	81r
Health insurance expenditures	year	553	91	81r
Insurance premium, family medical care	month	396.06	1/95	41s
Medical services expenditures	year	559	91	81r
Medical supplies expenditures	year	80	91	81r
Household Goods				
Floor coverings, expenditures	year	158	91	81r
Furniture, expenditures	year	341	91	81r
Household equipment, misc. expenditures	year	363	91	81r
Household expenditures, miscellaneous	year	194	91	81r
Household furnishings and equipment, expenditures	year	1158	91	81r
Household operations expenditures	year	378	91	81r
Household textiles, expenditures	year	88	91	81r
Housekeeping supplies, expenditures	year	426	91	81r
Laundry and cleaning supplies, expenditures	year	122	91	81r
Postage and stationery, expenditures	year	134	91	81r
Housing				
Add garage/carport		11,614	3/95	74r
Add room(s)		16,816	3/95	74r
Apartment condominium or co-op, median	unit	96700	12/94	62r
Dwellings (owned), expenditures	year	3305	91	81r
Enclose porch/patio/breezeway		2,980	3/95	74r
Finish room in basement/attic		4,330	3/95	74r
Home, existing, single-family, median	unit	161600	12/94	62r
Maintenance, repairs, insurance, and other housing expenditures	year	569	91	81r
Mortgage interest and charges expenditures	year	1852	91	81r
Princ. & int., mortgage, median-price exist. sing.-family home	mo.	765	12/94	62r
Property taxes expenditures	year	884	91	81r
Redesign, restructure more than half of home's interior		2,750	3/95	74r
Rental units expenditures	year	1832	91	81r
Insurance and Pensions				
Auto insurance, private passenger	year	1094.56	12/94	71s
Insurance and pensions, personal, expenditures	year	2690	91	81r
Insurance, life and other personal, expenditures	year	341	91	81r
Pensions and Social Security, expenditures	year	2349	91	81r
Legal Assistance				
Estate planning, law-firm partner	hr.	375.00	10/93	12r
Legal work, law firm associate	hour	78		10r
Legal work, law firm partner	hour	183		10r
Personal Services				
Personal services expenditures	year	184	91	81r

Trenton, NJ - continued

Item	Per	Value	Date	Ref.
Restaurant Food				
Dining expenditures, family	week	34.26	94	73r
Taxes				
Taxes, Federal income, expenditures	year	2409	91	81r
Taxes, personal, expenditures	year	3094	91	81r
Taxes, State and local income, expenditures	year	620	91	81r
Transportation				
Cars and trucks purchased, new	year	1170	91	81r
Cars and trucks purchased, used	year	739	91	81r
Driver's learning permit fee	perm	5.00	1/94	84s
Driver's license fee	orig	16.00	1/94	84s
Driver's license fee, duplicate	lic	3.00	1/94	84s
Driver's license reinstatement fee, min.	susp	30.00	1/94	85s
Driver's license renewal fee	renew	16.00	1/94	84s
Identification card, nondriver	card	5.50	1/94	83s
Motorcycle learning permit fee	perm	5.00	1/94	84s
Motorcycle license fee	orig	8.00	1/94	84s
Motorcycle license fee, duplicate	lic	3.00	1/94	84s
Motorcycle license renewal fee	renew	8.00	1/94	84s
Public transportation expenditures	year	430	91	81r
Transportation expenditures, total	year	4810	91	81r
Vehicle finance charges	year	238	91	81r
Vehicle insurance expenditures	year	630	91	81r
Vehicle maintenance and repairs expenditures	year	532	91	81r
Vehicle purchases	year	1920	91	81r
Vehicle rental, leases, licenses, etc. expenditures	year	193	91	81r
Vehicles purchased, other than cars and trucks	year	11	91	81r
Utilities				
Electricity expenditures	year	695	91	81r
Utilities, fuels, and public services, total expenditures	year	1981	91	81r
Water and other public services, expenditures	year	154	91	81r
Weddings				
Bridal attendants' gowns	event	750	10/93	76r
Bridal gown	event	852	10/93	76r
Bridal headpiece and veil	event	167	10/93	76r
Bride's wedding band	event	708	10/93	76r
Clergy	event	224	10/93	76r
Engagement ring	event	2756	10/93	76r
Flowers	event	863	10/93	76r
Formal wear for groom	event	106	10/93	76r
Groom's attendants' formal wear	event	530	10/93	76r
Groom's wedding band	event	402	10/93	76r
Music	event	600	10/93	76r
Photography	event	1088	10/93	76r
Shoes for bride	event	50	10/93	76r
Videography	event	483	10/93	76r
Wedding invitations and announcements	event	342	10/93	76r
Wedding reception	event	7000	10/93	76r

Tucson, AZ

Item	Per	Value	Date	Ref.
Composite, ACCRA index		99.70	12/94	2c
Alcoholic Beverages				
Beer, Miller Lite, Bud, 12-oz., ex deposit	6	3.62	12/94	2c
J & B Scotch	750-ml.	14.45	12/94	2c
Wine, Gallo Chablis blanc	1.5-lit	4.26	12/94	2c
Appliances				
Appliances (major), expenditures	year	160	91	81r
Average annual exp.				
Food, health care, personal goods, services	year	32461	91	81r

Values are in dollars or fractions of dollars. In the column headed *Ref*, references are shown to sources. Each reference is followed by a letter. These refer to the geographical level for which data were reported: s=State, r=Region, and c=City or metro. The abbreviation *ex* is used to mean *except* or *excluding*; *exp* stands for *expenditures*. For other abbreviations and further explanations, please see the Introduction.

Tucson, AZ - continued

Item	Per	Value	Date	Ref.
Charity				
Cash contributions, expenditures	year	975	91	81r
Clothing				
Apparel, men and boys, total expenditures	year	467	91	81r
Apparel, women and girls, total expenditures	year	737	91	81r
Footwear, expenditures	year	270	91	81r
Jeans, man's denim		29.99	12/94	2c
Shirt, man's dress shirt		27.69	12/94	2c
Undervest, boy's size 10-14, cotton	3	6.19	12/94	2c
Communications				
Long-distance telephone rate, day, addl. min., 1-10 mi.	min.	0.10	12/93	9s
Long-distance telephone rate, day, initial min., 1-10 mi.	min.	0.24	12/93	9s
Newspaper subscription, dly. and Sun. delivery	month	11.74	12/94	2c
Phone line, single, business, field visit	inst	56.00	12/93	9s
Phone line, single, business, no field visit	inst	56.00	12/93	9s
Phone line, single, residence, field visit	inst	46.50	12/93	9s
Phone line, single, residence, no field visit	inst	46.50	12/93	9s
Telephone bill, family of four	month	17.95	12/94	2c
Telephone service, expenditures	year	611	91	81r
Telephone, residential, flat rate	mo.	12.40	12/93	8c
Education				
Board, 4-year private college/university	year	2044	8/94	80s
Board, 4-year public college/university	year	1904	8/94	80s
Education, total expenditures	year	375	91	81r
Room, 4-year private college/university	year	1617	8/94	80s
Room, 4-year public college/university	year	1739	8/94	80s
Total cost, 4-year private college/university	year	9542	8/94	80s
Total cost, 4-year public college/university	year	5462	8/94	80s
Tuition, 2-year public college/university, in-state	year	729	8/94	80s
Tuition, 4-year private college/university, in-state	year	5881	8/94	80s
Tuition, 4-year public college/university, in-state	year	1819	8/94	80s
Energy and Fuels				
Energy, combined forms, 1800 sq. ft.	mo.	114.40	12/94	2c
Energy, exc. electricity, 1800 sq. ft.	mo.	31.37	12/94	2c
Fuel oil and other fuels, expenditures	year	33	91	81r
Gas, cooking, 10 therms	month	11.43	2/94	65c
Gas, cooking, 30 therms	month	23.26	2/94	65c
Gas, cooking, 50 therms	month	35.13	2/94	65c
Gas, heating, winter, 100 therms	month	64.76	2/94	65c
Gas, heating, winter, average use	month	54.09	2/94	65c
Gas, natural, expenditures	year	212	91	81r
Gas, reg unlead, taxes inc., cash, self-service	gal	1.09	12/94	2c
Gasoline and motor oil purchased	year	1115	91	81r
Gasoline, unleaded midgrade	gallon	1.36	4/93	82r
Gasoline, unleaded premium	gallon	1.43	4/93	82r
Gasoline, unleaded regular	gallon	1.23	4/93	82r
Entertainment				
Bowling, evening rate	game	1.99	12/94	2c
Concert ticket, Pearl Jam group	perf	20.00	94	50r
Entertainment, total expenditures	year	1853	91	81r
Fees and admissions, expenditures	year	482	91	81r
Monopoly game, Parker Brothers', No. 9	game	11.20	12/94	2c
Movie	adm	6.75	12/94	2c
Pets, toys, playground equipment, expenditures	year	299	91	81r
Reading, expenditures	year	164	91	81r
Televisions, radios, and sound equipment, expenditures	year	528	91	81r
Tennis balls, yellow, Wilson or Penn, 3	can	2.22	12/94	2c
Funerals				
Burial, immediate, container provided by funeral home		1360.49	1/95	54r
Cards, acknowledgment		11.24	1/95	54r

Tucson, AZ - continued

Item	Per	Value	Date	Ref.
Funerals - continued				
Casket, minimum alternative		232.73	1/95	54r
Cosmetology, hair care, etc.		114.13	1/95	54r
Cremation, direct, container provided by funeral home		1027.08	1/95	54r
Embalming		286.24	1/95	54r
Funeral, funeral home		315.60	1/95	54r
Funeral, other facility		303.08	1/95	54r
Graveside service		423.83	1/95	54r
Hearse, local		133.12	1/95	54r
Limousine, local		99.10	1/95	54r
Memorial service		442.57	1/95	54r
Service charge, professional, nondeclinable		840.16	1/95	54r
Visitation and viewing		168.50	1/95	54r
Groceries				
Groceries, ACCRA Index		99.60	12/94	2c
Apples, Red Delicious	lb.	0.72	12/94	82r
Baby food, strained vegetables, lowest price	4-4.5 oz.	0.29	12/94	2c
Bacon, sliced	lb.	1.73	12/94	82r
Bananas	lb.	0.24	12/94	2c
Bananas	lb.	0.52	12/94	82r
Beef or hamburger, ground	lb.	1.59	12/94	2c
Beef purchases	year	241	91	81r
Beverage purchases, alcoholic	year	328	91	81r
Beverage purchases, nonalcoholic	year	234	91	81r
Bologna, all beef or mixed	lb.	2.33	12/94	82r
Bread, white	24-oz.	0.82	12/94	2c
Bread, white, pan	lb.	0.81	12/94	82r
Carrots, short trimmed and topped	lb.	0.43	12/94	82r
Cereals and bakery products purchases	year	392	91	81r
Cereals and cereals products purchases	year	139	91	81r
Cheese, Kraft grated Parmesan	8-oz.	3.47	12/94	2c
Chicken breast, bone-in	lb.	2.04	12/94	82r
Chicken, fresh, whole	lb.	0.95	12/94	82r
Chicken, whole fryer	lb.	0.89	12/94	2c
Cigarettes, Winston, Kings	carton	14.49	12/94	2c
Coffee, 100%, ground roast, all sizes	lb.	4.48	12/94	82r
Coffee, vacuum-packed	13 oz.	3.70	12/94	2c
Corn Flakes, Kellogg's or Post Toasties	18 oz.	2.70	12/94	2c
Corn, frozen, whole kernel, lowest price	10 oz.	0.68	12/94	2c
Dairy products (other) purchases	year	182	91	81r
Eggs, Grade A large	dozen	0.81	12/94	2c
Fish and seafood purchases	year	94	91	81r
Flour, white, all purpose	lb.	0.21	12/94	82r
Food purchases, food eaten at home	year	2749	91	81r
Foods purchased away from home, not prepared by consumer	year	1909	91	81r
Fruits and vegetables purchases	year	459	91	81r
Grapefruit	lb.	0.56	12/94	82r
Ground beef, 100% beef	lb.	1.31	12/94	82r
Ham, boneless, exc. canned	lb.	2.46	12/94	82r
Ice cream, prepackaged, bulk, regular	1/2 gal.	2.57	12/94	82r
Lemons	lb.	1.00	12/94	82r
Lettuce, iceberg	lb.	0.93	12/94	82r
Lettuce, iceberg	head	0.83	12/94	2c
Margarine, Blue Bonnet or Parkay cubes	lb.	0.69	12/94	2c
Meats, poultry, fish, and eggs purchases	year	700	91	81r
Milk and cream (fresh) purchases	year	155	91	81r
Milk, whole	1/2 gal.	1.45	12/94	2c
Orange juice, frozen concentrate 12-oz. can	16 oz.	1.52	12/94	82r
Orange juice, Minute Maid frozen	12-oz.	1.14	12/94	2c
Oranges, Navel	lb.	0.56	12/94	82r
Peaches, halves or slices, Hunt's, Del Monte, or Libby's	29-oz.	1.45	12/94	2c
Peas, sweet, Del Monte or Green Giant	15-17 oz.	0.61	12/94	2c
Pork chops, center cut, bone-in	lb.	3.30	12/94	82r
Pork purchases	year	122	91	81r
Potato chips	16-oz.	3.03	12/94	82r
Potatoes, frozen, French fried	lb.	0.77	12/94	82r

Values are in dollars or fractions of dollars. In the column headed *Ref*, references are shown to sources. Each reference is followed by a letter. These refer to the geographical level for which data were reported: s = State, r = Region, and c = City or metro. The abbreviation *ex* is used to mean *except* or *excluding*; *exp* stands for *expenditures*. For other abbreviations and further explanations, please see the Introduction.

Tucson, AZ - continued

Item	Per	Value	Date	Ref.
Groceries				
Potatoes, white	lb.	0.35	12/94	82r
Potatoes, white or red	10-lb. sack	1.14	12/94	2c
Rice, white, long grain, uncooked	lb.	0.54	12/94	82r
Round roast, USDA choice, boneless	lb.	2.92	12/94	82r
Sausage, Jimmy Dean, 100% pork	lb.	3.32	12/94	2c
Shortening, vegetable oil blends	lb.	0.80	12/94	82r
Shortening, vegetable, Crisco	3-lb.	2.74	12/94	2c
Soft drink, Coca Cola, ex deposit	2 lit	1.21	12/94	2c
Spaghetti and macaroni	lb.	1.02	12/94	82r
Steak, round, graded & ungraded, exc. USDA prime & choice	lb.	3.13	12/94	82r
Steak, sirloin, USDA choice, boneless	lb.	4.07	12/94	82r
Steak, t-bone	lb.	4.01	12/94	2c
Sugar and other sweets, eaten at home, expenditures	year	105	91	81r
Sugar, cane or beet	4 lbs.	1.42	12/94	2c
Sugar, white, all sizes	lb.	0.38	12/94	82r
Tobacco products and smoking supplies, total expenditures	year	221	91	81r
Tomatoes, field grown	lb.	1.45	12/94	82r
Tomatoes, Hunt's or Del Monte	14.5 oz.	0.77	12/94	2c
Tuna, chunk, light	lb.	2.18	12/94	82r
Tuna, chunk, light, oil-packed	6.125-6.5 oz.	0.71	12/94	2c
Goods and Services				
Miscellaneous goods and services, ACCRA Index		99.60	12/94	2c
Health Care				
Health care, ACCRA Index		106.80	12/94	2c
Antibiotic ointment, Polysporin	1.5 oz.	4.49	12/94	2c
Childbirth, Cesarean delivery, hospital charge	birth	6059.00	12/91	69r
Childbirth, Cesarean delivery, physician charge	birth	2248.00	12/91	69r
Childbirth, normal delivery, hospital charge	birth	3006.00	12/91	69r
Childbirth, normal delivery, physician charge	birth	1634.00	12/91	69r
Dentist's fee, adult teeth cleaning and periodic oral exam	visit	51.20	12/94	2c
Doctor's fee, routine exam, established patient	visit	39.80	12/94	2c
Drugs, expenditures	year	230	91	81r
Health care, total expenditures	year	1544	91	81r
Health insurance expenditures	year	558	91	81r
Hospital care, semiprivate room	day	521.80	12/94	2c
Insurance premium, family medical care	month	364.71	1/95	41s
Medical services expenditures	year	676	91	81r
Medical supplies expenditures	year	80	91	81r
Surgery, open-heart	proc	37818.00	1/93	14r
Household Goods				
Appl. repair, service call, wash mach	min. lab. chg.	21.78	12/94	2c
Floor coverings, expenditures	year	79	91	81r
Furniture, expenditures	year	352	91	81r
Household equipment, misc. expenditures	year	614	91	81r
Household expenditures, miscellaneous	year	294	91	81r
Household furnishings and equipment, expenditures	year	1416	91	81r
Household operations expenditures	year	580	91	81r
Household textiles, expenditures	year	113	91	81r
Housekeeping supplies, expenditures	year	447	91	81r
Laundry and cleaning supplies, expenditures	year	114	91	81r
Laundry detergent, Tide Ultra, Bold, or Cheer	42 oz.	3.77	12/94	2c
Postage and stationery, expenditures	year	145	91	81r
Tissues, facial, Kleenex brand	175	1.05	12/94	2c

Tucson, AZ - continued

Item	Per	Value	Date	Ref.
Housing				
Housing, ACCRA Index		100.00	12/94	2c
Add garage/carport		6,422	3/95	74r
Add room(s)		26,583	3/95	74r
Apartment condominium or co-op, median	unit	105300	12/94	62r
Dwellings (owned), expenditures	year	3932	91	81r
Enclose porch/patio/breezeway		5,382	3/95	74r
Finish room in basement/attic		3,911	3/95	74r
Home, existing, single-family, median	unit	178600	12/94	62r
Home, existing, single-family, median	unit	91.40	12/94	62c
House payment, principal and interest, 25% down payment	mo.	749	12/94	2c
House, 1800 sq ft, 8000 sq ft lot, new, urban, utilities	total	120875	12/94	2c
Maintenance, repairs, insurance, and other housing expenditures	year	591	91	81r
Mortgage interest and charges expenditures	year	2747	91	81r
Mtge. rate, incl. points and orig. fee, 30-year conv. fixed or ARM	mo.	9.30	12/94	2c
Princ. & int., mortgage, median-price exist. sing.-family home	mo.	845	12/94	62r
Property taxes expenditures	year	594	91	81r
Redesign, restructure more than half of home's interior		5,467	3/95	74r
Rent, apartment, 2 br., 1 1/2-2 baths, unfurnished, water	mo.	576	12/94	2c
Rental units expenditures	year	2077	91	81r
Insurance and Pensions				
Auto insurance, private passenger	year	782.68	12/94	71s
Insurance and pensions, personal, expenditures	year	3042	91	81r
Insurance, life and other personal, expenditures	year	298	91	81r
Pensions and Social Security, expenditures	year	2744	91	81r
Legal Assistance				
Legal work, law firm associate	hour	91		10r
Legal work, law firm partner	hour	151		10r
Personal Goods				
Shampoo, Alberto VO5	15-oz.	1.06	12/94	2c
Toothpaste, Crest or Colgate	6-7 oz.	1.86	12/94	2c
Personal Services				
Dry cleaning, man's 2-pc. suit		7.57	12/94	2c
Haircut, man's barbershop, no styling		10.90	12/94	2c
Haircut, woman's shampoo, trim, blow-dry		19.50	12/94	2c
Personal services expenditures	year	286	91	81r
Restaurant Food				
Chicken, fried, thigh and drumstick		2.15	12/94	2c
Dining expenditures, family	week	32.25	94	73r
Hamburger with cheese	1/4 lb.	1.99	12/94	2c
Pizza, Pizza Hut or Pizza Inn	12-13 in.	8.19	12/94	2c
Taxes				
Tax, cigarettes	year	368.00	10/93	43s
Taxes, Federal income, expenditures	year	2946	91	81r
Taxes, personal, expenditures	year	3791	91	81r
Taxes, State and local income, expenditures	year	791	91	81r
Transportation				
Transportation, ACCRA Index		93.40	12/94	2c
Bus fare, one-way	trip	0.75	12/95	1c
Bus fare, up to 10 miles	one-way	0.75	12/94	2c
Cars and trucks purchased, new	year	1231	91	81r
Cars and trucks purchased, used	year	915	91	81r
Driver's learning permit fee	perm	7.00	1/94	84s
Driver's license fee	orig	7.00	1/94	84s
Driver's license fee, duplicate	lic	4.00	1/94	84s
Driver's license reinstatement fee, min.	susp	10.00	1/94	85s
Driver's license renewal fee	renew	7.00	1/94	84s
Identification card, nondriver	card	5.00	1/94	83s

Values are in dollars or fractions of dollars. In the column headed *Ref*, references are shown to sources. Each reference is followed by a letter. These refer to the geographical level for which data were reported: s = State, r = Region, and c = City or metro. The abbreviation *ex* is used to mean *except* or *excluding*; *exp* stands for *expenditures*. For other abbreviations and further explanations, please see the Introduction.

Tucson, AZ - continued

Item	Per	Value	Date	Ref.
Transportation				
Motorcycle learning permit fee	perm	7.00	1/94	84s
Motorcycle license fee	orig	7.00	1/94	84s
Motorcycle license fee, duplicate	lic	4.00	1/94	84s
Motorcycle license renewal fee	renew	7.00	1/94	84s
Public transportation expenditures	year	375	91	81r
Tire balance, computer or spin bal., front	wheel	6.30	12/94	2c
Transportation expenditures, total	year	5527	91	81r
Vehicle finance charges	year	287	91	81r
Vehicle insurance expenditures	year	624	91	81r
Vehicle maintenance and repairs expenditures	year	695	91	81r
Vehicle purchases	year	2174	91	81r
Vehicle rental, leases, licenses, etc. expenditures	year	257	91	81r
Vehicles purchased, other than cars and trucks	year	28	91	81r
Utilities				
Utilities, ACCRA Index		100.60	12/94	2c
Electricity expenditures	year	616	91	81r
Electricity, (part.), other, 1800 sq. ft., new home	mo.	83.03	12/94	2c
Electricity, summer, 250 KWh	month	26.41	8/93	64c
Electricity, summer, 500 KWh	month	48.99	8/93	64c
Electricity, summer, 750 KWh	month	71.57	8/93	64c
Electricity, summer, 1000 KWh	month	94.15	8/93	64c
Utilities, fuels, and public services, total expenditures	year	1681	91	81r
Water and other public services, expenditures	year	209	91	81r
Weddings				
Bridal attendants' gowns	event	750	10/93	76r
Bridal gown	event	852	10/93	76r
Bridal headpiece and veil	event	167	10/93	76r
Bride's wedding band	event	708	10/93	76r
Clergy	event	224	10/93	76r
Engagement ring	event	2756	10/93	76r
Flowers	event	863	10/93	76r
Formal wear for groom	event	106	10/93	76r
Groom's attendants' formal wear	event	530	10/93	76r
Groom's wedding band	event	402	10/93	76r
Music	event	600	10/93	76r
Photography	event	1088	10/93	76r
Shoes for bride	event	50	10/93	76r
Videography	event	483	10/93	76r
Wedding invitations and announcements	event	342	10/93	76r
Wedding reception	event	7000	10/93	76r

Tulsa, OK

Item	Per	Value	Date	Ref.
Composite, ACCRA index		91.00	12/94	2c
Alcoholic Beverages				
Beer, Miller Lite, Bud, 12-oz., ex deposit	6	3.86	12/94	2c
J & B Scotch	750-ml.	15.21	12/94	2c
Wine, Gallo Chablis blanc	1.5-lit	5.33	12/94	2c
Appliances				
Appliances (major), expenditures	year	153	91	81r
Average annual exp.				
Food, health care, personal goods, services	year	27020	91	81r
Charity				
Cash contributions, expenditures	year	839	91	81r
Clothing				
Apparel, men and boys, total expenditures	year	380	91	81r
Apparel, women and girls, total expenditures	year	660	91	81r
Footwear, expenditures	year	193	91	81r
Jeans, man's denim		27.79	12/94	2c
Shirt, man's dress shirt		31.50	12/94	2c
Undervest, boy's size 10-14, cotton	3	5.29	12/94	2c

Tulsa, OK - continued

Item	Per	Value	Date	Ref.
Communications				
Long-distance telephone rate, day, addl. min., 1-10 mi.	min.	0.07	12/93	9s
Long-distance telephone rate, day, initial min., 1-10 mi.	min.	0.12	12/93	9s
Newspaper subscription, dly. and Sun. delivery	month	9.00	12/93	2c
Phone line, single, business, field visit	inst	82.75	12/93	9s
Phone line, single, business, no field visit	inst	82.75	12/93	9s
Phone line, single, residence, field visit	inst	44.45	12/93	9s
Phone line, single, residence, no field visit	inst	44.45	12/93	9s
Telephone bill, family of four	month	19.69	12/94	2c
Telephone service, expenditures	year	616	91	81r
Telephone, residential, flat rate	mo.	12.07	12/93	8c
Education				
Board, 4-year private college/university	year	1974	8/94	80s
Board, 4-year public college/university	year	1502	8/94	80s
Education, total expenditures	year	319	91	81r
Room, 4-year private college/university	year	1618	8/94	80s
Room, 4-year public college/university	year	876	8/94	80s
Total cost, 4-year private college/university	year	10801	8/94	80s
Total cost, 4-year public college/university	year	4023	8/94	80s
Tuition, 2-year public college/university, in-state	year	1095	8/94	80s
Tuition, 4-year private college/university, in-state	year	7210	8/94	80s
Tuition, 4-year public college/university, in-state	year	1645	8/94	80s
Energy and Fuels				
Energy, combined forms, 1800 sq. ft.	mo.	102.42	12/94	2c
Energy, exc. electricity, 1800 sq. ft.	mo.	36.91	12/94	2c
Fuel oil and other fuels, expenditures	year	56	91	81r
Gas, natural, expenditures	year	150	91	81r
Gas, reg unlead, taxes inc., cash, self-service	gal	0.94	12/94	2c
Gasoline and motor oil purchased	year	1152	91	81r
Gasoline, unleaded midgrade	gallon	1.21	4/93	82r
Gasoline, unleaded premium	gallon	1.30	4/93	82r
Gasoline, unleaded regular	gallon	1.10	4/93	82r
Entertainment				
Bowling, evening rate	game	2.13	12/94	2c
Concert ticket, Pearl Jam group	perf	20.00	94	50r
Entertainment, total expenditures	year	1266	91	81r
Fees and admissions, expenditures	year	306	91	81r
Monopoly game, Parker Brothers', No. 9	game	8.95	12/94	2c
Movie	adm	5.90	12/94	2c
Pets, toys, playground equipment, expenditures	year	271	91	81r
Reading, expenditures	year	131	91	81r
Televisions, radios, and sound equipment, expenditures	year	439	91	81r
Tennis balls, yellow, Wilson or Penn, 3	can	2.47	12/94	2c
Funerals				
Burial, immediate, container provided by funeral home		1574.60	1/95	54r
Cards, acknowledgment		22.24	1/95	54r
Casket, minimum alternative		239.41	1/95	54r
Cosmetology, hair care, etc.		91.04	1/95	54r
Cremation, direct, container provided by funeral home		1085.15	1/95	54r
Embalming		281.30	1/95	54r
Funeral, funeral home		323.04	1/95	54r
Funeral, other facility		327.58	1/95	54r
Graveside service		355.19	1/95	54r
Hearse, local		141.89	1/95	54r
Limousine, local		99.40	1/95	54r
Memorial service		284.67	1/95	54r
Service charge, professional, nondeclinable		904.06	1/95	54r
Visitation and viewing		187.04	1/95	54r

Values are in dollars or fractions of dollars. In the column headed *Ref*, references are shown to sources. Each reference is followed by a letter. These refer to the geographical level for which data were reported: s = State, r = Region, and c = City or metro. The abbreviation *ex* is used to mean *except* or *excluding*; *exp* stands for *expenditures*. For other abbreviations and further explanations, please see the Introduction.

Tulsa, OK - continued

Item	Per	Value	Date	Ref.
Groceries				
Groceries, ACCRA Index		92.30	12/94	2c
Apples, Red Delicious	lb.	0.73	12/94	82r
Baby food, strained vegetables, lowest price	4-4.5 oz.	0.27	12/94	2c
Bacon, sliced	lb.	1.67	12/94	82r
Bananas	lb.	0.38	12/94	2c
Bananas	lb.	0.42	12/94	82r
Beef or hamburger, ground	lb.	1.20	12/94	2c
Beef purchases	year	213	91	81r
Beverage purchases, alcoholic	year	249	91	81r
Beverage purchases, nonalcoholic	year	207	91	81r
Bologna, all beef or mixed	lb.	2.27	12/94	82r
Bread, white	24-oz.	0.67	12/94	2c
Bread, white, pan	lb.	0.68	12/94	82r
Cabbage	lb.	0.42	12/94	82r
Carrots, short trimmed and topped	lb.	0.53	12/94	82r
Cereals and bakery products purchases	year	345	91	81r
Cereals and cereals products purchases	year	127	91	81r
Cheddar cheese, natural	lb.	3.58	12/94	82r
Cheese, Kraft grated Parmesan	8-oz.	3.45	12/94	2c
Chicken breast, bone-in	lb.	1.71	12/94	82r
Chicken, fresh, whole	lb.	0.78	12/94	82r
Chicken, whole fryer	lb.	0.66	12/94	2c
Chuck roast, USDA choice, boneless	lb.	2.26	12/94	82r
Cigarettes, Winston, Kings	carton	15.27	12/94	2c
Coffee, vacuum-packed	13 oz.	3.44	12/94	2c
Corn Flakes, Kellogg's or Post Toasties	18 oz.	2.14	12/94	2c
Corn, frozen, whole kernel, lowest price	10 oz.	0.68	12/94	2c
Crackers, soda, salted	lb.	1.27	12/94	82r
Cucumbers	lb.	0.65	12/94	82r
Dairy products (other) purchases	year	141	91	81r
Eggs, Grade A large	dozen	0.74	12/94	2c
Eggs, Grade A large	dozen	0.87	12/94	82r
Fish and seafood purchases	year	72	91	81r
Flour, white, all purpose	lb.	0.23	12/94	82r
Food purchases, food eaten at home	year	2381	91	81r
Foods purchased away from home, not prepared by consumer	year	1696	91	81r
Frankfurters, all meat or all beef	lb.	1.74	12/94	82r
Fruits and vegetables purchases	year	380	91	81r
Grapefruit	lb.	0.45	12/94	82r
Grapes, Thompson seedless	lb.	2.30	12/94	82r
Ground beef, 100% beef	lb.	1.37	12/94	82r
Ground chuck, 100% beef	lb.	1.97	12/94	82r
Ham, boneless, exc. canned	lb.	2.54	12/94	82r
Ice cream, prepackaged, bulk, regular	1/2 gal.	2.47	12/94	82r
Lemons	lb.	1.02	12/94	82r
Lettuce, iceberg	lb.	0.96	12/94	82r
Lettuce, iceberg	head	0.81	12/94	2c
Margarine, Blue Bonnet or Parkay cubes	lb.	0.53	12/94	2c
Margarine, stick	lb.	0.77	12/94	82r
Meats, poultry, fish, and eggs purchases	year	655	91	81r
Milk and cream (fresh) purchases	year	130	91	81r
Milk, whole	1/2 gal.	1.29	12/94	2c
Orange juice, frozen concentrate 12-oz. can	16 oz.	1.36	12/94	82r
Orange juice, Minute Maid frozen	12-oz.	1.01	12/94	2c
Oranges, Navel	lb.	0.54	12/94	82r
Peaches, halves or slices, Hunt's, Del Monte, or Libby's	29-oz.	1.33	12/94	2c
Pears, Anjou	lb.	0.81	12/94	82r
Peas, sweet, Del Monte or Green Giant	15-17 oz.	0.55	12/94	2c
Pork chops, center cut, bone-in	lb.	3.07	12/94	82r
Pork purchases	year	142	91	81r
Potato chips	16-oz.	3.15	12/94	82r
Potatoes, frozen, French fried .	lb.	0.82	12/94	82r
Potatoes, white	lb.	0.34	12/94	82r
Potatoes, white or red	10-lb. sack	1.71	12/94	2c
Rice, white, long grain, uncooked	lb.	0.48	12/94	82r

Tulsa, OK - continued

Item	Per	Value	Date	Ref.
Groceries - continued				
Round roast, USDA choice, boneless	lb.	2.91	12/94	82r
Sausage, fresh	lb.	1.82	12/94	82r
Sausage, Jimmy Dean, 100% pork	lb.	2.45	12/94	2c
Shortening, vegetable oil blends	lb.	0.75	12/94	82r
Shortening, vegetable, Crisco	3-lb.	2.04	12/94	2c
Soft drink, Coca Cola, ex deposit	2 lit	1.03	12/94	2c
Spaghetti and macaroni	lb.	0.87	12/94	82r
Steak, rib eye, USDA choice, boneless	lb.	6.85	12/94	82r
Steak, round, graded & ungraded, exc. USDA prime & choice	lb.	2.96	12/94	82r
Steak, round, USDA choice, boneless	lb.	3.17	12/94	82r
Steak, sirloin, USDA choice, boneless	lb.	4.12	12/94	82r
Steak, t-bone	lb.	4.90	12/94	2c
Steak, T-bone, USDA choice, bone-in	lb.	5.63	12/94	82r
Sugar and other sweets, eaten at home, expenditures	year	93	91	81r
Sugar, cane or beet	4 lbs.	1.35	12/94	2c
Sugar, white, all sizes	lb.	0.39	12/94	82r
Tobacco products and smoking supplies, total expenditures	year	286	91	81r
Tomatoes, field grown	lb.	1.36	12/94	82r
Tomatoes, Hunt's or Del Monte	14.5 oz.	0.76	12/94	2c
Tuna, chunk, light	lb.	1.94	12/94	82r
Tuna, chunk, light, oil-packed	6.125-6.5 oz.	0.69	12/94	2c
Turkey, frozen, whole	lb.	0.96	12/94	82r
Yogurt, natural, fruit flavored	8 oz.	0.58	12/94	82r
Goods and Services				
Miscellaneous goods and services, ACCRA Index		97.70	12/94	2c
Health Care				
Health care, ACCRA Index		96.80	12/94	2c
Adenosine, emergency room	treat	100.00	95	23r
Antibiotic ointment, Polysporin	1.5 oz.	3.98	12/94	2c
Bladder tap, superpubic, infant, emergency room	treat	119.00	95	23r
Blood analysis, emergency room	treat	25.00	95	23r
Blood tests, abdominal pain, emergency room	treat	25.00	95	23r
Burn dressing, emergency room	treat	266.00	95	23r
Cardiology interpretation, emergency room	treat	26.00	95	23r
Chest X-ray, emergency room	treat	78.00	95	23r
Childbirth, Cesarean delivery, hospital charge	birth	5462.00	12/91	69r
Childbirth, Cesarean delivery, physician charge	birth	2228.00	12/91	69r
Childbirth, normal delivery, hospital charge	birth	2943.00	12/91	69r
Childbirth, normal delivery, physician charge	birth	1619.00	12/91	69r
Defibrillation pads, emergency room	treat	6.00	95	23r
Dentist's fee, adult teeth cleaning and periodic oral exam	visit	54.20	12/94	2c
Doctor's fee, routine exam, established patient	visit	41.20	12/94	2c
Drugs, expenditures	year	297	91	81r
Gastric tube insertion, nasal, emergency room	treat	25.00	95	23r
Health care, total expenditures	year	1600	91	81r
Health insurance expenditures	year	637	91	81r
Heart monitor, emergency room	treat	40.00	95	23r
Hospital care, semiprivate room	day	289.60	12/94	2c
Insurance premium, family medical care	month	373.98	1/95	41s
Intravenous fluids, emergency room	treat	130.00	95	23r
Intravenous fluids, emergency room	liter	26.00	95	23r
Intravenous line, central, emergency room	treat	342.00	95	23r
Liver function tests, abdominal pain, emergency room	treat	26.00	95	23r
Medical care charges, total, emergency room, third-degree burns	treat	2101.00	95	23r
Medical care charges, total, emergency, infant with fever	treat	628.00	95	23r

Values are in dollars or fractions of dollars. In the column headed *Ref*, references are shown to sources. Each reference is followed by a letter. These refer to the geographical level for which data were reported: s = State, r = Region, and c = City or metro. The abbreviation *ex* is used to mean *except* or *excluding*; *exp* stands for expenditures. For other abbreviations and further explanations, please see the Introduction.

Tulsa, OK - continued

Item	Per	Value	Date	Ref.
Health Care				
Medical services expenditures	year	573	91	81r
Medical supplies expenditures	year	93	91	81r
Morphine, emergency room	treat	34.00	95	23r
Nursing care and facilities charges, emergency room	treat	252.00	95	23r
Nursing care and facilities charges, emergency, infant with fever	treat	252.00	95	23r
Nursing care and facilities charges, emergency, third-degree burns	treat	861.00	95	23r
Physician's charges, emergency, infant with fever	treat	212.00	95	23r
Physician's charges, emergency, third-degree burns	treat	372.00	95	23r
Physician's fee, emergency room	treat	372.00	95	23r
Physician's fee, general practitioner	visit	51.20	12/93	60r
Surgery, open-heart	proc	42374.00	1/93	14r
Ultrasound, abdominal, emergency room	treat	276.00	95	23r
Urinalysis, emergency room	treat	20.00	95	23r
Urinalysis, infant, emergency room	treat	20.00	95	23r
X-rays, emergency room	treat	78.00	95	23r
Household Goods				
Appl. repair, service call, wash mach	min. lab. chg.	35.78	12/94	2c
Floor coverings, expenditures	year	48	91	81r
Furniture, expenditures	year	280	91	81r
Household equipment, misc. expenditures	year	342	91	81r
Household expenditures, miscellaneous	year	256	91	81r
Household furnishings and equipment, expenditures	year	988	91	81r
Household operations expenditures	year	468	91	81r
Household textiles, expenditures	year	95	91	81r
Housekeeping supplies, expenditures	year	380	91	81r
Laundry and cleaning supplies, expenditures	year	109	91	81r
Laundry detergent, Tide Ultra, Bold, or Cheer	42 oz.	3.94	12/94	2c
Postage and stationery, expenditures	year	105	91	81r
Tissues, facial, Kleenex brand	175	1.26	12/94	2c
Housing				
Housing, ACCRA Index		83.50	12/94	2c
Add garage/carport		6,980	3/95	74r
Add room(s)		11,403	3/95	74r
Apartment condominium or co-op, median	unit	68600	12/94	62r
Dwellings (owned), expenditures	year	2428	91	81r
Enclose porch/patio/breezeway		4,572	3/95	74r
Finish room in basement/attic		3,794	3/95	74r
Home, existing, single-family, median	unit	120200	12/94	62r
Home, existing, single-family, median	unit	73.30	12/94	62c
House payment, principal and interest, 25% down payment	mo.	643	12/94	2c
House, 1800 sq ft, 8000 sq ft lot, new, urban, utilities	total	104988	12/94	2c
Maintenance, repairs, insurance, and other housing expenditures	year	531	91	81r
Mortgage interest and charges expenditures	year	1506	91	81r
Mtge. rate, incl. points and orig. fee, 30-year conv. fixed or ARM	mo.	9.17	12/94	2c
Princ. & int., mortgage, median-price exist. sing.-family home	mo.	540	12/94	62r
Property taxes expenditures	year	391	91	81r
Redesign, restructure more than half of home's interior		17,641	3/95	74r
Rent, apartment, 2 br., 1 1/2-2 baths, unfurnished, 950 sq ft, water	mo.	432	12/94	2c
Rental units expenditures	year	1264	91	81r
Insurance and Pensions				
Auto insurance, private passenger	year	604.38	12/94	71s
Insurance and pensions, personal, expenditures	year	2395	91	81r

Tulsa, OK - continued

Item	Per	Value	Date	Ref.
Insurance and Pensions - continued				
Insurance, life and other personal, expenditures	year	368	91	81r
Pensions and Social Security, expenditures	year	2027	91	81r
Personal Goods				
Shampoo, Alberto VO5	15-oz.	1.25	12/94	2c
Toothpaste, Crest or Colgate	6-7 oz.	1.77	12/94	2c
Personal Services				
Dry cleaning, man's 2-pc. suit		5.60	12/94	2c
Haircut, man's barbershop, no styling		7.30	12/94	2c
Haircut, woman's shampoo, trim, blow-dry		18.20	12/94	2c
Personal services expenditures	year	212	91	81r
Restaurant Food				
Chicken, fried, thigh and drumstick		1.99	12/94	2c
Dining expenditures, family	week	33.83	94	73r
Hamburger with cheese	1/4 lb.	1.89	12/94	2c
Pizza, Pizza Hut or Pizza Inn	12-13 in.	7.77	12/94	2c
Taxes				
Tax, cigarettes	year	382.00	10/93	43s
Taxes, Federal income, expenditures	year	2275	91	81r
Taxes, personal, expenditures	year	2715	91	81r
Taxes, State and local income, expenditures	year	365	91	81r
Transportation				
Transportation, ACCRA Index		81.90	12/94	2c
Bus fare, one-way	trip	0.75	12/95	1c
Cars and trucks purchased, new	year	1306	91	81r
Cars and trucks purchased, used	year	942	91	81r
Driver's learning permit fee	perm	19.00	1/94	84s
Driver's license fee	orig	19.00	1/94	84s
Driver's license fee, duplicate	lic	5.00	1/94	84s
Driver's license reinstatement fee, min.	susp	75.00	1/94	85s
Driver's license renewal fee	renew	15.00	1/94	84s
Identification card, nondriver	card	7.00	1/94	83s
Motorcycle license fee	orig	19.00	1/94	84s
Motorcycle license fee, duplicate	lic	5.00	1/94	84s
Motorcycle license renewal fee	renew	15.00	1/94	84s
Public transportation expenditures	year	249	91	81r
Tire balance, computer or spin bal., front	wheel	5.40	12/94	2c
Transportation expenditures, total	year	5307	91	81r
Vehicle finance charges	year	346	91	81r
Vehicle insurance expenditures	year	544	91	81r
Vehicle maintenance and repairs expenditures	year	600	91	81r
Vehicle purchases	year	2275	91	81r
Vehicle rental, leases, licenses, etc. expenditures	year	141	91	81r
Vehicles purchased, other than cars and trucks	year	27	91	81r
Utilities				
Utilities, ACCRA Index		92.60	12/94	2c
Electricity expenditures	year	950	91	81r
Electricity, (part.), other, 1800 sq. ft., new home	mo.	65.51	12/94	2c
Electricity, summer, 250 KWh	month	22.44	8/93	64c
Electricity, summer, 500 KWh	month	38.00	8/93	64c
Electricity, summer, 750 KWh	month	53.55	8/93	64c
Electricity, summer, 1000 KWh	month	69.11	8/93	64c
Utilities, fuels, and public services, total expenditures	year	2000	91	81r
Water and other public services, expenditures	year	227	91	81r
Weddings				
Bridal attendants' gowns	event	750	10/93	76r
Bridal gown	event	852	10/93	76r
Bridal headpiece and veil	event	167	10/93	76r
Bride's wedding band	event	708	10/93	76r
Clergy	event	224	10/93	76r
Engagement ring	event	2756	10/93	76r

Values are in dollars or fractions of dollars. In the column headed *Ref*, references are shown to sources. Each reference is followed by a letter. These refer to the geographical level for which data were reported: s = State, r = Region, and c = City or metro. The abbreviation *ex* is used to mean *except* or *excluding*; *exp* stands for *expenditures*. For other abbreviations and further explanations, please see the Introduction.

Tulsa, OK - continued

Item	Per	Value	Date	Ref.
Weddings				
Flowers	event	863	10/93	76r
Formal wear for groom	event	106	10/93	76r
Groom's attendants' formal wear	event	530	10/93	76r
Groom's wedding band	event	402	10/93	76r
Music	event	600	10/93	76r
Photography	event	1088	10/93	76r
Shoes for bride	event	50	10/93	76r
Videography	event	483	10/93	76r
Wedding invitations and announcements	event	342	10/93	76r
Wedding reception	event	7000	10/93	76r

Tuscaloosa, AL

Item	Per	Value	Date	Ref.
Appliances				
Appliances (major), expenditures	year	153	91	81r
Average annual exp.				
Food, health care, personal goods, services	year	27020	91	81r
Charity				
Cash contributions, expenditures	year	839	91	81r
Clothing				
Apparel, men and boys, total expenditures	year	380	91	81r
Apparel, women and girls, total expenditures	year	660	91	81r
Footwear, expenditures	year	193	91	81r
Communications				
Long-distance telephone rate, day, addl. min., 1-10 mi.	min.	0.09	12/93	9s
Long-distance telephone rate, day, initial min., 1-10 mi.	min.	0.11	12/93	9s
Phone line, single, business, field visit	inst	69.00	12/93	9s
Phone line, single, business, no field visit	inst	69.00	12/93	9s
Phone line, single, residence, field visit	inst	40.00	12/93	9s
Phone line, single, residence, no field visit	inst	40.00	12/93	9s
Telephone service, expenditures	year	616	91	81r
Education				
Board, 4-year private college/university	year	2072	8/94	80s
Board, 4-year public college/university	year	1706	8/94	80s
Education, total expenditures	year	319	91	81r
Room, 4-year private college/university	year	1607	8/94	80s
Room, 4-year public college/university	year	1598	8/94	80s
Total cost, 4-year private college/university	year	10664	8/94	80s
Total cost, 4-year public college/university	year	5287	8/94	80s
Tuition, 2-year public college/university, in-state	year	1110	8/94	80s
Tuition, 4-year private college/university, in-state	year	6985	8/94	80s
Tuition, 4-year public college/university, in-state	year	1983	8/94	80s
Energy and Fuels				
Fuel oil and other fuels, expenditures	year	56	91	81r
Gas, natural, expenditures	year	150	91	81r
Gasoline and motor oil purchased	year	1152	91	81r
Gasoline, unleaded midgrade	gallon	1.21	4/93	82r
Gasoline, unleaded premium	gallon	1.30	4/93	82r
Gasoline, unleaded regular	gallon	1.10	4/93	82r
Entertainment				
Concert ticket, Pearl Jam group	perf	20.00	94	50r
Entertainment, total expenditures	year	1266	91	81r
Fees and admissions, expenditures	year	306	91	81r
Pets, toys, playground equipment, expenditures	year	271	91	81r
Reading, expenditures	year	131	91	81r
Televisions, radios, and sound equipment, expenditures	year	439	91	81r
Funerals				
Burial, immediate, container provided by funeral home		1298.96	1/95	54r
Cards, acknowledgment		21.26	1/95	54r

Tuscaloosa, AL - continued

Item	Per	Value	Date	Ref.
Funerals - continued				
Casket, minimum alternative		204.95	1/95	54r
Cosmetology, hair care, etc.		85.40	1/95	54r
Cremation, direct, container provided by funeral home		1054.77	1/95	54r
Embalming		287.71	1/95	54r
Funeral, funeral home		269.18	1/95	54r
Funeral, other facility		272.88	1/95	54r
Graveside service		302.54	1/95	54r
Hearse, local		122.08	1/95	54r
Limousine, local		80.31	1/95	54r
Memorial service		277.66	1/95	54r
Service charge, professional, nondeclinable		896.65	1/95	54r
Visitation and viewing		232.39	1/95	54r
Groceries				
Apples, Red Delicious	lb.	0.73	12/94	82r
Bacon, sliced	lb.	1.67	12/94	82r
Bananas	lb.	0.42	12/94	82r
Beef purchases	year	213	91	81r
Beverage purchases, alcoholic	year	249	91	81r
Beverage purchases, nonalcoholic	year	207	91	81r
Bologna, all beef or mixed	lb.	2.27	12/94	82r
Bread, white, pan	lb.	0.68	12/94	82r
Cabbage	lb.	0.42	12/94	82r
Carrots, short trimmed and topped	lb.	0.53	12/94	82r
Cereals and bakery products purchases	year	345	91	81r
Cereals and cereals products purchases	year	127	91	81r
Cheddar cheese, natural	lb.	3.58	12/94	82r
Chicken breast, bone-in	lb.	1.71	12/94	82r
Chicken, fresh, whole	lb.	0.78	12/94	82r
Chuck roast, USDA choice, boneless	lb.	2.26	12/94	82r
Crackers, soda, salted	lb.	1.27	12/94	82r
Cucumbers	lb.	0.65	12/94	82r
Dairy products (other) purchases	year	141	91	81r
Eggs, Grade A large	dozen	0.87	12/94	82r
Fish and seafood purchases	year	72	91	81r
Flour, white, all purpose	lb.	0.23	12/94	82r
Food purchases, food eaten at home	year	2381	91	81r
Foods purchased away from home, not prepared by consumer	year	1696	91	81r
Frankfurters, all meat or all beef	lb.	1.74	12/94	82r
Fruits and vegetables purchases	year	380	91	81r
Grapefruit	lb.	0.45	12/94	82r
Grapes, Thompson seedless	lb.	2.30	12/94	82r
Ground beef, 100% beef	lb.	1.37	12/94	82r
Ground chuck, 100% beef	lb.	1.97	12/94	82r
Ham, boneless, exc. canned	lb.	2.54	12/94	82r
Ice cream, prepackaged, bulk, regular	1/2 gal.	2.47	12/94	82r
Lemons	lb.	1.02	12/94	82r
Lettuce, iceberg	lb.	0.96	12/94	82r
Margarine, stick	lb.	0.77	12/94	82r
Meats, poultry, fish, and eggs purchases	year	655	91	81r
Milk and cream (fresh) purchases	year	130	91	81r
Orange juice, frozen concentrate 12-oz. can	16 oz.	1.36	12/94	82r
Oranges, Navel	lb.	0.54	12/94	82r
Pears, Anjou	lb.	0.81	12/94	82r
Pork chops, center cut, bone-in	lb.	3.07	12/94	82r
Pork purchases	year	142	91	81r
Potato chips	16-oz.	3.15	12/94	82r
Potatoes, frozen, French fried	lb.	0.82	12/94	82r
Potatoes, white	lb.	0.34	12/94	82r
Rice, white, long grain, uncooked	lb.	0.48	12/94	82r
Round roast, USDA choice, boneless	lb.	2.91	12/94	82r
Sausage, fresh	lb.	1.82	12/94	82r
Shortening, vegetable oil blends	lb.	0.75	12/94	82r
Spaghetti and macaroni	lb.	0.87	12/94	82r
Steak, rib eye, USDA choice, boneless	lb.	6.85	12/94	82r
Steak, round, graded & ungraded, exc. USDA prime & choice	lb.	2.96	12/94	82r
Steak, round, USDA choice, boneless	lb.	3.17	12/94	82r
Steak, sirloin, USDA choice, boneless	lb.	4.12	12/94	82r
Steak, T-bone, USDA choice, bone-in	lb.	5.63	12/94	82r

Values are in dollars or fractions of dollars. In the column headed *Ref*, references are shown to sources. Each reference is followed by a letter. These refer to the geographical level for which data were reported: s = State, r = Region, and c = City or metro. The abbreviation *ex* is used to mean *except* or *excluding*; *exp* stands for *expenditures*. For other abbreviations and further explanations, please see the Introduction.

Tuscaloosa, AL - continued

Item	Per	Value	Date	Ref.
Groceries				
Sugar and other sweets, eaten at home, expenditures	year	93	91	81r
Sugar, white, all sizes	lb.	0.39	12/94	82r
Tobacco products and smoking supplies, total expenditures	year	286	91	81r
Tomatoes, field grown	lb.	1.36	12/94	82r
Tuna, chunk, light	lb.	1.94	12/94	82r
Turkey, frozen, whole	lb.	0.96	12/94	82r
Yogurt, natural, fruit flavored	8 oz.	0.58	12/94	82r
Health Care				
Adenosine, emergency room	treat	100.00	95	23r
Bladder tap, superpubic, infant, emergency room	treat	119.00	95	23r
Blood analysis, emergency room	treat	25.00	95	23r
Blood tests, abdominal pain, emergency room	treat	25.00	95	23r
Burn dressing, emergency room	treat	266.00	95	23r
Cardiology interpretation, emergency room	treat	26.00	95	23r
Chest X-ray, emergency room	treat	78.00	95	23r
Childbirth, Cesarean delivery, hospital charge	birth	5462.00	12/91	69r
Childbirth, Cesarean delivery, physician charge	birth	2228.00	12/91	69r
Childbirth, normal delivery, hospital charge	birth	2943.00	12/91	69r
Childbirth, normal delivery, physician charge	birth	1619.00	12/91	69r
Defibrillation pads, emergency room	treat	6.00	95	23r
Drugs, expenditures	year	297	91	81r
Gastric tube insertion, nasal, emergency room	treat	25.00	95	23r
Health care, total expenditures	year	1600	91	81r
Health insurance expenditures	year	637	91	81r
Heart monitor, emergency room	treat	40.00	95	23r
Insurance premium, family medical care	month	360.67	1/95	41s
Intravenous fluids, emergency room	treat	130.00	95	23r
Intravenous fluids, emergency room	liter	26.00	95	23r
Intravenous line, central, emergency room	treat	342.00	95	23r
Liver function tests, abdominal pain, emergency room	treat	26.00	95	23r
Medical care charges, total, emergency room, third-degree burns	treat	2101.00	95	23r
Medical care charges, total, emergency, infant with fever	treat	628.00	95	23r
Medical services expenditures	year	573	91	81r
Medical supplies expenditures	year	93	91	81r
Morphine, emergency room	treat	34.00	95	23r
Nursing care and facilities charges, emergency room	treat	252.00	95	23r
Nursing care and facilities charges, emergency, infant with fever	treat	252.00	95	23r
Nursing care and facilities charges, emergency, third-degree burns	treat	861.00	95	23r
Physician's charges, emergency, infant with fever	treat	212.00	95	23r
Physician's charges, emergency, third-degree burns	treat	372.00	95	23r
Physician's fee, emergency room	treat	372.00	95	23r
Physician's fee, general practitioner	visit	51.20	12/93	60r
Surgery, open-heart	proc	42374.00	1/93	14r
Ultrasound, abdominal, emergency room	treat	276.00	95	23r
Urinalysis, emergency room	treat	20.00	95	23r
Urinalysis, infant, emergency room	treat	20.00	95	23r
X-rays, emergency room	treat	78.00	95	23r
Household Goods				
Floor coverings, expenditures	year	48	91	81r
Furniture, expenditures	year	280	91	81r
Household equipment, misc. expenditures	year	342	91	81r
Household expenditures, miscellaneous	year	256	91	81r
Household furnishings and equipment, expenditures	year	988	91	81r
Household operations expenditures	year	468	91	81r
Household textiles, expenditures	year	95	91	81r

Tuscaloosa, AL - continued

Item	Per	Value	Date	Ref.
Household Goods - continued				
Housekeeping supplies, expenditures	year	380	91	81r
Laundry and cleaning supplies, expenditures	year	109	91	81r
Postage and stationery, expenditures	year	105	91	81r
Housing				
Add garage/carport		6,980	3/95	74r
Add room(s)		11,403	3/95	74r
Apartment condominium or co-op, median	unit	68600	12/94	62r
Dwellings (owned), expenditures	year	2428	91	81r
Enclose porch/patio/breezeway		4,572	3/95	74r
Finish room in basement/attic		3,794	3/95	74r
Home, existing, single-family, median	unit	120200	12/94	62r
Maintenance, repairs, insurance, and other housing expenditures	year	531	91	81r
Mortgage interest and charges expenditures	year	1506	91	81r
Princ. & int., mortgage, median-price exist. sing.-family home	mo.	540	12/94	62r
Property taxes expenditures	year	391	91	81r
Redesign, restructure more than half of home's interior		17,641	3/95	74r
Rental units expenditures	year	1264	91	81r
Insurance and Pensions				
Auto insurance, private passenger	year	604.07	12/94	71s
Insurance and pensions, personal, expenditures	year	2395	91	81r
Insurance, life and other personal, expenditures	year	368	91	81r
Pensions and Social Security, expenditures	year	2027	91	81r
Personal Services				
Personal services expenditures	year	212	91	81r
Restaurant Food				
Dining expenditures, family	week	33.83	94	73r
Taxes				
Taxes, Federal income, expenditures	year	2275	91	81r
Taxes, personal, expenditures	year	2715	91	81r
Taxes, State and local income, expenditures	year	365	91	81r
Transportation				
Cars and trucks purchased, new	year	1306	91	81r
Cars and trucks purchased, used	year	942	91	81r
Driver's learning permit fee	perm	20.00	1/94	84s
Driver's license fee	orig	20.00	1/94	84s
Driver's license fee, duplicate	lic	5.00	1/94	84s
Driver's license reinstatement fee, min.	susp	50.00	1/94	85s
Driver's license renewal fee	renew	20.00	1/94	84s
Identification card, nondriver	card	20.00	1/94	83s
Motorcycle license fee	orig	20.00	1/94	84s
Motorcycle license fee, duplicate	lic	5.00	1/94	84s
Motorcycle license renewal fee	renew	20.00	1/94	84s
Public transportation expenditures	year	249	91	81r
Transportation expenditures, total	year	5307	91	81r
Vehicle finance charges	year	346	91	81r
Vehicle insurance expenditures	year	544	91	81r
Vehicle maintenance and repairs expenditures	year	600	91	81r
Vehicle purchases	year	2275	91	81r
Vehicle rental, leases, licenses, etc. expenditures	year	141	91	81r
Vehicles purchased, other than cars and trucks	year	27	91	81r
Utilities				
Electricity expenditures	year	950	91	81r
Utilities, fuels, and public services, total expenditures	year	2000	91	81r
Water and other public services, expenditures	year	227	91	81r
Weddings				
Bridal attendants' gowns	event	750	10/93	76r
Bridal gown	event	852	10/93	76r

Values are in dollars or fractions of dollars. In the column headed *Ref*, references are shown to sources. Each reference is followed by a letter. These refer to the geographical level for which data were reported: s=State, r=Region, and c=City or metro. The abbreviation *ex* is used to mean *except* or *excluding*; *exp* stands for *expenditures*. For other abbreviations and further explanations, please see the Introduction.

Tuscaloosa, AL - continued

Item	Per	Value	Date	Ref.
Weddings				
Bridal headpiece and veil	event	167	10/93	76r
Bride's wedding band	event	708	10/93	76r
Clergy	event	224	10/93	76r
Engagement ring	event	2756	10/93	76r
Flowers	event	863	10/93	76r
Formal wear for groom	event	106	10/93	76r
Groom's attendants' formal wear	event	530	10/93	76r
Groom's wedding band	event	402	10/93	76r
Music	event	600	10/93	76r
Photography	event	1088	10/93	76r
Shoes for bride	event	50	10/93	76r
Videography	event	483	10/93	76r
Wedding invitations and announcements	event	342	10/93	76r
Wedding reception	event	7000	10/93	76r

Twin Falls, ID

Item	Per	Value	Date	Ref.
Composite, ACCRA index		97.70	12/94	2c
Alcoholic Beverages				
Beer, Miller Lite, Bud, 12-oz., ex deposit	6	3.89	12/94	2c
J & B Scotch	750-ml.	18.85	12/94	2c
Wine, Gallo Chablis blanc	1.5-lit	4.99	12/94	2c
Clothing				
Jeans, man's denim		26.57	12/94	2c
Shirt, man's dress shirt		30.00	12/94	2c
Undervest, boy's size 10-14, cotton	3	5.22	12/94	2c
Communications				
Newspaper subscription, dly. and Sun. delivery	month	13.04	12/94	2c
Telephone bill, family of four	month	16.00	12/94	2c
Telephone, residential, flat rate	mo.	11.04	12/93	8c
Energy and Fuels				
Energy, combined forms, 1800 sq. ft.	mo.	81.89	12/94	2c
Energy, exc. electricity, 1800 sq. ft.	mo.	42.70	12/94	2c
Gas, reg unlead, taxes inc., cash, self-service	gal	1.24	12/94	2c
Entertainment				
Bowling, evening rate	game	1.63	12/94	2c
Monopoly game, Parker Brothers', No. 9	game	11.32	12/94	2c
Movie	adm	5.50	12/94	2c
Tennis balls, yellow, Wilson or Penn, 3	can	2.29	12/94	2c
Groceries				
Groceries, ACCRA Index		101.00	12/94	2c
Baby food, strained vegetables, lowest price	4-4.5 oz.	0.29	12/94	2c
Bananas	lb.	0.50	12/94	2c
Beef or hamburger, ground	lb.	1.86	12/94	2c
Bread, white	24-oz.	0.70	12/94	2c
Cheese, Kraft grated Parmesan	8-oz.	3.76	12/94	2c
Chicken, whole fryer	lb.	0.82	12/94	2c
Cigarettes, Winston, Kings	carton	15.71	12/94	2c
Coffee, vacuum-packed	13 oz.	4.26	12/94	2c
Corn Flakes, Kellogg's or Post Toasties	18 oz.	2.18	12/94	2c
Corn, frozen, whole kernel, lowest price	10 oz.	0.54	12/94	2c
Eggs, Grade A large	dozen	0.78	12/94	2c
Lettuce, iceberg	head	0.73	12/94	2c
Margarine, Blue Bonnet or Parkay cubes	lb.	0.54	12/94	2c
Milk, whole	1/2 gal.	1.48	12/94	2c
Orange juice, Minute Maid frozen	12-oz.	1.34	12/94	2c
Peaches, halves or slices, Hunt's, Del Monte, or Libby's	29-oz.	1.30	12/94	2c
Peas, sweet, Del Monte or Green Giant	15-17 oz.	0.63	12/94	2c
Potatoes, white or red	10-lb. sack	1.40	12/94	2c
Sausage, Jimmy Dean, 100% pork	lb.	3.23	12/94	2c

Item	Per	Value	Date	Ref.
Groceries - continued				
Shortening, vegetable, Crisco	3-lb.	2.32	12/94	2c
Soft drink, Coca Cola, ex deposit	2 lit	1.16	12/94	2c
Steak, t-bone	lb.	4.22	12/94	2c
Sugar, cane or beet	4 lbs.	1.32	12/94	2c
Tomatoes, Hunt's or Del Monte	14.5 oz.	0.59	12/94	2c
Tuna, chunk, light, oil-packed	6.125-6.5 oz.	0.86	12/94	2c
Goods and Services				
Miscellaneous goods and services, ACCRA Index		100.30	12/94	2c
Health Care				
Health care, ACCRA Index		93.70	12/94	2c
Antibiotic ointment, Polysporin	1.5 oz.	4.22	12/94	2c
Dentist's fee, adult teeth cleaning and periodic oral exam	visit	51.00	12/94	2c
Doctor's fee, routine exam, established patient	visit	34.67	12/94	2c
Hospital care, semiprivate room	day	367.50	12/94	2c
Household Goods				
Appl. repair, service call, wash mach	min. lab. chg.	27.50	12/94	2c
Laundry detergent, Tide Ultra, Bold, or Cheer	42 oz.	3.26	12/94	2c
Tissues, facial, Kleenex brand	175	1.09	12/94	2c
Housing				
Housing, ACCRA Index		99.60	12/94	2c
House payment, principal and interest, 25% down payment	mo.	765	12/94	2c
House, 1800 sq ft, 8000 sq ft lot, new, urban, utilities	total	122333	12/94	2c
Mtge. rate, incl. points and orig. fee, 30-year conv. fixed or ARM	mo.	9.40	12/94	2c
Personal Goods				
Shampoo, Alberto VO5	15-oz.	1.16	12/94	2c
Toothpaste, Crest or Colgate	6-7 oz.	1.92	12/94	2c
Personal Services				
Dry cleaning, man's 2-pc. suit		6.42	12/94	2c
Haircut, man's barbershop, no styling		7.33	12/94	2c
Haircut, woman's shampoo, trim, blow-dry		16.33	12/94	2c
Restaurant Food				
Chicken, fried, thigh and drumstick		2.59	12/94	2c
Hamburger with cheese	1/4 lb.	1.99	12/94	2c
Pizza, Pizza Hut or Pizza Inn	12-13 in.	8.95	12/94	2c
Transportation				
Transportation, ACCRA Index		100.00	12/94	2c
Tire balance, computer or spin bal., front	wheel	5.82	12/94	2c
Utilities				
Utilities, ACCRA Index		74.20	12/94	2c
Electricity, (part.), other, 1800 sq. ft., new home	mo.	39.19	12/94	2c

Tyler, TX

Item	Per	Value	Date	Ref.
Composite, ACCRA index		100.20	12/94	2c
Alcoholic Beverages				
Beer, Miller Lite, Bud, 12-oz., ex deposit	6	3.97	12/94	2c
J & B Scotch	750-ml.	18.22	12/94	2c
Wine, Gallo Chablis blanc	1.5-lit	4.72	12/94	2c
Appliances				
Appliances (major), expenditures	year	153	91	81r

Values are in dollars or fractions of dollars. In the column headed *Ref*, references are shown to sources. Each reference is followed by a letter. These refer to the geographical level for which data were reported: s=State, r=Region, and c=City or metro. The abbreviation *ex* is used to mean *except* or *excluding*; *exp* stands for expenditures. For other abbreviations and further explanations, please see the Introduction.

Tyler, TX - continued

Item	Per	Value	Date	Ref.
Average annual exp.				
Food, health care, personal goods, services	year	27020	91	81r
Charity				
Cash contributions, expenditures	year	839	91	81r
Clothing				
Apparel, men and boys, total expenditures	year	380	91	81r
Apparel, women and girls, total expenditures	year	660	91	81r
Footwear, expenditures	year	193	91	81r
Jeans, man's denim		30.59	12/94	2c
Shirt, man's dress shirt		38.62	12/94	2c
Undervest, boy's size 10-14, cotton	3	4.39	12/94	2c
Communications				
Long-distance telephone rate, day, addl. min., 1-10 mi.	min.	0.08	12/93	9s
Long-distance telephone rate, day, initial min., 1-10 mi.	min.	0.10	12/93	9s
Newspaper subscription, dly. and Sun. delivery	month	11.00	12/94	2c
Phone line, single, business, field visit	inst	71.90	12/93	9s
Phone line, single, business, no field visit	inst	57.30	12/93	9s
Phone line, single, residence, field visit	inst	52.95	12/93	9s
Phone line, single, residence, no field visit	inst	38.35	12/93	9s
Telephone bill, family of four	month	15.36	12/94	2c
Telephone service, expenditures	year	616	91	81r
Telephone, residential, flat rate	mo.	9.10	12/93	8c
Education				
Board, 4-year private college/university	year	2084	8/94	80s
Board, 4-year public college/university	year	1675	8/94	80s
Education, total expenditures	year	319	91	81r
Room, 4-year private college/university	year	1840	8/94	80s
Room, 4-year public college/university	year	1756	8/94	80s
Total cost, 4-year private college/university	year	11876	8/94	80s
Total cost, 4-year public college/university	year	4935	8/94	80s
Tuition, 2-year public college/university, in-state	year	625	8/94	80s
Tuition, 4-year private college/university, in-state	year	7952	8/94	80s
Tuition, 4-year public college/university, in-state	year	1503	8/94	80s
Energy and Fuels				
Energy, combined forms, 1800 sq. ft.	mo.	147.43	12/94	2c
Energy, exc. electricity, 1800 sq. ft.	mo.	32.17	12/94	2c
Fuel oil and other fuels, expenditures	year	56	91	81r
Gas, natural, expenditures	year	150	91	81r
Gas, reg unlead, taxes inc., cash, self-service	gal	1.11	12/94	2c
Gasoline and motor oil purchased	year	1152	91	81r
Gasoline, unleaded midgrade	gallon	1.21	4/93	82r
Gasoline, unleaded premium	gallon	1.30	4/93	82r
Gasoline, unleaded regular	gallon	1.10	4/93	82r
Entertainment				
Bowling, evening rate	game	2.40	12/94	2c
Concert ticket, Pearl Jam group	perf	20.00	94	50r
Entertainment, total expenditures	year	1266	91	81r
Fees and admissions, expenditures	year	306	91	81r
Monopoly game, Parker Brothers', No. 9	game	11.29	12/94	2c
Movie	adm	5.67	12/94	2c
Pets, toys, playground equipment, expenditures	year	271	91	81r
Reading, expenditures	year	131	91	81r
Televisions, radios, and sound equipment, expenditures	year	439	91	81r
Tennis balls, yellow, Wilson or Penn, 3	can	2.49	12/94	2c
Funerals				
Burial, immediate, container provided by funeral home		1574.60	1/95	54r
Cards, acknowledgment		22.24	1/95	54r
Casket, minimum alternative		239.41	1/95	54r
Cosmetology, hair care, etc.		91.04	1/95	54r

Tyler, TX - continued

Item	Per	Value	Date	Ref.
Funerals - continued				
Cremation, direct, container provided by funeral home		1085.15	1/95	54r
Embalming		281.30	1/95	54r
Funeral, funeral home		323.04	1/95	54r
Funeral, other facility		327.58	1/95	54r
Graveside service		355.19	1/95	54r
Hearse, local		141.89	1/95	54r
Limousine, local		99.40	1/95	54r
Memorial service		284.67	1/95	54r
Service charge, professional, nondeclinable		904.06	1/95	54r
Visitation and viewing		187.04	1/95	54r
Groceries				
Groceries, ACCRA Index		89.20	12/94	2c
Apples, Red Delicious	lb.	0.73	12/94	82r
Baby food, strained vegetables, lowest price	4-4.5 oz.	0.25	12/94	2c
Bacon, sliced	lb.	1.67	12/94	82r
Bananas	lb.	0.37	12/94	2c
Bananas	lb.	0.42	12/94	82r
Beef or hamburger, ground	lb.	1.19	12/94	2c
Beef purchases	year	213	91	81r
Beverage purchases, alcoholic	year	249	91	81r
Beverage purchases, nonalcoholic	year	207	91	81r
Bologna, all beef or mixed	lb.	2.27	12/94	82r
Bread, white	24-oz.	0.63	12/94	2c
Bread, white, pan	lb.	0.68	12/94	82r
Cabbage	lb.	0.42	12/94	82r
Carrots, short trimmed and topped	lb.	0.53	12/94	82r
Cereals and bakery products purchases	year	345	91	81r
Cereals and cereals products purchases	year	127	91	81r
Cheddar cheese, natural	lb.	3.58	12/94	82r
Cheese, Kraft grated Parmesan	8-oz.	3.43	12/94	2c
Chicken breast, bone-in	lb.	1.71	12/94	82r
Chicken, fresh, whole	lb.	0.78	12/94	82r
Chicken, whole fryer	lb.	0.65	12/94	2c
Chuck roast, USDA choice, boneless	lb.	2.26	12/94	82r
Cigarettes, Winston, Kings	carton	16.48	12/94	2c
Coffee, vacuum-packed	13 oz.	3.15	12/94	2c
Corn Flakes, Kellogg's or Post Toasties	18 oz.	2.00	12/94	2c
Corn, frozen, whole kernel, lowest price	10 oz.	0.68	12/94	2c
Crackers, soda, salted	lb.	1.27	12/94	82r
Cucumbers	lb.	0.65	12/94	82r
Dairy products (other) purchases	year	141	91	81r
Eggs, Grade A large	dozen	0.74	12/94	2c
Eggs, Grade A large	dozen	0.87	12/94	82r
Fish and seafood purchases	year	72	91	81r
Flour, white, all purpose	lb.	0.23	12/94	82r
Food purchases, food eaten at home	year	2381	91	81r
Foods purchased away from home, not prepared by consumer	year	1696	91	81r
Frankfurters, all meat or all beef	lb.	1.74	12/94	82r
Fruits and vegetables purchases	year	380	91	81r
Grapefruit	lb.	0.45	12/94	82r
Grapes, Thompson seedless	lb.	2.30	12/94	82r
Ground beef, 100% beef	lb.	1.37	12/94	82r
Ground chuck, 100% beef	lb.	1.97	12/94	82r
Ham, boneless, exc. canned	lb.	2.54	12/94	82r
Ice cream, prepackaged, bulk, regular	1/2 gal.	2.47	12/94	82r
Lemons	lb.	1.02	12/94	82r
Lettuce, iceberg	lb.	0.96	12/94	82r
Lettuce, iceberg	head	0.84	12/94	2c
Margarine, Blue Bonnet or Parkay cubes	lb.	0.52	12/94	2c
Margarine, stick	lb.	0.77	12/94	82r
Meats, poultry, fish, and eggs purchases	year	655	91	81r
Milk and cream (fresh) purchases	year	130	91	81r
Milk, whole	1/2 gal.	1.40	12/94	2c
Orange juice, frozen concentrate 12-oz. can	16 oz.	1.36	12/94	82r
Orange juice, Minute Maid frozen	12-oz.	1.09	12/94	2c
Oranges, Navel	lb.	0.54	12/94	82r

Values are in dollars or fractions of dollars. In the column headed *Ref*, references are shown to sources. Each reference is followed by a letter. These refer to the geographical level for which data were reported: s=State, r=Region, and c=City or metro. The abbreviation *ex* is used to mean *except* or *excluding*; *exp* stands for expenditures. For other abbreviations and further explanations, please see the Introduction.

Tyler, TX - continued

Item	Per	Value	Date	Ref.
Groceries				
Peaches, halves or slices, Hunt's, Del Monte, or Libby's	29-oz.	1.36	12/94	2c
Pears, Anjou	lb.	0.81	12/94	82r
Peas, sweet, Del Monte or Green Giant	15-17 oz.	0.46	12/94	2c
Pork chops, center cut, bone-in	lb.	3.07	12/94	82r
Pork purchases	year	142	91	81r
Potato chips	16-oz.	3.15	12/94	82r
Potatoes, frozen, French fried	lb.	0.82	12/94	82r
Potatoes, white	lb.	0.34	12/94	82r
Potatoes, white or red	10-lb. sack	2.28	12/94	2c
Rice, white, long grain, uncooked	lb.	0.48	12/94	82r
Round roast, USDA choice, boneless	lb.	2.91	12/94	82r
Sausage, fresh	lb.	1.82	12/94	82r
Sausage, Jimmy Dean, 100% pork	lb.	2.16	12/94	2c
Shortening, vegetable oil blends	lb.	0.75	12/94	82r
Shortening, vegetable, Crisco	3-lb.	2.10	12/94	2c
Soft drink, Coca Cola, ex deposit	2 lit	1.04	12/94	2c
Spaghetti and macaroni	lb.	0.87	12/94	82r
Steak, rib eye, USDA choice, boneless	lb.	6.85	12/94	82r
Steak, round, graded & ungraded, exc. USDA prime & choice	lb.	2.96	12/94	82r
Steak, round, USDA choice, boneless	lb.	3.17	12/94	82r
Steak, sirloin, USDA choice, boneless	lb.	4.12	12/94	82r
Steak, t-bone	lb.	4.99	12/94	2c
Steak, T-bone, USDA choice, bone-in	lb.	5.63	12/94	82r
Sugar and other sweets, eaten at home, expenditures	year	93	91	81r
Sugar, cane or beet	4 lbs.	1.43	12/94	2c
Sugar, white, all sizes	lb.	0.39	12/94	82r
Tobacco products and smoking supplies, total expenditures	year	286	91	81r
Tomatoes, field grown	lb.	1.36	12/94	82r
Tomatoes, Hunt's or Del Monte	14.5 oz.	0.62	12/94	2c
Tuna, chunk, light	lb.	1.94	12/94	82r
Tuna, chunk, light, oil-packed	6.125-6.5 oz.	0.64	12/94	2c
Turkey, frozen, whole	lb.	0.96	12/94	82r
Yogurt, natural, fruit flavored	8 oz.	0.58	12/94	82r
Goods and Services				
Miscellaneous goods and services, ACCRA Index		104.90	12/94	2c
Health Care				
Health care, ACCRA Index		95.60	12/94	2c
Adenosine, emergency room	treat	100.00	95	23r
Antibiotic ointment, Polysporin	1.5 oz.	3.94	12/94	2c
Bladder tap, superpubic, infant, emergency room	treat	119.00	95	23r
Blood analysis, emergency room	treat	25.00	95	23r
Blood tests, abdominal pain, emergency room	treat	25.00	95	23r
Burn dressing, emergency room	treat	266.00	95	23r
Cardiology interpretation, emergency room	treat	26.00	95	23r
Chest X-ray, emergency room	treat	78.00	95	23r
Childbirth, Cesarean delivery, hospital charge	birth	5462.00	12/91	69r
Childbirth, Cesarean delivery, physician charge	birth	2228.00	12/91	69r
Childbirth, normal delivery, hospital charge	birth	2943.00	12/91	69r
Childbirth, normal delivery, physician charge	birth	1619.00	12/91	69r
Defibrillation pads, emergency room	treat	6.00	95	23r
Dentist's fee, adult teeth cleaning and periodic oral exam	visit	48.20	12/94	2c
Doctor's fee, routine exam, established patient	visit	39.00	12/94	2c
Drugs, expenditures	year	297	91	81r
Gastric tube insertion, nasal, emergency room	treat	25.00	95	23r
Health care, total expenditures	year	1600	91	81r

Tyler, TX - continued

Item	Per	Value	Date	Ref.
Health Care - continued				
Health insurance expenditures	year	637	91	81r
Heart monitor, emergency room	treat	40.00	95	23r
Hospital care, semiprivate room	day	385.00	12/94	2c
Insurance premium, family medical care	month	389.25	1/95	41s
Intravenous fluids, emergency room	treat	130.00	95	23r
Intravenous fluids, emergency room	liter	26.00	95	23r
Intravenous line, central, emergency room	treat	342.00	95	23r
Liver function tests, abdominal pain, emergency room	treat	26.00	95	23r
Medical care charges, total, emergency room, third-degree burns	treat	2101.00	95	23r
Medical care charges, total, emergency, infant with fever	treat	628.00	95	23r
Medical services expenditures	year	573	91	81r
Medical supplies expenditures	year	93	91	81r
Morphine, emergency room	treat	34.00	95	23r
Nursing care and facilities charges, emergency room	treat	252.00	95	23r
Nursing care and facilities charges, emergency, infant with fever	treat	252.00	95	23r
Nursing care and facilities charges, emergency, third-degree burns	treat	861.00	95	23r
Physician's charges, emergency, infant with fever	treat	212.00	95	23r
Physician's charges, emergency, third-degree burns	treat	372.00	95	23r
Physician's fee, emergency room	treat	372.00	95	23r
Physician's fee, general practitioner	visit	51.20	12/93	60r
Surgery, open-heart	proc	42374.00	1/93	14r
Ultrasound, abdominal, emergency room	treat	276.00	95	23r
Urinalysis, emergency room	treat	20.00	95	23r
Urinalysis, infant, emergency room	treat	20.00	95	23r
X-rays, emergency room	treat	78.00	95	23r
Household Goods				
Appl. repair, service call, wash mach	min. lab. chg.	30.61	12/94	2c
Floor coverings, expenditures	year	48	91	81r
Furniture, expenditures	year	280	91	81r
Household equipment, misc. expenditures	year	342	91	81r
Household expenditures, miscellaneous	year	256	91	81r
Household furnishings and equipment, expenditures	year	988	91	81r
Household operations expenditures	year	468	91	81r
Household textiles, expenditures	year	95	91	81r
Housekeeping supplies, expenditures	year	380	91	81r
Laundry and cleaning supplies, expenditures	year	109	91	81r
Laundry detergent, Tide Ultra, Bold, or Cheer	42 oz.	2.96	12/94	2c
Postage and stationery, expenditures	year	105	91	81r
Tissues, facial, Kleenex brand	175	0.96	12/94	2c
Housing				
Housing, ACCRA Index		96.80	12/94	2c
Add garage/carport		6,980	3/95	74r
Add room(s)		11,403	3/95	74r
Apartment condominium or co-op, median	unit	68600	12/94	62r
Dwellings (owned), expenditures	year	2428	91	81r
Enclose porch/patio/breezeway		4,572	3/95	74r
Finish room in basement/attic		3,794	3/95	74r
Home, existing, single-family, median	unit	120200	12/94	62r
House payment, principal and interest, 25% down payment	mo.	733	12/94	2c
House, 1800 sq ft, 8000 sq ft lot, new, urban, utilities	total	117700	12/94	2c
Maintenance, repairs, insurance, and other housing expenditures	year	531	91	81r
Mortgage interest and charges expenditures	year	1506	91	81r
Mtge. rate, incl. points and orig. fee, 30-year conv. fixed or ARM	mo.	9.35	12/94	2c

Values are in dollars or fractions of dollars. In the column headed *Ref*, references are shown to sources. Each reference is followed by a letter. These refer to the geographical level for which data were reported: s = State, r = Region, and c = City or metro. The abbreviation *ex* is used to mean *except* or *excluding*; *exp* stands for expenditures. For other abbreviations and further explanations, please see the Introduction.

Tyler, TX - continued

Item	Per	Value	Date	Ref.
Housing				
Princ. & int., mortgage, median-price exist. sing.-family home	mo.	540	12/94	62r
Property taxes expenditures	year	391	91	81r
Redesign, restructure more than half of home's interior		17,641	3/95	74r
Rent, apartment, 2 br., 1 1/2-2 baths, unfurnished, 950 sq ft, water	mo.	535	12/94	2c
Rental units expenditures	year	1264	91	81r
Insurance and Pensions				
Auto insurance, private passenger	year	785.78	12/94	71s
Insurance and pensions, personal, expenditures	year	2395	91	81r
Insurance, life and other personal, expenditures	year	368	91	81r
Pensions and Social Security, expenditures	year	2027	91	81r
Personal Goods				
Shampoo, Alberto VO5	15-oz.	0.98	12/94	2c
Toothpaste, Crest or Colgate	6-7 oz.	2.10	12/94	2c
Personal Services				
Dry cleaning, man's 2-pc. suit		5.34	12/94	2c
Haircut, man's barbershop, no styling		8.19	12/94	2c
Haircut, woman's shampoo, trim, blow-dry		24.00	12/94	2c
Personal services expenditures	year	212	91	81r
Restaurant Food				
Chicken, fried, thigh and drumstick		2.12	12/94	2c
Dining expenditures, family	week	33.83	94	73r
Hamburger with cheese	1/4 lb.	1.89	12/94	2c
Pizza, Pizza Hut or Pizza Inn	12-13 in.	8.99	12/94	2c
Taxes				
Tax, cigarettes	year	584.00	10/93	43s
Taxes, Federal income, expenditures	year	2275	91	81r
Taxes, personal, expenditures	year	2715	91	81r
Taxes, State and local income, expenditures	year	365	91	81r
Transportation				
Transportation, ACCRA Index		94.40	12/94	2c
Cars and trucks purchased, new	year	1306	91	81r
Cars and trucks purchased, used	year	942	91	81r
Driver's learning permit fee	perm	5.00	1/94	84s
Driver's license fee	orig	16.00	1/94	84s
Driver's license fee, duplicate	lic	10.00	1/94	84s
Driver's license reinstatement fee, min.	susp	50.00	1/94	85s
Driver's license renewal fee	renew	16.00	1/94	84s
Identification card, nondriver	card	10.00	1/94	83s
Motorcycle learning permit fee	perm	5.00	1/94	84s
Motorcycle license fee	orig	16.00	1/94	84s
Motorcycle license fee, duplicate	lic	10.00	1/94	84s
Motorcycle license renewal fee	renew	21.00	1/94	84s
Public transportation expenditures	year	249	91	81r
Tire balance, computer or spin bal., front	wheel	6.00	12/94	2c
Transportation expenditures, total	year	5307	91	81r
Vehicle finance charges	year	346	91	81r
Vehicle insurance expenditures	year	544	91	81r
Vehicle maintenance and repairs expenditures	year	600	91	81r
Vehicle purchases	year	2275	91	81r
Vehicle rental, leases, licenses, etc. expenditures	year	141	91	81r
Vehicles purchased, other than cars and trucks	year	27	91	81r
Utilities				
Utilities, ACCRA Index		124.30	12/94	2c
Electricity expenditures	year	950	91	81r
Electricity, (part.), other, 1800 sq. ft., new home	mo.	115.26	12/94	2c
Utilities, fuels, and public services, total expenditures	year	2000	91	81r

Tyler, TX - continued

Item	Per	Value	Date	Ref.
Utilities - continued				
Water and other public services, expenditures	year	227	91	81r
Weddings				
Bridal attendants' gowns	event	750	10/93	76r
Bridal gown	event	852	10/93	76r
Bridal headpiece and veil	event	167	10/93	76r
Bride's wedding band	event	708	10/93	76r
Clergy	event	224	10/93	76r
Engagement ring	event	2756	10/93	76r
Flowers	event	863	10/93	76r
Formal wear for groom	event	106	10/93	76r
Groom's attendants' formal wear	event	530	10/93	76r
Groom's wedding band	event	402	10/93	76r
Music	event	600	10/93	76r
Photography	event	1088	10/93	76r
Shoes for bride	event	50	10/93	76r
Videography	event	483	10/93	76r
Wedding invitations and announcements	event	342	10/93	76r
Wedding reception	event	7000	10/93	76r

Utica-Rome, NY

Item	Per	Value	Date	Ref.
Composite, ACCRA index		105.80	12/94	2c
Alcoholic Beverages				
Beer, Miller Lite, Bud, 12-oz., ex deposit	6	4.99	12/94	2c
J & B Scotch	750-ml.	19.33	12/94	2c
Wine, Gallo Chablis blanc	1.5-lit	6.09	12/94	2c
Appliances				
Appliances (major), expenditures	year	145	91	81r
Average annual exp.				
Food, health care, personal goods, services	year	29496	91	81r
Charity				
Cash contributions, expenditures	year	708	91	81r
Clothing				
Apparel, men and boys, total expenditures	year	416	91	81r
Apparel, women and girls, total expenditures	year	744	91	81r
Footwear, expenditures	year	305	91	81r
Jeans, man's denim		35.59	12/94	2c
Shirt, man's dress shirt		26.30	12/94	2c
Undervest, boy's size 10-14, cotton	3	5.09	12/94	2c
Communications				
Long-distance telephone rate, day, addl. min., 1-10 mi.	min.	4.00	12/93	9s
Long-distance telephone rate, day, initial min., 1-10 mi.	min.	14.90	12/93	9s
Newspaper subscription, dly. and Sun. delivery	month	14.35	12/94	2c
Phone line, single, business, field visit	inst	143.26	12/93	9s
Phone line, single, business, no field visit	inst	106.05	12/93	9s
Phone line, single, residence, field visit	inst	85.46	12/93	9s
Phone line, single, residence, no field visit	inst	55.00	12/93	9s
Telephone bill, family of four	month	32.92	12/94	2c
Telephone service, expenditures	year	589	91	81r
Telephone, residential, flat rate	mo.	16.65	12/93	8c
Education				
Board, 4-year private college/university	year	2918	8/94	80s
Board, 4-year public college/university	year	2177	8/94	80s
Education, total expenditures	year	593	91	81r
Room, 4-year private college/university	year	3302	8/94	80s
Room, 4-year public college/university	year	2624	8/94	80s
Total cost, 4-year private college/university	year	18451	8/94	80s
Total cost, 4-year public college/university	year	7723	8/94	80s
Tuition, 2-year public college/university, in-state	year	2112	8/94	80s
Tuition, 4-year private college/university, in-state	year	12231	8/94	80s

Values are in dollars or fractions of dollars. In the column headed *Ref*, references are shown to sources. Each reference is followed by a letter. These refer to the geographical level for which data were reported: s=State, r=Region, and c=City or metro. The abbreviation *ex* is used to mean *except* or *excluding*; *exp* stands for expenditures. For other abbreviations and further explanations, please see the Introduction.

Utica-Rome, NY - continued

Item	Per	Value	Date	Ref.
Education				
Tuition, 4-year public college/university, in-state	year	2921	8/94	80s
Energy and Fuels				
Energy, combined forms, 1800 sq. ft.	mo.	148.23	12/94	2c
Energy, exc. electricity, 1800 sq. ft.	mo.	70.24	12/94	2c
Fuel oil and other fuels, expenditures	year	257	91	81r
Gas, natural, expenditures	year	285	91	81r
Gas, reg unlead, taxes inc., cash, self-service	gal	1.21	12/94	2c
Gasoline and motor oil purchased	year	867	91	81r
Gasoline, unleaded midgrade	gallon	1.32	4/93	82r
Gasoline, unleaded premium	gallon	1.40	4/93	82r
Gasoline, unleaded regular	gallon	1.19	4/93	82r
Entertainment				
Bowling, evening rate	game	1.78	12/94	2c
Entertainment, total expenditures	year	1331	91	81r
Fees and admissions, expenditures	year	398	91	81r
Monopoly game, Parker Brothers', No. 9	game	11.99	12/94	2c
Movie	adm	5.60	12/94	2c
Pets, toys, playground equipment, expenditures	year	270	91	81r
Reading, expenditures	year	171	91	81r
Televisions, radios, and sound equipment, expenditures	year	429	91	81r
Tennis balls, yellow, Wilson or Penn, 3	can	2.71	12/94	2c
Funerals				
Burial, immediate, container provided by funeral home		1370.36	1/95	54r
Cards, acknowledgment		17.72	1/95	54r
Casket, minimum alternative		192.52	1/95	54r
Cosmetology, hair care, etc.		139.56	1/95	54r
Cremation, direct, container provided by funeral home		1049.24	1/95	54r
Embalming		387.57	1/95	54r
Funeral, funeral home		278.77	1/95	54r
Funeral, other facility		275.85	1/95	54r
Graveside service		213.08	1/95	54r
Hearse, local		157.27	1/95	54r
Limousine, local		146.45	1/95	54r
Memorial service		271.02	1/95	54r
Service charge, professional, nondeclinable		943.58	1/95	54r
Visitation and viewing		322.86	1/95	54r
Groceries				
Groceries, ACCRA Index		109.80	12/94	2c
Apples, Red Delicious	lb.	0.78	12/94	82r
Baby food, strained vegetables, lowest price	4-4.5 oz.	0.33	12/94	2c
Bacon, sliced	lb.	2.24	12/94	82r
Bananas	lb.	0.52	12/94	2c
Bananas	lb.	0.49	12/94	82r
Beef or hamburger, ground	lb.	1.80	12/94	2c
Beef purchases	year	226	91	81r
Beverage purchases, alcoholic	year	332	91	81r
Beverage purchases, nonalcoholic	year	213	91	81r
Bread, white	24-oz.	0.85	12/94	2c
Bread, white, pan	lb.	0.80	12/94	82r
Butter, salted, Grade AA, stick	lb.	1.67	12/94	82r
Carrots, short trimmed and topped	lb.	0.51	12/94	82r
Cereals and bakery products purchases	year	407	91	81r
Cereals and cereals products purchases	year	132	91	81r
Cheese, Kraft grated Parmesan	8-oz.	3.09	12/94	2c
Chicken breast, bone-in	lb.	2.22	12/94	82r
Chicken, fresh, whole	lb.	1.05	12/94	82r
Chicken, whole fryer	lb.	0.97	12/94	2c
Chuck roast, USDA choice, boneless	lb.	2.74	12/94	82r
Cigarettes, Winston, Kings	carton	20.91	12/94	2c
Coffee, 100%, ground roast, all sizes	lb.	4.61	12/94	82r
Coffee, vacuum-packed	13 oz.	3.96	12/94	2c
Corn Flakes, Kellogg's or Post Toasties	18 oz.	2.05	12/94	2c
Corn, frozen, whole kernel, lowest price	10 oz.	0.74	12/94	2c

Utica-Rome, NY - continued

Item	Per	Value	Date	Ref.
Groceries - continued				
Dairy products (other) purchases	year	161	91	81r
Eggs, Grade A large	dozen	0.82	12/94	2c
Eggs, Grade A large	dozen	1.12	12/94	82r
Fish and seafood purchases	year	112	91	81r
Food purchases, food eaten at home	year	2599	91	81r
Foods purchased away from home, not prepared by consumer	year	2024	91	81r
Fruits and vegetables purchases	year	444	91	81r
Grapefruit	lb.	0.44	12/94	82r
Grapes, Thompson seedless	lb.	2.24	12/94	82r
Ground chuck, 100% beef	lb.	1.67	12/94	82r
Ice cream, prepackaged, bulk, regular	1/2 gal.	2.93	12/94	82r
Lemons	lb.	1.06	12/94	82r
Lettuce, iceberg	lb.	0.92	12/94	82r
Lettuce, iceberg	head	0.99	12/94	2c
Margarine, Blue Bonnet or Parkay cubes	lb.	0.62	12/94	2c
Meats, poultry, fish, and eggs purchases	year	751	91	81r
Milk and cream (fresh) purchases	year	152	91	81r
Milk, whole	1/2 gal.	1.23	12/94	2c
Orange juice, frozen concentrate 12-oz. can	16 oz.	1.92	12/94	82r
Orange juice, Minute Maid frozen	12-oz.	1.37	12/94	2c
Oranges, Navel	lb.	0.56	12/94	82r
Peaches, halves or slices, Hunt's, Del Monte, or Libby's	29-oz.	1.59	12/94	2c
Peas, sweet, Del Monte or Green Giant	15-17 oz.	0.65	12/94	2c
Pork chops, center cut, bone-in	lb.	3.09	12/94	82r
Pork purchases	year	130	91	81r
Potatoes, white	lb.	0.37	12/94	82r
Potatoes, white or red	10-lb. sack	2.19	12/94	2c
Rib roast, USDA choice, bone-in	lb.	4.98	12/94	82r
Round roast, USDA choice, boneless	lb.	2.93	12/94	82r
Sausage, Jimmy Dean, 100% pork	lb.	3.40	12/94	2c
Shortening, vegetable oil blends	lb.	1.03	12/94	82r
Shortening, vegetable, Crisco	3-lb.	2.77	12/94	2c
Soft drink, Coca Cola, ex deposit	2 lit	0.99	12/94	2c
Spaghetti and macaroni	lb.	0.84	12/94	82r
Steak, round, USDA choice, boneless	lb.	3.48	12/94	82r
Steak, sirloin, USDA choice, bone-in	lb.	3.38	12/94	82r
Steak, sirloin, USDA choice, boneless	lb.	4.81	12/94	82r
Steak, t-bone	lb.	5.91	12/94	2c
Sugar and other sweets, eaten at home, expenditures	year	89	91	81r
Sugar, cane or beet	4 lbs.	1.64	12/94	2c
Sugar, white, all sizes	lb.	0.46	12/94	82r
Tobacco products and smoking supplies, total expenditures	year	279	91	81r
Tomatoes, field grown	lb.	1.56	12/94	82r
Tomatoes, Hunt's or Del Monte	14.5 oz.	0.77	12/94	2c
Tuna, chunk, light	lb.	2.09	12/94	82r
Tuna, chunk, light, oil-packed	6.125-6.5 oz.	0.76	12/94	2c
Goods and Services				
Miscellaneous goods and services, ACCRA Index		103.70	12/94	2c
Health Care				
Health care, ACCRA Index		107.30	12/94	2c
Antibiotic ointment, Polysporin	1.5 oz.	4.06	12/94	2c
Childbirth, Cesarean delivery, hospital charge	birth	6334.00	12/91	69r
Childbirth, Cesarean delivery, physician charge	birth	2234.00	12/91	69r
Childbirth, normal delivery, hospital charge	birth	3225.00	12/91	69r
Childbirth, normal delivery, physician charge	birth	1623.00	12/91	69r
Dentist's fee, adult teeth cleaning and periodic oral exam	visit	48.00	12/94	2c

Values are in dollars or fractions of dollars. In the column headed *Ref*, references are shown to sources. Each reference is followed by a letter. These refer to the geographical level for which data were reported: s = State, r = Region, and c = City or metro. The abbreviation *ex* is used to mean *except* or *excluding*; *exp* stands for expenditures. For other abbreviations and further explanations, please see the Introduction.

Utica-Rome, NY - continued

Item	Per	Value	Date	Ref.
Health Care				
Doctor's fee, routine exam, established patient	visit	55.00	12/94	2c
Drugs, expenditures	year	205	91	81r
Health care, total expenditures	year	1396	91	81r
Health insurance expenditures	year	553	91	81r
Hospital care, semiprivate room	day	341.87	12/94	2c
Insurance premium, family medical care	month	384.24	1/95	41s
Medical services expenditures	year	559	91	81r
Medical supplies expenditures	year	80	91	81r
Household Goods				
Appl. repair, service call, wash mach	min. lab. chg.	26.60	12/94	2c
Floor coverings, expenditures	year	158	91	81r
Furniture, expenditures	year	341	91	81r
Household equipment, misc. expenditures	year	363	91	81r
Household expenditures, miscellaneous	year	194	91	81r
Household furnishings and equipment, expenditures	year	1158	91	81r
Household operations expenditures	year	378	91	81r
Household textiles, expenditures	year	88	91	81r
Housekeeping supplies, expenditures	year	426	91	81r
Laundry and cleaning supplies, expenditures	year	122	91	81r
Laundry detergent, Tide Ultra, Bold, or Cheer	42 oz.	3.57	12/94	2c
Postage and stationery, expenditures	year	134	91	81r
Tissues, facial, Kleenex brand	175	1.16	12/94	2c
Housing				
Housing, ACCRA Index		96.00	12/94	2c
Add garage/carport		11,614	3/95	74r
Add room(s)		16,816	3/95	74r
Apartment condominium or co-op, median	unit	96700	12/94	62r
Dwellings (owned), expenditures	year	3305	91	81r
Enclose porch/patio/breezeway		2,980	3/95	74r
Finish room in basement/attic		4,330	3/95	74r
Home, existing, single-family, median	unit	161600	12/94	62r
House payment, principal and interest, 25% down payment	mo.	706	12/94	2c
House, 1800 sq ft, 8000 sq ft lot, new, urban, utilities	total	112250	12/94	2c
Maintenance, repairs, insurance, and other housing expenditures	year	569	91	81r
Mortgage interest and charges expenditures	year	1852	91	81r
Mtge. rate, incl. points and orig. fee, 30-year conv. fixed or ARM	mo.	9.48	12/94	2c
Princ. & int., mortgage, median-price exist. sing.-family home	mo.	765	12/94	62r
Property taxes expenditures	year	884	91	81r
Redesign, restructure more than half of home's interior		2,750	3/95	74r
Rent, apartment, 2 br., 1 1/2-2 baths, unfurnished, 950 sq ft, water	mo.	591	12/94	2c
Rental units expenditures	year	1832	91	81r
Insurance and Pensions				
Auto insurance, private passenger	year	985.07	12/94	71s
Insurance and pensions, personal, expenditures	year	2690	91	81r
Insurance, life and other personal, expenditures	year	341	91	81r
Pensions and Social Security, expenditures	year	2349	91	81r
Legal Assistance				
Estate planning, law-firm partner	hr.	375.00	10/93	12r
Legal work, law firm associate	hour	78		10r
Legal work, law firm partner	hour	183		10r
Personal Goods				
Shampoo, Alberto VO5	15-oz.	1.19	12/94	2c
Toothpaste, Crest or Colgate	6-7 oz.	1.95	12/94	2c

Item	Per	Value	Date	Ref.
Personal Services				
Dry cleaning, man's 2-pc. suit		7.75	12/94	2c
Haircut, man's barbershop, no styling		7.50	12/94	2c
Haircut, woman's shampoo, trim, blow-dry		15.40	12/94	2c
Personal services expenditures	year	184	91	81r
Restaurant Food				
Chicken, fried, thigh and drumstick		2.34	12/94	2c
Dining expenditures, family	week	34.26	94	73r
Hamburger with cheese	1/4 lb.	1.99	12/94	2c
Pizza, Pizza Hut or Pizza Inn	12-13 in.	8.10	12/94	2c
Taxes				
Taxes, Federal income, expenditures	year	2409	91	81r
Taxes, personal, expenditures	year	3094	91	81r
Taxes, State and local income, expenditures	year	620	91	81r
Transportation				
Transportation, ACCRA Index		108.50	12/94	2c
Bus fare, up to 10 miles	one-way	0.60	12/94	2c
Cars and trucks purchased, new	year	1170	91	81r
Cars and trucks purchased, used	year	739	91	81r
Driver's learning permit fee	perm	10.00	1/94	84s
Driver's license fee	orig	32.00-37.00	1/94	84s
Driver's license fee, duplicate	lic	7.25	1/94	84s
Driver's license reinstatement fee, min.	susp	25.00	1/94	85s
Driver's license renewal fee	renew	22.25	1/94	84s
Identification card, nondriver	card	6.25	1/94	83s
Motorcycle license fee	orig	32.00-37.00	1/94	84s
Motorcycle license fee, duplicate	lic	7.25	1/94	84s
Motorcycle license renewal fee	renew	22.25	1/94	84s
Public transportation expenditures	year	430	91	81r
Tire balance, computer or spin bal., front	wheel	8.29	12/94	2c
Transportation expenditures, total	year	4810	91	81r
Vehicle finance charges	year	238	91	81r
Vehicle insurance expenditures	year	630	91	81r
Vehicle maintenance and repairs expenditures	year	532	91	81r
Vehicle purchases	year	1920	91	81r
Vehicle rental, leases, licenses, etc. expenditures	year	193	91	81r
Vehicles purchased, other than cars and trucks	year	11	91	81r
Utilities				
Utilities, ACCRA Index		137.00	12/94	2c
Electricity expenditures	year	695	91	81r
Electricity, (part.), other, 1800 sq. ft., new home	mo.	77.99	12/94	2c
Utilities, fuels, and public services, total expenditures	year	1981	91	81r
Water and other public services, expenditures	year	154	91	81r
Weddings				
Bridal attendants' gowns	event	750	10/93	76r
Bridal gown	event	852	10/93	76r
Bridal headpiece and veil	event	167	10/93	76r
Bride's wedding band	event	708	10/93	76r
Clergy	event	224	10/93	76r
Engagement ring	event	2756	10/93	76r
Flowers	event	863	10/93	76r
Formal wear for groom	event	106	10/93	76r
Groom's attendants' formal wear	event	530	10/93	76r
Groom's wedding band	event	402	10/93	76r
Music	event	600	10/93	76r
Photography	event	1088	10/93	76r
Shoes for bride	event	50	10/93	76r
Videography	event	483	10/93	76r
Wedding invitations and announcements	event	342	10/93	76r
Wedding reception	event	7000	10/93	76r

Values are in dollars or fractions of dollars. In the column headed *Ref*, references are shown to sources. Each reference is followed by a letter. These refer to the geographical level for which data were reported: s = State, r = Region, and c = City or metro. The abbreviation *ex* is used to mean *except* or *excluding*; *exp* stands for expenditures. For other abbreviations and further explanations, please see the Introduction.

Valdosta, GA

Item	Per	Value	Date	Ref.
Composite, ACCRA index		93.80	12/94	2c
Alcoholic Beverages				
Beer, Miller Lite, Bud, 12-oz., ex deposit	6	4.10	12/94	2c
J & B Scotch	750-ml.	18.19	12/94	2c
Wine, Gallo Chablis blanc	1.5-lit	6.00	12/94	2c
Clothing				
Jeans, man's denim		30.66	12/94	2c
Shirt, man's dress shirt		28.17	12/94	2c
Undervest, boy's size 10-14, cotton	3	4.64	12/94	2c
Communications				
Newspaper subscription, dly. and Sun. delivery	month	10.35	12/94	2c
Telephone bill, family of four	month	18.69	12/94	2c
Telephone, residential, flat rate	mo.	11.20	12/93	8c
Energy and Fuels				
Energy, combined forms, 1800 sq. ft.	mo.	124.18	12/94	2c
Gas, reg unlead, taxes inc., cash, self-service	gal	1.01	12/94	2c
Entertainment				
Bowling, evening rate	game	2.00	12/94	2c
Monopoly game, Parker Brothers', No. 9	game	11.23	12/94	2c
Movie	adm	5.00	12/94	2c
Tennis balls, yellow, Wilson or Penn, 3	can	1.92	12/94	2c
Groceries				
Groceries, ACCRA Index		95.30	12/94	2c
Baby food, strained vegetables, lowest price	4-4.5 oz.	0.31	12/94	2c
Bananas	lb.	0.39	12/94	2c
Beef or hamburger, ground	lb.	1.51	12/94	2c
Bread, white	24-oz.	0.80	12/94	2c
Cheese, Kraft grated Parmesan	8-oz.	3.06	12/94	2c
Chicken, whole fryer	lb.	0.71	12/94	2c
Cigarettes, Winston, Kings	carton	13.89	12/94	2c
Coffee, vacuum-packed	13 oz.	3.41	12/94	2c
Corn Flakes, Kellogg's or Post Toasties	18 oz.	2.30	12/94	2c
Corn, frozen, whole kernel, lowest price	10 oz.	0.58	12/94	2c
Eggs, Grade A large	dozen	0.69	12/94	2c
Lettuce, iceberg	head	0.74	12/94	2c
Margarine, Blue Bonnet or Parkay cubes	lb.	0.56	12/94	2c
Milk, whole	1/2 gal.	1.36	12/94	2c
Orange juice, Minute Maid frozen	12-oz.	1.13	12/94	2c
Peaches, halves or slices, Hunt's, Del Monte, or Libby's	29-oz.	1.33	12/94	2c
Peas, sweet, Del Monte or Green Giant	15-17 oz.	0.49	12/94	2c
Potatoes, white or red	10-lb. sack	2.74	12/94	2c
Sausage, Jimmy Dean, 100% pork	lb.	2.36	12/94	2c
Shortening, vegetable, Crisco	3-lb.	2.56	12/94	2c
Soft drink, Coca Cola, ex deposit	2 lit	1.18	12/94	2c
Steak, t-bone	lb.	5.51	12/94	2c
Sugar, cane or beet	4 lbs.	1.48	12/94	2c
Tomatoes, Hunt's or Del Monte	14.5 oz.	0.52	12/94	2c
Tuna, chunk, light, oil-packed	6.125-6.5 oz.	0.65	12/94	2c
Goods and Services				
Miscellaneous goods and services, ACCRA Index		97.00	12/94	2c
Health Care				
Health care, ACCRA Index		94.00	12/94	2c
Antibiotic ointment, Polysporin	1.5 oz.	3.96	12/94	2c
Dentist's fee, adult teeth cleaning and periodic oral exam	visit	52.00	12/94	2c
Doctor's fee, routine exam, established patient	visit	43.33	12/94	2c
Hospital care, semiprivate room	day	230.00	12/94	2c

Valdosta, GA - continued

Item	Per	Value	Date	Ref.
Household Goods				
Appl. repair, service call, wash mach	min. lab. chg.	37.48	12/94	2c
Laundry detergent, Tide Ultra, Bold, or Cheer	42 oz.	2.78	12/94	2c
Tissues, facial, Kleenex brand	175	0.98	12/94	2c
Housing				
Housing, ACCRA Index		83.10	12/94	2c
House payment, principal and interest, 25% down payment	mo.	622	12/94	2c
House, 1800 sq ft, 8000 sq ft lot, new, urban, utilities	total	100518	12/94	2c
Mtge. rate, incl. points and orig. fee, 30-year conv. fixed or ARM	mo.	9.29	12/94	2c
Rent, apartment, 2 br., 1 1/2-2 baths, unfurnished, 950 sq ft, water	mo.	481	12/94	2c
Personal Goods				
Shampoo, Alberto VO5	15-oz.	1.00	12/94	2c
Toothpaste, Crest or Colgate	6-7 oz.	1.98	12/94	2c
Personal Services				
Dry cleaning, man's 2-pc. suit		6.38	12/94	2c
Haircut, man's barbershop, no styling		6.33	12/94	2c
Haircut, woman's shampoo, trim, blow-dry		19.33	12/94	2c
Restaurant Food				
Chicken, fried, thigh and drumstick		2.02	12/94	2c
Hamburger with cheese	1/4 lb.	1.92	12/94	2c
Pizza, Pizza Hut or Pizza Inn	12-13 in.	7.99	12/94	2c
Transportation				
Transportation, ACCRA Index		99.70	12/94	2c
Tire balance, computer or spin bal., front	wheel	7.67	12/94	2c
Utilities				
Utilities, ACCRA Index		108.70	12/94	2c
Electricity, 1800 sq. ft., new home	mo.	124.18	12/94	2c

Vallejo-Fairfield-Napa, CA

Item	Per	Value	Date	Ref.
Appliances				
Appliances (major), expenditures	year	160	91	81r
Average annual exp.				
Food, health care, personal goods, services	year	32461	91	81r
Charity				
Cash contributions, expenditures	year	975	91	81r
Clothing				
Apparel, men and boys, total expenditures	year	467	91	81r
Apparel, women and girls, total expenditures	year	737	91	81r
Footwear, expenditures	year	270	91	81r
Communications				
Long-distance telephone rate, day, addl. min., 1-10 mi.	min.	0.07	12/93	9s
Long-distance telephone rate, day, initial min., 1-10 mi.	min.	0.17	12/93	9s
Phone line, single, business, field visit	inst	70.75	12/93	9s
Phone line, single, business, no field visit	inst	70.75	12/93	9s
Phone line, single, residence, field visit	inst	34.75	12/93	9s
Phone line, single, residence, no field visit	inst	34.75	12/93	9s
Telephone service, expenditures	year	611	91	81r
Education				
Board, 4-year private college/university	year	2945	8/94	80s
Board, 4-year public college/university	year	2321	8/94	80s
Education, total expenditures	year	375	91	81r
Room, 4-year private college/university	year	3094	8/94	80s
Room, 4-year public college/university	year	2812	8/94	80s
Student fee, university	year	21.00	93	18s
Total cost, 4-year private college/university	year	19321	8/94	80s

Values are in dollars or fractions of dollars. In the column headed *Ref*, references are shown to sources. Each reference is followed by a letter. These refer to the geographical level for which data were reported: s=State, r=Region, and c=City or metro. The abbreviation *ex* is used to mean *except* or *excluding*; *exp* stands for expenditures. For other abbreviations and further explanations, please see the Introduction.

Vallejo-Fairfield-Napa, CA - continued

Item	Per	Value	Date	Ref.
Education				
Total cost, 4-year public college/university	year	7511	8/94	80s
Tuition, 2-year public college/university, in-state	year	345	8/94	80s
Tuition, 4-year private college/university, in-state	year	13282	8/94	80s
Tuition, 4-year public college/university, in-state	year	2378	8/94	80s
Energy and Fuels				
Fuel oil and other fuels, expenditures	year	33	91	81r
Gas, natural, expenditures	year	212	91	81r
Gasoline and motor oil purchased	year	1115	91	81r
Gasoline, unleaded midgrade	gallon	1.36	4/93	82r
Gasoline, unleaded premium	gallon	1.43	4/93	82r
Gasoline, unleaded regular	gallon	1.23	4/93	82r
Entertainment				
Concert ticket, Pearl Jam group	perf	20.00	94	50r
Entertainment, total expenditures	year	1853	91	81r
Fees and admissions, expenditures	year	482	91	81r
Pets, toys, playground equipment, expenditures	year	299	91	81r
Reading, expenditures	year	164	91	81r
Televisions, radios, and sound equipment, expenditures	year	528	91	81r
Funerals				
Burial, immediate, container provided by funeral home		1382.70	1/95	54r
Cards, acknowledgment		21.87	1/95	54r
Casket, minimum alternative		128.54	1/95	54r
Cosmetology, hair care, etc.		119.69	1/95	54r
Cremation, direct, container provided by funeral home		1030.62	1/95	54r
Embalming		255.42	1/95	54r
Funeral, funeral home		437.38	1/95	54r
Funeral, other facility		444.46	1/95	54r
Graveside service		338.46	1/95	54r
Hearse, local		147.50	1/95	54r
Limousine, local		130.33	1/95	54r
Memorial service		553.16	1/95	54r
Service charge, professional, nondeclinable		859.15	1/95	54r
Visitation and viewing		93.23	1/95	54r
Groceries				
Apples, Red Delicious	lb.	0.72	12/94	82r
Bacon, sliced	lb.	1.73	12/94	82r
Bananas	lb.	0.52	12/94	82r
Beef purchases	year	241	91	81r
Beverage purchases, alcoholic	year	328	91	81r
Beverage purchases, nonalcoholic	year	234	91	81r
Bologna, all beef or mixed	lb.	2.33	12/94	82r
Bread, white, pan	lb.	0.81	12/94	82r
Carrots, short trimmed and topped	lb.	0.43	12/94	82r
Cereals and bakery products purchases	year	392	91	81r
Cereals and cereals products purchases	year	139	91	81r
Chicken breast, bone-in	lb.	2.04	12/94	82r
Chicken, fresh, whole	lb.	0.95	12/94	82r
Coffee, 100%, ground roast, all sizes	lb.	4.48	12/94	82r
Dairy products (other) purchases	year	182	91	81r
Fish and seafood purchases	year	94	91	81r
Flour, white, all purpose	lb.	0.21	12/94	82r
Food purchases, food eaten at home	year	2749	91	81r
Foods purchased away from home, not prepared by consumer	year	1909	91	81r
Fruits and vegetables purchases	year	459	91	81r
Grapefruit	lb.	0.56	12/94	82r
Ground beef, 100% beef	lb.	1.31	12/94	82r
Ham, boneless, exc. canned	lb.	2.46	12/94	82r
Ice cream, prepackaged, bulk, regular	1/2 gal.	2.57	12/94	82r
Lemons	lb.	1.00	12/94	82r
Lettuce, iceberg	lb.	0.93	12/94	82r
Meats, poultry, fish, and eggs purchases	year	700	91	81r

Vallejo-Fairfield-Napa, CA - continued

Item	Per	Value	Date	Ref.
Groceries - continued				
Milk and cream (fresh) purchases	year	155	91	81r
Orange juice, frozen concentrate 12-oz. can	16 oz.	1.52	12/94	82r
Oranges, Navel	lb.	0.56	12/94	82r
Pork chops, center cut, bone-in	lb.	3.30	12/94	82r
Pork purchases	year	122	91	81r
Potato chips	16-oz.	3.03	12/94	82r
Potatoes, frozen, French fried	lb.	0.77	12/94	82r
Potatoes, white	lb.	0.35	12/94	82r
Rice, white, long grain, uncooked	lb.	0.54	12/94	82r
Round roast, USDA choice, boneless	lb.	2.92	12/94	82r
Shortening, vegetable oil blends	lb.	0.80	12/94	82r
Spaghetti and macaroni	lb.	1.02	12/94	82r
Steak, round, graded & ungraded, exc. USDA prime & choice	lb.	3.13	12/94	82r
Steak, sirloin, USDA choice, boneless	lb.	4.07	12/94	82r
Sugar and other sweets, eaten at home, expenditures	year	105	91	81r
Sugar, white, all sizes	lb.	0.38	12/94	82r
Tobacco products and smoking supplies, total expenditures	year	221	91	81r
Tomatoes, field grown	lb.	1.45	12/94	82r
Tuna, chunk, light	lb.	2.18	12/94	82r
Health Care				
Childbirth, Cesarean delivery, hospital charge	birth	6059.00	12/91	69r
Childbirth, Cesarean delivery, physician charge	birth	2248.00	12/91	69r
Childbirth, normal delivery, hospital charge	birth	3006.00	12/91	69r
Childbirth, normal delivery, physician charge	birth	1634.00	12/91	69r
Drugs, expenditures	year	230	91	81r
Health care, total expenditures	year	1544	91	81r
Health insurance expenditures	year	558	91	81r
Insurance premium, family medical care	month	380.27	1/95	41s
Medical services expenditures	year	676	91	81r
Medical supplies expenditures	year	80	91	81r
Surgery, open-heart	proc	37818.00	1/93	14r
Household Goods				
Floor coverings, expenditures	year	79	91	81r
Furniture, expenditures	year	352	91	81r
Household equipment, misc. expenditures	year	614	91	81r
Household expenditures, miscellaneous	year	294	91	81r
Household furnishings and equipment, expenditures	year	1416	91	81r
Household operations expenditures	year	580	91	81r
Household textiles, expenditures	year	113	91	81r
Housekeeping supplies, expenditures	year	447	91	81r
Laundry and cleaning supplies, expenditures	year	114	91	81r
Postage and stationery, expenditures	year	145	91	81r
Housing				
Add garage/carport		6,422	3/95	74r
Add room(s)		26,583	3/95	74r
Apartment condominium or co-op, median	unit	105300	12/94	62r
Dwellings (owned), expenditures	year	3932	91	81r
Enclose porch/patio/breezeway		5,382	3/95	74r
Finish room in basement/attic		3,911	3/95	74r
Home, existing, single-family, median	unit	178600	12/94	62r
Maintenance, repairs, insurance, and other housing expenditures	year	591	91	81r
Mortgage interest and charges expenditures	year	2747	91	81r
Princ. & int., mortgage, median-price exist. sing.-family home	mo.	845	12/94	62r
Property taxes expenditures	year	594	91	81r
Redesign, restructure more than half of home's interior		5,467	3/95	74r
Rental units expenditures	year	2077	91	81r
Insurance and Pensions				
Auto insurance, private passenger	year	892.80	12/94	71s
Insurance and pensions, personal, expenditures	year	3042	91	81r

Values are in dollars or fractions of dollars. In the column headed *Ref*, references are shown to sources. Each reference is followed by a letter. These refer to the geographical level for which data were reported: s=State, r=Region, and c=City or metro. The abbreviation *ex* is used to mean *except* or *excluding*; *exp* stands for expenditures. For other abbreviations and further explanations, please see the Introduction.

Vallejo-Fairfield-Napa, CA - continued

Item	Per	Value	Date	Ref.
Insurance and Pensions				
Insurance, life and other personal, expenditures	year	298	91	81r
Pensions and Social Security, expenditures	year	2744	91	81r
Legal Assistance				
Legal work, law firm associate	hour	91		10r
Legal work, law firm partner	hour	151		10r
Personal Services				
Personal services expenditures	year	286	91	81r
Restaurant Food				
Dining expenditures, family	week	32.25	94	73r
Taxes				
Taxes, Federal income, expenditures	year	2946	91	81r
Taxes, personal, expenditures	year	3791	91	81r
Taxes, State and local income, expenditures	year	791	91	81r
Transportation				
Cars and trucks purchased, new	year	1231	91	81r
Cars and trucks purchased, used	year	915	91	81r
Driver's learning permit fee	perm	12.00	1/94	84s
Driver's license fee	orig	12.00	1/94	84s
Driver's license fee, duplicate	lic	12.00	1/94	84s
Driver's license reinstatement fee, min.	susp	15.00	1/94	85s
Driver's license renewal fee	renew	12.00	1/94	84s
Identification card, nondriver	card	6.00	1/94	83s
Motorcycle learning permit fee	perm	12.00	1/94	84s
Motorcycle license fee	orig	12.00	1/94	84s
Motorcycle license fee, duplicate	lic	12.00	1/94	84s
Motorcycle license renewal fee	renew	12.00	1/94	84s
Public transportation expenditures	year	375	91	81r
Transportation expenditures, total	year	5527	91	81r
Vehicle finance charges	year	287	91	81r
Vehicle insurance expenditures	year	624	91	81r
Vehicle maintenance and repairs expenditures	year	695	91	81r
Vehicle purchases	year	2174	91	81r
Vehicle rental, leases, licenses, etc. expenditures	year	257	91	81r
Vehicles purchased, other than cars and trucks	year	28	91	81r
Utilities				
Electricity expenditures	year	616	91	81r
Utilities, fuels, and public services, total expenditures	year	1681	91	81r
Water and other public services, expenditures	year	209	91	81r
Weddings				
Bridal attendants' gowns	event	750	10/93	76r
Bridal gown	event	852	10/93	76r
Bridal headpiece and veil	event	167	10/93	76r
Bride's wedding band	event	708	10/93	76r
Clergy	event	224	10/93	76r
Engagement ring	event	2756	10/93	76r
Flowers	event	863	10/93	76r
Formal wear for groom	event	106	10/93	76r
Groom's attendants' formal wear	event	530	10/93	76r
Groom's wedding band	event	402	10/93	76r
Music	event	600	10/93	76r
Photography	event	1088	10/93	76r
Shoes for bride	event	50	10/93	76r
Videography	event	483	10/93	76r
Wedding invitations and announcements	event	342	10/93	76r
Wedding reception	event	7000	10/93	76r

Vancouver, WA

Item	Per	Value	Date	Ref.
Appliances				
Appliances (major), expenditures	year	160	91	81r
Average annual exp.				
Food, health care, personal goods, services	year	32461	91	81r
Charity				
Cash contributions, expenditures	year	975	91	81r
Clothing				
Apparel, men and boys, total expenditures	year	467	91	81r
Apparel, women and girls, total expenditures	year	737	91	81r
Footwear, expenditures	year	270	91	81r
Communications				
Long-distance telephone rate, day, addl. min., 1-10 mi.	min.	0.01	12/93	9s
Long-distance telephone rate, day, initial min., 1-10 mi.	min.	0.15	12/93	9s
Phone line, single, business, field visit	inst	48.00	12/93	9s
Phone line, single, business, no field visit	inst	48.00	12/93	9s
Phone line, single, residence, field visit	inst	31.00	12/93	9s
Phone line, single, residence, no field visit	inst	31.00	12/93	9s
Telephone service, expenditures	year	611	91	81r
Education				
Board, 4-year private college/university	year	1928	8/94	80s
Board, 4-year public college/university	year	2194	8/94	80s
Education, total expenditures	year	375	91	81r
Room, 4-year private college/university	year	2455	8/94	80s
Room, 4-year public college/university	year	1952	8/94	80s
Total cost, 4-year private college/university	year	16332	8/94	80s
Total cost, 4-year public college/university	year	6483	8/94	80s
Tuition, 2-year public college/university, in-state	year	1141	8/94	80s
Tuition, 4-year private college/university, in-state	year	11949	8/94	80s
Tuition, 4-year public college/university, in-state	year	2337	8/94	80s
Energy and Fuels				
Fuel oil and other fuels, expenditures	year	33	91	81r
Gas, natural, expenditures	year	212	91	81r
Gasoline and motor oil purchased	year	1115	91	81r
Gasoline, unleaded midgrade	gallon	1.36	4/93	82r
Gasoline, unleaded premium	gallon	1.43	4/93	82r
Gasoline, unleaded regular	gallon	1.23	4/93	82r
Entertainment				
Concert ticket, Pearl Jam group	perf	20.00	94	50r
Entertainment, total expenditures	year	1853	91	81r
Fees and admissions, expenditures	year	482	91	81r
Pets, toys, playground equipment, expenditures	year	299	91	81r
Reading, expenditures	year	164	91	81r
Televisions, radios, and sound equipment, expenditures	year	528	91	81r
Funerals				
Burial, immediate, container provided by funeral home		1382.70	1/95	54r
Cards, acknowledgment		21.87	1/95	54r
Casket, minimum alternative		128.54	1/95	54r
Cosmetology, hair care, etc.		119.69	1/95	54r
Cremation, direct, container provided by funeral home		1030.62	1/95	54r
Embalming		255.42	1/95	54r
Funeral, funeral home		437.38	1/95	54r
Funeral, other facility		444.46	1/95	54r
Graveside service		338.46	1/95	54r
Hearse, local		147.50	1/95	54r
Limousine, local		130.33	1/95	54r
Memorial service		553.16	1/95	54r
Service charge, professional, nondeclinable		859.15	1/95	54r
Visitation and viewing		93.23	1/95	54r

Values are in dollars or fractions of dollars. In the column headed *Ref*, references are shown to sources. Each reference is followed by a letter. These refer to the geographical level for which data were reported: s=State, r=Region, and c=City or metro. The abbreviation *ex* is used to mean *except* or *excluding*; *exp* stands for expenditures. For other abbreviations and further explanations, please see the Introduction.

Vancouver, WA - continued

Item	Per	Value	Date	Ref.
Groceries				
Apples, Red Delicious	lb.	0.72	12/94	82r
Bacon, sliced	lb.	1.73	12/94	82r
Bananas	lb.	0.52	12/94	82r
Beef purchases	year	241	91	81r
Beverage purchases, alcoholic	year	328	91	81r
Beverage purchases, nonalcoholic	year	234	91	81r
Bologna, all beef or mixed	lb.	2.33	12/94	82r
Bread, white, pan	lb.	0.81	12/94	82r
Carrots, short trimmed and topped	lb.	0.43	12/94	82r
Cereals and bakery products purchases	year	392	91	81r
Cereals and cereals products purchases	year	139	91	81r
Chicken breast, bone-in	lb.	2.04	12/94	82r
Chicken, fresh, whole	lb.	0.95	12/94	82r
Coffee, 100%, ground roast, all sizes	lb.	4.48	12/94	82r
Dairy products (other) purchases	year	182	91	81r
Fish and seafood purchases	year	94	91	81r
Flour, white, all purpose	lb.	0.21	12/94	82r
Food purchases, food eaten at home	year	2749	91	81r
Foods purchased away from home, not prepared by consumer	year	1909	91	81r
Fruits and vegetables purchases	year	459	91	81r
Grapefruit	lb.	0.56	12/94	82r
Ground beef, 100% beef	lb.	1.31	12/94	82r
Ham, boneless, exc. canned	lb.	2.46	12/94	82r
Ice cream, prepackaged, bulk, regular	1/2 gal.	2.57	12/94	82r
Lemons	lb.	1.00	12/94	82r
Lettuce, iceberg	lb.	0.93	12/94	82r
Meats, poultry, fish, and eggs purchases	year	700	91	81r
Milk and cream (fresh) purchases	year	155	91	81r
Orange juice, frozen concentrate 12-oz. can	16 oz.	1.52	12/94	82r
Oranges, Navel	lb.	0.56	12/94	82r
Pork chops, center cut, bone-in	lb.	3.30	12/94	82r
Pork purchases	year	122	91	81r
Potato chips	16-oz.	3.03	12/94	82r
Potatoes, frozen, French fried	lb.	0.77	12/94	82r
Potatoes, white	lb.	0.35	12/94	82r
Rice, white, long grain, uncooked	lb.	0.54	12/94	82r
Round roast, USDA choice, boneless	lb.	2.92	12/94	82r
Shortening, vegetable oil blends	lb.	0.80	12/94	82r
Spaghetti and macaroni	lb.	1.02	12/94	82r
Steak, round, graded & ungraded, exc. USDA prime & choice	lb.	3.13	12/94	82r
Steak, sirloin, USDA choice, boneless	lb.	4.07	12/94	82r
Sugar and other sweets, eaten at home, expenditures	year	105	91	81r
Sugar, white, all sizes	lb.	0.38	12/94	82r
Tobacco products and smoking supplies, total expenditures	year	221	91	81r
Tomatoes, field grown	lb.	1.45	12/94	82r
Tuna, chunk, light	lb.	2.18	12/94	82r
Health Care				
Childbirth, Cesarean delivery, hospital charge	birth	6059.00	12/91	69r
Childbirth, Cesarean delivery, physician charge	birth	2248.00	12/91	69r
Childbirth, normal delivery, hospital charge	birth	3006.00	12/91	69r
Childbirth, normal delivery, physician charge	birth	1634.00	12/91	69r
Drugs, expenditures	year	230	91	81r
Health care, total expenditures	year	1544	91	81r
Health insurance expenditures	year	558	91	81r
Insurance premium, family medical care	month	382.32	1/95	41s
Medical services expenditures	year	676	91	81r
Medical supplies expenditures	year	80	91	81r
Surgery, open-heart	proc	37818.00	1/93	14r
Household Goods				
Floor coverings, expenditures	year	79	91	81r
Furniture, expenditures	year	352	91	81r
Household equipment, misc. expenditures	year	614	91	81r
Household expenditures, miscellaneous	year	294	91	81r

Vancouver, WA - continued

Item	Per	Value	Date	Ref.
Household Goods - continued				
Household furnishings and equipment, expenditures	year	1416	91	81r
Household operations expenditures	year	580	91	81r
Household textiles, expenditures	year	113	91	81r
Housekeeping supplies, expenditures	year	447	91	81r
Laundry and cleaning supplies, expenditures	year	114	91	81r
Postage and stationery, expenditures	year	145	91	81r
Housing				
Add garage/carport		6,422	3/95	74r
Add room(s)		26,583	3/95	74r
Apartment condominium or co-op, median	unit	105300	12/94	62r
Dwellings (owned), expenditures	year	3932	91	81r
Enclose porch/patio/breezeway		5,382	3/95	74r
Finish room in basement/attic		3,911	3/95	74r
Home, existing, single-family, median	unit	178600	12/94	62r
Maintenance, repairs, insurance, and other housing expenditures	year	591	91	81r
Mortgage interest and charges expenditures	year	2747	91	81r
Princ. & int., mortgage, median-price exist. sing.-family home	mo.	845	12/94	62r
Property taxes expenditures	year	594	91	81r
Redesign, restructure more than half of home's interior		5,467	3/95	74r
Rental units expenditures	year	2077	91	81r
Insurance and Pensions				
Auto insurance, private passenger	year	711.57	12/94	71s
Insurance and pensions, personal, expenditures	year	3042	91	81r
Insurance, life and other personal, expenditures	year	298	91	81r
Pensions and Social Security, expenditures	year	2744	91	81r
Legal Assistance				
Legal work, law firm associate	hour	91		10r
Legal work, law firm partner	hour	151		10r
Personal Services				
Personal services expenditures	year	286	91	81r
Restaurant Food				
Dining expenditures, family	week	32.25	94	73r
Taxes				
Taxes, Federal income, expenditures	year	2946	91	81r
Taxes, personal, expenditures	year	3791	91	81r
Taxes, State and local income, expenditures	year	791	91	81r
Transportation				
Cars and trucks purchased, new	year	1231	91	81r
Cars and trucks purchased, used	year	915	91	81r
Driver's learning permit fee	perm	4.00	1/94	84s
Driver's license fee	orig	21.00	1/94	84s
Driver's license fee, duplicate	lic	5.00	1/94	84s
Driver's license reinstatement fee, min.	susp	20.00-50.00	1/94	85s
Driver's license renewal fee	renew	14.00	1/94	84s
Identification card, nondriver	card	4.00	1/94	83s
Motorcycle license fee	orig	8.00	1/94	84s
Motorcycle license renewal fee	renew	7.50	1/94	84s
Public transportation expenditures	year	375	91	81r
Transportation expenditures, total	year	5527	91	81r
Vehicle finance charges	year	287	91	81r
Vehicle insurance expenditures	year	624	91	81r
Vehicle maintenance and repairs expenditures	year	695	91	81r
Vehicle purchases	year	2174	91	81r
Vehicle rental, leases, licenses, etc. expenditures	year	257	91	81r
Vehicles purchased, other than cars and trucks	year	28	91	81r

Values are in dollars or fractions of dollars. In the column headed *Ref*, references are shown to sources. Each reference is followed by a letter. These refer to the geographical level for which data were reported: s = State, r = Region, and c = City or metro. The abbreviation *ex* is used to mean *except* or *excluding*; *exp* stands for expenditures. For other abbreviations and further explanations, please see the Introduction.

Vancouver, WA - continued

Item	Per	Value	Date	Ref.
Utilities				
Electricity expenditures	year	616	91	81r
Utilities, fuels, and public services, total expenditures	year	1681	91	81r
Water and other public services, expenditures	year	209	91	81r
Weddings				
Bridal attendants' gowns	event	750	10/93	76r
Bridal gown	event	852	10/93	76r
Bridal headpiece and veil	event	167	10/93	76r
Bride's wedding band	event	708	10/93	76r
Clergy	event	224	10/93	76r
Engagement ring	event	2756	10/93	76r
Flowers	event	863	10/93	76r
Formal wear for groom	event	106	10/93	76r
Groom's attendants' formal wear	event	530	10/93	76r
Groom's wedding band	event	402	10/93	76r
Music	event	600	10/93	76r
Photography	event	1088	10/93	76r
Shoes for bride	event	50	10/93	76r
Videography	event	483	10/93	76r
Wedding invitations and announcements	event	342	10/93	76r
Wedding reception	event	7000	10/93	76r

Vermillion, SD

Item	Per	Value	Date	Ref.
Composite, ACCRA index		94.80	12/94	2c
Alcoholic Beverages				
Beer, Miller Lite, Bud, 12-oz., ex deposit	6	3.79	12/94	2c
J & B Scotch	750-ml.	18.74	12/94	2c
Wine, Gallo Chablis blanc	1.5-lit	5.49	12/94	2c
Clothing				
Jeans, man's denim		25.99	12/94	2c
Shirt, man's dress shirt		25.99	12/94	2c
Undervest, boy's size 10-14, cotton	3	4.49	12/94	2c
Communications				
Newspaper subscription, dly. and Sun. delivery	month	13.04	12/94	2c
Telephone bill, family of four	month	20.20	12/94	2c
Telephone, residential, flat rate	mo.	12.70	12/93	8c
Energy and Fuels				
Energy, combined forms, 1800 sq. ft.	mo.	85.89	12/94	2c
Energy, exc. electricity, 1800 sq. ft.	mo.	43.35	12/94	2c
Gas, reg unlead, taxes inc., cash, self-service	gal	1.19	12/94	2c
Entertainment				
Bowling, evening rate	game	1.85	12/94	2c
Monopoly game, Parker Brothers', No. 9	game	13.74	12/94	2c
Movie	adm	4.50	12/94	2c
Tennis balls, yellow, Wilson or Penn, 3	can	2.99	12/94	2c
Groceries				
Groceries, ACCRA Index		101.40	12/94	2c
Baby food, strained vegetables, lowest price	4-4.5 oz.	0.40	12/94	2c
Bananas	lb.	0.33	12/94	2c
Beef or hamburger, ground	lb.	1.29	12/94	2c
Bread, white	24-oz.	0.85	12/94	2c
Cheese, Kraft grated Parmesan	8-oz.	3.14	12/94	2c
Chicken, whole fryer	lb.	0.84	12/94	2c
Cigarettes, Winston, Kings	carton	15.45	12/94	2c
Coffee, vacuum-packed	13 oz.	3.45	12/94	2c
Corn Flakes, Kellogg's or Post Toasties	18 oz.	2.03	12/94	2c
Corn, frozen, whole kernel, lowest price	10 oz.	0.81	12/94	2c
Eggs, Grade A large	dozen	0.63	12/94	2c
Lettuce, iceberg	head	0.83	12/94	2c
Margarine, Blue Bonnet or Parkay cubes	lb.	0.78	12/94	2c
Milk, whole	1/2 gal.	1.30	12/94	2c

Vermillion, SD - continued

Item	Per	Value	Date	Ref.
Groceries - continued				
Orange juice, Minute Maid frozen	12-oz.	1.27	12/94	2c
Peaches, halves or slices, Hunt's, Del Monte, or Libby's	29-oz.	1.51	12/94	2c
Peas, sweet, Del Monte or Green Giant	15-17 oz.	0.59	12/94	2c
Potatoes, white or red	10-lb. sack	2.29	12/94	2c
Sausage, Jimmy Dean, 100% pork	lb.	2.90	12/94	2c
Shortening, vegetable, Crisco	3-lb.	2.56	12/94	2c
Soft drink, Coca Cola, ex deposit	2 lit	1.22	12/94	2c
Steak, t-bone	lb.	4.94	12/94	2c
Sugar, cane or beet	4 lbs.	1.42	12/94	2c
Tomatoes, Hunt's or Del Monte	14.5 oz.	0.78	12/94	2c
Tuna, chunk, light, oil-packed	6.125-6.5 oz.	0.66	12/94	2c
Goods and Services				
Miscellaneous goods and services, ACCRA Index		97.40	12/94	2c
Health Care				
Health care, ACCRA Index		96.90	12/94	2c
Antibiotic ointment, Polysporin	1.5 oz.	4.89	12/94	2c
Dentist's fee, adult teeth cleaning and periodic oral exam	visit	52.67	12/94	2c
Doctor's fee, routine exam, established patient	visit	39.33	12/94	2c
Hospital care, semiprivate room	day	296.00	12/94	2c
Household Goods				
Appl. repair, service call, wash mach	min. lab. chg.	35.00	12/94	2c
Laundry detergent, Tide Ultra, Bold, or Cheer	42 oz.	3.67	12/94	2c
Tissues, facial, Kleenex brand	175	0.97	12/94	2c
Housing				
Housing, ACCRA Index		91.60	12/94	2c
House payment, principal and interest, 25% down payment	mo.	719	12/94	2c
House, 1800 sq ft, 8000 sq ft lot, new, urban, utilities	total	117000	12/94	2c
Mtge. rate, incl. points and orig. fee, 30-year conv. fixed or ARM	mo.	9.20	12/94	2c
Rent, apartment, 2 br., 1 1/2-2 baths, unfurnished, 950 sq ft, water	mo.	435	12/94	2c
Personal Goods				
Shampoo, Alberto VO5	15-oz.	1.46	12/94	2c
Toothpaste, Crest or Colgate	6-7 oz.	2.33	12/94	2c
Personal Services				
Dry cleaning, man's 2-pc. suit		6.75	12/94	2c
Haircut, man's barbershop, no styling		7.25	12/94	2c
Haircut, woman's shampoo, trim, blow-dry		16.50	12/94	2c
Restaurant Food				
Chicken, fried, thigh and drumstick		1.73	12/94	2c
Hamburger with cheese	1/4 lb.	2.04	12/94	2c
Pizza, Pizza Hut or Pizza Inn	12-13 in.	7.49	12/94	2c
Transportation				
Transportation, ACCRA Index		95.50	12/94	2c
Tire balance, computer or spin bal., front	wheel	5.50	12/94	2c
Utilities				
Utilities, ACCRA Index		80.20	12/94	2c
Electricity, (part.), other, 1800 sq. ft., new home	mo.	42.54	12/94	2c

Values are in dollars or fractions of dollars. In the column headed *Ref*, references are shown to sources. Each reference is followed by a letter. These refer to the geographical level for which data were reported: s = State, r = Region, and c = City or metro. The abbreviation *ex* is used to mean *except* or *excluding*; *exp* stands for *expenditures*. For other abbreviations and further explanations, please see the Introduction.

Victoria, TX

Item	Per	Value	Date	Ref.
Composite, ACCRA index		92.50	12/94	2c
Alcoholic Beverages				
Beer, Miller Lite, Bud, 12-oz., ex deposit	6	3.75	12/94	2c
J & B Scotch	750-ml.	16.60	12/94	2c
Wine, Gallo Chablis blanc	1.5-lit	4.89	12/94	2c
Appliances				
Appliances (major), expenditures	year	153	91	81r
Average annual exp.				
Food, health care, personal goods, services	year	27020	91	81r
Charity				
Cash contributions, expenditures	year	839	91	81r
Clothing				
Apparel, men and boys, total expenditures	year	380	91	81r
Apparel, women and girls, total expenditures	year	660	91	81r
Footwear, expenditures	year	193	91	81r
Jeans, man's denim		24.66	12/94	2c
Shirt, man's dress shirt		29.83	12/94	2c
Undervest, boy's size 10-14, cotton	3	3.47	12/94	2c
Communications				
Long-distance telephone rate, day, addl. min., 1-10 mi.	min.	0.08	12/93	9s
Long-distance telephone rate, day, initial min., 1-10 mi.	min.	0.10	12/93	9s
Newspaper subscription, dly. and Sun. delivery	month	8.00	12/94	2c
Phone line, single, business, field visit	inst	71.90	12/93	9s
Phone line, single, business, no field visit	inst	57.30	12/93	9s
Phone line, single, residence, field visit	inst	52.95	12/93	9s
Phone line, single, residence, no field visit	inst	38.35	12/93	9s
Telephone bill, family of four	month	15.18	12/94	2c
Telephone service, expenditures	year	616	91	81r
Education				
Board, 4-year private college/university	year	2084	8/94	80s
Board, 4-year public college/university	year	1675	8/94	80s
Education, total expenditures	year	319	91	81r
Room, 4-year private college/university	year	1840	8/94	80s
Room, 4-year public college/university	year	1756	8/94	80s
Total cost, 4-year private college/university	year	11876	8/94	80s
Total cost, 4-year public college/university	year	4935	8/94	80s
Tuition, 2-year public college/university, in-state	year	625	8/94	80s
Tuition, 4-year private college/university, in-state	year	7952	8/94	80s
Tuition, 4-year public college/university, in-state	year	1503	8/94	80s
Energy and Fuels				
Energy, combined forms, 1800 sq. ft.	mo.	140.10	12/94	2c
Energy, exc. electricity, 1800 sq. ft.	mo.	33.47	12/94	2c
Fuel oil and other fuels, expenditures	year	56	91	81r
Gas, natural, expenditures	year	150	91	81r
Gas, reg unlead, taxes inc., cash, self-service	gal	1.03	12/94	2c
Gasoline and motor oil purchased	year	1152	91	81r
Gasoline, unleaded midgrade	gallon	1.21	4/93	82r
Gasoline, unleaded premium	gallon	1.30	4/93	82r
Gasoline, unleaded regular	gallon	1.10	4/93	82r
Entertainment				
Bowling, evening rate	game	1.98	12/94	2c
Concert ticket, Pearl Jam group	perf	20.00	94	50r
Entertainment, total expenditures	year	1266	91	81r
Fees and admissions, expenditures	year	306	91	81r
Monopoly game, Parker Brothers', No. 9	game	12.10	12/94	2c
Movie	adm	4.75	12/94	2c
Pets, toys, playground equipment, expenditures	year	271	91	81r
Reading, expenditures	year	131	91	81r

Victoria, TX - continued

Item	Per	Value	Date	Ref.
Entertainment - continued				
Televisions, radios, and sound equipment, expenditures	year	439	91	81r
Tennis balls, yellow, Wilson or Penn, 3	can	2.21	12/94	2c
Funerals				
Burial, immediate, container provided by funeral home		1574.60	1/95	54r
Cards, acknowledgment		22.24	1/95	54r
Casket, minimum alternative		239.41	1/95	54r
Cosmetology, hair care, etc.		91.04	1/95	54r
Cremation, direct, container provided by funeral home		1085.15	1/95	54r
Embalming		281.30	1/95	54r
Funeral, funeral home		323.04	1/95	54r
Funeral, other facility		327.58	1/95	54r
Graveside service		355.19	1/95	54r
Hearse, local		141.89	1/95	54r
Limousine, local		99.40	1/95	54r
Memorial service		284.67	1/95	54r
Service charge, professional, nondeclinable		904.06	1/95	54r
Visitation and viewing		187.04	1/95	54r
Groceries				
Groceries, ACCRA Index		82.50	12/94	2c
Apples, Red Delicious	lb.	0.73	12/94	82r
Baby food, strained vegetables, lowest price	4-4.5 oz.	0.25	12/94	2c
Bacon, sliced	lb.	1.67	12/94	82r
Bananas	lb.	0.32	12/94	2c
Bananas	lb.	0.42	12/94	82r
Beef or hamburger, ground	lb.	0.98	12/94	2c
Beef purchases	year	213	91	81r
Beverage purchases, alcoholic	year	249	91	81r
Beverage purchases, nonalcoholic	year	207	91	81r
Bologna, all beef or mixed	lb.	2.27	12/94	82r
Bread, white	24-oz.	0.49	12/94	2c
Bread, white, pan	lb.	0.68	12/94	82r
Cabbage	lb.	0.42	12/94	82r
Carrots, short trimmed and topped	lb.	0.53	12/94	82r
Cereals and bakery products purchases	year	345	91	81r
Cereals and cereals products purchases	year	127	91	81r
Cheddar cheese, natural	lb.	3.58	12/94	82r
Cheese, Kraft grated Parmesan	8-oz.	3.36	12/94	2c
Chicken breast, bone-in	lb.	1.71	12/94	82r
Chicken, fresh, whole	lb.	0.78	12/94	82r
Chicken, whole fryer	lb.	0.52	12/94	2c
Chuck roast, USDA choice, boneless	lb.	2.26	12/94	82r
Cigarettes, Winston, Kings	carton	16.39	12/94	2c
Coffee, vacuum-packed	13 oz.	3.31	12/94	2c
Corn Flakes, Kellogg's or Post Toasties	18 oz.	2.34	12/94	2c
Corn, frozen, whole kernel, lowest price	10 oz.	0.65	12/94	2c
Crackers, soda, salted	lb.	1.27	12/94	82r
Cucumbers	lb.	0.65	12/94	82r
Dairy products (other) purchases	year	141	91	81r
Eggs, Grade A large	dozen	0.64	12/94	2c
Eggs, Grade A large	dozen	0.87	12/94	82r
Fish and seafood purchases	year	72	91	81r
Flour, white, all purpose	lb.	0.23	12/94	82r
Food purchases, food eaten at home	year	2381	91	81r
Foods purchased away from home, not prepared by consumer	year	1696	91	81r
Frankfurters, all meat or all beef	lb.	1.74	12/94	82r
Fruits and vegetables purchases	year	380	91	81r
Grapefruit	lb.	0.45	12/94	82r
Grapes, Thompson seedless	lb.	2.30	12/94	82r
Ground beef, 100% beef	lb.	1.37	12/94	82r
Ground chuck, 100% beef	lb.	1.97	12/94	82r
Ham, boneless, exc. canned	lb.	2.54	12/94	82r
Ice cream, prepackaged, bulk, regular	1/2 gal.	2.47	12/94	82r
Lemons	lb.	1.02	12/94	82r
Lettuce, iceberg	lb.	0.96	12/94	82r
Lettuce, iceberg	head	0.73	12/94	2c

Values are in dollars or fractions of dollars. In the column headed *Ref*, references are shown to sources. Each reference is followed by a letter. These refer to the geographical level for which data were reported: s=State, r=Region, and c=City or metro. The abbreviation *ex* is used to mean *except* or *excluding*; *exp* stands for expenditures. For other abbreviations and further explanations, please see the Introduction.

Victoria, TX - continued

Item	Per	Value	Date	Ref.
Groceries				
Margarine, Blue Bonnet or Parkay cubes	lb.	0.49	12/94	2c
Margarine, stick	lb.	0.77	12/94	82r
Meats, poultry, fish, and eggs purchases	year	655	91	81r
Milk and cream (fresh) purchases	year	130	91	81r
Milk, whole	1/2 gal.	1.04	12/94	2c
Orange juice, frozen concentrate 12-oz. can	16 oz.	1.36	12/94	82r
Orange juice, Minute Maid frozen	12-oz.	1.04	12/94	2c
Oranges, Navel	lb.	0.54	12/94	82r
Peaches, halves or slices, Hunt's, Del Monte, or Libby's	29-oz.	1.27	12/94	2c
Pears, Anjou	lb.	0.81	12/94	82r
Peas, sweet, Del Monte or Green Giant	15-17 oz.	0.48	12/94	2c
Pork chops, center cut, bone-in	lb.	3.07	12/94	82r
Pork purchases	year	142	91	81r
Potato chips	16-oz.	3.15	12/94	82r
Potatoes, frozen, French fried	lb.	0.82	12/94	82r
Potatoes, white	lb.	0.34	12/94	82r
Potatoes, white or red	10-lb. sack	1.57	12/94	2c
Rice, white, long grain, uncooked	lb.	0.48	12/94	82r
Round roast, USDA choice, boneless	lb.	2.91	12/94	82r
Sausage, fresh	lb.	1.82	12/94	82r
Sausage, Jimmy Dean, 100% pork	lb.	2.29	12/94	2c
Shortening, vegetable oil blends	lb.	0.75	12/94	82r
Shortening, vegetable, Crisco	3-lb.	1.97	12/94	2c
Soft drink, Coca Cola, ex deposit	2 lit	1.09	12/94	2c
Spaghetti and macaroni	lb.	0.87	12/94	82r
Steak, rib eye, USDA choice, boneless	lb.	6.85	12/94	82r
Steak, round, graded & ungraded, exc. USDA prime & choice	lb.	2.96	12/94	82r
Steak, round, USDA choice, boneless	lb.	3.17	12/94	82r
Steak, sirloin, USDA choice, boneless	lb.	4.12	12/94	82r
Steak, t-bone	lb.	4.22	12/94	2c
Steak, T-bone, USDA choice, bone-in	lb.	5.63	12/94	82r
Sugar and other sweets, eaten at home, expenditures	year	93	91	81r
Sugar, cane or beet	4 lbs.	1.28	12/94	2c
Sugar, white, all sizes	lb.	0.39	12/94	82r
Tobacco products and smoking supplies, total expenditures	year	286	91	81r
Tomatoes, field grown	lb.	1.36	12/94	82r
Tomatoes, Hunt's or Del Monte	14.5 oz.	0.49	12/94	2c
Tuna, chunk, light	lb.	1.94	12/94	82r
Tuna, chunk, light, oil-packed	6.125-6.5 oz.	0.49	12/94	2c
Turkey, frozen, whole	lb.	0.96	12/94	82r
Yogurt, natural, fruit flavored	8 oz.	0.58	12/94	82r
Goods and Services				
Miscellaneous goods and services, ACCRA Index		95.20	12/94	2c
Health Care				
Health care, ACCRA Index		91.00	12/94	2c
Adenosine, emergency room	treat	100.00	95	23r
Antibiotic ointment, Polysporin	1.5 oz.	3.51	12/94	2c
Bladder tap, superpubic, infant, emergency room	treat	119.00	95	23r
Blood analysis, emergency room	treat	25.00	95	23r
Blood tests, abdominal pain, emergency room	treat	25.00	95	23r
Burn dressing, emergency room	treat	266.00	95	23r
Cardiology interpretation, emergency room	treat	26.00	95	23r
Chest X-ray, emergency room	treat	78.00	95	23r
Childbirth, Cesarean delivery, hospital charge	birth	5462.00	12/91	69r
Childbirth, Cesarean delivery, physician charge	birth	2228.00	12/91	69r
Childbirth, normal delivery, hospital charge	birth	2943.00	12/91	69r
Childbirth, normal delivery, physician charge	birth	1619.00	12/91	69r

Victoria, TX - continued

Item	Per	Value	Date	Ref.
Health Care - continued				
Defibrillation pads, emergency room	treat	6.00	95	23r
Dentist's fee, adult teeth cleaning and periodic oral exam	visit	49.00	12/94	2c
Doctor's fee, routine exam, established patient	visit	39.80	12/94	2c
Drugs, expenditures	year	297	91	81r
Gastric tube insertion, nasal, emergency room	treat	25.00	95	23r
Health care, total expenditures	year	1600	91	81r
Health insurance expenditures	year	637	91	81r
Heart monitor, emergency room	treat	40.00	95	23r
Hospital care, semiprivate room	day	293.67	12/94	2c
Insurance premium, family medical care	month	389.25	1/95	41s
Intravenous fluids, emergency room	treat	130.00	95	23r
Intravenous fluids, emergency room	liter	26.00	95	23r
Intravenous line, central, emergency room	treat	342.00	95	23r
Liver function tests, abdominal pain, emergency room	treat	26.00	95	23r
Medical care charges, total, emergency room, third-degree burns	treat	2101.00	95	23r
Medical care charges, total, emergency, infant with fever	treat	628.00	95	23r
Medical services expenditures	year	573	91	81r
Medical supplies expenditures	year	93	91	81r
Morphine, emergency room	treat	34.00	95	23r
Nursing care and facilities charges, emergency room	treat	252.00	95	23r
Nursing care and facilities charges, emergency, infant with fever	treat	252.00	95	23r
Nursing care and facilities charges, emergency, third-degree burns	treat	861.00	95	23r
Physician's charges, emergency, infant with fever	treat	212.00	95	23r
Physician's charges, emergency, third-degree burns	treat	372.00	95	23r
Physician's fee, emergency room	treat	372.00	95	23r
Physician's fee, general practitioner	visit	51.20	12/93	60r
Surgery, open-heart	proc	42374.00	1/93	14r
Ultrasound, abdominal, emergency room	treat	276.00	95	23r
Urinalysis, emergency room	treat	20.00	95	23r
Urinalysis, infant, emergency room	treat	20.00	95	23r
X-rays, emergency room	treat	78.00	95	23r
Household Goods				
Appl. repair, service call, wash mach	min. lab. chg.	37.68	12/94	2c
Floor coverings, expenditures	year	48	91	81r
Furniture, expenditures	year	280	91	81r
Household equipment, misc. expenditures	year	342	91	81r
Household expenditures, miscellaneous	year	256	91	81r
Household furnishings and equipment, expenditures	year	988	91	81r
Household operations expenditures	year	468	91	81r
Household textiles, expenditures	year	95	91	81r
Housekeeping supplies, expenditures	year	380	91	81r
Laundry and cleaning supplies, expenditures	year	109	91	81r
Laundry detergent, Tide Ultra, Bold, or Cheer	42 oz.	3.20	12/94	2c
Postage and stationery, expenditures	year	105	91	81r
Tissues, facial, Kleenex brand	175	0.88	12/94	2c
Housing				
Housing, ACCRA Index		87.00	12/94	2c
Add garage/carport		6,980	3/95	74r
Add room(s)		11,403	3/95	74r
Apartment condominium or co-op, median	unit	68600	12/94	62r
Dwellings (owned), expenditures	year	2428	91	81r
Enclose porch/patio/breezeway		4,572	3/95	74r
Finish room in basement/attic		3,794	3/95	74r
Home, existing, single-family, median	unit	120200	12/94	62r

Values are in dollars or fractions of dollars. In the column headed *Ref*, references are shown to sources. Each reference is followed by a letter. These refer to the geographical level for which data were reported: s=State, r=Region, and c=City or metro. The abbreviation *ex* is used to mean *except* or *excluding*; *exp* stands for expenditures. For other abbreviations and further explanations, please see the Introduction.

Victoria, TX - continued

Item	Per	Value	Date	Ref.
Housing				
House payment, principal and interest, 25% down payment	mo.	646	12/94	2c
House, 1800 sq ft, 8000 sq ft lot, new, urban, utilities	total	104533	12/94	2c
Maintenance, repairs, insurance, and other housing expenditures	year	531	91	81r
Mortgage interest and charges expenditures	year	1506	91	81r
Mtge. rate, incl. points and orig. fee, 30-year conv. fixed or ARM	mo.	9.27	12/94	2c
Princ. & int., mortgage, median-price exist. sing.-family home	mo.	540	12/94	62r
Property taxes expenditures	year	391	91	81r
Redesign, restructure more than half of home's interior		17,641	3/95	74r
Rent, apartment, 2 br., 1 1/2-2 baths, unfurnished, 950 sq ft, water	mo.	519	12/94	2c
Rental units expenditures	year	1264	91	81r
Insurance and Pensions				
Auto insurance, private passenger	year	785.78	12/94	71s
Insurance and pensions, personal, expenditures	year	2395	91	81r
Insurance, life and other personal, expenditures	year	368	91	81r
Pensions and Social Security, expenditures	year	2027	91	81r
Personal Goods				
Shampoo, Alberto VO5	15-oz.	0.85	12/94	2c
Toothpaste, Crest or Colgate	6-7 oz.	1.52	12/94	2c
Personal Services				
Dry cleaning, man's 2-pc. suit		5.41	12/94	2c
Haircut, man's barbershop, no styling		8.25	12/94	2c
Haircut, woman's shampoo, trim, blow-dry		22.62	12/94	2c
Personal services expenditures	year	212	91	81r
Restaurant Food				
Chicken, fried, thigh and drumstick		1.94	12/94	2c
Dining expenditures, family	week	33.83	94	73r
Hamburger with cheese	1/4 lb.	1.99	12/94	2c
Pizza, Pizza Hut or Pizza Inn	12-13 in.	9.39	12/94	2c
Taxes				
Tax, cigarettes	year	584.00	10/93	43s
Taxes, Federal income, expenditures	year	2275	91	81r
Taxes, personal, expenditures	year	2715	91	81r
Taxes, State and local income, expenditures	year	365	91	81r
Transportation				
Transportation, ACCRA Index		95.50	12/94	2c
Cars and trucks purchased, new	year	1306	91	81r
Cars and trucks purchased, used	year	942	91	81r
Driver's learning permit fee	perm	5.00	1/94	84s
Driver's license fee	orig	16.00	1/94	84s
Driver's license fee, duplicate	lic	10.00	1/94	84s
Driver's license reinstatement fee, min.	susp	50.00	1/94	85s
Driver's license renewal fee	renew	16.00	1/94	84s
Identification card, nondriver	card	10.00	1/94	83s
Motorcycle learning permit fee	perm	5.00	1/94	84s
Motorcycle license fee	orig	16.00	1/94	84s
Motorcycle license fee, duplicate	lic	10.00	1/94	84s
Motorcycle license renewal fee	renew	21.00	1/94	84s
Public transportation expenditures	year	249	91	81r
Tire balance, computer or spin bal., front	wheel	6.81	12/94	2c
Transportation expenditures, total	year	5307	91	81r
Vehicle finance charges	year	346	91	81r
Vehicle insurance expenditures	year	544	91	81r
Vehicle maintenance and repairs expenditures	year	600	91	81r
Vehicle purchases	year	2275	91	81r
Vehicle rental, leases, licenses, etc. expenditures	year	141	91	81r
Vehicles purchased, other than cars and trucks	year	27	91	81r

Victoria, TX - continued

Item	Per	Value	Date	Ref.
Utilities				
Utilities, ACCRA Index		118.50	12/94	2c
Electricity expenditures	year	950	91	81r
Electricity, (part.), other, 1800 sq. ft., new home	mo.	106.63	12/94	2c
Utilities, fuels, and public services, total expenditures	year	2000	91	81r
Water and other public services, expenditures	year	227	91	81r
Weddings				
Bridal attendants' gowns	event	750	10/93	76r
Bridal gown	event	852	10/93	76r
Bridal headpiece and veil	event	167	10/93	76r
Bride's wedding band	event	708	10/93	76r
Clergy	event	224	10/93	76r
Engagement ring	event	2756	10/93	76r
Flowers	event	863	10/93	76r
Formal wear for groom	event	106	10/93	76r
Groom's attendants' formal wear	event	530	10/93	76r
Groom's wedding band	event	402	10/93	76r
Music	event	600	10/93	76r
Photography	event	1088	10/93	76r
Shoes for bride	event	50	10/93	76r
Videography	event	483	10/93	76r
Wedding invitations and announcements	event	342	10/93	76r
Wedding reception	event	7000	10/93	76r

Vineland-Millville-Bridgeton, NJ

Item	Per	Value	Date	Ref.
Appliances				
Appliances (major), expenditures	year	145	91	81r
Average annual exp.				
Food, health care, personal goods, services	year	29496	91	81r
Charity				
Cash contributions, expenditures	year	708	91	81r
Clothing				
Apparel, men and boys, total expenditures	year	416	91	81r
Apparel, women and girls, total expenditures	year	744	91	81r
Footwear, expenditures	year	305	91	81r
Communications				
Long-distance telephone rate, day, addl. min., 1-10 mi.	min.	0.03	12/93	9s
Long-distance telephone rate, day, initial min., 1-10 mi.	min.	0.09	12/93	9s
Phone line, single, business, field visit	inst	98.50	12/93	9s
Phone line, single, business, no field visit	inst	79.50	12/93	9s
Phone line, single, residence, field visit	inst	56.50	12/93	9s
Phone line, single, residence, no field visit	inst	42.00	12/93	9s
Telephone service, expenditures	year	589	91	81r
Education				
Board, 4-year private college/university	year	2841	8/94	80s
Board, 4-year public college/university	year	1956	8/94	80s
Education, total expenditures	year	593	91	81r
Room, 4-year private college/university	year	2999	8/94	80s
Room, 4-year public college/university	year	2778	8/94	80s
Total cost, 4-year private college/university	year	18264	8/94	80s
Total cost, 4-year public college/university	year	8252	8/94	80s
Tuition, 2-year public college/university, in-state	year	1539	8/94	80s
Tuition, 4-year private college/university, in-state	year	12423	8/94	80s
Tuition, 4-year public college/university, in-state	year	3518	8/94	80s
Energy and Fuels				
Fuel oil and other fuels, expenditures	year	257	91	81r
Gas, natural, expenditures	year	285	91	81r
Gasoline and motor oil purchased	year	867	91	81r
Gasoline, unleaded midgrade	gallon	1.32	4/93	82r

Values are in dollars or fractions of dollars. In the column headed *Ref*, references are shown to sources. Each reference is followed by a letter. These refer to the geographical level for which data were reported: s=State, r=Region, and c=City or metro. The abbreviation *ex* is used to mean *except* or *excluding*; *exp* stands for expenditures. For other abbreviations and further explanations, please see the Introduction.

Vineland-Millville-Bridgeton, NJ - continued

Item	Per	Value	Date	Ref.
Energy and Fuels				
Gasoline, unleaded premium	gallon	1.40	4/93	82r
Gasoline, unleaded regular	gallon	1.19	4/93	82r
Entertainment				
Entertainment, total expenditures	year	1331	91	81r
Fees and admissions, expenditures	year	398	91	81r
Pets, toys, playground equipment, expenditures	year	270	91	81r
Reading, expenditures	year	171	91	81r
Televisions, radios, and sound equipment, expenditures	year	429	91	81r
Funerals				
Burial, immediate, container provided by funeral home		1370.36	1/95	54r
Cards, acknowledgment		17.72	1/95	54r
Casket, minimum alternative		192.52	1/95	54r
Cosmetology, hair care, etc.		139.56	1/95	54r
Cremation, direct, container provided by funeral home		1049.24	1/95	54r
Embalming		387.57	1/95	54r
Funeral, funeral home		278.77	1/95	54r
Funeral, other facility		275.85	1/95	54r
Graveside service		213.08	1/95	54r
Hearse, local		157.27	1/95	54r
Limousine, local		146.45	1/95	54r
Memorial service		271.02	1/95	54r
Service charge, professional, nondeclinable		943.58	1/95	54r
Visitation and viewing		322.86	1/95	54r
Groceries				
Apples, Red Delicious	lb.	0.78	12/94	82r
Bacon, sliced	lb.	2.24	12/94	82r
Bananas	lb.	0.49	12/94	82r
Beef purchases	year	226	91	81r
Beverage purchases, alcoholic	year	332	91	81r
Beverage purchases, nonalcoholic	year	213	91	81r
Bread, white, pan	lb.	0.80	12/94	82r
Butter, salted, Grade AA, stick	lb.	1.67	12/94	82r
Carrots, short trimmed and topped	lb.	0.51	12/94	82r
Cereals and bakery products purchases	year	407	91	81r
Cereals and cereals products purchases	year	132	91	81r
Chicken breast, bone-in	lb.	2.22	12/94	82r
Chicken, fresh, whole	lb.	1.05	12/94	82r
Chuck roast, USDA choice, boneless	lb.	2.74	12/94	82r
Coffee, 100%, ground roast, all sizes	lb.	4.61	12/94	82r
Dairy products (other) purchases	year	161	91	81r
Eggs, Grade A large	dozen	1.12	12/94	82r
Fish and seafood purchases	year	112	91	81r
Food purchases, food eaten at home	year	2599	91	81r
Foods purchased away from home, not prepared by consumer	year	2024	91	81r
Fruits and vegetables purchases	year	444	91	81r
Grapefruit	lb.	0.44	12/94	82r
Grapes, Thompson seedless	lb.	2.24	12/94	82r
Ground chuck, 100% beef	lb.	1.67	12/94	82r
Ice cream, prepackaged, bulk, regular	1/2 gal.	2.93	12/94	82r
Lemons	lb.	1.06	12/94	82r
Lettuce, iceberg	lb.	0.92	12/94	82r
Meats, poultry, fish, and eggs purchases	year	751	91	81r
Milk and cream (fresh) purchases	year	152	91	81r
Orange juice, frozen concentrate 12-oz. can	16 oz.	1.92	12/94	82r
Oranges, Navel	lb.	0.56	12/94	82r
Pork chops, center cut, bone-in	lb.	3.09	12/94	82r
Pork purchases	year	130	91	81r
Potatoes, white	lb.	0.37	12/94	82r
Rib roast, USDA choice, bone-in	lb.	4.98	12/94	82r
Round roast, USDA choice, boneless	lb.	2.93	12/94	82r
Shortening, vegetable oil blends	lb.	1.03	12/94	82r
Spaghetti and macaroni	lb.	0.84	12/94	82r
Steak, round, USDA choice, boneless	lb.	3.48	12/94	82r
Steak, sirloin, USDA choice, bone-in	lb.	3.38	12/94	82r
Steak, sirloin, USDA choice, boneless	lb.	4.81	12/94	82r

Vineland-Millville-Bridgeton, NJ - continued

Item	Per	Value	Date	Ref.
Groceries - continued				
Sugar and other sweets, eaten at home, expenditures	year	89	91	81r
Sugar, white, all sizes	lb.	0.46	12/94	82r
Tobacco products and smoking supplies, total expenditures	year	279	91	81r
Tomatoes, field grown	lb.	1.56	12/94	82r
Tuna, chunk, light	lb.	2.09	12/94	82r
Health Care				
Childbirth, Cesarean delivery, hospital charge	birth	6334.00	12/91	69r
Childbirth, Cesarean delivery, physician charge	birth	2234.00	12/91	69r
Childbirth, normal delivery, hospital charge	birth	3225.00	12/91	69r
Childbirth, normal delivery, physician charge	birth	1623.00	12/91	69r
Drugs, expenditures	year	205	91	81r
Health care, total expenditures	year	1396	91	81r
Health insurance expenditures	year	553	91	81r
Insurance premium, family medical care	month	396.06	1/95	41s
Medical services expenditures	year	559	91	81r
Medical supplies expenditures	year	80	91	81r
Household Goods				
Floor coverings, expenditures	year	158	91	81r
Furniture, expenditures	year	341	91	81r
Household equipment, misc. expenditures	year	363	91	81r
Household expenditures, miscellaneous	year	194	91	81r
Household furnishings and equipment, expenditures	year	1158	91	81r
Household operations expenditures	year	378	91	81r
Household textiles, expenditures	year	88	91	81r
Housekeeping supplies, expenditures	year	426	91	81r
Laundry and cleaning supplies, expenditures	year	122	91	81r
Postage and stationery, expenditures	year	134	91	81r
Housing				
Add garage/carport		11,614	3/95	74r
Add room(s)		16,816	3/95	74r
Apartment condominium or co-op, median	unit	96700	12/94	62r
Dwellings (owned), expenditures	year	3305	91	81r
Enclose porch/patio/breezeway		2,980	3/95	74r
Finish room in basement/attic		4,330	3/95	74r
Home, existing, single-family, median	unit	161600	12/94	62r
Maintenance, repairs, insurance, and other housing expenditures	year	569	91	81r
Mortgage interest and charges expenditures	year	1852	91	81r
Princ. & int., mortgage, median-price exist. sing.-family home	mo.	765	12/94	62r
Property taxes expenditures	year	884	91	81r
Redesign, restructure more than half of home's interior		2,750	3/95	74r
Rental units expenditures	year	1832	91	81r
Insurance and Pensions				
Auto insurance, private passenger	year	1094.56	12/94	71s
Insurance and pensions, personal, expenditures	year	2690	91	81r
Insurance, life and other personal, expenditures	year	341	91	81r
Pensions and Social Security, expenditures	year	2349	91	81r
Legal Assistance				
Estate planning, law-firm partner	hr.	375.00	10/93	12r
Legal work, law firm associate	hour	78		10r
Legal work, law firm partner	hour	183		10r
Personal Services				
Personal services expenditures	year	184	91	81r
Restaurant Food				
Dining expenditures, family	week	34.26	94	73r
Taxes				
Taxes, Federal income, expenditures	year	2409	91	81r
Taxes, personal, expenditures	year	3094	91	81r

Values are in dollars or fractions of dollars. In the column headed *Ref*, references are shown to sources. Each reference is followed by a letter. These refer to the geographical level for which data were reported: s=State, r=Region, and c=City or metro. The abbreviation *ex* is used to mean *except* or *excluding*; *exp* stands for expenditures. For other abbreviations and further explanations, please see the Introduction.

Vineland-Millville-Bridgeton, NJ - continued

Item	Per	Value	Date	Ref.
Taxes				
Taxes, State and local income, expenditures	year	620	91	81r
Transportation				
Cars and trucks purchased, new	year	1170	91	81r
Cars and trucks purchased, used	year	739	91	81r
Driver's learning permit fee	perm	5.00	1/94	84s
Driver's license fee	orig	16.00	1/94	84s
Driver's license fee, duplicate	lic	3.00	1/94	84s
Driver's license reinstatement fee, min.	susp	30.00	1/94	85s
Driver's license renewal fee	renew	16.00	1/94	84s
Identification card, nondriver	card	5.50	1/94	83s
Motorcycle learning permit fee	perm	5.00	1/94	84s
Motorcycle license fee	orig	8.00	1/94	84s
Motorcycle license fee, duplicate	lic	3.00	1/94	84s
Motorcycle license renewal fee	renew	8.00	1/94	84s
Public transportation expenditures	year	430	91	81r
Transportation expenditures, total	year	4810	91	81r
Vehicle finance charges	year	238	91	81r
Vehicle insurance expenditures	year	630	91	81r
Vehicle maintenance and repairs expenditures	year	532	91	81r
Vehicle purchases	year	1920	91	81r
Vehicle rental, leases, licenses, etc. expenditures	year	193	91	81r
Vehicles purchased, other than cars and trucks	year	11	91	81r
Utilities				
Electricity expenditures	year	695	91	81r
Utilities, fuels, and public services, total expenditures	year	1981	91	81r
Water and other public services, expenditures	year	154	91	81r
Weddings				
Bridal attendants' gowns	event	750	10/93	76r
Bridal gown	event	852	10/93	76r
Bridal headpiece and veil	event	167	10/93	76r
Bride's wedding band	event	708	10/93	76r
Clergy	event	224	10/93	76r
Engagement ring	event	2756	10/93	76r
Flowers	event	863	10/93	76r
Formal wear for groom	event	106	10/93	76r
Groom's attendants' formal wear	event	530	10/93	76r
Groom's wedding band	event	402	10/93	76r
Music	event	600	10/93	76r
Photography	event	1088	10/93	76r
Shoes for bride	event	50	10/93	76r
Videography	event	483	10/93	76r
Wedding invitations and announcements	event	342	10/93	76r
Wedding reception	event	7000	10/93	76r

Visalia, CA

Item	Per	Value	Date	Ref.
Composite, ACCRA index		110.10	12/94	2c
Alcoholic Beverages				
Beer, Miller Lite, Bud, 12-oz., ex deposit	6	4.17	12/94	2c
J & B Scotch	750-ml.	17.85	12/94	2c
Wine, Gallo Chablis blanc	1.5-lit	4.91	12/94	2c
Appliances				
Appliances (major), expenditures	year	160	91	81r
Average annual exp.				
Food, health care, personal goods, services	year	32461	91	81r
Charity				
Cash contributions, expenditures	year	975	91	81r
Clothing				
Apparel, men and boys, total expenditures	year	467	91	81r
Apparel, women and girls, total expenditures	year	737	91	81r
Footwear, expenditures	year	270	91	81r

Visalia, CA - continued

Item	Per	Value	Date	Ref.
Clothing - continued				
Jeans, man's denim		33.40	12/94	2c
Shirt, man's dress shirt		33.40	12/94	2c
Undervest, boy's size 10-14, cotton	3	5.39	12/94	2c
Communications				
Long-distance telephone rate, day, addl. min., 1-10 mi.	min.	0.07	12/93	9s
Long-distance telephone rate, day, initial min., 1-10 mi.	min.	0.17	12/93	9s
Newspaper subscription, dly. and Sun. delivery	month	11.25	12/94	2c
Phone line, single, business, field visit	inst	70.75	12/93	9s
Phone line, single, business, no field visit	inst	70.75	12/93	9s
Phone line, single, residence, field visit	inst	34.75	12/93	9s
Phone line, single, residence, no field visit	inst	34.75	12/93	9s
Telephone bill, family of four	month	12.12	12/94	2c
Telephone service, expenditures	year	611	91	81r
Telephone, residential, flat rate	mo.	8.35	12/93	8c
Education				
Board, 4-year private college/university	year	2945	8/94	80s
Board, 4-year public college/university	year	2321	8/94	80s
Education, total expenditures	year	375	91	81r
Room, 4-year private college/university	year	3094	8/94	80s
Room, 4-year public college/university	year	2812	8/94	80s
Student fee, university	year	21.00	93	18s
Total cost, 4-year private college/university	year	19321	8/94	80s
Total cost, 4-year public college/university	year	7511	8/94	80s
Tuition, 2-year public college/university, in-state	year	345	8/94	80s
Tuition, 4-year private college/university, in-state	year	13282	8/94	80s
Tuition, 4-year public college/university, in-state	year	2378	8/94	80s
Energy and Fuels				
Energy, combined forms, 1800 sq. ft.	mo.	134.52	12/94	2c
Energy, exc. electricity, 1800 sq. ft.	mo.	34.46	12/94	2c
Fuel oil and other fuels, expenditures	year	33	91	81r
Gas, natural, expenditures	year	212	91	81r
Gas, reg unlead, taxes inc., cash, self-service	gal	1.22	12/94	2c
Gasoline and motor oil purchased	year	1115	91	81r
Gasoline, unleaded midgrade	gallon	1.36	4/93	82r
Gasoline, unleaded premium	gallon	1.43	4/93	82r
Gasoline, unleaded regular	gallon	1.23	4/93	82r
Entertainment				
Bowling, evening rate	game	2.50	12/94	2c
Concert ticket, Pearl Jam group	perf	20.00	94	50r
Entertainment, total expenditures	year	1853	91	81r
Fees and admissions, expenditures	year	482	91	81r
Monopoly game, Parker Brothers', No. 9	game	12.43	12/94	2c
Movie	adm	5.75	12/94	2c
Pets, toys, playground equipment, expenditures	year	299	91	81r
Reading, expenditures	year	164	91	81r
Televisions, radios, and sound equipment, expenditures	year	528	91	81r
Tennis balls, yellow, Wilson or Penn, 3	can	2.83	12/94	2c
Funerals				
Burial, immediate, container provided by funeral home		1382.70	1/95	54r
Cards, acknowledgment		21.87	1/95	54r
Casket, minimum alternative		128.54	1/95	54r
Cosmetology, hair care, etc.		119.69	1/95	54r
Cremation, direct, container provided by funeral home		1030.62	1/95	54r
Embalming		255.42	1/95	54r
Funeral, funeral home		437.38	1/95	54r
Funeral, other facility		444.46	1/95	54r
Graveside service		338.46	1/95	54r
Hearse, local		147.50	1/95	54r

Values are in dollars or fractions of dollars. In the column headed *Ref*, references are shown to sources. Each reference is followed by a letter. These refer to the geographical level for which data were reported: s=State, r=Region, and c=City or metro. The abbreviation *ex* is used to mean *except* or *excluding*; *exp* stands for *expenditures*. For other abbreviations and further explanations, please see the Introduction.

Visalia, CA - continued

Item	Per	Value	Date	Ref.
Funerals				
Limousine, local		130.33	1/95	54r
Memorial service		553.16	1/95	54r
Service charge, professional, nondeclinable		859.15	1/95	54r
Visitation and viewing		93.23	1/95	54r
Groceries				
Groceries, ACCRA Index		110.50	12/94	2c
Apples, Red Delicious	lb.	0.72	12/94	82r
Baby food, strained vegetables, lowest price	4-4.5 oz.	0.40	12/94	2c
Bacon, sliced	lb.	1.73	12/94	82r
Bananas	lb.	0.39	12/94	2c
Bananas	lb.	0.52	12/94	82r
Beef or hamburger, ground	lb.	1.39	12/94	2c
Beef purchases	year	241	91	81r
Beverage purchases, alcoholic	year	328	91	81r
Beverage purchases, nonalcoholic	year	234	91	81r
Bologna, all beef or mixed	lb.	2.33	12/94	82r
Bread, white	24-oz.	1.16	12/94	2c
Bread, white, pan	lb.	0.81	12/94	82r
Carrots, short trimmed and topped	lb.	0.43	12/94	82r
Cereals and bakery products purchases	year	392	91	81r
Cereals and cereals products purchases	year	139	91	81r
Cheese, Kraft grated Parmesan	8-oz.	3.67	12/94	2c
Chicken breast, bone-in	lb.	2.04	12/94	82r
Chicken, fresh, whole	lb.	0.95	12/94	82r
Chicken, whole fryer	lb.	0.90	12/94	2c
Cigarettes, Winston, Kings	carton	16.04	12/94	2c
Coffee, 100%, ground roast, all sizes	lb.	4.48	12/94	82r
Coffee, vacuum-packed	13 oz.	3.59	12/94	2c
Corn Flakes, Kellogg's or Post Toasties	18 oz.	2.60	12/94	2c
Corn, frozen, whole kernel, lowest price	10 oz.	0.80	12/94	2c
Dairy products (other) purchases	year	182	91	81r
Eggs, Grade A large	dozen	1.10	12/94	2c
Fish and seafood purchases	year	94	91	81r
Flour, white, all purpose	lb.	0.21	12/94	82r
Food purchases, food eaten at home	year	2749	91	81r
Foods purchased away from home, not prepared by consumer	year	1909	91	81r
Fruits and vegetables purchases	year	459	91	81r
Grapefruit	lb.	0.56	12/94	82r
Ground beef, 100% beef	lb.	1.31	12/94	82r
Ham, boneless, exc. canned	lb.	2.46	12/94	82r
Ice cream, prepackaged, bulk, regular	1/2 gal.	2.57	12/94	82r
Lemons	lb.	1.00	12/94	82r
Lettuce, iceberg	lb.	0.93	12/94	82r
Lettuce, iceberg	head	0.67	12/94	2c
Margarine, Blue Bonnet or Parkay cubes	lb.	0.77	12/94	2c
Meats, poultry, fish, and eggs purchases	year	700	91	81r
Milk and cream (fresh) purchases	year	155	91	81r
Milk, whole	1/2 gal.	1.32	12/94	2c
Orange juice, frozen concentrate 12-oz. can	16 oz.	1.52	12/94	82r
Orange juice, Minute Maid frozen	12-oz.	1.57	12/94	2c
Oranges, Navel	lb.	0.56	12/94	82r
Peaches, halves or slices, Hunt's, Del Monte, or Libby's	29-oz.	1.42	12/94	2c
Peas, sweet, Del Monte or Green Giant	15-17 oz.	0.68	12/94	2c
Pork chops, center cut, bone-in	lb.	3.30	12/94	82r
Pork purchases	year	122	91	81r
Potato chips	16-oz.	3.03	12/94	82r
Potatoes, frozen, French fried	lb.	0.77	12/94	82r
Potatoes, white	lb.	0.35	12/94	82r
Potatoes, white or red	10-lb. sack	1.87	12/94	2c
Rice, white, long grain, uncooked	lb.	0.54	12/94	82r
Round roast, USDA choice, boneless	lb.	2.92	12/94	82r
Sausage, Jimmy Dean, 100% pork	lb.	2.59	12/94	2c
Shortening, vegetable oil blends	lb.	0.80	12/94	82r
Shortening, vegetable, Crisco	3-lb.	2.73	12/94	2c
Soft drink, Coca Cola, ex deposit	2 lit	1.21	12/94	2c

Visalia, CA - continued

Item	Per	Value	Date	Ref.
Groceries - continued				
Spaghetti and macaroni	lb.	1.02	12/94	82r
Steak, round, graded & ungraded, exc. USDA prime & choice	lb.	3.13	12/94	82r
Steak, sirloin, USDA choice, boneless	lb.	4.07	12/94	82r
Steak, t-bone	lb.	4.83	12/94	2c
Sugar and other sweets, eaten at home, expenditures	year	105	91	81r
Sugar, cane or beet	4 lbs.	1.66	12/94	2c
Sugar, white, all sizes	lb.	0.38	12/94	82r
Tobacco products and smoking supplies, total expenditures	year	221	91	81r
Tomatoes, field grown	lb.	1.45	12/94	82r
Tomatoes, Hunt's or Del Monte	14.5 oz.	0.79	12/94	2c
Tuna, chunk, light	lb.	2.18	12/94	82r
Tuna, chunk, light, oil-packed	6.125-6.5 oz.	0.70	12/94	2c
Goods and Services				
Miscellaneous goods and services, ACCRA Index		110.60	12/94	2c
Health Care				
Health care, ACCRA Index		106.40	12/94	2c
Antibiotic ointment, Polysporin	1.5 oz.	4.48	12/94	2c
Childbirth, Cesarean delivery, hospital charge	birth	6059.00	12/91	69r
Childbirth, Cesarean delivery, physician charge	birth	2248.00	12/91	69r
Childbirth, normal delivery, hospital charge	birth	3006.00	12/91	69r
Childbirth, normal delivery, physician charge	birth	1634.00	12/91	69r
Dentist's fee, adult teeth cleaning and periodic oral exam	visit	53.60	12/94	2c
Doctor's fee, routine exam, established patient	visit	41.20	12/94	2c
Drugs, expenditures	year	230	91	81r
Health care, total expenditures	year	1544	91	81r
Health insurance expenditures	year	558	91	81r
Hospital care, semiprivate room	day	460.00	12/94	2c
Insurance premium, family medical care	month	380.27	1/95	41s
Medical services expenditures	year	676	91	81r
Medical supplies expenditures	year	80	91	81r
Surgery, open-heart	proc	37818.00	1/93	14r
Household Goods				
Appl. repair, service call, wash mach	min. lab. chg.	40.30	12/94	2c
Floor coverings, expenditures	year	79	91	81r
Furniture, expenditures	year	352	91	81r
Household equipment, misc. expenditures	year	614	91	81r
Household expenditures, miscellaneous	year	294	91	81r
Household furnishings and equipment, expenditures	year	1416	91	81r
Household operations expenditures	year	580	91	81r
Household textiles, expenditures	year	113	91	81r
Housekeeping supplies, expenditures	year	447	91	81r
Laundry and cleaning supplies, expenditures	year	114	91	81r
Laundry detergent, Tide Ultra, Bold, or Cheer	42 oz.	3.97	12/94	2c
Postage and stationery, expenditures	year	145	91	81r
Tissues, facial, Kleenex brand	175	1.10	12/94	2c
Housing				
Housing, ACCRA Index		109.70	12/94	2c
Add garage/carport		6,422	3/95	74r
Add room(s)		26,583	3/95	74r
Apartment condominium or co-op, median	unit	105300	12/94	62r
Dwellings (owned), expenditures	year	3932	91	81r
Enclose porch/patio/breezeway		5,382	3/95	74r
Finish room in basement/attic		3,911	3/95	74r
Home, existing, single-family, median	unit	178600	12/94	62r

Values are in dollars or fractions of dollars. In the column headed *Ref*, references are shown to sources. Each reference is followed by a letter. These refer to the geographical level for which data were reported: s = State, r = Region, and c = City or metro. The abbreviation *ex* is used to mean *except* or *excluding*; *exp* stands for *expenditures*. For other abbreviations and further explanations, please see the Introduction.

Visalia, CA - continued

Item	Per	Value	Date	Ref.
Housing				
House payment, principal and interest, 25% down payment	mo.	873	12/94	2c
House, 1800 sq ft, 8000 sq ft lot, new, urban, utilities	total	141975	12/94	2c
Maintenance, repairs, insurance, and other housing expenditures	year	591	91	81r
Mortgage interest and charges expenditures	year	2747	91	81r
Mtge. rate, incl. points and orig. fee, 30-year conv. fixed or ARM	mo.	9.22	12/94	2c
Princ. & int., mortgage, median-price exist. sing.-family home	mo.	845	12/94	62r
Property taxes expenditures	year	594	91	81r
Redesign, restructure more than half of home's interior		5,467	3/95	74r
Rent, apartment, 2 br., 1 1/2-2 baths, unfurnished, 950 sq ft, water	mo.	485	12/94	2c
Rental units expenditures	year	2077	91	81r
Insurance and Pensions				
Auto insurance, private passenger	year	892.80	12/94	71s
Insurance and pensions, personal, expenditures	year	3042	91	81r
Insurance, life and other personal, expenditures	year	298	91	81r
Pensions and Social Security, expenditures	year	2744	91	81r
Legal Assistance				
Legal work, law firm associate	hour	91		10r
Legal work, law firm partner	hour	151		10r
Personal Goods				
Shampoo, Alberto VO5	15-oz.	1.36	12/94	2c
Toothpaste, Crest or Colgate	6-7 oz.	2.49	12/94	2c
Personal Services				
Dry cleaning, man's 2-pc. suit		6.95	12/94	2c
Haircut, man's barbershop, no styling		7.60	12/94	2c
Haircut, woman's shampoo, trim, blow-dry		24.80	12/94	2c
Personal services expenditures	year	286	91	81r
Restaurant Food				
Chicken, fried, thigh and drumstick		2.49	12/94	2c
Dining expenditures, family	week	32.25	94	73r
Hamburger with cheese	1/4 lb.	1.89	12/94	2c
Pizza, Pizza Hut or Pizza Inn	12-13 in.	8.59	12/94	2c
Taxes				
Taxes, Federal income, expenditures	year	2946	91	81r
Taxes, personal, expenditures	year	3791	91	81r
Taxes, State and local income, expenditures	year	791	91	81r
Transportation				
Transportation, ACCRA Index		109.70	12/94	2c
Bus fare, one-way	trip	1.03	12/95	1c
Cars and trucks purchased, new	year	1231	91	81r
Cars and trucks purchased, used	year	915	91	81r
Driver's learning permit fee	perm	12.00	1/94	84s
Driver's license fee	orig	12.00	1/94	84s
Driver's license fee, duplicate	lic	12.00	1/94	84s
Driver's license reinstatement fee, min.	susp	15.00	1/94	85s
Driver's license renewal fee	renew	12.00	1/94	84s
Identification card, nondriver	card	6.00	1/94	83s
Motorcycle learning permit fee	perm	12.00	1/94	84s
Motorcycle license fee	orig	12.00	1/94	84s
Motorcycle license fee, duplicate	lic	12.00	1/94	84s
Motorcycle license renewal fee	renew	12.00	1/94	84s
Public transportation expenditures	year	375	91	81r
Tire balance, computer or spin bal., front	wheel	7.50	12/94	2c
Transportation expenditures, total	year	5527	91	81r
Vehicle finance charges	year	287	91	81r
Vehicle insurance expenditures	year	624	91	81r
Vehicle maintenance and repairs expenditures	year	695	91	81r
Vehicle purchases	year	2174	91	81r

Visalia, CA - continued

Item	Per	Value	Date	Ref.
Transportation - continued				
Vehicle rental, leases, licenses, etc. expenditures	year	257	91	81r
Vehicles purchased, other than cars and trucks	year	28	91	81r
Utilities				
Utilities, ACCRA Index		112.10	12/94	2c
Electricity expenditures	year	616	91	81r
Electricity, (part.), other, 1800 sq. ft., new home	mo.	100.06	12/94	2c
Utilities, fuels, and public services, total expenditures	year	1681	91	81r
Water and other public services, expenditures	year	209	91	81r
Weddings				
Bridal attendants' gowns	event	750	10/93	76r
Bridal gown	event	852	10/93	76r
Bridal headpiece and veil	event	167	10/93	76r
Bride's wedding band	event	708	10/93	76r
Clergy	event	224	10/93	76r
Engagement ring	event	2756	10/93	76r
Flowers	event	863	10/93	76r
Formal wear for groom	event	106	10/93	76r
Groom's attendants' formal wear	event	530	10/93	76r
Groom's wedding band	event	402	10/93	76r
Music	event	600	10/93	76r
Photography	event	1088	10/93	76r
Shoes for bride	event	50	10/93	76r
Videography	event	483	10/93	76r
Wedding invitations and announcements	event	342	10/93	76r
Wedding reception	event	7000	10/93	76r

Waco, TX

Item	Per	Value	Date	Ref.
Composite, ACCRA index		92.30	12/94	2c
Alcoholic Beverages				
Beer, Miller Lite, Bud, 12-oz., ex deposit	6	3.89	12/94	2c
J & B Scotch	750-ml.	16.95	12/94	2c
Wine, Gallo Chablis blanc	1.5-lit	4.74	12/94	2c
Appliances				
Appliances (major), expenditures	year	153	91	81r
Average annual exp.				
Food, health care, personal goods, services	year	27020	91	81r
Charity				
Cash contributions, expenditures	year	839	91	81r
Clothing				
Apparel, men and boys, total expenditures	year	380	91	81r
Apparel, women and girls, total expenditures	year	660	91	81r
Footwear, expenditures	year	193	91	81r
Jeans, man's denim		25.92	12/94	2c
Shirt, man's dress shirt		30.88	12/94	2c
Undervest, boy's size 10-14, cotton	3	4.32	12/94	2c
Communications				
Long-distance telephone rate, day, addl. min., 1-10 mi.	min.	0.08	12/93	9s
Long-distance telephone rate, day, initial min., 1-10 mi.	min.	0.10	12/93	9s
Newspaper subscription, dly. and Sun. delivery	month	11.50	12/94	2c
Phone line, single, business, field visit	inst	71.90	12/93	9s
Phone line, single, business, no field visit	inst	57.30	12/93	9s
Phone line, single, residence, field visit	inst	52.95	12/93	9s
Phone line, single, residence, no field visit	inst	38.35	12/93	9s
Telephone bill, family of four	month	17.56	12/94	2c
Telephone service, expenditures	year	616	91	81r

Values are in dollars or fractions of dollars. In the column headed *Ref*, references are shown to sources. Each reference is followed by a letter. These refer to the geographical level for which data were reported: s=State, r=Region, and c=City or metro. The abbreviation *ex* is used to mean *except* or *excluding*; *exp* stands for expenditures. For other abbreviations and further explanations, please see the Introduction.

Waco, TX - continued

Item	Per	Value	Date	Ref.
Education				
Board, 4-year private college/university	year	2084	8/94	80s
Board, 4-year public college/university	year	1675	8/94	80s
Education, total expenditures	year	319	91	81r
Room, 4-year private college/university	year	1840	8/94	80s
Room, 4-year public college/university	year	1756	8/94	80s
Total cost, 4-year private college/university	year	11876	8/94	80s
Total cost, 4-year public college/university	year	4935	8/94	80s
Tuition, 2-year public college/university, in-state	year	625	8/94	80s
Tuition, 4-year private college/university, in-state	year	7952	8/94	80s
Tuition, 4-year public college/university, in-state	year	1503	8/94	80s
Energy and Fuels				
Energy, combined forms, 1800 sq. ft.	mo.	142.35	12/94	2c
Energy, exc. electricity, 1800 sq. ft.	mo.	32.62	12/94	2c
Fuel oil and other fuels, expenditures	year	56	91	81r
Gas, natural, expenditures	year	150	91	81r
Gas, reg unlead, taxes inc., cash, self-service	gal	1.08	12/94	2c
Gasoline and motor oil purchased	year	1152	91	81r
Gasoline, unleaded midgrade	gallon	1.21	4/93	82r
Gasoline, unleaded premium	gallon	1.30	4/93	82r
Gasoline, unleaded regular	gallon	1.10	4/93	82r
Entertainment				
Bowling, evening rate	game	2.29	12/94	2c
Concert ticket, Pearl Jam group	perf	20.00	94	50r
Entertainment, total expenditures	year	1266	91	81r
Fees and admissions, expenditures	year	306	91	81r
Monopoly game, Parker Brothers', No. 9	game	9.95	12/94	2c
Movie	adm	5.50	12/94	2c
Pets, toys, playground equipment, expenditures	year	271	91	81r
Reading, expenditures	year	131	91	81r
Televisions, radios, and sound equipment, expenditures	year	439	91	81r
Tennis balls, yellow, Wilson or Penn, 3	can	2.08	12/94	2c
Funerals				
Burial, immediate, container provided by funeral home		1574.60	1/95	54r
Cards, acknowledgment		22.24	1/95	54r
Casket, minimum alternative		239.41	1/95	54r
Cosmetology, hair care, etc.		91.04	1/95	54r
Cremation, direct, container provided by funeral home		1085.15	1/95	54r
Embalming		281.30	1/95	54r
Funeral, funeral home		323.04	1/95	54r
Funeral, other facility		327.58	1/95	54r
Graveside service		355.19	1/95	54r
Hearse, local		141.89	1/95	54r
Limousine, local		99.40	1/95	54r
Memorial service		284.67	1/95	54r
Service charge, professional, nondeclinable		904.06	1/95	54r
Visitation and viewing		187.04	1/95	54r
Groceries				
Groceries, ACCRA Index		86.80	12/94	2c
Apples, Red Delicious	lb.	0.73	12/94	82r
Baby food, strained vegetables, lowest price	4-4.5 oz.	0.26	12/94	2c
Bacon, sliced	lb.	1.67	12/94	82r
Bananas	lb.	0.31	12/94	2c
Bananas	lb.	0.42	12/94	82r
Beef or hamburger, ground	lb.	1.03	12/94	2c
Beef purchases	year	213	91	81r
Beverage purchases, alcoholic	year	249	91	81r
Beverage purchases, nonalcoholic	year	207	91	81r
Bologna, all beef or mixed	lb.	2.27	12/94	82r
Bread, white	24-oz.	0.57	12/94	2c
Bread, white, pan	lb.	0.68	12/94	82r
Cabbage	lb.	0.42	12/94	82r

Waco, TX - continued

Item	Per	Value	Date	Ref.
Groceries - continued				
Carrots, short trimmed and topped	lb.	0.53	12/94	82r
Cereals and bakery products purchases	year	345	91	81r
Cereals and cereals products purchases	year	127	91	81r
Cheddar cheese, natural	lb.	3.58	12/94	82r
Cheese, Kraft grated Parmesan	8-oz.	3.28	12/94	2c
Chicken breast, bone-in	lb.	1.71	12/94	82r
Chicken, fresh, whole	lb.	0.78	12/94	82r
Chicken, whole fryer	lb.	0.68	12/94	2c
Chuck roast, USDA choice, boneless	lb.	2.26	12/94	82r
Cigarettes, Winston, Kings	carton	16.02	12/94	2c
Coffee, vacuum-packed	13 oz.	3.47	12/94	2c
Corn Flakes, Kellogg's or Post Toasties	18 oz.	2.37	12/94	2c
Corn, frozen, whole kernel, lowest price	10 oz.	0.68	12/94	2c
Crackers, soda, salted	lb.	1.27	12/94	82r
Cucumbers	lb.	0.65	12/94	82r
Dairy products (other) purchases	year	141	91	81r
Eggs, Grade A large	dozen	0.71	12/94	2c
Eggs, Grade A large	dozen	0.87	12/94	82r
Fish and seafood purchases	year	72	91	81r
Flour, white, all purpose	lb.	0.23	12/94	82r
Food purchases, food eaten at home	year	2381	91	81r
Foods purchased away from home, not prepared by consumer	year	1696	91	81r
Frankfurters, all meat or all beef	lb.	1.74	12/94	82r
Fruits and vegetables purchases	year	380	91	81r
Grapefruit	lb.	0.45	12/94	82r
Grapes, Thompson seedless	lb.	2.30	12/94	82r
Ground beef, 100% beef	lb.	1.37	12/94	82r
Ground chuck, 100% beef	lb.	1.97	12/94	82r
Ham, boneless, exc. canned	lb.	2.54	12/94	82r
Ice cream, prepackaged, bulk, regular	1/2 gal.	2.47	12/94	82r
Lemons	lb.	1.02	12/94	82r
Lettuce, iceberg	lb.	0.96	12/94	82r
Lettuce, iceberg	head	0.74	12/94	2c
Margarine, Blue Bonnet or Parkay cubes	lb.	0.51	12/94	2c
Margarine, stick	lb.	0.77	12/94	82r
Meats, poultry, fish, and eggs purchases	year	655	91	81r
Milk and cream (fresh) purchases	year	130	91	81r
Milk, whole	1/2 gal.	1.15	12/94	2c
Orange juice, frozen concentrate 12-oz. can	16 oz.	1.36	12/94	82r
Orange juice, Minute Maid frozen	12-oz.	1.05	12/94	2c
Oranges, Navel	lb.	0.54	12/94	82r
Peaches, halves or slices, Hunt's, Del Monte, or Libby's	29-oz.	1.36	12/94	2c
Pears, Anjou	lb.	0.81	12/94	82r
Peas, sweet, Del Monte or Green Giant	15-17 oz.	0.51	12/94	2c
Pork chops, center cut, bone-in	lb.	3.07	12/94	82r
Pork purchases	year	142	91	81r
Potato chips	16-oz.	3.15	12/94	82r
Potatoes, frozen, French fried	lb.	0.82	12/94	82r
Potatoes, white	lb.	0.34	12/94	82r
Potatoes, white or red	10-lb. sack	1.67	12/94	2c
Rice, white, long grain, uncooked	lb.	0.48	12/94	82r
Round roast, USDA choice, boneless	lb.	2.91	12/94	82r
Sausage, fresh	lb.	1.82	12/94	82r
Sausage, Jimmy Dean, 100% pork	lb.	2.23	12/94	2c
Shortening, vegetable oil blends	lb.	0.75	12/94	82r
Shortening, vegetable, Crisco	3-lb.	2.08	12/94	2c
Soft drink, Coca Cola, ex deposit	2 lit	0.98	12/94	2c
Spaghetti and macaroni	lb.	0.87	12/94	82r
Steak, rib eye, USDA choice, boneless	lb.	6.85	12/94	82r
Steak, round, graded & ungraded, exc. USDA prime & choice	lb.	2.96	12/94	82r
Steak, round, USDA choice, boneless	lb.	3.17	12/94	82r
Steak, sirloin, USDA choice, boneless	lb.	4.12	12/94	82r
Steak, t-bone	lb.	4.69	12/94	2c
Steak, T-bone, USDA choice, bone-in	lb.	5.63	12/94	82r

Values are in dollars or fractions of dollars. In the column headed *Ref*, references are shown to sources. Each reference is followed by a letter. These refer to the geographical level for which data were reported: s=State, r=Region, and c=City or metro. The abbreviation *ex* is used to mean *except* or *excluding*; *exp* stands for *expenditures*. For other abbreviations and further explanations, please see the Introduction.

Waco, TX - continued

Item	Per	Value	Date	Ref.
Groceries				
Sugar and other sweets, eaten at home, expenditures	year	93	91	81r
Sugar, cane or beet	4 lbs.	1.31	12/94	2c
Sugar, white, all sizes	lb.	0.39	12/94	82r
Tobacco products and smoking supplies, total expenditures	year	286	91	81r
Tomatoes, field grown	lb.	1.36	12/94	82r
Tomatoes, Hunt's or Del Monte	14.5 oz.	0.67	12/94	2c
Tuna, chunk, light	lb.	1.94	12/94	82r
Tuna, chunk, light, oil-packed	6.125-6.5 oz.	0.55	12/94	2c
Turkey, frozen, whole	lb.	0.96	12/94	82r
Yogurt, natural, fruit flavored	8 oz.	0.58	12/94	82r
Goods and Services				
Miscellaneous goods and services, ACCRA Index		96.40	12/94	2c
Health Care				
Health care, ACCRA Index		85.40	12/94	2c
Adenosine, emergency room	treat	100.00	95	23r
Antibiotic ointment, Polysporin	1.5 oz.	3.83	12/94	2c
Bladder tap, superpubic, infant, emergency room	treat	119.00	95	23r
Blood analysis, emergency room	treat	25.00	95	23r
Blood tests, abdominal pain, emergency room	treat	25.00	95	23r
Burn dressing, emergency room	treat	266.00	95	23r
Cardiology interpretation, emergency room	treat	26.00	95	23r
Chest X-ray, emergency room	treat	78.00	95	23r
Childbirth, Cesarean delivery, hospital charge	birth	5462.00	12/91	69r
Childbirth, Cesarean delivery, physician charge	birth	2228.00	12/91	69r
Childbirth, normal delivery, hospital charge	birth	2943.00	12/91	69r
Childbirth, normal delivery, physician charge	birth	1619.00	12/91	69r
Defibrillation pads, emergency room	treat	6.00	95	23r
Dentist's fee, adult teeth cleaning and periodic oral exam	visit	44.40	12/94	2c
Doctor's fee, routine exam, established patient	visit	35.75	12/94	2c
Drugs, expenditures	year	297	91	81r
Gastric tube insertion, nasal, emergency room	treat	25.00	95	23r
Health care, total expenditures	year	1600	91	81r
Health insurance expenditures	year	637	91	81r
Heart monitor, emergency room	treat	40.00	95	23r
Hospital care, semiprivate room	day	293.50	12/94	2c
Insurance premium, family medical care	month	389.25	1/95	41s
Intravenous fluids, emergency room	treat	130.00	95	23r
Intravenous fluids, emergency room	liter	26.00	95	23r
Intravenous line, central, emergency room	treat	342.00	95	23r
Liver function tests, abdominal pain, emergency room	treat	26.00	95	23r
Medical care charges, total, emergency room, third-degree burns	treat	2101.00	95	23r
Medical care charges, total, emergency, infant with fever	treat	628.00	95	23r
Medical services expenditures	year	573	91	81r
Medical supplies expenditures	year	93	91	81r
Morphine, emergency room	treat	34.00	95	23r
Nursing care and facilities charges, emergency room	treat	252.00	95	23r
Nursing care and facilities charges, emergency, infant with fever	treat	252.00	95	23r
Nursing care and facilities charges, emergency, third-degree burns	treat	861.00	95	23r
Physician's charges, emergency, infant with fever	treat	212.00	95	23r
Physician's charges, emergency, third-degree burns	treat	372.00	95	23r
Physician's fee, emergency room	treat	372.00	95	23r

Waco, TX - continued

Item	Per	Value	Date	Ref.
Health Care - continued				
Physician's fee, general practitioner	visit	51.20	12/93	60r
Surgery, open-heart	proc	42374.00	1/93	14r
Ultrasound, abdominal, emergency room	treat	276.00	95	23r
Urinalysis, emergency room	treat	20.00	95	23r
Urinalysis, infant, emergency room	treat	20.00	95	23r
X-rays, emergency room	treat	78.00	95	23r
Household Goods				
Appl. repair, service call, wash mach	min. lab. chg.	31.98	12/94	2c
Floor coverings, expenditures	year	48	91	81r
Furniture, expenditures	year	280	91	81r
Household equipment, misc. expenditures	year	342	91	81r
Household expenditures, miscellaneous	year	256	91	81r
Household furnishings and equipment, expenditures	year	988	91	81r
Household operations expenditures	year	468	91	81r
Household textiles, expenditures	year	95	91	81r
Housekeeping supplies, expenditures	year	380	91	81r
Laundry and cleaning supplies, expenditures	year	109	91	81r
Laundry detergent, Tide Ultra, Bold, or Cheer	42 oz.	3.57	12/94	2c
Postage and stationery, expenditures	year	105	91	81r
Tissues, facial, Kleenex brand	175	0.95	12/94	2c
Housing				
Housing, ACCRA Index		80.50	12/94	2c
Add garage/carport		6,980	3/95	74r
Add room(s)		11,403	3/95	74r
Apartment condominium or co-op, median	unit	68600	12/94	62r
Dwellings (owned), expenditures	year	2428	91	81r
Enclose porch/patio/breezeway		4,572	3/95	74r
Finish room in basement/attic		3,794	3/95	74r
Home, existing, single-family, median	unit	120200	12/94	62r
House payment, principal and interest, 25% down payment	mo.	562	12/94	2c
House, 1800 sq ft, 8000 sq ft lot, new, urban, utilities	total	90225	12/94	2c
Maintenance, repairs, insurance, and other housing expenditures	year	531	91	81r
Mortgage interest and charges expenditures	year	1506	91	81r
Mtge. rate, incl. points and orig. fee, 30-year conv. fixed or ARM	mo.	9.36	12/94	2c
Princ. & int., mortgage, median-price exist. sing.-family home	mo.	540	12/94	62r
Property taxes expenditures	year	391	91	81r
Redesign, restructure more than half of home's interior		17,641	3/95	74r
Rent, apartment, 2 br., 1 1/2-2 baths, unfurnished, 950 sq ft, water	mo.	582	12/94	2c
Rental units expenditures	year	1264	91	81r
Insurance and Pensions				
Auto insurance, private passenger	year	785.78	12/94	71s
Insurance and pensions, personal, expenditures	year	2395	91	81r
Insurance, life and other personal, expenditures	year	368	91	81r
Pensions and Social Security, expenditures	year	2027	91	81r
Personal Goods				
Shampoo, Alberto VO5	15-oz.	0.99	12/94	2c
Toothpaste, Crest or Colgate	6-7 oz.	1.62	12/94	2c
Personal Services				
Dry cleaning, man's 2-pc. suit		5.24	12/94	2c
Haircut, man's barbershop, no styling		7.20	12/94	2c
Haircut, woman's shampoo, trim, blow-dry		17.50	12/94	2c
Personal services expenditures	year	212	91	81r
Restaurant Food				
Chicken, fried, thigh and drumstick		2.38	12/94	2c
Dining expenditures, family	week	33.83	94	73r

Values are in dollars or fractions of dollars. In the column headed *Ref*, references are shown to sources. Each reference is followed by a letter. These refer to the geographical level for which data were reported: s=State, r=Region, and c=City or metro. The abbreviation *ex* is used to mean *except* or *excluding*; *exp* stands for *expenditures*. For other abbreviations and further explanations, please see the Introduction.

Waco, TX - continued

Item	Per	Value	Date	Ref.
Restaurant Food				
Hamburger with cheese	1/4 lb.	1.89	12/94	2c
Pizza, Pizza Hut or Pizza Inn	12-13 in.	8.09	12/94	2c
Taxes				
Tax, cigarettes	year	584.00	10/93	43s
Taxes, Federal income, expenditures	year	2275	91	81r
Taxes, personal, expenditures	year	2715	91	81r
Taxes, State and local income, expenditures	year	365	91	81r
Transportation				
Transportation, ACCRA Index		101.60	12/94	2c
Bus fare, one-way	trip	0.75	12/95	1c
Cars and trucks purchased, new	year	1306	91	81r
Cars and trucks purchased, used	year	942	91	81r
Driver's learning permit fee	perm	5.00	1/94	84s
Driver's license fee	orig	16.00	1/94	84s
Driver's license fee, duplicate	lic	10.00	1/94	84s
Driver's license reinstatement fee, min.	susp	50.00	1/94	85s
Driver's license renewal fee	renew	16.00	1/94	84s
Identification card, nondriver	card	10.00	1/94	83s
Motorcycle learning permit fee	perm	5.00	1/94	84s
Motorcycle license fee	orig	16.00	1/94	84s
Motorcycle license fee, duplicate	lic	10.00	1/94	84s
Motorcycle license renewal fee	renew	21.00	1/94	84s
Public transportation expenditures	year	249	91	81r
Tire balance, computer or spin bal., front	wheel	7.40	12/94	2c
Transportation expenditures, total	year	5307	91	81r
Vehicle finance charges	year	346	91	81r
Vehicle insurance expenditures	year	544	91	81r
Vehicle maintenance and repairs expenditures	year	600	91	81r
Vehicle purchases	year	2275	91	81r
Vehicle rental, leases, licenses, etc. expenditures	year	141	91	81r
Vehicles purchased, other than cars and trucks	year	27	91	81r
Utilities				
Utilities, ACCRA Index		121.90	12/94	2c
Electricity expenditures	year	950	91	81r
Electricity, (part.), other, 1800 sq. ft., new home	mo.	109.73	12/94	2c
Utilities, fuels, and public services, total expenditures	year	2000	91	81r
Water and other public services, expenditures	year	227	91	81r
Weddings				
Bridal attendants' gowns	event	750	10/93	76r
Bridal gown	event	852	10/93	76r
Bridal headpiece and veil	event	167	10/93	76r
Bride's wedding band	event	708	10/93	76r
Clergy	event	224	10/93	76r
Engagement ring	event	2756	10/93	76r
Flowers	event	863	10/93	76r
Formal wear for groom	event	106	10/93	76r
Groom's attendants' formal wear	event	530	10/93	76r
Groom's wedding band	event	402	10/93	76r
Music	event	600	10/93	76r
Photography	event	1088	10/93	76r
Shoes for bride	event	50	10/93	76r
Videography	event	483	10/93	76r
Wedding invitations and announcements	event	342	10/93	76r
Wedding reception	event	7000	10/93	76r

Warner Robins, GA

Item	Per	Value	Date	Ref.
Composite, ACCRA index		94.80	12/94	2c
Alcoholic Beverages				
Beer, Miller Lite, Bud, 12-oz., ex deposit	6	4.19	12/94	2c

Warner Robins, GA - continued

Item	Per	Value	Date	Ref.
Alcoholic Beverages - continued				
J & B Scotch	750-ml.	16.51	12/94	2c
Wine, Gallo Chablis blanc	1.5-lit	5.35	12/94	2c
Clothing				
Jeans, man's denim		26.06	12/94	2c
Shirt, man's dress shirt		32.84	12/94	2c
Undervest, boy's size 10-14, cotton	3	4.30	12/94	2c
Communications				
Newspaper subscription, dly. and Sun. delivery	month	12.18	12/94	2c
Telephone bill, family of four	month	20.45	12/94	2c
Telephone, residential, flat rate	mo.	13.55	12/93	8c
Energy and Fuels				
Energy, combined forms, 1800 sq. ft.	mo.	116.52	12/94	2c
Gas, reg unlead, taxes inc., cash, self-service	gal	1.01	12/94	2c
Entertainment				
Bowling, evening rate	game	2.50	12/94	2c
Monopoly game, Parker Brothers', No. 9	game	11.94	12/94	2c
Movie	adm	5.50	12/94	2c
Tennis balls, yellow, Wilson or Penn, 3	can	2.94	12/94	2c
Groceries				
Groceries, ACCRA Index		96.90	12/94	2c
Baby food, strained vegetables, lowest price	4-4.5 oz.	0.33	12/94	2c
Bananas	lb.	0.39	12/94	2c
Beef or hamburger, ground	lb.	1.71	12/94	2c
Bread, white	24-oz.	0.77	12/94	2c
Cheese, Kraft grated Parmesan	8-oz.	3.38	12/94	2c
Chicken, whole fryer	lb.	0.75	12/94	2c
Cigarettes, Winston, Kings	carton	13.67	12/94	2c
Coffee, vacuum-packed	13 oz.	3.35	12/94	2c
Corn Flakes, Kellogg's or Post Toasties	18 oz.	2.32	12/94	2c
Corn, frozen, whole kernel, lowest price	10 oz.	0.79	12/94	2c
Eggs, Grade A large	dozen	0.74	12/94	2c
Lettuce, iceberg	head	0.95	12/94	2c
Margarine, Blue Bonnet or Parkay cubes	lb.	0.59	12/94	2c
Milk, whole	1/2 gal.	1.39	12/94	2c
Orange juice, Minute Maid frozen	12-oz.	1.05	12/94	2c
Peaches, halves or slices, Hunt's, Del Monte, or Libby's	29-oz.	1.11	12/94	2c
Peas, sweet, Del Monte or Green Giant	15-17 oz.	0.53	12/94	2c
Potatoes, white or red	10-lb. sack	2.79	12/94	2c
Sausage, Jimmy Dean, 100% pork	lb.	2.17	12/94	2c
Shortening, vegetable, Crisco	3-lb.	2.43	12/94	2c
Soft drink, Coca Cola, ex deposit	2 lit	1.11	12/94	2c
Steak, t-bone	lb.	5.43	12/94	2c
Sugar, cane or beet	4 lbs.	1.52	12/94	2c
Tomatoes, Hunt's or Del Monte	14.5 oz.	0.62	12/94	2c
Tuna, chunk, light, oil-packed	6.125-6.5 oz.	0.67	12/94	2c
Goods and Services				
Miscellaneous goods and services, ACCRA Index		101.40	12/94	2c
Health Care				
Health care, ACCRA Index		88.80	12/94	2c
Antibiotic ointment, Polysporin	1.5 oz.	3.74	12/94	2c
Dentist's fee, adult teeth cleaning and periodic oral exam	visit	49.80	12/94	2c
Doctor's fee, routine exam, established patient	visit	41.00	12/94	2c
Hospital care, semiprivate room	day	207.00	12/94	2c

Values are in dollars or fractions of dollars. In the column headed *Ref*, references are shown to sources. Each reference is followed by a letter. These refer to the geographical level for which data were reported: s=State, r=Region, and c=City or metro. The abbreviation *ex* is used to mean *except* or *excluding*; *exp* stands for expenditures. For other abbreviations and further explanations, please see the Introduction.

Warner Robins, GA - continued

Item	Per	Value	Date	Ref.
Household Goods				
Appl. repair, service call, wash mach	min. lab. chg.	25.88	12/94	2c
Laundry detergent, Tide Ultra, Bold, or Cheer	42 oz.	3.06	12/94	2c
Tissues, facial, Kleenex brand	175	1.00	12/94	2c
Housing				
Housing, ACCRA Index		85.70	12/94	2c
House payment, principal and interest, 25% down payment	mo.	633	12/94	2c
House, 1800 sq ft, 8000 sq ft lot, new, urban, utilities	total	103375	12/94	2c
Mtge. rate, incl. points and orig. fee, 30-year conv. fixed or ARM	mo.	9.17	12/94	2c
Rent, apartment, 2 br., 1 1/2-2 baths, unfurnished, 950 sq ft, water	mo.	521	12/94	2c
Personal Goods				
Shampoo, Alberto VO5	15-oz.	0.92	12/94	2c
Toothpaste, Crest or Colgate	6-7 oz.	1.83	12/94	2c
Personal Services				
Dry cleaning, man's 2-pc. suit		6.48	12/94	2c
Haircut, man's barbershop, no styling		9.00	12/94	2c
Haircut, woman's shampoo, trim, blow-dry		24.80	12/94	2c
Restaurant Food				
Chicken, fried, thigh and drumstick		2.19	12/94	2c
Hamburger with cheese	1/4 lb.	1.92	12/94	2c
Pizza, Pizza Hut or Pizza Inn	12-13 in.	7.99	12/94	2c
Transportation				
Transportation, ACCRA Index		90.50	12/94	2c
Tire balance, computer or spin bal., front	wheel	6.18	12/94	2c
Utilities				
Utilities, ACCRA Index		104.00	12/94	2c
Electricity, 1800 sq. ft., new home	mo.	116.52	12/94	2c

Washington, DC, MD, VA

Item	Per	Value	Date	Ref.
Composite, ACCRA index		132.40	12/94	2c
Alcoholic Beverages				
Beer	bottle	2.65	94	35c
Beer, Miller Lite, Bud, 12-oz., ex deposit	6	4.10	12/94	2c
J & B Scotch	750-ml.	19.69	12/94	2c
Wine, Gallo Chablis blanc	1.5-lit	5.81	12/94	2c
Appliances				
Appliances (major), expenditures	year	157	91	81c
Average annual exp.				
Food, health care, personal goods, services	year	38560	91	81c
Business				
Bank fee, bad check	check	24.00	12/93	5c
Dinner and tip, hotel, corporate rate	night	32.00	2/94	15c
Hotel room, corporate rate	night	111.00	2/94	15c
Business Fees				
Lawyer's license fee	lic	250.00	93	66c
Charity				
Cash contributions, expenditures	year	1524	91	81c
Child Care				
Child care, for-profit daycare center	week	101.00	12/94	28c
Clothing				
Apparel, men and boys, total expenditures	year	582	91	81c
Apparel, women and girls, total expenditures	year	1016	91	81c
Footwear, expenditures	year	334	91	81c
Jeans, man's denim		31.60	12/94	2c
Shirt, dress, men's	shirt	0.00	1/92	44c

Washington, DC, MD, VA - continued

Item	Per	Value	Date	Ref.
Clothing - continued				
Shirt, man's dress shirt		28.72	12/94	2c
Undervest, boy's size 10-14, cotton	3	3.23	12/94	2c
Communications				
Newspaper subscription, dly. and Sun. delivery	month	10.44	12/94	2c
Phone line, single, business, field visit	inst	0.00	12/93	9c
Phone line, single, business, no field visit	inst	66.03	12/93	9c
Phone line, single, residence, field visit	inst	0.00	12/93	9c
Phone line, single, residence, no field visit	inst	30.76	12/93	9c
Telephone bill, family of four	month	21.04	12/94	2c
Telephone service, expenditures	year	699	91	81c
Telephone, residential, flat rate	mo.	14.60	12/93	8c
Education				
Board, 4-year private college/university	year	2455	8/94	80c
Education, total expenditures	year	933	91	81c
Room, 4-year private college/university	year	3554	8/94	80c
Total cost, 4-year private college/university	year	18620	8/94	80c
Tuition, 4-year private college/university, in-state	year	12610	8/94	80c
Tuition, 4-year public college/university, in-state	year	974	8/94	80c
Energy and Fuels				
Electricity	500 KWh	43.80	12/94	82c
Energy, combined forms, 1800 sq. ft.	mo.	120.34	12/94	2c
Energy, exc. electricity, 1800 sq. ft.	mo.	50.19	12/94	2c
Fuel oil #2	gallon	1.05	12/94	82c
Fuel oil and other fuels, expenditures	year	103	91	81c
Gas	gal.	1.16	1/92	44c
Gas, cooking, 10 therms	month	12.45	2/94	65c
Gas, cooking, 30 therms	month	27.64	2/94	65c
Gas, cooking, 50 therms	month	42.83	2/94	65c
Gas, heating, winter, 100 therms	month	84.06	2/94	65c
Gas, heating, winter, average use	month	177.50	2/94	65c
Gas, natural, expenditures	year	230	91	81c
Gas, piped	40 therms	37.87	12/94	82c
Gas, piped	100 therms	81.37	12/94	82c
Gas, piped	therm	0.84	12/94	82c
Gas, reg unlead, taxes inc., cash, self-service	gal	1.22	12/94	2c
Gasoline and motor oil purchased	year	1007	91	81c
Gasoline, unleaded midgrade	gallon	1.31	4/93	82c
Gasoline, unleaded premium	gallon	1.39	4/93	82c
Gasoline, unleaded regular	gallon	1.21	4/93	82c
Entertainment				
Bowling, evening rate	game	2.85	12/94	2c
Entertainment supplies, equipment, and services, misc. expenditures	year	265	91	81c
Entertainment, total expenditures	year	1714	91	81c
Fees and admissions, expenditures	year	538	91	81c
Monopoly game, Parker Brothers', No. 9	game	10.99	12/94	2c
Movie	adm	6.87	12/94	2c
Movie ticket, adult	ticket	6.50	1/92	44c
Pets, toys, playground equipment, expenditures	year	283	91	81c
Reading, expenditures	year	246	91	81c
Televisions, radios, and sound equipment, expenditures	year	628	91	81c
Tennis balls, yellow, Wilson or Penn, 3	can	2.22	12/94	2c
Funerals				
Burial, immediate, container provided by funeral home		1370.36	1/95	54r
Cards, acknowledgment		14.83	1/95	54r
Casket, minimum alternative		192.52	1/95	54r
Cosmetology, hair care, etc.		102.27	1/95	54r
Cremation, direct, container provided by funeral home		1065.64	1/95	54r

Values are in dollars or fractions of dollars. In the column headed *Ref*, references are shown to sources. Each reference is followed by a letter. These refer to the geographical level for which data were reported: s = State, r = Region, and c = City or metro. The abbreviation *ex* is used to mean *except* or *excluding*; *exp* stands for expenditures. For other abbreviations and further explanations, please see the Introduction.

Washington, DC, MD, VA - continued

Item	Per	Value	Date	Ref.
Funerals				
Embalming		304.29	1/95	54r
Funeral, funeral home		287.83	1/95	54r
Funeral, other facility		284.14	1/95	54r
Graveside service		349.13	1/95	54r
Hearse, local		132.27	1/95	54r
Limousine, local		98.45	1/95	54r
Memorial service		270.59	1/95	54r
Service charge, professional, nondeclinable		933.59	1/95	54r
Visitation and viewing		225.83	1/95	54r
Groceries				
Groceries, ACCRA Index		116.60	12/94	2c
Baby food, strained vegetables, lowest price	4-4.5 oz.	0.46	12/94	2c
Bananas	lb.	0.48	12/94	2c
Beef or hamburger, ground	lb.	1.94	12/94	2c
Beef purchases	year	172	91	81c
Beverage purchases, alcoholic	year	363	91	81c
Beverage purchases, nonalcoholic	year	229	91	81c
Big Mac hamburger	burger	2.17	94	35c
Bread, white	24-oz.	0.87	12/94	2c
Cereals and bakery products purchases	year	363	91	81c
Cereals and cereal products purchases	year	138	91	81c
Cheese, Kraft grated Parmesan	8-oz.	3.55	12/94	2c
Chicken, whole fryer	lb.	1.02	12/94	2c
Cigarettes, Winston, Kings	carton	15.93	12/94	2c
Coffee, vacuum-packed	13 oz.	3.86	12/94	2c
Corn Flakes, Kellogg's or Post Toasties	18 oz.	2.73	12/94	2c
Corn, frozen, whole kernel, lowest price	10 oz.	0.87	12/94	2c
Dairy products (other) purchases	year	178	91	81c
Eggs, Grade A large	dozen	0.84	12/94	2c
Fish and seafood purchases	year	115	91	81c
Food purchases, food eaten at home	year	2559	91	81c
Foods purchased away from home, not prepared by consumer	year	2193	91	81c
Fruits and vegetables purchases	year	465	91	81c
Lettuce, iceberg	head	0.91	12/94	2c
Margarine, Blue Bonnet or Parkay cubes	lb.	0.88	12/94	2c
Meats, poultry, fish, and eggs purchases	year	611	91	81c
Milk and cream (fresh) purchases	year	105	91	81c
Milk, 2%	gal.	2.26	1/92	44c
Milk, whole	1/2 gal.	1.39	12/94	2c
Orange juice, Minute Maid frozen	12-oz.	1.51	12/94	2c
Peaches, halves or slices, Hunt's, Del Monte, or Libby's	29-oz.	1.58	12/94	2c
Peas, sweet, Del Monte or Green Giant	15-17 oz.	0.65	12/94	2c
Pork purchases	year	105	91	81c
Potatoes, white or red	10-lb. sack	2.70	12/94	2c
Rental rate, 2-bedroom apartment	month	0.00	1/92	44c
Sausage, Jimmy Dean, 100% pork	lb.	2.77	12/94	2c
Shortening, vegetable, Crisco	3-lb.	3.15	12/94	2c
Soft drink, Coca Cola, ex deposit	2 lit	1.11	12/94	2c
Steak, t-bone	lb.	6.20	12/94	2c
Sugar and other sweets, eaten at home, purchases	year	110	91	81c
Sugar, cane or beet	4 lbs.	1.59	12/94	2c
Tobacco products and smoking supplies, total expenditures	year	199	91	81c
Tomatoes, Hunt's or Del Monte	14.5 oz.	0.81	12/94	2c
Tuna, chunk, light, oil-packed	6.125-6.5 oz.	0.87	12/94	2c
Goods and Services				
Miscellaneous goods and services, ACCRA Index		104.90	12/94	2c
Health Care				
Health care, ACCRA Index		122.50	12/94	2c
Antibiotic ointment, Polysporin	1.5 oz.	4.53	12/94	2c
Birth, normal delivery	del	2,605	11/93	93c

Washington, DC, MD, VA - continued

Item	Per	Value	Date	Ref.
Health Care - continued				
Broken arm treatment	treat	528	11/93	93c
Delivery, uncomplicated, total charge	birth	9070	1/93	24c
Delivery, uncomplicated, vaginal, hospital charge	birth	5080	1/93	24c
Delivery, uncomplicated, vaginal, physician's charge	birth	3990	1/93	24c
Dentist's fee, adult teeth cleaning and periodic oral exam	visit	63.00	12/94	2c
Doctor's fee, routine exam, established patient	visit	59.70	12/94	2c
Drugs, expenditures	year	265	91	81c
Health care, total expenditures	year	1962	91	81c
Health insurance expenditures	year	687	91	81c
Hospital care, semiprivate room	day	340.80	12/94	2c
Hospital cost	adm	7,743	2/94	72c
Insurance premium, family medical care	month	450.14	1/95	41c
Medical services expenditures	year	893	91	81c
Medical supplies expenditures	year	117	91	81c
Physical exam, well baby	check-up	52	11/93	93c
Physical, complete	phys	121	11/93	93c
Surgery, open-heart	surg	6,230	11/93	93c
Household Goods				
Appl. repair, service call, wash mach	min. lab. chg.	37.49	12/94	2c
Floor coverings, expenditures	year	47	91	81c
Furniture, expenditures	year	362	91	81c
Household equipment, misc., expenditures	year	660	91	81c
Household expenditures, miscellaneous	year	309	91	81c
Household furnishings and equipment, expenditures	year	1460	91	81c
Household operations expenditures	year	603	91	81c
Household textiles, expenditures	year	139	91	81c
Housekeeping supplies, expenditures	year	463	91	81c
Laundry and cleaning supplies, expenditures	year	115	91	81c
Laundry detergent, Tide Ultra, Bold, or Cheer	42 oz.	4.30	12/94	2c
Postage and stationery, expenditures	year	129	91	81c
Tissues, facial, Kleenex brand	175	1.23	12/94	2c
Housing				
Housing, ACCRA Index		182.10	12/94	2c
Car rental	day	48.00	5/95	95c
Dwellings (owned), expenditures	year	4806	91	81c
Home, existing, single-family, median	unit	155.80	12/94	62c
Home, purchase price	unit	199.10	3/93	26c
Hotel room	day	165.00	5/95	95c
House payment, principal and interest, 25% down payment	mo.	1412	12/94	2c
House, 1800 sq ft, 8000 sq ft lot, new, urban, utilities	total	233583	12/94	2c
Maintenance, repairs, insurance, and other housing expenditures	year	675	91	81c
Mortgage interest and charges expenditures	year	3312	91	81c
Mtge. rate, incl. points and orig. fee, 30-year conv. fixed or ARM	mo.	9.02	12/94	2c
Property taxes expenditures	year	819	91	81c
Rent, apartment, 2 br., 1 1/2-2 baths, unfurnished, 950 sq ft, water	mo.	913	12/94	2c
Rent, office space	sq. ft.	12.90	93	57c
Rental units expenditures	year	2462	900/00/ 91	81c
Insurance and Pensions				
Auto insurance, private passenger	year	1001.09	12/94	71c
Insurance and pensions, personal, expenditures	year	4266	91	81c
Insurance, life and other personal, expenditures	year	429	91	81c
Pensions and Social Security, expenditures	year	3837	91	81c

Values are in dollars or fractions of dollars. In the column headed *Ref*, references are shown to sources. Each reference is followed by a letter. These refer to the geographical level for which data were reported: s = State, r = Region, and c = City or metro. The abbreviation *ex* is used to mean *except* or *excluding*; *exp* stands for expenditures. For other abbreviations and further explanations, please see the Introduction.

Washington, DC, MD, VA - continued

Item	Per	Value	Date	Ref.
Personal Goods				
Personal care products and services, total expenditures	year	509	91	81c
Shampoo, Alberto VO5	15-oz.	1.20	12/94	2c
Toothpaste, Crest or Colgate	6-7 oz.	2.34	12/94	2c
Personal Services				
Dry cleaning, man's 2-pc. suit		6.29	12/94	2c
Dry cleaning, woman's dress	dress	10.50	1/92	44c
Haircut, man's barbershop, no styling		11.40	12/94	2c
Haircut, woman's shampoo, trim, blow-dry		26.20	12/94	2c
Personal services expenditures	year	294	91	81c
Restaurant Food				
Big Mac, small fries, medium drink	meal	3.17	1/92	44c
Chicken, fried, thigh and drumstick		2.34	12/94	2c
Hamburger with cheese	1/4 lb.	1.97	12/94	2c
Pizza, Pizza Hut or Pizza Inn	12-13 in.	8.57	12/94	2c
Taxes				
Tax rate, residential property, month	$100	0.91	1/92	79c
Taxes, Federal income, expenditures	year	5102	91	81c
Taxes, personal, expenditures	year	6922	91	81c
Taxes, State and local income, expenditures	year	1705	91	81c
Transportation				
Transportation, ACCRA Index		135.90	12/94	2c
Bus fare, one-way	trip	0.81	12/95	1c
Bus fare, up to 10 miles	one-way	3.00	12/94	2c
Cars and trucks purchased, new	year	1991	91	81c
Cars and trucks purchased, used	year	480	91	81c
Driver's learning permit fee	perm	10.00	1/94	84c
Driver's license fee	orig	20.00	1/94	84c
Driver's license fee, duplicate	lic	5.00	1/94	84c
Driver's license reinstatement fee, min.	susp	75.00	1/94	85c
Driver's license renewal fee	renew	20.00	1/94	84c
Identification card, nondriver	card	15.00	1/94	83c
Motorcycle learning permit fee	perm	10.00	1/94	84c
Motorcycle license fee	orig	20.00	1/94	84c
Motorcycle license fee, duplicate	lic	5.00	1/94	84c
Motorcycle license renewal fee	renew	20.00	1/94	84c
parking, long-term lot, airport	3 days	21.00	1/92	44c
Public transportation expenditures	year	582	91	81c
Railway fare, commuter rail, one-way	trip	3.30	12/95	1c
Railway fare, heavy rail, one-way	trip	1.00	12/95	1c
Tire balance, computer or spin bal., front	wheel	8.33	12/94	2c
Transportation expenditures, total	year	6192	91	81c
Vehicle expenses, miscellaneous	year	2131	91	81c
Vehicle finance charges	year	339	91	81c
Vehicle insurance expenditures	year	735	91	81c
Vehicle maintenance and repairs expenditures	year	780	91	81c
Vehicle purchases	year	2471	91	81c
Vehicle rental, leases, licenses, etc. expenditures	year	277	91	81c
Utilities				
Utilities, ACCRA Index		107.30	12/94	2c
Electricity	KWh	0.08	12/94	82c
Electricity expenditures	year	693	91	81c
Electricity, (part.), other, 1800 sq. ft., new home	mo.	70.15	12/94	2c
Electricity, summer, 250 KWh	month	13.07	8/93	64c
Electricity, summer, 500 KWh	month	31.78	8/93	64c
Electricity, summer, 750 KWh	month	59.94	8/93	64c
Electricity, summer, 1000 KWh	month	88.10	8/93	64c
Utilities, fuels, and public services, total expenditures	year	1905	91	81c
Water and other public services, expenditures	year	181	91	81c
Weddings				
Bridal attendants' gowns	event	750	10/93	76r
Bridal gown	event	852	10/93	76r

Washington, DC, MD, VA - continued

Item	Per	Value	Date	Ref.
Weddings - continued				
Bridal headpiece and veil	event	167	10/93	76r
Bride's wedding band	event	708	10/93	76r
Clergy	event	224	10/93	76r
Engagement ring	event	2756	10/93	76r
Flowers	event	863	10/93	76r
Formal wear for groom	event	106	10/93	76r
Groom's attendants' formal wear	event	530	10/93	76r
Groom's wedding band	event	402	10/93	76r
Music	event	600	10/93	76r
Photography	event	1088	10/93	76r
Shoes for bride	event	50	10/93	76r
Videography	event	483	10/93	76r
Wedding invitations and announcements	event	342	10/93	76r
Wedding reception	event	7000	10/93	76r

Waterloo-Cedar Falls, IA

Item	Per	Value	Date	Ref.
Appliances				
Appliances (major), expenditures	year	131	91	81r
Average annual exp.				
Food, health care, personal goods, services	year	25935	91	81r
Charity				
Cash contributions, expenditures	year	745	91	81r
Clothing				
Apparel, men and boys, total expenditures	year	332	91	81r
Apparel, women and girls, total expenditures	year	578	91	81r
Footwear, expenditures	year	164	91	81r
Communications				
Long-distance telephone rate, day, addl. min., 1-10 mi.	min.	0.11	12/93	9s
Long-distance telephone rate, day, initial min., 1-10 mi.	min.	0.21	12/93	9s
Phone line, single, business, field visit	inst	50.00	12/93	9s
Phone line, single, business, no field visit	inst	50.00	12/93	9s
Phone line, single, residence, field visit	inst	35.00	12/93	9s
Phone line, single, residence, no field visit	inst	35.00	12/93	9s
Telephone service, expenditures	year	547	91	81r
Education				
Board, 4-year private college/university	year	1971	8/94	80s
Board, 4-year public college/university	year	1562	8/94	80s
Education, total expenditures	year	394	91	81r
Room, 4-year private college/university	year	1707	8/94	80s
Room, 4-year public college/university	year	1526	8/94	80s
Total cost, 4-year private college/university	year	14510	8/94	80s
Total cost, 4-year public college/university	year	5440	8/94	80s
Tuition, 2-year public college/university, in-state	year	1612	8/94	80s
Tuition, 4-year private college/university, in-state	year	10832	8/94	80s
Tuition, 4-year public college/university, in-state	year	2352	8/94	80s
Energy and Fuels				
Fuel oil and other fuels, expenditures	year	83	91	81r
Gas, natural, expenditures	year	373	91	81r
Gasoline and motor oil purchased	year	1000	91	81r
Gasoline, unleaded midgrade	gallon	1.15	4/93	82r
Gasoline, unleaded premium	gallon	1.23	4/93	82r
Gasoline, unleaded regular	gallon	1.07	4/93	82r
Entertainment				
Entertainment, total expenditures	year	1356	91	81r
Fees and admissions, expenditures	year	347	91	81r
Pets, toys, playground equipment, expenditures	year	270	91	81r
Reading, expenditures	year	160	91	81r
Televisions, radios, and sound equipment, expenditures	year	433	91	81r

Values are in dollars or fractions of dollars. In the column headed *Ref*, references are shown to sources. Each reference is followed by a letter. These refer to the geographical level for which data were reported: s=State, r=Region, and c=City or metro. The abbreviation *ex* is used to mean *except* or *excluding*; *exp* stands for *expenditures*. For other abbreviations and further explanations, please see the Introduction.

Waterloo-Cedar Falls, IA - continued

Item	Per	Value	Date	Ref.
Funerals				
Burial, immediate, container provided by funeral home		1348.78	1/95	54r
Cards, acknowledgment		21.20	1/95	54r
Casket, minimum alternative		182.83	1/95	54r
Cosmetology, hair care, etc.		133.11	1/95	54r
Cremation, direct, container provided by funeral home		1101.95	1/95	54r
Embalming		314.45	1/95	54r
Funeral, funeral home		304.88	1/95	54r
Funeral, other facility		301.37	1/95	54r
Graveside service		290.59	1/95	54r
Hearse, local		137.37	1/95	54r
Limousine, local		82.84	1/95	54r
Memorial service		316.57	1/95	54r
Service charge, professional, nondeclinable		1099.00	1/95	54r
Visitation and viewing		209.25	1/95	54r
Groceries				
Apples, Red Delicious	lb.	0.68	12/94	82r
Bacon, sliced	lb.	1.88	12/94	82r
Bananas	lb.	0.41	12/94	82r
Beef purchases	year	197	91	81r
Beef, stew, boneless	lb.	2.52	12/94	82r
Beverage purchases, alcoholic	year	293	91	81r
Beverage purchases, nonalcoholic	year	203	91	81r
Bologna, all beef or mixed	lb.	2.12	12/94	82r
Bread, white, pan	lb.	0.76	12/94	82r
Cabbage	lb.	0.44	12/94	82r
Carrots, short trimmed and topped	lb.	0.44	12/94	82r
Cereals and bakery products purchases	year	347	91	81r
Cereals and cereals products purchases	year	119	91	81r
Cheddar cheese, natural	lb.	3.28	12/94	82r
Chicken breast, bone-in	lb.	1.61	12/94	82r
Chicken, fresh, whole	lb.	0.89	12/94	82r
Chuck roast, USDA choice, boneless	lb.	2.33	12/94	82r
Coffee, 100%, ground roast, all sizes	lb.	4.28	12/94	82r
Cookies, chocolate chip	lb.	2.72	12/94	82r
Dairy products (other) purchases	year	148	91	81r
Eggs, Grade A large	dozen	0.76	12/94	82r
Fish and seafood purchases	year	61	91	81r
Flour, white, all purpose	lb.	0.22	12/94	82r
Food purchases, food eaten at home	year	2313	91	81r
Foods purchased away from home, not prepared by consumer	year	1709	91	81r
Fruits and vegetables purchases	year	372	91	81r
Grapefruit	lb.	0.47	12/94	82r
Grapes, Thompson seedless	lb.	2.15	12/94	82r
Ground beef, 100% beef	lb.	1.37	12/94	82r
Ground chuck, 100% beef	lb.	1.81	12/94	82r
Ham, boneless, exc. canned	lb.	2.16	12/94	82r
Ice cream, prepackaged, bulk, regular	1/2 gal.	2.48	12/94	82r
Lemons	lb.	1.08	12/94	82r
Lettuce, iceberg	lb.	0.81	12/94	82r
Margarine, stick	lb.	0.81	12/94	82r
Meats, poultry, fish, and eggs purchases	year	591	91	81r
Milk and cream (fresh) purchases	year	132	91	81r
Orange juice, frozen concentrate 12-oz. can	16 oz.	1.41	12/94	82r
Oranges, Navel	lb.	0.56	12/94	82r
Peanut butter, creamy, all sizes	lb.	1.81	12/94	82r
Pork chops, center cut, bone-in	lb.	2.76	12/94	82r
Pork purchases	year	130	91	81r
Potato chips	16-oz.	2.81	12/94	82r
Potatoes, frozen, French fried	lb.	0.83	12/94	82r
Potatoes, white	lb.	0.28	12/94	82r
Round roast, USDA choice, boneless	lb.	2.90	12/94	82r
Shortening, vegetable oil blends	lb.	0.88	12/94	82r
Spaghetti and macaroni	lb.	0.78	12/94	82r
Steak, rib eye, USDA choice, boneless	lb.	6.15	12/94	82r
Steak, round, graded & ungraded, exc. USDA prime & choice	lb.	2.72	12/94	82r
Steak, round, USDA choice, boneless	lb.	3.02	12/94	82r
Steak, sirloin, USDA choice, boneless	lb.	3.85	12/94	82r

Waterloo-Cedar Falls, IA - continued

Item	Per	Value	Date	Ref.
Groceries - continued				
Steak, T-bone, USDA choice, bone-in	lb.	5.38	12/94	82r
Sugar and other sweets, eaten at home, expenditures	year	91	91	81r
Sugar, white, all sizes	lb.	0.36	12/94	82r
Tobacco products and smoking supplies, total expenditures	year	298	91	81r
Tomatoes, field grown	lb.	1.36	12/94	82r
Tuna, chunk, light	lb.	1.94	12/94	82r
Turkey, frozen, whole	lb.	0.96	12/94	82r
Yogurt, natural, fruit flavored	8 oz.	0.62	12/94	82r
Health Care				
Childbirth, Cesarean delivery, hospital charge	birth	5101.00	12/91	69r
Childbirth, Cesarean delivery, physician charge	birth	2234.00	12/91	69r
Childbirth, normal delivery, hospital charge	birth	2891.00	12/91	69r
Childbirth, normal delivery, physician charge	birth	1623.00	12/91	69r
Drugs, expenditures	year	248	91	81r
Health care, total expenditures	year	1336	91	81r
Health insurance expenditures	year	550	91	81r
Insurance premium, family medical care	month	395.98	1/95	41s
Medical services expenditures	year	457	91	81r
Medical supplies expenditures	year	82	91	81r
Household Goods				
Floor coverings, expenditures	year	105	91	81r
Furniture, expenditures	year	291	91	81r
Household equipment, misc. expenditures	year	341	91	81r
Household expenditures, miscellaneous	year	162	91	81r
Household furnishings and equipment, expenditures	year	1042	91	81r
Household operations expenditures	year	365	91	81r
Household textiles, expenditures	year	101	91	81r
Housekeeping supplies, expenditures	year	390	91	81r
Laundry and cleaning supplies, expenditures	year	110	91	81r
Postage and stationery, expenditures	year	115	91	81r
Housing				
Add garage/carport		8,479	3/95	74r
Add room(s)		21,347	3/95	74r
Apartment condominium or co-op, median	unit	87100	12/94	62r
Bathroom addition, average cost	add	9734.00	3/95	13r
Bathroom remodeling, average cost	remod	6414.00	3/95	13r
Bedroom, master suite addition, average cost	add	27122.00	3/95	13r
Deck addition, average cost	add	6665.00	3/95	13r
Dwellings (owned), expenditures	year	2566	91	81r
Enclose porch/patio/breezeway		4,556	3/95	74r
Exterior remodeling, average cost	remod	15395.00	3/95	13r
Family room addition, average cost	add	27658.00	3/95	13r
Finish room in basement/attic		5,074	3/95	74r
Home, existing, single-family, median	unit	106500	12/94	62r
Kitchen remodeling, major, average cost	remod	17084.00	3/95	13r
Kitchen remodeling, minor, average cost	remod	5804.00	3/95	13r
Maintenance, repairs, insurance, and other housing expenditures	year	484	91	81r
Mortgage interest and charges expenditures	year	1443	91	81r
Office, home addition, average cost	add	8121.00	3/95	13r
Princ. & int., mortgage, median-price exist. sing.-family home	mo.	515	12/94	62r
Property taxes expenditures	year	639	91	81r
Redesign, restructure more than half of home's interior		9,114	3/95	74r
Rental units expenditures	year	1200	91	81r
Sun-space addition, average cost	add	23768.00	3/95	13r
Wing addition, two-story, average cost	add	50410.00	3/95	13r
Insurance and Pensions				
Auto insurance, private passenger	year	467.45	12/94	71s
Insurance and pensions, personal, expenditures	year	2408	91	81r

Values are in dollars or fractions of dollars. In the column headed *Ref*, references are shown to sources. Each reference is followed by a letter. These refer to the geographical level for which data were reported: s=State, r=Region, and c=City or metro. The abbreviation *ex* is used to mean *except* or *excluding*; *exp* stands for expenditures. For other abbreviations and further explanations, please see the Introduction.

Waterloo-Cedar Falls, IA - continued

Item	Per	Value	Date	Ref.
Insurance and Pensions				
Insurance, life and other personal, expenditures	year	355	91	81r
Pensions and Social Security, expenditures	year	2053	91	81r
Legal Assistance				
Legal work, law firm associate	hour	90		10r
Legal work, law firm partner	hour	139		10r
Personal Services				
Personal services expenditures	year	203	91	81r
Restaurant Food				
Dining expenditures, family	week	30.03	94	73r
Taxes				
Taxes, Federal income, expenditures	year	1756	91	81r
Taxes, personal, expenditures	year	2426	91	81r
Taxes, State and local income, expenditures	year	568	91	81r
Transportation				
Cars and trucks purchased, new	year	891	91	81r
Cars and trucks purchased, used	year	1155	91	81r
Driver's learning permit fee	perm	6.00	1/94	84s
Driver's license fee	orig	0.00	1/94	84s
Driver's license fee, duplicate	lic	3.00	1/94	84s
Driver's license reinstatement fee, min.	susp	20.00	1/94	85s
Driver's license renewal fee	renew	0.00	1/94	84s
Identification card, nondriver	card	5.00	1/94	83s
Motorcycle learning permit fee	perm	8.00	1/94	84s
Motorcycle license fee	orig	8.00	1/94	84s
Motorcycle license fee, duplicate	lic	3.00	1/94	84s
Motorcycle license renewal fee	renew	8.00	1/94	84s
Public transportation expenditures	year	209	91	81r
Transportation expenditures, total	year	4792	91	81r
Vehicle finance charges	year	300	91	81r
Vehicle insurance expenditures	year	485	91	81r
Vehicle maintenance and repairs expenditures	year	534	91	81r
Vehicle purchases	year	2068	91	81r
Vehicle rental, leases, licenses, etc. expenditures	year	197	91	81r
Vehicles purchased, other than cars and trucks	year	22	91	81r
Utilities				
Electricity expenditures	year	668	91	81r
Utilities, fuels, and public services, total expenditures	year	1838	91	81r
Water and other public services, expenditures	year	167	91	81r
Weddings				
Bridal attendants' gowns	event	750	10/93	76r
Bridal gown	event	852	10/93	76r
Bridal headpiece and veil	event	167	10/93	76r
Bride's wedding band	event	708	10/93	76r
Clergy	event	224	10/93	76r
Engagement ring	event	2756	10/93	76r
Flowers	event	863	10/93	76r
Formal wear for groom	event	106	10/93	76r
Groom's attendants' formal wear	event	530	10/93	76r
Groom's wedding band	event	402	10/93	76r
Music	event	600	10/93	76r
Photography	event	1088	10/93	76r
Shoes for bride	event	50	10/93	76r
Videography	event	483	10/93	76r
Wedding invitations and announcements	event	342	10/93	76r
Wedding reception	event	7000	10/93	76r

Wausau, WI

Item	Per	Value	Date	Ref.
Composite, ACCRA index		103.40	12/94	2c
Alcoholic Beverages				
Beer, Miller Lite, Bud, 12-oz., ex deposit	6	3.29	12/94	2c
J & B Scotch	750-ml.	15.06	12/94	2c
Wine, Gallo Chablis blanc	1.5-lit	4.49	12/94	2c
Appliances				
Appliances (major), expenditures	year	131	91	81r
Average annual exp.				
Food, health care, personal goods, services	year	25935	91	81r
Charity				
Cash contributions, expenditures	year	745	91	81r
Clothing				
Apparel, men and boys, total expenditures	year	332	91	81r
Apparel, women and girls, total expenditures	year	578	91	81r
Footwear, expenditures	year	164	91	81r
Jeans, man's denim		30.76	12/94	2c
Shirt, man's dress shirt		32.00	12/94	2c
Undervest, boy's size 10-14, cotton	3	3.72	12/94	2c
Communications				
Long-distance telephone rate, day, addl. min., 1-10 mi.	min.	0.10	12/93	9s
Long-distance telephone rate, day, initial min., 1-10 mi.	min.	0.15	12/93	9s
Newspaper subscription, dly. and Sun. delivery	month	11.52	12/94	2c
Phone line, single, business, field visit	inst	64.65	12/93	9s
Phone line, single, business, no field visit	inst	64.65	12/93	9s
Phone line, single, residence, field visit	inst	33.05	12/93	9s
Phone line, single, residence, no field visit	inst	33.05	12/93	9s
Telephone bill, family of four	month	23.44	12/94	2c
Telephone service, expenditures	year	547	91	81r
Telephone, residential, flat rate	mo.	6.00	12/93	8c
Education				
Board, 4-year private college/university	year	2145	8/94	80s
Board, 4-year public college/university	year	1303	8/94	80s
Education, total expenditures	year	394	91	81r
Room, 4-year private college/university	year	1576	8/94	80s
Room, 4-year public college/university	year	1631	8/94	80s
Total cost, 4-year private college/university	year	13902	8/94	80s
Total cost, 4-year public college/university	year	5252	8/94	80s
Tuition, 2-year public college/university, in-state	year	1557	8/94	80s
Tuition, 4-year private college/university, in-state	year	10181	8/94	80s
Tuition, 4-year public college/university, in-state	year	2318	8/94	80s
Energy and Fuels				
Energy, combined forms, 1800 sq. ft.	mo.	91.51	12/94	2c
Energy, exc. electricity, 1800 sq. ft.	mo.	48.23	12/94	2c
Fuel oil and other fuels, expenditures	year	83	91	81r
Gas, cooking, winter, 10 therms	month	9.80	2/94	65c
Gas, cooking, winter, 30 therms	month	21.39	2/94	65c
Gas, cooking, winter, 50 therms	month	32.98	2/94	65c
Gas, heating, winter, 100 therms	month	61.96	2/94	65c
Gas, heating, winter, average use	month	106.01	2/94	65c
Gas, natural, expenditures	year	373	91	81r
Gas, reg unlead, taxes inc., cash, self-service	gal	1.06	12/94	2c
Gasoline and motor oil purchased	year	1000	91	81r
Gasoline, unleaded midgrade	gallon	1.15	4/93	82r
Gasoline, unleaded premium	gallon	1.23	4/93	82r
Gasoline, unleaded regular	gallon	1.07	4/93	82r
Entertainment				
Bowling, evening rate	game	1.83	12/94	2c
Entertainment, total expenditures	year	1356	91	81r
Fees and admissions, expenditures	year	347	91	81r
Monopoly game, Parker Brothers', No. 9	game	10.32	12/94	2c

Values are in dollars or fractions of dollars. In the column headed *Ref*, references are shown to sources. Each reference is followed by a letter. These refer to the geographical level for which data were reported: s=State, r=Region, and c=City or metro. The abbreviation *ex* is used to mean *except* or *excluding*; *exp* stands for expenditures. For other abbreviations and further explanations, please see the Introduction.

Wausau, WI - continued

Item	Per	Value	Date	Ref.
Entertainment				
Movie	adm	5.50	12/94	2c
Pets, toys, playground equipment, expenditures	year	270	91	81r
Reading, expenditures	year	160	91	81r
Televisions, radios, and sound equipment, expenditures	year	433	91	81r
Tennis balls, yellow, Wilson or Penn, 3	can	2.11	12/94	2c
Funerals				
Burial, immediate, container provided by funeral home		1268.31	1/95	54r
Cards, acknowledgment		26.12	1/95	54r
Casket, minimum alternative		198.03	1/95	54r
Cosmetology, hair care, etc.		122.19	1/95	54r
Cremation, direct, container provided by funeral home		977.81	1/95	54r
Embalming		334.00	1/95	54r
Funeral, funeral home		321.16	1/95	54r
Funeral, other facility		317.73	1/95	54r
Graveside service		292.48	1/95	54r
Hearse, local		153.20	1/95	54r
Limousine, local		123.52	1/95	54r
Memorial service		356.30	1/95	54r
Service charge, professional, nondeclinable		968.24	1/95	54r
Visitation and viewing		332.66	1/95	54r
Groceries				
Groceries, ACCRA Index		101.60	12/94	2c
Apples, Red Delicious	lb.	0.68	12/94	82r
Baby food, strained vegetables, lowest price	4-4.5 oz.	0.42	12/94	2c
Bacon, sliced	lb.	1.88	12/94	82r
Bananas	lb.	0.37	12/94	2c
Bananas	lb.	0.41	12/94	82r
Beef or hamburger, ground	lb.	1.52	12/94	2c
Beef purchases	year	197	91	81r
Beef, stew, boneless	lb.	2.52	12/94	82r
Beverage purchases, alcoholic	year	293	91	81r
Beverage purchases, nonalcoholic	year	203	91	81r
Bologna, all beef or mixed	lb.	2.12	12/94	82r
Bread, white	24-oz.	0.79	12/94	2c
Bread, white, pan	lb.	0.76	12/94	82r
Cabbage	lb.	0.44	12/94	82r
Carrots, short trimmed and topped	lb.	0.44	12/94	82r
Cereals and bakery products purchases	year	347	91	81r
Cereals and cereals products purchases	year	119	91	81r
Cheddar cheese, natural	lb.	3.28	12/94	82r
Cheese, Kraft grated Parmesan	8-oz.	3.12	12/94	2c
Chicken breast, bone-in	lb.	1.61	12/94	82r
Chicken, fresh, whole	lb.	0.89	12/94	82r
Chicken, whole fryer	lb.	0.99	12/94	2c
Chuck roast, USDA choice, boneless	lb.	2.33	12/94	82r
Cigarettes, Winston, Kings	carton	17.17	12/94	2c
Coffee, 100%, ground roast, all sizes	lb.	4.28	12/94	82r
Coffee, vacuum-packed	13 oz.	3.41	12/94	2c
Cookies, chocolate chip	lb.	2.72	12/94	82r
Corn Flakes, Kellogg's or Post Toasties	18 oz.	2.26	12/94	2c
Corn, frozen, whole kernel, lowest price	10 oz.	0.65	12/94	2c
Dairy products (other) purchases	year	148	91	81r
Eggs, Grade A large	dozen	0.65	12/94	2c
Eggs, Grade A large	dozen	0.76	12/94	82r
Fish and seafood purchases	year	61	91	81r
Flour, white, all purpose	lb.	0.22	12/94	82r
Food purchases, food eaten at home	year	2313	91	81r
Foods purchased away from home, not prepared by consumer	year	1709	91	81r
Fruits and vegetables purchases	year	372	91	81r
Grapefruit	lb.	0.47	12/94	82r
Grapes, Thompson seedless	lb.	2.15	12/94	82r
Ground beef, 100% beef	lb.	1.37	12/94	82r
Ground chuck, 100% beef	lb.	1.81	12/94	82r
Ham, boneless, exc. canned	lb.	2.16	12/94	82r

Item	Per	Value	Date	Ref.
Groceries - continued				
Ice cream, prepackaged, bulk, regular	1/2 gal.	2.48	12/94	82r
Lemons	lb.	1.08	12/94	82r
Lettuce, iceberg	lb.	0.81	12/94	82r
Lettuce, iceberg	head	0.77	12/94	2c
Margarine, Blue Bonnet or Parkay cubes	lb.	0.64	12/94	2c
Margarine, stick	lb.	0.81	12/94	82r
Meats, poultry, fish, and eggs purchases	year	591	91	81r
Milk and cream (fresh) purchases	year	132	91	81r
Milk, whole	1/2 gal.	1.07	12/94	2c
Orange juice, frozen concentrate 12-oz. can	16 oz.	1.41	12/94	82r
Orange juice, Minute Maid frozen	12-oz.	1.29	12/94	2c
Oranges, Navel	lb.	0.56	12/94	82r
Peaches, halves or slices, Hunt's, Del Monte, or Libby's	29-oz.	1.38	12/94	2c
Peanut butter, creamy, all sizes	lb.	1.81	12/94	82r
Peas, sweet, Del Monte or Green Giant	15-17 oz.	0.48	12/94	2c
Pork chops, center cut, bone-in	lb.	2.76	12/94	82r
Pork purchases	year	130	91	81r
Potato chips	16-oz.	2.81	12/94	82r
Potatoes, frozen, French fried	lb.	0.83	12/94	82r
Potatoes, white	lb.	0.28	12/94	82r
Potatoes, white or red	10-lb. sack	1.49	12/94	2c
Round roast, USDA choice, boneless	lb.	2.90	12/94	82r
Sausage, Jimmy Dean, 100% pork	lb.	2.62	12/94	2c
Shortening, vegetable oil blends	lb.	0.88	12/94	82r
Shortening, vegetable, Crisco	3-lb.	2.64	12/94	2c
Soft drink, Coca Cola, ex deposit	2 lit	1.23	12/94	2c
Spaghetti and macaroni	lb.	0.78	12/94	82r
Steak, rib eye, USDA choice, boneless	lb.	6.15	12/94	82r
Steak, round, graded & ungraded, exc. USDA prime & choice	lb.	2.72	12/94	82r
Steak, round, USDA choice, boneless	lb.	3.02	12/94	82r
Steak, sirloin, USDA choice, boneless	lb.	3.85	12/94	82r
Steak, t-bone	lb.	5.53	12/94	2c
Steak, T-bone, USDA choice, bone-in	lb.	5.38	12/94	82r
Sugar and other sweets, eaten at home, expenditures	year	91	91	81r
Sugar, cane or beet	4 lbs.	1.30	12/94	2c
Sugar, white, all sizes	lb.	0.36	12/94	82r
Tobacco products and smoking supplies, total expenditures	year	298	91	81r
Tomatoes, field grown	lb.	1.36	12/94	82r
Tomatoes, Hunt's or Del Monte	14.5 oz.	0.76	12/94	2c
Tuna, chunk, light	lb.	1.94	12/94	82r
Tuna, chunk, light, oil-packed	6.125-6.5 oz.	0.75	12/94	2c
Turkey, frozen, whole	lb.	0.96	12/94	82r
Yogurt, natural, fruit flavored	8 oz.	0.62	12/94	82r
Goods and Services				
Miscellaneous goods and services, ACCRA Index		96.80	12/94	2c
Health Care				
Health care, ACCRA Index		107.60	12/94	2c
Antibiotic ointment, Polysporin	1.5 oz.	4.10	12/94	2c
Childbirth, Cesarean delivery, hospital charge	birth	5101.00	12/91	69r
Childbirth, Cesarean delivery, physician charge	birth	2234.00	12/91	69r
Childbirth, normal delivery, hospital charge	birth	2891.00	12/91	69r
Childbirth, normal delivery, physician charge	birth	1623.00	12/91	69r
Dentist's fee, adult teeth cleaning and periodic oral exam	visit	52.00	12/94	2c
Doctor's fee, routine exam, established patient	visit	56.80	12/94	2c
Drugs, expenditures	year	248	91	81r
Health care, total expenditures	year	1336	91	81r

Values are in dollars or fractions of dollars. In the column headed *Ref*, references are shown to sources. Each reference is followed by a letter. These refer to the geographical level for which data were reported: s=State, r=Region, and c=City or metro. The abbreviation *ex* is used to mean *except* or *excluding*; *exp* stands for *expenditures*. For other abbreviations and further explanations, please see the Introduction.

Wausau, WI - continued

Item	Per	Value	Date	Ref.
Health Care				
Health insurance expenditures	year	550	91	81r
Hospital care, semiprivate room	day	263.50	12/94	2c
Insurance premium, family medical care	month	378.79	1/95	41s
Medical services expenditures	year	457	91	81r
Medical supplies expenditures	year	82	91	81r
Household Goods				
Appl. repair, service call, wash mach	min. lab. chg.	32.77	12/94	2c
Floor coverings, expenditures	year	105	91	81r
Furniture, expenditures	year	291	91	81r
Household equipment, misc. expenditures	year	341	91	81r
Household expenditures, miscellaneous	year	162	91	81r
Household furnishings and equipment, expenditures	year	1042	91	81r
Household operations expenditures	year	365	91	81r
Household textiles, expenditures	year	101	91	81r
Housekeeping supplies, expenditures	year	390	91	81r
Laundry and cleaning supplies, expenditures	year	110	91	81r
Laundry detergent, Tide Ultra, Bold, or Cheer	42 oz.	3.73	12/94	2c
Postage and stationery, expenditures	year	115	91	81r
Tissues, facial, Kleenex brand	175	0.98	12/94	2c
Housing				
Housing, ACCRA Index		121.50	12/94	2c
Add garage/carport		8,479	3/95	74r
Add room(s)		21,347	3/95	74r
Apartment condominium or co-op, median	unit	87100	12/94	62r
Bathroom addition, average cost	add	9734.00	3/95	13r
Bathroom remodeling, average cost	remod	6414.00	3/95	13r
Bedroom, master suite addition, average cost	add	27122.00	3/95	13r
Deck addition, average cost	add	6665.00	3/95	13r
Dwellings (owned), expenditures	year	2566	91	81r
Enclose porch/patio/breezeway		4,556	3/95	74r
Exterior remodeling, average cost	remod	15395.00	3/95	13r
Family room addition, average cost	add	27658.00	3/95	13r
Finish room in basement/attic		5,074	3/95	74r
Home, existing, single-family, median	unit	106500	12/94	62r
House payment, principal and interest, 25% down payment	mo.	961	12/94	2c
House, 1800 sq ft, 8000 sq ft lot, new, urban, utilities	total	154000	12/94	2c
Kitchen remodeling, major, average cost	remod	17084.00	3/95	13r
Kitchen remodeling, minor, average cost	remod	5804.00	3/95	13r
Maintenance, repairs, insurance, and other housing expenditures	year	484	91	81r
Mortgage interest and charges expenditures	year	1443	91	81r
Mtge. rate, incl. points and orig. fee, 30-year conv. fixed or ARM	mo.	9.38	12/94	2c
Office, home addition, average cost	add	8121.00	3/95	13r
Princ. & int., mortgage, median-price exist. sing.-family home	mo.	515	12/94	62r
Property taxes expenditures	year	639	91	81r
Redesign, restructure more than half of home's interior		9,114	3/95	74r
Rent, apartment, 2 br., 1 1/2-2 baths, unfurnished, 950 sq ft, water	mo.	557	12/94	2c
Rental units expenditures	year	1200	91	81r
Sun-space addition, average cost	add	23768.00	3/95	13r
Wing addition, two-story, average cost	add	50410.00	3/95	13r
Insurance and Pensions				
Auto insurance, private passenger	year	554.10	12/94	71s
Insurance and pensions, personal, expenditures	year	2408	91	81r
Insurance, life and other personal, expenditures	year	355	91	81r
Pensions and Social Security, expenditures	year	2053	91	81r

Wausau, WI - continued

Item	Per	Value	Date	Ref.
Legal Assistance				
Legal work, law firm associate	hour	90		10r
Legal work, law firm partner	hour	139		10r
Personal Goods				
Shampoo, Alberto VO5	15-oz.	0.91	12/94	2c
Toothpaste, Crest or Colgate	6-7 oz.	1.80	12/94	2c
Personal Services				
Dry cleaning, man's 2-pc. suit		6.84	12/94	2c
Haircut, man's barbershop, no styling		7.25	12/94	2c
Haircut, woman's shampoo, trim, blow-dry		16.70	12/94	2c
Personal services expenditures	year	203	91	81r
Restaurant Food				
Chicken, fried, thigh and drumstick		2.18	12/94	2c
Dining expenditures, family	week	30.03	94	73r
Hamburger with cheese	1/4 lb.	1.79	12/94	2c
Pizza, Pizza Hut or Pizza Inn	12-13 in.	8.49	12/94	2c
Taxes				
Taxes, Federal income, expenditures	year	1756	91	81r
Taxes, personal, expenditures	year	2426	91	81r
Taxes, State and local income, expenditures	year	568	91	81r
Transportation				
Transportation, ACCRA Index		85.90	12/94	2c
Bus fare, up to 10 miles	one-way	0.75	12/94	2c
Cars and trucks purchased, new	year	891	91	81r
Cars and trucks purchased, used	year	1155	91	81r
Driver's learning permit fee	perm	20.00	1/94	84s
Driver's license fee	orig	10.00	1/94	84s
Driver's license fee, duplicate	lic	4.00	1/94	84s
Driver's license reinstatement fee, min.	susp	50.00	1/94	85s
Driver's license renewal fee	renew	10.00	1/94	84s
Identification card, nondriver	card	4.00	1/94	83s
Motorcycle license fee	orig	4.00	1/94	84s
Motorcycle license fee, duplicate	lic	4.00	1/94	84s
Motorcycle license renewal fee	renew	4.00	1/94	84s
Public transportation expenditures	year	209	91	81r
Tire balance, computer or spin bal., front	wheel	5.15	12/94	2c
Transportation expenditures, total	year	4792	91	81r
Vehicle finance charges	year	300	91	81r
Vehicle insurance expenditures	year	485	91	81r
Vehicle maintenance and repairs expenditures	year	534	91	81r
Vehicle purchases	year	2068	91	81r
Vehicle rental, leases, licenses, etc. expenditures	year	197	91	81r
Vehicles purchased, other than cars and trucks	year	22	91	81r
Utilities				
Utilities, ACCRA Index		86.80	12/94	2c
Electricity expenditures	year	668	91	81r
Electricity, (part.), other, 1800 sq. ft., new home	mo.	43.28	12/94	2c
Utilities, fuels, and public services, total expenditures	year	1838	91	81r
Water and other public services, expenditures	year	167	91	81r
Weddings				
Bridal attendants' gowns	event	750	10/93	76r
Bridal gown	event	852	10/93	76r
Bridal headpiece and veil	event	167	10/93	76r
Bride's wedding band	event	708	10/93	76r
Clergy	event	224	10/93	76r
Engagement ring	event	2756	10/93	76r
Flowers	event	863	10/93	76r
Formal wear for groom	event	106	10/93	76r
Groom's attendants' formal wear	event	530	10/93	76r
Groom's wedding band	event	402	10/93	76r
Music	event	600	10/93	76r

Values are in dollars or fractions of dollars. In the column headed *Ref*, references are shown to sources. Each reference is followed by a letter. These refer to the geographical level for which data were reported: s = State, r = Region, and c = City or metro. The abbreviation *ex* is used to mean *except* or *excluding*; *exp* stands for expenditures. For other abbreviations and further explanations, please see the Introduction.

Wausau, WI - continued

Item	Per	Value	Date	Ref.
Weddings				
Photography	event	1088	10/93	76r
Shoes for bride	event	50	10/93	76r
Videography	event	483	10/93	76r
Wedding invitations and announcements	event	342	10/93	76r
Wedding reception	event	7000	10/93	76r

Weatherford, TX

Item	Per	Value	Date	Ref.
Composite, ACCRA index		90.20	12/94	2c
Alcoholic Beverages				
Beer, Miller Lite, Bud, 12-oz., ex deposit	6	4.14	12/94	2c
J & B Scotch	750-ml.	17.94	12/94	2c
Wine, Gallo Chablis blanc	1.5-lit	4.94	12/94	2c
Clothing				
Jeans, man's denim		29.50	12/94	2c
Shirt, man's dress shirt		25.62	12/94	2c
Undervest, boy's size 10-14, cotton	3	3.45	12/94	2c
Communications				
Newspaper subscription, dly. and Sun. delivery	month	10.95	12/94	2c
Telephone bill, family of four	month	22.25	12/94	2c
Energy and Fuels				
Energy, combined forms, 1800 sq. ft.	mo.	119.97	12/94	2c
Energy, exc. electricity, 1800 sq. ft.	mo.	9.54	12/94	2c
Gas, reg unlead, taxes inc., cash, self-service	gal	1.16	12/94	2c
Entertainment				
Bowling, evening rate	game	2.15	12/94	2c
Monopoly game, Parker Brothers', No. 9	game	11.08	12/94	2c
Movie	adm	4.50	12/94	2c
Tennis balls, yellow, Wilson or Penn, 3	can	2.74	12/94	2c
Groceries				
Groceries, ACCRA Index		90.20	12/94	2c
Baby food, strained vegetables, lowest price	4-4.5 oz.	0.27	12/94	2c
Bananas	lb.	0.40	12/94	2c
Beef or hamburger, ground	lb.	1.12	12/94	2c
Bread, white	24-oz.	0.66	12/94	2c
Cheese, Kraft grated Parmesan	8-oz.	3.34	12/94	2c
Chicken, whole fryer	lb.	0.70	12/94	2c
Cigarettes, Winston, Kings	carton	16.15	12/94	2c
Coffee, vacuum-packed	13 oz.	3.45	12/94	2c
Corn Flakes, Kellogg's or Post Toasties	18 oz.	1.96	12/94	2c
Corn, frozen, whole kernel, lowest price	10 oz.	0.67	12/94	2c
Eggs, Grade A large	dozen	0.66	12/94	2c
Lettuce, iceberg	head	0.61	12/94	2c
Margarine, Blue Bonnet or Parkay cubes	lb.	0.53	12/94	2c
Milk, whole	1/2 gal.	1.37	12/94	2c
Orange juice, Minute Maid frozen	12-oz.	1.21	12/94	2c
Peaches, halves or slices, Hunt's, Del Monte, or Libby's	29-oz.	1.41	12/94	2c
Peas, sweet, Del Monte or Green Giant	15-17 oz.	0.50	12/94	2c
Potatoes, white or red	10-lb. sack	1.90	12/94	2c
Sausage, Jimmy Dean, 100% pork	lb.	2.23	12/94	2c
Shortening, vegetable, Crisco	3-lb.	2.22	12/94	2c
Soft drink, Coca Cola, ex deposit	2 lit	0.94	12/94	2c
Steak, t-bone	lb.	4.90	12/94	2c
Sugar, cane or beet	4 lbs.	1.30	12/94	2c
Tomatoes, Hunt's or Del Monte	14.5 oz.	0.65	12/94	2c
Tuna, chunk, light, oil-packed	6.125-6.5 oz.	0.66	12/94	2c

Weatherford, TX - continued

Item	Per	Value	Date	Ref.
Goods and Services				
Miscellaneous goods and services, ACCRA Index		98.10	12/94	2c
Health Care				
Health care, ACCRA Index		83.90	12/94	2c
Antibiotic ointment, Polysporin	1.5 oz.	3.92	12/94	2c
Dentist's fee, adult teeth cleaning and periodic oral exam	visit	43.80	12/94	2c
Doctor's fee, routine exam, established patient	visit	35.00	12/94	2c
Hospital care, semiprivate room	day	280.00	12/94	2c
Household Goods				
Appl. repair, service call, wash mach	min. lab. chg.	36.25	12/94	2c
Laundry detergent, Tide Ultra, Bold, or Cheer	42 oz.	3.29	12/94	2c
Tissues, facial, Kleenex brand	175	0.93	12/94	2c
Housing				
Housing, ACCRA Index		74.10	12/94	2c
House payment, principal and interest, 25% down payment	mo.	544	12/94	2c
House, 1800 sq ft, 8000 sq ft lot, new, urban, utilities	total	87600	12/94	2c
Mtge. rate, incl. points and orig. fee, 30-year conv. fixed or ARM	mo.	9.32	12/94	2c
Rent, apartment, 2 br., 1 1/2-2 baths, unfurnished, 950 sq ft, water	mo.	460	12/94	2c
Personal Goods				
Shampoo, Alberto VO5	15-oz.	1.08	12/94	2c
Toothpaste, Crest or Colgate	6-7 oz.	1.90	12/94	2c
Personal Services				
Dry cleaning, man's 2-pc. suit		5.24	12/94	2c
Haircut, man's barbershop, no styling		6.99	12/94	2c
Haircut, woman's shampoo, trim, blow-dry		21.40	12/94	2c
Restaurant Food				
Chicken, fried, thigh and drumstick		2.30	12/94	2c
Hamburger with cheese	1/4 lb.	1.79	12/94	2c
Pizza, Pizza Hut or Pizza Inn	12-13 in.	9.14	12/94	2c
Transportation				
Transportation, ACCRA Index		99.70	12/94	2c
Tire balance, computer or spin bal., front	wheel	6.42	12/94	2c
Utilities				
Utilities, ACCRA Index		107.90	12/94	2c
Electricity, (part.), other, 1800 sq. ft., new home	mo.	110.43	12/94	2c

West Palm Beach-Boca Raton-Delray Beach, FL

Item	Per	Value	Date	Ref.
Composite, ACCRA index		110.30	12/94	2c
Alcoholic Beverages				
Beer, Miller Lite, Bud, 12-oz., ex deposit	6	4.16	12/94	2c
J & B Scotch	750-ml.	17.57	12/94	2c
Wine, Gallo Chablis blanc	1.5-lit	5.94	12/94	2c
Appliances				
Appliances (major), expenditures	year	153	91	81r
Average annual exp.				
Food, health care, personal goods, services	year	27020	91	81r
Charity				
Cash contributions, expenditures	year	839	91	81r
Clothing				
Apparel, men and boys, total expenditures	year	380	91	81r
Apparel, women and girls, total expenditures	year	660	91	81r

Values are in dollars or fractions of dollars. In the column headed *Ref*, references are shown to sources. Each reference is followed by a letter. These refer to the geographical level for which data were reported: s=State, r=Region, and c=City or metro. The abbreviation *ex* is used to mean *except* or *excluding*; *exp* stands for expenditures. For other abbreviations and further explanations, please see the Introduction.

West Palm Beach-Boca Raton-Delray Beach, FL - continued

Item	Per	Value	Date	Ref.
Clothing				
Footwear, expenditures	year	193	91	81r
Jeans, man's denim		33.40	12/94	2c
Shirt, man's dress shirt		30.99	12/94	2c
Undervest, boy's size 10-14, cotton	3	6.98	12/94	2c
Communications				
Long-distance telephone rate, day, addl. min., 1-10 mi.	min.	0.08	12/93	9s
Long-distance telephone rate, day, initial min., 1-10 mi.	min.	0.15	12/93	9s
Newspaper subscription, dly. and Sun. delivery	month	11.04	12/94	2c
Phone line, single, business, field visit	inst	86.00	12/93	9s
Phone line, single, business, no field visit	inst	54.50	12/93	9s
Phone line, single, residence, field visit	inst	76.00	12/93	9s
Phone line, single, residence, no field visit	inst	44.50	12/93	9s
Telephone bill, family of four	month	15.10	12/94	2c
Telephone service, expenditures	year	616	91	81r
Telephone, residential, flat rate	mo.	10.30	12/93	8c
Credit Cards				
Fee, conventional credit card, secured	year	25.00	1/95	96c
Education				
Bar examination preparatory course	course	500.00-100	94	17s
Board, 4-year private college/university	year	2123	8/94	80s
Board, 4-year public college/university	year	2101	8/94	80s
Education, total expenditures	year	319	91	81r
Room, 4-year private college/university	year	2242	8/94	80s
Room, 4-year public college/university	year	1970	8/94	80s
Total cost, 4-year private college/university	year	13853	8/94	80s
Total cost, 4-year public college/university	year	5855	8/94	80s
Tuition, 2-year public college/university, in-state	year	1076	8/94	80s
Tuition, 4-year private college/university, in-state	year	9287	8/94	80s
Tuition, 4-year public college/university, in-state	year	1784	8/94	80s
Energy and Fuels				
Energy, combined forms, 1800 sq. ft.	mo.	112.78	12/94	2c
Fuel oil and other fuels, expenditures	year	56	91	81r
Gas, cooking, 10 therms	month	14.17	2/94	65c
Gas, cooking, 30 therms	month	26.51	2/94	65c
Gas, cooking, 50 therms	month	38.85	2/94	65c
Gas, heating, winter, 100 therms	month	69.71	2/94	65c
Gas, heating, winter, average use	month	29.60	2/94	65c
Gas, natural, expenditures	year	150	91	81r
Gas, reg unlead, taxes inc., cash, self-service	gal	1.25	12/94	2c
Gasoline and motor oil purchased	year	1152	91	81r
Gasoline, unleaded midgrade	gallon	1.21	4/93	82r
Gasoline, unleaded premium	gallon	1.30	4/93	82r
Gasoline, unleaded regular	gallon	1.10	4/93	82r
Entertainment				
Bowling, evening rate	game	2.60	12/94	2c
Concert ticket, Pearl Jam group	perf	20.00	94	50r
Entertainment, total expenditures	year	1266	91	81r
Fees and admissions, expenditures	year	306	91	81r
Monopoly game, Parker Brothers', No. 9	game	13.49	12/94	2c
Movie	adm	5.90	12/94	2c
Pets, toys, playground equipment, expenditures	year	271	91	81r
Reading, expenditures	year	131	91	81r
Televisions, radios, and sound equipment, expenditures	year	439	91	81r
Tennis balls, yellow, Wilson or Penn, 3	can	2.35	12/94	2c
Funerals				
Burial, immediate, container provided by funeral home		1370.36	1/95	54r
Cards, acknowledgment		14.83	1/95	54r
Casket, minimum alternative		192.52	1/95	54r

West Palm Beach-Boca Raton-Delray Beach, FL - continued

Item	Per	Value	Date	Ref.
Funerals - continued				
Cosmetology, hair care, etc.		102.27	1/95	54r
Cremation, direct, container provided by funeral home		1065.64	1/95	54r
Embalming		304.29	1/95	54r
Funeral, funeral home		287.83	1/95	54r
Funeral, other facility		284.14	1/95	54r
Graveside service		349.13	1/95	54r
Hearse, local		132.27	1/95	54r
Limousine, local		98.45	1/95	54r
Memorial service		270.59	1/95	54r
Service charge, professional, nondeclinable		933.59	1/95	54r
Visitation and viewing		225.83	1/95	54r
Groceries				
Groceries, ACCRA Index		101.90	12/94	2c
Apples, Red Delicious	lb.	0.73	12/94	82r
Baby food, strained vegetables, lowest price	4-4.5 oz.	0.33	12/94	2c
Bacon, sliced	lb.	1.67	12/94	82r
Bananas	lb.	0.37	12/94	2c
Bananas	lb.	0.42	12/94	82r
Beef or hamburger, ground	lb.	1.77	12/94	2c
Beef purchases	year	213	91	81r
Beverage purchases, alcoholic	year	249	91	81r
Beverage purchases, nonalcoholic	year	207	91	81r
Bologna, all beef or mixed	lb.	2.27	12/94	82r
Bread, white	24-oz.	0.71	12/94	2c
Bread, white, pan	lb.	0.68	12/94	82r
Cabbage	lb.	0.42	12/94	82r
Carrots, short trimmed and topped	lb.	0.53	12/94	82r
Cereals and bakery products purchases	year	345	91	81r
Cereals and cereals products purchases	year	127	91	81r
Cheddar cheese, natural	lb.	3.58	12/94	82r
Cheese, Kraft grated Parmesan	8-oz.	3.00	12/94	2c
Chicken breast, bone-in	lb.	1.71	12/94	82r
Chicken, fresh, whole	lb.	0.78	12/94	82r
Chicken, whole fryer	lb.	1.13	12/94	2c
Chuck roast, USDA choice, boneless	lb.	2.26	12/94	82r
Cigarettes, Winston, Kings	carton	18.05	12/94	2c
Coffee, vacuum-packed	13 oz.	4.00	12/94	2c
Corn Flakes, Kellogg's or Post Toasties	18 oz.	2.39	12/94	2c
Corn, frozen, whole kernel, lowest price	10 oz.	0.66	12/94	2c
Crackers, soda, salted	lb.	1.27	12/94	82r
Cucumbers	lb.	0.65	12/94	82r
Dairy products (other) purchases	year	141	91	81r
Eggs, Grade A large	dozen	0.71	12/94	2c
Eggs, Grade A large	dozen	0.87	12/94	82r
Fish and seafood purchases	year	72	91	81r
Flour, white, all purpose	lb.	0.23	12/94	82r
Food purchases, food eaten at home	year	2381	91	81r
Foods purchased away from home, not prepared by consumer	year	1696	91	81r
Frankfurters, all meat or all beef	lb.	1.74	12/94	82r
Fruits and vegetables purchases	year	380	91	81r
Grapefruit	lb.	0.45	12/94	82r
Grapes, Thompson seedless	lb.	2.30	12/94	82r
Ground beef, 100% beef	lb.	1.37	12/94	82r
Ground chuck, 100% beef	lb.	1.97	12/94	82r
Ham, boneless, exc. canned	lb.	2.54	12/94	82r
Ice cream, prepackaged, bulk, regular	1/2 gal.	2.47	12/94	82r
Lemons	lb.	1.02	12/94	82r
Lettuce, iceberg	lb.	0.96	12/94	82r
Lettuce, iceberg	head	1.03	12/94	2c
Margarine, Blue Bonnet or Parkay cubes	lb.	0.56	12/94	2c
Margarine, stick	lb.	0.77	12/94	82r
Meats, poultry, fish, and eggs purchases	year	655	91	81r
Milk and cream (fresh) purchases	year	130	91	81r
Milk, whole	1/2 gal.	1.44	12/94	2c
Orange juice, frozen concentrate 12-oz. can	16 oz.	1.36	12/94	82r
Orange juice, Minute Maid frozen	12-oz.	1.10	12/94	2c
Oranges, Navel	lb.	0.54	12/94	82r

Values are in dollars or fractions of dollars. In the column headed *Ref*, references are shown to sources. Each reference is followed by a letter. These refer to the geographical level for which data were reported: s = State, r = Region, and c = City or metro. The abbreviation *ex* is used to mean *except* or *excluding*; *exp* stands for *expenditures*. For other abbreviations and further explanations, please see the Introduction.

West Palm Beach-Boca Raton-Delray Beach, FL - continued

Item	Per	Value	Date	Ref.
Groceries				
Peaches, halves or slices, Hunt's, Del Monte, or Libby's	29-oz.	1.22	12/94	2c
Pears, Anjou	lb.	0.81	12/94	82r
Peas, sweet, Del Monte or Green Giant	15-17 oz.	0.51	12/94	2c
Pork chops, center cut, bone-in	lb.	3.07	12/94	82r
Pork purchases	year	142	91	81r
Potato chips	16-oz.	3.15	12/94	82r
Potatoes, frozen, French fried	lb.	0.82	12/94	82r
Potatoes, white	lb.	0.34	12/94	82r
Potatoes, white or red	10-lb. sack	2.79	12/94	2c
Rice, white, long grain, uncooked	lb.	0.48	12/94	82r
Round roast, USDA choice, boneless	lb.	2.91	12/94	82r
Sausage, fresh	lb.	1.82	12/94	82r
Sausage, Jimmy Dean, 100% pork	lb.	2.39	12/94	2c
Shortening, vegetable oil blends	lb.	0.75	12/94	82r
Shortening, vegetable, Crisco	3-lb.	2.78	12/94	2c
Soft drink, Coca Cola, ex deposit	2 lit	0.98	12/94	2c
Spaghetti and macaroni	lb.	0.87	12/94	82r
Steak, rib eye, USDA choice, boneless	lb.	6.85	12/94	82r
Steak, round, graded & ungraded, exc. USDA prime & choice	lb.	2.96	12/94	82r
Steak, round, USDA choice, boneless	lb.	3.17	12/94	82r
Steak, sirloin, USDA choice, boneless	lb.	4.12	12/94	82r
Steak, t-bone	lb.	6.24	12/94	2c
Steak, T-bone, USDA choice, bone-in	lb.	5.63	12/94	82r
Sugar and other sweets, eaten at home, expenditures	year	93	91	81r
Sugar, cane or beet	4 lbs.	1.49	12/94	2c
Sugar, white, all sizes	lb.	0.39	12/94	82r
Tobacco products and smoking supplies, total expenditures	year	286	91	81r
Tomatoes, field grown	lb.	1.36	12/94	82r
Tomatoes, Hunt's or Del Monte	14.5 oz.	0.58	12/94	2c
Tuna, chunk, light	lb.	1.94	12/94	82r
Tuna, chunk, light, oil-packed	6.125-6.5 oz.	0.55	12/94	2c
Turkey, frozen, whole	lb.	0.96	12/94	82r
Yogurt, natural, fruit flavored	8 oz.	0.58	12/94	82r
Goods and Services				
Miscellaneous goods and services, ACCRA Index		109.90	12/94	2c
Health Care				
Health care, ACCRA Index		102.10	12/94	2c
Adenosine, emergency room	treat	100.00	95	23r
Antibiotic ointment, Polysporin	1.5 oz.	4.29	12/94	2c
Bladder tap, superpubic, infant, emergency room	treat	119.00	95	23r
Blood analysis, emergency room	treat	25.00	95	23r
Blood tests, abdominal pain, emergency room	treat	25.00	95	23r
Burn dressing, emergency room	treat	266.00	95	23r
Cardiology interpretation, emergency room	treat	26.00	95	23r
Chest X-ray, emergency room	treat	78.00	95	23r
Childbirth, Cesarean delivery, hospital charge	birth	5462.00	12/91	69r
Childbirth, Cesarean delivery, physician charge	birth	2228.00	12/91	69r
Childbirth, normal delivery, hospital charge	birth	2943.00	12/91	69r
Childbirth, normal delivery, physician charge	birth	1619.00	12/91	69r
Defibrillation pads, emergency room	treat	6.00	95	23r
Dentist's fee, adult teeth cleaning and periodic oral exam	visit	51.17	12/94	2c
Doctor's fee, routine exam, established patient	visit	46.67	12/94	2c
Drugs, expenditures	year	297	91	81r
Gastric tube insertion, nasal, emergency room	treat	25.00	95	23r
Health care, total expenditures	year	1600	91	81r

West Palm Beach-Boca Raton-Delray Beach, FL - continued

Item	Per	Value	Date	Ref.
Health Care - continued				
Health insurance expenditures	year	637	91	81r
Heart monitor, emergency room	treat	40.00	95	23r
Hospital care, semiprivate room	day	325.20	12/94	2c
Insurance premium, family medical care	month	301.92	1/95	41s
Intravenous fluids, emergency room	treat	130.00	95	23r
Intravenous fluids, emergency room	liter	26.00	95	23r
Intravenous line, central, emergency room	treat	342.00	95	23r
Liver function tests, abdominal pain, emergency room	treat	26.00	95	23r
Medical care charges, total, emergency room, third-degree burns	treat	2101.00	95	23r
Medical care charges, total, emergency, infant with fever	treat	628.00	95	23r
Medical services expenditures	year	573	91	81r
Medical supplies expenditures	year	93	91	81r
Morphine, emergency room	treat	34.00	95	23r
Nursing care and facilities charges, emergency room	treat	252.00	95	23r
Nursing care and facilities charges, emergency, infant with fever	treat	252.00	95	23r
Nursing care and facilities charges, emergency, third-degree burns	treat	861.00	95	23r
Physician's charges, emergency, infant with fever	treat	212.00	95	23r
Physician's charges, emergency, third-degree burns	treat	372.00	95	23r
Physician's fee, emergency room	treat	372.00	95	23r
Physician's fee, general practitioner	visit	51.20	12/93	60r
Surgery, open-heart	proc	42374.00	1/93	14r
Ultrasound, abdominal, emergency room	treat	276.00	95	23r
Urinalysis, emergency room	treat	20.00	95	23r
Urinalysis, infant, emergency room	treat	20.00	95	23r
X-rays, emergency room	treat	78.00	95	23r
Household Goods				
Appl. repair, service call, wash mach	min. lab. chg.	40.40	12/94	2c
Floor coverings, expenditures	year	48	91	81r
Furniture, expenditures	year	280	91	81r
Household equipment, misc. expenditures	year	342	91	81r
Household expenditures, miscellaneous	year	256	91	81r
Household furnishings and equipment, expenditures	year	988	91	81r
Household operations expenditures	year	468	91	81r
Household textiles, expenditures	year	95	91	81r
Housekeeping supplies, expenditures	year	380	91	81r
Laundry and cleaning supplies, expenditures	year	109	91	81r
Laundry detergent, Tide Ultra, Bold, or Cheer	42 oz.	2.78	12/94	2c
Postage and stationery, expenditures	year	105	91	81r
Tissues, facial, Kleenex brand	175	1.17	12/94	2c
Housing				
Housing, ACCRA Index		118.00	12/94	2c
Add garage/carport		6,980	3/95	74r
Add room(s)		11,403	3/95	74r
Apartment condominium or co-op, median	unit	68600	12/94	62r
Dwellings (owned), expenditures	year	2428	91	81r
Enclose porch/patio/breezeway		4,572	3/95	74r
Finish room in basement/attic		3,794	3/95	74r
Home, existing, single-family, median	unit	120200	12/94	62r
Home, existing, single-family, median	unit	120.00	12/94	62c
House payment, principal and interest, 25% down payment	mo.	876	12/94	2c
House, 1800 sq ft, 8000 sq ft lot, new, urban, utilities	total	146333	12/94	2c
Maintenance, repairs, insurance, and other housing expenditures	year	531	91	81r
Mortgage interest and charges expenditures	year	1506	91	81r
Mtge. rate, incl. points and orig. fee, 30-year conv. fixed or ARM	mo.	9.16	12/94	2c

Values are in dollars or fractions of dollars. In the column headed *Ref*, references are shown to sources. Each reference is followed by a letter. These refer to the geographical level for which data were reported: s=State, r=Region, and c=City or metro. The abbreviation *ex* is used to mean *except* or *excluding*; *exp* stands for expenditures. For other abbreviations and further explanations, please see the Introduction.

West Palm Beach-Boca Raton-Delray Beach, FL - continued

Item	Per	Value	Date	Ref.
Housing				
Princ. & int., mortgage, median-price exist. sing.-family home	mo.	540	12/94	62r
Property taxes expenditures	year	391	91	81r
Redesign, restructure more than half of home's interior		17,641	3/95	74r
Rent, apartment, 2 br., 1 1/2-2 baths, unfurnished, 950 sq ft, water	mo.	705	12/94	2c
Rental units expenditures	year	1264	91	81r
Insurance and Pensions				
Auto insurance, private passenger	year	753.93	12/94	71s
Insurance and pensions, personal, expenditures	year	2395	91	81r
Insurance, life and other personal, expenditures	year	368	91	81r
Pensions and Social Security, expenditures	year	2027	91	81r
Personal Goods				
Shampoo, Alberto VO5	15-oz.	0.94	12/94	2c
Toothpaste, Crest or Colgate	6-7 oz.	1.59	12/94	2c
Personal Services				
Dry cleaning, man's 2-pc. suit		7.78	12/94	2c
Haircut, man's barbershop, no styling		12.40	12/94	2c
Haircut, woman's shampoo, trim, blow-dry		24.40	12/94	2c
Personal services expenditures	year	212	91	81r
Restaurant Food				
Chicken, fried, thigh and drumstick		2.40	12/94	2c
Dining expenditures, family	week	33.83	94	73r
Hamburger with cheese	1/4 lb.	1.98	12/94	2c
Pizza, Pizza Hut or Pizza Inn	12-13 in.	7.99	12/94	2c
Taxes				
Taxes, Federal income, expenditures	year	2275	91	81r
Taxes, personal, expenditures	year	2715	91	81r
Taxes, State and local income, expenditures	year	365	91	81r
Transportation				
Transportation, ACCRA Index		119.40	12/94	2c
Bus fare, one-way	trip	1.00	12/95	1c
Cars and trucks purchased, new	year	1306	91	81r
Cars and trucks purchased, used	year	942	91	81r
Driver's learning permit fee	perm	20.00	1/94	84s
Driver's license fee	orig	20.00	1/94	84s
Driver's license fee, duplicate	lic	10.00	1/94	84s
Driver's license reinstatement fee, min.	susp	25.00	1/94	85s
Driver's license renewal fee	renew	15.00	1/94	84s
Identification card, nondriver	card	3.00	1/94	83s
Motorcycle learning permit fee	perm	20.00	1/94	84s
Motorcycle license fee	orig	20.00	1/94	84s
Motorcycle license fee, duplicate	lic	10.00	1/94	84s
Motorcycle license renewal fee	renew	15.00	1/94	84s
Public transportation expenditures	year	249	91	81r
Tire balance, computer or spin bal., front	wheel	8.79	12/94	2c
Transportation expenditures, total	year	5307	91	81r
Vehicle finance charges	year	346	91	81r
Vehicle insurance expenditures	year	544	91	81r
Vehicle maintenance and repairs expenditures	year	600	91	81r
Vehicle purchases	year	2275	91	81r
Vehicle rental, leases, licenses, etc. expenditures	year	141	91	81r
Vehicles purchased, other than cars and trucks	year	27	91	81r
Utilities				
Utilities, ACCRA Index		97.40	12/94	2c
Electricity expenditures	year	950	91	81r
Electricity, 1800 sq. ft., new home	mo.	112.78	12/94	2c
Utilities, fuels, and public services, total expenditures	year	2000	91	81r
Water and other public services, expenditures	year	227	91	81r

West Palm Beach-Boca Raton-Delray Beach, FL - continued

Item	Per	Value	Date	Ref.
Weddings				
Bridal attendants' gowns	event	750	10/93	76r
Bridal gown	event	852	10/93	76r
Bridal headpiece and veil	event	167	10/93	76r
Bride's wedding band	event	708	10/93	76r
Clergy	event	224	10/93	76r
Engagement ring	event	2756	10/93	76r
Flowers	event	863	10/93	76r
Formal wear for groom	event	106	10/93	76r
Groom's attendants' formal wear	event	530	10/93	76r
Groom's wedding band	event	402	10/93	76r
Music	event	600	10/93	76r
Photography	event	1088	10/93	76r
Shoes for bride	event	50	10/93	76r
Videography	event	483	10/93	76r
Wedding invitations and announcements	event	342	10/93	76r
Wedding reception	event	7000	10/93	76r

Wheeling, WV, OH

Item	Per	Value	Date	Ref.
Appliances				
Appliances (major), expenditures	year	153	91	81r
Average annual exp.				
Food, health care, personal goods, services	year	27020	91	81r
Charity				
Cash contributions, expenditures	year	839	91	81r
Clothing				
Apparel, men and boys, total expenditures	year	380	91	81r
Apparel, women and girls, total expenditures	year	660	91	81r
Footwear, expenditures	year	193	91	81r
Communications				
Long-distance telephone rate, day, addl. min., 1-10 mi.	min.	0.13	12/93	9s
Long-distance telephone rate, day, initial min., 1-10 mi.	min.	0.26	12/93	9s
Phone line, single, business, field visit	inst	0.00	12/93	9s
Phone line, single, business, no field visit	inst	96.90	12/93	9s
Phone line, single, residence, field visit	inst	0.00	12/93	9s
Phone line, single, residence, no field visit	inst	42.00	12/93	9s
Telephone service, expenditures	year	616	91	81r
Education				
Board, 4-year private college/university	year	2166	8/94	80s
Board, 4-year public college/university	year	1968	8/94	80s
Education, total expenditures	year	319	91	81r
Room, 4-year private college/university	year	1745	8/94	80s
Room, 4-year public college/university	year	1847	8/94	80s
Total cost, 4-year private college/university	year	13220	8/94	80s
Total cost, 4-year public college/university	year	5691	8/94	80s
Tuition, 2-year public college/university, in-state	year	1247	8/94	80s
Tuition, 4-year private college/university, in-state	year	9310	8/94	80s
Tuition, 4-year public college/university, in-state	year	1875	8/94	80s
Energy and Fuels				
Fuel oil and other fuels, expenditures	year	56	91	81r
Gas, natural, expenditures	year	150	91	81r
Gasoline and motor oil purchased	year	1152	91	81r
Gasoline, unleaded midgrade	gallon	1.21	4/93	82r
Gasoline, unleaded premium	gallon	1.30	4/93	82r
Gasoline, unleaded regular	gallon	1.10	4/93	82r
Entertainment				
Concert ticket, Pearl Jam group	perf	20.00	94	50r
Entertainment, total expenditures	year	1266	91	81r
Fees and admissions, expenditures	year	306	91	81r
Pets, toys, playground equipment, expenditures	year	271	91	81r
Reading, expenditures	year	131	91	81r

Values are in dollars or fractions of dollars. In the column headed *Ref*, references are shown to sources. Each reference is followed by a letter. These refer to the geographical level for which data was reported: s=State, r=Region, and c=City or metro. The abbreviation *ex* is used to mean *except* or *excluding*; *exp* stands for expenditures. For other abbreviations and further explanations, please see the Introduction.

Wheeling, WV, OH - continued

Item	Per	Value	Date	Ref.
Entertainment				
Televisions, radios, and sound equipment, expenditures	year	439	91	81r
Funerals				
Burial, immediate, container provided by funeral home		1370.36	1/95	54r
Cards, acknowledgment		14.83	1/95	54r
Casket, minimum alternative		192.52	1/95	54r
Cosmetology, hair care, etc.		102.27	1/95	54r
Cremation, direct, container provided by funeral home		1065.64	1/95	54r
Embalming		304.29	1/95	54r
Funeral, funeral home		287.83	1/95	54r
Funeral, other facility		284.14	1/95	54r
Graveside service		349.13	1/95	54r
Hearse, local		132.27	1/95	54r
Limousine, local		98.45	1/95	54r
Memorial service		270.59	1/95	54r
Service charge, professional, nondeclinable		933.59	1/95	54r
Visitation and viewing		225.83	1/95	54r
Groceries				
Apples, Red Delicious	lb.	0.73	12/94	82r
Bacon, sliced	lb.	1.67	12/94	82r
Bananas	lb.	0.42	12/94	82r
Beef purchases	year	213	91	81r
Beverage purchases, alcoholic	year	249	91	81r
Beverage purchases, nonalcoholic	year	207	91	81r
Bologna, all beef or mixed	lb.	2.27	12/94	82r
Bread, white, pan	lb.	0.68	12/94	82r
Cabbage	lb.	0.42	12/94	82r
Carrots, short trimmed and topped	lb.	0.53	12/94	82r
Cereals and bakery products purchases	year	345	91	81r
Cereals and cereals products purchases	year	127	91	81r
Cheddar cheese, natural	lb.	3.58	12/94	82r
Chicken breast, bone-in	lb.	1.71	12/94	82r
Chicken, fresh, whole	lb.	0.78	12/94	82r
Chuck roast, USDA choice, boneless	lb.	2.26	12/94	82r
Crackers, soda, salted	lb.	1.27	12/94	82r
Cucumbers	lb.	0.65	12/94	82r
Dairy products (other) purchases	year	141	91	81r
Eggs, Grade A large	dozen	0.87	12/94	82r
Fish and seafood purchases	year	72	91	81r
Flour, white, all purpose	lb.	0.23	12/94	82r
Food purchases, food eaten at home	year	2381	91	81r
Foods purchased away from home, not prepared by consumer	year	1696	91	81r
Frankfurters, all meat or all beef	lb.	1.74	12/94	82r
Fruits and vegetables purchases	year	380	91	81r
Grapefruit	lb.	0.45	12/94	82r
Grapes, Thompson seedless	lb.	2.30	12/94	82r
Ground beef, 100% beef	lb.	1.37	12/94	82r
Ground chuck, 100% beef	lb.	1.97	12/94	82r
Ham, boneless, exc. canned	lb.	2.54	12/94	82r
Ice cream, prepackaged, bulk, regular	1/2 gal.	2.47	12/94	82r
Lemons	lb.	1.02	12/94	82r
Lettuce, iceberg	lb.	0.96	12/94	82r
Margarine, stick	lb.	0.77	12/94	82r
Meats, poultry, fish, and eggs purchases	year	655	91	81r
Milk and cream (fresh) purchases	year	130	91	81r
Orange juice, frozen concentrate 12-oz. can	16 oz.	1.36	12/94	82r
Oranges, Navel	lb.	0.54	12/94	82r
Pears, Anjou	lb.	0.81	12/94	82r
Pork chops, center cut, bone-in	lb.	3.07	12/94	82r
Pork purchases	year	142	91	81r
Potato chips	16-oz.	3.15	12/94	82r
Potatoes, frozen, French fried	lb.	0.82	12/94	82r
Potatoes, white	lb.	0.34	12/94	82r
Rice, white, long grain, uncooked	lb.	0.48	12/94	82r
Round roast, USDA choice, boneless	lb.	2.91	12/94	82r
Sausage, fresh	lb.	1.82	12/94	82r
Shortening, vegetable oil blends	lb.	0.75	12/94	82r

Wheeling, WV, OH - continued

Item	Per	Value	Date	Ref.
Groceries - continued				
Spaghetti and macaroni	lb.	0.87	12/94	82r
Steak, rib eye, USDA choice, boneless	lb.	6.85	12/94	82r
Steak, round, graded & ungraded, exc. USDA prime & choice	lb.	2.96	12/94	82r
Steak, round, USDA choice, boneless	lb.	3.17	12/94	82r
Steak, sirloin, USDA choice, boneless	lb.	4.12	12/94	82r
Steak, T-bone, USDA choice, bone-in	lb.	5.63	12/94	82r
Sugar and other sweets, eaten at home, expenditures	year	93	91	81r
Sugar, white, all sizes	lb.	0.39	12/94	82r
Tobacco products and smoking supplies, total expenditures	year	286	91	81r
Tomatoes, field grown	lb.	1.36	12/94	82r
Tuna, chunk, light	lb.	1.94	12/94	82r
Turkey, frozen, whole	lb.	0.96	12/94	82r
Yogurt, natural, fruit flavored	8 oz.	0.58	12/94	82r
Health Care				
Adenosine, emergency room	treat	100.00	95	23r
Bladder tap, superpubic, infant, emergency room	treat	119.00	95	23r
Blood analysis, emergency room	treat	25.00	95	23r
Blood tests, abdominal pain, emergency room	treat	25.00	95	23r
Burn dressing, emergency room	treat	266.00	95	23r
Cardiology interpretation, emergency room	treat	26.00	95	23r
Chest X-ray, emergency room	treat	78.00	95	23r
Childbirth, Cesarean delivery, hospital charge	birth	5462.00	12/91	69r
Childbirth, Cesarean delivery, physician charge	birth	2228.00	12/91	69r
Childbirth, normal delivery, hospital charge	birth	2943.00	12/91	69r
Childbirth, normal delivery, physician charge	birth	1619.00	12/91	69r
Defibrillation pads, emergency room	treat	6.00	95	23r
Drugs, expenditures	year	297	91	81r
Gastric tube insertion, nasal, emergency room	treat	25.00	95	23r
Health care, total expenditures	year	1600	91	81r
Health insurance expenditures	year	637	91	81r
Heart monitor, emergency room	treat	40.00	95	23r
Intravenous fluids, emergency room	treat	130.00	95	23r
Intravenous fluids, emergency room	liter	26.00	95	23r
Intravenous line, central, emergency room	treat	342.00	95	23r
Liver function tests, abdominal pain, emergency room	treat	26.00	95	23r
Medical care charges, total, emergency room, third-degree burns	treat	2101.00	95	23r
Medical care charges, total, emergency, infant with fever	treat	628.00	95	23r
Medical services expenditures	year	573	91	81r
Medical supplies expenditures	year	93	91	81r
Morphine, emergency room	treat	34.00	95	23r
Nursing care and facilities charges, emergency room	treat	252.00	95	23r
Nursing care and facilities charges, emergency, infant with fever	treat	252.00	95	23r
Nursing care and facilities charges, emergency, third-degree burns	treat	861.00	95	23r
Physician's charges, emergency, infant with fever	treat	212.00	95	23r
Physician's charges, emergency, third-degree burns	treat	372.00	95	23r
Physician's fee, emergency room	treat	372.00	95	23r
Physician's fee, general practitioner	visit	51.20	12/93	60r
Surgery, open-heart	proc	42374.00	1/93	14r
Ultrasound, abdominal, emergency room	treat	276.00	95	23r
Urinalysis, emergency room	treat	20.00	95	23r
Urinalysis, infant, emergency room	treat	20.00	95	23r
X-rays, emergency room	treat	78.00	95	23r
Household Goods				
Floor coverings, expenditures	year	48	91	81r
Furniture, expenditures	year	280	91	81r

Values are in dollars or fractions of dollars. In the column headed *Ref*, references are shown to sources. Each reference is followed by a letter. These refer to the geographical level for which data were reported: s=State, r=Region, and c=City or metro. The abbreviation *ex* is used to mean *except* or *excluding*; *exp* stands for expenditures. For other abbreviations and further explanations, please see the Introduction.

Wheeling, WV, OH - continued

Item	Per	Value	Date	Ref.
Household Goods				
Household equipment, misc. expenditures	year	342	91	81r
Household expenditures, miscellaneous	year	256	91	81r
Household furnishings and equipment, expenditures	year	988	91	81r
Household operations expenditures	year	468	91	81r
Household textiles, expenditures	year	95	91	81r
Housekeeping supplies, expenditures	year	380	91	81r
Laundry and cleaning supplies, expenditures	year	109	91	81r
Postage and stationery, expenditures	year	105	91	81r
Housing				
Add garage/carport		6,980	3/95	74r
Add room(s)		11,403	3/95	74r
Apartment condominium or co-op, median	unit	68600	12/94	62r
Dwellings (owned), expenditures	year	2428	91	81r
Enclose porch/patio/breezeway		4,572	3/95	74r
Finish room in basement/attic		3,794	3/95	74r
Home, existing, single-family, median	unit	120200	12/94	62r
Maintenance, repairs, insurance, and other housing expenditures	year	531	91	81r
Mortgage interest and charges expenditures	year	1506	91	81r
Princ. & int., mortgage, median-price exist. sing.-family home	mo.	540	12/94	62r
Property taxes expenditures	year	391	91	81r
Redesign, restructure more than half of home's interior		17,641	3/95	74r
Rental units expenditures	year	1264	91	81r
Insurance and Pensions				
Auto insurance, private passenger	year	696.89	12/94	71s
Insurance and pensions, personal, expenditures	year	2395	91	81r
Insurance, life and other personal, expenditures	year	368	91	81r
Pensions and Social Security, expenditures	year	2027	91	81r
Personal Services				
Personal services expenditures	year	212	91	81r
Restaurant Food				
Dining expenditures, family	week	33.83	94	73r
Taxes				
Taxes, Federal income, expenditures	year	2275	91	81r
Taxes, personal, expenditures	year	2715	91	81r
Taxes, State and local income, expenditures	year	365	91	81r
Transportation				
Cars and trucks purchased, new	year	1306	91	81r
Cars and trucks purchased, used	year	942	91	81r
Driver's learning permit fee	perm	4.00	1/94	84s
Driver's license fee	orig	10.50	1/94	84s
Driver's license fee, duplicate	lic	5.00	1/94	84s
Driver's license renewal fee	renew	10.50	1/94	84s
Identification card, nondriver	card	5.00	1/94	83s
Motorcycle learning permit fee	perm	5.00	1/94	84s
Motorcycle license fee	orig	10.00	1/94	84s
Motorcycle license fee, duplicate	lic	5.00	1/94	84s
Motorcycle license renewal fee	renew	10.00	1/94	84s
Public transportation expenditures	year	249	91	81r
Transportation expenditures, total	year	5307	91	81r
Vehicle finance charges	year	346	91	81r
Vehicle insurance expenditures	year	544	91	81r
Vehicle maintenance and repairs expenditures	year	600	91	81r
Vehicle purchases	year	2275	91	81r
Vehicle rental, leases, licenses, etc. expenditures	year	141	91	81r
Vehicles purchased, other than cars and trucks	year	27	91	81r
Utilities				
Electricity expenditures	year	950	91	81r
Electricity, summer, 250 KWh	month	27.23	8/93	64s

Wheeling, WV, OH - continued

Item	Per	Value	Date	Ref.
Utilities - continued				
Electricity, summer, 500 KWh	month	36.96	8/93	64s
Electricity, summer, 750 KWh	month	52.76	8/93	64s
Electricity, summer, 1000 KWh	month	68.52	8/93	64s
Utilities, fuels, and public services, total expenditures	year	2000	91	81r
Water and other public services, expenditures	year	227	91	81r
Weddings				
Bridal attendants' gowns	event	750	10/93	76r
Bridal gown	event	852	10/93	76r
Bridal headpiece and veil	event	167	10/93	76r
Bride's wedding band	event	708	10/93	76r
Clergy	event	224	10/93	76r
Engagement ring	event	2756	10/93	76r
Flowers	event	863	10/93	76r
Formal wear for groom	event	106	10/93	76r
Groom's attendants' formal wear	event	530	10/93	76r
Groom's wedding band	event	402	10/93	76r
Music	event	600	10/93	76r
Photography	event	1088	10/93	76r
Shoes for bride	event	50	10/93	76r
Videography	event	483	10/93	76r
Wedding invitations and announcements	event	342	10/93	76r
Wedding reception	event	7000	10/93	76r

Wichita, KS

Item	Per	Value	Date	Ref.
Composite, ACCRA index		94.80	12/94	2c
Alcoholic Beverages				
Beer, Miller Lite, Bud, 12-oz., ex deposit	6	4.15	12/94	2c
J & B Scotch	750-ml.	17.99	12/94	2c
Wine, Gallo Chablis blanc	1.5-lit	4.83	12/94	2c
Appliances				
Appliances (major), expenditures	year	131	91	81r
Average annual exp.				
Food, health care, personal goods, services	year	25935	91	81r
Charity				
Cash contributions, expenditures	year	745	91	81r
Clothing				
Apparel, men and boys, total expenditures	year	332	91	81r
Apparel, women and girls, total expenditures	year	578	91	81r
Footwear, expenditures	year	164	91	81r
Jeans, man's denim		27.85	12/94	2c
Shirt, dress, men's	shirt	27.00	1/92	44c
Shirt, man's dress shirt		29.79	12/94	2c
Undervest, boy's size 10-14, cotton	3	3.51	12/94	2c
Communications				
Long-distance telephone rate, day, addl. min., 1-10 mi.	min.	0.09	12/93	9s
Long-distance telephone rate, day, initial min., 1-10 mi.	min.	0.18	12/93	9s
Newspaper subscription, dly. and Sun. delivery	month	16.04	12/94	2c
Phone line, single, business, field visit	inst	57.40	12/93	9s
Phone line, single, business, no field visit	inst	57.40	12/93	9s
Phone line, single, residence, field visit	inst	39.00	12/93	9s
Phone line, single, residence, no field visit	inst	39.00	12/93	9s
Telephone bill, family of four	month	17.66	12/94	2c
Telephone service, expenditures	year	547	91	81r
Telephone, residential, flat rate	mo.	11.35	12/93	8c
Education				
Board, 4-year private college/university	year	2084	8/94	80s
Board, 4-year public college/university	year	1709	8/94	80s
Education, total expenditures	year	394	91	81r
Room, 4-year private college/university	year	1458	8/94	80s
Room, 4-year public college/university	year	1605	8/94	80s

Values are in dollars or fractions of dollars. In the column headed *Ref*, references are shown to sources. Each reference is followed by a letter. These refer to the geographical level for which data were reported: s = State, r = Region, and c = City or metro. The abbreviation *ex* is used to mean *except* or *excluding*; *exp* stands for *expenditures*. For other abbreviations and further explanations, please see the Introduction.

Wichita, KS - continued

Item	Per	Value	Date	Ref.
Education				
Total cost, 4-year private college/university	year	11145	8/94	80s
Total cost, 4-year public college/university	year	5236	8/94	80s
Tuition, 2-year public college/university, in-state	year	960	8/94	80s
Tuition, 4-year private college/university, in-state	year	7602	8/94	80s
Tuition, 4-year public college/university, in-state	year	1921	8/94	80s
Energy and Fuels				
Energy, combined forms, 1800 sq. ft.	mo.	101.68	12/94	2c
Energy, exc. electricity, 1800 sq. ft.	mo.	30.07	12/94	2c
Fuel oil and other fuels, expenditures	year	83	91	81r
Gas	gal.	1.13	1/92	44c
Gas, cooking, 10 therms	month	10.28	2/94	65c
Gas, cooking, 30 therms	month	19.85	2/94	65c
Gas, cooking, 50 therms	month	29.41	2/94	65c
Gas, heating, winter, 100 therms	month	53.34	2/94	65c
Gas, heating, winter, average use	month	113.53	2/94	65c
Gas, natural, expenditures	year	373	91	81r
Gas, reg unlead, taxes inc., cash, self-service	gal	0.99	12/94	2c
Gasoline and motor oil purchased	year	1000	91	81r
Gasoline, unleaded midgrade	gallon	1.15	4/93	82r
Gasoline, unleaded premium	gallon	1.23	4/93	82r
Gasoline, unleaded regular	gallon	1.07	4/93	82r
Entertainment				
Bowling, evening rate	game	2.43	12/94	2c
Entertainment, total expenditures	year	1356	91	81r
Fees and admissions, expenditures	year	347	91	81r
Monopoly game, Parker Brothers', No. 9	game	10.12	12/94	2c
Movie	adm	5.75	12/94	2c
Movie ticket, adult	ticket	6.00	1/92	44c
Pets, toys, playground equipment, expenditures	year	270	91	81r
Reading, expenditures	year	160	91	81r
Televisions, radios, and sound equipment, expenditures	year	433	91	81r
Tennis balls, yellow, Wilson or Penn, 3	can	2.20	12/94	2c
Funerals				
Burial, immediate, container provided by funeral home		1348.78	1/95	54r
Cards, acknowledgment		21.20	1/95	54r
Casket, minimum alternative		182.83	1/95	54r
Cosmetology, hair care, etc.		133.11	1/95	54r
Cremation, direct, container provided by funeral home		1101.95	1/95	54r
Embalming		314.45	1/95	54r
Funeral, funeral home		304.88	1/95	54r
Funeral, other facility		301.37	1/95	54r
Graveside service		290.59	1/95	54r
Hearse, local		137.37	1/95	54r
Limousine, local		82.84	1/95	54r
Memorial service		316.57	1/95	54r
Service charge, professional, nondeclinable		1099.00	1/95	54r
Visitation and viewing		209.25	1/95	54r
Groceries				
Groceries, ACCRA Index		88.40	12/94	2c
Apples, Red Delicious	lb.	0.68	12/94	82r
Baby food, strained vegetables, lowest price	4-4.5 oz.	0.30	12/94	2c
Bacon, sliced	lb.	1.88	12/94	82r
Bananas	lb.	0.35	12/94	2c
Bananas	lb.	0.41	12/94	82r
Beef or hamburger, ground	lb.	1.02	12/94	2c
Beef purchases	year	197	91	81r
Beef, stew, boneless	lb.	2.52	12/94	82r
Beverage purchases, alcoholic	year	293	91	81r
Beverage purchases, nonalcoholic	year	203	91	81r
Bologna, all beef or mixed	lb.	2.12	12/94	82r
Bread, white	24-oz.	0.58	12/94	2c

Wichita, KS - continued

Item	Per	Value	Date	Ref.
Groceries - continued				
Bread, white, pan	lb.	0.76	12/94	82r
Cabbage	lb.	0.44	12/94	82r
Carrots, short trimmed and topped	lb.	0.44	12/94	82r
Cereals and bakery products purchases	year	347	91	81r
Cereals and cereals products purchases	year	119	91	81r
Cheddar cheese, natural	lb.	3.28	12/94	82r
Cheese, Kraft grated Parmesan	8-oz.	3.47	12/94	2c
Chicken breast, bone-in	lb.	1.61	12/94	82r
Chicken, fresh, whole	lb.	0.89	12/94	82r
Chicken, whole fryer	lb.	0.64	12/94	2c
Chuck roast, USDA choice, boneless	lb.	2.33	12/94	82r
Cigarettes, Winston, Kings	carton	15.18	12/94	2c
Coffee, 100%, ground roast, all sizes	lb.	4.28	12/94	82r
Coffee, vacuum-packed	13 oz.	3.18	12/94	2c
Cookies, chocolate chip	lb.	2.72	12/94	82r
Corn Flakes, Kellogg's or Post Toasties	18 oz.	2.35	12/94	2c
Corn, frozen, whole kernel, lowest price	10 oz.	0.66	12/94	2c
Dairy products (other) purchases	year	148	91	81r
Eggs, Grade A large	dozen	0.58	12/94	2c
Eggs, Grade A large	dozen	0.76	12/94	82r
Fish and seafood purchases	year	61	91	81r
Flour, white, all purpose	lb.	0.22	12/94	82r
Food purchases, food eaten at home	year	2313	91	81r
Foods purchased away from home, not prepared by consumer	year	1709	91	81r
Fruits and vegetables purchases	year	372	91	81r
Grapefruit	lb.	0.47	12/94	82r
Grapes, Thompson seedless	lb.	2.15	12/94	82r
Ground beef, 100% beef	lb.	1.37	12/94	82r
Ground chuck, 100% beef	lb.	1.81	12/94	82r
Ham, boneless, exc. canned	lb.	2.16	12/94	82r
Ice cream, prepackaged, bulk, regular	1/2 gal.	2.48	12/94	82r
Lemons	lb.	1.08	12/94	82r
Lettuce, iceberg	lb.	0.81	12/94	82r
Lettuce, iceberg	head	0.79	12/94	2c
Margarine, Blue Bonnet or Parkay cubes	lb.	0.53	12/94	2c
Margarine, stick	lb.	0.81	12/94	82r
Meats, poultry, fish, and eggs purchases	year	591	91	81r
Milk and cream (fresh) purchases	year	132	91	81r
Milk, 2%	gal.	1.70	1/92	44c
Milk, whole	1/2 gal.	1.33	12/94	2c
Orange juice, frozen concentrate 12-oz. can	16 oz.	1.41	12/94	82r
Orange juice, Minute Maid frozen	12-oz.	1.32	12/94	2c
Oranges, Navel	lb.	0.56	12/94	82r
Peaches, halves or slices, Hunt's, Del Monte, or Libby's	29-oz.	1.32	12/94	2c
Peanut butter, creamy, all sizes	lb.	1.81	12/94	82r
Peas, sweet, Del Monte or Green Giant	15-17 oz.	0.48	12/94	2c
Pork chops, center cut, bone-in	lb.	2.76	12/94	82r
Pork purchases	year	130	91	81r
Potato chips	16-oz.	2.81	12/94	82r
Potatoes, frozen, French fried	lb.	0.83	12/94	82r
Potatoes, white	lb.	0.28	12/94	82r
Potatoes, white or red	10-lb. sack	1.57	12/94	2c
Rental rate, 2-bedroom apartment	month	380.00	1/92	44c
Round roast, USDA choice, boneless	lb.	2.90	12/94	82r
Sausage, Jimmy Dean, 100% pork	lb.	2.80	12/94	2c
Shortening, vegetable oil blends	lb.	0.88	12/94	82r
Shortening, vegetable, Crisco	3-lb.	2.16	12/94	2c
Soft drink, Coca Cola, ex deposit	2 lit	1.03	12/94	2c
Spaghetti and macaroni	lb.	0.78	12/94	82r
Steak, rib eye, USDA choice, boneless	lb.	6.15	12/94	82r
Steak, round, graded & ungraded, exc. USDA prime & choice	lb.	2.72	12/94	82r
Steak, round, USDA choice, boneless	lb.	3.02	12/94	82r
Steak, sirloin, USDA choice, boneless	lb.	3.85	12/94	82r
Steak, t-bone	lb.	4.73	12/94	2c
Steak, T-bone, USDA choice, bone-in	lb.	5.38	12/94	82r

Values are in dollars or fractions of dollars. In the column headed *Ref*, references are shown to sources. Each reference is followed by a letter. These refer to the geographical level for which data were reported: s = State, r = Region, and c = City or metro. The abbreviation *ex* is used to mean *except* or *excluding*; *exp* stands for expenditures. For other abbreviations and further explanations, please see the Introduction.

Wichita, KS - continued

Item	Per	Value	Date	Ref.
Groceries				
Sugar and other sweets, eaten at home, expenditures	year	91	91	81r
Sugar, cane or beet	4 lbs.	1.14	12/94	2c
Sugar, white, all sizes	lb.	0.36	12/94	82r
Tobacco products and smoking supplies, total expenditures	year	298	91	81r
Tomatoes, field grown	lb.	1.36	12/94	82r
Tomatoes, Hunt's or Del Monte	14.5 oz.	0.67	12/94	2c
Tuna, chunk, light	lb.	1.94	12/94	82r
Tuna, chunk, light, oil-packed	6.125-6.5 oz.	0.53	12/94	2c
Turkey, frozen, whole	lb.	0.96	12/94	82r
Yogurt, natural, fruit flavored	8 oz.	0.62	12/94	82r
Goods and Services				
Miscellaneous goods and services, ACCRA Index		97.40	12/94	2c
Health Care				
Health care, ACCRA Index		107.40	12/94	2c
Antibiotic ointment, Polysporin	1.5 oz.	4.00	12/94	2c
Childbirth, Cesarean delivery, hospital charge	birth	5101.00	12/91	69r
Childbirth, Cesarean delivery, physician charge	birth	2234.00	12/91	69r
Childbirth, normal delivery, hospital charge	birth	2891.00	12/91	69r
Childbirth, normal delivery, physician charge	birth	1623.00	12/91	69r
Dentist's fee, adult teeth cleaning and periodic oral exam	visit	55.50	12/94	2c
Doctor's fee, routine exam, established patient	visit	42.65	12/94	2c
Drugs, expenditures	year	248	91	81r
Health care, total expenditures	year	1336	91	81r
Health insurance expenditures	year	550	91	81r
Hospital care, semiprivate room	day	456.25	12/94	2c
Insurance premium, family medical care	month	370.49	1/95	41s
Medical services expenditures	year	457	91	81r
Medical supplies expenditures	year	82	91	81r
Household Goods				
Appl. repair, service call, wash mach	min. lab. chg.	33.54	12/94	2c
Floor coverings, expenditures	year	105	91	81r
Furniture, expenditures	year	291	91	81r
Household equipment, misc. expenditures	year	341	91	81r
Household expenditures, miscellaneous	year	162	91	81r
Household furnishings and equipment, expenditures	year	1042	91	81r
Household operations expenditures	year	365	91	81r
Household textiles, expenditures	year	101	91	81r
Housekeeping supplies, expenditures	year	390	91	81r
Laundry and cleaning supplies, expenditures	year	110	91	81r
Laundry detergent, Tide Ultra, Bold, or Cheer	42 oz.	2.94	12/94	2c
Postage and stationery, expenditures	year	115	91	81r
Tissues, facial, Kleenex brand	175	0.89	12/94	2c
Housing				
Housing, ACCRA Index		94.30	12/94	2c
Add garage/carport		8,479	3/95	74r
Add room(s)		21,347	3/95	74r
Apartment condominium or co-op, median	unit	87100	12/94	62r
Bathroom addition, average cost	add	9734.00	3/95	13r
Bathroom remodeling, average cost	remod	6414.00	3/95	13r
Bedroom, master suite addition, average cost	add	27122.00	3/95	13r
Deck addition, average cost	add	6665.00	3/95	13r
Dwellings (owned), expenditures	year	2566	91	81r
Enclose porch/patio/breezeway		4,556	3/95	74r
Exterior remodeling, average cost	remod	15395.00	3/95	13r
Family room addition, average cost	add	27658.00	3/95	13r

Wichita, KS - continued

Item	Per	Value	Date	Ref.
Housing - continued				
Finish room in basement/attic		5,074	3/95	74r
Home, existing, single-family, median	unit	106500	12/94	62r
Home, existing, single-family, median	unit	72.50	12/94	62c
House payment, principal and interest, 25% down payment	mo.	738	12/94	2c
House, 1800 sq ft, 8000 sq ft lot, new, urban, utilities	total	119858	12/94	2c
Kitchen remodeling, major, average cost	remod	17084.00	3/95	13r
Kitchen remodeling, minor, average cost	remod	5804.00	3/95	13r
Maintenance, repairs, insurance, and other housing expenditures	year	484	91	81r
Mortgage interest and charges expenditures	year	1443	91	81r
Mtge. rate, incl. points and orig. fee, 30-year conv. fixed or ARM	mo.	9.22	12/94	2c
Office, home addition, average cost	add	8121.00	3/95	13r
Princ. & int., mortgage, median-price exist. sing.-family home	mo.	515	12/94	62r
Property taxes expenditures	year	639	91	81r
Redesign, restructure more than half of home's interior		9,114	3/95	74r
Rent, apartment, 2 br., 1 1/2-2 baths, unfurnished, 950 sq ft, water	mo.	455	12/94	2c
Rental units expenditures	year	1200	91	81r
Sun-space addition, average cost	add	23768.00	3/95	13r
Wing addition, two-story, average cost	add	50410.00	3/95	13r
Insurance and Pensions				
Auto insurance, private passenger	year	526.96	12/94	71s
Insurance and pensions, personal, expenditures	year	2408	91	81r
Insurance, life and other personal, expenditures	year	355	91	81r
Pensions and Social Security, expenditures	year	2053	91	81r
Legal Assistance				
Legal work, law firm associate	hour	90		10r
Legal work, law firm partner	hour	139		10r
Personal Goods				
Shampoo, Alberto VO5	15-oz.	1.08	12/94	2c
Toothpaste, Crest or Colgate	6-7 oz.	1.60	12/94	2c
Personal Services				
Dry cleaning, man's 2-pc. suit		6.54	12/94	2c
Dry cleaning, woman's dress	dress	7.00	1/92	44c
Haircut, man's barbershop, no styling		9.69	12/94	2c
Haircut, woman's shampoo, trim, blow-dry		20.12	12/94	2c
Personal services expenditures	year	203	91	81r
Restaurant Food				
Big Mac, small fries, medium drink	meal	3.50	1/92	44c
Chicken, fried, thigh and drumstick		1.94	12/94	2c
Dining expenditures, family	week	30.03	94	73r
Hamburger with cheese	1/4 lb.	1.83	12/94	2c
Pizza, Pizza Hut or Pizza Inn	12-13 in.	7.99	12/94	2c
Taxes				
Tax rate, residential property, month	$100	1.76	1/92	79c
Taxes, Federal income, expenditures	year	1756	91	81r
Taxes, personal, expenditures	year	2426	91	81r
Taxes, State and local income, expenditures	year	568	91	81r
Transportation				
Transportation, ACCRA Index		93.10	12/94	2c
Bus fare, up to 10 miles	one-way	0.85	12/94	2c
Cars and trucks purchased, new	year	891	91	81r
Cars and trucks purchased, used	year	1155	91	81r
Driver's learning permit fee	perm	3.00	1/94	84s
Driver's license fee	orig	12.00	1/94	84s
Driver's license fee, duplicate	lic	5.00	1/94	84s
Driver's license reinstatement fee, min.	susp	25.00	1/94	85s
Driver's license renewal fee	renew	9.00	1/94	84s
Identification card, nondriver	card	6.00	1/94	83s

Values are in dollars or fractions of dollars. In the column headed *Ref*, references are shown to sources. Each reference is followed by a letter. These refer to the geographical level for which data were reported: s=State, r=Region, and c=City or metro. The abbreviation *ex* is used to mean *except* or *excluding*; *exp* stands for expenditures. For other abbreviations and further explanations, please see the Introduction.

Wichita, KS - continued

Item	Per	Value	Date	Ref.
Transportation				
Motorcycle license fee	orig	9.00	1/94	84s
Motorcycle license fee, duplicate	lic	5.00	1/94	84s
Motorcycle license renewal fee	renew	6.00	1/94	84s
parking, long-term lot, airport	3 days	15.00	1/92	44c
Public transportation expenditures	year	209	91	81r
Tire balance, computer or spin bal., front	wheel	6.80	12/94	2c
Transportation expenditures, total	year	4792	91	81r
Vehicle finance charges	year	300	91	81r
Vehicle insurance expenditures	year	485	91	81r
Vehicle maintenance and repairs expenditures	year	534	91	81r
Vehicle purchases	year	2068	91	81r
Vehicle rental, leases, licenses, etc. expenditures	year	197	91	81r
Vehicles purchased, other than cars and trucks	year	22	91	81r
Utilities				
Utilities, ACCRA Index		90.60	12/94	2c
Electricity expenditures	year	668	91	81r
Electricity, (part.), other, 1800 sq. ft., new home	mo.	71.61	12/94	2c
Electricity, summer, 250 KWh	month	31.17	8/93	64c
Electricity, summer, 500 KWh	month	53.56	8/93	64c
Electricity, summer, 750 KWh	month	79.80	8/93	64c
Electricity, summer, 1000 KWh	month	106.42	8/93	64c
Utilities, fuels, and public services, total expenditures	year	1838	91	81r
Water and other public services, expenditures	year	167	91	81r
Weddings				
Bridal attendants' gowns	event	750	10/93	76r
Bridal gown	event	852	10/93	76r
Bridal headpiece and veil	event	167	10/93	76r
Bride's wedding band	event	708	10/93	76r
Clergy	event	224	10/93	76r
Engagement ring	event	2756	10/93	76r
Flowers	event	863	10/93	76r
Formal wear for groom	event	106	10/93	76r
Groom's attendants' formal wear	event	530	10/93	76r
Groom's wedding band	event	402	10/93	76r
Music	event	600	10/93	76r
Photography	event	1088	10/93	76r
Shoes for bride	event	50	10/93	76r
Videography	event	483	10/93	76r
Wedding invitations and announcements	event	342	10/93	76r
Wedding reception	event	7000	10/93	76r

Wichita Falls, TX

Item	Per	Value	Date	Ref.
Composite, ACCRA index		92.90	12/94	2c
Alcoholic Beverages				
Beer, Miller Lite, Bud, 12-oz., ex deposit	6	3.80	12/94	2c
J & B Scotch	750-ml.	18.22	12/94	2c
Wine, Gallo Chablis blanc	1.5-lit	4.78	12/94	2c
Appliances				
Appliances (major), expenditures	year	153	91	81r
Average annual exp.				
Food, health care, personal goods, services	year	27020	91	81r
Charity				
Cash contributions, expenditures	year	839	91	81r
Clothing				
Apparel, men and boys, total expenditures	year	380	91	81r
Apparel, women and girls, total expenditures	year	660	91	81r
Footwear, expenditures	year	193	91	81r
Jeans, man's denim		28.59	12/94	2c
Shirt, man's dress shirt		29.30	12/94	2c
Undervest, boy's size 10-14, cotton	3	4.78	12/94	2c

Wichita Falls, TX - continued

Item	Per	Value	Date	Ref.
Communications				
Long-distance telephone rate, day, addl. min., 1-10 mi.	min.	0.08	12/93	9s
Long-distance telephone rate, day, initial min., 1-10 mi.	min.	0.10	12/93	9s
Newspaper subscription, dly. and Sun. delivery	month	11.50	12/94	2c
Phone line, single, business, field visit	inst	71.90	12/93	9s
Phone line, single, business, no field visit	inst	57.30	12/93	9s
Phone line, single, residence, field visit	inst	52.95	12/93	9s
Phone line, single, residence, no field visit	inst	38.35	12/93	9s
Telephone bill, family of four	month	15.34	12/94	2c
Telephone service, expenditures	year	616	91	81r
Telephone, residential, flat rate	mo.	9.10	12/93	8c
Education				
Board, 4-year private college/university	year	2084	8/94	80s
Board, 4-year public college/university	year	1675	8/94	80s
Education, total expenditures	year	319	91	81r
Room, 4-year private college/university	year	1840	8/94	80s
Room, 4-year public college/university	year	1756	8/94	80s
Total cost, 4-year private college/university	year	11876	8/94	80s
Total cost, 4-year public college/university	year	4935	8/94	80s
Tuition, 2-year public college/university, in-state	year	625	8/94	80s
Tuition, 4-year private college/university, in-state	year	7952	8/94	80s
Tuition, 4-year public college/university, in-state	year	1503	8/94	80s
Energy and Fuels				
Energy, combined forms, 1800 sq. ft.	mo.	141.93	12/94	2c
Energy, exc. electricity, 1800 sq. ft.	mo.	44.06	12/94	2c
Fuel oil and other fuels, expenditures	year	56	91	81r
Gas, natural, expenditures	year	150	91	81r
Gas, reg unlead, taxes inc., cash, self-service	gal	1.08	12/94	2c
Gasoline and motor oil purchased	year	1152	91	81r
Gasoline, unleaded midgrade	gallon	1.21	4/93	82r
Gasoline, unleaded premium	gallon	1.30	4/93	82r
Gasoline, unleaded regular	gallon	1.10	4/93	82r
Entertainment				
Bowling, evening rate	game	2.10	12/94	2c
Concert ticket, Pearl Jam group	perf	20.00	94	50r
Entertainment, total expenditures	year	1266	91	81r
Fees and admissions, expenditures	year	306	91	81r
Monopoly game, Parker Brothers', No. 9	game	11.90	12/94	2c
Movie	adm	5.25	12/94	2c
Pets, toys, playground equipment, expenditures	year	271	91	81r
Reading, expenditures	year	131	91	81r
Televisions, radios, and sound equipment, expenditures	year	439	91	81r
Tennis balls, yellow, Wilson or Penn, 3	can	2.36	12/94	2c
Funerals				
Burial, immediate, container provided by funeral home		1574.60	1/95	54r
Cards, acknowledgment		22.24	1/95	54r
Casket, minimum alternative		239.41	1/95	54r
Cosmetology, hair care, etc.		91.04	1/95	54r
Cremation, direct, container provided by funeral home		1085.15	1/95	54r
Embalming		281.30	1/95	54r
Funeral, funeral home		323.04	1/95	54r
Funeral, other facility		327.58	1/95	54r
Graveside service		355.19	1/95	54r
Hearse, local		141.89	1/95	54r
Limousine, local		99.40	1/95	54r
Memorial service		284.67	1/95	54r
Service charge, professional, nondeclinable		904.06	1/95	54r
Visitation and viewing		187.04	1/95	54r

Values are in dollars or fractions of dollars. In the column headed *Ref*, references are shown to sources. Each reference is followed by a letter. These refer to the geographical level for which data were reported: s = State, r = Region, and c = City or metro. The abbreviation *ex* is used to mean *except* or *excluding*; *exp* stands for expenditures. For other abbreviations and further explanations, please see the Introduction.

Wichita Falls, TX - continued

Item	Per	Value	Date	Ref.
Groceries				
Groceries, ACCRA Index		95.10	12/94	2c
Apples, Red Delicious	lb.	0.73	12/94	82r
Baby food, strained vegetables, lowest price	4-4.5 oz.	0.29	12/94	2c
Bacon, sliced	lb.	1.67	12/94	82r
Bananas	lb.	0.39	12/94	2c
Bananas	lb.	0.42	12/94	82r
Beef or hamburger, ground	lb.	1.25	12/94	2c
Beef purchases	year	213	91	81r
Beverage purchases, alcoholic	year	249	91	81r
Beverage purchases, nonalcoholic	year	207	91	81r
Bologna, all beef or mixed	lb.	2.27	12/94	82r
Bread, white	24-oz.	0.55	12/94	2c
Bread, white, pan	lb.	0.68	12/94	82r
Cabbage	lb.	0.42	12/94	82r
Carrots, short trimmed and topped	lb.	0.53	12/94	82r
Cereals and bakery products purchases	year	345	91	81r
Cereals and cereals products purchases	year	127	91	81r
Cheddar cheese, natural	lb.	3.58	12/94	82r
Cheese, Kraft grated Parmesan	8-oz.	3.67	12/94	2c
Chicken breast, bone-in	lb.	1.71	12/94	82r
Chicken, fresh, whole	lb.	0.78	12/94	82r
Chicken, whole fryer	lb.	0.79	12/94	2c
Chuck roast, USDA choice, boneless	lb.	2.26	12/94	82r
Cigarettes, Winston, Kings	carton	14.98	12/94	2c
Coffee, vacuum-packed	13 oz.	3.38	12/94	2c
Corn Flakes, Kellogg's or Post Toasties	18 oz.	2.43	12/94	2c
Corn, frozen, whole kernel, lowest price	10 oz.	0.80	12/94	2c
Crackers, soda, salted	lb.	1.27	12/94	82r
Cucumbers	lb.	0.65	12/94	82r
Dairy products (other) purchases	year	141	91	81r
Eggs, Grade A large	dozen	0.75	12/94	2c
Eggs, Grade A large	dozen	0.87	12/94	82r
Fish and seafood purchases	year	72	91	81r
Flour, white, all purpose	lb.	0.23	12/94	82r
Food purchases, food eaten at home	year	2381	91	81r
Foods purchased away from home, not prepared by consumer	year	1696	91	81r
Frankfurters, all meat or all beef	lb.	1.74	12/94	82r
Fruits and vegetables purchases	year	380	91	81r
Grapefruit	lb.	0.45	12/94	82r
Grapes, Thompson seedless	lb.	2.30	12/94	82r
Ground beef, 100% beef	lb.	1.37	12/94	82r
Ground chuck, 100% beef	lb.	1.97	12/94	82r
Ham, boneless, exc. canned	lb.	2.54	12/94	82r
Ice cream, prepackaged, bulk, regular	1/2 gal.	2.47	12/94	82r
Lemons	lb.	1.02	12/94	82r
Lettuce, iceberg	lb.	0.96	12/94	82r
Lettuce, iceberg	head	0.84	12/94	2c
Margarine, Blue Bonnet or Parkay cubes	lb.	0.64	12/94	2c
Margarine, stick	lb.	0.77	12/94	82r
Meats, poultry, fish, and eggs purchases	year	655	91	81r
Milk and cream (fresh) purchases	year	130	91	81r
Milk, whole	1/2 gal.	1.42	12/94	2c
Orange juice, frozen concentrate 12-oz. can	16 oz.	1.36	12/94	82r
Orange juice, Minute Maid frozen	12-oz.	1.16	12/94	2c
Oranges, Navel	lb.	0.54	12/94	82r
Peaches, halves or slices, Hunt's, Del Monte, or Libby's	29-oz.	1.38	12/94	2c
Pears, Anjou	lb.	0.81	12/94	82r
Peas, sweet, Del Monte or Green Giant	15-17 oz.	0.56	12/94	2c
Pork chops, center cut, bone-in	lb.	3.07	12/94	82r
Pork purchases	year	142	91	81r
Potato chips	16-oz.	3.15	12/94	82r
Potatoes, frozen, French fried	lb.	0.82	12/94	82r
Potatoes, white	lb.	0.34	12/94	82r
Potatoes, white or red	10-lb. sack	1.90	12/94	2c
Rice, white, long grain, uncooked	lb.	0.48	12/94	82r

Wichita Falls, TX - continued

Item	Per	Value	Date	Ref.
Groceries - continued				
Round roast, USDA choice, boneless	lb.	2.91	12/94	82r
Sausage, fresh	lb.	1.82	12/94	82r
Sausage, Jimmy Dean, 100% pork	lb.	2.49	12/94	2c
Shortening, vegetable oil blends	lb.	0.75	12/94	82r
Shortening, vegetable, Crisco	3-lb.	2.26	12/94	2c
Soft drink, Coca Cola, ex deposit	2 lit	1.43	12/94	2c
Spaghetti and macaroni	lb.	0.87	12/94	82r
Steak, rib eye, USDA choice, boneless	lb.	6.85	12/94	82r
Steak, round, graded & ungraded, exc. USDA prime & choice	lb.	2.96	12/94	82r
Steak, round, USDA choice, boneless	lb.	3.17	12/94	82r
Steak, sirloin, USDA choice, boneless	lb.	4.12	12/94	82r
Steak, t-bone	lb.	4.77	12/94	2c
Steak, T-bone, USDA choice, bone-in	lb.	5.63	12/94	82r
Sugar and other sweets, eaten at home, expenditures	year	93	91	81r
Sugar, cane or beet	4 lbs.	1.42	12/94	2c
Sugar, white, all sizes	lb.	0.39	12/94	82r
Tobacco products and smoking supplies, total expenditures	year	286	91	81r
Tomatoes, field grown	lb.	1.36	12/94	82r
Tomatoes, Hunt's or Del Monte	14.5 oz.	0.74	12/94	2c
Tuna, chunk, light	lb.	1.94	12/94	82r
Tuna, chunk, light, oil-packed	6.125-6.5 oz.	0.69	12/94	2c
Turkey, frozen, whole	lb.	0.96	12/94	82r
Yogurt, natural, fruit flavored	8 oz.	0.58	12/94	82r
Goods and Services				
Miscellaneous goods and services, ACCRA Index		97.60	12/94	2c
Health Care				
Health care, ACCRA Index		88.30	12/94	2c
Adenosine, emergency room	treat	100.00	95	23r
Antibiotic ointment, Polysporin	1.5 oz.	3.79	12/94	2c
Bladder tap, superpubic, infant, emergency room	treat	119.00	95	23r
Blood analysis, emergency room	treat	25.00	95	23r
Blood tests, abdominal pain, emergency room	treat	25.00	95	23r
Burn dressing, emergency room	treat	266.00	95	23r
Cardiology interpretation, emergency room	treat	26.00	95	23r
Chest X-ray, emergency room	treat	78.00	95	23r
Childbirth, Cesarean delivery, hospital charge	birth	5462.00	12/91	69r
Childbirth, Cesarean delivery, physician charge	birth	2228.00	12/91	69r
Childbirth, normal delivery, hospital charge	birth	2943.00	12/91	69r
Childbirth, normal delivery, physician charge	birth	1619.00	12/91	69r
Defibrillation pads, emergency room	treat	6.00	95	23r
Dentist's fee, adult teeth cleaning and periodic oral exam	visit	40.67	12/94	2c
Doctor's fee, routine exam, established patient	visit	40.50	12/94	2c
Drugs, expenditures	year	297	91	81r
Gastric tube insertion, nasal, emergency room	treat	25.00	95	23r
Health care, total expenditures	year	1600	91	81r
Health insurance expenditures	year	637	91	81r
Heart monitor, emergency room	treat	40.00	95	23r
Hospital care, semiprivate room	day	322.00	12/94	2c
Insurance premium, family medical care	month	389.25	1/95	41s
Intravenous fluids, emergency room	treat	130.00	95	23r
Intravenous fluids, emergency room	liter	26.00	95	23r
Intravenous line, central, emergency room	treat	342.00	95	23r
Liver function tests, abdominal pain, emergency room	treat	26.00	95	23r
Medical care charges, total, emergency room, third-degree burns	treat	2101.00	95	23r
Medical care charges, total, emergency, infant with fever	treat	628.00	95	23r

Values are in dollars or fractions of dollars. In the column headed *Ref*, references are shown to sources. Each reference is followed by a letter. These refer to the geographical level for which data were reported: s=State, r=Region, and c=City or metro. The abbreviation *ex* is used to mean *except* or *excluding*; *exp* stands for expenditures. For other abbreviations and further explanations, please see the Introduction.

Wichita Falls, TX - continued

Item	Per	Value	Date	Ref.
Health Care				
Medical services expenditures	year	573	91	81r
Medical supplies expenditures	year	93	91	81r
Morphine, emergency room	treat	34.00	95	23r
Nursing care and facilities charges, emergency room	treat	252.00	95	23r
Nursing care and facilities charges, emergency, infant with fever	treat	252.00	95	23r
Nursing care and facilities charges, emergency, third-degree burns	treat	861.00	95	23r
Physician's charges, emergency, infant with fever	treat	212.00	95	23r
Physician's charges, emergency, third-degree burns	treat	372.00	95	23r
Physician's fee, emergency room	treat	372.00	95	23r
Physician's fee, general practitioner	visit	51.20	12/93	60r
Surgery, open-heart	proc	42374.00	1/93	14r
Ultrasound, abdominal, emergency room	treat	276.00	95	23r
Urinalysis, emergency room	treat	20.00	95	23r
Urinalysis, infant, emergency room	treat	20.00	95	23r
X-rays, emergency room	treat	78.00	95	23r
Household Goods				
Appl. repair, service call, wash mach	min. lab. chg.	34.50	12/94	2c
Floor coverings, expenditures	year	48	91	81r
Furniture, expenditures	year	280	91	81r
Household equipment, misc. expenditures	year	342	91	81r
Household expenditures, miscellaneous	year	256	91	81r
Household furnishings and equipment, expenditures	year	988	91	81r
Household operations expenditures	year	468	91	81r
Household textiles, expenditures	year	95	91	81r
Housekeeping supplies, expenditures	year	380	91	81r
Laundry and cleaning supplies, expenditures	year	109	91	81r
Laundry detergent, Tide Ultra, Bold, or Cheer	42 oz.	3.69	12/94	2c
Postage and stationery, expenditures	year	105	91	81r
Tissues, facial, Kleenex brand	175	1.02	12/94	2c
Housing				
Housing, ACCRA Index		79.70	12/94	2c
Add garage/carport		6,980	3/95	74r
Add room(s)		11,403	3/95	74r
Apartment condominium or co-op, median	unit	68600	12/94	62r
Dwellings (owned), expenditures	year	2428	91	81r
Enclose porch/patio/breezeway		4,572	3/95	74r
Finish room in basement/attic		3,794	3/95	74r
Home, existing, single-family, median	unit	120200	12/94	62r
House payment, principal and interest, 25% down payment	mo.	611	12/94	2c
House, 1800 sq ft, 8000 sq ft lot, new, urban, utilities	total	98946	12/94	2c
Maintenance, repairs, insurance, and other housing expenditures	year	531	91	81r
Mortgage interest and charges expenditures	year	1506	91	81r
Mtge. rate, incl. points and orig. fee, 30-year conv. fixed or ARM	mo.	9.26	12/94	2c
Princ. & int., mortgage, median-price exist. sing.-family home	mo.	540	12/94	62r
Property taxes expenditures	year	391	91	81r
Redesign, restructure more than half of home's interior		17,641	3/95	74r
Rent, apartment, 2 br., 1 1/2-2 baths, unfurnished, 950 sq ft, water	mo.	419	12/94	2c
Rental units expenditures	year	1264	91	81r
Insurance and Pensions				
Auto insurance, private passenger	year	785.78	12/94	71s
Insurance and pensions, personal, expenditures	year	2395	91	81r
Insurance, life and other personal, expenditures	year	368	91	81r

Wichita Falls, TX - continued

Item	Per	Value	Date	Ref.
Insurance and Pensions - continued				
Pensions and Social Security, expenditures	year	2027	91	81r
Personal Goods				
Shampoo, Alberto VO5	15-oz.	0.98	12/94	2c
Toothpaste, Crest or Colgate	6-7 oz.	1.76	12/94	2c
Personal Services				
Dry cleaning, man's 2-pc. suit		5.52	12/94	2c
Haircut, man's barbershop, no styling		5.67	12/94	2c
Haircut, woman's shampoo, trim, blow-dry		16.40	12/94	2c
Personal services expenditures	year	212	91	81r
Restaurant Food				
Chicken, fried, thigh and drumstick		2.16	12/94	2c
Dining expenditures, family	week	33.83	94	73r
Hamburger with cheese	1/4 lb.	1.75	12/94	2c
Pizza, Pizza Hut or Pizza Inn	12-13 in.	8.70	12/94	2c
Taxes				
Tax, cigarettes	year	584.00	10/93	43s
Taxes, Federal income, expenditures	year	2275	91	81r
Taxes, personal, expenditures	year	2715	91	81r
Taxes, State and local income, expenditures	year	365	91	81r
Transportation				
Transportation, ACCRA Index		91.40	12/94	2c
Bus fare, up to 10 miles	one-way	0.75	12/94	2c
Cars and trucks purchased, new	year	1306	91	81r
Cars and trucks purchased, used	year	942	91	81r
Driver's learning permit fee	perm	5.00	1/94	84s
Driver's license fee	orig	16.00	1/94	84s
Driver's license fee, duplicate	lic	10.00	1/94	84s
Driver's license reinstatement fee, min.	susp	50.00	1/94	85s
Driver's license renewal fee	renew	16.00	1/94	84s
Identification card, nondriver	card	10.00	1/94	83s
Motorcycle learning permit fee	perm	5.00	1/94	84s
Motorcycle license fee	orig	16.00	1/94	84s
Motorcycle license fee, duplicate	lic	10.00	1/94	84s
Motorcycle license renewal fee	renew	21.00	1/94	84s
Public transportation expenditures	year	249	91	81r
Tire balance, computer or spin bal., front	wheel	6.00	12/94	2c
Transportation expenditures, total	year	5307	91	81r
Vehicle finance charges	year	346	91	81r
Vehicle insurance expenditures	year	544	91	81r
Vehicle maintenance and repairs expenditures	year	600	91	81r
Vehicle purchases	year	2275	91	81r
Vehicle rental, leases, licenses, etc. expenditures	year	141	91	81r
Vehicles purchased, other than cars and trucks	year	27	91	81r
Utilities				
Utilities, ACCRA Index		120.00	12/94	2c
Electricity expenditures	year	950	91	81r
Electricity, (part.), other, 1800 sq. ft., new home	mo.	97.87	12/94	2c
Utilities, fuels, and public services, total expenditures	year	2000	91	81r
Water and other public services, expenditures	year	227	91	81r
Weddings				
Bridal attendants' gowns	event	750	10/93	76r
Bridal gown	event	852	10/93	76r
Bridal headpiece and veil	event	167	10/93	76r
Bride's wedding band	event	708	10/93	76r
Clergy	event	224	10/93	76r
Engagement ring	event	2756	10/93	76r
Flowers	event	863	10/93	76r
Formal wear for groom	event	106	10/93	76r
Groom's attendants' formal wear	event	530	10/93	76r
Groom's wedding band	event	402	10/93	76r

Values are in dollars or fractions of dollars. In the column headed *Ref*, references are shown to sources. Each reference is followed by a letter. These refer to the geographical level for which data were reported: s = State, r = Region, and c = City or metro. The abbreviation *ex* is used to mean *except* or *excluding*; *exp* stands for expenditures. For other abbreviations and further explanations, please see the Introduction.

Wichita Falls, TX - continued

Item	Per	Value	Date	Ref.
Weddings				
Music	event	600	10/93	76r
Photography	event	1088	10/93	76r
Shoes for bride	event	50	10/93	76r
Videography	event	483	10/93	76r
Wedding invitations and announcements	event	342	10/93	76r
Wedding reception	event	7000	10/93	76r

Wilkes-Barre, PA

Item	Per	Value	Date	Ref.
Composite, ACCRA index		97.70	12/94	2c
Alcoholic Beverages				
Beer, Miller Lite, Bud, 12-oz., ex deposit	6	5.45	12/94	2c
J & B Scotch	750-ml.	16.99	12/94	2c
Wine, Gallo Chablis blanc	1.5-lit	5.99	12/94	2c
Appliances				
Appliances (major), expenditures	year	145	91	81r
Average annual exp.				
Food, health care, personal goods, services	year	29496	91	81r
Charity				
Cash contributions, expenditures	year	708	91	81r
Clothing				
Apparel, men and boys, total expenditures	year	416	91	81r
Apparel, women and girls, total expenditures	year	744	91	81r
Footwear, expenditures	year	305	91	81r
Jeans, man's denim		32.07	12/94	2c
Shirt, man's dress shirt		25.38	12/94	2c
Undervest, boy's size 10-14, cotton	3	3.34	12/94	2c
Communications				
Long-distance telephone rate, day, addl. min., 1-10 mi.	min.	0.08	12/93	9s
Long-distance telephone rate, day, initial min., 1-10 mi.	min.	0.15	12/93	9s
Newspaper subscription, dly. and Sun. delivery	month	9.35	12/94	2c
Phone line, single, business, field visit	inst	75.00	12/93	9s
Phone line, single, business, no field visit	inst	75.00	12/93	9s
Phone line, single, residence, field visit	inst	40.00	12/93	9s
Phone line, single, residence, no field visit	inst	40.00	12/93	9s
Telephone bill, family of four	month	15.03	12/94	2c
Telephone service, expenditures	year	589	91	81r
Telephone, residential, flat rate	mo.	21.00	12/93	8c
Education				
Board, 4-year private college/university	year	2714	8/94	80s
Board, 4-year public college/university	year	1899	8/94	80s
Education, total expenditures	year	593	91	81r
Room, 4-year private college/university	year	2720	8/94	80s
Room, 4-year public college/university	year	2063	8/94	80s
Total cost, 4-year private college/university	year	18118	8/94	80s
Total cost, 4-year public college/university	year	8278	8/94	80s
Tuition, 2-year public college/university, in-state	year	1671	8/94	80s
Tuition, 4-year private college/university, in-state	year	12684	8/94	80s
Tuition, 4-year public college/university, in-state	year	4316	8/94	80s
Energy and Fuels				
Energy, combined forms, 1800 sq. ft.	mo.	112.04	12/94	2c
Energy, exc. electricity, 1800 sq. ft.	mo.	59.54	12/94	2c
Fuel oil and other fuels, expenditures	year	257	91	81r
Gas, natural, expenditures	year	285	91	81r
Gas, reg unlead, taxes inc., cash, self-service	gal	1.14	12/94	2c
Gasoline and motor oil purchased	year	867	91	81r
Gasoline, unleaded midgrade	gallon	1.32	4/93	82r
Gasoline, unleaded premium	gallon	1.40	4/93	82r
Gasoline, unleaded regular	gallon	1.19	4/93	82r

Wilkes-Barre, PA - continued

Item	Per	Value	Date	Ref.
Entertainment				
Bowling, evening rate	game	2.01	12/94	2c
Entertainment, total expenditures	year	1331	91	81r
Fees and admissions, expenditures	year	398	91	81r
Monopoly game, Parker Brothers', No. 9	game	11.33	12/94	2c
Movie	adm	5.87	12/94	2c
Pets, toys, playground equipment, expenditures	year	270	91	81r
Reading, expenditures	year	171	91	81r
Televisions, radios, and sound equipment, expenditures	year	429	91	81r
Tennis balls, yellow, Wilson or Penn, 3	can	2.16	12/94	2c
Funerals				
Burial, immediate, container provided by funeral home		1370.36	1/95	54r
Cards, acknowledgment		17.72	1/95	54r
Casket, minimum alternative		192.52	1/95	54r
Cosmetology, hair care, etc.		139.56	1/95	54r
Cremation, direct, container provided by funeral home		1049.24	1/95	54r
Embalming		387.57	1/95	54r
Funeral, funeral home		278.77	1/95	54r
Funeral, other facility		275.85	1/95	54r
Graveside service		213.08	1/95	54r
Hearse, local		157.27	1/95	54r
Limousine, local		146.45	1/95	54r
Memorial service		271.02	1/95	54r
Service charge, professional, nondeclinable		943.58	1/95	54r
Visitation and viewing		322.86	1/95	54r
Groceries				
Groceries, ACCRA Index		107.40	12/94	2c
Apples, Red Delicious	lb.	0.78	12/94	82r
Baby food, strained vegetables, lowest price	4-4.5 oz.	0.38	12/94	2c
Bacon, sliced	lb.	2.24	12/94	82r
Bananas	lb.	0.53	12/94	2c
Bananas	lb.	0.49	12/94	82r
Beef or hamburger, ground	lb.	1.77	12/94	2c
Beef purchases	year	226	91	81r
Beverage purchases, alcoholic	year	332	91	81r
Beverage purchases, nonalcoholic	year	213	91	81r
Bread, white	24-oz.	0.83	12/94	2c
Bread, white, pan	lb.	0.80	12/94	82r
Butter, salted, Grade AA, stick	lb.	1.67	12/94	82r
Carrots, short trimmed and topped	lb.	0.51	12/94	82r
Cereals and bakery products purchases	year	407	91	81r
Cereals and cereals products purchases	year	132	91	81r
Cheese, Kraft grated Parmesan	8-oz.	3.46	12/94	2c
Chicken breast, bone-in	lb.	2.22	12/94	82r
Chicken, fresh, whole	lb.	1.05	12/94	82r
Chicken, whole fryer	lb.	1.01	12/94	2c
Chuck roast, USDA choice, boneless	lb.	2.74	12/94	82r
Cigarettes, Winston, Kings	carton	15.95	12/94	2c
Coffee, 100% ground roast, all sizes	lb.	4.61	12/94	82r
Coffee, vacuum-packed	13 oz.	3.72	12/94	2c
Corn Flakes, Kellogg's or Post Toasties	18 oz.	2.45	12/94	2c
Corn, frozen, whole kernel, lowest price	10 oz.	0.73	12/94	2c
Dairy products (other) purchases	year	161	91	81r
Eggs, Grade A large	dozen	0.87	12/94	2c
Eggs, Grade A large	dozen	1.12	12/94	82r
Fish and seafood purchases	year	112	91	81r
Food purchases, food eaten at home	year	2599	91	81r
Foods purchased away from home, not prepared by consumer	year	2024	91	81r
Fruits and vegetables purchases	year	444	91	81r
Grapefruit	lb.	0.44	12/94	82r
Grapes, Thompson seedless	lb.	2.24	12/94	82r
Ground chuck, 100% beef	lb.	1.67	12/94	82r
Ice cream, prepackaged, bulk, regular	1/2 gal.	2.93	12/94	82r
Lemons	lb.	1.06	12/94	82r
Lettuce, iceberg	lb.	0.92	12/94	82r

Values are in dollars or fractions of dollars. In the column headed *Ref*, references are shown to sources. Each reference is followed by a letter. These refer to the geographical level for which data were reported: s=State, r=Region, and c=City or metro. The abbreviation *ex* is used to mean *except* or *excluding*; *exp* stands for *expenditures*. For other abbreviations and further explanations, please see the Introduction.

Wilkes-Barre, PA - continued

Item	Per	Value	Date	Ref.
Groceries				
Lettuce, iceberg	head	0.91	12/94	2c
Margarine, Blue Bonnet or Parkay cubes	lb.	0.66	12/94	2c
Meats, poultry, fish, and eggs purchases	year	751	91	81r
Milk and cream (fresh) purchases	year	152	91	81r
Milk, whole	1/2 gal.	1.21	12/94	2c
Orange juice, frozen concentrate 12-oz. can	16 oz.	1.92	12/94	82r
Orange juice, Minute Maid frozen	12-oz.	1.41	12/94	2c
Oranges, Navel	lb.	0.56	12/94	82r
Peaches, halves or slices, Hunt's, Del Monte, or Libby's	29-oz.	1.46	12/94	2c
Peas, sweet, Del Monte or Green Giant	15-17 oz.	0.65	12/94	2c
Pork chops, center cut, bone-in	lb.	3.09	12/94	82r
Pork purchases	year	130	91	81r
Potatoes, white	lb.	0.37	12/94	82r
Potatoes, white or red	10-lb. sack	2.45	12/94	2c
Rib roast, USDA choice, bone-in	lb.	4.98	12/94	82r
Round roast, USDA choice, boneless	lb.	2.93	12/94	82r
Sausage, Jimmy Dean, 100% pork	lb.	2.66	12/94	2c
Shortening, vegetable oil blends	lb.	1.03	12/94	82r
Shortening, vegetable, Crisco	3-lb.	2.47	12/94	2c
Soft drink, Coca Cola, ex deposit	2 lit	0.97	12/94	2c
Spaghetti and macaroni	lb.	0.84	12/94	82r
Steak, round, USDA choice, boneless	lb.	3.48	12/94	82r
Steak, sirloin, USDA choice, bone-in	lb.	3.38	12/94	82r
Steak, sirloin, USDA choice, boneless	lb.	4.81	12/94	82r
Steak, t-bone	lb.	5.71	12/94	2c
Sugar and other sweets, eaten at home, expenditures	year	89	91	81r
Sugar, cane or beet	4 lbs.	1.56	12/94	2c
Sugar, white, all sizes	lb.	0.46	12/94	82r
Tobacco products and smoking supplies, total expenditures	year	279	91	81r
Tomatoes, field grown	lb.	1.56	12/94	82r
Tomatoes, Hunt's or Del Monte	14.5 oz.	0.80	12/94	2c
Tuna, chunk, light	lb.	2.09	12/94	82r
Tuna, chunk, light, oil-packed	6.125-6.5 oz.	0.77	12/94	2c
Goods and Services				
Miscellaneous goods and services, ACCRA Index		93.10	12/94	2c
Health Care				
Health care, ACCRA Index		97.50	12/94	2c
Antibiotic ointment, Polysporin	1.5 oz.	4.15	12/94	2c
Childbirth, Cesarean delivery, hospital charge	birth	6334.00	12/91	69r
Childbirth, Cesarean delivery, physician charge	birth	2234.00	12/91	69r
Childbirth, normal delivery, hospital charge	birth	3225.00	12/91	69r
Childbirth, normal delivery, physician charge	birth	1623.00	12/91	69r
Dentist's fee, adult teeth·cleaning and periodic oral exam	visit	53.00	12/94	2c
Doctor's fee, routine exam, established patient	visit	38.40	12/94	2c
Drugs, expenditures	year	205	91	81r
Health care, total expenditures	year	1396	91	81r
Health insurance expenditures	year	553	91	81r
Hospital care, semiprivate room	day	357.50	12/94	2c
Insurance premium, family medical care	month	349.05	1/95	41s
Medical services expenditures	year	559	91	81r
Medical supplies expenditures	year	80	91	81r
Household Goods				
Appl. repair, service call, wash mach	min. lab. chg.	29.91	12/94	2c
Floor coverings, expenditures	year	158	91	81r
Furniture, expenditures	year	341	91	81r
Household equipment, misc. expenditures	year	363	91	81r

Wilkes-Barre, PA - continued

Item	Per	Value	Date	Ref.
Household Goods - continued				
Household expenditures, miscellaneous	year	194	91	81r
Household furnishings and equipment, expenditures	year	1158	91	81r
Household operations expenditures	year	378	91	81r
Household textiles, expenditures	year	88	91	81r
Housekeeping supplies, expenditures	year	426	91	81r
Laundry and cleaning supplies, expenditures	year	122	91	81r
Laundry detergent, Tide Ultra, Bold, or Cheer	42 oz.	3.35	12/94	2c
Postage and stationery, expenditures	year	134	91	81r
Tissues, facial, Kleenex brand	175	1.13	12/94	2c
Housing				
Housing, ACCRA Index		100.20	12/94	2c
Add garage/carport		11,614	3/95	74r
Add room(s)		16,816	3/95	74r
Apartment condominium or co-op, median	unit	96700	12/94	62r
Dwellings (owned), expenditures	year	3305	91	81r
Enclose porch/patio/breezeway		2,980	3/95	74r
Finish room in basement/attic		4,330	3/95	74r
Home, existing, single-family, median	unit	161600	12/94	62r
House payment, principal and interest, 25% down payment	mo.	797	12/94	2c
House, 1800 sq ft, 8000 sq ft lot, new, urban, utilities	total	132667	12/94	2c
Maintenance, repairs, insurance, and other housing expenditures	year	569	91	81r
Mortgage interest and charges expenditures	year	1852	91	81r
Mtge. rate, incl. points and orig. fee, 30-year conv. fixed or ARM	mo.	8.96	12/94	2c
Princ. & int., mortgage, median-price exist. sing.-family home	mo.	765	12/94	62r
Property taxes expenditures	year	884	91	81r
Redesign, restructure more than half of home's interior		2,750	3/95	74r
Rent, apartment, 2 br., 1 1/2-2 baths, unfurnished, 950 sq ft, water	mo.	444	12/94	2c
Rental units expenditures	year	1832	91	81r
Insurance and Pensions				
Auto insurance, private passenger	year	721.50	12/94	71s
Insurance and pensions, personal, expenditures	year	2690	91	81r
Insurance, life and other personal, expenditures	year	341	91	81r
Pensions and Social Security, expenditures	year	2349	91	81r
Legal Assistance				
Estate planning, law-firm partner	hr.	375.00	10/93	12r
Legal work, law firm associate	hour	78		10r
Legal work, law firm partner	hour	183		10r
Personal Goods				
Shampoo, Alberto VO5	15-oz.	0.99	12/94	2c
Toothpaste, Crest or Colgate	6-7 oz.	1.90	12/94	2c
Personal Services				
Dry cleaning, man's 2-pc. suit		6.50	12/94	2c
Haircut, man's barbershop, no styling		6.33	12/94	2c
Haircut, woman's shampoo, trim, blow-dry		15.57	12/94	2c
Personal services expenditures	year	184	91	81r
Restaurant Food				
Chicken, fried, thigh and drumstick		2.29	12/94	2c
Dining expenditures, family	week	34.26	94	73r
Hamburger with cheese	1/4 lb.	1.26	12/94	2c
Pizza, Pizza Hut or Pizza Inn	12-13 in.	7.99	12/94	2c
Taxes				
Taxes, Federal income, expenditures	year	2409	91	81r
Taxes, personal, expenditures	year	3094	91	81r
Taxes, State and local income, expenditures	year	620	91	81r

Values are in dollars or fractions of dollars. In the column headed *Ref*, references are shown to sources. Each reference is followed by a letter. These refer to the geographical level for which data were reported: s = State, r = Region, and c = City or metro. The abbreviation *ex* is used to mean *except* or *excluding*; *exp* stands for expenditures. For other abbreviations and further explanations, please see the Introduction.

Wilkes-Barre, PA - continued

Item	Per	Value	Date	Ref.
Transportation				
Transportation, ACCRA Index		91.00	12/94	2c
Bus fare, up to 10 miles	one-way	1.25	12/94	2c
Cars and trucks purchased, new	year	1170	91	81r
Cars and trucks purchased, used	year	739	91	81r
Driver's learning permit fee	perm	27.00	1/94	84s
Driver's license fee	orig	0.00	1/94	84s
Driver's license fee, duplicate	lic	7.00	1/94	84s
Driver's license reinstatement fee, min.	susp	25.00	1/94	85s
Driver's license renewal fee	renew	0.00	1/94	84s
Identification card, nondriver	card	5.00	1/94	83s
Motorcycle learning permit fee	perm	27.00	1/94	84s
Motorcycle license fee	orig	0.00	1/94	84s
Motorcycle license fee, duplicate	lic	7.00	1/94	84s
Motorcycle license renewal fee	renew	0.00	1/94	84s
Public transportation expenditures	year	430	91	81r
Tire balance, computer or spin bal., front	wheel	4.45	12/94	2c
Transportation expenditures, total	year	4810	91	81r
Vehicle finance charges	year	238	91	81r
Vehicle insurance expenditures	year	630	91	81r
Vehicle maintenance and repairs expenditures	year	532	91	81r
Vehicle purchases	year	1920	91.	81r
Vehicle rental, leases, licenses, etc. expenditures	year	193	91	81r
Vehicles purchased, other than cars and trucks	year	11	91	81r
Utilities				
Utilities, ACCRA Index		96.80	12/94	2c
Electricity expenditures	year	695	91	81r
Electricity, (part.), other, 1800 sq. ft., new home	mo.	52.50	12/94	2c
Utilities, fuels, and public services, total expenditures	year	1981	91	81r
Water and other public services, expenditures	year	154	91	81r
Weddings				
Bridal attendants' gowns	event	750	10/93	76r
Bridal gown	event	852	10/93	76r
Bridal headpiece and veil	event	167	10/93	76r
Bride's wedding band	event	708	10/93	76r
Clergy	event	224	10/93	76r
Engagement ring	event	2756	10/93	76r
Flowers	event	863	10/93	76r
Formal wear for groom	event	106	10/93	76r
Groom's attendants' formal wear	event	530	10/93	76r
Groom's wedding band	event	402	10/93	76r
Music	event	600	10/93	76r
Photography	event	1088	10/93	76r
Shoes for bride	event	50	10/93	76r
Videography	event	483	10/93	76r
Wedding invitations and announcements	event	342	10/93	76r
Wedding reception	event	7000	10/93	76r

Williamsport, PA

Item	Per	Value	Date	Ref.
Composite, ACCRA index		100.60	12/94	2c
Alcoholic Beverages				
Beer, Miller Lite, Bud, 12-oz., ex deposit	6	5.87	12/94	2c
J & B Scotch	750-ml.	16.99	12/94	2c
Wine, Gallo Chablis blanc	1.5-lit	5.99	12/94	2c
Appliances				
Appliances (major), expenditures	year	145	91	81r
Average annual exp.				
Food, health care, personal goods, services	year	29496	91	81r
Charity				
Cash contributions, expenditures	year	708	91	81r

Williamsport, PA - continued

Item	Per	Value	Date	Ref.
Clothing				
Apparel, men and boys, total expenditures	year	416	91	81r
Apparel, women and girls, total expenditures	year	744	91	81r
Footwear, expenditures	year	305	91	81r
Jeans, man's denim		31.16	12/94	2c
Shirt, man's dress shirt		26.40	12/94	2c
Undervest, boy's size 10-14, cotton	3	3.31	12/94	2c
Communications				
Long-distance telephone rate, day, addl. min., 1-10 mi.	min.	0.08	12/93	9s
Long-distance telephone rate, day, initial min., 1-10 mi.	min.	0.15	12/93	9s
Newspaper subscription, dly. and Sun. delivery	month	8.26	12/94	2c
Phone line, single, business, field visit	inst	75.00	12/93	9s
Phone line, single, business, no field visit	inst	75.00	12/93	9s
Phone line, single, residence, field visit	inst	40.00	12/93	9s
Phone line, single, residence, no field visit	inst	40.00	12/93	9s
Telephone bill, family of four	month	15.42	12/94	2c
Telephone service, expenditures	year	589	91	81r
Telephone, residential, flat rate	mo.	21.00	12/93	8c
Education				
Board, 4-year private college/university	year	2714	8/94	80s
Board, 4-year public college/university	year	1899	8/94	80s
Education, total expenditures	year	593	91	81r
Room, 4-year private college/university	year	2720	8/94	80s
Room, 4-year public college/university	year	2063	8/94	80s
Total cost, 4-year private college/university	year	18118	8/94	80s
Total cost, 4-year public college/university	year	8278	8/94	80s
Tuition, 2-year public college/university, in-state	year	1671	8/94	80s
Tuition, 4-year private college/university, in-state	year	12684	8/94	80s
Tuition, 4-year public college/university, in-state	year	4316	8/94	80s
Energy and Fuels				
Energy, combined forms, 1800 sq. ft.	mo.	126.76	12/94	2c
Fuel oil and other fuels, expenditures	year	257	91	81r
Gas, natural, expenditures	year	285	91	81r
Gas, reg unlead, taxes inc., cash, self-service	gal	1.17	12/94	2c
Gasoline and motor oil purchased	year	867	91	81r
Gasoline, unleaded midgrade	gallon	1.32	4/93	82r
Gasoline, unleaded premium	gallon	1.40	4/93	82r
Gasoline, unleaded regular	gallon	1.19	4/93	82r
Entertainment				
Bowling, evening rate	game	1.87	12/94	2c
Entertainment, total expenditures	year	1331	91	81r
Fees and admissions, expenditures	year	398	91	81r
Monopoly game, Parker Brothers', No. 9	game	12.09	12/94	2c
Movie	adm	5.50	12/94	2c
Pets, toys, playground equipment, expenditures	year	270	91	81r
Reading, expenditures	year	171	91	81r
Televisions, radios, and sound equipment, expenditures	year	429	91	81r
Tennis balls, yellow, Wilson or Penn, 3	can	2.05	12/94	2c
Funerals				
Burial, immediate, container provided by funeral home		1370.36	1/95	54r
Cards, acknowledgment		17.72	1/95	54r
Casket, minimum alternative		192.52	1/95	54r
Cosmetology, hair care, etc.		139.56	1/95	54r
Cremation, direct, container provided by funeral home		1049.24	1/95	54r
Embalming		387.57	1/95	54r
Funeral, funeral home		278.77	1/95	54r
Funeral, other facility		275.85	1/95	54r
Graveside service		213.08	1/95	54r
Hearse, local		157.27	1/95	54r

Values are in dollars or fractions of dollars. In the column headed *Ref*, references are shown to sources. Each reference is followed by a letter. These refer to the geographical level for which data were reported: s = State, r = Region, and c = City or metro. The abbreviation *ex* is used to mean *except* or *excluding*; *exp* stands for expenditures. For other abbreviations and further explanations, please see the Introduction.

Williamsport, PA - continued

Item	Per	Value	Date	Ref.
Funerals				
Limousine, local		146.45	1/95	54r
Memorial service		271.02	1/95	54r
Service charge, professional, nondeclinable		943.58	1/95	54r
Visitation and viewing		322.86	1/95	54r
Groceries				
Groceries, ACCRA Index		101.70	12/94	2c
Apples, Red Delicious	lb.	0.78	12/94	82r
Baby food, strained vegetables, lowest price	4-4.5 oz.	0.38	12/94	2c
Bacon, sliced	lb.	2.24	12/94	82r
Bananas	lb.	0.49	12/94	2c
Bananas	lb.	0.49	12/94	82r
Beef or hamburger, ground	lb.	1.61	12/94	2c
Beef purchases	year	226	91	81r
Beverage purchases, alcoholic	year	332	91	81r
Beverage purchases, nonalcoholic	year	213	91	81r
Bread, white	24-oz.	0.81	12/94	2c
Bread, white, pan	lb.	0.80	12/94	82r
Butter, salted, Grade AA, stick	lb.	1.67	12/94	82r
Carrots, short trimmed and topped	lb.	0.51	12/94	82r
Cereals and bakery products purchases	year	407	91	81r
Cereals and cereals products purchases	year	132	91	81r
Cheese, Kraft grated Parmesan	8-oz.	3.42	12/94	2c
Chicken breast, bone-in	lb.	2.22	12/94	82r
Chicken, fresh, whole	lb.	1.05	12/94	82r
Chicken, whole fryer	lb.	0.77	12/94	2c
Chuck roast, USDA choice, boneless	lb.	2.74	12/94	82r
Cigarettes, Winston, Kings	carton	16.19	12/94	2c
Coffee, 100%, ground roast, all sizes	lb.	4.61	12/94	82r
Coffee, vacuum-packed	13 oz.	2.08	12/94	2c
Corn Flakes, Kellogg's or Post Toasties	18 oz.	2.71	12/94	2c
Corn, frozen, whole kernel, lowest price	10 oz.	0.69	12/94	2c
Dairy products (other) purchases	year	161	91	81r
Eggs, Grade A large	dozen	0.79	12/94	2c
Eggs, Grade A large	dozen	1.12	12/94	82r
Fish and seafood purchases	year	112	91	81r
Food purchases, food eaten at home	year	2599	91	81r
Foods purchased away from home, not prepared by consumer	year	2024	91	81r
Fruits and vegetables purchases	year	444	91	81r
Grapefruit	lb.	0.44	12/94	82r
Grapes, Thompson seedless	lb.	2.24	12/94	82r
Ground chuck, 100% beef	lb.	1.67	12/94	82r
Ice cream, prepackaged, bulk, regular	1/2 gal.	2.93	12/94	82r
Lemons	lb.	1.06	12/94	82r
Lettuce, iceberg	lb.	0.92	12/94	82r
Lettuce, iceberg	head	0.95	12/94	2c
Margarine, Blue Bonnet or Parkay cubes	lb.	0.71	12/94	2c
Meats, poultry, fish, and eggs purchases	year	751	91	81r
Milk and cream (fresh) purchases	year	152	91	81r
Milk, whole	1/2 gal.	1.18	12/94	2c
Orange juice, frozen concentrate 12-oz. can	16 oz.	1.92	12/94	82r
Orange juice, Minute Maid frozen	12-oz.	1.39	12/94	2c
Oranges, Navel	lb.	0.56	12/94	82r
Peaches, halves or slices, Hunt's, Del Monte, or Libby's	29-oz.	1.30	12/94	2c
Peas, sweet, Del Monte or Green Giant	15-17 oz.	0.62	12/94	2c
Pork chops, center cut, bone-in	lb.	3.09	12/94	82r
Pork purchases	year	130	91	81r
Potatoes, white	lb.	0.37	12/94	82r
Potatoes, white or red	10-lb. sack	2.63	12/94	2c
Rib roast, USDA choice, bone-in	lb.	4.98	12/94	82r
Round roast, USDA choice, boneless	lb.	2.93	12/94	82r
Sausage, Jimmy Dean, 100% pork	lb.	3.65	12/94	2c
Shortening, vegetable oil blends	lb.	1.03	12/94	82r
Shortening, vegetable, Crisco	3-lb.	2.53	12/94	2c
Soft drink, Coca Cola, ex deposit	2 lit	1.15	12/94	2c
Spaghetti and macaroni	lb.	0.84	12/94	82r

Williamsport, PA - continued

Item	Per	Value	Date	Ref.
Groceries - continued				
Steak, round, USDA choice, boneless	lb.	3.48	12/94	82r
Steak, sirloin, USDA choice, bone-in	lb.	3.38	12/94	82r
Steak, sirloin, USDA choice, boneless	lb.	4.81	12/94	82r
Steak, t-bone	lb.	4.81	12/94	2c
Sugar and other sweets, eaten at home, expenditures	year	89	91	81r
Sugar, cane or beet	4 lbs.	1.47	12/94	2c
Sugar, white, all sizes	lb.	0.46	12/94	82r
Tobacco products and smoking supplies, total expenditures	year	279	91	81r
Tomatoes, field grown	lb.	1.56	12/94	82r
Tomatoes, Hunt's or Del Monte	14.5 oz.	0.74	12/94	2c
Tuna, chunk, light	lb.	2.09	12/94	82r
Tuna, chunk, light, oil-packed	6.125-6.5 oz.	0.63	12/94	2c
Goods and Services				
Miscellaneous goods and services, ACCRA Index		97.30	12/94	2c
Health Care				
Health care, ACCRA Index		98.00	12/94	2c
Antibiotic ointment, Polysporin	1.5 oz.	4.59	12/94	2c
Childbirth, Cesarean delivery, hospital charge	birth	6334.00	12/91	69r
Childbirth, Cesarean delivery, physician charge	birth	2234.00	12/91	69r
Childbirth, normal delivery, hospital charge	birth	3225.00	12/91	69r
Childbirth, normal delivery, physician charge	birth	1623.00	12/91	69r
Dentist's fee, adult teeth cleaning and periodic oral exam	visit	52.67	12/94	2c
Doctor's fee, routine exam, established patient	visit	37.00	12/94	2c
Drugs, expenditures	year	205	91	81r
Health care, total expenditures	year	1396	91	81r
Health insurance expenditures	year	553	91	81r
Hospital care, semiprivate room	day	372.50	12/94	2c
Insurance premium, family medical care	month	349.05	1/95	41s
Medical services expenditures	year	559	91	81r
Medical supplies expenditures	year	80	91	81r
Household Goods				
Appl. repair, service call, wash mach	min. lab. chg.	32.47	12/94	2c
Floor coverings, expenditures	year	158	91	81r
Furniture, expenditures	year	341	91	81r
Household equipment, misc. expenditures	year	363	91	81r
Household equipment, miscellaneous	year	194	91	81r
Household furnishings and equipment, expenditures	year	1158	91	81r
Household operations expenditures	year	378	91	81r
Household textiles, expenditures	year	88	91	81r
Housekeeping supplies, expenditures	year	426	91	81r
Laundry and cleaning supplies, expenditures	year	122	91	81r
Laundry detergent, Tide Ultra, Bold, or Cheer	42 oz.	2.73	12/94	2c
Postage and stationery, expenditures	year	134	91	81r
Tissues, facial, Kleenex brand	175	1.03	12/94	2c
Housing				
Housing, ACCRA Index		103.60	12/94	2c
Add garage/carport		11,614	3/95	74r
Add room(s)		16,816	3/95	74r
Apartment condominium or co-op, median	unit	96700	12/94	62r
Dwellings (owned), expenditures	year	3305	91	81r
Enclose porch/patio/breezeway		2,980	3/95	74r
Finish room in basement/attic		4,330	3/95	74r
Home, existing, single-family, median	unit	161600	12/94	62r
House payment, principal and interest, 25% down payment	mo.	828	12/94	2c

Values are in dollars or fractions of dollars. In the column headed *Ref*, references are shown to sources. Each reference is followed by a letter. These refer to the geographical level for which data were reported: s=State, r=Region, and c=City or metro. The abbreviation *ex* is used to mean *except* or *excluding*; *exp* stands for *expenditures*. For other abbreviations and further explanations, please see the Introduction.

Williamsport, PA - continued

Item	Per	Value	Date	Ref.
Housing				
House, 1800 sq ft, 8000 sq ft lot, new, urban, utilities	total	132800	12/94	2c
Maintenance, repairs, insurance, and other housing expenditures	year	569	91	81r
Mortgage interest and charges expenditures	year	1852	91	81r
Mtge. rate, incl. points and orig. fee, 30-year conv. fixed or ARM	mo.	9.38	12/94	2c
Princ. & int., mortgage, median-price exist. sing.-family home	mo.	765	12/94	62r
Property taxes expenditures	year	884	91	81r
Redesign, restructure more than half of home's interior		2,750	3/95	74r
Rent, apartment, 2 br., 1 1/2-2 baths, unfurnished, 950 sq ft, water	mo.	447	12/94	2c
Rental units expenditures	year	1832	91	81r
Insurance and Pensions				
Auto insurance, private passenger	year	721.50	12/94	71s
Insurance and pensions, personal, expenditures	year	2690	91	81r
Insurance, life and other personal, expenditures	year	341	91	81r
Pensions and Social Security, expenditures	year	2349	91	81r
Legal Assistance				
Estate planning, law-firm partner	hr.	375.00	10/93	12r
Legal work, law firm associate	hour	78		10r
Legal work, law firm partner	hour	183		10r
Personal Goods				
Shampoo, Alberto VO5	15-oz.	1.13	12/94	2c
Toothpaste, Crest or Colgate	6-7 oz.	2.00	12/94	2c
Personal Services				
Dry cleaning, man's 2-pc. suit		7.13	12/94	2c
Haircut, man's barbershop, no styling		5.36	12/94	2c
Haircut, woman's shampoo, trim, blow-dry		16.43	12/94	2c
Personal services expenditures	year	184	91	81r
Restaurant Food				
Chicken, fried, thigh and drumstick		2.43	12/94	2c
Dining expenditures, family	week	34.26	94	73r
Hamburger with cheese	1/4 lb.	1.97	12/94	2c
Pizza, Pizza Hut or Pizza Inn	12-13 in.	7.99	12/94	2c
Taxes				
Taxes, Federal income, expenditures	year	2409	91	81r
Taxes, personal, expenditures	year	3094	91	81r
Taxes, State and local income, expenditures	year	620	91	81r
Transportation				
Transportation, ACCRA Index		96.70	12/94	2c
Bus fare, one-way	trip	1.00	12/95	1c
Cars and trucks purchased, new	year	1170	91	81r
Cars and trucks purchased, used	year	739	91	81r
Driver's learning permit fee	perm	27.00	1/94	84s
Driver's license fee	orig	0.00	1/94	84s
Driver's license fee, duplicate	lic	7.00	1/94	84s
Driver's license reinstatement fee, min.	susp	25.00	1/94	85s
Driver's license renewal fee	renew	0.00	1/94	84s
Identification card, nondriver	card	5.00	1/94	83s
Motorcycle learning permit fee	perm	27.00	1/94	84s
Motorcycle license fee	orig	0.00	1/94	84s
Motorcycle license fee, duplicate	lic	7.00	1/94	84s
Motorcycle license renewal fee	renew	0.00	1/94	84s
Public transportation expenditures	year	430	91	81r
Tire balance, computer or spin bal., front	wheel	5.89	12/94	2c
Transportation expenditures, total	year	4810	91	81r
Vehicle finance charges	year	238	91	81r
Vehicle insurance expenditures	year	630	91	81r
Vehicle maintenance and repairs expenditures	year	532	91	81r
Vehicle purchases	year	1920	91	81r

Williamsport, PA - continued

Item	Per	Value	Date	Ref.
Transportation - continued				
Vehicle rental, leases, licenses, etc. expenditures	year	193	91	81r
Vehicles purchased, other than cars and trucks	year	11	91	81r
Utilities				
Utilities, ACCRA Index		108.40	12/94	2c
Electricity expenditures	year	695	91	81r
Electricity, 1800 sq. ft., new home	mo.	126.76	12/94	2c
Utilities, fuels, and public services, total expenditures	year	1981	91	81r
Water and other public services, expenditures	year	154	91	81r
Weddings				
Bridal attendants' gowns	event	750	10/93	76r
Bridal gown	event	852	10/93	76r
Bridal headpiece and veil	event	167	10/93	76r
Bride's wedding band	event	708	10/93	76r
Clergy	event	224	10/93	76r
Engagement ring	event	2756	10/93	76r
Flowers	event	863	10/93	76r
Formal wear for groom	event	106	10/93	76r
Groom's attendants' formal wear	event	530	10/93	76r
Groom's wedding band	event	402	10/93	76r
Music	event	600	10/93	76r
Photography	event	1088	10/93	76r
Shoes for bride	event	50	10/93	76r
Videography	event	483	10/93	76r
Wedding invitations and announcements	event	342	10/93	76r
Wedding reception	event	7000	10/93	76r

Wilmington, DE

Item	Per	Value	Date	Ref.
Composite, ACCRA index		110.30	12/94	2c
Alcoholic Beverages				
Beer, Miller Lite, Bud, 12-oz., ex deposit	6	4.02	12/94	2c
J & B Scotch	750-ml.	14.23	12/94	2c
Wine, Gallo Chablis blanc	1.5-lit	5.56	12/94	2c
Appliances				
Appliances (major), expenditures	year	153	91	81r
Average annual exp.				
Food, health care, personal goods, services	year	27020	91	81r
Charity				
Cash contributions, expenditures	year	839	91	81r
Child Care				
Child care, for-profit daycare center	week	91.00	12/94	28c
Clothing				
Apparel, men and boys, total expenditures	year	380	91	81r
Apparel, women and girls, total expenditures	year	660	91	81r
Footwear, expenditures	year	193	91	81r
Jeans, man's denim		31.78	12/94	2c
Shirt, man's dress shirt		29.62	12/94	2c
Undervest, boy's size 10-14, cotton	3	4.00	12/94	2c
Communications				
Long-distance telephone rate, day, addl. min., 1-10 mi.	min.	0.10	12/93	9s
Long-distance telephone rate, day, initial min., 1-10 mi.	min.	0.13	12/93	9s
Newspaper subscription, dly. and Sun. delivery	month	14.35	12/94	2c
Phone line, single, business, field visit	inst	46.00	12/93	9s
Phone line, single, business, no field visit	inst	46.00	12/93	9s
Phone line, single, residence, field visit	inst	36.00	12/93	9s
Phone line, single, residence, no field visit	inst	36.00	12/93	9s
Telephone bill, family of four	month	13.89	12/94	2c
Telephone service, expenditures	year	616	91	81r
Telephone, residential, flat rate	mo.	2.25	12/93	8c

Values are in dollars or fractions of dollars. In the column headed *Ref*, references are shown to sources. Each reference is followed by a letter. These refer to the geographical level for which data were reported: s=State, r=Region, and c=City or metro. The abbreviation *ex* is used to mean *except* or *excluding*; *exp* stands for expenditures. For other abbreviations and further explanations, please see the Introduction.

Wilmington, DE - continued

Item	Per	Value	Date	Ref.
Credit Cards				
Fee, conventional credit card, secured	year	20.00	1/95	96c
Education				
Board, 4-year private college/university	year	1275	8/94	80s
Board, 4-year public college/university	year	1937	8/94	80s
Education, total expenditures	year	319	91	81r
Room, 4-year private college/university	year	2507	8/94	80s
Room, 4-year public college/university	year	2190	8/94	80s
Total cost, 4-year private college/university	year	10700	8/94	80s
Total cost, 4-year public college/university	year	7811	8/94	80s
Tuition, 4-year private college/university, in-state	year	6917	8/94	80s
Tuition, 4-year public college/university, in-state	year	3684	8/94	80s
Energy and Fuels				
Energy, combined forms, 1800 sq. ft.	mo.	136.67	12/94	2c
Fuel oil and other fuels, expenditures	year	56	91	81r
Gas, cooking, 10 therms	month	10.36	2/94	65c
Gas, cooking, 30 therms	month	24.19	2/94	65c
Gas, cooking, 50 therms	month	38.02	2/94	65c
Gas, heating, winter, 100 therms	month	68.50	2/94	65c
Gas, heating, winter, average use	month	82.89	2/94	65c
Gas, natural, expenditures	year	150	91	81r
Gas, reg unlead, taxes inc., cash, self-service	gal	1.13	12/94	2c
Gasoline and motor oil purchased	year	1152	91	81r
Gasoline, unleaded midgrade	gallon	1.21	4/93	82r
Gasoline, unleaded premium	gallon	1.30	4/93	82r
Gasoline, unleaded regular	gallon	1.10	4/93	82r
Entertainment				
Bowling, evening rate	game	2.76	12/94	2c
Concert ticket, Pearl Jam group	perf	20.00	94	50r
Entertainment, total expenditures	year	1266	91	81r
Fees and admissions, expenditures	year	306	91	81r
Monopoly game, Parker Brothers', No. 9	game	12.24	12/94	2c
Movie	adm	5.85	12/94	2c
Pets, toys, playground equipment, expenditures	year	271	91	81r
Reading, expenditures	year	131	91	81r
Televisions, radios, and sound equipment, expenditures	year	439	91	81r
Tennis balls, yellow, Wilson or Penn, 3	can	2.15	12/94	2c
Funerals				
Burial, immediate, container provided by funeral home		1370.36	1/95	54r
Cards, acknowledgment		14.83	1/95	54r
Casket, minimum alternative		192.52	1/95	54r
Cosmetology, hair care, etc.		102.27	1/95	54r
Cremation, direct, container provided by funeral home		1065.64	1/95	54r
Embalming		304.29	1/95	54r
Funeral, funeral home		287.83	1/95	54r
Funeral, other facility		284.14	1/95	54r
Graveside service		349.13	1/95	54r
Hearse, local		132.27	1/95	54r
Limousine, local		98.45	1/95	54r
Memorial service		270.59	1/95	54r
Service charge, professional, nondeclinable		933.59	1/95	54r
Visitation and viewing		225.83	1/95	54r
Groceries				
Groceries, ACCRA Index		119.10	12/94	2c
Apples, Red Delicious	lb.	0.73	12/94	82r
Baby food, strained vegetables, lowest price	4-4.5 oz.	0.38	12/94	2c
Bacon, sliced	lb.	1.67	12/94	82r
Bananas	lb.	0.51	12/94	2c
Bananas	lb.	0.42	12/94	82r
Beef or hamburger, ground	lb.	1.86	12/94	2c
Beef purchases	year	213	91	81r
Beverage purchases, alcoholic	year	249	91	81r

Wilmington, DE - continued

Item	Per	Value	Date	Ref.
Groceries - continued				
Beverage purchases, nonalcoholic	year	207	91	81r
Bologna, all beef or mixed	lb.	2.27	12/94	82r
Bread, white	24-oz.	0.96	12/94	2c
Bread, white, pan	lb.	0.68	12/94	82r
Cabbage	lb.	0.42	12/94	82r
Carrots, short trimmed and topped	lb.	0.53	12/94	82r
Cereals and bakery products purchases	year	345	91	81r
Cereals and cereals products purchases	year	127	91	81r
Cheddar cheese, natural	lb.	3.58	12/94	82r
Cheese, Kraft grated Parmesan	8-oz.	4.01	12/94	2c
Chicken breast, bone-in	lb.	1.71	12/94	82r
Chicken, fresh, whole	lb.	0.78	12/94	82r
Chicken, whole fryer	lb.	1.07	12/94	2c
Chuck roast, USDA choice, boneless	lb.	2.26	12/94	82r
Cigarettes, Winston, Kings	carton	15.45	12/94	2c
Coffee, vacuum-packed	13 oz.	3.79	12/94	2c
Corn Flakes, Kellogg's or Post Toasties	18 oz.	2.70	12/94	2c
Corn, frozen, whole kernel, lowest price	10 oz.	0.87	12/94	2c
Crackers, soda, salted	lb.	1.27	12/94	82r
Cucumbers	lb.	0.65	12/94	82r
Dairy products (other) purchases	year	141	91	81r
Eggs, Grade A large	dozen	0.98	12/94	2c
Eggs, Grade A large	dozen	0.87	12/94	82r
Fish and seafood purchases	year	72	91	81r
Flour, white, all purpose	lb.	0.23	12/94	82r
Food purchases, food eaten at home	year	2381	91	81r
Foods purchased away from home, not prepared by consumer	year	1696	91	81r
Frankfurters, all meat or all beef	lb.	1.74	12/94	82r
Fruits and vegetables purchases	year	380	91	81r
Grapefruit	lb.	0.45	12/94	82r
Grapes, Thompson seedless	lb.	2.30	12/94	82r
Ground beef, 100% beef	lb.	1.37	12/94	82r
Ground chuck, 100% beef	lb.	1.97	12/94	82r
Ham, boneless, exc. canned	lb.	2.54	12/94	82r
Ice cream, prepackaged, bulk, regular	1/2 gal.	2.47	12/94	82r
Lemons	lb.	1.02	12/94	82r
Lettuce, iceberg	lb.	0.96	12/94	82r
Lettuce, iceberg	head	0.96	12/94	2c
Margarine, Blue Bonnet or Parkay cubes	lb.	0.97	12/94	2c
Margarine, stick	lb.	0.77	12/94	82r
Meats, poultry, fish, and eggs purchases	year	655	91	81r
Milk and cream (fresh) purchases	year	130	91	81r
Milk, whole	1/2 gal.	1.27	12/94	2c
Orange juice, frozen concentrate 12-oz. can	16 oz.	1.36	12/94	82r
Orange juice, Minute Maid frozen	12-oz.	1.82	12/94	2c
Oranges, Navel	lb.	0.54	12/94	82r
Peaches, halves or slices, Hunt's, Del Monte, or Libby's	29-oz.	1.53	12/94	2c
Pears, Anjou	lb.	0.81	12/94	82r
Peas, sweet, Del Monte or Green Giant	15-17 oz.	0.64	12/94	2c
Pork chops, center cut, bone-in	lb.	3.07	12/94	82r
Pork purchases	year	142	91	81r
Potato chips	16-oz.	3.15	12/94	82r
Potatoes, frozen, French fried	lb.	0.82	12/94	82r
Potatoes, white	lb.	0.34	12/94	82r
Potatoes, white or red	10-lb. sack	2.94	12/94	2c
Rice, white, long grain, uncooked	lb.	0.48	12/94	82r
Round roast, USDA choice, boneless	lb.	2.91	12/94	82r
Sausage, fresh	lb.	1.82	12/94	82r
Sausage, Jimmy Dean, 100% pork	lb.	3.65	12/94	2c
Shortening, vegetable oil blends	lb.	0.75	12/94	82r
Shortening, vegetable, Crisco	3-lb.	3.02	12/94	2c
Soft drink, Coca Cola, ex deposit	2 lit	1.12	12/94	2c
Spaghetti and macaroni	lb.	0.87	12/94	82r
Steak, rib eye, USDA choice, boneless	lb.	6.85	12/94	82r
Steak, round, graded & ungraded, exc. USDA prime & choice	lb.	2.96	12/94	82r

Values are in dollars or fractions of dollars. In the column headed *Ref*, references are shown to sources. Each reference is followed by a letter. These refer to the geographical level for which data were reported: s = State, r = Region, and c = City or metro. The abbreviation *ex* is used to mean *except* or *excluding*; *exp* stands for expenditures. For other abbreviations and further explanations, please see the Introduction.

Wilmington, DE - continued

Item	Per	Value	Date	Ref.
Groceries				
Steak, round, USDA choice, boneless	lb.	3.17	12/94	82r
Steak, sirloin, USDA choice, boneless	lb.	4.12	12/94	82r
Steak, t-bone	lb.	6.69	12/94	2c
Steak, T-bone, USDA choice, bone-in	lb.	5.63	12/94	82r
Sugar and other sweets, eaten at home, expenditures	year	93	91	81r
Sugar, cane or beet	4 lbs.	1.50	12/94	2c
Sugar, white, all sizes	lb.	0.39	12/94	82r
Tobacco products and smoking supplies, total expenditures	year	286	91	81r
Tomatoes, field grown	lb.	1.36	12/94	82r
Tomatoes, Hunt's or Del Monte	14.5 oz.	0.82	12/94	2c
Tuna, chunk, light	lb.	1.94	12/94	82r
Tuna, chunk, light, oil-packed	6.125-6.5 oz.	0.87	12/94	2c
Turkey, frozen, whole	lb.	0.96	12/94	82r
Yogurt, natural, fruit flavored	8 oz.	0.58	12/94	82r
Goods and Services				
Miscellaneous goods and services, ACCRA Index		104.80	12/94	2c
Health Care				
Health care, ACCRA Index		119.70	12/94	2c
Adenosine, emergency room	treat	100.00	95	23r
Antibiotic ointment, Polysporin	1.5 oz.	4.23	12/94	2c
Bladder tap, superpubic, infant, emergency room	treat	119.00	95	23r
Blood analysis, emergency room	treat	25.00	95	23r
Blood tests, abdominal pain, emergency room	treat	25.00	95	23r
Burn dressing, emergency room	treat	266.00	95	23r
Cardiology interpretation, emergency room	treat	26.00	95	23r
Chest X-ray, emergency room	treat	78.00	95	23r
Childbirth, Cesarean delivery, hospital charge	birth	5462.00	12/91	69r
Childbirth, Cesarean delivery, physician charge	birth	2228.00	12/91	69r
Childbirth, normal delivery, hospital charge	birth	2943.00	12/91	69r
Childbirth, normal delivery, physician charge	birth	1619.00	12/91	69r
Defibrillation pads, emergency room	treat	6.00	95	23r
Dentist's fee, adult teeth cleaning and periodic oral exam	visit	74.20	12/94	2c
Doctor's fee, routine exam, established patient	visit	38.60	12/94	2c
Drugs, expenditures	year	297	91	81r
Gastric tube insertion, nasal, emergency room	treat	25.00	95	23r
Health care, total expenditures	year	1600	91	81r
Health insurance expenditures	year	637	91	81r
Heart monitor, emergency room	treat	40.00	95	23r
Hospital care, semiprivate room	day	508.50	12/94	2c
Insurance premium, family medical care	month	485.01	1/95	41s
Intravenous fluids, emergency room	treat	130.00	95	23r
Intravenous fluids, emergency room	liter	26.00	95	23r
Intravenous line, central, emergency room	treat	342.00	95	23r
Liver function tests, abdominal pain, emergency room	treat	26.00	95	23r
Medical care charges, total, emergency room, third-degree burns	treat	2101.00	95	23r
Medical care charges, total, emergency, infant with fever	treat	628.00	95	23r
Medical services expenditures	year	573	91	81r
Medical supplies expenditures	year	93	91	81r
Morphine, emergency room	treat	34.00	95	23r
Nursing care and facilities charges, emergency room	treat	252.00	95	23r
Nursing care and facilities charges, emergency, infant with fever	treat	252.00	95	23r
Nursing care and facilities charges, emergency, third-degree burns	treat	861.00	95	23r

Wilmington, DE - continued

Item	Per	Value	Date	Ref.
Health Care - continued				
Physician's charges, emergency, infant with fever	treat	212.00	95	23r
Physician's charges, emergency, third-degree burns	treat	372.00	95	23r
Physician's fee, emergency room	treat	372.00	95	23r
Physician's fee, general practitioner	visit	51.20	12/93	60r
Surgery, open-heart	proc	42374.00	1/93	14r
Ultrasound, abdominal, emergency room	treat	276.00	95	23r
Urinalysis, emergency room	treat	20.00	95	23r
Urinalysis, infant, emergency room	treat	20.00	95	23r
X-rays, emergency room	treat	78.00	95	23r
Household Goods				
Appl. repair, service call, wash mach	min. lab. chg.	39.98	12/94	2c
Floor coverings, expenditures	year	48	91	81r
Furniture, expenditures	year	280	91	81r
Household equipment, misc. expenditures	year	342	91	81r
Household expenditures, miscellaneous	year	256	91	81r
Household furnishings and equipment, expenditures	year	988	91	81r
Household operations expenditures	year	468	91	81r
Household textiles, expenditures	year	95	91	81r
Housekeeping supplies, expenditures	year	380	91	81r
Laundry and cleaning supplies, expenditures	year	109	91	81r
Laundry detergent, Tide Ultra, Bold, or Cheer	42 oz.	3.61	12/94	2c
Postage and stationery, expenditures	year	105	91	81r
Tissues, facial, Kleenex brand	175	1.24	12/94	2c
Housing				
Housing, ACCRA Index		112.40	12/94	2c
Add garage/carport		6,980	3/95	74r
Add room(s)		11,403	3/95	74r
Apartment condominium or co-op, median	unit	68600	12/94	62r
Dwellings (owned), expenditures	year	2428	91	81r
Enclose porch/patio/breezeway		4,572	3/95	74r
Finish room in basement/attic		3,794	3/95	74r
Home, existing, single-family, median	unit	120200	12/94	62r
House payment, principal and interest, 25% down payment	mo.	882	12/94	2c
House, 1800 sq ft, 8000 sq ft lot, new, urban, utilities	total	146620	12/94	2c
Maintenance, repairs, insurance, and other housing expenditures	year	531	91	81r
Mortgage interest and charges expenditures	year	1506	91	81r
Mtge. rate, incl. points and orig. fee, 30-year conv. fixed or ARM	mo.	8.96	12/94	2c
Princ. & int., mortgage, median-price exist. sing.-family home	mo.	540	12/94	62r
Property taxes expenditures	year	391	91	81r
Redesign, restructure more than half of home's interior		17,641	3/95	74r
Rent, apartment, 2 br., 1 1/2-2 baths, unfurnished, 950 sq ft, water	mo.	534	12/94	2c
Rental units expenditures	year	1264	91	81r
Insurance and Pensions				
Auto insurance, private passenger	year	813.00	12/94	71s
Insurance and pensions, personal, expenditures	year	2395	91	81r
Insurance, life and other personal, expenditures	year	368	91	81r
Pensions and Social Security, expenditures	year	2027	91	81r
Personal Goods				
Shampoo, Alberto VO5	15-oz.	1.51	12/94	2c
Toothpaste, Crest or Colgate	6-7 oz.	2.23	12/94	2c
Personal Services				
Dry cleaning, man's 2-pc. suit		6.23	12/94	2c
Haircut, man's barbershop, no styling		8.00	12/94	2c

Values are in dollars or fractions of dollars. In the column headed *Ref*, references are shown to sources. Each reference is followed by a letter. These refer to the geographical level for which data were reported: s=State, r=Region, and c=City or metro. The abbreviation *ex* is used to mean *except* or *excluding*; *exp* stands for expenditures. For other abbreviations and further explanations, please see the Introduction.

Wilmington, DE - continued

Item	Per	Value	Date	Ref.
Personal Services				
Haircut, woman's shampoo, trim, blow-dry		17.62	12/94	2c
Personal services expenditures	year	212	91	81r
Restaurant Food				
Chicken, fried, thigh and drumstick		2.29	12/94	2c
Dining expenditures, family	week	33.83	94	73r
Hamburger with cheese	1/4 lb.	1.89	12/94	2c
Pizza, Pizza Hut or Pizza Inn	12-13 in.	8.99	12/94	2c
Taxes				
Tax rate, residential property, month	$100	0.94	1/92	79c
Taxes, Federal income, expenditures	year	2275	91	81r
Taxes, personal, expenditures	year	2715	91	81r
Taxes, State and local income, expenditures	year	365	91	81r
Transportation				
Transportation, ACCRA Index		97.50	12/94	2c
Bus fare, one-way	trip	1.15	12/95	1c
Cars and trucks purchased, new	year	1306	91	81r
Cars and trucks purchased, used	year	942	91	81r
Driver's learning permit fee	perm	12.50	1/94	84s
Driver's license fee	orig	12.50	1/94	84s
Driver's license fee, duplicate	lic	10.00	1/94	84s
Driver's license reinstatement fee, min.	susp	25.00	1/94	85s
Driver's license renewal fee	renew	12.50	1/94	84s
Identification card, nondriver	card	5.00	1/94	83s
Motorcycle learning permit fee	perm	12.50	1/94	84s
Motorcycle license fee	orig	12.50	1/94	84s
Motorcycle license fee, duplicate	lic	10.00	1/94	84s
Motorcycle license renewal fee	renew	12.50	1/94	84s
Public transportation expenditures	year	249	91	81r
Tire balance, computer or spin bal., front	wheel	6.33	12/94	2c
Transportation expenditures, total	year	5307	91	81r
Vehicle finance charges	year	346	91	81r
Vehicle insurance expenditures	year	544	91	81r
Vehicle maintenance and repairs expenditures	year	600	91	81r
Vehicle purchases	year	2275	91	81r
Vehicle rental, leases, licenses, etc. expenditures	year	141	91	81r
Vehicles purchased, other than cars and trucks	year	27	91	81r
Utilities				
Utilities, ACCRA Index		115.00	12/94	2c
Electricity expenditures	year	950	91	81r
Electricity, 1800 sq. ft., new home	mo.	136.67	12/94	2c
Electricity, summer, 250 KWh	month	28.58	8/93	64c
Electricity, summer, 500 KWh	month	52.35	8/93	64c
Electricity, summer, 750 KWh	month	76.13	8/93	64c
Electricity, summer, 1000 KWh	month	99.09	8/93	64c
Utilities, fuels, and public services, total expenditures	year	2000	91	81r
Water and other public services, expenditures	year	227	91	81r
Weddings				
Bridal attendants' gowns	event	750	10/93	76r
Bridal gown	event	852	10/93	76r
Bridal headpiece and veil	event	167	10/93	76r
Bride's wedding band	event	708	10/93	76r
Clergy	event	224	10/93	76r
Engagement ring	event	2756	10/93	76r
Flowers	event	863	10/93	76r
Formal wear for groom	event	106	10/93	76r
Groom's attendants' formal wear	event	530	10/93	76r
Groom's wedding band	event	402	10/93	76r
Music	event	600	10/93	76r
Photography	event	1088	10/93	76r
Shoes for bride	event	50	10/93	76r
Videography	event	483	10/93	76r
Wedding invitations and announcements	event	342	10/93	76r
Wedding reception	event	7000	10/93	76r

Winston-Salem, NC

Item	Per	Value	Date	Ref.
Composite, ACCRA index		97.50	12/94	2c
Alcoholic Beverages				
Beer, Miller Lite, Bud, 12-oz., ex deposit	6	3.63	12/94	2c
J & B Scotch	750-ml.	18.60	12/94	2c
Wine, Gallo Chablis blanc	1.5-lit	4.31	12/94	2c
Appliances				
Appliances (major), expenditures	year	153	91	81r
Average annual exp.				
Food, health care, personal goods, services	year	27020	91	81r
Charity				
Cash contributions, expenditures	year	839	91	81r
Clothing				
Apparel, men and boys, total expenditures	year	380	91	81r
Apparel, women and girls, total expenditures	year	660	91	81r
Footwear, expenditures	year	193	91	81r
Jeans, man's denim		25.77	12/94	2c
Shirt, man's dress shirt		31.79	12/94	2c
Undervest, boy's size 10-14, cotton	3	4.08	12/94	2c
Communications				
Long-distance telephone rate, day, addl. min., 1-10 mi.	min.	0.10	12/93	9s
Long-distance telephone rate, day, initial min., 1-10 mi.	min.	0.16	12/93	9s
Newspaper subscription, dly. and Sun. delivery	month	10.00	12/94	2c
Phone line, single, business, field visit	inst	62.50	12/93	9s
Phone line, single, business, no field visit	inst	62.50	12/93	9s
Phone line, single, residence, field visit	inst	42.75	12/93	9s
Phone line, single, residence, no field visit	inst	42.75	12/93	9s
Telephone bill, family of four	month	16.56	12/94	2c
Telephone service, expenditures	year	616	91	81r
Education				
Board, 4-year private college/university	year	2069	8/94	80s
Board, 4-year public college/university	year	1627	8/94	80s
Education, total expenditures	year	319	91	81r
Room, 4-year private college/university	year	1824	8/94	80s
Room, 4-year public college/university	year	1669	8/94	80s
Total cost, 4-year private college/university	year	13505	8/94	80s
Total cost, 4-year public college/university	year	4704	8/94	80s
Tuition, 2-year public college/university, in-state	year	577	8/94	80s
Tuition, 4-year private college/university, in-state	year	9612	8/94	80s
Tuition, 4-year public college/university, in-state	year	1409	8/94	80s
Energy and Fuels				
Energy, combined forms, 1800 sq. ft.	mo.	112.27	12/94	2c
Fuel oil and other fuels, expenditures	year	56	91	81r
Gas, natural, expenditures	year	150	91	81r
Gas, reg unlead, taxes inc., cash, self-service	gal	1.12	12/94	2c
Gasoline and motor oil purchased	year	1152	91	81r
Gasoline, unleaded midgrade	gallon	1.21	4/93	82r
Gasoline, unleaded premium	gallon	1.30	4/93	82r
Gasoline, unleaded regular	gallon	1.10	4/93	82r
Entertainment				
Bowling, evening rate	game	2.73	12/94	2c
Concert ticket, Pearl Jam group	perf	20.00	94	50r
Entertainment, total expenditures	year	1266	91	81r
Fees and admissions, expenditures	year	306	91	81r
Monopoly game, Parker Brothers', No. 9	game	10.95	12/94	2c
Movie	adm	5.00	12/94	2c
Pets, toys, playground equipment, expenditures	year	271	91	81r
Reading, expenditures	year	131	91	81r
Televisions, radios, and sound equipment, expenditures	year	439	91	81r

Values are in dollars or fractions of dollars. In the column headed *Ref*, references are shown to sources. Each reference is followed by a letter. These refer to the geographical level for which data were reported: s = State, r = Region, and c = City or metro. The abbreviation *ex* is used to mean *except* or *excluding*; *exp* stands for expenditures. For other abbreviations and further explanations, please see the Introduction.

Winston-Salem, NC - continued

Item	Per	Value	Date	Ref.
Entertainment				
Tennis balls, yellow, Wilson or Penn, 3	can	2.30	12/94	2c
Funerals				
Burial, immediate, container provided by funeral home		1370.36	1/95	54r
Cards, acknowledgment		14.83	1/95	54r
Casket, minimum alternative		192.52	1/95	54r
Cosmetology, hair care, etc.		102.27	1/95	54r
Cremation, direct, container provided by funeral home		1065.64	1/95	54r
Embalming		304.29	1/95	54r
Funeral, funeral home		287.83	1/95	54r
Funeral, other facility		284.14	1/95	54r
Graveside service		349.13	1/95	54r
Hearse, local		132.27	1/95	54r
Limousine, local		98.45	1/95	54r
Memorial service		270.59	1/95	54r
Service charge, professional, nondeclinable		933.59	1/95	54r
Visitation and viewing		225.83	1/95	54r
Groceries				
Groceries, ACCRA Index		97.10	12/94	2c
Apples, Red Delicious	lb.	0.73	12/94	82r
Baby food, strained vegetables, lowest price	4-4.5 oz.	0.39	12/94	2c
Bacon, sliced	lb.	1.67	12/94	82r
Bananas	lb.	0.49	12/94	2c
Bananas	lb.	0.42	12/94	82r
Beef or hamburger, ground	lb.	1.49	12/94	2c
Beef purchases	year	213	91	81r
Beverage purchases, alcoholic	year	249	91	81r
Beverage purchases, nonalcoholic	year	207	91	81r
Bologna, all beef or mixed	lb.	2.27	12/94	82r
Bread, white	24-oz.	0.71	12/94	2c
Bread, white, pan	lb.	0.68	12/94	82r
Cabbage	lb.	0.42	12/94	82r
Carrots, short trimmed and topped	lb.	0.53	12/94	82r
Cereals and bakery products purchases	year	345	91	81r
Cereals and cereals products purchases	year	127	91	81r
Cheddar cheese, natural	lb.	3.58	12/94	82r
Cheese, Kraft grated Parmesan	8-oz.	3.18	12/94	2c
Chicken breast, bone-in	lb.	1.71	12/94	82r
Chicken, fresh, whole	lb.	0.78	12/94	82r
Chicken, whole fryer	lb.	0.74	12/94	2c
Chuck roast, USDA choice, boneless	lb.	2.26	12/94	82r
Cigarettes, Winston, Kings	carton	13.13	12/94	2c
Coffee, vacuum-packed	13 oz.	3.31	12/94	2c
Corn Flakes, Kellogg's or Post Toasties	18 oz.	2.44	12/94	2c
Corn, frozen, whole kernel, lowest price	10 oz.	0.63	12/94	2c
Crackers, soda, salted	lb.	1.27	12/94	82r
Cucumbers	lb.	0.65	12/94	82r
Dairy products (other) purchases	year	141	91	81r
Eggs, Grade A large	dozen	0.88	12/94	2c
Eggs, Grade A large	dozen	0.87	12/94	82r
Fish and seafood purchases	year	72	91	81r
Flour, white, all purpose	lb.	0.23	12/94	82r
Food purchases, food eaten at home	year	2381	91	81r
Foods purchased away from home, not prepared by consumer	year	1696	91	81r
Frankfurters, all meat or all beef	lb.	1.74	12/94	82r
Fruits and vegetables purchases	year	380	91	81r
Grapefruit	lb.	0.45	12/94	82r
Grapes, Thompson seedless	lb.	2.30	12/94	82r
Ground beef, 100% beef	lb.	1.37	12/94	82r
Ground chuck, 100% beef	lb.	1.97	12/94	82r
Ham, boneless, exc. canned	lb.	2.54	12/94	82r
Ice cream, prepackaged, bulk, regular	1/2 gal.	2.47	12/94	82r
Lemons	lb.	1.02	12/94	82r
Lettuce, iceberg	lb.	0.96	12/94	82r
Lettuce, iceberg	head	0.89	12/94	2c
Margarine, Blue Bonnet or Parkay cubes	lb.	0.57	12/94	2c
Margarine, stick	lb.	0.77	12/94	82r

Winston-Salem, NC - continued

Item	Per	Value	Date	Ref.
Groceries - continued				
Meats, poultry, fish, and eggs purchases	year	655	91	81r
Milk and cream (fresh) purchases	year	130	91	81r
Milk, whole	1/2 gal.	1.42	12/94	2c
Orange juice, frozen concentrate 12-oz. can	16 oz.	1.36	12/94	82r
Orange juice, Minute Maid frozen	12-oz.	1.13	12/94	2c
Oranges, Navel	lb.	0.54	12/94	82r
Peaches, halves or slices, Hunt's, Del Monte, or Libby's	29-oz.	1.32	12/94	2c
Pears, Anjou	lb.	0.81	12/94	82r
Peas, sweet, Del Monte or Green Giant	15-17 oz.	0.48	12/94	2c
Pork chops, center cut, bone-in	lb.	3.07	12/94	82r
Pork purchases	year	142	91	81r
Potato chips	16-oz.	3.15	12/94	82r
Potatoes, frozen, French fried	lb.	0.82	12/94	82r
Potatoes, white	lb.	0.34	12/94	82r
Potatoes, white or red	10-lb. sack	2.71	12/94	2c
Rice, white, long grain, uncooked	lb.	0.48	12/94	82r
Round roast, USDA choice, boneless	lb.	2.91	12/94	82r
Sausage, fresh	lb.	1.82	12/94	82r
Sausage, Jimmy Dean, 100% pork	lb.	2.29	12/94	2c
Shortening, vegetable oil blends	lb.	0.75	12/94	82r
Shortening, vegetable, Crisco	3-lb.	2.53	12/94	2c
Soft drink, Coca Cola, ex deposit	2 lit	1.15	12/94	2c
Spaghetti and macaroni	lb.	0.87	12/94	82r
Steak, rib eye, USDA choice, boneless	lb.	6.85	12/94	82r
Steak, round, graded & ungraded, exc. USDA prime & choice	lb.	2.96	12/94	82r
Steak, round, USDA choice, boneless	lb.	3.17	12/94	82r
Steak, sirloin, USDA choice, boneless	lb.	4.12	12/94	82r
Steak, t-bone	lb.	5.63	12/94	2c
Steak, T-bone, USDA choice, bone-in	lb.	5.63	12/94	82r
Sugar and other sweets, eaten at home, expenditures	year	93	91	81r
Sugar, cane or beet	4 lbs.	1.44	12/94	2c
Sugar, white, all sizes	lb.	0.39	12/94	82r
Tobacco products and smoking supplies, total expenditures	year	286	91	81r
Tomatoes, field grown	lb.	1.36	12/94	82r
Tomatoes, Hunt's or Del Monte	14.5 oz.	0.55	12/94	2c
Tuna, chunk, light	lb.	1.94	12/94	82r
Tuna, chunk, light, oil-packed	6.125-6.5 oz.	0.62	12/94	2c
Turkey, frozen, whole	lb.	0.96	12/94	82r
Yogurt, natural, fruit flavored	8 oz.	0.58	12/94	82r
Goods and Services				
Miscellaneous goods and services, ACCRA Index		96.70	12/94	2c
Health Care				
Health care, ACCRA Index		91.80	12/94	2c
Adenosine, emergency room	treat	100.00	95	23r
Antibiotic ointment, Polysporin	1.5 oz.	4.19	12/94	2c
Bladder tap, superpubic, infant, emergency room	treat	119.00	95	23r
Blood analysis, emergency room	treat	25.00	95	23r
Blood tests, abdominal pain, emergency room	treat	25.00	95	23r
Burn dressing, emergency room	treat	266.00	95	23r
Cardiology interpretation, emergency room	treat	26.00	95	23r
Chest X-ray, emergency room	treat	78.00	95	23r
Childbirth, Cesarean delivery, hospital charge	birth	5462.00	12/91	69r
Childbirth, Cesarean delivery, physician charge	birth	2228.00	12/91	69r
Childbirth, normal delivery, hospital charge	birth	2943.00	12/91	69r
Childbirth, normal delivery, physician charge	birth	1619.00	12/91	69r
Defibrillation pads, emergency room	treat	6.00	95	23r

Values are in dollars or fractions of dollars. In the column headed *Ref*, references are shown to sources. Each reference is followed by a letter. These refer to the geographical level for which data were reported: s=State, r=Region, and c=City or metro. The abbreviation *ex* is used to mean *except* or *excluding*; *exp* stands for expenditures. For other abbreviations and further explanations, please see the Introduction.

Winston-Salem, NC - continued

Item	Per	Value	Date	Ref.
Health Care				
Dentist's fee, adult teeth cleaning and periodic oral exam	visit	54.00	12/94	2c
Doctor's fee, routine exam, established patient	visit	39.20	12/94	2c
Drugs, expenditures	year	297	91	81r
Gastric tube insertion, nasal, emergency room	treat	25.00	95	23r
Health care, total expenditures	year	1600	91	81r
Health insurance expenditures	year	637	91	81r
Heart monitor, emergency room	treat	40.00	95	23r
Hospital care, semiprivate room	day	216.00	12/94	2c
Insurance premium, family medical care	month	405.45	1/95	41s
Intravenous fluids, emergency room	treat	130.00	95	23r
Intravenous fluids, emergency room	liter	26.00	95	23r
Intravenous line, central, emergency room	treat	342.00	95	23r
Liver function tests, abdominal pain, emergency room	treat	26.00	95	23r
Medical care charges, total, emergency room, third-degree burns	treat	2101.00	95	23r
Medical care charges, total, emergency, infant with fever	treat	628.00	95	23r
Medical services expenditures	year	573	91	81r
Medical supplies expenditures	year	93	91	81r
Morphine, emergency room	treat	34.00	95	23r
Nursing care and facilities charges, emergency room	treat	252.00	95	23r
Nursing care and facilities charges, emergency, infant with fever	treat	252.00	95	23r
Nursing care and facilities charges, emergency, third-degree burns	treat	861.00	95	23r
Physician's charges, emergency, infant with fever	treat	212.00	95	23r
Physician's charges, emergency, third-degree burns	treat	372.00	95	23r
Physician's fee, emergency room	treat	372.00	95	23r
Physician's fee, general practitioner	visit	51.20	12/93	60r
Surgery, open-heart	proc	42374.00	1/93	14r
Ultrasound, abdominal, emergency room	treat	276.00	95	23r
Urinalysis, emergency room	treat	20.00	95	23r
Urinalysis, infant, emergency room	treat	20.00	95	23r
X-rays, emergency room	treat	78.00	95	23r
Household Goods				
Appl. repair, service call, wash mach	min. lab. chg.	26.39	12/94	2c
Floor coverings, expenditures	year	48	91	81r
Furniture, expenditures	year	280	91	81r
Household equipment, misc. expenditures	year	342	91	81r
Household expenditures, miscellaneous	year	256	91	81r
Household furnishings and equipment, expenditures	year	988	91	81r
Household operations expenditures	year	468	91	81r
Household textiles, expenditures	year	95	91	81r
Housekeeping supplies, expenditures	year	380	91	81r
Laundry and cleaning supplies, expenditures	year	109	91	81r
Laundry detergent, Tide Ultra, Bold, or Cheer	42 oz.	2.67	12/94	2c
Postage and stationery, expenditures	year	105	91	81r
Tissues, facial, Kleenex brand	175	0.99	12/94	2c
Housing				
Housing, ACCRA Index		99.20	12/94	2c
Add garage/carport		6,980	3/95	74r
Add room(s)		11,403	3/95	74r
Apartment condominium or co-op, median	unit	68600	12/94	62r
Dwellings (owned), expenditures	year	2428	91	81r
Enclose porch/patio/breezeway		4,572	3/95	74r
Finish room in basement/attic		3,794	3/95	74r
Home, existing, single-family, median	unit	120200	12/94	62r
Home, existing, single-family, median	unit	98.90	12/94	62c
Home, purchase price	unit	101.20	3/93	26c

Winston-Salem, NC - continued

Item	Per	Value	Date	Ref.
Housing - continued				
House payment, principal and interest, 25% down payment	mo.	792	12/94	2c
House, 1800 sq ft, 8000 sq ft lot, new, urban, utilities	total	129400	12/94	2c
Maintenance, repairs, insurance, and other housing expenditures	year	531	91	81r
Mortgage interest and charges expenditures	year	1506	91	81r
Mtge. rate, incl. points and orig. fee, 30-year conv. fixed or ARM	mo.	9.16	12/94	2c
Princ. & int., mortgage, median-price exist. sing.-family home	mo.	540	12/94	62r
Property taxes expenditures	year	391	91	81r
Redesign, restructure more than half of home's interior		17,641	3/95	74r
Rent, apartment, 2 br., 1 1/2-2 baths, unfurnished, 950 sq ft, water	mo.	430	12/94	2c
Rental units expenditures	year	1264	91	81r
Insurance and Pensions				
Auto insurance, private passenger	year	528.43	12/94	71s
Insurance and pensions, personal, expenditures	year	2395	91	81r
Insurance, life and other personal, expenditures	year	368	91	81r
Pensions and Social Security, expenditures	year	2027	91	81r
Personal Goods				
Shampoo, Alberto VO5	15-oz.	1.05	12/94	2c
Toothpaste, Crest or Colgate	6-7 oz.	1.90	12/94	2c
Personal Services				
Dry cleaning, man's 2-pc. suit		6.75	12/94	2c
Haircut, man's barbershop, no styling		7.60	12/94	2c
Haircut, woman's shampoo, trim, blow-dry		25.40	12/94	2c
Personal services expenditures	year	212	91	81r
Restaurant Food				
Chicken, fried, thigh and drumstick		2.09	12/94	2c
Dining expenditures, family	week	33.83	94	73r
Hamburger with cheese	1/4 lb.	1.81	12/94	2c
Pizza, Pizza Hut or Pizza Inn	12-13 in.	7.99	12/94	2c
Taxes				
Taxes, Federal income, expenditures	year	2275	91	81r
Taxes, personal, expenditures	year	2715	91	81r
Taxes, State and local income, expenditures	year	365	91	81r
Transportation				
Transportation, ACCRA Index		99.20	12/94	2c
Bus fare, one-way	trip	0.70	12/95	1c
Bus fare, one-way	trip	0.75	12/95	1c
Cars and trucks purchased, new	year	1306	91	81r
Cars and trucks purchased, used	year	942	91	81r
Driver's learning permit fee	perm	10.00	1/94	84s
Driver's license fee	orig	10.00	1/94	84s
Driver's license fee, duplicate	lic	5.00	1/94	84s
Driver's license reinstatement fee, min.	susp	25.00	1/94	85s
Driver's license renewal fee	renew	10.00	1/94	84s
Fine, safety belt violation	ticket	25.00	95	56s
Identification card, nondriver	card	10.00	1/94	83s
Motorcycle license fee	orig	5.00	1/94	84s
Public transportation expenditures	year	249	91	81r
Tire balance, computer or spin bal., front	wheel	6.70	12/94	2c
Transportation expenditures, total	year	5307	91	81r
Vehicle finance charges	year	346	91	81r
Vehicle insurance expenditures	year	544	91	81r
Vehicle maintenance and repairs expenditures	year	600	91	81r
Vehicle purchases	year	2275	91	81r
Vehicle rental, leases, licenses, etc. expenditures	year	141	91	81r
Vehicles purchased, other than cars and trucks	year	27	91	81r

Values are in dollars or fractions of dollars. In the column headed *Ref*, references are shown to sources. Each reference is followed by a letter. These refer to the geographical level for which data were reported: s = State, r = Region, and c = City or metro. The abbreviation *ex* is used to mean *except* or *excluding*; *exp* stands for *expenditures*. For other abbreviations and further explanations, please see the Introduction.

Winston-Salem, NC - continued

Item	Per	Value	Date	Ref.
Utilities				
Utilities, ACCRA Index		98.00	12/94	2c
Electricity expenditures	year	950	91	81r
Electricity, 1800 sq. ft., new home	mo.	112.27	12/94	2c
Utilities, fuels, and public services, total expenditures	year	2000	91	81r
Water and other public services, expenditures	year	227	91	81r
Weddings				
Bridal attendants' gowns	event	750	10/93	76r
Bridal gown	event	852	10/93	76r
Bridal headpiece and veil	event	167	10/93	76r
Bride's wedding band	event	708	10/93	76r
Clergy	event	224	10/93	76r
Engagement ring	event	2756	10/93	76r
Flowers	event	863	10/93	76r
Formal wear for groom	event	106	10/93	76r
Groom's attendants' formal wear	event	530	10/93	76r
Groom's wedding band	event	402	10/93	76r
Music	event	600	10/93	76r
Photography	event	1088	10/93	76r
Shoes for bride	event	50	10/93	76r
Videography	event	483	10/93	76r
Wedding invitations and announcements	event	342	10/93	76r
Wedding reception	event	7000	10/93	76r

Worcester, MA

Item	Per	Value	Date	Ref.
Appliances				
Appliances (major), expenditures	year	145	91	81r
Average annual exp.				
Food, health care, personal goods, services	year	29496	91	81r
Charity				
Cash contributions, expenditures	year	708	91	81r
Clothing				
Apparel, men and boys, total expenditures	year	416	91	81r
Apparel, women and girls, total expenditures	year	744	91	81r
Footwear, expenditures	year	305	91	81r
Communications				
Long-distance telephone rate, day, addl. min., 1-10 mi.	min.	0.09	12/93	9s
Long-distance telephone rate, day, initial min., 1-10 mi.	min.	0.19	12/93	9s
Phone line, single, business, field visit	inst	27.50	12/93	9s
Phone line, single, business, no field visit	inst	93.02	12/93	9s
Phone line, single, residence, field visit	inst	27.50	12/93	9s
Phone line, single, residence, no field visit	inst	37.07	12/93	9s
Telephone service, expenditures	year	589	91	81r
Education				
Board, 4-year private college/university	year	3179	8/94	80s
Board, 4-year public college/university	year	2035	8/94	80s
Education, total expenditures	year	593	91	81r
Room, 4-year private college/university	year	3369	8/94	80s
Room, 4-year public college/university	year	2290	8/94	80s
Total cost, 4-year private college/university	year	21346	8/94	80s
Total cost, 4-year public college/university	year	8467	8/94	80s
Tuition, 2-year public college/university, in-state	year	2361	8/94	80s
Tuition, 4-year private college/university, in-state	year	14797	8/94	80s
Tuition, 4-year public college/university, in-state	year	4142	8/94	80s
Energy and Fuels				
Fuel oil and other fuels, expenditures	year	257	91	81r
Gas, natural, expenditures	year	285	91	81r
Gasoline and motor oil purchased	year	867	91	81r
Gasoline, unleaded midgrade	gallon	1.32	4/93	82r
Gasoline, unleaded premium	gallon	1.40	4/93	82r

Worcester, MA - continued

Item	Per	Value	Date	Ref.
Energy and Fuels - continued				
Gasoline, unleaded regular	gallon	1.19	4/93	82r
Entertainment				
Entertainment, total expenditures	year	1331	91	81r
Fees and admissions, expenditures	year	398	91	81r
Pets, toys, playground equipment, expenditures	year	270	91	81r
Reading, expenditures	year	171	91	81r
Televisions, radios, and sound equipment, expenditures	year	429	91	81r
Funerals				
Burial, immediate, container provided by funeral home		1507.89	1/95	54r
Cards, acknowledgment		18.10	1/95	54r
Casket, minimum alternative		133.03	1/95	54r
Cosmetology, hair care, etc.		114.12	1/95	54r
Cremation, direct, container provided by funeral home		1309.19	1/95	54r
Embalming		320.97	1/95	54r
Funeral, funeral home		327.61	1/95	54r
Funeral, other facility		314.81	1/95	54r
Graveside service		286.11	1/95	54r
Hearse, local		158.95	1/95	54r
Limousine, local		149.45	1/95	54r
Memorial service		315.94	1/95	54r
Service charge, professional, nondeclinable		1148.43	1/95	54r
Visitation and viewing		249.66	1/95	54r
Groceries				
Apples, Red Delicious	lb.	0.78	12/94	82r
Bacon, sliced	lb.	2.24	12/94	82r
Bananas	lb.	0.49	12/94	82r
Beef purchases	year	226	91	81r
Beverage purchases, alcoholic	year	332	91	81r
Beverage purchases, nonalcoholic	year	213	91	81r
Bread, white, pan	lb.	0.80	12/94	82r
Butter, salted, Grade AA, stick	lb.	1.67	12/94	82r
Carrots, short trimmed and topped	lb.	0.51	12/94	82r
Cereals and bakery products purchases	year	407	91	81r
Cereals and cereals products purchases	year	132	91	81r
Chicken breast, bone-in	lb.	2.22	12/94	82r
Chicken, fresh, whole	lb.	1.05	12/94	82r
Chuck roast, USDA choice, boneless	lb.	2.74	12/94	82r
Coffee, 100%, ground roast, all sizes	lb.	4.61	12/94	82r
Dairy products (other) purchases	year	161	91	81r
Eggs, Grade A large	dozen	1.12	12/94	82r
Fish and seafood purchases	year	112	91	81r
Food purchases, food eaten at home	year	2599	91	81r
Foods purchased away from home, not prepared by consumer	year	2024	91	81r
Fruits and vegetables purchases	year	444	91	81r
Grapefruit	lb.	0.44	12/94	82r
Grapes, Thompson seedless	lb.	2.24	12/94	82r
Ground chuck, 100% beef	lb.	1.67	12/94	82r
Ice cream, prepackaged, bulk, regular	1/2 gal.	2.93	12/94	82r
Lemons	lb.	1.06	12/94	82r
Lettuce, iceberg	lb.	0.92	12/94	82r
Meats, poultry, fish, and eggs purchases	year	751	91	81r
Milk and cream (fresh) purchases	year	152	91	81r
Orange juice, frozen concentrate 12-oz. can	16 oz.	1.92	12/94	82r
Oranges, Navel	lb.	0.56	12/94	82r
Pork chops, center cut, bone-in	lb.	3.09	12/94	82r
Pork purchases	year	130	91	81r
Potatoes, white	lb.	0.37	12/94	82r
Rib roast, USDA choice, bone-in	lb.	4.98	12/94	82r
Round roast, USDA choice, boneless	lb.	2.93	12/94	82r
Shortening, vegetable oil blends	lb.	1.03	12/94	82r
Spaghetti and macaroni	lb.	0.84	12/94	82r
Steak, round, USDA choice, boneless	lb.	3.48	12/94	82r
Steak, sirloin, USDA choice, bone-in	lb.	3.38	12/94	82r
Steak, sirloin, USDA choice, boneless	lb.	4.81	12/94	82r

Values are in dollars or fractions of dollars. In the column headed *Ref*, references are shown to sources. Each reference is followed by a letter. These refer to the geographical level for which data were reported: s = State, r = Region, and c = City or metro. The abbreviation *ex* is used to mean *except* or *excluding*; *exp* stands for *expenditures*. For other abbreviations and further explanations, please see the Introduction.

Worcester, MA - continued

Item	Per	Value	Date	Ref.
Groceries				
Sugar and other sweets, eaten at home, expenditures	year	89	91	81r
Sugar, white, all sizes	lb.	0.46	12/94	82r
Tobacco products and smoking supplies, total expenditures	year	279	91	81r
Tomatoes, field grown	lb.	1.56	12/94	82r
Tuna, chunk, light	lb.	2.09	12/94	82r
Health Care				
Childbirth, Cesarean delivery, hospital charge	birth	6334.00	12/91	69r
Childbirth, Cesarean delivery, physician charge	birth	2234.00	12/91	69r
Childbirth, normal delivery, hospital charge	birth	3225.00	12/91	69r
Childbirth, normal delivery, physician charge	birth	1623.00	12/91	69r
Drugs, expenditures	year	205	91	81r
Health care, total expenditures	year	1396	91	81r
Health insurance expenditures	year	553	91	81r
Insurance premium, family medical care	month	457.38	1/95	41s
Medical services expenditures	year	559	91	81r
Medical supplies expenditures	year	80	91	81r
Household Goods				
Floor coverings, expenditures	year	158	91	81r
Furniture, expenditures	year	341	91	81r
Household equipment, misc. expenditures	year	363	91	81r
Household expenditures, miscellaneous	year	194	91	81r
Household furnishings and equipment, expenditures	year	1158	91	81r
Household operations expenditures	year	378	91	81r
Household textiles, expenditures	year	88	91	81r
Housekeeping supplies, expenditures	year	426	91	81r
Laundry and cleaning supplies, expenditures	year	122	91	81r
Postage and stationery, expenditures	year	134	91	81r
Housing				
Add garage/carport		11,614	3/95	74r
Add room(s)		16,816	3/95	74r
Apartment condominium or co-op, median	unit	96700	12/94	62r
Dwellings (owned), expenditures	year	3305	91	81r
Enclose porch/patio/breezeway		2,980	3/95	74r
Finish room in basement/attic		4,330	3/95	74r
Home, existing, single-family, median	unit	161600	12/94	62r
Maintenance, repairs, insurance, and other housing expenditures	year	569	91	81r
Mortgage interest and charges expenditures	year	1852	91	81r
Princ. & int., mortgage, median-price exist. sing.-family home	mo.	765	12/94	62r
Property taxes expenditures	year	884	91	81r
Redesign, restructure more than half of home's interior		2,750	3/95	74r
Rental units expenditures	year	1832	91	81r
Insurance and Pensions				
Auto insurance, private passenger	year	1009.56	12/94	71s
Insurance and pensions, personal, expenditures	year	2690	91	81r
Insurance, life and other personal, expenditures	year	341	91	81r
Pensions and Social Security, expenditures	year	2349	91	81r
Legal Assistance				
Estate planning, law-firm partner	hr.	375.00	10/93	12r
Legal work, law firm associate	hour	78		10r
Legal work, law firm partner	hour	183		10r
Personal Services				
Personal services expenditures	year	184	91	81r
Restaurant Food				
Dining expenditures, family	week	34.26	94	73r
Taxes				
Taxes, Federal income, expenditures	year	2409	91	81r
Taxes, personal, expenditures	year	3094	91	81r

Worcester, MA - continued

Item	Per	Value	Date	Ref.
Taxes - continued				
Taxes, State and local income, expenditures	year	620	91	81r
Transportation				
Cars and trucks purchased, new	year	1170	91	81r
Cars and trucks purchased, used	year	739	91	81r
Driver's learning permit fee	perm	15.00	1/94	84s
Driver's license fee	orig	50.00	1/94	84s
Driver's license fee, duplicate	lic	15.00	1/94	84s
Driver's license renewal fee	renew	43.75	1/94	84s
Identification card, nondriver	card	15.00	1/94	83s
Motorcycle license fee	orig	50.00	1/94	84s
Motorcycle license fee, duplicate	lic	15.00	1/94	84s
Motorcycle license renewal fee	renew	43.75	1/94	84s
Public transportation expenditures	year	430	91	81r
Transportation expenditures, total	year	4810	91	81r
Vehicle finance charges	year	238	91	81r
Vehicle insurance expenditures	year	630	91	81r
Vehicle maintenance and repairs expenditures	year	532	91	81r
Vehicle purchases	year	1920	91	81r
Vehicle rental, leases, licenses, etc. expenditures	year	193	91	81r
Vehicles purchased, other than cars and trucks	year	11	91	81r
Utilities				
Electricity expenditures	year	695	91	81r
Utilities, fuels, and public services, total expenditures	year	1981	91	81r
Water and other public services, expenditures	year	154	91	81r
Weddings				
Bridal attendants' gowns	event	750	10/93	76r
Bridal gown	event	852	10/93	76r
Bridal headpiece and veil	event	167	10/93	76r
Bride's wedding band	event	708	10/93	76r
Clergy	event	224	10/93	76r
Engagement ring	event	2756	10/93	76r
Flowers	event	863	10/93	76r
Formal wear for groom	event	106	10/93	76r
Groom's attendants' formal wear	event	530	10/93	76r
Groom's wedding band	event	402	10/93	76r
Music	event	600	10/93	76r
Photography	event	1088	10/93	76r
Shoes for bride	event	50	10/93	76r
Videography	event	483	10/93	76r
Wedding invitations and announcements	event	342	10/93	76r
Wedding reception	event	7000	10/93	76r

Worcester County, MD

Item	Per	Value	Date	Ref.
Composite, ACCRA index		110.30	12/94	2c
Alcoholic Beverages				
Beer, Miller Lite, Bud, 12-oz., ex deposit	6	3.99	12/94	2c
J & B Scotch	750-ml.	17.94	12/94	2c
Wine, Gallo Chablis blanc	1.5-lit	6.79	12/94	2c
Clothing				
Jeans, man's denim		41.00	12/94	2c
Shirt, man's dress shirt		34.50	12/94	2c
Undervest, boy's size 10-14, cotton	3	4.59	12/94	2c
Communications				
Newspaper subscription, dly. and Sun. delivery	month	15.65	12/94	2c
Telephone bill, family of four	month	16.95	12/94	2c
Energy and Fuels				
Energy, combined forms, 1800 sq. ft.	mo.	161.98	12/94	2c
Gas, reg unlead, taxes inc., cash, self-service	gal	1.16	12/94	2c

Values are in dollars or fractions of dollars. In the column headed *Ref*, references are shown to sources. Each reference is followed by a letter. These refer to the geographical level for which data were reported: s = State, r = Region, and c = City or metro. The abbreviation *ex* is used to mean *except* or *excluding*; *exp* stands for expenditures. For other abbreviations and further explanations, please see the Introduction.

Worcester County, MD - continued

Item	Per	Value	Date	Ref.
Entertainment				
Bowling, evening rate	game	2.37	12/94	2c
Monopoly game, Parker Brothers', No. 9	game	11.66	12/94	2c
Movie	adm	7.00	12/94	2c
Tennis balls, yellow, Wilson or Penn, 3	can	3.58	12/94	2c
Groceries				
Groceries, ACCRA Index		102.50	12/94	2c
Baby food, strained vegetables, lowest price	4-4.5 oz.	0.37	12/94	2c
Bananas	lb.	0.41	12/94	2c
Beef or hamburger, ground	lb.	1.51	12/94	2c
Bread, white	24-oz.	0.69	12/94	2c
Cheese, Kraft grated Parmesan	8-oz.	3.46	12/94	2c
Chicken, whole fryer	lb.	0.81	12/94	2c
Cigarettes, Winston, Kings	carton	15.86	12/94	2c
Coffee, vacuum-packed	13 oz.	3.86	12/94	2c
Corn Flakes, Kellogg's or Post Toasties	18 oz.	2.61	12/94	2c
Corn, frozen, whole kernel, lowest price	10 oz.	0.62	12/94	2c
Eggs, Grade A large	dozen	0.86	12/94	2c
Lettuce, iceberg	head	0.84	12/94	2c
Margarine, Blue Bonnet or Parkay cubes	lb.	0.82	12/94	2c
Milk, whole	1/2 gal.	1.31	12/94	2c
Orange juice, Minute Maid frozen	12-oz.	1.44	12/94	2c
Peaches, halves or slices, Hunt's, Del Monte, or Libby's	29-oz.	1.41	12/94	2c
Peas, sweet, Del Monte or Green Giant	15-17 oz.	0.53	12/94	2c
Potatoes, white or red	10-lb. sack	2.94	12/94	2c
Sausage, Jimmy Dean, 100% pork	lb.	2.57	12/94	2c
Shortening, vegetable, Crisco	3-lb.	2.31	12/94	2c
Soft drink, Coca Cola, ex deposit	2 lit	0.96	12/94	2c
Steak, t-bone	lb.	5.32	12/94	2c
Sugar, cane or beet	4 lbs.	1.39	12/94	2c
Tomatoes, Hunt's or Del Monte	14.5 oz.	0.75	12/94	2c
Tuna, chunk, light, oil-packed	6.125-6.5 oz.	0.69	12/94	2c
Goods and Services				
Miscellaneous goods and services, ACCRA Index		119.10	12/94	2c
Health Care				
Health care, ACCRA Index		94.90	12/94	2c
Antibiotic ointment, Polysporin	1.5 oz.	4.07	12/94	2c
Dentist's fee, adult teeth cleaning and periodic oral exam	visit	44.33	12/94	2c
Doctor's fee, routine exam, established patient	visit	42.00	12/94	2c
Hospital care, semiprivate room	day	364.50	12/94	2c
Household Goods				
Appl. repair, service call, wash mach	min. lab. chg.	43.65	12/94	2c
Laundry detergent, Tide Ultra, Bold, or Cheer	42 oz.	3.16	12/94	2c
Tissues, facial, Kleenex brand	175	1.14	12/94	2c
Housing				
Housing, ACCRA Index		102.50	12/94	2c
House payment, principal and interest, 25% down payment	mo.	779	12/94	2c
House, 1800 sq ft, 8000 sq ft lot, new, urban, utilities	total	127500	12/94	2c
Mtge. rate, incl. points and orig. fee, 30-year conv. fixed or ARM	mo.	9.13	12/94	2c
Rent, apartment, 2 br., 1 1/2-2 baths, unfurnished, 950 sq ft, water	mo.	560	12/94	2c
Personal Goods				
Shampoo, Alberto VO5	15-oz.	1.07	12/94	2c
Toothpaste, Crest or Colgate	6-7 oz.	2.31	12/94	2c

Worcester County, MD - continued

Item	Per	Value	Date	Ref.
Personal Services				
Dry cleaning, man's 2-pc. suit		6.90	12/94	2c
Haircut, man's barbershop, no styling		8.00	12/94	2c
Haircut, woman's shampoo, trim, blow-dry		19.67	12/94	2c
Restaurant Food				
Chicken, fried, thigh and drumstick		2.52	12/94	2c
Hamburger with cheese	1/4 lb.	2.34	12/94	2c
Pizza, Pizza Hut or Pizza Inn	12-13 in.	8.19	12/94	2c
Transportation				
Transportation, ACCRA Index		103.30	12/94	2c
Tire balance, computer or spin bal., front	wheel	7.00	12/94	2c
Utilities				
Utilities, ACCRA Index		136.60	12/94	2c
Electricity, 1800 sq. ft., new home	mo.	161.98	12/94	2c

Yakima, WA

Item	Per	Value	Date	Ref.
Composite, ACCRA index		104.10	12/94	2c
Alcoholic Beverages				
Beer, Miller Lite, Bud, 12-oz., ex deposit	6	3.69	12/94	2c
J & B Scotch	750-ml.	18.95	12/94	2c
Wine, Gallo Chablis blanc	1.5-lit	4.82	12/94	2c
Appliances				
Appliances (major), expenditures	year	160	91	81r
Average annual exp.				
Food, health care, personal goods, services	year	32461	91	81r
Charity				
Cash contributions, expenditures	year	975	91	81r
Clothing				
Apparel, men and boys, total expenditures	year	467	91	81r
Apparel, women and girls, total expenditures	year	737	91	81r
Footwear, expenditures	year	270	91	81r
Jeans, man's denim		28.79	12/94	2c
Shirt, man's dress shirt		31.50	12/94	2c
Undervest, boy's size 10-14, cotton	3	3.89	12/94	2c
Communications				
Long-distance telephone rate, day, addl. min., 1-10 mi.	min.	0.01	12/93	9s
Long-distance telephone rate, day, initial min., 1-10 mi.	min.	0.15	12/93	9s
Newspaper subscription, dly. and Sun. delivery	month	9.50	12/94	2c
Phone line, single, business, field visit	inst	48.00	12/93	9s
Phone line, single, business, no field visit	inst	48.00	12/93	9s
Phone line, single, residence, field visit	inst	31.00	12/93	9s
Phone line, single, residence, no field visit	inst	31.00	12/93	9s
Telephone bill, family of four	month	15.12	12/94	2c
Telephone service, expenditures	year	611	91	81r
Telephone, residential, flat rate	mo.	9.75	12/93	8c
Education				
Board, 4-year private college/university	year	1928	8/94	80s
Board, 4-year public college/university	year	2194	8/94	80s
Education, total expenditures	year	375	91	81r
Room, 4-year private college/university	year	2455	8/94	80s
Room, 4-year public college/university	year	1952	8/94	80s
Total cost, 4-year private college/university	year	16332	8/94	80s
Total cost, 4-year public college/university	year	6483	8/94	80s
Tuition, 2-year public college/university, in-state	year	1141	8/94	80s
Tuition, 4-year private college/university, in-state	year	11949	8/94	80s
Tuition, 4-year public college/university, in-state	year	2337	8/94	80s

Values are in dollars or fractions of dollars. In the column headed *Ref*, references are shown to sources. Each reference is followed by a letter. These refer to the geographical level for which data were reported: s = State, r = Region, and c = City or metro. The abbreviation *ex* is used to mean *except* or *excluding*; *exp* stands for expenditures. For other abbreviations and further explanations, please see the Introduction.

Yakima, WA - continued

Item	Per	Value	Date	Ref.
Energy and Fuels				
Energy, combined forms, 1800 sq. ft.	mo.	83.86	12/94	2c
Fuel oil and other fuels, expenditures	year	33	91	81r
Gas, natural, expenditures	year	212	91	81r
Gas, reg unlead, taxes inc., cash, self-service	gal	1.27	12/94	2c
Gasoline and motor oil purchased	year	1115	91	81r
Gasoline, unleaded midgrade	gallon	1.36	4/93	82r
Gasoline, unleaded premium	gallon	1.43	4/93	82r
Gasoline, unleaded regular	gallon	1.23	4/93	82r
Entertainment				
Bowling, evening rate	game	1.92	12/94	2c
Concert ticket, Pearl Jam group	perf	20.00	94	50r
Entertainment, total expenditures	year	1853	91	81r
Fees and admissions, expenditures	year	482	91	81r
Monopoly game, Parker Brothers', No. 9	game	9.99	12/94	2c
Movie	adm	6.00	12/94	2c
Pets, toys, playground equipment, expenditures	year	299	91	81r
Reading, expenditures	year	164	91	81r
Televisions, radios, and sound equipment, expenditures	year	528	91	81r
Tennis balls, yellow, Wilson or Penn, 3	can	2.32	12/94	2c
Funerals				
Burial, immediate, container provided by funeral home		1382.70	1/95	54r
Cards, acknowledgment		21.87	1/95	54r
Casket, minimum alternative		128.54	1/95	54r
Cosmetology, hair care, etc.		119.69	1/95	54r
Cremation, direct, container provided by funeral home		1030.62	1/95	54r
Embalming		255.42	1/95	54r
Funeral, funeral home		437.38	1/95	54r
Funeral, other facility		444.46	1/95	54r
Graveside service		338.46	1/95	54r
Hearse, local		147.50	1/95	54r
Limousine, local		130.33	1/95	54r
Memorial service		553.16	1/95	54r
Service charge, professional, nondeclinable		859.15	1/95	54r
Visitation and viewing		93.23	1/95	54r
Groceries				
Groceries, ACCRA Index		103.50	12/94	2c
Apples, Red Delicious	lb.	0.72	12/94	82r
Baby food, strained vegetables, lowest price	4-4.5 oz.	0.23	12/94	2c
Bacon, sliced	lb.	1.73	12/94	82r
Bananas	lb.	0.59	12/94	2c
Bananas	lb.	0.52	12/94	82r
Beef or hamburger, ground	lb.	1.33	12/94	2c
Beef purchases	year	241	91	81r
Beverage purchases, alcoholic	year	328	91	81r
Beverage purchases, nonalcoholic	year	234	91	81r
Bologna, all beef or mixed	lb.	2.33	12/94	82r
Bread, white	24-oz.	0.69	12/94	2c
Bread, white, pan	lb.	0.81	12/94	82r
Carrots, short trimmed and topped	lb.	0.43	12/94	82r
Cereals and bakery products purchases	year	392	91	81r
Cereals and cereals products purchases	year	139	91	81r
Cheese, Kraft grated Parmesan	8-oz.	3.72	12/94	2c
Chicken breast, bone-in	lb.	2.04	12/94	82r
Chicken, fresh, whole	lb.	0.95	12/94	82r
Chicken, whole fryer	lb.	0.97	12/94	2c
Cigarettes, Winston, Kings	carton	19.39	12/94	2c
Coffee, 100%, ground roast, all sizes	lb.	4.48	12/94	82r
Coffee, vacuum-packed	13 oz.	3.83	12/94	2c
Corn Flakes, Kellogg's or Post Toasties	18 oz.	2.07	12/94	2c
Corn, frozen, whole kernel, lowest price	10 oz.	0.70	12/94	2c
Dairy products (other) purchases	year	182	91	81r
Eggs, Grade A large	dozen	0.88	12/94	2c
Fish and seafood purchases	year	94	91	81r
Flour, white, all purpose	lb.	0.21	12/94	82r
Food purchases, food eaten at home	year	2749	91	81r

Yakima, WA - continued

Item	Per	Value	Date	Ref.
Groceries - continued				
Foods purchased away from home, not prepared by consumer	year	1909	91	81r
Fruits and vegetables purchases	year	459	91	81r
Grapefruit	lb.	0.56	12/94	82r
Ground beef, 100% beef	lb.	1.31	12/94	82r
Ham, boneless, exc. canned	lb.	2.46	12/94	82r
Ice cream, prepackaged, bulk, regular	1/2 gal.	2.57	12/94	82r
Lemons	lb.	1.00	12/94	82r
Lettuce, iceberg	lb.	0.93	12/94	82r
Lettuce, iceberg	head	0.80	12/94	2c
Margarine, Blue Bonnet or Parkay cubes	lb.	0.66	12/94	2c
Meats, poultry, fish, and eggs purchases	year	700	91	81r
Milk and cream (fresh) purchases	year	155	91	81r
Milk, whole	1/2 gal.	1.49	12/94	2c
Orange juice, frozen concentrate 12-oz. can	16 oz.	1.52	12/94	82r
Orange juice, Minute Maid frozen	12-oz.	1.07	12/94	2c
Oranges, Navel	lb.	0.56	12/94	82r
Peaches, halves or slices, Hunt's, Del Monte, or Libby's	29-oz.	1.38	12/94	2c
Peas, sweet, Del Monte or Green Giant	15-17 oz.	0.70	12/94	2c
Pork chops, center cut, bone-in	lb.	3.30	12/94	82r
Pork purchases	year	122	91	81r
Potato chips	16-oz.	3.03	12/94	82r
Potatoes, frozen, French fried	lb.	0.77	12/94	82r
Potatoes, white	lb.	0.35	12/94	82r
Potatoes, white or red	10-lb. sack	1.63	12/94	2c
Rice, white, long grain, uncooked	lb.	0.54	12/94	82r
Round roast, USDA choice, boneless	lb.	2.92	12/94	82r
Sausage, Jimmy Dean, 100% pork	lb.	3.45	12/94	2c
Shortening, vegetable oil blends	lb.	0.80	12/94	82r
Shortening, vegetable, Crisco	3-lb.	2.29	12/94	2c
Soft drink, Coca Cola, ex deposit	2 lit	1.58	12/94	2c
Spaghetti and macaroni	lb.	1.02	12/94	82r
Steak, round, graded & ungraded, exc. USDA prime & choice	lb.	3.13	12/94	82r
Steak, sirloin, USDA choice, boneless	lb.	4.07	12/94	82r
Steak, t-bone	lb.	5.19	12/94	2c
Sugar and other sweets, eaten at home, expenditures	year	105	91	81r
Sugar, cane or beet	4 lbs.	1.20	12/94	2c
Sugar, white, all sizes	lb.	0.38	12/94	82r
Tobacco products and smoking supplies, total expenditures	year	221	91	81r
Tomatoes, field grown	lb.	1.45	12/94	82r
Tomatoes, Hunt's or Del Monte	14.5 oz.	0.72	12/94	2c
Tuna, chunk, light	lb.	2.18	12/94	82r
Tuna, chunk, light, oil-packed	6.125-6.5 oz.	0.79	12/94	2c
Goods and Services				
Miscellaneous goods and services, ACCRA Index		100.50	12/94	2c
Health Care				
Health care, ACCRA Index		116.70	12/94	2c
Antibiotic ointment, Polysporin	1.5 oz.	3.99	12/94	2c
Childbirth, Cesarean delivery, hospital charge	birth	6059.00	12/91	69r
Childbirth, Cesarean delivery, physician charge	birth	2248.00	12/91	69r
Childbirth, normal delivery, hospital charge	birth	3006.00	12/91	69r
Childbirth, normal delivery, physician charge	birth	1634.00	12/91	69r
Dentist's fee, adult teeth cleaning and periodic oral exam	visit	86.25	12/94	2c
Doctor's fee, routine exam, established patient	visit	34.60	12/94	2c
Drugs, expenditures	year	230	91	81r
Health care, total expenditures	year	1544	91	81r

Values are in dollars or fractions of dollars. In the column headed *Ref*, references are shown to sources. Each reference is followed by a letter. These refer to the geographical level for which data were reported: s=State, r=Region, and c=City or metro. The abbreviation *ex* is used to mean *except* or *excluding*; *exp* stands for expenditures. For other abbreviations and further explanations, please see the Introduction.

Yakima, WA - continued

Item	Per	Value	Date	Ref.
Health Care				
Health insurance expenditures	year	558	91	81r
Hospital care, semiprivate room	day	370.50	12/94	2c
Insurance premium, family medical care	month	382.32	1/95	41s
Medical services expenditures	year	676	91	81r
Medical supplies expenditures	year	80	91	81r
Surgery, open-heart	proc	37818.00	1/93	14r
Household Goods				
Appl. repair, service call, wash mach	min. lab. chg.	38.96	12/94	2c
Floor coverings, expenditures	year	79	91	81r
Furniture, expenditures	year	352	91	81r
Household equipment, misc. expenditures	year	614	91	81r
Household expenditures, miscellaneous	year	294	91	81r
Household furnishings and equipment, expenditures	year	1416	91	81r
Household operations expenditures	year	580	91	81r
Household textiles, expenditures	year	113	91	81r
Housekeeping supplies, expenditures	year	447	91	81r
Laundry and cleaning supplies, expenditures	year	114	91	81r
Laundry detergent, Tide Ultra, Bold, or Cheer	42 oz.	3.72	12/94	2c
Postage and stationery, expenditures	year	145	91	81r
Tissues, facial, Kleenex brand	175	1.14	12/94	2c
Housing				
Housing, ACCRA Index		116.00	12/94	2c
Add garage/carport		6,422	3/95	74r
Add room(s)		26,583	3/95	74r
Apartment condominium or co-op, median	unit	105300	12/94	62r
Dwellings (owned), expenditures	year	3932	91	81r
Enclose porch/patio/breezeway		5,382	3/95	74r
Finish room in basement/attic		3,911	3/95	74r
Home, existing, single-family, median	unit	178600	12/94	62r
House payment, principal and interest, 25% down payment	mo.	795	12/94	2c
House, 1800 sq ft, 8000 sq ft lot, new, urban, utilities	total	128000	12/94	2c
Maintenance, repairs, insurance, and other housing expenditures	year	591	91	81r
Mortgage interest and charges expenditures	year	2747	91	81r
Mtge. rate, incl. points and orig. fee, 30-year conv. fixed or ARM	mo.	9.32	12/94	2c
Princ. & int., mortgage, median-price exist. sing.-family home	mo.	845	12/94	62r
Property taxes expenditures	year	594	91	81r
Redesign, restructure more than half of home's interior		5,467	3/95	74r
Rent, apartment, 2 br., 1 1/2-2 baths, unfurnished, 950 sq ft, water	mo.	550	12/94	2c
Rental units expenditures	year	2077	91	81r
Insurance and Pensions				
Auto insurance, private passenger	year	711.57	12/94	71s
Insurance and pensions, personal, expenditures	year	3042	91	81r
Insurance, life and other personal, expenditures	year	298	91	81r
Pensions and Social Security, expenditures	year	2744	91	81r
Legal Assistance				
Legal work, law firm associate	hour	91		10r
Legal work, law firm partner	hour	151		10r
Personal Goods				
Shampoo, Alberto VO5	15-oz.	1.07	12/94	2c
Toothpaste, Crest or Colgate	6-7 oz.	1.85	12/94	2c
Personal Services				
Dry cleaning, man's 2-pc. suit		6.54	12/94	2c
Haircut, man's barbershop, no styling		7.56	12/94	2c
Haircut, woman's shampoo, trim, blow-dry		19.40	12/94	2c
Personal services expenditures	year	286	91	81r

Yakima, WA - continued

Item	Per	Value	Date	Ref.
Restaurant Food				
Chicken, fried, thigh and drumstick		2.19	12/94	2c
Dining expenditures, family	week	32.25	94	73r
Hamburger with cheese	1/4 lb.	2.06	12/94	2c
Pizza, Pizza Hut or Pizza Inn	12-13 in.	8.99	12/94	2c
Taxes				
Taxes, Federal income, expenditures	year	2946	91	81r
Taxes, personal, expenditures	year	3791	91	81r
Taxes, State and local income, expenditures	year	791	91	81r
Transportation				
Transportation, ACCRA Index		98.20	12/94	2c
Bus fare, one-way	trip	0.35	12/95	1c
Bus fare, up to 10 miles	one-way	0.35	12/94	2c
Cars and trucks purchased, new	year	1231	91	81r
Cars and trucks purchased, used	year	915	91	81r
Driver's learning permit fee	perm	4.00	1/94	84s
Driver's license fee	orig	21.00	1/94	84s
Driver's license fee, duplicate	lic	5.00	1/94	84s
Driver's license reinstatement fee, min.	susp	20.00-50.00	1/94	85s
Driver's license renewal fee	renew	14.00	1/94	84s
Identification card, nondriver	card	4.00	1/94	83s
Motorcycle license fee	orig	8.00	1/94	84s
Motorcycle license renewal fee	renew	7.50	1/94	84s
Public transportation expenditures	year	375	91	81r
Tire balance, computer or spin bal., front	wheel	6.45	12/94	2c
Transportation expenditures, total	year	5527	91	81r
Vehicle finance charges	year	287	91	81r
Vehicle insurance expenditures	year	624	91	81r
Vehicle maintenance and repairs expenditures	year	695	91	81r
Vehicle purchases	year	2174	91	81r
Vehicle rental, leases, licenses, etc. expenditures	year	257	91	81r
Vehicles purchased, other than cars and trucks	year	28	91	81r
Utilities				
Utilities, ACCRA Index		75.10	12/94	2c
Electricity expenditures	year	616	91	81r
Electricity, 1800 sq. ft., new home	mo.	83.86	12/94	2c
Electricity, summer, 250 KWh	month	12.74	8/93	64c
Electricity, summer, 500 KWh	month	21.73	8/93	64c
Electricity, summer, 750 KWh	month	32.48	8/93	64c
Electricity, summer, 1000 KWh	month	44.41	8/93	64c
Utilities, fuels, and public services, total expenditures	year	1681	91	81r
Water and other public services, expenditures	year	209	91	81r
Weddings				
Bridal attendants' gowns	event	750	10/93	76r
Bridal gown	event	852	10/93	76r
Bridal headpiece and veil	event	167	10/93	76r
Bride's wedding band	event	708	10/93	76r
Clergy	event	224	10/93	76r
Engagement ring	event	2756	10/93	76r
Flowers	event	863	10/93	76r
Formal wear for groom	event	106	10/93	76r
Groom's attendants' formal wear	event	530	10/93	76r
Groom's wedding band	event	402	10/93	76r
Music	event	600	10/93	76r
Photography	event	1088	10/93	76r
Shoes for bride	event	50	10/93	76r
Videography	event	483	10/93	76r
Wedding invitations and announcements	event	342	10/93	76r
Wedding reception	event	7000	10/93	76r

Values are in dollars or fractions of dollars. In the column headed *Ref*, references are shown to sources. Each reference is followed by a letter. These refer to the geographical level for which data were reported: s=State, r=Region, and c=City or metro. The abbreviation *ex* is used to mean *except* or *excluding*; *exp* stands for *expenditures*. For other abbreviations and further explanations, please see the Introduction.

York, PA

Item	Per	Value	Date	Ref.
Composite, ACCRA index		99.90	12/94	2c
Alcoholic Beverages				
Beer, Miller Lite, Bud, 12-oz., ex deposit	6	5.34	12/94	2c
J & B Scotch	750-ml.	16.99	12/94	2c
Wine, Gallo Chablis blanc	1.5-lit	5.99	12/94	2c
Appliances				
Appliances (major), expenditures	year	145	91	81r
Average annual exp.				
Food, health care, personal goods, services	year	29496	91	81r
Charity				
Cash contributions, expenditures	year	708	91	81r
Clothing				
Apparel, men and boys, total expenditures	year	416	91	81r
Apparel, women and girls, total expenditures	year	744	91	81r
Footwear, expenditures	year	305	91	81r
Jeans, man's denim		30.99	12/94	2c
Shirt, man's dress shirt		35.30	12/94	2c
Undervest, boy's size 10-14, cotton	3	3.29	12/94	2c
Communications				
Long-distance telephone rate, day, addl. min., 1-10 mi.	min.	0.08	12/93	9s
Long-distance telephone rate, day, initial min., 1-10 mi.	min.	0.15	12/93	9s
Newspaper subscription, dly. and Sun. delivery	month	10.00	12/94	2c
Phone line, single, business, field visit	inst	75.00	12/93	9s
Phone line, single, business, no field visit	inst	75.00	12/93	9s
Phone line, single, residence, field visit	inst	40.00	12/93	9s
Phone line, single, residence, no field visit	inst	40.00	12/93	9s
Telephone bill, family of four	month	22.56	12/94	2c
Telephone service, expenditures	year	589	91	81r
Education				
Board, 4-year private college/university	year	2714	8/94	80s
Board, 4-year public college/university	year	1899	8/94	80s
Education, total expenditures	year	593	91	81r
Room, 4-year private college/university	year	2720	8/94	80s
Room, 4-year public college/university	year	2063	8/94	80s
Total cost, 4-year private college/university	year	18118	8/94	80s
Total cost, 4-year public college/university	year	8278	8/94	80s
Tuition, 2-year public college/university, in-state	year	1671	8/94	80s
Tuition, 4-year private college/university, in-state	year	12684	8/94	80s
Tuition, 4-year public college/university, in-state	year	4316	8/94	80s
Energy and Fuels				
Energy, combined forms, 1800 sq. ft.	mo.	114.75	12/94	2c
Energy, exc. electricity, 1800 sq. ft.	mo.	59.58	12/94	2c
Fuel oil and other fuels, expenditures	year	257	91	81r
Gas, natural, expenditures	year	285	91	81r
Gas, reg unlead, taxes inc., cash, self-service	gal	1.12	12/94	2c
Gasoline and motor oil purchased	year	867	91	81r
Gasoline, unleaded midgrade	gallon	1.32	4/93	82r
Gasoline, unleaded premium	gallon	1.40	4/93	82r
Gasoline, unleaded regular	gallon	1.19	4/93	82r
Entertainment				
Bowling, evening rate	game	2.29	12/94	2c
Entertainment, total expenditures	year	1331	91	81r
Fees and admissions, expenditures	year	398	91	81r
Monopoly game, Parker Brothers', No. 9	game	10.48	12/94	2c
Movie	adm	5.63	12/94	2c
Pets, toys, playground equipment, expenditures	year	270	91	81r
Reading, expenditures	year	171	91	81r
Televisions, radios, and sound equipment, expenditures	year	429	91	81r

York, PA - continued

Item	Per	Value	Date	Ref.
Entertainment - continued				
Tennis balls, yellow, Wilson or Penn, 3	can	2.05	12/94	2c
Funerals				
Burial, immediate, container provided by funeral home		1370.36	1/95	54r
Cards, acknowledgment		17.72	1/95	54r
Casket, minimum alternative		192.52	1/95	54r
Cosmetology, hair care, etc.		139.56	1/95	54r
Cremation, direct, container provided by funeral home		1049.24	1/95	54r
Embalming		387.57	1/95	54r
Funeral, funeral home		278.77	1/95	54r
Funeral, other facility		275.85	1/95	54r
Graveside service		213.08	1/95	54r
Hearse, local		157.27	1/95	54r
Limousine, local		146.45	1/95	54r
Memorial service		271.02	1/95	54r
Service charge, professional, nondeclinable		943.58	1/95	54r
Visitation and viewing		322.86	1/95	54r
Groceries				
Groceries, ACCRA Index		97.00	12/94	2c
Apples, Red Delicious	lb.	0.78	12/94	82r
Baby food, strained vegetables, lowest price	4-4.5 oz.	0.38	12/94	2c
Bacon, sliced	lb.	2.24	12/94	82r
Bananas	lb.	0.35	12/94	2c
Bananas	lb.	0.49	12/94	82r
Beef or hamburger, ground	lb.	1.33	12/94	2c
Beef purchases	year	226	91	81r
Beverage purchases, alcoholic	year	332	91	81r
Beverage purchases, nonalcoholic	year	213	91	81r
Bread, white	24-oz.	0.71	12/94	2c
Bread, white, pan	lb.	0.80	12/94	82r
Butter, salted, Grade AA, stick	lb.	1.67	12/94	82r
Carrots, short trimmed and topped	lb.	0.51	12/94	82r
Cereals and bakery products purchases	year	407	91	81r
Cereals and cereals products purchases	year	132	91	81r
Cheese, Kraft grated Parmesan	8-oz.	3.20	12/94	2c
Chicken breast, bone-in	lb.	2.22	12/94	82r
Chicken, fresh, whole	lb.	1.05	12/94	82r
Chicken, whole fryer	lb.	0.72	12/94	2c
Chuck roast, USDA choice, boneless	lb.	2.74	12/94	82r
Cigarettes, Winston, Kings	carton	15.76	12/94	2c
Coffee, 100%, ground roast, all sizes	lb.	4.61	12/94	82r
Coffee, vacuum-packed	13 oz.	3.48	12/94	2c
Corn Flakes, Kellogg's or Post Toasties	18 oz.	2.42	12/94	2c
Corn, frozen, whole kernel, lowest price	10 oz.	0.71	12/94	2c
Dairy products (other) purchases	year	161	91	81r
Eggs, Grade A large	dozen	0.70	12/94	2c
Eggs, Grade A large	dozen	1.12	12/94	82r
Fish and seafood purchases	year	112	91	81r
Food purchases, food eaten at home	year	2599	91	81r
Foods purchased away from home, not prepared by consumer	year	2024	91	81r
Fruits and vegetables purchases	year	444	91	81r
Grapefruit	lb.	0.44	12/94	82r
Grapes, Thompson seedless	lb.	2.24	12/94	82r
Ground chuck, 100% beef	lb.	1.67	12/94	82r
Ice cream, prepackaged, bulk, regular	1/2 gal.	2.93	12/94	82r
Lemons	lb.	1.06	12/94	82r
Lettuce, iceberg	lb.	0.92	12/94	82r
Lettuce, iceberg	head	0.85	12/94	2c
Margarine, Blue Bonnet or Parkay cubes	lb.	0.66	12/94	2c
Meats, poultry, fish, and eggs purchases	year	751	91	81r
Milk and cream (fresh) purchases	year	152	91	81r
Milk, whole	1/2 gal.	1.22	12/94	2c
Orange juice, frozen concentrate 12-oz. can	16 oz.	1.92	12/94	82r
Orange juice, Minute Maid frozen	12-oz.	1.17	12/94	2c
Oranges, Navel	lb.	0.56	12/94	82r

Values are in dollars or fractions of dollars. In the column headed *Ref*, references are shown to sources. Each reference is followed by a letter. These refer to the geographical level for which data were reported: s=State, r=Region, and c=City or metro. The abbreviation *ex* is used to mean *except* or *excluding*; *exp* stands for *expenditures*. For other abbreviations and further explanations, please see the Introduction.

York, PA - continued

Item	Per	Value	Date	Ref.
Groceries				
Peaches, halves or slices, Hunt's, Del Monte, or Libby's	29-oz.	1.26	12/94	2c
Peas, sweet, Del Monte or Green Giant	15-17 oz.	0.46	12/94	2c
Pork chops, center cut, bone-in	lb.	3.09	12/94	82r
Pork purchases	year	130	91	81r
Potatoes, white	lb.	0.37	12/94	82r
Potatoes, white or red	10-lb. sack	1.97	12/94	2c
Rib roast, USDA choice, bone-in	lb.	4.98	12/94	82r
Round roast, USDA choice, boneless	lb.	2.93	12/94	82r
Sausage, Jimmy Dean, 100% pork	lb.	2.92	12/94	2c
Shortening, vegetable oil blends	lb.	1.03	12/94	82r
Shortening, vegetable, Crisco	3-lb.	2.59	12/94	2c
Soft drink, Coca Cola, ex deposit	2 lit	1.06	12/94	2c
Spaghetti and macaroni	lb.	0.84	12/94	82r
Steak, round, USDA choice, boneless	lb.	3.48	12/94	82r
Steak, sirloin, USDA choice, bone-in	lb.	3.38	12/94	82r
Steak, sirloin, USDA choice, boneless	lb.	4.81	12/94	82r
Steak, t-bone	lb.	5.59	12/94	2c
Sugar and other sweets, eaten at home, expenditures	year	89	91	81r
Sugar, cane or beet	4 lbs.	1.33	12/94	2c
Sugar, white, all sizes	lb.	0.46	12/94	82r
Tobacco products and smoking supplies, total expenditures	year	279	91	81r
Tomatoes, field grown	lb.	1.56	12/94	82r
Tomatoes, Hunt's or Del Monte	14.5 oz.	0.73	12/94	2c
Tuna, chunk, light	lb.	2.09	12/94	82r
Tuna, chunk, light, oil-packed	6.125-6.5 oz.	0.64	12/94	2c
Goods and Services				
Miscellaneous goods and services, ACCRA Index		101.40	12/94	2c
Health Care				
Health care, ACCRA Index		94.20	12/94	2c
Antibiotic ointment, Polysporin	1.5 oz.	4.23	12/94	2c
Childbirth, Cesarean delivery, hospital charge	birth	6334.00	12/91	69r
Childbirth, Cesarean delivery, physician charge	birth	2234.00	12/91	69r
Childbirth, normal delivery, hospital charge	birth	3225.00	12/91	69r
Childbirth, normal delivery, physician charge	birth	1623.00	12/91	69r
Dentist's fee, adult teeth cleaning and periodic oral exam	visit	55.20	12/94	2c
Doctor's fee, routine exam, established patient	visit	33.60	12/94	2c
Drugs, expenditures	year	205	91	81r
Health care, total expenditures	year	1396	91	81r
Health insurance expenditures	year	553	91	81r
Hospital care, semiprivate room	day	340.67	12/94	2c
Insurance premium, family medical care	month	349.05	1/95	41s
Medical services expenditures	year	559	91	81r
Medical supplies expenditures	year	80	91	81r
Household Goods				
Appl. repair, service call, wash mach	min. lab. chg.	33.59	12/94	2c
Floor coverings, expenditures	year	158	91	81r
Furniture, expenditures	year	341	91	81r
Household equipment, misc. expenditures	year	363	91	81r
Household expenditures, miscellaneous	year	194	91	81r
Household furnishings and equipment, expenditures	year	1158	91	81r
Household operations expenditures	year	378	91	81r
Household textiles, expenditures	year	88	91	81r
Housekeeping supplies, expenditures	year	426	91	81r
Laundry and cleaning supplies, expenditures	year	122	91	81r

York, PA - continued

Item	Per	Value	Date	Ref.
Household Goods - continued				
Laundry detergent, Tide Ultra, Bold, or Cheer	42 oz.	3.06	12/94	2c
Postage and stationery, expenditures	year	134	91	81r
Tissues, facial, Kleenex brand	175	1.03	12/94	2c
Housing				
Housing, ACCRA Index		98.80	12/94	2c
Add garage/carport		11,614	3/95	74r
Add room(s)		16,816	3/95	74r
Apartment condominium or co-op, median	unit	96700	12/94	62r
Dwellings (owned), expenditures	year	3305	91	81r
Enclose porch/patio/breezeway		2,980	3/95	74r
Finish room in basement/attic		4,330	3/95	74r
Home, existing, single-family, median	unit	161600	12/94	62r
House payment, principal and interest, 25% down payment	mo.	766	12/94	2c
House, 1800 sq ft, 8000 sq ft lot, new, urban, utilities	total	126938	12/94	2c
Maintenance, repairs, insurance, and other housing expenditures	year	569	91	81r
Mortgage interest and charges expenditures	year	1852	91	81r
Mtge. rate, incl. points and orig. fee, 30-year conv. fixed or ARM	mo.	9.00	12/94	2c
Princ. & int., mortgage, median-price exist. sing.-family home	mo.	765	12/94	62r
Property taxes expenditures	year	884	91	81r
Redesign, restructure more than half of home's interior		2,750	3/95	74r
Rent, apartment, 2 br., 1 1/2-2 baths, unfurnished, 950 sq ft, water	mo.	495	12/94	2c
Rental units expenditures	year	1832	91	81r
Insurance and Pensions				
Auto insurance, private passenger	year	721.50	12/94	71s
Insurance and pensions, personal, expenditures	year	2690	91	81r
Insurance, life and other personal, expenditures	year	341	91	81r
Pensions and Social Security, expenditures	year	2349	91	81r
Legal Assistance				
Estate planning, law-firm partner	hr.	375.00	10/93	12r
Legal work, law firm associate	hour	78		10r
Legal work, law firm partner	hour	183		10r
Personal Goods				
Shampoo, Alberto VO5	15-oz.	1.37	12/94	2c
Toothpaste, Crest or Colgate	6-7 oz.	2.23	12/94	2c
Personal Services				
Dry cleaning, man's 2-pc. suit		7.01	12/94	2c
Haircut, man's barbershop, no styling		7.80	12/94	2c
Haircut, woman's shampoo, trim, blow-dry		15.80	12/94	2c
Personal services expenditures	year	184	91	81r
Restaurant Food				
Chicken, fried, thigh and drumstick		2.24	12/94	2c
Dining expenditures, family	week	34.26	94	73r
Hamburger with cheese	1/4 lb.	1.87	12/94	2c
Pizza, Pizza Hut or Pizza Inn	12-13 in.	7.99	12/94	2c
Taxes				
Taxes, Federal income, expenditures	year	2409	91	81r
Taxes, personal, expenditures	year	3094	91	81r
Taxes, State and local income, expenditures	year	620	91	81r
Transportation				
Transportation, ACCRA Index		103.30	12/94	2c
Bus fare, one-way	trip	1.10	12/95	1c
Bus fare, up to 10 miles	one-way	1.10	12/94	2c
Cars and trucks purchased, new	year	1170	91	81r
Cars and trucks purchased, used	year	739	91	81r
Driver's learning permit fee	perm	27.00	1/94	84s
Driver's license fee	orig	0.00	1/94	84s

Values are in dollars or fractions of dollars. In the column headed *Ref*, references are shown to sources. Each reference is followed by a letter. These refer to the geographical level for which data were reported: s=State, r=Region, and c=City or metro. The abbreviation *ex* is used to mean *except* or *excluding*; *exp* stands for *expenditures*. For other abbreviations and further explanations, please see the Introduction.

York, PA - continued

Item	Per	Value	Date	Ref.
Transportation				
Driver's license fee, duplicate	lic	7.00	1/94	84s
Driver's license reinstatement fee, min.	susp	25.00	1/94	85s
Driver's license renewal fee	renew	0.00	1/94	84s
Identification card, nondriver	card	5.00	1/94	83s
Motorcycle learning permit fee	perm	27.00	1/94	84s
Motorcycle license fee	orig	0.00	1/94	84s
Motorcycle license fee, duplicate	lic	7.00	1/94	84s
Motorcycle license renewal fee	renew	0.00	1/94	84s
Public transportation expenditures	year	430	91	81r
Tire balance, computer or spin bal., front	wheel	7.09	12/94	2c
Transportation expenditures, total	year	4810	91	81r
Vehicle finance charges	year	238	91	81r
Vehicle insurance expenditures	year	630	91	81r
Vehicle maintenance and repairs expenditures	year	532	91	81r
Vehicle purchases	year	1920	91	81r
Vehicle rental, leases, licenses, etc. expenditures	year	193	91	81r
Vehicles purchased, other than cars and trucks	year	11	91	81r
Utilities				
Utilities, ACCRA Index		104.10	12/94	2c
Electricity expenditures	year	695	91	81r
Electricity, (part.), other, 1800 sq. ft., new home	mo.	55.17	12/94	2c
Utilities, fuels, and public services, total expenditures	year	1981	91	81r
Water and other public services, expenditures	year	154	91	81r
Weddings				
Bridal attendants' gowns	event	750	10/93	76r
Bridal gown	event	852	10/93	76r
Bridal headpiece and veil	event	167	10/93	76r
Bride's wedding band	event	708	10/93	76r
Clergy	event	224	10/93	76r
Engagement ring	event	2756	10/93	76r
Flowers	event	863	10/93	76r
Formal wear for groom	event	106	10/93	76r
Groom's attendants' formal wear	event	530	10/93	76r
Groom's wedding band	event	402	10/93	76r
Music	event	600	10/93	76r
Photography	event	1088	10/93	76r
Shoes for bride	event	50	10/93	76r
Videography	event	483	10/93	76r
Wedding invitations and announcements	event	342	10/93	76r
Wedding reception	event	7000	10/93	76r

Youngstown, OH

Item	Per	Value	Date	Ref.
Composite, ACCRA index		93.50	12/94	2c
Alcoholic Beverages				
Beer, Miller Lite, Bud, 12-oz., ex deposit	6	4.15	12/94	2c
J & B Scotch	750-ml.	18.90	12/94	2c
Wine, Gallo Chablis blanc	1.5-lit	5.47	12/94	2c
Appliances				
Appliances (major), expenditures	year	131	91	81r
Average annual exp.				
Food, health care, personal goods, services	year	25935	91	81r
Charity				
Cash contributions, expenditures	year	745	91	81r
Clothing				
Apparel, men and boys, total expenditures	year	332	91	81r
Apparel, women and girls, total expenditures	year	578	91	81r
Footwear, expenditures	year	164	91	81r
Jeans, man's denim		29.99	12/94	2c
Shirt, man's dress shirt		28.62	12/94	2c
Undervest, boy's size 10-14, cotton	3	2.90	12/94	2c

Youngstown, OH - continued

Item	Per	Value	Date	Ref.
Communications				
Long-distance telephone rate, day, addl. min., 1-10 mi.	min.	0.16	12/93	9s
Long-distance telephone rate, day, initial min., 1-10 mi.	min.	0.32	12/93	9s
Newspaper subscription, dly. and Sun. delivery	month	8.70	12/94	2c
Phone line, single, business, field visit	inst	55.42	12/93	9s
Phone line, single, business, no field visit	inst	55.42	12/93	9s
Phone line, single, residence, field visit	inst	30.38	12/93	9s
Phone line, single, residence, no field visit	inst	30.38	12/93	9s
Telephone bill, family of four	month	21.29	12/94	2c
Telephone service, expenditures	year	547	91	81r
Telephone, residential, flat rate	mo.	15.25	12/93	8c
Education				
Board, 4-year private college/university	year	2241	8/94	80s
Board, 4-year public college/university	year	1625	8/94	80s
Education, total expenditures	year	394	91	81r
Room, 4-year private college/university	year	2118	8/94	80s
Room, 4-year public college/university	year	2103	8/94	80s
Total cost, 4-year private college/university	year	15444	8/94	80s
Total cost, 4-year public college/university	year	6987	8/94	80s
Tuition, 2-year public college/university, in-state	year	2076	8/94	80s
Tuition, 4-year private college/university, in-state	year	11085	8/94	80s
Tuition, 4-year public college/university, in-state	year	3259	8/94	80s
Energy and Fuels				
Energy, combined forms, 1800 sq. ft.	mo.	124.09	12/94	2c
Energy, exc. electricity, 1800 sq. ft.	mo.	40.75	12/94	2c
Fuel oil and other fuels, expenditures	year	83	91	81r
Gas, natural, expenditures	year	373	91	81r
Gas, reg unlead, taxes inc., cash, self-service	gal	1.02	12/94	2c
Gasoline and motor oil purchased	year	1000	91	81r
Gasoline, unleaded midgrade	gallon	1.15	4/93	82r
Gasoline, unleaded premium	gallon	1.23	4/93	82r
Gasoline, unleaded regular	gallon	1.07	4/93	82r
Entertainment				
Bowling, evening rate	game	1.84	12/94	2c
Entertainment, total expenditures	year	1356	91	81r
Fees and admissions, expenditures	year	347	91	81r
Monopoly game, Parker Brothers', No. 9	game	9.93	12/94	2c
Movie	adm	6.00	12/94	2c
Pets, toys, playground equipment, expenditures	year	270	91	81r
Reading, expenditures	year	160	91	81r
Televisions, radios, and sound equipment, expenditures	year	433	91	81r
Tennis balls, yellow, Wilson or Penn, 3	can	2.26	12/94	2c
Funerals				
Burial, immediate, container provided by funeral home		1268.31	1/95	54r
Cards, acknowledgment		26.12	1/95	54r
Casket, minimum alternative		198.03	1/95	54r
Cosmetology, hair care, etc.		122.19	1/95	54r
Cremation, direct, container provided by funeral home		977.81	1/95	54r
Embalming		334.00	1/95	54r
Funeral, funeral home		321.16	1/95	54r
Funeral, other facility		317.73	1/95	54r
Graveside service		292.48	1/95	54r
Hearse, local		153.20	1/95	54r
Limousine, local		123.52	1/95	54r
Memorial service		356.30	1/95	54r
Service charge, professional, nondeclinable		968.24	1/95	54r
Visitation and viewing		332.66	1/95	54r
Groceries				
Groceries, ACCRA Index		97.50	12/94	2c

Values are in dollars or fractions of dollars. In the column headed *Ref*, references are shown to sources. Each reference is followed by a letter. These refer to the geographical level for which data were reported: s=State, r=Region, and c=City or metro. The abbreviation *ex* is used to mean *except* or *excluding*; *exp* stands for expenditures. For other abbreviations and further explanations, please see the Introduction.

Youngstown, OH - continued

Item	Per	Value	Date	Ref.
Groceries				
Apples, Red Delicious	lb.	0.68	12/94	82r
Baby food, strained vegetables, lowest price	4-4.5 oz.	0.32	12/94	2c
Bacon, sliced	lb.	1.88	12/94	82r
Bananas	lb.	0.39	12/94	2c
Bananas	lb.	0.41	12/94	82r
Beef or hamburger, ground	lb.	1.29	12/94	2c
Beef purchases	year	197	91	81r
Beef, stew, boneless	lb.	2.52	12/94	82r
Beverage purchases, alcoholic	year	293	91	81r
Beverage purchases, nonalcoholic	year	203	91	81r
Bologna, all beef or mixed	lb.	2.12	12/94	82r
Bread, white	24-oz.	0.69	12/94	2c
Bread, white, pan	lb.	0.76	12/94	82r
Cabbage	lb.	0.44	12/94	82r
Carrots, short trimmed and topped	lb.	0.44	12/94	82r
Cereals and bakery products purchases	year	347	91	81r
Cereals and cereals products purchases	year	119	91	81r
Cheddar cheese, natural	lb.	3.28	12/94	82r
Cheese, Kraft grated Parmesan	8-oz.	3.33	12/94	2c
Chicken breast, bone-in	lb.	1.61	12/94	82r
Chicken, fresh, whole	lb.	0.89	12/94	82r
Chicken, whole fryer	lb.	0.97	12/94	2c
Chuck roast, USDA choice, boneless	lb.	2.33	12/94	82r
Cigarettes, Winston, Kings	carton	14.73	12/94	2c
Coffee, 100%, ground roast, all sizes	lb.	4.28	12/94	82r
Coffee, vacuum-packed	13 oz.	4.24	12/94	2c
Cookies, chocolate chip	lb.	2.72	12/94	82r
Corn Flakes, Kellogg's or Post Toasties	18 oz.	2.15	12/94	2c
Corn, frozen, whole kernel, lowest price	10 oz.	0.75	12/94	2c
Dairy products (other) purchases	year	148	91	81r
Eggs, Grade A large	dozen	0.70	12/94	2c
Eggs, Grade A large	dozen	0.76	12/94	82r
Fish and seafood purchases	year	61	91	81r
Flour, white, all purpose	lb.	0.22	12/94	82r
Food purchases, food eaten at home	year	2313	91	81r
Foods purchased away from home, not prepared by consumer	year	1709	91	81r
Fruits and vegetables purchases	year	372	91	81r
Grapefruit	lb.	0.47	12/94	82r
Grapes, Thompson seedless	lb.	2.15	12/94	82r
Ground beef, 100% beef	lb.	1.37	12/94	82r
Ground chuck, 100% beef	lb.	1.81	12/94	82r
Ham, boneless, exc. canned	lb.	2.16	12/94	82r
Ice cream, prepackaged, bulk, regular	1/2 gal.	2.48	12/94	82r
Lemons	lb.	1.08	12/94	82r
Lettuce, iceberg	lb.	0.81	12/94	82r
Lettuce, iceberg	head	0.87	12/94	2c
Margarine, Blue Bonnet or Parkay cubes	lb.	0.60	12/94	2c
Margarine, stick	lb.	0.81	12/94	82r
Meats, poultry, fish, and eggs purchases	year	591	91	81r
Milk and cream (fresh) purchases	year	132	91	81r
Milk, whole	1/2 gal.	1.26	12/94	2c
Orange juice, frozen concentrate 12-oz. can	16 oz.	1.41	12/94	82r
Orange juice, Minute Maid frozen	12-oz.	1.27	12/94	2c
Oranges, Navel	lb.	0.56	12/94	82r
Peaches, halves or slices, Hunt's, Del Monte, or Libby's	29-oz.	1.48	12/94	2c
Peanut butter, creamy, all sizes	lb.	1.81	12/94	82r
Peas, sweet, Del Monte or Green Giant	15-17 oz.	0.51	12/94	2c
Pork chops, center cut, bone-in	lb.	2.76	12/94	82r
Pork purchases	year	130	91	81r
Potato chips	16-oz.	2.81	12/94	82r
Potatoes, frozen, French fried	lb.	0.83	12/94	82r
Potatoes, white	lb.	0.28	12/94	82r
Potatoes, white or red	10-lb. sack	1.87	12/94	2c
Round roast, USDA choice, boneless	lb.	2.90	12/94	82r
Sausage, Jimmy Dean, 100% pork	lb.	2.79	12/94	2c

Item	Per	Value	Date	Ref.
Groceries - continued				
Shortening, vegetable oil blends	lb.	0.88	12/94	82r
Shortening, vegetable, Crisco	3-lb.	2.38	12/94	2c
Soft drink, Coca Cola, ex deposit	2 lit	0.99	12/94	2c
Spaghetti and macaroni	lb.	0.78	12/94	82r
Steak, rib eye, USDA choice, boneless	lb.	6.15	12/94	82r
Steak, round, graded & ungraded, exc. USDA prime & choice	lb.	2.72	12/94	82r
Steak, round, USDA choice, boneless	lb.	3.02	12/94	82r
Steak, sirloin, USDA choice, boneless	lb.	3.85	12/94	82r
Steak, t-bone	lb.	5.68	12/94	2c
Steak, T-bone, USDA choice, bone-in	lb.	5.38	12/94	82r
Sugar and other sweets, eaten at home, expenditures	year	91	91	81r
Sugar, cane or beet	4 lbs.	1.19	12/94	2c
Sugar, white, all sizes	lb.	0.36	12/94	82r
Tobacco products and smoking supplies, total expenditures	year	298	91	81r
Tomatoes, field grown	lb.	1.36	12/94	82r
Tomatoes, Hunt's or Del Monte	14.5 oz.	0.76	12/94	2c
Tuna, chunk, light	lb.	1.94	12/94	82r
Tuna, chunk, light, oil-packed	6.125-6.5 oz.	0.63	12/94	2c
Turkey, frozen, whole	lb.	0.96	12/94	82r
Yogurt, natural, fruit flavored	8 oz.	0.62	12/94	82r
Goods and Services				
Miscellaneous goods and services, ACCRA Index		89.20	12/94	2c
Health Care				
Health care, ACCRA Index		83.40	12/94	2c
Antibiotic ointment, Polysporin	1.5 oz.	3.48	12/94	2c
Childbirth, Cesarean delivery, hospital charge	birth	5101.00	12/91	69r
Childbirth, Cesarean delivery, physician charge	birth	2234.00	12/91	69r
Childbirth, normal delivery, hospital charge	birth	2891.00	12/91	69r
Childbirth, normal delivery, physician charge	birth	1623.00	12/91	69r
Dentist's fee, adult teeth cleaning and periodic oral exam	visit	46.40	12/94	2c
Doctor's fee, routine exam, established patient	visit	32.60	12/94	2c
Drugs, expenditures	year	248	91	81r
Health care, total expenditures	year	1336	91	81r
Health insurance expenditures	year	550	91	81r
Hospital care, semiprivate room	day	300.40	12/94	2c
Insurance premium, family medical care	month	350.73	1/95	41s
Medical services expenditures	year	457	91	81r
Medical supplies expenditures	year	82	91	81r
Household Goods				
Appl. repair, service call, wash mach	min. lab. chg.	28.59	12/94	2c
Floor coverings, expenditures	year	105	91	81r
Furniture, expenditures	year	291	91	81r
Household equipment, misc. expenditures	year	341	91	81r
Household expenditures, miscellaneous	year	162	91	81r
Household furnishings and equipment, expenditures	year	1042	91	81r
Household operations expenditures	year	365	91	81r
Household textiles, expenditures	year	101	91	81r
Housekeeping supplies, expenditures	year	390	91	81r
Laundry and cleaning supplies, expenditures	year	110	91	81r
Laundry detergent, Tide Ultra, Bold, or Cheer	42 oz.	2.99	12/94	2c
Postage and stationery, expenditures	year	115	91	81r
Tissues, facial, Kleenex brand	175	1.04	12/94	2c
Housing				
Housing, ACCRA Index		95.80	12/94	2c
Add garage/carport		8,479	3/95	74r

Youngstown, OH - continued

Item	Per	Value	Date	Ref.
Housing				
Add room(s)		21,347	3/95	74r
Apartment condominium or co-op, median	unit	87100	12/94	62r
Bathroom addition, average cost	add	9734.00	3/95	13r
Bathroom remodeling, average cost	remod	6414.00	3/95	13r
Bedroom, master suite addition, average cost	add	27122.00	3/95	13r
Deck addition, average cost	add	6665.00	3/95	13r
Dwellings (owned), expenditures	year	2566	91	81r
Enclose porch/patio/breezeway		4,556	3/95	74r
Exterior remodeling, average cost	remod	15395.00	3/95	13r
Family room addition, average cost	add	27658.00	3/95	13r
Finish room in basement/attic		5,074	3/95	74r
Home, existing, single-family, median	unit	106500	12/94	62r
Home, existing, single-family, median	unit	61.90	12/94	62c
House payment, principal and interest, 25% down payment	mo.	757	12/94	2c
House, 1800 sq ft, 8000 sq ft lot, new, urban, utilities	total	123000	12/94	2c
Kitchen remodeling, major, average cost	remod	17084.00	3/95	13r
Kitchen remodeling, minor, average cost	remod	5804.00	3/95	13r
Maintenance, repairs, insurance, and other housing expenditures	year	484	91	81r
Mortgage interest and charges expenditures	year	1443	91	81r
Mtge. rate, incl. points and orig. fee, 30-year conv. fixed or ARM	mo.	9.23	12/94	2c
Office, home addition, average cost	add	8121.00	3/95	13r
Princ. & int., mortgage, median-price exist. sing.-family home	mo.	515	12/94	62r
Property taxes expenditures	year	639	91	81r
Redesign, restructure more than half of home's interior		9,114	3/95	74r
Rent, apartment, 2 br., 1 1/2-2 baths, unfurnished, 950 sq ft, water	mo.	438	12/94	2c
Rental units expenditures	year	1200	91	81r
Sun-space addition, average cost	add	23768.00	3/95	13r
Wing addition, two-story, average cost	add	50410.00	3/95	13r
Insurance and Pensions				
Auto insurance, private passenger	year	550.52	12/94	71s
Insurance and pensions, personal, expenditures	year	2408	91	81r
Insurance, life and other personal, expenditures	year	355	91	81r
Pensions and Social Security, expenditures	year	2053	91	81r
Legal Assistance				
Legal work, law firm associate	hour	90		10r
Legal work, law firm partner	hour	139		10r
Personal Goods				
Shampoo, Alberto VO5	15-oz.	0.92	12/94	2c
Toothpaste, Crest or Colgate	6-7 oz.	1.88	12/94	2c
Personal Services				
Dry cleaning, man's 2-pc. suit		5.57	12/94	2c
Haircut, man's barbershop, no styling		8.50	12/94	2c
Haircut, woman's shampoo, trim, blow-dry		11.80	12/94	2c
Personal services expenditures	year	203	91	81r
Restaurant Food				
Chicken, fried, thigh and drumstick		2.19	12/94	2c
Dining expenditures, family	week	30.03	94	73r
Hamburger with cheese	1/4 lb.	0.89	12/94	2c
Pizza, Pizza Hut or Pizza Inn	12-13 in.	8.00	12/94	2c
Taxes				
Taxes, Federal income, expenditures	year	1756	91	81r
Taxes, personal, expenditures	year	2426	91	81r
Taxes, State and local income, expenditures	year	568	91	81r
Transportation				
Transportation, ACCRA Index		87.20	12/94	2c
Bus fare, one-way	trip	0.70	12/95	1c
Cars and trucks purchased, new	year	891	91	81r

Youngstown, OH - continued

Item	Per	Value	Date	Ref.
Transportation - continued				
Cars and trucks purchased, used	year	1155	91	81r
Driver's learning permit fee	perm	3.00	1/94	84s
Driver's license fee	orig	5.00	1/94	84s
Driver's license fee, duplicate	lic	1.50	1/94	84s
Driver's license reinstatement fee, min.	susp	12.50-100.00	1/94	85s
Driver's license renewal fee	renew	5.00	1/94	84s
Identification card, nondriver	card	2.50	1/94	83s
Motorcycle learning permit fee	perm	3.00	1/94	84s
Motorcycle license fee	orig	5.00	1/94	84s
Motorcycle license fee, duplicate	lic	1.50	1/94	84s
Motorcycle license renewal fee	renew	5.00	1/94	84s
Public transportation expenditures	year	209	91	81r
Tire balance, computer or spin bal., front	wheel	5.57	12/94	2c
Transportation expenditures, total	year	4792	91	81r
Vehicle finance charges	year	300	91	81r
Vehicle insurance expenditures	year	485	91	81r
Vehicle maintenance and repairs expenditures	year	534	91	81r
Vehicle purchases	year	2068	91	81r
Vehicle rental, leases, licenses, etc.	year	197	91	81r
Vehicles purchased, other than cars and trucks	year	22	91	81r
Utilities				
Utilities, ACCRA Index		110.40	12/94	2c
Electricity expenditures	year	668	91	81r
Electricity, (part.), other, 1800 sq. ft., new home	mo.	83.34	12/94	2c
Utilities, fuels, and public services, total expenditures	year	1838	91	81r
Water and other public services, expenditures	year	167	91	81r
Weddings				
Bridal attendants' gowns	event	750	10/93	76r
Bridal gown	event	852	10/93	76r
Bridal headpiece and veil	event	167	10/93	76r
Bride's wedding band	event	708	10/93	76r
Clergy	event	224	10/93	76r
Engagement ring	event	2756	10/93	76r
Flowers	event	863	10/93	76r
Formal wear for groom	event	106	10/93	76r
Groom's attendants' formal wear	event	530	10/93	76r
Groom's wedding band	event	402	10/93	76r
Music	event	600	10/93	76r
Photography	event	1088	10/93	76r
Shoes for bride	event	50	10/93	76r
Videography	event	483	10/93	76r
Wedding invitations and announcements	event	342	10/93	76r
Wedding reception	event	7000	10/93	76r

Yuba City, CA

Item	Per	Value	Date	Ref.
Appliances				
Appliances (major), expenditures	year	160	91	81r
Average annual exp.				
Food, health care, personal goods, services	year	32461	91	81r
Charity				
Cash contributions, expenditures	year	975	91	81r
Clothing				
Apparel, men and boys, total expenditures	year	467	91	81r
Apparel, women and girls, total expenditures	year	737	91	81r
Footwear, expenditures	year	270	91	81r
Communications				
Long-distance telephone rate, day, addl. min., 1-10 mi.	min.	0.07	12/93	9s
Long-distance telephone rate, day, initial min., 1-10 mi.	min.	0.17	12/93	9s

Values are in dollars or fractions of dollars. In the column headed *Ref*, references are shown to sources. Each reference is followed by a letter. These refer to the geographical level for which data were reported: s = State, r = Region, and c = City or metro. The abbreviation *ex* is used to mean *except* or *excluding*; *exp* stands for *expenditures*. For other abbreviations and further explanations, please see the Introduction.

Yuba City, CA - continued

Item	Per	Value	Date	Ref.
Communications				
Phone line, single, business, field visit	inst	70.75	12/93	9s
Phone line, single, business, no field visit	inst	70.75	12/93	9s
Phone line, single, residence, field visit	inst	34.75	12/93	9s
Phone line, single, residence, no field visit	inst	34.75	12/93	9s
Telephone service, expenditures	year	611	91	81r
Education				
Board, 4-year private college/university	year	2945	8/94	80s
Board, 4-year public college/university	year	2321	8/94	80s
Education, total expenditures	year	375	91	81r
Room, 4-year private college/university	year	3094	8/94	80s
Room, 4-year public college/university	year	2812	8/94	80s
Student fee, university	year	21.00	93	18s
Total cost, 4-year private college/university	year	19321	8/94	80s
Total cost, 4-year public college/university	year	7511	8/94	80s
Tuition, 2-year public college/university, in-state	year	345	8/94	80s
Tuition, 4-year private college/university, in-state	year	13282	8/94	80s
Tuition, 4-year public college/university, in-state	year	2378	8/94	80s
Energy and Fuels				
Fuel oil and other fuels, expenditures	year	33	91	81r
Gas, natural, expenditures	year	212	91	81r
Gasoline and motor oil purchased	year	1115	91	81r
Gasoline, unleaded midgrade	gallon	1.36	4/93	82r
Gasoline, unleaded premium	gallon	1.43	4/93	82r
Gasoline, unleaded regular	gallon	1.23	4/93	82r
Entertainment				
Concert ticket, Pearl Jam group	perf	20.00	94	50r
Entertainment, total expenditures	year	1853	91	81r
Fees and admissions, expenditures	year	482	91	81r
Pets, toys, playground equipment, expenditures	year	299	91	81r
Reading, expenditures	year	164	91	81r
Televisions, radios, and sound equipment, expenditures	year	528	91	81r
Funerals				
Burial, immediate, container provided by funeral home		1382.70	1/95	54r
Cards, acknowledgment		21.87	1/95	54r
Casket, minimum alternative		128.54	1/95	54r
Cosmetology, hair care, etc.		119.69	1/95	54r
Cremation, direct, container provided by funeral home		1030.62	1/95	54r
Embalming		255.42	1/95	54r
Funeral, funeral home		437.38	1/95	54r
Funeral, other facility		444.46	1/95	54r
Graveside service		338.46	1/95	54r
Hearse, local		147.50	1/95	54r
Limousine, local		130.33	1/95	54r
Memorial service		553.14	1/95	54r
Service charge, professional, nondeclinable		859.15	1/95	54r
Visitation and viewing		93.23	1/95	54r
Groceries				
Apples, Red Delicious	lb.	0.72	12/94	82r
Bacon, sliced	lb.	1.73	12/94	82r
Bananas	lb.	0.52	12/94	82r
Beef purchases	year	241	91	81r
Beverage purchases, alcoholic	year	328	91	81r
Beverage purchases, nonalcoholic	year	234	91	81r
Bologna, all beef or mixed	lb.	2.33	12/94	82r
Bread, white, pan	lb.	0.81	12/94	82r
Carrots, short trimmed and topped	lb.	0.43	12/94	82r
Cereals and bakery products purchases	year	392	91	81r
Cereals and cereals products purchases	year	139	91	81r
Chicken breast, bone-in	lb.	2.04	12/94	82r
Chicken, fresh, whole	lb.	0.95	12/94	82r
Coffee, 100%, ground roast, all sizes	lb.	4.48	12/94	82r
Dairy products (other) purchases	year	182	91	81r

Yuba City, CA - continued

Item	Per	Value	Date	Ref.
Groceries - continued				
Fish and seafood purchases	year	94	91	81r
Flour, white, all purpose	lb.	0.21	12/94	82r
Food purchases, food eaten at home	year	2749	91	81r
Foods purchased away from home, not prepared by consumer	year	1909	91	81r
Fruits and vegetables purchases	year	459	91	81r
Grapefruit	lb.	0.56	12/94	82r
Ground beef, 100% beef	lb.	1.31	12/94	82r
Ham, boneless, exc. canned	lb.	2.46	12/94	82r
Ice cream, prepackaged, bulk, regular	1/2 gal.	2.57	12/94	82r
Lemons	lb.	1.00	12/94	82r
Lettuce, iceberg	lb.	0.93	12/94	82r
Meats, poultry, fish, and eggs purchases	year	700	91	81r
Milk and cream (fresh) purchases	year	155	91	81r
Orange juice, frozen concentrate 12-oz. can	16 oz.	1.52	12/94	82r
Oranges, Navel	lb.	0.56	12/94	82r
Pork chops, center cut, bone-in	lb.	3.30	12/94	82r
Pork purchases	year	122	91	81r
Potato chips	16-oz.	3.03	12/94	82r
Potatoes, frozen, French fried	lb.	0.77	12/94	82r
Potatoes, white	lb.	0.35	12/94	82r
Rice, white, long grain, uncooked	lb.	0.54	12/94	82r
Round roast, USDA choice, boneless	lb.	2.92	12/94	82r
Shortening, vegetable oil blends	lb.	0.80	12/94	82r
Spaghetti and macaroni	lb.	1.02	12/94	82r
Steak, round, graded & ungraded, exc. USDA prime & choice	lb.	3.13	12/94	82r
Steak, sirloin, USDA choice, boneless	lb.	4.07	12/94	82r
Sugar and other sweets, eaten at home, expenditures	year	105	91	81r
Sugar, white, all sizes	lb.	0.38	12/94	82r
Tobacco products and smoking supplies, total expenditures	year	221	91	81r
Tomatoes, field grown	lb.	1.45	12/94	82r
Tuna, chunk, light	lb.	2.18	12/94	82r
Health Care				
Childbirth, Cesarean delivery, hospital charge	birth	6059.00	12/91	69r
Childbirth, Cesarean delivery, physician charge	birth	2248.00	12/91	69r
Childbirth, normal delivery, hospital charge	birth	3006.00	12/91	69r
Childbirth, normal delivery, physician charge	birth	1634.00	12/91	69r
Drugs, expenditures	year	230	91	81r
Health care, total expenditures	year	1544	91	81r
Health insurance expenditures	year	558	91	81r
Insurance premium, family medical care	month	380.27	1/95	41s
Medical services expenditures	year	676	91	81r
Medical supplies expenditures	year	80	91	81r
Surgery, open-heart	proc	37818.00	1/93	14r
Household Goods				
Floor coverings, expenditures	year	79	91	81r
Furniture, expenditures	year	352	91	81r
Household equipment, misc. expenditures	year	614	91	81r
Household expenditures, miscellaneous	year	294	91	81r
Household furnishings and equipment, expenditures	year	1416	91	81r
Household operations expenditures	year	580	91	81r
Household textiles, expenditures	year	113	91	81r
Housekeeping supplies, expenditures	year	447	91	81r
Laundry and cleaning supplies, expenditures	year	114	91	81r
Postage and stationery, expenditures	year	145	91	81r
Housing				
Add garage/carport		6,422	3/95	74r
Add room(s)		26,583	3/95	74r
Apartment condominium or co-op, median	unit	105300	12/94	62r
Dwellings (owned), expenditures	year	3932	91	81r
Enclose porch/patio/breezeway		5,382	3/95	74r
Finish room in basement/attic		3,911	3/95	74r
Home, existing, single-family, median	unit	178600	12/94	62r

Values are in dollars or fractions of dollars. In the column headed *Ref*, references are shown to sources. Each reference is followed by a letter. These refer to the geographical level for which data were reported: s = State, r = Region, and c = City or metro. The abbreviation *ex* is used to mean *except* or *excluding*; *exp* stands for *expenditures*. For other abbreviations and further explanations, please see the Introduction.

Yuba City, CA - continued

Item	Per	Value	Date	Ref.
Housing				
Maintenance, repairs, insurance, and other housing expenditures	year	591	91	81r
Mortgage interest and charges expenditures	year	2747	91	81r
Princ. & int., mortgage, median-price exist. sing.-family home	mo.	845	12/94	62r
Property taxes expenditures	year	594	91	81r
Redesign, restructure more than half of home's interior		5,467	3/95	74r
Rental units expenditures	year	2077	91	81r
Insurance and Pensions				
Auto insurance, private passenger	year	892.80	12/94	71s
Insurance and pensions, personal, expenditures	year	3042	91	81r
Insurance, life and other personal, expenditures	year	298	91	81r
Pensions and Social Security, expenditures	year	2744	91	81r
Legal Assistance				
Legal work, law firm associate	hour	91		10r
Legal work, law firm partner	hour	151		10r
Personal Services				
Personal services expenditures	year	286	91	81r
Restaurant Food				
Dining expenditures, family	week	32.25	94	73r
Taxes				
Taxes, Federal income, expenditures	year	2946	91	81r
Taxes, personal, expenditures	year	3791	91	81r
Taxes, State and local income, expenditures	year	791	91	81r
Transportation				
Cars and trucks purchased, new	year	1231	91	81r
Cars and trucks purchased, used	year	915	91	81r
Driver's learning permit fee	perm	12.00	1/94	84s
Driver's license fee	orig	12.00	1/94	84s
Driver's license fee, duplicate	lic	12.00	1/94	84s
Driver's license reinstatement fee, min.	susp	15.00	1/94	85s
Driver's license renewal fee	renew	12.00	1/94	84s
Identification card, nondriver	card	6.00	1/94	83s
Motorcycle learning permit fee	perm	12.00	1/94	84s
Motorcycle license fee	orig	12.00	1/94	84s
Motorcycle license fee, duplicate	lic	12.00	1/94	84s
Motorcycle license renewal fee	renew	12.00	1/94	84s
Public transportation expenditures	year	375	91	81r
Transportation expenditures, total	year	5527	91	81r
Vehicle finance charges	year	287	91	81r
Vehicle insurance expenditures	year	624	91	81r
Vehicle maintenance and repairs expenditures	year	695	91	81r
Vehicle purchases	year	2174	91	81r
Vehicle rental, leases, licenses, etc. expenditures	year	257	91	81r
Vehicles purchased, other than cars and trucks	year	28	91	81r
Utilities				
Electricity expenditures	year	616	91	81r
Utilities, fuels, and public services, total expenditures	year	1681	91	81r
Water and other public services, expenditures	year	209	91	81r
Weddings				
Bridal attendants' gowns	event	750	10/93	76r
Bridal gown	event	852	10/93	76r
Bridal headpiece and veil	event	167	10/93	76r
Bride's wedding band	event	708	10/93	76r
Clergy	event	224	10/93	76r
Engagement ring	event	2756	10/93	76r
Flowers	event	863	10/93	76r
Formal wear for groom	event	106	10/93	76r
Groom's attendants' formal wear	event	530	10/93	76r
Groom's wedding band	event	402	10/93	76r

Yuba City, CA - continued

Item	Per	Value	Date	Ref.
Weddings - continued				
Music	event	600	10/93	76r
Photography	event	1088	10/93	76r
Shoes for bride	event	50	10/93	76r
Videography	event	483	10/93	76r
Wedding invitations and announcements	event	342	10/93	76r
Wedding reception	event	7000	10/93	76r

Yuma, AZ

Item	Per	Value	Date	Ref.
Composite, ACCRA index		95.30	12/94	2c
Alcoholic Beverages				
Beer, Miller Lite, Bud, 12-oz., ex deposit	6	3.43	12/94	2c
J & B Scotch	750-ml.	14.54	12/94	2c
Wine, Gallo Chablis blanc	1.5-lit	4.24	12/94	2c
Appliances				
Appliances (major), expenditures	year	160	91	81r
Average annual exp.				
Food, health care, personal goods, services	year	32461	91	81r
Charity				
Cash contributions, expenditures	year	975	91	81r
Clothing				
Apparel, men and boys, total expenditures	year	467	91	81r
Apparel, women and girls, total expenditures	year	737	91	81r
Footwear, expenditures	year	270	91	81r
Jeans, man's denim		25.66	12/94	2c
Shirt, man's dress shirt		28.75	12/94	2c
Undervest, boy's size 10-14, cotton	3	4.89	12/94	2c
Communications				
Long-distance telephone rate, day, addl. min., 1-10 mi.	min.	0.10	12/93	9s
Long-distance telephone rate, day, initial min., 1-10 mi.	min.	0.24	12/93	9s
Newspaper subscription, dly. and Sun. delivery	month	9.00	12/94	2c
Phone line, single, business, field visit	inst	56.00	12/93	9s
Phone line, single, business, no field visit	inst	56.00	12/93	9s
Phone line, single, residence, field visit	inst	46.50	12/93	9s
Phone line, single, residence, no field visit	inst	46.50	12/93	9s
Telephone bill, family of four	month	17.39	12/94	2c
Telephone service, expenditures	year	611	91	81r
Telephone, residential, flat rate	mo.	12.40	12/93	8c
Education				
Board, 4-year private college/university	year	2044	8/94	80s
Board, 4-year public college/university	year	1904	8/94	80s
Education, total expenditures	year	375	91	81r
Room, 4-year private college/university	year	1617	8/94	80s
Room, 4-year public college/university	year	1739	8/94	80s
Total cost, 4-year private college/university	year	9542	8/94	80s
Total cost, 4-year public college/university	year	5462	8/94	80s
Tuition, 2-year public college/university, in-state	year	729	8/94	80s
Tuition, 4-year private college/university, in-state	year	5881	8/94	80s
Tuition, 4-year public college/university, in-state	year	1819	8/94	80s
Energy and Fuels				
Energy, combined forms, 1800 sq. ft.	mo.	123.86	12/94	2c
Fuel oil and other fuels, expenditures	year	33	91	81r
Gas, natural, expenditures	year	212	91	81r
Gas, reg unlead, taxes inc., cash, self-service	gal	1.22	12/94	2c
Gasoline and motor oil purchased	year	1115	91	81r
Gasoline, unleaded midgrade	gallon	1.36	4/93	82r
Gasoline, unleaded premium	gallon	1.43	4/93	82r
Gasoline, unleaded regular	gallon	1.23	4/93	82r

Values are in dollars or fractions of dollars. In the column headed *Ref*, references are shown to sources. Each reference is followed by a letter. These refer to the geographical level for which data were reported: s = State, r = Region, and c = City or metro. The abbreviation *ex* is used to mean *except* or *excluding*; *exp* stands for expenditures. For other abbreviations and further explanations, please see the Introduction.

Yuma, AZ - continued

Item	Per	Value	Date	Ref.
Entertainment				
Bowling, evening rate	game	2.55	12/94	2c
Concert ticket, Pearl Jam group	perf	20.00	94	50r
Entertainment, total expenditures	year	1853	91	81r
Fees and admissions, expenditures	year	482	91	81r
Monopoly game, Parker Brothers', No. 9	game	10.27	12/94	2c
Movie	adm	6.00	12/94	2c
Pets, toys, playground equipment, expenditures	year	299	91	81r
Reading, expenditures	year	164	91	81r
Televisions, radios, and sound equipment, expenditures	year	528	91	81r
Tennis balls, yellow, Wilson or Penn, 3	can	2.30	12/94	2c
Funerals				
Burial, immediate, container provided by funeral home		1360.49	1/95	54r
Cards, acknowledgment		11.24	1/95	54r
Casket, minimum alternative		232.73	1/95	54r
Cosmetology, hair care, etc.		114.13	1/95	54r
Cremation, direct, container provided by funeral home		1027.08	1/95	54r
Embalming		286.24	1/95	54r
Funeral, funeral home		315.60	1/95	54r
Funeral, other facility		303.08	1/95	54r
Graveside service		423.83	1/95	54r
Hearse, local		133.12	1/95	54r
Limousine, local		99.10	1/95	54r
Memorial service		442.57	1/95	54r
Service charge, professional, nondeclinable		840.16	1/95	54r
Visitation and viewing		168.50	1/95	54r
Groceries				
Groceries, ACCRA Index		99.90	12/94	2c
Apples, Red Delicious	lb.	0.72	12/94	82r
Baby food, strained vegetables, lowest price	4-4.5 oz.	0.31	12/94	2c
Bacon, sliced	lb.	1.73	12/94	82r
Bananas	lb.	0.39	12/94	2c
Bananas	lb.	0.52	12/94	82r
Beef or hamburger, ground	lb.	1.36	12/94	2c
Beef purchases	year	241	91	81r
Beverage purchases, alcoholic	year	328	91	81r
Beverage purchases, nonalcoholic	year	234	91	81r
Bologna, all beef or mixed	lb.	2.33	12/94	82r
Bread, white	24-oz.	0.77	12/94	2c
Bread, white, pan	lb.	0.81	12/94	82r
Carrots, short trimmed and topped	lb.	0.43	12/94	82r
Cereals and bakery products purchases	year	392	91	81r
Cereals and cereals products purchases	year	139	91	81r
Cheese, Kraft grated Parmesan	8-oz.	3.77	12/94	2c
Chicken breast, bone-in	lb.	2.04	12/94	82r
Chicken, fresh, whole	lb.	0.95	12/94	82r
Chicken, whole fryer	lb.	0.88	12/94	2c
Cigarettes, Winston, Kings	carton	14.47	12/94	2c
Coffee, 100%, ground roast, all sizes	lb.	4.48	12/94	82r
Coffee, vacuum-packed	13 oz.	3.63	12/94	2c
Corn Flakes, Kellogg's or Post Toasties	18 oz.	2.71	12/94	2c
Corn, frozen, whole kernel, lowest price	10 oz.	0.70	12/94	2c
Dairy products (other) purchases	year	182	91	81r
Eggs, Grade A large	dozen	0.73	12/94	2c
Fish and seafood purchases	year	94	91	81r
Flour, white, all purpose	lb.	0.21	12/94	82r
Food purchases, food eaten at home	year	2749	91	81r
Foods purchased away from home, not prepared by consumer	year	1909	91	81r
Fruits and vegetables purchases	year	459	91	81r
Grapefruit	lb.	0.56	12/94	82r
Ground beef, 100% beef	lb.	1.31	12/94	82r
Ham, boneless, exc. canned	lb.	2.46	12/94	82r
Ice cream, prepackaged, bulk, regular	1/2 gal.	2.57	12/94	82r
Lemons	lb.	1.00	12/94	82r
Lettuce, iceberg	lb.	0.93	12/94	82r

Yuma, AZ - continued

Item	Per	Value	Date	Ref.
Groceries - continued				
Lettuce, iceberg	head	0.67	12/94	2c
Margarine, Blue Bonnet or Parkay cubes	lb.	0.68	12/94	2c
Meats, poultry, fish, and eggs purchases	year	700	91	81r
Milk and cream (fresh) purchases	year	155	91	81r
Milk, whole	1/2 gal.	1.27	12/94	2c
Orange juice, frozen concentrate 12-oz. can	16 oz.	1.52	12/94	82r
Orange juice, Minute Maid frozen	12-oz.	1.21	12/94	2c
Oranges, Navel	lb.	0.56	12/94	82r
Peaches, halves or slices, Hunt's, Del Monte, or Libby's	29-oz.	1.45	12/94	2c
Peas, sweet, Del Monte or Green Giant	15-17 oz.	0.53	12/94	2c
Pork chops, center cut, bone-in	lb.	3.30	12/94	82r
Pork purchases	year	122	91	81r
Potato chips	16-oz.	3.03	12/94	82r
Potatoes, frozen, French fried	lb.	0.77	12/94	82r
Potatoes, white	lb.	0.35	12/94	82r
Potatoes, white or red	10-lb. sack	1.67	12/94	2c
Rice, white, long grain, uncooked	lb.	0.54	12/94	82r
Round roast, USDA choice, boneless	lb.	2.92	12/94	82r
Sausage, Jimmy Dean, 100% pork	lb.	3.29	12/94	2c
Shortening, vegetable oil blends	lb.	0.80	12/94	82r
Shortening, vegetable, Crisco	3-lb.	2.52	12/94	2c
Soft drink, Coca Cola, ex deposit	2 lit	1.09	12/94	2c
Spaghetti and macaroni	lb.	1.02	12/94	82r
Steak, round, graded & ungraded, exc. USDA prime & choice	lb.	3.13	12/94	82r
Steak, sirloin, USDA choice, boneless	lb.	4.07	12/94	82r
Steak, t-bone	lb.	4.92	12/94	2c
Sugar and other sweets, eaten at home, expenditures	year	105	91	81r
Sugar, cane or beet	4 lbs.	1.30	12/94	2c
Sugar, white, all sizes	lb.	0.38	12/94	82r
Tobacco products and smoking supplies, total expenditures	year	221	91	81r
Tomatoes, field grown	lb.	1.45	12/94	82r
Tomatoes, Hunt's or Del Monte	14.5 oz.	0.79	12/94	2c
Tuna, chunk, light	lb.	2.18	12/94	82r
Tuna, chunk, light, oil-packed	6.125-6.5 oz.	0.77	12/94	2c
Goods and Services				
Miscellaneous goods and services, ACCRA Index		98.20	12/94	2c
Health Care				
Health care, ACCRA Index		96.40	12/94	2c
Antibiotic ointment, Polysporin	1.5 oz.	4.01	12/94	2c
Childbirth, Cesarean delivery, hospital charge	birth	6059.00	12/91	69r
Childbirth, Cesarean delivery, physician charge	birth	2248.00	12/91	69r
Childbirth, normal delivery, hospital charge	birth	3006.00	12/91	69r
Childbirth, normal delivery, physician charge	birth	1634.00	12/91	69r
Dentist's fee, adult teeth cleaning and periodic oral exam	visit	44.60	12/94	2c
Doctor's fee, routine exam, established patient	visit	36.00	12/94	2c
Drugs, expenditures	year	230	91	81r
Health care, total expenditures	year	1544	91	81r
Health insurance expenditures	year	558	91	81r
Hospital care, semiprivate room	day	495.00	12/94	2c
Insurance premium, family medical care	month	364.71	1/95	41s
Medical services expenditures	year	676	91	81r
Medical supplies expenditures	year	80	91	81r
Surgery, open-heart	proc	37818.00	1/93	14r
Household Goods				
Appl. repair, service call, wash mach	min. lab. chg.	35.20	12/94	2c

Values are in dollars or fractions of dollars. In the column headed *Ref*, references are shown to sources. Each reference is followed by a letter. These refer to the geographical level for which data were reported: s = State, r = Region, and c = City or metro. The abbreviation *ex* is used to mean *except* or *excluding*; *exp* stands for *expenditures*. For other abbreviations and further explanations, please see the Introduction.

Yuma, AZ - continued

Item	Per	Value	Date	Ref.
Household Goods				
Floor coverings, expenditures	year	79	91	81r
Furniture, expenditures	year	352	91	81r
Household equipment, misc. expenditures	year	614	91	81r
Household expenditures, miscellaneous	year	294	91	81r
Household furnishings and equipment, expenditures	year	1416	91	81r
Household operations expenditures	year	580	91	81r
Household textiles, expenditures	year	113	91	81r
Housekeeping supplies, expenditures	year	447	91	81r
Laundry and cleaning supplies, expenditures	year	114	91	81r
Laundry detergent, Tide Ultra, Bold, or Cheer	42 oz.	3.76	12/94	2c
Postage and stationery, expenditures	year	145	91	81r
Tissues, facial, Kleenex brand	175	0.96	12/94	2c
Housing				
Housing, ACCRA Index		80.80	12/94	2c
Add garage/carport		6,422	3/95	74r
Add room(s)		26,583	3/95	74r
Apartment condominium or co-op, median	unit	105300		62r
Dwellings (owned), expenditures	year	3932	91	81r
Enclose porch/patio/breezeway		5,382	3/95	74r
Finish room in basement/attic		3,911	3/95	74r
Home, existing, single-family, median	unit	178600		62r
House payment, principal and interest, 25% down payment	mo.	582	12/94	2c
House, 1800 sq ft, 8000 sq ft lot, new, urban, utilities	total	93100	12/94	2c
Maintenance, repairs, insurance, and other housing expenditures	year	591	91	81r
Mortgage interest and charges expenditures	year	2747	91	81r
Mtge. rate, incl. points and orig. fee, 30-year conv. fixed or ARM	mo.	9.40	12/94	2c
Princ. & int., mortgage, median-price exist. sing.-family home	mo.	845	12/94	62r
Property taxes expenditures	year	594	91	81r
Redesign, restructure more than half of home's interior		5,467	3/95	74r
Rent, apartment, 2 br., 1 1/2-2 baths, unfurnished, 950 sq ft, water	mo.	532	12/94	2c
Rental units expenditures	year	2077	91	81r
Insurance and Pensions				
Auto insurance, private passenger	year	782.68	12/94	71s
Insurance and pensions, personal, expenditures	year	3042	91	81r
Insurance, life and other personal, expenditures	year	298	91	81r
Pensions and Social Security, expenditures	year	2744	91	81r
Legal Assistance				
Legal work, law firm associate	hour	91		10r
Legal work, law firm partner	hour	151		10r
Personal Goods				
Shampoo, Alberto VO5	15-oz.	1.13	12/94	2c
Toothpaste, Crest or Colgate	6-7 oz.	1.82	12/94	2c
Personal Services				
Dry cleaning, man's 2-pc. suit		7.18	12/94	2c
Haircut, man's barbershop, no styling		5.38	12/94	2c
Haircut, woman's shampoo, trim, blow-dry		22.00	12/94	2c
Personal services expenditures	year	286	91	81r
Restaurant Food				
Chicken, fried, thigh and drumstick		2.32	12/94	2c
Dining expenditures, family	week	32.25	94	73r
Hamburger with cheese	1/4 lb.	1.99	12/94	2c
Pizza, Pizza Hut or Pizza Inn	12-13 in.	8.19	12/94	2c
Taxes				
Tax, cigarettes	year	368.00	10/93	43s
Taxes, Federal income, expenditures	year	2946	91	81r

Yuma, AZ - continued

Item	Per	Value	Date	Ref.
Taxes - continued				
Taxes, personal, expenditures	year	3791	91	81r
Taxes, State and local income, expenditures	year	791	91	81r
Transportation				
Transportation, ACCRA Index		109.80	12/94	2c
Cars and trucks purchased, new	year	1231	91	81r
Cars and trucks purchased, used	year	915	91	81r
Driver's learning permit fee	perm	7.00	1/94	84s
Driver's license fee	orig	7.00	1/94	84s
Driver's license fee, duplicate	lic	4.00	1/94	84s
Driver's license reinstatement fee, min.	susp	10.00	1/94	85s
Driver's license renewal fee	renew	7.00	1/94	84s
Identification card, nondriver	card	5.00	1/94	83s
Motorcycle learning permit fee	perm	7.00	1/94	84s
Motorcycle license fee	orig	7.00	1/94	84s
Motorcycle license fee, duplicate	lic	4.00	1/94	84s
Motorcycle license renewal fee	renew	7.00	1/94	84s
Public transportation expenditures	year	375	91	81r
Tire balance, computer or spin bal., front	wheel	7.59	12/94	2c
Transportation expenditures, total	year	5527	91	81r
Vehicle finance charges	year	287	91	81r
Vehicle insurance expenditures	year	624	91	81r
Vehicle maintenance and repairs expenditures	year	695	91	81r
Vehicle purchases	year	2174	91	81r
Vehicle rental, leases, licenses, etc. expenditures	year	257	91	81r
Vehicles purchased, other than cars and trucks	year	28	91	81r
Utilities				
Utilities, ACCRA Index		107.50	12/94	2c
Electricity expenditures	year	616	91	81r
Electricity, 1800 sq. ft., new home	mo.	123.86	12/94	2c
Utilities, fuels, and public services, total expenditures	year	1681	91	81r
Water and other public services, expenditures	year	209	91	81r
Weddings				
Bridal attendants' gowns	event	750	10/93	76r
Bridal gown	event	852	10/93	76r
Bridal headpiece and veil	event	167	10/93	76r
Bride's wedding band	event	708	10/93	76r
Clergy	event	224	10/93	76r
Engagement ring	event	2756	10/93	76r
Flowers	event	863	10/93	76r
Formal wear for groom	event	106	10/93	76r
Groom's attendants' formal wear	event	530	10/93	76r
Groom's wedding band	event	402	10/93	76r
Music	event	600	10/93	76r
Photography	event	1088	10/93	76r
Shoes for bride	event	50	10/93	76r
Videography	event	483	10/93	76r
Wedding invitations and announcements	event	342	10/93	76r

Values are in dollars or fractions of dollars. In the column headed *Ref*, references are shown to sources. Each reference is followed by a letter. These refer to the geographical level for which data were reported: s = State, r = Region, and c = City or metro. The abbreviation *ex* is used to mean *except* or *excluding*; *exp* stands for expenditures. For other abbreviations and further explanations, please see the Introduction.

LIST OF SOURCES

This section shows all sources used in *American Cost of Living Survey*, 2nd Edition. Numerals in bold on the left are those found in the data tables in the column marked Ref. Notes to the data are also provided as shown in the source.

1 *1995 APTA Transit Fare Summary.* Washington, D.C.: American Public Transit Association (APTA), 1995. *Notes:* Some of the figures shown are averages based on fares charged by two or more public transportation systems. For additional information contact: American Public Transit Association, 1201 New York Ave. N.W., Suite 400, Washington, DC 20005 (202) 898-4129.

2 *ACCRA Cost of Living Index*, Fourth Quarter 1994, vol. 27, no. 4.: Price Reports. Louisville, KY: American Chambers of Commerce Research Association (ACCRA), 1995. *Notes:* Copyright 1994, ACCRA. Reproduced by permission. ACCRA is a nonprofit organization promoting excellence in research for community and economic development. *ACCRA Cost of Living Index* has been published quarterly without interruption since 1968. For additional information contact: ACCRA, P.O. Box 6749, Louisville, KY 40206-6749. The quarterly report is available by subscription for $115 per year. Single copies may be purchased for $58 each.

3 Andrews, Edmund L. "No-holds-barred battle for long-distance calls." *New York Times.* 21 January 1995, p.1.

4 Anundsen, Kristin. "Small business for small change." *PC World.* July 1995, p. 260.

5 "Bad check fees called 'gouging'." *USA TODAY.* 10-12 December 1993, p. 1A.

6 Barge, Jeff, "Defenders seek parity in pay, caseloads." *ABA Journal.* December 1994, p. 73.

7 Barron, James, "Rental companies to limit free mileage." *New York Times.* 8 June 1995, p. B1.

8 *Bell Operating Companies Exchange Service Telephone Rates,* December 31, 1993. Washington, D.C.: National Association of Regulatory Utility Commissioners (NARUC), 1994. *Notes:* Copyright 1994, Bellcore, Inc. Used by permission. This material can be ordered for $47.50 plus a 10% shipping and handling fee from: NARUC, 1102 ICC Building, P.O. Box 684, Washington, DC 20044-0684 (202) 898-2200.

9 *Bell Operating Companies Long Distance Message Telephone Rates,* December 31, 1993. Washington, D.C.: National Association of Regulatory Utility Commissioners (NARUC), 1994. *Notes:* Copyright 1994, Bellcore, Inc. Used by permission. This material can be ordered for $37.50 plus a 10% shipping and handling fee from: NARUC, 1102 ICC Building, P.O. Box 684, Washington, DC 20044-0684 (202) 898-2200.

10 "Billing the time." *ABA Journal.* March 1994, p. 73. *Notes:* Figures are from a Gallup Organization survey based on a random sample of 400 ABA (American Bar Association) members. The national averages are $153 per hour for law firm partners and $91 per hour for law firm associates.

11 Clark, Michelle A. "Home sweet home in the eighth district." *Regional Economist.* April 1994, p. 12.

12 Clash, James M. "Reversal of fortunates." *Forbes.* 18 October 1993, p. 108.

13 Colborn, Marge. "Before you pick a project, look at the cost and the payback." *Detroit News.* 25 March 1995, p. 24D. *Note:* Figures are from a 60-city "Cost vs. Value" survey conducted by *Remodeling* magazine.

14 "Competition costs money in Colorado's open-heart surgery market." *Denver Business Journal.* 12-18 November 1993, p. 47.

15 Conlon, Michael. "Hotel rates are holding steady." *St. Louis Post-Dispatch.* Business Plus. 21 February 1994, p. 23.

16 "The cost of industrial water use." *Water Environment Technology.* January 1995, p. 13.

17 Curriden, Mark. "Bar scholarships for blacks cause stir." *ABA Journal.* February 1994, p. 34. *Note:* Price includes discount offered by providers of the course.

18 DeBenedictis, Don J. "Some university fees voluntary: Like lawyers, students don't have to fund objectionable speech, court rules." *ABA Journal.* May 1993, p. 30. *Note:* Fee is paid by students of the University of California.

19 DeBenedictis, Don J., "How long is too long?" *ABA Journal.* October 1993, p. 76.

20 Deck, Cecilia. "Sorting out the winners and losers in the great drug store war." *Detroit Free Press.* 20 February 1995, p. 11F.

21 Diesenhouse, Susan. "A market for primary homes on the Cape." *New York Times.* 21 May 1995, p. 27.

22 Einhorn, Erin, "Saving for those extra costs poses tough test for students." *Detroit News.* 5 June 1995, 10D.

23 Elber, Lynn. "Tell 'ER' doctor where it hurts: In the wallet." *Detroit Free Press.* 25 May 1995, p. 6C. *Note:* Figures shown are an estimate of charges by a nonprofit hospital in a midsize city in the South.

24 Evans, Sandra. "A look at the bill." *Washington Post Health.* 29 November 1994, p. 13.

25 Federal Communications Commission. Industry Analysis Division. Common Carrier Bureau. *Telephone Rates Update 1991.* Washington, D.C.: Federal Communications Commission, 1992, n.p. *Note:* Prices include surcharges and taxes.

26 Federal Housing Finance Board. *News.* Washington, D.C.: Federal Housing Finance Board. FHFB 93-21 (MIRS), April 1993, p. 1.

27 Fidrini, Phillip. "Economy demographics boost demand." *USA TODAY.* 4 November 1994, p.2B. *Note:* Figure given for Ogden, Utah, is the price of a vacation condominium.

28 "Financial Briefs: Where child care is--and isn't--a bargain." *Medical Economics.* 25 January 1993, p. 22.

29 Gainor, Paul E. "A buyer's market: can a savvy consumer on a tight budget really stuff his car and then himself after just one trip downtown?" *Detroit News.* 13 June 1995, p. 1B. *Note:* Figures shown are from Eastern Market, a farmers' market center in Detroit, Michigan.

30 Giblen, Gary M. "A view from Wall Street: Supercenter insights from on high." *Grocery Marketing.* April 1995, p. 33. *Note:* Figures shown are an average of prices in from three to five stores.

31   "The Globetrotter's indispensable index." *Travel Holiday.* December 1994/January 1995, p. 30.

32   "The Globetrotter's indispensable index." *Travel Holiday.* February 1995, p. 30.

33   "The Globetrotter's indispensable index." *Travel Holiday.* July/August 1994, p. 32.

34   "The Globetrotter's indispensable index." *Travel Holiday.* March 1995, p. 30.

35   "The Globetrotter's indispensable index." *Travel Holiday.* October 1994, p. 36.

36   "The Globetrotter's indispensable index." *Travel Holiday.* September 1994, p. 24.

37   Greengard, Samuel. " Holy pocketbook! (Cost of living in Los Angeles, California)." *Los Angeles Magazine.* July 1993, vol. 38, no. 7, p. 64.

38   Hansell, Saul. "Bane of banks: those educated consumers." *New York Times.* 5 June 1995, p. A1.

39   Hansell, Saul. "Citibank will end most fees on electronic transactions." *New York Times.* 24 May 1995, p. C1.

40   Hays, Constance L., "Increasing shift work challenges child care." *New York Times.* 8 June 1995, p. B5.

41   "HMOs: an industry snapshot." *Business & Health.* January 1995, p. 18. *Note:* No data were available for the states of Mississippi and Montana.

42 "How baby care prices compare at four chains." *Non-Foods Merchandising.* June 1994, p. 21.

43 "How smokers will pay." *Business Week.* 11 October 1993, p. 43.

44 Howard, Michelle B. "Is the grass greener, or just costlier? Survey compares living costs: are movies that much better in Louisville?" *Cincinnati Business Courier.* 6-12 January 1992, p. 3.

45 Kaplan, Joel. "The great escape: the joys and woes of resort town practice." *ABA Journal.* August 1993, p. 72.

46 Laabs, Jennifer J. "Relocation: smooth moves." *Personnel Journal.* February 1994, p. 68.

47 Lam, Tina. "Cost of going to Tiger games climbs." *Detroit Free Press.* 6 April 1994, p. 5C.

48 Larabee, John. "There's still time to send kids to camp." *Detroit News.* 22 June 1995, p. 6D.

49 Lavin, Douglas and Robert Johnson. "Prices for rental cars are set to climb sharply--again." *Wall Street Journal.* 29 September 1993, p. B1.

50 Letters. "Encore to Ticketmaster." *ABA Journal.* December 1994, p. 10.

51 McClellan, Barbara. "It's 'I do' to budget chapels." *Detroit News.* 2 June 1995, p. 8D.

52 *Meetings & Conventions.* May 1993, p. 101.

53 Miller, Lisa. "Takeoffs and Landings: Ride up, bike down." *Wall Street Journal.* 16 June 1995, p. B9.

54 National Funeral Directors Association (NFDA). *FTC Mandated General Price List.* Milwaukee, WI: National Funeral Directors Association, 1995, unpublished data. *Notes:* The average professional service charge in large cities was $1040; in small cities, towns, and rural areas, $938. All prices given were in effect as of January 1, 1995.

55 Noble, Kenneth. "What's doing in Los Angeles." *New York Times.* 25 June 1995. Sec. 5, p. 1.

56 O'Donnell, Jayne. "North Carolina in driver's seat on safety." *USA TODAY.* 16 June 1995, p.2A.

57 Pacelle, Mitchell. "Office vacancy decline gives landlords little relief." *Wall Street Journal.* 4 February 1994, p. B4.

58 Partch, Ken, "When Supermarkets Collide," *Supermarket Business.* May 1994, p. 26. *Note:* Figures shown are an average of prices in from four to six stores.

59 "Professional briefs: Managed care isn't always the cheapest alternative." *Medical Economics.* 26 April 1993, p. 22.

60 "Random price index." *USA TODAY.* 14 January 1994, p. 2B.

61 "Ranking cabs." *Economist.* 2 April 1994, p. 57.

62 *Real Estate Outlook: Market Trends & Insights,* vol. 2, no. 4. Washington, D.C.: National Association of Realtors, June 1995, pp. 13-16. *Notes:* Copyright 1995, National Association of Realtors. Used by permission. California values courtesy of California Association of Realtors. Editorial questions may be addressed to: Kate Anderson at (202) 383-1216. Subscription rates for 12 issues of *Real Estate Outlook* are $95 for members of the National Association of Realtors (NAR); $135 for nonmembers.

63 Reeves, Pamela. "Home buyers can expect to pay a wide variety of fees in closing costs." *Detroit News.* 12 June 1995, p. 6F.

64 *Residential Electric Bills, Summer 1993.* Washington, D.C.: National Association of Regulatory Utility Commissioners (NARUC), 1994. *Notes:* Rates are calculated for the largest area in each utility's service area. The state of Nebraska does not regulate retail electric rates. This material can be ordered for $32.50 plus a 10% shipping and handling fee from NARUC, 1102 ICC Building, P.O. Box 684, Washington, DC 20044-0684 (202) 898-2200.

65 *Residential Gas Bills, Winter 1993-94.* Washington, D.C.: National Association of Regulatory Utility Commissioners (NARUC), 1994. *Notes:* Rates are calculated for the largest area in each utility's service area. Bill computations are based on the rate schedule applicable to the majority of a utility's space heating and non-space heating customers within each state. The total bill includes the base rate, the purchased gas adjustment charge, and all taxes except sales taxes not covered by the utility for the tax imposing authority. The state of Nebraska does not regulate natural gas prices. Figures shown for Wichita, Kansas, are an average of typical monthly bills for two utility companies. This material can be ordered for $30 plus a 10% shipping and handling fee from NARUC, 1102 ICC Building, P.O. Box 684, Washington, DC 20044-0684 (202) 898-2200.

66 Reske, Henry J. "D.C. considers tax on professionals: Beleaguered governments increasingly eye lawyers as revenue source." *ABA Journal.* May 1993, p. 27.

67 Sack, Kevin. "What's doing in Saratoga." *New York Times.* 2 July 1995, Sec. 5, p. 1.

68 Slezak, Michael. "Big Y's: Remedy for congestion." *SN (Supermarket News).* 5 September 1994, p. 36.

69 *Source Book of Health Insurance Data 1993.* "Charges for Selected Surgical Procedures, by Geographic Area 1992." Washington, D.C.: Health Insurance Association of America (HIAA). Copyright 1994, Health Insurance Association of America (HIAA). Used by permission. *Note:* For additional information contact HIAA, 1025 Connecticut Ave., N.W., Washington, DC 20036-3998. To order the *Source Book,* call (800) 828-0111.

70 Spano, Susan. "In Missouri, history and barbecue." *New York Times.* 21 May 1995, p. 6.

71 *State Average Expenditures & Premiums for Personal Automobile Insurance in 1993.* Kansas City, MO: National Association of Insurance Commissioners (NAIC), 1995, Table 1. *Notes:* Copyright 1995, National Association of Insurance Commissioners (NAIC). Used by permission. Figures shown are averages of liability, collision, and comprehensive insurance combined. This publication can be ordered for $25 from National Association of Insurance Commissioners (NAIC), 120 W. 12th Street, Suite 1100, Kansas City, MO 64105-1925 (816) 842-3600.

72 "Stats: cost per hospital admission." *Health Care Weekly Review.* 14 February 1994, p. 3.

73 "Survey results at a glance." *Restaurants & Institutions.* 1 October 1994, p. 49.

74 Sutton, Rodney K. "Remodeling trends revealed: professionally installed kitchen, bath projects on tap for consumers." *BSHC.* March 1995, p. 29.

75 Thomas, Jr., Emory. "Many hot Olympic tickets are already gone." *Wall Street Journal.* 25 April 1995, sec. B, p.1.

76 "Today's Tip." *Detroit Free Press.* 27 May 1994, p. 3C. *Notes:* Reception costs include hall, caterers, and liquor. Figures given for formal wear for groom and for groom's attendants are for rental only. Expenses are based on a national average total cost of $17470.

77 Tompor, Susan, "Map out your travel plans when renting cars." *Detroit News.* 12 June 1995, p. 3F. *Note:* Fee shown is based on a trip to Phoenix, Arizona.

78 "Typical area mortgage payment falls $122 in 2 years." *Detroit News.* 21 January 1994, p. 1E.

79 U.S. Bureau of the Census. *Statistical Abstract of the United States 1994.* 114th edition. Washington, D.C.: U.S. Government Printing Office, 1995, p. 310.

80 U.S. Department of Education. National Center for Education Statistics. *Digest of Education Statistics 1993.* Washington, D.C.: U.S. Government Printing Office, October 1994, p. 313. *Notes:* Data reflect average charges for the entire academic year. Tuition and fees are weighted by the number of full-time-equivalent undergraduate students in 1992, but are not adjusted to reflect student residency. Room and board figures are based on full-time students.

81 U.S. Department of Labor. Bureau of Labor Statistics. *Consumer Expenditure Survey 1990-91.* Washington, D.C.: U.S. Government Printing Office, September 1993, p. 86.

82 U.S. Department of Labor. Bureau of Labor Statistics. *CPI Detailed Report: Data for December 1994.* Washington, D.C.: U.S. Government Printing Office, January 1995, p. 93.

83 U.S. Department of Transportation. Federal Highway Administration. Office of Highway Information Management. *1994 Driver License Administration Requirements and Fees.* Table DL-104A. FHWA-PL-94-030. Washington, D.C.: U.S. Department of Transportation, June 1994.

84 U.S. Department of Transportation. Federal Highway Administration. Office of Highway Information Management. *1994 Driver License Administration Requirements and Fees.* Table DL-105. FHWA-PL-94-030. Washington, D.C.: U.S. Department of Transportation, June 1994. *Note:* In Alabama, the fee is $15 for second and subsequently issued licenses; in Jefferson County, Alabama, there is an additional fee of 25 cents local issuance for all permits and licenses. In California, there is a $30 dollar charge for a retest of driving skills for Class A, B, or CDL Class C.

85 U.S. Department of Transportation. Federal Highway Administration. Office of Highway Information Management. *1994 Driver License Administration Requirements and Fees.* Table DL-106A. FHWA-PL-94-030. Washington, D.C.: U.S. Department of Transportation, June 1994.

86 USA Snapshots. "Costliest big cities for driving." *USA TODAY.* 3 May 1995, p. 1A.

87 USA Snapshots. "Don't even think of parking here!" *USA TODAY.* 3 December 1993, p. 1A.

88 USA Snapshots. "Shop for your doc." *USA TODAY.* 10 January 1994, p. 1A.

89 USA Snapshots. "Six cheapest cities for driving." *USA TODAY.* 4 May 1995, p. 1A.

90 USA Snapshots: "Immunization Prices." *USA TODAY.* 26 August 1993, p. 1A.

91 Waddell, Ray. "Family price index rates FECs a bargain." *Amusement Business.* 9-15 May 1994, p. 42.

92 Wagner, Karen. "Career Option: Practice in a small town." *Barrister Magazine,* Fall 1993, p. 7.

93 *Washington Post Health.* 30 November 1993, p. 5.

94 "The week in healthcare: Consumers are comparing prices as they shop to pick HMOs in hot markets--study." *Modern Healthcare.* 4 April 1994, p. 26.

95 "What the average room and car will cost next week." *Wall Street Journal.* 12 May 1995, p. B9.

96 "Where are the country's best credit-card deals?" *Consumers Digest.* March/April 1995, p. 50. *Note:* Figure shown is an average of fees charged by three institutions.